CENTURY READINGS
IN ENGLISH LITERATURE

CENTURY READINGS

in English Literature

Edited and Annotated by

John W. Cunliffe, D.Lit.
Professor of English and Director Emeritus of the School of Journalism, Columbia University

J. F. A. Pyre, Ph.D.
Professor of English, University of Wisconsin

Karl Young, Ph.D.
Professor of English, Yale University

The Fourth Edition

NEW YORK : D. APPLETON-CENTURY COMPANY : LONDON
INCORPORATED

COPYRIGHT, 1937, BY

D. APPLETON-CENTURY COMPANY, INC.

All rights reserved. This book, or parts thereof, must not be reprinted in any form without permission of the publisher.

339

COPYRIGHT, 1910, 1925, 1929, BY THE CENTURY CO.

COPYRIGHT, 1937, BY JOHN WILLIAM CUNLIFFE

PRINTED IN U. S. A.

PREFACE

Century Readings in English Literature, when it was first published in 1910, was a pioneer effort to provide an organized basis for the systematic teaching or study of English literature as a whole from the earliest period to the present. The Editors were all at that time professors in the Department of English of the University of Wisconsin, and they brought to the development of the new method the enthusiasm and ambition of youth, testing it first in their classes in the university, and perfecting it by almost daily consultation with each other and with their colleagues. The results obtained encouraged them to believe that their scheme of instruction could be extended to other universities and colleges with advantage to English teaching generally, and the publication of Century Readings in English Literature was the outcome.

The success of the book was immediate and surpassed all expectations. Hardly a year has passed since without the appearance of imitations which adopted with more or less modification the method, the selections, and even the title. But the publication of competing volumes, by widening the field for books of this character and possibly by stimulating the Editors to further efforts, only served to increase the circulation of Century Readings, which easily kept its place at the head of the procession.

Each succeeding issue has given occasion for additions and improvements, and this Fourth Edition has afforded the opportunity not only for a revision and enlargement of the selections from twentieth century authors but for the introduction of a new feature in the illustrations, which have been chosen with the same regard to accuracy and educational value as has been given to the text.

The Editors wish to record their sincere gratitude to many teachers of English who have helped them with suggestions, and especially to their Wisconsin colleagues, Professors William Ellery Leonard and R. E. N. Dodge, to the former for the use of his translation of 'Beowulf' (Century Co.) and to the latter for the use of the Cambridge text of Spenser (Houghton Mifflin Co.). They are also indebted to the generosity of numerous authors and publishers, who have permitted the reproduction of a large amount of copyright material. They wish, in particular, to make the following acknowledgments:

G. W. Armitage and the *Manchester Guardian* for the poem 'Lancashire.'
D. Appleton & Co., for 'Emancipation: Black and White' by T. H. Huxley.
Brentano's, for 'The Case for the Critic-Dramatist' by George Bernard Shaw.
Cambridge University Press, for 'All the Hills and Vales Along' by Charles Hamilton Sorley.
The Century Co., for the translation of 'Pearl.'
The Century Magazine, for 'William and Mary' by Max Beerbohm.

Country Life, for 'The Defenders' by John Drinkwater; 'The Wykhamist' by Nora Griffiths.

George H. Doran Company, Publishers, for 'Salary Earning Girls' from 'Our Women' by Arnold Bennett, copyright 1920.

Doubleday, Doran & Company, Inc., for 'At Sea' from 'Jesting Pilate' by Aldous Huxley, copyright 1926 by George H. Doran Company.

Doubleday, Page & Co., for 'The Ballad of Iskander' by James Elroy Flecker.

E. P. Dutton & Co., for 'My First Visit to Buenos Ayres' by W. H. Hudson, by permission, copyright 1918 by E. P. Dutton & Co.; 'The Spires of Oxford' by Winifred M. Letts; 'The Old Huntsman' by Siegfried Sassoon, by permission, copyright 1918 by E. P. Dutton & Co.

A. C. Fifield, for 'Leisure,' 'Money,' 'Sheep' and 'The Muse' by William H. Davies from 'Collected Poems by W. H. Davies.'

Four Seas Company, for 'The Mountainy Singer' by Joseph Campbell.

Harcourt, Brace and Company, Inc., for 'The Last Years,' from 'Queen Victoria' by Lytton Strachey, copyright 1921 by Harcourt, Brace and Company, Inc.; 'The *Boston Evening Transcript*,' 'Aunt Helen,' and 'Cousin Nancy' by T. S. Eliot; and 'The Patron and the Crocus' by Virginia Woolf.

Harcourt, Brace and Howe, for 'English Hills,' 'Happy is England Now' by John Freeman.

Harper & Bros., for 'With the Marseilles Pilots' by Joseph Conrad; 'The Contemporary Novel' by H. G. Wells.

The Harrovian, for 'A Harrow Grave in Flanders' by Lord Crewe.

Henry Holt & Co., for 'The Plougher' and 'What the Shuiler Said as She Lay by the Fire in the Farmer's House' by Padraic Colum; 'All That's Past' and 'Miss Loo' by Walter de la Mare; 'Sowing,' 'Bright Clouds' and 'The Gallows' by Edward Thomas; 'Romance and Realism' by Hugh Walpole.

Houghton Mifflin Company, for 'For the Fallen' by Laurence Binyon, and for 'England after the War' from 'The People's King' by John Buchan, Lord Tweedsmuir.

B. W. Huebsch, Inc., for 'The Bride' and 'Study' by D. H. Lawrence (copyrighted).

Mitchell Kennerley, for selections from 'The Note Books' by Samuel Butler, and 'The South Country' by Hilaire Belloc.

Alfred A. Knopf, Inc., for 'Not Dead' by Robert Graves.

John Lane Co., for 'The Old Vicarage, Grantchester' and 'The Soldier' by Rupert Brooke; 'The Return of the Barbarian' and 'The Wife of Flanders' by G. K. Chesterton; 'Thirty Bob a Week' by John Davidson; 'A Shropshire Lad' by A. E. Housman; 'Clifton Chapel,' 'Drake's Drum' and 'Vitai Lampada' by Sir Henry Newbolt; 'Revenge for Rheims' by Stephen Phillips; 'Wordsworth's Grave' by Sir William Watson.

The Macmillan Company, for 'The Earth Breath' by 'A. E.'; 'His Father,' 'The Question,' and 'Raining' by Wilfred Wilson Gibson; 'Afterwards,' 'For Life I had Never Cared Greatly' and 'The Coming of the End' by Thomas Hardy; 'Eve' and 'The Bull' by Ralph Hodgson; 'The Island of Skyros' and 'Sea-Fever' by John Masefield; 'What Tomas An Buile Said in a Pub' by James Stephens; 'Into the Twilight,' 'The Lake Isle of Innisfree,' 'Red Hanrahan's Song about Ireland,' and 'Song from the Land of Heart's Desire' by William Butler Yeats.

The Poetry Bookshop, for 'Over the Brazier' by Robert Graves; 'Milk for the Cat,' 'Suburb,' 'The Rebellious Vine,' and 'Change of Mind' by Harold Monro.

The Poetry Review, for 'The Airman' by Gregg Goddard.

G. P. Putnam's Sons, for 'Soldier, Soldier' by Maurice Hewlett.

Grant Richards, for 'Socks' by Jessie Pope.

Charles Scribner's Sons, for 'The Lost Dog' by John Galsworthy; 'Parted,' 'The Lady Poverty' and 'The Shepherdess,' by Alice Meynell.

Sidgwick & Jackson, for 'A Girl's Song,' by Katharine Tynan.

Frederick A. Stokes Co., for 'The Search Lights' by Alfred Noyes.

The London *Times*, for 'How Sleep the Brave' by Walter de la Mare; 'Into Battle' by Julian Grenfell.

The Westminster Gazette, for 'Many Sisters to Many Brothers' by Rose Macaulay.

CONTENTS

EARLY ENGLISH LITERATURE

	PAGE
HISTORICAL INTRODUCTION	3

Beowulf
(In Modern Verse) ... 5

Sir Gawain and the Green Knight (c. 1375)
(In Modern Prose) ... 38

Pearl (c. 1375)
(In Modern Verse) ... 59

The Chester Plays
Noah's Flood (In Modern Verse) ... 65
The Banns ... 70

CHAUCER TO THE RENAISSANCE

HISTORICAL INTRODUCTION AND TABLE OF DATES ... 71

Geoffrey Chaucer (c. 1340–1400)
The Canterbury Tales: The Prologue ... 74
　　　　　　　　　The Nun's Priest's Tale ... 81
Chaucers Wordes unto Adam, his Owne Scriveyn ... 86
Lak of Stedfastnesse ... 86
The Compleint of Chaucer to his Empty Purse ... 87
Truth ... 87

Sir Thomas Malory (c. 1395–1471)
Le Morte D'Arthur ... 88

Anonymous
The Nutbrowne Maide (c. 1500) ... 101

English and Scottish Popular Ballads
Robin Hood and Guy of Gisborne ... 105
Robin Hood's Death and Burial ... 108
The Battle of Otterburn ... 108
Captain Car or Edom O Gordon ... 111
The Wife of Usher's Well ... 113
Kemp Owyne ... 113
The Dæmon Lover ... 114
Lord Randal ... 114
Sir Patrick Spens ... 115
Thomas Rymer ... 115
Bonny Barbara Allan ... 116
The Twa Sisters ... 116
The Cruel Brother ... 117
Edward ... 118

THE ELIZABETHAN AGE

HISTORICAL INTRODUCTION AND TABLE OF DATES ... 119

Sir Thomas Wyatt (1503?–1542)
Sonnets ... 121
'Forget not yet' ... 122
An Earnest Suit to his Unkind Mistress ... 122
The Lover Complaineth the Unkindness of his Love ... 122
The Lover Sendeth his Complaints ... 123
Of the Mean and Sure Estate ... 123

Henry Howard, Earl of Surrey (1517?–1547)
Sonnets ... 125
Complaint of the Absence of Her Lover ... 126
A Praise of his Love ... 127
Description of the Restless State of a Lover ... 127
Of the Death of Sir T[homas] W[yatt] ... 127
Virgil's Æneid, Book II ... 128

Thomas Sackville, Lord Buckhurst (1536–1608)
The Induction ... 129

Roger Ascham (1515–1568)
The Schoolmaster, Book I ... 135

John Lyly (1554?–1606)
Euphues and his England ... 139
Songs from the Plays ... 142

Sir Philip Sidney (1554–1586)
An Apology for Poetry ... 144
Astrophel and Stella ... 150
Song: The Nightingale ... 152
Love is Dead ... 152
Dorus to Pamela (*from Arcadia*) ... 152
A Ditty ... 152

Hakluyt's Voyages
Dedicatory Epistle ... 153
The Last Fight of the *Revenge* ... 154
Linschoten's Testimony ... 157
The Loss of Sir Humphrey Gilbert ... 157
A Report of Virginia ... 159
Drake in California ... 160

Edmund Spenser (1552–1599)
The Shepheardes Calendar: Februarie ... 161
　　　　　　　　　　　　October ... 164
The Faerie Queene: Canto I ... 166
　　　　　　　Canto II ... 171
Amoretti ... 176
Epithalamion ... 177
Prothalamion ... 181

ELIZABETHAN LYRICS

George Gascoigne (1525?–1577)
A Strange Passion of a Lover ... 184

Sir Edward Dyer (1550?–1607)
My Mind to Me a Kingdom Is ... 185

Sir Walter Raleigh (1552?–1618)
The Silent Lover ... 185
His Pilgrimage ... 185
A Vision upon this Conceit of the Faery Queen ... 186
The Conclusion ... 186

George Peele (c. 1557–1596)
Song (*from The Arraignment of Paris*) ... 186

vii

CONTENTS

Harvestmen A-Singing (*from The Old Wives' Tale*) 187
Robert Greene (*1560–1592*)
    Songs 187
Robert Southwell (*1561?–1595*)
    The Burning Babe 188
Samuel Daniel (*1562–1619*)
    Sonnets (*from Delia*) 189
Michael Drayton (*1563–1631*)
    Sonnets (*from Idea*) 190
    To the Virginian Voyage 191
    To the Cambro-Britons and their Harp 191
Christopher Marlowe (*1564–1593*)
    Hero and Leander: The First Sestiad 192
William Shakespeare (*1564–1616*)
    Venus and Adonis 194
    Sonnets 198
    Songs from the Plays 203
Thomas Dekker (*c. 1572–c. 1632*)
    O Sweet Content (*from Patient Grissell*) 204
England's Helicon (*1600*)
    Phyllida and Corydon 204
    As It Fell upon a Day 205
    To Colin Clout 205
    The Shepherd's Commendation of his Nymph 205
    The Herdman's Happy Life 206
    A Nymph's Disdain of Love 206
    Rosalind's Madrigal 206

THE SEVENTEENTH CENTURY

HISTORICAL INTRODUCTION AND TABLE OF DATES 207

SEVENTEENTH CENTURY LYRICS

Thomas Campion (*1567–1620*)
    When Thou Must Home 210
    Basia 210
    A Renunciation 210
    Sic Transit 210
Ben Jonson (*1573?–1637*)
    Song to Celia 210
    Song: To Celia 210
    Hymn to Diana 211
    To Heaven 211
    The Triumph of Charis 211
    An Epitaph on Salathiel Pavy 211
    Epitaph on Elizabeth L. H. 212
    To the Memory of My Beloved, Master William Shakespeare 212
John Donne (*1573–1631*)
    Song ('Go and catch a falling star') 212
    The Indifferent 213
    The Canonization 213
    The Dream 213
    Love's Deity 214
    The Funeral 214
    The Computation 214
    Forget 214
    Death 215
    A Hymn to God the Father 215

John Fletcher (*1579–1625*)
    Love's Emblems 215
    Melancholy 215
    Song to Bacchus 215
    Beauty Clear and Fair 215
    Weep No More 216
    Aspatia's Song 216
Francis Beaumont (*1584–1616*)
    On the Life of Man 216
    Lines on the Tombs in Westminster 216
George Wither (*1588–1667*)
    The Lover's Resolution 216
    When We are upon the Seas 217
    The Prayer of Old Age 217
William Browne (*1591–1643*)
    On the Countess Dowager of Pembroke 217
Robert Herrick (*1591–1674*)
    The Argument of His Book 217
    Corinna's Going A-Maying 218
    Upon Julia's Clothes 218
    To the Virgins 218
    To Daffodils 219
    To Music 219
    The Night-Piece, to Julia 219
    An Ode for Ben Jonson 219
    A Thanksgiving to God for His House 219
    Grace for a Child 220
    His Prayer for Absolution 220
Francis Quarles (*1592–1644*)
    An Ecstasy 220
George Herbert (*1593–1633*)
    Virtue 220
    Love 221
    The Collar 221
    The Quip 221
    The World 221
    The Pulley 222
James Shirley (*1596–1666*)
    The Glories of Our Blood and State 222
Thomas Carew (*1598?–1639?*)
    Song ('Ask me no more') 222
    Song ('Would you know what's soft?') 222
    The Protestation 223
    Persuasions to Joy: A Song 223
    Ingrateful Beauty Threatened 223
    An Epitaph 223
Sir William Davenant (*1606–1668*)
    Song ('The lark now leaves his wat'ry nest,') 223
    Praise and Prayer 223
Edmund Waller (*1606–1687*)
    The Story of Phœbus and Daphne Applied 224
    To Phyllis 224
    On a Girdle 224
    Go, Lovely Rose! 224
Sir John Suckling (*1609–1642*)
    A Doubt of Martyrdom 224
    The Constant Lover 225
    Why so Pale and Wan? 225
Richard Crashaw (*1613?–1649*)
    In the Holy Nativity of our Lord God 225

CONTENTS

Sir John Denham (1615–1669)
    Cooper's Hill 226
    On Mr. Abraham Cowley's Death 227

Richard Lovelace (1618–1658)
    To Lucasta, Going to the Wars 227
    To Althea, from Prison 227
    The Rose 228
    To Lucasta 228

Abraham Cowley (1618–1667)
    The Swallow 228
    The Wish 228

Andrew Marvel (1621–1678)
    The Garden 229
    To his Coy Mistress 229

Henry Vaughan (1622–1695)
    The Retreat 230
    The World 230
    Departed Friends 231

Charles Sackville, Earl of Dorset (1638–1706)
    Song ('To all you ladies now at land') .. 231

John Wilmot, Earl of Rochester (1647–1680)
    On Charles II 232

Francis Bacon (1561–1626)
    Essays 233

Sir Thomas Browne (1605–1682)
    Religio Medici 245
    Hydriotaphia, Urn-burial 253

Isaak Walton (1593–1683)
    The Complete Angler: Chapter IV 256

Thomas Fuller (1608–1661)
    The Life of Sir Francis Drake 261

Jeremy Taylor (1613–1667)
    The Faith and Patience of the Saints ... 265

John Bunyan (1628–1688)
    The Pilgrim's Progress 269

John Milton (1608–1674)
    On Shakespeare 279
    L'Allegro 280
    Il Penseroso 281
    Lycidas 282
    Sonnets 284
    Paradise Lost: Book I 286
                  Book II 294
    Areopagitica 299

John Dryden (1631–1700)
    Absalom and Achitophel 304
    Alexander's Feast, or The Power of Music 307
    An Essay of Dramatic Poesy 309

Samuel Pepys (1633–1703)
    The Diary of Samuel Pepys 318

THE EIGHTEENTH CENTURY

HISTORICAL INTRODUCTION AND TABLE OF DATES 323

Daniel Defoe (1661–1731)
    The True-Born Englishman 325
    The Shortest Way with the Dissenters ... 326
    Preface to the Review 332
    The Education of Women 335

Jonathan Swift (1667–1745)
    A Tale of a Tub 337
    A Meditation upon a Broomstick 347
    A Modest Proposal 347

Sir Richard Steele (1672–1729)
    Essays from The Tatler 351
    Essays from The Spectator 352

Joseph Addison (1672–1719)
    Essays from The Spectator 361

Alexander Pope (1688–1744)
    An Essay on Criticism 375
    The Rape of the Lock 381
    Epistle to Dr. Arbuthnot 388

James Thomson (1700–1748)
    Summer 393
    Autumn 394
    Winter 394
    A Hymn 395
    The Castle of Indolence: Book I 396

Thomas Gray (1716–1771)
    Sonnet on the Death of Mr. Richard West 399
    An Ode on a Distant Prospect of Eton College 399
    Hymn to Adversity 400
    Elegy Written in a Country Churchyard .. 401
    The Progress of Poesy 402
    The Bard 404
    The Fatal Sisters 405
    Letters 406

William Collins (1721–1759)
    Dirge in Cymbeline 411
    Ode ('How sleep the brave') 411
    Ode to Evening 411
    Ode to Simplicity 412
    The Passions 412
    Ode on the Death of Mr. Thomson 414

Thomas Chatterton (1752–1770)
    An Excellent Ballad of Charity 415
    Mynstrelles Songe (*from Ælla*) 416

Oliver Goldsmith (1728–1774)
    Song ('When lovely woman') 417
    The Deserted Village 417
    The Retaliation 421

Samuel Johnson (1709–1784)
    The Life of Addison 423
    Letters 436
    The Vanity of Human Wishes 437

James Boswell (1740–1795)
    The Life of Johnson 439

Edmund Burke (1729–1797)
    The Speech for Conciliation with the Colonies 457

Edward Gibbon (1737–1794)
    The Decline and Fall of the Roman Empire: Chapter LXVIII 465

HYMNS OF THE 18TH CENTURY

Thomas Ken (1637–1711) 475
Isaac Watts (1674–1748) 475
Charles Wesley (1707–1788) 476

CONTENTS

	PAGE
John Fawcett (1739–1817)	478
Augustus Montague Toplady (1740–1778)	478
Edward Perronet (1726–1792)	478
William Cowper (1731–1800)	
Walking with God	479
Table Talk	479
The Task	480
On the Receipt of my Mother's Picture	482
Sonnet to Mrs. Unwin	483
On the Loss of the Royal George	483
The Castaway	484
Letters	484
George Crabbe (1754–1832)	
The Village: Book I	489
William Blake (1757–1827)	
To Spring	493
To the Muses	493
Mad Song	494
The Piper	494
The Shepherd	494
The Little Black Boy	494
Cradle Song (from Songs of Innocence)	495
Cradle Song (from Songs of Experience)	495
A Dream	495
The Divine Image	495
The Chimney Sweeper	496
The Clod and the Pebble	496
The Tiger	496
Ah Sunflower	496
Nurse's Song	496
From Milton ('And did those feet in ancient time')	496
Robert Burns (1759–1796)	
Song: Mary Morison	497
Song: My Nanie, O	498
Song: Green Grow the Rashes	498
Lines to John Lapraik	498
To a Mouse	498
The Cotter's Saturday Night	499
Address to the Deil	501
A Bard's Epitaph	502
Of A' the Airts the Wind Can Blaw	502
Go Fetch to Me a Pint o' Wine	503
Auld Lang Syne	503
John Anderson My Jo	503
Tam Glen	503
To Mary in Heaven	504
Tam O'Shanter	504
Willie Brewed a Peck o' Maut	506
A Winter Night	506
Highland Mary	506
Flow Gently, Sweet Afton	507
Bonie Doon	507
Duncan Gray	507
Scots Wha Hae	508
A Man's a Man for A' That	508

THE ROMANTIC REVIVAL

	PAGE
HISTORICAL INTRODUCTION AND TABLE OF DATES	509
William Wordsworth (1770–1850)	
Preface to Lyrical Ballads	512
The Prelude: Book I	522
Lines Composed a Few Miles above Tintern Abbey	524
Strange Fits of Passion Have I Known	525
She Dwelt among the Untrodden Ways	525
I Traveled among Unknown Men	526
Three Years She Grew in Sun and Shower	526
A Slumber Did My Spirit Seal	526
Michael	526
My Heart Leaps Up When I Behold	531
The Sparrow's Nest	531
To the Cuckoo	531
Resolution and Independence	531
To a Young Lady	533
She Was a Phantom of Delight	533
Yarrow Unvisited	533
The Solitary Reaper	534
I Wandered Lonely as a Cloud	534
To a Skylark	535
Elegiac Stanzas	535
Ode to Duty	536
Character of the Happy Warrior	536
Ode on Intimations of Immortality from Recollections of Early Childhood	537
Sonnets	539
Samuel Taylor Coleridge (1772–1834)	
Biographia Literaria: Chapters X and XIV	544
The Rime of the Ancient Mariner	553
Christabel	559
Kubla Khan	565
Frost at Midnight	565
Humility the Mother of Charity	566
Epitaph	566
Charles Lamb (1775–1834)	
The Old Familiar Faces	567
Mackery End in Hertfordshire	567
Dream-Children: A Reverie	570
A Chapter on Ears	571
A Dissertation upon Roast Pig	574
Sir Walter Scott (1771–1832)	
Marmion: Canto VI	577
Soldier, Rest!	584
George Noel Gordon, Lord Byron (1788–1824)	
Sonnet on Chillon	585
Childe Harold: Canto III	586
Canto IV	591
The Vision of Judgment	596
Don Juan: Canto III	599
Canto IV	602
Percy Bysshe Shelley (1792–1822)	
Hymn to Intellectual Beauty	607
Ozymandias	608
Stanzas Written in Dejection, Near Naples	608
Prometheus Unbound: Act IV	609
Ode to the West Wind	616
The Indian Serenade	617
The Cloud	617
To a Skylark	618
A Lament	619
To —— ('Music, when soft voices die')	619
Adonais	619
To Night	625
To ('One word is too often profaned')	625
With a Guitar, to Jane	625

CONTENTS

Lines: When the Lamp is Shattered........ 626
A Dirge................................. 626

John Keats (1795–1821)
Keen, Fitful Gusts Are Whispering Here and There........................... 627
On First Looking into Chapman's Homer... 627
Endymion: Book I, Proem................ 627
The Eve of St. Agnes.................... 628
Ode ('Bards of Passion and of Mirth')...... 632
Robin Hood............................. 632
Lines on the Mermaid Tavern............. 633
Ode on a Grecian Urn.................... 633
Ode to a Nightingale..................... 634
Ode on Melancholy...................... 635
To Autumn.............................. 635
Hyperion: Book I........................ 635
In a Drear-Nighted December............. 639
La Belle Dame Sans Merci................ 639
On Seeing the Elgin Marbles.............. 639
On the Sea.............................. 639
To One who Has Been Long in City Pent... 640
To Chatterton........................... 640
When I Have Fears that I May Cease to Be 640
Bright Star! Would I Were Steadfast as Thou Art............................. 640

OTHER POETS OF THE ROMANTIC REVIVAL

Robert Southey (1774–1843)
The Battle of Blenheim................... 641

Walter Savage Landor (1775–1864)
Rose Aylmer............................ 642
Mild is the Parting Year................. 642
Past Ruined Ilion........................ 642
The Death of Artemidora................. 642
Dirce................................... 642
On Lucretia Borgia's Hair................ 642
Memory and Pride....................... 642
The Love of Other Years................. 643
To Robert Browning..................... 643
On Timely Death........................ 643
To Age.................................. 643
On his Seventy-Fifth Birthday............ 643

Thomas Campbell (1777–1844)
Ye Mariners of England.................. 643

Thomas Moore (1779–1852)
Oft in the Stilly Night................... 644
The Harp that Once Through Tara's Halls.. 644

Leigh Hunt (1784–1859)
Rondeau................................ 644

Thomas Love Peacock (1785–1866)
The Men of Gotham..................... 644
The War-Song of Dinas Vawr............. 645
The Friar's Song........................ 645

Charles Wolfe (1791–1823)
The Burial of Sir John Moore............. 645

John Keble (1792–1866)
United States........................... 646

Thomas Hood (1799–1845)
Fair Ines............................... 646
The Bridge of Sighs..................... 647
The Song of the Shirt................... 648

Winthrop Mackworth Praed (1802–1839)
The Belle of the Ball-Room............... 648
A Letter of Advice...................... 649

William Barnes (1801–1886)
Blackmwore Maidens..................... 650
The Surprise............................ 651

Thomas Lovell Beddoes (1803–1849)
Dream-Pedlary.......................... 651
Ballad of Human Life.................... 652
To Sea, To Sea!......................... 652
Dirge ('If thou wilt ease thine heart')...... 652
Song ('Old Adam, the carrion crow')...... 652

William Hazlitt (1778–1830)
On Going a Journey..................... 653

Thomas De Quincey (1785–1859)
Confessions of an English Opium Eater..... 658

Thomas Babington Macaulay (1800–1859)
The Romance of History................. 665
The History of England: Volume I, Chapter III............................. 670

THE VICTORIAN ERA

HISTORICAL INTRODUCTION AND TABLE OF DATES......................... 675

John Henry, Cardinal Newman (1801–1890)
The Idea of a University: Discourse VI..... 678

Thomas Carlyle (1795–1881)
The French Revolution: Volume I, Book V, Chapter VI............................ 687
Past and Present: Book III, Chapters XI and XII................................. 691

John Ruskin (1819–1900)
Traffic................................. 695

Alfred, Lord Tennyson (1809–1892)
Mariana................................ 705
Song ('A spirit haunts the year's last hours') 706
The Poet............................... 706
The Lady of Shalott..................... 707
The Palace of Art....................... 708
A Dream of Fair Women................. 712
Saint Agnes' Eve........................ 715
You Ask Me, Why, Though Ill at Ease..... 715
Of Old Sat Freedom on the Heights........ 716
Sir Galahad............................. 716
A Farewell............................. 717
Morte D'Arthur......................... 717
Ulysses................................ 720
Locksley Hall........................... 720
Break, Break, Break..................... 724
The Poet's Song......................... 724
Songs (*from The Princess*).............. 724
In Memoriam A. H. H................... 725
Maud: A Monodrama.................... 727
Song (*from Guinevere*)................. 733
Tithonus............................... 734
Milton................................. 734
Northern Farmer, Old Style.............. 735
The Revenge........................... 736
To Virgil............................... 738

CONTENTS

	PAGE
'Frater Ave Atque Vale'	738
Crossing the Bar	738

Robert Browning (1812–1889)
Songs (*from Pippa Passes*)	740
My Last Duchess	740
Count Gismond	741
Incident of the French Camp	742
The Italian in England	742
The Lost Leader	744
Home-Thoughts from Abroad	744
Home-Thoughts from the Sea	744
Saul	745
Love Among the Ruins	751
A Woman's Last Word	751
A Toccata of Galuppi's	752
My Star	753
The Last Ride Together	753
Memorabilia	754
'De Gustibus'	754
Andrea Del Sarto	755
The Guardian-Angel	757
A Grammarian's Funeral	758
One Word More	760
Abt Vogler	762
Rabbi Ben Ezra	764
Prospice	766
Herve Riel	766
The Two Poets of Croisic: Prologue	768
Epilogue	768
Pheidippides	769
Cavalier Tunes	772
Asolando: Epilogue	772

Matthew Arnold (1822–1888)
The Study of Poetry	773
Shakespeare	785
The Forsaken Merman	785
The Buried Life	786
Self-Dependence	787
Morality	788
Sohrab and Rustum	788
The Scholar Gipsy	797
Requiescat	800
Rugby Chapel	800
Dover Beach	802

Dante Gabriel Rossetti (1828–1882)
My Sister's Sleep	803
The Blessed Damozel	804
Francesca da Rimini	805
Love's Nocturn	805
The Cloud Confines	807
Three Shadows	807
The King's Tragedy	807
Sonnets (*from The House of Life*)	816

William Morris (1834–1896)
The Earthly Paradise	819
Atalanta's Race	820
The Lady of the Land	827

Algernon Charles Swinburne (1837–1909)
Choruses (*from Atalanta in Calydon*)	833
The Garden of Proserpine	836
Hertha	836
A Forsaken Garden	839
Thalassius	840
Étude Réaliste	842

	PAGE
The Roundel	842
On a Country Road	843
Cor Cordium	843
'Non Dolet'	843
On the Deaths of Thomas Carlyle and George Eliot	843
Christopher Marlowe	844
A Match	844

George Meredith (1828–1909)
Love in the Valley	845
The Last Words of Juggling Jerry	848
The Old Chartist	849
France, 1870	850
The Lark Ascending	854
The Woods of Westermain	855
Modern Love	859

OTHER VICTORIAN POETS

Elizabeth Barrett Browning (1806–1861)
Sonnets from the Portuguese	860

Edward Fitzgerald (1809–1883)
The Rubáiyát of Omar Khayyám	862

William Makepeace Thackeray (1811–1863)
At the Church Gate	862
The End of the Play	862

Arthur Hugh Clough (1819–1861)
Qua Cursum Ventus	863
Whither Depart the Brave	864
Where Lies the Land	864
Ah! Yet Consider it Again!	864
In the Depths	864
The Latest Decalogue	864
Say not the Struggle Nought Availeth	865
Life is Struggle	865

Frederick Locker-Lampson (1821–1895)
To My Grandmother	865
My Mistress's Boots	866

Coventry Patmore (1823–1896)
The Spirit's Epochs	866
The Married Lover	866
If I Were Dead	867

Sidney Dobell (1824–1874)
America	867

Christina Rossetti (1830–1894)
Song ('When I am dead, my dearest')	867
Remember	867
Abnegation	868
Trust	868
Up-Hill	868

Charles Stuart Calverley (1831–1884)
Companions	868

Austin Dobson (1840–1921)
A Dead Letter	869

James Thomson (1834–1882)
Melencolia (*from The City of Dreadful Night*)	870

Arthur O'Shaughnessy (1844–1881)
Has Summer Come without the Rose	871
Ode ('We are the music makers')	871

Robert Bridges (1844–1930)
The Growth of Love	871
Moonlight	872

CONTENTS

	PAGE
Alice Meynell (1848–1922)	
Parted	872
The Lady Poverty	872
The Shepherdess	872
William Ernest Henley (1849–1903)	
Out of the Night that Covers Me	872
Pro Rege Nostro	873
Sir William Watson (1856–1935)	
Wordsworth's Grave	873
John Davidson (1857–1909)	
Thirty Bob a Week	873
Francis Thompson (1859–1907)	
The Hound of Heaven	875
Alfred Edward Housman (1859–1936)	
A Shropshire Lad:	
IV. Reveille	876
V.	877
XXXI. The New Mistress	877
XLI.	877
XLIX.	877
Sir Henry Newbolt (1862–)	
Drake's Drum	878
Vitaï Lampada	878
Clifton Chapel	878
Rudyard Kipling (1865–1936)	
The Ballad of East and West	879
Danny Deever	880
Recessional	881
William Butler Yeats (1865–)	
The Lake Isle of Innisfree	881
Into the Twilight	881
Red Hanrahan's Song about Ireland	882
Song (*from The Land of Heart's Desire*)	882
'A. E.' [George Russell] (1862–1935)	
The Earth Breath	882
Thomas Henry Huxley (1825–1895)	
Emancipation—Black and White	884
Samuel Butler (1835–1902)	
The Note-books	887
Young People	887
The Family	888
Unconscious Humor	888
Homer's *Odyssey*	888
Melchisedec	888
Bacon for Breakfast	888
God and Man	888
The Homeric Deity and the *Pall Mall Gazette*	889
Good Breeding the Summum Bonum	889
Advice to the Young	889
Religion	889
Heaven and Hell	889
Priggishness	889
Lohengrin	889
Swells	889
Science and Religion	889
Gentleman	890
The Finest Men	890
On Being a Swell All Round	890
Money	890
A Luxurious Death	890
Money, Health and Reputation	890
Solicitors	890
Doctors	890
Priests	890
Walter Horatio Pater (1839–1894)	
Style	891
Robert Louis Stevenson (1850–1894)	
The Foreigner at Home	902
A Child's Garden of Verses:	
Whole Duty of Children	907
Bed in Summer	907
System	907
Happy Thought	907
To Auntie	907
In the States	907
Heather Ale	907
George Moore (1852–1933)	
The Organization of Art	909
George Bernard Shaw (1856–)	
The Case for the Critic Dramatist	912

THE TWENTIETH CENTURY

HISTORICAL INTRODUCTION AND TABLE OF DATES ... 915

EARLY TWENTIETH-CENTURY PROSE

Joseph Conrad (1857–1924)	
With the Marseilles Pilots	917
H. G. Wells (1866–)	
The Contemporary Novel	921
John Galsworthy (1867–1933)	
The Lost Dog	925
Arnold Bennett (1867–1931)	
Salary Earning Girls	927

GEORGIAN PROSE

Gilbert K. Chesterton (1873–1936)	
The Return of the Barbarian	929
Max Beerbohm (1872–)	
William and Mary	934
W. H. Hudson (1841–1922)	
My First Visit to Buenos Ayres	939
Lytton Strachey (1880–1932)	
The Last Years of Queen Victoria	943
Hugh Walpole (1884–)	
Romance and Realism	948
Aldous Huxley (1894–)	
At Sea	950
T. S. Eliot (1888–)	
The Criticism of Poetry	951
Virginia Woolf	
The Patron and the Crocus	954
John Buchan, Lord Tweedsmuir (1875–)	
England after the War	955

TWENTIETH-CENTURY POETRY

John Masefield (1874–)	
Sea-Fever	959
Hilaire Belloc (1870–)	
The South Country	959

CONTENTS

Walter de la Mare (1873–)
   All That's Past ... 960
   Miss Loo ... 960

Rupert Brooke (1887–1915)
   The Old Vicarage, Grantchester ... 961

James Elroy Flecker (1884–1915)
   The Ballad of Iskander ... 962

POEMS OF THE GREAT WAR

Laurence Binyon
   For the Fallen ... 964

Rupert Brooke
   The Soldier ... 964

Gilbert K. Chesterton
   The Wife of Flanders ... 964

Robert Offley Ashburton, Lord Crewe
   A Harrow Grave in Flanders ... 965

Walter de la Mare
   'How Sleep the Brave' ... 965

John Drinkwater
   The Defenders ... 965

W. W. Gibson
   Raining ... 965
   The Question ... 965
   His Father ... 965

Gregg Goddard
   The Airman ... 966

Julian Grenfell
   Into Battle ... 966

Nora Griffiths
   The Wykhamist ... 966

Maurice Hewlett
   Soldier, Soldier ... 966

Winifred M. Letts
   The Spires of Oxford ... 967

Rose Macaulay
   Many Sisters to Many Brothers ... 967

John Masefield
   The Island of Skyros ... 967

Alfred Noyes
   The Searchlights ... 968

Stephen Phillips
   Revenge for Rheims ... 968

Jessie Pope
   Socks ... 968

Charles Hamilton Sorley
   'All the Hills and Vales Along' ... 969

Katharine Tynan
   A Girl's Song ... 969

Iolo Aneurin Williams
   From a Flemish Graveyard ... 969

AFTER THE WAR

G. W. Armitage
   Lancashire ... 970

Joseph Campbell (1881–)
   I Am the Mountainy Singer ... 973

Padraic Colum (1881–)
   The Plougher ... 973
   What the Shuiler Said as She Lay by the Fire in the Farmer's House ... 973

William H. Davies (1870–)
   Leisure ... 974
   Money ... 974
   Sheep ... 974
   The Muse ... 974

T. S. Eliot (1888–)
   The *Boston Evening Transcript* ... 974
   Aunt Helen ... 975
   Cousin Nancy ... 975

John Freeman (1880–1929)
   English Hills ... 975
   Happy is England Now ... 975

Robert Graves (1895–)
   Not Dead ... 975
   Over the Brazier ... 976

Thomas Hardy (1840–1928)
   For Life I Had Never Cared Greatly ... 976
   Afterwards ... 976
   The Coming of the End ... 977

Ralph Hodgson (1879–)
   Eve ... 977
   The Bull ... 978

D. H. Lawrence (1885–1931)
   The Bride ... 979
   Study ... 979

Susan L. Mitchell
   Ambition in Cuffe Street ... 980
   How Would It Be? ... 980

Harold Monro (1879–1932)
   The Rebellious Vine ... 980
   Change of Mind ... 980
   Suburb ... 981
   Milk for the Cat ... 981

Siegfried Sassoon (1886–)
   The Old Huntsman ... 982

James Stephens (1882–)
   What Thomas An Buile Said in a Pub ... 984

Edward Thomas (1878–1917)
   Sowing ... 984
   Bright Clouds ... 984
   The Gallows ... 984

NOTES ... 985
INDEX OF AUTHORS ... 1089
INDEX OF ILLUSTRATIONS ... 1098
INDEX OF TITLES ... 1091
INDEX OF FIRST LINES ... 1099
MAP ... *Inside Back Cover*

LIST OF ILLUSTRATIONS

	PAGE
First Page of Beowulf MS.	xvii
From the unique copy in the British Museum	
Chaucer (From a fifteenth-century MS. British Museum)	xviii
Caxton's Malory (Morte d'Arthur, First Edition 1485)	xix

The text may be modernized as follows:

'that ever I heard speak of. I have espied thy King met never yet with worshipful man, but tell him I will have his head without he do me homage.' Then the messenger departed. 'Now is there any here,' said Arthur, 'that knoweth King Ryons?' Then answered a knight that hight Naram, 'Sire, I know the King well; he is a passing good man of his body as few be living, and a passing proud man; and, Sire, doubt ye not he will make war on you with a mighty puissance.' 'Well,' said Arthur, 'I shall ordain for him in short time.'

Chapter XXVIII

Then King Arthur let send for all the children born on May-day begotten of lords and born of ladies, for Merlin told King Arthur that he that should destroy him should be born on May-day, wherefore he sent for them all upon pain of death. And so there were found many lords' sons, and all were sent unto the King, and so was Mordred sent by King Lot's wife, and all were put in a ship to the sea, and some were four weeks old, and some less. And so by fortune the ship drove unto a castle, and was all toriven, and destroyed the most part, save that Mordred was cast up, and a good man found him, and nourished him till he was fourteen years old, and then he brought him to the Court, as it rehearseth afterward toward the end of the Death of Arthur. So many lords and barons of this realm were displeased, for their children were so lost, and many put the blame on Merlin more than on Arthur; so what for dread and for love they held their peace. But when the messenger came to King Ryons, then was he angry out of measure, and provided himself with a great host, as it rehearseth after in the book of Balin the Savage that followeth next after, how by adventure Balin got the sword.

Book First ends
Book Second begins

After the death of Uther Pendragon reigned Arthur his son, the which had great war in his days for to get all England into his hand. For there were many kings within the realm of England, and in Wales, Scotland, and Cornwall. So it befell on a time when King Arthur

Hakluyt's Voyages (Title Page of First Edition, 1589)	xx
Sir Walter Raleigh	xxi
Edmund Spenser	xxii
Dedication of the Faerie Queene (Second Edition, 1596)	xxiii
Shakespeare's Bust in Stratford Church	xxiv
First Folio Title Page (1623)	xxv
Sir Philip Sidney	xxvi
John Donne	xxvii
Francis Bacon (Robed as Lord Chancellor)	xxviii
Bacon's Essays Title Page First Edition (1597)	xxix
John Milton	xxx
Paradise Lost Title Page First Edition (1667)	xxxi
John Bunyan	xxxii
Pilgrim's Progress Title Page (1678)	xxxiii

LIST OF ILLUSTRATIONS

	PAGE
John Dryden	xxxiv
Samuel Pepys	xxxv
Daniel Defoe	xxxvi
Jonathan Swift	xxxvii
Alexander Pope	xxxviii
Thomas Gray	xxxix
Johnson, Boswell, Goldsmith, Burke	xl
Boswell's Johnson Title Page First Edition (1791)	xli
William Cowper	xlii
Robert Burns	xliii
Lyrical Ballads Second Edition (1800)	xliv
William Wordsworth as a Young Man	xlv
Samuel Taylor Coleridge at Twenty-three	xlvi
Sir Walter Scott	xlvii
Charles Lamb	xlviii
Lord Byron	xlix
Percy Bysshe Shelley	l
John Keats in His Sitting Room at Hampstead	li
Lord Macaulay	lii
Thomas Carlyle in 1865	liii
Cardinal Newman	liv
John Ruskin in Old Age	lv
Lord Tennyson	lvi
Robert Browning at Forty-seven	lvii
Matthew Arnold	lviii
Algernon Charles Swinburne	lix
Robert Louis Stevenson	lx
Wells, Kipling, Bennett, Galsworthy	lxi
Bernard Shaw	lxii
Lytton Strachey	lxiii
John Masefield, Aldous Huxley, Virginia Woolf, D. H. Lawrence	lxiv

HWÆT WE GARDE

na ingear dagum. þeod cyninga
þrym gefrunon huða æþelingas elle[n]
fremedon. oft scyld scefing sceaþe[na]
þreatum monegũ mægþum meodo setl[a]
ofteah egsode eorl syððan ærest w[earð]
fea sceaft funden he þæs frofre geba[d]
weox under wolcnum weorð myndum þah
oð þ him æghwylc þara ymb sittendra
ofer hron rade hyran scolde gomban
gyldan þ wæs god cyning. ðæm eafera wæs
æfter cenned geong in geardum þone god
sende folce tofrofre fyren ðearfe on
geat þ hie ær drugon aldor ..ase lange
hwile him þæs lif frea wuldres weald[end]
worold are forgeaf beowulf wæs breme
blæd wide sprang scyld.. eafera scede
landum in. Swa sceal .... geong
.e gewyrcean fromum feoh....... on fæder ......

FIRST PAGE OF BEOWULF MS

xviii

CHAUCER

that euer I herd spoke of / I haue aspyed / thy kynge met ne=
uer yet with worshipful man / but telle hym / I wyll haue his
hede without he doo me homage / thenne the messager departed
¶ Now is there ony here said Arthur that knoweth kyng Ry
ons / thenne ansuerd a knyght that hyght Naram / Syre I kno
we the kynge wel / he is a passyng good man of his body / as
fewe ben lyuynge / and a passyng prowde man / and sir doubte
ye not / he wille make warre on yow with a myghty puyssa=
unce / wel said Arthur I shall ordeyne for hym in short tyme

¶ Capitulum xxviij

THenne kyng arthur lete sende for al the children born on
may day begoten of lordes & born of ladyes / for Merlyn
told kynge Arthur that he that shold destroye hym / shold be
borne in may day / wherfor he sent for hem all vpon payn of deth
and so ther were founde many lordes sones / and all were sente
vnto the kynge / and soo was Mordred sente by kyng Lotts
wyf / and all were put in a ship to the see / and some were iiij
wekes old and some lasse / And so by fortune the shyp drofe
vnto a castel and was al to ryuen and destroyed the most part
sauf that Mordred was cast vp and a good man fonde hym /
and nouryshed hym tyl he was xiiij yere olde / & thenne he
brought hym to the Court / as it rehercith afterward toward
the ende of the deth of Arthur / So many lordes and barons of
this reame were displeasyd / for her children were so lost / and
many put the wyte on Merlyn more than on Arthur / so what
for drede and for loue they helde their pees / But whanne the
messager came to kynge Ryons / thenne was he wood oute of
mesure and purueyed hym for a grete hoost as it rehercyth af=
ter in the book of Balyn le sauuage that foloweth next after /
how by aduenture Balyn gat the swerd

¶ Explicit liber primus
¶ Incipit liber secundus

AFter the dethe of Vtherpendragon regned Ar=
thur his sone / the whiche had grete werre in his
dayes for to gete al Englond in to his hand /
For there were many kynges within the real=
me of Englond and in walys / Scotland / and
Cornewaille / Soo it befelle on a tyme / whanne kyng Arthur

CAXTON'S MALORY, PAGE 75

THE PRINCIPALL NAVIGATIONS, VOIA-
GES AND DISCOVERIES OF THE
English nation, made by Sea or ouer Land,

to the most remote and farthest distant Quarters of
the earth at any time within the compasse
of these 1500. yeeres: Deuided into three
seuerall parts, according to the positions of the Regions wherun-
to they were directed.

The first, conteining the personall trauels of the English vnto *Iudæa, Syria, A-rabia,* the riuer *Euphrates, Babylon, Balsara,* the *Persian* Gulfe, *Ormuz, Chaul, Goa, India,* and many Islands adioyning to the South parts of *Asia*: together with the like vnto *Egypt,* the chiefest ports and places of *Africa* within and without the Streight of *Gibraltar,* and about the famous Promontorie of *Buona Esperança.*

The second, comprehending the worthy discoueries of the English towards the North and Northeast by Sea, as of *Lapland, Scrikfinia, Corelia,* the Baie of *S. Nicholas,* the Isles of *Colgoieue, Vaigats,* and *Noua Zembla* toward the great riuer *Ob,* with the mightie Empire of *Russia,* the *Caspian* Sea, *Georgia, Armenia, Media, Persia, Boghar* in *Bactria,* & diuers kingdoms of *Tartaria.*

The third and last, including the English valiant attempts in searching almost all the corners of the vaste and new world of *America,* from 73. degrees of Northerly latitude Southward, to *Meta Incognita, Newfoundland,* the maine of *Virginia,* the point of *Florida,* the Baie of *Mexico,* all the Inland of *Noua Hispania,* the coast of *Terra firma, Brasill,* the riuer of *Plate,* to the Streight of *Magellan:* and through it, and from it in the South Sea to *Chili, Peru, Xalisco,* the Gulfe of *California, Noua Albion* vpon the backside of *Canada,* further then euer any Christian hitherto hath pierced.

Whereunto is added the last most renowmed *English* Nauigation,
round about the whole Globe of the Earth.

By Richard Hakluyt Master of Artes, and Student sometime
of Christ-church in Oxford.

Imprinted at London by GEORGE BISHOP
and RALPH NEWBERIE, Deputies to
CHRISTOPHER BARKER, Printer to the
Queenes most excellent Maiestie.

1589.

SIR WALTER RALEIGH

EDMUND SPENSER

TO
THE MOST HIGH,
MIGHTIE
And
MAGNIFICENT
EMPRESSE RENOV-
MED FOR PIETIE, VER-
TVE, AND ALL GRATIOVS
GOVERNMENT ELIZABETH BY
THE GRACE OF GOD QVEENE
OF ENGLAND FRAVNCE AND
IRELAND AND OF VIRGI-
NIA, DEFENDOVR OF THE
FAITH, &c. H·ER MOST
HVMBLE SERVAVNT
EDMVND SPENSER
DOTH IN ALL HV-
MILITIE DEDI-
CATE, PRE-
SENT
AND CONSECRATE THESE
HIS LABOVRS TO LIVE
VVITH THE ETERNI-
TIE OF HER
FAME.

DEDICATION OF THE FAERIE QUEENE, SECOND EDITION (1596)

SHAKESPEARE'S BUST IN STRATFORD CHURCH

Mr. WILLIAM SHAKESPEARES
COMEDIES, HISTORIES, & TRAGEDIES.

Published according to the True Originall Copies.

Martin Droeshout sculpsit London.

LONDON
Printed by Isaac Iaggard, and Ed. Blount. 1623.

xxvi

SIR PHILIP SIDNEY

JOHN DONNE

FRANCIS BACON, LORD VERULAM

Essayes.

Religious Meditations.

Places of perswasion and disswasion.

Seene and allowed.

At LONDON,
Printed for Humfrey Hooper, and are
to be sold at the blacke Beare
in Chauncery Lane.
1 5 9 7.

TITLE PAGE OF BACON'S ESSAYS, FIRST EDITION

Paradise lost.

A POEM

Written in
TEN BOOKS

By *JOHN MILTON*.

Licenſed and Entred according to Order.

LONDON

Printed, and are to be ſold by *Peter Parker* under *Creed* Church neer *Aldgate*; And by *Robert Boulter* at the *Turks Head* in *Biſhopſgate-ſtreet*; And *Matthias Walker*, under St. *Dunſtons* Church in *Fleet-ſtreet*, 1667.

THE
Pilgrim's Progress
FROM
THIS WORLD,
TO
That which is to come:

Delivered under the Similitude of a
DREAM

Wherein is Discovered,
The manner of his setting out,
His Dangerous Journey; And safe
Arrival at the Desired Countrey.

I have used Similitudes, Hos. 12. 10.

By *John Bunyan.*

Licensed and Entred according to Order.

LONDON,
Printed for *Nath.* Ponder at the *Peacock*
in the *Poultrey* near *Cornhil*, 1678.

JOHN DRYDEN

SAMUEL PEPYS

DANIEL DEFOE

JONATHAN SWIFT

ALEXANDER POPE

THOMAS GRAY

JOHNSON   BOSWELL

GOLDSMITH   BURKE

THE LIFE
OF
SAMUEL JOHNSON, LL.D.

COMPREHENDING

AN ACCOUNT OF HIS STUDIES
AND NUMEROUS WORKS,
IN CHRONOLOGICAL ORDER;

A SERIES OF HIS EPISTOLARY CORRESPONDENCE
AND CONVERSATIONS WITH MANY EMINENT PERSONS;

AND

VARIOUS ORIGINAL PIECES OF HIS COMPOSITION,
NEVER BEFORE PUBLISHED.

THE WHOLE EXHIBITING A VIEW OF LITERATURE AND LITERARY MEN
IN GREAT-BRITAIN, FOR NEAR HALF A CENTURY,
DURING WHICH HE FLOURISHED.

IN TWO VOLUMES.

BY JAMES BOSWELL, Esq.

——— *Quò fit ut* OMNIS
Votiva pateat veluti descripta tabella
VITA SENIS.——— HORAT.

VOLUME THE FIRST.

LONDON:
PRINTED BY HENRY BALDWIN,
FOR CHARLES DILLY, IN THE POULTRY.
M DCC XCI.

XLII

WILLIAM COWPER

ROBERT BURNS

LYRICAL BALLADS,

WITH

OTHER POEMS.

IN TWO VOLUMES.

By W. WORDSWORTH.

Quam nihil ad genium, Papiniane, tuum!

VOL. I.

SECOND EDITION.

LONDON:

PRINTED FOR T. N. LONGMAN AND O. REES, PATERNOSTER-ROW,

BY BIGGS AND CO. BRISTOL.

1800.

WILLIAM WORDSWORTH

xlvi

SAMUEL TAYLOR COLERIDGE

SIR WALTER SCOTT

CHARLES LAMB

LORD BYRON

L

Percy B Shelley.

JOHN KEATS

LORD MACAULAY

Thomas Carlyle (Chelsea, 1865)

John H Newman

JOHN RUSKIN

LORD TENNYSON

ROBERT BROWNING

MATTHEW ARNOLD

ALGERNON CHARLES SWINBURNE

ROBERT LOUIS STEVENSON

WELLS

KIPLING

BENNETT

GALSWORTHY

G Bernard Shaw

LXiii

LYTTON STRACHEY

JOHN MASEFIELD

ALDOUS HUXLEY

VIRGINIA WOOLF

D. H. LAWRENCE

CENTURY READINGS
IN ENGLISH LITERATURE

EARLY ENGLISH LITERATURE

THE beginnings of English literature are to be found among certain groups of Teutonic peoples—Angles, Saxons, and Jutes—who, in a succession of migrations during the fifth and sixth centuries, left the Continent, invaded Britain, and took possession of the southern half of the island. These Anglo-Saxon colonizers were heathen, worshiping Germanic deities such as Woden and Thor. They formed a number of separate settlements, which, by the seventh century, were organized into some seven or eight distinct kingdoms; and these, in the ninth century, were united, more or less effectually, under Egbert, as over-lord. The Angles—who may have outnumbered the other invading tribes—eventually gave their name to the whole island, and to the language that developed there out of the several related Germanic dialects.

In the early cultural history of England the most important occurrence was the introduction of Christianity, during the sixth and seventh centuries, through the labors of Saint Augustine and his missionaries in the south, and of Irish monks in the north. Numerous monasteries were established throughout the country, and it is in these religious houses that much of our earliest English literature was written down. Since the monks were inevitably hostile to the pagan literature of the original Germanic settlers, their impulse was either to suppress it or to Christianize it. Hence virtually all of the earliest compositions in English which survive have a more or less Christian aspect.

Among the poems which are essentially heathen, and least affected by Christian elements, may be mentioned *The Seafarer*, *The Wanderer*, *The Ruins*, *The Fight at Finnsburg*, *Deor's Lament*, and *Widsith* ('Far-Wanderer'). In the last of these, a professional minstrel, or 'scop,' relates his wanderings from country to country, and hall to hall, and thus gives us some impression of the circumstances under which heathen poetry was written and sung. Of immensely larger range than these shorter poems is the epic, *Beowulf*.

The purely Christian poetry of the early English period is best represented by the so-called Cædmonian poems, which are chiefly versifications of parts of the Biblical *Genesis*, *Exodus*, and *Book of Daniel*. These poems were formerly ascribed to a cowherd, named Cædmon, in the monastery of Whitby, who lived in the seventh century, and who is known to have written Biblical paraphrases. The surviving pieces mentioned above, however, are no longer attributed to this particular author. During the eighth century a highly cultivated poet, Cynewulf, wrote his *Crist*, *Elene*, *Juliana*, and possibly other Christian compositions. With these religious works may be associated the prose translations of Latin works, made by King Alfred (871–901), the most interesting of which is *On the Consolation of Philosophy*, from the original of Boethius. Alfred's productions, however, belong more properly to learning rather than to literature.

All the early English poetry mentioned above is written in an alliterative meter, of which the unit is a long line, of an irregular number of syllables, divided into two parts. Each part has two particularly strong metrical accents, and the two divisions of the long line are bound together by alliteration: that is, by beginning two or three of the accented syllables with the same consonant, or with a vowel sound. Although the alliterative meter ceased to be common after the eleventh century, it was employed in certain important poems down to the sixteenth century, and the riming of initial sounds of words has been occasionally used as a form of poetical ornament in still more recent compositions.

The first period of English, or Anglo-Saxon, literature was brought to a close with the coming of the Normans under William the Conqueror in 1066. This new conquest had a momentous effect upon English society and letters through bringing them into closer relation with the culture of the Continent. The Normans brought with them the civilization of France, including a feudal system of government, a large body of literature and learning, new metrical forms, and a fresh literary refinement. The eventual effect upon the English language was the simplifying of its grammar, and the addition to it of numerous words and phrases of French origin. In its structure and common vocabulary the language remained English, but the elaborate system of inflections which had prevailed before the Norman Conquest gradually disappeared. The introduction of new metrical forms into England effected a compromise between the alliteration, accent, and irregularity in the number of syllables in the earlier English verse, and the rime, unstressed movement, and syllabic regularity of the French. The result was the use of rime, the retention of accent, and the regularizing of the number of syllables. The eventual refinement of these characteristics is seen in the verse of Chaucer.

Of the new forms of literature cultivated in England during several centuries following the Norman Conquest the most significant is romance. A romance may be described as a fictitious story of heroic, marvelous, or supernatural incidents, derived from history or from popular tradition, and written at considerable length, either in verse or in prose, by a conscious literary artist, for refined and courtly readers. In accordance with their subjects the great majority of the writings of this sort fall into four large divisions, or cycles. A considerable number of romances treat stories from antiquity, such as those concerning Alexander, Æneas, and the cities of Thebes and Troy. Others, such as *The Geste of King Horn*, *Havelok the Dane*, *Guy of Warwick*, and *Bevis of Hampton*, deal with distinctively English themes. A third group recount the adventures of French national heroes, such as Charlemagne and Roland. Most acceptable of all to most modern readers, finally, are the romances of Celtic origin and French fashioning which present the courtly life and achievements of King Arthur and the knights of the Round Table. To this last group belongs *Sir Gawain and the Green Knight*, generally regarded as among the finest of mediæval literary productions. The ideals of conduct embodied in the romances as a whole belong to the system known as chivalry. The chivalric hero is usually of noble birth, and skilled in the arts of war. His normal occupations are adventurous wanderings, in the course of which he frequently rescues ladies in distress, kills monsters, participates in tournaments, and serves his lord in battle. In his acts he is guided chiefly by his refined devotion to religion and to womankind.

Beside romances the early period of English literature provided a considerable body of shorter narratives, such as *exempla*, or anecdotes for enlivening sermons, *fabliaux*, or versified short stories from the lower ranges of contemporary society, and short romantic tales more or less similar in tone to the romances themselves. A perennial feeling for music produced a variety of songs, religious, amorous, satirical, and patriotic. Formal religious works took such forms as collections of sermons, manuals of instruction, and legends of saints. Religious doctrine is attractively combined with personal feeling in the unique elegy known as *Pearl*. With the Church one must associate also the beginnings of English drama. The earliest dramatic performances were simple accompaniments of Christian worship, written in Latin. Eventually, however, they were put into English and were enlarged in scope under secular auspices outside the Church, the result being plays like *Noah's Flood*, acted upon large wagons in the open air by the craft guilds of Chester.

BEOWULF

BEOWULF, the hero of this poem, may have been a real person. Although he does not actually appear in sober history, his uncle, Hygelac of the poem, is identified with an historical Scandinavian leader who invaded the land of his enemies on the Lower Rhine during the early part of the sixth century (See Section XXXIV of the text below). Even though the uncle was disastrously defeated in this foray, the nephew may have acquired fame through deeds of which no authentic record is preserved. The chief adventures of Beowulf in the poem before us, however, arise not from history but from a widely distributed folk-tale, according to which a young hero has victorious encounters with two supernatural beings, one in a dwelling above ground, and the other beneath the surface of the earth. For the further glorifying of the hero the Anglo-Saxon poet added the somewhat conventional tale of his encounter with a dragon. As the result of this combining of folk-tales and historical events we can discern in *Beowulf* some four separate episodes: (1) a fight with Grendel, (2) a fight with Grendel's mother, (3) the triumphant return of the hero to his home, and (4) a fight with a dragon. After having been recounted in Scandinavian countries these stories, in a metrical form, were probably brought to Britain by Anglians during the latter part of the sixth century. At the end of the seventh century, or the beginning of the eighth, an Anglo-Saxon poet composed *Beowulf* in virtually the form now preserved for us in a manuscript of the tenth century. This author was a sophisticated man of letters writing for a courtly audience. To him we attribute both the somewhat elaborate poetical language and the Christian coloring of the narrative. This Christian element, it will be observed, is applied to the poem somewhat superficially and incongruously; it is not an organic part of the narrative. The genuine vitality of the epic is pagan.

BEOWULF
THE OPENING

WHAT ho! We've heard the glory ·
                  of Spear-Danes, clansmen-kings,
Their deeds of olden story,— ·
                  how fought the æthelings!
Often Scyld Scefing   ·   reft his foemen all,
Reft the tribes at wassail ·
                  of bench and mead in hall.
Smote the jarls with terror; ·
                  gat good recompense 5
For that he came a foundling, ·
                  a child with no defense:
He waxed beneath the welkin, ·
                  grew in honors great,
Till each and every people, ·
                  of those around who sate
Off beyond the whale-road, ·
                  to him was underling,
To him must tender toll-fee. ·
                  That was a goodly King! 10

UNTO him thereafter,   ·   was an heir y-born,
Within his gates a youngling, ·
                  whom God that folk forlorn
For recompense was sending.
                  He marked the grievous wrong,
How they of old had suffered, ·
                  without a prince so long.

And so the Wonder-Wielder, ·
                  the Lord of Life, fulfilled 15
For them world's weal and honor, ·
                  through him, the heir of Scyld.
For famous was this Beowulf, ·
                  and far and wide there came
O'er the lands of Scandia ·
                  the vaunting of his name.
So shall youth achieve it, ·
                  with good works before,
With bold gifts and largesse, ·
                  from his father's store, 20
That in old age after, ·
                  when the wars may come,
Willing comrades, liegemen loyal, ·
                  may stand by at home.
Praiseful deed will bring good speed ·
                  in what clan soe'er.

THEN did Scyld betake him, ·
                  when his hour was there,
The stout and staunch betook himself ·
                  to his Lord's good care. 25
Then away they bore him ·
                  to the sea-tides,—did,
They, his loving clansmen, · as himself had bid,
Whilst he wielded speech-craft, ·
                  he, the Scyldings' friend,
Prince so long who ruled them, · dear to the end.
There in haven stood she, ·
                  her prow a rounded ring, 30

Icy and out-bound, · barge of the Ætheling.
Laid they then the dear Chief, ·
    Bracelet-Breaker of old,
Mighty King, by the mast there, ·
    within the good ship's hold.
And full many a treasure, ·
    many a shining thing,
They fetched from ways afar off, ·
    for his journeying. 35
Never heard I tell of · keel more fairly dight
With the warrior-weapons ·
    and the weeds of fight,
With the blades and byrnies. · On his bosom lay
Treasure to fare with him · far o'er floods away.
Methinks not less a lading ·
    of lordly gifts they gave 40
Than those who sent him whilom ·
    a lone babe o'er the wave.
O'er his head they set, too, ·
    golden banner steep,
Let the billows bear him, · gave him to the deep.
Theirs were souls of sorrow, ·
    theirs were hearts to weep.
And no man can say sooth,— ·
    none in halls of state, 45
None of battle-bold ones,— ·
    who took up that freight.

THE FIRST PART

I

RULED Beowulf, the Scylding, ·
    in burg for many a year,
Famed among the people, · a folk-king dear
(His father was ta'en elsewhere, ·
    that chief from home was ta'en),
Until for him there woke a son, ·
    the high Halfdane. 50
And Halfdane, named the Agèd ·
    and the Fierce-in-fray,
O'er the gracious Scyldings held, ·
    all his life, the sway.
And, lo, for him four children ·
    (to count them as they be)
Awoke unto the world's light: ·
    warrior-leaders three,
Heorogar, and Hrothgar, ·
    and Halga, named the good; 55
And daughter, queen (says story) ·
    in Sweden o'er the flood.

Now was there given to Hrothgar ·
    such valor in the van,
Such honor in the onset, ·
    that all his kin-of-clan
Eagerly obeyed him, ·
    till waxed around his throne
Host of comrade-tribesmen, ·
    warrior-youths well-grown 60
It came into his mood then ·
    to bid his serfs up-raise

A hall-chamber, a mead-house, ·
    a mightier far for praise
Than sons of men e'er heard of, ·
    and then within the hall
Unto young and unto old ·
    to deal his treasures all,
Such as God had lent him, ·
    except men's lives and lands. 65
To many tribes (I've heard too) ·
    he gave his wide commands
Around this earth to deck it, ·
    this folkstead, with their hands.
Nor was it long thereafter, ·
    men saw its finished frame,
The greatest of hall-houses: ·
    Heorot was the name
That he whose word was mighty ·
    had fashioned for the same. 70
He failed not of his vaunting, ·
    he dealt the rings thereby,
The treasure at carousal. ·
    Heorot towered high,
With stag-horn on each gable ·
    . . . waiting its fiery fate,
The burning after battle; ·
    nor far the day when hate,
After old feuds, should waken, ·
    once more betwixt the twain— 75
Betwixt the daughter's father ·
    and him her wedded thane.
But now that bold Hobgoblin, ·
    who dwelt in fenways dark,
Ill bore the sullen grievance ·
    that he each day must hark
To revel loud at banquet. ·
    The noise of harp was there,
In hall clear song of singer. ·
    He spake who knew full fair 80
To tell mankind's beginning, ·
    how God Almighty wrought
The earth, that shining lea-land, ·
    which waters fold about;
Quoth how God set, triumphant, ·
    the sun and the moon
As lights to lighten landsfolk; ·
    how he adornèd soon
With leaf and limb the fold all; ·
    and eke created birth 85
For every kind that moveth ·
    on ocean, air, or earth.

So lived the troop of tribesmen, ·
    in revel, wise and well,
Till One began to do misdeed— ·
    this selfsame Fiend of hell.
And that grim Hobgoblin ·
    was Grendel named by men,
Great Stalker of the marches, ·
    who held the moor and fen; 90
Housed with the brood of giants ·
    this joyless Wight the while,

After Lord Creator ·
    had doomed his damned exile.
(Upon Cain's kin the Eternal ·
    avengèd Abel's blood.
Cain gat no mirth from murder; ·
    God banished him from good,
Afar from man, for sin's sake. ·
    Thence woke the monster-brood, 95
Ettins, elves, and ogres, ·
    and giants, too, that warred
So long with God, who paid them ·
    at last their fit reward.)

II

THEN fared he forth, did Grendel, ·
    to seek at dead of night
The high house, how the Ring-Danes,
    after their beer, were dight.
The æthelings he found there, ·
    aslumber after mirth; 100
Naught they knew of sorrow, ·
    naught of human dearth.
The Creature of damnation, ·
    the grim, the greedy One,
The fierce One in his fury, ·
    was ready there anon;
And, where they rested, reft he ·
    thirty, thane by thane,
And thence went faring homeward, ·
    of his plunder fain, 105
With his fill of slaughter, · to seek his lairs again.

IN the dawning, at the daybreak, ·
    arose of men the wail,
A mickle morning-uproar, ·
    after their yester-ale,
When Grendel's strength in battle ·
    to sons of men was plain.
Blitheless sate the high Prince, ·
    the Ætheling so good; 110
That strong Heart stricken sate, ·
    o'er lost thanes abroad,
What time the court set eyes on ·
    the cursèd Monster's trail,—
Too strong that strife for Danefolk, ·
    too long the bane and bale.

EFTSOONS, but one night after, ·
    was he at work once more,
With more of loathly slaughter, ·
    nor mourned a whit therefor, 115
A whit for feud and foul deed— ·
    in sin was he so bound!
Then might ye mark full many ·
    who somewhat further found
Resting-places elsewhere,— ·
    in outer bowers their bed,
When, by so clear a token, ·
    to them was soothly said
The hate of this new Hall-Thane. ·
    More far, more tight, all such 120
Did keep themselves thereafter ·
    who 'scaped that devil's clutch!
So ruled he and so ravaged, ·
    in wrong the one 'gainst all,
Till idle stood and empty · that excelling hall.
Mickle long the while was: · twelve winters' tide
Hrothgar dreed disaster, ·
    woes with never end, 125
Sorrows unbounded, · he, the Scyldings' Friend.
And the mournful tidings ·
    to courts and kingdoms wide
In gleemen's ballads travelled, ·
    how Grendel's hate defied
Hrothgar forever, · how for many a year
Grendel waged his warfare, ·
    strife of ceaseless fear; 130
Would not, by a peace-pact, ·
    set the Danemen free,
Would not with the Æthelings ·
    e'er compound for fee.
And still less might any ·
    of the Wise-men wot,
'Gainst those paws of pillage, ·
    help for Hrothgar's lot.
The grisly Wretch kept reaving ·
    youth and age of breath; 135
He lurked, he lured them darkly, ·
    that skulking Shade of Death;
Made, through nights eternal, ·
    misty moors his home;
Though beyond man's ken the haunts, ·
    where Hell's wizards roam.
Such a tale of terrors, ·
    such heap of hard despite
Wrought this Foe of mankind, ·
    Stalker lone by night. 140
Heorot Hall, the gold-bright, ·
    was his dusky den.
(Yet not his the power— ·
    God forbade him then!—
E'er to greet the gift-stool, · e'er to come anear
Throne itself of Hrothgar, ·
    nor partake its cheer.)
And so soul of Hrothgar, ·
    Scylding good and great, 145
Long was wracked and broken.
    And chiefs together sate
Oft at rede, devising, · what to do were best,
For such stout-hearted clansmen, ·
    against such awful guest.

WHILES at their idol-temples ·
    they vowed their offerings fair,
And conjured the Soul-Destroyer, ·
    for help in folk-despair. 150
Such was their devil-practice, ·
    and hope of these heathen men,
'Twas Hell in their hearts they remembered; ·
    and God was not in their ken.
The Doomsman of Deeds, they wist not; ·
    wist not the Lord of Love;

Nor worshipped the Wielder-of-Wonders, ·
    the Helm of the Heavens above.
Woe to the soul that perversely ·
    shall fling to the fiery pit, 155
Never to ween of comfort, ·
    never to change a whit;
Weal to the soul that after ·
    the day of his death is come
May seek the Lord and crave there ·
    in arms of the Father a home.

III

AND so the son of Halfdane ·
    was carked by cares which bide,
Nor might the brave and wise One ·
    the sorrow turn aside: 160
Too big the strife for Danefolk, ·
    too long the bale and bane,
This hugest of night-horrors, ·
    that on his people came.
Far in his home, that good man, ·
    among the Geatish breeds,
Hyglac's thane and nephew, ·
    got word of Grendel's deeds.
Of all mankind the strongest ·
    in might and main was he, 165
In the days of this our life here, ·
    high-born and free.
Bade make ready for him · a rider-of-the-sea;
Quoth, he'd seek this War-King, ·
    o'er the swan-road, he!—
Seek this noble Chieftain, ·
    'for that 't is men he needs.'
The canny carls did chide him ·
    (though he to them was dear) 170
Little for his faring; ·
    nay, rather spake him cheer,
Him the battle-brave One, ·
    and looked for omens clear.
The Good One of the Geatfolk ·
    now picked his comrades keen:
When he sought his timbered vessel, ·
    he was one of bold fifteen;
And well he kenned the coast-marks, ·
    wise in sailor-craft. 175

THE boat ere long they launchèd, ·
    under the bluffs abaft;
The ready warriors clambered ·
    over the wave-tossed side;
Against the sands the breakers ·
    were writhing with the tide;
On the breast of the bark the heroes ·
    bore their bright array,
Their battle-gear so gorgeous. ·
    They pushed the bark away, 180
Away on its eager voyage. ·
    The well-braced floater flew,
The foamy-necked, the bird-like, ·
    before the winds that blew,
Over the waves of the waters— ·
    till, after the risen sun
Of the next day, the curved prow ·
    her course so well had run
That these faring-men the land saw, ·
    the cliffs aglow o'er the deep, 185
Broad sea promontories, · high hills steep.
Ocean now was o'er-wandered, ·
    now was their voyaging o'er.
Thence clomb the Weder-clansmen ·
    speedily up on the shore;
Anchored well their sea-wood, ·
    whilst their armor clanked,
Their mailèd sarks of battle; ·
    God Almighty thanked 190
Because for them the sea-paths ·
    had not been made too hard.

THEN from the wall the Watchman, ·
    the Scylding set to guard
The water-cliffs, espied them ·
    over the gangway bear
Their glittering shields of linden, ·
    their ready fighting-gear.
His wits were seized with wonder, ·
    what men were these indeed! 195
Down to the strand he gat him, ·
    riding on a steed;
Henchman, he, of Hrothgar,— ·
    mightily did shake
With his hands his spear-shaft, ·
    and in parley spake:
'What are ye, ye mail-clad, ·
    what armor-bearing braves,
Who lead a keel so high-prowed ·
    hither o'er the waves, 200
O'er the ocean causeway? ·
    I've been out-post long,
Long I've held the sea-watch, · lest a pirate throng
In their fleet might some time ·
    do our Daneland wrong.
Here have strangers never ·
    made them more at home;
Yet to you no word-of-leave ·
    from my kin hath come, 205
No consent from braves here. · Never did I view
O'er earth a mightier jarlman, ·
    than is one of you,—
That Hero in his harness: ·
    yon Man in weapons dight,
He is no mere retainer, · if tells his face aright,
His peerless port and presence! ·
    But know I must your kin, 210
Your home, before from hence ye ·
    (as if some spies ye bin)
Farther fare on Daneland. ·
    Ye boatmen of the brine,
Ye far-off dwellers, hear now ·
    this simple thought of mine:
'T were best forthwith ye tell me ·
    whence your comings be!'

IV

Him answered then the eldest, ·
          the war-band Leader, he, 215
His chest of words unlocking: ·
          'Of Geatish kin are we,
And Hyglac's hearth-fellows. ·
          Wide was my father's fame;
The high-born Warrior-Chieftain, ·
          and Ecgtheow his name.
He tarried many winters ·
          before he fared away
From his courts, an old man; ·
          and wide o'er earth today 220
Him the wise remember. ·
          In faithful mood we come
Seeking the son of Halfdane, ·
          thy Folk-King at home.
Be to us good of guidance. ·
          To Danemen's monarch bold,
We have a mickle errand,— ·
          which must not lurk untold:
Thou wottest if it be so, ·
          as we have heard for sooth, 225
That 'mongst ye Danes some dusky ·
          Scather without ruth,
Some Doer in the dark night, ·
          is dealing spite uncouth,
Dastard shame and carnage. ·
          I can in generous mood
Teach a rede to Hrothgar, ·
          how he, the sage and good,
This Fiend may overmaster,— ·
          if e'er to be it is 230
That toil and teen shall alter, ·
          help come to him and his,
And seething cares grow cooler; ·
          or else forevermore
He tholeth days of sorrow, ·
          dearth so sad and sore,
Whilst there upon its high-place ·
          the best of halls shall bide.'

The Watchman, doughty servitor, ·
          from his steed replied: 235
'Behooveth the keen shieldman, ·
          he who thinketh well,
'Twixt words and works the tokens ·
          cunningly to tell.
I hear this band is friendly ·
          unto the great Scylding:
Bear forth your weeds and weapons; ·
          I'll guide you to my King,
And bid my faithful kin-thanes ·
          'gainst aught of foes to guard 240
Your boat upon the beach here, ·
          this floater newly-tarred,
Till once more, o'er the sea-streams, ·
          the curved-neck timber bear
To Weder-mark the dear men,— ·
          those to whomsoe'er
It shall be granted safely ·
          to bide the coming fray.'

They gat them, then, to fare forth; ·
          at rest the floater lay, 245
On hawser fast at anchor, ·
          broad-breasted ship ashore.
O'er cheek-guards shone the golden ·
          body of the boar—
Flashing, fire-hardened, ·
          keeping a life-guard o'er
The battle-eager Hero. · Together on they sped,
Until they saw the gold-bright ·
          high hall timberèd. 250
Under the wide heavens, ·
          where'er men dwell, was that
The fairest of all houses ·
          wherein King Hrothgar sat;
The light whereof went streaming ·
          out o'er many lands.
Then showed their Guide that gleaming ·
          burg of battle-bands;
Bade their march be forward, ·
          thither where he show'th; 255
Reined around his palfrey, ·
          words thereafter quoth:
'Time for me to fare back; · in his mercy may
The Almighty Father · keep ye safe alway
On your voyage and venture. ·
          I will to the coast,
There to hold my sea-watch ·
          'gainst a hostile host.' 260

V

The street was laid with bright stones; ·
          the road led on the band;
The battle-byrnies shimmered, ·
          the hard, the linked-by-hand;
The iron-rings, the gleaming, ·
          amid their armor sang,
Whilst thither, in dread war-gear, ·
          to hall they marched alang;
The ocean-weary warriors ·
          set down their bucklers wide, 265
Their shields, so hard and hardy, ·
          against that House's side;
They stacked points up, these seamen, ·
          their ash-wood, gray-tipped spears;
And bent to bench, as clankèd ·
          their byrnies, battle-gears—
An iron-troop well-weaponed! ·
          Then proud a Dane forthwith
Did of these men-at-arms there ·
          enquire the kin and kith: 270
'Ye bear these plated bucklers ·
          hither from what realms;
These pilèd shafts of onset, ·
          gray sarks, and visored helms?
The Henchman and the Herald ·
          of Hrothgar, lo, am I!

Never so many strangers ·
                I 've seen of mood more high.
I ween that 't is for prowess, ·
                and not for exile far, 275
That 't is indeed for glory, ·
                that ye have sought Hrothgár.'

THE valor-famed, the proud Prince ·
                of Weders, made reply,
As, hardy under helmet, ·
                he spake his words thereby:
'We 're Hyglac's board-fellows, ·
                Beowulf my name.
I would to son of Halfdane ·
                my errand here proclaim, 280
To the great King, thy Master, ·
                if he but thinketh meet
To grant to us that we may · one so goodly greet.'

WULFGAR made a speech then ·
                (Prince of the Wendels, he,
For soul of war and wisdom ·
                renowned exceedingly):
'Fain will I ask the Danes' Friend, ·
                the Lord of all Scyldíngs, 285
As to the boon thou beggest,— ·
                will ask the Breaker-of-Rings,
My ever-glorious Sovran, ·
                touching this thy quest,
And quickly fetch such answer ·
                as he, the good, deems best.'

IN haste he hied him thither ·
                where King Hrothgar sate,
The old man, the hoary, ·
                with his jarls in state. 290
He strode, the valor-famèd, ·
                until he stood before
The shoulders of his dear King— ·
                O he knew courtly lore!
Wulfgar made a speech then ·
                to his chief, Hrothgár:
'Hither have there ferried, · coming from afar
O'er the ocean stretches, · Geatfolk to our hall;
Him who is their eldest · Beowulf they call. 296
These men-at-arms the boon beg ·
                that they, my Chief, of thee
May ask and hear a word now: ·
                O gracious Hrothgar, be
Not niggard of replyings! ·
                They in their warrior-dress
Of jarlman's fairest favor ·
                are worthy, as I guess,— 300
And he who led them hither ·
                is doughty prince indeed.'

VI

HROTHGAR made his speech then, ·
                Helm of the Scylding-Breed:
'I knew him as a child once; ·
                Ecgtheow his father old,
To whom, at home, Geat Hrethel, ·
                his only daughter gave;
And now is Ecgtheow's offspring, ·
                hither come, the bold, 305
And seeketh now the faithful ·
                friend across the wave.
Of yore those seamen told me, ·
                who bore to Geatmen's land
Thither in thanks my royal gifts, ·
                that he in grip-of-hand,
He, the keen-at-contest, had ·
                the clinch of thirty thanes.
Him holy God in mercy sent, ·
                methinks, to us West-Danes 310
Against the greed of Grendel. ·
                This goodly youth unto,
I trust to proffer treasure ·
                for this his derring-do.
Be speedy, bid them enter ·
                to see our banded thanes,
Say eke to them in right words ·
                they 're welcome guests to Danes.'

THEN went to doorway Wulfgar, ·
                and spake he from within: 315
'My high Lord, King of East-Danes, ·
                bids say he knows your kin;
And that ye are to him all, ·
                from o'er the ocean crests,
Ye hardy-hearted seamen, ·
                hither welcome guests.
Now may ye under visors · wend in warrior-gear
To see our Hrothgar, leaving ·
                your battle-bucklers here, 320
Your ash-woods, shafts-of-slaughter, ·
                to bide the parley's close.'

UPROSE the mighty Geat then; ·
                ringed around him, rose
His valiant throng of thanemen. ·
                Some remained without,
Guarding their martial trappings, ·
                as bade their chieftain stout.
They hied them in together, ·
                where the Herald led, 325
Under roof of Heorot. · The Hero strode ahead,
The stout One under helmet, ·
                till at the hearth he stood.

BEOWULF made his speech then ·
                (shone his corslet good,
A cunning net-work woven ·
                by olden wit of smith):
'Hail and health, O Hrothgar! ·
                Of Hyglac's kin and kith 330
Am I, who've gained in young days ·
                glories not a few.
Afar this thing of Grendel ·
                on my home-turf I knew.
Sea-farers say it standeth, · this excelling hall,
Idle and empty   ·   unto each and all,

When under heaven's hollows ·
                the evening-light is hid. 335
So my best of henchmen, ·
                my canny carls, they did
Teach me, Sovran Hrothgar, ·
                that I should seek thee out,
For that so well they wotted ·
                this strength of mine how stout.
Themselves had they seen me ·
                from sore straits come alive,
Blood-flecked from foemen, ·
                where I'd bounden five, 340
Killed the kin of ettins, ·   out upon the main
By night had smote the nicors, ·
                suffered stress and pain,
Avenged their hate of Geatmen— ·
                (they hoped to harry us!)—
And crunched and crushed those grim ones. ·
                And now with Grendel thus,
With the Grisly, this Giant, ·
                alone I'd hold debate. 345
So now, O Prince of Bright-Danes, ·
                thou Shelter-of-the-Great,
Of thee one boon I'm begging: ·
                O Scyldings' Bulwark-Bar,
Deny not, noble Folk-Friend, ·
                now I have come so far,
That I alone with mine here, ·
                who still would share my lot,
This throng of hardy thanemen, ·
                may purge thee Heorot. 350
Eke have I learned this Terror, ·
                in wanton mood and vain,
Recketh not of weapons. ·
                Therefore will I disdain
(Thus Hyglac's heart, my Master's, ·
                may it rejoice through me)
To bear or sword or broad shield, ·
                that yellow disk, to strife.
With grip I'll grasp this Grendel, ·
                and we'll contend for life, 355
A loather 'gainst a loather. ·
                The one whom death shall hale,
Let him believe the Lord's doom. ·
                He will, if he prevail,
Methinketh, in that war-hall, ·
                eat unfearingly
The Geatfolk, as so often ·
                the Danishmen did he.
No need for thee to hide, then, ·
                this head of mine or veil; 360
He'll have me, sprent with gore, if ·
                't is I whom Death shall hale;
He'll bear his bloody quarry, ·
                he'll think to taste his prey;
He'll eat—this lonely Stalker— ·
                unmournfully away;
He'll track with me his fen-lair: ·
                the need will ne'er be thine
In death to have the care of ·
                the body which was mine. 365

Send Hygelac this war-coat, ·
                which wardeth now my breast
(Of all men's battle-byrnies ·
                the brightest and the best)—
If that Hild should hale me— ·
                Hrethel left in trust,
And smith Weland worked it. ·
                Wyrd goeth as she must.'

VII

HROTHGAR made his speech then, ·
                Helm of Scylding-Breeds: 370
'Us hast thou sought, friend Beowulf, ·
                because of ancient deeds,
Because too of thy kindness. ·
                Thy father, when by hand
Heatholaf he slew there · in the Wylfings' land,
The worst of feuds awakened. ·
                Then might his Weder-kin,
For fear of Wylfings' harryings, ·
                take not Ecgtheow in. 375
Thence he sought the South-Danes, ·
                over the sea-surging,
Us, the Glory-Scyldings, ·
                what time I first was King
Of Danefolk and in youth held ·
                this kingdom jewelèd,
This treasure-burg of heroes. ·
                For Heorogar was dead,
Yes, he, my elder brother, ·
                bairn of Halfdane high, 380
Was not among the living— ·
                a better man than I!
Thereafter I compounded · the feud for a fee:
I sent unto the Wylfings, ·
                over the ridge of the sea,
Goodly gifts and olden, ·
                and oaths he sware to me.

SORROW for soul of me 't is · to tell to any one
What shame to me, what dread spite, ·
                in Heorot Grendel's done 386
With his thoughts of hatred; ·
                is my folk-on-floor,
My warrior throng of house-carls, ·
                almost no more.
Them hath Wyrd away swept ·
                into Grendel's greed.
Yet can God that Scather mad ·
                turn from his deed! 390
Full oft across their ale-cups ·
                my men-at-arms would pledge,
When beer had roused their bosoms, ·
                to bide with fierce sword-edge,
Within these walls of wassail, ·
                Grendel's coming-on.
But then would be this mead-house, ·
                when the day would dawn,
This lordly chamber, gore-stained ·
                at the morning-tide; 395

Boards of all its benches ·
                with blood be-spattered wide,
With battle-blood this hall here. ·
                I had of trusty men,
Of dear and doughty, fewer— ·
                since death had taken them.
Sit thee now to banquet, ·
                the cords of speech untie,
Tell us of thy victor-vaunt, ·
                as whets thy soul thereby.' 400

  Then for Geatish tribesmen, ·
                close together all,
Was a bench made ready · in the wassail-hall.
There the stout-in-spirit ·
                went to take their seat,
Proud of this their prowess. ·
                A henchman did as meet,
Mindful he to bear round ·
                the figured ale-tankárd, 405
And pour to each the clear mead. ·
                Whiles would sing a bard,
Clear of voice in Heorot. ·
                Revelled there the thanes—
A host of happy heroes, · Wederfolk and Danes.

VIII

Unferth made his speech then, ·
                at Hrothgar's feet who sate;
Let loose that bairn of Ecglaf ·
                his secret grudge of hate. 410
Beowulf's quest, bold seaman, ·
                to him was mickle spite,
Because he might not own it ·
                that any other wight
Ever in this Middle-Yard ·
                more deeds of bravery
Had done beneath the heavens ·
                than himself had he:
'Art thou, then, that Beowulf, ·
                who strove with Breca, thou, 415
Who on the deep contested ·
                in swimming hard enow!—
When in your pride ye twain did ·
                attempt the waters wide,
And risked in rash vain-glory ·
                your lives upon the tide?
Nor might not any man then, ·
                whether lief or loath,
From fearful voyage dissuade ye, ·
                from breasting seaward both; 420
There ye stretched your arms out ·
                ocean streams among,
Measured ye the mere's path, ·
                drew with your hands along,
Bounded over the billows. ·
                Flood was asurge with foam,
With the waves of winter. ·
                Ye on the water's home,
Seven nights ye swinkèd. ·
                He outstripped in stroke! 425

Had the more of might, he! ·
                Him, when morrow broke,
Surf up-cast by Heathoreams. ·
                He sought his home therewith,
He, beloved of clansmen; ·
                sought dear Bronding-kith,
And his own fair stronghold, ·
                where he had a folk,
Had a town and treasures. ·
                All his vaunt 'gainst thee 430
Did the son of Beanstan · fulfil faithfully!
So I ween for thee now · worser outcome there
(Though in battle-onset, ·
                though in grim warfare,
E'er wert thou so doughty!), ·
                if thou durst abide,
For coming-close of Grendel, ·
                one night-long tide.' 435

  Beowulf made his speech then, ·
                the son of Ecgtheow, he:
'Aplenty hast thou prated, ·
                beer-drunken as thou be,
Friend Unferth, about Breca,— ·
                his feat hast told at length.
But truth I hold it, mine was ·
                a mightier ocean-strength,
A bigger toil in the billows, ·
                than any other man's. 440
We twain, when still but younglings, ·
                had talked and pledged our plans
To risk (we were but boys then) ·
                our lives far out to sea.
We did as we had vowed to! ·
                Our naked swords had we,
Our hardy swords, in hands there, ·
                on breasting seaward both,
To fend us from the whale-fish. ·
                He could no whit from me 445
Float o'er the sea-flood swifter— ·
                and I from him was loath.
Thus were we twain together ·
                five nights upon the wave,
Till surge and weltering waters ·
                us both asunder drave;
The coldest of all weathers, ·
                dark night and northern blast,
Blew battle-grim against us; ·
                fierce were the floods we passed; 450
Roused was the wrath of mere-fish; ·
                but there against the foe
My mail-coat, hard and hand-linked, ·
                helped me even so!
My braided sark-of-battle ·
                lay about my breast,
My corslet gold-adornèd. ·
                Me bottom-ward did wrest
A spotted Devil-Scather— ·
                fast held the Grim his grip! 455
But unto me was given ·
                to pierce with swordsmanship,

Aye, with the blade-of-battle, ·
                the Monster of the brine.
The mighty Mere-Beast foundered ·
                through this hand of mine!

IX

THUS the loathly lurkers ·
                pressed me sore and oft.
I served them with my dear sword ·
                in ways not soft. 460
For those foul devisers ·
                the hope of fill was o'er—
To eat me, to sit round · a feast on ocean's floor!
But upon the morrow, · wounded by the glaive,
They were lying up along ·
                the leavings of the wave,
Put to sleep by sword there— ·
                ne'er to thwart again 465
Sailor-folk in ferrying · the fords of the main.
From the east a light rose— ·
                God's beacon bright;
The rolling seas subsided, · so that see I might
Headlands and windy walls. ·
                Wyrd will often save
A jarl who is no fey man, · if he be but brave.
And so to me 'twas granted ·
                that with sword I slew 471
Nine there of the Nicors. · Nay, I never knew
Under the vault of the heavens ·
                by night a fight more fierce,
Nor on the streams of the ocean ·
                a man put to it worse.
Way-weary, yet I 'scapèd ·
                the clutch of monsters fell; 475
And the sea up-cast me, ·
                flood-tide and swell,
On the land of Finn-men. · Never about thee
Such straits of strife, such terrors ·
                of sword-blades heard I tell;
Ne'er yet at war-play Breca, ·
                nor neither one of ye,
Did deed so bold with bloody brands— ·
                nor boast thereof I will— 480
Though thou forsooth thy brothers, ·
                thy kin-of-heart, didst kill!
(Whence curse of hell awaits thee, ·
                though good thy wit may be.)
I say to thee in sooth now, · thou of Ecglaf son,
That Grendel ne'er so many ·
                gruesome things had done,
The Grisly ne'er such havoc ·
                in Heorot to thy King, 485
If thought of thine, if soul of thine, ·
                were grim as thy telling.
But he hath found he needeth ·
                fear or feud or stroke
Little from thy people, ·
                the Victor-Scylding folk!
He taketh the forced pledges, ·
                unsparingly he rends.

He hath his lust of slaughter, ·
                he puts to sleep, he sends,— 490
He recketh not of any · contest with the Dane.
But speedily 't is mine now ·
                to show him might and main,
The warrior-work of Geatmen! ·
                Let him go who can
Blithe to mead tomorrow— ·
                when o'er bairns of man
Shineth from the southward, ·
                on other day begun, 495
Once more that light-of-morning, ·
                the sky-girt sun.

THEN the Prince of Bright-Danes, ·
                the Treasure-Breaker, he,
The old-haired and war-famed, ·
                had his time of glee.
Now in help he trusted; · from Beowulf he caught,
He, his people's Shepherd, ·
                the firm-resolvèd thought. 500
Then was there heroes' laughter; ·
                and rang the shout and song,
And merry speech was bandied; ·
                and then stepped forth along
Wealhtheow, Queen of Hrothgar, ·
                mindful of manners all,
And gold-bedight she greeted ·
                the guest-men in the hall.
And then the high-born Lady ·
                erst gave the cup in hand 505
To him who was the Warder ·
                of East-Danes' fatherland;
And him she bade be blithesome ·
                at the bout-of-beer,
Him beloved of clansmen. ·
                He took with goodly cheer
The banquet and the beaker, ·
                the King of victory-fame.
Then round the hall to each and all ·
                she stepped, the Helmings' Dame, 510
And gave to young and older ·
                the goblet rich-beseen,
Till came the happy moment ·
                when in hall the Queen,
Crown-bedight and high-souled, ·
                the cup to Beowulf bore.
She greeted the Geats' lord; ·
                God she thanked therefor,
Wise in her word-craft, ·
                that her wish had thriven 515
That she could trust some jarlman ·
                for help 'gainst horrors given.
He took the cup from Wealhtheow, ·
                a warsman fierce-to-smite;
And then he offered answer, · eager for the fight.

BEOWULF made his speech then, ·
                bairn of Ecgtheow, he:
'When with my troop of tribesmen, ·
                I mounted on the sea. 520

And sate me in my sailor-boat, ·
                  I had this thought in me:
Either to work for all time ·
                  thy people's will at last,
Or to fall afighting · in grip of Grendel fast.
Firm am I to do my · jarlman's deed withal,
Or to dree my end-of-days · in this mead-hall.'

    THOSE words well pleased that woman,— ·
                the Geatman's battle-vows; 526
And gold-bedight she went, then, ·
                to sit beside her spouse,
Folk-Queen high-born. ·
                And once again there be
Brave words spoken, · and hall-men in glee,
And uproar of victor-folk— ·
                until the King anon 530
Would seek his evening resting-place, ·
                Halfdane's Son.
He knew that battle waited ·
                the fiend on that high floor,
After they the sun-light · could see no more,
After the dun night · was over all about,
And the shapes of shadow ·
                should come aprowling out, 535
Wan beneath the welkin. ·
                Together rose the clan;
Then Hrothgar greeted Beowulf, ·
                man wishing luck to man,
Gave him of that wine-house ·
                the power and sway, and swore:
'Never have I trusted · to any man before,—
Not since I could heave up ·
                hand and shield of me,— 540
This brave house of Danemen, ·
                until now to thee.
Have now and hold it— · this excelling hall!
Remember thy glory,— ·
                make known thy might to all!
Watch against the Wrathful! ·
                Each wish of thine I'll do,
If with thy life thou see'st ·
                this deed of daring through.' 545

X

THEN did Hrothgar hie him, ·
                the Scyldings' Bulwark-Bar,
Forth from the mead-hall ·
                with his band-of-war;
Wished that Warrior-Chieftain ·
                Wealhtheow for to seek,
His Queen for his bed-mate. ·
                The King-of-Glory there
Over against Grendel ·
                (so men had heard him speak) 550
Had set a chamber-warder; ·
                whose special task was care
Of him, the Danemen's Monarch, ·
                in keeping ogre-guard.
Truly, the Geatish Leader ·
                trusted well the Lord,
And his own proud mettle. ·
                His mail he then undid,
From his head his helmet, ·
                gave his figured sword 555
(That goodliest of iron-things) ·
                to his man and bid
Watch and ward his war-gear. ·
                Then his boast he said,
Beowulf, the brave Geat, · ere he clomb to bed:
'Not poorer in battle-prowess, ·
                do I reckon me,
In the works of warfare, · than is Grendel, he!
So not with sword I purpose ·
                to spill his life tonight, 561
To put to sleep the Monster, ·
                though indeed I might.
Those goodly arts he knows not ·
                whereby to cut at me,
To hew against my buckler, ·
                though so bold he be
In the works of combat. · But this eventide 565
To both of us behooveth ·
                leave the blade aside,
If he durst to seek out · a lack-weapon fray,
And holy Lord, the wise God, ·
                thereafter either way
Let him decree the glory · as him-thinketh best.'

    AND then the Keen-in-contest ·
                laid him down to rest; 570
And in the pillow sank, then, ·
                that Jarlman's cheek and head;
And many a brisk one round him ·
                bent to his hall-bed—
Many an ocean-warrior. · Not any of the band
Thought 't would e'er be his to seek ·
                from here his fatherland,
The dear folk, or free-burg, ·
                that fostered him and bore; 575
But they had heard that ere now ·
                more than many a man
Slaughter-death had taken off ·
                of the Danish clan.
But unto them the Lord gave ·
                the webs of weal-in-war,
Gave unto the Weders · aid and comfort so
That, through the strength of One, they ·
                all o'ercame their foe,— 580
Through his might of selfhood. ·
                'T is known that God, the Giver,
Hath wielded over mankind ·
                forever and forever.

    STRIDING through the wan night, ·
                the Shadow-Stalker stepped;
The holders of that hornèd house, ·
                the shooting-men, they slept—
All, save only one there. ·
                'T was known to men that he, 585
That ghostly Scather, might not, ·
                against the Lord's decree,

Draw them down to Darkness. ·
     Watching the foe to smite,
In wrath the Geatman bided ·
     the issue of the fight.

XI

And now from out the moorland, ·
     under the misty slopes,
Came astalking Grendel— ·
     God's anger on his hopes. 590
That Scather foul was minded ·
     to snare of human kin
Some one, or sundry, · that high hall within.
Under the welkin strode he, ·
     until full well he spied
The wine-house, the gold-hall, ·
     with fret-work glittering wide.
Nor was that the first time ·
     Hrothgar's home he sought. 595
Yet never in his life-days, · late or early, aught
Like this harsh welcome found he ·
     from thanemen in the hall.
He came afooting onward · to the house withal,
This warring One that ever ·
     had been from bliss out-cast;
Forthwith the door sprang open, ·
     with forged-bolts though fast, 600
When with his paws he pressed it; ·
     yea, then, on bale-work bent,
Swoln as he was with fury, ·
     that house's mouth he rent.
Anon the Fiend was treading ·
     the shining floor in there;
On he moved in anger; ·
     from eyes of him did glare,
Unto fire likest, · a light unfair. 605
He saw within the chamber ·
     many a man asleep,—
Kinsman band together, · of clanfolk a heap;
Laughed his mood, was minded ·
     that Hobgoblin grim,
Ere the dawn to sunder ·
     each his life from limb,
Now that fill-of-feeding ·
     he weened awaited him! 610
But Wyrd it was that would not ·
     longer grant him might
To seize on more of mankind ·
     after that same night.

Was watching he, the stalwart ·
     Kin of Hygelac,
How with grip the Grisly ·
     would go at his attack.
He had no thought, this Goblin, ·
     that business to put off; 615
But pounced upon a sleeping man, ·
     starting quick enough!
Unthwartedly he slit him, ·
     bit his bone-box, drunk

From his veins the blood of him, ·
     gulped him chunk by chunk,
Till soon, then, he had there ·
     this un-living Gea·
Altogether eaten down, · even to hands and feet
Then stepped he forth and nearer, ·
     and pawed by bed to nim 621
The hardy-headed Hero, · reaching toward him
With his claws be-deviled: ·
     with thoughts that boded harm.
Beowulf received him, · propped upon an arm,
But soon he found, did Grendel,— ·
     this Herdsman-over-crimes,— 625
That never in this Middle-World, ·
     this earth of many climes
He'd met a mightier hand-grip ·
     in any man than here.
Afeared in mood and spirit, ·
     small help he gat from fear!
Was bent on making-off, ho!— ·
     out to the dark would flee,
Would seek the din of devils! ·
     Not now in Heorot he 630
Fared as in the old-days!— ·
     And then the Bold-in-pride,
Hygelac's Thane, remembered ·
     his speech of eventide.
Up he stood and grasped him ·
     so tight the fingers cracked.
The Ettin started outward— ·
     the Jarl upon him packed.
The monstrous One was minded, ·
     whereso'er he may, 635
To fling himself but farther, ·
     and from thence away
To flee to boggy dingles; ·
     his fingers' power he wist
Was in the grip of Grim One. ·
     That was a sorry quest
Whereon the Scather Grendel ·
     to Heorot Hall had pressed.
The lordly room resounded; ·
     and all the Danes did quail, 640
Those warrior jarls of walled-town, ·
     lest reft for aye of ale.
Wroth were the ramping twain there, ·
     those warders of the house;
The chamber rang with uproar; ·
     mickle wonder 't was
How the wine-hall held out ·
     'gainst shock of fighters there,
How adown did fall not ·
     that earthly dwelling fair. 645
But inside and outside ·
     it was too firmly wrought,
With the bands of iron, ·
     forged by cunning thought.
I've heard that many a mead-bench, ·
     with gold gilded o'er,
There where tugged the foemen, ·
     started from the floor.

So had weened the wise ones ·
                of the Scyldings erst 650
That never any man by force ·
                might asunder burst
That brave house and bone-bright, ·
                nor by craft might split—
Save that bosoming fire ·
                in flame should swallow it.

  Up there rose a shriek then, ·
                strange enough o'night;
On each and every North-Dane ·
                seized a grisly fright, 655
On each who from the wall there ·
                heard that 'well-a-way'—
Heard this God-Forsaker ·
                chant his gruesome lay,
His song of loss-in-battle, ·
                heard bewail his wound
This Grendel, Hell's Bondsman. ·
                For held him tightly bound
That man who was of all men ·
                between the seas confessed, 660
In the days of this our life here, ·
                in strength the mightiest.

XII

The jarls' Defender would not, ·
                forsooth with a will,
Let him loose aliving— · him who came to kill,
Deeming not his life-days · of use to any folk.
More than once did jarlman ·
                of Beowulf try a stroke 665
With his father's falchion, · fain the life to ward
Of the famèd Chieftain, · their great Lord.
They wist not, these warsmen, ·
                these hardy-headed few,
The while they fell asmiting ·
                and thought the while to hew
On this side, on that side, · seeking soul to kill,
That best of earthly iron blades, ·
                nor never battle-bill, 671
This accursèd Scather · could hurt or harm:
For over victor-weapons · he had cast a charm,
Over every sword-edge. · Yet his passing-o'er,
In the days of his life here, · was to be full sore;
And this alien Elf-Thing · was to fare afar 676
To the under-places · where the devils are.
For he had found, had Grendel,— ·
                this Striver against God,—
Who in such merry mood of old ·
                so oft on man had trod,
That his bulk-of-body ·
                would not help him moe, 680
Now Hygelac's stout Kinsman ·
                held his fore-paw so!
Was each unto the other · alive a loathly thing.
A body-sore he gat there, ·
                this wretched Ogreling:
There showed upon his shoulder ·
                a cureless wound anon:

His sinews sprang asunder; ·
                from socket burst the bone. 685
To Beowulf was given · the glory of the fray;
And Grendel was to flee hence, ·
                sick-to-death, away,—
Off under fen-slopes, · off to dens of gloom.
He wist, O well he wist it, ·
                his end-of-life had come,
His full tale of days now.—·
                The wish of Danemen all, 690
After that gory set-to, · had come to pass withal.

  He had now y-cleansèd, ·
                he who came from far,
The Wise-Head and Stout-Heart, ·
                the House of high Hrothgár,
Had freed it now from fury. ·
                His night-work made him glad,
His deed of might and glory. ·
                The Geatmen's Leader had 695
Now before the East-Danes ·
                fulfilled his vaunting there,—
Aye, all ills amended · and the carking care,
Which they had dreed aforetime, ·
                and by stress and strain
Long been doomed to suffer— ·
                more than little pain.
Of this there was a token, ·
                clear enough in proof, 700
When the Victor-Fighter · under the gabled roof
Hung on high the fore-paw, ·
                the arm and shoulder grim—
And there ye had together ·
                all Grendel's clutching-limb!

XIII

Then there was at morning ·
                —so I 've heard the tale—
Round about the gift-hall · many a man-of-mail.
Thither fared the folk-chiefs, ·
                near and far asunder, 706
All along the wide-ways, ·
                for to view the wonder,—
The traces of the loathed Thing. ·
                Seemed his passing-out
Not a grievous sorrow · to any thereabout, 709
Any who were viewing ·
                now the craven's trail—
How he, weary-hearted, · beaten in the bout,
Death-doomed and routed, · off away from here
Made for very life his tracks ·
                to the Nicors' mere.
Yonder were the waters · weltering with blood;
Mingled all with hot gore, ·
                surged the gruesome flood; 715
With battle-spatter rolled the deep, ·
                where the death-doomed then
Laid forlorn his body down, ·
                his heathen soul, in fen—
There did Hell receive him! ·

HOME on horse anew
Rode the old companions, • many a younger too,
Back from merry journey, •
     bold men back from mere, 720
Warriors on the white steeds. •
     Then was sounded clear
Beowulf's deed of daring: •
     all said it o'er and o'er,
That south or north none other, •
     from shore to farthest shore,
Betwixt the seas none other, •
     beneath the sky's domain,
Was better man to bear shield •
     or worthier to reign. 725
(Nor they by this belied not •
     their Friend in anything,
Hrothgar, their gracious Lord—
     but that was goodly King!)

WHILES these doughty warsmen •
     let leap their fallow bays,
Let run a race where fairest •
     seemed the country-ways;
Whiles a thane of Hrothgar,— •
     a man of boasts was he, 730
Stored with olden sagas, •
     and deft at balladry,—
Found one good word for other •
     and bound them soothfully;
So too this scop made mention •
     right well of Beowulf's quest,
And had good speed at speaking •
     his phrases artfullest,
Linking words together. 735

* * * *

So homeward, oft a-racing, •
     these warriors old and young
With swift horses followed •
     the fallow paths along.
Now was the sun-of-morning urged •
     higher up the skies;
Went many a bold retainer •
     to see the wondrous prize
At the high hall Heorot. •
     The King himself no less, 740
The Warder of the ring-hoard, •
     famed for worthiness,
From out the wedding-bowers •
     strode in royal sheen,
Girt by many clansmen; •
     and, lo, with him the Queen
With troop of maidens measured •
     the mead-path to the scene.

XIV

HROTHGAR made a speech then; •
     he walked unto the hall; 745
Stood upon the fore-steps; •
     looked at roof so tall,
So garnishèd with gold-work; •
     at Grendel's paw looked he:

'Thanks to the All-Wielder •
     at once for what I see!
From Grendel have I suffered •
     such gruesome plight and plunder:
But ever God he worketh •
     wonder upon wonder— 750
He is the King-of-Glory! • It was but now that I
Weened no boot for sorrows • for me until I die,
When stood this best of houses •
     battle-sprent with gore,
A sorrow spread so widely • for every councillor
Who weened they might not ever •
     save from Fiends-of-murk, 755
From ogres and from demons, •
     this great folk-work.
Now hath a thane by Lord's might •
     a deed put through
That we for all our cunning •
     erewhile could never do.
Well can she say, that woman •
     (if yet she be on earth)
Who gave, among the tribes of men, •
     to such an offspring birth, 760
That olden God was kindly •
     to her in child-bearing.
Now Beowulf, best of battlers, •
     to my heart's fostering
For mine own son I'll take thee. •
     Guard it well from now,
This our new-born kinship! •
     Never lack shalt thou
For aught of world's desires •
     whereover I have power. 765
Full oft did I for less deed •
     of old a largesse shower,
Rewards from out my treasure, •
     upon a punier swain,
A slacker one at slaughter. •
     By thine own might and main
Thou hast thyself achieved •
     that thy name shall live
Forever unto ages. • May the All-Wielder give
Reward of good unto thee, •
     as ever he hath done.' 771

BEOWULF made a speech then, •
     who was of Ecgtheow son:
'We wrought that work of warfare, •
     that fight, with goodly will;
Boldly we dared the might of •
     that mystic Thing-of-ill.
O I would the rather • that thou his very self 775
Hadst seen in his trappings, •
     that weary, wavering Elf!
Swift I thought to pin him •
     with my clutches firm
Down upon a bed of death, •
     that he in vain should squirm,
Dying under hand-grip— • unless his body fled.
That flight I could not hinder— •
     God willed him free instead. 780

To him, this Life-Destroyer, ·
    I clave not well enough—
He was too strong at foot-work, ·
    this Fiend in making-off!
To save his life, however, ·
    he left his fingers back,
His arm and his shoulder, ·
    as witness of his track! 784
Yet by this the creature · not any comfort wins;
None the longer lives he, · harried by his sins.
But him his sore hath bounden ·
    fast by bonds of bale,
In a gripe of anguish. · There abide he shall,
Outlawed by evil, · the day of doom so grim,
Waiting how the shining Judge ·
    wills to sentence him!' 790

 Then Unferth, son of Ecglaf, ·
    he was less noisy wight,
In brag of works of battle, ·
    when, thanks to this man's might,
The æthelings were gazing ·
    that high roof along
At paw and foeman's fingers— ·
    and foreward there they hung,
Each of the claws in place there, ·
    unto steel most like— 795
That heathen creature's hand-spur, ·
    that warrior's eery spike.
The gazers vowed no brave man's ·
    good old blade soever
Might touch him, might the Monster's ·
    bloody fight-paw sever.

XV

 Then quick the hest was given. ·
    Within was Heorot then
By many hands bedeckèd. ·
    Of women and of men 800
Aye, full many were there ·
    who did make ready all
That wine-house and guest-room. ·
    Gleamed on every wall
Woven hangings, gold-gay— ·
    of wondrous sights so much,
For each and every mortal ·
    of those who gaze at such.
It had been greatly battered, ·
    that building brave and bright, 805
Though all within-ward bounden ·
    by bands of iron tight;
And the door-hinges rended; ·
    the roof alone held out
Sound all-together, ·
    when Grendel turned about,
That Ogre in his fleeing, ·
    outlawed by deeds of ill,
And of his life in wanhope. ·
    Ah, let each try who will, 810
It is not over-easy · to flee away from death!

But each of bairns of mankind, ·
    each who beareth breath,
Each who dwelleth on the ground, ·
    shall seek, as fate shall force,
The place made ready for him, ·
    where his body-corse
Shall sleep upon its resting-bed, ·
    when the feasting's done. 815

 'T was time and tide when hall-ward hied ·
    Halfdane's son;
The King himself, this Hrothgar, ·
    would in the revel share.
Ne'er heard I tell of tribesmen ·
    themselves who better bare
Around their treasure-giver, · in a goodlier press.
They bent them to the benches, ·
    owners of success! 820
Merrily they feasted; · took again, again,
Cheerily the mead-cup. ·
    And kinsmen still withal
Were both of those stout-hearted ones ·
    in that high hall—
Hrothgar and Hrothulf. ·
    Within was Heorot then
Filled alone with friends all— ·
    never in those times 825
Had the folk of Scyldings ·
    wrought the traitor-crimes.

 Then the bairn of Halfdane, ·
    to Beowulf he gave
A banneret of gold-work, ·
    broidered on a stave,
A helmet and a byrnie, · as meed of victory.
And a glorious jewelled sword ·
    many there did see 830
Borne unto the Hero. · Standing forth on floor,
Beowulf received the cup; ·
    that warrior-band before,
He needed not to suffer shame ·
    for these gifts of price.
I have not known many ·
    to give in friendlier wise
To others on the ale-bench ·
    golden treasures four! 835
Across the crown of the helmet, ·
    a ridge outside there rose,
Of wires interwoven, ·
    to guard the head from blows,
Lest the files'-remainders, ·
    the battle-hardened glaive,
Too fiercely might scathe it, ·
    what time the brave
Behind his shield should hie him ·
    forth against his foes. 840
Bade them the jarlmen's Bulwark ·
    bring adown the hall
Horses eight, with golden plate ·
    upon the cheeks of all.
On one a saddle rested · with jewel-work replete,

Shining with deft devices— ·
                that was the battle-seat
Of Hrothgar, the high King, ·
            when Halfdane's son would fare 845
Forth unto the sword-play; ·
                and in the vanward ne'er
Failed his famous valor, ·
              while round him fell the slain!
And then the Lord of Ingwines ·
              to Beowulf gave the twain,
The horses and the weapons, ·
              as his to have and hold—
Bade him well enjoy them! ·
              Hrothgar, the bold,
The Hoard-Guard of heroes, ·
            so manfully paid back, 851
With horses and with treasures, ·
              Beowulf's attack,
That none who 'll speak the truth aright ·
            can blame for any lack.

XVI

Then, too, the Lord of jarlmen ·
            at mead-bench bestowed
On each who had with Beowulf ·
            taken the ocean-road 855
Some treasure, some heirloom, ·
            and bade with gold requite
The death of him whom Grendel ·
            had foully slain that night—
As more of them he fain had slain, ·
            except that God, the good,
And the man's own courage, ·
            for them that wyrd withstood.
The Judge then ruled all races ·
            even as he doth yet— 860
So best is alway insight, ·
            and forethought of wit.
How much of lief and loathly ·
            shall fall to each man's life
Who long makes earth his dwelling here ·
            in these days of strife!

Now was there chant and music, ·
            together linked as one,
Before the Army-Chieftain, · Halfdane's Son.
The merry harp was fingered, ·
            the lay was lilted free, 866
As Hrothgar's bard by mead-bench ·
            sang in hall his glee.

* * *

            Sung was now the lay,
The harp-chant of gleeman. ·
            Mirth arose once more,
Loud rang the bench-joy. ·
            Cup-bearers did pour 870
Wine from jars-of-wonder. ·
            Forth came Wealhtheow there,
Walking under golden crown, ·
            to where the friendly pair,
The nephew and the uncle, sate: ·
            then was their kinship still at one,
Each unto the other true: ·
            And Spokesman Unferth, Ecglaf's son,
Sate at the feet of Scyldings' King. ·
            Both trusted still his spirit bold, 875
That he was man of courage keen; ·
            though he unto his kin of old
Were not at sword-play merciful. ·

        And then the Dame of Scyldings spake:
'Breaker-of-Rings and Free-Lord mine, ·
            now this beaker take;
Be thou blithe of spirit, ·
            thou Gold-Friend in hall;
Bespeak the Geats in happy words, ·
            such as behooves withal; 880
Be gladsome to the Geatmen, ·
            and not forgetful be
Of good gifts anear or far ·
            which now thou havest free.
'T was told me, this warrior ·
            thou 'dst take for son to thee.
This bright ring-chamber, ·
            this Heorot, is restored;
Use, while still thou mayest, ·
            thy times for fair reward; 885
And leave unto thy kinsmen ·
            the folk and the state,
When 't is thine to fare forth, ·
            to greet eternal fate.
I know my gladsome Hrothulf— ·
            that 't is his will to be
Gracious to these boys of ours, ·
            if earlier thou than he,
O thou Friend of Scyldings, ·
            leavest the world behind. 890
I ween, with goodness he 'll requite ·
            the offspring of us two,
If he all that remembers · that you and I did do
For him when erst a youngling, ·
            with gifts and honors kind.'

Thereat to bench she turned her ·
            where her lads were then,
Hrethric and Hrothmund, ·
            with bairns of fighting men— 895
The youth all together. ·
            There sate the doughty Thane,
Beowulf, the Geatman, ·
            between the brothers twain.

XVII

To him she bare the goblet, ·
            and friendly words spake she,
And armlets twain of twisted gold ·
            she proffered graciously,
And rings and a war-coat, ·
            and best of collars too 900
That ever on earth I heard of. ·

* * *

The hall rang out in glee;
Wealhtheow made a speech then; ·
  before the band spake she:
'Have joy of this collar, ·
  with weal, belovèd Youth!
This war-coat use, my Beowulf—·
  a royal gift in sooth— 905
Thrive thou well and show thee ·
  ever strong and free,
And unto these my boys here ·
  kind in counsels be:
For that will I be mindful ·
  of recompense to thee!
Thou hast done so doughtily ·
  that for many a year
Men shall do thee honor ·
  both from far and near, 910
As widely as the sea-waves ·
  wash each windy wall;
As long as ever thou livest ·
  to thee may good befall!
I wish thee well with treasures! ·
  Unto this my boy
In deeds of thine be helpful, ·
  guarding him his joy!
Here is each jarl to other ·
  true and mild of mood, 915
Faithful to his Overlord; ·
  all the thanes are good,
The folk at one and ready, ·
  the revelling fighters free.
Do thou as I bid thee.' ·

  Unto her seat went she.
Here was the best of feastings; ·
  here drank of wine the bold;
They wist not Wyrd was walking, ·
  this grim Fate of old, 920
Forth for many a jarl there. ·
  When the eve had come
And Hrothgar had hied him ·
  unto his own home—
Unto his rest, the Chieftain—·
  then did guard the floor
A goodly count of jarlmen ·
  as oft they did before.
The bench-boards they bare off; ·
  and through the hall did strew 925
The beddings and the bolsters. ·
  And of that boisterous crew
Was one to rest who laid him—·
  ne'er to wake anew.
At heads they set their bucklers ·
  their war-wood bright.
On bench above each ætheling ·
  there was plain to sight 929
The steep battle-helmets, · the byrnies of rings,
The spear-shafts sturdy. · For these æthelings
Were wont to be full often · ready for the fray
At home or on a harrying,—·
  be whichever it may,—
Even on such of seasons ·
  as when befell some stroke
Against their Lord and Master. ·
  That was a doughty folk! 935

THE SECOND PART

XVIII

Sank they to sleep then; ·
  was one who purchased sore
His rest there of evening—·
  as oft had chanced before,
Ever since this Grendel made ·
  Gold-Hall his home,
And wrought there at wrong deeds ·
  till his end did come—
His death after sinnings. ·
  And now 't was seen by men, 940
And far and wide reported, ·
  that an Avenger then
Yet survived the Monster,—·
  that all the time Another
Survived this battle-sorrow: ·
  Grendel's own Mother,
The She-Thing, the Witch-Wife, ·
  her pang was mourning near,
She who needs must make her ·
  home in grisly mere, 945
In the cold sea-currents—·
  after the times when Cain
An only brother, his father's son, ·
  with the sword had slain.
Outlaw, marked for murder, ·
  he fled the joys of folk,
Haunted the wildernesses. · So from him awoke
The breed of fated goblins; ·
  of these was Grendel kin, 950
That Horror, that Outcast—·
  who Heorot Hall within
Had found that watchful Human, ·
  awaiting the fight.
There the Ogre gripped him, ·
  but of his strength of might
Beowulf was mindful—·
  to him God's precious gift—
And trusted the Almighty ·
  for grace and cheer and shift. 955
Thereby he overcame the Foe; ·
  this Troll of Hell he strook,
Who slunk off acringing, · of his joys forsook,
For to see his death-place—·
  this Foe of mankind.

And now his greedy, gloomy ·
  Mother was of mind
To go on quest of sorrow, ·
  to wreak the death of her son. 960
She came then to Heorot, ·
  where around the floor

The Ring-Danes were sleeping. ·
                Then came to jarls anon
Return of olden evils, · when athrough the door
Burst the Mother of Grendel! ·
                But this was a terror less,
Less by as much as less is ·
                a woman's war-prowéss, 965
The battling might of maidens, ·
                than a man in fighting dress
(Whenever his falchion, banded, ·
                anvil-beat by the sledge,
His sword with blood bestainèd, ·
                cleaves with its doughty edge
Down through the foeman's boar-crest, ·
                over the helmet's crown).
Then in the hall of Hrothgar, ·
                many a blade was drawn, 970
Swords from over the benches; ·
                many a buckler tall
Was lifted tight in the hand there! ·
                Never a man in hall
Thought of his helm or corslet— ·
                on whom that fear did fall.
Hers was a sudden hasting— ·
                hers was a turning about
To save her life in the open, ·
                knowing herself found out. 975
But speedily the Ogress · had seizèd tightly then
One of the Danish house-carls, ·
                as off she fled to fen;
Hrothgar's dearest Hero ·
                in vassal's rank was he,
A mighty shield-warrior, ·
                between the sea and sea,
A fighter of a sure renown ·
                whom in his rest killed she. 980
And Beowulf was absent,— ·
                for to the Geatman bold
Another lodge allotted was ·
                after the gifts of gold.
Uproar was in Heorot. · Away with her she bore
The famous paw of Grendel, ·
                dripping with its gore.
Sorrow was renewèd ·
                within their homes once more. 985
'T was an exchange right grievous, ·
                where either side must pay
With the lives of loved ones. ·

                Then that Warsman gray,
Old King Hrothgar,   ·   had a heart of pain,
Knowing this Prince was lifeless, ·
                dead this dearest Thane.
Speedily to bower · was Beowulf fetched away,
The victory-blessèd Hero. ·
                And just at dawn of day 991
He wended with his jarlmen, ·
                this champion Ætheling,
Himself with his comrades, ·
                to where abode the King,
Waiting if All-Wielder · might ever will to show

To him a turn-for-better · after the spell of woe.
Strode along the floor, then, ·
                this Man, the brave-in-brawl, 996
With his hand-companions, ·
                whilst sounded planks in hall,
To greet with words the Wise One, ·
                and ask the Ingwines' Sire
If he had slept a quiet night · after his desire.

XIX

Hrothgar made a speech then, ·
                Helm of the Scylding-Brood:
'Nay, ask not after joyance! · Sorrow is renewed
Unto the folk of Daneland. ·
                Dead is now another— 1001
Æscher, of Yrmenlaf ·
                who was the elder brother,
My councillor, my wise-man, ·
                and comrade at my right
Whenever our heads we warded ·
                amidst of the fight,
As clashed the foot-foemen, ·
                and rang the boar-crest— 1005
A jarl should be like Æscher, ·
                an ætheling the best.
Him hath the hand in Heorot ·
                of roving Death-Sprite slain,
And I wot not whither ·
                its backward-ways 't has ta'en,
In its prey exulting,   ·   of its feasting fain.
She hath the feud avengèd ·
                whereby on yester-night 1010
Thou slewest so grimly Grendel ·
                by gripping him so tight—
Because he rent and ravaged ·
                too long my folk in strife.
He fell at last in battle, · paying with his life;
And now hath come another ·
                Scather lorn and lewd,
Who would avenge her offspring— ·
                and farther bears the feud: 1015
So that indeed it seemeth · unto many a thane,
Who weepeth for his Ring-Giver, ·
                a hard heart-bane;
Low lies the hand that wrought ye ·
                your every wish so well.

I 've heard my land-dwellers, ·
                my folk's householders, tell
They 'd seen a pair of such ones, ·
                alien Sprites obscure, 1020
Mickle Border-Stalkers, · haunting the moor.
And of these the One was— ·
                as far as guess they might—
The likeness of a woman; ·
                the other wretched Wight
Trod his tracks of exile · in a man's own mien,
Save that he was bigger ·
                than man hath ever been— 1025
Whom the landfolk named · Grendel of yore.

Knew they not the father—·
                      whether theretofore
Ever he 'd begotten   ·   any troll-kin more.

   THEIR haunts are secret places, ·
                      the wolf-slopes dim,
The headlands windy, · the fen-ways grim, 1030
Where the mountain waterfall · downward away
Floweth under crag-head, ·
                      under mists of spray.
And the mere it standeth ·
                      off some mile or more:
Over it there hangeth · a forest frosted hoar;
A wood, fast-rooted, · the water over-hoods;
Each night is seen a wonder weird— ·
                      a fire on the floods! 1036
There lives no man so wise on earth ·
                      whoso its bottom sounds:
Though the heath-ranger, ·
                      harried by the hounds,
The hart, strong of antlers, · hunted far in flight,
May seek this woodsy thicket, ·
                      he 'll rather yield his sprite, 1040
His life upon the brink there, ·
                      than plunge for safety in.
A spot uncanny is it; ·
                      whence wan to welkin spin
Welter of foam and waters, ·
                      when the winds begin
Astirring the foul weather— ·
                      till the air is murk,
And the heaven weepeth. ·

          AGAIN we wait thy work, 1045
Thine and thine only! ·
                      That land not yet thou know'st,
The fearsome spot whereunder ·
                      thou 'lt find that damnèd Ghost—
Seek it, if thou darest! · For this fight to thee
I 'll give, as even erst I did, · twisted gold in fee,
Aye, mine olden treasure, ·
                      if back thou com'st to me.' 1050

              XX

BEOWULF made a speech then, ·
                      son of Ecgtheow, he:
'Sorrow not, thou Sage One,— ·
                      for each it better be
That his friend he wreaketh ·
                      than bemourn him late.
Our end of life in world here · we must all await;
Let who is able win him · glory ere his death;
In after-years for warrior dead ·
                      that chiefly profiteth. 1056
Arise thou Kingdom's Warden! ·
                      Speedily let us hie
Of this Kin of Grendel · the trail for to spy.
This to thee I promise: ·
                      She 'll refuge in no rest—
Neither in earth's bosom · nor in hill-forést,
Nor in sea-bottom, · wheresoe'er she go! 1061
For this day have patience · in thine every woe,
As I ween thou wilt have.' ·

          UPLEAPT the Graybeard now;
Thanked the Lord Almighty ·
                      for what this man did vow.
Then Hrothgar's horse was bridled, ·
                      his steed with braided mane; 1065
Stately rode the royal Sage; ·
                      and afoot his train
Of shield-bearers was stepping. ·
                      Wide was there to see
Her tracks across the wood-ways, ·
                      her trail along the lea,
Whither fared she forward ·
                      over the murky moor,
And with her bare the dead man, ·
                      the best of kin-thanes sure 1070
Of all who once with Hrothgar ·
                      warded well the home.
Then the Son of æthelings · now did over-roam
The narrow-passes, · the steep cliff-stone,
The close defiles and · the paths unknown,
The beetling cragheads, · the Nicors' den. 1075
All ahead he hastened with · a few wise men
For to view the region, · till a sudden he
Found the joyless forest, ·
                      found the mountain tree,
Leaning o'er the hoar cliff. · Under the wood,
Blood-stained and troubled, ·
                      there the waters stood. 1080
Unto the friends of Scyldings, ·
                      unto every Dane,
It was a thing of sorrow, ·
                      a burden of heart's pain,
Aye, to many a clansman ·
                      a grief it was and dread,
When, upon the sea-cliff, ·
                      they met with Æscher's head!

   THE flood with blood was boiling, ·
                      yes, with the hot gore; 1085
The folk saw down upon it; ·
                      the horn was singing o'er
Its battle-blast of onset. · The band all sate;
They watched along the water ·
                      the sea-worms great,
Monsters of the dragon-breed, ·
                      trying there the sea,
And on the foreland ledges · Nicors lying free
(Who 're wont at early morning ·
                      their grievous quest to take 1091
Out upon the sail-road)— ·
                      and wild-beast and snake.
Bitter and puffed with anger, ·
                      they hastened away—
They had heard that clangor, ·
                      the war-horn's lay.
One did the Geatish Leader ·
                      with arrow-bow from shore 1095
Berob of life forever · and of the waves' uproar.

The warrior-shaft, the hardy, ·
          unto his heart went home—
He whom death had taken swam ·
          more sluggish on the foam!
Speedily on the billows ·
          with barbed boar-spears
They pressed him so sorely, ·
          they harried him so fierce, 1100
And dragged him up the ledges, ·
          this wave-tossing Ranger.
The marvelling warriors looked upon ·
          the grim and grisly Stranger.

GIRDED himself, did Beowulf, ·
          with his jarlman's weeds;
Naught for his life he mournèd. ·
          His coat of mail must needs,
Bright with deft devices, ·
          be trying the sea-quest— 1105
This hand-woven byrnie big, ·
          that girt his bony-chest,
So never a grip-in-battle ·
          might do his bosom scath,
Nor life be hurt by vengeful grasp ·
          of this Thing-of-Wrath.
The head of him was guarded ·
          by the helmet white
That soon must seek the sounding surge ·
          and stir the deeps below: 1110
With lordly bands 't was bounden, ·
          with treasure-work 't was dight,
As the weapon-smith had wrought it ·
          in days of long ago,
And wondrously had decked it ·
          and set with shapes of boar,
That brand nor blade of battle ·
          might bite it nevermore.

NOR was that the smallest ·
          of helps to mighty deed 1115
Which Spokesman of Hrothgar ·
          had loaned him in his need:
A good sword hafted, · and Hrunting its name,
Of all old heirlooms · the first it was in fame.
The edge of it was iron, ·
          etched with twig and spray,
Hardened by the battle-blood; ·
          ne'er did it betray 1120
Any man that clasped it ·
          with hand amid the fray,—
Any man that dared to go · on war-paths away,
To folk-stead of foemen. ·
          Nor this the first time now
That Hrunting-sword of Unferth ·
          in mighty works should dow.
In sooth the bairn of Ecglaf, ·
          great though his prowess be, 1125
Remembered not his speech of late ·
          when drunk with wine was he,—
Now as he lent his weapon ·
          to a stouter swordsman here.

Himself he durst not hazard ·
          his own life in the mere,
Nor dree a warrior's duty. ·
          And thus he lost the fame,
The glory of a doughty deed. ·
          For the Other 't was not so, 1130
When he himself had girded ·
          for battle with the Foe.

XXI

BEOWULF made his speech then, ·
          bairn of Ecgtheow, he:
'Bethink thee now, thou mighty ·
          son of Halfdane's name,
Gold-Friend of house-carls, ·
          Sovran wise and free,
Bethink thee, now I 'm girt for quest, ·
          what we twain spake before: 1135
If for thy need, O Hrothgar, ·
          my life I should give o'er,
That thou to me wouldst ever be, ·
          when I 'm no longer here,
Still in the place of a father; · every trusty fere,
Each of these my kin-thanes, ·
          do thou as guardian tend,
If once the battle take me; ·
          and likewise, O my Friend, 1140
These treasures that thou gavest me ·
          unto my Master send.
Then Hygelac, son of Hrethel, ·
          may ken from all this gold,
Aye, see, when he beholdeth ·
          these giftings rich and old,
That I indeed had found me ·
          a Treasure-Giver bright,
And had my joy in him and his ·
          so long as still I might. 1145
And let thou, too, thy Unferth, ·
          that far-famed soul,
Have the olden heirloom, ·
          the sword with wavy scroll,
Hard of edge and jewelled. ·
          In Hrunting will I trust
To work my doom of glory— ·
          or I die the death I must.'

AFTER these his words the Geat, ·
          Beowulf, in pride 1150
Hastened in his valor. ·
          No answer would he bide.
The billows took the Battle-Man. ·
          'T was a while of the day
Ere he arrived the sea-floor ·
          where the Monster lay.
And soon this grim and greedy ·
          She-Thing ravin-fierce,
That held the stretches of the floods ·
          a hundred half-years, 1155
Found that there some one of men ·
          from up above had sought

The dwelling-place of eldritch-wights. ·
     Against him then she caught,
With grisly claws she gripped him. ·
      His warrior-body sound
Thereby no whit she scathèd. ·
     His mail did shield him round
So that reach she might not, ·
    with loathly fingers stark, 1160
Athrough his army-corslet, ·
      his linkèd battle-sark.
Then as she to the bottom came, ·
    this She-Wolf of the sea,
She bore unto her own home ·
    the Chieftain-of-the-Rings,
In such a wise he might not, ·
     albeit so wroth was he,
Ever wield his weapons. ·
    And many monstrous Things 1165
Mauled him in the maelstrom, ·
     many a sea-beast tried,
With its battling tushes, ·
     to burst his sark aside,
And swarmed upon their Troubler. ·
    Then was the Jarl aware
That he was in some hall of hate— ·
    he knew not what or where—
In which not any water ·
     could scathe him at all,
Nor floods in onrush touch him ·
     because of roofèd hall; 1171
And he saw a light of fire, ·
     a brightly flashing flare.
And Beowulf had a look then ·
    upon this deep-sea Troll,
This mighty Mere-Woman. ·
     Then up with sword and soul
He made a sudden onset, ·
    nor hand delayed the stroke, 1175
And on her head the ringèd blade ·
     its greedy war-song woke,
But, lo, the Stranger found then ·
     his flasher-in-the-fray
Would bite not, would scathe not ·
     the life it sought today,
For Hrunting's edge was failing ·
     the Chief in his distress,
Though often in the old days ·
     it had endured the press, 1180
And cloven many a helmet, ·
    and war-coat of the fey:
This was the first of all times ·
     that low its glory lay.
Again had he but one thought,— ·
    nor courage did he lack,—
Still mindful of valor, · this Kin of Hygelac!
In wrath the Champion hurlèd ·
     the fretted blade away, 1185
Bound on hilt with ring-work, ·
     till there on earth it lay.
That stout sword and steel-edged; ·
    and on main strength relied,

The might of his old hand-grip. ·
     So must a man of pride,
Whenever he bethinks him ·
     to win in battle-strife
Praises everlasting, · nor careth for his life. 1190
The Chieftain of the Geatfolk,— ·
    who mourned not at the feud,—
Graspèd by her mane of hair ·
     Grendel's Mother lewd.
This hardy son of battle,— ·
     so did his anger swell,—
Flung the deadly She-Wolf ·
     till to ground she fell.
Speedily thereafter, · with her grip so grim, 1195
She gave him goodly payment ·
     and laid her hold on him.
And then with heart aweary, ·
    this Fighter fierce and lone
Stumbled in his footing, ·
    that there he tumbled prone.
Then on the Stranger in her hall ·
    The Mother squatted down,
And forth she drew her dagger, ·
    broad of blade and brown. 1200
She would wreak her bairn now, ·
     her only child this day;
But on the Geatman's shoulders ·
    the woven breast-mail lay,
And that withstood the inthrust ·
     of point and edge at last.
For then the son of Ecgtheow ·
    to under-earth had passed,
Had not his battle-byrnie, ·
    his war-mesh stout and broad, 1205
To him its help y-given, · and had not holy God,
The Ruler, he, of Heaven, ·
     justly swayed the fight—
The wise Lord with his award— ·
    when Beowulf stood upright.

XXII

For saw he 'mongst the war-gear ·
     one victorious bill,
An old sword of ettins, ·
    with edges doughty still, 1210
The pick and choice of weapons, ·
    a warsman's prize indeed;
But more than any other man ·
    might bear in battle-need—
Good and brave to look on, ·
     the giants' handicraft.
The Bold One of the Scyldings ·
    he seized its belted haft;
And, battle-grim and savage, ·
    the ringèd blade he drew; 1215
And, of his life all hopeless, ·
     in fury smote so true
That it gripped her sorely · unto the neck, oho!
And brake in twain its bone-rings. ·
    The sword was keen to go

Athrough her doomèd body. ·
     She crumpled in the murk.
The old sword was bloody. ·
     The Hero liked his work. 1220

AND the gleam out-blazèd, ·
     within there stood a light,
As from heaven shineth ·
     the sky's Candle bright.
He looked about the dwelling, ·
     he turned him to the wall,
He heaved by hilt the weapon, ·
     this hardiest sword of all;
Wroth and with but *one* thought, ·
     the Thane of Hygelac— 1225
With its edge not useless ·
     for such a man's attack!—
Speedily was of a will · to pay that Grendel back
For his many onslaughts ·
     made on folk West-Dane,
Mickle more than one time, ·
     when asleep he'd slain
Hrothgar's hearth-fellows, ·
     and slumbering eat with jaws 1230
Fifteen of Danish folk ·
     and fifteen borne in claws
Outward, his ghastly prey. ·
     For Beowulf, the dread,
Paid him his award for that, ·
     where he beheld on bed
Grendel, the battle-weary, · lying lorn of life,
Ev'n by scathe he'd gotten ·
     in Heorot at the strife. 1235
The corse did spring asunder; ·
     it dreed a blow, though dead,
Oho, a swinging war-stroke,— ·
     and off was carved the head!

THE wise carls that with Hrothgar ·
     sate peering at the flood
Soon saw the surges swirling, ·
     the sea all stained with blood,
The white-haired ones together ·
     about the brave Man speak: 1240
Saying they ween the Ætheling ·
     no more will come to seek,
In the pride of victory, · their glorious Overlord,
Since him it seemed to many ·
     the Sea-Wolf had devoured.
Then came the day's ninth hour; ·
     the Scyldings left the ness;
The Gold-Friend of clansmen, ·
     Hrothgar, hied him home; 1245
Only the Geatish strangers ·
     sate in their distress,
Sick at heart with longing, ·
     and stared upon the foam.
They wished but never weened to see ·
     their dear Lord's self again.

THEN the sword, the war-bill, ·
     'gan wondrously to wane
In icicles of battle, ·
     by goblin-gore accurst: 1250
Likest to ice it melted, ·
     when God, the Father, first
The bands of frost doth loosen, ·
     unfettering stream and pool,—
He 's Lord of times and seasons, ·
     and very sooth his rule!
The Chieftain of the Weder-Geats ·
     he took not from the lair
Not any goods of treasure ·
     (though saw he many there), 1255
Except the head of Grendel ·
     and hilt so bravely dight:
The fretted blade had burnt away, ·
     the sword had melted quite—
So hot had been the blood of her, ·
     so poison-fierce withal
Had been this eldritch Ogress ·
     that died there in the hall.
But he who in the combat ·
     did bide the demon-slaughter 1260
Soon was at his swimming, ·
     up-diving through the water.

CLEANSED were surge and stretches wide, ·
     where the grim Mere-Wife
Had left this fleeting world of ours ·
     and her days of life.
The sea-farer's Safe-guard, ·
     this Stout-Heart of toil,
Came striking out to landward, ·
     fain of his sea-spoil, 1265
Fain of his booty-burden. ·
     Went to meet him then
His staunch troop of tribesmen, ·
     thanked the God of men,
Rejoiced in him their Leader ·
     to see him sound again.
Helm and mail of Hero ·
     they loosened with a will;
The waters under welkin, ·
     the bloody pool was still; 1270
Forth they fared in foot-prints, ·
     these happy æthelings;
The earth-way, the known road, ·
     they measured, bold as kings.
They bare the head from sea-cliff, ·
     a load for each, though stout,
And four upon the spear-pole ·
     scarce lifted it about
Onward to the Gold-Hall, · till into hall bedene
They came, these brave-in-battle, ·
     these Geatmen, the fourteen. 1276
Their Chieftain in a mighty mood ·
     amid them trod the mead,
Till he, as first of clansmen, ·
     this Man so keen of deed,
Hero, battle-hardy, · with glory honorèd,
Came to greet his Hrothgar. ·
     And now is Grendel's head 1280

XXIII

Borne by hair where warriors drink,— ·
                    to jarls and Lady there
A gruesome vision wondrous. ·
                    The Danes upon it stare.

BEOWULF made his speech then, ·
                    son of Ecgtheow, he:
'Lo, thou Son of Halfdane, ·
                    with joy we 've brought to thee,
As token of glory, · this spoil thou here dost see,
O Sovran of the Scyldings. ·
                    I barely 'scaped with life; 1286
Unsoftly did I risk the work ·
                    in under-water strife;
Straight had the battle ended, ·
                    had God not been my shield,
For Hrunting in the combat ·
                    I might in no wise wield,
Though doughty be that weapon. ·
                    But he, mankind's Defender, 1290
Gave me upon the wall to see, ·
                    hanging in its splendor,
A huge sword of old times. · (Oft and oft withal
The Father guides the friendless.) ·
                    I drew that sword from wall,
Then slew I at the onset, ·
                    when my chance was good,
The Wardens of that under-house. ·
                    But so sprang the blood, 1295
The hottest gore of slaughter, ·
                    that the fretted blade,
The battle-bill, was burnt all. ·
                    From my foes I made,
Bearing thence the hilt away. ·
                    I wreaked the crimes of hell,
The death-fall of Danishmen, ·
                    as was fit and well.
I promise thee in Heorot · a sleep care-free, 1300
With band of thy retainers, ·
                    each who follows thee,
Of the older, of the younger; ·
                    and ever from that quarter,
O Sovran of the Scyldings, ·
                    release from dread of slaughter
For these here, thy jarlmen, ·
                    as erst 't was thine to dree.'

THEN was that hilt, the golden, ·
                    the giants' work of yore, 1305
Giv'n to hand of the old King, ·
                    the Battle-Leader hoar;
After the fall of devils, ·
                    to Hrothgar's keep it fell—
This work of wonder-smithmen; ·
                    yea, when this Heart-of-Hell,
God's Foeman, murder-guilty, ·
                    this world of ours gave o'er
(And eke this Grendel's Mother), ·
                    it passed into the power 1310
Of him, the best of World-Kings ·
                    of all between the seas
Who e'er on Scandia's island dealt ·
                    men their golden fees.

HROTHGAR made his speech then; ·
                    on hilt he cast his eyes,
Relic of the olden time, ·
                    whereon was writ the rise
Of that far-off warfare, ·
                    when o'erwhelmed the flood 1315
And the ocean's outpour ·
                    once the giants' brood:
They bore themselves too boldly, ·
                    a folk estranged from God;
For this the Lord made end-award ·
                    by whelming under wave.
So on the golden sword-guard, ·
                    in many a runic stave,
Was marked aright and set and said ·
                    for whom was wrought of yore 1320
That best of steel with twinèd hilt, ·
                    and etched with dragons o'er.

THEN spake wise Son of Halfdane— ·
                    and still were all the throng:
'Lo, one, like me, who 's warded ·
                    a kingdom long and long,
And for his folk still worketh ·
                    the right and the sooth,
One who remembers all of old, ·
                    may say this thing indeed: 1325
That here 's a very jarlman ·
                    born of better breed.
Thy fame shall be uplifted, · my belovèd youth,
Among all peoples, Beowulf, ·
                    over the wide ways;
And thou shalt hold thy prowess ·
                    with wisdom all thy days;
My troth to thee will I fulfill, ·
                    e'en as we spake before. 1330
Thou 'lt be unto thy people ·
                    an aid forevermore,
A help unto the heroes.'

* * *

XXIV

* * *

WENT to seek his seat then, ·
                    the Geat so free of sorrow,
As the Wise One bade him. ·
                    And now, as erst, again
The feast was dight so fairly ·
                    for valor-famous men, 1335
The sitters in that hall-house. . . . . ·
                    The helmet of the night
Darkened dusky o'er the band. ·
                    Arose each warrior-wight;
The hoary agèd Scylding ·
                    was fain to seek his bed;

The Geat did list him passing well ·
                to lay to rest his head,
He, the famous Shieldman. ·
             And soon the Thane-in-hall— 1340
Who tended with meet courtesy ·
                the Hero's needments all
(Ev'n as these ocean-farers ·
                were worthy of the best)—
Led forth the Hero come from far, ·
                weary from his quest.
So rested he, the Great-Heart. ·
             That House it towered high,
Broad-roofed, gold-bright. ·
             Within it slept the guest, 1345
Until the black raven · with his blithesome cry
Boded the Joy-of-Heaven. ·
             Onward came the Bright,
The Shine that follows shadow. ·
             Hastened every wight;
Æthelings were eager · back to folk to fare;
The Big-Heart would take ship ·
              far away from there. 1350
Bade he then, this Brave One, ·
             Unferth Hrunting bear,
Bade him take his sword again, ·
              the iron blade so lief;
Thanked him for the loan thereof; ·
              quoth, he counted it
A friend-in-war, a good and great; ·
              belied he not a whit
The edge of Unferth's falchion. ·
             That was a gallant chief! 1355
And when the braves were forward, ·
              ready in their gear,
Then stepped he forth, the Hero, ·
              he to Danes so dear,
To where was there the Other ·
              high on kingly seat,
And then this battling Ætheling ·
              did his Hrothgar greet.

XXV

Beowulf made his speech then, ·
            son of Ecgtheow, he: 1360
'Lo, we far-comers, · we farers on the sea,
Have a will to say now · we 'd seek our Hygelac.
Thou hast been a goodly host; ·
            in nothing did we lack.
O Lord of men, if ever · I may this earth upon
Earn me of thy heart's love ·
            more than yet I 've done, 1365
By aught of work-of-battle, · I 'll ready be anon.
If across the long seas, · ever I should hear
That the dwellers round about ·
            burden thee with fear,
As the haters of thy realm ·
            have done of yester-year,
I 'll bring to thee a thousand thanes, ·
            braves for help to thee.' 1370

* * *

Thereto the Son of Halfdane, ·
            whom 'Shield of jarls' they call,
To Beowulf presented · treasures twelve in hall.
And bade him with these giftings ·
            his own, his dear domain
To seek in weal and safety, ·
            and quickly come again.
And then the Lord of Scyldings, ·
            the King of birth so high, 1375
Kissed the best of æthelings ·
            and clasped his neck thereby;
The tears they were afalling ·
            from him, the old man hoar;—
Two likelihoods he thought of—·
            but one of them the more:
That never thereafter ·
            might they each other scan,
Proud men in parley. ·
            So lief was him this man
That now his breast's upheaving ·
            seemed too much to bear; 1381
Bound within his bosom ·
            a secret longing there
After the man beloved · burned into his blood.

But Beowulf thence away ·
            the grass-plain trod,
War-man, gold-proud, · fain of treasure-fee.
There at anchor riding, · a goer-on-the-sea 1386
Was its master biding. ·
            And marching to the main,
The Geatmen spoke of Hrothgar's boon ·
            again and yet again.
That was a King all spotless . . . ·
            till from his joys of strength
Eld, that scathes so many men, ·
            took him too at length. 1390

* * *

THE THIRD PART

XXVI

* * *

It came to pass in after-days, ·
            when Hygelac lay dead
After the battle-clashings, ·
            and battle-swords had sped
Heardred, his offspring, ·
            under the sheltering shield,
(What time the hardy foeman, ·
            the Scylfings, fierce in field,
Had sought him in the vanguard, ·
            and laid him low with grame, 1395
Nephew of Hereric), · that Beowulf became
Ruler of the broad realms. · Fifty winters told,
He reigned till now an agèd King, ·
            a Folk-Ward old.
'T was then that in the dark nights, ·
            a Thing began to lord—

A Dragon on a hollow heath, ·
        who watched there a hoard, 1400
A steep stone-barrow. · A path thereunder lay,
By sons of men unguessed of. ·
        There within did stray
Some nameless man or other,
        who with hand did nim
From out the heathen Hoard, whilst ·
        slept the Dragon grim,
A goblet, a golden one, · nor gave it back to him,
Albeit was thus defrauded ·
        its Keeper thievishly. . . . 1406
Then the folk in burgs around ·
        found how wroth was he!

XXVII

But not of own accord there, ·
        not of his own will,
Brake he the Serpent's Hoard there, ·
        who did the Drake such ill;
But he, a slave of some one ·
        of human fellowship, 1410
Seeking forlorn for cover, ·
        fled his master's whip,
And into the cave he entered, ·
        a man by guilt oppressed.
Anon he gazed with terror, ·
        he, the stranger guest;
Yet, even amid the horror, ·
        he, the wretched wight,
Espied the jewelled goblet. ·
        Was plain, besides, to sight 1415
Many a treasure olden · in that house-of-earth,
Precious heirlooms golden ·
        of kinsmen of high birth,
Which some jarl or other, · in the days of yore,
Taking thought, had hidden ·
        there forevermore.
All his kin aforetime · death away had taken,
And he alone of warrior-host ·
        lingering there forsaken, 1421
A watcher, friends bewailing, ·
        weened like theirs his doom,—
That soon he too must leave each ·
        glad heirloom.
Ready to hand a barrow new ·
        lay by ness and moor,
Hard-by the sea-waves, · secret and secure. 1425
The Warden-of-Rings did thither ·
        the jarl-treasure bear,
Of plated gold a goodly deal, ·
        worth the hiding there.

Quoth he then in few words: ·
        'Earth, now hold,
Now that warriors can not, ·
        the jarlmen's gold— 1429
Lo, from thee did brave men · get it all of old.
Battle-death hath taken, · body-bale hath slain
Every sturdy fighter, · each folk-thane,
Of all who saw the joy in hall— ·
        ne'er to see again.
None have I who'll wield the sword, ·
        none who'll burnish fair
The golden-plated tankard, ·
        the drink-stoup rare: 1435
All the valiant noblemen ·
        are gone . . . else . . . where.
From helmet hard, with gold dight, ·
        the platings shall depart;
The burnishers are sleeping ·
        who should prepare with art
The casques for every onset. ·
        E'en so the army-coat,
That braved amid the battle ·
        bite of steel on throat 1440
Over the clashing bucklers, ·
        shall crumble with its bearer;
Yea, the ringèd byrnie, ·
        shall with its warrior-wearer
Fare afar no longer · on the hero's frame.
Never joy of harp now, · the glee-wood's game;
Never now the good hawk ·
        swingeth through the hall; 1445
Never now the swift horse ·
        beateth court or stall;
Of my kith hath battle-death ·
        sent . . . forth . . . all.'

Thus, with soul of sorrow, ·
        alone he mourned the rest;
By day and night he wandered, ·
        blitheless of breast,
Till waves of death o'erwhelmed him. ·
        His Hoard of dead delight 1450
That old Dusk-Scather, ·
        who flieth in the night,
Enfolded in fire, · found all open there,—
That naked Poison-Dragon, ·
        who, burning through the air,
Seeketh out the barrows. · Him the folk on fold
Dreadeth very sorely. ·
        He needs must seek, I'm told, 1455
For hoards within the earth ·
        and guard the heathen gold,
A Worm of many winters— ·
        no good thereby gets he!
So this Plague-of-people ·
        for winters hundreds three,
This Drake so huge and mighty, ·
        held within the ground
His own hoard-cavern, ·
        until the man who found 1460
Roused his wrath in bosom. ·
        The golden tankard then
He bare unto his Master; ·
        and begged for peace again
Of him, his angry Owner. ·
        Thus plundered was the den,
The hoard of booty lessened. ·
        The wretch received his boon.

His lord now first did look upon ·
    the olden work of men; 1465
And when the Worm awoke, there was ·
     a new woe soon.
Along the stone he snuffed there, ·
    this Stark-Heart dread,
And found the foeman's footprints, ·
   who with secret tread
Had stepped there too forward ·
    near his Dragon-head.
(Thus may a man not fey yet ·
  survive, where'er he trod, 1470
Woe and ways of exile ·
  who owns the grace of God.)
Greedily the Hoard-Ward ·
   sought along the ground
To find the man who gave his heart ·
·   asleep so sore a wound;
Hot and fierce, he circled
    the barrow all around;
But in that barren moorland ·
   not any man he found. 1475
Yet war was in his marrow, ·
  on battle-work his thought,—
Whiles darted into barrow, ·
   the precious flagon sought.
Soon he found that some man ·
   had searchèd out his gold,
His treasure-trove so lordly. ·
   Though restive he and bold,
The Hoard-Ward bided ·
  until the evening came; 1480
Awrath the barrow's Keeper ·
   would requite with flame
The dear drink-flagon. . . . ·
    Now the day was fled,
To the joy of Dragon. · Blazing now he sped,
Folded in fire, · forth from the wall.
That was a beginning · horrible for all; 1485
And folk within that Kingdom ·
   soon thereafter kenned
In fate of their Ring-Giver ·
    thereof the awful end.

XXVIII

THEN began the Stranger One ·
   forth his gleeds to spew,
And burn the bright homesteads; ·
    the glare ablazing flew,
Frightful to landsfolk. · Nothing living there
Would he leave, this loathly One, ·
    Flier-in-the-air. 1491
The warfare of the great Worm ·
   wide about was clear,
The rancor of this Ravager, · afar and anear,—
How this fell Destroyer · the folk of Geatish kin
Hated and hounded. · He shot to Hoard within,
To his hidden King's-hall, ·
   ere the morning came. 1496
The dwellers in the land he 'd ·
   lapped about with flame,
With brand and with bale-fire. ·
   He trusted in his mound,
His wall and his warfare. ·
   His trust in vain he found.

THEN was unto Beowulf ·
   the horror made known, 1500
Speedily and soothly, · that the home his own,
The goodliest of dwellings, ·
    the Geat's gift-throne,
In fiery surge had melted. ·
    That to this good King
Was a grief in bosom, · the worst of sorrowing.
The Wise One he weenèd ·
   that he the Wielder might 1505
Bitterly have angered, · breaking olden right
Of the Lord eternal. · Welled his bosom sore
With thoughts of black foreboding, ·
   as ne'er his wont before.
From beyond the water-land, ·
   the Fire-Drake with gleeds
Now had laid in ashes · the fastness of the ledes,
The stronghold of Geatmen. ·
   The Warrior-King for this, 1511
The Sovran of the Weders, planned ·
   how vengeance should be his.
He, the clansmen's Bulwark, ·
    Lord of jarlmen, he,
Bade them work a wondrous shield, ·
    all of iron firm—
For well he wist that linden, ·
   wood of forest tree, 1515
Could help him not against the flames ·
   of that great Worm.
He needs must now be meeting, ·
   this King of passing worth,
His end of days, the fleeting, ·
   and his life on earth—
And the Dragon with him, ·
  though long he held the Hoard.
Yet there he scorned, did Beowulf, ·
   the Geats' Ring-Lord, 1520
To follow the Far-Flier ·
   with troops of spear and sword.
He dreaded not the contest, ·
   despised the Dragon's war,
His vigor and his valor; · because so oft before,
He 'd passed so many perils, · clashes in the van,
Hazarded so many straits, · since as victor-man,
He 'd cleansed the hall of Hrothgar, ·
   and at the grapple erst 1526
Battling crushed the Grendel-kin— ·
    that breed accurst.

   * * *

XXIX

   * * *

BEOWULF made his speech then; ·
   spake a vaunting word,
Even for the last time: · 'Lo, I dared my fill

Of battles in my youth, I. · Now this day I will,
The folk's old Warden, · dare another still, 1531
And do a deed of glory,   ·   if this Pest-of-all
Forth will come to seek me ·
       from his earth-hall.'

Then each man he greeted, ·
      the helmet-bearers grim,
Even for the final time, · his fellows dear to him:
'No sword would I bear me, ·
   no weapon to this Snake, 1536
If I only wist how   ·   to get upon the Drake
The boasted grip of arm that I ·
      once on Grendel got.
But yonder I do fear me   ·   battle-fire hot,
Reek of breath and poison. ·
     And so I have on me 1540
Shield-board and byrnie. ·
     No foot-breadth I'll flee
From the barrow's Keeper. ·
      Us twain it shall befall,
Even as Wyrd allotteth, ·
      fighting at the wall—
Wyrd who is the master   ·   ever of us all.
My mood is bold and I forbear ·
    my boast against this Flyer. 1545
Bide ye by the barrow,   ·   in your war-attire,
Ye heroes in your harness, ·
      awaiting which of twain
Shall better bear the onset · and the battle-pain.
This quest is not for you now, ·
    but mine alone the meed
To match a might with Monster ·
     and do a jarlman's deed. 1550
I'll win this gold with prowess, ·
    or war shall take me hence—
The death-bale take the fighting man, ·
      your dear Prince.'

Upstood beside his buckler ·
     this Man-at-arms so stark,
Hardy under helmet. · He bore his battle-sark
Down beneath the stone-cliff. ·
     He trusted at the test 1555
The strength of one man only— ·
    not that a craven's quest!
Then he who'd passed in hardihood ·
     unscathed so many blows,
So many battle-rushes ·
    where clashed afoot the foes,
Espied by the wall there   ·   a stone-arch stout,
Whence a stream was breaking ·
     from the barrow out. 1560
The billows of that burn there ·
     were hot with fierce fire;
Nor that under-passage, · to the Hoard nigher,
Might he any while endure, ·
     for the Dragon's flare.
From his breast he let then · a word forth fare,
He, the Prince of Weder-Geats, ·
     swelling in his ire. 1565

The Stark-Heart stormèd. ·
     His battle-clear tone
Went aringing inward   ·   under the hoar stone.
Dragon-hate was rousèd; ·
     the Hoard-Ward knew
'T was indeed the voice of man. ·
     Now between the two
Was no time for peace-pact! ·
    First from out the gloom 1570
Burst the breath of Monster, · hot battle-fume,
The hollow earth resounded. ·
     Against the grisly Guest
Beowulf in barrow   ·   swung his shield to chest;
Then Ring-Bow in heart was · ready for the test.
But the goodly War-King ·
    had drawn his sword for blow, 1575
An old-time heirloom,   ·   with edge not slow.
Each with thoughts of murder felt ·
      terror of his foe.
Stern of mood, the Chieftain stood ·
     against his buckler high.
The Worm now arched its back amain. ·
     The Mailed One waited nigh.
With body bowed it burned and glode, ·
     hastening to its fate; 1580
But shield did fend in life and limb ·
     the King so good and great
A briefer while than wish of him ·
      did thereby await:
For there 't was his to struggle ·
     the first time and day
In such a wise as Wyrd denies ·
     victory in the fray.
He had his hand uplifted, ·
    he, the Geatish Lord; 1585
Hard smote the grisly Foeman ·
     with the ancient sword;
But, lo, its edge did crumble, ·
     brown upon the bone,
And bit there too slackly · for need of Hero lone,
In the press of sore distress. ·
     The barrow's Keeper then
After that battle-swingeing ·
     was mad of mood again; 1590
He scattered fires of slaughter; ·
     and wide sprang the flame.
The Gold-Friend of Geatmen ·
     bragged no victory-fame.
His war-bill weakened,   ·   naked in the feud,
As it ever ought not,   ·   an iron passing good.
That was no easy faring ·
     back o'er cavern's ground 1595
For the Kin of Ecgtheow,   ·   the far-renownèd.
'T was his against his will now ·
     to make his home elsewhere,
To leave the life that's loaned us, ·
     as every man must fare.
Anon the infuriate Foemen ·
     again together drew;
Heartened himself the Hoard-Ward, ·
     and belched his breath anew; 1600

And he who once had wielded ·
                      over a folk as Sire
Was laboring now in sore straits, ·
                      folded round with fire.
Nor stood about him staunchly ·
                      his own fighting crew,
The bairns of the æthelings; ·
                      but to the woods they flew,
And there they saved their bodies. ·
                      On one of them this wrought 1605
Cark and care of spirit: · there is never aught
Can alter loyal kinship ·
                      for man of noble thought.

XXX

HIGHT was that one Wiglaf, ·
                      the son of Weohstan,
And Lord of the Scylfings, · belovèd Shield-man,
Ælfhere's kinsman. · His Liege-Lord he saw
Under his casque of battle ·
                      front that flaming maw. 1611
Then he recalled the giftings ·
                      from him his Lord and Head,—
The lands of the Waegmundings, ·
                      the rich homestead,
And each of all the folk-rights ·
                      his father used to wield.
No longer might he hold back; ·
                      his fingers clasped the shield, 1615
The wood of yellow linden; ·
                      his olden sword he drew.

* * *

                      AND now in battle-strife
'T was Wiglaf's for the first time ·
                      to serve beside his Lord.
Nor did his spirit soften, ·
                      nor did his father's sword
Weaken in the war-fare— ·
                      as soon he found, the Drake, 1620
When once they 'd met together! ·
                      Wiglaf he spake;
Said to comrades sagely, ·
                      as sorrow sore he dreed:
'The time I well remember, ·
                      as we took the mead,
How we vowed in beer-hall ·
                      to him who gave us rings,
Vowed unto our Overlord, ·
                      that we, his æthelings, 1625
Would requite for war-gear, ·
                      for hard sword and helm,
If need like this should haply · ever overwhelm.
For this it was he chose us, ·
                      us for this his quest,
Of his own will, and deemed us ·
                      worth the glorious test.
And gave to me these treasures, ·
                      because he counted us 1630
Good spear-wielders, · helmets valorous,
Albeit our Lord was minded, ·
                      as Fender of his folk,
Himself alone to compass ·
                      for us the victor-stroke,
Since he of men hath compassed ·
                      most of glory-fray,
Most of deeds of daring. · Now is come the day
Our Master needs the prowess ·
                      of war-men good. 1636
Let us hasten to him, · to help his hardihood,
Whilst the heat is round him, ·
                      the grim horror-fire.
Of me, at least, God wotteth ·
                      it is my dear desire
That flame embrace this body mine ·
                      with his who gave me gold. 1640
Methinketh it unseemly ·
                      our bucklers home to bring
Before we fell the foe and ·
                      save the Weders' King.
Well I wot it suits not · with all his deeds of old
That he, alone of Geatland's ·
                      tried men and bold,
Should suffer this sorrow ·
                      and sink in battle down. 1645
Sword, helm, byrnie, shield, ·
                      between us shall be one.'

THEN strode he through the slaughter-reek ·
                      with casque upon his head,
To be the standby of his Lord. ·
                      A few words he said:
'Beowulf, belovèd, · hold here, hold,
Even as in young days · sworest thou of old 1650
Ne'er to let thy glory fall, ·
                      so long as life should be.
'T is thine, O steadfast Ætheling, ·
                      famed in bravery,
To guard thee now with all thy prow. ·
                      I will succor thee.'

AT the words the Worm came ·
                      a second time in ire,
Shining in the surging flame, ·
                      Stranger fierce and dire, 1655
To seek his Foes, the loathèd men. ·
                      Was burnt in waves of fire
His buckler to the very boss. ·
                      Nor yet his byrnie might
Serve to shelter Wiglaf, ·
                      the young Spear-Wight.
So dodged the Youth right speedily ·
                      his Kinsman's shield behind,
Now his own was all consumed ·
                      by the fury-wind. 1660
Then again the War-King ·
                      his glory called to mind,
And smote he then by main-strength ·
                      with his battle-glaive,
That, under impulse of his hate, ·
                      to the head it drave.

But Nægling was shivered: ·
     failed him in the fray,
This the sword of Beowulf, ·
    etched and old and gray. 1665
To him it was not given ·
    that any edge of brand
Him could help at battle; ·
    so strong his arm and hand,
As I have heard the story, ·
    that every blade so'er
He overtaxed in swinging it, ·
    when he to battle bare
A weapon wondrous hardy. ·
   'T would stead him not a whit. 1670

Then was the People-Scather, ·
    a third time too,
This bold Fire-Dragon, · mindful to do;
He rushed upon the Hero, ·
    where his chance was fit,
Hot and battle-ugly. · All the neck he bit
With his bitter fang-teeth. ·
   To death the Geat was hurt, 1675
Bloodied o'er with his own gore, ·
    in welling wave and spurt.

XXXI

Then at the need of Beowulf, · as I heard tell,
The Jarlman upstanding ·
    proved his prowess well,
His craft and his keenness, ·
    as his indeed by birth.
He made not for the Monster's head; ·
   but in his will and worth, 1680
His hand was all but burnt away, ·
    the while he helped his Kin,
As pierce he did the flamy Drake ·
    from under, up and in,—
This Hero in his harness. ·
    Deep the sword it ran,
Gleaming and gold-dight. · And the fire began
To slacken thereafter. ·
   The King himself once more 1685
Girt his wits together. · His war-knife he drew,
Biting and battle-sharp, ·
    which on his sark he wore.
The Weder down the middle then ·
    slit the Worm in two.
So they felled the Dragon, ·
    the fiery head and wings.
The dauntless twain the Pest had slain, ·
    Kinsman-Æthelings. 1690
Each warrior it behooveth · like Wiglaf to be,
Each thane at need of liege-lord. ·
    But for the King was this
The last of victor-hours · by any deed of his,
The last of work in world here. ·
    The wound he had to dree
From the Snake of under-earth ·
    began to burn and swell; 1695
And soon he found a poison · balefully did well
Deep in breast within him. ·
    Walked the King along,
Till by the wall he sate him, ·
    thinking, on the mould;
He looked upon the giants' works,— ·
    the earth-house old
With arches there-under ·
    on posts stone-strong.
Then with hands his Wiglaf, ·
    retainer without peer, 1700
Laved him with water, · his Overlord dear,
Laved the bleeding Hero, ·
    battle-worn and drear,
And loosened him his helmet. ·

    Beowulf replied,
Spake, in spite of deadly wound ·
    pitifully wide;
Well he weened his time was come, ·
    his earth-joys passed, 1706
His tale of days all taken, ·
    and death anearing fast:
'Now would I give over, · now unto my son,
To offspring, my war-weeds, ·
    if me were granted one—
An heir from my body, ·
    to wear them when I died. 1710
I have ruled this people · fifty winters' tide;
Nor is there any folk-king ·
    of all who dwell around
That durst me touch with sword of his, ·
    or me with terrors hound.
I bided in my homeland · my appointed while;
Well mine own I warded; ·
    nor practiced feud and wile; 1715
Nor sware, I guess, not many ·
    broken oaths of guile.
Of all of this my joy I have, ·
    though ill of wounds within,
Since me the God of men may not ·
    charge with murdered kin,
When life my body leaveth. . . . .
    Go, now, quick,
To look upon the Hoard there ·
    under the hoar stone, 1720
Wiglaf, belovèd, ... ·
    now the Worm is prone,
And sleepeth, reft of treasure-trove, ·
    from the sword so sick.
Wiglaf, hasten now, · that I may once behold
These riches of the foretime, · ·
    these master-stores of gold. . . .
Yea, that once with gladness ·
    I may look upon
The bright and cunning jewels. ·
    For softlier anon, 1726
After that golden seeing, ·
    I 'll leave behind, I know,
My life and the lordship ·
    I held from long ago.'

XXXII

Then the son of Weohstan, · as I heard tell,
Swiftly stirred to wish and word ·
        of him whose wound was fell, 1730
Of him the battle-sick Man; ·
        and under barrow's roof
Took himself and ring-mesh, ·
        his woven sark of proof.
And then that dauntless Thane-man ·
        saw with victor-pride,
On passing where his Chieftain sate, ·
        store of gems inside:
Saw the gold glisten · on the ground then, 1735
Wonders on the wall there, ·
        and the Dragon's den,
Flier old by twilight, · of standing jars a sight,
Vessels of the men of yore, ·
        with none to burnish bright,
Bereft of their adornments. · Many a helmet old
There was lying rusty, · and arm-rings of gold,
Artfully twisted. · (Riches so rare, 1741
Such booty in a barrow, · may easily ensnare
Any one of mankind, · hide it whosoe'er.)
And also saw he hanging · over Hoard on high
A banner all golden, · wefted cunningly, 1745
Of handiwork a wonder. ·
        And from it streamed a light,
Whereby the cavern's bottom ·
        well perceive he might,
And well o'er-count the prizes. ·
        But saw not there within
Any sign of Serpent— · sword had taken him.

Then, as I heard the story, ·
        did one Man alone 1750
Reave the Hoard from olden mound, ·
        the giants' work of stone;
With beakers and with platters, ·
        as his choice would seek,
He laded his bosom. · He took the banner eke,
Brightest of beacons. · The old King's bill—
O its edge was iron!— · a while ago did kill 1755
Him who had defended ·
        so long the treasure-found,
And spread o' midnights terror-flames, ·
        billowing fiercely round,
Hot before the Hoard there, ·
        until he died of wound.
Hastened now the Herald, · eager to go back,
Spurred by splendor-booty. ·
        Him a doubt did rack 1760
Whether he, the high-souled, ·
        would meet alive once more
The Sovran of the Weders, ·
        weakened now so sore,
There upon the moor-stead ·
        where him he 'd left before.

Then Wiglaf with the treasures ·
        found his King and Friend,
His glorious Chief, ableeding, ·
        near his life's end. 1765
Again he plashed with water; ·
        until the point of word
Pierced athrough the breast-hoard ·
        of Beowulf, the old,
And spake he in his grieving, ·
        with gaze upon the gold:
'For this splendor-booty ·
        be thanks unto the Lord,
Unto the King-of-Glory, ·
        for what I here behold, 1770
To God, the everlasting, ·
        in that 't is mine to give
Such gifts unto my people, · while an hour I live.
Now have I bartered · for the hoard of gold
The end of this my old life. ·
        Look ye well, my fere,
To my people's needs now. · I 'm no longer here.
Bid the battle-bold men · build a mound to me,
Shining, after death-pyre, ·
        on foreland by the sea; 1777
Out upon Whale's Ness, · it shall lift on high,
Reminder to my people · of the man was I,
That ever thereafter · sailor-folk will hail 1780
"Beowulf's Barrow" ·
        when home from far they sail,
O'er the misty ocean, · past the Ness-of-Whale.'

From his neck he doffed then, ·
        he, the Sturdy-Souled,
And gave to his Retainer, · a collar of gold;
Gave the young Spearman ·
        his helmet gold-bedight, 1785
His ring and his byrnie; ·
        bade him use them right:
'Thou art only remnant · of our common line,
The Kin of the Waegmundings, · Wiglaf mine.
Wyrd has swept before ye ·
        all my stock and stem,
The jarlmen in their glory. · I must after them.'
The last of words was that for which ·
        that agèd Heart had breath, 1791
Ere he chose the bale-fire, ·
        the hot waves of death.
And so from breast of Beowulf ·
        the soul took flight
To seek the just award of souls ·
        soothfast in the right.

XXXIII

Then it went O sorely · with the young Friend,
When he saw his dearest · at his life's end, 1796
Faring so pitiful— · his King upon the ground.
But lay the Slayer likewise, ·
        wasted with a wound,
Of his life bereavèd, · Earth-Drake vile—
No longer crook-bow worm could lord ·
        o'er the treasure-pile, 1800
Since the edge of iron, ·
        forged by hammer's play.

Blade so hard and battle-scarred, ·
                had ta'en him far away.
Thus the Wide-Flier, · from his wound so still,
Sprawled upon the mould there, ·
                nigh his hoard-hill.
Nevermore o' midnights ·
            would he disport in air, 1805
Or, proud of his prizes, · show his shadow there.
But he to earth had fallen, ·
                by the work of hands
Of a Battle-Leader. · Forsooth, in all the lands
But few, however hardy ·
                and dauntless of deed,
Have thriven when they bravèd ·
            the breath of Poison-Breed, 1810
Or when they laid their hands on ·
                a drake's ring-hall,
If once they found the Warden ·
                watching by the wall,
Crouching at the barrow— · few, as I recall.
This deal of lordly goods was bought ·
              by Beowulf's own death;
And each from out this fleeting life ·
                yielded up his breath. 1815

Ere long the battle-laggards, ·
              the troth-breaking men,
The woodland abandoned, · together the ten,
That durst not there awhile ago ·
              put their spears in play
For Beowulf, their Liege-Lord, ·
              in his mickle needs;
But each one bore his buckler ·
            and his battle-weeds, 1820
Shambling and shame-faced, ·
              to where the Old One lay.
And they looked on Wiglaf. ·
              He o'erwearied kneeled
At his Master's shoulder, ·
              he, so brave with shield;
Would waken him with water. ·
              But help was none thereby,
And the Youth he might not, ·
            though yearned he so to try, 1825
Hold on earth the life of him ·
            whom God had willed should die.
God, the mighty Deemster, · wielded his will
Then o'er deeds of human kind ·
              as he doeth still.
There was in the young Thane ·
            an answer grim withal,
Nor hard of understanding, ·
            to those cowards all. 1830

Wiglaf made a speech then, ·
              son of Weohstan,
Gazing broken-hearted · at each hated man:
'Lo, whoso will speak sooth, · can say one thing:
That, when he gave ye good gear, ·
              he, your Lord and King,
Gave the battle-harness · ye are standing in,
He threw away those war-weeds, ·
              unto shame and sin, 1836
When the fight befell him— ·
            and oft enough withal
Bestowed he at the ale-bench ·
              on sitters in the hall,
This King unto his clansmen, ·
              helm and byrnie-gear,
The finest he could find for ye, ·
              from afar or near. 1840
In sooth had he, your Folk-King, ·
              little cause to vaunt
Of comrades in this conquest! ·
            But God was kind to grant,
The Wielder over victories, ·
              that with knife, alone,
When he had need of valor, ·
            he laid the Monster prone.
Little could I offer · of aid at the fight, 1845
Yet I helped my Kinsman · beyond my might.
When I struck the deadly ·
              Foeman with my sword,
Thereby was he the weaker ·
            and the slower poured
The fire from the wits of him. ·
              Of helpers, small the sum
That thronged around the Chieftain ·
            when his hour had come. 1850
How shall fail forever · for your Kin abhorred
The getting of the gold-rings, ·
              the gifting of the sword,
All the mirth of land of birth. ·
              Every man shall roam,
Beggared of his freehold, ·
              from his burg and home,
When æthelings from far away ·
            shall hear your deed of blame, 1855
This your flight, ye cowards. ·
            For one of jarlman's name,
Death itself is better · than a life of shame.'

XXXIV

Then Wiglaf bade a Herald ·
              the war-work to declare
Yonder at the fastness · o'er the sea-cliff there,
Where the band of shieldmen ·
            had sat in brooding pain 1860
All the long morning, · between doubts twain:
The end of their belovèd, or . . . ·
              his coming-home again.
Of these new tidings · the Rider to the ness
Was silent touching little; · nay, in soothfastness
He told out the story · in ears of all the band:
'Now is he, Joy-Giver · of the Weder-land, 1866
The Sovran of the Geatmen, ·
              on the couch-of-death,—
He woneth on the slaughter-bed, ·
            from Dragon's tooth and breath.
Is lying there beside him ·
              the Queller of the Good,

Sick with thrusts of dagger; •
           for with the sword he could 1870
Work no wound soever, •
           upon the Monster's hide.
Wiglaf is sitting,   •   Beowulf beside,
Weohstan's youngling, •
           the quick beside the dead.
Holdeth he with heart's woe •
           a watch at his head,
O'er loved Lord and loathed Drake. •
           Now our folk may wait 1875
Anew a while of warfare • when our Prince's fate
Unto Franks and Frisians • shall be widely told.
Started was this quarrel • grievously of old,
When Hygelac to Frisian land •
           afaring came with fleet.
And him the Hetwaras • did in battle beat, 1880
And valiantly achievèd • by their over-might
That he, the byrnie-breasted, •
           bowed and fell in fight—
To give unto his chivalry •
           no more the treasures bright.

        * * *

        XXXV

        * * *

Now is best that thither •
           we hasten with speed
To look upon our people's Sire, •
           and Beowulf to bring 1885
Onward to the funeral pyre, •
           who gave us ring by ring.
Nor shall a portion only •
           melt with the man so bold,
But there is a hoard of treasures, •
           and there is countless gold,
Purchased forsooth at a grim price,— •
           circlet and sword and pelf,
Bought us now at the latest •
           with life of the King himself. 1890
These shall the fire devour, •
           these shall the flame enfold;
Never a jarl shall bear him •
           a token dear of the King,
No beautiful girl shall wear gem •
           on neck in a noble ring;
But each, of the gold bereavèd, •
           each in a mood of pain,
Shall wander the lands of strangers, •
           over and over again, 1895
Now that the Army-Leader •
           hath lowered his laughter here,
His mirth and the joy of his revel. •
           For this shall many a spear,
Iron-cold in the morning, •
           be lifted up in the arm,
Clasped in the clansman's fingers; •
           and never the harper's charm
Shall waken these of our warriors. •
           Nay, but the raven wan, 1900
Fluttering over the fallen, •
           shall utter his croak anon,
Telling unto the eagle •
           how he at his feasting sped,
The while with the wolf together •
           he tore away on the dead.'

Thus it was the Warsman •
           the loathly tidings said;
Little was he lying • in words or doom ahead.
Together rose the band then, •
           with tears of sorrow-stress, 1906
Blitheless they betook them •
           under Eagles' Ness,
To gaze upon the wonder. •
           They found o'er sandy shore
Him who gave the rings to them •
           in the times before
Lifeless on his bed of rest. •
           His ending-day had been 1910
Unto him, the dauntless, •
           the Prince of Weder-kin,
Unto him, the Warrior-King, •
           a death of wondrous dying.
But erst had they espied there •
           a stranger creature lying—
The Serpent him beside there, •
           loathed for flame and flying.
That Drake, the grim and grisly, •
           was scorched by fire about; 1915
Fifty foot he measured long, • all stretched out.
Aloft he 'd had his joy of air •
           in night-times past,
And down again had gone to den. •
           In death now fast,
He would use his earthly lair • nevermore at last.
The jars and the goblets •
           were standing by him here, 1920
And platters here were lying, •
           and good swords dear,
Rusted and eaten through, • even as of old
They 'd housèd in earth's bosom •
           a thousand winters told.
This heritage had magic might: •
           this by-gone mortals' gold
Had been by spells encircled, •
           that none of human kind 1925
Could ever touch that treasure-hall, •
           save him whom God designed
(The Sooth-King of victories, •
           Helper, he, of men),
Whomsoe'er he deemèd fit •
           to open hoard and den.

        XXXVI

        * * *

Wiglaf made a speech then, • son of Weohstan:
'Many a jarl must often, • for will of one man,
Suffer a great bitterness— • even now as we.
Nor might we rede our lief Lord, •
           Shepherd of the free, 1932

Not to greet that Gold-Guard, ·
                but to let him lie
Yonder where he long was ·
                and dwell his cavern by,
Ever unto world's end. · But Beowulf, not he!—
Held he to his high fate. ·
        The Hoard is ours to see, 1936
Albeit grimly gotten. · Too strong the destiny
That thither lured our Folk-King. ·
                I was in the hall,
And of that chambered treasure ·
                had my look at all;
When by chance I 'd found there, ·
                none too pleasantly, 1940
A pathway in and under · that earth-wall.
With hands I seized me swiftly, ·
                from the treasure-store,
A burthen big and mickle; ·
                and hither out I bore
Back unto my own King. · Quick as yet was he,
Wise, with wits about him, ·
                and spake he full and free, 1945
The Agèd in his anguish, ·
                and sent farewells to ye,
And bade ye that ye build him, ·
                for deeds of him, your Friend,
A barrow, a high one, · yonder on land's end,
Memorial, mickle barrow, ·
                where his pyre shall be—
For worthiest warrior was he, ·
                wide across the earth, 1950
Whilst still he wielded burg-wealth, ·
                of all of human birth.
Let us hasten yonder · to seek and see anew
Under wall the wonder— ·
                the heap I 'll show to you;
Where of rings and broad gold ·
                anear enough ye 'll view.
Be the bier ready, · ordered anon, 1955
By our coming back here; · we will bear him on,
Our own Lord, our dear man, ·
                to where for long and late
In the Wielder's shelter · he 'll abide his fate.'

Then the Boy of Weohstan, ·
                Hero battle-stout,
Bade order many warriors ·
                of homesteads round about 1960
Thither to fetch the bale-wood ·
                from far for him, the Great,
Him, the people's Ruler: ·
                'Now shall fire devour,
As wax the murky flames now, ·
                the fighters' Man-of-power,
Him who oft abided · of old the iron-shower,
When the storm of arrows, ·
                speeded by the strings, 1965
Shot above the shield-wall ·
                swift on feathered wings,
And shaft fulfilled its duty ·
                and drave the barb to goal.'

Of sooth, the son of Weohstan, ·
                Wiglaf, wise of soul,
Chose from out the followers ·
                thane-men of the King's,
The seven best together, ·
                and under roof of hate 1970
Went he with the warriors, ·
                himself as one of eight,
And one who walked ahead there ·
                bare a torch in hand.
Nor was there any drawing-lots ·
                among that eager band
For who that Hoard should pillage, ·
                when they saw in hall
It resting reft of Keeper · and lost it lying all.
And little were they mourning, ·
                as out they carried fast 1976
The treasure-trove, the priceless. ·
                The Dragon, eke, they cast,
The Worm, over the wall-cliff,— ·
                let the wave take,
Let the flood embosom ·
                the Hoard-Ward Drake.
The æthelings they piled a wain ·
                with twisted gold beyond a guess, 1980
And bare the hoary Hero on, · up Whale's Ness.

XXXVII

Then for him the Geats made ·
                the pyre, firm on earth,
And hung it with helmets, ·
                with byrnies a-sheen,
And with battle-bucklers, ·
                as his prayer had been.
And they laid amid it ·
                the Prince of wondrous worth, 1985
Laid their Lord belovèd, ·
                weeping in their dearth.
And upon the hill-top · the warriors awoke
The mightiest of bale-fires. ·
                Rose the wood-smoke,
Swart above the blazing. · And the roar of flame
Blended was with wailing, ·
                as still the winds became, 1990
Till, hot unto his heart, it broke ·
                the Geat's bone-frame.
Unglad of mood, in grief they mourned ·
                their great Chief dead.
And his Wife, with hair bound, ·
                her song of sorrow said,
Over and over: · how 't was hers to dread
Days of harm and hardship, ·
                warriors' fall and grame, 1995
The terror of the raider, · captivity and shame.

The sky the reek had swallowed. ·
                The Weders raised thereby
A mound upon the headland, ·
                that was broad and high,
Seen afar from ocean · by sailors on their ways,

And built the battle-bold One •
                a beacon in ten days. 2000
Around the brands and ashes •
                a wall they ran and wrought,
The worthiest contriving •
                of men of wisest thought.
And in the barrow set they •
                ring and gem and plate,
And all the splendor-booty • out of hoard of late
Forth their hands had taken, •
                urged by heads of hate. 2005
They gave the wealth of jarlmen •
                to earth for to hold,
Now where yet it liveth, •
                in the mould, the gold,
As useless unto mortals   •   as it was of old.

    THEN around the mound rode, •
                with cry and call,
Bairns of the æthelings,   •   twelve of all, 2010
To mourn for their Master, •
                their sorrow to sing,
Framing a word-chant, • speaking of the King:
They vaunted his earlship, •
                they honored doughtily
His wonder-works of glory.   •   Let it ever be,
That heart of man shall cherish •
                and word of man shall praise 2015
The Master-Friend, when in the end •
                his spirit goes its ways.
So the Geatish clansmen •
                bemoanèd their dearth,
The passing-forth of Beowulf, •
                these comrades of his hearth,
Calling him a World-King, •
                the mildest under crown,
And to his kin the kindest, •
                and keenest for renown. 2020

SIR GAWAIN AND THE GREEN KNIGHT (c. 1375)

The romantic stories cherished by the Norman conquerors of England found equal favor, in the course of time, among the English. In England the romances flourished especially during the fourteenth century, the finest of them, the anonymous *Sir Gawain and the Green Knight*, having been written about the year 1375. In this Arthurian poem are combined two stories which no doubt were originally separate: (1) the challenge to Sir Gawain's bravery through the beheading incident and the compact with the Green Knight, and (2) the test of his honor and chastity through the wife of his host of the castle. Although the English author probably drew the materials for his story directly from French sources, and ultimately, in part, from Celtic, many of the structural and rhetorical excellencies of the present poem are certainly his own. A tale of daring, loyalty, courtesy, and religious devotion is here recounted with a refinement and gentility scarcely to be exceeded. The charm of chivalry is felt throughout. The poet's power of language is shown best, perhaps, in the description of the scenery through which Sir Gawain wanders, —the landscape, not of conventional story, but of Arthur's own Britain.

SIR GAWAIN AND THE GREEN KNIGHT

I

After the siege and the assault of Troy, when that burg was destroyed and burnt to ashes, and the traitor tried for his treason, the noble Æneas and his kin sailed forth to become princes and patrons of well-nigh all the Western Isles. Thus Romulus built Rome (and gave to the city his own name, which it bears even to this day); and Ticius turned him to Tuscany; and Langobard raised him up dwellings in Lombardy; and Felix Brutus sailed far over the French flood, and founded the kingdom of Britain, wherein have been war and waste and wonder, and bliss and bale, ofttimes since.

And in that kingdom of Britain have been wrought more gallant deeds than in any other; but of all British kings Arthur was the most valiant, as I have heard tell; therefore will I set forth a wondrous adventure that fell out in his time. And if ye will listen to me, but for a little while, I will tell it even as it stands in story stiff and strong, fixed in the letter, as it hath long been known in the land.

King Arthur lay at Camelot upon a Christmas-tide, with many a gallant lord and lovely lady, and all the noble brotherhood of the Round Table. There they held rich revels with gay talk and jest; one while they would ride forth to joust and tourney, and again back to the court to make carols; for there was the feast holden fifteen days with all the mirth that men could devise, song and glee, glorious to hear, in the daytime, and dancing at night. Halls and chambers were crowded with noble guests, the bravest of knights and the loveliest of ladies, and Arthur himself was the comeliest king that ever held a court. For all this fair folk were in their youth, the fairest and most fortunate under heaven, and the king himself of such fame that it were hard now to name so valiant a hero.

Now the New Year had but newly come in, and on that day a double portion was served on the high table to all the noble guests, and thither came the king with all his knights, when the service in the chapel had been sung to an end. And they greeted each other for the New Year, and gave rich gifts, the one to the other (and they that received them were not wroth, that may ye well believe!), and the maidens laughed and made mirth till it was time to get them to meat. Then they washed and sat them down to the feasting in fitting rank and order, and Guinevere the queen, gaily clad, sat on the high daïs. Silken was her seat, with a fair canopy over her head, of rich tapestries of Tars, embroidered, and studded with costly gems; fair she was to look upon, with her shining gray eyes, a fairer woman might no man boast himself of having seen.

But Arthur would not eat till all were served, so full of joy and gladness was he, even as a child; he liked not either to lie long, or to sit long at meat, so worked upon him his young blood and his wild brain. And another custom he had also, that came of his nobility, that he would never eat upon an high day till he had been advised of some knightly deed, or some strange and marvelous tale, of his ancestors, or of arms, or of other ventures. Or till some stranger knight should seek of him leave to joust with one of the Round Table, that they might set their lives in jeopardy, one against another, as fortune might favor them. Such was the king's custom when he sat in hall at each high feast with his noble knights; therefore on that New Year tide, he abode, fair of face, on the throne, and made much mirth withal.

Thus the king sat before the high tables, and spake of many things; and there good Sir Gawain was seated by Guinevere the queen, and on her other side sat Agravain, *à la dure main;* both were the king's sister's sons and full gallant knights. And at the end of the table was Bishop Bawdewyn, and Ywain, King Urien's son, sat at the other side alone. These were worthily served on the daïs, and at the lower tables sat many valiant knights. Then they bare the first course with the blast of trumpets and waving of banners, with the sound of drums and pipes, of song and lute, that many a heart was uplifted at the melody. Many were the dainties, and rare the meats; so great was the plenty they might scarce find room on the board to set on the dishes. Each helped himself as he liked best, and to each two were twelve dishes, with great plenty of beer and wine.

Now I will say no more of the service, but that ye may know there was no lack, for there drew near a venture that the folk might well have left their labor to gaze upon. As the sound of the music ceased, and the first course had been fitly served, there came in at the hall door one terrible to behold, of stature greater than any on earth; from neck to loin so strong and thickly made, and with limbs so long and so great that he seemed even as a giant. And yet he was but a man, only the mightiest that might mount a steed; broad of chest and shoulders and slender of waist, and all his features of like fashion; but men marveled much at his color, for he rode even as a knight, yet was green all over.

For he was clad all in green, with a straight coat, and a mantle above; all decked and lined with fur was the cloth and the hood that was thrown back from his locks and lay on his shoulders. Hose had he of the same green, and spurs of bright gold with silken fastenings richly worked; and all his vesture was verily green. Around his waist and his saddle were bands with fair stones set upon silken work, 't were too long to tell of all the trifles that were embroidered thereon—birds and insects in gay gauds of green and gold. All the trappings of his steed were of metal of like enamel, even the stirrups that he stood in stained of the same, and stirrups and saddle-bow alike gleamed and shone with green stones. Even the steed on which he rode was of the same hue, a green horse, great and strong, and hard to hold, with broidered bridle, meet for the rider.

The knight was thus gaily dressed in green, his hair falling around his shoulders; on his breast hung a beard, as thick and green as a bush, and the beard and the hair of his head were clipped all round above his elbows. The lower part of his sleeves was fastened with clasps in the same wise as a king's mantle. The horse's mane was crisp and plaited with many a knot folded in with gold thread about the fair green, here a twist of the hair, here another of gold. The tail was twined in like manner, and both were bound about with a band of bright green set with many a precious stone; then they were tied aloft in a cunning knot, whereon rang many bells of burnished gold. Such a steed might no other ride, nor had such ever been looked upon in that hall ere that time; and all who saw that knight spake and said that a man might scarce abide his stroke.

The knight bore no helm nor hauberk, neither gorget nor breast-plate, neither shaft nor buckler to smite nor to shield, but in one hand he had a holly-bough, that is greenest when the groves are bare, and in his other an axe, huge and uncomely, a cruel weapon in fashion, if one would picture it. The head was an ell-yard long, the metal all of green steel and gold, the blade burnished bright, with a broad edge, as well shapen to shear as a sharp razor. The steel was set into a strong staff, all bound round with iron, even to the end, and engraved with green in cunning work. A lace was twined about it, that looped at the head, and all adown the handle it was clasped with tassels on buttons of bright green richly broidered.

The knight rideth through the entrance of the hall, driving straight to the high daïs, and greeted no man, but looked ever upwards; and the first words he spake were, 'Where is the ruler of this folk? I would gladly look upon that hero, and have speech with him.' He cast his eyes on the knights, and mustered them up and down, striving ever to see who of them was of most renown.

Then was there great gazing to behold that chief, for each man marveled what it might mean that a knight and his steed should have even such a hue as the green grass; and that seemed even greener than green enamel on bright gold. All looked on him as he stood, and drew near unto him, wondering greatly what he might be; for many marvels had they seen, but none such as this, and phantasm and faërie did the folk deem it. Therefore were the gallant knights slow to answer, and gazed astounded, and sat stone still in a deep silence through that goodly hall, as if a slumber were fallen upon them. I deem it was not all for doubt, but some for courtesy that they might give ear unto his errand.

Then Arthur beheld this adventurer before his high daïs, and knightly he greeted him, for fearful was he never. 'Sir,' he said, 'thou art welcome to this place—lord of this hall am I, and men call me Arthur. Light thee down, and tarry awhile, and what thy will is, that shall we learn after.'

'Nay,' quoth the stranger, 'so help me he that sitteth on high, 'twas not mine errand to tarry any while in this dwelling; but the praise of this thy folk and thy city is lifted up on high, and thy warriors are holden for the best and the most valiant of those who ride mail-clad to the fight. The wisest and the worthiest of this world are they, and well proven in all knightly sports. And here, as I have heard tell, is fairest courtesy; therefore have I come hither as at this time. Ye may be sure by the branch that I bear here that I come in peace, seeking no strife. For had I willed to journey in warlike guise I have at home both hauberk and helm, shield and shining spear, and other weapons to mine hand, but since I seek no war, my raiment is that of peace. But if thou be as bold as all men tell, thou wilt freely grant me the boon I ask.'

And Arthur answered, 'Sir Knight, if thou cravest battle here thou shalt not fail for lack of a foe.'

And the knight answered, 'Nay, I ask no fight; in faith here on the benches are but beardless children; were I clad in armor on my steed there is no man here might match me. Therefore I ask in this court but a Christmas jest, for that it is Yule-tide, and New Year, and there are here many fain for sport. If any one in this hall holds himself so hardy, so bold both of blood and brain, as to dare strike me one stroke for another, I will give him as a gift this axe, which is heavy enough, in sooth, to handle as he may list, and I will abide the first blow, unarmed as I sit. If any knight be so bold as to prove my words, let him come swiftly to me here, and take this weapon; I quit claim to it, he may keep it as his own, and I will abide his stroke, firm on the floor. Then shalt thou give me the right to deal him another, the respite of a year and a day shall he have. Now haste, and let see whether any here dare say aught.'

Now if the knights had been astounded at the first, yet stiller were they all, high and low, when they had heard his words. The knight on his steed straightened himself in the saddle, and rolled his eyes fiercely round the hall; red they gleamed under his green and bushy brows. He frowned and twisted his beard, waiting to see who should rise, and when none answered he cried aloud in mockery, 'What, is this Arthur's hall, and these the knights whose renown hath run through many realms? Where are now your pride and your conquests, your wrath, and anger, and mighty words? Now are the praise and the renown of the Round Table overthrown by one man's speech, since all keep silence for dread ere ever they have seen a blow!'

With that he laughed so loudly that the blood rushed to the king's fair face for very shame; he waxed wroth, as did all his knights, and sprang to his feet, and drew near to the stranger and said, 'Now by heaven, foolish is thy asking, and thy folly shall find its fitting answer. I know no man aghast at thy great words. Give me here thine axe and I shall grant thee the boon thou hast asked.' Lightly he sprang to him and caught at his hand, and the knight, fierce of aspect, lighted down from his charger.

Then Arthur took the axe and gripped the haft, and swung it round, ready to strike. And the knight stood before him, taller by the head than any in the hall; he stood, and stroked his beard, and drew down his coat, no more dismayed for the king's threats than if one had brought him a drink of wine.

Then Gawain, who sat by the queen, leaned forward to the king and spake, 'I beseech ye, my lord, let this venture be mine. Would ye but bid me rise from this seat, and stand by your side, so that my liege lady thought it not ill, then would I come to your counsel before this goodly court. For I think it not seemly when such challenges be made in your hall that ye yourself should undertake it, while there are many bold knights who sit beside ye, none are there, methinks, of readier will under heaven, or more valiant in open field. I am the weakest, I wot, and the feeblest of wit, and it will be the less loss of my life if ye seek sooth. For save that ye are mine uncle, naught is there in me to praise, no virtue is there in my body save your blood, and since this challenge is such folly that it beseems ye not to take it, and I have asked it from ye first, let it fall to me, and if I bear myself ungallantly, then let all this court blame me.'

Then they all spake with one voice that the king should leave this venture and grant it to Gawain.

Then Arthur commanded the knight to rise, and he rose up quickly and knelt down before the king, and caught hold of the weapon; and the king loosed his hold of it, and lifted up his hand, and gave him his blessing, and bade him be strong both of heart and hand. 'Keep thee well, nephew,' quoth Arthur, 'that thou give him but the one blow, and if thou redest him rightly I trow thou shalt well abide the stroke he may give thee after.'

Gawain stepped to the stranger, axe in hand, and he, never fearing, awaited his coming. Then the Green Knight spake to Sir Gawain, 'Make we our covenant ere we go further. First, I ask thee, knight, what is thy name? Tell me truly, that I may know thee.'

'In faith,' quoth the good knight, 'Gawain am I, who give thee this buffet, let what may come of it; and at this time twelvemonth will I take another at thine hand with whatsoever weapon thou wilt, and none other.'

Then the other answered again, 'Sir Gawain, so may I thrive as I am fain to take this buffet at thine hand,' and he quoth further, 'Sir Gawain, it liketh me well that I shall take at thy fist that which I have asked here, and thou hast readily and truly rehearsed all the covenant that I asked of the king, save that thou shalt swear me, by thy troth, to seek me thyself wherever thou hopest that I may be found, and win thee such reward as thou dealest me to-day, before this folk.'

'Where shall I seek thee?' quoth Gawain. 'Where is thy place? By him that made me, I wot never where thou dwellest, nor know I thee, knight, thy court, nor thy name. But teach me truly all that pertaineth thereto, and tell me thy name, and I shall use all my wit to win my way thither, and that I swear thee for sooth, and by my sure troth.'

'That is enough in the New Year, it needs no more,' quoth the Green Knight to the gallant Gawain, 'if I tell thee truly when I have taken the blow, and thou hast smitten me; then will I teach thee of my house and home, and mine own name, then mayest thou ask thy road and keep covenant. And if I waste no words then farest thou the better, for thou canst dwell in thy land, and seek no further. But take now thy toll, and let see how thou strikest.'

'Gladly will I,' quoth Gawain, handling his axe.

Then the Green Knight swiftly made him ready, he bowed down his head, and laid his long locks on the crown that his bare neck might be seen. Gawain gripped his axe and raised it on high, the left foot he set forward on the floor, and let the blow fall lightly on the bare neck. The sharp edge of the blade sundered the bones, smote through the neck, and clave it in two, so that the edge of the steel bit on the ground, and the fair head fell to the earth that many struck it with their feet as it rolled forth. The blood spurted forth, and glistened on the green raiment, but the knight neither faltered nor fell; he started forward with out-stretched hand, and caught the head, and lifted it up; then he turned to his steed, and took hold of the bridle, set his foot in the stirrup, and mounted. His head he held by the hair, in his hand. Then he seated himself in his saddle as if naught ailed him, and he were not headless. He turned his steed about, the grim corpse bleeding freely the while, and they who looked upon him doubted them much for the covenant.

For he held up the head in his hand, and turned the face towards them that sat on the high daïs, and it lifted up the eyelids and looked upon them and spake as ye shall hear. 'Look, Gawain, that thou art ready to go as thou hast promised, and seek loyally till thou find me, even as thou hast sworn in this hall in the hearing of these knights. Come thou, I charge thee, to the Green Chapel; such a stroke as thou hast dealt thou hast deserved, and it shall be promptly paid thee on New Year's morn. Many men know me as the knight of the Green Chapel, and if thou askest, thou shalt not fail to find me. Therefore it behooves thee to come, or to yield thee as recreant.'

With that he turned his bridle, and galloped out at the hall door, his head in his hands, so that the sparks flew from beneath his horse's hoofs. Whither he went none knew, no more than they wist whence he had come; and the king and Gawain they gazed and laughed, for in sooth this had proved a greater marvel than any they had known aforetime.

Though Arthur the king was astonished at his heart, yet he let no sign of it be seen, but spake in courteous wise to the fair queen: 'Dear lady, be not dismayed, such craft is well suited to Christmas-tide when we seek jesting, laughter, and song, and fair carols of knights and ladies. But now I may well get me to meat, for I have seen a marvel I may not forget.' Then he looked on Sir Gawain, and said gaily, 'Now, fair nephew, hang up thine axe, since it has hewn enough,' and they hung it on the dossal above the daïs, where all men might look on it for a marvel, and by its true token tell of the wonder. Then the twain sat them down together, the king and the good knight, and men served them with a double portion, as was the share of the noblest, with all manner of meat and of minstrelsy. And they spent that day in gladness, but Sir Gawain must well bethink him of the heavy venture to which he had set his hand.

II

This beginning of adventures had Arthur at the New Year; for he yearned to hear gallant tales, though his words were few when he sat at the feast. But now had they stern work on hand. Gawain was glad to begin the jest in the hall, but ye need have no marvel if the end be heavy. For though a man be merry in mind when he has well drunk, yet a year runs full swiftly, and the beginning but rarely matches the end.

For Yule was now over-past, and the year after, each season in its turn following the other. For after Christmas comes crabbed Lent, that will have fish for flesh and simpler cheer. But then the weather of the world chides with winter; the cold withdraws itself, the clouds uplift, and the rain falls in warm showers on the fair plains. Then the flowers come forth, meadows and grove are clad in green, the birds make ready to build, and sing sweetly for solace of the soft summer that follows thereafter. The blossoms bud and blow in the hedgerows rich and rank, and noble notes enough are heard in the fair woods.

After the season of summer, with the soft winds, when zephyr breathes lightly on seeds and herbs, joyous indeed is the growth that waxes thereout when the dew drips from the leaves beneath the blissful glance of the bright sun. But then comes harvest, and hardens the grain, warning it to wax ripe ere the winter. The drought drives the dust on high, flying over the face of the land; the angry wind of the welkin wrestles with the sun; the leaves fall from the trees and light upon the ground, and all brown are the groves that but now were green, and ripe is the fruit that once was flower. So the year passes into many yesterdays, and winter comes again, as it needs no sage to tell us.

When the Michaelmas moon was come in with warnings of winter, Sir Gawain bethought him full oft of his perilous journey. Yet till All Hallows Day he lingered with Arthur, and on that day they made a great feast for the hero's sake, with much revel and richness of the Round Table. Courteous knights and comely ladies, all were in sorrow for the love of that knight, and though they spake no word of it, many were joyless for his sake.

And after meat, sadly Sir Gawain turned to his uncle, and spake of his journey, and said, 'Liege lord of my life, leave from you I crave. Ye know well how the matter stands without more words; to-morrow am I bound to set forth in search of the Green Knight.'

Then came together all the noblest knights, Ywain and Erec, and many another. Sir Dodinel le Sauvage, the Duke of Clarence, Launcelot and Lionel, and Lucan the Good, Sir Bors and Bedivere, valiant knights both, and many another hero, with Sir Mador de la Porte, and they all drew near, heavy at heart, to take counsel with Sir Gawain. Much sorrow and weeping was there in the hall to think that so worthy a knight as Gawain should wend his way to seek a deadly blow, and should no more wield his sword in fight. But the knight made ever good cheer, and said, 'Nay, wherefore should I shrink? What may a man do but prove his fate?'

He dwelt there all that day, and on the morn he arose and asked betimes for his armor; and they brought it unto him on this wise: first, a rich carpet was stretched on the floor (and brightly did the gold gear glitter upon it), then the knight stepped upon it, and handled the steel; clad he was in a doublet of silk, with a close hood, lined fairly throughout. Then they set the steel shoes upon his feet, and wrapped his legs with greaves, with polished knee-caps, fastened with knots of gold. Then they cased his thighs in cuisses closed with thongs, and brought him the byrnie of bright steel rings sewn upon a fair stuff. Well burnished braces they set on each arm with good elbow-pieces, and gloves of mail, and all the goodly gear that should shield him in his need. And they cast over all a rich surcoat, and set the golden spurs on his heels, and girt him with a trusty sword fastened with a silken bawdrick. When he was thus clad his harness was costly, for the least loop or latchet gleamed with gold. So armed as he was he harkened Mass and made his offering at the high altar. Then he came to the king, and the knights of his court, and courteously took leave of lords and ladies, and they kissed him, and commended him to Christ.

With that was Gringalet ready, girt with a saddle that gleamed gaily with many golden fringes, enriched and decked anew for the venture. The bridle was all barred about with bright gold buttons, and all the covertures and trappings of the steed, the crupper and the rich skirts, accorded with the saddle; spread fair with the rich red gold that glittered and gleamed in the rays of the sun.

Then the knight called for his helmet, which was well lined throughout, and set it high on his head, and hasped it behind. He wore a light kerchief over the ventail, that was broidered and studded with fair gems on a broad silken ribbon, with birds of gay color, and many a turtle and true-lover's knot interlaced thickly, even as many a maiden had wrought diligently for seven winters long. But the circlet which crowned his helmet was yet more precious, being adorned with a device in diamonds. Then they brought him his shield, which was of bright red, with the pentangle painted thereon in gleaming gold. And why that noble prince bare the pentangle I am minded to tell you, though my tale tarry thereby. It is a sign that Solomon set ere-while, as betokening truth; for it is a figure with five points and each line overlaps the other, and nowhere hath it beginning or end, so that in English it is called 'the endless knot.' And therefore was it well suiting to this knight and to his arms, since Gawain was faithful in five and five-fold, for pure was he as gold, void of all villainy and endowed with all virtues. Therefore he bare the pentangle on shield and surcoat as truest of heroes and gentlest of knights.

For first he was faultless in his five senses; and his five fingers never failed him; and all his trust upon earth was in the five wounds that Christ bare on the cross, as the Creed tells. And wherever this knight found himself in stress of battle he deemed well that he drew his strength from the five joys which the Queen of Heaven had of her Child. And for this cause did he bear an image of Our Lady on the one half of his shield, that whenever he looked upon it he might not lack for aid. And the fifth five that the hero used were frankness and fellowship above all, purity and courtesy that never failed him, and compassion that surpasses all; and in these five virtues was that hero wrapped and clothed. And all these, five-fold, were linked one in the other, so that they had no end, and were fixed on five points that never failed, neither at any side were they joined or sundered, nor could ye find beginning or end. And therefore on his shield was the knot shapen, red-gold upon red, which is the pure pentangle. Now was Sir Gawain ready, and he took his lance in hand, and bade them all farewell, he deemed it had been for ever.

Then he smote the steed with his spurs, and sprang on his way, so that sparks flew from the stones after him. All that saw him were grieved at heart, and said one to the other, 'By Christ, 't is great pity that one of such noble life should be lost! I' faith 't were not easy to find his equal upon earth. The king had done better to have wrought more warily. Yonder knight should have been made a duke; a gallant leader of men is he, and such a fate had beseemed him better than to be hewn in pieces at the will of an elfish man, for mere pride. Who ever knew a king to take such counsel as to risk his knights on a Christmas jest?' Many were the tears that flowed from their eyes when that goodly knight rode from the hall. He made no delaying, but went his way swiftly, and rode many a wild road, as I heard say in the book.

So rode Sir Gawain through the realm of Logres, on an errand that he held for no jest. Often he lay companionless at night, and must lack the fare that he liked. No comrade had he save his steed, and none save God with whom to take counsel. At length he drew nigh to North Wales, and left the isles of Anglesey on his left hand, crossing over the fords by the foreland over at Holyhead, till he came into the wilderness of Wirral, where but few dwell who love God and man of true heart. And ever he asked, as he fared, of all whom he met, if they had heard any tidings of a Green Knight in the country thereabout, or of a Green

Chapel? And all answered him, Nay, never in their lives had they seen any man of such a hue. And the knight wended his way by many a strange road and many a rugged path, and the fashion of his countenance changed full often ere he saw the Green Chapel.

Many a cliff did he climb in that unknown land, where afar from his friends he rode as a stranger. Never did he come to a stream or a ford but he found a foe before him, and that one so marvelous, so foul and fell, that it behooved him to fight. So many wonders did that knight behold, that it were too long to tell the tenth part of them. Sometimes he fought with dragons and wolves; sometimes with wild men that dwelt in the rocks; another while with bulls, and bears, and wild boars, or with giants of the high moorland that drew near to him. Had he not been a doughty knight, enduring, and of well-proved valor, and a servant of God, doubtless he had been slain, for he was oft in danger of death. Yet he cared not so much for the strife; what he deemed worse was when the cold clear water was shed from the clouds, and froze ere it fell on the fallow ground. More nights than enough he slept in his harness on the bare rocks, near slain with the sleet, while the stream leapt bubbling from the crest of the hills, and hung in hard icicles over his head.

Thus in peril and pain, and many a hardship, the knight rode alone till Christmas Eve, and in that tide he made his prayer to the Blessed Virgin that she would guide his steps and lead him to some dwelling. On that morning he rode by a hill, and came into a thick forest, wild and drear; on each side were high hills, and thick woods below them of great hoar oaks, a hundred together, of hazel and hawthorn with their trailing boughs inter-twined, and rough ragged moss spreading everywhere. On the bare twigs the birds chirped piteously, for pain of the cold. The knight upon Gringalet rode lonely beneath them, through marsh and mire, much troubled at heart lest he should fail to see the service of the Lord, who on that self-same night was born of a maiden for the cure of our grief; and therefore he said, sighing, 'I beseech thee, Lord, and Mary thy gentle Mother, for some shelter where I may hear Mass, and thy matins at morn. This I ask meekly, and thereto I pray my Paternoster, Ave, and Credo.' Thus he rode praying, and lamenting his misdeeds, and he crossed himself, and said, 'May the Cross of Christ speed me.'

Now that knight had crossed himself but thrice ere he was aware in the wood of a dwelling within a moat, above a lawn, on a mound surrounded by many mighty trees that stood round the moat. 'T was the fairest castle that ever a knight owned; built in a meadow with a park all about it, and a spiked palisade, closely driven, that enclosed the trees for more than two miles. The knight was ware of the hold from the side, as it shone through the oaks. Then he lifted off his helmet, and thanked Christ and Saint Julian that they had courteously granted his prayer, and hearkened to his cry. 'Now,' quoth the knight, 'I beseech ye, grant me fair hostel.' Then he pricked Gringalet with his golden spurs, and rode gaily towards the great gate, and came swiftly to the bridge end.

The bridge was drawn up and the gates close shut; the walls were strong and thick, so that they might fear no tempest. The knight on his charger abode on the bank of the deep double ditch that surrounded the castle. The walls were set deep in the water, and rose aloft to a wondrous height; they were of hard hewn stone up to the corbels, which were adorned beneath the battlements with fair carvings, and turrets set in between with many a loophole; a better barbican Sir Gawain had never looked upon. And within he beheld the high hall, with its tower and many windows with carven cornices, and chalk-white chimneys on the turreted roofs that shone fair in the sun. And everywhere, thickly scattered on the castle battlements, were pinnacles, so many that it seemed as if it were all wrought out of paper, so white was it.

The knight on his steed deemed it fair enough, if he might come to be sheltered within it to lodge there while that the holy-day lasted. He called aloud, and soon there came a porter of kindly countenance, who stood on the wall and greeted this knight and asked his errand.

'Good sir,' quoth Gawain, 'wilt thou go mine errand to the high lord of the castle, and crave for me lodging?'

'Yea, by Saint Peter,' quoth the porter. 'In sooth I trow that ye be welcome to dwell here so long as it may like ye.'

Then he went, and came again swiftly, and many folk with him to receive the knight. They let down the great drawbridge, and came forth and knelt on their knees on the cold earth to give him worthy welcome. They held wide open the great gates, and courteously he bade them rise, and rode over the bridge. Then men came to him and held his stirrup while he dismounted, and took and stabled his steed. There came down knights and squires to bring the guest with joy to the hall. When he raised his helmet there were many to take it from his hand, fain to serve him, and they took from him sword and shield.

Sir Gawain gave good greeting to the noble and the mighty men who came to do him honor. Clad in his shining armor they led him to the hall, where a great fire burnt brightly on the floor; and the lord of the household came forth from his chamber to meet the hero fitly. He spake to the knight, and said: 'Ye are welcome to do here as it likes ye. All that is here is your own to have at your will and disposal.'

'Gramercy!' quoth Gawain, 'may Christ requite ye.'

As friends that were fain each embraced the other; and Gawain looked on the knight who greeted him so kindly, and thought 't was a bold warrior that owned that burg.

Of mighty stature he was, and of high age; broad and flowing was his beard, and of a bright hue. He was stalwart of limb, and strong in his stride, his face fiery red, and his speech free: in sooth he seemed one well fitted to be a leader of valiant men.

Then the lord led Sir Gawain to a chamber, and commanded folk to wait upon him, and at his bidding there came men enough who brought the guest to a fair bower. The bedding was noble, with curtains of pure silk wrought with gold, and wondrous coverings of fair cloth all embroidered. The curtains ran on ropes with rings of red gold, and the walls were hung with carpets of Orient, and the same spread on the floor. There with mirthful speeches they took from the guest his byrnie and all his shining armor, and brought him rich robes of the choicest in its stead. They were long and flowing, and became him well, and when he was clad in them all who looked on the hero thought that surely God had never made a fairer knight: he seemed as if he might be a prince without peer in the field where men strive in battle.

Then before the hearth-place, whereon the fire burned, they made ready a chair for Gawain, hung about with cloth and fair cushions; and there they cast around him a mantle of brown samite, richly embroidered and furred within with costly skins of ermine, with a hood of the same, and he seated himself in that rich seat, and warmed himself at the fire, and was cheered at heart. And while he sat thus, the serving men set up a table on trestles, and covered it with a fair white cloth, and set thereon salt-cellar, and napkin, and silver spoons; and the knight washed at his will, and set him down to meat.

The folk served him courteously with many dishes seasoned of the best, a double portion. All kinds of fish were there, some baked in bread, some broiled on the embers, some sodden, some stewed and savored with spices, with all sorts of cunning devices to his taste. And often he called it a feast, when they spake gaily to him all together, and said, 'Now take ye this penance, and it shall be for your amendment.' Much mirth thereof did Sir Gawain make.

Then they questioned that prince courteously of whence he came; and he told them that he was of the court of Arthur, who is the rich royal king of the Round Table, and that it was Gawain himself who was within their walls, and would keep Christmas with them, as the chance had fallen out. And when the lord of the castle heard those tidings he laughed aloud for gladness, and all men in that keep were joyful that they should be in the company of him to whom belonged all fame, and valor, and courtesy, and whose honor was praised above that of all men on earth. Each said softly to his fellow, 'Now shall we see courteous bearing, and the manner of speech befitting courts. What charm lieth in gentle speech shall we learn without asking, since here we have welcomed the fine father of courtesy. God has surely shown us his grace since he sends us such a guest as Gawain! When men shall sit and sing, blithe for Christ's birth, this knight shall bring us to the knowledge of fair manners, and it may be that hearing him we may learn the cunning speech of love.'

By the time the knight had risen from dinner it was near nightfall. Then chaplains took their way to the chapel, and rang loudly, even as they should, for the solemn evensong of the high feast. Thither went the lord, and the lady also, and entered with her maidens into a comely closet, and thither also went Gawain. Then the lord took him by the sleeve and led him to a seat, and called him by his name, and told him he was of all men in the world the most welcome. And Sir Gawain thanked him truly, and each kissed the other, and they sat gravely together throughout the service.

Then was the lady fain to look upon that knight; and she came forth from her closet with many fair maidens. The fairest of ladies was she in face, and figure, and coloring, fairer even than Guinevere, so the knight thought. She came through the chancel to greet the hero; another lady held her by the left hand, older than she, and seemingly of high estate, with many nobles about her. But unlike to look upon were those ladies, for if the younger were fair, the elder was yellow. Rich red were the cheeks of the one, rough and wrinkled those of the other; the kerchiefs of the one were broidered with many glistening pearls, her throat and neck bare, and whiter than the snow that lies on the hills; the neck of the other was swathed in a gorget, with a white wimple over her black chin. Her forehead was wrapped in silk with many folds, worked with knots, so that naught of her was seen save her black brows, her eyes, her nose, and her lips, and those were bleared, and ill to look upon. A worshipful lady in sooth one might call her! In figure was she short and broad, and thickly made—far fairer to behold was she whom she led by the hand.

When Gawain beheld that fair lady, who looked at him graciously, with leave of the lord he went towards them, and, bowing low, he greeted the elder, but the younger and fairer he took lightly in his arms, and kissed her courteously, and greeted her in knightly wise. Then she hailed him as friend, and he quickly prayed to be counted as her servant, if she so willed. Then they took him between them, and talking, led him to the chamber, to the hearth, and bade them bring spices, and they brought them in plenty with the good wine that was wont to be drunk at such seasons. Then the lord sprang to his feet and bade them make merry, and took off his hood, and hung it on a spear, and bade him win the worship thereof who should make most mirth that Christmastide. 'And I shall try, by my faith, to fool it with the best, by the help of my friends, ere I lose my raiment.' Thus with gay words the lord made trial to gladden Gawain with jests that night, till it was time to bid them light the tapers, and Sir Gawain took leave of them and gat him to rest.

In the morn when all men call to mind how Christ our Lord was born on earth to die for us, there is joy, for his sake, in all dwellings of the world; and so was there here on that day. For high feast was held, with many dainties and cunningly cooked messes. On the daïs sat gallant men, clad in their best. The ancient dame sat on the high seat, with the lord of the castle beside her. Gawain and the fair lady sat together, even in the midst of the board when the feast was served; and so throughout all the hall each sat in his degree, and was served in order. There was meat, there was mirth, there was much joy, so that to tell thereof would take me too long, though peradventure I might strive to declare it. But Gawain and that fair lady had much joy of each other's company through her sweet words and courteous converse. And there was music made before each prince, trumpets and drums, and merry pipings; each man hearkened his minstrel, and they too hearkened theirs.

So they held high feast that day and the next, and the third day thereafter, and the joy on Saint John's Day was fair to hearken, for 't was the last of the feast and the guests would depart in the gray of the morning. Therefore they awoke early, and drank wine, and danced fair carols, and at last, when it was late, each man took his leave to wend early on his way. Gawain would bid his host farewell, but the lord took him by the hand, and led him to his own chamber beside the hearth, and there he thanked him for the favor he had shown him in honoring his dwelling at that high season, and gladdening his castle with his fair countenance. 'I wis, sir, that while I live I shall be held the worthier that Gawain has been my guest at God's own feast.'

'Gramercy, sir,' quoth Gawain, 'in good faith, all the honor is yours, may the High King give it you, and I am but at your will to work your behest, inasmuch as I am beholden to you in great and small by rights.'

Then the lord did his best to persuade the knight to tarry with him, but Gawain answered that he might in no wise do so. Then the host asked him courteously what stern behest had driven him at the holy season from the king's court, to fare all alone, ere yet the feast was ended?

'Forsooth,' quoth the knight, 'ye say but the truth: 't is a high quest and a pressing that hath brought me afield, for I am summoned myself to a certain place, and I know not whither in the world I may wend to find it; so help me Christ, I would give all the kingdom of Logres an I might find it by New Year's morn. Therefore, sir, I make request of you that ye tell me truly if ye ever heard word of the Green Chapel, where it may be found, and the Green Knight that keeps it. For I am pledged by solemn compact sworn between us to meet that knight at the New Year if so I were on life; and of that same New Year it wants but little—I' faith, I would look on that hero more joyfully than on any other fair sight! Therefore, by your will, it behooves me to leave you, for I have but barely three days, and I would as fain fall dead as fail of mine errand.'

Then the lord quoth, laughing, 'Now must ye needs stay, for I will show you your goal, the Green Chapel, ere your term be at an end, have ye no fear! But ye can take your ease, friend, in your bed, till the fourth day, and go forth on the first of the year and come to that place at midmorn to do as ye will. Dwell here till New Year's Day, and then rise and set forth, and ye shall be set in the way; 't is not two miles hence.'

Then was Gawain glad, and he laughed gaily. 'Now I thank you for this above all else. Now my quest is achieved I will dwell here at your will, and otherwise do as ye shall ask.'

Then the lord took him, and set him beside him, and bade the ladies be fetched for their greater pleasure, tho' between themselves they had solace. The lord, for gladness, made merry jest, even as one who wist not what to do for joy; and he cried aloud to the knight, 'Ye have promised to do the thing I bid ye: will ye hold to this behest, here, at once?'

'Yea, forsooth,' said that true knight, 'while I abide in your burg I am bound by your behest.'

'Ye have traveled from far,' said the host, 'and since then ye have waked with me, ye are not well refreshed by rest and sleep, as I know. Ye shall therefore abide in your chamber, and lie at your ease to-morrow at Mass-tide, and go to meat when ye will with my wife, who shall sit with you, and comfort you with her company till I return; and I shall rise early and go forth to the chase.' And Gawain agreed to all this courteously.

'Sir knight,' quoth the host, 'we will make a covenant. Whatsoever I win in the wood shall be yours, and whatever may fall to your share, that shall ye exchange for it. Let us swear, friend, to make this exchange, however our hap may be, for worse or for better.'

'I grant ye your will,' quoth Gawain the good; 'if ye list so to do, it liketh me well.'

'Bring hither the wine-cup, the bargain is made,' so said the lord of that castle. They laughed each one, and drank of the wine, and made merry, these lords and ladies, as it pleased them. Then with gay talk and merry jest they rose, and stood, and spoke softly, and kissed courteously, and took leave of each other. With burning torches, and many a serving-man, was each led to his couch; yet ere they gat them to bed the old lord oft repeated their covenant, for he knew well how to make sport.

III

FULL early, ere daylight, the folk rose up; the guests who would depart called their grooms, and they made them ready, and saddled the steeds, tightened up the girths, and trussed up their mails. The knights, all arrayed for riding, leapt up lightly, and took their bridles, and each rode his way as pleased him best.

The lord of the land was not the last. Ready for the chase, with many of his men, he ate a sop hastily when he had heard Mass, and then with blast of the bugle fared forth to the field. He and his nobles were to horse ere daylight glimmered upon the earth.

Then the huntsmen coupled their hounds, unclosed the kennel door, and called them out. They blew three blasts gaily on the bugles, the hounds bayed fiercely, and they that would go a-hunting checked and chastised them. A hundred hunters there were of the best, so I have heard tell. Then the trackers gat them to the trysting-place and uncoupled the hounds, and the forest rang again with their gay blasts.

At the first sound of the hunt the game quaked for fear, and fled, trembling, along the vale. They betook them to the heights, but the liers in wait turned them back with loud cries; the harts they let pass them, and the stags with their spreading antlers, for the lord had forbidden that they should be slain, but the hinds and the does they turned back, and drave down into the valleys. Then might ye see much shooting of arrows. As the deer fled under the boughs a broad whistling shaft smote and wounded each sorely, so that, wounded and bleeding, they fell dying on the banks. The hounds followed swiftly on their tracks, and hunters, blowing the horn, sped after them with ringing shouts as if the cliffs burst asunder. What game escaped those that shot was run down at the outer ring. Thus were they driven on the hills, and harassed at the waters, so well did the men know their work, and the greyhounds were so great and swift that they ran them down as fast as the hunters could slay them. Thus the lord passed the day in mirth and joyfulness, even to nightfall.

So the lord roamed the woods, and Gawain that good knight, lay ever a-bed, curtained about, under the costly coverlet, while the daylight gleamed on the walls. And as he lay half slumbering, he heard a little sound at the door, and he raised his head, and caught back a corner of the curtain, and waited to see what it might be. It was the lovely lady, the lord's wife; she shut the door softly behind her, and turned towards the bed; and Gawain was shamed, laid him down softly and made as if he slept. And she came lightly to the bedside, within the curtain, and sat herself down beside him, to wait till he wakened. The knight lay there awhile, and marveled within himself what her coming might betoken; and he said to himself, ''T were more seemly if I asked her what hath brought her hither.' Then he made feint to waken, and turned towards her, and opened his eyes as one astonished, and crossed himself; and she looked on him laughing, with her cheeks red and white, lovely to behold, and small smiling lips.

'Good morrow, Sir Gawain,' said that fair lady; 'ye are but a careless sleeper, since one can enter thus. Now are ye taken unawares, and lest ye escape me I shall bind you in your bed; of that be ye assured!' Laughing, she spake these words.

'Good morrow, fair lady,' quoth Gawain blithely. 'I will do your will, as it likes me well. For I yielded me readily, and pray your grace, and that is best, by my faith, since I needs must do so.' Thus he jested again, laughing. 'But an ye would, fair lady, grant me this grace that ye pray your prisoner to rise. I would get me from bed, and array me better, then could I talk with ye in more comfort.'

'Nay, forsooth, fair sir,' quoth the lady, 'ye shall not rise, I will rede ye better. I shall keep ye here, since ye can do no other, and talk with my knight whom I have captured. For I know well that ye are Sir Gawain, whom all the world worships, wheresoever ye may ride. Your honor and your courtesy are praised by lords and ladies, by all who live. Now ye are here and we are alone, my lord and his men are afield; the serving men in their beds, and my maidens also, and the door shut upon us. And since in this hour I have him that all men love, I shall use my time well with speech, while it lasts. Ye are welcome to my company, for it behooves me in sooth to be your servant.'

'In good faith,' quoth Gawain, 'I think me that I am not him of whom ye speak, for unworthy am I of such service as ye here proffer. In sooth, I were glad if I might set myself by word or service to your pleasure; a pure joy would it be to me!'

'In good faith, Sir Gawain,' quoth the gay lady, 'the praise and the prowess that pleases all ladies I lack them not, nor hold them light; yet are there ladies enough who would liever now have the knight in their hold, as I have ye here, to dally with your courteous words, to bring them comfort and to ease their cares, than much of the treasure and the gold that are theirs. And now, through the grace of Him who upholds the heavens, I have wholly in my power that which they all desire!'

Thus the lady, fair to look upon, made him great cheer, and Sir Gawain, with modest words, answered her again: 'Madam,' he quoth, 'may Mary requite ye, for in good faith I have found in ye a noble frankness. Much courtesy have other folk shown me, but the honor they have done me is naught to the worship of yourself, who knoweth but good.'

'By Mary,' quoth the lady, 'I think otherwise; for were I worth all the women alive, and had I the wealth of the world in my hand, and might choose me a lord to my liking, then, for all that I have seen in ye, Sir Knight, of beauty and courtesy and blithe semblance, and for all that I have hearkened and hold for true, there should be no knight on earth to be chosen before ye.'

'Well I wot,' quoth Sir Gawain, 'that ye have chosen a better; but I am proud that ye should so prize me; and as your servant do I hold ye my sovereign, and your knight am I, and may Christ reward ye.'

So they talked of many matters till mid-morn was past, and ever the lady made as though she loved him, and the knight turned her speech aside. For though she were the brightest of maidens, yet had he forborne to show her love for the danger that awaited him and the blow that must be given without delay.

Then the lady prayed her leave from him, and he granted it readily. And she gave him good-day, with laughing glance, but he must needs marvel at her words:

'Now He that speeds fair speech reward ye this disport; but that ye be Gawain my mind misdoubts me greatly.'

'Wherefore?' quoth the knight quickly, fearing lest he had lacked in some courtesy.

And the lady spake: 'So true a knight as Gawain is holden, and one so perfect in courtesy, would never have tarried so long with a lady but he would of his courtesy have craved a kiss at parting.'

Then quoth Gawain, 'I wot I will do even as

it may please ye, and kiss at your commandment, as a true knight should who forbears to ask for fear of displeasure.'

At that she came near and bent down and kissed the knight, and each commended the other to Christ, and she went forth from the chamber softly.

Then Sir Gawain rose and called his chamberlain and chose his garments, and when he was ready he gat him forth to Mass, and then went to meat, and made merry all day till the rising of the moon, and never had a knight fairer lodging than had he with those two noble ladies, the elder and the younger.

And ever the lord of the land chased the hinds through holt and heath till eventide, and then with much blowing of bugles and baying of hounds they bore the game homeward; and by the time daylight was done all the folk had returned to that fair castle. And when the lord and Sir Gawain met together, then were they both well pleased. The lord commanded them all to assemble in the great hall, and the ladies to descend with their maidens, and there, before them all, he bade the men fetch in the spoil of the day's hunting, and he called unto Gawain, and counted the tale of the beasts, and showed them unto him, and said, 'What think ye of this game, Sir Knight? Have I deserved of ye thanks for my woodcraft?'

'Yea, I wis,' quoth the other, 'here is the fairest spoil I have seen this seven year in the winter season.'

'And all this do I give ye, Gawain,' quoth the host, 'for by accord of covenant ye may claim it as your own.'

'That in sooth,' quoth the other, 'I grant you that same; and I have fairly won this within walls, and with as good will do I yield it to ye.' With that he clasped his hands round the lord's neck and kissed him as courteously as he might. 'Take ye here my spoils, no more have I won; ye should have it freely, though it were greater than this.'

''T is good,' said the host, 'gramercy thereof. Yet were I fain to know where ye won this same favor, and if it were by your own wit?'

'Nay,' answered Gawain, 'that was not in the bond. Ask me no more: ye have taken what was yours by right, be content with that.'

They laughed and jested together, and sat them down to supper, where they were served with many dainties; and after supper they sat by the hearth, and wine was served out to them; and oft in their jesting they promised to observe on the morrow the same covenant that they had made before and whatever chance might betide, to exchange their spoil, be it much or little, when they met at night. Thus they renewed their bargain before the whole court, and then the night-drink was served, and each courteously took leave of the other and gat him to bed.

By the time the cock had crowed thrice the lord of the castle had left his bed; Mass was sung and meat fitly served. The folk were forth to the wood ere the day broke, with hound and horn they rode over the plain, and uncoupled their dogs among the thorns. Soon they struck on the scent, and the hunt cheered on the hounds who were first to seize it, urging them with shouts. The others hastened to the cry, forty at once, and there rose such a clamor from the pack that the rocks rang again. The huntsmen spurred them on with shouting and blasts of the horn; and the hounds drew together to a thicket betwixt the water and a high crag in the cliff beneath the hillside. There where the rough rock fell ruggedly they, the huntsmen, fared to the finding, and cast about round the hill and the thicket behind them. The knights wist well what beast was within, and would drive him forth with the bloodhounds. And as they beat the bushes, suddenly over the beaters there rushed forth a wondrous great and fierce boar, long since had he left the herd to roam by himself. Grunting, he cast many to the ground, and fled forth at his best speed, without more mischief. The men hallooed loudly and cried, 'Hay! Hay!' and blew the horns to urge on the hounds, and rode swiftly after the boar. Many a time did he turn to bay and tare the hounds, and they yelped and howled shrilly. Then the men made ready their arrows and shot at him, but the points were turned on his thick hide, and the barbs would not bite upon him, for the shafts shivered in pieces, and the head but leapt again wherever it hit.

But when the boar felt the stroke of the arrows he waxed mad with rage, and turned on the hunters and tare many, so that, affrighted, they fled before him. But the lord on a swift steed pursued him, blowing his bugle; as a gallant knight he rode through the woodland chasing the boar till the sun grew low.

So did the hunters this day, while Sir Gawain lay in his bed lapped in rich gear; and the lady forgat not to salute him, for early was she at his side, to cheer his mood.

She came to the bedside and looked on the knight, and Gawain gave her fit greeting, and she greeted him again with ready words, and sat her by his side and laughed, and with a sweet look she spoke to him:

'Sir, if ye be Gawain, I think it a wonder that ye be so stern and cold, and care not for the courtesies of friendship, but if one teach ye to know them ye cast the lesson out of your mind. Ye have soon forgotten what I taught ye yesterday, by all the truest tokens that I knew!'

'What is that?' quoth the knight. 'I trow I know not. If it be sooth that ye say, then is the blame mine own.'

'But I taught ye of kissing,' quoth the fair lady. 'Wherever a fair countenance is shown him, it behooves a courteous knight quickly to claim a kiss.'

'Nay, my dear,' said Sir Gawain, 'cease that speech; that durst I not do lest I were denied, for if I were forbidden I wot I were wrong did I further entreat.'

'I' faith,' quoth the lady merrily, 'ye may not be forbid, ye are strong enough to constrain by strength an ye will, were any so discourteous as to give ye denial.'

'Yea, by heaven,' said Gawain, 'ye speak well; but threats profit little in the land where I dwell, and so with a gift that is given not of good will! I am at your commandment to kiss when ye like, to take or to leave as ye list.'

Then the lady bent her down and kissed him courteously.

And as they spake together she said, 'I would learn somewhat from ye, and ye would not be wroth, for young ye are and fair, and so courteous and knightly as ye are known to be, the head of all chivalry, and versed in all wisdom of love and war—'t is ever told of true knights how they adventured their lives for their true love, and endured hardships for her favors, and avenged her with valor, and eased her sorrows, and brought joy to her bower; and ye are the fairest knight of your time, and your fame and your honor are everywhere, yet I have sat by ye here twice, and never a word have I heard of love! Ye who are so courteous and skilled in such love ought surely to teach one so young and unskilled some little craft of true love! Why are ye so unlearned who are otherwise so famous? Or is it that ye deemed me unworthy to hearken to your teaching? For shame, Sir Knight! I come hither alone and sit at your side to learn of ye some skill; teach me of your wit, while my lord is from home.'

'In good faith,' quoth Gawain, 'great is my joy and my profit that so fair a lady as ye are should deign to come hither, and trouble ye with so poor a man, and make sport with your knight with kindly countenance, it pleaseth me much. But that I, in my turn, should take it upon me to tell of love and such like matters to ye who know more by half, or a hundred fold, of such craft than I do, or ever shall in all my lifetime, by my troth 't were folly indeed! I will work your will to the best of my might as I am bounden, and evermore will I be your servant, so help me Christ!'

Then often with guile she questioned that knight that she might win him to woo her, but he defended himself so fairly that none might in any wise blame him, and naught but bliss and harmless jesting was there between them. They laughed and talked together till at last she kissed him, and craved her leave of him, and went her way.

Then the knight rose and went forth to Mass, and afterward dinner was served and he sat and spake with the ladies all day. But the lord of the castle rode ever over the land chasing the wild boar, that fled through the thickets, slaying the best of his hounds and breaking their backs in sunder; till at last he was so weary he might run no longer, but made for a hole in a mound by a rock. He got the mound at his back and faced the hounds, whetting his white tusks and foaming at the mouth. The huntsmen stood aloof, fearing to draw nigh him; so many of them had been already wounded that they were loath to be torn with his tusks, so fierce he was and mad with rage. At length the lord himself came up, and saw the beast at bay, and the men standing aloof. Then quickly he sprang to the ground and drew out a bright blade, and waded through the stream to the boar.

When the beast was aware of the knight with weapon in hand, he set up his bristles and snorted loudly, and many feared for their lord lest he should be slain. Then the boar leapt upon the knight so that beast and man were one atop of the other in the water; but the boar had the worst of it, for the man had marked, even as he sprang, and set the point of his brand to the beast's chest, and drove it up to the hilt, so that the heart was split in twain, and the boar fell snarling, and was swept down by the water to where a hundred hounds seized on him, and the men drew him to shore for the dogs to slay.

Then was there loud blowing of horns and

baying of hounds, the huntsmen smote off the boar's head, and hung the carcass by the four feet to a stout pole, and so went on their way homewards. The head they bore before the lord himself, who had slain the beast at the ford by force of his strong hand.

It seemed him o'er long ere he saw Sir Gawain in the hall, and he called, and the guest came to take that which fell to his share. And when he saw Gawain the lord laughed aloud, and bade them call the ladies and the household together, and he showed them the game, and told them the tale, how they hunted the wild boar through the woods, and of his length and breadth and height; and Sir Gawain commended his deeds and praised him for his valor, well proven, for so mighty a beast had he never seen before.

Then they handled the huge head, and the lord said aloud, 'Now, Gawain, this game is your own by sure covenant, as ye right well know.'

'"T is sooth,' quoth the knight, 'and as truly will I give ye all I have gained.' He took the host round the neck, and kissed him courteously twice. 'Now are we quits,' he said 'this eventide, of all the covenants that we made since I came hither.'

And the lord answered, 'By Saint Giles, ye are the best I know; ye will be rich in a short space if ye drive such bargains!'

Then they set up the tables on trestles, and covered them with fair cloths, and lit waxen tapers on the walls. The knights sat and were served in the hall, and much game and glee was there round the hearth, with many songs, both at supper and after; song of Christmas, and new carols, with all the mirth one may think of. And ever that lovely lady sat by the knight, and with still stolen looks made such feint of pleasing him, that Gawain marveled much, and was wroth with himself, but he could not for his courtesy return her fair glances, but dealt with her cunningly, however she might strive to wrest the thing.

When they had tarried in the hall so long as it seemed them good, they turned to the inner chamber and the wide hearthplace, and there they drank wine, and the host proffered to renew the covenant for New Year's Eve; but the knight craved leave to depart on the morrow, for it was nigh to the term when he must fulfil his pledge. But the lord would withhold him from so doing, and prayed him to tarry, and said, 'As I am a true knight I swear my troth that ye shall come to the Green Chapel to achieve your task on New Year's morn, long before prime. Therefore abide ye in your bed, and I will hunt in this wood, and hold ye to the covenant to exchange with me against all the spoil I may bring hither. For twice have I tried ye, and found ye true, and the morrow shall be the third time and the best. Make we merry now while we may, and think on joy, for misfortune may take a man whensoever it wills.'

Then Gawain granted his request, and they brought them drink, and they gat them with lights to bed.

Sir Gawain lay and slept softly, but the lord, who was keen on woodcraft, was afoot early. After Mass he and his men ate a morsel, and he asked for his steed; all the knights who should ride with him were already mounted before the hall gates.

'T was a fair frosty morning, for the sun rose red in ruddy vapor, and the welkin was clear of clouds. The hunters scattered them by a forest side, and the rocks rang again with the blast of their horns. Some came on the scent of a fox, and a hound gave tongue; the huntsmen shouted, and the pack followed in a crowd on the trail. The fox ran before them, and when they saw him they pursued him with noise and much shouting, and he wound and turned through many a thick grove, often cowering and hearkening in a hedge. At last by a little ditch he leapt out of a spinney, stole away slily by a copse path, and so out of the wood and away from the hounds. But he went, ere he wist, to a chosen tryst, and three started forth on him at once, so he must needs double back, and betake him to the wood again.

Then was it joyful to hearken to the hounds; when all the pack had met together and had sight of their game they made as loud a din as if all the lofty cliffs had fallen clattering together. The huntsmen shouted and threatened, and followed close upon him so that he might scarce escape, but Reynard was wily, and he turned and doubled upon them, and led the lord and his men over the hills, now on the slopes, now in the vales, while the knight at home slept through the cold morning beneath his costly curtains.

But the fair lady of the castle rose betimes, and clad herself in a rich mantle that reached even to the ground, left her throat and her fair neck bare, and was bordered and lined with costly furs. On her head she wore no golden circlet, but a network of precious stones, that gleamed and shone through her tresses in clusters of twenty together. Thus she came into the chamber, closed the door after her, and set open a window, and called to him gaily, 'Sir Knight, how may ye sleep? The morning is so fair.'

Sir Gawain was deep in slumber, and in his dream he vexed him much for the destiny that should befall him on the morrow, when he should meet the knight at the Green Chapel, and abide his blow; but when the lady spake he heard her, and came to himself, and roused from his dream and answered swiftly. The lady came laughing, and kissed him courteously, and he welcomed her fittingly with a cheerful countenance. He saw her so glorious and gaily dressed, so faultless of features and complexion, that it warmed his heart to look upon her.

They spake to each other smiling, and all was bliss and good cheer between them. They exchanged fair words, and much happiness was therein, yet was there a gulf between them, and she might win no more of her knight, for that gallant prince watched well his words—he would neither take her love, nor frankly refuse it. He cared for his courtesy, lest he be deemed churlish, and yet more for his honor lest he be traitor to his host. 'God forbid,' quoth he to himself, 'that it should so befall.' Thus with courteous words did he set aside all the special speeches that came from her lips.

Then spake the lady to the knight, 'Ye deserve blame if ye hold not that lady who sits beside ye above all else in the world, if ye have not already a love whom ye hold dearer, and like better, and have sworn such firm faith to that lady that ye care not to loose it—and that am I now fain to believe. And now I pray ye straitly that ye tell me that in truth, and hide it not.'

And the knight answered, 'By Saint John' (and he smiled as he spake) 'no such love have I, nor do I think to have yet awhile.'

'That is the worst word I may hear,' quoth the lady, 'but in sooth I have mine answer; kiss me now courteously, and I will go hence; I can but mourn as a maiden that loves much.'

Sighing, she stooped down and kissed him, and then she rose up and spake as she stood, 'Now, dear, at our parting do me this grace: give me some gift, if it were but thy glove, that I may bethink me of my knight, and lessen my mourning.'

'Now, I wis,' quoth the knight, 'I would that I had here the most precious thing that I possess on earth that I might leave ye as love-token, great or small, for ye have deserved forsooth more reward than I might give ye. But it is not to your honor to have at this time a glove for reward as gift from Gawain, and I am here on a strange errand, and have no man with me, nor mails with goodly things—that mislikes me much, lady, at this time; but each man must fare as he is taken, if for sorrow and ill.'

'Nay, knight highly honored,' quoth that lovesome lady, 'though I have naught of yours, yet shall ye have somewhat of mine.' With that she reached him a ring of red gold with a sparkling stone therein, that shone even as the sun (wit ye well, it was worth many marks); but the knight refused it, and spake readily,

'I will take no gift, lady, at this time. I have none to give, and none will I take.'

She prayed him to take it, but he refused her prayer, and sware in sooth that he would not have it.

The lady was sorely vexed, and said, 'If ye refuse my ring as too costly, that ye will not be so highly beholden to me, I will give you my girdle as a lesser gift.' With that she loosened a lace that was fastened at her side, knit upon her kirtle under her mantle. It was wrought of green silk, and gold, only braided by the fingers, and that she offered to the knight, and besought him though it were of little worth that he would take it, and he said nay, he would touch neither gold nor gear ere God give him grace to achieve the adventure for which he had come hither. 'And therefore, I pray ye, displease ye not, and ask me no longer, for I may not grant it. I am dearly beholden to ye for the favor ye have shown me, and ever, in heat and cold, will I be your true servant.'

'Now,' said the lady, 'ye refuse this silk, for it is simple in itself, and so it seems, indeed; lo, it is small to look upon and less in cost, but whoso knew the virtue that is knit therein he would, peradventure, value it more highly. For whatever knight is girded with this green lace, while he bears it knotted about him there is no man under heaven can overcome him, for he may not be slain for any magic on earth.'

Then Gawain bethought him, and it came into his heart that this were a jewel for the jeopardy that awaited him when he came to the Green Chapel to seek the return blow—could he so order it that he should escape unslain, 't were a craft worth trying. Then he bare with her chiding, and let her say her say, and she pressed the girdle on him and prayed him to take it, and he granted her prayer, and she gave it him with good will, and besought him for her sake never to reveal it but to hide it loyally from her lord; and the knight agreed that never should any man know it, save they two alone. He thanked her often and heartily, and she kissed him for the third time.

Then she took her leave of him, and when she was gone Sir Gawain rose, and clad him in rich attire, and took the girdle, and knotted it round him, and hid it beneath his robes. Then he took his way to the chapel, and sought out a priest privily and prayed him to teach him better how his soul might be saved when he should go hence; and there he shrived him, and showed his misdeeds, both great and small, and besought mercy and craved absolution; and the priest assoiled him, and set him as clean as if doomsday had been on the morrow. And afterwards Sir Gawain made him merry with the ladies, with carols, and all kinds of joy, as never he did but that one day, even to nightfall; and all the men marveled at him, and said that never since he came thither had he been so merry.

Meanwhile the lord of the castle was abroad chasing the fox; awhile he lost him, and as he rode through a spinney he heard the hounds near at hand, and Reynard came creeping through a thick grove, with all the pack at his heels. Then the lord drew out his shining brand, and cast it at the beast, and the fox swerved aside for the sharp edge, and would have doubled back, but a hound was on him ere he might turn, and right before the horse's feet they all fell on him, and worried him fiercely, snarling the while.

Then the lord leapt from his saddle, and caught the fox from the jaws, and held it aloft over his head, and hallooed loudly, and many brave hounds bayed as they beheld it; and the hunters hied them thither, blowing their horns; all that bare bugles blew them at once, and all the others shouted. 'T was the merriest meeting that ever men heard, the clamor that was raised at the death of the fox. They rewarded the hounds, stroking them and rubbing their heads, and took Reynard and stripped him of his coat; then blowing their horns, they turned them homewards, for it was nigh nightfall.

The lord was gladsome at his return, and found a bright fire on the hearth, and the knight beside it, the good Sir Gawain, who was in joyous mood for the pleasure he had had with the ladies. He wore a robe of blue, that reached even to the ground, and a surcoat richly furred, that became him well. A hood like to the surcoat fell on his shoulders, and all alike were done about with fur. He met the host in the midst of the floor, and jesting, he greeted him, and said, 'Now shall I be first to fulfil our covenant which we made together when there was no lack of wine.' Then he embraced the knight, and kissed him thrice, as solemnly as he might.

'Of a sooth,' quoth the other, 'ye have good luck in the matter of this covenant, if ye made a good exchange!'

'Yet, it matters naught of the exchange,' quoth Gawain, 'since what I owe is swiftly paid.'

'Marry,' said the other, 'mine is behind, for I have hunted all this day, and naught have I got but this foul foxskin, and that is but poor payment for three such kisses as ye have here given me.'

'Enough,' quoth Sir Gawain, 'I thank ye, by the Rood.'

Then the lord told them of his hunting, and how the fox had been slain.

With mirth and minstrelsy, and dainties at their will, they made them as merry as a folk well might till it was time for them to sever, for at last they must needs betake them to their beds. Then the knight took his leave of the lord, and thanked him fairly.

'For the fair sojourn that I have had here at this high feast may the High King give ye honor. I give ye myself, as one of your servants, if ye so like; for I must needs, as ye know, go hence with the morn, and ye will give me, as ye promised, a guide to show me the way to the Green Chapel, an God will suffer me on New Year's Day to deal the doom of my weird.'

'By my faith,' quoth the host, 'all that ever I promised, that shall I keep with good will.' Then he gave him a servant to set him in the way, and lead him by the downs, that he should have no need to ford the stream, and should fare by the shortest road through the groves; and Gawain thanked the lord for the honor done him. Then he would take leave of the ladies, and courteously he kissed them, and spake, praying them to receive his thanks, and they made like reply; then with many sighs they commended him to Christ, and he departed courteously from that fold. Each man that he met he thanked him for his service and his solace, and the pains he had been at to do his will; and each found it as hard to part from the knight as if he had ever dwelt with him.

Then they led him with torches to his chamber, and brought him to his bed to rest. That he slept soundly I may not say, for the morrow gave him much to think on. Let him rest awhile, for he was near that which he sought, and if ye will but listen to me I will tell ye how it fared with him thereafter.

IV

Now the New Year drew nigh, and the night passed, and the day chased the darkness, as is God's will; but wild weather wakened therewith. The clouds cast the cold to the earth, with enough of the north to slay them that lacked clothing. The snow drave smartly, and the whistling wind blew from the heights, and made great drifts in the valleys. The knight, lying in his bed, listened, for though his eyes were shut, he might sleep but little, and hearkened every cock that crew.

He arose ere the day broke, by the light of a lamp that burned in his chamber, and called to his chamberlain, bidding him bring his armor and saddle his steed. The other gat him up, and fetched his garments, and robed Sir Gawain.

First he clad him in his clothes to keep off the cold, and then in his harness, which was well and fairly kept. Both hauberk and plates were well burnished, the rings of the rich byrnie freed from rust, and all as fresh as at first, so that the knight was fain to thank them. Then he did on each piece, and bade them bring his steed, while he put the fairest raiment on himself; his coat with its fair cognizance, adorned with precious stones upon velvet, with broidered seams, and all furred within with costly skins. And he left not the lace, the lady's gift, that Gawain forgot not, for his own good. When he had girded on his sword he wrapped the gift twice about him, swathed around his waist. The girdle of green silk set gaily and well upon the royal red cloth, rich to behold, but the knight ware it not for pride of the pendants, polished though they were with fair gold that gleamed brightly on the ends, but to save himself from sword and knife, when it behooved him to abide his hurt without question. With that the hero went forth, and thanked that kindly folk full often.

Then was Gringalet ready, that was great and strong, and had been well cared for and tended in every wise; in fair condition was that proud steed, and fit for a journey. Then Gawain went to him, and looked on his coat, and said by his sooth, 'There is a folk in this place that thinketh on honor; much joy may they have, and the lord who maintains them, and may all good betide that lovely lady all her life long. Since they for charity cherish a guest, and hold honor in their hands, may he who holds the heaven on high requite them, and also ye all. And if I might live anywhile on earth, I would give ye full reward, readily, if so I might.' Then he set foot in the stirrup and bestrode his steed, and his squire gave him his shield, which he laid on his shoulder. Then he smote Gringalet with his golden spurs, and the steed pranced on the stones and would stand no longer.

By that his man was mounted, who bare his spear and lance, and Gawain quoth, 'I commend this castle to Christ, may he give it ever good fortune.' Then the drawbridge was let down, and the broad gates unbarred and opened on both sides; the knight crossed himself, and passed through the gateway, and praised the porter, who knelt before the prince, and gave him good-day, and commended him to God. Thus the knight went on his way with the one man who should guide him to that dread place where he should receive rueful payment.

The two went by hedges where the boughs were bare, and climbed the cliffs where the cold clings. Naught fell from the heavens, but 't was ill beneath them; mist brooded over the moor and hung on the mountains; each hill had a cap, a great cloak, of mist. The streams foamed and bubbled between their banks, dashing sparkling on the shores where they shelved downwards. Rugged and dangerous was the way through the woods, till it was time for the sun-rising. Then were they on a high hill; the snow lay white beside them, and the man who rode with Gawain drew rein by his master.

'Sir,' he said, 'I have brought ye hither, and now ye are not far from the place that ye have sought so specially. But I will tell ye for sooth, since I know ye well, and ye are such a knight as I well love, would ye follow my counsel ye would fare the better. The place whither ye go is accounted full perilous, for he who liveth in that waste is the worst on earth, for he is strong and fierce; and loveth to deal mighty blows; taller he is than any man on earth, and greater of frame than any four in Arthur's court, or in any other. And this is his custom at the Green Chapel; there may no man pass by that place, however proud his arms, but he does him to death by force of his hand, for he is a discourteous knight, and shows no mercy. Be he churl or chaplain who rides by that chapel, monk or mass-priest, or any man else, he thinks it as pleasant to slay them as to pass alive himself. Therefore, I tell ye, as sooth as ye sit in saddle, if ye come there and that knight know it, ye shall be slain, though ye had twenty lives; trow me that truly! He has dwelt here full long and seen many a combat; ye may not defend ye against his blows. Therefore, good Sir Gawain, let the man be, and get ye away some other road; for God's sake seek ye another land, and there may Christ speed ye! And I will hie me home again, and I promise ye further that I will swear by God and the saints, or any other oath ye please, that I will keep counsel faithfully, and never let any wit the tale that ye fled for fear of any man.'

'Gramercy,' quoth Gawain, but ill-pleased. 'Good fortune be his who wishes me good, and that thou wouldst keep faith with me I will believe; but didst thou keep it never so truly, an I passed here and fled for fear as thou sayest, then were I a coward knight, and might not be held guiltless. So I will to the chapel let chance what may, and talk with that man, even as I may list, whether for weal or for woe as fate may have it. Fierce though he may be in fight, yet God knoweth well how to save his servants.'

'Well,' quoth the other, 'now that ye have said so much that ye will take your own harm on yourself, and ye be pleased to lose your life, I will neither let nor keep ye. Have here your helm and the spear in your hand, and ride down this same road beside the rock till ye come to the bottom of the valley, and there look a little to the left hand, and ye shall see in that vale the chapel, and the grim man who keeps it. Now fare ye well, noble Gawain; for all the gold on earth I would not go with ye nor bear ye fellowship one step further.' With that the man turned his bridle into the wood, smote the horse with his spurs as hard as he could, and galloped off, leaving the knight alone.

Quoth Gawain, 'I will neither greet nor moan, but commend myself to God, and yield me to his will.'

Then the knight spurred Gringalet, and rode adown the path close in by a bank beside a grove. So he rode through the rough thicket, right into the dale, and there he halted, for it seemed him wild enough. No sign of a chapel could he see, but high and burnt banks on either side and rough rugged crags with great stones above. An ill-looking place he thought it.

Then he drew in his horse and looked round to seek the chapel, but he saw none and thought it strange. Then he saw as it were a mound on a level space of land by a bank beside the stream where it ran swiftly; the water bubbled within as if boiling. The knight turned his steed to the mound, and lighted down and tied the rein to the branch of a linden; and he turned to the mound and walked round it, questioning with himself what it might be. It had a hole at the end and at either side, and was overgrown with clumps of grass, and it was hollow within as an old cave or the crevice of a crag; he knew not what it might be.

'Ah,' quoth Gawain, 'can this be the Green Chapel? Here might the devil say his matins at midnight! Now I wis there is wizardry here. 'T is an ugly oratory, all overgrown with grass, and 't would well beseem that fellow in green to say his devotions on devil's wise. Now feel I in five wits, 't is the foul fiend himself who hath set me this tryst, to destroy me here! This is a chapel of mischance: ill-luck betide it, 't is the cursedest kirk that ever I came in!'

Helmet on head and lance in hand, he came up to the rough dwelling, when he heard over the high hill beyond the brook, as it were in a bank, a wondrous fierce noise, that rang in the cliff as if it would cleave asunder. 'T was as if one ground a scythe on a grindstone, it whirred and whetted like water on a mill-wheel and rushed and rang, terrible to hear.

'By God,' quoth Gawain, 'I trow that gear is preparing for the knight who will meet me here. Alas! naught may help me, yet should my life be forfeit, I fear not a jot!' With that he called aloud. 'Who waiteth in this place to give me tryst? Now is Gawain come hither: if any man will aught of him let him hasten hither now or never.'

'Stay,' quoth one on the bank above his head, 'and ye shall speedily have that which I promised ye.' Yet for a while the noise of whetting went on ere he appeared, and then he came forth from a cave in the crag with a fell weapon, a Danish axe newly dight, wherewith to deal the blow. An evil head it had, four feet large, no less, sharply ground, and bound to the handle by the lace that gleamed brightly. And the knight himself was all green as before, face and foot, locks and beard, but now he was afoot. When he came to the water he would not wade it, but sprang over with the pole of his axe, and strode boldly over the bent that was white with snow.

Sir Gawain went to meet him, but he made no low bow. The other said, 'Now, fair sir, one may trust thee to keep tryst. Thou art welcome, Gawain, to my place. Thou hast timed thy coming as befits a true man. Thou knowest the covenant set between us: at this time twelve months agone thou didst take that which fell to thee, and I at this New Year will readily requite thee. We are in this valley, verily alone, here are no knights to sever us, do what we will. Have off thy helm from thine head, and have here thy pay; make me no more talking than I did then when thou didst strike off my head with one blow.'

'Nay,' quoth Gawain, 'by God that gave me life, I shall make no moan whatever befall me, but make thou ready for the blow and I shall stand still and say never a word to thee, do as thou wilt.'

With that he bent his head and showed his neck all bare, and made as if he had no fear, for he would not be thought a-dread.

Then the Green Knight made him ready, and grasped his grim weapon to smite Gawain. With all his force he bore it aloft with a mighty feint of slaying him: had it fallen as straight as he aimed he who was ever doughty of deed had been slain by the blow. But Gawain swerved aside as the axe came gliding down to slay him as he stood, and shrank a little with the shoulders, for the sharp iron. The other heaved up the blade and rebuked the prince with many proud words:

'Thou art not Gawain,' he said, 'who is held so valiant, that never feared he man by hill or vale, but thou shrinkest for fear ere thou feelest hurt. Such cowardice did I never hear of Gawain! Neither did I flinch from thy blow, or make strife in King Arthur's hall. My head fell to my feet, and yet I fled not; but thou didst wax faint of heart ere any harm befell. Wherefore must I be deemed the braver knight.'

Quoth Gawain, 'I shrank once, but so will I no more; though an my head fall on the stones I cannot replace it. But haste, Sir Knight, by thy faith, and bring me to the point, deal me my destiny, and do it out of hand, for I will stand thee a stroke and move no more till thine axe have hit me—my troth on it.'

'Have at thee, then,' quoth the other, and heaved aloft the axe with fierce mien, as if he were mad. He struck at him fiercely but wounded him not, withholding his hand ere it might strike him.

Gawain abode the stroke, and flinched in no limb, but stood still as a stone or the stump of a tree that is fast rooted in the rocky ground with a hundred roots.

Then spake gaily the man in green, 'So now thou hast thine heart whole it behooves me to smite. Hold aside thy hood that Arthur gave thee, and keep thy neck thus bent lest it cover it again.'

Then Gawain said angrily, 'Why talk on thus? Thou dost threaten too long. I hope thy heart misgives thee.'

'For sooth,' quoth the other, 'so fiercely thou speakest I will no longer let thine errand wait its reward.' Then he braced himself to strike, frowning with lips and brow, 't was no marvel that it pleased but ill him who hoped for no rescue. He lifted the axe lightly and let it fall with the edge of the blade on the bare neck. Though he struck swiftly, it hurt him no more than on the one side where it severed the skin. The sharp blade cut into the flesh so that the blood ran over his shoulder to the ground. And when the knight saw the blood staining the snow, he sprang forth, swift-foot, more than a spear's length, seized his helmet and set it on his head, cast his shield over his shoulder, drew out his bright sword, and spake boldly (never since he was born was he half so blithe), 'Stop, Sir Knight, bid me no more blows. I have stood a stroke here without flinching, and if thou give me another, I shall requite thee, and give thee as good again. By the covenant made betwixt us in Arthur's hall but one blow falls to me here. Halt, therefore.'

Then the Green Knight drew off from him and leaned on his axe, setting the shaft on the ground, and looked on Gawain as he stood all armed and faced him fearlessly—at heart it pleased him well. Then he spake merrily in a loud voice, and said to the knight, 'Bold sir, be not so fierce; no man here hath done thee wrong, nor will do, save by covenant, as we made at Arthur's court. I promised thee a blow and thou hast it—hold thyself well paid! I release thee of all other claims. If I had been so minded I might perchance have given thee a rougher buffet. First I menaced thee with a feigned one, and hurt thee not for the covenant that we made in the first night, and which thou didst hold truly. All the gain didst thou give me as a true man should. The other feint I proffered thee for the morrow: my fair wife kissed thee, and thou didst give me her kisses—for both those days I gave thee two blows without scathe—true man, true return. But the third time thou didst fail, and therefore hadst thou that blow. For 't is *my* weed thou wearest, that same woven girdle, my own wife wrought it, that do I wot for sooth. Now know I well thy kisses, and thy conversation, and the wooing of my wife, for 't was mine own doing. I sent her to try thee, and in sooth I think thou art the most faultless knight that ever trod earth. As a pearl among white peas is of more worth than they, so is Gawain, i' faith, by other knights. But thou didst lack a little, Sir Knight, and wast wanting in loyalty, yet that was for no evil work, nor for wooing neither, but because thou lovedst thy life—therefore I blame thee the less.'

Then the other stood a great while, still sorely angered and vexed within himself; all the blood flew to his face, and he shrank for shame as the Green Knight spake; and the first words he said were, 'Cursed be ye, cowardice and covetousness, for in ye is the destruction of virtue.' Then he loosed the girdle, and gave it to the knight. 'Lo, take there the falsity, may foul befall it! For fear of thy blow cowardice bade me make friends with covetousness and forsake the customs of largess and loyalty, which befit all knights. Now am I faulty and false and have been afeared: from treachery and untruth come sorrow and care. I avow to thee, Sir Knight, that I have ill done; do then thy will. I shall be more wary hereafter.'

Then the other laughed and said gaily, 'I wot I am whole of the hurt I had, and thou hast made such free confession of thy misdeeds, and hast so borne the penance of mine axe edge, that I hold thee absolved from that sin, and purged as clean as if thou hadst never sinned since thou wast born. And this girdle that is wrought with gold and green, like my raiment, do I give thee, Sir Gawain, that thou mayest think upon this chance when thou goest forth among princes of renown, and keep this for a token of the adventure of the Green Chapel, as it chanced between chivalrous knights. And thou shalt come again with me to my dwelling and pass the rest of this feast in gladness.' Then the lord laid hold of him, and said, 'I wot we shall soon make peace with my wife, who was thy bitter enemy.'

'Nay, forsooth,' said Sir Gawain, and seized his helmet and took it off swiftly, and thanked the knight: 'I have fared ill, may bliss betide thee, and may he who rules all things reward thee swiftly. Commend me to that courteous lady, thy fair wife, and to the other my honored ladies, who have beguiled their knight with skilful craft. But 't is no marvel if one be made a fool and brought to sorrow by women's wiles, for so was Adam beguiled by one, and Solomon by many, and Samson all too soon, for Delilah dealt him his doom; and David thereafter was wedded with Bathsheba, which brought him much sorrow—if one might love a woman and believe her not, 't were great gain! And since all they were beguiled by women, methinks 't is the less blame to me that I was misled! But as for thy girdle, that will I take with good will, not for gain of the gold, nor for samite, nor silk, nor the costly pendants, neither for weal nor for worship, but in sign of my frailty. I shall look upon it when I ride in renown and remind myself of the fault and faintness of the flesh; and so when pride uplifts me for prowess of arms, the sight of this lace shall humble my heart. But one thing would I pray, if it displease thee not: since thou art lord of yonder land wherein I have dwelt, tell me what thy rightful name may be, and I will ask no more.'

'That will I truly,' quoth the other. 'Bernlak de Hautdesert am I called in this land. Morgain le Fay dwelleth in mine house, and through knowledge of clerkly craft hath she taken many. For long time was she the mistress of Merlin, who knew well all you knights of the court. Morgain the goddess is she called therefore, and there is none so haughty but she can bring him low. She sent me in this guise to yon fair hall to test the truth of the renown that is spread abroad of the valor of the Round Table. She taught me this marvel to betray your wits, to vex Guinevere and fright her to death by the man who spake with his head in his hand at the high table. That is she who is at home, that ancient lady, she is even thine aunt, Arthur's half-sister, the daughter of the Duchess of Tintagel, who afterward married King Uther. Therefore I bid thee, knight, come to thine aunt, and make merry in thine house; my folk love thee, and I wish thee as well as any man on earth, by my faith, for thy true dealing.'

But Sir Gawain said nay, he would in no wise do so; so they embraced and kissed, and commended each other to the Prince of Paradise, and parted right there, on the cold ground. Gawain on his steed rode swiftly to the king's hall, and the Green Knight got him whithersoever he would.

Sir Gawain, who had thus won grace of his life, rode through wild ways on Gringalet; oft he lodged in a house, and oft without, and many adventures did he have and came off victor full often, as at this time I cannot relate in tale. The hurt that he had in his neck was healed, he bare the shining girdle as a baldric bound by his side, and made fast with a knot 'neath his left arm, in token that he was taken in a fault—and thus he came in safety again to the court.

Then joy awakened in that dwelling when the king knew that the good Sir Gawain was come, for he deemed it gain. King Arthur kissed the knight, and the queen also, and many valiant knights sought to embrace him. They asked him how he had fared, and he told them all that had chanced to him—the adventure of the chapel, the fashion of the knight, the love of the lady—at last of the lace. He showed them the wound in the neck which he won for his disloyalty at the hand of the knight; the blood flew to his face for shame as he told the tale.

'Lo, lady,' he quoth, and handled the lace, 'this is the bond of the blame that I bear in my neck, this is the harm and the loss I have suffered, the cowardice and covetousness in which I was caught, the token of my covenant in which I was taken. And I must needs wear it so long as I live, for none may hide his harm, but undone it may not be, for if it hath clung to thee once, it may never be severed.'

Then the king comforted the knight, and the court laughed loudly at the tale, and all made accord that the lords and the ladies who belonged to the Round Table, each hero among them, should wear bound about him a baldric of bright green for the sake of Sir Gawain. And to this was agreed all the honor of the Round Table, and he who ware it was honored the more thereafter, as it is testified in the book of romance. That in Arthur's days this adventure befell, the book of Brutus bears witness. For since that bold knight came hither first, and the siege and the assault were ceased at Troy, I wis

    Many a venture herebefore
        Hath fallen such as this:
    May He that bare the crown of thorn
        Bring us unto His bliss.
                    Amen.

PEARL (c.1375)

Pearl is found in the same manuscript with *Sir Gawain and the Green Knight*, and is commonly ascribed to the same author; but it differs entirely from this romance in its nature. *Pearl* is essentially not a narrative, but an elegy. The lament is uttered by a mature person, possibly a father, and the object of his sorrow is a beloved young girl, perhaps a daughter, who had died before reaching the age of two years. Though the poem is elegiac in its intention, it takes the form of a vision of the other world. This vision falls into three parts. In the first, the mourner recounts his falling asleep upon the grave of the child, and the departure of his spirit to a marvelous landscape in the midst of which appears the beloved maiden arrayed in supernatural brilliance (Stanzas I to XIX below). The second part consists in a long dialogue in which the transfigured maiden conveys to the dreamer a substantial amount of theological instruction (Stanzas XX to XL). Finally in the third part the poet recounts his vision of the New Jerusalem, and his awaking from his dream (Stanzas XLI to XLIII). Aside from its remarkable theological learning, most of which is omitted from Dr. Mitchell's translation, the poem is notable, if not unique, among medieval works in England for descriptive beauty and sincerity of personal feeling.

PEARL

I

Pearl, for a prince's pleasance fair enow,
Right cleanly housed in gold so clear,
No orient pearl I dare avow
Was ever yet her precious peer.
So rounded, in such rare array, 5
So small, of smoothen comeliness,
I judged her of all jewels gay
As singly set in singleness.
Lost in mine arbor,—woe is me!
'Neath earth she lies with grass o'ergrown, 10
I mourn love's sweet anxiety
That spotless pearl had made my own.

II

There have I tarried ofttimes where below
It left my sight, to seek again the joy
That once was wont to scatter all my woe, 15
And lift my life above the world's annoy.
About my heart do ceaseless sorrows throng,
That constant grief must ever constant be—
Yet, thought I, never was so sweet a song
As the still hours thither brought to me. 20
Ah me! what thoughts are mine! I sit and dream
Of those fair colors clad, alas! in clay.
O earth! why hast thou marred this tender theme—
My spotless pearl, that was mine own alway?

III

What lavish fragrance here is spread 25
By herb and flower, newly won!
Of blossoms white and blue and red,
No gayer rise to greet the sun.
Here nor fruit nor flower may fade,
Where passed my pearl to night of ground; 30
From dead grain cometh fruitful blade,
Else never wheat had harvest found.
Ever 't is good that good doth bring,
Such seemly seed it faileth not;
Here ever-fragrant flowers shall spring 35
O'er thee, my pearl without a spot.

IV

That place I sweeten with gentle rhyme,
I came to, where was my arbor green,
In the high season of August time,
When corn is cut with the sickle keen. 40
Where pearl lay under the grassy mead,
Shadowed it was with leafage green,
Gillyflower, ginger, and gromwell seed,
And peonies powdered all between.
Fair and seemly the sight was seen, 45
Fairer fragrance earth knoweth not;
Worthily won it was, I ween,
Of pearl, the precious, without a spot.

V

I gazed, my hands together pressed,
For, chilled with care and sorrow caught, 50
My heart beat wildly in my breast,
Though reason sager counsel taught.
I wept my pearl in earthy cell,
And timid reason fought with doubt;
Though Christ did comfort me full well, 55
Weak will with woe me cast about.
Such soothing scents the air did fill
That, lulled on this rose-peopled plot,
By sleep o'ercome, I rested still
Above my pearl without a spot. 60

VI

Thence sped my spirit far through space,
My body tranced upon the ground,
My soul's quick ghost by God's sure grace
Adventuring where be marvels found.
I wist not where on earth that place 65
With cloven cliffs, so high and sheer,
But toward a wood I set my face,
Borne whither radiant rocks appear.
Their light more golden than the sun,
A gleaming glory glinted thence: 70
Was never web of mortals spun
So wondrous fair to mortal sense.

VII

The hill-sides there were brightly crowned
With crystal cliffs so clear of kind,
And wood-sides, set with boles around, 75
Shone blue as is the blue of Inde.
On every branch, with light between,
The leaves of quivering silver hung;
Through gleaming glades with shimmering sheen
The light fell glistering them among. 80
The gravel rolled upon the shore
Was precious pearls of Orient
The sun's bright beams were pale before
That sight so fair of wonderment.

VIII

My spirit there forgot its woe, 85
So wondrous were those charmed hills.
Rare flavored fruits thereon did grow,
Fit food to cure all human ills.
In fair accord the birds flew by,
Like wingèd flames, both great and small, 90
Nor cittern string nor minstrelsy
Might hope to match their joyous call:
For when the air their red wings beat,
Full choir sang they rapturously.
No greater joy a man could greet 95
Than this to hear, and that to see.

IX

Past all that eye of man has seen,
Past any wealth of words he hath,
The beauty of those wood-ways green,
The witchery of that wooing path. 100
Still on I pressed, as one who goes
Companioned by a joyous mood,
Through deepening dells where richly rose
Fair flowers by winsome breezes wooed.
Hedge-rows and marsh where wild fowl breed 105
I saw, and lo! a golden band—
A wonder that did all exceed—
A sunlit river cleft the strand.

X

O marvellous river, broad and deep,
With banks that beam with beryl bright! 110
As music sweet the waters sweep,
Or gently murmur low and light.
From darkened depths shone jewels fine,
As gleams through glowing glass the light,
As quivering stars in the welkin shine, 115
When tired men sleep of a winter night.
Each little stone that stream below
Was emerald green, or sapphire gent;
From them the light did leap and glow,
To daze a man with wonderment. 120

XI

Wondrous glamour of down and vale,
Wood and water and noble plain,
Did build me bliss and made me hale,
Routed sorrow and cured my pain.
Low bowed beside the stream I strayed. 125
With breed of joys my mind was glad;
The more I walked by mere and glade,
More strength of joy my spirit had.
Fortune fares where likes she still,
Sends she solace or evil sore, 130
The wight on whom she works her will
Hath ever of either more and more.

XII

More and more, and yet far more,
I longed to see beyond the strand;
For if 't was fair on the nearer shore, 135
More lovelike was that farther land.
I stayed my steps,—I stood at gaze,
To find a ford I sought,—alas!
Beside the strand, as in a maze,
I won not any way to pass. 140
Though peril in my path might stand,
I recked not, where such treasures were;
But fresh delights were nigh at hand,
That did my wondering spirit stir.

XIII

What wonder more did daunt my sight?   145
I saw beyond that mystic mere
A shining cliff of crystal bright,
With royal rays, as morning clear.
At foot there sat a little maid—
A maid of grace, and debonair;   150
In glistening white was she arrayed,
Well known long ere I saw her there.
More radiant than refinèd gold,
She stood in sunshine on the shore.
Long did my sight that vision hold,   155
And more I knew her, more and more.

XIV

Long feasted I on her dear face,
The lissome curves her figure wore,
Until the gladness of her grace
My heart's guest was as ne'er before.   160
Her gentle name I fain had called,
But stayed was I with wonderment,
So strange the place I stood appalled,
My eager gaze upon her bent.
Then turned on me her visage fair,—   165
As ivory white the face she wore.
Heart-struck was I to see her there,
And still I loved her more and more.

XV

Yearning had I by dread opposed.
I stood full still, I durst not call,   170
With eyes wide open and mouth full closed,
Like to a well-trained hawk in hall.
Hope had I for my soul's behoof;
Fear had I it might thus befall,
That she I longed for might stay aloof,   175
Or pass forever beyond recall.
Lo! uprose that child of grace,
Slender, small, and seemly slight,—
Rose right royal with lifted face,
A precious maid, with pearls bedight.   180

XVI

When, fresh as dewy fleur-de-lys,
Adown the bank she moved toward me,
High fortuned he on earth that sees
Such peerless pearls of empery.
As white as snow her amice gleams,   185
Her waist a lustrous broidery
Of pearls a man might see in dreams,
But never else on earth could see.
Full ample hung her sleeves, I ween;
Twain braided they with pearlës bright.   190
Her kirtle green alike was seen,
With pearls of price around bedight.

XVII

A crown did wear that maiden girl
Of margerys, and none other stone.
High pinnacled, of clear white pearl,   195
It glowed with flowers wrought thereon.
Her head no other gem did grace;
Her hair half hid her neck from view.
In statelihood of mighty place
She stood more white than whale tooth's hue.   200
Her loosened locks, that gold exceed,   201
Flowed wandering, o'er her shoulders curled;
Though dark their gold, they scarce did need
For contrast fair her robe impearled.

XVIII

Bravely broidered was every hem,   205
On sleeve and vest fair broidery lay
Of white pearls and no other gem,
And glossy shone her white array.
A wonder pearl without a taint
Lay moon-white where her bodice met;   210
Soul of man might falter and faint
Ere mind of man its price could set.
Tongue of man might ne'er be sure
With fitting words to tell aright
How spotless white and virgin pure   215
Was that rare pearl, my soul's delight.

XIX

Decked with pearls, that precious piece
Of Heaven's make came down the strand;
My grief won wings of glad release
When that I saw her nearer stand.   220
None else of kin were dear as she,
And joyful then was my surprise
When seemed it she would speak to me,
And courteous bowed in woman wise.
She doffed her crown of jewels bright,   225
With low obeisance bending blithe.
Leave to answer that pearl of light
Made worth it well to be alive.

XX

'O Pearl, so gay with pearls,' quoth I,—
'O Pearl that in my loneliness   230
Art yearned for when at night I lie
Sole comrade of my own distress,—
Since over thee the grasses twine,
No love to mine with love replies.
May liking, love, and joy be thine,—   235
The strifeless bourne of Paradise.
Such weird as brought thee hither here,
With plight of sorrow hath me undone;
Now are we twayned that were so dear,
And in love's life were but as one.'   240

XXI

High crowned with pearls of Orient,
Looked up at me with fair blue eyes
That gracious maid with grave intent,
And sober spake in courtly wise.
'Sir, the tale is by half mistold   245
To say thy pearl is all perdue,
That a comely coffer in guard doth hold,
In flowered gardens, gay to view,
Where she may ever dwell and play,
Where sin nor sorrow come never near.   250
Safe should such treasury seem alway
If thou didst love thy jewel dear.

XXII

'Gentle sir,' said the maiden gem,
'Why do men jest? Distraught ye be.
Three words hast said, and all of them   255
Forsooth are folly,—yea, all the three.
Thou knowest not what thy words may mean;
Quick words thy tardy wits outfly.
Dost surely think that I here am seen
Because thou seest with mortal eye.   260
Thou sayest, too, that thou, alas!
May bide with me in this domain.
The way this stream to freely pass
No living wight may know to gain.

XXIII

'Small praise that man would have of me   265
That trusts the wisdom of the eye.
Much to be blamed and graceless he
That thinks the Lord could speak a lie,—
Our Lord who promised thy life to raise,
Though fortune bid thy body die!   270
Ye read his words in crooked ways
To trust alone what sees the eye:
And that is a fault of haughtiness
Doth ill a righteous man beseem,
To trow no tale has worthiness   275
Unless his reason so may deem.

XXIV

'Think now thyself if it be well
Of God such words as thine to say.
Dost think in this fair land to dwell?
Methinks 't were better his leave to pray: 280
And yet might fail thine eager quest.
Ere thou shalt pass that watery way
Thou first must find another rest,
And cold must lie thy corse in clay;
For it was marred in Paradise,   285
Where our yore-father wrought it loss,—
Through dreary death thy journey lies
Ere God will give thee leave to cross.

XXV

'Thou thinkest sorrow is nought but dole.
Why dost thou make this vain pretence?   290
For lesser loss the wailing soul
May lose far more than he laments.
Shouldst rather hold thee blessed by it,
And love thy God in weal and woe,
For anger helpeth thee no whit,   295
And man must bear what all must know.
Though thou shouldst prance as any doe,
And fret and chafe in mad unrest,
Thou canst not any further go,—
Abide thou must what He thinks best.'   300

XXVI

Then spake I to that demoiselle—
'Let not my Lord be wroth with me.
As from a spring quick waters well,
Leaps forth my speech so wild and free.
My lonely heart is sorrow-scarred,   305
In misericorde of Christ I rest,
Rebuke me not with words so hard,
Forlorn am I, adored and best.
Thy kindly comfort me afford
With piteous thinking upon this—   310
Of care and me ye made accord
Who once were ground of all my bliss.

XXVII

'Thou hast been both my bale and bliss,
But greater is the bale I moan.
On every field my pearl I miss,   315
I wist not where my pearl has flown.
With clearer sight is sorrow eased.
Ere parting came we were at one.
Forbid it, God, we be displeased,
Though meet we not beneath the sun,   320
Though tender sweet thy courtesy,
I am but earth, my joy is gone;
Gone every hope of help for me
Save mercy of Christ, Marie, and John.

XXVIII

'I seek thee with thy comrade, joy.   325
Ah, think of me when thou art glad;
Sad hours my ageing life annoy,
A lonely man bereft and sad.
But now, within thy presence here
I fain would bide, and patient wait   330
That ye may tell—ah, pearl most dear—
What life ye have both early and late.
Full glad am I that thy estate
Is changed to worship and to weal;
Where thou hast passed to lofty state—   335
There lies the only joy I feel.'

XXIX

'To know if here the life is led
Be glad, will that thy grief assuage.
Thou knowest when thy pearl lay dead
Full young was I, of tender age.   340
Lo! I am bride of Christ the Lamb!
Through sacred Godhead wedded sure;
A crownèd queen of bliss I am,
Through days that shall for aye endure.
Who have his love do hold in fee   345
This heritage. I am his alone;
His priceless glory is to me
The source of every joy I own.'

XXX

'Ah, Pearl of bliss, can this be true?
Let not my error bid me rue.   350
Art thou the Queen of heaven's blue
That all the world does honour to?
Art her we worship, the spring of grace,
Who bare a Child of virgin flower?
Ah, none can take her crown and place,   355
That pass her not in worth and power.
For singleness of gentillesse
We call her phenix of Araby,—
The bird none match in stateliness,
Like to that Queen of Courtesy.'   360

XXXI

'Ay, Queen of Courtesy!' she said;
And lowly knelt and hid her face.
'Matchless mother and merriest maid!
Blest beginner of all our grace.'
Then rose she up and 'gan to speak,   365
And looked at me across the space.
'Though many find what here they seek,
None here may take another's place.
The heavens do her empire make,
Of earth and hell the Queen is she;   370
Her heritage may no one take,
For she is Queen of Courtesy.'

XXXII

'Yea, courtesy, I well believe,
And charity do here belong.
Let not my words thy goodness grieve—   375
To me thy speech still seemeth wrong.
Thyself to set so high in heaven
As queen to make of one so young—
What honor more might him be given
That in the world by grief was wrung,   380
And bought his bliss by years of bale—
Yea, lived in penance wearily?
No lesser honor him could fail
Than King be crowned by courtesy.

XXXIII

'Such courtesy too free appears,   385
If that be sooth which thou dost say.
On earth were thine but two brief years,
Never couldst thou God please or pray,
Knew never neither pater nor creed,—
But queen outright on thy death day,—   390
I may not trow it, so God me speed,
That God should rule so wrong a way.
Countess or demoiselle, par ma fay,
Were fair to be in heaven's estate,
Or else a lady of less array,—   395
But queen! it were too high a fate.'

XXXIV

'His goodness hath nor mete nor bound,'
Said then to me this worthsome wight;
'For all is truth where he is found,
Nought can he do but that is right.   400
This Matthew doth for thee express,
Writ clear in gospel sooth aright,
Ensampled plain for easy guess,
A parable of heavenly light.'
'My realm,' saith Christ, 'is like, on high,   405
A lord's that had a vineyard fair,
When lo! the vintage time was nigh,
And men must to his vines repair.

XXXV

'Right well his men the season know,
So up full early that lord arose   410
To send them where his vines did grow,
And unto some did there propose
A penny a day to be their gain.
With this accord forthwith they go,
And toil and labor with honest pain,   415
And prune and carry, go to and fro.
At noon this lord the market seeks,
And finds men standing idle here.
"Why stand ye idle?" thus he speaks
"Now know ye not the time of year?"   420

XXXVI

' "We hither came ere day begun,"
This was their answer, one and all.
"Here have we stood since rose the sun,
And no man yet on us doth call."
"Go to my vineyard, work aright,   425
And rest ye sure," that lord did say,
"What wages fair ye earn by night,
In very sooth I will surely pay."
Into his vines they went and wrought,
The while he came, and came again,   430
And new men into his vineyard brought,
Until the day was on the wane.

XXXVII

'At close of day, at evensong,
An hour before the sun had fled,
He saw there idle men and strong,   435
And unto them he gently said:
"Why stand ye idle all day long?"
"No man," they said, "has come to hire."
"Go to my vines, ye yeomen strong,
And work your best, as I desire."   440
Soon the world grew dusk and gray,
The sun went down, it waxèd late;
He summoned them to take their pay—
The hour had come for which they wait.

XXXVIII

'That lord well knew the time of day,   445
And bade his steward pay them all.
"Give every man his proper pay;
And that no blame on me may fall,
Set ye all of them in a row,
And give alike a penny to each.   450
Begin with him that stands most low,
Until the first his wage shall reach."
Thereon the first did quick complain:
"My lord, we toiled full long and sore;
These last have had but little pain,   455
Our wage should justly be far more."

XXXIX

'Then said this lord, "In sooth, I try
To use mine own as seemeth meet.
Why turn on me an evil eye,
Who justice seek and no man cheat?"   460
Quoth Christ, "I now do thus decree,
The first shall be the last, and those
Who latest came the first shall be,—
Of many called but few be chose."
Thus do poor men win their way,   465
Though late they come and low their state;
If brief has been their labor day,
The more of grace doth them await.

XL

'More bliss have I, and joy herein
Of ladyship, and life's delight,   470
Than all the men on earth might win
If all they sought were theirs by right.
Although the night was nigh at hand
When came I to the vines at even,
Among the first God bade me stand,   475
And fullest wage to me was given.
Yet others waited there in vain,
Who toiled and sweated long of yore,
And still no wage repaid their pain,
And may not for a year or more.'   480

XLI

The Lamb's delight none doubted there.
Though seemed he hurt and wounded sore,
Yet glorious glad his glances were,
And nought of pain his semblance bore.
I looked among his radiant host,   485
Quick with eternal life,—and lo!
I saw my pearlës gentle ghost,
I loved and lost so long ago.
Lord! much of mirth that maiden made
Among her peers, so pure and white.   490
I yearned to cross—all unafraid,
So longed my love—so dear the sight.

XLII

Delight held captive eye and ear;
My mortal mind toward madness drave,
I would be there where stayed my dear,   495
Beyond that river's mystic wave.
Methought that none would do so ill
As me to halt, if now I tried;
And if at start none checked my will,
Fain would I venture though I died.   500
Anon, from bold resolve I fell
When I would take that peril's chance;
In that rash mood I dare not dwell—
Not so my Prince's fair pleasance.

XLIII

It pleased not God that I come near,   505
Or think to cross that guarding mere,
Aghast I stood, alone with fear—
Alone, and she no longer here.
For, as I stood beside the stream,
I wakened in that arbor's shade.   510
Gone was the gladness of my dream!
My head was on that hillock laid
Where over her the roses grow.
Heartsore I lay upon the sod,
And to myself I murmured low: 515
'Blest be my maid in care of God.'

* * *

THE CHESTER PLAYS

The drama of the Middle Ages in Western Europe was prevailingly religious, and in the hands of the Church it normally appeared in the form of relatively brief scenes written in Latin and presented by the clergy in close association with the liturgy. Although our records are scanty, we may be sure that liturgical plays of this sort were performed in England from the tenth century to the fourteenth, and even later. By the fourteenth century, however, the religious drama had largely passed from within the church into secular surroundings outside. In the new circumstances the language employed was English, the actors were chiefly laymen, and the dramatic incidents were sometimes taken from other than religious sources. Under the auspices of associations of guilds this English religious drama usually took the form of large cycles of short plays, the typical cycle including the whole of sacred history, beginning with the Fall of the Angels and the Creation, proceeding through parts of the Old and New Testaments, and ending with the Last Judgment. This kind of drama is well exemplified by the Chester Plays, which were presented by the guilds of Chester from time to time during the fourteenth, fifteenth, and sixteenth centuries. The twenty-five separate plays of this cycle were commonly performed on the first three weekdays of Whitsuntide: nine on Monday, nine on Tuesday, and seven on Wednesday. Each play was assigned to a separate guild, or group of guilds, and the remarkable aptness of some of these assignments is shown by the fact that *Noah's Flood*, printed below, was played by the carriers of water from the River Dee, on the banks of which the city of Chester stands. Each play was performed upon a wagon, or 'pageant,' described in the records as 'a high place made like a house, with two rooms, being open on the top. [In] the lower room they apparelled and dressed themselves, and in the higher room they played.' Each pageant-wagon was drawn about the city and halted at each of the several stations where its play was to be presented. The way in which the succession of wagons was managed is well described in one of the Chester manuscripts: 'The places where they played them was in every street. They began first at the Abbey gates, and when the pageant was played, it was wheeled to the High Cross, before the Mayor; and so to every street, and so every street had a pageant playing before them till all the pageants for the day appointed were played. And when one pageant was near ended, word was brought from street to street, that so the [next] might come in place thereof, exceeding orderly. And all the streets had their pageant before them, all at one time playing together.' In *Noah's Flood* the farcical rôle of Noah's wife illustrates the freedom and levity with which the unknown playwrights of the cycles occasionally enlivened the Biblical narrative, and tolerantly mingled the comic and the serious.

NOAH'S FLOOD

THE WATERLEADERS AND DRAWERS OF DEE

First, in some high place, or in the clouds, if it may be done, GOD *speaks to* NOAH *standing with all his family outside the ark.*

GOD

I, GOD, that all the world have wrought,
Heaven and earth, and all of nought,
I see my people in deed and thought
   Are foully set in sin.
My ghost shall not remain in man   5
That through fleshly liking is my fone,
But till six score years be gone,
   To look if they will blyn.

Man that I made I will destroy,
Beast, worm, and fowl that fly,   10
For on earth they do me annoy,
   The folk that are thereon;
It harms me so hurtfully,
The malice now that does multiply
That sore it grieveth me inwardly   15
   That ever I made man.

Therefore, Noah, my servant free,
That righteous man art, as I see
A ship right soon thou shalt make thee
   Of trees both dry and light;   20
Little chambers therein do make,
And binding pitch also do take:
Within and out do thou not slake
   To anoint it through thy might,

Three hundred cubits it shall be long, 25
And fifty of breadth, to make it strong,
Of height fifty, the range do thou fonge;
   Thus measure it about.
One window fashion through thy wit,
One cubit of length and breadth make it; 30
Upon the side a door shall sit,
   For to come in and out.

Eating places make thou also,
Three roofed chambers, one or two,
For with water I think to flow 35
   Man that I did make;
Destroyed all the world shall be,
Save thou, thy wife, and thy sons three,
And all their wives also with thee,
   Shall saved be for thy sake. 40

NOAH

Ah, Lord, I thank thee loud and still,
That to me art in such good will,
And sparest me and my house to spill,
   As now I soothly find;
Thy bidding, Lord, I shall fulfill, 45
And never more thee grieve nor grill,
That such a grace hast sent me till,
   Among all mankind.

       [NOAH *speaks to his family.*]

Have done, you men and women all!
Help, for aught that may befall, 50
To make this ship, chamber and hall,
   As God hath bidden us do.

SHEM

Father, I am already bowne:
An axe I have here, by my crown,
As sharp as any in all this town, 55
   For to go thereto.

HAM

I have a hatchet wonder keen
To bite right well, as may be seen;
A better ground one, as I ween
   Is not in all this town. 60

JAPHET

And I can well now make a pin,
And with this hammer knock it in;
Go and work without more din,
   And I am ready bowne.

NOAH'S WIFE

And we shall bring the timber too 65
For we may nothing other do:
Women be weak to undergo
   Any great travail.

SHEM'S WIFE

Here is a right good chopping-block,
On this you may well hew and knock; 70
Shall none be idle in this flock,
   Nor now may no man fail.

HAM'S WIFE

And I will go to gather slich
The ship here for to clean and pitch:
Anointed it must be each stitch, 75
   Board, tree, and pin.

JAPHET'S WIFE

And I will gather chips up here
To make a fire for you in fere,
And for to dight you your dinner
   Against that you come in. 80

Then they make motions as if they were working with various tools.

NOAH

Now in the name of God I will begin
To make the ship that we shall go in,
That we be ready for to swim
   At the coming of the flood:
These boards I join up here together 85
To keep us safe from all the weather,
That we may row both hither and thither,
   And safe be from this flood.

Of this tree will I make the mast,
Tied with cables that will last, 90
With a sailyard for each blast,
   And each thing in their kind;
With topcastle and bowsprit,
With cords and ropes I have all meet
To sail forth at the next weete: 95
   This ship is at an end.

Then NOAH and all his family again make motions of working with various tools.

Wife, in this castle we shall be kept;
My children and thou I would in leapt.

NOAH'S WIFE

In faith, Noah, I had as lief thou slept.
   For all thy frankish fare, 100
I will not do after thy rede.

NOAH

Good wife, do now as I thee bid.

NOAH'S WIFE

By Christ! not ere I see more need,
   Though thou stand all the day and stare.

NOAH

Lord, that women be crabbed aye, 105
And never are meek, that dare I say;
This is well seen by me today
   In witness of you each one.
Good wife, let be all this bere
That thou makest in this place here, 110
For all they ween thou art master—
   And so thou art, by St. John!

GOD

Noah, take thou thy company,
And in the ship hie that you be,
For none so righteous man to me 115
   Is now on earth living.
Of clean beasts do thou with thee take
Seven and seven, ere thou slake,
He and she, and make to make,
   Quickly in do thou bring. 120

Of beasts unclean, two and two,
Male and female, without mo,
Of clean fowls seven also,
   The he and she together;
Of fowls unclean, two and no more, 125
As I of beasts did say before,
That shall be saved through my lore,
   Against I send the weather.

Of all the meats that must be eaten
Into the ship look there be getten, 130
For that no way may be forgetten,
   And do all this bydene,
To sustain man and beast therein,
Aye till this water cease and blyn.
This world is filled full of sin, 135
   And that is now well seen.

Seven days be yet coming,
You shall have space them in to bring;
After that is my liking
   Mankind for to annoy: 140
Forty days and forty nights
Rain shall fall for their unrights,
And what I have made through my mights,
   Now think I to destroy.

NOAH

Lord, at your bidding I am bayne; 145
Since nothing else your grace will gain,
It will I fulfill fain,
   For gracious I thee find.
A hundred winters and twenty
This ship making tarried have I, 150
If through amendment thy mercy
   Would fall unto mankind.

      [NOAH *summons his family.*]

Have done, you men and women all!
Hie you, lest this water fall.
That each beast were in his stall, 155
   And into the ship brought!
Of clean beasts seven there shall be,
Of unclean two, this God bade me.
This flood is nigh, well may we see;
   Therefore tarry you not. 160

Then NOAH *shall enter the ark, and his family shall exhibit and name all the animals painted on sheets of parchment, and after each one has spoken his part, he shall go into the ark, except* NOAH'S WIFE. *The animals painted must conform to the words spoken. And thus let the first son begin.*

SHEM

Sir, here are lions, leopards in,
Horses, mares, oxen, and swine,
Goats, calves, sheep, and kine,
   Here sitting thou mayst see.

HAM

Camels, asses, men may find, 165
Buck, doe, hart, and hind,
And beasts of all manner of kind
   Here be, it seems to me.

JAPHET

Take here cats, and dogs too,
Otter, fox, fulmart also, 170
Hares hopping gaily can go,
   Have cowle here for to eat.

NOAH'S WIFE

And here are bears, and wolves set,
Apes, and owls, and marmoset.
Weasels, squirrels, and ferret; 175
   Here they eat their meat.

SHEM'S WIFE

Yet more beasts are in this house:
Here the cats make it full crowse,
Here a rat and here a mouse,
   They all stand nigh together. 180

HAM'S WIFE

And here fowls, both less and more:
Herons, cranes, and bittour,
Swans, peacocks; and them before
   Meat for this weather.

JAPHET'S WIFE

Here are cocks and kites and crows,   185
Rooks and ravens, many rows;
Ducks, curlews: whoever knows
   Each one in his kind?
And here are doves and ducks and drakes,
Redshanks, running through the lakes;   190
And each fowl that language makes
   In this ship men find.

NOAH

Wife, come in! why standest thou here?
Thou art ever froward, dare I swear.
Come in, on God's half! time it were,   195
   For fear lest that we drown.

NOAH'S WIFE

Yea, sir, set up your sail,
And row forth with evil hail!
For without any fail
   I will not from this town.   200

Unless I have my gossips every one
One foot further I will not gone;
They shall not drown here, by St. John!
   If I may save their life!
They loved me full well, by Christ!   205
Unless thou'lt let them in thy chest,
Row forth, Noah, whither thou list,
   And get thee a new wife.

NOAH

Shem, son, lo! thy mother is wraw:
Forsooth, such another I do not know!   210

SHEM

Father, I'll fetch her in, I trow,
   Without any fail.
   [*Goes to where his mother is sitting.*]
Mother, my father after thee sent,
And bids thee into yon ship wend.
Look up and see the wind,   215
   For we be ready to sail.

NOAH'S WIFE

Son, go back to him and say,
I will not come therein today.

NOAH

Come in, wife, in twenty devils' way!
   Or else stand there without.   220

HAM

Shall we all fetch her in?

NOAH

Yea, sons, in Christ's blessing and mine!
I would you hied you betime,
   For of this flood I am in doubt.

THE GOOD GOSSIPS [*Singing*]

The flood comes in full fleeting fast,   225
On every side it spreadeth full far;
For fear of drowning I am aghast,
   Good gossip, let us draw near.
And let us drink ere we depart,
For oftentimes we have done so;   230
For at a draught thou drink'st a quart,
   And so will I do ere I go.

JAPHET

Mother, we pray you altogether,
For we are here, your own childer,
Come into the ship for fear of the weather,   235
   For his love that you bought.

NOAH'S WIFE

That will I not for all your call,
Unless I have my gossips all.

SHEM

In faith, mother, yet you shall,
   Whether you will or not!   240
      Then she will go.

NOAH

Welcome, wife, into this boat!

NOAH'S WIFE

And have thou that for thy mote!
   She deals NOAH *a blow.*

NOAH

Aha, marry, this is hot!
   It is good to be still.
Ah, children, methinks my boat removes!   245
Our tarrying here hugely me grieves;
Over the land the water spreads,—
   God do as he will!

Ah, great God, that art so good;
Who works not thy will is wood.   250
Now all this world is in a flood,
   As I see well in sight;
This window I will shut anon,
And into my chamber will I gone,
Till this water, so great one,   255
   Be slakèd through thy might.

Then let NOAH close the window of the ark, and after remaining within for a short time, let them sing the psalm, 'Save me, O God.' Then let NOAH open the window and look out.

Now forty days are fully gone.
Send a raven I will anon,
To see if earth or tree or stone,
  Be dry in any place;   260
And if this fowl come not again,
It is a sign, the sooth to sayne,
That dry it is on hill or plain,
  And God hath done some grace.

Then let him send forth a raven, and taking a dove in his hands, let him speak.

Ah, Lord, where'er this raven be,   265
Somewhere is dry, right well I see.
But yet a dove, by my loyalty,
  After I will send.
Thou wilt turn again to me,

* * *

For of all fowls that may fly,   270
  Thou art most meek and hend.

Then let him send forth the dove. And there shall be on the ship another dove bearing an olive branch in its mouth, which some one shall let down from the mast by a cord into NOAH'S hand. And afterwards let NOAH speak.

Ah, Lord, blessed be thou aye,
That me hast comforted thus today!
By this sight I may well say
  This flood begins to cease: 275
My sweet dove to me brought has
A branch of olive from some place;
This betokeneth God has done us some grace,
  And is a sign of peace.

Ah, Lord, honorèd may thou be!   280
All earth dries now, I see,
But yet till thou commandest me,
  Hence will I not hie.
All this water is away;
Therefore as soon as I may,   285
Sacrifice I shall do in fay
  To thee devoutly.

GOD

Noah, take thy wife anon,
And thy children every one;
Out of the ship thou shalt gone   290
  And they all with thee;
Beasts and all that can fly
Out anon they shall hie,
On earth to grow and multiply;
  I will that it so be.   295

NOAH

Lord, I thank thee, through thy might,
Thy bidding shall be done in hight,
And as fast as I may dight
  I will do thee honor,
And to thee offer sacrifice.   300
Therefore comes in all wise,
For of these beasts here that be his
  Offer I will this store.

Then coming forth from the ark with all his family, NOAH shall take his animals and fowls and make an offering, and slay them.

Lord God in majesty,
That such grace hast granted me   305
Where all was lost, safe to be,
  Therefore now I am bowne,
My wife, my children, my company,
With sacrifice to honor thee,
With beasts and fowls, as thou mayst see.   310
  I offer here right soon.

GOD

Noah, to me thou art full able,
And thy sacrifice acceptable,
For I have found thee true and stable;
  On thee now must I myn.   315
Curse the earth will I no more
For man's sin that grieves me sore,
For of youth man full yore
  Has been inclined to sin.

You shall now grow and multiply,   320
And earth again you edify;
Each beast and fowl that may fly
  Shall be afraid of you;
And fish in sea that may flytte
Shall sustain you, I you behite;   325
To eat of them do you not let,
  That clean be you may know.

Whereas you have eaten before
Grass and roots since you were bore,
Of clean beasts, less and more,   330
  I give you leave to eat;
Save blood and flesh both in fere
Of wrong dead carrion that is here:
Eat not of that in no manner,
  For that aye shall you let.   335

Manslaughter also you shall flee,
For that is not pleasant to me.
Who sheds blood, he or she,
  Any where amongst mankind,
That blood foully shed shall be,   340
And vengeance have that men shall see.
Therefore beware now all ye,
  You fall not in that sin.

A foreword now with thee I make,
And all thy seed too for thy sake, 345
From such vengeance for to slake,
  For now I have my will;
Here I promise thee a hest:
That man nor woman, fowl nor beast
With water, while the world shall last, 350
  I will no more spill.

My bow between you and me
In the firmament shall be,
By very token that you may see
  That such vengeance shall cease; 355
That man nor woman shall never more
Be wasted by water as is before;

But for sin, that grieveth me sore,
  Therefore this vengeance was.

Where clouds in the welkin been 360
That same bow shall now be seen,
In token that my wrath and teen
  Shall never thus wreaked be;
The string is turned toward you,
And toward me is bent the bow, 365
That such weather shall never show,
  And this I promise thee.

My blessing now I give thee here,
To thee, Noah, my servant dear,
For vengeance shall no more appear. 370
And now, farewell, my darling dear.

END OF THE THIRD PAGEANT

THE BANNS WHICH ARE READ BEFORE THE BEGINNING OF THE PLAYS OF CHESTER

REVEREND Lords and ladies all,
  That at this time here assembled be,
By this message understand you shall
  That some time there was mayor of this city
Sir John Arnway, knight, who most worthily 5
Contented himself to set out in play
The device of one Don Rondall, monk of Chester Abbey.

This monk,—monk-like in Scriptures well seen,
  In stories learnèd with the best sort,—
In pageants set forth apparently to all eyen 10
  The Old and New Testament with lively comfort,
  Intermingling therewith, only to make sport,
Some things not warranted by any writ,
Which to glad the hearers he would men to take it.

This matter he abbrevited into plays twenty-four, 15
And every play of the matter gave but a taste,
Leaving for better learning the circumstance to accomplish;
  For all his proceedings may appear to be in haste,
  Yet altogether unprofitable his labor he did not waste; 19
For at this day and ever he deserveth the fame
Which all monks deserve, professing that name.

These stories of the Testament at this time you know
  In a common English tongue never read or heard; 23
Yet thereof in these pageants to make open show
  This monk, though monk, was nothing afraid
  With fear of hanging, burning, or cutting off head,

To set out that all may discern and see;
And part good are left, believe you me.

As in this city divers years they have been set out,
  So at this time of Pentecost, called Whitsuntide, 30
Although to all the city follow labor and cost,
  Yet, God giving leave, that time shall you in play
  For three days together, beginning on Monday,
See these pageants played to the best of their skill,
Where to supply all wants shall be no wants of good will. 35

* * *

Now you worshipful Tanners, that of custom old
  The fall of Lucifer did set out,
Some writers awarrant your matter; therefore be bold
  Erstly to play the same to all the rout;
  And if any thereof stand in any doubt, 40
Your author his author hath. Your show let be
Good speech, fine players, with apparel comely.

Of the Drapers, you wealthy company
  The creation of the world, Adam, and Eve
According to your wealth set out wealthily 45
  And how Cain his brother Abel his life did bereave.

The good simple Water-leaders and Drawers of Dee,
  See that your ark in all points be prepared.
Of Noah and his children the whole story,
  And of the universal flood by you shall be played. 50

* * *

FROM CHAUCER TO THE RENAISSANCE

SO great was the freshness, force, and charm of the poetry of Geoffrey Chaucer (c.1340–1400), and so pervasive was his influence during the generations immediately following him, that we very naturally use his name to mark the beginning of a new period of English literature. In his writings we discern signs of a passing from medieval to modern times. During his life occurred events stirring enough to arouse skepticism concerning the older social and political order, and to stimulate reflection upon the possibility of changes in the practical realities of life. In the year 1337 began a succession of conflicts with France which lasted for more than a century, and which are known collectively as the Hundred Years' War. The victories of Crécy (1346) and of Poitiers (1356) aroused English patriotism through pride in England as a power on the Continent. Profound economic changes at home were brought about by the increasing influence of the middle and lower classes of society. The emancipation of the laboring class was hastened especially by the plague which afflicted the country during the years 1348 and 1349, destroying a large proportion of the workers, and enhancing the economic and political status of those who survived. The agitations which followed those years culminated in the Peasants' Revolt of 1381, which secured at least royal promises of relief for the laborers. Ecclesiastical unrest, engendered by obvious elements of corruption in the Church, led to a revolt against papal authority by John Wycliffe and by the Lollards who propagated his heresies.

Within the period of Chaucer's life occurred a marked change also in the status of the English language. During the two centuries preceding the fourteenth, the nobles and gentry of Norman descent had spoken French, and had looked with some contempt upon the native tongue used by the mass of the people. At the time of Chaucer's birth, however, the nobler classes in increasing numbers were adopting English even in their schools, and in 1362 a formal statute ordered that it be substituted for French in pleadings in courts of law. Thus the great body of Englishmen were brought into oral communication with their rulers.

Although the stir of contemporary occurrences is seldom mentioned in Chaucer's poems explicitly, he occasionally alludes to passing events, and follows the general drift of thought in his day through his increasing tendency toward a realistic treatment of common humanity. He made full use of medieval tales and narrative devices, but he refashioned them freely, presented them concisely, and enlivened them with humor; and in his maturest work he drew the portraits and explored the psychology of the folk about him, in a manner which we like to call modern.

The immediate contemporaries of Chaucer treated social conditions and external events of their own time with a directness that he did not attempt. *The Vision of Piers Plowman* (three versions, c.1362, c.1377, c.1397), traditionally ascribed to a certain William Langland, is, in its most striking parts, a direct satirical attack upon the vices and foibles of the several social classes. Chaucer's personal friend, John Gower (1330?–1408), devoted the most significant of his works, the Latin *Vox Clamantis*, to an account of the Peasants' Revolt of 1381, and to general reflections arising therefrom. His one long English poem, *Confessio Amantis*, is remotely analogous to Chaucer's *Canterbury Tales*, in that it encloses in a frame-work a large number of stories. Both in its design and in its narrative detail, however, this poem lacks the human appeal of Chaucer's.

During the century that followed Chaucer's death, English poetry was largely under his influence. His power, indeed, has been felt in our literature almost continuously from his day to our own. His immediate successors, however, although they avowedly imitate him, do not reflect his qualities in a highly distinguished form. Thomas Occleve and John Lydgate are usually remembered rather for their expressed devotion to their "master Chaucer" than for their actual literary accomplishments. During the century after Chaucer's death his most successful disciples were the Scottish poets, King James the First (1394–1437) and Robert Henryson (c.1425–c.1500). *The King's Quair* of the former beautifully recounts a stirring story, and Henryson's *Testament of Cresseid*, continuing the story of Chaucer's *Troilus and Criseyde*, has often been declared the finest poem written in the British Isles between Chaucer and Spenser.

The single English work of the fifteenth century most generally known to modern readers is the prose compilation of Arthurian narratives made by Sir Thomas Malory (c.1395–1471) under the title, *Le Morte d'Arthur*. This work is especially important as being the most comprehensive collection of Arthurian stories in our language, and the source from which modern poets have frequently drawn. From it Tennyson derived much of the matter treated in his *Idylls of the King*. The *Morte d'Arthur* admirably exemplifies the persistent interest of English readers in medieval romance.

With the close of the fifteenth century we associate the body of popular poetry known as ballads. Since these poems belong essentially to the folk, and were handed down orally from generation to generation, the date of their origin cannot be determined. Certain ballads, however, can be traced back into the Middle Ages; and the end of that period is a sufficiently appropriate place for bringing them into notice.

NOTEWORTHY DATES

ENGLISH LITERATURE AND HISTORY		FOREIGN LITERATURE AND HISTORY	
1307–27	Edward II	1265–1321	Dante Alighieri
1330?–1408	John Gower	1304–64	Francesco Petrarch
1327–77	Edward III	1313–75	Giovanni Boccaccio
1337–1453	Hundred Years' War	1337–1410	Jean Froissart
c.1340–1400	Geoffrey Chaucer	1346	Battle of Crécy
1348	Black Death	1356	Battle of Poitiers
c.1362–c.1397	*Piers the Plowman*	1360	Peace of Brétigny
c.1368–c.1450	Thomas Occleve	1364–80	Charles V, of France
c.1370–c.1450	John Lydgate		
c.1375	*Sir Gawain*		
c.1375	*Pearl*		
1377–99	Richard II	1380–1422	Charles VI, of France
1381	Peasants' rebellion		
c.1382	Wycliffe's English Bible		
1390	Gower's *Confessio Amantis*	1391–1465	Charles d'Orléans
c.1395–1471	Sir Thomas Malory		
1399–1413	Henry IV		
1413–22	Henry V	1415	Battle of Agincourt
1422–61	Henry VI	1422–61	Charles VII, of France
c.1425–c.1500	Robert Henryson	1431–c.1484	François Villon
1461–83	Edward IV	1453	Fall of Constantinople
1483	Edward V		
1483–85	Richard III	1483–98	Charles VIII, of France
1485	Malory's *Morte d'Arthur* pub.		
c.1500	*The Nutbrowne Maide*	1492	Columbus discovers America

GEOFFREY CHAUCER (c.1340–1400)

Our earliest records concerning Geoffrey Chaucer show that in April, 1357, as a youth of some seventeen years or more, he was occupied, perhaps as page, in the household of Elizabeth, wife of Prince Lionel, son of Edward III, where he continued to serve throughout that year and probably into the next. During this service Chaucer accompanied the princess to Hatfield, in Yorkshire, to London, and probably to other parts of England. We surmise that he witnessed more than one brilliant chivalric entertainment, and that at Hatfield, during Christmastide of 1357, he met his future friend and patron, John of Gaunt. During the year 1359 Chaucer was a soldier in the army of Edward III, in France. Having been taken prisoner, not far from Reims, he was released through a ransom to which the king himself contributed a substantial sum. After the conclusion of this military expedition, with the Peace of Brétigny, May 8, 1360, Chaucer returned to England, where he seems to have increased in favor at court, for in 1367 he was granted a life pension of twenty marks as a valet of the king. During the next ten or fifteen years he took part in a considerable number of diplomatic missions to the Continent, of which the most noteworthy, from a literary point of view, were a secret embassy to Genoa and Florence (Dec., 1372 to May, 1373), and a mission to Milan (May to September, 1378). Although both Petrarch and Boccaccio were living at the time of Chaucer's first visit to Italy, we have no evidence that the English poet met either of them. To these Italian journeys, however, may have been due, in large measure, his subsequent devotion to Italian literature. Aside from his diplomatic employment, the poet had official duties at home in connection with the customs of the port of London. In 1374 he was appointed controller of the customs and subsidy on wools, hides, and wool-fells at the port of London, and in 1382 he received the additional appointment of the controllership of the petty customs. In the autumn of 1386 Chaucer sat for a short time in Parliament as a knight of the shire for Kent. At the end of this same year he lost, or perhaps resigned, his official positions in the customs. Whether this change was brought about by political misfortune or by Chaucer's desire for other employment, in his altered circumstances he probably had increased leisure for literary work, and between 1386 and 1389 he may have written a considerable part of *The Canterbury Tales*. In this latter year he was again in the service of the government as clerk of the king's works, and although the loss of this employment, in 1391, may have reduced his income considerably, a royal pension of twenty pounds in 1394, and a yearly gift of a butt of wine in 1398, may be presumed to have relieved any impending distress. When Henry IV, son of Chaucer's old friend, John of Gaunt, came to the throne in 1399, the poet promptly addressed to him a ballade entitled, *The Compleint of Chaucer to his Empty Purse*. To this graceful form of begging the new king responded readily with a pension of forty marks, along with a confirmation of the annuity of twenty pounds which had been granted in 1394. Chaucer spent his last days, then, in comparative comfort, and on his death, October 25, 1400, he was buried in the part of the south transept of Westminster Abbey, which has since become 'The Poets' Corner.'

Although the exact chronology of most of Chaucer's works is far from certain, the literary influences under which he wrote are rather clearly defined. As a courtier, diplomat, and man of affairs he was familiar with literary fashions, at home and abroad, and embodied them freely in his writings. His first works are imitations or translations of French poems esteemed at court both in France and in England. To an early stage of his career is assigned his translation of at least part of the *Roman de la Rose*, a French poem composed during the thirteenth century, and popular in the fourteenth. French in its conception is *The Book of the Duchess*, written as an elegy upon the death, in 1369, of Blanche, wife of John of Gaunt. Upon French models Chaucer composed his early poem, *A.B.C.*, and numerous pieces 'that highten balades, roundels, virelayes.' *The Parliament of Fowls*, written, probably, in 1381 or 1382, to celebrate the betrothal or marriage of Richard II and Princess Anne of Bohemia, is conspicuously influenced by French poetical taste. During the period of his journeys to Italy, or before, Chaucer acquired a new source of literary inspiration in the works of Dante, Petrarch, and Boccaccio. Although from Dante and Petrarch his borrowings in detail are few, his extensive verbal obligations to Boccaccio are seen in *Troilus and Criseyde*, written about 1383, and in the *Knight's Tale*. *The House of Fame*, written, perhaps, about 1379, clearly shows the general influence of Dante, as well as of French allegorical poetry. To the last fifteen years of Chaucer's life may be assigned *The Legend of Good Women* and *The Canterbury Tales*. Although in these works he used a multiplicity of sources, and employed a variety of poetical styles, old and new, the poems themselves reveal a striking advance in English vigor and in literary originality.

THE CANTERBURY TALES

THE PROLOGUE

Whan that Aprille with his shoures soote
The droghte of Marche hath percèd to the roote,
And bathèd every veyne in swich licour,
Of which vertu engendrèd is the flour;
When Zephirus eek with his swete breeth   5
Inspirèd hath in every holt and heeth
The tendre croppes, and the yonge sonne
Hath in the Ram his halfe cours y-ronne,
And smale fowles maken melodye,
That slepen al the night with open yë,   10
(So priketh hem nature in hir corages):
Than longen folk to goon on pilgrimages,
And palmers for to seken straunge strondes,
To ferne halwes, couthe in sondry londes;
And specially, from every shires ende   15
Of Engelond, to Caunterbury they wende,
The holy blisful martir for to seke,
That hem hath holpen, whan that they were seke.

Bifel that, in that sesoun on a day,
In Southwerk at the Tabard as I lay   20
Redy to wenden on my pilgrimage
To Caunterbury with ful devout corage,
At night was come in-to that hostelrye
Wel nyne and twenty in a compaignye,
Of sondry folk, by aventure y-falle   25
In felawshipe, and pilgrims were they alle,
That toward Caunterbury wolden ryde;
The chambres and the stables weren wyde,
And wel we weren esèd atte beste.
And shortly, whan the sonne was to reste,   30
So hadde I spoken with hem everichon,
That I was of hir felawshipe anon,
And made forward erly for to ryse,
To take our wey, ther as I yow devyse.

But natheles, whyl I have tyme and space,
Er that I ferther in this tale pace,   36
Me thinketh it acordaunt to resoun,
To telle yow al the condicioun
Of ech of hem, so as it semèd me,   39
And whiche they weren, and of what degree;
And eek in what array that they were inne;
And at a knight than wol I first biginne.

A Knight ther was, and that a worthy man,
That fro the tyme that he first bigan
To ryden out, he lovèd chivalrye,   45
Trouthe and honour, fredom and curteisye.
Ful worthy was he in his lordes werre,
And thereto hadde he riden (no man ferre)
As wel in cristendom as hethenesse,
And evere honourèd for his worthinesse.   50
At Alisaundre he was, whan it was wonne;
Ful ofte tyme he hadde the bord bigonne
Aboven alle naciouns in Pruce.
In Lettow hadde he reysèd and in Ruce,
No cristen man so ofte of his degree.   55
In Gernade at the sege eek hadde he be
Of Algezir, and riden in Belmarye.
At Lyeys was he, and at Satalye,
Whan they were wonne; and in the Grete See
At many a noble aryve hadde he be.   60
At mortal batailles hadde he been fiftene,
And foughten for our feith at Tramissene
In listes thryes, and ay slayn his foo.
This ilke worthy knight hadde been also
Somtyme with the lord of Palatye,   65
Ageyn another hethen in Turkye:
And everemore he hadde a sovereyn prys.
And though that he were worthy, he was wys,
And of his port as meek as is a mayde.
He nevere yet no vileinye ne sayde   70
In al his lyf, un-to no maner wight.
He was a verray parfit gentil knight.
But for to tellen yow of his array,
His hors were goode, but he was nat gay.
Of fustian he werèd a gipoun   75
Al bismotered with his habergeoun.
For he was late y-come from his viage,
And wente for to doon his pilgrimage.

With him ther was his sone, a yong Squyer,
A lovyer, and a lusty bacheler,   80
With lokkes crulle, as they were leyd in presse.
Of twenty yeer of age he was, I gesse.
Of his stature he was of evene lengthe,
And wonderly delivere, and greet of strengthe.
And he hadde been somtyme in chivachye,   85
In Flaundres, in Artoys, and Picardye,
And born him wel, as of so litel space,
In hope to stonden in his lady grace.
Embrouded was he, as it were a mede
Al ful of fresshe floures, whyte and rede.   90
Singinge he was, or floytinge, al the day;
He was as fresh as is the month of May.
Short was his goune, with sleves longe and wyde.
Wel coude he sitte on hors, and faire ryde.
He coude songes make and wel endyte,   95
Iuste and eek daunce, and wel purtreye and wryte.
So hote he lovede, that by nightertale
He sleep namore than doth a nightingale.
Curteys he was, lowly, and servisable,
And carf biforn his fader at the table.   100

A Yeman hadde he, and servaunts namo
At that tyme, for him liste ryde so;
And he was clad in cote and hood of grene;
A sheef of pecok arwes brighte and kene

Under his belt he bar ful thriftily, 105
(Wel coude he dresse his takel yemanly:
His arwes droupèd noght with fetheres lowe),
And in his hand he bar a mighty bowe.
A not-heed hadde he, with a broun visage.
Of wode-craft wel coude he al the usage. 110
Upon his arm he bar a gay bracer,
And by his syde a swerd and a bokeler,
And on that other syde a gay daggere,
Harneisèd wel, and sharp as point of spere;
A Cristofre on his brest of silver shene. 115
An horn he bar, the bawdrik was of grene;
A forster was he, soothly, as I gesse.

Ther was also a Nonne, a Prioresse,
That of hir smyling was ful simple and coy;
Hir gretteste ooth was but by sëynt Loy; 120
And she was clepèd madame Eglentyne.
Ful wel she song the service divyne,
Entunèd in hir nose ful semely;
And Frensh she spak ful faire and fetisly,
After the scole of Stratford atte Bowe, 125
For Frensh of Paris was to hir unknowe.
At mete wel y-taught was she with-alle;
She leet no morsel from hir lippes falle,
Ne wette hir fingres in hir sauce depe.
Wel coude she carie a morsel, and wel kepe, 130
That no drope ne fille up-on hir brest.
In curteisye was set ful moche hir lest.
Hir over lippe wypèd she so clene,
That in hir coppe was no ferthing sene
Of grece, whan she dronken hadde hir draughte.
Ful semely after hir mete she raughte, 136
And sikerly she was of greet disport,
And ful pleasunt, and amiable of port,
And peynèd hir to countrefete chere
Of court, and been estatlich of manere, 140
And to ben holden digne of reverence.
But, for to speken of hir conscience,
She was so charitable and so pitous,
She wolde wepe, if that she sawe a mous
Caught in a trappe, if it were deed or bledde. 145
Of smale houndes had she, that she fedde
With rostèd flesh, or milk and wastel breed.
But sore weep she if oon of hem were deed,
Or if men smoot it with a yerde smerte:
And al was conscience and tendre herte. 150
Ful semely hir wimpel pinchèd was;
Hir nose tretys; hir eyen greye as glas;
Hir mouth ful smal, and ther-to softe and reed;
But sikerly she hadde a fair forheed.
It was almost a spanne brood, I trowe; 155
For, hardily, she was nat undergrowe.
Ful fetis was hir cloke, as I was war.
Of smal coral aboute hir arm she bar
A peire of bedes, gauded al with grene;
And ther-on heng a broche of gold ful shene, 160
On which ther was first write a crownèd A,
And after, *Amor vincit omnia.*

Another Nonne with hir hadde she,
That was hir chapeleyne, and Preestes thre.

A Monk ther was, a fair for the maistrye, 165
An out-rydere, that lovede venerye;
A manly man, to been an abbot able.
Ful many a deyntee hors hadde he in stable:
And, whan he rood, men mighte his brydel here
Ginglen in a whistling wynd as clere, 170
And eek as loude as doth the chapel-belle,
Ther as this lord was keper of the celle.
The reule of seint Maure or of seint Beneit,
By-cause that it was old and som-del streit,
This ilke monk leet olde thinges pace, 175
And held after the newe world the space.
He yaf nat of that text a pullèd hen,
That seith, that hunters been nat holy men;
Ne that a monk, whan he is cloisterlees,
Is liknèd til a fish that is waterlees; 180
This is to seyn, a monk out of his cloistre.
But thilke text held he nat worth an oistre.
And I seyde his opinioun was good.
What sholde he studie, and make him-selven wood,
Upon a book in cloistre alwey to poure, 185
Or swinken with his handes, and laboure,
As Austin bit? How shal the world be servèd?
Lat Austin have his swink to him reservèd.
Therfor he was a pricasour aright;
Grehoundes he hadde, as swifte as fowel in flight; 190
Of priking and of hunting for the hare
Was al his lust, for no cost wolde he spare.
I seigh his sleves purfiled at the hond
With grys, and that the fyneste of a lond;
And, for to festne his hood under his chin, 195
He hadde of gold y-wroght a curious pin:
A love-knot in the gretter ende ther was.
His heed was balled, that shoon as any glas.
And eek his face, as he hadde been anoint.
He was a lord ful fat and in good point; 200
His eyen stepe, and rollinge in his heed,
That stemèd as a forneys of a leed;
His botes souple, his hors in greet estat.
Now certeinly he was a fair prelat;
He was nat pale as a for-pynèd goost. 205
A fat swan loved he best of any roost.
His palfrey was as broun as is a berye.

A Frere ther was, a wantown and a merye.
A limitour, a ful solempne man.
In alle the ordres foure is noon that can 210
So moche of daliaunce and fair langage.
He hadde maad ful many a mariage
Of yonge wommen, at his owne cost.
Un-to his ordre he was a noble post.
Ful wel biloved and famulier was he 215
With frankeleyns over-al in his contree,
And eek with worthy wommen of the toun:
For he had power of confessioun,
As seyde him-self, more than a curat,
For of his ordre he was licentiat. 220
Ful swetely herde he confessioun,
And plesaunt was his absolucioun;

He was an esy man to yeve penaunce
Ther as he wiste to han a good pitaunce;
For unto a povre ordre for to yive   225
Is signe that a man is wel y-shrive.
For if he yaf, he dorste make avaunt,
He wiste that a man was repentaunt.
For many a man so hard is of his herte,
He may nat wepe al-thogh him sore smerte. 230
Therfore, in stede of weping and preyeres,
Men moot yeve silver to the povre freres.
His tipet was ay farsèd ful of knyves
And pinnes, for to yeven faire wyves.
And certeinly he hadde a mery note;   235
Wel coude he singe and pleyen on a rote.
Of yeddings he bar utterly the prys.
His nekke whyt was as the flour-de-lys.
There-to he strong was as a champioun.
He knew the tavernes wel in every toun, 240
And everich hostiler and tappestere
Bet than a lazar or a beggestere;
For un-to swich a worthy man as he
Acorded nat, as by his facultee,
To have with seke lazars aqueyntaunce.   245
It is nat honest, it may nat avaunce
For to delen with no swich poraille,
But al with riche and sellers of vitaille.
And over-al, ther as profit sholde aryse,
Curteys he was, and lowly of servyse.   250
Ther nas no man nowher so vertuous.
He was the beste beggere in his hous;
For thogh a widwe hadde noght a sho,
So plesaunt was his *In principio*,
Yet wolde he have a ferthing, er he wente 255
His purchas was well bettre than his rente.
And rage he coude as it were right a whelpe
In love-dayes ther coude he mochel helpe.
For ther he was nat lyk a cloisterer,
With a thredbare cope, as is a povre scoler 260
But he was lyk a maister or a pope.
Of double worsted was his semi-cope,
That rounded as a belle out of the presse.
Somwhat he lipsèd, for his wantownesse,
To make his English swete up-on his tonge;
And in his harping, whan that he had songe, 266
His eyen twinklèd in his heed aright,
As doon the sterres in the frosty night.
This worthy limitour was cleped Huberd.

A MARCHANT was ther with a forkèd berd,
In mottelee, and hye on horse he sat,   271
Up-on his heed a Flaundrish bever hat;
His botes claspèd faire and fetisly.
His resons he spak ful solempnely,
Sowninge alway thencrees of his winning. 275
He wolde the see were kept for any thing
Bitwixe Middelburgh and Orewelle.
Wel coude he in eschaunge sheelds selle.
This worthy man ful wel his wit bisette;
Ther wiste no wight that he was in dette, 280
So estatly was he of his governaunce,
With his bargaynes, and with his chevisaunce.

For sothe he was a worthy man with-alle,
But sooth to seyn, I noot how men him calle.

A CLERK ther was of Oxenford also,   285
That un-to logik hadde longe y-go.
As lene was his hors as is a rake,
And he nas nat right fat, I undertake;
But lokèd holwe, and ther-to soberly.
Ful thredbar was his overest courtepy;   290
For he had geten him yet no benefice,
Ne was so worldly for to have office.
For him was levere have at his beddes heed
Twenty bokes, clad in blak or reed
Of Aristotle and his philosophye,   295
Than robes riche, or fithele, or gay sautrye.
But al be that he was a philosophre,
Yet hadde he but litel gold in cofre;
But al that he mighte of his frendes hente,
On bokes and on lerninge he it spente,   300
And bisily gan for the soules preye
Of hem that yaf him wher-with to scoleye.
Of studie took he most cure and most hede.
Noght o word spak he more than was nede,
And that was seyd in forme and reverence, 305
And short and quik, and ful of hy sentence.
Sowninge in moral vertu was his speche,
And gladly wolde he lerne, and gladly teche.

A SERGEANT OF THE LAWE, war and wys,
That often hadde been at the parvys,   310
Ther was also, ful riche of excellence.
Discreet he was, and of greet reverence:
He semèd swich, his wordes weren so wyse,
Iustice he was ful often in assyse,
By patente, and by pleyn commissioun;   315
For his science, and for his heigh renoun
Of fees and robes hadde he many oon.
So greet a purchasour was nowher noon.
Al was fee simple to him in effect,
His purchasing mighte nat been infect.   320
Nowher so bisy a man as he ther nas,
And yet he semèd bisier than he was.
In termes hadde he caas and domes alle,
That from the tyme of king William were falle.
Therto he coude endyte, and make a thing, 325
Ther coude no wight pinche at his wryting;
And every statut coude he pleyn by rote.
He rood but hoomly in a medlee cote
Girt with a ceint of silk, with barres smale;
Of his array telle I no lenger tale.   330

A FRANKELEYN was in his compaignye;
Whyt was his berd, as is the dayesye.
Of his complexion he was sangwyn.
Wel loved he by the morwe a sop in wyn.
To liven in delyt was evere his wone,   335
For he was Epicurus owne sone,
That heeld opinioun that pleyn delyt
Was verraily felicitee parfyt.
An housholdere, and that a greet, was he;
Seynt Iulian he was in his contree.   340
His breed, his ale, was alwey after oon;

A bettre envyned man was nevere noon.
With-oute bake mete was nevere his hous,
Of fish and flesh, and that so plentevous,
It snewèd in his hous of mete and drinke,   345
Of alle deyntees that men coude thinke.
After the sondry sesons of the yeer,
So chaungèd he his mete and his soper.
Ful many a fat partrich hadde he in mewe,
And many a breem and many a luce in stewe.
Wo was his cook, but-if his sauce were   351
Poynaunt and sharp, and redy al his gere.
His table dormant in his halle alway
Stood redy covered al the longe day.
At sessiouns ther was he lord and sire.   355
Ful ofte tyme he was knight of the shire.
An anlas and a gipser al of silk
Heng at his girdel, whyt as morne milk.
A shirreve hadde he been, and a countour;
Was nowher such a worthy vavasour.   360

   An HABERDASSHER and a CARPENTER,
A WEBBE, a DYERE, and a TAPICER,
And they were clothèd alle in o liveree,
Of a solempne and greet fraternitee.
Ful fresh and newe hir gere apykèd was;   365
Hir knyves were y-chapèd noght with bras,
But al with silver wrought ful clene and weel.
Hir girdles and hir pouches everydeel.
Wel semèd ech of hem a fair burgeys,
To sitten in a yeldhalle on a deys.   370
Everich, for the wisdom that he can,
Was shaply for to been an alderman.
For catel hadde they ynogh and rente,
And eek hir wyves wolde it wel assente;
And elles certein were they to blame.   375
It is ful fair to been y-clept *ma dame*,
And goon to vigilyës al bifore,
And have a mantel roialliche y-bore.

   A COOK they hadde with hem for the nones,
To boille chiknes with the mary-bones,   380
And poudre-marchant tart, and galingale.
Wel coude he knowe a draughte of London ale.
He coude roste, and sethe, and broille, and frye,
Maken mortreux, and wel bake a pye.
But greet harm was it, as it thoughte me,   385
That on his shine a mormal hadde he;
For blankmanger, that made he with the beste.

   A SHIPMAN was ther, woning fer by weste:
For aught I woot, he was of Dertemouthe.
He rood up-on a rouncy, as he couthe,   390
In a gowne of falding to the knee.
A daggere hanging on a laas hadde he
Aboute his nekke under his arm adoun.
The hote somer had maad his hewe al broun;
And, certeinly, he was a good felawe.   395
Ful many a draughte of wyn had he y-drawe
From Burdeux-ward, whyl that the chapman sleep.
Of nyce conscience took he no keep.
If that he faught, and hadde the hyer hond,
By water he sente hem hoom to every lond.   400
But of his craft to rekene wel his tydes,
His stremes and his daungers him bisydes,
His herberwe and his mone, his lodemenage,
Ther nas noon swich from Hulle to Cartage.
Hardy he was, and wys to undertake;   405
With many a tempest hadde his berd been shake.
He knew wel alle the havenes, as they were,
From Gootlond to the cape of Finistere,
And every cryke in Britayne and in Spayne;
His barge y-clepèd was the Maudelayne.   410

   With us ther was a DOCTOUR OF PHISYK,
In al this world ne was ther noon him lyk
To speke of phisik and of surgerye;
For he was grounded in astronomye.
He kepte his pacient a ful greet del   415
In houres, by his magik naturel.
Wel coude he fortunen the ascendent
Of his images for his pacient.
He knew the cause of everich maladye,
Were it of hoot or cold, or moiste, or drye,   420
And where engendrèd, and of what humour;
He was a verrey parfit practisour.
The cause y-knowe, and of his harm the rote,
Anon he yaf the seke man his bote.
Ful redy hadde he his apothecaries,   425
To sende him drogges, and his letuaries,
For ech of hem made other for to winne;
Hir frendschipe nas nat newe to biginne.
Wel knew he the olde Esculapius,
And Deiscorides, and eek Rufus;   430
Old Ypocras, Haly, and Galien;
Serapion, Razis, and Avicen;
Averrois, Damascien, and Constantyn;
Bernard, and Gatesden, and Gilbertyn.
Of his diete mesurable was he,   435
For it was of no superfluitee,
But of greet norissing and digestible.
His studie was but litel on the Bible.
In sangwin and in pers he clad was al,
Lynèd with taffata and with sendal;   440
And yet he was but esy of dispence;
He kepte that he wan in pestilence.
For gold in phisik is a cordial,
Therfor he lovede gold in special.

   A good WYF was ther of bisyde BATHE,   445
But she was som-del deef, and that was scathe,
Of cloth-making she hadde swiche an haunt,
She passèd hem of Ypres and of Gaunt.
In al the parisshe wyf ne was ther noon
That to the offring bifore hir sholde goon;   450
And if ther dide, certeyn, so wrooth was she,
That she was out of alle charitee.
Hir coverchiefs ful fyne were of ground;
I dorste swere they weyeden ten pound
That on a Sonday were upon hir heed.   455
Hir hosen weren of fyn scarlet reed,
Ful streite y-teyd, and shoos ful moiste and newe.

Bold was hir face, and fair, and reed of hewe.
She was a worthy womman al hir lyve,
Housbondes at chirche-dore she hadde fyve, 460
Withouten other compaignye in youthe;
But thereof nedeth nat to speke as nouthe.
And thryes hadde she been at Ierusalem;
She hadde passèd many a straunge streem;
At Rome she hadde been, and at Boloigne, 465
In Galice at seint Iame, and at Coloigne.
She coude moche of wandring by the weye.
Gat-tothèd was she, soothly for to seye.
Up-on an amblere esily she sat,
Y-wimplèd wel, and on hir heed an hat 470
As brood as is a bokeler or a targe;
A foot-mantel aboute hir hipes large,
And on hir feet a paire of spores sharpe.
In felaweschip wel coude she laughe and carpe.
Of remedies of love she knew per-chaunce, 475
For she coude of that art the olde daunce.

A good man was ther of religioun,
And was a povre PERSOUN of a toun;
But riche he was of holy thoght and werk.
He was also a lernèd man, a clerk, 480
That Cristes gospel trewely wolde preche;
His parisshens devoutly wolde he teche.
Benigne he was, and wonder diligent,
And in adversitee ful pacient;
And swich he was y-prevèd ofte sythes. 485
Ful looth were him to cursen for his tythes,
But rather wolde he yeven, out of doute,
Un-to his povre parisshens aboute
Of his offring, and eek of his substaunce.
He coude in litel thing han suffisaunce. 490
Wyd was his parisshe, and houses fer a-sonder,
But he ne lafte nat, for reyn ne thonder,
In siknes nor in meschief to visyte
The ferreste in his parisshe, moche and lyte,
Up-on his feet, and in his hand a staf, 495
This noble ensample to his sheep he yaf,
That first he wroghte, and afterward he taughte;
Out of the gospel he tho wordes caughte;
And this figure he added eek ther-to,
That if gold ruste, what shal yren do? 500
For if a preest be foul, on whom we truste,
No wonder is a lewèd man to ruste;
And shame it is, if a preest take keep,
A [dirty] shepherde and a clene sheep.
Wel oghte a preest ensample for to yive, 505
By his clennesse, how that his sheep shold live.
He sette nat his benefice to hyre,
And leet his sheep encombrèd in the myre,
And ran to London, un-to sëynt Poules,
To seken him a chaunterie for soules, 510
Or with a bretherhed to been withholde;
But dwelte at hoom, and kepte wel his folde
So that the wolf ne made it nat miscarie;
He was a shepherde and no mercenarie.
And though he holy were, and vertuous, 515
He was to sinful man nat despitous,
Ne of his speche daungerous ne digne,

But in his teching discreet and benigne.
To drawen folk to heven by fairnesse
By good ensample, this was his bisynesse: 520
But it were any persone obstinat,
What so he were, of heigh or lowe estat,
Him wolde he snibben sharply for the nones.
A bettre preest, I trowe that nowher non is.
He wayted after no pompe and reverence, 525
Ne maked him a spycèd conscience,
But Cristes lore, and his apostles twelve,
He taughte, but first he folwèd it him-selve.

   With him ther was a PLOWMAN, was his brother,
That hadde y-lad of dong ful many a fother,
A trewe swinkere and a good was he, 531
Livinge in pees and parfit charitee.
God loved he best with al his hole herte
At alle tymes, thogh him gamed or smerte,
And thanne his neighebour right as himselve.
He wolde thresshe, and ther-to dyke and delve,
For Cristes sake, for every povre wight, 537
Withouten hyre, if it lay in his might.
His tythes payèd he ful faire and wel,
Bothe of his propre swink and his catel. 540
In a tabard he rood upon a mere.

   Ther was also a Reve and a Millere,
A Somnour and a Pardoner also,
A Maunciple, and my-self; ther were namo.

   The MILLER was a stout carl, for the nones,
Ful big he was of braun, and eek of bones; 546
That provèd wel, for over-al ther he cam,
At wrastling he wolde have alwey the ram.
He was short-sholdrèd, brood, a thikke knarre
Ther nas no dore that he nolde heve of harre,
Or breke it, at a renning, with his heed. 551
His berd as any sowe or fox was reed,
And ther-to brood, as though it were a spade.
Up-on the cop right of his nose he hade
A werte, and ther-on stood a tuft of heres, 555
Reed as the bristles of a sowes eres;
His nose-thirles blake were and wyde.
A swerd and bokeler bar he by his syde;
His mouth as greet was as a greet forneys.
He was a Ianglere and a goliardeys, 560
And that was most of sinne and harlotryes.
Wel coude he stelen corn, and tollen thryes;
And yet he hadde a thombe of gold, pardee.
A whyt cote and a blew hood werèd he.
A baggepype wel coude he blowe and sowne,
And therwithal he broghte us out of towne.

   A gentil MAUNCIPLE was ther of a temple, 567
Of which achatours mighte take exemple
For to be wyse in bying of vitaille.
For whether that he payde, or took by taille,
Algate he wayted so in his achat, 571
That he was ay biforn and in good stat.
Now is nat that of God a ful fair grace,
That swich a lewèd mannes wit shal pace
The wisdom of an heep of iernèd men? 575

Of maistres hadde he mo than thryes ten,
That were of lawe expert and curious;
Of which ther were a doseyn in that hous,
Worthy to been stiwardes of rente and lond
Of any lord that is in Engelond, 580
To make him live by his propre good,
In honour dettelees, but he were wood,
Or live as scarsly as him list desire;
And able for to helpen al a shire
In any cas that mighte falle or happe; 585
And yit this maunciple sette hir aller cappe.

The Reve was a sclendre colerik man,
His berd was shave as ny as ever he can.
His heer was by his eres round y-shorn.
His top was dokkèd lyk a preest biforn. 590
Ful longe were his legges, and ful lene,
Y-lyk a staf, ther was no calf y-sene.
Wel coude he kepe a gerner and a binne;
Ther was noon auditour coude on him winne.
Wel wiste he, by the droghte, and by the reyn,
The yeldying of his seed, and of his greyn. 596
His lordes sheep, his neet, his dayerye,
His swyn, his hors, his stoor, and his pultrye,
Was hoolly in this reves governing,
And by his covenaunt yaf the rekening, 600
Sin that his lord was twenty yeer of age;
Ther coude no man bringe him in arrerage.
Ther nas baillif, ne herde, ne other hyne
That he ne knew his sleighte and his covyne;
They were adrad of him, as of the deeth. 605
His woning was ful fair up-on an heeth,
With grene treës shadwèd was his place.
He coude bettre than his lord purchace.
Ful riche he was astorèd prively,
His lord wel coude he plesen subtilly, 610
To yeve and lene him of his owne good,
And have a thank, and yet a cote, and hood.
In youthe he lernèd hadde a good mister;
He was a wel good wrighte, a carpenter.
This reve sat up-on a ful good stot, 615
That was al pomely grey, and highte Scot.
A long surcote of pers up-on he hade,
And by his syde he bar a rusty blade.
Of Northfolk was this reve, of which I telle,
Bisyde a toun men clepen Baldeswelle. 620
Tukkèd he was, as is a frere, aboute,
And evere he rood the hindreste of our route.

A Somnour was ther with us in that place,
That hadde a fyr-reed cherubinnes face,
For sawceflem he was, with eyen narwe. 625
As hoot he was, and lecherous as a sparwe,
With scallèd browes blake, and pilèd berd;
Of his visage children were aferd.
Ther nas quik-silver, litarge, ne brimstoon,
Boras, ceruce, ne oille of tartre noon, 630
Ne oynement that wolde clense and byte,
That him mighte helpen of his whelkes whyte,
Ne of the knobbes sittinge on his chekes.
Wel loved he garleek, oynons, and eek lekes,
And for to drinken strong wyn, reed as blood. 635
Thanne wolde he speke, and crye as he were wood.
And whan that he wel dronken hadde the wyn,
Than wolde he speke no word but Latyn.
A fewe termes hadde he, two or thre,
That he had lernèd out of som decree; 640
No wonder is, he herde it al the day;
And eek ye knowen wel, how that a Iay
Can clepen 'Watte,' as well as can the pope.
But who-so coude in other thing him grope,
Thanne hadde he spent al his philosophye; 645
Ay '*Questio quid iuris*' wolde he crye.
He was a gentil harlot and a kynde;
A bettre felawe sholde men noght fynde.
He wolde suffre for a quart of wyn
A good felawe to have his concubyn 650
A twelf-month, and excuse him atte fulle:
And prively a finch eek coude he pulle.
And if he fond owher a good felawe,
He wolde techen him to have non awe,
In swich cas, of the erchedeknes curs, 655
But-if a mannes soule were in his purs;
For in his purs he sholde y-punisshed be.
'Purs is the erchedeknes helle,' seyde he.
But wel I woot he lyèd right in dede;
Of cursing oghte ech gulty man him drede— 660
For curs wol slee right as assoilling saveth—
And also war him of a *significavit*.
In daunger hadde he at his owne gyse
The yonge girles of the diocyse,
And knew hir counseil, and was al hir reed. 665
A gerland hadde he set up-on his heed,
As greet as it were for an ale-stake;
A bokeler hadde he maad him of a cake.

With him ther rood a gentil Pardoner
Of Rouncivale, his frend and his compeer, 670
That streight was comen fro the court of Rome.
Ful loude he song, 'Come hider, love, to me.'
This somnour bar to him a stif burdoun,
Was nevere trompe of half so greet a soun.
This pardoner hadde heer as yelow as wex, 675
But smothe it heng, as doth a strike of flex;
By ounces henge his lokkes that he hadde,
And there-with he his shuldres oversprádde;
But thinne it lay, by colpons oon and oon;
But hood, for Iolitee, ne wered he noon, 680
For it was trussèd up in his walet.
Him thoughte he rood al of the newe Iet;
Dischevele, save his cappe, he rood al bare.
Swiche glaringe eyen hadde he as an hare.
A vernicle hadde he sowèd on his cappe. 685
His walet lay biforn him in his lappe,
Bret-ful of pardoun come from Rome al hoot.
A voys he hadde as smal as hath a goot.
No berd hadde he, ne nevere sholde have.
As smothe it was as it were late y-shave; 690

* * *

But of his craft, fro Berwik into Ware,
Ne was ther swich another pardoner.
For in his male he hadde a pilwe-beer,

Which that, he seyde, was our lady veyl: 695
He seyde he hadde a gobet of the seyl
That sëynt Peter hadde, whan that he wente
Up-on the see, til Iesu Crist him hente.
He hadde a croys of latoun, ful of stones,
And in a glas he hadde pigges bones. 700
But with thise relikes, whan that he fond
A povre person dwelling up-on lond,
Up-on a day he gat him more moneye
Than that the person gat in monthes tweye.
And thus with feynèd flaterye and Iapes, 705
He made the person and the peple his apes
But trewely to tellen, atte laste,
He was in chirche a noble ecclesiaste.
Wel coude he rede a lessoun or a storie,
But alderbest he song an offertorie; 710
For wel he wiste, whan that song was songe,
He moste preche, and wel affyle his tonge.
To winne silver, as he ful wel coude;
Therefore he song so meriely and loude.

Now have I told you shortly, in a clause, 715
Thestat, tharray, the nombre, and eek the cause
Why that assemblèd was this compaignye
In Southwerk, at this gentil hostelrye,
That highte the Tabard, faste by the Belle.
But now is tyme to yow for to telle 720
How that we baren us that ilke night,
Whan we were in that hostelrye alight.
And after wol I telle of our viage,
And al the remenaunt of our pilgrimage.
But first I pray yow of your curteisye, 725
That ye narette it nat my vileinye,
Thogh that I pleynly speke in this matere,
To telle yow hir wordes and hir chere;
Ne thogh I speke hir wordes proprely.
For this ye knowen al-so wel as I, 730
Who-so shal telle a tale after a man,
He moot reherce, as ny as evere he can,
Everich a word, if it be in his charge,
Al speke he never so rudeliche and large;
Or elles he moot telle his tale untrewe, 735
Or feyne thing, or fynde wordes newe.
He may nat spare, al-thogh he were his brother;
He moot as wel seye o word as another.
Crist spak him-self ful brode in holy writ,
And wel ye woot, no vileinye is it. 740
Eek Plato seith, who-so that can him rede,
The wordes mote be cosin to the dede
Also I prey yow to foryeve it me,
Al have I nat set folk in hir degree
Here in this tale, as that they sholde stonde;
My wit is short, ye may wel understonde. 746

Greet chere made our hoste us everichon,
And to the soper sette he us anon;
And servèd us with vitaille at the beste.
Strong was the wyn, and wel to drinke us leste. 750
A semely man our hoste was with-alle
For to han been a marshal in an halle;

A large man he was with eyen stepe,
A fairer burgeys was ther noon in Chepe:
Bold of his speche, and wys, and wel y-taught,
And of manhood him lakkede right naught. 756
Eek thereto he was right a mery man,
And after soper pleyen he bigan,
And spak of mirthe amonges othere thinges,
Whan that we hadde maad our rekeninges; 760
And seyde thus: 'Now, lordinges, trewely
Ye ben to me right welcome hertely:
For by my trouthe, if that I shal nat lye,
I ne saugh this yeer so mery a compaignye
At ones in this herberwe as is now. 765
Fayn wolde I doon yow mirthe, wiste I how.
And of a mirthe I am right now bithoght,
To doon yow ese, and it shal coste noght.

'Ye goon to Caunterbury; God yow spede,
The blisful martir quyte yow your mede. 770
And wel I woot, as ye goon by the weye,
Ye shapen yow to talen and to pleye;
For trewely, confort ne mirthe is noon
To ryde by the weye doumb as a stoon;
And therfore wol I maken yow disport, 775
As I seyde erst, and doon yow som confort.
And if yow lyketh alle, by oon assent,
Now for to stonden at my Iugement,
And for to werken as I shal yow seye,
To-morwe, whan ye ryden by the weye, 780
Now, by my fader soule, that is deed,
But ye be merye, I wol yeve yow myn heed.
Hold up your hond, withoute more speche.'
Our counsèil was nat longe for to seche;
Us thoughte it was noght worth to make it wys, 785
And grauntèd him with-outen more avys,
And bad him seye his verdit, as him leste.

'Lordinges,' quod he, 'now herkneth for the beste;
But tak it not, I prey yow, in desdeyn;
This is the poynt, to speken short and pleyn,
That ech of yow, to shorte with our weye, 791
In this viage, shal telle tales tweye,
To Caunterbury-ward, I mene it so,
And hom-ward he shal tellen othere two,
Of aventures that whylom han bifalle. 795
And which of yow that bereth him best of alle,
That is to seyn, that telleth in this cas
Tales of best sentence and most solas,
Shal han a soper at our aller cost
Here in this place, sitting by this post, 800
Whan that we come agayn fro Caunterbury.
And for to make yow the more mery,
I wol my-selven gladly with yow ryde,
Right at myn owne cost, and be your gyde.
And who-so wol my Iugement withseye 805
Shal paye al that we spenden by the weye
And if ye vouche-sauf that it be so,
Tel me anon, with-outen wordes mo,
And I wol erly shape me therfore.'

This thing was graunted, and our othes swore
With ful glad herte, and preyden him also 811
That he wold vouche-sauf for to do so,
And that he wolde been our governour,
And of our tales Iuge and reportour,
And sette a soper at a certeyn prys; 815
And we wold reulèd been at his devys,
In heigh and lowe; and thus, by oon assent,
We been acorded to his Iugement.
And ther-up-on the wyn was fet anoon;
We dronken, and to reste wente echoon, 820
With-outen any lenger taryinge.
A-morwe, whan that day bigan to springe,
Up roos our host, and was our aller cok,
And gadrede us togidre, alle in a flok,
And forth we riden, a litel more than pas, 825
Un-to the watering of seint Thomas.
And there our host bigan his hors areste,
And seyde; 'Lordinges, herkneth if yow leste.
Ye woot your forward, and I it yow recorde.
If even-song and morwe-song acorde, 830
Lat se now who shal telle the firste tale.
As evere mote I drinke wyn or ale,
Who-so be rebel to my Iugement
Shal paye for al that by the weye is spent.
Now draweth cut, er that we ferrer twinne; 835
He which that hath the shortest shal beginne.'
'Sire knight,' quod he, 'my maister and my lord,
Now draweth cut, for that is myn acord.
Cometh neer,' quod he, 'my lady prioresse;
And ye, sir clerk, lat be your shamfastnesse,
Ne studieth noght; ley hond to, every man.'

Anon to drawen every wight bigan, 842
And shortly for to tellen, as it was,
Were it by aventure, or sort, or cas,
The sothe is this, the cut fil to the knight, 845
Of which ful blythe and glad was every wight;
And telle he moste his tale, as was resoun,
By forward and by composicioun,
As ye han herd; what nedeth wordes mo?
And whan this goode man saugh it was so, 850
As he that wys was and obedient
To kepe his forward by his free assent,
He seyde: 'Sin I shal beginne the game,
What, welcome be the cut, a Goddes name!
Now lat us ryde, and herkneth what I seye.' 855

And with that word we riden forth our weye;
And he bigan with right a mery chere
His tale anon, and seyde in this mannere.

* * *

THE NUN'S PRIEST'S TALE

A POVRE widwe somdel stope in age,
Was whylom dwelling in a narwe cotage,
Bisyde a grove, stondyng in a dale.
This widwe, of which I telle yow my tale,
Sin thilke day that she was last a wyf, 5
In pacience ladde a ful simple lyf,
For litel was hir catel and hir rente;
By housbondrye, of such as God hir sente,
She fond hir-self, and eek hir doghtren two.
Three large sowes hadde she, and namo, 10
Three kyn, and eek a sheep that highte Malle.
Ful sooty was hir bour, and eek hir halle,
In which she eet ful many a sclendre meel.
Of poynaunt sauce hir neded never a deel.
No deyntee morsel passèd thrugh hir throte; 15
Hir dyete was accordant to hir cote.
Repleccioun ne made hir nevere syk;
Attempree dyete was al hir phisyk,
And exercyse, and hertes suffisaunce.
The goute lette hir no-thing for to daunce, 20
Ne poplexye shente nat hir heed;
No wyn ne drank she, neither whyt ne reed;
Hir bord was servèd most with whyt and blak,
Milk and broun breed, in which she fond no lak,
Seynd bacoun, and somtyme an ey or tweye, 25
For she was as it were a maner deye.

A yerd she hadde, enclosèd al aboute
With stikkes, and a drye dich with-oute,
In which she hadde a cok, hight Chauntecleer,
In al the land of crowing nas his peer. 30
His vois was merier than the merye orgon
On messe-dayes that in the chirche gon;
Wel sikerer was his crowing in his logge,
Than is a clokke, or an abbey orlogge.
By nature knew he ech ascencioun 35
Of equinoxial in thilke toun;
For whan degrees fiftene were ascended,
Thanne crew he, that it mighte nat ben amended.
His comb was redder than the fyn coral,
And batailed, as it were a castel-wal. 40
His bile was blak, and as the Ieet it shoon;
Lyk asur were his legges, and his toon;
His nayles whytter than the lilie flour,
And lyk the burnèd gold was his colour.
This gentil cok hadde in his governaunce 45
Sevene hennes, for to doon al his pleasaunce,
Whiche were his sustres and his paramours,
And wonder lyk to him, as of colours,
Of whiche the faireste hewèd on hir throte
Was clepèd faire damoysele Pertelote. 50
Curteys she was, discreet, and debonaire,
And compaignable, and bar hir-self so faire,
Sin thilke day that she was seven night old,
That trewely she hath the herte in hold
Of Chauntecleer loken in every lith; 55
He loved hir so, that wel him was therwith.
But such a Ioye was it to here hem singe,
Whan that the brighte sonne gan to springe,
In swete accord, 'my lief is faren in londe.'
For thilke tyme, as I have understonde, 60
Bestes and briddes coude speke and singe.

And so bifel, that in a dawenynge,
As Chauntecleer among his wyves alle
Sat on his perche, that was in the halle,
And next him sat this faire Pertelote, 65

This Chauntecleer gan gronen in his throte,
As man that in his dreem is drecchèd sore.
And whan that Pertelote thus herde him rore,
She was agast, and seyde, 'O herte deere,
What eyleth yow, to grone in this manere?   70
Ye ben a verray sleper, fy for shame!'
And he answerde and seyde thus, 'Madame,
I pray yow, that ye take it nat agrief:
By God, me mette I was in swich meschief
Right now, that yet myn herte is sore afright.
Now God,' quod he, 'my swevene rede aright,   76
And keep my body out of foul prisoun!
Me mette, how that I romèd up and doun
Withinne our yerde, wher as I saugh a beste,
Was lyk an hound, and wolde han maad areste
Upon my body, and wolde han had me deed.   81
His colour was bitwixe yelwe and reed;
And tippèd was his tail, and bothe his eres
With blak, unlyk the remenant of his heres;
His snowte smal, with glowinge eyen tweye.   85
Yet of his look for fere almost I deye;
This causèd me my groning, douteles.'

'Avoy!' quod she, 'fy on yow, herteles!
Allas!' quod she, 'for, by that God above,
Now han ye lost myn herte and al my love;   90
I can nat love a coward, by my feith.
For certes, what so any womman seith,
We alle desyren, if it mighte be,
To han housbondes hardy, wyse, and free,
And secree, and no nigard, ne no fool,   95
Ne him that is agast of every tool,
Ne noon avauntour, by that God above!
How dorste ye sayn for shame unto youre love,
That any thing mighte make yow aferd?
Have ye no mannes herte, and han a berd?   100
Allas! and conne ye been agast of swevenis?
No-thing, God wot, but vanitee, in sweven is.
Swevenes engendren of repleccioms,
And ofte of fume, and of compleccions,
Whan humours been to habundant in a wight.
Certes this dreem, which ye han met to-night,
Cometh of the grete superfluitee   107
Of youre rede *colera*, pardee,
Which causeth folk to dremen in here dremes
Of arwes, and of fyr with rede lemes,   110
Of grete bestes, that they wol hem byte,
Of contek, and of whelpes grete and lyte;
Right as the humour of malencolye
Causeth ful many a man, in sleep, to crye,
For fere of blake beres, or boles blake,   115
Or elles, blake develes wole him take.
Of othere humours coude I telle also,
That werken many a man in sleep ful wo;
But I wol passe as lightly as I can.

'Lo Catoun, which that was so wys a man,   120
Seyde he nat thus, ne do no fors of dremes?
Now, sire,' quod she, 'whan we flee fro the bemes,
For Goddes love, as tak som laxatyf;
Up peril of my soule, and of my lyf,
I counseille yow the beste, I wol nat lye,   125
That both of colere, and of malencolye
Ye purge yow; and for ye shul nat tarie,
Though in this toun is noon apotecarie,
I shal my-self to herbes techen yow,
That shul ben for your hele, and for your prow;
And in our yerd tho herbes shal I fynde,   131
The whiche han of here propretee, by kynde,
To purgen yow binethe, and eek above.
Forget not this, for Goddes owene love!
Ye been ful colerik of compleccioun.   135
Ware the sonne in his ascencioun
Ne fynde yow nat repleet of humours hote;
And if it do, I dar wel leye a grote,
That ye shul have a fevere terciane,
Or an agu, that may be youre bane.   140
A day or two ye shul have digestyves
Of wormes, er ye take your laxatyves,
Of lauriol, centaure, and fumetere,
Or elles of ellebor, that groweth there,
Of catapuce, or of gaytres beryis,   145
Of erbe yve, growing in our yerd, that mery is;
Pekke hem up right as they growe, and ete hem in.
Be mery, housbond, for your fader kyn!
Dredeth no dreem; I can say yow namore.'

'Madame,' quod he, '*graunt mercy* of your lore.   150
But natheles, as touching daun Catoun,
That hath of wisdom such a gret renoun,
Though that he bad no dremes for to drede,
By God, men may in olde bokes rede
Of many a man, more of auctoritee   155
Than evere Catoun was, so moot I thee,
That al the revers seyn of this sentence,
And han wel founden by experience,
That dremes ben significaciouns,
As wel of Ioye as tribulaciouns   160
That folk enduren in this lyf present.
Ther nedeth make of this noon argument;
The verray preve sheweth it in dede.
Oon of the gretteste auctours that men rede
Seith thus, that whylom two felawes wente   165
On pilgrimage, in a ful good entente;
And happèd so, they come into a toun,
Where as ther was swich congregacioun
Of peple, and eek so streit of herbergage,
That they ne founde as muche as o cotage   170
In which they bothe mighte y-loggèd be.
Wherfor thay mosten, of necessitee,
As for that night, departen compaignye;
And ech of hem goth to his hostelrye,
And took his logging as it wolde falle.   175
That oon of hem was loggèd in a stalle,
Fer in a yerd, with oxen of the plough;
That other man was loggèd wel y-nough,
As was his aventure, or his fortune,
That us governeth alle as in commune.   180
And so bifel, that, long er it were day,
This man mette in his bed, ther as he lay,

How that his felawe gan up-on him calle,
And seyde, "Allas! for in an oxes stalle
This night I shal be mordrèd ther I lye.   185
Now help me, dere brother, or I dye;
In alle haste com to me," he sayde.
This man out of his sleep for fere abrayde:
But whan that he was waknèd of his sleep,
He turnèd him, and took of this no keep,   190
Him thoughte his dreem nas but a vanitee.
Thus twyes in his sleping dremèd he.
And atte thridde tyme yet his felawe
Com, as him thoughte, and seide, "I am now slawe;
Bihold my bloody woundes, depe and wyde!
Arys up erly in the morwe-tyde,   196
And at the west gate of the toun," quod he,
"A carte ful of donge ther shaltow see,
In which my body is hid ful prively;
Do thilke carte arresten boldely.   200
My gold causèd my mordre, sooth to sayn;"
And tolde him every poynt how he was slayn,
With a ful pitous face, pale of hewe.
And truste wel, his dreem he fond ful trewe;
For on the morwe, as sone as it was day,   205
To his felawes in he took the way;
And whan that he cam to this oxes stalle,
After his felawe he bigan to calle.
The hostiler answerde him anon,
And seyde, "Sire, your felawe is agon,   210
As sone as day he wente out of the toun."
This man gan fallen in suspecioun,
Remembring on his dremes that he mette,
And forth he goth, no lenger wolde he lette,
Unto the west gate of the toun, and fond   215
A dong-carte, as it were to donge lond,
That was arrayèd in that same wyse
As ye han herd the dede man devyse;
And with an hardy herte he gan to crye
Vengeaunce and Iustice of this felonye:—   220
"My felawe mordrèd is this same night,
And in this carte he lyth gapinge upright.
I crye out on the ministres," quod he,
"That sholden kepe and reulen this citee;
Harrow! allas! her lyth my felawe slayn!"   225
What sholde I more un-to this tale sayn?
The peple out-sterte, and caste the cart to grounde,
And in the middel of the dong they founde
The dede man, that mordrèd was al newe.

'O blisful God, that art so Iust and trewe!   230
Lo, how that thou biwreyest mordre alway!
Mordre wol out, that se we day by day.
Mordre is so wlatsom and abhominable
To God, that is so Iust and resonable,
That he ne wol nat suffre it helèd be;   235
Though it abyde a yeer, or two, or three,
Mordre wol out, this my conclusioun.
And right anoon, ministres of that toun
Han hent the carter, and so sore him pynèd,
And eek the hostiler so sore engynèd,   240
That thay biknewe hir wikkednesse anoon,
And were an-hangèd by the nekke-boon.

'Here may men seen that dremes been to drede.
And certes, in the same book I rede,
Right in the nexte chapitre after this,   245
(I gabbe nat, so have I Ioye or blis,)
Two men that wolde han passèd over see,
For certeyn cause, in-to a fer contree,
If that the wind ne hadde been contrarie,
That made hem in a citee for to tarie,   250
That stood ful mery upon an haven-syde.
But on a day, agayn the even-tyde,
The wind gan chaunge, and blew right as hem leste.
Iolif and glad they wente un-to hir reste,
And casten hem ful erly for to saille;   255
But to that oo man fel a greet mervaille.
That oon of hem, in sleping as he lay,
Him mette a wonder dreem, agayn the day;
Him thoughte a man stood by his beddes syde,
And him comaunded, that he sholde abyde,   260
And seyde him thus, "If thou to-morwe wende,
Thou shalt be dreynt; my tale is at an ende."
He wook, and tolde his felawe what he mette,
And preyde him his viage for to lette;
As for that day, he preyde him to abyde.   265
His felawe, that lay by his beddes syde,
Gan for to laughe, and scornèd him ful faste.
"No dreem," quod he, "may so myn herte agaste,
That I wol lette for to do my thinges.
I sette not a straw by thy dreminges,   270
For swevenes been but vanitees and Iapes.
Men dreme al-day of owles or of apes,
And eek of many a mase therwithal;
Men dreme of thing that nevere was ne shal,
But sith I see that thou wolt heer abyde,   275
And thus for-sleuthen wilfully thy tyde,
God wot it reweth me; and have good day."
And thus he took his leve, and wente his way.
But er that he hadde halfe his cours y-seylèd,
Noot I nat why, ne what mischaunce it eylèd,
But casuelly the shippes botme rente,   281
And ship and man under the water wente
In sighte of othere shippes it byside,
That with hem seylèd at the same tyde.
And therfor, faire Pertelote so dere,   285
By swiche ensamples olde maistow lere,
That no man sholde been to recchelees
Of dremes, for I sey thee, doutelees,
That many a dreem ful sore is for to drede.

'Lo, in the lyf of seint Kenelm, I rede,   290
That was Kenulphus sone, the noble king
Of Mercenrike, how Kenelm mette a thing;
A lyte er he was mordrèd, on a day,
His mordre in his avisioun he say.
His norice him expounèd every del   295
His swevene, and bad him for to kepe him wel
For traisoun; but he nas but seven yeer old.

And therefore litel tale hath he told
Of any dreem, so holy was his herte.
By God, I hadde levere than my sherte 300
That ye had rad his legende, as have I.
Dame Pertelote, I sey yow trewely,
Macrobeus, that writ the avisioun
In Affrike of the worthy Cipioun,
Affermeth dremes, and seith that they been 305
Warning of thinges that men after seen.
And forther-more, I pray yow loketh wel
In the olde testament, of Daniel,
If he held dremes any vanitee.
Reed eek of Ioseph, and ther shul ye see 310
Wher dremes ben somtyme (I sey nat alle)
Warning of thinges that shul after falle.
Loke of Egipt the king, daun Pharao,
His bakere and his boteler also,
Wher they ne felte noon effect in dremes. 315
Who so wol seken actes of sondry remes,
May rede of dremes many a wonder thing.

'Lo Cresus, which that was of Lyde king,
Mette he nat that he sat upon a tree,
Which signified he sholde anhangèd be? 320
Lo heer Andromacha, Ectores wyf,
That day that Ector sholde lese his lyf,
She dremèd on the same night biforn,
How that the lyf of Ector sholde be lorn,
If thilke day he wente in-to bataille; 325
She warnèd him, but it mighte nat availle;
He wente for to fighte natheles,
But he was slayn anoon of Achilles.
But thilke tale is al to long to telle,
And eek it is ny day, I may nat dwelle. 330
Shortly I seye, as for conclusioun,
That I shal han of this avisoun
Adversitee; and I seye forther-more,
That I ne telle of laxatyves no store,
For they ben venimous, I woot it wel; 335
I hem defye, I love hem nevere a del.

'Now let us speke of mirthe, and stinte al this;
Madame Pertelote, so have I blis,
Of o thing God hath sent me large grace;
For whan I see the beautee of your face, 340
Ye ben so scarlet-reed aboute youre yën,
It maketh al my drede for to dyen;
For, also siker as *In principio*,
Mulier est hominis confusio;
Madame, the sentence of this Latin is— 345
Womman is mannes Ioye and al his blis.

* * *

I am so ful of Ioye and of solas 350
That I defye bothe sweven and dreem.'
And with that word he fley doun fro the beem,
For it was day, and eek his hennes alle;
And with a chuk he gan hem for to calle,
For he had founde a corn, lay in the yerd. 355
Roial he was, he was namore aferd;

* * *

He loketh as it were a grim leoun;
And on his toos he rometh up and doun, 360
Him deynèd not to sette his foot to grounde.
He chukketh, whan he hath a corn y-founde,
And to him rennen thanne his wyves alle.
Thus roial, as a prince is in his halle,
Leve I this Chauntecleer in his pasture; 365
And after wol I telle his aventure.

Whan that the month in which the world bigan,
That highte March, whan God first makèd man,
Was complet, and y-passèd were also,
Sin March bigan, thritty dayes and two, 370
Bifel that Chauntecleer, in al his pryde,
His seven wyves walking by his syde,
Caste up his eyen to the brighte sonne,
That in the signe of Taurus hadde y-ronne
Twenty degrees and oon, and somwhat more;
And knew by kynde, and by noon other lore, 376
That it was pryme, and crew with blisful stevene.
'The sonne,' he sayde, 'is clomben up on hevene
Fourty degrees and oon, and more, y-wis.
Madame Pertelote, my worldes blis, 380
Herkneth thise blisful briddes how they singe,
And see the fresshe floures how they springe;
Ful is myn hert of revel and solas.'
But sodeinly him fil a sorweful cas;
For evere the latter ende of Ioye is wo. 385
God woot that worldly Ioye is sone ago;
And if a rethor coude faire endyte,
He in a chronique saufly mighte it write,
As for a sovereyn notabilitee.
Now every wys man, lat him herkne me; 390
This storie is al-so trewe, I undertake,
As is the book of Launcelot de Lake,
That wommen holde in ful gret reverence.
Now wol I torne agayn to my sentence.

A col-fox, ful of sly iniquitee, 395
That in the grove hadde wonèd yeres three,
By heigh imaginacioun forn-cast,
The same night thurgh-out the hegges brast
Into the yerd, ther Chauntecleer the faire
Was wont, and eek his wyves, to repaire; 400
And in a bed of wortes stille he lay,
Til it was passèd undern of the day,
Wayting his tyme on Chauntecleer to falle
As gladly doon thise homicydes alle,
That in awayt liggen to mordre men. 405
O false mordrer, lurking in thy den!
O newe Scariot, newe Genilon!
False dissimilour, O Greek Sinon,
That broghtest Troye al outrely to sorwe!
O Chauntecleer, acursèd be that morwe, 410
That thou into that yerd flough fro the bemes!
Thou were ful wel y-warnèd by thy dremes,
That thilke day was perilous to thee.
But what that God forwot mot nedes be,
After the opinioun of certeyn clerkis. 415
Witnesse on him, that any perfit clerk is,

That in scole is gret altercacioun
In this matere, and greet disputisoun,
And hath ben of an hundred thousand men
But I ne can not bulte it to the bren, 420
As can the holy doctour Augustyn,
Or Boece, or the bishop Bradwardyn,
Whether that Goddes worthy forwiting
Streyneth me nedely for to doon a thing,
(Nedely clepe I simple necessitee); 425
Or elles, if free choys be graunted me
To do that same thing, or do it noght,
Though God forwot it, er that it was wroght;
Or if his witing streyneth nevere a del
But by necessitee condicionel. 430
I wol not han to do of swich matere;
My tale is of a cok, as ye may here,
That took his counseil of his wyf, with sorwe,
To walken in the yerd upon that morwe
That he had met the dreem, that I of tolde 435
Wommennes counseils been ful ofte colde;
Wommannes counseil broghte us first to wo,
And made Adam fro paradys to go,
Ther as he was ful mery, and wel at ese.
But for I noot, to whom it mighte displese, 440
If I counseil of wommen wolde biame,
Passe over, for I seyde it in my game.
Rede auctours, wher they trete of swich matere,
And what thay seyn of wommen ye may here.
Thise been the cokkes wordes, and nat myne;
I can noon harme of no woman divyne. 446

Faire in the sond, to bathe hire merily,
Lyth Pertelote, and alle hir sustres by,
Agayn the sonne; and Chauntecleer so free
Song merier than the mermayde in the see;
For Phisiologus seith sikerly, 451
How that they singen wel and merily.
And so bifel, that as he caste his yë,
Among the wortes, on a boterflye,
He was war of this fox that lay ful lowe. 455
No-thing ne liste him thanne for to crowe,
But cryde anon, 'cok, cok,' and up he sterte,
As man that was affrayèd in his herte.
For naturelly a beest desyreth flee
Fro his contrarie, if he may it see, 460
Though he never erst had seyn it with his yë.

This Chauntecleer, whan he gan him espye,
He wolde han fled, but that the fox anon
Seyde, 'Gentil sire, allas! wher wol ye gon?
Be ye affrayed of me that am your freend? 465
Now certes, I were worse than a feend,
If I to yow wolde harm or vileinye.
I am nat come your counseil for tespye;
But trewely, the cause of my cominge
Was only for to herkne how that ye singe. 470
For trewely ye have as mery a stevene,
As eny aungel hath, that is in hevene;
Therwith ye han in musik more felinge
Than hadde Boece, or any that can singe.
My lord your fader (God his soule blesse!) 475
And eek your moder, of hir gentilesse,
Han in myn hous y-been, to my gret ese;
And certes, sire, ful fayn wolde I yow plese.
But for men speke of singing, I wol saye,
So mote I brouke wel myn eyen tweye, 480
Save yow, I herde nevere man so singe,
As dide your fader in the morweninge;
Certes, it was of herte, al that he song.
And for to make his voys the more strong,
He wolde so peyne him, that with both his yën
He moste winke, so loude he wolde cryen, 486
And stonden on his tiptoon therwithal,
And strecche forth his nekke long and smal,
And eek he was of swich discrecioun,
That ther nas no man in no regioun 490
That him in song or wisdom mighte passe.
I have weel rad in daun Burnel the Asse,
Among his vers, how that ther was a cok,
For that a prestes sone yaf him a knok
Upon his leg, whyl he was yong and nyce, 495
He made him for to lese his benefyce.
But certeyn, ther nis no comparisoun
Bitwix the wisdom and discrecioun
Of your fader, and of his subtiltee.
Now singeth, sire, for seinte charitee, 500
Let se, conne ye your fader countrefete?'
This Chauntecleer his winges gan to bete,
As man that coude his tresoun nat espye,
So was he ravisshed with his flaterye.

Allas! ye lordes, many a fals flatour 505
Is in your courtes, and many a losengeour
That plesen yow wel more, by my feith,
Than he that soothfastnesse unto yow seith.
Redeth Ecclesiaste of flaterye;
Beth war, ye lordes, of hir trecherye. 510

This Chauntecleer stood hye up-on his toos,
Strecching his nekke, and held his eyen cloos,
And gan to crowe loude for the nones;
And daun Russel the fox sterte up at ones.
And by the gargat hente Chauntecleer, 515
And on his bak toward the wode him beer,
For yet ne was ther no man that him sewèd.
O destinee, that mayst nat ben eschewèd!
Allas, that Chauntecleer fleigh fro the bemes!
Allas, his wyf ne roghte nat of dremes! 520
And on a Friday fil al this meschaunce.
O Venus, that art goddesse of plesaunce,
Sin that thy servant was this Chauntecleer,
And in thy service dide al his poweer,
More for delyt, than world to multiplye, 525
Why woldestow suffre him on thy day to dye?
O Gaufred, dere mayster soverayn,
That, whan thy worthy king Richard was slayn
With shot, compleynedest his deth so sore,
Why ne hadde I now thy sentence and thy lore,
The Friday for to chide, as diden ye? 531
(For on a Friday soothly slayn was he.)
Than wolde I shewe yow how that I coude pleyne
For Chauntecleres drede, and for his peyne.

Certes, swich cry ne lamentacioun 535
Was nevere of ladies maad, whan Ilioun
Was wonne, and Pirrus with his streite swerd,
Whan he hadde hent king Priam by the berd,
And slayn him (as sath us *Eneydos*),
As maden alle the hennes in the clos, 540
Whan they had seyn of Chauntecleer the sighte.
But sovereynly dame Pertelote shrighte,
Ful louder than dide Hasdrubales wyf,
Whan that hir housbond hadde lost his lyf,
And that the Romayns hadde brend Cartage,
She was so ful of torment and of rage, 546
That wilfully into the fyr she sterte,
And brende hir-selven with a stedfast herte.
O woful hennes, right so cryden ye,
As, whan that Nero brende the citee 550
Of Rome, cryden senatoures wyves,
For that hir housbondes losten alle hir lyves;
Withouten gilt this Nero hath hem slayn.
Now wol I torne to my tale agayn:

This sely widwe, and eek hir doghtres two, 555
Herden thise hennes crye and maken wo,
And out at dores sterten thay anoon,
And syen the fox toward the grove goon,
And bar upon his bak the cok away;
And cryden, 'Out! harrow! and weylaway! 560
Ha, ha, the fox!' and after him they ran,
And eek with staves many another man;
Ran Colle our dogge, and Talbot, and Gerland,
And Malkin, with a distaf in hir hand;
Ran cow and calf, and eek the verry hogges 565
So were they fered for berking of the dogges
And shouting of the men and wimmen eke,
They ronne so, hem thoughte hir herte breke.
They yelleden as feendes doon in helle;
The dokes cryden as men wolde hem quelle; 570
The gees for fere flowen over the trees;
Out of the hyve cam the swarm of bees;
So hidous was the noyse, a! *benedicite!*
Certes, he Iakke Straw, and his meynee,
Ne maden nevere shoutes half so shrille, 575
Whan that they wolden any Fleming kille,
As thilke day was maad upon the fox.
Of bras thay broghten bemes, and of box,
Of horn, of boon, in whiche they blewe and
poupèd,
And therwithal thay shrykèd and they houpèd;
It semèd as that hevene sholde falle. 581
Now, gode men, I pray yow herkneth alle!

Lo, how fortune turneth sodeinly
The hope and pryde eek of hir enemy!
This cok, that lay upon the foxes bak, 585
In al his drede, un-to the fox he spak,
And seyde, 'Sire, if that I were as ye,
Yet sholde I seyn (as wis God helpe me),
"Turneth agayn, ye proude cherles alle!
A verray pestilence up-on yow falle! 590
Now am I come un-to this wodes syde,
Maugree your heed, the cok shal heer abyde;
I wol him ete in feith, and that anon."'

The fox answerde, 'In feith, it shal be don,'
And as he spak that word, al sodeinly 595
This cok brak from his mouth deliverly,
And heighe up-on a tree he fleigh anon.
And whan the fox saugh that he was y-gon,
'Allas!' quod he, 'O Chauntecleer, allas!
I have to yow,' quod he, 'y-doon trespas, 600
In-as-muche as I makèd yow aferd,
Whan I yow hente, and broghte out of the yerd;
But, sire, I dide it in no wikke entente;
Com doun, and I shal telle yow what I mente.
I shal seye sooth to yow, God help me so.' 605
'Nay than,' quod he, 'I shrewe us bothe two,
And first I shrewe my-self, bothe blood and
bones,
If thou bigyle me ofter than ones.
Thou shalt namore, thurgh thy flaterye
Do me to singe and winke with myn yë. 610
For he that winketh, whan he sholde see,
Al wilfully, God lat him never thee!'
'Nay,' quod the fox, 'but God yive him mes-
chaunce,
That is so undiscreet of governaunce,
That iangleth whan he sholde holde his pees.' 615

Lo, swich it is for to be recchelees,
And necligent, and truste on flaterye.
But ye that holden this tale a folye,
As of a fox, or of a cok and hen,
Taketh the moralitee, good men. 620
For seint Paul seith, that al that writen is,
To our doctryne it is y-write, y-wis.
Taketh the fruyt, and lat the chaf be stille.

Now, gode God, if that it be thy wille, 624
As seith my lord, so make us alle good men;
And bringe us to his heighe blisse. Amen.

CHAUCERS WORDES UNTO ADAM HIS OWNE SCRIVEYN

ADAM scriveyn, if ever it thee bifalle
Boece or Troilus to wryten newe,
Under thy lokkes thou most have the scalle,
But after my making thou wryte trewe.
So ofte a daye I mot thy werk renewe, 5
Hit to correcte and eek to rubbe and scrape;
And al is through thy negligence and rape.

LAK OF STEDFASTNESSE

BALADE

SOM tyme this world was so stedfast and stable
That mannes word was obligacioun,
And now hit is so fals and deceivable,
That word and deed, as in conclusioun,
Ben no-thing lyk, for turnèd up so doun 5
Is al this world for mede and wilfulnesse,
That al is lost, for lak of stedfastnesse.

What maketh this world to be so variable
But lust that folk have in dissensioun?
Among us now a man is holde unable, 10
But-if he can, by som collusioun,
Don his neighbour wrong or oppressioun.
What causeth this, but wilful wrecchednesse,
That al is lost, for lak of stedfastnesse?

Trouthe is put doun, resoun is holden fable;
Vertu hath now no dominacioun, 16
Pitee exyled, no man is merciable.
Through covetyse is blent discrecioun;
The world hath mad a permutacioun
Fro right to wrong, fro trouthe to fikelnesse, 20
That al is lost, for lak of stedfastnesse.

Lenvoy to King Richard

O prince, desyre to be honourable,
Cherish thy folk and hate extorcioun!
Suffre no thing, that may be reprevable 25
To thyn estat, don in thy regioun.
Shew forth thy swerd of castigacioun,
Dred God, do law, love trouthe and worthi-
  nesse,
And wed thy folk agein to stedfastnesse.

THE COMPLEINT OF CHAUCER TO HIS EMPTY PURSE

To you, my purse, and to non other wight
Compleyne I, for ye be my lady dere!
I am so sory, now that ye be light;
For certes, but ye make me hevy chere,
Me were as leef be leyd up-on my bere; 5
For whiche un-to your mercy thus I crye:
Beth hevy ageyn, or elles mot I dye!

Now voucheth sauf this day, or hit be night,
That I of you the blisful soun may here,
Or see your colour lyk the sonne bright, 10
That of yelownesse hadde never pere.
Ye be my lyf, ye be myn hertes stere,
Quene of comfort and of good companye:
Beth hevy ageyn, or elles mot I dye!

Now purs, that be to me my lyves light, 15
And saveour, as doun in this world here,
Out of this toune help me through your might,
Sin that ye wole nat been my tresorere;
For I am shave as nye as any frere.
But yit I pray un-to your curtesye: 20
Beth hevy ageyn, or elles mot I dye!

Lenvoy de Chaucer

O conquerour of Brutes Albioun!
Which that by lyne and free eleccioun
Ben verray king, this song to you I sende; 25
And ye, that mowen al our harm amende,
Have minde up-on my supplicacioun!

TRUTH

BALADE DE BON CONSEYL

FLEE fro the prees, and dwelle with sothfastnesse,
Suffyce unto thy good, though hit be smal;
For hord hath hate, and climbing tikelnesse,
Prees hath envye, and wele blent overal;
Savour no more than thee bihove shal; 5
Werk wel thyself, that other folk canst rede;
And trouthe shal delivere, hit is no drede.

Tempest thee noght al croked to redresse,
In trust of hir that turneth as a bal:
Gret reste stant in litel besinesse; 10
And eek be war to sporne ageyn an al;
Stryve noght, as doth the krokke with the wal.
Daunte thyself, that dauntest otheres dede;
And trouthe shal delivere, hit is no drede.

That thee is sent, receyve in buxumnesse, 15
The wrastling for this worlde axeth a fal.
Her nis non hoom, her nis but wildernesse:
Forth, pilgrim, forth! Forth, beste, out of thy stal!
Know thy contree, look up, thank God of al;
Hold the hye wey, and lat thy gost thee lede: 20
And trouthe shal delivere, hit is no drede.

Envoy

Therfore, thou vache, leve thyn old wrecched-
  nesse
Unto the worlde; leve now to be thral;
Crye him mercy, that of his hy goodnesse
Made thee of noght, and in especial 25
Draw unto him, and pray in general
For thee, and eek for other, hevenlich mede;
And trouthe shal delivere, hit is no drede.

SIR THOMAS MALORY (c.1395–1471)

The life of the author of the *Morte d'Arthur* was long, turbulent, and not entirely blameless. He was born about 1395, lived at Newbold Revel, in Warwickshire, and was knighted. As a member of the retinue of Richard Beauchamp, Earl of Warwick, he accompanied this 'father of courtesy' to France, and saw extensive military service there. He may have been present at the burning of Joan of Arc at Rouen in 1431. In 1445 Malory represented Warwickshire in Parliament. Somewhat later he was legally prosecuted upon a formidable array of charges, the validity of which is left in uncertainty. The outcome of his alleged crimes was his continuous, or almost continuous, imprisonment in London from 1457 to 1460. He appears to have been in prison also when he wrote the *Morte d'Arthur*, between March, 1469, and March, 1470. He died on March fourteenth, 1471, and was buried in the Grey Friars' sanctuary in London. Whatever his legal misdemeanors may have been, Malory was 'a gentleman of an ancient house and a soldier,' belonging to the most highly cultivated society of his time. He had ready access to literary works, and was, it would seem, well endowed for producing the chivalric compilation through which he is now best known. It may well be that some of the incidents and numerous descriptive details in the *Morte d'Arthur* are reflections from Malory's own adventurous life.

William Caxton (c.1422–1491) deserves a place by the side of Malory in the literary history of the fifteenth century not only because he edited and published the *Morte d'Arthur*, but also because he brought into print numerous other works of romance. After a considerable period of activity as a merchant, Caxton began his career as printer, translator, and editor by issuing at Bruges, about 1475, the first book printed in English, *The Recuyell of the Histories of Troy*. Caxton translated this work himself, from the French of Raoul le Fevre. In 1476 he returned to England, and set up his press in Westminster, where he finished printing, on November 18, 1477, *The Dictes and Sayings of the Philosophers*, the first dated book issued in England. From his press in Westminster Caxton issued some seventy-one separate works, of which Malory's *Morte d'Arthur* was the fifty-second.

LE MORTE D'ARTHUR

PREFACE OF WILLIAM CAXTON

After that I had accomplished and finished divers histories, as well of contemplation as of other historical and worldly acts of great conquerors and princes, and also certain books of ensamples and doctrine, many noble and divers gentlemen of this realm of England came and demanded me, many and ofttimes, wherefore that I have not do made and enprint the noble history of the Sangreal, and of the most renowned christian king, first and chief of the three best christian and worthy, King Arthur, which ought most to be remembered among us Englishmen to-fore all other christian kings. For it is notoriously known through the universal world that there be nine worthy and the best that ever were. That is to wit three paynims, three Jews, and three christian men. As for the paynims they were to-fore the Incarnation of Christ, which were named, the first, Hector of Troy, of whom the history is come both in ballad and in prose; the second, Alexander the Great; and the third, Julius Cæsar, Emperor of Rome, of whom the histories be well known and had. And as for the three Jews which also were to-fore the Incarnation of our Lord, of whom the first was Duke Joshua which brought the children of Israel into the land of behest; the second, David, King of Jerusalem; and the third, Judas Maccabæus: of these three the Bible rehearseth all their noble histories and acts. And since the said Incarnation have been three noble christian men stalled and admitted through the universal world into the number of the nine best and worthy, of whom was first the noble Arthur, whose noble acts I purpose to write in this present book here following. The second was Charlemagne, or Charles the Great, of whom the history is had in many places, both in French and English; and the third and last was Godfrey of Boloine, of whose acts and life I made a book unto the excellent prince and king of noble memory, King Edward the Fourth.

The said noble gentlemen instantly required me to enprint the history of the said noble king and conqueror, King Arthur, and of his knights, with the history of the Sangreal, and of the death and ending of the said Arthur; affirming that I ought rather to enprint his acts and noble feats, than of Godfrey of Boloine, or any of the other eight, considering that he was a man born within this realm, and king and emperor of the same; and that there be in French divers and many noble volumes of his acts, and also of his knights. To whom I answered, that divers men hold opinion that there was no such Arthur, and that all such books as been made of him be feigned and fables, because that some chronicles make of him no mention, nor remember him no thing, nor of his knights. Whereto they answered, and one in special said, that in him that should say or think that there was never such a king called Arthur, might well be aretted great folly and blindness; for he said that there were many evidences of the contrary: first ye may see his sepulture in the monastery of Glastonbury. And also in *Polichronicon*, in the fifth book the sixth chapter, and in the seventh book the twenty-third chapter, where his body was buried, and after found, and translated into the said monastery. Ye shall see also in the history of Bochas, in his book *De Casu Principum*, part of his noble acts, and also of his fall. Also Galfridus in his British book recounteth his life; and in divers places of England many remembrances be yet of him and shall remain perpetually, and also of his knights. First in the Abbey of Westminster, at Saint Edward's shrine, remaineth the print of his seal in red wax closed in beryl, in which is written *Patricius Arthurus, Britannie, Gallie, Germanie, Dacie, Imperator*. Item in the castle of Dover ye may see Gawaine's skull and Craddock's mantle: at Winchester the Round Table: in other places Launcelot's sword and many other things. Then all these things considered, there can no man reasonably gainsay but there was a king of this land named Arthur. For in all places, christian and heathen, he is reputed and taken for one of the nine worthy, and the first of the three christian men. And also he is more spoken of beyond the sea, more books made of his noble acts, than there be in England, as well in Dutch, Italian, Spanish, and Greek, as in French. And yet of record remain in witness of him in Wales, in the town of Camelot, the great stones and marvelous works of iron, lying under the grov̥d, and royal vaults, which divers now living have seen. Wherefore it is a marvel why he is no more renowned in his own country, save only it accordeth to the Word of God, which saith that no man is accept for a prophet in his own country.

Then all these things foresaid alleged, I could not well deny but that there was such a noble king named Arthur, and reputed one of the nine worthy, and first and chief of the christian men; and many noble volumes be made of him and of his noble knights in French, which I have seen and read beyond the sea, which be not had in our maternal tongue, but in Welsh be many and also in French, and some in English, but nowhere nigh all. Wherefore, such as have late been drawn out briefly into English I have after the simple conning that God hath sent to me, under the favor and correction of all noble lords and gentlemen, emprised to enprint a book of the noble histories of the said King Arthur, and of certain of his knights, after a copy unto me delivered, which copy Sir Thomas Malory did take out of certain books of French, and reduced it into English. And I, according to my copy, have done set it in enprint, to the intent that noble men may see and learn the noble acts of chivalry, the gentle and virtuous deeds that some knights used in those days, by which they came to honor; and how they that were vicious were punished and oft put to shame and rebuke; humbly beseeching all noble lords and ladies, with all other estates, of what estate or degree they been of, that shall see and read in this said book and work, that they take the good and honest acts in their remembrance, and to follow the same. Wherein they shall find many joyous and pleasant histories, and noble and renowed acts of humanity, gentleness, and chivalries. For herein may be seen noble chivalry, courtesy, humanity, friendliness, hardiness, love, friendship, cowardice, murder, hate, virtue, and sin. Do after the good and leave the evil, and it shall bring you to good fame and renown. And for to pass the time this book shall be pleasant to read in; but for to give faith and belief that all is true that is contained herein, ye be at your liberty; but all is written for our doctrine, and for to beware that we fall not to vice nor sin; but to exercise and follow virtue; by which we may come and attain to good fame and renown in this life, and after this short and transitory life, to come unto everlasting bliss in heaven, the which he grant us that reigneth in heaven, the blessed Trinity. Amen. . . .

BOOK XXI

CHAPTER I

HOW SIR MORDRED PRESUMED AND TOOK ON HIM TO BE KING OF ENGLAND, AND WOULD HAVE MARRIED THE QUEEN, HIS UNCLE'S WIFE

As Sir Mordred was ruler of all England, he did do make letters as though that they came from beyond the sea, and the letters specified that King Arthur was slain in battle with Sir Launcelot. Wherefore Sir Mordred made a parliament, and called the lords together, and there he made them to choose him king; and so was he crowned at Canterbury, and held a feast there fifteen days; and afterward he drew him unto Winchester, and there he took the Queen Guenever, and said plainly that he would wed her which was his uncle's wife and his father's wife. And so he made ready for the feast, and a day prefixed that they should be wedded; wherefore Queen Guenever was passing heavy. But she durst not discover her heart, but spake fair, and agreed to Sir Mordred's will. Then she desired of Sir Mordred for to go to London, to buy all manner of things that longed unto the wedding. And because of her fair speech, Sir Mordred trusted her well enough, and gave her leave to go. And so when she came to London, she took the Tower of London, and suddenly in all haste possible she stuffed it with all manner of victual, and well garnished it with men, and so kept it. Then when Sir Mordred wist and understood how he was beguiled, he was passing wroth out of measure. And a short tale for to make, he went and laid a mighty siege about the Tower of London, and made many great assaults thereat, and threw many great engines unto them, and shot great guns. But all might not prevail Sir Mordred, for Queen Guenever would never for fair speech nor for foul, would never trust to come in his hands again. Then came the Bishop of Canterbury, the which was a noble clerk and an holy man, and thus he said to Sir Mordred: 'Sir, what will ye do? will ye first displease God and sithen shame yourself, and all knighthood? Is not King Arthur your uncle, no farther but your mother's brother, and on her himself King Arthur begat you upon his own sister, therefore, how may you wed your father's wife? Sir,' said the noble clerk, 'leave this opinion or I shall curse you with book and bell and candle.' 'Do thou thy worst,' said Sir Mordred, 'wit thou well I shall defy thee.' 'Sir,' said the bishop, 'and wit you well I shall not fear me to do that me ought to do. Also where ye noise where my lord Arthur is slain, and that is not so, and therefore ye will make a foul work in this land.' 'Peace, thou false priest,' said Sir Mordred,' for an thou chafe me any more, I shall make strike off thy head.' So the bishop departed and did the cursing in the most orgulist wise that might be done. And then Sir Mordred sought the Bishop of Canterbury, for to have slain him. Then the bishop fled, and took part of his goods with him, and went nigh unto Glastonbury; and there he was as priest hermit in a chapel, and lived in poverty and in holy prayers, for well he understood that mischievous war was at hand.

Then Sir Mordred sought on Queen Guenever by letters and sonds, and by fair means and foul means, for to have her to come out of the Tower of London; but all this availed not, for she answered him shortly, openly and privily, that she had liefer slay herself than to be married with him. Then came word to Sir Mordred that King Arthur had araised the siege for Sir Launcelot, and he was coming homeward with a great host, to be avenged upon Sir Mordred; wherefore Sir Mordred made write writs to all the barony of this land, and much people drew to him. For then was the common voice among them that with Arthur was none other life but war and strife, and with Sir Mordred was great joy and bliss. Thus was Sir Arthur depraved and evil said of. And many there were that King Arthur had made up of naught, and given them lands, might not then say him a good word. Lo ye all Englishmen, see ye not what a mischief here was! for he that was the most king and knight of the world, and most loved the fellowship of noble knights, and by him they were all upholden, now might not these Englishmen hold them content with him. Lo thus was the old custom and usage of this land; and also men say that we of this land have not yet lost nor forgotten that custom and usage. Alas, this is a great default of us Englishmen, for there may no thing please us no term. And so fared the people at that time, they were better pleased with Sir Mordred than they were with King Arthur; and much people drew unto Sir Mordred, and said they would abide with him for better and for worse. And so Sir Mordred drew with a great host to Dover, for there he heard say that Sir Arthur would arrive, and so he thought to beat his own father from his lands; and the most part of all England held with Sir Mordred, the people were so new-fangle.

CHAPTER II

HOW AFTER THAT KING ARTHUR HAD TIDINGS, HE RETURNED AND CAME TO DOVER, WHERE SIR MORDRED MET HIM TO LET HIS LANDING; AND OF THE DEATH OF SIR GAWAINE

AND so as Sir Mordred was at Dover with his host, there came King Arthur with a great navy of ships, and galleys, and carracks. And there was Sir Mordred ready awaiting upon his landing, to let his own father to land upon the land that he was king over. Then there was launching of great boats and small, and full of noble men of arms; and there was much slaughter of gentle knights, and many a full bold baron was laid full low, on both parties. But King Arthur was so courageous that there might no manner of knights let him to land, and his knights fiercely followed him; and so they landed maugre Sir Mordred and all his power, and put Sir Mordred aback, that he fled and all his people.

So when this battle was done, King Arthur let bury his people that were dead. And then was noble Sir Gawaine found in a great boat, lying more than half dead. When Sir Arthur wist that Sir Gawaine was laid so low, he went unto him; and there the king made sorrow out of measure, and took Sir Gawaine in his arms, and thrice he there swooned. And then when he awaked, he said: 'Alas, Sir Gawaine, my sister's son, here now thou liest, the man in the world that I loved most; and now is my joy gone, for now, my nephew Sir Gawaine, I will discover me unto your person: in Sir Launcelot and you I most had my joy, and mine affiance, and now have I lost my joy of you both; wherefore all mine earthly joy is gone from me.' 'Mine uncle King Arthur,' said Sir Gawaine, 'wit you well my death-day is come, and all is through mine own hastiness and wilfulness; for I am smitten upon the old wound the which Sir Launcelot gave me, on the which I feel well I must die; and had Sir Launcelot been with you as he was, this unhappy war had never begun; and of all this am I causer, for Sir Launcelot and his blood, through their prowess, held all your cankered enemies in subjection and danger. And now,' said Sir Gawaine, 'ye shall miss Sir Launcelot. But, alas, I would not accord with him, and therefore,' said Sir Gawaine, 'I pray you, fair uncle, that I may have paper, pen, and ink, that I may write to Sir Launcelot a cedle with mine own hands.' And then when paper and ink was brought, then Gawaine was set up weakly by King Arthur, for he was shriven a little to-fore; and then he wrote thus, as the French book maketh mention: 'Unto Sir Launcelot, flower of all noble knights that ever I heard of or saw by my days, I, Sir Gawaine, King Lot's son of Orkney, sister's son unto the noble King Arthur, send thee greeting, and let thee have knowledge that the tenth day of May I was smitten upon the old wound that thou gavest me afore the city of Benwick, and through the same wound that thou gavest me I am come to my death-day. And I will that all the world wit, that I, Sir Gawaine, knight of the Table Round, sought my death, and not through thy deserving, but it was mine own seeking; wherefore I beseech thee, Sir Launcelot, to return again unto this realm, and see my tomb, and pray some prayer, more or less, for my soul. And this same day that I wrote this cedle, I was hurt to the death in the same wound, the which I had of thy hand, Sir Launcelot; for of a more nobler man might I not be slain. Also, Sir Launcelot, for all the love that ever was betwixt us, make no tarrying, but come over the sea in all haste, that thou mayest with thy noble knights rescue that noble king that made thee knight, that is my lord Arthur; for he is full straitly bestead with a false traitor, that is my half-brother, Sir Mordred; and he hath let crown him king, and would have wedded my lady Queen Guenever, and so had he done had she not put herself in the Tower of London. And so the tenth day of May last past, my lord Arthur and we all landed upon them at Dover; and there we put that false traitor, Sir Mordred, to flight, and there it misfortuned me to be stricken upon thy stroke. And at the date of this letter was written, but two hours and a half afore my death, written with mine own hand, and so subscribed with part of my heart's blood. And I require thee, most famous knight of the world, that thou wilt see my tomb.' And then Sir Gawaine wept, and King Arthur wept; and then they swooned both. And when they awaked both, the king made Sir Gawaine to receive his Saviour. And then Sir Gawaine prayed the king for to send for Sir Launcelot, and to cherish him above all other knights. And so at the hour of noon

Sir Gawaine yielded up the spirit; and then the king let inter him in a chapel within Dover Castle; and there yet all men may see the skull of him, and the same wound is seen that Sir Launcelot gave him in battle. Then was it told the king that Sir Mordred had pight a new field upon Barham Down. And upon the morn the king rode thither to him, and there was a great battle betwixt them, and much people was slain on both parties; but at the last, Sir Arthur's party stood best, and Sir Mordred and his party fled unto Canterbury.

CHAPTER III

HOW AFTER, SIR GAWAINE'S GHOST APPEARED TO KING ARTHUR, AND WARNED HIM THAT HE SHOULD NOT FIGHT THAT DAY

AND then the king let search all the towns for his knights that were slain, and interred them; and salved them with soft salves that so sore were wounded. Then much people drew unto King Arthur. And then they said that Sir Mordred warred upon King Arthur with wrong. And then King Arthur drew him with his host down by the seaside westward toward Salisbury; and there was a day assigned betwixt King Arthur and Sir Mordred, that they should meet upon a down beside Salisbury, and not far from the seaside; and this day was assigned on a Monday after Trinity Sunday, whereof King Arthur was passing glad, that he might be avenged upon Sir Mordred. Then Sir Mordred araised much people about London, for they of Kent, Southsex, and Surrey, Estsex, and of Southfolk, and of Northfolk, held the most part with Sir Mordred; and many a full noble knight drew unto Sir Mordred and to the king: but they that loved Sir Launcelot drew unto Sir Mordred.

So upon Trinity Sunday at night, King Arthur dreamed a wonderful dream, and that was this: that him seemed he sat upon a chaflet in a chair, and the chair was fast to a wheel, and thereupon sat King Arthur in the richest cloth of gold that might be made; and the king thought there was under him, far from him, an hideous deep black water, and therein were all manner of serpents, and worms, and wild beasts, foul and horrible; and suddenly the king thought the wheel turned up-so-down, and he fell among the serpents and every beast took him by a limb; and then the king cried as he lay on his bed and slept: 'Help!' And then knights, squires, and yeomen awaked the king; and then he was so amazed that he wist not where he was; and then he fell a-slumbering again, not sleeping nor thoroughly waking. So the king seemed verily that there came Sir Gawaine unto him with a number of fair ladies with him. And when King Arthur saw him, then he said: 'Welcome, my sister's son; I weened thou hadst been dead, and now I see thee alive, much am I beholding unto almighty Jesu. O fair nephew and my sister's son, what be these ladies that hither be come with you?' 'Sir,' said Sir Gawaine, 'all these be ladies for whom I have foughten when I was man living, and all these are those that I did battle for in righteous quarrel; and God hath given them that grace at their great prayer, because I did battle for them, that they should bring me hither unto you: thus much hath God given me leave, for to warn you of your death; for an ye fight as to-morn with Sir Mordred, as ye both have assigned, doubt ye not ye must be slain, and the most part of your people on both parties. And for the great grace and goodness that almighty Jesu hath unto you, and for pity of you, and many more other good men there shall be slain, God hath sent me to you of his special grace, to give you warning that in no wise ye do battle as tomorn, but that ye take a treaty for a month day; and proffer you largely, so as to-morn to be put in a delay. For within a month shall come Sir Launcelot with all his noble knights, and rescue you worshipfully, and slay Sir Mordred, and all that ever will hold with him.' Then Sir Gawaine and all the ladies vanished.

And anon the king called upon his knights, squires, and yeomen, and charged them wightly to fetch his noble lords and wise bishops unto him. And when they were come, the king told them his avision, what Sir Gawaine had told him, and warned him that if he fought on the morn he should be slain. Then the king commanded Sir Lucan the Butler, and his brother Sir Bedivere, with two bishops with them, and charged them in any wise, an they might, 'Take a treaty for a month day with Sir Mordred, and spare not, proffer him lands and goods as much as ye think best.' So then they departed, and came to Sir Mordred, where he had a grim host of an hundred thousand men. And there they entreated Sir Mordred long time; and at the last Sir Mordred was agreed for to have Cornwall and Kent, by Arthur's days: after, all England, after the days of King Arthur.

CHAPTER IV

HOW BY MISADVENTURE OF AN ADDER THE BATTLE BEGAN, WHERE MORDRED WAS SLAIN, AND ARTHUR HURT TO THE DEATH

Then were they condescended that King Arthur and Sir Mordred should meet betwixt both their hosts, and everych of them should bring fourteen persons; and they came with this word unto Arthur. Then said he: 'I am glad that this is done:' and so he went into the field. And when Arthur should depart, he warned all his host that an they see any sword drawn: 'Look ye come on fiercely, and slay that traitor, Sir Mordred, for I in no wise trust him.' In like wise Sir Mordred warned his host that: 'An ye see any sword drawn, look that ye come on fiercely, and so slay all that ever before you standeth; for in no wise I will not trust for this treaty, for I know well my father will be avenged on me.' And so they met as their appointment was, and so they were agreed and accorded thoroughly; and wine was fetched, and they drank. Right soon came an adder out of a little heath bush, and it stung a knight on the foot. And when the knight felt him stung, he looked down and saw the adder, and then he drew his sword to slay the adder, and thought of none other harm. And when the host on both parties saw that sword drawn, then they blew beams, trumpets, and horns, and shouted grimly. And so both hosts dressed them together. And King Arthur took his horse, and said: 'Alas, this unhappy day!' and so rode to his party. And Sir Mordred in like wise. And never was there seen a more dolefuller battle in no christian land; for there was but rushing and riding, foining and striking, and many a grim word was there spoken either to other, and many a deadly stroke. But ever King Arthur rode throughout the battle of Sir Mordred many times, and did full nobly as a noble king should, and at all times he fainted never; and Sir Mordred that day put him in devoir, and in great peril. And thus they fought all the long day, and never stinted till the noble knights were laid to the cold earth; and ever they fought still till it was near night, and by that time was there an hundred thousand laid dead upon the down. Then was Arthur wood wroth out of measure, when he saw his people so slain from him.

Then the king looked about him, and then was he ware, of all his host and of all his good knights, were left no more alive but two knights; that one was Sir Lucan the Butler, and his brother Sir Bedivere, and they were full sore wounded. 'Jesu mercy,' said the king, 'where are all my noble knights become? Alas that ever I should see this doleful day, for now,' said Arthur, 'I am come to mine end. But would to God that I wist where were that traitor Sir Mordred, that hath caused all this mischief.' Then was King Arthur ware where Sir Mordred leaned upon his sword among a great heap of dead men. 'Now give me my spear,' said Arthur unto Sir Lucan, 'for yonder I have espied the traitor that all this woe hath wrought.' 'Sir, let him be,' said Sir Lucan, 'for he is unhappy; and if ye pass this unhappy day, ye shall be right well revenged upon him. Good lord, remember ye of your night's dream, and what the spirit of Sir Gawaine told you this night, yet God of his great goodness hath preserved you hitherto. Therefore, for God's sake, my lord, leave off by this, for, blessed be God, ye have won the field, for here we be three alive, and with Sir Mordred is none alive; and if ye leave off now, this wicked day of destiny is past.' 'Tide me death, betide me life,' saith the king, 'now I see him yonder alone he shall never escape mine hands, for at a better avail shall I never have him.' 'God speed you well,' said Sir Bedivere.

Then the king gat his spear in both his hands, and ran toward Sir Mordred, crying: 'Traitor, now is thy death-day come.' And when Sir Mordred heard Sir Arthur, he ran until him with his sword drawn in his hand. And there King Arthur smote Sir Mordred under the shield, with a foin of his spear, throughout the body, more than a fathom. And when Sir Mordred felt that he had his death wound, he thrust himself with the might that he had up to the bur of King Arthur's spear. And right so he smote his father Arthur, with his sword holden in both his hands, on the side of the head, that the sword pierced the helmet and the brain-pan, and therewithal Sir Mordred fell stark dead to the earth; and the noble Arthur fell in a swoon to the earth, and there he swooned ofttimes. And Sir Lucan the Butler, and Sir Bedivere, ofttimes heaved him up. And so weakly they led him betwixt them both, to a little chapel not far from the seaside. And when the king was there, he thought him well eased.

Then heard they people cry in the field. 'Now go, thou, Sir Lucan,' said the king, 'and do me to wit what betokens that noise in the field.' So Sir Lucan departed, for he was grievously wounded in many places. And so as he yede, he saw and hearkened by the moonlight, how that pillers and robbers were come into the field, to pill and to rob many a full noble knight of brooches, and beads, of many a good ring, and of many a rich jewel; and who that were not dead all out, there they slew them for their harness and their riches. When Sir Lucan understood this work, he came to the king as soon as he might, and told him all what he had heard and seen. 'Therefore by my rede,' said Sir Lucan, 'it is best that we bring you to some town.' 'I would it were so,' said the king.

CHAPTER V

HOW KING ARTHUR COMMANDED TO CAST HIS SWORD EXCALIBUR INTO THE WATER, AND HOW HE WAS DELIVERED TO LADIES IN A BARGE

'But I may not stand, mine head works so. Ah, Sir Launcelot,' said King Arthur, 'this day have I sore missed thee: alas, that ever I was against thee, for now have I my death, whereof Sir Gawaine me warned in my dream.' Then Sir Lucan took up the king the one part, and Sir Bedivere the other part, and in the lifting the king swooned; and Sir Lucan fell in a swoon with the lift, that the part of his guts fell out of his body, and therewith the noble knight's heart brast. And when the king awoke, he beheld Sir Lucan, how he lay foaming at the mouth, and part of his guts lay at his feet. 'Alas,' said the king, 'this is to me a full heavy sight, to see this noble duke so die for my sake, for he would have holpen me, that had more need of help than I. Alas, he would not complain him, his heart was so set to help me: now Jesu have mercy upon his soul!' Then Sir Bedivere wept for the death of his brother. 'Leave this mourning and weeping,' said the king, 'for all this will not avail me, for wit thou well, an I might live myself, the death of Sir Lucan would grieve me evermore; but my time hieth fast,' said the king. 'Therefore,' said Arthur unto Sir Bedivere, 'take thou Excalibur, my good sword, and go with it to yonder waterside, and when thou comest there, I charge thee throw my sword in that water, and come again and tell me what thou there seest.' 'My lord,' said Bedivere, 'your commandment shall be done, and lightly bring you word again.'

So Sir Bedivere departed, and by the way he beheld that noble sword, that the pommel and the haft was all of precious stones; and then he said to himself: 'If I throw this rich sword in the water, thereof shall never come good, but harm and loss.' And then Sir Bedivere hid Excalibur under a tree. And so, as soon as he might, he came again unto the king, and said he had been at the water, and had thrown the sword in the water. 'What saw thou there?' said the king. 'Sir,' he said, 'I saw nothing but waves and winds.' 'That is untruly said of thee,' said the king, 'therefore go thou lightly again, and do my commandment; as thou art to me lief and dear, spare not, but throw it in.' Then Sir Bedivere returned again, and took the sword in his hand; and then him thought sin and shame to throw away that noble sword, and so eft he hid the sword, and returned again, and told to the king that he had been at the water, and done his commandment. 'What saw thou there?' said the king. 'Sir,' he said, 'I saw nothing but the waters wap and waves wan.' 'Ah, traitor untrue,' said King Arthur, 'now hast thou betrayed me twice. Who would have weened that, thou that hast been to me so lief and dear? and thou art named a noble knight, and would betray me for the richness of the sword. But now go again lightly, for thy long tarrying putteth me in great jeopardy of my life, for I have taken cold. And but if thou do now as I bid thee, if ever I may see thee, I shall slay thee with mine own hands; for thou wouldst for my rich sword see me dead.'

Then Sir Bedivere departed, and went to the sword, and lightly took it up, and went to the water side; and there he bound the girdle about the hilts, and then he threw the sword as far into the water as he might; and there came an arm and an hand above the water and met it, and caught it, and so shook it thrice and brandished, and then vanished away the hand with the sword in the water. So Sir Bedivere came again to the king, and told him what he saw. 'Alas,' said the king, 'help me hence, for I dread me I have tarried over long.' Then Sir Bedivere took the king upon his back, and so went with him to that water side. And when they were at the water side, even fast by the bank hoved a little barge with many fair ladies in it, and among them all was a queen, and all they had black hoods, and all they wept and shrieked when they saw King Arthur. 'Now put me into the barge,' said the king. And so he did softly; and there received him three queens with great mourning; and so they set them down, and in one of their laps King Arthur laid his head.

And then that queen said: 'Ah, dear brother, why have ye tarried so long from me? alas, this wound on your head hath caught over-much cold.' And so then they rowed from the land, and Sir Bedivere beheld all those ladies go from him. Then Sir Bedivere cried: 'Ah, my lord Arthur, what shall become of me, now ye go from me and leave me here alone among mine enemies?' 'Comfort thyself,' said the king, 'and do as well as thou mayest, for in me is no trust for to trust in; for I will into the vale of Avilion to heal me of my grievous wound: and if thou hear never more of me, pray for my soul.' But ever the queens and ladies wept and shrieked, that it was pity to hear. And as soon as Sir Bedivere had lost the sight of the barge, he wept and wailed, and so took the forest; and so he went all that night, and in the morning he was ware betwixt two holts hoar, of a chapel and an hermitage.

CHAPTER VI

HOW SIR BEDIVERE FOUND HIM ON THE MORROW DEAD IN AN HERMITAGE, AND HOW HE ABODE THERE WITH THE HERMIT

Then was Sir Bedivere glad, and thither he went: and when he came into the chapel, he saw where lay an hermit groveling on all four, there fast by a tomb was new graven. When the hermit saw Sir Bedivere he knew him well, for he was but little to-fore Bishop of Canterbury, that Sir Mordred flemed. 'Sir,' said Bedivere, 'what man is there interred that ye pray so fast for?' 'Fair son,' said the hermit, 'I wot not verily, but by deeming. But this night, at midnight, here came a number of ladies, and brought hither a dead corpse, and prayed me to bury him; and here they offered an hundred tapers, and they gave me an hundred besants.' 'Alas,' said Sir Bedivere, 'that was my lord King Arthur, that here lieth buried in this chapel.' Then Sir Bedivere swooned; and when he awoke he prayed the hermit he might abide with him still there, to live with fasting and prayers. 'For from hence will I never go,' said Sir Bedivere, 'by my will, but all the days of my life here to pray for my lord Arthur.' 'Ye are welcome to me,' said the hermit, 'for I know ye better than ye ween that I do. Ye are the bold Bedivere, and the full noble duke, Sir Lucan the Butler, was your brother.' Then Sir Bedivere told the hermit all as ye have heard to-fore. So there bode Sir Bedivere with the hermit that was to-fore Bishop of Canterbury, and there Sir Bedivere put upon him poor clothes, and served the hermit full lowly in fasting and in prayers.

Thus of Arthur I find never more written in books that be authorized, nor more of the very certainty of his death heard I never read, but thus was he led away in a ship wherein were three queens; that one was King Arthur's sister, Queen Morgan le Fay; the other was the Queen of Northgalis; the third was the Queen of the Waste Lands. Also there was Nimue, the chief lady of the lake, that had wedded Pelleas the good knight; and this lady had done much for King Arthur, for she would never suffer Sir Pelleas to be in no place where he should be in danger of his life; and so he lived to the uttermost of his days with her in great rest. More of the death of King Arthur could I never find, but that ladies brought him to his burials; and such one was buried there, that the hermit bare witness that some time was Bishop of Canterbury, but yet the hermit knew not in certain that he was verily the body of King Arthur: for this tale Sir Bedivere, knight of the Table Round, made it to be written.

CHAPTER VII

OF THE OPINION OF SOME MEN OF THE DEATH OF KING ARTHUR; AND HOW QUEEN GUENEVER MADE HER A NUN IN ALMESBURY

Yet some men say in many parts of England that King Arthur is not dead, but had by the will of our Lord Jesu into another place; and men say that he shall come again, and he shall win the holy cross. I will not say it shall be so, but rather I will say: here in this world he changed his life. But many men say that there is written upon his tomb this verse: *Hic jacet Arthurus, Rex quondam, Rexque futurus* [Here lies Arthur, king once, and king to be]. Thus leave I here Sir Bedivere with the hermit, that dwelled that time in a chapel beside Glastonbury, and there was his hermitage. And so they lived in their prayers, and fastings, and great abstinence.

And when Queen Guenever understood that King Arthur was slain, and all the noble knights, Sir Mordred and all the remnant, then the queen stole away, and five ladies with her, and so she went to Almesbury; and there she let make herself a nun, and ware white clothes and black, and great penance she took, as ever did sinful lady in this land, and never creature could make her merry; but lived in fasting, prayers, and alms-deeds, that all manner of people marveled how virtuously she was changed. Now leave we Queen Guenever in Almesbury, a nun in white clothes and black, and there she was abbess and ruler, as reason would; and turn we from her, and speak we of Sir Launcelot du Lake.

CHAPTER VIII

HOW WHEN SIR LAUNCELOT HEARD OF THE DEATH OF KING ARTHUR, AND OF SIR GAWAINE, AND OTHER MATTERS, HE CAME INTO ENGLAND

AND when he heard in his country that Sir Mordred was crowned king in England, and made war against King Arthur, his own father, and would let him to land in his own land; also it was told Sir Launcelot how that Sir Mordred had laid siege about the Tower of London, because the queen would not wed him; then was Sir Launcelot wroth out of measure, and said to his kinsmen: 'Alas, that double traitor Sir Mordred, now me repenteth that ever he escaped my hands, for much shame hath he done unto my lord Arthur; for all I feel by the doleful letter that my lord Sir Gawaine sent me, on whose soul Jesu have mercy, that my lord Arthur is full hard bestead. Alas,' said Sir Launcelot, 'that ever I should live to hear that most noble king that made me knight thus to be overset with his subject in his own realm. And this doleful letter that my lord, Sir Gawaine, hath sent me afore his death, praying me to see his tomb, wit you well his doleful words shall never go from mine heart, for he was a full noble knight as ever was born; and in an unhappy hour was I born that ever I should have that unhap to slay first Sir Gawaine, Sir Gaheris the good knight, and mine own friend Sir Gareth, that full noble knight. Alas, I may say I am unhappy,' said Sir Launcelot, 'that ever I should do thus unhappily', and, 'alas, yet might I never have hap to slay that traitor, Sir Mordred.' 'Leave your complaints,' said Sir Bors, 'and first revenge you of the death of Sir Gawaine; and it will be well done that ye see Sir Gawaine's tomb, and secondly that ye revenge my lord Arthur, and my lady, Queen Guenever.' 'I thank you,' said Sir Launcelot, 'for ever ye will my worship.' Then they made them ready in all the haste that might be, with ships and galleys, with Sir Launcelot and his host to pass into England. And so he passed over the sea till he came to Dover, and there he landed with seven kings, and the number was hideous to behold. Then Sir Launcelot spered of men of Dover where was King Arthur become. Then the people told him how that he was slain, and Sir Mordred and an hundred thousand died on a day; and how Sir Mordred gave King Arthur there the first battle at his landing, and there was good Sir Gawaine slain; and on the morn Sir Mordred fought with the king upon Barham Down, and there the king put Sir Mordred to the worse. 'Alas,' said Sir Launcelot, 'this is the heaviest tidings that ever came to me. Now, fair sirs,' said Sir Launcelot, 'shew me the tomb of Sir Gawaine.' And then certain people of the town brought him into the Castle of Dover, and shewed him the tomb. Then Sir Launcelot kneeled down and wept, and prayed heartily for his soul. And that night he made a dole, and all they that would come had as much flesh, fish, wine and ale, and every man and woman had twelve pence, come who would. Thus with his own hand dealt he this money, in a mourning gown; and ever he wept, and prayed them to pray for the soul of Sir Gawaine. And on the morn all the priests and clerks that might be gotten in the country were there, and sang mass of *Requiem;* and there offered first Sir Launcelot, and he offered an hundred pound; and then the seven kings offered forty pound apiece; and also there was a thousand knights, and each of them offered a pound; and the offering dured from morn till night, and Sir Launcelot lay two nights on his tomb in prayers and weeping. Then on the third day Sir Launcelot called the kings, dukes, earls, barons, and knights, and said thus: 'My fair lords, I thank you all of your coming into this country with me, but we came too late, and that shall repent me while I live, but against death may no man rebel. But sithen it is so,' said Sir Launcelot, 'I will myself ride and seek my lady, Queen Guenever, for as I hear say she hath had great pain and much disease; and I heard say that she is fled into the West. Therefore ye all shall abide me here, and but if I come again within fifteen days, then take your ships and your fellowship, and depart into your country, for I will do as I say to you.'

CHAPTER IX

HOW SIR LAUNCELOT DEPARTED TO SEEK THE QUEEN GUENEVER, AND HOW HE FOUND HER AT ALMESBURY

THEN came Sir Bors de Ganis, and said: 'My lord, Sir Launcelot, what think ye for to do, now to ride in this realm? wit ye well ye shall find few friends.' 'Be as be may,' said Sir Launcelot, 'keep you still here, for I will forth on my journey, and no man nor child shall go with me.' So it was no boot to strive, but he departed and rode westerly, and there he sought a seven or eight days; and at the last he came to a nunnery, and then was Queen Guenever ware of Sir Launcelot as he walked in the cloister. And when she saw him there she swooned thrice, that all the ladies and gentlewomen had work enough to hold the queen up. So when she might speak, she called ladies and gentlewomen to her, and said: 'Ye marvel, fair ladies, why I make this fare. Truly,' she said, 'it is for the sight of yonder knight that yonder standeth; wherefore I pray you all call him to me.' When Sir Launcelot was brought to her, then she said to all the ladies: 'Through this man and me hath all this war been wrought, and the death of the most noblest knights of the world; for through our love that we have loved together is my most noble lord slain. Therefore, Sir Launcelot, wit thou well I am set in such a plight to get my soul-heal; and yet I trust through God's grace that after my death to have a sight of the blessed face of Christ, and at doomsday to sit on his right side, for as sinful as ever I was are saints in heaven. Therefore, Sir Launcelot, I require thee and beseech thee heartily, for all the love that ever was betwixt us, that thou never see me more in the visage; and I command thee, on God's behalf, that thou forsake my company, and to thy kingdom thou turn again, and keep well thy realm from war and wrack; for as well as I have loved thee, mine heart will not serve me to see thee, for through thee and me is the flower of kings and knights destroyed; therefore, Sir Launcelot, go to thy realm, and there take thee a wife, and live with her with joy and bliss; and I pray thee heartily, pray for me to our Lord that I may amend my misliving.' 'Now, sweet madam,' said Sir Launcelot, 'would ye that I should now return again unto my country, and there to wed a lady? Nay, madam, wit you well that shall I never do, for I shall never be so false to you of that I have promised; but the same destiny that ye have taken you to, I will take me unto, for to please Jesu, and ever for you I cast me specially to pray.' 'If thou wilt do so,' said the queen, 'hold thy promise, but I may never believe but that thou wilt turn to the world again.' 'Well, madam,' said he, 'ye say as pleaseth you, yet wist you me never false of my promise, and God defend but I should forsake the world as ye have done. For in the quest of the Sangreal I had forsaken the vanities of the world had not your lord been. And if I had done so at that time, with my heart, will, and thought, I had passed all the knights that were in the Sangreal except Sir Galahad, my son. And therefore, lady, sithen ye have taken you to perfection, I must needs take me to perfection, of right. For I take record of God, in you I have had mine earthly joy; and if I had found you now so disposed, I had cast to have had you into mine own realm.

CHAPTER X

HOW SIR LAUNCELOT CAME TO THE HERMITAGE WHERE THE ARCHBISHOP OF CANTERBURY WAS, AND HOW HE TOOK THE HABIT ON HIM

'BUT sithen I find you thus disposed, I ensure you faithfully, I will ever take me to penance, and pray while my life lasteth, if I may find any hermit, either gray or white, that will receive me. Wherefore, madam, I pray you kiss me and never no more.' 'Nay,' said the queen, 'that shall I never do, but abstain you from such works;' and they departed. But there was never so hard an hearted man but he would have wept to see the dolor that they made; for there was lamentation as they had been stung with spears; and many times they swooned, and the ladies bare the queen to her chamber.

And Sir Launcelot awoke, and went and took his horse, and rode all that day and all night in a forest, weeping. And at the last he was ware of an hermitage and a chapel stood betwixt two cliffs; and then he heard a little bell ring to mass, and thither he rode and alighted, and tied his horse to the gate, and heard mass. And he that sang mass was the Bishop of Canterbury. Both the bishop and Sir Bedivere knew Sir Launcelot, and they spake together after mass. But when Sir Bedivere had told his tale all whole, Sir Launcelot's heart almost brast for sorrow, and Sir Launcelot threw his arms abroad, and said: 'Alas, who may trust this world.' And then he kneeled down on his knee, and prayed the bishop to shrive him and assoil him. And then he besought the bishop that he might be his brother. Then the bishop said: 'I will gladly'; and there he put an habit upon Sir Launcelot, and there he served God day and night with prayers and fastings.

Thus the great host abode at Dover. And then Sir Lionel took fifteen lords with him, and rode to London to seek Sir Launcelot; and there Sir Lionel was slain and many of his lords. Then Sir Bors de Ganis made the great host for to go home again; and Sir Bors, Sir Ector de Maris, Sir Blamore, Sir Bleoberis, with more other of Sir Launcelot's kin, took on them to ride all England overthwart and endlong, to seek Sir Launcelot. So Sir Bors by fortune rode so long till he came to the same chapel where Sir Launcelot was; and so Sir Bors heard a little bell knell, that rang to mass; and there he alighted and heard mass. And when mass was done, the bishop, Sir Launcelot, and Sir Bedivere, came to Sir Bors. And when Sir Bors saw Sir Launcelot in that manner clothing, then he prayed the Bishop that he might be in the same suit. And so there was an habit put upon him, and there he lived in prayers and fasting. And within half a year, there was come Sir Galihud, Sir Galihodin, Sir Blamore, Sir Bleoberis, Sir Villiars, Sir Clarras, and Sir Gahalantine. So all these seven noble knights there abode still. And when they saw Sir Launcelot had taken him to such perfection, they had no lust to depart, but took such an habit as he had. Thus they endured in great penance six years; and then Sir Launcelot took the habit of priesthood of the bishop, and a twelvemonth he sang mass. And there was none of these other knights but they read in books, and holp for to sing mass, and rang bells, and did bodily all manner of service. And so their horses went where they would, for they took no regard of no worldly riches. For when they saw Sir Launcelot endure such penance, in prayers, and fastings, they took no force what pain they endured, for to see the noblest knight of the world take such abstinence that he waxed full lean. And thus upon a night, there came a vision to Sir Launcelot, and charged him, in remission of his sins, to haste him unto Almesbury: 'And by then thou come there, thou shalt find Queen Guenever dead. And therefore take thy fellows with thee, and purvey them of an horse bier, and fetch thou the corpse of her, and bury her by her husband, the noble King Arthur.' So this avision came to Sir Launcelot thrice in one night.

CHAPTER XI

HOW SIR LAUNCELOT WENT WITH HIS SEVEN FELLOWS TO ALMESBURY, AND FOUND THERE QUEEN GUENEVER DEAD, WHOM THEY BROUGHT TO GLASTONBURY

THEN Sir Launcelot rose up or day, and told the hermit. 'It were well done,' said the hermit, 'that ye made you ready, and that you disobey not the avision.' Then Sir Launcelot took his seven fellows with him, and on foot they yede from Glastonbury to Almesbury, the which is little more than thirty mile. And thither they came within two days, for they were weak and feeble to go. And when Sir Launcelot was come to Almesbury within the nunnery, Queen Guenever died but half an hour afore. And the ladies told Sir Launcelot that Queen Guenever told them all or she passed, that Sir Launcelot had been priest near a twelvemonth, 'And hither he cometh as fast as he may to fetch my corpse; and beside my lord, King Arthur, he shall bury me.' Wherefore the queen said in hearing of them all: 'I beseech Almighty God that I may never have power to see Sir Launcelot with my worldly eyes.' 'And thus,' said all the ladies, 'was ever her prayer these two days, till she was dead.' Then Sir Launcelot saw her visage, but he wept not greatly, but sighed. And so he did all the observance of the service himself, both the *Dirige*, and on the morn he sang mass. And there was ordained an horse bier; and so with an hundred torches ever brenning about the corpse of the queen, and ever Sir Launcelot with his seven fellows went about the horse bier, singing and reading many an holy orison, and frankincense upon the corpse incensed. Thus Sir Launcelot and his seven fellows went on foot from Almesbury unto Glastonbury. And when they were come to the chapel and the hermitage, there she had a *Dirige*, with great devotion. And on the morn, the hermit that sometime was Bishop of Canterbury sang the mass of *Requiem* with great devotion. And Sir Launcelot was the first that offered, and then also his seven fellows. And then she was wrapped in cered cloth of Raines, from the top to the toe, in thirtyfold; and after she was put in a web of lead, and then in a coffin of marble. And when she was put in the earth, Sir Launcelot swooned, and lay long still, while the hermit came and awaked him, and said: 'Ye be to blame, for ye displease God with such manner of sorrow-making.' 'Truly,' said Sir Launcelot, 'I trust I do not displease God, for he knoweth mine intent. For my sorrow was not, nor is not, for any rejoicing of sin, but my sorrow may never have end. For when I remember of her beauty, and of her noblesse, that was both with her king and with her, so when I saw his corpse and her corpse so lie together, truly mine heart would not serve to sustain my careful body. Also when I remember me how by my default, mine orgulity, and my pride, that they were both laid full low, that were peerless that ever was living of christian people, wit you well,' said Sir Launcelot, 'this remembered, of their kindness and mine unkindness, sank so to mine heart, that I might not sustain myself.' So the French book maketh mention.

CHAPTER XII

HOW SIR LAUNCELOT BEGAN TO SICKEN, AND AFTER DIED, WHOSE BODY WAS BORNE TO JOYOUS GARD FOR TO BE BURIED

THEN Sir Launcelot never after ate but little meat, ne drank, till he was dead. For then he sickened more and more, and dried, and dwined away. For the Bishop nor none of his fellows might not make him to eat, and little he drank, that he was waxen by a cubit shorter than he was, that the people could not know him. For evermore, day and night, he prayed, but sometime he slumbered a broken sleep; ever he was lying groveling on the tomb of King Arthur and Queen Guenever. And there was no comfort that the Bishop, nor Sir Bors, nor none of his fellows, could make him, it availed not. So within six weeks after, Sir Launcelot fell sick, and lay in his bed; and then he sent for the Bishop that there was hermit, and all his true fellows. Then Sir Launcelot said with dreary steven: 'Sir Bishop, I pray you give to me all my rites that longeth to a christian man.' 'It shall not need you,' said the hermit and all his fellows, 'it is but heaviness of your blood; ye shall be well mended by the grace of God to-morn.' 'My fair lords,' said Sir Launcelot, 'wit you well my careful body will into the earth, I have warning more than now I will say; therefore give me my rites.' So when he was houseled and anealed, and had all that a christian man ought to have, he prayed the bishop that his fellows might bear his body to Joyous Gard. Some men say it was Alnwick, and some men say it was Bamborough. 'Howbeit,' said Sir Launcelot, 'me repenteth sore, but I made mine avow sometime, that in Joyous Gard I would be buried. And because of breaking of mine avow, I pray you all, lead me thither.' Then there was weeping and wringing of hands among his fellows.

So at a season of the night they all went to their beds, for they all lay in one chamber. And so after midnight, against day, the Bishop [that] then was hermit, as he lay in his bed asleep, he fell upon a great laughter. And therewith all the fellowship awoke, and came to the Bishop, and asked him what he ailed. 'Ah, Jesu mercy,' said the bishop, 'why did ye awake me? I was never in all my life so merry and so well at ease.' 'Wherefore?' said Sir Bors. 'Truly,' said the Bishop, 'here was Sir Launcelot with me with more angels than ever I saw men in one day. And I saw the angels heave up Sir Launcelot unto heaven, and the gates of heaven opened against him.' 'It is but dretching of swevens,' said Sir Bors, 'for I doubt not Sir Launcelot aileth nothing but good.' 'It may well be,' said the Bishop; 'go ye to his bed, and then shall ye prove the sooth.' So when Sir Bors and his fellows came to his bed, they found him stark dead, and he lay as he had smiled, and the sweetest savor about him that ever they felt.

Then was there weeping and wringing of hands, and the greatest dole they made that ever made men. And on the morn the Bishop did his mass of *Requiem;* and after, the Bishop and all the nine knights put Sir Launcelot in the same horse bier that Queen Guenever was laid in to-fore that she was buried. And so the Bishop and they all together went with the body of Sir Launcelot daily, till they came to Joyous Gard; and ever they had an hundred torches brenning about him. And so within fifteen days they came to Joyous Gard. And there they laid his corpse in the body of the quire, and sang and read many psalters and prayers over him and about him. And ever his visage was laid open and naked, that all folks might behold him. For such was the custom in those days, that all men of worship should so lie with open visage till that they were buried. And right thus as they were at their service, there came Sir Ector de Maris, that had seven years sought all England, Scotland, and Wales, seeking his brother, Sir Launcelot.

CHAPTER XIII

HOW SIR ECTOR FOUND SIR LAUNCELOT HIS BROTHER DEAD, AND HOW CONSTANTINE REIGNED NEXT AFTER ARTHUR; AND OF THE END OF THIS BOOK

AND when Sir Ector heard such noise and light in the quire of Joyous Gard, he alighted and put his horse from him, and came into the quire, and there he saw men sing and weep. And all they knew Sir Ector, but he knew not them. Then went Sir Bors unto Sir Ector, and told him how there lay his brother, Sir Launcelot, dead; and then Sir Ector threw his shield, sword, and helm from him. And when he beheld Sir Launcelot's visage, he fell down in a swoon. And when he waked, it were hard any tongue to tell the doleful complaints that he made for his brother. 'Ah Launcelot,' he said, 'thou were head of all Christian knights, and now I dare say,' said Sir Ector, 'thou Sir Launcelot, there thou liest, that thou were never matched of earthly knight's hand. And thou were the courteoust knight that ever bare shield. And thou were the truest friend to thy lover that ever bestrad horse. And thou were the truest lover of a sinful man that ever loved woman. And thou were the kindest man that ever struck with sword. And thou were the goodliest person that ever came among press of knights. And thou was the meekest man and the gentlest that ever ate in hall among ladies. And thou were the sternest knight to thy mortal foe that ever put spear in the rest.' Then there was weeping and dolor out of measure.

Thus they kept Sir Launcelot's corpse aloft fifteen days, and then they buried it with great devotion. And then at leisure they went all with the Bishop of Canterbury to his hermitage, and there they were together more than a month. Then Sir Constantine, that was Sir Cador's son of Cornwall, was chosen king of England. And he was a full noble knight, and worshipfully he ruled this realm. And then this King Constantine sent for the Bishop of Canterbury, for he heard say where he was. And so he was restored unto his bishopric, and left that hermitage. And Sir Bedivere was there ever still hermit to his life's end. Then Sir Bors de Ganis, Sir Ector de Maris, Sir Gahalantine, Sir Galihud, Sir Galihodin, Sir Blamore, Sir Bleoberis, Sir Villiars le Valiant, Sir Clarrus of Clermont, all these knights drew them to their countries. Howbeit King Constantine would have had them with him, but they would not abide in this realm. And there they all lived in their countries as holy men. And some English books make mention that they went never out of England after the death of Sir Launcelot, but that was but favor of makers. For the French book maketh mention, and is authorized, that Sir Bors, Sir Ector, Sir Blamore, and Sir Bleoberis, went into the Holy Land thereas Jesu Christ was quick and dead, and anon as they had stablished their lands. For the book saith, so Sir Launcelot commanded them for to do, or ever he passed out of this world. And these four knights did many battles upon the miscreants or Turks. And there they died upon a Good Friday for God's sake.

Here is the end of the book of King Arthur, and of his noble knights of the Round Table, that when they were whole together there was ever an hundred and forty. And here is the end of the death of Arthur. I pray you all, gentlemen and gentlewomen that readeth this book of Arthur and his knights, from the beginning to the ending, pray for me while I am alive, that God send me good deliverance, and when I am dead, I pray you all pray for my soul. For this book was ended the ninth year of the reign of King Edward the Fourth, by Sir Thomas Maleore, knight, as Jesu help him for his great might, as he is the servant of Jesu both day and night.

Thus endeth this noble and joyous book entitled Le Morte Darthur. Notwithstanding it treateth of the birth, life, and acts of the said King Arthur of his noble knights of the Round Table, their marvelous enquests and adventures, the achieving of the Sangreal, and in the end the dolorous death and departing out of this world of them all. Which book was reduced into English by Sir Thomas Malory, knight, as afore is said, and by me divided into twenty-one books, chaptered and enprinted, and finished in the abbey, Westminster, the last day of July, the year of our Lord MCCCCLXXXV.

Caxton me fieri fecit.

THE NUTBROWNE MAIDE (c.1500)

This charming anonymous lyric, worthy in itself of a conspicuous place in any collection of English poetry, serves significantly as a link between an earlier and a later period. In its suggestion of the 'débat' form, it recalls the Middle Ages; in versification and sentiment, it is definitely modern.

THE NUTBROWNE MAIDE

[HE]

Be it right or wrong, these men among on women do complaine,
Affermyng this, how that it is a labour spent in vaine
To love them wele, for never a dele they love a man agayne;
For lete a man do what he can ther favour to attayne,
Yet yf a newe do them pursue, ther furst trew lover than   5
Laboureth for nought, and from her thought he is a bannished man.

[SHE]

I say not nay but that all day it is bothe writ and sayde
That woman's fayth is, as who sayth, all utterly decayed;
But nevertheless, right good witnes in this case might be layde,
That they love trewe and contynew,—recorde the Nutbrowne Maide,   10
Whiche from her love, whan, her to prove, he cam to make his mone,
Wolde not departe, for in her herte she lovyd but hym allone.

[HE]

Than betwene us lete us discusse what was all the maner
Betwene them too, we wyl also telle all the peyne and fere
That she was in. Now I begynne, see that ye me answere.   15
Wherefore [all] ye that present be, I pray you geve an eare.
I am a knyght, I cum be nyght, as secret as I can,
Sayng, 'Alas! thus stondyth the case: I am a bannisshed man.'

[SHE]

And I your wylle for to fulfylle, in this wyl not refuse,
Trusting to shewe, in wordis fewe, that men have an ille use,   20
To ther owne shame wymen to blame, and causeles them accuse.
Therfore to you I answere now, alle wymen to excuse:
'Myn own hert dere, with you what chiere? I prey you telle anoon;
For in my mynde of all mankynde I love but you allon.'

[HE]

It stondith so, a deed is do wherof moche harme shal growe.   25
My destenye is for to dey a shamful dethe, I trowe,
Or ellis to flee; the ton must bee, none other wey I knowe
But to withdrawe as an outlaw and take me to my bowe.
Wherfore, adew, my owne hert trewe, none other red I can;
For I muste to the grene wode goo, alone, a bannysshed man.   30

[SHE]

O Lorde, what is this worldis blisse, that chaungeth as the mone?
My somers day in lusty May is derked before the none.
I here you saye 'farwel;' nay, nay, we departe not soo sone.
Why say ye so? wheder wyl ye goo? alas! what have ye done?
Alle my welfare to sorow and care shulde chaunge if ye were gon;   35
For in my mynde of all mankynde I love but you alone.

101

[HE]

I can beleve it shal you greve, and somwhat you distrayne;
But aftyrwarde your paynes harde within a day or tweyne
Shal sone aslake, and ye shal take confort to you agayne.
Why shuld ye nought? for to take thought, your labur were in vayne.   40
And thus I do, and pray you, too, as hertely as I can;
For I muste too the grene wode goo, alone, a bannysshed man.

[SHE]

Now syth that ye have shewed to me the secret of your mynde,
I shal be playne to you agayne, lyke as ye shal me fynde;
Syth it is so that ye wyll goo, I wol not leve behynde;   45
Shal never be sayd the Nutbrowne Mayd was to her love unkind.
Make you redy, for soo am I, all though it were anoon;
For in my mynde of all mankynde I love but you alone.

[HE]

Yet I you rede to take good hede, what men wyl thinke and sey;
Of yonge and olde it shal be told that ye be gone away,   50
Your wanton wylle for to fulfylle, in grene wood you to play,
And that ye myght from your delyte noo lenger make delay.
Rather than ye shuld thus for me be called an ylle woman,
Yet wolde I to the grenewodde goo, alone, a banysshed man.

[SHE]

Though it be songe of olde and yonge that I shuld be to blame,   55
Theirs be the charge that speke so large in hurting of my name;
For I wyl prove that feythful love it is devoyd of shame,
In your distresse and hevynesse to parte wyth you the same;
And sure all thoo that doo not so, trewe lovers ar they noon;
But in my mynde of all mankynde I love but you alone.   60

[HE]

I counsel yow, remembre how it is noo maydens lawe
Nothing to dought, but to renne out to wod with an outlawe;
For ye must there in your hande bere a bowe to bere and drawe,
And as a theef thus must ye lyeve ever in drede and awe,
By whiche to yow gret harme myght grow; yet had I lever than   65
That I had too the grenewod goo, alone, a banysshyd man.

[SHE]

I thinke not nay, but as ye saye, it is noo maydens lore;
But love may make me for your sake, as ye have said before,
To com on fote, to hunte and shote to gete us mete and store;
For soo that I your company may have, I aske noo more;   70
From whiche to parte, it makith myn herte as colde as ony ston;
For in my mynde of all mankynde I love but you alone.

[HE]

For an outlawe this is the lawe, that men hym take and binde,
Wythout pytee hangèd to bee, and waver wyth the wynde.
Yf I had neede, as God forbede, what rescous coude ye finde?   75
For sothe I trowe, you and your bowe shuld drawe for fere behynde;
And noo merveyle, for lytel avayle were in your councel than;
Wherfore I too the woode wyl goo, alone, a banysshed man.

[SHE]

Ful wel knowe ye that wymen bee ful febyl for to fyght;
Noo womanhed is it indeede to bee bolde as a knight;   80
Yet in suche fere yf that ye were, amonge enemys day and nyght,
I wolde wythstonde, with bowe in hande, to greeve them as I myght,
And you to save, as wymen have, from deth many one;
For in my mynde of all mankynde I love but you alone.

[HE]

Yet take good hede, for ever I drede that ye coude not sustein   85
The thorney wayes, the depe valeis, the snowe, the frost, the reyn,
The colde, the hete; for, drye or wete, we must lodge on the playn,
And, us aboove, noon other rove but a brake, bussh, or twayne;

Whiche sone shulde greve you, I beleve, and
    ye wolde gladly than
That I had too the grenewode goo, alone, a
    banysshyd man.   90

[SHE]

Syth I have here been partynere with you of
    joy and blysse,
I muste also parte of your woo endure, as
    reason is;
Yet am I sure of oo plesure, and shortly it is
    this.
That where ye bee, me semeth, perdé, I coude
    not fare amysse.
Wythout more speche, I you beseche that we
    were soon agone;   95
For in my mynde of all mankynde I love but
    you alone.

[HE]

Yf ye goo thedyr, ye must consider, whan ye
    have lust to dyne,
Ther shel no mete be fore to gete, nor drinke,
    bere, ale, ne wine,
Ne shetis clene to lye betwene, made of thred
    and twyne,
Noon other house but levys and bowes, to
    kever your hed and myn.   100
Loo! myn herte swete, this ylle dyet shuld
    make you pale and wan;
Wherfore I to the wood wyl goo, alone, a
    banysshid man.

[SHE]

Amonge the wylde dere suche an archier as men
    say that ye bee
Ne may not fayle of good vitayle, where is so
    grete plenté;
And watir cleere of the ryvere shal be ful swete
    to me,   105
Wyth whiche in hele I shal right wele endure,
    as ye shal see;
And, er we goo, a bed or too I can provide
    anoon;
For in my mynde of all mankynde I love but
    you alone.

[HE]

Loo! yet before ye must doo more, yf ye wyl
    goo with me,—
As cutte your here up by your ere, your kirtel
    by the knee,   110
Wyth bowe in hande, for to withstonde your
    enmys, yf nede be,
And this same nyght before daylight to wood-
    ward wyl I flee;
And if ye wyl all this fulfylle, doo it shortely
    as ye can;
Ellis wil I to the grenewode goo, alone, a
    banysshyd man.

[SHE]

I shal, as now, do more for you than longeth
    to womanhede,   115
To short my here, a bowe to bere to shote in
    tyme of nede.
O my swete moder, before all other, for you have
    I most drede;
But now adiew! I must ensue, where fortune
    duth me leede:
All this make ye; now lete us flee, the day cums
    fast upon;
For in my mynde of all mankynde I love but
    you alone.   120

[HE]

Nay, nay, not soo, ye shal not goo! and I shal
    telle you why:
Your appetyte is to be lyght of love, I wele
    aspie;
For right as ye have sayd to me, in lykewise
    hardely
Ye wolde answere, whosoever it were, in way of
    company.
It is sayd of olde, 'sone hote, sone colde,' and
    so is a woman;   125
Wherfore I too the woode wyl goo, alone a
    banysshid man.

[SHE]

Yef ye take hede, yet is noo nede, suche wordis
    to say bee me,
For oft ye preyd, and longe assayed, or I you
    lovid, perdé!
And though that I of auncestry a barons
    doughter bee,
Yet have you proved how I you loved, a squyer
    of lowe degree,   130
And ever shal, what so befalle, to dey therfore
    anoon;
For in my mynde of all mankynde I love but
    you alone.

[HE]

A barons childe to be begyled, it were a curssèd
    dede,
To be felaw with an outlawe, almyghty God
    forbede!
Yet bettyr were the power squyer alone to
    forest yede,   135
Than ye shal saye, another day, that be my
    wyked dede
Ye were betrayed; wherfore, good maide, the
    best red that I can,
Is that I too the greenewode goo, alone, a
    banysshed man.

[SHE]

Whatsoever befalle, I never shal of this thing
    you upbraid;
But yf ye goo and leve me so, than have ye me
    betraied.   140

Remembre you wele how that ye dele, for yf
    ye, as ye sayde,
Be so unkynde to leve behynd your love, the
    Notbrowne Maide,
Trust me truly that I shal dey sone after ye be
    gone;
For in my mynde of all mankynde I love but
    you alone.

[HE]

Yef that ye went, ye shulde repent, for in the
    forest now   145
I have purveid me of a maide, whom I love more
    than you,—
Another fayrer than ever ye were, I dare it wel
    avowe;
And of you bothe, eche shulde be wrothe with
    other, as I trowe.
It were myn ease to lyve in pease; so wyl I, yf
    I can;
Wherfore I to the wode wyl goo, alone, a
    banysshid man.   150

[SHE]

Though in the wood I undirstode ye had a
    paramour,
All this may nought remeve my thought, but
    that I wil be your;
And she shal fynde me soft and kynde, and
    curteis every our,
Glad to fulfylle all that she wylle commaunde
    me, to my power;
For had ye, loo! an hundred moo, yet wolde
    I be that one;   155
For in my mynde of all mankynde I love but
    you alone.

[HE]

Myn oune dere love, I see the prove that ye
    be kynde and trewe;
Of mayde and wyf, in all my lyf, the best that
    ever I knewe!
Be mery and glad, be no more sad, the case is
    chaungèd newe;
For it were ruthe that for your trouth you
    shuld have cause to rewe.   160
Be not dismayed, whatsoever I sayd, to you
    whan I began,
I wyl not too the grenewod goo, I am noo
    banysshyd man.

[SHE]

Theis tidingis be more glad to me than to be
    made a quene,
Yf I were sure they shuld endure; but it is
    often seen,
When men wyl breke promyse, they speke the
    wordis on the splene.   165
Ye shape some wyle, me to begyle, and stele
    fro me, I wene.
Then were the case wurs than it was, and I
    more woo-begone;
For in my mynde of all mankynde I love but
    you alone.

[HE]

Ye shall not nede further to drede, I wyl not
    disparage
You, God defende, sith you descende of so
    grete a lynage.   170
Nou understonde, to Westmerlande, whiche is
    my herytage,
I wyle you bringe, and wyth a rynge, be wey
    of maryage,
I wyl you take, and lady make, as shortly as I
    can;
Thus have ye wone an erles son, and not a
    banysshyd man.

Here may ye see that wymen be in love meke,
    kinde, and stable,   175
Late never man repreve them than, or calle them
    variable,
But rather prey God that we may to them be con-
    fortable,
Whiche somtyme provyth suche as he loveth, yf
    they be charitable.
For sith men wolde that wymen shode be meke
    to them echeon,
Moche more ought they to God obey, and serve
    but hym alone.   180

ENGLISH AND SCOTTISH POPULAR BALLADS

The popular ballad is a short, anonymous poem, in simple meter, recounting a simple narrative, and adapted, originally, for singing to a recurrent melody. The true ballad usually shows no traces of individual authorship: the story is told impersonally, without a suggestion of sentiment or reflection from the storyteller. Ballads probably originated often in a naïve, homogeneous community under such circumstances that they might fairly be said to have been composed not by any single person, but by the community as a whole. Such compositions may be thought of as beginning in a choral throng, in which one person after another contributes an improvised verse, couplet, or short stanza to a simple but gradually increasing story. Under such conditions the story grows by 'incremental repetition'; that is, in making his contribution, each singer in succession both repeats a part of the preceding utterance, and adds to the story a new incident, or element, of his own. After adding their parts to the narrative, the successive singers disappear as individuals, leaving as a result a simple narrative poem which is thenceforth regarded as the product not of one person, or of particular persons, but of the whole gathering. Although such a process of composition can be fairly inferred, no extant ballad shows so simple a form as would result immediately from such communal authorship. Since all true ballads are transmitted orally, variations in style and alterations of the narrative are inevitable; and in the recorded forms of some ballads the hand of a dominating and cultivated individual may be surmised. A large proportion of the ballads actually preserved do, however, bear marks of their ultimate communal origin; and all ballads worthy of the name are the genuine possession of a body of the folk. The circumstances of their origin and transmission seem to explain the chief formal characteristics of popular ballads: refrain, repetition, and dialogue.

From the fact that ballads are transmitted orally, and are committed to writing only by happy accident, the body of preserved and published ballads of any people will represent, inevitably, only a small proportion of the whole sum of such poems produced during the history of that people. The English language, including Scottish, is fortunate in the preservation of at least three hundred and six ballads. Although the greater part of these are recorded only in comparatively modern documents, many of the stories themselves are of very ancient origin. The oldest English ballad completely recorded dates from the thirteenth century. The most important of ballad manuscripts, the so-called Percy Folio, was written about the year 1650. Only some eleven of our ballads are preserved in documents older than the seventeenth century.

ROBIN HOOD AND GUY OF GISBORNE

1. When shawes beene sheene, and shradds full fayre,
    And leeves both large and longe,
  It is merry, walking in the fayre fforrest,
    To heare the small birds songe.

2. The woodweele sang, and wold not cease, 5
    Amongst the leaves a lyne;
  And it is by two wight yeomen.
    By deare God, that I meane.

* * *

3. 'Me thought they did mee beate and binde,
    And tooke my bowe mee froe; 10
  If I bee Robin alive in this lande,
    I'le be wrocken on both them towe.'

4. 'Sweavens are swift, master,' quoth John,
    'As the wind that blowes ore a hill;
  Ffor if itt be never soe lowde this night, 15
    To-morrow it may be still.'

5. 'Buske yee, bowne yee, my merry men all,
    Ffor John shall goe with mee;
  For I'le goe seeke yond wight yeomen
    In greenwood where they bee.' 20

6. They cast on their gowne of greene,
    A shooting gone are they,
  Untill they came to the merry greenwood,
    Where they had gladdest bee;
  There were they ware of a wight yeoman,
    His body leaned to a tree. 26

7. A sword and a dagger he wore by his side,
    Had beene many a mans bane,
  And he was cladd in his capull-hyde,
    Topp, and tayle, and mayne. 30

8. 'Stand you still, master,' quoth Litle John,
    'Under this trusty tree,
  And I will goe to yond wight yeoman,
    To know his meaning trulye.

9. 'A, John, by me thou setts noe store, 35
   And that's a ffarley thinge;
   How offt send I my men beffore,
   And tarry my-selfe behinde?

10. 'It is noe cunning a knave to ken,
    And a man but heare him speake; 40
    And itt were not for bursting of my bowe,
    John, I wold thy head breake.'

11. But often words they breeden bale;
    That parted Robin and John.
    John is gone to Barnesdale, 45
    The gates he knowes eche one.

12. And when hee came to Barnesdale,
    Great heavinesse there hee hadd;
    He ffound two of his fellowes
    Were slaine both in a slade, 50

13. And Scarlett a-ffoote flyinge was,
    Over stockes and stone,
    For the sheriffe with seven score men
    Fast after him is gone.

14. 'Yett one shoote I'le shoote,' sayes Litle John, 55
    'With Crist his might and mayne;
    I'le make yond fellow that flyes soe fast
    To be both glad and ffaine.'

15. John bent up a good veiwe bow,
    And ffetteled him to shoote; 60
    The bow was made of a tender boughe,
    And fell downe to his foote.

16. 'Woe worth thee, wicked wood,' sayd Litle John,
    'That ere thou grew on a tree!
    Ffor this day thou art my bale, 65
    My boote when thou shold bee!'

17. This shoote it was but looselye shott,
    The arrowe flew in vaine,
    And it mett one of the sheriffes men;
    Good William a Trent was slaine. 70

18. It had beene better for William a Trent
    To hange upon a gallowe
    Then for to lye in the greenwoode,
    There slaine with an arrowe.

19. And it is sayd, when men be mett, 75
    Six can doe more then three:
    And they have tane Litle John,
    And bound him ffast to a tree.

20. 'Thou shalt be drawen by dale and downe,'
    quoth the sheriffe,
    'And hanged hye on a hill:' 80
    'But thou may ffayle,' quoth Litle John,
    'If itt be Christs owne will.'

21. Let us leave talking of Litle John,
    For hee is bound fast to a tree,
    And talke of Guy and Robin Hood 85
    In the green woode where they bee.

22. How these two yeomen together they mett,
    Under the leaves of lyne,
    To see what marchandise they made
    Even at that same time. 90

23. 'Good morrow, good fellow,' quoth Sir Guy;
    'Good morrow, good ffellow,' quoth hee;
    'Methinkes by this bow thou beares in thy hand,
    A good archer thou seems to bee.'

24. 'I am wilfull of my way,' quoth Sir Guye, 95
    'And of my morning tyde:'
    'I'le lead thee through the wood,' quoth Robin,
    'Good ffellow, I'le be thy guide.'

25. 'I seeke an outlaw,' quoth Sir Guye,
    'Men call him Robin Hood; 100
    I had rather meet with him upon a day
    Than forty pound of golde.'

26. 'If you tow mett, itt wold be seene whether were better
    Afore yee did part awaye;
    Let us some other pastime find, 105
    Good ffellow, I thee pray.

27. 'Let us some other masteryes make,
    And wee will walke in the woods even;
    Wee may chance meet with Robin Hoode
    Att some unsett steven.' 110

28. They cutt them downe the summer shroggs
    Which grew both under a bryar,
    And sett them three score rood in twinn,
    To shoote the prickes full neare.

29. 'Leade on, good ffellow,' sayd Sir Guye, 115
    'Lead on, I doe bidd thee:'
    'Nay, by my faith,' quoth Robin Hood,
    'The leader thou shalt bee.'

30. The first good shoot that Robin ledd,
    Did not shoote an inch the pricke ffroe;
    Guy was an archer good enoughe, 121
    But he cold neere shoote soe.

31. The second shoote Sir Guy shott,
    He shott within the garlande;
    But Robin Hoode shott it better then hee,
    For he clove the good pricke-wande 126

32. 'Gods blessing on thy heart!' sayes Guye,
    'Goode ffellow, thy shooting is goode;
    For an thy hart be as good as thy hands,
    Thou were better then Robin Hood. 130

33. 'Tell me thy name, good ffellow,' quoth Guy,
    'Under the leaves of lyne:'
    'Nay, by my faith,' quoth good Robin,
    'Till thou have told me thine.'

34. 'I dwell by dale and downe,' quoth Guye,
    'And I have done many a curst turne; 136
    And he that calles me by my right name,
    Calles me Guye of good Gysborne.'

35. 'My dwelling is in the wood,' sayes Robin;
    'By thee I set right nought; 140
    My name is Robin Hood of Barnesdale,
    A ffellow thou has long sought.'

36. He that had neither beene a kithe nor kin
    Might have seene a full fayre sight,
    To see how together these yeomen went,
    With blades both browne and bright; 146

37. To have seene how these yeomen together fought
    Two howers of a summers day;
    Itt was neither Guy nor Robin Hood
    That ffettled them to flye away. 150

38. Robin was reacheles on a roote,
    And stumbled at that tyde,
    And Guy was quicke and nimble withall,
    And hitt him ore the left side.

39. 'Ah, deere Lady!' sayd Robin Hoode, 155
    'Thou art both mother and may!
    I thinke it was never mans destinye
    To dye before his day.'

40. Robin thought on Our Lady deere,
    And soone leapt up againe, 160
    And thus he came with an awkwarde stroke;
    Good Sir Guy hee has slayne.

41. He tooke Sir Guys head by the hayre,
    And sticked itt on his bowes end:
    'Thou hast beene traytor all thy liffe, 165
    Which thing must have an ende.'

42. Robin pulled forth an Irish kniffe,
    And nicked Sir Guy in the fface,
    That hee was never on a woman borne
    Cold tell who Sir Guye was. 170

43. Saies, 'Lye there, lye there, good Sir Guye,
    And with me be not wrothe;
    If thou have had the worse stroakes at my hand,
    Thou shalt have the better cloathe.'

44. Robin did off his gowne of greene, 175
    Sir Guye hee did it throwe;
    And hee put on that capull-hyde
    That cladd him topp to toe.

45. 'The bowe, the arrowes, and litle horne,
    And with me now I'le beare; 180
    Ffor now I will goe to Barnesdale
    To see how my men doe ffare.'

46. Robin sett Guyes horne to his mouth
    A lowd blast in it he did blow;
    That beheard the sheriffe of Nottingham,
    As he leaned under a lowe. 186

47. 'Hearken! hearken!' sayd the sheriffe,
    'I heard noe tydings but good;
    For yonder I heare Sir Guyes horne blowe,
    For he hath slaine Robin Hoode. 190

48. 'For yonder I heare Sir Guyes horne blow,
    Itt blowes soe well in tyde,
    For yonder comes that wighty yeoman,
    Cladd in his capull-hyde.

49. 'Come hither, thou good Sir Guy, 195
    Aske of mee what thou wilt have:'
    'I'le none of thy gold,' sayes Robin Hood,
    'Nor I'le none of itt have.

50. 'But now I have slaine the master,' he sayd,
    'Let me goe strike the knave; 200
    This is all the reward I aske,
    Nor noe other will I have.'

51. 'Thou art a madman,' said the shiriffe,
    'Thou sholdest have had a knights ffee;
    Seeing thy asking hath beene soe badd,
    Well granted it shall be.' 206

52. But Litle John heard his master speake,
    Well he knew that was his steven;
    'Now shall I be loset,' quoth Litle John,
    'With Christs might in heaven.' 210

53. But Robin hee hyed him towards Litle John,
    Hee thought hee wold loose him belive;
    The sheriffe and all his companye
    Fast after him did drive.

54. 'Stand abacke! stand abacke!' sayd Robin;
    'Why draw you mee soe neere? 216
    Itt was never the use in our countrye
    Ones shrift another shold heere.'

55. But Robin pulled forth an Irysh kniffe,
    And losed John hand and ffoote, 220
    And gave him Sir Guyes bow in his hand,
    And bade it be his boote.

56. But John tooke Guyes bow in his hand—
    His arrowes were rawstye by the roote;
    The sherriffe saw Litle John draw a bow 225
    And ffettle him to shoote.

57. Towards his house in Nottingam
    He ffled full fast away,
    And soe did all his companye,
    Not one behind did stay.   230

58. But he cold neither soe fast goe,
    Nor away soe fast runn,
    But Litle John, with an arrow broade,
    Did cleave his heart in twinn.

ROBIN HOOD'S DEATH AND BURIAL

1. WHEN Robin Hood and Little John
    Down a down a down a down
   Went oer yon bank of broom,
   Said Robin Hood bold to Little John,
   'We have shot for many a pound.'   5
   Hey down, a down, a down.

2. 'But I am not able to shoot one shot more,
    My broad arrows will not flee;
    But I have a cousin lives down below,
    Please God, she will bleed me.'   10

3. Now Robin he is to fair Kirkly gone,
    As fast as he can win;
    But before he came there, as we do hear,
    He was taken very ill.

4. And when he came to fair Kirkly-hall,
    He knocked all at the ring,   16
    But none was so ready as his cousin herself
    For to let bold Robin in.

5. 'Will you please to sit down, cousin Robin,'
    she said,
    'And drink some beer with me?'   20
    'No, I will neither eat nor drink,
    Till I am blooded by thee.'

6. 'Well, I have a room, cousin Robin,' she
    said,
    'Which you did never see,
    And if you please to walk therein,   25
    You blooded by me shall be.'

7. She took him by the lily-white hand,
    And led him to a private room,
    And there she blooded bold Robin Hood,
    While one drop of blood would run
    down.   30

8. She blooded him in a vein of the arm,
    And locked him up in the room;
    Then did he bleed all the live-long day,
    Until the next day at noon.

9. He then bethought him of a casement
    there,   35
    Thinking for to get down;
    But was so weak he could not leap,
    He could not get him down.

10. He then bethought him of his bugle-horn,
    Which hung low down to his knee;   40
    He set his horn unto his mouth,
    And blew out weak blasts three.

11. Then Little John, when hearing him,
    As he sat under a tree,
    'I fear my master is now near dead, 45
    He blows so wearily.'

12. Then Little John to fair Kirkly is gone,
    As fast as he can dree;
    But when he came to Kirkly-hall,
    He broke locks two or three: 50

13. Until he came bold Robin to see,
    Then he fell on his knee;
    'A boon, a boon,' cries Little John,
    'Master, I beg of thee.'

14. 'What is that boon,' said Robin Hood, 55
    'Little John, thou begs of me?'
    'It is to burn fair Kirkly-hall,
    And all their nunnery.'

15. 'Now nay, now nay,' quoth Robin Hood,
    'That boon I 'll not grant thee;   60
    I never hurt woman in all my life,
    Nor men in woman's company.

16. 'I never hurt fair maid in all my time,
    Nor at mine end shall it be;
    But give me my bent bow in my hand, 65
    And a broad arrow I 'll let flee
    And where this arrow is taken up,
    There shall my grave digged be.

17. 'Lay me a green sod under my head,
    And another at my feet;   70
    And lay my bent bow by my side,
    Which was my music sweet;
    And make my grave of gravel and green,
    Which is most right and meet.

18. 'Let me have length and breadth enough,
    With a green sod under my head;   76
    That they may say, when I am dead,
    Here lies bold Robin Hood.'

19. These words they readily granted him,
    Which did bold Robin please: 80
    And there they buried bold Robin Hood,
    Within the fair Kirkleys.

THE BATTLE OF OTTERBURN

1. YT felle abowght the Lamasse tyde,
   Whan husbondes wynnes ther haye,
   The dowghtye Dowglasse bowynd hym to
   ryde,
   In Ynglond to take a praye.

2. The yerlle of Fyffe, wythowghten stryffe,
   He bowynd hym over Sulway;
   The grete wolde ever to-gether ryde;
   That raysse they may rewe for aye.

3. Over Hoppertope hyll they cam in,
   And so down by Rodclyffe crage;
   Upon Grene Lynton they lighted dowyn,
   Styrande many a stage.

4. And boldely brente Northomberlond,
   And haryed many a towyn;
   They dyd owr Ynglyssh men grete wrange,
   To battell that were not bowyn.

5. Then spake a berne upon the bent,
   Of comforte that was not colde,
   And sayd, 'We have brente Northomberlond,
   We have all welth in holde.

6. 'Now we have haryed all Bamborowe schyre,
   All the welth in the worlde have wee;
   I rede we ryde to Newe Castell,
   So styll and stalworthlye.'

7. Upon the morowe, when it was day,
   The standerds schone fulle bryght;
   To the Newe Castell they toke the waye,
   And thether they cam full ryght.

8. Syr Henry Perssy laye at the New Castell,
   I tell yow wythowtten drede;
   He had byn a march-man all hys dayes,
   And kepte Barwyke upon Twede.

9. To the Newe Castell when they cam,
   The Skottes they cryde on hyght,
   'Syr Hary Perssy, and thow byste within,
   Com to the fylde, and fyght.

10. 'For we have brente Northomberlonde,
    Thy erytage good and ryght,
    And syne my logeyng I have take,
    Wyth my brande dubbyd many a knyght.'

11. Syr Harry Perssy cam to the walles,
    The Skottyssch oste for to se,
    And sayd, 'And thow hast brente Northomberlond,
    Full sore it rewyth me.

12. 'Yf thou hast haryed all Bamborowe schyre,
    Thow hast done me grete envye;
    For the trespasse thow hast me done,
    The tone of us schall dye.'

13. 'Where schall I byde the?' sayd the Dowglas,
    'Or where wylte thow com to me?'
    'At Otterborne, in the hygh way,
    Ther mast thow well logeed be.

14. 'The roo full rekeles ther sche rinnes,
    To make the game and glee;
    The fawken and the fesaunt both,
    Amonge the holtes on hye.

15. 'Ther mast thow have thy welth at wyll,
    Well loogèd ther mast be;
    Yt schall not be long or I com the tyll,'
    Sayd Syr Harry Perssye.

16. 'Ther schall I byde the,' sayd the Dowglas,
    'By the fayth of my bodye.'
    'Thether schall I com,' sayd Syr Harry Perssy
    'My trowth I plyght to the.'

17. A pype of wyne he gave them over the walles,
    For soth as I yow saye;
    Ther he mayd the Dowglasse drynke,
    And all hys ost that daye.

18. The Dowglas turnyd hym homewarde agayne,
    For soth withowghten naye;
    He toke his logeyng at Oterborne,
    Upon a Wedynsday.

19. And ther he pyght hys standerd dowyn,
    Hys gettyng more and lesse,
    And syne he warned hys men to goo
    To chose ther geldynges gresse.

20. A Skottysshe knyght hoved upon the bent,
    A wache I dare well saye;
    So was he ware on the noble Perssy,
    In the dawnyng of the daye.

21. He prycked to hys pavyleon-dore,
    As faste as he myght ronne;
    'Awaken, Dowglas,' cryed the knyght,
    'For hys love that syttes in trone.

22. 'Awaken, Dowglas,' cryed the knyght,
    'For thow maste waken wyth wynne;
    Yender have I spyed the prowde Perssye,
    And seven stondardes wyth hym.'

23. 'Nay by my trowth,' the Dowglas sayed,
    'It ys but a faynèd taylle;
    He durst not loke on my brede banner
    For all Ynglonde so haylle.

24. 'Was I not yesterdaye at the Newe Castell,
    That stondes so fayre on Tyne?
    For all the men the Perssy had,
    He coude not garre me ones to dyne.'

25. He stepped owt at his pavelyon-dore,
    To loke and it were lesse:
    'Araye yow, lordynges, one and all,
    For here bygynnes no peysse.

26. 'The yerle of Mentaye, thow arte my eme,
       The forwarde I gyve to the:
    The yerlle of Huntlay, cawte and kene,
       He schall be wyth the.

27. 'The lorde of Bowghan, in armure bryght,
       On the other hand he schall be;   106
    Lord Jhonstoune and Lorde Maxwell,
       They to schall be wyth me.

28. 'Swynton, fayre fylde upon your pryde!
       To batell make yow bowen   110
    Syr Davy Skotte, Syr Water Stewarde,
       Syr Jhon of Agurstone!'

29. The Perssy cam byfore hys oste,
       Wych was ever a gentyll knyght;
    Upon the Dowglas lowde can he crye,   115
       'I wyll holde that I have hyght.

30. 'For thou haste brente Northomberlonde,
       And done me grete envye;
    For thys trespasse thou hast me done,
       The tone of us schall dye.'   120

31. The Dowglas answerde hym agayne,
       Wyth grett wurdes upon hye,
    And sayd, 'I have twenty agaynst thy one,
       Byholde, and thou maste see.'

32. Wyth that the Perssy was grevyd sore,   125
       For soth as I yow saye;
    He lyghted dowyn upon his foote,
       And schoote hys horsse clene awaye.

33. Every man sawe that he dyd soo,
       That ryall was ever in rowght;   130
    Every man schoote hys horsse hym froo,
       And lyght hym rowynde abowght.

34. Thus Syr Hary Perssye toke the fylde,
       For soth as I yow saye;
    Jhesu Cryste in hevyn on hyght   135
       Dyd helpe hym well that daye.

35. But nyne thowzand, ther was no moo,
       The cronykle wyll not layne;
    Forty thowsande of Skottes and fowre
       That day fowght them agayne.   140

36. But when the batell bygane to joyne,
       In hast ther cam a knyght;
    The letters fayre furth hath he tayne,
       And thus he sayd full ryght:

37. 'My lorde your father he gretes yow well,
       Wyth many a noble knyght;   146
    He desyres yow to byde
       That he may see thys fyght.

38. 'The Baron of Grastoke ys com out of the west,
       With hym a noble companye;   150
    All they loge at your fathers thys nyght,
       And the batell fayne wolde they see.'

39. 'For Jhesus love,' sayd Syr Harye Perssy,
       'That dyed for yow and me,
    Wende to my lorde my father agayne,   155
       And saye thow sawe me not with yee.

40. 'My trowth ys plyght to yonne Skottysh knyght,
       It nedes me not to layne,
    That I schulde byde hym upon thys bent,
       And I have hys trowth agayne.   160

41. 'And if that I weynde of thys growende,
       For soth, onfowghten awaye,
    He wolde me call but a kowarde knyght
       In hys londe another daye.

42. 'Yet had I lever to be rynde and rente,   165
       By Mary, that mykkel maye,
    Then ever my manhood schulde be reprovyd
       Wyth a Skotte another daye.

43. 'Wherefore schote, archars, for my sake,
       And let scharpe arowes flee;   170
    Mynstrells, playe up for your waryson,
       And well quyt it schall bee.

44. 'Every man thynke on hys trewe-love,
       And marke hym to the Trenité;
    For to God I make myne avowe   175
       Thys day wyll I not flee.'

45. The blodye harte in the Dowglas armes,
       Hys standerde stood on hye,
    That every man myght full well knowe;
       By syde stode starrës thre.   180

46. The whyte lyon on the Ynglyssh perte,
       For soth as I yow sayne,
    The lucettes and the cressawntes both;
       The Skottes faught them agayne.

47. Upon Sent Androwe lowde can they crye,
       And thrysse they schowte on hyght,   186
    And syne merked them one owr Ynglysshe men,
       As I have tolde yow ryght.

48. Sent George the bryght, owr Ladyes knyght,
       To name they were full fayne;   190
    Owr Ynglyssh men they cryde on hyght,
       And thrysse the schowtte agayne.

49. Wyth that scharpe arowes bygan to flee,
       I tell yow in sertayne;
    Men of armes bygane to joyne,   195
       Many a dowghty man was ther slayne.

50. The Perssy and the Dowglas mette,
    That ether of other was fayne;
    They swapped together whyll that the swette,
    Wyth swordes of fyne collayne: 200

51. Tyll the bloode from ther bassonnettes ranne,
    As the roke doth in the rayne;
    'Yelde the to me,' sayd the Dowglas,
    'Or elles thow schalt be slayne.

52. 'For I see by thy bryght bassonet,   205
    Thow arte sum man of myght;
    And so I do by thy burnysshed brande;
    Thow arte an yerle, or elles a knyght.'

53. 'By my good faythe,' sayd the noble Perssye,
    'Now haste thow rede full ryght;   210
    Yet wyll I never yelde me to the
    Whyll I may stonde and fyght.'

54. They swapped together whyll that they swette,
    Wyth swordës scharpe and long;
    Ych on other so faste thee beette,   215
    Tyll ther helmes cam in peyses dowyn.

55. The Perssy was a man of strengheth,
    I tell yow in thys stounde;
    He smote the Dowglas at the swordës length
    That he felle to the growynde.   220

56. The sworde was scharpe, and sore can byte,
    I tell yow in sertayne;
    To the harte he cowde hym smyte,
    Thus was the Dowglas slayne.

57. The stonderdes stode styll on eke a syde,
    Wyth many a grevous grone;   226
    Ther they fowght the day, and all the nyght,
    And many a dowghty man was slayne.

58. Ther was no freke that ther wolde flye,
    But styffely in stowre can stond,   230
    Ychone hewyng on other whyll they myght drye,
    Wyth many a baylleful bronde.

59. Ther was slayne upon the Skottës syde,
    For soth and sertenly,
    Syr James a Dowglas ther was slayne,   235
    That day that he cowde dye.

60. The yerlle of Mentaye he was slayne,
    Grysely groned upon the growynd;
    Syr Davy Skotte, Syr Water Stewarde,
    Syr Jhon of Agurstoune.   240

61. Syr Charllës Morrey in that place,
    That never a fote wold flee;
    Syr Hewe Maxwell, a lord he was,
    Wyth the Dowglas dyd he dye.

62. Ther was slayne upon the Skottës syde,
    For soth as I yow saye,   246
    Of fowre and forty thowsande Scottes
    Went but eyghtene awaye.

63. Ther was slayne upon the Ynglysshe syde,
    For soth and sertenlye,   250
    A gentell knyght, Syr Jhon Fechewe,
    Yt was the more pety.

64. Syr James Hardbotell ther was slayne,
    For hym ther hartes were sore;
    The gentyll Lovell ther was slayne,   255
    That the Perssys standerd bore.

65. Ther was slayne upon the Ynglyssh pert
    For soth as I yow saye,
    Of nyne thowsand Ynglyssh men
    Fvye hondert cam awaye.   260

66. The other were slayne in the fylde;
    Cryste kepe ther sowlles from wo!
    Seyng ther was so fewe fryndes
    Agaynst so many a foo.

67. Then on the morne they mayde them beerys   265
    Of byrch and haysell graye;
    Many a wydowe, wyth wepyng teyres,
    Ther makes they fette awaye.

68. Thys fraye bygan at Otterborne,
    Bytwene the nyght and the day;   270
    Ther the Dowglas lost hys lyffe,
    And the Perssy was lede awaye.

69. Then was ther a Scottysh prisoner tayne,
    Syr Hewe Mongomery was hys name;
    For soth as I yow saye,   275
    He borowed the Perssy home agayne.

70. Now let us all for the Perssy praye
    To Jhesu most of myght,
    To bryng hys sowlle to the blysse of heven,
    For he was a gentyll knyght.   280

CAPTAIN CAR or EDOM O GORDON

1. It befell at Martynmas,
    When wether waxed colde,
    Captaine Care said to his men,
    'We must go take a holde.'
    Syck, sike, and to-towe sike,   5
    And sike and like to die;
    The sikest nighte that ever I abode,
    God Lord have mercy on me!

2. 'Haille, master, and wether you will,
    And wether ye like it best;' 10
  'To the castle of Crecrynbroghe,
    And there we will take our reste.'

3. 'I knowe where is a gay castle,
    Is builded of lyme and stone;
  Within their is a gay ladie, 15
    Her lord is riden and gone.'

4. The ladie she lend on her castle-walle,
    She lokèd upp and downe;
  There was she ware of an host of men,
    Come riding to the towne. 20

5. 'Se yow, my meri men all,
    And se yow what I see?
  Yonder I see an host of men,
    I muse who they shold bee.'

6. She thought he had ben her wed lord, 25
    As he comd riding home;
  Then was it traitur Captaine Care
    The lord of Ester-towne.

7. They were no soner at supper sett,
    Then after said the grace, 30
  Or Captaine Care and all his men
    Were lighte aboute the place.

8. 'Gyve over thi howsse, thou lady gay,
    And I will make the a bande;
  To-nighte thou shall ly within my armes, 35
    To-morrowe thou shall ere my lande.'

9. Then bespacke the eldest sonne,
    That was both whitt and redde:
  'O mother dere, geve over your howsse,
    Or elles we shalbe deade.' 40

10. 'I will not geve over my hous,' she saithe,
    'Not for feare of my lyffe;
  It shalbe talked throughout the land,
    The slaughter of a wyffe.'

11. 'Fetch me my pestilett, 45
    And charge me my gonne,
  That I may shott at this bloddy butcher,
    The lord of Easter-towne.'

12. Styfly upon her wall she stode,
    And lett the pellettes flee; 50
  But then she myst the blody bucher,
    And she slew other three.

13. 'I will not geve over my hous,' she saithe,
    'Netheir for lord nor lowne;
  Nor yet for traitour Captaine Care, 55
    The lord of Easter-towne.

14. 'I desire of Captaine Care,
    And all his bloodye band,
  That he would save my eldest sonne,
    The eare of all my lande.' 60

15. 'Lap him in a shete,' he sayth,
    'And let him downe to me,
  And I shall take him in my armes,
    His waran shall I be.'

16. The captayne sayd unto him selfe; 65
    Wyth sped, before the rest,
  He cut his tonge out of his head,
    His hart out of his brest.

17. He lapt them in a handkerchef,
    And knet it of knotes three, 70
  And cast them over the castell-wall,
    At that gay ladye.

18. 'Fye upon the, Captayne Care,
    And all thy bloddy band!
  For thou hast slayne my eldest sonne, 75
    The ayre of all my land.'

19. Then bespake the yongest sonne,
    That sat on the nurses knee,
  Sayth, 'Mother gay, geve over your house;
    It smoldereth me.' 80

20. 'I wold geve my gold,' she saith,
    'And so I wolde my ffee,
  For a blaste of the westryn wind,
    To dryve the smoke from thee.'

21. 'Fy upon the, John Hamleton, 85
    That ever I paid the hyre!
  For thou hast broken my castle-wall,
    And kyndled in the ffyre.'

22. The lady gate to her close parler,
    The fire fell aboute her head; 90
  She toke up her children thre,
    Seth, 'Babes, we are all dead.'

23. Then bespake the hye steward,
    That is of hye degree;
  Saith, 'Ladie gay, you are in close, 95
    Wether ye fighte or flee.'

24. Lord Hamleton dremd in his dream,
    In Carvall where he laye,
  His halle were all of fyre,
    His ladie slayne or daye. 100

25. 'Busk and bowne, my mery men all,
    Even and go ye with me;
  For I dremd that my haal was on fyre,
    My lady slayne or day.'

26. He buskt him and bownd hym, 105
    And like a worthi knighte;
  And when he saw his hall burning,
    His harte was no dele lighte.

27. He sett a trumpett till his mouth,
    He blew as it plesd his grace; 110
  Twenty score of Hamlentons
    Was light aboute the place.

28. 'Had I knowne as much yesternighte
    As I do to-daye,
    Captaine Care and all his men
    Should not have gone so quite.   115

29. 'Fye upon the, Captaine Care,
    And all thy blody bande!
    Thou haste slayne my lady gay,
    More wurth then all thy lande.   120

30. 'If thou had ought eny ill will,' he saith,
    'Thou shoulde have taken my lyffe,
    And have saved my children thre,
    All and my lovesome wyffe.'

THE WIFE OF USHER'S WELL

1. There lived a wife at Usher's Well,
   And a wealthy wife was she;
   She had three stout and stalwart sons,
   And sent them oer the sea.

2. They hadna been a week from her,   5
   A week but barely ane,
   Whan word came to the carline wife
   That her three sons were gane.

3. They hadna been a week from her,
   A week but barely three,   10
   Whan word came to the carlin wife
   That her sons she'd never see.

4. 'I wish the wind may never cease,
   Nor fashes in the flood,
   Till my three sons come hame to me,   15
   In earthly flesh and blood.'

5. It fell about the Martinmass,
   When nights are lang and mirk,
   The carlin wife's three sons came hame,
   And their hats were o the birk.   20

6. It neither grew in syke nor ditch,
   Nor yet in ony sheugh;
   But at the gates o Paradise,
   That birk grew fair eneugh.

       * * *

7. 'Blow up the fire, my maidens,   25
   Bring water from the well;
   For a' my house shall feast this night,
   Since my three sons are well.'

8. And she has made to them a bed,
   She's made it large and wide,   30
   And she's taen her mantle her about,
   Sat down at the bed-side.

       * * *

9. Up then crew the red, red cock,
   And up and crew the gray;
   The eldest to the youngest said,   35
   ''Tis time we were away.'

10. The cock he hadna crawd but once,
    And clapped his wings at al,
    When the youngest to the eldest said,
    'Brother, we must awa.   40

11. 'The cock doth craw, the day doth daw,
    The channerin worm doth chide;
    Gin we be mist out o our place,
    A sair pain we maun bide.

12. 'Faer ye weel, my mother dear!   45
    Fareweel to barn and byre!
    And fare ye weel, the bonny lass
    That kindles my mother's fire!'

KEMP OWYNE

1. Her mother died when she was young,
   Which gave her cause to make great moan;
   Her father married the warst woman
   That ever lived in Christendom.

2. She servèd her with foot and hand,   5
   In every thing that she could dee,
   Till once, in an unlucky time,
   She threw her in ower Craigy's sea.

3. Says, 'Lie you there, dove Isabel,
   And all my sorrows lie with thee;   10
   Till Kemp Owyne come ower the sea,
   And borrow you with kisses three
   Let all the warld do what they will,
   Oh borrowed shall you never be!'

4. Her breath grew strang, her hair grew lang,
   And twisted thrice about the tree,   16
   And all the people, far and near,
   Thought that a savage beast was she.

5. These news did come to Kemp Owyne,
   Where he lived, far beyond the sea;   20
   He hasted him to Craigy's sea,
   And on the savage beast lookd he.

6. Her breath was strang, her hair was lang,
   And twisted was about the tree,
   And with a swing she came about: 25
   'Come to Craigy's sea, and kiss with me.

7. 'Here is a royal belt,' she cried,
   'That I have found in the green sea;
   And while your body it is on,
   Drawn shall your blood never be;   30
   But if you touch me, tail or fin,
   I vow my belt your death shall be.'

8. He stepped in, gave her a kiss,
   The royal belt he brought him wi;
   Her breath was strang, her hair was lang,
   And twisted twice about the tree,   36
   And with a swing she came about:
   'Come to Craigy's sea, and kiss with me.

9. 'Here is a royal ring,' she said,
   'That I have found in the green sea;   40
And while your finger it is on,
   Drawn shall your blood never be;
But if you touch me, tail or fin,
   I swear my ring your death shall be.'

10. He stepped in, gave her a kiss,   45
   The royal ring he brought him wi;
Her breath was strang, her hair was lang,
   And twisted ance about the tree,
And with a swing she came about:
   'Come to Craigy's sea, and kiss with me.'

11. 'Here is a royal brand,' she said,   51
   'That I have found in the green sea;
And while your body it is on,
   Drawn shall your blood never be;
But if you touch me, tail or fin,   55
   I swear my brand your death shall be.'

12. He stepped in, gave her a kiss,
   The royal brand he brought him wi;
Her breath was sweet, her hair grew short,
   And twisted nane about the tree,   60
And smilingly she came about,
   As fair a woman as fair could be.

THE DÆMON LOVER

1. 'O WHERE have you been, my long, long love,
   This long seven years and mair?'
'O I 'm come to seek my former vows
   Ye granted me before.'

2. 'O hold your tongue of your former vows, 5
   For they will breed sad strife;
O hold your tongue of your former vows,
   For I am become a wife.'

3. He turned him right and round about,
   And the tear blinded his ee: 10
'I wad never hae trodden on Irish ground,
   If it had not been for thee.

4. 'I might hae had a king's daughter,
   Far, far beyond the sea;
I might have had a king's daughter,   15
   Had it not been for love o thee.'

5. 'If ye might have had a king's daughter,
   Yersel ye had to blame;
Ye might have had taken the king's daughter,
   For ye kend that I was nane.   20

6. 'If I was to leave my husband dear,
   And my two babes also,
O what have you to take me to,
   If with you I should go?'

7. 'I hae seven ships upon the sea—   25
   The eighth brought me to land—
With four-and-twenty bold mariners,
   And music on every hand.'

8. She has taken up her two little babes,
   Kissd them baith cheek and chin: 30
'O fair ye weel, my ain two babes,
   For I 'll never see you again.'

9. She set her foot upon the ship,
   No mariners could she behold;
But the sails were o the taffetie,   35
   And the masts o the beaten gold.

10. She had not sailed a league, a league,
   A league but barely three,
When dismal grew his countenance,
   And drumlie grew his ee.   40

11. They had not saild a league, a league,
   A league but barely three,
Until she espied his cloven foot,
   And she wept right bitterlie.

12. 'O hold your tongue of your weeping,' says he,   45
   'Of your weeping now let me be;
I will shew you how the lilies grow
   On the banks of Italy.'

13. 'O what hills are yon, yon pleasant hills,
   That the sun shines sweetly on?'   50
'O yon are the hills of heaven,' he said,
   'Where you will never win.'

14. 'O whaten a mountain is yon,' she said,
   'All so dreary wi frost and snow?'
'O yon is the mountain of hell,' he cried,
   'Where you and I will go.'   56

15. He strack the tap-mast wi his hand,
   The fore-mast wi his knee,
And he brake that gallant ship in twain,
   And sank her in the sea.   60

LORD RANDAL

1. 'O WHERE hae ye been, Lord Randal, my son?
   O where hae ye been, my handsome young man?'
'I hae been to the wild wood; mother, make my bed soon,
   Fir I 'm weary wi hunting, and fain wald lie down.'

2. 'Where gat ye your dinner, Lord Randal,
      my son?   5
   Where gat ye your dinner, my handsome
      young man?'
   'I dined wi my true-love; mother, make
      my bed soon,
   For I 'm weary wi hunting, and fain wald
      lie down.'

3. 'What gat ye to your dinner, Lord Randal,
      my son?
   What gat ye to your dinner, my handsome
      young man?'   10
   'I gat eels boiled in broo; mother, make my
      bed soon,
   For I 'm weary wi hunting, and fain wald
      lie down.'

4. 'What became of your bloodhounds, Lord
      Randal, my son?
   What became of your bloodhounds, my
      handsome young man?'
   'O they swelld and they died; mother,
      make my bed soon,   15
   For I 'm weary wi hunting, and fain wald
      lie down.'

5. 'O I fear ye are poisond, Lord Randal, my
      son!
   O I fear ye are poisond, my handsome
      young man!'
   'O yes! I am poisond; mother, make my
      bed soon,
   For I 'm sick at the heart and I fain wald
      lie down.'   20

SIR PATRICK SPENS

1. THE king sits in Dumferling toune,
      Drinking the blude-reid wine:
   'O whar will I get guid sailor,
      To sail this schip of mine?'

2. Up and spak an eldern knicht,   5
      Sat at the kings richt kne:
   'Sir Patrick Spence is the best sailor,
      That sails upon the se.'

3. The king has written a braid letter,
      And signd it wi his hand,   10
   And sent it to Sir Patrick Spence,
      Was walking on the sand.

4. The first line that Sir Patrick red,
      A loud lauch laughèd he;
   The next line that Sir Patrick red,   15
      The teir blinded his ee.

5. 'O wha is this has don this deid,
      This ill deid don to me,
   To send me out this time o' the yeir,
      To sail upon the se!   20

6. 'Mak hast, mak haste, my mirry men all,
      Our guid schip sails the morne:'
   'O say na sae, my master deir,
      For I feir a deadlie storme.

7. 'Late, late yestreen I saw the new moone,
      Wi the auld moone in hir arme,   26
   And I feir, I feir, my deir master,
      That we will cum to harme.'

8. O our Scots nobles wer richt laith
      To weet their cork-heild schoone;   30
   Bot lang owre a' the play wer playd,
      Thair hats they swam aboone.

9. O lang, lang may their ladies sit,
      Wi thair fans into their hand,
   Or eir they se Sir Patrick Spence   35
      Cum sailing to the land.

10. O lang, lang may the ladies stand,
      Wi thair gold kems in their hair,
    Waiting for thar ain deir lords,
      For they 'll se thame na mair.   40

11. Haf owre, haf owre to Aberdour,
      It 's fiftie fadom deip,
    And thair lies guid Sir Patrick Spence,
      Wi the Scots lords at his feit.

THOMAS RYMER

1. TRUE Thomas lay oer yond grassy bank,
      And he beheld a ladie gay,
   A ladie that was brisk and bold,
      Come riding oer the fernie brae.

2. Her skirt was of the grass-green silk,   5
      Her mantel of the velvet fine,
   At ilka tett of her horse's mane
      Hung fifty silver bells and nine.

3. True Thomas he took off his hat
      And bowed him low down till his knee: 10
   'All hail, thou mighty Queen of Heaven!
      For your peer on earth I never did see.'

4. 'O no, O no, True Thomas,' she says,
      'That name does not belong to me;
   I am but the queen of fair Elfland,   15
      And I 'm come here for to visit thee.

          * * *

5. 'But ye maun go wi me now, Thomas,
      True Thomas, ye maun go wi me,
   For ye maun serve me seven years,
      Thro weel or wae as may chance to be.' 20

6. She turned about her milk-white steed,
     And took True Thomas up behind,
   And aye wheneer her bridle rang,
     The steed flew swifter than the wind.

7. For forty days and forty nights
     He wade thro red blude to the knee,
   And he saw neither sun nor moon,
     But heard the roaring of the sea.

8. O they rade on and further on,
     Until they came to a garden green:
   'Light down, light down, ye ladie free,
     Some of that fruit let me pull to thee.'

9. 'O no, O no, True Thomas,' she says,
     'That fruit maun not be touched by thee,
   For a' the plagues that are in hell
     Light on the fruit of this countrie.

10. 'But I have a loaf here in my lap,
      Likewise a bottle of claret wine,
    And here ere we go farther on,
      We 'll rest a while, and ye may dine.'

11. When he had eaten and drunk his fill,
      'Lay down your head upon my knee,'
    The lady sayd, 'ere we climb yon hill,
      And I will show you fairlies three.

12. 'O see ye not yon narrow road,
      So thick beset wi thorns and briers?
    That is the path of righteousness,
      Tho after it but few enquires.

13. 'And see not ye that braid braid road,
      That lies across yon lillie leven?
    That is the path of wickedness,
      Tho some call it the road to heaven.

14. 'And see ye not that bonny road,
      Which winds about the fernie brae?
    That is the road to fair Elfland,
      Where you and I this night maun gae.

15. 'But Thomas, ye maun hold your tongue,
      Whatever ye may hear or see,
    For gin ae word you should chance to speak,
      You will neer get back to your ain countrie.'

16. He has gotten a coat of the even cloth,
      And a pair of shoes of velvet green,
    And till seven years were past and gone
      True Thomas on earth was never seen.

BONNY BARBARA ALLAN

1. It was in and about the Martinmas time,
     When the green leaves were a falling,
   That Sir John Græme, in the West Country,
     Fell in love with Barbara Allan.

2. He sent his man down through the town,
     To the place where she was dwelling:
   'O haste and come to my master dear,
     Gin ye be Barbara Allan.'

3. O hooly, hooly rose she up,
     To the place where he was lying,
   And when she drew the curtain by,
     'Young man, I think you 're dying.'

4. 'O it's I 'm sick, and very, very sick,
     And 't is a' for Barbara Allan:'
   'O the better for me ye 's never be,
     Tho your heart's blood were a spilling.

5. 'O dinna ye mind, young man,' said she,
     'When ye was in the tavern a drinking,
   That ye made the healths gae round and round,
     And slighted Barbara Allan?'

6. He turnd his face unto the wall,
     And death was with him dealing:
   'Adieu, adieu, my dear friends all,
     And be kind to Barbara Allan.'

7. And slowly, slowly raise she up,
     And slowly, slowly left him,
   And sighing said, she could not stay,
     Since death of life had reft him.

8. She had not gane a mile but twa,
     When she heard the dead-bell ringing,
   And every jow that the dead-bell geid,
     It cryd, Woe to Barbara Allan!

9. 'O mother, mother, make my bed!
     O make it saft and narrow!
   Since my love died for me to-day,
     I 'll die for him to-morrow.'

THE TWA SISTERS

1. There was twa sisters in a bowr,
     Edinburgh, Edinburgh
   There was twa sisters in a bowr,
     Stirling for ay
   There was twa sisters in a bowr,
   There came a knight to be their wooer,
     Bonny Saint Johnston stands upon Tay.

2. He courted the eldest wi glove an ring,
   But he lovd the youngest above a' thing.

3. He courted the eldest wi brotch an knife,
   But lovd the youngest as his life.

4. The eldest she was vexèd sair,
   And much envied her sister fair.

5. Into her bowr she could not rest,
   Wi grief an spite she almos brast. 15

6. Upon a morning fair an clear,
   She cried upon her sister dear:

7. 'O sister, come to yon sea stran,
   An see our father's ships come to lan.'

8. She's taen her by the milk-white han, 20
   An led her down to yon sea stran.

9. The youngest stood upon a stane,
   The eldest came an threw her in,

10. She tooke her by the middle sma,
    And dashd her bonny back to the jaw. 25

11. 'O sister, sister, tak my han,
    An Ise mack you heir to a' my lan.

12. 'O sister, sister, tak my middle,
    An yes get my goud and my gouder girdle.

13. 'O sister, sister, save my life, 30
    An I swear Ise never be nae man's wife.'

14. 'Foul fa the han that I should tacke,
    It twind me an my wardles make.

15. 'Your cherry cheeks an yallow hair
    Gars me gae maiden for evermair.' 35

16. Sometimes she sank, an sometimes she swam,
    Till she came down yon bonny mill-dam.

17. O out it came the miller's son,
    An saw the fair maid swimmin in.

18. 'O father, father, draw your dam, 40
    Here's either a mermaid or a swan.'

19. The miller quickly drew the dam,
    An there he found a drownd woman.

20. You coudna see her yallow hair
    For gold and pearle that were so rare. 45

21. You coudna see her middle sma
    For gouden girdle that was sae braw.

22. You coudna see her fingers white,
    For gouden rings that was sae gryte.

23. An by there came a harper fine, 50
    That harpèd to the king at dine.

24. When he did look that lady upon,
    He sighd and made a heavy moan.

25. He's taen three locks o her yallow hair,
    And wi them strung his harp sae fair. 55

26. The first tune he did play and sing,
    Was, 'Farewell to my father the king.'

27. The nextin tune that he played syne,
    Was, 'Farewell to my mother the queen.'

28. The lasten tune that he playd then, 60
    Was, 'Wae to my sister, fair Ellen.'

THE CRUEL BROTHER

1. THERE was three ladies played at the ba,
   With a hey ho and a lillie gay
   There came a knight and played oer them a'.
   As the primrose spreads so sweetly.

2. The eldest was baith tall and fair, 5
   But the youngest was beyond compare.

3. The midmost had a graceful mien,
   But the youngest lookd like beautie's queen.

4. The knight bowd low to a' the three,
   But to the youngest he bent his knee. 10

5. The ladie turned her head aside,
   The knight he wooed her to be his bride.

6. The ladie blushed a rosy red,
   And sayd, 'Sir knight, I'm too young to wed.'

7. 'O ladie fair, give me your hand, 15
   And I'll make you ladie of a' my land.'

8. 'Sir knight, ere ye my favor win,
   You maun get consent frae a' my kin.'

9. He's got consent frae her parents dear,
   And likewise frae her sisters fair. 20

10. He's got consent frae her kin each one,
    But forgot to spiek to her brother John.

11. Now, when the wedding day was come,
    The knight would take his bonny bride home.

12. And many a lord and many a knight 25
    Came to behold that ladie bright.

13. And there was nae man that did her see
    But wished himself bridegroom to be.

14. Her father dear led her down the stair,
    And her sisters twain they kissd her there.

15. Her mother dear led her thro the closs,
    And her brother John set her on her horse.

16. She leaned her oer the saddle-bow,
    To give him a kiss ere she did go.

17. He has taen a knife, baith lang and sharp,
    And stabbed that bonny bride to the heart.

18. She hadno ridden half thro the town,
    Until her heart's blude staind her gown.

19. 'Ride softly on,' says the best young man,
    'For I think our bonny bride looks pale and wan.'

20. 'O lead me gently up yon hill,
    And I'll there sit down, and make my will.'

21. 'O what will you leave to your father dear?'
    'The silver-shode steed that brought me here.'

22. 'What will you leave to your mother dear?'
    'My velvet pall and my silken gear.'

23. 'What will you leave to your sister Anne?'
    'My silken scarf and my gowden fan.'

24. 'What will you leave to your sister Grace?'
    'My bloody cloaths to wash and dress.'

25. 'What will you leave to your brother John?'
    'The gallows-tree to hang him on.'

26. 'What will you leave to your brother John's wife?'
    'The wilderness to end her life.'

27. This ladie fair in her grave was laid,
    And many a mass was oer her said.

28. But it would have made your heart right sair,
    To see the bridegroom rive his haire.

EDWARD

1. 'Why dois your brand sae drap wi bluid,
        Edward, Edward,
    Why dois your brand sae drap wi bluid,
        And why sae sad gang yee O?'
    'O I hae killed my hauke sae guid,
        Mither, mither,
    O I hae killed my hauke sae guid,
        And I had nae mair bot hee O.'

2. 'Your haukis bluid was nevir sae reid,
        Edward, Edward,
    Your haukis bluid was nevir sae reid,
        My deir son I tell thee O.'
    'O I hae killed my reid-roan steid,
        Mither, mither,
    O I hae killed my reid-roan steid,
        That erst was sae fair and frie O.'

3. 'Your steid was auld, and ye hae got mair,
        Edward, Edward,
    Your steid was auld, and ye hae got mair,
        Sum other dule ye drie O.'
    'O I hae killed my fadir deir,
        Mither, mither.
    O I hae killed my fadir deir,
        Alas, and wae is mee O!'

4. 'And whatten penance wul ye drie for that,
        Edward, Edward,
    And whatten penance will ye drie for that?
        My deir son, now tell me O.'
    'Ile set my feit in yonder boat,
        Mither, mither,
    Ile set my feit in yonder boat,
        And Ile fare ovir the sea O.'

5. 'And what wul ye doe wi your towirs and your ha,
        Edward, Edward?
    And what wul you doe wi your towirs and your ha,
        That were sae fair to see O?'
    'Ile let thame stand tul they doun fa,
        Mither, mither,
    Ile let thame stand tul they down fa,
        For here nevir mair maun I bee O.'

6. 'And what wul ye leive to your bairns and your wife,
        Edward, Edward?
    And what wul ye leive to your bairns and your wife,
        Whan ye gang ovir the sea O?'
    'The warldis room, late them beg thrae life,
        Mither, mither,
    The warldis room, late them beg thrae life,
        For thame nevir mair wul I see O.'

7. 'And what wul ye leive to your ain mither deir,
        Edward, Edward?
    And what wul ye leive to your ain mither deir?
        My deir son, now tell me O.'
    'The curse of hell frae me sall ye beir,
        Mither, mither,
    The curse of hell frae me sall ye beir,
        Sic counseils ye gave to me O.'

THE ELIZABETHAN AGE

ALTHOUGH Queen Elizabeth's reign occupied only the latter half of the sixteenth century (1558-1603), the literary brilliance manifested under this sovereign justifies our using the term 'Elizabethan Age' to designate the whole period of a hundred years or more during which English literature was transformed by the movement of European thought known as the Renaissance. Fundamentally this movement was a revival, or 'rebirth,' of interest in the mundane powers of man, and in his earthly surroundings. It may be regarded as an emphatic departure from the medieval minimizing of the importance of man's intellect and sensuous life, and as a fresh assertion of human worldliness. The date at which English literature first reflects the ideas of the Renaissance cannot, of course, be determined; but we may fairly say that in England their influence was fully felt about the beginning of the sixteenth century.

Among the more important aspects of this new view of life is its paganism. It encouraged the enjoyment of all human capacities, the cultivation of earthly beauty, and the perfecting of life as a purely human concern. This new attitude was supported, and in some measure created, by the rediscovery of the writings of pagan antiquity. Between the years 1490 and 1520 such scholars as Thomas Linacre, William Grocyn, John Colet, and Erasmus established in England the teaching of the classics of Greece and Rome, and thus opened to English readers a new realm of non-Christian philosophy and art. This renewed study of Greek and Latin literature is usually referred to as the Revival of Learning, and those who participated in it are often called Humanists. The effect of their teaching may be seen in Sir Thomas More's *Utopia* (Latin, 1516; English translation, 1551), which advocates living 'according to nature,' or in *The Schoolmaster*, of Roger Ascham (1515-1568).

Another potent element in Renaissance thought is its encouragement of independent, scientific inquiry. This spirit of investigation is most vividly manifested in voyages of discovery, which are stirringly recorded in the pages of Hakluyt and in poems such as Michael Drayton's *To the Virginian Voyage*. A more profound effect of this impulse toward intellectual exploration appeared within the sphere of organized religion. When men rebelled against the traditional guidance of the medieval Church, and asserted their right to search for truth through their own intellects, the result was Protestantism. The Protestant revolt from Roman authority is pervasively reflected in much of Elizabethan literature, and quite explicitly in the writings of Roger Ascham and Edmund Spenser.

The introduction of new ideas into England was accompanied by a marked refinement of life in general and of letters in particular. The study of the literature of antiquity, and increasing contact with Continental life, and a notable economic prosperity under Tudor sovereigns all contributed to what may be called the aristocratic aspect of Renaissance life in the island. A more elegant form of worldly life was reflected in more refined forms of literary expression. This formal refinement appears, for example, in the sonnet, a form of versification introduced from the Continent by the courtly poets, Sir Thomas Wyatt and the Earl of Surrey, and practiced by a notable succession of writers including Sidney, Spenser, Drayton, and Shakespeare. With the new verse-forms was adopted also a more self-conscious phraseology characterized by 'conceits,' or exaggerated figures of speech. Prose also developed highly sophisticated styles, the most conspicuous of which is that called 'Euphuism,' from its use by John Lyly in his novel, *Euphues* (1578, 1580).

Among the more general aspects of the English Renaissance may be noticed, finally, its spirit of nationalism. The renewed interest in men's mundane concerns aroused in Englishmen an increasing desire to develop and protect their national life. During the latter part of the sixteenth century this patriotic feeling was solidified by a general political loyalty to a great sovereign, and by such stirring events as the defeat of the Spanish Armada in 1588.

All the aspects of the Renaissance described above are reflected with especial cogency in Elizabethan drama. This, the greatest literary achievement of the age, was not a sudden creation, but the culmination of a long development. The earliest English religious plays, such as those of Chester, had been gradually secularized through the inclusion of comic and worldly elements, and eventually gave way before other medieval dramatic types such as moral plays and farces, and especially before the classical and romantic conceptions of tragedy and comedy introduced from the Continent during the course of the sixteenth century. From such dramatic antecedents arose the plays of Shakespeare's immediate predecessors and early competitors: John Lyly (1554?–1606), George Peele (c. 1557–1596), Thomas Kyd (1558–1594), Robert Greene (1560–1592), and Christopher Marlowe (1564–1593). Aided by the examples of these able writers, but relying chiefly upon his own genius, Shakespeare created the dramas which have given to the Elizabethan age its lasting preëminence. In them are found the most potent portrayals of human emotion known to art, along with expressions of the most significant elements in Renaissance thinking: a vivid sense of earthly beauty, a consciousness of expanding intellectual and geographical horizons, a refinement of literary style, and an ardent patriotism.

NOTEWORTHY DATES

ENGLISH LITERATURE AND HISTORY		FOREIGN LITERATURE AND HISTORY	
1478–1535	Sir Thomas More	1465?–1536	Desiderius Erasmus
1485–1509	Henry VII	1474–1533	Ludovico Ariosto
1503?–42	Sir Thomas Wyatt	1495?–1553	François Rabelais
1509–47	Henry VIII		
1515–68	Roger Ascham		
1516	More's *Utopia*	1517–32	German Reformation
1517?–47	Earl of Surrey	1524–85	Pierre de Ronsard
1536–1608	Thomas Sackville	1533–92	Michel Eyquem de Montaigne
1547–53	Edward VI	1544–95	Torquato Tasso
1552–99	Edmund Spenser	1545–63	Council of Trent
1552?–1618	Sir Walter Raleigh	1547–1616	Miguel de Cervantes
1553–58	Queen Mary	c. 1548–1600	Giordano Bruno
1554–86	Sir Philip Sidney	1554	Bandello's *Novelle*
1554?–1606	John Lyly		
1557	Tottel's *Miscellany*	1556–98	Philip II, of Spain
1558–1603	Queen Elizabeth		
1561–1626	Francis Bacon	1564–1642	Galileo
1564–93	Christopher Marlowe	1565	Cinthio's *Hecatommithi*
1564–1616	William Shakespeare		
1576	First London Theatre	1572	Massacre of St. Bartholomev
1578, 80	Lyly's *Euphues*		
1579	Spenser's *Shepherd's Calendar*		
1588	Spanish Armada defeated	1589–1610	Henry IV, of France
1590, 96	Spenser's *Faerie Queene*		
1597	Bacon's *Essays*		
1599	Globe Theatre built	1598	Edict of Nantes

SIR THOMAS WYATT (1503?–1542)

Wyatt was preëminently a courtier. Well educated at Cambridge, and, possibly, also at Oxford, he began his career at court in several offices connected with the person of the king, from which he advanced speedily to diplomatic services, during the period 1525-1540, in France, Italy, Spain, and Flanders. In 1536, Wyatt was knighted, and in 1542, he represented Kent in Parliament. A vigorous tradition persists that Wyatt was attached to the English court not only through his official appointments, but also, indirectly, as the youthful lover of Anne Boleyn.

Well-read in Italian, French, and classical literature, Wyatt deliberately formed his style by imitating Italian and French models. He is conspicuous in the history of English literature chiefly from the fact that he introduced into English the sonnet form, with its refining influence upon English meter and diction. Several of Wyatt's sonnets are direct translations from Petrarch, upon whom, throughout, he drew largely for his rime-scheme, his vocabulary, and his conventional ideas. Besides sonnets, Wyatt wrote other lyrics, epigrams, satires, and devotional verse. In his lyrics other than sonnets, is found his finest work. A collection of Wyatt's poems was printed in *Songs and Sonnets written by the right honorable Lord Henry Howard, late Earl of Surrey, and others*, published by Richard Tottel in 1557, and commonly known as *Tottel's Miscellany*.

SONNET

THE LOVER FOR SHAME-FASTNESS HIDETH HIS DESIRE WITHIN HIS FAITHFUL HEART

The long love that in my thought I harbor,
And in my heart doth keep his residence,
Into my face presseth with bold pretence,
And there campeth displaying his banner.

She that me learns to love and to suffer,   5
And wills that my trust, and lust's negligence
Be reined by reason, shame, and reverence,
With his hardiness takes displeasure.

Wherewith love to the heart's forest he fleeth,
Leaving his enterprise with pain and cry,   10
And there him hideth, and not appeareth.
What may I do, when my master feareth?
But in the field with him to live and die?
For good is the life, ending faithfully.

SONNET

THE LOVER COMPARETH HIS STATE TO A SHIP IN PERILOUS STORM TOSSED ON THE SEA

My galley chargèd with forgetfulness
Thorough sharp seas, in winter nights doth pass,
'Tween rock and rock; and eke my foe, alas,
That is my lord, steereth with cruelness,

And every hour, a thought in readiness,   5
As though that death were light in such a case.
An endless wind doth tear the sail apace
Of forcèd sighs, and trusty fearfulness.

A rain of tears, a cloud of dark disdain
Hath done the wearied cords great hinderance,
Wreathèd with error, and with ignorance.   11
The stars be hid that led me to this pain;
Drowned is reason that should be my comfort,
And I remain, despairing of the port.

SONNET

THE LOVER HAVING DREAMED OF ENJOYING OF HIS LOVE, COMPLAINETH THAT THE DREAM IS NOT EITHER LONGER OR TRUER

Unstable dream, according to the place,
Be steadfast once, or else at least be true.
By tasted sweetness make me not to rue
The sudden loss of thy false feignèd grace.

By good respect in such a dangerous case   5
Thou broughtst not her into these tossing seas,
But madest my spirit to live, my care t'encrease,
My body in tempest her delight t'embrace.

The body dead, the spirit had his desire;
Painless was th' one, the other in delight.   10
Why then, alas! did it not keep it right,
But thus return to leap into the fire,
And where it was at wish, could not remain?
Such mocks of dreams do turn to deadly pain!

SONNET

A RENOUNCING OF LOVE

Farewell, Love, and all thy laws for ever!
Thy baited hooks shall tangle me no more:
Senec and Plato call me from thy lore
To perfect wealth my wit for to endeavor.

In blind error when I did perséver, 5
Thy sharp repulse, that pricketh aye so sore,
Taught me in trifles that I set no store;
But 'scape forth thence, since liberty is lever.

Therefore, farewell! go trouble younger hearts,
And in me claim no more authority. 10
With idle youth go use thy property,
And thereon spend thy many brittle darts;
For hitherto though I have lost my time,
Me list no longer rotten boughs to climb.

'FORGET NOT YET!'

THE LOVER BESEECHETH HIS MISTRESS NOT TO FORGET HIS STEADFAST FAITH AND TRUE INTENT

FORGET not yet the tried intent
Of such a truth as I have meant;
My great travail so gladly spent,
    Forget not yet!

Forget not yet when first began 5
The weary life ye know, since whan
The suit, the service none tell can;
    Forget not yet!

Forget not yet the great assays,
The cruel wrong, the scornful ways, 10
The painful patience in delays,
    Forget not yet!

Forget not! O, forget not this,
How long ago hath been, and is,
The mind that never meant amiss— 15
    Forget not yet!

Forget not then thine own approved,
The which so long hath thee so loved,
Whose steadfast faith yet never moved:
    Forget not this! 20

AN EARNEST SUIT TO HIS UNKIND MISTRESS NOT TO FORSAKE HIM

AND wilt thou leave me thus?
Say nay, say nay, for shame!
To save thee from the blame
Of all my grief and grame.
And wilt thou leave me thus? 5
    Say nay! say nay!

And wilt thou leave me thus,
That hath loved thee so long
In wealth and woe among:
And is thy heart so strong 10
As for to leave me thus?
    Say nay! say nay!

And wilt thou leave me thus,
That hath given thee my heart
Never for to depart 15
Neither for pain nor smart:
And wilt thou leave me thus?
    Say nay! say nay!

And wilt thou leave me thus,
And have no more pity 20
Of him that loveth thee?
Alas, thy cruelty!
And wilt thou leave me thus?
    Say nay! say nay!

THE LOVER COMPLAINETH THE UNKINDNESS OF HIS LOVE

MY lute, awake, perform the last
Labor that thou and I shall waste,
And end that I have now begun,
And when this song is sung and past,
My lute, be still, for I have done. 5

As to be heard where ear is none,
As lead to grave in marble stone,
My song may pierce her heart as soon.
Should we then sigh, or sing, or moan?
No, no, my lute, for I have done. 10

The rocks do not so cruelly
Repulse the waves continually,
As she my suit and affection;
So that I am past remedy,
Whereby my lute and I have done. 15

Proud of the spoil that thou hast got
Of simple hearts through Lovës shot,
By whom unkind thou hast them won,
Think not he hath his bow forgot,
Although my lute and I have done. 20

Vengeance shall fall on thy disdain
That makest but game on earnest pain.
Think not alone under the sun
Unquit to cause thy lovers playn,
Although my lute and I have done. 25

May chance thee lie withered and old
In winter nights that are so cold,
Playing in vain unto the moon;
Thy wishes then dare not be told.
Care then who list, for I have done. 30

And then may chance thee to repent
The time that thou hast lost and spent
To cause thy lovers sigh and swoon;
Then shalt thou know beauty but lent,
And wish and want, as I have done. 35

Now cease, my lute, this is the last
Labor that thou and I shall waste,
And ended is that we begun.
Now is the song both sung and past,
My lute, be still, for I have done.   40

THE LOVER SENDETH HIS COMPLAINTS AND TEARS TO SUE FOR GRACE

Pass forth, my wonted cries,
  Those cruel ears to pierce,
Which in most hateful wise
  Do still my plaints reverse.
Do you, my tears, also   5
  So wet her barren heart,
That pity there may grow,
  And cruelty depart.

For though hard rocks among
  She seems to have been bred,   10
And of the tiger long
  Been nourishèd and fed;
Yet shall that nature change,
  If pity once win place,
Whom as unknown and strange   15
  She now away doth chace.

And as the water soft,
  Without forcing or strength,
Where that it falleth oft,
  Hard stones doth pierce at length;   20
So in her stony heart
  My plaints at last shall grave,
And, rigor set apart,
  Win grant of that I crave.

Wherefore, my plaints, present   25
  Still so to her my suit,
As ye, through her assent,
  May bring to me some fruit.
And as she shall me prove,
  So bid her me regard,   30
And render love for love,
  Which is a just reward.

OF THE MEAN AND SURE ESTATE

WRITTEN TO JOHN POINS

My mother's maids, when they did sew and spin,
  They sung sometime a song of the field mouse
That, for because her livelihood was but thin,
Would needs go seek her townish sister's house.
  She thought herself endurèd too much pain; 5
The stormy blasts her cave so sore did souse
That when the furrows swimmèd with the rain,
  She must lie cold and wet in sorry plight;
And worse than that, bare meat there did remain

To comfort her when she her house had dight;
  Sometime a barley corn; sometime a bean, 11
For which she labored hard both day and night
In harvest time whilst she might go and glean;
  And when her store was stroyèd with the flood,
Then welaway! for she undone was clean.   15
Then was she fain to take, instead of food,
  Sleep, if she might, her hunger to beguile.

'My sister,' quoth she, 'hath a living good,
And hence from me she dwelleth not a mile.
  In cold and storm she lieth warm and dry 20
In bed of down, the dirt doth not defile
Her tender foot, she laboreth not as I.
  Richly she feedeth, and at the rich man's cost,
And for her meat she needs not crave nor cry.
By sea, by land, of the delicates, the most 25
  Her cater seeks and spareth for no peril,
She feedeth on boiled bacon, meat, and roast,
And hath thereof neither charge nor travail; 28
  And, when she list, the liquor of the grape
Doth glad her heart till that her belly swell.'

And at this journey she maketh but a jape;
  So forth she goeth, trusting of all this wealth
With her sister her part so for to shape,
That if she might keep herself in health,
  To live a lady while her life doth last. 35

And to the door now is she come by stealth,
And with her foot anon she scrapeth full fast.
  Th' other, for fear, durst not well scarce appear,
Of every noise so was the wretch aghast.
At last she askèd softly who was there,   40
  And in her language as well as she could.
'Peep!' quoth the other sister, 'I am here.'
'Peace,' quoth the town mouse, 'why speakest thou so loud?'
  And by the hand she took her fair and well.
'Welcome,' quoth she, 'my sister, by the Rood!' 45
She feasted her, that joy it was to tell
  The fare they had; they drank the wine so clear,
And, as to purpose now and then it fell,
She cheerèd her with 'How, sister, what cheer!'

Amid this joy befell a sorry chance,   50
  That, welaway! the stranger bought full dear
The fare she had, for, as she looked askance,
Under a stool she spied two steaming eyes
  In a round head with sharp ears. In France
Was never mouse so feared, for, though unwise
  Had not y-seen such a beast before,   56
Yet had nature taught her after her guise
To know her foe and dread him evermore.
  The towny mouse fled, she knew whither to go;
Th' other had no shift, but wonders sore 60

Feared of her life. At home she wished her tho,
　And to the door, alas! as she did skip,
　　The heaven it would, lo! and eke her chance was so,
At the threshold her silly foot did trip;
　And ere she might recover it again,　　65
　The traitor cat had caught her by the hip,
And made her there against her will remain,
　That had forgot her poor surety and rest
　　For seeming wealth wherein she thought to reign.

Alas, my Poins, how men do seek the best　70
　And find the worst by error as they stray!
　And no marvel; when sight is so opprest,
And blinds the guide, anon out of the way
　Goeth guide and all in seeking quiet life.
　O wretched minds, there is no gold that may
Grant that you seek; no war, no peace, no strife.　　76
　No, no, although thy head were hooped with gold,
　Sergeant with mace, halberd, sword, nor knife,
Cannot repulse the care that follow should.
　Each kind of life hath with him his disease.
　Live in delight even as thy lust would,　81
And thou shalt find, when lust doth most thee please,
　It irketh straight, and by itself doth fade.
　A small thing is it that may thy mind appease.
None of ye all there is that is so mad　85

To seek for grapes on brambles or on briars;
　Nor none, I trow, that hath his wit so bad
To set his hay for conies over rivers,
　Nor ye set not a drag-net for an hare;
　And yet the thing that most is your desire
Ye do mis-seek with more travail and care.　91
　Make plain thine heart, that it be not knotted
　With hope or dread, and see thy will be bare
From all effects whom vice hath ever spotted.
　Thyself content with that is thee assigned,
　And use it well that is to thee allotted.　96
Then seek no more out of thyself to find
　The thing that thou hast sought so long before,
　For thou shalt feel it sticking in thy mind.
Mad, if ye list to continue your sore,　100
　Let present pass and gape on time to come,
　And deep yourself in travail more and more.

Henceforth, my Poins, this shall be all and some,
　These wretched fools shall have naught else of me;
　But to the great God and to his high dome,
None other pain pray I for them to be,　106
　But, when the rage doth lead them from the right,
　That, looking backward, virtue they may see,
Even as she is so goodly fair and bright,
　And whilst they clasp their lusts in arms across,　110
　Grant them, good Lord, as thou mayst of thy might,
To fret inward for losing such a loss.

HENRY HOWARD, EARL OF SURREY (1517?–1547)

Henry Howard, or, as he is commonly called, Surrey, was, like Wyatt, actively connected with the English court. His courtly occupations, however, were not so much administrative and diplomatic as military and chivalric. From his early years up to manhood, Surrey was the companion of princes, and more than once his elders bargained for his marriage with a princess. As a boy of some fifteen years, Surrey accompanied the king to France, and remained eleven months at the French court. At the age of twenty, by striking a courtier who had accused him of seditious intentions, he landed himself in confinement for a few months at Windsor. These months Surrey spent in versifying, a diversion for which he had been well prepared by previous practice and by considerable reading in classical and contemporary literature. After having distinguished himself from time to time in jousts, he was made Knight of the Garter in 1541. Surrey's impulsive and adventurous spirit, which established him as 'the most foolish proud boy that is in England,' led him to eminent military service in France, during which he called forth the king's reprimand by exposing himself needlessly to danger. By numerous angry and trenchant utterances, he eventually brought upon himself the charge of treason, which he vigorously denied, but which led, ultimately, to his beheading on Tower Hill, January 21, 1547.

Although Surrey composed verse during most of his life-time, his poems first appeared in print in 1557, when Richard Tottel published *Songs and Sonnets written by the right honorable Lord Henry Howard, late Earl of Surrey, and others*. During the same year appeared Surrey's translation of the second and fourth books of Virgil's *Æneid*, a translation in which blank verse is used for the first time, in any notable way, in English. Although Surrey was the poetical disciple of his friend Wyatt, he excelled his master in range of subject, in refinement and variety of versification, and in delicacy of feeling.

SONNET

DESCRIPTION OF SPRING, WHEREIN EACH THING RENEWS, SAVE ONLY THE LOVER

The soote season that bud and bloom forth brings,
With green hath clad the hill and eke the vale;
The nightingale with feathers new she sings;
The turtle to her make hath told her tale:

Summer is come, for every spray now springs;
The hart hath hung his old head on the pale; 6
The buck in brake his winter coat he flings;
The fishes flete with new repairèd scale;

The adder all her slough away she slings;
The swift swallow pursueth the flies smale; 10
The busy bee her honey now she mings.
Winter is worn, that was the flowers' bale:
And thus I see among these pleasant things
Each care decays, and yet my sorrow springs!

SONNET

COMPLAINT OF A LOVER REBUKED

Love, that liveth and reigneth in my thought,
That built his seat within my captive breast,
Clad in the arms wherein with me he fought,
Oft in my face he doth his banner rest.

She that me taught to love, and suffer pain, 5
My doubtful hope and eke my hot desire
With shamefast cloak to shadow and refrain,
Her smiling grace converteth straight to ire.

The coward Love then to the heart apace
Taketh his flight, whereas he lurks and plains,
His purpose lost, and dare not show his face 11
For my lord's guilt thus faultless bide I pains.
Yet from my lord shall not my foot remove;
Sweet is his death that takes his end by love.

SONNET

DESCRIPTION AND PRAISE OF HIS LOVE GERALDINE

From Tuscan came my lady's worthy race;
Fair Florence was sometime her ancient seat;
The Western isle whose pleasant shore doth face
Wild Camber's cliffs did give her lively heat;

Fostered she was with milk of Irish breast; 5
Her sire, an earl; her dame, of princes' blood;
From tender years, in Britain she doth rest,
With a king's child, where she tasteth costly food;

Hunsdon did first present her to mine eyen;
Bright is her hue, and Geraldine she hight; 10

Hampton me taught to wish her first for mine;
And Windsor, alas, doth chase me from her sight:
Her beauty of kind, her virtues from above.
Happy is he that can obtain her love!

SONNET

COMPLAINT OF THE LOVER DISDAINED

In Cyprus springs, whereas dame Venus dwelt,
A well so hot, that whoso tastes the same,
Were he of stone, as thawèd ice should melt,
And kindled find his breast with firèd flame;

Whose moist poison dissolvèd hath my heart. 5
With creeping fire my cold limbs are suppresst,
Feeleth the heart that harbored freedom, smart:
Endless despair long thraldom hath imprest.

Another well of frozen ice is found,
Whose chilling venom of repugnant kind, 10
The fervent heat doth quench of Cupid's wound,
And with the spot of change infects the mind;
Whereof my dear hath tasted, to my pain:
Whereby my service grows into disdain.

SONNET

A COMPLAINT BY NIGHT OF THE LOVER NOT BELOVED

Alas, so all things now do hold their peace!
Heaven and earth disturbèd in nothing;
The beasts, the air, the birds their song do cease,
The nightès chair the stars about doth bring.

Calm is the sea; the waves work less and less; 5
So am not I, whom love, alas, doth wring,
Bringing before my face the great increase
Of my desires, whereat I weep and sing,

In joy and woe, as in a doubtful ease.
For my sweet thoughts sometime do pleasure bring; 10
But by and by, the cause of my disease
Gives me a pang, that inwardly doth sting,
When that I think what grief it is again,
To live and lack the thing should rid my pain.

SONNET

VOW TO LOVE FAITHFULLY HOWSOEVER HE BE REWARDED

Set me whereas the sun doth parch the green,
Or where his beams do not dissolve the ice;
In temperate heat, where he is felt and seen;
In presence prest of people, mad or wise;

Set me in high, or yet in low degree; 5
In longest night, or in the longest day;
In clearest sky, or where clouds thickest be;
In lusty youth, or when my hairs are gray:

Set me in heaven, in earth, or else in hell,
In hill, or dale, or in the foaming flood; 10
Thrall, or at large, alive whereso I dwell;
Sick or in health, in evil fame or good;
Hers will I be, and only with this thought
Content myself, although my chance be naught.

COMPLAINT OF THE ABSENCE OF HER LOVER BEING UPON THE SEA

O happy dames! that may embrace
   The fruit of your delight:
Help to bewail the woeful case,
   And eke the heavy plight,
Of me, that wonted to rejoice 5
   The fortune of my pleasant choice:
Good ladies, help to fill my mourning voice.

In ship freight with rememberance
   Of thoughts and pleasures past,
He sails that hath in governance 10
   My life, while it will last;
With scalding sighs, for lack of gale,
   Furthering his hope, that is his sail,
Toward me, the sweet port of his avail.

Alas, how oft in dreams I see 15
   Those eyes that were my food;
Which sometime so delighted me,
   That yet they do me good;
Wherewith I wake with his return,
   Whose absent flame did make me burn: 20
But when I find the lack, Lord, how I mourn!

When other lovers in arms across,
   Rejoice their chief delight,
Drownèd in tears to mourn my loss,
   I stand the bitter night 25
In my window, where I may see
   Before the winds how the clouds flee:
Lo, what a mariner love hath made me!

And in green waves when the salt flood
   Doth rise by rage of wind, 30
A thousand fancies in that mood,
   Assail my restless mind.
Alas, now drencheth my sweet foe,
   That with the spoil of my heart did go,
And left me; but, alas, why did he so? 35

And when the seas wax calm again,
   To chase from me annoy,
My doubtful hope doth cause me pain;
   So dread cuts off my joy.
Thus is my wealth mingled with woe, 40
   And of each thought a doubt doth grow;
Now he comes! Will he come? Alas, no, no!

A PRAISE OF HIS LOVE

**WHEREIN HE REPROVETH THEM THAT COMPARE
THEIR LADIES WITH HIS**

Give place, ye lovers, here before
    That spent your boasts and brags in vain;
My lady's beauty passeth more
    The best of yours, I dare well sayn,
Than doth the sun the candle light,   5
Or brightest day the darkest night.

And thereto hath a troth as just
    As had Penelope the fair;
For what she saith, ye may it trust
    As it by writing sealèd were: 10
And virtues hath she many mo
Than I with pen have skill to show.

I could rehearse, if that I would,
    The whole effect of Nature's plaint,
When she had lost the perfect mold,   15
    The like to whom she could not paint:
With wringing hands, how she did cry,
And what she said, I know it, I.

I know she swore with raging mind,
    Her kingdom only set apart,   20
There was no loss by law of kind
    That could have gone so near her heart.
And this was chiefly all her pain:
    She could not make the like again.

Sith Nature thus gave her the praise,   25
    To be the chiefest work she wrought;
In faith, methink, some better ways
    On your behalf might well be sought,
Than to compare, as ye have done,
To match the candle with the sun.   30

DESCRIPTION OF THE RESTLESS STATE OF A LOVER

The sun hath twice brought forth his tender green
    And clad the earth in lively lustiness,
Once have the winds the trees despoilèd clean,
    And new again begins their cruelness,
Since I have hid under my breast the harm   5
    That never shall recover healthfulness.
The winter's hurt recovers with the warm,
    The parchèd green restored is with the shade.
What warmth, alas, may serve for to disarm
The frozen heart that mine in flame hath made?
    What cold again is able to restore   11
My fresh green years, that wither thus and fade?
Alas, I see, nothing hath hurt so sore,
    But time in time reduceth a return;
In time, my harm increaseth more and more,
And seems to have my cure always in scorn.   16

Strange kinds of death, in life that I do try,
    At hand to melt, far off in flame to burn;
And like as time list to my cure apply,
    So doth each place my comfort clean refuse.
All thing alive that seeth the heavens with eye   21
With cloak of night may cover and excuse
    Itself from travail of the day's unrest,
Save I, alas, against all others' use,
That then stir up the torments of my breast,   25
    And curse each star as causer of my fate.
And when the sun hath eke the dark opprest,
And brought the day, it doth nothing abate
    The travails of mine endless smart and pain;
For then, as one that hath the light in hate,   30
I wish for night, more covertly to plain,
    And me withdraw from every haunted place,
Lest by my cheer my chance appear too plain.
And in my mind I measure, pace by pace,
    To seek the place where I myself had lost,
That day that I was tangled in the lace,   36
In seeming slack, that knitteth ever most.
    But never yet the travail of my thought
Of better state could catch a cause to boast;
For if I found, sometime that I have sought,   40
    Those stars by whom I trusted of the port,
My sails do fall, and I advance right naught,
As anchored fast, my spirits do all resort
    To stand agazed, and sink in more and more
The deadly harm which she doth take in sport.   45
Lo, if I seek, how do I find my sore!
    And if I flee I carry with me still
The venomed shaft, which doth his force restore
    By haste of flight, and I may plain my fill
Unto myself, unless this careful song   50
    Print in your heart some parcel of my teen;
For I, alas, in silence all too long
    Of mine old hurt yet feel the wound but green.
Rue on my life, or else your cruel wrong   54
Shall well appear, and by my death be seen!

OF THE DEATH OF SIR T. W.

[SIR THOMAS WYATT]

W. resteth here, that quick could never rest;
Whose heavenly gifts, encreasèd by disdain,
And virtue sank the deeper in his breast;
Such profit he by envy could obtain.

A head where wisdom mysteries did frame;   5
Whose hammers beat still in that lively brain
As on a stithe where that some work of fame
Was daily wrought to turn to Britain's gain.

A visage stern and mild, where both did grow,
Vice to condemn, in virtue to rejoice;   10
Amid great storms, whom grace assurèd so
To live upright and smile at fortune's choice.

A hand that taught what might be said in rime;
That reft Chaucer the glory of his wit:
A mark, the which (unperfected, for time)   15
Some may approach, but never none shall hit.

A tongue that served in foreign realms his king;
Whose courteous talk to virtue did enflame
Each noble heart; a worthy guide to bring
Our English youth by travail unto fame.   20

An eye whose judgment none affect could blind,
Friends to allure, and foes to reconcile;
Whose piercing look did represent a mind
With virtue fraught, reposèd, void of guile.

A heart where dread was never so imprest,   25
To hide the thought that might the truth advance;
In neither fortune lost, nor yet represt,
To swell in wealth, or yield unto mischance.

A valiant corse, where force and beauty met;
Happy, alas, too happy, but for foes!   30
Lived, and ran the race that Nature set:
Of manhood's shape, where she the mold did lose.

But to the heavens that simple soul is fled,
Which left with such as covet Christ to know
Witness of faith that never shall be dead,   35
Sent for our health, but not receivèd so.

Thus for our guilt, this jewel have we lost;
The earth his bones, the heavens possess his ghost!

VIRGIL'S ÆNEID

BOOK II

They whisted all, with fixèd face attent,
When Prince Æneas from the royal seat
Thus gan to speak:
    O Queen, it is thy will
I should renew a woe cannot be told;
How that the Greeks did spoil and overthrow
The Phrygian wealth and wailful realm of Troy.   6
Those ruthful things that I myself beheld,
And whereof no small part fell to my share;
Which to express, who could refrain from tears?
What Myrmidon? or yet what Dolopës?   10
What stern Ulysses' wagèd soldier?
And lo! moist night now from the welkin falls,
And stars declining counsel us to rest;

But since so great is thy delight to hear
Of our mishaps and Troyës last decay,   15
Though to record the same my mind abhors
And plaint eschews, yet thus will I begin:
 The Greekës chieftains, all irked with the war,
Wherein they wasted had so many years,
And oft repulsed by fatal destiny,   20
A huge horse made, high raisèd like a hill,
By the divine science of Minerva—
Of cloven fir compacted were his ribs,
For their return a feignèd sacrifice—
The fame whereof so wandered it at point.   25
In the dark bulk they closed bodies of men
Chosen by lot, and did enstuff by stealth
The hollow womb with armèd soldiers.
 There stands in sight an isle hight Tenedon,
Rich, and of fame while Priam's kingdom stood,
Now but a bay and road unsure for ship.   31
Hither them secretly the Greeks withdrew,
Shrouding themselves under the desert shore;
And, weening we they had been fled and gone,
And with that wind had fet the land of Greece,
Troy discharged her long continued dole.   36
The gates cast up, we issued out to play,
The Greekish camp desirous to behold,
The places void and the forsaken coasts.
Here Pyrrhus' band, there fierce Achilles pight;
Here rode their ships, there did their battles join.   41
Astonied some the scathful gift beheld,
Behight by vow unto the chaste Minerve,
All wondering at the hugeness of the horse.
 And first of all, Timœtes gan advise   45
Within the walls to lead and draw the same,
And place it eke amid the palace court,
Whether of guile, or Troyës fate it would.
Capys, with some of judgment more discreet,
Willed it to drown, or underset with flame,   50
The suspect present of the Greeks' deceit,
Or bore and gauge the hollow caves uncouth;
So diverse ran the giddy people's mind.
 Lo! foremost of a rout that followed him,
Kindled Laöcoön hasted from the tower,   55
Crying far off: 'O wretched citizens,
What so great kind of frenzy fretteth you?
Deem ye the Greeks, our enemies, to be gone?
Or any Greekish gifts can you suppose
Devoid of guile? Is so Ulysses known?   60
Either the Greeks are in this timber hid,
Or this an engine is to annoy our walls,
To view our towers, and overwhelm our town.
Here lurks some craft. Good Troyans give no trust
Unto this horse, for, whatsoever it be,   65
I dread the Greeks, yea, when they offer gifts.'

* * *

THOMAS SACKVILLE, LORD BUCKHURST (1536–1608)

About the year 1553, certain English printers projected a continuation of John Lydgate's *Fall of Princes*, a version of Boccaccio's *De Casibus Virorum Illustrium*, the design of these printers being to add stories of famous unfortunates from the period with which Boccaccio ended 'unto this presente time.' The project, under the general title *A Mirror for Magistrates*, was printed in gradually enlarged editions between the years 1555 and 1610. Although probably not a partner to the original plan, Sackville early became an associate and a contributor. *The Induction*, written as an introduction to such stories as he should contribute, and *The Complaint of Henry, Duke of Buckingham*, the only 'tragedy' actually contributed by Sackville, appeared in the edition of 1563.

The Induction is commonly accounted one of the best achievements in English poetry between Chaucer and Spenser. Although in writing his description of the lower world Sackville evidently had in mind both the sixth book of Virgil's *Æneid* and medieval allegory, the superb vivifying of such abstractions as Remorse of Conscience, Dread, Revenge, and the like, is to be credited to the genius of the English poet. Sackville owes his inspiration, perhaps, to Virgil, and his verse form, certainly, to Chaucer; his masterly control of his material and his power of phrasing are surely his own.

THE INDUCTION

The wrathful Winter, 'proaching on apace,
With blustering blasts had all ybared the treen,
And old Saturnus, with his frosty face,
With chilling cold had pierced the tender green;
The mantles rent, wherein enwrappèd been   5
The gladsome groves that now lay overthrown,
The tapets torn, and every bloom down blown.

The soil, that erst so seemly was to seen,
Was all despoilèd of her beauty's hue;
And soote fresh flowers, wherewith the summer's queen   10
Had clad the earth, now Boreas' blasts down blew;
And small fowls flocking, in their song did rue
The winter's wrath, wherewith each thing defaced
In woeful wise bewailed the summer past.

Hawthorn had lost his motley livery,   15
The naked twigs were shivering all for cold,
And dropping down the tears abundantly;
Each thing, methought, with weeping eye me told
The cruel season, bidding me withhold
Myself within; for I was gotten out   20
Into the fields, whereas I walked about.

When lo, the night with misty mantles spread,
Gan dark the day, and dim the azure skies;
And Venus in her message Hermes sped
To bloody Mars, to will him not to rise,   25
While she herself approached in speedy wise;
And Virgo hiding her disdainful breast,
With Thetis now had laid her down to rest.

Whiles Scorpio dreading Sagittarius' dart,
Whose bow prest bent in fight, the string had slipped,   30
Down slid into the ocean flood apart,
The Bear, that in the Irish seas had dipped
His grisly feet, with speed from thence he whipped:
For Thetis, hasting from the Virgin's bed,
Pursued the Bear, that ere she came was fled.   35

And Phaëton now, near reaching to his race
With glist'ring beams, gold streaming where they bent,
Was prest to enter in his resting place:
Erythius, that in the cart first went,
Had even now attained his journey's stent: 40
And, fast declining, hid away his head,
While Titan couched him in his purple bed.

And pale Cynthea, with her borrowed light,
Beginning to supply her brother's place
Was past the noonstead six degrees in sight,   45
When sparkling stars amid the heaven's face,
With twinkling light shone on the earth apace,
That, while they brought about the nightës chare,
The dark had dimmed the day ere I was ware.

And sorrowing I to see the summer flowers,   50
The lively green, the lusty leas forlorn,
The sturdy trees so shattered with the showers,
The fields so fade, that flourished so beforn,
It taught me well, all earthly things be born
To die the death, for naught long time may last;
The summer's beauty yields to winter's blast.   56

Then looking upward to the heaven's leams,
With nightës stars thick powdered everywhere,
Which erst so glistened with the golden streams
That cheerful Phœbus spread down from his sphere,
Beholding dark oppressing day so near: 61
The sudden sight reducèd to my mind,
The sundry changes that in earth we find.

That musing on this worldly wealth in thought,
Which comes, and goes, more faster than we see
The flickering flame that with the fire is wrought,
My busy mind presented unto me   67
Such fall of peers as in this realm had be;
That oft I wished some would their woes descrive,
To warn the rest whom fortune left alive.   70

And straight forth stalking with redoubled pace,
For that I saw the night drew on so fast,
In black all clad, there fell before my face
A piteous wight, whom woe had all forewaste;
Forth from her eyen the crystal tears out brast;
And sighing sore, her hands she wrung and fold,   76
Tare all her hair, that ruth was to behold.

Her body small, forewithered, and forespent,
As is the stalk that summer's drought oppressed;
Her welkèd face with woeful tears besprent;   80
Her color pale; and, as it seemed her best,
In woe and plaint reposèd was her rest;
And, as the stone that drops of water wears,
So dented were her cheeks with fall of tears.

Her eyes swollen with flowing streams afloat,
Wherewith, her looks thrown up full piteously,
Her forceless hands together oft she smote,   87
With doleful shrieks, that echoed in the sky;
Whose plaint such sighs did straight accompany,
That, in my doom, was never man did see   90
A wight but half so woe-begone as she.

I stood aghast, beholding all her plight,
'Tween dread and dolor, so distrained in heart,
That, while my hairs upstarted with the sight,
The tears outstreamed for sorrow of her smart:
But, when I saw no end that could apart   96
The deadly dewle which she so sore did make,
With doleful voice then thus to her I spake:

'Unwrap thy woes, whatever wight thou be, 99
And stint in time to spill thyself with plaint;
Tell what thou art, and whence, for well I see
Thou canst not dure, with sorrow thus attaint:'
And, with that word of sorrow, all forefaint
She lookèd up, and, prostrate as she lay,
With piteous sound, lo, thus she gan to say: 105

'Alas, I wretch, whom thus thou seest distrained
With wasting woes, that never shall aslake,
Sorrow I am, in endless torments pained
Among the Furies in the infernal lake,
Where Pluto, god of hell, so grisly black,   110
Doth hold his throne, and Lethe's deadly taste
Doth reave remembrance of each thing forepast:

'Whence come I am, the dreary destiny
And luckless lot for to bemoan of those
Whom fortune, in this maze of misery,   115
Of wretched chance, most woeful mirrors chose;
That, when thou seest how lightly they did lose
Their pomp, their power, and that they thought most sure,
Thou mayst soon deem no earthly joy may dure.'

Whose rueful voice no sooner had out brayed
Those woeful words wherewith she sorrowed so,   121
But out, alas, she shright, and never stayed,
Fell down, and all to-dashed herself for woe:
The cold pale dread my limbs gan overgo,
And I so sorrowed at her sorrows eft,   125
That, what with grief and fear, my wits were reft.

I stretched myself, and straight my heart revives,
That dread and dolor erst did so appale;
Like him that with the fervent fever strives, 129
When sickness seeks his castle health to scale;
With gathered spirits so forced I fear to avale:
And, rearing her, with anguish all foredone,
My spirits returned, and then I thus begun:

'O Sorrow, alas, sith Sorrow is thy name,   134
And that to thee this drear doth well pertain,
In vain it were to seek to cease the same:
But, as a man himself with sorrow slain,
So I, alas, do comfort thee in pain,
That here in sorrow art foresunk so deep,   139
That at thy sight I can but sigh and weep.'

I had no sooner spoken of a stike,
But that the storm so rumbled in her breast,
As Æolus could never roar the like;
And showers down rainèd from her eyen so fast,
That all bedrent the place, till at the last,   145
Well easèd they the dolor of her mind,
As rage of rain doth swage the stormy wind:

For forth she pacèd in her fearful tale:
'Come, come,' quoth she, 'and see what I shall show,
Come, hear the plaining and the bitter bale 150
Of worthy men by Fortune overthrow:
Come thou, and see them ruing all in row,

They were but shades that erst in mind thou rolled:
Come, come with me, thine eyes snall them behold.'

What could these words but make me more aghast, 155
To hear her tell whereon I mused whilere?
So was I mazed therewith, till, at the last,
Musing upon her words, and what they were,
All suddenly well lessoned was my fear;
For to my mind returnèd, how she telled 160
Both what she was, and where her won she held.

Whereby I knew that she a goddess was
And, therewithal, resorted to my mind
My thought, that late presented me the glass
Of brittle state, of cares that here we find, 165
Of thousand woes to silly men assigned:
And how she now bid me come and behold,
To see with eye that erst in thought I rolled.

Flat down I fell, and with all reverence
Adorèd her, perceiving now that she, 170
A goddess, sent by godly providence,
In earthly shape thus showed herself to me,
To wail and rue this world's uncertainty:
And, while I honored thus her godhead's might
With plaining voice these words to me she shright: 175

'I shall thee guide first to the grisly lake,
And thence unto the blissful place of rest,
Where thou shall see, and hear, the plaint they make
That whilom here bare swing among the best:
This shall thou see: but great is the unrest 180
That thou must bide, before thou canst attain
Unto the dreadful place where these remain.'

And, with these words, as I upraisèd stood,
And gan to follow her that straight forth paced,
Ere I was ware, into a desert wood 185
We now were come, where, hand in hand embraced,
She led the way, and through the thick so traced,
As, but I had been guided by her might,
It was no way for any mortal wight.

But lo, while thus amid the desert dark 190
We passèd on with steps and pace unmeet,
A rumbling roar, confused with howl and bark
Of dogs, shook all the ground under our feet,
And struck the din within our ears so deep,
As, half distraught, unto the ground I fell, 195
Besought return, and not to visit hell.

But she, forthwith, uplifting me apace,
Removed my dread, and, with a steadfast mind,
Bade me come on; for here was now the place,
The place where we our travail end should find: 200

Wherewith I rose, and to the place assigned
Astoined I stalk, when straight we approached near
The dreadful place, that you will dread to hear.

An hideous hole all vast, withouten shape,
Of endless depth, o'erwhelmed with ragged stone, 205
With ugly mouth, and grisly jaws doth gape,
And to our sight confounds itself in one:
Here entered we, and yeding forth, anon
An horrible loathly lake we might discern,
As black as pitch, that clepèd is Avern: 210

A deadly gulf, where naught but rubbish grows,
With foul black swelth in thickened lumps that lies,
Which up in th' air such stinking vapors throws,
That over there may fly no fowl but dies
Choked with the pestilent savors that arise: 215
Hither we come; whence forth we still did pace,
In dreadful fear amid the dreadful place:

And, first, within the porch and jaws of hell,
Sat deep Remorse of Conscience, all besprent
With tears; and to herself oft would she tell 220
Her wretchedness, and cursing never stent
To sob and sigh; but ever thus lament,
With thoughtful care, as she that, all in vain,
Would wear, and waste continually in pain.

Her eyes unsteadfast, rolling here and there,
Whirled on each place, as place that vengeance brought, 226
So was her mind continually in fear,
Tossed and tormented with the tedious thought
Of those detested crimes which she had wrought;
With dreadful cheer, and looks thrown to the sky, 230
Wishing for death, and yet she could not die.

Next saw we Dread, all trembling how he shook,
With foot uncertain, proffered here and there:
Benumbed of speech, and, with a ghastly look,
Searched every place, all pale and dead for fear,
His cap borne up with staring of his hair, 236
'Stoined and amazed at his own shade for dread,
And fearing greater dangers than was need.

And next, within the entry of this lake,
Sat fell Revenge, gnashing her teeth for ire, 240
Devising means how she may vengeance take,
Never in rest, till she have her desire:
But frets within so far forth with the fire
Of wreaking flames, that now determines she
To die by death, or venged by death to be. 245

When fell Revenge, with bloody foul pretence
Had showed herself, as next in order set,
With trembling limbs we softly parted thence,

Till in our eyes another sight we met:
When from my heart a sigh forthwith I fet,
Ruing, alas! upon the woeful plight 251
Of Misery, that next appeared in sight.

His face was lean, and somedeal pined away,
And eke his hands consumèd to the bone,
But what his body was, I cannot say, 255
For on his carcass raiment had he none,
Save clouts and patches, piecèd one by one;
With staff in hand, and scrip on shoulders cast,
His chief defence against the winter's blast.

His food, for most, was wild fruits of the tree, 260
Unless sometimes some crumbs fell to his share,
Which in his wallet long, God wot, kept he,
As on the which full daint'ly would he fare:
His drink, the running stream; his cup, the bare
Of his palm closed; his bed, the hard cold ground: 265
To this poor life was Misery ybound.

Whose wretched state when we had well beheld,
With tender ruth on him, and on his fears,
In thoughtful cares forth then our pace we held;
And, by and by, another shape appears, 270
Of greedy Care, still brushing up the breres,
His knuckles knobbed, his flesh deep dented in,
With tawèd hands, and hard ytannèd skin.

The morrow gray no sooner hath begun
To spread his light, even peeping in our eyes,
When he is up, and to his work yrun: 276
But let the night's black misty mantles rise,
And with foul dark never so much disguise
The fair bright day, yet ceaseth he no while,
But hath his candles to prolong his toil. 280

By him lay heavy Sleep, the cousin of Death,
Flat on the ground, and still as any stone,
A very corpse, save yielding forth a breath:
Small keep took he, whom Fortune frownèd on,
Or whom she lifted up into the throne 285
Of high renown; but, as a living death,
So, dead alive, of life he drew the breath.

The body's rest, the quiet of the heart,
The travail's ease, the still night's fear was he,
And of our life in earth the better part; 290
Reaver of sight, and yet in whom we see
Things oft that tide, and oft that never be;
Without respect, esteeming equally
King Crœsus' pomp, and Irus' poverty.

And next, in order sad, Old Age we found: 295
His beard all hoar, his eyes hollow and blind,
With drooping cheer still poring on the ground,
As on the place where Nature him assigned
To rest, when that the Sisters had untwined
His vital thread, and ended with their knife 300
The fleeting course of fast declining life.

There heard we him with broke and hollow plaint
Rue with himself his end approaching fast,
And all for naught his wretched mind torment
With sweet remembrance of his pleasures past,
And fresh delights of lusty youth forewaste;
Recounting which, how would he sob and shriek,
And to be young again of Jove beseek! 308

But and the cruel fates so fixèd be,
That time forepast cannot return again, 310
This one request of Jove yet prayèd he:
That, in such withered plight, and wretched pain,
As eld, accompanied with his loathsome train,
Had brought on him, all were it woe and grief,
He might a while yet linger forth his life, 315
And not so soon descend into the pit,
Where Death, when he the mortal corpse hath slain,
With reckless hand in grave doth cover it,
Thereafter never to enjoy again 319
The gladsome light, but in the ground ylain,
In the depth of darkness waste and wear to naught,
As he had never into the world been brought.

But who had seen him sobbing, how he stood
Unto himself, and how he would bemoan 324
His youth forepast, as though it wrought him good
To talk of youth, all were his youth foregone,
He would have mused, and marveled much, whereon
This wretched Age should life desire so fain,
And knows full well life doth but length his pain.

Crookbacked he was, tooth-shaken, and bleareyed, 330
Went on three feet, and sometime crept on four,
With old lame bones that rattled by his side,
His scalp all pilled, and he with eld forlore:
His withered fist still knocking at Death's door,
Fumbling, and driveling, as he draws his breath: 335
For brief, the shape and messenger of Death.

And fast by him pale Malady was placed,
Sore sick in bed, her color all foregone,
Bereft of stomach, savor, and of taste,
Ne could she brook no meat, but broths alone:
Her breath corrupt, her keepers every one 341
Abhorring her, her sickness past recure,
Detesting physic, and all physic's cure.

But, oh, the doleful sight that then we see!
We turned our look, and, on the other side, 345
A grisly shape of Famine might we see,

With greedy looks, and gaping mouth that cried
And roared for meat, as she should there have died;
Her body thin and bare as any bone, 349
Whereto was left naught but the case alone.

And that, alas, was gnawn on every where,
All full of holes, that I ne might refrain
From tears, to see how she her arms could tear,
And with her teeth gnash on the bones in vain,
When, all for naught, she fain would so sustain
Her starven corpse, that rather seemed a shade,
Than any substance of a creature made. 357

Great was her force, whom stone wall could not stay,
Her tearing nails snatching at all she saw;
With gaping jaws, that by no means ymay 360
Be satisfied from hunger of her maw,
But eats herself as she that hath no law:
Gnawing, alas, her carcass all in vain,
Where you may count each sinew, bone, and vein.

On her while we thus firmly fixed our eyes, 365
That bled for ruth of such a dreary sight,
Lo, suddenly she shrieked in so huge wise,
As made hell-gates to shiver with the might:
Wherewith, a dart we saw, how it did light
Right on her breast, and, therewithal, pale Death 370
Enthrilling it, to reave her of her breath.

And by and by, a dumb dead corpse we saw,
Heavy and cold, the shape of Death aright,
That daunts all earthly creatures to his law;
Against whose force in vain it is to fight: 375
Ne peers, ne princes, nor no mortal wight,
No towns, ne realms, cities, ne strongest tower,
But all, perforce, must yield unto his power.

His dart, anon, out of the corpse he took,
And in his hand (a dreadful sight to see) 380
With great triumph eftsoons the same he shook,
That most of all my fears affrayèd me:
His body dight with naught but bones, pardé.
The naked shape of man there saw I plain,
All save the flesh, the sinew, and the vein. 385

Lastly, stood War, in glittering arms yclad,
With visage grim, stern looks, and blackly hued;
In his right hand a naked sword he had,
That to the hilts was all with blood imbrued;
And in his left (that kings and kingdoms rued)
Famine and fire he held, and therewithal 391
He razèd towns, and threw down towers and all.

Cities he sacked, and realms that whilom flowered
In honor, glory, and rule, above the best,
He overwhelmed, and all their fame devoured,
Consumed, destroyed, wasted and never ceased,
Till he their wealth, their name, and all oppressed: 397
His face forehewed with wounds, and by his side
There hung his targe, with gashes deep and wide.

In mids of which, depainted there, we found
Deadly Debate, all full of snaky hair, 401
That with a bloody fillet was ybound,
Out breathing naught but discord everywhere:
And round about were portrayed, here and there,
The hugy hosts, Darius and his power, 405
His kings, princes, his peers, and all his flower,

Whom great Macedo vanquished there in sight,
With deep slaughter, despoiling all his pride,
Pierced through his realms, and daunted all his might:
Duke Hannibal beheld I there beside, 410
In Canna's field, victor how he did ride,
And woeful Romans that in vain withstood,
And consul Paulus covered all in blood.

Yet saw I more the fight at Thrasimene,
And Treby field, and eke when Hannibal 415
And worthy Scipio last in arms were seen
Before Carthago gate, to cry for all
The world's empire, to whom it should befall:
There saw I Pompey and Cæsar clad in arms,
Their hosts allied and all their civil harms: 420

With conquerors' hands, forebathed in their own blood,
And Cæsar weeping over Pompey's head;
Yet saw I Sulla and Marius where they stood,
Their great cruelty, and the deep bloodshed
Of friends: Cyrus I saw and his host dead, 425
And how the queen with great despite hath flung
His head in blood of them she overcome.

Xerxes, the Persian king, yet saw I there,
With his huge host, that drank the rivers dry,
Dismounted hills, and made the vales uprear, 430
His host and all yet saw I slain, pardé:
Thebës I saw, all razed how it did lie
In heaps of stones, and Tyrus put to spoil,
With walls and towers flat evened with the soil.

But Troy, alas, methought, above them all, 435
It made mine eyes in very tears consume:
When I beheld the woeful word befall,
That by the wrathful will of gods was come;
And Jove's unmovèd sentence and foredoom
On Priam king, and on his town so bent, 440
I could not lin, but I must there lament.

And that the more, sith destiny was so stern
As, force perforce, there might no force avail,
But she must fall: and, by her fall, we learn,

That cities, towers, wealth, world, and all shall
    quail: 445
No manhood, might, nor nothing might prevail;
All were there prest full many a prince, and
    peer,
And many a knight that sold his death full dear.

Not worthy Hector, worthiest of them all,
Her hope, her joy, his force is now for naught:
O Troy, Troy, Troy, there is no boot but bale,
The hugy horse within thy walls is brought; 452
Thy turrets fall, thy knights, that whilom fought
In arms amid the field, are slain in bed,
Thy gods defiled, and all thy honor dead. 455

The flames up spring, and cruelly they creep
From wall to roof, till all to cinders waste:
Some fire the houses where the wretches sleep,
Some rush in here, some run in there as fast;
In every where or sword or fire they taste: 460
The walls are torn, the towers whirled to the
    ground;
There is no mischief but may there be found.

Cassandra yet there saw I how they haled
From Pallas' house, with sperkled tress undone,
Her wrists fast bound, and with Greeks' rout
    empaled: 465
And Priam eke, in vain how he did run
To arms, whom Pyrrhus with despite hath done
To cruel death, and bathed him in the baign
Of his son's blood, before the altar slain.

But how can I describe the doleful sight, 470
That in the shield so livelike fair did shine?
Sith in this world, I think was never wight
Could have set forth the half, not half so fine:
I can no more, but tell how there is seen
Fair Ilium fall in burning red gledes down, 475
And, from the soil, great Troy, Neptunus' town.

Herefrom when scarce I could mine eyes with-
    draw,
That filled with tears as doth the springing well,
We passèd on so far forth till we saw
Rude Acheron, a loathsome lake to tell, 480
That boils and bubs up swelth as black as hell;
Where grisly Charon, at their fixèd tide,
Still ferries ghosts unto the farther side.

The agèd God no sooner Sorrow spied,
But, hasting straight unto the bank apace, 485
With hollow call unto the rout he cried,
To swerve apart, and give the goddess place:
Straight it was done, when to the shore we pace,
Where, hand in hand as we then linkèd fast,
Within the boat we are together placed. 490

And forth we launch full fraughted to the brink:
When, with the unwonted weight, the rusty keel
Began to crack as if the same should sink:
We hoise up mast and sail, that in a while
We fetched the shore, where scarcely we had
    while 495
For to arrive, but that we heard anon
A three-sound bark confounded all in one.

We had not long forth passed, but that we saw
Black Cerberus, the hideous hound of hell,
With bristles reared, and with a three-mouthed
    jaw 500
Foredinning the air with his horrible yell,
Out of the deep dark cave where he did dwell.
The goddess straight he knew, and by and by,
He peased and couched, while that we passèd
    by.

Thence come we to the horror and the hell, 505
The large great kingdoms, and the dreadful
    reign
Of Pluto in his throne where he did dwell,
The wide waste places, and the hugy plain,
The wailings, shrieks, and sundry sorts of pain,
The sighs, the sobs, the deep and deadly groan;
Earth, air, and all, resounding plaint and
    moan. 511

Here puled the babes, and here the maids unwed
With folded hands their sorry chance bewailed;
Here wept the guiltless slain, and lovers dead,
That slew themselves when nothing else availed;
A thousand sorts of sorrows here, that wailed
With sighs, and tears, sobs, shrieks, and all
    yfear, 517
That, of, alas, it was a hell to hear.

We staid us straight, and with a rueful fear,
Beheld this heavy sight; while from mine eyes
The vapored tears down stillèd here and there,
And Sorrow eke, in far more woeful wise, 522
Took on with plaint, upheaving to the skies
Her wretched hands, that, with her cry, the rout
Gan all in heaps to swarm us round about. 525

'Lo here' quoth Sorrow, 'princes of renown,
That whilom sat on top of Fortune's wheel,
Now laid full low; like wretches whirlèd down,
Even with one frown, that stayed but with a
    smile:
And now behold the thing that thou, erewhile,
Saw only in thought; and, what thou now shalt
    hear, 531
Recount the same to kesar, king, and peer.'

    * * *

ROGER ASCHAM (1515-1568)

Ascham was prepared for his career by gentle birth and by a thorough humanistic education at St. John's College, Cambridge. His studying of Greek resulted in his being one of the most enthusiastic advocates of the new classical learning. In 1531, he became a fellow of St. John's College, and subsequently held the appointments of reader in Greek and of public orator. Ascham's *Toxophilus* (1545), full of patriotism, learning, and human feeling, won for him the favor of Henry VIII, who granted him a pension, later renewed by Edward VI. In 1548, he became tutor of the Princess Elizabeth, and, soon after, secretary to an embassy to the court of Charles V. He became secretary to Queen Mary, and later received preferment from Queen Elizabeth. Ascham's vigorous humanism is emphatically expressed in his *Schoolmaster*, written late in life, and published posthumously in 1570.

THE SCHOOLMASTER

From BOOK I

But I am afraid that over-many of our travelers into Italy do not eschew the way to Circe's Court, but go and ride, and run, and fly thither; they make great haste to come to her; they make great suit to serve her; yea, I could point out some with my finger that never had gone out of England but only to serve Circe in Italy. Vanity and vice and any licence to ill living in England was counted stale and rude unto them. And so, being mules and horses before they went, returned very swine and asses home again; yet everywhere very foxes with subtle and busy heads; and where they may, very wolves with cruel malicious hearts. A marvelous monster, which, for filthiness of living, for dulness to learning himself, for wiliness in dealing with others, for malice in hurting without cause, should carry at once, in one body, the belly of a swine, the head of an ass, the brain of a fox, the womb of a wolf. If you think we judge amiss and write too sore against you, hear what the Italian saith of the Englishman, what the master reporteth of the scholar; who uttereth plainly what is taught by him, and what is learned by you, saying, '*Inglese Italianato è un diabolo incarnato*,' that is to say, you remain men in shape and fashion, but become devils in life and condition. This is not the opinion of one for some private spite, but the judgment of all in a common proverb, which riseth of that learning and those manners which you gather in Italy: a good schoolhouse of wholesome doctrine, and worthy masters of commendable scholars, where the master had rather defame himself for his teaching, than not shame his scholar for his learning. A good nature of the master, and fair conditions of the scholars. And now choose you, you Italian Englishmen, whether you will be angry with us for calling you monsters, or with the Italians for calling you devils, or else with your own selves that take so much pains and go so far to make yourselves both. If some yet do not well understand what is an Englishman Italianated, I will plainly tell him. He that by living and traveling in Italy bringeth home into England out of Italy the religion, the learning, the policy, the experience, the manners of Italy. That is to say, for religion, papistry or worse; for learning, less, commonly, than they carried out with them; for policy, a factious heart, a discoursing head, a mind to meddle in all men's matters; for experience, plenty of new mischiefs never known in England before; for manners, variety of vanities and change of filthy living. These be the enchantments of Circe, brought out of Italy to mar men's manners in England; much by example of ill life, but more by precepts of fond books of late translated out of Italian into English, sold in every shop in London, commended by honest titles, the sooner to corrupt honest manners; dedicated over-boldly to virtuous and honorable personages, the easier to beguile simple and innocent wits. It is pity that those which have authority and charge to allow and disallow books to be printed, be no more circumspect herein than they are. Ten sermons at Paul's Cross do not so much good for moving men to true doctrine, as one of those books do harm with enticing men to ill living. Yea, I say farther, those books tend not so much to corrupt honest living, as they do to subvert true religion. More papists be made by your merry books of Italy than by your earnest books of Louvain. And because our great physicians do wink at the matter, and make no count of this sore, I, though not admitted one of their fellowship, yet having been many years a prentice to God's true religion, and trust to continue a poor journeyman therein all days of my life, for the duty I owe and love I bear both to true doctrine and honest living, though I have no authority to amend the sore myself, yet I will declare my good-will to discover the sore to others.

St. Paul saith that sects and ill opinions be the works of the flesh and fruits of sin. This is spoken no more truly for the doctrine than sensible for the reason. And why? For ill doings breed ill thinkings. And of corrupted manners spring perverted judgments. And how? There be in man two special things: man's will, man's mind. Where will inclineth to goodness, the mind is bent to truth. Where will is carried from goodness to vanity, the mind is soon drawn from truth to false opinion. And so the readiest way to entangle the mind with false doctrine is first to entice the will to wanton living. Therefore, when the busy and open papists abroad could not by their contentious books turn men in England fast enough from truth and right judgment in doctrine, then the subtle and secret papists at home procured bawdy books to be translated out of the Italian tongue, whereby over-many young wills and wits, allured to wantonness, do now boldly contemn all severe books that sound to honesty and godliness. In our forefathers' time, when papistry, as a standing pool, covered and overflowed all England, few books were read in our tongue, saving certain books [of] chivalry, as they said, for pastime and pleasure, which, as some say, were made in monasteries by idle monks or wanton canons: as one, for example, *Morte Arthur*, the whole pleasure of which book standeth in two special points—in open manslaughter and bold bawdry. In which book those be counted the noblest knights that do kill most men without any quarrel, and commit foulest adulteries by subtlest shifts: as Sir Launcelot with the wife of King Arthur, his master; Sir Tristram with the wife of King Mark, his uncle; Sir Lamerock with the wife of King Lot, that was his own aunt. This is good stuff for wise men to laugh at, or honest men to take pleasure at! Yet I know when God's Bible was banished the court, and *Morte Arthur* received into the prince's chamber. What toys the daily reading of such a book may work in the will of a young gentleman or a young maid that liveth wealthily and idly, wise men can judge and honest men do pity. And yet ten *Morte Arthurs* do not the tenth part so much harm as one of these books made in Italy and translated in England. They open not fond and common ways to vice, but such subtle, cunning, new, and diverse shifts to carry young wills to vanity and young wits to mischief, to teach old bawds new school-points, as the simple head of an Englishman is not able to invent, nor never was heard of in England before; yea, when papistry overflowed all. Suffer these books to be read, and they shall soon displace all books of godly learning. For they, carrying the will to vanity and marring good manners, shall easily corrupt the mind with ill opinions and false judgment in doctrine: first, to think nothing of God himself—one special point that is to be learned in Italy and Italian books. And that which is most to be lamented, and therefore more needful to be looked to, there be more of these ungracious books set out in print within these few months than have been seen in England many score years before. And because our Englishmen made Italians cannot hurt but certain persons and in certain places, therefore these Italian books are made English to bring mischief enough openly and boldly to all states, great and mean, young and old, everywhere.

And thus you see how will enticed to wantonness doth easily allure the mind to false opinions; and how corrupt manners in living, breed false judgment in doctrine; how sin and fleshliness bring forth sects and heresies. And, therefore, suffer not vain books to breed vanity in men's wills, if you would have God's truth take root in men's minds.

That Italian that first invented the Italian proverb against our Englishmen Italianated, meant no more their vanity in living than their lewd opinion in religion. For in calling them devils, he carrieth them clean from God; and yet he carrieth them no farther than they willingly go themselves—that is, where they may freely say their minds—to the open contempt of God and all godliness, both in living and doctrine.

And how? I will express how, not by a fable

of Homer, nor by the philosophy of Plato, but by a plain truth of God's Word, sensibly uttered by David thus: 'These men, *abominabiles facti in studiis suis*, think verily and sing gladly the verse before, *Dixit insipiens in corde suo, non est Deus*'—that is to say, they giving themselves up to vanity, shaking off the motions of grace, driving from them the fear of God, and running headlong into all sin, first lustily contemn God, then scornfully mock his Word, and also spitefully hate and hurt all well-willers thereof. Then they have in more reverence the *Triumphs* of Petrarch than the *Genesis* of Moses. They make more account of Tully's *Offices* than St. Paul's *Epistles;* of a tale in Boccaccio than a story of the Bible. Then they count as fables the holy mysteries of Christian religion. They make Christ and his Gospel only serve civil policy. Then neither religion cometh amiss to them. In time they be promoters of both openly: in place, again, mockers of both privily, as I wrote once in a rude rime:—

Now new, now old, now both, now neither,
To serve the world's course, they care not with whether.

For where they dare, in company where they like, they boldly laugh to scorn both protestant and papist. They care for no Scripture; they make no count of general councils; they contemn the consent of the church; they pass for no doctors; they mock the Pope; they rail on Luther; they allow neither side; they like none, but only ourselves. The mark they shoot at, the end they look for, the heaven they desire, is only their own present pleasure and private profit: whereby they plainly declare of whose school, of what religion they be—that is, epicures in living and ἄθεοι [godless] in doctrine. This last word is no more unknown now to plain Englishmen than the person was unknown some time in England, until some Englishman took pains to fetch that devilish opinion out of Italy. These men, thus Italianated abroad cannot abide our godly Italian church at home; they be not of that parish; they be not of that fellowship; they like not that preacher; they hear not his sermons, except sometimes for company they come thither to hear the Italian tongue naturally spoken, not to hear God's doctrine truly preached.

And yet these men in matters of divinity openly pretend a great knowledge, and have privately to themselves a very compendious understanding of all, which, nevertheless, they will utter when and where they list. And that is this: all the mysteries of Moses, the whole law and ceremonies, the Psalms and prophets, Christ and his Gospel, God and the devil, heaven and hell, faith, conscience, sin, death, and all they shortly wrap up, they quickly expound with this one half verse of Horace:

Credat Judæus Apella.
[Let the Jew Apella believe it]

Yet though in Italy they may freely be of no religion, as they are in England in very deed to, nevertheless, returning home into England, they must countenance the profession of the one or the other, however inwardly they laugh to scorn both. And though for their private matters they can follow, fawn, and flatter noble personages contrary to them in all respects, yet commonly they ally themselves with the worst papists, to whom they be wedded, and do well agree together in three proper opinions: in open contempt of God's Word; in a secret security of sin; and in a bloody desire to have all taken away by sword and burning that be not of their faction. They that do read with indifferent judgment Pygius and Machiavelli, two indifferent patriarchs of these two religions, do know full well what I say true.

Ye see what manners and doctrine our Englishmen fetch out of Italy. For, finding no other there, they can bring no other hither. And, therefore, many godly and excellent learned Englishmen, not many years ago, did make a better choice, when open cruelty drove them out of this country, to place themselves there where Christ's doctrine, the fear of God, punishment of sin, and discipline of honesty were had in special regard.

I was once in Italy myself; but I thank God my abode there was but nine days. And yet I saw in that little time, in one city, more liberty to sin than ever I heard tell of in our noble city of London in nine years. I saw it was there as free to sin not only without all punishment, but also without any man's marking, as it is free in the city of London to choose without all blame whether a man lust to wear shoe or pantocle. And good cause why; for, being unlike in truth of religion, they must needs be unlike in honesty of living. For blessed be Christ, in our city of London commonly the commandments of God be more diligently taught, and the service of God more reverently used, and that daily in many private men's houses, than they be in Italy once a week in their common churches; where making ceremonies to delight the eye, and vain sounds to please the ear, do quite thrust out of the churches all service of God in spirit and truth. Yea, the Lord Mayor of London, being but a civil officer, is commonly, for his time, more diligent in punishing sin, the bent enemy against God and good order, than all the bloody inquisitors in Italy be in seven years. For their care and charge is not to punish sin, not to amend manners, not to purge doctrine, but only to watch and oversee that Christ's true religion set no sure footing where the Pope hath any jurisdiction. I learned, when I was at Venice, that there it is counted good policy, when there be four or five brethren of one family, one only to marry, and all the rest to welter with as little shame in open lechery as swine do here in the common mire. Yea, there be as fair houses of religion, as great provision, as diligent officers to keep up this misorder, as Bridewell is and all the masters there to keep down misorder. And, therefore, if the Pope himself do not only grant pardons to further these wicked purposes abroad in Italy, but also (although this present Pope in the beginning made some show of misliking thereof) assign both meed and merit to the maintenance of stews and brothelhouses at home in Rome, then let wise men think Italy a safe place for wholesome doctrine and godly manners, and a fit school for young gentlemen of England to be brought up in!

Our Italians bring home with them other faults from Italy, though not so great as this of religion, yet a great deal greater than many good men can well bear. For commonly they come home common contemners of marriage and ready persuaders of all others to the same; not because they love virginity, nor yet because they hate pretty young virgins, but, being free in Italy to go whithersoever lust will carry them, they do not like that law and honesty should be such a bar to their like liberty at home in England. And yet they be the greatest makers of love, the daily dalliers, with such pleasant words, with such smiling and secret countenances, with such signs, tokens, wagers, purposed to be lost before they were purposed to be made, with bargains of wearing colors, flowers, and herbs, to breed occasion of ofter meeting of him and her, and bolder talking of this and that, etc. And although I have seen some, innocent of all ill and staid in all honesty, that have used these things without all harm, without all suspicion of harm, yet these knacks were brought first into England by them that learned them before in Italy in Circe's Court; and how courtly courtesies soever they be counted now, yet, if the meaning and manners of some that do use them were somewhat amended, it were no great hurt neither to themselves nor to others.

Another property of this our English Italians is to be marvelous singular in all their matters: singular in knowledge, ignorant of nothing; so singular in wisdom (in their own opinion) as scarce they count the best counselor the prince hath comparable with them; common discoursers of all matters; busy searchers of most secret affairs; open flatterers of great men; privy mislikers of good men; fair speakers, with smiling countenances and much courtesy openly to all men; ready backbiters, sore nippers, and spiteful reporters privily of good men. And being brought up in Italy in some free city, as all cities be there, where a man may freely discourse against what he will, against whom he lust, against any prince, against any government, yea, against God himself and his whole religion; where he must be either Guelph or Ghibelin, either French or Spanish, and always compelled to be of some party, of some faction, he shall never be compelled to be of any religion; and if he meddle not over-much with Christ's true religion, he shall have free liberty to embrace all religions, and become, if he lust, at once, without any let or punishment, Jewish, Turkish, papish, and devilish.

A young gentleman thus bred up in this goodly school, to learn the next and ready way to sin, to have a busy head, a factious heart, a talkative tongue, fed with discoursing of factions, led to contemn God and his religion, shall come home into England but very ill taught, either to be an honest man himself, a quiet subject to his prince, or willing to serve God under the obedience of true doctrine, or within the order of honest living.

I know none will be offended with this my general writing, but only such as find themselves guilty privately therein: who shall have good leave to be offended with me, until they begin to amend themselves. I touch not them that be good; and I say too little of them that be not; and so, though not enough for their deserving, yet sufficiently for this time, and more else when if occasion so require.

* * *

JOHN LYLY (1554?–1606)

Of the events of Lyly's life little is known. After taking his degree from Oxford, thus securing for himself the somewhat invidious title of 'university wit,' he supported himself in London by his pen. Although his nine plays had an important influence in the development of pre-Shakespearean drama, and although they represent his most valuable contribution to English literature, Lyly is best known, probably, through the extravagant style of his *Euphues, the Anatomy of Wit* (1578) and *Euphues and his England* (1580). These two works, usually referred to in combination as *Euphues*, constitute, ostensibly, a romance. The story, however, meager at best, is almost infinitely attenuated by letters, 'model' conversations, and moral preachments. The interest of *Euphues*,—an interest more curious and historical than human,—lies in its unremitting artificiality of style, characterized especially by balance, alliteration, punning, citation of examples from classical antiquity, and fantastic references to natural history.

From EUPHUES AND HIS ENGLAND

This queen being deceased, Elizabeth, being of the age of twenty-two years, of more beauty than honor, and yet of more honor than any earthly creature, was called from a prisoner to be a prince, from the castle to the crown, from the fear of losing her head, to be supreme head. And here, ladies, it may be you will move a question, why this noble lady was either in danger of death, or cause of distress, which, had you thought to have passed in silence, I would, notwithstanding, have revealed.

This lady all the time of her sister's reign was kept close, as one that tendered not those proceedings which were contrary to her conscience, who, having divers enemies, endured many crosses, but so patiently as in her deepest sorrow she would rather sigh for the liberty of the Gospel than her own freedom. Suffering her inferiors to triumph over her, her foes to threaten her, her dissembling friends to undermine her, learning in all this misery only the patience that Zeno taught Eretricus to bear and forbear, never seeking revenge, but, with good Lycurgus, to lose her own eye rather than to hurt another's eye.

But being now placed in the seat royal, she first of all established religion, banished popery, advanced the Word, that before was so much defaced, who having in her hand the sword to revenge, used rather bountifully to reward, being as far from rigor when she might have killed, as her enemies were from honesty when they could not, giving a general pardon when she had cause to use particular punishments, preferring the name of pity before the remembrance of perils, thinking no revenge more princely than to spare when she might spill, to stay when she might strike, to proffer to save with mercy when she might have destroyed with justice. Here is the clemency worthy commendation and admiration, nothing inferior to the gentle disposition of Aristides, who, after his exile, did not so much as note them that banished him, saying with Alexander that there can be nothing more noble than to do well to those that deserve ill.

This mighty and merciful queen, having many bills of private persons that sought beforetime to betray her, burnt them all, resembling Julius Cæsar, who, being presented with the like complaints of his commons, threw them into the fire, saying that he had rather not know the names of rebels than have occasion to revenge, thinking it better to be ignorant of those that hated him than to be angry with them.

This clemency did her Majesty not only show at her coming to the throne, but also throughout her whole government, when she hath spared to shed their bloods that sought to spill hers, not racking the laws to extremity, but mitigating the rigor with mercy, insomuch as it may be said of that royal monarch as it was of Antoninus, surnamed the godly Emperor, who reigned many years without the effusion of blood. What greater virtue can there be in a prince than mercy; what greater praise than to abate the edge which she should whet, to pardon where she should punish, to reward where she should revenge?

I myself being in England when her Majesty was for her recreation in her barge upon the Thames, heard of a gun that was shot off, though of the party unwittingly, yet to her noble person dangerously, which fact she most graciously pardoned, accepting a just excuse before a great amends, taking more grief for her poor bargeman, that was a little hurt, than care for herself that stood in greatest hazard. O rare example of pity, O singular spectacle of piety.

Divers besides have there been which by private conspiracies, open rebellions, close wiles, cruel witchcrafts, have sought to end her life, which saveth all their lives, whose practices by the divine providence of the Almighty, have ever been disclosed, insomuch that he hath kept her safe in the whale's belly when her subjects went about to throw her into the sea, preserved her in the hot oven, when her enemies increased the fire, not suffering a hair to fall from her, much less any harm to fasten upon her. These injuries and treasons of her subjects, these policies and undermining of foreign nations so little moved her, that she would often say, 'Let them know that, though it be not lawful for them to speak what they list, yet it is lawful for us to do with them what we list,' being always of that merciful mind, which was in Theodosius, who wished rather that he might call the dead to life than put the living to death, saying with Augustus when she should set her hand to any condemnation, 'I would to God we could not write.' Infinite were the examples that might be alleged, and almost incredible, whereby she hath shown herself a lamb in meekness, when she had cause to be a lion in might, proved a dove in favor, when she was provoked to be an eagle in fierceness, requiting injuries with benefits, revenging grudges with gifts, in highest majesty bearing the lowest mind, forgiving all that sued for mercy, and forgetting all that deserved justice.

O divine nature, O heavenly nobility, what thing can there more be required in a prince, than in greatest power to show greatest patience, in chiefest glory to bring forth chiefest grace, in abundance of all earthly pomp to manifest abundance of all heavenly piety? O fortunate England that hath such a Queen, ungrateful if thou pray not for her, wicked if thou do not love her, miserable if thou lose her.

* * *

Touching the beauty of this prince, her countenance, her personage, her majesty, I cannot think that it may be sufficiently commended, when it cannot be too much marveled at; so that I am constrained to say as Praxitiles did, when he began to paint Venus and her son, who doubted whether the world could afford colors good enough for two such fair faces, and I, whether our tongue can yield words to blaze that beauty, the perfection whereof none can imagine; which seeing it is so, I must do like those that want a clear sight, who, being not able to discern the sun in the sky, are enforced to behold it in the water. Zeuxis, having before him fifty fair virgins of Sparta whereby to draw one amiable Venus, said that fifty more fairer than those could not minister sufficient beauty to show the goddess of beauty; therefore, being in despair either by art to shadow her, or by imagination to comprehend her, he drew in a table a fair temple, the gates open, and Venus going in so as nothing could be perceived but her back, wherein he used such cunning that Apelles himself, seeing this work, wished that Venus would turn her face, saying that if it were in all parts agreeable to the back, he would become apprentice to Zeuxis, and slave to Venus. In the like manner fareth it with me, for having all the ladies in Italy, more than fifty hundred, whereby to color Elizabeth, I must say with Zeuxis that as many more will not suffice, and therefore in as great an agony paint her court with her back towards you, for that I cannot by art portray her beauty, wherein, though I want the skill to do it as Zeuxis did, yet viewing it narrowly, and comparing it wisely, you all will say that if her face be answerable to her back, you will like my handicraft and become her handmaids. In the mean season, I leave you gazing until she turn her face, imagining her to be such a one as nature framed to that end, that no art should imitate, wherein she hath proved herself to be exquisite, and painters to be apes.

This beautiful mold when I beheld to be indued with chastity, temperance, mildness, and all other good gifts of nature (as hereafter shall appear), when I saw her to surpass all in beauty, and yet a virgin, to excel all in piety, and yet a prince, to be inferior to none in all the lineaments of the body, and yet superior to every one in all gifts of the mind, I began thus to pray, that as she hath lived forty years a virgin in great majesty, so she may live four score years a mother with great joy, that as with her we have long time had peace and plenty, so by her we may ever have quietness and abundance, wishing this even from the bottom of a heart that wisheth well to England, though feareth ill, that either the world may end before she die, or she live to see her children's children in the world; otherwise how tickle their state is that now triumph, upon what a twist they hang that now are in honor, they that live shall see, which I to think on, sigh! But God for his mercy's sake, Christ for his merits' sake, the Holy Ghost for his name's sake, grant to that realm comfort without any ill chance, and the prince they have without any other change, that the longer she liveth, the sweeter she may smell, like the bird Ibis, that she may be triumphant in victories, like the palm tree, fruitful in her age like the vine, in all ages prosperous, to all men gracious, in all places glorious, so that there be no end of her praise until the end of all flesh.

Thus did I often talk with myself, and wish with mine whole soul.

Why should I talk of her sharp wit, excellent wisdom, exquisite learning, and all other qualities of the mind, wherein she seemeth as far to excel those that have been accounted singular, as the learned have surpassed those that have been thought simple.

In questioning, not inferior to Nicaulia, the queen of Saba, that did put so many hard doubts to Solomon; equal to Nicostrata in the Greek tongue, who was thought to give precepts for the better perfection; more learned in the Latin than Amalasunta; passing Aspasia in philosophy, who taught Pericles; exceeding in judgment Themistoclea, who instructed Pythagoras. Add to these qualities, those that none of these had; the French tongue, the Spanish, the Italian, not mean in every one, but excellent in all; readier to correct escapes in those languages than to be controlled; fitter to teach others than learn of any; more able to add new rules than to err in the old, insomuch as there is no ambassador that cometh into her court but she is willing and able both to understand his message and utter her mind; not like unto the kings of Assyria, who answered ambassadors by messengers, while they themselves either dally in sin or snort in sleep. Her godly zeal to learning, with her great skill, hath been so manifestly approved that I cannot tell whether she deserve more honor for her knowledge, or admiration for her courtesy, who in great pomp hath twice directed her progress unto the universities, with no less joy to the students than glory to her state. Here, after long and solemn disputations in law, physic, and divinity, not as one wearied with scholars' arguments, but wedded to their orations, when every one feared to offend in length, she in her own person, with no less praise to her Majesty than delight to her subjects, with a wise and learned conclusion, both gave them thanks, and put herself to pains. O noble pattern of a princely mind, not like to the kings of Persia, who in their progresses did nothing else but cut sticks to drive away the time, nor like the delicate lives of the Sybarites, who would not admit any art to be exercised within their city that might make the least noise. Her wit so sharp, that if I should repeat the apt answers, the subtle questions, the fine speeches, the pithy sentences, which on the sudden she hath uttered, they would rather breed admiration than credit. But such are the gifts that the living God hath indued her withal, that look in what art or language, wit or learning, virtue or beauty any one hath particularly excelled most, she only hath generally exceeded every one in all, insomuch that there is nothing to be added that either man would wish in a woman, or God doth give to a creature.

I let pass her skill in music, her knowledge in all the other sciences, whenas I fear lest by my simplicity I should make them less than they are, in seeking to show how great they are, unless I were praising her in the gallery of Olympia, where giving forth one word, I might hear seven.

But all these graces, although they be to be wondered at, yet her politic government, her prudent counsel, her zeal to religion, her clemency to those that submit, her stoutness to those that threaten, so far exceed all other virtues that they are more easy to be marveled at than imitated.

Two and twenty years hath she borne the sword with such justice, that neither offenders could complain of rigor, nor the innocent of wrong; yet so tempered with mercy as malefactors have been sometimes pardoned upon hope of grace, and the injured requited to ease their grief, insomuch that in the whole course of her glorious reign, it could never be said that either the poor were oppressed without remedy, or the guilty repressed without cause, bearing this engraven in her noble heart, that justice without mercy were extreme injury, and pity without equity, plain partiality, and that it is as great tyranny not to mitigate laws, as iniquity to break them.

Her care for the flourishing of the Gospel hath well appeared whenas neither the curses of the Pope (which are blessings to good people) nor the threatenings of kings (which are perilous to a prince) nor the persuasions of papists (which are honey to the mouth) could either fear her or allure her to violate the holy league contracted with Christ, or to maculate the blood of the ancient Lamb, which is Christ. But always constant in the true faith, she hath to the exceeding joy of her subjects, to the unspeakable comfort of her soul, to the great glory of God, established that religion the maintenance whereof she rather seeketh to confirm by fortitude, than leave off for fear, knowing that there is nothing smelleth sweeter to the Lord than a sound spirit, which neither the hosts of the ungodly nor the horror of death can either remove or move.

This Gospel with invincible courage, with rare constancy, with hot zeal, she hath maintained in her own countries without change, and defended against all kingdoms that sought change insomuch that all nations round about her, threatening alteration, shaking swords, throwing fire, menacing famine, murder, destruction, desolation, she only hath stood like a lamp on the top of a hill, not fearing the blasts of the sharp winds, but trusting in his providence that rideth upon the wings of the four winds. Next followeth the love she beareth to her subjects, who no less tendereth them than the apple of her own eye, showing herself a mother to the afflicted, a physician to the sick, a sovereign and mild governess to all.

Touching her magnanimity, her majesty, her estate royal, there was neither Alexander, nor Galba the Emperor, nor any, that might be compared with her.

This is she that, resembling the noble queen of Navarre, useth the marigold for her flower, which at the rising of the sun openeth her leaves, and at the setting shutteth them, referring all her actions and endeavors to him that ruleth the sun. This is that Cæsar, that first bound the crocodile to the palm tree, bridling those that sought to rein her. This is that good pelican, that to feed her people spareth not to rend her own person. This is that mighty eagle, that hath thrown dust into the eyes of the hart that went about to work destruction to her subjects, into whose wings although the blind beetle would have crept, and so being carried into her nest, destroyed her young ones, yet hath she with the virtue of her feathers, consumed that fly in his own fraud. She hath exiled the swallow that sought to spoil the grasshopper, and given bitter almonds to the ravenous wolves that endeavored to devour the silly lambs, burning even with the breath of her mouth like the princely stag, the serpents that were engendered by the breath of the huge elephant, so that now all her enemies are as whist as the bird Attagen, who never singeth any tune after she is taken, nor they being so overtaken.

But whither do I wade, ladies, as one forgetting himself, thinking to sound the depth of her virtues with a few fathoms, when there is no bottom; for I know not how it cometh to pass that, being in this labyrinth, I may sooner lose myself than find the end.

Behold, ladies, in this glass a queen, a woman, a virgin in all gifts of the body, in all graces of the mind, in all perfection of either, so far to excel all men, that I know not whether I may think the place too bad for her to dwell among men.

To talk of other things in that court were to bring eggs after apples, or after the setting out of the sun, to tell a tale of a shadow.

But this I say, that all offices are looked to with great care, that virtue is embraced of all, vice hated, religion daily increased, manners reformed, that whoso seeth the place there, will think it rather a church for divine service than a court for princes' delight.

This is the glass, ladies, wherein I would have you gaze, wherein I took my whole delight; imitate the ladies in England, amend your manners, rub out the wrinkles of the mind, and be not curious about the weams in the face. As for their Elizabeth, since you can neither sufficiently marvel at her, nor I praise her, let us all pray for her, which is the only duty we can perform, and the greatest that we can proffer.

Yours to command,
EUPHUES.

* * *

APELLES' SONG

From ALEXANDER AND CAMPASPE

CUPID and my Campaspe played
At cards for kisses; Cupid paid.
He stakes his quiver, bows and arrows,
His mother's doves and team of sparrows;
Loses them too; then down he throws
The coral of his lip, the rose
Growing on 's cheek (but none knows how);

With these, the crystal of his brow,
And then the dimple of his chin;
All these did my Campaspe win.   10
At last he set her both his eyes;
She won, and Cupid blind did rise.
O Love, has she done this to thee?
What shall, alas! become of me?

SPRING'S WELCOME

From Alexander and Campaspe

What bird so sings, yet so does wail?
O 't is the ravished nightingale.
'Jug, jug, jug, jug, tereu,' she cries,
And still her woes at midnight rise.
Brave prick-song! who is 't now we hear?   5
None but the lark so shrill and clear;
Now at heaven's gates she claps her wings,
The morn not waking till she sings.
Hark, hark, with what a pretty throat
Poor robin redbreast tunes his note!   10
Hark how the jolly cuckoos sing,
'Cuckoo,' to welcome in the spring!
'Cuckoo,' to welcome in the spring!

SAPPHO'S SONG

From Sappho and Phao

O cruel Love! on thee I lay
My curse, which shall strike blind the day:
Never may sleep with velvet hand
Charm thine eyes with sacred wand;
Thy jailors still be hopes and fears;   5
Thy prison-mates groans, sighs, and tears;
Thy play to wear out weary times,
Fantastic passions, vows, and rimes;
Thy bread be frowns; thy drink be gall;
Such as when you Phao call;   10
The bed thou liest on be despair;
Thy sleep, fond dreams; thy dreams, long care;
Hope (like thy fool) at thy bed's head,
Mock thee, till madness strikes thee dead,   14

As, Phao, thou dost me, with thy proud eyes.
In thee poor Sappho lives, in thee she dies.

SONG

From Gallathea

TELUSA

O yes, O yes! if any maid
Whom leering Cupid has betrayed
To frowns of spite, to eyes of scorn,
And would in madness now see torn
The boy in pieces,

ALL THREE

      Let her come   5
Hither, and lay on him her doom.

EUROTA

O yes, O yes! has any lost
A heart which many a sigh hath cost;
Is any cozened of a tear
Which, as a pearl, disdain does wear?   10

ALL THREE

Here stands the thief; let her but come
Hither, and lay on him her doom.

LARISSA

Is any one undone by fire,
And turned to ashes through desire?
Did ever any lady weep,   15
Being cheated of her golden sleep
Stol'n by sick thoughts?

ALL THREE

      The pirate's found
And in her tears he shall be drowned.
Read this indictment, let him hear
What he 's to trust to. Boy, give ear!

SIR PHILIP SIDNEY (1554-1586)

SIDNEY's parents were Sir Henry Sidney, subsequently Lord Deputy in Ireland, and Lady Mary Dudley, daughter of the Duke of Northumberland. After an agreeable schooling at Shrewsbury, Sidney took up residence at Christ Church, Oxford, a residence which he cut short in order to travel abroad, after the fashion of young men of rank. At the time of the Massacre of St. Bartholomew, August 23-4, 1572, he was in Paris, and subsequently his travels, during about four years, extended to Germany, Italy, and other parts of the Continent. Of these travels, one interesting legacy is his Latin correspondence with the distinguished Huguenot, Hubert Languet. In 1576-1577, Sidney was abroad on a diplomatic mission to the Emperor Rudolf II. As a courtier he was esteemed and honored on the Continent, both for his personal charm and for his genuine talent. Although he was a favorite of Queen Elizabeth, his opposition to her proposed marriage with the Duke of Anjou may have been the cause of his retirement, for a time, to Wilton, where he wrote *Arcadia*, a pastoral romance (published 1590), in honor of his sister, the Countess of Pembroke, and *An Apology for Poetry* (published 1595). During this period of retirement, also, he may have begun writing the sonnets and songs addressed to Penelope Devereux, and published, in 1591, as *Astrophel and Stella*. In 1582, Sidney was knighted by the queen, who is said to have interfered later against his being offered the Polish crown. In 1585, the queen appointed him governor of Flushing, on the coast of the Netherlands. During the siege of Zutphen, in an expedition to intercept a Spanish convoy, he was mortally wounded, and died, October 17, 1586.

Short-lived as he was, Sidney acquired a substantial place in English literature as a masterly poet of the courtly order, as a charming romancer, and as a gentle but firm critic. The charm of his poetry and romance extended even to his criticism, and gave to his somewhat too orthodox canons and moral restrictions, a permanent allurement of frankness, gentleness, and humor.

From AN APOLOGY FOR POETRY

But since I have run so long a career in this matter, methinks, before I give my pen a full stop, it shall be but a little more lost time to inquire, why England, the mother of excellent minds, should be grown so hard a step-mother to poets, who certainly in wit ought to pass all others, since all only proceeds from their wit, being, indeed, makers of themselves, not takers of others. How can I but exclaim,

Musa, mihi causas memora, quo numine læso?
[Muse, bring to my mind the reasons: for the injury of what divinity?]

Sweet poesy! that hath anciently had kings, emperors, senators, great captains, such as besides a thousand others, David, Adrian, Sophocles, Germanicus, not only to favor poets, but to be poets; and of our nearer times can present for her patrons, a Robert, King of Sicily; the great King Francis of France; King James of Scotland; such cardinals as Bembus and Bibiena; such famous preachers and teachers as Beza and Melancthon; so learned philosophers as Fracastorius and Scaliger; so great orators as Pontanus and Muretus; so piercing wits as George Buchanan; so grave councilors as, besides many, but before all, that Hospital of France, than whom, I think, that realm never brought forth a more accomplished judgment, more firmly builded upon virtue; I say these, with numbers of others, not only to read others' poesies, but to poetize for others' reading: that poesy, thus embraced in all other places, should only find in our time a hard welcome in England, I think the very earth laments it, and therefore decks our soil with fewer laurels than it was accustomed. For heretofore poets have in England also flourished; and, which is to be noted, even in those times when the trumpet of Mars did sound loudest. And now that an over-faint quietness should seem to strew the house for poets, they are almost in as good reputation as the mountebanks at Venice. Truly, even that, as of the one side it giveth great praise to poesy, which, like Venus (but to better purpose), had rather be troubled in the net with Mars, than enjoy the homely quiet of Vulcan; so serves it for a piece of a reason why they are less grateful to idle England, which now can scarce endure the pain of a pen. Upon this necessarily followeth that base men with servile wits undertake it, who think it enough if they can be rewarded of the printer; and so as Epaminondas is said, with the honor of his virtue, to have made an office by his exercising it, which before was contemptible, to become highly respected; so these men, no more but setting their names to it, by their own disgracefulness, disgrace the most graceful poesy. For now, as if all the Muses were got with child, to bring forth bastard poets, without any commission, they do post over the banks of Helicon, until they make their readers more weary than post-horses; while, in the meantime, they,

Queis meliore luto finxit præcordia Titan,
[Whose heart-strings the Titan fastened with a better clay]

are better content to suppress the outflowings of their wit than by publishing them to be accounted knights of the same order.

But I that, before ever I durst aspire unto the dignity, am admitted into the company of the paper-blurrers, do find the very true cause of our wanting estimation is want of desert, taking upon us to be poets in despite of Pallas. Now, wherein we want desert, were a thankworthy labor to express. But if I knew, I should have mended myself; but as I never desired the title, so have I neglected the means to come by it; only, overmastered by some thoughts, I yielded an inky tribute unto them. Marry, they that delight in poesy itself, should seek to know what they do, and how they do, and, especially, look themselves in an unflattering glass of reason, if they be inclinable unto it.

For poesy must not be drawn by the ears, it must be gently led, or rather it must lead; which was partly the cause that made the ancient learned affirm it was a divine gift, and no human skill, since all other knowledges lie ready for any that have strength of wit; a poet no industry can make, if his own genius be not carried into it. And therefore is it an old proverb, *Orator fit, poeta nascitur* [The orator is made, the poet born]. Yet confess I always, that, as the fertilest ground must be manured, so must the highest flying wit have a Dædalus to guide him. That Dædalus, they say, both in this and in other, hath three wings to bear itself up into the air of due commendation; that is, art, imitation, and exercise. But these, neither artificial rules, nor imitative patterns, we much cumber ourselves withal. Exercise, indeed, we do, but that very forebackwardly; for where we should exercise to know, we exercise as having known; and so is our brain delivered of much matter which never was begotten by knowledge. For there being two principal parts, matter to be expressed by words, and words to express the matter, in neither we use art or imitation rightly. Our matter is *quodlibet* [what you will], indeed, although wrongly, performing Ovid's verse,

Quicquid conabor dicere, versus erit;
[Whatever I shall try to say will be verse]

never marshaling it into any assured rank, that almost the readers cannot tell where to find themselves.

Chaucer, undoubtedly, did excellently in his *Troilus and Criseyde;* of whom, truly, I know not whether to marvel more, either that he in that misty time could see so clearly, or that we in this clear age go so stumblingly after him. Yet had he great wants, fit to be forgiven in so reverend antiquity. I account the *Mirror for Magistrates* meetly furnished of beautiful parts. And in the Earl of Surrey's lyrics, many things tasting of a noble birth, and worthy of a noble mind. The *Shepherd's Calendar* hath much poetry in its eclogues, indeed, worthy the reading, if I be not deceived. That same framing of its style to an old rustic language, I dare not allow; since neither Theocritus in Greek, Virgil in Latin, nor Sannazaro in Italian, did affect it. Besides these, I do not remember to have seen but few (to speak boldly) printed that have poetical sinews in them. For proof whereof, let but most of the verses be put in prose, and then ask the meaning, and it will be found that one verse did but beget another, without ordering at the first what should be at the last; which becomes a confused mass of words, with a tinkling sound of rime, barely accompanied with reason.

Our tragedies and comedies (not without cause, cried out against) observing rules neither of honest civility nor of skilful poetry, excepting *Gorboduc* (again I say of those that I have seen), which notwithstanding, as it is full of stately speeches and well-sounding phrases, climbing to the height of Seneca's style, and as full of notable morality, which it does most delightfully teach, and so obtain the very end of poesy; yet, in truth, it is very defective in the circumstances, which grieves me, because it might not remain as an exact model of all tragedies. For it is faulty both in place and time, the two necessary companions of all corporal actions. For where the stage should always represent but one place, and the uttermost time presupposed in it should be, both by Aristotle's precept, and common reason, but one day, there is both many days and many places inartificially imagined.

But if it be so in *Gorboduc*, how much more in all the rest? where you shall have Asia of the one side, and Afric of the other, and so many other under kingdoms, that the player, when he comes in, must ever begin with telling where he is, or else the tale will not be conceived. Now you shall have three ladies walk to gather flowers, and then we must believe the stage to be a garden. By and by, we hear news of shipwreck in the same place, and then we are to blame if we accept it not for a rock. Upon the back of that comes out a hideous monster, with fire and smoke, and then the miserable beholders are bound to take it for a cave; while, in the meantime, two armies fly in, represented with four swords and bucklers, and then, what hard heart will not receive it for a pitched field?

Now, of time they are much more liberal; for ordinary it is, that two young princes fall in love; after many traverses she is got with child; delivered of a fair boy; he is lost, groweth a man, falls in love, and is ready to get another child; and all this in two hours' space; which, how absurd it is in sense, even sense may imagine; and art hath taught and all ancient examples justified, and at this day the ordinary players in Italy will not err in. Yet will some bring in an example of the *Eunuch* in Terence, that containeth matter of two days, yet far short of twenty years. True it is, and so was it to be played in two days, and so fitted to the time it set forth. And though Plautus have in one place done amiss, let us hit it with him, and not miss with him.

But they will say, How then shall we set forth a story which contains both many places and many times? And do they not know that a tragedy is tied to the laws of poesy, and not of history; not bound to follow the story, but having liberty either to feign a quite new matter, or to frame the history to the most tragical conveniency? Again many things may be told, which cannot be showed: if they know the difference betwixt reporting and representing. As, for example, I may speak, though I am here, of Peru, and in speech digress from that to the description of Calicut; but in action I cannot represent it without Pacolet's horse. And so was the manner the ancients took, by some *Nuntius* [Messenger] to recount things done in former time, or other place.

Lastly, if they will represent an history, they must not, as Horace saith, begin *ab ovo*, [from the egg] but they must come to the principal point of that one action which they will represent. By example this will be best expressed. I have a story of young Polydorus, delivered, for safety's sake, with great riches, by his father Priamus to Polymnestor, King of Thrace, in the Trojan war time. He, after some years, hearing the overthrow of Priamus, for to make the treasure his own, murdereth the child; the body of the child is taken up by Hecuba; she, the same day, findeth a sleight to be revenged most cruelly of the tyrant. Where, now, would one of our tragedy-writers begin, but with the delivery of the child? Then should he sail over into Thrace, and so spend I know not how many years, and travel numbers of places. But where doth Euripides? Even with the finding of the body; leaving the rest to be told by the spirit of Polydorus. This needs no further to be enlarged; the dullest wit may conceive it.

But besides these gross absurdities, how all their plays be neither right tragedies nor right comedies, mingling kings and clowns, not because the matter so carrieth it, but thrust in clowns by head and shoulders to play a part in majestical matters, with neither decency nor discretion; so as neither the admiration and commiseration, nor the right sportfulness, is by their mongrel tragi-comedy obtained. I know Apuleius did somewhat so, but that is a thing recounted with space of time, not represented in one moment: and I know the ancients have one or two examples of tragi-comedies, as Plautus hath *Amphitruo*. But, if we mark them well, we shall find that they never, or very daintily, match hornpipes and funerals. So falleth it out, that, having, indeed, no right comedy in that comical part of our tragedy, we have nothing but scurrility, unworthy of any chaste ears; or some extreme show of doltishness, indeed fit to lift up a loud laughter, and nothing else; where the whole tract of a comedy should be full of delight as the tragedy should be still maintained in a well-raised admiration.

But our comedians think there is no delight without laughter, which is very wrong; for though laughter may come with delight, yet cometh it not of delight, as though delight should be the cause of laughter; but well may one thing breed both together. Nay, in themselves, they have, as it were, a kind of contrariety. For delight we scarcely do, but in things that have a conveniency to ourselves, or to the general nature. Laughter almost ever cometh of things most disproportioned to ourselves and nature: delight hath a joy in it, either permanent or present; laughter hath only a scornful tickling. For example: we are ravished with delight to see a fair woman, and yet are far from being moved to laughter; we laugh at deformed creatures, wherein certainly we cannot delight; we delight in good chances; we laugh at mischances; we delight to hear the happiness of our friends or country, at which he were worthy to be laughed at that would laugh: we shall, contrarily, laugh sometimes to find a matter quite mistaken, and go down the hill against the bias, in the mouth of some such men, as for the respect of them, one shall be heartily sorry, yet he cannot choose but laugh, and so is rather pained than delighted with laughter. Yet deny I not, but that they may go well together; for, as in Alexander's picture well set out, we delight without laughter, and in twenty mad antics we laugh without delight: so in Hercules, painted with his great beard and furious countenance, in a woman's attire, spinning at Omphale's commandment, it breedeth both delight and laughter; for the representing of so strange a power in love procures delight, and the scornfulness of the action stirreth laughter.

But I speak to this purpose, that all the end of the comical part be not upon such scornful matters as stir laughter only, but mix with it that delightful teaching which is the end of poesy. And the great fault, even in that point of laughter, and forbidden plainly by Aristotle, is, that they stir laughter in sinful things, which are rather execrable than ridiculous; or in miserable, which are rather to be pitied than scorned. For what is it to make folks gape at a wretched beggar, and a beggarly clown; or against the law of hospitality, to jest at strangers, because they speak not English so well as we do? what do we learn? since it is certain,

> *Nil habet infelix paupertas durius in se,*
> *Quam quod ridiculos, homines facit.*
> [Of all the griefs that harass the distrest,
> Sure the most bitter is a scornful jest]

But rather a busy loving courtier, a heartless threatening Thraso; a self-wise-seeming schoolmaster; a wry-transformed traveler: these, if we saw walk in stage names, which we play naturally, therein were delightful laughter, and teaching delightfulness: as in the other, the tragedies of Buchanan do justly bring forth a divine admiration.

But I have lavished out too many words of this play matter; I do it, because, as they are excelling parts of poesy, so is there none so much used in England, and none can be more pitifully abused; which, like an unmannerly daughter, showing a bad education, causeth her mother Poesy's honesty to be called in question.

Other sorts of poetry, almost have we none, but that lyrical kind of songs and sonnets, which, if the Lord gave us so good minds, how well it might be employed, and with how heavenly fruits, both private and public in singing the praises of the immortal beauty, the immortal goodness of that God, who giveth us hands to write, and wits to conceive; of which we might well want words, but never matter; of which we could turn our eyes to nothing, but we should ever have new budding occasions. But, truly, many of such writings as come under the banner of irresistible love, if I were a mistress, would never persuade me they were in love; so coldly they apply fiery speeches, as men that had rather read lovers' writings, and so caught up certain swelling phrases, which hang together—like a man which once told me, 'the wind was at northwest and by south,' because he would be sure to name winds enough—than that, in truth, they feel those passions, which easily, as I think, may be bewrayed by the same forcibleness, or *energia* (as the Greeks call it), of the writer. But let this be a sufficient, though short note, that we miss the right use of the material point of poesy.

Now for the outside of it, which is words, or, as I may term it, diction, it is even well worse; so is that honey-flowing matron Eloquence, appareled, or rather disguised, in a courtesan-like painted affectation. One time with so far-fetched words, that may seem monsters, but must seem strangers to any poor Englishman: another time with coursing of a letter, as if they were bound to follow the method of a dictionary: another time with figures and flowers, extremely winter-starved.

But I would this fault were only peculiar to versifiers, and had not as large possession among prose printers: and, which is to be marveled, among many scholars, and, which is to be pitied, among some preachers. Truly, I could wish (if at least I might be so bold to wish, in a thing beyond the reach of my capacity) the diligent imitators of Tully and Demosthenes, most worthy to be imitated, did not so much keep Nizolian paper-books of their figures and phrases, as by attentive translation, as it were, devour them whole, and make them wholly theirs. For now they cast sugar and spice upon every dish that is served to the table: like those Indians, not content to wear earrings at the fit and natural place of the ears, but they will thrust jewels through their nose and lips, because they will be sure to be fine. Tully, when he was to drive out Catiline, as it were with a thunderbolt of eloquence, often used the figure of repetition.

Vivit. Vivit? imo in Senatum venit, etc.
[He lives. Lives? nay comes to the Senate]

Indeed, inflamed with a well-grounded rage, he would have his words, as it were, double out of his mouth; and so do that artificially which we see men do in choler naturally. And we, having noted the grace of those words, hale them in sometimes to a familiar epistle, when it were too much choler to be choleric.

How well, store of 'similiter cadences' doth sound with the gravity of the pulpit, I would but invoke Demosthenes' soul to tell, who with a rare daintiness useth them. Truly, they have made me think of the sophister, that with too much subtlety would prove two eggs three, and, though he might be counted a sophister, had none for his labor. So these men bringing in such a kind of eloquence, well may they obtain an opinion of a seeming fineness, but persuade few, which should be the end of their fineness.

Now for similitudes in certain printed discourses, I think all herbalists, all stories of beasts, fowls, and fishes are rifled up, that they come in multitudes to wait upon any of our conceits, which certainly is as absurd a surfeit to the ears as is possible. For the force of a similitude not being to prove anything to a contrary disputer, but only to explain to a willing hearer: when that is done, the rest is a most tedious prattling, rather overswaying the memory from the purpose whereto they were applied, than any whit informing the judgment, already either satisfied, or by similitudes not to be satisfied.

For my part, I do not doubt, when Antonius and Crassus, the great forefathers of Cicero in eloquence, the one (as Cicero testifieth of them) pretended not to know art, the other not to set by it, because with a plain sensibleness they might win credit of popular ears, which credit is the nearest step to persuasion (which persuasion is the chief mark of oratory); I do not doubt, I say, but that they used these knacks very sparingly; which who doth generally use, any man may see, doth dance to his own music; and so to be noted by the audience, more careful to speak curiously than to speak truly. Undoubtedly (at least to my opinion, undoubtedly) I have found in divers small-learned courtiers a more sound style than in some professors of learning; of which I can guess no other cause, but that the courtier following that which by practice he findeth fittest to nature, therein (though he know it not) doth according to art, though not by art: where the other, using art to show art, and not to hide art (as in these cases he should do), flieth from nature, and indeed abuseth art.

But what! methinks I deserve to be pounded for straying from poetry to oratory: but both have such an affinity in the wordish considerations, that I think this digression will make my meaning receive the fuller understanding: which is not to take upon me to teach poets how they should do, but only finding myself sick among the rest, to show some one or two spots of the common infection grown among the most part of writers; that, acknowledging ourselves somewhat awry, we may bend to the right use both of matter and manner: whereto our language giveth us great occasion, being, indeed, capable of any excellent exercising of it. I know some will say, it is a mingled language: and why not so much the better, taking the best of both the other? Another will say, it wanteth grammar. Nay, truly, it hath that praise, that it wanteth not grammar; for grammar it might have, but it needs it not; being so easy in itself, and so void of those cumbersome differences of cases, genders, moods, and tenses; which, I think, was a piece of the Tower of Babylon's curse, that a man should be put to school to learn his mother tongue. But for the uttering sweetly and properly the conceits of the mind, which is the end of speech, that hath it equally with any other tongue in the world, and is particularly happy in compositions of two or three words together, near the Greek, far beyond the Latin; which is one of the greatest beauties can be in a language.

Now, of versifying there are two sorts, the one ancient, the other modern; the ancient marked the quantity of each syllable, and according to that, framed its verse; the modern, observing only number, with some regard of the accent, the chief life of it standeth in that like sounding of the words, which we call rime. Whether of these be the more excellent, would bear many speeches; the ancient, no doubt more fit for music, both words and tune observing quantity; and more fit lively to express divers passions, by the low and lofty sound of the well-weighed syllable. The latter, likewise, with his rime striketh a certain music to the ear; and, in fine, since it doth delight, though by another way, it obtains the same purpose; there being in either, sweetness, and wanting in neither, majesty. Truly the English, before any other vulgar language I know, is fit for both sorts; for, for the ancient, the Italian is so full of vowels, that it must ever be cumbered with elisions. The Dutch so of the other side with consonants, that they cannot yield the sweet sliding fit for a verse. The French, in his whole language, hath not one word that hath its accent in the last syllable, saving two, called antepenultima; and little more hath the Spanish; and, therefore, very gracelessly may they use dactyls. The English is subject to none of these defects.

Now for rime, though we do not observe quantity, yet we observe the accent very precisely, which other languages either cannot do, or will not do so absolutely. That cæsura, or breathing-place, in the midst of the verse, neither Italian nor Spanish have, the French and we never almost fail of. Lastly, even the very rime itself the Italian cannot put in the last syllable, by the French named the masculine rime, but still in the next to the last, which the French call the female; or the next before that, which the Italians term *sdrucciola*: the example of the former is, *buono, suono*; of the *sdrucciola* is, *femina, semina*. The French, of the other side, hath both the male, as *bon, son*, and the female, as *plaise, taise*; but the *sdrucciola* he hath not; where the English hath all three, as 'due,' 'true,' 'father,' 'rather,' 'motion,' 'potion'; with much more which might be said, but that I find already the triflingness of this discourse is much too much enlarged.

So that since the ever praiseworthy poesy is full of virtue-breeding delightfulness, and void of no gift that ought to be in the noble name of learning; since the blames laid against it are either false or feeble; since the cause why it is not esteemed in England is the fault of poet-apes, not poets; since, lastly, our tongue is most fit to honor poesy, and to be honored by poesy; I conjure you all that have had the evil luck to read this ink-wasting toy of mine, even in the name of the Nine Muses, no more to scorn the sacred mysteries of poesy; no more to laugh at the name of poets, as though they were next inheritors to fools; no more to jest at the reverend title of a rimer; but to believe, with Aristotle, that they were the ancient treasurers of the Grecians' divinity; to believe, with Bembus, that they were the first bringers in of all civility; to believe, with Scaliger, that no philosopher's precepts can sooner make you an honest man, than the reading of Virgil; to believe, with Clauserus, the translator of Cornutus, that it pleased the heavenly deity by Hesiod and Homer, under the veil of fables, to give us all knowledge, logic, rhetoric, philosophy natural and moral, and *Quid non?* [Why not] to believe, with me, that there are many mysteries contained in poetry, which of purpose were written darkly, lest by profane wits it should be abused; to believe, with Landin, that they are so beloved of the gods that whatsoever they write proceeds of a divine fury. Lastly, to believe themselves, when they tell you they will make you immortal by their verses.

Thus doing, your names shall flourish in the printers' shops: thus doing, you shall be of kin to many a poetical preface: thus doing, you shall be most fair, most rich, most wise, most all: you shall dwell upon superlatives: thus doing, though you be *Libertino patre natus* [Born of a freedman father], you shall suddenly grow *Herculea proles* [Descendant of Hercules],

Si quid mea Carmina possunt:
[If my poems are good for anything]

Thus doing, your soul shall be placed with Dante's Beatrice, or Virgil's Anchises.

But if (fie of such a but!) you be born so near the dull-making cataract of Nilus, that you cannot hear the planet-like music of poetry; if you have so earth-creeping a mind, that it cannot lift itself up to look to the sky of poetry, or rather, by a certain rustical disdain, will become such a Mome, as to be a Momus of poetry; then, though I will not wish unto you the ass's ears of Midas, nor to be driven by a poet's verses, as Bubonax was, to hang himself; nor to be rimed to death, as is said to be done in Ireland; yet thus much curse I must send you in the behalf of all poets; that while you live, you live in love, and never get favor, for lacking skill of a sonnet; and when you die, your memory die from the earth for want of an epitaph.

ASTROPHEL AND STELLA

I

Loving in truth, and fain in verse my love to show,
That she, dear she, might take some pleasure of my pain—
Pleasure might cause her read, reading might make her know,
Knowledge might pity win, and pity grace obtain—

I sought fit words to paint the blackest face of woe, 5
Studying inventions fine, her wits to entertain,
Oft turning others' leaves, to see if thence would flow
Some fresh and fruitful showers upon my sunburnt brain.

But words came halting forth, wanting Invention's stay;
Invention, Nature's child, fled step-dame Study's blows; 10
And others' feet still seemed but strangers' in my way.
Thus, great with child to speak, and helpless in my throes,
Biting my truant pen, beating myself for spite;
'Fool,' said my Muse to me, 'look in thy heart, and write.'

VII

When Nature made her chief work, Stella's eyes,
In color black why wrapt she beams so bright?
Would she, in beamy black, like painter wise,
Frame daintiest luster, mixed of shades and light?

Or did she else that sober hue devise, 5
In object best to knit and strength our sight;
Lest, if no veil these brave gleams did disguise,
They, sunlike, should more dazzle than delight?

Or would she her miraculous power show,
That, whereas black seems Beauty's contrary, 10
She even in black doth make all beauties flow?
Both so, and thus,—she, minding Love should be
Placed ever there, gave him this mourning weed
To honor all their deaths which for her bleed.

XV

You that do search for every purling spring
Which from the ribs of old Parnassus flows,
And every flower, not sweet perhaps, which grows
Near thereabouts, into your poesy wring;

You that do dictionary's method bring 5
Into your rimes, running in rattling rows;
You that poor Petrarch's long-deceasèd woes
With new-born sighs and denizened wit do sing;

You take wrong ways; those far-fet helps be such
As to bewray a want of inward touch, 10
And sure, at length stolen goods do come to light:
But if, both for your love and skill, your name
You seek to nurse at fullest breasts of Fame,
Stella behold, and then begin to endite.

XXI

Your words, my friend, right healthful caustics, blame
My young mind marred, whom Love doth windlass so;
That mine own writings, like bad servants, show
My wits quick in vain thoughts, in virtue, lame;

That Plato I read for naught but-if he tame 5
Such coltish years; that to my birth I owe
Nobler desires, lest else that friendly foe,
Great Expectation, wear a train of shame:

For since mad March great promise made of me,
If now the May of my years much decline, 10
What can be hoped my harvest-time will be?
Sure, you say well, 'Your wisdom's golden mine
Dig deep with Learning's spade.' Now tell me this—
Hath this world aught so fair as Stella is?

XXXI

With how sad steps, O Moon, thou climb'st the skies!
How silently, and with how wan a face!
What, may it be that even in heavenly place
That busy archer his sharp arrows tries!

Sure, if that long-with-love-acquainted eyes 5
Can judge of love, thou feel'st a lover's case,
I read it in thy looks; thy languished grace,
To me, that feel the like, thy state descries.

Then, even of fellowship, O Moon, tell me,
Is constant love deemed there but want of wit?
Are beauties there as proud as here they be? 11
Do they above love to be loved, and yet
Those lovers scorn whom that love doth possess?
Do they call virtue there ungratefulness?

XXXII

Morpheus, the lively son of deadly Sleep,
Witness of life to them that living die,
A prophet oft, and oft an history,
A poet eke, as humors fly or creep;
Since thou in me so sure a power dost keep, 5
That never I with closed-up sense do lie,
But by thy work my Stella I descry,
Teaching blind eyes both how to smile and weep;
Vouchsafe, of all acquaintance, this to tell,
Whence hast thou ivory, rubies, pearl, and gold, 10
To show her skin, lips, teeth, and head so well?
'Fool!' answers he; 'no Indes such treasures hold;
But from thy heart, while my sire charmeth thee,
Sweet Stella's image I do steal to me.'

XXXIX

Come, Sleep! O Sleep, the certain knot of peace,
The baiting-place of wits, the balm of woe,
The poor man's wealth, the prisoner's release,
Th' indifferent judge between the high and low;
With shield of proof shield me from out the press 5
Of those fierce darts Despair at me doth throw:
O make in me those civil wars to cease·
I will good tribute pay, if thou do so.
Take thou of me smooth pillows, sweetest bed,
A chamber deaf of noise and blind of light, 10
A rosy garland and a weary head:
And if these things, as being thine by right,
Move not thy heavy grace, thou shalt in me,
Livelier than elsewhere, Stella's image see.

XLI

Having this day my horse, my hand, my lance
Guided so well that I obtained the prize,
Both by the judgment of the English eyes
And of some sent from that sweet enemy, France; 4
Horsemen my skill in horsemanship advance,
Townsfolk, my strength; a daintier judge applies
His praise to sleight which from good use doth rise;
Some lucky wits impute it but to chance;
Others, because of both sides I do take
My blood from them who did excel in this, 10
Think Nature me a man-at-arms did make.
How far they shot awry! the true cause is,
Stella looked on, and from her heavenly face
Sent forth the beams which made so fair my race.

LXIV

No more! My Dear, no more these counsels try!
O give my passions leave to run their race!
Let Fortune lay on me her worst disgrace!
Let folk o'ercharged with brain, against me cry!
Let clouds bedim my face, break in mine eye! 5
Let me no steps but of lost labor trace!
Let all the earth in scorn recount my case;
But do not will me from my love to fly!
I do not envy Aristotle's wit;
Nor do aspire to Cæsar's bleeding fame; 10
Nor ought do care, though some above me sit;
Nor hope, nor wish another course to frame:
But that which once may win thy cruel heart.
Thou art my wit, and thou my virtue art.

CVII

Stella, since thou so right a princess art
Of all the powers which life bestows on me;
That ere by them ought undertaken be,
The first resort unto that sovereign part.
Sweet, for a while give respite to my heart, 5
Which pants as though it still should leap to thee;
And on my thoughts give thy lieutenancy
To this great cause, which needs both use and art.
And as a queen, who from her presence sends
Whom she employs, dismiss from thee my wit!
Till it have wrought what thy own will attends. 11
On servants' shame oft master's blame doth sit.
O let not fools in me thy works reprove;
And scorning, say, 'See, what it is to love!'

ELEVENTH SONG

'Who is it that this dark night
  Underneath my window plaineth?'
It is one who from thy sight
  Being, ah! exiled, disdaineth
Every other vulgar light. 5

'Why, alas! and are you he?
  Be not yet those fancies changèd?'
Dear, when you find change in me,
  Though from me you be estrangèd,
Let my change to ruin be. 10

'Well, in absence this will die;
  Leave to see, and leave to wonder.'
Absence sure will help, if I
  Can learn how myself to sunder
From what in my heart doth lie. 15

'But time will these thoughts remove;
  Time doth work what no man knoweth.
Time doth as the subject prove;
  With time still the affection groweth
In the faithful turtle-dove. 20

'What if we new beauties see?
  Will not they stir new affection?'
I will think they pictures be,
  (Image-like, of saint's perfection)
Poorly counterfeiting thee. 25

'But your reason's purest light
  Bids you leave such minds to nourish.'
Dear, do reason no such spite;
  Never doth thy beauty flourish
More than in my reason's sight. 30

'But the wrongs Love bears will make
  Love at length leave undertaking.'
No, the more fools it do shake,
  In the ground of so firm making,
Deeper still they drive the stake. 35

'Peace, I think that some give ear!
  Come no more, lest I get anger!'
Bliss, I will my bliss forbear;
  Fearing, sweet, you to endanger;
But my soul shall harbor there. 40

'Well, be gone! be gone, I say,
  Lest that Argus' eyes perceive you!'
O unjust is Fortune's sway,
  Which can make me thus to leave you;
And from louts to run away. 45

SONG: THE NIGHTINGALE

The nightingale, as soon as April bringeth
Unto her rested sense a perfect waking,
While late bare earth, proud of new clothing, springeth,
Sings out her woes, a thorn her song-book making,
And mournfully bewailing, 5
Her throat in tunes expresseth
What grief her breast oppresseth
For Tereus' force on her chaste will prevailing.
O Philomela fair, O take some gladness,
That here is juster cause of painful sadness: 10
Thine earth now springs, mine fadeth;
Thy thorn without, my thorn my heart invadeth.

LOVE IS DEAD

Ring out your bells, let mourning shows be spread;
  For Love is dead:
All Love is dead, infected
With plague of deep disdain:
  Worth, as naught worth, rejected, 5
And Faith fair scorn doth gain.
    From so ungrateful fancy,
    From such a female franzie,
    From them that use men thus,
    Good Lord, deliver us! 10

Weep, neighbors, weep; do you not hear it said
  That Love is dead?
His death-bed, peacock's folly;
His winding-sheet is shame;
  His will, false-seeming holy; 15
His sole exec'tor, blame.
    From so ungrateful fancy,
    From such a female franzie,
    From them that use men thus,
    Good Lord, deliver us! 20

Let dirge be sung, and trentals rightly read,
  For Love is dead:
Sir Wrong his tomb ordaineth:
My mistress' marble heart;
  Which epitaph containeth, 25
'Her eyes were once his dart.'
    From so ungrateful fancy,
    From such a female franzie,
    From them that use men thus,
    Good Lord, deliver us! 30

Alas, I lie: rage hath this error bred;
  Love is not dead;
Love is not dead, but sleepeth
In her unmatchèd mind,
  Where she his counsel keepeth, 35
Till due deserts she find.
    Therefore from so vile fancy,
    To call such wit a franzie,
    Who Love can temper thus,
    Good Lord, deliver us! 40

DORUS TO PAMELA

From Arcadia

My sheep are thoughts, which I both guide and serve;
Their pasture is fair hills of fruitless love,
On barren sweets they feed, and feeding sterve.
I wail their lot, but will not other prove;
My sheep-hook is wan hope, which all upholds;
My weeds, desire, cut out in endless folds; 6
What wool my sheep shall bear, whilst thus they live,
In you it is, you must the judgment give.

A DITTY

My true-love hath my heart, and I have his,
By just exchange one to the other given:
I hold his dear, and mine he cannot miss,
There never was a better bargain driven:
  My true-love hath my heart, and I have his. 5

His heart in me keeps him and me in one,
My heart in him his thoughts and senses guides:
He loves my heart, for once it was his own,
I cherish his because in me it bides: 9
  My true-love hath my heart, and I have his.

HAKLUYT'S VOYAGES

RICHARD HAKLUYT (1553-1616) has been well termed by Professor Raleigh 'the Homer of our heroic age'; yet his aim was not so much to record great deeds as to inspire them, to urge his countrymen to explore and colonize unknown countries, to encourage trade with the distant parts of the earth, and to furnish maps and other helps to navigation. A clergyman and a student, he had no experience of the adventures he described and prompted; but he was much more than a mere compiler. He brought to his self-appointed task the devotion and enthusiasm of a lofty purpose, and must be given a high rank among those who founded the British Empire and established the Anglo-Saxon race beyond the seas. It was fortunate for posterity that the Elizabethan age of commercial enterprise and romantic adventure found a chronicler with leisure and ability to save its achievements from oblivion, for the voyagers themselves were, as a rule, too busy making history to write it. Grenville's desperate resolution, Gilbert's religious valor, and Drake's restless daring would have been lost to literature, and perhaps even to history, if we had had to depend on their own records. Raleigh ...st be mentioned as a conspicuous exception; he combined with the spirit of adventure a literary power which makes his narratives a strange contrast to the matter-of-fact or garrulous reports of his less gifted fellows.

DEDICATORY EPISTLE TO SIR FRANCIS WALSINGHAM

(From the first edition of the Voyages, 1589)

RIGHT honorable, I do remember that being a youth, and one of her Majesty's scholars at Westminster, that fruitful nursery, it was my hap to visit the chamber of Mr. Richard Hakluyt, my cousin, a gentleman of the Middle Temple, well known unto you, at a time when I found lying open upon his board certain books of cosmography, with a universal map. He, seeing me somewhat curious in the view thereof, began to instruct my ignorance by showing me the division of the earth into three parts after the old account, and then according to the latter, and better distribution, into more. He pointed with his wand to all the known seas, gulfs, bays, straits, capes, rivers, empires, kingdoms, dukedoms, and territories of each part, with declaration also of their special commodities, and particular wants, which, by the benefit of traffic and intercourse of merchants, are plentifully supplied. From the map he brought me to the Bible, and turning to the 107th Psalm, directed me to the 23rd and 24th verses, where I read, that they which go down to the sea in ships and occupy by the great waters, they see the works of the Lord, and his wonders in the deep, &c. Which words of the prophet, together with my cousin's discourse (things of high and rare delight to my young nature), took in me so deep an impression that I constantly resolved, if ever I were preferred to the university, where better time and more convenient place might be ministered for these studies, I would by God's assistance prosecute that knowledge and kind of literature, the doors whereof, after a sort, were so happily opened before me.

According to which my resolution, when, not long after, I was removed to Christ Church in Oxford, my exercises of duty first performed, I fell to my intended course, and by degrees read over whatsoever printed or written discoveries and voyages I found extant either in the Greek, Latin, Italian, Spanish, Portugal, French, or English languages, and in my public lectures was the first that produced and showed both the old imperfectly composed, and the new lately reformed maps, globes, spheres, and other instruments of this art for demonstration in the common schools, to the singular pleasure and general contentment of my auditory. In continuance of time, and by reason principally of my insight in this study, I grew familiarly acquainted with the chiefest captains at sea, the greatest merchants, and the best mariners of our nation; by which means having gotten somewhat more than common knowledge, I passed at length the narrow seas into France with Sir Edward Stafford, her Majesty's careful and discreet Ligier, where during my five years' abode with him in his dangerous and chargeable residence in her Highness' service, I both heard in speech, and read in books other nations miraculously extolled for their discoveries and notable enterprises by sea, but the English of all others for their sluggish security, and continual neglect of the like attempts, especially in so long and happy a time of peace, either ignominiously reported, or exceedingly condemned; which singular opportunity, if some other people, our neighbors, had been blessed with, their protestations are often and vehement, they would far otherwise have used. . . . Thus both hearing and reading the obloquy of our nation, and finding few or none of our own men able to reply herein; and further, not seeing any man to have care to recommend to the world the industrious labors and painful travels of our countrymen: for stopping the mouths of the reproachers, myself being the last winter returned from France with the honorable the Lady Sheffield, for her passing good behavior highly esteemed in all the French court, determined notwithstanding all difficulties to undertake the burden of that work wherein all others pretended either ignorance or lack of leisure, or want of sufficient argument, whereas (to speak truly) the huge toil and the small profit to ensue were the chief causes of the refusal. I call the work a burden in consideration that these voyages lay so dispersed, scattered, and hidden in several hucksters' hands, that I now wonder at myself to see how I was able to endure the delays, curiosity, and backwardness of many from whom I was to receive my originals, so that I have just cause to make that complaint of the maliciousness of divers in our time which Pliny made of the men of his age: *At nos elaborata iis abscondere atque supprimere cupimus, et fraudare vitam etiam alienis bonis, &c.* [But we desire to hide away and suppress their achievements, and to rob life even of the glories of others.]

To harp no longer upon this string, and to speak a word of that just commendation which our nation do indeed deserve: it cannot be denied, but as in all former ages they have been men full of activity, stirrers abroad, and searchers of the remote parts of the world, so in this most famous and peerless government of her most excellent Majesty, her subjects, through the special assistance and blessing of God, in searching the most opposite corners and quarters of the world, and to speak plainly, in compassing the vast globe of the earth more than once, have excelled all the nations and people of the earth. For which of the kings of this land before her Majesty had their banners ever seen in the Caspian sea? which of them hath ever dealt with the emperor of Persia as her Majesty hath done, and obtained for her merchants large and loving privileges? who ever saw, before this regiment, an English Ligier in the stately porch of the Grand Signor at Constantinople? who ever found English consuls and agents at Tripolis in Syria, at Aleppo, at Babylon, at Balsara, and which is more, who ever heard of Englishman at Goa before now? what English ships did heretofore ever anchor in the mighty river of Plate? pass and repass the unpassable (in former opinion) Strait of Magellan, range along the coast of Chili, Peru, and all the backside of Nova Hispania, further than any Christian ever passed, traverse the mighty breadth of the South Sea, land upon the Luzones in despite of the enemy, enter into alliance, amity, and traffic with the princes of the Moluccas and the isle of Java, double the famous cape of Bona Speranza, arrive at the isle of St. Helena, and last of all return home most richly laden with the commodities of China, as the subjects of this now flourishing monarchy have done?

* * *

THE LAST FIGHT OF THE REVENGE

(From 'a report of the truth of the fight about the isles of Azores, the last of August, 1591, betwixt the *Revenge*, one of her Majesty's ships and an armada of the king of Spain. Penned by the honorable Sir Walter Raleigh, knight.')

THE Lord Thomas Howard with six of her Majesty's ships, six victualers of London, the bark *Raleigh*, and two or three other pinnaces riding at anchor near unto Flores, one of the westerly islands of the Azores, the last of August in the afternoon, had intelligence by one Captain Middleton of the approach of the Spanish armada. Which Middleton, being in a very good sailer, had kept them company three days before, of good purpose both to discover their forces the more, as also to give advice to my Lord Thomas of their approach. He had no sooner delivered the news but the fleet was in sight; many of our ships' companies were on shore in the island, some providing ballast for their ships, others filling of water and refreshing themselves from the land with such things as they could, either for money, or by force, recover. By reason whereof, our ships being all pestered and rummaging, every thing out of order, very light for want of ballast, and that which was most to our disadvantage, the one half part of the men of every ship sick and utterly unserviceable; for in the *Revenge* there were ninety diseased, in the *Bonaventure* not so many in health as could handle her mainsail. For had not twenty men been taken out of a bark of Sir George Carey's, his being commanded to be sunk, and those appointed to her, she had hardly ever recovered England. The rest, for the most part, were in little better state. The names of her Majesty's ships were these, as followeth: the *Defiance*, which was admiral; the *Revenge*, viceadmiral; the *Bonaventure*, commanded by Captain Cross; the *Lion* by George Fenner; the *Foresight* by Mr. Thomas Vavasour; and the *Crane* by Duffield. The *Foresight* and the *Crane* being but small ships, only the others were of the middle size; the rest, besides the bark *Raleigh*, commanded by Captain Thin, were victualers, and of small force or none. The Spanish fleet, having shrouded their approach by reason of the island, were now so soon at hand as our ships had scarce time to weigh their anchors, but some of them were driven to let slip their cables and set sail. Sir Richard Grenville was the last that weighed, to recover the men that were upon the island, which otherwise had been lost. The Lord Thomas with the rest very hardly recovered the wind, which Sir Richard Grenville not being able to do, was persuaded by the master and others to cut his mainsail and cast about, and to trust to the sailing of the ship, for the squadron of Seville were on his weather bow. But Sir Richard utterly refused to turn from the enemy, alleging that he would rather choose to die than to dishonor himself, his country, and her Majesty's ship, persuading his company that he would pass through the two squadrons in despite of them and enforce those of Seville to give him way. Which he performed upon divers of the foremost, who, as the mariners term it, sprang their luff, and fell under the lee of the *Revenge*. But the other course had been the better, and might right well have been answered in so great an impossibility of prevailing. Notwithstanding, out of the greatness of his mind, he could not be persuaded. In the meanwhile, as he attended those which were nearest him, the great *San Philip*, being in the wind of him and coming towards him, becalmed his sails in such sort, as the ship could neither make way nor feel the helm; so huge and high charged was the Spanish ship, being of a thousand and five hundred tons. Who after laid the *Revenge* aboard. When he was thus bereft of his sails, the ships that were under his lee, luffing up, also laid him aboard, of which the next was the admiral of the Biscayans, a very mighty and puissant ship commanded by Brittandona. The said *Philip* carried three tiers of ordnance on a side, and eleven pieces in every tier. She shot eight forth right out of her chase, besides those of her stern ports.

After the *Revenge* was entangled with this *Philip*, four others boarded her, two on her larboard, and two on her starboard. The fight, thus beginning at three of the clock in the afternoon, continued very terrible all that evening. But the great *San Philip*, having received the lower tier of the *Revenge*, discharged with crossbar shot, shifted herself with all diligence from her sides, utterly misliking her first entertainment. Some say that the ship foundered, but we cannot report it for truth, unless we were assured. The Spanish ships were filled with companies of soldiers, —in some two hundred besides the mariners, in some five, in others eight hundred. In ours there were none at all beside the mariners but the servants of the commanders and some few voluntary gentlemen only. After many interchanged volleys of great ordnance and small shot, the Spaniards deliberated to enter the *Revenge*, and made divers attempts, hoping to force her by the multitudes of their armed soldiers and musketeers, but were still repulsed again and again, and at all times beaten back into their own ships, or into the seas. In the beginning of the fight, the *George Noble* of London, having received some shot through her by the armadas, fell under the lee of the *Revenge*, and asked Sir Richard what he would command him, being but one of the victualers and of small force. Sir Richard bade him save himself, and leave him to his fortune. After the fight had thus, without intermission, continued while the day lasted and some hours of the night, many of our men were slain and hurt, and one of the great galleons of the armada, and the admiral of the hulks both sunk, and in many other of the Spanish ships great slaughter was made. Some write that Sir Richard was very dangerously hurt almost in the beginning of the fight, and lay speechless for a time ere he recovered. But two of the *Revenge's* own company brought home in a ship of Lima from the islands, examined by some of the lords and others, affirmed that he was never so wounded as that he forsook the upper deck, till an hour before midnight, and then, being shot into the body with a musket, as he was dressing was again shot into the head, and withal his surgeon wounded to death. This agreeth also with an examination, taken by Sir Francis Godolphin, of four other mariners of the same ship, being returned, which examination the said Sir Francis sent unto Master William Killigrew, of her Majesty's privy chamber.

But to return to the fight: the Spanish ships which attempted to board the *Revenge*, as they were wounded and beaten off, so always others came in their places, she having never less than two mighty galleons by her sides and aboard her. So that ere the morning, from three of the clock the day before, there had fifteen several armadas assailed her; and all so ill approved their entertainment as they were by the break of day far more willing to hearken to a composition than hastily to make any more assaults or entries. But as the day increased, so our men decreased; and as the light grew more and more, by so much more grew our discomforts. For none appeared in sight but enemies, saving one small ship called the *Pilgrim*, commanded by Jacob Whiddon, who hovered all night to see the success, but in the morning, bearing with the *Revenge*, was hunted like a hare amongst many ravenous hounds, but escaped.

All the powder of the *Revenge* to the last barrel was now spent, all her pikes broken, forty of her best men slain, and the most part of the rest hurt. In the beginning of the fight she had but one hundred free from sickness, and fourscore and ten sick, laid in hold upon the ballast: a small troop to man such a ship, and a weak garrison to resist so mighty an army. By those hundred all was sustained, the volleys, boardings, and enterings of fifteen ships of war, besides those which beat her at large. On the contrary, the Spanish were always supplied with soldiers brought from every squadron, all manner of arms and powder at will. Unto ours there remained no comfort at all, no hope, no supply either of ships, men, or weapons; the masts all beaten overboard, all her tackle cut asunder, her upper work altogether razed, and in effect evened she was with the water, but the very foundation or bottom of a ship, nothing being left overhead, either for flight or defence. Sir Richard, finding himself in this distress, and unable any longer to make resistance, having endured, in this fifteen hours' fight, the assault of fifteen several armadas, all by turns aboard him, and by estimation eight hundred shot of great artillery, besides many assaults and entries; and that himself and the ship must needs be possessed by the enemy, who were now all cast in a ring round about him, (the *Revenge* not able to move one way or other, but as she was moved with the waves and billows of the sea), commanded the master gunner, whom he knew to be a most resolute man, to split and sink the ship, that thereby nothing might remain of glory or victory to the Spaniards, seeing in so many hours' fight, and with so great a navy, they were not able to take her, having had fifteen hours' time, above ten thousand men, and fifty and three sail of men-of-war to perform it withal; and persuaded the company, or as many as he could induce, to yield themselves unto God and to the mercy of none else; but as they had, like valiant resolute men, repulsed so many enemies, they should not now shorten the honor of their nation by prolonging their own lives for a few hours or a few days. The master gunner readily condescended and divers others; but the captain and the master were of another opinion, and besought Sir Richard to have care of them, alleging that the Spaniard would be as ready to entertain a composition as they were willing to offer the same, and that there being divers sufficient and valiant men yet living, and whose wounds were not mortal, they might do their country and prince acceptable service hereafter. And whereas Sir Richard had alleged that the Spaniards should never glory to have taken one ship of her Majesty, seeing they had so long and so notably defended themselves, they answered, that the ship had six foot water in hold, three shot under water, which were so weakly stopped as with the first working of the sea, she must needs sink, and was besides so crushed and bruised as she could never be removed out of the place.

And as the matter was thus in dispute, and Sir Richard refusing to hearken to any of those reasons, the master of the *Revenge* (while the captain won unto him the greater party) was convoyed aboard the General Don Alfonso Bazan. Who (finding none over hasty to enter the *Revenge* again, doubting lest Sir Richard would have blown them up and himself, and perceiving by the report of the master of the *Revenge* his dangerous disposition) yielded that all their lives should be saved, the company sent for England, and the better sort to pay such reasonable ransom as their estate would bear, and in the mean season to be free from galley or imprisonment. To this he so much the rather condescended as well, as I have said, for fear of further loss and mischief to themselves, as also for the desire he had to recover Sir Richard Grenville, whom for his notable valor he seemed greatly to honor and admire.

* * *

From LINSCHOTEN'S TESTIMONY

THE 13th of September the said armada arrived at the island of Corvo, where the Englishmen with about 16 ships as then lay, staying for the Spanish fleet, whereof some or the most part were come, and there the English were in good hope to have taken them. But when they perceived the king's army to be strong, the admiral, being the Lord Thomas Howard, commanded his fleet not to fall upon them, nor any of them once to separate their ships from him, unless he gave commission so to do. Notwithstanding the vice-admiral, Sir Richard Grenville, being in the ship called the *Revenge*, went into the Spanish fleet and shot among them, doing them great hurt, and thinking the rest of the company would have followed; which they did not, but left him there, and sailed away. The cause why could not be known. Which the Spaniards perceiving, with 7 or 8 ships they boarded her, but she withstood them all, fighting with them, at the least 12 hours together, and sunk two of them, one being a new double fly-boat of 600 tons, and admiral of the fly-boats, the other a Biscayan. But in the end, by reason of the number that came upon her, she was taken, but to their great loss, for they had lost in fighting and by drowning above 400 men, and of the English were slain about 100, Sir Richard Grenville himself being wounded in his brain, whereof afterwards he died. He was carried into the ship called *San Paul*, wherein was the admiral of the fleet, Don Alonzo de Bazan. There his wounds were dressed by the Spanish surgeons, but Don Alonzo himself would neither see him nor speak with him. All the rest of the captains and gentlemen went to visit him, and to comfort him in his hard fortune, wondering at his courage and stout heart, for that he showed not any sign of faintness nor changing of color. But feeling the hour of death to approach, he spake these words in Spanish, and said: Here die I, Richard Grenville, with a joyful and quiet mind, for that I have ended my life as a true soldier ought to do, that hath fought for his country, queen, religion, and honor, whereby my soul most joyful departeth out of this body, and shall always leave behind it an everlasting fame of a valiant and true soldier, that hath done his duty, as he was bound to do. When he had finished these or such other like words, he gave up the ghost, with great and stout courage, and no man could perceive any true sign of heaviness in him.

* * *

THE LOSS OF SIR HUMPHREY GILBERT

(From 'a report of the voyage and success thereof, attempted in the year of our Lord, 1583, by Sir Humphrey Gilbert, knight, with other gentlemen assisting him in that action, intended to discover and to plant Christian inhabitants in place convenient, upon those large and ample countries extended northward from the cape of Florida, lying under very temperate climes, esteemed fertile and rich in minerals, yet not in the actual possession of any Christian prince, written by Mr. Edward Haie, gentleman, and principal actor in the same voyage, who alone continued to the end, and by God's special assistance returned home with his retinue safe and entire.')

So upon Saturday in the afternoon, the 31st of August, we changed our course and returned back for England, at which very instant, even in winding about, there passed along between us and towards the land which we now forsook, a very lion to our seeming, in shape, hair, and color, not swimming after the manner of a beast, by moving of his feet, but rather sliding upon the water with his whole body (excepting the legs) in sight; neither yet diving under, and again rising above the water, as the manner is of whales, dolphins, tunnies, porpoises, and all other fish, but confidently showing himself above water without hiding. Notwithstanding, we presented ourselves in open view and gesture to amaze him, as all creatures will be commonly at a sudden gaze and sight of men. Thus he passed along turning his head to and fro, yawning and gaping wide, with ugly demonstration of long teeth and glaring eyes, and to bid us a farewell (coming right against the *Hind*) he sent forth a horrible voice, roaring or bellowing as doth a lion, which spectacle we all beheld so far as we were able to discern the same, as men prone to wonder at every strange thing, as this doubtless was, to see a lion in the ocean sea, or fish in shape of a lion. What opinion others had thereof, and chiefly the general himself, I forbear to deliver. But he took it for *bonum omen* [a good omen], rejoicing that he was to war against such an enemy, if it were the devil.

The wind was large for England at our return, but very high, and the sea rough, insomuch as the frigate wherein the general went was almost swallowed up.

Monday in the afternoon (Sept. 2), we passed in the sight of Cape Race, having made as much way in little more than two days and nights back again, as before we had done in eight days from Cape Race unto the place where our ship perished which hindrance thitherward and speed back again, is to be imputed unto the swift current, as well as to the winds, which we had more large in our return.

This Monday the general came aboard the *Hind* to have the surgeon of the *Hind* to dress his foot, which he hurt by treading upon a nail. At what time we comforted each other with hope of hard success to be all past, and of the good to come. So agreeing to carry out lights always by night, that we might keep together, he departed into his frigate, being by no means to be entreated to tarry in the *Hind*, which had been more for his security. Immediately after followed a sharp storm which we overpassed for that time. Praised be God.

The weather fair, the general came aboard the *Hind* again to make merry together with the captain, master, and company, which was the last meeting, and continued there from morning until night. During which time there passed sundry discourses, touching affairs past and to come, lamenting greatly the loss of his great ship, more of the men, but most of all of his books and notes, and what else I know not; for which he was out of measure grieved, the same doubtless being some matter of more importance than his books, which I could not draw from him, yet by circumstance I gathered the same to be the ore which Daniel the Saxon had brought unto him in the New-found-land. Whatsoever it was, the remembrance touched him so deep as not able to contain himself, he beat his boy in great rage, even at the same time, so long after the miscarrying of the great ship, because upon a fair day, when we were becalmed upon the coast of the New-found-land, near unto Cape Race, he sent his boy aboard the admiral to fetch certain things, amongst which, this being chief, was yet forgotten, and left behind. After which time, he could never conveniently send again aboard the great ship; much less he doubted her ruin so near at hand.

Herein my opinion was better confirmed diversely, and by sundry conjectures, which maketh me have the greater hope of this rich mine. For whereas the general had never before good conceit of these north parts of the world, now his mind was wholly fixed upon the New-found-land. And as before he refused not to grant assignments liberally to them that required the same into these north parts, now he became contrarily affected, refusing to make any so large grants, especially of St. John's, which certain English merchants made suit for, offering to employ their money and travel upon the same. Yet neither by their own suit, nor of others of his own company, whom he seemed willing to pleasure, it could be obtained.

Also laying down his determination in the spring following, for disposing of his voyage then to be re-attempted, he assigned the captain and master of the *Golden Hind* unto the south discovery, and reserved unto himself the north, affirming that this voyage had won his heart from the south, and that he was now become a northern man altogether.

Last, being demanded what means he had at his arrival in England to compass the charges of so great preparation as he intended to make the next spring, having determined upon two fleets, one for the south, another for the north: Leave that to me (he replied), I will ask a penny of no man. I will bring good tidings unto her Majesty, who will be so gracious to lend me 10,000 pounds, willing us therefore to be of good cheer, for he did thank God (he said) with all his heart for that he had seen, the same being enough for us all, and that we needed not to seek any further. And these last words he would often repeat, with demonstration of great fervency of mind, being himself very confident and settled in belief of inestimable good by this voyage, which the greater number of his followers nevertheless mistrusted altogether, not being made partakers of those secrets, which the general kept unto himself. Yet all of them that are living may be witnesses of his words and protestations, which sparingly I have delivered.

Leaving the issue of this good hope unto God, who knoweth the truth only, and can at his good pleasure bring the same to light, I will hasten to the end of this tragedy, which must be knit up in the person of our general. And as it was God's ordinance upon him, even so the vehement persuasion and entreaty of his friends could nothing avail to divert him from a wilful resolution of going through in his frigate, which was overcharged upon their decks, with fights, nettings, and small artillery, too cumbersome for so small a boat that was to pass through the ocean sea at that season of the year, when by course we might expect much storm of foul weather, whereof indeed we had enough.

But when he was entreated by the captain, master, and other his well-willers of the *Hind*, not to venture in the frigate, this was his answer: I will not forsake my little company going homeward, with whom I have passed so many storms and perils. And in very truth, he was urged to be so over hard, by hard reports given of him, that he was afraid of the sea, albeit this was rather rashness than advised resolution, to prefer the wind of a vain report to the weight of his own life.

Seeing he would not bend to reason, he had provision out of the *Hind*, such as was wanting aboard his frigate. And so we committed him to God's protection, and set him aboard his pinnace, we being more than 300 leagues onward of our way home.

By that time we had brought the islands of Azores south of us; yet we then keeping much to the north, until we had got into the height and elevation of England, we met with very foul weather and terrible seas, breaking short and high, pyramid wise. The reason whereof seemed to proceed either of hilly grounds, high and low, within the sea, (as we see hills and dales upon the land), upon which the seas do mount and fall; or else the cause proceedeth of diversity of winds, shifting often in sundry points, all which having power to move the great ocean, which again is not presently settled, so many seas do encounter together as there had been diversity of winds. Howsoever it cometh to pass, men which all their life time had occupied the sea, never saw more outrageous seas. We had also upon our mainyard, an apparition of a little fire by night, which seamen do call Castor and Pollux. But we had only one, which they take an evil sign of more tempest; the same is usual in storms.

Monday the ninth of September, in the afternoon, the frigate was near cast away, oppressed by waves; yet at that time recovered; and giving forth signs of joy, the general sitting abaft with a book in his hand, cried out unto us in the *Hind* (so oft as we did approach within hearing): We are as near to heaven by sea as by land. Reiterating the same speech, well beseeming a soldier, resolute in Jesus Christ, as I can testify he was.

The same Monday night, about twelve of the clock, or not long after, the frigate being ahead of us in the *Golden Hind*, suddenly her lights were out, whereof, as it were in a moment, we lost the sight, and withal our watch cried, the general was cast away, which was too true. For in that moment, the frigate was devoured and swallowed up of the sea. Yet still we looked out all that night and ever after, until we arrived upon the coast of England, omitting no small sail at sea, unto which we gave not the tokens between us agreed upon, to have perfect knowledge of each other, if we should at any time be separated.

In great torment of weather and peril of drowning, it pleased God to send safe home the *Golden Hind*, which arrived in Falmouth, the 22nd day of September, being Sunday, not without as great danger escaped in a flaw, coming from the southeast, with such thick mist that we could not discern land, to put in right with the haven.

A REPORT OF VIRGINIA

(From 'a brief and true report of the new-found land of Virginia, of the commodities there found and to be raised, as well merchantable as others. Written by Thomas Heriot, servant to Sir Walter Raleigh, a member of the colony and there employed in discovering a full twelvemonth.')

THERE is an herb which is sowed apart by itself, and is called by the inhabitants *uppowoc*. In the West Indies it hath divers names, according to the several places and countries where it groweth and is used; the Spaniards generally call it *tobacco*. The leaves thereof being dried and brought into powder, they use to take the fume or smoke thereof by sucking it, through pipes made of clay, into their stomach and head, from whence it purgeth superfluous phlegm and other gross humors, and opens all the pores and passages of the body; by which means the use thereof not only preserveth the body from obstructions, but also (if any be, so that they have not been of too long continuance) in short time breaketh them, whereby their bodies are notably preserved in health, and know not many grievous diseases, wherewithal we in England are often times afflicted.

This *uppowoc* is of so precious estimation amongst them, that they think their gods are marvelously delighted therewith. Whereupon sometimes they make hallowed fires, and cast some of the powder therein for a sacrifice. Being in a storm upon the waters, to pacify their gods, they cast some up into the air and into the water. So a weir for fish being newly set up, they cast some therein and into the air. Also, after an escape of danger, they cast some into the air likewise; but all done with strange gestures, stamping, sometime dancing, clapping of hands, holding up of hands, and staring up into the heavens, uttering therewithal, and chattering strange words and noises.

We ourselves, during the time we were there, used to suck it after their manner, as also since our return, and have found many rare and wonderful experiments of the virtues thereof, of which the relation would require a volume by itself. The use of it by so many of late, men and women of great calling, as else, and some learned physicians also, is sufficient witness.

* * *

DRAKE IN CALIFORNIA

(From 'the famous voyage of Sir Francis Drake into the South Sea, and therehence about the whole globe of the earth begun in the year of our Lord, 1577.')

THE fifth day of June, being in 43 degrees towards the pole Arctic, we found the air so cold that our men, being grievously pinched with the same, complained of the extremity thereof; and the further we went, the more the cold increased upon us. Whereupon we thought it best for that time to seek the land, and did so, finding it not mountainous, but low plain land, till we came within 38 degrees towards the Line. In which height it pleased God to send us into a fair and good bay, with a good wind to enter the same.

In this bay we anchored, and the people of the country, having their houses close by the water's side, showed themselves unto us, and sent a present to our general.

When they came unto us, they greatly wondered at the things that we brought, but our general (according to his natural and accustomed humanity) courteously entreated them, and liberally bestowed on them necessary things to cover their nakedness, whereupon they supposed us to be gods, and would not be persuaded to the contrary. The presents which they sent to our general were feathers and cauls of network.

Their houses are digged round about with earth, and have from the uttermost brims of the circle clifts of wood set upon them, joining close together at the top like a spire steeple, which by reason of that closeness are very warm.

Their beds is the ground with rushes strewed on it, and lying about the house, have the fire in the midst. The men go naked, the women take bulrushes and comb them after the manner of hemp, and thereof make their loose garments, which being knit about their middles, hang down about their hips, having also about their shoulders a skin of deer with the hair upon it. These women are very obedient and serviceable to their husbands.

After they were departed from us, they came and visited us the second time and brought with them feathers and bags of tobacco for presents. And when they came to the top of the hill (at the bottom whereof we had pitched our tents) they stayed themselves, where one appointed for speaker wearied himself with making a long oration, which done, they left their bows upon the hill, and came down with their presents.

In the meantime the women, remaining on the hill, tormented themselves lamentably, tearing their flesh from their cheeks, whereby we perceived that they were about a sacrifice. In the meantime our general with his company went to prayer and to reading of the Scriptures, at which exercise they were attentive, and seemed greatly to be affected with it. But when they were come unto us, they restored again unto us those things which before we bestowed upon them.

The news of our being there being spread through the country, the people that inhabited round about came down, and amongst them the king himself, a man of goodly stature and comely personage, with many other tall and warlike men; before whose coming were sent two ambassadors to our general to signify that their king was coming, in doing of which message their speech was continued about half an hour. This ended, they by signs requested our general to send some thing by their hand to their king as a token that his coming might be in peace, wherein our general having satisfied them, they returned with glad tidings to their king, who marched to us with a princely majesty, the people crying continually after their manner; and as they drew near unto us, so did they strive to behave themselves in their actions with comeliness.

* * *

EDMUND SPENSER (1552-1599)

ALTHOUGH Spenser's father was 'a gentleman by birth,' he seems to have lacked adequate resources for bringing up his son. In spite of insufficient means, however, Spenser received a thoroughly good education, first as a 'poor scholar' in the Merchant Tailors' School in London, under Richard Mulcaster, and later, during seven years, as a sizar, or needy student, at Pembroke Hall, Cambridge. At the university he gained not only a high standing in classical studies, but also the permanent friendship of Gabriel Harvey, Fellow of Pembroke, the Hobbinol of Spenser's pastoral verse. After leaving the university, in 1576, Spenser seems to have retired for a year or so into the country, where, according to a persistent tradition, he met the Rosalind of the *Shepherd's Calendar*. He began his active career as a private secretary, first, perhaps, to Sir Henry Sidney, in Ireland, certainly to Bishop Young of Rochester, in 1578, and finally to the Earl of Leicester, in 1579. In this last position he met Leicester's nephew, Sir Philip Sidney, and Sir Edward Dyer, with both of whom he formed an intimate literary and personal friendship. His friendship with Sidney, Spenser recorded in *Astrophel: A Pastoral Elegy* (1595). Under Leicester's roof was completed the *Shepherd's Calendar*, published in 1579. The enthusiastic reception of the poem among men of letters promptly established Spenser as the chief of English poets then living. In 1580, Spenser went to Ireland as secretary to the lord deputy, Arthur Grey, and, except for two visits to England, he remained in Ireland until a month before his death. In 1581, he became clerk of the faculties in the Court of Chancery, and in the succeeding years prospered sufficiently to acquire land and to buy the office of clerk of the council of Munster, in 1588, when, probably, he began to reside upon his new estate at Kilcolman Castle. In 1589, Sir Walter Raleigh visited Spenser, who showed him the first three books of the *Faery Queen*, and who departed with his eminent visitor during that same year for London, there to present his work to the queen and to publish it. If the poet expected reward in the form of a government office in London, he was disappointed, for in 1591, after obtaining a pension of fifty pounds, he returned home. Raleigh's visit and the sojourn in London are reflected in *Colin Clout's Come Home Again* (1595). After his return to Ireland, Spenser seems to have worked assiduously upon the *Faery Queen*, for the second three books were completed before June 11, 1594, when he married Elizabeth Boyle, the inspiration of the *Amoretti* and of *Epithalamion*. In 1596, Spenser again visited London, to publish Books IV-VI of the *Faery Queen*, and, no doubt, to seek office—once more unsuccessfully. To this London visit is assigned the writing of the *Four Hymns*, the *Prothalamion*, and the prose tract, *View of the Present State of Ireland*. In this last work the poet vigorously records his contempt for the Irish, a contempt that must have grown into bitter hatred when, in 1598, Irish rebels burned Kilcolman Castle and drove Spenser and his family to Cork. After having prepared for the queen an account of the situation in Ireland, Spenser set out with dispatches for London, where he died, January 16, 1599.

From THE SHEPHEARDES CALENDAR, FEBRUARIE

ÆGLOGA SECUNDA

CUDDIE. THENOT.

CUDDIE

AH for pittie! wil rancke winters rage
These bitter blasts never ginne tasswage?
The kene cold blowes through my beaten hyde,
All as I were through the body gryde.
My ragged rontes all shiver and shake. 5
As doen high towers in an earthquake:
They wont in the wind wagge their wrigle tailes,
Perke as peacock: but nowe it avales.

THENOT

Lewdly complainest thou, laesie ladde,
Of winters wracke, for making thee sadde. 10
Must not the world wend in his commun course,
From good to badd, and from badde to worse,
From worse unto that is worst of all,
And then returne to his former fall?
Who will not suffer the stormy time, 15
Where will he live tyll the lusty prime?
Selfe have I worne out thrise threttie yeares,
Some in much joy, many in many teares;
Yet never complained of cold nor heate,

Of sommers flame, nor of winters threat; 20
Ne ever was to fortune foeman,
But gently tooke that ungently came:
And ever my flocke was my chiefe care;
Winter or sommer they mought well fare.

CUDDIE

No marveile, Thenot, if thou can beare 25
Cherefully the winters wrathfull cheare:
For age and winter accord full nie,
This chill, that cold, this crooked, that wrye;
And as the lowring wether lookes downe,
So semest thou like Good Fryday to frowne. 30
But my flowring youth is foe to frost,
My shippe unwont in stormes to be tost.

THENOT

The soveraigne of seas he blames in vaine,
That, once seabeate, will to sea againe.
So loytring live you little heardgroomes, 35
Keeping your beastes in the budded broomes:
And when the shining sunne laugheth once,
You deemen the spring is come attonce.
Tho gynne you, fond flyes, the cold to scorne,
And crowing in pypes made of greene corne, 40
You thinken to be lords of the yeare.
But eft, when ye count you freed from feare,
Comes the breme winter with chamfred browes,
Full of wrinkles and frostie furrowes,
Drerily shooting his stormy darte, 45
Which cruddles the blood, and pricks the harte.
Then is your carelesse corage accoied,
Your careful heards with cold bene annoied:
Then paye you the price of your surquedrie,
With weeping, and wayling, and misery. 50

CUDDIE

Ah, foolish old man! I scorne thy skill,
That wouldest me my springing youngth to spil.
I deeme thy braine emperished bee
Through rusty elde, that hath rotted thee:
Or sicker thy head veray tottie is, 55
So on thy corbe shoulder it leanes amisse.
Now thy selfe hast lost both lopp and topp,
Als my budding braunch thou wouldest cropp:
But were thy yeares greene, as now bene myne,
To other delights they would encline. 60
Tho wouldest thou learne to caroll of love,
And hery with hymnes thy lasses glove:
Tho wouldest thou pype of Phyllis prayse:
But Phyllis is myne for many dayes:
I wonne her with a grydle of gelt, 65
Embost with buegle about the belt:
Such an one shepeheards woulde make full faine,
Such an one would make thee younge againe.

THENOT

Thou art a fon, of thy love to boste;
All that is lent to love wyll be lost. 70

CUDDIE

Seest howe brag yond bullocke beares,
So smirke, so smoothe, his prickèd eares?
His hornes bene as broade as rainebowe bent,
His dewelap as lythe as lasse of Kent.
See howe he venteth into the wynd. 75
Weenest of love is not his mynd?
Seemeth thy flocke thy counsell can,
So lustlesse bene they, so weake, so wan,
Clothed with cold, and hoary wyth frost.
Thy flocks father his corage hath lost: 80
Thy ewes, that wont to have blowen bags,
Like wailefull widdowes hangen their crags:
The rather lambes bene starved with cold,
All for their maister is lustlesse and old.

THENOT

Cuddie, I wote thou kenst little good, 85
So vainely tadvaunce thy headlessehood.
For youngth is a bubble blown up with breath,
Whose witt is weakenesse, whose wage is death,
Whose way is wildernesse, whose ynne penaunce,
And stoopegallaunt age, the hoste of greevaunce. 90
But shall I tel thee a tale of truth,
Which I cond of Tityrus in my youth,
Keeping his sheepe on the hils of Kent?

CUDDIE

To nought more, Thenot, my mind is bent,
Then to heare novells of his devise: 95
They bene so well thewed, and so wise,
What ever that good old man bespake.

THENOT

Many meete tales of youth did he make,
And some of love, and some of chevalrie:
But none fitter then this to applie. 100
Now listen a while, and hearken the end.
  There grewe an agèd tree on the greene,
A goodly Oake sometime had it bene,
With armes full strong and largely displayd,
But of their leaves they were disarayde: 105
The bodie bigge, and mightely pight,
Throughly rooted, and of wonderous hight:
Whilome had bene the king of the field,
And mochell mast to the husband did yielde,
And with his nuts larded many swine. 110
But now the gray mosse marred his rine,
His barèd boughs were beaten with stormes,
His toppe was bald, and wasted with wormes,
His honor decayed, his braunches sere.
  Hard by his side grewe a bragging Brere, 115
Which proudly thrust into thelement,
And seemed to threat the firmament.
Yt was embellisht with blossomes fayre,
And thereto aye wonned to repayre 119
The shepheards daughters, to gather flowres,
To peinct their girlonds with his colowres:

And in his small bushes used to shrowde
The sweete nightingale singing so lowde:
Which made this foolish Brere wexe so bold,
That on a time he cast him to scold 125
And snebbe the good Oake, for he was old.
  'Why standst there,' quoth he, 'thou brutish blocke?
Nor for fruict nor for shadowe serves thy stocke.
Seest how fresh my flowers bene spredde,
Dyed in lilly white and cremsin redde, 130
With leaves engrained in lusty greene
Colours meete to clothe a mayden queene?
Thy wast bignes but combers the grownd,
And dirks the beauty of my blossomes round.
The mouldie mosse, which thee accloieth, 135
My sinamon smell too much annoieth.
Wherefore soone, I rede thee, hence remove,
Least thou the price of my displeasure prove.'
So spake this bold Brere with great disdaine:
Little him answered the Oake againe, 140
But yielded, with shame and greefe adawed,
That of a weede he was overawed.
  Yt chaunced after upon a day,
The husbandman selfe to come that way,
Of custome for to survewe his grownd, 145
And his trees of state in compasse rownd.
Him when the spitefull Brere had espyed,
Causlesse complained, and lowdly cryed
Unto his lord, stirring up sterne strife:
  'O my liege Lord, the god of my life, 150
Pleaseth you ponder your suppliants plaint,
Caused of wrong, and cruell constraint,
Which I your poore vassall dayly endure:
And but your goodnes the same recure,
Am like for desperate doole to dye, 155
Through felonous force of mine enemie.'
  Greatly aghast with this piteous plea,
Him rested the goodman on the lea,
And badde the Brere in his plaint proceede.
With painted words tho gan this proude weede
(As most usen ambitious folke) 161
His colowred crime with craft to cloke.
  'Ah my soveraigne, lord of creatures all,
Thou placer of plants both humble and tall,
Was not I planted of thine owne hand, 165
To be the primrose of all thy land,
With flowring blossomes to furnish the prime,
And scarlot berries in sommer time?
How falls it then, that this faded Oake,
Whose bodie is sere, whose braunches broke, 170
Whose naked armes stretch unto the fyre,
Unto such tyrannie doth aspire;
Hindering with his shade my lovely light,
And robbing me of the swete sonnes sight?
So beate his old boughes my tender side, 175
That oft the bloud springeth from wounds wyde:
Untimely my flowres forced to fall,
That bene the honor of your coronall.
And oft he lets his cancker wormes light
Upon my braunches, to worke me more spight:

And oft his hoarie locks downe doth cast, 181
Where with my fresh flowretts bene defast.
For this, and many more such outrage,
Craving your goodlihead to aswage
The ranckorous rigour of his might, 185
Nought aske I, but onely to hold my right;
Submitting me to your good sufferance,
And praying to be garded from greevance.'
  To this the Oake cast him to replie
Well as he couth: but his enemie 190
Had kindled such coles of displeasure,
That the good man noulde stay his leasure,
But home him hasted with furious heate,
Encreasing his wrath with many a threate.
His harmefull hatchet he hent in hand, 195
(Alas, that it so ready should stand!)
And to the field alone he speedeth,
(Ay little helpe to harme there needeth.)
Anger nould let him speake to the tree,
Enaunter his rage mought cooled bee; 200
But to the roote bent his sturdy stroke,
And made many wounds in the wast Oake.
The axes edge did oft turne againe,
As halfe unwilling to cutte the graine:
Semed, the sencelesse yron dyd feare, 205
Or to wrong holy eld did forbeare.
For it had bene an auncient tree,
Sacred with many a mysteree,
And often crost with the priestes crewe,
And often halowed with holy water dewe. 210
But sike fancies weren foolerie,
And broughten this Oake to this miserye.
For nought mought they quitten him from decay:
For fiercely the goodman at him did laye.
The blocke oft groned under the blow, 215
And sighed to see his neare overthrow.
In fine, the steele had pierced his pitth:
Tho downe to the earth he fell forthwith:
His wonderous weight made the grounde to quake,
Thearth shronke under him, and seemed to shake. 220
There lyeth the Oake, pitied of none.
  Now stands the Brere like a lord alone,
Puffed up with pryde and vaine pleasaunce:
But all this glee had no continuaunce.
For eftsones winter gan to approche, 225
The blustring Boreas did encroche,
And beate upon the solitarie Brere:
For nowe no succoure was seene him nere.
Now gan he repent his pryde to late:
For naked left and disconsolate, 230
The byting frost nipt his stalke dead,
The watrie wette weighed downe his head,
And heaped snowe burdned him so sore,
That nowe upright he can stand no more:
And being downe, is trodde in the durt 235
Of cattell, and brouzed, and sorely hurt.
Such was thend of this ambitious Brere,
For scorning eld—

CUDDIE

Now I pray thee, shepheard, tel it not forth:
Here is a long tale, and little worth.   240
So longe have I listened to thy speche,
That graffèd to the ground is my breche:
My hartblood is welnigh frorne, I feele,
And my galage growne fast to my heele:
But little ease of thy lewd tale I tasted.   245
Hye thee home, shepheard, the day is nigh wasted.

THENOTS EMBLEME.

Iddio, perchè è vecchio,
Fa suoi al suo essempio.

CUDDIES EMBLEME.

Niuno vecchio
Spaventa Iddio.

OCTOBER

ÆGLOGA DECIMA

PIERCE. CUDDIE.

PIERS

Cuddie, for shame! hold up thy heavye head,
And let us cast with what delight to chace
And weary thys long lingring Phœbus race.
Whilome thou wont the shepheards laddes to leade
In rymes, in ridles, and in bydding base: 5
Now they in thee, and thou in sleepe art dead.

CUDDIE

Piers, I have pypèd erst so long with payne,
That all mine oten reedes bene rent and wore:
And my poore Muse hath spent her sparèd store,
Yet little good hath got, and much lesse gayne.
Such pleasaunce makes the grashopper so poore,
And ligge so layd, when winter doth her straine.   12

The dapper ditties that I wont devise,
To feede youthes fancie and the flocking fry,
Delighten much: what I the bett forthy?   15
They han the pleasure, I a sclender prise:
I beate the bush, the byrds to them doe flye:
What good thereof to Cuddie can arise?

PIERS

Cuddie, the prayse is better then the price,
The glory eke much greater then the gayne: 20
O what an honor is it, to restraine
The lust of lawlesse youth with good advice,
Or pricke them forth with pleasaunce of thy vaine,
Whereto thou list their traynèd willes entice!
Soone as thou gynst to sette thy notes in frame,   25
O how the rurall routes to thee doe cleave!
Seemeth thou doest their soule of sense bereave,
All as the shepheard, that did fetch his dame
From Plutoes balefull bowre withouten leave:
His musicks might the hellish hound did tame.

CUDDIE

So praysen babes the peacoks spotted traine, 31
And wondren at bright Argus blazing eye;
But who rewards him ere the more forthy,
Or feedes him once the fuller by a graine?
Sike prayse is smoke, that sheddeth in the skye,
Sike words bene wynd, and wasten soone in vayne.   36

PIERS

Abandon then the base and viler clowne:
Lyft up thy selfe out of the lowly dust,
And sing of bloody Mars, of wars, of giusts:
Turne thee to those that weld the awful crowne,   40
To doubted knights, whose woundlesse armour rusts,
And helmes unbruzèd wexen dayly browne.

There may thy Muse display her fluttryng wing,
And stretch her selfe at large from east to west:
Whither thou list in fayre Elisa rest,   45
Or if thee please in bigger notes to sing,
Advaunce the worthy whome shee loveth best,
That first the white beare to the stake did bring.

And when the stubborne stroke of stronger stounds
Has somewhat slackt the tenor of thy string,   50
Of love and lustihead tho mayst thou sing,
And carol lowde, and leade the myllers rownde,
All were Elisa one of thilke same ring.
So mought our Cuddies name to heaven sownde.

CUDDIE

Indeede the Romish Tityrus, I heare,   55
Through his Mecœnas left his oaten reede,
Whereon he earst had taught his flocks to feede,
And laboured lands to yield the timely eare,
And eft did sing of warres and deadly drede,
So as the heavens did quake his verse to here.   60

But ah! Mecœnas is yclad in claye,
And great Augustus long ygoe is dead,
And all the worthies liggen wrapt in leade,
That matter made for poets on to play:
For, ever, who in derring doe were dreade,   65
The loftie verse of hem was lovèd aye.

But after vertue gan for age to stoupe,
And mighty manhode brought a bedde of ease,
The vaunting poets found nought worth a pease,

To put in preace emong the learnèd troupe. 70
Tho gan the streames of flowing wittes to cease,
And sonnebright honour pend in shamefull coupe.

And if that any buddes of poesie
Yet of the old stocke gan to shoote agayne,
Or it mens follies mote be forst to fayne, 75
And rolle with rest in rymes of rybaudrye,
Or, as it sprong, it wither must agayne:
Tom Piper makes us better melodie.

PIERS

O pierlesse Poesye, where is then thy place?
If nor in princes pallace thou doe sitt, 80
(And yet is princes pallace the most fitt)
Ne brest of baser birth doth thee embrace.
Then make thee winges of thine aspyring wit,
And, whence thou camst, flye backe to heaven apace.

CUDDIE

Ah, Percy! it is all to weake and wanne, 85
So high to sore, and make so large a flight;
Her peecèd pyneons bene not so in plight:
For Colin fittes such famous flight to scanne:
He, were he not with love so ill bedight,
Would mount as high and sing as soote as swanne. 90

PIERS

Ah, fon! for love does teach him climbe so hie,
And lyftes him up out of the loathsome myre:
Such immortall mirrhor as he doth admire
Would rayse ones mynd above the starry skie,
And cause a caytive corage to aspire; 95
For lofty love doth loath a lowly eye.

CUDDIE

All otherwise the state of poet stands:
For lordly Love is such a tyranne fell,
That, where he rules, all power he doth expell.
The vaunted verse a vacant head demaundes,
Ne wont with crabbèd Care the Muses dwell: 101
Unwisely weaves, that takes two webbes in hand.

Who ever casts to compasse weightye prise,
And thinks to throwe out thondring words of threate,
Let powre in lavish cups and thriftie bitts of meate; 105
For Bacchus fruite is frend to Phœbus wise,
And then with wine the braine begins to sweate,
The nombers flowe as fast as spring doth ryse.

Thou kenst not, Percie, howe the ryme should rage.
O if my temples were distaind with wine, 110
And girt in girlonds of wild yvie twine,
How I could reare the Muse on stately stage,
And teache her tread aloft in buskin fine,
With queint Bellona in her equipage!

But ah! my corage cooles ere it be warme; 115
Forthy content us in thys humble shade,
Where no such troublous tydes han us assayde.
Here we our slender pipes may safely charme.

PIERS

And when my gates shall han their bellies layd,
Cuddie shall have a kidde to store his farme.

CUDDIES EMBLEME.

Agitante calescimus illo, &c.

THE FAERIE QUEENE

THE FIRST BOOKE OF THE FAERIE QUEENE,
CONTAYNING THE LEGEND OF THE KNIGHT
OF THE RED CROSSE OR OF HOLINESSE

I

Lo! I the man, whose muse whylome did maske,
As time her taught, in lowly shephards weeds,
Am now enforst, a farre unfitter taske,
For trumpets sterne to chaunge mine oaten reeds,
And sing of knights and ladies gentle deeds; 5
Whose praises having slept in silence long,
Me, all too meane, the sacred Muse areeds
To blazon broade emongst her learnèd throng:
Fierce warres and faithfull loves shall moralize my song.

II

Helpe then, O holy virgin, chiefe of nyne, 10
Thy weaker novice to performe thy will;
Lay forth out of thine everlasting scryne
The antique rolles, which there lye hidden still,
Of Faerie knights, and fayrest Tanaquill,
Whom that most noble Briton Prince so long 15
Sought through the world, and suffered so much ill,
That I must rue his undeservèd wrong:
O helpe thou my weake wit, and sharpen my dull tong.

III

And thou, most dreaded impe of highest Jove,
Faire Venus sonne, that with thy cruell dart 20
At that good knight so cunningly didst rove,
That glorious fire it kindled in his hart,
Lay now thy deadly heben bowe apart,
And with thy mother mylde come to mine ayde:
Come both, and with you bring triumphant Mart, 25
In loves and gentle jollities arraid,
After his murdrous spoyles and bloudie rage allayd.

IV

And with them eke, O Goddesse heavenly bright,
Mirrour of grace and majestie divine,
Great Ladie of the greatest Isle, whose light 30
Like Phœbus lampe throughout the world doth shine,
Shed thy faire beames into my feeble eyne,
And raise my thoughts, too humble and too vile,
To thinke of that true glorious type of thine,
The argument of mine afflicted stile: 35
The which to heare vouchsafe, O dearest dread, a while.

CANTO I

The patrone of true Holinesse
Foule Errour doth defeate:
Hypocrisie, him to entrappe,
Doth to his home entreate.

I

A gentle knight was pricking on the plaine,
Ycladd in mightie armes and silver shielde,
Wherein old dints of deepe woundes did remaine,
The cruell markes of many a bloody fielde;
Yet armes till that time did he never wield: 5
His angry steede did chide his foming bitt,
As much disdayning to the curbe to yield:
Full jolly knight he seemd, and faire did sitt,
As one for knightly giusts and fierce encounters fitt.

II

But on his brest a bloodie crosse he bore, 10
The deare remembrance of his dying Lord,
For whose sweete sake that glorious badge he wore,
And dead as living ever him ador'd:
Upon his shield the like was also scor'd,
For soveraine hope, which in his helpe he had: 15
Right faithful true he was in deede and word,
But of his cheere did seeme too solemne sad;
Yet nothing did he dread, but ever was ydrad.

III

Upon a great adventure he was bond,
That greatest Gloriana to him gave, 20
That greatest glorious queene of Faery Lond,
To winne him worshippe, and her grace to have,
Which of all earthly thinges he most did crave;
And ever as he rode his hart did earne
To prove his puissance in battell brave 25
Upon his foe, and his new force to learne;
Upon his foe, a dragon horrible and stearne.

IV

A lovely ladie rode him faire beside,
Upon a lowly asse more white then snow,
Yet she much whiter, but the same did hide 30
Under a vele, that wimpled was full low,
And over all a blacke stole shee did throw:
As one that inly mournd, so was she sad,
And heavie sate upon her palfrey slow:
Seemèd in heart some hidden care she had; 35
And by her in a line a milkewhite lambe she lad.

V

So pure and innocent, as that same lambe,
She was in life and every vertuous lore,
And by descent from royall lynage came
Of ancient kinges and queenes, that had of yore 40
Their scepters stretcht from east to westerne shore,
And all the world in their subjection held,
Till that infernall feend with foule uprore
Forwasted all their land, and them expeld:
Whom to avenge, she had this knight from far compeld.

VI

Behind her farre away a dwarfe did lag,
That lasie seemd, in being ever last,
Or wearièd with bearing of her bag
Of needments at his backe. Thus as they past,
The day with cloudes was suddeine overcast, 50
And angry Jove an hideous storme of raine
Did poure into his lemans lap so fast,
That everie wight to shrowd it did constrain,
And this faire couple eke to shroud themselves were fain.

VII

Enforst to seeke some covert nigh at hand, 55
A shadie grove not farr away they spide,
That promist ayde the tempest to withstand:
Whose loftie trees, yclad with sommers pride,
Did spred so broad, that heavens light did hide,
Not perceable with power of any starr; 60
And all within were pathes and alleies wide,
With footing worne, and leading inward farr:
Faire harbour that them seemes, so in they entred ar.

VIII

And foorth they passe, with pleasure forward led,
Joying to heare the birdes sweete harmony, 65
Which, therein shrouded from the tempest dred,
Seemd in their song to scorne the cruell sky.
Much can they praise the trees so straight and hy,
The sayling pine, the cedar proud and tall,
The vine-propp elme, the poplar never dry, 70
The builder oake, sole king of forrests all,
The aspine good for staves, the cypresse funerall,

IX

The laurell, meed of mightie conquerours
And poets sage, the firre that weepeth still,
The willow worne of forlorne paramours, 75

The eugh obedient to the benders will,
The birch for shaftes, the sallow for the mill,
The mirrhe sweete bleeding in the bitter wound,
The warlike beech, the ash for nothing ill,
The fruitfull olive, and the platane round, 80
The carver holme, the maple seeldom inward sound.

X

Led with delight, they thus beguile the way,
Untill the blustring storme is overblowne;
When, weening to returne whence they did stray,
They cannot finde that path, which first was showne, 85
But wander too and fro in waies unknowne,
Furthest from end then, when they neerest weene,
That makes them doubt, their wits be not their owne:
So many pathes, so many turnings seene,
That which of them to take, in diverse doubt they been. 90

XI

At last resolving forward still to fare,
Till that some end they finde, or in or out,
That path they take, that beaten seemd most bare,
And like to lead the labyrinth about;
Which when by tract they hunted had through-out, 95
At length it brought them to a hollowe cave,
Amid the thickest woods. The champion stout
Eftsoones dismounted from his courser brave,
And to the dwarfe a while his needlesse spere he gave.

XII

'Be well aware,' quoth then that ladie milde, 100
'Least suddaine mischiefe ye too rash provoke:
The danger hid, the place unknowne and wilde,
Breedes dreadfull doubts: oft fire is without smoke,
And perill without show: therefore your stroke,
Sir knight, with-hold, till further tryall made.'
'Ah, ladie,' sayd he, 'shame were to revoke 106
The forward footing for an hidden shade:
Vertue gives her selfe light, through darkenesse for to wade.'

XIII

'Yea, but,' quoth she, 'the perill of this place
I better wot then you; though nowe too late 110
To wish you backe returne with foule disgrace,
Yet wisedome warnes, whilest foot is in the gate,
To stay the steppe, ere forcèd to retrate.
This is the wandring wood, this Errours den,
A monster vile, whom God and man does hate: 115
Therefore I read beware.' 'Fly, fly!' quoth then
The fearefull dwarfe: 'this is no place for living men.'

XIV

But full of fire and greedy hardiment,
The youthfull knight could not for ought be staide,
But forth unto the darksom hole he went, 120
And lookèd in: his glistring armor made
A litle glooming light, much like a shade,
By which he saw the ugly monster plaine,
Halfe like a serpent horribly displaide,
But th' other halfe did womans shape retaine, 125
Most lothsom, filthie, foule, and full of vile disdaine.

XV

And as she lay upon the durtie ground,
Her huge long taile her den all overspred,
Yet was in knots and many boughtes upwound,
Pointed with mortall sting. Of her there bred 130
A thousand yong ones, which she dayly fed,
Sucking upon her poisnous dugs, eachone
Of sundrie shapes, yet all ill favorèd:
Soone as that uncouth light upon them shone,
Into her mouth they crept, and suddain all were gone. 135

XVI

Their dam upstart, out of her den effraide,
And rushèd forth, hurling her hideous taile
About her cursèd head, whose folds displaid
Were stretcht now forth at length without entraile.
She lookt about, and seeing one in mayle, 140
Armèd to point, sought backe to turne againe;
For light she hated as the deadly bale,
Ay wont in desert darknes to remaine,
Where plain none might her see, nor she see any plaine.

XVII

Which when the valiant elfe perceiv'd, he lept
As lyon fierce upon the flying pray, 146
And with his trenchand blade her boldly kept
From turning backe, and forcèd her to stay:
Therewith enrag'd she loudly gan to bray,
And turning fierce, her speckled taile advaunst, 150
Threatning her angrie sting, him to dismay:
Who, nought aghast, his mightie hand enhaunst:
The stroke down from her head unto her shoulder glaunst.

XVIII

Much daunted with that dint, her sence was dazed,
Yet kindling rage her selfe she gathered round,
And all attonce her beastly bodie raizd 156
With doubled forces high above the ground:
Tho, wrapping up her wrethèd sterne arownd,
Lept fierce upon his shield, and her huge traine
All suddenly about his body wound, 160

XIX

That hand or foot to stirr he strove in vaine:
God helpe the man so wrapt in Errours endlesse traine.

XIX

His lady, sad to see his sore constraint,
Cride out, 'Now, now, sir knight, shew what ye bee;
Add faith unto your force, and be not faint: 165
Strangle her, els she sure will strangle thee.'
That when he heard, in great perplexitie,
His gall did grate for griefe and high disdaine;
And knitting all his force, got one hand free,
Wherewith he grypt her gorge with so great paine, 170
That soone to loose her wicked bands did her constraine.

XX

Therewith she spewd out of her filthie maw
A floud of poyson horrible and blacke,
Full of great lumps of flesh and gobbets raw,
Which stunck so vildly, that it forst him slacke
His grasping hold, and from her turne him backe: 176
Her vomit full of bookes and papers was,
With loathy frogs and toades, which eyes did lacke,
And creeping sought way in the weedy gras:
Her filthie parbreake all the place defilèd has. 180

XXI

As when old father Nilus gins to swell
With timely pride above the Ægyptian vale,
His fattie waves doe fertile slime outwell,
And overflow each plaine and lowly dale:
But when his later spring gins to avale, 185
Huge heapes of mudd he leaves, wherin there breed
Ten thousand kindes of creatures, partly male
And partly femall, of his fruitful seed;
Such ugly monstrous shapes elswhere may no man reed.

XXII

The same so sore annoyèd has the knight, 190
That, welnigh chokèd with the deadly stinke,
His forces faile, ne can no lenger fight.
Whose corage when the feend perceivd to shrinke,
She pourèd forth out of her hellish sinke
Her fruitfull cursèd spawne of serpents small, 195
Deformèd monsters, fowle, and blacke as inke,
Which swarming all about his legs did crall,
And him encombred sore, but could not hurt at all.

XXIII

As gentle shepheard in sweete eventide,
When ruddy Phebus gins to welke in west, 200
High on an hill, his flocke to vewen wide,
Markes which doe byte their hasty supper best;
A cloud of cumbrous gnattes doe him molest,
All striving to infixe their feeble stinges,
That from their noyance he no where can rest, 205
But with his clownish hands their tender wings
He brusheth oft, and oft doth mar their murmurings.

XXIV

Thus ill bestedd, and fearefull more of shame
Then of the certeine perill he stood in,
Halfe furious unto his foe he came, 210
Resolvd in minde all suddenly to win,
Or soone to lose, before he once would lin;
And stroke at her with more then manly force,
That from her body, full of filthie sin,
He raft her hatefull heade without remorse: 215
A streame of cole black blood forth gushèd from her corse.

XXV

Her scattred brood, soone as their parent deare
They saw so rudely falling to the ground,
Groning full deadly, all with troublous feare,
Gathred themselves about her body round, 220
Weening their wonted entrance to have found
At her wide mouth: but being there withstood,
They flockèd all about her bleeding wound,
And suckèd up their dying mothers bloud,
Making her death their life, and eke her hurt their good. 225

XXVI

That detestable sight him much amazde,
To see th' unkindly impes, of heaven accurst,
Devoure their dam; on whom while so he gazd,
Having all satisfide their bloudy thurst,
Their bellies swolne he saw with fulnesse burst,
And bowels gushing forth; well worthy end 231
Of such as drunke her life, the which them nurst!
Now needeth him no lenger labour spend;
His foes have slaine themselves, with whom he should contend.

XXVII

His lady, seeing all that chaunst, from farre, 235
Approcht in hast to greet his victorie,
And saide, 'Faire knight, borne under happie starre,
Who see your vanquisht foes before you lye,
Well worthie be you of that armory,
Wherein ye have great glory wonne this day, 240
And proov'd your strength on a strong enimie,
Your first adventure: many such I pray,
And henceforth ever wish that like succeed it may.'

XXVIII

Then mounted he upon his steede againe,
And with the lady backward sought to wend: 245
That path he kept which beaten was most plaine,

Ne ever would to any by way bend,
But still did follow one unto the end,
The which at last out of the wood them brought.
So forward on his way (with God to frend) 250
He passèd forth, and new adventure sought:
Long way he traveilèd, before he heard of ought.

XXIX

At length they chaunst to meet upon the way
An agèd sire, in long blacke weedes yclad,
His feete all bare, his beard all hoarie gray, 255
And by his belte his booke he hanging had;
Sober he seemde, and very sagely sad,
And to the ground his eyes were lowly bent,
Simple in shew, and voide of malice bad,
And all the way he prayèd as he went, 260
And often knockt his brest, as one that did repent.

XXX

He faire the knight saluted, louting low,
Who faire him quited, as that courteous was;
And after askèd him, if he did know
Of straunge adventures, which abroad did pas. 265
'Ah! my dear sonne,' quoth he, 'how should, alas!
Silly old man, that lives in hidden cell,
Bidding his beades all day for his trespas,
Tydings of warre and worldly trouble tell?
With holy father sits not with such thinges to mell. 270

XXXI

'But if of daunger, which hereby doth dwell,
And homebredd evil ye desire to heare,
Of a straunge man I can you tidings tell,
That wasteth all his countrie farre and neare.'
'Of such,' saide he, 'I chiefly doe inquere, 275
And shall you well rewarde to shew the place,
In which that wicked wight his dayes doth weare:
For to all knighthood it is foule disgrace,
That such a cursèd creature lives so long a space.'

XXXII

'Far hence,' quoth he, 'in wastefull wildernesse,
His dwelling is, by which no living wight 281
May ever passe, but thorough great distresse.'
'Now,' saide the ladie, 'draweth toward night,
And well I wote, that of your later fight
Ye all forwearied be: for what so strong, 285
But, wanting rest, will also want of might?
The Sunne, that measures heaven all day long,
At night doth baite his steedes the ocean waves emong.

XXXIII

'Then with the Sunne take, sir, your timely rest,
And with new day new worke at once begin: 290
Untroubled night, they say, gives counsell best.'
'Right well, sir knight, ye have advisèd bin,'

Quoth then that agèd man; 'the way to win
Is wisely to advise: now day is spent;
Therefore with me ye may take up your in 295
For this same night.' The knight was well content:
So with that godly father to his home they went.

XXXIV

A litle lowly hermitage it was,
Downe in a dale, hard by a forests side,
Far from resort of people, that did pas 300
In traveill to and froe: a litle wyde
There was an holy chappell edifyde,
Wherein the hermite dewly wont to say
His holy thinges each morne and even-tyde:
Thereby a christall streame did gently play, 305
Which from a sacred fountaine wellèd forth alway.

XXXV

Arrivèd there, the little house they fill,
Ne looke for entertainment, where none was:
Rest is their feast, and all thinges at their will;
The noblest mind the best contentment has. 310
With faire discourse the evening so they pas:
For that olde man of pleasing wordes had store,
And well could file his tongue as smooth as glas:
He told of saintes and popes, and evermore
He strowd an Ave-Mary after and before. 315

XXXVI

The drouping night thus creepeth on them fast,
And the sad humor loading their eye liddes,
As messenger of Morpheus, on them cast
Sweet slombring deaw, the which to sleep them biddes:
Unto their lodgings then his guestes he riddes:
Where when all drownd in deadly sleepe he findes, 321
He to his studie goes, and there amiddes
His magick bookes and artes of sundrie kindes,
He seekes out mighty charmes, to trouble sleepy minds.

XXXVII

Then choosing out few words most horrible, 325
(Let none them read) thereof did verses frame;
With which and other spelles like terrible,
He bad awake blacke Plutoes griesly dame,
And cursèd heven, and spake reproachful shame
Of highest God, the Lord of life and light: 330
A bold bad man, that dar'd to call by name
Great Gorgon, prince of darknes and dead night,
At which Cocytus quakes, and Styx is put to flight.

XXXVIII

And forth he cald out of deepe darknes dredd
Legions of sprights, the which, like litle flyes 335
Fluttring about his ever damnèd hedd,
Awaite whereto their service he applyes,

To aide his friendes, or fray his enimies:
Of those he chose out two, the falsest twoo,
And fittest for to forge true-seeming lyes; 340
The one of them he gave a message too,
The other by him selfe staide, other worke to doo.

XXXIX

He, making speedy way through spersèd ayre,
And through the world of waters wide and deepe,
To Morpheus house doth hastily repaire. 345
Amid the bowels of the earth full steepe,
And low, where dawning day doth never peepe,
His dwelling is; there Tethys his wet bed
Doth ever wash, and Cynthia still doth steepe
In silver deaw his ever-drouping hed, 350
Whiles sad Night over him her mantle black doth spred.

XL

Whose double gates he findeth lockèd fast,
The one faire fram'd of burnisht yvory,
The other all with silver overcast; 354
And wakeful dogges before them farre doe lye,
Watching to banish Care their enimy,
Who oft is wont to trouble gentle Sleepe.
By them the sprite doth passe in quietly,
And unto Morpheus comes, whom drownèd deepe
In drowsie fit he findes: of nothing he takes keepe. 360

XLI

And more, to lulle him in his slumber soft,
A trickling streame from high rock tumbling downe,
And ever drizling raine upon the loft,
Mixt with a murmuring winde, much like the sowne
Of swarming bees, did cast him in a swowne: 365
No other noyse, nor peoples troublous cryes,
As still are wont t'annoy the wallèd towne,
Might there be heard: but carelesse Quiet lyes,
Wrapt in eternall silence farre from enimyes.

XLII

The messenger approching to him spake, 370
But his waste wordes retourned to him in vaine:
So sound he slept, that nought mought him awake.
Then rudely he him thrust, and pusht with paine,
Whereat he gan to stretch: but he againe
Shooke him so hard, that forcèd him to speake.
As one then in a dreame, whose dryer braine 376
Is tost with troubled sights and fancies weake,
He mumbled soft, but would not all his silence breake.

XLIII

The sprite then gan more boldly him to wake,
And threatened unto him the dreaded name
Of Hecate: whereat he gan to quake, 381
And, lifting up his lompish head, with blame
Halfe angrie askèd him, for what he came.
'Hether,' quoth he, 'me Archimago sent,
He that the stubborne sprites can wisely tame; 385
He bids thee to him send for his intent
A fit false dreame, that can delude the sleepers sent.'

XLIV

The god obayde, and calling forth straight way
A diverse dreame out of his prison darke,
Delivered it to him, and downe did lay 390
His heavie head, devoide of careful carke;
Whose sences all were straight benumbd and starke.
He, backe returning by the yvorie dore,
Remounted up as light as cheareful larke,
And on his litle winges the dreame he bore 395
In hast unto his lord, where he him left afore.

XLV

Who all this while, with charmes and hidden artes,
Had made a lady of that other spright,
And fram'd of liquid ayre her tender partes,
So lively and so like in all mens sight, 400
That weaker sence it could have ravisht quight:
The maker selfe, for all his wondrous witt,
Was nigh beguilèd with so goodly sight:
Her all in white he clad, and over it
Cast a black stole, most like to seeme for Una fit. 405

XLVI

Now when that ydle dreame was to him brought,
Unto that Elfin knight he bad him fly,
Where he slept soundly, void of evil thought,
And with false shewes abuse his fantasy,
In sort as he him schoolèd privily: 410
And that new creature, borne without her dew,
Full of the makers guyle, with usage sly
He taught to imitate that lady trew,
Whose semblance she did carrie under feignèd hew.

XLVII

Thus well instructed, to their worke they haste, 415
And comming where the knight in slomber lay,
The one upon his hardie head him plaste,
And made him dreame of loves and lustfull play,
That nigh his manly hart did melt away,
Bathèd in wanton blis and wicked joy. 420
Then seemèd him his lady by him lay,
And to him playnd, how that false wingèd boy
Her chaste hart had subdewd to learne Dame Pleasures toy.

XLVIII

And she her selfe, of beautie soveraigne queene,
Fayre Venus, seemde unto his bed to bring   425
Her, whom he, waking, evermore did weene
To bee the chastest flowre that aye did spring
On earthly braunch, the daughter of a king,
Now a loose leman to vile service bound:
And eke the Graces seemèd all to sing   430
Hymen iö Hymen, dauncing all around,
Whylst freshest Flora her with yvie girlond
  crownd.

XLIX

In this great passion of unwonted lust,
Or wonted feare of doing ought amis,
He started up, as seeming to mistrust   435
Some secret ill, or hidden foe of his:
Lo! there before his face his ladie is,
Under blacke stole hyding her bayted hooke,
And as halfe blushing offred him to kis,
With gentle blandishment and lovely looke,
Most like that virgin true, which for her knight
  him took.   441

L

All cleane dismayed to see so uncouth sight,
And halfe enragèd at her shamelesse guise,
He thought have slaine her in his fierce de-
  spight;
But hastie heat tempring with sufferance
  wise,   445
He stayde his hand, and gan himselfe advise
To prove his sense, and tempt her faignèd truth.
Wringing her hands in wemens pitteous wise,
Tho can she weepe, to stirre up gentle ruth,
Both for her noble blood, and for her tender
  youth.   450

LI

And sayd, 'Ah sir, my liege lord and my love,
Shall I accuse the hidden cruell fate,
And mightie causes wrought in heaven above,
Or the blind god, that doth me thus amate,
For hopèd love to winne me certaine hate?   455
Yet thus perforce he bids me do, or die
Die is my dew: yet rew my wretched state
You, whom my hard avenging destinie
Hath made judge of my life or death indiffer-
  ently.

LII

'Your owne deare sake forst me at first to
  leave   460
My fathers kingdom'—There she stopt with
  teares;
Her swollen hart her speech seemed to bereave;
And then againe begonne: 'My weaker yeares,
Captiv'd to fortune and frayle worldly feares,
Fly to your fayth for succour and sure ayde: 465
Let me not die in languor and long teares.'

LIII

'Why, dame,' quoth he, 'what hath ye thus
  dismayd?
What frayes ye, that were wont to comfort me
  affrayd?'

LIII

'Love of your selfe,' she saide, 'and deare con-
  straint,
Lets me not sleepe, but waste the wearie
  night   470
In secret anguish and unpittied plaint,
Whiles you in careless sleepe are drownèd
  quight.'
Her doubtfull words made that redoubted knight
Suspect her truth: yet since no' untruth he knew,
Her fawning love with foule disdainefull
  spight   475
He would not shend, but said, 'Deare dame, I
  rew,
That for my sake unknowne such griefe unto
  you grew.

LIV

'Assure your selfe, it fell not all to ground;
For all so deare as life is to my hart,
I deeme your love, and hold me to you bound;
Ne let vaine feares procure your needlesse
  smart,   481
Where cause is none, but to your rest depart'
Not all content, yet seemd she to appease
Her mournfull plaintes, beguilèd of her art,
And fed with words, that could not chose but
  please;   485
So slyding softly forth, she turnd as to her ease.

LV

Long after lay he musing at her mood,
Much griev'd to thinke that gentle dame so
  light,
For whose defence he was to shed his blood.
At last dull wearines of former fight   490
Having yrockt a sleepe his irkesome spright,
That troublous dreame gan freshly tosse his
  braine
With bowres, and beds, and ladies deare delight:
But when he saw his labour all was vaine,
With that misformèd spright he backe returnd
  againe.   495

CANTO II

*The guilefull great enchaunter parts
The Redcrosse Knight from Truth:
Into whose stead faire Falshood steps,
And workes him woefull ruth.*

I

By this the northerne wagoner had set
His sevenfold teme behind the stedfast starre,
That was in ocean waves yet never wet,
But firme is fixt, and sendeth light from farre

To al that in the wide deepe wandring arre: 5
And chearefull Chaunticlere with his note shrill
Had warnèd once, that Phœbus fiery carre
In hast was climbing up the easterne hill,
Full envious that night so long his roome did fill:

II

When those accursèd messengers of hell, 10
That feigning dreame, and that faire-forgèd spright,
Came to their wicked maister, and gan tel
Their bootelesse paines, and ill succeeding night:
Who, all in rage to see his skilfull might
Deluded so, gan threaten hellish paine 15
And sad Proserpines wrath, them to affright.
But when he saw his threatning was but vaine,
He cast about, and searcht his baleful bokes againe.

III

Eftsoones he tooke that miscreated faire,
And that false other spright, on whom he spred
A seeming body of the subtile aire, 21
Like a young squire, in loves and lustyhed
His wanton daies that ever loosely led,
Without regard of armes and dreaded fight:
Those twoo he tooke, and in a secrete bed, 25
Covered with darkenes and misdeeming night,
Them both together laid, to joy in vaine delight.

IV

Forthwith he runnes with feignèd faithfull hast
Unto his guest, who, after troublous sights
And dreames, gan now to take more sound repast; 30
Whom suddenly he wakes with fearful frights,
As one aghast with feends or damnèd sprights,
And to him cals: 'Rise, rise, unhappy swaine,
That here wex old in sleepe, whiles wicked wights
Have knit themselves in Venus shameful chaine; 35
Come see, where your false lady doth her honor staine.'

V

All in amaze he suddenly up start
With sword in hand, and with the old man went;
Who soone him brought into a secret part,
Where that false couple were full closely ment 40
In wanton lust and leud embracement:
Which when he saw, he burnt with gealous fire,
The eie of reason was with rage yblent,
And would have slaine them in his furious ire,
But hardly was restreinèd of that agèd sire. 45

VI

Retourning to his bed in torment great,
And bitter anguish of his guilty sight,
He could not rest, but did his stout heart eat,
And wast his inward gall with deepe despight,
Yrkesome of life, and too long lingring night. 50
At last faire Hesperus in highest skie
Had spent his lampe, and brought forth dawning light;
Then up he rose, and clad him hastily;
The dwarfe him brought his steed: so both away do fly.

VII

Now when the rosy fingred Morning faire, 55
Weary of agèd Tithones saffron bed,
Had spred her purple robe through deawy aire,
And the high hils Titan discoverèd,
The royall virgin shooke of drousyhed,
And rising forth out of her baser bowre, 60
Lookt for her knight, who far away was fled,
And for her dwarfe, that wont to wait each howre:
Then gan she wail and weepe, to see that woeful stowre.

VIII

And after him she rode with so much speede,
As her slowe beast could make; but all in vaine: 65
For him so far had borne his light-foot steede,
Prickèd with wrath and fiery fierce disdaine,
That him to follow was but fruitlesse paine;
Yet she her weary limbes would never rest,
But every hil and dale, each wood and plaine,
Did search, sore grievèd in her gentle brest, 71
He so ungently left her, whome she lovèd best.

IX

But subtill Archimago, when his guests
He saw divided into double parts,
And Una wandring in woods and forrests, 75
Th' end of his drift, he praisd his divelish arts,
That had such might over true meaning harts:
Yet rests not so, but other meanes doth make,
How he may worke unto her further smarts:
For her he hated as the hissing snake, 80
And in her many troubles did most pleasure take.

X

He then devisde himselfe how to disguise;
For by his mighty science he could take
As many formes and shapes in seeming wise,
As ever Proteus to himselfe could make: 85
Sometime a fowle, sometime a fish in lake,
Now like a foxe, now like a dragon fell,
That of himselfe he ofte for feare would quake,
And oft would flie away. O who can tell
The hidden powre of herbes, and might of magick spel? 90

XI

But now seemde best, the person to put on
Of that good knight, his late beguilèd guest:
In mighty armes he was yclad anon,
And silver shield; upon his coward brest

A bloody crosse, and on his craven crest 95
A bounch of heares discoloured diversly:
Full jolly knight he seemde, and wel addrest,
And when he sate uppon his courser free,
Saint George himselfe ye would have deemèd him to be.

XII

But he, the knight whose semblaunt he did beare, 100
The true Saint George, was wandred far away,
Still flying from his thoughts and gealous feare;
Will was his guide, and griefe led him astray.
At last him chaunst to meete upon the way
A faithlesse Sarazin, all armde to point, 105
In whose great shield was writ with letters gay
Sans foy: full large of limbe and every joint
He was, and carèd not for God or man a point.

XIII

Hee had a faire companion of his way,
A goodly lady clad in scarlot red, 110
Purfled with gold and pearle of rich assay;
And like a Persian mitre on her hed
Shee wore, with crowns and owches garnishèd,
The which her lavish lovers to her gave:
Her wanton palfrey all was overspred 115
With tinsell trappings, woven like a wave,
Whose bridle rung with golden bels and bosses brave.

XIV

With faire disport and courting dalliaunce
She intertainde her lover all the way:
But when she saw the knight his speare advaunce 120
Shee soone left of her mirth and wanton play,
And bad her knight addresse him to the fray:
His foe was nigh at hand. He, prickte with pride
And hope to winne his ladies hearte that day,
Forth spurrèd fast: adowne his coursers side 125
The red bloud trickling staind the way, as he did ride.

XV

The Knight of the Redcrosse, when him he spide
Spurring so hote with rage dispiteous,
Gan fairely couch his speare, and towards ride:
Soone meete they both, both fell and furious,
That, daunted with theyr forces hideous, 131
Their steeds doe stagger, and amazèd stand,
And eke themselves, too rudely rigorous,
Astonied with the stroke of their owne hand,
Doe backe rebutte, and ech to other yealdeth land. 135

XVI

As when two rams, stird with ambitious pride,
Fight for the rule of the rich fleecèd flocke,
Their hornèd fronts so fierce on either side
Doe meete, that, with the terror of the shocke
Astonied, both stand sencelesse as a blocke, 140
Forgetfull of the hanging victory:
So stood these twaine, unmovèd as a rocke,
Both staring fierce, and holding idely
The broken reliques of their former cruelty.

XVII

The Sarazin, sore daunted with the buffe, 145
Snatcheth his sword, and fiercely to him flies;
Who well it wards, and quyteth cuff with cuff:
Each others equall puissaunce envies,
And through their iron sides with cruell spies
Does seeke to perce: repining courage yields 150
No foote to foe. The flashing fier flies,
As from a forge, out of their burning shields,
And streams of purple bloud new dies the verdant fields.

XVIII

'Curse on that Crosse,' quoth then the Sarazin,
'That keepes thy body from the bitter fitt! 155
Dead long ygoe, I wote, thou haddest bin,
Had not that charme from thee forwarnèd itt:
But yet I warne thee now assurèd sitt,
And hide thy head.' Therewith upon his crest
With rigor so outrageous he smitt, 160
That a large share it hewd out of the rest,
And glauncing downe his shield, from blame him fairely blest.

XIX

Who thereat wondrous wroth, the sleeping spark
Of native vertue gan eftsoones revive,
And at his haughty helmet making mark, 165
So hugely stroke, that it the steele did rive,
And cleft his head. He, tumbling downe alive,
With bloudy mouth his mother earth did kis,
Greeting his grave: his grudging ghost did strive
With the fraile flesh; at last it flitted is, 170
Whether the soules doe fly of men that live amis.

XX

The lady, when she saw her champion fall,
Like the old ruines of a broken towre,
Staid not to waile his woefull funerall,
But from him fled away with all her powre; 175
Who after her as hastily gan scowre,
Bidding the dwarfe with him to bring away
The Sarazins shield, signe of the conqueroure.
Her soone he overtooke, and bad to stay,
For present cause was none of dread her to dismay. 180

XXI

Shee, turning backe with ruefull countenaunce,
Cride, 'Mercy, mercy, sir, vouchsafe to showe
On silly dame, subject to hard mischaunce,
And to your mighty wil!' Her humblesse low,

In so ritch weedes and seeming glorious show, 185
Did much emmove his stout heroïcke heart,
And said, 'Deare dame, your suddein over-
  throw
Much rueth me; but now put feare apart,
And tel, both who ye be, and who that tooke
  your part.'

XXII

Melting in teares, then gan shee thus lament: 190
'The wreched woman, whom unhappy howre
Hath now made thrall to your commandement,
Before that angry heavens list to lowre,
And Fortune false betraide me to your powre,
Was, (O what now availeth that I was?)   195
Borne the sole daughter of an emperour,
He that the wide west under his rule has,
And high hath set his throne where Tiberis doth
  pas.

XXIII

'He, in the first flowre of my freshest age,
Betrothèd me unto the onely haire   200
Of a most mighty king, most rich and sage;
Was never prince so faithfull and so faire,
Was never prince so meeke and debonaire;
But ere my hopèd day of spousall shone,
My dearest lord fell from high honors staire, 205
Into the hands of hys accursèd fone,
And cruelly was slaine, that shall I ever mone.

XXIV

'His blessed body, spoild of lively breath,
Was afterward, I know not how, convaid
And fro me hid: of whose most innocent death
When tidings came to mee, unhappy maid, 211
O how great sorrow my sad soule assaid!
Then forth I went his woefull corse to find,
And many yeares throughout the world I straid,
A virgin widow, whose deepe wounded mind
With love, long time did languish as the striken
  hind.   216

XXV

'At last it chauncèd this proud Sarazin
To meete me wandring; who perforce me led
With him away, but yet could never win
The fort, that ladies hold in soveraigne dread. 220
There lies he now with foule dishonor dead,
Who, whilse he livde, was callèd proud Sansfoy:
The eldest of three brethren, all three bred
Of one bad sire, whose youngest is Sansjoy,
And twixt them both was born the bloudy bold
  Sansloy.   225

XXVI

'In this sad plight, friendlesse, unfortunate,
Now miserable I Fidessa dwell,
Craving of you, in pitty of my state,
To doe none ill, if please ye not doe well.'
He in great passion al this while did dwell, 230
More busying his quicke eies, her face to view,
Then his dull eares, to heare what shee did tell;
And said, 'Faire lady, hart of flint would rew
The undeservèd woes and sorrows which ye
  shew.

XXVII

'Henceforth in safe assuraunce may ye rest, 235
Having both found a new friend you to aid,
And lost an old foe, that did you molest:
Better new friend then an old foe is said.'
With chaunge of chear the seeming simple maid
Let fal her eien, as shamefast, to the earth, 240
And yeelding soft, in that she nought gain-
  said,
So forth they rode, he feining seemely merth,
And shee coy lookes: so dainty, they say, maketh
  derth.

XXVIII

Long time they thus together traveilèd,
Til, weary of their way, they came at last   245
Where grew two goodly trees, that faire did
  spred
Their armes abroad, with gray mosse overcast,
And their greene leaves, trembling with every
  blast,
Made a calme shadowe far in compasse round:
The fearefull shepheard, often there aghast, 250
Under them never sat, ne wont there sound
His merry oaten pipe, but shund th' unlucky
  ground.

XXIX

But this good knight, soone as he them can spie,
For the coole shade him thither hastly got:
For golden Phœbus, now ymounted hie,   255
From fiery wheeles of his faire chariot
Hurlèd his beame so scorching cruell hot,
That living creature mote it not abide;
And his new lady it endurèd not.
There they alight, in hope themselves to hide 260
From the fierce heat, and rest their weary limbs
  a tide.

XXX

Faire seemely pleasaunce each to other makes,
With goodly purposes, there as they sit:
And in his falsèd fancy he her takes
To be the fairest wight that livèd yit;   265
Which to expresse, he bends his gentle wit,
And thinking of those braunches greene to
  frame
A girlond for her dainty forehead fit,
He pluckt a bough; out of whose rifte there
  came
Smal drops of gory bloud, that trickled down
  the same.   270

XXXI

Therewith a piteous yelling voice was heard,
Crying, 'O spare with guilty hands to teare
My tender sides in this rough rynd embard;
But fly, ah! fly far hence away, for feare

'Least to you hap that happened to me heare, 275
And to this wretched lady, my deare love;
O too deare love, love bought with death too deare!'
Astond he stood, and up his heare did hove,
And with that suddein horror could no member move.

XXXII

At last, whenas the dreadfull passion 280
Was overpast, and manhood well awake,
Yet musing at this straunge occasion,
And doubting much his sence, he thus bespake:
'What voice of damnèd ghost from Limbo lake,
Or guilefull spright wandring in empty aire, 285
Both which fraile men doe oftentimes mistake,
Sends to my doubtful eares these speaches rare,
And ruefull plaints, me bidding guiltlesse blood to spare?'

XXXIII

Then groning deep: 'Nor damnèd ghost,' quoth he,
'Nor guileful spirite to thee these words doth speake, 290
But once a man, Fradubio, now a tree;
Wretched man, wretched tree! whose natuie weake
A cruell witch, her cursèd will to wreake,
Hath thus transformed, and plast in open plaines,
Where Boreas doth blow full bitter bleake, 295
And scorching sunne does dry my secret vaines:
For though a tree I seme, yet cold and heat me paines.'

XXXIV

'Say on, Fradubio, then, or man or tree,'
Quoth then the knight; 'by whose mischievous arts
Art thou misshapèd thus, as now I see? 300
He oft finds med'cine who his griefe imparts;
But double griefs afflict concealing harts,
As raging flames who striveth to suppresse.'
'The author then,' said he, 'of all my smarts,
Is one Duessa, a false sorceresse, 305
That many errant knights hath broght to wretchednesse.

XXXV

'In prime of youthly yeares, when corage hott
The fire of love and joy of chevalree
First kindled in my brest, it was my lott
To love this gentle lady, whome ye see 310
Now not a lady, but a seeming tree;
With whome as once I rode accompanyde,
Me chauncèd of a knight encountred bee,
That had a like faire lady by his syde;
Lyke a faire lady, but did fowle Duessa hyde. 315

XXXVI

'Whose forgèd beauty he did take in hand
All other dames to have exceded farre;
I in defence of mine did likewise stand,
Mine, that did then shine as the morning starre:
So both to batteill fierce arraungèd arre; 320
In which his harder fortune was to fall
Under my speare; such is the dye of warre:
His lady, left as a prise martiall,
Did yield her comely person, to be at my call.

XXXVII

'So doubly lov'd of ladies unlike faire, 325
Th' one seeming such, the other such indeede,
One day in doubt I cast for to compare,
Whether in beauties glorie did exceede;
A rosy girlond was the victors meede.
Both seemde to win, and both seemde won to bee, 330
So hard the discord was to be agreede:
Frælissa was as faire as faire mote bee,
And ever false Duessa seemde as faire as shee.

XXXVIII

'The wicked witch, now seeing all this while
The doubtfull ballaunce equally to sway, 335
What not by right, she cast to win by guile;
And by her hellish science raisd streight way
A foggy mist, that overcast the day,
And a dull blast, that, breathing on her face,
Dimmèd her former beauties shining ray, 340
And with foule ugly forme did her disgrace:
Then was she fayre alone, when none was faire in place.

XXXIX

'Then cride she out, "Fye, fye! deformèd wight,
Whose borrowed beautie now appeareth plaine
To have before bewitchèd all mens sight; 345
O leave her soone, or let her soone be slaine."
Her loathly visage viewing with disdaine,
Eftsoones I thought her such as she me told,
And would have kild her; but with faignèd paine
The false witch did my wrathfull hand withhold: 350
So left her, where she now is turnd to treën mould.

XL

'Thensforth I tooke Duessa for my dame,
And in the witch unweeting joyd long time,
Ne ever wist but that she was the same:
Till on a day (that day is everie prime, 355
When witches wont do penance for their crime)
I chaunst to see her in her proper hew,
Bathing her selfe in origane and thyme:
A filthy foule old woman I did vew,
That ever to have toucht her I did deadly rew.

XLI

'Her neather partes misshapen, monstruous, 361
Were hidd in water, that I could not see,
But they did seeme more foule and hideous,
Then womans shape man would beleeve to bee,
Thensforth from her most beastly companie 365
I gan refraine, in minde to slipp away,
Soone as appeard safe opportunitie:
For danger great, if not assurd decay,
I saw before mine eyes, if I were knowne to stray.

XLII

'The divelish hag, by chaunges of my cheare, 370
Perceiv'd my thought; and drownd in sleepie night,
With wicked herbes and oyntments did besmeare
My body all, through charmes and magicke might,
That all my senses were bereavèd quight:
Then brought she me into this desert waste, 375
And by my wretched lovers side me pight,
Where now enclosed in wooden wals full faste,
Banisht from living wights, our wearie daies we waste.'

XLIII

'But how long time,' said then the Elfin knight,
'Are you in this misformèd hous to dwell?' 380
'We may not chaunge,' quoth he, 'this evill plight
Till we be bathèd in a living well;
That is the terme prescribèd by the spell.'
'O how,' sayd he, 'mote I that well out find, 384
That may restore you to your wonted well?'
'Time and suffisèd fates to former kynd
Shall us restore; none else from hence may us unbynd.'

XLIV

The false Duessa, now Fidessa hight,
Heard how in vaine Fradubio did lament,
And knew well all was true. But the good knight 390
Full of sad feare and ghastly dreriment,
When all this speech the living tree had spent,
The bleeding bough did thrust into the ground,
That from the blood he might be innocent,
And with fresh clay did close the wooden wound: 395
Then turning to his lady, dead with feare her fownd.

XLV

Her seeming dead he fownd with feignèd feare,
As all unweeting of that well she knew,
And paynd himselfe with busie care to reare
Her out of carelesse swowne. Her eyelids blew,
And dimmèd sight, with pale and deadly hew, 401
At last she up gan lift: with trembling cheare
Her up he tooke, too simple and too trew,
And oft her kist. At length, all passèd feare,
He set her on her steede, and forward forth did beare. 405

* * *

AMORETTI

I

HAPPY ye leaves! when as those lilly hands,
Which hold my life in their dead doing might,
Shall handle you, and hold in loves soft bands,
Lyke captives trembling at the victors sight.

And happy lines! on which, with starry light, 5
Those lamping eyes will deigne sometimes to look,
And reade the sorrowes of my dying spright,
Written with teares in harts close bleeding book.

And happy rymes! bath'd in the sacred brooke
Of Helicon, whence she derivèd is, 10
When ye behold that angels blessèd looke,
My soules long lackèd foode my heavens blis.

Leaves, lines, and rymes, seeke her to please alone,
Whom if ye please, I care for other none.

VIII

MORE then most faire, full of the living fire
Kindled above unto the Maker neere:
No eies, but joyes, in which al powers conspire,
That to the world naught else be counted deare:

Thrugh your bright beams doth not the blinded guest 5
Shoot out his darts to base affections wound;
But angels come, to lead fraile mindes to rest
In chast desires, on heavenly beauty bound.

You frame my thoughts, and fashion me within,
You stop my toung, and teach my hart to speake, 10
You calme the storme that passion did begin,
Strong thrugh your cause, but by your vertue weak.

Dark is the world where your light shinèd never;
Well is he borne that may behold you ever.

XXIV

WHEN I behold that beauties wonderment,
And rare perfection of each goodly part,
Of Natures skill the onely complement,
I honor and admire the Makers art.

But when I feele the bitter balefulle smart 5
Which her fayre eyes unwares doe worke in mee,
That death out of theyr shiny beames doe dart,
I thinke that I a new Pandora see;

Whom all the gods in councell did agree,
Into this sinfull world from heaven to send, 10
That she to wicked men a scourge should bee,
For all their faults with which they did offend.

But since ye are my scourge, I will intreat
That for my faults ye will me gently beat.

XXXIV

Lyke as a ship, that through the ocean wyde
By conduct of some star doth make her way,
Whenas a storme hath dimd her trusty guyde,
Out of her course doth wander far astray;
So I, whose star, that wont with her bright ray 5
Me to direct, with cloudes is overcast,
Doe wander now in darknesse and dismay,
Through hidden perils round about me plast.
Yet hope I well, that when this storme is past,
My Helice, the lodestar of my lyfe, 10
Will shine again, and looke on me at last,
With lovely light to cleare my cloudy grief.
Till then I wander carefull comfortlesse,
In secret sorrow and sad pensivenesse.

LXIII

After long stormes and tempests sad assay,
Which hardly I endurèd heretofore,
In dread of death, and daungerous dismay,
With which my silly barke was tossèd sore,
I doe at length descry the happy shore, 5
In which I hope ere long for to arryve:
Fayre soyle it seemes from far, and fraught with store
Of all that deare and daynty is alyve.
Most happy he that can at last atchyve
The joyous safety of so sweet a rest; 10
Whose least delight sufficeth to deprive
Remembrance of all paines which him opprest.
All paines are nothing in respect of this,
All sorrowes short that gaine eternall blisse.

LXX

Fresh Spring, the herald of loves mighty king,
In whose cote-armour richly are displayd
All sorts of flowers the which on earth do spring,
In goodly colours gloriously arrayd,
Goe to my love, where she is carelesse layd, 5
Yet in her winters bowre, not well awake;
Tell her the joyous time wil not be staid,
Unlesse she doe him by the forelock take:
Bid her therefore her selfe soone ready make,
To wayt on Love amongst his lovely crew, 10
Where every one that misseth then her make
Shall be by him amearst with penance dew.
Make hast therefore, sweet love, whilest it is prime;
For none can call againe the passèd time.

LXXII

Oft when my spirit doth spred her bolder winges,
In mind to mount up to the purest sky,
It down is weighd with thoght of earthly things,
And clogd with burden of mortality:
Where, when that soverayne beauty it doth spy,
Resembling heavens glory in her light, 6
Drawne with sweet pleasures bayt, it back doth fly,
And unto heaven forgets her former flight.
There my fraile fancy, fed with full delight,
Doth bath in blisse, and mantleth most at ease;
Ne thinks of other heaven, but how it might 11
Her harts desire with most contentment please.
Hart need not wish none other happinesse,
But here on earth to have such hevens blisse.

LXXIX

Men call you fayre, and you doe credit it,
For that your selfe ye dayly such doe see;
But the trew fayre, that is the gentle wit
And vertuous mind, is much more praysd of me.
For all the rest, how ever fayre it be, 5
Shall turne to nought and loose that glorious hew;
But onely that is permanent, and free
From frayle corruption, that doth flesh ensew.
That is true beautie: that doth argue you
To be divine, and borne of heavenly seed, 10
Deriv'd from that fayre Spirit from whom al true
And perfect beauty did at first proceed.
He onely fayre, and what he fayre hath made;
All other fayre, lyke flowres, untymely fade.

EPITHALAMION

Ye learnèd sisters, which have oftentimes
Beene to me ayding, others to adorne,
Whom ye thought worthy of your gracefull rymes,
That even the greatest did not greatly scorne
To heare theyr names sung in your simple layes,
But joyèd in theyr praise; 6
And when ye list your owne mishaps to mourne,
Which death, or love, or fortunes wreck did rayse,
Your string could soone to sadder tenor turne,
And teach the woods and waters to lament 10
Your doleful dreriment:
Now lay those sorrowfull complaints aside,
And having all your heads with girland crownd,
Helpe me mine owne loves prayses to resound;
Ne let the same of any be envide: 15
So Orpheus did for his owne bride:
So I unto my selfe alone will sing;
The woods shall to me answer, and my eccho ring.

Early, before the worlds light giving lampe
His golden beame upon the hils doth spred, 20
Having disperst the nights unchearefull dampe,
Doe ye awake, and, with fresh lustyhed,
Go to the bowre of my belovèd love,
   My truest turtle dove:
Bid her awake; for Hymen is awake, 25
And long since ready forth his maske to move,
With his bright tead that flames with many a flake,
And many a bachelor to waite on him,
   In theyr fresh garments trim.
Bid her awake therefore, and soone her dight, 30
For lo! the wishèd day is come at last,
That shall, for al the paynes and sorrowes past,
Pay to her usury of long delight:
   And whylest she doth her dight,
Doe ye to her of joy and solace sing, 35
That all the woods may answer, and your eccho ring.

Bring with you all the nymphes that you can heare,
Both of the rivers and the forrests greene,
And of the sea that neighbours to her neare,
Al with gay girlands goodly wel beseene. 40
And let them also with them bring in hand
   Another gay girland,
For my fayre love, of lillyes and of roses,
Bound truelove wize with a blew silke riband.
And let them make great store of bridale poses,
And let them eeke bring store of other flowers, 46
   To deck the bridale bowers.
And let the ground whereas her foot shall tread,
For feare the stones her tender foot should wrong,
Be strewed with fragrant flowers all along, 50
And diapred lyke the discolored mead.
Which done, doe at her chamber dore awayt,
   For she will waken strayt;
The whiles doe ye this song unto her sing
The woods shall to you answer, and your eccho ring. 55

Ye nymphes of Mulla, which with carefull heed
The silver scaly trouts doe tend full well,
And greedy pikes which use therein to feed,
(Those trouts and pikes all others doo excell)
And ye likewise which keepe the rushy lake, 60
   Where none doo fishes take,
Bynd up the locks the which hang scattered light,
And in his waters, which your mirror make,
Behold your faces as the christall bright,
That when you come whereas my love doth lie,
   No blemish she may spie. 66
And eke ye lightfoot mayds which keepe the dere
That on the hoary mountayne use to towre,
And the wylde wolves, which seeke them to devoure,
With your steele darts doo chace from comming neer, 70
   Be also present heere,
To helpe to decke her, and to help to sing,
That all the woods may answer, and your eccho ring.

Wake now, my love, awake! for it is time:
The rosy Morne long since left Tithones bed, 75
All ready to her silver coche to clyme,
And Phœbus gins to shew his glorious hed.
Hark how the cheerefull birds do chaunt theyr laies,
   And carroll of loves praise!
The merry larke hir mattins sings aloft, 80
The thrush replyes, the mavis descant playes,
The ouzell shrills, the ruddock warbles soft,
So goodly all agree, with sweet consent,
   To this dayes merriment.
Ah! my deere love, why doe ye sleepe thus long, 85
When meeter were that ye should now awake,
T'awayt the comming of your joyous make,
And hearken to the birds love-learnèd song,
   The deawy leaves among?
For they of joy and pleasance to you sing, 90
That all the woods them answer, and theyr eccho ring.

My love is now awake out of her dreame,
And her fayre eyes, like stars that dimmèd were
With darksome cloud, now shew theyr goodly beames
More bright then Hesperus his head doth rere.
Come now, ye damzels, daughters of delight, 96
   Helpe quickly her to dight.
But first come ye, fayre Houres, which were begot,
In Joves sweet paradice, of Day and Night,
Which doe the seasons of the year allot, 100
   And al that ever in this world is fayre
   Do make and still repayre.
And ye three handmayds of the Cyprian Queene,
The which doe still adorne her beauties pride,
Helpe to addorne my beautifullest bride: 105
And as ye her array, still throw betweene
   Some graces to be seene:
And as ye use to Venus, to her sing,
The whiles the woods shal answer, and your eccho ring.

Now is my love all ready forth to come: 110
Let all the virgins therefore well awayt,
And ye fresh boyes, that tend upon her groome,
Prepare your selves, for he is comming strayt.
Set all your things in seemely good aray,
   Fit for so joyfull day, 115
The joyfulst day that ever sunne did see.
Faire Sun, shew forth thy favourable ray,
And let thy lifull heat not fervent be,
For feare of burning her sunshyny face,
   Her beauty to disgrace. 120
O fayrest Phœbus, father of the Muse,
If ever I did honour thee aright,
Or sing the thing that mote thy mind delight,

Doe not thy servants simple boone refuse,
But let this day, let this one day be myne, 125
  Let all the rest be thine.
Then I thy soverayne prayses loud wil sing,
That all the woods shal answer, and theyr
  eccho ring.

Harke how the minstrels gin to shrill aloud
Their merry musick that resounds from far, 130
The pipe, the tabor, and the trembling croud,
That well agree withouten breach or jar,
But most of all the damzels doe delite,
  When they their tymbrels smyte,
And thereunto doe daunce and carrol sweet,
That all the sences they doe ravish quite, 136
The whyles the boyes run up and downe the
  street,
Crying aloud with strong confusèd noyce,
As if it were one voyce.
'Hymen, Iö Hymen, Hymen,' they do shout, 140
That even to the heavens theyr shouting shrill
Doth reach, and all the firmament doth fill;
To which the people, standing all about,
As in approvance doe thereto applaud,
  And loud advaunce her laud, 145
And evermore they 'Hymen, Hymen' sing,
That al the woods them answer, and theyr
  eccho ring.

Loe! where she comes along with portly pace,
Lyke Phœbe, from her chamber of the east,
Arysing forth to run her mighty race, 150
Clad all in white, that seemes a virgin best.
So well it her beseemes, that ye would weene
  Some angell she had beene.
Her long loose yellow locks lyke golden wyre,
Sprinckled with perle, and perling flowres a-
  tweene, 155
Doe lyke a golden mantle her attyre,
And being crownèd with a girland greene,
  Seeme lyke some mayden queene.
Her modest eyes, abashèd to behold
So many gazers as on her do stare, 160
Upon the lowly ground affixèd are;
Ne dare lift up her countenance too bold,
But blush to heare her prayses sung so loud,
  So farre from being proud.
Nathlesse doe ye still loud her prayses sing, 165
That all the woods may answer, and your eccho
  ring.

Tell me, ye merchants daughters, did ye see
So fayre a creature in your towne before,
So sweet, so lovely, and so mild as she,
Adornd with beautyes grace and vertues store?
Her goodly eyes lyke saphyres shining bright, 171
  Her forehead yvory white,
Her cheekes lyke apples which the sun hath
  rudded,
Her lips lyke cherryes charming men to byte,
Her brest like to a bowle of creame uncrudded, 175
  Her paps lyke lyllies budded,

Her snowie necke lyke to a marble towre,
And all her body like a pallace fayre,
Ascending uppe, with many a stately stayre,
To honors seat and chastities sweet bowre. 180
Why stand ye still, ye virgins, in amaze,
  Upon her so to gaze,
Whiles ye forget your former lay to sing,
To which the woods did answer, and your eccho
  ring.

But if ye saw that which no eyes can see, 185
The inward beauty of her lively spright,
Garnisht with heavenly guifts of high degree,
Much more then would ye wonder at that sight,
And stand astonisht lyke to those which red
  Medusaes mazeful hed. 190
There dwels sweet Love and constant Chastity,
Unspotted Fayth, and comely Womanhood,
Regard of Honour, and mild Modesty;
There Vertue raynes as queene in royal throne,
  And giveth lawes alone, 195
The which the base affections doe obay,
And yeeld theyr services unto her will;
Ne thought of thing uncomely ever may
Thereto approch to tempt her mind to ill.
Had ye once seene these her celestial threa-
  sures, 200
  And unrevealèd pleasures,
Then would ye wonder, and her prayses sing,
That al the woods should answer, and your echo
  ring.

Open the temple gates unto my love,
Open them wide that she may enter in, 205
And all the postes adorne as doth behove,
And all the pillours deck with girlands trim,
For to receyve this saynt with honour dew,
  That commeth in to you.
With trembling steps and humble reverence, 210
She commeth in before th' Almighties vew:
Of her, ye virgins, learne obedience,
When so ye come into those holy places,
  To humble your proud faces.
Bring her up to th' high altar, that she may 215
The sacred ceremonies there partake,
The which do endlesse matrimony make;
And let the roring organs loudly play
The praises of the Lord in lively notes,
  The whiles with hollow throates 220
The choristers the joyous antheme sing,
That al the woods may answere, and their
  eccho ring.

Behold, whiles she before the altar stands,
Hearing the holy priest that to her speakes,
And blesseth her with his two happy hands, 225
How the red roses flush up in her cheekes,
And the pure snow with goodly vermill stayne,
  Like crimsin dyde in grayne:
That even th' angels, which continually
About the sacred altare doe remaine, 230
Forget their service and about her fly,

Ofte peeping in her face, that seemes more fayre,
   The more they on it stare.
But her sad eyes, still fastened on the ground,
Are governèd with goodly modesty,   235
That suffers not one looke to glaunce awry,
Which may let in a little thought unsownd.
Why blush ye, love, to give to me your hand,
   The pledge of all our band?
Sing, ye sweet angels, Alleluya sing,   240
That all the woods may answere, and your
   eccho ring.

Now al is done; bring home the bride againe,
Bring home the triumph of our victory,
Bring home with you the glory of her gaine,
With joyance bring her and with jollity.   245
Never had man more joyfull day then this,
   Whom heaven would heape with blis.
Make feast therefore now all this live long day;
This day for ever to me holy is;
Poure out the wine without restraint or stay,   250
Poure not by cups, but by the belly full,
   Poure out to all that wull,
And sprinkle all the postes and wals with wine,
That they may sweat, and drunken be withall.
Crowne ye God Bacchus with a coronall.   255
And Hymen also crowne with wreathes of vine;
And let the Graces daunce unto the rest,
   For they can doo it best:
The whiles the maydens doe theyr carroll sing,
The which the woods shal answer, and theyr
   eccho ring.   260

Ring ye the bels, ye yong men of the towne,
And leave your wonted labors for this day:
This day is holy; doe ye write it downe,
That ye for ever it remember may.
This day the sunne is in his chiefest hight,   265
   With Barnaby the bright,
From whence declining daily by degrees,
He somewhat loseth of his heat and light,
When once the Crab behind his back he sees.
But for this time it ill ordained was,   270
To chose the longest day in all the yeare,
And shortest night, when longest fitter weare:
Yet never day so long, but late would passe.
Ring ye the bels, to make it weare away,
   And bonefires make all day,   275
And daunce about them, and about them sing:
That all the woods may answer, and your
   eccho ring.

Ah! when will this long weary day have end,
And lende me leave to come unto my love?
How slowly do the houres theyr numbers spend!
How slowly does sad Time his feathers move!   281
Hast thee, O fayrest planet, to thy home
   Within the westerne fome:
Thy tyrèd steedes long since have need of rest.
Long though it be, at last I see it gloome,   285
And the bright evening star with golden creast
   Appeare out of the east.

Fayre childe of beauty, glorious lampe of love,
That all the host of heaven in rankes doost lead,
And guydest lovers through the nightes dread,
How chearefully thou lookest from above,   291
And seemst to laugh atweene thy twinkling light,
   As joying in the sight
Of these glad many, which for joy doe sing,
That all the woods them answer, and their echo
   ring!   295

Now ceasse, ye damsels, your delights forepast;
Enough is it that all the day was youres:
Now day is doen, and night is nighing fast:
Now bring the bryde into the brydall boures.
The night is come, now soone her disaray,   300
   And in her bed her lay;
Lay her in lillies and in violets,
And silken courteins over her display,
And odourd sheetes, and Arras coverlets.
Behold how goodly my faire love does ly,   305
   In proud humility!
Like unto Maia, when as Jove her tooke
In Tempe, lying on the flowry gras,
Twixt sleepe and wake, after she weary was
With bathing in the Acidalian brooke.   310
Now it is night, ye damsels may be gon,
   And leave my love alone.
And leave likewise your former lay to sing:
The woods no more shal answere, nor your echo
   ring.

Now welcome, night! thou night so long expected,   315
That long daies labour doest at last defray,
And all my cares, which cruell Love collected,
Hast sumd in one, and cancellèd for aye:
Spread thy broad wing over my love and me,
   That no man may us see,   320
And in thy sable mantle us enwrap,
From feare of perrill and foule horror free.
Let no false treason seeke us to entrap,
Nor any dread disquiet once annoy
   The safety of our joy: 325
But let the night be calme and quietsome,
Without tempestuous storms or sad afray:
Lyke as when Jove with fayre Alcmena lay,
When he begot the great Tirynthian groome:
Or lyke as when he with thy selfe did lie,   330
   And begot Majesty.
And let the mayds and yongmen cease to sing:
Ne let the woods them answer, nor theyr eccho
   ring.

Let no lamenting cryes, nor dolefull teares,
Be heard all night within, nor yet without: 335
Ne let false whispers, breeding hidden feares,
Breake gentle sleepe with misconceivèd dout.
Let no deluding dreames, nor dreadfull sights,
   Make sudden sad affrights;
Ne let house-fyres, nor lightnings helplesse
   harmes,   340
Ne let the Pouke, nor other evill sprights,

Ne let mischivous witches with theyr charmes,
Ne let hob goblins, names whose sense we see not,
  Fray us with things that be not.
Let not the shriech oule, nor the storke be heard, 345
Nor the night raven that still deadly yels,
Nor damnèd ghosts cald up with mighty spels,
Nor griesly vultures make us once affeard:
Ne let th' unpleasant quyre of frogs still kroking
  Make us to wish theyr choking. 350
Let none of these theyr drery accents sing;
Ne let the woods them answer, nor theyr eccho ring.

But let stil Silence trew night watches keepe,
That sacred Peace may in assurance rayne,
And tymely Sleep, when it is tyme to sleepe, 355
May poure his limbs forth on your pleasant playne,
The whiles an hundred little wingèd loves,
  Like divers fethered doves,
Shall fly and flutter round about our bed,
And in the secret darke, that none reproves, 360
Their prety stealthes shall worke, and snares shal spread
To filch away sweet snatches of delight,
  Conceald through covert night.
Ye sonnes of Venus, play your sports at will:
For greedy Pleasure, careless of your toyes, 365
Thinks more upon her paradise of joyes,
  Then what ye do, albe it good or ill.
All night therefore attend your merry play,
  For it will soone be day:
Now none doth hinder you, that say or sing,
Ne will the woods now answer, nor your eccho ring. 371

Who is the same which at my window peepes?
Or whose is that faire face that shines so bright?
Is it not Cinthia, she that never sleepes,
But walkes about high heaven al the night? 375
O fayrest goddesse, do thou not envy
  My love with me to spy:
For thou likewise didst love, though now unthought,
And for a fleece of woll, which privily
The Latmian shephard once unto thee brought,
  His pleasures with thee wrought. 381
Therefore to us be favorable now;
And sith of wemens labours thou hast charge,
And generation goodly dost enlarge,
Encline thy will t' effect our wishfull vow, 385
And the chast wombe informe with timely seed,
  That may our comfort breed:
Till which we cease our hopefull hap to sing,
Ne let the woods us answere, nor our eccho ring.

And thou, great Juno, which with awful might
The lawes of wedlock still dost patronize, 391
And the religion of the faith first plight
With sacred rites hast taught to solemnize,
And eeke for comfort often callèd art
  Of women in their smart, 395
Eternally bind thou this lovely band,
And all thy blessings unto us impart.
And thou, glad Genius, in whose gentle hand
The bridale bowre and geniall bed remaine,
  Without blemish or staine, 400
And the sweet pleasures of theyr loves delight
With secret ayde doest succour and supply,
Till they bring forth the fruitfull progeny,
Send us the timely fruit of this same night.
And thou, fayre Hebe, and thou, Hymen free, 405
  Grant that it may so be.
Til which we cease your further prayse to sing,
Ne any woods shal answer, nor your eccho ring.

And ye high heavens, the temple of the gods,
In which a thousand torches flaming bright 410
Doe burne, that to us wretched earthly clods
In dreadful darknesse lend desirèd light,
And all ye powers which in the same remayne,
  More then we men can fayne,
Poure out your blessing on us plentiously, 415
And happy influence upon us raine,
That we may raise a large posterity,
Which from the earth, which they may long possesse
  With lasting happinesse,
Up to your haughty pallaces may mount, 420
And for the guerdon of theyr glorious merit,
May heavenly tabernacles there inherit,
Of blessed saints for to increase the count.
So let us rest, sweet love, in hope of this,
And cease till then our tymely joyes to sing:
The woods no more us answer, nor our eccho ring. 426

Song, made in lieu of many ornaments
With which my love should duly have bene dect,
Which cutting off through hasty accidents,
Ye would not stay your dew time to expect, 430
  But promist both to recompens,
Be unto her a goodly ornament,
And for short time an endlesse moniment.

PROTHALAMION

Calme was the day, and through the trembling ayre
Sweete breathing Zephyrus did softly play,
A gentle spirit, that lightly did delay
Hot Titans beames, which then did glyster fayre:
  When I, whom sullein care, 5
Through discontent of my long fruitlesse stay

In princes court, and expectation vayne
Of idle hopes, which still doe fly away,
Like empty shaddowes, did aflict my brayne,
    Walkt forth to ease my payne   10
Along the shoare of silver streaming Themmes;
Whose rutty bancke, the which his river hemmes,
Was paynted all with variable flowers,
And all the meades adornd with daintie gemmes,
    Fit to decke maydens bowres,   15
    And crowne their paramours,
Against the brydale day, which is not long:
    Sweete Themmes, runne softly, till I end my song.

There, in a meadow, by the rivers side,
A flocke of nymphes I chauncèd to espy,   20
All lovely daughters of the flood thereby,
With goodly greenish locks all loose untyde,
    As each had bene a bryde:
And each one had a little wicker basket,
Made of fine twigs entraylèd curiously,   25
In which they gathered flowers to fill their flasket;
And with fine fingers cropt full feateously
    The tender stalkes on hye.
Of every sort, which in that meadow grew,
They gathered some; the violet pallid blew,   30
The little dazie, that at evening closes,
The virgin lillie, and the primrose trew,
    With store of vermeil roses,
    To decke their bridegromes posies
Against the brydale day, which was not long: 35
    Sweete Themmes, runne softly, till I end my song.

With that I saw two swannes of goodly hewe
Come softly swimming downe along the lee;
Two fairer birds I yet did never see:
The snow which doth the top of Pindus strew 40
    Did never whiter shew,
Nor Jove himselfe, when he a swan would be
For love of Leda, whiter did appear:
Yet Leda was, they say, as white as he,
Yet not so white as these, nor nothing neare: 45
    So purely white they were,
That even the gentle streame, the which them bare,
Seem'd foule to them, and bad his billowes spare
To wet their silken feathers, least they might
Soyle their fayre plumes with water not so fayre,
    And marre their beauties bright,   51
    That shone as heavens light,
Against their brydale day, which was not long:
    Sweete Themmes, runne softly, till I end my song.

Eftsoones the nymphes, which now had flowers their fill,   55
Ran all in haste to see that silver brood,
As they came floating on the christal flood;

Whom when they sawe, they stood amazèd still,
    Their wondring eyes to fill.
Them seem'd they never saw a sight so fayre, 60
Of fowles so lovely, that they sure did deeme
Them heavenly borne, or to be that same payre
Which through the skie draw Venus silver teeme;
    For sure they did not seeme
To be begot of any earthly seede,   65
But rather angels or of angels breede:
Yet were they bred of Somers-heat, they say,
In sweetest season, when each flower and weede
    The earth did fresh aray;
    So fresh they seem'd as day,   70
Even as their brydale day, which was not long:
    Sweete Themmes, runne softly, till I end my song.

Then forth they all out of their baskets drew
Great store of flowers, the honour of the field,
That to the sense did fragrant odours yield, 75
All which upon those goodly birds they threw,
    And all the waves did strew,
That like old Peneus waters they did seeme,
When downe along by pleasant Tempes shore,
Scattred with flowres, through Thessaly they streeme,   80
That they appeare, through lillies plenteous store,
    Like a brydes chamber flore.
Two of those nymphes, meane while, two garlands bound
Of freshest flowres which in that mead they found,
The which presenting all in trim array,   85
Their snowie foreheads therewithall they crownd,
    Whil'st one did sing this lay,
    Prepar'd against that day,
Against their brydale day, which was not long:
    Sweete Themmes, runne softly, till I end my song.   90

'Ye gentle birdes, the worlds faire ornament,
And heavens glorie, whom this happie hower
Doth leade unto your lovers blissfull bower,
Joy may you have and gentle hearts content
    Of your loves couplement: 95
And let faire Venus, that is Queene of Love,
With her heart-quelling sonne upon you smile,
Whose smile, they say, hath vertue to remove
All loves dislike, and friendships faultie guile
    For ever to assoile.   100
Let endlesse peace your steadfast hearts accord,
And blessèd plentie wait upon your bord;
And let your bed with pleasures chast abound,
That fruitfull issue may to you afford,
    Which may your foes confound,   105
    And make your joyes redound,
Upon your brydale day, which is not long:
    Sweete Themmes, run softlie, till I end my song.'

So ended she; and all the rest around
To her redoubled that her undersong, 110
Which said, their bridale daye should not be long.
And gentle Eccho from the neighbour ground
Their accents did resound.
So forth those joyous birdes did passe along,
Adowne the lee, that to them murmurde low, 115
As he would speake, but that he lackt a tong,
Yeat did by signes his glad affection show,
  Making his streame run slow.
And all the foule which in his flood did dwell
Gan flock about these twaine, that did excell 120
The rest so far as Cynthia doth shend
The lesser starres. So they, enrangèd well,
  Did on those two attend,
  And their best service lend,
Against their wedding day, which was not long: 125
  Sweete Themmes, run softly, till I end my song.

At length they all to mery London came,
To mery London, my most kyndly nurse,
That to me gave this lifes first native sourse:
Though from another place I take my name,
  An house of auncient fame. 131
There when they came, whereas those bricky towres,
The which on Themmes brode agèd backe doe ryde,
Where now the studious lawyers have their bowers,
There whylome wont the Templer Knights to byde, 135
  Till they decayd through pride:
Next whereunto there standes a stately place,
Where oft I gaynèd giftes and goodly grace
Of that great lord which therein wont to dwell,
Whose want too well now feeles my freendles case: 140
  But ah! here fits not well
  Olde woes, but joyes to tell,
Against the bridale daye, which is not long:
  Sweete Themmes, runne softly, till I end my song.

Yet therein, now doth lodge a noble peer,
Great Englands glory and the worlds wide wonder, 146
Whose dreadfull name late through all Spaine did thunder,
And Hercules two pillors standing neere
Did make to quake and feare.
Faire branch of honor, flower of chevalrie, 150
That fillest England with thy triumphes fame,
Joy have thou of thy noble victorie,
And endlesse happinesse of thine owne name
  That promiseth the same:
That through thy prowesse and victorious armes 155
Thy country may be freed from forraine harmes;
And great Elisaes glorious name may ring
Through al the world, fil'd with thy wide alarmes,
  Which some brave Muse may sing
  To ages following, 160
Upon the brydale day, which is not long:
  Sweete Themmes, runne softly, till I end my song.

From those high towers this noble lord issuing,
Like radiant Hesper when his golden hayre
In th' ocean billows he hath bathèd fayre, 165
Descended to the rivers open vewing,
  With a great traine ensuing.
Above the rest were goodly to bee seene
Two gentle knights of lovely face and feature,
Beseeming well the bower of anie queene, 170
With gifts of wit and ornaments of nature,
Fit for so goodly stature:
That like the twins of Jove they seem'd in sight,
Which decke the bauldricke of the heavens bright.
They two, forth pacing to the rivers side, 175
Received those two faire brides, their loves delight,
  Which, at th' appointed tyde,
  Each one did make his bryde,
Against their brydale day, which is not long:
  Sweete Themmes, runne softly, till I end my song. 180

ELIZABETHAN LYRICS

As a whole, the brilliant lyrical effluence of the Elizabethan period may fairly be regarded as the product of English courtly life, and particularly, in its beginning, the product of the Renaissance court of Henry VIII. Wyatt and Surrey were conspicuous courtiers, and scarcely one of the contributors to *Tottel's Miscellany* (1557) was free from court influence. An inevitable result of courtliness in literature is convention, a too conscious refinement, and, often, a baffling veil of literary pretence. These qualities are salient and inherent in the Elizabethan sonnet. After its introduction into English literature by Sir Thomas Wyatt, and after its chastening in the hands of Surrey and others, this poetical form was first used in masterly fashion by Sir Philip Sidney in his *Astrophel and Stella*, the earliest sonnet sequence in English, composed a good while before its publication in 1591. During the decade 1590–1600, the sonnet was, apparently, the prevailing literary fashion, a fashion to which Shakespeare submitted without restraint. Of the total number of these sonnets—which 'far exceeds two thousand'—the larger proportion are found in sonnet collections, or sonnet sequences, of which the most important, after those of Shakespeare and Sidney, are the following: *Delia* (1592), by Samuel Daniel; *Idea* (1594), by Michael Drayton; and *Amoretti* (1595), by Edmund Spenser. With few exceptions, these sonnets, like those of Wyatt and Surrey, are imitations of Continental models.

But since lyric is essentially the expression of personal emotion, the lyrist inevitably breaks out, at times, into a frank, intimate, and spontaneous utterance which is of all sorts of expression the most immediately pleasurable. Free, fresh, and various are the lyrics found in the series of miscellanies which began with *Tottel's Miscellany*, and continued with *The Paradise of Dainty Devices* (1576), *A Gorgeous Gallery of Gallant Inventions* (1578), *A Handful of Pleasant Delights* (1584), *The Phœnix' Nest* (1593), *The Passionate Pilgrim* (1599), *England's Helicon* (1600), and Francis Davison's *Poetical Rhapsody* (1602). In one or other of these collections are represented the chief lyrical writers of the Elizabethan period.

In a group apart from the lyrical miscellanies, though not conspicuously different from some of them in content, may be reckoned the Elizabethan song books. William Byrd's *Psalms, Sonnets and Songs of Sadness and Piety* (1587) and *Songs of Sundry Natures* (1589) were followed, during the next two or three decades, by some scores of similar collections, such as John Dowland's *The First Book of Songs or Airs* (1597), Thomas Campion's *A Book of Airs* (1601), and Francis Pilkington's *Second Set of Madrigals* (1624). Along with the songs in song books should be mentioned those that delightfully enliven many of the plays of the period, eminently those of Lyly and of Shakespeare.

GEORGE GASCOIGNE
(1525?–1577)

A STRANGE PASSION OF A LOVER

Amid my bale I bathe in bliss,
  I swim in heaven, I sink in hell:
I find amends for every miss,
  And yet my moan no tongue can tell.
I live and love, what would you more?   5
As never lover lived before.

I laugh sometimes with little lust,
  So jest I oft and feel no joy;
Mine eye is builded all on trust,
  And yet mistrust breeds mine annoy.   10
I live and lack, I lack and have;
I have and miss the thing I crave.

These things seem strange, yet are they true.
  Believe me, sweet, my state is such,
One pleasure which I would eschew,   15
  Both slakes my grief and breeds my grutch.
So doth one pain which I would shun,
Renew my joys where grief begun.

Then like the lark that passed the night
  In heavy sleep with cares opprest;   20
Yet when she spies the pleasant light,
  She sends sweet notes from out her breast.
So sing I now because I think
How joys approach, when sorrows shrink.

And as fair Philomene again   25
  Can watch and sing when others sleep;
And taketh pleasure in her pain,
  To wray the woe that makes her weep.
So sing I now for to bewray
The loathsome life I lead alway.   30

The which to thee, dear wench, I write,
    That know'st my mirth, but not my moan·
I pray God grant thee deep delight,
    To live in joys when I am gone.
I cannot live; it will not be: 35
I die to think to part from thee.

SIR EDWARD DYER
(1550?–1607)
MY MIND TO ME A KINGDOM IS

My mind to me a kingdom is,
    Such present joys therein I find
That it excels all other bliss
    That earth affords or grows by kind:
Though much I want which most would have, 5
Yet still my mind forbids to crave.

No princely pomp, no wealthy store,
    No force to win the victory,
No wily wit to salve a sore,
    No shape to feed a loving eye;   10
To none of these I yield as thrall:
For why? My mind doth serve for all.

I see how plenty [surfeits] oft,
    And hasty climbers soon do fall;
I see that those which are aloft   15
    Mishap doth threaten most of all;
They get with toil, they keep with fear:
Such cares my mind could never bear.

Content to live, this is my stay;
    I seek no more than may suffice; 20
I press to bear no haughty sway;
    Look, what I lack my mind supplies:
Lo, thus I triumph like a king,
Content with that my mind doth bring.

Some have too much, yet still do crave; 25
    I little have, and seek no more.
They are but poor, though much they have,
    And I am rich with little store:
They poor, I rich; they beg, I give;
They lack, I leave; they pine, I live. 30

I laugh not at another's loss;
    I grudge not at another's pain;
No worldly waves my mind can toss;
    My state at one doth still remain:
I fear no foe, I fawn no friend;   35
I loathe not life, nor dread my end.

Some weigh their pleasure by their lust,
    Their wisdom by their rage of will;
Their treasure is their only trust;
    A cloakèd craft their store of skill: 40
But all the pleasure that I find
Is to maintain a quiet mind.

My wealth is health and perfect ease;
    My conscience clear my chief defence;
I neither seek by bribes to please,   45
    Nor by deceit to breed offence:
Thus do I live; thus will I die;
Would all did so as well as I!

SIR WALTER RALEIGH
(1552?–1618)
THE SILENT LOVER

I

Passions are likened best to floods and streams:
    The shallow murmur, but the deep are dumb.
So, when affection yields discourse, it seems
    The bottom is but shallow whence they come.
They that are rich in words, in words discover 5
That they are poor in that which makes a lover.

II

Wrong not, sweet empress of my heart,
    The merit of true passion,
With thinking that he feels no smart,
    That sues for no compassion.

Silence in love bewrays more woe   5
    Than words, though ne'er so witty:
A beggar that is dumb, you know,
    May challenge double pity.

Then wrong not, dearest to my heart,
    My true, though secret passion; 10
He smarteth most that hides his smart,
    And sues for no compassion.

HIS PILGRIMAGE

Give me my scallop-shell of quiet,
    My staff of faith to walk upon,
My scrip of joy, immortal diet,
    My bottle of salvation,
My gown of glory, hope's true gauge;   5
And thus I'll take my pilgrimage.

Blood must be my body's balmer;
    No other balm will there be given;
Whilst my soul, like a quiet palmer,
    Traveleth towards the land of heaven, 10
Over the silver mountains,
Where spring the nectar fountains.
    There will I kiss
    The bowl of bliss;
And drink mine everlasting fill   15
Upon every milken hill.
My soul will be a-dry before;
But, after, it will thirst no more.

Then by that happy blissful day
  More peaceful pilgrims I shall see,   20
That have cast off their rags of clay,
  And walk appareled fresh like me.
    I'll take them first,
    To quench their thirst
  And taste of nectar suckets,   25
    At those clear wells
    Where sweetness dwells,
Drawn up by saints in crystal buckets.

  And when our bottles and all we
Are filled with immortality,   30
Then the blessèd paths we'll travel,
Strowed with rubies thick as gravel;
Ceilings of diamonds, sapphire floors,
High walls of coral, and pearly bowers.

  From thence to heaven's bribeless hall,   35
Where no corruptèd voices brawl;
No conscience molten into gold;
No forged accuser bought or sold;
No cause deferred, no vain-spent journey,
For there Christ is the King's attorney,   40
Who pleads for all, without degrees,
And he hath angels but no fees.

  And when the grand twelve million jury
Of our sins, with direful fury,
Against our souls black verdicts give,   45
Christ pleads his death; and then we live.

  Be Thou my speaker, taintless pleader!
Unblotted lawyer! true proceeder!
Thou giv'st salvation, even for alms,
Not with a bribèd lawyer's palms.   50

  And this is mine eternal plea
To him that made heaven and earth and sea:
That, since my flesh must die so soon,
And want a head to dine next noon,
Just at the stroke, when my veins start and
    spread,   55
Set on my soul an everlasting head!

Then am I ready, like a palmer fit,
To tread those blest paths; which before I writ.

A VISION UPON THIS CONCEIT OF THE FAERY QUEEN

METHOUGHT I saw the grave where Laura lay,
Within that temple where the vestal flame
Was wont to burn: and, passing by that way,
To see that buried dust of living fame,

Whose tomb fair Love and fairer Virtue kept,   5
All suddenly I saw the Faery Queen;
At whose approach the soul of Petrarch wept,
And from thenceforth those graces were not
    seen,

For they this queen attendèd; in whose stead
Oblivion laid him down on Laura's hearse.   10
Hereat the hardest stones were seen to bleed,
And groans of buried ghosts the heavens did
    pierce:
Where Homer's sprite did tremble all for grief,
And cursed the access of that celestial thief.

THE CONCLUSION

EVEN such is time, that takes in trust
  Our youth, our joys, our all we have,
And pays us but with earth and dust;
  Who, in the dark and silent grave,
When we have wandered all our ways,   5
Shuts up the story of our days:
But from this earth, this grave, this dust,
My God shall raise me up, I trust.

GEORGE PEELE
(c. 1557–1596)

SONG
From THE ARRAIGNMENT OF PARIS

ŒNONE

FAIR and fair, and twice so fair,
  As fair as any may be;
The fairest shepherd on our green,
  A love for any lady.

PARIS

Fair and fair, and twice so fair,   5
  As fair as any may be;
Thy love is fair for thee alone,
  And for no other lady.

ŒNONE

My love is fair, my love is gay,
As fresh as bin the flowers in May,   10
And of my love my roundelay,
  My merry, merry roundelay,
Concludes with Cupid's curse,—
  'They that do change old love for new,
Pray gods they change for worse!'   15

AMBO SIMUL.

They that do change, etc.

ŒNONE

Fair and fair, etc.

PARIS

Fair and fair, etc.
Thy love is fair, etc.

ŒNONE

My love can pipe, my love can sing,   20
My love can many a pretty thing,
And of his lovely praises ring

My merry, merry roundelays,
    Amen to Cupid's curse,—
'They that do change,' etc.   25

        PARIS
They that do change, etc.

        AMBO
Fair and fair, etc.

HARVESTMEN A-SINGING

From THE OLD WIVES' TALE

ALL ye that lovely lovers be,
Pray you for me:
Lo, here we come a-sowing, a-sowing,
And sow sweet fruits of love;
In your sweet hearts well may it prove!   5

Lo, here we come a-reaping, a-reaping,
To reap our harvest-fruit!
And thus we pass the year so long,
And never be we mute.

ROBERT GREENE
(1560–1592)

SONG

From THE FAREWELL TO FOLLY

SWEET are the thoughts that savor of content;
    The quiet mind is richer than a crown;
Sweet are the nights in careless slumber spent;
    The poor estate scorns fortune's angry frown:
Such sweet content, such minds, such sleep, such
    bliss,   5
Beggars enjoy, when princes oft do miss.

The homely house that harbors quiet rest;
    The cottage that affords no pride nor care;
The mean that 'grees with country music best;
    The sweet consort of mirth and music's fare;
Obscurèd life sets down a type of bliss: 11
A mind content both crown and kingdom is.

PHILOMELA'S ODE

From PHILOMELA

SITTING by a river's side,
Where a silent stream did glide,
Muse I did of many things
That the mind in quiet brings.
I gan think how some men deem   5
Gold their god; and some esteem
Honor is the chief content
That to man in life is lent.
And some others do contend,
Quiet none like to a friend.   10
Others hold there is no wealth
Compared to a perfect health.

Some man's mind in quiet stands,
When he is lord of many lands.
But I did sigh, and said all this   15
Was but a shade of perfect bliss;
And in my thoughts I did approve,
Naught so sweet as is true love.
Love 'twixt lovers passeth these,
When mouth kisseth and heart 'grees,   20
With folded arms and lips meeting,
Each soul another sweetly greeting;
For by the breath the soul fleeteth,
And soul with soul in kissing meeteth.
If love be so sweet a thing,   25
That such happy bliss doth bring,
Happy is love's sugared thrall,
But unhappy maidens all,
Who esteem your virgin blisses
Sweeter than a wife's sweet kisses.   30
No such quiet to the mind
As true love with kisses kind;
But if a kiss prove unchaste,
Then is true love quite disgraced.
Though love be sweet, learn this of me   35
No sweet love but honesty.

SONG

From MENAPHON

Weep not, my wanton, smile upon my knee,
When thou art old there's grief enough for thee.
    Mother's wag, pretty boy,
    Father's sorrow, father's joy;
    When thy father first did see   5
    Such a boy by him and me,
    He was glad, I was woe,
    Fortune changèd made him so,
    When he left his pretty boy
    Last his sorrow, first his joy.   10

Weep not, my wanton, smile upon my knee,
When thou art old there's grief enough for thee.
    Streaming tears that never stint,
    Like pearl-drops from a flint,
    Fell by course from his eyes,   15
    That one another's place supplies;
    Thus he grieved in every part,
    Tears of blood fell from his heart,
    When he left his pretty boy,
    Father's sorrow, father's joy.   20

Weep not, my wanton, smile upon my knee,
When thou art old there's grief enough for thee.
    The wanton smiled, father wept,
    Mother cried, baby leapt;
    More he crowed, more he cried,   25
    Nature could not sorrow hide:
    He must go, he must kiss
    Child and mother, baby bless,
    For he left his pretty boy,
    Father's sorrow, father's joy.   30

Weep not, my wanton, smile upon my knee,
When thou art old there's grief enough for thee.

SONG

From Menaphon

Some say Love,
Foolish Love,
    Doth rule and govern all the gods:
I say Love,
Inconstant Love,   5
    Sets men's senses far at odds.
Some swear Love,
Smooth-faced Love,
    Is sweetest sweet that men can have:
I say Love,   10
Sour Love,
    Makes virtue yield as beauty's slave.
A bitter sweet, a folly worst of all,
That forceth wisdom to be folly's thrall.

Love is sweet,   15
Wherein sweet?
    In fading pleasures that do pain.
Beauty sweet:
Is that sweet
    That yieldeth sorrow for a gain?   20
If Love's sweet,
Herein sweet,
    That minutes' joys are monthly woes:
'Tis not sweet,
That is sweet   25
    Nowhere but where repentance grows.
Then love who list, if beauty be so sour;
Labor for me, Love rest in prince's bower.

THE SHEPHERD'S WIFE'S SONG

From The Mourning Garment

Ah, what is love? It is a pretty thing,
As sweet unto a shepherd as a king;
    And sweeter too:
For kings have cares that wait upon a crown,
And cares can make the sweetest love to frown. 5
    Ah then, ah then,
If country loves such sweet desires do gain,
What lady would not love a shepherd swain?

His flocks are folded, he comes home at night,
As merry as a king in his delight;   10
    And merrier too:
For kings bethink them what the state require,
Where shepherds careless carol by the fire.
    Ah then, ah then,
If country loves such sweet desires do gain,   15
What lady would not love a shepherd swain?

He kisseth first, then sits as blithe to eat
His cream and curds as doth the king his meat;
    And blither too:
For kings have often fears when they do sup, 20
Where shepherds dread no poison in their cup.
    Ah then, ah then,
If country loves such sweet desires do gain,
What lady would not love a shepherd swain?

To bed he goes, as wanton then, I ween,   25
As is a king in dalliance with a queen;
    More wanton too:
For kings have many griefs affects to move,
Where shepherds have no greater grief than love.
    Ah then, ah then,   30
If country loves such sweet desires do gain,
What lady would not love a shepherd swain?

Upon his couch of straw he sleeps as sound,
As doth the king upon his bed of down;
    More sounder too: 35
For cares cause kings full oft their sleep to spill,
Where weary shepherds lie and snort their fill.
    Ah then, ah then,
If country loves such sweet desires do gain,
What lady would not love a shepherd swain?   40

Thus with his wife he spends the year, as blithe
As doth the king at every tide or sithe;
    And blither too:
For kings have wars and broils to take in hand
When shepherds laugh and love upon the land.
    Ah then, ah then,   46
If country loves such sweet desires do gain,
What lady would not love a shepherd swain?

ROBERT SOUTHWELL
(1561?-1595)

THE BURNING BABE

As I in hoary winter's night stood shivering in the snow,
Surprised I was with sudden heat which made my heart to glow;
And lifting up a fearful eye to view what fire was near,
A pretty babe, all burning bright, did in the air appear,
Who scorchèd with exceeding heat such floods of tears did shed,   5
As though his floods should quench his flames with what his tears were fed;
'Alas!' quoth he, 'but newly born in fiery heats I fry,
Yet none approach to warm their hearts or feel my fire but I!
My faultless breast the furnace is, the fuel wounding thorns;
Love is the fire and sighs the smoke, the ashes shame and scorns;   10

The fuel Justice layeth on, and Mercy blows
    the coals;
The metal in this furnace wrought are men's
    defilèd souls;
For which, as now on fire I am, to work them to
    their good,
So will I melt into a bath, to wash them in my
    blood:'
With this he vanished out of sight, and swiftly
    shrunk away,   15
And straight I callèd unto mind that it was
    Christmas-day.

SAMUEL DANIEL
(1562–1619)

SONNETS *from* DELIA

XIX

RESTORE thy treasure to the golden ore;
Yield Cytherea's son those arcs of love;
Bequeath the heavens the stars that I adore,
And to the orient do thy pearls remove.

Yield thy hands' pride unto the ivory white;   5
To Arabian odors give thy breathing sweet;
Restore thy blush unto Aurora bright;
To Thetis give the honor of thy feet.

Let Venus have the graces she resigned;
And thy sweet voice yield to Hermonius' spheres:
But yet restore thy fierce and cruel mind   11
To Hyrcan tigers and to ruthless bears.
Yield to the marble thy hard heart again;
So shalt thou cease to plague and I to pain.

XXIII

FALSE Hope prolongs my ever certain grief,
Traitor to me, and faithful to my Love.
A thousand times it promised me relief,
Yet never any true effect I prove.

Oft, when I find in her no truth at all,   5
I banish her, and blame her treachery:
Yet, soon again, I must her back recall,
As one that dies without her company.

Thus often, as I chase my Hope from me
Straightway, she hastes her unto Delia's eyes: 10
Fed with some pleasing look, there shall she be;
And so sent back. And thus my fortune lies.
Looks feed my Hope, Hope fosters me in vain;
Hopes are unsure, when certain is my pain.

XXVIII

OFT do I marvel, whether Delia's eyes
Are eyes, or else two radiant stars that shine?
For how could Nature ever thus devise
Of earth, on earth, a substance so divine?

Stars, sure, they are, whose motions rule desires;
And calm and tempest follow their aspects: 6
Their sweet appearing still such power inspires,
That makes the world admire so strange effects.

Yet whether fixed or wandering stars are they,
Whose influence rules the orb of my poor heart?
Fixed, sure, they are, but wandering, make me
    stray   11
In endless errors, whence I cannot part.
Stars, then, not eyes, move you, with milder
    view,
Your sweet aspect on him that honors you!

XXXVIII

THOU canst not die, whilst any zeal abound
In feeling hearts, that can conceive these lines:
Though thou, a Laura, hast no Petrarch found;
In base attire, yet, clearly, Beauty shines.

And I, though born within a colder clime,   5
Do feel mine inward heat as great, I know it.
He never had more faith, although more rime:
I love as well, though he could better show it.

But I may add one feather to thy fame,
To help her flight throughout the fairest Isle; 10
And if my pen could more enlarge thy name,
Then should'st thou live in an immortal style.
For though that Laura better limnèd be,
Suffice, thou shalt be loved as well as she!

XLIX

CARE-CHARMER Sleep, son of the sable Night,
Brother to Death, in silent darkness born:
Relieve my anguish, and restore the light;
With dark forgetting of my care, return!

And let the day be time enough to mourn   5
The shipwreck of my ill-adventured youth:
Let waking eyes suffice to wail their scorn,
Without the torment of the night's untruth.

Cease, dreams, the images of day-desires,
To model forth the passions of the morrow;   10
Never let rising sun approve you liars,
To add more grief to aggravate my sorrow.
Still let me sleep, embracing clouds in vain;
And never wake to feel the day's disdain.

L

LET others sing of Knights and Paladins
In agèd accents and untimely words;
Paint shadows in imaginary lines
Which well the reach of their high wits records:

But I must sing of thee, and those fair eyes   5
Authentic shall my verse in time to come;
When yet th' unborn shall say, 'Lo, where she
    lies
Whose beauty made him speak that else was
    dumb.'

These are the arcs, the trophies I erect,
That fortify thy name against old age;   10
And these thy sacred virtues must protect
Against the dark, and Time's consuming rage.
Though the error of my youth in them appear,
Suffice they show I lived and loved thee dear.

MICHAEL DRAYTON
(1563-1631)

SONNETS *from* IDEA

TO THE READER OF THESE SONNETS

INTO these loves, who but for passion looks,
At this first sight, here let him lay them by,
And seek elsewhere in turning other books,
Which better may his labor satisfy.

No far-fetched sigh shall ever wound my breast;
Love from mine eye a tear shall never wring;
Nor in 'Ah me's!' my whining sonnets drest!
A libertine! fantasticly I sing!

My verse is the true image of my mind,
Ever in motion, still desiring change;
And as thus, to variety inclined,
So in all humors sportively I range!
My Muse is rightly of the English strain,
That cannot long one fashion entertain.

IV

BRIGHT Star of Beauty, on whose eyelids sit
A thousand nymph-like and enamored Graçes,
The Goddesses of Memory and Wit,
Which there in order take their several places;

In whose dear bosom, sweet delicious Love
Lays down his quiver, which he once did bear,
Since he that blessèd paradise did prove;
And leaves his mother's lap, to sport him there.

Let others strive to entertain with words!
My soul is of a braver mettle made:
I hold that vile, which vulgar wit affords;
In me's that faith which time cannot invade!
Let what I praise be still made good by you!
Be you most worthy, whilst I am most true!

IX

As other men, so I myself, do muse
Why in this sort I wrest invention so?
And why these giddy metaphors I use,
Leaving the path the greater part do go?

I will resolve you. I am lunatic!
And ever this in madmen you shall find,
What they last thought of, when the brain grew sick,
In most distraction, they keep that in mind.

Thus talking idly, in this Bedlam fit,
Reason and I, you must conceive, are twain;
'Tis nine years now, since first I lost my wit.
Bear with me, then, though troubled be my brain!
What diet and correction, men distraught,
Not too far past, may to their wits be brought.

XX

AN evil Spirit (your Beauty) haunts me still,
Wherewith, alas, I have been long possest;
Which ceaseth not to attempt me to each ill,
Nor give me once, but one poor minute's rest.

In me it speaks, whether I sleep or wake;
And when by means to drive it out I try,
With greater torments then it me doth take,
And tortures me in most extremity.

Before my face, it lays down my despairs,
And hastes me on unto a sudden death;
Now tempting me to drown myself in tears,
And then in sighing to give up my breath.
Thus am I still provoked to every evil,
By this good-wicked Spirit, sweet Angel-Devil.

XLIV

WHILST thus my pen strives to eternize thee,
Age rules my lines with wrinkles in my face,
Where, in the map of all my misery,
Is modeled out the world of my disgrace;

Whilst in despite of tyrannizing times,
Medea-like, I make thee young again,
Proudly thou scorn'st my world-outwearing rimes,
And murder'st Virtue with thy coy disdain!

And though in youth my youth untimely perish
To keep thee from oblivion and the grave,
Ensuing ages yet my rimes shall cherish,
Where I entombed, my better part shall save;
And though this earthly body fade and die,
My name shall mount upon Eternity!

LXI

SINCE there's no help, come, let us kiss and part!
Nay, I have done; you get no more of me!
And I am glad, yea, glad, with all my heart,
That thus so cleanly I myself can free.

Shake hands for ever! Cancel all our vows!
And when we meet at any time again,
Be it not seen in either of our brows,
That we one jot of former love retain!

Now at the last gasp of Love's latest breath,
When, his pulse failing, Passion speechless lies;
When Faith is kneeling by his bed of death,
And Innocence is closing up his eyes,—
Now, if thou wouldst, when all have given him over,
From death to life thou might'st him yet recover!

ODE XI
TO THE VIRGINIAN VOYAGE

You brave heroic minds,
Worthy your country's name,
  That honor still pursue;
  Go and subdue!
Whilst loitering hinds   5
Lurk here at home with shame.

Britons, you stay too long;
Quickly aboard bestow you!
  And with a merry gale
  Swell your stretched sail,   10
With vows as strong
As the winds that blow you!

Your course securely steer,
West-and-by-south forth keep!
  Rocks, lee-shores, nor shoals,   15
  When Eolus scowls,
You need not fear,
So absolute the deep.

And, cheerfully at sea,
Success you still entice,   20
  To get the pearl and gold;
  And ours to hold,
Virginia,
Earth's only Paradise.

Where Nature hath in store   25
Fowl, venison, and fish;
  And the fruitful'st soil,—
  Without your toil,
Three harvests more,
All greater than your wish.   30

And the ambitious vine
Crowns with his purple mass
  The cedar reaching high
  To kiss the sky,
The cypress, pine,   35
And useful sassafras.

To whom, the Golden Age
Still Nature's laws doth give:
  Nor other cares attend,
  But them to defend   40
From winter's rage,
That long there doth not live.

When as the luscious smell
Of that delicious land,
  Above the seas that flows,   45
  The clear wind throws,
Your hearts to swell,
Approaching the dear strand.

In kenning of the shore
(Thanks to God first given!)   50
  O you, the happiest men,
  Be frolic then!
Let cannons roar,
Frightening the wide heaven!

And in regions far,   55
Such heroes bring ye forth
  As those from whom we came!
  And plant our name
Under that star
Not known unto our North!   60

And as there plenty grows
The laurel everywhere,
  Apollo's sacred tree,
  You may it see
A poet's brows   65
To crown, that may sing there.

Thy Voyages attend,
Industrious Hakluyt!
  Whose reading shall inflame
  Men to seek fame;   70
And much commend
To after times thy wit.

ODE XII
TO THE CAMBRO-BRITONS AND THEIR HARP HIS BALLAD OF AGINCOURT

Fair stood the wind for France,
When we our sails advance;
Nor now to prove our chance
  Longer will tarry;
But putting to the main,   5
At Caux, the mouth of Seine,
With all his martial train
  Landed King Harry.

And taking many a fort,
Furnished in warlike sort,   10
Marcheth towards Agincourt
  In happy hour;
Skirmishing, day by day,
With those that stopped his way,
Where the French general lay   15
  With all his power.

Which, in his height of pride,
King Henry to deride,
His ransom to provide,
  To the King sending;   20
Which he neglects the while,
As from a nation vile,
Yet, with an angry smile,
  Their fall portending.

And turning to his men,   25
Quoth our brave Henry then:
'Though they to one be ten
  Be not amazed!
Yet have we well begun:
Battles so bravely won   30
Have ever to the sun
  By Fame been raised!

'And for myself,' quoth he,
'This my full rest shall be:
England ne'er mourn for me,   35
  Nor more esteem me!
Victor I will remain,
Or on this earth lie slain;
Never shall she sustain
  Loss to redeem me!   40

'Poitiers and Cressy tell,
When most their pride did swell,
Under our swords they fell.
  No less our skill is,
Than when our Grandsire great,   45
Claiming the regal seat,
By many a warlike feat
  Lopped the French lilies.'

The Duke of York so dread
The eager vanward led;   50
With the main, Henry sped
  Amongst his henchmen;
Exeter had the rear,
A braver man not there!
O Lord, how hot they were   55
  On the false Frenchmen!

They now to fight are gone;
Armor on armor shone;
Drum now to drum did groan:
  To hear, was wonder;   60
That, with the cries they make,
The very earth did shake;
Trumpet to trumpet spake;
  Thunder to thunder.

Well it thine age became,   65
O noble Erpingham,
Which didst the signal aim
  To our hid forces!
When, from a meadow by,
Like a storm suddenly,   70
The English archery
  Stuck the French horses.

With Spanish yew so strong;
Arrows a cloth-yard long,
That like to serpents stung,   75
  Piercing the weather.
None from his fellow starts;
But, playing manly parts,
And like true English hearts,
  Stuck close together.   80

When down their bows they threw,
And forth their bilboes drew,
And on the French they flew:
  Not one was tardy.
Arms were from shoulders sent,   85
Scalps to the teeth were rent,
Down the French peasants went:
  Our men were hardy.

This while our noble King,
His broad sword brandishing,   90
Down the French host did ding,
  As to o'erwhelm it.
And many a deep wound lent;
His arms with blood besprent,
And many a cruel dent   95
  Bruisèd his helmet.

Gloucester, that duke so good,
Next of the royal blood,
For famous England stood
  With his brave brother.   100
Clarence, in steel so bright,
Though but a maiden knight,
Yet in that furious fight
  Scarce such another!

Warwick in blood did wade;   105
Oxford, the foe invade,
And cruel slaughter made,
  Still as they ran up.
Suffolk his axe did ply;
Beaumont and Willoughby   110
Bare them right doughtily;
  Ferrers, and Fanhope.

Upon Saint Crispin's Day
Fought was this noble fray;
Which Fame did not delay   115
  To England to carry.
O, when shall English men
With such acts fill a pen?
Or England breed again
  Such a King Harry?   120

CHRISTOPHER MARLOWE
(1564–1593)

HERO AND LEANDER

From THE FIRST SESTIAD

On Hellespont, guilty of true love's blood,
In view and opposite two cities stood,
Sea-borderers, disjoined by Neptune's might;
The one Abydos, the other Sestos hight.
At Sestos Hero dwelt; Hero the fair,   5
Whom young Apollo courted for her hair,
And offered as a dower his burning throne,
Where she should sit, for men to gaze upon.
The outside of her garments were of lawn,
The lining purple silk, with gilt stars drawn;   10
Her wide sleeves green, and bordered with a
  grove,
Where Venus in her naked glory strove
To please the careless and disdainful eyes
Of proud Adonis, that before her lies;
Her kirtle blue, whereon was many a stain,   15
Made with the blood of wretched lovers slain.

Upon her head she ware a myrtle wreath,
From whence her veil reached to the ground beneath;
Her veil was artificial flowers and leaves,
Whose workmanship both man and beast deceives. 20
Many would praise the sweet smell as she past,
When 'twas the odor which her breath forth cast;
And there, for honey, bees have sought in vain,
And, beat from thence, have lighted there again.
About her neck hung chains of pebblestone, 25
Which, lightened by her neck, like diamonds shone.
She ware no gloves; for neither sun nor wind
Would burn or parch her hands, but, to her mind,
Or warm or cool them, for they took delight
To play upon those hands, they were so white.
Buskins of shells, all silvered, usèd she, 31
And branched with blushing coral to the knee;
Where sparrows perched of hollow pearl and gold,
Such as the world would wonder to behold:
Those with sweet water oft her handmaid fills, 35
Which as she went, would chirrup through the bills.
Some say, for her the fairest Cupid pined,
And, looking in her face, was strooken blind.
But this is true; so like was one the other,
As he imagined Hero was his mother; 40
And oftentimes into her bosom flew,
About her naked neck his bare arms threw,
And laid his childish head upon her breast,
And, with still panting rock, there took his rest.
So lovely-fair was Hero, Venus' nun, 45
As Nature wept, thinking she was undone,
Because she took more from her than she left,
And of such wondrous beauty her bereft:
Therefore, in sign her treasure suffered wrack,
Since Hero's time hath half the world been black. 50

Amorous Leander, beautiful and young
(Whose tragedy divine Musæus sung),
Dwelt at Abydos; since him dwelt there none
For whom succeeding times make greater moan.
His dangling tresses, that were never shorn, 55
Had they been cut, and unto Colchos borne,
Would have allured the venturous youth of Greece
To hazard more than for the golden fleece.
Fair Cynthia wished his arms might be her sphere;
Grief makes her pale, because she moves not there. 60
His body was as straight as Circe's wand;
Jove might have sipt out nectar from his hand.
Even as delicious meat is to the taste,
So was his neck in touching, and surpast

The white of Pelops' shoulder: I could tell ye, 65
How smooth his breast was, and how white his belly;
And whose immortal fingers did imprint
That heavenly path with many a curious dint
That runs along his back; but my rude pen
Can hardly blazon forth the loves of men, 70
Much less of powerful gods: let it suffice
That my slack Muse sings of Leander's eyes;
Those orient cheeks and lips, exceeding his
That leapt into the water for a kiss
Of his own shadow, and, despising many, 75
Died ere he could enjoy the love of any.
Had wild Hippolytus Leander seen,
Enamored of his beauty had he been.
His presence made the rudest peasant melt,
That in the vast uplandish country dwelt; 80
The barbarous Thracian soldier, moved with naught,
Was moved with him, and for his favor sought.
Some swore he was a maid in man's attire,
For in his looks were all that men desire,—
A pleasant-smiling cheek, a speaking eye, 85
A brow for love to banquet royally;
And such as knew he was a man, would say,
'Leander, thou art made for amorous play;
Why art thou not in love, and loved of all?
Though thou be fair, yet be not thine own thrall.' 90

The men of wealthy Sestos every year,
For his sake whom their goddess held so dear,
Rose-cheeked Adonis, kept a solemn feast.
Thither resorted many a wandering guest
To meet their loves; such as had none at all, 95
Came lovers home from this great festival;
For every street, like to a firmament,
Glistered with breathing stars, who, where they went,
Frighted the melancholy earth, which deemed
Eternal heaven to burn, for so it seemed 100
As if another Phaëton had got
The guidance of the sun's rich chariot.
But, far above the loveliest, Hero shined,
And stole away th' enchanted gazer's mind;
For like sea-nymphs' inveigling harmony, 105
So was her beauty to the standers by;
Nor that night-wandering, pale, and watery star
(When yawning dragons draw her thirling car
From Latmus' mount up to the gloomy sky,
Where, crowned with blazing light and majesty,
She proudly sits) more over-rules the flood 111
Than she the hearts of those that near her stood.
Even as, when gaudy nymphs pursue the chase,
Wretched Ixion's shaggy-footed race,
Incensed with savage heat, gallop amain 115
From steep pine-bearing mountains to the plain,

So ran the people forth to gaze upon her,
And all that viewed her were enamored on her.
And as, in fury of a dreadful fight,
Their fellows being slain or put to flight,   120
Poor soldiers stand with fear of death deadstrooken,
So at her presence all surprised and tooken,
Await the sentence of her scornful eyes;
He whom she favors lives; the other dies.
There might you see one sigh; another rage;   125
And some, their violent passions to assuage,
Compile sharp satires; but, alas, too late!
For faithful love will never turn to hate.
And many, seeing great princes were denied,
Pined as they went, and thinking on her died.   130
On this feast-day—O cursèd day and hour!—
Went Hero thorough Sestos, from her tower
To Venus' temple, where unhappily,
As after chanced, they did each other spy.
So fair a church as this had Venus none: 135
The walls were of discolored jasper-stone,
Wherein was Proteus carved; and overhead
A lively vine of green sea-agate spread,
Where by one hand light-headed Bacchus hung,
And with the other wine from grapes outwrung.
Of crystal shining fair the pavement was;   141
The town of Sestos called it Venus' glass:
There might you see the gods in sundry shapes,
Committing heady riots, incest, rapes:

* * *

Blood-quaffing Mars, heaving the iron net,   145
Which limping Vulcan and his Cyclops set:
Love kindling fire, to burn such towns as Troy:
Silvanus weeping for the lovely boy
That now is turned into a cypress-tree,
Under whose shade the wood-gods love to be.   150
And in the midst a silver altar stood:
There Hero, sacrificing turtles' blood,
Vailed to the ground, veiling her eyelids close;
And modestly they opened as she rose.
Thence flew Love's arrow with the golden head;
And thus Leander was enamorèd.   156
Stone-still he stood, and evermore he gazed,
Till with the fire that from his countenance blazed
Relenting Hero's gentle heart was strook:
Such force and virtue hath an amorous look.   160

It lies not in our power to love or hate,
For will in us is over-ruled by fate.
When two are stript long ere the course begin,
We wish that one should lose, the other win;
And one especially do we affect   165
Of two gold ingots, like in each respect:
The reason no man knows, let it suffice,
What we behold is censured by our eyes.
Where both deliberate, the love is slight:
Who ever loved, that loved not at first sight?   170

WILLIAM SHAKESPEARE
(1564–1616)

From VENUS AND ADONIS

Lo, here the gentle lark, weary of rest,
From his moist cabinet mounts up on high,
And wakes the morning, from whose silver breast
The sun ariseth in his majesty;
   Who doth the world so glorious behold   5
   That cedar-tops and hills seem burnished gold.

Venus salutes him with this fair good-morrow:
'O thou clear god, and patron of all light,
From whom each lamp and shining star doth borrow
The beauteous influence that makes him bright,   10
   There lives a son that sucked an earthly mother,
   May lend thee light, as thou dost lend to other.'

This said, she hasteth to a myrtle grove,
Musing the morning is so much o'erworn,
And yet she hears no tidings of her love: 15
She hearkens for his hounds and for his horn:
   Anon she hears them chant it lustily,
   And all in haste she coasteth to the cry.

And as she runs, the bushes in the way
Some catch her by the neck, some kiss her face,
Some twine about her thigh to make her stay: 21
She wildly breaketh from their strict embrace,
   Like a milch doe, whose swelling dugs do ache,
   Hasting to feed her fawn hid in some brake.

By this, she hears the hounds are at a bay;   25
Whereat she starts, like one that spies an adder
Wreathed up in fatal folds just in his way,
The fear whereof doth make him shake and shudder;
   Even so the timorous yelping of the hounds
   Appals her senses and her spirit confounds.   30

For now she knows it is no gentle chase,
But the blunt boar, rough bear, or lion proud,
Because the cry remaineth in one place,
Where fearfully the dogs exclaim aloud:
   Finding their enemy to be so curst,   35
   They all strain courtesy who shall cope him first.

This dismal cry rings sadly in her ear,
Through which it enters to surprise her heart;
Who, overcome by doubt and bloodless fear,
With cold-pale weakness numbs each feeling part: 40
   Like soldiers, when their captain once doth yield,
   They basely fly and dare not stay the field.

Thus stands she in a trembling ecstasy;
Till, cheering up her senses all dismayed,
She tells them 'tis a causeless fantasy, 45
And childish error, that they are afraid;
  Bids them leave quaking, bids them fear no
    more:—
  And with that word she spied the hunted
    boar,

Whose frothy mouth, bepainted all with red,
Like milk and blood being mingled both to-
    gether, 50
A second fear through all her sinews spread,
Which madly hurries her she knows not whither:
  This way she runs, and now she will no
    further,
  But back retires to rate the boar for murther.

A thousand spleens bear her a thousand ways: 55
She treads the path that she untreads again;
Her more than haste is mated with delays,
Like the proceedings of a drunken brain,
  Full of respects, yet naught at all respecting;
  In hand with all things, naught at all effect-
    ing. 60

Here kenneled in a brake she finds a hound,
And asks the weary caitiff for his master,
And there another licking of his wound,
'Gainst venomed sores the only sovereign plas-
    ter;
  And here she meets another sadly scowling 65
  To whom she speaks, and he replies with
    howling.

When he hath ceased his ill-resounding noise,
Another flap-mouthed mourner, black and grim,
Against the welkin volleys out his voice,
Another and another answer him, 70
  Clapping their proud tails to the ground
    below,
  Shaking their scratched ears, bleeding as they
    go.

Look, how the world's poor people are amazed
At apparitions, signs, and prodigies,
Whereon with fearful eyes they long have gazed,
Infusing them with dreadful prophecies; 76
  So she at these sad signs draws up her breath
  And sighing it again, exclaims on Death.

'Hard-favored tyrant, ugly, meager, lean,
Hateful divorce of love,'—thus chides she
    Death,— 80
'Grim-grinning ghost, earth's worm, what dost
    thou mean
To stifle beauty and to steal his breath,
  Who when he lived, his breath and beauty set
  Gloss on the rose, smell to the violet?

'If he be dead,—O no, it cannot be, 85
Seeing his beauty, thou shouldst strike at it:—
O yes, it may; thou hast no eyes to see,
But hatefully at random dost thou hit.
  Thy mark is feeble age, but thy false dart
  Mistakes that aim and cleaves an infant's
    heart. 90

'Hadst thou but bid beware, then he had spoke,
And, hearing him, thy power had lost his power.
The Destinies will curse thee for this stroke;
They bid thee crop a weed, thou pluck'st a
    flower:
  Love's golden arrow at him should have fled,
  And not Death's ebon dart, to strike him
    dead. 96

'Dost thou drink tears, that thou provok'st
    such weeping?
What may a heavy groan advantage thee?
Why hast thou cast into eternal sleeping
Those eyes that taught all other eyes to see? 100
  Now Nature cares not for thy mortal vigor,
  Since her best work is ruined with thy rigor.'

Here overcome, as one full of despair,
She vailed her eyelids, who, like sluices, stopt
The crystal tide that from her two cheeks fair
In the sweet channel of her bosom dropt; 106
  But through the flood-gates breaks the silver
    rain,
  And with his strong course opens them again.

O, how her eyes and tears did lend and borrow!
Her eyes seen in the tears, tears in her eye; 110
Both crystals, where they viewed each other's
    sorrow,
Sorrow that friendly sighs sought still to dry;
  But like a stormy day, now wind, now rain,
  Sighs dry her cheeks, tears make them wet
    again.

Variable passions throng her constant woe, 115
As striving who should best become her grief;
All entertained, each passion labors so,
That every present sorrow seemeth chief,
  But none is best: then join they all together,
  Like many clouds consulting for foul weather.

By this, far off she hears some huntsman
    hallo; 121
A nurse's song ne'er pleased her babe so well:
The dire imagination she did follow
This sound of hope doth labor to expel;
  For now reviving joy bids her rejoice, 125
  And flatters her it is Adonis' voice.

Whereat her tears began to turn their tide,
Being prisoned in her eye like pearls in glass;
Yet sometimes falls an orient drop beside,
Which her cheek melts, as scorning it should
    pass, 130

To wash the foul face of the sluttish ground,
Who is but drunken when she seemeth drowned.

O hard-believing love, how strange it seems
Not to believe, and yet too credulous!
Thy weal and woe are both of them extremes; 135
Despair and hope makes thee ridiculous:
  The one doth flatter thee in thoughts unlikely,
  In likely thoughts the other kills thee quickly.

Now she unweaves the web that she hath wrought;
Adonis lives, and Death is not to blame; 140
It was not she that called him all to naught:
Now she adds honors to his hateful name;
  She clepes him king of graves and grave for kings,
  Imperious supreme of all mortal things.

'No, no,' quoth she, 'sweet Death, I did but jest; 145
Yet pardon me I felt a kind of fear
When-as I met the boar, that bloody beast,
Which knows no pity, but is still severe;
  Then, gentle shadow,—truth I must confess,—
  I railed on thee, fearing my love's decease. 150

'T is not my fault: the boar provoked my tongue;
Be wreaked on him, invisible commander;
'T is he, foul creature, that hath done thee wrong;
I did but act, he 's author of thy slander;
  Grief hath two tongues, and never woman yet
  Could rule them both without ten women's wit.' 156

Thus hoping that Adonis is alive,
Her rash suspect she doth extenuate;
And that his beauty may the better thrive,
With Death she humbly doth insinuate; 160
  Tells him of trophies, statues, tombs, and stories;
  His victories, his triumphs, and his glories.

'O Jove,' quoth she, 'how much a fool was I
To be of such a weak and silly mind
To wail his death who lives and must not die 165
Till mutual overthrow of mortal kind!
  For he being dead, with him is beauty slain,
  And, beauty dead, black chaos comes again.

'Fie, fie, fond love, thou art as full of fear
As one with treasure laden, hemmed with thieves; 170
Trifles, unwitnessèd with eye or ear,
Thy coward heart with false bethinking grieves.'
  Even at this word she hears a merry horn,
  Whereat she leaps that was but late forlorn.

As falcon to the lure, away she flies; 175
The grass stoops not, she treads on it so light;
And in her haste unfortunately spies
The foul boar's conquest on her fair delight;
  Which seen, her eyes, as murdered with the view,
  Like stars ashamed of day, themselves withdrew; 180

Or, as the snail, whose tender horns being hit,
Shrinks backward in his shelly cave with pain,
And there, all smothered up, in shade doth sit,
Long after fearing to creep forth again;
  So, at his bloody view, her eyes are fled 185
  Into the deep dark cabins of her head:

Where they resign their office and their light
To the disposing of her troubled brain;
Who bids them still consort with ugly night,
And never wound the heart with looks again; 190
  Who, like a king perplexèd in his throne,
  By their suggestion gives a deadly groan.

Whereat each tributary subject quakes;
As when the wind, imprisoned in the ground,
Struggling for passage, earth's foundation shakes, 195
Which with cold terror doth men's minds confound.
  This mutiny each part doth so surprise
  That from their dark beds once more leap her eyes;

And, being opened, threw unwilling light
Upon the wide wound that the boar had trenched 200
In his soft flank; whose wonted lily white
With purple tears, that his wound wept, was drenched.
  No flower was nigh, no grass, herb, leaf, or weed,
  But stole his blood and seemed with him to bleed.

This solemn sympathy poor Venus noteth; 205
Over one shoulder doth she hang her head;
Dumbly she passions, franticly she doteth;
She thinks he could not die, he is not dead:
  Her voice is stopt, her joints forget to bow;
  Her eyes are mad that they have wept till now. 210

Upon his hurt she looks so steadfastly,
That her sight dazzling makes the wound seem three;
And then she reprehends her mangling eye,
That makes more gashes where no breach should be:
  His face seems twain, each several limb is doubled; 215
  For oft the eye mistakes, the brain being troubled.

'My tongue cannot express my grief for one,
And yet,' quoth she, 'behold two Adons dead!
My sighs are blown away, my salt tears gone,
Mine eyes are turned to fire, my heart to lead:
  Heavy heart's lead, melt at mine eyes' red
    fire!   221
  So shall I die by drops of hot desire.

'Alas, poor world, what treasure hast thou lost!
What face remains alive that's worth the view-
    ing?
Whose tongue is music now? what canst thou
    boast   225
Of things long since, or anything ensuing?
  The flowers are sweet, their colors fresh and
    trim;
  But true-sweet beauty lived and died with
    him.

'Bonnet nor veil henceforth no creature wear!
Nor sun nor wind will ever strive to kiss you: 230
Having no fair to lose, you need not fear;
The sun doth scorn you and the wind doth hiss
    you:
  But when Adonis lived, sun and sharp air
  Lurked like two thieves, to rob him of his
    fair.

'And therefore would he put his bonnet on, 235
Under whose brim the gaudy sun would peep;
The wind would blow it off and, being gone,
Play with his locks: then would Adonis weep;
  And straight, in pity of his tender years,
  They both would strive who first should dry
    his tears.   240

'To see his face the lion walked along
Behind some hedge, because he would not fear
    him;
To recreate himself when he hath sung,
The tiger would be tame and gently hear him;
  If he had spoke, the wolf would leave his prey
  And never fright the silly lamb that day. 246

'When he beheld his shadow in the brook,
The fishes spread on it their golden gills;
When he was by, the birds such pleasure took,
That some would sing, some other in their bills
  Would bring him mulberries and ripe-red
    cherries;   251
  He fed them with his sight, they him with
    berries.

'But this foul, grim, and urchin-snouted boar,
Whose downward eye still looketh for a grave,
Ne'er saw the beauteous livery that he wore;
Witness the entertainment that he gave: 256
  If he did see his face, why then I know
  He thought to kiss him, and hath killed him
    so.

''Tis true, 'tis true; thus was Adonis slain:
He ran upon the boar with his sharp spear, 260
Who did not whet his teeth at him again,
But by a kiss thought to persuade him there;
  And nuzzling in his flank, the loving swine
  Sheathed unaware the tusk in his soft groin.

'Had I been toothed like him, I must confess, 265
With kissing him I should have killed him first;
But he is dead, and never did he bless
My youth with his; the more am I accurst.'
  With this, she falleth in the place she stood,
  And stains her face with his congealèd blood.

She looks upon his lips, and they are pale; 271
She takes him by the hand, and that is cold;
She whispers in his ears a heavy tale,
As if they heard the woeful words she told;
  She lifts the coffer-lids that close his eyes, 275
  Where, lo, two lamps, burnt out, in darkness
    lies;

Two glasses, where herself herself beheld
A thousand times, and now no more reflect;
Their virtue lost, wherein they late excelled,
And every beauty robbed of his effect: 280
  'Wonder of time,' quoth she, 'this is my spite,
  That, thou being dead, the day should yet be
    light.

'Since thou art dead, lo, here I prophesy:
Sorrow on love hereafter shall attend:
It shall be waited on with jealousy,   285
Find sweet beginning, but unsavory end,
  Ne'er settled equally, but high or low,
  That all love's pleasure shall not match his
    woe.

'It shall be fickle, false, and full of fraud,
Bud and be blasted in a breathing-while; 290
The bottom poison, and the top o'erstrawed
With sweets that shall the truest sight beguile:
  The strongest body shall it make most weak,
  Strike the wise dumb and teach the fool to
    speak.

'It shall be sparing and too full of riot   295
Teaching decrepit age to tread the measures;
The staring ruffian shall it keep in quiet,
Pluck down the rich, enrich the poor with
    treasures;
  It shall be raging-mad and silly-mild,
  Make the young old, the old become a child.

'It shall suspect where is no cause of fear; 301
It shall not fear where it should most mistrust;
It shall be merciful and too severe,
And most deceiving when it seems most just;
  Perverse it shall be where it shows most to-
    ward;   305
  Put fear to valor, courage to the coward.

'It shall be cause of war and dire events,
And set dissension 'twixt the son and sire;
Subject and servile to all discontents,
As dry combustious matter is to fire: 310
   Sith in his prime Death doth my love destroy,
   They that love best their loves shall not enjoy.'

By this, the boy that by her side lay killed
Was melted like a vapor from her sight,
And in his blood that on the ground lay spilled,
A purple flower sprung up, chequered with white, 316
   Resembling well his pale cheeks and the blood
   Which in round-drops upon their whiteness stood.

She bows her head, the new-sprung flower to smell,
Comparing it to her Adonis' breath, 320
And says, within her bosom it shall dwell,
Since he himself is reft from her by death:
   She crops the stalk, and in the breach appears
   Green dropping sap, which she compares to tears.

'Poor flower,' quoth she, 'this was thy father's guise— 325
Sweet issue of a more sweet-smelling sire—
For every little grief to wet his eyes:
To grow unto himself was his desire,
   And so 't is thine; but know, it is as good
   To wither in my breast as in his blood. 330

'Here was thy father's bed, here in my breast;
Thou art the next of blood, and 't is thy right:
Lo, in this hollow cradle take thy rest,
My throbbing heart shall rock thee day and night;
   There shall not be one minute in an hour 335
   Wherein I will not kiss my sweet love's flower.'

Thus weary of the world, away she hies,
And yokes her silver doves; by whose swift aid
Their mistress mounted through the empty skies
In her light chariot quickly is conveyed; 340
   Holding their course to Paphos, where their queen
   Means to immure herself and not be seen.

SONNETS

XII

When I do count the clock that tells the time,
And see the brave day sunk in hideous night;
When I behold the violet past prime,
And sable curls all silvered o'er with white;

When lofty trees I see barren of leaves, 5
Which erst from heat did canopy the herd,
And summer's green all girded up in sheaves
Borne on the bier with white and bristly beard,

Then of thy beauty do I question make,
That thou among the wastes of time must go, 10
Since sweets and beauties do themselves forsake
And die as fast as they see others grow;
And nothing 'gainst Time's scythe can make defence
Save breed, to brave him when he takes thee hence.

XV

When I consider every thing that grows
Holds in perfection but a little moment,
That this huge stage presenteth naught but shows
Whereon the stars in secret influence comment;

When I perceive that men as plants increase, 5
Cheerèd and checked even by the self-same sky,
Vaunt in their youthful sap, at height decrease,
And wear their brave state out of memory:

Then the conceit of this inconstant stay
Sets you most rich in youth before my sight, 10
Where wasteful Time debateth with Decay,
To change your day of youth to sullied night;
And all in war with Time for love of you,
As he takes from you, I engraft you new.

XVIII

Shall I compare thee to a summer's day?
Thou art more lovely and more temperate:
Rough winds do shake the darling buds of May,
And summer's lease hath all too short a date:

Sometime too hot the eye of heaven shines 5
And often is his gold complexion dimmed;
And every fair from fair sometime declines,
By chance or nature's changing course untrimmed;

But thy eternal summer shall not fade
Nor lose possession of that fair thou owest; 10
Nor shall Death brag thou wander'st in his shade,
When in eternal lines to time thou growest:
So long as men can breathe or eyes can see,
So long lives this and this gives life to thee.

XXV

Let those who are in favor with their stars
Of public honor and proud titles boast,
Whilst I, whom fortune of such triumph bars,
Unlooked for joy in that I honor most.

Great princes' favorites their fair leaves spread 5
But as the marigold at the sun's eye,
And in themselves their pride lies buried,
For at a frown they in their glory die.

The painful warrior famousèd for fight,
After a thousand victories once foiled, 10
Is from the book of honor razèd quite,
And all the rest forgot for which he toiled:

Then happy I, that love and am beloved
Where I may not remove nor be removed.

XXIX

When in disgrace with fortune and men's eyes,
I all alone beweep my outcast state
And trouble deaf heaven with my bootless cries
And look upon myself and curse my fate,

Wishing me like to one more rich in hope, 5
Featured like him, like him with friends possessed,
Desiring this man's art and that man's scope,
With what I most enjoy contented least;

Yet in these thoughts myself almost despising,
Haply I think on thee, and then my state, 10
Like to the lark at break of day arising
From sullen earth, sings hymns at heaven's gate;
For thy sweet love remembered such wealth brings
That then I scorn to change my state with kings.

XXX

When to the sessions of sweet silent thought
I summon up remembrance of things past,
I sigh the lack of many a thing I sought,
And with old woes new wail my dear time's waste:

Then can I drown an eye, unused to flow, 5
For precious friends hid in death's dateless night,
And weep afresh love's long since canceled woe,
And moan the expense of many a vanished sight:

Then can I grieve at grievances foregone,
And heavily from woe to woe tell o'er 10
The sad account of fore-bemoanèd moan,
Which I new pay as if not paid before.
But if the while I think on thee, dear friend,
All losses are restored and sorrows end.

XXXIII

Full many a glorious morning have I seen
Flatter the mountain-tops with sovereign eye,
Kissing with golden face the meadows green,
Gilding pale streams with heavenly alchemy;

Anon permit the basest clouds to ride 5
With ugly rack on his celestial face,
And from the forlorn world his visage hide,
Stealing unseen to west with this disgrace:

Even so my sun one early morn did shine
With all-triumphant splendor on my brow; 10
But out, alack! he was but one hour mine;
The region cloud hath masked him from me now.
Yet him for this my love no whit disdaineth;
Suns of the world may stain when heaven's sun staineth. 14

LIV

O, how much more doth beauty beauteous seem
By that sweet ornament which truth doth give!
The rose looks fair, but fairer we it deem
For that sweet odor which doth in it live.

The canker blooms have full as deep a dye 5
As the perfumèd tincture of the roses,
Hang on such thorns, and play as wantonly
When summer's breath their maskèd buds discloses;

But, for their virtue only is their show,
They live unwooed and unrespected fade, 10
Die to themselves. Sweet roses do not so;
Of their sweet deaths are sweetest odors made:
And so of you, beauteous and lovely youth,
When that shall fade, my verse distills your truth.

LV

Not marble, nor the gilded monuments
Of princes, shall outlive this powerful rime;
But you shall shine more bright in these contents
Than unswept stone besmeared with sluttish time.

When wasteful war shall statues overturn, 5
And broils root out the work of masonry,
Nor Mars his sword nor war's quick fire shall burn
The living record of your memory.

'Gainst death and all-oblivious enmity
Shall you pace forth; your praise shall still find room 10
Even in the eyes of all posterity
That wear this world out to the ending doom.
So, till the judgment that yourself arise,
You live in this, and dwell in lovers' eyes.

LX

Like as the waves make towards the pebbled shore,
So do our minutes hasten to their end;
Each changing place with that which goes before,
In sequent toil all forwards do contend.

Nativity, once in the main of light, 5
Crawls to maturity, wherewith being crowned,
Crookèd eclipses 'gainst his glory fight,
And Time that gave doth now his gift confound.

Time doth transfix the flourish set on youth
And delves the parallels in beauty's brow, 10
Feeds on the rarities of nature's truth,
And nothing stands but for his scythe to mow:
And yet to times in hope my verse shall stand,
Praising thy worth, despite his cruel hand.

LXIV

When I have seen by Time's fell hand defaced
The rich proud cost of outworn buried age;

When sometime lofty towers I see down-razed
And brass eternal slave to mortal rage;

When I have seen the hungry ocean gain 5
Advantage on the kingdom of the shore,
And the firm soil win of the watery main,
Increasing store with loss and loss with store;

When I have seen such interchange of state,
Or state itself confounded to decay; 10
Ruin hath taught me thus to ruminate,
That Time will come and take my love away.

This thought is as a death, which cannot choose
But weep to have that which it fears to lose.

LXV

Since brass, nor stone, nor earth, nor boundless sea,
But sad mortality o'er-sways their power,
How with this rage shall beauty hold a plea,
Whose action is no stronger than a flower?

O, how shall summer's honey breath hold out 5
Against the wreckful siege of battering days,
When rocks impregnable are not so stout,
Nor gates of steel so strong, but Time decays?

O fearful meditation! where, alack,
Shall Time's best jewel from Time's chest lie hid? 10
Or what strong hand can hold his swift foot back?
Or who his spoil of beauty can forbid?
O, none, unless this miracle have might,
That in black ink my love may still shine bright.

LXVI

Tired with all these, for restful death I cry,—
As, to behold desert a beggar born,
And needy nothing trimmed in jollity,
And purest faith unhappily forsworn,

And gilded honor shamefully misplaced, 5
And maiden virtue rudely strumpeted,
And right perfection wrongfully disgraced,
And strength by limping sway disablèd,

And art made tongue-tied by authority,
And folly doctor-like controlling skill, 10
And simple truth miscalled simplicity.
And captive good attending captain ill:
Tired with all these, from these would I be gone,
Save that, to die, I leave my love alone.

LXXI

No longer mourn for me when I am dead
Than you shall hear the surley sullen bell
Give warning to the world that I am fled
From this vile world, with vilest worms to dwell:

Nay, if you read this line, remember not 5
The hand that writ it; for I love you so
That I in your sweet thoughts would be forgot
If thinking on me then should make you woe.

O, if, I say, you look upon this verse
When I perhaps compounded am with clay, 10
Do not so much as my poor name rehearse,
But let your love even with my life decay,
Lest the wise world should look into your moan
And mock you with me after I am gone.

LXXIII

That time of year thou mayst in me behold
When yellow leaves, or none, or few, do hang
Upon those boughs which shake against the cold,
Bare ruined choirs, where late the sweet birds sang.

In me thou see'st the twilight of such day 5
As after sunset fadeth in the west,
Which by and by black night doth take away,
Death's second self, that seals up all in rest.

In me thou see'st the glowing of such fire
That on the ashes of his youth doth lie, 10
As the death-bed whereon it must expire,
Consumed with that which it was nourished by.
This thou perceiv'st, which makes thy love more strong,
To love that well which thou must leave ere long.

LXXVI

Why is my verse so barren of new pride,
So far from variation or quick change?
Why with the time do I not glance aside
To new-found methods and to compounds strange?

Why write I still all one, ever the same, 5
And keep invention in a noted weed,
That every word doth almost tell my name,
Showing their birth and where they did proceed?

O, know, sweet love, I always write of you,
And you and love are still my argument; 10
So all my best is dressing old words new,
Spending again what is already spent:
For as the sun is daily new and old,
So is my love still telling what is told.

XCVII

How like a winter hath my absence been
From thee, the pleasure of the fleeting year!
What freezings have I felt, what dark days seen!
What old December's bareness everywhere!

And yet this time removed was summer's time, 5
The teeming autumn, big with rich increase,
Bearing the wanton burden of the prime,
Like widowed wombs after their lord's decease:

Yet this abundant issue seemed to me
But hope of orphans and unfathered fruit; 10
For summer and his pleasures wait on thee,
And, thou away, the very birds are mute;

Or, if they sing, 't is with so dull a cheer
That leaves look pale, dreading the winter's near.

XCVIII

From you have I been absent in the spring,
When proud-pied April dressed in all his trim
Hath put a spirit of youth in every thing,
That heavy Saturn laughed and leaped with him.
Yet nor the lays of birds nor the sweet smell 5
Of different flowers in odor and in hue
Could make me any summer's story tell,
Or from their proud lap pluck them where they grew;
Nor did I wonder at the lily's white,
Nor praise the deep vermilion in the rose; 10
They were but sweet, but figures of delight,
Drawn after you, you pattern of all those.
Yet seemed it winter still, and, you away,
As with your shadow, I with these did play.

XCIX

The forward violet thus did I chide:
Sweet thief, whence didst thou steal thy sweet that smells,
If not from my love's breath? The purple pride
Which on thy soft cheek for complexion dwells
In my love's veins thou hast too grossly dyed. 5
The lily I condemnèd for thy hand,
And buds of marjoram had stol'n thy hair.
The roses fearfully on thorns did stand,
One blushing shame, another white despair;
A third, nor red nor white, had stol'n of both 10
And to his robbery had annexed thy breath;
But, for his theft, in pride of all his growth
A vengeful canker eat him up to death.
More flowers I noted, yet I none could see
But sweet or color it had stol'n from thee. 15

CIV

To me, fair friend, you never can be old,
For as you were when first your eye I eyed,
Such seems your beauty still. Three winters cold
Have from the forests shook three summers' pride,
Three beauteous springs to yellow autumn turned 5
In process of the seasons have I seen,
Three April perfumes in three hot Junes burned
Since first I saw you fresh, which yet are green.
Ah! yet doth beauty, like a dial-hand,
Steal from his figure and no pace perceived; 10
So your sweet hue, which methinks still doth stand,
Hath motion and mine eye may be deceived:
For fear of which, hear this, thou age unbred:
Ere you were born was beauty's summer dead.

CVI

When in the chronicle of wasted time
I see descriptions of the fairest wights,
And beauty making beautiful old rime
In praise of ladies dead and lovely knights,
Then, in the blazon of sweet beauty's best, 5
Of hand, of foot, of lip, of eye, of brow,
I see their antique pen would have expressed
Even such a beauty as you master now.
So all their praises are but prophecies
Of this our time, all you prefiguring; 10
And, for they looked but with divining eyes,
They had not skill enough your worth to sing:
For we, which now behold these present days,
Have eyes to wonder, but lack tongues to praise.

CVII

Not mine own fears, nor the prophetic soul
Of the wide world dreaming on things to come,
Can yet the lease of my true love control,
Supposed as forfeit to a confined doom.
The mortal moon hath her eclipse endured 5
And the sad augurs mock their own presage;
Incertainties now crown themselves assured
And peace proclaims olives of endless age.
Now with the drops of this most balmy time
My love looks fresh, and Death to me subscribes, 10
Since, spite of him, I 'll live in this poor rime,
While he insults o'er dull and speechless tribes:
And thou in this shalt find thy monument,
When tyrants' crests and tombs of brass are spent.

CIX

O, never say that I was false of heart,
Though absence seemed my flame to qualify.
As easy might I from myself depart
As from my soul, which in thy breast doth lie:
That is my home of love: if I have ranged, 5
Like him that travels I return again,
Just to the time, not with the time exchanged,
So that myself bring water for my stain.
Never believe, though in my nature reigned
All frailties that besiege all kinds of blood, 10
That it could so preposterously be stained,
To leave for nothing all thy sum of good;
For nothing this wide universe I call,
Save thou, my rose; in it thou art my all.

CX

Alas, 'tis true I have gone here and there
And made myself a motley to the view,
Gored mine own thoughts, sold cheap what is most dear,
Made old offences of affections new;

Most true it is that I have looked on truth 5
Askance and strangely; but, by all above,
These blenches gave my heart another youth,
And worse essays proved thee my best of love.

Now all is done, have what shall have no end:
Mine appetite I never more will grind 10
On newer proof, to try an older friend,
A god in love, to whom I am confined.
Then give me welcome, next my heaven the best,
Even to thy pure and most most loving breast.

CXI

O, for my sake do you with Fortune chide,
The guilty goddess of my harmful deeds,
That did not better for my life provide
Than public means which public manners breeds.

Thence comes it that my name receives a brand,
And almost thence my nature is subdued 6
To what it works in, like the dyer's hand.
Pity me then and wish I were renewed;

Whilst, like a willing patient, I will drink
Potions of eisel 'gainst my strong infection; 10
No bitterness that I will bitter think,
Nor double penance, to correct correction
Pity me then, dear friend, and I assure ye
Even that your pity is enough to cure me.

CXVI

Let me not to the marriage of true minds
Admit impediments. Love is not love
Which alters when it alteration finds,
Or bends with the remover to remove:

O, no! it is an ever-fixèd mark 5
That looks on tempests and is never shaken;
It is the star to every wandering bark,
Whose worth's unknown, although his height be taken.

Love's not Time's fool, though rosy lips and cheeks
Within his bending sickle's compass come; 10
Love alters not with his brief hours and weeks,
But bears it out even to the edge of doom.
If this be error and upon me proved,
I never writ, nor no man ever loved.

CXIX

What potions have I drunk of Siren tears,
Distilled from limbecks foul as hell within,
Applying fears to hopes and hopes to fears,
Still losing when I saw myself to win!

What wretched errors hath my heart committed, 5
Whilst it hath thought itself so blessèd never!
How have mine eyes out of their spheres been fitted
In the distraction of this madding fever!

O benefit of ill! now I find true
That better is by evil still made better; 10
And ruined love, when it is built anew,
Grows fairer than at first, more strong, far greater.
So I return rebuked to my content,
And gain by ills thrice more than I have spent.

CXXVIII

How oft, when thou, my music, music play'st,
Upon that blessèd wood whose motion sounds
With thy sweet fingers, when thou gently sway'st
The wiry concord that mine ear confounds,

Do I envy those jacks that nimble leap 5
To kiss the tender inward of thy hand,
Whilst my poor lips, which should that harvest reap,
At the wood's boldness by thee blushing stand!

To be so tickled, they would change their state
And situation with those dancing chips, 10
O'er whom thy fingers walk with gentle gait,
Making dead wood more blest than living lips.
Since saucy jacks so happy are in this,
Give them thy fingers, me thy lips to kiss.

CXXX

My mistress' eyes are nothing like the sun;
Coral is far more red than her lips' red;
If snow be white, why then her breasts are dun;
If hairs be wires, black wires grow on her head.

I have seen roses damasked, red and white, 5
But no such roses see I in her cheeks;
And in some perfumes is there more delight
Than in the breath that from my mistress reeks.

I love to hear her speak, yet well I know
That music hath a far more pleasing sound; 10
I grant I never saw a goddess go;
My mistress, when she walks, treads on the ground:
And yet, by heaven, I think my love as rare
As any she belied with false compare.

CXLVI

Poor soul, the center of my sinful earth,
Thrall to these rebel powers that thee array,
Why dost thou pine within and suffer dearth,
Painting thy outward walls so costly gay?

Why so large cost, having so short a lease, 5
Dost thou upon thy fading mansion spend?
Shall worms, inheritors of this excess,
Eat up thy charge? is this thy body's end?

Then, soul, live thou upon thy servant's loss,
And let that pine to aggravate thy store; 10
Buy terms divine in selling hours of dross;
Within be fed, without be rich no more:
So shalt thou feed on Death, that feeds on men,
And Death once dead, there's no more dying then.

SONGS FROM THE PLAYS

From Love's Labor's Lost

When icicles hang by the wall,
   And Dick the shepherd blows his nail,
And Tom bears logs into the hall,
   And milk comes frozen home in pail,
When blood is nipped and ways be foul,   5
Then nightly sings the staring owl,
   'Tu-whit, tu-who!' a merry note,
While greasy Joan doth keel the pot.

When all aloud the wind doth blow,
   And coughing drowns the parson's saw,   10
And birds sit brooding in the snow,
   And Marian's nose looks red and raw,
When roasted crabs hiss in the bowl,
Then nightly sings the staring owl,
   'Tu-whit, tu-who!' a merry note,   15
While greasy Joan doth keel the pot.

From Two Gentlemen of Verona

Who is Silvia? what is she,
   That all our swains commend her?
Holy, fair, and wise is she;
   The heaven such grace did lend her,
That she might admirèd be.   5

Is she kind as she is fair?
   For beauty lives with kindness.
Love doth to her eyes repair
   To help him of his blindness,
And, being helped, inhabits there.   10

Then to Silvia let us sing,
   That Silvia is excelling;
She excels each mortal thing
   Upon the dull earth dwelling:
To her let us garlands bring.   15

From The Merchant of Venice

   Tell me, where is fancy bred,
   Or in the heart, or in the head?
   How begot, how nourishèd!
      Reply, reply.
   It is engendered in the eyes,   5
   With gazing fed; and fancy dies
   In the cradle where it lies:
   Let us all ring fancy's knell;
   I'll begin it,—Ding-dong, bell.
      Ding, dong, bell.   10

From As You Like It

Under the greenwood tree
   Who loves to lie with me,
   And turn his merry note
   Unto the sweet bird's throat,
Come hither! come hither! come hither!   5
   Here shall he see
      No enemy
But winter and rough weather.

Who doth ambition shun
   And loves to live i' the sun,   10
   Seeking the food he eats
   And pleased with what he gets,
Come hither! come hither! come hither!
   Here shall he see
      No enemy   15
But winter and rough weather.

From As You Like It

Blow, blow, thou winter wind!
Thou art not so unkind
   As man's ingratitude;
Thy tooth is not so keen,
Because thou art not seen,   5
   Although thy breath be rude.

Heigh ho! sing, heigh ho! unto the green holly:
Most friendship is feigning, most loving mere
   folly:
   Then, heigh ho, the holly!
   This life is most jolly.   10

Freeze, freeze, thou bitter sky!
That dost not bite so nigh
   As benefits forgot;
Though thou the waters warp,
Thy sting is not so sharp   15
   As friend remembered not.

Heigh ho! sing, heigh ho! etc.

From Much Ado About Nothing

Sigh no more, ladies, sigh no more!
   Men were deceivers ever,
One foot in sea and one on shore,
   To one thing constant never:
Then sigh not so, but let them go,   5
   And be you blithe and bonny,
Converting all your sounds of woe
   Into Hey nonny, nonny!

Sing no more ditties, sing no moe
   Of dumps so dull and heavy!   10
The fraud of men was ever so,
   Since summer first was leafy:
Then sigh not so, but let them go,
   And be you blithe and bonny,
Converting all your sounds of woe   15
   Into Hey nonny, nonny!

From Twelfth Night

O Mistress mine, where are you roaming?
O, stay and hear; your true love's coming,
   That can sing both high and low:
Trip no further, pretty sweeting,
Journeys end in lovers meeting,   5
   Every wise man's son doth know.

What is love? 't is not hereafter;
Present mirth hath present laughter;
  What 's to come is still unsure:
In delay there lies no plenty;   10
Then come kiss me, sweet and twenty,
  Youth 's a stuff will not endure.

From MEASURE FOR MEASURE

TAKE, O, take those lips away,
  That so sweetly were forsworn;
And those eyes, the break of day,
  Lights that do mislead the morn:
But my kisses bring again.   5
                 Bring again;
Seals of love, but sealed in vain,
                 Sealed in vain!

From CYMBELINE

HARK, hark! the lark at heaven's gate sings,
  And Phœbus 'gins arise,
His steeds to water at those springs
  On chaliced flowers that lies;
And winking Mary-buds begin   5
  To ope their golden eyes;
With every thing that pretty is,
  My lady sweet, arise!
    Arise, arise!

From CYMBELINE

FEAR no more the heat o' th' sun,
  Nor the furious winter's rages;
Thou thy worldly task hast done,
  Home art gone, and ta'en thy wages:
Golden lads and girls all must,   5
  As chimney-sweepers, come to dust.

Fear no more the frown o' th' great;
  Thou art past the tyrant's stroke;
Care no more to clothe and eat;
  To thee the reed is as the oak;   10
The Scepter, Learning, Physic, must
  All follow this, and come to dust.

Fear no more the lightning-flash,
  Nor th' all-dreaded thunder-stone;
Fear not slander, censure rash;   15
  Thou hast finished joy and moan;
All lovers young, all lovers must
  Consign to thee, and come to dust.

No exorciser harm thee!
  Nor no witchcraft charm thee!   20
Ghost unlaid forbear thee!
  Nothing ill come near thee!
Quiet consummation have;
  And renownèd be thy grave!

ARIEL'S SONG

From THE TEMPEST

FULL fathom five thy father lies:
  Of his bones are coral made;
Those are pearls that were his eyes;
  Nothing of him that doth fade
But doth suffer a sea-change   5
Into something rich and strange.
Sea-nymphs hourly ring his knell:
                 Ding-dong!
Hark! now I hear them,—Ding-dong, bell!

THOMAS DEKKER
(c. 1572–c. 1632)

SONG

From PATIENT GRISSELL

ART thou poor, yet hast thou golden slumbers?
    O sweet content!
Art thou rich, yet is thy mind perplexed?
    O punishment!
Dost thou laugh to see how fools are vexed 5
To add to golden numbers, golden numbers?
    O sweet content! O sweet, O sweet content!
    Work apace, apace, apace, apace;
    Honest labor bears a lovely face;
Then hey nonny nonny, hey nonny nonny! 10

Canst drink the waters of the crispèd spring?
    O sweet content!
Swimm'st thou in wealth, yet sink'st in thine
    own tears?
    O punishment!
Then he that patiently want's burden bears 15
No burden bears, but is a king, a king!
    O sweet content! O sweet, O sweet content!
    Work apace, apace, apace, apace;
    Honest labor bears a lovely face;
Then hey nonny nonny, hey nonny nonny! 20

ENGLAND'S HELICON
(1600)

PHYLLIDA AND CORYDON

IN the merry month of May,
In a morn by break of day,
Forth I walked by the wood-side,
When as May was in her pride:
There I spièd all alone,   5
Phyllida and Corydon.

Much ado there was, God wot!
He would love and she would not.
She said, never man was true;
He said, none was false to you.   10
He said, he had loved her long;
She said, love should have no wrong.
Corydon would kiss her then;
She said, maids must kiss no men.

Till they did for good and all;
Then she made the shepherd call
All the heavens to witness truth:
Never loved a truer youth.
Thus with many a pretty oath,
Yea and nay, and faith and troth,
Such as silly shepherds use
When they will not love abuse,
Love which had been long deluded,
Was with kisses sweet concluded;
And Phyllida, with garlands gay,
Was made the Lady of the May.
                N. BRETON

AS IT FELL UPON A DAY

As it fell upon a day,
In the merry month of May,
Sitting in a pleasant shade,
Which a group of myrtles made,
Beasts did leap and birds did sing,
Trees did grow and plants did spring,
Everything did banish moan,
Save the nightingale alone;
She, poor bird, as all forlorn,
Leaned her breast against a thorn,
And there sung the dolefull'st ditty,
That to hear it was great pity.
'Fie, fie, fie!' now would she cry;
'Teru, teru!' by-and-by.
That to hear her so complain
Scarce I could from tears refrain;
For her griefs so lively shown
Made me think upon mine own.
Ah, thought I, thou mourn'st in vain,
None takes pity on thy pain.
Senseless trees, they cannot hear thee;
Ruthless beasts, they will not cheer thee;
King Pandion he is dead,
All thy friends are lapped in lead;
All thy fellow birds do sing,
Careless of thy sorrowing;
Even so, poor bird, like thee,
None alive will pity me.
                IGNOTO

TO COLIN CLOUT

BEAUTY sat bathing in a spring,
  Where fairest shades did hide her;
The winds blew calm, the birds did sing,
  The cool streams ran beside her.
My wanton thoughts enticed mine eye,
  To see what was forbidden;
But better memory said, fie:
  So, vain desire was chidden.
  Hey nonny, nonny, etc.

Into a slumber then I fell,
  When fond Imagination
Seemed to see, but could not tell,
  Her feature or her fashion.
But even as babes in dreams do smile,
  And sometimes fall a-weeping,
So I awaked, as wise this while
  As when I fell a-sleeping.
  Hey nonny, nonny, etc.
                SHEPHERD TONY

THE SHEPHERD'S COMMENDATION OF HIS NYMPH

WHAT shepherd can express
The favor of her face,
To whom in this distress
I do appeal for grace?
  A thousand Cupids fly
  About her gentle eye.

From which each throws a dart
That kindleth soft sweet fire
Within my sighing heart,
Possessèd by desire;
  No sweeter life I try
  Than in her love to die.

The lily in the field,
That glories in his white,
For pureness now must yield,
And render up his right;
  Heaven pictured in her face
  Doth promise joy and grace.

Fair Cynthia's silver light,
That beats on running streams,
Compares not with her white,
Whose hairs are all sunbeams.
  So bright my nymph doth shine
  As day unto my eyne.

With this there is a red,
Exceeds the damask-rose,
Which in her cheeks is spread,
Where every favor grows;
  In sky there is no star,
  But she surmounts it far.

When Phœbus from the bed
Of Thetis doth arise,
The morning blushing red,
In fair carnation-wise,
  He shows in my nymph's face
  As queen of every grace.

This pleasant lily white,
This taint of roseate red,
This Cynthia's silver light,
This sweet fair Dea spread,
  These sunbeams in mine eye,
  These beauties make me die.
                EARL OF OXFORD

THE HERDMAN'S HAPPY LIFE

What pleasure have great princes
    More dainty to their choice
Than herdmen wild, who careless
    In quiet life rejoice?
And fortune's fate not fearing,
Sing sweet in summer morning.

Their dealings plain and rightful,
    Are void of all deceit;
They never know how spiteful
    It is to kneel and wait
On favorite presumptuous,
Whose pride is vain and sumptuous.

All day their flocks each tendeth,
    At night they take their rest,
More quiet than who sendeth
    His ship into the east,
Where gold and pearl are plenty,
But getting very dainty.

For lawyers and their pleading,
    They 'steem it not a straw;
They think that honest meaning,
    Is of itself a law;
Where conscience judgeth plainly,
They spend no money vainly.

Oh, happy who thus liveth!
    Not caring much for gold;
With clothing which sufficeth,
    To keep him from the cold.
Though poor and plain his diet,
Yet merry it is and quiet.
      Out of Mr. Bird's Set Songs

A NYMPH'S DISDAIN OF LOVE

'Hey, down, a down!' did Dian sing,
    Amongst her virgins sitting;
'Than love there is no vainer thing,
    For maidens most unfitting.'
And so think I, with a down, down, derry.

When women knew no woe,
    But lived themselves to please,
Men's feigning guiles they did not know,
    The ground of their disease.
Unborn was false suspect,
    No thought of jealousy;
From wanton toys and fond affect,
    The virgin's life was free.

'Hey, down, a down!' did Dian sing, etc.

At length men used charms,
    To which what maids gave ear,
Embracing gladly endless harms,
    Anon enthrallèd were.
Thus women welcomed woe,
    Disguised in name of love,
A jealous hell, a painted show:
    So shall they find that prove.

'Hey, down, a down!' did Dian sing,
    Amongst her virgins sitting;
'Than love there is no vainer thing,
    For maidens most unfitting.'
And so think I, with a down, down, derry.
                    Ignoto

ROSALIND'S MADRIGAL

Love in my bosom like a bee,
    Doth suck his sweet;
Now with his wings he plays with me,
    Now with his feet.
Within mine eyes he makes his nest,
His bed amidst my tender breast;
My kisses are his daily feast,
And yet he robs me of my rest.
    Ah, wanton, will ye?

And if I sleep, then percheth he,
    With pretty slight,
And makes his pillow of my knee,
    The livelong night.
Strike I my lute, he tunes the string;
He music plays if I but sing;
He lends me every lovely thing;
Yet cruel he my heart doth sting.
    Whist, wanton, still ye!

Else I with roses every day
    Will whip ye hence,
And bind ye, when ye long to play,
    For your offence.
I'll shut my eyes to keep ye in,
I'll make you fast it for your sin,
I'll count your power not worth a pin,
Alas! what hereby shall I win
    If he gainsay me?

What if I beat the wanton boy
    With many a rod?
He will repay me with annoy,
    Because a god.
Then sit thou safely on my knee,
And let thy bower my bosom be;
Lurk in mine eyes, I like of thee.
O Cupid! so thou pity me,
    Spare not, but play thee.
                    Thomas Lodge

THE SEVENTEENTH CENTURY

THE first third of the seventeenth century witnessed the culmination of the vast creative impulse which had its rise in the great days of Elizabeth. And it felt the first swell of a new wave of moral conviction and fierce spiritual energy which was to spend its force mainly in the fighting out of practical issues, and in a rationalization of them, rather than in that serene realization of life which finds expression in the forms of pure literature. England was under Stuart kings for a large part of the century, and their policies forced the English people into a protracted struggle for the preservation of constitutional government and the supremacy of the Protestant religion. Though political in origin, the controversy was far-reaching. It drove men into hostile camps, opposing them on terms of their inbred tastes and basic philosophies of life. It drove some of them over the seas to found fresh nations in another hemisphere. It brought high officials to the block, and inspired humblest citizens to stake goods, home, life itself, for moral issues. While this contest was in progress its issues were never very remote from the consciousness of Englishmen, and practically everything written in that time is directly concerned with them, or is colored by them.

One of the triumphs of Elizabeth's long reign had been her success in keeping religious hostilities suspended amongst her own subjects, whilst the nations of the Continent were being torn by civil wars and ravaged by invasions in the name of religion. By the time of James's accession, Protestantism had been quietly gaining ground for two generations, and was so mixed with the instincts of the average Englishman as to be almost synonymous with patriotism. Catholicism, on the other hand, would be instinctively associated with the institutions and morals of its champions on the continent—Spain first, and later, France. To insular Protestants it suggested absolute sovereigns, luxurious courts, religious inquisitions, and cruel wars of aggression.

The extreme anti-Catholic wing of English Protestantism was the Puritan party. In its beginnings, Puritanism was essentially a moral awakening, an indefinable spirit, which arose within the established church. But it soon took on independent theological, political, and social implications. Deriving their theology from Calvin, the Puritans championed a democratic type of government, for both church and state, defying episcopacy in the one, and government by royal prerogative and court favorites in the other. Since the worldliness of the mother church was their main object of attack, the very idea of a state-controlled religion was abhorrent to them. They quarreled with the established church on this ground, and even more with its forms of worship. For the English service had not completely discarded the ceremonials of the Mass; and a large ingredient of Puritan 'zeal' was a superstitious abhorrence of anything in religious dress or observance that savored of Romanism. Socially, also, the Puritans became a class apart. Recruited mainly from the middle and professional classes, they adopted a drabness and uniformity of dress and manners. At James's court, and later, the liveliness and magnificence of the Renaissance was fast degenerating into licentiousness and effeminate display, and the Puritan expressed in his person a manly contempt for a foppishness which he associated with luxury and vice.

The tension between crown and parliament, increasingly acute under James I (1603-1625), came to open rupture under Charles I, and, in 1642, broke into armed conflict between Royalist and Parliamentary forces. The king was eventually captured, tried for treason, and solemnly executed (1649). The sacrilege of the act sent a shudder through Christendom; but it was a lucid reply to the doctrine of the divinity of kings. England was promptly proclaimed a free Commonwealth and, after a brief experience of purely Parliamentary rule, Oliver Cromwell, having declined the style of 'King,' was made 'Lord Protector.' When Cromwell died, the Commonwealth crumbled, and there was a burst of Royalist fervor, resulting in 'the Restoration' of Charles II (1660).

His reign was scandalous. Charles was lazy, unscrupulous, and luxurious. His court was an elegant brothel. His foreign policy was ignoble and treacherous. The question of his successor kept the nation in a turmoil. The king had no legitimate offspring, and his brother, the Duke of York, was a professed Catholic. Even respectable Royalists looked back upon the firm and dignified, if harsh, rule of Cromwell, as upon a worthier day. Yet Charles kept his throne for a quarter century and died in his bed, wittily, as he had lived. His brother, James II, was more candid and less successful. He carried things with a high hand, but was frightened from the throne and from the realm before three years were out. He fled in haste when his son-in-law, the dour but able William of Orange, landed on the English coast in response to a cordial invitation from James's subjects. Thus was ushered in the final 'Protestant Revolution' (1688).

The arrangements entered into between William and Parliament, preparatory to his acceptance of the crown—as co-sovereign with his wife, Mary—laid the foundations of modern English constitutional government. England was not quite done with the Stuarts; but they were to be known henceforth as 'Pretenders.' Henceforth, also, even real kings were to be of less consequence; the will of the people, of more.

NOTEWORTHY DATES

ENGLISH LITERATURE AND HISTORY		FOREIGN LITERATURE AND HISTORY	
1603–25	James I	1602	Biron's Conspiracy
1605	Gunpowder Plot	1605	Cervantes' *Don Quixote*
1608–74	John Milton	1606–84	Pierre Corneille
1611	King James Bible	1610–43	Louis XIII, of France
1612	Bacon's *Essays* (enlarged)	1618	Thirty Years' War
1616	Death of Shakespeare	1622–73	Molière
1623	First Folio of Shakespeare	1620	Landing of the Pilgrims
1625	Bacon's *Essays* (enlarged)	1624	Richelieu's ministry
1625–49	Charles I	1630	Massachusetts Bay Colony
1631–1700	John Dryden	1632	Death of Gustavus Adolphus
1633	Laud, Archbishop		
1634	Milton's *Comus*	1635	French Academy founded
1637	Jonson died	1636	Corneille's *Le Cid*
1638	Milton's *Lycidas*	1639–99	Jean Baptiste Racine
1642	London Theatres closed		
1644	Milton's *Areopagitica*	1648	Treaty of Westphalia
1649–60	Commonwealth and Protectorate		
1653–58	Cromwell, Protector	1654	Vondel's *Lucifer*
1660–85	Charles II		
1662	Royal Society founded	1661–1715	Louis XIV, of France
1667	Milton's *Paradise Lost*	1664	Molière's *Tartuffe*
1681	Dryden's *Absalom and Achitophel*	1674	Boileau's *Art Poétique*
1685–89	James II		
1689–1702	William and Mary		
1700	Congreve's *Way of the World*	1697	Treaty of Ryswick

SEVENTEENTH CENTURY LYRICS

The factionalism which embittered the minds of Englishmen during the seventeenth century was not favorable to the practice of literature as a fine art. A man of preëminent genius, like Milton, might claim to have emerged from the conflict 'with voice unchanged to hoarse or mute'; yet we need but to glance at Milton's own career to see how the conflict could disrupt the life and modify the talent of a man of letters. The temper of the times tended to draw men of literary gifts into partisan debate or to drive them into retreat. Neither condition was friendly to the perpetuation of the more vital types of literature that had flourished in the preceding age, or the begetting of new kinds to take their place. For more general reasons, also, in England, as elsewhere in Europe, the gorgeous day of the Renaissance was about over. The splendid exuberance of fantasy and form, in which felicity atoned for extravagance, was slipping into esoteric quaintness or tortured ingenuity and was being superseded by a more scholarly and self-conscious artistry, which aimed at a rational content, at clarity and symmetry of form, and a certain terseness and innateness of ornament. The decadence of the Renaissance impulse is seen in the English drama. Here, the penetrating passion of Shakespeare's supreme tragedies and the bold magnificence of his greater contemporaries was succeeded by searching and ingenious, but furtive and over-curious, studies of crime and erotic passion; while the gayety and glow of romantic comedy gave way to analytic satire, to a cold and coarse realism, or at worst, to mere obscene buffoonery. It was upon a drama of jaded beauty and spent wit that the Puritans closed the theaters in 1642.

These conditions were less disastrous to the short flights of the lyrist than to forms of literature requiring a more sustained effort of imagination. The seventeenth century produced an abundance of charming lyrical poetry. The gift was widely diffused, and, very frequently, we have two or three exquisite pieces from authors who have left hardly anything else of note. The stream of song, so abundant and fresh in the preceding age, was not, then, hushed; but its quality gradually changed. The 'melodious bursts' of the Elizabethans have a seemingly accidental magic, reminding us of genuine folk song; despite the superficial learning with which they are frequently decorated, they are true 'wood-notes wild,' Shakespeare's with the rest. The lyrics of the seventeenth century have a more rehearsed air. Though graceful and sincere, they are more obviously the product of artifice. There is more logic in their behavior, which smacks of an acquaintance with the more sophisticated Latin poets, with Horace and Catullus, and with Martial. As for native models, one discerns somewhat clearly, among the lyrics of the earlier part of the century, at least three poetical manners, which emanated, respectively, from Edmund Spenser, Ben Jonson, and John Donne.

The sensuous beauty, playful imagery, and fluent melody of Spenser are clearly present in the poems of William Browne and George Wither, and in the earlier poems of Milton. Jonson's fine finish, poise, and chastened sweetness are a forming and refining influence in the shorter lyrics of Robert Herrick, Thomas Carew, John Suckling, and Richard Lovelace. In John Donne, incisive and intricate thinking finds fantastic, mordant, and sometimes harsh, expression in far-fetched analogies and mystifying metaphors, and in subtle, original, sometimes violent, rhythms. The poetical apparatus of Donne, often, and his fancy, still more often, are essential in the passionate, soaring, and mystical outbursts of George Herbert, Richard Crashaw, and Henry Vaughan, and in the fantastic ingenuities of Francis Quarles.

Around the middle of the century appears a new departure in the development given to the 'closed' heroic couplet by Edmund Waller, John Denham, and Andrew Marvell. This verse-form, best adapted to epic and satire, had no important influence upon lyric, except, indirectly, through repression. Abraham Cowley is perhaps related to this group, though he wrote little in couplet form and is about equally 'the last of the fantastics' and an innovator of the new rationalism. The rationalistic tendency, which more and more became the trend of seventeenth century thought, had its inevitable effect upon the lyrical impulse and, by the close of the century, had virtually silenced it. A genuine, if shallow, vein of lyricism still lingered among the 'wits' of the Restoration, voicing, not passion or impassioned fancy, but polite gallantry, compliment, or satirical disdain. Some of the verses of the Earl of Dorset and the Earl of Rochester, finished and epigrammatic, rather accurately strike the pitch of what is commonly called *vers de société*.

THOMAS CAMPION
(1567-1620)

WHEN THOU MUST HOME

When thou must home to shades of underground,
    And there arrived, a new admirèd guest,
The beauteous spirits do engirt thee round,
    White Iope, blithe Helen, and the rest,
To hear the stories of thy finished love   5
From that smooth tongue whose music hell can move;

Then wilt thou speak of banqueting delights,
    Of masques and revels which sweet youth did make,
Of journeys and great challenges of knights,
    And all these triumphs for thy beauty's sake;   10
When thou hast told these honours done to thee,
Then tell, O tell, how thou didst murder me.

BASIA

Turn back, you wanton flyer,
    And answer my desire
        With mutual greeting.
Yet bend a little nearer,—
    True beauty still shines clearer   5
        In closer meeting!
Hearts with hearts delighted
    Should strive to be united,
Each other's arms with arms enchaining,—
        Hearts with a thought,   10
Rosy lips with a kiss still entertaining.

    What harvest half so sweet is
    As still to reap the kisses
        Grown ripe in sowing?
    And straight to be receiver   15
    Of that which thou art giver,
        Rich in bestowing?
    There's no strict observing
    Of times' or seasons' swerving,
There is ever one fresh spring abiding;—   20
        Then what we sow
With our lips let us reap, love's gains dividing.

A RENUNCIATION

Thou art not fair, for all thy red and white,
    For all those rosy ornaments in thee,—
Thou art not sweet, though made of mere delight,
    Nor fair, nor sweet—unless thou pity me!
I will not soothe thy fancies; thou shalt prove   5
That beauty is no beauty without love.

Yet love not me, nor seek not to allure
    My thoughts with beauty, were it more divine:
Thy smiles and kisses I cannot endure,
    I'll not be wrapped up in those arms of thine:
Now show it, if thou be a woman right—   11
Embrace and kiss and love me, in despite!

SIC TRANSIT

Come, cheerful day, part of my life to me;
    For while thou view'st me with thy fading light
Part of my life doth still depart with thee,
    And I still onward haste to my last night:
Time's fatal wings do ever forward fly—   5
So every day we live, a day we die.

But O ye nights ordained for barren rest,
    How are my days deprived of life in you
When heavy sleep my soul hath dispossest,
    By feignèd death life sweetly to renew!   10
Part of my life in that, you life deny:
So every day we live, a day we die.

BEN JONSON
(1573?-1637)

SONG TO CELIA

Drink to me only with thine eyes,
    And I will pledge with mine;
Or leave a kiss but in the cup,
    And I'll not look for wine.
The thirst that from the soul doth rise   5
    Doth ask a drink divine;
But might I of Jove's nectar sup,
    I would not change for thine.

I sent thee late a rosy wreath,
    Not so much honoring thee   10
As giving it a hope, that there
    It could not withered be.
But thou thereon didst only breathe,
    And sent'st it back to me;   14
Since when it grows, and smells, I swear,
    Not of itself, but thee.

SONG: TO CELIA

Come, my Celia, let us prove,
While we can, the sports of love.
Time will not be ours for ever;
He, at length, our good will sever;
Spend not then his gifts in vain: 5
Suns that set may rise again;
But if once we lose this light,
'T is with us perpetual night.

Why should we defer our joys?
Fame and rumor are but toys.
Cannot we delude the eyes
Of a few poor household spies?
Or his easier ears beguile,
Thus removèd by our wile?
'T is no sin love's fruits to steal;
But the sweet theft to reveal,
To be taken, to be seen,
These have crimes accounted been.

HYMN TO DIANA

Queen and Huntress, chaste and fair,
    Now the sun is laid to sleep,
Seated in thy silver chair
    State in wonted manner keep:
*Hesperus entreats thy light
Goddess excellently bright.*

Earth, let not thy envious shade
    Dare itself to interpose;
Cynthia's shining orb was made
    Heaven to clear when day did close:
*Bless us then with wishèd sight,
Goddess excellently bright.*

Lay thy bow of pearl apart
    And thy crystal-shining quiver;
Give unto the flying hart
    Space to breathe, how short soever:
*Thou that mak'st a day of night,
Goddess excellently bright!*

TO HEAVEN

Good and great God! can I not think of thee,
But it must straight my melancholy be?
Is it interpreted in me disease,
That, laden with my sins, I seek for ease?
O be thou witness, that the reins dost know
And hearts of all, if I be sad for show;
And judge me after, if I dare pretend
To aught but grace, or aim at other end.
As thou art all, so be thou all to me,
First, midst, and last, converted One and Three!
My faith, my hope, my love; and, in this state,
My judge, my witness, and my advocate!
Where have I been this while exiled from thee,
And whither rapt, now thou but stoop'st to me?
Dwell, dwell here still! O, being everywhere,
How can I doubt to find thee ever here?
I know my state, both full of shame and scorn,
Conceived in sin, and unto labor born,
Standing with fear, and must with horror fall,
And destined unto judgment, after all.
I feel my griefs too, and there scarce is ground
Upon my flesh t' inflict another wound;
Yet dare I not complain or wish for death,
With holy Paul, lest it be thought the breath
Of discontent; or that these prayers be
For weariness of life, not love of thee.

THE TRIUMPH OF CHARIS

See the chariot at hand here of Love,
    Wherein my Lady rideth!
Each that draws is a swan or a dove,
    And well the car Love guideth.
As she goes, all hearts do duty
    Unto her beauty;
And enamored, do wish, so they might
    But enjoy such a sight,
That they still were to run by her side,
Through swords, through seas, whither she would ride.

Do but look on her eyes, they do light
    All that Love's world compriseth!
Do but look on her hair, it is bright
    As Love's star when it riseth!
Do but mark, her forehead 's smoother
    Than words that soothe her;
And from her arched brows, such a grace
    Sheds itself through the face
As alone there triumphs to the life
All the gain, all the good, of the elements' strife

Have you seen but a bright lily grow
    Before rude hands have touched it?
Have you marked but the fall of the snow
    Before the soil hath smutched it?
Have you felt the wool of the beaver?
    Or swan's down ever?
Or have smelt o' the bud of the briar?
    Or the nard in the fire?
Or have tasted the bag of the bee?
Oh so white! Oh so soft! Oh so sweet is she!

AN EPITAPH ON SALATHIEL PAVY

Weep with me, all you that read
    This little story:
And know, for whom a tear you shed
    Death's self is sorry.
'T was a child that so did thrive
    In grace and feature,
As heaven and nature seemed to strive
    Which owned the creature.
Years he numbered scarce thirteen
    When fates turned cruel,
Yet three filled zodiacs had he been
    The stage's jewel;
And did act, what now we moan,
    Old men so duly,
As, sooth, the Parcæ thought him one,
    He played so truly.
So, by error, to his fate
    They all consented;
But viewing him since, alas, too late!
    They have repented;
And have sought, to give new birth,
    In baths to steep him;
But being so much too good for earth,
    Heaven vows to keep him.

EPITAPH ON ELIZABETH L. H.

Would'st thou hear what man can say
In a little? Reader, stay.

    Underneath this stone doth lie
As much beauty as could die:
Which in life did harbor give   5
To more virtue than doth live.

    If at all she had a fault,
Leave it buried in this vault.
One name was Elizabeth,
The other, let it sleep with death!   10
Fitter, where it died, to tell,
Than that it lived at all. Farewell!

TO THE MEMORY OF MY BELOVED, MASTER WILLIAM SHAKESPEARE

To draw no envy, Shakespeare, on thy name,
Am I thus ample to thy book and fame;
While I confess thy writings to be such
As neither man, nor muse, can praise too much.
'T is true, and all men's suffrage. But these ways   5
Were not the paths I meant unto thy praise;
For silliest ignorance on these may light,
Which, when it sounds at best, but echoes right;
Or blind affection, which doth ne'er advance
The truth, but gropes, and urgeth all by chance;
Or crafty malice might pretend this praise,   11
And think to ruin, where it seemed to raise.
These are, as some infamous bawd or whore
Should praise a matron. What could hurt her more?
But thou art proof against them, and, indeed,   15
Above the ill fortune of them, or the need.

    I therefore will begin. Soul of the age!
The applause, delight, the wonder of our stage!
My Shakespeare, rise! I will not lodge thee by
Chaucer, or Spenser, or bid Beaumont lie   20
A little further, to make thee a room:
Thou art a monument without a tomb,
And art alive still while thy book doth live
And we have wits to read and praise to give.
That I not mix thee so, my brain excuses,   25
I mean with great, but disproportioned Muses;
For if I thought my judgment were of years,
I should commit thee surely with thy peers,
And tell how far thou didst our Lyly outshine,
Or sporting Kyd, or Marlowe's mighty line.   30
And though thou hadst small Latin and less Greek,
From thence to honor thee, I would not seek
For names; but call forth thundering Æschylus,
Euripides, and Sophocles to us;
Pacuvius, Accius, him of Cordova dead,   35
To life again, to hear thy buskin tread,
And shake a stage; or, when thy socks were on,
Leave thee alone for the comparison
Of all that insolent Greece or haughty Rome
Sent forth, or since did from their ashes come.   40
Triumph, my Britain, thou hast one to show
To whom all scenes of Europe homage owe.
He was not of an age, but for all time!
And all the Muses still were in their prime,
When, like Apollo, he came forth to warm   45
Our ears, or like a Mercury to charm!
Nature herself was proud of his designs
And joyed to wear the dressing of his lines!
Which were so richly spun, and woven so fit,
As, since, she will vouchsafe no other wit.   50
The merry Greek, tart Aristophanes,
Neat Terence, witty Plautus, now not please;
But antiquated and deserted lie,
As they were not of Nature's family.

    Yet must I not give Nature all; thy art,   55
My gentle Shakespeare, must enjoy a part.
For though the poet's matter nature be,
His art doth give the fashion; and, that he
Who casts to write a living line, must sweat,
(Such as thine are) and strike the second heat   60
Upon the Muses' anvil; turn the same
(And himself with it) that he thinks to frame,
Or, for the laurel, he may gain a scorn;
For a good poet's made, as well as born.
And such wert thou!
                Look how the father's face   65
Lives in his issue, even so the race
Of Shakespeare's mind and manners brightly shines
In his well turnèd, and true filèd lines;
In each of which he seems to shake a lance,
As brandished at the eyes of ignorance.   70

    Sweet Swan of Avon! what a sight it were
To see thee in our waters yet appear,
And make those flights upon the banks of Thames,
That so did take Eliza, and our James!
But stay, I see thee in the hemisphere   75
Advanced, and made a constellation there!
Shine forth, thou Star of poets, and with rage
Or influence, chide or cheer the drooping stage,
Which, since thy flight from hence, hath mourn'd like night,
And despairs day, but for thy volume's light.   80

JOHN DONNE
(1573–1631)

SONG

    Go and catch a falling star,
        Get with child a mandrake root,
    Tell me where all past years are,
        Or who cleft the devil's foot;

Teach me to hear mermaids singing, 5
  To keep off envy's stinging,
    And find
    What wind
Serves to advance an honest mind.

If thou be'st born to strange sights, 10
  Things invisible go see,
Ride ten thousand days and nights
  Till Age snow white hairs on thee;
Thou, when thou return'st, wilt tell me
All strange wonders that befell thee, 15
    And swear
    No where
Lives a woman true and fair.

If thou find'st one, let me know;
  Such a pilgrimage were sweet. 20
Yet do not; I would not go,
  Though at next door we might meet.
Though she were true when you met her,
And last till you write your letter,
    Yet she 25
    Will be
False, ere I come, to two or three.

THE INDIFFERENT

I can love both fair and brown;
Her whom abundance melts, and her whom want betrays;
Her who loves loneness best, and her who masks and plays;
Her whom the country formed, and whom the town;
Her who believes, and her who tries; 5
Her who still weeps with spongy eyes,
And her who is dry cork and never cries.
I can love her, and her, and you, and you;
I can love any, so she be not true.

Will no other vice content you? 10
Will it not serve your turn to do as did your mothers?
Or have you all old vices spent and now would find out others?
Or doth a fear that men are true torment you?
O we are not, be not you so;
Let me—and do you—twenty know; 15
Rob me, but bind me not, and let me go.
Must I, who came to travel thorough you,
Grow your fixed subject, because you are true?

Venus heard me sigh this song;
And by love's sweetest part, variety, she swore,
She heard not this till now; it should be so no more. 21
She went, examined, and returned ere long,
And said, 'Alas! some two or three
Poor heretics in love there be,
Which think to stablish dangerous constancy. 25
But I have told them, "Since you will be true,
You shall be true to them who're false to you."'

THE CANONIZATION

For God's sake hold your tongue, and let me love;
  Or chide my palsy, or my gout;
  My five gray hairs, or ruined fortune flout;
With wealth your state, your mind with arts improve;
  Take you a course, get you a place, 5
  Observe his Honor, or his Grace;
Or the king's real, or his stampèd face
  Contemplate; what you will, approve,
  So you will let me love.

Alas! alas! who's injured by my love? 10
  What merchant's ships have my sighs drowned?
  Who says my tears have overflowed his ground?
When did my colds a forward spring remove?
  When did the heats which my veins fill
  Add one more to the plaguy bill? 15
Soldiers find wars, and lawyers find out still
  Litigious men, which quarrels move,
  Though she and I do love.

Call's what you will, we are made such by love;
  Call her one, me another fly, 20
  We're tapers too, and at our own cost die,
And we in us find th' eagle and the dove.
  The phœnix riddle hath more wit
  By us; we two being one, are it;
So, to one neutral thing both sexes fit. 25
  We die and rise the same, and prove
  Mysterious by this love.

We can die by it, if not live by love,
  And if unfit for tomb or hearse
  Our legend be, it will be fit for verse; 30
And if no piece of chronicle we prove,
  We'll build in sonnets pretty rooms;
  As well a well-wrought urn becomes
The greatest ashes, as half-acre tombs,
  And by these hymns all shall approve 35
  Us canonized for love;

And thus invoke us, 'You, whom reverend love
  Made one another's hermitage;
  You, to whom love was peace, that now is rage;
Who did the whole world's soul contract, and drove 40
  Into the glasses of your eyes;
  So made such mirrors, and such spies,
That they did all to you epitomize—
  Countries, towns, courts beg from above
  A pattern of your love.' 45

THE DREAM

Dear love, for nothing less than thee
Would I have broke this happy dream;
  It was a theme
For reason, much too strong for fantasy.

Therefore, thou waked'st me wisely; yet 5
My dream thou brok'st not, but continued'st it.
Thou art so true that thoughts of thee suffice
To make dreams truths, and fables histories;
Enter these arms, for since thou thought'st it best
Not to dream all my dream, let's act the rest. 10

As lightning, or a taper's light,
Thine eyes, and not thine noise, waked me;
    Yet I thought thee—
For thou lov'st truth—an angel, at first sight;
But when I saw thou saw'st my heart, 15
And knew'st my thoughts beyond an angel's art,
When thou knew'st what I dreamt, when thou knew'st when
Excess of joy would wake me, and cam'st then,
I must confess it could not choose but be
Profane to think thee anything but thee. 20

Coming and staying showed thee thee,
But rising makes me doubt that now
    Thou art not thou.
That love is weak where fear's as strong as he;
'Tis not all spirit pure and brave 25
If mixture it of fear, shame, honor have.
Perchance as torches, which must ready be,
Men light and put out, so thou deal'st with me.
Thou cam'st to kindle, go'st to come: then I
Will dream that hope again, but else would die. 30

LOVE'S DEITY

I LONG to talk with some old lover's ghost
  Who died before the god of love was born.
I cannot think that he who then loved most
  Sunk so low as to love one which did scorn.
But since this god produced a destiny, 5
And that vice-nature, custom, lets it be,
  I must love her that loves not me.

Sure they which made him god, meant not so much,
  Nor he in his young godhead practised it.
But when an even flame two hearts did touch, 10
  His office was indulgently to fit
Actives to passives. Correspondency
Only his subject was; it cannot be
  Love till I love her who loves me.

But every modern god will now extend 15
  His vast prerogative as far as Jove.
To rage, to lust, to write to, to commend,
  All is the purlieu of the god of love.
O! were we wakened by this tyranny
To ungod this child again, it could not be 20
  I should love her who loves not me.

Rebel and atheist too, why murmur I,
  As though I felt the worst that love could do?
Love may make me leave loving, or might try
  A deeper plague, to make her love me too; 25
Which, since she loves before, I'm loth to see.
Falsehood is worse than hate; and that must be,
  If she whom I love, should love me.

THE FUNERAL

WHOEVER comes to shroud me, do not harm
    Nor question much
That subtle wreath of hair about mine arm;
The mystery, the sign you must not touch,
    For 'tis my outward soul, 5
Viceroy to that which, unto heav'n being gone,
    Will leave this to control
And keep these limbs, her provinces, from dissolution.

For if the sinewy thread my brain lets fall
    Through every part 10
Can tie those parts, and make me one of all;
Those hairs, which upward grew, and strength and art
Have from a better brain,
Can better do't: except she meant that I
    By this should know my pain, 15
As prisoners then are manacled, when they're condemned to die.

Whate'er she meant by't, bury it with me,
    For since I am
Love's martyr, it might breed idolatry
If into other hands these reliques came. 20
    As 't was humility
T' afford to it all that a soul can do,
    So 't is some bravery
That, since you would have none of me, I bury some of you.

THE COMPUTATION

FOR my first twenty years, since yesterday,
I scarce believed thou couldst be gone away;
For forty more I fed on favors past,
And forty on hopes, that thou wouldst they might last;
Tears drowned one hundred, and sighs blew out two; 5
A thousand I did neither think nor do.
Or not divide, all being one thought of you;
Or in a thousand more, forgot that too.
Yet call not this long life; but think that I
Am, by being dead, immortal; can ghosts die? 10

FORGET

IF poisonous minerals, and if that tree
Whose fruit threw death on else immortal us,
If lecherous goats, if serpents envious
Cannot be damned, alas! why should I be?

Why should intent or reason, born in me, 5
Make sins, else equal, in me more heinous?
And, mercy being easy and glorious
To God, in his stern wrath why threatens he?

But who am I, that dare dispute with thee?
O God, O! of thine only worthy blood   10
And my tears make a heavenly Lethean flood,
And drown in it my sin's black memory.
That thou remember them, some claim as debt;
I think it mercy if thou wilt forget.

DEATH

Death, be not proud, though some have callèd thee
Mighty and dreadful, for thou art not so;
For those whom thou think'st thou dost overthrow
Die not, poor Death; nor yet canst thou kill me.
From rest and sleep, which but thy picture be,   5
Much pleasure; then from thee much more must flow;
And soonest our best men with thee do go—
Rest of their bones and souls' delivery!
Thou'rt slave to fate, chance, kings, and desperate men,   9
And dost with poison, war, and sickness dwell;
And poppy or charms can make us sleep as well
And better than thy stroke. Why swell'st thou then?
One short sleep past, we wake eternally,
And Death shall be no more: Death, thou shalt die!   14

A HYMN TO GOD THE FATHER

Wilt thou forgive that sin where I begun,
  Which was my sin, though it were done before?
Wilt thou forgive that sin through which I run,
  And do run still, though still I do deplore?
When thou hast done, thou hast not done;   5
  For I have more.

Wilt thou forgive that sin which I have won
  Others to sin, and made my sins their door?
Wilt thou forgive that sin which I did shun
  A year or two, but wallowed in a score?   10
When thou hast done, thou hast not done;
  For I have more.

I have a sin of fear, that when I've spun
  My last thread, I shall perish on the shore;
But swear by thyself that at my death thy Son
  Shall shine as he shines now and heretofore; 16
And having done that, thou hast done;
  I fear no more.

JOHN FLETCHER
(1579–1625)
LOVE'S EMBLEMS

Now the lusty spring is seen;
  Golden yellow, gaudy blue,
  Daintily invite the view,
Everywhere on every green,
Roses blushing as they blow,   5
  And enticing men to pull
Lilies whiter than the snow,
  Woodbines of sweet honey full:
All love's emblems, and all cry,
'Ladies, if not plucked, we die.'   10

Yet the lusty spring hath stayed;
  Blushing red and purest white
  Daintily to love invite
Every woman, every maid.
Cherries kissing as they grow,   15
  And inviting men to taste,
Apples even ripe below,
  Winding gently to the waist:
All love's emblems, and all cry,
'Ladies, if not plucked, we die.'   20

MELANCHOLY

Hence, all you vain delights,
As short as are the nights
  Wherein you spend your folly!
There's naught in this life sweet,
If man were wise to see 't,   5
  But only melancholy;
  O sweetest melancholy!
Welcome, folded arms and fixèd eyes,
A sigh that piercing mortifies,
A look that's fastened to the ground,   10
A tongue chained up without a sound!
Fountain heads and pathless groves,
Places which pale passion loves!
Moonlight walks, when all the fowls
Are warmly housed save bats and owls!   15
A midnight bell, a parting groan,
These are the sounds we feed upon.
Then stretch our bones in a still gloomy valley;
Nothing's so dainty sweet as lovely melancholy.

SONG TO BACCHUS

God Lyæus, ever young,
Ever honored, ever sung;
Stained with blood of lusty grapes.
In a thousand lusty shapes,
Dance upon the mazer's brim,   5
In the crimson liquor swim;
From thy plenteous hand divine
Let a river run with wine;
God of youth, let this day here
Enter neither care nor fear!   10

BEAUTY CLEAR AND FAIR

Beauty clear and fair,
  Where the air
Rather like a perfume dwells;
  Where the violet and the rose
  Their blue veins and blush disclose,   5
And come to honor nothing else.

Where to live near,
    And planted there,
Is to live, and still live new;
    Where to gain a favor is   10
More than light, perpetual bliss—
Make me live by serving you.

Dear, again back recall
    To this light
A stranger to himself and all;   15
    Both the wonder and the story
    Shall be yours, and eke the glory:
I am your servant, and your thrall.

WEEP NO MORE

Weep no more, nor sigh, nor groan,
Sorrow calls no time that's gone;
Violets plucked the sweetest rain
Makes not fresh nor grow again;
Trim thy locks, look cheerfully;   5
Fate's hid ends eyes cannot see;
Joys as wingèd dreams fly fast,
Why should sadness longer last?
Grief is but a wound to woe;
Gentlest fair, mourn, mourn no mo.   10

ASPATIA'S SONG

Lay a garland on my hearse
    Of the dismal yew;
Maidens, willow branches bear;
    Say, I dièd true.

My love was false, but I was firm   5
    From my hour of birth.
Upon my buried body lie
    Lightly, gentle earth!

FRANCIS BEAUMONT
(1584–1616)

ON THE LIFE OF MAN

Like to the falling of a star,
Or as the flights of eagles are,
Or like the fresh spring's gaudy hue,
Or silver drops of morning dew,
Or like a wind that chafes the flood,   5
Or bubbles which on water stood:
Even such is man, whose borrowed light
Is straight called in and paid to night:
The wind blows out, the bubble dies,
The spring intombed in autumn lies;   10
The dew's dried up, the star is shot,
The flight is past, and man forgot.

LINES ON THE TOMBS IN WESTMINSTER

Mortality, behold and fear!
What a change of flesh is here!
Think how many royal bones
Sleep within this heap of stones;
Here they lie had realms and lands,   5
Who now want strength to stir their hands;
Where from their pulpits sealed with dust
They preach, 'In greatness is no trust.'
Here's an acre sown indeed
With the richest royal'st seed   10
That the earth did e'er suck in,
Since the first man died for sin;
Here the bones of birth have cried,
'Though gods they were, as men they died.'
Here are sands, ignoble things,   15
Dropt from the ruined sides of kings.
Here's a world of pomp and state,
Buried in dust, once dead by fate.

GEORGE WITHER
(1588–1667)

THE LOVER'S RESOLUTION

Shall I, wasting in despair,
Die, because a woman's fair?
Or make pale my cheeks with care,
'Cause another's rosy are?
Be she fairer than the day,   5
Or the flowery meads in May!
    If she be not so to me,
    What care I how fair she be?

Should my heart be grieved or pined,
'Cause I see a woman kind?   10
Or a well disposèd nature
Joinèd with a lovely feature?
Be she meeker, kinder than
Turtle dove, or pelican!
    If she be not so to me,   15
    What care I how kind she be?

Shall a woman's virtues move
Me to perish for her love?
Or her well deserving known,
Make me quite forget mine own?   20
Be she with that goodness blest
Which may gain her name of best!
    If she be not such to me,
    What care I how good she be?

'Cause her fortune seems too high,   25
Shall I play the fool, and die?
Those that bear a noble mind,
Where they want of riches find,

Think 'What, with them, they would do
That, without them, dare to woo!'   30
    And unless that mind I see,
    What care I though great she be?

Great, or good, or kind, or fair,
I will ne'er the more despair!
If she love me (this believe!)   35
I will die, ere she shall grieve!
If she slight me, when I woo,
I can scorn, and let her go!
    For if she be not for me,
    What care I for whom she be?   40

WHEN WE ARE UPON THE SEAS

From HALLELUJAH

ON those great waters now I am,
    Of which I have been told,
That whosoever thither came
    Should wonders there behold.
In this unsteady place of fear,   5
    Be present, Lord, with me;
For in these depths of water here,
    I depths of danger see.

A stirring courser now I sit,
    A headstrong steed I ride,   10
That champs and foams upon the bit
    Which curbs his lofty pride.
The softest whistling of the winds
    Doth make him gallop fast;
And as their breath increased he finds   15
    The more he maketh haste.

Take thou, Oh Lord! the reins in hand,
    Assume our Master's room;
Vouchsafe thou at our helm to stand,
    And pilot to become.   20
Trim thou the sails, and let good speed
    Accompany our haste;
Sound thou the channels at our need
    And anchor for us cast.

A fit and favorable wind   25
    To further us, provide;
And let it wait on us behind,
    Or lackey by our side.
From sudden gusts, from storms, from sands,
    And from the raging wave;   30
From shallows, rocks, and pirates' hands,
    Men, goods, and vessel save.

Preserve us from the wants, the fear,
    And sickness of the seas;
But chiefly from our sins, which are   35
    A danger worse than these.
Lord! let us, also, safe arrive
    Where we desire to be;
And for thy mercies let us give
    Due thanks and praise to thee.   40

THE PRAYER OF OLD AGE

From HALLELUJAH

As this my carnal robe grows old,
Soiled, rent, and worn by length of years,
Let me on that by faith lay hold
Which man in life immortal wears:
    So sanctify my days behind,   5
    Do let my manners be refined,
That when my soul and flesh must part,
There lurk no terrors in my heart.

So shall my rest be safe and sweet
When I am lodgèd in my grave;   10
And when my soul and body meet,
A joyful meeting they shall have;
    Their essence, then, shall be divine,
    This muddy flesh shall starlike shine,
And God shall that fresh youth restore   15
Which will abide for evermore.

WILLIAM BROWNE
(1591–1643)

ON THE COUNTESS DOWAGER OF PEMBROKE

UNDERNEATH this sable hearse
Lies the subject of all verse:
Sidney's sister, Pembroke's mother:
Death, ere thou hast slain another
Fair and learned and good as she,   5
Time shall throw a dart at thee.

Marble piles let no man raise
To her name: for after days
Some kind woman, born as she,
Reading this, like Niobe   10
Shall turn marble, and become
Both her mourner and her tomb.

ROBERT HERRICK
(1591–1674)

THE ARGUMENT OF HIS BOOK

I SING of brooks, of blossoms, birds and bowers,
Of April, May, of June and July-flowers;
I sing of May-poles, hock-carts, wassails, wakes,
Of bridegrooms, brides, and of their bridal cakes;
I write of youth, of love, and have access   5
By these to sing of cleanly wantonness;
I sing of dews, of rains, and, piece by piece,
Of balm, of oil, of spice and ambergris;
I sing of times trans-shifting, and I write
How roses first came red and lilies white;   10

I write of groves, of twilights, and I sing
The court of Mab, and of the Fairy King;
I write of hell; I sing (and ever shall)
Of heaven, and hope to have it after all.

CORINNA'S GOING A-MAYING

Get up, get up for shame, the blooming morn
Upon her wings presents the god unshorn.
   See how Aurora throws her fair
     Fresh-quilted colors through the air:
   Get up, sweet slug-a-bed, and see   5
   The dew bespangling herb and tree.
Each flower has wept and bowèd toward the east
Above an hour since: yet you not dressed;
   Nay! not so much as out of bed?
   When all the birds have matins said   10
   And sung their thankful hymns, 'tis sin,
   Nay, profanation, to keep in,
Whenas a thousand virgins on this day
Spring, sooner than the lark, to fetch in May.

Rise, and put on your foliage, and be seen   15
To come forth, like the spring-time, fresh and green,
   And sweet as Flora. Take no care
   For jewels for your gown or hair:
   Fear not; the leaves will strew
   Gems in abundance upon you: 20
Besides, the childhood of the day has kept,
Against you come, some orient pearls unwept;
   Come and receive them while the light
   Hangs on the dew-locks of the night:
   And Titan on the eastern hill   25
   Retires himself, or else stands still
Till you come forth. Wash, dress, be brief in praying:
Few beads are best when once we go a-Maying.

Come, my Corinna, come; and, coming mark   29
How each field turns a street, each street a park
   Made green and trimmed with trees; see how
   Devotion gives each house a bough
   Or branch: each porch, each door ere this
   An ark, a tabernacle is,
Made up of white-thorn, neatly interwove;   35
As if here were those cooler shades of love.
   Can such delights be in the street
   And open fields and we not see't?
   Come, we'll abroad; and let's obey
   The proclamation made for May: 40
And sin no more, as we have done, by staying;
But, my Corinna, come, let's go a-Maying.

There's not a budding boy or girl this day
But is got up, and gone to bring in May.
   A deal of youth, ere this, is come   45
   Back, and with white-thorn laden home.
   Some have despatched their cakes and cream
   Before that we have left to dream:
And some have wept, and wooed, and plighted troth,
And chose their priest, ere we can cast off sloth:
   Many a green-gown has been given;   51
   Many a kiss, both odd and even:
   Many a glance too has been sent
   From out the eye, love's firmament;
Many a jest told of the keys betraying   55
This night, and locks picked, yet we're not a-Maying.

Come, let us go while we are in our prime;
And take the harmless folly of the time.
   We shall grow old apace, and die
   Before we know our liberty.   60
   Our life is short, and our days run
   As fast away as does the sun;
And, as a vapor or a drop of rain,
Once lost, can ne'er be found again,
   So when or you or I are made   65
   A fable, song, or fleeting shade,
   All love, all liking, all delight
   Lies drowned with us in endless night.
Then while time serves, and we are but decaying,
Come, my Corinna, come let's go a-Maying.   70

UPON JULIA'S CLOTHES

Whenas in silks my Julia goes,
Then, then, methinks, how sweetly flows
The liquefaction of her clothes.

Next, when I cast mine eyes, and see
That brave vibration, each way free,   5
O, how that glittering taketh me!

TO THE VIRGINS TO MAKE MUCH OF TIME

Gather ye rosebuds while ye may,
   Old Time is still aflying;
And this same flower that smiles to-day,
   To-morrow will be dying.

The glorious lamp of heaven, the sun,   5
   The higher he's a-getting,
The sooner will his race be run,
   And nearer he's to setting.

That age is best which is the first,
   When youth and blood are warmer;   10
But being spent, the worse and worst
   Times still succeed the former.

Then be not coy, but use your time,
   And while ye may, go marry;
For, having lost but once your prime,   15
   You may forever tarry.

TO DAFFODILS

Fair Daffodils, we weep to see
    You haste away so soon;
As yet the early rising sun
    Has not attained his noon.
        Stay, stay, 5
      Until the hasting day
        Has run
    But to the even-song;
And, having prayed together, we
    Will go with you along. 10

We have short time to stay, as you,
    We have as short a spring;
As quick a growth to meet decay,
    As you, or anything.
        We die 15
    As your hours do, and dry
        Away,
    Like to the summer's rain;
Or as the pearls of morning's dew,
    Ne'er to be found again. 20

TO MUSIC

Charm me asleep, and melt me so
    With thy delicious numbers,
That being ravished, hence I go
    Away in easy slumbers.
Ease my sick head, 5
And make my bed,
    Thou power that canst sever
From me this ill;
And quickly still,
    Though thou not kill 10
My fever.

Thou sweetly canst convert the same
    From a consuming fire,
Into a gentle-licking flame,
    And make it thus expire. 15
Then make me weep
My pains asleep,
    And give me such reposes
That I, poor I,
May think, thereby, 20
I live and die
    'Mongst roses.

Fall on me like a silent dew,
    Or like those maiden showers,
Which, by the peep of day, do strew 25
    A baptism o'er the flowers.
Melt, melt my pains
With thy soft strains;
    That having ease me given,
With full delight, 30
I leave this light,
And take my flight
    For heaven.

THE NIGHT-PIECE, TO JULIA

Her eyes the glowworm lend thee,
    The shooting stars attend thee;
        And the elves also,
        Whose little eyes glow
Like the sparks of fire, befriend thee. 5

No Will-o'-th'-Wisp mislight thee,
Nor snake or slowworm bite thee;
        But on, on thy way,
        Not making a stay,
Since ghost there's none to affright thee. 10

Let not the dark thee cumber;
What though the moon does slumber?
        The stars of the night
        Will lend thee their light,
Like tapers clear, without number. 15

Then, Julia, let me woo thee,
Thus, thus to come unto me;
        And when I shall meet
        Thy silvery feet,
My soul I'll pour into thee. 20

AN ODE FOR BEN JONSON

        Ah, Ben!
      Say how or when
    Shall we, thy guests,
Meet at those lyric feasts,
      Made at the Sun, 5
    The Dog, the Triple Tun;
Where we such clusters had,
As made us nobly wild, not mad?
And yet each verse of thine
Out-did the meat, out-did the frolic wine. 10

        My Ben!
      Or come again,
      Or send to us
    Thy wit's great overplus;
    But teach us yet 15
    Wisely to husband it,
    Lest we that talent spend;
And having once brought to an end
    That precious stock, the store
Of such a wit the world should have no more. 20

A THANKSGIVING TO GOD FOR HIS HOUSE

    Lord, thou hast given me a cell
        Wherein to dwell,
    A little house, whose humble roof
        Is weather-proof,
    Under the spars of which I lie 5
        Both soft and dry;

Where thou, my chamber for to ward,
    Hast set a guard
Of harmless thoughts to watch and keep
    Me, while I sleep.   10
Low is my porch, as is my fate,
    Both void of state;
And yet the threshold of my door
    Is worn by th' poor,
Who thither come and freely get   15
    Good words, or meat
Like as my parlor, so my hall
    And kitchen's small;
A little buttery, and therein
    A little bin,   20
Which keeps my little loaf of bread
    Unchipped, unflead;
Some brittle sticks of thorn or briar
    Make me a fire,
Close by whose living coal I sit,   25
    And glow like it.
Lord, I confess, too, when I dine,
    The pulse is thine,
And all those other bits that be
    There placed by thee;   30
The worts, the purslain, and the mess
    Of water-cress,
Which of thy kindness thou hast sent;
    And my content
Makes those, and my belovèd beet,   35
    To be more sweet.
'T is thou that crown'st my glittering hearth
    With guiltless mirth,
And giv'st me wassail bowls to drink,
    Spiced to the brink.   40
Lord, 'tis thy plenty-dropping hand
    That soils my land,
And giv'st me, for my bushel sown,
    Twice ten for one;
Thou mak'st my teeming hen to lay   45
    Her egg each day;
Besides my healthful ewes to bear
    Me twins each year;
The while the conduits of my kine
    Run cream, for wine.   50
All these, and better thou dost send
    Me, to this end,
That I should render, for my part,
    A thankful heart,
Which, fired with incense, I resign,   55
    As wholly thine;
But the acceptance, that must be,
    My Christ, by thee.

GRACE FOR A CHILD

Here, a little child, I stand,
Heaving up my either hand:
Cold as paddocks though they be,
Here I lift them up to thee,
For a benison to fall   5
On our meat, and on us all.
    Amen.

HIS PRAYER FOR ABSOLUTION

For those my unbaptizèd rimes,
Writ in my wild unhallowed times,
For every sentence, clause, and word,
That's not inlaid with thee, my Lord
Forgive me, God, and blot each line   5
Out of my book that is not thine.
But if 'mongst all, thou find'st here one
Worthy thy benediction,
That one of all the rest shall be
The glory of my work and me.   10

FRANCIS QUARLES
(1592–1644)

AN ECSTASY

E'en like two little bank-dividing brooks,
    That wash the pebbles with their wanton streams,
And having ranged and search'd a thousand nooks,
    Meet both at length in silver-breasted Thames,
Where in a greater current they conjoin: 5
So I my Best-belovèd's am; so He is mine.

E'en so we met; and after long pursuit,
    E'en so we joined; we both became entire;
No need for either to renew a suit,
    For I was flax, and He was flames of fire: 10
Our firm-united souls did more than twine;
So I my Best-belovèd's am; so He is mine.

If all those glittering monarchs, that command
    The servile quarters of this earthly ball,
Should tender in exchange their shares of land,   15
    I would not change my fortunes for them all:
Their wealth is but a counter to my coin:
The world's but theirs; but my Belovèd's mine.

GEORGE HERBERT
(1593–1633)

VIRTUE

Sweet day, so cool, so calm, so bright,
    The bridal of the earth and sky!
The dew shall weep thy fall to-night;
    For thou must die.

Sweet rose, whose hue, angry and brave,   5
    Bids the rash gazer wipe his eye,
Thy root is ever in its grave,
    And thou must die.

Sweet spring, full of sweet days and roses,
    A box where sweets compacted lie,   10
My music shows ye have your closes,
    And all must die.

Only a sweet and virtuous soul,
    Like seasoned timber, never gives;
But though the whole world turn to coal,   15
    Then chiefly lives.

LOVE

Love bade me welcome; yet my soul drew back,
    Guilty of dust and sin,
But quick-eyed Love, observing me grow slack
    From my first entrance in,
Drew nearer to me, sweetly questioning,   5
    If I lacked anything.

'A guest,' I answered, 'worthy to be here:'
    Love said, 'You shall be he.'
'I, the unkind, ungrateful? Ah, my dear,
    I cannot look on thee!'   10
Love took my hand and smiling did reply,
    'Who made the eyes but I?'

'Truth, Lord; but I have marred them: let my shame
    Go where it doth deserve.'
'And know you not,' says Love, 'who bore the blame?'   15
    'My dear, then I will serve.'
'You must sit down,' says Love, 'and taste my meat.'
    So I did sit and eat.

THE COLLAR

I struck the board, and cried, 'No more;
    I will abroad!
What! shall I ever sigh and pine?
    My lines and life are free; free as the road,
Loose as the wind, as large as store.   5
    Shall I be still in suit?
Have I no harvest but a thorn
    To let me blood, and not restore
What I have lost with cordial fruit?
    Sure there was wine   10
Before my sighs did dry it; there was corn
    Before my tears did drown it;
Is the year only lost to me?
    Have I no bays to crown it,
No flowers, no garlands gay? all blasted,   15
    All wasted?
Not so, my heart, but there is fruit,
    And thou hast hands.
Recover all thy sigh-blown age
On double pleasures; leave thy cold dispute   20
Of what is fit and not; forsake thy cage,
    Thy rope of sands
Which petty thoughts have made; and made to thee
    Good cable, to enforce and draw,
        And be thy law,   25
While thou didst wink and wouldst not see.
    Away! take heed;
        I will abroad.
Call in thy death's head there, tie up thy fears:
    He that forbears   30
    To suit and serve his need
        Deserves his load.'
But as I raved, and grew more fierce and wild
    At every word,
Methought I heard one calling, 'Child';   35
    And I replied, 'My Lord.'

THE QUIP

The merry World did on a day
    With his train-bands and mates agree
To meet together where I lay,
    And all in sport to jeer at me.

First Beauty crept into a rose,   5
    Which when I pluckt not, 'Sir,' said she,
'Tell me, I pray, whose hands are those?'
    But Thou shalt answer, Lord, for me.

Then Money came, and chinking still,
    'What tune is this, poor man?' said he: 10
'I heard in Music you had skill;'
    But Thou shalt answer, Lord, for me.

Then came brave Glory puffing by
    In silks that whistled, who but he!
He scarce allowed me half an eye;   15
    But Thou shalt answer, Lord, for me.

Then came quick Wit and Conversation,
    And he would needs a comfort be,
And, to be short, make an oration:
    But Thou shalt answer, Lord, for me.   20

Yet when the hour of Thy design
    To answer these fine things shall come,
Speak not at large; say, 'I am Thine,'
    And then they have their answer home.

THE WORLD

Love built a stately house, where Fortune came;
    And spinning fancies, she was heard to say
That her fine cobwebs did support the frame,
Whereas they were supported by the same;
    But Wisdom quickly swept them all away.   5

Then Pleasure came, who, liking not the fashion,
    Began to make balconies, terraces,
Till she had weakened all by alteration;
But reverend laws, and many a proclamation,
    Reformèd all at length with menaces.   10

Then entered Sin, and with that sycamore
    Whose leaves first sheltered man from
        drought and dew,
Working and winding slily evermore,
The inward walls and summers cleft and tore;
    But Grace shored these, and cut that as it
        grew.   15

Then Sin combined with Death in a firm band
    To raze the building to the very floor:
Which they effected, none could them with-
        stand;
But Love and Grace took Glory by the hand,
    And built a braver palace than before. 20

THE PULLEY

When God at first made man,
Having a glass of blessing standing by;
'Let us,' said he, 'pour on him all we can:
Let the world's riches, which dispersèd lie,
    Contract into a span.'   5

So Strength first made a way;
Then Beauty flowed; then Wisdom, Honor,
    Pleasure.
When almost all was out, God made a stay,
Perceiving that alone, of all his treasure,
    Rest in the bottom lay.   10

'For if I should,' said he,
'Bestow this jewel also on my creature,
He would adore my gifts instead of me,
And rest in Nature, not the God of Nature;
    So both should losers be.   15

'Yet let him keep the rest,
But keep them with repining restlessness;
    Let him be rich and weary, that at least,
If goodness lead him not, yet weariness
    May toss him to my breast.'   20

JAMES SHIRLEY
(1596–1666)

THE GLORIES OF OUR BLOOD AND STATE

The glories of our blood and state
    Are shadows, not substantial things;
There is no armor against fate;
    Death lays his icy hand on kings:
        Sceptre and crown   5
        Must tumble down,
And in the dust be equal made
With the poor crooked scythe and spade.

Some men with swords may reap the field,
    And plant fresh laurels where they kill: 10
But their strong nerves at last must yield;
    They tame but one another still:
        Early or late
        They stoop to fate,
And must give up their murmuring breath 15
When they, pale captives, creep to death.

The garlands wither on your brow;
    Then boast no more your mighty deeds;
Upon Death's purple altar now
    See where the victor-victim bleeds: 20
        Your heads must come
        To the cold tomb;
Only the actions of the just
Smell sweet, and blossom in their dust.

THOMAS CAREW
(1598?–1639?)

SONG

Ask me no more where Jove bestows,
When June is past, the fading rose,
For in your beauty's orient deep
These flowers, as in their causes, sleep.

Ask me no more whither do stray   5
The golden atoms of the day,
For, in pure love, heaven did prepare
Those powders to enrich your hair.

Ask me no more whither doth haste
The nightingale when May is past,   10
For in your sweet dividing throat
She winters and keeps warm her note.

Ask me no more where those stars light
That downwards fall in dead of night,
For in your eyes they sit, and there   15
Fixèd become as in their sphere.

Ask me no more if east or west
The Phœnix builds her spicy nest,
For unto you at last she flies,
And in your fragrant bosom dies.   20

SONG

Would you know what's soft? I dare
Not bring you to the down, or air,
Nor to stars to show what's bright,
Nor to snow to teach you white;

Nor, if you would music hear,   5
Call the orbs to take your ear;
Nor, to please your sense, bring forth
Bruisèd nard, or what's more worth;

Or on food were your thoughts placed,
Bring you nectar for a taste;   10
Would you have all these in one,
Name my mistress, and 'tis done.

THE PROTESTATION

No more shall meads be decked with flowers,
Nor sweetness dwell in rosy bowers,
Nor greenest buds on branches spring,
Nor warbling birds delight to sing,
Nor April violets paint the grove,   5
If I forsake my Celia's love.

The fish shall in the ocean burn,
And fountains sweet shall bitter turn,
The humble oak no flood shall know
When floods shall highest hills o'erflow,   10
Black Lethe shall oblivion leave,
If e'er my Celia I deceive.

Love shall his bow and shaft lay by,
And Venus' doves want wings to fly,
The Sun refuse to show his light,   15
And day shall then be turned to night,
And in that night no star appear,
If once I leave my Celia dear.

Love shall no more inhabit earth,
Nor lovers more shall love for worth,   20
Nor joy above in heaven dwell,
Nor pain torment poor souls in hell,
Grim death no more shall horrid prove,
If e'er I leave bright Celia's love.

PERSUASIONS TO JOY: A SONG

If the quick spirits in your eye
Now languish and anon must die;
If every sweet and every grace
Must fly from that forsaken face;
   Then, Celia, let us reap our joys   5
   Ere Time such goodly fruit destroys.

Or if that golden fleece must grow
For ever free from agèd snow;
If those bright suns must know no shade
Nor your fresh beauties ever fade;   10
   Then fear not, Celia, to bestow
   What, still being gathered, still must grow.

Thus either Time his sickle brings
In vain, or else in vain his wings.

INGRATEFUL BEAUTY THREATENED

Know, Celia, since thou art so proud,
   'T was I that gave thee thy renown.
Thou hadst in the forgotten crowd
   Of common beauties lived unknown,
Had not my verse extolled thy name,   5
   And with it imped the wings of Fame.

That killing power is none of thine:
   I gave it to thy voice and eyes;
Thy sweets, thy graces, all are mine;
   Thou art my star, shin'st in my skies;   10
Then dart not from thy borrowed sphere
Lightning on him that fixed thee there.

Tempt me with such affrights no more,
   Lest what I made I uncreate;
Let fools thy mystic form adore,   15
   I know thee in thy mortal state.
Wise poets, that wrapt Truth in tales,
Knew her themselves through all her veils

AN EPITAPH

This little vault, this narrow room,
Of love and beauty is the tomb;
The dawning beam, that 'gan to clear
Our cloudèd sky, lies darkened here,
For ever set to us: by death   5
Sent to enflame the world beneath.
'T was but a bud, yet did contain
More sweetness than shall spring again;
A budding star, that might have grown
Into a sun when it had blown.   10
This hopeful beauty did create
New life in love's declining state;
But now his empire ends, and we
From fire and wounding darts are free;
   His brand, his bow, let no man fear: 15
   The flames, the arrows, all lie here.

SIR WILLIAM DAVENANT
(1606-1668)

SONG

The lark now leaves his wat'ry nest,
   And climbing, shakes his dewy wings.
He takes this window for the East,
   And to implore your light he sings—
Awake, awake! the morn will never rise   5
Till she can dress her beauty at your eyes.

The merchant bows unto the seaman's star,
   The ploughman from the sun his season takes;
But still the lover wonders what they are
   Who look for day before his mistress wakes.   10
Awake, awake! break thro' your veils of lawn!
And draw your curtains, and begin the dawn!

PRAISE AND PRAYER

Praise is devotion fit for mighty minds,
   The diff'ring world's agreeing sacrifice;
Where Heaven divided faiths united finds:
   But prayer in various discord upward flies.

For Prayer the ocean is where diversely 5
  Men steer their course, each to a sev'ral coast;
Where all our interests so discordant be
  That half beg winds by which the rest are lost.

By penitence when we ourselves forsake,
  'Tis but in wise design on piteous Heaven; 10
In praise we nobly give what God may take,
  And are, without a beggar's blush, forgiven.

EDMUND WALLER
(1606-1687)

THE STORY OF PHŒBUS AND DAPHNE APPLIED

Thyrsis, a youth of the inspirèd train,
Fair Sacharissa loved, but loved in vain.
Like Phœbus sung the no less amorous boy;
Like Daphne she, as lovely, and as coy!
With numbers he the flying nymph pursues, 5
With numbers such as Phœbus' self might use!
Such is the chase when Love and Fancy leads,
O'er craggy mountains, and through flowery meads;
Invoked to testify the lover's care,
Or form some image of his cruel fair. 10
Urged with his fury, like a wounded deer,
O'er these he fled; and now approaching near,
Had reached the nymph with his harmonious lay,
Whom all his charms could not incline to stay.
Yet, what he sung in his immortal strain, 15
Though unsuccessful, was not sung in vain;
All, but the nymph that should redress his wrong,
Attend his passion, and approve his song.
Like Phœbus thus, acquiring unsought praise,
He catched at love, and filled his arms with bays. 20

TO PHYLLIS

Phyllis! why should we delay
Pleasures shorter than the day?
Could we (which we never can)
Stretch our lives beyond their span,
Beauty like a shadow flies, 5
And our youth before us dies.
Or would youth and beauty stay,
Love hath wings, and will away.
Love hath swifter wings than Time;
Change in love to heaven does climb. 10
Gods that never change their state,
Vary oft their love and hate.

  Phyllis! to this truth we owe
All the love betwixt us two.
Let not you and I inquire 15
What has been our past desire;
On what shepherds you have smiled,
Or what nymphs I have beguiled;
Leave it to the planets too,
What we shall hereafter do; 20
For the joys we now may prove,
Take advice of present love.

ON A GIRDLE

That which her slender waist confined,
Shall now my joyful temples bind;
No monarch but would give his crown,
His arms might do what this has done.

It was my heaven's extremest sphere, 5
The pale which held that lovely deer.
My joy, my grief, my hope, my love,
Did all within this circle move!

A narrow compass! and yet there
Dwelt all that's good, and all that's fair; 10
Give me but what this ribband bound,
Take all the rest the sun goes round.

GO, LOVELY ROSE!

Go, lovely Rose!
Tell her that wastes her time and me,
  That now she knows,
When I resemble her to thee,
How sweet and fair she seems to be. 5

Tell her that's young,
And shuns to have her graces spied,
  That hadst thou sprung
In deserts, where no men abide,
Thou must have uncommended died. 10

Small is the worth
Of beauty from the light retired;
  Bid her come forth,
Suffer herself to be desired,
And not blush so to be admired. 15

Then die! that she
The common fate of all things rare
  May read in thee;
How small a part of time they share
That are so wondrous sweet and fair! 20

SIR JOHN SUCKLING
(1609-1642)

A DOUBT OF MARTYRDOM

O for some honest lover's ghost,
  Some kind unbodied post
    Sent from the shades below!
I strangely long to know
Whether the noble chaplets wear 5
Those that their mistress' scorn did bear
  Or those that were used kindly.

For whatsoe'er they tell us here
  To make those sufferings dear,
    'Twill there, I fear, be found   10
    That to the being crowned
T' have loved alone will not suffice,
  Unless we also have been wise
    And have our loves enjoyed.

What posture can we think him in   15
  That, here unloved, again
    Departs, and 's thither gone
    Where each sits by his own?
Or how can that Elysium be
Where I my mistress still must see   20
    Circled in other's arms?

For there the judges all are just,
  And Sophonisba must
    Be his whom she held dear,
    Not his who loved her here.   25
The sweet Philoclea, since she died,
  Lies by her Pirocles his side,
    Not by Amphialus.

Some bays, perchance, or myrtle bough
  For difference crowns the brow   30
    Of those kind souls that were
    The noble martyrs here:
And if that be the only odds
  (As who can tell?), ye kinder gods,
    Give me the woman here!   35

THE CONSTANT LOVER

Out upon it, I have loved
  Three whole days together!
And am like to love three more,
  If it prove fair weather.

Time shall moult away his wings   5
  Ere he shall discover
In the whole wide world again
  Such a constant lover.

But the spite on 't is, no praise
  Is due at all to me: 10
Love with me had made no stays,
  Had it any been but she.

Had it any been but she,
  And that very face,
There had been at least ere this   15
  A dozen dozen in her place

WHY SO PALE AND WAN?

Why so pale and wan, fond lover?
  Prithee, why so pale?
Will, when looking well can't move her,
  Looking ill prevail?
  Prithee, why so pale?   5

Why so dull and mute, young sinner?
  Prithee, why so mute?
Will, when speaking well can't win her,
  Saying nothing do 't?
  Prithee, why so mute?   10

Quit, quit for shame! This will not move;
  This cannot take her.
If of herself she will not love,
  Nothing can make her:
  The devil take her!   15

RICHARD CRASHAW
(1613?–1649)

IN THE HOLY NATIVITY OF OUR LORD GOD

A HYMN SUNG AS BY THE SHEPHERDS

CHORUS

Come, we shepherds, whose blest sight
Hath met Love's noon in Nature's night;
Come, lift we up our loftier song
And wake the sun that lies too long.

To all our world of well-stol'n joy   5
He slept, and dreamt of no such thing;
  While we found out heaven's fairer eye
And kissed the cradle of our King.
Tell him he rises now, too late
To show us aught worth looking at.   10

Tell him we now can show him more
Than he e'er showed to mortal sight;
  Than he himself e'er saw before;
Which to be seen needs not his light.
Tell him, Tityrus, where th' hast been   15
Tell him, Thyrsis, what th' hast seen.

TITYRUS

Gloomy night embraced the place
Where the noble infant lay,
  The babe looked up and showed his face;
In spite of darkness, it was day.   20
It was thy day, sweet! and did rise
Not from the east, but from thine eyes.

CHORUS

It was thy day, sweet, etc.

THYRSIS

Winter chid aloud; and sent
The angry North to wage his wars.   25
  The North forgot his fierce intent;
And left perfumes instead of scars.
By those sweet eyes' persuasive powers,
Where he meant frost he scattered flowers.

CHORUS
By those sweet eyes', etc.

BOTH
We saw thee in thy balmy nest,
Young dawn of our Eternal Day!
　We saw thine eyes break from their east
And chase the trembling shades away.
We saw thee, and we blest the sight,
We saw thee by thine own sweet light.

TITYRUS
Poor World, said I, what wilt thou do
To entertain this starry stranger?
　Is this the best thou canst bestow?
A cold, and not too cleanly, manger?
Contend, the powers of heaven and earth,
To fit a bed for this huge birth!

CHORUS
Contend the powers, etc.

THYRSIS
Proud World, said I; cease your contest
And let the mighty babe alone;
　The phœnix builds the phœnix' nest,
Love's architecture is his own;
The babe whose birth embraves this morn,
Made his own bed e'er he was born.

CHORUS
The babe whose, etc.

TITYRUS
I saw the curled drops, soft and slow,
Come hovering o'er the place's head;
　Off'ring their whitest sheets of snow
To furnish the fair infant's bed.
Forbear, said I; be not too bold,
Your fleece is white, but 't is too cold.

CHORUS
Forbear, said I, etc.

THYRSIS
I saw the obsequious seraphim
Their rosy fleece of fire bestow,
　For well they now can spare their wing,
Since heaven itself lies here below.
Well done, said I; but are you sure
Your down so warm, will pass for pure?

CHORUS
Well done, said I, etc.

TITYRUS
No, no, your king's not yet to seek
Where to repose his royal head;
　See, see how soon his new-bloomed cheek
'Twixt's mother's breasts is gone to bed!
Sweet choice, said we! no way but so
Not to lie cold, yet sleep in snow.

CHORUS
Sweet choice, said we, etc.

BOTH
We saw thee in thy balmy nest,
Bright dawn of our Eternal Day!
　We saw thine eyes break from their east
And chase the trembling shades away.
We saw thee, and we blest the sight,
We saw thee by thine own sweet light.

CHORUS
We saw thee, etc.

FULL CHORUS
Welcome all wonders in one night!
Eternity shut in a span,
　Summer in winter, day in night,
Heaven in earth, and God in man.
Great Little One, whose all-embracing birth
Lifts earth to heaven, stoops heaven to earth!

Welcome, though nor to gold nor silk,
To more than Cæsar's birthright is;
　Two sister-seas of virgin-milk
With many a rarely-tempered kiss
That breathes at once both maid and mother,
Warms in the one, cools in the other.

Welcome, though not to those gay flies
Gilded i' th' beams of earthly kings,
　Slippery souls in smiling eyes,
But to poor shepherds, homespun things,
Whose wealth's their flock, whose wit's to be
Well read in their simplicity.

Yet when young April's husband showers
Shall bless the fruitful Maia's bed,
　We'll bring the first-born of her flowers
To kiss thy feet and crown thy head.
To thee, dread Lamb! Whose love must keep
The shepherds, more than they the sheep.

To thee, meek Majesty! soft King
Of simple graces and sweet loves!
　Each of us his lamb will bring,
Each his pair of silver doves!
Till burnt at last in fire of thy fair eyes,
Ourselves become our own best sacrifice!

SIR JOHN DENHAM
(1615–1669)

From COOPER'S HILL

My eye, descending from the hill, surveys
Where Thames amongst the wanton valleys strays;
Thames, the most loved of all the Ocean's sons,
By his old sire, to his embraces runs.

Hasting to pay his tribute to the sea, 5
Like mortal life to meet eternity;
Though with those streams he no resemblance hold,
Whose foam is amber, and their gravel gold,
His genuine and less guilty wealth t' explore,
Search not his bottom, but survey his shore, 10
O'er which he kindly spreads his spacious wing,
And hatches plenty for th' ensuing spring;
Nor then destroys it with too fond a stay,
Like mothers which their infants overlay,
Nor, with a sudden and impetuous wave, 15
Like profuse kings, resumes the wealth he gave;
No unexpected inundations spoil
The mower's hopes, nor mock the ploughman's toil,
But godlike his unwearied bounty flows,
First loves to do, then loves the good he does;
Nor are his blessings to his banks confined, 21
But free and common as the sea or wind;
When he to boast or to disperse his stores,
Full of the tributes of his grateful shores,
Visits the world, and in his flying towers, 25
Brings home to us, and makes both Indies ours,
Finds wealth where 't is, bestows it where it wants,
Cities in deserts, woods in cities plants;
So that to us no thing, no place is strange,
While his fair bosom is the world's exchange. 30
O could I flow like thee, and make thy stream
My great example, as it is my theme!
Though deep, yet clear, though gentle, yet not dull,
Strong without rage, without o'erflowing full.

* * *

ON MR. ABRAHAM COWLEY'S DEATH AND BURIAL AMONGST THE ANCIENT POETS

Old Chaucer, like the morning star,
To us discovers day from far.
His light those mists and clouds dissolved,
Which our dark nation long involved;
But he descending to the shades, 5
Darkness again the age invades.
Next, like Aurora, Spenser rose,
Whose purple blush the day foreshows;
The other three, with his own fires
Phœbus, the poets' god inspires; 10
By Shakespeare's, Jonson's, Fletcher's lines,
Our stage's luster Rome's outshines:
These poets near our princes sleep,
And in one grave their mansion keep;
They lived to see so many days, 15
Till time had blasted all their bays;
But cursèd be the fatal hour
That plucked the fairest, sweetest flower
That in the muses' garden grew,
And amongst withered laurels threw. 20

Time, which made them their fame outlive,
To Cowley scarce did ripeness give.
Old mother wit, and Nature, gave
Shakespeare and Fletcher all they have;
In Spenser, and in Jonson, Art 25
Of slower Nature got the start;
But both in him so equal are,
None knows which bears the happiest share;
To him no author was unknown,
Yet what he wrote was all his own; 30
He melted not the ancient gold,
Nor, with Ben Jonson, did make bold
To plunder all the Roman stores
Of poets, and of orators:
Horace's wit, and Virgil's state, 35
He did not steal, but emulate:
And when he would like them appear,
Their garb, but not their clothes, did wear:
He not from Rome alone, but Greece,
Like Jason brought the golden fleece; 40
To him that language, though to none
Of th' others, as his own was known.
On a stiff gale, as Flaccus sings,
The Theban swan extends his wings,
When through th' ethereal clouds he flies, 45
To the same pitch our swan doth rise.
Old Pindar's flights by him are reached,
When on that gale his wings are stretched.
His fancy and his judgment such,
Each to the other seemed too much, 50
His severe judgment, giving law,
His modest fancy, kept in awe,
As rigid husbands jealous are
When they believe their wives too fair.

* * *

RICHARD LOVELACE
(1618–1658)

TO LUCASTA, GOING TO THE WARS

Tell me not, Sweet, I am unkind,
  That from the nunnery
Of thy chaste breast and quiet mind
  To war and arms I fly.

True, a new mistress now I chase, 5
  The first foe in the field;
And with a stronger faith embrace
  A sword, a horse, a shield.

Yet this inconstancy is such
  As thou too shalt adore; 10
I could not love thee, Dear, so much,
  Loved I not Honor more.

TO ALTHEA, FROM PRISON

When Love with unconfinèd wings
  Hovers within my gates,
And my divine Althea brings
  To whisper at the grates;

When I lie tangled in her hair
   And fettered to her eye,
The birds that wanton in the air
   Know no such liberty.

When flowing cups run swiftly round
   With no allaying Thames,
Our careless heads with roses bound,
   Our hearts with loyal flames;
When thirsty grief in wine we steep,
   When healths and draughts go free,
Fishes that tipple in the deep
   Know no such liberty.

When, like committed linnets, I
   With shriller throat will sing
The sweetness, mercy, majesty,
   And glories of my king;
When I shall voice aloud how good
   He is, how great should be,
Enlargèd winds, that curl the flood,
   Know no such liberty.

Stone walls do not a prison make,
   Nor iron bars a cage;
Minds innocent and quiet take
   That for an hermitage;
If I have freedom in my love
   And in my soul am free,
Angels alone, that soar above,
   Enjoy such liberty.

THE ROSE

Sweet, serene, sky-like flower,
Haste to adorn her bower,
   From thy long cloudy bed
   Shoot forth thy damask head.

New-startled blush of Flora,
The grief of pale Aurora
   (Who will contest no more),
   Haste, haste to strew her floor!

Vermilion ball that's given
From lip to lip in heaven,
   Love's couch's coverled,
   Haste, haste to make her bed.

Dear offspring of pleased Venus
And jolly plump Silenus,
   Haste, haste to deck the hair
   Of th' only sweetly fair!

See! rosy is her bower,
Her floor is all this flower,
   Her bed a rosy nest
   By a bed of roses pressed!

But early as she dresses,
Why fly you her bright tresses?
   Ah! I have found, I fear,—
   Because her cheeks are near.

TO LUCASTA

Lucasta, frown, and let me die!
   But smile, and, see, I live!
The sad indifference of your eye
   Both kills and doth reprieve;
You hide our fate within its screen;
   We feel our judgment, e'er we hear;
So in one picture I have seen
   An angel here, the devil there!

ABRAHAM COWLEY
(1618–1667)

THE SWALLOW

Foolish Prater, what do'st thou
So early at my window do
With thy tuneless serenade?
Well't had been had Tereus made
Thee as dumb as Philomel:
There his knife had done but well.
In thy undiscovered nest
Thou dost all the winter rest,
And dreamest o'er thy summer joys,
Free from the stormy season's noise:
Free from th' ill thou'st done to me;
Who disturbs, or seeks out thee?
Had'st thou all the charming notes
Of the wood's poetic throats,
All thy art could never pay
What thou'st ta'en from me away;
Cruel bird, thou'st ta'en away
A dream out of my arms to-day,
A dream that ne'er must equaled be
By all that waking eyes may see.
Thou this damage to repair,
Nothing half so sweet or fair,
Nothing half so good can'st bring,
Though men say, 'Thou bring'st the spring.'

THE WISH

Well then! I now do plainly see
This busy world and I shall ne'er agree.
The very honey of all earthly joy
Does of all meats the soonest cloy;
   And they, methinks, deserve my pity
Who for it can endure the stings,
The crowd and buzz and murmurings,
   Of this great hive, the city.

Ah, yet, ere I descend to the grave
May I a small house and large garden have;
And a few friends, and many books, both true,
Both wise, and both delightful too!
   And since love ne'er will from me flee,
A mistress moderately fair,
And good as guardian angels are,
   Only beloved and loving me.

O fountains! when in you shall I
Myself eased of unpeaceful thoughts espy?
O fields! O woods! when, when shall I be made
    The happy tenant of your shade? 20
      Here's the spring-head of pleasure's flood:
    Here's wealthy Nature's treasury,
    Where all the riches lie that she
      Has coined and stamped for good.

Pride and ambition here 25
Only in far-fetched metaphors appear;
Here naught but winds can hurtful murmurs
    scatter,
And naught but Echo flatter.
      The gods, when they descended, hither
From heaven did always choose their way: 30
    And therefore we may boldly say
    That 'tis the way, too, thither.

How happy here should I
And one dear She live, and embracing die!
She who is all the world, and can exclude 35
    In deserts solitude.
      I should have then this only fear:
Lest men, when they my pleasures see,
Should hither throng to live like me,
    And so make a city here. 40

ANDREW MARVEL
(1621–1678)

THE GARDEN

How vainly men themselves amaze,
To win the palm, the oak, or bays,
And their incessant labors see
Crowned from some single herb or tree
Whose short and narrow-vergèd shade 5
Does prudently their toils upbraid,
While all the flowers and trees do close
To weave the garlands of repose!

Fair Quiet, have I found thee here,
And Innocence, thy sister dear? 10
Mistaken long, I sought you then
In busy companies of men.
Your sacred plants, if here below,
Only among the plants will grow;
Society is all but rude 15
To this delicious solitude.

No white nor red was ever seen
So amorous as this lovely green.
Fond lovers, cruel as their flame,
Cut in these trees their mistress' name. 20
Little, alas! they know or heed,
How far these beauties hers exceed!
Fair trees! wheres'e'r your barks I wound
No name shall but your own be found.

When we have run our passion's heat, 25
Love hither makes his best retreat.
The gods, that mortal beauty chase,
Still in a tree did end their race;
Apollo hunted Daphne so,
Only that she might laurel grow; 30
And Pan did after Syrinx speed,
Not as a nymph, but for a reed.

What wondrous life is this I lead!
Ripe apples drop about my head;
The luscious clusters of the vine 35
Upon my mouth do crush their wine;
The nectarine, and curious peach,
Into my hands themselves do reach;
Stumbling on melons, as I pass,
Insnared with flowers, I fall on grass. 40

Meanwhile the mind, from pleasure less,
Withdraws into its happiness;—
The mind, that ocean where each kind
Does straight its own resemblance find;
Yet it creates, transcending these, 45
Far other worlds, and other seas,
Annihilating all that's made
To a green thought in a green shade.

Here at the fountain's sliding foot,
Or at some fruit-tree's mossy root, 50
Casting the body's vest aside,
My soul into the boughs does glide:
There, like a bird, it sits and sings,
Then whets and combs its silver wings,
And, till prepared for longer flight, 55
Waves in its plumes the various light.

Such was that happy garden-state,
While man there walked without a mate
After a place so pure and sweet.
What other help could yet be meet! 60
But 'twas beyond a mortal's share
To wander solitary there:
Two paradises 'twere in one,
To live in paradise alone.

How well the skilful gardener drew 65
Of flowers, and herbs, this dial new;
Where, from above, the milder sun
Does through a fragrant zodiac run,
And, as it works, the industrious bee
Computes its time as well as we! 70
How could such sweet and wholesome hours
Be reckoned but with herbs and flowers?

TO HIS COY MISTRESS

Had we but world enough, and time,
This coyness, Lady, were no crime,
We would sit down and think which way
To walk and pass our long love's day.
Thou by the Indian Ganges' side 5
Shouldst rubies find; I by the tide

Of Humber would complain. I would
Love you ten years before the Flood,
And you should, if you please, refuse
Till the conversion of the Jews.
My vegetable love should grow
Vaster than empires, and more slow;
An hundred years should go to praise
Thine eyes and on thy forehead gaze;
Two hundred to adore each breast,
But thirty thousand to the rest;
An age at least to every part,
And the last age should show your heart.
For, Lady, you deserve this state,
Nor would I love at lower rate.

   But at my back I always hear
Time's wingèd chariot hurrying near;
And yonder all before us lie
Deserts of vast eternity.
Thy beauty shall no more be found,
Nor, in thy marble vault, shall sound
My echoing song; then worms shall try
That long preserved virginity,
And your quaint honor turn to dust,
And into ashes all my lust:
The grave's a fine and private place,
But none, I think, do there embrace.

   Now therefore, while the youthful hue
Sits on thy skin like morning dew,
And while thy willing soul transpires
At every pore with instant fires,
Now let us sport us while we may,
And now, like amorous birds of prey,
Rather at once our time devour
Than languish in his slow-chapt power.
Let us roll all our strength and all
Our sweetness up into one ball,
And tear our pleasures with rough strife
Thorough the iron gates of life:
Thus, though we cannot make our sun
Stand still, yet we will make him run.

HENRY VAUGHAN
(1622-1695)

THE RETREAT

HAPPY those early days, when I
Shined in my angel-infancy!
Before I understood this place
Appointed for my second race,
Or taught my soul to fancy aught
But a white, celestial thought;
When yet I had not walked above
A mile or two from my first love,
And looking back, at that short space,
Could see a glimpse of his bright face;
When on some gilded cloud or flower
My gazing soul would dwell an hour,
And in those weaker glories spy
Some shadows of eternity;
Before I taught my tongue to wound
My conscience with a sinful sound,
Or had the black art to dispense,
A several sin to every sense,
But felt through all this fleshly dress
Bright shoots of everlastingness.

   O, how I long to travel back,
And tread again that ancient track,
That I might once more reach that plain,
Where first I left my glorious train;—
From whence the enlightened spirit sees
That shady city of palm trees.
But ah! my soul with too much stay
Is drunk, and staggers in the way!
Some men a forward motion love,
But I by backward steps would move;
And when this dust falls to the urn,
In that state I came, return.

THE WORLD

I SAW Eternity the other night,
Like a great ring of pure and endless light,
   All calm, as it was bright;
And round beneath it, Time, in hours, days, years,
   Driv'n by the spheres
Like a vast shadow moved; in which the world
   And all her train were hurled.
The doting lover in his quaintest strain
   Did there complain;
Near him, his lute, his fancy, and his flights,
   Wit's four delights,
With gloves, and knots, the silly snares of pleasure,
   Yet his dear treasure,
All scattered lay, while he his eyes did pour
   Upon a flower.

The darksome statesman, hung with weights and woe,
   Like a thick, midnight-fog, moved there so slow,
   He did not stay, nor go;
Condemning thoughts, like sad eclipses, scowl
   Upon his soul,
And clouds of crying witnesses without
   Pursued him with one shout.
Yet digged the mole, and lest his ways be found,
   Worked under ground,
Where he did clutch his prey; but one did see
   That policy;
Churches and altars fed him; perjuries
   Were gnats and flies;
It rained about him blood and tears, but he
   Drank them as free.

The fearful miser on a heap of rust
Sat pining all his life there, did scarce trust
    His own hands with the dust,
Yet would not place one piece above, but lives
    In fear of thieves.   35
Thousands there were as frantic as himself,
    And hugged each one his pelf;
The downright epicure placed heaven in sense,
    And scorned pretence;
While others, slipt into a wide excess,   40
    Said little less;
The weaker sort, slight, trivial wares enslave,
    Who think them brave;
And poor, despisèd Truth sat counting by
    Their victory.   45

Yet some, who all this while did weep and sing,
And sing and weep, soared up into the ring;
    But most would use no wing.
O fools, said I, thus to prefer dark night
    Before true light!   50
To live in grots and caves, and hate the day
    Because it shows the way,
The way, which from this dead and dark abode
    Leads up to God;
A way there you might tread the sun, and be   55
    More bright than he!
But, as I did their madness so discuss,
    One whispered thus
'This ring the Bridegroom did for none provide,
    But for his bride.'   60

DEPARTED FRIENDS

They are all gone into the world of light!
    And I alone sit lingering here;
Their very memory is fair and bright,
    And my sad thoughts doth clear.

It glows and glitters in my cloudy breast,   5
    Like stars upon some gloomy grove,
Or those faint beams in which this hill is drest,
    After the sun's remove.

I see them walking in an air of glory,
    Whose light doth trample on my days: 10
My days, which are at best but dull and hoary,
    Mere glimmering and decays.

O holy Hope! and high Humility,
    High as the heavens above!
These are your walks, and you have showed them me,   15
    To kindle my cold love.

Dear, beauteous Death! the jewel of the just,
    Shining nowhere, but in the dark,
What mysteries do lie beyond thy dust,
    Could man outlook that mark!   20

He that hath found some fledged bird's nest,
    may know
At first sight if the bird be flown;
But what fair well or grove he sings in now,
    That is to him unknown.

And yet, as angels in some brighter dreams   25
    Call to the soul, when man doth sleep,
So some strange thoughts transcend our wonted themes,
    And into glory peep.

If a star were confined into a tomb,
    The captive flames must needs burn there;   30
But when the hand that locked her up, gives room,
    She'll shine through all the sphere.

O Father of eternal life, and all
    Created glories under Thee,
Resume Thy spirit from this world of thrall   35
    Into true liberty.

Either disperse these mists, which blot and fill
    My perspective still as they pass;
Or else remove me hence unto that hill,
    Where I shall need no glass.   40

CHARLES SACKVILLE
EARL OF DORSET
(1638-1706)

SONG

To all you ladies now at land
    We men at sea indite;
But first would have you understand
    How hard it is to write:
The Muses now, and Neptune too,   5
We must implore to write to you—
    With a fa, la, la, la, la!

For though the Muses should prove kind,
    And fill our empty brain,
Yet if rough Neptune rouse the wind   10
    To wave the azure main,
Our paper, pen, and ink, and we,
Roll up and down our ships at sea—
    With a fa, la, la, la, la!

Then if we write not by each post,   15
    Think not we are unkind;
Nor yet conclude our ships are lost
    By Dutchmen or by wind:
Our tears we'll send a speedier way,
The tide shall bring them twice a day—   20
    With a fa, la, la, la, la!

The King with wonder and surprise
  Will swear the seas grow bold,
Because the tides will higher rise
  Than e'er they did of old;   25
But let him know it is our tears
Bring floods of grief to Whitehall stairs—
    With a fa, la, la, la, la!

Should foggy Opdam chance to know
  Our sad and dismal story,   30
The Dutch would scorn so weak a foe,
  And quit their fort at Goree;
For what resistance can they find
From men who've left their hearts behind?—
    With a fa, la, la, la, la!   35

Let wind and weather do its worst,
  Be you to us but kind;
Let Dutchmen vapor, Spaniards curse,
  No sorrow we shall find;
'Tis then no matter how things go,   40
Or who's our friend, or who's our foe—
    With a fa, la, la, la, la!

To pass our tedious hours away
  We throw a merry main,
Or else at serious ombre play;   45
  But why should we in vain
Each other's ruin thus pursue?
We were undone when we left you—
    With a fa, la, la, la, la!

But now our fears tempestuous grow   50
  And cast our hopes away,
Whilst you, regardless of our woe,
  Sit careless at a play,
Perhaps permit some happier man
To kiss your hand, or flirt your fan—   55
    With a fa, la, la, la, la!

When any mournful tune you hear
  That dies in every note,
As if it sighed with each man's care
  For being so remote,   60
Think then how often love we've made
To you, when all those tunes were played—
    With a fa, la, la, la, la!

In justice you cannot refuse
  To think of our distress,   65
When we for hopes of honor lose
  Our certain happiness:
All those designs are but to prove
Ourselves more worthy of your love—
    With a fa, la, la, la, la!   70

And now we've told you all our loves,
  And likewise all our fears,
In hopes this declaration moves
  Some pity for our tears:
Let's hear of no inconstancy—   75
We have too much of that at sea—
    With a fa, la, la, la, la!

JOHN WILMOT
EARL OF ROCHESTER
(1647–1680)

ON CHARLES II

Here lies our Sovereign Lord the King,
  Whose word no man relies on,
Who never said a foolish thing,
  Nor ever did a wise one.

FRANCIS BACON (1561–1626)

Bacon was connected through both his parents with the governing classes. His father was Lord Keeper of the Great Seal, and the Queen used to call the boy her 'young Lord Keeper.' At twelve he went to Trinity College, Cambridge, and as a youth he studied law at Gray's Inn. He was in the diplomatic service at Paris when his father died, leaving him but ill provided for. In 1584 he was elected to the House of Commons, but in spite of conspicuous ability and powerful connections, his political preferment was slow. He became Solicitor-General in 1607, Attorney-General 1613, Privy Councillor 1616, Lord Keeper 1617, Lord Chancellor and Baron Verulam 1618, Viscount St. Albans 1621. But hostile political influences in this last year brought about his fall. He was accused of bribery, and admitted receiving gifts, but denied that they had influenced him in the administration of justice. He was deprived of all his offices, fined £40,000, imprisoned, and excluded from court and parliament. All the penalties except the last were immediately remitted by the King, but he was not allowed to return to public life. He retired to the estate he had inherited from his elder brother, and gave himself to literature and philosophy, which had always occupied his leisure. While still a young man, he said, 'I have as vast contemplative ends as I have moderate civil ends: for I have taken all knowledge to be my province.' *The Advancement of Learning*, published in English in 1605, is mainly an attempt to review what was then known; the *Novum Organum* (in Latin, 1620) is an exposition of the means by which the bounds of knowledge may be extended. His philosophical work was of great influence on account of the stress he laid on observation of facts and the testing of hypothesis by experiment. He met his death through a chill contracted by leaving his coach on a winter's day to gather snow to stuff a fowl in order to try the effect of cold on the preservation of meat. His *History of Henry VII* (1622) is an important work, but his most notable contribution to literature was the *Essays*—a title probably suggested by the French *Essais* of Montaigne (1580). Bacon's first edition of ten essays appeared in 1597, an enlarged edition, containing thirty-eight, in 1612, and the final issue (fifty-eight essays) in 1625. Though they reveal only at times the philosophical bent of Bacon's genius, they illustrate fully the extraordinary keenness of his mind, his practical worldly wisdom, and the terse incisiveness of his style.

ESSAYS

OF TRUTH — No. 1

'What is truth?' said jesting Pilate; and would not stay for an answer. Certainly there be that delight in giddiness, and count it a bondage to fix a belief, affecting free-will in thinking, as well as in acting. And though the sects of philosophers of that kind be gone, yet there remain certain discoursing wits which are of the same veins, though there be not so much blood in them as was in those of the ancients. But it is not only the difficulty and labor which men take in finding out of truth; nor again, that when it is found, it imposeth upon men's thoughts, that doth bring lies in favor: but a natural though corrupt love of the lie itself. One of the later school of the Grecians examineth the matter, and is at a stand to think what should be in it, that men should love lies: where neither they make for pleasure, as with poets; nor for advantage, as with the merchant; but for the lie's sake. But I cannot tell: this same truth is a naked and open daylight, that doth not show the masques, and mummeries, and triumphs of the world half so stately and daintily as candle-lights. Truth may perhaps come to the price of a pearl, that showeth best by day; but it will not rise to the price of a diamond or carbuncle, that showeth best in varied lights. A mixture of a lie doth ever add pleasure. Doth any man doubt that if there were taken out of men's minds vain opinions, flattering hopes, false valuations, imaginations as one would, and the like, but it would leave the minds of a number of men poor shrunken things, full of melancholy and indisposition, and unpleasing to themselves? One of the fathers, in great severity, called poesy *vinum dæmonum* [devils' wine], because it filleth the imagination, and yet it is but with the shadow of a lie. But it is not the lie that passeth through the mind, but the lie that sinketh in and settleth in it that doth the hurt, such as we spake of before. But howsoever these things are thus in men's depraved judgments and affections, yet truth, which only doth judge itself, teacheth that the inquiry of truth, which is the love-making, or wooing of it; the knowledge of truth, which is the presence of it; and the belief of truth, which is the enjoying of it, is the sovereign good of human nature. The first creature of God, in the works of the days, was the light of the sense; the last was the light of reason; and his Sabbath work, ever since, is the illumination of his spirit. First he breathed light upon the face of the matter, or chaos; then he breathed light into the face of man; and still he breatheth and inspireth light into the face of his chosen. The poet, that beautified the sect, that was otherwise inferior to the rest, saith yet excellently well, 'It is a pleasure to stand upon the shore, and to see ships tost upon the sea; a pleasure to stand in the window of a castle, and to see a battle, and the adventures thereof below; but no pleasure is comparable to the standing upon the vantage ground of truth (a hill not to be commanded, and where the air is always clear and serene), and to see the errors, and wanderings, and mists, and tempests, in the vale below'; so always that this prospect be with pity, and not with swelling or pride. Certainly it is heaven upon earth to have a man's mind move in charity, rest in providence, and turn upon the poles of truth.

To pass from theological and philosophical truth to the truth of civil business, it will be acknowledged, even by those that practice it not, that clear and round dealing is the honor of man's nature, and that mixture of falsehood is like alloy in coin of gold and silver, which may make the metal work the better, but it embaseth it; for these winding and crooked courses are the goings of the serpent, which goeth basely upon the belly, and not upon the feet. There is no vice that doth so cover a man with shame as to be found false and perfidious; and therefore Montaigne saith prettily, when he inquired the reason why the word of the lie should be such a disgrace, and such an odious charge, 'If it be well weighed, to say that a man lieth, is as much as to say that he is brave towards God, and a coward towards man.' For a lie faces God, and shrinks from man. Surely the wickedness of falsehood and breach of faith cannot possibly be so highly expressed as in that it shall be the last peal to call the judgments of God upon the generations of men: it being foretold, that when Christ cometh, 'he shall not find faith upon the earth.'

OF ADVERSITY — No. 5

It was a high speech of Seneca, after the manner of the Stoics, that 'the good things which belong to prosperity are to be wished, but the good things that belong to adversity are to be admired.' *Bona rerum secundarum optabilia, adversarum mirabilia.* Certainly if miracles be the command over Nature, they appear most in adversity. It is yet a higher speech of his than the other, much too high for a heathen, 'It is true greatness to have in one the frailty of a man and the security of a God' (*Vere magnum, habere fragilitatem hominis, securitatem Dei*). This would have done better in poesy, where transcendencies are more allowed. And the poets, indeed, have been busy with it; for it is in effect the thing which is figured in that strange fiction of the ancient poets which seemeth not to be without mystery; nay, and to have some approach to the state of a Christian: that Hercules, when he went to unbind Prometheus, by whom human nature is represented, sailed the length of the great ocean in an earthen pot or pitcher; lively describing Christian resolution that saileth in the frail bark of the flesh through the waves of the world. But to speak in a mean, the virtue of prosperity is temperance, the virtue of adversity is fortitude, which in morals is the more heroical virtue. Prosperity is the blessing of the Old Testament, adversity is the blessing of the New, which carrieth the greater benediction and the clearer revelation of God's favor. Yet, even in the Old Testament, if you listen to David's harp you shall hear as many hearse-like airs as carols. And the pencil of the Holy Ghost hath labored more in describing the afflictions of Job than the felicities of Solomon. Prosperity is not without many fears and distastes, and adversity is not without comforts and hopes. We see in needleworks and embroideries it is more pleasing to have a lively work upon a sad and solemn ground than to have a dark and melancholy work upon a lightsome ground. Judge, therefore, of the pleasure of the heart by the pleasure of the eye. Certainly virtue is like precious odors, most fragrant when they are incensed or crushed; for prosperity doth best discover vice, but adversity doth best discover virtue.

OF PARENTS AND CHILDREN — No. 7

The joys of parents are secret, and so are their griefs and fears; they cannot utter the one, nor they will not utter the other. Children sweeten labors, but they make misfortunes more bitter; they increase the cares of life, but they mitigate the remembrance of death. The perpetuity by generation is common to beasts; but memory, and merit, and noble works are proper to men; and surely a man shall see the noblest works and foundations have proceeded from childless men, which have sought to express the images of their minds where those of their bodies have failed; so that care of posterity is most in them that have no posterity. They that are the first raisers of their houses are most indulgent towards their children, beholding them as the continuance, not only of their kind, but of their work, and so both children and creatures.

The difference in affection of parents towards their several children is many times unequal, and sometimes unworthy, especially in the mother; as Solomon saith, 'A wise son rejoiceth the father, but an ungracious son shames the mother.' A man shall see, where there is a house full of children, one or two of the eldest respected, and the youngest made wantons; but in the midst, some that are as it were forgotten, who, many times, nevertheless, prove the best. The illiberality of parents, in allowance towards their children, is a harmful error, and makes them base, acquaints them with shifts, makes them sort with mean company, and makes them surfeit more when they come to plenty; and therefore the proof is best when men keep their authority towards their children, but not their purse. Men have a foolish manner (both parents, and schoolmasters, and servants), in creating and breeding an emulation between brothers during childhood, which many times sorteth to discord when they are men, and disturbeth families. The Italians make little difference between children and nephews, or near kinsfolk; but so they be of the lump they care not, though they pass not through their own body. And, to say truth, in nature it is much a like matter; insomuch that we see a nephew sometimes resembleth an uncle, or a kinsman, more than his own parent, as the blood happens. Let parents choose betimes the vocations and courses they mean their children should take, for then they are most flexible; and let them not too much apply themselves to the disposition of their children, as thinking they will take best to that which they have most mind to. It is true, that if the affection, or aptness, of the children be extraordinary, then it is good not to cross it; but generally the precept is good: *Optimum elige, suave et facile illud faciet consuetudo* [Choose the best; custom will make it pleasant and easy]. Younger brothers are commonly fortunate, but seldom or never where the elder are disinherited.

OF MARRIAGE AND SINGLE LIFE No. 8

He that hath wife and children hath given hostages to fortune; for they are impediments to great enterprises, either of virtue or mischief. Certainly the best works, and of greatest merit for the public, have proceeded from the unmarried or childless men, which, both in affection and means, have married and endowed the public. Yet it were great reason that those that have children should have greatest care of future times, unto which they know they must transmit their dearest pledges.

Some there are, who, though they lead a single life, yet their thoughts do end with themselves, and account future times impertinences; nay, there are some other that account wife and children but as bills of charges. Nay, more, there are some foolish rich covetous men that take a pride in having no children, because they may be thought so much the richer; for, perhaps, they have heard some talk, 'Such a one is a great rich man,' and another except to it, 'Yea, but he hath a great charge of children,' as if it were an abatement to his riches. But the most ordinary cause of a single life is liberty, especially in certain self-pleasing and humorous minds, which are so sensible of every restraint, as they will go near to think their girdles and garters to be bonds and shackles. Unmarried men are best friends, best masters, best servants, but not always best subjects, for they are light to run away, and almost all fugitives are of that condition. A single life doth well with churchmen, for charity will hardly water the ground where it must first fill a pool. It is indifferent for judges and magistrates, for if they be facile and corrupt you shall have a servant five times worse than a wife. For soldiers, I find the generals commonly, in their hortatives, put men in mind of their wives and children. And I think the despising of marriage amongst the Turks maketh the vulgar soldier more base. Certainly, wife and children are a kind of discipline of humanity; and single men, though they be many times more charitable, because their means are less exhaust, yet, on the other side, they are more cruel and hard-hearted, good to make severe inquisitors, because their tenderness is not so oft called upon. Grave natures, led by custom, and therefore constant, are commonly loving husbands; as was said of Ulysses, '*Vetulam suam prætulit immortalitati*' [He preferred his old wife to immortality]. Chaste women are often proud and froward, as presuming upon the merit of their chastity. It is one of the best bonds, both of chastity and obedience, in the wife if she think her husband wise, which she will never do if she find him jealous. Wives are young men's mistresses, companions for middle age, and old men's nurses; so as a man may have a quarrel to marry when he will. But yet he was reputed one of the wise men that made answer to the question when a man should marry, 'A young man not yet, an elder man not at all.' It is often seen that bad husbands have very good wives; whether it be that it raiseth the price of their husband's kindness when it comes, or that the wives take a pride in their patience; but this never fails, if the bad husbands were of their own choosing, against their friends' consent; for then they will be sure to make good their own folly.

OF LOVE — No. 10

THE stage is more beholden to love than the life of man. For as to the stage love is ever a matter of comedies and now and then of tragedies, but in life it doth much mischief, sometimes like a siren, sometimes like a fury. You may observe that amongst all the great and worthy persons whereof the memory remaineth, either ancient or recent, there is not one that hath been transported to the mad degree of love, which shows that great spirits and great business do keep out this weak passion. You must except, nevertheless, Marcus Antonius, the half-partner of the empire of Rome, and Appius Claudius, the decemvir and lawgiver; whereof the former was indeed a voluptuous man and inordinate, but the latter was an austere and wise man; and therefore it seems, though rarely, that love can find entrance, not only into an open heart, but also into a heart well fortified, if watch be not well kept. It is a poor saying of Epicurus: *Satis magnum alter alteri theatrum sumus* [We are to each other a theater large enough], as if man, made for the contemplation of heaven and all noble objects, should do nothing but kneel before a little idol and make himself subject, though not of the mouth, as beasts are, yet of the eye, which was given him for higher purposes. It is a strange thing to note the excess of this passion, and how it braves the nature and value of things by this, that the speaking in a perpetual hyperbole is comely in nothing but in love. Neither is it merely in the phrase; for whereas it hath been well said that the arch-flatterer, with whom all the petty flatterers have intelligence, is a man's self, certainly the lover is more. For there was never proud man thought so absurdly well of himself as the lover doth of the person loved, and, therefore, it was well said that it is impossible to love and to be wise. Neither doth this weakness appear to others only, and not to the party loved, but to the loved most of all, except the love be reciprocal. For it is a true rule that love is ever rewarded either with the reciproque or with an inward and secret contempt; by how much the more men ought to beware of this passion, which loseth not only other things but itself. As for the other losses, the poet's relation doth well figure them, that he that preferred Helena quitted the gifts of Juno and Pallas; for whosoever esteemeth too much of amorous affection quitteth both riches and wisdom. This passion hath its floods in the very times of weakness, which are great prosperity and great adversity (though this latter hath been less observed), both which times kindle love and make it more fervent, and, therefore, show it to be the child of folly. They do best who, if they cannot but admit love, yet make it keep quarter, and sever it wholly from their serious affairs and actions of life; for if it check once with business, it troubleth men's fortunes and maketh men that they can nowise be true to their own ends. I know not how, but martial men are given to love; I think it is but as they are given to wine, for perils commonly ask to be paid in pleasures. There is in man's nature a secret inclination and motion towards love of others, which, if it be not spent upon some one or a few, doth naturally spread itself towards many, and maketh men become humane and charitable, as it is seen sometimes in friars. Nuptial love maketh mankind, friendly love perfecteth it, but wanton love corrupteth and embaseth it.

OF BOLDNESS — No. 12

IT is a trivial grammar-school text, but yet worthy a wise man's consideration: question was asked of Demosthenes, what was the chief part of an orator? He answered, Action: what next? Action: what next again? Action. He said it that knew it best, and had by nature himself no advantage in that he commended. A strange thing, that that part of an orator which is but superficial, and rather the virtue of a player, should be placed so high above those other noble parts, of invention, elocution, and the rest—nay, almost alone, as if it were all in all. But the reason is plain. There is in human nature generally more of the fool than of the wise; and, therefore, those faculties by which the foolish part of men's minds is taken are most potent. Wonderful like is the case of boldness in civil business. What first?—Boldness. What second and third?—Boldness. And yet boldness is a child of ignorance and baseness, far inferior to other parts. But, nevertheless, it doth fascinate and bind hand and foot those that are either shallow in judgment or weak in courage, which are the greatest part—yea, and prevaileth with wise men at weak times. Therefore, we see it hath done wonders in popular states, but with senates and princes less; and more ever upon the first entrance of bold persons into action than soon after; for boldness is an ill keeper of promise. Surely, as there are mountebanks for the natural body, so there are mountebanks for the politic body; men that undertake great cures, and perhaps have been lucky in two or three experiments, but want the grounds of science, and therefore cannot hold out—nay, you shall see a bold fellow many times do Mahomet's miracle. Mahomet made the people believe that he would call a hill to him, and from the top of it offer up his prayers for the observers of his law. The people assembled; Mahomet called the hill to come to him again and again; and when the hill stood still he was never a whit abashed, but said, 'If the hill will not come to Mahomet, Mahomet will go to the hill.' So these men, when they have promised great matters, and failed most shamefully, yet, if they have the perfection of boldness, they will but slight it over, and make a turn, and no more ado. Certainly to men of great judgment bold persons are a sport to behold—nay, and to the vulgar also boldness hath somewhat of the ridiculous; for if absurdity be the subject of laughter, doubt you not but great boldness is seldom without some absurdity. Especially it is a sport to see when a bold fellow is out of countenance, for that puts his face into a most shrunken and wooden posture, as needs it must, for in bashfulness the spirits do a little go and come; but with bold men, upon like occasion, they stand at a stay, like a stale at chess, where it is no mate, but yet the game cannot stir; but this last were fitter for a satire than for a serious observation. This is well to be weighed, that boldness is ever blind: for it seeth not dangers and inconveniences. Therefore it is ill in counsel, good in execution; so that the right use of bold persons is that they never command in chief, but be seconds, and under the direction of others. For in counsel it is good to see dangers; and in execution not to see them, except they be very great.

OF SUPERSTITION — No. 17

It were better to have no opinion of God at all, than such an opinion as is unworthy of him; for the one is unbelief, the other is contumely: and certainly superstition is the reproach of the Deity. Plutarch saith well to that purpose: 'Surely,' saith he, 'I had rather a great deal, men should say there was no such a man at all as Plutarch, than that they should say that there was one Plutarch, that would eat his children as soon as they were born'; as the poets speak of Saturn. And as the contumely is greater towards God, so the danger is greater towards men. Atheism leaves a man to sense, to philosophy, to natural piety, to laws, to reputation—all which may be guides to an outward moral virtue, though religion were not; but superstition dismounts all these, and erecteth an absolute monarchy in the minds of men. Therefore atheism did never perturb states; for it makes men wary of themselves, as looking no further; and we see the times inclined to atheism, as the time of Augustus Cæsar, were civil times; but superstition hath been the confusion of many states, and bringeth in a new *primum mobile*, that ravisheth all the spheres of government. The master of superstition is the people; and in all superstition wise men follow fools; and arguments are fitted to practice in a reversed order. It was gravely said, by some of the prelates in the Council of Trent, where the doctrine of the schoolmen bare great sway, that the schoolmen were like astronomers, which did feign eccentrics and epicycles, and such engines of orbs, to save the phenomena, though they knew there were no such things; and, in like manner, that the schoolmen had framed a number of subtle and intricate axioms and theorems to save the practice of the church. The causes of superstition are pleasing and sensual rites and ceremonies, excess of outward and pharisaical holiness, over-great reverence of traditions, which cannot but load the church; the stratagems of prelates for their own ambition and lucre; the favoring too much of good intentions, which openeth the gate to conceits and novelties; the taking an aim at divine matters by human, which cannot but breed mixture of imaginations; and, lastly, barbarous times, especially joined with calamities and disasters. Superstition without a veil is a deformed thing, for as it addeth deformity to an ape to be so like a man, so the similitude of superstition to religion makes it the more deformed. And as wholesome meat corrupteth to little worms, so good forms and orders corrupt into a number of petty observances. There is a superstition in avoiding superstition, when men think to do best if they go farthest from the superstition formerly received. Therefore care would be had that, as it fareth in ill purgings, the good be not taken away with the bad, which commonly is done when the people is the reformer.

OF WISDOM FOR A MAN'S SELF — No. 23

An ant is a wise creature for itself, but it is a shrewd thing in an orchard or garden; and certainly men that are great lovers of themselves waste the public. Divide with reason between self-love and society; and be so true to thyself as thou be not false to others, especially to thy king and country. It is a poor center of a man's actions, himself. It is right earth; for that only stands fast upon its own center; whereas all things that have affinity with the heavens move upon the center of another, which they benefit. The referring of all to a man's self is more tolerable in a sovereign prince, because themselves are not only themselves, but their good and evil is at the peril of the public fortune: but it is a desperate evil in a servant to a prince, or a citizen in a republic; for whatsoever affairs pass such a man's hands, he crooketh them to his own ends, which must needs be often eccentric to the ends of his master or state. Therefore, let princes or states choose such servants as have not this mark, except they mean their service should be made but the accessory. That which maketh the effect more pernicious is that all proportion is lost. It were disproportion enough for the servant's good to be preferred before the master's; but yet it is a greater extreme, when a little good of the servant shall carry things against a great good of the master's. And yet that is the case of bad officers, treasurers, ambassadors, generals, and other false and corrupt servants, which set a bias upon their bowl, of their own petty ends and envies, to the overthrow of their master's great and important affairs. And for the most part, the good such servants receive is after the model of their own fortune, but the hurt they sell for that good is after the model of their master's fortune. And certainly it is the nature of extreme self-lovers, as they will set a house on fire and it were but to roast their eggs; and yet these men many times hold credit with their masters, because their study is but to please them, and profit themselves; and for either respect they will abandon the good of their affairs.

Wisdom for a man's self is, in many branches thereof, a depraved thing; it is the wisdom of rats, that will be sure to leave a house somewhat before it fall; it is the wisdom of the fox, that thrusts out the badger, who digged and made room for him; it is the wisdom of crocodiles, that shed tears when they would devour. But that which is specially to be noted is that those which (as Cicero says of Pompey) are *sui amantes sine rivali* [lovers of themselves without a rival] are many times unfortunate; and whereas they have all their time sacrificed to themselves, they become in the end themselves sacrifices to the inconstancy of fortune, whose wings they thought by their self-wisdom to have pinioned.

OF DISPATCH — No. 25

Affected dispatch is one of the most dangerous things to business that can be. It is like that which the physicians call *predigestion*, or hasty digestion, which is sure to fill the body full of crudities and secret seeds of diseases. Therefore measure not dispatch by the times of sitting, but by the advancement of the business. And as in races, it is not the large stride, or high lift, that makes the speed, so in business, the keeping close to the matter, and not taking of it too much at once, procureth dispatch. It is the care of some, only to come off speedily for the time, or to contrive some false periods of business, because they may seem men of dispatch; but it is one thing to abbreviate by contracting, another by cutting off; and business so handled at several sittings or meetings goeth commonly backward and forward in an unsteady manner. I knew a wise man that had it for a byword, when he saw men hasten to a conclusion, 'Stay a little, that we may make an end the sooner.'

On the other side, true dispatch is a rich thing; for time is the measure of business, as money is of wares; and business is bought at a dear hand where there is small dispatch. The Spartans and Spaniards have been noted to be of small dispatch: *Mi venga la muerte de Spagna*, 'Let my death come from Spain,' for then it will be sure to be long in coming.

Give good hearing to those that give the first information in business; and rather direct them in the beginning than interrupt them in the continuance of their speeches; for he that is put out of his own order will go forward and backward, and be more tedious while he waits upon his memory, than he could have been if he had gone on in his own course. But sometimes it is seen that the moderator is more troublesome than the actor.

Iterations are commonly loss of time; but there is no such gain of time as to iterate often the state of the question; for it chaseth away many a frivolous speech as it is coming forth. Long and curious speeches are as fit for dispatch as a robe or mantle with a long train is for a race. Prefaces, and passages, and excusations, and other speeches of reference to the person are great wastes of time; and though they seem to proceed of modesty, they are bravery. Yet beware of being too material when there is any impediment or obstruction in men's wills; for pre-occupation of mind ever requireth preface of speech, like a fomentation to make the unguent enter.

Above all things, order and distribution, and singling out of parts is the life of dispatch, so as the distribution be not too subtle; for he that doth not divide will never enter well into business, and he that divideth too much will never come out of it clearly. To choose time is to save time; and an unseasonable motion is but beating the air. There be three parts of business—the preparation, the debate, or examination, and the perfection; whereof, if you look for dispatch, let the middle only be the work of many, and the first and last the work of few. The proceeding upon somewhat conceived in writing doth for the most part facilitate dispatch; for though it should be wholly rejected, yet that negative is more pregnant of direction than an indefinite, as ashes are more generative than dust.

OF SEEMING WISE — No. 26

It hath been an opinion that the French are wiser than they seem, and the Spaniards seem wiser than they are. But howsoever it be between nations, certainly it is so between man and man. For as the Apostle saith of godliness, 'having a show of godliness, but denying the power thereof,' so certainly there are in points of wisdom and sufficiency that do nothing or little very solemnly — *magno conatu nugas* [trifles with great effort]. It is a ridiculous thing, and fit for a satire to persons of judgment, to see what shifts these formalists have, and what prospectives to make superficies to seem body that hath depth and bulk. Some are so close and reserved as they will not show their wares but by a dark light, and seem always to keep back somewhat; and when they know within themselves they speak of that they do not well know would, nevertheless, seem to others to know of that which they may not well speak. Some help themselves with countenance and gesture, and are wise by signs, as Cicero saith of Piso, that when he answered him he fetched one of his brows up to his forehead and bent the other down to his chin—*respondes, altero ad frontem sublato altero ad mentum depresso supercilio, crudelitatem tibi non placere.* Some think to bear it by speaking a great word and being peremptory, and go on and take by admittance that which they cannot make good. Some, whatsoever is beyond their reach, will seem to despise or make light of it as impertinent or curious, and so would have their ignorance seem judgment. Some are never without a difference, and commonly, by amusing men with a subtlety, blanch the matter, of whom A. Gellius saith, *Hominem delirum, qui verborum minutiis rerum frangit pondera* [a foolish man who breaks up important business with small points about words]. Of which kind also Plato, in his *Protagoras*, bringeth in Prodicus in scorn, and maketh him make a speech that consisteth of distinctions from the beginning to the end. Generally, such men, in all deliberations, find ease to be of the negative side, and affect a credit to object and foretell difficulties; for when propositions are denied, there is an end of them; but if they be allowed, it requireth a new work; which false point of wisdom is the bane of business. To conclude, there is no decaying merchant, or inward beggar, hath so many tricks to uphold the credit of their wealth, as these empty persons have to maintain the credit of their sufficiency. Seeming wise men may make shift to get opinion; but let no man choose them for employment; for, certainly, you were better take for business a man somewhat absurd than over-formal.

OF EXPENSE — No. 28

RICHES are for spending, and spending for honor and good actions. Therefore extraordinary expense must be limited by the worth of the occasion; for voluntary undoing may be as well for a man's country as for the kingdom of heaven. But ordinary expense ought to be limited by a man's estate, and governed with such regard as it be within his compass, and not subject to deceit and abuse of servants, and ordered to the best show, that the bills may be less than the estimation abroad. Certainly, if a man will keep but of even hand, his ordinary expenses ought to be but to the half of his receipts, and if he think to wax rich, but to the third part. It is no baseness for the greatest to descend and look into their own estate. Some forbear it, not upon negligence alone, but doubting to bring themselves into melancholy, in respect they shall find it broken. But wounds cannot be cured without searching. He that cannot look into his own estate at all had need both choose well them whom he employeth, and change them often, for new are more timorous and less subtle. He that can look into his estate but seldom, it behoveth him to turn all to certainties. A man had need, if he be plentiful in some kind of expense, to be as saving again in some other: as if he be plentiful in diet, to be saving in apparel; if he be plentiful in the hall, to be saving in the stable; and the like. For he that is plentiful in expenses of all kinds will hardly be preserved from decay. In clearing of a man's estate, he may as well hurt himself in being too sudden, as in letting it run on too long, for hasty selling is commonly as disadvantageable as interest. Besides, he that clears at once will relapse, for, finding himself out of straits, he will revert to his customs; but he that cleareth by degrees induceth a habit of frugality, and gaineth as well upon his mind as upon his estate. Certainly, who hath a state to repair may not despise small things: and, commonly, it is less dishonorable to abridge petty charges than to stoop to petty gettings. A man ought warily to begin charges which, once begun, will continue; but in matters that return not, he may be more magnificent.

OF DISCOURSE — No. 32

SOME in their discourse desire rather commendation of wit, in being able to hold all arguments, than of judgment, in discerning what is true; as if it were a praise to know what might be said, and not what should be thought. Some have certain commonplaces and themes, wherein they are good, and want variety; which kind of poverty is for the most part tedious, and, when it is once perceived, ridiculous. The honorablest part of talk is to give the occasion; and again to moderate, and pass to somewhat else, for then a man leads the dance. It is good in discourse and speech of conversation to vary and intermingle speech of the present occasion with arguments, tales with reasons, asking of questions with telling of opinions, and jest with earnest, for it is a dull thing to tire, and as we say now, to jade anything too far. As for jest, there be certain things which ought to be privileged from it, namely, religion, matters of state, great persons, any man's present business of importance, and any case that deserveth pity. Yet there be some that think their wits have been asleep, except they dart out somewhat that is piquant and to the quick: that is a vein which would be bridled.

Parce, puer, stimulis, et fortius utere loris.
[Spare, boy, the whip, and tighter hold the reins.]

And generally men ought to find the difference between saltness and bitterness. Certainly he that hath a satirical vein, as he maketh others afraid of his wit, so he had need be afraid of others' memory. He that questioneth much shall learn much and content much; but especially if he apply his questions to the skill of the persons whom he asketh, for he shall give them occasion to please themselves in speaking, and himself shall continually gather knowledge. But let his questions not be troublesome, for that is fit for a poser. And let him be sure to leave other men their turns to speak. Nay, if there be any that would reign, and take up all the time, let him find means to take them off and to bring others on; as musicians used to do with those that danced too long galliards. If you dissemble sometimes your knowledge of that you are thought to know, you shall be thought another time to know that you know not. Speech of a man's self ought to be seldom and well chosen. I knew one was wont to say in scorn, 'He must needs be a wise man, he speaks so much of himself.' And there is but one case wherein a man may commend himself with good grace, and that is in commending virtue in another, especially if it be such a virtue whereunto himself pretendeth. Speech of touch towards others should be sparingly used, for discourse ought to be as a field, without coming home to any man. I knew two noblemen of the west part of England, whereof the one was given to scoff, but kept ever royal cheer in his house. The other would ask of those that had been at the other's table, 'Tell truly, was there never a flout or dry blow given?' To which the guest would answer, such and such a thing passed. The lord would say, 'I thought he would mar a good dinner.' Discretion of speech is more than eloquence, and to speak agreeably to him with whom we deal is more than to speak in good words or in good order. A good continued speech, without a good speech of interlocution, shows slowness; and a good reply, or second speech, without a good settled speech, showeth shallowness and weakness. As we see in beasts, that those that are weakest in the course are yet nimblest in the turn, as it is betwixt the greyhound and the hare. To use too many circumstances ere one come to the matter is wearisome; to use none at all is blunt.

OF RICHES — No. 34

I CANNOT call riches better than the baggage of virtue. The Roman word is better, *impedimenta*, for as the baggage is to an army so is riches to virtue. It cannot be spared, nor left behind, but it hindereth the march, yea, and the care of it sometimes loseth or disturbeth the victory. Of great riches there is no real use, except it be in the distribution; the rest is but conceit. So saith Solomon, 'Where much is, there are many to consume it; and what hath the owner but the sight of it with his eyes?' The personal fruition in any man cannot reach to feel great riches; there is a custody of them, or a power of dole and donative of them, or a fame of them, but no solid use to the owner. Do you not see what feigned prices are set upon little stones and rarities? And what works of ostentation are undertaken, because there might seem to be some use of great riches? But then you will say, they may be of use, to buy men out of dangers or troubles. As Solomon saith, 'Riches are as a stronghold in the imagination of the rich man.' But this is excellently expressed, that it is in imagination, and not always in fact. For certainly great riches have sold more men than they have bought out. Seek not proud riches, but such as thou mayest get justly, use soberly, distribute cheerfully, and leave contentedly. Yet have no abstract or friarly contempt of them, but distinguish, as Cicero saith well of Rabirius Posthumus, *In studio rei amplificandæ, apparebat, non avaritiæ prædam, sed instrumentum bonitati quæri* [In his efforts to increase his wealth, it was clear that he did not seek a prey for avarice but an instrument for doing good]. Hearken also to Solomon, and beware of hasty gathering of riches: *Qui festinat ad divitias, non erit insons* [He that maketh haste to be rich shall not be innocent]. The poets feign that when Plutus (which is riches) is sent from Jupiter, he limps, and goes slowly, but when he is sent from Pluto, he runs, and is swift of foot; meaning that riches gotten by good means and just labor pace slowly, but when they come by the death of others (as by the course of inheritance, testaments, and the like), they come tumbling upon a man: but it might be applied likewise to Pluto taking him for the devil; for when riches come from the devil (as by fraud, and oppression, and unjust means) they come upon speed. The ways to enrich are many, and most of them foul; parsimony is one of the best, and yet is not innocent, for it withholdeth men from works of liberality and charity. The improvement of the ground is the most natural obtaining of riches, for it is our great mother's blessing, the earth's; but it is slow: and yet, where men of great wealth do stoop to husbandry, it multiplieth riches exceedingly. I knew a nobleman in England that had the greatest audits of any man in my time, —a great grazier, a great sheep master, a great timber man, a great collier, a great corn master, a great lead man, and so of iron and a number of the like points of husbandry; so as the earth seemed a sea to him in respect of the perpetual importation. It was truly observed by one, 'That himself came very hardly to a little riches, and very easily to great riches'; for when a man's stock is come to that, that he can expect the prime of markets, and overcome those bargains, which for their greatness are few men's money, and be partner in the industries of younger men, he cannot but increase mainly. The gains of ordinary trades and vocations are honest, and furthered by two things chiefly: by diligence, and by a good name for good and fair dealing; but the gains of bargains are of a more doubtful nature, when men shall wait upon others' necessity; broke by servants, and instruments to draw them on; put off others cunningly that would be better chapmen, and the like practices, which are crafty and naught. As for the chopping of bargains, when a man buys not to hold, but to sell over again, that commonly grindeth double, both upon the seller and upon the buyer. Sharings do greatly enrich, if the hands be well chosen that are trusted. Usury is the certainest means of gain, though one of the worst, as that whereby a man doth eat his bread *in sudori vultus alieni* [in the sweat of another man's brow]; and besides, doth plough upon Sundays. But yet certain though it be, it hath flaws, for that the scriveners and brokers do value unsound men, to serve their own turn. The fortune in being the first in an invention, or in a privilege, doth cause sometimes a wonderful overgrowth in riches, as it was with the first sugarman in the Canaries. Therefore, if a man can play the true logician, to have as well judgment as invention, he may do great matters, especially if the times be fit. He that resteth upon gains certain shall hardly grow to great riches. And he that puts all upon adventures, doth oftentimes break, and come to poverty: it is good therefore to guard adventures with certainties that may uphold losses. Monopolies, and co-emption of wares for resale, where they are not restrained, are great means to enrich, especially if the party have intelligence what things are like to come into request, and so store himself beforehand. Riches gotten by service, though it be of the best rise, yet when they are gotten by flattery, feeding humors, and other servile conditions, they may be placed amongst the worst. As for fishing for testaments and executorships, as Tacitus saith of Seneca, *Testamenta et orbos tanquam indagine capi* [he took in bequests and wardships as with a net]; it is yet worse, by how much men submit themselves to meaner persons than in service. Believe not much them that seem to despise riches, for they despise them that despair of them, and none worse when they come to them. Be not penny-wise; riches have wings, and sometimes they fly away of themselves, sometimes they must be set flying to bring in more. Men leave their riches either to their kindred, or to the public; and moderate portions prosper best in both. A great estate left to an heir is as a lure to all the birds of prey round about to seize on him, if he be not the better stablished in years and judgments. Likewise glorious gifts and foundations are like sacrifices without salt, and but the painted sepulchers of alms, which soon will putrefy and corrupt inwardly. Therefore measure not thine advancements by quantity, but frame them by measure: and defer not charities till death; for, certainly, if a man weigh it rightly, he that doth so is rather liberal of another man's than of his own.

OF YOUTH AND AGE — No. 42

A MAN that is young in years may be old in hours if he have lost no time. But that happeneth rarely. Generally youth is like the first cogitations, not so wise as the second. For there is a youth in thoughts as well as in ages. And yet the invention of young men is more lively than that of old; and imaginations stream into their minds, better and, as it were, more divinely. Natures that have much heat, and great and violent desires and perturbations, are not ripe for action till they have passed the meridian of their years, as it was with Julius Cæsar and Septimius Severus, of the latter of whom it is said, *Juventutem egit erroribus, imo furoribus plenam* [he spent a youth full of errors, and even of acts of madness]. And yet he was the ablest emperor almost of all the list. But reposed natures may do well in youth, as it is seen in Augustus Cæsar, Cosmos, Duke of Florence, Gaston de Fois, and others. On the other side, heat and vivacity in age is an excellent composition for business. Young men are fitter to invent than to judge, fitter for execution than for counsel, and fitter for new projects than for settled business. For the experience of age, in things that fall within the compass of it, directeth them; but in new things abuseth them. The errors of young men are the ruin of business; but the errors of aged men amount but to this, that more might have been done, or sooner. Young men, in the conduct and manage of actions, embrace more than they can hold; stir more than they can quiet; fly to the end, without consideration of the means and degrees; pursue some few principles, which they have chanced upon, absurdly; care not to innovate, which draws unknown inconveniences; use extreme remedies at first; and, that which doubleth all errors, will not acknowledge or retract them, like an unready horse, that will neither stop nor turn. Men of age object too much, consult too long, adventure too little, repent too soon, and seldom drive business home to the full period, but content themselves with a mediocrity of success. Certainly it is good to compound employments of both, for that will be good for the present, because the virtues of either age may correct the defects of both; and good for succession, that young men may be learners, while men in age are actors; and, lastly, good for extern accidents, because authority followeth old men, and favor and popularity youth. But for the moral part perhaps youth will have the preëminence, as age hath for the politic. A certain rabbin upon the text, 'Your young men shall see visions, and your old men shall dream dreams,' inferreth that young men are admitted nearer to God than old, because vision is a clearer revelation than a dream. And certainly the more a man drinketh of the world the more it intoxicateth; and age doth profit rather in the powers of understanding than in the virtues of the will and affections. There be some have an over-early ripeness in their years, which fadeth betimes; these are, first, such as have brittle wits, the edge whereof is soon turned—such as was Hermogenes, the rhetorician, whose books are exceeding subtle, who afterwards waxed stupid. A second sort is of those that have some natural dispositions, which have better grace in youth than in age, such as is a fluent and luxuriant speech, which becomes youth well, but not age; so Tully saith of Hortensius, *Idem manebat, neque idem decebat* [He continued the same, when it was no longer becoming]. The third is of such as take too high a strain at the first, and are magnanimous more than tract of years can uphold; as was Scipio Africanus, of whom Livy saith in effect, *Ultima primis cedebant* [His end fell below his beginning].

OF NEGOTIATING — No. 47

It is generally better to deal by speech than by letter, and by the mediation of a third than by a man's self. Letters are good, when a man would draw an answer by letter back again; or when it may serve for a man's justification afterwards to produce his own letter; or where it may be danger to be interrupted, or heard by pieces. To deal in person is good, when a man's face breedeth regard, as commonly with inferiors; or in tender cases, where a man's eye upon the countenance of him with whom he speaketh may give him a direction how far to go; and generally, where a man will reserve to himself liberty, either to disavow or to expound. In choice of instruments, it is better to choose men of a plainer sort, that are like to do that that is committed to them, and to report back again faithfully the success, than those that are cunning to contrive out of other men's business somewhat to grace themselves, and will help the matter in report, for satisfaction sake. Use also such persons as affect the business wherein they are employed, for that quickeneth much; and such as are fit for the matter, as bold men for expostulation, fair-spoken men for persuasion, crafty men for inquiry and observation, froward and absurd men for business that doth not well bear out itself. Use also such as have been lucky, and prevailed before in things wherein you have employed them; for that breeds confidence, and they will strive to maintain their prescription.

It is better to sound a person with whom one deals, afar off, than to fall upon the point at first, except you mean to surprise him by some short question. It is better dealing with men in appetite, than with those that are where they would be. If a man deal with another upon conditions, the start or first performance is all; which a man cannot reasonably demand, except either the nature of the thing be such which must go before; or else a man can persuade the other party, that he shall still need him in some other thing: or else that he be counted the honester man. All practice is to discover, or to work. Men discover themselves in trust, in passion, at unawares; and of necessity, when they would have somewhat done, and cannot find an apt pretext. If you would work any man, you must either know his nature and fashions, and so lead him, or his ends, and so persuade him, or his weakness and disadvantages, and so awe him, or those that have interest in him, and so govern him. In dealing with cunning persons, we must ever consider their ends to interpret their speeches, and it is good to say little to them, and that which they least look for. In all negotiations of difficulty a man may not look to sow and reap at once, but must prepare business, and so ripen it by degrees.

OF STUDIES — No. 50

Studies serve for delight, for ornament, and for ability. Their chief use for delight is in privateness and retiring; for ornament is in discourse; and for ability is in the judgment and disposition of business. For expert men can execute, and perhaps judge of particulars, one by one; but the general counsels and the plots and marshalling of affairs come best from those that are learned. To spend too much time in studies is sloth; to use them too much for ornament is affectation; to make judgment wholly by their rules is the humor of a scholar. They perfect nature, and are perfected by experience. For natural abilities are like natural plants, that need pruning by study; and studies themselves do give forth directions too much at large, except they be bounded in by experience. Crafty men contemn studies, simple men admire them, and wise men use them. For they teach not their own use; but that is a wisdom without them, and above them, won by observation. Read not to contradict and confute; nor to believe and take for granted; nor to find talk and discourse; but to weigh and consider. Some books are to be tasted, others to be swallowed, and some few to be chewed and digested—that is, some books are to be read only in parts, others to be read, but not curiously, and some few to be read wholly, and with diligence and attention. Some books also may be read by deputy, and extracts made of them by others; but that would be only in the less important arguments and the meaner sort of books; else distilled books are like common distilled waters, flashy things. Reading maketh a full man, conference a ready man, and writing an exact man. And therefore if a man write little he had need have a great memory; if he confer little he had need have a present wit; and if he read little he had need have much cunning to seem to know that he doth not. Histories make men wise, poets witty, the mathematics subtle, natural philosophy deep, moral grave, logic and rhetoric able to contend, *Abeunt studia in mores* [Studies develop into habits]. Nay, there is no stond or impediment in the wit but may be wrought out by fit studies, like as diseases of the body may have appropriate exercises. Bowling is good for the stone and reins, shooting for the lungs and breast, gentle walking for the stomach, riding for the head, and the like. So if a man's wit be wandering, let him study the mathematics, for in demonstrations, if his wit be called away never so little, he must begin again; if his wit be not apt to distinguish or find differences, let him study the schoolmen, for they are *cymini sectores* [hair-splitters]; if he be not apt to beat over matters and to call up one thing to prove and illustrate another, let him study the lawyer's cases. So every defect of the mind may have a special receipt.

SIR THOMAS BROWNE (1605-1682)

BROWNE is described by Mr. Saintsbury as 'the greatest prose-writer perhaps, when all things are taken together, in the whole range of English,' and all critics are agreed that he is one of the greatest. He was educated at Winchester and Oxford, studied medicine abroad, and took his doctor's degree at Leyden. He was only thirty when he wrote the work by which he is best known, *Religio Medici*, or A Physician's Religion. Circulated at first in manuscript, it was twice printed surreptitiously in 1642, and an authorized edition was published in 1643. It at once attracted attention and was translated into Latin, Dutch, French, and German. In 1637 Browne settled at Norwich, and there he spent the rest of his life in the enjoyment of a wide fame, both as a scholar and as a physician. He was knighted when Charles II visited the city in 1671. He wrote a great deal, and left many tracts, which were published after his death. His most considerable work is an exposure of popular superstitions entitled *Pseudodoxia Epidemica* or Vulgar and Common Errors (1648). Ten years later appeared *Hydriotaphia Urn Burial, or a Discourse of the Sepulchral Urns lately found in Norfolk* and *The Garden of Cyrus, or the Quincuncial Lozenge, net-work plantations of the Ancients, artificially, naturally, mystically considered*. Of the latter Coleridge says that Browne finds 'quincunxes in heaven above, quincunxes in earth below, quincunxes in the mind of man, quincunxes in tones, in optic nerves, in roots of trees, in leaves, in everything.' Browne has, however, much rarer virtues than curious learning and quaintness of phrase: he discloses a lofty nature, and expresses the deep thoughts of an unusually well-balanced mind in a style not merely clear and dignified, but rich with a sustained and subtle harmony as of solemn music.

RELIGIO MEDICI

THE FIRST PART

FOR my religion though there be several circumstances that might persuade the world I have none at all, as the general scandal of my profession, the natural course of my studies, the indifferency of my behavior and discourse in matters of religion, neither violently defending one, nor with that common ardor and contention opposing another; yet in despite hereof, I dare, without usurpation, assume the honorable style of a Christian. Not that I merely owe this title to the font, my education, or clime wherein I was born, as being bred up either to confirm those principles my parents instilled into my understanding, or by a general consent proceed in the religion of my country: but having in my riper years and confirmed judgment, seen and examined all, I find myself obliged by the principles of grace, and the law of mine own reason, to embrace no other name but this: neither doth herein my zeal so far make me forget the general charity I owe unto humanity, as rather to hate than pity Turks, Infidels, and (what is worse) Jews; rather contenting myself to enjoy that happy style, than maligning those who refuse so glorious a title.

But because the name of a Christian is become too general to express our faith, there being a geography of religion as well as lands, and every clime distinguished not only by their laws and limits, but circumscribed by their doctrines and rules of faith; to be particular, I am of that reformed new-cast religion, wherein I dislike nothing but the name; of the same belief our Savior taught, the apostles disseminated, the fathers authorized, and the martyrs confirmed, but by the sinister ends of princes, the ambition and avarice of prelates, and the fatal corruption of times, so decayed, impaired, and fallen from its native beauty, that it required the careful and charitable hands of these times to restore it to its primitive integrity. Now the accidental occasion whereupon, the slender means whereby, the low and abject condition of the person by whom so good a work was set on foot, which in our adversaries beget contempt and scorn, fills me with wonder, and is the very same objection the insolent pagans first cast at Christ and his disciples.

Yet have I not so shaken hands with those desperate resolutions, who had rather venture at large their decayed bottom, than bring her in to be new trimmed in the dock; who had rather promiscuously retain all, than abridge any, and obstinately be what they are, than what they have been, as to stand in diameter and swords point with them. We have reformed from them, not against them; for omitting those improperations, and terms of scurrility betwixt us, which only difference our affections, and not our cause, there is between us one common name and appellation, one faith and necessary body of principles common to us both. And therefore I am not scrupulous to converse and live with them, to enter their churches in defect of ours, and either pray with them, or for them. I could never perceive any rational consequence from those many texts which prohibit the Children of Israel to pollute themselves with the temples of the heathens; we being all Christians, and not divided by such detested impieties as might profane our prayers, or the place wherein we make them; or that a resolved conscience may not adore her Creator anywhere, especially in places devoted to his service; where if their devotions offend him, mine may please him; if theirs profane it, mine may hallow it; holy-water and crucifix (dangerous to the common people) deceive not my judgment, nor abuse my devotion at all. I am, I confess, naturally inclined to that which misguided zeal terms superstition: my common conversation I do acknowledge austere, my behavior full of rigor, sometimes not without morosity; yet at my devotion I love to use the civility of my knee, my hat, and hand, with all those outward and sensible motions which may express or promote my invisible devotion. I should violate my own arm rather than a church, nor willingly deface the name of saint or martyr. At the sight of a cross or crucifix I can dispense with my hat, but scarce with the thought or memory of my Savior: I cannot laugh at, but rather pity the fruitless journeys of pilgrims, or contemn the miserable condition of friars; for though misplaced in circumstances, there is something in it of devotion. I could never hear the Ave-Mary bell[1] without an elevation, or think it a sufficient warrant, because they erred in one circumstance, for me to err in all, that is, in silence and dumb contempt. Whilst therefore they direct their devotions to her, I offer mine to God, and rectify the errors of their prayers, by rightly ordering mine own. At a solemn procession I have wept abundantly, while my consorts, blind with opposition and prejudice, have fallen into an excess of scorn and laughter. There are questionless, both in Greek, Roman, and African churches, solemnities and ceremonies, whereof the wiser zeals do make a Christian use, and stand condemned by us, not as evil in themselves, but as allurements and baits of superstition to those vulgar heads that look asquint on the face of truth, and those unstable judgments that cannot consist in the narrow point and center of virtue without a reel or stagger to the circumference.

As there were many reformers, so likewise many reformations; every country proceeding in a particular way and method, according as their national interest, together with their constitution and clime inclined them; some angrily, and with extremity; others calmly, and with mediocrity, not rending but easily dividing the community, and leaving an honest possibility of a reconciliation; which though peaceable spirits do desire, and may conceive that revolution of time and the mercies of God may effect, yet that judgment that shall consider the present antipathies between the two extremes, their contrarieties in condition, affection and opinion, may with the same hopes expect a union in the poles of heaven.

But to difference myself nearer, and draw into a lesser circle: there is no church, whose every part so squares unto my conscience; whose articles, constitutions, and customs, seem so consonant unto reason, and as it were framed to my particular devotion, as this whereof I hold my belief, the Church of England, to whose faith I am a sworn subject; and therefore in a double obligation subscribe unto her articles, and endeavor to observe her constitutions. Whatsoever is beyond, as points indifferent, I observe according to the rules of my private reason, or the humor and fashion of my devotion; neither believing this, because Luther affirmed it, or disproving that, because Calvin hath disavouched it. I condemn not all things in the Council of Trent, nor approve all in the Synod of Dort. In brief, where the Scripture is silent, the church is my text; where that speaks, 'tis but my comment: where there is a joint silence of both, I borrow not the rules of my religion from Rome or Geneva, but the dictates of my own reason. It is an unjust scandal of our adversaries, and a gross error in ourselves,

---

[1] A church bell that tolls every day at six and twelve of the clock; at the hearing whereof, every one in what place soever, either of house or street, betakes himself to his prayer, which is commonly directed to the Virgin.

to compute the nativity of our religion from Henry the Eighth, who though he rejected the Pope, refused not the faith of Rome, and effected no more than what his own predecessors desired and assayed in ages past, and was conceived the state of Venice would have attempted in our days. It is as uncharitable a point in us to fall upon those popular scurrilities and opprobrious scoffs of the Bishop of Rome, to whom as temporal prince, we owe the duty of good language. I confess there is a cause of passion between us; by his sentence I stand excommunicated, heretic is the best language he affords me; yet can no ear witness, I ever returned him the name of Antichrist, Man of sin, or Whore of Babylon. It is the method of charity to suffer without reaction: those usual satires and invectives of the pulpit may perchance produce a good effect on the vulgar, whose ears are opener to rhetoric than logic; yet do they in no wise confirm the faith of wiser believers, who know that a good cause needs not to be pardoned by passion, but can sustain itself upon a temperate dispute.

I could never divide myself from any man upon the difference of an opinion, or be angry with his judgment for not agreeing with me in that, from which within a few days I should dissent myself. I have no genius to disputes in religion, and have often thought it wisdom to decline them, especially upon a disadvantage, or when the cause of truth might suffer in the weakness of my patronage. Where we desire to be informed, 'tis good to contest with men above ourselves; but to confirm and establish our opinions, 'tis best to argue with judgments below our own, that the frequent spoils and victories over their reasons, may settle in ourselves an esteem and confirmed opinion of our own. Every man is not a proper champion for truth, nor fit to take up the gauntlet in the cause of verity. Many from the ignorance of these maxims, and an inconsiderate zeal unto truth, have too rashly charged the troops of error, and remain as trophies unto the enemies of truth. A man may be in as just possession of truth as of a city, and yet be forced to surrender; 'tis therefore far better to enjoy her with peace, than to hazard her on a battle. If therefore there rise any doubts in my way, I do forget them, or at least defer them, till my better settled judgment and more manly reason be able to resolve them, for I perceive every man's own reason is his best Œdipus, and will upon a reasonable truce find a way to loose those bonds wherewith the subtleties of error have enchained our more flexible and tender judgments. In philosophy, where truth seeme double faced, there is no man more paradoxical than myself; but in divinity I love to keep the road; and though not in an implicit, yet an humble faith, follow the great wheel of the church, by which I move, not reserving any proper poles or motion from the epicycle of my own brain. By this means I have no gap for heresy, schisms, or errors, of which at present I hope I shall not injure truth to say I have no taint or tincture. I must confess my greener studies have been polluted with two or three, not any begotten in the latter centuries, but old and obsolete such as could never have been revived but by such extravagant and irregular heads as mine. For indeed heresies perish not with their authors, but like the river Arethusa, though they lose their currents in one place, they rise up again in another. One general council is not able to extirpate one single heresy; it may be cancelled for the present, but revolution of time, and the like aspects from heaven, will restore it, when it will flourish till it be condemned again. For as though there were metempsychosis, and the soul of one man passed into another; opinions do find after certain revolutions men and minds like those that first begat them. To see ourselves again, we need not look for Plato's year:[1] every man is not only himself; there hath been many Diogenes, and as many Timons, though but few of that name; men are lived over again, the world is now as it was in ages past; there was none then, but there hath been some one since that parallels him, and as it were his revived self.

* * *

As for those wingy mysteries in divinity, and airy subtleties in religion, which have unhinged the brains of better heads, they never stretched the *pia mater* of mine; methinks there be not impossibilities enough in religion, for an active faith; the deepest mysteries ours contains, have not only been illustrated, but maintained by syllogism, and the rule of reason: I love to lose myself in a mystery, to pursue my reason to an *O altitudo!* 'Tis my solitary recreation to pose my apprehension with those involved enigmas and riddles of the Trinity, with incarnation and resurrection. I can answer all the objections of Satan and my rebellious rea-

---

[1] A revolution of certain thousand years, when all things should return unto their former estate, and he be teaching again in his school as when he delivered this opinion.

son, with that odd resolution I learned of Tertullian, *Certum est quia impossibile est* [It is certain because it is impossible]. I desire to exercise my faith in the difficultest point; for to credit ordinary and visible objects, is not faith, but persuasion. Some believe the better for seeing Christ's sepulcher; and when they have seen the Red Sea, doubt not of the miracle. Now contrarily, I bless myself, and am thankful that I lived not in the days of miracles, that I never saw Christ nor his disciples. I would not have been one of those Israelites that passed the Red Sea, nor one of Christ's patients on whom he wrought his wonders; then had my faith been thrust upon me; nor should I enjoy that greater blessing pronounced to all that believe and saw not. 'Tis an easy and necessary belief, to credit what our eye and sense hath examined: I believe he was dead and buried, and rose again; and desire to see him in his glory, rather than to contemplate him in his cenotaph or sepulcher. Nor is this much to believe; as we have reason, we owe this faith unto history: they only had the advantage of a bold and noble faith, who lived before his coming, who upon obscure prophecies and mystical types could raise a belief, and expect apparent impossibilities.

* * *

Thus there are two books from whence I collect my divinity; besides that written one of God, another of his servant nature, that universal and public manuscript, that lies expansed unto the eyes of all; those that never saw him in the one, have discovered him in the other: this was the scripture and theology of the heathens; the natural motion of the sun made them more admire him, than its supernatural station did the Children of Israel; the ordinary effects of nature wrought more admiration in them, than in the other all his miracles; surely the heathens knew better how to join and read these mystical letters, than we Christians, who cast a more careless eye on these common hieroglyphics, and disdain to suck divinity from the flowers of nature. Nor do I so forget God as to adore the name of nature; which I define not with the schools, to be the principle of motion and rest, but that straight and regular line, that settled and constant course the wisdom of God hath ordained the actions of his creatures, according to their several kinds. To make a revolution every day, is the nature of the sun, because of that necessary course which God hath ordained it, from which it cannot swerve but by a faculty from that voice which first did give it motion. Now this course of nature God seldom alters or perverts, but like an excellent artist hath so contrived his work, that with the selfsame instrument, without a new creation, he may effect his obscurest designs. Thus he sweeteneth the water with a word, preserveth the creatures in the ark, which the blast of his mouth might have as easily created. For God is like a skilful geometrician, who when more easily, and with one stroke of his compass he might describe or divide a right line, had yet rather do this in a circle or longer way; according to the constituted and fore-laid principles of his art. Yet this rule of his he doth sometimes pervert, to acquaint the world with his prerogative, lest the arrogancy of our reason should question his power, and conclude he could not. And thus I call the effects of nature the works of God, whose hand and instrument she only is; and therefore to ascribe his actions unto her, is to devolve the honor of the principal agent, upon the instrument; which if with reason we may do, then let our hammers rise up and boast they have built our houses, and our pens receive the honor of our writing. I hold there is a general beauty in the works of God, and therefore no deformity in any kind of species of creature whatsoever: I cannot tell by what logic we call a toad, a bear, or an elephant ugly, they being created in those outward shapes and figures which best express those actions of their inward forms. And having passed that general visitation of God, who saw that all that he had made was good, that is, conformable to his will, which abhors deformity, and is the rule of order and beauty; there is no deformity but in monstrosity, wherein notwithstanding there is a kind of beauty. Nature so ingeniously contriving the irregular parts, as they become sometimes more remarkable than the principal fabric. To speak yet more narrowly, there was never anything ugly or mis-shapen but the chaos; wherein notwithstanding, to speak strictly, there was no deformity, because no form, nor was it yet impregnant by the voice of God. Now nature is not at variance with art, nor art with nature; they being both servants of his providence. Art is the perfection of nature: were the world now as it was the sixth day, there were yet a chaos. Nature hath made one world, and art another. In brief, all things are artificial; for nature is the art of God.

* * *

I am naturally bashful, nor hath conversation, age, or travel been able to effront, or enharden me; yet I have one part of modesty, which I have seldom discovered in another, that is (to speak truly) I am not so much afraid of death, as ashamed thereof; 't is the very disgrace and ignominy of our natures, that in a moment can so disfigure us, that our nearest friends, wife and children stand afraid and start at us. The birds and beasts of the field, that before in a natural fear obeyed us, forgetting all allegiance begin to prey upon us. This very conceit hath in a tempest disposed and left me willing to be swallowed up in the abyss of waters; wherein I had perished unseen, unpitied, without wondering eyes, tears of pity, lectures of mortality, and none had said, *Quantum mutatus ab illo* [How much changed from what he was]! Not that I am ashamed of the anatomy of my parts, or can accuse nature for playing the bungler in any part of me, or my own vicious life for contracting any shameful disease upon me, whereby I might not call myself as wholesome a morsel for the worms as any.

Some upon the courage of a fruitful issue, wherein, as in the truest chronicle, they seem to outlive themselves, can with greater patience away with death. This conceit and counterfeit subsisting in our progenies, seems to be a mere fallacy, unworthy the desires of a man, that can but conceive a thought of the next world; who, in a nobler ambition, should desire to live in his substance in heaven, rather than his name and shadow in the earth. And therefore at my death I mean to take a total adieu of the world, not caring for a monument, history, or epitaph, not so much as the memory of my name to be found anywhere, but in the universal register of God. I am not yet so cynical, as to approve the testament of Diogenes,[1] nor do I altogether allow that rodomontado of Lucan:

> *Cælo tegitur, qui non habet urnam.*
> He that unburied lies, wants not his hearse,
> For unto him a tomb's the universe.

But commend in my calmer judgment, those ingenuous intentions that desire to sleep by the urns of [their] fathers, and strive to go the nearest way unto corruption. I do not envy the temper of crows and daws, nor the numerous and weary days of our fathers before the flood. If there be any truth in astrology, I may outlive a jubilee; as yet I have not seen one revolution of Saturn, nor hath my pulse beat thirty years; and yet excepting one, have seen the ashes, and left underground, all the kings of Europe; have been contemporary to three emperors, four grand signiors, and as many popes. Methinks I have outlived myself, and begin to be weary of the sun; I have shaken hands with delight: in my warm blood and canicular days, I perceive I do anticipate the vices of age. The world to me is but a dream or mock show, and we all therein but pantalones and antics, to my severer contemplations.

It is not, I confess, an unlawful prayer to desire to surpass the days of our Savior, or wish to outlive that age wherein he thought fittest to die; yet if (as divinity affirms) there shall be no gray hairs in heaven, but all shall rise in the perfect state of men, we do but outlive those perfections in this world, to be recalled unto them by a greater miracle in the next, and run on here but to be retrograde hereafter. Were there any hopes to outlive vice, or a point to be superannuated from sin, it were worthy our knees to implore the days of Methuselah. But age doth not rectify, but incurvate our natures, turning bad dispositions into worser habits, and (like diseases) brings on incurable vices; for every day as we grow weaker in age, we grow stronger in sin; and the number of our days doth but make our sins innumerable. The same vice committed at sixteen, is not the same, though it agrees in all other circumstances, as at forty, but swells and doubles from that circumstance of our ages, wherein, besides the constant and inexcusable habit of transgressing, the maturity of our judgment cuts off pretense unto excuse or pardon. Every sin the oftener it is committed, the more it acquireth in the quality of evil; as it succeeds in time, so it proceeds in degrees of badness; for as they proceed they ever multiply, and like figures in arithmetic, the last stands for more than all that went before it. And though I think no man can live well once, but he that could live twice, yet for my own part I would not live over my hours past, or begin again the thread of my days: not upon Cicero's ground, because I have lived them well, but for fear I should live them worse. I find my growing judgment daily instruct me how to be better, but my untamed affections and confirmed vitiosity makes me daily do worse; I find in my confirmed age the same sins I discovered in my

---

[1] Who willed his friend not to bury him, but hang him up with a staff in his hand to fright away the crows.

youth; I committed many then because I was a child, and because I commit them still, I am yet an infant. Therefore I perceive a man may be twice a child before the days of dotage, and stand in need of Æson's bath before threescore.

And truly there goes a great deal of providence to produce a man's life unto three score. There is more required than an able temper for those years; though the radical humor contain in it sufficient oil for seventy, yet I perceive in some it gives no light past thirty: men assign not all the causes of long life, that write whole books thereof. They that found themselves on the radical balsam, or vital sulphur of the parts, determine not why Abel lived not so long as Adam. There is therefore a secret glome or bottom of our days; 't is his wisdom to determine them, but his perpetual and waking providence that fulfils and accomplisheth them; wherein the spirits, ourselves, and all the creatures of God in a secret and disputed way do execute his will. Let them not therefore complain of immaturity that die about thirty; they fall but like the whole world, whose solid and well-composed substance must not expect the duration and period of its constitution. When all things are completed in it, its age is accomplished; and the last and general fever may as naturally destroy it before six thousand, as me before forty. There is therefore some other hand that twines the thread of life than that of nature. We are not only ignorant in antipathies and occult qualities; our ends are as obscure as our beginnings. The line of our days is drawn by night, and the various effects therein by a pencil that is invisible: wherein though we confess our ignorance, I am sure we do not err if we say it is the hand of God.

* * *

The Second Part

Now for that other virtue of charity, without which faith is a mere notion, and of no existence, I have ever endeavored to nourish the merciful disposition and humane inclination I borrowed from my parents, and regulate it to the written and prescribed laws of charity; and if I hold the true anatomy of myself, I am delineated and naturally framed to such a piece of virtue. For I am of a constitution so general, that it comforts and sympathizeth with all things; I have no antipathy, or rather idiosyncrasy, in diet, humor, air, anything: I wonder not at the French for their dishes of frogs, snails, and toadstools; nor at the Jews for locusts and grasshoppers; but being amongst them, make them my common viands; and I find they agree with my stomach as well as theirs. I could digest a salad gathered in a churchyard, as well as in a garden. I cannot start at the presence of a serpent, scorpion, lizard, or salamander: at the sight of a toad or viper, I find in me no desire to take up a stone to destroy them. I feel not in myself those common antipathies that I can discover in others: those national repugnances do not touch me, nor do I behold with prejudice the French, Italian, Spaniard, and Dutch; but where I find their actions in balance with my countrymen's, I honor, love, and embrace them in the same degree. I was born in the eighth climate, but seem for to be framed and constellated unto all: I am no plant that will not prosper out of a garden: all places, all airs make unto me one country; I am in England, everywhere, and under any meridian. I have been shipwrecked, yet am not enemy with the sea or winds; I can study, play, or sleep in a tempest. In brief, I am averse from nothing; my conscience would give me the lie if I should absolutely detest or hate any essence but the devil; or so at least abhor anything, but that we might come to composition. If there be any among those common objects of hatred I do contemn and laugh at, it is that great enemy of reason, virtue, and religion, the multitude; that numerous piece of monstrosity, which taken asunder seem men, and the reasonable creatures of God; but confused together, make but one great beast, and a monstrosity more prodigious than Hydra. It is no breach of charity to call these fools; it is the style all holy writers have afforded them, set down by Solomon in canonical Scripture, and a point of our faith to believe so. Neither in the name of multitude do I only include the base and minor sort of people; there is a rabble even amongst the gentry, a sort of plebeian heads, whose fancy moves with the same wheel as these; men in the same level with mechanics, though their fortunes do somewhat gild their infirmities, and their purses compound for their follies. But as in casting account, three or four men together come short in account of one man placed by himself below them: so neither are a troop of these ignorant Doradoes, of that true esteem and value, as many a forlorn person, whose condition doth place them below their feet. Let us speak like politicians, there is a nobility without heraldry, a natural dignity, whereby one man is ranked with another; another filed before him, according to the quality of his desert, and preëminence of his good parts: though the corruption of these times, and the bias of present practice wheel another way. Thus it was in the first and primitive commonwealths, and is yet in the integrity and cradle of well-ordered polities, till corruption getteth ground, ruder desires laboring after that which wiser generations contemn, every one having a liberty to amass and heap up riches, and they a license or faculty to do or purchase anything.

* * *

To do no injury, nor take none, was a principle, which to my former years, and impatient affections, seemed to contain enough of morality; but my more settled years, and Christian constitution, have fallen upon severer resolutions. I can hold there is no such thing as injury; that if there be, there is no such injury as revenge, and no such revenge as the contempt of an injury; that to hate another, is to malign himself; that the truest way to love another, is to despise ourselves. I were unjust unto mine own conscience, if I should say I am at variance with anything like myself. I find there are many pieces in this one fabric of man: this frame is raised upon a mass of antipathies. I am one methinks, but as the world; wherein notwithstanding there are a swarm of distinct essences, and in them another world of contrarieties; we carry private and domestic enemies within, public and more hostile adversaries without. The devil, that did but buffet St. Paul, plays methinks at sharp with me. Let me be nothing, if within the compass of myself I do not find the battle of Lepanto, passion against reason, reason against faith, faith against the devil, and my conscience against all. There is another man within me, that's angry with me, rebukes, commands, and dastards me. I have no conscience of marble, to resist the hammer of more heavy offenses; nor yet so soft and waxen, as to take the impression of each single peccadillo or scape of infirmity: I am of a strange belief, that it is as easy to be forgiven some sins, as to commit some others. For my original sin, I hold it to be washed away in my baptism; for my actual transgressions, I compute and reckon with God but from my last repentance, sacrament, or general absolution; and therefore am not terrified with the sins or madness of my youth. I thank the goodness of God, I have no sins that want a name. I am not singular in offenses; my transgressions are epidemical, and from the common breath of our corruption. For there are certain tempers of body, which, matched with a humorous depravity of mind, do hatch and produce vitiosities, whose newness and monstrosity of nature admits no name. . . . For the heavens are not only fruitful in new and unheard-of stars, the earth in plants and animals; but men's minds also in villainy and vices. Now the dulness of my reason, and the vulgarity of my disposition, never prompted my invention, nor solicited my affection unto any of those. Yet even those common and quotidian infirmities that so necessarily attend me, and do seem to be my very nature, have so dejected me, so broken the estimation that I should have otherwise of myself, that I repute myself the most abjectest piece of mortality. Divines prescribe a fit of sorrow to repentance; there goes indignation, anger, sorrow, hatred, into mine: passions of a contrary nature, which neither seem to suit with this action, nor my proper constitution. It is no breach of charity to ourselves, to be at variance with our vices; nor to abhor that part of us, which is an enemy to the ground of charity, our God; wherein we do but imitate our great selves, the world, whose divided antipathies and contrary faces do yet carry a charitable regard unto the whole by their particular discords, preserving the common harmony, and keeping in fetters those powers, whose rebellions once masters might be the ruin of all.

I thank God, amongst those millions of vices I do inherit and hold from Adam, I have escaped one, and that a mortal enemy to charity, the first and [father-sin], not only of man, but of the devil, pride; a vice whose name is comprehended in a monosyllable, but in its nature not circumscribed with a world. I have escaped it in a condition that can hardly avoid it. Those petty acquisitions and reputed perfections that advance and elevate the conceits of other men add no feathers unto mine. I have seen a grammarian tower and plume himself over a single line in Horace, and show more pride in the construction of one ode, than the author in the composure of the whole book. For my own part, besides the jargon and *patois* of several provinces, I understand no less than six languages; yet I protest I have no higher conceit of myself, than had our fathers before the confusion of Babel, when there was but one language in the world, and none to boast himself either linguist or critic. I have not only seen several countries, beheld the nature of their climes, the chorography of their provinces, topography of their cities, but understood their several laws, customs, and policies; yet cannot all this persuade the dulness of my spirit unto such an opinion of myself, as I behold in nimbler and conceited heads, that never looked a degree beyond their nests. I know the names, and somewhat more, of all the constellations in my horizon; yet I have seen a prating mariner, that could only name the pointers and the north star, out-talk me, and conceit himself a whole sphere above me. I know most of the plants of my country and of those about me; yet methinks I do not know so many as when I did but know a hundred, and had scarcely ever simpled further than Cheapside. For indeed, heads of capacity, and such as are not full with a handful, or easy measure of knowledge, think they know nothing, till they know all; which being impossible, they fall upon the opinion of Socrates, and only know they know not anything. I cannot think that Homer pined away upon the riddle of the fisherman, or that Aristotle, who understood the uncertainty of knowledge, and confessed so often the reason of man too weak for the works of nature, did ever drown himself upon the flux and reflux of Euripus. We do but learn to-day, what our better advanced judgments will unteach to-morrow; and Aristotle doth not instruct us, as Plato did him; that is, to confute himself. I have run through all sorts, yet find no rest in any: though our first studies and junior endeavors may style us Peripatetics, Stoics, or Academics, yet I perceive the wisest heads prove, at last, almost all skeptics, and stand like Janus in the field of knowledge. I have therefore one common and authentic philosophy I learned in the schools, whereby I discourse and satisfy the reason of other men; another more reserved, and drawn from experience, whereby I content mine own. Solomon, that complained of ignorance in the height of knowledge, hath not only humbled my conceits, but discouraged my endeavors. There is yet another conceit that hath sometimes made me shut my books, which tells me it is a vanity to waste our days in the blind pursuit of knowledge; it is but attending a little longer, and we shall enjoy that by instinct and infusion, which we endeavor at here by labor and inquisition. It is better to sit down in a modest ignorance; and rest contented with the natural blessing of our own reasons, than buy the uncertain knowledge of this life, with sweat and vexation, which death gives every fool gratis, and is an accessory of our glorification.

I was never yet once, and commend their resolutions who never marry twice: not that I disallow of second marriage; as neither in all cases of polygamy, which considering some times, and the unequal number of both sexes, may be also necessary. The whole world was made for man, but the twelfth part of man for woman: man is the whole world, and the breath of God; woman the rib, and crooked piece of man. . . . I speak not in prejudice, nor am averse from that sweet sex, but naturally amorous of all that is beautiful; I can look a whole day with delight upon a handsome picture, though it be but of a horse. It is my temper, and I like it the better, to affect all harmony; and sure there is music even in the beauty, and the silent note which Cupid strikes, far sweeter than the sound of an instrument. For there is a music wherever there is a harmony, order or proportion; and thus far we may maintain the music of the spheres: for those well-ordered motions, and regular paces, though they give no sound unto the ear, yet to the understanding they strike a note most full of harmony. Whosoever is harmonically composed, delights in harmony; which makes me much distrust the symmetry of those heads which declaim against all church-music. For myself, not only from my obedience, but my particular genius, I do embrace it: for even that vulgar and tavern-music, which makes one man merry, another mad, strikes in me a deep fit of devotion, and a profound contemplation of the first composer. There is something in it of divinity more than the ear discovers: it is a hieroglyphical and shadowed lesson of the whole world, and creatures of God; such a melody to the ear, as the whole world well understood, would afford the understanding. In brief, it is a sensible fit of that harmony, which intellectually sounds in the ears of God. I will not say with Plato, the soul is a harmony, but harmonical, and hath its nearest sympathy unto music: thus some whose temper of body agrees, and humors the constitution of their souls, are born poets, though indeed all are naturally inclined unto rhythm. This made Tacitus in the very first line of his story, fall upon a verse,[1] and Cicero

---

[1] *Urbem Romam in principio reges habuere.*

the worst of poets, but declaiming for a poet, falls in the very first sentence upon a perfect hexameter.[2] I feel not in me those sordid and unchristian desires of my profession; I do not secretly implore and wish for plagues, rejoice at famines, revolve ephemerides and almanacs, in expectation of malignant aspects, fatal conjunctions and eclipses: I rejoice not at unwholesome springs, nor unseasonable winters; my prayer goes with the husbandman's; I desire everything in its proper season, that neither men nor the times be put out of temper. Let me be sick myself, if sometimes the malady of my patient be not a disease unto me; I desire rather to cure his infirmities than my own necessities: where I do him no good, methinks it is scarce honest gain; though I confess 't is but the worthy salary of our well-intended endeavors. I am not only ashamed, but heartily sorry, that besides death, there are diseases incurable; yet not for my own sake, or that they be beyond my art, but for the general cause and sake of humanity, whose common cause I apprehend as mine own. And to speak more generally, those three noble professions which all civil commonwealths do honor are raised upon the fall of Adam, and are not exempt from their infirmities; there are not only diseases incurable in physic, but cases indissolvable in laws, vices incorrigible in divinity. If general councils may err, I do not see why particular courts should be infallible; their perfectest rules are raised upon the erroneous reasons of man; and the laws of one do but condemn the rules of another; as Aristotle oft-times the opinions of his predecessors, because, though agreeable to reason, yet were not consonant to his own rules, and logic of his proper principles. Again, to speak nothing of the sin against the Holy Ghost, whose cure not only, but whose nature is unknown; I can cure the gout or stone in some, sooner than divinity, pride, or avarice in others. I can cure vices by physic, when they remain incurable by divinity; and shall obey my pills, when they contemn their precepts. I boast nothing, but plainly say, we all labor against our own cure; for death is the cure of all diseases. There is no catholicon or universal remedy I know but this, which though nauseous to queasy stomachs, yet to prepared appetites is nectar, and a pleasant potion of immortality.

* * *

[1] *Pro Archia Poeta: In qua me non inficior mediocriter esse.*

From HYDRIOTAPHIA. URN-BURIAL

WHAT song the Syrens sang, or what name Achilles assumed when he hid himself among women, though puzzling questions,[2] are not beyond all conjecture. What time the persons of these ossuaries entered the famous nations of the dead,[3] and slept with princes and counsellors, might admit a wide solution. But who were the proprietaries of these bones, or what bodies these ashes made up, were a question above antiquarism, not to be resolved by man, nor easily perhaps by spirits, except we consult the provincial guardians, or tutelary observators. Had they made as good provision for their names as they have done for their relics, they had not so grossly erred in the art of perpetuation. But to subsist in bones, and be but pyramidally extant, is a fallacy in duration. Vain ashes, which, in the oblivion of names, persons, times and sexes, have found unto themselves a fruitless continuation, and only arise unto late posterity as emblems of mortal vanities, antidotes against pride, vain-glory, and madding vices! Pagan vain-glories, which thought the world might last forever, had encouragement for ambition, and finding no *Atropos* unto the immortality of their names, were never damped with the necessity of oblivion. Even old ambitions had the advantage of ours in the attempts of their vain-glories, who acting early, and before the probable meridian of time, have by this time found great accomplishment of their designs, whereby the ancient heroes have already out-lasted their monuments and mechanical preservations. But in this latter scene of time we cannot expect such mummies unto our memories, when ambition may fear the prophecy of Elias;[4] and Charles the Fifth can never hope to live within two Methuselahs of Hector.[5]

And therefore restless inquietude for the diuturnity of our memories unto present considerations seems a vanity almost out of date, and a superannuated piece of folly. We cannot hope to live so long in our names as some have done in their persons: one face of Janus holds no proportion to the other. 'T is too late to be ambitious. The great mutations of

[2] The puzzling questions of Tiberius unto grammarians. Marcel. *Donatus in Suet.*
[3] κλυτὰ ἔθνεα νεκρῶν.—Hom. *Job.*
[4] That the world may last but six thousand years.
[5] Hector's fame lasting above two lives of Methuselah, before that famous prince was extant.

the world are acted, or time may be too short for our designs. To extend our memories by monuments, whose death we daily pray for, and whose duration we cannot hope without injury to our expectations in the advent of the last day, were a contradiction to our beliefs. We, whose generations are ordained in this setting part of time, are providentially taken off from such imaginations; and, being necessitated to eye the remaining particle of futurity, are naturally constituted unto thoughts of the next world, and cannot excusably decline the consideration of that duration which maketh pyramids pillars of snow, and all that's past a moment.

Circles and right lines limit and close all bodies, and the mortal right-lined circle[1] must conclude and shut up all. There is no antidote against the opium of time, which temporally considereth all things. Our fathers find their graves in our short memories, and sadly tell us how we may be buried in our survivors. Gravestones tell truth scarce forty years.[2] Generations pass while some trees stand, and old families last not three oaks. To be read by bare inscriptions, like many in Gruter,[3] to hope for eternity by enigmatical epithets or first letters of our names, to be studied by antiquaries who we were, and have new names given us like many of the mummies, are cold consolations unto the students of perpetuity, even by everlasting languages.

To be content that times to come should only know there was such a man, not caring whether they knew more of him, was a frigid ambition in Cardan,[4] disparaging his horoscopal inclination and judgment of himself. Who cares to subsist like Hippocrates' patients, or Achilles' horses in Homer, under naked nominations, without deserts and noble acts, which are the balsam of our memories, the *entelechia* and soul of our subsistences? To be nameless in worthy deed exceeds an infamous history. The Canaanitish woman lives more happily without a name, than Herodias with one. And who had not rather have been the good thief, than Pilate?

But the iniquity of oblivion blindly scattereth her poppy, and deals with the memory of men without distinction to merit of perpetuity. Who can but pity the founder of the pyramids? Herostratus lives that burnt the temple of Diana; he is almost lost that built it. Time hath spared the epitaph of Adrian's horse, confounded that of himself. In vain we compute our felicities by the advantage of our good names, since bad have equal durations; and Thersites is like to live as long as Agamemnon, without the favor of the everlasting register. Who knows whether the best of men be known? or whether there be not more remarkable persons forgot, than any that stand remembered in the known account of time? The first man had been as unknown as the last, and Methuselah's long life had been his only chronicle.

Oblivion is not to be hired: the greater part must be content to be as though they had not been, to be found in the register of God, not in the record of man. Twenty-seven names make up the first story, and the recorded names ever since contain not one living century. The number of the dead long exceedeth all that shall live. The night of time far surpasseth the day, and who knows when was the equinox? Every hour adds unto that current arithmetic, which scarce stands one moment. And since death must be the *Lucina* of life, and even pagans could doubt whether thus to live were to die; since our longest sun sets at right descensions, and makes but winter arches, and therefore it cannot be long before we lie down in darkness, and have our light in ashes; since the brother of death daily haunts us with dying mementoes, and time, that grows old itself, bids us hope no long duration: diuturnity is a dream and folly of expectation.

Darkness and light divide the course of time, and oblivion shares with memory a great part even of our living beings; we slightly remember our felicities, and the smartest strokes of affliction leave but short smart upon us. Sense endureth no extremities, and sorrows destroy us or themselves. To weep into stones are fables. Afflictions induce callosities, miseries are slippery, or fall like snow upon us, which notwithstanding is no stupidity. To be ignorant of evils to come, and forgetful of evils past, is a merciful provision in nature, whereby we digest the mixture of our few and evil days, and our delivered senses not relapsing into cutting remembrances, our sorrows are not kept raw by the edge of repetitions. A great part of antiquity contented their hopes of subsistency with a transmigration of their souls. A good

---

[1] ϴ The character of death.

[2] Old ones being taken up and other bodies laid under them.

[3] *Gruteri Inscriptiones Antiquæ.*

[4] *Cuperem notum esse quòd sim, non opto ut sciatur qualis sim.—Card. in vita propria.*

way to continue their memories, while having the advantage of plural successions, they could not but act something remarkable in such variety of beings, and enjoying the fame of their passed selves, make accumulation of glory unto their last durations. Others, rather than be lost in the uncomfortable night of nothing, were content to recede into the common being, and make one particle of the public soul of all things, which was no more than to return into their unknown and divine original again. Egyptian ingenuity was more unsatisfied, contriving their bodies in sweet consistencies to attend the return of their souls. But all was vanity,[1] feeding the wind, and folly. The Egyptian mummies, which Cambyses or time hath spared, avarice now consumeth. Mummy is become merchandise, Mizraim cures wounds, and Pharaoh is sold for balsams.

In vain do individuals hope for immortality, or any patent from oblivion, in preservations below the moon; men have been deceived even in their flatteries above the sun, and studied conceits to perpetuate their names in heaven. The various cosmography of that part hath already varied the names of contrived constellations; Nimrod is lost in Orion, and Osiris in the dog-star. While we look for incorruption in the heavens, we find they are but like the earth; durable in their main bodies, alterable in their parts: whereof, beside comets and new stars, perspectives begin to tell tales; and the spots that wander about the sun, with Phæthon's favor, would make clear conviction.

There is nothing strictly immortal but immortality; whatever hath no beginning may be confident of no end: (all others have a dependent being, and within the reach of destruction) which is the peculiar of that necessary essence that cannot destroy itself; and the highest strain of omnipotency, to be so powerfully constituted, as not to suffer even from the power of itself. But the sufficiency of Christian immortality frustrates all earthly glory, and the quality of either state after death makes a folly of posthumous memory. God, who can only destroy our souls, and hath assured our resurrection, either of our bodies or names hath directly promised no duration; wherein there is so much of chance, that the boldest expectants have found unhappy frustration; and to hold long subsistence, seems but a scape in oblivion. But man is a noble animal, splendid in ashes, and pompous in the grave, solemnizing nativities and deaths with equal luster nor omitting ceremonies of bravery in the infamy of his nature.

Life is a pure flame, and we live by an invisible sun within us. A small fire sufficeth for life, great flames seemed too little after death, while men vainly affected precious pyres, and to burn like Sardanapalus. But the wisdom of funeral laws found the folly of prodigal blazes, and reduced undoing fires, unto the rule of sober obsequies, wherein few could be so mean as not to provide wood, pitch, a mourner, and an urn.

Five languages secured not the epitaph of Gordianus. The man of God lives longer without a tomb than any by one, invisibly interred by angels, and adjudged to obscurity, though not without some marks directing human discovery. Enoch and Elias, without either tomb or burial, in an anomalous state of being, are the great examples of perpetuity in their long and living memory, in strict account being still on this side death, and having a late part yet to act upon this stage of earth. If in the decretory term of the world we shall not all die, but be changed, according to received translation, the last day will make but few graves; at least quick resurrections will anticipate lasting sepultures: some graves will be opened before they be quite closed, and Lazarus be no wonder, when many that feared to die shall groan that they can die but once. The dismal state is the second and living death, when life puts despair on the damned; when men shall wish the coverings of mountains, not of monuments, and annihilation shall be courted.

[1] *Omnia vanitas et pastio venti, νομὴ ἀνέμου καὶ βόσκησις, ut olim Aquila et Symmachus. v. Drus. Eccles.*

* * *

ISAAK WALTON (1593-1683)

The *Complete Angler* (1653) is one of the best established of the English classics, holding its place through succeeding ages by its unaffected simplicity and charming naturalness. Its author, when he was not fishing and enjoying country sights and sounds, was a London linen draper with many pleasant friendships, including some of the leading men of the time; his life was happy and uneventful.

THE COMPLETE ANGLER

CHAPTER IV

OBSERVATIONS OF THE NATURE AND BREEDING OF THE TROUT, AND HOW TO FISH FOR HIM; AND THE MILKMAID'S SONG

PISCATOR [ANGLER]. THE trout is a fish highly valued both in this and foreign nations: he may be justly said, as the old poet said of wine, and we English say of venison, to be a generous fish: a fish that is so like the buck that he also has his seasons; for it is observed, that he comes in and goes out of season with the stag and buck. Gesner says his name is of a German offspring, and says he is a fish that feeds clean and purely, in the swiftest streams, and on the hardest gravel; and that he may justly contend with all fresh-water fish, as the mullet may with all sea-fish, for precedency and daintiness of taste, and that being in right season, the most dainty palates have allowed precedency to him.

And before I go further in my discourse, let me tell you, that you are to observe, that as there be some barren does that are good in summer, so there be some barren trouts that are good in winter; but there are not many that are so, for usually they be in their perfection in the month of May, and decline with the buck. Now you are to take notice that in several countries, as in Germany and in other parts, compared to ours, fish differ much in their bigness and shape, and other ways, and so do trouts: it is well known that in the Lake Leman, the Lake of Geneva, there are trouts taken of three cubits long, as is affirmed by Gesner, a writer of good credit; and Mercator says the trouts that are taken in the Lake of Geneva are a great part of the merchandise of that famous city. And you are further to know that there be certain waters that breed trouts remarkable both for their number and smallness. I know a little brook in Kent that breeds them to a number incredible, and you may take them twenty or forty in an hour, but none greater than about the size of a gudgeon: there are also in divers rivers, especially that relate to or be near to the sea, as Winchester or the Thames about Windsor, a little trout called a samlet or skegger trout (in both which places I have caught twenty or forty at a standing), that will bite as fast and as freely as minnows; these be by some taken to be young salmons; but in those waters they never grow to be bigger than a herring.

There is also in Kent, near to Canterbury, a trout called there a Fordidge trout, a trout that bears the name of the town where it is usually caught, that is accounted the rarest of fish: many of them near the bigness of salmon, but known by their different color; and in their best season they cut very white; and none of these have been known to be caught with an angle, unless it were one that was caught by Sir George Hastings, an excellent angler, and now with God: and he hath told me, he thought *that* trout bit not for hunger but wantonness; and it is rather to be believed, because both he then, and many others before him, have been curious to search into their bellies, what the food was by which they lived, and have found out nothing by which they might satisfy their curiosity.

Concerning which you are to take notice that it is reported by good authors that grasshoppers and some fish have no mouths, but are nourished and take breath by the porousness of their gills, man knows not how: and this may be believed, if we consider that when the raven hath hatched her eggs, she takes no further care, but leaves her young ones to the care of the God of nature, who is said, in the Psalms, 'to feed the young ravens that call upon him.' And they be kept alive and fed by dew, or worms that breed in their nests, or some other ways that we mortals know not; and this may be believed of the Fordidge trout, which, as it is said of the stork (Jerem. viii. 7), that 'he knows his season,' so he knows his times, I think almost his day of coming into that river out of the sea, where he lives, and, it is like, feeds nine months of the year, and fasts three in the river of Fordidge. And you are to note that those townsmen are very punctual in observing the time of beginning to fish for them, and boast much that their river affords a trout that exceeds all others. And just so does Sussex boast of several fish: as namely, a Shelsey cockle, a Chichester lobster, an Arundel mullet, and an Amerly trout.

And now for some confirmation of the Fordidge trout: you are to know that this trout is thought to eat nothing in the fresh water; and it may be better believed, because it is well known that swallows and bats and wagtails, which are called half-year birds, and not seen to fly in England for six months in the year, but about Michaelmas leave us for a better climate than this; yet some of them that have been left behind their fellows, have been found many thousands at a time, in hollow trees, or clay caves; where they have been observed to live and sleep out the whole winter without meat; and so Albertus observes, that there is one kind of frog that hath her mouth naturally shut up about the end of August, and that she lives so all the winter; and though it be strange to some, yet it is known to too many among us to be doubted.

And so much for these Fordidge trouts, which never afford an angler sport, but either live their time of being in the fresh water, by their meat formerly got in the sea (not unlike the swallow or frog), or by the virtue of the fresh water only; or, as the birds of Paradise and the chameleon are said to live by the sun and the air.

There is also in Northumberland a trout called a bull trout, of a much greater length and bigness than any in the southern parts. And there are, in many rivers that relate to the sea, salmon trouts, as much different from others, both in shape and in their spots, as we see sheep in some countries differ one from another in their shape and bigness, and in the fineness of their wool. And certainly, as some pastures breed larger sheep, so do some rivers, by reason of the ground over which they run, breed larger trouts.

Now the next thing that I will commend to your consideration is that the trout is of a more sudden growth than other fish. Concerning which, you are also to take notice that he lives not so long as the perch and divers other fishes do, as Sir Francis Bacon hath observed in his History of Life and Death.

And now you are to take notice that he is not like the crocodile, which if he lives never so long, yet always thrives till his death; but 'tis not so with the trout; for after he is come to his full growth, he declines in his body, and keeps his bigness or thrives only in his head till his death. And you are to know that he will about, especially before, the time of his spawning, get almost miraculously through weirs and floodgates against the streams; even through such high and swift places as is almost incredible. Next, that the trout usually spawns about October or November, but in some rivers a little sooner or later; which is the more observable, because most other fish spawn in the spring or summer, when the sun hath warmed both the earth and the water, and made it fit for generation. And you are to note, that he continues many months out of season; for it may be observed of the trout, that he is like the buck or the ox, that will not be fat in many months, though he go in the very same pasture that horses do, which will be fat in one month; and so you may observe that most other fishes recover strength, and grow sooner fat and in season, than the trout doth.

And next you are to note that till the sun gets to such a height as to warm the earth and the water, the trout is sick and lean, and lousy, and unwholesome; for you shall in winter find him to have a big head, and then to be lank, and thin, and lean; at which time many of them have sticking on them sugs, or trout-lice, which is a kind of worm, in shape like a clove or pin, with a big head, and sticks close to him and sucks his moisture: those I think the trout breeds himself, and never thrives till he free himself from them, which is when warm weather comes; and then, as he grows stronger, he gets from the dead, still water, into the sharp streams and the gravel, and there rubs off these worms or lice; and then as he grows stronger, so he gets into swifter and swifter streams, and there lies at the watch for any fly or minnow that comes near to him; and he especially loves the May-fly, which is bred of the cod-worm or caddis; and these make the trout bold and lusty, and he is usually fatter and better meat at that end of that month [May] than at any time of the year.

Now you are to know that it is observed that usually the best trouts are either red or yellow; though some (as the Fordidge trout) be white and yet good; but that is not usual: and it is a note observable, that the female trout hath usually a less head and a deeper body than the male trout, and is usually the better meat. And note that a hogback and a little head to either trout, salmon, or any other fish, is a sign that that fish is in season.

But yet you are to note that as you see some willows or palm-trees bud and blossom sooner than others do, so some trouts be in rivers sooner in season; and as some hollies or oaks are longer before they cast their leaves, so are some trouts in rivers longer before they go out of season.

And you are to note that there are several kinds of trouts; but these several kinds are not considered but by very few men; for they go under the general name of trouts; just as pigeons do in most places; though it is certain there are tame and wild pigeons; and of the tame, there be helmets and runts, and carriers and cropers, and indeed too many to name. Nay, the Royal Society have found and published lately that there be thirty and three kinds of spiders; and yet all, for aught I know, go under that one general name of spider. And it is so with many kinds of fish, and of trouts especially, which differ in their bigness and shape and spots and color. The great Kentish hens may be an instance, compared to other hens. And, doubtless, there is a kind of small trout, which will never thrive to be big, that breeds very many more than others do, that be of a larger size; which you may rather believe if you consider that the little wren and titmouse will have twenty young ones at a time, when usually the noble hawk or the musical thrassel or blackbird exceed not four or five.

And now you shall see me try my skill to catch a trout; and at my next walking, either this evening or to-morrow morning, I will give you direction how you yourself shall fish for him.

VENATOR [The HUNTER]. Trust me, master, I see now it is a harder matter to catch a trout than a chub; for I have put on patience and followed you these two hours, and not seen a fish stir, neither at your minnow nor your worm.

PISCATOR [The ANGLER]. Well, scholar, you must endure worse luck some time, or you will never make a good angler. But what say you now? There is a trout now, and a good one too, if I can but hold him, and two or three more turns more will tire him. Now you see he lies still, and the sleight is to land him. Reach me that landing-net; so, sir, now he is mine own. What say you now? is not this worth all my labor and your patience?

VEN. On my word, master, this is a gallant trout: what shall we do with him?

PISC. Marry, e'en eat him to supper; we'll go to my hostess, from whence we came; she told me, as I was going out of door, that my brother Peter, a good angler and a cheerful companion, had sent word that he would lodge there tonight, and bring a friend with him. My hostess has two beds, and I know you and I may have the best; we'll rejoice with my brother Peter and his friend, tell tales, or sing ballads, or make a catch, or find some harmless sport to content us and pass away a little time, without offense to God or man.

VEN. A match, good master, let's go to that house, for the linen looks white and smells of lavender, and I long to lie in a pair of sheets that smells so. Let's be going, good master, for I am hungry again with fishing.

PISC. Nay, stay a little, good scholar. I caught my last trout with a worm; now I will put on a minnow, and try a quarter of an hour about yonder trees for another; and so walk towards our lodging. Look you, scholar, thereabout we shall have a bite presently or not at all. Have with you, sir! o' my word I have hold of him. Oh! it is a great logger-headed chub; come hang him upon that willow twig, and let's be going. But turn out of the way a little, good scholar, towards yonder high honeysuckle hedge; there we'll sit and sing, whilst this shower falls so gently upon the teeming earth, and gives yet a sweeter smell to the lovely flowers that adorn these verdant meadows.

Look! under that broad beech-tree I sat down, when I was last this way a-fishing. And the birds in the adjoining grove seemed to have a friendly contention with an echo, whose dead voice seemed to live in a hollow tree, near to the brow of that primrose hill. There I sat viewing the silver streams glide silently towards their center, the tempestuous sea; yet sometimes opposed by rugged roots and pebble-stones, which broke their waves, and turned them into foam. And sometimes I beguiled time by viewing the harmless lambs; some leaping securely in the cool shade, whilst others sported themselves in the cheerful sun; and saw others craving comfort from the swollen udders of their bleating dams. As I thus sat, these and other sights had so fully possessed my soul with content, that I thought, as the poet hath happily expressed it,

> I was for that time lifted above earth,
> And possessed joys not promised in my birth.

As I left this place, and entered into the next field, a second pleasure entertained me; 'twas a handsome milkmaid, that had not yet attained so much age and wisdom as to load her mind with any fears of many things that will never be as too many men too often do; but she cast away all care, and sang like a nightingale: her voice was good, and the ditty fitted for it: it was that smooth song which was made by Kit Marlow, now at least fifty years ago; and the milkmaid's mother sang an answer to it, which was made by Sir Walter Raleigh in his younger days.

They were old-fashioned poetry, but choicely good; I think much better than the strong lines that are now in fashion in this critical age. Look yonder; on my word, yonder they both be a-milking again. I will give her the chub, and persuade them to sing those two songs to us.

God speed you, good woman! I have been a-fishing and am going to Bleak Hall to my bed, and having caught more fish than will sup myself and friend, I will bestow this upon you and your daughter, for I use to sell none.

MILK-WOMAN. Marry, God requite you, sir, and we'll eat it cheerfully; and if you come this way a-fishing two months hence, a grace of God, I'll give you a syllabub of new verjuice in a new made hay-cock for it, and my Maudlin shall sing you one of her best ballads; for she and I both love all anglers, they be such honest, civil, quiet men: in the meantime will you drink a draft of red cow's milk? you shall have it freely.

PISC. No, I thank you; but, I pray, do us a courtesy that shall stand you and your daughter in nothing, and yet we will think ourselves still something in your debt; it is but to sing us a song that was sung by your daughter when I last passed over this meadow, about eight or nine days since.

MILK-WOMAN. What song was it, I pray? Was it *Come, shepherds, deck your heads?* or, *As at noon Dulcina rested?* or, *Phillida flouts me?* or, *Chevy Chase?* or, *Johnny Armstrong?* or, *Troy Town?*

PISC. No, it is none of those; it is a song that your daughter sang the first part, and you sang the answer to it.

MILK-WOMAN. Oh. I know it now. I learned it the first part in my golden age, when I was about the age of my poor daughter; and the latter part, which indeed fits me best now, but two or three years ago, when the cares of the world began to take hold of me: but you shall, God willing, hear them both, and sung as well as we can, for we both love anglers. Come, Maudlin, sing the first part to the gentlemen with a merry heart, and I'll sing the second, when you have done.

THE MILKMAID'S SONG

> Come, live with me, and be my love,
> And we will all the pleasures prove
> That valleys, groves, or hills, or field,
> Or woods and steepy mountains yield;
>
> Where we will sit upon the rocks,
> And see the shepherds feed our flocks
> By shallow rivers, to whose falls
> Melodious birds sing madrigals.
>
> And I will make thee beds of roses,
> And then a thousand fragrant posies.
> A cap of flowers, and a kirtle
> Embroidered all with leaves of myrtle;
>
> A gown made of the finest wool
> Which from our pretty lambs we pull;
> Slippers lined choicely for the cold,
> With buckles of the purest gold;
>
> A belt of straw and ivy-buds,
> With coral clasps and amber studs:
> And if these pleasures may thee move,
> Come, live with me, and be my love.
>
> Thy silver dishes for thy meat,
> As precious as the gods do eat,
> Shall on an ivory table be
> Prepared each day for thee and me.
>
> The shepherd swains shall dance and sing,
> For thy delight, each May morning.
> If these delights thy mind may move,
> Then live with me, and be my love.

VEN. Trust me, master, it is a choice song, and sweetly sung by honest Maudlin. I now see it was not without cause that our good Queen Elizabeth did so often wish herself a milkmaid all the month of May, because they are not troubled with fears and cares, and sing sweetly all the day and sleep securely all the night; and without doubt, honest, innocent, pretty Maudlin does so. I'll bestow Sir Thomas Overbury's milkmaid's wish upon her, 'That she may die in the spring, and being dead, may have good store of flowers stuck round about her winding-sheet.'

THE MILKMAID'S MOTHER'S ANSWER

If all the world and love were young,
And truth in every shepherd's tongue,
These pretty pleasures might me move
To live with thee, and be thy love.

But time drives flocks from field to fold,
When rivers rage and rocks grow cold;
Then Philomel becometh dumb,
And age complains of care to come.

The flowers do fade, and wanton fields
To wayward winter reckoning yields.
A honey tongue, a heart of gall,
Is fancy's spring, but sorrow's fall.

Thy gowns, thy shoes, thy beds of roses,
Thy cap, thy kirtle, and thy posies,
Soon break, soon wither, soon forgotten,
In folly ripe, in reason rotten.

Thy belt of straw and ivy-buds,
Thy coral clasps and amber studs,
All these in me no means can move
To come to thee, and be thy love.

What should we talk of dainties then,
Of better meat than's fit for men?
These are but vain; that's only good
Which God hath blest, and sent for food.

But could youth last and love still breed,
Had joys no date nor age no need;
Then those delights my mind might move
To live with thee, and be thy love.

* * *

Pisc. Well sung, good woman; I thank you. I'll give you another dish of fish one of these days, and then beg another song of you. Come, scholar, let Maudlin alone; do not you offer to spoil her voice. Look, yonder comes mine hostess, to call us to supper. How now? Is my brother Peter come?

Hostess. Yes, and a friend with him, they are both glad to hear that you are in these parts, and long to see you, and long to be at supper, for they be very hungry.

THOMAS FULLER (1608-1661)

FULLER retained more than his contemporaries of the Elizabethan quaintness and humor. Although a clergyman and an army chaplain during the Civil War, he was not a keen partisan, and kept his position at Waltham Abbey under the Commonwealth. At the Restoration he was made chaplain to the king, and would have become a bishop, if he had not been suddenly carried off by a fever. His chief works were *The Holy State* (1642) and *The Worthies of England*, published the year after his death.

THE LIFE OF SIR FRANCIS DRAKE

From THE HOLY STATE

BK. II, CH. XXI

FRANCIS DRAKE was born nigh South Tavistock in Devonshire, and brought up in Kent; God dividing the honor betwixt two counties, that the one might have his birth, and the other his education. His father, being a minister, fled into Kent, for fear of the Six Articles, wherein the sting of Popery still remained in England, though the teeth thereof were knocked out, and the Pope's supremacy abolished. Coming into Kent, he bound his son Francis apprentice to the master of a small bark, which traded into France and Zealand, where he underwent a hard service; and pains, with patience in his youth, did knit the joints of his soul, and made them more solid and compacted. His master, dying unmarried, in reward of his industry, bequeathed his bark unto him for a legacy.

For some time he continued his master's profession; but the narrow seas were a prison for so large a spirit, born for greater undertakings. He soon grew weary of his bark; which would scarce go alone, but as it crept along by the shore: wherefore, selling it, he unfortunately ventured most of his estate with Captain John Hawkins into the West Indies, in 1567; whose goods were taken by the Spaniards at St. John de Ulva, and he himself scarce escaped with life: the king of Spain being so tender in those parts, that the least touch doth wound him; and so jealous of the West Indies, his wife, that willingly he would have none look upon her: he therefore used them with the greater severity.

Drake was persuaded by the minister of his ship, that he might lawfully recover in value of the king of Spain, and repair his losses upon him anywhere else. The case was clear in sea-divinity; and few are such infidels, as not to believe doctrines which make for their own profit. Whereupon Drake, though a poor private man, hereafter undertook to revenge himself on so mighty a monarch; who, as not contented that the sun riseth and setteth in his dominions, may seem to desire to make all his own where he shineth. And now let us see how a dwarf, standing on the mount of God's providence, may prove an overmatch for a giant.

After two or three several voyages to gain intelligence in the West Indies, and some prizes taken, at last he effectually set forward from Plymouth with two ships, the one of seventy, the other twenty-five tons, and seventy-three men and boys in both. He made with all speed and secrecy to Nombre de Dios, as loath to put the town to too much charge (which he knew they would willingly bestow) in providing beforehand for his entertainment; which city was then the granary of the West Indies, wherein the golden harvest brought from Panama was hoarded up till it could be conveyed into Spain. They came hard aboard the shore, and lay quiet all night, intending to attempt the town in the dawning of the day.

But he was forced to alter his resolution, and assault it sooner; for he heard his men muttering amongst themselves of the strength and greatness of the town: and when men's heads are once fly-blown with buzzes of suspicion, the vermin multiply instantly, and one jealousy begets another. Wherefore, he raised them from their nest before they had hatched their fears; and, to put away those conceits, he persuaded them it was day-dawning when the moon rose, and instantly set on the town, and won it, being unwalled. In the market-place the Spaniards saluted them with a volley of shot; Drake returned their greeting with a flight of arrows, the best and ancient English compliment, which drave their enemies away. Here Drake received a dangerous wound, though he valiantly concealed it a long time; knowing if his heart stooped, his men's would fall, and loath to leave off the action, wherein if so bright an opportunity once setteth, it seldom riseth again. But at length his men forced him to return to his ship, that his wound might be dressed; and this unhappy accident defeated the whole design. Thus victory sometimes slips through their fingers who have caught it in their hands.

But his valor would not let him give over the project as long as there was either life or warmth in it; and therefore, having received intelligence from the negroes called Symerons, of many mules'-lading of gold and silver, which was to be brought from Panama, he, leaving competent numbers to man his ships, went on land with the rest, and bestowed himself in the woods by the way as they were to pass, and so intercepted and carried away an infinite mass of gold. As for the silver, which was not portable over the mountains, they digged holes in the ground and hid it therein.

There want not those who love to beat down the price of every honorable action, though they themselves never mean to be chapmen. These cry up Drake's fortune herein to cry down his valor; as if this his performance were nothing, wherein a golden opportunity ran his head, with his long forelock, into Drake's hands beyond expectation. But, certainly, his resolution and unconquerable patience deserved much praise, to adventure on such a design, which had in it just no more probability than what was enough to keep it from being impossible. Yet I admire not so much at all the treasure he took, as at the rich and deep mine of God's providence.

Having now full freighted himself with wealth, and burnt at the House of Crosses above two hundred thousand pounds' worth of Spanish merchandise, he returned with honor and safety into England, and, some years after (December 13th, 1577) undertook that his famous voyage about the world, most accurately described by our English authors: and yet a word or two thereof will not be amiss.

Setting forward from Plymouth, he bore up for Cabo-verd, where, near to the island of St. Jago, he took prisoner Nuno de Silva, an experienced Spanish pilot, whose direction he used in the coasts of Brazil and Magellan Straits, and afterwards safely landed him at Guatulco in New Spain. Hence they took their course to the island of Brava; and hereabouts they met with those tempestuous winds whose only praise is, that they continue not an hour, in which time they change all the points of the compass. Here they had great plenty of rain, poured (not, as in other places, as it were out of sieves, but) as out of spouts, so that a butt of water falls down in a place; which, notwithstanding, is but a courteous injury in that hot climate far from land, and where otherwise fresh water cannot be provided. Then cutting the Line, they saw the face of that heaven which earth hideth from us, but therein only three stars of the first greatness, the rest few and small compared to our hemisphere; as if God, on purpose, had set up the best and biggest candles in that room wherein his civilest guests are entertained.

Sailing the south of Brazil, he afterwards passed the Magellan Straits (August 20th, 1578) and then entered *Mare Pacificum* [the Pacific Ocean], came to the southernmost land at the height of 55½ latitudes; thence directing his course northward, he pillaged many Spanish towns, and took rich prizes of high value in the kingdoms of Chili, Peru, and New Spain. Then, bending eastwards, he coasted China, and the Moluccas, where, by the king of Terrenate, a true gentleman Pagan, he was most honorably entertained. The king told them, they and he were all of one religion in this respect,—that they believed not in gods made of stocks and stones, as did the Portugals. He furnished them also with all necessaries that they wanted.

On January 9th following (1579), his ship, having a large wind and a smooth sea, ran aground on a dangerous shoal, and struck twice on it; knocking twice at the door of death, which, no doubt, had opened the third time. Here they stuck, from eight o'clock at night till four the next afternoon, having ground too much, and yet too little to land on; and water too much, and yet too little to sail in. Had God (who, as the wise man saith, 'holdeth the winds in his fist,' Prov. xxx. 4) but opened his little finger, and let out the smallest blast, they had undoubtedly been cast away; but there blew not any wind all the while. Then they, conceiving aright that the best way to lighten the ship was, first, to ease it of the burden of their sins by true repentance, humbled themselves, by fasting, under the hand of God.

Afterwards they received the communion, dining on Christ in the sacrament, expecting no other than to sup with him in heaven. Then they cast out of their ship six great pieces of ordnance, threw overboard as much wealth as would break the heart of a miser to think on it, with much sugar, and packs of spices, making a caudle of the sea round about. Then they betook themselves to their prayers, the best lever at such a dead lift indeed; and it pleased God, that the wind, formerly their mortal enemy, became their friend; which, changing from the starboard to the larboard of the ship, and rising by degrees, cleared them off to the sea again,—for which they returned unfeigned thanks to Almighty God.

By the Cape of Good Hope and west of Africa, he returned safe into England, and (November 3rd, 1580) landed at Plymouth (being almost the first of those that made a thorough light through the world), having, in his whole voyage though a curious searcher after the time, lost one day through the variation of several climates. He feasted the queen in his ship at Dartford, who knighted him for his service. Yet it grieved him not a little, that some prime courtiers refused the gold he offered them, as gotten by piracy. Some of them would have been loath to have been told, that they had *aurum Tholosanum* [gold of Spain] in their own purses. Some think that they did it to show that their envious pride was above their covetousness, who of set purpose did blur the fair copy of his performance, because they would not take pains to write after it.

I pass by his next West-Indian voyage (1585), wherein he took the cities of St. Jago, St. Domingo, Carthagena, and St. Augustine in Florida; as also his service performed in 1588, wherein he, with many others, helped to the waning of that half-moon, which sought to govern all the motion of our sea. I haste to his last voyage.

Queen Elizabeth, in 1595, perceiving that the only way to make the Spaniard a cripple forever, was to cut his sinews of war in the West Indies, furnished Sir Francis Drake, and Sir John Hawkins, with six of her own ships, besides twenty-one ships and barks of their own providing, containing in all two thousand five hundred men and boys, for some service on America. But, alas! this voyage was marred before begun. For, so great preparations being too big for a cover, the king of Spain knew of it, and sent a caraval of adviso to the West Indies; so that they had intelligence three weeks before the fleet set forth of England, either to fortify or remove their treasure; whereas, in other of Drake's voyages, not two of his own men knew whither he went; and managing such a design is like carrying a mine in war,—if it hath any vent, all is spoiled. Besides, Drake and Hawkins, being in joint commission, hindered each other. The latter took himself to be inferior rather in success than skill; and the action was unlike to prosper when neither would follow, and both could not handsomely go abreast. It vexed old Hawkins, that his counsel was not followed, in present sailing to America, but that they spent time in vain in assaulting the Canaries; and the grief that his advice was slighted, say some, was the cause of his death. Others impute it to the sorrow he took for the taking of his bark called 'the Francis,' which five Spanish frigates had intercepted. But when the same heart hath two mortal wounds given it together, it is hard to say which of them killeth.

Drake continued his course for Porto Rico; and, riding within the road, a shot from the Castle entered the steerage of the ship, took away the stool from under him as he sat at supper, wounded Sir Nicholas Clifford, and Brute Brown to death. 'Ah, dear Brute!' said Drake, 'I could grieve for thee, but now is no time for me to let down my spirits.' And, indeed, a soldier's most proper bemoaning a friend's death in war, is in revenging it. And, sure, as if grief had made the English furious, they soon after fired five Spanish ships of two hundred tons apiece, in despite of the Castle.

America is not unfitly resembled to an hour-glass, which hath a narrow neck of land (suppose it the hole where the sand passeth), betwixt the parts thereof,—Mexicana and Peruana. Now, the English had a design to march by land over this Isthmus, from Porto Rico to Panama, where the Spanish treasure was laid up. Sir Thomas Baskerville, general of the land-forces, undertook the service with seven hundred and fifty armed men. They marched through deep ways, the Spaniards much annoying them with shot out of the woods. One fort in the passage they assaulted in vain, and heard two others were built to stop them, besides Panama itself. They had so much of this breakfast they thought they should surfeit of a dinner and supper of the same. No hope of conquest, except with cloying the jaws of death, and thrusting men on the mouth of the cannon. Wherefore, fearing to find the proverb true, that 'gold may be bought too dear,' they returned to their ships. Drake afterwards fired Nombre de Dios, and many other petty towns (whose treasure the Spaniards had conveyed away), burning the empty casks, when their precious liquor was run out before, and then prepared for their returning home.

Great was the difference betwixt the Indian cities now, from what they were when Drake first haunted these coasts. At first, the Spaniards here were safe and secure, counting their treasure sufficient to defend itself, the remoteness thereof being the greatest (almost only) resistance, and the fetching of it more than the fighting for it. Whilst the king of Spain guarded the head and heart of his dominions in Europe, he left his long legs in America open to blows; till, finding them to smart, being beaten black and blue by the English, he learned to arm them at last, fortifying the most important of them to make them impregnable.

Now began Sir Francis's discontent to feed upon him. He conceived, that expectation, a merciless usurer, computing each day since his departure, exacted an interest and return of honor and profit proportionable to his great preparations, and transcending his former achievements. He saw that all the good which he had done in this voyage, consisted in the evil he had done to the Spaniards afar off, whereof he could present but small visible fruits in England. These apprehensions, accompanying, if not causing, the disease of the flux, wrought his sudden death, January 28th, 1595. And sickness did not so much untie his clothes, as sorrow did rend at once the robe of his mortality asunder. He lived by the sea, died on it, and was buried in it. Thus an extempore performance (scarce heard to be begun before we hear it is ended!) comes off with better applause, or miscarries with less disgrace, than a long-studied and openly-premeditated action. Besides, we see how great spirits, having mounted to the highest pitch of performance, afterwards strain and break their credits in striving to go beyond it. Lastly, God oftentimes leaves the brightest men in an eclipse, to show that they do but borrow their luster from his reflexion. We will not justify all the actions of any man, though of a tamer profession than a sea-captain, in whom civility is often counted preciseness. For the main, we say that this our captain was a religious man towards God and his houses (generally sparing churches where he came), chaste in his life, just in his dealings, true of his word, and merciful to those that were under him, hating nothing so much as idleness, and therefore, lest his soul should rust in peace: at spare hours he brought fresh water to Plymouth. Careful he was for posterity (though men of his profession have as well an ebb of riot, as a float of fortune) and providently raised a worshipful family of his kindred. In a word: should those that speak against him fast till they fetch their bread where he did his, they would have a good stomach to eat it.

JEREMY TAYLOR (1613-1667)

Mr. Saintsbury, whose praise of Browne's prose style is quoted on page 245, says in another place that 'on the whole no one in English prose has so much command of the enchanter's wand as Jeremy Taylor'; and critical authority is, indeed, much divided as to the stylistic excellences of the two writers. Taylor's inferiority is more in thought than in expression, and he has the disadvantage of writing from the point of view of the theologian or cleric: Browne is a layman and has a touch of modern skepticism.

Taylor was the son of a barber, spent many years at Cambridge and Oxford, became a clergyman at Uppingham, in Rutlandshire, and lost his rectory under the Commonwealth. He retired to Wales, and there composed *The Liberty of Prophesying*, a plea for toleration against Presbyterian bigotry (1647), *Holy Living* (1650), *Holy Dying* (1651), *A Course of Sermons for all the Sundays of the Year* (1651), and *The Golden Grove*, a manual of private devotion for young people (1655).

THE FAITH AND PATIENCE OF THE SAINTS

From A SERMON

PREACHED AT GOLDEN GROVE

The state of the Gospel is a state of sufferings, not of temporal prosperities. This was foretold by the prophets: 'A fountain shall go out of the house of the Lord *et irrigabit torrentum spinarum* (so it is in the Vulgar Latin), and it shall water the torrent of thorns,' that is, the state or time of the Gospel, which, like a torrent, shall carry all the world before it, and, like a torrent, shall be fullest in ill weather; and by its banks shall grow nothing but thorns and briers, sharp afflictions, temporal infelicities, and persecution. This sense of the words is more fully explained in the book of the prophet Isaiah. 'Upon the ground of my people shall thorns and briers come up; how much more in all the houses of the city of rejoicing?' Which prophecy is the same in the style of the prophets, that my text is in the style of the Apostles. The house of God shall be watered with the dew of heaven, and there shall spring up briers in it: 'Judgment must begin there;' but how much more 'in the houses of the city of rejoicing?' how much more amongst 'them that are at ease in Sion,' that serve their desires, that satisfy their appetites, that are given over to their own heart's lust, that so serve themselves that they never serve God, that 'dwell in the city of rejoicing?' They are like Dives, whose portion was in this life, 'who went in fine linen, and fared deliciously every day:' they, indeed, trample upon their briers and thorns, and suffer them not to grow in their houses; but the roots are in the ground, and they are reserved for fuel of wrath in the day of everlasting burning. Thus, you see, it was prophesied, now see how it was performed; Christ was the captain of our sufferings, and he began.

He entered into the world with all the circumstances of poverty. He had a star to illustrate his birth; but a stable for his bedchamber, and a manger for his cradle. The angels sang hymns when he was born; but he was cold and cried, uneasy and unprovided. He lived long in the trade of a carpenter; he, by whom God made the world, had in his first years the business of a mean and ignoble trade. He did good wherever he went; and almost wherever he went, was abused. He deserved heaven for his obedience, but found a cross in his way thither: and if ever any man had reason to expect fair usages from God, and to be dandled in the lap of ease, softness, and a prosperous fortune, he it was only that could deserve that, or anything that can be good. But after he had chosen to live a life of virtue, of poverty, and labor, he entered into a state of death, whose shame and trouble was great enough to pay for the sins of the whole world. And I shall choose to express this mystery in the words of Scripture. He died not by a single or a sudden death, but he was the 'Lamb slain from the beginning of the world:' for he was massacred in Abel, saith St. Paulinus; he was tossed upon the waves of the sea in the person of Noah; it was he that went out of his country, when Abraham was called from Charran, and wandered from his native soil; he was offered up in Isaac, persecuted in Jacob, betrayed in Joseph, blinded in Samson, affronted in Moses, sawed in Isaiah, cast into the dungeon with Jeremiah: for all these were types of Christ suffering. And then his passion continued even after his resurrection. For it is he that suffers in all his members; it is he that 'endures the contradiction of all sinners'; it is he that is 'the lord of life,' and is 'crucified again, and put to open shame' in all the sufferings of his servants, and sins of rebels, and defiances of apostates and renegadoes, and violence of tyrants, and injustice of usurpers, and the persecutions of his church. It is he that is stoned in St. Stephen, flayed in the person of St. Bartholomew; he was roasted upon St. Laurence's gridiron, exposed to lions in St. Ignatius, burnt in St. Polycarp, frozen in the lake where stood forty martyrs of Cappadocia. '*Unigenitus enim Dei ad peragendum mortis suæ sacramentum consummavit omne genus humanarum passionum*' said St. Hilary; 'the sacrament of Christ's death is not to be accomplished but by suffering all the sorrows of humanity.'

All that Christ came for was, or was mingled with, sufferings; for all those little joys which God sent, either to re-create his person, or to illustrate his office, were abated or attended with afflictions, God being more careful to establish in him the covenant of sufferings than to refresh his sorrows. Presently after the angels had finished their hallelujahs, he was forced to fly to save his life; and the air became full of shrieks of the desolate mothers of Bethlehem for their dying babes. God had no sooner made him illustrious with a voice from heaven and the descent of the Holy Ghost upon him in the waters of baptism, but he was delivered over to be tempted and assaulted by the devil in the wilderness. His transfiguration was a bright ray of glory; but then also he entered into a cloud, and was told a sad story what he was to suffer at Jerusalem. And upon Palm Sunday, when he rode triumphantly into Jerusalem, and was adorned with the acclamations of a king and a god, he wet the palms with his tears, sweeter than the drops of manna, or the little pearls of heaven that descended upon Mount Hermon; weeping, in the midst of this triumph, over obstinate, perishing, and malicious Jerusalem. For this Jesus was like the rainbow, which God set in the clouds as a sacrament to confirm a promise and establish a grace; he was half made of the glories of the light, and half of the moisture of a cloud; in his best days he was but half triumph and half sorrow: he was sent to tell of his Father's mercies, and that God intended to spare us; but appeared not but in the company or in the retinue of a shower and of foul weather. But I need not tell that Jesus, beloved of God, was a suffering person: that which concerns this question most is that he made for us a covenant of sufferings: his doctrines were such as expressly, and by consequent, enjoin and suppose sufferings and a state of affliction; his very promises were sufferings; his beatitudes were sufferings; his rewards and his arguments to invite men to follow him were only taken from sufferings in this life and the reward of sufferings hereafter.

For if we sum up the commandments of Christ, we shall find humility, mortification, self-denial, repentance, renouncing the world, mourning, taking up the cross, dying for him, patience and poverty, to stand in the chiefest rank of Christian precepts, and in the direct order to heaven: 'He that will be my disciple, must deny himself, and take up his cross and follow me.' We must follow him that was crowned with thorns and sorrows, him that was drenched in Cedron, nailed upon the cross, that deserved all good, and suffered all evil: that is the sum of Christian religion, as it distinguishes from all the religions in the world. To which we may add the express precept recorded by St. James: 'Be afflicted, and mourn, and weep; let your laughter be turned into mourning, and your joy into weeping.' You see the commandments: will you also see the promises? These they are. 'In the world ye shall have tribulation; in me, ye shall have peace:—Through many tribulations ye shall enter into heaven:—He that loseth father and mother, wives and children, houses and lands, for my name's sake and the Gospel, shall receive a hundred fold in this life, with persecution:' that is part of his reward: and, 'He chastiseth every son that he receiveth;—if ye be exempt from sufferings, ye are bastards, and not sons.' These are some of Christ's promises: will you see some of Christ's blessings that he gives his church? 'Blessed are the poor: blessed are the hungry and thirsty: blessed are they that mourn: blessed are the humble:

blessed are the persecuted.' Of the eight beatitudes, five of them have temporal misery and meanness, or an afflicted condition for their subject. Will you at last see some of the rewards which Christ hath propounded to his servants, to invite them to follow him? 'When I am lifted up, I will draw all men after me:' when Christ is 'lifted up, as Moses lift up the serpent in the wilderness,' that is, lifted upon the cross, then 'he will draw us after him.' 'To you it is given for Christ,' saith St. Paul, when he went to sweeten and flatter the Philippians: well, what is given to them? some great favors, surely; true; 'It is not only given you that you believe in Christ,' though that be a great matter, 'but also that you suffer for him,' that is the highest of your honor. And therefore, saith St. James, 'My brethren, count it all joy when ye enter into divers temptations:' and St. Peter; 'Communicating with the sufferings of Christ, rejoice.' And St. James again: 'We count them blessed that have suffered:' and St. Paul, when he gives his blessing to the Thessalonians, useth this form of prayer; 'Our Lord direct your hearts in the charity of God, and in the patience and sufferings of Christ.' So that if we will serve the king of sufferings, whose crown was of thorns, whose scepter was a reed of scorn, whose imperial robe was a scarlet of mockery, whose throne was the cross, we must serve him in sufferings, in poverty of spirit, in humility and mortification; and for our reward we shall have persecution, and all its blessed consequents. '*Atque hoc est esse Christianum*' [And this is to be a Christian].

Since this was done in the green tree, what might we expect should be done in the dry? Let us, in the next place, consider how God hath treated his saints and servants in the descending ages of the Gospel: that if the best of God's servants were followers of Jesus in this covenant of sufferings, we may not think it strange concerning the fiery trial, as if some new thing had happened to us. For as the Gospel was founded in sufferings, we shall also see it grow in persecutions; and as Christ's blood did cement the corner-stones and the first foundation; so the blood and sweat, the groans and sighings, the afflictions and mortifications, of saints and martyrs, did make the superstructures, and must at last finish the building.

If we begin with the apostles, who were to persuade the world to become Christian, and to use proper arguments of invitations, we shall find that they never offered an argument of temporal prosperity; they never promised empires and thrones on earth, nor riches, nor temporal power: and it would have been soon confuted, if they who were whipped and imprisoned, banished and scattered, persecuted and tormented, should have promised sunshine days to others which they could not to themselves. Of all the apostles there was not one that died a natural death but only St. John; and did he escape? Yes: but he was put into a cauldron of scalding lead and oil before the Porta Latina in Rome, and escaped death by miracle, though no miracle was wrought to make him escape the torture. And, besides this, he lived long in banishment, and that was worse than St. Peter's chains. '*Sanctus Petrus in vinculis, et Johannes ante Portam Latinam*' [Saint Peter in chains, and John before the Latin Gate], were both days of martyrdom, and church-festivals. And after a long and laborious life, and the affliction of being detained from his crown, and his sorrows for the death of his fellow-disciples, he died full of days and sufferings. And when St. Paul was taken into the apostolate, his commissions were signed in these words: 'I will shew unto him how great things he must suffer for my name:' And his whole life was a continual suffering. '*Quotidie morior*' was his motto, 'I die daily;' and his lesson that he daily learned was, to 'know Christ Jesus, and him crucified;' and all his joy was 'to rejoice in the cross of Christ;' and the changes of his life were nothing but the changes of his sufferings and the variety of his labors. For though Christ hath finished his own sufferings for expiation of the world: yet there are ὑστερήματα θλιψέων, portions that are behind of the sufferings of Christ, which must be filled up by his body, the church; and happy are they that put in the greatest symbol: for 'in the same measure you are partakers of the sufferings of Christ, in the same shall ye be also of the consolation.' And therefore, concerning St. Paul, as it was also concerning Christ, there is nothing or but very little in Scripture relating to his person and chances of his private life, but his labors and persecutions; as if the Holy Ghost did think nothing fit to stand upon record for Christ but sufferings.

And now began to work the greatest glory of the divine providence; here was the case of Christianity at stake. The world was rich and prosperous, learned and full of wise men; the Gospel was preached with poverty and persecution, in simplicity of discourse, and in demonstration of the Spirit: God was on one side, and the Devil on the other; they each of them dressed up their city; Babylon upon earth, Jerusalem from above. The Devil's city was full of pleasure, triumphs, victories, and cruelty; good news, and great wealth; conquest over kings, and making nations tributary: they 'bound kings in chains, and the nobles with links of iron;' and the inheritance of the earth was theirs: the Romans were lords over the greatest part of the world; and God permitted to the Devil the firmament and increase, the wars and the success of that people, giving to him an entire power of disposing the great change of the world, so as might best increase their greatness and power; and he therefore did it, because all the power of the Roman greatness was a professed enemy to Christianity. And on the other side, God was to build up Jerusalem, and the kingdom of the Gospel; and he chose to build it of hewn stone, cut and broken; the apostles he chose for preachers, and they had no learning; women and mean people were the first disciples, and they had no power; the Devil was to lose his kingdom, and he wanted no malice: and therefore he stirred up, and, as well as he could, he made active all the power of Rome, and all the learning of the Greeks, and all the malice of barbarous people, and all the prejudice and the obstinacy of the Jews, against this doctrine and institution, which preached, and promised, and brought, persecution along with it. On the one side, there was '*scandalum crucis*' [the offence of the cross]; on the other, '*patientia sanctorum*' [the patience of the saints], and what was the event? They that had overcome the world, could not strangle Christianity. But so have I seen the sun with a little ray of distant light challenge all the power of darkness, and without violence and noise, climbing up the hill, hath made night so to retire that its memory was lost in the joys and spritefulness of the morning: and Christianity without violence or armies, without resistance and self-preservation, without strength or human eloquence, without challenging of privileges or fighting against tyranny, without alteration of government and scandal of princes, with its humility and meekness, with toleration and patience, with obedience and charity, with praying and dying, did insensibly turn the world into Christian, and persecution into victory.

JOHN BUNYAN (1628-1688)

THE greatest of English allegorical writers was a Bedfordshire tinker. 'I never went to school to Aristotle or Plato, but was brought up at my father's house in a very mean condition, among a company of poor countrymen,' he tells us in his autobiography, *Grace abounding to the Chief of Sinners* (1666). As a matter of fact, he was not a conspicuously bad character, the worst faults of which he can accuse himself being fondness for dancing, bell-ringing, and other sports and pastimes, and a habit of profanity, for which he acquired a local reputation. All this was changed, however, by his marriage, about the age of twenty, to a godly wife, who brought about his conversion. He became famous as a preacher, to the great displeasure of the regular clergy, who were 'angry with the tinker because he strove to mend souls as well as kettles and pans.' After the Restoration, when the old laws against dissenters were revived, he was arrested for holding religious services, and remained in prison for the next twelve years; he made laces for the support of his family, preached to his fellow-prisoners, studied the Bible and Foxe's Book of Martyrs, and wrote a large number of religious tracts. It was apparently during a later imprisonment that he wrote *The Pilgrim's Progress*, the first part of which was published in 1678 and became immediately popular. After two other allegorical stories—from one point of view religious tracts, from another, novels—*The Life and Death of Mr. Badman* and *The Holy War*—he wrote the second part of *Pilgrim's Progress* (1684), completing the pilgrimage of Christian, his wife Christiana, and their children. In his later years he was active as a nonconformist minister (his congregation met in a barn at Bedford) and he was known in the surrounding country as 'Bishop Bunyan'; his fame as a preacher spread to London, where he drew great crowds together on his occasional visits, and attracted the attention of royalty; but it is only in recent years that Bunyan's literary merits have been fully appreciated—his power of imagination and realistic description, and the forthright directness of his style.

From THE PILGRIM'S PROGRESS

Now I saw in my dream, that the highway up which Christian was to go, was fenced on either side with a wall, and that wall was called Salvation.[1] Up this way, therefore, did burdened Christian run, but not without great difficulty, because of the load on his back.

He ran thus till he came at a place somewhat ascending, and upon that place stood a cross, and a little below, in the bottom, a sepulcher. So I saw in my dream, that just as Christian came up with the cross, his burden loosed from off his shoulders, and fell from off his back, and began to tumble, and so continued to do, till it came to the mouth of the sepulcher, where it fell in, and I saw it no more.

Then was Christian glad and lightsome, and said, with a merry heart, 'He hath given me rest by his sorrow, and life by his death.' Then he stood still awhile to look and wonder; for it was very surprising to him, that the sight of the cross should thus ease him of his burden. He looked, therefore, and looked again, even till the springs that were in his head sent the waters down his cheeks.[2] Now, as he stood looking and weeping, behold three Shining Ones came to him and saluted him with 'Peace be to thee.' So the first said to him, 'Thy sins be forgiven thee!'[3] the second stripped him of his rags, and clothed him 'with change of raiment;'[4] the third also set a mark in his forehead, and gave him a roll with a seal upon it, which he bade him look on as he ran, and that he should give it in at the Celestial Gate.[5] So they went their way. Then Christian gave three leaps for joy, and went on singing —

Thus far I did come laden with my sin;
Nor could aught ease the grief that I was in
Till I came hither: What a place is this!
Must here be the beginning of my bliss?
Must here the burden fall from off my back?
Must here the strings that bound it to me crack?
Blest cross! blest sepulcher! blest rather be
The man that there was put to shame for me!

[1] Zec. xii. 10.   [2] Zec. xii. 10.   [3] Mar. ii. 5.   [4] Zec. iii. 4.   [5] Ep. i. 13.

I saw then in my dream, that he went on thus, even until he came at a bottom, where he saw, a little out of the way, three men fast asleep, with fetters upon their heels. The name of the one was Simple, another Sloth, and the third Presumption.

Christian then seeing them lie in this case, went to them, if peradventure he might awake them, and cried, You are like them that sleep on the top of a mast, for the Dead Sea is under you—a gulf that hath no bottom.[1] Awake, therefore, and come away; be willing also, and I will help you off with your irons. He also told them, If he that 'goeth about like a roaring lion' comes by, you will certainly become a prey to his teeth.[2] With that they looked upon him, and began to reply in this sort: Simple said, 'I see no danger;' Sloth said, 'Yet a little more sleep;' and Presumption said, 'Every fat must stand upon its own bottom.' And so they lay down to sleep again, and Christian went on his way.

Yet was he troubled to think that men in that danger should so little esteem the kindness of him that so freely offered to help them, both by awakening of them, counseling of them, and proffering to help them off with their irons. And as he was troubled thereabout he espied two men come tumbling over the wall, on the left hand of the narrow way; and they made up apace to him. The name of the one was Formalist, and the name of the other Hypocrisy. So, as I said, they drew up unto him, who thus entered with them into discourse.

CHRISTIAN. Gentlemen, whence came you, and whither go you?

FORMALIST and HYPOCRISY. We were born in the land of Vain-glory, and are going for praise to Mount Zion.

CHR. Why came you not in at the gate, which standeth at the beginning of the way? Know you not that it is written, that he that cometh not in by the door, 'but climbeth up some other way, the same is a thief and a robber?'[3]

FORM. and HYP. They said, That to go to the gate for entrance was, by all their countrymen, counted too far about; and that, therefore, their usual way was to make a short cut of it, and to climb over the wall, as they had done.

CHR. But will it not be counted a trespass against the Lord of the city whither we are bound, thus to violate his revealed will?

FORM. and HYP. They told him, that, as for that, he needed not to trouble his head thereabout; for what they did, they had custom for; and could produce, if need were, testimony that would witness it for more than a thousand years.

CHR. But, said Christian, will your practice stand a trial at law?

FORM. and HYP. They told him, That custom, it being of so long a standing as above a thousand years, would doubtless, now be admitted as a thing legal by any impartial judge; and besides, said they, if we get into the way, what's matter which way we get in? if we are in, we are in; thou art but in the way, who, as we perceived, came in at the gate; and we are also in the way, that came tumbling over the wall; wherein, now, is thy condition better than ours?

CHR. I walk by the rule of my Master; you walk by the rude working of your fancies. You are counted thieves already, by the Lord of the way; therefore, I doubt you will not be found true men at the end of the way. You come in by yourselves, without his direction; and shall go out by yourselves, without his mercy.

To this they made him but little answer; only they bid him look to himself. Then I saw that they went on every man in his way, without much conference one with another; save that these two men told Christian, that as to laws and ordinances, they doubted not but they should as conscientiously do them as he; therefore, said they, we see not wherein thou differest from us, but by the coat that is on thy back, which was, as we trow, given thee by some of thy neighbors, to hide the shame of thy nakedness.

CHR. By laws and ordinances you will not be saved, since you came not in by the door.[4] And as for this coat that is on my back, it was given me by the Lord of the place whither I go; and that, as you say, to cover my nakedness with. And I take it as a token of his kindness to me; for I had nothing but rags before. And, besides, thus I comfort myself as I go: Surely, think I, when I come to the gate of the city, the Lord thereof will know me for good, since I have his coat on my back—a coat that he gave me freely in the day that he stripped me of my rags. I have, moreover, a mark in my forehead, of which, perhaps, you have taken no notice, which one of my Lord's most intimate associates fixed there in the day that my burden fell off my shoulders. I will tell

---

[1] Pr. xxiii. 34.　　[2] Pe. v. 5.　　[3] Ja. x. 1.　　[4] Ga. ii. 15.

you, moreover, that I had then given me a roll, sealed, to comfort me by reading, as I go on the way; I was also bid to give it in at the Celestial Gate, in token of my certain going in after it; all which things, I doubt, you want, and want them because you came not in at the gate.

To these things they gave him no answer; only they looked upon each other, and laughed. Then I saw that they went on all, save that Christian kept before, who had no more talk but with himself, and that sometimes sighingly and sometimes comfortably; also he would be often reading in the roll that one of the Shining Ones gave him, by which he was refreshed.

I beheld, then, that they all went on till they came to the foot of the Hill Difficulty; at the bottom of which was a spring. There were also in the same place two other ways besides that which came straight from the gate; one turned to the left hand, and the other to the right, at the bottom of the hill; but the narrow way lay right up the hill, and the name of the going up the side of the hill is called Difficulty. Christian now went to the spring, and drank thereof, to refresh himself,[1] and then began to go up the hill, saying—

> The hill, though high, I covet to ascend,
> The difficulty will not me offend;
> For I perceive the way to life lies here.
> Come, pluck up heart, let's neither faint nor fear;
> Better, though difficult, the right way to go,
> Than wrong, though easy, where the end is woe.

The other two also came to the foot of the hill; but when they saw that the hill was steep and high, and that there were two other ways to go; and supposing also that these two ways might meet again, with that up which Christian went, on the other side of the hill; therefore they were resolved to go in those ways. Now the name of one of those ways was Danger, and the name of the other Destruction. So the one took the way which is called Danger, which led him into a great wood, and the other took directly up the way to Destruction, which led him into a wide field, full of dark mountains, where he stumbled and fell, and rose no more.

I looked, then, after Christian, to see him go up the hill, where I perceived he fell from running to going, and from going to clambering upon his hands and his knees, because of the steepness of the place. Now, about the midway to the top of the hill was a pleasant arbor, made by the Lord of the hill for the refreshing of weary travelers; thither, therefore, Christian got, where also he sat down to rest him. Then he pulled his roll out of his bosom, and read therein to his comfort; he also now began afresh to take a review of the coat or garment that was given him as he stood by the cross. Thus pleasing himself awhile, he at last fell into a slumber, and thence into a fast sleep, which detained him in that place until it was almost night; and in his sleep his roll fell out of his hand. Now, as he was sleeping, there came one to him, and awaked him, saying, 'Go to the ant, thou sluggard; consider her ways, and be wise.'[2] And with that Christian suddenly started up, and sped him on his way, and went apace, till he came to the top of the hill.

Now, when he was got up to the top of the hill, there came two men running to meet him amain; the name of the one was Timorous, and of the other Mistrust; to whom Christian said, Sirs, what's the matter? You run the wrong way. Timorous answered, that they were going to the City of Zion, and had got up that difficult place; but, said he, the further we go, the more danger we meet with; wherefore we turned, and are going back again.

Yes, said Mistrust, for just before us lie a couple of lions in the way, whether sleeping or waking we know not, and we could not think. if we came within reach, but they would presently pull us in pieces.

CHR. Then said Christian, You make me afraid, but whither shall I fly to be safe? If I go back to mine own country, *that* is prepared for fire and brimstone, and I shall certainly perish there. If I can get to the Celestial City, I am sure to be in safety there. I must venture. To go back is nothing but death; to go forward is fear of death, and life everlasting beyond it. I will yet go forward. So Mistrust and Timorous ran down the hill, and Christian went on his way. But, thinking again of what he heard from the men, he felt in his bosom for his roll, that he might read therein, and be comforted; but he felt, and found it not. Then was Christian in great distress, and knew not what to do; for he wanted that which used to relieve him, and that which should have been his pass into the Celestial City. Here therefore, he began to be much perplexed, and knew not what to do. At last, he bethought himself, that he had slept in the arbor that is on the side of the hill; and,

[1] Is. xlix. 10.   [2] Pr. vi. 6.

falling down upon his knees, he asked God forgiveness for that his foolish fact, and then went back to look for his roll. But all the way he went back, who can sufficiently set forth the sorrow of Christian's heart! Sometimes he sighed, sometimes he wept, and oftentimes he chid himself for being so foolish to fall asleep in that place, which was erected only for a little refreshment for his weariness. Thus, therefore, he went back, carefully looking on this side, and on that, all the way as he went, if happily he might find his roll, that had been his comfort so many times in his journey. He went thus, till he came again within sight of the arbor where he sat and slept; but that sight renewed his sorrow the more, by bringing again, even afresh, his evil of sleeping into his mind.[1] Thus, therefore, he now went on bewailing his sinful sleep, saying, 'O wretched man that I am!' that I should sleep in the day-time! that I should sleep in the midst of difficulty! that I should so indulge the flesh, as to use that rest for ease to my flesh, which the Lord of the hill hath erected only for the relief of the spirits of pilgrims!

How many steps have I took in vain! Thus it happened to Israel, for their sin; they were sent back again by the way of the Red Sea; and I am made to tread those steps with sorrow, which I might have trod with delight, had it not been for this sinful sleep. How far might I have been on my way by this time! I am made to tread those steps thrice over, which I needed not to have trod but once; yea, now also I am like to be benighted, for the day is almost spent. O that I had not slept!

Now by this time he was come to the arbor again, where for a while he sat down and wept; but at last, as Christian would have it, looking sorrowfully down under the settle, there he espied his roll; the which he, with trembling and haste, catched up, and put it into his bosom. But who can tell how joyful this man was when he had gotten his roll again! for this roll was the assurance of his life and acceptance at the desired haven. Therefore he laid it up in his bosom, gave thanks to God for directing his eye to the place where it lay, and with joy and tears betook himself again to his journey. But oh, how nimbly now did he go up the rest of the hill! Yet, before he got up, the sun went down upon Christian; and this made him again recall the vanity of his sleeping to his remembrance; and thus he again began to condole with himself. O thou sinful sleep! how, for thy sake am I like to be benighted in my journey! I must walk without the sun; darkness must cover the path of my feet; and I must hear the noise of the doleful creatures, because of my sinful sleep.[2] Now also he remembered the story that Mistrust and Timorous told him of, how they were frighted with the sight of the lions. Then said Christian to himself again, These beasts range in the night for their prey; and if they should meet with me in the dark, how should I shift them? How should I escape being by them torn in pieces? Thus he went on his way. But while he was thus bewailing his unhappy miscarriage, he lift up his eyes, and behold there was a very stately palace before him, the name of which was Beautiful; and it stood just by the highway side.

So I saw in my dream, that he made haste and went forward, that if possible he might get lodging there. Now before he had gone far, he entered into a very narrow passage, which was about a furlong off of the porter's lodge; and looking very narrowly before him as he went, he espied two lions in the way. Now, thought he, I see the dangers that Mistrust and Timorous were driven back by. (The lions were chained, but he saw not the chains.) Then he was afraid, and thought also himself to go back after them, for he thought nothing but death was before him. But the porter at the lodge, whose name is Watchful, perceiving that Christian made a halt as if he would go back, cried unto him, saying, Is thy strength so small?[3] Fear not the lions, for they are chained, and are placed there for trial of faith where it is, and for discovery of those that have none. Keep in the midst of the path, and no hurt shall come unto thee.

Then I saw that he went on, trembling for fear of the lions, but taking good heed to the directions of the porter; he heard them roar, but they did him no harm. Then he clapped his hands, and went on till he came and stood before the gate, where the porter was. Then said Christian to the porter, Sir, what house is this? and may I lodge here to-night? The porter answered, This house was built by the Lord of the hill, and he built it for the relief and security of pilgrims. The porter also asked whence he was, and whither he was going.

CHR. I am come from the City of Destruction, and am going to Mount Zion; but because the sun is now set, I desire, if I may, to lodge here to-night.

---

[1] Re. ii. 5: 1 Th. v. 7, 8.   [2] 1 Th. v. 6, 7   [3] Mar. xiii. 34–37.

PORTER. What is your name?

CHR. My name is now Christian, but my name at the first was Graceless; I came of the race of Japheth, whom God will persuade to dwell in the tents of Shem.[1]

POR. But how doth it happen that you come so late? The sun is set.

CHR. I had been here sooner, but that, 'wretched man that I am!' I slept in the arbor that stands on the hill-side; nay, I had, notwithstanding that, been here much sooner, but that, in my sleep, I lost my evidence, and came without it to the brow of the hill; and then feeling for it, and finding it not, I was forced, with sorrow of heart, to go back to the place where I slept my sleep, where I found it, and now I am come.

POR. Well, I will call out one of the virgins of this place, who will, if she likes your talk, bring you in to the rest of the family, according to the rules of the house. So Watchful, the porter, rang a bell, at the sound of which came out at the door of the house, a grave and beautiful damsel, named Discretion, and asked why she was called.

The porter answered, This man is in a journey from the City of Destruction to Mount Zion, but being weary and benighted, he asked me if he might lodge here to-night; so I told him I would call for thee, who, after discourse had with him, mayest do as seemeth thee good, even according to the law of the house.

Then she asked him whence he was, and whither he was going; and he told her. She asked him also how he got into the way; and he told her. Then she asked him what he had seen and met with in the way; and he told her. And last she asked his name; so he said, It is Christian, and I have so much the more a desire to lodge here to-night, because, by what I perceive, this place was built by the Lord of the hill, for the relief and security of pilgrims. So she smiled, but the water stood in her eyes; and after a little pause, she said, I will call forth two or three more of the family. So she ran to the door, and called out Prudence, Piety, and Charity, who, after a little more discourse with him, had him in to the family; and many of them meeting him at the threshold of the house, said, 'Come in, thou blessed of the Lord;' this house was built by the Lord of the hill, on purpose to entertain such pilgrims in. Then he bowed his head, and followed them into the house. So when he was come in and sat down,

[1] Ge. ix. 23.

they gave him something to drink, and consented together, that until supper was ready, some of them should have some particular discourse with Christian, for the best improvement of time; and they appointed Piety, and Prudence, and Charity to discourse with him; and thus they began:

PIETY. Come, good Christian, since we have been so loving to you, to receive you into our house this night, let us, if perhaps we may better ourselves thereby, talk with you of all things that have happened to you in your pilgrimage.

CHR. With a very good will, and I am glad that you are so well disposed.

PIETY. What moved you at first to betake yourself to a pilgrim's life?

CHR. I was driven out of my native country, by a dreadful sound that was in mine ears; to wit, that unavoidable destruction did attend me, if I abode in that place where I was.

PIETY. But how did it happen that you came out of your country this way?

CHR. It was as God would have it; for when I was under the fears of destruction, I did not know whither to go; but by chance there came a man, even to me, as I was trembling and weeping, whose name is Evangelist, and he directed me to the wicket-gate, which else I should never have found, and so set me into the way that hath led me directly to this house.

PIETY. But did you not come by the house of the Interpreter?

CHR. Yes, and did see such things there, the remembrance of which will stick by me as long as I live; especially three things, to wit, how Christ, in despite of Satan, maintains his work of grace in the heart; how the man had sinned himself quite out of hopes of God's mercy; and also the dream of him that thought in his sleep the day of judgment was come.

PIETY. Why, did you hear him tell his dream?

CHR. Yes, and a dreadful one it was. I thought it made my heart ache as he was telling of it; but yet I am glad I heard it.

PIETY. Was that all that you saw at the house of the Interpreter?

CHR. No; he took me and had me where he showed me a stately palace, and how the people were clad in gold that were in it; and how there came a venturous man and cut his way through the armed men that stood in the door to keep him out; and how he was bid to come in, and win eternal glory. Methought those things did ravish my heart! I would have staid at that good man's house a twelvemonth, but that I knew I had further to go.

PIETY. And what saw you else in the way?

CHR. Saw! why, I went but a little further, and I saw one, as I thought in my mind, hang bleeding upon the tree; and the very sight of him made my burden fall off my back (for I groaned under a very heavy burden), but then it fell down from off me. It was a strange thing to me, for I never saw such a thing before; yea, and while I stood looking up, for then I could not forbear looking, three Shining Ones came to me. One of them testified that my sins were forgiven me; another stripped me of my rags, and gave me this broidered coat which you see; and the third set the mark which you see in my forehead, and gave me this sealed roll. (And with that he plucked it out of his bosom.)

PIETY. But you saw more than this, did you not?

CHR. The things that I have told you were the best, yet some other matters I saw, as, namely, I saw three men, Simple, Sloth, and Presumption, lie asleep a little out of the way, as I came, with irons upon their heels; but do you think I could awake them? I also saw Formality and Hypocrisy come tumbling over the wall, to go, as they pretended, to Zion, but they were quickly lost, even as I myself did tell them; but they would not believe. But above all, I found it hard work to get up this hill, and as hard to come by the lions' mouths; and truly if it had not been for the good man, the porter that stands at the gate, I do not know but that after all I might have gone back again; but now, I thank God I am here, and I thank you for receiving of me.

Then Prudence thought good to ask him a few questions, and desired his answer to them.

PRUD. Do you not think sometimes of the country from whence you came?

CHR. Yes, but with much shame and detestation: 'truly if I had been mindful of that country from whence I came out, I might have had opportunity to have returned; but now I desire a better country, that is, an heavenly.'[1]

PRUD. Do you not yet bear away with you some of the things that then you were conversant withal?

CHR. Yes, but greatly against my will; especially my inward and carnal cogitations, with which all my countrymen, as well as myself, were delighted; but now all those things are my grief; and might I but choose mine own things, I would choose never to think of those things more; but when I would be doing of that which is best, that which is worst is with me.[2]

PRUD. Do you not find sometimes, as if those things were vanquished, which at other times are your perplexity?

CHR. Yes, but that is but seldom; but they are to me golden hours, in which such things happen to me.

PRUD. Can you remember by what means you find your annoyances at times, as if they were vanquished?

CHR. Yes; when I think what I saw at the cross, that will do it; and when I look upon my broidered coat, that will do it; also when I look into the roll that I carry in my bosom, that will do it; and when my thoughts wax warm about whither I am going, that will do it.

PRUD. And what is it that makes you so desirous to go to Mount Zion?

CHR. Why, there I hope to see him alive that did hang dead on the cross; and there I hope to be rid of all those things that to this day are in me an annoyance to me; there, they say, there is no death; and there I shall dwell with such company as I like best.[3] For, to tell you truth, I love him, because I was by him eased of my burden; and I am weary of my inward sickness. I would fain be where I shall die no more, and with the company that shall continually cry, 'Holy, holy, holy.'

Then said Charity to Christian, Have you a family? Are you a married man?

CHR. I have a wife and four small children.

CHAR. And why did you not bring them along with you?

CHR. Then Christian wept, and said, Oh how willingly would I have done it! but they were all of them utterly averse to my going on pilgrimage.

CHAR. But you should have talked to them, and have endeavored to have shown them the danger of being behind.

CHR. So I did; and told them also what God had shown to me of the destruction of our city; 'but I seemed to them as one that mocked,' and they believed me not.[4]

CHAR. And did you pray to God that he would bless your counsel to them?

CHR. Yes, and that with much affection; for you must think that my wife and poor children were very dear unto me.

[1] He. xi. 15, 16.   [2] Ro. vii.   [3] Is. xxv. 8; Re. xxi. 4.   [4] Ge. xix. 14.

CHAR. But did you tell them of your own sorrow, and fear of destruction? for I suppose that destruction was visible enough to you.

CHR. Yes, over, and over, and over. They might also see my fears in my countenance, in my tears, and also in my trembling under the apprehension of the judgment that did hang over our heads; but all was not sufficient to prevail with them to come with me.

CHAR. But what could they say for themselves, why they came not?

CHR. Why, my wife was afraid of losing this world, and my children were given to the foolish delights of youth; so what by one thing, and what by another, they left me to wander in this manner alone.

CHAR. But did you not, with your vain life, damp all that you by words used by way of persuasion to bring them away with you?

CHR. Indeed, I cannot commend my life; for I am conscious to myself of many failings therein; I know also, that a man by his conversation may soon overthrow, what by argument or persuasion he doth labor to fasten upon others for their good. Yet this I can say, I was very wary of giving them occasion, by any unseemly action, to make them averse to going on pilgrimage. Yea, for this very thing, they would tell me I was too precise, and that I denied myself of things, for their sakes, in which they saw no evil. Nay, I think I may say, that if what they saw in me did hinder them, it was my great tenderness in sinning against God, or of doing any wrong to my neighbor.

CHAR. Indeed Cain hated his brother, 'because his own works were evil, and his brother's righteous;'[1] and if thy wife and children have been offended with thee for this, they thereby show themselves to be implacable to good, and 'thou hast delivered thy soul from their blood.'[2]

Now I saw in my dream, that thus they sat talking together until supper was ready. So when they had made ready, they sat down to meat. Now the table was furnished 'with fat things, and with wine that was well refined:' and all their talk at the table was about the Lord of the hill; as, namely, about what he had done, and wherefore he did what he did, and why he had builded that house. And by what they said, I perceived that he had been a great warrior, and had fought with and slain 'him that had the power of death,' but not without great danger to himself, which made me love him the more.[3]

For, as they said, and as I believe (said Christian), he did it with the loss of much blood; but that which put glory of grace into all he did, was, that he did it out of pure love to his country. And besides, there were some of them of the household that said they had seen and spoke with him since he did die on the cross; and they have attested that they had it from his own lips, that he is such a lover of poor pilgrims, that the like is not to be found from the east to the west.

They, moreover, gave an instance of what they affirmed, and that was, he had stripped himself of his glory, that he might do this for the poor; and that they heard him say and affirm, 'that he would not dwell in the mountain of Zion alone.' They said, moreover, that he had made many pilgrims princes, though by nature they were beggars born, and their original had been the dunghill.[4]

Thus they discoursed together till late at night; and after they had committed themselves to their Lord for protection, they betook themselves to rest: the Pilgrim they laid in a large upper chamber, whose window opened toward the sunrising; the name of the chamber, was Peace; where he slept till break of day, and then he awoke and sang—

Where am I now? Is this the love and care
Of Jesus for the men that pilgrims are?
Thus to provide! that I should be forgiven!
And dwell already the next door to heaven!

So, in the morning, they all got up; and after some more discourse, they told him that he should not depart till they had shown him the rarities of that place. And first, they had him into the study, where they showed him records of the greatest antiquity; in which, as I remember my dream, they showed him first the pedigree of the Lord of the hill, that he was the son of the Ancient of Days, and came by that eternal generation. Here also was more fully recorded the acts that he had done, and the names of many hundreds that he had taken into his service; and how he had placed them in such habitations, that could neither by length of days, nor decays of nature, be dissolved.

Then they read to him some of the worthy acts that some of his servants had done: as, how they had 'subdued kingdoms, wrought righteousness, obtained promises, stopped the mouths of

---

[1] 1 Jn. iii. 12.   [2] Eze. III. 19.   [3] He. ii. 14 15.   [4] 1 Sa. ii. 8: Ps. cxiii. 7.

lions, quenched the violence of fire, escaped the edge of the sword, out of weakness were made strong, waxed valiant in fight, and turned to flight the armies of the aliens.'[1]

They then read again in another part of the records of the house, where it was showed how willing their Lord was to receive into his favor any, even any, though they in time past had offered great affronts to his person and proceedings. Here also were several other histories of many other famous things of all which Christian had a view; as of things both ancient and modern; together with prophecies and predictions of things that have their certain accomplishment, both to the dread and amazement of enemies, and the comfort and solace of pilgrims.

The next day they took him and had him into the armory, where they showed him all manner of furniture, which their Lord had provided for pilgrims, as sword, shield, helmet, breastplate, all-prayer, and shoes that would not wear out. And there was here enough of this to harness out as many men, for the service of their Lord, as there be stars in the heaven for multitude.

They also showed him some of the engines with which some of his servants had done wonderful things. They showed him Moses' rod; the hammer and nail with which Jael slew Sisera; the pitchers, trumpets, and lamps, too, with which Gideon put to flight the armies of Midian. Then they showed him the ox's goad wherewith Shamgar slew six hundred men. They showed him, also, the jaw-bone with which Samson did such mighty feats. They showed him, moreover, the sling and stone with which David slew Goliath of Gath; and the sword, also, with which their Lord will kill the Man of Sin, in the day that he shall rise up to the prey. They showed him, besides, many excellent things, with which Christian was much delighted. This done, they went to their rest again.

Then I saw in my dream, that, on the morrow, he got up to go forward; but they desired him to stay till the next day also; and then, said they, we will, if the day be clear, show you the Delectable Mountains, which, they said, would yet further add to his comfort, because they were nearer the desired haven than the place where at present he was; so he consented and stayed. When the morning was up, they had him to the top of the house, and bid him look south; so he did; and, behold, at a great distance, he saw a most pleasant mountainous country, beautified with woods, vineyards, fruits of all sorts, flowers also, with springs and fountains, very delectable to behold.[2] Then he asked the name of the country. They said it was Immanuel's Land; and it is as common, said they, as this hill is, to and for all the pilgrims. And when thou comest there, from thence, said they, thou mayest see to the gate of the Celestial City, as the shepherds that live there will make appear.

Now, he bethought himself of setting forward, and they were willing he should. But first, said they, let us go again into the armory. So they did; and when he came there, they harnessed him from head to foot with what was of proof, lest, perhaps, he should meet with assaults in the way. He being, therefore, thus accoutred, walketh out with his friends to the gate, and there he asked the porter if he saw any pilgrims pass by. Then the porter answered, Yes.

CHR. Pray, did you know him? said he.

POR. I asked his name, and he told me it was Faithful.

CHR. Oh, said Christian, I know him; he is my townsman, my near neighbor; he comes from the place where I was born. How far do you think he may be before?

POR. He is got by this time below the hill.

CHR. Well, said Christian, good Porter, the Lord be with thee, and add to all thy blessings much increase, for the kindness that thou hast showed to me.

Then he began to go forward; but Discretion, Piety, Charity and Prudence, would accompany him down to the foot of the hill. So they went on together, reiterating their former discourses, till they came to go down the hill. Then, said Christian, as it was difficult coming up, so, so far as I can see, it is dangerous going down. Yes, said Prudence, so it is, for it is a hard matter for a man to go down into the Valley of Humiliation, as thou art now, and to catch no slip by the way; therefore, said they, are we come out to accompany thee down the hill. So he began to go down, but very warily; yet he caught a slip or two.

Then I saw in my dream that these good companions, when Christian was gone to the bottom of the hill, gave him a loaf of bread, a bottle of wine, and a cluster of raisins; and then he went on his way.

---

[1] He. xl. 33, 34. [2] Is. xxxiii. 16, 17.

But now in this Valley of Humiliation, poor Christian was hard put to it; for he had gone but a little way, before he espied a foul fiend coming over the field to meet him; his name is Apollyon. Then did Christian begin to be afraid, and to cast in his mind whether to go back or to stand his ground. But he considered again that he had no armor for his back; and, therefore, thought that to turn the back to him might give him the greater advantage, with ease to pierce him with his darts. Therefore he resolved to venture and stand his ground; for, thought he, had I no more in mine eye than the saving of my life, it would be the best way to stand.

So he went on, and Apollyon met him. Now the monster was hideous to behold; he was clothed with scales, like a fish (and they are his pride), he had wings like a dragon, feet like a bear, and out of his belly came fire and smoke, and his mouth was as the mouth of a lion. When he was come up to Christian, he beheld him with a disdainful countenance, and thus began to question with him.

APOL. Whence come you? and whither are you bound?

CHR. I am come from the City of Destruction, which is the place of all evil, and am going to the City of Zion.

APOL. By this I perceive thou art one of my subjects, for all that country is mine, and I am the prince and god of it. How is it, then, that thou hast run away from thy king? Were it not that I hope thou mayest do me more service, I would strike thee now, at one blow, to the ground.

CHR. I was born, indeed, in your dominions, but your service was hard, and your wages such as a man could not live on, 'for the wages of sin is death;'[1] therefore, when I was come to years, I did as other considerate persons do, look out, if, perhaps, I might mend myself.

APOL. There is no prince that will thus lightly lose his subjects, neither will I as yet lose thee; but since thou complainest of thy service and wages, be content to go back; what our country will afford, I do here promise to give thee.

CHR. But I have let myself to another, even to the King of princes; and how can I, with fairness, go back with thee?

APOL. Thou hast done in this according to the proverb, 'Changed a bad for a worse;' but it is ordinary for those that have professed themselves his servants, after a while to give him the slip, and return again to me. Do thou so too, and all shall be well.

CHR. I have given him my faith, and sworn my allegiance to him; how, then, can I go back from this, and not be hanged as a traitor?

APOL. Thou didst the same to me, and yet I am willing to pass by all, if now thou wilt yet turn again and go back.

CHR. What I promised thee was in my nonage; and, besides, I count the Prince under whose banner now I stand is able to absolve me; yea, and to pardon also what I did as to my compliance with thee; and besides, O thou destroying Apollyon! to speak truth, I like his service, his wages, his servants, his government, his company, and country, better than thine; and, therefore, leave off to persuade me further; I am his servant, and I will follow him.

APOL. Consider again, when thou art in cool blood, what thou art like to meet with in the way that thou goest. Thou knowest that, for the most part, his servants come to an ill end, because they are transgressors against me and my ways. How many of them have been put to shameful deaths! and, besides, thou countest his service better than mine, whereas he never came yet from the place where he is to deliver any that served him out of their hands; but as for me, how many times, as all the world very well knows, have I delivered, either by power or fraud, those that have faithfully served me, from him and his, though taken by them; and so I will deliver thee.

CHR. His forbearing at present to deliver them is on purpose to try their love, whether they will cleave to him to the end; and as for the ill end thou sayest they come to, that is most glorious in their account; for, for present deliverance, they do not much expect it, for they stay for their glory, and then they shall have it, when their Prince comes in his and the glory of the angels.

APOL. Thou hast already been unfaithful in thy service to him; and how dost thou think to receive wages of him?

CHR. Wherein, O Apollyon! have I been unfaithful to him?

APOL. Thou didst faint at first setting out, when thou wast almost choked in the Gulf of Despond; thou didst attempt wrong ways to be rid of thy burden, whereas thou shouldst have stayed till thy Prince had taken it off; thou didst sinfully sleep, and lose thy choice thing; thou wast, also, almost persuaded to go

---

[1] Ro. vi. 23.

back, at the sight of the lions; and when thou talkest of thy journey, and of what thou hast heard and seen, thou art inwardly desirous of vain-glory in all that thou sayest or doest.

CHR. All this is true, and much more which thou hast left out; but the Prince, whom I serve and honor, is merciful, and ready to forgive; but, besides, these infirmities possessed me in thy country, for there I sucked them in; and I have groaned under them, been sorry for them, and have obtained pardon of my Prince.

APOL. Then Apollyon broke out into a grievous rage, saying, I am an enemy to this Prince; I hate his person, his laws, and people; I am come out on purpose to withstand thee.

CHR. Apollyon, beware what you do; for I am in the king's highway, the way of holiness; therefore take heed to yourself.

APOL. Then Apollyon straddled quite over the whole breadth of the way, and said, I am void of fear in this matter: prepare thyself to die; for I swear by my infernal den, that thou shalt go no further; here will I spill thy soul.

And with that he threw a flaming dart at his breast; but Christian had a shield in his hand, with which he caught it, and so prevented the danger of that.

Then did Christian draw; for he saw it was time to bestir him: and Apollyon as fast made at him, throwing darts as thick as hail; by the which, notwithstanding all that Christian could do to avoid it, Apollyon wounded him in his head, his hand, and foot. This made Christian give a little back; Apollyon, therefore, followed his work amain, and Christian again took courage and resisted as manfully as he could. This sore combat lasted for above half a day, even till Christian was almost quite spent; for you must know, that Christian, by reason of his wounds, must needs grow weaker and weaker.

Then Apollyon, espying his opportunity, began to gather up close to Christian, and wrestling with him, gave him a dreadful fall; and with that, Christian's sword flew out of his hand. Then said Apollyon, I am sure of thee now. And with that he had almost pressed him to death; so that Christian began to despair of life: but as God would have it, while Apollyon was fetching of his last blow, thereby to make a full end of this good man, Christian nimbly reached out his hand for his sword, and caught it, saying, 'Rejoice not against me, O mine enemy: when I fall, I shall arise;' [1] and with that gave him a deadly thrust, which made him give back, as one that had received his mortal wound. Christian perceiving that, made at him again, saying, 'Nay, in all these things we are more than conquerors, through him that loved us.' [2] And with that Apollyon spread forth his dragon's wings, and sped him away, that Christian for a season saw him no more.[3]

In this combat no man can imagine, unless he had seen and heard as I did, what yelling and hideous roaring Apollyon made all the time of the fight—he spake like a dragon; and, on the other side, what sighs and groans burst from Christian's heart. I never saw him all the while give so much as one pleasant look, till he perceived he had wounded Apollyon with his two-edged sword; then, indeed, he did smile and look upward; but it was the dreadfulest sight that ever I saw.

So when the battle was over, Christian said, 'I will here give thanks to him that delivered me out of the mouth of the lion, to him that did help me against Apollyon.' And so he did.

* * *

[1] Mi. vii. 8. [2] Ro. viii. 37. [3] Ja. iv. 7.

JOHN MILTON (1608-1674)

MILTON belonged to a London Puritan family, and when he went up to Cambridge at the end of James I's reign, it was with the intention of becoming a clergyman of the Church of England, in which the Puritans were then a party, hoping to substitute in it government by presbyters, elected by church councils, for government by bishops, appointed by the king. Changes in the administration of the national church under Charles I as well as the development of Milton's own opinions led him to abandon this purpose, towards which all his early training was directed. He has described his serious and studious boyhood in lines 201-7 of *Paradise Regained*, Book I. He was deeply versed not only in Greek and Latin, but also in Hebrew, and in French and Italian, but his early poems show no sign of the mingling of Christianity and paganism which is characteristic of Renaissance thought. On the other hand, he did not share the later Puritan intolerance of innocent amusements. Two of his earlier poems, *Arcades* (c. 1630-33) and *Comus* (1634) and one of his latest, *Samson Agonistes* (pub. 1671), were in dramatic form; in 1630 he wrote a poem in praise of Shakespeare for the folio edition of the plays (see below), and in *L'Allegro* he speaks appreciatively of both Shakespeare's and Jonson's comedies (see p. 281). After seven years at Christ's College, where on account of his almost girlish beauty he was known as 'our fair lady of Christ's,' he retired for further study to Horton in Buckinghamshire, where his principal early poems were written (1632-37). He then traveled on the Continent to complete his education (1638-39), and was recalled by the political crisis preceding the outbreak of the Civil War. 'I thought it base,' he wrote later, 'to be traveling for amusement abroad while my fellow citizens were fighting for liberty at home.' Milton fought, not with the sword, but with the pen. He perceived that 'there were three species of liberty which are essential to the happiness of social life—religious, domestic and civil.' In 1641-42 he took an active part in the controversy that was raging as to the government of the Church by bishops, which appeared to him contrary to religious liberty. His marriage in 1643 to Mary Powell, daughter of a Cavalier and half his own age, turned out unhappily; she found life with the poet and pamphleteer 'very solitary' and too 'philosophical,' and after a month's experience of it returned to her father's house. This led Milton to publish a series of pamphlets in favor of divorce, and he was said to be contemplating a marriage with Miss Davis, the 'virtuous young lady' of Sonnet IX (see p. 282) but, when this came to his wife's ears, she sought and obtained a reconciliation. In 1644 he wrote two important tracts—one on education, and another on the freedom of the press (*Areopagitica*). In 1649 he took up the defence of the Commonwealth for the execution of Charles I, and as Latin Secretary to the Council of State continued his task with a devotion which involved the sacrifice of his eye-sight (see Sonnets, pp. 285-6). His pen was still active on behalf of religious toleration and republican government when the Restoration drove him into hiding; he was arrested, but suffered no harm beyond a short imprisonment and the burning of his books by the hangman. He lost, of course, his Latin secretaryship, and the destruction of some of his property by the fire of London brought him into straitened circumstances; but his tastes were simple, and bating 'not a jot of heart or hope' he returned to his studies. He wrote a history, a logic, a Latin grammar, a compendium of theology; but the great works of his later years were *Paradise Lost* (published 1667), and *Paradise Regained* and *Samson Agonistes* (1671). He chose the subject of *Paradise Lost* out of some hundred which he jotted down about 1640, and wrote a small part of it, but the great design was interrupted by the Civil War, resumed in 1658, and completed in 1663 or 1665.

ON SHAKESPEARE

What needs my Shakespeare for his honored bones
The labor of an age in pilèd stones?
Or that his hallowed relics should be hid
Under a star-ypointing pyramid?
Dear son of memory, great heir of fame,   5
What need'st thou such weak witness of thy name?
Thou in our wonder and astonishment
Hast built thyself a livelong monument.
For whilst, to the shame of slow-endeavoring art,
Thy easy numbers flow, and that each heart   10
Hath from the leaves of thy unvalued book
Those Delphic lines with deep impression took,
Then thou, our fancy of itself bereaving,
Dost make us marble with too much conceiving,
And so sepulchered in such pomp dost lie   15
That kings for such a tomb would wish to die.
                                          (1632)

L'ALLEGRO

Hence, loathèd Melancholy,
Of Cerberus and blackest midnight born
  In Stygian cave forlorn,
'Mongst horrid shapes, and shrieks, and sights unholy!
  Find out some uncouth cell   5
Where brooding Darkness spreads his jealous wings
  And the night raven sings;
There, under ebon shades and low-browed rocks
  As ragged as thy locks,
In dark Cimmerian desert ever dwell.   10

But come, thou goddess fair and free,
In heaven yclept Euphrosyne,
And by men heart-easing Mirth,
Whom lovely Venus, at a birth
With two sister Graces more,   15
To ivy-crownèd Bacchus bore:
Or whether (as some sages sing)
The frolic wind that breathes the spring,
Zephyr with Aurora playing
As he met her once a-Maying,   20
There, on beds of violets blue
And fresh-blown roses washed in dew,
Filled her with thee, a daughter fair,
So buxom, blithe, and debonair.

  Haste thee, nymph, and bring with thee   25
Jest, and youthful jollity,
Quips, and cranks, and wanton wiles,
Nods, and becks, and wreathèd smiles,
Such as hang on Hebe's cheek
And love to live in dimple sleek;   30
Sport that wrinkled Care derides,
And Laughter holding both his sides.
Come, and trip it, as you go
On the light fantastic toe;
And in thy right hand lead with thee   35
The mountain nymph, sweet Liberty;
And, if I give thee honor due,
Mirth, admit me of thy crew,
To live with her, and live with thee,
In unreprovèd pleasures free: 40

  To hear the lark begin his flight,
And, singing, startle the dull night,
From his watch-tower in the skies,
Till the dappled dawn doth rise;
Then to come, in spite of sorrow,   45
And at my window bid good-morrow,
Through the sweet-briar, or the vine,
Or the twisted eglantine;
While the cock, with lively din,
Scatters the rear of darkness thin,   50
And to the stack, or the barn-door,
Stoutly struts his dames before;
Oft listening how the hounds and horn
Cheerly rouse the slumbering morn,
From the side of some hoar hill,   55
Through the high wood echoing shrill;

Some time walking, not unseen,
By hedgerow elms, on hillocks green,
Right against the eastern gate
Where the great sun begins his state   60
Robed in flames and amber light,
The clouds in thousand liveries dight;
While the ploughman, near at hand,
Whistles o'er the furrowed land,
And the milkmaid singeth blithe,   65
And the mower whets his scythe,
And every shepherd tells his tale
Under the hawthorn in the dale.

  Straight mine eye hath caught new pleasures,
Whilst the landscape round it measures: 70
Russet lawns, and fallows gray,
Where the nibbling flocks do stray;
Mountains on whose barren breast
The laboring clouds do often rest;
Meadows trim, with daisies pied,   75
Shallow brooks, and rivers wide;
Towers and battlements it sees
Bosomed high in tufted trees,
Where, perhaps, some beauty lies,
The cynosure of neighboring eyes.   80

  Hard by, a cottage chimney smokes
From betwixt two agèd oaks,
Where Corydon and Thyrsis met,
Are at their savory dinner set
Of herbs, and other country messes,   85
Which the neat-handed Phyllis dresses;
And then in haste her bower she leaves,
With Thestylis to bind the sheaves,
Or, if the earlier season lead,
To the tanned haycock in the mead.   90

  Sometimes, with secure delight,
The upland hamlets will invite,
When the merry bells ring round,
And the jocund rebecks sound
To many a youth and many a maid   95
Dancing in the checkered shade,
And young and old come forth to play
On a sunshine holyday,
Till the livelong daylight fail;
Then to the spicy nut-brown ale,   100
With stories told of many a feat:
How fairy Mab the junkets eat;
She was pinched, and pulled she said;
And he, by friar's lantern led,
Tells how the drudging goblin sweat   105
To earn his cream-bowl duly set,
When, in one night, ere glimpse of morn,
His shadowy flail hath threshed the corn
That ten day-laborers could not end;
Then lies him down the lubber fiend,   110
And, stretched out all the chimney's length,
Basks at the fire his hairy strength,
And, crop-full, out of doors he flings,
Ere the first cock his matin rings.
Thus done the tales, to bed they creep,   115
By whispering winds soon lulled asleep.

Towered cities please us then,
And the busy hum of men,
Where throngs of knights and barons bold,
In weeds of peace high triumphs hold, 120
With store of ladies, whose bright eyes
Rain influence, and judge the prize
Of wit or arms, while both contend
To win her grace whom all commend.
There let Hymen oft appear 125
In saffron robe, with taper clear,
And pomp, and feast, and revelry,
With mask and antique pageantry;
Such sights as youthful poets dream
On summer eves by haunted stream. 130
Then to the well-trod stage anon,
If Jonson's learnèd sock be on,
Or sweetest Shakespeare, Fancy's child,
Warble his native wood-notes wild.

And ever, against eating cares, 135
Lap me in soft Lydian airs
Married to immortal verse,
Such as the meeting soul may pierce
In notes with many a winding bout
Of linkèd sweetness long drawn out, 140
With wanton heed and giddy cunning,
The melting voice through mazes running,
Untwisting all the chains that tie
The hidden soul of harmony;
That Orpheus' self may heave his head, 145
From golden slumber on a bed
Of heaped elysian flowers, and hear
Such strains as would have won the ear
Of Pluto to have quite set free
His half-regained Eurydice. 150

These delights if thou canst give,
Mirth, with thee I mean to live.

(1645)

IL PENSEROSO

Hence, vain deluding joys,
The brood of Folly, without father bred!
How little you bested,
Or fill the fixèd mind with all your toys!
Dwell in some idle brain, 5
And fancies fond with gaudy shapes possess
As thick and numberless
As the gay motes that people the sunbeams,
Or likest hovering dreams,
The fickle pensioners of Morpheus' train. 10

But, hail! thou goddess sage and holy,
Hail, divinest Melancholy,
Whose saintly visage is too bright
To hit the sense of human sight,
And, therefore, to our weaker view, 15
O'erlaid with black, staid Wisdom's hue;
Black, but such as in esteem
Prince Memnon's sister might beseem,
Or that starred Ethiop queen that strove
To set her beauty's praise above 20
The sea-nymphs, and their powers offended,
Yet thou art higher far descended;
Thee bright-haired Vesta, long of yore,
To solitary Saturn bore;
His daughter she; in Saturn's reign 25
Such mixture was not held a stain.
Oft in glimmering bowers and glades
He met her, and in secret shades
Of woody Ida's inmost grove,
Whilst yet there was no fear of Jove. 30

Come, pensive nun, devout and pure,
Sober, steadfast, and demure,
All in a robe of darkest grain
Flowing with majestic train,
And sable stole of cypress lawn 35
Over thy decent shoulders drawn.
Come, but keep thy wonted state,
With even step, and musing gait,
And looks commèrcing with the skies,
Thy rapt soul sitting in thine eyes: 40
There, held in holy passion still,
Forget thyself to marble, till,
With a sad leaden downward cast,
Thou fix them on the earth as fast.
And join with thee calm Peace and Quiet, 45
Spare Fast, that oft with gods doth diet,
And hears the Muses, in a ring,
Aye round about Jove's altar sing.
And add to these retirèd Leisure,
That in trim gardens takes his pleasure. 50
But first, and chiefest, with thee bring,
Him that yon soars on golden wing,
Guiding the fiery-wheelèd throne,
The cherub Contemplation;
And the mute silence hist along, 55
'Less Philomel will deign a song,
In her sweetest saddest plight,
Smoothing the rugged brow of Night,
While Cynthia checks her dragon yoke
Gently o'er the accustomed oak. 60

Sweet bird, that shunn'st the noise of folly,
Most musical, most melancholy!
Thee, chantress, oft, the woods among,
I woo, to hear thy even-song;
And, missing thee, I walk unseen 65
On the dry smooth-shaven green,
To behold the wandering moon
Riding near her highest noon,
Like one that had been led astray
Through the heaven's wide pathless way, 70
And oft, as if her head she bowed,
Stooping through a fleecy cloud.

Oft, on a plat of rising ground,
I hear the far-off curfew sound
Over some wide watered shore, 75
Swinging slow with sullen roar;
Or, if the air will not permit,
Some still, removèd place will fit,

Where glowing embers through the room
Teach light to counterfeit a gloom; 80
Far from all resort of mirth,
Save the cricket on the hearth,
Or the bellman's drowsy charm
To bless the doors from nightly harm.

    Or let my lamp, at midnight hour, 85
Be seen in some high lonely tower
Where I may oft outwatch the Bear
With thrice great Hermes, or unsphere
The spirit of Plato, to unfold
What worlds or what vast regions hold 90
The immortal mind that hath forsook
Her mansion in this fleshly nook,
And of those demons that are found
In fire, air, flood, or underground,
Whose power hath a true consent, 95
With planet or with element.
Sometime let gorgeous Tragedy,
In sceptered pall, come sweeping by,
Presenting Thebes, or Pelops' line,
Or the tale of Troy divine, 100
Or what (though rare) of later age
Ennobled hath the buskined stage.

    But, O, sad virgin! that thy power
Might raise Musæus from his bower;
Or bid the soul of Orpheus sing 105
Such notes as, warbled to the string,
Drew iron tears down Pluto's cheek,
And made hell grant what love did seek;
Or call up him that left half told
The story of Cambuscan bold, 110
Of Camball, and of Algarsife,
And who had Canacè to wife
That owned the virtuous ring and glass,
And of the wondrous horse of brass,
On which the Tartar king did ride; 115
And if aught else great bards beside
In sage and solemn tunes have sung,
Of tourneys, and of trophies hung,
Of forests, and enchantments drear,
Where more is meant than meets the ear. 120

    Thus, Night, oft see me in thy pale career,
Till civil-suited Morn appear,
Not tricked and frounced as she was wont
With the Attic boy to hunt,
But kerchieft in a comely cloud, 125
While rocking winds are piping loud;
Or ushered with a shower still,
When the gust hath blown his fill,
Ending on the rustling leaves,
With minute drops from off the eaves. 130
And, when the sun begins to fling
His flaring beams, me, goddess, bring
To archèd walks of twilight groves,
And shadows brown, that Sylvan loves,
Of pine, or monumental oak, 135
Where the rude axe with heavèd stroke
Was never heard the nymphs to daunt
Or fright them from their hallowed haunt.
There in close covert by some brook,
Where no profaner eye may look, 140
Hide me from day's garish eye,
While the bee, with honied thigh,
That at her flowery work doth sing,
And the waters murmuring,
With such concert as they keep, 145
Entice the dewy-feathered sleep;
And let some strange mysterious dream
Wave at his wings, in airy stream
Of lively portraiture displayed,
Softly on my eyelids laid. 150
And, as I wake, sweet music breathe
Above, about, or underneath,
Sent by some spirit to mortals good,
Or the unseen genius of the wood.

    But let my due feet never fail 155
To walk the studious cloister's pale,
And love the high embowèd roof,
With antique pillars massy proof,
And storied windows richly dight,
Casting a dim religious light: 160
There let the pealing organ blow
To the full-voiced choir below
In service high and anthems clear
As may with sweetness, through mine ear,
Dissolve me into ecstasies, 165
And bring all heaven before mine eyes.

    And may at last my weary age
Find out the peaceful hermitage,
The hairy gown and mossy cell,
Where I may sit and rightly spell 170
Of every star that heaven doth shew,
And every herb that sips the dew,
Till old experience do attain
To something like prophetic strain.

    These pleasures, Melancholy, give, 175
And I with thee will choose to live.

(1645)

LYCIDAS

Yet once more, O ye laurels, and once more,
Ye myrtles brown, with ivy never sere,
I come, to pluck your berries harsh and crude,
    And with forced fingers rude
Shatter your leaves before the mellowing year.
Bitter constraint and sad occasion dear 6
Compels me to disturb your season due;
For Lycidas is dead, dead ere his prime,
Young Lycidas, and hath not left his peer;
Who would not sing for Lycidas? He knew 10
Himself to sing, and build the lofty rime.
He must not float upon his watery bier
Unwept, and welter to the parching wind
Without the meed of some melodious tear.

Begin, then, sisters of the sacred well   15
That from beneath the seat of Jove doth spring:
Begin, and somewhat loudly sweep the string;
Hence with denial vain, and coy excuse:
So may some gentle muse
With lucky words favor my destined urn.   20
    And as he passes, turn,
And bid fair peace be to my sable shroud!

For we were nursed upon the self-same hill,
Fed the same flock, by fountain, shade, and rill.
Together both, ere the high lawns appeared   25
Under the opening eyelids of the morn,
We drove a-field, and both together heard
What time the gray-fly winds her sultry horn,
Battening our flocks with the fresh dews of night,
Oft till the star that rose at evening bright   30
Toward heaven's descent had sloped his westering wheel.
Meanwhile the rural ditties were not mute;
    Tempered to the oaten flute
Rough satyrs danced, and fauns with cloven heel
From the glad sound would not be absent long:
And old Damœtas loved to hear our song.   36

But, oh! the heavy change, now thou art gone,
Now thou art gone and never must return!
Thee, shepherd, thee the woods, and desert caves,
With wild thyme and the gadding vine o'ergrown   40
    And all their echoes, mourn:
The willows, and the hazel copses green,
    Shall now no more be seen
Fanning their joyous leaves to thy soft lays.
As killing as the canker to the rose,   45
Or taint-worm to the weanling herds that graze,
Or frost to flowers, that their gay wardrobe wear,
    When first the white-thorn blows;
Such, Lycidas, thy loss to shepherd's ear.

Where were ye, Nymphs, when the remorseless deep   50
Closed o'er the head of your loved Lycidas?
For neither were ye playing on the steep
Where your old bards, the famous Druids, lie,
Nor on the shaggy top of Mona high,
Nor yet where Deva spreads her wizard stream:
    Ah me! I fondly dream,   56
'Had ye been there': . . . for what could that have done?
What could the Muse herself that Orpheus bore,
The Muse herself, for her enchanting son
Whom universal nature did lament,   60
When by the rout that made the hideous roar
His gory visage down the stream was sent,
Down the swift Hebrus to the Lesbian shore?

Alas! what boots it with incessant care
To tend the homely, slighted, shepherd's trade,
And strictly meditate the thankless Muse?   66
Were it not better done, as others use,
To sport with Amaryllis in the shade,
Or with the tangles of Neæra's hair?
Fame is the spur that the clear spirit doth raise
(That last infirmity of noble mind)   71
To scorn delights and live laborious days:
But the fair guerdon when we hope to find,
And think to burst out into sudden blaze,
Comes the blind Fury with the abhorrèd shears
And slits the thin-spun life. 'But not the praise,'   76
Phœbus replied, and touched my trembling ears:
'Fame is no plant that grows on mortal soil,
    Nor in the glistering foil
Set off to the world, nor in broad rumor lies,   80
But lives and spreads aloft by those pure eyes
And perfect witness of all-judging Jove:
As he pronounces lastly on each deed,
Of so much fame in heaven expect thy meed.'

O fountain Arethuse, and thou honored flood,
Smooth-sliding Mincius, crowned with vocal reeds,   86
That strain I heard was of a higher mood.
    But now my oat proceeds,
And listens to the herald of the sea
    That came in Neptune's plea;   90
He asked the waves, and asked the felon winds,
What hard mishap hath doomed this gentle swain?
And questioned every gust, of rugged wings,
That blows from off each beakèd promontory:
    They know not of his story: 95
And sage Hippotades their answer brings,
That not a blast was from his dungeon strayed,
The air was calm, and on the level brine
Sleek Panopè with all her sisters played.
It was that fatal and perfidious bark,   100
Built in the eclipse, and rigged with curses dark,
That sunk so low that sacred head of thine.

Next, Camus, reverend sire, went footing slow,
His mantle hairy, and his bonnet sedge
Inwrought with figures dim and on the edge   105
Like to that sanguine flower inscribed with woe.
'Ah! who hath reft,' quoth he, 'my dearest pledge?'
    Last came, and last did go,
The pilot of the Galilean lake.
Two massy keys he bore, of metals twain,   110
The golden opes, the iron shuts amain.
He shook his mitered locks, and stern bespake:
'How well could I have spared for thee, young swain,
Enow of such as, for their bellies' sake
Creep, and intrude, and climb into the fold!   115
Of other care they little reckoning make

Than how to scramble at the shearers' feast
And shove away the worthy bidden guest;
Blind mouths! that scarce themselves know
    how to hold
A sheep-hook, or have learned aught else the
    least   120
That to the faithful herdsman's art belongs!
What recks it them? What need they? They
    are sped,
And, when they list, their lean and flashy songs
Grate on their scrannel pipes of wretched straw;
The hungry sheep look up, and are not fed, 125
But, swoln with wind and the rank mist they
    draw,
Rot inwardly, and foul contagion spread;
Besides what the grim wolf, with privy paw,
Daily devours apace, and nothing said.
But that two-handed engine at the door   130
Stands ready to smite once, and smite no more.'

    Return, Alphëus, the dread voice is past,
That shrunk thy streams; return, Sicilian Muse,
And call the vales, and bid them hither cast
Their bells and flowerets of a thousand hues. 135
Ye valleys low, where the mild whispers use
Of shades and wanton winds, and gushing
    brooks,
On whose fresh lap the swart star sparely looks,
Throw hither all your quaint enameled eyes
That on the green turf suck the honeyed
    showers,   140
And purple all the ground with vernal flowers.
Bring the rathe primrose that forsaken dies,
The tufted crow-toe, and pale jessamine,
The white pink, and the pansy freaked with jet,
The glowing violet,   145
The musk-rose, and the well-attired woodbine,
With cowslips wan that hang the pensive head,
And every flower that sad embroidery wears;
Bid amaranthus all his beauty shed,
And daffodillies fill their cups with tears,   150
To strew the laureate hearse where Lycid lies.
For so, to interpose a little ease,
Let our frail thoughts dally with false surmise:
Ah me! whilst thee the shores and sounding seas
Wash far away, where'er thy bones are hurled;
Whether beyond the stormy Hebrides,   156
Where thou, perhaps under the whelming tide,
Visit'st the bottom of the monstrous world;
Or whether thou, to our moist vows denied,
Sleep'st by the fable of Bellerus old,   160
Where the great vision of the guarded mount
Looks toward Namancos and Bayona's hold:
Look homeward, angel, now, and melt with
    ruth;
And, O ye dolphins, waft the hapless youth.

    Weep no more, woeful shepherds, weep no
    more,   165
For Lycidas, your sorrow, is not dead,
Sunk though he be beneath the watery floor.
So sinks the day-star in the ocean-bed,
And yet anon repairs his drooping head,
And tricks his beams, and, with new spangled
    ore,   170
Flames in the forehead of the morning sky:
So Lycidas sunk low, but mounted high,
Through the dear might of Him that walked
    the waves,
Where, other groves and other streams along,
With nectar pure his oozy locks he laves,   175
And hears the unexpressive nuptial song
In the blest kingdoms meek of joy and love.
There entertain him all the saints above,
In solemn troops and sweet societies
That sing, and, singing, in their glory move, 180
And wipe the tears for ever from his eyes.
Now, Lycidas, the shepherds weep no more;
Henceforth thou art the genius of the shore
In thy large recompense, and shalt be good
To all that wander in that perilous flood.   185

    Thus sang the uncouth swain to the oaks and
    rills,
While the still morn went out with sandals
    gray;
He touched the tender stops of various quills,
With eager thought warbling his Doric lay;
And now the sun had stretched out all the hills.
And now was dropt into the western bay;   191
At last he rose, and twitched his mantle blue:
To-morrow to fresh woods and pastures new.
    (1638)

SONNETS

When the Assault was Intended to the City

Captain or colonel, or knight in arms,
Whose chance on these defenseless doors may
    seize,
If deed of honor did thee ever please,
Guard them, and him within protect from
    harms.

He can requite thee; for he knows the charms 5
That call fame on such gentle acts as these,
And he can spread thy name o'er lands and seas,
Whatever clime the sun's bright circle warms.

Lift not thy spear against the Muses' bower:
The great Emathian conqueror bid spare   10
The house of Pindarus, when temple and tower
Went to the ground; and the repeated air
Of sad Electra's poet had the power
To save the Athenian walls from ruin bare.
    (1645)

To a Virtuous Young Lady

Lady, that in the prime of earliest youth
Wisely hast shunned the broad way and the
    green,
And with those few art eminently seen
That labor up the hill of heavenly truth,

The better part with Mary and with Ruth 5
Chosen thou hast; and they that overween,
And at thy growing virtues fret their spleen,
No anger find in thee, but pity and ruth.

Thy care is fixed, and zealously attends
To fill thy odorous lamp with deeds of light, 10
And hope that reaps not shame. Therefore be sure
Thou, when the Bridegroom with his feastful friends
Passes to bliss at the mid-hour of night,
Hast gained thy entrance, virgin wise and pure.
(1645)

On the Detraction which Followed upon my Writing Certain Treatises

A book was writ of late called *Tetrachordon*,
And woven close, both matter, form, and style;
The subject new: it walked the town a while,
Numbering good intellects; now seldom pored on.
Cries the stall-reader, 'Bless us! what a word on
A title page is this!' and some in file 6
Stand spelling false, while one might walk to Mile-
End Green. Why, is it harder, sirs, than *Gordon*,

Colkitto, or *Macdonnel*, or *Galasp?*
Those rugged names to our like mouths grow sleek 10
That would have made Quintilian stare and gasp.
Thy age, like ours, O soul of Sir John Cheke,
Hated not learning worse than toad or asp,
When thou taught'st Cambridge and King Edward Greek.
(1673)

On the Same

I did but prompt the age to quit their clogs
By the known rules of ancient liberty,
When straight a barbarous noise environs me
Of owls and cuckoos, asses, apes, and dogs;

As when those hinds that were transformed to frogs 5
Railed at Latona's twin-born progeny,
Which after held the sun and moon in fee.
But this is got by casting pearl to hogs,

That bawl for freedom in their senseless mood,
And still revolt when truth would set them free.
License they mean when they cry Liberty; 11
For who loves that must first be wise and good;
But from that mark how far they rove we see,
For all this waste of wealth and loss of blood.
(1673)

To the Lord General Cromwell, May 1652
On the Proposals of Certain Ministers at the Committee for Propagation of the Gospel

Cromwell, our chief of men, who through a cloud
Not of war only, but detractions rude,
Guided by faith and matchless fortitude,
To peace and truth thy glorious way hast ploughed,

And on the neck of crownèd Fortune proud 5
Hast reared God's trophies, and his work pursued,
While Darwen stream, with blood of Scots imbrued,
And Dunbar field, resounds thy praises loud,

And Worcester's laureate wreath: yet much remains
To conquer still; Peace hath her victories 10
No less renowned than War: new foes arise,
Threatening to bind our souls with secular chains.
Help us to save free conscience from the paw
Of hireling wolves, whose Gospel is their maw.
(Written, 1652)

On the Late Massacre in Piedmont

Avenge, O Lord, thy slaughtered saints, whose bones
Lie scattered on the Alpine mountains cold;
Even them who kept thy truth so pure of old,
When all our fathers worshipped stocks and stones,

Forget not: in thy book record their groans 5
Who were thy sheep, and in their ancient fold
Slain by the bloody Piedmontese, that rolled
Mother with infant down the rocks. Their moans

The vales redoubled to the hills, and they
To heaven. Their martyred blood and ashes sow 10
O'er all the Italian fields, where still doth sway
The triple Tyrant that from these may grow
A hundredfold, who, having learnt thy way,
Early may fly the Babylonian woe.
(1673)

On his Blindness

When I consider how my light is spent
Ere half my days in this dark world and wide,
And that one talent which is death to hide
Lodged with me useless, though my soul more bent

To serve therewith my Maker, and present 5
My true account, lest he returning chide,
'Doth God exact day-labor, light denied?'
I fondly ask. But Patience, to prevent

That murmur, soon replies, 'God doth not need
Either man's work or his own gifts. Who best 10
Bear his mild yoke, they serve him best. His state
Is kingly: thousands at his bidding speed,
And post o'er land and ocean without rest;
They also serve who only stand and wait.'
(1673)

To Cyriack Skinner

Cyriack, this three years' day these eyes, though clear,
To outward view, of blemish or of spot,
Bereft of light, their seeing have forgot;
Nor to their idle orbs doth sight appear
Of sun, or moon, or star, throughout the year, 5
Or man, or woman. Yet I argue not
Against Heaven's hand or will, nor bate a jot
Of heart or hope, but still bear up and steer

Right onward. What supports me, dost thou ask?
The conscience, friend, to have lost them over-plied 10
In liberty's defense, my noble task,
Of which all Europe rings from side to side.

This thought might lead me through the world's vain mask
Content, though blind, had I no better guide.

On His Deceased Wife

Methought I saw my late espousèd saint
Brought to me like Alcestis from the grave,
Whom Jove's great son to her glad husband gave,
Rescued from Death by force, though pale and faint.

Mine, as whom washed from spot of childbed taint 5
Purification in the old law did save,
And such as yet once more I trust to have
Full sight of her in heaven without restraint,

Came vested all in white, pure as her mind.
Her face was veiled; yet to my fancied sight 10
Love, sweetness, goodness, in her person shined
So clear as in no face with more delight.
But, oh! as to embrace me she inclined,
I waked, she fled, and day brought back my night. (1673)

PARADISE LOST

BOOK I

The Argument

This First Book proposes, first in brief, the whole subject,—Man's disobedience, and the loss thereupon of Paradise, wherein he was placed: then touches the prime cause of his fall,—the serpent, or rather Satan in the serpent; who, revolting from God, and drawing to his side many legions of angels, was, by the command of God, driven out of heaven, with all his crew, into the great deep. Which action passed over, the poem hastens into the midst of things, presenting Satan, with his angels, now fallen into hell, described here, not in the center (for heaven and earth may be supposed as yet not made, certainly not yet accursed), but in a place of utter darkness, fitliest called Chaos: here Satan with his angels, lying on the burning lake, thunderstruck and astonished, after a certain space recovers, as from confusion, calls up him who next in order and dignity lay by him. They confer of their miserable fall; Satan awakens all his legions, who lay till then in the same manner confounded. They rise; their numbers; array of battle; their chief leaders named, according to the idols known afterwards in Canaan and the countries adjoining. To these Satan directs his speech, comforts them with hope yet of regaining heaven, but tells them lastly of a new world and new kind of creature to be created, according to an ancient prophecy, or report, in heaven—for, that the angels were long before this visible creation, was the opinion of many ancient fathers. To find out the truth of this prophecy, and what to determine thereon, he refers to a full council. What his associates thence attempt. Pandemonium, the palace of Satan, rises, suddenly built out of the deep: the infernal peers there sit in council

Of Man's first disobedience, and the fruit
Of that forbidden tree, whose mortal taste
Brought death into the world, and all our woe,
With loss of Eden, till one greater Man
Restore us, and regain the blissful seat, 5
Sing, heavenly Muse, that on the secret top
Of Oreb, or of Sinai, did'st inspire
That shepherd, who first taught the chosen seed,
In the beginning how the heavens and earth
Rose out of chaos: or, if Sion hill 10
Delight thee more, and Siloa's brook that flowed
Fast by the oracle of God, I thence
Invoke thy aid to my adventurous song,
That with no middle flight intends to soar
Above the Aonian mount, while it pursues 15
Things unattempted yet in prose or rime.

And chiefly thou, O Spirit, that dost prefer
Before all temples the upright heart and pure,
Instruct me, for thou know'st; thou from the first
Wast present, and, with mighty wings outspread, 20
Dove-like, sat'st brooding on the vast abyss,
And mad'st it pregnant: what in me is dark,
Illumine; what is low, raise and support;
That to the height of this great argument
I may assert eternal Providence, 25
And justify the ways of God to men.

Say first—for heaven hides nothing from thy view,
Nor the deep tract of hell—say first, what cause
Moved our grand Parents, in that happy state,
Favored of Heaven so highly, to fall off 30
From their Creator, and transgress his will
For one restraint, lords of the world besides.
Who first seduced them to that foul revolt?

The infernal Serpent; he it was, whose guile,
Stirred up with envy and revenge, deceived 35
The mother of mankind; what time his pride
Had cast him out from heaven, with all his host
Of rebel angels; by whose aid, aspiring
To set himself in glory above his peers,
He trusted to have equaled the Most High, 40
If he opposed; and, with ambitious aim
Against the throne and monarchy of God,
Raised impious war in heaven, and battle proud,
With vain attempt. Him the Almighty Power
Hurled headlong flaming from the ethereal sky,
With hideous ruin and combustion, down 46
To bottomless perdition; there to dwell
In adamantine chains and penal fire,
Who durst defy the Omnipotent to arms.

Nine times the space that measures day and night 50
To mortal men, he with his horrid crew
Lay vanquished, rolling in the fiery gulf,
Confounded, though immortal. But his doom
Reserved him to more wrath; for now the thought
Both of lost happiness and lasting pain 55
Torments him; round he throws his baleful eyes,
That witnessed huge affliction and dismay,
Mixed with obdurate pride, and steadfast hate.
At once, as far as angels' ken, he views
The dismal situation waste and wild. 60
A dungeon horrible, on all sides round,
As one great furnace, flamed; yet from those flames
No light; but rather darkness visible
Served only to discover sights of woe,
Regions of sorrow, doleful shades, where peace
And rest can never dwell; hope never comes 66
That comes to all; but torture without end
Still urges, and a fiery deluge, fed
With ever-burning sulphur unconsumed.

Such place eternal justice had prepared 70
For those rebellious; here their prison ordained
In utter darkness, and their portion set
As far removed from God and light of heaven,
As from the center thrice to the utmost pole. 74
O, how unlike the place from whence they fell!

There the companions of his fall, o'erwhelmed
With floods and whirlwinds of tempestuous fire,
He soon discerns; and weltering by his side
One next himself in power, and next in crime,

Long after known in Palestine, and named 80
Beëlzebub. To whom the arch-enemy,
And thence in heaven called Satan, with bold words
Breaking the horrid silence, thus began:

'If thou beest he—but O, how fall'n! how changed
From him who, in the happy realms of light, 85
Clothed with transcendent brightness, didst outshine
Myriads, though bright! If he, whom mutual league,
United thoughts and counsels, equal hope
And hazard in the glorious enterprise,
Joined with me once, now misery hath joined 90
In equal ruin; into what pit thou seest
From what height fall'n, so much the stronger proved
He with his thunder: and till then who knew
The force of those dire arms? Yet not for those,
Nor what the potent victor in his rage 95
Can else inflict, do I repent or change,
Though changed in outward luster, that fixed mind,
And high disdain from sense of injured merit,
That with the Mightiest raised me to contend,
And to the fierce contention brought along 100
Innumerable force of spirits armed,
That durst dislike his reign, and, me preferring,
His utmost power with adverse power opposed
In dubious battle on the plains of heaven,
And shook his throne. What though the field be lost? 105
All is not lost; the unconquerable will,
And study of revenge, immortal hate,
And courage never to submit or yield,
And what is else not to be overcome;
That glory never shall his wrath or might 110
Extort from me. To bow and sue for grace
With suppliant knee, and deify his power
Who from the terror of this arm so late
Doubted his empire—that were low indeed,
That were an ignominy, and shame beneath 115
This downfall; since, by fate, the strength of gods,
And this empyreal substance, cannot fail:
Since, through experience of this great event,
In arms not worse, in foresight much advanced,
We may with more successful hope resolve 120
To wage by force or guile eternal war,
Irreconcilable to our grand foe,
Who now triumphs, and, in the excess of joy
Sole reigning, holds the tyranny of heaven.' 124

So spake the apostate angel, though in pain,
Vaunting aloud, but racked with deep despair
And him thus answered soon his bold compeer:

'O prince, O chief of many-thronèd powers,
That led the embattled seraphim to war
Under thy conduct, and in dreadful deeds 130

Fearless, endangered heaven's perpetual King,
And put to proof his high supremacy,
Whether upheld by strength, or chance, or fate;
Too well I see, and rue the dire event,
That with sad overthrow, and foul defeat, 135
Hath lost us heaven, and all this mighty host
In horrible destruction laid thus low,
As far as gods and heavenly essences
Can perish: for the mind and spirit remain
Invincible, and vigor soon returns, 140
Though all our glory extinct, and happy state
Here swallowed up in endless misery.
But what if he our Conqueror (whom I now
Of force believe Almighty, since no less
Than such could have o'erpowered such force
  as ours) 145
Have left us this our spirit and strength entire,
Strongly to suffer and support our pains,
That we may so suffice his vengeful ire,
Or do him mightier service as his thralls
By right of war, whate'er his business be, 150
Here in the heart of hell to work in fire,
Or do his errands in the gloomy deep?
What can it then avail, though yet we feel
Strength undiminished, or eternal being
To undergo eternal punishment?' 155

   Whereto with speedy words the arch-fiend
     replied:
'Fallen cherub, to be weak is miserable,
Doing or suffering; but of this be sure,
To do aught good never will be our task,
But ever to do ill our sole delight, 160
As being the contrary to his high will
Whom we resist. If then his providence
Out of our evil seek to bring forth good,
Our labor must be to pervert that end,
And out of good still to find means of evil, 165
Which ofttimes may succeed, so as perhaps
Shall grieve him, if I fail not, and disturb
His inmost counsels from their destined aim.
But see, the angry Victor hath recalled
His ministers of vengeance and pursuit 170
Back to the gates of heaven; the sulphurous
   hail,
Shot after us in storm, o'erblown, hath laid
The fiery surge, that from the precipice
Of heaven received us falling; and the thunder,
Winged with red lightning and impetuous rage,
Perhaps hath spent his shafts, and ceases now
To bellow through the vast and boundless deep.
Let us not slip the occasion, whether scorn 178
Or satiate fury yield it from our foe.
Seest thou yon dreary plain, forlorn and wild,
The seat of desolation, void of light, 181
Save what the glimmering of these livid flames
Casts pale and dreadful? Thither let us tend
From off the tossing of these fiery waves;
There rest, if any rest can harbor there; 185
And, re-assembling our afflicted powers,
Consult how we may henceforth most offend
Our enemy; our own loss how repair;
How overcome this dire calamity;
What reinforcement we may gain from hope;
If not, what resolution from despair.' 191

   Thus Satan, talking to his nearest mate,
With head uplift above the wave, and eyes
That sparkling blazed; his other parts besides
Prone on the flood, extended long and large, 195
Lay floating many a rood; in bulk as huge
As whom the fables name of monstrous size,
Titanian, or Earth-born, that warred on Jove;
Briareos or Typhon, whom the den
By ancient Tarsus held; or that sea-beast 200
Leviathan, which God of all his works,
Created hugest that swim the ocean stream.
Him, haply, slumbering on the Norway foam,
The pilot of some small night-foundered skiff,
Deeming some island, oft, as seamen tell, 205
With fixèd anchor in his scaly rind
Moors by his side under the lee, while night
Invests the sea, and wishèd morn delays:
So stretched out huge in length the arch-fiend
   lay
Chained on the burning lake: nor ever thence
Had risen, or heaved his head; but that the will
And high permission of all-ruling Heaven 212
Left him at large to his own dark designs;
That with reiterated crimes he might
Heap on himself damnation, while he sought 213
Evil to others; and, enraged, might see
How all his malice served but to bring forth
Infinite goodness, grace, and mercy, shown
On man by him seduced; but on himself 219
Treble confusion, wrath, and vengeance poured.

   Forthwith upright he rears from off the pool
His mighty stature; on each hand the flames,
Driven backward, slope their pointing spires,
   and rolled
In billows, leave i' the midst a horrid vale. 224
Then with expanded wings he steers his flight
Aloft, incumbent on the dusky air,
That felt unusual weight; till on dry land
He lights, if it were land that ever burned
With solid, as the lake with liquid fire;
And such appeared in hue, as when the force 230
Of subterranean wind transports a hill
Torn from Pelorus, or the shattered side
Of thundering Etna, whose combustible
And fuelled entrails thence conceiving fire,
Sublimed with mineral fury, aid the winds, 235
And leave a singèd bottom, all involved
With stench and smoke: such resting found the
   sole
Of unblest feet. Him followed his next mate:
Both glorying to have 'scaped the stygian flood
As gods, and by their own recovered strength,
Not by the sufferance of supernal power. 241

   'Is this the region, this the soil, the clime,'
Said then the lost archangel, 'this the seat

That we must change for heaven; this mournful gloom
For that celestial light? Be it so, since he, 245
Who now is Sovereign, can dispose and bid
What shall be right: farthest from him is best,
Whom reason hath equaled, force hath made supreme
Above his equals. Farewell, happy fields,
Where joy for ever dwells! Hail, horrors! hail
Infernal world! and thou profoundest hell, 251
Receive thy new possessor—one who brings
A mind not to be changed by place or time:
The mind is its own place, and in itself
Can make a heaven of hell, a hell of heaven. 255
What matter where, if I be still the same,
And what I should be; all but less than he
Whom thunder hath made greater? Here at least
We shall be free: the Almighty hath not built
Here for his envy, will not drive us hence: 260
Here we may reign secure, and, in my choice,
To reign is worth ambition, though in hell;
Better to reign in hell, than serve in heaven.
But wherefore let we then our faithful friends,
The associates and co-partners of our loss, 265
Lie thus astonished on the oblivious pool,
And call them not to share with us their part
In this unhappy mansion; or once more
With rallied arms to try what may be yet
Regained in heaven, or what more lost in hell?'

So Satan spake, and him Beëlzebub 271
Thus answered: 'Leader of those armies bright,
Which, but the Omnipotent, none could have foiled,
If once they hear that voice, their liveliest pledge
Of hope in fears and dangers, heard so oft 275
In worst extremes, and on the perilous edge
Of battle when it raged, in all assaults
Their surest signal, they will soon resume
New courage and revive; though now they lie
Groveling and prostrate on yon lake of fire, 280
As we erewhile, astounded and amazed;
No wonder, fall'n such a pernicious height.'

He scarce had ceased, when the superior fiend
Was moving toward the shore: his ponderous shield
Ethereal temper, massy, large, and round, 285
Behind him cast; the broad circumference
Hung on his shoulders like the moon, whose orb
Through optic glass the Tuscan artist views
At evening, from the top of Fesolè,
Or in Valdarno, to descry new lands, 290
Rivers, or mountains, in her spotty globe.
His spear, to equal which the tallest pine
Hewn on Norwegian hills, to be the mast
Of some great admiral, were but a wand,
He walked with, to support uneasy steps 295
Over the burning marl, not like those steps
On heaven's azure, and the torrid slime

Smote on him sore besides, vaulted with fire:
Nathless he so endured, till on the beach
Of that inflamèd sea he stood, and called 300
His legions, angel forms, who lay entranced,
Thick as autumnal leaves, that strew the brooks
In Vallombrosa, where the Etrurian shades,
High over-arched, embower; or scattered sedge
Afloat, when with fierce winds Orion armed 305
Hath vexed the Red Sea coast, whose waves o'erthrew
Busiris and his Memphian chivalry,
While with perfidious hatred they pursued
The sojourners of Goshen, who beheld
From the safe shore their floating carcasses 310
And broken chariot-wheels; so thick bestrewn,
Abject and lost lay these, covering the flood,
Under amazement of their hideous change.

He called so loud, that all the hollow deep
Of hell resounded. 'Princes, potentates, 315
Warriors, the flower of heaven, once yours, now lost,
If such astonishment as this can seize
Eternal spirits; or have ye chosen this place
After the toil of battle to repose
Your wearied virtue, for the ease you find 320
To slumber here, as in the vales of heaven?
Or in this abject posture have ye sworn
To adore the Conqueror? who now beholds
Cherub and seraph rolling in the flood
With scattered arms and ensigns, till anon 325
His swift pursuers from heaven-gates discern
The advantage, and descending, tread us down
Thus drooping, or with linkèd thunderbolts
Transfix us to the bottom of this gulf?
Awake, arise, or be for ever fall'n!' 330

They heard, and were abashed, and up they sprung
Upon the wing; as when men, wont to watch
On duty, sleeping found by whom they dread,
Rouse and bestir themselves ere well awake.
Nor did they not perceive the evil plight 335
In which they were, or the fierce pains not feel;
Yet to their general's voice they soon obeyed,
Innumerable. As when the potent rod
Of Amram's son, in Egypt's evil day,
Waved round the coast, up called a pitchy cloud
Of locusts, warping on the eastern wind, 341
That o'er the realm of impious Pharaoh hung
Like night, and darkened all the land of Nile:
So numberless were those bad angels seen
Hovering on wing under the cope of hell, 345
'Twixt upper, nether, and surrounding fires;
Till, at a signal given, the uplifted spear
Of their great sultan waving to direct
Their course, in even balance down they light
On the firm brimstone, and fill all the plain: 350
A multitude like which the populous north
Poured never from her frozen loins, to pass
Rhine or the Danube, when her barbarous sons

Came like a deluge on the south and spread
Beneath Gibraltar to the Libyan sands.   355

    Forthwith from every squadron and each
        band
The heads and leaders thither haste where stood
Their great commander; godlike shapes and
    forms
Excelling human; princely dignities;
And powers that erst in heaven sat on thrones,
Though of their names in heavenly records now
Be no memorial; blotted out and rased   362
By their rebellion from the books of life.
Nor had they yet among the sons of Eve
Got them new names; till, wandering o'er the
    earth,   365
Through God's high sufferance, for the trial of
    man,
By falsities and lies the greater part
Of mankind they corrupted to forsake
God their Creator, and the invisible
Glory of him that made them, to transform   370
Oft to the image of a brute, adorned
With gay religions, full of pomp and gold,
And devils to adore for deities:
Then were they known to men by various
    names,
And various idols through the heathen world.

    Say, Muse, their names then known, who first,
        who last,   376
Roused from the slumber on that fiery couch,
At their great emperor's call, as next in worth,
Came singly where he stood on the bare strand,
While the promiscuous crowd stood yet aloof.

    The chief were those who from the pit of hell,
Roaming to seek their prey on earth, durst fix
Their seats long after next the seat of God,   383
Their altars by his altar, gods adored
Among the nations round, and durst abide   385
Jehovah thundering out of Sion, throned
Between the cherubim; yea, often placed
Within his sanctuary itself their shrines,
Abominations; and with cursed things
His holy rites and solemn feasts profaned,   390
And with their darkness durst affront his light.
First, Moloch, horrid king, besmeared with
    blood
Of human sacrifice, and parents' tears;
Though, for the noise of drums and timbrels
    loud,
Their children's cries unheard, that passed
    through fire   395
To his grim idol. Him the Ammonite
Worshipped in Rabba and her watery plain,
In Argob and in Basan, to the stream
Of utmost Arnon. Nor content with such
Audacious neighborhood, the wisest heart   400
Of Solomon he led by fraud to build
His temple right against the temple of God,
On that opprobrious hill; and made his grove
The pleasant valley of Hinnom, Tophet thence
And black Gehenna called, the type of hell.   405

    Next, Chemos, the obscene dread of Moab's
        sons,
From Aroer to Nebo, and the wild
Of southmost Abarim; in Heseb0n
And Horonáim, Seon's realm, beyond
The flowery dale of Sibma clad with vines,   410
And Eleälë to the asphaltic pool;
Peor his other name, when he enticed
Israel in Sittim, on their march from Nile,
To do him wanton rites, which cost them woe.
Yet thence his lustful orgies he enlarged   415
Even to that hill of scandal, by the grove
Of Moloch homicide: lust hard by hate;
Till good Josiah drove them thence to hell.

    With these came they who, from the border-
        ing flood
Of old Euphrates to the brook that parts   420
Egypt from Syrian ground, had general names
Of Baälim and Ashtaroth; those male,
These feminine; for spirits, when they please,
Can either sex assume, or both; so soft
And uncompounded is their essence pure;   425
Not tied or manacled with joint or limb,
Nor founded on the brittle strength of bones,
Like cumbrous flesh; but, in what shape they
    choose,
Dilated or condensed, bright or obscure,
Can execute their aëry purposes,   430
And works of love or enmity fulfil.
For those the race of Israel oft forsook
Their living Strength, and unfrequented left
His righteous altar, bowing lowly down
To bestial gods; for which their heads as low   435
Bowed down in battle, sunk before the spear
Of despicable foes.

            With these in troop
Came Astoreth, whom the Phenicians called
Astartè, queen of heaven, with crescent horns;
To whose bright image nightly by the moon   440
Sidonian virgins paid their vows and songs;
In Sion also not unsung, where stood
Her temple on the offensive mountain, built
By that uxorious king, whose heart, though
    large,
Beguiled by fair idolatresses, fell   445
To idols foul. Thammuz came next behind,
Whose annual wound in Lebanon allured
The Syrian damsels to lament his fate
In amorous ditties all a summer's day;
While smooth Adonis from his native rock   450
Ran purple to the sea, supposed with blood
Of Thammuz yearly wounded; the love-tale
Infected Sion's daughters with like heat;
Whose wanton passions in the sacred porch
Ezekiel saw, when, by the vision led,   455
His eye surveyed the dark idolatries
Of alienated Judah. Next came one
Who mourned in earnest, when the captive ark

Maimed his brute image, head and hands lopped off
In his own temple, on the grunsel edge, 460
Where he fell flat, and shamed his worshippers;
Dagon his name, sea-monster, upward man
And downward fish; yet had his temple high
Reared in Azotus, dreaded through the coast
Of Palestine, in Gath and Ascalon, 465
And Accaron and Gaza's frontier bounds.

Him followed Rimmon, whose delightful seat
Was fair Damascus, on the fertile banks
Of Abbana and Pharphar, lucid streams.
He also 'gainst the house of God was bold: 470
A leper once he lost, and gained a king;
Ahaz his sottish conqueror, whom he drew
God's altar to disparage and displace
For one of Syrian mode, whereon to burn
His odious offerings, and adore the gods 475
Whom he had vanquished.
           After these appeared
A crew who, under names of old renown,
Osiris, Isis, Orus, and their train,
With monstrous shapes and sorceries abused
Fanatic Egypt and her priests, to seek 480
Their wandering gods disguised in brutish forms
Rather than human. Nor did Israel 'scape
The infection, when their borrowed gold composed
The calf in Oreb; and the rebel king
Doubled that sin in Bethel and in Dan, 485
Likening his Maker to the grazèd ox—
Jehovah, who in one night, when he passed
From Egypt marching, equaled with one stroke
Both her first-born and all her bleating gods.

Belial came last, than whom a spirit more lewd 490
Fell not from heaven, or more gross to love
Vice for itself; to him no temple stood,
Or altar smoked; yet who more oft than he
In temples and at altars, when the priest
Turns atheist, as did Eli's sons, who filled 495
With lust and violence the house of God?
In courts and palaces he also reigns,
And in luxurious cities, where the noise
Of riot ascends above their loftiest towers,
And injury and outrage: and when night 500
Darkens the streets, then wander forth the sons
Of Belial, flown with insolence and wine.
Witness the streets of Sodom, and that night
In Gibeah, when the hospitable door
Exposed a matron, to avoid worse rape. 505

These were the prime in order and in might:
The rest were long to tell, though far renowned,
The Ionian gods—of Javan's issue held
Gods, yet confessed later than heaven and earth,
Their boasted parents: Titan, heaven's first-born 510
With his enormous brood, and birthright seized
By younger Saturn; he from mightier Jove,
His own and Rhea's son, like measure found;
So Jove usurping reigned: these first in Crete
And Ida known, thence on the snowy top 515
Of cold Olympus ruled the middle air,
Their highest heaven; or on the Delphian cliff,
Or in Dodona, and through all the bounds
Of Doric land: or who with Saturn old
Fled over Adria to the Hesperian fields, 520
And o'er the Celtic roamed the utmost isles.

All these and more came flocking, but with looks
Downcast and damp; yet such wherein appeared
Obscure some glimpse of joy, to have found their chief
Not in despair, to have found themselves not lost 525
In loss itself; which on his countenance cast
Like doubtful hue; but he, his wonted pride
Soon recollecting, with high words, that bore
Semblance of worth, not substance, gently raised
Their fainting courage, and dispelled their fears. 530
Then straight commands that at the warlike sound
Of trumpets loud and clarions be upreared
His mighty standard; that proud honor claimed
Azazel as his right, a cherub tall;
Who forthwith from the glittering staff unfurled 535
The imperial ensign; which, full high advanced,
Shone like a meteor, streaming to the wind,
With gems and golden luster rich emblazed,
Seraphic arms and trophies, all the while
Sonorous metal blowing martial sounds: 540
At which the universal host up-sent
A shout, that tore hell's concave, and beyond
Frighted the reign of Chaos and old Night.

All in a moment through the gloom were seen
Ten thousand banners rise into the air. 545
With orient colors waving; with them rose
A forest huge of spears; and thronging helms
Appeared, and serried shields in thick array
Of depth immeasurable; anon they move
In perfect phalanx to the Dorian mood 550
Of flutes and soft recorders; such as raised
To height of noblest temper heroes old
Arming to battle, and instead of rage,
Deliberate valor breathed, firm and unmoved
With dread of death to flight or foul retreat; 555
Nor wanting power to mitigate and 'suage
With solemn touches troubled thoughts, and chase
Anguish, and doubt, and fear, and sorrow, and pain
From mortal or immortal minds. Thus they,
Breathing united force, with fixèd thought, 560
Moved on in silence, to soft pipes, that charmed

Their painful steps o'er the burnt soil: and now
Advanced in view they stand; a horrid front
Of dreadful length and dazzling arms, in guise
Of warriors old with ordered spear and shield,
Awaiting what command their mighty chief 566
Had to impose: he through the armèd files
Darts his experienced eye, and soon traverse
The whole battalion views, their order due,
Their visages and stature as of gods; 570
Their number last he sums. And now his heart
Distends with pride, and hardening in his strength
Glories: for never since created man
Met such embodied force as, named with these,
Could merit more than that small infantry 575
Warred on by cranes: though all the giant brood
Of Phlegra with the heroic race were joined
That fought at Thebes and Ilium, on each side
Mixed with auxiliar gods; and what resounds
In fable or romance of Uther's son 580
Begirt with British and Armoric knights;
And all who since, baptized or infidel,
Jousted in Aspramont, or Montalban,
Damascus, or Morocco, or Trebizond,
Or whom Biserta sent from Afric shore, 585
When Charlemagne with all his peerage fell
By Fontarabbia. Thus far these beyond
Compare of mortal prowess, yet observed
Their dread commander; he, above the rest
In shape and gesture proudly eminent, 590
Stood like a tower; his form had yet not lost
All its original brightness; nor appeared
Less than archangel ruined, and the excess
Of glory obscured: as when the sun, new risen,
Looks through the horizontal misty air 595
Shorn of his beams, or from behind the moon,
In dim eclipse, disastrous twilight sheds
On half the nations, and with fear of change
Perplexes monarchs. Darkened so, yet shone
Above them all the archangel; but his face 600
Deep scars of thunder had entrenched; and care
Sat on his faded cheek; but under brows
Of dauntless courage, and considerate pride
Waiting revenge; cruel his eye, but cast
Signs of remorse and passion, to behold 605
The fellows of his crime, the followers rather
(Far other once beheld in bliss), condemned
For ever now to have their lot in pain;
Millions of spirits for his fault amerced
Of heaven, and from eternal splendors flung 610
For his revolt; yet faithful how they stood,
Their glory withered; as when heaven's fire
Hath scathed the forest oaks, or mountain pines,
With singèd top their stately growth, though bare, 614
Stands on the blasted heath. He now prepared
To speak; whereat their doubled ranks they bend
From wing to wing, and half enclose him round

With all his peers: attention held them mute.
Thrice he essayed, and thrice, in spite of scorn,
Tears, such as angels weep, burst forth; at last
Words, interwove with sighs, found out their way. 621

'O myriads of immortal spirits! O powers
Matchless, but with the Almighty; and that strife
Was not inglorious, though the event was dire,
As this place testifies, and this dire change, 625
Hateful to utter! but what power of mind,
Foreseeing or presaging, from the depth
Of knowledge, past or present, could have feared
How such united force of gods, how such
As stood like these, could ever know repulse? 630
For who can yet believe, though after loss,
That all these puissant legions, whose exile
Hath emptied heaven, shall fail to reascend
Self-raised, and repossess their native seat?
For me, be witness all the host of heaven, 635
If counsels different, or dangers shunned
By me, have lost our hopes. But he who reigns
Monarch in heaven, till then as one secure
Sat on this throne upheld by old repute,
Consent or custom; and his regal state 640
Put forth at full, but still his strength concealed,
Which tempted our attempt, and wrought our fall.
Henceforth his might we know, and know our own;
So as not either to provoke, or dread
New war, provoked; our better part remains,
To work in close design, by fraud or guile, 646
What force effected not; that he no less
At length from us may find, who overcomes
By force, hath overcome but half his foe.
Space may produce new worlds; whereof so rife
There went a fame in heaven that he ere long
Intended to create, and therein plant 652
A generation, whom his choice regard
Should favor equal to the sons of heaven:
Thither, if but to pry, shall be perhaps 655
Our first eruption; thither, or elsewhere;
For this infernal pit shall never hold
Celestial spirits in bondage, nor the abyss
Long under darkness cover. But these thoughts
Full counsel must mature; peace is despaired;
For who can think submission? War, then, war, 661
Open or understood, must be resolved.'

He spake; and, to confirm his words, outflew
Millions of flaming swords, drawn from the thighs
Of mighty cherubim; the sudden blaze 665
Far round illumined hell; highly they raged
Against the Highest, and fierce with graspèd arms
Clashed on their sounding shields the din of war,
Hurling defiance toward the vault of heaven.

There stood a hill not far, whose grisly top 670
Belched fire and rolling smoke; the rest entire
Shone with a glossy scurf, undoubted sign
That in his womb was hid metallic ore,
The work of sulphur. Thither, wing'd with speed,
A numerous brigade hastened: as when bands
Of pioneers, with spade and pickaxe armed, 676
Forerun the royal camp, to trench a field,
Or cast a rampart. Mammon led them on:
Mammon, the least erected spirit that fell
From heaven; for even in heaven his looks and
    thoughts 680
Were always downward bent, admiring more
The riches of heaven's pavement, trodden gold,
Than aught, divine or holy, else enjoyed
In vision beatific; by him first
Men also, and by his suggestion taught, 685
Ransacked the center, and with impious hands
Rifled the bowels of their mother earth
For treasures, better hid. Soon had his crew
Opened into the hill a spacious wound,
And digged out ribs of gold. Let none admire
That riches grow in hell; that soil may best 691
Deserve the precious bane. And here let those
Who boast in mortal things, and wondering tell
Of Babel, and the works of Memphian kings,
Learn how their greatest monuments of fame,
And strength and art, are easily outdone 696
By spirits reprobate, and in an hour
What in an age they with incessant toil
And hands innumerable scarce perform.

Nigh on the plain, in many cells prepared, 700
That underneath had veins of liquid fire
Sluiced from the lake, a second multitude
With wondrous art founded the massy ore,
Severing each kind, and scummed the bullion
    dross;
A third as soon had formed within the ground
A various mold, and from the boiling cells, 706
By strange conveyance, filled each hollow nook,
As in an organ, from one blast of wind,
To many a row of pipes the sound-board
    breathes.
Anon, out of the earth a fabric huge 710
Rose like an exhalation, with the sound
Of dulcet symphonies and voices sweet,
Built like a temple, where pilasters round
Were set, and Doric pillars overlaid
With golden architrave; nor did there want 715
Cornice or frieze, with bossy sculptures graven:
The roof was fretted gold. Not Babylon,
Nor great Alcairo, such magnificence
Equaled in all their glories, to enshrine
Belus or Serapis their gods, or seat 720
Their kings, when Egypt with Assyria strove
In wealth and luxury. The ascending pile
Stood fixed her stately height: and straight the
    doors,
Opening their brazen folds, discover, wide
Within, her ample spaces, o'er the smooth 725
And level pavement; from the archèd roof,
Pendent by subtle magic, many a row
Of starry lamps and blazing cressets, fed
With naphtha and asphaltus, yielded light
As from a sky. The hasty multitude 730
Admiring entered; and the work some praise,
And some the architect: his hand was known
In heaven by many a towered structure high
Where sceptered angels held their residence,
And sat as princes; whom the supreme King 735
Exalted to such power, and gave to rule,
Each in his hierarchy, the orders bright.
Nor was his name unheard or unadored
In ancient Greece; and in Ausonian land
Men called him Mulciber; and how he fell 740
From heaven they fabled, thrown by angry Jove
Sheer o'er the crystal battlements: from morn
To noon he fell, from noon to dewy eve,
A summer's day; and with the setting sun
Dropped from the zenith like a falling star, 745
On Lemnos, th' Ægean isle: thus they relate,
Erring; for he with this rebellious rout
Fell long before; nor aught availed him now
To have built in heaven high towers; nor did he
    'scape
By all his engines, but was headlong sent 750
With his industrious crew to build in hell.

    Meanwhile, the wingèd heralds, by command
Of sovereign power, with awful ceremony
And trumpet's sound, throughout the host pro-
    claim
A solemn council, forthwith to be held 755
At Pandemonium, the high capital
Of Satan and his peers: their summons called
From every band and squarèd regiment
By place or choice the worthiest; they anon,
With hundreds and with thousands, trooping
    came, 760
Attended; all access was thronged; the gates
And porches wide, but chief the spacious hall
(Though like a covered field, where champions
    bold
Wont ride in armed, and at the soldan's chair
Defied the best of paynim chivalry 765
To mortal combat, or career with lance),
Thick swarmed, both on the ground and in the
    air,
Brushed with the hiss of rustling wings. As bees
In spring-time, when the sun with Taurus rides,
Pour forth their populous youth about the hive
In clusters; they among fresh dews and flowers
Fly to and fro, or on the smoothèd plank, 772
The suburb of their straw-built citadel,
New rubbed with balm, expatiate, and confer
Their state affairs; so thick the aëry crowd 775
Swarmed and were straitened; till, the signal
    given,
Behold a wonder! They, but now who seemed
In bigness to surpass earth's giant sons,
Now less than smallest dwarfs, in narrow room

Throng numberless, like that Pygmëan race 780
Beyond the Indian mount, or faëry elves,
Whose midnight revels, by a forest side
Or fountain, some belated peasant sees,
Or dreams he sees, while over head the moon
Sits arbitress, and nearer to the earth 785
Wheels her pale course; they, on their mirth
    and dance
Intent, with jocund music charm his ear;
At once with joy and fear his heart rebounds.
Thus incorporeal spirits to smallest forms
Reduced their shapes immense, and were at
    large, 790
Though without number still, amidst the hall
Of that infernal court. But far within,
And in their own dimensions, like themselves,
The great seraphic lords and cherubim
In close recess and secret conclave sat; 795
A thousand demi-gods on golden seats
Frequent and full. After short silence then,
And summons read, the great consult began.

BOOK II

The Argument

The consultation begun, Satan debates whether another battle be to be hazarded for the recovery of Heaven: some advise it, others dissuade: a third proposal is preferred, mentioned before by Satan, to search the truth of that prophecy or tradition in Heaven concerning another world, and another kind of creature equal or not much inferior to themselves, about this time to be created: their doubt who should be sent on this difficult search: Satan their chief undertakes alone the voyage, is honored and applauded. The council thus ended, the rest betake them several ways, and to several employments, as their inclinations lead them, to entertain the time till Satan return. He passes on his journey to Hell-gates, finds them shut, and who sat there to guard them, by whom at length they are opened, and discover to him the great gulf between Hell and Heaven; with what difficulty he passes through, directed by Chaos, the power of that place, to the sight of this new world which he sought.

High on a throne of royal state, which far
Outshone the wealth of Ormus and of Ind,
Or where the gorgeous East, with richest hand,
Showers on her kings barbaric pearl and gold,
Satan exalted sat, by merit raised 5
To that bad eminence; and, from despair
Thus high uplifted beyond hope, aspires
Beyond thus high, insatiate to pursue
Vain war with Heaven; and, by success un-
    taught,
His proud imaginations thus displayed: 10

'Powers and dominions, deities of heaven;
For since no deep within her gulf can hold
Immortal vigor, though oppressed and fallen,
I give not heaven for lost. From this descent
Celestial virtues rising, will appear 15
More glorious and more dread than from no fall,
And trust themselves to fear no second fate.
Me, though just right, and the fixed laws of
    heaven,
Did first create your leader; next, free choice,
With what besides, in council or in fight, 20
Hath been achieved of merit; yet this loss,
Thus far at least recovered, hath much more
Established in a safe unenvied throne,
Yielded with full consent. The happier state
In heaven, which follows dignity, might draw 25
Envy from each inferior; but who here
Will envy whom the highest place exposes
Foremost to stand against the Thunderer's aim,
Your bulwark, and condemns to greatest share
Of endless pain? Where there is then no good 30
For which to strive, no strife can grow up there
From faction; for none sure will claim in hell
Precèdence; none whose portion is so small
Of present pain, that with ambitious mind
Will covet more. With this advantage, then, 35
To union, and firm faith, and firm accord,
More than can be in heaven, we now return
To claim our just inheritance of old.
Surer to prosper than prosperity
Could have assured us; and, by what best way,
Whether of open war or covert guile, 41
We now debate; who can advise, may speak.'

He ceased; and next him Moloch, sceptered
    king,
Stood up, the strongest and the fiercest spirit
That fought in heaven, now fiercer by despair.
His trust was with the Eternal to be deemed 46
Equal in strength; and rather than be less,
Cared not to be at all; with that care lost
Went all his fear: of God, or hell, or worse,
He recked not; and these words thereafter
    spake: 50

'My sentence is for open war: of wiles,
More unexpert, I boast not; them let those
Contrive who need, or when they need, not
    now.
For, while they sit contriving, shall the rest,
Millions that stand in arms, and longing wait 55
The signal to ascend, sit lingering here
Heaven's fugitives, and for their dwelling-place
Accept this dark, opprobrious den of shame,
The prison of his tyranny who reigns
By our delay? No, let us rather choose, 60
Armed with hell-flames and fury, all at once,
O'er heaven's high towers to force resistless way,
Turning our tortures into horrid arms
Against the torturer; when, to meet the noise
Of his almighty engine, he shall hear 65
Infernal thunder; and, for lightning, see
Black fire and horror shot with equal rage
Among his angels; and his throne itself
Mixed with Tartarean sulphur, and strange fire,
His own invented torments.
    But perhaps 70
The way seems difficult and steep to scale

With upright wing against a higher foe.
Let such bethink them, if the sleepy drench
Of that forgetful lake benumb not still,
That in our proper motion we ascend 75
Up to our native seat; descent and fall
To us is adverse. Who but felt of late,
When the fierce foe hung on our broken rear
Insulting, and pursued us through the deep,
With what compulsion and laborious flight 80
We sunk thus low? The ascent is easy then;
The event is feared; should we again provoke
Our stronger, some worse way his wrath may find
To our destruction; if there be in hell
Fear to be worse destroyed; what can be worse
Than to dwell here, driven out from bliss, condemned 86
In this abhorrèd deep to utter woe;
Where pain of unextinguishable fire
Must exercise us without hope of end,
The vassals of his anger, when the scourge 90
Inexorable, and the torturing hour,
Calls us to penance? More destroyed than thus,
We should be quite abolished, and expire.
What fear we, then? what doubt we to incense
His utmost ire? which, to the height enraged, 95
Will either quite consume us, and reduce
To nothing this essential (happier far
Than miserable to have eternal being),
Or, if our substance be indeed divine,
And cannot cease to be, we are at worst 100
On this side nothing; and by proof we feel
Our power sufficient to disturb his heaven,
And with perpetual inroads to alarm,
Though inaccessible, his fatal throne;
Which, if not victory, is yet revenge.' 105

He ended frowning, and his look denounced
Desperate revenge, and battle dangerous
To less than gods. On the other side uprose
Belial, in act more graceful and humane;
A fairer person lost not heaven; he seemed 110
For dignity composed, and high exploit:
But all was false and hollow, though his tongue
Dropt manna, and could make the worse appear
The better reason, to perplex and dash
Maturest counsels: for his thoughts were low:
To vice industrious, but to nobler deeds 116
Timorous and slothful; yet he pleased the ear,
And with persuasive accent thus began:

'I should be much for open war, O peers,
As not behind in hate; if what was urged 120
Main reason to persuade immediate war,
Did not dissuade me most, and seem to cast
Ominous conjecture on the whole success
When he who most excels in fact of arms,
In what he counsels and in what excels 125
Mistrustful, grounds his courage on despair
And utter dissolution as the scope
Of all his aim, after some dire revenge.

First, what revenge? The towers of heaven are filled
With armèd watch, that render all access 130
Impregnable; oft on the bordering deep
Encamp their legions; or, with obscure wing,
Scout far and wide into the realm of night,
Scorning surprise. Or could we break our way
By force, and at our heels all hell should rise 135
With blackest insurrection, to confound
Heaven's purest light; yet our great enemy
All incorruptible, would on his throne
Sit unpolluted, and the ethereal mold,
Incapable of stain, would soon expel 140
Her mischief, and purge off the baser fire,
Victorious. Thus repulsed, our final hope
Is flat despair: we must exasperate
The Almighty Victor to spend all his rage,
And that must end us; that must be our cure,
To be no more. Sad cure! for who would lose,
Though full of pain, this intellectual being, 147
Those thoughts that wander through eternity,
To perish rather, swallowed up and lost
In the wide womb of uncreated night, 150
Devoid of sense and motion? And who knows,
Let this be good, whether our angry foe
Can give it, or will ever? how he can,
Is doubtful; that he never will, is sure.
Will he, so wise, let loose at once his ire 155
Belike through impotence, or unaware,
To give his enemies their wish, and end
Them in his anger whom his anger saves
To punish endless? "Wherefore cease we then?"
Say they who counsel war. "We are decreed,
Reserved, and destined to eternal woe; 161
Whatever doing, what can we suffer more,
What can we suffer worse?" Is this then worst,
Thus sitting, thus consulting, thus in arms?
What, when we fled amain, pursued, and struck
With heaven's afflicting thunder, and besought
The deep to shelter us? this hell then seemed 167
A refuge from those wounds; or when we lay
Chained on the burning lake? that sure was worse.
What if the breath that kindled those grim fires,
Awaked, should blow them into sevenfold rage,
And plunge us in the flames? or, from above, 172
Should intermitted vengeance arm again
His red right hand to plague us? What if all
Her stores were opened, and this firmament 175
Of hell should spout her cataracts of fire,
Impendent horrors, threatening hideous fall
One day upon our heads; while we, perhaps,
Designing or exhorting glorious war,
Caught in a fiery tempest, shall be hurled 180
Each on his rock transfixed, the sport and prey
Of racking whirlwinds; or for ever sunk
Under yon boiling ocean, wrapt in chains;
There to converse with everlasting groans,
Unrespited, unpitied, unreprieved, 185
Ages of hopeless end? This would be worse.

War, therefore, open or concealed, alike
My voice dissuades; for what can force or guile
With him, or who deceive his mind, whose eye
Views all things at one view? He from heaven's height 190
All these our motions vain sees and derides:
Not more almighty to resist our might,
Than wise to frustrate all our plots and wiles.
Shall we then live thus vile, the race of heaven
Thus trampled, thus expelled, to suffer here 195
Chains and these torments? Better these than worse,
By my advice; since fate inevitable
Subdues us, and omnipotent decree,
The victor's will. To suffer, as to do,
Our strength is equal, nor the law unjust 200
That so ordains; this was at first resolved,
If we were wise, against so great a foe
Contending, and so doubtful what might fall.

'I laugh, when those who at the spear are bold
And venturous, if that fail them, shrink and fear 205
What yet they know must follow, to endure
Exile, or ignominy, or bonds, or pain,
The sentence of their conqueror; this is now
Our doom; which if we can sustain and bear,
Our supreme foe in time may much remit 210
His anger; and perhaps, thus far removed,
Not mind us not offending, satisfied
With what is punished; whence these raging fires
Will slacken, if his breath stir not their flames.
Our purer essence then will overcome 215
Their noxious vapor; or, inured, not feel;
Or, changed at length, and to the place conformed
In temper and in nature, will receive
Familiar the fierce heat, and void of pain;
This horror will grow mild, this darkness light;
Besides what hope the never-ending flight 221
Of future days may bring, what chance, what change
Worth waiting; since our present lot appears
For happy though but ill, for ill not worst,
If we procure not to ourselves more woe.' 225

Thus Belial, with words clothed in reason's garb,
Counseled ignoble ease, and peaceful sloth,
Not peace; and after him thus Mammon spake:

'Either to disenthrone the King of heaven
We war, if war be best, or to regain 230
Our own right lost: him to unthrone we then
May hope, when everlasting fate shall yield
To fickle chance, and Chaos judge the strife:
The former, vain to hope, argues as vain
The latter; for what place can be for us 235
Within heaven's bound, unless heaven's Lord supreme
We overpower? Suppose he should relent,
And publish grace to all, on promise made
Of new subjection; with what eyes could we
Stand in his presence humble, and receive 240
Strict laws imposed, to celebrate his throne
With warbled hymns, and to his Godhead sing
Forced hallelujahs, while he lordly sits
Our envied sovereign, and his altar breathes
Ambrosial odors and ambrosial flowers, 245
Our servile offerings? This must be our task
In heaven, this our delight; how wearisome
Eternity so spent, in worship paid
To whom we hate! Let us not then pursue
By force impossible, by leave obtained 250
Unacceptable, though in heaven, our state
Of splendid vassalage; but rather seek
Our own good from ourselves, and from our own
Live to ourselves, though in this vast recess,
Free, and to none accountable, preferring 255
Hard liberty before the easy yoke
Of servile pomp. Our greatness will appear
Then most conspicuous, when great things of small,
Useful of hurtful, prosperous of adverse,
We can create; and in what place soe'er 260
Thrive under evil, and work ease out of pain,
Through labor and endurance. This deep world
Of darkness do we dread?. How oft amidst
Thick clouds and dark doth heaven's all-ruling Sire
Choose to reside, his glory unobscured, 265
And with the majesty of darkness round
Covers his throne; from whence deep thunders roar,
Mustering their rage, and heaven resembles hell!
As he our darkness, cannot we his light
Imitate when we please? This desert soil 270
Wants not her hidden luster, gems and gold;
Nor want we skill or art, from whence to raise
Magnificence; and what can heaven show more?
Our torments also may in length of time
Become our elements; these piercing fires 275
As soft as now severe, our temper changed
Into their temper; which must needs remove
The sensible of pain. All things invite
To peaceful counsels, and the settled state
Of order, how in safety best we may 280
Compose our present evils, with regard
Of what we are, and where; dismissing quite
All thoughts of war. Ye have what I advise.'

He scarce had finished, when such murmur filled
The assembly, as when hollow rocks retain 285
The sound of blustering winds which all night long
Had roused the sea, now with hoarse cadence lull
Seafaring men o'er-watched, whose bark by chance
Or pinnace anchors in a craggy bay

After the tempest: such applause was heard 290
As Mammon ended, and his sentence pleased,
Advising peace; for such another field
They dreaded worse than hell; so much the fear
Of thunder and the sword of Michael
Wrought still within them, and no less desire 295
To found this nether empire, which might rise
By policy, and long process of time,
In emulation opposite to heaven.

Which when Beëlzebub perceived, than whom,
Satan except, none higher sat, with grave 300
Aspect he rose, and in his rising seemed
A pillar of state; deep on his front engraven
Deliberation sat, and public care;
And princely counsel in his face yet shone,
Majestic, though in ruin; sage he stood. 305
With Atlantean shoulders fit to bear
The weight of mightiest monarchies; his look
Drew audience and attention still as night
Or summer's noontide air, while thus he spake:

'Thrones and imperial powers, offspring of heaven, 310
Ethereal virtues! or these titles now
Must we renounce, and, changing style, be called
Princes of hell, for so the popular vote
Inclines, here to continue and build up here
A growing empire; doubtless, while we dream,
And know not that the King of heaven hath doomed 316
This place our dungeon; not our safe retreat
Beyond his potent arm; to live exempt
From heaven's high jurisdiction, in new league
Banded against his throne, but to remain 320
In strictest bondage, though thus far removed,
Under the inevitable curb, reserved
His captive multitude: for he, be sure,
In height or depth, still first and last will reign
Sole king, and of his kingdom lose no part 325
By our revolt, but over hell extend
His empire, and with iron scepter rule
Us here, as with his golden those in heaven.
What sit we then projecting peace and war?
War hath determined us, and foiled with loss
Irreparable; terms of peace yet none 331
Vouchsafed or sought; for what peace will be given
To us enslaved but custody severe,
And stripes, and arbitrary punishment
Inflicted? and what peace can we return, 335
But to our power hostility and hate,
Untamed reluctance, and revenge, though slow,
Yet ever plotting how the Conqueror least
May reap his conquest, and may least rejoice
In doing what we most in suffering feel? 340

'Nor will occasion want, nor shall we need
With dangerous expedition to invade
Heaven, whose high walls fear no assault or siege,
Or ambush from the deep. What if we find
Some easier enterprise? There is a place 345
(If ancient and prophetic fame in heaven
Err not), another world, the happy seat
Of some new race, called Man, about this time
To be created like to us, though less
In power and excellence, but favored more 350
Of him who rules above; so was his will
Pronounced among the gods; and by an oath
That shook heaven's whole circumference confirmed.
Thither let us bend all our thoughts, to learn
What creatures there inhabit, of what mold 355
Or substance, how endued, and what their power,
And where their weakness, how attempted best,
By force or subtlety. Though heaven be shut,
And heaven's high Arbitrator sit secure
In his own strength, this place may lie exposed,
The utmost border of his kingdom, left 361
To their defense who hold it; here perhaps
Some advantageous act may be achieved
By sudden onset; either with hell-fire
To waste his whole creation, or possess 365
All as our own, and drive, as we were driven,
The puny habitants; or, if not drive,
Seduce them to our party, that their God
May prove their foe, and with repenting hand
Abolish his own works. This would surpass 370
Common revenge, and interrupt his joy
In our confusion, and our joy upraise
In his disturbance, when his darling sons,
Hurled headlong to partake with us, shall curse
Their frail original and faded bliss, 375
Faded so soon. Advise, if this be worth
Attempting, or to sit in darkness here
Hatching vain empires.'
Thus Beëlzebub
Pleaded his devilish counsel, first devised
By Satan, and in part proposed; for whence 380
But from the author of all ill could spring
So deep a malice, to confound the race
Of mankind in one root, and earth with hell
To mingle and involve, done all to spite
The great Creator? But their spite still serves
His glory to augment. The bold design 386
Pleased highly those infernal states, and joy
Sparkled in all their eyes: with full assent
They vote: whereat his speech he thus renews:

'Well have ye judged, well ended long debate,
Synod of gods, and, like to what ye are, 391
Great things resolved, which from the lowest deep
Will once more lift us up, in spite of fate,
Nearer our ancient seat: perhaps in view
Of those bright confines, whence, with neighboring arms, 395
And opportune excursion, we may chance
Re-enter heaven; or else in some mild zone
Dwell, not unvisited of heaven's fair light,
Secure; and at the brightening orient beam
Purge off this gloom; the soft delicious air, 400
To heal the scar of these corrosive fires.

Shall breathe her balm. But first, whom shall
    we send
In search of this new world? whom shall we find
Sufficient? who shall tempt with wandering feet
The dark, unbottomed, infinite abyss,   405
And through the palpable obscure find out
His uncouth way, or spread his aëry flight,
Upborne with indefatigable wings,
Over the vast abrupt, ere he arrive
The happy isle? What strength, what art, can
    then   410
Suffice, or what evasion bear him safe
Through the strict senteries and stations thick
Of angels watching round? Here he had need
All circumspection, and we now no less
Choice in our suffrage; for, on whom we send,
The weight of all, and our last hope relies.'   416

  This said, he sat; and expectation held
His look suspense, awaiting who appeared
To second, or oppose, or undertake
The perilous attempt: but all sat mute,   420
Pondering the danger with deep thoughts; and
    each
In other's countenance read his own dismay,
Astonished: none among the choice and prime
Of those heaven-warring champions could be
    found
So hardy as to proffer or accept,   425
Alone, the dreadful voyage; till at last
Satan, whom now transcendent glory raised
Above his fellows, with monarchal pride,
Conscious of highest worth, unmoved thus
    spake:

  'O progeny of heaven! empyreal thrones!   430
With reason hath deep silence and demur
Seized us, though undismayed. Long is the way
And hard, that out of hell leads up to light;
Our prison strong; this huge convex of fire,
Outrageous to devour, immures us round   435
Ninefold; and gates of burning adamant,
Barred over us, prohibit all egress.
These passed, if any pass, the void profound
Of unessential night receives him next,
Wide-gaping, and with utter loss of being   440
Threatens him plunged in that abortive gulf.
If thence he 'scape into whatever world
Or unknown region, what remains him less
Than unknown dangers and as hard escape?
But I should ill become this throne, O peers,   445
And this imperial sovereignty, adorned
With splendor, armed with power, if aught pro-
    posed
And judged of public moment, in the shape
Of difficulty or danger, could deter
Me from attempting. Wherefore do I assume
These royalties, and not refuse to reign,   451
Refusing to accept as great a share
Of hazard as of honor, due alike
To him who reigns, and so much to him due
Of hazard more, as he above the rest   455

High honored sits? Go, therefore, mighty
    powers,
Terror of heaven, though fallen; intend at home
(While here shall be our home) what best may
    ease
The present misery, and render hell
More tolerable; if there be cure or charm   460
To respite, or deceive, or slack the pain
Of this ill mansion; intermit no watch
Against a wakeful foe, while I abroad
Through all the coasts of dark destruction seek
Deliverance for us all: this enterprise   465
None shall partake with me.' Thus saying, rose
The monarch, and prevented all reply;
Prudent, lest from his resolution raised
Others among the chief might offer now
(Certain to be refused) what erst they feared;
And, so refused, might in opinion stand   471
His rivals; winning cheap the high repute
Which he through hazard huge must earn.
    But they
Dreaded not more the adventure than his voice
Forbidding; and at once with him they rose.   475
Their rising all at once was as the sound
Of thunder heard remote. Towards him they
    bend
With awful reverence prone; and as a god
Extol him equal to the Highest in heaven.
Nor failed they to express how much they
    praised   480
That for the general safety he despised
His own: for neither do the spirits damned
Lose all their virtue; lest bad men should boast
Their specious deeds on earth, which glory
    excites
Or close ambition varnished o'er with zeal.   485

  Thus they their doubtful consultations dark
Ended, rejoicing in their matchless chief:
As when from mountain-tops the dusky clouds
Ascending, while the north wind sleeps, o'er-
    spread
Heaven's cheerful face, the louring element   490
Scowls o'er the darkened landscape snow or
    shower;
If chance the radiant sun, with farewell sweet,
Extend his evening beam, the fields revive,
The birds their notes renew, and bleating herds
Attest their joy, that hill and valley rings.   495

  O shame to men! devil with devil damned
Firm concord holds, men only disagree
Of creatures rational, though under hope
Of heavenly grace; and, God proclaiming peace,
Yet live in hatred, enmity, and strife   500
Among themselves, and levy cruel wars,
Wasting the earth, each other to destroy:
As if (which might induce us to accord)
Man had not hellish foes enough besides,
That day and night for his destruction wait.   505

    *   *   *   (1667)

From AREOPAGITICA

A SPEECH FOR THE LIBERTY OF UNLICENSED PRINTING, TO THE PARLIAMENT OF ENGLAND

Lords and Commons of England, consider what nation it is whereof ye are, and whereof ye are the governors: a nation not slow and dull, but of a quick, ingenious, and piercing spirit, acute to invent, subtle and sinewy to discourse, not beneath the reach of any point the highest that human capacity can soar to. Therefore the studies of learning in her deepest sciences have been so ancient and so eminent among us, that writers of good antiquity and ablest judgment have been persuaded that even the school of Pythagoras and the Persian wisdom took beginning from the old philosophy of this island. And that wise and civil Roman, Julius Agricola, who governed once here for Cæsar, preferred the natural wits of Britain, before the labored studies of the French. Nor is it for nothing that the grave and frugal Transylvanian sends out yearly from as far as the mountainous borders of Russia, and beyond the Hercynian wilderness, not their youth, but their staid men, to learn our language, and our theologic arts. Yet that which is above all this, the favor and the love of Heaven we have great argument to think in a peculiar manner propitious and propending towards us. Why else was this nation chosen before any other, that out of her as out of Sion should be proclaimed and sounded forth the first tidings and trumpet of Reformation to all Europe? And had it not been the obstinate perverseness of our prelates against the divine and admirable spirit of Wyclif, to suppress him as a schismatic and innovator, perhaps neither the Bohemian Huss and Jerome, no, nor the name of Luther, or of Calvin had been ever known: the glory of reforming all our neighbors had been completely ours. But now, as our obdurate clergy have with violence demeaned the matter, we are become hitherto the latest and the backwardest scholars, of whom God offered to have made us the teachers. Now once again by all concurrence of signs, and by the general instinct of holy and devout men, as they daily and solemnly express their thoughts, God is decreeing to begin some new and great period in his church, even to the reforming of Reformation itself: what does he then but reveal himself to his servants, and as his manner is, first to his Englishmen; I say as his manner is, first to us, though we mark not the method of his counsels, and are unworthy. Behold now this vast city: a city of refuge, the mansion house of liberty, encompassed and surrounded with his protection. The shop of war hath not there more anvils and hammers waking, to fashion out the plates and instruments of armed justice in defense of beleaguered truth, than there be pens and heads there, sitting by their studious lamps, musing, searching, revolving new notions and ideas wherewith to present, as with their homage and their fealty, the approaching Reformation; others as fast reading, trying all things, assenting to the force of reason and convincement. What could a man require more from a nation so pliant and so prone to seek after knowledge? What wants there to such a towardly and pregnant soil, but wise and faithful laborers, to make a knowing people, a nation of prophets, of sages, and of worthies? We reckon more than five months yet to harvest; there need not be five weeks; had we but eyes to lift up, the fields are white already. Where there is much desire to learn, there of necessity will be much arguing, much writing, many opinions; for opinion in good men is but knowledge in the making. Under these fantastic terrors of sect and schism, we wrong the earnest and zealous thirst after knowledge and understanding which God hath stirred up in this city. What some lament of, we rather should rejoice at, should rather praise this pious forwardness among men, to reassume the ill-deputed care of their religion into their own hands again. A little generous prudence, a little forbearance of one another, and some grain of charity might win all these diligences to join, and unite in one general and brotherly search after truth, could we but forgo this prelatical tradition of crowding free consciences and Christian liberties into canons and precepts of men. I doubt not, if some great and worthy stranger should come among us, wise to discern the mold and temper of a people, and how to govern it, observing the high hopes and aims, the diligent alacrity of our extended thoughts and reasonings in the pursuance of truth and freedom, but that he would cry out as Pyrrhus did, admiring the Roman docility and courage, 'If such were my Epirots, I would not despair the greatest design that could be attempted to make a church or kingdom happy.' Yet these are the men cried out against for schismatics and sectaries; as if, while the temple of the

Lord was building, some cutting, some squaring the marble, others hewing the cedars, there should be a sort of irrational men who would not consider there must be many schisms and many dissections made in the quarry and in the timber, ere the house of God can be built. And when every stone is laid artfully together, it cannot be united into a continuity, it can but be contiguous in this world; neither can every piece of the building be of one form; nay, rather the perfection consists in this, that out of many moderate varieties and brotherly dissimilitudes that are not vastly disproportional, arises the goodly and the graceful symmetry that commends the whole pile and structure. Let us therefore be more considerate builders, more wise in spiritual architecture, when great reformation is expected. For now the time seems come, wherein Moses the great prophet may sit in heaven rejoicing to see that memorable and glorious wish of his fulfilled, when not only our seventy elders, but all the Lord's people, are become prophets. No marvel then though some men, and some good men too, perhaps, but young in goodness, as Joshua then was, envy them. They fret, and out of their own weakness are in agony, lest those divisions and subdivisions will undo us. The adversary again applauds, and waits the hour, when they have branched themselves out (saith he) small enough into parties and partitions, then will be our time. Fool! he sees not the firm root, out of which we all grow, though into branches; nor will beware until he see our small divided maniples cutting through at every angle of his ill-united and unwieldy brigade. And that we are to hope better of all these supposed sects and schisms, and that we shall not need that solicitude (honest perhaps though over-timorous) of them that vex in this behalf, but shall laugh in the end, at those malicious applauders of our differences, I have these reasons to persuade me.

First, when a city shall be as it were besieged and blocked about, her navigable river infested, inroads and incursions round, defiance and battle oft rumored to be marching up even to her walls and suburb trenches, that then the people, or the greater part, more than at other times, wholly taken up with the study of highest and most important matters to be reformed, should be disputing, reasoning, reading, inventing, discoursing, even to a rarity and admiration, things not before discoursed or written of, argues first a singular good will, contentedness and confidence in your prudent foresight, and safe government, Lords and Commons; and from thence derives itself to a gallant bravery and well grounded contempt of their enemies, as if there were no small number of as great spirits among us, as his was, who when Rome was nigh besieged by Hannibal, being in the city, bought that piece of ground at no cheap rate, whereon Hannibal himself encamped his own regiment. Next, it is a lively and cheerful presage of our happy success and victory. For as in a body, when the blood is fresh, the spirits pure and vigorous, not only to vital, but to rational faculties, and those in the acutest and the pertest operations of wit and subtlety, it argues in what good plight and constitution the body is, so when the cheerfulness of the people is so sprightly up, as that it has, not only wherewith to guard well its own freedom and safety, but to spare, and to bestow upon the solidest and sublimest points of controversy and new invention, it betokens us not degenerated, nor drooping to a fatal decay, but casting off the old and wrinkled skin of corruption to outlive these pangs and wax young again, entering the glorious ways of truth and prosperous virtue destined to become great and honorable in these latter ages. Methinks I see in my mind a noble and puissant nation, rousing herself like a strong man after sleep, and shaking her invincible locks. Methinks I see her as an eagle mewing her mighty youth, and kindling her undazzled eyes at the full midday beam; purging and unscaling her long-abused sight at the fountain itself of heavenly radiance; while the whole noise of timorous and flocking birds, with those also that love the twilight, flutter about, amazed at what she means, and in their envious gabble would prognosticate a year of sects and schisms.

What should ye do then, should ye suppress all this flowery crop of knowledge and new light sprung up and yet springing daily in this city, should ye set an oligarchy of twenty engrossers over it, to bring a famine upon our minds again, when we shall know nothing but what is measured to us by their bushel? Believe it, Lords and Commons, they who counsel ye to such a suppressing, do as good as bid ye suppress yourselves; and I will soon show how. If it be desired to know the immediate cause of all this free writing and free speaking, there cannot be assigned a truer than your own mild, and free, and humane government; it is the liberty, Lords and Commons, which your own valorous and happy counsels have purchased us, liberty which is the nurse of all great wits. This is that which hath rarefied and enlightened our spirits like the influence of heaven; this is that which hath enfranchised, enlarged, and lifted up our apprehensions degrees above themselves. Ye cannot make us now less capable, less knowing, less eagerly pursuing of the truth, unless ye first make yourselves, that made us so, less the lovers, less the founders of our true liberty. We can grow ignorant again, brutish, formal, and slavish, as ye found us; but you then must first become that which ye cannot be, oppressive, arbitrary, and tyrannous, as they were from whom ye have freed us. That our hearts are now more capacious, our thoughts more erected to the search and expectation of greatest and exactest things, is the issue of your own virtue propagated in us; ye cannot suppress that unless ye reinforce an abrogated and merciless law, that fathers may despatch at will their own children. And who shall then stick closest to ye, and excite others? not he who takes up arms for coat and conduct, and his four nobles of danegelt. Although I dispraise not the defense of just immunities, yet love my peace better, if that were all. Give me the liberty to know, to utter, and to argue freely according to conscience, above all liberties.

What would be best advised, then, if it be found so hurtful and so unequal to suppress opinions for the newness, or the unsuitableness to a customary acceptance, will not be my task to say. I only shall repeat what I have learned from one of your own honorable number, a right noble and pious lord, who, had he not sacrificed his life and fortunes to the church and commonwealth, we had not now missed and bewailed a worthy and undoubted patron of this argument. Ye know him I am sure; yet I for honor's sake, and may it be eternal to him, shall name him the Lord Brook. He writing of episcopacy and by the way treating of sects and schisms, left ye his vote, or rather now the last words of his dying charge, which I know will ever be of dear and honored regard with ye, so full of meekness and breathing charity, that next to his last testament, who bequeathed love and peace to his disciples, I cannot call to mind where I have read or heard words more mild and peaceful. He there exhorts us to hear with patience and humility those, however they be miscalled, that desire to live purely, in such a use of God's ordinances, as the best guidance of their conscience gives them, and to tolerate them, though in some disconformity to ourselves. The book itself will tell us more at large, being published to the world, and dedicated to the Parliament by him who both for his life and for his death deserves that what advice he left be not laid by without perusal.

And now the time in special is, by privilege to write and speak what may help to the further discussing of matters in agitation. The temple of Janus with his two controversal faces might now not unsignificantly be set open. And though all the winds of doctrine were let loose to play upon the earth, so Truth be in the field, we do injuriously by licensing and prohibiting to misdoubt her strength. Let her and Falsehood grapple; who ever knew Truth put to the worse, in a free and open encounter? Her confuting is the best and surest suppressing. He who hears what praying there is for light and clearer knowledge to be sent down among us, would think of other matters to be constituted beyond the discipline of Geneva, framed and fabricked already to our hands. Yet when the new light which we beg for shines in upon us, there be who envy and oppose, if it come not first in at their casements. What a collusion is this, whenas we are exhorted by the wise man to use diligence, to seek for wisdom as for hidden treasures early and late, that another order shall enjoin us to know nothing but by statute? When a man hath been laboring the hardest labor in the deep mines of knowledge, hath furnished out his findings in all their equipage, drawn forth his reasons as it were a battle ranged, scattered and defeated all objections in his way, calls out his adversary into the plain, offers him the advantage of wind and sun, if he please, only that he may try the matter by dint of argument—for his opponents then to skulk, to lay ambushments, to keep a narrow bridge of licensing where the challenger should pass, though it be valor enough in soldiership, is but weakness and cowardice in the wars of Truth. For who knows not that Truth is strong, next to the Almighty; she needs no policies, no stratagems, no licensings to make her victorious; those are the shifts and the defenses that error uses against her power: give her but room, and do not bind her when she sleeps, for then she speaks not true, as the old Proteus did, who spake oracles only when he was caught and bound, but then rather she turns herself into all shapes, except her own, and perhaps tunes her voice according to the time, as Micaiah did before Ahab, until she be adjured into her own likeness. Yet it is not impossible that she may have more shapes than one. What else is all that rank of things indifferent, wherein Truth may be on this side, or on the other, without being unlike herself? What but a vain shadow else is the abolition of those ordinances, that hand-writing nailed to the cross, what great purchase is this Christian liberty which Paul so often boasts of? His doctrine is, that he who eats or eats not, regards a day or regards it not, may do either to the Lord. How many other things might be tolerated in peace, and left to conscience, had we but charity, and were it not the chief stronghold of our hypocrisy to be ever judging one another. I fear yet this iron yoke of outward conformity hath left a slavish print upon our necks; the ghost of a linen decency yet haunts us. We stumble and are impatient at the least dividing of one visible congregation from another, though it be not in fundamentals; and through our forwardness to suppress, and our backwardness to recover any enthralled piece of truth out of the grip of custom, we care not to keep truth separated from truth, which is the fiercest rent and disunion of all. We do not see that while we still affect by all means a rigid external formality, we may as soon fall again into a gross conforming stupidity, a stark and dead congealment of wood, and hay, and stubble forced and frozen together, which is more to the sudden degenerating of a church than many subdichotomies of petty schisms. Not that I can think well of every light separation, or that all in a church is to be expected gold and silver and precious stones. It is not possible for man to sever the wheat from the tares, the good fish from the other fry; that must be the angels' ministry at the end of mortal things. Yet if all cannot be of one mind, (as who looks they should be?) this doubtless is more wholesome, more prudent, and more Christian that many be tolerated, rather than all compelled. I mean not tolerated popery, and open superstition, which, as it extirpates all religions and civil supremacies, so itself should be extirpate, provided first that all charitable and compassionate means be used to win and regain the weak and the misled: that also which is impious or evil absolutely either against faith or manners, no law can possibly permit that intends not to unlaw itself. But those neighboring differences, or rather indifferences, are what I speak of, whether in some point of doctrine or of discipline, which though they may be many, yet need not interrupt the unity of Spirit, if we could but find among us the bond of peace. In the meanwhile if any one would write, and bring his helpful hand to the slow-moving reformation which we labor under, if Truth have spoken to him before others, or but seemed at least to speak, who hath so bejesuited us that we should trouble that man with asking license to do so worthy a deed? and not consider this, that if it come to prohibiting, there is not aught more likely to be prohibited than truth itself; whose first appearance to our eyes bleared and dimmed with prejudice and custom, is more unsightly and unplausible than many errors, even as the person is of many a great man slight and contemptible to see to. And what do they tell us vainly of new opinions, when this very opinion of theirs, that none must be heard but whom they like, is the worst and newest opinion of all others; and is the chief cause why sects and schisms do so much abound, and true knowledge is kept at distance from us; besides yet a greater danger which is in it. For when God shakes a kingdom with strong and healthful commotions to a general reforming, 't is not untrue that many sectaries and false teachers are then busiest in seducing; but yet more true it is, that God then raises to his own work men of rare abilities, and more than common industry, not only to look back and revise what hath been taught heretofore, but to gain further and go on, some new enlightened steps in the discovery of truth. For such is the order of God's enlightening his church, to dispense and deal out by degrees his beam, so as our earthly eyes may best sustain it. Neither is God appointed and confined, where and out of what place these his chosen shall be first heard to speak; for he sees not as man sees, chooses not as man chooses, lest we should devote ourselves again to set places, and assemblies, and outward callings of men; planting our faith one while in the old Convocation House, and another while in the Chapel at Westminster; when all the faith and religion that shall be there canonized, is not sufficient without plain convincement, and the charity of patient instruction to supple the least bruise of conscience, to edify the meanest Christian, who desires to walk in the Spirit, and not in the letter of human trust, for all the number of voices that can be there made—no, though Harry VII himself there, with all his liege tombs about him, should lend them voices from the dead, to swell their number. And if the men be erroneous who appear to be the leading schismatics, what withholds us but our sloth, our self-will, and distrust in the right cause, that we do not give them gentle meetings and gentle dismissions, that we debate not and examine the matter thoroughly with liberal and frequent audience; if not for their sakes, yet for our own? Seeing no man who hath tasted learning, but will confess the many ways of profiting by those who, not contented with stale receipts, are able to manage and set forth new positions to the world. And were they but as the dust and cinders of our feet, so long as in that notion they may yet serve to polish and brighten the armory of Truth, even for that respect they were not utterly to be cast away. But if they be of those whom God hath fitted for the special use of these times with eminent and ample gifts, and those perhaps neither among the Priests, nor among the Pharisees, and we in the haste of a precipitant zeal shall make no distinction, but resolve to stop their mouths, because we fear they come with new and dangerous opinions, as we commonly forejudge them ere we understand them, no less than woe to us, while thinking thus to defend the Gospel, we are found the persecutors.

There have been not a few since the beginning of this Parliament, both of the Presbytery and others, who by their unlicensed books to the contempt of an Imprimatur first broke that triple ice clung about our hearts, and taught the people to see day. I hope that none of those were the persuaders to renew upon us this bondage which they themselves have wrought so much good by contemning. But if neither the check that Moses gave to young Joshua, nor the countermand which our Savior gave to young John, who was so ready to prohibit those whom he thought unlicensed, be not enough to admonish our Elders, how unacceptable to God their testy mood of prohibiting is; if neither their own remembrance what evil hath abounded in the Church by this let of licensing, and what good they themselves have begun by transgressing it, be not enough, but that they will persuade, and execute the most Dominican part of the Inquisition over us, and are already with one foot in the stirrup so active at suppressing, it would be no unequal distribution in the first place to suppress the suppressors themselves: whom the change of their condition hath puffed up, more than their late experience of harder times hath made wise.

And as for regulating the Press, let no man think to have the honor of advising ye better than yourselves have done in that order published next before this, 'that no book be printed, unless the printer's and the author's name, or at least the printer's be registered.' Those which otherwise come forth, if they be found mischievous and libelous, the fire and the executioner will be the timeliest and the most effectual remedy, that man's prevention can use. For this authentic Spanish policy of licensing books, if I have said aught, will prove the most unlicensed book itself within a short while; and was the immediate image of a Star Chamber decree to that purpose made in those very times when that court did the rest of those her pious works, for which she is now fallen from the stars with Lucifer. Whereby ye may guess what kind of state prudence, what love of the people, what care of religion or good manners there was at the contriving, although with singular hypocrisy it pretended to bind books to their good behavior. And how it got the upper hand of your precedent order, so well constituted before, if we may believe those men whose profession gives them cause to inquire most, it may be doubted there was in it the fraud of some old patentees and monopolizers in the trade of bookselling; who under pretense of the poor in their Company not to be defrauded, and the just retaining of each man his several copy (which God forbid should be gainsaid), brought divers glossing colors to the House; which were indeed but colors, and serving to no end except it be to exercise a superiority over their neighbors, men who do not therefore labor in an honest profession to which learning is indebted, that they should be made other men's vassals. Another end is thought was aimed at by some of them in procuring by petition this order, that having power in their hands, malignant books might the easier 'scape abroad, as the event shows. But of these sophisms and elenchs of merchandise I skill not. This I know, that errors in a good government and in a bad are equally almost incident; for what magistrate may not be misinformed, and much the sooner, if liberty of printing be reduced into the power of a few; but to redress willingly and speedily what hath been erred, and in highest authority to esteem a plain advertisement more than others have done a sumptuous bribe, is a virtue (honored Lords and Commons) answerable to your highest actions, and whereof none can participate but greatest and wisest men.   (1644)

JOHN DRYDEN (1631-1700)

DRYDEN came of a good Northamptonshire family, and was educated at Westminster School and Trinity College, Cambridge. He was only eighteen when his first verses were published, but his first poem of importance was in commemoration of the death of Oliver Cromwell. Dryden's dependence as a professional writer on the party in power made his financial position insecure, hampered his genius, and ruined his reputation for consistency: his eulogy of Cromwell was followed almost immediately by poems in celebration of Charles II. The reopening of the theaters after the Restoration gave him a less equivocal opportunity for the exercise of his talents, and he led the way in the development of the new comedy (largely indebted to the French) and the heroic play with its preposterous characters and incidents and extravagant rant. After defending and perfecting the rimed couplet as a medium for tragedy, he turned to blank verse in *All for Love* (1678), founded upon Shakespeare's *Anthony and Cleopatra*, and generally accounted Dryden's best play. Meanwhile he had won distinction in other ways; his *Essay of Dramatic Poesy* (1668) is remarkable both for its literary insight and its vigorous and lucid style, which had an important influence on the development of English prose. In 1670 he was appointed Poet Laureate and Historiographer with a salary of £200, which relieved his immediate necessities, but was not enough to save him from financial difficulties. The political intrigues at the end of Charles II's reign gave occasion for the bitter satirical poem *Absalom and Achitophel* (1681) which in its own kind of poetry remains unsurpassed. *Religio Laici* (1682), a poem in defense of the Church of England, was discounted by the author's conversion to Roman Catholicism on the accession of James II, though most students of Dryden's life and writings hold that his change of view was sincere. *The Hind and the Panther*, a plea for the poet's newly adopted faith, appeared in 1687. The Revolution of 1688 deprived Dryden of his offices, and he was dependent for the rest of his life upon his pen. He returned to the stage with *Don Sebastian* (1690), one of his best tragedies, wrote excellent prologues and epilogues for the plays of other men, and worked hard at criticism and translations. After enjoying for many years the literary leadership of his time, he was buried in the Poets' Corner at Westminster Abbey.

ABSALOM AND ACHITOPHEL

From PART I

Of all this numerous progeny was none
So beautiful, so brave, as Absalon:
Whether, inspir'd by some diviner lust,
His father got him with a greater gust;
Or that his conscious destiny made way,   5
By manly beauty, to imperial sway.
Early in foreign fields he won renown,
With kings and states allied to Israel's crown:
In peace the thoughts of war he could remove,
And seem'd as he were only born for love.   10
Whate'er he did, was done with so much ease,
In him alone 't was natural to please:
His motions all accompanied with grace;
And paradise was open'd in his face.
With secret joy indulgent David view'd   15
His youthful image in his son renew'd:
To all his wishes nothing he denied;
And made the charming Annabel his bride.
What faults he had (for who from faults is free?)
His father could not, or he would not see.   20
Some warm excesses which the law forbore.
Were construed youth that purg'd by boiling o'er,
And Ammon's murder, by a specious name,
Was call'd a just revenge for injur'd fame.
Thus prais'd and lov'd the noble youth remain'd,   25
While David, undisturb'd, in Sion reign'd.

But life can never be sincerely blest;
Heav'n punishes the bad, and proves the best.
The Jews, a headstrong, moody, murm'ring race,
As ever tried th' extent and stretch of grace;   30
God's pamper'd people, whom, debauch'd with ease,
No king could govern, nor no God could please,
(Gods they had tried of every shape and size,
That god-smiths could produce, or priests devise:)
These Adam-wits, too fortunately free,   35
Began to dream they wanted liberty;
And when no rule, no precedent was found,
Of men by laws less circumscrib'd and bound;

They led their wild desires to woods and caves,
And thought that all but savages were slaves. 40
They who, when Saul was dead, without a blow,
Made foolish Ishbosheth the crown forgo;
Who banish'd David did from Hebron bring,
And with a general shout proclaim'd him king:
Those very Jews, who, at their very best, 45
Their humor more than loyalty express'd,
Now wonder'd why so long they had obey'd
An idol monarch, which their hands had made;
Thought they might ruin him they could create,
Or melt him to that golden calf, a State. 50
But these were random bolts; no form'd design,
Nor interest made the factious crowd to join:
The sober part of Israel, free from stain,
Well knew the value of a peaceful reign;
And, looking backward with a wise affright, 55
Saw seams of wounds, dishonest to the sight:
In contemplation of whose ugly scars
They curs'd the memory of civil wars.
The moderate sort of men, thus qualified,
Inclin'd the balance to the better side; 60
And David's mildness manag'd it so well,
The bad found no occasion to rebel.
But when to sin our bias'd nature leans,
The careful Devil is still at hand with means;
And providently pimps for ill desires. 65
The Good Old Cause reviv'd, a plot requires:
Plots, true or false, are necessary things,
To raise up commonwealths, and ruin kings.

Th' inhabitants of old Jerusalem
Were Jebusites; the town so call'd from them;
And theirs the native right— 71
But when the chosen people grew more strong,
The rightful cause at length became the wrong;
And every loss the men of Jebus bore,
They still were thought God's enemies the more. 75
Thus worn and weaken'd, well or ill content,
Submit they must to David's government:
Impoverish'd and depriv'd of all command,
Their taxes doubled as they lost their land;
And, what was harder yet to flesh and blood, 80
Their gods disgrac'd, and burnt like common wood.
This set the heathen priesthood in a flame;
For priests of all religions are the same:
Of whatsoe'er descent their godhead be,
Stock, stone, or other homely pedigree, 85
In his defense his servants are as bold
As if he had been born of beaten gold.
The Jewish rabbins, tho' their enemies,
In this conclude them honest men and wise;
For 't was their duty, all the learned think, 90
T' espouse his cause, by whom they eat and drink.
From hence began that Plot, the nation's curse,
Bad in itself, but represented worse;
Rais'd in extremes, and in extremes decried;
With oaths affirm'd, with dying vows denied; 95
Not weigh'd or winnow'd by the multitude;
But swallow'd in the mass, unchew'd and crude.
Some truth there was, but dash'd and brew'd with lies,
To please the fools, and puzzle all the wise.
Succeeding times did equal folly call, 100
Believing nothing, or believing all.
Th' Egyptian rites the Jebusites embrac'd;
Where gods were recommended by their taste.
Such sav'ry deities must needs be good,
As serv'd at once for worship and for food. 105
By force they could not introduce these gods,
For ten to one in former days was odds;
So fraud was us'd (the sacrificer's trade):
Fools are more hard to conquer than persuade.
Their busy teachers mingled with the Jews, 110
And rak'd for converts even the court and stews:
Which Hebrew priests the more unkindly took,
Because the fleece accompanies the flock.
Some thought they God's anointed meant to slay
By guns, invented since full many a day: 115
Our author swears it not; but who can know
How far the Devil and Jebusites may go?
This Plot, which fail'd for want of common sense,
Had yet a deep and dangerous consequence:
For, as when raging fevers boil the blood, 120
The standing lake soon floats into a flood,
And ev'ry hostile humor, which before
Slept quiet in its channels, bubbles o'er;
So several factions from this first ferment
Work up to foam, and threat the government.
Some by their friends, more by themselves thought wise, 126
Oppos'd the pow'r to which they could not rise.
Some had in courts been great, and thrown from thence,
Like fiends were harden'd in impenitence.
Some, by their monarch's fatal mercy, grown
From pardon'd rebels kinsmen to the throne, 131
Were rais'd in pow'r and public office high;
Strong bands, if bands ungrateful men could tie.

Of these the false Achitophel was first;
A name to all succeeding ages curst: 135
For close designs and crooked counsels fit;
Sagacious, bold, and turbulent of wit;
Restless, unfix'd in principles and place;
In pow'r unpleas'd, impatient of disgrace.
A fiery soul, which, working out its way, 140
Fretted the pigmy body to decay,
And o'er-inform'd the tenement of clay.
A daring pilot in extremity;
Pleas'd with the danger, when the waves went high,
He sought the storms; but, for a calm unfit, 145
Would steer too nigh the sands, to boast his wit.
Great wits are sure to madness near allied,
And thin partitions do their bounds divide;
Else why should he, with wealth and honor blest,

Refuse his age the needful hours of rest? 150
Punish a body which he could not please;
Bankrupt of life, yet prodigal of ease?
And all to leave what with his toil he won,
To that unfeather'd two-legg'd thing, a son;
Got, while his soul did huddled notions try; 155
And born a shapeless lump, like anarchy.
In friendship false, implacable in hate;
Resolv'd to ruin or to rule the State.
To compass this the triple bond he broke;
The pillars of the public safety shook; 160
And fitted Israel for a foreign yoke:
Then seiz'd with fear, yet still affecting fame,
Usurp'd a patriot's all-atoning name.
So easy still it proves in factious times,
With public zeal to cancel private crimes. 165
How safe is treason, and how sacred ill,
Where none can sin against the people's will!
Where crowds can wink, and no offense be known,
Since in another's guilt they find their own!
Yet fame deserv'd no enemy can grudge; 170
The statesman we abhor, but praise the judge.
In Israel's courts ne'er sat an Abbethdin
With more discerning eyes, or hands more clean;
Unbrib'd, unsought, the wretched to redress;
Swift of dispatch, and easy of access. 175
O, had he been content to serve the crown,
With virtues only proper to the gown;
Or had the rankness of the soil been freed
From cockle, that oppress'd the noble seed;
David for him his tuneful harp had strung, 180
And Heav'n had wanted one immortal song.
But wild Ambition loves to slide, not stand,
And Fortune's ice prefers to Virtue's land.
Achitophel, grown weary to possess
A lawful fame, and lazy happiness, 185
Disdain'd the golden fruit to gather free,
And lent the crowd his arm to shake the tree.
Now, manifest of crimes contriv'd long since,
He stood at bold defiance with his prince;
Held up the buckler of the people's cause 190
Against the crown, and skulk'd behind the laws.
The wish'd occasion of the Plot he takes;
Some circumstances finds, but more he makes.
By buzzing emissaries fills the ears
Of list'ning crowds with jealousies and fears 195
Of arbitrary counsels brought to light,
And proves the king himself a Jebusite.
Weak arguments! which yet he knew full well
Were strong with people easy to rebel.
For, govern'd by the moon, the giddy Jews 200
Tread the same track when she the prime renews;
And once in twenty years, their scribes record,
By natural instinct they change their lord.
Achitophel still wants a chief, and none
Was found so fit as warlike Absalom. 205
Not that he wish'd his greatness to create,
(For politicians neither love nor hate,)
But, for he knew his title not allow'd,
Would keep him still depending on the crowd:
That kingly pow'r, thus ebbing out, might be 210
Drawn to the dregs of a democracy.

* * *

To further this, Achitophel unites
The malcontents of all the Israelites;
Whose differing parties he could wisely join,
For several ends, to serve the same design. 215
The best, (and of the princes some were such,)
Who thought the pow'r of monarchy too much;
Mistaken men, and patriots in their hearts;
Not wicked, but seduc'd by impious arts.
By these the springs of property were bent, 220
And wound so high, they crack'd the government.
The next for interest sought t' embroil the State,
To sell their duty at a dearer rate;
And make their Jewish markets of the throne,
Pretending public good, to serve their own. 225
Others thought kings an useless heavy load,
Who cost too much, and did too little good.
These were for laying honest David by,
On principles of pure good husbandry.
With them join'd all th' haranguers of the throng, 230
That thought to get preferment by the tongue.
Who follow next, a double danger bring,
Not only hating David, but the king:
The Solymæan rout, well-vers'd of old
In godly faction, and in treason bold; 235
Cow'ring and quaking at a conqu'ror's sword;
But lofty to a lawful prince restor'd;
Saw with disdain an Ethnic plot begun,
And scorn'd by Jebusites to be outdone.
Hot Levites headed these; who, pull'd before 240
From th' ark, which in the Judges' days they bore,
Resum'd their cant, and with a zealous cry
Pursued their old belov'd Theocracy:
Where Sanhedrim and priest enslav'd the nation,
And justified their spoils by inspiration: 245
For who so fit for reign as Aaron's race,
If once dominion they could found in grace!
These led the pack; tho' not of surest scent,
Yet deepest mouth'd against the government.
A numerous host of dreaming saints succeed, 250
Of the true old enthusiastic breed:
'Gainst form and order they their pow'r employ,
Nothing to build, and all things to destroy.
But far more numerous was the herd of such,
Who think too little, and who talk too much. 255
These, out of mere instinct, they knew not why,
Ador'd their fathers' God and property;
And, by the same blind benefit of fate,
The Devil and the Jebusite did hate:
Born to be sav'd, even in their own despite, 260
Because they could not help believing right.
Such were the tools; but a whole Hydra more
Remains, of sprouting heads too long to score.

Some of their chiefs were princes of the land:
In the first rank of these did Zimri stand; 265
A man so various, that he seem'd to be
Not one, but all mankind's epitome:
Stiff in opinions, always in the wrong;
Was everything by starts, and nothing long;
But, in the course of one revolving moon, 270
Was chymist, fiddler, statesman, and buffoon:
Then all for women, painting, riming, drinking,
Besides ten thousand freaks that died in thinking.
Blest madman, who could every hour employ,
With something new to wish, or to enjoy! 275
Railing and praising were his usual themes;
And both (to shew his judgment) in extremes:
So over-violent, or over-civil,
That every man, with him, was God or Devil.
In squand'ring wealth was his peculiar art; 280
Nothing went unrewarded but desert.
Beggar'd by fools, whom still he found too late,
He had his jest, and they had his estate.
He laugh'd himself from court; then sought relief
By forming parties, but could ne'er be chief; 285
For, spite of him, the weight of business fell
On Absalom and wise Achitophel:
Thus, wicked but in will, of means bereft,
He left not faction, but of that was left.
(1681)

* * *

From PART II

Now stop your noses, readers, all and some,
For here's a tun of midnight work to come,
Og from a treason-tavern rolling home;
Round as a globe, and liquor'd ev'ry chink,
Goodly and great he sails behind his link. 5
With all this bulk there's nothing lost in Og,
For ev'ry inch that is not fool, is rogue:
A monstrous mass of foul corrupted matter,
As all the devils had spew'd to make the batter.
When wine has given him courage to blaspheme, 10
He curses God, but God before curs'd him;
And if man could have reason, none has more,
That made his paunch so rich, and him so poor.
With wealth he was not trusted, for Heav'n knew
What 't was of old to pamper up a Jew; 15
To what would he on quail and pheasant swell,
That ev'n on tripe and carrion could rebel?
But tho' Heav'n made him poor, (with rev'rence speaking,)
He never was a poet of God's making.
The midwife laid her hand on his thick skull, 20
With this prophetic blessing: *Be thou dull!*
Drink, swear, and roar, forbear no lewd delight
Fit for thy bulk, do anything but write:
Thou art of lasting make, like thoughtless men,
A strong nativity—but for the pen; 25
Eat opium, mingle arsenic in thy drink,
Still thou mayst live, avoiding pen and ink.
I see, I see, 't is counsel given in vain,
For treason botch'd in rime will be thy bane;
Rime is the rock on which thou art to wreck, 30
'T is fatal to thy fame and to thy neck:
Why should thy meter good King David blast?
A psalm of his will surely be thy last.
Dar'st thou presume in verse to meet thy foes,
Thou whom the penny pamphlet foil'd in prose?
Doeg, whom God for mankind's mirth has made, 36
O'ertops thy talent in thy very trade;
Doeg to thee, thy paintings are so coarse,
A poet is, tho' he's the poets' horse.
A double noose thou on thy neck dost pull, 40
For writing treason, and for writing dull;
To die for faction is a common evil,
But to be hang'd for nonsense is the devil.
Hadst thou the glories of thy kind express'd,
Thy praises had been satire at the best; 45
But thou in clumsy verse, unlick'd, unpointed,
Hast shamefully defied the Lord's anointed.
I will not rake the dunghill of thy crimes,
For who would read thy life that reads thy rimes?
But of King David's foes, be this the doom: 50
May all be like the young man Absalom;
And for my foes, may this their blessing be:
To talk like Doeg, and to write like thee.
(1682)

* * *

ALEXANDER'S FEAST

ALEXANDER'S FEAST
OR THE POWER OF MUSIC

A SONG IN HONOR OF ST. CECILIA'S DAY

I

'T was at the royal feast for Persia won
  By Philip's warlike son:
    Aloft in awful state
    The godlike hero sate
      On his imperial throne; 5
His valiant peers were placed around;
Their brows with roses and with myrtles bound
(So should desert in arms be crowned).
    The lovely Thais, by his side,
    Sate like a blooming Eastern bride, 10
    In flower of youth and beauty's pride.
     Happy, happy, happy pair!
       None but the brave,
       None but the brave,
  None but the brave deserves the fair. 15

CHORUS

Happy, happy, happy pair, etc.

2

Timotheus, placed on high
    Amid the tuneful quire,
    With flying fingers touched the lyre:
The trembling notes ascend the sky,   20
    And heavenly joys inspire
The song began from Jove,
Who left his blissful seats above
(Such is the power of mighty love).
A dragon's fiery form belied the god: 25
Sublime on radiant spires he rode,
When he to fair Olympia pressed:
And while he sought her snowy breast,
Then round her slender waist he curled,
And stamped an image of himself, a sovereign
    of the world.   30
The listening crowd admire the lofty sound,
A present deity, they shout around;
A present deity the vaulted roofs rebound:
    With ravished ears
    The monarch hears,   35
    Assumes the god,
    Affects to nod,
    And seems to shake the spheres.

CHORUS

With ravished ears, etc.

3

The praise of Bacchus then the sweet musician
    sung,   40
Of Bacchus ever fair, and ever young.
    The jolly god in triumph comes;
    Sound the trumpets, beat the drums;
    Flushed with a purple grace
    He shows his honest face: 45
Now give the hautboys breath; he comes, he
    comes.
    Bacchus, ever fair and young,
    Drinking joys did first ordain;
    Bacchus' blessings are a treasure,
    Drinking is the soldier's pleasure;   50
    Rich the treasure,
    Sweet the pleasure,
    Sweet is pleasure after pain.

CHORUS

Bacchus' blessings are a treasure, etc.

4

Soothed with the sound the king grew vain;   55
    Fought all his battles o'er again;
And thrice he routed all his foes, and thrice he
    slew the slain.
    The master saw the madness rise,
    His glowing cheeks, his ardent eyes;
And while he heaven and earth defied,   60
Changed his hand, and checked his pride.
    He chose a mournful Muse,
    Soft pity to infuse;
    He sung Darius great and good,
    By too severe a fate,   65
    Fallen, fallen, fallen, fallen,
    Fallen from his high estate,
    And weltering in his blood;
    Deserted at his utmost need
By those his former bounty fed!   70
On the bare earth exposed he lies,
With not a friend to close his eyes.
With downcast looks the joyless victor sate,
    Revolving in his altered soul
    The various turns of chance below;   75
    And, now and then, a sigh he stole,
    And tears began to flow.

CHORUS

Revolving in his altered soul, etc.

5

    The mighty master smiled to see
    That love was in the next degree: 80
    'T was but a kindred sound to move,
    For pity melts the mind to love.
    Softly sweet in Lydian measures,
    Soon he soothed his soul to pleasures.
    War, he sung, is toil and trouble;   85
    Honor but an empty bubble;
    Never ending, still beginning,
    Fighting still, and still destroying:
    If the world be worth thy winning,
    Think, O think it worth enjoying: 90
    Lovely Thais sits beside thee,
    Take the good the gods provide thee.
The many rend the skies with loud applause;
So love was crowned, but Music won the cause.
    The prince, unable to conceal his pain,   95
    Gazed on the fair
    Who caused his care,
    And sighed and looked, sighed and looked,
    Sighed and looked, and sighed again;
At length, with love and wine at once oppressed,
The vanquished victor sunk upon her breast.   101

CHORUS

The prince, unable to conceal his pain, etc.

6

    Now strike the golden lyre again;
    A louder yet, and yet a louder strain.
Break his bands of sleep asunder,   105
And rouse him, like a rattling peal of thunder.
    Hark, hark, the horrid sound
    Has raised up his head;
    As awaked from the dead,
    And amazed, he stares around.   110
Revenge, revenge, Timotheus cries,
    See the Furies arise;
    See the snakes that they rear,
    How they hiss in their hair,

And the sparkles that flash from their eyes! 115
    Behold a ghastly band,
    Each a torch in his hand!
Those are Grecian ghosts, that in battle were slain,
    And unburied remain
    Inglorious on the plain: 120
    Give the vengeance due
    To the valiant crew.
Behold how they toss their torches on high,
    How they point to the Persian abodes,
    And glittering temples of their hostile gods.
The princes applaud with a furious joy; 126
And the king seized a flambeau with zeal to destroy;
    Thais led the way,
    To light him to his prey,
And, like another Helen, fired another Troy. 130

CHORUS

And the king seized a flambeau with zeal to destroy, etc.

7

Thus long ago,
    Ere heaving bellows learned to blow,
    While organs yet were mute,
    Timotheus, to his breathing flute 135
    And sounding lyre,
Could swell the soul to rage, or kindle soft desire.
    At last divine Cecilia came,
    Inventress of the vocal frame;
The sweet enthusiast, from her sacred store, 140
    Enlarged the former narrow bounds,
    And added length to solemn sounds,
With Nature's mother-wit, and arts unknown before.
    Let old Timotheus yield the prize,
    Or both divide the crown: 145
    He raised a mortal to the skies;
    She drew an angel down.

GRAND CHORUS

At last divine Cecilia came, etc. (1697)

AN ESSAY OF DRAMATIC POESY

It was that memorable day, in the first summer of the late war, when our navy engaged the Dutch—a day wherein the two most mighty and best appointed fleets which any age had ever seen, disputed the command of the greater half of the globe, the commerce of nations, and the riches of the universe. While these vast floating bodies, on either side, moved against each other in parallel lines, and our countrymen, under the happy conduct of his royal highness, went breaking, by little and little, into the line of the enemies, the noise of the cannon from both navies reached our ears about the city; so that all men being alarmed with it, and in a dreadful suspense of the event, which they knew was then deciding, every one went following the sound as his fancy led him. And leaving the town almost empty, some took towards the Park, some cross the river, others down it; all seeking the noise in the depth of silence.

Among the rest, it was the fortune of Eugenius, Crites, Lisideius, and Neander, to be in company together: three of them persons whom their wit and quality have made known to all the town; and whom I have chosen to hide under these borrowed names, that they may not suffer by so ill a relation as I am going to make of their discourse.

Taking then a barge, which a servant of Lisideius had provided for them, they made haste to shoot the bridge, and left behind them that great fall of waters which hindered them from hearing what they desired; after which, having disengaged themselves from many vessels which rode at anchor in the Thames, and almost blocked up the passage towards Greenwich, they ordered the watermen to let fall their oars more gently; and then every one favoring his own curiosity with a strict silence, it was not long ere they perceived the air to break about them like the noise of distant thunder, or of swallows in a chimney: those little undulations of sound, though almost vanishing before they reached them, yet still seeming to retain somewhat of their first horror which they had betwixt the fleets.

After they had attentively listened till such time as the sound by little and little went from them, Eugenius, lifting up his head, and taking notice of it, was the first who congratulated to the rest that happy omen of our nation's victory: adding, that we had but this to desire in confirmation of it, that we might hear no more of that noise which was now leaving the English coast.

When the rest had concurred in the same opinion, Crites (a person of a sharp judgment, and somewhat a too delicate taste in wit, which the world have mistaken in him for ill nature), said, smiling to us, that if the concernment of this battle had not been so exceeding great, he could scarce have wished the victory at the price he knew he must pay for it, in being subject to the reading and hearing of so many ill verses as he was sure would be made on that subject. Adding, that no argument could 'scape some of those eternal rimers, who watch a battle with more diligence than the ravens and birds of prey; and the worst of them surest to be first in upon the quarry; while the better able, either out of modesty writ not at all, or set that due value upon their poems, as to let them be often desired, and long expected.

There are some of those impertinent people of whom you speak (answered Lisideius) who, to my knowledge, are already so provided, either way, that they can produce not only a panegyric upon the victory, but, if need be, a funeral elegy on the duke; wherein, after they have crowned his valor with many laurels, they will at last deplore the odds under which he fell, concluding, that his courage deserved a better destiny.

* * *

There are so few who write well, in this age (said Crites), that methinks any praises should be welcome. They neither rise to the dignity of the last age, nor to any of the ancients: and we may cry out of the writers of this time, with more reason than Petronius of his, *Pace vestra liceat dixisse, primi omnium eloquentiam perdidistis:* You have debauched the true old poetry so far, that Nature, which is the soul of it, is not in any of your writings!

If your quarrel (said Eugenius) to those who now write, be grounded only upon your reverence to antiquity, there is no man more ready to adore those great Greeks and Romans than I am; but, on the other side, I cannot think so contemptibly of the age in which I live, or so dishonorably of my own country, as not to judge we equal the ancients in most kinds of poesy, and in some surpass them. Neither know I any reason why I may not be as zealous for the reputation of our age, as we find the ancients themselves were in reference to those who lived before them. For you hear your Horace saying,

*Indignor quidquam reprehendi, non quia crasse
Compositum, illepideve putetur, sed quia nuper.*

[I am indignant when anything is blamed, not because it is thought badly or inelegantly written, but because it is new.]

And after:

*Si meliora dies, ut vina, poemata reddit,
Scire velim, pretium chartis quotus arroget annus?*

[If time makes poems better, as it does wines, I should like to know what length of years gives value to writings.]

But I see I am engaging in a wide dispute, where the arguments are not like to reach close on either side; for poesy is of so large an extent, and so many, both of the ancients and moderns, have done well in all kinds of it, that in citing one against the other, we shall take up more time this evening, than each man's occasions will allow him. Therefore I would ask Crites to what part of poesy he would confine his arguments, and whether he would defend the general cause of the ancients against the moderns, or oppose any age of the moderns against this of ours.

Crites, a little while considering upon this demand, told Eugenius, that if he pleased he would limit their dispute to dramatic poesy; in which he thought it not difficult to prove, either that the ancients were superior to the moderns, or the last age to this of ours.

Eugenius was somewhat surprised, when he heard Crites make choice of that subject. For aught I see (said he), I have undertaken a harder province than I imagined; for, though I never judged the plays of the Greek or Roman poets comparable to ours, yet, on the other side, those we now see acted come short of many which were written in the last age. But my comfort is, if we are overcome, it will be only by our own countrymen; and if we yield to them in this one part of poesy, we more surpass them in all the other; for in the epic or lyric way, it will be hard for them to show us one such amongst them, as we have many now living, or who lately were. They can produce nothing so courtly writ, or which expresses so much the conversation of a gentleman, as Sir John Suckling; nothing so even, sweet, and flowing, as Mr. Waller; nothing so majestic, so correct, as Sir John Denham; nothing so elevated, so copious, and full of spirit, as Mr. Cowley. As for the Italian, French, and Spanish plays, I can make it evident that those who now write surpass them; and that the drama is wholly ours.

All of them were thus far of Eugenius his opinion, that the sweetness of English verse was never understood or practised by our fathers; even Crites himself did not much oppose it. And every one was willing to acknowledge how much our poesy is improved, by the happiness of some writers yet living, who first taught us to mold our thoughts into easy and significant words, to retrench the superfluities of expression, and to make our rime so properly a part of the verse, that it should never mislead the sense, but itself be led and governed by it.

Eugenius was going to continue this discourse,

when Lisideius told him that it was necessary, before they proceeded further, to take a standing measure of their controversy; for how was it possible to be decided, who wrote the best plays, before we know what a play should be? But, this once agreed on by both parties, each might have recourse to it, either to prove his own advantages, or to discover the failings of his adversary.

He had no sooner said this, but all desired the favor of him to give the definition of a play; and they were the more importunate, because neither Aristotle, nor Horace, nor any other, who had writ of that subject, had ever done it.

Lisideius, after some modest denials, at last confessed he had a rude notion of it; indeed rather a description than a definition; but which served to guide him in his private thoughts, when he was to make a judgment of what others writ; that he conceived a play ought to be, 'A just and lively image of human nature, representing its passions and humors, and the changes of fortune to which it is subject, for the delight and instruction of mankind.'

This definition (though Crites raised a logical objection against it—that it was only *a genere et fine*, and so not altogether perfect) was yet well received by the rest; and after they had given order to the waterman to turn their barge, and row softly, that they might take the cool of the evening in their return, Crites, being desired by the company to begin, spoke on behalf of the ancients, in this manner:

If confidence presage a victory, Eugenius, in his own opinion, has already triumphed over the ancients: nothing seems more easy to him than to overcome those whom it is our greatest praise to have imitated well; for we do not only build upon their foundations, but by their models. Dramatic poesy had time enough, reckoning from Thespis (who first invented it) to Aristophanes, to be born, to grow up, and to flourish in maturity. It has been observed of arts and sciences, that in one and the same century they have arrived to great perfection; and no wonder, since every age has a kind of universal genius, which inclines those that live in it to some particular studies. The work then being pushed on by many hands, must of necessity go forward.

Is it not evident, in these last hundred years (when the study of philosophy has been the business of all the virtuosi in Christendom), that almost a new nature has been revealed to us? that more errors of the school have been detected, more useful experiments in philosophy have been made, more noble secrets in optics, medicine, anatomy, astronomy, discovered, than in all those credulous and doting ages from Aristotle to us? So true it is, that nothing spreads more fast than science, when rightly and generally cultivated.

Add to this, the more than common emulation that was in those times, of writing well; which though it be found in all ages and all persons that pretend to the same reputation, yet poesy being then in more esteem than now it is, had greater honors decreed to the professors of it, and consequently the rivalship was more high between them. They had judges ordained to decide their merit, and prizes to reward it; and historians have been diligent to record of Æschylus, Euripides, Sophocles, Lycophron, and the rest of them, both who they were that vanquished in these wars of the theater, and how often they were crowned; while the Asian kings and Grecian commonwealths scarce afforded them a nobler subject than the unmanly luxuries of a debauched court, or giddy intrigues of a factious city. *Alit æmulatio ingenia*, (says Paterculus) *et nunc invidia, nunc admiratio incitationem accendit:* Emulation is the spur of wit; and sometimes envy, sometimes admiration, quickens our endeavors.

But now since the rewards of honor are taken away, that virtuous emulation is turned into direct malice; yet so slothful, that it contents itself to condemn and cry down others, without attempting to do better. 'T is a reputation too unprofitable, to take the necessary pains for it; yet wishing they had it, that desire is incitement enough to hinder others from it. And this, in short, Eugenius, is the reason, why you have now so few good poets, and so many severe judges. Certainly, to imitate the ancients well, much labor and long study is required; which pains, I have already shown, our poets would want encouragement to take, if yet they had ability to go through the work. Those ancients have been faithful imitators, and wise observers of that nature which is so torn and ill represented in our plays; they have handed down to us a perfect resemblance of her; which we, like ill copiers, neglecting to look on, have rendered monstrous, and disfigured. But, that you may know how much you are indebted to those your masters, and be ashamed to have so ill requited them, I must remember you, that all the rules by which we practise the drama at this day (either such as relate to the justness and symmetry of the plot; or the episodical ornaments, such as descriptions, narrations, and other beauties, which are not essential to the play) were delivered to us from the observations which Aristotle made, of those poets, who either lived before him, or were his contemporaries. We have added nothing of our own, except we have the confidence to say, our wit is better; of which none boast in this our age, but such as understand not theirs. Of that book which Aristotle has left us, περὶ τῆς Ποιητικῆς, Horace his *Art of Poetry*, is an excellent comment, and, I believe, restores to us that Second Book of his concerning comedy, which is wanting in him.

Out of these two have been extracted the famous rules which the French call *les trois unités*, or the three unities, which ought to be observed in every regular play; namely, of time, place, and action.

The unity of time they comprehend in twenty-four hours, the compass of a natural day, or as near as it can be contrived; and the reason of it is obvious to every one,—that the time of the feigned action, or fable of the play, should be proportioned as near as can be to the duration of that time in which it is represented. Since therefore all plays are acted on the theater in a space of time much within the compass of twenty-four hours, that play is to be thought the nearest imitation of nature, whose plot or action is confined within that time. And by the same rule which concludes this general proportion of time, it follows that all the parts of it are (as near as may be) to be equally subdivided; namely, that one act take not up the supposed time of half a day, which is out of proportion to the rest; since the other four are then to be straitened within the compass of the remaining half: for it is unnatural, that one act, which being spoken or written, is not longer than the rest, should be supposed longer by the audience. It is therefore the poet's duty, to take care, that no act should be imagined to exceed the time in which it is represented on the stage; and that the intervals and inequalities of time be supposed to fall out between the acts.

This rule of time, how well it has been observed by the ancients, most of their plays will witness. You see them in their tragedies (wherein to follow this rule is certainly most difficult), from the very beginning of their plays, falling close into that part of the story which they intend for the action, or principal object of it, leaving the former part to be delivered by narration: so that they set the audience, as it were, at the post where the race is to be concluded; and saving them the tedious expectation of seeing the poet set out and ride the beginning of the course, they suffer you not to behold him, till he is in sight of the goal, and just upon you.

For the second unity, which is that of place, the ancients meant by it, that the scene ought to be continued through the play, in the same place where it was laid in the beginning; for the stage, on which it is represented, being but one and the same place, it is unnatural to conceive it many; and those far distant from one another. I will not deny, but by the variation of painted scenes, the fancy (which in these cases will contribute to its own deceit) may sometimes imagine it several places, with some appearance of probability; yet it still carries the greater likelihood of truth, if those places be supposed so near each other, as in the same town or city, which may all be comprehended under the larger denomination of one place; for a greater distance will bear no proportion to the shortness of time which is allotted, in the acting, to pass from one of them to another. For the observation of this, next to the ancients, the French are to be most commended. They tie themselves so strictly to the unity of place, that you never see in any of their plays, a scene changed in the middle of an act: if the act begins in a garden, a street, or chamber, 't is ended in the same place; and that you may know it to be the same, the stage is so supplied with persons, that it is never empty all the time: he who enters second, has business with him who was on before; and before the second quits the stage, a third appears who has business with him. This Corneille calls *la liaison des scènes*, the continuity or joining of the scenes; and 't is a good mark of a well-contrived play, when all the persons are known to each other, and every one of them has some affairs with all the rest.

As for the third unity, which is that of action, the ancients meant no other by it than what the logicians do by their *finis*, the end or scope of any action; that which is the first in intention, and last in execution. Now the poet is to aim at one great and complete action, to the carrying on of which all things in his play, even the very obstacles, are to be subservient; and the reason of this is as evident as any of the former.

For two actions equally labored and driven on by the writer, would destroy the unity of the poem; it would be no longer one play, but two: not but that there may be many actions in a play, as Ben Jonson has observed in his *Discoveries;* but they must be all subservient to the great one, which our language happily expresses in the name of underplots: such as in Terence's *Eunuch* is the difference and reconcilement of Thais and Phædria, which is not the chief business of the play, but promotes the marriage of Chærea and Chremes's sister, principally intended by the poet. There ought to be but one action (says Corneille), that is, one complete action, which leaves the mind of the audience in a full repose; but this cannot be brought to pass, but by many other imperfect actions, which conduce to it, and hold the audience in a delightful suspense of what will be.

If by these rules (to omit many other drawn from the precepts and practice of the ancients) we should judge our modern plays, 't is probable that few of them would endure the trial: that which should be the business of a day, takes up in some of them an age; instead of one action, they are the epitomes of a man's life, and for one spot of ground (which the stage should represent) we are sometimes in more countries than the map can show us.

But if we allow the ancients to have contrived well, we must acknowledge them to have written better. Questionless we are deprived of a great stock of wit in the loss of Menander among the Greek poets, and Cæcilius, Afranius, and Varius, among the Romans. We may guess at Menander's excellency, by the plays of Terence, who translated some of them; and yet wanted so much of him, that he was called by C. Cæsar the half-Menander; and may judge of Varius, by the testimonies of Horace, Martial, and Velleius Paterculus. 'T is probable that these, could they be recovered, would decide the controversy; but so long as Aristophanes and Plautus are extant, while the tragedies of Euripides, Sophocles, and Seneca, are in our hands, I can never see one of those plays which are now written, but it increases my admiration of the ancients. And yet I must acknowledge further, that to admire them as we ought, we should understand them better than we do. Doubtless many things appear flat to us, the wit of which depended on some custom or story, which never came to our knowledge; or perhaps on some criticism in their language, which being so long dead, and only remaining in their books, 't is not possible they should make us understand perfectly. To read Macrobius, explaining the propriety and elegancy of many words in Virgil, which I had before passed over without consideration, as common things, is enough to assure me, that I ought to think the same of Terence; and that in the purity of his style (which Tully so much valued, that he ever carried his works about him), there is yet left in him great room for admiration, if I knew but where to place it. In the meantime, I must desire you to take notice, that the greatest man of the last age (Ben Jonson) was willing to give place to them in all things: he was not only a professed imitator of Horace, but a learned plagiary of all the others; you track him everywhere in their snow. If Horace, Lucan, Petronius Arbiter, Seneca, and Juvenal, had their own from him, there are few serious thoughts which are new in him; you will pardon me, therefore, if I presume he loved their fashion, when he wore their clothes. But since I have otherwise a great veneration for him, and you, Eugenius, prefer him above all other poets, I will use no farther argument to you than his example: I will produce before you Father Ben, dressed in all the ornaments and colors of the ancients; you will need no other guide to our party, if you follow him; and whether you consider the bad plays of our age, or regard the good plays of the last, both the best and worst of the modern poets will equally instruct you to admire the ancients.

Crites had no sooner left speaking, but Eugenius, who had waited with some impatience for it, thus began:

I have observed in your speech, that the former part of it is convincing, as to what the moderns have profited by the rules of the ancients; but in the latter you are careful to conceal how much they have excelled them. We own all the helps we have from them, and want neither veneration nor gratitude, while we acknowledge that to overcome them we must make use of the advantages we have received from them; but to these assistances we have joined our own industry; for, had we sat down with a dull imitation of them, we might then have lost somewhat of the old perfection, but never acquired any that was new. We draw not therefore after their lines, but those of nature; and having the life before us, besides the experience of all they knew, it is no wonder if we hit some airs and features which they have missed. I deny not what you urge of arts and sciences, that they flourished in some ages more than others; but your instance in philosophy makes for me: for if natural causes be more known now than in the time of Aristotle, because more studied, it follows that poesy and other arts may, with the same pains, arrive still nearer to perfection; and, that granted, it will rest for you to prove that they wrought more perfect images of human life, than we; which seeing in your discourse you have avoided to make good, it shall now be my task to show you some part of their defects, and some few excellencies of the moderns. And I think there is none among us can imagine I do it enviously, or with purpose to detract from them; for what interest of fame or profit can the living lose by the reputation of the dead? On the other side, it is a great truth which Velleius Paterculus affirms: *Audita visis libentius laudamus; et præsentia invidia, præterita admiratione prosequimur; et his nos obrui, illis instrui credimus* [We praise things reported more willingly than those seen; and things of the present we pursue with envy, those of the past with admiration, believing ourselves to be hindered by the former and helped by the latter]. That praise or censure is certainly the most sincere, which unbribed posterity shall give us.

Be pleased then, in the first place, to take notice, that the Greek poesy, which Crites has affirmed to have arrived to perfection in the reign of the old comedy, was so far from it, that the distinction of it into acts was not known to them; or if it were, it is yet so darkly delivered to us, that we cannot make it out.

All we know of it is, from the singing of their chorus; and that too is so uncertain, that in some of their plays we have reason to conjecture they sung more than five times. Aristotle indeed divides the integral parts of a play into four. First, the *Protasis*, or entrance, which gives light only to the characters of the persons, and proceeds very little into any part of the action. Secondly, the *Epitasis*, or working up of the plot; where the play grows warmer, the design or action of it is drawing on, and you see something promising that it will come to pass. Thirdly, the *Catastasis*, called by the Romans, *Status*, the height and full growth of the play: we may call it properly the counter-turn, which destroys that expectation, embroils the action in new difficulties, and leaves you far distant from that hope in which it found you; as you may have observed in a violent stream, resisted by a narrow passage,—it runs round to an eddy, and carries back the waters with more swiftness than it brought them on. Lastly, the *Catastrophe*, which the Grecians called λύσις, the French *le dénouement*, and we the discovery, or unraveling of the plot: there you see all things settling again upon their first foundations, and, the obstacles which hindered the design or action of the play once removed, it ends with that resemblance of truth and nature, that the audience are satisfied with the conduct of it. Thus this great man delivered to us the image of a play; and I must confess it is so lively, that from thence much light has been derived to the forming it more perfectly into acts and scenes; but what poet first limited to five the number of the acts, I know not; only we see it so firmly established in the time of Horace, that he gives it for a rule in comedy: —*Neu brevior quinto, neu sit productior actu* [Let it be neither shorter nor longer than five acts]. So that you see the Grecians cannot be said to have consummated this art; writing rather by entrances, than by acts, and having rather a general indigested notion of a play, than knowing how, and where to bestow the particular graces of it.

But since the Spaniards at this day allow but three acts, which they call *jornadas*, to a play, and the Italians in many of theirs follow them, when I condemn the ancients, I declare it is not altogether because they have not five acts to every play, but because they have not confined themselves to one certain number; it is building a house without a model; and when they succeeded in such undertakings, they ought to have sacrificed to Fortune, not to the Muses.

Next, for the plot, which Aristotle called τὸ μῦθος, and often τῶν πραγμάτων σύνθεσις, and from him the Romans Fabula, it has already been judiciously observed by a late writer, that in their tragedies it was only some tale derived from Thebes or Troy, or at least something that happened in those two ages; which was worn so thread-bare by the pens of all the epic poets, and even by tradition itself of the talkative Greeklings (as Ben Jonson calls them), that before it came upon the stage, it was already known to all the audience; and the people, so soon as ever they heard the name of Œdipus, knew as well as the poet, that he had killed his father by a mistake, and committed incest with his mother, before the play; that they were now to hear of a great plague, an oracle, and the ghost of Laius; so that they sat with a yawning kind of expectation, till he was to come with his eyes pulled out, and speak a hundred or more verses in a tragic tone, in complaint of his misfortunes. But one Œdipus, Hercules, or Medea, had been tolerable; poor people, they escaped not so good cheap; they had still the *chapon bouillé* [boiled chicken] set before them, till their appetites were cloyed with the same dish, and, the novelty being gone, the pleasure vanished; so that one main end of dramatic poesy in its definition, which was to cause delight, was of consequence destroyed.

In their comedies, the Romans generally borrowed their plots from the Greek poets; and theirs was commonly a little girl stolen or wandered from her parents, brought back unknown to the city, there got with child by some lewd young fellow, who, by the help of his servant, cheats his father; and when her time comes to cry *Juno Lucina, fer opem* [Help me, O goddess of childbearing]! one or other sees a little box or cabinet which was carried away with her, and so discovers her to her friends, if some god do not prevent it, by coming down in a machine, and taking the thanks of it to himself.

By the plot you may guess much of the characters of the persons. An old father, who would willingly, before he dies, see his son well married; his debauched son, kind in his nature to his mistress, but miserably in want of money; a servant or slave, who has so much wit to strike in with him, and help to dupe his father; a braggadocio captain, a parasite, and a lady of pleasure.

As for the poor honest maid, on whom the story is built, and who ought to be one of the principal actors in the play, she is commonly a mute in it; she has the breeding of the old Elizabeth way, which was for maids to be seen, and not to be heard; and it is enough you know she is willing to be married, when the fifth act requires it.

These are plots built after the Italian mode of houses,—you see through them all at once; the characters are indeed the imitations of nature, but so narrow, as if they had imitated only an eye or an hand, and did not dare to venture on the lines of a face, or the proportion of a body.

But in how strait a compass soever they have bounded their plots and characters, we will pass it by, if they have regularly pursued them, and perfectly observed those three unities of time, place, and action; the knowledge of which you say is derived to us from them. But, in the first place, give me leave to tell you, that the unity of place, however it might be practised by them, was never any of their rules: we neither find it in Aristotle, Horace, or any who have written of it, till in our age the French poets first made it a precept of the stage. The unity of time, even Terence himself, who was the best and most regular of them, has neglected: his *Heautontimorumenos*, or Self-punisher, takes up visibly two days, says Scaliger; the two first acts concluding the first day, the three last the day ensuing; and Euripides, in tying himself to one day, has committed an absurdity never to be forgiven him; for in one of his tragedies he has made Theseus go from Athens to Thebes, which was about forty English miles, under the walls of it to give battle, and appear victorious in the next act; and yet, from the time of his departure to the return of the Nuntius, who gives the relation of his victory, Æthra and the Chorus have but thirty-six verses; which is not for every mile a verse.

The like error is as evident in Terence his *Eunuch*, when Laches, the old man, enters by mistake into the house of Thais; where, betwixt his exit, and the entrance of Pythias, who comes to give ample relation of the disorders he has raised within, Parmeno, who was left upon the stage, has not above five lines to speak. *C'est bien employer un temps si court* [This is making good use of so short a time], says the French poet, who furnished me with one of the observations: and almost all their tragedies will afford us examples of the like nature.

It is true, they have kept the continuity, or, as you called it, *liaison des scènes*, somewhat better: two do not perpetually come in together, talk, and go out together; and other two succeed them, and do the same throughout the act, which the English call by the name of single scenes; but the reason is, because they have seldom above two or three scenes, properly so called, in every act; for it is to be accounted a new scene, not only every time the stage is empty, but every person who enters, though to others, makes it so; because he introduces a new business. Now the plots of their plays being narrow, and the persons few, one of their acts was written in a less compass than one of our well-wrought scenes: and yet they are often deficient even in this. To go no farther than Terence, you find in the *Eunuch*, Antipho entering single in the midst of the third act, after Chremes and Pythias were gone off: in the same play you have likewise Dorias beginning the fourth act alone; and after she has made a relation of what was done at the Soldier's entertainment (which by the way was very inartificial, because she was presumed to speak directly to the audience, and to acquaint them with what was necessary to be known, but yet should have been so contrived by the poet, as to have been told by persons of the drama to one another, and so by them to have come to the knowledge of the people), she quits the stage, and Phædria enters next, alone likewise: he also gives you an account of himself, and of his returning from the country, in monologue; to which unnatural way of narration Terence is subject in all his plays. In his *Adelphi*, or Brothers, Syrus and Demea enter after the scene was broken by the departure of Sostrata, Geta, and Canthara; and indeed you can scarce look into any of his comedies, where you will not presently discover the same interruption.

But as they have failed both in laying of their plots, and in the management, swerving from the rules of their own art, by misrepresenting nature to us, in which they have ill satisfied one intention of a play, which was delight; so in the instructive part they have erred worse: instead of punishing vice, and rewarding virtue, they have often shown a prosperous wickedness, and an unhappy piety: they have set before us a bloody image of revenge in Medea, and given her dragons to convey her safe from punishment; a Priam and Astyanax murdered, and Cassandra ravished, and the lust and murder ending in the victory of him who acted them. In short, there is no indecorum in any of our modern plays, which, if I would excuse, I could not shadow with some authority from the ancients.

And one further note of them let me leave you: tragedies and comedies were not writ then, as they are now, promiscuously, by the same person; but he who found his genius bending to the one, never attempted the other way. This is so plain, that I need not instance to you that Aristophanes, Plautus, Terence, never, any of them, writ a tragedy; Æschylus, Euripides, Sophocles, and Seneca never meddled with comedy. The sock and buskin were not worn by the same poet. Having, then, so much care to excel in one kind, very little is to be pardoned them if they miscarried in it. And this would lead me to the consideration of their wit, had not Crites given me sufficient warning not to be too bold in my judgment of it; because, the languages being dead, and many of the customs and little accidents on which it depended lost to us, we are not competent judges of it. But though I grant that, here and there, we may miss the application of a proverb or a custom, yet a thing well said will be wit in all languages; and, though it may lose something in the translation, yet to him who reads it in the original, 't is still the same: he has an idea of its excellency, though it cannot pass from his mind into any other expression or words than those in which he finds it.

* * *

As Neander was beginning to examine *The Silent Woman*, Eugenius, earnestly regarding him: I beseech you, Neander (said he), gratify the company, and me in particular, so far as, before you speak of the play, to give us a character of the author; and tell us frankly your opinion, whether you do not think all writers, both French and English, ought to give place to him?

I fear (replied Neander) that, in obeying your commands, I shall draw some envy on myself. Besides, in performing them, it will be first necessary to speak somewhat of Shakespeare and Fletcher, his rivals in poesy; and one of them, in my opinion, at least his equal, perhaps his superior.

To begin then with Shakespeare. He was the man who of all modern, and perhaps ancient poets, had the largest and most comprehensive soul. All the images of nature were still present to him, and he drew them not laboriously, but luckily: when he describes anything, you more than see it, you feel it too. Those who accuse him to have wanted learning, give him the greater commendation: he was naturally learned; he needed not the spectacles of books to read nature; he looked inwards, and found her there. I cannot say he is everywhere alike; were he so, I should do him injury to compare him with the greatest of mankind. He is many times flat, insipid; his comic wit degenerating into clenches, his serious swelling into bombast. But he is always great, when some great occasion is presented to him: no man can say, he ever had a fit subject for his wit, and did not then raise himself as high above the rest of poets,

Quantum lenta solent inter viburna cupressi.
[As the cypresses tower above low-growing shrubs.]

The consideration of this made Mr. Hales of Eton say, that there was no subject of which any poet ever writ, but he would produce it much better done in Shakespeare; and however others are now generally preferred before him, yet the age wherein he lived, which had contemporaries with him, Fletcher and Jonson, never equaled them to him in their esteem: and in the last king's court, when Ben's reputation was at highest, Sir John Suckling, and with him the greater part of the courtiers, set our Shakespeare far above him.

Beaumont and Fletcher, of whom I am next to speak, had with the advantage of Shakespeare's wit, which was their precedent, great natural gifts, improved by study; Beaumont especially being so accurate a judge of plays, that Ben Jonson, while he lived, submitted all his writings to his censure, and 't is thought, used his judgment in correcting, if not contriving all his plots. What value he had for him, appears by the verses he writ to him; and therefore I need speak no farther of it. The first play that brought Fletcher and him in esteem, was their *Philaster;* for before that, they had written two or three very unsuccessfully: as the like is reported of Ben Jonson, before he writ *Every Man in his Humor.* Their plots were generally more regular than Shakespeare's, especially those which were made before Beaumont's death; and they understood and imitated the conversation of gentlemen much better; whose wild debaucheries, and quickness of wit in repartees, no poet before them could paint as they have done. Humor, which Ben Jonson derived from particular persons, they made it not their business to describe; they represented all the passions very lively, but above all, love. I am apt to believe the English language in them arrived to its highest perfection; what words have since been taken in, are rather superfluous than ornamental. Their plays are now the most pleasant and frequent entertainments of the stage; two of theirs being acted through the year for one of Shakespeare's or Jonson's: the reason is, because there is a certain gaiety in their comedies, and pathos in their more serious plays, which suits generally with all men's humors. Shakespeare's language is likewise a little obsolete, and Ben Jonson's wit comes short of theirs.

As for Jonson, to whose character I am now arrived, if we look upon him while he was himself (for his last plays were but his dotages), I think him the most learned and judicious writer which any theater ever had. He was a most severe judge of himself, as well as others. One cannot say he wanted wit, but rather that he was frugal of it. In his works you find little to retrench or alter. Wit and language, and humor also in some measure, we had before him; but something of art was wanting to the drama, till he came. He managed his strength to more advantage than any who preceded him. You seldom find him making love in any of his scenes, or endeavoring to move the passions; his genius was too sullen and saturnine to do it gracefully, especially when he knew he came after those who had performed both to such a height. Humor was his proper sphere; and in that he delighted most to represent mechanic people. He was deeply conversant in the ancients, both Greek and Latin, and he borrowed boldly from them: there is scarce a poet or historian among the Roman authors of those times, whom he has not translated in *Sejanus* and *Catiline.* But he has done his robberies so openly, that one may see he fears not to be taxed by any law. He invades authors like a monarch; and what would be theft in other poets, is only victory in him. With the spoils of these writers he so represents old Rome to us, in its rites, ceremonies, and customs, that if one of their poets had written either of his tragedies, we had seen less of it than in him. If there was any fault in his language, it was, that he weaved it too closely and laboriously, in his comedies especially: perhaps, too, he did a little too much Romanize our tongue, leaving the words which he translated almost as much Latin as he found them; wherein, though he learnedly followed their language, he did not enough comply with the idiom of ours. If I would compare him with Shakespeare, I must acknowledge him the more correct poet, but Shakespeare the greater wit. Shakespeare was the Homer, or father of our dramatic poets; Jonson was the Virgil, the pattern of elaborate writing; I admire him, but I love Shakespeare. To conclude of him; as he has given us the most correct plays, so in the precepts which he has laid down in his *Discoveries,* we have as many and profitable rules for perfecting the stage, as any wherewith the French can furnish us.

* * *

(1668)

SAMUEL PEPYS (1633–1703)

SAMUEL PEPYS became a clerk of the Navy Board in 1660, and rose to be Secretary of the Admiralty, retiring with a competence, on the change of government in 1689. His famous *Diary*, which covers the years from 1660 to 1669, was kept in shorthand, and is a remarkable deposit of immediate impressions, owing much of its charm to the complete artlessness with which it was set down, rather than to any literary art or intention of its author. But, though in no sense a man of letters, Pepys was undoubtedly a man of parts; he was lively, inquisitive, his interests were uncommonly varied, and he had unsurpassed opportunities for observing the leading persons and events of his day. The unique unconstraint of the *Diary* may be accounted for by the complete privacy with which it was kept. The popular notion of Pepys, as a mere gossip, is a misconception. A more just idea of his character and a glimpse of a very different kind of diary may be gained from the following entry in the *Diary* of John Evelyn:

'*26th May* 1703.—This day died Mr. Sam. Pepys, a very worthy, industrious, and curious person, none in England exceeding him in knowledge of the Navy, in which he had passed through all the most considerable offices (clerk of the Acts, and secretary of the Admiralty), all which he performed with great integrity. When King James II. went out of England, he laid down his office, and would serve no more, but withdrawing himself from all public affairs, he lived at Clapham with his partner Mr. Hewer, formerly his clerk, in a very noble house and sweet place, where he enjoyed the fruit of his labours in great prosperity. He was universally beloved, hospitable, generous, learned in many things, skilled in music, a very great cherisher of learned men of whom he had the conversation. His library and collection of other curiosities were of the most considerable, the models of ships especially. Besides what he published of an account of the Navy, as he found and left it, he had for divers years under his hand the *History of the Navy*, or *Navalia* as he called it; but how far advanced, and what will follow of his, is left, I suppose, to his sister's son Mr. Jackson, a young gentleman whom Mr. Pepys had educated in all sorts of useful learning, sending him to travel abroad, from whence he returned with extraordinary accomplishments, and worthy to be heir. Mr. Pepys had been for near forty years so much my particular friend, that Mr. Jackson sent me complete mourning, desiring me to be one to hold up the pall at his magnificent obsequies, but my indisposition hindered me from doing him this last office.'

From THE DIARY OF SAMUEL PEPYS

THE LANDING OF CHARLES II

May 25, 1660.—By the morning we were come close to the land, and everybody made ready to get on shore. The King and the two Dukes did eat their breakfast before they went, and there being set some ship's diet, they eat of nothing else but pease and pork, and boiled beef. Dr. Clerke, who eat with me, told me how the King had given 50*l*. to Mr. Shepley for my Lord's servants, and 500*l*. among the officers and common men of the ship. I spoke to the Duke of York about business, who called me Pepys by name, and upon my desire did promise me his future favour. Great expectation of the King's making some Knights, but there was none. About noon (though the brigantine that Beale made was there ready to carry him) yet he would go in my Lord's barge with the two Dukes. Our Captn. steered, and my Lord went along bare with him. I went, and Mr. Mansell, and one of the King's footmen, and a dog that the King loved, in a boat by ourselves, and so got on shore when the King did, who was received by General Monk with all imaginable love and respect at his entrance upon the land of Dover. Infinite the crowd of people and the horsemen, citizens, and noblemen of all sorts. The Mayor of the town come and gave him his white staffe, the badge of his place, which the King did give him again. The Mayor also presented him from the town a very rich Bible, which he took and said it was the thing that he loved above all things in the world. A canopy was provided for him to stand under, which he did, and talked awhile with General Monk and others, and so into a stately coach there set for him, and so away through the towne towards Canterbury, without making any stay at Dover. The shouting and joy expressed by all is past imagination. Seeing that my Lord did not stir out of his barge, I got into a boat and so into his barge. My Lord almost transported with joy that he had done all this without any the least blur or obstruction in the world, that could give offence to any, and with the great honour he thought it would be to him. Being overtook by the brigantine, my Lord and we went out of our barge into it, and so went on board with Sir W. Batten and the Vice and Rear-Admirals. At night I supped with the Captn., who told me what the King had given us. My Lord returned late, and at his coming did give me order to cause the marke to be gilded, and a Crowne and C. R. to be made at the head of the coach table, where the King to-day with his own hand did marke his height, which accordingly I caused the painter to do, and is now done as is to be seen.

May 26, 1660.—My Lord dined with the Vice-Admiral to-day, (who is as officious, poor man! as any spaniel can be; but I believe all to no purpose, for I believe he will not hold his place;) so I dined commander at the coach table.

PLAYS AND PLAYERS

October 11, 1660.—To walk in St. James's Park, where we observed the several engines at work to draw up water, with which sight I was very much pleased. Above all the rest, I liked that which Mr. Greatorex brought, which do carry up the water with a great deal of ease. Here, in the Park, we met with Mr. Salisbury, who took Mr. Creed and me to the Cockpit to see 'The Moore of Venice,' which was well done. Burt acted the Moore; by the same token, a very pretty lady that sat by me, called out, to see Desdemona smothered.

March 1, 1661.—After dinner Mr. Shepley and I in private talking about my Lord's intentions to go speedily into the country, but to what end we know not. We fear he is to go to sea with his fleet now preparing. But we wish that he could get his 4000*l.* per annum settled before he do go. To White-fryars, and saw 'The Bondman' acted; an excellent play and well done. But above all that ever I saw, Betterton do the Bondman the best.

March 2, 1661.—After dinner I went to the theatre, where I found so few people (which is strange, and the reason I do not know) that I went out again, and so to Salsbury Court, where the house as full as could be; and it seems it was a new play, 'The Queen's Maske,' wherein there are some good humours: among others, a good jeer to the old story of the Siege of Troy, making it to be a common country tale. But above all it was strange to see so little a boy as that was to act Cupid, which is one of the greatest parts in it.

March 23, 1661.—To the Red Bull (where I had not been since plays come up again) up to the tireing-room, where strange the confusion and disorder that there is among them in fitting themselves, especially here, where the clothes are very poore, and the actors but common fellows. At last into the pitt, where I think there was not above ten more than myself, and not one hundred in the whole house. And the play, which is called 'All's Lost by Lust,' poorly done; and with so much disorder, among others, in the musique-room the boy that was to sing a song, not singing it right, his master fell about his eares and beat him so, that it put the whole house in an uproar.

April 20, 1661.—To the Cockpitt; and there, by the favour of one Mr. Bowman, he and I got in, and there saw the King and Duke of York and his Duchesse, (which is a plain woman, and like her mother, my Lady Chancellor). And so saw 'The Humersome Lieutenant' acted before the King, but not very well done. But my pleasure was great to see the manner of it, and so many great beauties, but above all Mrs. Palmer, with whom the King do discover a great deal of familiarity.

August 27, 1661.—My wife and I to the theatre, and there saw 'The Joviall Crew,' where the King, Duke and Duchesse, and Madame Palmer, were; and my wife, to her great content, had a full sight of them all the while.

October 2, 1662.—At night hearing that there was a play at the Cockpit, (and my Lord Sandwich, who come to town last night, at it,) I do go thither, and by very great fortune did follow four or five gentlemen who were carried to a little private door in a wall, and so crept through a narrow place and come into one of the boxes next the King's, but so as I could not see the King or Queene, but many of the fine ladies, who yet are not really so handsome generally as I used to take them to be, but that they are finely dressed. Then we saw 'The Cardinall,' a tragedy I had never seen before, nor is there any great matter in it. The company that come in with me into the box, were all Frenchmen that could speak no English, but Lord! what sport they made to ask a pretty lady that they got among them that understood both French and English to make her tell them what the actors said.

March 2, 1667.—AFTER dinner with my wife to the King's house to see 'The Mayden Queene,' a new play of Dryden's, mightily commended for the regularity of it, and the strain and wit: and the truth is, there is a comical part done by Nell, which is Florimell, that I never can hope ever to see the like done again by man or woman. The King and Duke of York were at the play. But so great performance of a comical part was never, I believe, in the world before as Nell do this, both as a mad girle, then most and best of all when she comes in like a young gallant; and hath the motions and carriage of a spark the most that ever I saw any man have. It makes me, I confess, admire her.

April 15, 1667.—To the King's house by chance, where a new play: so full as I never saw it; I forced to stand all the while close to the very door till I took cold, and many people went away for want of room. The King and Queene and Duke of York and Duchesse there, and all the Court, and Sir W. Coventry. The play called, 'The Change of Crownes:' a play of Ned Howard's, the best that I ever saw at that house, being a great play and serious; only Lacy did act the country-gentleman come up to Court, who do abuse the Court with all the imaginable wit and plainness about selling of places, and doing every thing for money. The play took very much. Thence I to my new bookseller's, and there bought 'Hooker's Polity,' the new edition, and 'Dugdale's History of the Inns of Court,' of which there was but a few saved out of the fire. Carried my wife to see the new play I saw yesterday: but there, contrary to expectation, I find 'The Silent Woman.'

April 16, 1667.—KNIPP tells me the King was so angry at the liberty taken by Lacy's part to abuse him to his face, that he commanded they should act no more, till Moone went and got leave for them to act again, but not this play. The King mighty angry; and it was bitter indeed, but very fine and witty. I never was more taken with a play than I am with this 'Silent Woman,' as old as it is, and as often as I have seen it. There is more wit in it than goes to ten new plays. Pierce told us the story how in good earnest the King is offended with the Duke of Richmond's marrying. and Mrs. Stewart's sending the King his jewels again. As she tells it, it is the noblest romance and example of a brave lady that ever I read in my life.

October 5, 1667.—To the King's house; and there going in met with Knipp, and she took us up into the tireing-rooms; and to the women's shift, where Nell was dressing herself, and was all unready, and is very pretty, prettier than I thought. And into the scene-room, and there sat down, and she gave us fruit: and here I read the questions to Knipp, while she answered me, through all her part of 'Flora's Figarys,' which was acted to-day. But, Lord! to see how they were both painted, would make a man mad, and did make me loath them; and what base company of men comes among them, and how lewdly they talk! And how poor the men are in clothes, and yet what a show they make on the stage by candle-light, is very observable. But to see how Nell cursed, for having so few people in the pit, was strange; the other house carrying away all the people at the new play, and is said now-a-days to have generally most company, as being better players. By and by into the pit, and there saw the play, which is pretty good.

ROYALTY ABROAD

July 13, 1663.—I MET the Queene-Mother walking in the Pell Mell, led by my Lord St. Alban's. And finding many coaches at the Gate, I found upon enquiry that the Duchesse is brought to bed of a boy; and hearing that the King and Queene are rode abroad with the Ladies of Honour to the Parke, and seeing a great crowd of gallants staying here to see their return, I also staid walking up and down. By and by the King and Queene, who looked in this dress (a white laced waistcoate and a crimson short pettycoate, and her hair dressed *à la negligence*) mighty pretty; and the King rode hand in hand with her. Here was also my Lady Castlemaine rode among the rest of the ladies; but the King took, methought, no notice of her; nor when she light, did any body press (as she seemed to expect, and staid for it,) to take her down, but was taken down by her own gentlemen. She looked mighty out of humour, and had a yellow plume in her hat, (which all took notice of,) and yet is very handsome, but very melancholy: nor did any body speak to her, or she so much as smile or speak to any body. I followed them up into

White Hall, and into the Queene's presence, where all the ladies walked, talking and fiddling with their hats and feathers, and changing and trying one another's by one another's heads, and laughing. But it was the finest sight to me, considering their great beautys, and dress, that ever I did see in all my life. But, above all, Mrs. Stewart in this dresse, with her hat cocked and a red plume, with her sweet eye, little Roman nose, and excellent taille, is now the greatest beauty I ever saw, I think, in my life; and, if ever woman can, do exceed my Lady Castlemaine, at least in this dress: nor do I wonder if the King changes, which I verily believe is the reason of his coldness to my Lady Castlemaine.

THE GREAT FIRE

September 2, 1666.—SOME of our maids sitting up late last night to get things ready against our feast to-day, Jane called us up about three in the morning, to tell us of a great fire they saw in the City. So I rose, and slipped on my nightgown, and went to her window; and thought it to be on the back-side of Marke-lane at the farthest; but, being unused to such fires as followed, I thought it far enough off; and so went to bed again, and to sleep. About seven rose again to dress myself, and there looked out at the window, and saw the fire not so much as it was, and further off. So to my closet to set things to rights, after yesterday's cleaning. By and by Jane comes and tells me that she hears that above 300 houses have been burned down to-night by the fire we saw, and that it is now burning down all Fish Street, by London Bridge. So I made myself ready presently, and walked to the Tower; and there got up upon one of the high places, Sir J. Robinson's little son going up with me; and there I did see the houses at that end of the bridge all on fire, and an infinite great fire on this and the other side the end of the bridge; which, among other people, did trouble me for poor little Michell and our Sarah on the bridge. So down, with my heart full of trouble, to the Lieutenant of the Tower, who tells me that it begun this morning in the King's baker's house in Pudding-lane, and that it hath burned down St. Magnus's Church and most part of Fish Street already. So I down to the waterside, and there got a boat, and through bridge, and there saw a lamentable fire. Poor Michell's house, as far as the Old Swan, already burned that way, and the fire running further, that, in a very little time, it got as far as the Steele-yard, while I was there. Every body endeavoring to remove their goods, and flinging them into the river, or bringing them into lighters that lay off; poor people staying in their houses as long as till the very fire touched them, and then running into boats, or clambering from one pair of stairs, by the waterside, to another. And, among other things, the poor pigeons, I perceive, were loth to leave their houses, but hovered about the windows and balconys, till they burned their wings, and fell down. Having staid, and in an hour's time seen the fire rage every way; and nobody, to my sight, endeavoring to quench it, but to remove their goods, and leave all to the fire; and, having seen it get as far as the Steele-yard, and the wind mighty high, and driving it into the City; and everything, after so long a drought, proving combustible, even the very stones of churches; and, among other things, the poor steeple by which pretty Mrs. —— lives, and whereof my old schoolfellow Elborough is parson, taken fire in the very top, and there burned till it fell down; I to White Hall, with a gentleman with me, who desired to go off from the Tower, to see the fire, in my boat; and there up to the King's closet in the Chapel, where people come about me, and I did give them an account dismayed them all, and word was carried in to the King. So I was called for, and did tell the King and Duke of York what I saw; and that, unless his Majesty did command houses to be pulled down, nothing could stop the fire. They seemed much troubled, and the King commanded me to go to my Lord Mayor from him, and command him to spare no houses, but to pull down before the fire every way. The Duke of York bid me tell him, that if he would have any more soldiers, he shall; and so did my Lord Arlington afterwards, as a great secret. Here meeting with Captain Cocke, I in his coach, which he lent me, and Creed with me to Paul's; and there walked along Watling Street, as well as I could, every creature coming away loaden with goods to save, and, here and there, sick people carried away in beds. Extraordinary good goods carried on carts and on backs. At last met my Lord Mayor in Canning Street, like a man spent, with a handkercher about his neck. To the King's message, he cried, like a fainting woman, 'Lord! what can I do? I am spent: people will not obey me. I have been pulling down houses; but the fire overtakes us faster than we can do it.' That he needed no more soldiers; and that, for himself, he must go and refresh himself, having been up all night. So he left me, and I him, and walked home; seeing people all almost distracted, and no manner of means used to quench the fire. The houses, too, so very thick thereabouts, and full of matter for burning, as pitch and tar, in Thames Street; and warehouses of oyle, and wines, and brandy, and other things. Here I saw Mr. Isaac Houblon, the handsome man, prettily dressed and dirty at his door at Dowgate, receiving some of his brother's things, whose houses were on fire; and, as he says, have been removed twice already; and he doubts, as it soon proved, that they must be, in a little time, removed from his house also, which was a sad consideration. And to see the churches all filling with goods by people who themselves should have been quietly there at this time. By this time, it was about twelve o'clock; and so home, and there find my guests, who were Mr. Wood and his wife, Barbary Shelden, and also Mr. Moone: she mighty fine, and her husband, for aught I see, a likely man.

* * *

IN WESTMINSTER ABBEY

February 23, 1669.—To Westminster Abbey, and there did see all the tombs very finely, having one with us alone (there being other company this day to see the tombs, it being Shrove-Tuesday:) and here we did see, by particular favour, the body of Queen Katherine of Valois; and I had the upper part of her body in my hands, and I did kiss her mouth, reflecting upon it that I did kiss a queene, and that this was my birth-day, thirty-six years old, that I did kiss a queene. But here this man, who seems to understand well, tells me that the saying is not true that she was never buried, for she was buried; only when Henry the Seventh built his chapel, she was taken up and laid in this wooden coffin; but I did there see that in it the body was buried in a leaden one, which remains under the body to this day.

'UP AND BY COACH'

May 1, 1669.—Up betimes. My wife extraordinary fine with her flowered tabby gown that she made two years ago, now laced exceeding pretty; and indeed was fine all over. And mighty earnest to go, though the day was very lowering; and she would have me put on my fine suit, which I did. And so anon we went alone through the town with our new liveries of serge, and the horses' manes and tails tied with red ribbons, and the standards thus gilt with varnish, and all clean, and green reines, that people did mightily look upon us; and the truth is, I did not see any coach more pretty, though more gay, than ours all the day; the day being unpleasing, though the Park full of coaches, but dusty, and windy, and cold, and now and then a little dribbling of rain; and what made it worse, there were so many hackney coaches as spoiled the sight of the gentlemen's; and so we had little pleasure.

FAREWELL TO THE DIARY

May 31, 1669.—Up very betimes, and continued all the morning with W. Hewer, upon examining and stating my accounts, in order to the fitting myself to go abroad beyond sea, which the ill condition of my eyes and my neglect for a year or two hath kept me behindhand in, and so as to render it very difficult now and troublesome to my mind to do it; but I this day made a satisfactory entrance therein. Had another meeting with the Duke of York at White Hall on yesterday's work, and made a good advance: and so being called by my wife, we to the Park, Mary Batelier, and a Dutch gentleman, a friend of hers, being with us. Thence to 'The World's End,' a drinking house by the Park; and there merry, and so home late. And thus ends all that I doubt I shall ever be able to do with my own eyes in the keeping of my Journall, I being not able to do it any longer, having done now so long as to undo my eyes almost every time that I take a pen in my hand; and therefore, whatever comes of it, I must forbear: and therefore resolve, from this time forward to have it kept by my people in long-hand, and must be contented to set down no more than is fit for them and all the world to know; or if there be any thing, I must endeavour to keep a margin in my book open, to add here and there a note in short-hand with my own hand. And so I betake myself to that course, which is almost as much as to see myself go into my grave: for which, and all the discomforts that will accompany my being blind, the good God prepare me!

S. P.

May 31, 1669.

THE EIGHTEENTH CENTURY

IN the one hundred and ten years that elapsed between the landing of William of Orange (1688) and Nelson's victory in the Battle of the Nile (1798), England advanced from an isolated and rather insignificant position in European affairs to that of an island empire, with 'dominion over palm and pine,' and a relation to the struggling nations of Europe not badly typified by the Rock of Gibraltar which France and Spain tried vainly to wrest from her grasp near the end of the century. At the beginning of the period, Louis XIV could refer to Charles II as *mon pensionnaire, le roi d'Angleterre*, and indicate his contempt by dressing all his lackeys in the costume which Charles had made fashionable at the English court; at its close, this 'nation of shop-keepers' was the chief stumbling-block in the path of Napoleon. The intervening period was, for Europe in general, one of restless intellectual activity, of bold and cynical inquiry into the foundations in reason and common-sense of traditional usages and institutions, followed by a mighty surge of prophetic aspiration and hope for mankind.

With intellectual progress came sweeping political changes and reversals in the relative importance of the European peoples. Spain, long the stronghold of obscurantism and reaction, sank gradually into the position of a backward nation. Austria was held temporarily at a standstill; while Prussia was forged almost out of nothingness into the powerful nation that was to be the means of raising Germany to a place of eminence in world affairs and world thought. For a good part of the century France remained the dominant nation of Europe; but The Grand Alliance, organized by William of Orange after he became king of England, had checked the aggressions of Louis XIV, and under Louis XV the *ancien régime* went rapidly to the dogs. England, with the aid of her colonies, drove France from the western hemisphere, while Clive and Hastings were loosening her hold upon India and confirming that of England. Unable to hold her acquisitions in the New World, France was reduced to the counter-stroke of assisting the American colonies to gain their independence. England received an expensive lesson in colonial administration, and the nucleus of a great nation was added to the world.

Meantime, in France, the inspired common-sense of Voltaire, Montesquieu, and the Encyclopedists, and the romantic radicalism of Rousseau had been undermining the superstitious traditionalism which alone supported the old régime. As the century closed, the French people were just emerging from the most terrific of internal revolutions and, with renewed vigor, were preparing, under Napoleon, again to try conclusions with England.

It must not be inferred that eighteenth-century England was in any sense a Utopia. To the eyes of the French Montesquieu, English institutions presented almost an ideal framework of popular government. In reality, it was only a framework, as yet; for so corrupt were the methods of constituting Parliament, and so shameless was the use of patronage, that the government was only in a very limited sense representative of the people. Yet even so, England had a head start over her Continental rivals, in that the English people, having passed through their revolutionary period in the preceding century, and having settled the principles upon which church and state were to be founded, were now disposed to adjourn further consideration of abstract principles and questions of conscience and devote their energies to the development of industry and trade, and to colonization and war so far as they related thereto. As a consequence of this attitude of mind and this concentration of effort, the wealth of the nation increased rapidly during the first half of the eighteenth century; but there was little of ideality in its politics or of spirituality in its religion. No English statesman has been more shrewd or more cynical than Walpole; the English clergy has never been so listless and useless as in his day; the tone of English literature, as a whole, has never been so smart, or so worldly, as in the Age of Pope.

Everything was done to promote the wealth of the nation, nothing to equalize its distribution. As England changed from an agricultural to a mining, manufacturing, and trading nation, some were enriched while others were impoverished. The invention of the steam-engine, the spinning jenny, and other machines, and the increase of mining, aggravated this maladjustment. The condition of the villager and the agricultural laborer became intolerable. Until the time of Pitt, no effective voice was raised for reform. But about the middle of the century there began a spiritual change. The conscience of the nation seemed to come to life and its soul to take fire. The impulse was apparent in the more idealistic policies and fiery patriotism of Pitt, and the popularity they won him; and, a little later, in the noble political utterances of Burke. It swept the masses like a prairie fire in the religious revival led by the Wesleys and others, penetrated and revivified the church, and produced practical results in the deep humanitarian movement of the ensuing era. It was an informing courage, no doubt, in the resplendent victories of Nelson and Wellington. And, not least, it found lasting expression in another great outburst of moral and imaginative beauty, in the poetry and fiction of the so-called Romantic Revival.

NOTEWORTHY DATES

ENGLISH LITERATURE AND HISTORY		FOREIGN LITERATURE AND HISTORY	
1702–14	Queen Anne	1694–1778	Voltaire
1704	Swift's *Tale of a Tub*	1704	Battle of Blenheim
1709–11	*The Tatler*	1709	Charles XII died
1711	Pope's *Essay on Criticism*	1712–78	Jean Jacques Rousseau
1711–12	*The Spectator*	1713	Treaty of Utrecht
1714–27	George I	1715–35	Le Sage's *Gil Blas*
1719	Defoe's *Robinson Crusoe*	1715–74	Louis XV, of France
1720	South Sea Bubble		
1721–42	Walpole's Ministry	1721	Montesquieu's *Lettres persanes*
1726	Swift's *Gulliver's Travels*		
1727–60	George II		
1728	Pope's *Dunciad*	1729–81	Gotthold Ephraim Lessing
1738	The Wesleys' *Hymns*		
1740	Richardson's *Pamela*	1740–86	Frederick the Great
1749	Fielding's *Tom Jones*	1749–1832	Johann Wolfgang von Goethe
1751	Gray's *Elegy*		
1755	Johnson's *Dictionary*	1756–63	Seven Years' War
1760–1820	George III		
1765	Percy's *Reliques*	1765	Stamp Act
1766	Goldsmith's *Vicar of Wakefield*	1766	Lessing's Laocoön
1775	Burke's *Speech on Conciliation*	1773	Goethe's *Götz*
1775	Sheridan's *The Rivals*	1774–92	Louis XVI, of France
1776–88	Gibbon's *Decline and Fall*	1776	Declaration of Independence
1779–81	Johnson's *Lives*		
1785	Cowper's *The Task*	1782	Schiller's *Die Räuber*
1786	Burns' *Poems* (Kilmarnock)	1789	Fall of the Bastille
1791	Boswell's *Life of Johnson*	1789–95	French Revolution
1798	*Lyrical Ballads*	1799	Napoleon First Consul

DANIEL DEFOE (1661-1731)

Defoe was the son of a nonconformist butcher, and attended a dissenting school where according to his own account, he received a sound training in English and other modern languages as well as in the classics. His master, Morton, was a man of advanced ideas in education, and afterwards became vice-president of Harvard College. Defoe took part in the rebellion of Monmouth, engaged unsuccessfully in trade, and welcomed the Revolution. When William III was attacked as a foreigner, Defoe took up his defence in a satirical poem, *The True-Born Englishman*, which ran through twenty-one editions and was sold in thousands in the streets. He published a number of political pamphlets, and one of them, *The Shortest Way with the Dissenters*, was so successful in its irony that it deceived both parties into accepting it as a serious plea for high church principles. When it became known that the author was a dissenter and that the tract was really a plea for toleration, the high church party were furious at the fraud practised upon them, and the dissenters were too sore and bewildered to defend him. Defoe was fined, imprisoned, and condemned to be exposed to public derision in the pillory (1703). But the people covered the pillory with flowers, drank his health, and bought copies of his *Hymn to the Pillory*, in which he denounced his antagonists as 'scandals to the times,' who 'are at a loss to find his guilt, and can't commit his crimes.' Defoe was not kept long in prison, and in 1704 he began the publication of the *Review*, which was continued till 1713 and marks an important advance in the development of journalism. As a journalist Defoe showed unwearied diligence, unsurpassed enterprise and resourcefulness, and a keen sense of popular interest. There are few features of the modern newspaper which are not represented in his writings. He wrote sometimes for one party, sometimes for another, and for some years he conducted Tory papers in the interests of the Whig government, by which he was employed in the secret service. His style is remarkably simple and direct, and the 'stories' he invented can hardly be distinguished from genuine narratives. Of his numerous works, which would make a considerable library if reprinted, the one which has earned most enduring popularity is *Robinson Crusoe* (1720), a realistic autobiography of a sailor cast away upon a desolate island. It has been translated into almost every literary language, has captivated readers of every stage of maturity, and has been followed by countless imitations.

From THE TRUE-BORN ENGLISHMAN

A true-born Englishman's a contradiction!
In speech, an irony; in fact, a fiction!
A banter made to be a test of fools!
Which those that use it, justly ridicules;
A metaphor invented to express   5
A man akin to all the universe!

For as the Scots, as learned men have said,
Throughout the world their wandering seed
    have spread,
So open-handed England, 't is believed,
Has all the gleanings of the world received.   10
Some think, of England 't was, our Savior meant
The Gospel should, to all the world be sent,
Since, when the blessed sound did hither reach,
They to all nations might be said to preach.

'T is well that virtue gives nobility;   15
How shall we else the want of birth and blood
    supply?
Since scarce one family is left alive,
Which does not from some foreigner derive.
Of sixty thousand English gentlemen
Whose names and arms in registers remain,   20
We challenge all our heralds to declare
Ten families which English Saxons are!

France justly boasts the ancient noble line
Of Bourbon, Montmorency, and Lorraine.
The Germans, too, their House of Austria show,
And Holland their invincible Nassau—   26
Lines which in heraldry were ancient grown,
Before the name of Englishman was known.
Even Scotland, too, her elder glory shows!
Her Gordons, Hamiltons, and her Monroes;   30
Douglas, Mackays, and Grahams, names well
    known
Long before ancient England knew her own.

But England, modern to the last degree,
Borrows or makes her own nobility;
And yet she boldly boasts of pedigree!   35
Repines that foreigners are put upon her,
And talks of her antiquity and honor!
Her S[ackvil]les, S[avi]les, C[eci]ls, Dela[me]res,
M[ohu]ns and M[ontag]ues, D[ura]s, and
    V[ee]res;

Not one have English names, yet all are English peers!
Your Houblons, Papillons, and Lethuliers
Pass now for true born English knights and squires,
And make good senate members, or lord mayors,
Wealth (howsoever got) in England, makes Lords, of mechanics! gentlemen, of rakes!
Antiquity and birth are needless here.
'T is impudence and money make a p[ee]r!

* * *

THE CONCLUSION

Then let us boast of ancestors no more,
Or deeds of heroes done in days of yore,
In latent records of the ages past,
Behind the rear of time, in long oblivion placed.
For if our virtues must in lines descend,
The merit with the families would end,
And intermixtures would most fatal grow,
For vice would be hereditary too;
The tainted blood would of necessity,
Involuntary wickedness convey!

Vice, like ill-nature, for an age or two,
May seem a generation to pursue:
But virtue seldom does regard the breed,
Fools do the wise, and wise men fools succeed.
What is it to us, what ancestors we had?
If good, what better? or what worse, if bad?
Examples are for imitation set,
Yet all men follow virtue with regret.

Could but our ancestors retrieve their fate,
And see their offspring thus degenerate;
How we contend for birth and names unknown,
And build on their past actions, not our own;
They'd cancel records, and their tombs deface,
And openly disown the vile degenerate race!
For fame of families is all a cheat;
'T is personal virtue only makes us great!

(1701)

THE SHORTEST WAY WITH THE DISSENTERS

SIR ROGER L'ESTRANGE tells us a story in his collection of Fables, of the cock and the horses. The cock was gotten to roost in the stable among the horses; and there being no racks or other conveniences for him, it seems he was forced to roost upon the ground. The horses jostling about for room and putting the cock in danger of his life, he gives them this grave advice, 'Pray, gentlefolks! let us stand still! for fear we should tread upon one another!'

There are some people in the world, who, now they are unperched, and reduced to an equality with other people, and under strong and very just apprehensions of being further treated as they deserve, begin with Esop's cock, to preach up peace and union and the Christian duty of moderation; forgetting that when they had the power in their hands, those graces were strangers in their gates!

It is now near fourteen years, that the glory and peace of the purest and most flourishing church in the world has been eclipsed, buffeted, and disturbed by a sort of men whom God in his providence has suffered to insult over her, and bring her down. These have been the days of her humiliation and tribulation. She has borne with an invincible patience the reproach of the wicked; and God has at last heard her prayers, and delivered her from the oppression of the stranger.

And now, they find their day is over, their power gone, and the throne of this nation possessed by a royal, English, true, and ever constant member of, and friend to, the Church of England. Now they find that they are in danger of the Church of England's just resentments. Now, they cry out, 'Peace!' 'Union!' 'Forbearance!' and 'Charity!': as if the Church had not too long harbored her enemies under her wing, and nourished the viperous brood, till they hiss and fly in the face of the mother that cherished them!

No, gentlemen, the time of mercy is past, your day of grace is over, you should have practised peace, and moderation, and charity, if you expected any yourselves.

We have heard none of this lesson for fourteen years past. We have been huffed and bullied with your Act of Toleration. You have told us you are the Church established by law, as well as others; have set up your canting synagogues at our church doors; and the Church and her members have been loaded with reproaches, with oaths, associations, abjurations, and what not! Where has been the mercy, the forbearance, the charity you have shown to tender consciences of the Church of England that could not take oaths as fast as you made them; that, having sworn allegiance to their lawful and rightful king, could not dispense with that oath, their king being still alive, and swear to your new hodge-podge of a Dutch government? These have been turned out of their livings, and they and their families left to starve; their estates double taxed to carry on a war they had no hand in, and you got nothing by!

What account can you give of the multitudes you have forced to comply, against their consciences, with your new sophistical politics, who, like new converts in France, sin because they cannot starve? And now the tables are turned upon you, you must not be persecuted! It is not a Christian spirit!

You have butchered one king, deposed another king, and made a mock king of a third, and yet, you could have the face to expect to be employed and trusted by the fourth! Anybody that did not know the temper of your party, would stand amazed at the impudence as well as the folly to think of it!

Your management of your Dutch monarch, whom you reduced to a mere King of Clubs, is enough to give any future princes such an idea of your principles as to warn them sufficiently from coming into your clutches; and, God be thanked, the Queen is out of your hands, knows you, and will have a care of you!

There is no doubt but the supreme authority of a nation has in itself a power, and a right to that power, to execute the laws upon any part of that nation it governs. The execution of the known laws of the land, and that with but a gentle hand neither, was all that the fanatical party of this land have ever called persecution. This they have magnified to a height that the sufferings of the Huguenots in France were not to be compared with them. Now to execute the known laws of a nation upon those who transgress them, after having first been voluntarily consenting to the making of those laws, can never be called persecution, but justice. But justice is always violence to the party offending, for every man is innocent in his own eyes.

The first execution of the laws against Dissenters in England was in the days of King James I; and what did it amount to? Truly, the worst they suffered was, at their own request, to let them go to New England, and erect a new colony; and give them great privileges, grants, and suitable powers; keep them under protection, and defend them against all invaders; and receive no taxes or revenue from them!

This was the cruelty of the Church of England. Fatal lenity! It was the ruin of that excellent prince, King Charles I. Had King James sent all the Puritans in England away to the West Indies, we had been a national unmixed church. The Church of England had been kept undivided and entire!

To requite the lenity of the father, they take up arms against the son, conquer, pursue, take, imprison, and at last put to death the anointed of God, and destroy the very being and nature of government: setting up a sordid impostor, who had neither title to govern, nor understanding to manage, but supplied that want, with power, bloody and desperate counsels and craft, without conscience.

Had not King James I withheld the full execution of the laws: had he given them strict justice, he had cleared the nation of them! And the consequences had been plain; his son had never been murdered by them, nor the monarchy overwhelmed. It was too much mercy shown them that was the ruin of his posterity, and the ruin of the nation's peace. One would think the Dissenters should not have the face to believe that we are to be wheedled and canted into peace and toleration, when they know that they have once requited us with a civil war, and once with an intolerable and unrighteous persecution, for our former civility.

Nay, to encourage us to be easy with them, it is apparent that they never had the upper hand of the Church but they treated her with all the severity, with all the reproach and contempt as was possible! What peace and what mercy did they show the loyal gentry of the Church of England, in the time of their triumphant Commonwealth? How did they put all the gentry of England to ransom, whether they were actually in arms for the king or not, making people compound for their estates, and starve their families! How did they treat the clergy of the Church of England, sequester the ministers, devour the patrimony of the Church and divide the spoil, by sharing the Church lands among their soldiers, and turning her clergy out to starve! Just such measure as they have meted, should be measured to them again!

Charity and love is the known doctrine of the Church of England, and it is plain she has put it in practice towards the Dissenters, even beyond what they ought, till she has been wanting to herself, and in effect unkind to her own sons; particularly, in the too much lenity of King James I, mentioned before. Had he so rooted the Puritans from the face of the land, which he had an opportunity early to have done, they had not had the power to vex the Church, as since they have done.

In the days of King Charles II, how did the

Church reward their bloody doings with lenity and mercy! Except the barbarous regicides of the pretended court of justice, not a soul suffered for all the blood in an unnatural war. King Charles came in all mercy and love, cherished them, preferred them, employed them, withheld the rigor of the law and oftentimes, even against the advice of his Parliament, gave them liberty of conscience; and how did they requite him? With the villainous contrivance to depose and murder him and his successor, at the Rye House Plot!

King James II, as if mercy was the inherent quality of the family, began his reign with unusual favor to them. Nor could their joining with the Duke of Monmouth against him, move him to do himself justice upon them. But that mistaken prince, thinking to win them by gentleness and love, proclaimed a universal liberty to them, and rather discountenanced the Church of England than them. How they requited him, all the world knows!

The late reign is too fresh in the memory of all the world to need a comment. How under pretense of joining with the Church in redressing some grievances, they pushed things to that extremity, in conjunction with some mistaken gentlemen, as to depose the late king; as if the grievance of the nation could not have been redressed but by the absolute ruin of the prince.

Here is an instance of their temper, their peace, and charity!

To what height they carried themselves during the reign of a king of their own, how they crept into all places of trust and profit; how they insinuated themselves into the favor of the king, and were at first preferred to the highest places in the nation, how they engrossed the ministry; and, above all, how pitifully they managed, is too plain to need any remarks.

But particularly, their mercy and charity, the spirit of union they tell us so much of, has been remarkable in Scotland. If any man would see the spirit of a Dissenter, let him look into Scotland. There, they made entire conquest of the Church, trampled down the sacred orders and suppressed the episcopal government, with an absolute, and, as they supposed, irretrievable victory; though it is possible they may find themselves mistaken!

Now it would be a very proper question to ask their impudent advocate, the *Observator*, 'Pray how much mercy and favor did the members of the Episcopal Church find in Scotland from the Scotch Presbyterian government?' And I shall undertake for the Church of England, that the Dissenters shall still receive as much here, though they deserve but little.

In a small treatise of *The Sufferings of the Episcopal Clergy in Scotland*, it will appear what usage they met with. How they not only lost their livings; but, in several places, were plundered and abused in their persons, the ministers that could not conform, were turned out with numerous families and no maintenance, and hardly charity enough left to relieve them with a bit of bread. The cruelties of the party were innumerable, and are not to be attempted in this short piece.

And now, to prevent the distant cloud which they perceive to hang over their heads from England, with a true Presbyterian policy, they put in for a union of nations—that England might unite their Church with the Kirk of Scotland, and their assembly of Scotch canting long-cloaks in our convocation. What might have been, if our fanatic Whiggish statesmen continued, God only knows; but we hope we are out of fear of that now.

It is alleged by some of the faction, and they have begun to bully us with it, that 'if we won't unite with them, they will not settle the Crown with us again; but when her Majesty dies, will choose a king for themselves!'

If they won't, we must make them; and it is not the first time we have let them know that we are able. The crowns of these kingdoms have not so far disowned the right of succession, but they may retrieve it again; and if Scotland thinks to come off from a successive to an elective state of government, England has not promised not to assist the right heir, and put him into possession, without any regards to their ridiculous settlements.

These are the gentlemen! these, their ways of treating the Church, both at home and abroad!

Now let us examine the reasons they pretend to give, why we should be favorable to them; why we should continue and tolerate them among us.

First. They are very numerous, they say. They are a great part of the nation, and we cannot suppress them!

To this, may be answered:

First. They are not so numerous as the Protestants in France: and yet the French king effectually cleared the nation of them at once; and we don't find he misses them at home!

But I am not of the opinion they are so numerous as is pretended. Their party is more numerous than their persons; and those mistaken people of the Church who are misled and deluded by their wheedling artifices to join with them, make their party the greater: but those will open their eyes when the government shall set heartily about the work, and come off from them, as some animals, which they say, always desert a house when it is likely to fall.

Secondly. The more numerous, the more dangerous; and therefore the more need to suppress them; and God has suffered us to bear them as goads in our sides, for not utterly extinguishing them long ago.

Thirdly. If we are to allow them, only because we cannot suppress them; then it ought to be tried, whether we can or not? And I am of opinion it is easy to be done, and could prescribe ways and means, if it were proper: but I doubt not the government will find effectual methods for the rooting of the contagion from the face of this land.

Another argument they use, which is this. That this is a time of war, and we have need to unite against the common enemy.

We answer, this common enemy had been no enemy, if they had not made him so. He was quiet, in peace, and no way disturbed and encroached upon us; and we know no reason we had to quarrel with him.

But further. We make no question but we are able to deal with this common enemy without their help: but why must we unite with them, because of the enemy? Will they go over to the enemy, if we do not prevent it, by a union with them? We are very well contented they should, and make no question, we shall be ready to deal with them and the common enemy too; and better without them than with them. Besides, if we have a common enemy, there is the more need to be secure against our private enemies. If there is one common enemy, we have the less need to have an enemy in our bowels!

It was a great argument some people used against suppressing the old money, that 'it was a time of war, and it was too great a risk for the nation to run. If we should not master it, we should be undone!' And yet the sequel proved the hazard was not so great, but it might be mastered, and the success was answerable. The suppressing the Dissenters is not a harder work, nor a work of less necessity to the public. We can never enjoy a settled, uninterrupted union and tranquillity in this nation, till the spirit of Whiggism, faction, and schism is melted down like the old money!

To talk of difficulty is to frighten ourselves with chimeras and notions of a powerful party, which are indeed a party without power. Difficulties often appear greater at a distance than when they are searched into with judgment, and distinguished from the vapors and shadows that attend them.

We are not to be frightened with it! This age is wiser than that, by all our own experience, and theirs too! King Charles I had early suppressed this party, if he had taken more deliberate measures. In short, it is not worth arguing, to talk of their arms. Their Monmouths and Shaftesburys and Argyles are gone! Their Dutch sanctuary is at an end! Heaven has made way for their destruction, and if we do not close with the divine occasion, we are to blame ourselves! and may hereafter remember that we had, once, an opportunity to serve the Church of England, by extirpating her implacable enemies; and having let slip the minute that Heaven presented, may experimentally complain, *post est occasio calva* [opportunity is bald behind].

Here are some popular objections in the way.

As first, the queen has promised them to continue them in their tolerated liberty; and has told us she will be a religious observer of her word.

What her Majesty will do we cannot help, but what, as the head of the Church, she ought to do, is another case. Her Majesty has promised to protect and defend the Church of England, and if she cannot effectually do that without the destruction of the Dissenters, she must, of course, dispense with one promise to comply with another.

But to answer this cavil more effectually. Her Majesty did never promise to maintain the toleration to the destruction of the Church; but it was upon supposition that it may be compatible with the well-being and safety of the Church, which she had declared she would take especial care of. Now if these two interests clash, it is plain her Majesty's intentions are to uphold, protect, defend, and establish the Church; and this, we conceive, is impossible.

Perhaps it may be said, that the Church is in no immediate danger from the Dissenters, and therefore it is time enough.

But this is a weak answer. For first: if the danger be real, the distance of it is no argument against, but rather a spur to quicken us to prevention, lest it be too late hereafter.

And secondly: here is the opportunity, and the only one, perhaps, that ever the Church had to secure herself and destroy her enemies.

The representatives of the nation have now an opportunity. The time is come which all good men have wished for, that the gentlemen of England may serve the Church of England, now they are protected and encouraged by a Church of England queen!

What will you do for your sister in the day that she shall be spoken for?

If ever you will establish the best Christian church in the world; if ever you will suppress the spirit of enthusiasm; if ever you will free the nation from the viperous brood that have so long sucked the blood of their mother; if ever you will leave your posterity free from faction and rebellion, this is the time! This is the time to pull up this heretical weed of sedition, that has so long disturbed the peace of the Church, and poisoned the good corn!

But, says another hot and cold objector, this is renewing fire and faggot, reviving the Act, *de heretico comburendo* [for the burning of heretics]. This will be cruelty in its nature, and barbarous to all the world.

I answer, it is cruelty to kill a snake or a toad in cold blood, but the poison of their nature makes it a charity to our neighbors to destroy those creatures, not for any personal injury received, but for prevention; not for the evil they have done, but the evil they may do. Serpents, toads, vipers, etc., are noxious to the body, and poison the sensitive life: their poison the soul, corrupt our posterity, ensnare our children, destroy the vitals of our happiness, our future felicity, and contaminate the whole mass!

Shall any law be given to such wild creatures? Some beasts are for sport, and the huntsmen give them the advantages of ground, but some are knocked on the head by all possible ways of violence and surprise.

I do not prescribe fire and faggot; but as Scipio said of Carthage, *Delenda est Carthago* [Carthage must be destroyed]! they are to be rooted out of this nation, if ever we will live in peace, serve God, or enjoy our own. As for the manner, I leave it to those hands who have a right to execute God's justice on the nation's and the Church's enemies.

But if we must be frighted from this justice, under these specious pretenses, and odious sense of cruelty, nothing will be effected. It will be more barbarous to our own children and dear posterity, when they shall reproach their fathers, as we ours, and tell us, 'You had an opportunity to root out this cursed race from the world under the favor and protection of a true Church of England queen, and out of your foolish pity, you spared them, because, forsooth, you would not be cruel! And now our Church is suppressed and persecuted, our religion trampled under foot, our estates plundered, our persons imprisoned, and dragged to gaols, gibbets, and scaffolds! Your sparing this Amalekite race is our destruction! Your mercy to them proves cruelty to your poor posterity!'

How just will such reflections be when our posterity shall fall under the merciless clutches of this uncharitable generation; when our Church shall be swallowed up in schism, faction, enthusiasm, and confusion; when our government shall be devolved upon foreigners, and our monarchy dwindled into a republic!

It would be more rational for us, if we must spare this generation, to summon our own to a general massacre; and as we have brought them into the world free, to send them out so; and not betray them to destruction by our supine negligence, and then cry, 'It is mercy!'

Moses was a merciful meek man; and yet with what fury did he run through the camp, and cut the throats of three and thirty thousand of his dear Israelites that were fallen into idolatry. What was the reason? It was mercy to the rest, to make these examples, to prevent the destruction of the whole army.

How many millions of future souls we save from infection and delusion, if the present race of poisoned spirits were purged from the face of the land!

It is vain to trifle in this matter. The light foolish handling of them by mulcts, fines, etc.; 't is their glory and their advantage! If the gallows instead of the counter, and the galleys instead of the fines were the reward of going to a conventicle to preach or hear, there would not be so many sufferers. The spirit of martyrdom is over. They that will go to church to be chosen sheriffs and mayors, would go to forty churches rather than be hanged!

If one severe law were made and punctually executed that whoever was found at a conventicle should be banished the nation, and the preacher be hanged, we should soon see an end of the tale. They would all come to church again, and one age would make us all one again.

To talk of five shillings a month for not coming to the sacrament, and one shilling per week, for not coming to church: this is such a way of converting people as was never known. This is selling them a liberty to transgress, for so much money.

If it be not a crime, why don't we give them full license? And if it be, no price ought to compound for the committing of it, for that is selling a liberty to people to sin against God and the government.

If it be a crime of the highest consequence, both against the peace and welfare of the nation, the glory of God, the good of the Church, and the happiness of the soul, let us rank it among capital offenses, and let it receive a punishment in proportion to it.

We hang men for trifles, and banish them for things not worth naming; but that an offense against God and the Church, against the welfare of the world, and the dignity of religion shall be bought off for five shillings: this is such a shame to a Christian government that it is with regret I transmit it to posterity.

If men sin against God, affront his ordinances, rebel against his church, and disobey the precepts of their superiors; let them suffer, as such capital crimes deserve. So will religion flourish, and this divided nation be once again united.

And yet the title of barbarous and cruel will soon be taken off from this law too. I am not supposing that all the Dissenters in England should be hanged or banished. But as in case of rebellions and insurrections, if a few of the ringleaders suffer, the multitude are dismissed; so a few obstinate people being made examples, there is no doubt but the severity of the law would find a stop in the compliance of the multitude.

To make the reasonableness of this matter out of question, and more unanswerably plain, let us examine for what it is that this nation is divided into parties and factions; and let us see how they can justify a separation; or we of the Church of England can justify our bearing the insults and inconveniences of the party.

One of their leading pastors, and a man of as much learning as most among them, in his *Answer* to a pamphlet entitled *An Enquiry into the Occasional Conformity*, hath these words, p. 27:—'Do the religion of the Church and the meeting houses make two religions? Wherein do they differ? The substance of the same religion is common to them both, and the modes and accidents are the things in which only they differ.' P. 28:—'Thirty-nine Articles are given us for the summary of our religion; thirty-six contain the substance of it wherein we agree; three are additional appendices, about which we have some differences.'

Now, if, as by their own acknowledgment, the Church of England is a true church, and the difference is only in a few 'modes and accidents,' why should we expect that they will suffer the gallows and galleys, corporal punishment and banishment, for these trifles? There is no question, but they will be wiser. Even their own principles won't bear them out in it.

They will certainly comply with the laws, and with reason. And though, at the first, severity may seem hard, the next age will feel nothing of it; the contagion will be rooted out. The disease being cured, there will be no need of the operation. But if they should venture to transgress, and fall into the pit, all the world must condemn their obstinacy, as being without ground from their own principles.

Thus the pretense of cruelty will be taken off, and the party actually suppressed, and the disquiets they have so often brought upon the nation, prevented.

Their numbers and their wealth make them haughty; and that is so far from being an argument to persuade us to forbear them, that it is a warning to us, without any more delay, to reconcile them to the unity of the Church, or remove them from us.

At present, Heaven be praised! they are not so formidable as they have been, and it is our own fault if ever we suffer them to be so. Providence and the Church of England seem to join in this particular, that now the destroyers of the nation's peace may be overturned; and to this end, the present opportunity seems to put into our hands.

To this end, her present Majesty seems reserved to enjoy the crown, that the ecclesiastic as well as civil rights of the nation may be restored by her hand.

To this end, the face of affairs has received such a turn in the process of a few months as never has been before. The leading men of the nation, the universal cry of the people, the unanimous request of the clergy agree in this, that the deliverance of our Church is at hand!

For this end, has Providence given such a parliament, such a convocation, such a gentry, and such a queen, as we never had before.

And what may be the consequences of a neglect of such opportunities? The succession of the crown has but a dark prospect. Another Dutch turn may make the hopes of it ridiculous, and the practice impossible. Be the house of our future princes ever so well inclined, they will be foreigners. Many years will be spent in suiting the genius of strangers to this crown, and the interests of the nation; and how many ages it may be before the English throne be filled with so much zeal and candor, so much tenderness and hearty affection to the Church, as we see it now covered with, who can imagine?

It is high time, then, for the friends of the Church of England to think of building up and establishing her in such a manner that she may be no more invaded by foreigners, nor divided by factions, schisms, and error.

If this could be done by gentle and easy methods, I should be glad: but the wound is corroded, the vitals begin to mortify, and nothing but amputation of members can complete the cure. All the ways of tenderness and compassion, all persuasive arguments have been made use of in vain.

The humor of the Dissenters has so increased among the people, that they hold the Church in defiance, and the house of God is an abomination among them. Nay, they have brought up their posterity in such prepossessed aversion to our holy religion, that the ignorant mob think we are all idolators and worshippers of Baal, and account it a sin to come within the walls of our churches. The primitive Christians were not more shy of a heathen temple, or of meat offered to idols, nor the Jews of swine's flesh, than some of our Dissenters are of the church and the divine service solemnized therein.

The obstinacy must be rooted out, with the profession of it. While the generation are left at liberty daily to affront God Almighty, and dishonor his holy worship, we are wanting in our duty to God, and to our mother, the Church of England.

How can we answer it to God, to the Church, and to our posterity, to leave them entangled with fanaticism, error, and obstinacy, in the bowels of the nation; to leave them an enemy in their streets, that, in time, may involve them in the same crimes, and endanger the utter extirpation of the religion of the nation.

What is the difference betwixt this, and being subject to the power of the Church of Rome, from whence we have reformed? If one be an extreme to the one hand, and one on another, it is equally destructive to the truth to have errors settled among us, let them be of what nature they will. Both are enemies of our Church, and of our peace; and why should it not be as criminal to admit an enthusiast as a Jesuit? Why should the papist with his seven sacraments be worse than the Quaker with no sacraments at all? Why should religious houses be more intolerable than meeting houses?

Alas, the Church of England! What with popery on one hand, and schismatics on the other, how has she been crucified between two thieves. Now, let us crucify the thieves!

Let her foundations be established upon the destruction of her enemies! The doors of mercy being always open to the returning part of the deluded people, let the obstinate be ruled with the rod of iron!

Let all true sons of so holy and oppressed a mother, exasperated by her afflictions, harden their hearts against those who have oppressed her.

And may God Almighty put it into the hearts of all the friends of truth, to lift up a standard against pride and Antichrist, that the posterity of the sons of error may be rooted out from the face of this land, for ever!

(1702)

PREFACE TO THE FIRST VOLUME OF THE REVIEW

WHEN authors present their works to the world, like a thief at the gallows, they make a speech to the people.

The author, indeed, has something like this to say, too, 'Good people all, take warning by me!' I have studied to inform and to direct the world, and what have I had for my labor?

Profit, the press would not allow; and therein I am not deceived, for I expected none. But good manners and good language, I thought I might expect, because I gave no other; and it were but just to treat mankind as we would be treated by them. But neither has this been paid me, in debt to custom and civility.

How often have my ears, my hands, and my head been to be pulled off! Impotent bullies! that attacked by truth, and their vices stormed, fill the air with rhodomontades and indecencies; but never show their faces to the resentment truth had a just cause to entertain for them.

I have passed through clouds of clamor, cavil, raillery, and objection; and have this satisfaction, that truth being the design, *Finis coronat* [The end crowns the work]!

I am never forward to value my own performances. 'Let another man's mouth praise thee!' said the Wise Man; but I cannot but own myself infinitely pleased, and more than satisfied that wise men read this paper with pleasure, own the just observations in it, and have voted it useful.

The first design I allow is not yet pursued, and indeed I must own the field is so large, the design so vast, and the necessary preliminaries so many that though I cannot yet pass for an old man, I must be so, if I live to go through with it.

This volume has passed through my descriptions of the French grandeur, with its influence on the affairs of Poland, Sweden, and Hungary. What assaults have I met with from the impatience of the readers; what uneasiness of friends, lest I was turned about to the enemy; I leave to their reading the sheets to discover.

How is this age unqualified to bear feeling truth, how unwilling to hear what we do not like, though ever so necessary to know!

And yet if this French monarchy were not very powerful, vastly strong, its power terrible, its increasing encroaching measures formidable; why do we (and justly too) applaud, extol, congratulate, and dignify the victorious Duke of Marlborough at such a rate? If it had been a mean and contemptible enemy, how shall we justify the English army's march through so many hazards; the nation's vast charge; the daily just concern in every article of this war; and (as I have frequently hinted), why not beat them, all this while?

They who have made, or may make, an ill use of the true plan of French greatness, which I have laid down, must place it to the account of their own corrupted prejudiced thoughts. My design is plain—to tell you the strength of your enemy, that you may fortify yourselves in due proportion, and not go out with your ten thousands against his twenty thousands.

In like manner, I think myself very oddly handled in the case of the Swedes and the Hungarians. How many complaints of ambassadors for the one, and of fellow Protestants for the other! And yet, after the whole story is finished, I have this felicity (than which no author can desire a greater) viz., not one thing I ever affirmed, but was exactly true; not one conjecture have I made, but has appeared to be rational; not one inference drawn, but the consequences have proved just; and not one thing guessed at, but what has come to pass.

I am now come home to England, and entered a little into our own affairs. Indeed, I have advanced some things as to trade, navies, seamen, etc., which some may think a little arrogant, because perfectly new. But as I have offered nothing but what I am always ready to make appear practicable, I finish my apology by saying to the world, 'Bring me to the test; and the rest, I leave to time.'

In the bringing the story of France down to the matter of trade, I confess myself surprisingly drawn into a vast wilderness of a subject so large that I know not where it will end. The misfortune of which is, that thinking to have finished it with this volume, I found myself strangely deceived, and indeed amazed, when I found the story of it intended to be the end of this volume, and hardly enough of it entered upon to say it is begun.

However, the volume being of necessity to be closed, I am obliged to content myself with taking what is here as an introduction to the next volume; and to give this notice, that the matter of our English trade appears to be a thing of such consequence to be treated of, so much pretended to, and so little understood, that nothing could be more profitable to the readers, more advantageous to the public interest of this nation, or more suitable to the greatness of this undertaking, than to make an essay at the evils, causes, and remedies of our general negoce.

I have been confirmed in my opinion of the consequences and benefit of this undertaking by a crowd of entreaties from persons of the best judgment, and some of extraordinary genius in these affairs; whose letters are my authority for this clause, and whose arguments are too forcible for me to resist.

And this is to me a sufficient apology for a vast digression from the affairs of France, which were really in my first design, and to which my title at first too straitly bound me.

Whoever shall live to see this undertaking finished, if the author (or some better pen after him) shall bring 20 or 30 volumes of this work on the stage, it will not look so preposterous as it seems now to have one whole volume to be employed on the most delightful as well as profitable subject of the English trade.

Things at short distance look large, and public patience is generally very short; but when remote, the case alters, and people see the reason of things in themselves. It is this remote prospect of affairs which I have before me. And this makes me not so much regard the uneasiness people show at the story being frequently broken abruptly, and running great lengths before it revolves upon itself again; but as time and the course of things will bring all about again, and make the whole to be of a piece with itself, I am content to wait the approbation of the readers, till such time as the thing itself forces it from the at present impatient readers.

Readers are strange judges when they see but part of the design. It is a new thing for an author to lay down his thoughts piece-meal. Importunate cavils assault him every day. They claim to be answered to-day! before tomorrow! and are so far from staying till the story is finished, that they can hardly stay till their letters come to hand, but follow the first with a second, that with clamor, and this sometimes with threatening scoffs, banters, and raillery!

Thus I am letter-baited by querists; and I think my trouble in writing civil private answers to teasing and querulous epistles, has been equal to, if not more troublesome than, all the rest of this work. Through these difficulties I steer with as much temper and steadiness as I can. I still hope to give satisfaction in the conclusion; and it is this alone that makes the continuing of the work tolerable to me. If I cannot, I have made my essay.

If those that know these things better than I would bless the world with further instructions, I shall be glad to see them, and very far from interrupting or discouraging them, as these do me.

Let not those gentlemen who are critics in style, in method, or manner, be angry, that I have never pulled off my cap to them, in humble excuse for my loose way of treating the world as to language, expression, and politeness of phrase. Matters of this nature differ from most things a man can write. When I am busied writing essays and matters of science, I shall address them for their aid, and take as much care to avoid their displeasure as becomes me; but when I am upon the subject of trade and the variety of casual story, I think myself a little loose from the bonds of cadence and perfections of style, and satisfy myself in my study to be explicit, easy, free, and very plain. And for all the rest, *Nec careo, nec curo* [I neither need it, nor pay attention to it]!

I had a design to say something on the entertaining part of this paper; but I have so often explained myself on that head, that I shall not trouble the world much about it.

When I first found the design of this paper (which had its birth *in tenebris*) [in darkness], I considered it would be a thing very historical, very long; and though it could be much better performed than ever I was likely to do it, this age had such natural aversion to a solemn and tedious affair, that however profitable, it would never be diverting, and the world would never read it.

To get over this difficulty, the secret hand (I make no doubt) that directed this birth into the world, dictated to make some sort of entertainment or amusement at the end of every paper, upon the immediate subject, then on the tongues of the town—which innocent diversion would hand on the more weighty and serious part of the design into the heads and thoughts of those to whom it might be useful.

I take this opportunity to assure the world that receiving or answering letters of doubts, difficulties, cases, and questions, as it is a work I think myself very meanly qualified for, so it was the remotest thing from my first design of anything in the world; and I could be heartily glad, if the readers of this paper would excuse me from it yet. But I see it cannot be, and the world will have it done. I have therefore done my best to oblige them; but as I have not one word to say for my performance that way, so I leave it where I found it, a mere circumstance casually and undesignedly annexed to the work, and a curiosity, though honestly endeavored to be complied with.

If the method I have taken in answering questions has pleased some wiser men more than I expected it would, I confess it is one of the chief reasons why I was induced to continue it.

I have constantly adhered to this rule in all my answers (and I refer my reader to his observation for the proof), that from the loosest and lightest questions, I endeavor to draw some useful inferences, and, if possible, to introduce something solid, and something solemn in applying it. The custom of the ancients in writing fables is my very laudable pattern for this; and my firm resolution, in all I write, to exalt virtue, expose vice, promote truth, and help men to serious reflection, is my first moving cause, and last directed end.

If any shall make ill use of, wrest, wrongly

interpret, wilfully or otherwise mistake the honest design of this work; let such wait for the end, when I doubt not, the author will be cleared by their own vote, their want of charity will appear, and they be self-condemned till they come to acknowledge their error, and openly to justify

Their humble servant, D. F.

(1705)

THE EDUCATION OF WOMEN
FROM AN ESSAY UPON PROJECTS

I HAVE often thought of it as one of the most barbarous customs in the world, considering us as a civilized and a Christian country, that we deny the advantages of learning to women. We reproach the sex every day with folly and impertinence; while I am confident, had they the advantages of education equal to us, they would be guilty of less than ourselves.

One would wonder, indeed, how it should happen that women are conversible at all, since they are only beholden to natural parts for all their knowledge. Their youth is spent to teach them to stitch and sew, or make baubles. They are taught to read, indeed, and perhaps to write their names, or so; and that is the height of a woman's education. And I would but ask any who slight the sex for their understanding, what is a man (a gentleman, I mean) good for, that is taught no more? I need not give instances, or examine the character of a gentleman, with a good estate, of a good family, and with tolerable parts; and examine what figure he makes for want of education.

The soul is placed in the body like a rough diamond, and must be polished, or the luster of it will never appear. And 't is manifest, that as the rational soul distinguishes us from brutes, so education carries on the distinction, and makes some less brutish than others. This is too evident to need any demonstration. But why then should women be denied the benefit of instruction? If knowledge and understanding had been useless additions to the sex, God Almighty would never have given them capacities; for he made nothing needless. Besides, I would ask such, what they can see in ignorance, that they should think it a necessary ornament to a woman? or how much worse is a wise woman than a fool? or what has the woman done to forfeit the privilege of being taught? Does she plague us with her pride and impertinence? Why did we not let her learn, that she might have had more wit? Shall we upbraid women with folly, when 't is only the error of this inhuman custom that hindered them from being made wiser?

The capacities of women are supposed to be greater, and their senses quicker than those of the men; and what they might be capable of being bred to, is plain from some instances of female wit, which this age is not without, which upbraids us with injustice, and looks as if we denied women the advantages of education, for fear they should vie with the men in their improvements. . . .

They should be taught all sorts of breeding suitable both to their genius and quality. And in particular, music and dancing, which it would be cruelty to bar the sex of because they are their darlings. But besides this, they should be taught languages, as particularly French and Italian, and I would venture the injury of giving a woman more tongues than one. They should, as a particular study, be taught all the graces of speech, and all the necessary air of conversation, which our common education is so defective in that I need not expose it. They should be brought to read books, and especially history; and so to read as to make them understand the world, and be able to know and judge of things when they hear of them.

To such whose genius would lead them to it, I would deny no sort of learning; but the chief thing, in general, is to cultivate the understandings of the sex, that they may be capable of all sorts of conversation; that their parts and judgments being improved, they may be as profitable in their conversation as they are pleasant.

Women, in my observation, have little or no difference in them, but as they are or are not distinguished by education. Tempers, indeed, may in some degree influence them, but the main distinguishing part is their breeding.

The whole sex are generally quick and sharp —I believe, I may be allowed to say, generally so: for you rarely see them lumpish and heavy when they are children, as boys will often be. If a woman be well bred, and taught the proper management of her natural wit, she proves generally very sensible and retentive.

And, without partiality, a woman of sense and manners is the finest and most delicate part of God's creation, the glory of her Maker, and the great instance of his singular regard to man, his darling creature, to whom he gave the best gift either God could bestow or man re ceive. And 't is the sordidest piece of folly and ingratitude in the world, to withhold from the sex the due luster which the advantages of education give to the natural beauty of their minds.

A woman well bred and well taught, furnished with the additional accomplishments of knowledge and behavior, is a creature without comparison. Her society is the emblem of sublimer enjoyments, her person is angelic, and her conversation heavenly. She is all softness and sweetness, peace, love, wit, and delight. She is every way suitable to the sublimest wish; and the man that has such a one to his portion, has nothing to do but to rejoice in her, and be thankful.

On the other hand, suppose her to be the very same woman, and rob her of the benefit of education, and it follows:—

If her temper be good, want of education makes her soft and easy.

Her wit, for want of teaching, makes her impertinent and talkative.

Her knowledge, for want of judgment and experience, makes her fanciful and whimsical.

If her temper be bad, want of breeding makes her worse; and she grows haughty, insolent, and loud.

If she be passionate, want of manners makes her a termagant and a scold, which is much at one with lunatic.

If she be proud, want of discretion (which still is breeding) makes her conceited, fantastic, and ridiculous.

And from these she degenerates to be turbulent, clamorous, noisy, nasty, the devil! . . .

The great distinguishing difference, which is seen in the world between men and women, is in their education; and this is manifested by comparing it with the difference between one man or woman, and another.

And herein it is that I take upon me to make such a bold assertion, that all the world are mistaken in their practice about women. For I cannot think that God Almighty ever made them so delicate, so glorious creatures, and furnished them with such charms, so agreeable and so delightful to mankind, with souls capable of the same accomplishments with men; and all, to be only stewards of our houses, cooks, and slaves.

Not that I am for exalting the female government in the least; but, in short, I would have men take women for companions, and educate them to be fit for it. A woman of sense and breeding will scorn as much to encroach upon the prerogative of man, as a man of sense will scorn to oppress the weakness of the woman. But if the women's souls were refined and improved by teaching, that word would be lost. To say, the weakness of the sex, as to judgment, would be nonsense; for ignorance and folly would be no more to be found among women than men.

I remember a passage, which I heard from a very fine woman. She had wit and capacity enough, an extraordinary shape and face, and a great fortune, but had been cloistered up all her time, and for fear of being stolen, had not had the liberty of being taught the common necessary knowledge of women's affairs. And when she came to converse in the world her natural wit made her so sensible of the want of education, that she gave this short reflection on herself: 'I am ashamed to talk with my very maids,' says she, 'for I don't know when they do right or wrong. I had more need go to school, than be married.'

I need not enlarge on the loss the defect of education is to the sex, nor argue the benefit of the contrary practice. 'T is a thing will be more easily granted than remedied. This chapter is but an essay at the thing; and I refer the practice to those happy days (if ever they shall be) when men shall be wise enough to mend it.

(1697)

JONATHAN SWIFT (1667-1745)

Swift was born in Dublin—a chance which all his life he chose to resent as the first of many insults of fortune. At Kilkenny Grammar School and at Trinity College, Dublin, where he was 'wild, witty, and poor,' he had to be supported by one relative, and for the next decade, he was a discontented dependent of another, Sir William Temple. During one of his disagreements with the latter, he left in a huff, crossed to Ireland, and went into holy orders. Dryden had crushed his poetic inclinations and incurred his lasting resentment by the solid remark, 'Cousin Swift, you will never be a poet.' He did not discover his genius for satire until about his thirtieth year, when he wrote *A Tale of a Tub* and *The Battle of the Books*. These were published anonymously in 1704, preceded and followed by a rapid volley of pamphlets upon subjects then in dispute. For about ten years, he spent much of his time in London, mingled with the reigning wits in their homes and clubs, amused his leisure with squibs and verses, and projected the Scriblerus Club whose chief members, besides himself, were Pope, Arbuthnot, Atterbury, Parnell and Gay. In 1710, personal interest united with conscience to engage him on the Tory side. He edited the *Examiner* (1710-11), threw himself ferociously into political intrigue, and, for a time, wielded an extraordinary personal influence. But, though he could dictate the preferment of bishops, the author of *A Tale of a Tub* was powerless to secure a high appointment for himself. He had to be content with the Deanery of St. Patrick's, at Dublin, whither after the disruption of the Tory party in 1714, he permanently retired,—an embittered and disappointed man. Ten years later, an undertaking suspected of being an attempt to exploit the Irish people by a scheme of debased coinage called forth the most angry, unscrupulous, and masterly of his controversial series, the *Letters of M. B. Drapier* (1724). Here, and in his *Modest Proposal for preventing the Children of Poor People from being a Burden to their Parents*, and similar ironical extravagances, he voiced his savage indignation at the unjust and heart-rending poverty of his adopted people. After the death of 'the unfortunate Stella' (Esther Johnson), Swift's powerful faculties began to show signs of derangement. 'I shall die at the top,' he had once said, pointing to a tree which had been blasted by lightning,—and the words were prophetic. Already, in the last portions of *Gulliver's Travels* (1726), we see the horrible evidences of 'a mind diseased.' In 1741, he became 'furiously insane,' then lapsed into idiocy, and at last was laid to rest in his own cathedral, in the city of his birth, 'where,' in the words of his epitaph, which he himself composed, 'ferocious indignation can no longer tear the heart'—

Ubi sæva indignatio
Cor ulterius lacerare nequit.

In dealing with Swift, it is never safe to forget the deadly purpose and 'intent to kill' which inspires his grim horseplay. He bitterly hated the world's shams and inconsistencies. His reckless and irreverent energy of thought and the acrid irony of his style made him dangerous to all he touched. His humor was like fire; what it played over, it consumed.

From A TALE OF A TUB

SECTION II

Once upon a time there was a man who had three sons by one wife, and all at a birth, neither could the midwife tell certainly which was the eldest. Their father died while they were young; and upon his death-bed, calling the lads to him, spoke thus:—

'Sons, because I have purchased no estate, nor was born to any, I have long considered of some good legacies to bequeath you; and at last, with much care, as well as expense, have provided each of you (here they are) a new coat. Now, you are to understand that these coats have two virtues contained in them; one is, that with good wearing they will last you fresh and sound as long as you live; the other is, that they will grow in the same proportion with your bodies, lengthening and widening of themselves, so as to be always fit. Here; let me see them on you before I die. So; very well; pray, children, wear them clean, and brush them often. You will find in my will[1] (here it is) full instructions in every particular concerning the wearing and management of your coats; wherein you must be very exact, to avoid the penalties I have appointed for every transgression or

[1] The New Testament. [The foot-notes, throughout, are Swift's.]

neglect, upon which your future fortunes will entirely depend. I have also commanded in my will that you should live together in one house like brethren and friends, for then you will be sure to thrive, and not otherwise.'

Here, the story says, this good father died, and the three sons went all together to seek their fortunes.

I shall not trouble you with recounting what adventures they met for the first seven years, any farther than by taking notice that they carefully observed their father's will, and kept their coats in very good order: that they traveled through several countries, encountered a reasonable quantity of giants, and slew certain dragons.

Being now arrived at the proper age for producing themselves, they came up to town, and fell in love with the ladies, but especially three, who about that time were in chief reputation; the Duchess d'Argent, Madame de Grands Titres, and the Countess d'Orgueil. On their first appearance our three adventurers met with a very bad reception; and soon with great sagacity guessing out the reason, they quickly began to improve in the good qualities of the town; they writ, and rallied, and rhymed, and sung, and said, and said nothing; they drank, and fought, and whored, and slept, and swore, and took snuff; they went to new plays on the first night, haunted the chocolate-houses, beat the watch, lay on bulks, and got claps; they bilked hackney-coachmen, ran in debt with shop-keepers, and lay with their wives; they killed bailiffs, kicked fiddlers down stairs, eat at Locket's, loitered at Will's; they talked of the drawing-room, and never came there; dined with lords they never saw; whispered a duchess, and spoke never a word; exposed the scrawls of their laundress for billets-doux of quality; came ever just from court, and were never seen in it; attended the levee *sub dio* [in the open air]; got a list of peers by heart in one company, and with great familiarity retailed them in another. Above all, they constantly attended those committees of senators who are silent in the house and loud in the coffee-house; where they nightly adjourn to chew the cud of politics, and are encompassed with a ring of disciples, who lie in wait to catch up their droppings. The three brothers had acquired forty other qualifications of the like stamp, too tedious to recount, and by consequence were justly reckoned the most accomplished persons in the town; but all would not suffice, and the ladies aforesaid continued still inflexible. To clear up which difficulty I must, with the reader's good leave and patience, have recourse to some points of weight, which the authors of that age have not sufficiently illustrated.

For about this time it happened a sect arose[1] whose tenets obtained and spread very far, especially in the *grand monde*, and among everybody of good fashion. They worshipped a sort of idol,[2] who, as their doctrine delivered, did daily create men by a kind of manufactory operation. This idol they placed in the highest parts of the house, on an altar erected about three foot; he was shown in the posture of a Persian emperor, sitting on a superficies, with his legs interwoven under him. This god had a goose for his ensign; whence it is that some learned men pretend to deduce his original from Jupiter Capitolinus. At his left hand, beneath the altar, hell seemed to open and catch at the animals the idol was creating; to prevent which, certain of his priests hourly flung in pieces of the uninformed mass, or substance, and sometimes whole limbs already enlivened, which that horrid gulf insatiably swallowed, terrible to behold. The goose was also held a subaltern divinity or *deus minorum gentium* [god of the lesser peoples], before whose shrine was sacrificed that creature whose hourly food is human gore, and who is in so great renown abroad for being the delight and favorite of the Egyptian Cercopithecus.[3] Millions of these animals were cruelly slaughtered every day to appease the hunger of that consuming deity. The chief idol was also worshipped as the inventor of the yard and needle; whether as the god of seamen, or on account of certain other mystical attributes, has not been sufficiently cleared.

The worshippers of this deity had also a system of their belief, which seemed to turn upon the following fundamentals. They held the universe to be a large suit of clothes, which invests everything; that the earth is invested by the air; the air is invested by the stars; and the stars are invested by the *primum mobile*. Look on this globe of earth, you will find it to be a very complete and fashionable dress. What is that which some call land but a fine coat

[1] This is an occasional satire upon dress and fashion, in order to introduce what follows.
[2] By this idol is meant a tailor.
[3] The Egyptians worshipped a monkey, which animal is very fond of eating lice, styled here creatures that feed on human gore.

faced with green? or the sea, but a waistcoat of water-tabby? Proceed to the particular works of the creation, you will find how curious journeyman Nature has been to trim up the vegetable beaux; observe how sparkish a periwig adorns the head of a beech, and what a fine doublet of white satin is worn by the birch. To conclude from all, what is man himself but a microcoat,[1] or rather a complete suit of clothes with all its trimmings? As to his body there can be no dispute; but examine even the acquirements of his mind, you will find them all contribute in their order towards furnishing out an exact dress: to instance no more; is not religion a cloak, honesty a pair of shoes worn out in the dirt, self-love a surtout, vanity a shirt, and conscience a pair of breeches? . . .

These postulata being admitted, it will follow in due course of reasoning that those beings, which the world calls improperly suits of clothes, are in reality the most refined species of animals; or, to proceed higher, that they are rational creatures or men. For, is it not manifest that they live, and move, and talk, and perform all other offices of human life? are not beauty, and wit, and mien, and breeding, their inseparable proprieties? in short, we see nothing but them, hear nothing but them. Is it not they who walk the streets, fill up parliament-, coffee-, play-, bawdy-houses? 'T is true, indeed, that these animals, which are vulgarly called suits of clothes, or dresses, do, according to certain compositions, receive different appellations. If one of them be trimmed up with a gold chain, and a red gown, and white rod, and a great horse, it is called a lord-mayor: if certain ermines and furs be placed in a certain position, we style them a judge; and so an apt conjunction of lawn and black satin we entitle a bishop.

Others of these professors, though agreeing in the main system, were yet more refined upon certain branches of it; and held that man was an animal compounded of two dresses, the natural and celestial suit, which were the body and the soul: that the soul was the outward, and the body the inward clothing; that the latter was *ex traduce*; but the former of daily creation and circumfusion; this last they proved by scripture, because in them we live, and move, and have our being; as likewise by philosophy, because they are all in all, and all in every part. Besides, said they, separate these two and you will find the body to be only a senseless unsavory carcase; by all which it is manifest that the outward dress must needs be the soul.

To this system of religion were tagged several subaltern doctrines, which were entertained with great vogue: as particularly the faculties of the mind were deduced by the learned among them in this manner; embroidery was sheer wit, gold fringe was agreeable conversation, gold lace was repartee, a huge long periwig was humor, and a coat full of powder was very good raillery —all which required abundance of *finesse* and *delicatesse* to manage with advantage, as well as a strict observance after times and fashions.

I have, with much pains and reading, collected out of ancient authors this short summary of a body of philosophy and divinity, which seems to have been composed by a vein and race of thinking very different from any other systems either ancient or modern. And it was not merely to entertain or satisfy the reader's curiosity, but rather to give him light into several circumstances of the following story; that, knowing the state of dispositions and opinions in an age so remote, he may better comprehend those great events which were the issue of them. I advise, therefore, the courteous reader to peruse with a world of application, again and again, whatever I have written upon this matter. And leaving these broken ends, I carefully gather up the chief thread of my story and proceed.

These opinions, therefore, were so universal, as well as the practices of them, among the refined part of court and town, that our three brother adventurers, as their circumstances then stood, were strangely at a loss. For, on the one side, the three ladies they addressed themselves to, whom we have named already, were at the very top of the fashion, and abhorred all that were below it but the breadth of a hair. On the other side, their father's will was very precise; and it was the main precept in it, with the greatest penalties annexed, not to add to or diminish from their coats one thread, without a positive command in the will. Now, the coats their father had left them were, 't is true, of very good cloth, and besides so neatly sewn, you would swear they were all of a piece; but at the same time very plain, and with little or no ornament: and it happened that before they were a month in town great shoulder-knots[2] came up— straight all the world was shoulder-knots—no

---

[1] Alluding to the word microcosm, or a little world, as man has been called by philosophers.

[2] By this is understood the first introducing of pageantry, and unnecessary ornaments in the Church, such as were neither for convenience nor edification, as a shoulder-knot, in which there is neither symmetry nor use.

approaching the ladies' *ruelles* without the *quota* of shoulder-knots. That fellow, cries one, has no soul; where is his shoulder-knot? Our three brethren soon discovered their want by sad experience, meeting in their walks with forty mortifications and indignities. If they went to the playhouse, the door-keeper showed them into the twelvepenny gallery; if they called a boat, says a waterman, 'I am first sculler'; if they stepped to the Rose to take a bottle, the drawer would cry, 'Friend, we sell no ale'; if they went to visit a lady, a footman met them at the door with 'Pray send up your message.' In this unhappy case they went immediately to consult their father's will, read it over and over, but not a word of the shoulder-knot. What should they do?—what temper should they find? —obedience was absolutely necessary, and yet shoulder-knots appeared extremely requisite. After much thought one of the brothers, who happened to be more book-learned than the other two, said he had found an expedient. "T is true,' said he, 'there is nothing here in this will, *totidem verbis* [in so many words], making mention of shoulder-knots: but I dare conjecture we may find them *inclusive*, or *totidem syllabis* [in so many syllables].' This distinction was immediately approved by all, and so they fell again to examine the will; but their evil star had so directed the matter that the first syllable was not to be found in the whole writing. Upon which disappointment, he who found the former evasion took heart, and said, 'Brothers, there are yet hopes; for though we cannot find them *totidem verbis*, nor *totidem syllabis*, I dare engage we shall make them out *tertio modo* [by a third method] or *totidem literis* [in so many letters].' This discovery was also highly commended, upon which they fell once more to the scrutiny, and picked out S, H, O, U, L, D, E, R; when the same planet, enemy to their repose, had wonderfully contrived that a K was not to be found. Here was a weighty difficulty! but the distinguishing brother, for whom we shall hereafter find a name, now his hand was in, proved by a very good argument that K was a modern, illegitimate letter, unknown to the learned ages, nor anywhere to be found in ancient manuscripts. "T is true,' said he, '*Calendæ* hath in Q. V. C.[1] been sometimes writ with a K, but erroneously; for in the best copies it ever spelt with a C. And, by consequence, it was a gross mistake in our language to spell "knot" with a "K"'; but that from henceforward he would take care it should be writ with a C. Upon this all farther difficulty vanished—shoulder-knots were made clearly out to be *jure paterno* [according to the law of the father], and our three gentlemen swaggered with as large and as flaunting ones as the best.

But, as human happiness is of a very short duration, so in those days were human fashions, upon which it entirely depends. Shoulder-knots had their time, and we must now imagine them in their decline; for a certain lord came just from Paris, with fifty yards of gold lace upon his coat, exactly trimmed after the court fashion of that month. In two days all mankind appeared closed up in bars of gold lace:[2] whoever durst peep abroad without his complement of gold lace was as scandalous as a ———, and as ill received among the women: what should our three knights do in this momentous affair? they had sufficiently strained a point already in the affair of shoulder-knots: upon recourse to the will, nothing appeared there but *altum silentium* [profound silence]. That of the shoulder-knots was a loose, flying, circumstantial point; but this of gold lace seemed too considerable an alteration without better warrant; it did *aliquo modo essentiæ adhærere* [in some manner belong to the essence of the matter], and therefore required a positive precept. But about this time it fell out that the learned brother aforesaid had read *Aristotelis dialectica*, and especially that wonderful piece *de interpretatione*, which has the faculty of teaching its readers to find out a meaning in everything but itself; like commentators on the Revelations, who proceed prophets without understanding a syllable of the text. 'Brothers,' said he, 'you are to be informed that of wills *duo sunt genera* [there are two kinds], nuncupatory[3] and scriptory: that in the scriptory will here before us there is no precept or mention about gold lace, *conceditur* [it is conceded] but *si idem affirmetur de nuncupatorio, negatur* [if the same is asserted of the nuncupatory, it is denied]. For, brothers, if you remember, we heard a fellow say when we were boys that he heard my father's man say, that he heard my father say, that he would advise his sons to get gold lace on their coats as soon as ever they could procure money to buy

---

[1] *Quibusdam veteribus codicibus;* i.e., in some ancient manuscripts.

[2] I cannot tell whether the author means any new innovation by this word, or whether it be only to introduce the new methods of forcing and perverting Scripture.

[3] By this is meant tradition, allowed by the Papists to have equal authority with the Scripture, or rather greater.

it.' 'By G——! that is very true,' cries the other; 'I remember it perfectly well,' said the third. And so without more ado they got the largest gold lace in the parish, and walked about as fine as lords.

A while after there came up all in fashion a pretty sort of flame-colored satin for linings;[1] and the mercer brought a pattern of it immediately to our three gentlemen; 'An please your worships,' said he, 'my lord C——[2] and Sir J. W. had linings out of this very piece last night: it takes wonderfully, and I shall not have a remnant left enough to make my wife a pincushion by to-morrow morning at ten o'clock.' Upon this they fell again to rummage the will, because the present case also required a positive precept—the lining being held by orthodox writers to be of the essence of the coat. After long search they could fix upon nothing to the matter in hand, except a short advice of their father in the will to take care of fire[3] and put out their candles before they went to sleep. This, though a good deal for the purpose, and helping very far towards self-conviction, yet not seeming wholly of force to establish a command (being resolved to avoid farther scruple as well as future occasion for scandal), says he that was the scholar, 'I remember to have read in wills of a codicil annexed, which is indeed a part of the will, and what it contains hath equal authority with the rest. Now, I have been considering of this same will here before us, and I cannot reckon it to be complete for want of such a codicil: I will therefore fasten one in its proper place very dexterously—I have had it by me some time—it was written by a dog-keeper of my grandfather's,[4] and talks a great deal, as good luck would have it, of this very flame-colored satin.' The project was immediately approved by the other two; an old parchment scroll was tagged on according to art in the form of a codicil annexed, and the satin bought and worn.

Next winter a player, hired for the purpose by the corporation of fringe-makers, acted his part in a new comedy, all covered with silver-fringe,[5] and, according to the laudable custom, gave rise to that fashion. Upon which the brothers, consulting their father's will, to their great astonishment found these words: '*item*, I charge and command my said three sons to wear no sort of silver fringe upon or about their said coats,' etc., with a penalty, in case of disobedience, too long here to insert. However, after some pause, the brother so often mentioned for his erudition, who was well skilled in criticisms, had found in a certain author, which he said should be nameless, that the same word which in the will is called fringe does also signify a broomstick: and doubtless ought to have the same interpretation in this paragraph. This another of the brothers disliked, because of that epithet silver, which could not, he humbly conceived, in propriety of speech be reasonably applied to a broomstick: but it was replied upon him that this epithet was understood in a mythological and allegorical sense. However, he objected again why their father should forbid them to wear a broomstick on their coats—a caution that seemed unnatural and impertinent; upon which he was taken up short, as one who spoke irreverently of a mystery, which doubtless was very useful and significant, but ought not to be over-curiously pried into or nicely reasoned upon. And, in short, their father's authority being now considerably sunk, this expedient was allowed to serve as a lawful dispensation for wearing their full proportion of silver fringe.

A while after was revived an old fashion, long antiquated, of embroidery with Indian figures of men, women, and children. Here they remembered but too well how their father had always abhorred this fashion; that he made several paragraphs on purpose, importing his utter detestation of it, and bestowing his everlasting curse to his sons whenever they should wear it. For all this, in a few days they appeared higher in the fashion than anybody else in the town. But they solved the matter by saying that these figures were not at all the same with those that

---

[1] This is a Purgatory, whereof he speaks more particularly hereafter; but here, only to shew how Scripture was perverted to prove it, which was done by giving equal authority with the canon to Apocrypha, called here a codicil annexed. It is likely the author, in every one of these changes in the brothers' dresses, refers to some particular error in the Church of Rome, though it is not easy, I think, to apply them all: but by this of flame-colored satin, is manifestly intended Purgatory; by gold lace may perhaps be understood, the lofty ornaments and plate in the churches; the shoulder-knots and silver fringe are not so obvious, at least to me; but the Indian figures of men, women, and children, plainly relate to the pictures in the Romish churches, of God like an old man, of the Virgin Mary, and our Savior as a child.

[2] This shews the time the author writ, it being about fourteen years since those two persons were reckoned the fine gentlemen of the town.

[3] That is, to take care of hell; and, in order to do that, to subdue and extinguish their lusts.

[4] I believe this refers to that part of the Apocrypha where mention is made of Tobit and his dog.

[5] This is certainly the farther introducing the pomps of habit and ornament.

were formerly worn and were meant in the will. Besides, they did not wear them in the sense as forbidden by their father; but as they were a commendable custom, and of great use to the public.[1] That these rigorous clauses in the will did therefore require some allowance and a favorable interpretation, and ought to be understood *cum grano salis* [with a grain of salt].

But fashions perpetually altering in that age, the scholastic brother grew weary of searching farther evasions, and solving everlasting contradictions. Resolved, therefore, at all hazards, to comply with the modes of the world, they concerted matters together, and agreed unanimously to lock up their father's will in a strong box, brought out of Greece or Italy (I have forgot which), and trouble themselves no farther to examine it, but only refer to its authority whenever they thought fit. In consequence whereof, a while after it grew a general mode to wear an infinite number of points, most of them tagged with silver: upon which the scholar pronounced, *ex cathedrâ* [from the bench], that points were absolutely *jure paterno*, as they might very well remember. 'T is true, indeed, the fashion prescribed somewhat more than were directly named in the will; however, that they, as heirs-general of their father, had power to make and add certain clauses for public emolument, though not deducible, *totidem verbis*, from the letter of the will, or else *multa absurda sequerentur* [many absurdities would follow]. This was understood for canonical, and therefore, on the following Sunday, they came to church all covered with points.

The learned brother, so often mentioned, was reckoned the best scholar in all that or the next street to it, insomuch as, having run something behindhand in the world, he obtained the favor of a certain lord[2] to receive him into his house, and to teach his children. A while after the lord died, and he, by long practice of his father's will, found the way of contriving a deed of conveyance of that house to himself and his heirs; upon which he took possession, turned the young squires out, and received his brothers in their stead.

* * *

SECTION IV

I HAVE now, with much pains and study, conducted the reader to a period where he must expect to hear of great revolutions. For no sooner had our learned brother, so often mentioned, got a warm house of his own over his head than he began to look big and take mightily upon him; insomuch that, unless the gentle reader, out of his great candor, will please a little to exalt his idea, I am afraid he will henceforth hardly know the hero of the play when he happens to meet him; his part, his dress, and his mien being so much altered.

He told his brothers he would have them to know that he was their elder, and consequently his father's sole heir; nay, a while after, he would not allow them to call him brother, but *Mr.* PETER, and then he must be styled *Father* PETER; and sometimes, *My Lord* PETER. To support this grandeur, which he soon began to consider could not be maintained without a better *fonde* than what he was born to, after much thought, he cast about at last to turn projector and virtuoso, wherein he so well succeeded, that many famous discoveries, projects and machines, which bear great vogue and practice at present in the world, are owing entirely to lord PETER'S invention. I will deduce the best account I have been able to collect of the chief among them, without considering much the order they came out in; because I think authors are not well agreed as to that point.

I hope, when this treatise of mine shall be translated into foreign languages (as I may without vanity affirm that the labor of collecting, the faithfulness in recounting, and the great usefulness of the matter to the public, will amply deserve that justice), that the worthy members of the several academies abroad, especially those of France and Italy, will favorably accept these humble offers for the advancement of universal knowledge. I do also advertise the most reverend fathers, the eastern missionaries, that I have, purely for their sakes, made use of such words and phrases as will best admit an easy turn into any of the oriental languages, especially the Chinese. And so I proceed with great content of mind, upon reflecting how much emolument this whole globe of the earth is likely to reap by my labors.

The first undertaking of lord Peter was, to purchase a large continent,[3] lately said to have been discovered in *terra australis incognita* [an unknown country to the south]. This tract of land he bought at a very great pennyworth from the discoverers themselves (though some pretend to doubt whether they had ever been

---

[1] Here they had no occasion to examine the will; they remembered.—*First Edition*.

[2] This was Constantine the Great, from whom the popes pretend a donation of St. Peter's patrimony, which they have never been able to produce.

[3] That is, Purgatory.

there), and then retailed it into several cantons to certain dealers, who carried over colonies, but were all shipwrecked in the voyage. Upon which lord Peter sold the said continent to other customers again, and again, and again, and again, with the same success.

The second project I shall mention was his sovereign remedy for the worms, especially those in the spleen. The patient was to eat nothing after supper for three nights:[1] as soon as he went to bed he was carefully to lie on one side, and when he grew weary to turn upon the other; he must also duly confine his two eyes to the same object. . . . These prescriptions diligently observed, the worms would void insensibly by perspiration, ascending through the brain.

A third invention was the erecting of a whispering-office for the public good and ease of all such as are hypochondriacal or troubled with the colic; as midwives,[2] small politicians, friends fallen out, repeating poets, lovers happy or in despair, bawds, privy-counsellors, pages, parasites, and buffoons; in short, of all such as are in danger of bursting with too much wind. An ass's head was placed so conveniently that the party affected might easily with his mouth accost either of the animal's ears; to which he was to apply close for a certain space, and by a fugitive faculty, peculiar to the ears of that animal, receive immediate benefit, either by eructation, or expiration, or evomitation.

Another very beneficial project of lord Peter's was an office of insurance for tobacco-pipes,[3] martyrs of the modern zeal, volumes of poetry, shadows, ——, and rivers; that these, nor any of these, shall receive damage by fire. Whence our friendly societies may plainly find themselves to be only transcribers from this original; though the one and the other have been of great benefit to the undertakers, as well as of equal to the public.

Lord PETER was also held the original author of puppets and raree-shows;[4] the great usefulness whereof being so generally known, I shall not enlarge farther upon this particular.

But another discovery for which he was much renowned, was his famous universal pickle. For, having remarked how your common pickle[5] in use among housewives was of no farther benefit than to preserve dead flesh and certain kinds of vegetables, Peter, with great cost as well as art, had contrived a pickle proper for houses, gardens, towns, men, women, children, and cattle; wherein he could preserve them as sound as insects in amber. Now, this pickle, to the taste, the smell, and the sight, appeared exactly the same with what is in common service for beef, and butter, and herrings, and has been often that way applied with great success; but, for its many sovereign virtues, was a quite different thing. For Peter would put in a certain quantity of his powder pimperlimpimp, after which it never failed of success. The operation was performed by spargefaction, in a proper time of the moon. The patient who was to be pickled, if it were a house, would infallibly be preserved from all spiders, rats, and weasels; if the party affected were a dog, he should be exempt from mange, and madness, and hunger. It also infallibly took away all scabs, and lice, and scalled heads from children, never hindering the patient from any duty, either at bed or board.

But of all Peter's rareties he most valued a certain set of bulls, whose race was by great fortune preserved in a lineal descent from those that guarded the golden fleece. Though some, who pretended to observe them curiously, doubted the breed had not been kept entirely chaste, because they had degenerated from their ancestors in some qualities, and had acquired others very extraordinary, by a foreign mixture. The bulls of Colchis are recorded to have brazen feet; but whether it happened by ill pasture and running, by an allay from intervention of other parents, from stolen intrigues; whether a weakness in their progenitors had impaired the seminal virtue, or by a decline necessary through a long course of time, the originals of nature being depraved in these latter sinful ages of the world; whatever was the cause, it is certain that lord Peter's bulls were extremely vitiated by the rust of time in the metal of their feet, which was now sunk into common lead. However, the terrible roaring peculiar to their lineage was preserved; as likewise that faculty of breathing out fire from their nostrils, which, notwithstanding, many of their detractors took to be a feat of art, to be nothing so terrible as it appeared, proceeding only from their usual course

---

[1] Here the author ridicules the penalties of the Church of Rome, which may be made as easy to the sinner as he pleases, provided he will pay for them accordingly.
[2] As likewise of all eavesdroppers, midwives, etc.—*First Edition.*
[3] This I take to be the office of indulgences, the gross abuses whereof first gave occasion for the Reformation.
[4] I believe are the monkeries and ridiculous processions, etc., among the papists.
[5] This is easily understood to be holy water, composed of the same ingredients with many other pickles.

of diet, which was of squibs and crackers.[1] However they had two peculiar marks, which extremely distinguished them from the bulls of Jason, and which I have not met together in the description of any other monster beside that in Horace:

   Varias inducere plumas;
   [putting on gay plumage.]
and
   Atrum desinat in piscem.
   [ending in a foul fish below.]

For these had fishes' tails, yet upon occasion could outfly any bird in the air. Peter put these bulls upon several employs. Sometimes he would set them a-roaring to fright naughty boys,[2] and make them quiet. Sometimes he would send them out upon errands of great importance; where, it is wonderful to recount (and perhaps the cautious reader may think much to believe it), an *appetitus sensibilis* [an appetite of the senses] deriving itself through the whole family from their noble ancestors, guardians of the golden fleece, they continued so extremely fond of gold, that if Peter sent them abroad, though it were only upon a compliment, they would roar, and spit, and belch, and snivel out fire, and keep a perpetual coil, till you flung them a bit of gold; but then, *pulveris exigui jactu* [by throwing on a little dust], they would grow calm and quiet as lambs. In short, whether by secret connivance or encouragement from their master, or out of their own liquorish affection to gold, or both, it is certain they were no better than a sort of sturdy, swaggering, beggars; and where they could not prevail to get an alms, would make women miscarry, and children fall into fits, who to this very day usually call sprights and hobgoblins by the name of bull-beggars. They grew at last so very troublesome to the neighborhood, that some gentlemen of the north-west got a parcel of right English bull-dogs, and baited them so terribly that they felt it ever after.

I must needs mention one more of lord Peter's projects, which was very extraordinary, and discovered him to be master of a high reach and profound invention. Whenever it happened that any rogue of Newgate was condemned to be hanged, Peter would offer him a pardon for a certain sum of money; which, when the poor caitiff had made all shifts to scrape up and send, his lordship would return a piece of paper in this form:—[3]

'To all mayors, sheriffs, jailors, constables, bailiffs, hangmen, etc. Whereas we are informed that A. B. remains in the hands of you, or some of you, under the sentence of death. We will and command you, upon sight hereof, to let the said prisoner depart to his own habitation, whether he stands condemned for murder, sodomy, rape, sacrilege, incest, treason, blasphemy, etc., for which this shall be your sufficient warrant; and if you fail hereof, G— d—mn you and yours to all eternity. And so we bid you heartily farewell.
   Your most humble
    Man's man,
     Emperor PETER.'

The wretches, trusting to this, lost their lives and money too.

I desire of those whom the learned among posterity will appoint for commentators upon this elaborate treatise, that they will proceed with great caution upon certain dark points, wherein all who are not *verè adepti* [genuine adepts] may be in danger to form rash and hasty conclusions, especially in some mysterious paragraphs, where certain *arcana* are joined for brevity sake, which in the operation must be divided. And I am certain that future sons of art will return large thanks to my memory for so grateful, so useful an *innuendo*.

It will be no difficult part to persuade the reader that so many worthy discoveries met with great success in the world; though I may justly assure him that I have related much the smallest number; my design having been only to single out such as will be of most benefit for public imitation, or which best serve to give some idea of the reach and wit of the inventor. And therefore it need not be wondered at if by this time lord Peter was become exceeding rich: but, alas! he had kept his brain so long and so violently upon the rack, that at last it shook itself, and began to turn round for a little ease. In short, what with pride, projects, and knavery, poor Peter was grown distracted, and conceived the strangest imaginations in the world. In the height of his fits, as it is usual with those who run mad out of pride, he would call himself God Almighty,[4] and sometimes Monarch of the

---

[1] These are the fulminations of the Pope, threatening hell and damnation to those princes who offend him.
[2] That is, kings who incurred his displeasure.
[3] This is a copy of a general pardon, signed *servus servorum* (slave of slaves).
[4] The Pope is not only allowed to be the vicar of Christ, but by several divines is called God upon earth, and other blasphemous titles.

Universe. I have seen him (says my author) take three old high-crowned hats,[1] and clap them all on his head three story high, with a huge bunch of keys at his girdle,[2] and an angling-rod in his hand. In which guise, whoever went to take him by the hand in the way of salutation, Peter with much grace, like a well-educated spaniel, would present them with his foot, and if they refused his civility, then he would raise it as high as their chaps, and give them a damned kick on the mouth, which hath ever since been called a salute. Whoever walked by without paying him their compliments, having a wonderful strong breath, he would blow their hats off into the dirt. Meantime his affairs at home went upside down, and his two brothers had a wretched time; where his first *boutade*[3] was to kick both their wives one morning out of doors, and his own too; and in their stead gave orders to pick up the first three strollers that could be met with in the streets. A while after he nailed up the cellar-door, and would not allow his brothers a drop of drink to their victuals.[4] Dining one day at an alderman's in the city, Peter observed him expatiating, after the manner of his brethren, in the praises of his sirloin of beef. 'Beef,' said the sage magistrate, 'is the king of meat; beef comprehends in it the quintessence of partridge, and quail, and venison, and pheasant, and plum-pudding, and custard.' When Peter came home he would needs take the fancy of cooking up this doctrine into use, and apply the precept, in default of a sirloin, to his brown loaf. 'Bread,' says he, 'dear brothers, is the staff of life; in which bread is contained, inclusive, the quintessence of beef, mutton, veal, venison, partridge, plum-pudding, and custard; and, to render all complete, there is intermingled a due quantity of water, whose crudities are also corrected by yeast or barm, through which means it becomes a wholesome fermented liquor, diffused through the mass of the bread.' Upon the strength of these conclusions, next day at dinner was the brown loaf served up in all the formality of a city feast. 'Come, brothers,' said Peter, 'fall to, and spare not; here is excellent good mutton; or hold, now my hand is in, I will help you.' At which word, in much ceremony, with fork and knife, he carves out two good slices of a loaf, and presents each on a plate to his brothers. The elder of the two, not suddenly entering into lord Peter's conceit, began with very civil language to examine the mystery. 'My lord,' said he, 'I doubt, with great submission, there may be some mistake.'—'What,' says Peter, 'you are pleasant; come then, let us hear this jest your head is so big with.'—'None in the world, my lord; but, unless I am very much deceived, your lordship was pleased a while ago to let fall a word about mutton, and I would be glad to see it with all my heart.'—'How,' said Peter, appearing in great surprise, 'I do not comprehend this at all.' Upon which the younger interposing to set the business aright, 'My lord,' said he, 'my brother, I suppose, is hungry, and longs for the mutton your lordship has promised us to dinner.'—'Pray,' said Peter, 'take me along with you; either you are both mad, or disposed to be merrier than I approve of; if you there do not like your piece I will carve you another; though I should take that to be the choice bit of the whole shoulder.' —'What then, my lord,' replied the first, 'it seems this is a shoulder of mutton all this while?' —'Pray, sir,' says Peter, 'eat your victuals, and leave off your impertinence, if you please, for I am not disposed to relish it at present': but the other could not forbear, being over-provoked at the affected seriousness of Peter's countenance: 'By G—, my lord,' said he, 'I can only say, that to my eyes, and fingers, and teeth, and nose, it seems to be nothing but a crust of bread.' Upon which the second put in his word: 'I never saw a piece of mutton in my life so nearly resembling a slice from a twelvepenny loaf.'—'Look ye, gentlemen,' cries Peter, in a rage; 'to convince you what a couple of blind, positive, ignorant, wilful puppies you are, I will use but this plain argument: by G—, it is true, good, natural mutton as any in Leadenhall-market; and G— confound you both eternally if you offer to believe otherwise.' Such a thundering proof as this left no farther room for objection; the two unbelievers began to gather and pocket up their mistake as hastily as they could. 'Why truly,' said the first, 'upon more mature consideration——' —'Ay,' says the other, interrupting him, 'now I have thought better on the thing, your lordship seems to have a great deal of reason.'—'Very well,' said Peter; 'here, boy, fill me a beer-glass of claret; here's to you both with all my heart.' The two brethren, much delighted to see him so readily appeased, returned their most humble thanks, and said they would

---

[1] The triple crown. [2] The keys of the Church.
[3] This word properly signifies a sudden jerk, or lash of a horse, when you do not expect it.
[4] The Pope's refusing the cup to the laity, persuading them that the blood is contained in the bread, and that the bread is the real and entire body of Christ.

be glad to pledge his lordship. 'That you shall,' said Peter; 'I am not a person to refuse you anything that is reasonable: wine, moderately taken, is a cordial; here is a glass a-piece for you; 't is true natural juice from the grape, none of your damned vintner's brewings.' Having spoke thus, he presented to each of them another large dry crust, bidding them drink it off, and not be bashful, for it would do them no hurt. The two brothers, after having performed the usual office in such delicate conjectures, of staring a sufficient period at lord Peter and each other, and finding how matters were likely to go, resolved not to enter on a new dispute, but let him carry the point as he pleased; for he was now got into one of his mad fits, and to argue or expostulate farther would only serve to render him a hundred times more untractable.

I have chosen to relate this worthy matter in all its circumstances, because it gave a principal occasion to that great and famous rupture [1] which happened about the same time among these brethren, and was never afterwards made up. But of that I shall treat at large in another section.

However, it is certain that lord Peter, even in his lucid intervals, was very lewdly given in his common conversation, extremely wilful and positive, and would at any time rather argue to the death than allow himself once to be in an error. Besides, he had an abominable faculty of telling huge palpable lies upon all occasions; and not only swearing to the truth, but cursing the whole company to hell if they pretended to make the least scruple of believing him. One time he swore he had a cow at home which gave as much milk at a meal as would fill three thousand churches; and, what was yet more extraordinary, would never turn sour. Another time he was telling of an old sign-post,[2] that belonged to his father, with nails and timber enough in it to build sixteen large men of war. Talking one day of Chinese wagons, which were made so light as to sail over mountains, 'Z—ds,' said Peter, 'where's the wonder of that? By G—, I saw a large house of lime and stone travel over sea and land (granting that it stopped sometimes to bait) above two thousand German leagues.' And that which was the good of it, he would swear desperately all the while that he never told a lie in his life; and at every word, 'By G—, gentlemen, I tell you nothing but the truth; and the d—l broil them eternally that will not believe me.'

In short, Peter grew so scandalous, that all the neighborhood began in plain words to say he was no better than a knave. And his two brothers, long weary of his ill-usage, resolved at last to leave him; but first they humbly desired a copy of their father's will, which had now lain by neglected time out of mind. Instead of granting this request he called them damned . . . rogues, traitors, and the rest of the vile names he could muster up. However, while he was abroad one day upon his projects, the two youngsters watched their opportunity, made a shift to come at the will,[3] and took a *copia vera* [true copy] by which they presently saw how grossly they had been abused; their father having left them equal heirs, and strictly commanded that whatever they got should lie in common among them all. Pursuant to which their next enterprise was to break open the cellar-door, and get a little good drink,[4] to spirit and comfort their hearts. In copying the will they had met another precept against whoring, divorce, and separate maintenance; upon which their next work [5] was to discard their concubines, and send for their wives. While all this was in agitation there enters a solicitor from Newgate, desiring lord Peter would please procure a pardon for a thief that was to be hanged to-morrow. But the two brothers told him he was a coxcomb to seek pardons from a fellow who deserved to be hanged much better than his client; and discovered all the method of that imposture in the same form I delivered it a while ago, advising the solicitor to put his friend upon obtaining a pardon from the king.[6] In the midst of all this clutter and revolution, in comes Peter with a file of dragoons at his heels,[7] and gathering from all hands what was in the wind, he and his gang, after several millions of scurrilities and curses, not very important here to repeat, by main force very fairly kicked them both out of doors,[8] and would never let them come under his roof from that day to this.

* * * (1704)

[3] Translated the Scriptures into the vulgar tongues.
[4] Administered the cup to the laity at the communion.
[5] Allowed the marriages of priests.
[6] Directed penitents not to trust to pardons and absolutions procured for money, but sent them to implore the mercy of God, from whence alone remission is to be obtained.
[7] By Peter's dragoons is meant the civil power, which those princes who were bigoted to the Romish superstition, employed against the reformers.
[8] The Pope shuts all who dissent from him out of the Church.

[1] By this rupture is meant the Reformation.
[2] By the sign-post is meant the cross of our Blessed Savior.

A MEDITATION UPON A BROOMSTICK

ACCORDING TO THE STYLE AND MANNER OF THE HON. ROBERT BOYLE'S MEDITATIONS

This single stick, which you now behold ingloriously lying in that neglected corner, I once knew in a flourishing state in a forest; it was full of sap, full of leaves, and full of boughs; but now in vain does the busy art of man pretend to vie with nature, by tying that withered bundle of twigs to its sapless trunk; 't is now at best but the reverse of what it was, a tree turned upside down, the branches on the earth, and the root in the air; 't is now handled by every dirty wench, condemned to do her drudgery, and, by a capricious kind of fate, destined to make other things clean, and be nasty itself; at length, worn to the stumps in the service of the maids, it is either thrown out of door, or condemned to the last use, of kindling a fire. When I beheld this, I sighed, and said within myself: *Surely Man is a Broomstick!* Nature sent him into the world strong and lusty, in a thriving condition, wearing his own hair on his head, the proper branches of this reasoning vegetable, until the axe of intemperance has lopped off his green boughs, and left him a withered trunk; he then flies to art, and puts on a periwig, valuing himself upon an unnatural bundle of hairs, all covered with powder, that never grew on his head; but now should this our broomstick pretend to enter the scene, proud of those birchen spoils it never bore, and all covered with dust, though the sweepings of the finest lady's chamber, we should be apt to ridicule and despise its vanity. Partial judges that we are of our own excellencies, and other men's defaults!

But a broomstick, perhaps you will say, is an emblem of a tree standing on its head; and pray, what is man but a topsy-turvy creature, his animal faculties perpetually mounted on his rational; his head where his heels should be, groveling on the earth! and yet, with all his faults, he sets up to be a universal reformer and corrector of abuses, a remover of grievances; rakes into every slut's corner of nature, bringing hidden corruption to the light, and raises a mighty dust where there was none before; sharing deeply all the while in the very same pollutions he pretends to sweep away: his last days are spent in slavery to women, and generally the least deserving, till, worn out to the stumps, like his brother besom, he is either kicked out of doors, or made use of to kindle flames for others to warm themselves by.   (1704)

A MODEST PROPOSAL

FOR PREVENTING THE CHILDREN OF POOR PEOPLE IN IRELAND FROM BEING A BURDEN TO THEIR PARENTS OR COUNTRY, AND FOR MAKING THEM BENEFICIAL TO THE PUBLIC

It is a melancholy object to those who walk through this great town or travel in the country, when they see the streets, the roads, and cabin doors, crowded with beggars of the female sex, followed by three, four, or six children, all in rags and importuning every passenger for an alms. These mothers, instead of being able to work for their honest livelihood, are forced to employ all their time in strolling to beg sustenance for their helpless infants: who as they grow up either turn thieves for want of work, or leave their dear native country to fight for the Pretender in Spain, or sell themselves to the Barbadoes.

I think it is agreed by all parties that this prodigious number of children in the arms, or on the backs, or at the heels of their mothers, and frequently of their fathers, is in the present deplorable state of the kingdom a very great additional grievance; and, therefore, whoever could find out a fair, cheap, and easy method of making these children sound, useful members of the commonwealth, would deserve so well of the public as to have his statue set up for a preserver of the nation.

But my intention is very far from being confined to provide only for the children of professed beggars; it is of a much greater extent, and shall take in the whole number of infants at a certain age who are born of parents in effect as little able to support them as those who demand our charity in the streets.

As to my own part, having turned my thoughts for many years upon this important subject, and maturely weighed the several schemes of other projectors, I have always found them grossly mistaken in the computation. It is true, a child just dropped from its dam may be supported by her milk for a solar year, with little other nourishment; at most not above the value of 2s., which the mother may certainly get, or the value in scraps, by her lawful occupation of begging; and it is exactly at one year old that I propose to provide for them in such a manner as instead of being a charge upon their parents or the parish, or wanting food and raiment for the rest of their lives, they shall on the contrary contribute to the feeding, and partly to the clothing, of many thousands.

There is likewise another great advantage

in my scheme, that it will prevent those voluntary abortions, and that horrid practice of women murdering their bastard children, alas! too frequent among us! sacrificing the poor innocent babes I doubt more to avoid the expense than the shame, which would move tears and pity in the most savage and inhuman breast.

The number of souls in this kingdom being usually reckoned one million and a half, of these I calculate there may be about two hundred thousand couple whose wives are breeders; from which number I subtract thirty thousand couples who are able to maintain their own children, although I apprehend there cannot be so many, under the present distresses of the kingdom; but this being granted, there will remain an hundred and seventy thousand breeders. I again subtract fifty thousand for those women who miscarry, or whose children die by accident or disease within the year. There only remains one hundred and twenty thousand children of poor parents annually born. The question therefore is, how this number shall be reared and provided for, which, as I have already said, under the present situation of affairs, is utterly impossible by all the methods hitherto proposed. For we can neither employ them in handicraft or agriculture: we neither build houses (I mean in the country) nor cultivate land: they can very seldom pick up a livelihood by stealing, till they arrive at six years old, except where they are of towardly parts, although I confess they learn the rudiments much earlier, during which time, they can however be properly looked upon only as probationers, as I have been informed by a principal gentleman in the county of Cavan, who protested to me that he never knew above one or two instances under the age of six, even in a part of the kingdom so renowned for the quickest proficiency in that art.

I am assured by our merchants, that a boy or a girl before twelve years old is no salable commodity; and even when they come to this age they will not yield above three pounds, or three pounds and half-a-crown at most on the exchange; which cannot turn to account either to the parents or kingdom, the charge of nutriment and rags having been at least four times that value.

I shall now therefore humbly propose my own thoughts, which I hope will not be liable to the least objection.

I have been assured by a very knowing American of my acquaintance in London, that a young healthy child well nursed is at a year old a most delicious, nourishing, and wholesome food, whether stewed, roasted, baked, or boiled; and I make no doubt that it will equally serve in a fricassee or a ragout.

I do therefore humbly offer it to public consideration that of the hundred and twenty thousand children already computed, twenty thousand may be reserved for breed, whereof only one-fourth part to be males; which is more than we allow to sheep, black cattle or swine; and my reason is, that these children are seldom the fruits of marriage, a circumstance not much regarded by our savages, therefore one male will be sufficient to serve four females. That the remaining hundred thousand may, at a year old, be offered in the sale to the persons of quality and fortune through the kingdom; always advising the mother to let them suck plentifully in the last month, so as to render them plump and fat for a good table. A child will make two dishes at an entertainment for friends; and when the family dines alone, the fore or hind quarter will make a reasonable dish, and seasoned with a little pepper or salt will be very good boiled on the fourth day, especially in winter.

I have reckoned upon a medium that a child just born will weigh 12 pounds, and in a solar year, if tolerably nursed, increaseth to 28 pounds.

I grant this food will be somewhat dear, and therefore very proper for landlords, who, as they have already devoured most of the parents, seem to have the best title to the children.

Infant's flesh will be in season throughout the year, but more plentiful in March, and a little before and after; for we are told by a grave author, an eminent French physician, that fish being a prolific diet, there are more children born in Roman Catholic countries about nine months after Lent than at any other season; therefore, reckoning a year after Lent, the markets will be more glutted than usual, because the number of popish infants is at least three to one in this kingdom: and therefore it will have one other collateral advantage, by lessening the number of papists among us.

I have already computed the charge of nursing a beggar's child (in which list I reckon all cottagers, laborers, and four-fifths of the farmers) to be about two shillings per annum, rags included; and I believe no gentleman would repine to give ten shillings for the carcass of a good fat child, which, as I have said, will make four dishes of excellent nutritive meat, when he hath only some particular friend or his own family to dine with him. Thus the squire will learn to be a good landlord, and grow popular among his tenants; the mother will have eight shillings net profit, and be fit for work till she produces another child.

Those who are more thrifty (as I must confess the times require) may flay the carcass; the skin of which artificially dressed will make admirable gloves for ladies, and summer boots for fine gentlemen.

As to our city of Dublin, shambles may be appointed for this purpose in the most convenient parts of it, and butchers we may be assured will not be wanting; although I rather recommend buying the children alive, and dressing them hot from the knife, as we do roasting pigs.

A very worthy person, a true lover of his country, and whose virtues I highly esteem, was lately pleased in discoursing on this matter to offer a refinement upon my scheme. He said that many gentlemen of this kingdom, having of late destroyed their deer, he conceived that the want of venison might be well supplied by the bodies of young lads and maidens, not exceeding fourteen years of age nor under twelve; so great a number of both sexes in every country being now ready to starve for want of work and service; and these to be disposed of by their parents, if alive, or otherwise by their nearest relations. But with due deference to so excellent a friend and so deserving a patriot, I cannot be altogether in his sentiments; for as to the males, my American acquaintance assured me, from frequent experience, that their flesh was generally tough and lean, like that of our schoolboys by continual exercise, and their taste disagreeable; and to fatten them would not answer the charge. Then as to the females, it would, I think, with humble submission be a loss to the public, because they soon would become breeders themselves; and besides, it is not improbable that some scrupulous people might be apt to censure such a practice (although indeed very unjustly), as a little bordering upon cruelty; which, I confess, hath always been with me the strongest objection against any project, however so well intended.

But in order to justify my friend, he confessed that this expedient was put into his head by the famous Psalmanazar, a native of the island Formosa, who came from thence to London above twenty years ago, and in conversation told my friend, that in his country when any young person happened to be put to death, the executioner sold the carcass to persons of quality as a prime dainty; and that in his time the body of a plump girl of fifteen, who was crucified for an attempt to poison the emperor, was sold to his imperial majesty's prime minister of state, and other great mandarins of the court, in joints from the gibbet, at four hundred crowns. Neither indeed can I deny, that if the same use were made of several plump young girls in this town, who without one single groat to their fortunes cannot stir abroad without a chair, and appear at playhouse and assemblies in foreign fineries which they never will pay for, the kingdom would not be the worse.

Some persons of a desponding spirit are in great concern about that vast number of poor people, who are aged, diseased, or maimed, and I have been desired to employ my thoughts what course may be taken to ease the nation of so grievous an encumbrance. But I am not in the least pain upon that matter, because it is very well known that they are every day dying and rotting by cold and famine, and filth and vermin, as fast as can be reasonably expected. And as to the young laborers, they are now in as hopeful a condition; they cannot get work, and consequently pine away for want of nourishment, to a degree that if at any time they are accidentally hired to common labor, they have not strength to perform it; and thus the country and themselves are happily delivered from the evils to come.

I have too long digressed, and therefore shall return to my subject. I think the advantages by the proposal which I have made are obvious and many, as well as of the highest importance.

For first, as I have already observed, it would greatly lessen the number of papists, with whom we are yearly overrun, being the principal breeders of the nation as well as our most dangerous enemies; and who stay at home on purpose with a design to deliver the kingdom to the Pretender, hoping to take their advantage by the absence of so many good protestants, who have chosen rather to leave their country than stay at home and pay tithes against their conscience to an episcopal curate.

Secondly, The poorer tenants will have something valuable of their own, which by law may be made liable to distress and help to pay their landlord's rent, their corn and cattle being already seized, and money a thing unknown.

Thirdly, Whereas the maintenance of an hundred thousand children, from two years old and upward, cannot be computed at less than ten shillings a-piece per annum, the nation's stock will be thereby increased fifty thousand pounds per annum, beside the profit of a new dish introduced to the tables of all gentlemen of fortune in the kingdom who have any refinement in taste. And the money will circulate among ourselves, the goods being entirely of our own growth and manufacture.

Fourthly. The constant breeders, beside the gain of eight shillings sterling per annum by the sale of their children, will be rid of the charge of maintaining them after the first year.

Fifthly, This food would likewise bring great custom to taverns; where the vintners will certainly be so prudent as to procure the best receipts for dressing it to perfection, and consequently have their houses frequented by all the fine gentlemen, who justly value themselves upon their knowledge in good eating: and a skilful cook, who understands how to oblige his guests, will contrive to make it as expensive as they please.

Sixthly, This would be a great inducement to marriage, which all wise nations have either encouraged by rewards or enforced by laws and penalties. It would increase the care and tenderness of mothers toward their children, when they were sure of a settlement for life to the poor babes, provided in some sort by the public, to their annual profit instead of expense. We should see an honest emulation among the married women, which of them could bring the fattest child to the market. Men would become as fond of their wives during the time of their pregnancy as they are now of their mares in foal, their cows in calf, their sows when they are ready to farrow; nor offer to beat or kick them (as is too frequent a practice) for fear of a miscarriage.

Many other advantages might be enumerated. For instance, the addition of some thousand carcasses in our exportation of barreled beef, the propagation of swine's flesh, and improvement in the art of making good bacon, so much wanted among us by the great destruction of pigs, too frequent at our tables; which are no way comparable in taste or magnificence to a well-grown, fat, yearling child, which roasted whole will make a considerable figure at a lord mayor's feast or any other public entertainment. But this and many others I omit, being studious of brevity.

* * *

After all, I am not so violently bent upon my own opinion as to reject any offer proposed by wise men, which shall be found equally innocent, cheap, easy, and effectual. But before something of that kind shall be advanced in contradiction to my scheme, and offering a better, I desire the author or authors will be pleased maturely to consider two points. First, as things now stand, how they will be able to find food and raiment for an hundred thousand useless mouths and backs. And secondly, there being a round million of creatures in human figure throughout this kingdom, whose whole subsistence put into a common stock would leave them in debt two millions of pounds sterling, adding those who are beggars by profession to the bulk of farmers, cottagers, and laborers, with their wives and children who are beggars in effect: I desire those politicians who dislike my overture, and may perhaps be so bold as to attempt an answer, that they will first ask the parents of these mortals, whether they would not at this day think it a great happiness to have been sold for food, at a year old in the manner I prescribe, and thereby have avoided such a perpetual scene of misfortunes as they have since gone through by the oppression of landlords, the impossibility of paying rent without money or trade, the want of common sustenance, with neither house nor clothes to cover them from the inclemencies of the weather, and the most inevitable prospect of entailing the like or greater miseries upon their breed for ever.

I profess, in the sincerity of my heart, that I have not the least personal interest in endeavoring to promote this necessary work, having no other motive than the public good of my country, by advancing our trade, providing for infants, relieving the poor, and giving some pleasure to the rich. I have no children by which I can propose to get a single penny; the youngest being nine years old, and my wife past child-bearing.

(1729)

SIR RICHARD STEELE (1672-1729)

STEELE, like Swift, was born in Dublin. He passed, with Addison, through Charterhouse School to Oxford, but soon left the university to seek his fortune in the army. By 1701, he had gained a captaincy in the Tower Guards and was a vivacious figure among the wits who haunted the coffee-houses, clubs, and theaters of London. Several comedies, in which he made a manly and effective effort to win a place for decency on the English stage, were still sprightly enough to sustain his reputation as a wit and good fellow. He was soon taken on by the government and, in 1707, was commissioned to write *The Gazette*. While officially 'keeping that paper very innocent and very insipid,' Steele discovered the possibilities of periodical writing. Two years later he began *The Tatler*, picking up as a disguise the character of a fictitious astrologer, Isaac Bickerstaff, which Swift had let drop after provoking the town to hilarious scoffing at one Partridge, an almanac-maker. Addison soon penetrated the disguise and was eagerly welcomed as a contributor. After about a year, Steele and Addison together devised the more commodious plan of *The Spectator*. The novel periodical created and supplied a new kind of literary demand. Its freedom from party bias, and the penetrating and yet urbane irony of its portrayals and criticisms of English manners gave it a wide appeal. *The Spectator* became a part of the 'tea-equipage' in London clubs and coffee-houses and wide-awake provincial homes. It turned out a valuable pecuniary asset; but the partnership did not last. Steele was a turbulent politician; Addison disapproved of his factious spirit; and, after the earlier numbers of *The Guardian* (1713), they ceased to collaborate. None of the later periodicals of either approximated the success of *The Spectator*. Steele was now approaching the liveliest part of his life. He had a stormy parliamentary experience, was made supervisor of the Drury Lane Theater, and George I knighted him for energetic championship of the Hanoverian succession.

His prosperity was brief, however. Through his opposition to the Peerage Bill (1719), he lost the support of his party and received some sore knocks from his old friend. He was frequently in money difficulties, and finally, broken in health as well as fortune, he took refuge in Wales, not as Swift venomously rimed, 'from perils of a hundred gaols,' but from the expenses of a London establishment, so that his debts might be paid before his death. Steele's Irish imprudences are sometimes exaggerated for the sake of contrasting him with Addison. He was not, in practice, above the fashionable vices of his times, and he was sinfully reckless in money matters. He was, nevertheless, a sincere champion of virtue and lover of piety; he was chivalrous toward women, generous and forgiving toward his friends, and intrepid where his political conscience was involved. The uncalculating prodigality and sweetness of his nature are reflected in his pages, and have made many besides Thackeray 'own to liking Dick Steele the man, and Dick Steele the author, much better than much better men and much better authors.'

From THE TATLER — No. 1
THE ADVERTISEMENT

THOUGH the other papers which are published for the use of the good people of England have certainly very wholesome effects and are laudable in their particular kinds, they do not seem to come up to the main design of such narrations, which, I humbly presume, should be principally intended for the use of politic persons, who are so public-spirited as to neglect their own affairs to look into transactions of state. Now these gentlemen, for the most part, being persons of strong zeal and weak intellects, it is both a charitable and necessary work to offer something whereby such worthy and well-affected members of the commonwealth may be instructed, after their reading, what to think; which shall be the end and purpose of this my paper, wherein I shall from time to time report and consider all matters of what kind soever that shall occur to me, and publish such my advices and reflections every Tuesday, Thursday and Saturday in the week, for the convenience of the post. I resolve also to have something which may be of entertainment to the fair sex, in honor of whom I have invented the title of this paper. I therefore earnestly desire all persons, without distinction, to take it in for the present *gratis*, and hereafter at the price of one penny, forbidding all hawkers to take more for it at their peril. And I desire all persons to consider that I am at a very great charge for proper materials for this work, as well as that, before I resolved upon it, I had settled a correspondence in all parts of the known and knowing world. And forasmuch as this globe is not trodden upon by mere drudges of business only, but that men of spirit and genius are justly to be esteemed as considerable agents in it, we shall not upon a dearth of news present you with musty foreign edicts, or dull proclamations, but shall divide our relation of the passages which occur in action or discourse throughout this town, as well as elsewhere, under such dates of places as may prepare you for the matter you are to expect, in the following manner:

All accounts of gallantry, pleasure, and entertainment shall be under the article of White's Chocolate-house; poetry, under that of Will's Coffee-house; learning, under the title of Grecian; foreign and domestic news, you will have from Saint James's Coffee-house; and what else I have to offer on any other subject shall be dated from my own apartment.

I once more desire my reader to consider that, as I cannot keep an ingenious man to go daily to Wills under twopence each day, merely for his charges; to White's under sixpence; nor to the Grecian, without allowing him some plain Spanish, to be as able as others at the learned table; and that a good observer cannot speak with even kidney at Saint James's without clean linen; I say, these considerations will, I hope, make all persons willing to comply with my humble request (when my *gratis* stock is exhausted) of a penny a piece; especially since they are sure of some proper amusement, and that it is impossible for me to want means to entertain them, having, besides the force of my own parts, the power of divination, and that I can, by casting a figure, tell you all that will happen before it comes to pass.

But this last faculty I shall use very sparingly, and speak but of few things until they are passed, for fear of divulging matters which may offend our superiors.

Tuesday, April 12, 1709.

* * *

From THE TATLER — No. 181

A RECOLLECTION

* * *

THE first sense of sorrow I ever knew was upon the death of my father, at which time I was not quite five years of age; but was rather amazed at what all the house meant than possessed with a real understanding why nobody was willing to play with me. I remember I went into the room where his body lay, and my mother sat weeping alone by it. I had my battledore in my hand, and fell a-beating the coffin, and calling 'Papa'; for I know not how, I had some slight idea that he was locked up there. My mother catched me in her arms, and transported beyond all patience of the silent grief she was before in, she almost smothered me in her embrace, and told me in a flood of tears, 'Papa could not hear me, and would play with me no more, for they were going to put him under ground, whence he could never come to us again.' She was a very beautiful woman, of a noble spirit, and there was a dignity in her grief amidst all the wildness of her transport, which, methought struck me with an instinct of sorrow which, before I was sensible of what it was to grieve, seized my very soul, and has made pity the weakness of my heart ever since. The mind in infancy is, methinks, like the body in embryo, and receives impressions so forcible that they are as hard to be removed by reason, as any mark with which a child is born is to be taken away by any future application. Hence it is that good-nature in me is no merit; but, having been so frequently overwhelmed with her tears before I knew the cause of any affliction, or could draw defenses from my own judgment, I imbibed commiseration, remorse, and an unmanly gentleness of mind, which has since insnared me into ten thousand calamities, and from whence I can reap no advantage, except it be that, in such a humor as I am now in, I can the better indulge myself in the softnesses of humanity, and enjoy that sweet anxiety which arises from the memory of past afflictions.

* * *

June 5, 1710.

From THE SPECTATOR — No. 2

THE CLUB

THE first of our society is a gentleman of Worcestershire, of ancient descent, a baronet, his name is Sir Roger de Coverley. His great grandfather was inventor of that famous country-dance which is called after him. All who know that shire are very well acquainted with the parts and merits of Sir Roger. He is a gentleman that is very singular in his behavior, but his singularities proceed from his good sense, and are contradictions to the manners of the world, only as he thinks the world is in the wrong. However, this humor creates him no enemies, for he does nothing with sourness or obstinacy; and his being unconfined to modes and forms, makes him but the readier and more capable to please and oblige all who know him. When he is in town, he lives in Soho Square. It is said, he keeps himself a bachelor, by reason he was crossed in love by a perverse beautiful widow of the next county to him. Before this disappointment, Sir Roger was what you call a fine gentleman, had often supped with my Lord Rochester and Sir George Etherege, fought a duel upon his first coming to town, and kicked Bully Dawson in a public coffee house for calling him youngster. But, being ill used by the above mentioned widow, he was very serious for a year and a half; and though, his temper being naturally jovial, he at last got over it, he grew careless of himself, and never dressed afterwards. He continues to wear a coat and doublet of the same cut that were in fashion at the time of his repulse, which, in his merry humors, he tells us, has been in and out twelve times since he first wore it. He is now in his fifty-sixth year, cheerful, gay, and hearty; keeps a good house both in town and country; a great lover of mankind: but there is such a mirthful cast in his behavior, that he is rather beloved than esteemed. His tenants grow rich, his servants look satisfied, all the young women profess love to him, and the young men are glad of his company; when he comes into a house, he calls the servants by their names, and talks all the way up stairs to a visit. I must not omit, that Sir Roger is a justice of the *quorum;* that he fills the chair at a quarter-sessions with great abilities, and three months ago, gained universal applause, by explaining a passage in the game-act.

The gentleman next in esteem and authority among us, is another bachelor, who is a member of the Inner Temple; a man of great probity, wit, and understanding; but he has chosen his place of residence rather to obey the direction of an old humorsome father, than in pursuit of his own inclinations. He was placed there to study the laws of the land, and is the most learned of any of the house in those of the stage. Aristotle and Longinus are much better understood by him than Littleton or Coke. The father sends up every post questions relating to marriage articles, leases and tenures, in the neighborhood; all which questions he agrees with an attorney to answer and take care of in the lump. He is studying the passions themselves, when he should be inquiring into the debates among men which arise from them. He knows the argument of each of the orations of Demosthenes and Tully; but not one case in the reports of our own courts. No one ever took him for a fool, but none, except his intimate friends, know he has a great deal of wit. This turn makes him at once both disinterested and agreeable; as few of his thoughts are drawn from business, they are most of them fit for conversation. His taste of books is a little too just for the age he lives in; he has read all, but approves of very few. His familiarity with the customs, manners, actions, and writings of the ancients, makes him a very delicate observer of what occurs to him in the present world. He is an excellent critic, and the time of the play is his hour of business; exactly at five he passes through New Inn, crosses through Russell court, and takes a turn at Will's, till the play begins; he has his shoes rubbed, and his periwig powdered at the barber's as you go into the Rose. It is for the good of the audience when he is at a play; for the actors have an ambition to please him.

The person of next consideration is Sir Andrew Freeport, a merchant of great eminence in the city of London. A person of indefatigable industry, strong reason, and great experience. His notions of trade are noble and generous, and (as every rich man has usually some sly way of jesting, which would make no great figure were he not a rich man) he calls the sea the British Common. He is acquainted with commerce in all its parts, and will tell you that it is a stupid and barbarous way to extend dominion by arms, for true power is to be got by arts and industry. He will often argue, that if this part of our trade were well cultivated, we should gain from one nation,—and if another, from another. I have heard him prove, that diligence makes more lasting acquisitions than valor, and that sloth has ruined more nations than the sword. He abounds in several frugal maxims, amongst which the greatest favorite is, 'A penny saved is a penny got.' A general trader of good sense is pleasanter company than a general scholar; and Sir Andrew having a natural unaffected eloquence, the perspicuity of his discourse gives the same pleasure that wit would in another man. He has made his fortunes himself; and says that England may be richer than other kingdoms, by as plain methods as he himself is richer than other men; though at the same time I can say this of him, that there is not a point in the compass but blows home a ship in which he is an owner.

Next to Sir Andrew in the club-room sits Captain Sentry, a gentleman of great courage, good understanding, but invincible modesty. He is one of those that deserve very well, but are very awkward at putting their talents within the observation of such as should take notice of them. He was some years a captain, and behaved himself with great gallantry in several engagements and at several sieges; but having a small estate of his own, and being next heir to Sir Roger, he has quitted a way of life, in which no man can rise suitably to his merit, who is not something of a courtier as well as a soldier. I have heard him often lament, that in a profession where merit is placed in so conspicuous a view, impudence should get the better of modesty. When he has talked to this purpose, I never heard him make a sour expression, but frankly confess that he left the world, because he was not fit for it. A strict honesty and an even regular behavior are in themselves obstacles to him that must press through crowds who endeavor at the same end with himself, the favor of a commander. He will, however, in his way of talk, excuse generals for not disposing according to men's desert, or inquiring into it: for, says he, that great man who has a mind to help me, has as many to break through to come at me, as I have to come at him: therefore, he will conclude, that the man who would make a figure, especially in a military way, must get over all false modesty, and assist his patron against the importunity of other pretenders, by a proper assurance in his own vindication. He says, it is a civil cowardice to be backward in asserting what you ought to expect, as it is a military fear to be slow in attacking when it is your duty. With this candor does the gentleman speak of himself and others. The same frankness runs through all his conversation. The military part of his life has furnished him with many adventures, in the relation of which he is very agreeable to the company; for he is never over-bearing, though accustomed to command men in the utmost degree below him; nor ever too obsequious, from an habit of obeying men highly above him.

But, that our society may not appear a set of humorists, unacquainted with the gallantries and pleasures of the age, we have among us the gallant Will Honeycomb, a gentleman who, according to his years, should be in the decline of his life, but, having ever been very careful of his person, and always had a very easy fortune, time has made but a very little impression, either by wrinkles on his forehead, or traces on his brain. His person is well turned, of a good height. He is very ready at that sort of discourse with which men usually entertain women. He has all his life dressed very well, and remembers habits as others do men. He can smile when one speaks to him, and laughs easily. He knows the history of every mode, and can inform you from what Frenchwomen our wives and daughters had this manner of curling their hair, that way of placing their hoods; and whose vanity to shew her foot made that part of the dress so short in such a year. In a word, all his conversation and knowledge have been in the female world; as other men of his age will take notice to you what such a minister said upon such and such an occasion, he will tell you, when the Duke of Monmouth danced at court, such a woman was then smitten, another was taken with him at the head of his troop in the Park. For all these important relations, he has ever about the same time received a kind glance or a blow of a fan from some celebrated beauty, mother of the present lord such-a-one.

This way of talking of his very much enlivens the conversation, among us of a more sedate turn; and I find there is not one of the company, but myself, who rarely speak at all, but speaks of him as of that sort of man who is usually called a well-bred fine gentleman. To conclude his character, where women are not concerned, he is an honest worthy man.

I cannot tell whether I am to account him whom I am next to speak of, as one of our company; for he visits us but seldom, but when he does, it adds to every man else a new enjoyment of himself. He is a clergyman, a very philosophic man, of general learning, great sanctity of life, and the most exact good breeding. He has the misfortune to be of a very weak constitution; and consequently cannot accept of such cares and business as preferments in his function would oblige him to; he is therefore among divines what a chamber-councillor is among lawyers. The probity of his mind, and the integrity of his life, create him followers, as being eloquent or loud advances others. He seldom introduces the subject he speaks upon; but we are so far gone in years that he observes, when he is among us, an earnestness to have him fall on some divine topic, which he always treats with much authority, as one who has no interest in this world, as one who is hastening to the object of all his wishes.

and conceives hope from his decays and infirmities. These are my ordinary companions.
Friday, March 2, 1710-11.

From THE SPECTATOR — No. 6
SIR ROGER ON MEN OF PARTS

I KNOW no evil under the sun so great as the abuse of the understanding, and yet there is no one vice more common. It has diffused itself through both sexes, and all qualities of mankind; and there is hardly that person to be found, who is not more concerned for the reputation of wit and sense, than honesty and virtue. But this unhappy affectation of being wise rather than honest, witty than good-natured, is the source of most of the ill habits of life. Such false impressions are owing to the abandoned writings of men of wit, and the awkward imitation of the rest of mankind.

For this reason, Sir Roger was saying last night, that he was of opinion that none but men of fine parts deserve to be hanged. The reflections of such men are so delicate upon all occurrences which they are concerned in, that they should be exposed to more than ordinary infamy and punishment, for offending against such quick admonitions as their own souls give them, and blunting the fine edge of their minds in such a manner, that they are no more shocked at vice and folly, than men of slower capacities. There is no greater monster in being, than a very ill man of great parts. He lives like a man in a palsy, with one side of him dead. While perhaps he enjoys the satisfaction of luxury, of wealth, of ambition, he has lost the taste of good will, of friendship, of innocence. Scare-crow, the beggar in Lincoln's-inn-fields, who disabled himself in his right leg, and asks alms all day to get himself a warm supper at night, is not half so despicable a wretch, as such a man of sense. The beggar has no relish above sensations; he finds rest more agreeable than motion; and while he has a warm fire, never reflects that he deserves to be whipped. Every man who terminates his satisfactions and enjoyments within the supply of his own necessities and passions is, says Sir Roger, in my eye as poor a rogue as Scarecrow. 'But,' continued he, 'for the loss of public and private virtue we are beholden to your men of fine parts forsooth; it is with them no matter what is done, so it be done with an air. But to me who am so whimsical in a corrupt age as to act according to nature and reason, a selfish man in the most shining circumstance and equipage, appears in the same condition with the fellow above mentioned, but more contemptible in proportion to what more he robs the public of and enjoys above him. I lay it down therefore for a rule, that the whole man is to move together; that every action of any importance, is to have a prospect of public good: and that the general tendency of our indifferent actions ought to be agreeable to the dictates of reason, of religion, of good breeding; without this, a man, as I have before hinted, is hopping instead of walking, he is not in his entire and proper motion.'

While the honest knight was thus bewildering himself in good starts, I looked intentively upon him, which made him, I thought, collect his mind a little. 'What I aim at,' says he, 'is, to represent, that I am of opinion, to polish our understandings and neglect our manners is of all things the most inexcusable. Reason should govern passion, but instead of that, you see, it is often subservient to it; and, as unaccountable as one would think it, a wise man is not always a good man.' This degeneracy is not only the guilt of particular persons, but also at some times of a whole people; and perhaps it may appear upon examination, that the most polite ages are the least virtuous. This may be attributed to the folly of admitting wit and learning as merit in themselves, without considering the application of them. By this means it becomes a rule, not so much to regard what we do, as how we do it. But this false beauty will not pass upon men of honest minds and true taste. Sir Richard Blackmore says, with as much good sense as virtue, 'It is a mighty dishonor and shame to employ excellent faculties and abundance of wit, to humor and please men in their vices and follies. The great enemy of mankind, notwithstanding his wit and angelic faculties, is the most odious being in the whole creation.' He goes on soon after to say, very generously, that he undertook the writing of his poem 'to rescue the Muses out of the hands of ravishers, to restore them to their sweet and chaste mansions, and to engage them in an employment suitable to their dignity.' This certainly ought to be the purpose of every man who appears in public, and whoever does not proceed upon that foundation, injures his country as fast as he succeeds in his studies. When modesty ceases to be the chief ornament of one sex, and integrity of the other, society is upon a wrong basis, and we shall be ever after without rules to guide our judgment in what is really becoming and ornamental. Nature and reason direct one thing, passion and humor another. To follow the dictates of these two latter, is going into a road that is both endless and intricate; when we pursue the other, our passage is delightful, and what we aim at easily attainable.

I do not doubt but England is at present as polite a nation as any in the world; but any man who thinks can easily see, that the affectation of being gay and in fashion, has very near eaten up our good sense and our religion. Is there anything so just as that mode and gallantry should be built upon exerting ourselves in what is proper and agreeable to the institutions of justice and piety among us? And yet is there anything more common, than that we run in perfect contradiction to them? All which is supported by no other pretension, than that it is done with what we call a good grace.

Nothing ought to be held laudable or becoming, but what nature itself should prompt us to think so. Respect to all kinds of superiors is founded, methinks, upon instinct; and yet what is so ridiculous as age? I make this abrupt transition to the mention of this vice, more than any other, in order to introduce a little story, which I think a pretty instance that the most polite age is in danger of being the most vicious.

'It happened at Athens, during a public representation of some play exhibited in honor of the commonwealth, that an old gentleman came too late for a place suitable to his age and quality. Many of the young gentlemen, who observed the difficulty and confusion he was in, made signs to him that they would accommodate him if he came where they sat. The good man bustled through the crowd accordingly; but when he came to the seats to which he was invited, the jest was to sit close and expose him, as he stood out of countenance, to the whole audience. The frolic went round all the Athenian benches. But on those occasions there were also particular places assigned for foreigners. When the good man skulked towards the boxes appointed for the Lacedæmonians, that honest people, more virtuous than polite, rose up all to a man, and with the greatest respect received him among them. The Athenians being suddenly touched with a sense of the Spartan virtue and their own degeneracy, gave a thunder of applause; and the old man cried out, "The Athenians understand what is good, but the Lacedæmonians practise it."'

Wednesday, March 17, 1710-11.

From THE SPECTATOR — No. 113

SIR ROGER IN LOVE

In my first description of the company in which I pass most of my time, it may be remembered, that I mentioned a great affliction which my friend Sir Roger had met with in his youth; which was no less than a disappointment in love. It happened this evening, that we fell into a very pleasing walk at a distance from his house. As soon as we came into it, 'It is,' quoth the good old man, looking round him with a smile, 'very hard, that any part of my land should be settled upon one who has used me so ill as the perverse widow did; and yet I am sure I could not see a sprig of any bough of this whole walk of trees, but I should reflect upon her and her severity. She has certainly the finest hand of any woman in the world. You are to know, this was the place wherein I used to muse upon her; and by that custom I can never come into it, but the same tender sentiments revive in my mind, as if I had actually walked with that beautiful creature under these shades. I have been fool enough to carve her name on the bark of several of these trees; so unhappy is the condition of men in love, to attempt the removing of their passion by the methods which serve only to imprint it deeper. She has certainly the finest hand of any woman in the world.'

Here followed a profound silence; and I was not displeased to observe my friend falling so naturally into a discourse which I had ever before taken notice he industriously avoided. After a very long pause, he entered upon an account of this great circumstance in his life, with an air which I thought raised my idea of him above what I had ever had before; and gave me the picture of that cheerful mind of his, before it received that stroke which has ever since affected his words and actions. But he went on as follows:—

'I came to my estate in my twenty-second year, and resolved to follow the steps of the most worthy of my ancestors who have inhabited this spot of earth before me, in all the methods of hospitality and good neighborhood, for the sake of my fame; and in country sports and recreations, for the sake of my health. In my twenty-third year I was obliged to serve as sheriff of the county; and in my servants, officers, and whole equipage, indulged the pleasure of a young man (who did not think ill of his own person) in taking that public occasion of showing my figure and behavior to advantage. You may easily imagine to yourself what appearance I made, who am pretty tall, ride well, and was very well dressed, at the head of a whole county, with music before me, a feather in my hat, and my horse well bitted. I can assure you I was not a little pleased with the kind looks and glances I had from all the balconies and windows as I rode to the hall where the assizes were held. But, when I came there, a beautiful creature in a widow's habit sat in a court to hear the event of a cause concerning her dower. This commanding creature (who was born for the destruction of all who behold her) put on such a resignation in her countenance, and bore the whispers of all around the court with such a pretty uneasiness, I warrant you, and then recovered herself from one eye to another, until she was perfectly confused by meeting something so wistful in all she encountered, that at last, with a murrain to her, she cast her bewitching eye upon me. I no sooner met it but I bowed like a great surprised booby; and knowing her cause to be the first which came on, I cried, like a captivated calf as I was, "Make way for the defendant's witnesses." This sudden partiality made all the county immediately see the sheriff also was become a slave to the fine widow. During the time her cause was upon trial, she behaved herself, I warrant you, with such a deep attention to her business, took opportunities to have little billets handed to her counsel, then would be in such a pretty confusion, occasioned, you must know, by acting before so much company, that not only I but the whole court was prejudiced in her favor; and all that the next heir to her husband had to urge was thought so groundless and frivolous, that when it came to her counsel to reply, there was not half so much said as every one besides in the court thought he could have urged to her advantage. You must understand, sir, this perverse woman is one of those unaccountable creatures that secretly rejoice in the admiration of men, but indulge themselves in no farther consequences. Hence it is that she has ever had a train of admirers, and she removes from her slaves in town to those in the country, according to the seasons of the year. She is a reading lady, and far gone in the pleasures of friendship. She is always accompanied by a confidante, who is witness to her daily protestations against our sex, and consequently a bar to her first steps towards love, upon the strength of her own maxims and declarations.

'However, I must needs say, this accomplished mistress of mine has distinguished me above the rest, and has been known to declare Sir Roger de Coverley was the tamest and most humane of all the brutes in the country. I was told she said so by one who thought he rallied me; and upon the strength of this slender encouragement of being thought least detestable, I made new liveries, new-paired my coach-horses, sent them all to town to be bitted, and taught to throw their legs well, and move all together, before I pretended to cross the country, and wait upon her. As soon as I thought my retinue suitable to the character of my fortune and youth, I set out from hence to make my addresses. The particular skill of this lady has ever been to inflame your wishes, and yet command respect. To make her mistress of this art, she has a greater share of knowledge, wit, and good sense than is usual even among men of merit. Then she is beautiful beyond the race of women. If you will not let her go on with a certain artifice with her eyes, and the skill of beauty, she will arm herself with her real charms, and strike you with admiration instead of desire. It is certain that if you were to behold the whole woman, there is that dignity in her aspect, that composure in her motion, that complacency in her manner, that if her form makes you hope, her merit makes you fear. But then again, she is such a desperate scholar that no country gentleman can approach her without being a jest. As I was going to tell you, when I came to her house, I was admitted to her presence with great civility; at the same time she placed herself to be first seen by me in such an attitude, as I think you call the posture of a picture, that she discovered new charms, and I at last came towards her with such an awe as made me speechless. This she no sooner observed but she made her advantage of it, and began a discourse to me concerning love and honor, as they both are followed by pretenders, and the real votaries to them. When she discussed these points in a discourse which, I verily believe, was as learned as the best philosopher in Europe could possibly make, she asked me whether she was so happy as to fall in with my sentiments on these important particulars. Her confidante sat by her, and on my being in the last confusion and silence, this malicious aid of hers turning to her, says, "I am very glad to observe Sir Roger pauses upon this subject, and seems resolved to deliver all his sentiments upon the matter when he pleases to speak." They both kept their countenances, and after I had sat half an hour meditating how to behave before such profound casuists, I rose up and took my leave. Chance has since that time thrown me very often in her way, and she as often directed a discourse to me which I do not understand. This barbarity has kept me ever at a distance from the most beautiful object my eyes ever beheld. It is thus also she deals with all mankind, and you must make love to her as you would conquer the sphinx, by posing her. But were she like other women, and that there were any talking to her, how constant must the pleasure of that man be, who could converse with a creature—But, after all, you may be sure her heart is fixed on some one or other: and yet I have been credibly informed—but who can believe half that is said!—They say she sings excellently; her voice in her ordinary speech has something in it inexpressibly sweet. You must know I dined with her at a public table the day after I first saw her, and she helped me to some tansy in the eye of all the gentlemen in the country. She has certainly the finest hand of any woman in the world. I can assure you, sir, were you to behold her, you would be in the same condition; for as her speech is music, her form is angelic. But I find I grow irregular while I am talking of her; but indeed it would be stupidity to be unconcerned at such perfection. Oh, the excellent creature! she is as inimitable to all women, as she is inaccessible to all men.'

I found my friend begin to rave, and insensibly led him towards the house, that we might be joined by some other company; and am convinced that the widow is the secret cause of all that inconsistency which appears in some parts of my friend's discourse; though he has so much command of himself as not directly to mention her, yet according to that of Martial, which one knows not how to render into English, *dum tacet hanc loquitur* [even when silent he talks of her].

* * *

Tuesday, July 10, 1711.

From THE SPECTATOR — No. 454

A DAY IN LONDON

IT is an expressible pleasure to know a little of the world, and to be of no character or significancy in it.

To be ever unconcerned, and ever looking on new objects with an endless curiosity, is a delight known only to those who are turned for speculation: nay, they who enjoy it must value things only as they are the objects of speculation, without drawing any worldly advantage to themselves from them, but just as they are what contribute to their amusement, or the improvement of the mind. I lay one night last week at Richmond; and being restless, not out of dissatisfaction, but a certain busy inclination one sometimes has, I rose at four in the morning, and took boat for London, with a resolution to rove by boat and coach for the next four-and-twenty hours, till the many different objects I must needs meet with should tire my imagination, and give me an inclination to a repose more profound than I was at that time capable of. I beg people's pardon for an odd humor I am guilty of, and was often that day, which is saluting any person whom I like, whether I know him or not. This is a particularity would be tolerated in me, if they considered that the greatest pleasure I know I receive at my eyes, and that I am obliged to an agreeable person for coming abroad into my view, as another is for a visit of conversation at their own houses.

The hours of the day and night are taken up in the cities of London and Westminster by people as different from each other as those who are born in different centuries. Men of six o'clock give way to those of nine, they of nine to the generation of twelve; and they of twelve disappear, and make room for the fashionable world, who have made two o'clock the noon of the day.

When we first put off from shore, we soon fell in with a fleet of gardeners, bound for the several market ports of London; and it was the most pleasing scene imaginable to see the cheerfulness with which those industrious people plied their way to a certain sale of their goods. The banks on each side are as well peopled, and beautified with as agreeable plantations, as any spot on the earth; but the Thames itself, loaded with the product of each shore, added very much to the landscape. It was very easy to observe by their sailing and the countenances of the ruddy virgins who were supercargoes, the parts of the town to which they were bound. There was an air in the purveyors for Covent Garden, who frequently converse with morning rakes, very unlike the seeming sobriety of those bound for Stocks Market.

Nothing remarkable happened in our voyage;

but I landed with ten sail of apricot-boats, at Strand Bridge, after having put in at Nine Elms, and taken in melons, consigned by Mr. Cuffe, of that place, to Sarah Sewell and Company, at their stall in Covent Garden. We arrived at Strand Bridge at six of the clock, and were unloading, when the hackney-coachmen of the foregoing night took their leave of each other at the Darkhouse, to go to bed before the day was too far spent. Chimney-sweepers passed by us as we made up to the market, and some raillery happened between one of the fruit-wenches and those black men about the Devil and Eve, with allusion to their several professions. I could not believe any place more entertaining than Covent Garden, where I strolled from one fruit-shop to another, with crowds of agreeable young women, around me, who were purchasing fruit for their respective families. It was almost eight of the clock before I could leave that variety of objects. I took coach and followed a young lady, who tripped into another just before me, attended by her maid. I saw immediately she was of the family of the Vainloves. There are a set of these, who, of all things, affect the play of blindman's-buff, and leading men into love for they know not whom, who are fled they know not where. This sort of woman is usually a jaunty slattern; she hangs on her clothes, plays her head, varies her posture, and changes place incessantly, and all with an appearance of striving at the same time to hide herself, and yet give you to understand she is in humor to laugh at you. You must have often seen the coachmen make signs with their fingers, as they drive by each other, to intimate how much they have got that day. They can carry on that language to give intelligence where they are driving. In an instant my coachman took the wink to pursue, and the lady's driver gave the hint that he was going through Longacre toward St. James's; while he whipped up James Street, we drove for King Street, to save the pass at St. Martin's Lane. The coachmen took care to meet, jostle, and threaten each other for way, and be entangled at the end of Newport Street and Longacre. The fright, you must believe, brought down the lady's coach-door, and obliged her, with her mask off, to inquire into the bustle,—when she sees the man she would avoid. The tackle of the coach-window is so bad she cannot draw it up again, and she drives on, sometimes wholly discovered, and sometimes half escaped, according to the accident of carriages in her way. One of these ladies keeps her seat in a hackney-coach as well as the best rider does on a managed horse. The laced shoe on her left foot, with a careless gesture, just appearing on the opposite cushion, held her both firm and in a proper attitude to receive the next jolt.

As she was an excellent coach-woman, many were the glances at each other which we had for an hour and a half in all parts of the town, by the skill of our drivers, till at last my lady was conveniently lost, with notice from her coachman to ours to make off, and he should hear where she went. This chase was now at an end, and the fellow who drove her came to us, and discovered that he was ordered to come again in an hour, for that she was a silk-worm. I was surprised with this phrase, but found it was a cant among the hackney fraternity for their best customers, women who ramble twice or thrice a week from shop to shop, to turn over all the goods in town without buying anything. The silk-worms are, it seems, indulged by the tradesmen; for, though they never buy, they are ever talking of new silks, laces, and ribbons, and serve the owners in getting them customers, as their common dunners do in making them pay.

The day of people of fashion began now to break, and carts and hacks were mingled with equipages of show and vanity, when I resolved to walk it, out of cheapness; but my unhappy curiosity is such, that I find it always my interest to take a coach, for some odd adventure among beggars, ballad-singers, or the like, detains and throws me into expense. It happened so immediately, for at the corner of Warwick Street, as I was listening to a new ballad, a ragged rascal, a beggar who knew me, came up to me, and began to turn the eyes of the good company upon me, by telling me he was extreme poor, and should die in the street for want of drink, except I immediately would have the charity to give him sixpence to go into the next ale-house and save his life. He urged with a melancholy face, that all his family had died of thirst. All the mob have humor, and two or three began to take the jest; by which Mr. Sturdy carried his point, and let me sneak off to a coach. As I drove along, it was a pleasing reflection to see the world so prettily checkered since I left Richmond, and the scene still filling with children of a new hour. This satisfaction increased as I moved towards the city; and gay signs, well-disposed streets, magnificent public structures, and wealthy shops adorned with contented faces, made the joy still rising till we came into the center of the city, and center of the world of trade, the Exchange of London. As other men in the crowds about me were pleased with their hopes and bargains, I found my account in observing them, in attention to their several interests. I, indeed, looked upon myself as the richest man that walked the Exchange that day; for my benevolence made me share the gains of every bargain that was made. It was not the least of my satisfaction in my survey, to go up stairs and pass the shops of agreeable females; to observe so many pretty hands busy in the folding of ribbons, and the utmost eagerness of agreeable faces in the sale of patches, pins, and wires, on each side of the counters, was an amusement in which I could longer have indulged myself, had not the dear creatures called to me, to ask what I wanted, when I could not answer, 'Only to look at you.' I went to one of the windows which opened to the area below, where all the several voices lost their distinction, and rose up in a confused humming, which created in me a reflection that could not come into the mind of any but of one a little too studious; for I said to myself with a kind of pun in thought, 'What nonsense is all the hurry of this world to those who are above it?' In these, or not much wiser thoughts, I had like to have lost my place at the chophouse, where every man, according to the natural bashfulness or sullenness of our nation, eats in a public room a mess of broth, or chop of meat, in dumb silence, as if they had no pretense to speak to each other on the foot of being men, except they were of each other's acquaintance.

I went afterward to Robin's, and saw people who had dined with me at the five-penny ordinary just before, give bills for the value of large estates; and could not but behold with great pleasure property lodged in and transferred in a moment from, such as would never be masters of half as much as is seemingly in them, and given from them, every day they live. But before five in the afternoon I left the city, came to my common scene of Covent Garden, and passed the evening at Will's in attending the discourses of several sets of people, who relieved each other within my hearing on the subjects of cards, dice, love, learning, and politics. The last subject kept me till I heard the streets in the possession of the bellman, who had now the world to himself, and cried, 'Past two o'clock.' This roused me from my seat; and I went to my lodgings, led by a light, whom I put into the discourse of his private economy, and made him give me an account of the charge, hazard, profit, and loss of a family that depended upon a link, with a design to end my trivial day with the generosity of sixpence, instead of a third part of that sum. When I came to my chambers, I writ down these minutes, but was at a loss what instruction I should propose to my reader from the enumeration of so many insignificant matters and occurrences; and I thought it of great use, if they could learn with me to keep their minds open to gratification, and ready to receive it from anything it meets with. This one circumstance will make every face you see give you the satisfaction you now take in beholding that of a friend; will make every object a pleasing one; will make all the good which arrives to any man an increase of happiness to yourself.

Monday, August 11, 1712.

JOSEPH ADDISON (1672-1719)

From a refined clerical home, Addison was sent to Charterhouse School and thence, at fifteen, to Oxford, where he distinguished himself as a scholar and rose to a fellowship at Magdalen College (1697-99). By his twenty-second year, he was known as a cultivated writer of English and Latin verses and Dryden had welcomed him to the world of letters. While he was considering the church, the Whig government, desiring to enlist the service of his pen, granted him a pension which enabled him to spend four years in study and travel on the Continent. Returning, in 1704, to a mean London lodging, he was directly sought out by the Whig leaders and commissioned to celebrate the recent victory of Marlborough at Blenheim. His poem, *The Campaign*, proved satisfactory, and he was rewarded with lucrative secretaryships, one of which took him to Ireland, where he was eminently successful and popular. Meantime, he had become a leader among the coffee-house wits and had won the friendship of Swift. He renewed his Charterhouse intimacy with Steele, was responsible for 'many applauded strokes' in the latter's comedy, *The Tender Husband* (1705), and contributed to *The Tatler* (1709), 42 of its 271 numbers. With Steele, he started *The Spectator* (1711-12) which appeared daily and ran to 555 numbers, of which Addison wrote 274. In *The Spectator*, Addison's genius found its aptest expression. No other periodical writing has ever combined, in so high a degree, immediate journalistic effectiveness and permanent literary charm. This success was promptly followed by that of his tragedy, *Cato* (1713), which, though intrinsically undramatic, became immensely famous because of its supposed political sentiments. When the Whigs returned to power, he was made chief secretary for Ireland; carried on, for a time, a party periodical called *The Freeholder;* became in 1716 commissioner for trade and the colonies, and, in 1717, secretary of state. Ill-health and, possibly, ill-success as a public speaker induced him to resign his post after a few months. In the midst of new literary plans and an unkind political squabble with his old friend Steele, he was cut off by death when only forty-seven years of age. A fine elegy, by his friend Tickell, gives us a good idea of his impressive night burial in Westminster Abbey.

Addison's central qualities are discretion and self-possession. He 'always preferred cheerfulness to mirth,' and those who look for sensational elements, whether in style or behavior, will find him tame. A profane person once pronounced him 'a parson in a tye-wig,' and another vindictively declared, 'One day or other you'll see that man a bishop.' But the chiefs of a witty and sociable age owned that, after the bottle had been round and among friends, he was the most delightful companion alive. As a writer, he profoundly influenced English manners and morals by demonstrating that urbanity and good breeding might be associated with learning, and that virtue is not incompatible with elegance and wit. Of his merit as a prose stylist, no one has spoken more roundly than Dr. Johnson in his measured statement, that 'Whoever wishes to attain an English style, familiar but not coarse, and elegant but not ostentatious, must give his days and nights to the volumes of Addison.'

From THE SPECTATOR — No. 1
THE SPECTATOR INTRODUCES HIMSELF

I have observed that a reader seldom peruses a book with pleasure, till he knows whether the writer of it be a black or a fair man, of a mild or choleric disposition, married or a bachelor, with other particulars of the like nature, that conduce very much to the right understanding of an author. To gratify this curiosity, which is so natural to a reader, I design this paper, and my next, as prefatory discourses to my following writings, and shall give some account in them of the several persons that are engaged in this work. As the chief trouble of compiling, digesting, and correcting, will fall to my share, I must do myself the justice to open the work with my own history. I was born to a small hereditary estate, which, according to the tradition of the village where it lies, was bounded by the same hedges and ditches in William the Conqueror's time that it is at present, and has been delivered down from father to son whole and entire, without the loss or acquisition of a single field or meadow, during the space of six hundred years. There runs a story in the family, that my mother, near the time of my birth, dreamed that her son was become a judge; whether this might proceed from a law-suit which was then depending in the family, or my father's being a justice of the peace, I cannot determine; for I am not so vain as to think it presaged any dignity that I should arrive at in my future life, though that was the interpretation which the neighborhood put upon it. The gravity of my behavior at my very first appearance in the world seemed to favor my mother's dream: for as she often told me, I threw away my rattle before I was two months old, and would not make use of my coral until they had taken away the bells from it.

As for the rest of my infancy, there being nothing in it remarkable, I shall pass it over in silence. I find, that during my nonage, I had the reputation of a very sullen youth, but was always a favorite of my schoolmaster, who used to say, that my parts were solid, and would wear well. I had not been long at the university, before I distinguished myself by a most profound silence; for, during the space of eight years, excepting in the public exercises of the college, I scarce uttered the quantity of an hundred words; and indeed do not remember that I ever spoke three sentences together in my whole life. Whilst I was in this learned body, I applied myself with so much diligence to my studies, that there are very few celebrated books, either in the learned or the modern tongues, which I am not acquainted with.

Upon the death of my father, I was resolved to travel into foreign countries, and therefore left the university, with the character of an odd unaccountable fellow, that had a great deal of learning, if I would but shew it. An insatiable thirst after knowledge carried me into all the countries of Europe, in which there was anything new or strange to be seen; nay, to such a degree was my curiosity raised, that having read the controversies of some great men concerning the antiquities of Egypt, I made a voyage to Grand Cairo, on purpose to take the measure of a pyramid; and as soon as I had set myself right in that particular, returned to my native country with great satisfaction.

I have passed my latter years in this city, where I am frequently seen in most public places, though there are not above half-a-dozen of my select friends that know me; of whom my next paper shall give a more particular account. There is no place of general resort, wherein I do not often make my appearance: sometimes I am seen thrusting my head into a round of politicians, at Will's, and listening with great attention to the narratives that are made in those little circular audiences. Sometimes I smoke a pipe at Child's, and whilst I seem attentive to nothing but the Postman, overhear the conversation of every table in the room. I appear on Sunday nights at St. James's coffee-house, and sometimes join the little committee of politics in the inner room, as one who comes there to hear and improve. My face is likewise very well known at the Grecian, the Cocoa-tree, and in the theaters both of Drury-Lane and the Hay-market. I have been taken for a merchant upon the exchange for above these ten years, and sometimes pass for a Jew in the assembly of stock-jobbers at Jonathan's: in short, wherever I see a cluster of people, I always mix with them, though I never open my lips but in my own club.

Thus I live in the world rather as a spectator of mankind, than as one of the species, by which means I have made myself a speculative statesman, soldier, merchant and artisan, without ever meddling with any practical part in life. I am very well versed in the theory of a husband or a father, and can discern the errors in the economy, business, and diversion of others, better than those who are engaged in them; as standers-by discover blots, which are apt to escape those who are in the game. I never espoused any party with violence, and am resolved to observe an exact neutrality between the whigs and tories, unless I shall be forced to declare myself by the hostilities of either side. In short, I have acted in all the parts of my life as a looker-on, which is the character I intend to preserve in this paper.

I have given the reader just so much of my history and character, as to let him see I am not altogether unqualified for the business I have undertaken. As for other particulars in my life and adventures, I shall insert them in following papers, as I shall see occasion. In the meantime, when I consider how much I have seen, read, and heard, I begin to blame my own taciturnity; and since I have neither time nor inclination, to communicate the fulness of my heart in speech, I am resolved to do it in writing, and to print myself out, if possible, before I die. I have been often told by my friends, that it is a pity so many useful discoveries which I have made should be in the possession of a silent man. For this reason, therefore, I shall publish a sheet-full of thoughts every morning, for the benefit of my contemporaries: and if I can any way contribute to the diversion or improvement of the country in which I live, I shall leave it when I am summoned out of it, with the secret satisfaction of thinking that I have not lived in vain.

There are three very material points which I have not spoken to in this paper; and which, for several important reasons, I must keep to myself, at least for some time: I mean, an account of my name, my age, and my lodgings. I must confess, I would gratify my reader in anything that is reasonable; but as for these three particulars, though I am sensible they might tend very much to the embellishment of my paper, I cannot yet come to a resolution of communicating them to the public. They would indeed draw me out of that obscurity which I have enjoyed for many years, and expose me in public places to several salutes and civilities, which have been always very disagreeable to me; for the greatest pain I can suffer, is the being talked to, and being stared at. It is for this reason likewise, that I keep my complexion and dress as very great secrets; though it is not impossible that I may make discoveries of both in the progress of the work I have undertaken.

After having been thus particular upon myself, I shall, in to-morrow's paper, give an account of those gentlemen who are concerned with me in this work; for, as I have before intimated, a plan of it is laid and concerted, as all other matters of importance are, in a club. However, as my friends have engaged me to stand in the front, those who have a mind to correspond with me may direct their letters to the Spectator, at Mr. Buckley's in Little Britain. For I must further acquaint the reader, that, though our club meet, only on Tuesdays and Thursdays, we have appointed a committee to sit every night, for the inspection of all such papers as may contribute to the advancement of the public weal.

Thursday, March 1, 1710–11.

From THE SPECTATOR — No. 112

A COUNTRY SUNDAY

I AM always very well pleased with a country Sunday, and think, if keeping holy the seventh day were only a human institution, it would be the best method that could have been thought of for the polishing and civilizing of mankind. It is certain the country people would soon degenerate into a kind of savages and barbarians, were there not such frequent returns of a stated time in which the whole village meet together with their best faces, and in their cleanliest habits, to converse with one another upon indifferent subjects, hear their duties explained to them, and join together in adoration of the Supreme Being. Sunday clears away the rust of the whole week, not only as it refreshes in their minds the notions of religion, but as it puts both the sexes upon appearing in their most agreeable forms, and exerting all such qualities as are apt to give them a figure in the eye of the village. A country fellow distinguishes himself as much in the churchyard, as a citizen does upon the Change, the whole parish-politics being generally discussed in that place either after sermon or before the bell rings.

My friend Sir Roger, being a good churchman, has beautified the inside of his church with several texts of his own choosing: he has likewise given a handsome pulpit-cloth, and railed in the communion table at his own expense. He has often told me, that at his coming to his estate he found his parishioners very irregular; and that in order to make them kneel and join in the responses, he gave every one of them a hassock and a common-prayer book: and at the same time employed an itinerant singing master, who goes about the country for that purpose, to instruct them rightly in the tunes of the psalms; upon which they now very much value themselves, and indeed outdo most of the country churches that I have ever heard.

As Sir Roger is landlord to the whole congregation, he keeps them in very good order, and will suffer nobody to sleep in it besides himself; for if, by chance, he has been surprised into a short nap at sermon, upon recovering out of it he stands up and looks about him, and if he sees anybody else nodding, either wakes them himself, or sends his servants to them. Several other of the old knight's particularities break out upon these occasions: sometimes he will be lengthening out a verse in the singing-psalms, half a minute after the rest of the congregation have done with it; sometimes, when he is pleased with the matter of his devotion, he pronounces 'Amen' three or four times to the same prayer; and sometimes stands up when everybody else is upon their knees, to count the congregation, or see if any of his tenants are missing.

I was yesterday very much surprised to hear my old friend, in the midst of the service, calling out to one John Matthews to mind what he was about, and not disturb the congregation. This

John Matthews it seems is remarkable for being an idle fellow, and at that time was kicking his heels for his diversion. This authority of the knight, though exerted in that odd manner which accompanies him in all circumstances of life, has a very good effect upon the parish, who are not polite enough to see any thing ridiculous in his behavior; besides that the general good sense and worthiness of his character makes his friends observe these little singularities as foils that rather set off than blemish his good qualities.

As soon as the sermon is finished, nobody presumes to stir till Sir Roger is gone out of the church. The knight walks down from his seat in the chancel between a double row of his tenants, that stand bowing to him on each side; and every now and then inquires how such a one's wife, or mother, or son, or father do, whom he does not see at church; which is understood as a secret reprimand to the person that is absent.

The chaplain has often told me, that upon a catechising day, when Sir Roger has been pleased with a boy that answers well, he has ordered a Bible to be given him next day for his encouragement; and sometimes accompanies it with a flitch of bacon to his mother. Sir Roger has likewise added five pounds a year to the clerk's place; and that he may encourage the young fellows to make themselves perfect in the church-service, has promised, upon the death of the present incumbent, who is very old, to bestow it according to merit.

The fair understanding between Sir Roger and his chaplain, and their mutual concurrence in doing good, is the more remarkable, because the very next village is famous for the differences and contentions that rise between the parson and the squire, who live in a perpetual state of war. The parson is always preaching at the squire, and the squire to be revenged on the parson never comes to church. The squire has made all his tenants atheists, and tithe-stealers; while the parson instructs them every Sunday in the dignity of his order, and insinuates to them in almost every sermon that he is a better man than his patron. In short, matters have come to such an extremity, that the squire had not said his prayers either in public or private this half year; and that the parson threatens him, if he does not mend his manners, to pray for him in the face of the whole congregation.

Feuds of this nature, though too frequent in the country, are very fatal to the ordinary people; who are so used to be dazzled with riches, that they pay as much deference to the understanding of a man of an estate, as of a man of learning: and are very hardly brought to regard any truth, how important soever it may be, that is preached to them, when they know there are several men of five hundred a year who do not believe it.

Monday, July 9, 1711.

From THE SPECTATOR — No. 122

SIR ROGER AT THE ASSIZES

A MAN's first care should be to avoid the reproaches of his own heart; his next, to escape the censures of the world: if the last interferes with the former, it ought to be entirely neglected; but otherwise there cannot be a greater satisfaction to an honest mind, than to see those approbations which it gives itself seconded by the applauses of the public: a man is more sure of conduct, when the verdict which he passes upon his own behavior is thus warranted and confirmed by the opinion of all that know him.

My worthy friend Sir Roger is one of those who is not only at peace within himself, but beloved and esteemed by all about him. He receives a suitable tribute for his universal benevolence to mankind, in the returns of affection and good-will, which are paid him by every one that lives within his neighborhood. I lately met with two or three odd instances of that general respect which is shewn to the good old knight. He would needs carry Will Wimble and myself with him to the county assizes: as we were upon the road Will Wimble joined a couple of plain men who rode before us, and conversed with them for some time; during which my friend Sir Roger acquainted me with their characters.

'The first of them,' says he, 'that has a spaniel by his side, is a yeoman of about an hundred pounds a year, an honest man: he is just within the game-act, and qualified to kill an hare or a pheasant: he knocks down his dinner with his gun twice or thrice a week: and by that means lives much cheaper than those who have not so good an estate as himself. He would be a good neighbor if he did not destroy so many partridges: in short he is a very sensible man; shoots flying; and has been several times foreman of the petty jury.

'That other that rides along with him is

Tom Touchy, a fellow famous for "taking the law" of everybody. There is not one in the town where he lives that he has not sued at a quarter-sessions. The rogue had once the impudence to go to law with the widow. His head is full of costs, damages, and ejectments: he plagued a couple of honest gentlemen so long for a trespass in breaking one of his hedges, till he was forced to sell the ground it enclosed to defray the charges of the prosecution: his father left him fourscore pounds a year; but he has cast and been cast so often, that he is not now worth thirty. I suppose he is going upon the old business of the willow tree.'

As Sir Roger was giving me this account of Tom Touchy, Will Wimble and his two companions stopped short till he came up to them. After having paid their respects to Sir Roger, Will told him that Mr. Touchy and he must appeal to him upon a dispute that arose between them. Will it seems had been giving his fellow-traveler an account of his angling one day in such a hole; when Tom Touchy, instead of hearing out his story, told him that Mr. such-a-one, if he pleased, might 'take the law of him' for fishing in that part of the river. My friend Sir Roger heard them both upon a round trot; and after having paused some time, told them, with the air of a man who would not give his judgment rashly, that 'much might be said on both sides.' They were neither of them dissatisfied with the knight's determination, because neither of them found himself in the wrong by it: upon which we made the best of our way to the assizes.

The court was set before Sir Roger came; but notwithstanding all the justices had taken their places upon the bench, they made room for the old knight at the head of them; who, for his reputation in the country, took occasion to whisper in the judge's ear, 'that he was glad his lordship had met with so much good weather in his circuit.' I was listening to the proceedings of the court with much attention, and infinitely pleased with that great appearance of solemnity which so properly accompanies such a public administration of our laws; when, after about an hour's sitting, I observed to my great surprise, in the midst of a trial, that my friend Sir Roger was getting up to speak. I was in some pain for him till I found he had acquitted himself of two or three sentences, with a look of much business and great intrepidity.

Upon his first rising the court was hushed, and a general whisper ran among the country people that Sir Roger 'was up.' The speech he made was so little to the purpose, that I shall not trouble my readers with an account of it; and I believe was not so much designed by the knight himself to inform the court, as to give him a figure in my eye, and keep up his credit in the country.

I was highly delighted, when the court rose, to see the gentlemen of the country gathering about my old friend, and striving who should compliment him most; at the same time that the ordinary people gazed upon him at a distance, not a little admiring his courage, that was not afraid to speak to the judge.

In our return home we met with a very odd accident; which I cannot forbear relating, because it shews how desirous all who know Sir Roger are of giving him marks of their esteem. When we were arrived upon the verge of his estate, we stopped at a little inn to rest ourselves and our horses. The man of the house had, it seems, been formerly a servant in the knight's family; and to do honor to his old master, had some time since, unknown to Sir Roger, put him up in a sign-post before the door; so that 'the Knight's Head' had hung out upon the road about a week before he himself knew anything of the matter. As soon as Sir Roger was acquainted with it, finding that his servant's indiscretion proceeded wholly from affection and good-will, he only told him that he had made him too high a compliment; and when the fellow seemed to think that could hardly be, added with a more decisive look, that it was too great an honor for any man under a duke; but told him at the same time, that it might be altered with a very few touches, and that he himself would be at the charge of it. Accordingly, they got a painter by the knight's directions to add a pair of whiskers to the face, and by a little aggravation of the features to change it into the *Saracen's Head*. I should not have known this story, had not the inn-keeper, upon Sir Roger's alighting, told him in my hearing, that his honor's head was brought back last night with the alterations that he had ordered to be made in it. Upon this my friend with his usual cheerfulness related the particulars abovementioned, and ordered the head to be brought into the room. I could not forbear discovering greater expressions of mirth than ordinary upon the appearance of this monstrous face, under which, notwithstanding it was made to frown and stare in a most extraordinary manner, I could still discover a distant resemblance of my old friend. Sir Roger, upon seeing me laugh, desired me to tell him truly if I thought it possible for people to know him in that disguise. I at first kept my usual silence: but upon the knight's conjuring me to tell him whether it was not still more like himself than a Saracen, I composed my countenance in the best manner I could, and replied 'That much might be said on both sides.'

These several adventures, with the knight's behavior in them, gave me as pleasant a day as ever I met with in any of my travels.

Friday, July 20, 1711.

From THE SPECTATOR — No. 131

TOWN AND COUNTRY

It is usual for a man who loves country sports to preserve the game on his own grounds, and divert himself upon those that belong to his neighbor. My friend Sir Roger generally goes two or three miles from his house, and gets into the frontiers of his estate, before he beats about in search of a hare or partridge, on purpose to spare his own fields, where he is always sure of finding diversion when the worst comes to the worst. By this means the breed about his house has time to increase and multiply besides that the sport is the more agreeable where the game is the harder to come at, and where it does not lie so thick as to produce any perplexity or confusion in the pursuit. For these reasons the country gentleman, like the fox, seldom preys near his own home.

In the same manner I have made a month's excursion out of town, which is the great field of game for sportsmen of my species, to try my fortune in the country, where I have started several subjects, and hunted them down, with some pleasure to myself, and I hope to others. I am here forced to use a great deal of diligence before I can spring anything to my mind, whereas in town, whilst I am following one character, it is ten to one but I am crossed in my way by another, and put up such a variety of odd creatures in both sexes, that they foil the scent of one another, and puzzle the chase. My greatest difficulty in the country is to find sport, and in town to choose it. In the mean time, as I have given a whole month's rest to the cities of London and Westminster, I promise myself abundance of new game upon my return thither.

It is indeed high time for me to leave the country, since I find the whole neighborhood begin to grow very inquisitive after my name and character; my love of solitude, taciturnity, and particular way of life, having raised a great curiosity in all these parts.

The notions which have been framed of me are various; some look upon me as very proud, some as very modest, and some as very melancholy. Will Wimble, as my friend the butler tells me, observing me very much alone, and extremely silent when I am in company, is afraid I have killed a man. The country people seem to suspect me for a conjurer; and some of them hearing of the visit which I made to Moll White, will needs have it that Sir Roger has brought down a cunning man with him, to cure the old woman, and free the country from her charms. So that the character which I go under in part of the neighborhood, is what they here call a 'white witch.'

A justice of peace, who lives about five miles off, and is not of Sir Roger's party, has, it seems, said twice or thrice at his table, that he wishes Sir Roger does not harbor a Jesuit in his house; and that he thinks the gentlemen of the country would do very well to make me give some account of myself.

On the other side, some of Sir Roger's friends are afraid the old knight is imposed upon by a designing fellow, and as they have heard that he converses very promiscuously when he is in town, do not know but he has brought down with him some discarded Whig, that is sullen, and says nothing because he is out of place.

Such is the variety of opinions which are here entertained of me, so that I pass among some for a disaffected person, and among others for a popish priest; among some for a wizard, and among others for a murderer; and all this for no other reason, that I can imagine, but because I do not hoot, and halloo, and make a noise. It is true, my friend Sir Roger tells them that it is my way, and that I am only a philosopher; but this will not satisfy them. They think there is more in me than he discovers, and that I do not hold my tongue for nothing.

For these and other reasons I shall set out for London to-morrow, having found by experience that the country is not a place for a person of my temper, who does not love jollity, and what they call good neighborhood. A man that is out of humor when an unexpected guest breaks in upon him, and does not care for sacrificing an afternoon to every chance comer,—that will be the master of his own time, and the pursuer of his own inclinations,—makes but a very unsociable figure in this kind of life. I shall therefore retire into the town, if I may make use of that phrase, and get into the crowd again as fast as I can, in order to be alone. I can there raise what speculations I please upon others without being observed myself, and at the same time enjoy all the advantages of company with all the privileges of solitude. In the meanwhile, to finish the month, and conclude these my rural speculations, I shall here insert a letter from my friend Will Honeycomb, who has not lived a month for these forty years out of the smoke of London, and rallies me after his way upon my country life.

'DEAR SPEC,

'I suppose this letter will find thee picking up daisies, or smelling to a lock of hay, or passing away thy time in some innocent country diversion of the like nature. I have however orders from the club to summon thee up to town, being all of us cursedly afraid thou wilt not be able to relish our company, after thy conversations with Moll White and Will Wimble. Pr'ythee don't send up any more stories of a cock and a bull, nor frighten the town with spirits and witches. Thy speculations begin to smell confoundedly of woods and meadows. If thou dost not come up quickly, we shall conclude that thou art in love with one of Sir Roger's dairy-maids. Service to the knight. Sir Andrew is grown the cock of the club since he left us, and if he does not return quickly, will make every mother's son of us commonwealth's men.

   'Dear Spec,
      'Thine eternally,
            'WILL HONEYCOMB.'
   Tuesday, July 31, 1711.

From THE SPECTATOR — No. 335

SIR ROGER AT THE PLAY

MY friend Sir Roger de Coverley, when we last met together at the club, told me that he had a great mind to see the new tragedy with me, assuring me at the same time, that he had not been at a play these twenty years. 'The last I saw,' said Sir Roger, 'was *The Committee*, which I should not have gone to neither, had not I been told before-hand that it was a good Church of England comedy.' He then proceeded to inquire of me who this 'Distressed Mother' was; and upon hearing that she was Hector's widow, he told me that her husband was a brave man, and that when he was a school-boy he had read his life at the end of the dictionary. My friend asked me, in the next place, if there would not be some danger in coming home late, in case the Mohocks should be abroad. 'I assure you,' says he, 'I thought I had fallen into their hands last night; for I observed two or three lusty black men that followed me half way up Fleet-street, and mended their pace behind me, in proportion as I put on to get away from them. You must know,' continued the knight, with a smile, 'I fancied they had a mind to *hunt* me; for I remember an honest gentleman in my neighborhood, who was served such a trick in King Charles II's time, for which reason he has not ventured himself in town ever since. I might have shewn them very good sport, had this been their design; for as I am an old fox-hunter, I should have turned and dodged, and nave played them a thousand tricks they had never seen in their lives before.' Sir Roger added, that if these gentlemen had any such intention, they did not succeed very well in it; 'for I threw them out,' says he, 'at the end of Norfolk-street, where I doubled the corner, and got shelter in my lodgings before they could imagine what was become of me. However,' says the knight, 'if Captain Sentry will make one with us to-morrow night, and if you will both of you call upon me about four o'clock, that we may be at the house before it is full, I will have my own coach in readiness to attend you, for John tells me he has got the fore-wheels mended.'

The captain, who did not fail to meet me there at the appointed hour, bid Sir Roger fear nothing, for that he had put on the same sword which he made use of at the battle of Steenkirk. Sir Roger's servants, and among the rest, my old friend the butler, had, I found, provided themselves with good oaken plants, to attend their master upon this occasion. When we had placed him in his coach, with myself at his left hand, the Captain before him, and his butler at the head of his footmen in the rear, we convoyed him in safety to the playhouse, where, having marched up the entry in good order, the Captain and I went in with him, and seated him betwixt us in the pit. As soon as the house was full, and the candles lighted, my old friend stood up and looked about him with that pleasure, which a mind seasoned with humanity naturally feels in itself, at the sight of a multitude of people who seem pleased with one another, and partake of the same common enter tainment. I could not but fancy myself, as the old man stood up in the middle of the pit, that he made a very proper center to a tragic audience. Upon the entering of Pyrrhus, the knight told me that he did not believe the king of France himself had a better strut. I was indeed very attentive to my old friend's remarks, because I looked upon them as a piece of natural criticism; and was well pleased to hear him, at the conclusion of almost every scene, telling me that he could not imagine how the play would end. One while he appeared much concerned for Andromache, and a little while after as much for Hermione; and was extremely puzzled to think what would become of Pyrrhus.

When Sir Roger saw Andromache's obstinate refusal to her lover's importunities, he whispered me in the ear, that he was sure she would never have him; to which he added, with a more than ordinary vehemence, 'You can't imagine, sir, what it is to have to do with a widow.' Upon Pyrrhus his threatening afterwards to leave her, the knight shook his head, and muttered to himself, 'Ay, do if you can.' This part dwelt so much upon my friend's imagination, that at the close of the third act, as I was thinking of something else, he whispered me in my ear, 'These widows, sir, are the most perverse creatures in the world. But pray,' says he, 'you that are a critic, is this play according to your dramatic rules, as you call them? Should your people in tragedy always talk to be understood? Why, there is not a single sentence in this play that I do not know the meaning of.'

The fourth act very unluckily began before I had time to give the old gentleman an answer: 'Well,' says the knight, sitting down with great satisfaction, 'I suppose we are now to see Hector's ghost.' He then renewed his attention, and from time to time fell a-praising the widow. He made, indeed, a little mistake as to one of her pages, whom at his first entering he took for Astyanax: but he quickly set himself right in that particular, though, at the same time, he owned he should have been very glad to have seen the little boy. 'Who,' says he, 'must needs be a very fine child by the account that is given of him.' Upon Hermione's going off with a menace to Pyrrhus, the audience gave a loud clap; to which Sir Roger added, 'On my word, a notable young baggage!'

As there was a very remarkable silence and stillness in the audience during the whole action, it was natural for them to take the opportunity of the intervals between the acts, to express their opinion of the players, and of their respective parts. Sir Roger hearing a cluster of them praise Orestes, struck in with them, and told them that he thought his friend Pylades was a very sensible man; as they were afterwards applauding Pyrrhus, Sir Roger put in a second time, 'And let me tell you,' says he, 'though he speak but little, I like the old fellow in whiskers as well as any of them.' Captain Sentry, seeing two or three wags who sat near us, lean with an attentive ear towards Sir Roger, and fearing lest they should smoke the knight, plucked him by the elbow, and whispered something in his ear, that lasted till the opening of the fifth act. The knight was wonderfully attentive to the account which Orestes gives of Pyrrhus his death, and at the conclusion of it told me, it was such a bloody piece of work, that he was glad it was not done upon the stage. Seeing afterwards Orestes in his raving fit, he grew more than ordinary serious, and took occasion to moralize (in his way) upon an evil conscience, adding, that Orestes, in his madness, looked as if he saw something.

As we were the first that came into the house, so we were the last that went out of it; being resolved to have a clear passage for our old friend, whom we did not care to venture among the justling of the crowd. Sir Roger went out fully satisfied with his entertainment, and we guarded him to his lodging in the same manner that we brought him to the playhouse; being highly pleased for my own part, not only with the performance of the excellent piece which had been presented, but with the satisfaction which it had given to the old man.

Tuesday, March 25, 1712.

From THE SPECTATOR — No. 517

THE DEATH OF SIR ROGER

WE last night received a piece of ill news at our club, which very sensibly afflicted every one of us. I question not but my readers themselves will be troubled at the hearing of it. To keep them no longer in suspense, Sir Roger de Coverley is *dead*. He departed this life at his house in the country, after a few weeks' sickness. Sir Andrew Freeport has a letter from one of his correspondents in those parts, that informs him the old man caught a cold at the county sessions, as he was very warmly promoting an address of his own penning, in which he succeeded according to his wishes. But this particular comes from a whig justice of peace, who was always Sir Roger's enemy and antagonist. I have letters both from the chaplain and Captain Sentry which mention nothing of it, but are filled with many particulars to the honor of the good old man. I have likewise a letter from the butler, who took so much care of me last summer when I was at the knight's house. As my friend the butler mentions, in the simplicity of his heart, several circumstances the others have passed over in silence, I shall give my reader a copy of his letter, without any alteration or diminution.

'HONORED SIR,

'Knowing that you was my old master's good friend, I could not forbear sending you the melancholy news of his death, which has afflicted the whole country as well as his poor servants, who loved him, I may say, better than we did our lives. I am afraid he caught his death the last county sessions, where he would go to see justice done to a poor widow woman, and her fatherless children, that had been wronged by a neighboring gentleman; for you know, sir, my good master was always the poor man's friend. Upon his coming home, the first complaint he made was, that he had lost his roast-beef stomach, not being able to touch a sirloin, which was served up according to custom; and you know he used to take great delight in it. From that time forward he grew worse and worse, but still kept a good heart to the last. Indeed we were once in great hope of his recovery, upon a kind message that was sent him from the widow lady whom he had made love to the forty last years of his life, but this only proved a lightning before death. He has bequeathed to this lady, as a token of his love, a great pearl necklace, and a couple of silver bracelets set with jewels, which belonged to my good old lady his mother: he has bequeathed the fine white gelding, that he used to ride a hunting upon, to his chaplain, because he thought he would be kind to him, and has left you all his books. He has, moreover, bequeathed to the chaplain a very pretty tenement with good lands about it. It being a very cold day when he made his will, he left for mourning, to every man in the parish, a great frize-coat, and to every woman a black riding-hood. It was a moving sight to see him take leave of his poor servants, commending us all for our fidelity, whilst we were not able to speak a word for weeping. As we most of us are grown gray-headed in our dear master's service, he has left us pensions and legacies, which we may live very comfortably upon the remaining part of our days. He has bequeathed a great deal more in charity, which is not yet come to my knowledge, and it is peremptorily said in the parish, that he has left money to build a steeple to the church; for he was heard to say some time ago that if he lived two years longer, Coverley church should have a steeple to it. The chaplain tells everybody that he made a very good end, and never speaks of him without tears. He was buried, according to his own directions, among the family of the Coverleys, on the left hand of his father Sir Arthur. The coffin was carried by six of his tenants, and the pall held up by six of the *quorum:* the whole parish followed the corpse with heavy hearts, and in their mourning suits, the men in frize, and the women in riding-hoods. Captain Sentry, my master's nephew, has taken possession of the hall-house and the whole estate. When my old master saw him a little before his death, he shook him by the hand, and wished him joy of the estate which was falling to him, desiring him only to make a good use of it, and to pay the several legacies, and the gifts of charity which he told him he had left as quit-rents upon the estate. The captain truly seems a courteous man, though he says but little. He makes much of those whom my master loved, and shews great kindness to the old house-dog, that you know my poor master was so fond of. It would have gone to your heart to have heard the moans the dumb creature made on the day of my master's death. He has never joyed himself since; no more has any of us. 'T was the melancholiest day for the poor people that ever happened in Worcestershire. This is all from,

'Honored Sir, your most sorrowful servant,
'EDWARD BISCUIT.

'P.S. My master desired, some weeks before he died, that a book which comes up to you by the carrier, should be given to Sir Andrew Freeport, in his name.'

This letter, notwithstanding the poor butler's manner of writing it, gave us such an idea of our good old friend, that upon the reading of it there was not a dry eye in the club. Sir Andrew, opening the book, found it to be a collection of acts of parliament. There was in particular the act of uniformity, with some passages in it marked by Sir Roger's own hand. Sir

Andrew found that they related to two or three points, which he had disputed with Sir Roger the last time he appeared at the club. Sir Andrew, who would have been merry at such an incident on another occasion, at the sight of the old man's hand-writing burst into tears, and put the book into his pocket. Captain Sentry informs me, that the knight has left rings and mourning for every one in the club.

Thursday, October 23, 1712.

From THE SPECTATOR — No. 81

PARTY PATCHES

ABOUT the middle of last winter I went to see an opera at the theater in the Hay-market, where I could not but take notice of two parties of very fine women, that had placed themselves in the opposite side-boxes, and seemed drawn up in a kind of battle-array one against another. After a short survey of them, I found they were Patched differently; the faces, on one hand, being spotted on the right side of the forehead, and those upon the other on the left: I quickly perceived that they cast hostile glances upon one another; and that their Patches were placed in those different situations, as party-signals to distinguish friends from foes. In the middle-boxes, between these two opposite bodies, were several ladies who patched indifferently on both sides of their faces, and seemed to sit there with no other intention but to see the opera. Upon enquiry I found, that the body of Amazons on my right hand were whigs, and those on my left, tories: and that those who had placed themselves in the middle-boxes were a neutral party, whose faces had not yet declared themselves. These last, however, as I afterwards found, diminished daily, and took their party with one side or the other; insomuch that I observed in several of them, the patches, which were before dispersed equally, are now all gone over to the whig or tory side of the face. The censorious say, that the men whose hearts are aimed at, are very often the occasions that one part of the face is thus dishonored, and lies under a kind of disgrace, while the other is so much set off and adorned by the owner; and that the Patches turn to the right or to the left, according to the principles of the man who is most in favor. But whatever may be the motives of a few fantastical coquettes, who do not Patch for the public good so much as for their own private advantage, it is certain, that there are several women of honor who Patch out of principle, and with an eye to the interest of their country. Nay, I am informed that some of them adhere so steadfastly to their party, and are so far from sacrificing their zeal for the public to their passion for any particular person, that in a late draught of marriage-articles a lady has stipulated with her husband, that whatever his opinions are, she shall be at liberty to patch on which sides she pleases.

I must here take notice that Rosalinda, a famous Whig partisan, has most unfortunately a very beautiful mole on the tory part of her forehead; which being very conspicuous, has occasioned many mistakes, and given an handle to her enemies to misrepresent her face, as though it had revolted from the whig interest. But, whatever this natural patch may seem to insinuate, it is well known that her notions of government are still the same. This unlucky mole, however, has misled several coxcombs; and like the hanging out of false colors, made some of them converse with Rosalinda in what they thought the spirit of her party, when on a sudden she has given them an unexpected fire, that has sunk them all at once. If Rosalinda is unfortunate in her mole, Nigranilla is as unhappy in a pimple, which forces her, against her inclinations, to patch on the whig side.

I am told that many virtuous matrons, who formerly have been taught to believe that this artificial spotting of the face was unlawful, are now reconciled by a zeal for their cause, to what they could not be prompted by a concern for their beauty. This way of declaring war upon one another, puts me in mind of what is reported of the tigress, that several spots rise in her skin when she is angry; or as Mr. Cowley has imitated the verses that stand as the motto of this paper,

—She swells with angry pride,
And calls forth all her spots on ev'ry side.

When I was in the theater the time above-mentioned, I had the curiosity to count the Patches on both sides, and found the Tory Patches to be about twenty stronger than the Whig; but to make amends for this small inequality, I the next morning found the whole puppet-shew filled with faces spotted after the whiggish manner. Whether or no the ladies had retreated hither in order to rally their forces, I cannot tell; but the next night they came in so great a body to the opera, that they out-numbered the enemy.

This account of Party-patches will, I am afraid, appear improbable to those who live at a distance from the fashionable world; but as it is a distinction of a very singular nature, and what perhaps may never meet with a parallel, I think I should not have discharged the office of a faithful SPECTATOR, had I not recorded it.

I have, in former papers, endeavored to expose this party-rage in women, as it only serves to aggravate the hatred and animosities that reign among men, and in a great measure deprives the fair sex of those peculiar charms with which nature has endowed them.

When the Romans and Sabines were at war, and just upon the point of giving battle, the women who were allied to both of them, interposed with so many tears and entreaties, that they prevented the mutual slaughter which threatened both parties, and united them together in a firm and lasting peace.

I would recommend this noble example to our British ladies, at a time when their country is torn with so many unnatural divisions, that if they continue, it will be a misfortune to be born in it. The Greeks thought it so improper for women to interest themselves in competitions and contentions, that for this reason, among others, they forbad them, under pain of death, to be present at the Olympic games, notwithstanding these were the public diversions of all Greece.

As our English women excel those of all nations in beauty, they should endeavor to outshine them in all other accomplishments proper to the sex, and to distinguish themselves as tender mothers and faithful wives, rather than as furious partisans. Female virtues are of a domestic turn. The family is the proper province for private women to shine in. If they must be showing their zeal for the public, let it not be against those who are perhaps of the same family, or at least of the same religion or nation, but against those who are the open, professed, undoubted enemies of their faith, liberty, and country. When the Romans were pressed with a foreign enemy, the ladies voluntarily contributed all their rings and jewels to assist the government under the public exigence, which appeared so laudable an action in the eyes of their countrymen, that from thenceforth it was permitted by a law to pronounce public orations at the funeral of a woman in praise of the deceased person, which till that time was peculiar to men. Would our English ladies, instead of sticking on a patch against those of their own country, show themselves so truly public-spirited as to sacrifice every one her necklace against the common enemy, what decrees ought not to be made in favor of them?

Since I am recollecting upon this subject such passages as occur to my memory out of ancient authors, I cannot omit a sentence in the celebrated funeral oration of Pericles, which he made in honor of those brave Athenians that were slain in a fight with the Lacedæmonians. After having addressed himself to the several ranks and orders of his countrymen, and shown them how they should behave themselves in the public cause, he turns to the female part of his audience; 'And as for you (says he) I shall advise you in very few words: Aspire only to those virtues that are peculiar to your sex; follow your natural modesty, and think it your greatest commendation not to be talked of one way or other.'

Saturday, June 2, 1711.

From THE SPECTATOR — No. 253

DETRACTION AMONG POETS

THERE is nothing which more denotes a great mind, than the abhorrence of envy and detraction. This passion reigns more among bad poets, than among any other set of men.

As there are none more ambitious of fame, than those who are conversant in poetry, it is very natural for such as have not succeeded in it, to depreciate the works of those who have. For since they cannot raise themselves to the reputation of their fellow-writers, they must endeavor to sink it to their own pitch, if they would still keep themselves upon a level with them.

The greatest wits that ever were produced in one age, lived together in so good an understanding, and celebrated one another with so much generosity, that each of them receives an additional luster from his contemporaries, and is more famous for having lived with men of so extraordinary a genius, than if he had himself been the sole wonder of the age. I need not tell my reader, that I here point at the reign of Augustus, and I believe he will be of my opinion, that neither Virgil nor Horace would have gained so great a reputation in the world, had they not been the friends and admirers of each other. Indeed all the great writers of that age, for whom singly we have so great an esteem, stand up together as vouchers for one another's reputation. But at the same time that Virgil was celebrated by Gallus, Propertius, Horace, Varius, Tucca, and Ovid, we know that Bavius and Mævius were his declared foes and calumniators.

In our own country a man seldom sets up for a poet, without attacking the reputation of all his brothers in the art. The ignorance of the moderns, the scribblers of the age, the decay of poetry, are the topics of detraction, with which he makes his entrance into the world; but how much more noble is the fame that is built on candor and ingenuity, according to those beautiful lines of Sir John Denham, in his poem on Fletcher's works!

> But whither am I strayed? I need not raise
> Trophies to thee from other men's dispraise:
> Nor is thy fame on lesser ruins built,
> Nor needs thy juster title the foul guilt
> Of eastern Kings, who to secure their reign
> Must have their brothers, sons, and kindred slain.

I am sorry to find that an author, who is very justly esteemed among the best judges, has admitted some strokes of this nature into a very fine poem, I mean *The Art of Criticism,* which was published some months since, and is a master-piece in its kind. The observations follow one another like those in Horace's *Art of Poetry,* without that methodical regularity which would have been requisite in a prose author. They are some of them uncommon, but such as the reader must assent to, when he sees them explained with that elegance and perspicuity in which they are delivered. As for those which are the most known, and the most received, they are placed in so beautiful a light, and illustrated with such apt allusions, that they have in them all the graces of novelty, and make the reader, who was before acquainted with them, still more convinced of their truth and solidity. And here give me leave to mention what Monsieur Boileau has so very well enlarged upon in the preface to his works, that wit and fine writing doth not consist so much in advancing things that are new, as in giving things that are known an agreeable turn. It is impossible for us, who live in the latter ages of the world, to make observations in criticism, morality, or in any art or science, which have not been touched upon by others. We have little else left us, but to represent the common sense of mankind in more strong, more beautiful, or more uncommon lights. If a reader examines Horace's *Art of Poetry,* he will find but very few precepts in it, which he may not meet with in Aristotle, and which were not commonly known by all the poets of the Augustan age. His way of expressing and applying them, not his invention of them, is what we are chiefly to admire.

For this reason I think there is nothing in the world so tiresome as the works of those critics who write in a positive dogmatic way, without either language, genius or imagination. If the reader would see how the best of the Latin critics writ, he may find their manner very beautifully described in the characters of Horace, Petronius, Quintilian, and Longinus, as they are drawn in the essay of which I am now speaking.

Since I have mentioned Longinus, who in his reflections has given us the same kind of sublime, which he observes in the several passages that occasioned them; I cannot but take notice, that our English author has after the same manner exemplified several of his precepts in the very precepts themselves. I shall produce two or three instances of this kind. Speaking of the insipid smoothness which some readers are so much in love with, he has the following verses:

> These EQUAL SYLLABLES alone require,
> Though oft the ear the OPEN VOWELS tire,
> While EXPLETIVES their feeble aid DO join,
> And ten low words oft creep in one dull line.

The gaping of the vowels in the second line, the expletive *do* in the third, and the ten monosyllables in the fourth, give such a beauty to this passage, as would have been very much admired in an ancient poet. The reader may observe the following lines in the same view:

> A NEEDLESS ALEXANDRINE ends the song,
> That like a wounded snake, drags its slow length along

And afterwards,

> 'T is not enough no harshness gives offense,
> The SOUND must seem an ECHO to the SENSE.
> SOFT is the strain when ZEPHYR gently blows,
> And the SMOOTH STREAM in SMOOTHER NUMBERS flows;
> But when loud surges lash the sounding shore,
> The HOARSE, ROUGH VERSE should like the TORRENT roar.
> When AJAX strives, some rock's vast weight to throw,
> The line too LABORS, and the words move SLOW:
> Not so, when swift CAMILLA scours the plain,
> Flies o'er th' unbending corn, and skims along the main.

The beautiful distich upon Ajax in the foregoing lines, puts me in mind of a description in Homer's *Odyssey.* . . . It would be endless to quote verses out of Virgil which have this particular kind of beauty in the numbers; but I may take an occasion in a future paper to shew several of them which have escaped the observation of others.

* * *

I cannot conclude this paper without taking notice, that we have three poems in our tongue, which are of the same nature, and each of them a masterpiece in its kind; the *Essay on Translated Verse*, the *Essay on the Art of Poetry*, and the *Essay upon Criticism*.

Thursday, December 20, 1711.

From THE SPECTATOR — No. 26

WESTMINSTER ABBEY

When I am in a serious humor, I very often walk by myself in Westminster Abbey; where the gloominess of the place and the use to which it is applied, with the solemnity of the building, and the condition of the people who lie in it, are apt to fill the mind with a kind of melancholy, or rather thoughtfulness, that is not disagreeable. I yesterday passed a whole afternoon in the churchyard, the cloisters, and the church, amusing myself with the tombstones and inscriptions that I met with in those several regions of the dead. Most of them recorded nothing else of the buried person, but that he was born upon one day, and died upon another, the whole history of his life being comprehended in those two circumstances, that are common to all mankind. I could not but look upon these registers of existence, whether of brass or marble, as a kind of satire upon the departed persons; who had left no other memorial of them, but that they were born and that they died. They put me in mind of several persons mentioned in the battles of heroic poems, who have sounding names given them, for no other reason but that they may be killed, and are celebrated for nothing but being knocked on the head.

Γλαυκόν τε Μέδοντά τε Θερσίλοχόν τε.—Hom.
Glaucumque, Medontaque, Thersilochumque.—Virg.

The life of these men is finely described in holy writ by 'the path of an arrow,' which is immediately closed up and lost.

Upon my going into the church, I entertained myself with the digging of a grave; and saw in every shovel-full of it that was thrown up, the fragment of a bone or skull intermixt with a kind of fresh moldering earth, that some time or other had a place in the composition of an human body. Upon this, I began to consider with myself what innumerable multitudes of people lay confused together under the pavement of that ancient cathedral; how men and women, friends and enemies, priests and soldiers, monks and prebendaries, were crumbled amongst one another, and blended together in the same common mass; how beauty, strength, and youth, with old-age, weakness and deformity, lay undistinguished in the same promiscuous heap of matter.

After having thus surveyed this great magazine of mortality, as it were, in the lump; I examined it more particularly by the accounts which I found on several of the monuments which are raised in every quarter of that ancient fabric. Some of them were covered with such extravagant epitaphs, that, if it were possible for the dead person to be acquainted with them, he would blush at the praises which his friends have bestowed upon him. There are others so excessively modest, that they deliver the character of the person departed in Greek or Hebrew, and by that means are not understood once in a twelvemonth. In the poetical quarter, I found there were poets who had no monuments, and monuments which had no poets. I observed indeed that the present war had filled the church with many of these uninhabited monuments, which had been erected to the memory of persons whose bodies were perhaps buried in the plains of Blenheim, or in the bosom of the ocean.

I could not but be very much delighted with several modern epitaphs, which are written with great elegance of expression and justness of thought, and therefore do honor to the living as well as to the dead. As a foreigner is very apt to conceive an idea of the ignorance or politeness of a nation, from the turn of their public monuments and inscriptions, they should be submitted to the perusal of men of learning and genius, before they are put in execution. Sir Cloudesly Shovel's monument has very often given me great offense: Instead of the brave, rough English admiral, which was the distinguishing character of that plain gallant man, he is represented on his tomb by the figure of a beau, dressed in a long periwig, and reposing himself upon velvet cushions under a canopy of state. The inscription is answerable to the Monument; for instead of celebrating the many remarkable actions he had performed in the service of his country, it acquaints us only with the manner of his death, in which it was impossible for him to reap any honor. The Dutch, whom we are apt to despise for want of genius, shew an infinitely greater taste of antiquity and politeness in their buildings and works of this nature, than what we meet with in those of our own country. The monuments of their admirals, which have been erected at the public expense, represent them like themselves; and are adorned with rostral crowns and naval ornaments, with beautiful festoons of sea-weed, shells, and coral.

But to return to our subject. I have left the repository of our English kings for the contemplation of another day, when I shall find my mind disposed for so serious an amusement. I know that entertainments of this nature are apt to raise dark and dismal thoughts in timorous minds, and gloomy imaginations; but for my own part, though I am always serious, I do not know what it is to be melancholy; and can therefore take a view of nature in her deep and solemn scenes, with the same pleasure as in her most gay and delightful ones. By this means I can improve myself with those objects, which others consider with terror. When I look upon the tombs of the great, every emotion of envy dies in me; when I read the epitaphs of the beautiful, every inordinate desire goes out; when I meet with the grief of parents upon a tomb-stone, my heart melts with compassion; when I see the tomb of the parents themselves, I consider the vanity of grieving for those whom we must quickly follow; when I see kings lying by those who deposed them, when I consider rival wits placed side by side, or the holy men that divided the world with their contests and disputes, I reflect with sorrow and astonishment on the little competitions, factions, and debates of mankind. When I read the several dates of the tombs, of some that died yesterday, and some six hundred years ago, I consider that great day when we shall all of us be contemporaries, and make our appearance together.

Friday, March 30, 1711.

ALEXANDER POPE (1688-1744)

Pope was born in London, the year of the Protestant Revolution. His parents, who were Catholics, shortly retired to a country home near Windsor Forest, and there the poet passed most of his boyhood. Deformed and sickly from his birth, he was reared with great tenderness and compliance and, after his twelfth year, was chiefly self-educated. He read widely and at random among English authors and was an eager, though inexact, student of the ancient classics. At a remarkably early age, he became avid of literary fame and displayed a talent for acquainting himself with the literary personalities of the day. Before he was twelve, he had visited Will's coffee-house in order to have a look at the great Dryden and, while yet a boy, had passed from the courting to the quarreling stage with Wycherley. His precocity as a verse-maker, which he never troubled himself to disparage, is celebrated in the well-known couplet:

> As yet a child, nor yet a fool to fame,
> I lisped in numbers for the numbers came.

He claimed to have written his *Pastorals* at sixteen. They were printed in 1709, and immediately attracted attention. His *Messiah* and his *Essay on Criticism* won the encomiums of *The Spectator* and admitted him to Addison's circle. *The Rape of the Lock* (1712-14) confirmed his reputation, and his translation of the *Iliad* (1715-18) and the *Odyssey* (completed 1726) procured him a competence. 'Thanks to Homer,' he 'could live and thrive, indebted to no prince or peer alive.' He purchased a villa on the Thames at Twickenham, and there spent the last twenty-five years of his life, improving his 'grotto,' and gardens, entertaining wits and social celebrities, and polishing off his rivals in finished satirical verse of which the monumental example is *The Dunciad*, published in 1728, but afterward much altered and amplified. His best known attempt at philosophical poetry is the superficial, but eminently quotable, *Essay on Man* (1732-34). Pope is chiefly valued for the smoothness and sweetness of his versification, and for his gift of turning into brief and memorable phrase 'what oft was thought, but ne'er so well expressed.' Though not a great poet in the highest sense of that term, he is often glowing and sometimes powerful in declamation; while for mischievous innuendo and sustained condensation and point he has no equal in English poetry. His satire, unlike Dryden's, is usually personal and frequently poisoned by the same envy and malice which impaired his character and conduct. 'Leave Pope as soon as you can; he is sure to play you some devilish trick else,' Addison wrote to Lady Montagu,—one victim of Pope's shiftiness to another. Pope's physical inferiority made him preternaturally sensitive and distorted his social outlook. He could be pitifully base and treacherous where his vanity was engaged, and his literary career was a tissue of trivial deceits and mean animosities. Yet we cannot but admire the indomitableness of the mind which, in spite of physical suffering and humiliation, fought its way by fair means and foul, to the chief place in the literature of its time.

AN ESSAY ON CRITICISM

I

'T is hard to say, if greater want of skill
Appear in writing or in judging ill;
But, of the two, less dangerous is the offense
To tire our patience, than mislead our sense.
Some few in that, but numbers err in this, 5
Ten censure wrong for one who writes amiss;
A fool might once himself alone expose,
Now one in verse makes many more in prose.

'T is with our judgments as our watches, none
Go just alike, yet each believes his own. 10
In poets as true genius is but rare,
True taste as seldom is the critic's share;
Both must alike from Heaven derive their light,
These born to judge, as well as those to write.
Let such teach others who themselves excel, 15
And censure freely who have written well.
Authors are partial to their wit, 't is true,
But are not critics to their judgment too?

Yet if we look more closely, we shall find
Most have the seeds of judgment in their mind:
Nature affords at least a glimmering light; 21
The lines, though touched but faintly, are drawn right.
But as the slightest sketch, if justly traced,
Is by ill-coloring but the more disgraced,
So by false learning is good sense defaced; 25
Some are bewildered in the maze of schools.

And some made coxcombs nature meant but
   fools.
In search of wit these lose their common sense,
And then turn critics in their own defense;
Each burns alike, who can, or cannot write,   30
Or with a rival's or an eunuch's spite.
All fools have still an itching to deride,
And fain would be upon the laughing side.
If Mævius scribble in Apollo's spite,
There are who judge still worse than he can
   write.   35

   Some have at first for wits, then poets passed,
Turned critics next, and proved plain fools at
   last.
Some neither can for wits nor critics pass,
As heavy mules are neither horse nor ass.
Those half-learned witlings, numerous in our
   isle,   40
As half-formed insects on the banks of Nile;
Unfinished things, one knows not what to call,
Their generation's so equivocal:
To tell 'em, would a hundred tongues require,
Or one vain wit's, that might a hundred tire.   45

   But you who seek to give and merit fame,
And justly bear a critic's noble name,
Be sure yourself and your own reach to know,
How far your genius, taste, and learning go;
Launch not beyond your depth, but be discreet,
And mark that point where sense and dulness
   meet.   51

   Nature to all things fixed the limits fit,
And wisely curbed proud man's pretending wit.
As on the land while here the ocean gains,
In other parts it leaves wide sandy plains;   55
Thus in the soul while memory prevails,
The solid power of understanding fails;
Where beams of warm imagination play,
The memory's soft figures melt away.
One science only will one genius fit;   60
So vast is art, so narrow human wit:
Not only bounded to peculiar arts,
But oft in those confined to single parts.
Like kings we lose the conquests gained before,
By vain ambition still to make them more;   65
Each might his several province well command,
Would all but stoop to what they understand.

   First follow Nature, and your judgment frame
By her just standard, which is still the same:
Unerring Nature, still divinely bright,   70
One clear, unchanged, and universal light,
Life, force, and beauty, must to all impart,
At once the source, and end, and test of Art.
Art from that fund each just supply provides,
Works without show, and without pomp pre-
   sides: 75
In some fair body thus the informing soul
With spirits feeds, with vigor fills the whole,
Each motion guides, and every nerve sustains;
Itself unseen, but in the effects, remains.

Some, to whom Heaven in wit has been profuse,
Want as much more, to turn it to its use;   81
For wit and judgment often are at strife,
Though meant each other's aid, like man and
   wife.
'T is more to guide than spur the Muse's steed;
Restrain his fury, than provoke his speed;   85
The wingèd courser, like a generous horse,
Shows most true mettle when you check his
   course.

   Those rules of old discovered, not devised,
Are Nature still, but Nature methodized;
Nature, like liberty, is but restrained   90
By the same laws which first herself ordained.

   Hear how learned Greece her useful rules in-
   dites,
When to repress, and when indulge our flights:
High on Parnassus' top her sons she showed,
And pointed out those arduous paths they trod;
Held from afar, aloft, the immortal prize,   96
And urged the rest by equal steps to rise.
Just precepts thus from great examples given,
She drew from them what they derived from
   Heaven.
The generous critic fanned the poet's fire,   100
And taught the world with reason to admire.
Then criticism the Muses' handmaid proved,
To dress her charms, and make her more be-
   loved:
But following wits from that intention strayed,
Who could not win the mistress, wooed the
   maid;   105
Against the poets their own arms they turned,
Sure to hate most the men from whom they
   learned.
So modern 'pothecaries, taught the art
By doctor's bills to play the doctor's part,
Bold in the practice of mistaken rules,   110
Prescribe, apply, and call their masters fools.
Some on the leaves of ancient authors prey,
Nor time nor moths e'er spoiled so much as they.
Some dryly plain, without invention's aid,
Write dull receipts, how poems may be made.
These leave the sense, their learning to display,
And those explain the meaning quite away.   117

   You, then, whose judgment the right course
   would steer,
Know well each ancient's proper character;
His fable, subject, scope in every page;   120
Religion, country, genius of his age:
Without all these at once before your eyes,
Cavil you may, but never criticise.
Be Homer's works your study and delight,
Read them by day, and meditate by night;   125
Thence form your judgment, thence your max-
   ims bring,
And trace the Muses upward to their spring.
Still with itself compared, his text peruse;
And let your comment be the Mantuan Muse.

When first young Maro in his boundless mind
A work to outlast immortal Rome designed, 131
Perhaps he seemed above the critic's law,
And but from nature's fountains scorned to draw:
But when to examine every part he came,
Nature and Homer were, he found, the same. 135
Convinced, amazed, he checks the bold design;
And rules as strict his labored work confine,
As if the Stagirite o'erlooked each line,
Learn hence for ancient rules a just esteem;
To copy nature is to copy them. 140

Some beauties yet no precepts can declare,
For there's a happiness as well as care.
Music resembles poetry, in each
Are nameless graces which no methods teach,
And which a master-hand alone can reach. 145
If, where the rules not far enough extend,
(Since rules were made but to promote their end)
Some lucky license answer to the full
The intent proposed, that license is a rule.
Thus Pegasus, a nearer way to take, 150
May boldly deviate from the common track;
From vulgar bounds with brave disorder part,
And snatch a grace beyond the reach of art,
Which without passing through the judgment, gains
The heart, and all its end at once attains. 155
In prospects thus, some objects please our eyes,
Which out of nature's common order rise,
The shapeless rock, or hanging precipice.
Great wits sometimes may gloriously offend,
And rise to faults true critics dare not mend. 160
But though the ancients thus their rules invade,
(As kings dispense with laws themselves have made)
Moderns, beware! or if you must offend
Against the precept, ne'er transgress its end;
Let it be seldom and compelled by need; 165
And have, at least, their precedent to plead.
The critic else proceeds without remorse,
Seizes your fame, and puts his laws in force.

I know there are, to whose presumptuous thoughts
Those freer beauties, even in them, seem faults.
Some figures monstrous and mis-shaped appear,
Considered singly, or beheld too near, 172
Which, but proportioned to their light or place,
Due distance reconciles to form and grace.
A prudent chief not always must display 175
His powers in equal ranks, and fair array,
But with the occasion and the place comply,
Conceal his force, nay, seem sometimes to fly.
Those oft are stratagems which errors seem,
Nor is it Homer nods, but we that dream. 180

Still green with bays each ancient altar stands,
Above the reach of sacrilegious hands;
Secure from flames, from envy's fiercer rage,
Destructive war, and all-involving age.
See, from each clime the learned their incense bring! 185
Hear, in all tongues, consenting peans ring!
In praise so just let every voice be joined,
And fill the general chorus of mankind.
Hail, bards triumphant! born in happier days;
Immortal heirs of universal praise! 190
Whose honors with increase of ages grow,
As streams roll down, enlarging as they flow;
Nations unborn your mighty names shall sound,
And worlds applaud that must not yet be found!
Oh, may some spark of your celestial fire, 195
The last, the meanest of your sons inspire,
(That on weak wings, from far, pursues your flights;
Glows while he reads, but trembles as he writes)
To teach vain wits a science little known,
To admire superior sense, and doubt their own!

II

Of all the causes which conspire to blind 201
Man's erring judgment, and misguide the mind,
What the weak head with strongest bias rules,
Is pride, the never-failing vice of fools.
Whatever nature has in worth denied, 205
She gives in large recruits of needful pride;
For as in bodies, thus in souls, we find
What wants in blood and spirits, swelled with wind:
Pride, where wit fails, steps in to our defense,
And fills up all the mighty void of sense. 210
If once right reason drives that cloud away,
Truth breaks upon us with resistless day.
Trust not yourself; but your defects to know,
Make use of every friend—and every foe.

A little learning is a dangerous thing; 215
Drink deep, or taste not the Pierian spring:
There shallow draughts intoxicate the brain,
And drinking largely sobers us again.
Fired at first sight with what the Muse imparts,
In fearless youth we tempt the heights of arts,
While from the bounded level of our mind, 221
Short views we take, nor see the lengths behind;
But more advanced, behold with strange surprise
New distant scenes of endless science rise!
So pleased at first the towering Alps we try, 225
Mount o'er the vales, and seem to tread the sky,
The eternal snows appear already past,
And the first clouds and mountains seem the last;
But, those attained, we tremble to survey
The growing labors of the lengthened way, 230
The increasing prospect tires our wandering eyes,
Hills peep o'er hills, and Alps on Alps arise!

A perfect judge will read each work of wit
With the same spirit that its author writ:
Survey the whole, nor seek slight faults to find
Where nature moves, and rapture warms the mind;   236
Nor lose, for that malignant dull delight,
The generous pleasure to be charmed with wit.
But in such lays as neither ebb, nor flow,
Correctly cold, and regularly low,   240
That shunning faults, one quiet tenor keep;
We cannot blame indeed, but we may sleep.
In wit, as nature, what affects our hearts
Is not the exactness of peculiar parts;
'T is not a lip, or eye, we beauty call,   245
But the joint force and full result of all.
Thus when we view some well-proportioned dome,
(The world's just wonder, and e'en thine, O Rome!)
No single parts unequally surprise,
All comes united to the admiring eyes;   250
No monstrous height, or breadth, or length appear;
The whole at once is bold, and regular.

Whoever thinks a faultless piece to see,
Thinks what ne'er was, nor is, nor e'er shall be.
In every work regard the writer's end,   255
Since none can compass more than they intend;
And if the means be just, the conduct true,
Applause, in spite of trivial faults, is due;
As men of breeding, sometimes men of wit,
To avoid great errors, must the less commit: 260
Neglect the rules each verbal critic lays,
For not to know some trifles, is a praise.
Most critics, fond of some subservient art,
Still make the whole depend upon a part:
They talk of principles, but notions prize,   265
And all to one loved folly sacrifice.

Once on a time, La Mancha's knight, they say,
A certain bard encountering on the way,
Discoursed in terms as just, with looks as sage,
As e'er could Dennis of the Grecian stage;   270
Concluding all were desperate sots and fools,
Who durst depart from Aristotle's rules.
Our author, happy in a judge so nice,
Produced his play, and begged the knight's advice;
Made him observe the subject, and the plot,   275
The manners, passions, unities, what not?
All which, exact to rule, were brought about,
Were but a combat in the lists left out.
'What! leave the combat out?' exclaims the knight;
Yes, or we must renounce the Stagirite.   280
'Not so, by Heaven' (he answers in a rage),
'Knights, squires, and steeds, must enter on the stage.'
So vast a throng the stage can ne'er contain.
'Then build a new, or act it in a plain.'

Thus critics, of less judgment than caprice,
Curious not knowing, not exact but nice,   286
Form short ideas; and offend in arts
(As most in manners) by a love to parts.

Some to conceit alone their taste confine,
And glittering thoughts struck out at every line;   290
Pleased with a work where nothing's just or fit;
One glaring chaos and wild heap of wit.
Poets like painters, thus unskilled to trace
The naked nature and the living grace,
With gold and jewels cover every part,   295
And hide with ornaments their want of art.
True wit is nature to advantage dressed,
What oft was thought, but ne'er so well expressed;
Something, whose truth convinced at sight we find,
That gives us back the image of our mind.   300
As shades more sweetly recommend the light,
So modest plainness sets off sprightly wit.
For works may have more wit than does 'em good,
As bodies perish thro' excess of blood.

Others for language all their care express,   305
And value books, as women, men, for dress:
Their praise is still,—the style is excellent:
The sense, they humbly take upon content.
Words are like leaves; and where they most abound,
Much fruit of sense beneath is rarely found;   310
False eloquence, like the prismatic glass,
Its gaudy colors spreads on every place;
The face of nature we no more survey,
All glares alike, without distinction gay: 314
But true expression, like the unchanging sun,
Clears and improves whate'er it shines upon,
It gilds all objects, but it alters none.
Expression is the dress of thought, and still
Appears more decent, as more suitable;
A vile conceit in pompous words expressed,   320
Is like a clown in regal purple dressed:
For different styles with different subjects sort,
As several garbs with country, town, and court.
Some by old words to fame have made pretense,
Ancients in phrase, mere moderns in their sense;   325
Such labored nothings, in so strange a style,
Amaze the unlearned, and make the learnèd smile.
Unlucky, as Fungoso in the play,
These sparks with awkward vanity display
What the fine gentlemen wore yesterday;   330
And but so mimic ancient wits at best,
As apes our grandsires, in their doublets dressed.
In words, as fashions, the same rule will hold;
Alike fantastic, if too new, or old:
Be not the first by whom the new are tried,   335
Nor yet the last to lay the old aside.

But most by numbers judge a poet's song;
And smooth or rough, with them, is right or wrong:
In the bright Muse though thousand charms conspire,
Her voice is all these tuneful fools admire;   340
Who haunt Parnassus but to please their ear,
Not mend their minds; as some to church repair,
Not for the doctrine, but the music there.
These equal syllables alone require,
Though oft the ear the open vowels tire;   345
While expletives their feeble aid do join;
And ten low words oft creep in one dull line:
While they ring round the same unvaried chimes,
With sure returns of still expected rhymes;   349
Where'er you find 'the cooling western breeze,'
In the next line, it 'whispers through the trees';
If crystal streams 'with pleasing murmurs creep,'
The reader's threatened (not in vain) with 'sleep':
Then, at the last and only couplet fraught   354
With some unmeaning thing they call a thought,
A needless Alexandrine ends the song,
That, like a wounded snake, drags its slow length along.
Leave such to tune their own dull rhymes, and know
What's roundly smooth or languishingly slow;
And praise the easy vigor of a line,   360
Where Denham's strength, and Waller's sweetness join.
True ease in writing comes from art, not chance,
As those move easiest who have learned to dance.
'T is not enough no harshness gives offense,
The sound must seem an echo to the sense: 365
Soft is the strain when Zephyr gently blows,
And the smooth stream in smoother numbers flows;
But when loud surges lash the sounding shore,
The hoarse, rough verse should like the torrent roar:
When Ajax strives some rock's vast weight to throw,   370
The line too labors, and the words move slow;
Not so, when swift Camilla scours the plain,
Flies o'er the unbending corn, and skims along the main.
Hear how Timotheus' varied lays surprise,
And bid alternate passions fall and rise!   375
While, at each change, the son of Libyan Jove
Now burns with glory, and then melts with love;
Now his fierce eyes with sparkling fury glow,
Now sighs steal out, and tears begin to flow: 379
Persians and Greeks like turns of nature found,
And the world's victor stood subdued by sound!
The power of music all our hearts allow,
And what Timotheus was, is Dryden now.

Avoid extremes; and shun the fault of such,
Who still are pleased too little or too much,   385
At every trifle scorn to take offense,
That always shows great pride, or little sense;
Those heads, as stomachs, are not sure the best,
Which nauseate all, and nothing can digest.
Yet let not each gay turn thy rapture move,   390
For fools admire, but men of sense approve:
As things seem large which we through mists descry,
Dulness is ever apt to magnify.

Some foreign writers, some our own despise;
The ancients only, or the moderns prize.   395
Thus wit, like faith, by each man is applied
To one small sect, and all are damned beside.
Meanly they seek the blessing to confine,
And force that sun but on a part to shine,
Which not alone the southern wit sublimes,   400
But ripens spirits in cold northern climes;
Which from the first has shone on ages past,
Enlights the present, and shall warm the last;
Though each may feel increases and decays,
And see now clearer and now darker days.   405
Regard not then if wit be old or new,
But blame the false, and value still the true.

Some ne'er advance a judgment of their own,
But catch the spreading notion of the town;
They reason and conclude by precedent,   410
And own stale nonsense which they ne'er invent.
Some judge of authors' names, not works, and then
Nor praise nor blame the writings, but the men.
Of all this servile herd the worst is he
That in proud dulness joins with quality.   415
A constant critic at the great man's board,
To fetch and carry nonsense for my lord.
What woeful stuff this madrigal would be,
In some starved hackney sonneteer, or me?
But let a lord once own the happy lines,   420
How the wit brightens; how the style refines!
Before his sacred name flies every fault,
And each exalted stanza teems with thought!

The vulgar thus through imitation err;
As oft the learned by being singular;   425
So much they scorn the crowd, that if the throng
By chance go right, they purposely go wrong;
So schismatics the plain believers quit,
And are but damned for having too much wit.
Some praise at morning what they blame at night;   430
But always think the last opinion right.
A Muse by these is like a mistress used,
This hour she's idolized, the next abused;
While their weak heads like towns unfortified,
'Twixt sense and nonsense daily change their side.   435
Ask them the cause; they're wiser still, they say;
And still to-morrow's wiser than to-day.

We think our fathers fools, so wise we grow;
Our wiser sons, no doubt, will think us so. 439
Once school-divines this zealous isle o'er-spread;
Who knew most Sentences, was deepest read;
Faith, Gospel, all seemed made to be disputed:
And none had sense enough to be confuted: 443
Scotists and Thomists, now in peace remain,
Amidst their kindred cobwebs in Duck Lane,
If faith itself has different dresses worn, 446
What wonder modes in wit should take their turn?
Oft, leaving what is natural and fit,
The current folly proves the ready wit;
And authors think their reputation safe, 450
Which lives as long as fools are pleased to laugh.

Some valuing those of their own side of mind,
Still make themselves the measure of mankind:
Fondly we think we honor merit then,
When we but praise ourselves in other men. 455
Parties in wit attend on those of state,
And public faction doubles private hate.
Pride, malice, folly, against Dryden rose,
In various shapes of parsons, critics, beaus;
But sense survived, when merry jests were past;
For rising merit will buoy up at last. 461
Might he return, and bless once more our eyes,
New Blackmores and new Milbourns must arise:
Nay, should great Homer lift his awful head,
Zoilus again would start up from the dead. 465
Envy will merit, as its shade, pursue;
But like a shadow, proves the substance true;
For envied wit, like Sol eclipsed, makes known
The opposing body's grossness, not its own.
When first that sun too powerful beams displays, 470
It draws up vapors which obscure its rays;
But ev'n those clouds at last adorn its way,
Reflect new glories, and augment the day.

Be thou the first true merit to defend,
His praise is lost, who stays till all commend.
Short is the date, alas, of modern rhymes, 476
And 't is but just to let them live betimes.
No longer now that golden age appears,
When patriarch-wits survived a thousand years:
Now length of fame (our second life) is lost, 480
And bare threescore is all ev'n that can boast;
Our sons their fathers' failing language see,
And such as Chaucer is, shall Dryden be.
So when the faithful pencil has designed
Some bright idea of the master's mind, 485
Where a new word leaps out at his command,
And ready nature waits upon his hand;
When the ripe colors soften and unite,
And sweetly melt into just shade and light;
When mellow years their full perfection give,
And each bold figure just begins to live, 491
The treacherous colors the fair art betray,
And all the bright creation fades away!

Unhappy wit, like most mistaken things,
Atones not for that envy which it brings. 495
In youth alone its empty praise we boast,
But soon the short-lived vanity is lost:
Like some fair flower the early spring supplies,
That gaily blooms, but even in blooming dies.
What is this wit, which must our cares employ?
The owner's wife, that other men enjoy; 501
Then most our trouble still when most admired,
And still the more we give, the more required;
Whose fame with pains we guard, but lose with ease,
Sure some to vex, but never all to please; 505
'T is what the vicious fear, the virtuous shun,
By fools 't is hated, and by knaves undone!

If wit so much from ignorance undergo,
Ah, let not learning too commence its foe!
Of old, those met rewards who could excel, 510
And such were praised who but endeavored well:
Though triumphs were to generals only due,
Crowns were reserved to grace the soldiers too.
Now, they who reach Parnassus' lofty crown,
Employ their pains to spurn some others down;
And while self-love each jealous writer rules, 516
Contending wits become the sport of fools:
But still the worst with most regret commend,
For each ill author is as bad a friend.
To what base ends, and by what abject ways,
Are mortals urged through sacred lust of praise!
Ah, ne'er so dire a thirst of glory boast, 522
Nor in the critic let the man be lost.
Good-nature and good-sense must ever join;
To err is human, to forgive, divine. 525

But if in noble minds some dregs remain
Not yet purged off, of spleen and sour disdain;
Discharge that rage on more provoking crimes,
Nor fear a dearth in these flagitious times.
No pardon vile obscenity should find, 530
Though wit and art conspire to move your mind;
But dulness with obscenity must prove
As shameful sure as impotence in love.
In the fat age of pleasure, wealth, and ease,
Sprung the rank weed, and thrived with large increase: 535
When love was all an easy Monarch's care;
Seldom at council, never in a war:
Jilts ruled the state, and statesmen farces writ;
Nay, wits had pensions, and young lords had wit:
The fair sat panting at a courtier's play, 540
And not a mask went unimproved away:
The modest fan was lifted up no more,
And virgins smiled at what they blushed before.
The following license of a foreign reign
Did all the dregs of bold Socinus drain; 545
Then unbelieving priests reformed the nation,
And taught more pleasant methods of salvation;
Where Heaven's free subjects might their rights dispute,
Lest God himself should seem too absolute;

Pulpits their sacred satire learned to spare, 550
And vice admired to find a flatterer there!
Encouraged thus, wit's Titans braved the skies,
And the press groaned with licensed blasphemies.
These monsters, critics! with your darts engage,
Here point your thunder, and exhaust your rage! 555

Yet shun their fault, who, scandalously nice,
Will needs mistake an author into vice;
All seems infected that the infected spy,
As all looks yellow to the jaundiced eye.

* * *

(1711)

THE RAPE OF THE LOCK

CANTO I

What dire offense from amorous causes springs,
What mighty contests rise from trivial things,
I sing—This verse to Caryl, Muse! is due:
This, even Belinda may vouchsafe to view:
Slight is the subject, but not so the praise, 5
If she inspire, and he approve my lays.

Say what strange motive, goddess! could compel
A well-bred lord to assault a gentle belle?
Oh, say what stranger cause, yet unexplored,
Could make a gentle belle reject a lord? 10
In tasks so bold, can little men engage,
And in soft bosoms dwells such mighty rage?

Sol through white curtains shot a timorous ray,
And oped those eyes that must eclipse the day:
Now lap-dogs give themselves the rousing shake, 15
And sleepless lovers, just at twelve, awake:
Thrice rung the bell, the slipper knocked the ground,
And the pressed watch returned a silver sound.
Belinda still her downy pillow pressed,
Her guardian sylph prolonged the balmy rest:
'T was he had summoned to her silent bed 21
The morning dream that hovered o'er her head;
A youth more glittering than a birth-night beau
(That e'en in slumber caused her cheek to glow),
Seemed to her ear his winning lips to lay, 25
And thus in whispers said, or seemed to say:

'Fairest of mortals, thou distinguished care
Of thousand bright inhabitants of air!
If e'er one vision touched thy infant thought,
Of all the nurse and all the priest have taught 30
Of airy elves by moonlight shadows seen,
The silver token, and the circled green,
Or virgins visited by angel powers,
With golden crowns and wreaths of heavenly flowers;
Hear and believe! thy own importance know, 35
Nor bound thy narrow views to things below.
Some secret truths, from learned pride concealed,
To maids alone and children are revealed:
What though no credit doubting wits may give?
The fair and innocent shall still believe. 40
Know, then, unnumbered spirits round thee fly,
The light militia of the lower sky:
These, though unseen, are ever on the wing,
Hang o'er the box, and hover round the Ring,
Think what an equipage thou hast in air, 45
And view with scorn two pages and a chair.
As now your own, our beings were of old,
And once enclosed in woman's beauteous mould;
Thence, by a soft transition, we repair
From earthly vehicles to these of air. 50
Think not, when woman's transient breath is fled,
That all her vanities at once are dead;
Succeeding vanities she still regards,
And though she plays no more, o'erlooking cards.
Her joy in gilded chariots, when alive, 55
And love of ombre, after death survive.
For when the fair in all their pride expire,
To their first elements their souls retire:
The sprites of fiery termagants in flame
Mount up, and take a salamander's name. 60
Soft yielding minds to water glide away,
And sip, with nymphs, their elemental tea.
The graver prude sinks downward to a gnome,
In search of mischief still on earth to roam.
The light coquettes in sylphs aloft repair, 65
And sport and flutter in the fields of air.

'Know further yet; whoever fair and chaste
Rejects mankind, is by some sylph embraced:
For spirits, freed from mortal laws, with ease
Assume what sexes and what shapes they please.
What guards the purity of melting maids, 71
In courtly balls, and midnight masquerades,
Safe from the treacherous friend, the daring spark,
The glance by day, the whisper in the dark,
When kind occasion prompts their warm desires, 75
When music softens, and when dancing fires?
'T is but their sylph, the wise celestials know,
Though honor is the word with men below.
Some nymphs there are, too conscious of their face,
For life predestined to the gnomes' embrace. 80
These swell their prospects and exalt their pride,
When offers are disdained, and love denied:
Then gay ideas crowd the vacant brain,
While peers, and dukes, and all their sweeping train,

And garters, stars, and coronets appear, 85
And in soft sounds "Your Grace" salutes their ear.
'T is these that early taint the female soul,
Instruct the eyes of young coquettes to roll,
Teach infant cheeks a bidden blush to know,
And little hearts to flutter at a beau. 90

'Oft, when the world imagine women stray,
The sylphs through mystic mazes guide their way,
Through all the giddy circle they pursue,
And old impertinence expel by new.
What tender maid but must a victim fall 95
To one man's treat, but for another's ball?
When Florio speaks, what virgin could withstand,
If gentle Damon did not squeeze her hand?
With varying vanities, from every part,
They shift the moving toyshop of their heart;
Where wigs with wigs, with sword-knots sword-knots strive, 101
Beaux banish beaux, and coaches coaches drive.
This erring mortals levity may call;
Oh, blind to truth! the sylphs contrive it all.

'Of these am I, who thy protection claim, 105
A watchful sprite, and Ariel is my name.
Late, as I ranged the crystal wilds of air,
In the clear mirror of thy ruling star
I saw, alas! some dread event impend,
Ere to the main this morning sun descend, 110
But Heaven reveals not what, or how, or where:
Warned by the sylph, O pious maid, beware!
This to disclose is all thy guardian can:
Beware of all, but most beware of man!'

He said; when Shock, who thought she slept too long, 115
Leaped up, and waked his mistress with his tongue.
'T was then, Belinda, if report say true,
Thy eyes first opened on a billet-doux;
Wounds, charms, and ardors were no sooner read,
But all the vision vanished from thy head. 120

And now, unveiled, the toilet stands displayed,
Each silver vase in mystic order laid.
First, robed in white, the nymph intent adores,
With head uncovered, the cosmetic powers.
A heavenly image in the glass appears. 125
To that she bends, to that her eyes she rears;
The inferior priestess, at her altar's side,
Trembling begins the sacred rites of pride.
Unnumbered treasures ope at once, and here
The various offerings of the world appear; 130
From each she nicely culls with curious toil,
And decks the goddess with the glittering spoil.
This casket India's glowing gems unlocks,
And all Arabia breathes from yonder box.
The tortoise here and elephant unite, 135
Transformed to combs, the speckled, and the white.
Here files of pins extend their shining rows,
Puffs, powders, patches, bibles, billet-doux.
Now awful beauty puts on all its arms;
The fair each moment rises in her charms, 140
Repairs her smiles, awakens every grace,
And calls forth all the wonders of her face;
Sees by degrees a purer blush arise,
And keener lightnings quicken in her eyes.
The busy sylphs surround their darling care, 145
These set the head, and those divide the hair,
Some fold the sleeve, whilst others plait the gown;
And Betty's praised for labors not her own.

CANTO II

Not with more glories, in the ethereal plain,
The sun first rises o'er the purpled main,
Than, issuing forth, the rival of his beams
Launched on the bosom of the silver Thames.
Fair nymphs, and well-dressed youths around her shone, 5
But every eye was fixed on her alone.
On her white breast a sparkling cross she wore,
Which Jews might kiss, and infidels adore.
Her lively looks a sprightly mind disclose,
Quick as her eyes, and as unfixed as those; 10
Favors to none, to all she smiles extends;
Oft she rejects, but never once offends.
Bright as the sun, her eyes the gazers strike,
And, like the sun, they shine on all alike.
Yet graceful ease, and sweetness void of pride,
Might hide her faults, if belles had faults to hide; 16
If to her share some female errors fall,
Look on her face, and you'll forget 'em all.

This nymph, to the destruction of mankind,
Nourished two locks, which graceful hung behind 20
In equal curls, and well conspired to deck
With shining ringlets the smooth ivory neck.
Love in these labyrinths his slaves detains,
And mighty hearts are held in slender chains.
With hairy springes, we the birds betray, 25
Slight lines of hair surprise the finny prey,
Fair tresses man's imperial race ensnare,
And beauty draws us with a single hair.

The adventurous baron the bright locks admired;
He saw, he wished, and to the prize aspired. 30
Resolved to win, he meditates the way,
By force to ravish, or by fraud betray;
For when success a lover's toil attends,
Few ask, if fraud or force attained his ends. 34

For this, ere Phœbus rose, he had implored
Propitious Heaven, and every power adored,

But chiefly Love—to Love an altar built,
Of twelve vast French romances, neatly gilt.
There lay three garters, half a pair of gloves;
And all the trophies of his former loves; 40
With tender billets-doux he lights the pyre,
And breathes three amorous sighs to raise the fire.
Then prostrate falls, and begs with ardent eyes
Soon to obtain, and long possess the prize:
The powers gave ear, and granted half his prayer, 45
The rest, the winds dispersed in empty air.

But now secure the painted vessel glides,
The sunbeams trembling on the floating tides:
While melting music steals upon the sky,
And softened sounds along the waters die; 50
Smooth flow the waves, the zephyrs gently play,
Belinda smiled, and all the world was gay.
All but the sylph—with careful thoughts oppressed,
The impending woe sat heavy on his breast.
He summons straight his denizens of air; 55
The lucid squadrons round the sails repair:
Soft o'er the shrouds aërial whispers breathe,
That seemed but zephyrs to the train beneath.
Some to the sun their insect wings unfold,
Waft on the breeze, or sink in clouds of gold; 60
Transparent forms, too fine for mortal sight,
Their fluid bodies half dissolved in light.
Loose to the wind their airy garments flew
Thin glittering textures of the filmy dew,
Dipt in the richest tincture of the skies, 65
Where light disports in ever-mingling dyes,
While every beam new transient colors flings,
Colors that change whene'er they wave their wings.
Amid the circle, on the gilded mast,
Superior by the head, was Ariel placed; 70
His purple pinions opening to the sun,
He raised his azure wand, and thus begun.

'Ye sylphs and sylphids, to your chief give ear!
Fays, fairies, genii, elves, and demons, hear!
Ye know the spheres, and various tasks assigned 75
By laws eternal to the aërial kind.
Some in the fields of purest ether play,
And bask and whiten in the blaze of day.
Some guide the course of wandering orbs on high,
Or roll the planets through the boundless sky.
Some less refined, beneath the moon's pale light 81
Pursue the stars that shoot athwart the night,
Or suck the mists in grosser air below,
Or dip their pinions in the painted bow,
Or brew fierce tempests on the wintry main, 85
Or o'er the glebe distil the kindly rain.
Others on earth o'er human race preside,
Watch all their ways, and all their actions guide:
Of these the chief, the care of nations own,
And guard with arms divine the British throne.

'Our humbler province is to tend the fair. 91
Not a less pleasing, though less glorious care;
To save the powder from too rude a gale,
Nor let the imprisoned essences exhale;
To draw fresh colors from the vernal flowers; 95
To steal from rainbows ere they drop in showers,
A brighter wash; to curl their waving hairs,
Assist their blushes, and inspire their airs;
Nay, oft in dreams, invention we bestow,
To change a flounce, or add a furbelow. 100

'This day, black omens threat the brightest fair
That e'er deserved a watchful spirit's care;
Some dire disaster, or by force, or slight;
But what, or where, the fates have wrapped in night.
Whether the nymph shall break Diana's law, 105
Or some frail china jar receive a flaw;
Or stain her honor, or her new brocade;
Forget her prayers, or miss a masquerade;
Or lose her heart, or necklace, at a ball;
Or whether Heaven has doomed that Shock must fall. 110
Haste, then, ye spirits! to your charge repair;
The fluttering fan be Zephyretta's care;
The drops to thee, Brillante, we consign;
And, Momentilla, let the watch be thine;
Do thou, Crispissa, tend her favorite lock; 115
Ariel himself shall be the guard of Shock.

'To fifty chosen sylphs, of special note,
We trust the important charge, the petticoat:
Oft have we known that seven-fold fence to fail,
Though stiff with hoops, and armed with ribs of whale; 120
Form a strong line about the silver bound,
And guard the wide circumference around.

'Whatever spirit, careless of his charge,
His post neglects, or leaves the fair at large,
Shall feel sharp vengeance soon o'ertake his sins, 125
Be stopped in vials, or transfixed with pins;
Or plunged in lakes of bitter washes lie,
Or wedged whole ages in a bodkin's eye:
Gums and pomatums shall his flight restrain,
While clogged he beats his silken wings in vain;
Or alum styptics with contracting power 131
Shrink his thin essence like a rivelled flower:
Or, as Ixion fixed, the wretch shall feel
The giddy motion of the whirling mill,
In fumes of burning chocolate shall glow, 135
And tremble at the sea that froths below!'

He spoke; the spirits from the sails descend;
Some, orb in orb, around the nymph extend;
Some thrid the mazy ringlets of her hair;
Some hang upon the pendants of her ear; 140
With beating hearts the dire event they wait,
Anxious, and trembling for the birth of fate.

CANTO III

Close by those meads, for ever crowned with flowers,
Where Thames with pride surveys his rising towers,
There stands a structure of majestic frame,
Which from the neighboring Hampton takes its name.
Here Britain's statesmen oft the fall foredoom 5
Of foreign tyrants and of nymphs at home;
Here thou, great Anna! whom three realms obey,
Dost sometimes counsel take—and sometimes tea.

Hither the heroes and the nymphs resort,
To taste awhile the pleasures of a court; 10
In various talk the instructive hours they passed,
Who gave the ball, or paid the visit last;
One speaks the glory of the British queen,
And one describes a charming Indian screen;
A third interprets motions, looks, and eyes; 15
At every word a reputation dies.
Snuff, or the fan, supply each pause of chat,
With singing, laughing, ogling, and all that.

Meanwhile, declining from the noon of day,
The sun obliquely shoots his burning ray; 20
The hungry judges soon the sentence sign,
And wretches hang that jurymen may dine;
The merchant from the Exchange returns in peace,
And the long labors of the toilet cease.
Belinda now, whom thirst of fame invites, 25
Burns to encounter two adventurous knights,
At ombre singly to decide their doom;
And swells her breast with conquests yet to come.
Straight the three bands prepare in arms to join,
Each band the number of the sacred nine. 30
Soon as she spreads her hand, the aërial guard
Descend, and sit on each important card:
First, Ariel perched upon a Matadore,
Then each, according to the rank they bore;
For sylphs, yet mindful of their ancient race, 35
Are, as when women, wondrous fond of place.

Behold, four kings in majesty revered,
With hoary whiskers and a forky beard;
And four fair queeens whose hands sustain a flower,
The expressive emblem of their softer power; 40
Four knaves in garbs succinct, a trusty band,
Caps on their heads, and halberts in their hand;
And parti-colored troops, a shining train,
Draw forth to combat on the velvet plain.

The skillful nymph reviews her force with care: 45
Let spades be trumps! she said, and trumps they were.

Now moved to war her sable Matadores,
In show like leaders of the swarthy Moors.
Spadillio first, unconquerable lord!
Led off two captive trumps, and swept the board. 50
As many more Manillio forced to yield,
And marched a victor from the verdant field.
Him Basto followed but his fate more hard
Gained but one trump and one plebeian card.
With his broad saber next, a chief in years, 55
The hoary majesty of spades appears,
Puts forth one manly leg, to sight revealed,
The rest, his many-colored robe concealed.
The rebel knave, who dares his prince engage,
Proves the just victim of his royal rage. 60
Even mighty Pam, that kings and queens o'erthrew,
And mowed down armies in the fights of Loo,
Sad chance of war! now destitute of aid,
Falls undistinguished by the victor spade!

Thus far both armies to Belinda yield; 65
Now to the baron fate inclines the field.
His warlike Amazon her host invades,
The imperial consort of the crown of spades,
The club's black tyrant first her victim died,
Spite of his haughty mien, and barbarous pride:
What boots the regal circle on his head, 71
His giant limbs, in state unwieldy spread;
That long behind he trails his pompous robe,
And, of all monarchs only grasps the globe?

The baron now his diamonds pours apace; 75
The embroidered king who shows but half his face,
And his refulgent queen, with powers combined,
Of broken troops an easy conquest find.
Clubs, diamonds, hearts, in wild disorder seen,
With throngs promiscuous strew the level green.
Thus when dispersed a routed army runs, 81
Of Asia's troops, and Afric's sable sons,
With like confusion different nations fly,
Of various habit, and of various dye,
The pierced battalions disunited fall, 85
In heaps on heaps; one fate o'erwhelms them all.

The knave of diamonds tries his wily arts,
And wins (oh, shameful chance!) the queen of hearts.
At this the blood the virgin's cheek forsook,
A livid paleness spreads o'er all her look; 90
She sees, and trembles at the approaching ill,
Just in the jaws of ruin, and codille.
And now (as oft in some distempered state)
On one nice trick depends the general fate,
An ace of hearts steps forth; the king unseen 95
Lurked in her hand, and mourned his captive queen:
He springs to vengeance with an eager pace,
And falls like thunder on the prostrate ace.
The nymph exulting fills with shouts the sky;
The walls, the wood, and long canals reply 100

Oh, thoughtless mortals! ever blind to fate,
Too soon dejected, and too soon elate.
Sudden, these honors shall be snatched away,
And cursed for ever this victorious day.

    For lo! the board with cups and spoons is crowned, 105
The berries crackle, and the mill turns round;
On shining altars of Japan they raise
The silver lamp; the fiery spirits blaze:
From silver spouts the grateful liquors glide,
While China's earth receives the smoking tide:
At once they gratify their scent and taste, 111
And frequent cups prolong the rich repast.
Straight hover round the fair her airy band;
Some, as she sipped, the fuming liquor fanned,
Some o'er her lap their careful plumes displayed, 115
Trembling, and conscious of the rich brocade.
Coffee (which makes the politician wise,
And see through all things with his half-shut eyes)
Sent up in vapors to the baron's brain
New stratagems the radiant lock to gain. 120
Ah, cease, rash youth! desist ere 't is too late,
Fear the just gods, and think of Scylla's fate!
Changed to a bird, and sent to flit in air,
She dearly pays for Nisus' injured hair!

    But when to mischief mortals bend their will,
How soon they find fit instruments of ill! 126
Just then Clarissa drew with tempting grace
A two-edged weapon from her shining case:
So ladies in romance assist their knight,
Present the spear, and arm him for the fight. 130
He takes the gift with reverence, and extends
The little engine on his finger's ends;
This just behind Belinda's neck he spread,
As o'er the fragrant steams she bends her head.
Swift to the lock a thousand sprites repair, 135
A thousand wings, by turns, blow back the hair;
And thrice they twitched the diamond in her ear;
Thrice she looked back, and thrice the foe drew near.
Just in that instant, anxious Ariel sought
The close recesses of the virgin's thought; 140
As on the nosegay in her breast reclined,
He watched the ideas rising in her mind,
Sudden he viewed, in spite of all her art,
An earthly lover lurking at her heart.
Amazed, confused, he found his power expired,
Resigned to fate, and with a sigh retired. 146

    The peer now spreads the glittering forfex wide,
To inclose the lock; now joins it, to divide.
Even then, before the fatal engine closed,
A wretched sylph too fondly interposed; 150
Fate urged the shears, and cut the sylph in twain,
(But airy substance soon unites again)
The meeting points the sacred hair dissever
From the fair head, for ever, and for ever!

Then flashed the living lightning from her eyes, 155
And screams of horror rend the affrighted skies.
Not louder shrieks to pitying Heaven are cast,
When husbands, or when lapdogs breathe their last;
Or when rich China vessels, fallen from high,
In glittering dust and painted fragments lie! 160

    'Let wreaths of triumph now my temples twine,'
(The victor cried), 'the glorious prize is mine!
While fish in streams, or birds delight in air,
Or in a coach and six the British fair,
As long as Atalantis shall be read, 165
Or the small pillow grace a lady's bed,
While visits shall be paid on solemn days,
When numerous wax-lights in bright order blaze,
While nymphs take treats, or assignations give,
So long my honor, name, and praise shall live!
What Time would spare, from steel receives its date, 171
And monuments, like men, submit to fate!
Steel could the labor of the gods destroy,
And strike to dust the imperial towers of Troy;
Steel could the works of mortal pride confound,
And hew triumphal arches to the ground. 176
What wonder then, fair nymph! thy hairs should feel
The conquering force of unresisted steel?'

CANTO IV

But anxious cares the pensive nymph oppressed,
And secret passions labored in her breast.
Not youthful kings in battle seized alive,
Not scornful virgins who their charms survive,
Not ardent lovers robbed of all their bliss, 5
Not ancient ladies when refused a kiss,
Not tyrants fierce that unrepenting die,
Not Cynthia when her manteau's pinned awry,
E'er felt such rage, resentment, and despair,
As thou, sad virgin, for thy ravished hair. 10
For, that sad moment, when the sylphs withdrew
And Ariel weeping from Belinda flew,
Umbriel, a dusky, melancholy sprite,
As ever sullied the fair face of light,
Down to the central earth, his proper scene, 15
Repaired to search the gloomy cave of Spleen.

    Swift on his sooty pinions flits the gnome,
And in a vapor reached the dismal dome.
No cheerful breeze this sullen region knows,
The dreaded east is all the wind that blows. 20
Here in a grotto, sheltered close from air,
And screened in shades from day's detested glare,
She sighs for ever on her pensive bed,

Pain at her side, and Megrim at her head.
Two handmaids wait the throne, alike in place,
But differing far in figure and in face.   26
Here stood Ill-nature like an ancient maid,
Her wrinkled form in black and white arrayed;
With store of prayers, for mornings, nights, and noons,
Her hand is filled; her bosom with lampoons.   30

   There Affectation, with a sickly mien,
Shows in her cheek the roses of eighteen,
Practiced to lisp, and hang the head aside,
Faints into airs, and languishes with pride,
On the rich quilt sinks with becoming woe,   35
Wrapped in a gown, for sickness, and for show.
The fair ones feel such maladies as these,
When each new night-dress gives a new disease.

A constant vapor o'er the palace flies;
Strange phantoms rising as the mists arise;   40
Dreadful, as hermit's dreams in haunted shades,
Or bright, as visions of expiring maids.
Now glaring fiends, and snakes on rolling spires,
Pale specters, gaping tombs, and purple fires:
Now lakes of liquid gold, Elysian scenes,   45
And crystal domes, and angels in machines.

   Unnumbered throngs on every side are seen,
Of bodies changed to various forms by Spleen.
Here living tea-pots stand, one arm held out,
One bent; the handle this, and that the spout:
A pipkin there, like Homer's tripod, walks;   51
Here sighs a jar, and there a goose-pie talks;
Men prove with child, as powerful fancy works,
And maids, turned bottles, call aloud for corks.

   Safe past the gnome through this fantastic band,   55
A branch of healing spleenwort in his hand.
Then thus addressed the power: 'Hail, wayward queen!
Who rule the sex, to fifty from fifteen:
Parent of vapors and of female wit,
Who give the hysteric, or poetic fit,   60
On various tempers act by various ways,
Make some take physic, others scribble plays;
Who cause the proud their visits to delay,
And send the godly in a pet to pray.
A nymph there is, that all thy power disdains,
And thousands more in equal mirth maintains.
But oh! if e'er thy gnome could spoil a grace,   67
Or raise a pimple on a beauteous face,
Like citron-waters matrons' cheeks inflame,
Or change complexions at a losing game;   70
If e'er with airy horns I planted heads,
Or rumpled petticoats, or tumbled beds,
Or caused suspicion when no soul was rude,
Or discomposed the head-dress of a prude,
Or e'er to costive lap-dog gave disease,   75
Which not the tears of brightest eyes could ease:
Hear me, and touch Belinda with chagrin,
That single act gives half the world the spleen.'

   The goddess with a discontented air
Seems to reject him, though she grants his prayer.   80
A wondrous bag with both her hands she binds,
Like that where once Ulysses held the winds;
There she collects the force of female lungs,
Sighs, sobs, and passions, and the war of tongues.
A vial next she fills with fainting fears,   85
Soft sorrows, melting griefs, and flowing tears.
The gnome rejoicing bears her gifts away,
Spreads his black wings, and slowly mounts to day.

   Sunk in Thalestris' arms the nymph he found,
Her eyes dejected and her hair unbound.   90
Full o'er their heads, the swelling bag he rent,
And all the furies issued at the vent.
Belinda burns with more than mortal ire,
And fierce Thalestris fans the rising fire.
'O wretched maid!' she spread her hands, and cried,   95
(While Hampton's echoes, 'Wretched maid!' replied)
'Was it for this you took such constant care
The bodkin, comb, and essence to prepare?
For this your locks in paper durance bound,   99
For this with torturing irons wreathed around?
For this with fillets strained your tender head,
And bravely bore the double loads of lead?
Gods! shall the ravisher display your hair,
While the fops envy, and the ladies stare!
Honor forbid! at whose unrivalled shrine   105
Ease, pleasure, virtue, all our sex resign.
Methinks already I your tears survey,
Already hear the horrid things they say,
Already see you a degraded toast,
And all your honor in a whisper lost!   110
How shall I, then, your helpless fame defend?
'T will then be infamy to seem your friend!
And shall this prize, the inestimable prize,
Exposed through crystal to the gazing eyes,
And heightened by the diamond's circling rays,
On that rapacious hand for ever blaze?   116
Sooner shall grass in Hyde Park Circus grow,
And wits take lodgings in the sound of Bow;
Sooner let earth, air, sea, to chaos fall,
Men, monkeys, lap-dogs, parrots, perish all!'

   She said; then raging to Sir Plume repairs,   121
And bids her beau demand the precious hairs.
(Sir Plume, of amber snuff-box justly vain,
And the nice conduct of a clouded cane)
With earnest eyes, and round unthinking face,
He first the snuff-box opened, then the case,   126
And thus broke out—'My lord, why, what the devil?
Z——ds! damn the lock! 'fore Gad, you must be civil!
Plague on't! 't is past a jest—nay prithee, pox!
Give her the hair,' he spoke, and rapped his box.   130

'It grieves me much,' replied the peer again,
'Who speaks so well should ever speak in vain.
But by this lock, this sacred lock, I swear,
(Which never more shall join its parted hair;
Which never more its honors shall renew, 135
Clipped from the lovely head where late it grew)
That while my nostrils draw the vital air,
This hand, which won it, shall for ever wear.'
He spoke, and speaking, in proud triumph spread
The long-contended honors of her head. 140

But Umbriel, hateful gnome! forbears not so;
He breaks the vial whence the sorrows flow.
Then see! the nymph in beauteous grief appears,
Her eyes half languishing, half drowned in tears;
On her heaved bosom hung her drooping head,
Which, with a sigh, she raised; and thus she said: 146

'For ever cursed be this detested day,
Which snatched my best, my favorite curl away!
Happy! ah, ten times happy had I been,
If Hampton Court these eyes had never seen!
Yet am not I the first mistaken maid, 151
By love of courts to numerous ills betrayed.
Oh, had I rather unadmired remained
In some lone isle or distant northern land;
Where the gilt chariot never marks the way, 155
Where none learn ombre, none e'er taste bohea!
There kept my charms concealed from mortal eye,
Like roses, that in deserts bloom and die.
What moved my mind with youthful lords to roam? 159
Oh, had I stayed, and said my prayers at home!
'T was this, the morning omens seemed to tell,
Thrice from my trembling hand the patch-box fell;
The tottering china shook without a wind.
Nay, Poll sat mute, and Shock was most unkind!
A sylph, too, warned me of the threats of fate,
In mystic visions, now believed too late! 166
See the poor remnants of these slighted hairs!
My hands shall rend what e'en thy rapine spares;
These in two sable ringlets taught to break,
Once gave new beauties to the snowy neck; 170
The sister lock now sits uncouth, alone,
And in its fellow's fate foresees its own;
Uncurled it hangs, the fatal shears demands,
And tempts once more, thy sacrilegious hands.
Oh, hadst thou, cruel! been content to seize 175
Hairs less in sight, or any hairs but these!'

CANTO V

She said: the pitying audience melt in tears.
But Fate and Jove had stopped the baron's ears.
In vain Thalestris with reproach assails,
For who can move when fair Belinda fails?
Not half so fixed the Trojan could remain, 5
While Anna begged and Dido raged in vain.
Then grave Clarissa graceful waved her fan;
Silence ensued, and thus the nymph began:

'Say, why are beauties praised and honored most,
The wise man's passion, and the vain man's toast? 10
Why decked with all that land and sea afford,
Why angels called, and angel-like adored?
Why round our coaches crowd the white-gloved beaux,
Why bows the side-box from its inmost rows?
How vain are all these glories, all our pains, 15
Unless good sense preserve what beauty gains:
That men may say, when we the front-box grace,
"Behold the first in virtue as in face!"
Oh! if to dance all night, and dress all day,
Charmed the smallpox, or chased old age away;
Who would not scorn what housewife's cares produce, 21
Or who would learn one earthly thing of use?
To patch, nay ogle, might become a saint,
Nor could it sure be such a sin to paint.
But since, alas! frail beauty must decay, 25
Curled or uncurled, since locks will turn to gray;
Since painted, or not painted, all shall fade,
And she who scorns a man must die a maid;
What then remains but well our power to use,
And keep good humor still whate'er we lose? 30
And trust me, dear! good humor can prevail,
When airs, and flights, and screams, and scolding fail.
Beauties in vain their pretty eyes may roll;
Charms strike the sight, but merit wins the soul.'

So spoke the dame, but no applause ensued;
Belinda frowned, Thalestris called her prude. 36
'To arms, to arms!' the fierce virago cries,
And swift as lightning to the combat flies.
All side in parties, and begin th' attack;
Fans clap, silks rustle, and tough whale-bones crack; 40
Heroes' and heroines' shouts confusedly rise,
And bass and treble voices strike the skies.
No common weapons in their hands are found,
Like gods they fight, nor dread a mortal wound.

So when bold Homer makes the gods engage,
And heavenly breasts with human passions rage;
'Gainst Pallas, Mars; Latona, Hermes arms;
And all Olympus rings with loud alarms: 48
Jove's thunder roars, Heaven trembles all around,
Blue Neptune storms, the bellowing deeps resound: 50
Earth shakes her nodding towers, the ground gives way,
And the pale ghosts start at the flash of day!

Triumphant Umbriel on a sconce's height
Clapped his glad wings, and sat to view the fight:
Propped on their bodkin spears, the sprites survey 55
The growing combat, or assist the fray.

While through the press enraged Thalestris flies,
And scatters death around from both her eyes,
A beau and witling perished in the throng,
One died in metaphor, and one in song. 60
'O cruel nymph! a living death I bear,'
Cried Dapperwit, and sunk beside his chair.
A mournful glance Sir Fopling upwards cast,
'Those eyes are made so killing'—was his last.
Thus on Meander's flowery margin lies 65
The expiring swan, and as he sings he dies.

When bold Sir Plume had drawn Clarissa down,
Chloe stepped in and killed him with a frown;
She smiled to see the doughty hero slain,
But, at her smile, the beau revived again. 70
Now Jove suspends his golden scales in air,
Weighs the men's wits against the lady's hair;
The doubtful beam long nods from side to side;
At length the wits mount up, the hairs subside.

See, fierce Belinda on the Baron flies, 75
With more than usual lightning in her eyes:
Nor feared the chief the unequal fight to try,
Who sought no more than on his foe to die.
But this bold lord with manly strength endued,
She with one finger and a thumb subdued: 80
Just where the breath of life his nostrils drew,
A charge of snuff the wily virgin threw;
The gnomes direct, to every atom just,
The pungent grains of titillating dust.
Sudden, with starting tears each eye o'erflows,
And the high dome re-echoes to his nose. 86

'Now meet thy fate,' incensed Belinda cried,
And drew a deadly bodkin from her side.
(The same, his ancient personage to deck,
Her great great grandsire wore about his neck,
In three seal-rings; which after, melted down, 91
Formed a vast buckle for his widow's gown:
Her infant grandame's whistle next it grew,
The bells she jingled, and the whistle blew;
Then in a bodkin graced her mother's hairs, 95
Which long she wore, and now Belinda wears.)

'Boast not my fall,' he cried, 'insulting foe!
Thou by some other shalt be laid as low,
Nor think to die dejects my lofty mind:
All that I dread is leaving you behind! 100
Rather than so, ah, let me still survive,
And burn in Cupid's flames—but burn alive.'

'Restore the lock!' she cries; and all around
'Restore the lock!' the vaulted roofs rebound.
Not fierce Othello in so loud a strain 105
Roared for the handkerchief that caused his pain.

But see how oft ambitious aims are crossed,
And chiefs contend till all the prize is lost!
The lock, obtained with guilt, and kept with pain,
In every place is sought, but sought in vain: 110
With such a prize no mortal must be blessed,
So Heaven decrees! with Heaven who can contest?

Some thought it mounted to the lunar sphere,
Since all things lost on earth are treasured there.
There heroes' wits are kept in ponderous vases,
And beaux' in snuff-boxes and tweezer cases. 116
There broken vows and death-bed alms are found,
And lovers' hearts with ends of riband bound,
The courtier's promises, and sick man's prayers,
The smiles of harlots, and the tears of heirs, 120
Cages for gnats, and chains to yoke a flea,
Dried butterflies, and tomes of casuistry.

But trust the Muse—she saw it upward rise,
Though marked by none but quick, poetic eyes:
(So Rome's great founder to the heavens withdrew, 125
To Proculus alone confessed in view)
A sudden star, it shot through liquid air,
And drew behind a radiant trail of hair.
Not Berenice's locks first rose so bright,
The heavens bespangling with dishevelled light.
The sylphs behold it kindling as it flies, 131
And pleased pursue its progress through the skies.

This the beau monde shall from the Mall survey,
And hail with music its propitious ray.
This the blest lover shall for Venus take, 135
And send up vows from Rosamonda's lake.
This Partridge soon shall view in cloudless skies,
When next he looks through Galileo's eyes;
And hence the egregious wizard shall foredoom
The fate of Louis and the fall of Rome. 140

Then cease, bright nymph! to mourn thy ravished hair,
Which adds new glory to the shining sphere!
Not all the tresses that fair head can boast,
Shall draw such envy as the lock you lost.
For, after all the murders of your eye, 145
When, after millions slain, yourself shall die:
When those fair suns shall set, as set they must,
And all those tresses shall be laid in dust,
This lock, the Muse shall consecrate to fame,
And 'midst the stars inscribe Belinda's name. 150

(1712, 1714)

From EPISTLE TO DR. ARBUTHNOT

POPE

SHUT, shut the door, good John! fatigued, I said;
Tie up the knocker, say I'm sick, I'm dead.

The Dog-star rages! nay, 't is past a doubt,
All Bedlam, or Parnassus, is let out:
Fire in each eye, and papers in each hand, 5
They rave, recite, and madden round the land.

   What walls can guard me, or what shades can hide?
They pierce my thickets, through my grot they glide;
By land, by water, they renew the charge,
They stop the chariot, and they board the barge.
No place is sacred, not the church is free; 11
E'en Sunday shines no Sabbath day to me:
Then from the Mint walks forth the man of rime,
Happy to catch me just at dinner-time.

   Is there a parson, much bemused in beer, 15
A maudlin poetess, a riming peer,
A clerk, foredoomed his father's soul to cross,
Who pens a stanza, when he should engross?
Is there, who, locked from ink and paper, scrawls
With desperate charcoal round his darkened walls? 20
All fly to Twit'nam, and in humble strain
Apply to me, to keep them mad or vain.
Arthur, whose giddy son neglects the laws,
Imputes to me and my damn'd works the cause:
Poor Cornus sees his frantic wife elope, 25
And curses wit, and poetry, and Pope.

   Friend to my life! (which did not you prolong,
The world had wanted many an idle song)
What drop or nostrum can this plague remove?
Or which must end me, a fool's wrath or love? 30
A dire dilemma! either way I'm sped:
If foes, they write, if friends, they read me dead.
Seized and tied down to judge, how wretched I!
Who can't be silent, and who will not lie.
To laugh, were want of goodness and of grace,
And to be grave, exceeds all power of face. 36
I sit with sad civility, I read
With honest anguish, and an aching head;
And drop at last, but in unwilling ears,
This saving counsel, 'Keep your piece nine years.' 40

   'Nine years!' cries he, who high in Drury Lane,
Lulled by soft zephyrs through the broken pane,
Rimes ere he wakes, and prints before term ends,
Obliged by hunger, and request of friends:
'The piece, you think, is incorrect? why, take it,
I'm all submission, what you 'd have it, make it.' 46

   Three things another's modest wishes bound,
My friendship, and a prologue, and ten pound.

   Pitholeon sends to me: 'You know his Grace,
I want a patron; ask him for a place.' 50
'Pitholeon libelled me'—'But here 's a letter
Informs you, sir, 't was when he knew no better.
Dare you refuse him? Curll invites to dine,
He'll write a journal, or he'll turn divine.'

   Bless me! a packet.—''T is a stranger sues, 55
A virgin tragedy, an orphan Muse.'
If I dislike it, 'Furies, death and rage!'
If I approve, 'Commend it to the stage.'
There (thank my stars) my whole commission ends,
The players and I are, luckily, no friends. 60
Fired that the house reject him, "Sdeath I'll print it,
And shame the fools——Your interest, sir, with Lintot!'
'Lintot, dull rogue! will think your price too much:'
'Not, sir, if you revise it, and retouch.'
All my demurs but double his attacks; 65
At last he whispers, 'Do; and we go snacks.'
Glad of a quarrel, straight I clap the door;
'Sir, let me see your works and you no more.'

   'T is sung, when Midas' ears began to spring,
(Midas, a sacred person and a king) 70
His very minister who spied them first,
(Some say his queen) was forced to speak, or burst.
And is not mine, my friend, a sorer case,
When every coxcomb perks them in my face?

ARBUTHNOT

   Good friend, forbear! you deal in dangerous things. 75
I'd never name queens, ministers, or kings;
Keep close to ears, and those let asses prick;
'T is nothing—

POPE

   Nothing? if they bite and kick?
Out with it, Dunciad! let the secret pass,
That secret to each fool, that he's an ass: 80
The truth once told (and wherefore should we lie?),
The Queen of Midas slept, and so may I.

   You think this cruel? take it for a rule,
No creature smarts so little as a fool.
Let peals of laughter, Codrus! round thee break,
Thou unconcerned canst hear the mighty crack:
Pit, box, and gallery in convulsions hurled, 87
Thou stand'st unshook amidst a bursting world.
Who shames a scribbler? break one cobweb through,
He spins the slight, self-pleasing thread anew: 90
Destroy his fib or sophistry, in vain,
The creature's at his dirty work again,
Throned in the centre of his thin designs,
Proud of a vast extent of flimsy lines!
Whom have I hurt? has poet yet, or peer, 95
Lost the arched eyebrow, or Parnassian sneer?

* * *

One dedicates in high heroic prose,
And ridicules beyond a hundred foes;
One from all Grub Street will my fame defend,
And, more abusive, calls himself my friend. 100
This prints my letters, that expects a bribe,
And others roar aloud, 'Subscribe, subscribe!'

There are, who to my person pay their court:
I cough like Horace, and, though lean, am short,
Ammon's great son one shoulder had too high,
Such Ovid's nose, and 'Sir! you have an eye'—
Go on, obliging creatures, make me see 107
All that disgraced my betters, met in me.
Say for my comfort, languishing in bed,
'Just so immortal Maro held his head:' 110
And when I die, be sure you let me know
Great Homer died three thousand years ago.

Why did I write? what sin to me unknown
Dipped me in ink, my parents', or my own?
As yet a child, nor yet a fool to fame, 115
I lisped in numbers, for the numbers came.
I left no calling for this idle trade,
No duty broke, no father disobeyed.
The Muse but served to ease some friend, not wife,
To help me through this long disease, my life, 120
To second, Arbuthnot! thy art and care,
And teach the being you preserved, to bear.

But why then publish? Granville the polite,
And knowing Walsh, would tell me I could write; 124
Well-natured Garth inflamed with early praise,
And Congreve loved, and Swift endured my lays;
The courtly Talbot, Somers, Sheffield, read;
E'en mitred Rochester would nod the head,
And St. John's self (great Dryden's friends before)
With open arms received one poet more. 130
Happy my studies, when by these approved!
Happier their author, when by these beloved!
From these the world will judge of men and books,
Not from the Burnets, Oldmixons, and Cookes.

Soft were my numbers; who could take offence 135
While pure description held the place of sense?
Like gentle Fanny's was my flowery theme,
A painted mistress, or a purling stream.
Yet then did Gildon draw his venal quill;—
I wished the man a dinner, and sat still. 140
Yet then did Dennis rave in furious fret;
I never answered—I was not in debt.
If want provoked, or madness made them print,
I waged no war with Bedlam or the Mint.

Did some more sober critic come aboard; 145
If wrong, I smiled; if right, I kissed the rod.
Pains, reading, study, are their just pretence,
And all they want is spirit, taste, and sense.
Commas and points they set exactly right,
And 't were a sin to rob them of their mite; 150
Yet ne'er one sprig of laurel graced these ribalds,
From slashing Bentley down to piddling Tibbalds.
Each wight, who reads not, and but scans and spells,
Each word-catcher, that lives on syllables,
E'en such small critics some regard may claim,
Preserved in Milton's or in Shakespeare's name.
Pretty! in amber to observe the forms 157
Of hairs, or straws, or dirt, or grubs, or worms!
The things, we know, are neither rich nor rare,
But wonder how the devil they got there. 160

Were others angry I excused them too;
Well might they rage, I gave them but their due.
A man's true merit 't is not hard to find;
But each man's secret standard in his mind,
That casting-weight pride adds to emptiness,
This, who can gratify? for who can guess? 166
The bard whom pilfered Pastorals renown,
Who turns a Persian tale for half a crown,
Just writes to make his barrenness appear,
And strains from hard-bound brains, eight lines a year; 170
He, who still wanting, though he lives on theft,
Steals much, spends little, yet has nothing left;
And he, who now to sense, now nonsense leaning,
Means not, but blunders round about a meaning;
And he, whose fustian's so sublimely bad, 175
It is not poetry, but prose run mad:
All these, my modest satire bade translate,
And owned that nine such poets made a Tate.
How did they fume, and stamp, and roar, and chafe!
And swear, not Addison himself was safe. 180

Peace to all such! but were there one whose fires
True genius kindles, and fair fame inspires;
Blessed with each talent and each art to please,
And born to write, converse, and live with ease:
Should such a man, too fond to rule alone, 185
Bear, like the Turk, no brother near the throne,
View him with scornful, yet with jealous eyes,
And hate for arts that caused himself to rise;
Damn with faint praise, assent with civil leer,
And without sneering, teach the rest to sneer;
Willing to wound, and yet afraid to strike, 191
Just hint a fault, and hesitate dislike;
Alike reserved to blame, or to commend,
A timorous foe, and a suspicious friend;
Dreading e'en fools, by flatterers besieged, 195
And so obliging, that he ne'er obliged;
Like Cato, give his little senate laws,
And sit attentive to his own applause;
While wits and Templars every sentence raise,
And wonder with a foolish face of praise— 200
Who but must laugh, if such a man there be?
Who would not weep, if Atticus were he!

What though my name stood rubric on the walls,
Or plastered posts, . . . in capitals?
Or smoking forth, a hundred hawkers' load, 205
On wings of winds came flying all abroad?
I sought no homage from the race that write;
I kept, like Asian monarchs, from their sight:
Poems I heeded (now be-rimed so long)
No more than thou, great George! a birthday song. 210
I ne'er with wits or witlings passed my days,
To spread about the itch of verse and praise;
Nor like a puppy, daggled through the town,
To fetch and carry sing-song up and down;
Nor at rehearsals sweat, and mouthed, and cried, 215
With handkerchief and orange at my side;
But sick of fops, and poetry, and prate,
To Bufo left the whole Castalian state.

Proud as Apollo on his forked hill,
Sat full-blown Bufo, puffed by every quill; 220
Fed with soft dedication all day long,
Horace and he went hand in hand in song.
His library (where busts of poets dead
And a true Pindar stood without a head)
Received of wits an undistinguished race, 225
Who first his judgment asked, and then a place,
Much they extolled his pictures, much his seat,
And flattered every day, and some days eat;
Till grown more frugal in his riper days,
He paid some bards with port, and some with praise; 230
To some a dry rehearsal was assigned;
And others (harder still) he paid in kind.
Dryden alone (what wonder?) came not nigh,
Dryden alone escaped this judging eye:
But still the great have kindness in reserve, 235
He helped to bury whom he helped to starve.

May some choice patron bless each grey goose quill!
May every Bavius have his Bufo still!
So, when a statesman wants a day's defence,
Or envy holds a whole week's war with sense, 240
Or simple pride for flattery makes demands,
May dunce by dunce be whistled off my hands!
Bless'd be the great! for those they take away,
And those they left me; for they left me Gay;
Left me to see neglected genius bloom, 245
Neglected die, and tell it on his tomb:
Of all thy blameless life the sole return
My verse, and Queensbury weeping o'er thy urn!

Oh, let me live my own, and die so too!
(To live and die is all I have to do!) 250
Maintain a poet's dignity and ease,
And see what friends, and read what books I please;
Above a patron, though I condescend
Sometimes to call a minister my friend.

I was not born for courts or great affairs; 255
I pay my debts, believe, and say my prayers;
Can sleep without a poem in my head,
Nor know, if Dennis be alive or dead.

Why am I asked what next shall see the light?
Heavens! was I born for nothing but to write?
Has life no joys for me? or (to be grave) 261
Have I no friend to serve, no soul to save?
'I found him close with Swift.'—'Indeed? no doubt,'
Cries prating Balbus, 'something will come out.'
'T is all in vain, deny it as I will. 265
'No, such a genius never can lie still;'
And then for mine obligingly mistakes
The first lampoon Sir Will or Bubo makes.
Poor guiltless I! and can I choose but smile,
When every coxcomb knows me by my style? 270

Curs'd be the verse, how well soe'er it flow,
That tends to make one worthy man my foe,
Give virtue scandal, innocence a fear,
Or from the soft-eyed virgin steal a tear!
But he who hurts a harmless neighbour's peace,
Insults fallen worth, or beauty in distress; 276
Who loves a lie, lame slander helps about;
Who writes a libel, or who copies out;
That fop, whose pride affects a patron's name,
Yet absent, wounds an author's honest fame; 280
Who can your merit selfishly approve,
And show the sense of it without the love;
Who has the vanity to call you friend,
Yet wants the honour, injured, to defend;
Who tells whate'er you think, whate'er you say,
And, if he lie not, must at least betray; 286
Who to the Dean and silver bell can swear,
And sees at Canons what was never there;
Who reads, but with a lust to misapply,
Make satire a lampoon, and fiction, lie: 290
A lash like mine no honest man shall dread,
But all such babbling blockheads in his stead.
Let Sporus tremble——

ARBUTHNOT

What? that thing of silk,
Sporus, that mere white curd of ass's milk?
Satire or sense, alas! can Sporus feel? 295
Who breaks a butterfly upon a wheel?

POPE

Yet let me flap this bug with gilded wings,
This painted child of dirt, that stinks and stings;
Whose buzz the witty and the fair annoys,
Yet wit ne'er tastes, and beauty ne'er enjoys:
So well-bred spaniels civilly delight 301
In mumbling of the game they dare not bite.
Eternal smiles his emptiness betray,
As shallow streams run dimpling all the way.
Whether in florid impotence he speaks, 305
And, as the prompter breathes, the puppet squeaks;

Or at the ear of Eve, familiar toad,
Half froth, half venom, spits himself abroad,
In puns, or politics, or tales, or lies,
Or spite, or smut, or rimes, or blasphemies. 310
His wit all see-saw, between that and this,
Now high, now low, now master up, now miss,
And he himself one vile antithesis.
Amphibious thing! that acting either part,
The trifling head, or the corrupted heart, 315
Fop at the toilet, flatterer at the board,
Now trips a lady, and now struts a lord.
Eve's tempter thus the rabbins have expressed,
A cherub's face, a reptile all the rest:
Beauty that shocks you, parts that none will trust, 320
Wit that can creep, and pride that licks the dust.

Not fortune's worshipper, nor fashion's fool,
Not lucre's madman, nor ambition's tool,
Not proud, nor servile;—be one poet's praise,
That, if he pleased, he pleased by manly ways:
That flattery, e'en to kings, he held a shame, 326
And thought a lie in verse or prose the same;
That not in fancy's maze he wandered long,
But stooped to truth, and moralized his song;
That not for fame, but virtue's better end, 330
He stood the furious foe, the timid friend,
The damning critic, half approving wit,
The coxcomb hit, or fearing to be hit;
Laughed at the loss of friends he never had, 334
The dull, the proud, the wicked, and the mad;
The distant threats of vengeance on his head,
The blow unfelt, the tear he never shed;
The tale revived, the lie so oft o'erthrown,
Th' imputed trash, and dullness not his own;
The morals blackened when the writings scape,
The libelled person, and the pictured shape; 341
Abuse, on all he loved, or loved him, spread,
A friend in exile, or a father dead;
The whisper, that to greatness still too near,
Perhaps, yet vibrates on his Sovereign's ear—
Welcome for thee, fair virtue! all the past; 346
For thee, fair virtue! welcome e'en the last!

ARBUTHNOT

But why insult the poor, affront the great?

POPE

A knave's a knave, to me, in every state:
Alike my scorn, if he succeed or fail, 350
Sporus at Court, or Japhet in a jail,
A hireling scribbler, or a hireling peer,
Knight of the post corrupt, or of the shire;
If on a pillory, or near a throne,
He gain his prince's ear, or lose his own. 355

Yet soft by nature, more a dupe than wit,
Sappho can tell you how this man was bit:
This dreaded satirist Dennis will confess
Foe to his pride, but friend to his distress:
So humble, he has knocked at Tibbald's door,
Has drunk with Cibber, nay has rimed for Moore. 361
Full ten years slandered, did he once reply?
Three thousand suns went down on Welsted's lie.
To please a mistress one aspersed his life;
He lashed him not, but let her be his wife. 365
Let Budgell charge low Grub Street on his quill;
And write whate'er he pleased, except his will;
Let the two Curlls of town and court, abuse
His father, mother, body, soul, and Muse.
Yet why? that father held it for a rule, 370
It was a sin to call our neighbour fool.

* * *

Of gentle blood (part shed in honour's cause,
While yet in Britain honour had applause)
Each parent sprung——

ARBUTHNOT
What fortune, pray?—

POPE
Their own,
And better got, than Bestia's from the throne.
Born to no pride, inheriting no strife, 376
Nor marrying discord in a noble wife,
Stranger to civil and religious rage,
The good man walked innoxious through his age.
No courts he saw, no suits would ever try, 380
Nor dared an oath, nor hazarded a lie.
Unlearn'd, he knew no schoolman's subtle art,
No language, but the language of the heart.
By nature honest, by experience wise,
Healthy by temperance, and by exercise; 385
His life, though long, to sickness passed unknown,
His death was instant, and without a groan.
O grant me thus to live, and thus to die!
Who sprung from kings shall know less joy than I.

O friend! may each domestic bliss be thine! 390
Be no unpleasing melancholy mine:
Me, let the tender office long engage,
To rock the cradle of reposing age,
With lenient arts extend a mother's breath,
Make languor smile, and smooth the bed of death, 395
Explore the thought, explain the asking eye,
And keep awhile one parent from the sky!
On cares like these if length of days attend,
May Heaven, to bless those days, preserve my friend,
Preserve him social, cheerful, and serene, 400
And just as rich as when he served a queen.

ARBUTHNOT
Whether that blessing be denied or given,
Thus far was right, the rest belongs to Heaven.

(1735)

JAMES THOMSON (1700–1748)

THOMSON was a Scotchman who, at the height of Pope's reign, went to seek his fortune in literary London. He arrived in need of a pair of shoes and lost the packet of recommendations which he had tied up in his handkerchief; but he was kindly received by his brother poets, and enjoyed sufficient patronage from the rich to preserve him from actual want. The four parts of *The Seasons* which appeared in rapid succession (1726–30) made his reputation, and a series of stiff tragedies in blank verse had a lukewarm success on the stage. Politically, he adhered to the opposition and was one of a group, including the poet Collins, which gathered around Lord Lyttleton at Hagley, under the 'precarious patronage' of Frederick, Prince of Wales. Thomson was an indolent man 'more fat than bard beseems,' luxurious and procrastinating, and the last fifteen years of his life originated little that was important. *The Castle of Indolence*, which commemorates the Hagley company, was begun in 1733, though not completed until two years before his death. Dull in unfamiliar society, Thomson was loyally and deeply beloved by those who intimately knew him. His warm and truthful delineations of nature and his resource in the older harmonies of English verse helped to inaugurate a new era in poetry. Notwithstanding these tendencies, Pope regarded him with respect and favor. In the next generation, Dr. Johnson abated his prejudice against blank verse in favor of *The Seasons*, and forgot his hostility to Spenserism in commenting on *The Castle of Indolence*. 'He thinks always as a man of genius; he looks round on Nature and on Life with the eye which Nature bestows only on a poet,' was Johnson's summary of his abilities.

From SUMMER

Low walks the sun, and broadens by degrees,
Just o'er the verge of day. The shifting clouds
Assembled gay, a richly gorgeous train,
In all their pomp attend his setting throne.
Air, earth, and ocean smile immense. And now,
As if his weary chariot sought the bowers 6
Of Amphitrite, and her tending nymphs—
So Grecian fable sung—he dips his orb;
Now half immersed; and now a golden curve
Gives one bright glance, then total disappears.

* * *

Confessed from yonder slow-extinguished clouds, 11
All ether softening, sober evening takes
Her wonted station in the middle air;
A thousand shadows at her beck. First this
She sends on earth; then that of deeper dye 15
Steals soft behind; and then a deeper still,
In circle following circle, gathers round,
To close the face of things. A fresher gale
Begins to wave the wood, and stir the stream,
Sweeping with shadowy gust the fields of corn:
While the quail clamors for his running mate. 21
Wide o'er the thistly lawn, as swells the breeze,
A whitening shower of vegetable down
Amusive floats. The kind impartial care
Of nature nought disdains: thoughtful to feed 25
Her lowest sons, and clothe the coming year,
From field to field the feathered seeds she wings.

His folded flock secure, the shepherd home
Hies merry-hearted; and by turns relieves
The ruddy milkmaid of her brimming pail; 30
The beauty whom perhaps his witless heart—
Unknowing what the joy-mixed anguish means—
Sincerely loves, by that best language shewn
Of cordial glances, and obliging deeds.
Onward they pass o'er many a panting height, 35
And valley sunk, and unfrequented; where
At fall of eve the fairy people throng,
In various game and revelry, to pass
The summer night, as village stories tell.
But far about they wander from the grave 40
Of him whom his ungentle fortune urged
Against his own sad breast to lift the hand
Of impious violence. The lonely tower
Is also shunned; whose mournful chambers hold—
So night-struck fancy dreams—the yelling ghost. 45
  Among the crooked lanes, on every hedge,
The glowworm lights his gem; and through the dark
A moving radiance twinkles. Evening yields
The world to night; not in her winter robe
Of massy Stygian woof, but loose arrayed 50
In mantle dun. A faint erroneous ray,
Glanced from the imperfect surfaces of things,
Flings half an image on the straining eye;
While wavering woods, and villages, and streams,

And rocks, and mountain-tops, that long retained 55
The ascending gleam, are all one swimming scene,
Uncertain if beheld. Sudden to heaven
Thence weary vision turns; where, leading soft
The silent hours of love, with purest ray
Sweet Venus shines; and from her genial rise, 60
When daylight sickens till it springs afresh,
Unrivaled reigns, the fairest lamp of night.

* * * (1727)

From AUTUMN

But see the fading many-colored woods,
Shade deepening over shade, the country round
Imbrown; a crowded umbrage dusk and dun,
Of every hue, from wan declining green
To sooty dark. These now the lonesome muse,
Low whispering, lead into their leaf-strewn walks, 6
And give the season in its latest view.

Meantime, light shadowing all, a sober calm
Fleeces unbounded ether: whose least wave
Stands tremulous, uncertain where to turn 10
The gentle current; while illumined wide,
The dewy-skirted clouds imbibe the sun,
And through their lucid veil his softened force
Shed o'er the peaceful world. Then is the time,
For those whom virtue and whom nature charm,
To steal themselves from the degenerate crowd,
And soar above this little scene of things: 17
To tread low-thoughted vice beneath their feet;
To soothe the throbbing passions into peace;
And woo lone Quiet in her silent walks. 20

Thus solitary, and in pensive guise,
Oft let me wander o'er the russet mead,
And through the saddened grove, where scarce is heard 23
One dying strain, to cheer the woodman's toil.
Haply some widowed songster pours his plaint,
Far, in faint warblings, through the tawny copse;
While congregated thrushes, linnets, larks,
And each wild throat, whose artless strains so late
Swelled all the music of the swarming shades,
Robbed of their tuneful souls, now shivering sit 30
On the dead tree, a dull despondent flock:
With not a brightness waving o'er their plumes,
And nought save chattering discord in their note.
O let not, aimed from some inhuman eye,
The gun the music of the coming year 35
Destroy; and harmless, unsuspecting harm,
Lay the weak tribes a miserable prey
In mingled murder, fluttering on the ground!

The pale descending year, yet pleasing still,
A gentler mood inspires; for now the leaf 40
Incessant rustles from the mournful grove;
Oft startling such as studious walk below,
And slowly circles through the waving air.
But should a quicker breeze amid the boughs
Sob, o'er the sky the leafy deluge streams; 45
Till choked, and matted with the dreary shower,
The forest walks, at every rising gale,
Roll wide the withered waste, and whistle bleak.
Fled is the blasted verdure of the fields;
And, shrunk into their beds, the flowery race 50
Their sunny robes resign. E'en what remained
Of stronger fruits falls from the naked tree;
And woods, fields, gardens, orchards all around,
The desolated prospect thrills the soul. . . .

The western sun withdraws the shortened day, 55
And humid evening, gliding o'er the sky,
In her chill progress, to the ground condensed
The vapor throws. Where creeping waters ooze,
Where marshes stagnate, and where rivers wind,
Cluster the rolling fogs, and swim along 60
The dusky-mantled lawn. Meanwhile the moon,
Full orbed, and breaking through the scattered clouds,
Shews her broad visage in the crimsoned east.
Turned to the sun direct her spotted disk,
Where mountains rise, umbrageous dales descend, 65
And caverns deep as optic tube descries,
A smaller earth, gives us his blaze again,
Void of its flame, and sheds a softer day.
Now through the passing clouds she seems to stoop,
Now up the pure cerulean rides sublime. 70
Wide the pale deluge floats, and streaming mild
O'er the skied mountain to the shadowy vale,
While rocks and floods reflect the quivering gleam;
The whole air whitens with a boundless tide
Of silver radiance trembling round the world. 75

* * * (1730)

From WINTER

Through the hushed air the whitening shower descends,
At first thin-wavering, till at last the flakes
Fall broad, and wide, and fast, dimming the day
With a continual flow. The cherished fields
Put on their winter robe of purest white: 5
'T is brightness all, save where the new snow melts
Along the mazy current. Low the woods
Bow their hoar head; and ere the languid sun
Faint from the west, emits his evening ray;
Earth's universal face, deep hid, and chill, 10

Is one wide dazzling waste, that buries wide
The works of man. Drooping, the laborer-ox
Stands covered o'er with snow, and then demands
The fruit of all his toil. The fowls of heaven,
Tamed by the cruel season, crowd around 15
The winnowing store, and claim the little boon
Which Providence assigns them. One alone,
The redbreast, sacred to the household gods,
Wisely regardful of the embroiling sky,
In joyless fields and thorny thickets, leaves 20
His shivering mates, and pays to trusted man
His annual visit. Half-afraid, he first
Against the window beats; then, brisk, alights
On the warm hearth; then hopping o'er the floor,
Eyes all the smiling family askance, 25
And pecks, and starts, and wonders where he is:
Till more familiar grown, the table crumbs
Attract his slender feet. The foodless wilds
Pour forth their brown inhabitants. The hare,
Though timorous of heart, and hard beset 30
By death in various forms, dark snares and dogs,
And more unpitying men, the garden seeks,
Urged on by fearless want. The bleating kine
Eye the bleak heaven, and next, the glistening earth,
With looks of dumb despair; then, sad dispersed,
Dig for the withered herb through heaps of snow. 36

* * *

As thus the snows arise, and foul and fierce
All winter drives along the darkened air,
In his own loose revolving fields the swain
Disastered stands; sees other hills ascend, 40
Of unknown joyless brow, and other scenes,
Of horrid prospect, shag the trackless plain;
Nor finds the river nor the forest, hid
Beneath the formless wild; but wanders on
From hill to dale, still more and more astray, 45
Impatient flouncing through the drifted heaps,
Stung with the thoughts of home; the thoughts of home
Rush on his nerves, and call their vigor forth
In many a vain attempt. How sinks his soul!
What black despair, what horror, fills his heart!
When for the dusky spot which fancy feigned,
His tufted cottage rising through the snow, 52
He meets the roughness of the middle waste,
Far from the track and blessed abode of man;
While round him night resistless closes fast, 55
And every tempest howling o'er his head,
Renders the savage wilderness more wild.
Then throng the busy shapes into his mind,
Of covered pits, unfathomably deep,
A dire descent! beyond the power of frost; 60
Of faithless bogs; of precipices huge
Smoothed up with snow; and what is land unknown,
What water of the still unfrozen spring,
In the loose marsh or solitary lake,
Where the fresh fountain from the bottom boils.
These check his fearful steps, and down he sinks
Beneath the shelter of the shapeless drift, 67
Thinking o'er all the bitterness of death,
Mixed with the tender anguish nature shoots
Through the wrung bosom of the dying man, 70
His wife, his children, and his friends, unseen.
In vain for him the officious wife prepares
The fire fair blazing, and the vestment warm:
In vain his little children, peeping out
Into the mingling storm, demand their sire 75
With tears of artless innocence. Alas!
Nor wife nor children more shall he behold,
Nor friends, nor sacred home. On every nerve
The deadly winter seizes, shuts up sense,
And o'er his inmost vitals creeping cold, 80
Lays him along the snows a stiffened corse,
Stretched out, and bleaching in the northern blast.

* * * (1726)

A HYMN

These, as they change, Almighty Father, these,
Are but the varied God. The rolling year
Is full of thee. Forth in the pleasing Spring
Thy beauty walks, thy tenderness and love.
Wide-flush the fields; the softening air is balm; 5
Echo the mountains round; the forest smiles;
And every sense, and every heart is joy.
Then comes thy glory in the summer-months,
With light and heart refulgent. Then thy sun
Shoots full perfection through the swelling year;
And oft thy voice in dreadful thunder speaks;
And oft at dawn, deep noon, or falling eve, 12
By brooks and groves, in hollow-whispering gales.
Thy bounty shines in autumn unconfined,
And spreads a common feast for all that lives. 15
In winter awful thou! with clouds and storms
Around thee thrown, tempest o'er tempest roll'd
Majestic darkness! on the whirlwind's wing,
Riding sublime, thou bidst the world adore,
And humblest Nature with thy northern blast.

Mysterious round! what skill, what force divine, 21
Deepfelt, in these appear! a simple train,
Yet so delightful mixed, with such kind art,
Such beauty and beneficence combined:
Shade, unperceived, so softening into shade; 25
And all so forming an harmonious whole;
That, as they still succeed, they ravish still.
But wandering oft, with brute unconscious gaze,
Man marks not thee, marks not the mighty hand,
That, ever-busy, wheels the silent spheres; 30
Works in the secret deep; shoots, steaming, thence
The fair profusion that o'erspreads the spring:

Flings from the sun direct the flaming day;
Feeds every creature; hurls the tempest forth;
And, as on earth this grateful change revolves,
With transport touches all the springs of life. 36

  Nature, attend! join every living soul,
Beneath the spacious temple of the sky,
In adoration join; and ardent raise
One general song! To him, ye vocal gales, 40
Breathe soft, whose spirit in your freshness breathes.
Oh, talk of him in solitary glooms,
Where o'er the rock the scarcely waving pine
Fills the brown shade with a religious awe,
And ye, whose bolder note is heard afar, 45
Who shake the astonished world, lift high to heaven
The impetuous song, and say from whom you rage.
His praise, ye brooks, attune, ye trembling rills;
And let me catch it as I muse along,
Ye headlong torrents, rapid and profound; 50
Ye softer floods, that lead the humid maze
Along the vale; and thou, majestic main,
A secret world of wonders in thyself,
Sound his stupendous praise, whose greater voice
Or bids you roar, or bids your roaring fall. 55
So roll your incense, herbs, and fruits, and flowers,
In mingled clouds to him, whose sun exalts,
Whose breath perfumes you, and whose pencil paints.
Ye forests, bend, ye harvests, wave to him;
Breathe your still song into the reaper's heart,
As home he goes beneath the joyous moon. 61
Ye that keep watch in heaven, as earth asleep
Unconscious lies, effuse your mildest beams;
Ye constellations, while your angels strike,
Amid the spangled sky, the silver lyre. 65
Great source of day! blest image here below
Of thy Creator, ever pouring wide,
From world to world, the vital ocean round,
On nature write with every beam his praise.
The thunder rolls: be hushed the prostrate world, 70
While cloud to cloud returns the solemn hymn.
Bleat out afresh, ye hills; ye mossy rocks,
Retain the sound; the broad responsive low,
Ye valleys, raise; for the Great Shepherd reigns,
And his unsuffering kingdom yet will come. 75
Ye woodlands, all awake; a boundless song
Burst from the groves; and when the restless day,
Expiring, lays the warbling world asleep,
Sweetest of birds! sweet Philomela, charm
The listening shades, and teach the night his praise. 80
Ye chief, for whom the whole creation smiles;
At once the head, the heart, the tongue of all,
Crown the great hymn! in swarming cities vast,
Assembled men to the deep organ join
The long resounding voice, oft breaking clear,
At solemn pauses, through the swelling base; 86
And, as each mingling flame increases each,
In one united ardor rise to heaven.
Or if you rather choose the rural shade,
And find a fane in every sacred grove, 90
There let the shepherd's lute, the virgin's lay,
The prompting seraph, and the poet's lyre,
Still sing the God of seasons as they roll.
For me, when I forget the darling theme,
Whether the blossom blows, the Summer ray 95
Russets the plain, inspiring Autumn gleams,
Or Winter rises in the blackening east—
Be my tongue mute, my fancy paint no more,
And, dead to joy, forget my heart to beat.

  Should fate command me to the furthest verge 100
Of the green earth, to distant barbarous climes,
Rivers unknown to song; where first the sun
Gilds Indian mountains, or his setting beam
Flames on the Atlantic isles, 't is nought to me;
Since God is ever present, ever felt, 105
In the void waste as in the city full;
And where he vital breathes, there must be joy.
When even at last the solemn hour shall come,
And wing my mystic flight to future worlds,
I cheerful will obey; there with new powers, 110
Will rising wonders sing. I cannot go
Where universal love not smiles around,
Sustaining all yon orbs, and all their suns;
From seeming evil still educing good,
And better thence again, and better still, 115
In infinite progression. But I lose
Myself in him, in light ineffable!
Come, then, expressive silence, muse his praise.

                                    (1730)

THE CASTLE OF INDOLENCE

BOOK I

O MORTAL man, who livest here by toil,
Do not complain of this thy hard estate;
That like an emmet thou must ever moil,
Is a sad sentence of an ancient date;
And, certes, there is for it reason great; 5
For, though sometimes it makes thee weep and wail,
And curse thy star, and early drudge and late,
Withouten that would come a heavier bale,
Loose life, unruly passions, and diseases pale.

In lowly dale, fast by a river's side, 10
With woody hill o'er hill encompassed round,
A most enchanting wizard did abide,
Than whom a fiend more fell is nowhere found.
It was, I ween, a lovely spot of ground:

And there a season atween June and May, 15
Half pranked with spring, with summer half imbrowned,
A listless climate made, where, sooth to say,
No living wight could work, ne carèd even for play.

Was nought around but images of rest: 19
Sleep-soothing groves, and quiet lawns between;
And flowery beds that slumberous influence kest,
From poppies breathed; and beds of pleasant green,
Where never yet was creeping creature seen.
Meantime unnumbered glittering streamlets played,
And hurlèd everywhere their waters sheen; 25
That, as they bickered through the sunny glade,
Though restless still themselves, a lulling murmur made.

Joined to the prattle of the purling rills,
Were heard the lowing herds along the vale,
And flocks loud bleating from the distant hills,
And vacant shepherds piping in the dale: 31
And now and then sweet Philomel would wail,
Or stock-doves 'plain amid the forest deep,
That drowsy rustled to the sighing gale;
And still a coil the grasshopper did keep; 35
Yet all these sounds yblent inclinèd all to sleep.

Full in the passage of the vale above,
A sable, silent, solemn forest stood,
Where nought but shadowy forms was seen to move,
As Idlesse fancied in her dreaming mood: 40
And up the hills, on either side, a wood
Of blackening pines, aye waving to and fro,
Sent forth a sleepy horror through the blood;
And where this valley winded out below,
The murmuring main was heard, and scarcely heard, to flow. 45

A pleasing land of drowsy-head it was,
Of dreams that wave before the half-shut eye:
And of gay castles in the clouds that pass,
For ever flushing round a summer sky:
There eke the soft delights, that witchingly 50
Instill a wanton sweetness through the breast,
And the calm pleasures, always hovered nigh;
But whate'er smacked of noyance or unrest,
Was far, far off expelled from this delicious nest.

* * *

The doors, that knew no shrill alarming bell, 55
Ne cursèd knocker plied by villain's hand,
Self-opened into halls, where, who can tell
What elegance and grandeur wide expand,
The pride of Turkey and of Persia land? 59
Soft quilts on quilts, on carpets carpets spread,
And couches stretched around in seemly band;
And endless pillows rise to prop the head;
So that each spacious room was one full-swelling bed.

And everywhere huge covered tables stood,
With wines high flavored and rich viands crowned; 65
Whatever sprightly juice or tasteful food
On the green bosom of this earth are found,
And all old ocean genders in his round;
Some hand unseen these silently displayed,
Even undemanded by a sign or sound; 70
You need but wish, and, instantly obeyed,
Fair ranged the dishes rose, and thick the glasses played.

The rooms with costly tapestry were hung,
Where was inwoven many a gentle tale;
Such as of old the rural poets sung, 75
Or of Arcadian or Sicilian vale:
Reclining lovers, in the lonely dale,
Poured forth at large the sweetly tortured heart;
Or, sighing tender passion, swelled the gale,
And taught charmed echo to resound their smart; 80
While flocks, woods, streams, around, repose and peace impart.

Those pleased the most, where, by a cunning hand,
Depainted was the patriarchal age;
What time Dan Abraham left the Chaldee land,
And pastured on from verdant stage to stage, 85
Where fields and fountains fresh could best engage.
Toil was not then. Of nothing took they heed,
But with wild beasts the sylvan war to wage,
And o'er vast plains their herds and flocks to feed;
Blest sons of nature they! true golden age indeed! 90

Sometimes the pencil, in cool airy halls,
Bade the gay bloom of vernal landscapes rise,
Or autumn's varied shades imbrown the walls;
Now the black tempest strikes the astonished eyes,
Now down the steep the flashing torrent flies; 95
The trembling sun now plays o'er ocean blue,
And now rude mountains frown amid the skies;
Whate'er Lorraine light-touched with softening hue,
Or savage Rosa dashed, or learnèd Poussin drew.

A certain music, never known before, 100
Here lulled the pensive melancholy mind,
Full easily obtained. Behoves no more,
But sidelong, to the gently waving wind,
To lay the well-tuned instrument reclined;
From which with airy flying fingers light, 105
Beyond each mortal touch the most refined,

The god of winds drew sounds of deep delight;
Whence, with just cause, the harp of Æolus it hight.

Ah me! what hand can touch the string so fine?
Who up the lofty diapason roll, 110
Such sweet, such sad, such solemn airs divine,
Then let them down again into the soul?
Now rising love they fanned; now pleasing dole
They breathed, in tender musings, through the heart;
And now a graver sacred strain they stole, 115
As when seraphic hands a hymn impart:
Wild warbling nature all, above the reach of art!

Such the gay splendor, the luxurious state
Of Caliphs old, who on the Tigris' shore,
In mighty Bagdad, populous and great, 120
Held their bright court, where was of ladies store;
And verse, love, music, still the garland wore;
When sleep was coy, the bard in waiting there
Cheered the lone midnight with the muse's lore;
Composing music bade his dreams be fair, 125
And music lent new gladness to the morning air.

Near the pavilions where we slept, still ran
Soft tinkling streams, and dashing waters fell,
And sobbing breezes sighed, and oft began—
So worked the wizard—wintry storms to swell,
As heaven and earth they would together mell;
At doors and windows threatening seemed to call 132
The demons of the tempest, growling fell.
Yet the least entrance found they none at all;
Whence sweeter grew our sleep, secure in massy hall. 135

And hither Morpheus sent his kindest dreams,
Raising a world of gayer tinct and grace;
O'er which were shadowy cast Elysian gleams,
That played in waving lights from place to place,
And shed a roseate smile on nature's face. 140
Not Titian's pencil e'er could so array,
So fleece with clouds the pure ethereal space;
Ne could it e'er such melting forms display,
As loose on flowery beds all languishingly lay.

No, fair illusions! artful phantoms, no! 145
My muse will not attempt your fairy-land:
She has no colors that like you can glow;
To catch your vivid scenes too gross her hand.
But sure it is, was ne'er a subtler band 149
Than these same guileful angel-seeming sprights
Who thus in dreams voluptuous, soft, and bland,
Poured all the Arabian heaven upon our nights,
And blessed them oft besides with more refined delights.

They were in sooth a most enchanting train,
Even feigning virtue; skilful to unite 155
With evil good, and strew with pleasure pain.
But for those fiends whom blood and broils delight,
Who hurl the wretch as if to hell outright
Down, down black gulfs where sullen waters sleep,
Or hold him clambering all the fearful night 160
On beetling cliffs, or pent in ruins deep—
They, till due time should serve, were bid far hence to keep.

Ye guardian spirits, to whom man is dear,
From these foul demons shield the midnight gloom!
Angels of fancy and of love, be near, 165
And o'er the wilds of sleep diffuse a bloom;
Evoke the sacred shades of Greece and Rome,
And let them virtue with a look impart!
But chief, awhile O! lend us from the tomb
Those long-lost friends for whom in love we smart, 170
And fill with pious awe and joy-mixt woe the heart!

* * * (1748)

THOMAS GRAY (1716-1771)

The life of Gray was singularly devoid of external incident. The records of a few personal ties, a little travel, and a few scattering and reluctant publications, alone give liveliness to the 'noiseless tenor' of his sequestered studies. At Eton he was noted for 'great delicacy and sometimes a too fastidious behavior,' but found sympathetic companions in Horace Walpole and Richard West. In 1734 he entered Pembroke Hall, Cambridge, and soon became a pensioner at Peterhouse. He devoted himself to classical literature, history, and modern languages, taking no degree on account of his dislike to mathematics. In 1739, on Walpole's invitation, Gray accompanied him to the continent and with great pleasure and profit, spent two years in Italy and France. Many of his Latin poems were written abroad and soon after his return he made his first trials in English verse. The death of his friend West, in 1742, deeply affected him and called forth the first sonnet of importance since those of Milton. About the same time, he began 'the far-famed *Elegy*,' while visiting his mother at Stoke, near Windsor. None of his poems was published until several years afterward. He now settled again at Peterhouse and when fifteen years later, he removed to Pembroke Hall, he referred to the incident as 'a sort of era in a life so barren of events as mine.' He graduated as LL.B. in 1744, but never entered the law. He made voluminous notes and collections for a History of English Poetry which was never written. Toward the end of his life he was appointed Professor of Modern History at Cambridge, but gave no lectures. A dozen poems in English, none long, were all that he published during his lifetime, and the two dozen fragments and fugitive pieces since collected add little to his fame.

By 1757 his reputation was such that he was offered, on the death of Colley Cibber, the poet laureateship; but he declined to be 'rat catcher to his Majesty.' Doctor Johnson, who is grudging in his estimate of Gray's genius, quotes without disparagement a statement that 'Perhaps he was the most learned man in Europe.' Gray was a precursor of the great romanticists in his taste for picturesque landscape, and he kept pace with the antiquarian movements of his time which were preparing the romantic revival. His *Letters*, which are among the best in the language, reveal the variety and enthusiasm of his interests. They also reveal a shrinking and fastidious taste dashed with piquant, half-cynical humor and not a little scholastic intolerance, and they help us to understand how the man who could write so tender and exquisite a poem as the *Elegy in a Country Churchyard* should have written so little else.

SONNET

ON THE DEATH OF MR. RICHARD WEST

In vain to me the smiling mornings shine,
And reddening Phœbus lifts his golden fire:
The birds in vain their amorous descant join;
Or cheerful fields resume their green attire:

These ears, alas! for other notes repine; 5
A different object do these eyes require:
My lonely anguish melts no heart but mine;
And in my breast the imperfect joys expire.

Yet morning smiles the busy race to cheer,
And new-born pleasure brings to happier men;
The fields to all their wonted tribute bear; 11
To warm their little loves the birds complain:
I fruitless mourn to him that cannot hear,
And weep the more, because I weep in vain.

(1744)

AN ODE

ON A DISTANT PROSPECT OF ETON COLLEGE

Ye distant spires, ye antique towers,
That crown the watery glade,
Where grateful Science still adores
Her Henry's holy Shade;
And ye, that from the stately brow 5
Of Windsor's heights the expanse below
Of grove, of lawn, of mead survey,
Whose turf, whose shade, whose flowers among
Wanders the hoary Thames along
His silver-winding way. 10

Ah, happy hills, ah, pleasing shade,
Ah, fields beloved in vain,
Where once my careless childhood strayed,
A stranger yet to pain!
I feel the gales, that from ye blow, 15
A momentary bliss bestow,
As waving fresh their gladsome wing,

399

My weary soul they seem to sooth,
And, redolent of joy and youth,
  To breathe a second spring.   20

Say, Father Thames, for thou hast seen
  Full many a sprightly race
Disporting on thy margent green
  The paths of pleasure trace,
Who foremost now delight to cleave   25
With pliant arm thy glassy wave?
  The captive linnet which enthrall?
What idle progeny succeed
To chase the rolling circle's speed,
  Or urge the flying ball?   30

While some on earnest business bent
  Their murmuring labors ply
'Gainst graver hours, that bring constraint
  To sweeten liberty:
Some bold adventurers disdain   35
The limits of their little reign,
  And unknown regions dare descry:
Still as they run they look behind,
They hear a voice in every wind,
  And snatch a fearful joy.   40

Gay hope is theirs by fancy fed,
  Less pleasing when possest;
The tear forgot as soon as shed,
  The sunshine of the breast:
Theirs buxom health of rosy hue,   45
Wild wit, invention ever-new,
  And lively cheer of vigor born;
The thoughtless day, the easy night,
The spirits pure, the slumbers light,
  That fly the approach of morn.   50

Alas, regardless of their doom,
  The little victims play!
No sense have they of ills to come,
  Nor care beyond to-day:
Yet see how all around 'em wait   55
The Ministers of human fate,
  And black Misfortune's baleful train!
Ah, shew them where in ambush stand
To seize their prey the murth'rous band!
  Ah, tell them, they are men!   60

These shall the fury Passions tear,
  The vultures of the mind,
Disdainful Anger, pallid Fear,
  And Shame that skulks behind;
Or pining Love shall waste their youth,   65
Or Jealousy with rankling tooth,
  That inly gnaws the secret heart,
And Envy wan, and faded Care,
Grim-visaged comfortless Despair,
  And Sorrow's piercing dart.   70

Ambition this shall tempt to rise,
  Then whirl the wretch from high,
To bitter Scorn a sacrifice,
  And grinning Infamy.

The stings of Falsehood those shall try,   75
And hard Unkindness, altered eye,
  That mocks the tear it forced to flow;
And keen Remorse with blood defiled,
And moody Madness laughing wild
  Amid severest woe.   80

Lo, in the vale of years beneath
  A griesly troop are seen,
The painful family of Death,
  More hideous than their Queen:
This racks the joints, this fires the veins,   85
That every laboring sinew strains,
  Those in the deeper vitals rage:
Lo, Poverty, to fill the band,
That numbs the soul with icy hand,
  And slow-consuming Age.   90

To each his sufferings: all are men,
  Condemned alike to groan,
The tender for another's pain;
  The unfeeling for his own.
Yet ah! why should they know their fate?   95
Since sorrow never comes too late,
  And happiness too swiftly flies.
Thought would destroy their paradise.
No more; where ignorance is bliss,
  'T is folly to be wise.   100

(1747)

HYMN TO ADVERSITY

Daughter of Jove, relentless power,
  Thou tamer of the human breast,
Whose iron scourge and torturing hour
  The bad affright, afflict the best!
Bound in thy adamantine chain,   5
The proud are taught to taste of pain,
And purple tyrants vainly groan
With pangs unfelt before, unpitied and alone.

When first thy sire to send on earth
  Virtue, his darling child, designed,   10
To thee he gave the heavenly birth,
  And bade to form her infant mind.
Stern rugged nurse! thy rigid lore
With patience many a year she bore:
What sorrow was, thou bad'st her know,   15
And from her own she learned to melt at others'
  woe.

Scared at thy frown terrific, fly
  Self-pleasing Folly's idle brood,
Wild Laughter, Noise, and thoughtless Joy,
  And leave us leisure to be good.   20
Light they disperse, and with them go
The summer friend, the flattering foe;
By vain Prosperity received,
To her they vow their truth, and are again be-
  lieved.

Wisdom in sable garb arrayed, 25
  Immersed in rapturous thought profound,
And Melancholy, silent maid,
  With leaden eye that loves the ground,
Still on thy solemn steps attend:
Warm Charity, the general friend, 30
  With Justice, to herself severe,
And Pity, dropping soft the sadly-pleasing tear.

Oh! gently on thy suppliant's head,
  Dread goddess, lay thy chastening hand!
Not in thy Gorgon terrors clad, 35
  Not circled with the vengeful band
(As by the impious thou art seen)
With thundering voice, and threatening mien,
  With screaming Horror's funeral cry,
Despair, and fell Disease, and ghastly Poverty:

Thy form benign, oh goddess, wear, 41
  Thy milder influence impart,
Thy philosophic train be there
  To soften, not to wound, my heart.
The generous spark extinct revive 45
Teach me to love, and to forgive,
Exact my own defects to scan,
What others are to feel, and know myself a Man.
                    (1753)

ELEGY

WRITTEN IN A COUNTRY CHURCH-YARD

The Curfew tolls the knell of parting day,
  The lowing herd wind slowly o'er the lea,
The plowman homeward plods his weary way,
  And leaves the world to darkness and to me.

Now fades the glimmering landscape on the sight, 5
  And all the air a solemn stillness holds,
Save where the beetle wheels his droning flight,
  And drowsy tinklings lull the distant folds;

Save that, from yonder ivy-mantled tower,
  The moping owl does to the moon complain
Of such, as wandering near her secret bower, 11
  Molest her ancient solitary reign.

Beneath those rugged elms, that yew-tree's shade,
  Where heaves the turf in many a mouldering heap,
Each in his narrow cell for ever laid, 15
  The rude forefathers of the hamlet sleep.

The breezy call of incense-breathing Morn,
  The swallow twittering from the straw-built shed,
The cock's shrill clarion, or the echoing horn,
  No more shall rouse them from their lowly bed. 20

For them no more the blazing hearth shall burn,
  Or busy housewife ply her evening care:
No children run to lisp their sire's return,
  Or climb his knees the envied kiss to share.

Oft did the harvest to their sickle yield, 25
  Their furrow oft the stubborn glebe has broke;
How jocund did they drive their team afield:
  How bowed the woods beneath their sturdy stroke!

Let not Ambition mock their useful toil,
  Their homely joys, and destiny obscure; 30
Nor Grandeur hear with a disdainful smile
  The short and simple annals of the poor.

The boast of heraldry, the pomp of power,
  And all that beauty, all that wealth e'er gave,
Awaits alike the inevitable hour. 35
  The paths of glory lead but to the grave.

Nor you, ye Proud, impute to These the fault,
  If Memory o'er their Tomb no Trophies raise,
Where through the long-drawn aisle and fretted vault
  The pealing anthem swells the note of praise.

Can storied urn or animated bust 41
  Back to its mansion call the fleeting breath?
Can Honor's voice provoke the silent dust,
  Or Flattery sooth the dull cold ear of Death?

Perhaps in this neglected spot is laid 45
  Some heart once pregnant with celestial fire;
Hands, that the rod of empire might have swayed,
  Or waked to ecstasy the living lyre.

But Knowledge to their eyes her ample page
  Rich with the spoils of time did ne'er unroll;
Chill Penury repressed their noble rage, 51
  And froze the genial current of the soul.

Full many a gem of purest ray serene,
  The dark unfathomed caves of ocean bear:
Full many a flower is born to blush unseen, 55
  And waste its sweetness on the desert air.

Some village Hampden, that with dauntless breast
  The little Tyrant of his fields withstood;
Some mute inglorious Milton here may rest,
  Some Cromwell guiltless of his country's blood. 60

The applause of listening senates to command,
  The threats of pain and ruin to despise,
To scatter plenty o'er a smiling land,
  And read their history in a nation's eyes,

Their lot forbade: nor circumscribed alone 65
  Their growing virtues, but their crimes confin'd;
Forbade to wade through slaughter to a throne,
  And shut the gates of mercy on mankind,

The struggling pangs of conscious truth to hide,
  To quench the blushes of ingenuous shame, 70
Or heap the shrine of Luxury and Pride
  With incense kindled at the Muse's flame.

Far from the madding crowd's ignoble strife,
  Their sober wishes never learned to stray;
Along the cool sequestered vale of life 75
  They kept the noiseless tenor of their way.

Yet even these bones from insult to protect,
  Some frail memorial still erected nigh,
With uncouth rhymes and shapeless sculpture decked,
  Implores the passing tribute of a sigh. 80

Their name, their years, spelt by the unlettered muse,
  The place of fame and elegy supply;
And many a holy text around she strews,
  That teach the rustic moralist to die.

For who to dumb Forgetfulness a prey, 85
  This pleasing anxious being e'er resigned,
Left the warm precincts of the cheerful day,
  Nor cast one longing lingering look behind?

On some fond breast the parting soul relies,
  Some pious drops the closing eye requires; 90
Ev'n from the tomb the voice of Nature cries,
  Ev'n in our Ashes live their wonted Fires.

For thee, who mindful of the unhonored Dead
  Dost in these lines their artless tale relate,
If chance, by lonely contemplation led, 95
  Some kindred Spirit shall inquire thy fate,

Haply some hoary-headed Swain may say,
  'Oft have we seen him at the peep of dawn
Brushing with hasty steps the dews away
  To meet the sun upon the upland lawn. 100

'There at the foot of yonder nodding beech
  That wreathes its old fantastic roots so high,
His listless length at noontide would he stretch,
  And pore upon the brook that babbles by.

'Hard by yon wood, now smiling as in scorn, 105
  Muttering his wayward fancies he would rove,
Now drooping, woeful wan, like one forlorn,
  Or crazed with care, or crossed in hopeless love.

'One morn I missed him on the customed hill,
  Along the heath and near his favorite tree; 110
Another came; nor yet beside the rill,
  Nor up the lawn, nor at the wood was he;

The next with dirges due in sad array
  Slow through the church-way path we saw him borne.
Approach and read (for thou can'st read) the lay, 115
  Graved on the stone beneath yon agèd thorn.'

THE EPITAPH

Here rests his head upon the lap of Earth
  A Youth to Fortune and to Fame unknown.
Fair Science frowned not on his humble birth,
  And Melancholy marked him for her own. 120

Large was his bounty, and his soul sincere,
  Heav'n did a recompense as largely send:
He gave to Misery all he had, a tear,
  He gained from Heaven ('t was all he wished) a friend.

No farther seek his merits to disclose, 125
  Or draw his frailties from their dread abode
(There they alike in trembling hope repose),
  The bosom of his Father and his God.

(1751)

THE PROGRESS OF POESY

A PINDARIC ODE

I

The Strophe

Awake, Æolian lyre, awake,
And give to rapture all thy trembling strings
From Helicon's harmonious springs
A thousand rills their mazy progress take:
  The laughing flowers, that round them blow, 5
  Drink life and fragrance as they flow.
Now the rich stream of music winds along
Deep, majestic, smooth, and strong,
Through verdant vales, and Ceres' golden reign:
Now rolling down the steep amain, 10
Headlong, impetuous, see it pour:
The rocks, and nodding groves rebellow to the roar.

The Antistrophe

  Oh! Sovereign of the willing soul,
Parent of sweet and solemn-breathing airs,
Enchanting shell! the sullen Cares, 15
And frantic Passions hear thy soft control.
  On Thracia's hills the Lord of War,
  Has curbed the fury of his car,
And dropped his thirsty lance at thy command.
Perching on the sceptered hand 20
Of Jove, thy magic lulls the feathered king
With ruffled plumes, and flagging wing:
Quenched in dark clouds of slumber lie
The terror of his beak, and lightnings of his eye.

The Epode

Thee the voice, the dance, obey, 25
Tempered to thy warbled lay.
O'er Idalia's velvet-green
The rosy-crownèd Loves are seen
On Cytherea's day
With antic Sports, and blue-eyed Pleasures, 30
Frisking light in frolic measures;
Now pursuing, now retreating.
Now in circling troops they meet:
To brisk notes in cadence beating
Glance their many-twinkling feet. 35
Slow melting strains their Queen's approach declare:
Where'er she turns the Graces homage pay
With arms sublime, that float upon the air,
In gliding state she wins her easy way:
O'er her warm cheek, and rising bosom, move
The bloom of young Desire, and purple light of Love. 41

II

The Strophe

MAN's feeble race what Ills await,
Labor, and Penury, the racks of Pain,
Disease, and Sorrow's weeping train,
And Death, sad refuge from the storms of Fate!
The fond complaint, my Song, disprove, 46
And justify the laws of Jove.
Say, has he given in vain the heavenly Muse?
Night, and all her sickly dews,
Her Specters wan, and Birds of boding cry, 50
He gives to range the dreary sky;
Till down the eastern cliffs afar
Hyperion's march they spy, and glittering shafts of war.

The Antistrophe

IN climes beyond the solar road,
Where shaggy forms o'er ice-built mountains roam, 55
The Muse has broke the twilight-gloom
To cheer the shivering Native's dull abode.
And oft, beneath the odorous shade
Of Chili's boundless forests laid,
She deigns to hear the savage Youth repeat 60
In loose numbers wildly sweet
Their feather-cinctured Chiefs, and dusky Loves.
Her track, where'er the Goddess roves,
Glory pursue, and generous Shame,
The unconquerable Mind, and Freedom's holy flame. 65

The Epode

Woods, that wave o'er Delphi's steep,
Isles, that crown the Ægean deep,
Fields, that cool Ilissus laves,
Or where Mæander's amber waves
In lingering Labyrinths creep, 70
How do your tuneful Echo's languish,
Mute, but to the voice of Anguish?
Where each old poetic Mountain
Inspiration breathed around:
Every shade and hallowed Fountain 75
Murmured deep a solemn sound:
Till the sad Nine in Greece's evil hour
Left their Parnassus for the Latian plains.
Alike they scorn the pomp of tyrant-Power,
And coward Vice, that revels in her chains, 80
When Latium had her lofty spirit lost,
They sought, O Albion! next thy sea-encircled coast.

III

The Strophe

FAR from the sun and summer-gale,
In thy green lap was Nature's Darling laid,
What time, where lucid Avon strayed, 85
To Him the mighty Mother did unveil
Her awful face: The dauntless Child
Stretched forth his little arms, and smiled.
This pencil take (she said) whose colors clear
Richly paint the vernal year: 90
Thine too these golden keys, immortal Boy!
This can unlock the gates of Joy;
Of Horror that, and thrilling Fears,
Or ope the sacred source of sympathetic Tears.

The Antistrophe

Nor second He, that rode sublime 95
Upon the seraph-wings of Ecstasy,
The secrets of the Abyss to spy.
He passed the flaming bounds of Place and Time:
The living Throne, the sapphire-blaze,
Where Angels tremble, while they gaze, 100
He saw; but blasted with excess of light,
Closed his eyes in endless night.
Behold, where Dryden's less presumptuous car,
Wide o'er the fields of Glory bear
Two Coursers of ethereal race, 105
With necks in thunder clothed, and long-resounding pace.

The Epode

Hark, his hands the lyre explore!
Bright-eyed Fancy hovering o'er
Scatters from her pictured urn
Thoughts that breathe, and words that burn. 110
But ah! 't is heard no more——
O Lyre divine, what daring Spirit
Wakes thee now? though he inherit
Nor the pride, nor ample pinion,
That the Theban Eagle bear 115
Sailing with supreme dominion
Through the azure deep of air:
Yet oft before his infant eyes would run
Such forms, as glitter in the Muse's ray

With orient hues, unborrowed of the Sun: 120
  Yet shall he mount, and keep his distant way
Beyond the limits of a vulgar fate,
Beneath the Good how far—but far above the
    Great.

              (1757)

THE BARD

A PINDARIC ODE

I

The Strophe

'RUIN seize thee, ruthless King!
Confusion on thy banners wait,
  Though fanned by Conquest's crimson wing
They mock the air with idle state.
  Helm, nor Hauberk's twisted mail, 5
  Nor even thy virtues, Tyrant, shall avail
To save thy secret soul from nightly fears,
From Cambria's curse, from Cambria's tears!'

Such were the sounds, that o'er the crested pride
Of the first Edward scattered wild dismay, 10
As down the steep of Snowdon's shaggy side
  He wound with toilsome march his long array.
Stout Gloster stood aghast in speechless trance;
To arms! cried Mortimer, and couched his quivering lance.

The Antistrophe

On a rock, whose haughty brow 15
Frowns o'er old Conway's foaming flood,
  Robed in the sable garb of woe,
With haggard eyes the Poet stood
  (Loose his beard, and hoary hair
Streamed, like a meteor, to the troubled air),
And with a Master's hand, and Prophet's fire, 21
Struck the deep sorrows of his lyre:

'Hark, how each giant-oak, and desert cave,
  Sighs to the torrent's awful voice beneath!
O'er thee, O King! their hundred arms they wave, 25
  Revenge on thee in hoarser murmurs breathe;
Vocal no more, since Cambria's fatal day,
To high-born Hoel's harp, or soft Llewellyn's
    lay.

The Epode

'Cold is Cadwallo's tongue,
That hushed the stormy main; 30
Brave Urien sleeps upon his craggy bed:
Mountains, ye mourn in vain
Modred, whose magic song
Made huge Plinlimmon bow his cloud-topped
    head.

'On dreary Arvon's shore they lie, 35
Smeared with gore, and ghastly pale:
Far, far aloof the affrighted ravens sail;
The famished Eagle screams, and passes by.

'Dear lost companions of my tuneful art,
Dear, as the light that visits these sad eyes, 40
Dear, as the ruddy drops that warm my heart,
Ye died amidst your dying country's cries—

'No more I weep. They do not sleep.
On yonder cliffs, a grisly band,
  I see them sit, they linger yet, 45
Avengers of their native land:
With me in dreadful harmony they join,
And weave with bloody hands the tissue of thy
    line:—

II

The Strophe

'WEAVE the warp, and weave the woof,
The winding sheet of Edward's race. 50
  Give ample room, and verge enough
The characters of hell to trace.
  Mark the year, and mark the night,
When Severn shall re-echo with affright
The shrieks of death, through Berkley's roofs
    that ring, 55
Shrieks of an agonizing King!

'She-Wolf of France, with unrelenting fangs.
  That tear'st the bowels of thy mangled Mate,
From thee be born, who o'er thy country hangs
  The scourge of Heav'n. What Terrors round
    him wait! 60
Amazement in his van, with Flight combined,
And Sorrow's faded form, and Solitude behind.

The Antistrophe

'Mighty Victor, mighty Lord,
Low on his funeral couch he lies!
  No pitying heart, no eye, afford 65
A tear to grace his obsequies.
  Is the sable Warrior fled?
Thy son is gone. He rests among the Dead.
The Swarm, that in thy noon-tide beam were
    born?
Gone to salute the rising Morn. 70

'Fair laughs the Morn, and soft the Zephyr
    blows,
  While proudly riding o'er the azure realm
In gallant trim the gilded Vessel goes;
  Youth on the prow, and Pleasure at the
    helm;
Regardless of the sweeping Whirlwind's sway,
That, hushed in grim repose, expects his
    evening-prey. 76

The Epode

'Fill high the sparkling bowl,
The rich repast prepare;
Reft of a crown, he yet may share the feast.
Close by the regal chair 80
Fell Thirst and Famine scowl
A baleful smile upon their baffled Guest.

'Heard ye the din of battle bray,
Lance to lance, and horse to horse?
Long years of havoc urge their destined course,
And through the kindred squadrons mow their
    way.   86

'Ye Towers of Julius, London's lasting shame,
With many a foul and midnight murther fed,
Revere his Consort's faith, his Father's fame,
And spare the meek Usurper's holy head.   90

'Above, below, the rose of snow,
Twined with her blushing foe, we spread:
  The bristled Boar in infant-gore
Wallows beneath the thorny shade.
Now, brothers, bending o'er the accursed loom
Stamp we our vengeance deep, and ratify his
    doom.   96

III

The Strophe

'EDWARD, lo! to sudden fate
(Weave we the woof. The thread is spun)
  Half of thy heart we consecrate.
(The web is wove. The work is done.)—   100
  Stay, oh stay! nor thus forlorn
  Leave me unblessed, unpitied, here to mourn!
In yon bright track, that fires the western skies,
  They melt, they vanish from my eyes.

'But oh! what solemn scenes on Snowdon's
    height   105
  Descending slow their glittering skirts unroll?
Visions of glory, spare my aching sight,
  Ye unborn Ages, crowd not on my soul!
No more our long-lost Arthur we bewail.
All-hail ye genuine Kings, Britannia's Issue,
    hail!   110

The Antistrophe

'Girt with many a baron bold
Sublime their starry fronts they rear;
  And gorgeous Dames, and Statesmen old
In bearded majesty, appear.
  In the midst a Form divine!   115
  Her eye proclaims her of the Briton-Line;
Her lion-port, her awe-commanding face,
  Attempered sweet to virgin-grace.

'What strings symphonious tremble in the air,
  What strains of vocal transport round her
    play!   120
Hear from the grave, great Taliessin, hear;
  They breathe a soul to animate thy clay.
Bright Rapture calls, and soaring, as she sings,
Waves in the eye of Heaven her many-colored
    wings.

The Epode

'The verse adorn again   125
Fierce War, and faithful Love,
And Truth severe, by fairy Fiction drest.

In buskined measures move
Pale Grief, and pleasing Pain,
With Horror, Tyrant of the throbbing breast.

'A Voice, as of the Cherub-Choir,   131
Gales from blooming Eden bear;
And distant warblings lessen on my ear,
That lost in long futurity expire.

'Fond impious Man, think'st thou, yon san-
    guine cloud,   135
Raised by thy breath, has quenched the Orb of
    day?
To-morrow he repairs the golden flood,
And warms the nations with redoubled ray.

'Enough for me: With joy I see
The different doom our Fates assign.   140
  Be thine Despair, and sceptered Care,
To triumph, and to die, are mine.'—
He spoke, and headlong from the mountain's
    height
Deep in the roaring tide he plunged to endless
    night.

                                         (1757)

THE FATAL SISTERS

AN ODE

FROM THE NORSE TONGUE

Now the storm begins to lower,
  (Haste, the loom of hell prepare,)
Iron-sleet of arrowy shower
  Hurtles in the darkened air.

Glittering lances are the loom,   5
  Where the dusky warp we strain,
Weaving many a soldier's doom,
  Orkney's woe, and Randver's bane.

See the grisly texture grow,
  ('T is of human entrails made,)   10
And the weights, that play below,
  Each a gasping warrior's head.

Shafts for shuttles, dipt in gore,
  Shoot the trembling cords along.
Sword, that once a monarch bore,   15
  Keep the tissue close and strong.

Mista black, terrific maid,
  Sangrida, and Hilda see,
Join the wayward work to aid:
  'T is the woof of victory.   20

Ere the ruddy sun be set,
  Pikes must shiver, javelins sing,
Blade with clattering buckler meet,
  Hauberk crash, and helmet ring.

(Weave the crimson web of war)
  Let us go, and let us fly,
Where our friends the conflict share,
  Where they triumph, where they die.

As the paths of fate we tread,
  Wading through the ensanguined field:
Gondula, and Geira, spread
  O'er the youthful king your shield.

We the reins to slaughter give,
  Ours to kill, and ours to spare:
Spite of danger he shall live.
  (Weave the crimson web of war.)

They, whom once the desert-beach
  Pent within its bleak domain,
Soon their ample sway shall stretch
  O'er the plenty of the plain.

Low the dauntless earl is laid,
  Gored with many a gaping wound:
Fate demands a nobler head;
  Soon a king shall bite the ground,

Long his loss shall Eirin weep,
  Ne'er again his likeness see;
Long her strains in sorrow steep,
  Strains of immortality!

Horror covers all the heath,
  Clouds of carnage blot the sun,
Sisters, weave the web of death;
  Sisters, cease, the work is done.

Hail the task, and hail the hands!
  Songs of joy and triumph sing!
Joy to the victorious bands;
  Triumph to the younger king.

Mortal, thou that hear'st the tale,
  Learn the tenor of our song.
Scotland, through each winding vale
  Far and wide the notes prolong.

Sisters, hence with spurs of speed:
  Each her thundering falchion wield;
Each bestride her sable steed.
  Hurry, hurry to the field.

(1768)

LETTERS

To Richard West

You must know that I do not take degrees, and, after this term, shall have nothing more of college impertinencies to undergo, which I trust will be some pleasure to you, as it is a great one to me. I have endured lectures daily and hourly since I came last, supported by the hopes of being shortly at full liberty to give myself up to my friends and classical companions, who, poor souls! though I see them fallen into great contempt with most people here, yet I cannot help sticking to them, and out of a spirit of obstinacy (I think) love them the better for it; and indeed, what can I do else? Must I plunge into metaphysics? Alas, I cannot see in the dark; nature has not furnished me with the optics of a cat. Must I pore upon mathematics? Alas, I cannot see in too much light; I am no eagle. It is very possible that two and two make four, but I would not give four farthings to demonstrate this ever so clearly; and if these be the profits of life, give me the amusements of it. The people I behold all around me, it seems, know all this and more, and yet I do not know one of them who inspires me with any ambition of being like him. Surely it was of this place, now Cambridge, but formerly known by the name of Babylon, that the prophet spoke when he said, 'the wild beasts of the desert shall dwell there, and their houses shall be full of doleful creatures, and owls shall build there, and satyrs shall dance there; their forts and towers shall be a den for ever, a joy of wild asses; there shall the great owl make her nest, and lay and hatch and gather under her shadow; it shall be a court of dragons; the screech owl also shall rest there, and find for herself a place of rest.' You see here is a pretty collection of desolate animals, which is verified in this town to a tittle, and perhaps it may also allude to your habitation, for you know all types may be taken by abundance of handles; however, I defy your owls to match mine.

* * *

Peterhouse, Dec. 1736.

To Mrs. Dorothy Gray

Lyons, Oct. 13, N.S. 1739.

It is now almost five weeks since I left Dijon, one of the gayest and most agreeable little cities of France, for Lyons, its reverse in all these particulars. It is the second in the kingdom in bigness and rank, the streets excessively narrow and nasty; the houses immensely high and large (that, for instance, where we are lodged, has twenty-five rooms on a floor, and that for five stories); it swarms with inhabitants like Paris itself, but chiefly a mercantile people, too much given up to commerce, to think of their own, much less of a stranger's diversions. We have no acquaintance in the town, but such English as happen to be passing through here, in their way to Italy and the south, which at present happen to be near thirty in number. It is a fortnight since we set out from hence upon a little excursion to Geneva. We took the longest road, which lies through Savoy, on purpose to see a famous monastery, called the Grand Chartreuse, and had no reason to think our time lost. After having travelled seven days very slow (for we did not change horses, it being impossible for a chaise to go post in these roads) we arrived at a little village, among the mountains of Savoy, called Echelles; from thence we proceeded on horses, who are used to the way, to the mountain of the Chartreuse. It is six miles to the top; the road runs winding up it, commonly not six feet broad; on one hand is the rock, with woods of pine-trees hanging over head; on the other, a monstrous precipice, almost perpendicular, at the bottom of which rolls a torrent, that sometimes tumbling among the fragments of stone that have fallen from on high, and sometimes precipitating itself down vast descents with a noise like thunder, which is still made greater by the echo from the mountains on each side, concurs to form one of the most solemn, the most romantic, and the most astonishing scenes I ever beheld. Add to this the strange views made by the craggs and cliffs on the other hand; the cascades that in many places throw themselves from the very summit down into the vale, and the river below; and many other particulars impossible to describe; you will conclude we had no occasion to repent our pains. This place St. Bruno chose to retire to, and upon its very top founded the aforesaid convent, which is the superior of the whole order. When we came there, the two fathers, who are commissioned to entertain strangers (for the rest must neither speak one to another, nor to any one else), received us very kindly; and set before us a repast of dried fish, eggs, butter, and fruits, all excellent in their kind, and extremely neat. They pressed us to spend the night there, and to stay some days with them; but this we could not do, so they led us about their house, which is, you must think, like a little city; for there are 100 fathers, besides 300 servants, that make their clothes, grind their corn, press their wine, and do everything among themselves. The whole is quiet, orderly, and simple; nothing of finery, but the wonderful decency, and the strange situation, more than supply the place of it. In the evening we descended by the same way, passing through many clouds that were then forming themselves on the mountain's side. Next day we continued our journey by Chamberry, which, though the chief city of the Dutchy, and residence of the King of Sardinia, when he comes into this part of his dominions, makes but a very mean and insignificant appearance; we lay at Aix, once famous for its hot baths, and the next night at Annecy; the day after, by noon, we got to Geneva.

* * *

To Thomas Wharton

I AM not lost; here am I at Stoke, whither I came on Tuesday, and shall be again in town on Saturday, and at Cambridge on Wednesday or Thursday, you may be anxious to know what has past. I wrote a note the night I came, and immediately received a very civil answer. I went the following evening to see the *party* (as Mrs. Foible says), was something abashed at his confidence: he came to meet me, kissed me on both sides with all the ease of one, who receives an acquaintance just come out of the country, squatted me into a *fauteuil*, began to talk of the town, and this and that and t'other, and continued with little interruption for three hours, when I took my leave very indifferently pleased, but treated with monstrous good-breeding, I supped with him next night (as he desired); Ashton was there, whose formalities tickled me inwardly, for he (I found) was to be angry about the letter I had wrote him. However in going home together our hackney-coach jumbled us into a sort of reconciliation: he hammered out somewhat like an excuse, and I received it very readily, because I cared not twopence, whether it were true or not, so we grew the best acquaintance imaginable, and I sate with him on Sunday some hours alone, when he informed me of abundance of anecdotes much to my satisfaction, and in short opened (I really believe) his heart to me, with that sincerity that I found I had still less reason to have a good opinion of him than (if possible) I ever had before. Next morning I breakfasted alone with Mr. Walpole; when we had all the *éclaircissement* I ever expected, and I left him far better satisfied than I have been hitherto. When I return I shall see him again.

[*Stoke-Pogis*], November, 1744.

To Horace Walpole

Stoke, June 12, 1750.

DEAR SIR,

As I live in a place, where even the ordinary tattle of the town arrives not till it is stale, and which produces no events of its own, you will not desire any excuse from me for writing so seldom, especially as of all people living I know you are the least a friend to letters spun out of one's own brains, with all the toil and constraint that accompanies sentimental productions. I have been here at Stoke a few days (where I shall continue good part of the summer); and having put an end to a thing, whose beginning you have seen long ago, I immediately send it you. You will, I hope, look upon it in the light of a thing with an end to it: a merit that most of my writings have wanted, and are like to want, but which this epistle I am determined shall not want, when it tells you that I am ever

Yours,
T. GRAY.

Not that I have done yet; but who could avoid the temptation of finishing so roundly and so cleverly, in the manner of good Queen Anne's days? Now I have talked of writings, I have seen a book which is by this time in the press, against Middleton (though without naming him), by Asheton. As far as I can judge from a very hasty reading, there are things in it new and ingenious, but rather too prolix, and the style here and there savouring too strongly of sermon. I imagine it will do him credit. So much for other people, now to *self* again. You are desired to tell me your opinion, if you can take the pains, of these lines. I am once more,

Ever yours.

To Horace Walpole

January, 1753.

I AM at present at Stoke, to which place I came at half an hour's warning upon the news I received of my mother's illness, and did not expect to have found her alive; but when I arrived she was much better, and continues so. I shall therefore be very glad to make you a visit at Strawberry Hill, whenever you give me notice of a convenient time. I am surprised at the print, which far surpasses my idea of London graving; the drawing itself was so finished that I suppose it did not require all the art I had imagined to copy it tolerably. My aunts, seeing me open your letter, took it to be a burying ticket, and asked whether anybody had left me a ring; and so they still conceive it to be, even with all their spectacles on. Heaven forbid they should suspect it to belong to any verses of mine,—they would burn me for a poet. . . . While I write this, I receive your second letter.—Sure you are not out of your wits! This I know, if you suffer my head to be printed, you will infallibly put me out of mine. I conjure you immediately to put a stop to any such design. Who is at the expense of engraving it, I know not; but if it be Dodsley, I will make up the loss to him. The thing as it was, I know, will make me ridiculous enough; but to appear in proper person, at the head of my works, consisting of half a dozen ballads in thirty pages, would be worse than the pillory. I do assure you, if I had received such a book, with such a frontispiece, without any warning, I believe it would have given me a palsy. Therefore I rejoice to have received this notice, and shall not be easy till you tell me all thoughts of it are laid aside. I am extremely in earnest, and cannot bear even the idea.

* * *

To the Rev. William Mason

Dec. 19, 1757.

THOUGH I very well know the bland, emollient, saponaceous qualities of both sack and silver, yet if any great man would say to me, 'I make you rat-catcher to his Majesty, with a salary of £300 a year and two butts of the best Malaga; and though it has been usual to catch a mouse or two, for form's sake, in public once a year, yet to you, sir, we shall not stand upon these things,' I cannot say I should jump at it. Nay, if they would drop the very name of the office, and call it Sinecure to the King's Majesty, I should still feel a little awkward, and think everybody I saw smelt a rat about me. But I do not pretend to blame any one else that has not the same sensations; for my part I would rather be sergeant trumpeter or pinmaker to the palace. Nevertheless I interest myself a little in the history of it, and rather wish somebody may accept it that will retrieve the credit of the thing, if it be retrievable, or ever had any credit. Rowe was, I think, the last man of character that had it. As to Settle, whom you mention, he belonged to my Lord Mayor, not to the king. Eusden was a person of great hopes in his youth, though at last he turned out a drunken parson. Dryden was as disgraceful to the office, from his character, as the poorest scribbler could have been from his verses. The office itself has always humbled the professor hitherto (even in an age when kings were somebody), if he were a poor writer by making him more conspicuous, and if he were a good one by setting him at war with the little fry of his own profession,—for there are poets little enough to envy even a poet laureate.

* * *.

To THOMAS WHARTON

WE set out then the 11th of September, and continuing along the Strath to the west passed through *Megill* (where is the tomb of *Queen Wanders, that was riven to dethe by staned-horses for nae gude that she did.* So the women there told me, I am sure), through Cowper of Angus, over the river Ila, then over a wide and dismal heath fit for an assembly of witches, till we came to a string of four lakes in a valley, whose deep blue waters, and green margin, with a gentleman's house or two seated on them in little groves, contrasted with the black desert in which they were enclosed. The ground now grew unequal; the hills more rocky seemed to close in upon us, till the road came to the brow of a steep descent, and (the sun then setting) between two woods of oak we saw far below us the river Tay come sweeping along at the bottom of a precipice, at least 150 feet deep, clear as glass, full to the brim, and very rapid in its course. It seemed to issue out of woods thick and tall, that rose on either hand, and were overhung by broken rocky crags of vast height; above them to the west, the tops of higher mountains appeared, on which the evening clouds reposed. Down by the side of the river, under the thickest shades is seated the town of Dunkeld; in the midst of it stands a round cathedral, the towers and shell of the building still entire; a little beyond it a large house of the Duke of Athol with its offices and gardens extends a mile beyond the town; and as his grounds were interrupted by the streets and roads, he has flung arches of communication across them, that add to the scenery of the place, which of itself is built of good white stone, and handsomely slated, so that no one would take it for a Scotch town till they came into it; here we passed the night. If I told you how, you would bless yourself.

Next day we set forward to Taymouth twenty-seven miles farther west; the road winding through beautiful woods, with the Tay almost always in full view to the right, being here from three to four hundred feet over. The Strath-Tay, from a mile to three miles or more wide, covered with corn, and spotted with groups of people, then in the midst of their harvest; on either hand a vast chain of rocky mountains, that changed their face, and opened something new every hundred yards, as the way turned, or the clouds passed. In short, altogether it was one of the most pleasing days I have passed these many years, and at every step I wished for you. At the close of the day we came to *Balloch*, so the place was called, but now for decency *Taymouth*; improperly enough, for here it is that the river issues out of Loch Tay (a glorious lake fifteen miles long, and one and a half broad), surrounded with prodigious mountains. There on its north-eastern brink impending over it, is the vast hill of Lawers; to the east is that monstrous creation of God, *Shekhallian* (*i.e.* the Maiden's Pap), spiring above the clouds. Directly west (beyond the end of the lake) *Beni-more* (the great mountain) rises to a most awful height, and looks down on the tomb of Fingal.

Lord Braidalbane's *policy* (so they call here all such ground as is laid out for pleasure) takes in about 2000 acres, of which his house, offices, and a deer-park about three miles round, occupy the plain or bottom, which is little above a mile in breadth; through it winds the Tay, which by means of a bridge I found here to be 156 feet over. His plantations and woods rise with the ground on either side of the vale, to the very summit of the enormous crags that overhang it; along them on the mountain's side runs a terrass one mile and a half long, that overlooks the course of the river. From several seats and temples perched on particular rocky eminences you command the lake for many miles in length, which turns like some huge river, and loses itself among the mountains that surround it. At its eastern extremity where the river issues out of it, on a peninsula, my lord has built a neat little town, and church, with a high square tower, and just before it lies a small round island in the lake covered with trees, amongst which are the ruins of some little religious house. Trees (by the way) grow here to great size and beauty. I saw four old chestnuts in the road, as you enter the park, of vast bulk and height. One beech tree I measured that was sixteen feet seven inches in the girth and (I guessed) near eighty feet in height. The gardener presented us with peaches, nectarines, and plums from the stone walls of the kitchen garden (for there are no brick nor hot walls); the peaches were good, the rest well tasted but scarce ripe. We had also golden-pippins from an espalier (not ripe), and a melon very well flavoured and fit to cut. Of the house I have little to say, it is a very good nobleman's house, handsomely furnished, and well kept, very comfortable to inhabit, but not worth going far to see. Of the earl's taste I have not much more to say, it is one of those noble situations that man cannot spoil; it is, however, certain that he has built an inn and a town just where his principal walks should have been, and in the most wonderful spot of ground that perhaps belongs to him.

In this inn however we lay, and next day returning down the river four miles, we passed it over a fine bridge, built at the expense of the government, and continued our way to Loije-Rait, just below which, in a most charming scene, the *Tummell*, which is here the larger river of the two, falls into the Tay. We ferried over the Tummell, in order to get into Marshal Wade's road (which leads from Dunkeld to Inverness), and continued our way along it toward the north. The road is excellent, but dangerous enough in conscience, the river often running directly under us at the bottom of a precipice 200 feet deep, sometimes masqued indeed by wood, that finds means to grow where I could not stand; but very often quite naked and without any defence: in such places we walked for miles together, partly for fear, and partly to admire the beauty of the country; which the beauty of the weather set off to the greatest advantage.

As evening came on, we approached the Pass of Gillikrankie, where in the year 1745 the Hessians with their prince at their head stopped short and refused to march a foot farther.

'*Vestibulum ante ipsum primisque in faucibus Orci,*'

stands the solitary mansion of Mr. Robinson of Faseley. Close by it rises a hill covered with oak, with grotesque masses of rock staring from among their trunks, like the sullen countenances of Fingal and all his family frowning on the little mortals of modern days. From between this hill and the adjacent mountains, pent in a narrow channel, comes roaring out the river Tummell, and falls headlong down, enclosed in white foam, which rises into a mist all round it.—But my paper is deficient, and I must say nothing of the pass itself, the black river Garry, the Blair of Athol, Mount Beni-gloe, my return (by another road) to Dunkeld, the Hermitage, the *Stra-Brann*, and the rumbling Brigg. In short, since I saw the Alps I have seen nothing sublime till now. In about a week I shall set forward by the Stirling road on my return all alone. Pray for me till I see you, for I dread Edinburgh and the itch; and expect to find very little in my way worth the perils I am to endure. My best compliments to Mrs. Wharton and the young ladies (including herself), and to Mr. and Mrs. Jonathan, if they are with you. Adieu!

I am ever yours,

T. G.

[*Glames*, Sept. 1765.]

To the Rev. Norton Nicholls

[Undated.]

It is long since that I heard you were gone in haste into Yorkshire on account of your mother's illness, and the same letter informed me that she was recovered, otherwise I had then wrote to you only to beg you would take care of her, and to inform you that I had discovered a thing very little known, which is, that in one's whole life one can never have any more than a single mother. You may think this is obvious, and (what you call) a trite observation. You are a green gosling! I was at the same age (very near) as wise as you, and yet I never discovered this (with full evidence and conviction I mean) till it was too late. It is thirteen years ago, and seems but as yesterday, and every day I live it sinks deeper into my heart. Many a corollary could I draw from this axiom for your use (not for my own), but I will leave you the merit of doing it for yourself. Pray tell me how your health is: I conclude it perfect, as I hear you offered yourself as a guide to Mr. Palgrave into the Sierra-Morena of Yorkshire. For me, I passed the end of May and all June in Kent, not disagreeably. In the west part of it, from every eminence, the eye catches some long reach of the Thames or Medway, with all their shipping; in the east the sea breaks in upon you, and mixes its white transient sails and glittering blue expanse with the deeper and brighter greens of the woods and corn. This sentence is so fine I am quite ashamed; but no matter! you must translate it into prose. Palgrave, if he heard it, would cover his face with his pudding sleeve.

* * *

WILLIAM COLLINS (1721-1759)

WILLIAM COLLINS was born at Chichester, Christmas Day, 1721, the son of a tradesman. He spent seven years at Winchester College and finished at the head of his form, thereby earning a scholarship at Magdalen College, Oxford, where he obtained his B.A. degree in 1743. He then became a literary adventurer in London, lounging about the theaters, coffee-houses, and book-shops, and indulging in the dissipations of the city. His reading was extensive, and his scholarship genuine and exact. He was passionately fond of music and poetry; but his acute distaste for ordinary men and routine pursuits unfitted him for practical life. At the age of thirty, he had made a wreck of his fortunes and of his health; his mind broke down, and he died, at the age of thirty-eight, having written practically nothing for a decade. It is characteristic of Collins, that his longest and most ambitious poem, the *Ode on the Popular Superstitions of the Scottish Highlands* was left unfinished. James Russell Lowell said of this poem, that it contained 'the whole Romantic School in its germ.' The poetry of Collins may, in fact, be said to owe its special quality to the union of a romantic spirit with classical taste and technique. In this respect, it somewhat resembles the poetry of Milton and, still more, that of Gray. One would like to steal for Collins what Matthew Arnold said of the latter, that he 'is the frailest of our classics; but he is a classic.'

DIRGE IN CYMBELINE

SUNG BY GUIDERUS AND ARVIRAGUS OVER FIDELE, SUPPOSED TO BE DEAD

To fair Fidele's grassy tomb
  Soft maids and village hinds shall bring
Each op'ning sweet, of earliest bloom,
  And rifle all the breathing spring.

No wailing ghost shall dare appear,   5
  To vex with shrieks this quiet grove;
But shepherd lads assemble here,
  And melting virgins own their love.

No wither'd witch shall here be seen,
  No goblins lead their nightly crew;   10
The female fays shall haunt the green,
  And dress thy grave with pearly dew.

The redbreast oft at ev'ning hours
  Shall kindly lend his little aid,
With hoary moss, and gather'd flow'rs,   15
  To deck the ground where thou art laid.

When howling winds, and beating rain,
  In tempests shake the sylvan cell,
Or midst the chase on ev'ry plain,
  The tender thought on thee shall dwell,   20

Each lonely scene shall thee restore.
  For thee the tear be duly shed:
Belov'd, till life could charm no more;
  And mourn'd, till Pity's self be dead.

(1744)

ODE

WRITTEN IN THE BEGINNING OF THE YEAR 1746

How sleep the brave who sink to rest
By all their country's wishes blest!
When Spring, with dewy fingers cold,
Returns to deck their hallow'd mold,
She there shall dress a sweeter sod   5
Than Fancy's feet have ever trod.

By fairy hands their knell is rung,
By forms unseen their dirge is sung;
There Honor comes, a pilgrim grey,
To bless the turf that wraps their clay;   10
And Freedom shall awhile repair,
To dwell a weeping hermit there!

ODE TO EVENING

IF ought of oaten stop, or pastoral song,
May hope, chaste Eve, to sooth thy modest ear,
  Like thy own solemn springs,
  Thy springs and dying gales,

O nymph reserv'd, while now the bright-hair'd
    sun   5
Sits in yon western tent, whose cloudy skirts,
  With brede ethereal wove,
  O'erhang his wavy bed:

Now air is hush'd, save where the weak-ey'd
    bat,
With short shrill shriek, flits by on leathern
    wing,   10
  Or where the beetle winds
  His small but sullen horn,

As oft he rises 'midst the twilight path,
Against the pilgrim borne in heedless hum:
   Now teach me, maid compos'd,   15
   To breathe some soften'd strain,

Whose numbers, stealing thro' thy dark'ning
   vale
May not unseemly with its stillness suit,
   As, musing slow, I hail
   Thy genial lov'd return!   20

For when thy folding-star arising shews
His paly circlet, at his warning lamp
   The fragrant Hours, the elves
   Who slept in flow'rs the day,

And many a nymph who wreaths her brows
   with sedge,   25
And sheds the fresh'ning dew, and, lovelier still
   The pensive Pleasures sweet,
   Prepare thy shadowy car.

Then lead, calm vot'ress, where some sheety
   lake
Cheers the lone heath, or some time-hallow'd pile
   Or upland fallows grey   31
   Reflect its last cool gleam.

But when chill blust'ring winds, or driving rain,
Forbid my willing feet, be mine the hut
   That from the mountain's side   35
   Views wilds, and swelling floods,

And hamlets brown, and dim-discover'd spires,
And hears their simple bell, and marks o'er all
   Thy dewy fingers draw
   The gradual dusky veil.   40

While Spring shall pour his show'rs, as oft he
   wont,
And bathe thy breathing tresses, meekest Eve;
   While Summer loves to sport
   Beneath thy ling'ring light;

While sallow Autumn fills thy lap with leaves;
Or Winter, yelling thro' the troublous air,   46
   Affrights thy shrinking train,
   And rudely rends thy robes;

So long, sure-found beneath the sylvan shed,
Shall Fancy, Friendship, Science, rose-lipp'd
   Health,   50
   Thy gentlest influence own,
   And hymn thy fav'rite name!
                          (1746)

ODE TO SIMPLICITY

O Thou, by nature taught
   To breathe her genuine thought,
In numbers warmly pure, and sweetly strong;
   Who first, on mountains wild,
   In fancy, loveliest child,   5
Thy babe, or pleasure's, nursed the powers of
   song!

Thou, who, with hermit heart,
   Disdain'st the wealth of art,
And gauds, and pageant weeds, and trailing pall;
   But com'st a decent maid,   10
   In Attic robe arrayed,
O chaste, unboastful nymph, to thee I call;

   By all the honeyed store
   On Hybla's thymy shore;
By all her blooms, and mingled murmurs dear;
   By her whose lovelorn woe,   16
   In evening musings slow,
Soothed sweetly sad Electra's poet's ear:

   By old Cephisus deep,
   Who spread his wavy sweep,   20
In warbled wanderings, round thy green retreat;
   On whose enameled side,
   When holy freedom died,
No equal haunt allured thy future feet.

   O sister meek of truth,   25
   To my admiring youth,
Thy sober aid and native charms infuse!
   The flowers that sweetest breathe,
   Though beauty culled the wreath,
Still ask thy hand to range their ordered hues.

   While Rome could none esteem   31
   But virtue's patriot theme,
You loved her hills, and led their laureat band:
   But stayed to sing alone
   To one distinguished throne;   35
And turned the face, and fled her altered land.

   No more, in hall or bower,
   The passions own thy power;
Love, only love, her forceless numbers mean:
   For thou hast left her shrine;   40
   Nor olive more, nor vine,
Shall gain thy feet to bless the servile scene.

   Though taste, though genius, bless
   To some divine excess,
Faints the cold work till thou inspire the whole;
   What each, what all supply,   46
   May court, may charm, our eye;
Thou, only thou, cans't raise the meeting soul!

   Of these let others ask,
   To aid some mighty task,   50
I only seek to find thy temperate vale;
   Where oft my reed might sound
   To maids and shepherds round,
And all thy sons, O Nature, learn my tale.
                          (1746)

THE PASSIONS

AN ODE FOR MUSIC

When Music, heav'nly maid, was young,
While yet in early Greece she sung,
The Passions oft, to hear her shell,
Throng'd around her magic cell,

Exulting, trembling, raging, fainting,   5
Possest beyond the Muse's painting;
By turns they felt the glowing mind
Disturb'd, delighted, rais'd, refin'd:
Till once, 't is said, when all were fir'd,
Fill'd with fury, rapt, inspir'd,   10
From the supporting myrtles round
They snatch'd her instruments of sound;
And as they oft had heard apart
Sweet lessons of her forceful art,
Each, for madness rul'd the hour,   15
Would prove his own expressive pow'r.

First Fear his hand, its skill to try,
  Amid the chords bewilder'd laid,
And back recoil'd, he knew not why,
  Ev'n at the sound himself had made.   20

Next Anger rush'd; his eyes, on fire,
  In lightnings own'd his secret stings;
In one rude clash he struck the lyre,
  And swept with hurried hand the strings.

With woeful measures wan Despair   25
  Low sullen sounds his grief beguil'd;
A solemn, strange, and mingled air;
  'T was sad by fits, by starts 't was wild.

But thou, O Hope, with eyes so fair,
  What was thy delightful measure?   30
  Still it whisper'd promis'd pleasure,
And bade the lovely scenes at distance hail!
  Still would her touch the strain prolong,
And from the rocks, the woods, the vale,
  She call'd on Echo still thro' all the song;   35
And where her sweetest theme she chose,
A soft responsive voice was heard at ev'ry close,
And Hope enchanted smil'd, and wav'd her
    golden hair.

And longer had she sung,—but with a frown
    Revenge impatient rose;   40
He threw his blood-stain'd sword in thunder
    down
  And with a with'ring look
  The war-denouncing trumpet took,
And blew a blast so loud and dread,
Were ne'er prophetic sounds so full of woe.   45
  And ever and anon he beat
  The doubling drum with furious heat;
And tho' sometimes, each dreary pause between,
  Dejected Pity, at his side,
  Her soul-subduing voice applied,   50
Yet still he kept his wild unalter'd mien,
While each strain'd ball of sight seem'd burst-
    ing from his head.

Thy numbers, Jealousy, to nought were fix'd,
  Sad proof of thy distressful state;
Of diff'ring themes the veering song was mix'd,
  And now it courted Love, now raving call'd
    on Hate.   56

With eyes uprais'd, as one inspir'd,
Pale Melancholy sate retir'd,
And from her wild sequester'd seat.
  In notes by distance made more sweet,   60
Pour'd thro' the mellow horn her pensive soul:
  And, dashing soft from rocks around,
  Bubbling runnels join'd the sound;
Thro' glades and glooms the mingled measure
    stole;
  Or o'er some haunted stream with fond delay
    Round an holy calm diffusing,   66
    Love of peace and lonely musing,
In hollow murmurs died away.

But oh, alter'd was its sprightlier tone,
When Cheerfulness, a nymph of healthiest hue,
  Her bow across her shoulder flung,   71
  Her buskins gemm'd with morning dew,
Blew an inspiring air, that dale and thicket
    rung,
  The hunter's call to faun and dryad known!
  The oak-crown'd sisters, and their chaste-
    ey'd queen,   75
  Satyrs, and sylvan boys, were seen,
  Peeping from forth their alleys green;
  Brown Exercise rejoic'd to hear,
And Sport leapt up, and seiz'd his beechen spear.

Last came Joy's ecstatic trial.   80
He, with viny crown advancing,
  First to the lively pipe his hand addrest;
But soon he saw the brisk awak'ning viol,
  Whose sweet entrancing voice he lov'd the
    best.
They would have thought, who heard the
    strain,   85
  They saw in Tempe's vale her native maids
  Amidst the vestal sounding shades,
To some unwearied minstrel dancing,
While, as his flying fingers kiss'd the strings,
Love fram'd with Mirth a gay fantastic
    round;   90
Loose were her tresses seen, her zone unbound,
  And he, amidst his frolic play,
  As if he would the charming air repay,
Shook thousand odors from his dewy wings.

O Music, sphere-descended maid,   95
Friend of Pleasure, Wisdom's aid,
Why, goddess, why, to us denied,
Lay'st thou thy ancient lyre aside?
As in that lov'd Athenian bow'r
You learn'd an all-commanding pow'r,   100
Thy mimic soul, O nymph endear'd,
Can well recall what then it heard.
Where is thy native simple heart,
Devote to Virtue, Fancy, Art?
Arise as in that elder time,   105
Warm, energic, chaste, sublime!
Thy wonders, in that godlike age,
Fill thy recording sister's page.—

'T is said, and I believe the tale,
Thy humblest reed could more prevail, 110
Had more of strength, diviner rage,
Than all which charms this laggard age,
Ev'n all at once together found,
Cecilia's mingled world of sound.
O, bid our vain endeavors, cease, 115
Revive the just designs of Greece,
Return in all thy simple state,
Confirm the tales her sons relate!

(1746)

ODE

ON THE DEATH OF MR. THOMSON

In yonder grave a druid lies,
  Where slowly winds the stealing wave;
The year's best sweets shall duteous rise
  To deck its poet's sylvan grave.

In yon deep bed of whispering reeds 5
  His airy harp shall now be laid,
That he, whose heart in sorrow bleeds,
  May love through life the soothing shade.

Then maids and youths shall linger here,
  And, while its sounds at distance swell, 10
Shall sadly seem in pity's ear
  To hear the woodland pilgrim's knell.

Remembrance oft shall haunt the shore
  When Thames in summer wreaths is drest,
And oft suspend the dashing oar, 15
  To bid his gentle spirit rest!

And oft, as ease and health retire
  To breezy lawn, or forest deep,
The friend shall view yon whitening spire,
  And 'mid the varied landscape weep. 20

But thou, who own'st that earthy bed,
  Ah! what will every dirge avail;
Or tears, which love and pity shed,
  That mourn beneath the gliding sail?

Yet lives there one whose heedless eye 25
  Shall scorn thy pale shrine glimmering near?
With him, sweet bard, may fancy die,
  And joy desert the blooming year.

But thou, lorn stream, whose sullen tide
  No sedge-crowned sisters now attend, 30
Now waft me from the green hill's side,
  Whose cold turf hides the buried friend!

And see—the fairy valleys fade;
  Dun night has veiled the solemn view!
Yet once again, dear parted shade, 35
  Meek nature's child, again adieu!

The genial meads, assigned to bless
  Thy life, shall mourn thy early doom;
Their hinds and shepherd-girls shall dress,
  With simple hands, thy rural tomb. 40

Long, long thy stone and pointed clay
  Shall melt the musing Briton's eyes;
O vales and wild woods! shall he say,
  In yonder grave your druid lies!

(1749)

THOMAS CHATTERTON (1752–1770)

THOMAS CHATTERTON spent most of his few years at Bristol, where his ancestors had been, for a century and a half, sextons of St. Mary Redcliffe. In the 'muniment room' of this church he pretended to have discovered the manuscripts of the poems which he gave to the world as those of a fifteenth century priest, Thomas Rowley. Some of his forgeries were clever enough to impose for a time upon Horace Walpole, though Gray readily detected the deception. In London, whither he had gone with the hope of living by his pen, the proud and morbidly precocious boy took his own life at the age of seventeen years and nine months. His strange hectic genius and the romantic tragedy of his death exercised a spell upon the poets of the next two generations. Artistically, Coleridge, Wordsworth, Shelley, Keats, and, less directly, Scott and Byron, all inherited in some measure from 'the marvelous boy, who perished in his pride'.

AN EXCELLENT BALLAD OF CHARITY

In Virgine the sultry Sun 'gan sheene
  And hot upon the meads did cast his ray:
The apple ruddied from its paly green,
  And the soft pear did bend the leafy spray;
  The pied chelàndry sang the livelong day: 5
'T was now the pride, the manhood of the year,
And eke the ground was dight in its most deft aumere.

The sun was gleaming in the mid of day,
  Dead still the air and eke the welkin blue,
When from the sea arist in drear array 10
  A heap of clouds of sable sullen hue,
  The which full fast unto the woodland drew,
Hiding at once the Sunnè's festive face;
And the black tempest swelled and gathered up apace.

Beneath an holm, fast by a pathway side 15
  Which did unto Saint Godwyn's convent lead,
A hapless pilgrim moaning did abide,
  Poor in his view, ungentle in his weed,
  Long breast-full of the miseries of need.
Where from the hailstorm could the beggar fly?
He had no housen there, nor any convent nigh.

Look in his gloomèd face; his sprite there scan,
  How woe-begone, how withered, sapless, dead! 23
Haste to thy church-glebe-house, accursèd man,
  Haste to thy coffin, thy sole slumbering-bed!
  Cold as the clay which will grow on thy head
Are Charity and Love among high elves; 27
The Knights and Barons live for pleasure and themselves.

The gathered storm is ripe; the big drops fall;
  The sunburnt meadows smoke and drink the rain; 30
The coming ghastness doth the cattle appal,
  And the full flocks are driving o'er the plain;
  Dashed from the clouds, the waters gush again;
The welkin opes, the yellow levin flies,
And the hot fiery steam in the wide flame-lowe dies. 35

List! now the thunder's rattling clamouring sound
  Moves slowly on, and then upswollen clangs,
Shakes the high spire, and lost, dispended, drown'd,
  Still on the affrighted ear of terror hangs;
  The winds are up; the lofty elm-tree swangs;
Again the levin and the thunder pours, 41
And the full clouds are burst at once in stormy showers.

Spurring his palfrey o'er the watery plain,
  The Abbot of Saint Godwyn's convent came;
His chapournette was drenchèd with the rain,
  His painted girdle met with mickle shame; 46
  He backwards told his bederoll at the same.
The storm increasèd, and he drew aside,
With the poor alms-craver near to the holm to bide.

His cope was all of Lincoln cloth so fine, 50
  With a gold button fastened near his chin;
His autremete was edged with golden twine,
  And his peak'd shoe a lordling's might have been;
  Full well it showed he counted cost no sin:
The trammels of the palfrey pleased his sight, 55
For the horse-milliner his head with roses dight.

'An alms, Sir Priest!' the drooping pilgrim said,
  'O let me wait within your convent-door

Till the sun shineth high above our head
   And the loud tempest of the air is o'er.   60
   Helpless and old am I, alas! and poor:
No house, nor friend, nor money in my pouch;
All that I call my own is this my silver crouch.'

'Varlet,' replied the Abbot, 'cease your din;
   This is no season alms and prayers to give; 65
My porter never lets a beggar in;
   None touch my ring who not in honour live.'
And now the sun with the black clouds did strive,
And shot upon the ground his glaring ray:
The Abbot spurred his steed, and eftsoons rode away.   70

Once more the sky was black, the thunder roll'd:
   Fast running o'er the plain a priest was seen,
Not dight full proud nor buttoned up in gold;
   His cope and jape were grey, and eke were clean;
A Limitour he was, of order seen;   75
And from the pathway side then turnèd he,
Where the poor beggar lay beneath the holmen tree.

'An alms, Sir Priest,' the drooping pilgrim said,
   'For sweet Saint Mary and your order's sake!'
The Limitour then loosened his pouch-thread 80
   And did thereout a groat of silver take;
   The needy pilgrim did for gladness shake.
'Here, take this silver, it may ease thy care;
We are God's stewards all,—nought of our own we bear.

'But ah! unhappy pilgrim, learn of me,   85
   Scarce any give a rentroll to their Lord:
Here, take my semicope,—thou'rt bare, I see;
   'T is thine; the Saints will give me my reward!'
He left the pilgrim and his way aborde.
Virgin and holy Saints who sit in gloure,   90
Or give the mighty will, or give the good man power!

               (1770)

MYNSTRELLES SONGE

From ÆLLA: A Tragycal Enterlude

O! synge untoe mie roundelaie,
O! droppe the brynie teare wythe mee,
Daunce ne moe atte hallie daie,
Lycke a reynynge [1] ryver bee;
   Mie love ys dedde,   5
   Gon to hys death-bedde,
   Al under the wyllowe tree.

Blacke hys cryne [2] as the wyntere nyghte,
Whyte hys rode [3] as the sommer snowe,
Rodde hys face as the mornynge lyghte,   10
Cale he lyes ynne the grave belowe;
   Mie love ys dedde,
   Gon to hys death-bedde,
   Al under the wyllowe tree.

Swote hys tyngue as the throstles note,   15
Quycke ynn daunce as thoughte canne bee,
Defte hys taboure, codgelle stote,
O! hee lyes bie the wyllowe tree:
   Mie love ys dedde,
   Gonne to hys death-bedde,   20
   Alle under the wyllowe tree.

Harke! the ravenne flappes hys wynge,
In the briered delle belowe;
Harke! the dethe-owle loude dothe syngg,
To the nyghte-mares as heie goe;   25
   Mie love ys dedde,
   Gonne to hys death-bedde,
   Al under the wyllowe tree.

See! the whyte moone sheenes onne hie;
Whyterre ys mie true loves shroude;   30
Whyterre yanne the mornynge skie,
Whyterre yanne the evenynge cloude;
   Mie love ys dedde,
   Gon to hys death-bedde,
   Al under the wyllowe tree.   35

Heere, uponne mie true loves grave,
Schalle the baren fleurs be layde,
Nee one hallie Seyncte to save
Al the celness of a mayde.
   Mie love ys dedde,   40
   Gonne to hys death-bedde,
   Alle under the wyllowe tree.

Wythe mie hondes I 'lle dente the brieres
Rounde his hallie corse to gre,
Ouphante fairie lyghte youre fyres,   45
Heere mie boddie stylle schalle bee.
   Mie love ys dedde,
   Gon to hys death-bedde,
   Al under the wyllowe tree.

Comme, wythe acorne-coppe & thorne,   50
Drayne mie hartys blodde awaie;
Lyfe & all yttes goode I scorne,
Daunce bie nete, or feaste by daie.
   Mie love ys dedde,
   Gon to hys death-bedde,   55
   Al under the wyllowe tree.

Waterre wytches, crownede wythe reytes, [4]
Bere mee to yer leathalle tyde.
I die; I comme; mie true love waytes.
Thos the damselle spake, and dyed.   60

               (1777)

---

[1] Running.   [2] Hair.   [3] Complexion.   [4] Water-flags.

OLIVER GOLDSMITH (1728-1774)

The author of *The Vicar of Wakefield* was the sixth of nine children of an Irish parson farmer and passed most of his boyhood in the little hamlet of Lissoy, which he afterward idealized in *The Deserted Village*. He was regarded as 'a stupid blockhead' in the village school and when, in 1749, he succeeded in taking a degree at Trinity College, Dublin, he was lowest on the list. For a number of years he showed little ability and still less inclination to fit himself to practical life. Rejected for holy orders, he taught school for a time and, soon disgusted, tried the law with the same result. He then spent several years in the nominal study of medicine, in the course of which, he made the grand tour of Europe, setting off it is said, 'with a guinea in his pocket, one shirt to his back, and a flute in his hand.' Finding his way to London, in 1756, he existed for a couple of years in a most haphazard manner, as 'chemist's' assistant, corrector of the press, struggling physician, usher in a school, and hack writer for the *Monthly Review*. The culmination of this period arrived when he borrowed a suit of clothes to present himself for examination as a hospital mate, failed in the examination, and pawned the clothes. Soon after this, his literary successes began. It was in 1764, that Johnson following close after a guinea with which he had responded to a message of distress, 'put the cork into the bottle' for which Goldsmith had promptly changed the guinea, carried off the manuscript of *The Vicar of Wakefield* to a bookseller, and relieved the author from arrest. *The Traveler* (1764) was now published and *The Deserted Village* (1770) confirmed the reputation which this had established. His two plays, *The Good Natured Man* (1768) and *She Stoops to Conquer* (1773) brought him five hundred pounds apiece; his *History of Animated Nature*, for which he had no qualification except the ability to write, secured him eight hundred pounds; and similar hack work was similarly paid; but such was his indiscretion that he was seldom long out of difficulty. He had in a high measure the prodigality, not uncommon among clever writers, of bestowing his entire stock of wisdom on the reader and reserving none for the conduct of life. Yet his follies, like those of Steele, were the indexes of a liberal and lovable nature. When he died, at the age of forty-six, leaving debts of two thousand pounds, there was as much tenderness as humor in Johnson's deep ejaculation: 'Was ever poet so trusted?'

SONG

From The Vicar of Wakefield

When lovely woman stoops to folly,
  And finds too late that men betray,
What charm can soothe her melancholy?
  What art can wash her guilt away?

The only art her guilt to cover,   5
  To hide her shame from every eye,
To give repentance to her lover,
  And wring his bosom, is—to die.

(1766)

THE DESERTED VILLAGE

Sweet Auburn! loveliest village of the plain;
Where health and plenty cheered the laboring swain,
Where smiling spring its earliest visit paid,
And parting summer's lingering blooms delayed:
Dear lovely bowers of innocence and ease,   5
Seats of my youth, when every sport could please,
How often have I loitered o'er thy green,
Where humble happiness endeared each scene!
How often have I paused on every charm,
The sheltered cot, the cultivated farm,   10
The never-failing brook, the busy mill,
The decent church that topped the neighboring hill,
The hawthorn bush, with seats beneath the shade,
For talking age and whispering lovers made!
How often have I blest the coming day,   15
When toil remitting lent its turn to play,
And all the village train, from labor free,
Led up their sports beneath the spreading tree,
While many a pastime circled in the shade,
The young contending as the old surveyed;   20
And many a gambol frolicked o'er the ground,
And sleights of art and feats of strength went round.
And still, as each repeated pleasure tired,
Succeeding sports the mirthful band inspired;
The dancing pair that simply sought renown,   25
By holding out to tire each other down;
The swain mistrustless of his smutted face,
While secret laughter tittered round the place;

The bashful virgin's side-long looks of love,
The matron's glance that would those looks reprove: 30
These were thy charms, sweet village! sports like these,
With sweet succession, taught even toil to please:
These round thy bowers their cheerful influence shed:
These were thy charms—but all these charms are fled.

Sweet smiling village, loveliest of the lawn, 35
Thy sports are fled, and all thy charms withdrawn;
Amidst thy bowers the tyrant's hand is seen,
And desolation saddens all thy green;
One only master grasps the whole domain,
And half a tillage stints thy smiling plain. 40
No more thy glassy brook reflects the day,
But, choked with sedges, works its weedy way;
Along thy glades, a solitary guest,
The hollow sounding bittern guards its nest;
Amidst thy desert walks the lapwing flies, 45
And tires their echoes with unvaried cries;
Sunk are thy bowers in shapeless ruin all,
And the long grass o'ertops the moldering wall;
And trembling, shrinking from the spoiler's hand,
Far, far away thy children leave the land. 50

Ill fares the land, to hastening ills a prey,
Where wealth accumulates, and men decay:
Princes and lords may flourish, or may fade;
A breath can make them, as a breath has made:
But a bold peasantry, their country's pride, 55
When once destroyed, can never be supplied.

A time there was, ere England's griefs began,
When every rood of ground maintained its man;
For him light labor spread her wholesome store,
Just gave what life required, but gave no more:
His best companions, innocence and health; 61
And his best riches, ignorance of wealth.

But times are altered; trade's unfeeling train
Usurp the land and dispossess the swain; 64
Along the lawn, where scattered hamlets rose,
Unwieldy wealth and cumbrous pomp repose,
And every want to opulence allied,
And every pang that folly pays to pride.
These gentle hours that plenty bade to bloom,
Those calm desires that asked but little room,
Those healthful sports that graced the peaceful scene, 71
Lived in each look, and brightened all the green;
These, far departing, seek a kinder shore,
And rural mirth and manners are no more.

Sweet Auburn! parent of the blissful hour, 75
Thy glades forlorn confess the tyrant's power.
Here, as I take my solitary rounds
Amidst thy tangling walks and ruined grounds,
And, many a year elapsed, return to view
Where once the cottage stood, the hawthorn grew, 80
Remembrance wakes with all her busy train,
Swells at my breast, and turns the past to pain.

In all my wanderings round this world of care,
In all my griefs—and God has given my share—
I still had hopes, my latest hours to crown, 85
Amidst these humble bowers to lay me down;
To husband out life's taper at the close,
And keep the flame from wasting by repose:
I still had hopes, for pride attends us still,
Amidst the swains to show my book-learned skill, 90
Around my fire an evening group to draw,
And tell of all I felt, and all I saw;
And, as an hare whom hounds and horns pursue,
Pants to the place from whence at first she flew,
I still had hopes, my long vexations past, 95
Here to return—and die at home at last.

O, blest retirement, friend to life's decline,
Retreats from care, that never must be mine,
How happy he who crowns in shades like these,
A youth of labor with an age of ease; 100
Who quits a world where strong temptations try,
And, since 't is hard to combat, learns to fly!
For him no wretches, born to work and weep,
Explore the mine, or tempt the dangerous deep;
No surly porter stands in guilty state, 105
To spurn imploring famine from the gate;
But on he moves to meet his latter end,
Angels around befriending Virtue's friend;
Bends to the grave with unperceived decay,
While resignation gently slopes the way; 110
And, all his prospects brightening to the last,
His heaven commences ere the world be past!

Sweet was the sound, when oft at evening's close
Up yonder hill the village murmur rose. 114
There, as I passed with careless steps and slow,
The mingling notes came softened from below;
The swain responsive as the milk-maid sung,
The sober herd that lowed to meet their young,
The noisy geese that gabbled o'er the pool,
The playful children just let loose from school,
The watch-dog's voice that bayed the whispering wind, 121
And the loud laugh that spoke the vacant mind;—
These all in sweet confusion sought the shade,
And filled each pause the nightingale had made.
But now the sounds of population fail, 125
No cheerful murmurs fluctuate in the gale,
No busy steps the grass-grown foot-way tread,
For all the bloomy flush of life is fled.
All but yon widowed, solitary thing,
That feebly bends beside the plashy spring: 130

She, wretched matron, forced in age, for bread,
To strip the brook with mantling cresses spread,
To pick her wintry faggot from the thorn,
To seek her nightly shed, and weep till morn;
She only left of all the harmless train,   135
The sad historian of the pensive plain.

   Near yonder copse, where once the garden smiled,
And still where many a garden flower grows wild;
There, where a few torn shrubs the place disclose,
The village preacher's modest mansion rose.   140
A man he was to all the country dear,
And passing rich with forty pounds a year;
Remote from towns he ran his godly race,
Nor e'er had changed, nor wished to change his place;
Unpracticed he to fawn, or seek for power,   145
By doctrines fashioned to the varying hour;
Far other aims his heart had learned to prize,
More skilled to raise the wretched than to rise.
His house was known to all the vagrant train;
He chid their wanderings but relieved their pain:
The long-remembered beggar was his guest,   151
Whose beard descending swept his aged breast;
The ruined spendthrift, now no longer proud,
Claimed kindred there, and had his claims allowed;
The broken soldier, kindly bade to stay,   155
Sat by the fire, and talked the night away,
Wept o'er his wounds or, tales of sorrow done,
Shouldered his crutch and showed how fields were won.
Pleased with his guests, the good man learned to glow,
And quite forgot their vices in their woe;   160
Careless their merits or their faults to scan
His pity gave ere charity began.

   Thus to relieve the wretched was his pride,
And e'en his failings leaned to Virtue's side;
But in his duty prompt at every call,   165
He watched and wept, he prayed and felt for all;
And, as a bird each fond endearment tries
To tempt its new-fledged offspring to the skies,
He tried each art, reproved each dull delay,
Allured to brighter worlds, and led the way.   170

   Beside the bed where parting life was laid,
And sorrow, guilt, and pain by turns dismayed,
The reverend champion stood. At his control
Despair and anguish fled the struggling soul;
Comfort came down the trembling wretch to raise,   175
And his last faltering accents whispered praise.

   At church, with meek and unaffected grace,
His looks adorned the venerable place;
Truth from his lips prevailed with double sway,
And fools, who came to scoff, remained to pray.
The service past, around the pious man,   181
With steady zeal, each honest rustic ran;
Even children followed with endearing wile,
And plucked his gown to share the good man's smile.
His ready smile a parent's warmth exprest;   185
Their welfare pleased him, and their cares distrest:
To them his heart, his love, his griefs were given,
But all his serious thoughts had rest in heaven.
As some tall cliff that lifts its awful form,
Swells from the vale, and midway leaves the storm,   190
Though round its breast the rolling clouds are spread,
Eternal sunshine settles on its head.

   Beside yon straggling fence that skirts the way,
With blossomed furze unprofitably gay,
There, in his noisy mansion, skilled to rule,   195
The village master taught his little school.
A man severe he was, and stern to view;
I knew him well, and every truant knew;
Well had the boding tremblers learned to trace
The day's disasters in his morning face;   200
Full well they laughed with counterfeited glee
At all his jokes, for many a joke had he;
Full well the busy whisper circling round
Conveyed the dismal tidings when he frowned.
Yet he was kind, or, if severe in aught,   205
The love he bore to learning was in fault;
The village all declared how much he knew:
'T was certain he could write, and cipher too;
Lands he could measure, terms and tides presage,
And even the story ran that he could gauge;   210
In arguing, too, the parson owned his skill,
For, even though vanquished, he could argue still;
While words of learned length and thundering sound
Amazed the gazing rustics ranged around;   214
And still they gazed, and still the wonder grew,
That one small head could carry all he knew.

   But past is all his fame. The very spot
Where many a time he triumphed, is forgot.
Near yonder thorn, that lifts its head on high,
Where once the sign-post caught the passing eye,
Low lies that house where nut-brown draughts inspired,   221
Where graybeard mirth and smiling toil retired,
Where village statesmen talked with looks profound,
And news much older than their ale went round.
Imagination fondly stoops to trace   225
The parlor splendors of that festive place:
The white-washed wall, the nicely sanded floor,
The varnished clock that clicked behind the door;
The chest contrived a double debt to pay,
A bed by night, a chest of drawers by day;   230

The pictures placed for ornament and use,
The twelve good rules, the royal game of goose;
The hearth, except when winter chilled the day,
With aspen boughs and flowers and fennel gay;
While broken tea-cups, wisely kept for show,
Ranged o'er the chimney, glistened in a row. 236

Vain transitory splendors! could not all
Reprieve the tottering mansion from its fall?
Obscure it sinks, nor shall it more impart 239
An hour's importance to the poor man's heart.
Thither no more the peasant shall repair
To sweet oblivion of his daily care;
No more the farmer's news, the barber's tale;
No more the woodman's ballad shall prevail; 244
No more the smith his dusky brow shall clear,
Relax his ponderous strength, and lean to hear;
The host himself no longer shall be found
Careful to see the mantling bliss go round;
Nor the coy maid, half willing to be prest,
Shall kiss the cup to pass it to the rest. 250

Yes! let the rich deride, the proud disdain,
These simple blessings of the lowly train;
To me more dear, congenial to my heart,
One native charm, than all the gloss of art.
Spontaneous joys, where Nature has its play,
The soul adopts, and owns their first born sway;
Lightly they frolic o'er the vacant mind, 257
Unenvied, unmolested, unconfined.
But the long pomp, the midnight masquerade,
With all the freaks of wanton wealth arrayed—
In these, ere triflers half their wish obtain, 261
The toiling pleasure sickens into pain;
And, even while fashion's brightest arts decoy,
The heart distrusting asks if this be joy.

Ye friends to truth, ye statesmen who survey
The rich man's joy increase, the poor's decay,
'T is yours to judge, how wide the limits stand
Between a splendid and an happy land. 268
Proud swells the tide with loads of freighted ore,
And shouting Folly hails them from her shore;
Hoards even beyond the miser's wish abound,
And rich men flock from all the world around.
Yet count our gains! This wealth is but a name
That leaves our useful products still the same.
Not so the loss. The man of wealth and pride
Takes up a space that many poor supplied; 276
Space for his lake, his park's extended bounds,
Space for his horses, equipage, and hounds:
The robe that wraps his limbs in silken sloth
Has robbed the neighboring fields of half their
    growth; 280
His seat, where solitary sports are seen,
Indignant spurns the cottage from the green:
Around the world each needful product flies,
For all the luxuries the world supplies;
While thus the land adorned for pleasure all 285
In barren splendor feebly waits the fall.
As some fair female unadorned and plain,
Secure to please while youth confirms her reign,
Slights every borrowed charm that dress supplies,
Nor shares with art the triumph of her eyes; 290
But when those charms are past, for charms are
    frail,
When time advances, and when lovers fail,
She then shines forth, solicitous to bless,
In all the glaring impotence of dress.
Thus fares the land by luxury betrayed: 295
In nature's simplest charms at first arrayed,
But verging to decline, its splendors rise,
Its vistas strike, its palaces surprise;
While, scourged by famine from the smiling
    land
The mournful peasant leads his humble band,
And while he sinks, without one arm to save, 301
The country blooms—a garden and a grave.

Where then, ah! where, shall poverty reside,
To 'scape the pressure of contiguous pride?
If to some common's fenceless limits strayed, 305
He drives his flock to pick the scanty blade,
Those fenceless fields the sons of wealth divide,
And even the bare-worn common is denied.

If to the city sped—what waits him there?
To see profusion that he must not share; 310
To see ten thousand baneful arts combined
To pamper luxury, and thin mankind;
To see those joys the sons of pleasure know
Extorted from his fellow-creature's woe.
Here while the courtier glitters in brocade, 315
There the pale artist plies the sickly trade;
Here while the proud their long-drawn pomps
    display,
There the black gibbet glooms beside the way.
The dome where pleasure holds her midnight
    reign,
Here, richly decked, admits the gorgeous train:
Tumultuous grandeur crowds the blazing
    square, 321
The rattling chariots clash, the torches glare.
Sure scenes like these no troubles e'er annoy!
Sure these denote one universal joy!
Are these thy serious thoughts?—Ah, turn thine
    eyes 325
Where the poor, houseless, shivering female lies.
She once, perhaps, in village plenty blest,
Has wept at tales of innocence distrest;
Her modest looks the cottage might adorn, 329
Sweet as the primrose peeps beneath the thorn;
Now lost to all; her friends, her virtue fled,
Near her betrayer's door she lays her head,
And, pinched with cold, and shrinking from the
    shower,
With heavy heart deplores that luckless hour,
When idly first, ambitious of the town, 335
She left her wheel and robes of country brown.

Do thine, sweet Auburn, thine, the loveliest
    train,
Do thy fair tribes participate her pain?

Even now, perhaps, by cold and hunger led,
At proud men's doors they ask a little bread! 340

Ah, no! To distant climes, a dreary scene,
Where half the convex world intrudes between,
Through torrid tracts with fainting steps they go,
Where wild Altama murmurs to their woe.
Far different there from all that charmed before 345
The various terrors of that horrid shore;
Those blazing suns that dart a downward ray,
And fiercely shed intolerable day;
Those matted woods, where birds forget to sing,
But silent bats in drowsy clusters cling; 350
Those poisonous fields with rank luxuriance crowned,
Where the dark scorpion gathers death around;
Where at each step the stranger fears to wake
The rattling terrors of the vengeful snake;
Where crouching tigers wait their hapless prey,
And savage men more murderous still than they; 356
While oft in whirls the mad tornado flies,
Mingling the ravaged landscape with the skies.
Far different these from every former scene,
The cooling brook, the grassy vested green, 360
The breezy covert of the warbling grove,
That only sheltered thefts of harmless love.

Good Heaven! what sorrows gloomed that parting day,
That called them from their native walks away;
When the poor exiles, every pleasure past, 365
Hung round the bowers, and fondly looked their last,
And took a long farewell, and wished in vain
For seats like these beyond the western main,
And shuddering still to face the distant deep,
Returned and wept, and still returned to weep.
The good old sire, the first prepared to go 371
To new found worlds, and wept for others' woe;
But for himself, in conscious virtue brave,
He only wished for worlds beyond the grave.
His lovely daughter, lovelier in her tears, 375
The fond companion of his helpless years,
Silent went next, neglectful of her charms,
And left a lover's for a father's arms.
With louder plaints the mother spoke her woes,
And blest the cot where every pleasure rose, 380
And kist her thoughtless babes with many a tear
And claspt them close, in sorrow doubly dear,
Whilst her fond husband strove to lend relief,
In all the silent manliness of grief.

O luxury! thou curst by Heaven's decree, 385
How ill exchanged are things like these for thee!
How do thy potions, with insidious joy,
Diffuse their pleasure only to destroy!
Kingdoms by thee, to sickly greatness grown,
Boast of a florid vigor not their own. 390
At every draught more large and large they grow,
A bloated mass of rank, unwieldy woe;
Till sapped their strength, and every part unsound,
Down, down, they sink, and spread a ruin round.

Even now the devastation is begun, 395
And half the business of destruction done;
Even now, methinks, as pondering here I stand,
I see the rural virtues leave the land.
Down where yon anchoring vessel spreads the sail,
That idly waiting flaps with every gale, 400
Downward they move, a melancholy band,
Pass from the shore, and darken all the strand.
Contented toil, and hospitable care,
And kind connubial tenderness, are there;
And piety with wishes placed above, 405
And steady loyalty, and faithful love.
And thou, sweet Poetry, thou loveliest maid,
Still first to fly where sensual joys invade;
Unfit in these degenerate times of shame 409
To catch the heart, or strike for honest fame;
Dear charming nymph, neglected and decried,
My shame in crowds, my solitary pride;
Thou source of all my bliss, and all my woe,
That found'st me poor at first, and keep'st me so;
Thou guide by which the nobler arts excel, 415
Thou nurse of every virtue, fare thee well!
Farewell, and oh! where'er thy voice be tried,
On Torno's cliffs, or Pambamarca's side,
Whether where equinoctial fervors glow,
Or winter wraps the polar world in snow, 420
Still let thy voice, prevailing over time,
Redress the rigors of the inclement clime;
Aid slighted truth with thy persuasive strain;
Teach erring man to spurn the rage of gain:
Teach him, that states of native strength possest, 425
Though very poor, may still be very blest;
That trade's proud empire hastes to swift decay,
As ocean sweeps the labored mole away;
While self-dependent power can time defy,
As rocks resist the billows and the sky. 430

(1770)

From THE RETALIATION

Here lies our good Edmund, whose genius was such,
We scarcely can praise it, or blame it too much;
Who, born for the universe, narrowed his mind,
And to party gave up what was meant for mankind:
Though fraught with all learning, yet straining his throat 5
To persuade Tommy Townshend to lend him a vote;

Who, too deep for his hearers, still went on re-
    fining,
And thought of convincing, while they thought
    of dining;
Though equal to all things, for all things unfit;
Too nice for a statesman, too proud for a wit; 10
For a patriot too cool; for a drudge disobedient;
And too fond of the right to pursue the expe-
    dient.
In short, 't was his fate, unemployed or in place,
    sir,
To eat mutton cold, and cut blocks with a razor.

* * *

   Here lies David Garrick, describe me who
    can,   15
An abridgment of all that was pleasant in man;
As an actor, confest without rival to shine;
As a wit, if not first, in the very first line;
Yet with talents like these, and an excellent
    heart,
The man had his failings, a dupe to his art;   20
Like an ill-judging beauty his colors he spread,
And beplastered with rouge his own natural red.
On the stage he was natural, simple, affecting,
'T was only that when he was off he was acting;
With no reason on earth to go out of his way   25
He turn'd and he varied full ten times a day:
Though secure of our hearts, yet confoundedly
    sick
If they were not his own by finessing and trick;
He cast off his friends as a huntsman his pack,
For he knew when he pleased he could whistle
    them back.   30
Of praise a mere glutton, he swallowed what
    came,
And the puff of a dunce he mistook it for fame;
Till his relish grown callous, almost to disease,
Who peppered the highest was surest to please.
But let us be candid, and speak out our mind: 35
If dunces applauded, he paid them in kind.

* * *

   Here Hickey reclines, a most blunt, pleasant
    creature,
And slander itself must allow him good nature:
He cherished his friend, and he relished a
    bumper;
Yet one fault he had, and that one was a
    thumper.   40
Perhaps you may ask if the man was a miser?
I answer, no, no, for he always was wiser:
Too courteous, perhaps, or obligingly flat?
His very worst foe can 't accuse him of that:
Perhaps he confided in men as they go,   45
And so was too foolishly honest? Ah no.
Then what was his failing? come, tell it, and,
    burn ye!
He was, could he help it?—a special attorney.

* * *

   Here Reynolds is laid, and, to tell you my
    mind,
He has not left a better or wiser behind: 50
His pencil was striking, resistless, and grand;
His manners were gentle, complying, and bland;
Still born to improve us in every part,
His pencil our faces, his manner our heart:
To coxcombs averse, yet most civilly steering, 55
When they judg'd without skill he was still hard
    of hearing:
When they talk'd of their Raphaels, Correggios,
    and stuff,
He shifted his trumpet, and only took snuff.

(1774)

SAMUEL JOHNSON (1709-1784)

Few personalities of famous men are so well-known to us as the personality of 'that great Cham of literature, Samuel Johnson.' The son of a poor Lichfield book-seller, Johnson had the advantages of the local grammar-school and a few poverty-stricken months at Pembroke College, Oxford; served for a time as usher in a boy's school; married for true love's sake, a woman much his senior; and set up a private academy near his native city. This enterprise proving neither agreeable nor profitable, in his twenty-eighth year, with little in his uncouth person, his ponderous genius, or in the sturdy independence of his character, to recommend him to the rich and fortunate, Johnson had the hardihood to seek a living among the penurious publishers and starving hack writers of London. For nearly a quarter of a century, he earned a precarious subsistence by huge 'odd jobs' of literature which now have little interest except as a part of his biography. The greatest of these, his *Dictionary of the English Language*, was published in 1755, after seven years of continuous labor. During a part of this time he had supported himself by writing *The Rambler* (1750-52), and, in ensuing years, *The Idler* (1759-60) and *Rasselas* (1759) helped to defray expenses while he was preparing his edition of Shakespeare (1765). He was now famous. A pension of three hundred pounds, granted by government in 1762, had relieved him from the pressure of necessity. Thereafter he wrote but little, and his social talents expanded. In 1764, he joined with Sir Joshua Reynolds in founding the renowned Literary Club which had the good fortune to gather to its convivial meetings such men as Burke, Goldsmith, Gibbon, Garrick, Adam Smith, the two Wartons, Bishop Percy of ballad fame, and many others whose names are still remembered. The previous year, Boswell had made his acquaintance and had begun to gather materials for the record of those 'nights and suppers of the gods' with which we are regaled in his *Life*. If we may trust Boswell's vivid and, apparently, accurate account, Johnson inspired in his comrades not only unusual affection, but a degree of respect which approximated reverence. His conversation was witty, powerful, and varied and gives us a higher idea of his genius than anything which he wrote. His eccentricities both of behavior and of opinion were extraordinary; but the prevailing impression left by Boswell's picture of his mind is one of massive common-sense, united with great depth and benignity of soul.

Johnson's most important contribution to literature is his *Lives of the Poets*, which he undertook toward the end of his life (1779-81), when his powers were in their fullness, and after years of polite conversation had chastened his style. They are the outpouring of a capacious mind stored by a lifetime of reading, and reflection. His judgments are often marred by his peculiar crochets of opinion or temper; but his sayings are almost always invigorating, for they are the abrupt utterances of an honest and strong man who knew much of the world and of letters.

THE LIFE OF ADDISON

Joseph Addison was born on the 1st of May, 1672, at Milston, of which his father, Lancelot Addison, was then rector, near Ambrosebury, in Wiltshire, and, appearing weak and unlikely to live, he was christened the same day. After the usual domestic education, which from the character of the father may be reasonably supposed to have given him strong impressions of piety, he was committed to the care of Mr. Naish at Ambrosebury, and afterwards of Mr. Taylor at Salisbury.

Not to name the school or the masters of men illustrious for literature, is a kind of historical fraud, by which honest fame is injuriously diminished: I would therefore trace him through the whole process of his education. In 1683, in the beginning of his twelfth year, his father, being made Dean of Lichfield, naturally carried his family to his new residence, and, I believe, placed him for some time, probably not long, under Mr. Shaw, then master of the school at Lichfield, father of the late Dr. Peter Shaw. Of this interval his biographers have given no account, and I know it only from a story of a 'barring-out,' told me, when I was a boy, by Andrew Corbet, of Shropshire, who had heard it from Mr. Pigot, his uncle.

The practice of 'barring-out' was a savage license, practiced in many schools to the end of the last century, by which the boys, when the periodical vacation drew near, growing petulant at the approach of liberty, some days before the time of regular recess, took possession of the school, of which they barred the doors, and bade their master defiance from the windows. It is not easy to suppose that on such occasions the master would do more than laugh; yet, if tradition may be credited, he often struggled hard to force or surprise the garrison. The master, when Pigot was a schoolboy, was 'barred out' at Lichfield; and the whole operation, as he said, was planned and conducted by Addison.

To judge better of the probability of this story, I have inquired when he was sent to the Chartreux; but, as he was not one of those who enjoyed the founder's benefaction, there is no account preserved of his admission. At the school of the Chartreux, to which he was removed either from that of Salisbury or Lichfield, he pursued his juvenile studies under the care of Dr. Ellis, and contracted that intimacy with Sir Richard Steele which their joint labors have so effectually recorded.

Of this memorable friendship the greater praise must be given to Steele. It is not hard to love those from whom nothing can be feared; and Addison never considered Steele as a rival; but Steele lived, as he confesses, under an habitual subjection to the predominating genius of Addison, whom he always mentioned with reverence, and treated with obsequiousness.

Addison, who knew his own dignity, could not always forbear to show it, by playing a little upon his admirer; but he was in no danger of retort; his jests were endured without resistance or resentment. But the sneer of jocularity was not the worst. Steele, whose imprudence of generosity, or vanity of profusion, kept him always incurably necessitous, upon some pressing exigence, in an evil hour, borrowed a hundred pounds of his friend probably without much purpose of repayment; but Addison, who seems to have had other notions of a hundred pounds, grew impatient of delay, and reclaimed his loan by an execution. Steele felt with great sensibility the obduracy of his creditor, but with emotions of sorrow rather than of anger.

In 1687 he was entered into Queen's College in Oxford, where, in 1689, the accidental perusal of some Latin verses gained him the patronage of Dr. Lancaster, afterwards Provost of Queen's College; by whose recommendation he was elected into Magdalen College as a demy, a term by which that society denominates those who are elsewhere called scholars: young men who partake of the founder's benefaction, and succeed in their order to vacant fellowships. Here he continued to cultivate poetry and criticism, and grew first eminent by his Latin compositions, which are indeed entitled to particular praise. He has not confined himself to the imitation of any ancient author, but has formed his style from the general language, such as a diligent perusal of the productions of different ages happened to supply. His Latin compositions seem to have had much of his fondness, for he collected a second volume of the *Musæ Anglicanæ*, perhaps for a convenient receptacle, in which all his Latin pieces are inserted, and where his poem on the Peace has the first place. He afterwards presented the collection to Boileau, who from that time 'conceived,' says Tickell, 'an opinion of the English genius for poetry.' Nothing is better known of Boileau than that he had an injudicious and peevish contempt of modern Latin, and therefore his profession of regard was probably the effect of his civility rather than approbation.

Three of his Latin poems are upon subjects on which perhaps he would not have ventured to have written in his own language:—*The Battle of the Pigmies and Cranes*, *The Barometer*, and *A Bowling-green*. When the matter is low or scanty, a dead language, in which nothing is mean because nothing is familiar, affords great conveniences; and by the sonorous magnificence of Roman syllables, the writer conceals penury of thought, and want of novelty, often from the reader and often from himself.

In his twenty-second year he first showed his power of English poetry by some verses addressed to Dryden; and soon afterwards published a translation of the greater part of the *Fourth Georgic* upon Bees; after which,—says Dryden, 'my latter swarm is hardly worth the hiving.' About the same time he composed the arguments prefixed to the several books of Dryden's *Virgil;* and produced an *Essay on the Georgics*, juvenile, superficial, and uninstructive, without much either of the scholar's learning or the critic's penetration. His next paper of verses contained a character of the principal English poets, inscribed to Henry Sacheverell, who was then, if not a poet, a writer of verses; as is shown by his version of a small part of Virgil's *Georgics*, published in the *Miscellanies;* and a Latin encomium on Queen Mary, in the *Musæ Anglicanæ*. These verses exhibit all the fondness of friendship; but, on one side or the other, friendship was afterwards too weak for the malignity of faction. In this poem is a very confident and discriminative character of Spenser, whose work he had then never read; so little sometimes is criticism the effect of judgment. It is necessary to inform the reader that about this time he was introduced by Congreve to Montague, then chancellor of the exchequer: Addison was then learning the trade of a courtier, and subjoined Montague as a poetical name to those of Cowley and of Dryden. By the influence of Mr. Montague, concurring, according to Tickell, with his natural modesty, he was diverted from his original design of entering into holy orders. Montague alleged the corruption of men who engaged in civil employments without liberal education; and declared that, though he was represented as an enemy to the church, he would never do it any injury but by withholding Addison from it.

Soon after (1695) he wrote a poem to King William, with a riming introduction addressed to Lord Somers. King William had no regard to elegance or literature; his study was only war; yet by a choice of ministers, whose disposition was very different from his own, he procured, without intention, a very liberal patronage to poetry. Addison was caressed both by Somers and Montague.

In 1697 appeared his Latin verses on the Peace of Ryswick, which he dedicated to Montague, and which was afterwards called, by Smith, 'the best Latin poem since the *Æneid*.' Praise must not be too rigorously examined; but the performance cannot be denied to be vigorous and elegant. Having yet no public employment, he obtained (in 1699) a pension of three hundred pounds a year, that he might be enabled to travel. He stayed a year at Blois, probably to learn the French language; and then proceeded in his journey to Italy, which he surveyed with the eyes of a poet. While he was traveling at leisure, he was far from being idle: for he not only collected his observations on the country, but found time to write his *Dialogues on Medals*, and four acts of *Cato*. Such, at least, is the relation of Tickell. Perhaps he only collected his materials and formed his plan. Whatever were his other employments in Italy, he there wrote the letter to Lord Halifax which is justly considered as the most elegant, if not the most sublime, of his poetical productions. But in about two years he found it necessary to hasten home; being, as Swift informs us, distressed by indigence, and compelled to become the tutor of a traveling squire, because his pension was not remitted.

At his return he published his Travels, with a dedication to Lord Somers. As his stay in foreign countries was short, his observations are such as might be supplied by a hasty view, and consist chiefly in comparisons of the present face of the country with the descriptions left us by the Roman poets, from whom he made preparatory collections, though he might have spared the trouble had he known that such collections had been made twice before by Italian authors. The most amusing passage of his book is his account of the minute republic of San Marino; of many parts it is not a very severe censure to say that they might have been written at home. His elegance of language, and variegation of prose and verse, however, gain upon the reader; and the book, though awhile neglected, became in time so much the favorite of the public that before it was reprinted it rose to five times its price.

When he returned to England (in 1702), with a meanness of appearance which gave testimony of the difficulties to which he had been reduced, he found his old patrons out of power, and was therefore, for a time, at full leisure for the cultivation of his mind; and a mind so cultivated gives reason to believe that little time was lost. But he remained not long neglected or useless. The victory at Blenheim (1704) spread triumph and confidence over the nation; and Lord Godolphin, lamenting to Lord Halifax that it had not been celebrated in a manner equal to the subject, desired him to propose it to some better poet. Halifax told him that there was no encouragement for genius; that worthless men were unprofitably enriched with public money, without any care to find or employ those whose appearance might do honor to their country. To this Godolphin replied that such abuses should in time be rectified; and that, if a man could be found capable of the task then proposed, he should not want an ample recompense. Halifax then named Addison, but required that the treasurer should apply to him in his own person. Godolphin sent the message by Mr. Boyle, afterwards Lord Carlton; and Addison, having undertaken the work, communicated it to the treasury while it was yet advanced no farther than the simile of the angel, and was immediately rewarded by succeeding Mr. Locke in the place of commissioner of appeals.

In the following year he was at Hanover with Lord Halifax: and the year after he was made under secretary of state, first to Sir Charles Hedges, and in a few months more to the Earl of Sunderland. About this time the prevalent taste for Italian operas inclined him to try what would be the effect of a musical drama in our own language. He therefore wrote the opera of *Rosamond*, which, when exhibited on the stage, was either hissed or neglected; but, trusting that the readers would do him more justice, he published it with an inscription to the Duchess of Marlborough—a woman without skill, or pretensions to skill, in poetry or literature. His dedication was therefore an instance of servile absurdity, to be exceeded only by Joshua Barnes's dedication of a Greek *Anacreon* to the Duke. His reputation had been somewhat advanced by *The Tender Husband*, a comedy which Steele dedicated to him, with a confession that he owed to him several of the most successful scenes. To this play Addison supplied a prologue.

When the Marquis of Wharton was appointed lord lieutenant of Ireland, Addison attended him as his secretary; and was made keeper of the records, in Birmingham's tower, with a salary of three hundred pounds a year. The office was little more than nominal, and the salary was agumented for his accommodation. Interest and faction allow little to the operation of particular dispositions or private opinions. Two men of personal characters more opposite than those of Wharton and Addison could not easily be brought together. Wharton was impious, profligate, and shameless; without regard, or appearance of regard, to right and wrong. Whatever is contrary to this may be said of Addison; but as agents of a party they were connected, and how they adjusted their other sentiments we cannot know.

Addison, must, however, not be too hastily condemned. It is not necessary to refuse benefits from a bad man when the acceptance implies no approbation of his crimes; nor has the subordinate officer any obligation to examine the opinions or conduct of those under whom he acts, except that he may not be made the instrument of wickedness. It is reasonable to suppose that Addison counteracted, as far as he was able, the malignant and blasting influence of the lieutenant; and that at least by his intervention some good was done, and some mischief prevented. When he was in office he made a law to himself, as Swift has recorded, never to remit his regular fees in civility to his friends: 'for,' said he, 'I may have a hundred friends; and if my fee be two guineas, I shall, by relinquishing my right, lose two hundred guineas, and no friend gain more than two; there is therefore no proportion between the good imparted and the evil suffered.' He was in Ireland when Steele, without any communication of his design, began the publication of *The Tatler;* but he was not long concealed; by inserting a remark on Virgil which Addison had given him he discovered himself. It is, indeed, not easy for any man to write upon literature or common life so as not to make himself known to those with whom he familiarly converses, and who are acquainted with his track of study, his favorite topic, his peculiar notions, and his habitual phrases.

If Steele desired to write in secret, he was not lucky; a single month detected him. His first *Tatler* was published April 22 (1709); and Addison's contribution appeared May 26. Tickell observes that *The Tatler* began and was concluded without his concurrence. This is doubtless literally true; but the work did not suffer much by his unconsciousness of its commencement, or his absence at its cessation; for he continued his assistance to December 23, and the paper stopped on January 2, 1710-11. He did not distinguish his pieces by any signature; and I know not whether his name was not kept secret till the papers were collected into volumes.

To *The Tatler*, in about two months, succeeded *The Spectator:* a series of essays of the same kind, but written with less levity, upon a more regular plan, and published daily. Such an undertaking showed the writers not to distrust their own copiousness of materials or facility of composition, and their performance justified their confidence. They found, however, in their progress many auxiliaries. To attempt a single paper was no terrifying labor; many pieces were offered, and many were received.

Addison had enough of the zeal of party; but Steele had at that time almost nothing else. *The Spectator*, in one of the first papers, showed the political tenets of its authors; but a resolution was soon taken of courting general approbation by general topics, and subjects on which faction had produced no diversity of sentiments; such as literature, morality, and familiar life. To this practice they adhered with few deviations. The ardor of Steele once broke out in praise of Marlborough; and when Dr. Fleetwood prefixed to some sermons a preface overflowing with whiggish opinions, that it might be read by the Queen, it was reprinted in *The Spectator*.

To teach the minuter decencies and inferior duties, to regulate the practice of daily conversation, to correct those depravities which are rather ridiculous than criminal, and remove those grievances which, if they produce no lasting calamities, impress hourly vexation, was first attempted by Casa in his book of *Manners*, and Castiglione in his *Courtier;* two books yet celebrated in Italy for purity and elegance, and which, if they are now less read, are neglected only because they have effected that reformation which their authors intended, and their precepts now are no longer wanted. Their usefulness to the age in which they were written is sufficiently attested by the translations which almost all the nations of Europe were in haste to obtain.

This species of instruction was continued, and perhaps advanced, by the French; among whom La Bruyère's *Manners of the Age* (though, as Boileau remarked, it is written without connection) certainly deserves great praise for liveliness of description and justness of observation.

Before *The Tatler* and *Spectator*, if the writers for the theater are excepted, England had no masters of common life. No writers had yet undertaken to reform either the savageness of neglect, or the impertinence of civility; to show when to speak, or to be silent; how to refuse, or how to comply. We had many books to teach us our more important duties, and to settle opinions in philosophy or politics; but an *arbiter elegantiarum*, a judge of propriety, was yet wanting, who should survey the track of daily conversation, and free it from thorns and prickles, which tease the passer, though they do not wound him. For this purpose nothing is so proper as the frequent publication of short papers, which we read, not as study, but amusement. If the subject be slight, the treatise likewise is short. The busy may find time, and the idle may find patience. This mode of conveying cheap and easy knowledge began among us in the civil war, when it was much the interest of either party to raise and fix the prejudices of the people. At that time appeared *Mercurius Aulicus, Mercurius Rusticus*, and *Mercurius Civicus*. It is said that when any title grew popular, it was stolen by the antagonist, who by this stratagem conveyed his notions to those who would not have received him had he not worn the appearance of a friend. The tumult of those unhappy days left scarcely any man leisure to treasure up occasional compositions; and so much were they neglected that a complete collection is nowhere to be found.

These Mercuries were succeeded by L'Estrange's *Observator;* and that by Lesley's *Rehearsal*, and perhaps by others; but hitherto nothing had been conveyed to the people, in this commodious manner, but controversy relating to the church or state; of which they taught many to talk, whom they could not teach to judge.

It has been suggested that the Royal Society was instituted soon after the Restoration to divert the attention of the people from public discontent. *The Tatler* and *Spectator* had the same tendency; they were published at a time when two parties—loud, restless, and violent, each with plausible declarations, and each perhaps without any distinct termination of its views—were agitating the nation; to minds heated with political contest they supplied cooler and more inoffensive reflections; and it is said by Addison, in a subsequent work, that they had a perceptible influence upon the conversation of that time, and taught the frolic and the gay to unite merriment with decency—an effect which they can never wholly lose while they continue to be among the first books by which both sexes are initiated in the elegances of knowledge.

The Tatler and *Spectator* adjusted, like Casa, the unsettled practice of daily intercourse by propriety and politeness; and, like La Bruyère, exhibited the characters and manners of the age. The personages introduced in these papers were not merely ideal; they were then known, and conspicuous in various stations. Of *The Tatler* that is told by Steele in his last paper; and of *The Spectator* by Budgell in the preface to *Theophrastus*, a book which Addison has recommended, and which he was suspected to have revised, if he did not write it. Of those portraits which may be supposed to be sometimes embellished, and sometimes aggravated, the originals are now partly known, and partly forgotten. But to say that they united the plans of two or three eminent writers, is to give them but a small part of their due praise; they superadded literature and criticism, and sometimes towered far above their predecessors; and taught, with great justness of argument and dignity of language, the most important duties and sublime truths. All these topics were happily varied with elegant fictions and refined allegories, and illuminated with different changes of style and felicities of invention.

It is recorded by Budgell, that of the characters feigned or exhibited in *The Spectator*, the favorite of Addison was Sir Roger de Coverley, of whom he had formed a very delicate and discriminated idea, which he would not suffer to be violated; and therefore when Steele had shown him innocently picking up a girl in the Temple, and taking her to a tavern, he drew upon himself so much of his friend's indignation that he was forced to appease him by a promise of forbearing Sir Roger for the time to come.

The reason which induced Cervantes to bring his hero to the grave, *para mi sola nacio Don Quixote, y yo para el* [for me alone was Don Quixote born, and I for him], made Addison declare, with undue vehemence of expression, that he would kill Sir Roger; being of opinion that they were born for one another, and that any other hand would do him wrong.

It may be doubted whether Addison ever filled up his original delineation. He describes his knight as having his imagination somewhat warped; but of this perversion he has made very little use. The irregularities in Sir Roger's conduct seem not so much the effects of a mind deviating from the beaten track of life, by the perpetual pressure of some overwhelming idea, as of habitual rusticity, and that negligence which solitary grandeur naturally generates. The variable weather of the mind, the flying vapors of incipient madness, which from time to time cloud reason without eclipsing it, it requires so much nicety to exhibit that Addison seems to have been deterred from prosecuting his own design.

To Sir Roger, who, as a country gentleman, appears to be a Tory, or, as it is gently expressed, an adherent to the landed interest, is opposed Sir Andrew Freeport, a new man, a wealthy merchant, zealous for the moneyed interest, and a Whig. Of this contrariety of opinions, it is probable more consequences were at first intended than could be produced when the resolution was taken to exclude party from the paper. Sir Andrew does but little, and that little seems not to have pleased Addison, who, when he dismissed him from the club, changed his opinions. Steele had made him, in the true spirit of unfeeling commerce, declare that he 'would not build an hospital for idle people'; but at last he buys land, settles in the country, and builds, not a manufactory, but an hospital for twelve old husbandmen —for men with whom a merchant has little acquaintance, and whom he commonly considers with little kindness.

Of essays thus elegant, thus instructive, and thus commodiously distributed, it is natural to suppose the approbation general, and the sale numerous. I once heard it observed that the sale may be calculated by the product of the tax, related in the last number to produce more than twenty pounds a week, and therefore stated at one-and-twenty pounds, or three pounds ten shillings a day: this, at a halfpenny a paper, will give sixteen hundred and eighty for the daily number. This sale is not great; yet this, if Swift be credited, was likely to grow less; for he declares that *The Spectator*, whom he ridicules for his endless mention of the *fair sex*, had before his recess wearied his readers.

The next year (1713), in which *Cato* came upon the stage, was the grand climacteric of Addison's reputation. Upon the death of Cato he had, as is said, planned a tragedy in the time of his travels, and had for several years the four first acts finished, which were shown to such as were likely to spread their admiration. They were seen by Pope and by Cibber, who relates that Steele, when he took back the copy, told him, in the despicable cant of literary modesty, that, whatever spirit his friend had shown in the composition, he doubted whether he would have courage sufficient to expose it to the censure of a British audience. The time, however, was now come when those who affected to think liberty in danger affected likewise to think that a stage-play might preserve it; and Addison was importuned, in the name of the tutelary deities of Britain, to show his courage and his zeal by finishing his design.

To resume his work he seemed perversely and unaccountably unwilling; and by a request, which perhaps he wished to be denied, desired Mr. Hughes to add a fifth act. Hughes supposed him serious; and, undertaking the supplement, brought in a few days some scenes for his examination; but he had in the meantime gone to work himself, and produced half an act, which he afterwards completed, but with brevity irregularly disproportionate to the foregoing parts, like a task performed with reluctance and hurried to its conclusion.

It may yet be doubted whether *Cato* was made public by any change of the author's purpose; for Dennis charged him with raising prejudices in his own favor by false positions of preparatory criticism, and with 'poisoning the town' by contradicting in *The Spectator* the established rule of poetical justice, because his own hero, with all his virtues, was to fall before a tyrant. The fact is certain; the motives we must guess.

Addison was, I believe, sufficiently disposed to bar all avenues against all danger. When

Pope brought him the prologue, which is properly accommodated to the play, there were these words, 'Britains, arise! be worth like this approved'; meaning nothing more than—Britons, erect and exalt yourselves to the approbation of public virtue. Addison was frighted, lest he should be thought a promoter of insurrection, and the line was liquidated to 'Britons, attend.'

Now 'heavily in clouds came on the day, the great, the important day,' when Addison was to stand the hazard of the theater. That there might, however, be left as little hazard as was possible, on the first night Steele, as himself relates, undertook to pack an audience. 'This,' says Pope, 'had been tried for the first time in favor of *The Distressed Mother*; and was now, with more efficacy, practiced for *Cato*.' The danger was soon over. The whole nation was at that time on fire with faction. The Whigs applauded every line in which liberty was mentioned, as a satire on the Tories; and the Tories echoed every clap, to show that the satire was unfelt. The story of Bolingbroke is well known; he called Booth to his box, and gave him fifty guineas for defending the cause of liberty so well against a perpetual dictator. 'The Whigs,' says Pope, 'design a second present, when they can accompany it with as good a sentence.'

The play, supported thus by the emulation of factious praise, was acted night after night for a longer time than, I believe, the public had allowed to any drama before; and the author, as Mrs. Porter long afterwards related, wandered through the whole exhibition behind the scenes with restless and unappeasable solicitude. When it was printed, notice was given that the Queen would be pleased if it was dedicated to her; 'but as he had designed that compliment elsewhere, he found himself obliged,' says Tickell, 'by his duty on the one hand, and his honor on the other, to send it into the world without any dedication.'

Human happiness has always its abatements; the brightest sunshine of success is not without a cloud. No sooner was *Cato* offered to the reader than it was attacked by the acute malignity of Dennis with all the violence of angry criticism. Dennis, though equally zealous, and probably by his temper more furious than Addison, for what they called liberty, and though a flatterer of the Whig Ministry, could not sit quiet at a successful play; but was eager to tell friends and enemies that they had misplaced their admirations. The world was too stubborn for instruction; with the fate of the censurer of Corneille's *Cid*, his animadversions showed his anger without effect, and *Cato* continued to be praised.

Pope had now an opportunity of courting the friendship of Addison by vilifying his old enemy, and could give resentment its full play without appearing to revenge himself. He therefore published *A Narrative of the Madness of John Dennis:* a performance which left the objections to the play in their full force, and therefore discovered more desire of vexing the critic than of defending the poet.

Addison, who was no stranger to the world, probably saw the selfishness of Pope's friendship; and, resolving that he should have the consequences of his officiousness to himself, informed Dennis by Steele that he was sorry for the insult; and that, whenever he should think fit to answer his remarks, he would do it in a manner to which nothing could be objected.

The greatest weakness of the play is in the scenes of love, which are said by Pope to have been added to the original plan upon a subsequent review, in compliance with the popular practice of the stage. Such an authority it is hard to reject; yet the love is so intimately mingled with the whole action that it cannot easily be thought extrinsic and adventitious; for if it were taken away, what would be left? Or how were the four acts filled in the first draft? At the publication the wits seemed proud to pay their attendance with encomiastic verses. The best are from an unknown hand, which will perhaps lose somewhat of their praise when the author is known to be Jeffreys.

Cato had yet other honors. It was censured as a party-play by a scholar of Oxford; and defended in a favorable examination by Dr. Sewel. It was translated by Salvini into Italian, and acted at Florence; and by the Jesuits of St. Omer's into Latin, and played by their pupils. Of this version a copy was sent to Mr. Addison: it is to be wished that it could be found, for the sake of comparing their version of the soliloquy with that of Bland.

A tragedy was written on the same subject by Des Champs, a French poet, which was translated with a criticism on the English play. But the translator and the critic are now forgotten. Dennis lived on unanswered, and therefore little read. Addison knew the policy of literature too well to make his enemy important by drawing the attention of the public upon a criticism which, though sometimes intemperate, was often irrefragable.

While *Cato* was upon the stage, another daily paper, called *The Guardian*, was published by Steele. To this Addison gave great assistance, whether occasionally or by previous engagement is not known. The character of Guardian was too narrow and too serious: it might properly enough admit both the duties and the decencies of life, but seemed not to include literary speculations, and was in some degree violated by merriment and burlesque. What had the Guardian of the Lizards to do with clubs of tall or of little men, with nests of ants, or with Strada's prolusions? Of this paper nothing is necessary to be said but that it found many contributors, and that it was a continuation of *The Spectator*, with the same elegance and the same variety, till some unlucky sparkle from a Tory paper set Steele's politics on fire, and wit at once blazed into faction. He was soon too hot for neutral topics, and quitted *The Guardian* to write *The Englishman*.

The papers of Addison are marked in *The Spectator* by one of the letters in the name of Clio, and in *The Guardian* by a hand; whether it was, as Tickell pretends to think, that he was unwilling to usurp the praise of others, or as Steele, with far greater likelihood, insinuates, that he could not without discontent impart to others any of his own. I have heard that his avidity did not satisfy itself with the air of renown, but that with great eagerness he laid hold on his proportion of the profits.

Many of these papers were written with powers truly comic, with nice discrimination of characters, and accurate observation of natural or accidental deviations from propriety; but it was not supposed that he had tried a comedy on the stage, till Steele after his death declared him the author of *The Drummer*. This, however, Steele did not know to be true by any direct testimony, for when Addison put the play into his hands, he only told him it was the work of a 'gentleman in the company,' and when it was received, as is confessed, with cold disapprobation, he was probably less willing to claim it. Tickell omitted it in his collection; but the testimony of Steele, and the total silence of any other claimant, has determined the public to assign it to Addison, and it is now printed with his other poetry. Steele carried *The Drummer* to the play-house, and afterwards to the press, and sold the copy for fifty guineas.

To the opinion of Steele may be added the proof supplied by the play itself, of which the characters are such as Addison would have delineated, and the tendency such as Addison would have promoted. That it should have been ill received would raise wonder, did we not daily see the capricious distribution of theatrical praise.

He was not all this time an indifferent spectator of public affairs. He wrote, as different exigences required (in 1707), *The present State of the War, and the Necessity of an Augmentation;* which, however judicious, being written on temporary topics, and exhibiting no peculiar powers, laid hold on no attention, and has naturally sunk by its own weight into neglect. This cannot be said of the few papers entitled *The Whig Examiner*, in which is employed all the force of gay malevolence and humorous satire. Of this paper, which just appeared and expired, Swift remarks, with exultation, that 'it is now down among the dead men.' He might well rejoice at the death of that which he could not have killed. Every reader of every party, since personal malice is past, and the papers which once inflamed the nation are read only as effusions of wit, must wish for more of the *Whig Examiners;* for on no occasion was the genius of Addison more vigorously exerted, and on none did the superiority of his powers more evidently appear. His *Trial of Count Tariff*, written to expose the treaty of commerce with France, lived no longer than the question that produced it.

Not long afterwards an attempt was made to revive *The Spectator*, at a time indeed by no means favorable to literature, when the succession of a new family to the throne filled the nation with anxiety, discord, and confusion; and either the turbulence of the times, or the satiety of the readers, put a stop to the publication after an experiment of eighty numbers, which were afterwards collected into an eighth volume, perhaps more valuable than any of those that went before it. Addison produced more than a fourth part; and the other contributors are by no means unworthy of appearing as his associates. The time that had passed during the suspension of *The Spectator*, though it had not lessened his power of humor, seems to have increased his disposition to seriousness: the proportion of his religious to his comic papers is greater than in the former series.

The Spectator, from its re-commencement, was published only three times a week; and no discriminative marks were added to the papers. To Addison, Tickell has ascribed twenty-three. *The Spectator* had many contributors; and Steele, whose negligence kept him always in a hurry, when it was his turn to furnish a paper, called loudly for the letters, of which Addison, whose materials were more, made little use—having recourse to sketches and hints, the product of his former studies, which he now reviewed and completed: among these are named by Tickell the Essays on Wit, those on the Pleasures of the Imagination, and the Criticism on Milton.

When the House of Hanover took possession of the throne, it was reasonable to expect that the zeal of Addison would be suitably rewarded. Before the arrival of King George, he was made secretary to the Regency, and was required by his office to send notice to Hanover that the Queen was dead, and that the throne was vacant. To do this would not have been difficult to any man but Addison, who was so overwhelmed with the greatness of the event, and so distracted by choice of expression, that the lords, who could not wait for the niceties of criticism, called Mr. Southwell, a clerk in the House, and ordered him to despatch the message. Southwell readily told what was necessary in the common style of business, and valued himself upon having done what was too hard for Addison. He was better qualified for *The Freeholder*, a paper which he published twice a week, from December 23, 1715, to the middle of the next year. This was undertaken in defense of the established Government, sometimes with argument, and sometimes with mirth. In argument he had many equals; but his humor was singular and matchless. Bigotry itself must be delighted with the Tory Fox-hunter. There are, however, some strokes less elegant and less decent; such as the *Pretender's Journal*, in which one topic of ridicule is his poverty. This mode of abuse had been employed by Milton against King Charles II.

Jacoboei
Centum exulantis viscera marsuppi regis.

[A hundred Jacobuses, dregs of the purse of an exiled king.]

And Oldmixon delights to tell of some alderman of London that he had more money than the exiled princes; but that which might be expected from Milton's savageness, or Oldmixon's meanness, was not suitable to the delicacy of Addison.

Steele thought the humor of *The Freeholder* too nice and gentle for such noisy times, and is reported to have said that the ministry made use of a lute, when they should have called for a trumpet.

This year (1716) he married the Countess Dowager of Warwick, whom he had solicited by a very long and anxious courtship, perhaps with behavior not very unlike that of Sir Roger to his disdainful widow; and who, I am afraid, diverted herself often by playing with his passion. He is said to have first known her by becoming tutor to her son. 'He formed,' said Tonson, 'the design of getting that lady from the time when he was first recommended into the family.' In what part of his life he obtained the recommendation, or how long, and in what manner he lived in the family, I know not. His advances at first, were certainly timorous, but grew bolder as his reputation and influence increased; till at last the lady was persuaded to marry him, on terms much like those on which a Turkish princess is espoused, to whom the Sultan is reported to pronounce, 'Daughter, I give thee this man for thy slave.' The marriage, if uncontradicted report can be credited, made no addition to his happiness; it neither found them nor made them equal. She always remembered her own rank, and thought herself entitled to treat with very little ceremony the tutor of her son. Rowe's ballad of *The Despairing Shepherd* is said to have been written, either before or after marriage, upon this memorable pair; and it is certain that Addison has left behind him no encouragement for ambitious love.

The year after (1717) he rose to his highest elevation, being made secretary of state. For this employment he might be justly supposed qualified by long practice of business, and by his regular ascent through other offices; but expectation is often disappointed; it is universally confessed that he was unequal to the duties of his place. In the House of Commons he could not speak, and therefore was useless to the defense of the government. 'In the office,' says Pope, 'he could not issue an order without losing his time in quest of fine expressions.' What he gained in rank he lost in credit; and finding by experience his own inability, was forced to solicit his dismission, with a pension of fifteen hundred pounds a year. His friends palliated this relinquishment, of which both friends and enemies knew the true reason, with an account of declining health, and the necessity of recess and quiet. He now returned to his vocation, and began to plan literary occupations for his future life. He purposed a tragedy on the death of Socrates, a story of which, as Tickell remarks, the basis is narrow, and to which I know not how love could have been appended. There would, however, have been no want either of virtue in the sentiments, or elegance in the language. He engaged in a nobler work, a *Defense of the Christian Religion*, of which part was published after his death; and he designed to have made a new poetical version of the Psalms.

These pious compositions Pope imputed to a selfish motive, upon the credit, as he owns, of Tonson; who, having quarreled with Addison, and not loving him, said that when he laid down the secretary's office he intended to take orders and obtain a bishopric; 'for,' said he, 'I always thought him a priest in his heart.'

That Pope should have thought this conjecture of Tonson worth remembrance, is a proof—but indeed, so far as I have found, the only proof—that he retained some malignity from their ancient rivalry. Tonson pretended but to guess it; no other mortal ever suspected it; and Pope might have reflected that a man who had been secretary of state in the ministry of Sunderland knew a nearer way to a bishopric than by defending religion or translating the Psalms.

It is related that he had once a design to make an *English Dictionary*, and that he considered Dr. Tillotson as the writer of highest authority. There was formerly sent to me by Mr. Locker, clerk of the Leathersellers' Company, who was eminent for curiosity and literature, a collection of examples selected from Tillotson's works, as Locker said, by Addison. It came too late to be of use, so I inspected it but slightly, and remember it indistinctly. I thought the passages too short. Addison, however, did not conclude his life in peaceful studies, but relapsed, when he was near his end, to a political dispute.

It so happened that (1718-19) a controversy was agitated with great vehemence between those friends of long continuance, Addison and Steele. It may be asked, in the language of Homer, what power or what cause could set them at variance. The subject of their dispute was of great importance. The Earl of Sunderland proposed an act called The Peerage Bill; by which the number of peers should be fixed, and the king restrained from any new creation of nobility, unless when an old family should be extinct. To this the lords would naturally agree; and the king, who was yet little acquainted with his own prerogative, and, as is now well known, almost indifferent to the possessions of the crown, had been persuaded to consent. The only difficulty was found among the commons, who were not likely to approve the perpetual exclusion of themselves and their posterity. The bill, therefore, was eagerly opposed, and, among others, by Sir Robert Walpole, whose speech was published.

The lords might think their dignity diminished by improper advancements, and particularly by the introduction of twelve new peers at once, to produce a majority of Tories in the last reign: an act of authority violent enough, yet certainly legal, and by no means to be compared with that contempt of national right with which some time afterwards, by the instigation of whiggism, the commons, chosen by the people for three years, chose themselves for seven. But, whatever might be the disposition of the lords, the people had no wish to increase their power. The tendency of the bill, as Steele observed in a letter to the Earl of Oxford, was to introduce an aristocracy: for a majority in the House of Lords, so limited, would have been despotic and irresistible.

To prevent this subversion of the ancient establishment, Steele, whose pen readily seconded his political passions, endeavored to alarm the nation by a pamphlet called *The Plebeian*. To this an answer was published by Addison, under the title of *The Old Whig*, in which it is not discovered that Steele was then known to be the advocate for the commons. Steele replied by a second *Plebeian*; and, whether by ignorance or by courtesy, confined himself to his question, without any personal notice of his opponent. Nothing hitherto was committed against the laws of friendship or proprieties of decency; but controvertists cannot long retain their kindness for each other. *The Old Whig* answered *The Plebeian*, and could not forbear some contempt of 'little Dicky, whose trade it was to write pamphlets.' Dicky, however, did not lose his settled veneration for his friend, but contented himself with quoting some lines of *Cato*, which were at once detection and reproof. The bill was laid aside during that session, and Addison died before the next, in which its commitment was rejected by two hundred and sixty-five to one hundred and seventy-seven.

Every reader surely must regret that these two illustrious friends, after so many years passed in confidence and endearment, in unity of interest, conformity of opinion, and fellowship of study, should finally part in acrimonious opposition. Such a controversy was *bellum plusquam civile* [worse than civil war], as Lucan expresses it. Why could not faction find other advocates? But among the uncertainties of the human state, we are doomed to number the instability of friendship. Of this dispute I have little knowledge but from the *Biographia Britannica*. *The Old Whig* is not inserted in Addison's works; nor is it mentioned by Tickell in his *Life;* why it was omitted, the biographers doubtless give the true reason: the fact was too recent, and those who had been heated in the contention were not yet cool.

The necessity of complying with times, and of sparing persons, is the great impediment of biography. History may be formed from permanent monuments and records; but lives can only be written from personal knowledge, which is growing every day less, and in a short time is lost for ever. What is known can seldom be immediately told; and when it might be told, it is no longer known. The delicate features of the mind, the nice discriminations of character, and the minute peculiarities of conduct, are soon obliterated; and it is surely better that caprice, obstinacy, frolic, and folly, however they might delight in the description, should be silently forgotten, than that, by wanton merriment and unseasonable detection, a pang should be given to a widow, a daughter, a brother, or a friend. As the process of these narratives is now bringing me among my contemporaries, I begin to feel myself 'walking upon ashes under which the fire is not extinguished,' and coming to the time of which it will be proper rather to say 'nothing that is false, than all that is true.'

The end of this useful life was now approaching. Addison had for some time been oppressed by shortness of breath, which was now aggravated by a dropsy; and, finding his danger pressing, he prepared to die comfortably to his own precepts and professions. During this lingering decay, he sent, as Pope relates, a message by the Earl of Warwick to Mr. Gay, desiring to see him. Gay, who had not visited him for some time before, obeyed the summons, and found himself received with great kindness. The purpose for which the interview had been solicited was then discovered. Addison told him that he had injured him; but that, if he recovered, he would recompense him. What the injury was he did not explain, nor did Gay ever know; but supposed that some preferment designed for him had, by Addison's intervention, been withheld.

Lord Warwick was a young man, of very irregular life, and perhaps of loose opinions. Addison, for whom he did not want respect, had very diligently endeavored to reclaim him, but his arguments and expostulations had no effect. One experiment, however, remained to be tried; when he found his life near its end, he directed the young lord to be called, and when he desired with great tenderness to hear his last injunctions, told him, 'I have sent for you that you may see how a Christian can die.' What effect this awful scene had on the earl, I know not; he likewise died himself in a short time.

In Tickell's excellent Elegy on his friend are these lines:—

> He taught us how to live; and, oh! too high
> The price of knowledge, taught us how to die—

in which he alludes, as he told Dr. Young, to this moving interview.

Having given directions to Mr. Tickell for the publication of his works, and dedicated them on his death-bed to his friend Mr. Craggs, he died June 17, 1719, at Holland House, leaving no child but a daughter.

Of his virtue it is a sufficient testimony that the resentment of party has transmitted no charge of any crime. He was not one of those who are praised only after death; for his merit was so generally acknowledged that Swift, having observed that his election passed without a contest, adds that if he had proposed himself for king he would hardly have been refused. His zeal for his party did not extinguish his kindness for the merit of his opponents; when he was secretary in Ireland, he refused to intermit his acquaintance with Swift. Of his habits or external manners, nothing is so often mentioned as that timorous or sullen taciturnity, which his friends called modesty by too mild a name. Steele mentions with great tenderness 'that remarkable bashfulness which is a cloak that hides and muffles merit'; and tells us that his abilities were covered only by modesty, which doubles the beauties which are seen, and gives credit and esteem to all that are concealed. Chesterfield affirms that 'Addison was the most timorous and awkward man that he ever saw.' And Addison, speaking of his own deficience in conversation used to say of himself that, with respect to intellectual wealth, 'he could draw bills for a thousand pounds, though he had not a guinea in his pocket.' That he wanted current coin for ready payment, and by that want was often obstructed and distressed; that he was oppressed by an improper and ungraceful timidity, every testimony concurs to prove; but Chesterfield's representation is doubtless hyperbolical. That man cannot be supposed very unexpert in the arts of conversation and practice of life who, without fortune or alliance, by his usefulness and dexterity became secretary of state, and who died at forty-seven, after having not only stood long in the highest rank of wit and literature, but filled one of the most important offices of state.

The time in which he lived had reason to lament his obstinacy of silence; 'for he was,' says Steele, 'above all men in that talent called humor, and enjoyed it in such perfection that I have often reflected, after a night spent with him apart from all the world, that I had had the pleasure of conversing with an intimate acquaintance of Terence and Catullus, who had all their wit and nature, heightened with humor more exquisite and delightful than any other man ever possessed.' This is the fondness of a friend; let us hear what is told us by a rival. 'Addison's conversation,' says Pope, 'had something in it more charming than I have found in any other man. But this was only when familiar: before strangers, or perhaps a single stranger, he preserved his dignity by a stiff silence.' This modesty was by no means inconsistent with a very high opinion of his own merit. He demanded to be the first name in modern wit; and, with Steele to echo him, used to depreciate Dryden, whom Pope and Congreve defended against them. There is no reason to doubt that he suffered too much pain from the prevalence of Pope's poetical reputation; nor is it without strong reason suspected that by some disingenuous acts he endeavored to obstruct it; Pope was not the only man whom he insidiously injured, though the only man of whom he could be afraid. His own powers were such as might have satisfied him with conscious excellence. Of very extensive learning he has indeed given no proofs. He seems to have had small acquaintance with the sciences, and to have read little except Latin and French; but of the Latin poets his *Dialogues on Medals* show that he had perused the works with great diligence and skill. The abundance of his own mind left him little need of adventitious sentiments; his wit always could suggest what the occasion demanded. He had read with critical eyes the important volume of human life, and knew the heart of man, from the depths of stratagem to the surface of affectation. What he knew he could easily communicate. 'This,' says Steele, 'was particular in this writer—that when he had taken his resolution, or made his plan for what he designed to write, he would walk about a room and dictate it into language with as much freedom and ease as any one could write it down, and attend to the coherence and grammar of what he dictated.'

Pope, who can be less suspected of favoring his memory, declares that he wrote very fluently, but was slow and scrupulous in correcting; that many of his *Spectators* were written very fast, and sent immediately to the press; and that it seemed to be for his advantage not to have time for much revisal. 'He would alter,' says Pope, 'anything to please his friends before publication, but would not re-touch his pieces afterwards; and I believe not one word in *Cato* to which I made an objection was suffered to stand.'

The last line of *Cato* is Pope's, having been originally written—

And oh! 't was this that ended Cato's life.

Pope might have made more objections to the six concluding lines. In the first couplet the words 'from hence' are improper; and the second line is taken from Dryden's Virgil. Of the next couplet, the first verse, being included in the second, is therefore useless; and in the third Discord is made to produce Strife.

Of the course of Addison's familiar day, before his marriage, Pope has given a detail. He had in the house with him Budgell, and perhaps Philips. His chief companions were Steele, Budgell, Philips, Carey, Davenant, and Colonel Brett. With one or other of these he always breakfasted. He studied all morning; then dined at a tavern; and went afterwards to Button's.

Button had been a servant in the Countess of Warwick's family, who, under the patronage of Addison, kept a coffee-house on the south side of Russell Street, about two doors from Covent Garden. Here it was that the wits of that time used to assemble. It is said when Addison had suffered any vexation from the countess, he withdrew the company from Button's house. From the coffee-house he went again to a tavern, where he often sat late, and drank too much wine. In the bottle discontent seeks for comfort, cowardice for courage, and bashfulness for confidence. It is not unlikely that Addison was first seduced to excess by the manumission which he obtained from the servile timidity of his sober hours. He that feels oppression from the presence of those to whom he knows himself superior will desire to set loose his powers of conversation; and who that ever asked succors from Bacchus was able to preserve himself from being enslaved by his auxiliary?

Among those friends it was that Addison displayed the elegance of his colloquial accomplishments, which may easily be supposed such as Pope represents them. The remark of Mandeville, who, when he had passed an evening in his company, declared that he was a parson in a tye-wig, can detract little from his character; he was always reserved to strangers, and was not incited to uncommon freedom by a character like that of Mandeville.

From any minute knowledge of his familiar manners the intervention of sixty years has now debarred us. Steele once promised Congreve and the public a complete description of his character; but the promises of authors are like the vows of lovers. Steele thought no more on his design, or thought on it with anxiety that at last disgusted him, and left his friend in the hands of Tickell.

One slight lineament of his character Swift has preserved. It was his practice, when he found any man invincibly wrong, to flatter his opinions by acquiescence, and sink him yet deeper in absurdity. This artifice of mischief was admired by Stella; and Swift seems to approve her admiration. His works will supply some information. It appears from his various pictures of the world, that, with all his bashfulness, he had conversed with many distinct classes of men, had surveyed their ways with very diligent observation, and marked with great acuteness the effects of different modes of life. He was a man in whose presence nothing reprehensible was out of danger; quick in discerning whatever was wrong or ridiculous, and not unwilling to expose it. 'There are,' says Steele, 'in his writings many oblique strokes upon some of the wittiest men of the age.' His delight was more to excite merriment than detestation; and he detects follies rather than crimes. If any judgment be made from his books of his moral character, nothing will be found but purity and excellence. Knowledge of mankind, indeed, less extensive than that of Addison, will show that to write, and to live, are very different. Many who praise virtue, do no more than praise it. Yet it is reasonable to believe that Addison's professions and practice were at no great variance, since amidst that storm of faction in which most of his life was passed, though his station made him conspicuous, and his activity made him formidable, the character given him by his friends was never contradicted by his enemies. Of those with whom interest or opinion united him he had not only the esteem, but the kindness; and of others whom the violence of opposition drove against him, though he might lose the love, he retained the reverence.

It is justly observed by Tickell that he employed wit on the side of virtue and religion. He not only made the proper use of wit himself, but taught it to others; and from his time it has been generally subservient to the cause of reason and of truth. He has dissipated the prejudice that had long connected gaiety with vice, and easiness of manners with laxity of principles. He has restored virtue to its dignity, and taught innocence not to be ashamed. This is an elevation of literary character 'above all Greek, above all Roman fame.' No greater felicity can genius attain than that of having purified intellectual pleasure, separated mirth from indecency, and wit from licentiousness; of having taught a succession of writers to bring elegance and gaiety to the aid of goodness; and, if I may use expressions yet more awful, of having 'turned many to righteousness.'

* * *

As a describer of life and manners, he must be allowed to stand perhaps the first of the first rank. His humor, which, as Steele observes, is peculiar to himself, is so happily diffused as to give the grace of novelty to domestic scenes and daily occurrences. He never 'outsteps the modesty of nature,' nor raises merriment or wonder by the violation of truth. His figures never divert by distortion nor amaze by aggravation. He copies life with so much fidelity that he can be hardly said to invent; yet his exhibitions have an air so much original, that it is difficult to suppose them not merely the product of imagination.

As a teacher of wisdom, he may be confidently followed. His religion has nothing in it enthusiastic or superstitious: he appears neither weakly credulous nor wantonly skeptical; his morality is neither dangerously lax nor impracticably rigid. All the enchantment of fancy, and all the cogency of argument, are employed to recommend to the reader his real interest, the care of pleasing the author of his being. Truth is shown sometimes as the phantom of a vision; sometimes appears half-veiled in an allegory; sometimes attracts regard in the robes of fancy; and sometimes steps forth in the confidence of reason. She wears a thousand dresses, and in all is pleasing.

Mille habet ornatus, mille decenter habet.

His prose is the model of the middle style; on grave subjects not formal, on light occasions not groveling; pure without scrupulosity, and exact without apparent elaboration; always equable, and always easy, without glowing words or pointed sentences. Addison never deviates from his track to snatch a grace; he seeks no ambitious ornaments, and tries no hazardous innovations. His page is always luminous, but never blazes in unexpected splendor.

It was apparently his principal endeavor to avoid all harshness and severity of diction; he is therefore sometimes verbose in his transitions and connections, and sometimes descends too much to the language of conversation; yet if his language had been less idiomatical it might have lost somewhat of its genuine Anglicism. What he attempted, he performed; he is never feeble, and he did not wish to be energetic; he is never rapid, and he never stagnates. His sentences have neither studied amplitude nor affected brevity; his periods, though not diligently rounded, are voluble and easy. Whoever wishes to attain an English style, familiar but not coarse, and elegant but not ostentatious, must give his days and nights to the volumes of Addison.

(1781)

LETTERS

To the Right Honorable
 the Earl of Chesterfield

February 7, 1755.

MY LORD:

I HAVE lately been informed by the proprietor of *The World*, that two papers, in which my *Dictionary* is recommended to the public, were written by your lordship. To be so distinguished is an honor which, being very little accustomed to favors from the great, I know not well how to receive, or in what terms to acknowledge.

When, upon some slight encouragement, I first visited your lordship, I was overpowered, like the rest of mankind, by the enchantment of your address; and I could not forbear to wish that I might boast myself '*Le vainqueur du vainqueur de la terre*' [conqueror of the conqueror of the earth]; that I might obtain that regard for which I saw the world contending; but I found my attendance so little encouraged, that neither pride nor modesty would suffer me to continue it. When I had once addressed your lordship in public, I had exhausted all the art of pleasing which a retired and uncourtly scholar can possess. I had done all that I could; and no man is well pleased to have his all neglected, be it ever so little.

Seven years, my lord, have now passed, since I waited in your outward rooms, or was repulsed from your door; during which time I have been pushing on my work through difficulties, of which it is useless to complain, and have brought it at last to the verge of publication, without one act of assistance, one word of encouragement, or one smile of favor. Such treatment I did not expect, for I never had a patron before.

The shepherd in Virgil grew at last acquainted with Love, and found him a native of the rocks.

Is not a patron, my lord, one who looks with unconcern on a man struggling for life in the water, and, when he has reached ground, encumbers him with help? The notice which you have been pleased to take of my labors, had it been early, had been kind; but it has been delayed till I am indifferent, and cannot enjoy it; till I am solitary, and cannot impart it; till I am known, and do not want it. I hope it is no very cynical asperity not to confess obligations where no benefit has been received, or to be unwilling that the public should consider me as owing that to a patron, which Providence has enabled me to do for myself.

Having carried on my work thus far with so little obligation to any favorer of learning, I shall not be disappointed though I should conclude it, if less be possible, with less; for I have been long wakened from that dream of hope, in which I once boasted myself with so much exultation,

My Lord,
 Your Lordship's most humble,
 Most obedient servant,
 SAM. JOHNSON.

MR. JAMES MACPHERSON:

I received your foolish and impudent letter. Any violence offered me I shall do my best to repel; and what I cannot do for myself the law shall do for me. I hope I shall never be deterred from detecting what I think a cheat, by the menaces of a ruffian.

What would you have me retract? I thought your book an imposture; I think it an imposture still. For this opinion I have given my reasons to the public, which I here dare you to refute. Your rage I defy. Your abilities, since your *Homer*, are not so formidable; and what I hear of your morals, inclines me to pay regard not to what you shall say, but to what you shall prove. You may print this if you will.

SAM. JOHNSON.

(1775)

To the Reverend Dr. Taylor,
    Ashbourne, Derbyshire
DEAR SIR:

What can be the reason that I hear nothing from you? I hope nothing disables you from writing. What I have seen, and what I have felt, gives me reason to fear everything. Do not omit giving me the comfort of knowing, that after all my losses I have yet a friend left.

I want every comfort. My life is very solitary and very cheerless. Though it has pleased God wonderfully to deliver me from the dropsy, I am yet very weak, and have not passed the door since the 13th of December. I hope for some help from warm weather, which will surely come in time.

I could not have the consent of physicians to go to church yesterday; I therefore received the holy sacrament at home, in the room where I communicated with dear Mrs. Williams, a little before her death. O! my friend, the approach of death is very dreadful. I am afraid to think on that which I know I cannot avoid. It is vain to look round and round for that help which cannot be had. Yet we hope and hope, and fancy that he who has lived to-day may live to-morrow. But let us learn to derive our hope only from God.

In the meantime let us be kind to one another. I have no friend now living but you and Mr. Hector, that was the friend of my youth. Do not neglect, dear Sir,

                Yours affectionately,
                      SAM. JOHNSON.
London, Easter Monday,
    April 12, 1784.

From THE VANITY OF HUMAN WISHES

LET observation, with extensive view,
Survey mankind, from China to Peru;
Remark each anxious toil, each eager strife,
And watch the busy scenes of crowded life;
Then say how hope and fear, desire and hate, 5
O'erspread with snares the clouded maze of fate,
Where wavering man, betrayed by venturous pride,
To tread the dreary paths without a guide;
As treacherous phantoms in the mist delude,
Shuns fancied ills, or chases airy good. 10
How rarely reason guides the stubborn choice,
Rules the bold hand, or prompts the suppliant voice.
How nations sink, by darling schemes oppressed,
When vengeance listens to the fool's request.
Fate wings with every wish the afflictive dart, 15
Each gift of nature, and each grace of art,
With fatal heat impetuous courage glows,
With fatal sweetness elocution flows,
Impeachment stops the speaker's powerful breath,
And restless fire precipitates on death. 20

But scarce observed, the knowing and the bold,
Fall in the general massacre of gold;
Wide-wasting pest! that rages unconfined,
And crowds with crimes the records of mankind;
For gold his sword the hireling ruffian draws, 25
For gold the hireling judge distorts the laws;
Wealth heaped on wealth, nor truth nor safety buys,
The dangers gather as the treasures rise.

Let history tell where rival kings command,
And dubious title shakes the maddened land; 30
When statutes glean the refuse of the sword,
How much more safe the vassal than the lord;
Low skulks the hind beneath the rage of power,
And leaves the wealthy traitor in the Tower,
Untouched his cottage, and his slumbers sound, 35
Though confiscation's vultures hover round.

* * *

In full-blown dignity, see Wolsey stand,
Law in his voice, and fortune in his hand:
To him the church, the realm, their powers consign;
Through him the rays of regal bounty shine: 40
Turned by his nod the stream of honor flows,
His smile alone security bestows:
Still to new heights his restless wishes tower;
Claim leads to claim, and power advances power;
Till conquest unresisted ceased to please, 45
And rights submitted, left him none to seize.
At length his sovereign frowns—the train of state
Mark the keen glance, and watch the sign to hate:
Where'er he turns he meets a stranger's eye,
His suppliants scorn him, and his followers fly;
Now drops at once the pride of awful state 51
The golden canopy, the glittering plate,
The regal palace, the luxurious board,
The liveried army, and the menial lord.
With age, with cares, with maladies oppressed,
He seeks the refuge of monastic rest. 56
Grief aids disease, remembered folly stings,
And his last sighs reproach the faith of kings.

Speak thou, whose thoughts at humble peace repine,
Shall Wolsey's wealth, with Wolsey's end be thine? 60

Or liv'st thou now, with safer pride content,
The wisest Justice on the banks of Trent?
For why did Wolsey, near the steeps of fate,
On weak foundations raise the enormous weight?
Why, but to sink beneath misfortune's blow, 65
With louder ruin to the gulfs below.

* * *

On what foundations stands the warrior's pride,
How just his hopes, let Swedish Charles decide;
A frame of adamant, a soul of fire,
No dangers fright him, and no labors tire; 70
O'er love, o'er fear, extends his wide domain,
Unconquered lord of pleasure and of pain.
No joys to him pacific scepters yield,
War sounds the trump, he rushes to the field;
Behold surrounding kings their powers combine,
And one capitulate, and one resign; 76
Peace courts his hand, but spreads her charms in vain;
'Think nothing gained,' he cries, 'till nought remain,
On Moscow's walls till Gothic standards fly,
And all be mine beneath the polar sky.' 80
The march begins in military state,
And nations on his eye suspended wait;
Stern famine guards the solitary coast,
And winter barricades the realms of frost:
He comes, nor want, nor cold, his course delay;
Hide, blushing glory, hide Pultowa's day: 86
The vanquished hero leaves his broken bands,
And shews his miseries in distant lands;
Condemned a needy supplicant to wait,
While ladies interpose, and slaves debate. 90
But did not Chance at length the error mend?
Did no subverted empire mark his end?
Did rival monarchs give the fatal wound?
Or hostile millions press him to the ground?
His fall was destined to a barren strand, 95
A petty fortress, and a dubious hand;
He left the name at which the world grew pale,
To point a moral, or adorn a tale.

* * *

Where then shall Hope and Fear their objects find?
Must dull suspense corrupt the stagnant mind?
Must helpless man, in ignorance sedate, 101
Roll darkling down the torrent of his fate?
Must no dislike alarm, no wishes rise,
No cries invoke the mercies of the skies?
Enquirer, cease; petitions yet remain 105
Which Heaven may hear, nor deem Religion vain.
Still raise for good the supplicating voice,
But leave to Heaven the measure and the choice.
Safe in his power whose eyes discern afar
The secret ambush of a specious prayer; 110
Implore his aid, in his decisions rest,
Secure, whate'er he gives, he gives the best.
Yet, when the sense of sacred presence fires,
And strong devotion to the skies aspires,
Pour forth thy fervors for a healthful mind, 115
Obedient passions, and a will resign'd;
For love, which scarce collective man can fill;
For patience, sovereign o'er transmuted ill;
For faith, that, panting for a happier seat,
Counts death kind Nature's signal of retreat. 120
These goods for man the laws of Heav'n ordain,
These goods he grants, who grants the power to gain;
With these celestial Wisdom calms the mind,
And makes the happiness she does not find.

(1749)

JAMES BOSWELL (1740-1795)

JAMES BOSWELL was the son of a Scotch laird at Auchinleck, in Ayrshire, and was prepared for the bar at Edinburgh and Glasgow. He also studied at Utrecht, later, entered the Middle Temple in London, and, in 1786, was admitted to the English bar. He traveled widely, cultivated assiduously the society of famous men, and made literary stock of their conversation and correspondence. During one of his tours he 'gratified his curiosity much in dining with Jean Jacques Rousseau,' then an exile 'in the wilds of Neufchâtel.' At another time, he got as far as Corsica, published an *Account* on his return, and, when Paoli, the Corsican patriot, took refuge in London in 1776, became his constant guest. But the acquaintance which was particularly fruitful for English literature was that with Dr. Samuel Johnson, begun in 1763 and lasting until Johnson's death. Boswell was gifted with a high degree of curiosity, acute perception and a retentive memory, and he early formed the habit of keeping an exact journal. It is reported of him that he would 'lay down his knife and fork, and take out his tablets to record a good anecdote.' In spite of toadyism and vanity and his habit of taking notes, he had the faculty of making himself agreeable as a companion and, in 1773, Johnson got him elected to the Literary Club, thus vastly extending his opportunities for observation. The same year, the two toured the Hebrides together. During this journey Boswell allowed Johnson to read portions of his journal, and the great man acknowledged that it was 'a very exact picture of a portion of his life.' The year after Johnson's death Boswell published his *Journal of a Tour to the Hebrides with Dr. Johnson*, and during the next few years, he brought to completion the *Life of Samuel Johnson, LL.D.* (1791). This remarkable book is as vital and intimate as a masterpiece of fiction and has the additional interest that it is an authentic transcript from the life of a great and influential man of peculiar social qualities, 'the whole exhibiting,' as the title page has it, 'a view of literature and literary men in Great Britain for near half a century, during which he flourished.'

From THE LIFE OF JOHNSON

THE accession of George the Third to the throne of these kingdoms, opened a new and brighter prospect to men of literary merit, who had been honored with no mark of royal favor in the preceding reign. His present Majesty's education in this country, as well as his taste and beneficence, prompted him to be the patron of science and the arts; and early this year, Johnson having been represented to him as a very learned and good man, without any certain provision, his Majesty was pleased to grant him a pension of three hundred pounds a year. The Earl of Bute, who was then prime minister, had the honor to announce this instance of his sovereign's bounty, concerning which, many and various stories, all equally erroneous, have been propagated; maliciously representing it as a political bribe to Johnson, to desert his avowed principles, and become the tool of a government which he held to be founded in usurpation. I have taken care to have it in my power to refute them from the most authentic information. Lord Bute told me that Mr. Wed- derburne, now Lord Loughborough, was the person who first mentioned this subject to him. Lord Loughborough told me that the pension was granted to Johnson solely as the reward of his literary merit, without any stipulation whatever, or even tacit understanding that he should write for the administration. His lordship added, that he was confident the political tracts which Johnson afterwards did write, as they were entirely consonant with his own opinions, would have been written by him though no pension had been granted to him.

Mr. Thomas Sheridan and Mr. Murphy, who then lived a good deal both with him and Mr. Wedderburne, told me that they previously talked with Johnson upon this matter, and that it was perfectly understood by all parties that the pension was merely honorary. Sir Joshua Reynolds told me, that Johnson called on him after his Majesty's intention had been notified to him, and said he wished to consult his friends as to the propriety of his accepting this mark of the royal favor, after the definitions which he had given in his *Dictionary* of 'pension' and 'pensioners.' He said he should not have Sir

Joshua's answer till next day, when he would call again, and desired he might think of it. Sir Joshua answered that he was clear to give his opinion then, that there could be no objection to his receiving from the king a reward for literary merit; and that certainly the definitions in his *Dictionary* were not applicable to him. Johnson, it should seem, was satisfied, for he did not call again till he had accepted the pension, and had waited on Lord Bute to thank him. He then told Sir Joshua that Lord Bute said to him expressly, 'It is not given you for anything you are to do, but what you have done.' His lordship, he said, behaved in the handsomest manner. He repeated the words twice, that he might be sure Johnson heard them, and thus set his mind perfectly at ease.

* * *

But I shall not detain my readers longer by any words of my own, on a subject on which I am happily enabled, by the favor of the Earl of Bute, to present them with what Johnson himself wrote; his lordship having been pleased to communicate to me a copy of the following letter to his father, which does great honor both to the writer and to the noble person to whom it is addressed:

'To the Right Honorable
   the Earl of Bute
                     July 20, 1762.

'My Lord—*When the bills were yesterday delivered to me by Mr. Wedderburne, I was informed by him of the future favors which his Majesty has, by your Lordship's recommendation, been induced to intend for me.*

'*Bounty always receives part of its value from the manner in which it is bestowed; your Lordship's kindness includes every circumstance that can gratify delicacy, or enforce obligation. You have conferred favors on a man who has neither alliance nor interest, who has not merited them by services, nor courted them by officiousness; you have spared him the shame of solicitation, and the anxiety of suspense.*

'*What has been thus elegantly given, will, I hope, be not reproachfully enjoyed; I shall endeavor to give your Lordship the only recompense which generosity desires,—the gratification of finding that your benefits are not improperly bestowed. I am, my Lord,*

     '*Your Lordship's most obliged,*
 '*Most obedient, and most humble servant,*
                             'SAM JOHNSON.'

This year his friend, Sir Joshua Reynolds, paid a visit of some weeks to his native county, Devonshire, in which he was accompanied by Johnson, who was much pleased with this jaunt, and declared he had derived from it a great accession of new ideas. He was entertained at the seats of several noblemen and gentlemen in the west of England,[1] but the greatest part of this time was passed at Plymouth, where the magnificence of the navy, the ship-building and all its circumstances, afforded him a grand subject for contemplation. The commissioner of the dock-yard paid him the compliment of ordering the yacht to convey him and his friend to the Eddystone, to which they accordingly sailed. But the weather was so tempestuous that they could not land.

* * *

Sir Joshua Reynolds, to whom I was obliged for my information concerning this excursion, mentions a very characteristical anecdote of Johnson while at Plymouth. Having observed that, in consequence of the dock-yard, a new town had arisen about two miles off as a rival to the old; and knowing, from his sagacity and just observation of human nature, that it is certain, if a man hates at all, he will hate his next neighbor, he concluded that this new and rising town could not but excite the envy and jealousy of the old, in which conjecture he was very soon confirmed; he, therefore, set himself resolutely on the side of the old town, the *established* town, in which his lot was cast, considering it as a kind of duty to *stand by* it. He accordingly entered warmly into its interests, and upon every occasion talked of the *dockers*, as the inhabitants of the new town were called, as upstarts and aliens. Plymouth is very plentifully supplied with water by a river brought into it from a great distance, which is so abundant that it runs to waste in the town. The Dock, or New-town, being totally destitute of water, petitioned Plymouth that a small portion of the conduit might be permitted to go to them, and this was now under consideration. Johnson, affecting to entertain the passions of the place, was violent in opposition; and half-laughing at

[1] At one of these seats Dr. Amyat, physician in London, told me he happened to meet him. In order to amuse him till dinner should be ready, he was taken out to walk in the garden. The master of the house, thinking it proper to introduce something scientific into the conversation, addressed him thus: 'Are you a botanist, Dr. Johnson?' 'No, sir,' answered Johnson, 'I am not a botanist; and (alluding no doubt to his near-sightedness), should I wish to become a botanist, I must first turn myself into a reptile.'

himself for his pretended zeal, where he had no concern, exclaimed, 'No, no; I am against the *dockers;* I am a Plymouth man. Rogues! let them die of thirst. They shall not have a drop!'

* * *

1763: Ætat. 54. In 1763, he furnished to *The Poetical Calendar*, published by Fawkes and Woty, a character of Collins, which he afterwards ingrafted into his entire life of that admirable poet, in the collection of lives which he wrote for the body of English poetry, formed and published by the booksellers of London. His account of the melancholy depression with which Collins was severely afflicted, and which brought him to his grave, is, I think, one of the most tender and interesting passages in the whole series of his writings.

* * *

This is to me a memorable year; for in it I had the happiness to obtain the acquaintance of that extraordinary man whose memoirs I am now writing: an acquaintance which I shall ever esteem as one of the most fortunate circumstances in my life. Though then but two-and-twenty, I had for several years read his works with delight and instruction, and had the highest reverence for their author, which had grown up in my fancy into a kind of mysterious veneration, by figuring to myself a state of solemn, elevated abstraction in which I supposed him to live in the immense metropolis of London. Mr. Gentleman, a native of Ireland, who passed some years in Scotland as a player, and as an instructor in the English language, a man whose talents and worth were depressed by misfortunes, had given me a representation of the figure and manner of DICTIONARY JOHNSON! as he was then generally called; and during my first visit to London, which was for three months in 1760, Mr. Derrick, the poet, who was Gentleman's friend and countryman, flattered me with hopes that he would introduce me to Johnson, an honor of which I was very ambitious. But he never found an opportunity, which made me doubt that he had promised to do what was not in his power; till Johnson, some years afterwards, told me, 'Derrick, sir, might very well have introduced you. I had a kindness for Derrick, and am sorry he is dead.'

In the summer of 1761 Mr. Thomas Sheridan was at Edinburgh, and delivered lectures upon the English language and public speaking to large and respectable audiences. I was often in his company, and heard him frequently expatiate upon Johnson's extraordinary knowledge, talents, and virtues, repeat his pointed sayings, describe his particularities, and boast of his being his guest sometimes till two or three in the morning. At his house I hoped to have many opportunities of seeing the sage, as Mr. Sheridan obligingly assured me I should not be disappointed.

When I returned to London in the end of 1762, to my surprise and regret I found an irreconcilable difference had taken place between Johnson and Sheridan. A pension of two hundred pounds a year had been given to Sheridan. Johnson, who thought slightingly of Sheridan's art, upon hearing that he was also pensioned, exclaimed, 'What! have they given *him* a pension? Then it is time for me to give up mine.' Whether this proceeded from a momentary indignation, as if it were an affront to his exalted merit that a player should be rewarded in the same manner with him, or was the sudden effect of a fit of peevishness, it was unluckily said, and indeed cannot be justified. Mr. Sheridan's pension was granted to him not as a player, but as a sufferer in the cause of government, when he was manager of the Theatre Royal in Ireland, when parties ran high in 1753. And it must also be allowed that he was a man of literature, and had considerably improved the arts of reading and speaking with distinctness and propriety.

* * *

Johnson complained that a man who disliked him repeated his sarcasm to Mr. Sheridan, without telling him what followed, which was, that after a pause he added, 'However, I am glad that Mr. Sheridan has a pension, for he is a very good man.' Sheridan could never forgive this hasty, contemptuous expression. It rankled in his mind; and though I informed him of all that Johnson said, and that he would be very glad to meet him amicably, he positively declined repeated offers which I made, and once went off abruptly from a house where he and I were engaged to dine, because he was told that Dr. Johnson was to be there.

I have no sympathetic feeling with such persevering resentment. It is painful when there is a breach between those who have lived together socially and cordially; and I wonder that there is not, in all such cases, a mutual wish that it should be healed. I could perceive that Mr. Sheridan was by no means satisfied with Johnson's acknowledging him to be a good man.

That could not soothe his injured vanity. I could not but smile, at the same time that I was offended, to observe Sheridan in *The Life of Swift*, which he afterwards published, attempting, in the writhings of his resentment, to depreciate Johnson, by characterizing him as 'A writer of gigantic fame in these days of little men'; that very Johnson whom he once so highly admired and venerated. This rupture with Sheridan deprived Johnson of one of his most agreeable resources for amusement in his lonely evenings; for Sheridan's well-informed, animated, and bustling mind never suffered conversation to stagnate; and Mrs. Sheridan was a most agreeable companion to an intellectual man. She was sensible, ingenious, unassuming, yet communicative. I recollect, with satisfaction, many pleasing hours which I passed with her under the hospitable roof of her husband, who was to me a very kind friend. Her novel, entitled *Memoirs of Miss Sydney Biddulph*, contains an excellent moral while it inculcates a future state of retribution; and what it teaches is impressed upon the mind by a series of as deep distress as can affect humanity, in the amiable and pious heroine who goes to her grave unrelieved, but resigned, and full of hope of 'heaven's mercy.' Johnson paid her this high compliment upon it: 'I know not, Madam, that you have a right, upon moral principles, to make your readers suffer so much.'

Mr. Thomas Davies, the actor, who then kept a bookseller's shop in Russell Street, Covent Garden, told me that Johnson was very much his friend, and came frequently to his house, where he more than once invited me to meet him; but by some unlucky accident or other he was prevented from coming to us. Mr. Thomas Davies was a man of good understanding and talents, with the advantage of a liberal education. Though somewhat pompous, he was an entertaining companion; and his literary performances have no inconsiderable share of merit. He was a friendly and very hospitable man. Both he and his wife, (who has been celebrated for her beauty), though upon the stage for many years, maintained an uniform decency of character; and Johnson esteemed them, and lived in as easy an intimacy with them, as with any family which he used to visit. Mr. Davies recollected several of Johnson's remarkable sayings, and was one of the best of the many imitators of his voice and manner, while relating them. He increased my impatience more and more to see the extraordinary man whose works I highly valued, and whose conversation was reported to be so peculiarly excellent.

At last, on Monday, the 16th of May, when I was sitting in Mr. Davies's back-parlor, after having drunk tea with him and Mrs. Davies, Johnson unexpectedly came into the shop; and Mr. Davies having perceived him, through the glass-door in the room in which we were sitting, advancing toward us,—he announced his awful approach to me, somewhat in the manner of an actor in the part of Horatio, when he addresses Hamlet on the appearance of his father's ghost, 'Look, my lord, it comes!' I found that I had a very perfect idea of Johnson's figure, from the portrait of him painted by Sir Joshua Reynolds soon after he had published his *Dictionary*, in the attitude of sitting in his easy chair in deep meditation. Mr. Davies mentioned my name, and respectfully introduced me to him. I was much agitated; and recollecting his prejudice against the Scotch, of which I had heard much, I said to Davies, 'Don't tell where I come from.'—'From Scotland,' cried Davies, roguishly. 'Mr. Johnson,' said I, 'I do indeed come from Scotland, but I cannot help it.' I am willing to flatter myself that I meant this as light pleasantry to soothe and conciliate him, and not as an humiliating abasement at the expense of my country. But however that might be, this speech was somewhat unlucky; for with that quickness of wit for which he was so remarkable, he seized the expression, 'come from Scotland,' which I used in the sense of being of that country; and, as if I had said that I had come away from it, or left it, retorted, 'That, sir, I find, is what a very great many of your countrymen cannot help.' This stroke stunned me a good deal; and when we had sat down, I felt myself not a little embarrassed, and apprehensive of what might come next. He then addressed himself to Davies: 'What do you think of Garrick? He has refused me an order for the play for Miss Williams, because he knows the house will be full, and that an order would be worth three shillings.' Eager to take any opening to get into conversation with him, I ventured to say, 'O sir, I cannot think Mr. Garrick would grudge such a trifle to you.' 'Sir,' said he, with a stern look, 'I have known David Garrick longer than you have done; and I know no right you have to talk to me on the subject.' Perhaps I deserved this check; for it was rather presumptuous in me, an entire stranger, to express any doubt of the justice of his animadversion upon his old acquaintance and pupil.[1] I now felt myself much mortified, and began to think that the hope which I had long indulged of obtaining his acquaintance was blasted. And, in truth, had not my ardor been uncommonly strong, and my resolution uncommonly persevering, so rough a reception might have deterred me from ever making any further attempts. Fortunately, however, I remained upon the field not wholly discomfited; and was soon rewarded by hearing some of his conversation, of which I preserved the following short minute, without remarking the questions and observations by which it was produced.

'People,' he remarked, 'may be taken in once, who imagine that an author is greater in private life than other men. Uncommon parts require uncommon opportunities, for their exertion.

'In barbarous society, superiority of parts is of real consequence. Great strength or great wisdom is of much value to an individual. But in more polished times there are people to do everything for money; and then there are a number of other superiorities, such as those of birth, and fortune, and rank, that dissipate men's attention, and leave no extraordinary share of respect for personal and intellectual superiority. This is wisely ordered by Providence, to preserve some equality among mankind.'

* * *

I was highly pleased with the extraordinary vigor of his conversation, and regretted that I was drawn away from it by an engagement at another place. I had, for a part of the evening, been left alone with him, and had ventured to make an observation now and then, which he received very civilly; so that I was satisfied that, though there was a roughness in his manner, there was no ill-nature in his disposition. Davies followed me to the door, and when I complained to him a little of the hard blows which the great man had given me, he kindly took upon him to console me by saying, 'Don't be uneasy. I can see he likes you very well.'

A few days afterwards I called on Davies, and asked him if he thought I might take the liberty of waiting on Mr. Johnson at his chambers in the Temple. He said I certainly might, and that Mr. Johnson would take it as a compliment. So, on Tuesday, the 24th day of May, after having been enlivened by the witty sallies of Messieurs Thornton, Wilkes, Churchill, and Lloyd, with whom I had passed the morning, I boldly repaired to Johnson. His chambers were on the first floor of No. 1, Inner Temple-lane, and I entered them with an impression given me by the Reverend Dr. Blair, of Edinburgh, who had been introduced to him not long before, and described his having 'found the Giant in his den'; an expression which, when I came to be pretty well acquainted with Johnson, I repeated to him, and he was diverted at this picturesque account of himself. Dr. Blair had been presented to him by Dr. James Fordyce. At this time the controversy concerning the pieces published by Mr. James Macpherson, as translations of Ossian, was at its height. Johnson had all along denied their authenticity; and, what was still more provoking to their admirers, maintained that they had no merit. The subject having been introduced by Dr. Fordyce, Dr. Blair, relying on the internal evidence of their antiquity, asked Dr. Johnson whether he thought any man of a modern age could have written such poems? Johnson replied, 'Yes, sir, many men, many women, and many children.' Johnson, at this time, did not know that Dr. Blair had just published a *Dissertation*, not only defending their authenticity, but seriously ranking them with the poems of Homer and Virgil; and when he was afterwards informed of this circumstance, he expressed some displeasure at Dr. Fordyce's having suggested the topic, and said, 'I am not sorry that they got thus much for their pains. Sir, it was like leading one to talk of a book, when the author is concealed behind the door.'

He received me very courteously; but it must be confessed that his apartment, and furniture, and morning dress, were sufficiently uncouth. His brown suit of clothes looked very rusty; he had on a little old shriveled unpowdered wig, which was too small for his head, his shirt-neck and knees of his breeches were loose; his black worsted stockings ill drawn up; and he had a pair of unbuckled shoes by way of slippers. But all these slovenly particularities were forgotten the moment that he began to talk. Some gentlemen, whom I do not recollect, were sitting with him; and when they went away, I also rose; but he said to me, 'Nay, don't go.' 'Sir,' said I,

---

[1] That this was a momentary sally against Garrick there can be no doubt; for at Johnson's desire he had, some years before, given a benefit-night at his theater to this very person, by which she had got two hundred pounds. Johnson, indeed, upon all other occasions, when I was in his company, praised the very liberal charity of Garrick. I once mentioned to him, 'It is observed, Sir, that you attack Garrick yourself, but will suffer nobody else to do it.' Johnson (smiling), 'Why, Sir, that is true.'

'I am afraid that I intrude upon you. It is benevolent to allow me to sit and hear you.' He seemed pleased with this compliment, which I sincerely paid him, and answered, 'Sir, I am obliged to any man who visits me.' I have preserved the following short minute of what passed this day:—

'Madness frequently discovers itself merely by unnecessary deviation from the usual modes of the world. My poor friend Smart showed the disturbance of his mind, by falling upon his knees, and saying his prayers in the street, or in any other unusual place. Now although, rationally speaking, it is greater madness not to pray at all, than to pray as Smart did, I am afraid there are so many who do not pray, that their understanding is not called in question.'

Concerning this unfortunate poet, Christopher Smart, who was confined in a madhouse, he had, at another time, the following conversation with Dr. Burney. BURNEY: 'How does poor Smart do, sir; is he likely to recover?'—JOHNSON: 'It seems as if his mind had ceased to struggle with the disease: for he grows fat upon it.'—BURNEY: 'Perhaps, sir, that may be from want of exercise.'—JOHNSON: 'No, sir; he has partly as much exercise as he used to have, for he digs in the garden. Indeed, before his confinement, he used for exercise to walk to the alehouse; but he was *carried* back again. I did not think he ought to be shut up. His infirmities were not noxious to society. He insisted on people praying with him, and I'd as lief pray with Kit Smart as any one else. Another charge was, that he did not love clean linen; and I have no passion for it.' Johnson continued: 'Mankind have a great aversion to intellectual labor; but even supposing knowledge to be easily attainable, more people would be content to be ignorant than would take even a little trouble to acquire it.

'The morality of an action depends on the motive from which we act. If I fling half-a-crown to a beggar, with intention to break his head, and he picks it up and buys victuals with it, the physical effect is good; but, with respect to me, the action is very wrong. So religious exercises, if not performed with an intention to please God, avail us nothing. As our Saviour says of those who perform them from other motives, "Verily they have their reward."

'The Christian religion has very strong evidences. It, indeed, appears in some degree strange to reason; but in History we have undoubted facts, against which, reasoning *à priori*, we have more arguments than we have for them; but then, testimony has great weight, and casts the balance. I would recommend to every man whose faith is yet unsettled, Grotius,—Dr. Pearson,—and Dr. Clarke.'

Talking of Garrick, he said, 'He is the first man in the world for sprightly conversation.'

When I rose a second time, he again pressed me to stay, which I did.

He told me, that he generally went abroad at four in the afternoon, and seldom came home till two in the morning. I took the liberty to ask if he did not think it wrong to live thus, and not make more use of his great talents. He owned it was a bad habit. On reviewing, at the distance of many years, my journal of this period, I wonder how, at my first visit, I ventured to talk to him so freely, and that he bore it with so much indulgence.

Before we parted, he was so good as to promise to favor me with his company one evening at my lodgings; and, as I took my leave, shook me cordially by the hand. It is almost needless to add, that I felt no little elation at having now so happily established an acquaintance of which I had been so long ambitious.

My readers will, I trust, excuse me for being thus minutely circumstantial, when it is considered that the acquaintance of Dr. Johnson was to me a most valuable acquisition, and laid the foundation of whatever instruction and entertainment they may receive from my collections concerning the great subject of the work which they are now perusing.

I did not visit him again till Monday, June 13, at which time I recollect no part of his conversation, except, that when I told him I had been to see Johnson ride upon three horses, he said, 'Such a man, sir, should be encouraged; for his performances show the extent of the human powers in one instance, and thus tend to raise our opinion of the faculties of man. He shows what may be attained by persevering application; so that every man may hope, that by giving as much application, although, perhaps, he may never ride three horses at a time, or dance upon a wire, yet he may be equally expert in whatever profession he has chosen to pursue.'

He again shook me by the hand at parting, and asked me why I did not come oftener to him. Trusting that I was now in his good graces, I answered, that he had not given me much encouragement, and reminded him of the check I had received from him at our first interview. 'Poh, poh!' said he, with a compla cent smile, 'never mind these things. Come to me as often as you can. I shall be glad to see you.'

I had learnt that his place of frequent resort was the Mitre tavern in Fleet-street, where he loved to sit up late, and I begged I might be allowed to pass an evening with him there soon, which he promised I should. A few days afterwards, I met him near Temple-bar about one o'clock in the morning, and asked if he would then go to the Mitre. 'Sir,' said he, 'it is too late, they won't let us in. But I'll go with you another night, with all my heart.'

A revolution of some importance in my plan of life had just taken place: for instead of procuring a commission in the foot guards, which was my own inclination, I had, in compliance with my father's wishes, agreed to study the law, and was soon to set out for Utrecht, to hear the lectures of an excellent civilian in that University, and then to proceed on my travels. Though very desirous of obtaining Dr. Johnson's advice and instructions on the mode of pursuing my studies, I was at this time so occupied, shall I call it? or so dissipated by the amusements of London, that our next meeting was not till Saturday, June 25, when, happening to dine at Clifton's eating-house, in Butcher-row, I was surprised to perceive Johnson come in and take his seat at another table. The mode of dining, or rather being fed, at such houses in London, is well known to many to be particularly unsocial, as there is no ordinary, or united company, but each person has his own mess, and is under no obligation to hold any intercourse with any one. A liberal and full-minded man, however, who loves to talk, will break through this churlish and unsocial restraint. Johnson and an Irish gentleman got into a dispute concerning the cause of some part of mankind being black. 'Why, sir,' said Johnson, 'it has been accounted for in three ways: either by supposing that they are the posterity of Ham, who was cursed, or that God at first created two kinds of men, one black, and another white, or that, by the heat of the sun, the skin is scorched, and so acquires a sooty hue. This matter has been much canvassed among naturalists, but has never been brought to any certain issue.' What the Irishman said is totally obliterated from my mind; but I remember that he became very warm and intemperate in his expressions; upon which Johnson rose, and quietly walked away. When he had retired, his antagonist took his revenge, as he thought by saying, 'He has a most ungainly figure, and an affectation of pomposity, unworthy of a man of genius.'

Johnson had not observed that I was in the room. I followed him, however, and he agreed to meet me in the evening at the Mitre. I called on him, and we went thither at nine. We had a good supper, and port wine, of which he then sometimes drank a bottle. The orthodox high-church sound of the Mitre,—the figure and manner of the celebrated Samuel Johnson,—the extraordinary power and precision of his conversation, and the pride, arising from finding myself admitted as his companion, produced a variety of sensations, and a pleasing elevation of mind beyond what I had ever before experienced. I find in my Journal the following minute of our conversation, which though it will give but a very faint notion of what passed, is, in some degree, a valuable record; and it will be curious in this view, as showing how habitual to his mind were some opinions which appear in his works.

'Colley Cibber, sir, was by no means a blockhead, but by arrogating to himself too much, he was in danger of losing that degree of estimation to which he was entitled. His friends gave out that he *intended* his Birthday Odes should be bad; but that was not the case, sir, for he kept them many months by him, and a few years before he died he showed me one of them, with great solicitude to render it as perfect as might be, and I made some corrections, to which he was not very willing to submit. I remember the following couplet in allusion to the King and himself:

Perched on the eagle's soaring wing,
The lowly linnet loves to sing.

Sir, he had heard something of the fabulous tale of the wren sitting upon the eagle's wing, and he had applied it to a linnet. Cibber's familiar style, however, was better than that which Whitehead had assumed. *Grand* nonsense is insupportable. Whitehead is but a little man to inscribe verses to players.'

I did not presume to controvert this censure, which was tinctured with his prejudice against players; but I could not help thinking that a dramatic poet might with propriety pay a compliment to an eminent performer, as Whitehead has very happily done in his verses to Mr. Garrick.

'Sir, I do not think Gray a first-rate poet. He has not a bold imagination, nor much command of words. The obscurity in which he has involved himself will not persuade us that he is sublime. His *Elegy in a Churchyard* has a happy selection of images, but I don't like what are called his great things. His Ode which begins

> Ruin seize thee, ruthless King,
> Confusion on thy banners wait!

has been celebrated for its abruptness, and plunging into the subject all at once. But such arts as these have no merit, unless when they are original. We admire them only once; and this abruptness has nothing new in it. We have had it often before. Nay, we have it in the old song of Johnny Armstrong:

> Is there ever a man in all Scotland,
> From the highest estate to the lowest degree.

And then, sir,

> Yes, there is a man in Westmoreland,
> And Johnny Armstrong they do him call.

There, now, you plunge at once into the subject. You have no previous narration to lead you to it. The two next lines in that Ode are, I think, very good:

> Though fanned by Conquest's crimson wing,
> They mock the air with idle state.

* * *

Finding him in a placid humor, and wishing to avail myself of the opportunity which I fortunately had of consulting a sage, to hear whose wisdom, I conceived, in the ardor of youthful imagination, that men filled with a noble enthusiasm for intellectual improvement would gladly have resorted from distant lands, —I opened my mind to him ingenuously, and gave him a little sketch of my life, to which he was pleased to listen with great attention.

I acknowledged that though educated very strictly in the principles of religion, I had for some time been misled into a certain degree of infidelity; but that I was come now to a better way of thinking, and was fully satisfied of the truth of the Christian revelation, though I was not clear as to every point considered to be orthodox. Being at all times a curious examiner of the human mind, and pleased with an undisguised display of what had passed in it, he called to me with warmth, 'Give me your hand, I have taken a liking to you.' He then began to descant upon the force of testimony, and the little we could know of final causes; so that the objections of, 'Why was it so?' or 'Why was it not so?' ought not to disturb us: adding, that he himself had at one period been guilty of a temporary neglect of religion, but that it was not the result of argument, but mere absence of thought.

After having given credit to reports of his bigotry, I was agreeably surprised when he expressed the following very liberal sentiment, which has the additional value of obviating an objection to our holy religion, founded upon the discordant tenets of Christians themselves: 'For my part, sir, I think all Christians, whether papists or protestants, agree in the essential articles, and that their differences are trivial, and rather political than religious.'

We talked of belief in ghosts. He said, 'Sir, I make a distinction between what a man may experience by the mere strength of his imagination, and what imagination cannot possibly produce. Thus, suppose I should think that I saw a form, and heard a voice cry, "Johnson, you are a very wicked fellow, and unless you repent you will certainly be punished"; my own unworthiness is so deeply impressed upon my mind, that I might *imagine* I thus saw and heard, and therefore I should not believe that an external communication had been made to me. But if a form should appear, and a voice should tell me that a particular man had died at a particular place, and a particular hour, a fact which I had no apprehension of, nor any means of knowing, and this fact, with all its circumstances, should afterwards be unquestionably proved, I should in that case be persuaded that I had supernatural intelligence imparted to me.'

Here it is proper, once for all, to give a true and fair statement of Johnson's way of thinking upon the question, whether departed spirits are ever permitted to appear in this world, or in any way to operate upon human life. He has been ignorantly misrepresented as weakly credulous upon that subject; and, therefore, though I feel an inclination to disdain and treat with silent contempt so foolish a notion concerning my illustrious friend, yet, as I find it has gained ground, it is necessary to refute it. The real fact then is, that Johnson had a very philosophical mind, and such a rational respect for testimony, as to make him submit his understanding to what was authentically proved, though he could not comprehend why it was so. Being thus disposed, he was willing to inquire into the truth of any relation of supernatural agency, a general belief of which has prevailed in all nations and ages. But so far was he from being the dupe of implicit faith, that he examined the matter with a jealous attention, and no man was more ready to refute its falsehood when he had discovered it. Churchill, in his poem entitled *The Ghost*, availed himself of the absurd credulity imputed to Johnson, and drew a caricature of him under the name of 'Pomposo,' representing him as one of the believers of the story of a ghost in Cock-lane, which, in the year 1762, had gained very general credit in London. Many of my readers, I am convinced, are to this hour under an impression that Johnson was thus foolishly deceived. It will therefore surprise them a good deal when they are informed upon undoubted authority, that Johnson was one of those by whom the imposture was detected. The story had become so popular, that he thought it should be investigated: and in this research he was assisted by the Rev. Dr. Douglas, now bishop of Salisbury, the great detector of impostures; who informs me that after the gentlemen who went and examined into the evidence were satisfied of its falsity, Johnson wrote in their presence an account of it, which was published in the newspapers and *Gentleman's Magazine*, and undeceived the world.

Our conversation proceeded. 'Sir,' said he, 'I am a friend to subordination as most conducive to the happiness of society. There is a reciprocal pleasure in governing and being governed.'

'Dr. Goldsmith is one of the first men we now have as an author, and he is a very worthy man too. He has been loose in his principles, but he is coming right.'

I mentioned Mallet's tragedy of *Elvira*, which had been acted the preceding winter at Drury-lane, and that the Honorable Andrew Erskine, Mr. Dempster, and myself, had joined in writing a pamphlet, entitled *Critical Strictures*, against it. That the mildness of Dempster's disposition had, however, relented; and he had candidly said, 'We have hardly a right to abuse this tragedy, for, bad as it is, how vain should either of us be to write one not near so good!' JOHNSON: 'Why, no sir; this is not just reasoning. You *may* abuse a tragedy, though you cannot write one. You may scold a carpenter who has made you a bad table, though you cannot make a table. It is not your trade to make tables.'

When I talked to him of the paternal estate to which I was heir, he said, 'Sir, let me tell you, that to be a Scotch landlord, where you have a number of families dependent upon you, and attached to you, is, perhaps, as high a situation as humanity can arrive at. A merchant upon the 'Change of London, with a hundred thousand pounds, is nothing; an English Duke, with an immense fortune, is nothing; he has no tenants who consider themselves as under his patriarchal care, and who will follow him to the field upon an emergency.'

* * *

I complained to him that I had not yet acquired much knowledge, and asked his advice as to my studies. He said, 'Don't talk of study, now. I will give you a plan; but it will require some time to consider of it.' 'It is very good of you,' I replied, 'to allow me to be with you thus. Had it been foretold to me some years ago that I should pass an evening with the author of the *Rambler*, how should I have exulted!' What I then expressed was sincerely from my heart. He was satisfied that it was, and cordially answered, 'Sir, I am glad we have met. I hope we shall pass many evenings, and mornings too, together.' We finished a couple of bottles of port, and sat till between one and two in the morning.

He wrote this year, in the *Critical Review*, the account of *Telemachus, a Mask*, by the Rev. George Graham, of Eton College. The subject of this beautiful poem was particularly interesting to Johnson, who had much experience of 'the conflict of opposite principles,' which he describes as 'the contention between pleasure and virtue, a struggle which will always be continued while the present system of nature shall subsist; nor can history or poetry exhibit more than pleasure triumphing over virtue, and virtue subjugating pleasure.'

As Dr. Oliver Goldsmith will frequently appear in this narrative, I shall endeavor to make my readers in some degree acquainted with his singular character. He was a native of Ireland, and a contemporary with Mr. Burke, at Trinity College, Dublin, but did not then give much promise of future celebrity. He, however, observed to Mr. Malone, that 'though he made no great figure in mathematics, which was a study in much repute there, he could turn an Ode of Horace into English better than any of them.' He afterwards studied physic in Edinburgh, and upon the Continent: and, I have been informed, was enabled to pursue his travels on foot, partly by demanding, at Universities, to enter the lists as a disputant, by which, according to the custom of many of them, he was entitled to the premium of a crown, when, luckily for him, his challenge was not accepted so that, as I once observed to Johnson, he *disputed* his passage through Europe. He then came to England,

and was employed successively in the capacities of an usher to an academy, a corrector of the press, a reviewer, and a writer for a newspaper. He had sagacity enough to cultivate assiduously the acquaintance of Johnson, and his faculties were gradually enlarged by the contemplation of such a model. To me and many others it appeared that he studiously copied the manner of Johnson, though, indeed, upon a smaller scale.

At this time I think he had published nothing with his name, though it was pretty generally known that *one Dr. Goldsmith* was the author of *An Inquiry into the present State of Polite Learning in Europe*, and of *The Citizen of the World*, a series of letters supposed to be written from London by a Chinese. No man had the art of displaying with more advantage, as a writer, whatever literary acquisitions he made. *Nihil quod tetigit non ornavit*[1] [There was nothing he touched he did not adorn]. His mind resembled a fertile but thin soil. There was a quick, but not a strong, vegetation, of whatever chanced to be thrown upon it. No deep root could be struck. The oak of the forest did not grow there; but the elegant shrubbery and the fragrant parterre appeared in gay succession. It has been generally circulated and believed that he was a mere fool in conversation; but, in truth, this has been greatly exaggerated. He had, no doubt, a more than common share of that hurry of ideas which we often find in his countrymen, and which sometimes produces a laughable confusion in expressing them. He was very much what the French call *un étourdi*, and from vanity and an eager desire of being conspicuous wherever he was, he frequently talked carelessly without knowledge of the subject, or even without thought. His person was short, his countenance coarse and vulgar, his deportment that of a scholar awkwardly affecting the easy gentleman. Those who were in any way distinguished, excited envy in him to so ridiculous an excess, that the instances of it are hardly credible. When accompanying two beautiful young ladies,[2] with their mother, on a tour in France, he was seriously angry that more attention was paid to them than to him; and once at the exhibition of the *Fantoccini* in London, when those who sat next to him observed with what dexterity a puppet was made to toss a pike, he could not bear that it should have such praise, and exclaimed, with some warmth, 'Pshaw! I can do it better myself.'[3]

He, I am afraid, had no settled system of any sort, so that his conduct must not be strictly scrutinized; but his affections were social and generous, and when he had money he gave it away very liberally. His desire of imaginary consequence predominated over his attention to truth. When he began to rise into notice, he said he had a brother who was dean of Durham, a fiction so easily detected, that it is wonderful how he should have been so inconsiderate as to hazard it. He boasted to me at this time of the power of his pen in commanding money, which I believe was true in a certain degree, though in the instance he gave he was by no means correct. He told me that he had sold a novel for four hundred pounds. This was his *Vicar of Wakefield*. But Johnson informed me that he had made the bargain for Goldsmith, and the price was sixty pounds. 'And, sir,' said he, 'a sufficient price too, when it was sold; for then the fame of Goldsmith had not been elevated, as it afterwards was, by his *Traveller;* and the bookseller had such faint hopes of profit by his bargain, that he kept the manuscript by him a long time, and did not publish it till after *The Traveller* had appeared. Then, to be sure, it was accidentally worth more money.'

Mrs. Piozzi and Sir John Hawkins have strangely misstated the history of Goldsmith's situation and Johnson's friendly interference, when this novel was sold. I shall give it authentically from Johnson's own exact narration:—'I received one morning a message from poor Goldsmith that he was in great distress, and, as it was not in his power to come to me, begging that I would come to him as soon as possible. I sent him a guinea, and promised to come to him directly. I accordingly went as soon as I was dressed, and found that his landlady had arrested him for his rent, at which he was in a violent passion. I perceived that he had already changed my guinea, and had got a bottle of Madeira and a glass before him. I put the cork into the bottle, desired he would be calm, and began to talk to him of the means by which he might be extricated. He then told me that he had a novel ready for the press, which he produced to me. I looked into it, and saw its merits; told the landlady I should re-

---

[1] See his epitaph in Westminster Abbey, written by Dr. Johnson.

[2] Miss Hornecks, one of whom is now married to Henry Bunbury, Esq., and the other to Colonel Gwyn.

[3] He went home with Mr. Burke to supper; and broke his shin by attempting to exhibit to the company how much better he could jump over a stick than the puppets.

turn; and, having gone to a bookseller, sold it for sixty pounds. I brought Goldsmith the money, and he discharged his rent, not without rating his landlady in a high tone for having used him so ill.'

My next meeting with Johnson was on Friday, the 1st of July, when he and I and Dr. Goldsmith supped at the Mitre.

* * *

He talked very contemptuously of Churchill's poetry, observing, that 'it had a temporary currency, only from its audacity of abuse, and being filled with living names, and that it would sink into oblivion.' I ventured to hint that he was not quite a fair judge, as Churchill had attacked him violently. JOHNSON: 'Nay sir, I am a very fair judge. He did not attack me violently till he found I did not like his poetry; and his attack on me shall not prevent me from continuing to say what I think of him, from an apprehension that it may be ascribed to resentment. No, sir, I called the fellow a blockhead at first, and I will call him a blockhead still. However, I will acknowledge that I have a better opinion of him now than I once had; for he has shown more fertility than I expected. To be sure, he is a tree that cannot produce good fruit: he only bears crabs. But, sir, a tree that produces a great many crabs, is better than a tree which produces only a few.'

* * *

Let me here apologize for the imperfect manner in which I am obliged to exhibit Johnson's conversation at this period. In the early part of my acquaintance with him, I was so wrapt in admiration of his extraordinary colloquial talents, and so little accustomed to his peculiar mode of expression, that I found it extremely difficult to recollect and record his conversation with its genuine vigor and vivacity. In progress of time, when my mind was, as it were, *strongly impregnated with the Johnsonian æther*, I could with much more facility and exactness, carry in my memory and commit to paper the exuberant variety of his wisdom and wit.

At this time *Miss* Williams, as she was then called, though she did not reside with him in the Temple under his roof, but had lodgings in Bolt-court, Fleet-street, had so much of his attention, that he every night drank tea with her before he went home, however late it might be, and she always sat up for him. This it may be conjectured, was not alone a proof of his regard for *her*, but of his own unwillingness to go into solitude, before that unseasonable hour at which he had habituated himself to expect the oblivion of repose. Dr. Goldsmith, being a privileged man, went with him this night, strutting away, and calling to me with an air of superiority, like that of an esoteric over an exoteric disciple of a sage of antiquity, 'I go to Miss Williams.' I confess, I then envied him this mighty privilege, of which he seemed so proud; but it was not long before I obtained the same mark of distinction.

* * *

On Wednesday, July 6, he was engaged to sup with me at my lodgings in Downing-street, Westminster. But on the preceding night my landlord having behaved very rudely to me and some company who were with me, I had resolved not to remain another night in his house. I was exceedingly uneasy at the awkward appearance I supposed I should make to Johnson and the other gentlemen whom I had invited, not being able to receive them at home, and being obliged to order supper at the Mitre. I went to Johnson in the morning and talked of it as a serious distress. He laughed and said, 'Consider, sir, how insignificant this will appear a twelvemonth hence.' Were this consideration to be applied to most of the little vexatious incidents of life, by which our quiet is too often disturbed, it would prevent many painful sensations. I have tried it frequently with good effect. 'There is nothing,' continued he, 'in this mighty misfortune; nay, we shall be better at the Mitre.' I told him that I had been at Sir John Fielding's office, complaining of my landlord, and had been informed that though I had taken my lodgings for a year, I might, upon proof of his bad behavior, quit them when I pleased, without being under an obligation to pay rent for any longer time than while I possessed them. The fertility of Johnson's mind could show itself even upon so small a matter as this. 'Why, sir,' said he, 'I suppose this must be the law, since you have been told so in Bow-street. But if your landlord could hold you to your bargain, and the lodgings should be yours for a year, you may certainly use them as you think fit. So, sir, you may quarter two life-guardsmen upon him; or you may send the greatest scoundrel you can find into your apartments; or you may say that you want to make some experiments in natural philosophy, and may burn a large quantity of assafœtida in his house.'

I had as my guests this evening at the Mitre Tavern, Dr. Johnson, Dr. Goldsmith, Mr. Thomas Davies, Mr. Eccles, an Irish gentleman for whose agreeable company I was obliged to Mr. Davies, and the Rev. Mr. John Ogilvie, who was desirous of being in company with my illustrious friend, while I, in my turn, was proud to have the honor of showing one of my countrymen upon what easy terms Johnson permitted me to live with him.

Goldsmith, as usual, endeavored with too much eagerness to *shine*, and disputed very warmly with Johnson against the well-known maxim of the British constitution, 'the king can do no wrong'; affirming that 'what was morally false could not be politically true; and as the king might, in the exercise of his regal power, command and cause the doing of what was wrong, it certainly might be said, in sense and in reason, that he could do wrong.' JOHNSON: 'Sir, you are to consider that in our constitution, according to its true principles, the king is the head, he is supreme; he is above everything, and there is no power by which he can be tried. Therefore, it is, sir, that we hold the king can do no wrong; that whatever may happen to be wrong in government, may not be above our reach by being ascribed to majesty. Redress is always to be had against oppression by punishing the immediate agents. The king, though he should command, cannot force a judge to condemn a man unjustly; therefore it is the judge whom we prosecute and punish. Political institutions are formed upon the consideration of what will most frequently tend to the good of the whole, although now and then exceptions may occur. Thus it is better in general that a nation should have a supreme legislative power, although it may at times be abused. And then, sir, there is this consideration, that *if the abuse be enormous, nature will rise up, and claiming her original rights, overturn a corrupt political system.*' I mark this animated sentence with peculiar pleasure, as a noble instance of that truly dignified spirit of freedom which ever glowed in his heart, though he was charged with slavish tenets by superficial observers; because he was at all times indignant against that false patriotism, that pretended love of freedom, that unruly restlessness, which is inconsistent with the stable authority of any good government. This generous sentiment, which he uttered with great fervor, struck me exceedingly, and stirred my blood to that pitch of fancied resistance, the possibility of which I am glad to keep in mind, but to which I trust I never shall be forced.

'Great abilities,' said he, 'are not requisite for an historian, for in historical composition all the greatest powers of the human mind are quiescent. He has facts ready to his hand, so there is no exercise of invention. Imagination is not required in any high degree; only about as much as is used in the lower kinds of poetry. Some penetration, accuracy, and coloring, will fit a man for the task, if he can give the application which is necessary.'

'Bayle's *Dictionary* is a very useful work for those to consult who love the biographical part of literature, which is what I love most.'

Talking of the eminent writers in Queen Anne's reign, he observed, 'I think Dr. Arbuthnot the first man among them. He was the most universal genius, being an excellent physician, a man of deep learning, and a man of much humor. Mr. Addison was, to be sure, a great man; his learning was not profound, but his morality, his humor, and his elegance of writing set him very high.'

Mr. Ogilvie was unlucky enough to choose for the topic of his conversation, the praises of his native country. He began with saying, that there was very rich land around Edinburgh. Goldsmith, who had studied physic there, contradicted this, very untruly, with a sneering laugh. Disconcerted a little by this, Mr. Ogilvie then took a new ground, where, I suppose, he thought himself perfectly safe; for he observed, that Scotland had a great many noble wild prospects. JOHNSON: 'I believe, sir, you have a great many. Norway, too, has noble wild prospects; and Lapland is remarkable for prodigious noble wild prospects. But, sir, let me tell you, the noblest prospect which a Scotchman ever sees is the high-road that leads him to England!' This unexpected and pointed sally produced a roar of applause. After all, however, those, who admire the rude grandeur of nature, cannot deny it to Caledonia.

On Saturday, July 9, I found Johnson surrounded with a numerous levee, but have not preserved any part of his conversation. On the 14th we had another evening by ourselves at the Mitre. It happening to be a very rainy night, I made some commonplace observations on the relaxation of nerves and depression of spirits which such weather occasioned; adding, however, that it was good for the vegetable creation. Johnson, who, as we have already seen, denied that the temperature of the air had any influence on the human frame, answered, with a smile of ridicule, 'Why, yes, sir, it is good for vegetables, and for the animals who eat those vegetables, and for the animals who eat those animals.' This observation of his, aptly enough introduced a good supper; and I soon forgot, in Johnson's company, the influence of a moist atmosphere.

Feeling myself now quite at ease as his companion, though I had all possible reverence for him, I expressed a regret that I could not be so easy with my father, though he was not much older than Johnson, and certainly, however respectable, had not more learning and greater abilities to depress me. I asked him the reason of this. JOHNSON: 'Why sir, I am a man of the world. I live in the world, and I take, in some degree, the color of the world as it moves along. Your father is a judge in a remote part of the island, and all his notions are taken from the old world. Besides, sir, there must always be a struggle between a father and a son, while one aims at power and the other at independence.' I said, I was afraid my father would force me to be a lawyer. JOHNSON: 'Sir, you need not be afraid of his forcing you to be a laborious practising lawyer; that is not in his power. For, as the proverb says, "One man may lead a horse to the water, but twenty cannot make him drink." He may be displeased that you are not what he wishes you to be; but that displeasure will not go far. If he insists only on your having as much law as is necessary for a man of property, and then endeavors to get you into parliament, he is quite in the right.'

He enlarged very convincingly upon the excellence of rime over blank verse in English poetry. I mentioned to him that Dr. Adam Smith, in his lectures upon composition, when I studied under him in the College of Glasgow, had maintained the same opinion strenuously, and I repeated some of his arguments. JOHNSON: 'Sir, I was once in company with Smith, and we did not take to each other; but had I known that he loved rime as much as you tell me he does, I should have HUGGED him.'

Talking of those who denied the truth of Christianity, he said: 'It is always easy to be on the negative side. If a man were now to deny that there is salt upon the table, you could not reduce him to an absurdity. Come, let us try this a little further. I deny that Canada is taken, and I can support my denial by pretty good arguments. The French are a much more numerous people than we; and it is not likely that they would allow us to take it. "But the ministry have assured us, in all the formality of *The Gazette*, that it is taken."—Very true. But the ministry have put us to an enormous expense by the war in America, and it is their interest to persuade us that we have got something for our money. "But the fact is confirmed by thousands of men who were at the taking of it." Ay, but these men have still more interest in deceiving us. They don't want that you should think the French have beat them, but that they have beat the French. Now suppose you should go over and find that it really is taken, that would only satisfy yourself; for when you come home we will not believe you. We will say, you have been bribed. Yet, sir, notwithstanding all these plausible objections, we have no doubt that Canada is really ours. Such is the weight of common testimony. How much stronger are the evidences of the Christian religion!'

'Idleness is a disease which must be combated; but I would not advise a rigid adherence to a particular plan of study. I myself have never persisted in any plan for two days together. A man ought to read just as inclination leads him; for what he reads as a task will do him little good. A young man should read five hours in a day, and so may acquire a great deal of knowledge.'

To such a degree of unrestrained frankness had he now accustomed me that in the course of this evening I talked of the numerous reflections which had been thrown out against him, on account of his having accepted a pension from his present Majesty. 'Why, sir,' said he, with a hearty laugh, 'it is a mighty foolish noise that they make.[1] I have accepted of a pension as a reward which has been thought due to my literary merit; and now that I have this pension, I am the same man in every respect that I have ever been; I retain the same principles. It is true, that I cannot now curse (smiling) the house of Hanover; nor would it be decent for me to drink King James's health in the wine that King George gives me money to pay for. But, sir, I think that the pleasure of cursing the house of Hanover, and drinking King James's health, are amply overbalanced by three hundred pounds a year.'

* * *

[1] When I mentioned the same idle clamor to him several years afterwards, he said, with a smile, 'I wish my pension were twice as large, that they might make twice as much noise.'

He recommended to me to keep a journal of my life, full and unreserved. He said it would be a very good exercise, and would yield me great satisfaction when the particulars were faded from my remembrance. I was uncommonly fortunate in having had a previous coincidence of opinion with him upon this subject, for I had kept such a journal for some time; and it was no small pleasure to me to have this to tell him, and to receive his approbation. He counseled me to keep it private, and said I might surely have a friend who would burn it in case of my death. From this habit I have been enabled to give the world so many anecdotes, which would otherwise have been lost to posterity. I mentioned that I was afraid I put into my journal too many little incidents. JOHNSON: 'There is nothing, sir, too little for so little a creature as man. It is by studying little things that we attain the great art of having as little misery, and as much happiness as possible.'

Next morning Mr. Dempster happened to call on me, and was so much struck even with the imperfect account which I gave him of Dr. Johnson's conversation, that to his honor be it recorded, when I complained that drinking port and sitting up late with him, affected my nerves for some time after, he said, 'One had better be palsied at eighteen, than not keep company with such a man.'

On Tuesday, July 18th, I found tall Sir Thomas Robinson sitting with Johnson. Sir Thomas said, that the king of Prussia valued himself upon three things: upon being a hero, a musician, and an author. JOHNSON: 'Pretty well, sir, for one man. As to his being an author, I have not looked at his poetry; but his prose is poor stuff. He writes just as you may suppose Voltaire's footboy to do, who has been his amanuensis. He has such parts as the valet might have, and about as much of the coloring of the style as might be got by transcribing his works.' When I was at Ferney, I repeated this to Voltaire in order to reconcile him somewhat to Johnson, whom he, in affecting the English mode of expression, had previously characterized as 'a superstitious dog;' but after hearing such a criticism on Frederick the Great, with whom he was then on bad terms, he exclaimed, 'An honest fellow!'

* * *

I again begged his advice as to my method of study at Utrecht. 'Come,' said he, 'let us make a day of it. Let us go down to Greenwich and dine, and talk of it there.' The following Saturday was fixed for this excursion.

As we walked along the Strand to-night, arm in arm, a woman of the town accosted us, in the usual enticing manner. 'No, no, my girl,' said Johnson, 'it won't do.' He, however, did not treat her with harshness; and we talked of the wretched life of such women, and agreed that much more misery than happiness, upon the whole, is produced by illicit commerce between the sexes.

On Saturday, July 30, Dr. Johnson and I took a sculler at the Temple-stairs, and set out for Greenwich. I asked him if he really thought a knowledge of the Greek and Latin languages an essential requisite to a good education. JOHNSON: 'Most certainly, sir; for those who know them have a very great advantage over those who do not. Nay, sir, it is wonderful what a difference learning makes upon people even in the common intercourse of life, which does not appear to be much connected with it.' 'And yet,' said I, 'people go through the world very well and carry on the business of life, to good advantage without learning.' JOHNSON: 'Why, sir, that may be true in cases where learning cannot possibly be of any use; for instance, this boy rows us as well without learning, as if he could sing the song of Orpheus to the Argonauts, who were the first sailors.' He then called to the boy, 'What would you give, my lad, to know about the Argonauts?' 'Sir,' said the boy, 'I would give what I have.' Johnson was much pleased with his answer, and we gave him a double fare. Dr. Johnson then turning to me, 'Sir,' said he, 'a desire of knowledge is the natural feeling of mankind; and every human being whose mind is not debauched, will be willing to give all that he has to get knowledge.'

We landed at the Old Swan, and walked to Billingsgate, where we took oars and moved smoothly along the silver Thames. It was a very fine day. We were entertained with the immense number and variety of ships that were lying at anchor, and with the beautiful country on each side of the river.

I talked of preaching, and of the great success which those called Methodists have. JOHNSON: 'Sir, it is owing to their expressing themselves in a plain and familiar manner, which is the only way to do good to the common people, and which clergymen of genius and learning ought to do from a principle of duty, when it is suited to their congregations; a practice, for which they will be praised by men of sense. To insist against drunkenness as a crime, because it debases reason: the noblest faculty of man, would be of no service to the common people, but to tell them that they may die in a fit of drunkenness and show them how dreadful that would be, cannot fail to make a deep impression. Sir, when your Scotch clergy give up their homely manner, religion will soon decay in that country.'

I was much pleased to find myself with Johnson at Greenwich, which he celebrates in his *London* as a favorite scene.

I had the poem in my pocket, and read the lines aloud with enthusiasm:

'On Thames's banks in silent thought we stood:
Where Greenwich smiles upon the silver flood:
Pleased with the seat which gave Eliza birth,
We kneel, and kiss the consecrated earth.'

He remarked that the structure of Greenwich hospital was too magnificent for a place of charity, and that its parts were too much detached, to make one great whole.

Buchanan, he said, was a very fine poet; and observe, that he was the first who complimented a lady, by ascribing to her the different perfections of the heathen goddesses; but that Johnstone improved upon this, by making his lady, at the same time, free from their defects.

He dwelt upon Buchanan's elegant verses to Mary Queen of Scots, *Nympha Caledoniæ*, [Nymph of Scotland] etc., and spoke with enthusiasm of the beauty of Latin verse. 'All the modern languages,' said he, 'cannot furnish so melodious a line as

Formosam resonare doces Amarillida silvas.
[You teach the woods to re-echo beauteous Amarillis.]'

Afterwards he entered upon the business of the day, which was to give me his advice as to a course of study. And here I am to mention with much regret that my record of what he said is miserably scanty. I recollect with admiration an animating blaze of eloquence, which roused every intellectual power in me to the highest pitch, but must have dazzled me so much that my memory could not preserve the substance of his discourse; for the note which I find of it is no more than this:—'He ran over the grand scale of human knowledge; advised me to select some particular branch to excel in, but to acquire a little of every kind.' The defect of my minutes will be fully supplied by a long letter upon the subject, which he favored me with after I had been some time at Utrecht, and which my readers will have the pleasure to peruse in its proper place.

We walked in the evening, in Greenwich Park. He asked me, I suppose, by way of trying my disposition, 'Is not this very fine?' Having no exquisite relish of the beauties of nature, and being more delighted with 'the busy hum of men,' I answered, 'Yes, sir, but not equal to Fleet-street.' JOHNSON: 'You are right, sir.'

I am aware that many of my readers may censure my want of taste. Let me, however, shelter myself under the authority of a very fashionable baronet in the brilliant world, who, on his attention being called to the fragrance of a May evening in the country, observed, 'This may be very well; but, for my part, I prefer the smell of a flambeau at the play-house.'

We stayed so long at Greenwich that our sail up the river, in our return to London, was by no means so pleasant as in the morning; for the night air was so cold that it made me shiver. I was the more sensible of it from having sat up all the night before recollecting and writing in my journal what I thought worthy of preservation; an exertion which during the first part of my acquaintance with Johnson, I frequently made. I remember having sat up four nights in one week, without being much incommoded in the daytime.

Johnson, whose robust frame was not in the least affected by the cold, scolded me, as if my shivering had been a paltry effeminacy, saying, 'Why do you shiver?' Sir William Scott, of the Commons, told me that when he complained of a headache in the post-chaise, as they were traveling together to Scotland, Johnson treated him in the same manner: 'At your age, sir, I had no headache.' It is not easy to make allowance for sensations in others, which we ourselves have not at the time.

We concluded the day at the Turk's Head coffee-house very sociably. He was pleased to listen to a particular account which I gave him of my family, and of its hereditary estate, as to the extent and population of which he asked questions, and made calculations; recommending at the same time, a liberal kindness to the tenantry, as people over whom the proprietor was placed by Providence. He took delight in hearing my description of the romantic seat of my ancestors. 'I must be there, sir,' said he. 'and we will live in the old castle; and if there is not a room in it remaining, we will build one.' I was highly flattered, but could scarcely indulge a hope that Auchinleck would indeed be honored by his presence, and celebrated by a description, as it afterward was, in his *Journey to the Western Islands*.

After we had again talked of my setting out for Holland, he said, 'I must see thee out of England; I will accompany you to Harwich.' I could not find words to express what I felt upon this unexpected and very great mark of his affectionate regard.

Next day, Sunday, July 31, I told him I had been that morning at a meeting of the people called Quakers, where I had heard a woman preach. JOHNSON: 'Sir, a woman's preaching is like a dog's walking on his hind legs. It is not done well; but you are surprised to find it done at all.'

On Tuesday, August 2 (the day of my departure from London having been fixed for the 5th), Dr. Johnson did me the honor to pass a part of the morning with me at my chambers. He said, 'that he always felt an inclination to do nothing.' I observed, that it was strange to think that the most indolent man in Britain had written the most laborious work, *The English Dictionary*.

I mentioned an imprudent publication, by a certain friend of his, at an early period of life, and asked him if he thought it would hurt him. JOHNSON: 'No, sir; not much. It may, perhaps, be mentioned at an election.'

I had now made good my title to be a privileged man, and was carried by him in the evening to drink tea with Miss Williams, whom, though under the misfortune of having lost her sight, I found to be agreeable in conversation, for she had a variety of literature, and expressed herself well; but her peculiar value was the intimacy in which she had long lived with Johnson, by which she was well acquainted with his habits, and knew how to lead him on to talk.

After tea he carried me to what he called his walk, which was a long narrow paved court in the neighborhood, overshadowed by some trees. There we sauntered a considerable time, and I complained to him that my love of London and of his company was such, that I shrunk almost from the thought of going away even to travel, which is generally so much desired by young men. He roused me by manly and spirited conversation. He advised me, when settled in any place abroad, to study with an eagerness after knowledge, and to apply to Greek an hour every day; and when I was moving about, to read diligently the great book of mankind.

On Wednesday, August 3, we had our last social evening at the Turk's Head coffee-house, before my setting out for foreign parts. I had the misfortune, before we parted, to irritate him unintentionally. I mentioned to him how common it was in the world to tell absurd stories of him, and to ascribe to him very strange sayings. JOHNSON: 'What do they make me say, sir?' BOSWELL: 'Why, sir, as an instance very strange indeed,' laughing heartily as I spoke, 'David Hume told me, you said that you would stand before a battery of cannon to restore the Convocation to its full powers.' Little did I apprehend that he had actually said this: but I was soon convinced of my error; for, with a determined look he thundered out, 'And would I not, sir? Shall the Presbyterian *Kirk* of Scotland have its General Assembly, and the Church of England be denied its Convocation?' He was walking up and down the room while I told him the anecdote; but, when he uttered this explosion of high-church zeal he had come close to my chair, and his eyes flashed with indignation. I bowed to the storm, and diverted the force of it, by leading him to expatiate on the influence which religion derived from maintaining the church with great external respectability.

I must not omit to mention that he this year wrote *The Life of Ascham*, and the Dedication to the Earl of Shaftesbury, prefixed to the edition of that writer's English works, published by Mr. Bennet.

On Friday, August 5, we set out early in the morning in the Harwich stagecoach. A fat elderly gentlewoman, and a young Dutchman, seemed the most inclined among us to conversation. At the inn where we dined, the gentlewoman said that she had done her best to educate her children; and particularly, that she had never suffered them to be a moment idle. JOHNSON: 'I wish, madam, you would educate me too; for I have been an idle fellow all my life.' 'I am sure, sir,' said she, 'you have not been idle.' JOHNSON: 'Nay, madam, it is very true: and that gentleman there, pointing to me, has been idle. He was idle at Edinburgh. His father sent him to Glasgow, where he continued to be idle. He then came to London, where he has been very idle; and now he is going to Utrecht, where he will be as idle as ever.' I asked him privately how he could expose me so. JOHNSON: 'Poh, poh!' said he, 'they knew nothing about you, and will think of it no more.' In the afternoon the gentlewoman talked violently against the Roman Catholics, and of the horrors of the inquisition. To the utter astonishment of all the passengers but myself, who knew that he could talk upon any side of a question, he defended the inquisition, and maintained that 'false doctrine should be checked on its first appearance; that the civil power should unite with the church in punishing those who dare to attack the established religion, and that such only were punished by the inquisition.' He had in his pocket, *Pomponius Mela de Situ Orbis*, in which he read occasionally, and seemed very intent upon ancient geography. Though by no means niggardly, his attention to what was generally right was so minute, that having observed at one of the stages that I ostentatiously gave a shilling to the coachman, when the custom was for each passenger to give only sixpence, he took me aside and scolded me, saying that what I had done would make the coachman dissatisfied with all the rest of the passengers, who gave him no more than his due.

* * *

Having stopped a night at Colchester, Johnson talked of that town with veneration, for having stood a siege for Charles the First. The Dutchman alone now remained with us. He spoke English tolerably well; and thinking to recommend himself to us by expatiating on the superiority of the criminal jurisprudence of this country over that of Holland, he inveighed against the barbarity of putting an accused person to the torture, in order to force a confession. But Johnson was as ready for this as for the inquisition. 'Why, sir, you do not, I find, understand the law of your own country. To torture in Holland is considered as a favor to an accused person; for no man is put to the torture there, unless there is as much evidence against him as would amount to conviction in England. An accused person, among you, therefore, has one chance more to escape punishment than those who are tried among us.'

At supper this night he talked of good eating with uncommon satisfaction. 'Some people,' said he, ' have a foolish way of not minding, or pretending not to mind, what they eat. For my part, I mind my belly very studiously and very carefully; for I look upon it, that he who does not mind his belly will hardly mind anything else.' He now appeared to me *Jean Bull philosophe*, and he was for the moment not only serious, but vehement, yet I have heard him, upon other occasions, talk with great contempt of people who were anxious to gratify their palates: and the 206th number of his *Rambler* is a masterly essay against gulosity. His practice, indeed, I must acknowledge, may be considered as casting the balance of his different opinions upon this subject; for I never knew any man who relished good eating more than he did. When at table he was totally absorbed in the business of the moment: his looks seemed riveted to his plate; nor would he, unless when in very high company, say one word, or even pay the least attention to what was said by others, till he had satisfied his appetite, which was so fierce, and indulged with such intenseness, that while in the act of eating, the veins of his forehead swelled, and generally a strong perspiration was visible. To those whose sensations were delicate, this could not but be disgusting; and it was doubtless not very suitable to the character of a philosopher, who should be distinguished by self-command. But it must be owned that Johnson, though he could be rigidly *abstemious*, was not a *temperate* man either in eating or drinking. He could refrain, but he could not use moderately. He told me that he had fasted two days without inconvenience, and that he had never been hungry but once. They who beheld with wonder how much he ate upon all occasions, when his dinner was to his taste, could not easily conceive what he must have meant by hunger; and not only was he remarkable for the extraordinary quantity which he ate, but he was, or affected to be, a man of very nice discernment in the science of cookery. He used to descant critically on the dishes which had been at table where he had dined or supped, and to recollect very minutely what he had liked. I remember when he was in Scotland, his praising '*Gordon's palates*' (a dish of palates at the Honorable Alexander Gordon's) with a warmth of expression which might have done honor to more important subjects. 'As for Maclaurin's imitation of a *made dish*, it was a wretched attempt.' He about the same time was so much displeased with the performances of a nobleman's French cook, that he exclaimed with vehemence, 'I'd throw such a rascal into the river;' and he then proceeded to alarm a lady at whose house he was to sup, by the following manifesto of his skill:—'I, madam, who live at a variety of good tables, am a much better judge of cookery, than any person who has a very tolerable cook, but lives much at home; for his palate is gradually adapted to the taste of his cook; whereas, madam, in trying by a wider range, I can more exquisitely judge.' When invited to dine, even with an intimate friend, he was not pleased if something better than a plain dinner was not prepared for him. I have heard him say on such an occasion, 'This was a good dinner enough to be sure; but it was not a dinner to *ask* a man to.' On the other hand, he was wont to express, with great glee, his satisfaction when he had been entertained quite to his mind.

While we were left by ourselves, after the Dutchman had gone to bed, Dr. Johnson talked of that studied behavior which many have recommended and practised. He disapproved of it; and said, 'I never considered whether I should be a grave man, or a merry man, but just let inclination, for the time, have its course.'

Next day we got to Harwich, to dinner; and my passage in the packet boat to Helvoetsluys being secured, and my baggage put on board, we dined at our inn by ourselves. I happened to say it would be terrible if he should not find a speedy opportunity of returning to London, and be confined in so dull a place. JOHNSON: 'Don't, sir, accustom yourself to use big words for little matters. It would *not* be *terrible*, though I *were* to be detained some time here.' The practice of using words of disproportionate magnitude, is, no doubt, too frequent everywhere; but, I think, most remarkable among the French, of which, all who have traveled in France must have been struck with innumerable instances.

We went and looked at the church, and having gone into it, and walked up to the altar, Johnson, whose piety was constant and fervent, sent me to my knees, saying, 'Now that you are going to leave your native country, recommend yourself to the protection of your Creator and Redeemer.'

After we came out of the church, we stood talking for some time together, of Bishop Berkeley's ingenious sophistry to prove the non-existence of matter, and that everything in the universe is merely ideal. I observed that, though we are satisfied his doctrine is not true, it is impossible to refute it. I never shall forget the alacrity with which Johnson answered, striking his foot with mighty force against a large stone, till he rebounded from it,—'I refute it *thus*.'

* * *

My revered friend walked down with me to the beach, where we embraced and parted with tenderness, and engaged to correspond by letters. I said, 'I hope, sir, you will not forget me in my absence.' JOHNSON: 'Nay, sir, it is more likely you should forget me, than that I should forget you.' As the vessel put out to sea, I kept my eyes upon him for a considerable time, while he remained rolling his majestic frame in his usual manner; and at last I perceived him walk back into the town, and he disappeared.

(1791)

* * *

EDMUND BURKE (1729-1797)

The career of Burke belongs to the history of English politics, its memorials to English literature. His father was a Dublin solicitor and a Protestant; his mother was a firm Catholic, and he spent a part of his school days under the tuition of a Quaker. He was himself brought up a Protestant, but on this as other subjects preserved a large and open mind. He took his bachelor's degree at Trinity College, Dublin, in 1748, and later read law at the Middle Temple in London. For upwards of a decade after his removal to England, in 1750, his ambition pointed to literature. In 1756 he published *A Vindication of Natural Society*, an ironical imitation of Bolingbroke intended to throw ridicule upon the political theories of that writer. 'Burke foresaw from the first,' an English statesman of our own day has said, 'what, if rationalism were allowed to run its course, would be the really great business of the second half of his century.' The same year he printed his youthful essay *On the Sublime and Beautiful* and three years later became editor of Dodsley's *Annual Register*. But his literary abilities soon marked him out for the public service. In some way, not very well understood, his financial disability was overcome, and he entered upon a career in Parliament, making his first speech in January, 1766. His *Observations on the Present State of the Nation* (1769) showed his grasp of economic detail, and his pamphlet, entitled, *Thoughts on the Present Discontents*, the following year, for the first time exhibited the full breadth of his political philosophy. Four years later the struggle with the American colonies which had been going on ever since Burke entered Parliament had reached the stage of threatened war. It was in the debate upon this great occasion that Burke's mastery of economic detail, and his broad and lucid command of principle were welded together by his gift of passionate exposition into the three documents of political philosophy which will be cherished wherever the race flourishes in whose language they were delivered. *The Speech on American Taxation* was given in April, 1774, *The Speech for Conciliation*, March 22, 1775, and the *Letter to the Sheriffs of Bristol* was issued in 1777. The other subjects upon which Burke distinguished himself as an orator were the impeachment of Warren Hastings and the incidents of the French Revolution. His views in regard to the latter were such as sometimes to perplex his party and his friends and he was often almost solitary in his position. In spite of Goldsmith's accusation that he 'to party gave up what was meant for mankind,' Burke's gifts were not those of the successful politician. He retired from Parliament in 1794, having wielded great power at times, but having won no official position of high dignity. His achievements were such as become increasingly lustrous with the passage of time.

From THE SPEECH FOR CONCILIATION WITH THE COLONIES

These, sir, are my reasons for not entertaining that high opinion of untried force, by which many gentlemen, for whose sentiments in other particulars I have great respect, seem to be so greatly captivated. But there is still behind a third consideration concerning this object, which serves to determine my opinion on the sort of policy which ought to be pursued in the management of America, even more than its population and its commerce, I mean its *temper and character*.

In this character of the Americans, a love of freedom is the predominating feature which marks and distinguishes the whole; and as an ardent is always a jealous affection, your colonies become suspicious, restive, and untractable, whenever they see the least attempt to wrest from them by force or shuffle from them by chicane, what they think the only advantage worth living for. This fierce spirit of liberty is stronger in the English colonies probably than in any other people of the earth; and this from a great variety of powerful causes; which, to understand the true temper of their minds, and the direction which this spirit takes, it will not be amiss to lay open somewhat more largely.

First, the people of the colonies are descendants of Englishmen. England, sir, is a nation which still I hope respects, and formerly adored, her freedom. The colonists emigrated from you, when this part of your character was most predominant; and they took this bias and direction the moment they parted from your hands. They are therefore not only devoted to liberty, but to liberty according to English ideas, and on English principles. Abstract liberty, like other mere abstractions, is not to be found. Liberty inheres in some sensible object; and every nation has formed to itself some favorite point, which by way of eminence becomes the criterion of their happiness. It happened, you know, sir, that the great contests for freedom in this country were from the earliest times chiefly upon the question of taxing. Most of the contests in the ancient commonwealths turned primarily on the right of election of magistrates; or on the balance among the several orders of the state. The question of money was not with them so immediate. But in England it was otherwise. On this point of taxes the ablest pens and most eloquent tongues have been exercised; the greatest spirits have acted and suffered. In order to give the fullest satisfaction concerning the importance of this point, it was not only necessary for those who in argument defended the excellence of the English constitution to insist on this privilege of granting money as a dry point of fact, and to prove that the right had been acknowledged in ancient parchments and blind usage to reside in a certain body called a House of Commons. They went much farther; they attempted to prove, and they succeeded, that in theory it ought to be so, from the particular nature of a House of Commons as an immediate representative of the people, whether the old records had delivered this oracle or not. They took infinite pains to inculcate, as a fundamental principle, that in all monarchies the people must in effect themselves, mediately or immediately, possess the power of granting their own money, or no shadow of liberty could subsist. The colonies draw from you, as with their lifeblood, these ideas and principles. Their love of liberty, as with you, fixed and attached on this specific point of taxing. Liberty might be safe, or might be endangered, in twenty other particulars, without their being much pleased or alarmed. Here they felt its pulse; and as they found that beat, they thought themselves sick or sound. I do not say whether they were right or wrong in applying your general arguments to their own cause. It is not easy indeed to make a monopoly of theorems and corollaries. The fact is, that they did thus apply those general arguments; and your mode of governing them, whether through lenity or indolence, through wisdom or mistake, confirmed them in the imagination, that they, as well as you, had an interest in these common principles.

They were further confirmed in this pleasing error by the form of their provincial legislative assemblies. The governments are popular in a high degree; some are merely popular; in all, the popular representative is the most weighty; and this share of the people in their ordinary government never fails to inspire them with lofty sentiments, and with a strong aversion from whatever tends to deprive them of their chief importance.

If anything were wanting to this necessary operation of the form of government, religion would have given it a complete effect. Religion, always a principle of energy, in this new people is no way worn out or impaired; and their mode of professing it is also one main cause of this free spirit. The people are Protestants; and of that kind which is the most adverse to all implicit submission of mind and opinion. This is a persuasion not only favorable to liberty, but built upon it. I do not think, sir, that the reason of this averseness in the dissenting churches, from all that looks like absolute government, is so much to be sought in their religious tenets as in their history. Every one knows that the Roman Catholic religion is at least coeval with most of the governments where it prevails; that it has generally gone hand in hand with them, and received great favor and every kind of support from authority. The Church of England too was formed from her cradle under the nursing care of regular government. But the dissenting interests have sprung up in direct opposition to all the ordinary powers of the world; and could justify that opposition only on a strong claim to natural liberty. Their very existence depended on the powerful and unremitted assertion of that claim. All Protestantism, even the most cold and passive, is a sort of dissent. But the religion most prevalent in our northern colonies is a refinement on the principle of resistance; it is the dissidence of dissent, and the Protestantism of the Protestant religion. This religion, under a variety of denominations agreeing in nothing but in the communion of the spirit of liberty, is predominant in most of the northern provinces, where the Church of England, notwithstanding its legal rights, is in reality no more than a sort of private sect, not composing most probably the tenth of the people. The colonists left England when this spirit was high, and in the emigrants was the highest of all, and even that stream of foreigners, which has been constantly flowing into these colonies, has, for the greatest part, been composed of dissenters from the establishments of their several countries, and have brought with them a temper and character far from alien to that of the people with whom they mixed.

Sir, I can perceive by their manner, that some gentlemen object to the latitude of this description, because in the southern colonies the Church of England forms a large body, and has a regular establishment. It is certainly true. There is, however, a circumstance attending these colonies, which, in my opinion, fully counterbalances this difference, and makes the spirit of liberty still more high and haughty than in those to the northward. It is, that in Virginia and the Carolinas they have a vast multitude of slaves. Where this is the case in any part of the world, those who are free are by far the most proud and jealous of their freedom. Freedom is to them not only an enjoyment, but a kind of rank and privilege. Not seeing there, that freedom, as in countries where it is a common blessing, and as broad and general as the air, may be united with much abject toil, with great misery, with all the exterior of servitude, liberty looks, amongst them, like something that is more noble and liberal. I do not mean, sir, to commend the superior morality of this sentiment, which has at least as much pride as virtue in it; but I cannot alter the nature of man. The fact is so; and these people of the southern colonies are much more strongly, and with a higher and more stubborn spirit, attached to liberty, than those to the northward. Such were all the ancient commonwealths; such were our Gothic ancestors; such in our days were the Poles; and such will be all masters of slaves who are not slaves themselves. In such a people, the haughtiness of domination combines with the spirit of freedom, fortifies it, and renders it invincible.

Permit me, sir, to add another circumstance in our colonies, which contributes no mean part towards the growth and effect of this untractable spirit. I mean their education. In no country perhaps in the world is the law so general a study. The profession itself is numerous and powerful; and in most provinces it takes the lead. The greater number of the deputies sent to the Congress were lawyers. But all who read (and most do read), endeavor to obtain some smattering in that science. I have been told by an eminent bookseller, that in no branch of his business, after tracts of popular devotion, were so many books as those on the law exported to the plantations. The colonists have now fallen into the way of printing them for their own use. I hear that they have sold nearly as many of Blackstone's Commentaries in America as in England. General Gage marks out this disposition very particularly in a letter on your table. He states that all the people in his government are lawyers, or smatterers in law; and that in Boston they have been enabled, by successful chicane, wholly to evade many parts of one of your capital penal constitutions. The smartness of debate will say that this knowledge ought to teach them more clearly the rights of legislature, their obligations to obedience, and the penalties of rebellion. All this is mighty well. But my honorable and learned friend on the floor, who condescends to mark what I say for animadversion, will disdain that ground. He has heard, as well as I, that when great honors and great emoluments do not win over this knowledge to the service of the state, it is a formidable adversary to government. If the spirit be not tamed and broken by these happy methods, it is stubborn and litigious. *Abeunt studia in mores* [studies develop into habits]. This study renders men acute, inquisitive, dexterous, prompt in attack, ready in defense, full of resources. In other countries, the people, more simple, and of a less mercurial cast, judge of an ill principle in government only by an actual grievance; here they anticipate the evil, and judge of the pressure of the grievance by the badness of the principle. They augur misgovernment at a distance; and snuff the approach of tyranny in every tainted breeze.

The last cause of this disobedient spirit in the colonies is hardly less powerful than the rest, as it is not merely moral, but laid deep in the natural constitution of things. Three thousand miles of ocean lie between you and them. No contrivance can prevent the effect of this distance in weakening government. Seas roll, and months pass, between the order and the execution; and the want of a speedy explanation of a single point is enough to defeat a whole system. You have, indeed, 'winged ministers of vengeance,' who carry your bolts in their pounces to the remotest verge of the sea. But there a power steps in, that limits the arrogance of raging passions and furious elements, and says, 'So far shalt thou go, and no farther.' Who are you, that you should fret and rage, and bite the chains of Nature?—nothing worse happens to you than does to all nations who have extensive empire; and it happens in all the forms into which empire can be thrown. In large bodies, the circulation of power must be less vigorous at the extremities. Nature has said it. The Turk cannot govern Egypt, and Arabia, and Kurdistan, as he governs Thrace; nor has he the same dominion in Crimea and Algiers which he has at Brusa and Smyrna. Despotism itself is obliged to truck and huckster. The Sultan gets such obedience as he can. He governs with a loose rein, that he may govern at all; and the whole of the force and vigor of his authority in his center is derived from a prudent relaxation in all his borders. Spain, in her provinces, is perhaps not so well obeyed as you are in yours. She complies too; she submits; she watches times. This is the immutable condition, the eternal law, of extensive and detached empire.

Then, sir, from these six capital sources; of descent; of form of government; of religion in the northern provinces; of manners in the southern; of education; of the remoteness of situation from the first mover of government; from all these causes a fierce spirit of liberty has grown up. It has grown with the growth of the people in your colonies, and increased with the increase of their wealth; a spirit, that unhappily meeting with an exercise of power in England, which, however lawful, is not reconcilable to any ideas of liberty, much less with theirs, has kindled this flame that is ready to consume us.

I do not mean to commend either the spirit in this excess, or the moral causes which produce it. Perhaps a more smooth and accommodating spirit of freedom in them would be more acceptable to us. Perhaps ideas of liberty might be desired more reconcilable with an arbitrary and boundless authority. Perhaps we might wish the colonists to be persuaded that their liberty is more secure when held in trust for them by us (as their guardians during a perpetual minority) than with any part of it in their own hands. The question is, not whether their spirit deserves praise or blame, but what, in the name of God, shall we do with it? You have before you the object, such as it is, with all its glories, with all its imperfections, on its head. You see the magnitude, the importance, the temper, the habits, the disorders. By all these considerations we are strongly urged to determine something concerning it. We are called upon to fix some rule and line for our future conduct, which may give a little stability to our politics, and prevent the return of such unhappy deliberations as the present. Every such return will bring the matter before us in a still more untractable form. For, what astonishing and incredible things have we not seen already! What monsters have not been generated from this unnatural contention! Whilst every principle of authority and resistance has been pushed, upon both sides, as far as it would go, there is nothing so solid and certain, either in reasoning or in practice, that has not been shaken. Until very lately, all authority in America seemed to be nothing but an emanation from yours. Even the popular part of the colony constitution derived all its activity, and its first vital movement, from the pleasure of the crown. We thought, sir, that the utmost which the discontented colonists could do was to disturb authority; we never dreamt they could of themselves supply it; knowing in general what an operose business it is to establish a government absolutely new. But having, for our purposes in this contention, resolved that none but an obedient assembly should sit; the humors of the people there finding all passage through the legal channel stopped, with great violence broke out another way. Some provinces have tried their experiment, as we have tried ours; and theirs has succeeded. They have formed a government sufficient for its purposes, without the bustle of a revolution, or the troublesome formality of an election. Evident necessity and tacit consent have done the business in an instant. So well they have done it, that Lord Dunmore—the account is among the fragments on your table—tells you that the new institution is infinitely better obeyed than the ancient government ever was in its most fortunate periods. Obedience is what makes government, and not the names by which it is called; not the name of Governor, as formerly, or Committee, as at present. This new government has originated directly from the people; and was not transmitted through any of the ordinary artificial media of a positive constitution. It was not a manufacture ready formed, and transmitted to them in that condition from England. The evil arising from hence is this, that the colonists having once found the possibility of enjoying the advantages of order in the midst of a struggle for liberty, such struggles will not henceforward seem so terrible to the settled and sober part of mankind as they had appeared before the trial.

Pursuing the same plan of punishing by the denial of the exercise of government to still greater lengths, we wholly abrogated the ancient government of Massachusetts. We were confident that the first feeling, if not the very prospect of anarchy, would instantly enforce a complete submission. The experiment was tried. A new, strange, unexpected phase of things appeared. Anarchy is found tolerable. A vast province has now subsisted, and subsisted in a considerable degree of health and vigor, for near a twelvemonth, without Governor, without public council, without judges, without executive magistrates. How long it will continue in this state, or what may rise out of this unheard-of situation, how can the wisest of us conjecture? Our late experience has taught us that many of those fundamental principles formerly believed infallible, are either not of the importance they were imagined to be; or that we have not at all adverted to some other far more important and far more powerful principles, which entirely overrule those we had considered as omnipotent. I am much against any further experiments, which tend to put to the proof any more of these allowed opinions, which contribute so much to the public tranquillity. In effect, we suffer as much at home by this loosening of all ties, and this concussion of all established opinions, as we do abroad. For, in order to prove that the Americans have no right to their liberties, we are every day endeavoring to subvert the maxims which preserve the whole spirit of our own. To prove that the Americans ought not to be free, we are obliged to depreciate the value of freedom itself; and we never seem to gain a paltry advantage over them in debate, without attacking some of those principles, or deriding some of those feelings, for which our ancestors have shed their blood.

But, sir, in wishing to put an end to pernicious experiments, I do not mean to preclude the fullest inquiry. Far from it. Far from deciding on a sudden or partial view, I would patiently go round and round the subject, and survey it minutely in every possible aspect. Sir, if I were capable of engaging you to an equal attention, I would state that, as far as I am capable of discerning, there are but three ways of proceeding relative to this stubborn spirit, which prevails in your colonies, and disturbs your government. These are: to change that spirit, as inconvenient, by removing the causes; to prosecute it as criminal; or, to comply with it as necessary. I would not be guilty of an imperfect enumeration; I can think of but these three. Another has indeed been started, that of giving up the colonies; but it met so slight a reception, that I do not think myself obliged to dwell a great while upon it. It is nothing but a little sally of anger, like the frowardness of peevish children, who, when they cannot get all they would have, are resolved to take nothing.

The first of these plans, to change the spirit as inconvenient, by removing the causes, I think is the most like a systematic proceeding. It is radical in its principle; but it is attended with great difficulties, some of them little short, as I conceive, of impossibilities. This will appear by examining into the plans which have been proposed.

As the growing population in the colonies is evidently one cause of their resistance, it was last session mentioned in both Houses, by men of weight, and received not without applause, that in order to check this evil, it would be proper for the crown to make no further grants of land. But to this scheme there are two objections. The first, that there is already so much unsettled land in private hands as to afford room for an immense future population, although the crown not only withheld its grants, but annihilated its soil. If this be the case, then the only effect of this avarice of desolation, this hoarding of a royal wilderness, would be to raise the value of the possessions in the hands of the great private monopolists, without any adequate check to the growing and alarming mischief of population.

But if you stopped your grants, what would be the consequence? The people would occupy without grants. They have already so occupied in many places. You cannot station garrisons in every part of these deserts. If you drive the people from one place, they will carry on their annual tillage, and remove with their flocks and herds to another. Many of the people in the back settlements are already little attached to particular situations. Already they have topped the Appalachian mountains. From thence they behold before them an immense plain, one vast, rich, level meadow; a square of five hundred miles. Over this they would wander without a possibility of restraint; they would change their manners with the habits of their life, would soon forget a government by which they were disowned; would become hordes of English Tartars; and pouring down upon your unfortified frontiers a fierce and irresistible cavalry, become masters of your governors and your counsellors, your collectors and comptrollers, and of all the slaves that adhered to them. Such would, and in no long time must, be the effect of attempting to forbid as a crime, and to suppress as an evil, the command and blessing of Providence, 'Increase and multiply.' Such would be the happy result of an endeavor to keep, as a lair of wild beasts, that earth which God, by an express charter, has *given to the children of men*. Far different, and surely much wiser, has been our policy hitherto. Hitherto we have invited our people, by every kind of bounty, to fixed establishments. We have invited the husbandman to look to authority for his title. We have taught him piously to believe in the mysterious virtue of wax and parchment. We have thrown each tract of land, as it was peopled, into districts, that the ruling power should never be wholly out of sight. We have settled all we could; and we have carefully attended every settlement with government.

Adhering sir, as I do, to this policy, as well as for the reasons I have just given, I think this new project of hedging-in population to be neither prudent nor practicable.

To impoverish the colonies in general, and in particular to arrest the noble course of their marine enterprises, would be a more easy task. I freely confess it. We have shown a disposition to a system of this kind; a disposition even to continue the restraint after the offence; looking on ourselves as rivals to our colonies, and persuaded that of course we must gain all that they shall lose. Much mischief we may certainly do. The power inadequate to all other things is often more than sufficient for this. I do not look on the direct and immediate power of the colonies to resist our violence as very formidable. In this, however, I may be mistaken. But when I consider that we have colonies for no purpose but to be serviceable to us, it seems to my poor understanding a little preposterous to make them unserviceable, in order to keep them obedient. It is, in truth, nothing more than the old, and, as I thought, exploded problem of tyranny, which proposes to beggar its subjects into submission. But remember, when you have completed your system of impoverishment, that Nature still proceeds in her ordinary course; that discontent will increase with misery; and that there are critical moments in the fortune of all states, when they who are too weak to contribute to your prosperity may be strong enough to complete your ruin. *Spoliatis arma supersunt* [Arms remain to the despoiled].

The temper and character which prevail in our colonies, are, I am afraid, unalterable by any human art. We cannot, I fear, falsify the pedigree of this fierce people, and persuade them that they are not sprung from a nation in whose veins the blood of freedom circulates. The language in which they would hear you tell them this tale would detect the imposition: your speech would betray you. An Englishman is the unfittest person on earth to argue another Englishman into slavery.

I think it is nearly as little in our power to change their republican religion as their free descent; or to substitute the Roman Catholic, as a penalty; or the Church of England, as an improvement. The mode of inquisition and dragooning is going out of fashion in the Old World, and I should not confide much to their efficacy in the New. The education of the Americans is also on the same unalterable bottom with their religion. You cannot persuade them to burn their books of curious science; to banish their lawyers from their courts of laws; or to quench the lights of their assemblies, by refusing to choose those persons who are best read in their privileges. It would be no less impracticable to think of wholly annihilating the popular assemblies, in which these lawyers sit. The army, by which we must govern in their place, would be far more chargeable to us; not quite so effectual; and perhaps, in the end, full as difficult to be kept in obedience.

With regard to the high aristocratic spirit of Virginia and the southern colonies, it has been proposed, I know, to reduce it, by declaring a general enfranchisement of their slaves. This project has had its advocates and panegyrists; yet I never could argue myself into any opinion of it. Slaves are often much attached to their masters. A general wild offer of liberty would not always be accepted. History furnishes few instances of it. It is sometimes as hard to persuade slaves to be free, as it is to compel freemen to be slaves; and in this auspicious scheme we should have both these pleasing tasks on our hands at once. But when we talk of enfranchisement, do we not perceive that the American master may enfranchise too, and arm servile hands in defence of freedom? A measure to which other people have had recourse more than once, and not without success, in a desperate situation of their affairs.

Slaves as these unfortunate black people are, and dull as all men are from slavery, must they not a little suspect the offer of freedom from that very nation which has sold them to their present masters? From that nation, one of whose causes of quarrel with those masters is their refusal to deal any more in that inhuman traffic? An offer of freedom from England would come rather oddly, shipped to them in an African vessel, which is refused an entry into the ports of Virginia or Carolina, with a cargo of three hundred Angola negroes. It would be curious to see the Guinea captain attempting at the same instant to publish his proclamation of liberty, and to advertise his sale of slaves.

But let us suppose all these moral difficulties got over. The ocean remains. You cannot pump this dry; and as long as it continues in its present bed, so long all the causes which weaken authority by distance will continue. 'Ye gods, annihilate but space and time, and make two lovers happy!' was a pious and passionate prayer; but just as reasonable as many of the serious wishes of very grave and solemn politicians.

If then, sir, it seems almost desperate to think of any alternative course for changing the moral causes, and not quite easy to remove the natural, which produce prejudices irreconcilable to the late exercise of our authority, but that the spirit infallibly will continue, and, continuing, will produce such effects as now embarrass us; the second mode under consideration is to prosecute that spirit in its overt acts as criminal.

At this proposition I must pause a moment. The thing seems a great deal too big for my ideas of jurisprudence. It should seem to my way of conceiving such matters, that there is a very wide difference in reason and policy between the mode of proceeding on the irregular conduct of scattered individuals, or even of bands of men, who disturb order within the state, and the civil dissensions which may, from time to time, on great questions, agitate the several communities which compose a great empire. It looks to me to be narrow and pedantic to apply the ordinary ideas of criminal justice to this great public contest. I do not know the method of drawing up an indictment against a whole people. I cannot insult and ridicule the feelings of millions of my fellow-creatures, as Sir Edward Coke insulted one excellent individual (Sir Walter Raleigh) at the bar. I hope I am not ripe to pass sentence on the gravest public bodies, entrusted with magistracies of great authority and dignity, and charged with the safety of their fellow-citizens, upon the very same title that I am. I really think that, for wise men, this is not judicious; for sober men, not decent; for minds tinctured with humanity, not mild and merciful.

Perhaps, sir, I am mistaken in my idea of an empire, as distinguished from a single state or kingdom. But my idea of it is this: that an empire is the aggregate of many states under one common head; whether this head be a monarch, or a presiding republic. It does, in such constitutions, frequently happen (and nothing but the dismal, cold, dead uniformity of servitude can prevent its happening) that the subordinate parts have many local privileges and immunities. Between these privileges and the supreme common authority the line may be extremely nice. Of course, disputes, often, too, very bitter disputes, and much ill blood, will arise. But though every privilege is an exemption (in the case) from the ordinary exercise of the supreme authority, it is no denial of it. The claim of the privilege seems rather, *ex vi termini* [by the meaning of the term], to imply a superior power. For to talk of the privileges of a state, or of a person, who has no superior, is hardly any better than speaking nonsense. Now, in such unfortunate quarrels among the component parts of a great political union of communities, I can scarcely conceive anything more completely imprudent than for the head of the empire to insist that, if any privilege is pleaded against his will, or his acts, his whole authority is denied; instantly to proclaim rebellion, to beat to arms, and to put the offending provinces under the ban. Will not this, sir, very soon teach the provinces to make no distinctions on their part? Will it not teach them that the government, against which a claim of liberty is tantamount to high treason, is a government to which submission is equivalent to slavery? It may not always be quite convenient to impress dependent communities with such an idea.

We are indeed, in all disputes with the colonies, by the necessity of things, the judge. It is true, sir. But I confess that the character of judge in my own cause is a thing that frightens me. Instead of filling me with pride, I am exceedingly humbled by it. I cannot proceed with a stern, assured, judicial confidence, until I find myself in something more like a judicial character. I must have these hesitations as long as I am compelled to recollect that, in my little reading upon such contests as these, the sense of mankind has, at least, as often decided against the superior as the subordinate power. Sir, let me add too, that the opinion of my having some abstract right in my favor would not put me much at my ease in passing sentence, unless I could be sure that there were no rights which, in their exercise under certain circumstances, were not the most odious of all wrongs, and the most vexatious of all injustice. Sir, these considerations have great weight with me, when I find things so circumstanced, that I see the same party at once a civil litigant against me in point of right; and a culprit before me, while I sit as a criminal judge on acts of his, whose moral quality is to be decided upon the merits of that very litigation. Men are every now and then put, by the complexity of human affairs, into strange situations; but justice is the same, let the judge be in what situation he will.

There is, sir, also a circumstance which convinces me that this mode of criminal proceeding is not (at least in the present stage of our contest) altogether expedient; which is nothing less than the conduct of those very persons who have seemed to adopt that mode, by lately declaring a rebellion in Massachusetts Bay, as they had formerly addressed to have traitors brought hither, under an Act of Henry the Eighth, for trial. For though rebellion is declared, it is not proceeded against as such; nor have any steps been taken towards the apprehension or conviction of any individual offender, either on our late or our former Address; but modes of public coercion have been adopted, and such as have much more resemblance to a sort of qualified hostility toward an independent power than the punishment of rebellious subjects. All this seems rather inconsistent; but it shows how difficult it is to apply these juridical ideas to our present case.

In this situation, let us seriously and coolly ponder. What is it we have got by all our menaces, which have been many and ferocious? What advantage have we derived from the penal laws we have rightly passed, and which, for the time, have been severe and numerous? What advances have we made towards our object, by the sending of a force which, by land and sea, is no contemptible strength? Has the disorder abated? Nothing less. When I see things in this situation, after such confident hopes, bold promises, and active exertions, I cannot for my life avoid a suspicion that the plan itself is not correctly right.

If then the removal of the causes of this spirit of American liberty be, for the greater part, or rather entirely, impracticable; if the ideas of criminal process be inapplicable, or if applicable, are in the highest degree inexpedient; what way yet remains? No way is open but the third and last—to comply with the American spirit as necessary; or, if you please, to submit to it as a necessary evil.

If we adopt this mode; if we mean to conciliate and concede; let us see of what nature the concession ought to be: to ascertain the nature of our concession we must look at their complaint. The colonies complain that they have not the characteristic mark and seal of British freedom. They complain that they are taxed in a parliament in which they are not represented. If you mean to satisfy them at all, you must satisfy them with regard to this complaint. If you mean to please any people, you must give them the boon which they ask; not what you may think better for them, but of a kind totally different. Such an act may be a wise regulation, but it is no concession; whereas our present theme is the mode of giving satisfaction.

* * *

Such is steadfastly my opinion of the absolute necessity of keeping up the concord of this empire by a unity of spirit, though in a diversity of operations, that, if I were sure the colonists had, at their leaving this country, sealed a regular compact of servitude; that they had solemnly abjured all the rights of citizens; that they had made a vow to renounce all ideas of liberty for them and their posterity to all generations; yet I should hold myself obliged to conform to the temper I found universally prevalent in my own day, and to govern two million of men, impatient of servitude, on the principles of freedom. I am not determining a point of law; I am restoring tranquillity; and the general character and situation of a people must determine what sort of government is fitted for them. That point nothing else can or ought to determine.

My idea, therefore, without considering whether we yield as matter of right, or grant as matter of favor, is to *admit the people of our colonies into an interest in the Constitution;* and, by recording that admission in the journals of parliament, to give them as strong an assurance as the nature of the thing will admit, that we mean for ever to adhere to that solemn declaration of systematic indulgence.

* * *

(1775)

EDWARD GIBBON (1737-1794)

The greatest of English historians was born not far from London, at Putney in Surrey, where his father lived the easy life of a country gentleman. Gibbon ascribed the success of his later years to the 'golden mediocrity' of his fortunes, which preserved him on the one hand from the seductions of pleasure and, on the other, from the need of earning a living. His childhood was sickly, his education was intermittent, and he was indulged in his bent for reading which soon settled to a passion for history. At an early age he had devoured everything in that department which was accessible in English and had begun to annex other languages in order that he might gratify his hunger for original documents. He was sent at fifteen to Magdalen College, Oxford, and has left a withering indictment of the neglect and incompetence which he encountered at that seat of learning. Left to himself, he fell under the influence of a Jesuit and was converted to Roman Catholicism; whereupon his father promptly deported him to Switzerland and placed him under the care of a Calvinist minister at Lausanne. Through constant practice in the defense of his faith he became familiar with its assailable points, and soon passed to the position of skepticism which he permanently occupied. He mastered the French language and the French method of study and became deeply imbued with the French rationalistic ideas of the period. By five years of great diligence under able direction he laid the foundation of his superb equipment for the task of his life. Returning to England, he published in the French language his first book, *Essai sur l'Étude de la Littérature* [Essay on the Study of Literature] (1761). To please his father he served for two years and a half as a captain of militia. The singleness of his ambition is well illustrated by his summary of these lost years: 'The discipline and evolutions of a modern battalion gave me a clearer notion of the phalanx and the legions, and the captain of the Hampshire grenadiers—the reader may smile—has not been useless to the historian of the Roman empire.' But of this and of his later career in Parliament he was impatient as of anything which did not contribute directly to his one ambition. From his early youth he had 'aspired to the character of a historian,' but he remained unsettled as to the field he should occupy until he found himself at Rome. 'In my journal, the place and the moment of the conception are recorded,' he tells us in his *Memoirs*, 'the fifteenth of October, 1764, in the close of the evening, as I sat musing in the church of the Zoccolanti or Franciscan friars, while they were singing vespers in the temple of Jupiter on the ruins of the Capitol.' Two years elapsed before he was able to set to work, twelve before the first volume was published in London, and another twelve before he laid down his pen at Lausanne. His *History of the Decline and Fall* had been his life, the one object toward which all his reading and experience were made to converge, and is the one subject of his *Memoirs*. He quietly finished his days at Lausanne, undoubtedly justified in his feeling that this achievement had been enough for one life. The substance of Gibbon's 'candid and rational inquiry into the human causes' of the religious growth which undermined the civilization of the ancient world, has not remained totally unassailed by the modern historian; nor is Gibbon's style perfect; but it is safe to say that no other Englishman has united in an equal degree abundance and accuracy of information, sense of historical perspective and proportion, vigor of narrative, and splendor of style.

From THE DECLINE AND FALL OF THE ROMAN EMPIRE

CHAPTER LXVIII

Of the triangle which composes the figure of Constantinople, the two sides along the sea were made inaccessible to an enemy: the Propontis by nature and the harbor by art. Between the two waters, the basis of the triangle, the land side was protected by a double wall and a deep ditch of the depth of one hundred feet. Against this line of fortification, which Phranza, an eyewitness, prolongs to the measure of six miles, the Ottomans directed their principal attack; and the emperor, after distributing the service and command of the most perilous stations, undertook the defence of the external wall. In the first days of the siege, the Greek soldiers 5 descended into the ditch, or sallied into the field; but they soon discovered that, in the proportion of their numbers, one Christian was of more value than twenty Turks; and, after these bold preludes, they were prudently content to 10 maintain the rampart with their missile weapons Nor should this prudence be accused of pusillanimity. The nation was indeed pusillanimous and base; but the last Constantine deserves the name of an hero: his noble band of volunteers was inspired with Roman virtue; and the foreign auxiliaries supported the honor of the Western chivalry. The incessant volleys of lances and arrows were accompanied with the smoke, the sound, and the fire of their musketry and cannon. Their small arms discharged at the same time either five or even ten balls of lead of the size of a walnut; and, according to the closeness of the ranks and the force of the powder, several breastplates and bodies were transpierced by the same shot. But the Turkish approaches were soon sunk in trenches or covered with ruins. Each day added to the science of the Christians; but their inadequate stock of gunpowder was wasted in the operations of each day. Their ordnance was not powerful either in size or number; and, if they possessed some heavy cannon, they feared to plant them on the walls, lest the aged structure should be shaken and overthrown by the explosion. The same destructive secret had been revealed to the Moslems; by whom it was employed with the superior energy of zeal, riches, and despotism. The great cannon of Mahomet has been separately noticed; an important and visible object in the history of the times: but that enormous engine was flanked by two fellows almost of equal magnitude; the long order of the Turkish artillery was pointed against the walls; fourteen batteries thundered at once on the most accessible places; and of one of these it is ambiguously expressed that it was mounted with one hundred and thirty guns, or that it discharged one hundred and thirty bullets. Yet, in the power and activity of the sultan, we may discern the infancy of the new science. Under a master who counted the moments, the great cannon could be loaded and fired no more than seven times in one day. The heated metal unfortunately burst; several workmen were destroyed; and the skill of an artist was admired, who bethought himself of preventing the danger and the accident, by pouring oil, after each explosion, into the mouth of the cannon.

The first random shots were productive of more sound than effect; and it was by the advice of a Christian that the engineers were taught to level their aim against the two opposite sides of the salient angles of a bastion. However imperfect, the weight and repetition of the fire made some impression on the walls; and the Turks, pushing their approaches to the edge of the ditch, attempted to fill the enormous chasm and to build a road to the assault. Innumerable fascines and hogsheads and trunks of trees were heaped on each other; and such was the impetuosity of the throng that the foremost and the weakest were pushed headlong down the precipice and instantly buried under the accumulated mass. To fill the ditch was the toil of the besiegers; to clear away the rubbish was the safety of the besieged; and, after a long and bloody conflict, the web that had been woven in the day was still unraveled in the night. The next resource of Mahomet was the practice of mines; but the soil was rocky; in every attempt he was stopped and undermined by the Christian engineers; nor had the art been yet invented of replenishing those subterraneous passages with gunpowder and blowing whole towers and cities into the air. A circumstance that distinguishes the siege of Constantinople is the reunion of the ancient and modern artillery. The cannon were intermingled with the mechanical engines for casting stones and darts; the bullet and the battering-ram were directed against the same walls; nor had the discovery of gunpowder superseded the use of the liquid and unextinguishable fire. A wooden turret of the largest size was advanced on rollers: this portable magazine of ammunition and fascines was protected by a threefold covering of bulls' hides; incessant volleys were securely discharged from the loop-holes; in the front, three doors were contrived for the alternate sally and retreat of the soldiers and workmen. They ascended by a staircase to the upper platform, and, as high as the level of that platform, a scaling-ladder could be raised by pulleys to form a bridge and grapple with the adverse rampart. By these various arts of annoyance, some as new as they were pernicious to the Greeks, the tower of St. Romanus was at length overturned: after a severe struggle, the Turks were repulsed from the breach and interrupted by darkness; but they trusted that with the return of light they should renew the attack with fresh vigor and decisive success. Of this pause of action, this interval of hope, each moment was improved by the activity of the emperor and Justiniani, who passed the night on the spot, and urged the labors which involved the safety of the church and city. At the dawn of day, the impatient sultan perceived, with astonishment and grief, that his wooden turret had been reduced to ashes: the ditch was cleared and restored; and the tower of St. Romanus was again strong and entire. He deplored the failure of his design; and uttered a profane exclamation that the word of the thirty-seven thousand prophets should not have compelled him to believe that such a work, in so short a time, should have been accomplished by the infidels.

The generosity of the Christian princes was cold and tardy; but, in the first apprehension of a siege, Constantine had negotiated, in the isles of the Archipelago, the Morea, and Sicily, the most indispensable supplies. As early as the beginning of April, five great ships, equipped for merchandise and war, would have sailed from the harbor of Chios, had not the wind blown obstinately from the north. One of these ships bore the Imperial flag; the remaining four belonged to the Genoese; and they were laden with wheat and barley, with wine, oil, and vegetables, and, above all, with soldiers and mariners, for the service of the capital. After a tedious delay, a gentle breeze, and, on the second day, a strong gale from the south, carried them through the Hellespont and the Propontis; but the city was already invested by sea and land; and the Turkish fleet, at the entrance of the Bosphorus, was stretched from shore to shore, in the form of a crescent, to intercept, or at least to repel, these bold auxiliaries. The reader who has present to his mind the geographical picture of Constantinople, will conceive and admire the greatness of the spectacle. The five Christian ships continued to advance with joyful shouts, and a full press both of sails and oars, against an hostile fleet of three hundred vessels; and the rampart, the camp, the coasts of Europe and Asia, were lined with innumerable spectators, who anxiously awaited the event of this momentous succor. At the first view that event could not appear doubtful: the superiority of the Moslems was beyond all measure or account; and, in a calm, their numbers and valor must inevitably have prevailed. But their hasty and imperfect navy had been created, not by the genius of the people, but by the will of the sultan: in the height of their prosperity, the Turks have acknowledged that, if God had given them the earth, he had left the sea to the infidels; and a series of defeats, a rapid progress of decay, has established the truth of their modest confession. Except eighteen galleys of some force, the rest of their fleet consisted of open boats, rudely constructed and awkwardly managed, crowded with troops and destitute of cannon; and, since courage arises in a great measure from the consciousness of strength, the bravest of the Janizaries might tremble on a new element. In the Christian squadron, five stout and lofty ships were guided by skilful pilots, and manned with the veterans of Italy and Greece, long practised in the arts and perils of the sea. Their weight was directed to sink or scatter the weak obstacles that impeded their passage: their artillery swept the waters; their liquid fire was poured on the heads of the adversaries who, with the design of boarding, presumed to approach them; and the winds and waves are always on the side of the ablest navigators. In this conflict, the Imperial vessel, which had been almost overpowered, was rescued by the Genoese; but the Turks, in a distant and closer attack, were twice repulsed with considerable loss. Mahomet himself sat on horseback on the beach, to encourage their valor by his voice and presence, by the promise of reward, and by fear more potent than the fear of the enemy. The passions of his soul, and even the gestures of his body, seemed to imitate the actions of the combatants; and, as if he had been the lord of nature, he spurred his horse with a fearless and impotent effort into the sea. His loud reproaches, and the clamors of the camp, urged the Ottomans to a third attack, more fatal and bloody than the two former; and I must repeat, though I cannot credit, the evidence of Phranza, who affirms, from their own mouth, that they lost above twelve thousand men in the slaughter of the day. They fled in disorder to the shores of Europe and Asia, while the Christian squadron, triumphant and unhurt, steered along the Bosphorus and securely anchored within the chain of the harbor. In the confidence of victory, they boasted that the whole Turkish power must have yielded to their arms; but the admiral, or captain bashaw, found some consolation for a painful wound in his eye, by representing that accident as the cause of his defeat. Baltha Ogli was a renegade of the race of the Bulgarian princes; his military character was tainted with the unpopular vice of avarice; and, under the despotism of the prince or people, misfortune is a sufficient evidence of guilt. His rank and services were annihilated by the displeasure of Mahomet. In the royal presence, the captain bashaw was extended on the ground by four slaves, and received one hundred strokes with a golden rod; his death had been pronounced; and he adored the clemency of the sultan, who was satisfied with the milder punishment of confiscation and exile. The introduction of this supply revived the hopes of the

Greeks, and accused the supineness of their Western allies. Amidst the deserts of Anatolia and the rocks of Palestine, the millions of the crusaders had buried themselves in a voluntary and inevitable grave; but the situation of the Imperial city was strong against her enemies, and accessible to her friends; and a rational and moderate armament of the maritime states might have saved the relics of the Roman name, and maintained a Christian fortress in the heart of the Ottoman empire. Yet this was the sole and feeble attempt for the deliverance of Constantinople; the more distant powers were insensible of its danger; and the ambassador of Hungary, or at least of Huniades, resided in the Turkish camp, to remove the fears, and to direct the operations, of the sultan.

It was difficult for the Greeks to penetrate the secret of the divan; yet the Greeks are persuaded that a resistance, so obstinate and surprising, had fatigued the perseverance of Mahomet. He began to meditate a retreat, and the siege would have been speedily raised, if the ambition and jealousy of the second vizir had not opposed the perfidious advice of Calil Bashaw, who still maintained a secret correspondence with the Byzantine court. The reduction of the city appeared to be hopeless, unless a double attack could be made from the harbor as well as from the land; but the harbor was inaccessible: an impenetrable chain was now defended by eight large ships, more than twenty of a smaller size, with several galleys and sloops; and instead of forcing this barrier, the Turks might apprehend a naval sally and a second encounter in the open sea. In this perplexity, the genius of Mahomet conceived and executed a plan of a bold and marvelous cast, of transporting by land his lighter vessels and military stores from the Bosphorus into the higher part of the harbor. The distance is about ten miles; the ground is uneven, and was overspread with thickets; and, as the road must be opened behind the suburb of Galata, their free passage or total destruction must depend on the option of the Genoese. But these selfish merchants were ambitious of the favor of being the last devoured; and the deficiency of art was supplied by the strength of obedient myriads. A level way was covered with a broad platform of strong and solid planks; and to render them more slippery and smooth, they were anointed with the fat of sheep and oxen. Fourscore light galleys and brigantines of fifty and thirty oars were disembarked on the Bosphorus shore. arranged successively on rollers, and drawn forwards by the power of men and pulleys. Two guides or pilots were stationed at the helm and the prow of each vessel: the sails were unfurled to the winds; and the labor was cheered by song and acclamation. In the course of a single night, this Turkish fleet painfully climbed the hill, steered over the plain, and was launched from the declivity into the shallow waters of the harbor, far above the molestation of the deeper vessels of the Greeks. The real importance of this operation was magnified by the consternation and confidence which it inspired; but the notorious, unquestionable fact was displayed before the eyes, and is recorded by the pens, of the two nations. A similar stratagem had been repeatedly practised by the ancients; the Ottoman galleys, I must again repeat, should be considered as large boats; and, if we compare the magnitude and the distance, the obstacles and the means, the boasted miracle has perhaps been equaled by the industry of our own times. As soon as Mahomet had occupied the upper harbor with a fleet and army, he constructed, in the narrowest part, a bridge, or rather mole, of fifty cubits in breadth and one hundred in length; it was formed of casks and hogsheads, joined with rafters linked with iron, and covered with a solid floor. On this floating battery he planted one of his largest cannon, while the fourscore galleys, with troops and scaling-ladders, approached the most accessible side, which had formerly been stormed by the Latin conquerors. The indolence of the Christians has been accused for not destroying these unfinished works; but their fire, by a superior fire, was controlled and silenced; nor were they wanting in a nocturnal attempt to burn the vessels as well as the bridge of the sultan. His vigilance prevented their approach; their foremost galliots were sunk or taken; forty youths, the bravest of Italy and Greece were inhumanly massacred at his command; nor could the emperor's grief be assuaged by the just though cruel retaliation of exposing from the walls the heads of two hundred and sixty Mussulman captives. After a siege of forty days, the fate of Constantinople could no longer be averted. The diminutive garrison was exhausted by a double attack; the fortifications, which had stood for ages against hostile violence, were dismantled on all sides by the Ottoman cannon; many breaches were opened; and near the gate of St. Romanus four towers had been leveled with the ground. For the payment of his feeble and mutinous troops, Constantine was compelled to despoil the churches, with the promise of a fourfold restitution; and his sacrilege offered a new reproach to the enemies of the union. A spirit of discord impaired the remnant of the Christian strength: the Genoese and Venetian auxiliaries asserted the pre-eminence of their respective service; and Justiniani and the Great Duke, whose ambition was not extinguished by the common danger, accused each other of treachery and cowardice.

During the siege of Constantinople, the words of peace and capitulation had been sometimes pronounced; and several embassies had passed between the camp and the city. The Greek emperor was humbled by adversity; and would have yielded to any terms compatible with religion and royalty. The Turkish sultan was desirous of sparing the blood of his soldiers; still more desirous of securing for his own use the Byzantine treasures; and he accomplished a sacred duty in presenting to the *Gabours* the choice of circumcision, of tribute, or of death. The avarice of Mahomet might have been satisfied with an annual sum of one hundred thousand ducats; but his ambition grasped the capital of the East; to the prince he offered a rich equivalent, to the people a free toleration or a safe departure: but, after some fruitless treaty, he declared his resolution of finding either a throne or a grave under the walls of Constantinople. A sense of honor and the fear of universal reproach forbade Palæologus to resign the city into the hands of the Ottomans; and he determined to abide the last extremities of war. Several days were employed by the sultan in the preparations of the assault; and a respite was granted by his favorite science of astrology, which had fixed on the twenty-ninth of May as the fortunate and fatal hour. On the evening of the twenty-seventh, he issued his final orders; assembled in his presence the military chiefs; and dispersed his heralds through the camp to proclaim the duty and the motives of the perilous enterprise. Fear is the first principle of a despotic government; and his menaces were expressed in the Oriental style, that the fugitives and deserters, had they the wings of a bird, should not escape from his inexorable justice. The greatest part of his bashaws and Janizaries were the offspring of Christian parents; but the glories of the Turkish name were perpetuated by successive adoption; and, in the gradual change of individuals, the spirit of a legion, a regiment, or an *oda* is kept alive by imitation and discipline. In this holy warfare, the Moslems were exhorted to purify their minds with prayer, their bodies with seven ablutions; and to abstain from food till the close of the ensuing day. A crowd of dervishes visited the tents, to instil the desire of martyrdom, and the assurance of spending an immortal youth amidst the rivers and gardens of paradise and in the embraces of the black-eyed virgins. Yet Mahomet principally trusted to the efficacy of temporal and visible rewards. A double pay was promised to the victorious troops: 'The city and the buildings,' said Mahomet, 'are mine; but I resign to your valor the captives and the spoil, the treasures of gold and beauty; be rich and be happy. Many are the provinces of my empire: the intrepid soldier who first ascends the walls of Constantinople shall be rewarded with the government of the fairest and most wealthy; and my gratitude shall accumulate his honors and fortunes above the measure of his own hopes.' Such various and potent motives diffused among the Turks a general ardor, regardless of life and impatient for action: the camp re-echoed with the Moslem shouts of 'God is God, there is but one God, and Mahomet is the apostle of God'; and the sea and land, from Galata to the seven towers, were illuminated by the blaze of their nocturnal fires.

Far different was the state of the Christians; who with loud and impotent complaints, deplored the guilt, or the punishment, of their sins. The celestial image of the Virgin had been exposed in solemn procession; but their divine patroness was deaf to their entreaties: they accused the obstinacy of the emperor for refusing a timely surrender; anticipated the horrors of their fate; and sighed for the repose and security of Turkish servitude. The noblest of the Greeks, and the bravest of the allies, were summoned to the palace, to prepare them, on the evening of the twenty-eighth, for the duties and dangers of the general assault. The last speech of Palæologus was the funeral oration of the Roman Empire: he promised, he conjured, and he vainly attempted to infuse the hope which was extinguished in his own mind. In this world all was comfortless and gloomy; and neither the gospel nor the church have proposed any conspicuous recompense to the heroes who fall in the service of their country. But the example of their prince and the confinement of a siege had armed these warriors with the courage of despair; and the pathetic scene is described by the feelings of the historian Phranza, who was himself present at this mournful assembly.

They wept, they embraced; regardless of their families and fortunes, they devoted their lives; and each commander, departing to his station, maintained all night a vigilant and anxious watch on the rampart. The emperor, and some faithful companions, entered the dome of St. Sophia, which in a few hours was to be converted into a mosque; and devoutly received, with tears and prayers, the sacrament of the holy communion. He reposed some moments in the place, which resounded with cries and lamentations; solicited the pardon of all whom he might have injured; and mounted on horseback to visit the guards and explore the motions of the enemy. The distress and fall of the last Constantine are more glorious than the long prosperity of the Byzantine Cæsars.

In the confusion of darkness an assailant may sometimes succeed; but, in this great and general attack, the military judgment and astrological knowledge of Mahomet advised him to expect the morning, the memorable twenty-ninth of May, in the fourteen hundred and fifty-third year of the Christian æra. The preceding night had been strenuously employed: the troops, the cannon, and the fascines were advanced to the edge of the ditch, which, in many parts, presented a smooth and level passage to the breach; and his fourscore galleys almost touched, with the prows and their scaling-ladders, the less defensible walls of the harbor. Under pain of death, silence was enjoined; but the physical laws of motion and sound are not obedient to discipline or fear; each individual might suppress his voice and measure his footsteps; but the march and labor of thousands must inevitably produce a strange confusion of dissonant clamors, which reached the ears of the watchmen of the towers. At daybreak, without the customary signal of the morning-gun, the Turks assaulted the city by sea and land: and the similitude of a twined or twisted thread has been applied to the closeness and continuity of their line of attack. The foremost ranks consisted of the refuse of the host, a voluntary crowd, who fought without order or command; of the feebleness of age or childhood, of peasants and vagrants, and of all who had joined the camp in the blind hope of plunder and martyrdom. The common impulse drove them onwards to the wall; the most audacious to climb were instantly precipitated; and not a dart, not a bullet of the Christians was idly wasted on the accumulated throng. But their strength and ammunition were exhausted in this laborious defence; the ditch was filled with the bodies of the slain; they supported the footsteps of their companions; and of this devoted vanguard the death was more serviceable than the life. Under their respective bashaws and sanjaks, the troops of Anatolia and Romania were successively led to the charge: their progress was various and doubtful; but, after a conflict of two hours, the Greeks still maintained and improved their advantage; and the voice of the emperor was heard, encouraging his soldiers to achieve, by a last effort, the deliverance of their country. In that fatal moment, the Janizaries arose, fresh, vigorous, and invincible. The sultan himself on horseback, with an iron mace in his hand, was the spectator and judge of their valor; he was surrounded by ten thousand of his domestic troops, whom he reserved for the decisive occasion; and the tide of battle was directed and impelled by his voice and eye. His numerous ministers of justice were posted behind the line, to urge, to restrain, and to punish; and, if danger was in the front, shame and inevitable death were in the rear of the fugitives. The cries of fear and of pain were drowned in the martial music of drums, trumpets, and attaballs; and experience has proved that the mechanical operation of sounds, by quickening the circulation of the blood and spirits, will act on the human machine more forcibly than the eloquence of reason and honor. From the lines, the galleys, and the bridge, the Ottoman artillery thundered on all sides; and the camp and city, the Greeks and the Turks, were involved in a cloud of smoke, which could only be dispelled by the final deliverance or destruction of the Roman empire. The single combats of the heroes of history or fable amuse our fancy and engage our affections: the skilful evolutions of war may inform the mind, and improve a necessary though pernicious science. But, in the uniform and odious pictures of a general assault, all is blood, and horror, and confusion; nor shall I strive, at the distance of three centuries and a thousand miles, to delineate a scene of which there could be no spectators, and of which the actors themselves were incapable of forming any just or adequate idea.

The immediate loss of Constantinople may be ascribed to the bullet, or arrow, which pierced the gauntlet of John Justiniani. The sight of his blood, and the exquisite pain, appalled the courage of the chief, whose arms and counsel were the firmest rampart of the city. As he withdrew from his station in quest of a surgeon, his flight was perceived and stopped by the indefatigable emperor. 'Your wound,' exclaimed Palæologus, 'is slight; the danger is pressing; your presence is necessary; and whither will you retire?' 'I will retire,' said the trembling Genoese, 'by the same road which God has opened to the Turks;' and at these words he hastily passed through one of the breaches of the inner wall. By this pusillanimous act, he stained the honors of a military life; and the few days which he survived in Galata, or the isle of Chios, were embittered by his own and the public reproach. His example was imitated by the greatest part of the Latin auxiliaries, and the defence began to slacken when the attack was pressed with redoubled vigor. The number of Ottomans was fifty, perhaps an hundred, times superior to that of the Christians; the double walls were reduced by the cannon to an heap of ruins; in a circuit of several miles, some places must be found more easy of access or more feebly guarded; and, if the besiegers could penetrate in a single point, the whole city was irrecoverably lost. The first who deserved the sultan's reward was Hassan, the Janizary, of gigantic stature and strength. With his scimitar in one hand and his buckler in the other, he ascended the outward fortification: of the thirty Janizaries, who were emulous of his valor, eighteen perished in the bold adventure. Hassan and his twelve companions had reached the summit: the giant was precipitated from the rampart; he rose on one knee, and was again oppressed by a shower of darts and stones. But his success had proved that the achievement was possible: the walls and towers were instantly covered with a swarm of Turks; and the Greeks, now driven from the vantage-ground, were overwhelmed by increasing multitudes. Amidst these multitudes, the emperor, who accomplished all the duties of a general and a soldier, was long seen, and finally lost. The nobles who fought round his person sustained, till their last breath, the honorable names of Palæologus and Cantacuzene: his mournful exclamation was heard, 'Cannot there be found a Christian to cut off my head?' and his last fear was that of falling alive into the hands of the infidels. The prudent despair of Constantine cast away purple; amidst the tumult, he fell by an unknown hand, and his body was buried under a mountain of the slain. After his death, resistance and order were no more; the Greeks fled towards the city; and many were pressed and stifled in the narrow pass of the gate of St. Romanus. The victorious Turks rushed through the breaches of the inner wall; and, as they advanced into the streets, they were soon joined by their brethren, who had forced the gate Phenar on the side of the harbor. In the first heat of the pursuit, about two thousand Christians were put to the sword; but avarice soon prevailed over cruelty; and the victors acknowledged that they should immediately have given quarter, if the valor of the emperor and his chosen bands had not prepared them for a similar opposition in every part of the capital. It was thus, after a siege of fifty-three days, that Constantinople, which had defied the power of Chosroes, the Chagan, and the caliphs, was irretrievably subdued by the arms of Mahomet the Second. Her empire only had been subverted by the Latins: her religion was trampled in the dust by the Moslem conquerors.

The tidings of misfortune fly with a rapid wing; yet such was the extent of Constantinople that the more distant quarters might prolong, some moments, the happy ignorance of their ruin. But in the general consternation, in the feelings of selfish or social anxiety, in the tumult and thunder of the assault, a *sleepless* night and morning must have elapsed; nor can I believe that many Grecian ladies were awakened by the Janizaries from a sound and tranquil slumber. On the assurance of the public calamity, the houses and convents were instantly deserted; and the trembling inhabitants flocked together in the streets, like an herd of timid animals, as if accumulated weakness could be productive of strength, or in the vain hope that amid the crowd each individual might be safe and invisible. From every part of the capital, they flowed into the church of St. Sophia: in the space of an hour, the sanctuary, the choir, the nave, the upper and lower galleries, were filled with the multitudes of fathers and husbands, of women and children, of priests, monks, and religious virgins: the doors were barred on the inside, and they sought protection from the sacred dome which they had so lately abhorred as a profane and polluted edifice. Their confidence was founded on the prophecy of an enthusiast or imposter, that one day the Turks would enter Constantinople, and pursue the Romans as far as the column of Constantine in the square before St. Sophia; but that this would be the term of their calamities; that an angel would descend from heaven, with a sword in his hand, and would deliver the empire, with that celestial weapon, to a poor man seated at the foot of the column. 'Take this sword,' would he say, 'and avenge the people of the Lord.' At these animating words, the Turks would instantly fly, and the victorious Romans would drive them from the West, and from all Anatolia, as far as the frontiers of Persia. It is on this occasion that Ducas, with some fancy and much truth, upbraids the discord and obstinacy of the Greeks. 'Had that angel appeared,' exclaims the historian, 'had he offered to exterminate your foes if you would consent to the union of the church, even then, in that fatal moment, you would have rejected your safety or have deceived your God.'

While they expected the descent of the tardy angel, the doors were broken with axes; and, as the Turks encountered no resistance, their bloodless hands were employed in selecting and securing the multitude of their prisoners. Youth, beauty, and the appearance of wealth attracted their choice; and the right of property was decided among themselves by a prior seizure, by personal strength, and by the authority of command. In the space of an hour, the male captives were bound with cords, the females with their veils and girdles. The senators were linked with their slaves; the prelates with the porters of the church; and young men of a plebeian class with noble maids, whose faces had been invisible to the sun and their nearest kindred. In this common captivity, the ranks of society were confounded; the ties of nature were cut asunder; and the inexorable soldier was careless of the father's groans, the tears of the mother, and the lamentations of the children. The loudest in their wailings were the nuns, who were torn from the altar with naked bosoms, outstretched hands, and disheveled hair; and we should piously believe that few could be tempted to prefer the vigils of the harem to those of the monastery. Of these unfortunate Greeks, of these domestic animals, whole strings were rudely driven through the streets; and, as the conquerors were eager to return for more prey, their trembling pace was quickened with menaces and blows. At the same hour, a similar rapine was exercised in all the churches and monasteries, in all the palaces and habitations of the capital; nor could any palace, however sacred or sequestered, protect the persons or the property of the Greeks. Above sixty thousand of this devoted people were transported from the city to the camp and fleet; exchanged or sold according to the caprice or interest of their masters, and dispersed in remote servitude through the provinces of the Ottoman empire.

* * *

The chain and entrance of the outward harbor was still occupied by the Italian ships of merchandise and war. They had signalized their valor in the siege: they embraced the moment of retreat, while the Turkish mariners were dissipated in the pillage of the city. When they hoisted sail the beach was covered with a suppliant and lamentable crowd; but the means of transportation were scanty; the Venetians and Genoese selected their countrymen; and, notwithstanding the fairest promises of the sultan, the inhabitants of Galata evacuated their houses and embarked with their most precious effects.

In the fall and the sack of great cities, an historian is condemned to repeat the tale of uniform calamity: the same effects must be produced by the same passions; and, when those passions may be indulged without control, small, alas! is the difference between civilized and savage man. Amidst the vague exclamations of bigotry and hatred, the Turks are not accused of a wanton or immoderate effusion of Christian blood; but, according to their maxims (the maxims of antiquity), the lives of the vanquished were forfeited; and the legitimate reward of the conqueror was derived from the service, the sale, or the ransom, of his captives of both sexes. The wealth of Constantinople had been granted by the sultan to his victorious troops; and the rapine of an hour is more productive than the industry of years. But, as no regular division was attempted of the spoil, the respective shares were not determined by merit; and the rewards of valor were stolen away by the followers of the camp, who had declined the toil and the danger of the battle. The narrative of their depredations could not afford either amusement or instruction: the total amount, in the last poverty of the empire, has been valued at four millions of ducats; and of this sum a small part was the property of the Venetians, the Genoese, the Florentines, and the merchants of Ancona. Of these foreigners, the stock was improved in quick and perpetual circulation; but the riches of the Greeks were displayed in the idle ostentation of palaces and wardrobes, or deeply buried in treasures of ingots and old coin, lest it should be demanded at their hands for the defence of their country. The profanation and plunder of the monasteries and churches excited the most tragic complaints. The dome of St. Sophia itself, the earthly heaven, the second firmament, the vehicle of the cherubim, the throne of the glory of God, was despoiled of the oblations of ages; and the gold and silver, the pearls and jewels, the vases and sacerdotal ornaments, were most wickedly converted to the service of mankind. After the divine images had been stripped of all that could be valuable to a profane eye, the canvas, or the wood, was torn, or broken, or burnt, or trod under foot, or applied, in the stables or the kitchen, to the vilest uses. The example of sacrilege was imitated, however, from the Latin conquerors of Constantinople; and the treatment which Christ, the Virgin, and the saints had sustained from the guilty Catholic might be inflicted by the zealous Mussulman on the monuments of idolatry. Perhaps, instead of joining the public clamor, a philosopher will observe that in the decline of the arts the workmanship could not be more valuable than the work, and that a fresh supply of visions and miracles would speedily be renewed by the craft of the priest and the credulity of the people. He will more seriously deplore the loss of the Byzantine libraries, which were destroyed or scattered in the general confusion: one hundred and twenty thousand manuscripts are said to have disappeared; ten volumes might be purchased for a single ducat; and the same ignominious price, too high perhaps for a shelf of theology, included the whole works of Aristotle and Homer, the noblest productions of the science and literature of ancient Greece. We may reflect with pleasure that an inestimable portion of our classic treasures was safely deposited in Italy; and that the mechanics of a German town had invented an art which derides the havoc of time and barbarism.

From the first hour of the memorable twenty-ninth of May, disorder and rapine prevailed in Constantinople till the eighth hour of the same day; when the sultan himself passed in triumph through the gate of St. Romanus. He was attended by his vizirs, bashaws, and guards, each of whom (says a Byzantine historian) was robust as Hercules, dexterous as Apollo, and equal in battle to any ten of the race of ordinary mortals. The conqueror gazed with satisfaction and wonder on the strange though splendid appearance of the domes and palaces, so dissimilar from the style of Oriental architecture. In the hippodrome, or *atmeidan*, his eye was attracted by the twisted column of the three serpents; and, as a trial of his strength, he shattered with his iron mace or battle-axe the under-jaw of one of these monsters, which in the eye of the Turks were the idols or talismans of the city. At the principal door of St. Sophia, he alighted from his horse and entered the dome; and such was his jealous regard for that monument of his glory that, on observing a zealous Mussulman in the act of breaking the marble pavement, he admonished him with his scimitar that, if the spoil and captives were granted to the soldiers, the public and private buildings had been reserved for the prince. By his command the metropolis of the Eastern church was transformed into a mosque: the rich and portable instruments of superstition had been removed; the crosses were thrown down; and the walls, which were covered with images and mosaics, were washed and purified and restored to a state of naked simplicity. On the same day, or on the ensuing Friday, the *muezin* or crier ascended the most lofty turret, and proclaimed the *ezan*, or public invitation, in the name of God and his prophet; the imam preached; and Mahomet the Second performed the *namaz* of prayer and thanksgiving on the great altar, where the Christian mysteries had so lately been celebrated before the last of the Cæsars. From St. Sophia he proceeded to the august but desolate mansion of an hundred successors of the great Constantine; but which, in a few hours, had been stripped of the pomp of royalty. A melancholy reflection on the vicissitudes of human greatness forced itself on his mind; and he repeated an elegant distich of Persian poetry, 'The spider has wove his web in the imperial palace; and the owl hath sung her watch-song on the towers of Afrasiab.'

* * *

(1788)

HYMNS OF THE EIGHTEENTH CENTURY

Of innumerable hymns that have appeared at one time and another in English hymn-books, a limited number have attained a degree of universality and permanence. That is, they appear in nearly all collections, and have been sung by Christian worshippers of all, or nearly all, varieties of belief, over a substantial period of time. The 'free congregational hymn,' however, is a relatively modern creation. Very few hymns now in general use are older than the early years of the eighteenth century. A few adaptations of German hymns, such as Luther's *Ein' Feste Burg*, and of some of the Latin canticles, still find a place in many hymn-books, and there are a few survivals of seventeenth-century compositions, though this applies more frequently to music than to words. Conspicuous additions to the store were made, of course, in the nineteenth century. But an impressive proportion of the best known English hymns belongs to the eighteenth century, and the 'hymn movement' is to be associated with the great evangelical revival which swept the British Isles and overflowed into the New World, about the middle of the century. The Wesleys and other evangelists of the Methodist movement did not, however, create the hymn, any more than they invented evangelism; they found it ready to their hand, adopted it, and gave it a new currency and force.

In 1707, Isaac Watts, a non-conformist minister of the sect known as Congregationalist, published his *Hymns and Spiritual Songs in Imitation of the Psalms*, which he followed with *Divine Songs* (1715), 'for Children,' and *Psalms of David Imitated in the Language of the New Testament* (1719). These publications are generally held to have determined the nature and form of the English hymn. Watts was considered to have made a daring departure in offering original hymns, made merely 'in imitation' of the divine songs of David, as substitutes for the literal translations of the *Psalms* which had been in use in English churches since the middle of the sixteenth century. In issuing his last volume, Watts felt called upon to defend his method, which consisted in discarding what was distant, and even repellant, in the imagery of the Old Testament, for an idiom more in accord with the experience and feelings of a modern Christian. There was really nothing distinctly new in this process, or in the form of Watts' hymns. The *Spiritual Songs* (1683) of John Mason, for instance, have the regular hymn structure, both as to thought and meter; while such songs as Mason's 'There is a Stream, which issues forth' or 'My lord, my love, was crucified,' have an evangelical tinge of phrase and feeling that refers us beyond Watts, to Wesley and Cowper. But Watts' hymns appeared when the time was ripe for such a departure, and were taken up and carried on the wave of the greatest religious revival of modern times.

As the technique of revivalism developed, congregational singing proved one of the most potent agencies for building up religious momentum and exerting the force of mass emotion upon the immediate 'experience' of individuals. The hymns of Watts served as a point of departure; but they were comparatively remote and ritualistic in tone. Evangelical leaders took to writing their own hymns, which were, in general, more fervid, intimate, and immediate; the products of particular excitements. Such are many of the hymns of Charles Wesley: personal, effusive, often mere impromptus; but fervent and sincere. Watts had written six hundred hymns; Wesley is said to have written over six thousand. And he was but one of scores of enthusiasts who frequently mistook religious excitement for literary inspiration, but occasionally made a happy hit. Toplady's 'Rock of Ages,' Perronet's 'Coronation,' Fawcett's 'Blest Be the Tie,' are fortunate effusions of this kind. We expect more literary security on the part of a poet like Cowper; but only three or four of his *Olney Hymns* are really fine poems, and even fewer are really good hymns.

'A good hymn,' Tennyson once declared, 'is the most difficult thing in the world to write.' It would be almost equally difficult, perhaps, to tell what constitutes a good hymn. Most famous hymns partly owe their persistence to the music to which they have been set. A hymn which has lived on its literary merits is usually noteworthy for breadth and simplicity of theme and treatment. The thought is likely to be obvious to the verge of commonplace. Only simple meters can survive; for the music must be within the compass of relatively untrained singers. The imagery, likewise, can better afford to be hackneyed than to seem far-fetched to ordinary minds. And, with all these limitations, the feeling expressed must be noble and large. These are no mean attributes of a literary manner. The literature of hymnody has been filtered through the favor of many generations. What survives will have something of the quality of folk-song, and a similar interest.

THOMAS KEN
(1637–1711)

DOXOLOGY

Praise God from whom all blessings flow;
Praise Him all creatures here below;
Praise Him above, ye heavenly host;
Praise Father, Son, and Holy Ghost.
(1695)

ISAAC WATTS
(1674–1748)

THERE IS A LAND

There is a land of pure delight,
   Where saints immortal reign,
Infinite day excludes the night,
   And pleasures banish pain.

There everlasting spring abides,   5
   And never withering flowers;
Death, like a narrow sea, divides
   This heavenly land from ours.

Sweet fields beyond the swelling flood
   Stand dressed in living green: 10
So to the Jews old Canaan stood,
   While Jordan rolled between.

But timorous mortals start and shrink
   To cross this narrow sea,
And linger shivering on the brink,   15
   And fear to launch away.

O, could we make our doubts remove,
   These gloomy doubts that rise,
And see the Canaan that we love
   With unbeclouded eyes,—   20

Could we but climb where Moses stood,
   And view the landscape o'er,—
Not Jordan's stream, nor death's cold flood,
   Should fright us from the shore.
(1709)

CHRIST CRUCIFIED

'And was crucified for us under Pontius Pilate; He suffered
and was buried.'

When I survey the wondrous cross
   On which the Prince of Glory died,
My richest gain I count but loss,
   And pour contempt on all my pride.

Forbid, it, Lord, that I should boast   5
   Save in the death of Christ, my God;
All the vain things that charm me most
   I sacrifice them to His Blood.

See from His head, His hands, His feet,
   Sorrow and love flow mingled down!   10
Did e'er such love and sorrow meet,
   Or thorns compose so rich a crown?

Were the whole realm of nature mine,
   That were a present far too small;
Love so amazing, so divine,   15
   Demands my soul, my life, my all.
(1709)

PSALM LXXII

Jesus shall reign where'er the sun
Does his successive journeys run;
His kingdom stretch from shore to shore,
Till moons shall wax and wane no more.

For him shall endless prayer be made,   5
And praises throng to crown His Head;
His Name, like sweet perfume, shall rise
With every morning sacrifice.

People and realms of every tongue
Dwell on His love with sweetest song,   10
And infant voices shall proclaim
Their early blessings on His Name.

Blessings abound where'er He reigns;
The prisoner leaps to lose his chains;
The weary find eternal rest,   15
And all the sons of want are blest.

Where He displays His healing power,
Death and the curse are known no more;
In Him the tribes of Adam boast
More blessings than their father lost.   20

Let every creature rise, and bring
Peculiar honors to our King;
Angels descend with songs again,
And earth repeat the long Amen!
(1719)

PSALM XC

Our God, our help in ages past,
   Our hope for years to come,
Our shelter from the stormy blast,
   And our eternal home:

Under the shadow of Thy Throne   5
   Thy saints have dwelt secure;
Sufficient is Thine arm alone,
   And our defence is sure.

Before the hills in order stood,
   Or earth received her frame,   10
From everlasting Thou art God,
   To endless years the same.

A thousand ages in Thy sight
  Are like an evening gone;
Short as the watch that ends the night   15
  Before the rising sun.

The busy tribes of flesh and blood,
  With all their lives and cares,
Are carried downwards by Thy flood,
  And lost in following years.   20

Time, like an ever-rolling stream,
  Bears all its sons away;
They fly forgotten, as a dream
  Dies at the opening day.

Our God, our help in ages past;   25
  Our hope for years to come;
Be Thou our guard while troubles last,
  And our eternal home!
                    (1719)

AGAINST QUARRELLING AND FIGHTING

Let dogs delight to bark and bite,
  For God hath made them so;
Let bears and lions growl and fight,
  For 't is their nature too.

But, children, you should never let   5
  Such angry passions rise;
Your little hands were never made
  To tear each other's eyes.

Let love through all your actions run,
  And all your words be mild;   10
Live like the blessed virgin's Son,
  That sweet and lovely child.

His soul was gentle as a lamb;
  And as His stature grew,
He grew in favour both with man,   15
  And God His Father too.

Now, Lord of all, He reigns above,
  And from His heavenly throne
He sees what children dwell in love,
  And marks them for His own.   20
                    (1715)

AGAINST IDLENESS AND MISCHIEF

How doth the little busy bee
  Improve each shining hour,
And gather honey all the day
  From every opening flower!

How skilfully she builds her cell!   5
  How neat she spreads the wax!
And labors hard to store it well
  With the sweet food she makes.

In works of labour or of skill,
  I would be busy too;   10
For Satan finds some mischief still
  For idle hands to do.

In books, or work, or healthful play,
  Let my first years be past,
That I may give for every day   15
  Some good account at last.
                    (1715)

From A CRADLE HYMN

Hush! my dear, lie still, and slumber,
  Holy angels guard thy bed!
Heavenly blessings without number
  Gently falling on thy head.

Sleep, my babe; thy food and raiment,   5
  House and home thy friends provide;
All without thy care or payment,
  All thy wants are well supplied.

How much better thou'rt attended
  Than the Son of God could be,   10
When from heaven He descended,
  And became a child like thee?

Soft and easy is thy cradle:
  Coarse and hard thy Saviour lay:
When His birthplace was a stable,   15
  And His softest bed was hay.

Blessed babe! what glorious features,
  Spotless, fair, divinely bright!
Must He dwell with brutal creatures?
  How could angels bear the sight?   20

Was there nothing but a manger
  Cursèd sinners could afford,
To receive the heavenly Stranger?
  Did they thus affront their Lord?

Soft, my child; I did not chide thee,   25
  Though my song might sound too hard;
'T is thy { Mother[1] / Nurse that } sits beside thee,
  And her arms shall be thy guard.
                    (1715)

CHARLES WESLEY
(1707–1788)

LOVE DIVINE

Love divine, all love excelling,
  Joy of heaven, to earth come down;
Fix in us Thy humble dwelling,
  All Thy faithful mercies crown:

---

[1] Here you may use the words, brother, sister, neighbour, friend, etc.

Jesus, Thou art all compassion,
    Pure, unbounded love Thou art;
Visit us with Thy salvation,
    Enter every trembling heart.

Breathe, O, breathe Thy loving spirit
    Into every troubled breast!
Let us all in Thee inherit,
    Let us find that second rest:
Take away our bent to sinning;
    Alpha and Omega be;
End of faith, as its beginning,
    Set our hearts at liberty.

Come, almighty to deliver,
    Let us all Thy grace receive;
Suddenly return, and never,
    Never more thy temples leave:
Thee we would be always blessing,
    Serve Thee as Thy hosts above,
Pray, and praise Thee without ceasing,
    Glory in Thy perfect love.

Finish then Thy new creation,
    Pure and spotless let us be;
Let us see Thy great salvation,
    Perfectly restored in Thee:
Changed from glory into glory,
    Till in heaven we take our place,
Till we cast our crowns before Thee,
    Lost in wonder, love, and praise.

CHRISTMAS CAROL

Hark! the herald angels sing,
  'Glory to the new-born King;
Peace on earth and mercy mild;
  God and sinners reconciled.'
Joyful, all ye nations, rise,
Join the triumph of the skies;
With th' angelic host proclaim,
  'Christ is born in Bethlehem.'

    Hark! the herald angels sing,
      'Glory to the new-born King.'

Christ, by highest heaven adored,
Christ, the everlasting Lord:
Late in time behold Him come,
Offspring of the Virgin's womb.
Veiled in flesh the Godhead see,
Hail the incarnate Deity!
Pleased as man with man to dwell;
Jesus, our Emmanuel!

Mild, He lays His glory by,
Born that man no more may die,
Born to raise the sons of earth,
Born to give them second birth.
Risen with healing in His wings,
Light and life to all He brings.

Hail, the Sun of righteousness!
Hail, the heaven-born Prince of Peace!

Come, Desire of nations, come!
Fix in us Thy humble home:
Rise, the woman's conquering seed,
Bruise in us the serpent's head;
Adam's likeness now efface,
Stamp Thine image in its place:
Second Adam from above,
Reinstate us in Thy love.

JESU, LOVER OF MY SOUL

Jesu, lover of my soul,
    Let me to Thy bosom fly,
While the nearer waters roll,
    While the tempest still is high!
Hide me, O my Saviour, hide,
    Till the storm of life is past,
Safe into the haven guide;
    O receive my soul at last!

Other refuge have I none;
    Hangs my helpless soul on Thee;
Leave, ah! leave me not alone,
    Still support and comfort me!
All my trust on Thee is stayed,
    All my help from Thee I bring:
Cover my defenceless head
    With the shadow of Thy wing!

Wilt Thou not regard my call?
    Wilt Thou not accept my prayer?
Lo! I sink, I faint, I fall!
    Lo! on Thee I cast my care!
Reach me out Thy gracious hand!
    While I of Thy strength receive,
Hoping against hope I stand,
    Dying, and behold I live!

Thou, O Christ, art all I want;
    More than all in Thee I find:
Raise the fallen, cheer the faint,
    Heal the sick, and lead the blind!
Just and holy is Thy Name;
    I am all unrighteousness;
False and full of sin I am,
    Thou art full of truth and grace.

Plenteous grace with Thee is found,
    Grace to cover all my sin;
Let the healing streams abound;
    Make and keep me pure within!
Thou of Life the Fountain art,
    Freely let me take of Thee;
Spring Thou up within my heart!
    Rise to all eternity!

(1740)

JOHN FAWCETT
(1739-1817)

BLEST BE THE TIE THAT BINDS

Blest be the tie that binds
  Our hearts in Christian love;
The fellowship of kindred minds
  Is like to that above.

Before our Father's throne
  We pour our ardent prayers;
Our fears, our hopes, our aims are one,
  Our comforts and our cares.

We share our mutual woes,
  Our mutual burdens bear;
And often for each other flows
  The sympathizing tear.

When we asunder part,
  It gives us inward pain;
But we shall still be joined in heart,
  And hope to meet again.

This glorious hope revives
  Our courage by the way;
While each in expectation lives
  And longs to see the day.

From sorrow, toil, and pain,
  And sin, we shall be free,
And perfect love and friendship reign
  Through all eternity.
      (1772)

AUGUSTUS MONTAGUE TOPLADY
(1740-1778)

ROCK OF AGES

Rock of Ages, cleft for me,
Let me hide myself in Thee!
Let the water and the blood,
From Thy riven side which flowed,
Be of sin the double cure,
Cleanse me from its guilt and power.

Not the labors of my hands
Can fulfil Thy law's demands;
Could my zeal no respite know,
Could my tears forever flow,
All for sin could not atone;
Thou must save, and Thou alone.

Nothing in my hand I bring;
Simply to Thy Cross I cling;
Naked, come to Thee for dress;
Helpless, look to Thee for grace;
Foul, I to Thy fountain fly;
Wash me, Saviour, or I die!

While I draw this fleeting breath,
When my eyelids close in death,
When I soar to worlds unknown,
See Thee on Thy judgment-throne;
Rock of Ages, cleft for me,
Let me hide myself in Thee!
      (1776)

EDWARD PERRONET
(1726-1792)

CORONATION

All hail the power of Jesus' name!
  Let angels prostrate fall;
Bring forth the royal diadem,
  And crown Him Lord of all.

Crown him, ye morning stars of light,
  Who fixed this floating ball;
Now hail the strength of Israel's might,
  And crown Him Lord of all.

Crown him, ye martyrs of our God,
  Who from His altar call;
Extol the stem of Jesse's rod,
  And crown Him Lord of all.

Ye chosen seed of Israel's race,
  Ye ransomed from the fall;
Hail Him, who saves you by His grace,
  And crown Him Lord of all.

Sinners, whose love can ne'er forget
  The wormwood and the gall,
Go, spread your trophies at His feet,
  And crown Him Lord of all.

Let every kindred, every tribe,
  On this terrestrial ball,
To Him all majesty ascribe,
  And crown Him Lord of all.

O! that with yonder sacred throng,
  We at His feet may fall;
We'll join the everlasting song,
  And crown Him Lord of all.

WILLIAM COWPER (1731–1800)

The son of a chaplain of George II, Cowper was derived on both sides from illustrious families and it is not unnatural to ascribe to race a certain touch of gentility in all he did or wrote. After seven years at Westminster School he was 'articled,' at eighteen, to a London attorney, with whom he spent three years, afterward going into residence in the Temple, and in 1754, he was called to the bar. His experiments in versification at this time, some of them addressed to his cousin Theodora, with whom he was in love, show few symptoms of the poetic originality which he long afterward evinced. Some of his early associates, too, Warren Hastings at Westminster, Thurlow, the fellow-clerk of his apprentice days, and the raucous and none too moral wits of the Nonsense Club, seem in their several ways incongruous associates for the shrinking and self-searching pietist whom we know in his later years. Cowper was too timid for the business of a lawyer and, in 1763, when he was thirty-two years of age, the dread of qualifying for a clerkship so preyed upon his mind that he became violently insane and attempted suicide. When he recovered, he determined to retire from the excitements of the world and found a retreat at Huntington, near Cambridge, where he entered the home of the Reverend Mr. Unwin and his wife and was converted to Methodism. On the death of Unwin, in 1767, Cowper removed with Mrs. Unwin to Olney, and here came under the influence of John Newton, with whom he joined in the writing of the *Olney Hymns*. Newton's strenuous fanaticism aggravated his religious mania and, in 1773, he again became mad and so remained for two years. On his recovery, along with other worldly diversions, such as gardening, cheerful conversation and the keeping of pet hares, which were discountenanced by his spiritual comforter, Cowper began to amuse himself by writing verses and found increasing satisfaction in the exercise. His first volume, containing *Table Talk* and other poems, was published in 1782. The liveliness of this period was increased by his acquaintance with Lady Austen, a bright young widow, who suggested the subjects of *The Task* and *The Diverting Ride of John Gilpin*. These poems, published in 1785, made his reputation national. The most exacting of his tasks, the translation of Homer, was brought to completion in 1791. He now began to sink, for the last time, under the cloud of despondency, suffering almost constantly from the conviction that he was a lost soul. Some of the darker and more intense of his short poems, such as *The Castaway*, belong to these unhappy years and were printed after his death. Cowper had a rare and intense, though not a rich nature. His gift of humor appears most conspicuously in his Letters, which some critics have not hesitated to pronounce the best in the language. Fidelity to nature and religious earnestness are the prevailing characteristics of his poetry. Byron's phrase, 'the quiet of a loving eye,' precisely fits Cowper's manner of looking about him, except in his most heightened moments.

From OLNEY HYMNS

WALKING WITH GOD
Gen. v. 24

Oh! for a closer walk with God,
  A calm and heavenly frame;
A light to shine upon the road
  That leads me to the Lamb!

Where is the blessedness I knew   5
  When first I saw the Lord?
Where is the soul-refreshing view
  Of Jesus and his word?

What peaceful hours I once enjoyed!
  How sweet their memory still!   10
But they have left an aching void
  The world can never fill.

Return, O holy Dove, return
  Sweet messenger of rest!
I hate the sins that made thee mourn   15
  And drove thee from my breast.

The dearest idol I have known,
  Whate'er that idol be,
Help me to tear it from thy throne,
  And worship only thee.   20

So shall my walk be close with God,
  Calm and serene my frame;
So purer light shall mark the road
  That leads me to the Lamb.

(1779)

From TABLE TALK

Pity religion has so seldom found
A skilful guide into poetic ground!
The flowers would spring where'er she deigned
  to stray,

And every Muse attend her in her way.
Virtue indeed meets many a rhyming friend, 5
And many a compliment politely penned;
But, unattired in that becoming vest
Religion weaves for her, and half undressed,
Stands in the desert, shivering and forlorn,
A wintry figure, like a withered thorn. 10
The shelves are full, all other themes are sped,
Hackneyed and worn to the last flimsy thread:
Satire has long since done his best, and cursed
And loathsome ribaldry has done his worst;
Fancy has sported all her powers away 15
In tales, in trifles, and in children's play;
And 't is the sad complaint, and almost true,
Whate'er we write, we bring forth nothing new.
'T were new indeed, to see a bard all fire,
Touched with a coal from Heaven, assume the lyre 20
And tell the world, still kindling as he sung,
With more than mortal music on his tongue,
That He, who died below, and reigns above,
Inspires the song, and that His name is Love.
(1782)

From THE TASK

BOOK I

PRAISE OF COUNTRY LIFE

For I have loved the rural walk through lanes
Of grassy swarth, close cropped by nibbling sheep,
And skirted thick with intertexture firm
Of thorny boughs; have loved the rural walk
O'er hills, through valleys, and by rivers' brink, 5
E'er since a truant boy I passed my bounds
T' enjoy a ramble on the banks of Thames;
And still remember, nor without regret
Of hours that sorrow since has much endeared,
How oft, my slice of pocket store consumed, 10
Still hung'ring, penniless and far from home,
I fed on scarlet hips and stony haws,
Or blushing crabs, or berries, that emboss
The bramble, black as jet, or sloes austere.
Hard fare! but such as boyish appetite 15
Disdains not; nor the palate, undepraved
By culinary arts, unsav'ry deems.
No SOFA then awaited my return;
Nor SOFA then I needed. Youth repairs
His wasted spirits quickly, by long toil 20
Incurring short fatigue; and, though our years
As life declines speed rapidly away,
And not a year but pilfers as he goes
Some youthful grace that age would gladly keep;
A tooth or auburn lock, and by degrees 25
Their length and color from the locks they spare;
Th' elastic spring of an unwearied foot
That mounts the stile with ease, or leaps the fence,
That play of lungs, inhaling and again
Respiring freely the fresh air, that makes 30
Swift pace or steep ascent no toil to me,
Mine have not pilfered yet; nor yet impaired
My relish of fair prospect; scenes that soothed
Or charmed me young, no longer young, I find
Still soothing and of pow'r to charm me still. 35
And witness, dear companion of my walks,
Whose arm this twentieth winter I perceive
Fast locked in mine, with pleasure such as love,
Confirmed by long experience of thy worth
And well-tried virtues, could alone inspire— 40
Witness a joy that thou hast doubled long.
Thou know'st my praise of nature most sincere,
And that my raptures are not conjured up
To serve occasions of poetic pomp,
But genuine, and art partner of them all. 45
How oft upon yon eminence our pace
Has slackened to a pause, and we have borne
The ruffling wind, scarce conscious that it blew,
While admiration, feeding at the eye,
And still unsated, dwelt upon the scene. 50
Thence with what pleasure have we just discerned
The distant plough slow moving, and beside
His lab'ring team, that swerved not from the track,
The sturdy swain diminished to a boy!
Here Ouse, slow winding through a level plain 55
Of spacious meads with cattle sprinkled o'er,
Conducts the eye along its sinuous course
Delighted. There, fast rooted in his bank,
Stand, never overlooked, our fav'rite elms,
That screen the herdsman's solitary hut; 60
While far beyond, and overthwart the stream
That, as with molten glass, inlays the vale,
The sloping land recedes into the clouds;
Displaying on its varied side the grace
Of hedge-row beauties numberless, square tow'r, 65
Tall spire, from which the sound of cheerful bells
Just undulates upon the list'ning ear,
Groves, heaths, and smoking villages remote.
Scenes must be beautiful, which, daily viewed,
Please daily, and whose novelty survives 70
Long knowledge and the scrutiny of years.
Praise justly due to those that I describe.

* * *

God made the country, and man made the town.
What wonder then that health and virtue, gifts
That can alone make sweet the bitter draught 75
That life holds out to all, should most abound
And least be threatened in the fields and groves?
Possess ye, therefore, ye who, borne about
In chariots and sedans, know no fatigue
But that of idleness, and taste no scenes 80
But such as art contrives, possess ye still
Your element; there only can ye shine,
There only minds like yours can do no harm.
Our groves were planted to console at noon

The pensive wand'rer in their shades. At eve 85
The moonbeam, sliding softly in between
The sleeping leaves, is all the light they wish,
Birds warbling all the music. We can spare
The splendor of your lamps; they but eclipse
Our softer satellite. Your songs confound 90
Our more harmonious notes: the thrush departs
Scared, and th' offended nightingale is mute.

BOOK II

OF SLAVERY

OH for a lodge in some vast wilderness,
Some boundless contiguity of shade,
Where rumor of oppression and deceit,
Of unsuccessful or successful war,
Might never reach me more! My ear is pained,
My soul is sick with every day's report 6
Of wrong and outrage with which earth is filled.
There is no flesh in man's obdurate heart,
It does not feel for man; the natural bond
Of brotherhood is severed as the flax 10
That falls asunder at the touch of fire.
He finds his fellow guilty of a skin
Not colored like his own, and, having power
To enforce the wrong, for such a worthy cause
Dooms and devotes him as his lawful prey. 15
Lands intersected by a narrow frith
Abhor each other. Mountains interposed
Make enemies of nations who had else
Like kindred drops been mingled into one.
Thus man devotes his brother, and destroys; 20
And worse than all, and most to be deplored,
As human nature's broadest, foulest blot,
Chains him, and tasks him, and exacts his sweat
With stripes that Mercy, with a bleeding heart,
Weeps when she sees inflicted on a beast. 25

Then what is man? And what man seeing this,
And having human feelings, does not blush
And hang his head, to think himself a man?
I would not have a slave to till my ground,
To carry me, to fan me while I sleep, 30
And tremble when I wake, for all the wealth
That sinews bought and sold have ever earned.
No: dear as freedom is, and in my heart's
Just estimation prized above all price,
I had much rather be myself the slave 35
And wear the bonds, than fasten them on him.

BOOK III

A STRICKEN DEER

I WAS a stricken deer that left the herd
Long since; with many an arrow deep infixed
My panting side was charged, when I withdrew
To seek a tranquil death in distant shades.
There was I found by One who had Himself 5
Been hurt by the archers. In His side He bore,
And in His hands and feet, the cruel scars.

With gentle force soliciting the darts,
He drew them forth, and healed and bade me
  live.
Since then, with few associates, in remote 10
And silent woods I wander, far from those
My former partners of the peopled scene;
With few associates, and not wishing more.

Here much I ruminate, as much I may,
With other views of men and manners now 15
Than once, and others of a life to come.
I see that all are wanderers, gone astray
Each in his own delusions; they are lost
In chase of fancied happiness, still wooed
And never won. Dream after dream ensues, 20
And still they dream that they shall still succeed,
And still are disappointed. Rings the world
With the vain stir. I sum up half mankind,
And add two-thirds of the remaining half,
And find the total of their hopes and fears 25
Dreams, empty dreams.

BOOK IV

NATURE AND POETRY

WOULD I had fallen upon those happier days
That poets celebrate; those golden times
And those Arcadian scenes that Maro sings,
And Sidney, warbler of poetic prose.
Nymphs were Dianas then, and swains had
  hearts 5
That felt their virtues. Innocence, it seems,
From courts dismissed, found shelter in the
  groves;
The footsteps of Simplicity, impressed
Upon the yielding herbage (so they sing),
Then were not all effaced. Then speech profane
And manners profligate were rarely found, 11
Observed as prodigies, and soon reclaimed.
Vain wish! those days were never: airy dreams
Sat for the picture; and the poet's hand,
Imparting substance to an empty shade, 15
Imposed a gay delirium for a truth.
Grant it: I still must envy them an age
That favored such a dream, in days like these
Impossible, when virtue is so scarce
That to suppose a scene where she presides 20
Is tramontane, and stumbles all belief.
No. We are polished now. The rural lass,
Whom once her virgin modesty and grace,
Her artless manners and her neat attire,
So dignified, that she was hardly less 25
Than the fair shepherdess of old romance,
Is seen no more. The character is lost.
Her head adorned with lappets pinned aloft
And ribbons streaming gay, superbly raised
And magnified beyond all human size, 30
Indebted to some smart wig-weaver's hand
For more than half the tresses it sustains;
Her elbows ruffled, and her tottering form

Ill propped upon French heels; she might be deemed
(But that the basket dangling on her arm   35
Interprets her more truly) of a rank
Too proud for dairy-work, or sale of eggs;
Expect her soon with foot-boy at her heels,
No longer blushing for her awkward load,
Her train and her umbrella all her care.   40

* * *

But slighted as it is, and by the great
Abandoned, and, which still I more regret,
Infected with the manners and the modes
It knew not once, the country wins me still.
I never framed a wish or formed a plan   45
That flattered me with hopes of earthly bliss,
But there I laid the scene. There early strayed
My fancy, ere yet liberty of choice
Had found me, or the hope of being free.
My very dreams were rural, rural too   50
The first-born efforts of my youthful muse,
Sportive, and jingling her poetic bells
Ere yet her ear was mistress of their powers.
No bard could please me but whose lyre was tuned
To Nature's praises. Heroes and their feats   55
Fatigued me, never weary of the pipe
Of Tityrus, assembling as he sang
The rustic throng beneath his favorite beech.
Then Milton had indeed a poet's charms:
New to my taste, his Paradise surpassed   60
The struggling efforts of my boyish tongue
To speak its excellence; I danced for joy.
I marveled much that, at so ripe an age
As twice seven years, his beauties had then first
Engaged my wonder, and admiring still,   65
And still admiring, with regret supposed
The joy half lost because not sooner found.
Thee, too, enamored of the life I loved,
Pathetic in its praise, in its pursuit
Determined, and possessing it at last   70
With transports such as favored lovers feel,
I studied, prized, and wished that I had known
Ingenious Cowley: and though now, reclaimed
By modern lights from an erroneous taste
I cannot but lament thy splendid wit   75
Entangled in the cobwebs of the schools,
I still revere thee, courtly though retired,
Though stretched at ease in Chertsey's silent bowers,
Not unemployed, and finding rich amends
For a lost world in solitude and verse.   80

(1785)

ON THE RECEIPT OF MY MOTHER'S PICTURE

OH, that those lips had language! Life has passed
With me but roughly since I heard thee last.
Those lips are thine—thy own sweet smile I see,
The same that oft in childhood solaced me;
Voice only fails, else how distinct they say,   5
'Grieve not, my child, chase all thy fears away!'
The meek intelligence of those dear eyes
(Blessed be the art that can immortalize,
The art that baffles Time's tyrannic claim   9
To quench it) here shines on me still the same.

Faithful remembrancer of one so dear,
O welcome guest, though unexpected here!
Who bidst me honor with an artless song,
Affectionate, a mother lost so long,
I will obey, not willingly alone,   15
But gladly, as the precept were her own:
And, while that face renews my filial grief,
Fancy shall weave a charm for my relief,
Shall steep me in Elysian reverie,
A momentary dream that thou art she.   20

My mother! when I learnt that thou wast dead
Say, wast thou conscious of the tears I shed?
Hovered thy spirit o'er thy sorrowing son,
Wretch even then, life's journey just begun?
Perhaps thou gavest me, though unfelt, a kiss:
Perhaps a tear, if souls can weep in bliss—   26
Ah, that maternal smile! It answers—Yes.
I heard the bell tolled on thy burial day,
I saw the hearse that bore thee slow away,
And turning from my nursery window, drew
A long, long sigh, and wept a last adieu!   31
But was it such?—It was.—Where thou art gone
Adieus and farewells are a sound unknown.
May I but meet thee on that peaceful shore,
The parting word shall pass my lips no more!   35
Thy maidens, grieved themselves at my concern,
Oft gave me promise of thy quick return.
What ardently I wished I long believed,
And, disappointed still, was still deceived.
By expectation every day beguiled,   40
Dupe of *to-morrow* even from a child.
Thus many a sad to-morrow came and went,
Till, all my stock of infant sorrow spent,
I learned at last submission to my lot;
But, though I less deplored thee, ne'er forgot.   45

Where once we dwelt our name is heard no more,
Children not thine have trod my nursery floor;
And where the gardener Robin, day by day,
Drew me to school along the public way,
Delighted with my bauble coach, and wrapped
In scarlet mantle warm, and velvet capped,   51
'T is now become a history little known,
That once we called the pastoral house our own.
Short-lived possession! but the record fair
That memory keeps, of all thy kindness there,
Still outlives many a storm that has effaced   56
A thousand other themes less deeply traced.
Thy nightly visits to my chamber made,
That thou mightst know me safe and warmly laid;

Thy morning bounties ere I left my home, 60
The biscuit, or confectionary plum;
The fragrant waters on my cheek bestowed
By thy own hand, till fresh they shone and glowed;
All this, and more endearing still than all,
Thy constant flow of love, that knew no fall, 65
Ne'er roughened by those cataracts and brakes
That humor interposed too often makes;
All this still legible in memory's page,
And still to be so to my latest age,
Adds joy to duty, makes me glad to pay 70
Such honors to thee as my numbers may;
Perhaps a frail memorial, but sincere,
Not scorned in heaven, though little noticed here.

Could Time, his flight reversed, restore the hours,
When, playing with thy vesture's tissued flowers, 75
The violet, the pink, and jessamine,
I pricked them into paper with a pin
(And thou wast happier than myself the while,
Wouldst softly speak, and stroke my head and smile),
Could those few pleasant days again appear, 80
Might one wish bring them, would I wish them here?
I would not trust my heart—the dear delight
Seems so to be desired, perhaps I might.—
But no—what here we call our life is such,
So little to be loved, and thou so much, 85
That I should ill requite thee to constrain
Thy unbound spirit into bonds again.

Thou, as a gallant bark from Albion's coast
(The storms all weathered and the ocean crossed)
Shoots into port at some well-havened isle, 90
Where spices breathe, and brighter seasons smile,
There sits quiescent on the floods that show
Her beauteous form reflected clear below,
While airs impregnated with incense play
Around her, fanning light her streamers gay; 95
So thou, with sails how swift! hast reached the shore,
'Where tempests never beat nor billows roar.'
And thy loved consort on the dangerous tide
Of life long since has anchored by thy side.
But me, scarce hoping to attain that rest, 100
Always from port withheld, always distressed—
Me howling blasts drive devious, tempest tost,
Sails ripped, seams opening wide, and compass lost,
And day by day some current's thwarting force
Sets me more distant from a prosperous course.
Yet, oh, the thought that thou art safe, and he!
That thought is joy, arrive what may to me. 107
My boast is not, that I deduce my birth
From loins enthroned and rulers of the earth;
But higher far my proud pretensions rise— 110
The son of parents passed into the skies!
And now, farewell—Time unrevoked has run
His wonted course, yet what I wished is done.
By contemplation's help, not sought in vain,
I seem to have lived my childhood o'er again;
To have renewed the joys that once were mine,
Without the sin of violating thine: 117
And, while the wings of Fancy still are free,
And I can view this mimic show of thee,
Time has but half succeeded in his theft— 120
Thyself removed, thy power to soothe me left.

(1798)

SONNET TO MRS. UNWIN

MARY! I want a lyre with other strings;
Such aid from Heaven as some have feigned they drew!
An eloquence scarce given to mortals, new,
And undebased by praise of meaner things!

That, ere through age or woe I shed my wings, 5
I may record thy worth, with honor due,
In verse as musical as thou art true,—
Verse, that immortalizes whom it sings!

But thou hast little need: there is a book,
By seraphs writ with beams of heavenly light, 10
On which the eyes of God not rarely look;
A chronicle of actions just and bright!
There all thy deeds, my faithful Mary, shine,
And since thou own'st that praise, I spare thee mine.

(1803)

ON THE LOSS OF THE ROYAL GEORGE

TOLL for the brave!
  The brave that are no more!
All sunk beneath the wave,
  Fast by their native shore!

Eight hundred of the brave, 5
  Whose courage well was tried,
Had made the vessel heel,
  And laid her on her side.

A land-breeze shook the shrouds,
  And she was overset; 10
Down went the Royal George,
  With all her crew complete.

Toll for the brave!
  Brave Kempenfelt is gone;
His last sea-fight is fought; 15
  His work of glory done.

It was not in the battle;
  No tempest gave the shock;
She sprang no fatal leak;
  She ran upon no rock. 20

His sword was in its sheath;
  His fingers held the pen,
When Kempenfelt went down
  With twice four hundred men.

Weigh the vessel up,
  Once dreaded by our foes!
And mingle with our cup
  The tears that England owes.

Her timbers yet are sound,
  And she may float again
Full charged with England's thunder,
  And plough the distant main.

But Kempenfelt is gone,
  His victories are o'er;
And he and his eight hundred
  Shall plough the wave no more.
              (1803)

THE CASTAWAY

Obscurest night involved the sky,
  The Atlantic billows roared,
When such a destined wretch as I,
  Washed headlong from on board,
Of friends, of hope, of all bereft,
His floating home for ever left.

No braver chief could Albion boast
  Than he with whom he went,
Nor ever ship left Albion's coast
  With warmer wishes sent.
He loved them both, but both in vain,
Nor him beheld, nor her again.

Not long beneath the whelming brine,
  Expert to swim, he lay;
Nor soon he felt his strength decline,
  Or courage die away;
But waged with death a lasting strife,
Supported by despair of life.

He shouted: nor his friends had failed
  To check the vessel's course,
But so the furious blast prevailed,
  That, pitiless perforce,
They left their outcast mate behind,
And scudded still before the wind.

Some succour yet they could afford,
  And such as storms allow,
The cask, the coop, the floated cord,
  Delayed not to bestow.
But he (they knew) nor ship nor shore,
Whate'er they gave, should visit more.

Nor, cruel as it seemed, could he
  Their haste himself condemn,
Aware that flight, in such a sea,
  Alone could rescue them;
Yet bitter felt it still to die
Deserted, and his friends so nigh.

He long survives, who lives an hour
  In ocean, self-upheld;
And so long he, with unspent power,
  His destiny repelled;
And ever, as the minutes flew,
Entreated help, or cried 'Adieu!'

At length, his transient respite past,
  His comrades, who before
Had heard his voice in every blast,
  Could catch the sound no more:
For then, by toil subdued, he drank
The stifling wave, and then he sank.

No poet wept him; but the page
  Of narrative sincere,
That tells his name, his worth, his age,
  Is wet with Anson's tear:
And tears by bards or heroes shed
Alike immortalize the dead.

I therefore purpose not, or dream,
  Descanting on his fate,
To give the melancholy theme
  A more enduring date:
But misery still delights to trace
Its semblance in another's case.

No voice divine the storm allayed,
  No light propitious shone,
When, snatched from all effectual aid,
  We perished, each alone:
But I beneath a rougher sea,
And whelmed in deeper gulfs than he.
              (1803)

LETTERS

To Joseph Hill

October 25, 1765.

Dear Joe—I am afraid the month of October has proved rather unfavourable to the *belle assemblée* at Southampton, high winds and continual rains being bitter enemies to that agreeable lounge, which you and I are equally fond of. I have very cordially betaken myself to my books and my fireside, and seldom leave them, unless for exercise. I have added another family to the number of those I was acquainted with when you were here. Their name is Unwin,—the most agreeable people imaginable; quite sociable, and as free from the ceremonious civility of country gentlefolks as any I ever met with. They treat me more like a near relation than a stranger, and their house is always open to me. The old gentleman carries me to Cambridge in his chaise. He is a man of learning and good sense, and as simple as Parson Adams. His wife has a very uncommon understanding, has read much to excellent purpose, and is more polite than a duchess. The son, who belongs to Cambridge, is a most amiable young man; and the daughter quite of a piece with the rest of the family. They see but little company, which suits me exactly; go when I will, I find a house full of peace and cordiality in all its parts, and am sure to hear no scandal, but such discourse instead of it as we are all better for. You remember Rousseau's description of an English morning; such are the mornings I spend with these good people; and the evenings differ from them in nothing, except that they are still more snug and quieter. Now I know them, I wonder that I liked Huntington so well before I knew them, and am apt to think I should find every place disagreeable that had not an Unwin belonging to it.

This incident convinces me of the truth of an observation I have often made, that when we circumscribe our estimate of all that is clever within the limits of our own acquaintance (which I at least have been always apt to do), we are guilty of a very uncharitable censure upon the rest of the world, and of a narrowness of thinking disgraceful to ourselves. Wapping and Redriff may contain some of the most amiable persons living, and such as one would go to Wapping and Redriff to make acquaintance with. You remember Gray's stanza:—

> Full many a gem of purest ray serene
> The deep unfathom'd caves of ocean bear;
> Full many a flower is born to blush unseen,
> And waste its sweetness on the desert air.

Yours, dear Joe,
W. C.

To the REV. WILLIAM UNWIN
October 31, 1779.

MY DEAR FRIEND—I wrote my last letter merely to inform you that I had nothing to say, in answer to which you have said nothing. I admire the propriety of your conduct, though I am a loser by it. I will endeavor to say something now, and shall hope for something in return.

I have been well entertained with Johnson's biography, for which I thank you: with one exception, and that a swinging one, I think he has acquitted himself with his usual good sense and sufficiency. His treatment of Milton is unmerciful to the last degree. A pensioner is not likely to spare a republican, and the Doctor, in order, I suppose to convince his royal patron of the sincerity of his monarchical principles, has belabored that great poet's character with the most industrious cruelty. As a man, he has hardly left him the shadow of one good quality. Churlishness in his private life, and a rancorous hatred of everything royal in his public, are the two colors with which he has smeared all the canvas. If he had any virtues, they are not to be found in the Doctor's picture of him, and it is well for Milton that some sourness in his temper is the only vice with which his memory has been charged; it is evident enough that if his biographer could have discovered more he would not have spared him. As a poet, he has treated him with severity enough, and has plucked one or two of the most beautiful feathers out of his Muse's wing, and trampled them under his great foot. He has passed sentence of condemnation upon *Lycidas*, and has taken occasion, from that charming poem, to expose to ridicule (what is indeed ridiculous enough) the childish prattlement of pastoral compositions, as if *Lycidas* was the prototype and pattern of them all. The liveliness of the description, the sweetness of the numbers, the classical spirit of antiquity, that prevails in it, go for nothing. I am convinced, by the way, that he has no ear for poetical numbers, or that it was stopped by prejudice against the harmony of Milton's. Was there ever anything so delightful as the music of the *Paradise Lost?* It is like that of a fine organ, has the fullest and the deepest tones of majesty, with all the softness and elegance of the Dorian flute; variety without end, and never equalled, unless perhaps by Virgil. Yet the Doctor has little or nothing to say upon this copious theme, but talks something about the unfitness of the English language for blank verse, and how apt it is, in the mouth of some readers, to degenerate into declamation. Oh! I could thrash his old jacket till I made his pension jingle in his pockets.

I could talk a good while longer, but I have no room. Our love attends yourself, Mrs. Unwin, and Miss Shuttleworth, not forgetting the two miniature pictures at your elbow.

Yours affectionately,
W. C.

To the REV. JOHN NEWTON
The Greenhouse, September 18, 1781.
* * *

I HAVE no objection in the world to your conveying a copy to Dr. Johnson; though I well know that one of his pointed sarcasms, if he should happen to be displeased, would soon find its way into all companies, and spoil the sale. He writes, indeed, like a man that thinks a great deal, and that sometimes thinks religiously; but report informs me that he has been severe enough in his animadversions on Dr. Watts, who was nevertheless, if I am in any degree a judge of verse, a man of true poetical ability: careless, indeed, for the most part, and inattentive too often to those niceties which constitute elegance of expression, but frequently sublime in his conceptions, and masterly in his execution. Pope, I have heard, had placed him once in the *Dunciad*, but on being advised to read before he judged him, was convinced that he deserved other treatment, and thrust somebody's blockhead into the gap, whose name, consisting of a monosyllable, happened to fit it. Whatever faults, however, I may be chargeable with as a poet, I cannot accuse myself of negligence. I never suffer a line to pass till I have made it as good as I can; and though my doctrines may offend this king of critics, he will not, I flatter myself, be disgusted by slovenly inaccuracy, either in the numbers, rhymes, or language. Let the rest take its chance. It is possible he may be pleased; and if he should, I shall have engaged on my side one of the best trumpeters in the kingdom. Let him only speak as favorably of me as he has spoken of Sir Richard Blackmore (who, though he shines in his poem called 'Creation,' has written more absurdities in verse than any writer of our country), and my success will be secured.

* * *

To Joseph Johnson, *Bookseller*

[December, 1784?]

I DID not write the line that has been tampered with hastily, or without due attention to the construction of it; and what appeared to me its only merit is, in its present state, entirely annihilated.

I know that the ears of modern verse writers are delicate to an excess, and their readers are troubled with the same squeamishness as themselves. So that if a line do not run as smooth as quicksilver, they are offended. A critic of the present day serves a poem as a cook does a dead turkey, when she fastens the legs of it to a post and draws out all the sinews. For this we may thank Pope; but unless we could imitate him in the closeness and compactness of his expression, as well as in the smoothness of his numbers, we had better drop the imitation, which serves no other purpose than to emasculate and weaken all we write. Give me a manly rough line, with a deal of meaning in it, rather than a whole poem full of musical periods, that have nothing but their oily smoothness to recommend them!

I have said thus much, as I hinted in the beginning, because I have just finished a much longer poem than the last, which our common friend will receive by the same messenger that has the charge of this letter. In that poem there are many lines which an ear so nice as the gentleman's who made the above-mentioned alteration would undoubtedly condemn; and yet (if I may be permitted to say it) they cannot be made smoother without being the worse for it. There is a roughness on a plum which nobody that understands fruit would rub off, though the plum would be much more polished without it. But, lest I tire you, I will only add that I wish you to guard me from all such meddling; assuring you that I always write as smoothly as I can; but that I never did, never will, sacrifice the spirit or sense of a passage to the sound of it.

To the Rev. John Newton

January 26, 1783.

MY DEAR FRIEND—It is reported among persons of the best intelligence at Olney—the barber, the schoolmaster, and the drummer of a corps quartered at this place—that the belligerent powers are at last reconciled, the articles of the treaty adjusted, and that peace is at the door. I saw this morning, at nine o'clock, a group of about twelve figures very closely engaged in a conference, as I suppose, upon the same subject. The scene of consultation was a blacksmith's shed, very comfortably screened from the wind, and directly opposed to the morning sun. Some held their hands behind them, some had them folded across their bosom, and others had thrust them into their breeches pockets. Every man's posture bespoke a pacific turn of mind; but the distance being too great for their words to reach me, nothing transpired. I am willing, however, to hope that the secret will not be a secret long, and that you and I, equally interested in the event, though not, perhaps, equally well informed, shall soon have an opportunity to rejoice in the completion of it. The powers of Europe have clashed with each other to a fine purpose; that the Americans, at length declared independent, may keep themselves so if they can; and that what the parties, who have thought proper to dispute upon that point, have wrested from each other in the course of the conflict may be, in the issue of it, restored to the proper owner. Nations may be guilty of a conduct that would render an individual infamous for ever, and yet carry their heads high, talk of their glory, and despise their neighbors. Your opinions and mine, I mean our political ones, are not exactly of a piece, yet I cannot think otherwise upon this subject than I have always done. England, more perhaps through the fault of her generals than her councils, has in some instances acted with a spirit of cruel animosity she was never chargeable with till now. But this is the worst that can be said. On the other hand, the Americans, who, if they had contented themselves with a struggle for lawful liberty, would have deserved applause, seem to me to have incurred the guilt of parricide by renouncing their parent, by making her ruin their favorite object, and by associating themselves with her worst enemy for the accomplishment of their purpose. France and, of course, Spain have acted a treacherous, a thievish part. They have stolen America from England, and whether they are able to possess themselves of that jewel or not hereafter, it was doubtless what they intended. Holland appears to me in a meaner light than any of them. They quarrelled with a friend for an enemy's sake. The French led them by the nose, and the English have thrashed them for suffering it. My view of the contest being, and having been always such, I have consequently brighter hopes for England than her situation some time since seemed to justify. She is the only injured party. America may perhaps call her the aggressor, but if she were so, America has not only repelled the injury, but done a greater. As to the rest, if perfidy, treachery, avarice, and ambition can prove their cause to have been a rotten one, those proofs are found upon them. I think, therefore, that whatever scourge may be prepared for England on some future day, her ruin is not yet to be expected.

Acknowledge, now, that I am worthy of a place under the shed I describe, and that I should make no small figure among the *quidnuncs* of Olney.

I wish the society you have formed may prosper. Your subjects will be of greater importance, and discussed with more sufficiency. The earth is a grain of sand, but the spiritual interests of man are commensurate with the heavens.

Pray remind Mr. Bull, who has too much genius to have a good memory, that he has an account to settle for Mrs. Unwin with her grocer, and give our love to him. Accept for yourself and Mrs. Newton your just share of the same commodity, with our united thanks for a very fine barrel of oysters. This, indeed, is rather commending the barrel than its contents. I should say, therefore, for a barrel of very fine oysters.

Yours, my dear friend, as ever,

W. C.

To Mrs. Bodham

Weston, February 27, 1790.

My Dearest Rose—Whom I thought withered and fallen from the stalk, but whom I find still alive: nothing could give me greater pleasure than to know it, and to learn it from yourself. I loved you dearly when you were a child, and love you not a jot the less for having ceased to be so. Every creature that bears any affinity to my mother is dear to me, and you, the daughter of her brother, are but one remove distant from her: I love you, therefore, and love you much, both for her sake and for your own. The world could not have furnished you with a present so acceptable to me as the picture which you have so kindly sent me. I received it the night before last, and viewed it with a trepidation of nerves and spirits somewhat akin to what I should have felt had the dear original presented herself to my embraces. I kissed it, and hung it where it is the last object that I see at night, and of course the first on which I open my eyes in the morning. She died when I had completed my sixth year; yet I remember her well, and am an ocular witness of the great fidelity of the copy. I remember, too, a multitude of the maternal tendernesses which I received from her, and which have endeared her memory to me beyond expression. There is in me, I believe, more of the Donne than of the Cowper; and though I love all of both names, and have a thousand reasons to love those of my own name, yet I feel the bond of nature draw me vehemently to your side. I was thought in the days of my childhood much to resemble my mother, and in my natural temper, of which at the age of fifty-eight I must be supposed a competent judge, can trace both her, and my late uncle, your father. Somewhat of his irritability, and a little I would hope both of his and her ——, I know not what to call it without seeming to praise myself, which is not my intention, but speaking to *you*, I will even speak out, and say *good nature*. Add to all this, I deal much in poetry, as did our venerable ancestor, the Dean of St. Paul's, and I think I shall have proved myself a Donne at all points. The truth is, that whatever I am, I love you all.

* * *

To Lady Hesketh

December 1, 1792.

I AM truly glad, my dearest coz, that the waters of Cheltenham have done thee good, and wish ardently that those of Bath may establish thy health, and prove the means of prolonging it many years, even till thou shalt become what thou wast called at a very early age, an old wench indeed. I have been a *pauvre misérable* ever since I came from Eartham, and was little better while there; so that whatever motive may incline me to travel again hereafter, it will not be the hope that my spirits will be much the better for it. Neither was Mrs. Unwin's health so much improved by that frisk of ours into Sussex, as I had hoped and expected. She is, however, tolerably well, but very far indeed from having recovered the effects of her last disorder.

My birthday—the sixty-first that I have numbered—has proved for once a propitious day to me; for on that day my spirits began to mend,—my nights became less hideous, and my days have been such of course.

I have heard nothing from Joseph, and having been always used to hear from him in November, am reduced to the dire necessity of supposing, with you, that he is heinously offended. Being in want of money, however, I wrote to him yesterday, and a letter which ought to produce a friendly answer; but whether it will or not is an affair at present of great uncertainty. Walter Bagot is offended too, and wonders that I would have any connection with so bad a man as the author of the Essay on Old Maids must necessarily be. Poor man! he has five sisters, I think, in that predicament, which makes *his* resentment rather excusable. Joseph, by the way, has two, and perhaps may be proportionally influenced by that consideration. Should that be the case, I have nothing left to do but to wish them all good husbands, since the reconciliation of my two friends seems closely connected with that contingency.

In making the first advances to your sister you have acted like yourself,—that is to say, like a good and affectionate sister, and will not, I hope, lose your reward. Rewarded in another world you will be, no doubt; but I should hope that you will not be altogether unrecompensed in this. Thou hast a heart, I know, that cannot endure to be long at enmity with any one; and were I capable of using thee never so ill, I am sure that in time you would sue to me for a pardon. Thou dost not want fire, but meekness is predominant in thee.

I was never so idle in my life, and never had so much to do. God knows when this will end, but I think of bestirring myself soon, and of putting on my Miltonic trammels once again. That once done, I shall not, I hope, put them off till the work is finished. I have written nothing lately but a sonnet to Romney, and a mortuary copy of verses for the town of Northampton, having been applied to by the new clerk for that purpose.

Johnson designs handsomely. You must pardon Johnson, and receive him into your best graces. He purposes to publish, together with my Homer, a new edition of my two volumes of poems, and to make me a present of the entire profits. They are to be handsome quartos, with an engraving of Abbott's picture of me prefixed. I have left myself neither time nor room for politics.

The French are a vain and childish people, and conduct themselves on this grand occasion with a levity and extravagance nearly akin to madness; but it would have been better for Austria and Prussia to let them alone. All nations have a right to choose their own modes of government; and the sovereignty of the people is a doctrine that evinces itself; for whenever the people choose to be masters, they always are so, and none can hinder them. God grant that we may have no revolution here; but unless we have a reform, we certainly shall. Depend upon it, my dear, the hour is come when power founded in patronage and corrupt majorities must govern this land no longer. Concessions, too, must be made to dissenters of every denomination. They have a right to them,—a right to all the privileges of Englishmen; and sooner or later, by fair means or by force, they will have them.

Adieu, my dearest coz. I have only time to add Mrs. U.'s most affectionate remembrances, and to conclude myself

Ever thine.

GEORGE CRABBE (1754-1832)

When Goldsmith sat down to sketch for all time the picture of his native village, it was after an absence of eighteen years and he saw it through a tinted haze of retrospect and soft sentimental reflection. Crabbe came to his task fresh from the hardships of his youth; he wrote 'with his eye on the object'; and he painted the cot 'as Truth will paint it and as Bards will not,' in all the reality of its hard and sordid detail. The *Village* was Aldborough, a rude fishing port on the 'frowning coast' of Suffolk. Here Crabbe was born, the eldest child of a collector of salt-duties. After a scattered education which consisted partly in loading butter and cheese in the neighboring port, he was apprenticed, at fourteen, to a surgeon near Bury St. Edmunds, who employed him in 'hoeing turnips.' After some years of study he set up as a surgeon in his native village; but his rewards were meager and he desired to marry. In the meantime, he had begun to cultivate the Muses and he resolved to try his lot in London. On the verge of starvation, he was taken up by Burke, who introduced him to his distinguished friends, aided the publication of his first successful poem, *The Library* (1781), and induced him to exchange the knife for the prayer-book. Returning to Aldborough as a curate, he became shortly after, through Burke's introduction, a protégé of the Duke of Rutland, and was never again in want. His literary fame, during most of his life, was based on *The Village*, which he published in 1783 and followed with a silence of twenty-four years, broken only by the publication of a trifling poem, *The Newspaper* (1785). During these years he wrote and destroyed large quantities of verse and a treatise on botany and busied himself with domestic life, but was especially occupied in healing both the minds and bodies of the poor of his various parishes. His second period of publication, beginning with *The Parish Register* (1807), including *The Borough* (1810) and *Tales in Verse* (1812), and concluding with *Tales of the Hall* (1819), brought him into the world of Wordsworth, Byron, and Scott. He outlived the second and died in the same year with the last.

Crabbe's powerful realism has been greatly admired by the men of his own craft. He has, as Tennyson said, 'a world of his own.' It is a far more populous world than that of Cowper or even of Wordsworth and it is not more unlovely than that of Burns; but he brought to its interpretation little of the tenderness of the first, the 'internal brightness' of the second, or the human tears and laughter of the third. We may be stunned or impressed by Crabbe's world, but we will never love it.

THE VILLAGE, Book I

The Village Life, and every care that reigns
O'er youthful peasants and declining swains;
What labor yields, and what, that labor past,
Age, in its hour of languor, finds at last;
What form the real Picture of the Poor,   5
Demand a song—the Muse can give no more.

  Fled are those times, when, in harmonious strains,
The rustic poet praised his native plains:
No shepherds now, in smooth alternate verse,
Their country's beauty or their nymphs rehearse;   10
Yet still for these we frame the tender strain,
Still in our lays fond Corydons complain,
And shepherds' boys their amorous pains reveal,
The only pains, alas! they never feel.

  On Mincio's banks, in Cæsar's bounteous reign,   15
If Tityrus found the Golden Age again,
Must sleepy bards the flattering dream prolong,
Mechanic echoes of the Mantuan song?
From Truth and Nature shall we widely stray,
Where Virgil, not where Fancy, leads the way?

  Yes, thus the Muses sing of happy swains,   21
Because the Muses never knew their pains;
They boast their peasants' pipes; but peasants now
Resign their pipes and plod behind the plough;
And few, amid the rural tribe, have time   25
To number syllables, and play with rime;
Save honest Duck, what son of verse could share
The poet's rapture and the peasant's care?
Or the great labors of the field degrade,
With the new peril of a poorer trade?   30

  From this chief cause these idle praises spring,
That themes so easy few forbear to sing;
For no deep thought the trifling subjects ask;
To sing of shepherds is an easy task;
The happy youth assumes the common strain,
A nymph his mistress, and himself a swain;   36

With no sad scenes he clouds his tuneful prayer,
But all, to look like her, is painted fair.

   I grant indeed that fields and flocks have charms
For him that grazes or for him that farms;   40
But when amid such pleasing scenes I trace
The poor laborious natives of the place,
And see the mid-day sun, with fervid ray,
On their bare heads and dewy temples play;
While some, with feebler heads, and fainter hearts   45
Deplore their fortune, yet sustain their parts—
Then shall I dare these real ills to hide,
In tinsel trappings of poetic pride?

   No; cast by Fortune on a frowning coast,   49
Which neither groves nor happy valleys boast;
Where other cares than those the Muse relates,
And other shepherds dwell with other mates;
By such examples taught, I paint the Cot,
As Truth will paint it, and as Bards will not.
Nor you, ye poor, of lettered scorn complain,   55
To you the smoothest song is smooth in vain;
O'ercome by labor, and bowed down by time,
Feel you the barren flattery of a rime?
Can poets soothe you, when you pine for bread,
By winding myrtles round your ruined shed?   60
Can their light tales your weighty griefs o'erpower,
Or glad with airy mirth the toilsome hour?

   Lo! where the heath, with withering brake grown o'er,
Lends the light turf that warms the neighboring poor;   64
From thence a length of burning sand appears,
Where the thin harvest waves its withered ears.
Rank weeds, that every art and care defy,
Reign o'er the land, and rob the blighted rye;
There thistles stretch their prickly arms afar,
And to the ragged infant threaten war;   70
There poppies, nodding, mock the hope of toil,
There the blue bugloss paints the sterile soil;
Hardy and high, above the slender sheaf,
The slimy mallow waves her silky leaf;
O'er the young shoot the charlock throws a shade,   75
And clasping tares cling round the sickly blade;
With mingled tints the rocky coasts abound,
And a sad splendor vainly shines around.
So looks the nymph whom wretched arts adorn,
Betrayed by man, then left for man to scorn;   80
Whose cheek in vain assumes the mimic rose,
While her sad eyes the troubled breast disclose:
Whose outward splendor is but folly's dress,
Exposing most when most it gilds distress.

   Here joyless roam a wild amphibious race,   85
With sullen woe displayed in every face;
Who, far from civil arts and social fly,
And scowl at strangers with suspicious eye.

   Here too the lawless merchant of the main
Draws from his plough the intoxicated swain;
Want only claimed the labor of the day,   91
But vice now steals his nightly rest away.

   Where are the swains, who, daily labor done,
With rural games played down the setting sun;
Who struck with matchless force the bounding ball,   95
Or made the ponderous quoit obliquely fall;
While some huge Ajax, terrible and strong,
Engaged some artful stripling of the throng,
And fell beneath him, foiled, while far around
Hoarse triumph rose, and rocks returned the sound?   100
Where now are these?—Beneath yon cliff they stand,
To show the freighted pinnace where to land;
To load the ready steed with guilty haste,
To fly in terror o'er the pathless waste,
Or, when detected, in their straggling course,   105
To foil their foes by cunning or by force;
Or, yielding part (which equal knaves demand),
To gain a lawless passport through the land.

   Here, wandering long, amid these frowning fields,
I sought the simple life that Nature yields;   110
Rapine and Wrong and Fear usurped her place,
And a bold, artful, surly, savage race;
Who, only skilled to take the finny tribe,
The yearly dinner, or septennial bribe,
Wait on the shore, and, as the waves run high,
On the tossed vessel bend their eager eye.   116
Which to their coast directs its vent'rous way;
Theirs or the ocean's miserable prey.

   As on their neighboring beach yon swallows stand,
And wait for favoring winds to leave the land;
While still for flight the ready wing is spread: 121
So waited I the favoring hour, and fled;
Fled from these shores where guilt and famine reign,
And cried, Ah! hapless they who still remain:
Who still remain to hear the ocean roar,   125
Whose greedy waves devour the lessening shore;
Till some fierce tide, with more imperious sway
Sweeps the low hut and all it holds away;
When the sad tenant weeps from door to door,
And begs a poor protection from the poor!   130

   But these are scenes where Nature's niggard hand
Gave a spare portion to the famished land;
Hers is the fault, if here mankind complain
Of fruitless toil and labor spent in vain;
But yet in other scenes more fair in view,   135
When Plenty smiles—alas! she smiles for few—
And those who taste not, yet behold her store,
Are as the slaves that dig the golden ore—
The wealth around them makes them doubly poor.

Or will you deem them amply paid in health, 140
Labor's fair child, that languishes with wealth?
Go, then! and see them rising with the sun,
Through a long course of daily toil to run;
See them beneath the Dog-star's raging heat,
When the knees tremble and the temples beat;
Behold them, leaning on their scythes, look o'er
The labor past, and toils to come explore; 147
See them alternate suns and showers engage,
And hoard up aches and anguish for their age;
Through fens and marshy moors their steps pursue, 150
When their warm pores imbibe the evening dew;
Then own that labor may as fatal be
To these thy slaves, as thine excess to thee.

Amid this tribe too oft a manly pride 154
Strives in strong toil the fainting heart to hide;
There may you see the youth of slender frame
Contend with weakness, weariness, and shame:
Yet, urged along, and proudly loth to yield,
He strives to join his fellows of the field;
Till long-contending nature droops at last, 160
Declining health rejects his poor repast,
His cheerless spouse the coming danger sees,
And mutual murmurs urge the slow disease.

Yet grant them health, 't is not for us to tell,
Though the head droops not, that the heart is well; 165
Or will you praise that homely, healthy fare,
Plenteous and plain, that happy peasants share!
Oh! trifle not with wants you cannot feel,
Nor mock the misery of a stinted meal;
Homely, not wholesome, plain, not plenteous, such 170
As you who praise, would never deign to touch.

Ye gentle souls, who dream of rural ease,
Whom the smooth stream and smoother sonnet please;
Go! if the peaceful cot your praises share,
Go look within, and ask if peace be there; 175
If peace be his, that drooping weary sire;
Or theirs, that offspring round their feeble fire;
Or hers, that matron pale, whose trembling hand
Turns on the wretched hearth the expiring brand.

Nor yet can Time itself obtain for these 180
Life's latest comforts, due respect and ease;
For yonder see that hoary swain, whose age
Can with no cares except its own engage;
Who, propped on that rude staff, looks up to see
The bare arms broken from the withering tree,
On which, a boy, he climbed the loftiest bough,
Then his first joy, but his sad emblem now. 187

He once was chief in all the rustic trade;
His steady hand the straightest furrow made;
Full many a prize he won, and still is proud
To find the triumphs of his youth allowed; 191

A transient pleasure sparkles in his eyes,
He hears and smiles, then thinks again and sighs;
For now he journeys to his grave in pain;
The rich disdain him; nay, the poor disdain:
Alternate masters now their slave command,
Urge the weak efforts of his feeble hand, 197
And, when his age attempts its task in vain,
With ruthless taunts, of lazy poor complain.

Oft may you see him, when he tends the sheep, 200
His winter charge, beneath the hillock weep;
Oft hear him murmur to the winds that blow
O'er his white locks and bury them in snow,
When, roused by rage and muttering in the morn,
He mends the broken edge with icy thorn:—

'Why do I live, when I desire to be 206
At once from life and life's long labor free?
Like leaves in spring, the young are blown away,
Without the sorrows of a slow decay;
I, like yon withered leaf, remain behind, 210
Nipped by the frost, and shivering in the wind;
There it abides till younger buds come on
As I, now all my fellow-swains are gone;
Then from the rising generation thrust,
It falls, like me, unnoticed to the dust. 215

'These fruitful fields, these numerous flocks I see,
Are others' gain, but killing cares to me;
To me the children of my youth are lords,
Cool in their looks, but hasty in their words:
Wants of their own demand their care; and who
Feels his own want and succors others too? 221
A lonely, wretched man, in pain I go,
None need my help, and none relieve my woe;
Then let my bones beneath the turf be laid,
And men forget the wretch they would not aid.'

Thus groan the old, till by disease oppressed,
They taste a final woe, and then they rest. 227

Theirs is yon House that holds the parish poor,
Whose walls of mud scarce bear the broken door;
There, where the putrid vapors, flagging, play, 230
And the dull wheel hums doleful through the day;
There children dwell who know no parents' care;
Parents, who know no children's love, dwell there!
Heart-broken matrons on their joyless bed
Forsaken wives, and mothers never wed; 235
Dejected widows with unheeded tears,
And crippled age with more than childhood fears;

The lame, the blind, and, far the happiest they!
The moping idiot, and the madman gay.

Here too the sick their final doom receive,
Here brought, amid the scenes of grief, to
   grieve,   241
Where the loud groans from some sad chamber
   flow,
Mixed with the clamors of the crowd below;
Here, sorrowing, they each kindred sorrow scan.
And the cold charities of man to man: 245
Whose laws indeed for ruined age provide,
And strong compulsion plucks the scrap from
   pride;
But still that scrap is bought with many a sigh,
And pride embitters what it can't deny.

Say, ye, oppressed by some fantastic woes,
Some jarring nerve that baffles your repose;   251
Who press the downy couch, while slaves ad-
   vance
With timid eye to read the distant glance;
Who with sad prayers the weary doctor tease,
To name the nameless ever new disease;   255
Who with mock patience dire complaints en-
   dure,
Which real pain and that alone can cure;
How would ye bear in real pain to lie,
Despised, neglected, left alone to die?
How would ye bear to draw your latest breath
Where all that's wretched paves the way for
   death?   261

Such is that room which one rude beam di-
   vides,
And naked rafters form the sloping sides;
Where the vile bands that bind the thatch are
   seen,
And lath and mud are all that lie between;   265
Save one dull pane, that, coarsely patched, gives
   way
To the rude tempest, yet excludes the day:
Here, on a matted flock, with dust o'erspread,
The drooping wretch reclines his languid head;
For him no hand the cordial cup applies,   270
Or wipes the tear that stagnates in his eyes;
No friends with soft discourse his pain beguile,
Or promise hope, till sickness wears a smile.

But soon a loud and hasty summons calls,
Shakes the thin roof, and echoes round the
   walls;   275
Anon, a figure enters, quaintly neat,
All pride and business, bustle and conceit;
With looks unaltered by these scenes of woe,
With speed that, entering, speaks his haste to go,
He bids the gazing throng around him fly,   280
And carries fate and physic in his eye:
A potent quack, long versed in human ills,
Who first insults the victim whom he kills;
Whose murd'rous hand a drowsy Bench pro-
   tect,
And whose most tender mercy is neglect.   285

Paid by the parish for attendance here,
He wears contempt upon his sapient sneer;
In haste he seeks the bed where Misery lies,
Impatience marked in his averted eyes;
And, some habitual queries hurried o'er,   290
Without reply, he rushes on the door:
His drooping patient, long inured to pain,
And long unheeded, knows remonstrance vain;
He ceases now the feeble help to crave
Of man; and silent sinks into the grave.   295

But ere his death some pious doubts arise,
Some simple fears, which 'bold bad' men de-
   spise;
Fain would he ask the parish priest to prove
His title certain to the joys above:
For this he sends the murmuring nurse, who
   calls   300
The holy stranger to these dismal walls:
And doth not he, the pious man, appear,
He, 'passing rich, with forty pounds a year?'
Ah! no; a shepherd of a different stock:
And far unlike him, feeds this little flock: 305
A jovial youth, who thinks his Sunday's task
As much as God or man can fairly ask;
The rest he gives to loves and labors light,
To fields the morning, and to feasts the night;
None better skilled the noisy pack to guide,   310
To urge their chase, to cheer them or to
   chide;
A sportsman keen, he shoots through half the
   day,
And, skilled at whist, devotes the night to play.
Then, while such honors bloom around his
   head,
Shall he sit sadly by the sick man's bed,   315
To raise the hope he feels not, or with zeal
To combat fears that e'en the pious feel?

* * *

Now to the church behold the mourners come,
Sedately torpid and devoutly dumb;   319
The village children now their games suspend,
To see the bier that bears their ancient friend:
For he was one in all their idle sport,
And like a monarch ruled their little court;
The pliant bow he formed, the flying ball,
The bat, the wicket, were his labors all;   325
Him now they follow to his grave, and stand,
Silent and sad, and gazing hand in hand;
While bending low, their eager eyes explore
The mingled relics of the parish poor.   329
The bell tolls late, the moping owl flies round,
Fear marks the flight and magnifies the sound.
The busy priest, detained by weightier care,
Defers his duty till the day of prayer;   333
And, waiting long, the crowd retire distressed,
To think a poor man's bones should lie un-
   blessed.

(1783)

WILLIAM BLAKE (1757–1827)

'I WALKED the other evening to the end of the heath and touched the sky with my finger.' Was the man inspired or mad who made this statement in fierce literalness, when bored by some scientific cant about 'the vastness of space'? One's answer to this question will determine one's attitude toward Blake. The ordinary biographical summary hardly seems to apply to him; yet undeniably, like the hero in the old song, 'This man was born, lived, drank, and died.' He was born in London, he spent his life there, he did not drink much and frequently had none too much to eat and wear, and in London he died, 'leaving the delusive Goddess Nature to her laws, to get into freedom from all law of the numbers, into the mind, in which every one is king and priest in his own house.' Yet this man who denied the validity of positive science and repudiated the reality of physical nature was a twofold artist, draughtsman and poet. After the bare rudiments of an education, he began at ten the study of drawing and almost as early, the writing of verses. At the age of fourteen he was apprenticed to the well-known engraver, Basire. About the same time he wrote some of his published poems. He first exhibited at the Royal Academy in 1780, and three years later brought out his first volume, *Poetical Sketches*, the only one of his publications which was printed in the ordinary manner. *Songs of Innocence* (1789), *Songs of Experience* (1794), and the series of enormous, crazed, difficult, or unintelligible Prophetic Books were all engraved upon plates and embellished with designs by himself. Other published designs and engravings of importance were those for Young's *Night Thoughts* (1797), Hayley's *Life of Cowper* (1803), Blair's *The Grave* (1808), the *Book of Job* (1825), and Dante (1824–27).

None of his accomplishments, whether in literature or design, brought him any considerable return in money or immediate fame. He lived most of his life in almost squalid poverty which he did not seem to mind and, when he had means, bestowed them with unstinted charity and without concern for the future. His conduct was fairly within the law of conventional society and government; his doctrines were revolutionary and extreme even for the age of revolution in which he lived. With all their wildness they are sometimes startlingly modern, and it is not unlikely that the world is yet to ring with some of his ideas. As a workman in lines he was strangely original and powerful, and has been compared with the greatest artists of design that ever lived; though often crudely careless or perverse he could draw with propriety and beauty when he chose, and with tremendous energy and suggestiveness. It would be hard to conceive of finer illustrations than his 'Winter' and 'Evening' for Cowper's *Task*. His poetry speaks for itself. Like his design it is often absurdly crude and at other times his speech is something more than mortal.

'When the stars threw down their spears '—

We happen upon a line like this and we seem to have heard a voice of other worlds.

TO SPRING

O THOU with dewy locks, who lookest down
Through the clear windows of the morning, turn
Thine angel eyes upon our western isle,
Which in full choir hails thy approach, O Spring!

The hills tell each other, and the listening   5
Valleys hear; all our longing eyes are turned
Up to thy bright pavilions: issue forth,
And let thy holy feet visit our clime.

Come o'er the eastern hills, and let our winds
Kiss thy perfumèd garments; let us taste   10
Thy morn and evening breath; scatter thy
    pearls
Upon our love-sick land that mourns for thee.

O deck her forth with thy fair fingers; pour
Thy soft kisses on her bosom; and put
Thy golden crown upon her languished head, 15
Whose modest tresses were bound up for thee.

                                    (1783)

TO THE MUSES

WHETHER on Ida's shady brow,
   Or in the chambers of the East,
The chambers of the sun, that now
   From ancient melody have ceased;

Whether in Heaven ye wander fair,   5
   Or the green corners of the earth,
Or the blue regions of the air
   Where the melodious winds have birth;

Whether on crystal rocks ye rove,
    Beneath the bosom of the sea   10
Wandering in many a coral grove,
    Fair Nine, forsaking Poetry!

How have you left the ancient love
    That bards of old enjoyed in you!
The languid strings do scarcely move!   15
    The sound is forced, the notes are few!
                    (1783)

MAD SONG

The wild winds weep,
    And the night is a-cold;
Come higher, Sleep;
    And my griefs enfold!
But lo! the morning peeps   5
    Over the eastern steeps,
And the rustling [birds] of dawn
    The earth do scorn.

Lo! to the vault
    Of paved heaven,   10
With sorrow fraught,
    My notes are driven:
They strike the ear of night,
    Make weep the eyes of day;
They make mad the roaring winds,   15
    And with tempests play.

Like a fiend in a cloud,
    With howling woe
After night I do crowd
    And with night will go;   20
I turn my back to the east
    From whence comforts have increased;
For light doth seize my brain
    With frantic pain.
                    (1783)

THE PIPER

Piping down the valleys wild,
    Piping songs of pleasant glee,
On a cloud I saw a child,
    And he laughing said to me:

'Pipe a song about a Lamb!'   5
    So I piped with merry cheer.
'Piper, pipe that song again;'
    So I piped: he wept to hear.

'Drop thy pipe, thy happy pipe;
    Sing thy songs of happy cheer:'   10
So I sang the same again,
    While he wept with joy to hear.

'Piper, sit thee down and write
    In a book, that all may read.'
So he vanished from my sight,   15
    And I plucked a hollow reed,

And I made a rural pen,
    And I stained the water clear,
And I wrote my happy songs
    Every child may joy to hear.   20
                    (1789)

THE SHEPHERD

How sweet is the shepherd's sweet lot!
    From the morn to the evening he strays,
He shall follow his sheep all the day,
    And his tongue shall be fillèd with praise.

For he hears the lamb's innocent call,   5
    And he hears the ewe's tender reply:
He is watchful while they are in peace,
    For they know when their shepherd is nigh.
                    (1789)

THE LITTLE BLACK BOY

My mother bore me in the southern wild,
    And I am black, but O my soul is white;
White as an angel is the English child,
    But I am black, as if bereaved of light.

My mother taught me underneath a tree,   5
    And, sitting down before the heat of day,
She took me on her lap and kissèd me,
    And, pointing to the east, began to say:

'Look on the rising sun—there God does live,
    And gives his light, and gives his heat away; 10
And flowers and trees and beasts and men receive
    Comfort in morning, joy in the noonday.

'And we are put on earth a little space,
    That we may learn to bear the beams of love;
And these black bodies and this sunburnt face 15
    Is but a cloud, and like a shady grove.

'For when our souls have learned the heat to bear,
    The cloud will vanish, we shall hear his voice,
Saying: "Come out from the grove, my love and care,
    And round my golden tent like lambs rejoice."'   20

Thus did my mother say, and kissèd me;
    And thus I say to little English boy.
When I from black, and he from white cloud free,
    And round the tent of God like lambs we joy,

I'll shade him from the heat, till he can bear 25
    To lean in joy upon our father's knee;
And then I'll stand and stroke his silver hair,
    And be like him, and he will then love me.
                    (1789)

CRADLE SONG

From SONGS OF INNOCENCE

SWEET dreams, form a shade
O'er my lovely infant's head;
Sweet dreams of pleasant streams
By happy, silent, moony beams.

Sweet sleep, with soft down
Weave thy brows an infant crown.
Sweet sleep, Angel mild,
Hover o'er my happy child.

Sweet smiles, in the night
Hover over my delight;
Sweet smiles, mother's smiles,
All the livelong night beguiles.

Sweet moans, dovelike sighs,
Chase not slumber from thy eyes.
Sweet moans, sweeter smiles,
All the dovelike moans beguiles.

Sleep, sleep, happy child,
All creation slept and smil'd;
Sleep, sleep, happy sleep,
While o'er thee thy mother weep.

Sweet babe, in thy face
Holy image I can trace.
Sweet babe, once like thee,
Thy Maker lay and wept for me.

Wept for me, for thee, for all,
When he was an infant small.
Thou his image ever see,
Heavenly face that smiles on thee,

Smiles on thee, on me, on all;
Who became an infant small.
Infant smiles are His own smiles;
Heaven and earth to peace beguiles.
(1789)

CRADLE SONG

From SONGS OF EXPERIENCE

SLEEP! sleep! beauty bright,
Dreaming o'er the joys of night;
Sleep! sleep! in thy sleep
Little sorrows sit and weep.

Sweet Babe, in thy face
Soft desires I can trace,
Secret joys and secret smiles,
Little pretty infant wiles.

As thy softest limbs I feel,
Smiles as of the morning steal
O'er thy cheek, and o'er thy breast
Where thy little heart does rest.

O! the cunning wiles that creep
In thy little heart asleep.
When thy little heart does wake
Then the dreadful lightnings break,

From thy cheek and from thy eye,
O'er the youthful harvests nigh.
Infant wiles and infant smiles
Heaven and Earth of peace beguiles.
(1794)

A DREAM

ONCE a dream did weave a shade
O'er my Angel-guarded bed,
That an emmet lost its way
Where on grass methought I lay.

Troubled, 'wildered, and forlorn,
Dark, benighted, travel-worn,
Over many a tangled spray,
All heart-broke I heard her say:

'O, my children! do they cry?
Do they hear their father sigh?
Now they look abroad to see:
Now return and weep for me.'

Pitying, I dropped a tear;
But I saw a glow-worm near,
Who replied: 'What wailing wight
Calls the watchman of the night?

'I am set to light the ground,
While the beetle goes his round:
Follow now the beetle's hum;
Little wanderer, hie thee home.'
(1789)

THE DIVINE IMAGE

To Mercy, Pity, Peace, and Love,
    All pray in their distress,
And to these virtues of delight
    Return their thankfulness.

For Mercy, Pity, Peace, and Love,
    Is God our Father dear;
And Mercy, Pity, Peace, and Love,
    Is man, his child and care.

For Mercy has a human heart;
    Pity, a human face;
And Love, the human form divine:
    And Peace, the human dress.

Then every man, of every clime,
    That prays in his distress,
Prays to the human form divine:
    Love, Mercy, Pity, Peace.

And all must love the human form,
  In heathen, Turk, or Jew.
Where Mercy, Love, and Pity dwell,
  There God is dwelling too.   20
              (1789)

THE CHIMNEY SWEEPER

A little black thing among the snow,
Crying 'weep! weep!' in notes of woe!
'Where are thy father and mother, say?'—
'They are both gone up to the church to pray.

'Because I was happy upon the heath,   5
And smiled among the winter's snow,
They clothèd me in the clothes of death,
And taught me to sing the notes of woe.

'And because I am happy and dance and sing,
They think they have done me no injury, 10
And are gone to praise God and his priest and
    king,
Who make up a heaven of our misery.'
              (1794)

THE CLOD AND THE PEBBLE

'Love seeketh not itself to please,
  Nor for itself hath any care,
But for another gives its ease,
  And builds a Heaven in Hell's despair.'

So sung a little clod of clay,   5
  Trodden with the cattle's feet,
But a pebble of the brook
  Warbled out these meters meet:

'Love seeketh only self to please,
  To bind another to its delight,   10
Joys in another's loss of ease,
  And builds a Hell in Heaven's despite.'
              (1794)

THE TIGER

Tiger! Tiger! burning bright
In the forests of the night,
What immortal hand or eye
Could frame thy fearful symmetry?

In what distant deeps or skies   5
Burnt the fire of thine eyes?
On what wings dare he aspire?
What the hand dare seize the fire?

And what shoulder, and what art,
Could twist the sinews of thy heart?   10
And when thy heart began to beat,
What dread hand? and what dread feet?

What the hammer? what the chain?
In what furnace was thy brain?
What the anvil? what dread grasp   15
Dare its deadly terrors clasp?

When the stars threw down their spears,
And watered heaven with their tears,
Did he smile his work to see?
Did he who made the Lamb make thee?   20

Tiger! Tiger! burning bright
In the forests of the night,
What immortal hand or eye
Dare frame thy fearful symmetry?
              (1794)

AH SUNFLOWER

Ah Sunflower, weary of time,
  Who countest the steps of the sun,
Seeking after that sweet golden clime
  Where the traveler's journey is done—

Where the youth pined away with desire, 5
  And the pale virgin, shrouded in snow,
Arise from their graves, and aspire
  Where my sunflower wishes to go!
              (1794)

NURSE'S SONG

When the voices of children are heard on the
    green
  And whisperings are in the dale,
The days of my youth rise fresh in my mind,
  My face turns green and pale.

Then come home, my children, the sun is gone
    down,   5
  And the dews of night arise;
Your spring and your day are wasted in play,
  And your winter and night in disguise.
              (1794)

From MILTON

And did those feet in ancient time
  Walk upon England's mountains green?
And was the holy Lamb of God
  On England's pleasant pastures seen?

And did the Countenance Divine   5
  Shine forth upon our clouded hills?
And was Jerusalem builded here
  Among these dark Satanic mills?

Bring me my bow of burning gold!
  Bring me my arrows of desire!   10
Bring me my spear! O clouds, unfold!
  Bring me my chariot of fire!

I will not cease from mental fight,
  Nor shall my sword sleep in my hand,
Till we have built Jerusalem   15
  In England's green and pleasant land.
              (1804)

ROBERT BURNS (1759-1796)

Burns was born near 'Alloway's auld haunted kirk' on the banks of the Doon, in a two-roomed cottage which his father had built with his own hands out of rough stone and clay. A storm blew down the gable a few days after his birth, and 'A blast o' Janwar' win' Blew hansel in on Robin.' 'No wonder that one ushered into the world amid such a tempest should be the victim of stormy passions,' Burns would afterward say. His father was a poor 'renter' who moved from one farm to another while Burns was growing up. Amid 'the unceasing moil of a galley slave,' he found time for the ordinary education of a Scotch peasant lad and added considerable reading in history and English poetry; but he had known many a weary day at the plow-tail and in harvest by the time he was fifteen. It was at this age, as he has told us, that he found himself partner in the harvest-field with 'a bonnie sweet sonsie lassie.' 'Among her love-inspiring qualities, she sung sweetly; and it was her favorite reel to which I attempted giving an embodied vehicle in rime. . . . Thus with me began love and poetry.'

Farming, love, and poetry were the staples of Burns's life from now on. He tried flax-dressing at Irvine, a town of some size near-by, but succeeded only in acquiring the bad habits of the place and soon returned to the farm and to poetry. After his father's death in 1784, he and his brother Gilbert moved to the farm of Mossgiel, and a little later he met Jean Armour, who after a long and irregular courtship became his wife. His first collection of poems was issued at Kilmarnock in 1786, and such was its immediate success that he went to Edinburgh and brought out a new edition the following winter. He was lionized for a season, but had bitterly to learn the difference between curiosity and social acceptance. From this publication he realized enough money to pay for a tour of the Highlands, contribute two hundred pounds to the needs of his brother, and stock a farm at Ellisland. Here he settled with his wife Jean, now regularly married, in December, 1788. But he had chosen his farm with a poet's rather than a farmer's eye, and shortly undertook to add to his earnings by securing a post in the excise at Dumfries, —'gauging auld wives' barrels,' he called it. His next course was to give up the farm and remove his family to town. It was a perilous position for one of his temperament. Too many 'trusty drouthy cronies' clustered around him; the 'social glass' became too frequent; 'thoughtless follies laid him low, and stained his name.'

Yet even during these years of decline in health and respectability his genius burned brightly. Many of the 'old Scots songs' with which his name is inseparably connected were given to the world at this time; many equally fine were not printed until after his death. Though it is totally uncritical to think of him as merely an unlettered natural singer, Burns never had the leisure or opportunity to become a highly cultivated poet in the English language or on the grand scale. He constantly falls back upon his native dialect for his most telling phrases and his most magical bursts; and he is at his best in those brief snatches, perfect in pitch and infinite in variety, for which—and for the passionate, imperfect, human bounty of his nature—the world so deeply loves him.

SONG: MARY MORISON

O Mary, at thy window be,
  It is the wish'd, the trysted hour!
Those smiles and glances let me see,
  That make the miser's treasure poor:
How blythely wad I bide the stoure,   5
  A weary slave frae sun to sun,
Could I the rich reward secure,
  The lovely Mary Morison.

Yestreen when to the trembling string
  The dance gaed thro' the lighted ha'   10
To thee my fancy took its wing,
  I sat, but neither heard nor saw:
Tho' this was fair, and that was braw,
  And yon the toast of a' the town,
I sigh'd, and said amang them a',   15
  'Ye are na Mary Morison.'

O Mary, canst thou wreck his peace,
  Wha for thy sake wad gladly die?
Or canst thou break that heart of his,
  Whase only faut is loving thee?   20
If love for love thou wilt na gie
  At least be pity to me shown:
A thought ungentle canna be
  The thought o' Mary Morison.

(1800)

SONG: MY NANIE, O

Behind yon hills where Lugar flows,
  'Mang moors an' mosses many, O,
The wintry sun the day has clos'd,
  An' I'll awa to Nanie, O.

The westlin wind blaws loud an' shill:
  The night's baith mirk an' rainy, O;
But I'll get my plaid an' out I'll steal,
  An' owre the hill to Nanie, O.

My Nanie's charming, sweet, an' young;
  Nae artfu' wiles to win ye, O:
May ill befa' the flattering tongue
  That wad beguile my Nanie, O.

Her face is fair, her heart is true,
  As spotless as she's bonie, O:
The op'ning gowan, wat wi' dew,
  Nae purer is than Nanie, O.

A country lad is my degree,
  An' few there be that ken me, O;
But what care I how few they be?
  I'm welcome aye to Nanie, O.

My riches a's my penny-fee,
  An' I maun guide it cannie, O;
But warl's gear ne'er troubles me,
  My thoughts are a' my Nanie, O.

Our auld guidman delights to view
  His sheep an' kye thrive bonie, O;
But, I'm as blythe that hauds his pleugh,
  And has nae care but Nanie, O.

Come weel, come woe, I care na by,
  I'll tak what Heav'n will sen' me, O;
Nae ither care in life hae I,
  But live, an love my Nanie, O.

(1787)

SONG: GREEN GROW THE RASHES

Chorus: *Green grow the rashes, O!*
  Green grow the rashes, O!
    The sweetest hours that e'er I spend
  Are spent amang the lasses, O.

There's nought but care on ev'ry han',
  In every hour that passes, O:
What signifies the life o' man,
  An 't were na for the lasses, O?

The war'ly race may riches chase,
  An' riches still may fly them, O;
An' tho' at last they catch them fast,
  Their hearts can ne'er enjoy them, O.

But gie me a cannie hour at e'en,
  My arms about my dearie, O;
An' war'ly cares, an' war'ly men,
  May a' gae tapsalteerie, O.

For you sae douce, ye sneer at this;
  Ye're nought but senseless asses, O:
The wisest man the warl' e'er saw,
  He dearly lov'd the lasses, O.

Auld Nature swears, the lovely dears
  Her noblest work she classes, O:
Her prentice han' she try'd on man,
  An' then she made the lasses, O.

(1803)

From LINES TO JOHN LAPRAIK

I am nae Poet, in a sense,
But just a Rhymer like by chance,
An' hae to learning nae pretence;
  Yet what the matter?
Whene'er my Muse does on me glance,
  I jingle at her.

Your critic-folk may cock their nose,
And say, 'How can you e'er propose,
You wha ken hardly verse frae prose,
  To mak a sang?'
But, by your leave, my learned foes,
  Ye're maybe wrang.

What's a' your jargon o' your schools,
Your Latin names for horns an' stools?
If honest nature made you fools.
  What sairs your grammars?
Ye'd better taen up spades and shools,
  Or knappin-hammers.

A set o' dull, conceited hashes
Confuse their brains in college classes!
They gang in stirks and come out asses,
  Plain truth to speak;
An' syne they think to climb Parnassus
  By dint o' Greek!

Gie me ae spark o' Nature's fire,
That's a' the learnin I desire;
Then, tho' I drudge thro' dub an' mire
  At pleugh or cart,
My Muse, though hamely in attire,
  May touch the heart.

* * *

(1786)

TO A MOUSE

ON TURNING UP HER NEST WITH THE PLOUGH,
NOVEMBER, 1785

Wee, sleekit, cow'rin, tim'rous beastie,
Oh, what a panic's in thy breastie!
Thou need na start awa sae hasty
  Wi' bickerin brattle!
I wad be laith to rin an' chase thee
  Wi' murd'rin pattle!

I'm truly sorry man's dominion
Has broken nature's social union,
An' justifies that ill opinion
    Which makes thee startle   10
At me, thy poor earth-born companion,
    An' fellow-mortal!

I doubt na, whyles, but thou may thieve:
What then? poor beastie, thou maun live!
A daimen icker in a thrave   15
    'S a sma' request;
I'll get a blessin wi' the lave,
    An' never miss 't!

Thy wee bit housie, too, in ruin!
Its silly wa's the win's are strewin   20
An' naething, now, to big a new ane,
    O' foggage green!
An' bleak December's winds ensuin
    Baith snell an' keen!

Thou saw the fields laid bare and waste,   25
An' weary winter comin fast,
An' cozie here beneath the blast
    Thou thought to dwell,
Till crash! the cruel coulter past
    Out thro' thy cell.   30

That wee bit heap o' leaves an' stibble
Has cost thee mony a weary nibble!
Now thou's turn'd out for a' thy trouble,
    But house or hald,
To thole the winter's sleety dribble   35
    An' cranreuch cauld!

But, Mousie, thou art no thy lane
In proving foresight may be vain:
The best laid schemes o' mice an' men
    Gang aft a-gley,   40
An' lea'e us nought but grief an' pain
    For promis'd joy.

Still thou art blest, compar'd wi' me!
The present only toucheth thee:
But, och! I backward cast my ee   45
    On prospects drear!
An' forward, tho' I canna see,
    I guess an' fear!

(1786)

THE COTTER'S SATURDAY NIGHT

INSCRIBED TO ROBERT AIKEN, ESQ.

> Let not Ambition mock their useful toil,
>   Their homely joys and destiny obscure;
> Nor Grandeur hear with a disdainful smile,
>   The short and simple annals of the poor
>   —GRAY.

My lov'd, my honored, much respected friend!
No mercenary bard his homage pays;
With honest pride, I scorn each selfish end:
My dearest meed a friend's esteem and praise.
To you I sing, in simple Scottish lays,   5
The lowly train in life's sequester'd scene;
The native feelings strong, the guileless ways;
What Aiken in a cottage would have been;
Ah! tho' his worth unknown, far happier there,
    I ween!

November chill blaws loud wi' angry sugh,   10
The short'ning winter day is near a close;
The miry beasts retreating frae the pleugh,
The black'ning trains o' craws to their repose;
The toil-worn Cotter frae his labor goes,—
This night his weekly moil is at an end,—   15
Collects his spades, his mattocks and his hoes,
Hoping the morn in ease and rest to spend,
And weary o'er the moor, his course does hameward bend.

At length his lonely cot appears in view,
Beneath the shelter of an agèd tree;   20
Th' expectant wee-things, toddlin, stacher through
To meet their dad, wi' flichterin noise an' glee.
His wee bit ingle, blinkin bonilie,
His clean hearth-stane, his thrifty wifie's smile,
The lisping infant prattling on his knee,   25
Does a' his weary kiaugh and care beguile,
An' makes him quite forget his labor an' his toil.

Belyve, the elder bairns come drappin in,
At service out amang the farmers roun';
Some ca the pleugh, some herd, some tentie rin
A cannie errand, to a neibor toun: 31
Their eldest hope, their Jenny, woman-grown,
In youthfu' bloom, love sparkling in her ee,
Comes hame, perhaps to shew a braw new gown,
Or deposite her sair-won penny-fee,   35
To help her parents dear, if they in hardship be.

With joy unfeign'd brothers and sisters meet,
An' each for other's weelfare kindly spiers:
The social hours, swift-wing'd, unnotic'd fleet;
Each tells the uncos that he sees or hears.   40
The parents, partial, eye their hopeful years;
Anticipation forward points the view;
The mother, wi' her needle an' her sheers,
Gars auld claes look amaist as weel's the new;
The father mixes a' wi' admonition due.   45

Their master's an' their mistress's command
The younkers a' are warnèd to obey;
An' mind their labors wi' an eydent hand,
An' ne'er tho' out o' sight, to jauk or play:
'An' O! be sure to fear the Lord alway,   50
An' mind your duty, duly, morn an' night!
Lest in temptation's path ye gang astray,
Implore his counsel and assisting might:
They never sought in vain that sought the Lord
    aright!'

But hark! a rap comes gently to the door. 55
Jenny, wha kens the meaning o' the same,
Tells how a neibor lad cam o'er the moor,
To do some errands, and convoy her hame.
The wily mother sees the conscious flame
Sparkle in Jenny's ee, and flush her cheek; 60
Wi' heart-struck, anxious care, inquires his name,
While Jenny hafflins is afraid to speak;
Weel pleas'd the mother hears it's nae wild worthless rake.

Wi' kindly welcome Jenny brings him ben,
A strappin youth; he takes the mother's eye; 65
Blythe Jenny sees the visit's no ill taen;
The father cracks of horses, pleughs, and kye.
The youngster's artless heart o'erflows wi' joy,
But, blate and laithfu', scarce can weel behave;
The mother wi' a woman's wiles can spy 70
What makes the youth sae bashfu' an' sae grave,
Weel-pleas'd to think her bairn's respected like the lave.

O happy love! where love like this is found!
O heart-felt raptures! bliss beyond compare!
I've pacèd much this weary, mortal round, 75
And sage experience bids me this declare—
'If Heaven a draught of heavenly pleasure spare,
One cordial in this melancholy vale,
'T is when a youthful, loving, modest pair,
In other's arms breathe out the tender tale, 80
Beneath the milk-white thorn that scents the ev'ning gale.'

Is there, in human form, that bears a heart,
A wretch! a villain! lost to love and truth!
That can with studied, sly, ensnaring art
Betray sweet Jenny's unsuspecting youth? 85
Curse on his perjur'd arts! dissembling smooth!
Are honor, virtue, conscience, all exil'd?
Is there no pity, no relenting ruth,
Points to the parents fondling o'er their child,
Then paints the ruin'd maid, and their distraction wild? 90

But now the supper crowns their simple board,
The halesome parritch, chief of Scotia's food;
The sowpe their only hawkie does afford,
That yont the hallan' snugly chows her cud.
The dame brings forth, in complimental mood,
To grace the lad, her weel-hain'd kebbuck fell, 96
And aft he's prest, an' aft he ca's it guid;
The frugal wifie, garrulous, will tell,
How 't was a towmond auld, sin' lint was i' the bell.

The cheerfu' supper done, wi' serious face, 100
They round the ingle form a circle wide;
The sire turns o'er with patriarchal grace
The big ha'-bible, ance his father's pride;
His bonnet re'rently is laid aside,
His lyart hafflets wearing thin and bare; 105
Those strains that once did sweet in Zion glide,
He wales a portion with judicious care;
And, 'Let us worship God,' he says with solemn air.

They chant their artless notes in simple guise;
They tune their hearts, by far the noblest aim:
Perhaps *Dundee's* wild-warbling measures rise,
Or plaintive *Martyrs*, worthy of the name, 112
Or noble *Elgin* beets the heaven-ward flame,
The sweetest far of Scotia's holy lays.
Compar'd with these, Italian trills are tame; 115
The tickl'd ear no heart-felt raptures raise;
Nae unison hae they with our Creator's praise.

The priest-like father reads the sacred page,—
How Abram was the friend of God on high;
Or Moses bade eternal warfare wage 120
With Amalek's ungracious progeny;
Or how the royal bard did groaning lie
Beneath the stroke of heaven's avenging ire;
Or Job's pathetic plaint, and wailing cry;
Or rapt Isaiah's wild, seraphic fire; 125
Or other holy seers that tune the sacred lyre.

Perhaps the Christian volume is the theme,—
How guiltless blood for guilty man was shed;
How he, who bore in heav'n the second name,
Had not on earth whereon to lay his head: 130
How his first followers and servants sped;
The precepts sage they wrote to many a land:
How he, who lone in Patmos banishèd,
Saw in the sun a mighty angel stand,
And heard great Bab'lon's doom pronounced by Heav'n's command. 135

Then kneeling down to Heaven's Eternal King,
The saint, the father, and the husband prays:
Hope 'springs exulting on triumphant wing,'
That thus they all shall meet in future days;
There ever bask in uncreated rays, 140
No more to sigh or shed the bitter tear,
Together hymning their Creator's praise,
In such society, yet still more dear,
While circling Time moves round in an eternal sphere.

Compar'd with this, how poor Religion's pride
In all the pomp of method and of art 146
When men display to congregations wide
Devotion's ev'ry grace except the heart!
The Pow'r, incens'd, the pageant will desert,
The pompous strain, the sacerdotal stole; 150
But haply in some cottage far apart
May hear, well pleased, the language of the soul,
And in his book of life the inmates poor enrol.

Then homeward all take off their sev'ral way;
The youngling cottagers retire to rest; 155

The parent-pair their secret homage pay,
And proffer up to Heav'n the warm request,
That he, who stills the raven's clam'rous nest
And decks the lily fair in flow'ry pride,
Would, in the way his wisdom sees the best, 160
For them and for their little ones provide;
But chiefly, in their hearts with grace divine
 preside.

From scenes like these old Scotia's grandeur
 springs,
That makes her lov'd at home, rever'd abroad;
Princes and lords are but the breath of kings, 165
'An honest man's the noblest work of God':
And certes, in fair Virtue's heavenly road,
The cottage leaves the palace far behind:
What is a lordling's pomp? a cumbrous load,
Disguising oft the wretch of human kind, 170
Studied in arts of hell, in wickedness refin'd!

O Scotia! my dear, my native soil!
For whom my warmest wish to Heaven is sent!
Long may thy hardy sons of rustic toil
Be blest with health, and peace, and sweet con-
 tent! 175
And, oh! may Heaven their simple lives prevent
From luxury's contagion, weak and vile!
Then, howe'er crowns and coronets be rent,
A virtuous populace may rise the while,
And stand a wall of fire around their much-
 lov'd isle. 180

O thou! who pour'd the patriotic tide
That stream'd thro' Wallace's undaunted heart,
Who dar'd to nobly stem tyrannic pride,
Or nobly die, the second glorious part,—
(The patriot's God peculiarly thou art, 185
His friend, inspirer, guardian, and reward!)
O never, never Scotia's realm desert,
But still the patriot, and the patriot-bard,
In bright succession raise, her ornament and
 guard!

      (1786)

ADDRESS TO THE DEIL

O THOU! whatever title suit thee,—
Auld Hornie, Satan, Nick, or Clootie!
Wha in yon cavern, grim an' sootie,
 Clos'd under hatches,
Spairges about the brunstane cootie 5
 To scaud poor wretches!

Hear me, auld Hangie, for a wee,
An' let poor damnèd bodies be;
I'm sure sma' pleasure it can gie,
 E'en to a deil. 10
To skelp an' scaud poor dogs like me,
 An' hear us squeel!

Great is thy pow'r, an' great thy fame;
Far ken'd an' noted is thy name;
An' tho' yon lowin heugh's thy hame, 15
 Thou travels far;
An' faith! thou's neither lag nor lame,
 Nor blate nor scaur.

Whyles, rangin like a roarin lion,
For prey a' holes an' corners tryin; 20
Whyles, on the strong-wing'd tempest flyin,
 Tirlin' the kirks;
Whyles, in the human bosom pryin,
 Unseen thou lurks.

I've heard my rev'rend grannie say, 25
In lanely glens ye like to stray;
Or whare auld ruin'd castles gray
 Nod to the moon,
Ye fright the nightly wand'rer's way
 Wi' eldritch croon. 30

When twilight did my grannie summon
To say her pray'rs, douce honest woman!
Aft yont the dike she's heard you bummin,
 Wi' eerie drone;
Or, rustlin, thro' the boortrees comin, 35
 Wi' heavy groan.

Ae dreary, windy, winter night,
The stars shot down wi' sklentin light,
Wi' you mysel I gat a fright
 Ayont the lough; 40
Ye like a rash-buss stood in sight
 Wi' waving sough.

The cudgel in my neive did shake,
Each bristl'd hair stood like a stake,
When wi' an eldritch, stoor 'Quaick, quaick,' 45
 Amang the springs,
Awa ye squatter'd like a drake,
 On whistlin wings.

Let warlocks grim an' wither'd hags
Tell how wi' you on ragweed nags 50
They skim the muirs an' dizzy crags
 Wi' wicked speed;
And in kirk-yards renew their leagues,
 Owre howket dead.

Thence, countra wives wi' toil an' pain 55
May plunge an' plunge the kirn in vain;
For oh! the yellow treasure's taen
 By witchin skill;
An' dawtet, twal-pint hawkie's gaen
 As yell's the bill. 60

Thence, mystic knots mak great abuse,
On young guidmen, fond, keen, an' crouse;
When the best wark-lume i' the house,
 By cantrip wit,
Is instant made no worth a louse, 65
 Just at the bit.

When thowes dissolve the snawy hoord,
An' float the jinglin icy-boord
Then water-kelpies haunt the foord
    By your direction, 70
An' nighted trav'lers are allur'd
    To their destruction.

And aft your moss-traversing spunkies
Decoy the wight that late and drunk is:
The bleezin, curst, mischievous monkeys 75
    Delude his eyes,
Till in some miry slough he sunk is,
    Ne'er mair to rise.

When mason's mystic word and grip
In storms an' tempests raise you up, 80
Some cock or cat your rage maun stop,
    Or, strange to tell,
The youngest brither ye wad whip
    Aff straught to hell!

Lang syne, in Eden's bonie yard, 85
When youthfu' lovers first were pair'd,
And all the soul of love they shar'd,
    The raptur'd hour,
Sweet on the fragrant flow'ry swaird,
    In shady bow'r; 90

Then you, ye auld sneck-drawin dog!
Ye cam to Paradise incog,
And play'd on man a cursed brogue,
    (Black be your fa'!)
And gied the infant warld a shog, 95
    Maist ruin'd a'.

D'ye mind that day, when in a bizz,
Wi' reeket duds and reestet gizz,
Ye did present your smoutie phiz
    Mang better folk, 100
An' sklented on the man of Uz
    Your spitefu' joke?

An' how ye gat him i' your thrall,
An' brak' him out o' house and hal',
While scabs and blotches did him gall, 105
    Wi' bitter claw,
An' lows'd his ill-tongued, wicked scaul,
    Was warst ava?

But a' your doings to rehearse,
Your wily snares an' fechtin fierce, 110
Sin' that day Michael did you pierce,
    Down to this time,
Wad ding a Lallan tongue, or Erse,
    In prose or rhyme.

An' now, auld Cloots, I ken ye're thinkin 115
A certain Bardie's rantin, drinkin,
Some luckless hour will send him linkin,
    To your black pit;
But faith! he'll turn a corner jinkin,
    An' cheat you yet. 120

But fare you weel, auld Nickie-ben!
O wad ye tak a thought an' men'!
Ye aiblins might—I dinna ken—
    Still hae a stake:
I'm wae to think upo' yon den, 125
    Ev'n for your sake!

(1786)

A BARD'S EPITAPH

Is there a whim-inspirèd fool,
Owre fast for thought, owre hot for rule,
Owre blate to seek, owre proud to snool?
    Let him draw near;
And owre this grassy heap sing dool, 5
    And drap a tear.

Is there a bard of rustic song,
Who, noteless, steals the crowds among,
That weekly this area throng?—
    Oh, pass not by! 10
But with a frater-feeling strong
    Here heave a sigh.

Is there a man whose judgment clear
Can others teach the course to steer,
Yet runs himself life's mad career 15
    Wild as the wave?—
Here pause—and thro' the starting tear
    Survey this grave.

The poor inhabitant below
Was quick to learn and wise to know, 20
And keenly felt the friendly glow
    And softer flame;
But thoughtless follies laid him low,
    And stain'd his name!

Reader, attend! whether thy soul 25
Soars fancy's flights beyond the pole,
Or darkling grubs this earthly hole
    In low pursuit;
Know, prudent, cautious self-control
    Is wisdom's root. 30

(1786)

OF A' THE AIRTS THE WIND CAN BLAW

Of a' the airts the wind can blaw
    I dearly like the west,
For there the bonie lassie lives,
    The lassie I lo'e best:
There's wild woods grow an' rivers row 5
    An' mony a hill between;
But day and night my fancy's flight
    Is ever wi' my Jean.

I see her in the dewy flow'rs,
    I see her sweet an' fair: 10
I hear her in the tunefu' birds,
    I hear her charm the air.

There's not a bonie flow'r that springs
   By fountain, shaw or green;
There's not a bonie bird that sings,   15
   But minds me o' my Jean.
                (1790)

GO FETCH TO ME A PINT O' WINE

Go fetch to me a pint o' wine,
   And fill it in a silver tassie;
That I may drink, before I go,
   A service to my bonie lassie:
The boat rocks at the pier o' Leith,   5
   Fu' loud the wind blaws frae the Ferry;
The ship rides by the Berwick-law,
   And I maun leave my bonie Mary.

The trumpets sound, the banners fly,
   The glittering spears are rankèd ready,   10
The shouts o' war are heard afar,
   The battle closes deep and bloody;
It's not the roar o' sea or shore
   Would mak me langer wish to tarry;
Nor shouts o' war that's heard afar—   15
   It's leaving thee, my bonie Mary!
                (1790)

AULD LANG SYNE

SHOULD auld acquaintance be forgot,
   And never brought to min'?
Should auld acquaintance be forgot
   And auld lang syne?

CHORUS: *For auld lang syne my dear,*   5
     For auld lang syne,
     We'll tak a cup o' kindness yet
     For auld lang syne.

And surely ye'll be your pint-stowp,
   And surely I'll be mine!   10
And we'll tak a cup o' kindness yet
   For auld lang syne.

We twa hae run about the braes,
   And pu'd the gowans fine;
But we've wander'd mony a weary fit   15
   Sin' auld lang syne.

We twa hae paidl't i' the burn,
   From mornin' sun till dine;
But seas between us braid hae roar'd
   Sin' auld lang syne.   20

And there's a hand, my trusty fier,
   And gie's a hand o' thine;
And we'll tak a right guid-willie waught
   For auld lang syne.
                (1796)

JOHN ANDERSON MY JO

JOHN ANDERSON my jo, John,
   When we were first acquent,
Your locks were like the raven,
   Your bonie brow was brent;
But now your brow is beld, John,   5
   Your locks are like the snaw;
But blessings on your frosty pow,
   John Anderson my jo.

John Anderson my jo, John,
   We clamb the hill thegither;   10
And monie a canty day, John,
   We've had wi' ane anither:
Now we maun totter down, John,
   And hand in hand we'll go,
And sleep thegither at the foot,   15
   John Anderson my jo.
                (1790)

TAM GLEN

MY heart is a-breaking, dear tittie,
   Some counsel unto me come len';
To anger them a' is a pity,
   But what will I do wi' Tam Glen?

I'm thinking, wi' sic a braw fellow,   5
   In poortith I might mak a fen':
What care I in riches to wallow,
   If I maunna marry Tam Glen?

There's Lowrie, the laird o' Dumeller,
   'Guid-day to you'—brute! he comes ben;
He brags and he blaws o' his siller,   11
   But when will he dance like Tam Glen?

My minnie does constantly deave me,
   And bids me beware o' young men;
They flatter, she says, to deceive me;   15
   But wha can think sae o' Tam Glen?

My daddie says, gin I'll forsake him,
   He'll gie me guid hunder marks ten:
But, if it's ordain'd I maun tak him,
   O, wha will I get but Tam Glen?   20

Yestreen at the valentines' dealing,
   My heart to my mou gied a sten:
For thrice I drew ane without failing,
   And thrice it was written, 'Tam Glen'!

The last Halloween I was waukin   25
   My droukit sark-sleeve, as ye ken:
His likeness cam up the house staukin,
   And the very gray breeks o' Tam Glen!

Come counsel, dear tittie, don't tarry;
   I'll gie ye my bonie black hen,   30
Gif ye will advise me to marry
   The lad I lo'e dearly, Tam Glen.
                (1790)

TO MARY IN HEAVEN

Thou ling'ring star, with less'ning ray,
    That lov'st to greet the early morn,
Again thou usher'st in the day
    My Mary from my soul was torn.
O Mary! dear departed shade!   5
    Where is thy place of blissful rest?
See'st thou thy lover lowly laid?
    Hear'st thou the groans that rend his breast?

That sacred hour can I forget,
    Can I forget the hallowed grove,   10
Where by the winding Ayr we met
    To live one day of parting love?
Eternity will not efface
    Those records dear of transports past,
Thy image at our last embrace—   15
    Ah! little thought we 't was our last!

Ayr, gurgling, kiss'd his pebbl'd shore,
    O'erhung with wild woods, thick'ning green;
The fragrant birch and hawthorn hoar
    Twin'd amorous round the raptur'd scene:
The flow'rs sprang wanton to be prest,   21
    The birds sang love on every spray,
Till too, too soon the glowing west
    Proclaim'd the speed of winged day.

Still o'er these scenes my mem'ry wakes,   25
    And fondly broods with miser care!
Time but th' impression stronger makes,
    As streams their channels deeper wear.
My Mary, dear departed shade!
    Where is thy place of blissful rest?   30
See'st thou thy lover lowly laid?
    Hear'st thou the groans that rend his breast?
                             (1790)

TAM O' SHANTER

A TALE

    Of Brownyis and of Bogillis full is this buke.
                                   —GAWIN DOUGLAS.

When chapman billies leave the street,
And drouthy neibors, neibors meet,
As market-days are wearing late,
And folk begin to tak the gate;
While we sit bousin at the nappy,   5
And gettin fou and unco happy,
We think na on the lang Scots miles,
The mosses, waters, slaps, and stiles,
That lie between us and our hame,
Whare sits our sulky, sullen dame,   10
Gathering her brows like gathering storm,
Nursing her wrath to keep it warm.

    This truth fand honest Tam o' Shanter,
As he frae Ayr ae night did canter:
(Auld Ayr, wham ne'er a town surpasses,   15
For honest men and bonnie lasses.)

O Tam! had'st thou but been sae wise
As taen thy ain wife Kate's advice!
She tauld thee weel thou was a skellum,
A bletherin, blusterin, drunken blellum;   20
That frae November till October,
Ae market-day thou was na sober;
That ilka melder wi' the miller,
Thou sat as lang as thou had siller;
That ev'ry naig was ca'd a shoe on,   25
The smith and thee gat roarin fou on;
That at the Lord's house, ev'n on Sunday,
Thou drank wi' Kirkton Jean till Monday.
She prophesied, that, late or soon,
Thou would be found deep drown'd in Doon; 30
Or catch't wi' warlocks in the mirk,
By Alloway's auld haunted kirk.

    Ah, gentle dames! it gars me greet,
To think how mony counsels sweet,
How mony lengthened sage advices,   35
The husband frae the wife despises!

    But to our tale:—Ae market night,
Tam had got planted unco right,
Fast by an ingle, bleezin finely,
Wi' reamin swats that drank divinely;   40
And at his elbow, Souter Johnie,
His ancient, trusty, drouthy crony:
Tam lo'ed him like a vera brither;
They had been fou for weeks thegither.
The night drave on wi' sangs and clatter; 45
And ay the ale was growing better;
The landlady and Tam grew gracious
Wi' secret favors, sweet, and precious:
The souter tauld his queerest stories;
The landlord's laugh was ready chorus: 50
The storm without might rair and rustle
Tam did na mind the storm a whistle.

    Care, mad to see a man sae happy,
E'en drown'd himself amang the nappy:
As bees flee hame wi' lades o' treasure, 55
The minutes wing'd their way wi' pleasure;
Kings may be blest, but Tam was glorious,
O'er a' the ills o' life victorious!

    But pleasures are like poppies spread,
You seize the flow'r, its bloom is shed;   60
Or like the snow falls in the river,
A moment white—then melts forever;
Or like the borealis race,
That flit ere you can point their place,
Or like the rainbow's lovely form   65
Evanishing amid the storm.
Nae man can tether time or tide:
The hour approaches Tam maun ride,—
That hour, o' night's black arch the keystane,
That dreary hour he mounts his beast in; 70
And sic a night he taks the road in,
As ne'er poor sinner was abroad in.

The wind blew as 't wad blawn its last;
The rattling show'rs rose on the blast;
The speedy gleams the darkness swallow'd; 75
Loud, deep, and lang the thunder bellow'd:
That night, a child might understand,
The Deil had business on his hand.

Weel mounted on his grey mear, Meg,—
A better never lifted leg,— 80
Tam skelpit on thro' dub and mire,
Despising wind and rain and fire;
Whiles holding fast his guid blue bonnet,
Whiles crooning o'er some auld Scots sonnet,
Whiles glowrin round wi' prudent cares, 85
Lest bogles catch him unawares.
Kirk-Alloway was drawing nigh,
Whare ghaists and houlets nightly cry.

By this time he was cross the ford,
Whare in the snaw the chapman smoor'd; 90
And past the birks and meikle stane,
Whare drucken Charlie brak's neck-bane;
And thro' the whins, and by the cairn,
Whare hunters fand the murder'd bairn;
And near the thorn, aboon the well, 95
Whare Mungo's mither hang'd hersel.
Before him Doon pours all his floods;
The doubling storm roars thro' the woods;
The lightnings flash from pole to pole,
Near and more near the thunders roll; 100
When, glimmering thro' the groaning trees,
Kirk-Alloway seemed in a bleeze:
Thro' ilka bore the beams were glancing,
And loud resounded mirth and dancing.

Inspiring bold John Barleycorn! 105
What dangers thou can'st make us scorn!
Wi' tippenny we fear nae evil;
Wi' usquebae we 'll face the devil!
The swats sae ream'd in Tammie's noddle,
Fair play, he car'd na deils a boddle. 110
But Maggie stood right sair astonish'd,
Till, by the heel and hand admonish'd,
She ventur'd forward on the light;
And, wow! Tam saw an unco sight!

Warlocks and witches in a dance; 115
Nae cotillon brent-new frae France,
But hornpipes, jigs, strathspeys, and reels
Put life and mettle in their heels:
A winnock bunker in the east,
There sat Auld Nick in shape o' beast; 120
A towzie tyke, black, grim, and large,
To gie them music was his charge;
He screw'd the pipes and gart them skirl,
Till roof and rafters a' did dirl.—
Coffins stood round like open presses, 125
That shaw'd the dead in their last dresses;
And by some devilish cantraip sleight
Each in its cauld hand held a light,
By which heroic Tam was able

To note upon the haly table 130
A murderer's banes in gibbet airns;
Twa span-lang, wee, unchristen'd bairns;
A thief, new-cutted frae the rape—
Wi' his last gasp his gab did gape;
Five tomahawks, wi' blude red-rusted; 135
Five scymitars, wi' murder crusted;
A garter, which a babe had strangled;
A knife, a father's throat had mangled;
Whom his ain son o' life bereft—
The grey hairs yet stack to the heft; 140
Wi' mair o' horrible and awfu,
Which ev'n to name wad be unlawfu'.

As Tammie glow'd, amaz'd and curious,
The mirth and fun grew fast and furious;
The piper loud and louder blew, 145
The dancers quick and quicker flew;
They reel'd, they set, they cross'd, they cleekit,
Till ilka carlin swat and reekit
And coost her duddies to the wark
And linket at it in her sark! 150

Now Tam, O Tam! had thae been queans,
A' plump and strapping in their teens!
Their sarks, instead o' creeshie flannen,
Been snaw-white seventeen hunder linen!—
Thir breeks o' mine, my only pair, 155
That ance were plush, o' gude blue hair,
I wad hae gien them aff my hurdies,
For ae blink o' the bonie burdies!

* * *

But Tam ken'd what was what fu' brawlie;
There was ae winsome wench and walie, 160
That night enlisted in the core
(Lang after ken'd on Carrick shore:
For mony a beast to dead she shot,
And perish'd mony a bonie boat,
And shook baith meikle corn and bear, 165
And kept the country-side in fear);
Her cutty sark o' Paisley harn,
That while a lassie she had worn,
In longitude tho' sorely scanty,
It was her best, and she was vauntie. 170
Ah! little kent thy reverend grannie,
That sark she coft for her wee Nannie,
Wi' twa pund Scots ('t was a' her riches),
Wad ever graced a dance o' witches!

But here my Muse her wing maun cow'r,
Sic flights are far beyond her pow'r; 176
To sing how Nannie lap and flang,
(A souple jad she was and strang,)
And how Tam stood like ane bewitch'd,
And thought his very een enrich'd; 180
Even Satan glowr'd and fidg'd fu' fain,
And hotch'd and blew wi' might and main:
Till first ae caper, syne anither,
Tam tint his reason a' thegither,
And roars out, 'Weel done, Cutty-sark!' 185
And in an instant all was dark:

And scarcely had he Maggie rallied,
When out the hellish legion sallied.

As bees bizz out wi' angry fyke,
When plundering herds assail their byke; 190
As open pussie's mortal foes,
When pop! she starts before their nose;
As eager runs the market-crowd,
When 'Catch the thief!' resounds aloud;
So Maggie runs, the witches follow, 195
Wi' mony an eldritch skriech and hollo.

Ah, Tam! ah, Tam! thou 'll get thy fairin!
In hell they 'll roast thee like a herrin!
In vain thy Kate awaits thy comin!
Kate soon will be a woefu' woman! 200
Now, do thy speedy utmost, Meg,
And win the key-stane of the brig:
There at them thou thy tail may toss,
A running stream they dare na cross.
But ere the key-stane she could make, 205
The fient a tail she had to shake!
For Nannie, far before the rest.
Hard upon noble Maggie prest,
And flew at Tam wi' furious ettle;
But little wist she Maggie's mettle— 210
Ae spring brought aff her master hale,
But left behind her ain grey tail.

* * *

(1793)

WILLIE BREWED A PECK O' MAUT

O, WILLIE brew'd a peck o' maut,
An' Rob an' Allan cam to see:
Three blyther hearts that lee-lang night
Ye wad na found in Christendie.

CHORUS: *We are na fou, we 're nae that fou,* 5
But just a drappie in our ee;
The cock may craw, the day may daw,
And aye we 'll taste the barley bree.

Here are we met, three merry boys,
Three merry boys, I trow, are we; 10
An' mony a night we've merry been,
And mony mae we hope to be!

It is the moon, I ken her horn,
That 's blinkin in the lift sae hie;
She shines sae bright to wile us hame, 15
But, by my sooth, she 'll wait a wee!

Wha first shall rise to gang awa',
A cuckold, coward loon is he!
Wha first beside his chair shall fa',
He is the king among us three! 20

(1790)

A WINTER NIGHT

Poor naked wretches, wheresoe'er you are,
That bide the pelting of this pitiless storm!
How shall your houseless heads and unfed sides,
Your looped and windowed raggedness, defend you
From seasons such as these?
—SHAKESPEARE.

WHEN biting Boreas, fell and doure,
Sharp shivers thro' the leafless bow'r;
When Phœbus gies a short lived glow'r
    Far south the lift,
Dim-darkening thro' the flaky show'r 5
    Or whirling drift;

Ae night the storm the steeples rocked,
Poor Labor sweet in sleep was locked,
While burns, wi' snawy wreaths up-choked,
    Wild-eddying swirl, 10
Or, thro' the mining outlet bocked,
    Down headlong hurl:

Listening the doors and winnocks rattle,
I thought me on the ourie cattle,
Or silly sheep, wha bide this brattle 15
    O' winter war,
An' through the drift, deep-lairing, sprattle
    Beneath a scaur.

Ilk happin bird—wee, helpless thing!—
That in the merry months o' spring 20
Delighted me to hear thee sing,
    What comes o' thee?
Whare wilt thou cow'r thy chittering wing
    An' close thy ee?

Ev'n you on murd'ring errands toil'd, 25
Lone from your savage homes exil'd,—
The blood-stain'd roost an' sheep-cot spoil'd
    My heart forgets,
While pitiless the tempest wild
    Sore on you beats. 30

* * *

(1787)

HIGHLAND MARY

YE banks, and braes, and streams around
    The castle o' Montgomery,
Green be your woods and fair your flowers,
    Your waters never drumlie!
There simmer first unfauld her robes, 5
    And there the langest tarry;
For there I took the last fareweel,
    O' my sweet Highland Mary.

How sweetly bloom'd the gay green birk,
    How rich the hawthorn's blossom, 10
As underneath their fragrant shade
    I clasp'd her to my bosom!

The golden hours, on angel wings,
    Flew o'er me and my dearie;
For dear to me as light and life,   15
    Was my sweet Highland Mary.

Wi' monie a vow and lock'd embrace
    Our parting was fu' tender;
And, pledging aft to meet again,
    We tore oursels asunder;   20
But O! fell death's untimely frost,
    That nipt my flower sae early!
Now green 's the sod, and cauld 's the clay,
    That wraps my Highland Mary!

O, pale, pale now, those rosy lips,   25
    I aft hae kiss'd sae fondly!
And closed for aye the sparkling glance,
    That dwelt on me sae kindly!
And mould'ring now in silent dust,
    That heart that lo'ed me dearly!   30
But still within my bosom's core
    Shall live my Highland Mary.
                          (1799)

FLOW GENTLY, SWEET AFTON

Flow gently, sweet Afton, among thy green braes,
Flow gently, I 'll sing thee a song in thy praise;
My Mary's asleep by thy murmuring stream,
Flow gently, sweet Afton, disturb not her dream.

Thou stock-dove, whose echo resounds thro' the glen.   5
Ye wild whistling blackbirds in yon thorny den,
Thou green-crested lapwing, thy screaming forbear,
I charge you disturb not my slumbering fair.

How lofty, sweet Afton, thy neighbouring hills,
Far mark'd with the courses of clear winding rills;   10
There daily I wander as noon rises high,
My flocks and my Mary's sweet cot in my eye.

How pleasant thy banks and green valleys below,
Where wild in the woodlands the primroses blow;
There oft, as mild Evening weeps over the lea,   15
The sweet-scented birk shades my Mary and me.

Thy crystal stream, Afton, how lovely it glides,
And winds by the cot where my Mary resides;
How wanton the waters her snowy feet lave,
As gathering sweet flow'rets she stems thy clear wave.   20

Flow gently, sweet Afton, among thy green braes,
Flow gently, sweet river, the theme of my lays;
My Mary's asleep by thy murmuring stream,
Flow gently, sweet Afton, disturb not her dream.

BONIE DOON

Ye flowery banks o' bonie Doon,
    How can ye blume sae fair?
How can ye chant, ye little birds,
    And I sae fu' o' care?

Thou 'll break my heart, thou bonie bird,   5
    That sings upon the bough;
Thou minds me o' the happy days,
    When my fause luve was true.

Thou 'll break my heart, thou bonie bird,
    That sings beside thy mate;   10
For sae I sat, and sae I sang,
    And wist na o' my fate.

Aft hae I rov'd by bonie Doon
    To see the wood-bine twine,
And ilka bird sang o' its luve,   15
    And sae did I o' mine.

Wi' lightsome heart I pu'd a rose
    Frae aff its thorny tree;
And my fause luver staw my rose
    But left the thorn wi' me.   20
                          (1808)

DUNCAN GRAY

Duncan Gray came here to woo,
    Ha, ha, the wooin o't!
On blythe Yule night when we were fou,
    Ha, ha, the wooin o't!
Maggie coost her head fu heigh,   5
Look'd asklent and unco skeigh,
Gart poor Duncan stand abeigh;
    Ha, ha, the wooin o't!

Duncan fleech'd, and Duncan pray'd;
    Ha, ha, the wooin o't!   10
Meg was deaf as Ailsa Craig,
    Ha, ha, the wooin o't!
Duncan sigh'd baith out and in,
Grat his een baith bleer't and blin'.
Spak o' lowpin owre a linn;   15
    Ha, ha, the wooin o't!

Time and chance are but a tide,
    Ha, ha, the wooin o't!
Slighted love is sair to bide,
    Ha, ha, the wooin o't!   20
'Shall I, like a fool,' quoth he,
'For a haughty hizzie die?
She may gae to—France for me!'
    Ha, ha, the wooin o't!

How it comes let doctors tell,   25
    Ha, ha, the wooin o't!
Meg grew sick as he grew hale,
    Ha, ha, the wooin o't!
Something in her bosom wrings,

For relief a sigh she brings; 30
And O! her een, they spak sic things!
   Ha, ha, the wooin o't!

Duncan was a lad o' grace,
   Ha, ha, the wooin o't!
Maggie's was a piteous case, 35
   Ha, ha, the wooin o't!
Duncan could na be her death,
Swelling pity smoor'd his wrath;
Now they're crouse and cantie baith;
   Ha, ha, the wooin o't! 40
               (1798)

SCOTS WHA HAE

Scots, wha hae wi' Wallace bled,
Scots, wham Bruce has aften led;
Welcome to your gory bed,
   Or to victory!
Now's the day, and now's the hour; 5
See the front o' battle lour;
See approach proud Edward's power—
   Chains and slavery!

Wha will be a traitor knave?
Wha can fill a coward's grave? 10
Wha sae base as be a slave?
   Let him turn and flee!
Wha for Scotland's king and law
Freedom's sword will strongly draw,
Freeman stand, or Freeman fa', 15
   Let him follow me!

By oppression's woes and pains
By your sons in servile chains!
We will drain our dearest veins,
   But they shall be free! 20
Lay the proud usurpers low!
Tyrants fall in every foe!
Liberty's in every blow!—
   Let us do or die!
               (1794)

A MAN'S A MAN FOR A' THAT

Is there, for honest poverty,
   That hings his head, an' a that?
The coward slave, we pass him by,
   We dare be poor for a' that!
      For a' that, an' a' that, 5
      Our toils obscure, an' a' that;
   The rank is but the guinea's stamp;
   The man's the gowd for a' that.

What tho' on hamely fare we dine,
   Wear hodden-gray, an' a' that; 10
Gie fools their silks, and knaves their wine,
   A man's a man for a' that.
      For a' that, an' a' that,
      Their tinsel show, an' a' that;
   The honest man, tho' e'er sae poor, 15
   Is king o' men for a' that.

Ye see yon birkie, ca'd a lord,
   Wha struts, an' stares, an' a' that;
Tho' hundreds worship at his word,
   He's but a coof for a' that. 20
      For a' that an' a' that,
      His riband, star, an' a' that
   The man o' independent mind,
   He looks and laughs at a' that.

A prince can mak a belted knight, 25
   A marquis, duke, an' a' that;
But an honest man's aboon his might,
   Guid faith he mauna fa' that!
      For a' that, an' a' that,
      Their dignities, an' a' that, 30
   The pith o' sense, an' pride o' worth,
   Are higher rank than a' that.

Then let us pray that come it may,
   As come it will for a' that,
That sense and worth, o'er a' the earth, 35
   May bear the gree, an' a' that.
      For a' that, an' a' that,
      It's coming yet, for a' that,
      That man to man, the warld o'er,
      Shall brothers be for a' that. 40
               (1800)

THE ROMANTIC REVIVAL

THE Romantic Revival was, in the main, a literary movement, although it extended in its later developments to music and the plastic arts, and became, indeed, a view of life. It was not confined to England, although English writers played leading parts in it, and its limits of time can hardly be definitely determined, as its fainter beginnings date back to the middle of the eighteenth century and its lingering effects continue almost to the end of the nineteenth. It is here used with special reference to the movement in English literature, of which the definite beginning may be fixed as the date of publication of *Lyrical Ballads* in 1798, and the end somewhat indefinitely assigned to the beginning of the Victorian Era in or about 1830.

In its origins the romantic movement was a return to the spirit and manner somewhat loosely associated with medieval romance. It was an escape from the sordid realities of contemporary life to the magic and mystery of a different age or a different sky. This phase of romanticism is admirably illustrated in Coleridge's *Rime of the Ancient Mariner*, *Christabel*, and *Kubla Khan*, and in *La Belle Dame sans Merci* of Keats. On its less mysterious side of sheer adventure and stirring narrative, romanticism found its best exponent in Sir Walter Scott, whose influence extended not merely to the literature of every country in Europe but to those of North and South America. In all these phases appeal was made to emotion rather than intelligence, and especially to the simple emotions, above all to the childlike one of wonder. A modern critic has defined romanticism as a social 'paramnesia'—a re-awakening in the adult memory of the recollections of an infantine or subconscious past.

This harking back to more primitive interests and emotions has been ascribed to the influence of Rousseau, with his idealizing of the state of nature and the virtues of the natural man. These ideas and other social forces found expression in the rebellion of the middle class and the peasants against the privileged orders which culminated in the French Revolution. As part of this general democratic impulse, literature transferred its appeal and its interests from the upper ranks to the humbler classes of society. Wordsworth, in the Preface to the second edition (1800) of *Lyrical Ballads*, sets forth the principal object of that famous collection of poems as the choosing of incidents and situations 'from common life,' and the relation or description of them 'in a selection of language really used by men.' It was a revolt not merely from the literary conventions of the eighteenth century but from its social and political standards. The lower classes in the eighteenth century literature are introduced mainly for the sake of comic relief or burlesque; in the nineteenth century the treatment is—again, with the necessary exceptions—mainly sympathetic. It was in the Victorian Era that most of the measures for the liberation, protection, and education of the working classes came to fruition, but it was in the earlier part of the century that a beginning was made—the first factory act passed, the rights of trades unions recognized, grants made for education, penal and poor law administration reformed, slavery in the British dominions abolished. Poverty was no longer regarded as a necessary part of the divine plan for the regeneration of mankind, and the great modern movement which we describe as 'humanitarian' got well under way. For all this the romantic writers were in large part responsible. The cry of the humble poor made vocal in the eighteenth century by Goldsmith, Crabbe, and Burns was repeated with ever more emphatic accents by Wordsworth, Ruskin, Carlyle, Mrs. Browning, and Tom Hood.

THE ROMANTIC REVIVAL — INTRODUCTION

Equally significant was the worship of nature to which Wordsworth first gave adequate expression in the *Lines composed a few miles above Tintern Abbey* and published in *Lyrical Ballads* in 1798. From the love of Nature of his boyish days, when 'the sounding cataract haunted him like a passion,' the poet rose to

> a sense sublime
> Of something far more deeply interfused,
> Whose dwelling is the light of setting suns,
> And the round ocean and the living air,
> And the blue sky, and in the mind of man.

This power to see natural objects in the light of eternity (*sub specie æternitatis*), to use the phrase of Spinoza, by whom Wordsworth and Coleridge were undoubtedly influenced (see p. 549), was not given to all their successors in English poetry, but the simple power to take delight in nature became a permanent possession of the English-speaking folk. It was not altogether a new gift; Chaucer had it and the Elizabethans had it. But the more sophisticated writers of the eighteenth century had almost lost it, though poets like Cowper and Burns gave promise of a better day.

This love of nature—especially in her wilder moods—we find often expressed in the poetry of Byron, who in other ways clings more closely to the eighteenth century tradition; he is obviously a satirist rather than an enthusiast. But he is characteristically romantic in his insistence upon his own ego; whether he exploits and parades his intellectual doubts and emotional sufferings in the person of Childe Harold or under the guise of other romantic adventurers, his real hero is always himself. This inflamed and inflated egoism is perhaps more characteristic of Continental than of English romanticism, but Byron was largely responsible for it. The passion for personal and national liberty, especially the freeing of oppressed nationalities, burns with a purer light in Shelley, and is carried on beyond the traditional limits of the Romantic Revival by Browning, Meredith, Swinburne, and many others.

NOTEWORTHY DATES

HISTORICAL	LITERARY
1800 Napoleon won Hohenlinden	1800 Preface to *Lyrical Ballads*
1802 Napoleon First Consul for life	1802 *Edinburgh Review*
1804 Napoleon Emperor	1805 Scott, *Lay of the Last Minstrel*
1805 Nelson died at Trafalgar	Schiller died
1807 Slave Trade abolished	1808 Goethe, *Faust*, Part I
1809 Napoleon won Wagram	1809 *Quarterly Review*
1810 Napoleon married Marie Louise	1810 Scott, *The Lady of the Lake*
1811 Prince of Wales Regent	1811 Jane Austen, *Sense and Sensibility*
1812 Retreat from Moscow	1812 Byron, *Childe Harold*, Cantos I–II
1813 Napoleon lost Leipzig	1813 Southey Poet Laureate
1814 Napoleon at Elba	1814 Scott, *Waverley*
1815 Waterloo, Napoleon at St. Helena	1821 Keats died at Rome
1819 Peterloo Massacre at Manchester	1822 Shelley died at Lerici
1820 GEORGE IV	1824 Byron died at Missolonghi
1825 Trades Unions legalized	1825 Macaulay, *Essay on Milton*
1829 Catholic Emancipation	1830 Tennyson, *Poems, Chiefly Lyrical*
1830 WILLIAM IV	1832 *Tracts for the Times*
Manchester & Liverpool Railway	Scott died. Goethe died
1832 First Reform Act	1833–'4 Carlyle, *Sartor Resartus*
Slavery abolished	
1834 Poor Law Reform. Education Grants	1834 Lamb died. Coleridge died
1835 Municipal Corporations Act	1835 Browning, *Paracelsus*

WILLIAM WORDSWORTH (1770-1850)

WORDSWORTH was born at Cockermouth in Cumberland, and educated at Hawkshead Grammar School between Esthwaite Water and Windermere in the Lake District, with which his whole life was closely connected. At St. John's College, Cambridge, according to his own account, he was neither among the 'loyal students faithful to their books,' nor among the 'honest dunces,' but one of the 'half-and-half idlers' who 'read lazily in trivial books,' amused themselves with athletic sports, 'and let the stars Come forth, perhaps, without one quiet thought.' In recollection, Wordsworth probably exaggerated his youthful idleness, for he read extensively, in both classical and modern languages, but he 'was not for that hour, nor for that place,' and he undoubtedly profited more, intellectually and spiritually, by his vacations in the Lake District and in France. He became a warm sympathizer with the French revolutionary movement, which deeply stirred his imagination. The declaration of war between France and England and the Reign of Terror in France cast him into deep melancholy, but he clung to his revolutionary principles until the Napoleonic despotism finally threw him back into agreement with his conservative fellow-countrymen. These events separated Wordsworth from the love of his ardent youth, Annette Vallon, who, in his absence from France, gave birth to a daughter. The little girl was acknowledged by Wordsworth and visited by him in France when peace between the two nations was restored. She was the 'dear child' who walked with him on the Calais sands, and whose memory is enshrined in one of his most famous sonnets, 'It is a beauteous evening, calm and free.'

In this spiritual crisis Wordsworth owed much to the companionship of his sister Dorothy, with whom he decided to retire from the world and devote himself to 'plain living and high thinking.' A legacy of £900 from a young admirer (Raisley Calvert) enabled the Wordsworths, who were living in the Lake District on milk and potatoes, to carry out this resolution, and in 1795 they took a cottage at Racedown, in Dorsetshire, where they were visited by Coleridge. In the autumn of 1797 the three friends took a long walk together in the Quantock Hills; and to pay the expenses of the excursion, the young men planned a small volume of poetry, which was published the following year by an obscure Bristol printer under the title of *Lyrical Ballads.* Containing Coleridge's *Ancient Mariner* and Wordsworth's *Lines written above Tintern Abbey*, it marked very distinctly the two new streams of influence which were to enrich English poetry throughout the nineteenth century, and it has come to be regarded as one of the most important events in the history of literature, although at the time it attracted little attention. In the same year (1798) the Wordsworths and Coleridge sailed for Germany, where the latter plunged deep into the study of German literature and philosophy, while Wordsworth began the composition of *The Prelude*, an account of his own poetical and spiritual development, which was finished in 1805, although withheld from publication until after his death.

In 1799 Wordsworth and his sister settled permanently in the Lake District, their home for the next nine years being Dove Cottage, Grasmere. In 1800 the payment of a long deferred debt to the family enabled Wordsworth to marry a lifelong friend, Mary Hutchison, sung by him in 'She was a phantom of delight' and other poems. In 1813 he was given a government sinecure as distributor of stamps, which brought him in £400 a year, and he was able to remove to a larger house at Rydal Mount, where he stayed until his death. Most of his work now recognized as of the highest excellence was published by 1807, though his longest poem, *The Excursion*, appeared in 1814; *The White Doe of Rylstone* and *Laodamia* in 1815; *The Waggoner* and *Peter Bell*, in 1819; the fine series of sonnets, *The River Duddon*, in 1820; and a less successful sequence, *Ecclesiastical Sketches*, in 1822. On the death of Southey in 1843, he was appointed Poet Laureate, and was in turn succeeded by Tennyson, who received 'the laurel greener from the brow, Of him who uttered nothing base.'

Wordsworth's most obvious service to English poetry was to free it from the bondage of the artificial diction which the school of Pope received as a tradition and hardened into a convention. Subsequent ages owe him a greater debt for opening their minds to truer and deeper relations with Nature, and their hearts to sympathy with simple things and simple people. But his greatest gift was neither a theory of diction nor a system of philosophy, but the union of high imaginative powers with a rare faculty of expression, which enabled him to enrich English poetry with priceless treasures. Matthew Arnold's conviction that 'the poetical performance of Wordsworth is after that of Shakespeare and Milton . . . undoubtedly the most considerable in our language from the Elizabethan age to the present time' has been confirmed by the judgment of later critics.

PREFACE TO LATER ISSUES OF 'LYRICAL BALLADS'

The first volume of these poems has already been submitted to general perusal. It was published as an experiment, which, I hoped, might be of some use to ascertain, how far, by fitting to metrical arrangement a selection of the real language of men in a state of vivid sensation, that sort of pleasure and that quantity of pleasure may be imparted, which a poet may rationally endeavor to impart.

* * *

Several of my friends are anxious for the success of these poems from a belief, that, if the views with which they were composed were indeed realized, a class of poetry would be produced well adapted to interest mankind permanently, and not unimportant in the quality and in the multiplicity of its moral relations: and on this account they have advised me to add a systematic defense of the theory upon which the poems were written. But I was unwilling to undertake the task, because I knew that on this occasion the reader would look coldly upon my arguments, since I might be suspected of having been principally influenced by the selfish and foolish hope of *reasoning* him into an approbation of these particular poems: and I was still more unwilling to undertake the task, because, adequately to display my opinions, and fully to enforce my arguments, would require a space wholly disproportionate to a preface. For to treat the subject with the clearness and coherence of which it is susceptible, it would be necessary to give a full account of the present state of the public taste in this country, and to determine how far this taste is healthy or depraved; which, again, could not be determined, without pointing out, in what manner language and the human mind act and react on each other, and without retracing the revolutions, not of literature alone, but likewise of society itself. I have therefore altogether declined to enter regularly upon this defense; yet I am sensible, that there would be some impropriety in abruptly obtruding upon the public, without a few words of introduction, poems so materially different from those upon which general approbation is at present bestowed.

It is supposed, that by the act of writing in verse an author makes a formal engagement that he will gratify certain known habits of association; that he not only thus apprises the reader that certain classes of ideas and expressions will be found in his book, but that others will be carefully excluded. This exponent or symbol held forth by metrical language must in different eras of literature have excited very different expectations: for example, in the age of Catullus, Terence, and Lucretius, and that of Statius or Claudian; and in our own country, in the age of Shakespeare and Beaumont and Fletcher, and that of Donne and Cowley, or Dryden, or Pope. I will not take upon me to determine the exact import of the promise which by the act of writing in verse an author, in the present day, makes to his reader; but it will undoubtedly appear to many persons that I have not fulfilled the terms of an engagement thus voluntarily contracted. They who have been accustomed to the gaudiness and inane phraseology of many modern writers, if they persist in reading this book to its conclusion, will, no doubt, frequently have to struggle with feelings of strangeness and awkwardness: they will look round for poetry, and will be induced to inquire by what species of courtesy these attempts can be permitted to assume that title. I hope therefore the reader will not censure me, for attempting to state what I have proposed to myself to perform; and also (as far as the limits of a preface will permit) to explain some of the chief reasons which have determined me in the choice of my purpose: that at least he may be spared any unpleasant feeling of disappointment, and that I myself may be protected from one of the most dishonorable accusations which can be brought against an author, namely, that of an indolence which prevents him from endeavoring to ascertain what is his duty, or, when his duty is ascertained, prevents him from performing it.

The principal object, then, proposed in these poems was to choose incidents and situations from common life, and to relate or describe them, throughout, as far as was possible, in a selection of language really used by men, and, at the same time, to throw over them a certain coloring of imagination, whereby ordinary things should be presented to the mind in an unusual aspect, and, further, and above all, to make these incidents and situations interesting by tracing in them, truly though not ostentatiously, the primary laws of our nature: chiefly, as far as regards the manner in which we associate ideas in a state of excitement. Humble and rustic life was generally chosen, because, in that condition, the essential passions of the heart find a better soil in which they can attain their maturity, are less under restraint, and speak a plainer and more emphatic language; because in that condition of life our elementary feelings co-exist in a state of greater simplicity, and, consequently, may be more accurately contemplated, and more forcibly communicated; because the manners of rural life germinate from those elementary feelings; and from the necessary character of rural occupations, are more easily comprehended, and are more durable; and, lastly, because in that condition the passions of men are incorporated with the beautiful and permanent forms of nature. The language, too, of these men is adopted (purified indeed from what appears to be its real defects, from all lasting and rational causes of dislike or disgust) because such men hourly communicate with the best objects from which the best part of language is originally derived; and because, from their rank in society and the sameness and narrow circle of their intercourse, being less under the influence of social vanity, they convey their feelings and notions in simple and unelaborated expressions. Accordingly such a language, arising out of repeated experience and regular feelings, is a more permanent, and a far more philosophical language, than that which is frequently substituted for it by poets, who think that they are conferring honor upon themselves and their art, in proportion as they separate themselves from the sympathies of men, and indulge in arbitrary and capricious habits of expression, in order to furnish food for fickle tastes, and fickle appetites, of their own creation.

I cannot, however, be insensible to the present outcry against the triviality and meanness, both of thought and language, which some of my contemporaries have occasionally introduced into their metrical compositions; and I acknowledge that this defect, where it exists, is more dishonorable to the writer's own character than false refinement or arbitrary innovation, though I should contend at the same time, that it is far less pernicious in the sum of its consequences. From such verses the poems in these volumes will be found distinguished at least by one mark of difference, that each of them has a worthy *purpose*. Not that I always began to write with a distinct purpose formally conceived; but habits of meditation have, I trust, so prompted and regulated my feelings, as that my descriptions of such objects as strongly excite those feelings, will be found to carry along with them a *purpose*. If this opinion is erroneous, I can have little right to the name of a poet. For all good poetry is the spontaneous overflow of powerful feelings: and though this be true, poems to which any value can be attached were never produced on any variety of subjects but by a man, who, being possessed of more than usual organic sensibility, had also thought long and deeply. For our continued influxes of feeling are modified and directed by our thoughts, which are indeed the representatives of all our past feelings; and, as by contemplating the relation of these general representatives to each other, we discover what is really important to men, so, by the repetition and continuance of this act, our feelings will be connected with important subjects, till at length, if we be originally possessed of much sensibility, such habits of mind will be produced, that, by obeying blindly and mechanically the impulses of those habits, we shall describe objects, and utter sentiments, of such a nature, and in such connection with each other, that the understanding of the reader must necessarily be in some degree enlightened, and his affections strengthened and purified.

I have said that each of these poems has a purpose. But it is proper that I should mention one other circumstance which distinguishes these poems from the popular poetry of the day; it is this, that the feeling therein developed gives importance to the action and situation, and not the action and situation to the feeling. My meaning will be rendered perfectly intelligible by referring my reader to the poems entitled *Poor Susan* and the *Childless Father*, particularly to the last stanza of the latter poem.

I will not suffer a sense of false modesty to prevent me from asserting, that I point my reader's attention to this mark of distinction, far less for the sake of these particular poems than from the general importance of the subject. The subject is indeed important! For the human mind is capable of being excited without the application of gross and violent stimulants; and he must have a very faint perception of its beauty and dignity who does not know this, and who does not further know, that one being is elevated above another, in proportion as he possesses this capability. It has therefore appeared to me, that to endeavor to produce or enlarge this capability is one of the best services in which, at any period, a writer can be engaged; but this service, excellent at all times, is especially so at the present day. For a multitude of causes, unknown to former times, are now acting with a combined force to blunt the discriminating powers of the mind, and unfitting it for all voluntary exertion, to reduce it to a state of almost savage torpor. The most effective of these causes are the great national events which are daily taking place, and the increasing accumulation of men in cities, where the uniformity of their occupations produces a craving for extraordinary incident, which the rapid communication of intelligence hourly gratifies. To this tendency of life and manners the literature and theatrical exhibitions of the country have conformed themselves. The invaluable works of our elder writers, I had almost said the works of Shakespeare and Milton, are driven into neglect by frantic novels, sickly and stupid German tragedies, and deluges of idle and extravagant stories in verse.—When I think upon this degrading thirst after outrageous stimulation, I am almost ashamed to have spoken of the feeble endeavor made in these volumes to counteract it; and, reflecting upon the magnitude of the general evil, I should be oppressed with no dishonorable melancholy, had I not a deep impression of certain inherent and indestructible qualities of the human mind, and likewise of certain powers in the great and permanent objects that act upon it, which are equally inherent and indestructible; and did I not further add to this impression a belief, that the time is approaching when the evil will be systematically opposed, by men of greater powers, and with far more distinguished success.

Having dwelt thus long on the subjects and aim of these poems, I shall request the reader's permission to apprise him of a few circumstances relating to their *style*, in order, among other reasons, that I may not be censured for not having performed what I never attempted. The reader will find that personifications of abstract ideas rarely occur in these volumes; and, I hope, are utterly rejected, as an ordinary device to elevate the style, and raise it above prose. I have proposed to myself to imitate, and, as far as is possible, to adopt the very language of men; and assuredly such personifications do not make any natural or regular part of that language. They are, indeed, a figure of speech occasionally prompted by passion, and I have made use of them as such; but I have endeavored utterly to reject them as a mechanical device of style, or as a family language which writers in meter seem to lay claim to by prescription. I have wished to keep my reader in the company of flesh and blood, persuaded that by so doing I shall interest him. Others who pursue a different track will interest him likewise; I do not interfere with their claim, but wish to prefer a different claim of my own. There will also be found in these pieces little of what is usually called poetic diction; as much pains has been taken to avoid it as is ordinarily taken to produce it; this has been done for the reason already alleged, to bring my language near to the language of men, and further, because the pleasure which I have proposed to myself to impart, is of a kind very different from that which is supposed by many persons to be the proper object of poetry. Without being culpably particular, I do not know how to give my reader a more exact notion of the style in which it was my wish and intention to write, than, by informing him that I have at all times endeavored to look steadily at my subject; consequently, there is, I hope in these poems little falsehood of description, and my ideas are expressed in language fitted to their respective importance. Something must have been gained by this practice, as it is friendly to one property of all good poetry, namely, good sense; but it has necessarily cut me off from a large portion of phrases and figures of speech which from father to son have long been regarded as the common inheritance of poets. I have also thought it expedient to restrict myself still further, having abstained from the use of many expressions, in themselves proper and beautiful, but which have been foolishly repeated by bad poets, till such feelings of disgust are connected with them as it is scarcely possible by any art of association to overpower.

If in a poem there should be found a series of lines, or even a single line, in which the language, though naturally arranged, and according to the strict laws of meter, does not differ from that of prose, there is a numerous class of critics who, when they stumble upon these prosaisms, as they call them, imagine that they have made a notable discovery, and exult over the poet as over a man ignorant of his own profession. Now these men would establish a canon of criticism which the reader will conclude he must utterly reject, if he wishes to be pleased with these pieces. And it would be a most easy task to prove to him, that not only the language of a large portion of every good poem, even of the most elevated character, must necessarily, except with reference to the meter, in no respect differ from that of good prose, but likewise that some of the most interesting parts of the best poems will be found to be strictly the language of prose, when prose is well written. The truth of this assertion might be demonstrated by innumerable passages from almost all the poetical writings, even of Milton himself. To illustrate the subject in a general manner, I will here adduce a short composition of Gray, who was at the head of those who, by their reasonings, have attempted to widen the space of separation betwixt prose and metrical composition, and was more than any other man curiously elaborate in the structure of his own poetic diction.

> In vain to me the smiling mornings shine,
> And reddening Phœbus lifts his golden fire;
> The birds in vain their amorous descant join,
> Or cheerful fields resume their green attire.
>
> These ears, alas! for other notes repine;
> *A different object do these eyes require;
> My lonely anguish melts no heart but mine;
> And in my breast the imperfect joys expire;*
> Yet morning smiles the busy race to cheer,
> And new-born pleasure brings to happier men;
> The fields to all their wonted tribute bear;
> To warm their little loves the birds complain.
> *I fruitless mourn to him that cannot hear,
> And weep the more because I weep in vain.*

It will easily be perceived, that the only part of this sonnet which is of any value is the lines printed in italics; it is equally obvious, that, except in the rime, and in the use of the single word 'fruitless' for fruitlessly, which is so far a defect, the language of these lines does in no respect differ from that of prose.

By the foregoing quotation I have shown that the language of prose may yet be well adapted to poetry; and it was previously asserted, that a large portion of the language of every good poem can in no respect differ from that of good prose. We will go further. It may be safely affirmed, that there neither is, nor can be, any essential difference between the language of prose and metrical composition. We are fond of tracing the resemblance between poetry and painting, and, accordingly, we call them sisters: but where shall we find bonds of connection sufficiently strict to typify the affinity betwixt metrical and prose composition? They both speak by and to the same organs; the bodies in which both of them are clothed may be said to be of the same substance, their affections are kindred, and almost identical, not necessarily differing in degree; poetry [1] sheds no tears 'such as angels weep' but natural and human tears; she can boast of no celestial ichor that distinguishes her vital juices from those of prose; the same human blood circulates through the veins of them both.

If it be affirmed that rime and metrical arrangement of themselves constitute a distinction which overturns what has just been said on the strict affinity of metrical language with that of prose, and paves the way for other artificial distinctions which the mind voluntarily admits, I answer that the language of such poetry as is here recommended is, as far as is possible, a selection of the language really spoken by men; that this selection, wherever it is made with true taste and feeling, will of itself form a distinction far greater than would at first be imagined, and will entirely separate the composition from the vulgarity and meanness of ordinary life; and, if meter be superadded thereto, I believe that a dissimilitude will be produced altogether sufficient for the gratification of a rational mind. What other distinction would we have? Whence is it to come? And where is it to exist? Not, surely, where the poet speaks through the mouths of his characters: it cannot be necessary here, either for elevation of style, or any of its supposed ornaments: for, if the poet's subject be judiciously chosen, it will naturally, and upon fit occasion, lead him to passions the language of which, if selected truly and judiciously, must necessarily be dignified and variegated, and alive with metaphors and figures. I forbear to speak of an incongruity which would shock the intelligent reader should the poet interweave any foreign splendor of his own with that which the passion naturally suggests: it is sufficient to say that such addition is unnecessary. And, surely, it is more probable that those passages, which with propriety abound with metaphors and figures, will have their due effect, if, upon other occasions where the passions are of a milder character, the style also be subdued and temperate.

But, as the pleasure which I hope to give by the poems now presented to the reader must depend entirely on just notions upon this subject, and, as it is in itself of high importance to our taste and moral feelings, I cannot content myself with these detached remarks. And if, in what I am about to say, it shall appear to some

---

[1] I here use the word 'poetry' (though against my own judgment) as opposed to the word 'prose,' and synonymous with metrical composition. But much confusion has been introduced into criticism by this contradistinction of poetry and prose, instead of the more philosophical one of poetry and matter of fact, or science. The only strict antithesis to prose is meter; nor is this, in truth, a *strict* antithesis; because lines and passages of meter so naturally occur in writing prose, that it would be scarcely possible to avoid them, even were it desirable.

that my labor is unnecessary, and that I am like a man fighting a battle without enemies, such persons may be reminded, that, whatever may be the language outwardly holden by men, a practical faith in the opinions which I am wishing to establish is almost unknown. If my conclusions are admitted, and carried as far as they must be carried if admitted at all, our judgments concerning the works of the greatest poets both ancient and modern will be far different from what they are at present, both when we praise, and when we censure: and our moral feelings influencing and influenced by these judgments will, I believe, be corrected and purified.

Taking up the subject, then, upon general grounds, let me ask what is meant by the word 'poet'? What is a poet? To whom does he address himself? And what language is to be expected from him? He is a man speaking to men: a man, it is true, endowed with more lively sensibility, more enthusiasm and tenderness, who has a greater knowledge of human nature, and a more comprehensive soul, than are supposed to be common among mankind; a man pleased with his own passions and volitions, and who rejoices more than other men in the spirit of life that is in him; delighting to contemplate similar volitions and passions as manifested in the goings-on of the universe, and habitually impelled to create them where he does not find them. To these qualities he has added, a disposition to be affected more than other men by absent things as if they were present; an ability of conjuring up in himself passions, which are indeed far from being the same as those produced by real events, yet (especially in those parts of the general sympathy which are pleasing and delightful) do more nearly resemble the passions produced by real events, than anything which, from the motions of their own minds merely, other men are accustomed to feel in themselves; whence, and from practice, he has acquired a greater readiness and power in expressing what he thinks and feels, and especially those thoughts and feelings which, by his own choice, or from the structure of his own mind, arise in him without immediate external excitement.

But, whatever portion of this faculty we may suppose even the greatest poet to possess, there cannot be a doubt but that the language which it will suggest to him must often, in liveliness and truth, fall far short of that which is uttered by men in real life, under the actual pressure of those passions, certain shadows of which the poet thus produces, or feels to be produced, in himself.

However exalted a notion we would wish to cherish of the character of a poet, it is obvious that, while he describes and imitates passions, his employment is in some degree mechanical, compared with the freedom and power of real and substantial action and suffering. So that it will be the wish of the poet to bring his feelings near to those of the persons whose feelings he describes, nay, for short spaces of time, perhaps, to let himself slip into an entire delusion, and even confound and identify his own feelings with theirs; modifying only the language which is thus suggested to him by a consideration that he describes for a particular purpose, that of giving pleasure. Here, then, he will apply the principle of selection which has been already insisted upon. He will depend upon this for removing what would otherwise be painful or disgusting in the passion; he will feel that there is no necessity to trick out or to elevate nature: and, the more industriously he applies this principle, the deeper will be his faith that no words, which *his* fancy or imagination can suggest, will be to be compared with those which are the emanations of reality and truth.

But it may be said by those who do not object to the general spirit of these remarks, that, as it is impossible for the poet to produce upon all occasions language as exquisitely fitted for the passion as that which the real passion itself suggests, it is proper that he should consider himself as in the situation of a translator, who does not scruple to substitute excellencies of another kind for those which are unattainable by him; and endeavors occasionally to surpass his original in order to make some amends for the general inferiority to which he feels that he must submit. But this would be to encourage idleness and unmanly despair. Further, it is the language of men who speak of what they do not understand; who talk of poetry as of a matter of amusement and idle pleasure; who will converse with us as gravely about a *taste* for poetry, as they express it, as if it were a thing as indifferent as a taste for rope-dancing, or frontiniac or sherry. Aristotle, I have been told, has said, that poetry is the most philosophic of all writing: it is so: its object is truth, not individual and local, but general, and operative; not standing upon external testimony, but carried alive into the heart by passion; truth which is its own testimony, which gives competence and confidence to the tribunal to which it appeals, and receives them from the same tribunal. Poetry is the image of man and nature. The obstacles which stand in the way of the fidelity of the biographer and historian and of their consequent utility, are incalculably greater than those which are to be encountered by the poet who comprehends the dignity of his art. The poet writes under one restriction only, namely, that of the necessity of giving immediate pleasure to a human being possessed of that information which may be expected from him, not as a lawyer, a physician, a mariner, an astronomer, or a natural philosopher, but as a man. Except this one restriction, there is no object standing between the poet and the image of things; between this, and the biographer and historian there are a thousand.

Nor let this necessity of producing immediate pleasure be considered as a degradation of the poet's art. It is far otherwise. It is an acknowledgment of the beauty of the universe, an acknowledgment the more sincere, because not formal, but indirect; it is a task light and easy to him who looks at the world in the spirit of love: further, it is a homage paid to the native and naked dignity of man, to the grand elementary principle of pleasure, by which he knows, and feels, and lives, and moves. We have no sympathy but what is propagated by pleasure: I would not be misunderstood; but wherever we sympathize with pain, it will be found that the sympathy is produced and carried on by subtle combinations with pleasure. We have no knowledge, that is, no general principles drawn from the contemplation of particular facts, but what has been built up by pleasure, and exists in us by pleasure alone. The man of science, the chemist and mathematician, whatever difficulties and disgusts they may have had to struggle with, know and feel this. However painful may be the objects with which the anatomist's knowledge is connected, he feels that his knowledge is pleasure; and where he has no pleasure he has no knowledge. What then does the poet? He considers man and the objects that surround him as acting and reacting upon each other, so as to produce an infinite complexity of pain and pleasure; he considers man in his own nature and in his ordinary life as contemplating this with a certain quantity of immediate knowledge, with certain convictions, intuitions, and deductions, which from habit acquire the quality of intuitions; he considers him as looking upon this complex scene of ideas and sensations, and finding everywhere objects that immediately excite in him sympathies which, from the necessities of his nature, are accompanied by an overbalance of enjoyment.

To this knowledge which all men carry about with them, and to these sympathies in which without any other discipline than that of our daily life, we are fitted to take delight, the poet principally directs his attention. He considers man and nature as essentially adapted to each other, and the mind of man as naturally the mirror of the fairest and most interesting qualities of nature. And thus the poet, prompted by this feeling of pleasure which accompanies him through the whole course of his studies, converses with general nature with affections akin to those which, through labor and length of time, the man of science has raised up in himself, by conversing with those particular parts of nature which are the objects of his studies. The knowledge both of the poet and the man of science is pleasure; but the knowledge of the one cleaves to us as a necessary part of our existence, our natural and inalienable inheritance; the other is a personal and individual acquisition, slow to come to us, and by no habitual and direct sympathy connecting us with our fellow-beings. The man of science seeks truth as a remote and unknown benefactor; he cherishes and loves it in his solitude: the poet, singing a song in which all human beings join with him, rejoices in the presence of truth as our visible friend and hourly companion. Poetry is the breath and finer spirit of all knowledge; it is the impassioned expression which is in the countenance of all science. Emphatically may it be said of the poet, as Shakespeare hath said of man, 'that he looks before and after.' He is the rock of defence of human nature; an upholder and preserver, carrying everywhere with him relationship and love. In spite of difference of soil and climate, of language and manners, of laws and customs, in spite of things silently gone out of mind, and things violently destroyed, the poet binds together by passion and knowledge the vast empire of human society, as it is spread over the whole earth, and over all time. The objects of the poet's thoughts are everywhere; though the eyes and senses of man are, it is true, his favorite guides, yet he will follow wheresoever he can find an atmosphere of sensation in which to move his wings. Poetry is the first and last of all knowledge—it is as immortal as the heart of man. If the labors of men of science should ever create any material revolution, direct or indirect, in our condition, and in the impressions which we habitually receive, the poet will sleep then no more than at present, but he will be ready to follow the steps of the man of science, not only in those general indirect effects, but he will be at his side, carrying sensation into the midst of the objects of the science itself. The remotest discoveries of the chemist, the botanist, or mineralogist, will be as proper objects of the poet's art as any upon which it can be employed, if the time should ever come when these things shall be familiar to us, and the relations under which they are contemplated by the followers of these respective sciences shall be manifestly and palpably material to us as enjoying and suffering beings. If the time should ever come when what is now called science, thus familiarized to men, shall be ready to put on, as it were, a form of flesh and blood, the poet will lend his divine spirit to aid the transfiguration, and will welcome the being thus produced, as a dear and genuine inmate of the household of man.—It is not, then, to be supposed that any one, who holds that sublime notion of poetry which I have attempted to convey, will break in upon the sanctity and truth of his pictures by transitory and accidental ornaments, and endeavor to excite admiration of himself by arts, the necessity of which must manifestly depend upon the assumed meanness of his subject.

What I have thus far said applies to poetry in general; but especially to those parts of composition where the poet speaks through the mouths of his characters; and upon this point it appears to authorize the conclusion, that there are few persons of good sense, who would not allow that the dramatic parts of composition are defective, in proportion as they deviate from the real language of nature, and are colored by a diction of the poet's own, either peculiar to him as an individual poet or belonging simply to poets in general, to a body of men who, from the circumstance of their compositions being in meter, it is expected will employ a particular language.

It is not, then, in the dramatic parts of composition that we look for this distinction of language; but still it may be proper and necessary where the poet speaks to us in his own person and character. To this I answer by referring my reader to the description which I have before given of a poet. Among the qualities which I have enumerated as principally conducing to form a poet, is implied nothing differing in kind from other men, but only in degree. The sum of what I have there said is, that the poet is chiefly distinguished from other men by a greater promptness to think and feel without immediate external excitement, and a greater power in expressing such thoughts and feelings as are produced in him in that manner. But these passions and thoughts and feelings are the general passions and thoughts and feelings of men. And with what are they connected? Undoubtedly with our moral sentiments and animal sensations, and with the causes which excite these; with the operations of the elements, and the appearances of the visible universe; with storm and sunshine, with the revolutions of the seasons, with cold and heat, with loss of friends and kindred, with injuries and resentments, gratitude and hope, with fear and sorrow. These, and the like, are the sensations and objects which the poet describes, as they are the sensations of other men, and the objects which interest them. The poet thinks and feels in the spirit of the passions of men. How, then, can his language differ in any material degree from that of all other men who feel vividly and see clearly? It might be *proved* that it is impossible. But supposing that this were not the case, the poet might then be allowed to use a peculiar language when expressing his feelings for his own gratification, or that of men like himself. But poets do not write for poets alone, but for men. Unless therefore we are advocates for that admiration which subsists upon ignorance, and that pleasure which arises from hearing what we do not understand, the poet must descend from this supposed height, and, in order to excite rational sympathy, he must express himself as other men express themselves. To this it may be added, that while he is only selecting from the real language of men, or, which amounts to the same thing, composing accurately in the spirit of such selection, he is treading upon safe ground, and we know what we are to expect from him. Our feelings are the same with respect to meter; for, as it may be proper to remind the reader, the distinction of meter is regular and uniform, and not, like that which is produced by what is usually called poetic diction, arbitrary, and subject to infinite caprices upon which no calculation whatever can be made. In the one case, the reader is utterly at the mercy of the poet respecting what imagery or diction he may choose to connect with the passion, whereas, in the other, the meter obeys certain laws, to which the poet and reader both willingly submit because they are certain, and because no interference is made by them with the passion but such as the concurring testimony of ages has shown to heighten and improve the pleasure which co-exists with it.

It will now be proper to answer an obvious question, namely, Why, professing these opinions, have I written in verse? To this, in addition to such answer as is included in what I have already said, I reply, in the first place, Because, however I may have restricted myself, there is still left open to me what confessedly constitutes the most valuable object of all writing, whether in prose or verse, the great and universal passions of men, the most general and interesting of their occupations, and the entire world of nature before me to supply endless combinations of forms and imagery. Now, supposing for a moment that whatever is interesting in these objects may be as vividly described in prose, why should I be condemned, for attempting to superadd to such description the charm, which, by the consent of all nations, is acknowledged to exist in metrical language? To this, by such as are yet unconvinced, it may be answered that a very small part of the pleasure given by poetry depends upon the meter, and that it is injudicious to write in meter, unless it be accompanied with the other artificial distinctions of style with which meter is usually accompanied, and that, by such deviation, more will be lost from the shock which will thereby be given to the reader's associations than will be counterbalanced by any pleasure which he can derive from the general power of numbers. In answer to those who still contend for the necessity of accompanying meter with certain appropriate colors of style in order to the accomplishment of its appropriate end, and who also, in my opinion, greatly underrate the power of meter in itself, it might, perhaps, as far as relates to these volumes, have been almost sufficient to observe, that poems are extant, written upon more humble subjects, and in a more naked and simple style than I have aimed at, which poems have continued to give pleasure from generation to generation. Now, if nakedness and simplicity be a defect, the fact here mentioned affords a strong presumption that poems somewhat less naked and simple are capable of affording pleasure at the present day; and, what I wished *chiefly* to attempt, at present, was to justify myself for having written under the impression of this belief.

But various causes might be pointed out why, when the style is manly, and the subject of some importance, words metrically arranged will long continue to impart such a pleasure to mankind as he who is sensible of the extent of that pleasure will be desirous to impart. The end of poetry is to produce excitement in coexistence with an overbalance of pleasure. Now, by the supposition, excitement is an unusual and irregular state of the mind; ideas and feelings do not, in that state, succeed each other in accustomed order. If the words, however, by which this excitement is produced be in themselves powerful, or the images and feelings have an undue proportion of pain connected with them, there is some danger that the excitement may be carried beyond its proper bounds. Now the co-presence of something regular, something to which the mind has been accustomed in various moods, and in a less excited state, cannot but have great efficacy in tempering and restraining the passion by an intertexture of ordinary feeling, and of feeling not strictly and necessarily connected with the passion. This is unquestionably true, and hence, though the opinion will at first appear paradoxical, from the tendency of meter to divest language, in a certain degree, of its reality, and thus to throw a sort of half consciousness of unsubstantial existence over the whole composition, there can be little doubt, but that more pathetic situations and sentiments, that is, those which have a greater proportion of pain connected with them, may be endured in metrical composition, especially in rime, than in prose. The meter of the old ballads is very artless: yet they contain many passages which would illustrate this opinion, and I hope, if the following poems be attentively perused, similar instances will be found in them. This opinion may be further illustrated by appealing to the reader's own experience of the reluctance with which he comes to the re-perusal of the distressful parts of Clarissa Harlowe, or the Gamester. While Shakespeare's writings, in the most pathetic scenes, never act upon us, as pathetic, beyond the bounds of pleasure—an effect which, in a much greater degree than might at first be imagined, is to be ascribed to small, but continual and regular impulses of pleasurable surprise from the metrical arrangement—on the other hand, (what it must be allowed will much more frequently happen,) if the poet's words should be incommensurate with the passion, and inadequate to raise the reader to a height of desirable excitement, then, (unless the poet's choice of his meter has been grossly injudicious), in the feelings of pleasure which the reader has been accustomed to connect with meter in general, and in the feeling, whether cheerful or melancholy, which he has been accustomed to connect with that particular movement of meter, there will be found something which will greatly contribute to impart passion to the words, and to effect the complex end which the poet proposes to himself.

If I had undertaken a systematic defense of the theory here maintained, it would have been my duty to develop the various causes upon which the pleasure received from metrical language depends. Among the chief of these causes is to be reckoned a principle which must be well known to those who have made any of the arts the object of accurate reflection; I mean the pleasure which the mind derives from the perception of similitude in dissimilitude. This principle is the great spring of the activity of our minds, and their chief feeder. From this principle the direction of the sexual appetite, and all the passions connected with it, take their origin: it is the life of our ordinary conversation; and upon the accuracy with which similitude in dissimilitude, and dissimilitude in similitude are perceived, depend our taste and our moral feelings. It would not be a useless employment to apply this principle to the consideration of meter, and to show that meter is hence enabled to afford much pleasure, and to point out in what manner that pleasure is produced. But my limits will not permit me to enter upon this subject, and I must content myself with a general summary.

I have said that poetry is the spontaneous overflow of powerful feelings; it takes its origin from emotion recollected in tranquillity; the emotion is contemplated, till, by a species of reaction, the tranquillity gradually disappears, and an emotion, kindred to that which was before the subject of contemplation, is gradually produced, and does itself actually exist in the mind. In this mood successful composition generally begins, and in a mood similar to this it is carried on; but the emotion of whatever kind, and in whatever degree, from various causes, is qualified by various pleasures, so that in describing any passions whatsoever, which are voluntarily described, the mind will, upon the whole, be in a state of enjoyment. If nature be thus cautious to preserve in a state of enjoyment a being so employed, the poet ought to profit by the lesson held forth to him, and ought especially to take care, that, whatever passions he communicates to his reader, those passions, if his reader's mind be sound and vigorous, should always be accompanied with an overbalance of pleasure. Now the music of harmonious metrical language, the sense of difficulty overcome, and the blind association of pleasure which has been previously received from works of rime or meter of the same or similar construction, an indistinct preception perpetually renewed of language closely resembling that of real life, and yet, in the circumstance of meter, differing from it so widely—all these imperceptibly make up a complex feeling of delight, which is of the most important use in tempering the painful feeling which is always found intermingled with powerful descriptions of the deeper passions. This effect is always produced in pathetic and impassioned poetry; while, in lighter compositions, the ease and gracefulness with which the poet manages his numbers are themselves confessedly a principal source of the gratification of the reader. All that it is *necessary* to say upon this subject, may be effected by affirming what few persons will deny, that, of two descriptions either of passions, manners, or characters, each of them equally well executed, the one in prose and the other in verse, the verse will be read a hundred times where the prose is read once.

Having thus explained a few of the reasons for writing in verse, and why I have chosen subjects from common life, and endeavored to bring my language near to the real language of men, if I have been too minute in pleading my own cause, I have at the same time been treating a subject of general interest; and for this reason a few words shall be added with reference solely to these particular poems, and to some defects which will probably be found in them. I am sensible that my associations must have sometimes been particular instead of general, and that, consequently, giving to things a false importance, I may have sometimes written upon unworthy subjects; but I am less apprehensive on this account, than that my language may frequently have suffered from those arbitrary connections of feelings and ideas with particular words and phrases, from which no man can altogether protect himself. Hence I have no doubt, that, in some instances, feelings, even of the ludicrous, may be given to my readers by expressions which appeared to me tender and pathetic. Such faulty expressions, were I convinced they were faulty at present, and that they must necessarily continue to be so, I would willingly take all reasonable pains to correct. But it is dangerous to make these alterations on the simple authority of a few individuals, or even of certain classes of men; for where the understanding of an author is not convinced, or his feelings altered, this cannot be done without great injury to himself: for his own feelings are his stay and support; and, if he set them aside in one instance, he may be induced to repeat this act till his mind shall lose all confidence in itself, and becomes utterly debilitated. To this it may be added, that the reader ought never to forget that he is himself exposed to the same errors as the poet, and, perhaps, in a much greater degree: for there can be no presumption in saying of most readers that it is not probable they will be so well acquainted with the various stages of meaning through which words have passed, or with the fickleness or stability of the relations of particular ideas to each other; and, above all, since they are so much less interested in the subject, they may decide lightly and carelessly.

Long as the reader has been detained, I hope he will permit me to caution him against a mode of false criticism which has been applied to poetry, in which the language closely resembles that of life and nature. Such verses have been triumphed over in parodies of which Dr. Johnson's stanza is a fair specimen.

> I put my hat upon my head
> And walked into the Strand,
> And there I met another man
> Whose hat was in his hand.

Immediately under these lines I will place one of the most justly-admired stanzas of the 'Babes in the Wood.'

> These pretty babes with hand in hand
> Went wandering up and down;
> But never more they saw the Man
> Approaching from the Town.

In both these stanzas the words, and the order of the words, in no respect differ from the most unimpassioned conversation. There are words in both, for example, 'The Strand,' and 'The Town,' connected with none but the most familiar ideas; yet the one stanza we admit as admirable, and the other as a fair example of the superlatively contemptible. Whence arises this difference? Not from the meter, not from the language, not from the order of the words; but the *matter* expressed in Dr. Johnson's stanza is contemptible. The proper method of treating trivial and simple verses, to which Dr. Johnson's stanza would be a fair parallelism, is not to say, This is a bad kind of poetry, or, This is not poetry; but, This wants sense; it is neither interesting in itself, nor can *lead* to anything interesting; the images neither originate in that sane state of feeling which arises out of thought, nor can excite thought or feeling in the reader. This is the only sensible manner of dealing with such verses Why trouble yourself about the species till you have previously decided upon the genus? Why take pains to prove that an ape is not a Newton, when it is self-evident that he is not a man?

I must make one request of my reader, which is, that in judging these poems he would decide by his own feelings genuinely, and not by reflection upon what will probably be the judgment of others. How common is it to hear a person say, 'I myself do not object to this style of composition, or this or that expression, but, to such and such classes of people, it will appear mean or ludicrous!' This mode of criticism, so destructive of all sound unadulterated judgment, is almost universal: let the reader then abide independently by his own feelings, and if he finds himself affected, let him not suffer such conjectures to interfere with his pleasure.

If an author, by any single composition, has impressed us with respect for his talents, it is useful to consider this as affording a presumption, that on other occasions where we have been displeased, he, nevertheless, may not have written ill or absurdly; and, further, to give him so much credit for this one composition as may induce us to review what has displeased us, with more care than we should otherwise have bestowed upon it. This is not only an act of justice, but, in our decisions upon poetry especially, may conduce, in a high degree, to the improvement of our own taste: for an *accurate* taste in poetry, and in all the other arts, as Sir Joshua Reynolds has observed, is an *acquired* talent, which can only be produced by thought and a long-continued intercourse with the best models of composition. This is mentioned, not with so ridiculous a purpose as to prevent the most inexperienced reader from judging for himself (I have already said that I wish him to judge for himself), but merely to temper the rashness of decision, and to suggest, that, if poetry be a subject on which much time has not been bestowed, the judgment may be erroneous; and that, in many cases, it necessarily will be so.

Nothing would, I know, have so effectually contributed to further the end which I have in view, as to have shown of what kind the pleasure is, and how that pleasure is produced, which is confessedly produced by metrical composition essentially different from that which I have here endeavored to recommend: for the reader will say that he has been pleased by such composition; and what more can be done for him? The power of any art is limited; and he will suspect, that, if it be proposed to furnish him with new friends, that can be only upon condition of his abandoning his old friends. Besides, as I have said, the reader is himself conscious of the pleasure which he has received from such composition, composition to which he has peculiarly attached the endearing name of poetry; and all men feel an habitual gratitude and something of an honorable bigotry for the objects which have long continued to please them; we not only wish to be pleased, but to be pleased in that particular way in which we have been accustomed to be pleased. There is in these feelings enough to resist a host of arguments; and I should be the less able to combat them successfully, as I am willing to allow, that, in order entirely to enjoy the poetry which I am recommending, it would be necessary to give up much of what is ordinarily enjoyed. But, would my limits have permitted me to point out how this pleasure is produced, many obstacles might have been removed, and the reader assisted in perceiving that the powers of language are not so limited as he may suppose; and that it is possible for poetry to give other enjoyments, of a purer, more lasting, and more exquisite nature. This part of the subject has not been altogether neglected; but it has not been so much my present aim to prove that the interest excited by some other kinds of poetry is less vivid, and less worthy of the nobler powers of the mind, as to offer reasons for presuming, that, if my purpose were fulfilled, a species of poetry would be produced, which is genuine poetry; in its nature well adapted to interest mankind permanently, and likewise important in the multiplicity and quality of its moral relations.

From what has been said, and from a perusal of the poems, the reader will be able clearly to perceive the object which I had in view; he will determine how far it has been attained; and, what is a much more important question, whether it be worth attaining; and upon the decision of these two questions will rest my claim to the approbation of the public.

(1800)

THE PRELUDE

From BOOK I

FAIR seed-time had my soul, and I grew up
Fostered alike by beauty and by fear:
Much favored in my birth-place, and no less
In that beloved Vale to which erelong
We were transplanted—there were we let loose 5
For sports of wider range. Ere I had told
Ten birth-days, when among the mountain slopes
Frost, and the breath of frosty wind, had snapped
The last autumnal crocus, 't was my joy
With store of springes o'er my shoulder hung 10
To range the open heights where woodcocks run
Along the smooth green turf. Through half the night,
Scudding away from snare to snare, I plied
That anxious visitation;—moon and stars
Were shining o'er my head. I was alone, 15
And seemed to be a trouble to the peace
That dwelt among them. Sometimes it befell
In these night wanderings, that a strong desire
O'erpowered my better reason, and the bird
Which was the captive of another's toil 20
Became my prey; and when the deed was done
I heard among the solitary hills
Low breathings coming after me, and sounds
Of undistinguishable motion, steps
Almost as silent as the turf they trod. 25

Nor less when spring had warmed the cultured Vale,
Moved we as plunderers where the mother-bird
Had in high places built her lodge; though mean
Our object and inglorious, yet the end
Was not ignoble. Oh! when I have hung 30
Above the raven's nest, by knots of grass
And half-inch fissures in the slippery rock
But ill sustained, and almost (so it seemed)
Suspended by the blast that blew amain,
Shouldering the naked crag, oh, at that time
While on the perilous ridge I hung alone, 36
With what strange utterance did the loud dry wind
Blow through my ear! the sky seemed not a sky
Of earth—and with what motion moved the clouds!

Dust as we are, the immortal spirit grows 40
Like harmony in music; there is a dark
Inscrutable workmanship that reconciles
Discordant elements, makes them cling together
In one society. How strange that all
The terrors, pains, and early miseries, 45
Regrets, vexations, lassitudes interfused
Within my mind, should e'er have borne a part,
And that a needful part, in making up
The calm existence that is mine when I
Am worthy of myself! Praise to the end! 50

Thanks to the means which Nature deigned to
    employ;
Whether her fearless visitings, or those
That came with soft alarm, like hurtless light
Opening the peaceful clouds; or she may use
Severer interventions, ministry 55
More palpable, as best might suit her aim.

One summer evening (led by her) I found
A little boat tied to a willow tree
Within a rocky cave, its usual home. 59
Straight I unloosed her chain, and stepping in
Pushed from the shore. It was an act of stealth
And troubled pleasure, nor without the voice
Of mountain-echoes did my boat move on;
Leaving behind her still, on either side,
Small circles glittering idly in the moon, 65
Until they melted all into one track
Of sparkling light. But now, like one who rows,
Proud of his skill, to reach a chosen point
With an unswerving line, I fixed my view
Upon the summit of a craggy ridge, 70
The horizon's utmost boundary; far above
Was nothing but the stars and the gray sky.
She was an elfin pinnace; lustily
I dipped my oars into the silent lake,
And, as I rose upon the stroke, my boat 75
Went heaving through the water like a swan;
When, from behind that craggy steep till then
The horizon's bound, a huge peak, black and
    huge,
As if with voluntary power instinct 79
Upreared its head. I struck and struck again,
And growing still in stature the grim shape
Towered up between me and the stars, and still,
For so it seemed, with purpose of its own
And measured motion like a living thing,
Strode after me. With trembling oars I turned,
And through the silent water stole my way 86
Back to the covert of the willow tree;
There in her mooring-place I left my bark,—
And through the meadows homeward went, in
    grave
And serious mood; but after I had seen 90
That spectacle, for many days, my brain
Worked with a dim and undetermined sense
Of unknown modes of being; o'er my thoughts
There hung a darkness, call it solitude
Or blank desertion. No familiar shapes 95
Remained, no pleasant images of trees,
Of sea or sky, no colors of green fields;
But huge and mighty forms that do not live
Like living men, moved slowly through the
    mind 99
By day, and were a trouble to my dreams.

WISDOM and Spirit of the universe!
Thou Soul that art the eternity of thought,
That givest to forms and images a breath
And everlasting motion, not in vain
By day or star-light thus from my first dawn 105
Of childhood didst thou intertwine for me

The passions that build up our human soul;
Not with the mean and vulgar works of man,
But with high objects, with enduring things—
With life and nature—purifying thus 110
The elements of feeling and of thought,
And sanctifying, by such discipline,
Both pain and fear, until we recognize
A grandeur in the beatings of the heart,
Nor was this fellowship vouchsafed to me 115
With stinted kindness. In November days,
When vapors rolling down the valley made
A lonely scene more lonesome, among woods,
At noon and 'mid the calm of summer nights,
When, by the margin of the trembling lake, 120
Beneath the gloomy hills homeward I went
In solitude, such intercourse was mine;
Mine was it in the fields both day and night,
And by the waters, all the summer long.

And in the frosty season, when the sun 125
Was set, and visible for many a mile
The cottage windows blazed through twilight
    gloom,
I heeded not their summons: happy time
It was indeed for all of us—for me
It was a time of rapture! Clear and loud 130
The village clock tolled six,—I wheeled about,
Proud and exulting like an untired horse
That cares not for his home. All shod with steel,
We hissed along the polished ice in games
Confederate, imitative of the chase 135
And woodland pleasures,—the resounding horn,
The pack loud chiming, and the hunted hare.
So through the darkness and the cold we flew,
And not a voice was idle; with the din
Smitten, the precipices rang aloud; 140
The leafless trees and every icy crag
Tinkled like iron; while far distant hills
Into the tumult sent an alien sound
Of melancholy not unnoticed, while the stars
Eastward were sparkling clear, and in the west
The orange sky of evening died away. 146
Not seldom from the uproar I retired
Into a silent bay, or sportively
Glanced sideway, leaving the tumultuous throng,
To cut across the reflex of a star 150
That fled, and, flying still before me, gleamed
Upon the glassy plain; and oftentimes,
When we had given our bodies to the wind,
And all the shadowy banks on either side
Came sweeping through the darkness, spinning
    still 155
The rapid line of motion, then at once
Have I, reclining back upon my heels,
Stopped short; yet still the solitary cliffs
Wheeled by me—even as if the earth had rolled
With visible motion her diurnal round! 160
Behind me did they stretch in solemn train,
Feebler and feebler, and I stood and watched
Till all was tranquil as a dreamless sleep.

                        (1850)

LINES

COMPOSED A FEW MILES ABOVE TINTERN ABBEY ON REVISITING THE BANKS OF THE WYE DURING A TOUR

JULY 13, 1798

FIVE years have past; five summers, with the length
Of five long winters! and again I hear
These waters, rolling from their mountain-springs
With a soft inland murmur.[1]—Once again
Do I behold these steep and lofty cliffs, 5
That on a wild secluded scene impress
Thoughts of more deep seclusion; and connect
The landscape with the quiet of the sky.
The day is come when I again repose
Here under this dark sycamore, and view 10
These plots of cottage-ground, these orchard-tufts,
Which at this season, with their unripe fruits,
Are clad in one green hue, and lose themselves
'Mid groves and copses. Once again I see
These hedgerows, hardly hedgerows, little lines 15
Of sportive wood run wild; these pastoral farms,
Green to the very door; and wreaths of smoke
Sent up in silence, from among the trees!
With some uncertain notice, as might seem,
Of vagrant dwellers in the houseless woods, 20
Or of some hermit's cave, where by his fire
The hermit sits alone.
     These beauteous forms,
Through a long absence, have not been to me
As is a landscape to a blind man's eye:
But oft, in lonely rooms, and mid the din 25
Of towns and cities, I have owed to them
In hours of weariness, sensations sweet,
Felt in the blood, and felt along the heart;
And passing even into my purer mind,
With tranquil restoration:—feelings, too, 30
Of unremembered pleasure: such perhaps,
As have no slight or trivial influence
On that best portion of a good man's life,
His little, nameless, unremembered acts
Of kindness and of love. Nor less, I trust, 35
To them I may have owed another gift,
Of aspect more sublime; that blessed mood,
In which the burden of the mystery,
In which the heavy and the weary weight
Of all this unintelligible world, 40
Is lightened:—that serene and blessed mood,
In which the affections gently lead us on,—
Until, the breath of this corporeal frame,
And even the motion of our human blood
Almost suspended, we are laid asleep 45
In body, and become a living soul:
While with an eye made quiet by the power

[1] The river is not affected by the tides a few miles above Tintern.

Of harmony, and the deep power of joy,
We see into the life of things.
       If this
Be but a vain belief, yet, oh! how oft— 50
In darkness, and amid the many shapes
Of joyless daylight; when the fretful stir
Unprofitable, and the fever of the world,
Have hung upon the beatings of my heart,
How oft, in spirit, have I turned to thee, 55
O sylvan Wye! Thou wanderer through the woods,
How often has my spirit turned to thee!

And now, with gleams of half-extinguished thought,
With many recognitions dim and faint,
And somewhat of a sad perplexity, 60
The picture of the mind revives again:
While here I stand, not only with the sense
Of present pleasure, but with pleasing thoughts
That in this moment there is life and food
For future years. And so I dare to hope. 65
Though, changed, no doubt, from what I was when first
I came among these hills; when like a roe
I bounded o'er the mountains, by the sides
Of the deep rivers, and the lonely streams,
Wherever nature led; more like a man 70
Flying from something that he dreads, than one
Who sought the thing he loved. For nature then
(The coarser pleasures of my boyish days,
And their glad animal movements all gone by)
To me was all in all.—I cannot paint 75
What then I was. The sounding cataract
Haunted me like a passion: the tall rock,
The mountain, and the deep and gloomy wood,
Their colors and their forms, were then to me
An appetite; a feeling and a love 80
That had no need of a remoter charm,
By thought supplied, nor any interest
Unborrowed from the eye.—That time is past,
And all its aching joys are now no more,
And all its dizzy raptures. Not for this 85
Faint I, nor mourn nor murmur; other gifts
Have followed; for such loss, I would believe,
Abundant recompense. For I have learned
To look on nature, not as in the hour
Of thoughtless youth; but hearing oftentimes 90
The still, sad music of humanity,
Nor harsh nor grating, though of ample power
To chasten and subdue. And I have felt
A presence that disturbs me with the joy
Of elevated thoughts; a sense sublime 95
Of something far more deeply interfused,
Whose dwelling is the light of setting suns,
And the round ocean and the living air,
And the blue sky, and in the mind of man:
A motion and a spirit, that impels 100
All thinking things, all objects of all thought,
And rolls through all things. Therefore am I still

A lover of the meadows and the woods,
And mountains; and of all that we behold 104
From this green earth; of all the mighty world
Of eye, and ear,—both what they half create,
And what perceive; well pleased to recognize
In nature and the language of the sense,
The anchor of my purest thoughts, the nurse,
The guide, the guardian of my heart, and soul
Of all my moral being.
                    Nor perchance, 111
If I were not thus taught, should I the more
Suffer my genial spirits to decay:
For thou art with me here upon the banks
Of this fair river; thou my dearest Friend, 115
My dear, dear Friend; and in thy voice I catch
The language of my former heart, and read
My former pleasures in the shooting lights
Of thy wild eyes. Oh! yet a little while
May I behold in thee what I was once, 120
My dear, dear Sister! and this prayer I make
Knowing that Nature never did betray
The heart that loved her; 't is her privilege
Through all the years of this our life, to lead
From joy to joy: for she can so inform 125
The mind that is within us, so impress
With quietness and beauty, and so feed
With lofty thoughts, that neither evil tongues,
Rash judgments, nor the sneers of selfish men,
Nor greetings where no kindness is, nor all 130
The dreary intercourse of daily life,
Shall e'er prevail against us, or disturb
Our cheerful faith that all which we behold
Is full of blessings. Therefore let the moon
Shine on thee in thy solitary walk; 135
And let the misty mountain-winds be free
To blow against thee: and, in after years,
When these wild ecstasies shall be matured
Into a sober pleasure; when thy mind
Shall be a mansion for all lovely forms, 140
Thy memory be as a dwelling-place
For all sweet sounds and harmonies; oh! then,
If solitude, or fear, or pain, or grief,
Should be thy portion, with what healing
      thoughts
Of tender joy wilt thou remember me, 145
And these my exhortations! Nor, perchance—
If I should be where I no more can hear
Thy voice, nor catch from thy wild eyes these
      gleams
Of past existence—wilt thou then forget
That on the banks of this delightful stream 150
We stood together; and that I, so long
A worshipper of Nature, hither came
Unwearied in that service: rather say
With warmer love—oh! with far deeper zeal
Of holier love. Nor wilt thou then forget, 155
That after many wanderings, many years
Of absence, these steep woods and lofty cliffs,
And this green pastoral landscape, were to me
More dear, both for themselves and for thy sake!
                                    (1798)

STRANGE FITS OF PASSION HAVE I KNOWN

Strange fits of passion have I known:
    And I will dare to tell,
But in the Lover's ear alone,
    What once to me befell.

When she I loved looked every day, 5
    Fresh as a rose in June,
I to her cottage bent my way,
    Beneath an evening moon.

Upon the moon I fixed my eye,
    All over the wide lea; 10
With quickening pace my horse drew nigh
    Those paths so dear to me.

And now we reached the orchard plot;
    And as we climbed the hill,
The sinking moon to Lucy's cot 15
    Came near and nearer still.

In one of those sweet dreams I slept,
    Kind Nature's gentlest boon!
And all the while my eyes I kept
    On the descending moon. 20

My horse moved on; hoof after hoof
    He raised, and never stopped:
When down behind the cottage roof,
    At once, the bright moon dropped. 24

What fond and wayward thought will slide
    Into a lover's head!—
'Oh, mercy!' to myself I cried,
    'If Lucy should be dead!'
                                (1800)

SHE DWELT AMONG THE UNTRODDEN WAYS

She dwelt among the untrodden ways
    Beside the springs of Dove,
A Maid whom there were none to praise,
    And very few to love.

A violet by a mossy stone 5
    Half-hidden from the eye!
Fair as a star, when only one
    Is shining in the sky.

She lived unknown, and few could know
    When Lucy ceased to be; 10
But she is in her grave, and, oh,
    The difference to me!
                                (1800)

I TRAVELED AMONG UNKNOWN MEN

I traveled among unknown men,
  In lands beyond the sea;
Nor, England! did I know till then
  What love I bore to thee.

'T is past, that melancholy dream!   5
  Nor will I quit thy shore
A second time; for still I seem
  To love thee more and more.

Among thy mountains did I feel
  The joy of my desire;   10
And she I cherished turned her wheel
  Beside an English fire.

Thy mornings showed, thy nights concealed
  The bowers where Lucy played;
And thine too is the last green field   15
  That Lucy's eyes surveyed.

                (1807)

THREE YEARS SHE GREW IN SUN AND SHOWER

Three years she grew in sun and shower,
Then Nature said, 'A lovelier flower
  On earth was never sown;
This Child I to myself will take,
She shall be mine, and I will make   5
  A Lady of my own.

'Myself will to my darling be
Both law and impulse: and with me
  The Girl, in rock and plain,
In earth and heaven, in glade and bower,   10
Shall feel an overseeing power
  To kindle or restrain.

'She shall be sportive as the fawn
That wild with glee across the lawn
  Or up the mountain springs;   15
And hers shall be the breathing balm,
And hers the silence and the calm
  Of mute insensate things.

'The floating clouds their state shall lend
To her; for her the willow bend;   20
  Nor shall she fail to see
Even in the motions of the Storm
Grace that shall mold the Maiden's form
  By silent sympathy.

'The stars of midnight shall be dear   25
To her; and she shall lean her ear
  In many a secret place
Where rivulets dance their wayward round,
And beauty born of murmuring sound
  Shall pass into her face.   30

'And vital feelings of delight
Shall rear her form to stately height,
  Her virgin bosom swell;
Such thoughts to Lucy I will give
While she and I together live   35
  Here in this happy dell.'

Thus Nature spake—The work was done—
How soon my Lucy's race was run!
  She died, and left to me
This heath, this calm, and quiet scene;   40
The memory of what has been,
  And never more will be.

                (1800)

A SLUMBER DID MY SPIRIT SEAL

A slumber did my spirit seal;
  I had no human fears:
She seemed a thing that could not feel
  The touch of earthly years.

No motion has she now, no force;   5
  She neither hears nor sees;
Rolled round in earth's diurnal course,
  With rocks, and stones, and trees.

                (1800)

MICHAEL

A PASTORAL POEM

If from the public way you turn your steps;
Up the tumultuous brook of Green-head Ghyll,
You will suppose that with an upright path
Your feet must struggle; in such bold ascent
The pastoral mountains front you face to face.   5
But courage! for around that boisterous brook
The mountains have all opened out themselves,
And made a hidden valley of their own.
No habitation can be seen: but they
Who journey thither find themselves alone   10
With a few sheep, with rocks and stones, and kites
That overhead are sailing in the sky.
It is in truth an utter solitude;
Nor should I have made mention of this Dell
But for one object which you might pass by,   15
Might see and notice not. Beside the brook
Appears a straggling heap of unhewn stones!
And to that simple object appertains,
A story unenriched with strange events,
Yet not unfit, I deem, for the fireside,   20
Or for the summer shade. It was the first
Of those domestic tales that spake to me
Of Shepherds, dwellers in the valleys, men
Whom I already loved;—not verily
For their own sakes, but for the fields and hills
Where was their occupation and abode.   26
And hence this Tale, while I was yet a Boy
Careless of books, yet having felt the power
Of Nature, by the gentle agency
Of natural objects led me on to feel   30

For passions that were not my own, and think
(At random and imperfectly indeed)
On man, the heart of man, and human life.
Therefore, although it be a history
Homely and rude, I will relate the same   35
For the delight of a few natural hearts;
And, with yet fonder feeling, for the sake
Of youthful Poets who among these hills
Will be my second self when I am gone.

Upon the forest-side in Grasmere Vale   40
There dwelt a Shepherd, Michael was his name;
An old man, stout of heart, and strong of limb.
His bodily frame had been from youth to age
Of an unusual strength: his mind was keen,
Intense, and frugal, apt for all affairs,   45
And in his shepherd's calling he was prompt
And watchful more than ordinary men.
Hence had he learned the meaning of all winds,
Of blasts of every tone; and, oftentimes,   49
When others heeded not, He heard the South
Make subterraneous music, like the noise
Of bagpipers on distant Highland hills.
The Shepherd, at such warning, of his flock
Bethought him, and he to himself would say,
'The winds are now devising work for me!'   55
And, truly, at all times, the storm, that drives
The traveler to a shelter, summoned him
Up to the mountains; he had been alone
Amid the heart of many thousand mists,
That came to him and left him on the heights.   60
So lived he till his eightieth year was past.
And grossly that man errs, who should suppose
That the green valleys, and the streams and rocks,
Were things indifferent to the Shepherd's thoughts.
Fields, where with cheerful spirits he had breathed   65
The common air; hills, which with vigorous step
He had so often climbed; which had impressed
So many incidents upon his mind
Of hardship, skill or courage, joy or fear;
Which like a book preserved the memory   70
Of the dumb animals, whom he had saved,
Had fed or sheltered, linking to such acts,
The certainty of honorable gain;
Those fields, those hills—what could they less?
—had laid
Strong hold on his affections, were to him   75
A pleasurable feeling of blind love,
The pleasure which there is in life itself.

His days had not been passed in singleness.
His Helpmate was a comely matron, old—
Though younger than himself full twenty years.
She was a woman of a stirring life,   81
Whose heart was in her house: two wheels she had
Of antique form, this large for spinning wool,
That small for flax; and if one wheel had rest,
It was because the other was at work.   85
The Pair had but one inmate in their house,
An only Child, who had been born to them
When Michael, telling o'er his years, began
To deem that he was old,—in shepherd's phrase,
With one foot in the grave. This only Son,   90
With two brave sheep-dogs tried in many a storm,
The one of an inestimable worth,
Made all their household. I may truly say,
That they were as a proverb in the vale
For endless industry. When day was gone,   95
And from their occupations out of doors
The Son and Father were come home, even then,
Their labor did not cease; unless when all
Turned to the cleanly supper-board, and there,
Each with a mess of pottage and skimmed milk,
Sat round the basket piled with oaten cakes,   101
And their plain home-made cheese. Yet when the meal
Was ended, Luke (for so the Son was named)
And his old father both betook themselves
To such convenient work as might employ   105
Their hands by the fire-side; perhaps to card
Wool for the Housewife's spindle, or repair
Some injury done to sickle, flail, or scythe,
Or other implement of house or field.   109

Down from the ceiling by the chimney's edge
That in our ancient uncouth country style
With huge and black projection overbrowed
Large space beneath, as duly as the light
Of day grew dim the Housewife hung a lamp;
An agèd utensil, which had performed   115
Service beyond all others of its kind.
Early at evening did it burn and late,
Surviving comrade of uncounted hours,
Which going by from year to year had found
And left the couple neither gay, perhaps,   120
Nor cheerful, yet with objects and with hopes,
Living a life of eager industry.
And now, when Luke had reached his eighteenth year
There by the light of this old lamp they sat,
Father and Son, while far into the night   125
The Housewife plied her own peculiar work,
Making the cottage through the silent hours
Murmur as with the sound of summer flies.
This light was famous in its neighborhood,
And was a public symbol of the life   130
That thrifty Pair had lived. For, as it chanced,
Their cottage on a plot of rising ground
Stood single, with large prospect, north and south,
High into Easedale, up to Dunmail-Raise,
And westward to the village near the lake;   135
And from this constant light, so regular
And so far seen, the House itself, by all
Who dwelt within the limits of the vale,
Both old and young, was named The Evening Star.   139

Thus living on through such a length of years,
The shepherd, if he loved himself, must needs
Have loved his Helpmate; but to Michael's heart
This son of his old age was yet more dear—
Less from instinctive tenderness, the same
Fond spirit that blindly works in the blood of all— 145
Than that a child, more than all other gifts,
That earth can offer to declining man
Brings hope with it, and forward looking thoughts,
And stirrings of inquietude, when they
By tendency of nature needs must fail. 150
Exceeding was the love he bare to him,
His heart and his heart's joy! For oftentimes
Old Michael, while he was a babe in arms,
Had done him female service, not alone
For pastime and delight, as is the use 155
Of fathers, but with patient mind enforced
To acts of tenderness; and he had rocked
His cradle as with a woman's gentle hand.

And, in a later time, ere yet the Boy
Had put on boy's attire, did Michael love, 160
Albeit of a stern unbending mind,
To have the Young one in his sight, when he
Wrought in the field, or on his shepherd's stool
Sat with a fettered sheep before him stretched,
Under the large old oak, that near his door, 165
Stood single, and, from matchless depth of shade,
Chosen for the Shearer's covert from the sun,
Thence in our rustic dialect was called
The Clipping Tree,[1] a name which yet it bears.
There, while they two were sitting in the shade,
With others round them, earnest all and blithe,
Would Michael exercise his heart with looks 172
Of fond correction and reproof bestowed
Upon the Child, if he disturbed the sheep
By catching at their legs, or with his shouts 175
Scared them, while they lay still beneath the shears.

And when by Heaven's good grace the boy grew up
A healthy Lad, and carried in his cheek
Two steady roses that were five years old,
Then Michael from a winter coppice cut 180
With his own hand a sapling, which he hooped
With iron, making it throughout in all
Due requisites a perfect shepherd's staff,
And gave it to the Boy; wherewith equipt
He as a watchman oftentimes was placed 185
At gate or gap, to stem or turn the flock;
And, to his office prematurely called,
There stood the urchin, as you will divine,
Something between a hindrance and a help;
And for this course not always, I believe, 190

[1] Clipping is the word used in the North of England for shearing.

Receiving from his Father hire of praise;
Though nought was left undone which staff or voice,
Or looks, or threatening gestures could perform.

But soon as Luke, full ten years old, could stand 194
Against the mountain blasts; and to the heights,
Not fearing toil, nor length of weary ways,
He with his Father daily went, and they
Were as companions, why should I relate
That objects which the Shepherd loved before
Were dearer now? that from the Boy there came
Feelings and emanations—things which were 201
Light to the sun and music to the wind;
And that the old Man's heart seemed born again.
Thus in his Father's sight the Boy grew up;
And now when he had reached his eighteenth year, 205
He was his comfort and his daily hope.

While in this sort the simple household lived
From day to day, to Michael's ear there came
Distressful tidings. Long before the time
Of which I speak, the Shepherd had been bound 210
In surety for his brother's son, a man
Of an industrious life, and ample means—
But unforeseen misfortunes suddenly
Had pressed upon him,—and old Michael now
Was summoned to discharge the forfeiture, 215
A grievous penalty, but little less
Than half his substance. This unlooked for claim
At the first hearing, for a moment took
More hope out of his life than he supposed
That any old man ever could have lost. 220
As soon as he had armed himself with strength
To look his trouble in the face, it seemed
The Shepherd's sole resource to sell at once
A portion of his patrimonial fields, 224
Such was his first resolve; he thought again,
And his heart failed him. 'Isabel,' said he,
Two evenings after he had heard the news,
'I have been toiling more than seventy years,
And in the open sunshine of God's love
Have we all lived; yet if these fields of ours 230
Should pass into a stranger's hand, I think
That I could not lie quiet in my grave.
Our lot is a hard lot; the sun himself
Has scarcely been more diligent than I;
And I have lived to be a fool at last 235
To my own family. An evil man
That was, and made an evil choice, if he
Were false to us; and if he were not false,
There are ten thousand to whom loss like this
Had been no sorrow. I forgive him—but 240
'T were better to be dumb, than to talk thus.
When I began, my purpose was to speak
Of remedies and of a cheerful hope.
Our Luke shall leave us, Isabel; the land

Shall not go from us, and it shall be free; 245
He shall possess it free as is the wind
That passes over it. We have, thou knowest,
Another kinsman—he will be our friend
In this distress. He is a prosperous man, 249
Thriving in trade—and Luke to him shall go,
And with his kinsman's help and his own thrift
He quickly will repair this loss, and then
He may return to us. If here he stay,
What can be done? Where every one is poor,
What can be gained?' At this the old Man paused, 255
And Isabel sat silent, for her mind
Was busy, looking back into past times.
There's Richard Bateman, thought she to herself,
He was a parish-boy—at the church-door
They made a gathering for him, shillings, pence,
And halfpennies, wherewith the neighbors bought 261
A basket, which they filled with pedlar's wares;
And with this basket on his arm, the lad
Went up to London, found a master there,
Who out of many chose the trusty boy 265
To go and overlook his merchandise
Beyond the seas: where he grew wondrous rich,
And left estates and monies to the poor,
And at his birthplace built a chapel floored 269
With marble, which he sent from foreign lands.
These thoughts, and many others of like sort,
Passed quickly through the mind of Isabel
And her face brightened. The old Man was glad,
And thus resumed:—'Well, Isabel! this scheme
These two days has been meat and drink to me.
Far more than we have lost is left us yet. 276
We have enough—I wish indeed that I
Were younger,—but this hope is a good hope.
Make ready Luke's best garments, of the best
Buy for him more, and let us send him forth 280
To-morrow, or the next day, or to-night:
If he *could* go, the Boy should go to-night.'

Here Michael ceased, and to the fields went forth
With a light heart. The Housewife for five days 284
Was restless morn and night, and all day long
Wrought on with her best fingers to prepare
Things needful for the journey of her son.
But Isabel was glad when Sunday came
To stop her in her work: for, when she lay
By Michael's side, she through the last two nights 290
Heard him, how he was troubled in his sleep:
And when they rose at morning she could see
That all his hopes were gone. That day at noon
She said to Luke, while they two by themselves
Were sitting at the door. 'Thou must not go:
We have no other Child but thee to lose, 296
None to remember—do not go away,
For if thou leave thy Father he will die.'
The Youth made answer with a jocund voice;
And Isabel, when she had told her fears, 300
Recovered heart. That evening her best fare
Did she bring forth, and all together sat
Like happy people round a Christmas fire.

With daylight Isabel resumed her work;
And all the ensuing week the house appeared
As cheerful as a grove in Spring: at length 306
The expected letter from their kinsman came,
With kind assurances that he would do
His utmost for the welfare of the Boy;
To which, requests were added, that forthwith
He might be sent to him. Ten times or more
The letter was read over; Isabel 312
Went forth to show it to the neighbors round;
Nor was there at that time on English land
A prouder heart than Luke's. When Isabel 315
Had to her house returned, the old Man said,
'He shall depart to-morrow.' To this word
The Housewife answered, talking much of things
Which, if at such short notice he should go,
Would surely be forgotten. But at length 320
She gave consent, and Michael was at ease.

Near the tumultuous brook of Green-head Ghyll,
In that deep valley, Michael had designed
To build a Sheep-fold; and, before he heard
The tidings of his melancholy loss, 325
For this same purpose he had gathered up
A heap of stones, which by the streamlet's edge
Lay thrown together, ready for the work.
With Luke that evening thitherward he walked;
And soon as they had reached the place he stopped, 330
And thus the old Man spake to him.—'My son,
To-morrow thou wilt leave me: with full heart
I look upon thee, for thou art the same
That wert a promise to me ere thy birth,
And all thy life hast been my daily joy. 335
I will relate to thee some little part
Of our two histories; 't will do thee good
When thou art from me, even if I should touch
On things thou canst not know of.—After thou
First cam'st into the world—as oft befalls 340
To new-born infants—thou didst sleep away
Two days, and blessings from thy Father's tongue
Then fell upon thee. Day by day passed on,
And still I loved thee with increasing love.
Never to living ear came sweeter sounds 345
Than when I heard thee by our own fireside
First uttering, without words, a natural tune;
While thou, a feeding babe, didst in thy joy
Sing at thy Mother's breast. Month followed month,
And in the open fields my life was passed 350
And on the mountains, else I think that thou
Hadst been brought up upon thy Father's knees.

But we were playmates, Luke: among these hills,
As well thou know'st, in us the old and young
Have played together, nor with me didst thou
Lack any pleasure which a boy can know.' 356
Luke had a manly heart; but at these words
He sobbed aloud. The old Man grasped his hand
And said, 'Nay, do not take it so—I see
That these are things of which I need not speak.
Even to the utmost I have been to thee 361
A kind and a good Father: and herein
I but repay a gift which I myself
Received at others' hands; for, though now old
Beyond the common life of man, I still 365
Remember them who loved me in my youth.
Both of them sleep together: here they lived
As all their forefathers had done; and when
At length their time was come, they were not loath
To give their bodies to the family mold. 370
I wished that thou shouldst live the life they lived.
But 't is a long time to look back, my Son,
And see so little gain from threescore years.
These fields were burdened when they came to me;
Till I was forty years of age, not more 375
Than half of my inheritance was mine.
I toiled and toiled; God blessed me in my work,
And till these three weeks past the land was free.
It looks as if it never could endure 379
Another Master. Heaven forgive me, Luke,
If I judge ill for thee, but it seems good
That thou shouldst go.' At this the old Man paused;
Then, pointing to the stones near which they stood,
Thus, after a short silence, he resumed:
'This was a work for us; and now, my son, 385
It is a work for me. But, lay one stone—
Here, lay it for me, Luke, with thine own hands.
Nay, Boy, be of good hope;—we both may live
To see a better day. At eighty-four 389
I still am strong and hale;—do thou thy part,
I will do mine.—I will begin again
With many tasks that were resigned to thee;
Up to the heights, and in among the storms,
Will I without thee go again, and do
All works which I was wont to do alone, 395
Before I knew thy face.—Heaven bless thee, Boy!
Thy heart these two weeks has been beating fast
With many hopes; it should be so—yes—yes—
I knew that thou couldst never have a wish
To leave me, Luke: thou hast been bound to me
Only by links of love: when thou art gone, 401
What will be left to us!—But, I forget
My purposes. Lay now the corner-stone,
As I requested; and, hereafter, Luke,
When thou art gone away, should evil men 405
Be thy companions, think of me, my Son,
And of this moment; hither turn thy thoughts,
And God will strengthen thee: amid all fear
And all temptation, Luke, I pray that thou
Mayst bear in mind the life thy Fathers lived,
Who, being innocent, did for that cause 411
Bestir them in good deeds. Now, fare thee well—
When thou return'st, thou in this place wilt see
A work which is not here: a covenant
'T will be between us—But, whatever fate 415
Befall thee, I shall love thee to the last,
And bear thy memory with me to the grave.'

The Shepherd ended here; and Luke stooped down,
And, as his Father had requested, laid 419
The first stone of the Sheep-fold. At the sight
The old Man's grief broke from him; to his heart
He pressed his Son, he kissèd him and wept;
And to the house together they returned.
Hushed was that House in peace, or seeming peace,
Ere the night fell;—with morrow's dawn the Boy 425
Began his journey, and when he had reached
The public way, he put on a bold face;
And all the neighbors as he passed their doors
Came forth with wishes and with farewell prayers,
That followed him till he was out of sight. 430

A good report did from their Kinsman come,
Of Luke and his well doing: and the Boy
Wrote loving letters, full of wondrous news,
Which, as the Housewife phrased it, were throughout
'The prettiest letters that were ever seen.' 435
Both parents read them with rejoicing hearts.
So, many months passed on: and once again
The Shepherd went about his daily work
With confident and cheerful thoughts; and now
Sometimes when he could find a leisure hour 440
He to that valley took his way, and there
Wrought at the sheep-fold. Meantime Luke began
To slacken in his duty; and at length
He in the dissolute city gave himself
To evil courses: ignominy and shame 445
Fell on him, so that he was driven at last
To seek a hiding-place beyond the seas.

There is a comfort in the strength of love;
'T will make a thing endurable, which else 449
Would overset the brain, or break the heart:
I have conversed with more than one who well
Remember the old Man, and what he was
Years after he had heard this heavy news.
His bodily frame had been from youth to age
Of an unusual strength. Among the rocks 455
He went, and still looked up to sun and cloud
And listened to the wind; and as before

Performed all kinds of labor for his sheep,
And for the land, his small inheritance.
And to that hollow dell from time to time   460
Did he repair, to build the fold of which
His flock had need. 'T is not forgotten yet
The pity which was then in every heart
For the old Man—and 't is believed by all
That many and many a day he thither went,
And never lifted up a single stone.   466

   There, by the Sheep-fold, sometimes was he seen
Sitting alone, or with his faithful Dog,
Then old, beside him, lying at his feet.   469
The length of full seven years from time to time
He at the building of this Sheep-fold wrought,
And left the work unfinished when he died.
Three years, or little more, did Isabel
Survive her Husband: at her death the estate
Was sold, and went into a stranger's hand.   475
The cottage which was named the Evening Star
Is gone—the ploughshare has been through the ground
On which it stood; great changes have been wrought
In all the neighborhood:—yet the oak is left   479
That grew beside their door; and the remains
Of the unfinished Sheep-fold may be seen
Beside the boisterous brook of Green-head Ghyll.
                        (1800)

MY HEART LEAPS UP WHEN I BEHOLD

My heart leaps up when I behold
  A rainbow in the sky:
So was it when my life began;
So is it now, I am a man:
So be it when I shall grow old,   5
  Or let me die!
The Child is father of the Man;
And I could wish my days to be
Bound each to each by natural piety.
                    (1807)

THE SPARROW'S NEST

BEHOLD, within the leafy shade,
Those bright blue eggs together laid!
On me the chance-discovered sight
Gleamed like a vision of delight.
I started—seeming to espy   5
  The home and sheltered bed,—
The Sparrow's dwelling, which, hard by
My Father's house, in wet or dry,
My sister Emmeline and I
  Together visited.   10
She looked at it, and seemed to fear it;
Dreading. tho' wishing to be near it;

Such heart was in her, being then
A little Prattler among men.
The Blessing of my later years   15
  Was with me when a boy:
She gave me eyes, she gave me ears;
And humble cares, and delicate fears;
A heart, the fountain of sweet tears;
  And love, and thought, and joy.   20
                    (1807)

TO THE CUCKOO

O BLITHE New-comer! I have heard,
  I hear thee and rejoice.
O Cuckoo! shall I call thee Bird,
  Or but a wandering Voice?

While I am lying on the grass   5
  Thy twofold shout I hear;
From hill to hill it seems to pass,
  At once far off, and near.

Though babbling only to the Vale,
  Of sunshine and of flowers,   10
Thou bringest unto me a tale
  Of visionary hours.

Thrice welcome, darling of the Spring!
  Even yet thou art to me
No bird, but an invisible thing,   15
  A voice, a mystery;

The same whom in my school-boy days
  I listened to; that Cry
Which made me look a thousand ways
  In bush, and tree, and sky.   20

To seek thee did I often rove
  Through woods and on the green;
And thou wert still a hope, a love;
  Still longed for, never seen.

And I can listen to thee yet;   25
  Can lie upon the plain
And listen, till I do beget
  That golden time again.

O blessed Bird! the earth we pace
  Again appears to be   30
An unsubstantial, faery place;
  That is fit home for Thee!
                    (1807)

RESOLUTION AND INDEPENDENCE

THERE was a roaring in the wind all night;
The rain came heavily and fell in floods;
But now the sun is rising calm and bright;
The birds are singing in the distant woods:
Over his own sweet voice the Stock-dove broods;

The Jay makes answer as the Magpie chatters; 6
And all the air is filled with pleasant noise of
   waters.

All things that love the sun are out of doors:
The sky rejoices in the morning's birth;
The grass is bright with rain-drops;—on the
   moors 10
The hare is running races in her mirth;
And with her feet she from the plashy earth
Raises a mist; that, glittering in the sun,
Runs with her all the way, wherever she doth
   run.

I was a Traveler then upon the moor; 15
I saw the hare that raced about with joy;
I heard the woods and distant waters roar,
Or heard them not, as happy as a boy:
The pleasant season did my heart employ:
My old remembrances went from me wholly; 20
And all the ways of men so vain and melancholy!

But, as it sometimes chanceth, from the might
Of joy in minds that can no further go,
As high as we have mounted in delight
In our dejection do we sink as low, 25
To me that morning did it happen so;
And fears, and fancies, thick upon me came;
Dim sadness—and blind thoughts, I knew not,
   nor could name.

I heard the sky-lark warbling in the sky;
And I bethought me of the playful hare: 30
Even such a happy child of earth am I;
Even as these blissful creatures do I fare;
Far from the world I walk, and from all care;
But there may come another day to me—
Solitude, pain of heart, distress, and poverty. 35

My whole life I have lived in pleasant thought,
As if life's business were a summer mood;
As if all needful things would come unsought
To genial faith, still rich in genial good;
But how can He expect that others should 40
Build for him, sow for him, and at his call
Love him, who for himself will take no heed at
   all?

I thought of Chatterton, the marvelous Boy,
The sleepless Soul that perished in his pride;
Of Him who walked in glory and in joy 45
Following his plough, along the mountainside:
By our own spirits are we deified:
We Poets in our youth begin in gladness;
But thereof come in the end despondency and
   madness.

Now, whether it were by peculiar grace, 50
A leading from above, a something given,
Yet it befell, that, in this lonely place,
When I with these untoward thoughts had
   striven,
Beside a pool bare to the eye of heaven

I saw a Man before me unawares: 55
The oldest man he seemed that ever wore gray
   hairs.

As a huge stone is sometimes seen to lie
Couched on the bald top of an eminence;
Wonder to all who do the same espy,
By what means it could thither come, and
   whence; 60
So that it seems a thing endued with sense:
Like a sea-beast crawled forth, that on a shelf
Of rock or sand reposeth, there to sun itself;

Such seemed this Man, not all alive nor dead,
Nor all asleep—in his extreme old age: 65
His body was bent double, feet and head
Coming together in life's pilgrimage;
As if some dire constraint of pain, or rage
Of sickness felt by him in times long past,
A more than human weight upon his frame had
   cast. 70

Himself he propped, limbs, body, and pale face,
Upon a long gray staff of shaven wood:
And, still as I drew near with gentle pace,
Upon the margin of that moorish flood
Motionless as a cloud the old Man stood; 75
That heareth not the loud winds when they call;
And moveth altogether, if it move at all.

At length, himself unsettling, he the pond
Stirred with his staff, and fixedly did look
Upon the muddy water, which he conned, 80
As if he had been reading in a book:
And now a stranger's privilege I took;
And, drawing to his side, to him did say,
'This morning gives us promise of a glorious
   day.'

A gentle answer did the old Man make, 85
In courteous speech which forth he slowly drew:
And him with further words I thus bespake,
'What occupation do you there pursue?
This is a lonesome place for one like you.'
Ere he replied, a flash of mild surprise 90
Broke from the sable orbs of his yet vivid eyes.

His words came feebly, from a feeble chest,
But each in solemn order followed each,
With something of a lofty utterance drest;
Choice word, and measured phrase, above the
   reach 95
Of ordinary men; a stately speech;
Such as grave Livers do in Scotland use,
Religious men, who give to God and man their
   dues.

He told, that to these waters he had come
To gather leeches, being old and poor: 100
Employment hazardous and wearisome!
And he had many hardships to endure:

From pond to pond he roamed, from moor ro moor;
Housing, with God's good help, by choice or chance;
And in this way he gained an honest maintenance.   105

The old Man still stood talking by my side;
But now his voice to me was like a stream
Scarce heard; nor word from word could I divide;
And the whole body of the man did seem
Like one whom I had met with in a dream;   110
Or like a man from some far region sent,
To give me human strength, by apt admonishment.

My former thoughts returned: the fear that kills;
And hope that is unwilling to be fed;
Cold, pain and labor, and all fleshly ills;   115
And mighty Poets in their misery dead.
Perplexed, and longing to be comforted,
My question eagerly did I renew,
'How is it that you live, and what is it you do?'

He with a smile did then his words repeat;   120
And said, that, gathering leeches, far and wide
He traveled; stirring thus about his feet
The waters of the pools where they abide.
'Once I could meet with them on every side;
But they have dwindled long by slow decay;   125
Yet still I persevere, and find them where I may.'

While he was talking thus, the lonely place,
The old Man's shape, and speech, all troubled me:
In my mind's eye I seemed to see him pace
About the weary moors continually,   130
Wandering about alone and silently.
While I these thoughts within myself pursued,
He, having made a pause, the same discourse renewed.

And soon with this he other matter blended,
Cheerfully uttered, with demeanor kind,   135
But stately in the main; and when he ended,
I could have laughed myself to scorn to find
In that decrepit Man so firm a mind.
'God,' said I, 'be my help and stay secure;
I'll think of the leech-gatherer on the lonely moor!'   140

(1807)

TO A YOUNG LADY

WHO HAD BEEN REPROACHED FOR TAKING LONG WALKS IN THE COUNTRY

Dear child of nature, let them rail!
There is a nest in a green dale,
  A harbor and a hold,
Where thou, a Wife and Friend, shalt see
Thy own heart-stirring days, and be   5
  A light to young and old.

There, healthy as a shepherd-boy,
And treading among flowers of joy,
  Which at no season fade,
Thou, while thy babes around thee cling,   10
Shalt show us how divine a thing
  A Woman may be made.

Thy thoughts and feelings shall not die,
Nor leave thee when gray hairs are nigh,
  A melancholy slave;   15
But an old age serene and bright,
And lovely as a Lapland night,
  Shall lead thee to thy grave.

(1807)

SHE WAS A PHANTOM OF DELIGHT

She was a Phantom of delight
When first she gleamed upon my sight;
A lovely Apparition, sent
To be a moment's ornament;
Her eyes as stars of Twilight fair;   5
Like Twilight's too, her dusky hair;
But all things else about her drawn
From May-time and the cheerful Dawn;
A dancing Shape, an Image gay,
To haunt, to startle, and waylay.   10

I saw her upon nearer view,
A Spirit, yet a Woman too!
Her household motions light and free,
And steps of virgin liberty;
A countenance in which did meet   15
Sweet records, promises as sweet;
A Creature not too bright or good
For human nature's daily food;
For transient sorrows, simple wiles,
Praise, blame, love, kisses, tears, and smiles.   20

And now I see with eye serene
The very pulse of the machine;
A Being breathing thoughtful breath,
A Traveler between life and death;
The reason firm, the temperate will,   25
Endurance, foresight, strength, and skill,
A perfect Woman, nobly planned,
To warn, to comfort, and command;
And yet a Spirit still, and bright
With something of angelic light.   30

(1807)

YARROW UNVISITED

See the various Poems the scene of which is laid upon the Banks of the Yarrow; in particular, the exquisite Ballad of Hamilton, beginning:

'Busk ye, busk ye, my bonny, bonny bride,
Busk ye, busk ye, my winsome Marrow!

From Stirling Castle we had seen
  The mazy Forth unraveled;
Had trod the banks of Clyde, and Tay,
  And with the Tweed had traveled:

And when we came to Clovenford,
Then said my *winsome Marrow*,
'Whate'er betide, we'll turn aside,
And see the Braes of Yarrow.'

'Let Yarrow folk, *frae* Selkirk town,
  Who have been buying, selling,
Go back to Yarrow, 't is their own;
  Each maiden to her dwelling!
On Yarrow's banks let herons feed,
Hares couch, and rabbits burrow!
But we will downward with the Tweed,
Nor turn aside to Yarrow'

'There's Gala Water, Leader Haughs,
  Both lying right before us;
And Dryburgh, where with chiming Tweed
  The lintwhites sing in chorus;
There's pleasant Teviotdale, a land
Made blithe with plough and harrow:
Why throw away a needful day
To go in search of Yarrow?

'What's Yarrow but a river bare,
  That glides the dark hills under?
There are a thousand such elsewhere
  As worthy of your wonder.'
Strange words they seemed of slight and scorn:
My True-love sighed for sorrow:
And looked me in the face, to think
I thus could speak of Yarrow!

'Oh! green,' said I, 'are Yarrow's holms,
  And sweet is Yarrow flowing!
Fair hangs the apple frae the rock,[1]
  But we will leave it growing.
O'er hilly path, and open Strath,
We'll wander Scotland thorough;
But, though so near, we will not turn
Into the dale of Yarrow.

'Let beeves and home-bred kine partake
  The sweets of Burn-mill meadow;
The swan on still St. Mary's Lake
  Float double, swan and shadow!
We will not see them; will not go,
To-day, nor yet to-morrow;
Enough if in our hearts we know
There's such a place as Yarrow.

'Be Yarrow stream unseen, unknown!
  It must, or we shall rue it:
We have a vision of our own;
  Ah! why should we undo it?
The treasured dreams of times long past,
We'll keep them, winsome Marrow!
For when we're there, although 't is fair,
'T will be another Yarrow!

[1] See Hamilton's ballad, as above.

'If Care, with freezing years should come,
  And wandering seem but folly,—
Should we be loath to stir from home,
  And yet be melancholy;
Should life be dull, and spirits low,
'T will soothe us in our sorrow,
That earth has something yet to show,
The bonny holms of Yarrow!'

(1807)

THE SOLITARY REAPER

BEHOLD her, single in the field,
  Yon solitary Highland Lass!
Reaping and singing by herself;
  Stop here, or gently pass!
Alone she cuts and binds the grain,
And sings a melancholy strain;
O listen! for the Vale profound
Is overflowing with the sound.

No Nightingale did ever chaunt
  More welcome notes to weary bands
Of travelers in some shady haunt,
  Among Arabian sands:
A voice so thrilling ne'er was heard
In spring-time from the Cuckoo-bird,
Breaking the silence of the seas
Among the farthest Hebrides.

Will no one tell me what she sings?—
  Perhaps the plaintive numbers flow
For old, unhappy, far-off things,
  And battles long ago:
Or is it some more humble lay,
Familiar matter of to-day?
Some natural sorrow, loss, or pain,
That has been, and may be again?

Whate'er the theme, the Maiden sang
  As if her song could have no ending;
I saw her singing at her work,
  And o'er the sickle bending;—
I listened, motionless and still;
And, as I mounted up the hill,
The music in my heart I bore,
Long after it was heard no more.

(1807)

WANDERED LONELY AS A CLOUD

I WANDERED lonely as a cloud
  That floats on high o'er vales and hills,
When all at once I saw a crowd,
  A host of golden daffodils;
Beside the lake, beneath the trees,
Fluttering and dancing in the breeze.

Continuous as the stars that shine
  And twinkle on the milky way,
They stretched in never-ending line
  Along the margin of a bay:
Ten thousand saw I at a glance,
Tossing their heads in sprightly dance.

The waves beside them danced, but they
  Outdid the sparkling waves in glee:—
A poet could not but be gay   15
  In such a jocund company:
I gazed—and gazed—but little thought
What wealth the show to me had brought.

For oft when on my couch I lie
  In vacant or in pensive mood,   20
They flash upon that inward eye
  Which is the bliss of solitude,
And then my heart with pleasure fills,
And dances with the daffodils.
                              (1807)

TO A SKY-LARK

Up with me! up with me into the clouds!
  For thy song, Lark, is strong;
Up with me, up with me into the clouds!
  Singing, singing,
With clouds and sky about thee ringing,   5
  Lift me, guide me till I find
That spot which seems so to thy mind.

I have walked through wildernesses dreary,
And to-day my heart is weary;
Had I now the wings of a Faery   10
Up to thee would I fly.
There is madness about thee, and joy divine
In that song of thine;
Lift me, guide me, high and high
To thy banqueting-place in the sky!   15

  Joyous as morning,
Thou art laughing and scorning;
Thou hast a nest for thy love and thy rest,
And, though little troubled with sloth,
Drunken Lark! thou wouldst be loath   20
To be such a traveler as I.
Happy, happy Liver,
With a soul as strong as a mountain river
Pouring out praise to the almighty Giver,
  Joy and jollity be with us both!   25

Alas! my journey, rugged and uneven,
Through prickly moors or dusty ways must
    wind;
But hearing thee, or others of thy kind,
As full of gladness and as free of heaven,
I, with my fate contented, will plod on,   30
And hope for higher raptures, when life's day
  is done.
                              (1807)

ELEGIAC STANZAS

SUGGESTED BY A PICTURE OF PEELE CASTLE IN
A STORM, PAINTED BY SIR GEORGE BEAUMONT

I WAS thy neighbor once, thou rugged Pile!
Four summer weeks I dwelt in sight of thee:
I saw thee every day; and all the while
Thy Form was sleeping on a glassy sea.

So pure the sky, so quiet was the air;   5
So like, so very like, was day to day!
Whene'er I looked, thy Image still was there;
It trembled, but it never passed away.

How perfect was the calm! it seemed no sleep;
No mood which season takes away or brings: 10
I could have fancied that the mighty Deep
Was even the gentlest of all gentle Things.

Ah! then, if mine had been the Painter's hand,
To express what then I saw; and add the gleam
The light that never was on sea or land,   15
The consecration and the Poet's dream;

I would have planted thee, thou hoary Pile!
Amid a world how different from this!
Beside a sea that could not cease to smile;
On tranquil land, beneath a sky of bliss.   20

Thou should'st have seemed a treasure-house
    divine
Of peaceful years; a chronicle of heaven;—
Of all the sunbeams that did ever shine
The very sweetest had to thee been given.

A Picture had it been of lasting ease,   25
Elysian quiet, without toil or strife;
No motion but the moving tide, a breeze,
Or merely silent Nature's breathing life.

Such, in the fond illusion of my heart,
Such Picture would I at that time have made:
And seen the soul of truth in every part;   31
A steadfast peace that might not be betrayed.

So once it would have been,—'t is so no more;
I have submitted to a new control:
A power is gone, which nothing can restore;
A deep distress hath humanized my Soul.   36

Not for a moment could I now behold
A smiling sea, and be what I have been:
The feeling of my loss will ne'er be old;
This, which I know, I speak with mind serene.

Then, Beaumont, Friend! who would have been
    the Friend,   41
If he had lived, of Him whom I deplore,
This work of thine I blame not, but commend;
This sea in anger, and that dismal shore.

Oh, 't is a passionate Work!—yet wise and well;
Well chosen is the spirit that is here;   46
That Hulk which labors in the deadly swell,
This rueful sky, this pageantry of fear!

And this huge Castle, standing here sublime,
I love to see the look with which it braves, 50
Cased in the unfeeling armor of old time
The lightning, the fierce wind, and trampling
    waves.

Farewell, farewell, the heart that lives alone,
Housed in a dream, at distance from the Kind!
Such happiness, wherever it be known,   55
Is to be pitied; for 't is surely blind.

But welcome fortitude, and patient cheer,
And frequent sights of what is to be borne!
Such sights, or worse, as are before me here.—
Not without hope we suffer and we mourn.   60
                        (1807)

ODE TO DUTY

Stern Daughter of the Voice of God!
  O Duty! if that name thou love,
Who art a light to guide, a rod
  To check the erring, and reprove;
Thou who art victory and law   5
When empty terrors overawe;
From vain temptations dost set free;
And calm'st the weary strife of frail humanity!

There are who ask not if thine eye
  Be on them; who, in love and truth,   10
Where no misgiving is, rely
  Upon the genial sense of youth;
Glad Hearts! without reproach or blot;
Who do thy work, and know it not:
Oh! if through confidence misplaced   15
They fail, thy saving arms, dread Power! around
    them cast.

Serene will be our days and bright,
  And happy will our nature be,
When love is an unerring light,
  And joy its own security.   20
And they a blissful course may hold
Even now, who, not unwisely bold,
Live in the spirit of this creed;
Yet seek thy firm support, according to their
    need.

I, loving freedom, and untried;   25
  No sport of every random gust,
Yet being to myself a guide,
  Too blindly have reposed my trust:
And oft, when in my heart was heard
Thy timely mandate, I deferred   30
The task, in smoother walks to stray;
But thee I now would serve more strictly, if I
    may.

Through no disturbance of my soul,
  Or strong compunction in me wrought,
I supplicate for thy control;   35
  But in the quietness of thought:
Me this uncharted freedom tires;
I feel the weight of chance-desires:
My hopes no more must change their name,
I long for a repose that ever is the same.   40

Stern Lawgiver! yet thou dost wear
  The Godhead's most benignant grace;
Nor know we anything so fair
  As is the smile upon thy face:
Flowers laugh before thee on their beds;   45
And fragrance in thy footing treads;
Thou dost preserve the stars from wrong;
And the most ancient heavens, through Thee,
    are fresh and strong.

To humbler functions, awful Power!
  I call thee: I myself commend   50
Unto thy guidance from this hour;
  Oh, let my weakness have an end!
Give unto me, made lowly wise,
The spirit of self-sacrifice;
The confidence of reason give;   55
And in the light of truth thy Bondman let me
    live!
                        (1807)

CHARACTER OF THE HAPPY WARRIOR

*Who is the happy Warrior? Who is he
That every man in arms should wish to be?*

It is the generous Spirit, who, when brought
Among the tasks of real life, hath wrought
Upon the plan that pleased his boyish thought:
Whose high endeavors are an inward light   6
That makes the path before him always bright:
Who, with a natural instinct to discern
What knowledge can perform, is diligent to
    learn;
Abides by this resolve, and stops not there,   10
But makes his moral being his prime care;
Who doomed to go in company with Pain,
And Fear, and Bloodshed, miserable train!
Turns his necessity to glorious gain;
In face of these doth exercise a power   15
Which is our human nature's highest dower;
Controls them and subdues, transmutes, be-
    reaves,
Of their bad influence, and their good receives;
By objects, which might force the soul to abate
Her feeling, rendered more compassionate;   20
Is placable—because occasions rise
So often that demand such sacrifice;
More skilful in self-knowledge, even more pure,
As tempted more; more able to endure,
As more exposed to suffering and distress;   25
Thence, also more alive to tenderness.

'T is he whose law is reason; who depends
Upon that law as on the best of friends;
Whence, in a state where men are tempted still
To evil for a guard against worse ill,   30
And what in quality or act is best
Doth seldom on a right foundation rest,
He labors good on good to fix, and owes

To virtue every triumph that he knows;
Who, if he rise to station of command, 35
Rises by open means; and there will stand
On honorable terms, or else retire,
And in himself possess his own desire;
Who comprehends his trust, and to the same
Keeps faithful with a singleness of aim; 40
And therefore does not stoop, nor lie in wait
For wealth, or honors or for worldly state;
Whom they must follow; on whose head must fall,
Like showers of manna, if they come at all:
Whose powers shed round him in the common strife, 45
Or mild concerns of ordinary life,
A constant influence, a peculiar grace;
But who, if he be called upon to face
Some awful moment to which Heaven has joined
Great issues, good or bad for human kind, 50
Is happy as a Lover; and attired
With sudden brightness, like a Man inspired;
And, through the heat of conflict keeps the law
In calmness made, and sees what he foresaw;
Or if an unexpected call succeed, 55
Come when it will, is equal to the need:

He who though thus endued as with a sense
And faculty for storm and turbulence,
Is yet a Soul whose master-bias leans
To homefelt pleasures and to gentle scenes; 60
Sweet images! which, wheresoe'er he be,
Are at his heart; and such fidelity
It is his darling passion to approve;
More brave for this, that he hath much to love:—

'T is, finally, the Man, who, lifted high 65
Conspicuous object in a Nation's eye,
Or left unthought-of in obscurity,—
Who, with a toward or untoward lot,
Prosperous or adverse, to his wish or not,
Plays, in the many games of life, that one 70
Where what he most doth value must be won:
Whom neither shape of danger can dismay,
Nor thought of tender happiness betray;
Who, not content that former worth stand fast,
Looks forward, persevering to the last, 75
From well to better, daily self-surpast:
Who, whether praise of him must walk the earth
For ever, and to noble deeds give birth,
Or he must fall to sleep without his fame,
And leave a dead unprofitable name, 80
Finds comfort in himself and in his cause;
And, while the mortal mist is gathering, draws
His breath in confidence of Heaven's applause:

*This is the happy Warrior; this is He
Whom every Man in arms should wish to be.* 85
(1807)

ODE
ON INTIMATIONS OF IMMORTALITY FROM RECOLLECTIONS OF EARLY CHILDHOOD

THERE was a time when meadow, grove and stream,
　The earth, and every common sight,
　　To me did seem
　　Apparelled in celestial light,
The glory and the freshness of a dream. 5
It is not now as it hath been of yore;—
　　Turn wheresoe'er I may,
　　By night or day,
The things which I have seen I now can see no more.

II

　　The rainbow comes and goes, 10
　　And lovely is the Rose,
　　The Moon doth with delight
Look round her when the heavens are bare,
　　Waters on a starry night
　　Are beautiful and fair; 15
　　The sunshine is a glorious birth;
　　But yet I know, where'er I go,
That there hath past away a glory from the earth.

III

Now, while the birds thus sing a joyous song,
　　And while the young lambs bound 20
　　　As to the tabor's sound,
To me alone there came a thought of grief:
A timely utterance gave that thought relief,
　　And I again am strong:
The cataracts blow their trumpets from the steep; 25
No more shall grief of mine the season wrong;
I hear the Echoes through the mountains throng,
The Winds come to me from the fields of sleep,
　　And all the earth is gay;
　　　Land and sea 30
　　Give themselves up to jollity,
　　And with the heart of May
　Doth every Beast keep holiday;—
　　Thou Child of Joy,
Shout round me, let me hear thy shouts, thou happy Shepherd-boy! 35

IV

Ye blessèd Creatures, I have heard the call
　Ye to each other make; I see
The heavens laugh with you in your jubilee;
　　My heart is at your festival,
　　My head hath its coronal, 40
The fulness of your bliss, I feel—I feel it all.
　　Oh evil day! if I were sullen
　　While Earth herself is adorning,
　　　This sweet May-morning,

And the Children are culling
    On every side,
In a thousand valleys far and wide,
Fresh flowers; while the sun shines warm,
And the Babe leaps up on his Mother's arm:—
    I hear, I hear, with joy I hear!
    —But there's a Tree, of many, one,
A single Field which I have looked upon,
Both of them speak of something that is gone:
    The Pansy at my feet
    Doth the same tale repeat:
Whither is fled the visionary gleam?
Where is it now, the glory and the dream?

V

Our birth is but a sleep and a forgetting:
The Soul that rises with us, our life's Star,
    Hath had elsewhere its setting,
    And cometh from afar:
    Not in entire forgetfulness,
    And not in utter nakedness,
But trailing clouds of glory do we come
    From God, who is our home:
Heaven lies about us in our infancy!
Shades of the prison-house begin to close
    Upon the growing Boy,
But he beholds the light, and whence it flows
    He sees it in his joy;
The Youth, who daily farther from the east
    Must travel, still is Nature's Priest,
    And by the vision splendid
    Is on his way attended;
At length the Man perceives it die away,
And fade into the light of common day.

VI

Earth fills her lap with pleasures of her own;
Yearnings she hath in her own natural kind,
And even with something of a Mother's mind,
    And no unworthy aim,
    The homely Nurse doth all she can
To make her Foster-child, her Inmate Man,
    Forget the glories he hath known,
And that imperial palace whence he came.

VII

Behold the Child among his new-born blisses,
A six years' Darling of a pigmy size!
See, where 'mid work of his own hand he lies,
Fretted by sallies of his mother's kisses,
With light upon him from his father's eyes!
See, at his feet, some little plan or chart,
Some fragment from his dream of human life,
Shaped by himself with newly-learnèd art;
    A wedding or a festival,
    A mourning or a funeral,
    And this hath now his heart,
    And unto this he frames his song:
    Then will he fit his tongue
To dialogues of business, love, or strife;
    But it will not be long
    Ere this be thrown aside,
    And with new joy and pride
The little Actor cons another part;
Filling from time to time his 'humorous stage'
With all the Persons, down to palsied Age,
That Life brings with her in her equipage;
    As if his whole vocation
    Were endless imitation.

VIII

Thou, whose exterior semblance doth belie
    Thy Soul's immensity;
Thou best Philosopher, who yet dost keep
Thy heritage, thou Eye among the blind,
That, deaf and silent, read'st the eternal deep,
Haunted for ever by the eternal mind,—
    Mighty Prophet! Seer blest!
    On whom those truths do rest,
Which we are toiling all our lives to find,
In darkness lost, the darkness of the grave;
Thou, over whom thy Immortality
Broods like the Day, a Master o'er a Slave,
A Presence which is not to be put by;
Thou little Child, yet glorious in the might
Of heaven-born freedom on thy being's height,
Why with such earnest pains dost thou provoke
The years to bring the inevitable yoke,
Thus blindly with thy blessedness at strife?
Full soon thy Soul shall have her earthly freight,
And custom lie upon thee with a weight,
Heavy as frost, and deep almost as life!

IX

    Oh joy! that in our embers
    Is something that doth live,
    That nature yet remembers
    What was so fugitive!
The thought of our past years in me doth breed
Perpetual benediction: not indeed
For that which is most worthy to be blest;
Delight and liberty, the simple creed
Of Childhood, whether busy or at rest,
With new-fledged hope still fluttering in his breast:—
    Not for these I raise
    The song of thanks and praise;
    But for those obstinate questionings
    Of sense and outward things,
    Fallings from us, vanishings;
    Blank misgivings of a Creature
Moving about in worlds not realized,
High instincts before which our mortal nature
Did tremble like a guilty thing surprised:
    But for those first affections,
    Those shadowy recollections,
    Which, be they what they may,
Are yet the fountain light of all our day,
Are yet a master light of all our seeing;
    Uphold us, cherish, and have power to make

Our noisy years seem moments in the being
Of the eternal Silence: truths that wake, 155
    To perish never;
Which neither listlessness, nor mad endeavor,
    Nor Man nor Boy,
Nor all that is at enmity with joy,
Can utterly abolish or destroy! 160
    Hence in a season of calm weather
    Though inland far we be,
Our Souls have sight of that immortal sea
    Which brought us hither,
    Can in a moment travel thither, 165
And see the Children sport upon the shore,
And hear the mighty waters rolling evermore.

X

Then sing, ye Birds, sing, sing a joyous song!
    And let the young Lambs bound
    As to the tabor's sound! 170
We in thought will join your throng,
    Ye that pipe and ye that play,
    Ye that through your hearts to-day
    Feel the gladness of the May!
What though the radiance which was once so bright 175
Be now for ever taken from my sight,
    Though nothing can bring back the hour
Of splendor in the grass, of glory in the flower;
    We will grieve not, rather find
    Strength in what remains behind; 180
    In the primal sympathy
    Which having been must ever be;
    In the soothing thoughts that spring
    Out of human suffering;
    In the faith that looks through death, 185
In years that bring the philosophic mind.

XI

And O, ye Fountains, Meadows, Hills, and Groves,
Forebode not any severing of our loves!
Yet in my heart of hearts I feel your might;
I only have relinquished one delight 190
To live beneath your more habitual sway.
I love the Brooks which down their channels fret,
Even more than when I tripped lightly as they;
The innocent brightness of a new-born Day
    Is lovely yet; 195
The Clouds that gather round the setting sun
Do take a sober coloring from an eye
That hath kept watch o'er man's mortality.
Another race hath been, and other palms are won.
Thanks to the human heart by which we live,
Thanks to its tenderness, its joys, and fears, 201
To me the meanest flower that blows can give
Thoughts that do often lie too deep for tears.
    (1807)

SONNET

NUNS FRET NOT AT THEIR CONVENT'S NARROW ROOM

NUNS fret not at their convent's narrow room;
And hermits are contented with their cells;
And students with their pensive citadels:
Maids at the wheel, the weaver at his loom,

Sit blithe and happy; bees that soar for bloom, 5
High as the highest Peak of Furness Fells,
Will murmur by the hour in foxglove bells:
In truth, the prison, unto which we doom

Ourselves, no prison is: and hence for me,
In sundry moods, 't was pastime to be bound 10
Within the sonnet's scanty plot of ground;
Pleased if some Souls (for such there needs must be)
Who have felt the weight of too much liberty,
Should find brief solace there, as I have found.
    (1807)

SONNET

COMPOSED UPON WESTMINSTER BRIDGE SEPTEMBER 3, 1802

EARTH has not anything to show more fair:
Dull would he be of soul who could pass by
A sight so touching in its majesty:
This city now doth like a garment wear

The beauty of the morning; silent, bare, 5
Ships, towers, domes, theaters, and temples lie
Open unto the fields, and to the sky;
All bright and glittering in the smokeless air.

Never did sun more beautifully steep
In his first splendor valley, rock, or hill; 10
Ne'er saw I, never felt, a calm so deep!
The river glideth at his own sweet will:
Dear God! the very houses seem asleep;
And all that mighty heart is lying still!
    (1807)

SONNET

COMPOSED BY THE SEA-SIDE NEAR CALAIS, AUGUST, 1802

FAIR Star of evening, Splendor of the west,
Star of my Country!—on the horizon's brink
Thou hangest, stooping, as might seem, to sink
On England's bosom: yet well pleased to rest,

Meanwhile, and be to her a glorious crest 5
Conspicuous to the Nations. Thou, I think,
Shouldst be my Country's emblem; and should'st wink,
Bright Star! with laughter on her banners, drest

In thy fresh beauty. There! that dusky spot
Beneath thee, that is England; there she lies. 10
Blessings be on you both! one hope, one lot,

One life, one glory! I with many a fear
For my dear Country, many heartfelt sighs,
Among men who do not love her, linger here.
(1807)

SONNET

IT IS A BEAUTEOUS EVENING, CALM AND FREE

It is a beauteous evening, calm and free.
The holy time is quiet as a Nun,
Breathless with adoration: the broad sun
Is sinking down in its tranquillity;

The gentleness of heaven broods o'er the sea; 5
Listen! the mighty Being is awake,
And doth with his eternal motion make
A sound like thunder—everlastingly.

Dear Child! dear Girl! that walkest with me here,
If thou appear untouched by solemn thought, 10
Thy nature is not therefore less divine:
Thou liest in Abraham's bosom all the year,
And worshipp'st at the Temple's inner shrine,
God being with thee when we know it not.
(1807)

SONNET

ON THE EXTINCTION OF THE VENETIAN REPUBLIC

Once did she hold the gorgeous east in fee;
And was the safeguard of the west: the worth
Of Venice did not fall below her birth,
Venice, the eldest Child of liberty.

She was a maiden City, bright and free; 5
No guile seduced, no force could violate;
And when she took unto herself a Mate,
She must espouse the everlasting Sea!

And what if she had seen those glories fade,
Those titles vanish, and that strength decay; 10
Yet shall some tribute of regret be paid
When her long life hath reached its final day:
Men are we, and must grieve when even the Shade
Of that which once was great, is passed away.
(1807)

TO TOUSSAINT L'OUVERTURE

Toussaint, the most unhappy man of men!
Whether the whistling Rustic tend his plough
Within thy hearing, or thy head be now
Pillowed in some deep dungeon's earless den;

O miserable Chieftain! where and when 5
Wilt thou find patience? Yet die not! do thou
Wear rather in thy bonds a cheerful brow:
Though fallen thyself, never to rise again,

Live, and take comfort. Thou hast left behind
Powers that will work for thee: air, earth, and skies; 10
There's not a breathing of the common wind
That will forget thee; thou hast great allies;
Thy friends are exultations, agonies,
And love, and man's unconquerable mind.
(1807)

SEPTEMBER, 1802, NEAR DOVER

Inland, within a hollow vale, I stood;
And saw, while sea was calm and air was clear,
The coast of France, the coast of France how near!
Drawn almost into frightful neighborhood.

I shrunk, for verily the barrier flood 5
Was like a lake, or river bright and fair,
A span of waters; yet what power is there!
What mightiness for evil and for good!

Even so doth God protect us if we be
Virtuous and wise. Winds blow, and waters roll, 10
Strength to the brave, and Power, and Deity,
Yet in themselves are nothing! One decree
Spake laws to *them*, and said that by the soul
Only the Nations shall be great and free!
(1807)

LONDON, 1802

Milton! thou shouldst be living at this hour:
England hath need of thee: she is a fen
Of stagnant waters; altar, sword, and pen,
Fireside, the heroic wealth of hall and bower,

Have forfeited their ancient English dower 5
Of inward happiness. We are selfish men;
Oh! raise us up, return to us again;
And give us manners, virtue, freedom, power.

Thy soul was like a Star, and dwelt apart;
Thou hadst a voice whose sound was like the sea; 10
Pure as the naked heavens, majestic, free,
So didst thou travel on life's common way,
In cheerful godliness; and yet thy heart
The lowliest duties on herself did lay.
(1807)

SONNET

IT IS NOT TO BE THOUGHT OF THAT THE FLOOD

It is not to be thought of that the Flood
Of British freedom, which, to the open sea
Of the world's praise, from dark antiquity
Hath flowed, 'with pomp of waters unwithstood,'

Roused though it be full often to a mood 5
Which spurns the check of salutary bands,
That this most famous Stream in bogs and sands
Should perish; and to evil and to good

Be lost for ever. In our halls is hung
Armory of the invincible knights of old: 10
We must be free or die, who speak the tongue
That Shakespeare spake: the faith and morals hold
Which Milton held. In everything we are sprung
Of earth's first blood, have titles manifold.
(1807)

SONNET

WHEN I HAVE BORNE IN MEMORY WHAT HAS TAMED

When I have borne in memory what has tamed
Great Nations, how ennobling thoughts depart
When men change swords for ledgers and desert
The student's bower for gold, some fears unnamed

I had, my Country!—am I to be blamed? 5
Now when I think of thee, and what thou art,
Verily, in the bottom of my heart,
Of those unfilial fears I am ashamed.

For dearly must we prize thee; we who find
In thee a bulwark for the cause of men; 10
And I by my affection was beguiled.
What wonder if a Poet now and then,
Among the many movements of his mind,
Felt for thee as a lover or a child!
(1807)

TO THE MEN OF KENT
OCTOBER, 1803

Vanguard of Liberty, ye men of Kent,
Ye children of a soil that doth advance
Her haughty brow against the coast of France,
Now is the time to prove your hardiment!

To France be words of invitation sent! 5
They from their fields can see the countenance
Of your fierce war, may ken the glittering lance
And hear you shouting forth your brave intent.

Left single, in bold parley, ye of yore,
Did from the Norman win a gallant wreath;
Confirmed the charters that were yours before;— 11
No parleying now! In Britain is one breath;
We are all with you now from shore to shore:
Ye men of Kent, 't is victory or death!
(1807)

SONNET

THOUGHT OF A BRITON ON THE SUBJUGATION OF SWITZERLAND

Two Voices are there; one is of the sea,
One of the mountains; each a mighty Voice:
In both from age to age thou didst rejoice,
They were thy chosen music, Liberty!

There came a Tyrant, and with holy glee 5
Thou fought'st against him; but hast vainly striven.
Thou from thy Alpine holds at length art driven,
Where not a torrent murmurs heard by thee.

Of one deep bliss thine ear hath been bereft; 9
Then cleave, O cleave to that which still is left;
For, high-souled Maid, what sorrow would it be
That Mountain floods should thunder as before,
And Ocean bellow from his rocky shore,
And neither awful Voice be heard by thee!
(1807)

THE WORLD IS TOO MUCH WITH US

The world is too much with us: late and soon,
Getting and spending, we lay waste our powers:
Little we see in Nature that is ours;
We have given our hearts away, a sordid boon!

This Sea that bares her bosom to the moon; 5
The winds that will be howling at all hours,
And are up-gathered now like sleeping flowers;
For this, for everything, we are out of tune;

It moves us not.—Great God! I'd rather be
A Pagan suckled in a creed outworn. 10
So might I, standing on this pleasant lea,
Have glimpses that would make me less forlorn;
Have sight of Proteus rising from the sea;
Or hear old Triton blow his wreathèd horn.
(1807)

AFTER-THOUGHT TO THE RIVER DUDDON

I thought of Thee, my partner and my guide,
As being past away. Vain sympathies!
For, backward, Duddon! as I cast my eyes,
I see what was, and is, and will abide;

Still glides the Stream, and shall for ever glide; 5
The Form remains, the Function never dies;
While we, the brave, the mighty, and the wise,
We Men, who in our morn of youth defied

The elements, must vanish;—be it so!
Enough, if something from our hands have power 10
To live, and act, and serve the future hour;
And if, as towards the silent tomb we go,
Through love, through hope, and faith's transcendent dower,
We feel that we are greater than we know.
(1820)

SONNET

INSIDE OF KING'S COLLEGE CHAPEL, CAMBRIDGE

Tax not the royal saint with vain expense,
With ill-matched aims the Architect who planned,
Albeit laboring for a scanty band
Of white-robed Scholars only, this immense

And glorious Work of fine intelligence! 5
Give all thou canst; high Heaven rejects the lore
Of nicely-calculated less or more;
So deemed the man who fashioned for the sense

These lofty pillars, spread that branching roof
Self-poised, and scooped into ten thousand cells, 10
Where light and shade repose, where music dwells
Lingering—and wandering on as loath to die;
Like thoughts whose very sweetness yieldeth proof
That they were born for immortality.
(1822)

CONTINUED

They dreamt not of a perishable home
Who thus could build. Be mine, in hours of fear
Or groveling thought, to seek a refuge here;
Or through the aisles of Westminster to roam;

Where bubbles burst, and folly's dancing foam 5
Melts, if it cross the threshold; where the wreath
Of awe-struck wisdom droops: or let my path
Lead to that younger Pile, whose sky-like dome

Hath typified by reach of daring art
Infinity's embrace; whose guardian crest, 10
The silent Cross, among the stars shall spread
As now, when She hath also seen her breast
Filled with mementos, satiate with its part
Of grateful England's overflowing Dead.
(1822)

SONNET

ON THE DEPARTURE OF SIR WALTER SCOTT FROM ABBOTSFORD FOR NAPLES

A trouble not of clouds, or weeping rain,
Nor of the setting sun's pathetic light
Engendered, hangs o'er Eildon's triple height:
Spirits of Power, assembled there, complain

For kindred Power departing from their sight; 5
While Tweed, best pleased in chanting a blithe strain,
Saddens his voice again, and yet again.
Lift up your hearts, ye Mourners! for the might

Of the whole world's good wishes with him goes;
Blessings and prayers in nobler retinue 10
Than sceptered King or laureled Conqueror knows,
Follow this wondrous Potentate. Be true,
Ye winds of ocean, and the midland sea,
Wafting your Charge to soft Parthenope!
(1835)

SONNET

'There!' said a Stripling, pointing with meet pride

'There!' said a Stripling, pointing with meet pride
Towards a low roof with green trees half concealed,
'Is Mossgiel Farm; and that's the very field
Where Burns ploughed up the Daisy.' Far and wide

A plain below stretched sea-ward, while, descried 5
Above sea-clouds, the Peaks of Arran rose;
And, by that simple notice, the repose
Of earth, sky, sea, and air, was vivified.

Beneath 'the random *bield* of clod or stone'
Myriads of daisies have shone forth in flower 10
Near the lark's nest, and in their natural hour
Have passed away, less happy than the One
That by the unwilling ploughshare died to prove
The tender charm of Poetry and Love.
(1835)

CONCLUSION

Most sweet it is with unuplifted eyes
To pace the ground if path be there or none,
While a fair region round the traveler lies,
Which he forbears again to look upon;

Pleased rather with some soft ideal scene, 5
The work of Fancy or some happy tone
Of meditation, slipping in between
The beauty coming and the beauty gone.

If Thought and Love desert us, from that day
Let us break off all commerce with the Muse; 10
With Thought and Love companions of our way,
Whate'er the senses take or may refuse
The Mind's internal heaven shall shed her dews
Of inspiration on the humblest lay.
(1835)

SAMUEL TAYLOR COLERIDGE (1772-1834)

COLERIDGE was the son of a Devonshire clergyman, about whose eccentricities some amusing stories are told. As a 'poor, friendless boy' he came to London at the age of ten, and entered Christ's Hospital, the famous charity school founded by Edward VI, at the same time as Charles Lamb, with whom he struck up a friendship which lasted as long as they lived. Coleridge was a dreamy, precocious youth, who talked neoplatonism and recited Homer and Pindar in Greek in the play ground. In 1791 he was admitted as a 'sizar,' or poor student, at Jesus College, Cambridge, which he left in his second year, encumbered with debt and disappointed in love, to enlist in a dragoon regiment under the name of Silas Tomkyn Cumberback. As he could not ride or clean his horse and accoutrements, he proved unsuccessful as a cavalry soldier, and after four months was sent back to the university. He left Cambridge without a degree in 1795, having already formed with Southey, who was at Oxford, the design of the Pantisocracy, an ideal community to be founded on the banks of the Susquehanna by twelve gentlemen and twelve ladies of good education and liberal principles. Southey and Coleridge did not go to America, but they married the two Misses Fricker, who were to have been their partners in the adventure. Mrs. Coleridge complained that her husband 'would walk up and down composing poetry when he ought to have been in bed,' and the union proved an ill-assorted one, but as Coleridge brought his bride to a cottage near Bristol unfurnished with groceries or kitchen ware, the fault was not entirely on her side. Coleridge was all his life terribly impractical, as his own story of the publication of *The Watchman* at this time, given below, abundantly shows. In the same year (1796), Coleridge made the acquaintance of Wordsworth, and the two poets formed a strong friendship, based upon mutual affection, admiration, and reverence. Wordsworth thought Coleridge 'the only wonderful man he had ever met'; Coleridge said of Wordsworth, 'I feel myself a little man by his side.' The two poets were very different in appearance and disposition. Wordsworth's tall, gaunt frame, his high ascetic forehead, stately expression and reserved manner contrasted sharply with Coleridge's stockish figure, awkward gait, and good-natured face with curly black hair and ardent gray eyes. For more than a year (1797-98) the two poets were constantly together, and their communion resulted, not only in the publication of *Lyrical Ballads*, as already related (p. 511), but in the permanent enrichment of each poetic nature by contact with another, richly though differently endowed. After transitory appearances as a Unitarian minister and a London journalist, Coleridge returned from his studies in Germany to publish his translation of Schiller's *Wallenstein* (1800), and to establish his family at Greta Hall, Keswick, a few miles from the Wordsworths. His lack of will power was increased by the habit of taking laudanum, which became fixed in 1803, and grew upon him to an alarming extent. Lamb described him in 1806 as 'an archangel, a little damaged'; a less humorous account says he was 'ill, penniless, and worse than homeless.' Another attempt at periodical publication, *The Friend* (1809), was no better managed, and no more successful than *The Watchman*. His lectures in London, begun about the same time, were more profitable, both to himself and to the public, in spite of his habit of lecturing on anything but the subject announced, and his occasional failure to come at all; the scattered notes he left behind contain some most valuable contributions to Shakespearean criticism. Unable to break himself of the opium habit, Coleridge in 1816 put himself under the care of Dr. Gillman, of Highgate, a London suburb, with whom he lived until his death. His poetic productivity had practically ceased years before, but he continued to write prose (*Biographia Literaria*, 1817; *Aids to Reflection*, 1825), and to pour forth the flood of impassioned and philosophical talk he had begun as a school boy at Christ's Hospital. Some of it is preserved in *Table Talk*, published after his death.

Coleridge had all the powers of a great poet except the ordinary virtues of concentration and continuity of purpose. The only great poem he succeeded in completing was the *Ancient Mariner*, on which he worked under the spur of Wordsworth's influence. He projected innumerable literary undertakings, most of which were not even begun. Yet his influence in producing what a modern critic has called 'the renascence of wonder' was as revolutionary as that of Wordsworth in another way; and if the change in poetry is rightly named 'the romantic revival,' Coleridge must be given a place by the side of his greater friend and fellow poet as one of the makers of the new era.

BIOGRAPHIA LITERARIA

From CHAPTER X

An imprudent man of common goodness of heart cannot but wish to turn even his imprudences to the benefit of others, as far as this is possible. If therefore any one of the readers of this semi-narrative should be preparing or intending a periodical work, I warn him, in the first place, against trusting in the number of names on his subscription list. For he cannot be certain that the names were put down by sufficient authority; or, should that be ascertained, it still remains to be known, whether they were not extorted by some over zealous friend's importunity; whether the subscriber had not yielded his name, merely from want of courage to answer, no; and with the intention of dropping the work as soon as possible. One gentleman procured me nearly a hundred names for *The Friend*, and not only took frequent opportunity to remind me of his success in his canvass, but labored to impress my mind with the sense of the obligation I was under to the subscribers; for, (as he very pertinently admonished me), 'fifty-two shillings a year was a large sum to be bestowed on one individual, where there were so many objects of charity with strong claims to the assistance of the benevolent.' Of these hundred patrons ninety threw up the publication before the fourth number, without any notice; though it was well known to them, that in consequence of the distance, and the slowness and irregularity of the conveyance, I was compelled to lay in a stock of stamped paper for at least eight weeks beforehand; each sheet of which stood me in five pence previously to its arrival at my printer's; though the subscription money was not to be received till the twenty-first week after the commencement of the work; and lastly, though it was in nine cases out of ten impracticable for me to receive the money for two or three numbers without paying an equal sum for the postage.

In confirmation of my first caveat, I will select one fact among many. On my list of subscribers, among a considerable number of names equally flattering, was that of an Earl of Cork, with his address. He might as well have been an Earl of Bottle, for aught I knew of him, who had been content to reverence the peerage *in abstracto*, rather than *in concretis*. Of course *The Friend* was regularly sent as far, if I remember right, as the eighteenth number; that is, till a fortnight before the subscription was to be paid. And lo! just at this time I received a letter from his lordship, reproving me in language far more lordly than courteous for my impudence in directing my pamphlets to him, who knew nothing of me or my work! Seventeen or eighteen numbers of which, however, his lordship was pleased to retain, probably for the culinary or post-culinary conveniences of his servants.

Secondly, I warn all others from the attempt to deviate from the ordinary mode of publishing a work by the trade. I thought indeed, that to the purchaser it was indifferent, whether thirty per cent. of the purchase-money went to the booksellers or to the government; and that the convenience of receiving the work by the post at his own door would give the preference to the latter. It is hard, I own, to have been laboring for years, in collecting and arranging the materials; to have spent every shilling that could be spared after the necessaries of life had been furnished, in buying books, or in journeys for the purpose of consulting them or of acquiring facts at the fountain head; then to buy the paper, pay for the printing, and the like, all at least fifteen per cent. beyond what the trade would have paid; and then after all to give thirty per cent. not of the net profits, but of the gross results of the sale, to a man who has merely to give the books shelf or warehouse room, and permit his apprentice to hand them over the counter to those who may ask for them; and this, too, copy by copy, although, if the work be on any philosophical or scientific subject, it may be years before the edition is sold off. All this, I confess, must seem a hardship, and one, to which the products of industry in no other mode of exertion are subject. Yet even this is better, far better, than to attempt in any way to unite the functions of author and publisher But the most prudent mode is to sell the copyright, at least of one or more editions, for the most that the trade will offer. By what only can a large remuneration be expected; but fifty pounds and ease of mind are of more real advantage to a literary man, than the chance of five hundred with the certainty of insult and degrading anxieties. I shall have been grievously misunderstood, if this statement should be interpreted as written with the desire of detracting from the character of booksellers or publishers The individuals did not make the laws and customs of their trade, but, as in every other trade, take them as they find them. Till the evil can be proved to be removable, and without the substitution of an equal or greater inconvenience, it were neither wise nor manly even to complain of it. But to use it as a pretext for speaking, or even for thinking, or feeling, unkindly or opprobriously of the tradesmen, as individuals, would be something worse than unwise or even unmanly; it would be immoral and calumnious. My motives point in a far different direction and to far other objects, as will be seen in the conclusion of the chapter.

A learned and exemplary old clergyman, who many years ago went to his reward followed by the regrets and blessings of his flock, published at his own expense two volumes octavo, entitled, *A New Theory of Redemption*. The work was most severely handled in *The Monthly* or *Critical Review*, I forget which; and this unprovoked hostility became the good old man's favorite topic of conversation among his friends. Well! (he used to exclaim,) in the second edition, I shall have an opportunity of exposing both the ignorance and the malignity of the anonymous critic. Two or three years however passed by without any tidings from the bookseller, who had undertaken the printing and publication of the work, and who was perfectly at his ease, as the author was known to be a man of large property. At length the accounts were written for; and in the course of a few weeks they were presented by the rider for the house, in person. My old friend put on his spectacles, and holding the scroll with no very firm hand, began—'*Paper, so much:* O moderate enough—not at all beyond my expectation! *Printing, so much:* well! moderate enough! *Stitching, covers, advertisements, carriage, and so forth, so much.*'—Still nothing amiss. *Selleridge* (for orthography is no necessary part of a bookseller's literary acquirements) £3. 3s. 'Bless me! only three guineas for the what d'ye call it—the *selleridge?*' 'No more, sir!' replied the rider. 'Nay, but that is *too* moderate!' rejoined my old friend. 'Only three guineas for *selling* a thousand copies of a work in two volumes?' 'O sir!' (cries the young traveler) 'you have mistaken the word. There have been none of them *sold*; they have been sent back from London long ago; and this £3. 3s. is for the *cellaridge*, or warehouse-room in our book cellar.' The work was in consequence preferred from the ominous cellar of the publisher's to the author's garret; and, on presenting a copy to an acquaintance, the old gentleman used to tell the anecdote with great humor and still greater good nature.

With equal lack of worldly knowledge, I was a far more than equal sufferer for it, at the very outset of my authorship. Toward the close of the first year from the time, that in an inauspicious hour I left the friendly cloisters, and the happy grove of quiet, ever honored Jesus College, Cambridge, I was persuaded by sundry philanthropists and Anti-polemists to set on foot a periodical work, entitled *The Watchman*, that, according to the general motto of the work, *all might know the truth, and that the truth might make us free!* In order to exempt it from the stamp-tax, and likewise to contribute as little as possible to the supposed guilt of a war against freedom, it was to be published on every eighth day, thirty-two pages, large octavo, closely printed, and price only four-pence. Accordingly with a flaming prospectus,—'*Knowledge is power,*' 'To cry the state of the political atmosphere,'—and so forth, I set off on a tour to the North, from Bristol to Sheffield, for the purpose of procuring customers, preaching by the way in most of the great towns, as a hireless volunteer, in a blue coat and white waistcoat, that not a rag of the woman of Babylon might be seen on me. For I was at that time and long after, though a Trinitarian (that is *ad normam Platonis*) in philosophy, yet a zealous Unitarian in religion; more accurately, I was a Psilanthropist, one of those who believe our Lord to have been the real son of Joseph, and who lay the main stress on the resurrection rather than on the crucifixion. O! never can I remember those days with either shame or regret. For I was most sincere, most disinterested. My opinions were indeed in many and most important points erroneous; but my heart was single. Wealth, rank, life itself then seemed cheap to me, compared with the interests of what I believed to be the truth, and the will of my Maker I cannot even accuse myself of having been actuated by vanity; for in the expansion of my enthusiasm I did not think of myself at all.

My campaign commenced at Birmingham; and my first attack was on a rigid Calvinist, a tallow-chandler by trade. He was a tall dingy man, in whom length was so predominant over breadth, that he might almost have been borrowed for a foundry poker. O that face! a face κατ' ἔμφασιν! I have it before me at this moment. The lank, black, twine-like hair, pingui-nitescent, cut in a straight line along the black stubble of his thin gunpowder eyebrows, that looked like a scorched after-math from a last week's shaving. His coat collar behind in perfect unison, both of color and luster, with the coarse yet glib cordage, which I suppose he called his hair, and which with a bend inward at the nape of the neck,—the only approach to flexure in his whole figure,—slunk in behind his waistcoat; while the countenance, lank, dark, very hard, and with strong perpendicular furrows, gave me a dim notion of some one looking at me through a used gridiron, all soot, grease, and iron! But he was one of the thorough-bred, a true lover of liberty, and, as I was informed, had proved to the satisfaction of many, that Mr. Pitt was one of the horns of the second beast in *The Revelations*, that *spake as a dragon*. A person, to whom one of my letters of recommendation had been addressed, was my introducer. It was a new event in my life, my first stroke in the new business I had undertaken of an author, yea, and of an author trading on his own account. My companion after some imperfect sentences and a multitude of hums and ha's abandoned the cause of his client; and I commenced an harangue of half an hour to Phileleutheros, the tallow-chandler, varying my notes, through the whole gamut of eloquence, from the ratiocinative to the declamatory, and in the latter from the pathetic to the indignant. I argued, I described, I promised, I prophesied; and beginning with the captivity of nations I ended with the near approach of the millennium, finishing the whole with some of my own verses describing that glorious state out of the Religious Musings:

> Such delights
> As float to earth, permitted visitants!
> When in some hour of solemn jubilee
> The massive gates of Paradise are thrown
> Wide open, and forth come in fragments wild
> Sweet echoes of unearthly melodies,
> And odors snatched from beds of amaranth,
> And they, that from the crystal river of life
> Spring up on freshened wing, ambrosial gales!

My taper man of lights listened with perseverant and praiseworthy patience, though, as I was afterwards told, on complaining of certain gales that were not altogether ambrosial, it was a melting day with him. 'And what, Sir,' he said, after a short pause, 'might the cost be?' 'Only four-pence,'—(O! how I felt the anticlimax, the abysmal bathos of that four-pence!) —'Only four-pence, Sir, each number, to be published on every eighth day.'—'That comes to a deal of money at the end of a year. And how much, did you say, there was to be for the money?'—'Thirty-two pages, Sir, large octavo, closely printed.'—'Thirty and two pages? Bless me! why except what I does in a family way on the Sabbath, that's more than I ever reads, Sir! all the year round. I am as great a one, as any man in Brummagem, Sir! for liberty and truth and all them sort of things, but as to this,—no offense, I hope, sir,—I must beg to be excused.'

So ended my first canvass: from causes that I shall presently mention, I made but one other application in person. This took place at Manchester to a stately and opulent wholesale dealer in cottons. He took my letter of introduction, and, having perused it, measured me from head to foot and again from foot to head, and then asked if I had any bill or invoice of the thing. I presented my prospectus to him He rapidly skimmed and hummed over the first side, and still more rapidly the second and concluding page; crushed it within his fingers and the palm of his hand; then most deliberately and significantly rubbed and smoothed one part against the other; and lastly putting it into his pocket turned his back on me with an '*over-run* with these articles!' and so without another syllable retired into his counting-house. And, I can truly say, to my unspeakable amusement.

This, I have said, was my second and last attempt. On returning baffled from the first, in which I had vainly essayed to repeat the miracle of Orpheus with the Brummagem patriot, I dined with the tradesman who had introduced me to him. After dinner he importuned me to smoke a pipe with him, and two or three other *illuminati* of the same rank. I objected, both because I was engaged to spend the evening with a minister and his friends, and because I had never smoked except once or twice in my lifetime, and then it was herb tobacco mixed with Oronooko. On the assurance, however, that the tobacco was equally mild, and seeing too that it was of a yellow color;—not forgetting the lamentable difficulty I have always experienced in saying, 'No,' and in abstaining from what the people about me were doing,—I took half a pipe, filling the lower half of the bowl with salt. I was soon however compelled to resign it, in consequence of a giddiness and distressful feeling in my eyes, which, as I had drunk but a single glass of ale, must, I knew, have been the effect of the tobacco. Soon after, deeming myself recovered, I sallied forth to my engagement; but the walk and the fresh air brought on all the symptoms again, and, I had scarcely entered the minister's drawing-room, and opened a small packet of letters, which he had received from Bristol for me; ere I sank back on the sofa in a sort of swoon rather than sleep. Fortunately I had found just time enough to inform him of the confused state of my feelings, and of the occasion. For here and thus I lay, my face like a wall that is white-washing, deathly pale and with the cold drops of perspiration running down it from my forehead, while one after another there dropped in the different gentlemen, who had been invited to meet, and spend the evening with me, to the number of from fifteen to twenty. As the poison of tobacco acts but for a short time, I at length awoke from insensibility, and looked round on the party, my eyes dazzled by the candles which had been lighted in the interim. By way of relieving my embarrassment one of the gentlemen began the conversation, with 'Have you seen a paper to-day, Mr. Coleridge?' 'Sir,' I replied, rubbing my eyes, 'I am far from convinced that a Christian is permitted to read either newspapers or any other works of merely political and temporary interest.' This remark, so ludicrously inapposite to, or rather, incongruous with, the purpose for which I was known to have visited Birmingham, and to assist me in which they were all then met, produced an involuntary and general burst of laughter; and seldom indeed have I passed so many delightful hours, as I enjoyed in that room from the moment of that laugh till an early hour the next morning. Never, perhaps, in so mixed and numerous a party have I since heard conversation sustained with such animation, enriched with such variety of information, and enlivened with such a flow of anecdote. Both then and afterwards they all joined in dissuading me from proceeding with my scheme; assured me in the most friendly and yet most flattering expressions, that neither was the employment fit for me, nor I fit for the employment. Yet, if I determined on persevering in it, they promised to exert themselves to the utmost to procure subscribers, and insisted that I should make no more applications in person, but carry on the canvass by proxy. The same hospitable reception, the same dissuasion, and, that failing, the same kind exertions in my behalf, I met with at Manchester, Derby, Nottingham, Sheffield,—indeed, at every place in which I took up my sojourn. I often recall with affectionate pleasure the many respectable men who interested themselves for me, a perfect stranger to them, not a few of whom I can still name among my friends. They will bear witness for me how opposite even then my principles were to those of Jacobinism or even of democracy, and can attest the strict accuracy of the statement which I have left on record in the tenth and eleventh numbers of *The Friend*.

From this remarkable tour I returned with nearly a thousand names on the subscription list of *The Watchman;* yet more than half convinced, that prudence dictated the abandonment of the scheme. But for this very reason I persevered in it; for I was at that period of my life so completely hag-ridden by the fear of being influenced by selfish motives, that to know a mode of conduct to be the dictate of prudence was a sort of presumptive proof to my feelings that the contrary was the dictate of duty. Accordingly, I commenced the work, which was announced in London by long bills in letters larger than had ever been seen before, and which, I have been informed, for I did not see them myself, eclipsed the glories even of the lottery puffs. But alas! the publication of the very first number was delayed beyond the day announced for its appearance. In the second number an essay against fast-days, with a most censurable application of a text from Isaiah for its motto, lost me near five hundred of my subscribers at one blow. In the two following numbers I made enemies of all my Jacobin and democratic patrons; for, disgusted by their infidelity, and their adoption of French morals with French *psilosophy;* and perhaps thinking that charity ought to begin nearest home; instead of abusing the government and the Aristocrats chiefly or entirely, as had been expected of me, I leveled my attacks at 'modern patriotism,' and even ventured to declare my belief, that whatever the motives of ministers might have been for the sedition, or as it was then the fashion to call them, the *gagging* bills, yet the bills themselves would produce an effect to be desired by all the true friends of freedom, as far as they should contribute to deter men from openly declaiming on subjects, the principles of which they had never bottomed and from 'pleading *to* the poor and ignorant, instead of pleading *for* them.' At the same time I avowed my conviction, that national education and a concurring spread of the Gospel were the indispensable condition of any true political melioration. Thus by the time the seventh number was published, I had the mortification—(but why should I say this, when in truth I cared too little for any thing that concerned my worldly interests to be at all mortified about it?)—of seeing the preceding numbers exposed in sundry old iron shops for a penny a piece. At the ninth number I dropped the work. But from the London publisher I could not obtain a shilling; he was a ———— and set me at defiance. From other places I procured but little, and after such delays as rendered that little worth nothing; and I should have been inevitably thrown into jail by my Bristol printer, who refused to wait even for a month, for a sum between eighty and ninety pounds, if the money had not been paid for me by a man by no means affluent, a dear friend, who attached himself to me from my first arrival at Bristol, who has continued my friend with a fidelity unconquered by time or even by my own apparent neglect; a friend from whom I never received an advice that was not wise, nor a remonstrance that was not gentle and affectionate.

Conscientiously an opponent of the first revolutionary war, yet with my eyes thoroughly opened to the true character and impotence of the favorers of revolutionary principles in England, principles which I held in abhorrence,—(for it was part of my political creed that whoever ceased to act as an individual by making himself a member of any society not sanctioned by his Government, forfeited the rights of a citizen)—a vehement Anti-Ministerialist, but after the invasion of Switzerland, a more vehement Anti-Gallican, and still more intensely an Anti-Jacobin, I retired to a cottage at Stowey, and provided for my scanty maintenance by writing verses for a London morning paper. I saw plainly that literature was not a profession, by which I could expect to live; for I could not disguise from myself, that, whatever my talents might or might not be in other respects, yet they were not of the sort that could enable me to become a popular writer, and that whatever my opinions might be in themselves, they were almost equidistant from all the three prominent parties, the Pittites, the Foxites, and the Democrats. Of the unsalable nature of my writings I had an amusing memento one morning from our own servant girl. For happening to rise at an earlier hour than usual, I observed her putting an extravagant quantity of paper into the grate in order to light the fire, and mildly checked her for her wastefulness; 'La, Sir!' (replied poor Nanny) 'why, it is only Watchmen.'

I now devoted myself to poetry and to the study of ethics and psychology; and so profound was my admiration at this time of Hartley's *Essay on Man*, that I gave his name to my firstborn. In addition to the gentleman, my neighbor, whose garden joined on to my little orchard, and the cultivation of whose friendship had been my sole motive in choosing Stowey for my residence, I was so fortunate as to acquire, shortly after my settlement there, an invaluable blessing in the society and neighborhood of one to whom I could look up with equal reverence, whether I regarded him as a poet, a philosopher, or a man. His conversation extended to almost all subjects, except physics and politics; with the latter he never troubled himself. Yet neither my retirement nor my utter abstraction from all the disputes of the day could secure me in those jealous times from suspicion and obloquy, which did not stop at me, but extended to my excellent friend, whose perfect innocence was even adduced as a proof of his guilt. One of the many busy sycophants of that day,—(I here use the word sycophant in its original sense, as a wretch who *flatters* the prevailing party by *informing* against his neighbors, under pretence that they are exporters of prohibited *figs* or fancies,—for the moral application of the term it matters not which)—one of these sycophantic law-mongrels, discoursing on the politics of the neighborhood, uttered the following deep remark: 'As to Coleridge, there is not so much harm in *him*, for he is a whirl-brain that talks whatever come uppermost; but that———! he is the *dark* traitor. *You never hear* HIM *say a syllable on the subject.*'

* * *

The dark guesses of some zealous *Quidnunc* met with so congenial a soil in the grave alarm of a titled Dogberry of our neighborhood, that a spy was actually sent down from the government *pour surveillance* of myself and friend. There must have been not only abundance, but variety of those 'honorable men' at the disposal of Ministers; for this proved a very honest fellow. After three weeks' truly Indian perseverance in tracking us, (for we were commonly together,) during all which time seldom were we out of doors, but he contrived to be within hearing,—and all the while utterly unsuspected; how indeed *could* such a suspicion enter our fancies?—he not only rejected Sir Dogberry's request that he would try yet a little longer, but declared to him his belief, that both my friend and myself were as good subjects, for aught he could discover to the contrary, as any in His Majesty's dominions. He had repeatedly hid himself, he said, for hours together behind a bank at the sea-side, (our favorite seat,) and overheard our conversation. At first he fancied, that we were aware of our danger; for he often heard me talk of one *Spy Nozy*, which he was inclined to interpret of himself, and of a remarkable feature belonging to him; but he was speedily convinced that it was the name of a man who had made a book and lived long ago. Our talk ran most upon books, and we were perpetually desiring each other to look at *this*, and to listen to *that;* but he could not catch a word about politics. Once he had joined me on the road; (this occurred as I was returning home alone from my friend's house, which was about three miles from my own cottage,) and, passing himself off as a traveler, he had entered into conversation with me, and talked of purpose in a democrat way in order to draw me out. The result, it appears, not only convinced him that I was no friend of Jacobinism; but, (he added), I had 'plainly made it out to be such a silly as well as wicked thing, that he felt ashamed though he had only *put it on.*' I distinctly remembered the occurrence, and had mentioned it immediately on my return, repeating what the traveler with his Bardolph nose had said, with my own answer; and so little did I suspect the true object of my 'tempter ere accuser,' that I expressed with no small pleasure my hope and belief that the conversation had been of some service to the poor misled malcontent. This incident therefore prevented all doubt as to the truth of the report, which through a friendly medium came to me from the master of the village inn, who had been ordered to entertain the Government gentleman in his best manner, but above all to be silent concerning such a person being in his house. At length he received Sir Dogberry's commands to accompany his guest at the final interview; and, after the absolving suffrage of the *gentleman honored with the confidence of Ministers,* answered, as follows, to the following queries: D. Well, landlord! and what do you know of the person in question? L. I see him often pass by with maister ———, my landlord, (*that is, the owner of the house*), and sometimes with the newcomers at Holford; but I never said a word to him or he to me. D. But do you not know that he has distributed papers and hand-bills of a seditious nature among the common people? L. No, your Honor! I never heard of such a thing. D. Have you not seen this Mr. Coleridge, or heard of his haranguing and talking to knots and clusters of the inhabitants?—What are you grinning at, sir? L. Beg your Honor's pardon! but I was only thinking, how they'd have stared at him. If what I have heard be true, your Honor! they would not have understood a word he said. When our Vicar was here, Dr. L., the master of the great school and Canon of Windsor, there was a great dinner party at maister ———'s; and one of the farmers that was there, told us that he and the Doctor talked real Hebrew Greek at each other for an hour together after dinner. D. Answer the question, sir! does he ever harangue the people? L. I hope your Honor ain't angry with me. I can say no more than I know. I never saw him talking with any one but my landlord, and our curate, and the strange gentleman. D. Has he not been seen wandering on the hills towards the Channel, and along the shore, with books and papers in his hand, taking charts and maps of the country? L. Why, as to that, your Honor! I own, I have heard; I am sure, I would not wish to say ill of any body; but it is certain, that I have heard—D. Speak out, man! don't be afraid, you are doing your duty to your King and Government. What have you heard? L. Why, folks do say, your Honor! as how that he is a *Poet,* and that he is going to put Quantock and all about here in print; and as they be so much together, I suppose that the strange gentleman has some *consarn* in the business.— So ended this formidable inquisition, the latter part of which alone requires explanation, and at the same time entitles the anecdote to a place in my literary life. I had considered it as a defect in the admirable poem of *The Task,* that the subject, which gives the title to the work, was not, and indeed could not be, carried on beyond the three or four first pages, and that, throughout the poem, the connections are frequently awkward, and the transitions abrupt and arbitrary. I sought for a subject that should give equal room and freedom for description, incident, and impassioned reflections on men, nature, and society, yet supply in itself a natural connection to the parts, and unity to the whole. Such a subject I conceived myself to have found in a stream, traced from its source in the hills among the yellow-red moss and conical glass-shaped tufts of bent, to the first break or fall, where its drops become audible, and it begins to form a channel; thence to the peat and turf barn, itself built of the same dark squares as it sheltered; to the sheepfold; to the first cultivated plot of ground; to the lonely cottage and its bleak garden won from the heath; to the hamlet, the villages, the market-town, the manufactories, and the seaport. My walks therefore were almost daily on top of Quantock, and among its sloping coombes. With my pencil and memorandum-book in my hand, I was *making studies*, as the artists call them, and often moulding my thoughts into verse, with the objects and imagery immediately before my senses. Many circumstances, evil and good, intervened to prevent the completion of the poem, which was to have been entitled *The Brook*. Had I finished the work, it was my purpose in the heat of the moment to have dedicated it to our then committee of public safety as containing the charts and maps, with which I was to have supplied the French Government in aid of their plans of invasion. And these too for a tract of coast that, from Clevedon to Minehead, scarcely permits the approach of a fishing-boat!

CHAPTER XIV

During the first year that Mr. Wordsworth and I were neighbors, our conversations turned frequently on the two cardinal points of poetry, the power of exciting the sympathy of the reader by a faithful adherence to the truth of nature, and the power of giving the interest of novelty by the modifying colors of imagination. The sudden charm, which accidents of light and shade, which moonlight or sunset, diffused over a known and familiar landscape, appeared to represent the practicability of combining both. These are the poetry of nature. The thought suggested itself (to which of us I do not recollect) that a series of poems might be composed of two sorts. In the one, the incidents and agents were to be, in part at least, supernatural; and the excellence aimed at was to consist in the interesting of the affections by the dramatic truth of such emotions, as would naturally accompany such situations, supposing them real. And real in this sense they have been to every human being who, from whatever source of delusion, has at any time believed himself under supernatural agency. For the second class, subjects were to be chosen from ordinary life; the characters and incidents were to be such as will be found in every village and its vicinity where there is a meditative and feeling mind to seek after them, or to notice them when they present themselves.

In this idea originated the plan of the *Lyrical Ballads*; in which it was agreed that my endeavors should be directed to persons and characters supernatural, or at least romantic; yet so as to transfer from our inward nature a human interest and a semblance of truth sufficient to procure for these shadows of imagination that willing suspension of disbelief for the moment, which constitutes poetic faith. Mr. Wordsworth, on the other hand, was to propose to himself as his object, to give the charm of novelty to things of every day, and to excite a feeling analogous to the supernatural, by awakening the mind's attention from the lethargy of custom, and directing it to the loveliness and the wonders of the world before us; an inexhaustible treasure, but for which, in consequence of the film of familiarity and selfish solicitude, we have eyes, yet see not, ears that hear not, and hearts that neither feel nor understand.

With this view I wrote the *Ancient Mariner*, and was preparing, among other poems, the *Dark Ladie*, and the *Christabel*, in which I should have more nearly realized my ideal than I had done in my first attempt. But Mr. Wordsworth's industry had proved so much more successful, and the number of his poems so much greater, that my compositions, instead of forming a balance, appeared rather an interpolation of heterogeneous matter. Mr. Wordsworth added two or three poems written in his own character, in the impassioned, lofty, and sustained diction which is characteristic of his genius. In this form the *Lyrical Ballads* were published; and were presented by him, as an experiment, whether subjects, which from their nature rejected the usual ornaments and extra-colloquial style of poems in general, might not be so managed in the language of ordinary life as to produce the pleasurable interest which it is the peculiar business of poetry to impart. To the second edition he added a preface of considerable length; in which, notwithstanding some passages of apparently a contrary import, he was understood to contend for the extension of this style to poetry of all kinds, and to reject as vicious and indefensible all phrases and forms of style that were not included in what he (unfortunately, I think, adopting an equivocal expression) called the language of real life. From this preface prefixed to poems in which it was impossible to deny the presence of original genius, however mistaken its direction might be deemed, arose the whole long-continued controversy. For from the conjunction of perceived power with supposed heresy I explain the inveteracy, and in some instances, I grieve to say, the acrimonious passions, with which the controversy has been conducted by the assailants.

Had Mr. Wordsworth's poems been the silly, the childish things which they were for a long time described as being; had they been really distinguished from the compositions of other poets merely by meanness of language, and inanity of thought; had they indeed contained nothing more than what is found in the parodies and pretended imitations of them; they must have sunk at once, a dead weight, into the slough of oblivion, and have dragged the preface along with them. But year after year increased the number of Mr. Wordsworth's admirers. They were found, too, not in the lower classes of the reading public, but chiefly among young men of strong sensibility and meditative minds; and their admiration (inflamed perhaps in some degree by opposition) was distinguished by its intensity, I might almost say, by its religious fervor. These facts, and the intellectual energy of the author, which was more or less consciously felt, where it was outwardly and even boisterously denied, meeting with sentiments of aversion to his opinions, and of alarm at their consequences, produced an eddy of criticism, which would of itself have borne up the poems by the violence with which it whirled them round and round. With many parts of this preface, in the sense attributed to them, and which the words undoubtedly seem to authorize, I never concurred; but, on the contrary, objected to them as erroneous in principle, and as contradictory (in appearance at least) both to other parts of the same preface and to the author's own practice in the greater number of the poems themselves. Mr. Wordsworth, in his recent collection, has, I find, degraded this prefatory disquisition to the end of his second volume, to be read or not at the reader's choice. But he has not, as far as I can discover, announced any change in his poetic creed. At all events, considering it as the source of a controversy, in which I have been honored more than I deserve by the frequent conjunction of my name with his, I think it expedient to declare, once for all, in what points I coincide with his opinions, and in what points I altogether differ. But in order to render myself intelligible, I must previously, in as few words as possible, explain my ideas, first, of a poem; and secondly, of poetry itself, in kind and in essence.

The office of philosophical disquisition consists in just distinction; while it is the privilege of the philosopher to preserve himself constantly aware that distinction is not division. In order to obtain adequate notions of any truth, we must intellectually separate its distinguishable parts; and this is the technical process of philosophy. But having so done, we must then restore them in our conceptions to the unity in which they actually coexist; and this is the result of philosophy. A poem contains the same elements as a prose composition; the difference, therefore, must consist in a different combination of them, in consequence of a different object proposed. According to the difference of the object will be the difference of the combination. It is possible that the object may be merely to facilitate the recollection of any given facts or observations by artificial arrangement; and the composition will be a poem, merely because it is distinguished from prose by meter, or by rime, or by both conjointly. In this, the lowest sense, a man might attribute the name of a poem to the well-known enumeration of the days in the several months:

> Thirty days hath September,
> April, June, and November, etc.

and others of the same class and purpose. And as a particular pleasure is found in anticipating the recurrence of sound and quantities, all compositions that have this charm superadded, whatever be their contents, *may* be entitled poems.

So much for the superficial form. A difference of object and contents supplies an additional ground of distinction. The immediate purpose may be the communication of truths: either of truth absolute and demonstrable, as in works of science; or of facts experienced and recorded, as in history. Pleasure, and that of the highest and most permanent kind, may result from the attainment of the end; but it is not itself the immediate end. In other works the communication of pleasure may be the immediate purpose; and though truth, either moral or intellectual, ought to be the ultimate end, yet this will distinguish the character of the author, not the class to which the work belongs. Blest indeed is that state of society, in which the immediate purpose would be baffled by the perversion of the proper ultimate end; in which no charm of diction or imagery could exempt the Bathyllus even of an Anacreon, or the Alexis of Virgil, from disgust and aversion!

But the communication of pleasure may be the immediate object of a work not metrically composed; and that object may have been in a high degree attained, as in novels and romances. Would then the mere superaddition of meter, with or without rime, entitle these to the name of poems? The answer is, that nothing can permanently please, which does not contain in itself the reason why it is so, and not otherwise. If meter be superadded, all other parts must be made consonant with it. They must be such as to justify the perpetual and distinct attention to each part, which an exact correspondent recurrence of accent and sound are calculated to excite. The final definition then, so deduced, may be thus worded. A poem is that species of composition, which is opposed to works of science, by proposing for its immediate object pleasure, not truth; and from all other species (having this object in common with it) it is discriminated by proposing to itself such delight from the whole, as is compatible with a distinct gratification from each component part.

Controversy is not seldom excited in consequence of the disputants' attaching each a different meaning to the same word; and in few instances has this been more striking than in disputes concerning the present subject. If a man chooses to call every composition a poem, which is rime, or measure, or both, I must leave his opinion uncontroverted. The distinction is at least competent to characterize the writer's intention. If it were subjoined, that the whole is likewise entertaining or affecting as a tale, or as a series of interesting reflections, I of course admit this as another fit ingredient of a poem, and an additional merit. But if the definition sought for be that of a legitimate poem, I answer, it must be one the parts of which mutually support and explain each other; all in their proportion harmonizing with, and supporting the purpose and known influences of metrical arrangement. The philosophic critics of all ages coincide with the ultimate judgment of all countries, in equally denying the praises of a just poem, on the one hand to a series of striking lines or distichs, each of which absorbing the whole attention of the reader to itself, disjoins it from its context, and makes it a separate whole, instead of a harmonizing part; and on the other hand, to an unsustained composition, from which the reader collects rapidly the general result unattracted by the component parts. The reader should be carried forward, not merely or chiefly by the mechanical impulse of curiosity, or by a restless desire to arrive at the final solution; but by the pleasurable activity of mind excited by the attractions of the journey itself. Like the motion of a serpent, which the Egyptians made the emblem of intellectual power; or like the path of sound through the air, at every step he pauses and half recedes, and from the retrogressive movement collects the force which again carries him onward, *Præcipitandus est liber spiritus* [The free spirit must be urged onward], says Petronius Arbiter most happily. The epithet, *liber*, here balances the preceding verb; and it is not easy to conceive more meaning condensed in fewer words.

But if this should be admitted as a satisfactory character of a poem, we have still to seek for a definition of poetry. The writings of Plato, and Bishop Taylor, and the *Theoria Sacra* of Burnet, furnish undeniable proofs that poetry of the highest kind may exist without meter, and even without the contra-distinguishing objects of a poem. The first chapter of Isaiah (indeed a very large proportion of the whole book) is poetry in the most emphatic sense; yet it would be not less irrational than strange to assert, that pleasure, and not truth, was the immediate object of the prophet. In short, whatever specific import we attach to the word poetry, there will be found involved in it, as a necessary consequence, that a poem of any length neither can be, nor ought to be, all poetry. Yet if a harmonious whole is to be produced, the remaining parts must be preserved in keeping with the poetry; and this can be no otherwise effected than by such a studied selection and artificial arrangement as will partake of one, though not a peculiar property of poetry. And this again can be no other than the property of exciting a more continuous and equal attention than the language of prose aims at, whether colloquial or written.

My own conclusions on the nature of poetry, in the strictest use of the word, have been in part anticipated in the preceding disquisition on the fancy and imagination. What is poetry? is so nearly the same question with, what is a poet? that the answer to the one is involved in the solution of the other. For it is a distinction resulting from the poetic genius itself, which sustains and modifies the images, thoughts, and emotions of the poet's own mind. The poet, described in ideal perfection, brings the whole soul of man into activity, with the subordination of its faculties to each other, according to their relative worth and dignity He diffuses a tone and spirit of unity, that blends, and (as it were) fuses, each into each, by that synthetic and magical power to which we have exclusively appropriated the name of imagination. This power, first put in action by the will and understanding, and retained under their irremissive, though gentle and unnoticed, control (*laxis effertur habenis* [he is borne with loose reins]), reveals itself in the balance or reconciliation of opposite or discordant qualities: of sameness, with difference; of the general, with the concrete; the idea, with the image; the individual, with the representative; the sense of novelty and freshness, with old and familiar objects; a more than usual state of emotion, with more than usual order; judgment ever awake and steady self-possession, with enthusiasm and feeling profound or vehement; and while it blends and harmonizes the natural and the artificial, still subordinates art to nature; the manner to the matter; and our admiration of the poet to our sympathy with the poetry. 'Doubtless,' as Sir John Davies observes of the soul (and his words may with slight alteration be applied, and even more appropriately, to the poetic imagination),—

Doubtless this could not be, but that she turns
Bodies to spirit by sublimation strange,
As fire converts to fire, the things it burns,
As we our food into our nature change.

From their gross matter she abstracts their forms,
And draws a kind of quintessence from things;
Which to her proper nature she transforms
To bear them light on her celestial wings.

Thus does she, when from individual states
She doth abstract the universal kinds;
Which then re-clothed in divers names and fates
Steal access through our senses to our minds.

Finally, good sense is the body of poetic genius, fancy its drapery, motion its life, and imagination the soul that is everywhere, and in each; and forms all into one graceful and intelligent whole.

(1817)

THE RIME OF THE ANCIENT MARINER

IN SEVEN PARTS

PART I

It is an ancient Mariner,
And he stoppeth one of three.
'By thy long gray beard and glittering eye,
Now wherefore stopp'st thou me?

'The Bridegroom's doors are opened wide,
And I am next of kin;
The guests are met, the feast is set:
May'st hear the merry din.'

He holds him with his skinny hand,
'There was a ship,' quoth he.
'Hold off! unhand me, graybeard loon!'
Eftsoons his hand dropt he.

He holds him with his glittering eye—
The Wedding-Guest stood still,
And listens like a three years' child:
The Mariner hath his will.

The Wedding-Guest sat on a stone:
He cannot choose but hear;
And thus spake on that ancient man,
The bright-eyed Mariner.

'The ship was cheered, the harbor cleared,
Merrily did we drop
Below the kirk, below the hill,
Below the lighthouse top.

'The sun came up upon the left,
Out of the sea came he!
And he shone bright, and on the right
Went down into the sea.

'Higher and higher every day,
Till over the mast at noon—'
The Wedding-Guest here beat his breast,
For he heard the loud bassoon.

The bride hath paced into the hall,
Red as a rose is she;
Nodding their heads before her goes
The merry minstrelsy.

The Wedding-Guest he beat his breast,
Yet he cannot choose but hear;
And thus spake on that ancient man,
The bright-eyed Mariner:

'And now the Storm-blast came, and he
Was tyrannous and strong:
He struck with his o'ertaking wings,
And chased us south along.

'With sloping masts and dipping prow,
As who pursued with yell and blow
Still treads the shadow of his foe,
And forward bends his head,
The ship drove fast, loud roared the blast,
And southward aye we fled.

'And now there came both mist and snow,
And it grew wondrous cold;
And ice, mast-high, came floating by,
As green as emerald.

'And through the drifts the snowy clifts　55
Did send a dismal sheen:
Nor shapes of men nor beasts we ken—
The ice was all between.

'The ice was here, the ice was there,
The ice was all around:　　　　　　　60
It cracked and growled, and roared and howled,
Like noises in a swound!

'At length did cross an Albatross:
Thorough the fog it came:
As if it had been a Christian soul,　65
We hailed it in God's name.

'It ate the food it ne'er had eat,
And round and round it flew.
The ice did split with a thunder-fit;
The helmsman steered us through!　70

'And a good south wind sprung up behind;
The Albatross did follow,
And every day, for food or play,
Came to the mariner's hollo!

'In mist or cloud, on mast or shroud,　75
It perched for vespers nine;
Whiles all the night, through fog-smoke white,
Glimmered the white moon-shine.'

'God save thee, ancient Mariner!
From the fiends, that plague thee thus!—　80
Why look'st thou so?'—'With my cross-bow
I shot the Albatross!'

PART II

'The Sun now rose upon the right:
Out of the sea came he,
Still hid in mist, and on the left　85
Went down into the sea.

'And the good south wind still blew behind,
But no sweet bird did follow,
Nor any day, for food or play,
Came to the mariner's hollo!　　　　90

'And I had done a hellish thing,
And it would work 'em woe;
For all averred, I had killed the bird
That made the breeze to blow.
Ah, wretch! said they, the bird to slay　95
That made the breeze to blow!

'Nor dim nor red, like God's own head,
The glorious Sun uprist:
Then all averred, I had killed the bird
That brought the fog and mist.　　　　100
'T was right, said they, such birds to slay,
That bring the fog and mist.

'The fair breeze blew, the white foam flew,
The furrow followed free:
We were the first that ever burst　105
Into that silent sea.

'Down dropt the breeze, the sails dropt down,
'T was sad as sad could be;
And we did speak only to break
The silence of the sea!　　　　　　　110

'All in a hot and copper sky,
The bloody Sun, at noon,
Right up above the mast did stand,
No bigger than the Moon.

'Day after day, day after day,　115
We stuck, nor breath nor motion;
As idle as a painted ship
Upon a painted ocean.

'Water, water, everywhere,
And all the boards did shrink;　　　　120
Water, water, everywhere,
Nor any drop to drink.

'The very deep did rot: O Christ!
That ever this should be!
Yea, slimy things did crawl with legs,　125
Upon the slimy sea.

'About, about, in reel and rout,
The death-fires danced at night;
The water, like a witch's oils,
Burnt green, and blue, and white.　　130

'And some in dreams assurèd were
Of the Spirit that plagued us so:
Nine fathom deep he had followed us,
From the land of mist and snow.

'And every tongue, through utter drought,　135
Was withered at the root;
We could not speak, no more than if
We had been choked with soot.

'Ah! well-a-day! what evil looks
Had I from old and young!　　　　　140
Instead of the cross, the Albatross
About my neck was hung.

PART III

'There passed a weary time. Each throat
Was parched, and glazed each eye.
A weary time! A weary time!　145
How glazed each weary eye!
When looking westward I beheld
A something in the sky.

'At first it seemed a little speck,
And then it seemed a mist:
It moved and moved, and took at last
A certain shape, I wist.

'A speck, a mist, a shape, I wist!
And still it neared and neared:
As if it dodged a water-sprite,
It plunged and tacked and veered.

'With throats unslaked, with black lips baked,
We could nor laugh nor wail;
Through utter drought all dumb we stood!
I bit my arm, I sucked the blood,
And cried, "A sail! a sail!"

'With throats unslaked, with black lips baked,
Agape they heard me call:
Gramercy! they for joy did grin,
And all at once their breath drew in,
As they were drinking all.

'"See! see (I cried) she tacks no more!
Hither to work us weal;
Without a breeze, without a tide,
She steadies with upright keel!"

'The western wave was all a-flame:
The day was well nigh done:
Almost upon the western wave
Rested the broad bright Sun;
When that strange shape drove suddenly
Betwixt us and the Sun.

'And straight the Sun was flecked with bars,
(Heaven's Mother send us grace!)
As if through a dungeon grate he peered,
With broad and burning face.

'Alas (thought I, and my heart beat loud)
How fast she nears and nears!
Are those her sails that glance in the Sun,
Like restless gossameres?

'Are those her ribs through which the Sun
Did peer, as through a grate?
And is that Woman all her crew?
Is that a Death? and are there two?
Is Death that woman's mate?

'Her lips were red, her looks were free,
Her locks were yellow as gold;
Her skin was as white as leprosy,
The Nightmare Life-in-Death was she,
Who thicks man's blood with cold.

'The naked hulk alongside came,
And the twain were casting dice;
"The game is done! I 've won, I 've won!"
Quoth she, and whistles thrice.

'The Sun's rim dips; the stars rush out:
At one stride comes the dark;
With far-heard whisper, o'er the sea,
Off shot the specter-bark.

'We listened and looked sideways up!
Fear at my heart, as at a cup,
My life-blood seemed to sip!

'The stars were dim, and thick the night,
The steersman's face by his lamp gleamed white;
From the sails the dew did drip—
Till clomb above the eastern bar
The hornèd Moon with one bright star
Within the nether tip.

'One after one, by the star-dogged Moon,
Too quick for groan or sigh,
Each turned his face with a ghastly pang,
And cursed me with his eye.

'Four times fifty living men,
(And I heard nor sigh nor groan)
With heavy thump, a lifeless lump,
They dropped down one by one.

'The souls did from their bodies fly—
They fled to bliss or woe!
And every soul, it passed me by,
Like the whiz of my cross-bow!'

PART IV

'I FEAR thee, ancient Mariner!
I fear thy skinny hand!
And thou art long, and lank, and brown,
As is the ribbed sea-sand.

'I fear thee and thy glittering eye,
And thy skinny hand, so brown.'—
'Fear not, fear not, thou Wedding-Guest!
This body dropt not down.

'Alone, alone, all, all alone,
Alone on a wide, wide sea!
And never a saint took pity on
My soul in agony.

'The many men, so beautiful!
And they all dead did lie:
And a thousand thousand slimy things
Lived on; and so did I.

'I looked upon the rotting sea,
And drew my eyes away;
I looked upon the rotting deck,
And there the dead men lay.

'I looked to heaven, and tried to pray;
But or ever a prayer had gusht,
A wicked whisper came, and made
My heart as dry as dust.

'I closed my lids, and kept them close,
And the balls like pulses beat;
For the sky and the sea, and the sea and the
    sky,   250
Lay like a load on my weary eye,
And the dead were at my feet.

'The cold sweat melted from their limbs,
Nor rot nor reek did they:
The look with which they looked on me   255
Had never passed away.

'An orphan's curse would drag to hell
A spirit from on high;
But oh! more horrible than that
Is the curse in a dead man's eye!   260
Seven days, seven nights, I saw that curse,
And yet I could not die.

'The moving Moon went up the sky,
And nowhere did abide:
Softly she was going up,   265
And a star or two beside—

'Her beams bemocked the sultry main,
Like April hoar-frost spread;
But where the ship's huge shadow lay,
The charmèd water burnt alway   270
A still and awful red.

'Beyond the shadow of the ship,
I watched the water-snakes:
They moved in tracks of shining white,
And when they reared, the elfish light   275
Fell off in hoary flakes.

'Within the shadow of the ship
I watched their rich attire:
Blue, glossy green, and velvet black,
They coiled and swam; and every track   280
Was a flash of golden fire.

'O happy living things! no tongue
Their beauty might declare:
A spring of love gushed from my heart,
And I blessed them unaware!   285
Sure my kind saint took pity on me,
And I blessed them unaware.

'The selfsame moment, I could pray;
And from my neck so free
The Albatross fell off, and sank   290
Like lead into the sea.

PART V

'Oh, sleep! it is a gentle thing,
Beloved from pole to pole!
To Mary Queen the praise be given!
She sent the gentle sleep from Heaven,   295
That slid into my soul.

'The silly buckets on the deck,
That had so long remained,
I dreamt that they were filled with dew;
And when I awoke, it rained.   300

'My lips were wet, my throat was cold,
My garments all were dank;
Sure I had drunken in my dreams,
And still my body drank.

'I moved, and could not feel my limbs: 305
I was so light—almost
I thought that I had died in sleep,
And was a blessèd ghost.

'And soon I heard a roaring wind:
It did not come anear;   310
But with its sound it shook the sails,
That were so thin and sere.

'The upper air burst into life!
And a hundred fire-flags sheen,
To and fro they were hurried about;   315
And to and fro, and in and out,
The wan stars danced between.

'And the coming wind did roar more loud,
And the sails did sigh like sedge;
And the rain poured down from one black cloud;
The Moon was at its edge.   321

'The thick black cloud was cleft, and still
The Moon was at its side:
Like waters shot from some high crag,
The lightning fell with never a jag,   325
A river steep and wide.

'The loud wind never reached the ship,
Yet now the ship moved on!
Beneath the lightning and the Moon
The dead men gave a groan.   330

'They groaned, they stirred, they all uprose,
Nor spake nor moved their eyes;
It had been strange, even in a dream,
To have seen those dead men rise.

'The helmsman steered, the ship moved on;
Yet never a breeze up-blew;   336
The mariners all 'gan work the ropes,
Where they were wont to do:
They raised their limbs like lifeless tools—
We were a ghastly crew.   340

'The body of my brother's son
Stood by me, knee to knee;
The body and I pulled at one rope,
But he said nought to me.'

'I fear thee, ancient Mariner!'   345
'Be calm, thou Wedding-Guest!
'T was not those souls that fled in pain,
Which to their corses came again,
But a troop of spirits blest:

'For when it dawned—they dropped their arms,
And clustered round the mast;
Sweet sounds rose slowly through their mouths,
And from their bodies passed.

'Around, around, flew each sweet sound,
Then darted to the Sun;
Slowly the sounds came back again,
Now mixed, now one by one.

'Sometimes a-dropping from the sky
I heard the skylark sing;
Sometimes all little birds that are,
How they seemed to fill the sea and air
With their sweet jargoning!

'And now 't was like all instruments,
Now like a lonely flute;
And now it is an angel's song,
That makes the heavens be mute.

'It ceased; yet still the sails made on
A pleasant noise till noon,
A noise like of a hidden brook
In the leafy month of June,
That to the sleeping woods all night
Singeth a quiet tune.

'Till noon we quietly sailed on,
Yet never a breeze did breathe:
Slowly and smoothly went the ship,
Moved onward from beneath.

'Under the keel nine fathom deep,
From the land of mist and snow,
The spirit slid; and it was he
That made the ship to go.
The sails at noon left off their tune,
And the ship stood still also.

'The Sun, right up above the mast,
Had fixed her to the ocean;
But in a minute she 'gan stir,
With a short uneasy motion—
Backwards and forwards half her length,
With a short uneasy motion.

'Then like a pawing horse let go,
She made a sudden bound:
It flung the blood into my head,
And I fell down in a swound.

'How long in that same fit I lay,
I have not to declare;
But ere my living life return'd,
I heard, and in my soul discern'd
Two voices in the air.

'"Is it he?" quoth one, "is this the man?
By Him who died on cross,
With his cruel bow he laid full low
The harmless Albatross.

'"The spirit who bideth by himself
In the land of mist and snow,
He loved the bird that loved the man
Who shot him with his bow."

'The other was a softer voice,
As soft as honey-dew:
Quoth he, "The man hath penance done,
And penance more will do."

PART VI

FIRST VOICE

'"But tell me, tell me! speak again
Thy soft response renewing—
What makes that ship drive on so fast?
What is the ocean doing?"

SECOND VOICE

'"Still as a slave before his lord,
The ocean hath no blast;
His great bright eye most silently
Up to the Moon is cast—

'"If he may know which way to go;
For she guides him, smooth or grim.
See, brother, see! how graciously
She looketh down on him."

FIRST VOICE

'"But why drives on that ship so fast,
Without or wave or wind?"

SECOND VOICE

'"The air is cut away before,
And closes from behind.

'"Fly brother, fly! more high, more high!
Or we shall be belated:
For slow and slow that ship will go,
When the Mariner's trance is abated."

'I woke, and we were sailing on,
As in a gentle weather:
'T was night, calm night, the moon was high;
The dead men stood together.

'All stood together on the deck,
For a charnel-dungeon fitter:
All fixed on me their stony eyes,
That in the Moon did glitter.

'The pang, the curse, with which they died,
Had never passed away:
I could not draw my eyes from theirs,
Nor turn them up to pray.

'And now this spell was snapt: once more
I viewed the ocean green,
And looked far forth, yet little saw
Of what had else been seen—

'Like one, that on a lonesome road
Doth walk in fear and dread,
And having once turned round, walks on,
And turns no more his head;
Because he knows a frightful fiend   450
Doth close behind him tread.

'But soon there breathed a wind on me,
Nor sound nor motion made:
Its path was not upon the sea,
In ripple or in shade.   455

'It raised my hair, it fanned my cheek
Like a meadow-gale of spring—
It mingled strangely with my fears,
Yet it felt like a welcoming.

'Swiftly, swiftly flew the ship,   460
Yet she sailed softly too:
Sweetly, sweetly blew the breeze—
On me alone it blew.

'Oh! dream of joy! is this indeed
The lighthouse top I see?   465
Is this the hill? is this the kirk?
Is this mine own countree?

'We drifted o'er the harbor-bar,
And I with sobs did pray—
"O let me be awake, my God!   470
Or let me sleep alway."

'The harbor-bay was clear as glass,
So smoothly it was strewn!
And on the bay the moonlight lay,
And the shadow of the Moon.   475

'The rock shone bright, the kirk no less,
That stands above the rock:
The moonlight steeped in silentness
The steady weathercock.

'And the bay was white with silent light,   480
Till rising from the same,
Full many shapes, that shadows were,
In crimson colors came.

'A little distance from the prow
Those crimson shadows were: 485
I turned my eyes upon the deck—
Oh, Christ! what saw I there!

'Each corse lay flat, lifeless and flat,
And, by the holy rood!
A man all light, a seraph-man,   490
On every corse there stood.

'This seraph-band, each waved his hand:
It was a heavenly sight!
They stood as signals to the land,
Each one a lovely light: 495

'This seraph-band, each waved his hand,
No voice did they impart—
No voice; but oh! the silence sank
Like music on my heart.

'But soon I heard the dash of oars,   500
I heard the pilot's cheer;
My head was turned perforce away,
And I saw a boat appear.

'The Pilot, and the Pilot's boy,
I heard them coming fast!   505
Dear Lord in Heaven! it was a joy
The dead men could not blast.

'I saw a third—I heard his voice:
It is the Hermit good!
He singeth loud his godly hymns   510
That he makes in the wood.
He'll shrieve my soul, he'll wash away
The Albatross's blood.

PART VII

'This Hermit good lives in that wood
Which slopes down to the sea.   515
How loudly his sweet voice he rears!
He loves to talk with mariners
That come from a far countree.

'He kneels at morn, and noon, and eve—
He hath a cushion plump: 520
It is the moss that wholly hides
The rotted old oak-stump.

'The skiff-boat neared: I heard them talk,
"Why, this is strange, I trow!
Where are those lights so many and fair,   525
That signal made but now?"

'"Strange, by my faith!" the Hermit said—
"And they answered not our cheer!
The planks looked warped! and see those sails,
How thin they are and sere!   530
I never saw aught like to them,
Unless perchance it were

'"Brown skeletons of leaves that lag
My forest-brook along:
When the ivy-tod is heavy with snow,   535
And the owlet whoops to the wolf below,
That eats the she-wolf's young."

'"Dear Lord! it hath a fiendish look"—
(The Pilot made reply)
"I am a-feared"—"Push on, push on!"   540
Said the Hermit cheerily.

'The boat came closer to the ship,
But I nor spake nor stirred;
The boat came close beneath the ship,
And straight a sound was heard.   545

'Under the water it rumbled on,
Still louder and more dread:
It reached the ship, it split the bay;
The ship went down like lead.

'Stunned by that loud and dreadful sound, 550
Which sky and ocean smote,
Like one that hath been seven days drowned,
My body lay afloat;
But swift as dreams, myself I found
Within the Pilot's boat. 555

'Upon the whirl, where sank the ship,
The boat spun round and round;
And all was still, save that the hill
Was telling of the sound.

'I moved my lips—the Pilot shrieked, 560
And fell down in a fit;
The holy Hermit raised his eyes,
And prayed where he did sit.

'I took the oars: the Pilot's boy,
Who now doth crazy go, 565
Laughed loud and long, and all the while
His eyes went to and fro.
"Ha! ha!" quoth he, "full plain I see,
The Devil knows how to row."

'And now, all in my own countree, 570
I stood on the firm land!
The Hermit stepped forth from the boat,
And scarcely he could stand.

' "O shrieve me, shrieve me, holy man!"
The Hermit crossed his brow. 575
"Say quick," quoth he, "I bid thee say—
What manner of man art thou?"

'Forthwith this frame of mine was wrenched
With a woeful agony,
Which forced me to begin my tale; 580
And then it left me free.

'Since then at an uncertain hour,
That agony returns;
And till my ghastly tale is told,
This heart within me burns. 585

'I pass, like night, from land to land;
I have strange power of speech;
That moment that his face I see,
I know the man that must hear me:
To him my tale I teach. 590

'What loud uproar bursts from that door:
The wedding-guests are there;
But in the garden-bower the bride
And bride-maids singing are;
And hark the little vesper bell, 595
Which biddeth me to prayer!

'O Wedding-Guest! this soul hath been
Alone on a wide wide sea:
So lonely 't was, that God himself
Scarce seemèd there to be. 600

'O sweeter than the marriage-feast,
'T is sweeter far to me,
To walk together to the kirk
With a goodly company!—

'To walk together to the kirk, 605
And all together pray,
While each to his great Father bends,
Old men, and babes, and loving friends,
And youths and maidens gay!

'Farewell, farewell! but this I tell 610
To thee, thou Wedding-Guest!
He prayeth well, who loveth well
Both man and bird and beast.

'He prayeth best, who loveth best
All things both great and small; 615
For the dear God who loveth us,
He made and loveth all.'

The Mariner, whose eye is bright,
Whose beard with age is hoar,
Is gone; and now the Wedding-Guest 620
Turned from the bridegroom's door.

He went like one that hath been stunned,
And is of sense forlorn:
A sadder and a wiser man
He rose the morrow morn. 625

(1798)

CHRISTABEL

PART I

'T is the middle of night by the castle clock
And the owls have awaken'd the crowing cock;
  Tu-whit!—Tu-whoo!
And hark, again! the crowing cock,
  How drowsily it crew. 5
Sir Leoline, the Baron rich,
Hath a toothless mastiff, which
From her kennel beneath the rock
Maketh answer to the clock,
Four for the quarters, and twelve for the hour;
Ever and aye, by shine and shower, 11
Sixteen short howls, not over loud;
Some say, she sees my lady's shroud.

Is the night chilly and dark?
The night is chilly, but not dark. 14
The thin gray cloud is spread on high,
It covers but not hides the sky.

The moon is behind, and at the full;
And yet she looks both small and dull.
The night is chill, the cloud is gray: 20
'T is a month before the month of May,
And the Spring comes slowly up this way.
The lovely lady, Christabel,
Whom her father loves so well,
What makes her in the wood so late, 25
A furlong from the castle gate?
She had dreams all yesternight
Of her own betrothèd knight;
And she in the midnight wood will pray
For the weal of her lover that's far away. 30

She stole along, she nothing spoke,
　The sighs she heaved were soft and low,
And naught was green upon the oak,
　But moss and rarest mistletoe:
She kneels beneath the huge oak tree, 35
And in silence prayeth she.

The lady sprang up suddenly,
　The lovely lady, Christabel!
It moaned as near, as near can be,
　But what it is she cannot tell.— 40
On the other side it seems to be,
Of the huge, broad-breasted, old oak tree.

The night is chill; the forest bare;
　Is it the wind that moaneth bleak?
There is not wind enough in the air 45
To move away the ringlet curl
　From the lovely lady's cheek—
There is not wind enough to twirl
The one red leaf, the last of its clan,
That dances as often as dance it can, 50
Hanging so light, and hanging so high,
On the topmost twig that looks up at the sky.

Hush, beating heart of Christabel!
Jesu, Maria, shield her well!
She folded her arms beneath her cloak, 55
And stole to the other side of the oak.
　What sees she there?

There she sees a damsel bright,
Drest in a silken robe of white,
That shadowy in the moonlight shone: 60
The neck that made that white robe wan,
Her stately neck, and arms were bare;
Her blue-veined feet unsandaled were;
And wildly glittered here and there
The gems entangled in her hair. 65
I guess, 't was frightful there to see
A lady so richly clad as she—
Beautiful exceedingly!

'*Mary mother, save me now!*'
Said Christabel, '*and who art thou?*' 70
The lady strange made answer meet,
And her voice was faint and sweet:—
'Have pity on my sore distress,
I scarce can speak for weariness:
Stretch forth thy hand, and have no fear!' 75
Said Christabel, 'How camest thou here?'
And the lady, whose voice was faint and sweet,
Did thus pursue her answer meet:—
'My sire is of a noble line,
And my name is Geraldine: 80
Five warriors seized me yestermorn,
Me, even me, a maid forlorn:
They choked my cries with force and fright,
And tied me on a palfrey white.
The palfrey was as fleet as wind, 85
And they rode furiously behind.
They spurred amain, their steeds were white:
And once we crossed the shade of night.
As sure as Heaven shall rescue me,
I have no thought what men they be; 90
Nor do I know how long it is
(For I have lain entranced, I wis)
Since one, the tallest of the five,
Took me from the palfrey's back,
A weary woman, scarce alive. 95
Some muttered words his comrades spoke:
He placed me underneath this oak;
He swore they would return with haste;
Whither they went I cannot tell—
I thought I heard, some minutes past, 100
Sounds as of a castle bell.
Stretch forth thy hand,' thus ended she,
'And help a wretched maid to flee.'

Then Christabel stretched forth her hand,
　And comforted fair Geraldine: 105
'O well, bright dame, may you command
　The service of Sir Leoline;
And gladly our stout chivalry
　Will he send forth, and friends withal,
To guide and guard you safe and free 110
　Home to your noble father's hall.'

She rose: and forth with steps they passed
That strove to be, and were not, fast.
Her gracious stars the lady blest,
　And thus spake on sweet Christabel: 115
'All our household are at rest,
　The hall as silent as the cell;
Sir Leoline is weak in health,
　And may not well awakened be,
But we will move as if in stealth; 120
　And I beseech your courtesy,
This night, to share your couch with me.'

They crossed the moat, and Christabel
Took the key that fitted well;
A little door she opened straight, 125
All in the middle of the gate;
The gate that was ironed within and without,
Where an army in battle array had marched out.
The lady sank, belike through pain,
And Christabel with might and main 130
Lifted her up, a weary weight.

Over the threshold of the gate:
Then the lady rose again,
And moved, as she were not in pain.

So, free from danger, free from fear, 135
They crossed the court: right glad they were.
And Christabel devoutly cried
To the Lady by her side;
'Praise we the Virgin all divine,
  Who hath rescued thee from thy distress!'
'Alas, alas!' said Geraldine, 141
  'I cannot speak for weariness.'
So, free from danger, free from fear,
They crossed the court: right glad they were.

Outside her kennel the mastiff old 145
Lay fast asleep, in moonshine cold.
The mastiff old did not awake,
Yet she an angry moan did make.
And what can ail the mastiff bitch?
Never till now she uttered yell 150
Beneath the eye of Christabel.
Perhaps it is the owlet's scritch:
For what can ail the mastiff bitch?

They passed the hall, that echoes still,
Pass as lightly as you will. 155
The brands were flat, the brands were dying,
Amid their own white ashes lying;
But when the lady passed, there came
A tongue of light, a fit of flame;
And Christabel saw the lady's eye, 160
And nothing else saw she thereby,
Save the boss of the shield of Sir Leoline tall,
Which hung in a murky old niche in the wall.
'O softly tread,' said Christabel,
'My father seldom sleepeth well.' 165
Sweet Christabel her feet doth bare,
And, jealous of the listening air,
They steal their way from stair to stair,
Now in glimmer, and now in gloom,
And now they pass the Baron's room, 170
As still as death, with stifled breath!
And now have reached her chamber door;
And now doth Geraldine press down
The rushes of the chamber floor.

The moon shines dim in the open air, 175
And not a moonbeam enters here.
But they without its light can see
The chamber carved so curiously,
  Carved with figures strange and sweet,
All made out of the carver's brain, 180
  For a lady's chamber meet:
The lamp with twofold silver chain
Is fastened to an angel's feet.
The silver lamp burns dead and dim;
But Christabel the lamp will trim. 185
  She trimmed the lamp, and made it bright,
And left it swinging to and fro,
  While Geraldine, in wretched plight,
Sank down upon the floor below.

'O weary lady, Geraldine, 190
I pray you, drink this cordial wine!
It is a wine of virtuous powers;
My mother made it of wild flowers.'
  'And will your mother pity me,
Who am a maiden most forlorn?' 195
Christabel answered—'Woe is me!
  She died the hour that I was born.
I have heard the gray-haired friar tell,
  How on her death-bed she did say,
That she should hear the castle-bell 200
  Strike twelve upon my wedding-day.
O mother dear! that thou wert here!'
'I would,' said Geraldine, 'she were!'

But soon, with altered voice, said she—
  'Off, wandering mother! Peak and pine!
I have power to bid thee flee.' 206
  Alas! what ails poor Geraldine?
Why stares she with unsettled eye?
Can she the bodiless dead espy?
And why with hollow voice cries she, 210
  'Off, woman, off! this hour is mine—
Though thou her guardian spirit be,
Off, woman, off! 't is given to me.'

Then Christabel knelt by the lady's side,
  And raised to heaven her eyes so blue— 215
'Alas!' said she, 'this ghastly ride—
  Dear lady! it hath wildered you!'
The lady wiped her moist cold brow.
And faintly said, ''T is over now!'
Again the wild-flower wine she drank: 220
Her fair large eyes 'gan glitter bright,
And from the floor, whereon she sank,
The lofty lady stood upright:
  She was most beautiful to see,
Like a lady of a far countrée. 225

  And thus the lofty lady spake—
'All they, who live in the upper sky,
  Do love you, holy Christabel!
And you love them, and for their sake,
  And for the good which me befell, 230
Even I in my degree will try,
  Fair maiden, to requite you well.
But now unrobe yourself; for I
Must pray, ere yet in bed I lie.'

Quoth Christabel, 'So let it be!' 235
And as the lady bade, did she.
Her gentle limbs did she undress
And lay down in her loveliness.

But through her brain, of weal and woe,
So many thoughts moved to and fro, 240
That vain it were her lids to close;
So half-way from the bed she rose,
And on her elbow did recline.
To look at the lady Geraldine.
Beneath the lamp the lady bowed, 245

And slowly rolled her eyes around;
Then drawing in her breath aloud,
  Like one that shuddered, she unbound
The cincture from beneath her breast:
Her silken robe, and inner vest, 250
Dropt to her feet, and full in view,
Behold! her bosom and half her side—
A sight to dream of, not to tell!
O shield her! shield sweet Christabel!

Yet Geraldine nor speaks nor stirs; 255
Ah! what a stricken look was hers!
Deep from within she seems half-way
To lift some weight with sick assay,
And eyes the maid and seeks delay;
Then suddenly, as one defied, 260
Collects herself in scorn and pride,
And lay down by the maiden's side!—
And in her arms the maid she took,
    Ah, well-a-day!
And with low voice and doleful look 265
    These words did say:

'In the touch of this bosom there worketh a
    spell,
Which is lord of thy utterance, Christabel!
Thou knowest to-night, and wilt know to-
    morrow,
This mark of my shame, this seal of my sorrow;
    But vainly thou warrest, 271
      For this is alone in
        Thy power to declare,
          That in the dim forest
Thou heard'st a low moaning, 275
And found'st a bright lady, surpassingly fair:
And didst bring her home with thee, in love and
    in charity,
To shield her and shelter her from the damp air.'

     The Conclusion to Part I

It was a lovely sight to see
The lady Christabel, when she 280
Was praying at the old oak tree.
    Amid the jagged shadows
    Of mossy leafless boughs,
    Kneeling in the moonlight,
      To make her gentle vows; 285
Her slender palms together prest,
Heaving sometimes on her breast;
Her face resigned to bliss or bale—
Her face, oh, call it fair not pale,
And both blue eyes more bright than clear,
Each about to have a tear. 291
With open eyes (ah, woe is me!)
Asleep, and dreaming fearfully,
Fearfully dreaming, yet, I wis,
Dreaming that alone, which is— 295
O sorrow and shame! Can this be she,
The lady, who knelt at the old oak tree?

And lo! the worker of these harms,
That holds the maiden in her arms,
Seems to slumber still and mild, 300
As a mother with her child.

A star hath set, a star hath risen,
  O Geraldine! since arms of thine
Have been the lovely lady's prison.
  O Geraldine! one hour was thine— 305
Thou'st had thy will! By tairn and rill,
The night-birds all that hour were still.
But now they are jubilant anew,
From cliff and tower, tu-whoo! tu-whoo!
Tu-whoo! tu-whoo! from wood and fell! 310

And see! the lady Christabel
Gathers herself from out her trance;
Her limbs relax, her countenance
Grows sad and soft; the smooth thin lids
Close o'er her eyes; and tears she sheds— 315
Large tears that leave the lashes bright!
And oft the while she seems to smile
As infants at a sudden light!
Yea, she doth smile, and she doth weep,
  Like a youthful hermitess, 320
  Beauteous in a wilderness,
Who, praying always, prays in sleep.
And, if she move unquietly,
Perchance, 't is but the blood so free
Comes back and tingles in her feet. 325
No doubt, she hath a vision sweet.
What if her guardian spirit 't were,
What if she knew her mother near?
But this she knows, in joys and woes,
That saints will aid if men will call: 330
For the blue sky bends over all.

             PART II

EACH matin bell, the Baron saith,
Knells us back to a world of death.
These words Sir Leoline first said,
When he rose and found his lady dead: 335
These words Sir Leoline will say
Many a morn to his dying day!

And hence the custom and law began
That still at dawn the sacristan,
Who duly pulls the heavy bell, 340
Five and forty beads must tell
Between each stroke—a warning knell,
Which not a soul can choose but hear
From Bratha Head to Wyndermere.
Saith Bracy the bard, 'So let it knell! 345
And let the drowsy sacristan
Still count as slowly as he can!'
There is no lack of such, I ween,
As well fill up the space between.
In Langdale Pike and Witch's Lair, 350
And Dungeon-ghyll so foully rent,

With ropes of rock and bells of air
Three sinful sextons' ghosts are pent,
Who all give back, one after t' other,
The death-note to their living brother; 355
And oft too, by the knell offended,
Just as their one! two! three! is ended,
The devil mocks the doleful tale
With a merry peal from Borrowdale.

The air is still! through mist and cloud 360
That merry peal comes ringing loud;
And Geraldine shakes off her dread,
And rises lightly from the bed;
Puts on her silken vestments white,
And tricks her hair in lovely plight, 365
And nothing doubting of her spell
Awakens the lady Christabel.
'Sleep you, sweet lady Christabel?
I trust that you have rested well.'

And Christabel awoke and spied 370
The same who lay down by her side—
O rather say, the same whom she
Raised up beneath the old oak tree!
Nay, fairer yet! and yet more fair!
For she belike hath drunken deep 375
Of all the blessedness of sleep!
And while she spake, her looks, her air,
Such gentle thankfulness declare,
That (so it seemed) her girded vests
Grew tight beneath her heaving breasts. 380
'Sure I have sinned!' said Christabel,
'Now heaven be praised if all be well!'
And in low faltering tones, yet sweet,
Did she the lofty lady greet
With such perplexity of mind 385
As dreams too lively leave behind.

So quickly she rose, and quickly arrayed
Her maiden limbs, and having prayed
That He, who on the cross did groan,
Might wash away her sins unknown, 390
She forthwith led fair Geraldine
To meet her sire, Sir Leoline.
The lovely maid and the lady tall
Are pacing both into the hall,
And pacing on through page and groom, 395
Enter the Baron's presence-room.

The Baron rose, and while he prest
His gentle daughter to his breast,
With cheerful wonder in his eyes
The lady Geraldine espies, 400
And gave such welcome to the same,
As might beseem so bright a dame!

But when he heard the lady's tale,
And when she told her father's name,
Why waxed Sir Leoline so pale, 405
Murmuring o'er the name again,
Lord Roland de Vaux of Tryermaine?
Alas! they had been friends in youth;

But whispering tongues can poison truth;
And constancy lives in realms above; 410
And life is thorny; and youth is vain;
And to be wroth with one we love
Doth work like madness in the brain.
And thus it chanced, as I divine,
With Roland and Sir Leoline. 415
Each spake words of high disdain
And insult to his heart's best brother:
They parted—ne'er to meet again!
But never either found another
To free the hollow heart from paining— 420
They stood aloof, the scars remaining,
Like cliffs which had been rent asunder;
A dreary sea now flows between.
But neither heat, nor frost, nor thunder,
Shall wholly do away, I ween, 425
The marks of that which once hath been.
Sir Leoline, a moment's space,
Stood gazing on the damsel's face:
And the youthful Lord of Tryermaine
Came back upon his heart again. 430

O then the Baron forgot his age,
His noble heart swelled high with rage;
He swore by the wounds in Jesu's side
He would proclaim it far and wide,
With trump and solemn heraldry, 435
  That they, who thus had wronged the dame
Were base as spotted infamy!
  'And if they dare deny the same,
My herald shall appoint a week,
And let the recreant traitors seek 440
  My tourney court—that there and then
I may dislodge their reptile souls
  From the bodies and forms of men!'
He spake: his eye in lightning rolls!
For the lady was ruthlessly seized; and he kenned 445
In the beautiful lady the child of his friend!

And now the tears were on his face,
  And fondly in his arms he took
Fair Geraldine who met the embrace,
  Prolonging it with joyous look. 450
Which when she viewed, a vision fell
Upon the soul of Christabel,
The vision of fear, the touch and pain!
She shrunk and shuddered, and saw again—
(*Ah, woe is me! Was it for thee,* 455
Thou gentle maid! such sights to see?)
  Again she saw that bosom old,
  Again she felt that bosom cold,
And drew in her breath with a hissing sound:
Whereat the Knight turned wildly round, 460
And nothing saw, but his own sweet maid
With eyes upraised, as one that prayed.

The touch, the sight, had passed away,
  And in its stead that vision blest,
Which comforted her after-rest, 465

While in the lady's arms she lay,
  Had put a rapture in her breast,
And on her lips and o'er her eyes
Spread smiles like light!
                     With new surprise,
'What ails then my belovèd child?'   470
The Baron said—His daughter mild
Made answer, 'All will yet be well!'
I ween, she had no power to tell
Aught else: so mighty was the spell.

Yet he who saw this Geraldine,   475
Had deemed her sure a thing divine.
Such sorrow with such grace she blended,
As if she feared she had offended
Sweet Christabel, that gentle maid!
And with such lowly tones she prayed   480
She might be sent without delay
Home to her father's mansion.
                     'Nay!
Nay, by my soul!' said Leoline.
'Ho! Bracy the brad, the charge be thine!
Go thou, with music sweet and loud,   485
And take two steeds with trappings proud,
And take the youth whom thou lov'st best
To bear thy harp, and learn thy song,
And clothe you both in solemn vest,
And over the mountains haste along,   490
Lest wandering folk, that are abroad,
Detain you on the valley road.

'And when he has crossed the Irthing flood,
My merry bard! he hastes, he hastes
Up Knorren Moor, through Halegarth Wood,
And reaches soon that castle good   496
Which stands and threatens Scotland's wastes.

'Bard Bracy! bard Bracy! your horses are fleet,
Ye must ride up the hall, your music so sweet,
More loud than your horses' echoing feet!   500
And loud and loud to Lord Roland call,
Thy daughter is safe in Langdale hall!
Thy beautiful daughter is safe and free—
Sir Leoline greets thee thus through me.
He bids thee come without delay   505
With all thy numerous array;
And take thy lovely daughter home:
And he will meet thee on the way
With all his numerous array
White with their panting palfreys' foam: 510
And, by mine honor! I will say,
That I repent me of the day
When I spake words of fierce disdain
To Roland de Vaux of Tryermaine!—
—For since that evil hour hath flown,   515
Many a summer's sun hath shone;
Yet ne'er found I a friend again
Like Roland de Vaux of Tryermaine.'

The lady fell, and clasped his knees,
Her face upraised, her eyes o'erflowing;   520
And Bracy replied, with faltering voice,
His gracious hail on all bestowing;
'Thy words, thou sire of Christabel,
Are sweeter than my harp can tell;
Yet might I gain a boon of thee,   525
This day my journey should not be,
So strange a dream hath come to me;
That I had vowed with music loud
To clear yon wood from thing unblest,
Warn'd by a vision in my rest!   530
For in my sleep I saw that dove,
That gentle bird, whom thou dost love,
And call'st by thy own daughter's name—
Sir Leoline! I saw the same,
Fluttering, and uttering fearful moan,   535
Among the green herbs in the forest alone.
Which when I saw and when I heard,
I wonder'd what might ail the bird;
For nothing near it could I see,
Save the grass and herbs underneath the old
    tree.'   540

* * *

Thus Bracy said: the Baron, the while,
Half-listening heard him with a smile;
Then turned to Lady Geraldine,
His eyes made up of wonder and love;
And said in courtly accents fine,   545
'Sweet maid, Lord Roland's beauteous dove,
With arms more strong than harp or song,
Thy sire and I will crush the snake!'
He kissed her forehead as he spake,
And Geraldine in maiden wise   550
Casting down her large bright eyes,
With blushing cheek and courtesy fine
She turned her from Sir Leoline;
Softly gathering up her train,
That o'er her right arm fell again;   555
And folded her arms across her chest,
And couched her head upon her breast,
And looked askance at Christabel—
Jesu, Maria, shield her well!

A snake's small eye blinks dull and shy,   560
And the lady's eyes they shrunk in her head,
Each shrunk up to a serpent's eye,
And with somewhat of malice, and more of
    dread,
At Christabel she look'd askance!—
One moment—and the sight was fled!   565
But Christabel in dizzy trance
Stumbling on the unsteady ground
Shuddered aloud, with a hissing sound;
And Geraldine again turned round,
And like a thing that sought relief,   570
Full of wonder and full of grief,
She rolled her large bright eyes divine
Wildly on Sir Leoline.

The maid, alas! her thoughts are gone,
She nothing sees—no sight but one!   575

The maid, devoid of guile and sin,
I know not how, in fearful wise,
So deeply had she drunken in
That look, those shrunken serpent eyes,
That all her features were resigned   580
To this sole image in her mind:
And passively did imitate
That look of dull and treacherous hate!
And thus she stood, in dizzy trance,
Still picturing that look askance   585
With forced unconscious sympathy
Full before her father's view—
As far as such a look could be
In eyes so innocent and blue!

And when the trance was o'er, the maid   590
Paused awhile, and inly prayed:
Then falling at the Baron's feet,
'By my mother's soul do I entreat
That thou this woman send away!'
She said: and more she could not say;   595
For what she knew she could not tell,
O'er-mastered by the mighty spell.

* * *

Within the Baron's heart and brain
If thoughts, like these, had any share,
They only swelled his rage and pain,   600
And did but work confusion there.
His heart was cleft with pain and rage,
His cheeks they quivered, his eyes were wild,
Dishonor'd thus in his old age;
Dishonor'd by his only child,   605
And all his hospitality
To the insulted daughter of his friend
By more than woman's jealousy
Brought thus to a disgraceful end—
He rolled his eye with stern regard   610
Upon the gentle ministrel bard,
And said in tones abrupt, austere—
'Why, Bracy! dost thou loiter here?
I bade thee hence!' The bard obeyed;
And turning from his own sweet maid,   615
The aged knight, Sir Leoline,
Led forth the lady Geraldine!
                              (1816)

KUBLA KHAN

In Xanadu did Kubla Khan
  A stately pleasure-dome decree:
  Where Alph, the sacred river, ran
  Through caverns measureless to man
    Down to a sunless sea.   5
So twice five miles of fertile ground
With walls and towers were girdled round:
And here were gardens bright with sinuous rills
Where blossomed many an incense-bearing
    tree;
And here were forests ancient as the hills, 10
Enfolding sunny spots of greenery.

But oh! that deep romantic chasm which
    slanted
Down the green hill athwart a cedarn cover!
A savage place! as holy and enchanted
As e'er beneath a waning moon was haunted 15
By woman wailing for her demon-lover!
And from this chasm, with ceaseless turmoil
    seething,
As if this earth in fast thick pants were breath-
    ing,
A mighty fountain momently was forced;
Amid whose swift half-intermitted burst   20
Huge fragments vaulted like rebounding hail,
Or chaffy grain beneath the thresher's flail:
And 'mid these dancing rocks at once and ever
It flung up momently the sacred river.
Five miles meandering with a mazy motion   25
Through wood and dale the sacred river ran,
Then reached the caverns measureless to man,
And sank in tumult to a lifeless ocean:
And 'mid this tumult Kubla heard from far
Ancestral voices prophesying war!   30

  The shadow of the dome of pleasure
      Floated midway on the waves;
  Where was heard the mingled measure
      From the fountain and the caves.
It was a miracle of rare device,   35
A sunny pleasure-dome with caves of ice!

    A damsel with a dulcimer
    In a vision once I saw:
    It was an Abyssinian maid,
    And on her dulcimer she played,   40
    Singing of Mount Abora.
    Could I revive within me
      Her symphony and song,
To such a deep delight 't would win me
That with music loud and long,   45
I would build that dome in air,
That sunny dome! those caves of ice!
And all who heard should see them there,
And all should cry, Beware! Beware!
His flashing eyes, his floating hair!   50
Weave a circle round him thrice,
And close your eyes with holy dread,
For he on honey-dew hath fed,
And drunk the milk of Paradise
                              (1816)

FROST AT MIDNIGHT

The frost performs its secret ministry,
Unhelped by any wind. The owlet's cry
Came loud—and hark, again! loud as before.
The inmates of my cottage, all at rest,
Have left me to that solitude, which suits   5
Abstruser musings: save that at my side
My cradled infant slumbers peacefully.
'T is calm indeed! so calm, that it disturbs
And vexes meditation with its strange

And extreme silentness. Sea, hill, and wood, 10
This populous village! Sea, and hill, and wood,
With all the numberless goings on of life
Inaudible as dreams! the thin blue flame
Lies on my low-burnt fire, and quivers not;
Only that film, which fluttered on the grate, 15
Still flutters there, the sole unquiet thing.
Methinks, its motion in this hush of nature
Gives it dim sympathies with me who live,
Making it a companionable form,
Whose puny flaps and freaks the idling Spirit 20
By its own moods interprets, every where
Echo or mirror seeking of itself,
And makes a toy of Thought.
       But O! how oft,
How oft, at school, with most believing mind, 25
Presageful, have I gazed upon the bars,
To watch that fluttering stranger! and as oft
With unclosed lids, already had I dreamt
Of my sweet birth-place, and the old church-
 tower,
Whose bells, the poor man's only music, rang 30
From morn to evening, all the hot Fair-day,
So sweetly, that they stirred and haunted me
With a wild pleasure, falling on mine ear
Most like articulate sounds of things to come!
So gazed I, till the soothing things I dreamt 35
Lulled me to sleep, and sleep prolonged my
 dreams!
And so I brooded all the following morn,
Awed by the stern preceptor's face, mine eye
Fixed with mock study on my swimming book:
Save if the door half opened, and I snatched 40
A hasty glance, and still my heart leaped up,
For still I hoped to see the stranger's face,
Townsman, or aunt, or sister more beloved,
My play-mate when we both were clothed alike!

Dear babe, that sleepest cradled by my side,
Whose gentle breathings, heard in this deep
 calm, 46
Fill up the interspersèd vacancies
And momentary pauses of the thought!
My babe so beautiful! it thrills my heart
With tender gladness, thus to look at thee, 50
And think that thou shalt learn far other lore
And in far other scenes! For I was reared
In the great city, pent 'mid cloisters dim,
And saw nought lovely but the sky and stars.
But thou, my babe! shalt wander like a breeze 55
By lakes and sandy shores, beneath the crags
Of ancient mountain, and beneath the clouds,
Which image in their bulk both lakes and shores
And mountain crags: so shalt thou see and hear
The lovely shapes and sounds intelligible 60
Of that eternal language, which thy God
Utters, who from eternity doth teach
Himself in all, and all things in himself.
Great universal Teacher! he shall mold
Thy spirit, and by giving make it ask. 65

Therefore all seasons shall be sweet to thee,
Whether the summer clothe the general earth
With greenness, or the redbreast sit and sing
Betwixt the tufts of snow on the bare branch
Of mossy apple-tree, while the nigh thatch 70
Smokes in the sun-thaw; whether the eavedrops
 fall
Heard only in the trances of the blast,
Or if the secret ministry of frost
Shall hang them up in silent icicles,
Quietly shining to the quiet Moon. 75
        (1798)

HUMILITY THE MOTHER OF CHARITY

FRAIL creatures are we all! To be the best
 Is but the fewest faults to have:—
Look thou then to thyself, and leave the rest
 To God, thy conscience, and the grave.
        (1830)

EPITAPH

STOP, Christian passer-by!—Stop, child of God,
And read with gentle breast. Beneath this sod
A poet lies, or that which once seemed he.—
O, lift one thought in prayer for S. T. C.;
That he who many a year with toil of breath 5
Found death in life, may here find life in death!
Mercy for praise—to be forgiven for fame
He asked, and hoped, through Christ.
      Do thou the same!
      (Nov. 9, 1833)

CHARLES LAMB (1775-1834)

There are few English authors with whose character and circumstances we may become so closely acquainted as with Charles Lamb's, on account of his habit of self-confession in his essays, his skill and charm as a letter-writer, and his many literary friendships. The first seven years of his life were spent at the Inner Temple, where his father had rooms as clerk and confidential servant to one of the barristers; for the next seven he was a 'blue coat boy' at Christ's Hospital, along with Coleridge. Lamb was passionately fond of London, where he passed nearly all his days, but in *Mackery End in Hertfordshire* and other essays he has given us delightful glimpses of holiday visits to the country home of his grandmother Field. It was on one of these visits that he fell in love with the 'fair Alice' of *Dream Children*, but this youthful romance was cruelly cut short. There was a strain of mental weakness in the family, and Lamb's mind gave way. Not long after his restoration, his sister Mary, the 'Bridget Elia' of the essays, in a sudden fit of insanity, was the cause of her mother's death; on her recovery it was necessary that some one should be responsible for her safe keeping, and to this task Charles devoted the rest of his life. At this time he was earning a small salary as a clerk in the office of the East India Company, and his first efforts in literature, apart from a few sonnets and other short poems, were directed to eking out their scanty income. *A Tale of Rosamund Gray*, published in 1798, had no great success; he could not get his tragedy, *John Woodvil*, put on the stage; his comedy, *Mr. H.*, was acted at Drury Lane and failed. He contributed 'witty paragraphs' to the morning papers at the rate of 'sixpence a joke, and it was thought pretty high, too,' as he tells us in the essay on *Newspapers Thirty-five Years Ago*. Fortune first smiled upon them in the *Tales from Shakespeare*, written for children by the brother and sister together, Charles taking the tragedies and Mary the comedies. His *Specimens of English Dramatists contemporary with Shakespeare* was an important contribution to the criticism of the Elizabethan drama, and his position in the world of letters was now well established. Leigh Hunt, Wordsworth, Southey, Keats, Hazlitt, De Quincey, and many other famous men were among his friends, and much of his leisure was spent in conversation and convivial meetings, from which he sometimes returned, as his sister says, 'very smoky and drinky.' His ready wit and unfailing kindliness endeared him to his friends, as the charm of his personality and the delicacy of his humor have to an ever-increasing circle of readers. His most characteristic work is found in the *Essays of Elia*, which appeared in the *London Magazine* from 1820 to 1826.

THE OLD FAMILIAR FACES

I have had playmates, I have had companions,
In my days of childhood, in my joyful schooldays;
All, all are gone, the old familiar faces.

I have been laughing, I have been carousing,
Drinking late, sitting late, with my bosom cronies; 5
All, all are gone, the old familiar faces.

I loved a love once, fairest among women;
Closed are her doors on me, I must not see her—
All, all are gone, the old familiar faces.

I have a friend, a kinder friend has no man; 10
Like an ingrate, I left my friend abruptly;
Left him, to muse on the old familiar faces.

Ghost-like I paced round the haunts of my childhood,
Earth seemed a desert I was bound to traverse,
Seeking to find the old familiar faces. 15

Friend of my bosom, thou more than a brother,
Why wert not thou born in my father's dwelling?
So might we talk of the old familiar faces—

How some they have died, and some they have left me,
And some are taken from me; all are departed;
All, all are gone, the old familiar faces. 21
(1798)

MACKERY END IN HERTFORDSHIRE

Bridget Elia has been my housekeeper for many a long year. I have obligations to Bridget, extending beyond the period of memory. We house together, old bachelor and maid, in a sort of double singleness; with such tolerable comfort, upon the whole, that I, for one, find in myself no sort of disposition to go out upon the mountains, with the rash king's offspring, to bewail my celibacy. We agree pretty well in our tastes and habits—yet so, as 'with a difference.' We are generally in harmony, with occasional bickerings—as it should be among near relations. Our sympathies are rather understood, than expressed; and once, upon my dissembling a tone in my voice more kind than ordinary, my cousin burst into tears, and complained that I was altered. We are both great readers in different directions. While I am hanging over (for the thousandth time) some passage in old Burton, or one of his strange contemporaries, she is abstracted in some modern tale, or adventure, whereof our common reading-table is daily fed with assiduously fresh supplies. Narrative teases me. I have little concern in the progress of events. She must have a story—well, ill, or indifferently told—so there be life stirring in it, and plenty of good or evil accidents. The fluctuations of fortune in fiction—and almost in real life—have ceased to interest, or operate but dully upon me. Out-of-the-way humors and opinions—heads with some diverting twist in them—the oddities of authorship please me most. My cousin has a native disrelish of anything that sounds odd or bizarre. Nothing goes down with her that is quaint, irregular, or out of the road of common sympathy. She 'holds Nature more clever.' I can pardon her blindness to the beautiful obliquities of the *Religio Medici;* but she must apologize to me for certain disrespectful insinuations, which she has been pleased to throw out latterly, touching the intellectuals of a dear favorite of mine, of the last century but one—the thrice noble, chaste, and virtuous, —but again somewhat fantastical, and original-brained, generous Margaret Newcastle.

It has been the lot of my cousin, oftener perhaps than I could have wished, to have had for her associates and mine, freethinkers—leaders, and disciples, of novel philosophies and systems; but she neither wrangles with, nor accepts, their opinions. That which was good and venerable to her, when a child, retains its authority over her mind still. She never juggles or plays tricks with her understanding.

We are both of us inclined to be a little too positive; and I have observed the result of our disputes to be almost uniformly this—that in matters of fact, dates, and circumstances, it turns out, that I was in the right, and my cousin in the wrong. But where we have differed upon moral points; upon something proper to be done, or let alone; whatever heat of opposition, or steadiness of conviction, I set out with, I am sure always, in the long run, to be brought over to her way of thinking.

I must touch upon the foibles of my kinswoman with a gentle hand, for Bridget does not like to be told of her faults. She hath an awkward trick (to say no worse of it) of reading in company: at which times she will answer *yes* or *no* to a question, without fully understanding its purport—which is provoking, and derogatory in the highest degree to the dignity of the putter of the said question. Her presence of mind is equal to the most pressing trials of life, but will sometimes desert her upon trifling occasions. When the purpose requires it, and is a thing of moment, she can speak to it greatly; but in matters which are not stuff of the conscience, she hath been known sometimes to let slip a word less seasonably.

Her education in youth was not much attended to; and she happily missed all that train of female garniture, which passeth by the name of accomplishments. She was tumbled early, by accident or design, into a spacious closet of good old English reading, without much selection or prohibition, and browsed at will upon that fair and wholesome pasturage. Had I twenty girls, they should be brought up exactly in this fashion. I know not whether their chance in wedlock might not be diminished by it; but I can answer for it, that it makes (if the worst come to the worst) most incomparable old maids.

In a season of distress, she is the truest comforter; but in the teasing accidents, and minor perplexities, which do not call out the *will* to meet them, she sometimes maketh matters worse by an excess of participation. If she does not always divide your trouble, upon the pleasanter occasions of life she is sure always to treble your satisfaction. She is excellent to be at play with, or upon a visit; but best, when she goes a journey with you.

We made an excursion together a few summers since, into Hertfordshire, to beat up the quarters of some of our less-known relations in that fine corn country.

The oldest thing I remember is Mackery End; or Mackarel End, as it is spelt, perhaps more properly, in some old maps of Hertfordshire: a farm-house,—delightfully situated within a gentle walk from Wheathampstead. I can just remember having been there, on a visit to a great-aunt, when I was a child, under the care of Bridget; who, as I have said, is older than myself by some ten years. I wish that I could throw into a heap the remainder of our joint existences, that we might share them in equal division. But that is impossible. The house was at that time in the occupation of a substantial yeoman, who had married my grandmother's sister. His name was Gladman. My grandmother was a Bruton, married to a Field. The Gladmans and the Brutons are still flourishing in that part of the county, but the Fields are almost extinct. More than forty years had elapsed since the visit I speak of; and, for the greater portion of that period, we had lost sight of the other two branches also. Who or what sort of persons inherited Mackery End—kindred or strange folk—we were afraid almost to conjecture, but determined some day to explore.

By somewhat a circuitous route, taking the noble park at Luton in our way from Saint Alban's, we arrived at the spot of our anxious curiosity about noon. The sight of the old farm-house, though every trace of it was effaced from my recollection, affected me with a pleasure which I had not experienced for many a year. For though *I* had forgotten it, *we* had never forgotten being there together, and we had been talking about Mackery End all our lives, till memory on my part became mocked with a phantom of itself, and I thought I knew the aspect of a place, which, when present, O how unlike it was to *that*, which I had conjured up so many times instead of it!

Still the air breathed balmily about it; the season was in the 'heart of June,' and I could say with the poet,

> But thou, that didst appear so fair
> To fond imagination,
> Dost rival in the light of day
> Her delicate creation!

Bridget's was more a waking bliss than mine, for she easily remembered her old acquaintance again—some altered features, of course, a little grudged at. At first, indeed, she was ready to disbelieve for joy; but the scene soon reconfirmed itself in her affections—and she traversed every outpost of the old mansion, to the wood-house, the orchard, the place where the pigeon-house had stood (house and birds were alike flown)—with a breathless impatience of recognition, which was more pardonable perhaps than decorous at the age of fifty odd. But Bridget in some things is behind her years.

The only thing left was to get into the house —and that was a difficulty which to me singly would have been insurmountable; for I am terribly shy in making myself known to strangers and out-of-date kinsfolk. Love, stronger than scruple, winged my cousin in without me; but she soon returned with a creature that might have sat to a sculptor for the image of Welcome. It was the youngest of the Gladmans; who, by marriage with a Bruton, had become mistress of the old mansion. A comely brood are the Brutons. Six of them, females, were noted as the handsomest young women in the county. But this adopted Bruton, in my mind, was better than they all—more comely. She was born too late to have remembered me. She just recollected in early life to have had her cousin Bridget once pointed out to her, climbing a stile. But the name of kindred, and of cousinship, was enough. Those slender ties, that prove slight as gossamer in the rending atmosphere of a metropolis, bind faster, as we found it, in hearty, homely, loving Hertfordshire. In five minutes we were as thoroughly acquainted as if we had been born and bred up together; were familiar, even to the calling each other by our Christian names. So Christians should call one another. To have seen Bridget, and her—it was like the meeting of the two scriptural cousins! There was a grace and dignity, an amplitude of form and stature, answering to her mind, in this farmer's wife, which would have shined in a palace—or so we thought it. We were made welcome by husband and wife equally—we, and our friend that was with us.—I had almost forgotten him—but B. F. will not so soon forget that meeting, if peradventure he shall read this on the far-distant shores where the kangaroo haunts. The fatted calf was made ready, or rather was already so, as if in anticipation of our coming; and, after an appropriate glass of native wine, never let me forget with what honest pride this hospitable cousin made us proceed to Wheathampstead, to introduce us (as some new-found rarity) to her mother and sister Gladmans, who did indeed know something more of us, at a time when she almost knew nothing.—With what corresponding kindness we were received by them also—how Bridget's memory, exalted by the occasion, warmed into a thousand half-obliterated recollections of things and persons, to my utter astonishment, and her own—and to the astoundment of B. F. who sat by, almost the only thing that was not a cousin there,—old effaced images of more than half-forgotten names and circumstances still crowding back upon her, as words written in lemon come out upon exposure to a friendly warmth,—when I forget all this, then may my country cousins forget me; and Bridget no more remember, that in the days of weakling infancy I was her tender charge—as I have been her care in foolish manhood since—in those pretty pastoral walks, long ago, about Mackery End, in Hertfordshire.

(1821)

DREAM-CHILDREN: A REVERIE

CHILDREN love to listen to stories about their elders, when *they* were children; to stretch their imagination to the conception of a traditionary great-uncle, or grandame, whom they never saw. It was in this spirit that my little ones crept about me the other evening to hear about their great-grandmother Field, who lived in a great house in Norfolk (a hundred times bigger than that in which they and papa lived) which had been the scene—so at least it was generally believed in that part of the country—of the tragic incidents which they had lately become familiar with from the ballad of the Children in the Wood. Certain it is that the whole story of the children and their cruel uncle was to be seen fairly carved out in wood upon the chimney-piece of the great hall, the whole story down to the Robin Redbreasts, till a foolish rich person pulled it down to set up a marble one of modern invention in its stead, with no story upon it. Here Alice put out one of her dear mother's looks, too tender to be called upbraiding. Then I went on to say, how religious and how good their great-grandmother Field was, how beloved and respected by everybody, though she was not indeed the mistress of this great house, but had only the charge of it (and yet in some respects she might be said to be the mistress of it too) committed to her by the owner, who preferred living in a newer and more fashionable mansion which he had purchased somewhere in the adjoining county; but still she lived in it in a manner as if it had been her own, and kept up the dignity of the great house in a sort while she lived, which afterwards came to decay, and was nearly pulled down, and all its old ornaments stripped and carried away to the owner's other house, where they were set up, and looked as awkward as if some one were to carry away the old tombs they had seen lately at the Abbey, and stick them up in Lady C.'s tawdry gilt drawing-room. Here John smiled, as much as to say, 'that would be foolish, indeed.' And then I told how, when she came to die, her funeral was attended by a concourse of all the poor, and some of the gentry too, of the neighborhood for many miles round, to show their respect for her memory, because she had been such a good and religious woman; so good indeed that she knew all the Psaltery by heart, ay, and a great part of the Testament besides. Here little Alice spread her hands. Then I told what a tall, upright, graceful person their great-grandmother Field once was; and how in her youth she was esteemed the best dancer—here Alice's little right foot played an involuntary movement, till upon my looking grave, it desisted—the best dancer, I was saying, in the county, till a cruel disease, called a cancer, came, and bowed her down with pain; but it could never bend her good spirits, or make them stoop, but they were still upright, because she was so good and religious. Then I told how she was used to sleep by herself in a lone chamber of the great lone house; and how she believed that an apparition of two infants was to be seen at midnight gliding up and down the great staircase near where she slept, but she said 'those innocents would do her no harm'; and how frightened I used to be, though in those days I had my maid to sleep with me, because I was never half so good or religious as she—and yet I never saw the infants. Here John expanded all his eyebrows and tried to look courageous. Then I told how good she was to all her grandchildren, having us to the great house in the holidays, where I in particular used to spend many hours by myself, in gazing upon the old busts of the twelve Cæsars, that had been emperors of Rome, till the old marble heads would seem to live again, or I to be turned into marble with them; how I never could be tired with roaming about that huge mansion, with its vast empty rooms, with their worn-out hangings, fluttering tapestry, and carved oaken panels, with the gilding almost rubbed out—sometimes in the spacious old-fashioned gardens, which I had almost to myself, unless when now and then a solitary gardening man would cross me—and how the nectarines and peaches hung upon the walls without my ever offering to pluck them, because they were forbidden fruit, unless now and then,—and because I had more pleasure in strolling about among the old melancholy-looking yew-trees, or the firs, and picking up the red berries, and the fir apples, which were good for nothing but to look at—or in lying about upon the fresh grass, with all the fine garden smells around me—or basking in the orangery, till I could almost fancy myself ripening too along with the oranges and the limes in that grateful warmth—or in watching the dace that darted to and fro in the fishpond, at the bottom of the garden, with here and there a great sulky pike hanging midway down the water in silent state, as if it mocked at their impertinent friskings,— I had more pleasure in these busy-idle diversions than in all the sweet flavors of peaches, nectarines, oranges, and such like common baits of children. Here John slyly deposited back upon the plate a bunch of grapes which, not unobserved by Alice, he had meditated dividing with her, and both seemed willing to relinquish them for the present as irrelevant. Then in somewhat a more heightened tone, I told how, though their great-grandmother Field loved all her grandchildren, yet in an especial manner she might be said to love their uncle, John L——, because he was so handsome and spirited a youth, and a king to the rest of us; and, instead of moping about in solitary corners, like some of us, he would mount the most mettlesome horse he could get, when but an imp no bigger than themselves, and make it carry him half over the county in a morning, and join the hunters when there were any out—and yet he loved the old great house and gardens too, but had too much spirit to be always pent up within their boundaries—and how their uncle grew up to man's estate as brave as he was handsome, to the admiration of everybody, but of their great-grandmother Field most especially; and how he used to carry me upon his back when I was a lame-footed boy—for he was a good bit older than me—many a mile when I could not walk for pain;—and how in after-life he became lame-footed too, and I did not always (I fear) make allowances enough for him when he was impatient, and in pain, nor remember sufficiently how considerate he had been to me when I was lame-footed; and how when he died, though he had not been dead an hour, it seemed as if he had died a great while ago, such a distance there is betwixt life and death; and how I bore his death as I thought pretty well at first, but afterwards it haunted and haunted me; and though I did not cry or take it to heart as some do, and as I think he would have done if I had died, yet I missed him all day long, and knew not till then how much I had loved him. I missed his kindness, and I missed his crossness, and wished him to be alive again, to be quarreling with him (for we quarreled sometimes), rather than not have him again, and was as uneasy without him, as he, their poor uncle, must have been when the doctor took off his limb. Here the children fell a-crying, and asked if their little mourning which they had on was not for uncle John, and they looked up, and prayed me not to go on about their uncle, but to tell them some stories about their pretty dead mother. Then I told how for seven long years, in hope sometimes, sometimes in despair, yet persisting ever, I courted the fair Alice W——n; and, as much as children could understand, I explained to them what coyness, and difficulty, and denial meant in maidens—when suddenly, turning to Alice, the soul of the first Alice looked out at her eyes with such a reality of representment, that I became in doubt which of them stood there before me, or whose that bright hair was; and while I stood gazing, both the children gradually grew fainter to my view, receding, and still receding till nothing at last but two mournful features were seen in the uttermost distance, which without speech, strangely impressed upon me the effects of speech: 'We are not of Alice, nor of thee, nor are we children at all. The children of Alice call Bartrum father. We are nothing; less than nothing, and dreams. We are only what might have been, and must wait upon the tedious shores of Lethe millions of ages before we have existence and a name'—and immediately awaking, I found myself quietly seated in my bachelor arm-chair, where I had fallen asleep, with the faithful Bridget unchanged by my side—but John L. (or James Elia) was gone for ever. (1822)

A CHAPTER ON EARS

I HAVE no ear.—

Mistake me not, reader,—nor imagine that I am by nature destitute of those exterior twin appendages, hanging ornaments, and (architectually speaking) handsome volutes to the human capital. Better my mother had never borne me. —I am, I think, rather delicately than copiously provided with those conduits; and I feel no disposition to envy the mule for his plenty, or the mole for her exactness, in those ingenious labyrinthine inlets—those indispensable side-intelligencers.

Neither have I incurred, or done anything to incur, with Defoe, that hideous disfigurement, which constrained him to draw upon assurance—to feel 'quite unabashed,' and at ease upon that article. I was never, I thank my stars, in the pillory; nor, if I read them aright, is it within the compass of my destiny, that I ever should be.

When therefore I say that I have no ear, you will understand me to mean—*for music.*—To say that this heart never melted at the concourse of sweet sounds, would be a foul self-libel.—'*Water parted from the sea*' never fails to move it strangely. So does '*In infancy.*' But they were used to be sung at her harpsichord (the old-fashioned instrument in vogue in those days) by a gentlewoman—the gentlest, sure, that ever merited the appellation—the sweetest—why should I hesitate to name Mrs. S——, once the blooming Fanny Weatheral of the Temple—who had power to thrill the soul of Elia, small imp as he was, even in his long coats; and to make him glow, tremble, and blush with a passion, that not faintly indicated the day-spring of that absorbing sentiment, which was afterwards destined to overwhelm and subdue his nature quite, for Alice W——n.

I even think that *sentimentally* I am disposed to harmony. But *organically* I am incapable of a tune. I have been practising '*God save the King*' all my life; whistling and humming of it over to myself in solitary corners; and am not yet arrived, they tell me, within many quavers of it. Yet hath the loyalty of Elia never been impeached.

I am not without suspicion that I have an undeveloped faculty of music within me. For, thrumming, in my mild way, on my friend A.'s piano, the other morning, while he was engaged in an adjoining parlor,—on his return he was pleased to say, '*he thought it could not be the maid!*' On his first surprise at hearing the keys touched in somewhat an airy and masterful way, not dreaming of me, his suspicions had lighted on *Jenny.* But a grace snatched from a superior refinement, soon convinced him that some being,—technically perhaps deficient, but higher informed from a principle common to all the fine arts,—had swayed the keys to a mood which Jenny, with all her (less cultivated) enthusiasm, could never have elicited from them. I mention this as a proof of my friend's penetration, and not with any view of disparaging Jenny.

Scientifically I could never be made to understand (yet have I taken some pains) what a note in music is; or how one note should differ from another. Much less in voices can I distinguish a soprano from a tenor. Only sometimes the thorough bass I contrive to guess at from its being supereminently harsh and disagreeable. I tremble, however, for my misapplication of the simplest terms of *that* which I disclaim. While I profess my ignorance, I scarce know what to *say* I am ignorant of. I hate, perhaps, by misnomers. *Sostenuto* and *adagio* stand in the like relation of obscurity to me; and *Sol, Fa, Mi, Re,* is as conjuring as *Baralipton.*

It is hard to stand alone—in an age like this,—(constituted to the quick and critical perception of all harmonious combinations, I verily believe, beyond all preceding ages, since Jubal stumbled upon the gamut)—to remain, as it were, singly unimpressible to the magic influences of an art which is said to have such an especial stroke at soothing, elevating, and refining the passions.—Yet, rather than break the candid current of my confessions, I must avow to you, that I have received a great deal more pain than pleasure from this so cried-up faculty.

I am constitutionally susceptible of noises. A carpenter's hammer in a warm summer noon, will fret me into more than midsummer madness. But those unconnected, unset sounds are nothing to the measured malice of music. The ear is passive to those single strokes; willingly enduring stripes, while it hath no task to con. To music it cannot be passive. It will strive—mine at least will—spite of its inaptitude, to thrid the maze; like an unskilled eye painfully poring upon hieroglyphics. I have sat through an Italian Opera, till, for sheer pain, and inexplicable anguish, I have rushed out into the noisiest places of the crowded streets, to solace myself with sounds, which I was not obliged to follow, and get rid of the distracting torment of endless, fruitless, barren attention! I take refuge in the unpretending assemblage of honest common-life sounds;—and the purgatory of the Enraged Musician becomes my paradise.

I have sat at an Oratorio (that profanation of the purposes of the cheerful playhouse) watching the faces of the auditory in the pit (what a contrast to Hogarth's Laughing Audience!) immovable, or affecting some faint emotion,—till (as some have said, that our occupations in the next world will be but a shadow of what delighted us in this) I have imagined myself in some cold theater in Hades, where some of the *forms* of the earthly one should be kept up, with none of the *enjoyment;* or like that—

Party in a parlor,
All silent, and all DAMNED!

Above all, those insufferable concertos, and pieces of music, as they are called, do plague and embitter my apprehension.—Words are something; but to be exposed to an endless battery of mere sounds; to be long a-dying, to lie stretched upon a rack of roses; to keep up languor by unintermitted effort; to pile honey upon sugar, and sugar upon honey, to an interminable tedious sweetness; to fill up sound with feeling, and strain ideas to keep pace with it; to gaze on empty frames, and be forced to make the pictures for yourself; to read a book *all stops*, and be obliged to supply the verbal matter; to invent extempore tragedies to answer to the vague gestures of an inexplicable rambling mime—these are faint shadows of what I have undergone from a series of the ablest-executed pieces of this empty *instrumental music.*

I deny not, that in the opening of a concert, I have experienced something vastly lulling and agreeable:—afterwards followeth the languor, and the oppression. Like that disappointing book in Patmos; or, like the comings on of melancholy, described by Burton, doth music make her first insinuating approaches:—'Most pleasant it is to such as are melancholy given, to walk alone in some solitary grove, betwixt wood and water, by some brook side, and to meditate upon some delightsome and pleasant subject, which shall affect him most, *amabilis insania,* and *mentis gratissimus error.* A most incomparable delight to build castles in the air, to go smiling to themselves, acting an infinite variety of parts, which they suppose, and strongly imagine, they act, or that they see done.—So delightsome these toys at first, they could spend whole days and nights without sleep, even whole years in such contemplations, and fantastical meditations, which are like so many dreams, and will hardly be drawn from them—winding and unwinding themselves as so many clocks, and still pleasing their humors, until at last the SCENE TURNS UPON A SUDDEN, and they being now habituated to such meditations and solitary places, can endure no company, can think of nothing but harsh and distasteful subjects. Fear, sorrow, suspicion, *subrusticus pudor*, discontent, cares, and weariness of life, surprise them on a sudden, and they can think of nothing else: continually suspecting, no sooner are their eyes open, but this infernal plague of melancholy seizeth on them, and terrifies their souls, representing some dismal object to their minds; which now, by no means, no labor, no persuasions, they can avoid, they cannot be rid of, they cannot resist.'

Something like this 'SCENE-TURNING' I have experienced at the evening parties, at the house of my good Catholic friend *Nov*——; who, by the aid of a capital organ, himself the most finished of players, converts his drawing-room into a chapel, his week days into Sundays, and these latter into minor heavens.[1]

When my friend commences upon one of those solemn anthems, which peradventure struck upon my heedless ear, rambling in the side aisles of the dim abbey, some five-and-thirty years since, waking a new sense, and putting a soul of old religion into my young apprehension—(whether it be *that*, in which the psalmist, weary of the persecutions of bad men, wisheth to himself dove's wings—or *that other* which, with a like measure of sobriety and pathos, inquireth by what means the young man shall best cleanse his mind)—a holy calm pervadeth me.—I am for the time

rapt above earth,
And possess joys not promised at my birth.

But when this master of the spell, not content to have laid a soul prostrate, goes on, in his power, to inflict more bliss than lies in her capacity to receive—impatient to overcome her 'earthly' with his 'heavenly,'—still pouring in, for protracted hours, fresh waves and fresh from the sea of sound, or from that inexhausted *German* ocean, above which, in triumphant progress, dolphin-seated, ride those Arions *Haydn* and *Mozart*, with their attendant Tritons *Bach*, *Beethoven*, and a countless tribe, whom to attempt to reckon up would but plunge me again in the deeps,—I stagger under the weight of harmony, reeling to and fro at my wit's end;—clouds, as of frankincense, oppress me—priests, altars, censers, dazzle before me—the genius of *his* religion hath me in her toils—a shadowy triple tiara invests the brow of my friend, late so naked, so ingenuous—he is Pope,—and by him sits, like as in the anomaly of dreams, a she-Pope too,—tri-coroneted like himself!—I am converted, and yet a Protestant;—at once *malleus hereticorum*, and myself grand heresiarch: or three heresies center in my person: I am Marcion, Ebion, and Cerinthus—Gog and Magog—

---

[1] 'I have been there, and still would go. 'T is like a little heaven below.'—*Dr. Watts.*

what not?—till the coming in of the friendly supper-tray dissipates the figment, and a draught of true Lutheran beer (in which chiefly my friend shows himself no bigot) at once reconciles me to the rationalities of a purer faith; and restores to me the genuine unterrifying aspects of my pleasant-countenanced host and hostess.

(1821)

A DISSERTATION UPON ROAST PIG

MANKIND, says a Chinese manuscript which my friend M. was obliging enough to read and explain to me, for the first seventy thousand ages ate their meat raw, clawing or biting it from the living animal, just as they do in Abyssinia to this day. This period is not obscurely hinted at by their great Confucius in the second chapter of his Mundane Mutations, where he designates a kind of golden age by the term Cho-fang, literally the Cooks' holiday. The manuscript goes on to say, that the art of roasting, or rather broiling (which I take to be the elder brother) was accidentally discovered in the manner following. The swine-herd, Ho-ti, having gone out into the woods one morning, as his manner was, to collect mast for his hogs, left his cottage in the care of his eldest son Bo-bo, a great lubberly boy, who being fond of playing with fire, as younkers of his age commonly are, let some sparks escape into a bundle of straw, which kindling quickly, spread the conflagration over every part of their poor mansion, till it was reduced to ashes. Together with the cottage (a sorry antediluvian makeshift of a building, you may think it), what was of much more importance, a fine litter of new-farrowed pigs, no less than nine in number, perished. China pigs have been esteemed a luxury all over the East from the remotest periods that we read of. Bo-bo was in the utmost consternation, as you may think, not so much for the sake of the tenement, which his father and he could easily build up again with a few dry branches, and the labor of an hour or two, at any time, as for the loss of the pigs. While he was thinking what he should say to his father, and wringing his hands over the smoking remnants of one of those untimely sufferers, an odor assailed his nostrils, unlike any scent which he had before experienced. What could it proceed from?—not from the burnt cottage—he had smelt that smell before—indeed this was by no means the first accident of the kind which had occurred through the negligence of this unlucky young firebrand. Much less did it resemble that of any known herb, weed, or flower. A premonitory moistening at the same time overflowed his nether lip. He knew not what to think. He next stooped down to feel the pig, if there were any signs of life in it. He burnt his fingers, and to cool them he applied them in his booby fashion to his mouth. Some of the crumbs of the scorched skin had come away with his fingers, and for the first time in his life (in the world's life indeed, for before him no man had known it) he tasted—*crackling!* Again he felt and fumbled at the pig. It did not burn him so much now, still he licked his fingers from a sort of habit. The truth at length broke into his slow understanding, that it was the pig that smelt so, and the pig that tasted so delicious; and, surrendering himself up to the new-born pleasure, he fell to tearing up whole handfuls of the scorched skin with the flesh next it, and was cramming it down his throat in his beastly fashion, when his sire entered amid the smoking rafters, armed with retributory cudgel, and finding how affairs stood, began to rain blows upon the young rogue's shoulders, as thick as hail-stones, which Bo-bo heeded not any more than if they had been flies. The tickling pleasure, which he experienced in his lower regions, had rendered him quite callous to any inconveniences he might feel in those remote quarters. His father might lay on, but he could not beat him from his pig, till he had fairly made an end of it, when, becoming a little more sensible of his situation, something like the following dialogue ensued.

'You graceless whelp, what have you got there devouring? Is it not enough that you have burnt me down three houses with your dog's tricks, and be hanged to you, but you must be eating fire, and I know not what—what have you got there, I say?'

'O father, the pig, the pig, do come and taste how nice the burnt pig eats.'

The ears of Ho-ti tingled with horror. He cursed his son and he cursed himself that ever he should beget a son that should eat burnt pig.

Bo-bo, whose scent was wonderfully sharpened since morning, soon raked out another pig, and fairly rending it asunder, thrust the lesser half by main force into the fists of Ho-ti, still shouting out, 'Eat, eat, eat the burnt pig, father, only taste,—O Lord,'—with suchlike barbarous ejaculations, cramming all the while as if he would choke.

Ho-ti trembled in every joint while he grasped the abominable thing, wavering whether he should not put his son to death for an unnatural young monster, when the crackling scorching his fingers, as it had done his son's, and applying the same remedy to them, he in his turn tasted some of its flavor, which, make what sour mouths he would for a pretense, proved not altogether displeasing to him. In conclusion (for the manuscript here is a little tedious) both father and son fairly sat down to the mess, and never left off till they had despatched all that remained of the litter.

Bo-bo was strictly enjoined not to let the secret escape, for the neighbors would certainly have stoned them for a couple of abominable wretches, who could think of improving upon the good meat which God had sent them. Nevertheless, strange stories got about. It was observed that Ho-ti's cottage was burnt down now more frequently than ever. Nothing but fires from this time forward. Some would break out in broad day, others in the night-time. As often as the sow farrowed, so sure was the house of Ho-ti to be in a blaze; and Ho-ti himself, which was the more remarkable, instead of chastising his son, seemed to grow more indulgent to him than ever. At length they were watched, the terrible mystery discovered, and father and son summoned to take their trial at Pekin, then an inconsiderable assize town. Evidence was given, the obnoxious food itself produced in court, and verdict about to be pronounced, when the foreman of the jury begged that some of the burnt pig, of which the culprits stood accused, might be handed into the box. He handled it, and they all handled it, and burning their fingers, as Bo-bo and his father had done before them, and nature prompting to each of them the same remedy, against the face of all the facts, and the clearest charge which judge had ever given,—to the surprise of the whole court, townsfolk, strangers, reporters, and all present—without leaving the box, or any manner of consultation whatever, they brought in a simultaneous verdict of Not Guilty.

The judge, who was a shrewd fellow, winked at the manifest iniquity of the decision; and, when the court was dismissed, went privily, and bought up all the pigs that could be had for love or money. In a few days his lordship's town house was observed to be on fire. The thing took wing, and now there was nothing to be seen but fires in every direction. Fuel and pigs grew enormously dear all over the districts. The insurance offices one and all shut up shop. People built slighter and slighter every day, until it was feared that the very science of architecture would in no long time be lost to the world. Thus this custom of firing houses continued, till in process of time, says my manuscript, a sage arose, like our Locke, who made a discovery, that the flesh of swine, or indeed of any other animal, might be cooked (*burnt*, as they called it) without the necessity of consuming a whole house to dress it. Then first began the rude form of a gridiron. Roasting by the string, or spit, came in a century or two later, I forget in whose dynasty. By such slow degrees, concludes the manuscript, do the most useful, and seemingly the most obvious arts, make their way among mankind.

Without placing too implicit faith in the account above given, it must be agreed, that if a worthy pretext for so dangerous an experiment as setting houses on fire (especially in these days) could be assigned in favor of any culinary object, that pretext and excuse might be found in ROAST PIG.

Of all the delicacies in the whole *mundus edibilis*, I will maintain it to be the most delicate —*princeps obsoniorum*.

I speak not of your grown porkers—things between pig and pork—those hobbydehoys— but a young and tender suckling—under a moon old—guiltless as yet of the sty—with no original speck of the *amor immunditiæ*, the hereditary failing of the first parent, yet manifest— his voice as yet not broken, but something between a childish treble, and a grumble—the mild forerunner, or *præludium*, of a grunt.

He must be roasted. I am not ignorant that our ancestors ate them seethed, or boiled—but what a sacrifice of the exterior tegument!

There is no flavor comparable, I will contend, to that of the crisp, tawny, well-watched, not over-roasted, *crackling*, as it is well called—the very teeth are invited to their share of the pleasure at this banquet in overcoming the coy, brittle resistance—with the adhesive oleaginous— O call it not fat—but an indefinable sweetness growing up to it—the tender blossoming of fat —fat cropped in the bud—taken in the shoot— in the first innocence—the cream and quintessence of the child-pig's yet pure food—the lean, no lean, but a kind of animal manna—or, rather, fat and lean (if it must be so) so blended and running into each other, that both together make but one ambrosian result, or common substance.

Behold him, while he is doing—it seemeth rather a refreshing warmth, than a scorching heat, that he is so passive to. How equably he twirleth round the string! Now he is just done. To see the extreme sensibility of that tender age, he hath wept out his pretty eyes—radiant jellies—shooting stars—

See him in the dish, his second cradle, how meek he lieth!—wouldst thou have had this innocent grow up to the grossness and indocility which too often accompany maturer swinehood? Ten to one he would have proved a glutton, a sloven, an obstinate, disagreeable animal—wallowing in all manner of filthy conversation—from these sins he is happily snatched away—

Ere sin could blight, or sorrow fade,
Death came with timely care—

his memory is odoriferous—no clown curseth, while his stomach half rejecteth, the rank bacon—no coalheaver bolteth him in reeking sausages—he hath a fair sepulcher in the grateful stomach of the judicious epicure—and for such a tomb might be content to die.

He is the best of sapors. Pineapple is great. She is indeed almost too transcendent—a delight, if not sinful, yet so like to sinning, that really a tender-conscienced person would do well to pause—too ravishing for mortal taste, she woundeth and excoriateth the lips that approach her—like lovers' kisses, she biteth—she is a pleasure bordering on pain from the fierceness and insanity of her relish—but she stoppeth at the palate—she meddleth not with the appetite—and the coarsest hunger might barter her consistently for a mutton chop.

Pig—let me speak his praise—is no less provocative of the appetite, than he is satisfactory to the criticalness of the censorious palate. The strong man may batten on him, and the weakling refuseth not his mild juices.

Unlike to mankind's mixed characters, a bundle of virtues and vices, inexplicably intertwisted, and not to be unraveled without hazard, he is—good throughout. No part of him is better or worse than another. He helpeth, as far as his little means extend, all around. He is the least envious of banquets. He is all neighbors' fare.

I am one of those who freely and ungrudgingly impart a share of the good things of this life which fall to their lot (few as mine are in this kind) to a friend. I protest I take as great an interest in my friend's pleasures, his relishes, and proper satisfactions, as in mine own. 'Presents,' I often say, 'endear Absents.' Hares, pheasants, partridges, snipes, barndoor chickens (those 'tame villatic fowl'), capons, plovers, brawn, barrels of oysters, I dispense as freely as I receive them. I love to taste them, as it were, upon the tongue of my friend. But a stop must be put somewhere. One would not, like Lear, 'give everything.' I make my stand upon pig. Methinks it is an ingratitude to the Giver of all good flavors, to extradomiciliate, or send out of the house, slightingly (under pretext of friendship, or I know not what), a blessing so particularly adapted, predestined, I may say, to my individual palate—It argues an insensibility.

* * *

Our ancestors were nice in their method of sacrificing these tender victims. We read of pigs whipt to death with something of a shock, as we hear of any other obsolete custom. The age of discipline is gone by, or it would be curious to inquire (in a philosophical light merely) what effect this process might have towards intenerating and dulcifying a substance, naturally so mild and dulcet as the flesh of young pigs. It looks like refining a violet. Yet we should be cautious, while we condemn the inhumanity, how we censure the wisdom of the practice. It might impart a gusto—

I remember an hypothesis, argued upon by the young students, when I was at St. Omer's, and maintained with much learning and pleasantry on both sides, 'Whether, supposing that the flavor of a pig who obtained his death by whipping (*per flagellationem extremam*) superadded a pleasure upon the palate of a man more intense than any possible suffering we can conceive in the animal, is man justified in using that method of putting the animal to death?' I forget the decision.

His sauce should be considered. Decidedly, a few bread crumbs, done up with his liver and brains, and a dash of mild sage. But, banish, dear Mrs. Cook, I beseech you, the whole onion tribe. Barbecue your whole hogs to your palate, steep them in shalots, stuff them out with plantations of the rank and guilty garlic; you cannot poison them, or make them stronger than they are—but consider, he is a weakling—a flower. (1822)

SIR WALTER SCOTT (1771-1832)

Scott's birthplace was Edinburgh. His father, a solicitor of creditable standing, had been the first of his family to adopt a town life, and Scott early evinced an innate attraction toward those ancestors who for centuries had linked their history with the stirring life of the Border. 'You will find me a rattle-skulled, half-lawyer, half-sportsman, through whose head a regiment of horse has been exercising since he was five years old,' he once wrote to a stranger. Lameness derived from a fever kept him inactive as a child and he was dreamy and fond of reading. As he grew up he entered robustly into outdoor sports; but his choicest pastime was cruising about the countryside after relics of folklore. Passing through the High-School and the College in Edinburgh, he studied law and, in 1792, became an advocate. His taste for country residence led him to settle on the Esk at Lasswade after his marriage in 1798, and from here as Sheriff of Selkirkshire, he removed to Ashestiel on the Tweed, in 1804. His *Border Minstrelsy* had appeared in 1802, and now his poems, *Lay of the Last Minstrel* (1805), *Marmion* (1808), *Lady of the Lake* (1810), and others in quick sequence began to supplement his profession as a means of livelihood. In 1812 he succeeded to a salary of £1300 as clerk of session, and he proceeded to materialize his dream of a feudal estate by purchasing, as nucleus, a hundred acres of rough land five miles down the Tweed at Abbotsford. Thither he removed with 'twenty-five cartloads of the veriest trash in nature, besides dogs, pigs, ponies, poultry, cows, calves'; he gives an amusing and significant account of 'the procession of my furniture, in which old swords, bows, targets, and lances, made a very conspicuous show. A family of turkeys was accommodated within the helmet of some *preux chevalier* of ancient border fame; and the very cows, for aught I know, were bearing banners and muskets.' From Abbotsford came the series of historical novels, beginning with *Waverley* (1814) and closing with *Castle Dangerous* (1831),—twenty-nine novels in half as many years. The quantity of energy which Scott poured into these works of fiction,—to say nothing of his edition of Swift and *Life of Napoleon*,—while discharging his official duties and engaging in all the activities of a country-gentleman, is almost inconceivable. In addition, the work of his last years was done in sharp adversity. Soon after his marriage he had entered into a secret partnership with James and John Ballantyne, publishers of Edinburgh, and this business had been complicated with that of Constable and Co. His partners were feeble managers; only the extraordinary success of the novels had tided over a crisis for several years. It is estimated that Scott's writings earned him, during his lifetime, nearly a million dollars; but his outlay at Abbotsford and in other directions had been excessively lavish, and greatly increased after he was knighted in 1820. The crash came in 1825; Constable, the Ballantynes, and Scott went down together. From the age of fifty-five to sixty, in spite of breaking health and failing imagination, he wrought doggedly with his pen to pay off £117,000 of debt. When the end came nearly half the debt remained; but this was extinguished by his copyrights after his death. In any event, Scott's character would have lived as one signally illustrious and lovable; his last years conferred upon it the quality of heroism. The real sweep and variety of his genius is denoted in his novels. His poetry is, nevertheless, animated and stirring, and well exemplifies his power of delineating, with bold, free strokes, scenic background and enterprising action.

From MARMION, CANTO VI

Not far advanced was morning day
When Marmion did his troop array
   To Surrey's camp to ride;
He had safe-conduct for his band
Beneath the royal seal and hand,   5
   And Douglas gave a guide.
The ancient earl with stately grace
Would Clara on her palfrey place,
And whispered in an undertone,
'Let the hawk stoop, his prey is flown.'   10
The train from out the castle drew,
But Marmion stopped to bid adieu:
   'Though something I might plain,' he said,
'Of cold respect to stranger guest,
Sent hither by your king's behest.   15
   While in Tantallon's towers I stayed,
Part we in friendship from your land,
And, noble earl, receive my hand.'—

But Douglas round him drew his cloak,
Folded his arms, and thus he spoke:— 20
'My manors, halls, and bowers shall still
Be open at my sovereign's will
To each one whom he lists, howe'er
Unmeet to be the owner's peer.
My castles are my king's alone, 25
From turret to foundation-stone—
The hand of Douglas is his own,
And never shall in friendly grasp
The hand of such as Marmion clasp.'

Burned Marmion's swarthy cheek like fire 30
And shook his very frame for ire,
  And—'This to me!' he said,
'An 't were not for thy hoary beard,
Such hand as Marmion's had not spared
  To cleave the Douglas' head! 35
And first I tell thee, haughty peer,
He who does England's message here,
Although the meanest in her state,
May well, proud Angus, be thy mate;
And, Douglas, more I tell thee here, 40
  Even in thy pitch of pride,
Here in thy hold, thy vassals near,—
Nay, never look upon your lord,
And lay your hands upon your sword,—
  I tell thee, thou'rt defied! 45
And if thou saidst I am not peer
To any lord in Scotland here,
Lowland or Highland, far or near,
  Lord Angus, thou hast lied!'
On the earl's cheek the flush of rage 50
O'ercame the ashen hue of age:
Fierce he broke forth,—'And darest thou then
To beard the lion in his den,
  The Douglas in his hall?
And hopest thou hence unscathed to go?— 55
No, by Saint Bride of Bothwell, no!
Up drawbridge, grooms—what, warder, ho!
  Let the portcullis fall,—'
Lord Marmion turned,—well was his need,—
And dashed the rowels in his steed, 60
Like arrow through the archway sprung
The ponderous grate behind him rung;
To pass there was such scanty room,
The bars descending razed his plume.

The steed along the drawbridge flies 65
Just as it trembled on the rise;
Not lighter does the swallow skim
Along the smooth lake's level brim:
And when Lord Marmion reached his band,
He halts, and turns with clenchèd hand, 70
And shout of loud defiance pours,
And shook his gauntlet at the towers.
'Horse! horse!' the Douglas cried, 'and chase!'
But soon he reigned his fury's pace:
'A royal messenger he came, 75
Though most unworthy of the name.—
A letter forged! Saint Jude to speed!

Did ever knight so foul a deed?[1]
At first in heart it liked me ill
When the king praised his clerkly skill. 80
Thanks to Saint Bothan, son of mine,
Save Gawain, ne'er could pen a line;
So swore I, and I swear it still,
Let my boy-bishop fret his fill.—
Saint Mary mend my fiery mood! 85
Old age ne'er cools the Douglas blood,
I thought to slay him where he stood.
'T is pity of him too,' he cried:
'Bold can he speak and fairly ride,
I warrant him a warrior tried.' 90
With this his mandate he recalls,
And slowly seeks his castle halls.

The day in Marmion's journey wore;
Yet, ere his passion's gust was o'er,
They crossed the heights of Stanrig-moor. 95
His troop more closely there he scanned,
And missed the Palmer from the band.
'Palmer or not,' young Blount did say,
'He parted at the peep of day;
Good sooth, it was in strange array.' 100
'In what array?' said Marmion quick.
'My lord, I ill can spell the trick;
But all night long with clink and bang
Close to my couch did hammers clang;
At dawn the falling drawbridge rang, 105
And from a loophole while I peep,
Old Bell-the-Cat came from the keep,
Wrapped in a gown of sables fair,
As fearful of the morning air;
Beneath, when that was blown aside, 110
A rusty shirt of mail I spied,
By Archibald won in bloody work
Against the Saracen and Turk;
Last night it hung not in the hall.
I thought some marvel would befall. 115
And next I saw them saddled lead
Old Cheviot forth, the earl's best steed,
A matchless horse, though something old,
Prompt in his paces, cool and bold.
I heard the Sheriff Sholto say 120
The earl did much the Master pray
To use him on the battle-day;
But he preferred'—'Nay, Henry, cease!
Thou sworn horse-courser, hold thy peace.—
Eustace, thou bear'st a brain—I pray, 125
What did Blount see at break of day?'

[1] Lest the reader should partake of the Earl's astonishment and consider the crime as inconsistent with the manners of the period, I have to remind him of the numerous forgeries (partly executed by a female assistant) devised by Robert of Artois, to forward his suit against the Countess Matilda; which, being detected, occasioned his flight into England, and proved the remote cause of Edward the Third's memorable wars in France. John Harding, also, was expressly hired by Edward IV to forge such documents as might appear to establish the claim of fealty asserted over Scotland by the English monarchs.

'In brief, my lord, we both descried—
For then I stood by Henry's side—
The Palmer mount and outwards ride
    Upon the earl's own favorite steed.   130
All sheathed he was in armor bright,
And much resembled that same knight
Subdued by you in Cotswold fight;
    Lord Angus wished him speed.'—
The instant that Fitz-Eustace spoke,   135
A sudden light on Marmion broke:—
'Ah! dastard fool, to reason lost!'
He muttered; ' 'T was nor fay nor ghost
I met upon the moonlight wold,
But living man of earthly mold,   140
    O dotage blind and gross!
Had I but fought as wont, one thrust
Had laid De Wilton in the dust,
    My path no more to cross.—
How stand we now?—he told his tale   145
To Douglas, and with some avail;
'T was therefore gloomed his rugged brow.—
Will Surrey dare to entertain
'Gainst Marmion charge disproved and vain?
    Small risk of that, I trow.   150
Yet Clare's sharp questions must I shun,
Must separate Constance from the nun—
Oh! what a tangled web we weave
When first we practise to deceive!
A Palmer too!—no wonder why   155
I felt rebuked beneath his eye;
I might have known there was but one
Whose look could quell Lord Marmion.'

Stung with these thoughts, he urged to speed
His troop, and reached at eve the Tweed,   160
Where Lennel's convent closed their march
There now is left but one frail arch,
    Yet mourn thou not its cells;
Our time a fair exchange has made:
Hard by, in hospitable shade   165
    A reverend pilgrim dwells,
Well worth the whole Bernardine brood
That e'er wore sandal, frock, or hood.
Yet did Saint Bernard's abbot there
Give Marmion entertainment fair,   170
And lodging for his train and Clare.
Next morn the baron climbed the tower,
To view afar the Scottish power,
    Encamped on Flodden edge;
The white pavilions made a show   175
Like remnants of the winter snow
    Along the dusky ridge.
Long Marmion looked:—at length his eye
Unusual movement might descry
    Amid the shifting lines;   180
The Scottish host drawn out appears,
For, flashing on the hedge of spears,
    The eastern sunbeam shines.
Their front now deepening, now extending,
Their flank inclining, wheeling, bending,   185
Now drawing back, and now descending,

The skilful Marmion well could know
They watched the motions of some foe
Who traversed on the plain below.
Even so it was. From Flodden ridge   190
    The Scots beheld the English host
    Leave Barmore-wood, their evening post,
    And heedful watched them as they crossed
The Till by Twisel Bridge.
    High sight it is and haughty, while   195
    They dive into the deep defile;
    Beneath the caverned cliff they fall,
    Beneath the castle's airy wall.
By rock, by oak, by hawthorn-tree.
    Troop after troop are disappearing;   200
    Troop after troop their banners rearing
Upon the eastern bank you see;
Still pouring down the rocky den
    Where flows the sullen Till,
And rising from the dim-wood glen,   205
Standards on standards, men on men,
    In slow succession still,
And sweeping o'er the Gothic arch,
And pressing on, in ceaseless march,
    To gain the opposing hill.   210
That morn, to many a trumpet clang,
Twisel! thy rock's deep echo rang,
And many a chief of birth and rank,
Saint Helen! at thy fountain drank.
Thy hawthorn glade, which now we see   215
In spring-tide bloom so lavishly,
Had then from many an axe its doom,
To give the marching columns room.
And why stands Scotland idly now,
Dark Flodden! on thy airy brow,   220
Since England gains the pass the while
And struggles through the deep defile?
What checks the fiery soul of James?
Why sits that champion of the dames
    Inactive on his steed,   225
And sees, between him and his land,
Between him and Tweed's southern strand,
    His host Lord Surrey lead?
What vails the vain knight-errant's brand?—
O Douglas, for thy leading wand!   230
    Fierce Randolph, for thy speed!
Oh! for one hour of Wallace wight,
Or well-skilled Bruce, to rule the fight
And cry, 'Saint Andrew and our right!'
Another sight had seen that morn,   235
From Fate's dark book a leaf been torn,
And Flodden had been Bannockbourne!—
The precious hour has passed in vain,
And England's host has gained the plain,
Wheeling their march and circling still   240
Around the base of Flodden hill.

Ere yet the bands met Marmion's eye,
Fitz-Eustace shouted loud and high,
'Hark! hark! my lord, an English drum!
And see ascending squadrons come   245
    Between Tweed's river and the hill,

Foot, horse, and cannon! Hap what hap,
My basnet to a prentice cap,
   Lord Surrey's o'er the Till!—
Yet more! yet more!—how fair arrayed   250
They file from out the hawthorn shade,
   And sweep so gallant by!
With all their banners bravely spread,
   And all their armor flashing high,
Saint George might waken from the dead,   255
   To see fair England's standards fly.'—
'Stint in thy prate,' quoth Blount, 'thou 'dst best,
And listen to our lord's behest.'—
With kindling brow Lord Marmion said,
'This instant be our band arrayed;   260
The river must be quickly crossed,
That we may join Lord Surrey's host.
If fight King James,—as well I trust
That fight he will, and fight he must,—
The Lady Clare behind our lines   265
Shall tarry while the battle joins.'

Himself he swift on horseback threw,
   Scarce to the abbot bade adieu,
Far less would listen to his prayer
To leave behind the helpless Clare.   270
Down to the Tweed his band he drew,
And muttered as the flood they view,
'The pheasant in the falcon's claw,
He scarce will yield to please a daw;
Lord Angus may the abbot awe,   275
So Clare shall bide with me.'
Then on that dangerous ford and deep
Where to the Tweed Leat's eddies creep,
   He ventured desperately:
And not a moment will he bide   280
Till squire or groom before him ride;
Headmost of all he stems the tide,
   And stems it gallantly.
Eustace held Clare upon her horse,
   Old Hubert led her rein,   285
Stoutly they braved the current's course,
And, though far downward driven perforce,
   The southern bank they gain.
Behind them straggling came to shore,
   As best they might, the train: 290
Each o'er his head his yew-bow bore,
   A caution not in vain;
Deep need that day that every string,
By wet unharmed, should sharply ring.
A moment then Lord Marmion stayed,   295
And breathed his steed, his men arrayed,
   Then forward moved his band,
Until, Lord Surrey's rear-guard won,
He halted by a cross of stone,
That on a hillock standing lone   300
   Did all the field command.

Hence might they see the full array
   Of either host for deadly fray;
Their marshaled lines stretched east and west,
   And fronted north and south.   305
And distant salutation passed
   From the loud cannon mouth;
Not in the close successive rattle
That breathes the voice of modern battle,
   But slow and far between.   310
The hillock gained, Lord Marmion stayed:
'Here, by this cross,' he gently said,
   'You well may view the scene.
Here shalt thou tarry, lovely Clare:
Oh! think of Marmion in thy prayer!—   315
Thou wilt not?—well, no less my care
Shall, watchful, for thy weal prepare.—
You, Blount and Eustace, are her guard,
   With ten picked archers of my train;
With England if the day go hard,   320
   To Berwick speed amain.—
But if we conquer, cruel maid,
My spoils shall at your feet be laid,
   When here we meet again.'
He waited not for answer there,   325
And would not mark the maid's despair,
   Nor heed the discontented look
From either squire, but spurred amain,
And dashing through the battle-plain,
   His way to Surrey took.   330

'The good Lord Marmion, by my life!
   Welcome to danger's hour!—
Short greeting serves in time of strife.—
   Thus have I ranged my power:
Myself will rule this central host,   335
   Stout Stanley fronts their right,
My sons command the vaward post,
   With Brian Tunstall, stainless knight;
Lord Dacre, with his horsemen light,
Shall be in rearward of the fight,   340
   And succor those that need it most.
Now gallant Marmion, well I know,
   Would gladly to the vanguard go;
Edmund, the Admiral, Tunstall there,
With thee their charge will blithely share;   345
There fight thine own retainers too
Beneath De Burg, thy steward true.'
'Thanks, noble Surrey!' Marmion said,
Nor further greeting there he paid,
But, parting like a thunderbolt,   350
   First in the vanguard made a halt,
Where such a shout there rose
Of 'Marmion! Marmion!' that the cry,
Up Flodden mountain shrilling high,
   Startled the Scottish foes.   355

Blount and Fitz-Eustace rested still
With Lady Clare upon the hill,
On which—for far the day was spent—
The western sunbeams now were bent;
The cry they heard, its meaning knew,   360
Could plain their distant comrades view:
   Sadly to Blount did Eustace say,
'Unworthy office here to stay!
No hope of gilded spurs to-day.—

But see! look up—on Flodden bent 365
The Scottish foe has fired his tent.'
  And sudden, as he spoke,
From the sharp ridges of the hill,
All downward to the banks of Till,
  Was wreathed in sable smoke. 370
Volumed and vast, and rolling far,
The cloud enveloped Scotland's war
  As down the hill they broke;
Nor martial shout, nor minstrel tone,
Announced their march; their tread alone, 375
  At times one warning trumpet blown,
  At times a stifled hum,
Told England, from his mountain-throne
  King James did rushing come.
Scarce could they hear or see their foes. 380
Until at weapon-point they close.—
They close in clouds of smoke and dust,
With sword-sway and with lance's thrust;
  And such a yell was there,
Of sudden and portentous birth, 385
As if men fought upon the earth,
  And fiends in upper air:
Oh! life and death were in the shout,
Recoil and rally, charge and rout,
  And triumph and despair. 390
Long looked the anxious squires; their eye
Could in the darkness nought descry.

At length the freshening western blast
Aside the shroud of battle cast;
And first the ridge of mingled spears 395
Above the brightening cloud appears,
And in the smoke the pennons flew,
As in the storm the white seamew.
Then marked they, dashing broad and far,
The broken billows of the war, 400
And plumèd crests of chieftains brave
Floating like foam upon the wave;
  But nought distinct they see:
Wide raged the battle on the plain;
Spears shook and falchions flashed amain; 405
Fell England's arrow-flight like rain;
Crests rose, and stooped, and rose again
  Wild and disorderly.
Amid the scene of tumult, high
They saw Lord Marmion's falcon fly; 410
And stainless Tunstall's banner white,
And Edmund Howard's lion bright,
Still bear them bravely in the fight,
  Although against them come
Of gallant Gordons many a one, 415
And many a stubborn Badenoch-man,
And many a rugged Border clan,
  With Huntly and with Home.—

Far on the left, unseen the while,
Stanley broke Lennox and Argyle, 420
Though there the western mountaineer
Rushed with bare bosom on the spear,
And flung the feeble targe aside,
And with both hands the broadsword plied.
'T was vain.—But Fortune, on the right, 425
With fickle smile cheered Scotland's fight.
Then fell that spotless banner white,
  The Howard's lion fell;
Yet still Lord Marmion's falcon flew
With wavering flight, while fiercer grew 430
  Around the battle-yell.
The Border slogan rent the sky!
A Home! a Gordon! was the cry:
  Loud were the clanging blows;
Advanced,—forced back,—now low, now high,
  The pennon sunk and rose; 436
As bends the bark's mast in the gale,
When rent are rigging, shrouds, and sail,
  It wavered mid the foes.
No longer Blount the view could bear: 440
'By heaven and all its saints! I swear
  I will not see it lost!
Fitz-Eustace, you with Lady Clare
May bid your beads and patter prayer,—
  I gallop to the host.' 445
And to the fray he rode amain,
Followed by all the archer train.
The fiery youth, with desperate charge,
Made for a space an opening large,—
  The rescued banner rose,— 450
But darkly closed the war around,
Like pine-tree rooted from the ground
  It sank among the foes.
Then Eustace mounted too,—yet stayed,
As loath to leave the helpless maid, 455
  When, fast as shaft can fly,
Bloodshot his eyes, his nostrils spread,
The loose rein dangling from his head,
Housing and saddle bloody red,
Lord Marmion's steed rushed by: 460
And Eustace, maddening at the sight,
  A look and sign to Clara cast
To mark he would return in haste,
Then plunged into the fight.

Ask me not what the maiden feels, 465
  Left in that dreadful hour alone:
Perchance her reason stoops or reels;
Perchance a courage, not her own,
  Braces her mind to desperate tone.—
The scattered van of England wheels;— 470
  She only said, as loud in air
The tumult roared, 'Is Wilton there?'—
  They fly, or, maddened by despair,
Fight but to die,—'Is Wilton there?'
With that, straight up the hill there rode 475
  Two horsemen drenched with gore,
And in their arms, a helpless load,
  A wounded knight they bore.
His hand still strained the broken brand;
His arms were smeared with blood and sand.
Dragged from among the horses' feet, 481
With dinted shield and helmet beat,
The falcon-crest and plumage gone.

Can that be haughty Marmion! . . .
Young Blount his armor did unlace, 485
And, gazing on his ghastly face,
  Said, 'By Saint George, he's gone!
That spear-wound has our master sped,
And see the deep cut on his head!
  Good-night to Marmion.'— 490
'Unnurtured Blount! thy brawling cease:
He opes his eyes,' said Eustace; 'peace!'

When, doffed his casque, he felt free air,
Around gan Marmion wildly stare:
'Where's Harry Blount? Fitz-Eustace where?
Linger ye here, ye hearts of hare! 495
Redeem my pennon,—charge again!
Cry, "Marmion to the rescue!"—Vain!
Last of my race, on battle-plain
That shout shall ne'er be heard again!— 500
Yet my last thought is England's—fly,
  To Dacre bear my signet-ring:
  Tell him his squadrons up to bring.—
Fitz-Eustace, to Lord Surrey hie:
  Tunstall lies dead upon the field, 505
  His lifeblood stains the spotless shield;
  Edmund is down; my life is reft;
  The Admiral alone is left.
Let Stanley charge with spur of fire,—
With Chester charge, and Lancashire, 510
Full upon Scotland's central host,
Or victory and England's lost.—
Must I bid twice?—hence, varlets fly!—
  Leave Marmion here alone—to die.'
They parted, and alone he lay; 515
  Clare drew her from the sight away,
Till pain wrung forth a lowly moan,
And half he murmured, 'Is there none
  Of all my halls have nurst,
Page, squire, or groom, one cup to bring 520
  Of blessèd water from the spring,
  To slake my dying thirst!'

O Woman! in our hours of ease
Uncertain, coy, and hard to please,
And variable as the shade 525
By the light quivering aspen made;
When pain and anguish wring the brow,
A ministering angel thou!—
Scarce were the piteous accents said,
When with the baron's casque the maid 530
  To the nigh streamlet ran:
Forgot were hatred, wrongs, and fears;
The plaintive voice alone she hears,
  Sees but the dying man.
She stooped her by the runnel's side, 535
  But in abhorrence backward drew;
For, oozing from the mountain's side
Where raged the war, a dark-red tide
  Was curdling in the streamlet blue.
Where shall she turn?—behold her mark 540
  A little fountain cell,
Where water, clear as diamond spark,
  In a stone basin fell.
Above, some half-worn letters say,

  𝔇𝔯𝔦𝔫𝔨· 𝔴𝔢𝔞𝔯𝔶· 𝔭𝔦𝔩𝔤𝔯𝔦𝔪· 𝔡𝔯𝔦𝔫𝔨· 𝔞𝔫𝔡· 𝔭𝔯𝔞𝔶·
  𝔉𝔬𝔯· 𝔱𝔥𝔢· 𝔨𝔦𝔫𝔡· 𝔰𝔬𝔲𝔩· 𝔬𝔣· 𝔖𝔦𝔟𝔶𝔩· 𝔊𝔯𝔢𝔶·
  𝔚𝔥𝔬· 𝔟𝔲𝔦𝔩𝔱· 𝔱𝔥𝔦𝔰· 𝔠𝔯𝔬𝔰𝔰· 𝔞𝔫𝔡· 𝔴𝔢𝔩𝔩·

She filled the helm and back she hied,
And with surprise and joy espied
  A monk supporting Marmion's head; 550
A pious man, whom duty brought
To dubious verge of battle fought,
  To shrive the dying, bless the dead.

Deep drank Lord Marmion of the wave,
And, as she stooped his brow to lave— 555
'Is it the hand of Clare,' he said,
'Or injured Constance, bathes my head?'
  Then, as remembrance rose,—
'Speak not to me of shrift or prayer!
  I must redress her woes. 560
Short space, few words, are mine to spare;
Forgive and listen, gentle Clare!'
  'Alas!' she said, 'the while.—
Oh! think of your immortal weal!
In vain for Constance is your zeal! 565
  She—died at Holy Isle.'—
Lord Marmion started from the ground
As light as if he felt no wound,
Though in the action burst the tide
In torrents from his wounded side. 570
'Then it was truth,' he said—'I knew
That the dark presage must be true.—
I would the Fiend, to whom belongs
The vengeance due to all her wrongs,
  Would spare me but a day! 575
For wasting fire, and dying groan,
And priests slain on the altar stone,
  Might bribe him for delay.
It may not be!—this dizzy trance—
Curse on yon base marauder's lance, 580
And doubly cursed my failing brand!
A sinful heart makes feeble hand.'
Then fainting down on earth he sunk,
Supported by the trembling monk.

With fruitless labor Clara bound 585
And strove to stanch the gushing wound:
The monk with unavailing cares
Exhausted all the Church's prayers.
Ever, he said, that close and near,
A lady's voice was in his ear, 590
And that the priest he could not hear;
  For that she ever sung,
'*In the lost battle borne down by the flying,
Where mingles war's rattle with groans of the
    dying!*'
  So the notes rung.— 595
'Avoid thee, Fiend!—with cruel hand
Shake not the dying sinner's sand!—
Oh! look, my son, upon yon sign
Of the Redeemer's grace divine;
  Oh! think on faith and bliss!— 600

By many a death-bed I have been,
And many a sinner's parting seen,
  But never aught like this.'
The war, that for a space did fail,
Now trebly thundering swelled the gale, 605
  And 'Stanley!' was the cry;—
A light on Marmion's visage spread,
  And fired his glazing eye;
With dying hand above his head
He shook the fragment of his blade, 610
  And shouted 'Victory!—
Charge, Chester, charge! On, Stanley, on!'
Were the last words of Marmion.

By this, though deep the evening fell,
Still rose the battle's deadly swell, 615
For still the Scots, around their king,
Unbroken, fought in desperate ring.
Where's now their victor vaward wing,
  Where Huntly, and where Home?—
O for a blast of that dread horn 620
On Fontarabian echoes borne,
  That to King Charles did come,
When Rowland brave, and Oliver,
And every paladin and peer,
  On Roncesvalles died! 625
Such blast might warn them, not in vain,
To quit the plunder of the slain,
And turn the doubtful day again,
  While yet on Flodden side,
Afar, the Royal Standard flies, 630
And round it toils, and bleeds, and dies,
  Our Caledonian pride!
In vain the wish—for far away,
While spoil and havoc mark their way,
Near Sybil's Cross the plunderers stray. 635
'O, Lady,' cried the Monk, 'away!'
  And placed her on her steed,
And led her to the chapel fair,
  Of Tillmouth upon Tweed.
There all the night they spent in prayer, 640
And at the dawn of morning, there
She met her kinsman, Lord Fitz-Clare.

But as they left the dark'ning heath,
More desperate grew the strife of death.
The English shafts in volleys hail'd, 645
In headlong charge their horse assail'd;
Front, flank, and rear, the squadrons sweep
To break the Scottish circle deep,
  That fought around their King.
But yet, though thick the shafts as snow, 650
Though charging knights like whirlwinds go,
Though bill-men ply the ghastly blow,
  Unbroken was the ring;
The stubborn spearmen still made good
Their dark impenetrable wood, 655
Each stepping where his comrade stood,
  The instant that he fell.
No thought was there of dastard flight;
Link'd in the serried phalanx tight,

Groom fought like noble, squire like knight, 660
  As fearlessly and well;
Till utter darkness closed her wing
O'er their thin host and wounded King.
Then skilful Surrey's sage commands
Led back from strife his shattered bands; 665
  And from the charge they drew,
As mountain-waves, from wasted lands,
  Sweep back to ocean blue.
Then did their loss his foeman know;
Their King, their Lords, their mightiest low,
They melted from the field as snow, 670
When streams are swol'n and south winds blow,
  Dissolves in silent dew.
Tweed's echoes heard the ceaseless plash,
  While many a broken band, 675
Disorder'd through her currents dash,
  To gain the Scottish land;
To town and tower, to down and dale,
To tell red Flodden's dismal tale,
And raise the universal wail. 680
Tradition, legend, tune, and song,
Shall many an age that tune prolong;
Still from the sire the son shall hear
Of the stern strife, and carnage drear,
  Of Flodden's fatal field, 685
Where shivered was fair Scotland's spear,
  And broken was her shield!

Day dawns upon the mountain's side:—
There, Scotland! lay thy bravest pride,
Chiefs, knights, and nobles, many a one: 690
The sad survivors all are gone.—
View not that corpse mistrustfully,
Defaced and mangled though it be;
Nor to yon Border castle high,
Look northward with upbraiding eye; 695
  Nor cherish hope in vain,
That, journeying far on foreign strand,
The Royal Pilgrim to his land
  May yet return again.
He saw the wreck his rashness wrought; 700
Reckless of life, he desperate fought,
  And fell on Flodden plain.
And well in death his trusty brand,
Firm clench'd within his manly hand,
Beseem'd the Monarch slain. 705
But, O! how chang'd since yon blithe night!—
Gladly I turn me from the sight,
  Unto my tale again.

Short is my tale:—Fitz-Eustace' care
A pierced and mangled body bare 710
To moated Lichfield's lofty pile;
And there, beneath the southern aisle,
A tomb, with Gothic sculpture fair,
Did long Lord Marmion's image bear,
(Now vainly for its site you look; 715
'Twas levell'd, when fanatic Brook
The fair cathedral stormed and took;
But, thanks to Heaven, and good Saint Chad,

A guerdon meet the spoiler had!)
There erst was martial Marmion found, 720
His feet upon a couchant hound,
 His hands to heaven upraised;
And all around, on scutcheon rich,
And tablet carved, and fretted niche,
 His arms and feats were blazed. 725
And yet, though all was carved so fair,
And priest for Marmion breathed the prayer,
The last Lord Marmion lay not there.
From Ettrick woods a peasant swain
Followed his lord to Flodden plain,— 730
One of those flowers, whom plaintive lay
In Scotland mourns as 'wede away':
Sore wounded, Sybil's Cross he spied,
And dragged him to its foot and died,
Close by the noble Marmion's side. 735
The spoilers stripp'd and gash'd the slain,
And thus their corpses were mista'en;
And thus, in the proud Baron's tomb,
The lowly woodsman took the room.

Less easy task it were, to show 740
Lord Marmion's nameless grave, and low.
 They dug his grave e'en where he lay,
  But every mark is gone;
 Time's wasting hand has done away
 The simple cross of Sybil Gray, 745
  And broke her font of stone;
But yet out from the little hill
Oozes the slender springlet still.
 Oft halts the stranger there,
For thence may best his curious eye 750
The memorable field descry;
 And shepherd boys repair
To seek the water-flag and rush,
And rest them by the hazel bush,
 And plait their garlands fair; 755
Nor dream they sit upon the grave
That holds the bones of Marmion brave.—
When thou shalt find the little hill,
With thy heart commune and be still.
If ever, in temptation strong, 760
Thou left'st the right path for the wrong;
If every devious step, thus trod,
Still led thee further from the road;
Dread thou to speak presumptuous doom
On noble Marmion's lowly tomb; 765

But say, 'He died a gallant knight,
With sword in hand, for England's right.'

* * *

        (1808)

SOLDIER, REST!

Soldier, rest! thy warfare o'er,
 Sleep the sleep that knows not breaking;
Dream of battled fields no more,
 Days of danger, nights of waking.
In our isle's enchanted hall, 5
 Hands unseen thy couch are strewing,
Fairy strains of music fall,
 Every sense in slumber dewing.
Soldier, rest! thy warfare o'er,
Dream of fighting fields no more; 10
Sleep the sleep that knows not breaking
Morn of toil, nor night of waking.

No rude sound shall reach thine ear,
 Armor's clang, or war-steed champing,
Trump nor pibroch summon here 15
 Mustering clan or squadron tramping.
Yet the lark's shrill fife may come
 At the daybreak from the fallow,
And the bittern sound his drum,
 Booming from the sedgy shallow. 20
Ruder sounds shall none be near,
Guards nor warders challenge here,
Here's no war-steed's neigh and champing,
Shouting clans of squadrons stamping.

Huntsman, rest! thy chase is done; 25
 While our slumbrous spells assail ye,
Dream not, with the rising sun,
 Bugles here shall sound reveillé.
Sleep! the deer is in his den;
 Sleep! thy hounds are by thee lying: 30
Sleep! nor dream in yonder glen
 How thy gallant steed lay dying.
Huntsman, rest! thy chase is done;
Think not of the rising sun,
For at dawning to assail ye 35
Here no bugles sound reveillé.

        (1810)

GEORGE NOEL GORDON, LORD BYRON (1788-1824)

BYRON's father, a military rake known as 'mad Jack Byron,' had squandered his wife's estate and terminated an ill-spent life within three years after the poet's birth in a London lodging house. His mother was a 'mad Gordon.' Byron therefore was half Scotch, and part of his childhood was spent in Scotland. His early training, chiefly at the hands of nurses and tutors, was incoherent and 'shabby-genteel.' When ten years of age he succeeded to the titles and estates of his uncle, 'the wicked Lord Byron' of Newstead. At Harrow (1801-5), in spite of a deformed ankle which the torture of surgeons had failed to correct and which his pride and sensitiveness converted into a curse, he was energetic in sports and laid the basis of those athletic habits which remained with him through life. While at Trinity College, Cambridge, he brought out his first volume of poems, *Hours of Idleness* (1807). To the ridicule of the *Edinburgh Review* he retorted angrily and with some vigor in his *English Bards and Scotch Reviewers* (1809), then left England for two years of travel in Spain, Greece and the Levant, and, on his return, published the first two cantos of *Childe Harold's Pilgrimage* (1812). The effect was electrical. Young, proud, traveled, mysteriously unhappy, romantically wicked, with a countenance of wild insolent beauty, a poet and a peer, Byron became the rage. Under such circumstances poetry is not critically scanned for its deeper elements. Byron's powers were sufficient for the occasion. From the midst of the social whirl into which he was caught up he extemporized tale after tale. *The Giaour, The Bride of Abydos, The Corsair, Lara*, followed each other in swift succession. Scott seemed local and tame, Marmion a schoolboy. Fashion followed and the critics fawned. Then came Byron's marriage, and a year later, his separation, and in 'one of those periodical spasms of British morality' his worshippers suddenly discovered that their idol had been a monster. Byron left England never to return alive. In Switzerland he met Shelley, and the two poets spent some months together among the Alps, an intimacy of great value to both, which they afterward renewed in Italy. From this time Byron's poetry, though still unequal, showed a deeper quality and his activity increased. The third canto of *Childe Harold, The Prisoner of Chillon*, and many short pieces of new sincerity and strength were finished, and *Manfred* begun, in Switzerland. In the autumn of 1816 he settled at Venice, and, except for short tours, remained there until in 1819 he removed to Ravenna in order to be near the Countess Guiccioli. He became domiciled with that lady in 1819, and in 1821 they moved to Pisa. Throughout his Italian residence Byron had been greatly interested in the plans for Italian independence, and had constantly given aid and comfort to the Carbonari. In 1823 he resolved to devote his fortune and services to the cause of Greek freedom, and it was while assisting in the organization of the patriot forces in Greece, that he succumbed to a fever at Missolonghi when only thirty-six years of age. During his seven years in Italy Byron had completed *Manfred* (1817) and written seven other dramas, and had added a fourth canto to *Childe Harold*. What was more important he had discovered in *Beppo* (1818) the serio-comic vein in which his real strength lay, had produced in *The Vision of Judgment* (1821) the sublimest of parodies, and in *Don Juan* (1819-23) his masterpiece. Few poets are so difficult to represent by selections as Byron. His lyrics do not exhibit him to advantage, and extracts from his more ambitious work give but a poor idea of his variety, sweep, and vitality. Great faults and great virtues 'antithetically mixed'; a spirit hampered by mal-direction, affectation, and self-sophistication, but when it gets free, giant and fine; an imagination full of clay and crudities, but volleying at times into prodigious passion, reality, and compass; this is Byron.

SONNET ON CHILLON

ETERNAL Spirit of the chainless Mind!
Brightest in dungeons, Liberty! thou art,
For there thy habitation is the heart—
The heart which love of thee alone can bind;

And when thy sons to fetters are consigned—   5
To fetters, and the damp vault's dayless gloom,
Their country conquers with their martyrdom,
And Freedom's fame finds wings on every wind.

Chillon! thy prison is a holy place,
And thy sad floor an altar—for 't was trod,   10
Until his very steps have left a trace
Worn, as if thy cold pavement were a sod,
By Bonnivard! May none those marks efface!
For they appeal from tyranny to God.

December 5, 1816.

From CHILDE HAROLD, CANTO III

Adieu to thee, fair Rhine! How long delighted
The stranger fain would linger on his way!
Thine is a scene alike where souls united
Or lonely Contemplation thus might stray;
And could the ceaseless vultures cease to prey   5
On self-condemning bosoms, it were here,
Where Nature, nor too somber nor too gay,
Wild but not rude, awful yet not austere,
Is to the mellow Earth as Autumn to the year.

Adieu to thee again! a vain adieu!   10
There can be no farewell to scene like thine;
The mind is colored by thy every hue;
And if reluctantly the eyes resign
Their cherished gaze upon thee, lovely Rhine!
'T is with the thankful heart of parting praise;
More mighty spots may rise, more glaring shine,
But none unite in one attaching maze   17
The brilliant, fair, and soft,—the glories of old days,

The negligently grand, the fruitful bloom
Of coming ripeness, the white city's sheen,   20
The rolling stream, the precipice's gloom,
The forest's growth and Gothic walls between,
The wild rocks shaped as they had turrets been,
In mockery of man's art; and these withal
A race of faces happy as the scene,   25
Whose fertile bounties here extend to all,
Still springing o'er thy banks, though Empires near them fall.

But these recede. Above me are the Alps,
The palaces of Nature, whose vast walls   29
Have pinnacled in clouds their snowy scalps,
And throned Eternity in icy halls
Of cold sublimity, where forms and falls
The avalanche—the thunderbolt of snow!
All that expands the spirit, yet appalls,
Gather around these summits, as to show   35
How earth may pierce to Heaven, yet leave vain man below.

But ere these matchless heights I dare to scan,
There is a spot should not be passed in vain,—
Morat! the proud, the patriot field! where man
May gaze on ghastly trophies of the slain,   40
Nor blush for those who conquered on that plain;
Here Burgundy bequeathed his tombless host,
A bony heap, through ages to remain,
Themselves their monument; the Stygian coast
Unsepulchered they roamed, and shrieked each wandering ghost.   45

While Waterloo with Cannæ's carnage vies,
Morat and Marathon twin names shall stand;
They were true Glory's stainless victories,
Won by the unambitious heart and hand
Of a proud, brotherly, and civic band,   50
All unbought champions in no princely cause
Of vice-entailed Corruption; they no land
Doomed to bewail the blasphemy of laws
Making kings' rights divine, by some Draconic clause.

By a lone wall a lonelier column rears   55
A gray and grief-worn aspect of old days:
'T is the last remnant of the wreck of years,
And looks as with the wild-bewildered gaze
Of one to stone converted by amaze,   59
Yet still with consciousness; and there it stands
Making a marvel that it not decays,
When the coeval pride of human hands,
Leveled Adventicum hath strewed her subject lands.

And there—oh! sweet and sacred be the name!—
Julia—the daughter, the devoted—gave   65
Her youth to Heaven; her heart, beneath a claim
Nearest to Heaven's, broke o'er a father's grave.
Justice is sworn 'gainst tears, and hers would crave
The life she lived in; but the judge was just,
And then she died on him she could not save.   70
Their tomb was simple, and without a bust,
And held within their urn one mind, one heart, one dust.

But these are deeds which should not pass away,
And names that must not wither though the earth
Forgets her empires with a just decay,   75
The enslavers and the enslaved, their death and birth;
The high, the mountain-majesty of worth
Should be, and shall, survivor of its woe,
And from its immortality look forth
In the sun's face, like yonder Alpine snow,   80
Imperishably pure beyond all things below.

Lake Leman woos me with its crystal face,
The mirror where the stars and mountains view
The stillness of their aspect in each trace
Its clear depth yields of their far height and hue;   85
There is too much of man here, to look through
With a fit mind the might which I behold;
But soon in me shall Loneliness renew
Thoughts hid, but not less cherished than of old,
Ere mingling with the herd had penned me in their fold.   90

To fly from, need not be to hate, mankind:
All are not fit with them to stir and toil,
Nor is it discontent to keep the mind
Deep in its fountain lest it overboil
In the hot throng, where we become the spoil   95
Of our infection, till too late and long
We may deplore and struggle with the coil,

In wretched interchange of wrong for wrong
Midst a contentious world, striving where none
    are strong.   99

There, in a moment we may plunge our years
In fatal penitence, and in the blight
Of our own soul turn all our blood to tears,
And color things to come with hues of Night;
The race of life becomes a hopeless flight
To those who walk in darkness: on the sea   105
The boldest steer but where their ports invite;
But there are wanderers o'er Eternity
Whose bark drives on and on, and anchored
    ne'er shall be.

Is it not better, then, to be alone,
And love Earth only for its earthly sake?   110
By the blue rushing of the arrowy Rhone,
Or the pure bosom of its nursing lake,
Which feeds it as a mother who doth make
A fair but froward infant her own care,
Kissing its cries away as these awake;—   115
Is it not better thus our lives to wear,
Than join the crushing crowd, doomed to inflict
    or bear?

I live not in myself, but I become
Portion of that around me; and to me
High mountains are a feeling, but the hum   120
Of human cities torture; I can see
Nothing to loathe in nature, save to be
A link reluctant in a fleshly chain,   123
Classed among creatures, when the soul can flee,
And with the sky, the peak, the heaving plain
Of ocean, or the stars, mingle, and not in vain.

And thus I am absorbed, and this is life:
I look upon the peopled desert past,
As on a place of agony and strife,
Where, for some sin, to sorrow I was cast,   130
To act and suffer, but remount at last
With a fresh pinion; which I feel to spring,
Though young, yet waxing vigorous as the blast
Which it would cope with, on delighted wing,
Spurning the clay-cold bonds which round our
    being cling.   135

And when, at length, the mind shall be all free
From what it hates in this degraded form,
Reft of its carnal life, save what shall be
Existent happier in the fly and worm—
When elements to elements conform,   140
And dust is as it should be, shall I not
Feel all I see, less dazzling, but more warm?
The bodiless thought? the Spirit of each spot?
Of which, even now, I share at times the im-
    mortal lot?   144

Are not the mountains, waves, and skies, a part
Of me and of my soul, as I of them?
Is not the love of these deep in my heart
With a pure passion? should I not contemn
All objects, if compared with these? and stem
A tide of suffering, rather than forego   150
Such feelings for the hard and worldly phlegm
Of those whose eyes are only turned below,
Gazing upon the ground, with thoughts which
    dare not glow?

But this is not my theme; and I return
To that which is immediate, and require   155
Those who find contemplation in the urn,
To look on One, whose dust was once all fire,
A native of the land where I respire
The clear air for a while—a passing guest
Where he became a being,—whose desire   160
Was to be glorious; 't was a foolish quest,
The which to gain and keep, he sacrificed all
    rest.

Here the self-torturing sophist, wild Rousseau,
The apostle of affliction, he who threw
Enchantment over passion, and from woe   165
Wrung overwhelming eloquence, first drew
The breath which made him wretched; yet he
    knew
How to make madness beautiful and cast
O'er erring deeds and thoughts a heavenly hue
Of words, like sunbeams, dazzling as they past
The eyes, which o'er them shed tears feelingly
    and fast.   171

His love was passion's essence:—as a tree
On fire by lightning, with ethereal flame
Kindled he was, and blasted; for to be
Thus, and enamored, were in him the same.   175
But his was not the love of living dame,
Nor of the dead who rise upon our dreams,
But of ideal beauty, which became
In him existence, and o'erflowing teems
Along his burning page, distempered though it
    seems.   180

This breathed itself to life in Julie, *this*
Invested her with all that 's wild and sweet;
This hallowed, too, the memorable kiss
Which every morn his fevered lip would greet,
From hers, who but with friendship his would
    meet;   185
But to that gentle touch through brain and
    breast
Flashed the thrilled spirit's love-devouring
    heat;
In that absorbing sigh perchance more blest
Than vulgar minds may be with all they seek
    possest.   189

His life was one long war with self-sought foes,
Or friends, by him self-banished; for his mind
Had grown Suspicion's sanctuary, and chose,
For its own cruel sacrifice, the kind,
'Gainst whom he raged with fury strange and
    blind.

But he was phrensied,—wherefore, who may
    know? 195
Since cause might be which skill could never
    find;
But he was phrensied by disease or woe,
To that worst pitch of all, which wears a rea-
    soning show.

For then he was inspired, and from him came,
As from the Pythian's mystic cave of yore, 200
Those oracles which set the world in flame,
Nor ceased to burn till kingdoms were no more:
Did he not this for France? which lay before
Bowed to the inborn tyranny of years?
Broken and trembling to the yoke she bore, 205
Till by the voice of him and his compeers
Roused up to too much wrath, which follows
    o'ergrown fears?

They made themselves a fearful monument!
The wreck of old opinions—things which grew,
Breathed from the birth of time: the veil they
    rent, 210
And what behind it lay, all earth shall view.
But good with ill they also overthrew,
Leaving but ruins, wherewith to rebuild
Upon the same foundation, and renew
Dungeons and thrones, which the same hour
    refilled, 215
As heretofore, because ambition was self-willed.

But this will not endure, nor be endured!
Mankind have felt their strength, and made
    it felt.
They might have used it better, but, allured
By their new vigor, sternly have they dealt 220
On one another; pity ceased to melt
With her once natural charities. But they
Who in oppression's darkness caved had dwelt,
They were not eagles, nourished with the day;
What marvel then, at times, if they mistook
    their prey? 225

What deep wounds ever closed without a scar?
The heart's bleed longest, and but heal to wear
That which disfigures it; and they who war
With their own hopes, and have been van-
    quished, bear
Silence, but not submission: in his lair 230
Fixed Passion holds his breath, until the hour
Which shall atone for years; none need despair:
It came, it cometh, and will come,—the power
To punish or forgive—in *one* we shall be slower.

Clear, placid Leman! thy contrasted lake, 235
With the wild world I dwelt in, is a thing
Which warns me, with its stillness, to forsake
Earth's troubled waters for a purer spring.
This quiet sail is as a noiseless wing
To waft me from distraction; once I loved 240
Torn ocean's roar, but thy soft murmuring

Sounds sweet as if a Sister's voice reproved,
That I with stern delights should e'er have been
    so moved.

It is the hush of night, and all between 244
Thy margin and the mountains, dusk, yet clear,
Mellowed and mingling, yet distinctly seen,
Save darkened Jura, whose capt heights appear
Precipitously steep; and drawing near,
There breathes a living fragrance from the shore,
Of flowers yet fresh with childhood; on the ear
Drops the light drip of the suspended oar, 251
Or chirps the grasshopper one good-night carol
    more.

He is an evening reveler, who makes
His life an infancy, and sings his fill;
At intervals, some bird from out the brakes 255
Starts into voice a moment, then is still.
There seems a floating whisper on the hill,
But that is fancy, for the starlight dews
All silently their tears of love instil,
Weeping themselves away, till they infuse 260
Deep into nature's breast the spirit of her hues.

Ye stars! which are the poetry of heaven!
If in your bright leaves we would read the fate
Of men and empires,—'t is to be forgiven,
That in our aspirations to be great, 265
Our destinies o'erleap their mortal state,
And claim a kindred with you; for ye are
A beauty and a mystery, and create
In us such love and reverence from afar,
That fortune, fame, power, life, have named
    themselves a star. 270

All heaven and earth are still—though not in
    sleep,
But breathless, as we grow when feeling most;
And silent, as we stand in thoughts too deep:—
All heaven and earth are still: From the high
    host 274
Of stars, to the lulled lake and mountain coast,
All is concentered in a life intense,
Where not a beam, nor air, nor leaf is lost,
But hath a part of being, and a sense
Of that which is of all Creator and defence.

Then stirs the feeling infinite, so felt 280
In solitude, where we are *least* alone;
A truth, which through our being then doth
    melt,
And purifies from self: it is a tone,
The soul and source of music, which makes
    known
Eternal harmony, and sheds a charm 285
Like to the fabled Cytherea's zone,
Binding all things with beauty:—'t would dis-
    arm
The specter Death, had he substantial power
    to harm.

Not vainly did the early Persian make
His altar the high places, and the peak 290
Of earth-o'ergazing mountains, and thus take
A fit and unwalled temple, there to seek
The Spirit, in whose honor shrines are weak,
Upreared of human hands. Come, and compare
Columns and idol-dwellings, Goth or Greek, 295
With Nature's realms of worship, earth and air,
Nor fix on fond abodes to circumscribe thy prayer!

The sky is changed!—and such a change! Oh, night,
And storm, and darkness, ye are wondrous strong,
Yet, lovely in your strength, as is the light 300
Of a dark eye in woman! Far along,
From peak to peak, the rattling crags among
Leaps the live thunder! Not from one lone cloud,
But every mountain now hath found a tongue,
And Jura answers, through her misty shroud,
Back to the joyous Alps, who call to her aloud!

And this is in the night:—Most glorious night!
Thou wert not sent for slumber! let me be 308
A sharer in thy fierce and far delight,—
A portion of the tempest and of thee! 310
How the lit lake shines, a phosphoric sea,
And the big rain comes dancing to the earth!
And now again 't is black—and now, the glee
Of the loud hills shakes with its mountain-mirth, 314
As if they did rejoice o'er a young earthquake's birth.

Now, where the swift Rhone cleaves his way between
Heights which appear as lovers who have parted
In hate, whose mining depths so intervene,
That they can meet no more, though broken-hearted;
Though in their souls, which thus each other thwarted, 320
Love was the very root of the fond rage
Which blighted their life's bloom, and then departed:
Itself expired, but leaving them an age
Of years all winters,—war within themselves to wage:

Now, where the quick Rhone thus hath cleft his way, 325
The mightiest of the storms hath ta'en his stand:
For here, not one, but many, make their play,
And fling their thunder-bolts from hand to hand,
Flashing and cast around; of all the band,
The brightest through these parted hills hath forked 330
His lightnings,—as if he did understand,
That in such gaps as desolation worked,
There the hot shaft should blast whatever therein lurked.

Sky, mountains, river, winds, lake, lightnings! ye! 334
With night, and clouds, and thunder, and a soul
To make these felt and feeling, well may be
Things that have made me watchful; the far roll
Of your departing voices, is the knoll
Of what in me is sleepless,—if I rest.
But where of ye, O tempests! is the goal? 340
Are ye like those within the human breast?
Or do ye find, at length, like eagles, some high nest?

Could I embody and unbosom now
That which is most within me,—could I wreak
My thoughts upon expression, and thus throw
Soul, heart, mind, passions, feelings, strong or weak, 346
All that I would have sought, and all I seek,
Bear, know, feel, and yet breathe—into *one* word,
And that one word were Lightning, I would speak;
But as it is, I live and die unheard, 350
With a most voiceless thought, sheathing it as a sword.

The morn is up again, the dewy morn,
With breath all incense, and with cheek all bloom,
Laughing the clouds away with playful scorn,
And living as if earth contained no tomb,— 355
And glowing into day: we may resume
The march of our existence: and thus I,
Still on thy shores, fair Leman! may find room
And food for meditation, nor pass by
Much, that may give us pause, if pondered fittingly. 360

Clarens! sweet Clarens, birthplace of deep Love!
Thine air is the young breath of passionate thought;
Thy trees take root in Love; the snows above
The very Glaciers have his colors caught,
And sunset into rose-hues sees them wrought 365
By rays which sleep there lovingly; the rocks,
The permanent crags, tell here of Love, who sought
In them a refuge from the worldly shocks,
Which stir and sting the soul with hope that woos, then mocks. 369

Clarens! by heavenly feet thy paths are trod,—
Undying Love's, who here ascends a throne
To which the steps are mountains; where the god
Is a pervading life and light,—so shown

Not on those summits solely, nor alone
In the still cave and forest; o'er the flower 375
His eye is sparkling, and his breath hath blown,
His soft and summer breath, whose tender power
Passes the strength of storms in their most desolate hour.

All things are here of *him;* from the black pines,
Which are his shade on high, and the loud roar
Of torrents, where he listeneth, to the vines 381
Which slope his green path downward to the shore,
Where the bowed waters meet him, and adore,
Kissing his feet with murmurs; and the wood,
The covert of old trees, with trunks all hoar, 385
But light leaves, young as joy, stands where it stood,
Offering to him, and his, a populous solitude;

A populous solitude of bees and birds,
And fairy-formed and many-colored things,
Who worship him with notes more sweet than words, 390
And innocently open their glad wings,
Fearless and full of life: the gush of springs,
And fall of lofty fountains, and the bend
Of stirring branches, and the bud which brings
The swiftest thought of beauty, here extend,
Mingling, and made by Love, unto one mighty end. 396

He who hath loved not, here would learn that lore,
And make his heart a spirit; he who knows
That tender mystery, will love the more; 399
For this is Love's recess, where vain men's woes,
And the world's waste, have driven him far from those,
For 't is his nature to advance or die;
He stands not still, but or decays, or grows
Into a boundless blessing, which may vie
With the immortal lights, in its eternity! 405

'T was not for fiction chose Rousseau this spot,
Peopling it with affections; but he found
It was the scene which Passion must allot
To the mind's purified beings; 't was the ground
Where early Love his Psyche's zone unbound,
And hallowed it with loveliness; 't is lone, 411
And wonderful, and deep, and hath a sound,
And sense, and sight of sweetness; here the Rhone
Hath spread himself a couch, the Alps have reared a throne. 414

Lausanne! and Ferney! ye have been the abodes
Of names which unto you bequeathed a name;
Mortals, who sought and found, by dangerous roads,
A path to perpetuity of fame:
They were gigantic minds, and their steep aim
Was, Titan-like, on daring doubts to pile 420
Thoughts which should call down thunder and the flame
Of Heaven again assailed, if Heaven the while
On man and man's research could deign do more than smile.

The one was fire and fickleness, a child
Most mutable in wishes, but in mind 425
A wit as various,—gay, grave, sage, or wild,—
Historian, bard, philosopher, combined;
He multiplied himself among mankind,
The Proteus of their talents: But his own
Breathed most in ridicule,—which, as the wind,
Blew where it listed, laying all things prone,—
Now to o'erthrow a fool, and now to shake a throne. 432

The other, deep and slow, exhausting thought,
And hiving wisdom with each studious year,
In meditation dwelt, with learning wrought, 435
And shaped his weapon with an edge severe,
Sapping a solemn creed with solemn sneer;
The lord of irony,—that master-spell,
Which stung his foes to wrath, which grew from fear,
And doomed him to the zealot's ready Hell, 440
Which answers to all doubts so eloquently well.

Yet, peace be with their ashes,—for by them,
If merited, the penalty is paid;
It is not ours to judge,—far less condemn;
The hour must come when such things shall be made 445
Known unto all, or hope and dread allayed
By slumber, on one pillow in the dust,
Which, thus much we are sure, must lie decayed;
And when it shall revive, as is our trust,
'T will be to be forgiven, or suffer what is just.

But let me quit man's works, again to read 451
His Maker's, spread around me, and suspend
This page, which from my reveries I feed,
Until it seems prolonging without end.
The clouds above me to the white Alps tend,
And I must pierce them, and survey whate'er
May be permitted, as my steps I bend 457
To their most great and growing region, where
The earth to her embrace compels the powers of air. 459

* * *

I have not loved the world, nor the world me;
I have not flattered its rank breath, nor bowed
To its idolatries a patient knee,
Nor coined my cheek to smiles, nor cried aloud
In worship of an echo; in the crowd 464
They could not deem me one of such; I stood
Among them, but not of them; in a shroud
Of thoughts which were not their thoughts, and still could,
Had I not filled my mind, which thus itself subdued.

I have not loved the world, nor the world me,—
But let us part fair foes; I do believe, 470
Though I have found them not, that there may be
Words which are things, hopes which will not deceive,
And virtues which are merciful, nor weave
Snares for the failing; I would also deem 474
O'er others' griefs that some sincerely grieve;
That two, or one, are almost what they seem,
That goodness is no name, and happiness no dream.

* * *

(1817)

From CHILDE HAROLD, CANTO IV

Oh Rome! my country! City of the soul!
The orphans of the heart must turn to thee,
Lone mother of dead empires! and control
In their shut breasts their petty misery.
What are our woes and sufferance? Come and see 5
The cypress, hear the owl, and plod your way
O'er steps of broken thrones and temples, Ye!
Whose agonies are evils of a day—
A world is at our feet as fragile as our clay.

The Niobe of nations! there she stands 10
Childless and crownless, in her voiceless woe;
An empty urn within her withered hands,
Whose holy dust was scattered long ago;
The Scipios' tomb contains no ashes now;
The very sepulchers lie tenantless 15
Of their heroic dwellers: dost thou flow,
Old Tiber! through a marble wilderness?
Rise, with thy yellow waves, and mantle her distress.

The Goth, the Christian, Time, War, Flood, and Fire,
Have dealt upon the seven-hilled city's pride; 20
She saw her glories star by star expire,
And up the steep barbarian monarchs ride,
Where the car climbed the Capitol; far and wide
Temple and tower went down, nor left a site:
Chaos of ruins! who shall trace the void, 25
O'er the dim fragments cast a lunar light,
And say, 'here was, or is,' where all is doubly night?

The double night of ages, and of her,
Night's daughter, Ignorance, hath wrapt and wrap
All round us; we but feel our way to err: 30
The ocean hath his chart, the stars their map,
And Knowledge spreads them on her ample lap;
But Rome is as the desert, where we steer
Stumbling o'er recollection; now we clap
Our hands, and cry 'Eureka!' it is clear— 35
When but some false mirage of ruin rises near.

Alas! the lofty city! and alas!
The trebly hundred triumphs! and the day
When Brutus made the dagger's edge surpass
The conqueror's sword in bearing fame away! 40
Alas, for Tully's voice, and Virgil's lay,
And Livy's pictured page! but these shall be
Her resurrection; all beside—decay.
Alas, for Earth, for never shall we see
That brightness in her eye she bore when Rome was free! 45

Oh thou, whose chariot rolled on Fortune's wheel,
Triumphant Sylla! Thou, who didst subdue
Thy country's foes ere thou wouldst pause to feel
The wrath of thy own wrongs, or reap the due
Of hoarded vengeance till thine eagles flew 50
O'er prostrate Asia;—thou, who with thy frown
Annihilated senates—Roman, too,
With all thy vices, for thou didst lay down
With an atoning smile a more than earthly crown—

The dictatorial wreath—couldst thou divine 55
To what would one day dwindle that which made
Thee more than mortal? and that so supine
By aught than Romans, Rome should thus be laid?
She who was named Eternal, and arrayed
Her warriors but to conquer—she who veiled 60
Earth with her haughty shadow, and displayed,
Until the o'er-canopied horizon failed,
Her rushing wings—Oh! she who was Almighty hailed.

Sylla was first of victors; but our own,
The sagest of usurpers, Cromwell!—he 65
Too swept off senates while he hewed the throne
Down to a block—immortal rebel! See
What crimes it costs to be a moment free,
And famous through all ages! but beneath
His fate the moral lurks of destiny; 70
His day of double victory and death
Beheld him win two realms, and happier, yield his breath.

The third of the same moon whose former course
Had all but crowned him, on the selfsame day
Deposed him gently from his throne of force, 75
And laid him with the earth's preceding clay.
And showed not Fortune thus how fame and sway,
And all we deem delightful, and consume
Our souls to compass through each arduous way,
Are in her eyes less happy than the tomb? 80
Were they but so in man's, how different were his doom!

And thou, dread statue? yet existent in
The austerest form of naked majesty,
Thou who beheldest, 'mid the assassin's din,

At thy bathed base the bloody Cæsar lie, 85
Folding his robe in dying dignity,
An offering to thine altar from the queen
Of gods and men, great Nemesis! did he die,
And thou, too, perish, Pompey? have ye been
Victors of countless kings, or puppets of a scene?

And thou, the thunder-stricken nurse of Rome!
She-wolf! whose brazen-imaged dugs impart 92
The milk of conquest yet within the dome
Where, as a monument of antique art,
Thou standest:—Mother of the mighty heart, 95
Which the great founder sucked from thy wild teat,
Scorched by the Roman Jove's ethereal dart,
And thy limbs black with lightning—dost thou yet
Guard thine immortal cubs, nor thy fond charge forget?

Thou dost; but all thy foster-babes are dead—
The men of iron; and the world hath reared 101
Cities from out their sepulchers: men bled
In imitation of the things they feared,
And fought and conquered, and the same course steered,
At apish distance; but as yet none have, 105
Nor could, the same supremacy have neared,
Save one vain man, who is not in the grave,
But, vanquished by himself, to his own slaves a slave—

The fool of false dominion—and a kind
Of bastard Cæsar, following him of old 110
With steps unequal; for the Roman's mind
Was modeled in a less terrestrial mold,
With passions fiercer, yet a judgment cold,
And an immortal instinct which redeemed
The frailties of a heart so soft, yet bold, 115
Alcides with the distaff now he seemed
At Cleopatra's feet,—and now himself he beamed,

And came—and saw—and conquered! But the man
Who would have tamed his eagles down to flee,
Like a trained falcon, in the Gallic van, 120
Which he, in sooth, long led to victory,
With a deaf heart, which never seemed to be
A listener to itself, was strangely framed;
With but one weakest weakness—vanity,
Coquettish in ambition, still he aimed— 125
At what? can he avouch or answer what he claimed?

And would be all or nothing—nor could wait
For the sure grave to level him; few years
Had fixed him with the Cæsars in his fate,
On whom we tread: For *this* the conqueror rears 130
The arch of triumph; and for this the tears

And blood of earth flow on as they have flowed,
An universal deluge, which appears
Without an ark for wretched man's abode,
And ebbs but to reflow! Renew thy rainbow, God! 135

What from this barren being do we reap?
Our senses narrow, and our reason frail,
Life short, and truth a gem which loves the deep,
And all things weighed in custom's falsest scale;
Opinion an omnipotence,—whose veil 140
Mantles the earth with darkness, until right
And wrong are accidents, and men grow pale
Lest their own judgments should become too bright,
And their free thoughts be crimes, and earth have too much light.

And thus they plod in sluggish misery, 145
Rotting from sire to son, and age to age,
Proud of their trampled nature, and so die,
Bequeathing their hereditary rage
To the new race of inborn slaves, who wage
War for their chains, and rather than be free, 150
Bleed gladiator-like, and still engage
Within the same arena where they see
Their fellows fall before, like leaves of the same tree.

I speak not of men's creeds—they rest between
Man and his Maker—but of things allowed,
Averred, and known, and daily, hourly seen—
The yoke that is upon us doubly bowed, 157
And the intent of tyranny avowed,
The edict of Earth's rulers, who are grown
The apes of him who humbled once the proud,
And shook them from their slumbers on the throne; 161
Too glorious, were this all his mighty arm had done.

Can tyrants but by tyrants conquered be,
And Freedom find no champion and no child
Such as Columbia saw arise when she 165
Sprung forth a Pallas, armed and undefiled?
Or must such minds be nourished in the wild,
Deep in the unpruned forest 'midst the roar
Of cataracts, where nursing Nature smiled
On infant Washington? Has earth no more 170
Such seeds within her breast, or Europe no such shore?

But France got drunk with blood to vomit crime,
And fatal have her Saturnalia been
To Freedom's cause, in every age and clime;
Because the deadly days which we have seen, 175
And vile Ambition, that built up between
Man and his hopes an adamantine wall,
And the base pageant last upon the scene,
Are grown the pretext for the eternal thrall
Which nips life's tree, and dooms man's worst— his second fall. 180

Yet, Freedom! yet thy banner, torn, but flying,
Streams, like the thunder-storm *against* the wind;
Thy trumpet voice, though broken now and dying,
The loudest still the tempest leaves behind;
Thy tree hath lost its blossoms, and the rind, 185
Chopped by the axe, looks rough and little worth,
But the sap lasts,—and still the seed we find
Sown deep, even in the bosom of the North;
So shall a better spring less bitter fruit bring forth.

There is a stern round tower of other days, 190
Firm as a fortress, with its fence of stone,
Such as an army's baffled strength delays,
Standing with half its battlements alone,
And with two thousand years of ivy grown,
The garland of eternity, where wave 195
The green leaves over all by time o'erthrown:—
What was this tower of strength? within its cave
What treasure lay so locked, so hid?—A woman's grave.

But who was she, the lady of the dead,
Tombed in a palace? Was she chaste and fair? 200
Worthy a king's or more—a Roman's bed?
What race of chiefs and heroes did she bear?
What daughter of her beauties was the heir?
How lived, how loved, how died she? Was she not
So honored—and conspicuously there, 205
Where meaner relics must not dare to rot,
Placed to commemorate a more than mortal lot?

Was she as those who love their lords, or they
Who love the lords of others? such have been
Even in the olden time, Rome's annals say. 210
Was she a matron of Cornelia's mien,
Or the light air of Egypt's graceful queen,
Profuse of joy—or 'gainst it did she war,
Inveterate in virtue? Did she lean
To the soft side of the heart, or wisely bar 215
Love from amongst her griefs?—for such the affections are.

Perchance she died in youth: it may be bowed
With woes far heavier than the ponderous tomb
That weighed upon her gentle dust, a cloud
Might gather o'er her beauty, and a gloom 220
In her dark eye, prophetic of the doom
Heaven gives its favorites—early death; yet shed
A sunset charm around her, and illume
With hectic light, the Hesperus of the dead,
Of her consuming cheek the autumnal leaf-like red. 225

Perchance she died in age—surviving all,
Charms, kindred, children—with the silver gray
On her long tresses, which might yet recall,
It may be, still a something of the day

When they were braided, and her proud array 230
And lovely form were envied, praised, and eyed
By Rome—But whither would Conjecture stray?
Thus much alone we know—Metella died,
The wealthiest Roman's wife: Behold his love or pride!

I know not why—but standing thus by thee 235
It seems as if I had thine inmate known,
Thou Tomb! and other days come back to me
With recollected music, though the tone
Is changed and solemn, like a cloudy groan
Of dying thunder on the distant wind; 240
Yet could I seat me by this ivied stone
Till I had bodied forth the heated mind,
Forms from the floating wreck which Ruin leaves behind;

And from the planks, far shattered o'er the rocks,
Built me a little bark of hope, once more 245
To battle with the ocean and the shocks
Of the loud breakers, and the ceaseless roar
Which rushes on the solitary shore
Where all lies foundered that was ever dear:
But could I gather from the wave-worn store 250
Enough for my rude boat, where should I steer?
There woos no home, nor hope, nor life, save what is here.

Then let the winds howl on! their harmony
Shall henceforth be my music, and the night
The sound shall temper with the owlets' cry, 255
As I now hear them, in the fading light
Dim o'er the bird of darkness' native site,
Answering each other on the Palatine,
With their large eyes, all glistening gray and bright,
And sailing pinions.—Upon such a shrine 260
What are our petty griefs?—let me not number mine.

Cypress and ivy, weed and wallflower grown
Matted and massed together, hillocks heaped
On what were chambers, arch crushed, column strown
In fragments, choked up vaults, and frescoes steeped 265
In subterranean damps, where the owl peeped,
Deeming it midnight:—Temples, baths, or halls?
Pronounce who can; for all that Learning reaped
From her research hath been, that these are walls—
Behold the Imperial Mount! 't is thus the mighty falls. 270

There is the moral of all human tales;
'T is but the same rehearsal of the past,
First Freedom and then Glory—when that fails,

Wealth, vice, corruption,—barbarism at last,
And history, with all her volumes vast, 275
Hath but *one* page—'t is better written here,
Where gorgeous Tyranny hath thus amassed
All treasures, all delights, that eye or ear,
Heart, soul could seek, tongue ask—Away with
  words! draw near,

Admire, exult, despise, laugh, weep,—for
  here 280
There is such matter for all feeling:—Man!
Thou pendulum betwixt a smile and tear,
Ages and realms are crowded in this span,
This mountain, whose obliterated plan
The pyramid of empires pinnacled 285
Of Glory's gewgaws shining in the van
Till the sun's rays with added flame were filled!
Where are its golden roofs? where those who
  dared to build?

Tully was not so eloquent as thou,
Thou nameless column with the buried base! 290
What are the laurels of the Cæsar's brow?
Crown me with ivy from his dwelling-place
Whose arch or pillar meets me in the face.
Titus or Trajan's? No—'t is that of Time;
Triumph, arch, pillar, all he doth displace 295
Scoffing; and apostolic statues climb
To crush the imperial urn, whose ashes slept
  sublime,

Buried in air, the deep blue sky of Rome,
And looking to the stars: they had contained
A spirit which with these would find a home, 300
The last of those who o'er the whole earth
  reigned,
The Roman globe, for after none sustained,
But yielded back his conquests:—he was more
Than a mere Alexander, and, unstained
With household blood and wine, serenely
  wore 305
His sovereign virtues—still we Trajan's name
  adore.

* * *

Arches on arches! as it were that Rome,
Collecting the chief trophies of her line,
Would build up all her triumphs in one dome,
Her Coliseum stands; the moonbeams shine
As 't were its natural torches, for divine 311
Should be the light which streams here, to illume
This long-explored but still exhaustless mine
Of contemplation; and the azure gloom
Of an Italian night, where the deep skies
  assume 315

Hues which have words, and speak to ye of
  heaven,
Floats o'er this vast and wondrous monument,
And shadows forth its glory. There is given
Unto the things of earth, which Time hath bent,
A spirit's feeling, and where he hath leant 320

His hand, but broke his scythe, there is a power
And magic in the ruined battlement,
For which the palace of the present hour
Must yield its pomp, and wait till ages are its
  dower.

Oh, Time! the beautifier of the dead, 325
Adorner of the ruin, comforter
And only healer when the heart hath bled;
Time! the corrector where our judgments err,
The test of truth, love—sole philosopher, 329
For all beside are sophists—from thy thrift,
Which never loses though it doth defer—
Time, the avenger! unto thee I lift
My hands, and eyes, and heart, and crave of
  thee a gift:

Amidst this wreck, where thou hast made a
  shrine
And temple more divinely desolate, 335
Among thy mightier offerings here are mine,
Ruins of years, though few, yet full of fate:
If thou hast ever seen me too elate,
Hear me not; but if calmly I have borne
Good, and reserved my pride against the
  hate 340
Which shall not whelm me, let me not have worn
This iron in my soul in vain—shall *they* not
  mourn?

And thou, who never yet of human wrong
Left the unbalanced scale, great Nemesis!
Here, where the ancient paid thee homage
  long— 345
Thou, who didst call the Furies from the abyss,
And round Orestes bade them howl and hiss
For that unnatural retribution—just,
Had it but been from hands less near—in this
Thy former realm, I call thee from the dust!
Dost thou not hear my heart?—Awake! thou
  shalt, and must. 351

It is not that I may not have incurred
For my ancestral faults or mine the wound
I bleed withal, and had it been conferred
With a just weapon, it had flowed unbound; 355
But now my blood shall not sink in the ground:
To thee I do devote it—*thou* shalt take
The vengeance, which shall yet be sought and
  found
Which if *I* have not taken for the sake—
But let that pass—I sleep, but thou shalt yet
  awake. 360

And if my voice break forth, 't is not that now
I shrink from what is suffered: let him speak
Who hath beheld decline upon my brow,
Or seen my mind's convulsion leave it weak;
But in this page a record will I seek. 365
Not in the air shall these my words disperse,
Though I be ashes; a far hour shall wreak

The deep prophetic fulness of this verse,
And pile on human heads the mountain of my curse!
That curse shall be Forgiveness,—Have I not— 370
Hear me, my mother Earth! behold it, Heaven!—
Have I not had to wrestle with my lot?
Have I not suffered things to be forgiven?
Have I not had my brain seared, my heart riven,
Hopes sapped, name blighted, Life's life lied away? 375
And only not to desperation driven,
Because not altogether of such clay
As rots into the souls of those whom I survey.

From mighty wrongs to petty perfidy
Have I not seen what human things could do?
From the loud roar of foaming calumny 381
To the small whisper of the as paltry few,
And subtler venom of the reptile crew,
The Janus glance of whose significant eye,
Learning to lie with silence, would *seem* true, 385
And without utterance, save the shrug or sigh,
Deal round to happy fools its speechless obloquy.

But I have lived, and have not lived in vain:
My mind may lose its force, my blood its fire,
And my frame perish even in conquering pain;
But there is that within me which shall tire 391
Torture and Time, and breathe when I expire;
Something unearthly, which they deem not of,
Like the remembered tone of a mute lyre,
Shall on their softened spirits sink, and move 395
In hearts all rocky now the late remorse of love.

The seal is set.—Now welcome, thou dread power!
Nameless, yet thus omnipotent, which here
Walk'st in the shadow of the midnight hour
With a deep awe, yet all distinct from fear; 400
Thy haunts are ever where the dead walls rear
Their ivy mantles, and the solemn scene
Derives from thee a sense so deep and clear
That we become a part of what has been,
And grow unto the spot, all-seeing but unseen.

And here the buzz of eager nations ran, 406
In murmured pity, or loud-roared applause,
As man was slaughtered by his fellow man.
And wherefore slaughtered? wherefore, but because
Such were the bloody Circus' genial laws, 410
And the imperial pleasure.—Wherefore not?
What matters where we fall to fill the maws
Of worms—on battle-plains or listed spot?
Both are but theaters where the chief actors rot.

I see before me the Gladiator lie: 415
He leans upon his hand—his manly brow
Consents to death, but conquers agony,
And his drooped head sinks gradually low—
And through his side the last drops, ebbing slow
From the red gash, fall heavy, one by one, 420
Like the first of a thunder-shower; and now
The arena swims around him—he is gone,
Ere ceased the inhuman shout which hailed the wretch who won.

He heard it, but he heeded not—his eyes
Were with his heart, and that was far away; 425
He recked not of the life he lost nor prize,
But where his rude hut by the Danube lay,
There were his young barbarians all at play,
There was their Dacian mother—he, their sire,
Butchered to make a Roman holiday— 430
All this rushed with his blood—Shall he expire
And unavenged? Arise! ye Goths, and glut your ire!

But here, where Murder breathed her bloody steam;
And here, where buzzing nations choked the ways,
And roared or murmured like a mountain stream 435
Dashing or winding as its torrent strays;
Here, where the Roman millions' blame or praise
Was death or life, the playthings of a crowd,
My voice sounds much—and fall the stars' faint rays
On the arena void—seats crushed—walls bowed— 440
And galleries, where my steps seem echoes strangely loud.

A ruin—yet what ruin!—from its mass
Walls, palaces, half-cities, have been reared;
Yet oft the enormous skeleton ye pass,
And marvel where the spoil could have appeared. 445
Hath it indeed been plundered, or but cleared?
Alas! developed, opens the decay,
When the colossal fabric's form is neared:
It will not bear the brightness of the day,
Which streams too much on all, years, man have reft away. 450

But when the rising moon begins to climb
Its topmost arch, and gently pauses there;
When the stars twinkle through the loops of time,
And the low night-breeze waves along the air
The garland-forest, which the gray walls wear,
Like laurels on the bald first Cæsar's head; 456
When the light shines serene but doth not glare,
Then in this magic circle raise the dead:
Heroes have trod this spot—'t is on their dust ye tread.

'While stands the Coliseum, Rome shall stand;
When falls the Coliseum, Rome shall fall, 461

And when Rome falls—the World.' From our
    own land
Thus spake the pilgrims o'er this mighty wall
In Saxon times, which we are wont to call
Ancient; and these three mortal things are still
On their foundations, and unaltered all;   466
Rome and her Ruin past Redemption's skill,
The world, the same wide den—of thieves, or
    what ye will.

     * * * (1818)

From THE VISION OF JUDGMENT

In the first year of freedom's second dawn
    Died George the Third; although no tyrant,
        one
Who shielded tyrants, till each sense withdrawn
    Left him nor mental nor external sun;
A better farmer ne'er brushed dew from lawn, 5
A worse king never left a realm undone!
He died—but left his subjects still behind,
One half as mad—and t' other no less blind.

He died! his death made no great stir on earth:
    His burial made some pomp; there was pro-
        fusion   10
Of velvet, gilding, brass, and no great dearth
    Of aught but tears—save those shed by col-
        lusion.
For these things may be bought at their true
    worth;
    Of elegy there was the due infusion—
Bought also; and the torches, cloaks and ban-
    ners,   15
Heralds, and relics of old Gothic manners,

Formed a sepulchral melodrame. Of all
    The fools who flocked to swell or see the show,
Who cared about the corpse? The funeral
    Made the attraction, and the black the woe.
There throbbed not there a thought which
    pierced the pall;   21
    And when the gorgeous coffin was laid low,
It seemed the mockery of hell to fold
The rottenness of eighty years in gold.

So mix his body with the dust! It might   25
    Return to what it *must* far sooner, were
The natural compound left alone to fight
    Its way back into earth, and fire, and air;
But the unnatural balsams merely blight
    What nature made him at his birth, as bare 30
As the mere million's base unmummied clay—
    Yet all his spices but prolong decay.

He's dead—and upper earth with him has done;
    He's buried: save the undertaker's bill,
Or lapidary scrawl, the world is gone   35
    For him, unless he left a German will;
But where's the proctor who will ask his son?

In whom his qualities are reigning still,
Except that household virtue, most uncommon,
Of constancy to a bad, ugly woman.   40

'God save the king!' It is a large economy
    In God to save the like; but if he will
Be saving, all the better; for not one am I
    Of those who think damnation better still:
I hardly know too if not quite alone am I   45
    In this small hope of bettering future ill
By circumscribing, with some slight restriction,
The eternity of hell's hot jurisdiction.

I know this is unpopular; I know
    'T is blasphemous; I know one may be
        damned   50
For hoping no one else may e'er be so;
    I know my catechism; I know we've crammed
With the best doctrines till we quite o'erflow;
    I know that all save England's church have
        shammed,
And that the other twice two hundred churches
And synagogues have made a *damned* bad pur-
    chase.   56

God help us all! God help me too! I am,
    God knows, as helpless as the devil can wish,
And not a whit more difficult to damn,
    Than is to bring to land a late-hooked fish, 60
Or to the butcher to purvey the lamb;
    Not that I'm fit for such a noble dish,
As one day will be that immortal fry
Of almost everybody born to die.

Saint Peter sat by the celestial gate,   65
    And nodded o'er his keys; when, lo! there
        came
A wondrous noise he had not heard of late—
    A rushing sound of wind, and stream and
        flame;
In short, a roar of things extremely great,
    Which would have made aught save a saint
        exclaim;   70
But he, with first a start and then a wink,
Said, 'There's another star gone out, I think!'

But ere he could return to his repose,
    A cherub flapped his right wing o'er his eyes—
At which St. Peter yawned, and rubbed his
    nose: 75
    'Saint porter,' said the angel, 'prithee rise!'
Waving a goodly wing, which glowed, as glows
    An earthly peacock's tail, with heavenly dyes:
To which the saint replied, 'Well, what's the
    matter?
Is Lucifer come back with all this clatter?'   80

'No,' quoth the cherub; 'George the Third is
    dead.'
    'And who *is* George the Third?' replied the
        apostle:

'*What George? what Third?*' 'The king of England,' said
  The angel. 'Well! he won't find kings to jostle
Him on his way; but does he wear his head? 85
  Because the last we saw here had a tussle,
And ne'er would have got into heaven's good graces,
  Had he not flung his head in all our faces.

'He was, if I remember, king of France;
  That head of his, which could not keep a crown 90
On earth, yet ventured in my face to advance
  A claim to those of martyrs—like my own;
If I had had my sword, as I had once
  When I cut ears off, I had cut him down;
But having but my *keys*, and not my brand, 95
I only knock'd his head from out his hand.

'And then he set up such a headless howl,
  That all the saints came out and took him in;
And there he sits by St. Paul, cheek by jowl;
  That fellow Paul—the parvenú! The skin
Of St. Bartholomew, which makes his cowl 101
  In heaven, and upon earth redeemed his sin,
So as to make a martyr, never sped
Better than did this weak and wooden head.

'But had it come up here upon its shoulders, 105
  There would have been a different tale to tell
The fellow-feeling in the saints' beholders
  Seems to have acted on them like a spell,
And so this very foolish head heaven solders
  Back on its trunk: it may be very well, 110
And seems the custom here, to overthrow
Whatever has been wisely done below.'

The angel answered, 'Peter! do not pout:
  The king who comes has head and all entire,
And never knew much what it was about— 115
  He did as doth the puppet—by its wire,
And will be judged like all the rest, no doubt:
  My business and your own is not to inquire
Into such matters, but to mind our cue—
Which is to act as we are bid to do.' 120

While thus they spake, the angelic caravan
  Arriving like a rush of mighty wind,
Cleaving the fields of space, as doth the swan
  Some silver stream (say Ganges, Nile or Inde,
Or Thames, or Tweed), and 'midst them an old man 125
  With an old soul, and both extremely blind,
Halted before the gate, and in his shroud
Seated their fellow traveler on a cloud.

But bringing up the rear of this bright host
  A Spirit of a different aspect waved 130
His wings, like thunder-clouds above some coast
  Whose barren beach with frequent wrecks is paved;

His brow was like the deep when tempest-tossed;
  Fierce and unfathomable thoughts engraved
Eternal wrath on his immortal face, 135
And *where* he gazed a gloom pervaded space.

As he drew near, he gazed upon the gate
  Ne'er to be entered more by him or Sin,
With such a glance of supernatural hate,
  As made Saint Peter wish himself within; 140
He pattered with his keys at a great rate,
  And sweated through his apostolic skin:
Of course his perspiration was but ichor,
Or some such other spiritual liquor.

The very cherubs huddled all together, 145
  Like birds when soars the falcon; and they felt
A tingling to the tip of every feather,
  And formed a circle like Orion's belt
Around their poor old charge; who scarce knew whither
  His guards had led him, though they gently dealt 150
With royal manes (for by many stories,
And true, we learn the angels all are Tories).

As things were in this posture, the gate flew
  Asunder, and the flashing of its hinges
Flung over space an universal hue 155
  Of many-colored flame, until its tinges
Reached even our speck of earth, and made a new
  Aurora borealis spread its fringes
O'er the North Pole; the same seen, when ice-bound, 159
By Captain Parry's crew, in 'Melville's Sound.'

And from the gate thrown open issued beaming
  A beautiful and mighty Thing of Light,
Radiant with glory, like a banner streaming
  Victorious from some world-o'erthrowing fight:
My poor comparisons must needs be teeming
  With earthly likenesses, for here the night 166
Of clay obscures our best conceptions, saving
Johanna Southcote, or Bob Southey raving.

'T was the archangel Michael; all men know
  The make of angels and archangels, since 170
There's scarce a scribbler has not one to show,
  From the fiends' leader to the angels' prince;
There also are some altar-pieces, though
  I really can't say that they much evince
One's inner notions of immortal spirits; 175
But let the connoisseurs explain *their* merits.

Michael flew forth in glory and in good;
  A goodly work of him from whom all glory
And good arise; the portal past—he stood;
  Before him the young cherubs and saints hoary— 180

(I say *young*, begging to be understood
 By looks, not years; and should be very sorry
To state, they were not older than St. Peter,
 But merely that they seemed a little sweeter).

The cherubs and the saints bowed down before
 That arch-angelic hierarch, the first   186
Of essences angelical, who wore
 The aspect of a god; but this ne'er nursed
Pride in his heavenly bosom, in whose core
 No thought, save for his Master's service, durst   190
Intrude, however glorified and high;
He knew him but the viceroy of the sky.

He and the somber, silent Spirit met—
 They knew each other both for good and ill;
Such was their power, that neither could forget
 His former friend and future foe; but still   196
There was a high, immortal, proud regret
 In either's eye, as if 't were less their will
Than destiny to make the eternal years
Their date of war, and their 'champ clos' the spheres.   200

But here they were in neutral space: we know
 From Job, that Satan hath the power to pay
A heavenly visit thrice a year or so;
 And that the 'sons of God,' like those of clay,
Must keep him company; and we might show
 From the same book, in how polite a way   206
The dialogue is held between the Powers
Of Good and Evil—but 't would take up hours.

And this is not a theologic tract,
 To prove with Hebrew and with Arabic,   210
If Job be allegory or a fact,
 But a true narrative; and thus I pick
From out the whole but such and such an act
 As sets aside the slightest thought of trick.
'T is every tittle true, beyond suspicion,   215
And accurate as any other vision.

The spirits were in neutral space, before
 The gate of heaven; like eastern thresholds is
The place where Death's grand cause is argued o'er,
 And souls despatched to that world or to this;
And therefore Michael and the other wore   221
 A civil aspect; though they did not kiss,
Yet still between his Darkness and his Brightness
There passed a mutual glance of great politeness.

The Archangel bowed, not like a modern beau,
 But with a graceful Oriental bend,   226
Pressing one radiant arm just where below
 The heart in good men is supposed to tend;
He turned as to an equal, not too low,
 But kindly; Satan met his ancient friend   230
With more hauteur, as might an old Castilian
Poor noble meet a mushroom rich civilian.

He merely bent his diabolic brow
 An instant; and then raising it, he stood
In act to assert his right or wrong, and show   235
 Cause why King George by no means could or should
Make out a case to be exempt from woe
 Eternal, more than other kings, endued
With better sense and hearts, whom history mentions,
Who long have 'paved hell with their good intentions.'   240

Michael began: 'What wouldst thou with this man,
 Now dead, and brought before the Lord? What ill
Hath he wrought since his mortal race began,
 That thou canst claim him? Speak! and do thy will,
If it be just: if in this earthly span   245
 He hath been greatly failing to fulfil
His duties as a king and mortal, say,
And he is thine; if not, let him have way.'

'Michael!' replied the Prince of Air, 'even here,
 Before the Gate of him thou servest, must   250
I claim my subject: and will make appear
 That as he was my worshipper in dust,
So shall he be in spirit, although dear
 To thee and thine, because nor wine nor lust
Were of his weaknesses; yet on the throne   255
He reigned o'er millions to serve me alone.

'Look to *our* earth, or rather *mine*; it was,
 Once, more thy Master's: but I triumph not
In this poor planet's conquest; nor, alas!
 Need he thou servest envy me my lot: 260
With all the myriads of bright worlds which pass
 In worship round him, he may have forgot
Yon weak creation of such paltry things:
I think few worth damnation save their kings,—

'And these but as a kind of quit-rent, to   265
 Assert my right as lord: and even had
I such an inclination, it were (as you
 Well know) superfluous; they are grown so bad,
That hell has nothing better left to do
 Than leave them to themselves: so much more mad   270
And evil by their own internal curse,
Heaven cannot make them better, nor I worse.

'Look to the earth, I said, and say again:
 When this old, blind, mad, helpless, weak, poor worm   274
Began in youth's first bloom and flush to reign,
 The world and he both wore a different form,
And much of earth and all the watery plain
 Of ocean called him king: through many a storm

His isles had floated on the abyss of time;
For the rough virtues chose them for their clime. 280

'He came to his scepter young; he leaves it old:
  Look to the state in which he found his realm,
And left it; and his annals too behold,
  How to a minion first he gave the helm;
How grew upon his heart a thirst for gold, 285
  The beggar's vice, which can but overwhelm
The meanest hearts; and for the rest, but glance
Thine eye along America and France.

'T is true, he was a tool from first to last
  (I have the workmen safe), but as a tool 290
So let him be consumed. From out the past
  Of ages, since mankind have known the rule
Of monarchs—from the bloody rolls amassed
  Of sin and slaughter—from the Cæsar's school,
Take the worst pupil; and produce a reign 295
More drenched with gore, more cumbered with the slain.

'He ever warred with freedom and the free:
  Nations as men, home subjects, foreign foes,
So that they uttered the word "Liberty!"
  Found George the Third their first opponent. Whose 300
History was ever stained as his will be
  With national and individual woes?
I grant his household abstinence; I grant
His neutral virtues, which most monarchs want;

'I know he was a constant consort; own 305
  He was a decent sire, and middling lord.
All this is much, and most upon a throne;
  As temperance, if at Apicius' board,
Is more than at an anchorite's supper shown.
  I grant him all the kindest can accord; 310
And this was well for him, but not for those
Millions who found him what oppression chose.

'The New World shook him off; the Old yet groans
  Beneath what he and his prepared, if not
Completed: he leaves heirs on many thrones
  To all his vices, without what begot 316
Compassion for him—his tame virtues; drones
  Who sleep, or despots who have now forgot
A lesson which shall be re-taught them, wake
Upon the thrones of earth; but let them quake!

'Five millions of the primitive, who hold 321
  The faith which makes ye great on earth, implored
A *part* of that vast *all* they held of old,—
  Freedom to worship—not alone your Lord,
Michael, but you, and you, Saint Peter! cold 325
  Must be your souls, if you have not abhorred
The foe to Catholic participation
In all the license of a Christian nation.

'True! he allowed them to pray God; but as
  A consequence of prayer, refused the law 330
Which would have placed them upon the same base
  With those who did not hold the saints in awe.'
But here Saint Peter started from his place,
  And cried, 'You may the prisoner withdraw:
Ere heaven shall ope her portals to this Guelph,
While I am guard, may I be damned myself! 336

'Sooner will I with Cerberus exchange
  My office (and *his* is no sinecure)
Than see this royal Bedlam bigot range 339
  The azure fields of heaven, of that be sure!'
'Saint!' replied Satan, 'you do well to avenge
  The wrongs he made your satellites endure;
And if to this exchange you should be given,
I'll try to coax *our* Cerberus up to heaven!'

Here Michael interposed: 'Good saint! and devil! 345
Pray, not so fast; you both outrun discretion.
Saint Peter! you were wont to be more civil!
  Satan, excuse this warmth of his expression,
And condescension to the vulgar's level;
  Even saints sometimes forget themselves in session. 350
Have you got more to say?'—'No.'— 'If you please,
I'll trouble you to call your witnesses.'

* * *   (1822)

From DON JUAN, CANTO III

THE ISLES OF GREECE

The isles of Greece, the isles of Greece!
  Where burning Sappho loved and sung,
Where grew the arts of war and peace,—
  Where Delos rose, and Phœbus sprung!
Eternal summer gilds them yet, 5
But all, except their sun, is set.

The Scian and the Teian muse,
  The hero's harp, the lover's lute,
Have found the fame your shores refuse:
  Their place of birth alone is mute 10
To sounds which echo further west
Than your sires' 'Islands of the Blest.'

The mountains look on Marathon—
  And Marathon looks on the sea;
And musing there an hour alone, 15
  I dreamed that Greece might still be free;
For standing on the Persian's grave,
I could not deem myself a slave.

A king sate on the rocky brow
  Which looks o'er sea-born Salamis; 20
And ships, by thousands, lay below,
  And men in nations;—all were his!
He counted them at break of day—
And when the sun set, where were they?

And where are they? and where art thou, 25
  My country? On thy voiceless shore
The heroic lay is tuneless now—
  The heroic bosom beats no more!
And must thy lyre, so long divine,
Degenerate into hands like mine? 30

'T is something, in the dearth of fame,
  Though linked among a fettered race,
To feel at least a patriot's shame,
  Even as I sing, suffuse my face;
For what is left the poet here? 35
For Greeks a blush—for Greece a tear.

Must *we* but weep o'er days more blest?
  Must *we* but blush?—Our fathers bled.
Earth! render back from out thy breast
  A remnant of our Spartan dead! 40
Of the three hundred grant but three,
To make a new Thermopylæ!

What, silent still? and silent all?
  Ah! no;—the voices of the dead
Sound like a distant torrent's fall, 45
  And answer, 'Let one living head,
But one arise,—we come, we come!'
'T is but the living who are dumb.

In vain—in vain: strike other chords:
  Fill high the cup with Samian wine! 50
Leave battles to the Turkish hordes,
  And shed the blood of Scio's vine!
Hark! rising to the ignoble call—
How answers each bold Bacchanal!

You have the Pyrrhic dance as yet: 55
  Where is the Pyrrhic phalanx gone?
Of two such lessons, why forget
  The nobler and the manlier one?
You have the letters Cadmus gave—
Think ye he meant them for a slave? 60

Fill high the bowl with Samian wine!
  We will not think of themes like these!
It made Anacreon's song divine;
  He served—but served Polycrates—
A tyrant; but our masters then 65
Were still, at least, our countrymen.

The tyrant of the Chersonese
  Was freedom's best and bravest friend;
That tyrant was Miltiades!
  Oh! that the present hour would lend 70
Another despot of the kind!
Such chains as his were sure to bind.

Fill high the bowl with Samian wine!
  On Suli's rock, and Parga's shore,
Exists the remnant of a line 75
  Such as the Doric mothers bore;
And there, perhaps, some seed is sown,
The Heracleidan blood might own.

Trust not for freedom to the Franks,
  They have a king who buys and sells; 80
In native swords and native ranks,
  The only hope of courage dwells:
But Turkish force, and Latin fraud,
Would break your shield, however broad.

Fill high the bowl with Samian wine! 85
  Our virgins dance beneath the shade—
I see their glorious black eyes shine;
  But gazing on each glowing maid,
My own the burning tear-drop laves,
To think such breasts must suckle slaves. 90

Place me on Sunium's marbled steep,
  Where nothing, save the waves and I,
May hear our mutual murmurs sweep;
  There, swan-like, let me sing and die:
A land of slaves shall ne'er be mine— 95
Dash down yon cup of Samian wine!

Thus sung, or would, or could, or should have sung,
  The modern Greek, in tolerable verse:
If not like Orpheus quite, when Greece was young,
  Yet in these times he might have done much worse: 100
His strain displayed some feeling—right or wrong;
  And feeling, in a poet, is the source
Of others' feeling; but they are such liars,
And take all colors—like the hands of dyers.

But words are things, and a small drop of ink,
  Falling like dew, upon a thought, produces 106
That which makes thousands, perhaps millions, think;
  'T is strange, the shortest letter which man uses
Instead of speech, may form a lasting link
Of ages; to what straits old Time reduces 110
Frail man when paper—even a rag like this,
Survives himself, his tomb, and all that 's his!

And when his bones are dust, his grave a blank,
  His station, generation, even his nation,
Become a thing, or nothing, save to rank 115
  In chronological commemoration,
Some dull MS. oblivion long has sank.
  Or graven stone found in a barrack's station
In digging the foundation of a closet,
May turn his name up, as a rare deposit. 120

And glory long has made the sages smile;
  'T is something, nothing, words, illusion, wind—
Depending more upon the historian's style
  Than on the name a person leaves behind:
Troy owes to Homer what whist owes to Hoyle:
The present century was growing blind 126

To the great Marlborough's skill in giving
    knocks,
Until his late Life by Archdeacon Coxe.

Milton's the prince of poets—so we say;
    A little heavy, but no less divine: 130
An independent being in his day—
    Learned, pious, temperate in love and wine;
But his life falling into Johnson's way,
    We're told this great high priest of all the
        Nine
Was whipt at college—a harsh sire—odd spouse,
For the first Mrs. Milton left his house.   136

All these are, *certes*, entertaining facts,
    Like Shakespeare's stealing deer, Lord Ba-
        con's bribes;
Like Titus' youth, and Cæsar's earliest acts;
    Like Burns (whom Doctor Currie well de-
        scribed);   140
Like Cromwell's pranks:—but although truth
        exacts
    These amiable descriptions from the scribes,
As most essential to their hero's story,
They do not much contribute to his glory.

All are not moralists, like Southey, when   145
    He prated to the world of 'Pantisocracy:'
Or Wordsworth unexcised, unhired, who then
    Seasoned his peddler poems with democracy;
Or Coleridge, long before his flighty pen
    Let to the Morning Post its aristocracy;   150
When he and Southey, following the same path,
Espoused two partners (milliners of Bath).

Such names at present cut a convict figure,
    The very Botany Bay in moral geography:
Their royal treason, renegado rigor,   155
    Are good manure for their more bare biogra-
        phy.
Wordsworth's last quarto, by the way, is bigger
    Than any since the birthday of typography:
A drowsy frowzy poem, called the 'Excursion,'
Writ in a manner which is my aversion.   160

* * *

T' our tale.—The feast was over, the slaves
        gone,
    The dwarfs and dancing girls had all retired:
The Arab lore and poet's song were done,
    And every sound of revelry expired;
The lady and her lover, left alone.   165
    The rosy flood of twilight's sky admired:
Ave Maria! o'er the earth and sea,
That heavenliest hour of Heaven is worthiest
    thee!

Ave Maria! blessed be the hour!
    The time, the clime, the spot, where I so oft
Have felt that moment in its fullest power   171
    Sink o'er the earth so beautiful and soft,
While swung the deep bell in the distant tower,
    Or the faint dying day-hymn stole aloft,
And not a breath crept through the rosy air,
And yet the forest leaves seemed stirred with
    prayer   176

Ave Maria! 't is the hour of prayer!
    Ave Maria! 't is the hour of love!
Ave Maria! may our spirits dare
    Look up to thine and to thy Son's above!
Ave Maria! oh, that face so fair!   181
    Those downcast eyes beneath the Almighty
        dove—
What though 't is but a pictured image strike,
That painting is no idol,—'t is too like.

Some kinder casuists are pleased to say,   185
    In nameless print—that I have no devotion;
But set those persons down with me to pray,
    And you shall see who has the properest no-
        tion
Of getting into heaven the shortest way;
    My altars are the mountains and the ocean,
Earth, air, stars,—all that springs from the
    great Whole,   191
Who hath produced, and will receive the soul.

Sweet hour of twilight!—in the solitude
    Of the pine forest and the silent shore
Which bounds Ravenna's immemorial wood,
    Rooted where once the Adrian wave flowed
        o'er,   196
To where the last Cæsarean fortress stood,
    Evergreen forest! which Boccaccio's lore
And Dryden's lay made haunted ground to me,
How have I loved the twilight hour and thee!

The shrill cicalas, people of the pine,   201
    Making their summer lives one ceaseless song,
Were the sole echoes, save my steed's and mine,
    And vesper bell's that rose the boughs along;
The specter huntsman of Onesti's line,   205
    His hell-dogs, and their chase, and the fair
        throng
Which learned from this example not to fly
From a true lover, shadowed my mind's eye.

O Hesperus! thou bringest all good things—
    Home to the weary, to the hungry cheer,   210
To the young bird the parent's brooding wings,
    The welcome stall to the o'erlabored steer;
Whate'er of peace about our hearthstone clings,
    Whate'er our household gods protect of dear,
Are gathered round us by thy look of rest;   215
Thou bring'st the child, too, to the mother's
    breast.

Soft hour! which wakes the wish and melts the
    heart
    Of those who sail the seas, on the first day
When they from their sweet friends are torn
    apart;
    Or fills with love the pilgrim on his way   220

As the far bell of vesper makes him start,
  Seeming to weep the dying day's decay;
Is this a fancy which our reason scorns?
Ah! surely nothing dies but something mourns!

When Nero perished by the justest doom   225
  Which ever the destroyer yet destroyed,
Amidst the roar of liberated Rome,
  Of nations freed, and the world overjoyed,
Some hands unseen strewed flowers upon his tomb:
  Perhaps the weakness of a heart not void   230
Of feeling for some kindness done, when power
  Had left the wretch an uncorrupted hour.

But I'm digressing; what on earth has Nero,
  Or any such like sovereign buffoons,
To do with the transactions of my hero,   235
  More than such madmen's fellow man—the moon's?
Sure my invention must be down at zero;
  And I grown one of many 'wooden spoons'
Of verse (the name with which we Cantabs please
To dub the last of honors in degrees).   240

* * *

DON JUAN, CANTO IV

NOTHING so difficult as a beginning
  In poesy, unless perhaps the end;
For oftentimes, when Pegasus seems winning
  The race, he sprains a wing, and down we tend,
Like Lucifer, when hurled from heaven for sinning;   5
  Our sin the same, and hard as his to mend,
Being pride, which leads the mind to soar too far,
Till our own weakness shows us what we are.

But Time, which brings all beings to their level,
  And sharp Adversity, will teach at last   10
Man, and—as we would hope—perhaps the devil,
  That neither of their intellects are vast:
While youth's hot wishes in our red veins revel,
  We know not this—the blood flows on too fast;
But as the torrent widens towards the ocean,
We ponder deeply on each past emotion.   16

As boy, I thought myself a clever fellow,
  And wished that others held the same opinion;
They took it up when my days grew more mellow,
  And other minds acknowledged my dominion:
Now my sere fancy 'falls into the yellow   21
  Leaf,' and Imagination droops her pinion,
And the sad truth which hovers o'er my desk
Turns what was once romantic to burlesque.

And if I laugh at any mortal thing,   25
  'T is that I may not weep; and if I weep,
'T is that our nature cannot always bring
  Itself to apathy, for we must steep
Our hearts first in the depth of Lethe's spring,
  Ere what we least wish to behold will sleep: 30
Thetis baptized her mortal son in Styx;
A mortal mother would on Lethe fix.

Some have accused me of a strange design
  Against the creed and morals of the land,
And trace it in this poem every line: 35
  I don't pretend that I quite understand
My own meaning when I would be *very* fine;
  But the fact is, that I have nothing planned
Unless it were to be a moment merry,
A novel word in my vocabulary.   40

To the kind reader of our sober clime,
  This way of writing will appear exotic:
Pulci was sire of the half-serious rhyme,
  Who sang when chivalry was more Quixotic,
And reveled in the fancies of the time,   45
  True knights, chaste dames, huge giants, kings despotic;
But all these, save the last, being obsolete,
I chose a modern subject as more meet.

How I have treated it, I do not know;
  Perhaps no better than they have treated me
Who have imputed such designs as show   51
  Not what they saw, but what they wished to see:
But if it gives them pleasure, be it so;
  This is a liberal age, and thoughts are free:
Meantime Apollo plucks me by the ear,   55
And tells me to resume my story here.

* * *

Now pillowed cheek to cheek, in loving sleep,
  Haidée and Juan their siesta took,
A gentle slumber, but it was not deep,
  For ever and anon a something shook   60
Juan, and shuddering o'er his frame would creep;
  And Haidée's sweet lips murmured like a brook
A wordless music, and her face so fair
Stirred with her dream, as rose-leaves with the air;

Or as the stirring of a deep clear stream   65
  Within an Alpine hollow, when the wind
Walks o'er it, was she shaken by the dream,
  The mystical usurper of the mind—
O'erpowering us to be whate'er may seem
  Good to the soul which we no more can bind: 70

Strange state of being! (for 't is still to be)
Senseless to feel, and with sealed eyes to see.

She dreamed of being alone on the seashore,
  Chained to a rock; she knew not how, but stir
She could not from the spot, and the loud roar   75
  Grew, and each wave rose roughly, threatening her;
And o'er her upper lip they seemed to pour,
  Until she sobbed for breath, and soon they were
Foaming o'er her lone head, so fierce and high—
Each broke to drown her, yet she could not die.   80

Anon—she was released; and then she strayed
  O'er the sharp shingles with her bleeding feet,
And stumbled almost every step she made:
  And something rolled before her in a sheet,
Which she must still pursue, howe'er afraid;   85
  'T was white and indistinct, nor stopped to meet
Her glance or grasp, for still she gazed and grasped,
And ran, but it escaped her as she clasped.

The dream changed:—in a cave she stood, its walls
  Were hung with marble icicles: the work   90
Of ages on its water-fretted halls,
  Where waves might wash, and seals might breed and lurk;
Her hair was dripping, and the very balls
  Of her black eyes seemed turned to tears, and mirk
The sharp rocks looked below each drop they caught,   95
Which froze to marble as it fell—she thought.

And wet, and cold, and lifeless, at her feet,
  Pale as the foam that frothed on his dead brow,
Which she essayed in vain to clear (how sweet
  Were once her cares, how idle seemed they now!)   100
Lay Juan, nor could aught renew the beat
  Of his quenched heart; and the sea-dirges low
Rang in her sad ears like a mermaid's song,
And that brief dream appeared a life too long.

And gazing on the dead, she thought his face   105
  Faded, or altered into something new—
Like to her father's features, till each trace
  More like and like to Lambro's aspect grew—
With all his keen worn look and Grecian grace;
  And starting, she awoke, and what to view?
O Powers of Heaven! what dark eye meets she there?   111
'T is—'t is her father's—fixed upon the pair!

Then shrieking, she arose, and shrieking fell,
  With joy and sorrow, hope and fear, to see
Him whom she deemed a habitant where dwell   115
The ocean buried, risen from death, to be
Perchance the death of one she loved too well:
  Dear as her father had been to Haidée,
It was a moment of that awful kind—
I have seen such—but must not call to mind   120

Up Juan sprang to Haidée's bitter shriek,
  And caught her falling, and from off the wall
Snatched down bis sabre, in hot haste to wreak
  Vengeance on him who was the cause of all;
Then Lambro, who till now forbore to speak,   125
  Smiled scornfully, and said, 'Within my call,
A thousand scimitars await the word;
Put up, young man, put up your silly sword.'

And Haidée clung around him: 'Juan, 't is—
  'T is Lambro—'t is my father! Kneel with me—   130
He will forgive us—yes—it must be—yes,
  Oh, dearest father, in this agony
Of pleasure and of pain—even while I kiss
  Thy garment's hem with transport, can it be
That doubt should mingle with my filial joy?   135
Deal with me as thou wilt, but spare this boy.'

High and inscrutable the old man stood,
  Calm in his voice, and calm within his eye—
Not always signs with him of calmest mood:
  He looked upon her, but gave no reply;   140
Then turned to Juan, in whose cheek the blood
  Oft came and went, as there resolved to die
In arms, at least, he stood in act to spring
On the first foe whom Lambro's call might bring.

'Young man, your sword!' So Lambro once more said;   145
  Juan replied, 'Not while this arm is free!'
The old man's cheek grew pale, but not with dread,
  But drawing from his belt a pistol, he
Replied, 'Your blood be then on your own head.'
  Then looked close at the flint, as if to see   150
'T was fresh—for he had lately used the lock—
And next proceeded quietly to cock.

It has a strange, quick jar upon the ear,
  That cocking of a pistol, when you know
A moment more will bring the sight to bear   155
  Upon your person, twelve yards off, or so;
A gentlemanly distance, not too near,
  If you have got a former friend for foe;
But after being fired at once or twice,
The ear becomes more Irish, and less nice.   160

Lambro presented, and one instant more
   Had stopped this canto, and Don Juan's breath,
When Haidée threw herself her boy before,
   Stern as her sire: 'On me,' she cried, 'let death
Descend—the fault is mine; this fatal shore 165
   He found—but sought not. I have pledged my faith;
I love him—I will die with him: I knew
   Your nature's firmness—know your daughter's too.'

A minute past, and she had been all tears,
   And tenderness, and infancy; but now 170
She stood as one who championed human fears—
   Pale, statue-like, and stern, she wooed the blow;
And tall beyond her sex, and their compeers,
   She drew up to her height, as if to show
A fairer mark; and with a fixed eye scanned
   Her father's face—but never stopped his hand. 176

He gazed on her, and she on him; 't was strange
   How like they looked! the expression was the same;
Serenely savage, with a little change
   In the large dark eye's mutual-darted flame;
For she, too, was as one who could avenge, 181
   If cause should be—a lioness, though tame:
Her father's blood, before her father's face
Boiled up, and proved her truly of his race.

I said they were alike, their features and 185
   Their stature differing but in sex and years;
Even to the delicacy of their hand
   There was resemblance, such as true blood wears;
And now to see them, thus divided, stand
   In fixed ferocity, when joyous tears, 190
And sweet sensations, should have welcomed both,
Show what the passions are in their full growth.

The father paused a moment, then withdrew
   His weapon, and replaced it; but stood still,
And looking on her, as to look her through, 195
   'Not *I*,' he said, 'have sought this stranger's ill;
Not *I* have made this desolation; few
   Would bear such outrage, and forbear to kill;
But I must do my duty—how thou hast
Done thine, the present vouches for the past. 200

'Let him disarm; or, by my father's head,
   His own shall roll before you like a ball!'
He raised his whistle, as the word he said,
   And blew, another answered to the call,
And, rushing in disorderly, though led, 205
   And armed from boot to turban, one and all,
Some twenty of his train came, rank on rank;
He gave the word—'Arrest or slay the Frank!'

Then, with a sudden movement, he withdrew
   His daughter; while compressed within his clasp, 210
'Twixt her and Juan interposed the crew;
   In vain she struggled in her father's grasp—
His arms were like a serpent's coil: then flew
   Upon their prey, as darts an angry asp,
The file of pirates; save the foremost, who 215
Had fallen, with his right shoulder half cut through.

The second had his cheek laid open; but
   The third, a wary, cool old sworder, took
The blow upon his cutlass, and then put
   His own well in: so well, ere you could look, 220
His man was floored, and helpless at his foot,
   With the blood running like a little brook,
From two smart sabre gashes, deep and red—
One on the arm, the other on the head.

And then they bound him where he fell, and bore
   Juan from the apartment: with a sign, 226
Old Lambro bade them take him to the shore,
   Where lay some ships which were to sail at nine.
They laid him in a boat, and plied the oar
   Until they reached some galliots, placed in line; 230
On board of one of these, and under hatches,
They stowed him, with strict orders to the watches.

The world is full of strange vicissitudes,
   And here was one exceedingly unpleasant:
A gentleman so rich in the world's goods, 235
   Handsome and young, enjoying all the present,
Just at the very time when he least broods
   On such a thing, is suddenly to sea sent,
Wounded and chained, so that he cannot move,
And all because a lady fell in love. 240

Here I must leave him, for I grow pathetic,
   Moved by the Chinese nymph of tears, green tea!
Than whom Cassandra was not more prophetic;
   For if my pure libations exceed three,
I feel my heart become so sympathetic, 245
   That I must have recourse to black Bohea:
'T is pity wine should be so deleterious,
For tea and coffee leave us much more serious,

Unless when qualified with thee, Cognac!
   Sweet Naiad of the Phlegethontic rill! 250
Ah, why the liver wilt thou thus attack,
   And make, like other nymphs, thy lovers ill?
I would take refuge in weak punch, but *rack*
   (In each sense of the word), whene'er I fill
My mild and midnight beakers to the brim, 255
Wakes me next morning with its synonym.

I leave Don Juan for the present, safe—
  Not sound, poor fellow, but severely wounded;
Yet could his corporal pangs amount to half
  Of those with which his Haidée's bosom bounded! 260
She was not one to weep, and rave, and chafe,
  And then give way, subdued, because surrounded;
Her mother was a Moorish maid, from Fez,
Where all is Eden, or a wilderness.

There the large olive rains its amber store 265
  In marble fonts; there grain, and flower, and fruit,
Gush from the earth, until the land runs o'er:
  But there, too, many a poison tree has root,
And midnight listens to the lion's roar,
  And long, long deserts scorch the camel's foot,
Or heaving, whelm the helpless caravan: 271
And as the soil is, so the heart of man.

Afric is all the sun's, and as her earth
  Her human clay is kindled: full of power
For good or evil, burning from its birth. 275
  The Moorish blood partakes the planet's hour,
And like the soil beneath, it will bring forth:
  Beauty and love were Haidée's mother's dower;
But her large dark eye showed deep Passion's force
Though sleeping like a lion near a source. 280

Her daughter, tempered with a milder ray,
  Like summer's clouds all silvery smooth and fair,
Till slowly charged with thunder, they display
  Terror to earth, and tempest to the air,
Had held till now her soft and milky way, 285
  But, overwrought with passion and despair,
The fire burst forth from her Numidian veins,
Even as the Simoom sweeps the blasted plains.

The last sight which she saw was Juan's gore,
  And he himself o'ermastered, and cut down;
His blood was running on the very floor, 291
  Where late he trod, her beautiful, her own;
Thus much she viewed an instant, and no more—
  Her struggles ceased with one convulsive groan;
On her sire's arm, which, until now, scarce held
Her, writhing, fell she, like a cedar felled. 296

A vein had burst, and her sweet lips' pure dyes
  Were dabbled with the deep blood which ran o'er;
And her head drooped, as when the lily lies
  O'ercharged with rain: her summoned handmaids bore 300
Their lady to her couch, with gushing eyes;
  Of herbs and cordials they produced their store,

But she defied all means they could employ,
Like one life could not hold, nor death destroy.

Days lay she in that state, unchanged, though chill— 305
  With nothing livid, still her lips were red:
She had no pulse, but death seemed absent still;
  No hideous sign proclaimed her surely dead;
Corruption came not, in each mind to kill
  All hope; to look upon her sweet face, bred 310
New thoughts of life, for it seemed full of soul—
She had so much, earth could not claim the whole.

The ruling passion, such as marble shows
  When exquisitely chiseled, still lay there,
But fixed as marble's unchanged aspect throws
  O'er the fair Venus, but forever fair; 316
O'er the Laocoön's all eternal throes,
  And ever-dying Gladiator's air,
Their energy, like life, forms all their fame,
Yet looks not life, for they are still the same. 320

She woke at length, but not as sleepers wake,
  Rather the dead, for life seemed something new,
A strange sensation which she must partake
  Perforce, since whatsoever met her view
Struck not on memory, though a heavy ache
  Lay at her heart, whose earliest beat, still true, 326
Brought back the sense of pain without the cause,
For, for a while, the furies made a pause.

She looked on many a face with vacant eye, 329
  On many a token, without knowing what;
She saw them watch her, without asking why,
  And recked not who around her pillow sat:
Not speechless, though she spoke not; not a sigh
  Relieved her thoughts; dull silence and quick chat 334
Were tried in vain by those who served; she gave
No sign, save breath, of having left the grave.

Her handmaids tended, but she heeded not;
  Her father watched, she turned her eyes away;
She recognized no being, and no spot,
  However dear, or cherished in their day; 340
They changed from room to room, but all forgot,
  Gentle, but without memory, she lay;
At length those eyes, which they would fain be weaning
Back to old thoughts, waxed full of fearful meaning.

And then a slave bethought her of a harp; 345
  The harper came and tuned his instrument.
At the first notes, irregular and sharp,
  On him her flashing eyes a moment bent,

Then to the wall she turned, as if to warp
  Her thoughts from sorrow through her heart
    re-sent; 350
And he began a long low island song
Of ancient days, ere tyranny grew strong.

Anon her thin wan fingers beat the wall,
  In time to his old tune: he changed the theme,
  And sung of love; the fierce name struck
    through all 355
  Her recollection; on her flashed the dream
Of what she was, and is, if ye could call
  To be so being: in a gushing stream
The tears rushed forth from her o'erclouded
    brain,
Like mountain mists, at length dissolved in rain.

Short solace, vain relief!—thought came too
    quick, 361
  And whirled her brain to madness; she arose,
  As one who ne'er had dwelt among the sick,
  And flew at all she met, as on her foes;
But no one ever heard her speak or shriek, 365
  Although her paroxysm drew towards its
    close:—
Hers was a frenzy which disdained to rave,
Even when they smote her, in the hope to save.

Yet she betrayed at times a gleam of sense;
  Nothing could make her meet her father's
    face, 370
Though on all other things with looks intense
  She gazed, but none she ever could retrace.
Food she refused, and raiment; no pretence
  Availed for either; neither change of place,
Nor time, not skill, nor remedy, could give her
Senses to sleep—the power seemed gone for-
    ever. 376

Twelve days and nights she withered thus; at
    last,
  Without a groan, or sigh, or glance, to show
A parting pang, the spirit from her past:
  And they who watched her nearest, could
    not know 380
The very instant, till the change that cast
  Her sweet face into shadow, dull and slow,
Glazed o'er her eyes—the beautiful, the black—
Oh! to possess such luster—and then lack!

Thus lived—thus died she; never more on her
  Shall sorrow light, or shame. She was not
    made 386
Through years or moons the inner weight to
    bear,
  Which colder hearts endure till they are laid
By age in earth; her days and pleasures were
  Brief but delightful—such as had not stayed
Long with her destiny; but she sleeps well 391
By the sea-shore, whereon she loved to dwell.

The isle is now all desolate and bare,
  Its dwellings down, its tenants passed away;
None but her own and father's grave is there,
  And nothing outward tells of human clay: 396
Ye could not know where lies a thing so fair,
  No stone is there to show, no tongue to say
What was: no dirge, except the hollow sea's,
Mourns o'er the beauty of the Cyclades. 400

* * *

(1821)

PERCY BYSSHE SHELLEY (1792–1822)

Shelley was the son of a country squire of large means whose utter inability to comprehend the nature of his son's convictions was an important factor in the latter's history. At Eton 'mad Shelley' became unpopular with the older boys for heading an insurrection against the school system of 'fagging,' and he had not been long at University College, Oxford, when he was expelled for circulating a revolutionary tract entitled *The Necessity of Atheism*. He was only nineteen when out of fancied chivalry he married Harriet Westbrooke, a schoolgirl of sixteen, much below him in social station. Angered by the first indiscretion, his father was permanently estranged by the second. These two children set off for Dublin, Shelley writing to a friend, 'We go to forward as much as we can the Catholic Emancipation.' Before setting out for the scene of destiny he had printed an *Address to the Irish People*, which he now published by dropping it from windows upon such passers-by as 'looked likely.' Shelley's ingenuous faith that men needed only to be shown the truth in order to follow it was doomed to cruel disillusion. For two or three years he wandered about the British Isles pushing his propaganda of freedom, and prosecuting irregular studies in philosophy and literature. His friend Hogg declared that a splendid library might have been formed out of the books which Shelley left scattered about the three kingdoms. In 1814, he separated from Harriet and, soon after, he fell passionately in love with Mary Godwin, daughter of the author of *Political Justice*. The feeling was returned and consistently with the tenets of all concerned, except Harriet and Shelley's father, Mary became his mate. Two years later, the wife whom he had abandoned ended her life by drowning. How far Shelley should be held culpable for this unhappy event is a moot point with his biographers. In 1818, he permanently left England for Italy, on account of his health and partly out of a fear lest the Lord Chancellor, who had already removed from his custody the children of his first marriage, might pass a similar judgment in regard to those of the second.

In Italy, for more reasons than one can pause to enumerate, Shelley's genius flowered; but only four years of it remained. Setting out in a small sailing boat he was overtaken by a squall in the bay of Lerici. A few days later his body was found embedded in the sand of the shore. In one pocket of his jacket was a volume of Sophocles, and in the other a volume of Keats, 'doubled back as if the reader, in the act of reading, had hastily thrust it away.'

A narration of the bare acts of Shelley's life leaves an impression of waywardness which is not altogether misleading. Those who were competent to judge agreed that his impulses were noble and high, that a purer spirit never breathed; but he suffered and made others suffer because he would not bind himself to the code by which society lives. To the common run of his contemporaries he was a fanatical monster; to many since it has seemed that his sufferings and errors were the fault of an irrationally organized world and that he himself belonged to a 'crowning race' of which he was 'a noble type, appearing ere the time was ripe.'

All of Shelley's poetry of importance was written after he met Mary Godwin. *Queen Mab* (1813) was a frantic poetical drama interesting only for its revolutionary doctrines. His genius first declared itself in *Alastor* (1815), and passages of great promise are scattered through his enormous revolutionary document, *The Revolt of Islam* (1817). But in Italy he matured with astonishing rapidity. To the year 1819 belonged *Prometheus Unbound*, his totally different *Cenci*, which some critics regard as the most distinguished poetical tragedy since the Elizabethans, and numerous fine lyrics, including the *Ode to the West Wind*. The year 1820 was notable chiefly for its lyrics, *To a Skylark* among them. In 1821, besides *Epipsychidion*, *Adonais*, and *Hellas*, came some of the most poignant of the short lyrics. *The Triumph of Life* was uncompleted when Shelley set out to sea on Monday, July 8, 1822.

No one can estimate Shelley for us but ourselves. This is true of all poetry, but preëminently so of Shelley's because it is so preëminently poetical. When it is best, it has little intellectual content. We do not, narrowly speaking, learn anything from Shelley; we surrender to an element.

HYMN TO INTELLECTUAL BEAUTY

The awful shadow of some unseen Power
   Floats though unseen amongst us,—visiting
This various world with as inconstant wing
As summer winds that creep from flower to flower;—
Like moonbeams that behind some piny mountain shower,   5
   It visits with inconstant glance
   Each human heart and countenance;

Like hues and harmonies of evening,—
   Like clouds in starlight widely spread,—
   Like memory of music fled,—   10
   Like aught that for its grace may be
Dear, and yet dearer for its mystery.

Spirit of Beauty, that dost consecrate
   With thine own hues all thou dost shine upon
   Of human thought or form,—where art thou gone?   15
Why dost thou pass away and leave our state,
This dim vast vale of tears, vacant and desolate?
   Ask why the sunlight not forever
   Weaves rainbows o'er yon mountain river,
Why aught should fail and fade that once is shown,   20
   Why fear and dream and death and birth
   Cast on the daylight of this earth
   Such gloom,—why man has such a scope
For love and hate, despondency and hope?

No voice from some sublimer world hath ever   25
   To sage or poet these responses given—
   Therefore the names of Dæmon, Ghost, and Heaven,
Remain the records of their vain endeavor,
Frail spells—whose uttered charm might not avail to sever,
   From all we hear and all we see,   30
   Doubt, chance, and mutability.
Thy light alone—like mist o'er mountains driven,
   Or music by the night wind sent,
   Through strings of some still instrument,
   Or moonlight on a midnight stream,   35
Gives grace and truth to life's unquiet dream.

Love, Hope, and Self-esteem, like clouds depart
   And come, for some uncertain moments lent.
   Man were immortal, and omnipotent,   39
Didst thou, unknown and awful as thou art,
Keep with thy glorious train firm state within his heart.
   Thou messenger of sympathies,
   That wax and wane in lovers' eyes—
Thou—that to human thought art nourishment,
   Like darkness to a dying flame!   45
   Depart not as thy shadow came,
   Depart not—lest the grave should be,
Like life and fear, a dark reality.

While yet a boy I sought for ghosts, and sped
   Through many a listening chamber, cave and ruin,   50
   And starlight wood, with fearful steps pursuing
Hopes of high talk with the departed dead.
I called on poisonous names with which our youth is fed;
   I was not heard—I saw them not—
   When musing deeply on the lot   55

Of life, at the sweet time when winds are wooing
   All vital things that wake to bring
   News of birds and blossoming,—
   Sudden, thy shadow fell on me;
I shrieked, and clasped my hands in ecstasy!   60
I vowed that I would dedicate my powers
   To thee and thine—have I not kept the vow?
   With beating heart and streaming eyes, even now
I call the phantoms of a thousand hours
Each from his voiceless grave: they have in visioned bowers   65
   Of studious zeal or love's delight
   Outwatched with me the envious night—
They know that never joy illumed my brow
   Unlinked with hope that thou wouldst free
   This world from its dark slavery,   70
   That thou—O awful Loveliness,
Wouldst give whate'er these words cannot express.

The day becomes more solemn and serene
   When noon is past—there is a harmony
   In autumn, and a luster in its sky,   75
Which through the summer is not heard or seen,
As if it could not be, as if it had not been!
   Thus let thy power, which like the truth
   Of nature on my passive youth
Descended, to my onward life supply   80
   Its calm—to one who worships thee,
   And every form containing thee,
   Whom, Spirit fair, thy spells did bind
To fear himself, and love all human kind.

(1819)

OZYMANDIAS

I met a traveler from an antique land
Who said: Two vast and trunkless legs of stone
Stand in the desert. Near them, on the sand,
Half sunk, a shattered visage lies, whose frown,
And wrinkled lip, and sneer of cold command,   5
Tell that its sculptor well those passions read
Which yet survive, (stamped on these lifeless things),
The hand that mocked them and the heart that fed;
And on the pedestal these words appear:
'My name is Ozymandias, king of kings;   10
Look on my works, ye Mighty, and despair!'
Nothing beside remains. Round the decay
Of that colossal wreck, boundless and bare,
The lone and level sands stretch far away.

(1819)

STANZAS

WRITTEN IN DEJECTION, NEAR NAPLES

The sun is warm, the sky is clear,
   The waves are dancing fast and bright,
Blue isles and snowy mountains wear
   The purple noon's transparent might,
   The breath of the moist earth is light,   5

Around its unexpanded buds:
  Like many a voice of one delight,
The winds, the birds, the ocean floods,
The City's voice itself is soft like Solitude's.

I see the Deep's untrampled floor   10
  With green and purple seaweeds strown:
I see the waves upon the shore,
  Like light dissolved in star-showers, thrown:
    I sit upon the sands alone,
The lightning of the noontide ocean   15
  Is flashing round me, and a tone
Arises from its measured motion,
How sweet! did any heart now share in my emotion.

Alas! I have nor hope nor health,
  Nor peace within nor calm around,   20
Nor that content surpassing wealth
  The sage in meditation found,
    And walked with inward glory crowned—
Nor fame, nor power, nor love, nor leisure.
  Others I see whom these surround—   25
Smiling they live, and call life pleasure;—
To me that cup has been dealt in another measure.

Yet now despair itself is mild,
  Even as the winds and waters are;
I could lie down like a tired child,   30
  And weep away the life of care
    Which I have borne and yet must bear,
Till death like sleep might steal on me,
  And I might feel in the warm air
My cheek grow cold, and hear the sea   35
Breathe o'er my dying brain its last monotony.

Some might lament that I were cold,
  As I when this sweet day is gone,
Which my lost heart, too soon grown old,
  Insults with this untimely moan;   40
    They might lament—for I am one
Whom men love not,—and yet regret,
  Unlike this day, which, when the sun
Shall on its stainless glory set,
Will linger, though enjoyed, like joy in memory
    yet.   45
(1842)

PROMETHEUS UNBOUND

ACT IV

SCENE, A PART OF THE FOREST NEAR THE CAVE OF PROMETHEUS. PANTHEA *and* IONE *are sleeping. They awaken gradually during the first song.*

VOICE OF UNSEEN SPIRITS

THE pale stars are gone!
For the sun, their swift shepherd,
  To their folds them compelling,
    In the depths of the dawn,
Hastes, in meteor-eclipsing array, and they flee
  Beyond his blue dwelling,   6
  As fawns flee the leopard.
    But where are ye?

A train of DARK FORMS *and* SHADOWS *passes by confusedly, singing.*

  Here, oh, here:
  We bear the bier   10
Of the Father of many a canceled year!
  Specters we
  Of the dead Hours be,
We bear Time to his tomb in eternity.

  Strew, oh, strew   15
  Hair, not yew!
Wet the dusty pall with tears, not dew!
  Be the faded flowers
  Of Death's bare bowers
Spread on the corpse of the King of Hours!   20

  Haste, oh, haste!
  As shades are chased,
Trembling, by day, from heaven's blue waste,
  We melt away,
  Like dissolving spray,   25
From the children of a diviner day,
  With the lullaby
  Of winds that die
On the bosom of their own harmony!

IONE

What dark forms were they?   30

PANTHEA

The past Hours weak and gray,
With the spoil which their toil
  Raked together
From the conquest but One could foil.

IONE

  Have they past?   35

PANTHEA

    They have past;
They outspeeded the blast,
While 't is said, they are fled:

IONE

Whither, oh, whither?

PANTHEA

To the dark, to the past, to the dead.   40

VOICE OF UNSEEN SPIRITS

Bright clouds float in heaven,
Dew-stars gleam on earth,
Waves assemble on ocean,
They are gathered and driven

By the storm of delight, by the panic of glee! 45
    They shake with emotion,
    They dance in their mirth.
        But where are ye?

    The pine boughs are singing,
    Old songs with new gladness, 50
    The billows and fountains
    Fresh music are flinging,
Like the notes of a spirit from land and from sea;
    The storms mock the mountains
    With the thunder of gladness. 55
        But where are ye?

        IONE

What charioteers are these?

        PANTHEA
        Where are their chariots?

    SEMICHORUS OF HOURS

The voice of the Spirits of Air and of Earth
    Have drawn back the figured curtain of sleep
Which covered our being and darkened our
        birth 61
In the deep.

        A VOICE
        In the deep?

      SEMICHORUS II
      Oh! below the deep.

      SEMICHORUS I

An hundred ages we had been kept 65
    Cradled in visions of hate and care,
And each one who waked as his brother slept,
Found the truth—

      SEMICHORUS II
    Worse than his visions were!

      SEMICHORUS I

We have heard the lute of Hope in sleep; 70
    We have known the voice of Love in dreams,
We have felt the wand of Power, and leap—

      SEMICHORUS I
    As the billows leap in the morning beams!

        CHORUS

Weave the dance on the floor of the breeze,
    Pierce with song heaven's silent light, 75
Enchant the day that too swiftly flees,
    To check its flight ere the cave of night.

Once the hungry Hours were hounds
    Which chased the day like a bleeding deer,
And it limped and stumbled with many wounds
    Through the nightly dells of the desert year.

But now, oh, weave the mystic measure 82
    Of music and dance, and shapes of light,
Let the Hours, and the spirits of might and
        pleasure,
    Like the clouds and sunbeams, unite. 85

        A VOICE
                Unite!
        PANTHEA
See, where the spirits of the human mind
Wrapt in sweet sounds, as in bright veils, ap-
    proach.

    CHORUS OF SPIRITS

    We join the throng
        Of the dance and the song, 90
By the whirlwind of gladness borne along:
    As the flying-fish leap
        From the Indian deep,
And mix with the sea-birds, half asleep.

    CHORUS OF HOURS

Whence come ye, so wild and so fleet, 95
For sandals of lightning are on your feet,
And your wings are soft and swift as thought,
And your eyes are as love which is veilèd not?

    CHORUS OF SPIRITS

    We come from the mind
        Of human kind 100
Which was late so dusk, and obscene, and blind.
    Now 't is an ocean
        Of clear emotion,
A heaven of serene and mighty motion;

    From that deep abyss 105
        Of wonder and bliss,
Whose caverns are crystal palaces;
    From these skiey towers
        Where Thought's crowned powers
Sit watching your dance, ye happy Hours! 110

    From the dim recesses
        Of woven caresses,
Where lovers catch ye by your loose tresses;
    From the azure isles;
        Where sweet Wisdom smiles 115
Delaying your ships with her siren wiles.

    From the temples high
        Of Man's ear and eye,
Roofed over Sculpture and Poesy;
    From the murmurings 120
        Of the unsealed springs
Where Science bedews his Dædal wings

    Years after years,
        Through blood and tears,
And a thick hell of hatreds, and hopes, and
        fears; 125
    We waded and flew
        And the islets were few
Where the bud-blighted flowers of happiness
    grew.

    Our feet now, every palm,
    Are sandaled with calm,   130
And the dew of our wings is a rain of balm;
    And, beyond our eyes,
    The human love lies
Which makes all it gazes on Paradise.

CHORUS OF SPIRITS AND HOURS

  Then weave the web of the mystic measure;
From the depths of the sky and the ends of the earth,   136
  Come, swift Spirits of might and of pleasure,
Fill the dance and the music of mirth,
As the waves of a thousand streams rush by
To an ocean of splendor and harmony!   140

CHORUS OF SPIRITS

    Our spoil is won,
    Our task is done,
We are free to dive, or soar, or run;
    Beyond and around,
    Or within the bound   145
Which clips the world with darkness round.

    We'll pass the eyes
    Of the starry skies
Into the hoar deep to colonize:
    Death, Chaos, and Night,   150
    From the sound of our flight,
Shall flee, like mist from a tempest's might.

    And Earth, Air, and Light,
    And the Spirit of Might,
Which drives round the stars in their fiery flight;   155
    And Love, Thought, and Breath,
    The powers that quell Death,
Wherever we soar shall assemble beneath.

    And our singing shall build
    In the void's loose field   160
A world for the Spirit of Wisdom to wield;
    We will take our plan
    From the new world of man,
And our work shall be called the Promethean.

CHORUS OF HOURS

Break the dance, and scatter the song;   165
Let some depart, and some remain.

SEMICHORUS I

We, beyond heaven, are driven along!

SEMICHORUS II

Us the enchantments of earth retain;

SEMICHORUS I

Ceaseless, and rapid, and fierce and free,
With the Spirits which build a new earth and sea,   170
And a heaven where yet heaven could never be.

SEMICHORUS II

Solemn, and slow, and serene, and bright,
Leading the Day and outspeeding the Night,
With the powers of a world of perfect light.

SEMICHORUS I

We whirl, singing loud, round the gathering sphere,   175
Till the trees, and the beasts, and the clouds appear
From its chaos made calm by love, not fear.

SEMICHORUS II

We encircle the ocean and mountains of earth,
And the happy forms of its death and birth
Change to the music of our sweet mirth.   180

CHORUS OF HOURS AND SPIRITS

Break the dance, and scatter the song,
  Let some depart, and some remain,
Wherever we fly we lead along,
In leashes, like starbeams, soft yet strong,
  The clouds that are heavy with love's sweet rain.   185

PANTHEA

  Ha! they are gone!

IONE

    Yet feel you no delight
From the past sweetness?

PANTHEA

    As the bare green hill
When some soft cloud vanishes into rain,   190
Laughs with a thousand drops of sunny water
To the unpavilioned sky!

IONE

    Even whilst we speak
New notes arise. What is that awful sound?

PANTHEA

'T is the deep music of the rolling world   195
Kindling within the strings of the waved air,
Æolian modulations.

IONE

    Listen too,
How every pause is filled with under notes,
Clear, silver, icy, keen, awakening tones,   200
Which pierce the sense, and live within the soul,
As the sharp stars pierce winter's crystal air
And gaze upon themselves within the sea.

PANTHEA

But see where through two openings in the forest
Which hanging branches overcanopy   205
And where two runnels of a rivulet,

Between the close moss violet-inwoven,
Have made their path of melody, like sisters
Who part with sighs that they may meet in smiles,
Turning their dear disunion to an isle   210
Of lovely grief, a wood of sweet sad thoughts;
Two visions of strange radiance float upon
The ocean-like enchantment of strong sound,
Which flows intenser, keener, deeper yet   214
Under the ground and through the windless air.

IONE

I see a chariot like that thinnest boat,
In which the mother of the months is borne
By ebbing night into her western cave,
When she upsprings from interlunar dreams,
O'er which is curved an orblike canopy   220
Of gentle darkness, and the hills and woods
Distinctly seen through that dusk airy veil,
Regard like shapes in an enchanter's glass;
Its wheels are solid clouds, azure and gold,
Such as the genii of the thunderstorm   225
Pile on the floor of the illumined sea
When the sun rushes under it: they roll
And move and grow as with an inward wind;
Within it sits a wingèd infant, white
Its countenance, like the whiteness of bright snow,   230
Its plumes are as feathers of sunny frost,
Its limbs gleam white, through the wind flowing folds
Of its white robe, woof of ethereal pearl.
Its hair is white, the brightness of white light
Scattered in strings; yet its two eyes are heavens
Of liquid darkness, which the Deity   236
Within seems pouring, as a storm is poured
From jaggèd clouds, out of their arrowy lashes,
Tempering the cold and radiant air around,
With fire that is not brightness: in its hand   240
It sways a quivering moonbeam, from whose point
A guiding power directs the chariot's prow
Over its wheelèd clouds, which as they roll
Over the grass, and flowers, and waves, wake sounds,
Sweet as a singing rain of silver dew.   245

PANTHEA

And from the other opening in the wood
Rushes, with loud and whirlwind harmony,
A sphere, which is as many thousand spheres,
Solid as crystal, yet through all its mass
Flow, as through empty space, music and light:
Ten thousand orbs involving and involved,   251
Purple and azure, white, and green, and golden,
Sphere within sphere; and every space between
Peopled with unimaginable shapes,
Such as ghosts dream dwell in the lampless deep,   255
Yet each inter-transpicuous, and they whirl
Over each other with a thousand motions,
Upon a thousand sightless axles spinning,
And with the force of self-destroying swiftness,
Intensely, slowly, solemnly roll on,   260
Kindling with mingled sounds, and many tones,
Intelligible words and music wild.
With mighty whirl the multitudinous orb
Grinds the bright brook into an azure mist
Of elemental subtlety; like light: 265
And the wild odor of the forest flowers,
The music of the living grass and air,
The emerald light of leaf-entangled beams
Round its intense yet self-conflicting speed,
Seem kneaded into one aërial mass   270
Which drowns the sense. Within the orb itself,
Pillowed upon its alabaster arms,
Like to a child o'erwearied with sweet toil,
On its own folded wings, and wavy hair,
The Spirit of the Earth is laid asleep,   275
And you can see its little lips are moving,
Amid the changing light of their own smiles,
Like one who talks of what he loves in dream.

IONE

'T is only mocking the orb's harmony.

PANTHEA

And from a star upon its forehead, shoot, 280
Like swords of azure fire, or golden spears
With tyrant-quelling myrtle overtwined,
Embleming heaven and earth united now,
Vast beams like spokes of some invisible wheel
Which whirl as the orb whirls, swifter than thought,   285
Filling the abyss with sun-like lightenings,
And perpendicular now, and now transverse,
Pierce the dark soil, and as they pierce and pass,
Make bare the secrets of the earth's deep heart;
Infinite mine of adamant and gold,   290
Valueless stones, and unimagined gems,
And caverns on crystalline columns poised
With vegetable silver overspread;
Wells of unfathomed fire, and water springs
Whence the great sea, even as a child is fed,   295
Whose vapors clothe earth's monarch mountain-tops
With kingly ermine snow. The beams flash on
And make appear the melancholy ruins
Of canceled cycles; anchors, beaks of ships;
Planks turned to marble; quivers, helms, and spears,   300
And gorgon-headed targes, and the wheels
Of scythèd chariots and the emblazonry
Of trophies, standards, and armorial beasts,
Round which death laughed, sepulchred emblems
Of dead destruction, ruin within ruin!   305
The wrecks beside of many a city vast,
Whose population which the earth grew over
Was mortal, but not human; see, they lie,
Their monstrous works, and uncouth skeletons,

Their statues, homes, and fanes: prodigious
    shapes   310
Huddled in gray annihilation, split,
Jammed in the hard, black deep; and over these,
The anatomies of unknown wingèd things,
And fishes which were isles of living scale,
And serpents, bony chains, twisted around   315
    The iron crags, or within heaps of dust
    To which the tortuous strength of their last
        pangs
Had crushed the iron crags; and over these
The jagged alligator, and the might
Of earth-convulsing behemoth, which once   320
Were monarch beasts, and on the slimy shores,
And weed-overgrown continents of earth,
Increased and multiplied like summer worms
On an abandoned corpse, till the blue globe
Wrapt deluge round it like a cloak, and they   325
Yelled, gasped, and were abolished; or some God
Whose throne was in a comet, passed, and cried,
Be not! And like my words they were no more.

THE EARTH

    The joy, the triumph, the delight, the mad-
        ness!
    The boundless, overflowing, bursting glad-
        ness,   330
The vaporous exultation not to be confined!
    Ha! ha! the animation of delight
    Which wraps me, like an atmosphere of light,
    And bears me as a cloud is borne by its own
        wind.

THE MOON

    Brother mine, calm wanderer,   335
    Happy globe of land and air,
Some Spirit is darted like a beam from thee.
    Which penetrates my frozen frame,
    And passes with the warmth of flame,
With love, and odor, and deep melody   340
        Through me, through me!

THE EARTH

Ha! ha! the caverns of my hollow mountains,
    My cloven fire-crags, sound-exulting foun-
        tains,
Laugh with a vast and inextinguishable laugh-
    ter.   344
    The oceans, and the deserts, and the abysses,
    And the deep air's unmeasured wildernesses,
Answer from all their clouds and billows, echo-
    ing after.
    They cry aloud as I do. Sceptered curse,
    Who all our green and azure universe
Threatenedst to muffle round with black de-
    struction, sending   350
    A solid cloud to rain hot thunderstones,
    And splinter and knead down my children's
        bones,
All I bring forth, to one void mass, battering
    and blending,—

Until each crag-like tower, and storied col-
    umn,
Palace, and obelisk, and temple solemn,   355
My imperial mountains crowned with cloud,
    and snow, and fire;
    My sea-like forests, every blade and blossom
    Which finds a grave or cradle in my bosom,
Were stamped by thy strong hate into a lifeless
    mire.

    How art thou sunk, withdrawn, covered,
        drunk up   360
    By thirsty nothing, as the brackish cup
Drained by a desert-troop, a little drop for all;
    And from beneath, around, within, above,
    Filling thy void annihilation, love
Burst in like light on caves cloven by the
    thunder-ball.   365

THE MOON

    The snow upon my lifeless mountains
    Is loosened into living fountains,
My solid oceans flow, and sing, and shine:
    A spirit from my heart bursts forth,
    It clothes with unexpected birth   370
My cold bare bosom: Oh! it must be thine
        On mine, on mine!

    Gazing on thee I feel, I know
    Green stalks burst forth, and bright flowers
        grow,
And living shapes upon my bosom move: 375
    Music is in the sea and air,
    Wingèd clouds soar here and there,
Dark with the rain new buds are dreaming of:
        'T is love, all love!

THE EARTH

    It interpenetrates my granite mass,   380
    Through tangled roots and trodden clay doth
        pass,
Into the utmost leaves and delicatest flowers;
    Upon the winds, among the clouds 't is spread,
    It wakes a life in the forgotten dead,
They breathe a spirit up from their obscurest
    bowers,   385

    And like a storm bursting its cloudy prison
    With thunder, and with whirlwind, has arisen
Out of the lampless caves of unimagined being:
    With earthquake shock and swiftness mak-
        ing shiver
    Thought's stagnant chaos, unremoved for
        ever,   390
Till hate, and fear, and pain, light-vanquished
    shadows, fleeing,

    Leave Man, who was a many-sided mirror,
    Which could distort to many a shape of error,
This true fair world of things, a sea reflecting
    love;   394

Which over all his kind as the sun's heaven
Gliding o'er ocean, smooth, serene and even
Darting from starry depths radiance and life, doth move,

Leave Man, even as a leprous child is left,
Who follows a sick beast to some warm cleft
Of rocks, through which the might of healing springs is poured; 400
Then when it wanders home with rosy smile,
Unconscious, and its mother fears awhile
It is a spirit, then, weeps on her child restored—

Man, oh, not men! a chain of linkèd thought,
Of love and might to be divided not, 405
Compelling the elements with adamantine stress;
As the sun rules, even with a tyrant's gaze,
The unquiet republic of the maze
Of planets, struggling fierce towards heaven's free wilderness—

Man, one harmonious soul of many a soul, 410
Whose nature is its own divine control,
Where all things flow to all, as rivers to the sea;
Familiar acts are beautiful through love;
Labor, and pain, and grief, in life's green grove
Sport like tame beasts, none knew how gentle they could be! 415

His will, with all mean passions, bad delights,
And selfish cares, its trembling satellites,
A spirit ill to guide, but mighty to obey,
Is as a tempest-wingèd ship whose helm
Love rules, through waves which dare not overwhelm, 420
Forcing life's wildest shores to own its sovereign sway.

All things confess his strength. Through the cold mass
Of marble and of color his dreams pass;
Bright threads whence mothers weave the robes their children wear;
Language is a perpetual orphic song, 425
Which rules with Dædal harmony a throng
Of thoughts and forms, which else senseless and shapeless were.

The lightning is his slave; heaven's utmost deep
Gives up her stars, and like a flock of sheep
They pass before his eyes, are numbered, and roll on! 430
The tempest is his steed, he strides the air;
And the abyss shouts from her depth laid bare,
Heaven, hast thou secrets? Man unveils me; I have none.

THE MOON

The shadow of white death has past
From my path in heaven at last 435
A clinging shroud of solid frost and sleep;
And through my newly-woven bowers
Wander happy paramours,
Less mighty, but as mild as those who keep
Thy vales more deep. 440

THE EARTH

As the dissolving warmth of dawn may fold
A half unfrozen dew-globe, green and gold,
And crystalline, till it becomes a wingèd mist,
And wanders up the vault of the blue day, 444
Outlives the noon, and on the sun's last ray
Hangs o'er the sea, a fleece of fire and amethyst.

THE MOON

Thou art folded, thou art lying
In the light which is undying,
Of thine own joy, and heaven's smile divine;
All suns and constellations shower 450
On thee a light, a life, a power
Which doth array thy sphere; thou pourest thine
   On mine, on mine!

THE EARTH

I spin beneath my pyramid of night,
Which points into the heavens dreaming delight, 455
Murmuring victorious joy in my enchanted sleep;
As a youth lulled in love-dreams faintly sighing,
Under the shadows of his beauty lying,
Which round his rest a watch of light and warmth doth keep.

THE MOON

As in the soft and sweet eclipse, 460
When soul meets soul on lovers' lips,
High hearts are calm, and brightest eyes are dull;
So when thy shadow falls on me,
Then am I mute and still, by thee
Covered: of thy love, Orb most beautiful, 465
   Full, oh, too full!

Thou art speeding round the sun,
Brightest world of many a one;
Green and azure sphere which shinest
With a light which is divinest 470
Among all the lamps of Heaven
To whom light and life is given;
I, thy crystal paramour,
Borne beside thee by a power
Like the polar Paradise, 475
Magnet-like of lovers' eyes;
I, a most enamored maiden
Whose weak brain is overladen

With the pleasure of her love,
Maniac-like around thee move 480
Gazing, an insatiate bride,
On thy form from every side
Like a Mænad, round the cup
Which Agavë lifted up
In the weird Cadmeian forest. 485
Brother, wheresoe'er thou soarest
I must hurry, whirl and follow
Through the heavens wide and hollow,
Sheltered by the warm embrace
Of thy soul from hungry space, 490
Drinking from thy sense and sight
Beauty, majesty, and might,
As a lover or chameleon
Grows like what it looks upon,
As a violet's gentle eye 495
Gazes on the azure sky
Until its hue grows like what it beholds,
As a gray and watery mist
Glows like solid amethyst
Athwart the western mountain it enfolds, 500
When the sunset sleeps
Upon its snow.

THE EARTH

And the weak day weeps
That it should be so.
Oh, gentle Moon, the voice of thy delight 505
Falls on me like thy clear and tender light
Soothing the seaman, borne the summer night,
Through isles for ever calm;
Oh, gentle Moon, thy crystal accents pierce
The caverns of my pride's deep universe, 510
Charming the tiger joy, whose tramplings fierce
Made wounds which need thy balm.

PANTHEA

I rise as from a bath of sparkling water,
A bath of azure light, among dark rocks,
Out of the stream of sound. 515

IONE

Ah me! sweet sister,
The stream of sound has ebbed away from us,
And you pretend to rise out of its wave,
Because your words fall like the clear, soft dew
Shaken from a bathing wood-nymph's limbs and
hair. 520

PANTHEA

Peace! peace! A mighty Power, which is as
darkness,
Is rising out of Earth, and from the sky
Is showered like night, and from within the air
Bursts, like eclipse which had been gathered up
Into the pores of sunlight: the bright visions, 525
Wherein the singing spirits rode and shone,
Gleam like pale meteors through a watery
night.

IONE

There is a sense of words upon mine ear.

PANTHEA

An universal sound like words: Oh, list! 530

DEMOGORGON

Thou, Earth, calm empire of a happy soul,
Sphere of divinest shapes and harmonies,
Beautiful orb! gathering as thou dost roll
The love which paves thy path along the
skies:

THE EARTH

I hear: I am as a drop of dew that dies. 535

DEMOGORGON

Thou, Moon, which gazest on the nightly Earth
With wonder, as it gazes upon thee;
Whilst each to men, and beasts, and the swift
birth
Of birds, is beauty, love, calm, harmony:

THE MOON

I hear: I am a leaf shaken by thee! 540

DEMOGORGON

Ye kings of suns and stars, Demons and Gods,
Ethereal Dominations, who possess
Elysian, windless, fortunate abodes
Beyond Heaven's constellated wilderness:

A VOICE FROM ABOVE

Our great Republic hears, we are blest, and
bless. 545

DEMOGORGON

Ye happy dead, whom beams of brightest verse
Are clouds to hide, not colors to portray,
Whether your nature is that universe
Which once ye saw and suffered—

A VOICE FROM BENEATH

Or as they 550
Whom we have left, we change and pass away.

DEMOGORGON

Ye elemental Genii, who have homes
From man's high mind even to the central
stone
Of sullen lead; from Heaven's star-fretted domes
To the dull weed some sea-worm battens on:

A CONFUSED VOICE

We hear: thy words waken Oblivion. 556

DEMOGORGON

Spirits, whose homes are flesh: ye beasts and
birds,
Ye worms, and fish; ye living leaves and buds;
Lightning and wind; and ye untamable herds,
Meteors and mists, which throng air's soli-
tudes:— 560

A VOICE

Thy voice to us is wind among still woods.

DEMOGORGON

Man, who wert once a despot and a slave;
  A dupe and a deceiver; a decay;
A traveler from the cradle to the grave
  Through the dim night of this immortal day:

ALL

Speak; thy strong words may never pass away.   566

DEMOGORGON

This is the day, which down the void abysm
At the Earth-born's spell yawns for Heaven's despotism,
  And Conquest is dragged captive through the deep:
Love, from its awful throne of patient power   570
  In the wise heart, from the last giddy hour
Of dead endurance, from the slippery, steep,
And narrow verge of crag-like agony, springs
And folds over the world its healing wings.   574

Gentleness, Virtue, Wisdom, and Endurance,
These are the seals of that most firm assurance
  Which bars the pit over Destruction's strength;
And if, with infirm hand, Eternity,
Mother of many acts and hours, should free
  The serpent that would clasp her with his length;   580
These are the spells by which to reassume
An empire o'er the disentangled doom.

To suffer woes which Hope thinks infinite;
To forgive wrongs darker than death or night;
  To defy Power, which seems omnipotent;   585
To love, and bear; to hope till Hope creates
From its own wreck the thing it contemplates;
  Neither to change, nor falter, nor repent;
This, like thy glory, Titan, is to be
Good, great and joyous, beautiful and free;   590
This is alone Life, Joy, Empire, and Victory.

(1820)

ODE TO THE WEST WIND

I

O, WILD West Wind, thou breath of Autumn's being,
  Thou, from whose unseen presence the leaves dead
  Are driven, like ghosts from an enchanter fleeing,

Yellow, and black, and pale, and hectic red,
  Pestilence-stricken multitudes: O, thou,   5
  Who chariotest to their dark wintry bed

The wingèd seeds, where they lie cold and low,
  Each like a corpse within its grave, until
  Thine azure sister of the spring shall blow

Her clarion o'er the dreaming earth, and fill   10
  (Driving sweet buds like flocks to feed in air)
  With living hues and odors plain and hill:

Wild Spirit, which art moving everywhere;
Destroyer and preserver; hear, O, hear!

II

THOU on whose stream, 'mid the steep sky's commotion,   15
  Loose clouds like earth's decaying leaves are shed,
  Shook from the tangled boughs of Heaven and Ocean,

Angels of rain and lightning: there are spread
  On the blue surface of thine airy surge,   19
  Like the bright hair uplifted from the head

Of some fierce Mænad, even from the dim verge
  Of the horizon to the zenith's height
  The locks of the approaching storm. Thou dirge

Of the dying year, to which this closing night
  Will be the dome of a vast sepulcher,   25
  Vaulted with all thy congregated might

Of vapors, from whose solid atmosphere
Black rain, and fire, and hail will burst: O, hear!

III

THOU who didst waken from his summer dreams
  The blue Mediterranean, where he lay,   30
  Lulled by the coil of his crystalline streams,

Beside a pumice isle in Baiæ's bay,
  And saw in sleep old palaces and towers
  Quivering within the wave's intenser day,

All overgrown with azure moss and flowers   35
  So sweet, the sense faints picturing them! Thou
  For whose path the Atlantic's level powers

Cleave themselves into chasms, while far below
  The sea-blooms and the oozy woods which wear
  The sapless foliage of the ocean, know   40

Thy voice, and suddenly grow gray with fear,
And tremble and despoil themselves: O, hear!

IV

If I were a dead leaf thou mightest bear;
  If I were a swift cloud to fly with thee;
  A wave to pant beneath thy power, and share

The impulse of thy strength, only less free   46
  Than thou, O, uncontrollable! If even
  I were as in my boyhood, and could be

The comrade of thy wanderings over heaven,
  As then, when to outstrip thy skiey speed 50
Scarce seemed a vision; I would ne'er have
    striven
As thus with thee in prayer in my sore need.
  Oh! lift me as a wave, a leaf, a cloud!
  I fall upon the thorns of life! I bleed!
A heavy weight of hours has chained and bowed
  One too like thee: tameless, and swift, and
    proud.   56

            v

Make me thy lyre, even as the forest is:
  What if my leaves are falling like its own!
  The tumult of thy mighty harmonies
Will take from both a deep, autumnal tone,
  Sweet though in sadness. Be thou, spirit
    fierce,   61
My spirit! Be thou me, impetuous one!
Drive my dead thoughts over the universe
  Like withered leaves to quicken a new birth!
  And, by the incantation of this verse,   65
Scatter, as from an unextinguished hearth
  Ashes and sparks, my words among mankind!
  Be through my lips to unawakened earth
The trumpet of a prophecy! O, wind,
If Winter comes, can Spring be far behind?   70
                (1820)

THE INDIAN SERENADE

I arise from dreams of thee
  In the first sweet sleep of night,
When the winds are breathing low,
  And the stars are shining bright:
I arise from dreams of thee,   5
  And a spirit in my feet
Hath led me—who knows how?
  To thy chamber window, Sweet!

The wandering airs they faint
  On the dark, the silent stream—   10
The Champak odors fail
  Like sweet thoughts in a dream;
The nightingale's complaint,
  It dies upon her heart;—
As I must on thine,   15
  O! belovèd as thou art!

O lift me from the grass!
  I die! I faint! I fail!
Let thy love in kisses rain
  On my lips and eyelids pale.   20
My cheek is cold and white, alas!
  My heart beats loud and fast;—
Oh! press it to thine own again,
  Where it will break at last.
                (1822)

THE CLOUD

I bring fresh showers for the thirsting flowers,
  From the seas and the streams;
I bear light shade for the leaves when laid
  In their noon-day dreams.
From my wings are shaken the dews that waken
  The sweet buds every one,   6
When rocked to rest on their mother's breast,
  As she dances about the sun.
I wield the flail of the lashing hail,
  And whiten the green plains under, 10
And then again I dissolve it in rain,
  And laugh as I pass in thunder.

I sift the snow on the mountains below,
  And their great pines groan aghast;
And all the night 't is my pillow white, 15
  While I sleep in the arms of the blast.
Sublime on the towers of my skiey bowers,
  Lightning my pilot sits;
In a cavern under is fettered the thunder,—
  It struggles and howls at fits;   20
Over earth and ocean, with gentle motion,
  This pilot is guiding me,
Lured by the love of the genii that move
  In the depths of the purple sea;
Over the rills, and the crags, and the hills, 25
  Over the lakes and the plains,
Wherever he dream, under mountain or stream,
  The Spirit he loves remains;
And I all the while bask in heaven's blue smile,
  Whilst he is dissolving in rains.   30

The sanguine sunrise, with his meteor eyes,
  And his burning plumes outspread,
Leaps on the back of my sailing rack,
  When the morning star shines dead,
As on the jag of a mountain crag,   35
  Which an earthquake rocks and swings,
An eagle alit one moment may sit
  In the light of its golden wings.
And when sunset may breathe, from the lit sea
    beneath,
  Its ardors of rest and of love,   40
And the crimson pall of eve may fall
  From the depth of heaven above,
With wings folded I rest, on mine airy nest,
  As still as a brooding dove.

That orbèd maiden with white fire laden,   45
  Whom mortals call the moon,
Glides glimmering o'er my fleece-like floor,
  By the midnight breezes strewn;
And wherever the beat of her unseen feet,
  Which only the angels hear,   50
May have broken the woof of my tent's thin
    roof,
  The stars peep behind her and peer;
And I laugh to see them whirl and flee,
  Like a swarm of golden bees,

When I widen the rent in my wind-built tent, 55
  Till the calm rivers, lakes, and seas,
Like strips of the sky fallen through me on high,
  Are each paved with the moon and these.

I bind the sun's throne with a burning zone,
  And the moon's with a girdle of pearl;   60
The volcanoes are dim, and the stars reel and swim,
  When the whirlwinds my banner unfurl.
From cape to cape, with a bridge-like shape,
  Over a torrent sea,
Sunbeam-proof, I hang like a roof,   65
  The mountains its columns be.
The triumphal arch through which I march
  With hurricane, fire, and snow,
When the powers of the air are chained to my chair,
  Is the million-colored bow;   70
The sphere-fire above its soft colors wove,
  While the moist earth was laughing below.

I am the daughter of earth and water,
  And the nursling of the sky;   74
I pass through the pores of the ocean and shores;
  I change, but I cannot die.
For after the rain when, with never a stain,
  The pavilion of heaven is bare,
And the winds and sunbeams with their convex gleams
  Build up the blue dome of air,   80
I silently laugh at my own cenotaph,
  And out of the caverns of rain,
Like a child from the womb, like a ghost from the tomb,
  I arise and unbuild it again.

(1820)

TO A SKYLARK

Hail to thee, blithe spirit!
  Bird thou never wert,
That from heaven, or near it,
  Pourest thy full heart
In profuse strains of unpremeditated art.   5

  Higher still and higher
    From the earth thou springest
  Like a cloud of fire;
    The blue deep thou wingest,
And singing still dost soar, and soaring ever singest.   10

  In the golden lightning
    Of the sunken sun,
  O'er which clouds are brightning,
    Thou dost float and run;
Like an unbodied joy whose race is just begun.   15

  The pale purple even
    Melts around thy flight;
  Like a star of heaven
    In the broad day-light
Thou art unseen, but yet I hear thy shrill delight,   20

  Keen as are the arrows
    Of that silver sphere,
  Whose intense lamp narrows
    In the white dawn clear,
Until we hardly see, we feel that it is there.

  All the earth and air   26
    With thy voice is loud,
  As, when night is bare,
    From one lonely cloud
The moon rains out her beams, and heaven is overflowed.   30

  What thou art we know not;
    What is most like thee?
  From rainbow clouds there flow not
    Drops so bright to see
As from thy presence showers a rain of melody.

  Like a poet hidden   36
    In the light of thought,
  Singing hymns unbidden,
    Till the world is wrought
To sympathy with hopes and fears it heeded not: 40

  Like a high-born maiden
    In a palace tower,
  Soothing her love-laden
    Soul in secret hour
With music sweet as love, which overflows her bower: 45

  Like a glow-worm golden
    In a dell of dew,
  Scattering unbeholden
    Its aërial hue
Among the flowers and grass which screen it from the view: 50

  Like a rose embowered
    In its own green leaves,
  By warm winds deflowered,
    Till the scent it gives
Makes faint with too much sweet these heavy-wingèd thieves.   55

  Sound of vernal showers
    On the twinkling grass,
  Rain-awakened flowers,
    All that ever was
Joyous, and clear, and fresh, thy music doth surpass.   60

Teach us, sprite or bird,
    What sweet thoughts are thine;
  I have never heard
    Praise of love or wine
That panted forth a flood of rapture so divine:

  Chorus Hymenæal,   66
    Or triumphal chaunt,
  Matched with thine, would be all
    But an empty vaunt,
A thing wherein we feel there is some hidden
    want.   70

  What objects are the fountains
    Of thy happy strain?
  What fields, or waves, or mountains?
    What shapes of sky or plain?
What love of thine own kind? what ignorance
    of pain?   75

  With thy clear keen joyance
    Languor cannot be—
  Shadow of annoyance
    Never came near thee:
Thou lovest—but ne'er knew love's sad satiety.

  Waking or asleep,   81
    Thou of death must deem
  Things more true and deep
    Than we mortals dream,
Or how could thy notes flow in such a crystal
    stream?   85

  We look before and after
    And pine for what is not:
  Our sincerest laughter
    With some pain is fraught;
Our sweetest songs are those that tell of saddest
    thought.   90

  Yet if we could scorn
    Hate, and pride, and fear;
  If we were things born
    Not to shed a tear,
I know not how thy joy we ever should come
    near.   95

  Better than all measures
    Of delightful sound—
  Better than all treasures
    That in books are found—
Thy skill to poet were, thou scorner of the
    ground!   100

  Teach me half the gladness
    That thy brain must know,
  Such harmonious madness
    From my lips would flow,
The world should listen then—as I am listening
    now.   105
        (1820)

A LAMENT

O WORLD! O life! O time!
  On whose last steps I climb
    Trembling at that where I had stood before;
When will return the glory of your prime?
    No more—Oh, never more!   5

Out of the day and night
  A joy has taken flight;
    Fresh spring, and summer, and winter hoar,
Move my faint heart with grief, but with delight
    No more—Oh, never more!   10
        (1824)

TO ——

Music, when soft voices die,
Vibrates in the memory—
Odors, when sweet violets sicken,
Live within the sense they quicken,

Rose leaves, when the rose is dead,   5
Are heaped for the belovèd's bed;
And so thy thoughts, when thou art gone,
Love itself shall slumber on.
        (1824)

ADONAIS

I WEEP for Adonais—he is dead!
O, weep for Adonais! though our tears
Thaw not the frost which binds so dear a head!
And thou, sad Hour, selected from all years
To mourn our loss, rouse thy obscure compeers,
And teach them thine own sorrow! Say: 'With
    me   6
Died Adonais; till the Future dares
Forget the Past, his fate and fame shall be
An echo and a light unto eternity!'

Where wert thou, mighty Mother, when he lay,
When thy Son lay, pierced by the shaft which
    flies   11
In darkness? where was lorn Urania
When Adonais died? With veilèd eyes,
'Mid listening Echoes, in her Paradise
She sate, while one, with soft enamored breath,
Rekindled all the fading melodies,   16
With which, like flowers that mock the corse
    beneath,
He had adorned and hid the coming bulk of
    death.

O, weep for Adonais—he is dead!
Wake, melancholy Mother, wake and weep!   20
Yet wherefore? Quench within their burning bed
Thy fiery tears, and let thy loud heart keep
Like his, a mute and uncomplaining sleep;

For he is gone, where all things wise and fair
Descend;—oh, dream not that the amorous
    Deep   25
Will yet restore him to the vital air;
Death feeds on his mute voice, and laughs at
    our despair.

Most musical of mourners, weep again!
Lament anew, Urania!—He died,—
Who was the Sire of an immortal strain,   30
Blind, old, and lonely, when his country's
    pride,
The priest, the slave, and the liberticide,
Trampled and mocked with many a loathèd rite
Of lust and blood; he went, unterrified,
Into the gulph of death; but his clear Sprite   35
Yet reigns o'er earth: the third among the sons
    of light.

Most musical of mourners, weep anew!
Not all to that bright station dared to climb;
And happier they their happiness who knew,
Whose tapers yet burn through that night of
    time   40
In which suns perished; others more sublime,
Struck by the envious wrath of man or God,
Have sunk, extinct in their refulgent prime;
And some yet live, treading the thorny road,
Which leads, through toil and hate, to Fame's
    serene abode.   45

But now, thy youngest, dearest one has perished,
The nursling of thy widowhood, who grew,
Like a pale flower by some sad maiden cherished,
And fed with true love tears, instead of dew;
Most musical of mourners, weep anew!   50
Thy extreme hope, the loveliest and the last,
The bloom, whose petals, nipped before they
    blew,
Died on the promise of the fruit, is waste;
The broken lily lies—the storm is overpast.

To that high Capital, where kingly Death   55
Keeps his pale court in beauty and decay,
He came; and bought, with price of purest
    breath,
A grave among the eternal.—Come away!
Haste, while the vault of blue Italian day
Is yet his fitting charnel-roof! while still   60
He lies, as if in dewy sleep he lay;
Awake him not! surely he takes his fill
Of deep and liquid rest, forgetful of all ill.

He will awake no more, oh, never more!—
Within the twilight chamber spreads apace,   65
The shadow of white Death, and at the door
Invisible Corruption waits to trace
His extreme way to her dim dwelling-place;
The eternal Hunger sits, but pity and awe
Soothe her pale rage, nor dares she to deface   70
So fair a prey, till darkness, and the law
Of change, shall o'er his sleep the mortal cur-
    tain draw.

O, weep for Adonais!—The quick Dreams,
The passion-wingèd Ministers of thought,
Who were his flocks, whom near the living
    streams   75
Of his young spirit he fed, and whom he taught
The love which was its music, wander not,—
Wander no more, from kindling brain to brain,
But droop there, whence they sprung; and
    mourn their lot
Round the cold heart, where, after their sweet
    pain,   80
They ne'er will gather strength, or find a home
    again.

And one with trembling hands clasps his cold
    head,
And fans him with her moonlight wings, and
    cries:
'Our love, our hope, our sorrow, is not dead;
See, on the silken fringe of his faint eyes,   85
Like dew upon a sleeping flower, there lies
A tear some Dream has loosened from his brain.'
Lost Angel of a ruined Paradise!
She knew not 't was her own; as with no stain
She faded, like a cloud which had outwept its
    rain.   90

One from a lucid urn of starry dew
Washed his light limbs as if embalming them:
Another clipped her profuse locks, and threw
The wreath upon him, like an anadem,
Which frozen tears instead of pearls begem;   95
Another in her wilful grief would break
Her bow and wingèd reeds, as if to stem
A greater loss with one which was more weak;
And dull the barbèd fire against his frozen
    cheek.

Another Splendor on his mouth alit,   100
That mouth, whence it was wont to draw the
    breath
Which gave it strength to pierce the guarded
    wit,
And pass into the panting heart beneath
With lightning and with music: the damp death
Quenched its caress upon his icy lips;   105
And, as a dying meteor stains a wreath
Of moonlight vapor, which the cold night clips,
It flushed through his pale limbs, and passed to
    its eclipse.

And others came . . . Desires and Adorations,
Wingèd Persuasions and veiled Destinies,   110
Splendors, and Glooms, and glimmering In-
    carnations
Of hopes and fears, and twilight Phantasies;
And Sorrow, with her family of Sighs,
And Pleasure, blind with tears, led by the gleam
Of her own dying smile instead of eyes,   115
Came in slow pomp;—the moving pomp might
    seem
Like pageantry of mist on an autumnal stream.

All he had loved, and molded into thought,
From shape, and hue, and odor, and sweet sound,
Lamented Adonais. Morning sought   120
Her eastern watch-tower, and her hair unbound,
Wet with the tears which should adorn the ground,
Dimmed the aërial eyes that kindle day;
Afar the melancholy thunder moaned,
Pale Ocean in unquiet slumber lay,   125
And the wild winds flew round, sobbing in their dismay.

Lost Echo sits amid the voiceless mountains,
And feeds her grief with his remembered lay,
And will no more reply to winds or fountains,
Or amorous birds perched on the young green spray,   130
Or herdsman's horn, or bell at closing day;
Since she can mimic not his lips, more dear
Than those for whose disdain she pined away
Into a shadow of all sounds;—a drear
Murmur, between their songs, is all the woodmen hear.   135

Grief made the young Spring wild, and she threw down
Her kindling buds, as if she Autumn were,
Or they dead leaves; since her delight is flown,
For whom should she have waked the sullen year?
To Phœbus was not Hyacinth so dear   140
Nor to himself Narcissus, as to both
Thou, Adonais: wan they stand and sere
Amid the faint companions of their youth,
With dew all turned to tears; odor, to sighing ruth.

Thy spirit's sister, the lorn nightingale,   145
Mourns not her mate with such melodious pain;
Not so the eagle, who like thee could scale
Heaven, and could nourish in the sun's domain
Her mighty youth with morning, doth complain,
Soaring and screaming round her empty nest,
As Albion wails for thee: the curse of Cain   151
Light on his head who pierced thy innocent breast,
And scared the angel soul that was its earthly guest!

Ah, woe is me! Winter is come and gone,
But grief returns with the revolving year;   155
The airs and streams renew their joyous tone;
The ants, the bees, the swallows reappear;
Fresh leaves and flowers deck the dead Seasons' bier;
The amorous birds now pair in every brake,
And build their mossy homes in field and brere;
And the green lizard, and the golden snake,   161
Like unimprisoned flames, out of their trance awake.

Through wood and stream and field and hill and Ocean
A quickening life from the Earth's heart has burst,
As it has ever done, with change and motion 165
From the great morning of the world when first
God dawned on Chaos; in its stream immersed
The lamps of Heaven flash with a softer light;
All baser things pant with life's sacred thirst;
Diffuse themselves; and spend in love's delight
The beauty and the joy of their renewèd might.

The leprous corpse touched by this spirit tender
Exhales itself in flowers of gentle breath;
Like incarnations of the stars, when splendor
Is changed to fragrance, they illumine death 175
And mock the merry worm that wakes beneath;
Naught we know, dies. Shall that alone which knows
Be as a sword consumed before the sheath
By sightless lightning?—the intense atom glows
A moment, then is quenched in a most cold repose.   180

Alas! that all we loved of him should be,
But for our grief, as if it had not been,
And grief itself be mortal! Woe is me!
Whence are we, and why are we? of what scene
The actors or spectators? Great and mean 185
Meet massed in death, who lends what life must borrow.
As long as skies are blue, and fields are green,
Evening must usher night, night urge the morrow,
Month follow month with woe, and year wake year to sorrow.

He will awake no more, oh, never more!   190
'Wake thou,' cried Misery, 'childless Mother, rise
Out of thy sleep, and slake, in thy heart's core,
A wound more fierce than his with tears and sighs.'
And all the Dreams that watched Urania's eyes,
And all the Echoes whom their sister's song 195
Had held in holy silence, cried: 'Arise!'
Swift as a Thought by the snake Memory stung,
From her ambrosial rest the fading Splendor sprung.

She rose like an autumnal Night, that springs
Out of the East, and follows wild and drear 200
The golden Day, which, on eternal wings,
Even as a ghost abandoning a bier,
Had left the Earth a corpse. Sorrow and fear
So struck, so roused, so rapt Urania;
So saddened round her like an atmosphere 205
Of stormy mist; so swept her on her way
Even to the mournful place where Adonais lay.

Out of her secret Paradise she sped,
Through camps and cities rough with stone and
    steel,
And human hearts, which to her aëry tread 210
Yielding not, wounded the invisible
Palms of her tender feet where'er they fell:
And barbèd tongues, and thoughts more sharp
    than they,
Rent the soft Form they never could repel,
Whose sacred blood, like the young tears of
    May, 215
Paved with eternal flowers that undeserving
    way.

In the death chamber for a moment Death,
Shamed by the presence of that living Might,
Blushed to annihilation, and the breath
Revisited those lips, and life's pale light 220
Flashed through those limbs, so late her dear
    delight.
'Leave me not wild and drear and comfortless,
As silent lightning leaves the starless night!
Leave me not!' cried Urania: her distress
Roused Death: Death rose and smiled, and met
    her vain caress. 225

'Stay yet awhile! speak to me once again;
Kiss me, so long but as a kiss may live;
And in my heartless breast and burning brain
That word, that kiss shall all thoughts else
    survive,
With food of saddest memory kept alive, 230
Now thou art dead, as if it were a part
Of thee, my Adonais! I would give
All that I am to be as thou now art!
But I am chained to Time, and cannot thence
    depart!

'Oh gentle child, beautiful as thou wert, 235
Why didst thou leave the trodden paths of men
Too soon, and with weak hands though mighty
    heart
Dare the unpastured dragon in his den?
Defenceless as thou wert, oh, where was then
Wisdom the mirrored shield, or scorn the spear?
Or hadst thou waited the full cycle, when 241
Thy spirit should have filled its crescent sphere,
The monsters of life's waste had fled from thee
    like deer.

'The herded wolves, bold only to pursue;
The obscene ravens, clamorous o'er the dead; 245
The vultures to the conqueror's banner true,
Who feed where Desolation first has fed,
And whose wings rain contagion;—how they
    fled,
When like Apollo, from his golden bow,
The Pythian of the age one arrow sped 250
And smiled!—The spoilers tempt no second
    blow;
They fawn on the proud feet that spurn them
    lying low.

'The sun comes forth, and many reptiles spawn;
He sets, and each ephemeral insect then
Is gathered into death without a dawn, 255
And the immortal stars awake again;
So is it in the world of living men:
A godlike mind soars forth, in its delight
Making earth bare and veiling heaven, and
    when
It sinks, the swarms that dimmed or shared its
    light 260
Leave to its kindred lamps the spirit's awful
    night.'

Thus ceased she: and the mountain shepherds
    came,
Their garlands sere, their magic mantles rent;
The Pilgrim of Eternity, whose fame
Over his living head like Heaven is bent, 265
An early but enduring monument,
Came, veiling all the lightnings of his song
In sorrow: from her wilds Ierne sent
The sweetest lyrist of her saddest wrong,
And love taught grief to fall like music from
    his tongue. 270

Midst others of less note, came one frail Form,
A phantom among men, companionless
As the last cloud of an expiring storm
Whose thunder is its knell; he, as I guess,
Had gazed on Nature's naked loveliness, 275
Actæon-like, and now he fled astray
With feeble steps o'er the world's wilderness,
And his own thoughts, along that rugged way,
Pursued, like raging hounds, their father and
    their prey.

A pardlike Spirit beautiful and swift— 280
A Love in desolation masked;—a Power
Girt round with weakness;—it can scarce uplift
The weight of the superincumbent hour;
It is a dying lamp, a falling shower,
A breaking billow;—even whilst we speak 285
Is it not broken? On the withering flower
The killing sun smiles brightly; on a cheek
The life can burn in blood, even while the heart
    may break.

His head was bound with pansies overblown,
And faded violets, white, and pied, and blue;
And a light spear topped with a cypress cone, 291
Round whose rude shaft dark ivy tresses grew
Yet dripping with the forest's noonday dew,
Vibrated, as the ever-beating heart
Shook the weak hand that grasped it; of that
    crew 295
He came the last, neglected and apart;
A herd-abandoned deer, struck by the hunter's
    dart.

All stood aloof, and at his partial moan
Smiled through their tears; well knew that
    gentle band
Who in another's fate now wept his own, 300

As, in the accents of an unknown land,
He sung new sorrow; sad Urania scanned
The Stranger's mien, and murmured: 'Who art
  thou?'
He answered not, but with a sudden hand
Made bare his branded and ensanguined brow,
Which was like Cain's or Christ's—Oh! that it
  should be so!   306

What softer voice is hushed over the dead?
Athwart what brow is that dark mantle thrown?
What form leans sadly o'er the white death-bed,
In mockery of monumental stone,   310
The heavy heart heaving without a moan?
If it be He, who, gentlest of the wise,
Taught, soothed, loved, honored the departed
  one,
Let me not vex with inharmonious sighs
The silence of that heart's accepted sacrifice. 315

Our Adonais has drunk poison—oh!
What deaf and viperous murderer could crown
Life's early cup with such a draught of woe?
The nameless worm would now itself disown:
It felt, yet could escape, the magic tone   320
Whose prelude held all envy, hate, and wrong,
But what was howling in one breast alone,
Silent with expectation of the song,
Whose master's hand is cold, whose silver lyre
  unstrung.

Live thou, whose infamy is not thy fame!   325
Live! fear no heavier chastisement from me,
Thou noteless blot on a remembered name!
But be thyself, and know thyself to be:
And ever at thy season be thou free
To spill the venom when thy fangs o'erflow: 330
Remorse and Self-contempt shall cling to thee;
Hot Shame shall burn upon thy secret brow,
And like a beaten hound tremble thou shalt—
  as now.

Nor let us weep that our delight is fled
Far from these carrion kites that scream below;
He wakes or sleeps with the enduring dead;   336
Thou canst not soar where he is sitting now.—
Dust to the dust! but the pure spirit shall flow
Back to the burning fountain whence it came,
A portion of the Eternal, which must glow   340
Through time and change, unquenchably the
  same,
Whilst thy cold embers choke the sordid hearth
  of shame.

Peace, peace! he is not dead, he doth not sleep—
He hath awakened from the dream of life—
'T is we who, lost in stormy visions, keep   345
With phantoms an unprofitable strife,
And in mad trance strike with our spirit's knife
Invulnerable nothings.—*We* decay
Like corpses in a charnel; fear and grief

Convulse us and consume us day by day,   350
And cold hopes swarm like worms within our
  living clay.

He has outsoared the shadow of our night;
Envy and calumny and hate and pain,
And that unrest which men miscall delight,
Can touch him not and torture not again;   355
From the contagion of the world's slow stain
He is secure, and now can never mourn
A heart grown cold, a head grown gray in vain;
Nor, when the spirit's self has ceased to burn,
With sparkless ashes load an unlamented urn.

He lives, he wakes—'t is Death is dead, not he;
Mourn not for Adonais.—Thou young Dawn, 362
Turn all thy dew to splendor, for from thee
The spirit thou lamentest is not gone;
Ye caverns and ye forests, cease to moan!   365
Cease, ye faint flowers and fountains, and thou
  Air,
Which like a mourning veil thy scarf hadst
  thrown
O'er the abandoned Earth, now leave it bare
Even to the joyous stars which smile on its
  despair!

He is made one with Nature: there is heard   370
His voice in all her music, from the moan
Of thunder, to the song of night's sweet bird;
He is a presence to be felt and known
In darkness and in light, from herb and stone,
Spreading itself where'er that Power may move
Which has withdrawn his being to its own;   376
Which wields the world with never wearied
  love,
Sustains it from beneath, and kindles it above.

He is a portion of the loveliness
Which once he made more lovely: he doth bear
His part, while the one Spirit's plastic stress 381
Sweeps through the dull dense world, compelling
  there
All new successions to the forms they wear;
Torturing the unwilling dross that checks its
  flight
To its own likeness, as each mass may bear; 385
And bursting in its beauty and its might
From trees and beasts and men into the
  Heaven's light.

The splendors of the firmament of time
May be eclipsed, but are extinguished not;
Like stars to their appointed height they climb
And death is a low mist which cannot blot   391
The brightness it may veil. When lofty thought
Lifts a young heart above its mortal lair,
And love and life contend in it, for what
Shall be its earthly doom, the dead live there 395
And move like winds of light on dark and
  stormy air.

The inheritors of unfulfilled renown
Rose from their thrones, built beyond mortal thought,
Far in the Unapparent.   Chatterton
Rose pale, his solemn agony had not   400
Yet faded from him; Sidney, as he fought
And as he fell and as he lived and loved,
Sublimely mild, a Spirit without spot,
Arose; and Lucan, by his death approved:
Oblivion, as they rose, shrank like a thing reproved.   405

And many more, whose names on Earth are dark
But whose transmitted effluence cannot die
So long as fire outlives the parent spark,
Rose, robed in dazzling immortality.
'Thou art become as one of us,' they cry,   410
'It was for thee yon kingless sphere has long
Swung blind in unascended majesty,
Silent alone amid an Heaven of Song.
Assume thy wingèd throne, thou Vesper of our throng!'

Who mourns for Adonais? oh, come forth,   415
Fond wretch! and know thyself and him aright.
Clasp with thy panting soul the pendulous Earth;
As from a center, dart thy spirit's light
Beyond all worlds, until its spacious might
Satiate the void circumference: then shrink   420
Even to a point within our day and night;
And keep thy heart light, lest it make thee sink,
When hope has kindled hope, and lured thee to the brink.

Or go to Rome, which is the sepulcher,
O, not of him, but of our joy: 't is nought   425
That ages, empires, and religions there
Lie buried in the ravage they have wrought;
For such as he can lend,—they borrow not
Glory from those who made the world their prey;
And he is gathered to the kings of thought   430
Who waged contention with their time's decay,
And of the past are all that cannot pass away.

Go thou to Rome,—at once the Paradise,
The grave, the city, and the wilderness;
And where its wrecks like shattered mountains rise   435
And flowering weeds and fragrant copses dress
The bones of Desolation's nakedness
Pass, till the Spirit of the spot shall lead
Thy footsteps to a slope of green access
Where, like an infant's smile, over the dead,   440
A light of laughing flowers along the grass is spread.

And gray walls moulder round, on which dull Time
Feeds, like slow fire upon a hoary brand,
And one keen pyramid with wedge sublime,
Pavilioning the dust of him who planned   445
This refuge for his memory, doth stand

Like flame transformed to marble; and beneath,
A field is spread, on which a newer band
Have pitched in Heaven's smile their camp of death,
Welcoming him we lose with scarce extinguished breath.   450

Here pause: these graves are all too young as yet
To have outgrown the sorrow which consigned
Its charge to each; and if the seal is set,
Here, on one fountain of a mourning mind,
Break it not thou! too surely shalt thou find   455
Thine own well full, if thou returnest home,
Of tears and gall.   From the world's bitter wind
Seek shelter in the shadow of the tomb.
What Adonais is, why fear we to become?

The One remains, the many change and pass;
Heaven's light forever shines, Earth's shadows fly;   461
Life, like a dome of many-colored glass,
Stains the white radiance of Eternity,
Until Death tramples it to fragments.—Die,
If thou wouldst be with that which thou dost seek!   465
Follow where all is fled!—Rome's azure sky,
Flowers, ruins, statues, music, words, are weak
The glory they transfuse with fitting truth to speak.

Why linger? why turn back, why shrink, my Heart?
Thy hopes are gone before: from all things here   470
They have departed; thou shouldst now depart!
A light is past from the revolving year,
And man, and woman; and what still is dear
Attracts to crush, repels to make thee wither.
The soft sky smiles,—the low wind whispers near;   475
'T is Adonais calls! oh, hasten thither,
No more let Life divide what Death can join together.

That Light whose smile kindles the Universe,
That Beauty in which all things work and move,
That Benediction which the eclipsing Curse   480
Of birth can quench not, that sustaining Love
Which, through the web of being blindly wove
By man and beast and earth and air and sea,
Burns bright or dim, as each are mirrors of
The fire for which all thirst, now beams on me,
Consuming the last clouds of cold mortality.   486

The breath whose might I have invoked in song
Descends on me; my spirit's bark is driven,
Far from the shore, far from the trembling throng
Whose sails were never to the tempest given;   490
The massy earth and spherèd skies are riven!
I am borne darkly, fearfully, afar:
Whilst burning through the inmost veil of Heaven,

The soul of Adonais, like a star,
Beacons from the abode where the Eternal
   are.   495
(1821)

TO NIGHT

Swiftly walk over the western wave,
    Spirit of Night!
Out of the misty eastern cave,
Where all the long and lone daylight,
Thou wovest dreams of joy and fear,   5
Which make thee terrible and dear,—
    Swift be thy flight!

Wrap thy form in a mantle gray,
    Star in-wrought!
Blind with thine hair the eyes of Day;   10
Kiss her until she be wearied out;
Then wander o'er city, and sea, and land,
Touching all with thine opiate wand—
    Come, long sought!

When I arose and saw the dawn,   15
    I sighed for thee;
When light rode high, and the dew was gone,
And noon lay heavy on flower and tree,
And the weary Day turned to his rest,
Lingering like an unloved guest,   20
    I sighed for thee.

Thy brother Death came, and cried,
    Wouldst thou me?
Thy sweet child Sleep, the filmy-eyed,
Murmured like a noon-tide bee,   25
Shall I nestle near thy side?
Wouldst thou me?—And I replied,
    No, not thee!

Death will come when thou art dead,
    Soon, too soon—   30
Sleep will come when thou art fled;
Of neither would I ask the boon
I ask of thee, belovèd Night—
Swift be thine approaching flight,
    Come soon, soon!   35
(1824)

TO ———

One word is too often profaned
    For me to profane it,
One feeling too falsely disdained
    For thee to disdain it.
One hope is too like despair   5
    For prudence to smother,
And pity from thee more dear
    Than that from another.

I can give not what men call love,
    But wilt thou accept not   10
The worship the heart lifts above
    And the Heavens reject not,

The desire of the moth for the star,
    Of the night for the morrow,
The devotion to something afar   15
    From the sphere of our sorrow?
(1824)

WITH A GUITAR, TO JANE

Ariel to Miranda.—Take
This slave of Music, for the sake
Of him who is the slave of thee,
And teach it all the harmony
In which thou canst, and only thou,   5
Make the delighted spirit glow,
Till joy denies itself again,
And, too intense, is turned to pain;
For by permission and command
Of thine own Prince Ferdinand,   10
Poor Ariel sends this silent token
Of more than ever can be spoken;
Your guardian spirit, Ariel, who,
From life to life, must still pursue
Your happiness;—for thus alone   15
Can Ariel ever find his own.
From Prospero's enchanted cell,
As the mighty verses tell,
To the throne of Naples, he
Lit you o'er the trackless sea,   20
Flitting on, your prow before,
Like a living meteor.
When you die, the silent Moon,
In her interlunar swoon,
Is not sadder in her cell   25
Than deserted Ariel.
When you live again on earth,
Like an unseen star of birth,
Ariel guides you o'er the sea
Of life from your nativity.   30
Many changes have been run,
Since Ferdinand and you begun
Your course of love, and Ariel still
Has tracked your steps, and served your will;
Now, in humbler, happier lot,   35
This is all remembered not;
And now, alas! the poor sprite is
Imprisoned, for some fault of his,
In a body like a grave;—
From you he only dares to crave,   40
For his service and his sorrow,
A smile to-day, a song to-morrow.

The artist who this idol wrought,
To echo all harmonious thought,
Felled a tree, while on the steep   45
The woods were in their winter sleep,
Rocked in that repose divine
On the wind-swept Apennine;
And dreaming, some of Autumn past,
And some of Spring approaching fast,   50
And some of April buds and showers,
And some of songs in July bowers,

And all of love; and so this tree,—
Oh, that such our death may be!—
Died in sleep, and felt no pain, 55
To live in happier form again:
From which, beneath Heaven's fairest star,
The artist wrought this loved Guitar,
And taught it justly to reply,
To all who question skilfully, 60
In language gentle as thine own;
Whispering in enamored tone
Sweet oracles of woods and dells,
And summer winds in sylvan cells;
For it had learnt all harmonies 65
Of the plains and of the skies,
Of the forests and the mountains,
And the many-voicèd fountains;
The clearest echoes of the hills,
The softest notes of falling rills, 70
The melodies of birds and bees,
The murmuring of summer seas,
And pattering rain, and breathing dew
And airs of evening; and it knew
That seldom-heard mysterious sound, 75
Which, driven on its diurnal round,
As it floats through boundless day,
Our world enkindles on its way—
All this it knows, but will not tell
To those who cannot question well 80
The spirit that inhabits it;
It talks according to the wit
Of its companions; and no more
Is heard than has been felt before,
By those who tempt it to betray 85
These secrets of an elder day:
But sweetly as its answers will
Flatter hands of perfect skill,
It keeps its highest, holiest tone
For our belovèd Jane alone. 90

(1832–1833)

LINES

WHEN THE LAMP IS SHATTERED

When the lamp is shattered
The light in the dust lies dead—
When the cloud is scattered
   The rainbow's glory is shed.
When the lute is broken, 5
Sweet tones are remembered not;
When the lips have spoken,
Loved accents are soon forgot.

As music and splendor
Survive not the lamp and the lute, 10
   The heart's echoes render
No song when the spirit is mute:—
   No song but sad dirges,
Like the wind through a ruined cell,
   Or the mournful surges 15
That ring the dead seaman's knell.

When hearts have once mingled
Love first leaves the well-built nest,
   The weak one is singled
To endure what it once possessed. 20
   O Love! who bewailest
The frailty of all things here,
   Why choose you the frailest
For your cradle, your home, and your bier?

   Its passions will rock thee 25
As the storms rock the ravens on high:
   Bright reason will mock thee,
Like the sun from a wintry sky.
   From thy nest every rafter
Will rot, and thine eagle home 30
   Leave thee naked to laughter,
When leaves fall and cold winds come.

(1824)

A DIRGE

Rough wind, that moanest loud
   Grief too sad for song;
Wild wind, when sullen cloud
   Knells all the night long;
Sad storm, whose tears are vain, 5
Bare woods, whose branches strain,
Deep caves and dreary main,—
   Wail, for the world's wrong!

(1824)

JOHN KEATS (1795-1821)

The parents of John Keats were living, at the time of his birth, at the Swan-and-Hoop stable in Finsbury, London. As a boy Keats was a sturdy fellow, with a hot temper, fond of fighting, fond of 'gold-finches, tomtits, minnows, mice, tickle-backs, dace, cock-salmons, and all the whole tribe of the bushes and the brooks.' It was toward the end of his schooldays that he was set dreaming by Spenser's *Faery Queen*. He persevered, however, in his medical studies, passed his surgeon's examination with credit, and proved a skilful operator. But he was excessively sensitive to the nervous strain incident to surgery and, also, he was pining for a poetic career, 'Like a sick eagle looking at the sky.' Early in 1816 he met Leigh Hunt and through him numerous poets and artists, including Shelley, Wordsworth, and the painter Haydon. Shelley took a lively interest in him and attempted to show him hospitality. Wordsworth, whom he admired highly, is said to have chilled him by remarking after Keats had recited his *Hymn to Pan* for the benefit of a company: 'A pretty piece of Paganism!' To Haydon he owed something of an initiation into art and an opportunity to lend thirty pounds. In May, 1816, Hunt published in his *Examiner* the sonnet 'O Solitude! if I with thee must dwell,' and Keats had, so to speak, his first taste of blood. He now gave himself with increasing constancy to composition. His first volume came in March, 1817, and a year later, *Endymion*. Chiefly because of Keats's friendship with Hunt, who was hated for his political opinions, these earlier volumes were sneeringly reviewed. Though Keats was indignant, it was by no means, '*The Quarterly*, so savage and tartarly' that killed him. Partly from nursing his brother Tom through his last illness and partly, perhaps, from inherited susceptibility he became a victim of consumption. A few months snatched from the grave, harassed by insufficient means, 'the law's delay,' and 'the pangs of disprized love,' produced the more mature and discreet work which lies between *Endymion* and his last sonnet ('Bright Star, would I were steadfast as thou art'), composed on shipboard as he was leaving for Italy to die. Brief as was Shelley's career, all his poems of recognized importance were written between his twenty-sixth and thirtieth years; the corresponding period of life Keats never knew. Yet his poetry is far more than the poetry of mere promise. Some of it is 'as final as Shakespeare.'

SONNET

KEEN, FITFUL GUSTS ARE WHISPERING HERE AND THERE

Keen, fitful gusts are whispering here and there
Among the bushes half leafless, and dry;
The stars look very cold about the sky,
And I have many miles on foot to fare.

Yet feel I little of the cool bleak air,   5
Or of the dead leaves rustling drearily,
Or of those silver lamps that burn on high,
Or of the distance from home's pleasant lair:

For I am brimful of the friendliness
That in a little cottage I have found;   10
Of fair-haired Milton's eloquent distress,
And all his love for gentle Lycid drowned;
Of lovely Laura in her light green dress,
And faithful Petrarch gloriously crowned.

(1816)

SONNET

ON FIRST LOOKING INTO CHAPMAN'S HOMER

Much have I traveled in the realms of gold
And many goodly states and kingdoms seen;
Round many western islands have I been
Which bards in fealty to Apollo hold.

Oft of one wide expanse had I been told   5
That deep-browed Homer ruled as his demesne;
Yet did I never breathe its pure serene
Till I heard Chapman speak out loud and bold:

Then felt I like some watcher of the skies
When a new planet swims into his ken;   10
Or like stout Cortez when with eagle eyes
He stared at the Pacific—and all his men
Looked at each other with a wild surmise—
Silent, upon a peak in Darien.

(1816)

From ENDYMION, BOOK I

PROEM

A thing of beauty is a joy for ever:
Its loveliness increases; it will never
Pass into nothingness; but still will keep
A bower quiet for us, and a sleep
Full of sweet dreams, and health, and quiet breathing.   5
Therefore, on every morrow, are we wreathing

A flowery band to bind us to the earth,
Spite of despondence, of the inhuman dearth
Of noble natures, of the gloomy days,
Of all the unhealthy and o'er-darkened ways   10
Made for our searching: yes, in spite of all,
Some shape of beauty moves away the pall
From our dark spirits. Such the sun, the moon,
Trees old and young, sprouting a shady boon
For simple sheep: and such are daffodils   15
With the green world they live in; and clear rills
That for themselves a cooling covert make
'Gainst the hot season; the mid-forest brake,
Rich with a sprinkling of fair musk-rose blooms:
And such too is the grandeur of the dooms   20
We have imagined for the mighty dead;
All lovely tales that we have heard or read:
An endless fountain of immortal drink,
Pouring unto us from the heaven's brink.

   Nor do we merely feel these essences   25
For one short hour; no, even as the trees
That whisper round a temple become soon
Dear as the temple's self, so does the moon,
The passion poesy, glories infinite,
Haunt us till they become a cheering light   30
Unto our souls, and bound to us so fast,
That, whether there be shine, or gloom o'ercast,
They alway must be with us, or we die.

   Therefore, 't is with full happiness that I
Will trace the story of Endymion.   35
The very music of the name has gone
Into my being, and each pleasant scene
Is growing fresh before me as the green
Of our own valleys: so I will begin
Now while I cannot hear the city's din;   40
Now while the early budders are just new,
And run in mazes of the youngest hue
About old forests; while the willow trails
Its delicate amber; and the dairy pails
Bring home increase of milk. And, as the year
Grows lush in juicy stalks, I 'll smoothly steer   46
My little boat, for many quiet hours,
With streams that deepen freshly into bowers.
Many and many a verse I hope to write,
Before the daisies, vermeil rimmed and white,
Hide in deep herbage; and ere yet the bees   51
Hum about globes of clover and sweet peas,
I must be near the middle of my story.
O may no wintry season, bare and hoary,
See it half finished; but let Autumn bold,   55
With universal tinge of sober gold,
Be all about me when I make an end.
And now at once, adventuresome, I send
My herald thought into a wilderness: 59
There let its trumpet blow, and quickly dress
My uncertain path with green, that I may speed
Easily onward, thorough flowers and weed.   62
                 (1818)

THE EVE OF ST. AGNES

St. Agnes' Eve—Ah, bitter chill it was!
The owl, for all his feathers, was a-cold;
The hare limped trembling through the frozen grass,
And silent was the flock in woolly fold:
Numb were the Beadsman's fingers, while he told   5
His rosary, and while his frosted breath,
Like pious incense from a censer old,
Seemed taking flight for heaven, without a death,
Past the sweet Virgin's picture, while his prayer he saith.

His prayer he saith, this patient, holy man   10
Then takes his lamp, and riseth from his knees,
And back returneth, meager, barefoot, wan,
Along the chapel aisle by slow degrees:
The sculptured dead, on each side, seem to freeze,
Emprisoned in black, purgatorial rails: 15
Knights, ladies, praying in dumb orat'ries,
He passeth by; and his weak spirit fails
To think how they may ache in icy hoods and mails.

Northward he turneth through a little door,
And scarce three steps, ere Music's golden tongue   20
Flattered to tears this aged man and poor;
But no—already had his deathbell rung;
The joys of all his life were said and sung:
His was harsh penance on St. Agnes' Eve:
Another way he went, and soon among   25
Rough ashes sat he for his soul's reprieve,
And all night kept awake, for sinners' sake to grieve.

That ancient Beadsman heard the prelude soft;
And so it chanced, for many a door was wide,
From hurry to and fro. Soon, up aloft,   30
The silver, snarling trumpets 'gan to chide:
The level chambers, ready with their pride,
Were glowing to receive a thousand guests:
The carvèd angels, ever eager-eyed,   34
Stared where upon their heads the cornice rests,
With hair blown back, and wings put crosswise on their breasts.

At length burst in the argent revelry,
With plume, tiara, and all rich array,
Numerous as shadows haunting fairily
The brain, new stuffed, in youth, with triumphs gay   40
Of old romance. These let us wish away,
And turn, sole-thoughted, to one Lady there,
Whose heart had brooded, all that wintry day,
On love, and winged St. Agnes' saintly care,
As she had heard old dames full many times declare   45

They told her how, upon St. Agnes' Eve,
Young virgins might have visions of delight,
And soft adorings from their loves receive
Upon the honeyed middle of the night
If ceremonies due they did aright; 50
As, supperless to bed they must retire,
And couch supine their beauties, lily white;
Nor look behind, nor sideways, but require
Of Heaven with upward eyes for all that they
   desire.

Full of this whim was thoughtful Madeline; 55
The music, yearning like a God in pain,
She scarcely heard: her maiden eyes divine,
Fixed on the floor, saw many a sweeping train
Pass by—she heeded not at all: in vain
Came many a tiptoe, amorous cavalier, 60
And back retired; not cooled by high disdain,
But she saw not: her heart was otherwhere:
She sighed for Agnes' dreams, the sweetest of
   the year.

She danced along with vague, regardless eyes, 64
Anxious her lips, her breathing quick and short:
The hallowed hour was near at hand: she sighs
Amid the timbrels, and the thronged resort
Of whisperers in anger, or in sport;
'Mid looks of love, defiance, hate, and scorn,
Hoodwinked with faery fancy; all amort, 70
Save to St. Agnes and her lambs unshorn,
And all the bliss to be before to-morrow morn.

So, purposing each moment to retire,
She lingered still. Meantime, across the moors,
Had come young Porphyro, with heart on fire 75
For Madeline. Beside the portal doors,
Buttressed from moonlight, stands he, and im-
   plores
All saints to give him sight of Madeline,
But for one moment in the tedious hours,
That he might gaze and worship all unseen; 80
Perchance speak, kneel, touch, kiss—in sooth
   such things have been.

He ventures in: let no buzzed whisper tell:
All eyes be muffled, or a hundred swords
Will storm his heart, Love's fev'rous citadel: 84
For him, those chambers held barbarian hordes,
Hyena foemen, and hot-blooded lords,
Whose very dogs would execrations howl
Against his lineage: not one breast affords
Him any mercy, in that mansion foul, 89
Save one old beldame, weak in body and in soul.

Ah, happy chance! the aged creature came,
Shuffling along with ivory-headed wand,
To where he stood, hid from the torch's flame,
Behind a broad hall-pillar, far beyond
The sound of merriment and chorus bland. 95
He startled her; but soon she knew his face,
And grasped his fingers in her palsied hand,

Saying, 'Mercy, Porphyro! hie thee from this
   place;
They are all here to-night, the whole blood-
   thirsty race!

Get hence! get hence! there's dwarfish Hilde-
   brand; 100
He had a fever late, and in the fit
He cursèd thee and thine, both house and land:
Then there's that old Lord Maurice, not a
   whit
More tame for his gray hairs—Alas me! flit!
Flit like a ghost away.'—'Ah, Gossip dear, 105
We're safe enough; here in this armchair sit.
And tell me how'—'Good Saints! not here, not
   here;
Follow me, child, or else these stones will be
   thy bier.'

He followed through a lowly archèd way,
Brushing the cobwebs with his lofty plume; 110
And as she muttered 'Well-a—well-a-day!'
He found him in a little moonlight room,
Pale, latticed, chill, and silent as a tomb.
'Now tell me where is Madeline,' said he,
'O tell me, Angela, by the holy loom 115
Which none but secret sisterhood may see,
When they St. Agnes' wool are weaving piously.'

'St. Agnes! Ah! it is St. Agnes' Eve—
Yet men will murder upon holy days:
Thou must hold water in a witch's sieve, 120
And be liege-lord of all the Elves and Fays,
To venture so; it fills me with amaze
To see thee, Porphyro—St. Agnes' Eve!
God's help! my lady fair the conjurer plays
This very night; good angels her deceive! 125
But let me laugh awhile, I've mickle time to
   grieve.'

Feebly she laugheth in the languid moon,
While Porphyro upon her face doth look,
Like puzzled urchin on an aged crone 129
Who keepeth closed a wond'rous riddle-book,
As spectacled she sits in chimney nook.
But soon his eyes grew brilliant, when she told
His lady's purpose; and he scarce could brook
Tears, at the thought of those enchantments
   cold,
And Madeline asleep in lap of legends old. 135

Sudden a thought came like a full-blown rose,
Flushing his brow, and in his painèd heart
Made purple riot: then doth he propose
A stratagem, that makes the beldame start:
'A cruel man and impious thou art: 140
Sweet lady, let her pray, and sleep, and dream
Alone with her good angels, far apart
From wicked men like thee. Go, go!—I deem
Thou canst not surely be the same that thou
   didst seem.'

'I will not harm her, by all saints I swear,' 145
Quoth Porphyro: 'O may I ne'er find grace
When my weak voice shall whisper its last prayer,
If one of her soft ringlets I displace,
Or look with ruffian passion in her face:
Good Angela, believe me by these tears: 150
Or I will, even in a moment's space,
Awake, with horrid shout, my foemen's ears,
And beard them, though they be more fanged than wolves and bears.'

'Ah! why wilt thou affright a feeble soul: 154
A poor, weak, palsy-stricken churchyard thing,
Whose passing-bell may ere the midnight toll;
Whose prayers for thee, each morn and evening,
Were never missed.' Thus plaining, doth she bring
A gentler speech from burning Porphyro;
So woful, and of such deep sorrowing, 160
That Angela gives promise she will do
Whatever he shall wish, betide her weal or woe.

Which was, to lead him, in close secrecy,
Even to Madeline's chamber, and there hide
Him in a closet, of such privacy 165
That he might see her beauty unespied,
And win perhaps that night a peerless bride,
While legioned fairies paced the coverlet,
And pale enchantment held her sleepy eyed.
Never on such a night have lovers met, 170
Since Merlin paid his Demon all the monstrous debt.

'It shall be as thou wishest,' said the Dame:
'All cates and dainties shall be stored there
Quickly on this feast-night: by the tambour frame 174
Her own lute thou wilt see: no time to spare,
For I am slow and feeble, and scarce dare
On such a catering trust my dizzy head.
Wait here, my child, with patience; kneel in prayer
The while: Ah! thou must needs the lady wed,
Or may I never leave my grave among the dead.' 180

So saying, she hobbled off with busy fear.
The lover's endless minutes slowly passed;
The dame returned, and whispered in his ear
To follow her; with agèd eyes aghast
From fright of dim espial. Safe at last, 185
Through many a dusky gallery, they gain
The maiden's chamber, silken, hushed, and chaste;
Where Porphyro took covert, pleased amain.
His poor guide hurried back with agues in her brain.

Her falt'ring hand upon the balustrade 190
Old Angela was feeling for the stair,
When Madeline, St. Agnes' charmèd maid,
Rose, like a missioned spirit, unaware:
With silver taper's light, and pious care,
She turned, and down the agèd gossip led 195
To a safe level matting. Now prepare,
Young Porphyro, for gazing on that bed;
She comes, she comes again, like ring-dove frayed and fled.

Out went the taper as she hurried in;
Its little smoke, in pallid moonshine, died: 200
She closed the door, she panted, all akin
To spirits of the air, and visions wide:
No uttered syllable, or, woe betide!
But to her heart, her heart was voluble,
Paining with eloquence her balmy side; 205
As though a tongueless nightingale should swell
Her throat in vain, and die, heart-stifled, in her dell.

A casement high and triple arched there was,
All garlanded with carven imag'ries
Of fruits, and flowers, and bunches of knot-grass. 210
And diamonded with panes of quaint device,
Innumerable of stains and splendid dyes,
As are the tiger-moth's deep-damasked wings;
And in the midst, 'mong thousand heraldries,
And twilight saints, and dim emblazonings, 215
A shielded scutcheon blushed with blood of queens and kings.

Full on this casement shone the wintry moon,
And threw warm gules on Madeline's fair breast,
As down she knelt for heaven's grace and boon;
Rose-bloom fell on her hands, together prest,
And on her silver cross soft amethyst, 221
And on her hair a glory, like a saint:
She seemed a splendid angel, newly drest,
Save wings, for heaven: Porphyro grew faint:
She knelt, so pure a thing, so free from mortal taint. 225

Anon his heart revives: her vespers done,
Of all its wreathèd pearls her hair she frees;
Unclasps her warmèd jewels one by one;
Loosens her fragrant bodice; by degrees
Her rich attire creeps rustling to her knees; 230
Half-hidden, like a mermaid in seaweed,
Pensive awhile she dreams awake, and sees,
In fancy, fair St. Agnes in her bed,
But dares not look behind, or all the charm is fled.

Soon, trembling in her soft and chilly nest, 235
In sort of wakeful swoon, perplexed she lay.
Until the poppied warmth of sleep oppressed
Her soothèd limbs, and soul fatigued away,
Flown, like a thought, until the morrow-day;
Blissfully havened both from joy and pain, 240
Clasped like a missal where swart Paynims pray;

Blinded alike from sunshine and from rain,
As though a rose should shut, and be a bud
   again.

Stolen to this paradise, and so entranced,
Porphyro gazed upon her empty dress,   245
And listened to her breathing, if it chanced
To wake into a slumberous tenderness;
Which when he heard, that minute did he bless,
And breathed himself: then from the closet
   crept,
Noiseless as fear in a wide wilderness,   250
And over the hushed carpet, silent, stepped,
And 'tween the curtains peeped, where, lo!—
   how fast she slept.

Then by the bed-side, where the faded moon
Made a dim, silver twilight, soft he set
A table, and, half-anguished, threw thereon   255
A cloth of woven crimson, gold, and jet:—
O for some drowsy Morphean amulet!
The boisterous, midnight, festive clarion,
The kettle-drum, and far-heard clarionet,
Affray his ears, though but in dying tone:—260
The hall door shuts again, and all the noise is
   gone.

And still she slept an azure-lidded sleep,
In blanchèd linen, smooth, and lavendered,
While he from forth the closet brought a heap
Of candied apple, quince, and plum, and gourd;
With jellies soother than the creamy curd.   266
And lucent syrops, tinct with cinnamon;
Manna and dates, in argosy transferred
From Fez; and spicèd dainties, every one,   269
From silken Samarcand to cedared Lebanon.

These delicates he heaped with glowing hand
On golden dishes and in baskets bright
Of wreathèd silver: sumptuous they stand
In the retired quiet of the night,   274
Filling the chilly room with perfume light.—
'And now, my love, my seraph fair, awake!
Thou art my heaven, and I thine eremite:
Open thine eyes, for meek St. Agnes' sake,
Or I shall drowse beside thee, so my soul doth
   ache.'   279

Thus whispering, his warm, unnervèd arm
Sank in her pillow. Shaded was her dream
By the dusk curtains:—'t was a midnight charm
Impossible to melt as icèd stream:
The lustrous salvers in the moonlight gleam:
Broad golden fringe upon the carpet lies: 285
It seemed he never, never could redeem
From such a stedfast spell his lady's eyes;
So mused awhile, entoiled in woofèd phantasies.

Awakening up, he took her hollow lute,—   289
Tumultuous,—and, in chords that tenderest be,
He played an ancient ditty, long since mute,

In Provence called, 'La belle dame sans mercy:'
Close to her ear touching the melody;—   293
Wherewith disturbed, she uttered a soft moan:
He ceased—she panted quick—and suddenly
Her blue affrayèd eyes wide open shone:
Upon his knees he sank, pale as smooth-sculp-
   tured stone.   297

Her eyes were open, but she still beheld,
Now wide awake, the vision of her sleep:
There was a painful change, that nigh expelled
The blisses of her dream so pure and deep   301
At which fair Madeline began to weep,
And moan forth witless words with many a sigh;
While still her gaze on Porphyro would keep;
Who knelt, with joinèd hands and piteous eye,
Fearing to move or speak, she looked so dream-
   ingly.   306

'Ah, Porphyro!' said she, 'but even now
Thy voice was at sweet tremble in mine ear,
Made tuneable with every sweetest vow;
And those sad eyes were spiritual and clear: 310
How changed thou art! how pallid, chill, and
   drear!
Give me that voice again, my Porphyro,
Those looks immortal, those complainings dear!
Oh, leave me not in this eternal woe,
For if thou diest, my Love, I know not where
   to go.'   315

Beyond a mortal man impassioned far
At these voluptuous accents, he arose,
Ethereal, flushed, and like a throbbing star
Seen mid the sapphire heaven's deep repose;
Into her dream he melted, as the rose   320
Blendeth its odor with the violet,—
Solution sweet: meantime the frost wind blows
Like Love's alarum pattering the sharp sleet
Against the window-panes; St. Agnes' moon
   hath set.

'T is dark; quick pattereth the flaw-blown sleet:
'This is no dream, my bride, my Madeline!' 326
'T is dark: the icèd gusts still rave and beat:
'No dream, alas! alas! and woe is mine!
Porphyro will leave me here to fade and pine.—
Cruel! what traitor could thee hither bring? 330
I curse not, for my heart is lost in thine,
Though thou forsakest a deceivèd thing;—
A dove forlorn and lost with sick unprunèd
   wing.'

'My Madeline! sweet dreamer! lovely bride!
Say, may I be for aye thy vassal blest?   335
Thy beauty's shield, heart-shaped and vermeil
   dyed?
Ah, silver shrine, here will I take my rest
After so many hours of toil and quest,
A famished pilgrim,—saved by a miracle.   339
Though I have found, I will not rob thy nest

Saving of thy sweet self; if thou think'st well
To trust, fair Madeline, to no rude infidel.

'Hark! 't is an elfin-storm from faery land,
Of haggard seeming, but a boon indeed:
Arise—arise! the morning is at hand;—   345
The bloated wassailers will never heed:—
Let us away, my love, with happy speed;
There are no ears to hear, or eyes to see,—
Drowned all in Rhenish and the sleepy mead;
Awake! arise! my love, and fearless be,   350
For o'er the southern moors I have a home for thee.'

She hurried at his words, beset with fears,
For there were sleeping dragons all around,
At glaring watch, perhaps, with ready spears—
Down the wide stairs a darkling way they found.—   355
In all the house was heard no human sound.
A chain-drooped lamp was flickering by each door;
The arras, rich with horseman, hawk, and hound,
Fluttered in the besieging wind's uproar;   359
And the long carpets rose along the gusty floor.

They glide, like phantoms, into the wide hall;
Like phantoms, to the iron porch, they glide;
Where lay the Porter, in uneasy sprawl,
With a huge empty flagon by his side:
The wakeful bloodhound rose, and shook his hide,   365
But his sagacious eye an inmate owns:
By one, and one, the bolts full easy slide:—
The chains lie silent on the footworn stones;—
The key turns, and the door upon its hinges groans.

And they are gone: ay, ages long ago   370
These lovers fled away into the storm.
That night the Baron dreamt of many a woe,
And all his warrior-guests, with shade and form
Of witch, and demon, and large coffin-worm,
Were long be-nightmared. Angela the old   375
Died palsy-twitched, with meager face deform;
The Beadsman, after thousand aves told,
For aye unsought for slept among his ashes cold.
(1820)

ODE

Bards of Passion and of Mirth,
Ye have left your souls on earth!
Have ye souls in heaven too,
Double-lived in regions new?
Yes, and those of heaven commune   5
With the spheres of sun and moon;
With the noise of fountains wond'rous,
And the parle of voices thund'rous;
With the whisper of heaven's trees
And one another, in soft ease   10

Seated on Elysian lawns
Browsed by none but Dian's fawns;
Underneath large blue-bells tented,
Where the daisies are rose-scented,
And the rose herself has got   15
Perfume which on earth is not;
Where the nightingale doth sing
Not a senseless, trancèd thing,
But divine melodious truth;
Philosophic numbers smooth;   20
Tales and golden histories
Of heaven and its mysteries.

Thus ye live on high, and then
On the earth ye live again;
And the souls ye left behind you   25
Teach us, here, the way to find you,
Where your other souls are joying,
Never slumbered, never cloying.
Here, your earth-born souls still speak
To mortals, of their little week;   30
Of their sorrows and delights;
Of their passions and their spites;
Of their glory and their shame;
What doth strengthen and what maim.
Thus ye teach us, every day,   35
Wisdom, though fled far away.

Bards of Passion and of Mirth,
Ye have left your souls on earth!
Ye have souls in heaven too,
Double-lived in regions new!   40
(1820)

ROBIN HOOD

No! those days are gone away,
And their hours are old and gray,
And their minutes buried all
Under the down-trodden pall
Of the leaves of many years: 5
Many times have winter's shears,
Frozen North, and chilling East,
Sounded tempests to the feast
Of the forest's whispering fleeces,
Since men knew nor rent nor leases.   10

No, the bugle sounds no more,
And the twanging bow no more;
Silent is the ivory shrill
Past the heath and up the hill;
There is no mid-forest laugh,   15
Where lone Echo gives the half
To some wight, amazed to hear
Jesting, deep in forest drear.

On the fairest time of June
You may go, with sun or moon,   20
Or the seven stars to light you,
Or the polar ray to right you;
But you never may behold
Little John, or Robin bold;

Never one, of all the clan,
Thrumming on an empty can
Some old hunting ditty, while
He doth his green way beguile
To fair hostess Merriment,
Down beside the pasture Trent;
For he left the merry tale
Messenger for spicy ale.

Gone, the merry morris din;
Gone, the song of Gamelyn;
Gone, the tough-belted outlaw
Idling in the 'grene shawe;'
All are gone away and past!
And if Robin should be cast
Sudden from his turfèd grave,
And if Marian should have
Once again her forest days,
She would weep, and he would craze:
He would swear, for all his oaks,
Fallen beneath the dockyard strokes,
Have rotted on the briny seas;
She would weep that her wild bees
Sang not to her—strange! that honey
Can't be got without hard money!

So it is: yet let us sing,
Honor to the old bow-string!
Honor to the bugle-horn!
Honor to the woods unshorn!
Honor to the Lincoln green!
Honor to the archer keen!
Honor to tight Little John,
And the horse he rode upon!
Honor to bold Robin Hood,
Sleeping in the underwood!
Honor to Maid Marian,
And to all the Sherwood-clan!
Though their days have hurried by,
Let us two a burden try.

(1820)

LINES ON THE MERMAID TAVERN

Souls of Poets dead and gone,
What Elysium have ye known,
Happy field or mossy cavern,
Choicer than the Mermaid Tavern?
Have ye tippled drink more fine
Than mine host's Canary wine?
Or are fruits of Paradise
Sweeter than those dainty pies
Of venison? O generous food!
Drest as though bold Robin Hood
Would, with his maid Marian,
Sup and bowse from horn and can.

I have heard that on a day
Mine host's sign-board flew away,
Nobody knew whither, till
An astrologer's old quill
To a sheepskin gave the story,
Said he saw you in your glory,
Underneath a new-old sign
Sipping beverage divine,
And pledging with contented smack
The Mermaid in the Zodiac.

Souls of Poets dead and gone,
What Elysium have ye known,
Happy field or mossy cavern,
Choicer than the Mermaid Tavern?

(1820)

ODE ON A GRECIAN URN

Thou still unravished bride of quietness,
  Thou foster-child of silence and slow time,
Sylvan historian, who canst thus express
  A flowery tale more sweetly than our rhyme:
What leaf-fringed legend haunts about thy shape
  Of deities or mortals, or of both,
    In Tempe or the dales of Arcady?
  What men or gods are these? What maidens loth?
What mad pursuit? What struggle to escape?
    What pipes and timbrels? What wild ecstasy?

Heard melodies are sweet, but those unheard
  Are sweeter; therefore, ye soft pipes, play on;
Not to the sensual ear, but, more endeared,
  Pipe to the spirit ditties of no tone:
Fair youth, beneath the trees, thou canst not leave
  Thy song, nor ever can those trees be bare;
    Bold Lover, never, never canst thou kiss
Though winning near the goal—yet, do not grieve;
    She cannot fade, though thou hast not thy bliss,
For ever wilt thou love, and she be fair!

Ah, happy, happy boughs! that cannot shed
  Your leaves, nor ever bid the Spring adieu;
And, happy melodist, unwearièd,
  For ever piping songs for ever new;
More happy love! more happy, happy love!
  For ever warm and still to be enjoyed,
    For ever panting, and for ever young;
All breathing human passion far above,
  That leaves a heart high-sorrowful and cloyed,
    A burning forehead, and a parching tongue.

Who are these coming to the sacrifice?
  To what green altar, O mysterious priest,
Lead'st thou that heifer lowing at the skies,
  And all her silken flanks with garlands dressed?

What little town by river or sea shore,   35
  Or mountain-built with peaceful citadel,
  Is emptied of this folk, this pious morn?
And, little town, thy streets for evermore
  Will silent be; and not a soul to tell
    Why thou art desolate, can e'er return.   40

O Attic shape! Fair attitude! with brede
  Of marble men and maidens over wrought,
With forest branches and the trodden weed;
  Thou, silent form, dost tease us out of thought
As doth eternity: Cold Pastoral!   45
  When old age shall this generation waste,
    Thou shalt remain, in midst of other woe
Than ours, a friend to man, to whom thou say'st,
  'Beauty is truth, truth beauty,'—that is all
    Ye know on earth, and all ye need to know.   50

                      (1820)

ODE TO A NIGHTINGALE

My heart aches, and a drowsy numbness pains
  My sense, as though of hemlock I had drunk,
Or emptied some dull opiate to the drains
  One minute past, and Lethe-wards had sunk:
'T is not through envy of thy happy lot,   5
  But being too happy in thine happiness,—
That thou, light wingèd Dryad of the trees,
    In some melodious plot
  Of beechen green, and shadows numberless,
Singest of summer in full-throated ease.   10

O for a draught of vintage! that hath been
  Cooled a long age in the deep-delved earth,
Tasting of Flora and the country green,
  Dance, and Provençal song, and sunburnt mirth!
O for a beaker full of the warm South,   15
  Full of the true, the blushful Hippocrene,
With beaded bubbles winking at the brim,
    And purple-stainèd mouth;
  That I might drink, and leave the world unseen,
And with thee fade away into the forest dim: 20

Fade far away, dissolve, and quite forget
  What thou among the leaves hast never known,
The weariness, the fever, and the fret
  Here, where men sit and hear each other groan;   24
Where palsy shakes a few, sad, last gray hairs,
  Where youth grows pale, and specter-thin, and dies;
Where but to think is to be full of sorrow
    And leaden-eyed despairs,
  Where Beauty cannot keep her lustrous eyes,
Or new Love pine at them beyond tomorrow.   30

Away! away! for I will fly to thee,
  Not charioted by Bacchus and his pards,
But on the viewless wings of Poesy,
  Though the dull brain perplexes and retards:
Already with thee! tender is the night,   35
  And haply the Queen-Moon is on her throne,
Clustered around by all her starry Fays;
    But here there is no light,
  Save what from heaven is with the breezes blown
Through verdurous glooms and winding mossy ways.   40

I cannot see what flowers are at my feet,
  Nor what soft incense hangs upon the boughs,
But, in embalmed darkness, guess each sweet
  Wherewith the seasonable month endows
The grass, the thicket, and the fruit-tree wild;   45
  White hawthorn, and the pastoral eglantine;
Fast fading violets covered up in leaves;
    And mid-May's eldest child,
  The coming musk-rose, full of dewy wine,
The murmurous haunt of flies on summer eves.

Darkling I listen; and, for many a time   51
  I have been half in love with easeful Death,
Called him soft names in many a musèd rhyme,
  To take into the air my quiet breath;
Now more than ever seems it rich to die,   55
  To cease upon the midnight with no pain,
While thou art pouring forth thy soul abroad
    In such an ecstasy!
  Still wouldst thou sing, and I have ears in vain—
To thy high requiem become a sod.   60

Thou wast not born for death, immortal Bird!
  No hungry generations tread thee down;
The voice I hear this passing night was heard
  In ancient days by emperor and clown:
Perhaps the self-same song that found a path   65
  Through the sad heart of Ruth, when, sick for home,
She stood in tears amid the alien corn:
    The same that oft-times hath
  Charmed magic casements, opening on the foam
Of perilous seas, in faery lands forlorn.   70

Forlorn! the very word is like a bell
  To toll me back from thee to my sole self!
Adieu! the fancy cannot cheat so well
  As she is famed to do, deceiving elf,
Adieu! adieu! thy plaintive anthem fades   75
  Past the near meadows, over the still stream,
Up the hill-side; and now 't is buried deep
    In the next valley-glades:
  Was it a vision, or a waking dream?
Fled is that music:—Do I wake or sleep?   80

                      (1819)

ODE ON MELANCHOLY

No, no, go not to Lethe, neither twist
  Wolf's-bane, tight-rooted, for its poisonous
    wine;
Nor suffer thy pale forehead to be kissed
  By nightshade, ruby grape of Proserpine;
Make not your rosary of yew-berries,   5
  Nor let the beetle, nor the death-moth be
    Your mournful Psyche, nor the downy owl
A partner in your sorrow's mysteries;
  For shade to shade will come too drowsily,
    And drown the wakeful anguish of the
      soul.   10

But when the melancholy fit shall fall
  Sudden from heaven like a weeping cloud,
That fosters the droop-headed flowers all,
  And hides the green hill in an April shroud:
Then glut thy sorrow on a morning rose,   15
  Or on the rainbow of a salt sandwave,
    Or on the wealth of globèd peonies;
Or if thy mistress some rich anger shows,
  Emprison her soft hand, and let her rave,   19
    And feed deep, deep upon her peerless eyes.

She dwells with Beauty—Beauty that must die;
  And Joy, whose hand is ever at his lips
Bidding adieu; and aching Pleasure nigh,
  Turning to poison while the bee-mouth sips:
Ay, in the very temple of Delight   25
  Veiled Melancholy has her sovran shrine,
    Though seen of none save him whose strenuous tongue
Can burst Joy's grape against his palate fine;
  His soul shall taste the sadness of her might,
    And be among her cloudy trophies hung.   30
      (1820)

TO AUTUMN

Season of mists and mellow fruitfulness,
  Close bosom friend of the maturing sun:
Conspiring with him how to load and bless
  With fruit the vines that round the thatch-eves run;
To bend with apples the mossed cottage-trees,   5
  And fill all fruit with ripeness to the core;
    To swell the gourd, and plump the hazel shells
With a sweet kernel; to set budding more,
  And still more, later flowers for the bees,   9
Until they think warm days will never cease,
  For Summer has o'er-brimmed their clammy cells.

Who hath not seen thee oft amid thy store?
  Sometimes whoever seeks abroad may find
Thee sitting careless on a granary floor,
  Thy hair soft-lifted by the winnowing wind;
Or on a half-reaped furrow sound asleep,   16
  Drowsed with the fume of poppies, while thy hook
  Spares the next swath and all its twinèd flowers:
And sometimes like a gleaner thou dost keep,
  Steady thy laden head across a brook;   20
  Or by a cider-press, with patient look,
    Thou watchest the last oozings hours by hours.

Where are the songs of Spring? Ay, where are they?
  Think not of them, thou hast thy music too,—
While barrèd clouds bloom the soft-dying day,
  And touch the stubble-plains with rosy hue;
Then in a wailful choir the small gnats mourn   27
  Among the river sallows, borne aloft
    Or sinking as the light wind lives or dies;
And full-grown lambs loud bleat from hilly bourn;   30
  Hedge-crickets sing: and now with treble soft
    The red-breast whistles from a garden-croft;
    And gathering swallows twitter in the skies.
      (1820)

HYPERION

A FRAGMENT

BOOK I

Deep in the shady sadness of a vale
Far sunken from the healthy breath of morn,
Far from the fiery noon, and eve's one star,
Sat gray-haired Saturn, quiet as a stone,
Still as the silence round about his lair;   5
Forest on forest hung about his head
Like cloud on cloud. No stir of air was there,
Not so much life as on a summer's day
Robs not one light seed from the feathered grass,
But where the dead leaf fell, there did it rest.   10
A stream went voiceless by, still deadened more
By reason of his fallen divinity
Spreading a shade: the Naiad 'mid her reeds
Pressed her cold finger closer to her lips.

Along the margin-sand large footmarks went,
No further than to where his feet had strayed   16
And slept there since. Upon the sodden ground
His old right hand lay nerveless, listless, dead,
Unsceptered; and his realmless eyes were closed;
While his bowed head seemed list'ning to the Earth,   20
His ancient mother, for some comfort yet.

  It seemed no force could wake him from his place;
But there came one, who with a kindred hand
Touched his wide shoulders, after bending low

With reverence, though to one who knew it not.
She was a Goddess of the infant world;
By her in stature the tall Amazon
Had stood a pigmy's height: she would have ta'en
Achilles by the hair and bent his neck;
Or with a finger stayed Ixion's wheel.
Her face was large as that of Memphian sphinx,
Pedestaled haply in a palace court,
When sages looked to Egypt for their lore.
But oh! how unlike marble was that face:
How beautiful, if sorrow had not made
Sorrow more beautiful than Beauty's self.
There was a listening fear in her regard,
As if calamity had but begun:
As if the vanward clouds of evil days
Had spent their malice, and the sullen rear
Was with its stored thunder laboring up.
One hand she pressed upon that aching spot
Where beats the human heart, as if just there,
Though an immortal, she felt cruel pain;
The other upon Saturn's bended neck
She laid, and to the level of his ear
Leaning with parted lips, some words she spake
In solemn tenor and deep organ tone:
Some mourning words, which in our feeble tongue
Would come in these like accents; O how frail
To that large utterance of the early Gods!
'Saturn, look up!—though wherefore, poor old King?
I have no comfort for thee, no, not one:
I cannot say, "O wherefore sleepest thou?"
For heaven is parted from thee, and the earth
Knows thee not, thus afflicted, for a God;
And ocean too, with all its solemn noise,
Has from thy scepter passed; and all the air
Is emptied of thine hoary majesty.
Thy thunder, conscious of the new command,
Rumbles reluctant o'er our fallen house;
And thy sharp lightning in unpractised hands
Scorches and burns our once serene domain.
O aching time! O moments big as years!
All as ye pass swell out the monstrous truth,
And press it so upon our weary griefs
That unbelief has not a space to breathe.
Saturn, sleep on:—O thoughtless, why did I
Thus violate thy slumbrous solitude?
Why should I ope thy melancholy eyes?
Saturn, sleep on! while at thy feet I weep.'

As when, upon a trancèd summer night,
Those green-robed senators of mighty woods,
Tall oaks, branch-charmèd by the earnest stars,
Dream, and so dream all night without a stir,
Save from one gradual solitary gust
Which comes upon the silence, and dies off,
As if the ebbing air had but one wave;
So came these words and went; the while in tears
She touched her fair large forehead to the ground,

Just where her falling hair might be outspread
A soft and silken mat for Saturn's feet.
One moon, with alteration slow, had shed
Her silver seasons four upon the night,
And still these two were postured motionless,
Like natural sculpture in cathedral cavern;
The frozen God still couchant on the earth,
And the sad Goddess weeping at his feet:
Until at length old Saturn lifted up
His faded eyes, and saw his kingdom gone,
And all the gloom and sorrow of the place,
And that fair kneeling Goddess; and then spake,
As with a palsied tongue, and while his beard
Shook horrid with such aspen-malady:
'O tender spouse of gold Hyperion,
Thea, I feel thee ere I see thy face;
Look up, and let me see our doom in it;
Look up, and tell me if this feeble shape
Is Saturn's; tell me, if thou hear'st the voice
Of Saturn; tell me, if this wrinkling brow,
Naked and bare of its great diadem,
Peers like the front of Saturn. Who had power
To make me desolate? whence came the strength?
How was it nurtured to such bursting forth,
While Fate seemed strangled in my nervous grasp?
But it is so; and I am smothered up,
And buried from all godlike exercise
Of influence benign on planets pale,
Of admonitions to the winds, and seas,
Of peaceful sway above man's harvesting,
And all those acts which Deity supreme
Doth ease its heart of love in.—I am gone
Away from my own bosom: I have left
My strong identity, my real self,
Somewhere between the throne, and where I sit
Here on this spot of earth. Search, Thea, search!
Open thine eyes eterne, and sphere them round
Upon all space: space starred, and lorn of light;
Space regioned with life-air; and barren void;
Spaces of fire, and all the yawn of hell.—
Search, Thea, search! and tell me, if thou seest
A certain shape or shadow, making way
With wings or chariot fierce to repossess
A heaven he lost erewhile: it must—it must
Be of ripe progress—Saturn must be King,
Yes, there must be a golden victory;
There must be Gods thrown down, and trumpets blown
Of triumph calm, and hymns of festival
Upon the gold clouds metropolitan,
Voices of soft proclaim, and silver stir
Of strings in hollow shells; and there shall be
Beautiful things made new, for the surprise
Of the sky-children; I will give command:
Thea! Thea! Thea! where is Saturn?'

This passion lifted him upon his feet,
And made his hands to struggle in the air,

His Druid locks to shake and ooze with sweat,
His eyes to fever out, his voice to cease.
He stood, and heard not Thea's sobbing deep;
A little time, and then again he snatched   140
Utterance thus.—'But cannot I create?
Cannot I form? Cannot I fashion forth
Another world, another universe,
To overbear and crumble this to nought?
Where is another chaos? Where?'—That word
Found way unto Olympus, and made quake   146
The rebel three.—Thea was startled up,
And in her bearing was a sort of hope,
As thus she quick-voiced spake, yet full of awe:

'This cheers our fallen house: come to our friends,   150
O Saturn! come away, and give them heart:
I know the covert, for thence came I hither.'
Thus brief; then with beseeching eyes she went
With backward footing through the shade a space:
He followed, and she turned to lead the way   155
Through agèd boughs, that yielded like the mist
Which eagles cleave upmounting from their nest.

Meanwhile in other realms big tears were shed,
More sorrow like to this, and such like woe,
Too huge for mortal tongue or pen of scribe;   160
The Titans fierce, self-hid, or prison-bound,
Groaned for the old allegiance once more,
And listened in sharp pain for Saturn's voice.
But one of the whole mammoth-brood still kept
His sov'reignty, and rule, and majesty;—   165
Blazing Hyperion on his orbèd fire
Still sat, still snuff'd the incense, teeming up
From man to the sun's God; yet unsecure:
For as among us mortals omens drear
Fright and perplex, so also shuddered he—   170
Not at dog's howl, or gloom-bird's hated screech,
Or the familiar visiting of one
Upon the first toll of his passing-bell,
Or prophesyings of the midnight lamp;
But horrors, portioned to a giant nerve,   175
Oft made Hyperion ache. His palace bright
Bastioned with pyramids of glowing gold,
And touched with shade of bronzèd obelisks,
Glared a blood-red through all its thousand courts,
Arches, and domes, and fiery galleries;   180
And all its curtains of Aurorian clouds
Flushed angerly: while sometimes eagle's wings,
Unseen before by Gods or wondering men,
Darkened the place; and neighing steeds were heard,
Not heard before by Gods or wondering men.
Also, when he would taste the spicy wreaths   186
Of incense, breathed aloft from sacred hills,
Instead of sweets, his ample palate took
Savor of poisonous brass and metal sick:
And so, when harbored in the sleepy west,   190
After the full completion of fair day,—
For rest divine upon exalted couch
And slumber in the arms of melody,
He paced away the pleasant hours of ease
With stride colossal, on from hall to hall;   195
While far within each aisle and deep recess,
His wingèd minions in close clusters stood,
Amazed and full of fear; like anxious men
Who on wide plains gather in panting troops,
When earthquakes jar their battlements and towers.   200
Even now, while Saturn, roused from icy trance,
Went step for step with Thea through the woods,
Hyperion, leaving twilight in the rear,
Came slope upon the threshold of the west;
Then, as was wont, his palace-door flew ope   205
In smoothest silence, save what solemn tubes,
Blown by the serious Zephyrs, gave of sweet
And wandering sounds, slow-breathèd melodies;
And like a rose in vermeil tint and shape,
In fragrance soft, and coolness to the eye,   210
That inlet to severe magnificence
Stood full blown, for the God to enter in.

He entered, but he entered full of wrath;
His flaming robes streamed out beyond his heels,
And gave a roar, as if of earthly fire,   215
That scared away the meek ethereal Hours
And made their dove-wings tremble. On he flared,
From stately nave to nave, from vault to vault,
Through bowers of fragrant and enwreathèd light,
And diamond-pavèd lustrous long arcades,   220
Until he reached the great main cupola;
There standing fierce beneath, he stamped his foot,
And from the basements deep to the high towers
Jarred his own golden region; and before
The quavering thunder thereupon had ceased,
His voice leapt out, despite of godlike curb,   226
To this result: 'O dreams of day and night!
O monstrous forms! O effigies of pain!
O specters busy in a cold, cold gloom!
O lank-eared Phantoms of black-weeded pools!
Why do I know ye? why have I seen ye? why   231
Is my eternal essence thus distraught
To see and to behold these horrors new?
Saturn is fallen, am I too to fall?
Am I to leave this haven of my rest,   235
This cradle of my glory, this soft clime,
This calm luxuriance of blissful light,
These crystalline pavilions, and pure fanes,
Of all my lucent empire? It is left
Deserted, void, nor any haunt of mine.   240
The blaze, the splendor, and the symmetry,
I cannot see—but darkness, death and darkness.
Even here, into my center of repose,
The shady visions come to domineer,
Insult, and blind, and stifle up my pomp.—   245

Fall!—No, by Tellus and her briny robes!
Over the fiery frontier of my realms
I will advance a terrible right arm,
Shall scare that infant thunderer, rebel Jove,
And bid old Saturn take his throne again.'— 250
He spake and ceased, the while a heavier threat
Held struggle with his throat but came not
    forth:
For as in theaters of crowded men
Hubbub increases more they call out 'Hush!'
So at Hyperion's words the Phantoms pale 255
Bestirred themselves, thrice horrible and cold;
And from the mirrored level where he stood
A mist arose, as from a scummy marsh.
At this, through all his bulk an agony
Crept gradual, from the feet unto the crown, 260
Like a lithe serpent vast and muscular
Making slow way, with head and neck convulsed
From over-strainèd might.   Releas'd, he fled
To the eastern gates, and full six dewy hours
Before the dawn in season due should blush, 265
He breathed fierce breath against the sleepy
    portals,
Cleared them of heavy vapors, burst them wide
Suddenly on the ocean's chilly streams.
The planet orb of fire, whereon he rode
Each day from east to west the heavens through,
Spun round in sable curtaining of clouds; 271
Not therefore veilèd quite, blindfold, and hid,
But ever and anon the glancing spheres,
Circles, and arcs, and broad-belting colure,
Glowed through, and wrought upon the muffling
    dark 275
Sweet-shapèd lightnings from the nadir deep
Up to the zenith,—hieroglyphics old,
Which sages and keen-eyed astrologers
Then living on the earth, with laboring thought
Won from the gaze of many centuries: 280
Now lost, save what we find in remnants huge
Of stone, or marble swart; their import gone,
Their wisdom long since fled. Two wings this orb
Possessed for glory, two fair argent wings,
Ever exalted at the God's approach: 285
And now, from forth the gloom their plumes
    immense
Rose, one by one, till all outspreaded were;
While still the dazzling globe maintained eclipse,
Awaiting for Hyperion's command.
Fain would he have commanded, fain took
    throne 290
And bid the day begin, if but for change.
He might not:—No, though a primeval God:
The sacred seasons might not be disturbed.
Therefore the operations of the dawn
Stayed in their birth, even as here 't is told 295
Those silver wings expanded sisterly,
Eager to sail their orb; the porches wide
Opened upon the dusk demesnes of night;
And the bright Titan, phrenzied with new woes,
Unused to bend, by hard compulsion bent 300
His spirit to the sorrow of the time;

And all along a dismal rack of clouds,
Upon the boundaries of day and night,
He stretched himself in grief and radiance faint.
There as he lay, the Heaven with its stars 305
Looked down on him with pity, and the voice
Of Cœlus, from the universal space,
Thus whispered low and solemn in his ear:
'O brightest of my children dear, earth-born
And sky-engendered, Son of Mysteries 310
All unrevealèd even to the powers
Which met at thy creating; at whose joy
And palpitations sweet, and pleasures soft,
I, Cœlus, wonder, how they came and whence;
And at the fruits thereof what shapes they be, 315
Distinct, and visible; symbols divine,
Manifestations of that beauteous life
Diffused unseen throughout eternal space;
Of these new-formed art thou, oh brightest
    child!
Of these, thy brethren and the Goddesses! 320
There is sad feud among ye, and rebellion
Of son against his sire. I saw him fall,
I saw my first-born tumbled from his throne!
To me his arms were spread, to me his voice
Found way from forth the thunders round his
    head! 325
Pale wox I and in vapors hid my face.
Art thou, too, near such doom? vague fear there
    is:
For I have seen my sons most unlike Gods.
Divine ye were created, and divine
In sad demeanor, solemn, undisturbed, 330
Unruffled like high Gods, ye lived and ruled:
Now I behold in you fear, hope, and wrath;
Actions of rage and passion; even as
I see them, on the mortal world beneath, 334
In men who die.—This is the grief, O Son!
Sad sign of ruin, sudden dismay, and fall!
Yet do thou strive; as thou art capable,
As thou canst move about, an evident God;
And canst oppose to each malignant hour
Ethereal presence:—I am but a voice; 340
My life is but the life of winds and tides,
No more than winds and tides can I avail:—
But thou canst.—Be thou therefore in the van
Of circumstance; yea, seize the arrow's barb 344
Before the tense string murmur.—To the earth!
For there thou wilt find Saturn, and his woes.
Meantime I will keep watch on thy bright sun,
And of thy seasons be a careful nurse.'—
Ere half this region-whisper had come down,
Hyperion arose, and on the stars 350
Lifted his curvèd lids, and kept them wide
Until it ceased; and still he kept them wide:
And still they were the same bright, patient
    stars.
Then with a slow incline of his broad breast,
Like to a diver in the pearly seas, 355
Forward he stooped over the airy shore,
And plunged all noiseless into the deep night.
                              (1820)

IN A DREAR-NIGHTED DECEMBER

In a drear-nighted December,
  Too happy, happy tree,
Thy branches ne'er remember
  Their green felicity:
The north cannot undo them,   5
With a sleety whistle through them;
Nor frozen thawings glue them
  From budding at the prime.

In a drear-nighted December,
  Too happy, happy brook,   10
Thy bubblings ne'er remember
  Apollo's summer look;
But with a sweet forgetting,
They stay their crystal fretting,
Never, never petting   15
  About the frozen time.

Ah! would 't were so with many
  A gentle girl and boy!
But were there ever any
  Writhed not at passèd joy   20
To know the change and feel it,
When there is none to heal it,
Nor numbèd sense to steal it,
  Was never said in rime.

(1829)

LA BELLE DAME SANS MERCI

BALLAD

O what can ail thee, knight-at-arms!
  Alone and palely loitering!
The sedge has withered from the lake,
  And no birds sing.

O what can ail thee, knight-at-arms!   5
  So haggard and so woe-begone?
The squirrel's granary is full,
  And the harvest's done.

I see a lily on thy brow
  With anguish moist and fever dew,   10
And on thy cheeks a fading rose
  Fast withereth too.

I met a lady in the meads,
  Full beautiful—a faery's child,
Her hair was long, her foot was light,   15
  And her eyes were wild.

I made a garland for her head,
  And bracelets too, and fragrant zone;
She looked at me as she did love,
  And made sweet moan.   20

I set her on my pacing steed,
  And nothing else saw all day long.
For sidelong would she bend, and sing
  A faery's song.

She found me roots of relish sweet,   25
  And honey wild, and manna dew,
And sure in language strange she said—
  'I love thee true.'

She took me to her elfin grot,
  And there she wept, and sighed full sore,   30
And there I shut her wild wild eyes
  With kisses four.

And there she lullèd me asleep,
  And there I dreamed—Ah! woe betide!
The latest dream I ever dreamed   35
  On the cold hill's side.

I saw pale kings and princes too,
  Pale warriors, death-pale were they all;
They cried—'La Belle Dame sans Merci
  Hath thee in thrall!'   40

I saw their starved lips in the gloam,
  With horrid warning gapèd wide,
And I awoke and found me here,
  On the cold hill's side.

And this is why I sojourn here,   45
  Alone and palely loitering,
Though the sedge is withered from the lake
  And no birds sing.

(1820)

ON SEEING THE ELGIN MARBLES

My spirit is too weak—mortality
Weighs heavily on me like unwilling sleep,
And each imagined pinnacle and steep
Of godlike hardship tells me I must die
Like a sick Eagle looking at the sky.   5
Yet 't is a gentle luxury to weep
That I have not the cloudy winds to keep,
Fresh for the opening of the morning's eye.
Such dim-conceivèd glories of the brain
Bring round the heart an undescribable feud;   10
So do these wonders a most dizzy pain,
That mingles Grecian grandeur with the rude
Wasting of old Time—with a billowy main—
A sun—a shadow of a magnitude.

(1817)

ON THE SEA

It keeps eternal whisperings around
Desolate shores, and with its mighty swell
Gluts twice ten thousand caverns, till the spell
Of Hecate leaves them their old shadowy sound.

Often 't is in such gentle temper found,   5
That scarcely will the very smallest shell
Be moved for days from whence it sometime
  fell,
When last the winds of heaven were unbound

Oh ye! who have your eye-balls vexed and tired,
Feast them upon the wideness of the Sea;   10
Oh ye! whose ears are dinned with uproar rude,
Or fed too much with cloying melody,—
Sit ye near some old cavern's mouth, and brood
Until ye start, as if the sea-nymphs quired!
(1848)

SONNET

TO ONE WHO HAS BEEN LONG IN CITY PENT

To one who has been long in city pent,
'T is very sweet to look into the fair
And open face of heaven,—to breathe a prayer
Full in the smile of the blue firmament.

Who is more happy, when, with heart's content,   5
Fatigued he sinks into some pleasant lair
Of wavy grass, and reads a debonair
And gentle tale of love and languishment?

Returning home at evening, with an ear
Catching the notes of Philomel,—an eye   10
Watching the sailing cloudlet's bright career,
He mourns that day so soon has glided by:
E'en like the passage of an angel's tear
That falls through the clear ether silently.
(1817)

SONNET

TO CHATTERTON

O Chatterton! how very sad thy fate!
Dear child of sorrow—son of misery!
How soon the film of death obscur'd that eye,
Whence Genius mildly flash'd, and high debate.

How soon that voice, majestic and elate,   5
Melted in dying numbers! Oh! how nigh
Was night to thy fair morning. Thou didst die
A half-blown flow'ret which cold blasts amate.

But this is past: thou art among the stars
Of highest Heaven: to the rolling spheres   10
Thou sweetly singest: nought thy hymning mars,

Above the ingrate world and human fears.
On earth the good man base detraction bars
From thy fair name, and waters it with tears.
(1848)

SONNET

WHEN I HAVE FEARS THAT I MAY CEASE TO BE

When I have fears that I may cease to be
Before my pen has gleaned my teeming brain,
Before high pilèd books, in charact'ry,
Hold like rich garners the full-ripened grain;

When I behold, upon the night's starred face,   5
Huge cloudy symbols of a high romance,
And think that I may never live to trace
Their shadows, with the magic hand of chance;

And when I feel, fair creature of an hour!
That I shall never look upon thee more,   10
Never have relish in the faery power
Of unreflecting love!—then on the shore
Of the wide world I stand alone, and think
Till Love and Fame to nothingness do sink.
(1848)

SONNET

BRIGHT STAR! WOULD I WERE STEADFAST AS THOU ART

Bright star! would I were steadfast as thou art—
Not in lone splendor hung aloft the night,
And watching, with eternal lids apart,
Like Nature's patient sleepless Eremite,

The moving waters at their priestlike task   5
Of pure ablution round earth's human shores,
Or gazing on the new soft fallen mask
Of snow upon the mountains and the moors—

No—yet still steadfast, still unchangeable,
Pillowed upon my fair love's ripening breast,   10
To feel for ever its soft fall and swell,
Awake for ever in a sweet unrest,
Still, still to hear her tender-taken breath,
And so live ever—or else swoon to death.
(1848)

OTHER POETS OF THE ROMANTIC REVIVAL

For lyric excellence the period between *Lyrical Ballads* (1798) and Tennyson's *Poems, Chiefly Lyrical* (1830) was as eminent as any in our history. Much of this excellence lies in the work of the greater poets, all of whom will perhaps live to after times for their short flights of song rather than by virtue of their ambitious work. Men of less notable power than the very greatest must particularly depend, for 'a perpetuity of fame,' upon those brief pieces or passages where their imperfect or less sustained genius gets for a moment a perfect, or happy, or distinctive utterance. Literature would be the poorer without these happier snatches of its less distinguished warblers, and the Romantic Revival is peculiarly rich in minor singers of this description. One grace of the minor singer is his frequent recognition of his minority, and his contentedness to sing in a light or a minor key, leaving the 'C Major of this life' to his robuster brethren. If he lack this self-denial or wisdom, time will not hesitate to do for him what he fails to do for himself. Thus, while Southey's obese epics are strangling in dust, we can still enjoy a ballad or two. Landor, with all his elegance and elevation may prove too great a tax on our patience unless we can select out a few choicely cut 'gems of purest ray,' sparkling with gallantry and gracious sentiment. There may be little hope of pleasure in Campbell's *Pleasures of Hope*; but his battle hymns can still bring a tingle to the blood which has any British infusion. The inimitable joviality of Peacock's songs will tempt some to read them in their setting, his novels. Tom Hood, for his humanitarian sympathy, his tragic insight, and his literary refinement when he throws off his Comic Almanac manner, will interest as long as greater and more fortunate poets. The busiest of us can afford to listen for an occasional moment to the bubbling pastoral music of Barnes, 'the Dorsetshire Burns.' We need not entangle ourselves among the fantastic situations and impossible characters of *Death's Jest Book* in order to feel Beddoes' tuneful diabolism; we may derive the essence of it from his dirges and night pieces.

ROBERT SOUTHEY
(1774–1843)

THE BATTLE OF BLENHEIM

It was a summer evening,
  Old Kaspar's work was done,
And he before his cottage door
  Was sitting in the sun,
And by him sported on the green   5
His little grandchild Wilhelmine.

She saw her brother Peterkin
  Roll something large and round,
Which he beside the rivulet
  In playing there had found;   10
He came to ask what he had found,
That was so large, and smooth, and round.

Old Kaspar took it from the boy,
  Who stood expectant by;
And then the old man shook his head,   15
  And with a natural sigh,
''T is some poor fellow's skull,' said he,
'Who fell in the great victory.

'I find them in the garden,
  For there's many here about;   20
And often when I go to plough,
  The ploughshare turns them out!
For many thousand men,' said he,
'Were slain in that great victory.'

'Now tell me what 't was all about,'   25
  Young Peterkin, he cries;
And little Wilhelmine looks up
  With wonder-waiting eyes;
'Now tell us all about the war,
And what they fought each other for.'   30

'It was the English,' Kaspar cried,
  'Who put the French to rout;
But what they fought each other for,
  I could not well make out;
But everybody said,' quoth he,   35
'That 't was a famous victory.

'My father lived at Blenheim then,
  Yon little stream hard by;
They burnt his dwelling to the ground,
  And he was forced to fly;   40
So with his wife and child he fled,
Nor had he where to rest his head.

'With fire and sword the country round
    Was wasted far and wide,
And many a childing mother then,   45
    And new-born baby died;
But things like that, you know, must be
At every famous victory.

'They say it was a shocking sight
    After the field was won;   50
For many thousand bodies here
    Lay rotting in the sun;
But things like that, you know, must be
After a famous victory.

'Great praise the Duke of Marlbro' won,   55
    And our good Prince Eugene.'
'Why 't was a very wicked thing!'
    Said little Wilhelmine.
'Nay, nay, my little girl,' quoth he,
'It was a famous victory.   60

'And everybody praised the Duke
    Who this great fight did win.'
'But what good came of it at last?'
    Quoth little Peterkin.
'Why that I cannot tell,' said he,   65
'But 't was a famous victory.'
                          (1805)

WALTER SAVAGE LANDOR
(1775–1864)

ROSE AYLMER

Ah, what avails the sceptered race,
    Ah, what the form divine!
What every virtue, every grace!
    Rose Aylmer, all were thine.
Rose Aylmer, whom these wakeful eyes   5
    May weep, but never see,
A night of memories and of sighs
    I consecrate to thee.
                          (1806)

MILD IS THE PARTING YEAR

Mild is the parting year, and sweet
    The odor of the falling spray;
Life passes on more rudely fleet,
    And balmless is its closing day.

I wait its close, I court its gloom,   5
    But mourn that never must there fall
Or on my breast or on my tomb
    The tear that would have soothed it all.
                          (1831)

PAST RUINED ILION

Past ruined Ilion Helen lives,
    Alcestis rises from the shades;
Verse calls them forth; 't is verse that gives
    Immortal youth to mortal maids.

Soon shall Oblivion's deepening veil   5
    Hide all the peopled hills you see,
The gay, the proud, while lovers hail
    These many summers you and me.
                          (1831)

THE DEATH OF ARTEMIDORA

'Artemidora! Gods invisible,
While thou art lying faint along the couch,
Have tied the sandal to thy slender feet
And stand beside thee, ready to convey
Thy weary steps where other rivers flow.   5
Refreshing shades will waft thy weariness
Away, and voices like thy own come near
And nearer, and solicit an embrace.'
    Artemidora sighed, and would have pressed
The hand now pressing hers, but was too weak.
Iris stood over her dark hair unseen   11
While thus Elpenor spake. He looked into
Eyes that had given light and life erewhile
To those above them, but now dim with tears
And wakefulness. Again he spake of joy   15
Eternal. At that word, that sad word, *joy*,
Faithful and fond her bosom heaved once more:
Her head fell back, and now a loud deep sob
Swelled through the darkened chamber; 't was
    not hers.
                          (1836)

DIRCE

Stand close around, ye Stygian set,
    With Dirce in one boat conveyed,
Or Charon, seeing, may forget
    That he is old, and she a shade.
                          (1836)

ON LUCRETIA BORGIA'S HAIR

Borgia, thou once wert almost too august
And high for adoration; now thou 'rt dust;
All that remains of thee these plaits unfold,
Calm hair meandering in pellucid gold.
                          (1837)

MEMORY AND PRIDE

'Do you remember me? or are you proud?'
Lightly advancing through her star-trimmed
    crowd,
Ianthe said, and looked into my eyes.

'A *yes*, a *yes*, to both: for Memory
  Where you but once have been must ever be,
    And at your voice Pride from his throne must
      rise.'
                                                   (1846)

THE LOVE OF OTHER YEARS

No, my own love of other years!
  No, it must never be.
Much rests with you that yet endears,
  Alas! but what with me?

Could those bright years o'er me revolve
  So gay, o'er you so fair,
The pearl of life we would dissolve
  And each the cup might share.

You show that truth can ne'er decay,
  Whatever fate befalls;
I, that the myrtle and the bay
  Shoot fresh on ruined walls.
                                                   (1846)

TO ROBERT BROWNING

There is delight in singing, though none hear
Beside the singer; and there is delight
In praising, tho' the praiser sit alone
And see the praised far off him, far above.

Shakespeare is not our poet, but the world's,
Therefore on him no speech! and brief for thee,
Browning! Since Chaucer was alive and hale,
No man hath walked along our roads with step

So active, so inquiring eye, or tongue
So varied in discourse. But warmer climes
Give brighter plumage, stronger wing: the
    breeze
Of Alpine heights thou playest with, borne on
Beyond Sorrento and Amalfi, where
The Siren waits thee, singing song for song.
                                                   (1846)

ON TIMELY DEATH

Is it not better at an early hour
  In its calm cell to rest the weary head,
While birds are singing and while blooms the
    bower,
  Than sit the fire out and go starved to bed?
                                                   (1846)

TO AGE

Welcome, old friend! These many years
  Have we lived door by door:
The Fates have laid aside their shears
  Perhaps for some few more.

I was indocile at an age
  When better boys were taught,
But thou at length hast made me sage,
  If I am sage in aught.

Little I know from other men,
  Too little they from me,
But thou hast pointed well the pen
  That writes these lines to thee.

Thanks for expelling Fear and Hope,
  One vile, the other vain;
One's scourge, the other's telescope,
  I shall not see again:

Rather what lies before my feet
  My notice shall engage—
He who hath braved Youth's dizzy heat
  Dreads not the frost of Age.
                                                   (1853)

ON HIS SEVENTY-FIFTH BIRTHDAY

I strove with none; for none was worth my
    strife,
  Nature I loved, and next to Nature, Art;
I warmed both hands before the fire of life,
  It sinks, and I am ready to depart.
                                                   (1853)

THOMAS CAMPBELL
(1777-1844)

YE MARINERS OF ENGLAND

A NAVAL ODE

Ye mariners of England
That guard our native seas,
Whose flag has braved a thousand years
The battle and the breeze!
Your glorious standard launch again
To match another foe,
  And sweep through the deep,
While the stormy winds do blow;
While the battle rages loud and long,
And the stormy winds do blow.

The spirits of your fathers
Shall start from every wave!—
For the deck it was their field of fame,
And Ocean was their grave:
Where Blake and mighty Nelson fell
Your manly hearts shall glow,
  As ye sweep through the deep,
While the stormy winds do blow;
While the battle rages loud and long,
And the stormy winds do blow.

Britannia needs no bulwark,
  No towers along the steep;
Her march is o'er the mountain waves,
  Her home is on the deep.
With thunders from her native oak   25
She quells the floods below—
  As they roar on the shore,
When the stormy winds do blow;
When the battle rages loud and long,
  And the stormy winds do blow.   30

The meteor flag of England
  Shall yet terrific burn,
Till danger's troubled night depart
  And the star of peace return.
Then, then, ye ocean-warriors!   35
Our song and feast shall flow
  To the fame of your name,
When the storm has ceased to blow;
When the fiery fight is heard no more,
  And the storm has ceased to blow.   40
                          (1801)

THOMAS MOORE
(1779–1852)

OFT IN THE STILLY NIGHT

Oft, in the stilly night,
  Ere Slumber's chain has bound me,
Fond Memory brings the light
  Of other days around me;
    The smiles, the tears,   5
    Of boyhood's years,
  The words of love then spoken;
    The eyes that shone,
    Now dimmed and gone,
  The cheerful hearts now broken!   10
Thus, in the stilly night,
  Ere Slumber's chain has bound me,
Sad Memory brings the light
  Of other days around me.

When I remember all   15
  The friends, so linked together,
I've seen around me fall,
  Like leaves in wintry weather;
    I feel like one
    Who treads alone   20
  Some banquet-hall deserted,
    Whose lights are fled,
    Whose garlands dead,
  And all but he departed!
Thus, in the stilly night,   25
  Ere Slumber's chain has bound me,
Sad Memory brings the light
  Of other days around me.
                          (1818)

THE HARP THAT ONCE THROUGH TARA'S HALLS

The harp that once through Tara's halls
  The soul of music shed,
Now hangs as mute on Tara's walls
  As if that soul were fled.
So sleeps the pride of former days,   5
  So glory's thrill is o'er,
And hearts that once beat high for praise
  Now feel that pulse no more!

No more to chiefs and ladies bright
  The harp of Tara swells;   10
The chord alone that breaks at night
  Its tale of ruin tells.
Thus Freedom now so seldom wakes,
  The only throb she gives
Is when some heart indignant breaks,   15
  To show that still she lives.
                          (1808)

LEIGH HUNT
(1784–1859)

RONDEAU

Jenny kissed me when we met,
  Jumping from the chair she sat in;
Time, you thief, who love to get
  Sweets into your list, put that in:
Say I'm weary, say I'm sad,   5
Say that health and wealth have missed me,
Say I'm growing old, but add,
  Jenny kissed me.
                          (1838)

THOMAS LOVE PEACOCK
(1785–1866)

THE MEN OF GOTHAM

Seamen three! what men be ye?
  Gotham's three Wise Men we be.
Whither in your bowl so free?
  To rake the moon from out the sea.
The bowl goes trim; the moon doth shine;   5
  And our ballast is old wine:
  And your ballast is old wine.

Who art thou, so fast adrift?
  I am he they call Old Care.
Here on board we will thee lift.   10
  No: I may not enter there.
Wherefore so? 'T is Jove's decree—
  In a bowl Care may not be:
  In a bowl Care may not be.

Fear ye not the waves that roll? 15
  No: in charmèd bowl we swim.
What the charm that floats the bowl?
  Water may not pass the brim.
The bowl goes trim; the moon doth shine;
  And our ballast is old wine: 20
  And your ballast is old wine.
(1818)

THE WAR-SONG OF DINAS VAWR

THE mountain sheep are sweeter,
  But the valley sheep are fatter;
We therefore deemed it meeter
  To carry off the latter.
We made an expedition; 5
  We met an host and quelled it;
We forced a strong position
  And killed the men who held it.

On Dyfed's richest valley,
  Where herds of kine were browsing, 10
We made a mighty sally,
  To furnish our carousing.
Fierce warriors rushed to meet us;
  We met them, and o'erthrew them:
They struggled hard to beat us, 15
  But we conquered them, and slew them.

As we drove our prize at leisure,
  The king marched forth to catch us:
His rage surpassed all measure,
  But his people could not match us. 20
He fled to his hall-pillars;
  And, ere our force we led off,
Some sacked his house and cellars,
  While others cut his head off.

We there, in strife bewildering, 25
  Spilt blood enough to swim in:
We orphaned many children
  And widowed many women.
The eagles and the ravens
  We glutted with our foemen: 30
The heroes and the cravens,
  The spearmen and the bowmen.

We brought away from battle,
  And much their land bemoaned them,
Two thousand head of cattle 35
  And the head of him who owned them:
Ednyfed, King of Dyfed,
  His head was borne before us;
His wine and beasts supplied our feasts,
  And his overthrow, our chorus. 40
(1829)

THE FRIAR'S SONG

THOUGH I be now a gray, gray friar,
  Yet I was once a hale young knight:
The cry of my dogs was the only choir
  In which my spirit did take delight.

Little I recked of matin bell, 5
  But drowned its toll with my clanging horn
And the only beads I loved to tell
  Were the beads of dew on the spangled thorn.

Little I reck of matin bell,
  But drown its toll with my clanging horn: 10
And the only beads I love to tell
  Are the beads of dew on the spangled thorn.

An archer keen I was withal,
  As ever did lean on greenwood tree;
And could make the fleetest roebuck fall, 15
  A good three hundred yards from me.
Though changeful time, with hand severe,
  Has made me now these joys forego,
Yet my heart bounds whene'er I hear
  Yoicks! hark away! and tally ho! 20

Though changeful time, with hand severe,
  Has made me now these joys forego,
Yet my heart bounds whene'er I hear
  Yoicks! hark away! and tally ho!
(1822)

CHARLES WOLFE
(1791–1823)

THE BURIAL OF SIR JOHN MOORE AT CORUNNA

NOT a drum was heard, not a funeral note,
  As his corse to the rampart we hurried;
Not a soldier discharged his farewell shot
  O'er the grave where our hero we buried.

We buried him darkly at dead of night, 5
  The sods with our bayonets turning;
By the struggling moonbeam's misty light,
  And the lantern dimly burning.

No useless coffin enclosed his breast,
  Not in sheet nor in shroud we wound him, 10
But he lay like a warrior taking his rest
  With his martial cloak around him.

Few and short were the prayers we said,
  And we spoke not a word of sorrow;
But we steadfastly gazed on the face that was dead,
    15
  And we bitterly thought of the morrow.

We thought as we hollowed his narrow bed,
  And smoothed down his lonely pillow,
That the foe and the stranger would tread o'er his head,
  And we far away on the billow! 20

Lightly they'll talk of the spirit that's gone,
  And o'er his cold ashes upbraid him,—
But little he'll reck, if they let him sleep on
  In the grave where a Briton has laid him.

But half of our weary task was done 25
  When the clock struck the hour for retiring;
And we heard the distant and random gun
  That the foe was sullenly firing.

Slowly and sadly we laid him down,
  From the field of his fame fresh and gory; 30
We carved not a line, and we raised not a stone—
  But we left him alone with his glory.
                              (1817)

JOHN KEBLE
(1792-1866)

UNITED STATES

Tyre of the *farther* West! be thou too warned,
Whose eagle wings thine own green world o'erspread,
Touching two Oceans: wherefore hast thou scorned
Thy fathers' God, O proud and full of bread?
  Why lies the Cross unhonored on thy ground 5
While in mid air thy stars and arrows flaunt?
That sheaf of darts, will it not fall unbound,
Except, disrobed of thy vain earthly vaunt,
Thou bring it to be blessed where Saints and Angels haunt?

The holy seed, by Heaven's peculiar grace, 10
Is rooted here and there in thy dark woods;
But many a rank weed round it grows apace,
And Mammon builds beside thy mighty floods,
  O'ertopping Nature, braving Nature's God;
O while thou yet hast room, fair fruitful land, 15
Ere war and want have stained thy virgin sod,
Mark thee a place on high, a glorious stand,
Whence Truth her sign may make o'er forest, lake, and strand.

Eastward, this hour, perchance thou turn'st thine ear,
Listening if haply with the surging sea, 20
Blend sounds of Ruin from a land once dear
To thee and Heaven. O trying hour for thee!
  Tyre mocked when Salem fell; where now is Tyre?
Heaven was against her. Nations thick as waves,
Burst o'er her walls, to Ocean doomed and fire: 25
And now the tideless water idly laves
Her towers, and lone sands heap her crownèd merchants' graves.
                              (1836)

THOMAS HOOD
(1799-1845)

FAIR INES

O saw ye not fair Ines?
  She's gone into the West,
To dazzle when the sun is down,
  And rob the world of rest;
She took our daylight with her, 5
  The smiles that we love best,
With morning blushes on her cheek,
  And pearls upon her breast.

O turn again, fair Ines,
  Before the fall of night, 10
For fear the Moon should shine alone,
  And stars unrivaled bright;
And blessèd will the lover be
  That walks beneath their light,
And breathes the love against thy cheek 15
  I dare not even write!

Would I had been, fair Ines,
  That gallant cavalier,
Who rode so gaily by thy side,
  And whispered thee so near!— 20
Were there no bonny dames at home
  Or no true lovers here,
That he should cross the seas to win
  The dearest of the dear?

I saw thee, lovely Ines, 25
  Descend along the shore,
With bands of noble gentlemen,
  And banners waved before;
And gentle youth and maidens gay,
  And snowy plumes they wore;— 30
It would have been a beauteous dream,
  —If it had been no more!

Alas, alas! fair Ines,
  She went away with song,
With Music waiting on her steps, 35
  And shoutings of the throng;
But some were sad and felt no mirth,
  But only Music's wrong,
In sounds that sang Farewell, Farewell
  To her you've loved so long. 40

Farewell, farewell, fair Ines!
  That vessel never bore
So fair a lady on its deck,
  Nor danced so light before,—
Alas for pleasure on the sea, 45
  And sorrow on the shore!
The smile that blest one lover's heart
  Has broken many more!
                              (1827)

THE BRIDGE OF SIGHS

One more Unfortunate,
  Weary of breath,
Rashly importunate,
  Gone to her death!

Take her up tenderly,
  Lift her with care;
Fashioned so slenderly,
  Young, and so fair!

Look at her garments
Clinging like cerements;
Whilst the wave constantly
  Drips from her clothing;
Take her up instantly,
  Loving, not loathing.

Touch her not scornfully;
Think of her mournfully,
  Gently and humanly,
Not of the stains of her;
All that remains of her
  Now is pure womanly.

Make no deep scrutiny
Into her mutiny
  Rash and undutiful:
Past all dishonor,
Death has left on her
  Only the beautiful.

Still, for all slips of hers,
  One of Eve's family—
Wipe those poor lips of hers
  Oozing so clammily.

Loop up her tresses
  Escaped from the comb,
Her fair auburn tresses;
Whilst wonderment guesses
  Where was her home?

Who was her father?
  Who was her mother?
Had she a sister?
  Had she a brother?
Or was there a dearer one
Still, and a nearer one
  Yet, than all other?

Alas! for the rarity
Of Christian charity
  Under the sun!
O, it was pitiful!
Near a whole city full,
  Home she had none.

Sisterly, brotherly,
Fatherly, motherly
  Feelings had changed:

Love, by harsh evidence,
Thrown from its eminence;
Even God's providence
  Seeming estranged.

Where the lamps quiver
So far in the river,
  With many a light
From window to casement,
From garret to basement,
She stood with amazement,
  Houseless by night.

The bleak wind of March
  Made her tremble and shiver;
But not the dark arch,
  Or the black flowing river:
Mad from life's history,
Glad to death's mystery,
  Swift to be hurled—
Anywhere, anywhere
  Out of the world!

In she plunged boldly—
No matter how coldly
  The rough river ran—
Over the brink of it,
Picture it—think of it,
  Dissolute Man!
Lave in it, drink of it,
  Then, if you can!

Take her up tenderly,
  Lift her with care;
Fashioned so slenderly,
  Young, and so fair!

Ere her limbs frigidly
  Stiffen too rigidly,
    Decently, kindly,
Smooth and compose them;
And her eyes, close them,
  Staring so blindly!

Dreadfully staring
  Through muddy impurity,
As when with the daring
Last look of despairing
  Fixed on futurity.

Perishing gloomily,
Spurred by contumely,
Cold inhumanity,
Burning insanity,
  Into her rest—
Cross her hands humbly,
As if praying dumbly,
  Over her breast!

Owning her weakness,
  Her evil behaviour,
And leaving with meekness,
  Her sins to her Saviour!

(1844)

THE SONG OF THE SHIRT

With fingers weary and worn,
  With eyelids heavy and red,
A woman sat, in unwomanly rags,
  Plying her needle and thread—
Stitch! stitch! stitch!   5
  In poverty, hunger, and dirt,
And still with a voice of dolorous pitch
  She sang the 'Song of the Shirt.'

'Work! work! work!
  While the cock is crowing aloof!   10
And work—work—work,
  Till the stars shine through the roof!
It's Oh! to be a slave
  Along with the barbarous Turk,
Where woman has never a soul to save,   15
  If this is Christian work

'Work—work—work,
  Till the brain begins to swim;
Work—work—work,
  Till the eyes are heavy and dim!   20
Seam, and gusset, and band,
  Band, and gusset, and seam,
Till over the buttons I fall asleep,
  And sew them on in a dream!

'Oh, Men, with Sisters dear!   25
  Oh, Men, with Mothers and Wives!
It is not linen you're wearing out
  But human creatures' lives!
Stitch—stitch—stitch,
  In poverty, hunger, and dirt,   30
Sewing at once, with a double thread,
  A Shroud as well as a Shirt.

'But why do I talk of Death?
  That Phantom of grisly bone,
I hardly fear its terrible shape,   35
  It seems so like my own—
It seems so like my own,
  Because of the fasts I keep;
Oh, God, that bread should be so dear,
  And flesh and blood so cheap!   40

'Work—work—work!
  My labor never flags;
And what are its wages? A bed of straw,
  A crust of bread—and rags.
That shattered roof—this naked floor—   45
  A table—a broken chair—
And a wall so blank, my shadow I thank
  For sometimes falling there!

'Work—work—work!
  From weary chime to chime,   50
Work—work—work,
  As prisoners work for crime!

Band, and gusset, and seam,
  Seam, and gusset, and band,
Till the heart is sick, and the brain benumbed, 55
  As well as the weary hand.

'Work—work—work,
  In the dull December light,
And work—work—work,
  When the weather is warm and bright—   60
While underneath the eaves
  The brooding swallows cling
As if to show me their sunny backs
  And twit me with the spring.

'Oh! but to breathe the breath   65
  Of the cowslip and primrose sweet—
With the sky above my head,
  And the grass beneath my feet;
For only one short hour
  To feel as I used to feel,   70
Before I knew the woes of want
  And the walk that costs a meal.

'Oh! but for one short hour!
  A respite however brief!
No blessèd leisure for Love or Hope,   75
  But only time for Grief!
A little weeping would ease my heart,
  But in their briny bed
My tears must stop, for every drop
  Hinders needle and thread!'   80

With fingers weary and worn,
  With eyelids heavy and red,
A woman sat, in unwomanly rags,
  Plying her needle and thread—
Stitch! stitch! stitch!   85
  In poverty, hunger, and dirt,
And still with a voice of dolorous pitch,—
Would that its tone could reach the Rich!—
  She sang this 'Song of the Shirt!'

(1843)

WINTHROP MACKWORTH PRAED
(1802–1839)

THE BELLE OF THE BALL-ROOM

Years—years ago, ere yet my dreams
  Had been of being wise or witty,—
Ere I had done with writing themes,
  Or yawned o'er this infernal Chitty;—
Years—years ago,—while all my joy   5
  Was in my fowling-piece and filly,—
In short, while I was yet a boy,
  I fell in love with Laura Lily.

I saw her at the County Ball:
  There, when the sounds of flute and fiddle
Gave signal sweet in that old hall   11
  Of hands across and down the middle,

Hers was the subtlest spell by far
  Of all that set young hearts romancing;
She was our queen, our rose, our star;   15
  And then she danced—O Heaven, her dancing!

Dark was her hair, her hand was white;
  Her voice was exquisitely tender;
Her eyes were full of liquid light;
  I never saw a waist so slender!   20
Her every look, her every smile,
  Shot right and left a score of arrows;
I thought 't was Venus from her isle,
  And wondered where she 'd left her sparrows.

She talked,—of politics or prayers,—   25
  Of Southey's prose or Wordsworth's sonnets,—
Of danglers—or of dancing bears,
  Of battles—or the last new bonnets,
By candlelight, at twelve o'clock,
  To me it mattered not a tittle,   30
If those bright lips had quoted Locke,
  I might have thought they murmured Little.

Through sunny May, through sultry June,
  I loved her with a love eternal;
I spoke her praises to the moon,   35
  I wrote them to the Sunday Journal:
My mother laughed; I soon found out
  That ancient ladies have no feeling:
My father frowned; but how should gout
  See any happiness in kneeling?   40

She was the daughter of a Dean,
  Rich, fat, and rather apoplectic;
She had one brother, just thirteen,
  Whose color was extremely hectic;
Her grandmother for many a year   45
  Had fed the parish with her bounty;
Her second cousin was a peer,
  And Lord Lieutenant of the County.

But titles, and the three per cents,
  And mortgages, and great relations,   50
And India bonds, and tithes, and rents,
  Oh, what are they to love's sensations?
Black eyes, fair forehead, clustering locks—
  Such wealth, such honors, Cupid chooses;
He cares as little for the Stocks,   55
  As Baron Rothschild for the Muses.

She sketched; the vale, the wood, the beach,
  Grew lovelier from her pencil's shading:
She botanized; I envied each
  Young blossom in her boudoir fading;   60
She warbled Handel; it was grand;
  She made the Catalani jealous:
She touched the organ; I could stand
  For hours and hours to blow the bellows.

She kept an album, too, at home,   65
  Well filled with all an album's glories;
Paintings of butterflies, and Rome,
  Patterns for trimmings, Persian stories;
Soft songs to Julia's cockatoo,
  Fierce odes to Famine and to Slaughter;   70
And autographs of Prince Leboo,
  And recipes for elder-water.

And she was flattered, worshipped, bored;
  Her steps were watched, her dress was noted,
Her poodle dog was quite adored,   75
  Her sayings were extremely quoted;
She laughed, and every heart was glad,
  As if the taxes were abolished;
She frowned, and every look was sad,
  As if the Opera were demolished.   80

She smiled on many, just for fun,—
  I knew that there was nothing in it;
I was the first—the only one
  Her heart had thought of for a minute.—
I knew it, for she told me so,   85
  In phrase which was divinely molded;
She wrote a charming hand,—and oh!
  How sweetly all her notes were folded!

Our love was like most other loves;—
  A little glow, a little shiver,   90
A rose-bud, and a pair of gloves,
  And 'Fly not yet'—upon the river;
Some jealousy of some one's heir,
  Some hopes of dying broken-hearted;
A miniature, a lock of hair,   95
  The usual vows,—and then we parted.

We parted; months and years rolled by;
  We met again four summers after:
Our parting was all sob and sigh;
  Our meeting was all mirth and laughter: 100
For in my heart's most secret cell
  There had been many other lodgers;
And she was not the ball-room's belle,
  But only—Mrs. Something Rogers!

(1844)

A LETTER OF ADVICE

FROM MISS MEDORA TREVILIAN, AT PADUA, TO MISS ARAMINTA VAVASOUR, IN LONDON

You tell me you 're promised a lover,
  My own Araminta, next week;
Why cannot my fancy discover
  The hue of his coat and his cheek?
Alas! if he look like another,   5
  A vicar, a banker, a beau,
Be deaf to your father and mother,
  My own Araminta, say 'No!'

Miss Lane, at her Temple of Fashion,
   Taught us both how to sing and to speak, 10
And we loved one another with passion,
   Before we had been there a week:
You gave me a ring for a token;
   I wear it wherever I go;
I gave you a chain,—is it broken? 15
   My own Araminta, say 'No!'

O think of our favorite cottage,
   And think of our dear Lalla Rookh!
How we shared with the milkmaids their pottage,
   And drank of the stream from the brook; 20
How fondly our loving lips faltered,
   'What further can grandeur bestow?'
My heart is the same;—is yours altered?
   My own Araminta, say 'No!'

Remember the thrilling romances 25
   We read on the bank in the glen;
Remember the suitors our fancies
   Would picture for both of us then.
They wore the red cross on their shoulder,
   They had vanquished and pardoned their foe— 30
Sweet friend, are you wiser or colder?
   My own Araminta, say 'No!'

You know, when Lord Rigmarole's carriage,
   Drove off with your Cousin Justine,
You wept, dearest girl, at the marriage, 35
   And whispered 'How base she has been!'
You said you were sure it would kill you,
   If ever your husband looked so;
And you will not apostatize,—will you?
   My own Araminta, say 'No!' 40

When I heard I was going abroad, love,
   I thought I was going to die;
We walked arm in arm to the road, love,
   We looked arm in arm to the sky;
And I said 'When a foreign postilion 45
   Has hurried me off to the Po,
Forget not Medora Trevilian:
   My own Araminta, say "No"!'

We parted! but sympathy's fetters
   Reach far over valley and hill; 50
I muse o'er your exquisite letters,
   And feel that your heart is mine still;
And he who would share it with me, love,—
   The richest of treasures below,—
If he's not what Orlando should be, love, 55
   My own Araminta, say 'No!'

If he wears a top-boot in his wooing,
   If he comes to you riding a cob,
If he talks of his baking or brewing,
   If he puts up his feet on the hob, 60
If he ever drinks port after dinner,
   If his brow or his breeding is low,
If he calls himself 'Thompson' or 'Skinner,'
   My own Araminta, say 'No!'

If he studies the news in the papers 65
   While you are preparing the tea,
If he talks of the damps or the vapors
   While moonlight lies soft on the sea,
If he's sleepy while you are capricious,
   If he has not a musical 'Oh!' 70
If he does not call Werther delicious,—
   My own Araminta, say 'No!'

If he ever sets foot in the City
   Among the stockbrokers and Jews,
If he has not a heart full of pity, 75
   If he don't stand six feet in his shoes,
If his lips are not redder than roses,
   If his hands are not whiter than snow,
If he has not the model of noses,—
   My own Araminta, say 'No!' 80

If he speaks of a tax or a duty,
   If he does not look grand on his knees,
If he's blind to a landscape of beauty,
   Hills, valleys, rocks, waters, and trees,
If he dotes not on desolate towers, 85
   If he likes not to hear the blast blow,
If he knows not the language of flowers,—
   My own Araminta, say 'No!'

He must walk—like a god of old story
   Come down from the home of his rest; 90
He must smile—like the sun in his glory
   On the buds he loves ever the best;
And oh! from its ivory portal
   Like music his soft speech must flow!—
If he speak, smile, or walk like a mortal, 95
   My own Araminta, say 'No!'

Don't listen to tales of his bounty,
   Don't hear what they say of his birth,
Don't look at his seat in the county,
   Don't calculate what he is worth; 100
But give him a theme to write verse on,
   And see if he turns out his toe;
If he's only an excellent person,—
   My own Araminta, say 'No!'

(1844)

WILLIAM BARNES
(1801–1886)

BLACKMWORE MAIDENS

The primrwose in the sheäde do blow,
   The cowslip in the zun,
The thyme upon the down do grow,
   The clote where streams do run;

An' where do pretty maidens grow
   An' blow, but where the tow'r
Do rise among the bricken tuns
   In Blackmwore by the Stour.

If you could zee their comely gaït,
   An' pretty feäces' smiles,
A-trippèn on so light o' waight,
   An' steppèn off the stiles;
A-gwain to church, as bells do swing
   An' ring 'ithin the tow'r,
You 'd own the pretty maidens' pleäce
   Is Blackmwore by the Stour.

If you vrom Wimborne took your road,
   To Stower or Paladore,
An' all the farmers' housen show'd
   Their daughters at the door;
You 'd cry to bachelors at hwome—
   'Here come: 'ithin an hour
You 'll vind ten maidens to your mind,
   In Blackmwore by the Stour.'

An' if you look'd 'ithin their door,
   To zee em in their pleäce,
A-doèn housework up avore
   Their smilèn mother's feäce;
You 'd cry—'Why, if a man would wive
   An' thrive, 'ithout a dow'r,
Then let en look en out a wife
   In Blackmwore by the Stour.'

As I upon my road did pass
   A school-house back in Maÿ,
There out upon the beäten grass
   Wer maidens at their plaÿ;
An' as the pretty souls did tweil
   An' smile, I cried, 'The flow'r
O' beauty, then, is still in bud
   In Blackmwore by the Stour.'

(1844)

THE SURPRISE

As there I left the road in May,
And took my way along a ground,
I found a glade with girls at play,
By leafy boughs close-hemmed around,
And there, with stores of harmless joys,
They plied their tongues, in merry noise;
Though little did they seem to fear
So queer a stranger might be near;
Teeh-hee! Look here! Hah! ha! Look there!
And oh! so playsome, oh! so fair.

And one would dance as one would spring,
Or bob or bow with leering smiles,
And one would swing, or sit and sing,
Or sew a stitch or two at whiles,
And one skipped on with downcast face,
All heedless, to my very place,
And there, in fright, in one foot out,
Made one dead step and turned about.
Heeh, hee, oh! oh! ooh! oo!—Look there!
And oh! so playsome, oh, so fair.

Away they scampered all, full speed,
By boughs that swung along their track,
As rabbits out of wood at feed,
At sight of men all scamper back.
And one pulled on behind her heel,
A thread of cotton, off her reel,
And oh! to follow that white clue,
I felt I fain could scamper too.
Teeh, hee, run here. Eeh! ee! Look there!
And oh! so playsome, oh! so fair.

(1868)

THOMAS LOVELL BEDDOES
(1803–1849)

DREAM-PEDLARY

If there were dreams to sell,
   What would you buy?
Some cost a passing bell;
   Some a light sigh,
That shakes from Life's fresh crown
Only a rose-leaf down.
If there were dreams to sell,
Merry and sad to tell,
And the crier rang the bell,
   What would you buy?

A cottage lone and still,
   With bowers nigh,
Shadowy, my woes to still,
   Until I die.
Such pearl from Life's fresh crown
Fain would I shake me down.
Were dreams to have at will,
This would best heal my ill,
   This would I buy.

But there were dreams to sell
   Ill didst thou buy;
Life is a dream, they tell,
   Waking, to die.
Dreaming a dream to prize,
Is wishing ghosts to rise;
And if I had the spell
To call the buried well,
   Which one would I?

If there are ghosts to raise,
   What shall I call,
Out of hell's murky haze,
   Heaven's blue pall?
Raise my loved long-lost boy,
To lead me to his joy.—
There are no ghosts to raise;
Out of death lead no ways;
   Vain is the call.

Know'st thou not ghosts to sue,
　No love thou hast.
Else lie, as I will do,　　　　　　　40
　And breathe thy last.
So out of Life's fresh crown
Fall like a rose-leaf down.
Thus are the ghosts to woo;
Thus are all dreams made true,　　45
　Ever to last!

(1851)

BALLAD OF HUMAN LIFE

When we were girl and boy together,
　We tossed about the flowers
And wreathed the blushing hours
Into a posy green and sweet.
　I sought the youngest, best,　　　5
　And never was at rest
Till I had laid them at thy fairy feet.
But the days of childhood they were fleet,
　And the blooming sweet-briar-breathed weather,
When we were boy and girl together.　10

Then we were lad and lass together,
　And sought the kiss of night
　Before we felt aright,
Sitting and singing soft and sweet.
　The dearest thought of heart　　15
　With thee 't was joy to part,
And the greater half was thine, as meet.
Still my eyelid's dewy, my veins they beat
　At the starry summer-evening weather,
When we were lad and lass together.　20

And we are man and wife together,
　Although thy breast, once bold
　With song, be closed and cold
Beneath flowers' roots and birds' light feet.
　Yet sit I by thy tomb,　　　　　25
　And dissipate the gloom
With songs of loving faith and sorrow sweet.
And fate and darkling grave kind dreams do cheat,
　That, while fair life, young hope, despair and death are,
We're boy and girl, and lass and lad, and man and wife together.　30

(1851)

TO SEA, TO SEA!

From Death's Jest Book

To sea, to sea! The calm is o'er;
　The wanton water leaps in sport,
And rattles down the pebbly shore;
　The dolphin wheels, the sea-cows snort,
And unseen Mermaids' pearly song　5
　Comes bubbling up, the weeds among.
Fling broad the sail, dip deep the oar;
　To sea, to sea! the calm is o'er.

To sea, to sea! our wide-winged bark
　Shall billowy cleave its sunny way,　10
And with its shadow, fleet and dark,
　Break the caved Triton's azure day,
Like mighty eagle soaring light
O'er antelopes on Alpine height.
The anchor heaves, the ship swings free,
The sails swell full. To sea, to sea!　16

(1850)

DIRGE

If thou wilt ease thine heart
　Of love and all its smart,
　　Then sleep, dear, sleep;
And not a sorrow
　Hang any tear on your eye-lashes;　5
　　Lie still and deep,
Sad soul, until the sea-wave washes
The rim o' the sun to-morrow,
　　In eastern sky.

But wilt thou cure thine heart　　10
　Of love and all its smart,
　　Then die, dear, die;
'T is deeper, sweeter,
　Than on a rose bank to lie dreaming
　　With folded eye;　　　　15
And then alone, amid the beaming
Of love's stars, thou 'lt meet her
　　In eastern sky.

(1850)

SONG

Old Adam, the carrion crow,
　The old crow of Cairo;
He sat in the shower, and let it flow
　Under his tail and over his crest;
　And through every feather　　5
　Leaked the wet weather;
And the bough swung under his nest;
　For his beak it was heavy with marrow.
Is that the wind dying? O no;
It's only two devils, that blow　　10
Through a murderer's bones, to and fro,
　　In the ghosts' moonshine.

Ho! Eve, my gray carrion wife,
　When we have supped on king's marrow,
Where shall we drink and make merry our life?
　Our nest it is Queen Cleopatra's skull,　16
　　'T is cloven and cracked,
　　And battered and hacked,
But with tears of blue eyes it is full:
Let us drink then, my raven of Cairo.　20
Is that the wind dying? O no;
It's only two devils, that blow
Through a murderer's bones, to and fro,
　　In the ghosts' moonshine.

(1850)

WILLIAM HAZLITT (1778-1830)

Hazlitt's father, a Unitarian minister at Maidstone, in Kent, sympathized so strongly with the American colonists in the revolutionary struggle that in 1783 he took his family to the United States, but after three years they returned to Wem in Shropshire, where the father had a small congregation and the son went to school. At Shrewsbury, in 1798, young Hazlitt heard Coleridge preach, and through him made the acquaintance of Wordsworth, and later of Charles Lamb, whose portrait he painted (now in the National Portrait Gallery). But from art Hazlitt soon turned to literature and journalism. He was in turn parliamentary reporter, dramatic critic, lecturer and essayist. He has not Coleridge's philosophical insight, or Lamb's whimsical charm, or De Quincey's copious and impressive rhetoric, but he shares with them the power of giving to a magazine article or an occasional lecture the permanent interest which marks the difference between journalism and literature. His *Dramatic Literature of the Age of Elizabeth* (1821) and other writings on associated subjects contributed perhaps as much as the work of any of the critics of the Romantic Revival to the appreciation and understanding of Shakespeare and his contemporaries. Hazlitt relied absolutely on his own judgment and the bare text; indeed it was his boast that he left off reading when he began to write.

Hazlitt quarreled with all his friends except Lamb, and made himself generally unpopular in his own time. It was said of him that he spoke well 'only of the dead.' He decried the popular hero of his time, the Duke of Wellington, and extolled his two pet idols, Napoleon and Rousseau. He scandalized his contemporaries by publishing a detailed account of his infatuation (a dozen years after his marriage) for the daughter of a lodging-house keeper, Sarah Walker; when Hazlitt obtained a Scotch divorce, Sarah refused to marry him, and he consoled himself with a well-to-do widow, who left him within a year of their marriage. He was undoubtedly a difficult man to get on with. A friend describes him as 'a pale anatomy of a man, sitting uneasily on half a chair, his anxious, highly intellectual face looking upon vacancy—emaciate, unstrung, inanimate.' In spite of a Bohemian existence, harassed by debt and anxiety, his final verdict on his deathbed was 'Well, I have had a happy life.' His repute as a critic and essayist has increased with time.

ON GOING A JOURNEY

One of the pleasantest things in the world is going a journey; but I like to go by myself. I can enjoy society in a room; but out of doors, nature is company enough for me. I am then never less alone than when alone.

'The fields his study, nature was his book.'

I cannot see the wit of walking and talking at the same time. When I am in the country, I wish to vegetate like the country. I am not for criticising hedgerows and black cattle. I go out of town in order to forget the town and all that is in it. There are those who for this purpose go to watering-places, and carry the metropolis with them. I like more elbow-room, and fewer incumbrances. I like solitude, when I give myself up to it, for the sake of solitude; nor do I ask for

'——a friend in my retreat,
Whom I may whisper solitude is sweet.'

The soul of a journey is liberty, perfect liberty, to think, feel, do just as one pleases. We go a journey chiefly to be free of all impediments and of all inconveniences; to leave ourselves behind, much more to get rid of others. It is because I want a little breathing-space to muse on indifferent matters, where Contemplation

'May plume her feathers and let grow her wings,
That in the various bustle of resort
Were all too ruffled, and sometimes impair'd,'

that I absent myself from the town for awhile, without feeling at a loss the moment I am left by myself. Instead of a friend in a post-chaise or in a Tilbury, to exchange good things with and vary the same stale topics over again, for once let me have a truce with impertinence. Give me the clear blue sky over my head, and the green turf beneath my feet, a winding road before me, and a three hours' march to dinner—and then to thinking! It is hard if I cannot start some game on these lone heaths. I laugh, I run, I leap, I sing for joy. From the point of yonder rolling cloud, I plunge into my past being, and revel there, as the sun-burnt Indian plunges headlong into the wave that wafts him to his native shore. Then long-forgotten things, like 'sunken wrack and sumless treasuries,' burst upon my eager sight, and I begin to feel, think, and be myself again. Instead of an awkward silence, broken by attempts at wit or dull commonplaces, mine is that undisturbed silence of the heart which alone is perfect eloquence. No one likes puns, alliterations, antitheses, argument, and analysis better than I do; but I sometimes had rather be without them. 'Leave, oh, leave me to my repose!' I have just now other business in hand, which would seem idle to you, but is with me 'very stuff of the conscience.' Is not this wild rose sweet without a comment? Does not this daisy leap to my heart set in its coat of emerald? Yet if I were to explain to you the circumstance that has so endeared it to me, you would only smile. Had I not better then keep it to myself, and let it serve me to brood over, from here to yonder craggy point, and from thence onward to the far-distant horizon? I should be but bad company all that way, and therefore prefer being alone. I have heard it said that you may, when the moody fit comes on, walk or ride on by yourself, and indulge your reveries. But this looks like a breach of manners, a neglect of others, and you are thinking all the time that you ought to rejoin your party. 'Out upon such half-faced fellowship,' say I. I like to be either entirely to myself, or entirely at the disposal of others; to talk or be silent, to walk or sit still, to be sociable or solitary. I was pleased with an observation of Mr. Cobbett's, that 'he thought it a bad French custom to drink our wine with our meals, and that an Englishman ought to do only one thing at a time.' So I cannot talk and think, or indulge in melancholy musing and lively conversation by fits and starts. 'Let me have a companion of my way,' says Sterne, 'were it but to remark how the shadows lengthen as the sun declines.' It is beautifully said: but in my opinion, this continual comparing of notes interferes with the involuntary impression of things upon the mind, and hurts the sentiment. If you only hint what you feel in a kind of dumb show, it is insipid: if you have to explain it, it is making a toil of a pleasure. You cannot read the book of nature, without being perpetually put to the trouble of translating it for the benefit of others. I am for the synthetical method on a journey, in preference to the analytical. I am content to lay in a stock of ideas then, and to examine and anatomize them afterwards. I want to see my vague notions float like the down of the thistle before the breeze, and not to have them entangled in the briars and thorns of controversy. For once, I like to have it all my own way; and this is impossible unless you are alone, or in such company as I do not covet. I have no objection to argue a point with any one for twenty miles of measured road, but not for pleasure. If you remark the scent of a beanfield crossing the road, perhaps your fellow-traveller has no smell. If you point to a distant object, perhaps he is short-sighted, and has to take out his glass to look at it. There is a feeling in the air, a tone in the color of a cloud which hits your fancy, but the effect of which you are unable to account for. There is then no sympathy, but an uneasy craving after it, and a dissatisfaction which pursues you on the way, and in the end probably produces ill humor. Now I never quarrel with myself, and take all my own conclusions for granted till I find it necessary to defend them against objections. It is not merely that you may not be of accord on the objects and circumstances that present themselves before you—these may recall a number of objects, and lead to associations too delicate and refined to be possibly communicated to others. Yet these I love to cherish, and sometimes still fondly clutch them, when I can escape from the throng to do so. To give way to our feelings before company, seems extravagance or affectation; and on the other hand, to have to unravel this mystery of our being at every turn, and to make others take an equal interest in it (otherwise the end is not answered) is a task to which few are competent. We must 'give it an understanding, but no tongue.' My old friend C———, however, could do both. He could go on in the most delightful explanatory way over hill and dale, a summer's day, and convert a landscape into a didactic poem or a Pindaric ode. 'He talked far above singing.' If I could so clothe my ideas in sounding and flowing words, I might perhaps wish to have some one with me to admire the swelling theme; or I could be more content, were it possible for me still to hear his echoing voice in the woods of All-Foxden. They had 'that fine madness in them which our first poets had;' and if they could have been caught by some rare instrument, would have breathed such strains as the following:

'———Here be woods as green
As any, air likewise as fresh and sweet
As when smooth Zephyrus plays on the fleet
Face of the curled stream, with flow'rs as many
As the young spring gives, and as choice as any;
Here be all new delights, cool streams and wells,

Arbours o'ergrown with woodbine, caves and dells;
Choose where thou wilt, while I sit by and sing,
Or gather rushes to make many a ring
For thy long fingers; tell thee tales of love,
How thy pale Phœbe, hunting in a grove,
First saw the boy Endymion, from whose eyes
She took eternal fire that never dies;
How she convey'd him softly in a sleep,
His temples bound with poppy, to the steep
Head of old Latmos, where she stoops each night,
Gilding the mountain with her brother's light,
To kiss her sweetest.'——
                    Faithful Shepherdess.

Had I words and images at command like these, I would attempt to wake the thoughts that lie slumbering on golden ridges in the evening clouds: but at the sight of nature my fancy, poor as it is, droops and closes up its leaves, like flowers at sunset. I can make nothing out on the spot:—I must have time to collect myself.—

In general, a good thing spoils out-of-door prospects: it should be reserved for Table-talk. L—— is for this reason, I take it, the worst company in the world out of doors; because he is the best within. I grant, there is one subject on which it is pleasant to talk on a journey; and that is, what one shall have for supper when we get to our inn at night. The open air improves this sort of conversation or friendly altercation, by setting a keener edge on appetite. Every mile of the road heightens the flavor of the viands we expect at the end of it. How fine it is to enter some old town, walled and turreted, just at the approach of night-fall, or to come to some straggling village, with the lights streaming through the surrounding gloom; and then after inquiring for the best entertainment that the place affords, to 'take one's ease at one's inn!' These eventful moments in our lives' history are too precious, too full of solid, heart-felt happiness to be frittered and dribbled away in imperfect sympathy. I would have them all to myself, and drain them to the last drop: they will do to talk of or to write about afterwards. What a delicate speculation it is, after drinking whole goblets of tea,

'The cups that cheer, but not inebriate,'

and letting the fumes ascend into the brain, to sit considering what we shall have for supper—eggs and a rasher, a rabbit smothered in onions, or an excellent veal-cutlet! Sancho in such a situation once fixed upon cow-heel; and his choice, though he could not help it, is not to be disparaged. Then in the intervals of pictured scenery and Shandean contemplation, to catch the preparation and the stir in the kitchen—*Procul, O procul este profani!* [Stand far off, ye unhallowed spirits!] These hours are sacred to silence and to musing, to be treasured up in the memory, and to feed the source of smiling thoughts hereafter. I would not waste them in idle talk; or if I must have the integrity of fancy broken in upon, I would rather it were by a stranger than a friend. A stranger takes his hue and character from the time and place; he is a part of the furniture and costume of an inn. If he is a Quaker, or from the West Riding of Yorkshire, so much the better. I do not even try to sympathize with him, and he breaks no squares. I associate nothing with my travelling companion but present objects and passing events. In his ignorance of me and my affairs, I in a manner forget myself. But a friend reminds one of other things, rips up old grievances, and destroys the abstraction of the scene. He comes in ungraciously between us and our imaginary character. Something is dropped in the course of conversation that gives a hint of your profession and pursuits; or from having some one with you that knows the less sublime portions of your history, it seems that other people do. You are no longer a citizen of the world: but your 'unhoused free condition is put into circumscription and confine.' The *incognito* of an inn is one of its striking privileges—'lord of one's-self, uncumber'd with a name.' Oh! it is great to shake off the trammels of the world and of public opinion—to lose our importunate, tormenting, everlasting personal identity in the elements of nature, and become the creature of the moment, clear of all ties—to hold to the universe only by a dish of sweet-breads, and to owe nothing but the score of the evening—and no longer seeking for applause and meeting with contempt, to be known by no other title than *the Gentleman in the parlor!* One may take one's choice of all characters in this romantic state of uncertainty as to one's real pretensions, and become indefinitely respectable and negatively right-worshipful. We baffle prejudice and disappoint conjecture; and from being so to others, begin to be objects of curiosity and wonder even to ourselves. We are no more those hackneyed commonplaces that we appear in the world: an inn restores us to the level of nature, and quits scores with society! I have certainly spent some enviable hours at inns—sometimes when I have been left entirely to myself, and have tried to solve some metaphysical problem, as once at Witham-common, where I found out the proof that likeness is not a case of the association of ideas—at other times, when there have been pictures in the room, as at St. Neot's (I think it was), where I first met with Gribelin's engravings of the Cartoons, into which I entered at once, and at a little inn on the borders of Wales, where there happened to be hanging some of Westall's drawings, which I compared triumphantly (for a theory that I had, not for the admired artist) with the figure of a girl who had ferried me over the Severn, standing up in the boat between me and the twilight—at other times I might mention luxuriating in books, with a peculiar interest in this way, as I remember sitting up half the night to read Paul and Virginia, which I picked up at an inn at Bridgewater, after being drenched in the rain all day; and at the same place I got through two volumes of Madame D'Arblay's Camilla. It was on the tenth of April, 1798, that I sat down to a volume of the New Eloise, at the inn at Llangollen, over a bottle of sherry and a cold chicken. The letter I chose was that in which St. Preux describes his feelings as he first caught a glimpse from the heights of the Jura of the Pays de Vaud, which I had brought with me as a *bon bouche* to crown the evening with. It was my birth-day, and I had for the first time come from a place in the neighbourhood to visit this delightful spot. The road to Llangollen turns off between Chirk and Wrexham; and on passing a certain point, you come all at once upon the valley, which opens like an amphitheatre, broad, barren hills rising in majestic state on either side, with 'green upland swells that echo to the bleat of flocks' below, and the river Dee babbling over its stony bed in the midst of them. The valley at this time 'glittered green with sunny showers,' and a budding ash-tree dipped its tender branches in the chiding stream. How proud, how glad I was to walk along the high road that overlooks the delicious prospect, repeating the lines which I have just quoted from Mr. Coleridge's poems. But besides the prospect which opened beneath my feet, another also opened to my inward sight, a heavenly vision, on which were written, in letters large as Hope could make them, these four words, LIBERTY, GENIUS, LOVE, VIRTUE; which have since faded into the light of common day, or mock my idle gaze.

'The beautiful is vanished, and returns not.'

Still I would return some time or other to this enchanted spot; but I would return to it alone. What other self could I find to share that influx of thoughts, of regret, and delight, the fragments of which I could hardly conjure up to myself, so much have they been broken and defaced! I could stand on some tall rock, and overlook the precipice of years that separates me from what I then was. I was at that time going shortly to visit the poet whom I have above named. Where is he now? Not only I myself have changed; the world, which was then new to me, has become old and incorrigible. Yet will I turn to thee in thought, O sylvan Dee, in joy, in youth and gladness as thou then wert; and thou shalt always be to me the river of Paradise, where I will drink of the waters of life freely!

There is hardly any thing that shows the short-sightedness or capriciousness of the imagination more than travelling does. With change of place we change our ideas; nay, our opinions and feelings. We can by an effort indeed transport ourselves to old and long-forgotten scenes, and then the picture of the mind revives again; but we forget those that we have just left. It seems that we can think but of one place at a time. The canvas of the fancy is but of a certain extent, and if we paint one set of objects upon it, they immediately efface every other. We cannot enlarge our conceptions, we only shift our point of view. The landscape bares its bosom to the enraptured eye, we take our fill of it, and seem as if we could form no other image of beauty or grandeur. We pass on, and think no more of it: the horizon that shuts it from our sight, also blots it from our memory like a dream. In travelling through a wild barren country, I can form no idea of a woody and cultivated one. It appears to me that all the world must be barren, like what I see of it. In the country we forget the town, and in town we despise the country. 'Beyond Hyde Park,' says Sir Fopling Flutter, 'all is a desert.' All that part of the map that we do not see before us is a blank. The world in our conceit of it is not much bigger than a nut-shell. It is not one prospect expanded into another, county joined to county, kingdom to kingdom, lands to sea, making an image voluminous and vast;—the mind can form no larger idea of space than the eye can take in at a single glance. The rest is a name written in a map, a calculation of arithmetic. For instance, what is the true signification of that immense mass of territory and population, known by the name of China to us? An inch of paste-board on a wooden globe, of no more account than a China orange! Things near us are seen of the size of life: things at a distance are diminished to the size of the understanding. We measure the universe by ourselves, and even comprehend the texture of our own being only piece-meal. In this way, however, we remember an infinity of things and places. The mind is like a mechanical instrument that plays a great variety of tunes, but it must play them in succession. One idea recalls another, but it at the same time excludes all others. In trying to renew old recollections, we cannot as it were unfold the whole web of our existence; we must pick out the single threads. So in coming to a place where we have formerly lived and with which we have intimate associations, every one must have found that the feeling grows more vivid the nearer we approach the spot, from the mere anticipation of the actual impression: we remember circumstances, feelings, persons, faces, names, that we had not thought of for years; but for the time all the rest of the world is forgotten!—To return to the question I have quitted above.

I have no objection to go to see ruins, aqueducts, pictures, in company with a friend or a party, but rather the contrary, for the former reason reversed. They are intelligible matters, and will bear talking about. The sentiment here is not tacit, but communicable and overt. Salisbury Plain is barren of criticism, but Stonehenge will bear a discussion antiquarian, picturesque, and philosophical. In setting out on a party of pleasure, the first consideration always is where we shall go to: in taking a solitary ramble, the question is what we shall meet with by the way. 'The mind is its own place;' nor are we anxious to arrive at the end of our journey. I can myself do the honors indifferently well to works of art and curiosity. I once took a party to Oxford with no mean *éclat*—shewed them that seat of the Muses at a distance,

'With glistening spires and pinnacles adorn'd'—

descanted on the learned air that breathes from the grassy quadrangles and stone walls of halls and colleges—was at home in the Bodleian; and at Blenheim quite superseded the powdered Cicerone that attended us, and that pointed in vain with his wand to common-place beauties in matchless pictures.—As another exception to the above reasoning, I should not feel confident in venturing on a journey in a foreign country without a companion. I should want at intervals to hear the sound of my own language. There is an involuntary antipathy in the mind of an Englishman to foreign manners and notions that requires the assistance of social sympathy to carry it off. As the distance from home increases, this relief, which was at first a luxury, becomes a passion and an appetite. A person would almost feel stifled to find himself in the deserts of Arabia without friends and countrymen: there must be allowed to be something in the view of Athens or old Rome that claims the utterance of speech; and I own that the Pyramids are too mighty for any simple contemplation. In such situations, so opposite to all one's ordinary train of ideas, one seems a species by one's-self, a limb torn off from society, unless one can meet with instant fellowship and support.—Yet I did not feel this want or craving very pressing once, when I first set my foot on the laughing shores of France. Calais was peopled with novelty and delight. The confused, busy murmur of the place was like oil and wine poured into my ears; nor did the mariners' hymn, which was sung from the top of an old crazy vessel in the harbor, as the sun went down, send an alien sound into my soul. I only breathed the air of general humanity. I walked over 'the vine-covered hills and gay regions of France,' erect and satisfied; for the image of man was not cast down and chained to the foot of arbitrary thrones: I was at no loss for language, for that of all the great schools of painting was open to me. The whole is vanished like a shade. Pictures, heroes, glory, freedom, all are fled: nothing remains but the Bourbons and the French people!—There is undoubtedly a sensation in travelling into foreign parts that is to be had nowhere else: but it is more pleasing at the time than lasting. It is too remote from our habitual associations to be a common topic of discourse or reference, and, like a dream or another state of existence, does not piece into our daily modes of life. It is an animated but a momentary hallucination. It demands an effort to exchange our actual for our ideal identity; and to feel the pulse of our old transports revive very keenly, we must 'jump' all our present comforts and connexions. Our romantic and itinerant character is not to be domesticated. Dr. Johnson remarked how little foreign travel added to the facilities of conversation in those who had been abroad. In fact, the time we have spent there is both delightful and in one sense instructive; but it appears to be cut out of our substantial, downright existence, and never to join kindly on to it. . . .

(1822)

THOMAS DE QUINCEY (1785-1859)

De Quincey's life was ill-regulated, almost from his infancy, in its material conditions. His education was interrupted by changes from one school to another, and at seventeen he ran away from the grammar school of his native city, Manchester, as he himself describes in the first of our extracts from the 'Confessions.' He made his way through Wales to London, where he wandered about in the streets and mixed with the lowest classes of society. After a year of this adventurous life he became an undergraduate at Oxford, but he gave little attention to the prescribed studies, and left without taking a degree. He spent a great deal of time on German, of which he had already learnt something from a chance meeting with a tourist during his wanderings in Wales, and he obtained a good knowledge of Kant and other philosophical writers. He wrote, years afterwards: 'Without breach of truth or modesty I may affirm that my life has been, on the whole, the life of a philosopher: from my birth I was made an intellectual creature; and intellectual in the highest sense my pursuits and pleasures have been, even from my schoolboy days.' In 1807 he paid a visit to Coleridge and escorted Mrs. Coleridge and her children to the Lake District, where he met Southey and Wordsworth, and settled down for some years, marrying the daughter of a Westmoreland farmer. In 1821 he removed to London and began his literary career by contributing the *Confessions of an English Opium Eater* to the *London Magazine*. His writings consist almost entirely of essays and reviews, written for various periodicals, and covering a wide range of subjects; many of them are on German literature, which at that time was interesting the British public. The latter part of his life was spent mainly in and about Edinburgh, where his daughter kept house for him. She says: 'He was not a reassuring man for nervous people to live with, as those nights were exceptions on which he did not set something on fire, the commonest incident being for someone to look up from book or work, to say casually: "Papa, your hair is on fire," of which a calm, "Is it, my love?" and a hand rubbing out of the blaze was all the notice taken.' His rooms were crowded with books and papers until they became uninhabitable and he moved elsewhere, leaving the accumulated store to the mercy of the landlady. He was incapable of managing money matters, and was often in prison for debt. He would ask for the loan of a small sum, imagining himself absolutely penniless when he had a £50 note in his pocket. His dress and his personal appearance were as odd as his habits; he was of very short stature, with a large head, and bright eyes. He had an extremely delicate ear for music and the harmonies of words; this in part accounts for the beauty of his prose style, which is molded on that of the great writers of the first half of the seventeenth century. He had a keenly analytic intellect, and some of his writings are highly philosophical and imaginative; but, like Lamb, as he himself said, he had 'a furious love for nonsense—headlong nonsense,' and the 'Confessions' need not be taken as literal accounts of actual fact.

From CONFESSIONS OF AN ENGLISH OPIUM EATER

I have often been asked how I first came to be a regular opium eater; and have suffered, very unjustly, in the opinion of my acquaintance, from being reputed to have brought upon myself all the sufferings which I shall have to record, by a long course of indulgence in this practice purely for the sake of creating an artificial state of pleasurable excitement. This, however, is a misrepresentation of my case. True it is, that for nearly ten years I did occasionally take opium for the sake of the exquisite pleasure it gave me: but, so long as I took it with this view, I was effectually protected from all material bad consequences, by the necessity of interposing long intervals between the several acts of indulgence, in order to renew the pleasurable sensations. It was not for the purpose of creating pleasure, but of 5 mitigating pain in the severest degree, that I first began to use opium as an article of daily diet. In the twenty-eighth year of my age, a most painful affection of the stomach, which I had first experienced about ten years before, 10 attacked me in great strength. This affection had originally been caused by extremities of hunger, suffered in my boyish days. During the season of hope and redundant happiness which succeeded (that is, from eighteen to twenty-four) it had slumbered; for the three following years it had revived at intervals; and now, under unfavorable circumstances, from depression of spirits, it attacked me with a violence that yielded to no remedies but opium. As the youthful sufferings, which first produced this derangement of the stomach, were interesting in themselves, and in the circumstances that attended them, I shall here briefly retrace them.

My father died when I was about seven years old, and left me to the care of four guardians. I was sent to various schools, great and small; and was very early distinguished for my classical attainments, especially for my knowledge of Greek. At thirteen I wrote Greek with ease; and at fifteen my command of that language was so great, that I not only composed Greek verses in lyric meters, but could converse in Greek fluently and without embarrassment—an accomplishment which I have not since met with in any scholar of my times, and which, in my case, was owing to the practice of daily reading off the newspapers into the best Greek I could furnish *extempore;* for the necessity of ransacking my memory and invention, for all sorts and combinations of periphrastic expressions, as equivalents for modern ideas, images, relations of things, etc., gave me a compass of diction which would never have been called out by a dull translation of moral essays, etc. 'That boy,' said one of my masters, pointing the attention of a stranger to me, 'that boy could harangue an Athenian mob, better than you and I could address an English one.' He who honored me with this eulogy was a scholar, 'and a ripe and good one;' and of all my tutors, was the only one whom I loved or reverenced. Unfortunately for me (and, as I afterwards learned, to this worthy man's great indignation) I was transferred to the care, first of a blockhead, who was in a perpetual panic, lest I should expose his ignorance; and finally, to that of a respectable scholar, at the head of a great school on an ancient foundation. This man had been appointed to his situation by —— College, Oxford; and was a sound, well-built scholar, but (like most men, whom I have known from that college) coarse, clumsy, and inelegant. A miserable contrast he presented, in my eyes, to the Etonian brilliancy of my favorite master; and beside, he could not disguise from my hourly notice, the poverty and meagerness of his understanding. It is a bad thing for a boy to be, and to know himself, far beyond his tutors, whether in knowledge or in power of mind. This was the case, so far as regarded knowledge at least, not with myself only, for the two boys who jointly with myself composed the first form were better Grecians than the head-master, though not more elegant scholars, nor at all more accustomed to sacrifice to the graces. When I first entered, I remember that we read Sophocles; and it was a constant matter of triumph to us, the learned triumvirate of the first form, to see our 'Archididascalus' (as he loved to be called) conning our lessons before we went up, and laying a regular train, with lexicon and grammar, for blowing up and blasting (as it were) any difficulties he found in the choruses; whilst *we* never condescended to open our books until the moment of going up, and were generally employed in writing epigrams upon his wig, or some such important matter. My two class-fellows were poor, and dependent for their future prospects at the university on the recommendation of the head-master; but I, who had a small patrimonial property, the income of which was sufficient to support me at college, wished to be sent thither immediately. I made earnest representations on the subject to my guardians, but all to no purpose. One, who was more reasonable, and had more knowledge of the world than the rest, lived at a distance; two of the other three resigned all their authority into the hands of the fourth; and this fourth with whom I had to negotiate, was a worthy man, in his way, but haughty, obstinate, and intolerant of all opposition to his will. After a certain number of letters and personal interviews, I found that I had nothing to hope for, not even a compromise of the matter, from my guardian; unconditional submission was what he demanded; and I prepared myself, therefore, for other measures. Summer was now coming on with hasty steps, and my seventeenth birthday was fast approaching; after which day I had sworn within myself that I would no longer be numbered amongst schoolboys. Money being what I chiefly wanted, I wrote to a woman of high rank, who, though young herself, had known me from a child, and had latterly treated me with great distinction, requesting that she would 'lend' me five guineas. For upwards of a week no answer came; and I was beginning to despond, when, at length, a servant put into my hands a double letter, with a coronet on the seal. The letter was kind and obliging; the fair writer was on the sea-coast, and in that way the delay had arisen; she enclosed double of what I had asked, and good-naturedly hinted that if I should *never* repay her, it would not absolutely ruin her. Now then, I was prepared for my scheme; ten guineas, added to about two which I had remaining from my pocket money, seemed to me sufficient for an indefinite length of time; and at that happy age, if no *definite* boundary can be assigned to one's power, the spirit of hope and pleasure makes it virtually infinite.

It is a just remark of Dr. Johnson's (and what cannot often be said of his remarks, it is a very feeling one), that we never do anything consciously for the last time (of things, that is, which we have long been in the habit of doing) without sadness of heart. This truth I felt deeply, when I came to leave ——, a place which I did not love, and where I had not been happy. On the evening before I left —— for ever, I grieved when the ancient and lofty school-room resounded with the evening service, performed for the last time in my hearing and at night, when the muster-roll of names was called over, and mine (as usual) was called first, I stepped forward, and, passing the head-master, who was standing by, I bowed to him, and looked earnestly in his face, thinking to myself, 'He is old and infirm, and in this world I shall not see him again.' I was right: I never *did* see him again, nor ever shall. He looked at me complacently, smiled good-naturedly, returned my salutation (or rather, my valediction), and we parted (though he knew it not) for ever. I could not reverence him intellectually; but he had been uniformly kind to me, and had allowed me many indulgences; and I grieved at the thought of the mortification I should inflict upon him.

The morning came which was to launch me into the world, and from which my whole succeeding life has, in many important points, taken its coloring. I lodged in the head-master's house, and had been allowed, from my first entrance, the indulgence of a private room, which I used both as a sleeping room and as a study. At half after three I rose, and gazed with deep emotion at the ancient towers of ——, 'drest in earliest light,' and beginning to crimson with the radiant luster of a cloudless July morning. I was firm and immovable in my purpose; but yet agitated by anticipation of uncertain danger and troubles; and, if I could have foreseen the hurricane and perfect hailstorm of affliction which soon fell upon me, well might I have been agitated. To this agitation the deep peace of the morning presented an affecting contrast, and in some degree a medicine. The silence was more profound than that of midnight; and to me the silence of a summer morning is more touching than all other silence, because, the light being broad and strong, as that of noon-day at other seasons of the year, it seems to differ from perfect day, chiefly because man is not yet abroad; and thus, the peace of nature, and of the innocent creatures of God, seems to be secure and deep, only so long as the presence of man, and his restless and unquiet spirit, are not there to trouble its sanctity. I dressed myself, took my hat and gloves, and lingered a little in the room. For the last year and a-half this room had been my 'pensive citadel;' here I had read and studied through all the hours of night; and, though true it was, that for the latter part of this time I, who was framed for love and gentle affections, had lost my gaiety and happiness, during the strife and fever of contention with my guardian; yet, on the other hand, as a boy, so passionately fond of books, and dedicated to intellectual pursuits, I could not fail to have enjoyed many happy hours in the midst of general dejection. I wept as I looked round on the chair, hearth, writing-table, and other familiar objects, knowing too certainly, that I looked upon them for the last time. Whilst I write this, it is eighteen years ago; and yet, at this moment, I see distinctly, as if it were yesterday, the lineaments and expression of the object on which I fixed my parting gaze; it was a picture of the lovely ——, which hung over the mantlepiece; the eyes and mouth of which were so beautiful, and the whole countenance so radiant with benignity and divine tranquillity, that I had a thousand times laid down my pen, or my book, to gather consolation from it, as a devotee from his patron saint. Whilst I was yet gazing upon it, the deep tones of —— clock proclaimed that it was four o'clock. I went up to the picture, kissed it, and then gently walked out, and closed the door for ever!

* * *

So blended and intertwisted in this life are occasions of laughter and of tears, that I cannot yet recall, without smiling, an incident which occurred at that time, and which had nearly put a stop to the immediate execution of my plan. I had a trunk of immense weight; for, besides my clothes, it contained nearly all my library. The difficulty was to get this removed to a carrier's; my room was at an aërial elevation in the house, and (what was worse) the staircase, which communicated with this angle of the building, was accessible only by a gallery which passed the head-master's chamber door. I was a favorite with all the servants; and, knowing that any of them would screen me, and act confidentially, I communicated my embarrassment to a groom of the head-master's. The groom swore he would do anything I wished; and, when the time arrived, went upstairs to bring the trunk down. This I feared was beyond the strength of any one man; however, the groom was a man

> Of Atlantean shoulders, fit to bear
> The weight of mightiest monarchies;

and had a back as spacious as Salisbury Plain. Accordingly he persisted in bringing down the trunk alone, whilst I stood waiting at the foot of the last flight, in anxiety for the event. For some time I heard him descending with slow and firm steps; but unfortunately, from his trepidation, as he drew near the dangerous quarter, within a few steps of the gallery, his foot slipped; and the mighty burden, falling from his shoulders, gained such increase of impetus at each step of the descent, that, on reaching the bottom, it trundled, or rather leaped, right across, with the noise of twenty devils, against the very bed-room door of the archididascalus. My first thought was that all was lost, and that my only chance for executing a retreat was to sacrifice my baggage. However, on reflection, I determined to abide the issue. The groom was in the utmost alarm, both on his own account and on mine; but, in spite of this, so irresistibly had the sense of the ludicrous in this unhappy *contretemps* taken possession of his fancy, that he sang out a long, loud and canorous peal of laughter, that might have wakened the Seven Sleepers. At the sound of this resonant merriment, within the very ears of insulted authority, I could not myself forbear joining in it; subdued to this, not so much by the unhappy *étourderie* of the trunk, as by the effect it had upon the groom. We both expected, as a matter of course, that Dr. —— would sally out of his room; for in general, if but a mouse stirred, he sprang out like a mastiff from the kennel. Strange to say, however, on this occasion, when the noise of laughter had ceased, no sound, or rustling even, was to be heard in the bed-room. Dr. —— had a painful complaint, which, sometimes keeping him awake, made his sleep, perhaps, when it *did* come, the deeper. Gathering courage from the silence, the groom hoisted his burden again, and accomplished the remainder of his descent, without accident. I waited until I saw the trunk placed on a wheel-barrow, and on its road to the carrier's; then, 'with Providence my guide,' I set off on foot—carrying a small parcel, with some articles of dress, under my arm; a favorite English poet in one pocket, and a small 12mo volume, containing about nine plays of Euripides, in the other.

* * *

If any man, poor or rich, were to say that he would tell us what had been the happiest day in his life, and the why and the wherefore, I suppose that we should all cry out—Hear him! hear him! As to the happiest *day*, that must be very difficult for any wise man to name; because any event that could occupy so distinguished a place in a man's retrospect of his life, or be entitled to have shed a special felicity on any one day, ought to be of such an enduring character as that (accidents apart) it should have continued to shed the same felicity, or one not distinguishably less, on many years together. To the happiest *lustrum*, however, or even to the happiest *year*, it may be allowed to any man to point without discountenance from wisdom. This year, in my case, reader, was the one which we have now reached; though it stood, I confess, as a parenthesis between years of a gloomier character. It was a year of brilliant water (to speak after the manner of jewelers), set as it were, and insulated, in the gloom and cloudy melancholy of opium. Strange as it may sound, I had a little before this time descended suddenly, and without any considerable effort, from 320 grains of opium (*i. e.*, eight [1] thousand drops of laudanum) per day to forty grains, or one-eighth part. Instantaneously, and as if by magic, the cloud of profoundest melancholy which rested upon my brain, like some black vapors that I have seen roll away from the summits of mountains, drew off in one day (νυχθήμερον); passed off with its murky banners as simultaneously as a ship that has been stranded, and is floated off by a spring-tide—

That moveth altogether, if it move at all.

[1] I here reckon twenty-five drops of laudanum as equivalent to one grain of opium, which, I believe, is the common estimate. However, as both may be considered variable quantities (the crude opium varying much in strength, and the tincture still more), I suppose that no infinitesimal accuracy can be had in such a calculation. Teaspoons vary as much in size as opium in strength. Small ones hold about 100 drops; so that 8,000 drops are about eighty times a teaspoonful. The reader sees how much I kept within Dr. Buchan's indulgent allowance.

Now, then, I was again happy; I now took only 1,000 drops of laudanum per day; and what was that? A latter spring had come to close up the season of youth; my brain performed its functions as healthily as ever before; I read Kant again, and again I understood him, or fancied that I did. Again my feelings of pleasure expanded themselves to all around me; and if any man from Oxford or Cambridge, or from neither, had been announced to me in my unpretending cottage, I should have welcomed him with as sumptuous a reception as so poor a man could offer. Whatever else was wanting to a wise man's happiness,—of laudanum I would have given him as much as he wished, and in a golden cup. And, by the way, now that I speak of giving laudanum away, I remember, about this time, a little incident, which I mention, because, trifling as it was, the reader will soon meet it again in my dreams, which it influenced more fearfully than could be imagined. One day a Malay knocked at my door. What business a Malay could have to transact amongst English mountains, I cannot conjecture; but possibly he was on his road to a seaport about forty miles distant.

The servant who opened the door to him was a young girl born and bred amongst the mountains, who had never seen an Asiatic dress of any sort; his turban, therefore, confounded her not a little; and, as it turned out, that his attainments in English were exactly of the same extent as hers in the Malay, there seemed to be an impassable gulf fixed between all communication of ideas, if either party had happened to possess any. In this dilemma, the girl, recollecting the reputed learning of her master (and, doubtless, giving me credit for a knowledge of all the languages of the earth, besides, perhaps, a few of the lunar ones), came and gave me to understand that there was a sort of demon below, whom she clearly imagined that my art could exorcise from the house. I did not immediately go down; but, when I did, the group which presented itself, arranged as it was by accident, though not very elaborate, took hold of my fancy and my eye in a way that none of the statuesque attitudes exhibited in the ballets at the Opera House, though so ostentatiously complex, had ever done. In a cottage kitchen, but paneled on the wall with dark wood that from age and rubbing resembled oak, and looking more like a rustic hall of entrance than a kitchen, stood the Malay—his turban and loose trousers of dingy white relieved upon the dark paneling; he had placed himself nearer to the girl than she seemed to relish; though her native spirit of mountain intrepidity contended with the feeling of simple awe which her countenance expressed as she gazed upon the tiger-cat before her. And a more striking picture there could not be imagined, than the beautiful English face of the girl, and its exquisite fairness, together with her erect and independent attitude, contrasted with the sallow and bilious skin of the Malay, enameled or veneered with mahogany, by marine air, his small, fierce, restless eyes, thin lips, slavish gestures and adorations. Half-hidden by the ferocious-looking Malay, was a little child from a neighboring cottage who had crept in after him, and was now in the act of reverting its head, and gazing upwards at the turban and the fiery eyes beneath it, whilst with one hand he caught at the dress of the young woman for protection. My knowledge of the Oriental tongues is not remarkably extensive, being indeed confined to two words—the Arabic word for barley, and the Turkish for opium (madjoon), which I have learned from Anastasius. And, as I had neither a Malay dictionary, nor even Adelung's *Mithridates*, which might have helped me to a few words, I addressed him in some lines from the Iliad; considering that, of such languages as I possessed, Greek, in point of longitude, came geographically nearest to an Oriental one. He worshipped me in a most devout manner, and replied in what I suppose was Malay. In this way I saved my reputation with my neighbors; for the Malay had no means of betraying the secret. He lay down upon the floor for about an hour, and then pursued his journey. On his departure I presented him with a piece of opium. To him, as an Orientalist, I concluded that opium must be familiar; and the expression of his face convinced me that it was. Nevertheless, I was struck with some little consternation when I saw him suddenly raise his hand to his mouth, and (in the schoolboy phrase) bolt the whole, divided into three pieces, at one mouthful. The quantity was enough to kill three dragoons and their horses; and I felt some alarm for the poor creature; but what could be done? I had given him the opium in compassion for his solitary life, on recollecting that if he had traveled on foot from London, it must be nearly three weeks since he could have exchanged a thought with any human being. I could not think of violating the laws of hospitality, by having him seized and drenched with an emetic, and thus frightening him into a notion that we were going to sacrifice him to some English idol. No: there was clearly no help for it;—he took his leave, and for some days I felt anxious; but as I never heard of any Malay being found dead, I became convinced that he was used [1] to opium: and that I must have done him the service I designed, by giving him one night of respite from the pains of wandering.

This incident I have digressed to mention, because this Malay (partly from the picturesque exhibition he assisted to frame, partly from the anxiety I connected with his image for some days) fastened afterwards upon my dreams, and brought other Malays with him worse than himself, that ran 'a-muck' [2] at me, and led me into a world of troubles. But to quit this episode, and to return to my intercalary year of happiness. I have said already, that on a subject so important to us all as happiness, we should listen with pleasure to any man's experience or experiments, even though he were but a plowboy, who cannot be supposed to have plowed very deep into such an intractable soil as that of human pains and pleasures, or to have conducted his researches upon any very enlightened principles. But I, who have taken happiness, both in a solid and a liquid shape, both boiled and unboiled, both East India and Turkey—who have conducted my experiments upon this interesting subject with a sort of galvanic battery—and have, for the general benefit of the world, inoculated myself, as it were, with the poison of 8,000 drops of laudanum per day (just, for the same reason, as a French surgeon inoculated himself lately with cancer—an English one, twenty years ago, with plague—and a third, I know not of what nation, with hydrophobia),— *I* (it will be admitted) must surely know what happiness is, if anybody does. And, therefore, I will here lay down an analysis of happiness; and as the most interesting mode of communicating it, I will give it, not didactically, but wrapped up and involved in a picture of one evening, as I spent every evening during the intercalary year when laudanum, though taken daily, was to me no more than the elixir of pleasure. This done, I shall quit the subject of happiness altogether, and pass to a very different one—the *pains of opium.*

Let there be a cottage, standing in a valley, eighteen miles from any town—no spacious valley, but about two miles long, by three quarters of a mile in average width; the benefit of which provision is, that all the families resident within its circuit will compose, as it were, one larger household personally familiar to your eye, and more or less interesting to your affections. Let the mountains be real mountains, between three and four thousand feet high; and the cottage a real cottage, not (as a witty author has it) 'a cottage with a double coach-house;' let it be, in fact (for I must abide by the actual scene), a white cottage, embowered with flowering shrubs, so chosen as to unfold a succession of flowers upon the walls, and clustering round the windows through all the months of spring, summer, and autumn—beginning, in fact, with May roses, and ending with jasmine. Let it, however, *not* be spring, nor summer, nor autumn— but winter in his sternest shape. This is a most important point in the science of happiness. And I am surprised to see people overlook it, and think it matter of congratulation that winter is going, or, if coming, is not likely to be a severe one. On the contrary, I put up a petition annually, for as much snow, hail, frost, or storm, of one kind or other, as the skies can possibly afford us. Surely everybody is aware of the divine pleasures which attend a winter fireside; candles at four o'clock, warm hearth-rugs, tea, a fair tea-maker, shutters closed, curtains flowing in ample draperies on the floor, whilst the wind and rain are raging audibly without,

And at the doors and windows seem to call,
As heaven and earth they would together mell;
Yet the least entrance find they none at all;
Whence sweeter grows our rest secure in massy hall.
—*Castle of Indolence.*

All these are items in the description of a winter evening, which must surely be familiar to everybody born in a high latitude. And it is evident that most of these delicacies, like ice-cream, require a very low temperature of the atmosphere to produce them: they are fruits

---

[1] This, however, is not a necessary conclusion; the varieties of effect produced by opium on different constitutions are infinite. A London Magistrate (Harriott's *Struggles through Life*, vol. iii, p. 391, Third Edition), has recorded that, on the first occasion of his trying laudanum for the gout, he took *forty* drops, the next night *sixty*, and on the fifth night *eighty*, without any effect whatever; and this at an advanced age. I have an anecdote from a country surgeon, however, which sinks Mr. Harriott's case into a trifle; and in my projected medical treatise on opium, which I will publish, provided the College of Surgeons will pay me for enlightening their benighted understandings upon this subject, I will relate it; but it is far too good a story to be published gratis.

[2] See the common accounts in any Eastern traveler or voyager of the frantic excesses committed by Malays who have taken opium, or are reduced to desperation by ill luck at gambling.

which cannot be ripened without weather stormy or inclement, in some way or other. I am not '*particular*,' as people say, whether it be snow, or black frost, or wind so strong, that (as Mr. —— says) 'you may lean your back against it like a post.' I can put up even with rain, provided it rains cats and dogs; but something of the sort I must have; and, if I have it not, I think myself in a manner ill-used; for why am I called on to pay so heavily for winter, in coals, and candles, and various privations that will occur even to gentlemen, if I am not to have the article good of its kind? No: a Canadian winter for my money; or a Russian one, where every man is but a co-proprietor with the north wind in the fee-simple of his own ears. Indeed, so great an epicure am I in this matter, that I cannot relish a winter night fully if it be much past St. Thomas's day, and have degenerated into disgusting tendencies to vernal appearances; no, it must be divided by a thick wall of dark nights from all return of light and sunshine. From the latter weeks of October to Christmas Eve, therefore, is the period during which happiness is in season, which, in my judgment, enters the room with the tea-tray; for tea, though ridiculed by those who are naturally of coarse nerves, or are become so from wine-drinking, and are not susceptible of influence from so refined a stimulant, will always be the favorite beverage of the intellectual; and, for my part, I would have joined Dr. Johnson in a *bellum internecinum* against Jonas Hanway, or any other impious person, who should presume to disparage it. But here, to save myself the trouble of too much verbal description, I will introduce a painter, and give him directions for the rest of the picture. Painters do not like white cottages, unless a good deal weather-stained; but as the reader now understands that it is a winter night, his services will not be required, except for the inside of the house.

Paint me, then, a room seventeen feet by twelve, and not more than seven and a half feet high. This, reader, is somewhat ambitiously styled, in my family, the drawing-room; but, being contrived 'a double debt to pay,' it is also, and more justly, termed the library; for it happens that books are the only articles of property in which I am richer than my neighbors. Of these I have about five thousand, collected gradually since my eighteenth year. Therefore, painter, put as many as you can into this room. Make it populous with books; and, furthermore, paint me a good fire; and furniture plain and modest, befitting the unpretending cottage of a scholar. And, near the fire paint me a tea-table; and (as it is clear that no creature can come to see one such a stormy night), place only two cups and saucers on the tea-tray; and, if you know how to paint such a thing symbolically, or otherwise, paint me an eternal tea-pot—eternal *á parte ante* and *á parte post;* for I usually drink tea from eight o'clock at night to four o'clock in the morning. And, as it is very unpleasant to make tea, or to pour it out for oneself, paint me a lovely young woman, sitting at the table. Paint her arms like Aurora's, and her smile like Hebe's.—But no, dear M——, not even in jest let me insinuate that thy power to illuminate my cottage rests upon a tenure so perishable as mere personal beauty; or that the witchcraft of angelic smiles lies within the empire of any earthly pencil. Pass, then, my good painter, to something more within its power; and the next article brought forward should naturally be myself—a picture of the Opium-eater, with his 'little golden receptacle of the pernicious drug' lying beside him on the table. As to the opium, I have no objection to see a picture of *that*, though I would rather see the original: you may paint it if you choose; but I apprise you, that no 'little' receptacle would, even in 1816, answer *my* purpose, who was at a distance from the 'stately Pantheon,' and all druggists (mortal or otherwise). No; you may as well paint the real receptacle, which was not of gold, but of glass, and as much like a wine-decanter as possible. Into this you may put a quart of ruby-colored laudanum: that, and a book of German Metaphysics placed by its side, will sufficiently attest my being in the neighborhood; but, as to myself,—there I demur.

* * * (1821)

THOMAS BABINGTON MACAULAY (1800-1859)

Macaulay's life is a remarkable story of successful endeavor. The son of a well-known philanthropist and anti-slavery agitator, he was a precocious boy, with a natural aptitude for literary composition and a phenomenal memory; he began a compendium of universal history at the age of seven, and repeated after a lapse of forty years a scrap of poetry he had read as a youth in a country newspaper and had not recalled in the interval; he knew *Paradise Lost* and *Pilgrim's Progress* by heart. He went in 1818 to Trinity College, Cambridge, and left with a fellowship which secured him a sufficient income for his personal wants for the next seven years. An essay on Milton he contributed to the *Edinburgh Review* in 1825 attracted the attention of the editor, Jeffrey, who said to him, 'The more I think, the less I can conceive where you picked up that style.' In 1830 he entered the House of Commons as member for Calne, and at once made his mark by a speech on the Reform Bill. The termination of his fellowship in 1831 put him in somewhat straitened circumstances, and he was obliged to sell the gold medals he had won at the university; but a way out of all financial difficulties was found in 1833 by his appointment as a member of the Supreme Council of India for five years at a salary of £10,000 a year. He did valuable work in India, reconstructing the educational system and drawing up a criminal code, beside doing an enormous amount of private reading. On his return home, he began his *History of England*, and published a collection of his essays, which at once obtained a very large sale. He was elected member for Edinburgh, and became Secretary for War, with a seat in the cabinet. The ministry fell in 1841, and in 1847 Macaulay was rejected by his constituency. He wrote a poem to the effect that literature had been his consolation under all the trials of life, 'of which,' says one biographer, 'it was rather difficult to make a respectable list.' The Edinburgh seat again becoming vacant, he was reelected without any exertion on his part, but he adhered to his determination to give the rest of his life to literature. The first two volumes of his History were published in 1848, the third and fourth in 1855; from the first it enjoyed very great popularity, and his publishers sent him a check for £20,000. He was raised to the peerage, and buried in Westminster Abbey. He never married, but was devoted to his sisters and their children; his nephew, Sir G. O. Trevelyan, wrote his life, and has attained a considerable reputation as a politician and man of letters.

Macaulay has not Lamb's delicate humor, or De Quincey's philosophical imagination. He disliked speculation, and his idea of history was to present accumulated facts with the attractiveness of fiction. His worst fault is a tendency to emphasize the commonplace—'blackening the chimney,' Sir Leslie Stephen calls it—but his judgment is generally sound, as far as it goes. His style has no subtle harmonies, but is admirable for mechanical excellences—orderly arrangement of material, careful paragraphing, and absolute clearness of statement. In these points he offers a better model for young writers than De Quincey, Carlyle, Ruskin, and other masters of a more elaborate style.

THE ROMANCE OF HISTORY

The best historians of later times have been seduced from truth, not by their imagination, but by their reason. They far excel their predecessors in the art of deducing general principles from facts. But unhappily they have fallen into the error of distorting facts to suit general principles. They arrive at a theory from looking at some of the phenomena; and the remaining phenomena they strain or curtail to suit the theory. For this purpose it is not necessary that they should assert what is absolutely false; for all questions in morals and politics are questions of comparison and degree. Any proposition which does not involve a contradiction in terms may by possibility be true; and if all the circumstances which raise a probability in its favor be stated and enforced, and those which lead to an opposite conclusion be omitted or lightly passed over, it may appear to be demonstrated. In every human character and transaction there is a mixture of good and evil: a little exaggeration, a little suppression, a judicious use of epithets, a watchful and searching skepticism with respect to the evidence on one side, a convenient credulity with respect to every report or tradition on the other, may easily make a saint of Laud, or a tyrant of Henry IV.

This species of misrepresentation abounds in the most valuable works of modern historians. Herodotus tells his story like a slovenly witness, who, heated by partialities and prejudices, unacquainted with the established rules of evidence, and uninstructed as to the obligations of his oath, confounds what he imagines with what he has seen and heard, and brings out facts, reports, conjectures, and fancies, in one mass. Hume is an accomplished advocate. Without positively asserting much more than he can prove, he gives prominence to all the circumstances which support his case; he glides lightly over those which are unfavorable to it; his own witnesses are applauded and encouraged; the statements which seem to throw discredit on them are controverted; the contradictions into which they fall are explained away; a clear and connected abstract of their evidence is given. Everything that is offered on the other side is scrutinized with the utmost severity; every suspicious circumstance is a ground for comment and invective; what cannot be denied is extenuated, or passed by without notice; concessions even are sometimes made: but this insidious candor only increases the effect of the vast mass of sophistry.

We have mentioned Hume as the ablest and most popular writer of his class; but the charge which we have brought against him is one to which all our most distinguished historians are in some degree obnoxious. Gibbon, in particular, deserves very severe censure. Of all the numerous culprits, however, none is more deeply guilty than Mr. Mitford. We willingly acknowledge the obligations which are due to his talents and industry. The modern historians of Greece had been in the habit of writing as if the world had learned nothing new during the last sixteen hundred years. Instead of illustrating the events which they narrated by the philosophy of a more enlightened age, they judged of antiquity by itself alone. They seemed to think that notions, long driven from every other corner of literature, had a prescriptive right to occupy this last fastness. They considered all the ancient historians as equally authentic. They scarcely made any distinction between him who related events at which he had himself been present and him who five hundred years after composed a philosophic romance for a society which had in the interval undergone a complete change. It was all Greek, and all true! The centuries which separated Plutarch from Thucydides seemed as nothing to men who lived in an age so remote. The distance of time produced an error similar to that which is sometimes produced by distance of place. There are many good ladies who think that all the people in India live together, and who charge a friend setting out for Calcutta with kind messages to Bombay. To Rollin and Barthelemi, in the same manner, all the classics were contemporaries.

Mr. Mitford certainly introduced great improvements; he showed us that men who wrote in Greek and Latin sometimes told lies; he showed us that ancient history might be related in such a manner as to furnish not only allusions to schoolboys, but important lessons to statesmen. From that love of theatrical effect and high-flown sentiment which had poisoned almost every other work on the same subject his book is perfectly free. But his passion for a theory was false, and far more ungenerous, led him substantially to violate truth in every page. Statements unfavorable to democracy are made with unhesitating confidence, and with the utmost bitterness of language. Every charge brought against a monarch or an aristocracy is sifted with the utmost care. If it cannot be denied, some palliating supposition is suggested; or we are at least reminded that some circumstances now unknown *may* have justified what at present appears unjustifiable. Two events are reported by the same author in the same sentence; their truth rests on the same testimony; but the one supports the darling hypothesis, and the other seems inconsistent with it. The one is taken and the other is left.

The practice of distorting narrative into a conformity with theory is a vice not so unfavorable as at first sight it may appear to the interests of political science. We have compared the writers who indulge in it to advocates; and we may add that their conflicting fallacies, like those of advocates, correct each other. It has always been held, in the most enlightened nations, that a tribunal will decide a judicial question most fairly when it has heard two able men argue, as unfairly as possible, on the two opposite sides of it; and we are inclined to think that this opinion is just. Sometimes, it is true, superior eloquence and dexterity will make the worse appear the better reason; but it is at least certain that the judge will be compelled to contemplate the case under two different aspects. It is certain that no important consideration will altogether escape notice.

This is at present the state of history. The

poet laureate appears for the Church of England, Lingard for the Church of Rome. Brodie has moved to set aside the verdicts obtained by Hume; and the cause in which Mitford succeeded is, we understand, about to be reheard. In the midst of these disputes, however, history proper, if we may use the term, is disappearing. The high, grave, impartial summing up of Thucydides is nowhere to be found.

While our historians are practising all the arts of controversy, they miserably neglect the art of narration, the art of interesting the affections and presenting pictures to the imagination. That a writer may produce these effects without violating truth is sufficiently proved by many excellent biographical works. The immense popularity which well-written books of this kind have acquired deserves the serious consideration of historians. Voltaire's Charles the Twelfth, Marmontel's Memoirs, Boswell's life of Johnson, Southey's account of Nelson, are perused with delight by the most frivolous and indolent. Whenever any tolerable book of the same description makes its appearance, the circulating libraries are mobbed; the book societies are in commotion; the new novel lies uncut; the magazines and newspapers fill their columns with extracts. In the meantime histories of great empires, written by men of eminent ability, lie unread on the shelves of ostentatious libraries.

The writers of history seem to entertain an aristocratical contempt for the writers of memoirs. They think it beneath the dignity of men who describe the revolutions of nations to dwell on the details which constitute the charm of biography. They have imposed on themselves a code of conventional decencies as absurd as that which has been the bane of the French drama. The most characteristic and interesting circumstances are omitted or softened down, because, as we are told, they are too trivial for the majesty of history. The majesty of history seems to resemble the majesty of the poor King of Spain, who died a martyr to ceremony because the proper dignitaries were not at hand to render him assistance.

That history would be more amusing if this etiquette were relaxed will, we suppose, be acknowledged. But would it be less dignified or less useful? What do we mean when we say that one past event is important and another insignificant? No past event has any intrinsic importance. The knowledge of it is valuable only as it leads us to form just calculations with respect to the future. A history which does not serve this purpose, though it may be filled with battles, treaties, and commotions, is as useless as the series of turnpike tickets collected by Sir Matthew Mite.

Let us suppose that Lord Clarendon, instead of filling hundreds of folio pages with copies of state papers in which the same assertions and contradictions are repeated till the reader is overpowered with weariness, had condescended to be the Boswell of the Long Parliament. Let us suppose that he had exhibited to us the wise and lofty self-government of Hampden, leading while he seemed to follow, and propounding unanswerable arguments in the strongest forms with the modest air of an inquirer anxious for information; the delusions which misled the noble spirit of Vane; the coarse fanaticism which concealed the yet loftier genius of Cromwell, destined to control a mutinous army and a factious people, to abase the flag of Holland, to arrest the victorious arms of Sweden, and to hold the balance firm between the rival monarchies of France and Spain. Let us suppose that he had made his Cavaliers and Roundheads talk in their own style; that he had reported some of the ribaldry of Rupert's pages, and some of the cant of Harrison and Fleetwood. Would not his work in that case have been more interesting? Would it not have been more accurate?

A history in which every particular incident may be true may on the whole be false. The circumstances which have most influence on the happiness of mankind, the changes of manners and morals, the transition of communities from poverty to wealth, from knowledge to ignorance, from ferocity to humanity—these are, for the most part, noiseless revolutions. Their progress is rarely indicated by what historians are pleased to call important events. They are not achieved by armies, or enacted by senates. They are sanctioned by no treaties, and recorded in no archives. They are carried on in every school, in every church, behind ten thousand counters, at ten thousand firesides. The upper current of society presents no certain criterion by which we can judge of the direction in which the under current flows. We read of defeats and victories. But we know that nations may be miserable amidst victories and prosperous amidst defeats. We read of the fall of wise ministers and of the rise of profligate favorites. But we must remember how small a proportion the good or evil effected by a single statesman can bear to the good or evil of a great social system.

Bishop Watson compares a geologist to a gnat mounted on an elephant, and laying down theories as to the whole internal structure of the vast animal, from the phenomena of the hide. The comparison is unjust to the geologists; but is very applicable to those historians who write as if the body politic were homogeneous, who look only on the surface of affairs, and never think of the mighty and various organization which lies deep below.

In the works of such writers as these, England, at the close of the Seven Years' War, is in the highest state of prosperity: at the close of the American war she is in a miserable and degraded condition; as if the people were not on the whole as rich, as well governed, and as well educated at the latter period as at the former. We have read books called Histories of England, under the reign of George the Second, in which the rise of Methodism is not even mentioned. A hundred years hence this breed of authors will, we hope, be extinct. If it should still exist, the late ministerial interregnum will be described in terms which will seem to imply that all government was at end; that the social contract was annulled; and that the hand of every man was against his neighbor until the wisdom and virtue of the new cabinet educed order out of the chaos of anarchy. We are quite certain that misconceptions as gross prevail at this moment respecting many important parts of our annals.

The effect of historical reading is analogous, in many respects, to that produced by foreign travel. The student, like the tourist, is transported into a new state of society. He sees new fashions. He hears new modes of expression. His mind is enlarged by contemplating the wide diversities of laws, of morals and of manners. But men may travel far, and return with minds as contracted as if they had never stirred from their own market-town. In the same manner, men may know the dates of many battles and the genealogies of many royal houses, and yet be no wiser. Most people look at past times as princes look at foreign countries. More than one illustrious stranger has landed on our island amidst the shouts of a mob, has dined with the King, has hunted with the master of the staghounds, has seen the Guards reviewed, and a knight of the garter installed, has cantered along Regent Street, has visited Saint Paul's, and noted down its dimensions; and has then departed, thinking that he has seen England. He has, in fact, seen a few public buildings, public men, and public ceremonies. But of the vast and complex system of society, of the fine shades of national character, of the practical operation of government and laws, he knows nothing. He who would understand these things rightly must not confine his observations to palaces and solemn days. He must see ordinary men as they appear in their ordinary business and in their ordinary pleasures. He must mingle in the crowds of the exchange and the coffeehouse. He must obtain admittance to the convivial table and the domestic hearth. He must bear with vulgar expressions. He must not shrink from exploring even the retreats of misery. He who wishes to understand the condition of mankind in former ages must proceed on the same principle. If he attends only to public transactions, to wars, congresses, and debates, his studies will be as unprofitable as the travels of those imperial, royal and serene sovereigns who form their judgment of our island from having gone in state to a few fine sights, and from having held formal conferences with a few great officers.

The perfect historian is he in whose work the character and spirit of an age is exhibited in miniature. He relates no fact, he attributes no expression to his characters, which is not authenticated by sufficient testimony. But, by judicious selection, rejection, and arrangement, he gives to truth those attractions which have been usurped by fiction. In his narrative a due subordination is observed: some transactions are prominent; others retire. But the scale on which he represents them is increased or diminished, not according to the dignity of the persons concerned in them, but according to the degree in which they elucidate the condition of society and the nature of man. He shows us the court, the camp, and the senate. But he shows us also the nation. He considers no anecdote, no peculiarity of manner, no familiar saying, as too insignificant for his notice which is not too insignificant to illustrate the operation of laws, of religion, and of education, and to mark the progress of the human mind. Men will not merely be described, but will be made intimately known to us. The changes of manners will be indicated, not merely by a few general phrases or a few extracts from statistical documents, but by appropriate images presented in every line.

If a man, such as we are supposing, should

write the history of England, he would assuredly not omit the battles, the sieges, the negotiations, the seditions, the ministerial changes. But with these he would intersperse the details which are the charm of historical romances. At Lincoln Cathedral there is a beautiful painted window, which was made by an apprentice out of the pieces of glass which had been rejected by his master. It is so far superior to every other in the church, that, according to the tradition, the vanquished artist killed himself from mortification. Sir Walter Scott, in the same manner, has used those fragments of truth which historians have scornfully thrown behind them in a manner which may well excite their envy. He has constructed out of their gleanings works which, even considered as histories, are scarcely less valuable than theirs. But a truly great historian would reclaim those materials which the novelist has appropriated. The history of the government, and the history of the people, would be exhibited in that mode in which alone they can be exhibited justly, in inseparable conjunction and intermixture. We should not then have to look for the wars and votes of the Puritans in Clarendon, and for their phraseology in Old Mortality; for one half of King James in Hume, and for the other half in the Fortunes of Nigel.

The early part of our imaginary history would be rich with coloring from romance, ballad, and chronicle. We should find ourselves in the company of knights such as those of Froissart, and of pilgrims such as those who rode with Chaucer from the Tabard. Society would be shown from the highest to the lowest,—from the royal cloth of state to the den of the outlaw; from the throne of the Legate to the chimney-corner where the begging friar regaled himself. Palmers, minstrels, crusaders,—the stately monastery, with the good cheer in its refectory and the high-mass in its chapel,—the manor-house, with its hunting and hawking,—the tournament, with the heralds and ladies, the trumpets and the cloth of gold,—would give truth and life to the representation. We should perceive, in a thousand slight touches, the importance of the privileged burgher, and the fierce and haughty spirit which swelled under the collar of the degraded villain. The revival of letters would not merely be described in a few magnificent periods. We should discern, in innumerable particulars, the fermentation of mind, the eager appetite for knowledge, which distinguished the sixteenth from the fifteenth century. In the Reformation we should see, not merely a schism which changed the ecclesiastical constitution of England and the mutual relations of the European powers, but a moral war which raged in every family, which set the father against the son, and the son against the father, the mother against the daughter, and the daughter against the mother. Henry would be painted with the skill of Tacitus. We should have the change of his character from his profuse and joyous youth to his savage and imperious old age. We should perceive the gradual progress of selfish and tyrannical passions in a mind not naturally insensible or ungenerous; and to the last we should detect some remains of that open and noble temper which endeared him to a people whom he oppressed, struggling with the hardness of despotism and the irritability of disease. We should see Elizabeth in all her weakness and in all her strength, surrounded by the handsome favorites whom she never trusted, and the wise old statesman whom she never dismissed, uniting in herself the most contradictory qualities of both her parents,—the coquetry, the caprice, the petty malice of Anne,—the haughty and resolute spirit of Henry. We have no hesitation in saying that a great artist might produce a portrait of this remarkable woman at least as striking as that in the novel of Kenilworth, without employing a single trait not authenticated by ample testimony. In the meantime, we should see arts cultivated, wealth accumulated, the conveniences of life improved. We should see the keeps, where nobles, insecure themselves, spread insecurity around them, gradually giving place to the halls of peaceful opulence, to the oriels of Longleat, and the stately pinnacles of Burleigh. We should see towns extended, deserts cultivated, the hamlets of fishermen turned into wealthy havens, the meal of the peasant improved, and his hut more commodiously furnished. We should see those opinions and feelings which produced the great struggle against the House of Stuart slowly growing up in the bosom of private families, before they manifested themselves in parliamentary debates. Then would come the Civil War. Those skirmishes on which Clarendon dwells so minutely would be told, as Thucydides would have told them, with perspicuous conciseness. They are merely connecting links. But the great characteristics of the age, the loyal enthusiasm of the brave English gentry, the fierce licentiousness of the swearing, dicing, drunken reprobates whose excesses disgraced the royal cause,—the austerity of the Presbyterian Sabbaths in the city, the extravagance of the independent preachers in the camp, the precise garb, the severe countenance, the petty scruples, the affected accent, the absurd names and phrases which marked the Puritans,—the valor, the policy, the public spirit, which lurked beneath these ungraceful disguises,—the dreams of the raving Fifth-monarchy-man, the dreams, scarcely less wild, of the philosophic republican, —all these would enter into the representation, and render it at once more exact and more striking.

The instruction derived from history thus written would be of a vivid and practical character. It would be received by the imagination as well as by the reason. It would be not merely traced on the mind, but branded into it. Many truths, too, would be learned, which can be learned in no other manner. As the history of states is generally written, the greatest and most momentous revolutions seem to come upon them like supernatural inflictions, without warning or cause. But the fact is, that such revolutions are almost always the consequences of moral changes, which have gradually passed on the mass of the community, and which ordinarily proceed far, before their progress is indicated by any public measure. An intimate knowledge of the domestic history of nations is therefore absolutely necessary to the prognosis of political events. A narrative, defective in this respect, is as useless as a medical treatise which should pass by all the symptoms attendant on the early stage of a disease and mention only what occurs when the patient is beyond the reach of remedies.

A historian such as we have been attempting to describe would indeed be an intellectual prodigy. In his mind, powers scarcely compatible with each other must be tempered into an exquisite harmony. We shall sooner see another Shakespeare or another Homer. The highest excellence to which any single faculty can be brought would be less surprising than such a happy and delicate combination of qualities. Yet the contemplation of imaginary models is not an unpleasant or useless employment of the mind. It cannot indeed produce perfection; but it produces improvement, and nourishes that generous and liberal fastidiousness which is not inconsistent with the strongest sensibility to merit, and which, while it exalts our conceptions of the art, does not render us unjust to the artist.

(1828)

THE HISTORY OF ENGLAND

(*From* Vol. I, Chap. III, On the State of England in 1685)

The coffee-house must not be dismissed with a cursory mention. It might, indeed, at that time have been not improperly called a most important political institution. No Parliament had sat for years. The municipal council of the city had ceased to speak the sense of the citizens. Public meetings, harangues, resolutions, and the rest of the modern machinery of agitation had not yet come into fashion. Nothing resembling the modern newspaper existed. In such circumstances the coffee-houses were the chief organs through which the public opinion of the metropolis vented itself.

The first of these establishments had been set up, in the time of the Commonwealth, by a Turkey merchant, who had acquired among the Mahometans a taste for their favorite beverage. The convenience of being able to make appointments in any part of the town, and of being able to pass evenings socially at a very small charge, was so great that the fashion spread fast. Every man of the upper or middle class went daily to his coffee-house to learn the news and to discuss it. Every coffee-house had one or more orators to whose eloquence the crowd listened with admiration, and who soon became, what the journalists of our time have been called, a fourth Estate of the realm. The court had long seen with uneasiness the growth of this new power in the state. An attempt had been made, during Danby's administration, to close the coffee-houses. But men of all parties missed their usual places of resort so much that there was a universal outcry. The government did not venture, in opposition to a feeling so strong and general, to enforce a regulation of which the legality might well be questioned. Since that time ten years had elapsed, and during those years the number and influence of the coffee-houses had been constantly increasing. Foreigners remarked that the coffee-house was that which especially distinguished London from all other cities; that the coffee-house was the Londoner's home, and that those who wished to find a gentleman commonly asked, not whether he lived in Fleet Street or Chancery Lane, but whether he frequented the Grecian or the Rainbow. Nobody was excluded from these places who laid down his penny at the bar. Yet every rank and profession, and every shade of religious and political opinion, had its own headquarters.

There were houses near Saint James's Park where fops congregated, their heads and shoulders covered with black or flaxen wigs, not less ample than those which are now worn by the Chancellor and by the Speaker of the House of Commons. The wig came from Paris; and so did the rest of the fine gentleman's ornaments, his embroidered coat, his fringed gloves, and the tassel which upheld his pantaloons. The conversation was in that dialect, which, long after it had ceased to be spoken in fashionable circles, continued, in the mouth of Lord Foppington, to excite the mirth of theaters.[1] The atmosphere was like that of a perfumer's shop. Tobacco in any other form than that of richly scented snuff was held in abomination. If any clown, ignorant of the usages of the house, called for a pipe, the sneers of the whole assembly and the short answers of the waiters soon convinced him that he had better go somewhere else. Nor, indeed, would he have had far to go. For, in general, the coffee-rooms reeked with tobacco like a guard-room; and strangers sometimes expressed their surprise that so many people should leave their own firesides to sit in the midst of eternal fog and stench. Nowhere was the smoking more constant than at Will's. That celebrated house, situated between Covent Garden and Bow Street, was sacred to polite letters. There the talk was about poetical justice and the unities of place and time. There was a faction for Perrault and the moderns, a faction for Boileau and the ancients. One group debated whether Paradise Lost ought not to have been in rime. To another an envious poetaster demonstrated that Venice Preserved ought to have been hooted from the stage. Under no roof was a greater variety of figures to be seen. There were earls in stars and garters, clergymen in cassocks and bands, pert Templars, sheepish lads from the universities, translators and index-makers in ragged coats of frieze. The great press was to get near the chair where John Dryden sat. In winter that chair was always in the warmest nook by the fire; in summer it stood in the balcony. To bow to the Laureate, and to hear his opinion of Racine's last tragedy or of Bossu's treatise on epic poetry, was thought a privilege. A pinch from his snuff-box was an honor sufficient to turn the head of a young enthusiast. There were coffee-houses where the first medical men might be consulted. Dr. John Radcliffe, who, in the year 1685, rose to the largest practice in London, came daily, at the hour when the Exchange was full, from his house in Bow Street, then a fashionable part of the capital, to Garraway's, and was to be found surrounded by surgeons and apothecaries, at a particular table. There were Puritan coffee-houses where no oath was heard, and where lank-haired men discussed election and reprobation through their noses; Jew coffee-houses where dark-eyed money changers from Venice and from Amsterdam greeted each other; and popish coffee-houses where, as good Protestants believed, Jesuits planned, over their cups, another great fire, and cast silver bullets to shoot the King.[2]

These gregarious habits had no small share in forming the character of the Londoner of that age. He was, indeed, a different being from the rustic Englishman. There was not then the intercourse which now exists between the two classes. Only very great men were in the habit of dividing the year between town and country. Few esquires came to the capital thrice in their lives. Nor was it yet the practice of all citizens in easy circumstances to breathe the fresh air of the fields and woods during some weeks of every summer. A cockney in a rural village was stared at as much as if he had intruded into a kraal of Hottentots. On the other hand, when the lord of a Lincolnshire or Shropshire manor appeared in Fleet Street, he was as easily distinguished from the resident population as a Turk or a Lascar. His dress, his gait, his accent, the manner in which he gazed at the shops, stumbled into the gutters, ran against the porters, and stood under the waterspouts, marked him out as an excellent subject for the operations of swindlers and banterers. Bullies jostled him into the kennel. Hackney coachmen splashed him from head to foot. Thieves explored with perfect security the huge pockets of his horseman's coat, while he stood entranced by the splendor of the Lord Mayor's show. Money-droppers, sore from the cart's tail, introduced

---

[1] The chief peculiarity of this dialect was that, in a large class of words, the O was pronounced like A. Thus Lord was pronounced Lard. See Vanbrugh's *Relapse*. Lord Sunderland was a great master of this court tune, as Roger North calls it; and Titus Oates affected it in the hope of passing for a fine gentleman. *Examen*, 77, 254.

[2] *Lettres sur les Anglois; Tom Brown's Tour; Ward's London Spy; The Character of a Coffee House,* 1673; *Rules and Orders of the Coffee House,* 1674; *Coffee Houses vindicated,* 1675; *A Satyr against Coffee; North's Examen,* 138; *Life of Guildford,* 152; *Life of Sir Dudley North,* 149; *Life of Dr. Radcliffe,* published by Curll in 1715. The liveliest description of Will's is in the *City and Country Mouse*. There is a remarkable passage about the influence of the coffee house orators in Halstead's *Succinct Genealogies,* printed in 1685.

themselves to him, and appeared to him the most honest friendly gentlemen that he had ever seen. Painted women, the refuse of Lewkner Lane and Whetstone Park, passed themselves on him for countesses and maids of honor. If he asked his way to Saint James's, his informants sent him to Mile End. If he went into a shop, he was instantly discerned to be a fit purchaser of everything that nobody else would buy, of second-hand embroidery, copper rings, and watches that would not go. If he rambled into any fashionable coffee-house, he became a mark for the insolent derision of fops and the grave waggery of Templars. Enraged and mortified, he soon returned to his mansion, and there, in the homage of his tenants and the conversation of his boon companions, found consolation for the vexations and humiliations which he had undergone. There he was once more a great man, and saw nothing above himself except when at the assizes he took his seat on the bench near the judge, or when at the muster of the militia he saluted the Lord Lieutenant.

The chief cause which made the fusion of the different elements of society so imperfect was the extreme difficulty which our ancestors found in passing from place to place. Of all inventions, the alphabet and the printing-press alone excepted, those inventions which abridge distance have done most for the civilization of our species. Every improvement of the means of locomotion benefits mankind morally and intellectually as well as materially, and not only facilitates the interchange of the various productions of nature and art, but tends to remove national and provincial antipathies, and to bind together all the branches of the great human family. In the seventeenth century the inhabitants of London were, for almost every practical purpose, farther from Reading than they now are from Edinburgh, and farther from Edinburgh than they now are from Vienna.

The subjects of Charles the Second were not, it is true, quite unacquainted with that principle which has, in our own time, produced an unprecedented revolution in human affairs, which has enabled navies to advance in face of wind and tide, and brigades of troops, attended by all their baggage and artillery, to traverse kingdoms at a pace equal to that of the fleetest race horse. The Marquess of Worcester had recently observed the expansive power of moisture rarefied by heat. After many experiments he had succeeded in constructing a rude steam engine, which he called a fire water work, and which he pronounced to be an admirable and most forcible instrument of propulsion.[1] But the Marquess was suspected to be a madman, and known to be a Papist. His inventions, therefore, found no favorable reception. His fire water work might, perhaps, furnish matter for conversation at a meeting of the Royal Society, but was not applied to any practical purpose. There were no railways, except a few made of timber, on which coals were carried from the mouths of the Northumbrian pits to the banks of the Tyne.[2] There was very little international communication by water. A few attempts had been made to deepen and embank the natural streams, but with slender success. Hardly a single navigable canal had been even projected. The English of that day were in the habit of talking with mingled admiration and despair of the immense trench by which Louis the Fourteenth had made a junction between the Atlantic and Mediterranean. They little thought that their country would, in the course of a few generations, be intersected, at the cost of private adventurers, by artificial rivers making up more than four times the length of the Thames, the Severn, and the Trent together.

It was by the highways that both travelers and goods generally passed from place to place; and those highways appear to have been far worse than might have been expected from the degree of wealth and civilization which the nation had even then attained. On the best lines of communication the ruts were deep, the descents precipitous, and the way often such as it was hardly possible to distinguish, in the dusk, from the uninclosed heath and fen which lay on both sides. Ralph Thoresby, the antiquary, was in danger of losing his way on the great North road, between Barnby Moor and Tuxford, and actually lost his way between Doncaster and York.[3] Pepys and his wife, traveling in their own coach, lost their way between Newbury and Reading. In the course of the same tour they lost their way near Salisbury, and were in danger of having to pass the night on the plain.[4] It was only in fine weather that the whole breadth of the road was available for wheeled vehicles. Often the mud lay deep on the right and the left; and only a narrow track of firm ground rose above the quagmire.[5]

[1] *Century of Inventions*, 1663, No. 68.
[2] North's *Life of Guildford*, 136.
[3] *Thoresby's Diary*, Oct. 21, 1680, Aug. 3, 1712.
[4] *Pepys's Diary*, June 12 and 16, 1668.
[5] *Pepys's Diary*, Feb. 28, 1660.

At such times obstructions and quarrels were frequent, and the path was sometimes blocked up during a long time by carriers, neither of whom would break the way. It happened, almost every day, that coaches stuck fast, until a team of cattle could be procured from some neighboring farm to tug them out of the slough. But in bad seasons the traveler had to encounter inconveniences still more serious. Thoresby, who was in the habit of traveling between Leeds and the capital, has recorded, in his Diary, such a series of perils and disasters as might suffice for a journey to the Frozen Ocean or to the Desert of Sahara. On one occasion he learned that the floods were out between Ware and London, that passengers had to swim for their lives, and that a higgler had perished in the attempt to cross. In consequence of these tidings he turned out of the high-road, and was conducted across some meadows, where it was necessary for him to ride to the saddle skirts in water.[1] In the course of another journey he narrowly escaped being swept away by an inundation of the Trent. He was afterwards detained at Stamford four days, on account of the state of the roads, and then ventured to proceed only because fourteen members of the House of Commons, who were going up in a body to Parliament with guides and numerous attendants, took him into their company.[2] On the roads of Derbyshire, travelers were in constant fear for their necks, and were frequently compelled to alight and lead their beasts.[3] The great route through Wales to Holyhead was in such a state that, in 1685, a viceroy, going to Ireland, was five hours in traveling fourteen miles, from Saint Asaph to Conway. Between Conway and Beaumaris he was forced to walk a great part of the way; and his lady was carried in a litter. His coach was, with much difficulty, and by the help of many hands, brought after him entire. In general, carriages were taken to pieces at Conway, and borne, on the shoulders of stout Welsh peasants, to the Menai Straits.[4] In some parts of Kent and Sussex none but the strongest horses could, in winter, get through the bog, in which, at every step, they sank deep. The markets were often inaccessible during several months. It is said that the fruits of the earth were sometimes suffered to rot in one place, while in another place, distant only a few miles, the supply fell far short of the demand. The wheeled carriages were, in this district, generally pulled by oxen.[5] When Prince George of Denmark visited the stately mansion of Petworth in wet weather, he was six hours in going nine miles; and it was necessary that a body of sturdy hinds should be on each side of his coach, in order to prop it. Of the carriages which conveyed his retinue, several were upset and injured. A letter from one of the party has been preserved, in which the unfortunate courtier complains that, during fourteen hours, he never once alighted except when his coach was overturned or stuck fast in the mud.[6]

One chief cause of the badness of the roads seems to have been the defective state of the law. Every parish was bound to repair the highways which passed through it. The peasantry were forced to give their gratuitous labor six days in the year. If this was not sufficient, hired labor was employed, and the expense was met by a parochial rate. That a route connecting two great towns, which have a large and thriving trade with each other, should be maintained at the cost of the rural population scattered between them is obviously unjust; and this injustice was peculiarly glaring in the case of the great North road, which traversed very poor and thinly inhabited districts, and joined very rich and populous districts. Indeed it was not in the power of the parishes of Huntingdonshire to mend a highway worn by the constant traffic between the West Riding of Yorkshire and London. Soon after the Restoration this grievance attracted the notice of Parliament; and an act, the first of our many turnpike acts, was passed, imposing a small toll on travelers and goods, for the purpose of keeping some parts of this important line of communication in good repair.[7] This innovation, however, excited many murmurs; and the other great avenues to the capital were long left under the old system. A change was at length effected, but not without much difficulty. For unjust and absurd taxation to which men are accustomed is often borne far more willingly than the most reasonable impost which is new. It was not till many toll bars had been violently pulled down, till the troops had in many districts been forced to act against the people, and till much blood

---

[1] *Thoresby's Diary*, May 17, 1695.
[2] *Ibid.*, Dec. 27, 1708.
[3] *Tour in Derbyshire*, by J. Browne, son of Sir Thomas Browne, 1662. *Cotton's Angler*, 1676.
[4] *Correspondence of Henry, Earl of Clarendon*, Dec. 30, 1685. Jan. 1, 1686.
[5] *Postlethwaite's Dict.*, Roads; History of Hawkhurst, in the *Bibliotheca Topographica Britannica*.
[6] *Annals of Queen Anne*, 1703, Appendix, No. 3.
[7] 15 *Car. II.* c. 1.

had been shed, that a good system was introduced.[1] By slow degrees reason triumphed over prejudice; and our island is now crossed in every direction by near thirty thousand miles of turnpike road.

On the best highways heavy articles were, in the time of Charles the Second, generally conveyed from place to place by stage wagons. In the straw of these vehicles nestled a crowd of passengers, who could not afford to travel by coach or on horseback, and who were prevented by infirmity, or by the weight of their luggage, from going on foot. The expense of transmitting heavy goods in this way was enormous. From London to Birmingham the charge was seven pounds a ton; from London to Exeter, twelve pounds a ton.[2] This was about fifteen pence a ton for every mile, more by a third than was afterwards charged on turnpike roads, and fifteen times what is now demanded by railway companies. The cost of conveyance amounted to a prohibitory tax on many useful articles. Coal in particular was never seen except in the districts where it was produced, or in the districts to which it could be carried by sea, and was indeed always known in the south of England by the name of sea coal.

On by-roads, and generally throughout the country north of York and west of Exeter, goods were carried by long trains of pack horses. These strong and patient beasts, the breed of which is now extinct, were attended by a class of men who seem to have borne much resemblance to the Spanish muleteers. A traveler of humble condition often found it convenient to perform a journey mounted on a pack saddle between two baskets, under the care of these hardy guides. The expense of this mode of conveyance was small. But the caravan moved at a foot's pace; and in winter the cold was often insupportable.[3]

The rich commonly traveled in their own carriages, with at least four horses. Cotton, the facetious poet, attempted to go from London to the Peak with a single pair, but found at Saint Albans that the journey would be insupportably tedious, and altered his plan.[4] A coach and six is in our time never seen, except as part of some pageant. The frequent mention therefore of such equipages in old books is likely to mislead us. We attribute to magnificence what was really the effect of a very disagreeable necessity. People, in the time of Charles the Second, traveled with six horses, because with a smaller number there was great danger of sticking fast in the mire. Nor were even six horses always sufficient. Vanbrugh, in the succeeding generation, described with great humor the way in which a country gentleman, newly chosen a member of Parliament, went up to London. On that occasion all the exertions of six beasts, two of which had been taken from the plough, could not save the family coach from being embedded in a quagmire.

* * *

[1] The evils of the old system are strikingly set forth in many petitions which appear in the *Commons' Journal* of 1725–26. How fierce an opposition was offered to the new system may be learned from the *Gentleman's Magazine* of 1749.

[2] *Postlethwaite's Dict.*, Roads.

[3] *Loidis and Elmete;* Marshall's *Rural Economy of England.* In 1739 Roderic Random came from Scotland to Newcastle on a pack horse.

[4] Cotton's *Epistle to J. Bradshaw.*

THE VICTORIAN ERA

THE Victorian Era was a rich and complex period, not easily described in a few sentences. Its main problem was twofold: (a) to reconcile the newly developed industrial system with the humanitarian principles inherited from the Romantic Revival, and (b) to adjust the traditional faith of orthodox Christianity to the new knowledge of geology and biology resulting from recent scientific research and the new knowledge of the Bible resulting from the critical study of the original documents.

The problem of the condition of labor and the problem of religious faith are prominent, sometimes one, sometimes both, in the writings of Newman, Carlyle, Ruskin, Tennyson, Browning, Matthew Arnold and William Morris, who all have suggestions—each differing from all the others—as to the mode of readjustment necessary for the solution of the social and intellectual dilemmas their generation had to face. Among the novelists Thackeray and Anthony Trollope accept the standards of their time, Dickens and Gissing draw attention to the conditions of the poor, George Eliot, Meredith, and Hardy present the new ideas somewhat guardedly in their fiction but directly and frankly in their poetry, Samuel Butler is in open revolt against orthodoxy in any form, and the later school of novelists which arose at the end of the Victorian Era takes the new ideas for granted.

This revolution in Victorian opinion goes back in its origins to scientific and critical study in France and Germany at an earlier date, but so far as England is concerned its beginning may be associated with the publication of Sir Charles Lyell's *Principles of Geology* in 1830–33, and its crisis with the publication of Darwin's *Origin of Species* in 1859; the new spirit of critical inquiry was shown by the translation of Strauss's *Life of Jesus* by George Eliot in 1846, and the publication of *Essays and Reviews* in 1860.

The industrial revolution also goes back to more remote causes—the application of steam to industry and the improvement of machinery for production and transportation in the later years of the eighteenth century and the earlier years of the nineteenth; but it was not until after the beginning of the Victorian Era that the development of the factory system gained so much ground as to make its influence evident in political and social life. The passing of the First Reform Act in 1832 is usually taken as marking the beginning of the new era, and it was only the first step in the extension of the suffrage which arrived at its culmination in 1928, when every adult man and woman in Great Britain became entitled to vote. The middle class, to which the landed aristocracy surrendered power at the beginning of the Victorian era, handed it on to the working class before that period was ended. Associated with this political revolution, we have the establishment of compulsory state-aided elementary education in 1870 and the subsequent extension of state aid to secondary education; the legal recognition of trade unionism, coöperative distribution, friendly societies and other efforts of the working people to help themselves; protection of the workers by law against the risk of accident, against sickness, against old age, against excessive hours and insanitary or dangerous conditions of labor. All these changes made England at the end of the nineteenth century probably the most democratic country in the world.

This political and social evolution had inevitably very considerable effects upon literature. The reading public, which had been aristocratic in character, shifted its center to the middle class, and ultimately to the masses; the provision of free libraries and the improvement of the means of production and distribution of cheap books and newspapers facilitated the change; fiction, which at the beginning of the Victorian era circulated in thousands or tens of thousands of copies, was later demanded in hundreds of thousands or even in millions. Cobbett noted as a curious fact that four corn mills in his neighborhood had been turned into paper mills, as if 'the poor souls had actually taken to eating books.' Burke's estimate of the reading public at eighty thousand at the end of the eighteenth century called for multiplication five or ten times by the middle of the nineteenth century. With the increase in the number of readers, literature became more and more journalistic, dealing with interests of the passing day.

The term 'Victorian' was often used in the first quarter of the twentieth century as an adjective of depreciation to signify anything out of fashion and therefore to be despised. As a matter of fact, the period is characterized by a steady and rapid growth on fundamental questions of politics, economics, natural science, ethics, and religious belief. Its weakest points were prudery as to matters of sex and intolerance of points of view diverging from the established conventions. At the beginning of the period the power of 'Mrs. Grundy,' resting upon middle class prejudice, and supported by the all-pervading influence of the squire and the parson, was supreme, and writers like Thackeray groaned over the conventional and sometimes hypocritical restrictions by which their artistic freedom was curtailed; but at the end of the period, with the admission of women to higher education and the learned professions, even more perhaps their use of the bicycle and the tennis racket, conventional restriction had already started on its way to the growing laxity of the twentieth century. These aspects of Victorianism are not peculiar to any latitude or longitude or to any particular epoch; they are still prevalent in many societies, Anglo-Saxon and other, in which a somewhat ascetic view of life finds its expression in conventional restraints upon intellectual liberty or social practice.

NOTEWORTHY DATES

HISTORICAL

1837 VICTORIA
1839 Chartist Riots
1846 Corn Laws Repealed
1851 International Exhibition
1854–5 Crimean War
1857 Indian Mutiny
1859 United Italy
1867 Second Reform Act
1869 Irish Church disestablished
1870 Elementary Education Act
1870–1 Franco-Prussian War
1872 Vote by Ballot
1875 Suez Canal shares bought
1876 Victoria Empress of India
1878 Treaty of Berlin
1884–5 Franchise Act
1886 Irish Home Rule Bill
1887 Victorian Jubilee
1893 Second Home Rule Bill
1897 Diamond Jubilee
1898 Sudan conquered
1899–1902 Boer War
1901 EDWARD VII

LITERARY

1837 Carlyle *French Revolution*
Dickens *Pickwick Papers*
1843 Wordsworth Poet Laureate
1846–8 Thackeray *Vanity Fair*
1850 Tennyson Poet Laureate
1855 Browning *Men and Women*
1859 Macaulay d. George Eliot *Adam Bede*
Darwin *Origin of Species*
1863 Thackeray died
1870 Dickens died
1871 Swinburne *Songs before Sunrise*
1872 Butler *Erewhon*
1874 Hardy *Far from the Madding Crowd*
1880 George Eliot died
1881 Carlyle died
1883 Stevenson *Treasure Island*
1888 Kipling *Plain Tales from the Hills*
1889 Browning died
1890 Newman died
1892 Tennyson died
1895 Conrad *Almayer's Folly*
1898 Shaw *Arms and the Man*
1900 Ruskin died

JOHN HENRY, CARDINAL NEWMAN (1801-1890)

THAT ferment of aspiration and unrest which produced in the nineteenth century so many forms of religious inquiry, the questioning faith of Tennyson's *In Memoriam,* Carlyle's turbid discontent with modern civilization and Ruskin's frantic anti-materialism, produced in John Henry Newman its most specialized and inspired searcher after spiritual grace,—in short, a religious genius. Newman was born in the City of London not far from the Bank. His father, a banker, was a man of cultivated tastes and is thought to have been of Jewish extraction. His mother came of a Huguenot family and Newman was instructed during his childhood in 'modified Calvinism.' As a youth he displayed singular intellectual restlessness combined with literary instinct and precocity. He was said to know the Bible by heart. His early passion for Scott provided his imagination with a background of medieval sympathies, and his memory with a piquant reference at a crucial point in the most close-knit controversy of his later life. In 1817 he entered Trinity College, Oxford, and won a scholarship at the end of his first year. The stirrings of the medieval movement were already beginning at Oxford when Newman became a fellow of Oriel College, its special home. After some terms at the law in London, Newman took orders in the Anglican church and by 1829 had become a tutor in Oriel and Vicar of St. Mary's. From contact with Hurrell Froude he soon grew deeply interested in the historic phases of Christianity; the new-old ideas of the Fathers 'came like music' to his 'inward ear,' and he conveyed them with burning effect into his clarion University Sermons at St. Mary's. In 1832, with Froude, he saw Rome; he came near to death from cholera, paid devout visits to many ancient churches, wrote at Palermo, 'O, that thy creed were sound, thou Church of Rome,' and on shipboard composed in the twilight of Roman Catholicism, *Lead Kindly Light,* which one of his critics has termed 'the "March" of the tractarian movement.' The Sunday after Newman reached England, John Keble preached in his pulpit at St. Mary's the sermon on *National Apostasy,* which is held to have precipitated the Tractarian movement. To meet the rationalistic liberalism and irreligion which were threatening the church from without, two movements, broadly speaking, were advocated within it;—one, in sympathy with the temper of the age, toward more latitude of doctrine and more practical activity; the other, reactionary, toward a more zealous adherence to the forms, traditions and earlier sanctities of the church. It was this latter course that Newman and his friends espoused in the *Tracts for the Times*. Of this movement Newman was the most powerful writer. In seeking to establish the historical continuity of the English church, he gradually convinced himself of the authenticity of Romanism. He was not yet aware of the approaching position of his own mind, when he examined the subject of Apostolic Succession in his famous *Tract Ninety* (1841). The dangerousness of his position did not remain undetected by others and aroused the utmost violence of passion. Newman was compelled to leave Oxford and, soon after, it became known that he had entered the Roman fold. What followed is indescribable. Families were broken up. The entire religious world was in a state of almost tragic excitement. Newman alone preserved his calm and what was considered an ominous silence. For twenty years he addressed himself chiefly to his own parish and the men of his adopted faith. Finally, in 1864, a supreme opportunity came for him to address from a point of advantage the public which had reviled him. Charles Kingsley in a review of Froude's *History of England,* went out of his way to accuse 'Father Newman' of having justified the principle of dishonesty in the Roman priesthood. In the complicated correspondence, which was afterwards published in full, Newman had all the honors. With resistless logic and dexterity and the perfect poise and sincerity of a Christian gentleman he left his assailant in an obvious position of reckless bigotry, wrong-headedness and untruth. Newman could now present to the English world the logic of his religious development, and this he did in his *Apologia pro Vita Sua* [Defense of his Life]. This is a telling presentation, full of acute personal interest, of the claims which an ancient and established religion can urge upon modern culture, and a justification of faith 'against the assaults of a fictitious enlightenment.' Upon the elevation of Pope Leo XIII, Newman was made, in 1879, a Cardinal of the Roman church.

Newman's prose style was a remarkable weapon in the hands of a controversialist. Pliant and strong, colloquial but never familiar, subtle and suave without the least insinuation of vulgar slyness, in command of all the nuances of delicate culture which it sparingly uses, it bends and thrusts like a beautifully tempered steel. Even should its matter cease to be of great interest, Newman's prose will always remain poignant for its classic purity and strength.

THE IDEA OF A UNIVERSITY

DISCOURSE VI

KNOWLEDGE VIEWED IN RELATION TO LEARNING

It were well if the English, like the Greek language, possessed some definite word to express, simply and generally, intellectual proficiency or perfection, such as 'health,' as used with reference to the animal frame, and ' virtue,' with reference to our moral nature. I am not able to find such a term;—talent, ability, genius, belong distinctly to the raw material, which is the subject-matter, not to that excellence which is the result of exercise and training. When we turn, indeed, to the particular kinds of intellectual perfection, words are forthcoming for our purpose, as, for instance, judgment, taste, and skill; yet even these belong, for the most part, to powers or habits bearing upon practice or upon art, and not to any perfect condition of the intellect, considered in itself. Wisdom, again, is certainly a more comprehensive word than any other, but it has a direct relation to conduct, and to human life. Knowledge, indeed, and science express purely intellectual ideas, but still not a state or quality of the intellect; for knowledge, in its ordinary sense, is but one of its circumstances, denoting a possession or a habit; and science has been appropriated to the subject-matter of the intellect, instead of belonging in English, as it ought to do, to the intellect itself. The consequence is that, on an occasion like this, many words are necessary, in order, first, to bring out and convey what surely is no difficult idea in itself,—that of the cultivation of the intellect as an end; next, in order to recommend what surely is no unreasonable object; and lastly, to describe and make the mind realize the particular perfection in which that object consists. Every one knows practically what are the constituents of health or of virtue; and every one recognizes health and virtue as ends to be pursued; it is otherwise with intellectual excellence, and this must be my excuse, if I seem to anyone to be bestowing a good deal of labor on a preliminary matter.

In default of a recognized term, I have called the perfection or virtue of the intellect by the name of philosophy, philosophical knowledge, enlargement of mind, or illumination; terms which are not uncommonly given to it by writers of this day: but, whatever name we bestow on it, it is, I believe, as a matter of history, the business of a university to make this intellectual culture its direct scope, or to employ itself in the education of the intellect,—just as the work of a hospital lies in healing the sick or wounded, of a riding or fencing school, or of a gymnasium, in exercising the limbs, of an almshouse, in aiding and solacing the old, of an orphanage, in protecting innocence, of a penitentiary, in restoring the guilty. I say, a university, taken in its bare idea, and before we view it as an instrument of the church, has this object and this mission; it contemplates neither moral impression nor mechanical production; it professes to exercise the mind neither in art nor in duty; its function is intellectual culture; here it may leave its scholars, and it has done its work when it has done as much as this. It educates the intellect to reason well in all matters, to reach out towards truth, and to grasp it.

This, I said in my foregoing discourse, was the object of a university, viewed in itself, and apart from the Catholic Church, or from the state, or from any other power which may use it; and I illustrated this in various ways. I said that the intellect must have an excellence of its own, for there was nothing which had not its specific good; that the word 'educate' would not be used of intellectual culture, as it is used, had not the intellect had an end of its own; that, had it not such an end, there would be no meaning in calling certain intellectual exercises 'liberal,' in contrast with 'useful,' as is commonly done; that the very notion of a philosophical temper implied it, for it threw us back upon research and system as ends in themselves, distinct from effects and works of any kind; that a philosophical scheme of knowledge, or system of sciences, could not, from the nature of the case, issue in any one definite art or pursuit, as its end; and that, on the other hand, the discovery and contemplation of truth, to which research and systematizing led, were surely sufficient ends, though nothing beyond them were added, and that they had ever been accounted sufficient by mankind.

Here then I take up the subject; and, having determined that the cultivation of the intellect is an end distinct and sufficient in itself, and that, so far as words go, it is an enlargement or illumination, I proceed to inquire what this mental breadth, or power, or light, or philosophy consists in. A hospital heals a broken limb or cures a fever: what does an institution effect, which professes the health, not of the body, not of the soul, but of the intellect? What is this good, which in former times, as well as our own, has been found worth the notice, the appropriation of the Catholic Church?

I have then to investigate, in the discourses which follow, those qualities and characteristics of the intellect in which its cultivation issues or rather consists; and, with a view of assisting myself in this undertaking, I shall recur to certain questions which have already been touched upon. These questions are three: viz. the relation of intellectual culture, first, to *mere knowledge*; secondly, to *professional* knowledge; and thirdly, to *religious* knowledge. In other words, are *acquirements* and *attainments* the scope of a university education? or *expertness in particular arts* and *pursuits?* or *moral and religious proficiency?* or something besides these three? These questions I shall examine in succession, with the purpose I have mentioned; and I hope to be excused, if, in this anxious undertaking, I am led to repeat what, either in these discourses or elsewhere, I have already put upon paper. And first, of *mere knowledge*, or learning, and its connection with intellectual illumination or philosophy.

I suppose the *prima-facie* view which the public at large would take of a university, considering it as a place of education, is nothing more or less than a place for acquiring a great deal of knowledge on a great many subjects. Memory is one of the first developed of the mental faculties; a boy's business when he goes to school is to learn, that is, to store up things in his memory. For some years his intellect is little more than an instrument for taking in facts, or a receptacle for storing them; he welcomes them as fast as they come to him; he lives on what is without; he has his eyes ever about him; he has a lively susceptibility of impressions; he imbibes information of every kind; and little does he make his own in a true sense of the word, living rather upon his neighbors all around him. He has opinions, religious, political and literary, and, for a boy, is very positive in them and sure about them; but he gets them from his schoolfellows, or his masters, or his parents, as the case may be. Such as he is in his other relations, such also is he in his school exercises; his mind is observant, sharp, ready, retentive; he is almost passive in the acquisition of knowledge. I say this in no disparagement of the idea of a clever boy. Geography, chronology, history, language, natural history, he heaps up the matter of these studies as treasures for a future day. It is the seven years of plenty with him: he gathers in by handfuls, like the Egyptians, without counting; and though, as time goes on, there is exercise for his argumentative powers in the elements of mathematics, and for his taste in the poets and orators, still, while at school, or at least, till quite the last years of his time, he acquires, and little more; and when he is leaving for the university, he is mainly the creature of foreign influences and circumstances, and made up of accidents, homogeneous or not, as the case may be. Moreover, the moral habits, which are a boy's praise, encourage and assist this result; that is, diligence, assiduity, regularity, despatch, persevering application; for these are the direct conditions of acquisition, and naturally lead to it. Acquirements, again, are emphatically producible, and at a moment; they are a something to show, both for master and scholar; an audience, even though ignorant themselves of the subjects of an examination, can comprehend when questions are answered and when they are not. Here again is a reason why mental culture is in the minds of men identified with the acquisition of knowledge.

The same notion possesses the public mind, when it passes on from the thought of a school to that of a university: and with the best of reasons so far as this, that there is no true culture without acquirements, and that philosophy presupposes knowledge. It requires a great deal of reading, or a wide range of information, to warrant us in putting forth our opinions on any serious subject; and without such learning the most original mind may be able indeed to dazzle, to amuse, to refute, to perplex, but not to come to any useful result or any trustworthy conclusion. There are indeed persons who profess a different view of the matter, and even act upon it. Every now and then you will find a person of vigorous or fertile mind, who relies upon his own resources, despises all former authors, and gives the world, with the utmost fearlessness, his view upon religion, or history, or any other popular subject. And his works may sell for a while; he may get a name in his day; but this will be all. His readers are sure to find on the long run that his doctrines are mere theories, and not the expression of facts, that they are chaff instead of bread, and then his popularity drops as suddenly as it rose.

Knowledge then is the indispensable condition of expansion of mind, and the instrument of attaining to it; this cannot be denied, it is ever to be insisted on; I begin with it as a first principle; however, the very truth of it carries men too far, and confirms to them the notion that it is the whole of the matter. A narrow mind is thought to be that which contains little knowledge; and an enlarged mind, that which holds a great deal; and what seems to put the matter beyond dispute is, the fact of the great number of studies which are pursued in a university, by its very profession. Lectures are given on every kind of subject; examinations are held; prizes awarded. There are moral, metaphysical, physical professors; professors of languages, of history, of mathematics, of experimental science. Lists of questions are published, wonderful for their range and depth, variety and difficulty; treatises are written, which carry upon their very face the evidence of extensive reading or multifarious information; what then is wanting for mental culture to a person of large reading and scientific attainments? what is grasp of mind but acquirement? where shall philosophical repose be found, but in the consciousness and enjoyment of large intellectual possessions?

And yet this notion is, I conceive, a mistake, and my present business is to show that it is one, and that the end of a liberal education is not mere knowledge, or knowledge considered in its *matter;* and I shall best attain my object, by actually setting down some cases, which will be generally granted to be instances of the process of enlightenment or enlargement of mind, and others which are not, and thus, by the comparison, you will be able to judge for yourselves, gentlemen, whether knowledge, that is, acquirement, is after all the real principle of the enlargement or whether that principle is not rather something beyond it.

For instance, let a person, whose experience has hitherto been confined to the more calm and unpretending scenery of these islands, whether here or in England, go for the first time into parts where physical nature puts on her wilder and more awful forms, whether at home or abroad, as into mountainous districts; or let one, who has ever lived in a quiet village, go for the first time to a great metropolis,—then I suppose he will have a sensation which perhaps he never had before. He has a feeling not in addition or increase of former feelings, but of something different in its nature. He will perhaps be borne forward, and find for a time that he has lost his bearings. He has made a certain progress, and he has a consciousness of mental enlargement; he does not stand where he did, he has a new center, and a range of thoughts to which he was before a stranger.

Again, the view of the heavens which the telescope opens upon us, if allowed to fill and possess the mind, may almost whirl it round and make it dizzy. It brings in a flood of ideas, and is rightly called an intellectual enlargement, whatever is meant by the term.

And so again, the sight of beasts of prey and other foreign animals, their strangeness, the originality (if I may use the term) of their forms and gestures and habits, and their variety and independence of each other, throw us out of ourselves into another creation, and as if under another Creator, if I may so express the temptation which may come on the mind. We seem to have new faculties, or a new exercise for our faculties, by this addition to our knowledge; like a prisoner, who, having been accustomed to wear manacles or fetters, suddenly finds his arms and legs free.

Hence physical science generally, in all its departments, as bringing before us the exuberant riches and resources, yet the orderly course, of the universe, elevates and excites the student, and at first, I may say, almost takes away his breath, while in time it exercises a tranquilizing influence upon him.

Again the study of history is said to enlarge and enlighten the mind, and why? because, as I conceive, it gives it a power of judging of passing events and of all events, and a conscious superiority over them, which before it did not possess.

And in like manner, what is called seeing the world, entering into active life, going into society, traveling, gaining acquaintance with the various classes of the community, coming into contact with the principles and modes of thought of various parties, interests, and races, their views, aims, habits and manners, their religious creeds and forms of worship,—gaining experience how various yet how alike men are, how low-minded, how bad, how opposed, yet how confident in their opinions; all this exerts a perceptible influence upon the mind, which it is impossible to mistake, be it good or be it bad, and is popularly called its enlargement.

And then again, the first time the mind comes across the arguments and speculations of unbelievers, and feels what a novel light they cast upon what he has hitherto accounted sacred; and still more, if it gives in to them and embraces them, and throws off as so much prejudice what it has hitherto held, and, as if waking from a dream, begins to realize to its imagination that there is now no such thing as law and the transgression of law, that sin is a phantom, and punishment a bugbear, that it is free to sin, free to enjoy the world and the flesh; and still further, when it does enjoy them, and reflects that it may think and hold just what it will, that 'the world is all before it where to choose,' and what system to build up as its own private persuasion; when this torrent of wilful thoughts rushes over and inundates it, who will deny that the fruit of the tree of knowledge, or what the mind takes for knowledge, has made it one of the gods, with a sense of expansion and elevation,—an intoxication in reality, still, so far as the subjective state of the mind goes, an illumination? Hence the fanaticism of individuals or nations, who suddenly cast off their Maker. Their eyes are opened; and, like the judgment-stricken king in the tragedy, they see two suns, and a magic universe, out of which they look back upon their former state of faith and innocence with a sort of contempt and indignation, as if they were then but fools, and the dupes of imposture.

On the other hand, religion has its own enlargement, and an enlargement, not of tumult, but of peace. It is often remarked of uneducated persons, who have hitherto thought little of the unseen world, that, on their turning to God, looking into themselves, regulating their hearts, reforming their conduct, and meditating on death and judgment, heaven and hell, they seem to become, in point of intellect, different beings from what they were. Before, they took things as they came, and thought no more of one thing than another. But now every event has a meaning; they have their own estimate of whatever happens to them; they are mindful of times and seasons, and compare the present with the past; and the world, no longer dull, monotonous, unprofitable, and hopeless, is a various and complicated drama, with parts and an object, and an awful moral.

Now from these instances, to which many more might be added, it is plain, first, that the communication of knowledge certainly is either a condition of the means of that sense of enlargement, or enlightenment of which at this day we hear so much in certain quarters: this cannot be denied; but next, it is equally plain, that such communication is not the whole of the process. The enlargement consists, not merely in the passive reception into the mind of a number of ideas hitherto unknown to it, but in the mind's energetic and simultaneous action upon and towards and among those new ideas, which are rushing in upon it. It is the action of a formative power, reducing to order and meaning the matter of our acquirements; it is a making the objects of our knowledge subjectively our own, or, to use a familiar word, it is a digestion of what we receive, into the substance of our previous state of thought; and without this no enlargement is said to follow. There is no enlargement, unless there be a comparison of ideas one with another, as they come before the mind, and a systematizing of them. We feel our minds to be growing and expanding *then*, when we not only learn, but refer what we learn to what we know already. It is not the mere addition to our knowledge that is the illumination; but the locomotion, the movement onwards, of that mental center, to which both what we know, and what we are learning, the accumulating mass of our acquirements, gravitates. And therefore a truly great intellect, and recognized to be such by the common opinion of mankind, such as the intellect of Aristotle, or of St. Thomas, or of Newton, or of Goethe (I purposely take instances within and without the Catholic pale, when I would speak of the intellect as such), is one which takes a connected view of old and new, past and present, far and near, and which has an insight into the influence of all these one on another; without which there is no whole and no center. It possesses the knowledge, not only of things, but also of their mutual and true relations; knowledge, not merely considered as acquirement but as philosophy.

Accordingly, when this analytical, distributive, harmonizing process is away, the mind experiences no enlargement, and is not reckoned as enlightened or comprehensive, whatever it may add to its knowledge. For instance, a great memory, as I have already said, does not make a philosopher, any more than a dictionary can be called a grammar. There are men who embrace in their minds a vast multitude of ideas, but with little sensibility about their real relations towards each other. These may be antiquarians, annalists, naturalists; they may be learned in the law; they may be versed in statistics; they are most useful in their own place; I should shrink from speaking disrespectfully of them; still, there is nothing in such attainments to guarantee the absence of narrowness of mind. If they are nothing more than well-read men, or men of information, they have not what specially deserves the name of culture of mind, or fulfils the type of liberal education.

In like manner, we sometimes fall in with persons who have seen much of the world, and of the men who, in their day, have played a conspicuous part in it, but who generalize nothing, and have no observation, in the true sense of the word. They abound in information in detail, curious and entertaining, about men and things; and, having lived under the influence of no very clear or settled principles, religious or political, they speak of every one and every thing, only as so many phenomena, which are complete in themselves, and lead to nothing, not discussing them, or teaching any truth, or instructing the hearer, but simply talking. No one would say that these persons, well informed as they are, had attained to any great culture of intellect or to philosophy.

The case is the same still more strikingly where the persons in question are beyond dispute men of inferior powers and deficient education. Perhaps they have been much in foreign countries, and they receive, in a passive, otiose, unfruitful way, the various facts which are forced upon them there. Seafaring men, for example, range from one end of the earth to the other; but the multiplicity of external objects, which they have encountered, forms no symmetrical and consistent picture upon their imagination; they see the tapestry of human life, as it were on the wrong side, and it tells no story. They sleep, and they rise up, and they find themselves, now in Europe, now in Asia; they see visions of great cities and wild regions; they are in the marts of commerce, or amid the islands of the South; they gaze on Pompey's Pillar, or on the Andes; and nothing which meets them carries them forward or backward, to any idea beyond itself. Nothing has a drift or relation; nothing has a history or a promise. Every thing stands by itself, and comes and goes in its turn, like the shifting scenes of a show, which leave the spectator where he was. Perhaps you are near such a man on a particular occasion, and expect him to be shocked or perplexed at something which occurs; but one thing is much the same to him as another, or, if he is perplexed, it is as not knowing what to say, whether it is right to admire, or to ridicule, or to disapprove, while conscious that some expression of opinion is expected from him; for in fact he has no standard of judgment at all, and no landmarks to guide him to a conclusion. Such is mere acquisition, and, I repeat, no one would dream of calling it philosophy.

Instances, such as these, confirm, by the contrast, the conclusion I have already drawn from those which preceded them. That only is true enlargement of mind which is the power of viewing many things at once as one whole, of referring them severally to their true place in the universal system, of understanding their respective values, and determining their mutual dependence. Thus is that form of universal knowledge, of which I have on a former occasion spoken, set up in the individual intellect, and constitutes its perfection. Possessed of this real illumination, the mind never views any part of the extended subject-matter of knowledge without recollecting that it is but a part, or without the associations which spring from this recollection. It makes everything in some sort lead to everything else; it would communicate the image of the whole to every separate portion, till that whole becomes in imagination like a spirit, everywhere pervading and penetrating its component parts, and giving them one definite meaning. Just as our bodily organs, when mentioned, recall their function in the body, as the word 'creation' suggests the Creator, and 'subjects' a sovereign, so, in the mind of the philosopher, as we are abstractedly conceiving of him, the elements of the physical and moral world, sciences, arts, pursuits, ranks, officers, events, opinions, individualities, are all viewed as one, with correlative functions, and as gradually by successive combinations converging, one and all, to the true center.

To have even a portion of this illuminative reason and true philosophy is the highest state to which nature can aspire, in the way of intellect; it puts the mind above the influences of chance and necessity, above anxiety, suspense, unsettlement, and superstition, which is the lot of the many. Men, whose minds are possessed with some one object, take exaggerated views of its importance, are feverish in the pursuit of it, make it the measure of things which are utterly foreign to it, and are startled and despond if it happens to fail them. They are ever in alarm or in transport. Those on the other hand who have no object or principle whatever to hold by, lose their way every step they take. They are thrown out, and do not know what to think or say, at every fresh juncture; they have no view of persons, or occurrences, or facts, which come suddenly upon them, and they hang upon the opinion of others for want of internal resources But the intellect, which has been disciplined to the perfection of its powers, which knows, and thinks while it knows, which has learned to leaven the dense mass of facts and events with the elastic force of reason, such an intellect cannot be partial, cannot be exclusive, cannot be impetuous, cannot be at a loss, cannot but be patient, collected, and majestically calm, because it discerns the end in every beginning, the origin in every end, the law in every interruption, the limit in each delay; because it ever knows where it stands, and how its path lies from one point to another. It is the τετράγωνος [four-square] of the Peripatetic, and has the *nil admirari* [to be moved by nothing] of the Stoic,—

Felix qui potuit rerum cognoscere causas,
Atque metus omnes, et inexorabile fatum
Subjecit pedibus, strepitumque Acherontis avari.

[Happy is he who has come to know the sequences of things, and is thus above all fear and the dread march of fate and the roar of greedy Acheron.]

There are men who, when in difficulties, originate at the moment vast ideas or dazzling projects; who, under the influence of excitement, are able to cast a light, almost as if from inspiration, on a subject or course of action which comes before them; who have a sudden presence of mind equal to any emergency, rising with the occasion, and an undaunted magnanimous bearing, and an energy and keenness which is but made intense by opposition. This is genius, this is heroism; it is the exhibition of a natural gift, which no culture can teach, at which no institution can aim: here, on the contrary, we are concerned, not with mere nature, but with training and teaching. That perfection of the intellect, which is the result of education, and its *beau ideal*, to be imparted to individuals in their respective measures, is the clear, calm, accurate vision and comprehension of all things, as far as the finite mind can embrace them, each in its place, and with its own characteristics upon it. It is almost prophetic from its knowledge of history; it is almost heart-searching from its knowledge of human nature; it has almost supernatural charity from its freedom from littleness and prejudice; it has almost the repose of faith, because nothing can startle it; it has almost the beauty and harmony of heavenly contemplation, so intimate is it with the eternal order of things and the music of the spheres.

And now, if I may take for granted that the true and adequate end of intellectual training and of a university is not learning or acquirement, but rather, is thought or reason exercised upon knowledge, or what may be called philosophy, I shall be in a position to explain the various mistakes which at the present day beset the subject of university education.

I say then, if we would improve the intellect, first of all, we must ascend; we cannot gain real knowledge on a level; we must generalize, we must reduce to method, we must have a grasp of principles, and group and shape our acquisitions by means of them. It matters not whether our field of operation be wide or limited; in every case, to command it, is to mount above it. Who has not felt the irritation of mind and impatience created by a deep, rich country, visited for the first time, with winding lanes, and high hedges, and green steeps, and tangled woods, and every thing smiling indeed, but in a maze? The same feeling comes upon us in a strange city, where we have no map of its streets. Hence you hear of practised travelers, when they first come into a place, mounting some high hill or church tower, by way of reconnoitering its neighborhood. In like manner, you must be above your knowledge, not under it, or it will oppress you; and the more you have of it, the greater will be the load. The learning of a Salmasius or a Burman, unless you are its master, will be your tyrant. *Imperat aut servit* [it rules or it serves]; if you can wield it with a strong arm, it is a great weapon; otherwise,

Vis consili expers mole ruit suâ.
[Brute force without intelligence falls by its own weight.]

You will be overwhelmed, like Tarpeia, by the heavy wealth which you have exacted from tributary generations.

Instances abound: there are authors who are as pointless as they are inexhaustible in their literary resources. They measure knowledge by bulk, as it lies in the rude block, without symmetry, without design. How many commentators are there on the classics, how many on Holy Scripture, from whom we rise up, wondering at the learning which has passed before us, and wondering why it passed! How many writers are there of Ecclesiastical history, such as Mosheim or Du Pin, who, breaking up their subject into details, destroy its life, and defraud us of the whole by their anxiety about the parts! The sermons, again, of the English divines in the seventeenth century, how often are they mere repertories of miscellaneous and officious learning! Of course Catholics also may read without thinking; and in their case, equally as with

Protestants, it holds good, that such knowledge is unworthy of the name, knowledge which they have not thought through, and thought out. Such readers are only possessed by their knowledge, not possessed of it; nay, in matter of fact they are often even carried away by it, without any volition of their own. Recollect, the memory can tyrannize, as well as the imagination. Derangement, I believe, has been considered as a loss of control over the sequence of ideas. The mind, once set in motion, is henceforth deprived of the power of initiation, and becomes the victim of a train of associations, one thought suggesting another, in the way of cause and effect, as if by a mechanical process, or some physical necessity. No one, who has had experience of men of studious habits, but must recognize the existence of a parallel phenomenon in the case of those who have over-stimulated the memory. In such persons reason acts almost as feebly and as impotently as in the madman; once fairly started on any subject whatever, they have no power of self-control; they passively endure the succession of impulses which are evolved out of the original exciting cause; they are passed on from one idea to another and go steadily forward, plodding along one line of thought in spite of the amplest concessions of the hearer, or wandering from it in endless digression in spite of his remonstrances. Now, if, as is very certain, no one would envy the madman the glow and originality of his conceptions, why must we extol the cultivation of that intellect, which is the prey, not indeed of barren fancies but of barren facts, of random intrusions from without, though not of morbid imaginations from within? And in thus speaking, I am not denying that a strong and ready memory is in itself a real treasure; I am not disparaging a well-stored mind, though it be nothing besides, provided it be sober, any more than I would despise a bookseller's shop:—it is of great value to others, even when not so to the owner. Nor am I banishing, far from it, the possessors of deep and multifarious learning from my ideal University; they adorn it in the eyes of men; I do but say that they constitute no type of the results at which it aims; that it is no great gain to the intellect to have enlarged the memory at the expense of faculties which are indisputably higher.

Nor indeed am I supposing that there is any great danger, at least in this day, of over-education; the danger is on the other side. I will tell you, gentlemen, what has been the practical error of the last twenty years,—not to load the memory of the student with a mass of undigested knowledge, but to force upon him so much that he has rejected all. It has been the error of distracting and enfeebling the mind by an unmeaning profusion of subjects; of implying that a smattering in a dozen branches of study is not shallowness, which it really is, but enlargement, which it is not; of considering an acquaintance with the learned names of things and persons and the possession of clever duodecimos, and attendance on eloquent lecturers, and membership with scientific institutions, and the sight of the experiments of a platform and the specimens of a museum, that all this was not dissipation of mind, but progress. All things now are to be learned at once, not first one thing, then another, not one well, but many badly. Learning is to be without exertion, without attention, without toil; without grounding, without advance, without finishing. There is to be nothing individual in it; and this, forsooth, is the wonder of the age. What the steam engine does with matter, the printing press is to do with the mind; it is to act mechanically, and the population is to be passively, almost unconsciously enlightened, by the mere multiplication and dissemination of volumes. Whether it be the school boy, or the school girl, or the youth at college, or the mechanic in the town, or the politician in the senate, all have been the victims in one way or other of this most preposterous and pernicious of delusions. Wise men have lifted up their voices in vain; and at length, lest their own institutions should be outshone and should disappear in the folly of the hour, they have been obliged, as far as they could with a good conscience, to humor a spirit which they could not withstand, and make temporizing concessions at which they could not but inwardly smile.

It must not be supposed that, because I so speak, therefore I have some sort of fear of the education of the people: on the contrary, the more education they have, the better, so that it is really education. Nor am I an enemy to the cheap publication of scientific and literary works, which is now in vogue: on the contrary, I consider it a great advantage, convenience, and gain; that is, to those to whom education has given a capacity for using them. Further, I consider such innocent recreations as science and literature are able to furnish will be a very fit occupation of the thoughts and the leisure of young persons, and may be made the means of keeping them from bad employments and bad companions. Moreover, as to that superficial acquaintance with chemistry, and geology, and astronomy, and political economy, and modern history, and biography, and other branches of knowledge, which periodical literature and occasional lectures and scientific institutions diffuse through the community, I think it a graceful accomplishment, and a suitable, nay, in this day a necessary accomplishment, in the case of educated men. Nor, lastly, am I disparaging or discouraging the thorough acquisition of any one of these studies, or denying that, as far as it goes, such thorough acquisition is a real education of the mind. All I say is, call things by their right names, and do not confuse together ideas which are essentially different. A thorough knowledge of one science and a superficial acquaintance with many, are not the same thing; a smattering of a hundred things or a memory for detail, is not a philosophical or comprehensive view. Recreations are not education; accomplishments are not education. Do not say, the people must be educated, when, after all, you only mean, amused, refreshed, soothed, put into good spirits and good humor, or kept from vicious excesses. I do not say that such amusements, such occupations of mind, are not a great gain; but they are not education. You may as well call drawing and fencing education as a general knowledge of botany or conchology. Stuffing birds or playing stringed instruments is an elegant pastime, and a resource to the idle, but it is not education; it does not form or cultivate the intellect. Education is a high word; it is the preparation for knowledge, and it is the imparting of knowledge in proportion to that preparation. We require intellectual eyes to know withal, as bodily eyes for sight. We need both objects and organs intellectual; we cannot gain them without setting about it; we cannot gain them in our sleep, or by haphazard. The best telescope does not dispense with eyes; the printing press or the lecture room will assist us greatly, but we must be true to ourselves, we must be parties in the work. A university is, according to the usual designation, an alma mater, knowing her children one by one, not a foundry, or a mint, or a treadmill.

I protest to you, gentlemen, that if I had to choose between a so-called university, which dispensed with residence and tutorial superintendence, and gave its degrees to any person who passed an examination in a wide range of subjects, and a university which had no professors or examinations at all, but merely brought a number of young men together for three or four years, and then sent them away as the University of Oxford is said to have done some sixty years since, if I were asked which of these two methods was the better discipline of the intellect,—mind, I do not say which is morally the better, for it is plain that compulsory study must be a good and idleness an intolerable mischief,—but if I must determine which of the two courses was the more successful in training, molding, enlarging the mind, which sent out men the more fitted for their secular duties, which produced better public men, men of the world, men whose names would descend to posterity, I have no hesitation in giving the preference to that university which did nothing, over that which exacted of its members an acquaintance with every science under the sun. And, paradox as this may seem, still if results be the test of systems, the influence of the public schools and colleges of England, in the course of the last century, at least will bear out one side of the contrast as I have drawn it. What would come, on the other hand, of the ideal systems of education which have fascinated the imagination of this age, could they ever take effect, and whether they would not produce a generation frivolous, narrow-minded, and resourceless, intellectually considered, is a fair subject for debate; but so far is certain, that the universities and scholastic establishments, to which I refer, and which did little more than bring together first boys and then youths in large numbers, these institutions, with miserable deformities on the side of morals, with a hollow profession of Christianity, and a heathen code of ethics,—I say, at least they can boast of a succession of heroes and statesmen, of literary men and philosophers, of men conspicuous for great natural virtues, for habits of business, for knowledge of life, for practical judgment, for cultivated tastes, for accomplishments, who have made England what it is,—able to subdue the earth, able to domineer over Catholics.

How is this to be explained? I suppose as follows: When a multitude of young men, keen, open-hearted, sympathetic, and observant, as young men are, come together and freely mix with each other, they are sure to learn one from another, even if there be no one to teach them; the conversation of all is a series of lectures to each, and they gain for themselves new ideas and views, fresh matter of thought, and distinct principles for judging and acting. day by day. An infant has to learn the meaning of the information which its senses convey to it, and this seems to be its employment. It fancies all that the eye presents to it to be close to it, till it actually learns the contrary, and thus by practice does it ascertain the relations and uses of those first elements of knowledge which are necessary for its animal existence. A parallel teaching is necessary for our social being, and it is secured by a large school or a college; and this effect may be fairly called in its own department an enlargement of mind. It is seeing the world on a small field with little trouble; for the pupils or students come from very different places, and with widely different notions, and there is much to generalize, much to adjust, much to eliminate, there are inter-relations to be defined, and conventional rules to be established, in the process, by which the whole assemblage is molded together, and gains one tone and one character.

Let it be clearly understood, I repeat it, that I am not taking into account moral or religious considerations; I am but saying that that youthful community will constitute a whole, it will embody a specific idea, it will represent a doctrine, it will administer a code of conduct, and it will furnish principles of thought and action. It will give birth to a living teaching, which in course of time will take the shape of a self-perpetuating tradition, or a *genius loci*, as it is sometimes called; which haunts the home where it has been born, and which imbues and forms more or less, and one by one, every individual who is successively brought under its shadow.

* * *

Nay, self-education in any shape, in the most restricted sense, is preferable to a system of teaching which, professing so much, really does so little for the mind. Shut your college gates against the votary of knowledge, throw him back upon the searchings and the efforts of his own mind; he will gain by being spared an entrance into your babel. Few indeed there are who can dispense with the stimulus and support of instructors, or will do anything at all, if left to themselves. And fewer still (though such great minds are to be found), who will not, from such unassisted attempts, contract a self-reliance and a self-esteem, which are not only moral evils, but serious hindrances to the attainment of truth. And next to none, perhaps, or none, who will not be reminded from time to time of the disadvantage under which they lie, by their imperfect grounding, by the breaks, deficiencies, and irregularities of their knowledge, by the eccentricity of opinion and the confusion of principle which they exhibit. They will be too often ignorant of what every one knows and takes for granted, of that multitude of small truths which fall upon the mind like dust, impalpable and ever accumulating; they may be unable to converse, they may argue perversely, they may pride themselves on their worst paradoxes or their grossest truisms, they may be full of their own mode of viewing things, unwilling to be put out of their way, slow to enter into the minds of others;—but, with these and whatever other liabilities upon their heads, they are likely to have more thought, more mind, more philosophy, more true enlargement, than those earnest but ill-used persons, who are forced to load their minds with a score of subjects against an examination, who have too much on their hands to indulge themselves in thinking or investigation, who devour premise and conclusion together with indiscriminate greediness, who hold whole sciences on faith, and commit demonstrations to memory, and who too often, as might be expected, when their period of education is passed, throw up all they have learned in disgust, having gained nothing really by their anxious labors, except perhaps the habit of application.

Yet such is the better specimen of the fruit of that ambitious system which has of late years been making way among us: for its result on ordinary minds, and on the common run of students, is less satisfactory still; they leave their place of education simply dissipated and relaxed by the multiplicity of subjects, which they have never really mastered, and so shallow as not even to know their shallowness. How much better, I say, is it for the active and thoughtful intellect, where such is to be found, to eschew the college and the university altogether, than to submit to a drudgery so ignoble, a mockery so contumelious! How much more profitable for the independent mind, after the mere rudiments of education, to range through a library at random, taking down books as they meet him, and pursuing the trains of thought which his mother wit suggests! How much healthier to wander into the fields, and there with the exiled prince to find 'tongues in the trees, books in the running brooks!'

* * * (1852)

THOMAS CARLYLE (1795–1881)

EARLY struggles and privations, followed by acute dyspepsia, embittered Carlyle's temper. The son of a Scottish stone-mason, he walked eighty miles from his native village of Ecclefechan to Edinburgh to study at the university and prepare himself for the ministry. This latter purpose was soon abandoned on account of unsettled religious convictions; after graduating he earned a scanty living by teaching and tried in vain to obtain various professorships. Having married Jane Baillie Welsh, a woman of brilliant wit and some property, he retired with her to the manor house of Craigenputtock, where for six years he studied German literature and philosophy and wrote essays for the reviews, among them his first great work, *Sartor Resartus*. Under the disguise of a translation from the papers of a German professor, it is an imaginative account of his own school and college experiences, his falling in love with Margaret Gordon of Prince Edward Island, who returned to that colony as wife of the governor, his spiritual and intellectual struggles, and his philosophy of life. It had just been published in *Fraser's Magazine*, when, in 1834, the Carlyles determined to risk their little all, and leave Craigenputtock for London. Carlyle chose a house in Cheyne Row, Chelsea, and kept it for the rest of his life. The peculiar style of *Sartor* did not commend it to the public. Fraser wrote that it excited 'universal disapprobation,' and several subscribers to the magazine refused to take it any longer. Carlyle was more fortunate in his next subject, 'The French Revolution,' suggested by John Stuart Mill. When the manuscript of the first volume was finished, Carlyle lent it to Mill to read; Mill lent it in turn to a friend, whose housemaid found it on the table one morning and lit the fire with it. Carlyle was in despair at the loss of so much labor; he felt incapable of doing the work over again, and spent three months in reading Marryat's novels before he could bend his energies to the unwelcome task. The book was completed in 1837, and at once won the favor of both critics and public. He was also successful about this time as a lecturer, and his wife said that the public had evidently made up its mind that 'Carlyle was worth keeping alive at a moderate rate.' One of the courses he gave, that 'On Heroes, Hero-worship, and the Heroic in History,' when published in 1841 became one of his most popular works; it contains in the shortest and simplest form Carlyle's favorite doctrine that the history of the world is at bottom the history of its great men. After setting forth his ideas on social and political questions in *Chartism* and *Past and Present*, he returned to the study of history, and his *Life and Letters of Oliver Cromwell* made a remarkable change in the current estimate of the great Protector. The labor of a dozen years is contained in his last historical work, *Frederick the Great* (published 1858–65). The year after this was completed, Mrs. Carlyle died suddenly in her carriage from the shock caused by an accident to her pet dog, which was run over when she was driving one afternoon in Hyde Park. Carlyle in heartbroken remorse determined to put on record not only his wife's virtues but his own unkindness to her. The publication of the record after his death injured his reputation, and led to a controversy which has not yet ended, the discretion and even the good faith of J. A. Froude, who edited the papers, being attacked by Carlyle's admirers.

THE FRENCH REVOLUTION

VOLUME I, BOOK V, CHAPTER VI

THE TAKING OF THE BASTILLE

BUT, to the living and the struggling, a new, Fourteenth morning dawns. Under all roofs of this distracted City is the nodus of a Drama, not untragical, crowding toward solution. The bustlings and preparings, the tremors and menaces; the tears that fell from old eyes! This day, my sons, ye shall quit you like men. By the memory of your fathers' wrongs; by the hope of your children's rights! Tyranny impends in red wrath: help for you is none, if not in your own right hands. This day ye must do or die.

From earliest light, a sleepless Permanent Committee has heard the old cry, now waxing almost frantic, mutinous: Arms! Arms! Provost Flesselles, or what traitors there are among you, may think of those Charleville Boxes. A hundred-and-fifty thousand of us, and but the third man furnished with so much as a pike! Arms are the one thing needful: with arms we are an unconquerable man-defying National Guard; without arms, a rabble to be whiffed with grape-shot.

Happily the word has arisen, for no secret car

be kept,—that there lie muskets at the Hôtel des Invalides. Thither will we: King's Procureur M. Ethys de Corny, and whatsoever of authority a Permanent Committee can lend, shall go with us. Besenval's Camp is there; perhaps he will not fire on us; if he kill us, we shall but die.

Alas! poor Besenval, with his troops melting away in that manner, has not the smallest humor to fire! At five o'clock this morning, as he lay dreaming, oblivious in the École Militaire, a 'figure' stood suddenly at his bedside; 'with face rather handsome, eyes inflamed, speech rapid and curt, air audacious:' such a figure drew Priam's curtains! The message and monition of the figure was that resistance would be hopeless; that if blood flowed, woe to him who shed it. Thus spoke the figure: and vanished. 'Withal there was a kind of eloquence that struck one.' Besenval admits that he should have arrested him, but did not. Who this figure with inflamed eyes, with speech rapid and curt, might be? Besenval knows, but mentions not. Camille Desmoulins? Pythagorean Marquis Valadi, inflamed with 'violent motions all night at the Palais Royal?' Fame names him 'Young M. Meillar'; then shuts her lips about him forever.

In any case, behold, about nine in the morning, our National Volunteers, rolling in long wide flood south-westward to the Hôtel des Invalides, in search of the one thing needful. King's Procureur M. Ethys de Corny and officials are there; the Curé of Saint-Étienne du Mont marches unpacific at the head of his militant Parish; the Clerks of the Basoche in red coats we see marching, now Volunteers of the Palais Royal;—National Volunteers, numerable by tens of thousands; of one heart and mind. The King's Muskets are the Nation's; think, old M. de Sombreuil, how, in this extremity, thou wilt refuse them! Old M. de Sombreuil would fain hold parley, send couriers, but it skills not: the walls are scaled, no Invalide firing a shot; the gates must be flung open. Patriotism rushes in tumultuous, from grunsel up to ridge-tile, through all rooms and passages; rummaging distractedly for arms. What cellar or what cranny can escape it? The arms are found; all safe there, lying packed in straw,—apparently with a view to being burnt! More ravenous than famishing lions over dead prey, the multitude, with clangor and vociferation, pounces on them; struggling, dashing, clutching,—to the jamming up, to the pressure, fracture, and probable extinction of the weaker Patriot. And so, with such protracted crash of deafening, most discordant Orchestra-music, the Scene is changed: and eight-and-twenty thousand sufficient firelocks are on the shoulders of as many National Guards, thereby out of darkness into fiery light.

Let Besenval look at the glitter of these muskets as they flash by! Gardes Françaises, it is said, have cannon leveled on him; ready to open, if need were, from the other side of the river. Motionless sits he; 'astonished,' one may flatter one's self, 'at the proud bearing (*fière contenance*) of the Parisians.' And now to the Bastille, ye intrepid Parisians! There grape-shot still threatens; thither all men's thoughts and steps are now tending.

Old De Launay, as we hinted, withdrew 'into his interior' soon after midnight of Sunday. He remains there ever since, hampered, as all military gentlemen now are, in the saddest conflict of uncertainties. The Hôtel-de-Ville 'invites' him to admit National Soldiers, which is a soft name for surrendering. On the other hand, his Majesty's orders were precise. His garrison is but eighty-two old Invalides, reinforced by thirty-two young Swiss; his walls, indeed, are nine feet thick; he has cannon and powder, but alas! only one day's provision of victuals. The city, too, is French, the poor garrison mostly French. Rigorous old De Launay, think what thou wilt do!

All morning, since nine, there has been a cry everywhere: To the Bastille! Repeated 'deputations of citizens' have been here, passionate for arms, whom De Launay has got dismissed by soft speeches through port-holes. Towards noon, Elector Thuriot de la Rosiere gains admittance, finds De Launay indisposed for surrender, nay, disposed for blowing up the place, rather. Thuriot mounts with him to the battlements; heaps of paving-stones, old iron, and missiles lie piled; cannon all duly leveled; in every embrasure a cannon,—only drawn back a little! But outwards, behold, O Thuriot, how the multitude flows on, welling through every street, tocsin furiously pealing, all drums beating the *générale;* the suburb Saint-Antoine rolling hitherward wholly as one man! Such vision (spectral, yet real) thou, O Thuriot, as from thy Mount of Vision, beholdest in this moment: prophetic of what other Phantasmagories and loud-gibbering Spectral Realities which thou yet beholdest not, but shalt! '*Que voulez-vous?*' said De Launay, turning pale at the sight, with an air of reproach, almost of menace. 'Monsieur,' said Thuriot, rising into the moral sublime, 'what mean *you*? Consider if I could not precipitate *both* of us from this height,'—say only a hundred feet, exclusive of the walled ditch! Whereupon De Launay fell silent. Thuriot shows himself from some pinnacle to comfort the multitude becoming suspicious, fremescent, then descends, departs with protest, with warning address also to the Invalides, on whom however it produces but a mixed, indistinct impression. The old heads are none of the clearest; besides, it is said, De Launay has been profuse of beverages (*prodigue des buissons*). They think they will not fire—if not fired on— if they can help it; but must, on the whole, be ruled considerably by circumstances.

Woe to thee, De Launay, in such an hour, if thou canst not, taking some one firm decision, *rule* circumstances! Soft speeches will not serve, hard grape-shot is questionable, but hovering between the two is *un*questionable. Ever wilder swells the tide of men; their infinite hum waxing ever louder, into imprecations, perhaps into crackle of stray musketry,—which latter, on walls nine feet thick, cannot do execution. The Outer Drawbridge has been lowered for Thuriot; new *deputation of citizens* (it is the third and noisiest of all) penetrates that way into the Outer Court; soft speeches producing no clearance of these, De Launay gives fire; pulls up his drawbridge. A slight sputter, which has *kindled* the too combustible chaos, made it a roaring fire-chaos! Bursts forth Insurrection, at sight of its own blood (for there were deaths by that sputter of fire), into endless, rolling explosion of musketry, distraction, execration;—and over head, from the fortress, let one great gun, with its grape-shot, go booming, to show what we *could* do. The Bastille is besieged!

On, then, all Frenchmen that have hearts in your bodies! Roar with all your throats of cartilage and metal, ye Sons of Liberty; stir spasmodically whatsoever of utmost faculty is in you, soul, body, or spirit; for it is the hour! Smite thou, Louis Tournay, cartwright of the Marais, old-soldier of the Regiment Dauphiné; smite at that Outer Drawbridge chain, though the fiery hail whistles round thee! Never, over nave or felloe, did thy axe strike such a stroke. Down with it, man; down with it to Orcus: let the whole accursed edifice sink thither, and tyranny be swallowed up forever! Mounted, some say, on the roof of the guard-room, some 'on bayonets stuck into joints of the wall,' Louis Tournay smites, brave Aubin Bonnemère (also an old soldier) seconding him; the chain yields, breaks; the huge Drawbridge slams down, thundering (*avec fracas*). Glorious! and yet, alas! it is still but the outworks. The Eight Grim Towers, with their *Invalide* musketry, their paving-stones and cannon-mouth, still soar aloft intact;—Ditch yawning impassable, stone-faced; the inner Drawbridge with its *back* toward us; the Bastille is still to take!

To describe this Siege of the Bastille (thought to be one of the most important in History) perhaps transcends the talent of mortals. Could one but, after infinite reading, get to understand so much as the plan of the building! But there is open Esplanade at the end of the Rue Saint-Antoine; there are such Forecourts (*Cour Avancé*), *Cour de l'Orme*, arched gateway (where Louis Tournay now fights); then new drawbridges, dormant-bridges, rampart-bastions, and the grim Eight Towers: a labyrinthic Mass, high-frowning there, of all ages from twenty years to four hundred and twenty;—beleaguered, in this its last hour, as we said, by mere Chaos come again! Ordnance of all calibres; throats of all capacities; men of all plans, every man his own engineer; seldom since the war of Pygmies and Cranes was there seen so anomalous a thing. Half-pay Elie is home for a suit of regimentals; no one would heed him in colored clothes; half-pay Hulin is haranguing Gardes Françaises in the Place de Grève. Frantic patriots pick up the grape-shots; bear them, still hot (or seemingly so), to the Hôtel-de-Ville:—Paris, you perceive, is to be burnt! Flesselles is 'pale to the very lips,' for the roar of the multitude grows deep. Paris wholly has got to the acme of its frenzy; whirled, all ways, by panic madness. At every street-barricade, there whirls simmering a minor whirlpool,—strengthening the barricade, since God knows what is coming; and all minor whirlpools play distractedly into that grand Fire-Maelstrom which is lashing round the Bastille.

And so it lashes and it roars. Cholat the wine-merchant has become an impromptu cannoneer. See Georget of the marine service, fresh from Brest, ply the King of Siam's cannon. Singular (if we were not used to the like). Georget lay, last night, taking his ease at his inn; the King of Siam's cannon also lay, knowing nothing of *him*, for a hundred years; yet now, at the right instant, they have got together, and discourse eloquent music. For hearing what was toward, Georget sprang from the Brest Diligence, and ran. Gardes Françaises, also, will be here, with real artillery: were not the walls so thick!—Upward from the Esplanade, horizontally from all neighboring roofs and windows, flashes one irregular deluge of musketry, without effect. The Invalides lie flat, firing comparatively at their ease from behind stone; hardly through port-holes show the tip of a nose. We fall, shot; and make no impression!

Let conflagration rage; of whatsoever is combustible! Guard-rooms are burnt, Invalides mess-rooms. A distracted 'Peruke-maker with two fiery torches' is for burning 'the saltpetres of the Arsenal,' had not a woman run screaming; had not a Patriot, with some tincture of Natural Philosophy, instantly struck the wind out of him (butt of musket on pit of stomach), overturned barrels, and stayed the devouring element. A young beautiful lady, seized, escaping, in these Outer Courts, and thought falsely to be De Launay's daughter, shall be burnt in De Launay's sight; she lies, swooned, on a *paillasse;* but again a Patriot—it is brave Aubin Bonnemère, the old soldier—dashes in, and rescues her. Straw is burnt; three cartloads of it, hauled hither, go up in white smoke; almost to the choking of Patriotism itself; so that Elie had, with singed brows, to drag back one cart, and Réole the 'gigantic haberdasher' another. Smoke as of Tophet; confusion as of Babel; noise as of the Crack of Doom!

Blood flows; the aliment of new madness. The wounded are carried into houses of the Rue Cerisaie; the dying leave their last mandate not to yield till the accursed Stronghold fall. And yet, alas! how fall? The walls are so thick! Deputations, three in number, arrive from the Hôtel-de-Ville; Abbé Fauchet (who was of one) can say with what almost superhuman courage of benevolence. These wave their Town-flag in the arched Gateway, and stand, rolling their drum, but to no purpose. In such Crack of Doom, De Launay cannot hear them, dare not believe them; they return, with justified rage, the whew of lead still singing in their ears. What to do? The Firemen are here, squirting with their fire-pumps on the Invalides cannon, to wet the touchholes; they unfortunately cannot squirt so high; but produce only clouds of spray. Individuals of classical knowledge propose *catapults*. Santerre, the sonorous Brewer of the Suburb Saint-Antoine, advises rather that the place be fired by a 'mixture of phosphorus and oil of turpentine spouted up through forcing-pumps.' O Spinola-Santerre, hast thou the mixture *ready*? Every man his own engineer! And still the fire-deluge abates not; even women are firing, and Turks; at least one woman (with her sweetheart), and one Turk. Gardes Françaises have come; real cannon, real cannoneers. Usher Maillard is busy; half-pay Elie, half-pay Hulin, rage in the midst of thousands.

How the great Bastille clock ticks (inaudible) in its Inner Court, there, at its ease, hour after hour; as if nothing special, for it or the world, were passing! It tolled One when the firing began, and is now pointing toward Five, and still the firing slakes not.—Far down, in their vaults, the seven Prisoners hear muffled din as of earthquakes; their Turnkeys answer vaguely.

Woe to thee, De Launay, with thy poor hundred Invalides! Broglie is distant, and his ears heavy; Besenval hears, but can send no help. One poor troop of Hussars has crept, reconnoitring, cautiously along the Quais, as far as the Pont Neuf. 'We are come to join you,' said the Captain; for the crowd seems shoreless. A large-headed dwarfish individual, of smoke-bleared aspect, shambles forward, opening his blue lips, for there is sense in him; and croaks, 'Alight then, and give up your arms!' The Hussar-Captain is too happy to be escorted to the barriers and dismissed on parole. Who the squat individual was? Men answer, It is M. Marat, author of the excellent pacific 'Avis au Peuple'! Great, truly, O thou remarkable Dogleech, is this thy day of emergence and newbirth; and yet this same day come four years!—But let the curtains of the Future hang.

What shall De Launay do? One thing only De Launay could have done: what he said he would do. Fancy him sitting, from the first, with lighted taper, within arm's-length of the Powder-Magazine; motionless, like old Roman Senator, or Bronze Lamp-holder; coldly apprising Thuriot, and all men, by a slight motion of his eye, what his resolution was:—Harmless he sat there, while unharmed; but the King's Fortress, meanwhile, could, might, would, or should in nowise be surrendered save to the King's Messenger; one old man's life is worthless, so it be lost with honor; but think, ye brawling *canaille*, how will it be when a whole Bastille springs skyward? In such statuesque, taper-holding attitude, one fancies De Launay might have left Thuriot, the red clerks of the Basoche, Curé of Saint-Stephen, and all the tagrag and bobtail of the world, to work their will!

And, yet, withal, he could not do it. Hast thou considered how each man's heart is so tremulously responsive to the hearts of all men? Hast thou noted how omnipotent is the very sound of many men? How their shriek of indignation palsies the strong soul; their howl of contumely withers with unfelt pangs? The Ritter Gluck confessed that the ground-tone of the noblest passage in one of his noblest Operas was the voice of the populace he had heard at Vienna, crying to their Kaiser, Bread! Bread! Great is the combined voice of men, the utterance of their *instincts*, which are truer than their *thoughts*; it is the greatest a man encounters, among the sounds and shadows which make up this World of Time. He who can resist that, has his footing somewhere *beyond* Time. De Launay could not do it. Distracted, he hovers between two; hopes in the middle of despair; surrenders not his Fortress; declares that he will blow it up, seizes torches to blow it up, and does not blow it. Unhappy old De Launay, it is the death-agony of thy Bastille and thee! Jail, Jailoring, and Jailor, all three, such as they may have been, must finish.

For four hours now has the World-Bedlam roared; call it the World-Chimæra, blowing fire! The poor Invalides have sunk under their battlements, or rise only with reversed muskets; they have made a white flag of napkins; go beating the *chamade*, or seeming to beat, for one can hear nothing. The very Swiss at the Portcullis look weary of firing; disheartened in the fire-deluge; a port-hole at the drawbridge is opened, as by one that would speak. See Huissier Maillard, the shifty man! On his plank swinging over the abyss of that stone ditch; plank resting on parapet, balanced by weight of Patriots, he hovers perilous; such a Dove toward such an Ark! Deftly, thou shifty Usher; one man already fell; and lies smashed, far down there, against the masonry! Usher Maillard falls not; deftly, unerring, he walks, with outspread palm. The Swiss holds a paper through his port-hole; the shifty Usher snatches it and returns. Terms of surrender, Pardon, immunity to all! Are they accepted? '*Foi d'officier*, On the word of an officer,' answers halfpay Hulin, or half-pay Elie—for men do not agree on it—'they are!' Sinks the drawbridge, —Usher Maillard bolting it when down; rushes in the living deluge; the Bastille is fallen! *Victoire! La Bastille est prise!*

(1837)

PAST AND PRESENT

BOOK III, CHAPTERS XI–XII

LABOR

FOR there is a perennial nobleness, and even sacredness, in Work. Were he never so benighted, forgetful of his high calling, there is always hope in a man that actually and earnestly works: in Idleness alone is there perpetual despair. Work, never so Mammonish, mean, *is* in communication with Nature; the real desire to get Work done will itself lead one more and more to truth, to Nature's appointments and regulations, which are truth.

The latest Gospel in this world is, Know thy work and do it. 'Know thyself': long enough has that poor 'self' of thine tormented thee; thou wilt never get to 'know' it, I believe! Think it not thy business, this of knowing thyself; thou art an unknowable individual: know what thou canst work at; and work at it, like a Hercules! That will be thy better plan.

It has been written, 'an endless significance lies in Work'; a man perfects himself by working. Foul jungles are cleared away, fair seedfields rise instead, and stately cities; and withal the man himself first ceases to be a jungle and foul unwholesome desert thereby. Consider how, even in the meanest sorts of Labor, the whole soul of a man is composed into a kind of real harmony, the instant he sets himself to work! Doubt, Desire, Sorrow, Remorse, Indignation, Despair itself, all these like helldogs lie beleaguering the soul of the poor dayworker, as of every man: but he bends himself with free valor against his task, and all these are stilled, all these shrink murmuring far off into their caves. The man is now a man. The blessed glow of Labor in him, is it not as purifying fire, wherein all poison is burnt up, and of sour smoke itself there is made bright blessed flame!

Destiny, on the whole, has no other way of cultivating us. A formless Chaos, once set it revolving, grows round and ever rounder; ranges itself, by mere force of gravity, into strata, spherical courses; is no longer a Chaos, but a round compacted World. What would become of the Earth, did she cease to revolve? In the poor old Earth, so long as she revolves, all inequalities, irregularities disperse themselves; all irregularities are incessantly becoming regular. Hast thou looked on the Potter's wheel,—one of the venerablest objects; old as the Prophet Ezechiel and far older? Rude lumps of clay, how they spin themselves up, by mere quick whirling, into beautiful circular dishes. And fancy the most assiduous Potter, but without his wheel; reduced to make dishes or rather amorphous botches, by mere kneading and baking! Even such a Potter were Destiny, with a human soul that would rest and lie at ease, that would not work and spin! Of an idle unrevolving man the kindest Destiny, like the most assiduous Potter without wheel, can bake and knead nothing other than a botch; let her spend on him what expensive coloring, what gilding and enameling she will, he is but a botch. Not a dish; no, a bulging, kneaded, crooked, shambling, squint-cornered, amorphous botch,—a mere enameled vessel of dishonor! Let the idle think of this.

Blessed is he who has found his work; let him ask no other blessedness. He has a work, a life-purpose; he has found it, and will follow it! How, as a free-flowing channel, dug and torn by noble force through the sour mud-swamp of one's existence, like an ever-deepening river there, it runs and flows;—draining-off the sour festering water, gradually from the root of the remotest grass-blade; making, instead of pestilential swamp, a green fruitful meadow with its clear-flowing stream. How blessed for the meadow itself, let the stream and *its* value be great or small! Labor is Life: from the inmost heart of the Worker rises his god-given Force, the sacred celestial Life-essence breathed into him by Almighty God; from his inmost heart awakens him to all nobleness,—to all knowledge, 'self-knowledge' and much else, so soon as Work fitly begins. Knowledge? The knowledge that will hold good in working, cleave thou to that; for Nature herself accredits that, says Yea to that. Properly thou hast no other knowledge but what thou hast got by working: the rest is yet all a hypothesis of knowledge; a thing to be argued of in schools, a thing floating in the clouds, in endless logic-vortices, till we try it and fix it. 'Doubt, of whatever kind, can be ended by Action alone.'

And again, hast thou valued Patience, Courage, Perseverance, Openness to light; readiness to own thyself mistaken, to do better next time? All these, all virtues, in wrestling with the dim brute Powers of Fact, in ordering of thy fellows in such wrestle, there and elsewhere not at all, thou wilt continually learn. Set down a brave Sir Christopher in the middle of black ruined Stone-heaps, of foolish unarchitectural Bishops, redtape Officials, idle Nell-Gwyn Defenders of the Faith; and see whether he will ever raise a Paul's Cathedral out of all that, yea or no! Rough, rude, contradictory are all things and persons, from the mutinous masons and Irish hodmen, up to the idle Nell-Gwyn Defenders, to blustering redtape Officials, foolish unarchitectural Bishops. All these things and persons are there not for Christopher's sake and his Cathedral's; they are there for their own sake mainly! Christopher will have to conquer and constrain all these,—if he be able. All these are against him. Equitable Nature herself, who carries her mathematics and architectonics not on the face of her, but deep in the hidden heart of her,—Nature herself is but partially for him; will be wholly against him, if he constrain her not! His very money, where is it to come from? The pious munificence of England lies far-scattered, distant, unable to speak, and say, 'I am here';—must be spoken to before it can speak. Pious munificence, and all help, is so silent, invisible like the gods; impediment, contradictions manifold are so loud and near! O brave Sir Christopher, trust thou in those notwithstanding, and front all these; understand all these; by valiant patience, noble effort, insight, by man's-strength, vanquish and compel all these,—and, on the whole, strike down victoriously the last topstone of that Paul's Edifice; thy monument for certain centuries, the stamp 'Great Man' impressed very legibly on Portland-stone there!—

Yes, all manner of help, and pious response from Men or Nature, is always what we call silent; cannot speak or come to light, till it be seen, till it be spoken to. Every noble work is at first 'impossible.' In very truth, for every noble work the possibilities will lie diffused through Immensity; inarticulate, undiscoverable except to faith. Like Gideon thou shalt spread out thy fleece at the door of thy tent; see whether under the wide arch of Heaven there be any bounteous moisture, or none. Thy heart and life-purpose shall be as a miraculous Gideon's fleece, spread out in silent appeal to Heaven: and from the kind Immensities, what from the poor unkind Localities and town and country Parishes there never could, blessed dew-moisture to suffice thee shall have fallen!

Work is of a religious nature:—work is of a *brave* nature; which it is the aim of all religion to be. All work of man is as the swimmer's: a waste ocean threatens to devour him; if he front it not bravely, it will keep its word. By incessant wise defiance of it, lusty rebuke and buffet of it, behold how it loyally supports him, bears him as its conqueror along. 'It is so,' says Goethe, 'with all things that man undertakes in this world.'

Brave Sea-captain, Norse Sea-king,—Columbus, my hero, royalest Sea-king of all! it is no friendly environment this of thine, in the waste deep waters; around thee mutinous discouraged souls, behind thee disgrace and ruin, before thee the unpenetrated veil of Night. Brother, these wild water-mountains, bounding from their deep bases (ten miles deep, I am told), are not entirely there on thy behalf! Meseems *they* have other work than floating thee forward:—and the huge Winds, that sweep from Ursa Major to the Tropics and Equators, dancing their giant-waltz through the kingdoms of Chaos and Immensity, they care little about filling rightly or filling wrongly the small shoulder-of-mutton sails in this cockle-skiff of thine! Thou art not among articulate-speaking friends, my brother; thou art among immeasurable dumb monsters, tumbling, howling wide as the world here. Secret, far off, invisible to all hearts but thine, there lies a help in them: see how thou wilt get at that. Patiently thou wilt wait till the mad Southwester spend itself, saving thyself by dextrous science of defense, the while: valiantly, with swift decision, wilt thou strike in, when the favoring East, the Possible, springs up. Mutiny of men thou wilt sternly repress; weakness, despondency, thou wilt cheerily encourage: thou wilt swallow down complaint, unreason, weariness, weakness of others and thyself;—how much wilt thou swallow down! There shall be a depth of Silence in thee, deeper than this Sea, which is but ten miles deep: a Silence unsoundable; known to God only. Thou shalt be a Great Man. Yes, my World-Soldier, thou of the World Marine-service,—thou wilt have to be *greater* than this tumultuous unmeasured World here round thee is; thou, in thy strong soul, as with wrestler's arms, shalt embrace it, harness it down; and make it bear thee on,— to new Americas, or whither God wills!

REWARD

'RELIGION,' I said; for, properly speaking, all true Work is Religion: and whatsoever Religion is not Work may go and dwell among the Brahmins, Antinomians, Spinning Dervishes, or where it will; with me it shall have no harbor. Admirable was that of the old Monks, '*Laborare est Orare*, Work is Worship.'

Older than all preached Gospels was this unpreached, inarticulate, but ineradicable, forever-enduring Gospel: Work, and therein have well-being. Man, Son of Earth and of Heaven, lies there not, in the innermost heart of thee, a Spirit of active Method, a Force for Work;—and burns like a painfully-smoldering fire, giving thee no rest till thou unfold it, till thou write it down in beneficent Facts around thee! What is unmethodic, waste, thou shalt make methodic, regulated, arable; obedient and productive to thee. Wheresoever thou findest Disorder, there is thy eternal enemy; attack him swiftly, subdue him; make Order of him, the subject not of Chaos, but of Intelligence, Divinity and Thee! The thistle that grows in thy path, dig it out, that a blade of useful grass, a drop of nourishing milk, may grow there instead. The waste cotton-shrub, gather its waste white down, spin it, weave it; that, in place of idle litter, there may be folded webs, and the naked skin of man be covered.

But above all, where thou findest Ignorance, Stupidity, Brute-mindedness,—yes, there, with or without Church-tithes and Shovel-hat, with or without Talfourd-Mahon Copyrights, or were it with mere dungeons and gibbets and crosses, attack it, I say; smite it wisely, unweariedly, and rest not while thou livest and it lives; but smite, smite, in the name of God! The Highest God, as I understand it, does audibly so command thee; still audibly, if thou have ears to hear. He, even He, with his *un*spoken voice, awfuler than any Sinai thunders or syllabled speech of Whirlwinds; for the SILENCE of deep Eternities, of Worlds from beyond the morning-stars, does it not speak to thee? The unborn Ages; the old Graves, with their long-moldering dust, the very tears that wetted it now all dry,— do not these speak to thee, what ear hath not heard? The deep Death-kingdoms, the Stars in their never-resting courses, all Space and all Time, proclaim it to thee in continual silent admonition. Thou too, if ever man should, shalt work while it is called To-day. For the Night cometh, wherein no man can work.

All true Work is sacred; in all true Work, were it but true hand-labor, there is something of divineness. Labor, wide as the Earth, has its summit in Heaven. Sweat of the brow; and up from that to sweat of the brain, sweat of the heart; which includes all Kepler calculations, Newton meditations, all Sciences, all spoken Epics, all acted Heroisms, Martyrdoms,—up to that 'Agony of bloody sweat,' which all men have called divine! O brother, if this is not 'worship,' then I say, the more pity for worship; for this is the noblest thing yet discovered under God's sky. Who art thou that complainest of thy life of toil? Complain not. Look up, my wearied brother; see thy fellow Workmen there, in God's Eternity; surviving there, they alone surviving: sacred Band of the Immortals, celestial Bodyguard of the Empire of Mankind. Even in the weak Human Memory they survive so long, as saints, as heroes, as gods; they alone surviving; peopling, they alone, the unmeasured solitudes of Time! To thee Heaven, though severe, is *not* unkind; Heaven is kind,—as a noble Mother; as that Spartan Mother, saying while she gave her son his shield, 'With it, my son, or upon it!' Thou too shalt return *home* in honor; to thy far-distant home, in honor; doubt it not,—if in the battle thou keep thy shield! Thou, in the Eternities and deepest Death-kingdoms, art not an alien; thou everywhere art a denizen! Complain not; the very Spartans did not *complain*.

And who art thou that braggest of thy life of Idleness; complacently showest thy bright gilt equipages; sumptuous cushions; appliances for folding of the hands to mere sleep? Looking up, looking down, around, behind or before, discernest thou, if it be not in Mayfair alone, any *idle* hero, saint, god, or even devil? Not a vestige of one. In the Heavens, in the Earth, in the Waters under the Earth, is none like unto thee. Thou art an original figure in this Creation; a denizen in Mayfair alone, in this extraordinary Century or Half-Century alone! One monster there is in the world: the idle man. What is his 'Religion'? That Nature is a Phantasm, where cunning beggary or thievery may sometimes find good victual. That God is a lie; and that Man and his Life are a lie.—Alas, alas, who of us *is* there that can say, I have worked? The faithfulest of us are unprofitable servants; the faithfulest of us know that best. The faithfulest of us may say, with sad and true old Samuel, 'Much of my life has been trifled away!' But he that has, and except 'on public occasions' professes to have, no function but that of going idle in a graceful or graceless manner; and of begetting sons to go idle; and to address Chief Spinners and Diggers, who at least *are* spinning and digging, 'Ye scandalous persons who produce too much'—My Corn-Law friends, on what imaginary still richer Eldorados, and true iron-spikes with law of gravitation, are ye rushing!

As to the Wages of Work there might innumerable things be said; there will and must yet innumerable things be said and spoken, in St. Stephen's and out of St. Stephen's; and gradually not a few things be ascertained and written, on Law-parchment, concerning this very matter:—'Fair day's-wages for a fair day's-work' is the most unrefusable demand! Money-wages 'to the extent of keeping your worker alive that he may work more'; these, unless you mean to dismiss him straightway out of this world, are indispensable alike to the noblest Worker and to the least noble!

One thing only I will say here, in special reference to the former class, the noble and noblest; but throwing light on all the other classes and their arrangements of this difficult matter: The 'wages' of every noble Work do yet lie in Heaven or else Nowhere. Not in Bank-of-England bills, in Owen's Labor-bank, or any most improved establishment of banking and money-changing, needest thou, heroic soul, present thy account of earnings. Human banks and labor-banks know thee not; or know thee after generations and centuries have passed away, and thou art clean gone from 'rewarding,'—all manner of bank-drafts, shop-tills, and Downing-street Exchequers lying very invisible, so far from thee! Nay, at bottom, dost thou need any reward? Was it thy aim and life-purpose to be filled with good things for thy heroism; to have a life of pomp and ease, and be what men call 'happy,' in this world, or in any other world? I answer for thee deliberately, No. The whole spiritual secret of the new epoch lies in this, that thou canst answer for thyself, with thy whole clearness of head and heart, deliberately, No!

* * *

(1843)

JOHN RUSKIN (1819-1900)

Ruskin's literary career divides itself into two periods: in the first, his supreme interest was art; in the second, his attention was chiefly directed to social problems and ethical teaching. When he was only seventeen his indignation was aroused by the current depreciation of the great landscape painter, Turner, to whom he wrote offering his pen in defence. The offer was declined, but this youthful project was realized in *Modern Painters*, the first volume of which Ruskin published when he was twenty-four, and the sixth when he was forty-one. His main principles are that truth is the standard of all excellence, and nature the inspiration of all great art; he applies these tests to establish the conclusion that Turner is the only perfect landscape painter the world has ever seen. In the midst of this undertaking, which was expanded far beyond its original object, Ruskin wrote *The Seven Lamps of Architecture*—(Sacrifice, Truth, Power, Beauty, Life, Memory, Obedience). He developed his ideas further in *The Stones of Venice*, in which he defended Gothic architecture on the same grounds as he had defended Turner—truthfulness and the love of nature. These works and the successive volumes of *Modern Painters* gave him an unprecedented position as an art critic, but he was already beginning to turn his attention to other subjects. He was greatly influenced by Carlyle, with whom he formed a close friendship; and he was deeply interested in the Workmen's College conducted by Maurice and Kingsley, writing for his pupils there *The Elements of Drawing* and *The Elements of Perspective*. In 1857 he said that the kind of painting they wanted in London was painting cheeks red with health, and in the same year he gave fuller utterance to his new ideas in a course of lectures at Manchester on 'The Political Economy of Art.' Four essays which appeared in *The Cornhill Magazine* in 1860 (afterwards republished under the title *Unto This Last*) were even more outspoken, and caused so much dissatisfaction that the editor refused to continue the series; *Fraser's Magazine* a little later took the same course with the papers now included in Ruskin's works as *Munera Pulveris*. He advocated the application of Christian principles to the organization of labor, and condemned the accepted political economy of the day as self-seeking and unsound. His idea of political economy was that it was not an abstract science, but 'a system of conduct founded on the sciences, and impossible, except under certain conditions of moral culture.' He accordingly devoted his main energies henceforth to arousing the upper classes to a sense of their duties to the poor, and helping the lower classes to realize their opportunities. To this end he wrote, gave his money, and labored with his own hands. *Time and Tide by Weare and Tyne* and *Fors Clavigera* are letters to workingmen; *Sesame and Lilies* and *The Crown of Wild Olive* are lectures delivered in various parts of England, dealing with political, social, and economical questions. He held the Professorship of Fine Art at Oxford for many years, and his courses there were the foundation of several of his later works on art; after his retirement he wrote a series of sketches of his past life under the title *Præterita* (things gone by). His last years were spent in seclusion at Brantwood, on the shores of Coniston Water in the Lake District. On his eightieth birthday Edward, Prince of Wales, headed an address which was signed by the most distinguished men of the time to assure Ruskin of their 'deepest respect and sincerest affection.' While there have been wide differences of opinion about his theories of art and his views of political economy and social reform, his entire singleness of aim and his preëminence as a writer of English prose are beyond dispute.

TRAFFIC

(*A lecture delivered in the Town Hall, Bradford, afterwards included in* The Crown of Wild Olive)

My good Yorkshire friends, you asked me down here among your hills that I might talk to you about this Exchange you are going to build: but earnestly and seriously asking you to pardon me, I am going to do nothing of the kind. I cannot talk, or at least can say very little, about this same Exchange. I must talk of quite other things, though not willingly;—I could not deserve your pardon, if when you invited me to speak on one subject, I *wilfully* spoke on another. But I cannot speak, to purpose, of anything about which I do not care; and most simply and sorrowfully I have to tell you, in the outset, that I do *not* care about this Exchange of yours.

If, however, when you sent me your invitation, I had answered, 'I won't come, I don't care about the Exchange of Bradford,' you would have been justly offended with me, not knowing the reasons of so blunt a carelessness. So I have come down, hoping that you will patiently let me tell you why, on this, and many other such occasions, I now remain silent, when formerly I should have caught at the opportunity of speaking to a gracious audience.

In a word, then, I do not care about this Exchange,—because *you* don't; and because you know perfectly well I cannot make you. Look at the essential conditions of the case, which you, as business men, know perfectly well, though perhaps you think I forget them. You are going to spend £30,000, which to you, collectively, is nothing; the buying a new coat is, as to the cost of it, a much more important matter of consideration to me than building a new Exchange is to you. But you think you may as well have the right thing for your money. You know there are a great many odd styles of architecture about; you don't want to do anything ridiculous; you hear of me, among others, as a respectable architectural man-milliner; and you send for me, that I may tell you the leading fashion; and what is, in our shops, for the moment, the newest and sweetest thing in pinnacles.

Now, pardon me for telling you frankly, you cannot have good architecture merely by asking people's advice on occasion. All good architecture is the expression of national life and character; and it is produced by a prevalent and eager national taste, or desire for beauty. And I want you to think a little of the deep significance of this word 'taste;' for no statement of mine has been more earnestly or oftener controverted than that good taste is essentially a moral quality. 'No,' say many of my antagonists, 'taste is one thing, morality is another. Tell us what is pretty: we shall be glad to know that; but we need no sermons even were you able to preach them, which may be doubted.'

Permit me, therefore, to fortify this old dogma of mine somewhat. Taste is not only a part and an index of morality—it is the ONLY morality. The first, and last, and closest trial question to any living creature is, 'What do you like?' Tell me what you like, and I'll tell you what you are. Go out into the street, and ask the first man or woman you meet, what their 'taste' is, and if they answer candidly, you know them, body and soul. 'You, my friend in the rags, with the unsteady gait, what do *you* like?' 'A pipe and a quartern of gin.' I know you. 'You, good woman, with the quick step and tidy bonnet, what do you like?' 'A swept hearth and a clean tea-table, and my husband opposite me, and a baby at my breast.' Good, I know you also. 'You, little girl with the golden hair and the soft eyes, what do you like?' 'My canary, and a run among the wood hyacinths.' 'You, little boy with the dirty hands and the low forehead, what do you like?' 'A shy at the sparrows, and a game at pitch farthing.' Good; we know them all now. What more need we ask?

'Nay,' perhaps you answer: 'we need rather to ask what these people and children do, than what they like. If they *do* right, it is no matter that they like what is wrong; and if they *do* wrong, it is no matter that they like what is right. Doing is the great thing; and it does not matter that the man likes drinking, so that he does not drink; nor that the little girl likes to be kind to her canary, if she will not learn her lessons; nor that the little boy likes throwing stones at the sparrows, if he goes to the Sunday School.' Indeed, for a short time, and in a provisional sense, this is true. For if, resolutely, people do what is right, in time they come to like doing it. But they only are in a right moral state when they *have* come to like doing it; and as long as they don't like it, they are still in a vicious state. The man is not in health of body who is always thinking of the bottle in the cupboard, though he bravely bears his thirst; but the man who heartily enjoys water in the morning and wine in the evening, each in its proper quantity and time. And the entire object of true education is to make people not merely *do* the right things, but *enjoy* the right things—not merely industrious, but to love industry—not merely learned, but to love knowledge—not merely pure, but to love purity—not merely just, but to hunger and thirst after justice.

But you may answer or think, 'Is the liking for outside ornaments,—for pictures, or statues, or furniture, or architecture,—a moral quality?' Yes, most surely, if a rightly set liking. Taste for *any* pictures or statues is not a moral quality, but taste for good ones is. Only here again we have to define the word 'good.' I don't mean by 'good,' clever—or learned—or difficult in the doing. Take a picture by Teniers, of sots quarreling over their dice: it is an entirely clever picture; so clever that nothing in its kind has ever been done equal to it; but it is also an entirely base and evil picture. It is an expression of delight in the prolonged contemplation of a vile thing, and delight in that is an 'unmannered,' or 'immoral' quality. It is 'bad taste' in the profoundest sense—it is the taste of the devils. On the other hand, a picture of Titian's, or a Greek statue, or a Greek coin, or a Turner landscape, expresses delight in the perpetual contemplation of a good and perfect thing. That is an entirely moral quality—it is the taste of the angels. And all delight in fine art, and all love of it, resolve themselves into simple love of that which deserves love. That deserving is the quality which we call 'loveliness'—(we ought to have an opposite word, hateliness, to be said of the things which deserve to be hated); and it is not an indifferent nor optional thing whether we love this or that; but it is just the vital function of all our being. What we *like* determines what we *are*, and is the sign of what we are; and to teach taste is inevitably to form character.

As I was thinking over this, in walking up Fleet Street the other day, my eye caught the title of a book standing open in a bookseller's window. It was—'On the necessity of the diffusion of taste among all classes.' 'Ah,' I thought to myself, 'my classifying friend, when you have diffused your taste, where will your classes be? The man who likes what you like, belongs to the same class with you, I think. Inevitably so. You may put him to other work if you choose; but, by the condition you have brought him into, he will dislike the other work as much as you would yourself. You get hold of a scavenger, or a costermonger, who enjoyed the Newgate Calendar for literature, and "Pop goes the Weasel" for music. You think you can make him like Dante and Beethoven? I wish you joy of your lessons; but if you do, you have made a gentleman of him:—he won't like to go back to his costermongering.'

And so completely and unexceptionally is this so, that, if I had time to-night, I could show you that a nation cannot be affected by any vice, or weakness, without expressing it, legibly, and forever, either in bad art, or by want of art; and that there is no national virtue, small or great, which is not manifestly expressed in all the art which circumstances enable the people possessing that virtue to produce. Take, for instance, your great English virtue of enduring and patient courage. You have at present in England only one art of any consequence—that is, iron-working. You know thoroughly well how to cast and hammer iron. Now, do you think in those masses of lava which you build volcanic cones to melt, and which you forge at the mouths of the Infernos you have created; do you think, on those iron plates, your courage and endurance are not written forever—not merely with an iron pen, but on iron parchment? And take also your great English vice—European vice—vice of all the world—vice of all other worlds that roll or shine in heaven, bearing with them yet the atmosphere of hell—the vice of jealousy, which brings competition into your commerce, treachery into your councils, and dishonor into your wars—that vice which has rendered for you, and for your next neighboring nation, the daily occupations of existence no longer possible, but with the mail upon your breasts and the sword loose in its sheath; so that at last, you have realized for all the multitudes of the two great peoples who lead the so-called civilization of the earth,—you have realized for them all, I say, in person and in policy, what was once true only of the rough Border riders of your Cheviot hills—

They carved at the meal
With gloves of steel,
And they drank the red wine through the helmet barred;—

do you think that this national shame and dastardliness of heart are not written as legibly on every rivet of your iron armor as the strength of the right hands that forged it?

Friends, I know not whether this thing be the more ludicrous or the more melancholy. It is quite unspeakably both. Suppose, instead of being now sent for by you, I had been sent for by some private gentleman, living in a suburban house, with his garden separated only by a fruit-wall from his next door neighbor's; and he had called me to consult with him on the furnishing of his drawing room. I begin looking about me, and find the walls rather bare; I think such and such a paper might be desirable—perhaps a little fresco here and there on the ceiling —a damask curtain or so at the windows. 'Ah,' says my employer, 'damask curtains, indeed! That's all very fine, but you know I can't afford that kind of thing just now!' 'Yet the world credits you with a splendid income!' 'Ah, yes,' says my friend, 'but do you know, at present, I am obliged to spend it nearly all in steel-traps?' 'Steel-traps! for whom?' 'Why, for that fellow on the other side of the wall, you know: we're very good friends, but we are obliged to keep our traps set on both sides of the wall; we could not possibly keep on friendly terms without them, and our spring guns. The worst of it is, we are both clever fellows enough; and there's never a day passes that we don't find out a new trap, or a new gun-barrel, or something; we spend about fifteen millions a year each in our traps, take it all together; and I don't see how we're to do with less.' A highly comic state of life for two private gentlemen! but for two nations, it seems to me, not wholly comic? Bedlam would be comic, perhaps, if there were only one madman in it; and your Christmas pantomine is comic, when there is only one clown in it; but when the whole world turns clown, and paints itself red with its own heart's blood instead of vermilion, it is something else than comic, I think.

Mind, I know a great deal of this is play, and willingly allow for that. You don't know what to do with yourselves for a sensation: foxhunting and cricketing will not carry you through the whole of this unendurably long mortal life: you liked pop-guns when you were schoolboys, and rifles and Armstrongs are only the same things better made: but then the worst of it is, that what was play to you when boys, was not play to the sparrows; and what is play to you now, is not play to the small birds of State neither; and for the black eagles, you are somewhat shy of taking shots at them, if I mistake not.

I must get back to the matter in hand, however. Believe me, without farther instance, I could show you, in all time, that every nation's vice, or virtue, was written in its art: the soldiership of early Greece; the sensuality of late Italy; the visionary religion of Tuscany; the splendid human energy and beauty of Venice. I have no time to do this tonight (I have done it elsewhere before now); but I proceed to apply the principle to ourselves in a more searching manner.

I notice that among all the new buildings which cover your once wild hills, churches and schools are mixed in due, that is to say, in large proportion, with your mills and mansions; and I notice also that the churches and schools are almost always Gothic, and the mansions and mills are never Gothic. Will you allow me to ask precisely the meaning of this? For, remember, it is peculiarly a modern phenomenon. When Gothic was invented, houses were Gothic as well as churches; and when the Italian style superseded the Gothic, churches were Italian as well as houses. If there is a Gothic spire to the cathedral of Antwerp, there is a Gothic belfry to the Hôtel de Ville at Brussels: if Inigo Jones builds an Italian Whitehall, Sir Christopher Wren builds an Italian St. Paul's. But now you live under one school of architecture, and worship under another. What do you mean by doing this? Am I to understand that you are thinking of changing your architecture back to Gothic; and that you treat your churches experimentally, because it does not matter what mistakes you make in a church? Or am I to understand that you consider Gothic a preeminently sacred and beautiful mode of building, which you think, like the fine frankincense, should be mixed for the tabernacle only, and reserved for your religious services? For if this be the feeling, though it may seem at first as if it were graceful and reverent, at the root of the matter, it signifies neither more nor less than that you have separated your religion from your life.

For consider what a wide significance this fact has; and remember that it is not you only, but all the people of England, who are behaving thus just now.

You have all got into the habit of calling the church 'the house of God.' I have seen, over the doors of many churches, the legend actually carved, '*This* is the house of God, and this is the gate of heaven.' Now, note where that legend comes from, and of what place it was first spoken. A boy leaves his father's house to go on a long journey on foot, to visit his uncle; he has to cross a wild hill-desert; just as if one of your own boys had to cross the wolds to visit an uncle at Carlisle. The second or third day your boy finds himself somewhere between Hawes and Brough, in the midst of the moors, at sunset. It is stony ground, and boggy; he cannot go one foot farther that night. Down he lies, to sleep, on Wharnside, where best he may, gathering a few of the stones together to put under his head;—so wild the place is, he cannot get anything but stones. And there, lying under the broad night, he has a dream; and he sees a ladder set up on the earth, and the top of it reaches to heaven, and the angels of God are seen ascending and descending upon it. And when he wakes out of his sleep, he says, 'How dreadful is this place; surely, this is none other than the house of God, and this is the gate of heaven.' This PLACE, observe; not this church; not this city; not this stone, even, which he puts up for a memorial—the piece of flint on which his head has lain. But this *place;* this windy slope of Wharnside; this moorland hollow, torrent-bitten, snow-blighted; this *any* place where God lets down the ladder. And how are you to know where that will be? or how are you to determine where it may be, but by being ready for it always? Do you know where the lightning is to fall next? You *do* know that, partly; you can guide the lightning; but you cannot guide the going forth of the Spirit, which is as that lightning when it shines from the east to the west.

But the perpetual and insolent warping of that strong verse to serve a merely ecclesiastical purpose, is only one of the thousand instances in which we sink back into gross Judaism. We call our churches 'temples.' Now, you know perfectly well they are *not* temples. They have never had, never can have, anything whatever to do with temples. They are 'synagogues'—'gathering places'—where you gather yourselves together as an assembly; and by not calling them so, you again miss the force of another mighty text—'Thou, when thou prayest, shalt not be as the hypocrites are; for they love to pray standing in the *churches*' (we should translate it), 'that they may be seen of men. But thou, when thou prayest, enter into thy closet, and when thou hast shut thy door, pray to thy Father,'—which is, not in chancel nor in aisle, but 'in secret.'

Now, you *feel*, as I say this to you—I know you feel—as if I were trying to take away the honor of your churches. Not so; I am trying to prove to you the honor of your houses and your hills; not that the Church is not sacred—but that the whole Earth is. I would have you feel, what careless, what constant, what infectious sin there is in all modes of thought, whereby, in calling your churches only 'holy,' you call your hearths and homes 'profane'; and have separated yourselves from the heathen by casting all your household gods to the ground, instead of recognizing, in the place of their many and feeble Lares, the presence of your One and Mighty Lord and Lar.

'But what has all this to do with our Exchange?' you ask me, impatiently. My dear friends, it has just everything to do with it; on these inner and great questions depend all the outer and little ones; and if you have asked me down here to speak to you, because you had before been interested in anything I have written, you must know that all I have yet said about architecture was to show this. The book I called 'The Seven Lamps' was to show that certain right states of temper and moral feeling were the magic powers by which all good architecture, without exception, had been produced. 'The Stones of Venice' had, from beginning to end, no other aim than to show that the Gothic architecture of Venice had arisen out of, and indicated in all its features, a state of pure national faith, and of domestic virtue; and that its Renaissance architecture had arisen out of, and in all its features indicated, a state of concealed national infidelity, and of domestic corruption. And now, you ask me what style is best to build in; and how can I answer, knowing the meaning of the two styles, but by another question—do you mean to build as Christians or as Infidels? And still more—do you mean to build as honest Christians or as honest Infidels? as thoroughly and confessedly either one or the other? You don't like to be asked such rude questions. I cannot help it; they are of much more importance than this Exchange business; and if they can be at once answered, the Exchange business settles itself in a moment But, before I press them farther, I must ask leave to explain one point clearly.

In all my past work, my endeavor has been to show that good architecture is essentially religious—the production of a faithful and virtuous, not of an infidel and corrupted people. But in the course of doing this, I have had also to show that good architecture is not *ecclesiastical*. People are so apt to look upon religion as the business of the clergy, not their own, that the moment they hear of anything depending on 'religion,' they think it must also have depended on the priesthood; and I have had to take what place was to be occupied between these two errors, and fight both, often with seeming contradiction. Good architecture is the work of good and believing men; therefore, you say, at least some people say, 'Good architecture must essentially have been the work of the clergy, not of the laity.' No—a thousand times no; good architecture [1] has always been the work of the commonalty, *not* of the clergy. What, you say, those glorious cathedrals—the pride of Europe —did their builders not form Gothic architecture? No; they corrupted Gothic architecture. Gothic was formed in the baron's castle, and the burgher's street. It was formed by the thoughts, and hands, and powers of free citizens and warrior kings. By the monk it was used as an instrument for the aid of his superstition; when that superstition became a beautiful madness, and the best hearts of Europe vainly dreamed and pined in the cloister, and vainly raged and perished in the crusade—through that fury of perverted faith and wasted war, the Gothic rose also to its loveliest, most fantastic, and, finally, most foolish dreams; and, in those dreams, was lost.

[1] And all other arts, for the most part; even of incredulous and secularly-minded commonalties.

I hope, now, that there is no risk of your misunderstanding me when I come to the gist of what I want to say to-night;—when I repeat, that every great national architecture has been the result and exponent of a great national religion. You can't have bits of it here, bits there —you must have it everywhere, or nowhere. It is not the monopoly of a clerical company—it is not the exponent of a theological dogma—it is not the hieroglyphic writing of an initiated priesthood; it is the manly language of a people inspired by resolute and common purpose, and rendering resolute and common fidelity to the legible laws of an undoubted God.

Now, there have as yet been three distinct schools of European architecture. I say, European, because Asiatic and African architectures belong so entirely to other races and climates, that there is no question of them here; only, in passing, I will simply assure you that whatever is good or great in Eygpt, and Syria, and India, is just good or great for the same reasons as the buildings on our side of the Bosphorus. We Europeans, then, have had three great religions: the Greek, which was the worship of the God of Wisdom and Power; the Medieval, which was the Worship of the God of Judgment and Consolation; the Renaissance, which was the worship of the God of Pride and Beauty; these three we have had—they are past,—and now, at last, we English have got a fourth religion, and a God of our own, about which I want to ask you. But I must explain these three old ones first.

I repeat, first, the Greeks essentially worshipped the God of Wisdom; so that whatever contended against their religion,—to the Jews a stumbling block,—was, to the Greeks—*Foolishness.*

The first Greek idea of Deity was that expressed in the word, of which we keep the remnant in our words '*Di*-urnal' and '*Di*-vine'— the god of *Day*, Jupiter the revealer. Athena is his daughter, but especially daughter of the Intellect, springing armed from the head. We are only with the help of recent investigation beginning to penetrate the depth of meaning couched under the Athenaic symbols: but I may note rapidly, that her ægis, the mantle with the serpent fringes, in which she often, in the best statues, is represented as folding up her left hand for better guard, and the Gorgon on her shield, are both representative mainly of the chilling horror and sadness (turning men to stone, as it were), of the outmost and superficial spheres of knowledge—that knowledge which separates, in bitterness, hardness, and sorrow, the heart of the full-grown man from the heart of the child. For out of imperfect knowledge spring terror, dissension, danger, and disdain; but from perfect knowledge, given by the full-revealed Athena, strength and peace, in sign of which she is crowned with the olive spray, and bears the resistless spear.

This, then, was the Greek conception of purest Deity, and every habit of life, and every form of his art developed themselves from the seeking this bright, serene, resistless wisdom; and setting himself, as a man, to do things evermore rightly and strongly; [1] not with any ardent affection or ultimate hope; but with a resolute and continent energy of will, as knowing that for failure there was no consolation, and for sin there was no remission. And the Greek architecture rose unerring, bright, clearly defined, and self-contained.

Next followed in Europe the great Christian faith, which was essentially the religion of Comfort. Its great doctrine is the remission of sins; for which cause it happens, too often, in certain phases of Christianity, that sin and sickness themselves are partly glorified, as if, the more you had to be healed of, the more divine was the healing. The practical result of this doctrine, in art, is a continual contemplation of sin and disease, and of imaginary states of purification from them; thus we have an architecture conceived in a mingled sentiment of melancholy and aspiration, partly severe, partly luxuriant, which will bend itself to every one of our needs, and every one of our fancies, and be strong or weak with us, as we are strong or weak ourselves. It is, of all architecture, the basest, when base people built it—of all, the noblest, when built by the noble.

And now note that both these religions— Greek and Medieval—perished by falsehood in their own main purpose. The Greek religion of Wisdom perished in a false philosophy—'Oppositions of science, falsely so called.' The Medieval religion of Consolation perished in false

---

[1] It is an error to suppose that the Greek worship, or seeking, was chiefly of Beauty. It was essentially of Rightness and Strength, founded on Forethought: the principal character of Greek art is not Beauty, but design: and the Dorian Apollo-worship and Athenian Virgin-worship are both expressions of adoration of divine Wisdom and Purity. Next to these great deities rank, in power over the national mind, Dionysus and Ceres, the givers of human strength and life: then, for heroic example, Hercules. There is no Venus-worship among the Greeks in the great times: and the Muses are essentially teachers of Truth, and of its harmonies. Compare *Aratra Pentelici*, § 200.

comfort; in remission of sins given lyingly. It was the selling of absolution that ended the Medieval faith; and I can tell you more, it is the selling of absolution which, to the end of time, will mark false Christianity. Pure Christianity gives her remission of sins only by *ending* them; but false Christianity gets her remission of sins by *compounding for* them. And there are many ways of compounding for them. We English have beautiful little quiet ways of buying absolution, whether in low Church, or high, far more cunning than any of Tetzel's trading.

Then, thirdly, there followed the religion of Pleasure, in which all Europe gave itself to luxury, ending in death. First, *bals masqués* in every saloon, and then guillotines in every square. And all these three worships issue in vast temple building. Your Greek worshipped Wisdom, and built you the Parthenon—the Virgin's temple. The Medieval worshipped Consolation, and built you Virgin temples also —but to our Lady of Salvation. Then the Revivalist worshipped beauty, of a sort, and built you Versailles, and the Vatican. Now, lastly, will you tell me what *we* worship, and what *we* build?

You know we are speaking always of the real, active, continual, national worship; that by which men act while they live; not that which they talk of when they die. Now, we have, indeed, a nominal religion, to which we pay tithes of property and sevenths of time; but we have also a practical and earnest religion, to which we devote nine-tenths of our property and sixth-sevenths of our time. And we dispute a great deal about the nominal religion; but we are all unanimous about this practical one, of which I think you will admit that the ruling goddess may be best generally described as the 'Goddess of Getting-on,' or 'Britannia of the Market.' The Athenians had an 'Athena Agoraia,' or Athena of the Market; but she was a subordinate type of their goddess, while our Britannia Agoraia is the principal type of ours. And all your great architectural works, are, of course, built to her. It is long since you built a great cathedral; and how you would laugh at me, if I proposed building a cathedral on the top of one of these hills of yours, to make it an Acropolis! But your railroad mounds, vaster than the walls of Babylon; your railroad stations, vaster than the temple of Ephesus, and innumerable; your chimneys how much more mighty and costly than cathedral spires! your harbor piers; your warehouses; your exchanges!—all these are built to your great Goddess of 'Getting-on'; and she has formed, and will continue to form, your architecture, as long as you worship her; and it is quite vain to ask me to tell you how to build to *her;* you know far better than I.

There might indeed, on some theories, be a conceivably good architecture for Exchanges— that is to say, if there were any heroism in the fact or deed of exchange, which might be typically carved on the outside of your building. For, you know, all beautiful architecture must be adorned with sculpture or painting; and for sculpture or painting, you must have a subject. And hitherto it has been a received opinion among the nations of the world that the only right subjects for either, were *heroisms* of some sort. Even on his pots and his flagons, the Greek put a Hercules slaying lions, or an Apollo slaying serpents, or Bacchus slaying melancholy giants, and earth-born despondencies. On his temples, the Greek put contests of great warriors in founding states, or of gods with evil spirits. On his houses and temples alike, the Christian put carvings of angels conquering devils; or of hero-martyrs exchanging this world for another; subjects inappropriate, I think, to our direction of exchange here. And the Master of Christians not only left his followers without any orders as to the sculpture of affairs of exchange on the outside of buildings, but gave some strong evidence of his dislike of affairs of exchange within them. And yet there might surely be a heroism in such affairs; and all commerce become a kind of selling of doves, not impious. The wonder has always been great to me that heroism has never been supposed to be in anywise consistent with the practice of supplying people with food, or clothes; but rather with that of quartering one's self upon them for food, and stripping them of their clothes. Spoiling of armor is a heroic deed in all ages; but the selling of clothes, old or new, has never taken any color of magnanimity. Yet one does not see why feeding the hungry and clothing the naked should ever become base business, even when engaged in on a large scale. If one could contrive to attach the notion of conquest to them anyhow! so that, supposing there were anywhere an obstinate race, who refused to be comforted, one might take some pride in giving them compulsory comfort![1] and as it were, 'occupying a country' with one's gifts, instead of one's armies? If one could only consider it as much a victory to get a barren field sown, as to

[1] Quite serious, all this, though it reads like jest.

get an eared field stripped; and contend who should build villages, instead of who should 'carry' them! Are not all forms of heroism, conceivable in doing these serviceable deeds? You doubt who is strongest? It might be ascertained by push of spade, as well as push of sword. Who is wisest? There are witty things to be thought of in planning other business than campaigns. Who is bravest? There are always the elements to fight with, stronger than men; and nearly as merciless.

The only absolutely and unapproachably heroic element in the soldier's work seems to be —that he is paid little for it—and regularly: while you traffickers, and exchangers, and others occupied in presumably benevolent business, like to be paid much for it—and by chance. I never can make out how it is that a *knight*-errant does not expect to be paid for his trouble, but a *peddler*-errant always does;—that people are willing to take hard knocks for nothing, but never to sell ribbons cheap;—that they are ready to go on fervent crusades to recover the tomb of a buried God, but never on any travels to fulfil the orders of a living one;—that they will go anywhere barefoot to preach their faith, but must be well bribed to practice it, and are perfectly ready to give the Gospel gratis, but never the loaves and fishes.[1]

If you choose to take the matter up on any such soldierly principle, to do your commerce, and your feeding of nations, for fixed salaries; and to be as particular about giving people the best food, and the best cloth, as soldiers are about giving them the best gunpowder, I could carve something for you on your exchange worth looking at. But I can only at present suggest decorating its frieze with pendent purses; and making its pillars broad at the base, for the sticking of bills. And in the innermost chambers of it there might be a statue of Britannia of the Market, who may have, perhaps advisably, a partridge for her crest, typical at once of her courage in fighting for noble ideas, and of her interest in game; and round its neck the inscription in golden letters, *Perdix fovit quæ non peperit*.[2] Then, for her spear, she might have a weaver's beam; and on her shield, instead of St. George's Cross, the Milanese boar, semi-fleeced, with the town of Gennesaret proper, in the field, and the legend 'In the best market,[3] and her corselet, of leather, folded over her heart in the shape of a purse, with thirty slits in it for a piece of money to go in at, on each day of the month. And I doubt not but that people would come to see your exchange, and its goddess, with applause.

Nevertheless, I want to point out to you certain strange characters in this goddess of yours. She differs from the great Greek and Medieval deities essentially in two things—first, as to the continuance of her presumed power; secondly, as to the extent of it.

1st, as to the Continuance.

The Greek Goddess of Wisdom gave continual increase of wisdom, as the Christian Spirit of Comfort (or Comforter) continual increase of comfort. There was no question, with these, of any limit or cessation of function. But with your Agora Goddess, that is just the most important question. Getting on—but where to? Gathering together—but how much? Do you mean to gather always—never to spend? If so, I wish you joy of your goddess, for I am just as well off as you, without the trouble of worshipping her at all. But if you do not spend, somebody else will—somebody else must. And it is because of this (among many other such errors) that I have fearlessly declared your so-called science of Political Economy to be no science; because, namely, it has omitted the study of exactly the most important branch of the business—the study of *spending*. For spend you must, and as much as you make, ultimately. You gather corn:—will you bury England under a heap of grain; or will you, when you have gathered, finally eat? You gather gold:—will you make your house-roofs of it, or pave your streets with it? That is still one way of spending it. But if you keep it, that you may get more, I'll give you more; I'll give you all the gold you want—all you can imagine—if you can tell me what you'll do with it. You shall have thousands of gold pieces;—thousands of thousands—millions—mountains, of gold: where will you keep them? Will you put an Olympus of silver upon a golden Pelion—make Ossa like a wart? Do you think the rain and dew would then come down to you, in the streams from such mountains, more blessedly than they will down the mountains which God has made for you, of moss and whinstone? But it is not gold that you want to gather! What is it? green-

---

[1] Please think over this paragraph, too briefly and antithetically put, but one of those which I am happiest in having written.

[2] Jerem. xvii. 11 (best in Septuagint and Vulgate). 'As the partridge, fostering what she brought not forth, so he that getteth riches, not by right, shall leave them in the midst of his days, and at his end shall be a fool.'

[3] Meaning fully, 'We have brought our pigs to it.'

backs? No; not those neither. What is it then —is it ciphers after a capital I? Cannot you practise writing ciphers, and write as many as you want? Write ciphers for an hour every morning, in a big book, and say every evening, I am worth all those naughts more than I was yesterday. Won't that do? Well, what in the name of Plutus is it you want? Not gold, not greenbacks, not ciphers after a capital I? You will have to answer, after all, 'No; we want, somehow or other, money's *worth*.' Well, what is that? Let your Goddess of Getting-on discover it, and let her learn to stay therein.

II. But there is yet another question to be asked respecting this Goddess of Getting-on. The first was of the continuance of her power; the second is of its extent.

Pallas and the Madonna were supposed to be all the world's Pallas, and all the world's Madonna. They could teach all men, and they could comfort all men. But, look strictly into the nature of the power of your Goddess of Getting-on; and you will find she is the Goddess—not of everybody's getting on—but only of somebody's getting on. This is a vital, or rather deathful, distinction. Examine it in your own ideal of the state of national life which this Goddess is to evoke and maintain. I asked you what it was, when I was last here;[1]—you have never told me. Now, shall I try to tell you?

Your ideal of human life then is, I think, that it should be passed in a pleasant undulating world, with iron and coal everywhere underneath it. On each pleasant bank of this world is to be a beautiful mansion, with two wings; and stables, and coach-houses; a moderately-sized park; a large garden and hothouses; and pleasant carriage drives through the shrubberies. In this mansion are to live the favored votaries of the Goddess; the English gentleman, with his gracious wife, and his beautiful family; always able to have the boudoir and the jewels for the wife, and the beautiful ball dresses for the daughters, and hunters for the sons, and a shooting in the Highlands for himself. At the bottom of the bank, is to be the mill; not less than a quarter of a mile long, with a steam engine at each end, and two in the middle, and a chimney three hundred feet high. In this mill are to be in constant employment from eight hundred to a thousand workers, who never drink, never strike, always go to church on Sunday, and always express themselves in respectful language.

[1] *The Two Paths*, p. 115 (small edition), and p. 99 of vol. x of the *Revised Series of the Entire Works*.

Is not that, broadly, and in the main features, the kind of thing you propose to yourselves? It is very pretty indeed, seen from above; not at all so pretty, seen from below. For, observe, while to one family this deity is indeed the Goddess of Getting-on, to a thousand families she is the Goddess of *not* Getting-on. 'Nay,' you say 'they have all their chance.' Yes, so has every one in a lottery, but there must always be the same number of blanks. 'Ah! but in a lottery it is not skill and intelligence which take the lead, but blind chance.' What then! do you think the old practice, that 'they should take who have the power, and they should keep who can,' is less iniquitous, when the power has become power of brains instead of fist? and that, though we may not take advantage of a child's or a woman's weakness, we may of a man's foolishness? 'Nay, but finally, work must be done, and some one must be at the top, some one at the bottom.' Granted, my friends. Work must always be, and captains of work must always be; and if you in the least remember the tone of any of my writings, you must know that they are thought unfit for this age, because they are always insisting on need of government, and speaking with scorn of liberty. But I beg you to observe that there is a wide difference between being captains or governors of work, and taking the profits of it. It does not follow, because you are general of an army, that you are to take all the treasure, or land, it wins (if it fight for treasure or land); neither, because you are king of a nation, that you are to consume all the profits of the nation's work. Real kings, on the contrary, are known invariably by their doing quite the reverse of this,—by their taking the least possible quantity of the nation's work for themselves. There is no test of real kinghood so infallible as that. Does the crowned creature live simply, bravely, unostentatiously? probably he *is* a King. Does he cover his body with jewels, and his table with delicates? in all probability he is *not* a King.

* * *

I know that none of this wrong is done with deliberate purpose. I know, on the contrary, that you wish your workmen well; that you do much for them, and that you desire to do more for them, if you saw your way to such benevolence safely. I know that even all this wrong and misery are brought about by a warped sense of duty, each of you striving to do his best; but unhappily, not knowing for whom this best should be done. And all our hearts have been betrayed by the plausible impiety of the modern economist, that 'To do the best for yourself, is finally to do the best for others.' Friends, our great Master said not so; and most absolutely we shall find this world is not made so. Indeed, to do the best for others, is finally to do the best for ourselves; but it will not do to have our eyes fixed on that issue. The Pagans had got beyond that. Hear what a Pagan says of this matter; hear what were, perhaps, the last written words of Plato,—if not the last actually written (for this we cannot know), yet assuredly in fact and power his parting words—in which, endeavoring to give full crowning and harmonious close to all his thoughts, and to speak the sum of them by the imagined sentence of the Great Spirit, his strength and his heart fail him, and the words cease, broken off forever.

They are at the close of the dialogue called 'Critias,' in which he describes, partly from real tradition, partly in ideal dream, the early state of Athens; and the genesis, and order, and religion, of the fabled isle of Atlantis; in which genesis he conceives the same first perfection and final degeneracy of man, which in our own Scriptural tradition is expressed by saying that the Sons of God intermarried with the daughters of men, for he supposes the earliest race to have been indeed the children of God; and to have corrupted themselves, until 'their spot was not the spot of his children.' And this, he says, was the end; that indeed 'through many generations, so long as the God's nature in them yet was full, they were submissive to the sacred laws, and carried themselves lovingly to all that had kindred with them in divineness; for their uttermost spirit was faithful and true, and in every wise great; so that, in *all meekness of wisdom, they dealt with each other*, and took all the chances of life; and despising all things except virtue, they cared little what happened day by day, and *bore lightly the burden* of gold and of possessions; for they saw that, if *only their common love and virtue increased, all these things would be increased together with them;* but to set their esteem and ardent pursuit upon material possession would be to lose that first, and their virtue and affection together with it. And by such reasoning, and what of the divine nature remained in them, they gained all this greatness of which we have already told; but when the God's part of them faded and became extinct, being mixed again and again, and effaced by the prevalent mortality; and the human nature at last exceeded, they then became unable to endure the courses of fortune; and fell into shapelessness of life, and baseness in the sight of him who could see, having lost everything that was fairest of their honor; while to the blind hearts which could not discern the true life, tending to happiness, it seemed that they were then chiefly noble and happy, being filled with all iniquity of inordinate possession and power. Whereupon, the God of gods, whose Kinghood is in laws, beholding a once just nation thus cast into misery, and desiring to lay such punishment upon them as might make them repent into restraining, gathered together all the gods into his dwelling-place, which from heaven's center overlooks whatever has part in creation; and having assembled them, he said'—

The rest is silence. Last words of the chief wisdom of the heathen, spoken of this idol of riches; this idol of yours; this golden image high by measureless cubits, set up where your green fields of England are furnace-burnt into the likeness of the plain of Dura: this idol, forbidden to us, first of all idols, by our own Master and faith; forbidden, to us also by every human lip that has ever, in any age or people, been accounted of as able to speak according to the purposes of God. Continue to make that forbidden deity your principal one, and soon no more art, no more science, no more pleasure will be possible. Catastrophe will come; or worse than catastrophe, slow moldering and withering into Hades. But if you can fix some conception of a true human state of life to be striven for—life good for all men as for yourselves—if you can determine some honest and simple order of existence; following those trodden ways of wisdom, which are pleasantness, and seeking her quiet and withdrawn paths, which are peace;[1]—then, and so sanctifying wealth into 'commonwealth,' all your art, your literature, your daily labors, your domestic affection, and citizen's duty, will join and increase into one magnificent harmony. You will know then how to build, well enough; you will build with stone well, but with flesh better; temples not made with hands, but riveted of hearts; and that kind of marble, crimson-veined, is indeed eternal.

[1] I imagine the Hebrew chant merely intends passionate repetition, and not a distinction of this somewhat fanciful kind; yet we may profitably make it in reading the English.

ALFRED, LORD TENNYSON (1809–1892)

TENNYSON was born at Somersby Rectory in Lincolnshire. The rich level landscape of the reclaimed fen district is clearly visible in his poems. He soon began to imitate the English masters of verse and the compositions 'written between 15 and 17' in *Poems by Two Brothers* (1827) show his transitory allegiance to Byron and Scott. At Trinity College, Cambridge, he took the Newdigate prize in 1829 with a blank verse poem on *Timbuctoo*, and the next year issued *Poems, Chiefly Lyrical*. Numerous collegians, of whom many were afterward eminent in scholarship and affairs, became his sworn admirers and steadily announced that a new poet had arrived. *Poems* (1833) showed a further advance in quality and scope, but this and the preceding volume were ridiculed by the reviews for certain obvious affectations and slips of taste and Tennyson waited nine years before publishing again. During this interval, he set himself with great earnestness to comprehend the thoughts and movements of his time, enriched his mind by constant study of the classics and of English literature, re-created the best of his old poems and composed with great deliberation his new ones. When his two volumes of 1842 appeared, such poems as *The Lady of Shalott* and *The Palace of Art* had been transformed and with them came *Ulysses*, *Morte d'Arthur*, *Locksley Hall* and many others of moderate length, every one exquisitely tempered and wrought. His reputation was immediately secure, and steadily increased during fifty years more of continuous authorship. In 1850 he received the 'laurel greener from the brows of him that uttered nothing base.' *The Princess* had already appeared and *In Memoriam* which had been growing since the death of his friend Arthur Hallam in 1833, now sealed his title not only to the laureateship but to the position of chief spiritual guide to his age. *Maud* (1855) represented something of a departure from his previous methods toward a less restrained style and a more vigorous grasp on the realities of life, a departure which he carried still farther in some of his 'ballads' and in realistic studies such as *The Northern Farmer*. The chief enterprise of his later years, however, was *The Idylls of the King*, at which he wrought from 1856–59, and again in 1868–72, when the poem became substantially complete. For nearly ten years his chief energies were given to the production of his seven dramas; of these *Queen Mary*, *Harold*, and *Becket* were all written by 1879, though the last was not published until several years later. From 1880 until his death in 1892 every few years added another volume of miscellaneous poems. At least in his lyrics, Tennyson's voice remained to the last, 'unchanged to hoarse or mute,' a 'clear call' with only a few dark overtones caught from the perplexities of the new era into which his life extended. In the few years since his death, we have moved fast and far from the platforms of the Victorian age; its problems are not our problems, and still less its solutions. Our interest, then, shifts more and more from Tennyson's 'message,' which was of his time, and attaches to the rich and instructed beauty of his art, which is imperishable.

MARIANA

WITH blackest moss, the flower-plots
   Were thickly crusted, one and all:
The rusted nails fell from the knots
   That held the pear to the gable-wall.
The broken sheds looked sad and strange; 5
   Unlifted was the clinking latch;
   Weeded and worn the ancient thatch
Upon the lonely moated grange.
     She only said, '*My life is dreary*,
        He cometh not,' she said: 10
     She said, '*I am aweary, aweary*,
        I would that I were dead!'

Her tears fell with the dews at even;
   Her tears fell ere the dews were dried;
She could not look on the sweet heaven, 15
   Either at morn or eventide.
After the flitting of the bats,
   When thickest dark did trance the sky,
   She drew her casement-curtain by,
And glanced athwart the glooming flats, 20
     She only said, '*The night is dreary*,
        He cometh not,' she said;
     She said, '*I am aweary, aweary*,
        I would that I were dead!'

Upon the middle of the night, 25
   Waking she heard the night-fowl crow:
The cock sung out an hour ere light;
   From the dark fen the oxen's low
Came to her: without hope of change,
   In sleep she seemed to walk forlorn, 30
   Till cold winds woke the gray-eyed morn

About the lonely moated grange.
    She only said, '*My life is dreary,*
      He cometh not,' she said;
    She said, '*I am aweary, aweary,*   35
      I would that I were dead!'

About a stone-cast from the wall
    A sluice with blackened waters slept
And o'er it many, round and small,
    The clustered marish-mosses crept.   40
Hard by a poplar shook alway,
    All silver-green with gnarlèd bark:
    For leagues no other tree did mark
The level waste, the rounding gray.
    She only said, '*The night is dreary,*   45
      He cometh not,' she said;
    She said, '*I am aweary, aweary,*
      I would that I were dead!'

And ever when the moon was low,
    And the shrill winds were up and away,   50
In the white curtain, to and fro,
    She saw the gusty shadow sway.
But when the moon was very low,
    And wild winds bound within their cell,
The shadow of the poplar fell   55
    Upon her bed, across her brow.
    She only said, '*My life is dreary,*
      He cometh not,' she said;
    She said, '*I am aweary, aweary,*
      I would that I were dead!'   60

All day within the dreamy house,
    The doors upon their hinges creaked;
The blue fly sung in the pane; the mouse
    Behind the moldering wainscot shrieked,
Or from the crevice peered about,   65
    Old faces glimmered through the doors,
    Old footsteps trod the upper floors,
Old voices called her from without.
    She only said, '*My life is dreary,*
      He cometh not,' she said;   70
    She said, '*I am aweary, aweary,*
      I would that I were dead!'

The sparrow's chirrup on the roof,
    The slow clock ticking, and the sound
Which to the wooing wind aloof   75
    The poplar made, did all confound
Her sense; but most she loathed the hour
    When the thick-moated sunbeam lay
    Athwart the chambers, and the day
Was sloping toward his western bower.   80
    Then, said she, '*I am very dreary,*
      He will not come,' she said;
    She wept '*I am aweary, aweary,*
      O God, that I were dead!'

                    (1830)

SONG

I

A SPIRIT haunts the year's last hours,
Dwelling amid these yellowing bowers:
    To himself he talks;
For at eventide, listening earnestly,
At his work you may hear him sob and sigh   5
    In the walks;
Earthward he boweth the heavy stalks
    Of the moldering flowers:
Heavily hangs the broad sunflower
    Over its grave i' the earth so chilly;   10
Heavily hangs the hollyhock,
    Heavily hangs the tiger-lily.

II

The air is damp, and hushed, and close,
As a sick man's room when he taketh repose
    An hour before death;   15
My very heart faints and my whole soul grieves
At the moist rich smell of the rotting leaves,
    And the breath
Of the fading edges of box beneath,
    And the year's last rose.   20
Heavily hangs the broad sunflower
    Over its grave i' the earth so chilly;
Heavily hangs the hollyhock,
    Heavily hangs the tiger-lily.

                    (1830)

THE POET

THE poet in a golden clime was born,
    With golden stars above;
Dowered with the hate of hate, the scorn of scorn,
    The love of love.

He saw through life and death, through good and ill,
    He saw through his own soul.   5
The marvel of the everlasting will,
    An open scroll,

Before him lay; with echoing feet he threaded
    The secretest walks of fame: 10
The viewless arrows of his thoughts were headed
    And winged with flame,

Like Indian reeds blown from his silver tongue,
    And of so fierce a flight,
From Calpe unto Caucasus they sung,   15
    Filling with light

And vagrant melodies the winds which bore
    Them earthward till they lit;
Then, like the arrow-seeds of the field flower,
    The fruitful wit   20

Cleaving took root, and springing forth anew
    Where'er they fell, behold,
Like to the mother plant in semblance grew
    A flower all gold,

And bravely furnished all abroad to fling   25
    The wingèd shafts of truth,
To throng with stately blooms the breathing spring,
    Of Hope and Youth.

So many minds did gird their orbs with beams,
    Though one did fling the fire;   30
Heaven flowed upon the soul in many dreams
    Of high desire.

Thus truth was multiplied on truth, the world
    Like one great garden showed,
And through the wreaths of floating dark upcurled,   35
    Rare sunrise flowed.

And Freedom reared in that august sunrise
    Her beautiful bold brow,
When rites and forms before his burning eyes
    Melted like snow.   40

There was no blood upon her maiden robes
    Sunned by those orient skies;
But round about the circles of the globes
    Of her keen eyes

And in her raiment's hem was traced in flame   45
    WISDOM, a name to shake
All evil dreams of power—a sacred name,
    And when she spake,

Her words did gather thunder as they ran,
    And as the lightning to the thunder   50
Which follows it, riving the spirit of man,
    Making earth wonder,

So was their meaning to her words. No sword
    Of wrath her right arm whirled,   54
But one poor poet's scroll, and with *his* word
    She shook the world.

                  (1830)

THE LADY OF SHALOTT

PART I

ON either side the river lie
Long fields of barley and of rye,
That clothe the wold and meet the sky;
And through the field the road runs by
    To many-towered Camelot;   5
And up and down the people go,
Gazing where the lilies blow
Round an island there below,
    The island of Shalott.

Willows whiten, aspens quiver,   10
Little breezes dusk and shiver
Through the wave that runs for ever
By the island in the river
    Flowing down to Camelot.
Four gray walls, and four gray towers,   15
Overlook a space of flowers,
And the silent isle imbowers
    The Lady of Shalott.

By the margin, willow-veiled,
Slide the heavy barges trailed   20
By slow horses; and unhailed
The shallop flitteth silken-sailed
    Skimming down to Camelot;
But who hath seen her wave her hand?
Or at the casement seen her stand?   25
Or is she known in all the land,
    The Lady of Shalott?

Only reapers, reaping early
In among the bearded barley,
Hear a song that echoes cheerly   30
From the river winding clearly,
    Down to towered Camelot;
And by the moon the reaper weary,
Piling sheaves in uplands airy,
Listening, whispers, ' 'T is the fairy   35
    Lady of Shalott.'

PART II

THERE she weaves by night and day
A magic web with colors gay.
She has heard a whisper say,
A curse is on her if she stay   40
    To look down to Camelot.
She knows not what the curse may be,
And so she weaveth steadily,
And little other care hath she,
    The Lady of Shalott.   45

And moving through a mirror clear
That hangs before her all the year,
Shadows of the world appear.
There she sees the highway near
    Winding down to Camelot;   50
There the river eddy whirls,
And there the surly village-churls,
And the red cloaks of market girls,
    Pass onward from Shalott.

Sometimes a troop of damsels glad,   55
An abbot on an ambling pad,
Sometimes a curly shepherd-lad,
Or long-haired page in crimson clad,
    Goes by to towered Camelot;
And sometimes through the mirror blue   60
The knights come riding two and two:
She hath no loyal knight and true,
    The Lady of Shalott.

But in her web she still delights
To weave the mirror's magic sights,   65
For often through the silent nights
A funeral, with plumes and lights
    And music, went to Camelot;
Or when the moon was overhead,
Came two young lovers lately wed;   70
'I am half sick of shadows,' said
    The Lady of Shalott.

PART III

A BOW-SHOT from her bower-eaves,
He rode between the barley-sheaves,
The sun came dazzling through the leaves, 75
And flamed upon the brazen greaves
    Of bold Sir Lancelot.
A red-cross knight for ever kneeled,
To a lady in his shield,
That sparkled in the yellow field, 80
    Beside remote Shalott.

The gemmy bridle glittered free,
Like to some branch of stars we see
Hung in the golden Galaxy.
The bridle bells rang merrily 85
    As he rode down to Camelot;
And from his blazoned baldric slung
A mighty silver bugle hung,
And as he rode his armor rung,
    Beside remote Shalott. 90

All in the blue unclouded weather
Thick-jeweled shone the saddle-leather,
The helmet and the helmet-feather
Burned like one burning flame together,
    As he rode down to Camelot; 95
As often through the purple night,
Below the starry clusters bright,
Some bearded meteor, trailing light,
    Moves over still Shalott.

His broad clear brow in sunlight glowed; 100
On burnished hooves his war-horse trode;
From underneath his helmet flowed
His coal-black curls as on he rode,
    As he rode down to Camelot.
From the bank and from the river 105
He flashed into the crystal mirror,
'Tirra lirra,' by the river
    Sang Sir Lancelot.

She left the web, she left the loom,
She made three paces through the room, 110
She saw the water-lily bloom,
She saw the helmet and the plume,
    She looked down at Camelot.
Out flew the web and floated wide;
The mirror cracked from side to side; 115
'The curse is come upon me,' cried
    The Lady of Shalott.

PART IV

IN the stormy east-wind straining,
The pale yellow woods were waning,
The broad stream in his banks complaining, 120
Heavily the low sky raining
    Over towered Camelot;
Down she came and found a boat
Beneath a willow left afloat,
And round about the prow she wrote 125
    The Lady of Shalott.

And down the river's dim expanse
Like some bold seër in a trance,
Seeing all his own mischance—
With a glassy countenance 130
    Did she look to Camelot.
And at the closing of the day
She loosed the chain, and down she lay;
The broad stream bore her far away,
    The Lady of Shalott, 135

Lying, robed in snowy white
That loosely flew to left and right—
The leaves upon her falling light—
Through the noises of the night
    She floated down to Camelot; 140
And as the boat-head wound along
The willowy hills and fields among,
They heard her singing her last song,
    The Lady of Shalott.

Heard a carol, mournful, holy, 145
Chanted loudly, chanted lowly,
Till her blood was frozen slowly
And her eyes were darkened wholly
    Turned to towered Camelot.
For ere she reached upon the tide 150
The first house by the water-side,
Singing in her song she died,
    The Lady of Shalott.

Under tower and balcony,
By garden-wall and gallery, 155
A gleaming shape she floated by,
Dead-pale between the houses high,
    Silent into Camelot.
Out upon the wharfs they came,
Knight, and burgher, lord and dame, 160
And round the prow they read her name,
    The Lady of Shalott.

Who is this? and what is here?
And in the lighted palace near
Died the sound of royal cheer; 165
And they crossed themselves for fear,
    All the knights at Camelot;
But Lancelot mused a little space;
He said, 'She has a lovely face;
God in his mercy lend her grace, 170
    The Lady of Shalott.'

(1833)

THE PALACE OF ART

I BUILT my soul a lordly pleasure-house,
    Wherein at ease for aye to dwell.
I said, 'O Soul, make merry and carouse,
    Dear soul, for all is well.'

A huge crag-platform, smooth as burnished
    brass, 5
I chose. The rangèd ramparts bright
From level meadow-bases of deep grass
    Suddenly scaled the light.

Thereon I built it firm. Of ledge or shelf
    The rock rose clear, or winding stair, 10
My soul would live alone unto herself
    In her high palace there.

And 'while the world runs round and round,'
    I said,
'Reign thou apart, a quiet king,
Still as, while Saturn whirls, his steadfast shade
    Sleeps on his luminous ring.' 16

To which my soul made answer readily:
    'Trust me, in bliss I shall abide
In this great mansion, that is built for me,
    So royal-rich and wide.' 20

* * *
* * *

Four courts I made, East, West, and South
    and North,
In each a squarèd lawn, wherefrom
The golden gorge of dragons spouted forth
    A flood of fountain-foam.

And round the cool green courts there ran a row
    Of cloisters, branched like mighty woods, 26
Echoing all night to that sonorous flow
    Of spouted fountain-floods.

And round the roofs a gilded gallery
    That lent broad verge to distant lands, 30
Far as the wild swan wings, to where the sky
    Dipped down to sea and sands.

From those four jets four currents in one swell
    Across the mountain streamed below
In misty folds, that floating as they fell, 35
    Lit up a torrent-bow.

And high on every peak a statue seemed
    To hang on tiptoe, tossing up
A cloud of incense of all odor steamed
    From out a golden cup. 40

So that she thought, 'And who shall gaze upon
    My palace with unblinded eyes,
While this great bow will waver in the sun,
    And that sweet incense rise?'

For that sweet incense rose and never failed, 45
    And, while day sank or mounted higher,
The light aërial gallery, golden-railed,
    Burnt like a *fringe* of fire.

Likewise the deep-set windows, stained and
    traced,
Would seem slow-flaming crimson fires 50
From shadowed grots of arches interlaced,
    And tipped with frost-like spires.

* * *
* * *

Full of long-sounding corridors it was,
    That over-vaulted grateful gloom,
Through which the livelong day my soul did
    pass, 55
    Well-pleased, from room to room.

Full of great rooms and small the palace stood,
    All various, each a perfect whole
From living Nature, fit for every mood
    And change of my still soul. 60

For some were hung with arras green and blue,
    Showing a gaudy summer-morn,
Where with puffed cheek the belted hunter blew
    His wreathèd bugle-horn.

One seemed all dark and red—a tract of sand, 65
    And some one pacing there alone,
Who paced for ever in a glimmering land,
    Lit with a low large moon.

One showed an iron coast and angry waves,
    You seemed to hear them climb and fall 70
And roar rock-thwarted under bellowing caves,
    Beneath the windy wall.

And one, a full-fed river winding slow
    By herds upon an endless plain,
The ragged rims of thunder brooding low, 75
    With shadow-streaks of rain.

And one, the reapers at their sultry toil.
    In front they bound the sheaves. Behind
Were realms of upland, prodigal in oil,
    And hoary to the wind. 80

And one a foreground black with stones and
    slags,
    Beyond, a line of heights, and higher
All barred with long white cloud the scornful
    crags,
    And highest, snow and fire.

And one, an English home—gray twilight
    poured 85
    On dewy pastures, dewy trees,
Softer than sleep—all things in order stored,
    A haunt of ancient Peace.

Nor these alone, but every landscape fair,
    As fit for every mood of mind, 90
Or gay, or grave, or sweet, or stern, was there,
    Not less than truth designed.

* * *
* * *

Or the maid-mother by a crucifix,
  In tracts of pasture sunny-warm,
Beneath branch-work of costly sardonyx,   95
  Sat smiling, babe in arm.

Or in a clear-walled city on the sea,
  Near gilded organ-pipes, her hair
Wound with white roses, slept Saint Cecily;
  An angel looked at her.   100

Or thronging all one porch of Paradise
  A group of Houris bowed to see
The dying Islamite, with hands and eyes
  That said, We wait for thee.

Or mythic Uther's deeply-wounded son   105
  In some fair space of sloping greens
Lay, dozing in the vale of Avalon,
  And watched by weeping queens.

Or hollowing one hand against his ear,
  To list a foot-fall, ere he saw   110
The wood-nymph, stayed the Ausonian king
    to hear
  Of wisdom and of law.

Or over hills with peaky tops engrailed,
  And many a tract of palm and rice,
The throne of Indian Cama slowly sailed   115
  A summer fanned with spice.

Or sweet Europa's mantle blew unclasped,
  From off her shoulder backward borne,
From one hand drooped a crocus; one hand
    grasped
  The mild bull's golden horn.   120

Or else flushed Ganymede, his rosy thigh
  Half-buried in the eagle's down,
Sole as a flying star shot through the sky
  Above the pillared town.

Nor these alone; but every legend fair   125
  Which the supreme Caucasian mind
Carved out of Nature for itself, was there,
  Not less than life, designed.

          * * *
          * * *

Then in the towers I placed great bells that
    swung,
  Moved of themselves, with silver sound;
And with choice paintings of wise men I hung
  The royal dais round.   132

For there was Milton like a seraph strong,
  Beside him Shakespeare bland and mild;
And there the world-worn Dante grasped his
    song,   135
  And somewhat grimly smiled.

And there the Ionian father of the rest;
  A million wrinkles carved his skin;
A hundred winters snowed upon his breast,
  From cheek and throat and chin.   140

Above, the fair hall-ceiling stately-set
  Many an arch high up did lift,
And angels rising and descending met
  With interchange of gift.

Below was all mosaic choicely planned   145
  With cycles of the human tale
Of this wide world, the times of every land
  So wrought, they will not fail.

The people here, a beast of burden slow,
  Toiled onward, pricked with goads and stings;
Here played, a tiger, rolling to and fro   151
  The heads and crowns of kings;

Here rose, an athlete, strong to break or bind
  All force in bonds that might endure,
And here once more like some sick man declined,
  And trusted any cure.   156

But over these she trod; and those great bells
  Began to chime. She took her throne;
She sat betwixt the shining oriels,
  To sing her songs alone.   160

And through the topmost oriels' colored flame
  Two godlike faces gazed below;
Plato the wise, and large-browed Verulam,
  The first of those who know.

And all those names that in their motion were
  Full-welling fountain-heads of change,   166
Betwixt the slender shafts were blazoned fair
  In diverse raiment strange:

Through which the lights, rose, amber, emerald,
    blue,
  Flushed in her temples and her eyes,   170
And from her lips, as morn from Memnon, drew
  Rivers of melodies.

No nightingale delighteth to prolong
  Her low preamble all alone,
More than my soul to hear her echoed song
  Throb through the ribbèd stone;   176

Singing and murmuring in her feastful mirth,
  Joying to feel herself alive,
Lord over Nature, lord of the visible earth,
  Lord of the senses five;   180

Communing with herself: 'All these are mine,
  And let the world have peace or wars,
'T is one to me.' She—when young night divine
  Crowned dying day with stars,

Making sweet close of his delicious toils— 185
  Lit light in wreaths and anadems,
And pure quintessences of precious oils
  In hollowed moons of gems,

To mimic heaven; and clapped her hands and cried,
  'I marvel if my still delight 190
In this great house so royal-rich and wide
  Be flattered to the height.

'O all things fair to sate my various eyes!
  O shapes and hues that please me well!
O silent faces of the Great and Wise, 195
  My Gods, with whom I dwell!

'O Godlike isolation which art mine,
  I can but count thee perfect gain,
What time I watch the darkening droves of swine
  That range on yonder plain. 200

'In filthy sloughs they roll a prurient skin,
  They graze and wallow, breed and sleep;
And oft some brainless devil enters in,
  And drives them to the deep.'

Then of the moral instinct would she prate 205
  And of the rising from the dead,
As hers by right of full-accomplished Fate;
  And at the last she said:

'I take possession of man's mind and deed.
  I care not what the sects may brawl, 210
I sit as God holding no form of creed,
  But contemplating all.'

    * * *
    * * *

Full oft the riddle of the painful earth
  Flashed through her as she sat alone,
Yet not the less held she her solemn mirth,
  And intellectual throne. 216

And so she throve and prospered; so three years
  She prospered; on the fourth she fell,
Like Herod, when the shout was in his ears,
  Struck through with pangs of hell. 220

Lest she should fail and perish utterly,
  God, before whom ever lie bare
The abysmal deeps of Personality,
  Plagued her with sore despair.

When she would think, where'er she turned her sight, 225
  The airy hand confusion wrought,
Wrote 'Mene, mene,' and divided quite
  The kingdom of her thought.

Deep dread and loathing of her solitude
  Fell on her, from which mood was born 230
Scorn of herself; again, from out that mood
  Laughter at her self-scorn.

'What! is not this my place of strength,' she said,
  'My spacious mansion built for me,
Whereof the strong foundation-stones were laid
  Since my first memory?' 236

But in dark corners of her palace stood
  Uncertain shapes; and unawares
On white-eyed phantasms weeping tears of blood,
  And horrible nightmares, 240

And hollow shades enclosing hearts of flame,
  And, with dim fretted foreheads all,
On corpses three-months-old at noon she came,
  That stood against the wall.

A spot of dull stagnation, without light 245
  Or power of movement, seemed my soul,
Mid onward-sloping motions infinite
  Making for one sure goal.

A still salt pool, locked in with bars of sand
  Left on the shore. that hears all night 250
The plunging seas draw backward from the land
  Their moon-led waters white.

A star that with the choral starry dance
  Joined not, but stood, and standing saw
The hollow orb of moving Circumstance 255
  Rolled round by one fixed law.

Back on herself her serpent pride had curled.
  'No voice,' she shrieked in that lone hall,
'No voice breaks thro' the stillness of this world:
  One deep, deep silence all!' 260

She, moldering with the dull earth's moldering sod,
  Inwrapt tenfold in slothful shame,
Lay there exilèd from eternal God,
  Lost to her place and name;

And death and life she hated equally, 265
  And nothing saw, for her despair,
But dreadful time, dreadful eternity,
  No comfort anywhere;

Remaining utterly confused with fears,
  And ever worse with growing time, 270
And ever unrelieved by dismal tears,
  And all alone in crime:

Shut up as in a crumbling tomb, girt round
  With blackness as a solid wall,
Far off she seemed to hear the dully sound 275
  Of human footsteps fall.

As in strange lands a traveler walking slow,
　In doubt and great perplexity,
A little before moonrise hears the low
　　Moan of an unknown sea;　　　280

And knows not if it be thunder, or a sound
　Of rocks thrown down, or one deep cry
Of great wild beasts; then thinketh, 'I have found
　　A new land, but I die.'

She howled aloud, 'I am on fire within.　285
　There comes no murmur of reply.
What is it that will take away my sin,
　　And save me lest I die?'

So when four years were wholly finished
　She threw her royal robes away.　290
'Make me a cottage in the vale,' she said,
　　'Where I may mourn and pray.

'Yet pull not down my palace towers, that are
　So lightly, beautifully built;
Perchance I may return with others there, 295
　　When I have purged my guilt.'

　　　　　(1833–1842)

A DREAM OF FAIR WOMEN

I READ, before my eyelids dropped their shade,
　The Legend of Good Women, long ago
Sung by the morning star of song, who made
　　His music heard below;

Dan Chaucer, the first warbler, whose sweet breath　5
　Preluded those melodious bursts that fill
The spacious times of great Elizabeth
　　With sounds that echo still.

And, for a while, the knowledge of his art
　Held me above the subject, as strong gales
Hold swollen clouds from raining, though my heart,　11
　　Brimful of those wild tales,

Charged both mine eyes with tears. In every land
　I saw, wherever light illumineth,
Beauty and anguish walking hand in hand　15
　　The downward slope to death.

Those far-renownèd brides of ancient song
　Peopled the hollow dark, like burning stars,
And I heard sounds of insult, shame, and wrong,
　　And trumpets blown for wars;　20

And clattering flints battered with clanging hoofs;
　And I saw crowds in columned sanctuaries,
And forms that passed at windows and on roofs
　　Of marble palaces;

Corpses across the threshold; heroes tall　25
　Dislodging pinnacle and parapet
Upon the tortoise creeping to the wall;
　　Lances in ambush set;

And high shrine-doors burst through with heated blasts　29
　That run before the fluttering tongues of fire;
White surf wind-scattered over sails and masts,
　　And ever climbing higher;

Squadrons and squares of men in brazen plates,
　Scaffolds, still sheets of water, divers woes,
Ranges of glimmering vaults with iron grates, 35
　　And hushed seraglios.

So shape chased shape as swift as, when to land
　Bluster the winds and tides the self-same way,
Crisp foam-flakes scud along the level sand,
　　Torn from the fringe of spray.　40

I started once, or seemed to start in pain,
　Resolved on noble things, and strove to speak,
As when a great thought strikes along the brain,
　　And flushes all the cheek.

And once my arm was lifted to hew down　45
　A cavalier from off his saddle-bow,
That bore a lady from a leaguered town;
　　And then, I know not how,

All those sharp fancies, by down-lapsing thought
　Streamed onward, lost their edges, and did creep　50
Rolled on each other, rounded, smoothed, and brought
　　Into the gulfs of sleep.

At last methought that I had wandered far
　In an old wood; fresh-washed in coolest dew
The maiden splendors of the morning star　55
　　Shook in the steadfast blue.

Enormous elm-tree boles did stoop and lean
　Upon the dusky brushwood underneath
Their broad curved branches, fledged with clearest green,
　　New from its silken sheath.　60

The dim red Morn had died, her journey done,
　And with dead lips smiled at the twilight plain,
Half-fallen across the threshold of the sun,
　　Never to rise again.

There was no motion in the dumb dead air,　65
　Not any song of bird or sound of rill;
Gross darkness of the inner sepulchre
　　Is not so deadly still

As that wide forest. Growths of jasmine turned
  Their humid arms festooning tree to tree, 70
And at the root through lush green grasses
    burned
    The red anemone.

I knew the flowers, I knew the leaves, I knew
  The tearful glimmer of the languid dawn
On those long, rank, dark wood-walks drenched
    in dew, 75
    Leading from lawn to lawn.

The smell of violets, hidden in the green,
  Poured back into my empty soul and frame
The times when I remember to have been
    Joyful and free from blame. 80

And from within me a clear undertone
  Thrilled through mine ears in that unblissful
    clime,
'Pass freely through; the wood is all thine own,
    Until the end of time.'

At length I saw a lady within call, 85
  Stiller than chiseled marble, standing there;
A daughter of the gods, divinely tall,
    And most divinely fair.

Her loveliness with shame and with surprise
  Froze my swift speech; she turning on my face
The star-like sorrows of immortal eyes, 91
    Spoke slowly in her place.

'I had great beauty; ask thou not my name:
  No one can be more wise than destiny.
Many drew swords and died. Where'er I came
    I brought calamity.' 96

'No marvel, sovereign lady: in fair field
  Myself for such a face had boldly died,'
I answered free; and turning I appealed
    To one that stood beside. 100

But she, with sick and scornful looks averse,
  To her full height her stately stature draws;
'My youth,' she said, 'was blasted with a curse:
    This woman was the cause.

'I was cut off from hope in that sad place 105
  Which men called Aulis in those iron years;
My father held his hand upon his face;
    I, blinded with my tears,

'Still strove to speak: my voice was thick with
    sighs
  As in a dream. Dimly I could descry 110
The stern black-bearded kings with wolfish eyes,
    Waiting to see me die.

'The high masts flickered as they lay afloat;
  The crowds, the temples, wavered, and the
    shore;

The bright death quivered at the victim's
    throat; 115
    Touched; and I knew no more.'

Whereto the other with a downward brow:
  'I would the white cold heavy-plunging foam,
Whirled by the wind, had rolled me deep below,
    Then when I left my home.' 120

Her slow full words sank through the silence
    drear,
  As thunder-drops fall on a sleeping sea:
Sudden I heard a voice that cried, 'Come here,
    That I may look on thee.'

I turning saw, throned on a flowery rise, 125
  One sitting on a crimson scarf unrolled;
A queen, with swarthy cheeks and bold black
    eyes,
    Brow-bound with burning gold.

She, flashing forth a haughty smile, began: 129
  'I governed men by change, and so I swayed
All moods. 'T is long since I have seen a man.
    Once, like the moon, I made

'The ever-shifting currents of the blood
  According to my humor ebb and flow.
I have no men to govern in this wood: 135
    That makes my only woe.

'Nay—yet it chafes me that I could not bend
  One will; nor tame and tutor with mine eye
That dull cold-blooded Cæsar. Prythee, friend,
    Where is Mark Antony? 140

'The man, my lover, with whom I rode sub-
    lime
  On Fortune's neck; we sat as God by God;
The Nilus would have risen before his time
    And flooded at our nod.

'We drank the Libyan Sun to sleep, and lit 145
  Lamps which out-burned Canopus. O, my
    life
In Egypt! O, the dalliance and the wit,
    The flattery and the strife,

'And the wild kiss, when fresh from war's
    alarms,
  My Hercules, my Roman Antony, 150
My mailèd Bacchus leaped into my arms,
    Contented there to die!

'And there he died: and when I heard my name
  Sighed forth with life, I would not brook my
    fear
Of the other: with a worm I balked his fame. 155
    What else was left? look here!'—

With that she tore her robe apart, and half
  The polished argent of her breast to sight
Laid bare. Thereto she pointed with a laugh,
    Showing the aspic's bite.— 160

'I died a Queen. The Roman soldier found
  Me lying dead, my crown about my brows,
A name for ever!—lying robed and crowned
  Worthy a Roman spouse.'

Her warbling voice, a lyre of widest range   165
  Struck by all passion, did fall down and
    glance
From tone to tone, and glided through all
    change
  Of liveliest utterance.

When she made pause I knew not for delight; 169
  Because with sudden motion from the ground
She raised her piercing orbs, and filled with light
  The interval of sound.   172

Still with their fires Love tipt his keenest darts:
  As once they drew into two burning rings
All beams of Love, melting the mighty hearts
  Of captains and of kings.   176

Slowly my sense undazzled. Then I heard
  A noise of some one coming through the lawn,
And singing clearer than the crested bird
  That claps his wings at dawn: 180

'The torrent brooks of hallowed Israel
  From craggy hollows pouring, late and soon,
Sound all night long, in falling through the dell,
  Far-heard beneath the moon.

'The balmy moon of blessed Israel   185
  Floods all the deep-blue gloom with beams
    divine;
All night the splintered crags that wall the dell
  With spires of silver shine.'   188

As one that museth where broad sunshine laves
  The lawn by some cathedral, through the door
Hearing the holy organ rolling waves
  Of sound on roof and floor

Within, and anthem sung, is charmed and tied
  To where he stands,—so stood I, when that
    flow
Of music left the lips of her that died   195
  To save her father's vow,

The daughter of the warrior Gileadite,
  A maiden pure; as when she went along
From Mizpah's towered gate with welcome
    light,
  With timbrel and with song.   200

My words leaped forth: 'Heaven heads the
    count of crimes
  With that wild oath.' She rendered answer
    high:
'Not so, nor once alone; a thousand times
  I would be born and die.   204

'Single I grew, like some green plant, whose root
  Creeps to the garden water-pipes beneath,
Feeding the flower; but ere my flower to fruit
  Changed, I was ripe for death.

'My God, my land, my father—these did move
  Me from my bliss of life, that Nature gave,
Lowered softly with a threefold cord of love 211
  Down to a silent grave.

'And I went mourning, "No fair Hebrew boy
  Shall smile away my maiden blame among
The Hebrew mothers"—emptied of all joy, 215
  Leaving the dance and song.

'Leaving the olive-gardens far below,
  Leaving the promise of my bridal bower,
The valleys of grape-loaded vines that glow
  Beneath the battled tower.   220

'The light white cloud swam over us. Anon
  We heard the lion roaring from his den;
We saw the large white stars rise one by one,
  Or, from the darkened glen,

'Saw God divide the night with flying flame,
  And thunder on the everlasting hills.   226
I heard him, for he spake, and grief became
  A solemn scorn of ills.

'When the next moon was rolled into the sky,
  Strength came to me that equaled my desire,
How beautiful a thing it was to die   231
  For God and for my sire!

'It comforts me in this one thought to dwell,
  That I subdued me to my father's will;
Because the kiss he gave me, ere I fell,   235
  Sweetens the spirit still.

'Moreover it is written that my race
  Hewed Ammon, hip and thigh, from Aroer
On Arnon unto Minneth.' Here her face
  Glowed, as I looked at her.   240

She locked her lips; she left me where I stood:
  'Glory to God,' she sang, and past afar,
Thridding the somber boskage of the wood
  Toward the morning-star.

Losing her carol I stood pensively,   245
  As one that from a casement leans his head,
When midnight bells cease ringing suddenly,
  And the old year is dead.

'Alas! alas!' a low voice, full of care,   249
  Murmured beside me: 'Turn and look on me;
I am that Rosamond, whom men call fair.
  If what I was I be.

'Would I had been some maiden coarse and
    poor!
  O me, that I should ever see the light!
Those dragon eyes of angered Eleanor   255
    Do hunt me, day and night.'

She ceased in tears, fallen from hope and trust;
  To whom the Egyptian: 'O, you tamely died!
You should have clung to Fulvia's waist, and
    thrust
    The dagger through her side.'   260

With that sharp sound the white dawn's creep-
    ing beams,
  Stolen to my brain dissolved the mystery
Of folded sleep. The captain of my dreams
    Ruled in the eastern sky.

Morn broadened on the borders of the dark 265
  Ere I saw her, who clasped in her last trance
Her murdered father's head, or Joan of Arc,
    A light of ancient France;   268

Or her who knew that Love can vanquish Death,
  Who kneeling, with one arm about her king,
Drew forth the poison with her balmy breath,
    Sweet as new buds in spring.

No memory labors longer from the deep   273
  Gold-mines of thought to lift the hidden ore
That glimpses, moving up, than I from sleep
    To gather and tell o'er   276

Each little sound and sight. With what dull
    pain
  Compassed, how eagerly I sought to strike
Into that wondrous track of dreams again!
    But no two dreams are like.   280

As when a soul laments, which hath been blest,
  Desiring what is mingled with past years,
In yearnings that can never be expressed
    By sighs or groans or tears;

Because all words, though culled with choicest
    art,   285
  Failing to give the bitter of the sweet,
Wither beneath the palate, and the heart
    Faints, faded by its heat.
                      (1833)

SAINT AGNES' EVE

DEEP on the convent-roof the snows
  Are sparkling to the moon:
My breath to heaven like vapor goes:
  May my soul follow soon!
The shadows of the convent-towers   5
  Slant down the snowy sward,
Still creeping with the creeping hours
  That lead me to my Lord:

Make thou my spirit pure and clear
  As are the frosty skies,   10
Or this first snowdrop of the year
  That in my bosom lies.

As these white robes are soiled and dark,
  To yonder shining ground;
As this pale taper's earthly spark,   15
  To yonder argent round;
So shows my soul before the Lamb,
  My spirit before thee;
So in mine earthly house I am,
  To that I hope to be.   20
Break up the heavens, O Lord! and far,
  Through all yon starlight keen,
Draw me, thy bride, a glittering star,
  In raiment white and clean.

He lifts me to the golden doors;   25
  The flashes come and go;
All heaven bursts her starry floors,
  And strows her lights below,
And deepens on and up! the gates
  Roll back, and far within   30
For me the Heavenly Bridegroom waits,
  To make me pure of sin.
The Sabbaths of Eternity,
  One Sabbath deep and wide—
A light upon the shining sea—   35
  The Bridegroom with his bride!
                      (1837)

YOU ASK ME, WHY, THOUGH ILL AT EASE

You ask me, why, though ill at ease,
  Within this region I subsist,
  Whose spirits falter in the mist,
And languish for the purple seas.

It is the land that freemen till,   5
  That sober-suited Freedom chose,
  The land, where girt with friends or foes
A man may speak the thing he will;

A land of settled government,
  A land of just and old renown,   10
  Where Freedom slowly broadens down
From precedent to precedent:

Where faction seldom gathers head,
  But, by degrees to fullness wrought,
  The strength of some diffusive thought   15
Hath time and space to work and spread.

Should banded unions persecute
  Opinion, and induce a time
  When single thought is civil crime,
And individual freedom mute,   20

Though power should make from land to land
  The name of Britain trebly great—
  Though every channel of the State
Should fill and choke with golden sand—

Yet waft me from the harbor-mouth,   25
  Wild wind! I seek a warmer sky,
  And I will see before I die
The palms and temples of the South.
                 (1842)

OF OLD SAT FREEDOM ON THE HEIGHTS

Of old sat Freedom on the heights,
  The thunders breaking at her feet:
Above her shook the starry lights:
  She heard the torrents meet.

There in her place she did rejoice,   5
  Self-gathered in her prophet-mind,
But fragments of her mighty voice
  Came rolling on the wind.

Then stepped she down through town and field
  To mingle with the human race,   10
And part by part to men revealed
  The fulness of her face—

Grave mother of majestic works,
  From her isle-altar gazing down,
Who, Godlike, grasps the triple forks,   15
  And, king-like, wears the crown:

Her open eyes desire the truth.
  The wisdom of a thousand years
Is in them. May perpetual youth
  Keep dry their light from tears;   20

That her fair form may stand and shine,
  Make bright our days and light our dreams,
Turning to scorn with lips divine
  The falsehood of extremes!
                 (1842)

SIR GALAHAD

My good blade carves the casques of men,
  My tough lance thrusteth sure,
My strength is as the strength of ten,
  Because my heart is pure.
The shattering trumpet shrilleth high,   5
  The hard brands shiver on the steel,
The splintered spear-shafts crack and fly,
  The horse and rider reel:
They reel, they roll in clanging lists,
  And when the tide of combat stands,   10
Perfume and flowers fall in showers,
  That lightly rain from ladies' hands.

How sweet are looks that ladies bend
  On whom their favors fall!
For them I battle till the end,   15
  To save from shame and thrall:
But all my heart is drawn above,
  My knees are bowed in crypt and shrine:
I never felt the kiss of love,
  Nor maiden's hand in mine.   20
More bounteous aspects on me beam,
  Me mightier transports move and thrill;
So keep I fair through faith and prayer
  A virgin heart in work and will.

When down the stormy crescent goes,   25
  A light before me swims,
Between dark stems the forest glows,
  I hear a noise of hymns:
Then by some secret shrine I ride;
  I hear a voice but none are there;   30
The stalls are void, the doors are wide,
  The tapers burning fair.
Fair gleams the snowy altar-cloth,
  The silver vessels sparkle clean,
The shrill bell rings, the censer swings,   35
  And solemn chants resound between.

Sometimes on lonely mountain-meres
  I find a magic bark;
I leap on board: no helmsman steers:
  I float till all is dark: 40
A gentle sound, an awful light!
  Three angels bear the holy Grail:
With folded feet, in stoles of white,
  On sleeping wings they sail.
Ah, blessed vision! blood of God!   45
  My spirit beats her mortal bars,
As down dark tides the glory slides,
  And star-like mingles with the stars.

When on my goodly charger borne
  Through dreaming towns I go,   50
The cock crows ere the Christmas morn,
  The streets are dumb with snow.
The tempest crackles on the leads,
  And, ringing, springs from brand and mail;
But o'er the dark a glory spreads,   55
  And gilds the driving hail.
I leave the plain, I climb the height;
  No branchy thicket shelter yields;
But blessèd forms in whistling storms
  Fly o'er waste fens and windy fields.   60

A maiden knight—to me is given
  Such hope, I know not fear;
I yearn to breathe the airs of heaven
  That often meet me here.
I muse on joy that will not cease,   65
  Pure spaces clothed in living beams,
Pure lilies of eternal peace,
  Whose odors haunt my dreams;

And, stricken by an angel's hand,
    This mortal armor that I wear,   70
This weight and size, this heart and eyes,
    Are touched, are turned to finest air.

The clouds are broken in the sky,
    And through the mountain-walls
A rolling organ-harmony   75
    Swells up, and shakes and falls.
Then move the trees, the copses nod,
    Wings flutter, voices hover clear:
'O just and faithful knight of God!
    Ride on! the prize is near.'   80
So pass I hostel, hall, and grange;
    By bridge and ford, by park and pale,
All-armed I ride, whate'er betide,
    Until I find the holy Grail.

            (1842)

A FAREWELL

Flow down, cold rivulet, to the sea,
    Thy tribute wave deliver:
No more by thee my steps shall be,
    For ever and for ever.

Flow, softly flow, by lawn and lea,   5
    A rivulet, then a river:
Nowhere by thee my steps shall be,
    For ever and for ever.

But here will sigh thine alder-tree,
    And here thine aspen shiver;   10
And here by thee will hum the bee,
    For ever and for ever.

A thousand suns will stream on thee,
    A thousand moons will quiver;
But not by thee my steps shall be,   15
    For ever and for ever.

            (1842)

MORTE D'ARTHUR

So all day long the noise of battle rolled
Among the mountains by the winter sea;
Until King Arthur's table, man by man,
Had fallen in Lyonnesse about their lord,
King Arthur; then, because his wound was deep,
The bold Sir Bedivere uplifted him,   6
Sir Bedivere, the last of all his knights,
And bore him to a chapel nigh the field,
A broken chancel with a broken cross,
That stood on a dark strait of barren land.   10
On one side lay the ocean, and on one
Lay a great water, and the moon was full.

    Then spake King Arthur to Sir Bedivere:
'The sequel of to-day unsolders all
The goodliest fellowship of famous knights   15
Whereof this world holds record. Such a sleep

They sleep—the men I loved. I think that we
Shall never more, at any future time,
Delight our souls with talk of knightly deeds,
Walking about the gardens and the halls   20
Of Camelot, as in the days that were.
I perish by this people which I made,—
Though Merlin sware that I should come again
To rule once more—but let what will be be,
I am so deeply smitten through the helm   25
That without help I cannot last till morn.
Thou therefore take my brand Excalibur,
Which was my pride; for thou rememberest how
In those old days, one summer noon, an arm
Rose up from out the bosom of the lake,   30
Clothed in white samite, mystic, wonderful,
Holding the sword—and how I rowed across
And took it, and have worn it, like a king;
And, wheresoever I am sung or told
In aftertime, this also shall be known;   35
But now delay not; take Excalibur,
And fling him far into the middle mere;
Watch what thou seest, and lightly bring me
    word.'

    To him replied the bold Sir Bedivere:
'It is not meet, Sir King, to leave thee thus,   40
Aidless, alone, and smitten through the helm.
A little thing may harm a wounded man.
Yet I thy hest will all perform at full,
Watch what I see, and lightly bring thee word.'

    So saying, from the ruined shrine he stept   45
And in the moon athwart the place of tombs,
Where lay the mighty bones of ancient men,
Old knights, and over them the sea-wind sang
Shrill, chill, with flakes of foam. He, stepping
    down
By zigzag paths, and juts of pointed rock,   50
Came on the shining levels of the lake.

There drew he forth the brand Excalibur,
And o'er him, drawing it, the winter moon,
Brightening the skirts of a long cloud, ran forth
And sparkled keen with frost against the hilt;   55
For all the haft twinkled with diamond sparks,
Myriads of topaz-lights, and jacinth work
Of subtlest jewelery. He gazed so long
That both his eyes were dazzled, as he stood,
This way and that dividing the swift mind,   60
In act to throw; but at the last it seemed
Better to leave Excalibur concealed
There in the many-knotted water-flags,
That whistled stiff and dry about the marge.
So strode he back slow to the wounded king.   65

    Then spake King Arthur to Sir Bedivere:
'Hast thou performed my mission which I gave?
What is it thou hast seen, or what hast heard?'

    And answer made the bold Sir Bedivere:
'I heard the ripple washing in the reeds,   70
And the wild water lapping on the crag.'

To whom replied King Arthur, faint and pale:
'Thou hast betrayed thy nature and thy name,
Not rendering true answer, as beseemed
Thy fealty, nor like a noble knight;   75
For surer sign had followed, either hand,
Or voice, or else a motion of the mere.
This is a shameful thing for men to lie.
Yet now, I charge thee, quickly go again
As thou art lief and dear, and do the thing   80
I bade thee, watch, and lightly bring me word.'

Then went Sir Bedivere the second time
Across the ridge, and paced beside the mere,
Counting the dewy pebbles, fixed in thought;
But when he saw the wonder of the hilt,   85
How curiously and strangely chased, he smote
His palms together, and he cried aloud:

'And if indeed I cast the brand away,
Surely a precious thing, one worthy note,
Should thus be lost forever from the earth,   90
Which might have pleased the eyes of many men.
What good should follow this, if this were done?
What harm, undone? deep harm to disobey,
Seeing obedience is the bond of rule.
Were it well to obey then, if a king demand   95
An act unprofitable, against himself?
The king is sick, and knows not what he does.
What record, or what relic of my lord
Should be to aftertime, but empty breath
And rumors of a doubt? but were this kept,   100
Stored in some treasure-house of mighty kings,
Some one might show it at a joust of arms,
Saying, "King Arthur's sword, Excalibur,
Wrought by the lonely maiden of the lake;
Nine years she wrought it, sitting in the deeps   105
Upon the hidden bases of the hills."
So might some old man speak in the aftertime
To all the people, winning reverence;
But now much honor and much fame were lost.'

So spake he, clouded with his own conceit,   110
And hid Excalibur the second time,
And so strode back slow to the wounded king.

Then spoke King Arthur, breathing heavily:
'What is it thou hast seen, or what hast heard?'

And answer made the bold Sir Bedivere: 115
'I heard the water lapping on the crag,
And the long ripple washing in the reeds.'

To whom replied King Arthur, much in wrath:
'Ah, miserable and unkind, untrue,
Unknightly, traitor-hearted! Woe is me!   120
Authority forgets a dying king,
Laid widowed of the power in his eye
That bowed the will. I see thee what thou art,
For thou, the latest-left of all my knights,
In whom should meet the offices of all,   125
Thou wouldst betray me for the precious hilt;
Either from lust of gold, or like a girl
Valuing the giddy pleasure of the eyes.
Yet, for a man may fail in duty twice,
And the third time may prosper, get thee hence;
But, if thou spare to fling Excalibur,   131
I will arise and slay thee with my hands.'

Then quickly rose Sir Bedivere, and ran,
And, leaping down the ridges lightly, plunged
Among the bulrush-beds, and clutched the sword,   135
And strongly wheeled and threw it. The great brand
Made lightnings in the splendor of the moon,
And flashing round and round, and whirled in an arch,
Shot like a streamer of the northern morn,
Seen where the moving isles of winter shock   140
By night, with noises of the northern sea.
So flashed and fell the brand Excalibur;
But ere he dipped the surface, rose an arm
Clothed in white samite, mystic, wonderful,   144
And caught him by the hilt, and brandished him
Three times, and drew him under in the mere.
And lightly went the other to the king.

Then spoke King Arthur, drawing thicker breath:
'Now see I by thine eyes that this is done.
Speak out: what is it thou hast heard, or seen?'

And answer made the bold Sir Bedivere: 151
'Sir King, I closed mine eyelids, lest the gems
Should blind my purpose, for I never saw,
Nor shall see, here or elsewhere, till I die,
Not though I live three lives of mortal men,   155
So great a miracle as yonder hilt.
Then with both hands I flung him, wheeling him;
But when I looked again, behold an arm,
Clothed in white samite, mystic, wonderful,
That caught him by the hilt, and brandished him   160
Three times, and drew him under in the mere.'

And answer made King Arthur, breathing hard:
'My end draws nigh; 't is time that I were gone.
Make broad thy shoulders to receive my weight,
And bear me to the margin; yet I fear   165
My wound hath taken cold, and I shall die.'

So saying, from the pavement he half rose,
Slowly, with pain, reclining on his arm,
And looking wistfully with wide blue eyes
As in a picture. Him Sir Bedivere   170
Remorsefully regarded through his tears,
And would have spoken, but he found not words,
Then took with care, and kneeling on one knee,
O'er both his shoulders drew the languid hands
And rising bore him through the place of tombs

But, as he walked, King Arthur panted hard,
Like one that feels a nightmare on his bed   177
When all the house is mute. So sighed the king,
Muttering and murmuring at his ear, 'Quick,
    quick!
I fear it is too late, and I shall die.'   180
But the other swiftly strode from ridge to ridge,
Clothed with his breath, and looking, as he
    walked,
Larger than human on the frozen hills.
He heard the deep behind him, and a cry
Before. His own thought drove him like a goad.
Dry clashed his harness in the icy caves   186
And barren chasms, and all to left and right
The bare black cliff clanged round him, as he
    based
His feet on juts of slippery crag that rang
Sharp-smitten with the dint of armèd heels—190
And on a sudden, lo! the level lake.
And the long glories of the winter moon.

  Then saw they how there hove a dusky barge,
Dark as a funeral scarf from stem to stern,
Beneath them; and descending they were
    ware   195
That all the decks were dense with stately forms
Black-stoled, black-hooded, like a dream—by
    these
Three queens with crowns of gold—and from
    them rose
A cry that shivered to the tingling stars,
And, as it were one voice, an agony   200
Of lamentation, like a wind that shrills
All night in a waste land, where no one comes,
Or hath come, since the making of the world.

  Then murmured Arthur, 'Place me in the
    barge,'
And to the barge they came. There those three
    queens   205
Put forth their hands, and took the king, and
    wept.
But she that rose the tallest of them all
And fairest, laid his head upon her lap,
And loosed the shattered casque, and chafed his
    hands,
And called him by his name, complaining loud,
And dropping bitter tears against his brow   211
Striped with dark blood; for all his face was
    white
And colorless, and like the withered moon
Smote by the fresh beam of the springing east;
And all his greaves and cuisses dashed with
    drops   215
Of onset; and the light and lustrous curls—
That made his forehead like a rising sun
High from the dais-throne—were parched with
    dust;
Or, clotted into points and hanging loose,
Mixed with the knightly growth that fringed
    his lips   220

So like a shattered column lay the king;
Not like that Arthur who, with lance in rest,
From spur to plume a star of tournament,
Shot through the lists at Camelot, and charged
Before the eyes of ladies and of kings.   225

  Then loudly cried the bold Sir Bedivere:
'Ah! my Lord Arthur, whither shall I go?
Where shall I hide my forehead and my eyes?
For now I see the true old times are dead,   229
When every morning brought a noble chance,
And every chance brought out a noble knight.
Such times have been not since the light that led
The holy Elders with the gift of myrrh.
But now the whole ROUND TABLE is dissolved
Which was an image of the mighty world;   235
And I, the last, go forth companionless,
And the days darken round me, and the years,
Among new men, strange faces, other minds.'

  And slowly answered Arthur from the barge:
'The old order changeth, yielding place to new,
And God fulfils himself in many ways,   241
Lest one good custom should corrupt the world.
Comfort thyself: what comfort is in me?
I have lived my life, and that which I have done
May he within himself make pure! but thou,   245
If thou shouldst never see my face again,
Pray for my soul. More things are wrought by
    prayer
Than this world dreams of. Wherefore, let thy
    voice
Rise like a fountain for me night and day.   249
For what are men better than sheep or goats
That nourish a blind life within the brain,
If, knowing God, they lift not hands of prayer
Both for themselves and those who call them
    friend?
For so the whole round earth is every way
Bound by gold chains about the feet of God.   255
But now farewell. I am going a long way
With these thou seëst—if indeed I go—
(For all my mind is clouded with a doubt)
To the island-valley of Avilion;
Where falls not hail, or rain, or any snow,   260
Nor ever wind blows loudly; but it lies
Deep-meadowed, happy, fair with orchard
    lawns
And bowery hollows crowned with summer sea,
Where I will heal me of my grievous wound.'

  So said he, and the barge with oar and sail 265
Moved from the brink, like some full-breasted
    swan
That, fluting a wild carol ere her death,
Ruffles her pure cold plume, and takes the flood
With swarthy webs. Long stood Sir Bedivere
Revolving many memories, till the hull   270
Looked one black dot against the verge of dawn,
And on the mere the wailing died away.

(1842)

ULYSSES

It little profits that an idle king,
By this still hearth, among these barren crags,
Matched with an agèd wife, I mete and dole
Unequal laws unto a savage race,
That hoard, and sleep, and feed, and know not
    me.   5
I cannot rest from travel; I will drink
Life to the lees. All times I have enjoyed
Greatly, have suffered greatly, both with those
That loved me, and alone; on shore, and when
Through scudding drifts the rainy Hyades   10
Vext the dim sea. I am become a name;
For always roaming with a hungry heart
Much have I seen and known,—cities of men
And manners, climates, councils, governments,
Myself not least, but honored of them all;   15
And drunk delight of battle with my peers,
Far on the ringing plains of windy Troy.
I am a part of all that I have met;
Yet all experience is an arch wherethro'
Gleams that untraveled world whose margin
    fades   20
For ever and for ever when I move.
How dull it is to pause, to make an end,
To rust unburnished, not to shine in use!
As though to breathe were life! Life piled on life
Were all too little, and of one to me   25
Little remains; but every hour is saved
From that eternal silence, something more,
A bringer of new things; and vile it were
For some three suns to store and hoard myself,
And this gray spirit yearning in desire   30
To follow knowledge like a sinking star,
Beyond the utmost bound of human thought.
This is my son, mine own Telemachus,
To whom I leave the scepter and the isle—
Well-loved of me, discerning to fulfil   35
This labor, by slow prudence to make mild
A rugged people, and through soft degrees
Subdue them to the useful and the good.
Most blameless is he, centered in the sphere
Of common duties, decent not to fail   40
In offices of tenderness, and pay
Meet adoration to my household gods,
When I am gone. He works his work, I mine.

    There lies the port; the vessel puffs her sail:
There gloom the dark, broad seas. My mari-
    ners,   45
Souls that have toiled and wrought, and thought
    with me—
That ever with a frolic welcome took
The thunder and the sunshine, and opposed
Free hearts, free foreheads—you and I are old;
Old age hath yet his honor and his toil.   50
Death closes all; but something ere the end,
Some work of noble note, may yet be done,
Not unbecoming men that strove with Gods.
The lights begin to twinkle from the rocks:
The long day wanes; the slow moon climbs; the
    deep   55
Moans round with many voices. Come, my
    friends,
'T is not too late to seek a newer world.
Push off, and sitting well in order smite
The sounding furrows; for my purpose holds
To sail beyond the sunset, and the baths   60
Of all the western stars, until I die.
It may be that the gulfs will wash us down;
It may be we shall touch the Happy Isles,
And see the great Achilles, whom we knew.
Though much is taken, much abides; and
    though   65
We are not now that strength which in old days
Moved earth and heaven, that which we are,
    we are;
One equal temper of heroic hearts,
Made weak by time and fate, but strong in will
To strive, to seek, to find, and not to yield.   70
(1842)

LOCKSLEY HALL

Comrades, leave me here a little, while as yet
    't is early morn:
Leave me here, and when you want me, sound
    upon the bugle-horn.

'T is the place, and all around it, as of old, the
    curlews call,
Dreary gleams about the moorland flying over
    Locksley Hall;

Locksley Hall, that in the distance overlooks
    the sandy tracts,   5
And the hollow ocean-ridges roaring into cata-
    racts.

Many a night from yonder ivied casement, ere
    I went to rest,
Did I look on great Orion sloping slowly to the
    West.

Many a night I saw the Pleiads, rising through
    the mellow shade,
Glitter like a swarm of fire-flies tangled in a
    silver braid.   10

Here about the beach I wandered, nourishing a
    youth sublime
With the fairy tales of science, and the long re-
    sult of Time;

When the centuries behind me like a fruitful
    land reposed;
When I clung to all the present for the promise
    that it closed:

When I dipped into the future far as human
    eye could see;   15
Saw the Vision of the world, and all the wonder
    that would be.—

In the Spring a fuller crimson comes upon the
    robin's breast;
In the Spring the wanton lapwing gets himself
    another crest;
In the Spring a livelier iris changes on the
    burnished dove;
In the Spring a young man's fancy lightly turns
    to thoughts of love.   20

Then her cheek was pale and thinner than
    should be for one so young,
And her eyes on all my motions with a mute
    observance hung.

And I said, 'My cousin Amy, speak, and speak
    the truth to me,
Trust me, cousin, all the current of my being
    sets to thee.'

On her pallid cheek and forehead came a color
    and a light,   25
As I have seen the rosy red flushing in the
    northern night.

And she turned—her bosom shaken with a
    sudden storm of sighs—
All the spirit deeply dawning in the dark of
    hazel eyes—

Saying, 'I have hid my feelings, fearing they
    should do me wrong';
Saying, 'Dost thou love me, cousin?' weeping,
    'I have loved thee long.'   30

Love took up the glass of time, and turned it
    in his glowing hands;
Every moment, lightly shaken, ran itself in
    golden sands.

Love took up the harp of Life, and smote on
    all the chords with might;
Smote the chord of Self, that, trembling, passed
    in music out of sight.

Many a morning on the moorland did we hear
    the copses ring,   35
And her whisper thronged my pulses with the
    fulness of the Spring.

Many an evening by the waters did we watch
    the stately ships,
And our spirits rushed together at the touching
    of the lips.

O my cousin, shallow-hearted! O my Amy,
    mine no more!
O the dreary, dreary moorland! O the barren,
    barren shore!   40

Falser than all fancy fathoms, falser than all
    songs have sung,
Puppet to a father's threat, and servile to a
    shrewish tongue!

Is it well to wish thee happy? having known
    me—to decline
On a range of lower feelings and a narrower
    heart than mine!

Yet it shall be; thou shalt lower to his level
    day by day,   45
What is fine within thee growing coarse to
    sympathize with clay.

As the husband is, the wife is; thou art mated
    with a clown,
And the grossness of his nature will have weight
    to drag thee down.

He will hold thee, when his passion shall have
    spent its novel force,
Something better than his dog, a little dearer
    than his horse.   50

What is this? his eyes are heavy; think not they
    are glazed with wine.
Go to him, it is thy duty; kiss him, take his
    hand in thine.

It may be my lord is weary, that his brain is
    overwrought;
Soothe him with thy finer fancies, touch him
    with thy lighter thought.

He will answer to the purpose, easy things to
    understand—   55
Better thou wert dead before me, though I slew
    thee with my hand!

Better thou and I were lying, hidden from the
    hearts' disgrace,
Rolled in one another's arms, and silent in a
    last embrace.

Cursèd be the social wants that sin against the
    strength of youth!
Cursèd be the social lies that warp us from the
    living truth!   60

Cursèd be the sickly forms that err from honest
    Nature's rule!
Cursèd be the gold that gilds the straitened
    forehead of the fool!

Well—'t is well that I should bluster!—hadst
    thou less unworthy proved—
Would to God—for I had loved thee more than
    ever wife was loved.

Am I mad, that I should cherish that which
    bears but bitter fruit?   65
I will pluck it from my bosom, though my heart
    be at the root.

Never, though my mortal summers to such
    length of years should come
As the many-wintered crow that leads the
    clanging rookery home.

Where is comfort? in division of the records of
    the mind?
Can I part her from herself, and love her as I
    knew her, kind?   70

I remember one that perished; sweetly did she
    speak and move;
Such a one do I remember, whom to look at was
    to love.

Can I think of her as dead, and love her for the
    love she bore?
No—she never loved me truly; love is love for
    evermore.

Comfort? comfort scorned of devils! this is truth
    the poet sings,   75
That a sorrow's crown of sorrow is remember-
    ing happier things.

Drug thy memories, lest thou learn it, lest thy
    heart be put to proof,
In the dead unhappy night, and when the rain
    is on the roof.

Like a dog, he hunts in dreams, and thou art
    staring at the wall,
Where the dying night-lamp flickers, and the
    shadows rise and fall.   30

Then a hand shall pass before thee, pointing to
    his drunken sleep,
To thy widowed marriage-pillows, to the tears
    that thou wilt weep.

Thou shalt hear the 'Never, never,' whispered
    by the phantom years,
And a song from out the distance in the ringing
    of thine ears;

And an eye shall vex thee, looking ancient kind-
    ness on thy pain.   85
Turn thee, turn thee on thy pillow; get thee to
    thy rest again.

Nay, but Nature brings thee solace; for a tender
    voice will cry.
'T is a purer life than thine, a lip to drain thy
    trouble dry.

Baby lips will laugh me down; my latest rival
    brings thee rest.
Baby fingers, waxen touches, press me from the
    mother's breast.   90

O, the child too clothes the father with a dear-
    ness not his due.
Half is thine and half is his; it will be worthy of
    the two.

O, I see thee old and formal, fitted to thy petty
    part,
With a little hoard of maxims preaching down
    a daughter's heart.

'They were dangerous guides, the feelings—she
    herself was not exempt—   95
Truly, she herself had suffered'—Perish in thy
    self-contempt!

Overlive it—lower yet—be happy! wherefore
    should I care?
I myself must mix with action, lest I wither by
    despair.

What is that which I should turn to, lighting
    upon days like these?
Every door is barred with gold, and opens but
    to golden keys.   100

Every gate is thronged with suitors, all the
    markets overflow.
I have but an angry fancy; what is that which I
    should do?

I had been content to perish, falling on the foe-
    man's ground,
When the ranks are rolled in vapor, and the
    winds are laid with sound.

But the jingling of the guinea helps the hurt
    that Honor feels,   105
And the nations do but murmur, snarling at
    each other's heels.

Can I but relive in sadness? I will turn that
    earlier page.
Hide me from my deep emotion, O thou won-
    drous Mother-Age!

Make me feel the wild pulsation that I felt be-
    fore the strife,
When I heard my days before me, and the
    tumult of my life;   110

Yearning for the large excitement that the com-
    ing years would yield,
Eager-hearted as a boy when first he leaves his
    father's field,

And at night along the dusky highway near and
    nearer drawn,
Sees in heaven the light of London flaring like
    a dreary dawn;

And his spirit leaps within him to be gone be-
    fore him then,   115
Underneath the light he looks at, in among the
    throngs of men;

Men, my brothers, men the workers, ever reap-
    ing something new;
That which they have done but earnest of the
    things that they shall do.

For I dipped into the future, far as human eye
    could see,
Saw the Vision of the world, and all the wonder
    that would be;   120

Saw the heavens fill with commerce, argosies of magic sails,
Pilot of the purple twilight, dropping down with costly bales;

Heard the heavens fill with shouting, and there rained a ghastly dew
From the nations' airy navies grappling in the central blue;

Far along the world-wide whisper of the south-wind rushing warm, 125
With the standards of the peoples plunging through the thunder-storm;

Till the war-drum throbbed no longer, and the battle-flags were furled
In the Parliament of man, the Federation of the world.

There the common sense of most shall hold a fretful realm in awe,
And the kindly earth shall slumber, lapped in universal law. 130

So I triumphed ere my passion sweeping through me left me dry,
Left me with the palsied heart, and left me with the jaundiced eye;

Eye, to which all order festers, all things here are out of joint;
Science moves, but slowly slowly, creeping on from point to point;

Slowly comes a hungry people, as a lion, creeping nigher, 135
Glares at one that nods and winks behind a slowly-dying fire.

Yet I doubt not through the ages one increasing purpose runs,
And the thoughts of men are widened with the process of the suns.

What is that to him that reaps not harvest of his youthful joys,
Though the deep heart of existence beat for ever like a boy's? 140

Knowledge comes, but wisdom lingers, and I linger on the shore,
And the individual withers, and the world is more and more.

Knowledge comes, but wisdom lingers, and he bears a laden breast,
Full of sad experience, moving toward the stillness of his rest.

Hark, my merry comrades call me, sounding on the bugle-horn, 145
They to whom my foolish passion were a target for their scorn:

Shall it not be scorn to me to harp on such a moldered string?
I am shamed through all my nature to have loved so slight a thing.

Weakness to be wroth with weakness! woman's pleasure, woman's pain—
Nature made them blinder motions bounded in a shallower brain: 150

Woman is the lesser man, and all thy passions, matched with mine,
Are as moonlight unto sunlight, and as water unto wine—

Here at least, where nature sickens, nothing. Ah, for some retreat
Deep in yonder shining Orient, where my life began to beat,

Where in wild Mahratta-battle fell my father evil-starred;— 155
I was left a trampled orphan, and a selfish uncle's ward.

Or to burst all links of habit—there to wander far away,
On from island unto island at the gateways of the day.

Larger constellations burning, mellow moons and happy skies,
Breadths of tropic shade and palms in cluster, knots of Paradise. 160

Never comes the trader, never floats an European flag,
Slides the bird o'er lustrous woodland, swings the trailer from the crag;

Droops the heavy-blossomed bower, hangs the heavy-fruited tree—
Summer isles of Eden lying in dark-purple spheres of sea.

There methinks would be enjoyment more than in this march of mind, 165
In the steamship, in the railway, in the thoughts that shake mankind.

There the passions cramped no longer shall have scope and breathing space;
I will take some savage woman, she shall rear my dusky race.

Iron-jointed, supple-sinewed, they shall dive, and they shall run,
Catch the wild goat by the hair, and hurl their lances in the sun; 170

Whistle back the parrot's call, and leap the rainbows of the brooks,
Not with blinded eyesight poring over miserable books—

Fool, again the dream, the fancy! but I *know* my words are wild,
But I count the gray barbarian lower than the Christian child.

I, to herd with narrow foreheads, vacant of our glorious gains, 175
Like a beast with lower pleasures, like a beast with lower pains!

Mated with a squalid savage—what to me were sun or clime!
I the heir of all the ages, in the foremost files of time—

I that rather held it better men should perish one by one,
Than that earth should stand at gaze like Joshua's moon in Ajalon! 180

Not in vain the distance beacons. Forward, forward let us range,
Let the great world spin for ever down the ringing grooves of change.

Through the shadow of the globe we sweep into the younger day;
Better fifty years of Europe than a cycle of Cathay.

Mother-Age,—for mine I knew not,—help me as when life begun; 185
Rift the hills, and roll the waters, flash the lightnings, weigh the sun.

O, I see the crescent promise of my spirit hath not set.
Ancient founts of inspiration well through all my fancy yet.

Howsoever these things be, a long farewell to Locksley Hall!
Now for me the woods may wither, now for me the roof-tree fall. 190

Comes a vapor from the margin, blackening over heath and holt,
Cramming all the blast before it, in its breast a thunderbolt.

Let it fall on Locksley Hall, with rain or hail, or fire or snow;
For the mighty wind arises, roaring seaward, and I go.

(1842)

BREAK, BREAK, BREAK

Break, break, break,
  On thy cold gray stones, O Sea!
And I would that my tongue could utter
  The thoughts that arise in me.

O well for the fisherman's boy, 5
  That he shouts with his sister at play!
O well for the sailor lad,
  That he sings in his boat on the bay!

And the stately ships go on
  To their haven under the hill; 10
But O for the touch of a vanished hand,
  And the sound of a voice that is still!

Break, break, break,
  At the foot of thy crags, O Sea!
But the tender grace of a day that is dead 15
  Will never come back to me.

(1842)

THE POET'S SONG

The rain had fallen, the Poet arose,
He passed by the town and out of the street,
A light wind blew from the gates of the sun,
And waves of shadow went over the wheat,
And he sat him down in a lonely place, 5
And chanted a melody loud and sweet,
That made the wild-swan pause in her cloud
And the lark drop down at his feet.

The swallow stopped as he hunted the fly,
  The snake slipped under a spray, 10
The wild hawk stood with the down on his beak,
  And stared, with his foot on the prey,
And the nightingale thought, 'I have sung many songs,
  But never a one so gay,
For he sings of what the world will be 15
  When the years have died away.'

(1842)

SONGS

From The Princess

Tears, idle tears, I know not what they mean,
Tears from the depth of some divine despair
Rise in the heart, and gather to the eyes,
In looking on the happy Autumn-fields,
And thinking of the days that are no more. 5

Fresh as the first beam glittering on a sail,
That brings our friends up from the underworld,
Sad as the last which reddens over one
That sinks with all we love below the verge;
So sad, so fresh, the days that are no more. 10

Ah, sad and strange as in dark summer dawns
The earliest pipe of half-awakened birds
To dying ears, when unto dying eyes
The casement slowly grows a glimmering square;
So sad, so strange, the days that are no more. 15

Dear as remembered kisses after death,
And sweet as those by hopeless fancy feigned
On lips that are for others; deep as love,
Deep as first love, and wild with all regret;
O Death in Life, the days that are no more!   20
   (1847)

THE splendor falls on castle walls
   And snowy summits old in story;
The long light shakes across the lakes,
   And the wild cataract leaps in glory.
Blow, bugle, blow, set the wild echoes flying,   5
Blow, bugle; answer, echoes, dying, dying, dying.

O, hark, O, hear! how thin and clear,
   And thinner, clearer, farther going!
O, sweet and far from cliff and scar
   The horns of Elfland faintly blowing!   10
Blow, let us hear the purple glens replying;
Blow, bugle; answer, echoes, dying, dying, dying.

O love, they die in yon rich sky,
   They faint on hill or field or river;
Our echoes roll from soul to soul,   15
   And grow for ever and for ever.
Blow, bugle, blow, set the wild echoes flying,
And answer, echoes, answer, dying, dying, dying.
   (1850)

THY voice is heard through rolling drums
   That beat to battle where he stands;
Thy face across his fancy comes,
   And gives the battle to his hands:
A moment, while the trumpets blow,   5
   He sees his brood about thy knee;
The next, like fire he meets the foe,
   And strikes him dead for thine and thee.
   (1850)

HOME they brought her warrior dead;
   She nor swooned nor uttered cry:
All her maidens, watching, said,
   'She must weep or she will die.'

Then they praised him, soft and low,   5
   Called him worthy to be loved,
Truest friend and noblest foe;
   Yet she neither spoke nor moved.

Stole a maiden from her place,
   Lightly to the warrior stepped,   10
Took the face-cloth from the face;
   Yet she neither moved nor wept.

Rose a nurse of ninety years,
   Set his child upon her knee—
Like summer tempest came her tears—   15
   '*Sweet my child, I live for thee.*'
   (1850)

ASK me no more: the moon may draw the sea;
   The cloud may stoop from heaven and take
      the shape,
   With fold to fold, of mountain or of cape;
But O too fond, when have I answered thee?
   Ask me no more.   5

Ask me no more: what answer should I give?
   I love not hollow cheek or faded eye:
Yet, O my friend, I will not have thee die!
Ask me no more, lest I should bid thee live;
   Ask me no more.   10

Ask me no more: thy fate and mine are sealed;
   I strove against the stream and all in vain;
Let the great river take me to the main.
No more, dear love, for at a touch I yield;
   Ask me no more.   15
   (1850)

IN MEMORIAM A. H. H.

OBIIT MDCCCXXXIII

STRONG Son of God, immortal Love,
   Whom we, that have not seen thy face,
   By faith, and faith alone, embrace,
Believing where we cannot prove;

Thine are these orbs of light and shade;   5
   Thou madest Life in man and brute;
   Thou madest Death; and lo, thy foot
Is on the skull which thou hast made.

Thou wilt not leave us in the dust;
   Thou madest man, he knows not why,   10
   He thinks he was not made to die;
And thou hast made him: thou art just.

Thou seemest human and divine,
   The highest, holiest manhood, thou:
   Our wills are ours, we know not how;   15
Our wills are ours, to make them thine.

Our little systems have their day,
   They have their day and cease to be;
   They are but broken lights of thee,
And thou, O Lord, art more than they.   20

We have but faith: we cannot know;
   For knowledge is of things we see;
   And yet we trust it comes from thee,
A beam in darkness: let it grow.

Let knowledge grow from more to more,   25
   But more of reverence in us dwell;
   That mind and soul, according well,
May make one music as before,

But vaster. We are fools and slight;
   We mock thee when we do not fear: 30
   But help thy foolish ones to bear;
Help thy vain worlds to bear thy light.

Forgive what seemed my sin in me;
  What seemed my worth since I began;
  For merit lives from man to man,   35
And not from man, O Lord, to thee.

Forgive my grief for one removed,
  Thy creature, whom I found so fair.
  I trust he lives in thee, and there
I find him worthier to be loved.   40

Forgive these wild and wandering cries,
  Confusions of a wasted youth;
  Forgive them where they fail in truth,
And in thy wisdom make me wise.

LII

O Sorrow, cruel fellowship,
  O Priestess in the vaults of Death,
  O sweet and bitter in a breath,
What whispers from thy lying lip?

'The stars,' she whispers, 'blindly run;   5
  A web is woven across the sky,
  From out waste places comes a cry,
And murmurs from the dying sun;

'And all the phantom, Nature, stands—
  With all the music in her tone,   10
  A hollow echo of my own,—
A hollow form with empty hands.'

And shall I take a thing so blind,
  Embrace her as my natural good;
  Or crush her, like a vice of blood,   15
Upon the threshold of the mind?

XIX

The Danube to the Severn gave
  The darkened heart that beat no more;
  They laid him by the pleasant shore,
And in the hearing of the wave.

There twice a day the Severn fills;   5
  The salt sea-water passes by,
  And hushes half the babbling Wye,
And makes a silence in the hills.

The Wye is hushed nor moved along,
  And hushed my deepest grief of all,   10
  When filled with tears that cannot fall,
I brim with sorrow drowning song.

The tide flows down, the wave again
  Is vocal in its wooded walls;
  My deeper anguish also falls,   15
And I can speak a little then.

XXVII

I envy not in any moods
  The captive void of noble rage,
  The linnet born within the cage,
That never knew the summer woods;

I envy not the beast that takes   5
  His license in the field of time,
  Unfettered by the sense of crime,
To whom a conscience never wakes;

Nor, what may count itself as blest,
  The heart that never plighted troth   10
  But stagnates in the weeds of sloth;
Nor any want-begotten rest.

I hold it true, whate'er befall;
  I feel it, when I sorrow most;
  'T is better to have loved and lost   15
Than never to have loved at all.

LV

The wish, that of the living whole
  No life may fail beyond the grave,
  Derives it not from what we have
The likest God within the soul?

Are God and Nature then at strife,   5
  That Nature lends such evil dreams?
  So careful of the type she seems,
So careless of the single life;

That I, considering everywhere
  Her secret meaning in her deeds,   10
  And finding that of fifty seeds
She often brings but one to bear,

I falter where I firmly trod,
  And falling with my weight of cares
  Upon the great world's altar-stairs,   15
That slope through darkness up to God,

I stretch lame hands of faith, and grope,
  And gather dust and chaff, and call
  To what I feel is Lord of all,
And faintly trust the larger hope.   20

LXIV

Dost thou look back on what hath been,
  As some divinely gifted man,
  Whose life in low estate began
And on a simple village green;

Who breaks his birth's invidious bar,   5
  And grasps the skirts of happy chance,
  And breasts the blows of circumstance,
And grapples with his evil star;

Who makes by force his merit known
  And lives to clutch the golden keys,   10
  To mold a mighty state's decrees,
And shape the whisper of the throne;

And moving up from high to higher,
  Becomes in Fortune's crowning slope
  The pillar of a people's hope,   15
The center of a world's desire;

Yet feels, as in a pensive dream,
  When all his active powers are still,
  A distant dearness in the hill,
A secret sweetness in the stream,   20

The limit of his narrower fate,
  While yet beside its vocal springs
  He played at counselors and kings
With one that was his earliest mate;

Who ploughs with pain his native lea   25
  And reaps the labor of his hands,
  Or in the furrow musing stands:
'Does my old friend remember me?'

LXVII

When on my bed the moonlight falls,
  I know that in thy place of rest
  By that broad water of the west
There comes a glory on the walls;

Thy marble bright in dark appears,   5
  As slowly steals a silver flame,
  Along the letters of thy name,
And o'er the number of thy years.

The mystic glory swims away;
  From off my bed the moonlight dies;   10
  And closing eaves of wearied eyes
I sleep till dusk is dipped in gray:

And then I know the mist is drawn
  A lucid veil from coast to coast,
  And in the dark church like a ghost   15
Thy tablet glimmers to the dawn.

LXXXVIII

Wild bird, whose warble, liquid sweet,
  Rings Eden through the budded quicks
  O, tell me where the senses mix,
O, tell me where the passions meet,

Whence radiate: fierce extremes employ   5
  Thy spirits in the darkening leaf,
  And in the midmost heart of grief
Thy passion clasps a secret joy;

And I—my harp would prelude woe—
  I cannot all command the strings,   10
  The glory of the sum of things
Will flash along the chords and go.

CXXIII

There rolls the deep where grew the tree.
  O earth, what changes hast thou seen!
  There where the long street roars, hath been
The stillness of the central sea.

The hills are shadows, and they flow   5
  From form to form, and nothing stands;
  They melt like mist, the solid lands,
Like clouds they shape themselves and go.

But in my spirit will I dwell,
  And dream my dream, and hold it true;   10
  For though my lips may breathe adieu,
I cannot think the thing farewell.

CXXX

Thy voice is on the rolling air;
  I hear thee where the waters run;
  Thou standest in the rising sun,
And in the setting thou art fair.

What art thou then? I cannot guess;   5
  But though I seem in star and flower,
  To feel thee some diffusive power,
I do not therefore love thee less.

My love involves the love before;
  My love is vaster passion now;   10
  Though mixed with God and Nature thou,
I seem to love thee more and more.

Far off thou art, but ever nigh;
  I have thee still, and I rejoice;
  I prosper, circled with thy voice;   15
I shall not lose thee though I die.

CXXXI

O living will that shalt endure
  When all that seems shall suffer shock,
  Rise in the spiritual rock,
Flow through our deeds and make them pure,

That we may lift from out of dust   5
  A voice as unto him that hears,
  A cry above the conquered years
To one that with us works, and trust,

With faith that comes of self-control,
  The truths that never can be proved   10
  Until we close with all we loved,
And all we flow from, soul in soul.

(1850)

* * *

MAUD; A MONODRAMA

PART I

I

I hate the dreadful hollow behind the little
    wood,
Its lips in the field above are dabbled with
    blood-red heath,
The red-ribbed ledges drip with a silent horror
    of blood,
And Echo there, whatever is asked her, answers
    'Death.'

For there in the ghastly pit long since a body
    was found,   5
His who had given me life—O father! O God!
    was it well?—

Mangled and flattened, and crushed, and dinted into the ground:
There yet lies the rock that fell with him when he fell.

Did he fling himself down? who knows? for a vast speculation had failed,
And ever he muttered and maddened, and ever wanned with despair, 10
And out he walked, when the wind like a broken worldling wailed,
And the flying gold of the ruined woodlands drove through the air.

I remember the time, for the roots of my hair were stirred
By a shuffled step, by a dead weight trailed, by a whispered fright,
And my pulses closed their gates with a shock on my heart as I heard 15
The shrill-edged shriek of a mother divide the shuddering night.

Villainy somewhere! whose? One says, we are villains all.
Not he: his honest fame should at least by me be maintained.
But that old man, now lord of the broad estate and the Hall,
Dropped off gorged from a scheme that had left us flaccid and drained. 20

Why do they prate of the blessings of Peace? we have made them a curse,
Pickpockets, each hand lusting for all that is not its own;
And lust of gain, in the spirit of Cain, is it better or worse
Than the heart of the citizen hissing in war on his own hearthstone?

But these are the days of advance, the works of the men of mind, 25
When who but a fool would have faith in a tradesman's ware or his word?
Is it peace or war? Civil war, as I think, and that of a kind
The viler, as underhand, not openly bearing the sword.

Sooner or later I too may passively take the print
Of the golden age—why not, I have neither hope nor trust; 30
May make my heart as a millstone, set my face as a flint,
Cheat and be cheated, and die; who knows? we are ashes and dust.

Peace sitting under her olive, and slurring the days gone by,
When the poor are hoveled, and hustled together, each sex, like swine,
When only the ledger lives, and when only not all men lie; 35
Peace in her vineyard—yes!—but a company forges the wine.

And the vitriol madness flushes up in the ruffian's head,
Till the filthy by-lane rings to the yell of the trampled wife,
And chalk and alum and plaster are sold to the poor for bread,
And the spirit of murder works in the very means of life, 40

And Sleep must lie down armed, for the villainous center-bits
Grind on the wakeful ear in the hush of the moonless nights,
While another is cheating the sick of a few last gasps, as he sits
To pestle a poisoned poison behind his crimson lights,

When a Mammonite mother kills her babe for a burial fee, 45
And Timour-Mammon grins on a pile of children's bones,
Is it peace or war? better, war! loud war by land and by sea,
War with a thousand battles, and shaking a hundred thrones.

For I trust if an enemy's fleet came yonder round by the hill,
And the rushing battle-bolt sang from the three-decker out of the foam, 50
That the smooth-faced snubnosed rogue would leap from his counter and till,
And strike, if he could, were it but with his cheating yardwand, home.—

What! am I raging alone as my father raged in his mood?
Must *I* too creep to the hollow and dash myself down and die
Rather than hold by the law that I made, nevermore to brood 55
On a horror of shattered limbs and a wretched swindler's lie?

Would there be sorrow for *me?* there was *love* in the passionate shriek,
Love for the silent thing that had made false haste to the grave—
Wrapt in a cloak, as I saw him, and thought he would rise and speak
And rave at the lie and the liar, ah, God, as he used to rave. 60

I am sick of the Hall, and the hill, I am sick of the moor and the main.
Why should I stay? can a sweeter chance ever come to me here?

O, having the nerves of motion as well as the
    nerves of pain,
Were it not wise if I fled from the place and
    the pit and the fear?

Workmen up at the Hall!—they are coming
    back from abroad;   65
The dark old place will be gilt by the touch of
    a millionaire;
I have heard, I know not whence, of the singular
    beauty of Maud;
I played with the girl when a child; she prom-
    ised then to be fair.

Maud with her venturous climbings, and tum-
    bles and childish escapes,
Maud the delight of the village, the ringing joy
    of the Hall,   70
Maud with her sweet purse-mouth when my
    father dangled the grapes,
Maud the beloved of my mother, the moon-
    faced darling of all,—

What is she now? My dreams are bad. She
    may bring me a curse,
No, there is fatter game on the moor; she will
    let me alone.
Thanks, for the fiend best knows whether
    woman or man be the worse.   75
I will bury myself in myself, and the Devil may
    pipe to his own.

III

COLD and clear-cut face, why come you so
    cruelly meek,
Breaking a slumber in which all spleenful folly
    was drowned,
Pale with the golden beam of an eyelash dead
    on the cheek,
Passionless, pale, cold face, star-sweet on a
    gloom profound;   80
Woman-like, taking revenge too deep for a
    transient wrong
Done but in thought to your beauty, and ever
    as pale as before
Growing and fading and growing upon me
    without a sound,
Luminous, gem-like, ghost-like, death-like, half
    the night long
Growing and fading and growing, till I could
    bear it no more,   85
But arose, and all by myself in my own dark
    garden ground,
Listening now to the tide in its broad-flung ship-
    wrecking roar,
Now to the scream of a maddened beach
    dragged down by the wave,
Walked in a wintry wind by a ghastly glimmer,
    and found
The shining daffodil dead, and Orion low in his
    grave.   90

V

A VOICE by the cedar tree
In the meadow under the Hall!
She is singing an air that is known to me,
A passionate ballad gallant and gay,
A martial song like a trumpet's call!   95
Singing alone in the morning of life,
In the happy morning of life and of May,
Singing of men that in battle array,
Ready in heart and ready in hand,
March with banner and bugle and fife,   100
To the death, for their native land.
Maud with her exquisite face,
And wild voice pealing up to the sunny sky,
And feet like sunny gems on an English green,
Maud in the light of her youth and her grace,
Singing of Death, and of Honor that cannot
    die,   106
Till I well could weep for a time so sordid and
    mean,
And myself so languid and base.

Silence, beautiful voice!
Be still, for you only trouble the mind   110
With a joy in which I cannot rejoice,
A glory I shall not find.
Still! I will hear you no more.
For your sweetness hardly leaves me a choice
But to move to the meadow and fall before 115
    Her feet on the meadow grass, and adore,
Not her, who is neither courtly nor kind,
Not her, not her, but a voice.

XI

O, LET the solid ground
    Not fail beneath my feet   120
Before my life has found
    What some have found so sweet;
Then let come what come may,
What matter if I go mad,
I shall have had my day.   125

Let the sweet heavens endure,
    Not close and darken above me
Before I am quite quite sure
    That there is one to love me;
Then let come what come may   130
To a life that has been so sad,
I shall have had my day.

XII

BIRDS in the high Hall-garden,
    When twilight was falling,
Maud, Maud, Maud, Maud,   135
    They were crying and calling.

Where was Maud? in our wood;
    And I—who else?—was with her,
Gathering woodland lilies,
    Myriads blow together.   140

Birds in our wood sang
  Ringing through the valleys,
Maud is here, here, here
  In among the lilies.

I kissed her slender hand,   145
  She took the kiss sedately;
Maud is not seventeen,
  But she is tall and stately.

I to cry out on pride
  Who have won her favor!   150
O, Maud were sure of heaven
  If lowliness could save her!

I know the way she went
  Home with her maiden posy,
For her feet have touched the meadows   155
  And left the daisies rosy.

Birds in the high Hall-garden
  Were crying and calling to her,
Where is Maud, Maud, Maud?
  One is come to woo her.   160

Look, a horse at the door,
  And little King Charley snarling!
Go back, my lord, across the moor,
  You are not her darling.

XVII

  Go not, happy day,   165
    From the shining fields,
  Go not, happy day,
    Till the maiden yields.
  Rosy is the West,
    Rosy is the South,   170
  Roses are her cheeks,
    And a rose her mouth.
  When the happy Yes
    Falters from her lips,
  Pass and blush the news   175
    Over glowing ships;
  Over blowing seas,
    Over seas at rest,
  Pass the happy news,
    Blush it through the West;   180
  Till the red man dance
    By his red cedar-tree,
  And the red man's babe
    Leap, beyond the sea.
  Blush from West to East,   185
    Blush from East to West,
  Till the West is East,
    Blush it through the West.
  Rosy is the West,
    Rosy is the South,   190
  Roses are her cheeks,
    And a rose her mouth.

XVIII

I HAVE led her home, my love, my only friend.
There is none like her, none.
And never yet so warmly ran my blood   195
And sweetly, on and on
Calming itself to the long-wished-for end,
Full to the banks, close on the promised good.

None like her, none.
Just now the dry-tongued laurels' pattering talk
Seemed her light foot along the garden walk,   201
And shook my heart to think she comes once
  more;
But even then I heard her close the door;
The gates of heaven are closed, and she is gone.

There is none like her, none,   205
Nor will be when our summers have deceased.
O, art thou sighing for Lebanon
In the long breeze that streams to thy delicious
    East,
Sighing for Lebanon,
Dark cedar, though thy limbs have here in-
  creased,   210
Upon a pastoral slope as fair,
And looking to the South and fed
With honeyed rain and delicate air,
And haunted by the starry head
Of her whose gentle will has changed my fate,
And made my life a perfumed altar-flame,   216
And over whom thy darkness must have spread
With such delight as theirs of old, thy great
Forefathers of the thornless garden, there
Shadowing the snow-limbed Eve from whom
  she came?   220

Here will I lie, while these long branches sway,
And you fair stars that crown a happy day
Go in and out as if at merry play,
Who am no more so all forlorn
As when it seemed far better to be born   225
To labor and the mattock-hardened hand
Than nursed at ease and brought to understand
A sad astrology, the boundless plan
That makes you tyrants in your iron skies,
Innumerable, pitiless, passionless eyes,   230
Cold fires, yet with power to burn and brand
His nothingness into man.
But now shine on, and what care I
Who in this stormy gulf have found a pearl
The countercharm of space and hollow sky,   235
And do accept my madness, and would die
To save from some slight shame one simple
  girl?—

Would die, for sullen-seeming Death may give
More life to Love than is or ever was
In our low world, where yet 't is sweet to live.
Let no one ask me how it came to pass;   241
It seems that I am happy, that to me
A livelier emerald twinkles in the grass,
A purer sapphire melts into the sea.

Not die, but live a life of truest breath, 245
And teach true life to fight with mortal wrongs,
O, why should Love, like men in drinking songs,
Spice his fair banquet with the dust of death?
Make answer, Maud my bliss,
Maud made my Maud by that long loving kiss,
Life of my life, wilt thou not answer this? 251
'The dusky strand of Death inwoven here
With dear Love's tie, makes Love himself more
    dear.'

Is that enchanted moan only the swell
Of the long waves that roll in yonder bay? 255
And hark the clock within, the silver knell
Of twelve sweet hours that past in bridal white,
And died to live, long as my pulses play;
But now by this my love has closed her sight,
And given false death her hand, and stolen away
To dreamful wastes where footless fancies dwell
Among the fragments of the golden day. 262
May nothing there her maiden grace affright!
Dear heart, I feel with thee the drowsy spell.
My bride to be, my evermore delight, 265
My own heart's heart, my ownest own, farewell;
It is but for a little space I go,
And ye meanwhile far over moor and fell
Beat to the noiseless music of the night!
Has our whole earth gone nearer to the glow
Of your soft splendors that you look so bright?
I have climbed nearer out of lonely Hell. 272
Beat, happy stars, timing with things below,
Beat with my heart more blest than heart can
    tell,
Blest, but for some dark undercurrent woe,
That seems to draw—but it shall not be so: 276
Let all be well, be well.

XXI

Rivulet crossing my ground,
And bringing me down from the Hall
This garden-rose that I found, 280
Forgetful of Maud and me,
And lost in trouble and moving round
Here at the head of a tinkling fall,
And trying to pass to the sea;
O rivulet, born at the Hall, 285
My Maud has sent it by thee—
If I read her sweet will right—
On a blushing mission to me,
Saying in odor and color, 'Ah, be
Among the roses to-night.' 290

XXII

Come into the garden, Maud,
    For the black bat, night, has flown,
Come into the garden, Maud,
    I am here at the gate alone;
And the woodbine spices are wafted abroad,
    And the musk of the rose is blown. 296

For a breeze of morning moves,
    And the planet of love is on high,
Beginning to faint in the light that she loves
    On a bed of daffodil sky, 300
To faint in the light of the sun she loves
    To faint in his light, and to die.

All night have the roses heard
    The flute, violin, bassoon;
All night has the casement jessamine stirred
    To the dancers dancing in tune; 306
Till a silence fell with the waking bird,
    And a hush with the setting moon.

I said to the lily, 'There is but one,
    With whom she has heart to be gay. 310
When will the dancers leave her alone?
    She is weary of dance and play.'
Now half to the setting moon are gone,
    And half to the rising day;
Low on the sand and loud on the stone 315
    The last wheel echoes away.

I said to the rose, 'The brief night goes
    In babble and revel and wine.
O young lord-lover, what sighs are those,
    For one that will never be thine? 320
But mine, but mine,' so I sware to the rose,
    'Forever and ever, mine.'

And the soul of the rose went into my blood,
    As the music clashed in the Hall;
And long by the garden lake I stood, 325
    For I heard your rivulet fall
From the lake to the meadow and on to the
    wood,
    Our wood, that is dearer than all;

From the meadow your walks have left so sweet
    That whenever a March-wind sighs 330
He sets the jewel-print of your feet
    In violets blue as your eyes,
To the woody hollows in which we meet
    And the valleys of Paradise.

The slender acacia would not shake 335
    One long milk-bloom on the tree;
The white lake-blossom fell into the lake
    As the pimpernel dozed on the lea;
But the rose was awake all night for your sake,
    Knowing your promise to me; 340
The lilies and roses were all awake,
    They sighed for the dawn and thee.

Queen rose of the rosebud garden of girls,
    Come hither, the dances are done,
In gloss of satin and glimmer of pearls, 345
    Queen lily and rose in one;
Shine out, little head, sunning over with curls,
    To the flowers, and be their sun.

There has fallen a splendid tear
    From the passion-flower at the gate, 350
She is coming, my dove, my dear;
    She is coming, my life, my fate.

The red rose cries, 'She is near, she is near;'
  And the white rose weeps, 'She is late;'
The larkspur listens, 'I hear, I hear;'
  And the lily whispers, 'I wait.'

She is coming, my own, my sweet;
  Were it ever so airy a tread,
My heart would hear her and beat,
  Were it earth in an earthy bed;
My dust would hear her and beat,
  Had I lain for a century dead;
Would start and tremble under her feet,
  And blossom in purple and red.

PART II

II

See what a lovely shell,
Small and pure as a pearl,
Lying close to my foot,
Frail, but a work divine,
Made so fairly well
With delicate spire and whorl,
How exquisitely minute,
A miracle of design!

What is it? a learned man
Could give it a clumsy name,
Let him name it who can,
The beauty would be the same.

The tiny cell is forlorn,
Void of the little living will
That made it stir on the shore.
Did he stand at the diamond door
Of his house in a rainbow frill?
Did he push, when he was uncurled,
A golden foot or a fairy horn
Through his dim water-world?

Slight, to be crushed with a tap
Of my finger-nail on the sand,
Small, but a work divine,
Frail, but of force to withstand,
Year upon year, the shock
Of cataract seas that snap
The three-decker's oaken spine
Athwart the ledges of rock,
Here on the Breton strand!

Breton, not Briton; here
Like a shipwrecked man on a coast
Of ancient fable and fear—
Plagued with a flitting to and fro,
A disease, a hard mechanic ghost
That never came from on high
Nor ever arose from below,
But only moves with the moving eye,
Flying along the land and the main—

Why should it look like Maud?
Am I to be overawed
By what I cannot but know
Is a juggle born of the brain?
Back from the Breton coast,
Sick of a nameless fear,
Back to the dark sea-line
Looking, thinking of all I have lost;
An old song vexes my ear;
But that of Lamech is mine.

For years, a measureless ill,
For years, for ever, to part—
But she, she would love me still;
And as long, O God, as she
Have a grain of love for me,
So long, no doubt, no doubt,
Shall I nurse in my dark heart,
However weary, a spark of will
Not to be trampled out.

Strange, that the mind, when fraught
With a passion so intense
One would think that it well
Might drown all life in the eye,—
That it should, by being so overwrought,
Suddenly strike on a sharper sense
For a shell, or a flower, little things
Which else would have been past by!
And now I remember, I,
When he lay dying there,
I noticed one of his many rings
(For he had many, poor worm) and thought
It is his mother's hair.

Who knows if he be dead?
Whether I need have fled?
Am I guilty of blood?
However this may be,
Comfort her, comfort her, all things good,
While I am over the sea!
Let me and my passionate love go by,
But speak to her all things holy and high,
Whatever happen to me!
Me and my harmful love go by;
But come to her waking, find her asleep,
Powers of the height, Powers of the deep,
And comfort her though I die.

III

Courage, poor heart of stone,
I will not ask thee why
Thou canst not understand
That thou art left for ever alone:
Courage, poor stupid heart of stone.—
Or, if I ask thee why,
Care not thou to reply;
She is but dead, and the time is at hand
When thou shalt more than die.

IV

O that 't were possible
After long grief and pain

To find the arms of my true love
Round me once again!   460
When I was wont to meet her
In the silent woody places
By the home that gave me birth,
We stood tranced in long embraces
Mixed with kisses sweeter, sweeter   465
Than anything on earth.

A shadow flits before me,
Not thou, but like to thee,
Ah Christ, that it were possible
For one short hour to see   470
The souls we loved, that they might tell us
What and where they be!

It leads me forth at evening,
It lightly winds and steals
In a cold white robe before me,   475
When all my spirit reels
At the shouts, the leagues of lights,
And the roaring of the wheels.

Half the night I waste in sighs,
Half in dreams I sorrow after   480
The delight of early skies;
In a wakeful doze I sorrow
For the hand, the lips, the eyes,
For the meeting of the morrow,
The delight of happy laughter,   485
The delight of low replies.

'T is a morning pure and sweet,
And a dewy splendor falls
On the little flower that clings
To the turrets and the walls;   490
'T is a morning pure and sweet,
And the light and shadow fleet;
She is walking in the meadow,
And the woodland echo rings;
In a moment we shall meet;   495
She is singing in the meadow,
And the rivulet at her feet
Ripples on in light and shadow
To the ballad that she sings.

Do I hear her sing as of old,   500
My bird with the shining head,
My own dove with the tender eye?
But there rings on a sudden, a passionate cry,
There is some one dying or dead,
And a sullen thunder is rolled;   505
For a tumult shakes the city,
And I wake, my dream is fled;
In the shuddering dawn, behold,
Without knowledge, without pity,
By the curtains of my bed   510
That abiding phantom cold!

Get thee hence, nor come again,
Mix not memory with doubt,
Pass, thou death-like type of pain,
Pass and cease to move about!   515
'T is the blot upon the brain
That *will* show itself without.

Then I rise, the eave-drops fall,
And the yellow vapors choke
The great city sounding wide;   520
The day comes, a dull red ball
Wrapt in drifts of lurid smoke
On the misty river-tide.

Through the hubbub of the market
I steal, a wasted frame;   525
It crosses here, it crosses there,
Through all that crowd confused and loud,
The shadow still the same;
And on my heavy eyelids
My anguish hangs like shame.   530

Alas, for her that met me,
That heard me softly call,
Came glimmering through the laurels
At the quiet evenfall,
In the garden by the turrets   535
Of the old manorial hall!

Would the happy spirit descend
From the realms of light and song,
In the chamber or the street,
As she looks among the blest,   540
Should I fear to greet my friend
Or to say 'Forgive the wrong,'
Or to ask her, 'Take me, sweet,
To the regions of thy rest?'

But the broad light glares and beats,   545
And the shadow flits and fleets
And will not let me be;
And I loathe the squares and streets,
And the faces that one meets,
Hearts with no love for me.   550
Always I long to creep
Into some still cavern deep,
There to weep, and weep, and weep
My whole soul out to thee.

(1855)

SONG

From GUINEVERE

'LATE, late, so late! and dark the night and chill!
Late, late, so late! but we can enter still.'
'*Too late, too late! ye cannot enter now.*'

'No light had we; for that we do repent;
And learning this, the bridegroom will relent.'
'*Too late, too late! ye cannot enter now.*'

'No light! so late! and dark and chill the night!
O, let us in, that we may find the light!'
'*Too late, too late! ye cannot enter now.*'

'Have we not heard the bridegroom is so sweet?
O, let us in, though late, to kiss his feet!'   11
'*No, no, too late! ye cannot enter now.*'

(1859)

TITHONUS

The woods decay, the woods decay and fall,
The vapors weep their burthen to the ground,
Man comes and tills the field and lies beneath,
And after many a summer dies the swan.
Me only cruel immortality   5
Consumes; I wither slowly in thine arms,
Here at the quiet limit of the world,
A white-haired shadow roaming like a dream
The ever-silent spaces of the East,
Far-folded mists, and gleaming halls of morn.   10
Alas! for this gray shadow, once a man—
So glorious in his beauty and thy choice,
Who madest him thy chosen, that he seemed
To his great heart none other than a God!
I asked thee, 'Give me immortality.'   15
Then didst thou grant mine asking with a smile,
Like wealthy men who care not how they give.
But thy strong Hours indignant worked their wills,
And beat me down and marred and wasted me,
And though they could not end me, left me maimed   20
To dwell in presence of immortal youth,
Immortal age beside immortal youth,
And all I was, in ashes. Can thy love,
Thy beauty, make amends, though even now,
Close over us, the silver star, thy guide,   25
Shines in those tremulous eyes that fill with tears
To hear me? Let me go; take back thy gift;
Why should a man desire in any way
To vary from the kindly race of men,
Or pass beyond the goal of ordinance   30
Where all should pause, as is most meet for all?

A soft air fans the cloud apart; there comes
A glimpse of that dark world where I was born.
Once more the old mysterious glimmer steals
From thy pure brows, and from thy shoulders pure,   35
And bosom beating with a heart renewed.
Thy cheek begins to redden through the gloom,
Thy sweet eyes brighten slowly close to mine,
Ere yet they blind the stars, and the wild team
Which love thee, yearning for thy yoke, arise,   40
And shake the darkness from their loosened manes,
And beat the twilight into flakes of fire.

Lo! ever thus thou growest beautiful
In silence, then before thine answer given
Departest, and thy tears are on my cheek.   45

Why wilt thou ever scare me with thy tears,
And make me tremble lest a saying learnt,
In days far-off, on that dark earth, be true?
'The Gods themselves cannot recall their gifts.'

Ay me! ay me! with what another heart   50
In days far-off, and with what other eyes
I used to watch—if I be he that watched—
The lucid outline forming round thee; saw
The dim curls kindle into sunny rings;
Changed with thy mystic change, and felt my blood   55
Glow with the glow that slowly crimsoned all
Thy presence and thy portals, while I lay,
Mouth, forehead, eyelids, growing dewy-warm
With kisses balmier than half-opening buds
Of April, and could hear the lips that kissed   60
Whispering I knew not what of wild and sweet,
Like that strange song I heard Apollo sing,
While Ilion like a mist rose into towers.

Yet hold me not for ever in thine East;
How can my nature longer mix with thine?
Coldly thy rosy shadows bathe me, cold   66
Are all thy lights, and cold my wrinkled feet
Upon thy glimmering thresholds, when the steam
Floats up from those dim fields about the homes
Of happy men that have the power to die,   70
And grassy barrows of the happier dead.
Release me, and restore me to the ground;
Thou seest all things, thou wilt see my grave;
Thou wilt renew thy beauty morn by morn;
I earth in earth forget these empty courts,   75
And thee returning on thy silver wheels.

(1860)

MILTON
(ALCAICS)

O mighty-mouthed inventor of harmonies,
O skilled to sing of Time or Eternity,
God-gifted organ-voice of England,
    Milton, a name to resound for ages:

Whose Titan angels, Gabriel, Abdiel,   5
Starred from Jehovah's gorgeous armories,
Tower, as the deep-domed empyrean
    Rings to the roar of an angel onset!

Me rather all that bowery loneliness,
The brooks of Eden mazily murmuring,   10
And bloom profuse and cedar arches
    Charm, as a wanderer out in ocean,

Where some refulgent sunset of India
Streams o'er a rich ambrosial ocean isle,
And crimson-hued the stately palm-woods   15
    Whisper in odorous heights of even.

(1863)

NORTHERN FARMER
OLD STYLE

Wheer 'asta beän saw long and meä liggin' 'ere aloän?
Noorse? thoort nowt o' a noorse; whoy, Doctor 's abeän an' agoän;
Says that I moänt 'a naw moor aäle, but I beänt a fool;
Git ma my aäle, fur I beänt a-gawin' to breäk my rule.

Doctors, they knaws nowt, fur a says what 's nawways true; 5
Naw soort o' koind o' use to saäy the things that a do.
I 've 'ed my point o' aäle ivry noight sin' I beän 'ere.
An' I 've 'ed my quart ivry market-noight for foorty year.

Parson 's a beän loikewoise, an' a sittin' ere o' my bed.
'The Amoighty 's a taäkin o' you to 'issén, my friend,' a said, 10
An' a towd ma my sins, an' 's toithe were due, an' I gied it in hond;
I done moy duty boy 'um, as I 'a done boy the lond.

Larn'd a ma' beä. I reckons I 'annot sa mooch to larn.
But a cast oop, thot a did, 'bout Bessy Marris's barne.
Thaw a knaws I hallus voäted wi' Squoire an' choorch an' staäte, 15
An' i' the woorst o' toimes I wur niver again the raäte.

An' I hallus coom'd to 's choorch afoor moy Sally wur deäd,
An' 'eärd 'um a bummin' awaäy loike a buzzard-clock ower my 'eäd,
An' I niver knaw'd whot a meän'd but I thowt a 'ad summut to saäy,
An' I thowt a said whot a owt to 'a said, an' I coom'd awaäy. 20

Bessy Marris's barne! tha knaws she laäid it to meä.
Mowt a beän, mayhap, for she wur a bad un, sheä.
'Siver, I kep 'um, I kep 'um, my lass, tha mun understond;
I done moy duty boy 'um, as I 'a done boy the lond.

But Parson a cooms an' a goäs, an' a says it eäsy an' freeä: 25
'The Amoighty 's a taäking o' you to 'issén, my friend,' says 'eä.

I weänt saäy men be loiars, thaw summun said it in 'aäste;
But 'e reäds wonn sarmin a weeäk, an' I 'a stubb'd Thurnaby waäste.

D' ya moind the waäste, my lass? naw, naw, tha was not born then;
Theer wur a boggle in it, I often 'eärd 'um mysén; 30
Moäst loike a butter-bump, fur I 'eärd 'um about an' about,
But I stubb'd 'um oop wi' the lot, an' raäved an' rembled 'um out.

Keäper's it wur; fo' they fun 'um theer a-laäid of 'is faäce
Down i' the woild 'enemies afoor I coom'd to the plaäce.
Noäks or Thimbleby—toäner 'ed shot 'um as dead as a naäil. 35
Noäks wur 'ang'd for it oop at 'soize—but git ma my aäle.

Dubbut looök at the waäste; theer warn't not feeäd for a cow;
Nowt at all but bracken an' fuzz, an' looök at it now—
Warn's worth nowt a haäcre, an' now theer 's lots o' feeäd,
Fourscoor yows upon it, an' some on it down i' seeäd.

Nobbut a bit on it 's left, an' I meän'd to 'a stubb'd it at fall,
Done it ta-year I meän'd, an' runn'd plow thruff it an' all,
If Godamoighty an' parson 'ud nobbut let ma aloän,—
Meä, wi' haäte hoonderd haäcre o' Squoire's, an lond o' my oän.

Do Godamoighty knaw what a's doing a-taäkin' o' meä? 45
I beänt wonn as saws 'ere a beän an' yonder a peä;
An' Squoire 'ull be sa mad an' all—a' dear, a' dear!
And I 'a managed for Squoire coom Michaelmas thutty year.

A mowt 'a taäen owd Joänes, as 'ant not a 'aäpoth o' sense,
Or a mowt a' taäen young Robins—a niver mended a fence; 50
But Godamoighty a moost taäke meä an taäke ma now,
Wi' aäf the cows to cauve an' Thurnaby hoälms to plow!

Looök 'ow quoloty smoiles when they seeäs ma a passin' boy,
Says to thessén, naw doubt, 'What a man a beä sewerlos!'

Fur they knaws what I beän to Squoire sin' fust
    a coom'd to the 'All;   55
I done moy duty by Squoire an' I done moy
    duty boy hall.

Squoire 's i' Lunnon, an' summun I reckons 'ull
    'a to wroite,
For whoä 's to howd the lond ater meä thot
    muddles ma quoit;
Sartin-sewer I beä thot a weänt niver give it to
    Joänes,
Naw, nor a moänt to Robins—a niver rembles
    the stoäns.   60

But summun 'ull come ater meä mayhap wi'
    'is kittle o' steäm
Huzzin' an' maäzin' the blessed feälds wi' the
    divil's oän teäm.
Sin' I mun doy I mun doy, thaw loife they says
    is sweet,
But sin' I mun doy I mun doy, for I couldn
    abeär to see it.

What atta stannin' theer fur, an' doesn bring
    ma the aäle?   65
Doctor's a 'toättler, lass, an a's hallus i' the
    owd taäle;
I weänt breäk rules fur Doctor, a knaws naw
    moor nor a floy;
Git ma my aäle, I tèll tha, an' if I mun doy
    I mun doy.

                    (1864)

THE REVENGE
A BALLAD OF THE FLEET

I

At Flores in the Azores Sir Richard Grenville
    lay,
And a pinnace, like a fluttered bird, came flying
    from far away;
'Spanish ships of war at sea! we have sighted
    fifty-three!'
Then sware Lord Thomas Howard: "Fore God
    I am no coward;
But I cannot meet them here, for my ships are
    out of gear,   5
And the half my men are sick. I must fly, but
    follow quick.
We are six ships of the line; can we fight with
    fifty-three?'

II

Then spake Sir Richard Grenville: 'I know
    you are no coward;
You fly them for a moment to fight with them
    again.
But I 've ninety men and more that are lying
    sick ashore.   10
I should count myself the coward if I left them,
    my Lord Howard,
To these Inquisition dogs and the devildoms of
    Spain.'

III

So Lord Howard passed away with five ships
    of war that day,
Till he melted like a cloud in the silent summer
    heaven;
But Sir Richard bore in hand all his sick men
    from the land   15
Very carefully and slow,
Men of Bideford in Devon,
And we laid them on the ballast down below:
For we brought them all aboard,
And they blest him in their pain, that they were
    not left to Spain,   20
To the thumb-screw and the stake, for the glory
    of the Lord.

IV

He had only a hundred seamen to work the ship
    and to fight
And he sailed away from Flores till the Span-
    iard came in sight,
With his huge sea-castles heaving upon the
    weather bow.
'Shall we fight or shall we fly?   25
Good Sir Richard, tell us now,
For to fight is but to die!
There 'll be little of us left by the time this sun
    be set.'
And Sir Richard said again: 'We be all good
    English men.
Let us bang these dogs of Seville, the children
    of the devil,   30
For I never turned my back upon Don or devil
    yet.'

V

Sir Richard spoke and he laughed, and we
    roared a hurrah, and so
The little Revenge ran on sheer into the heart
    of the foe,
With her hundred fighters on deck, and her
    ninety sick below;
For half of their fleet to the right and half to
    the left were seen,   35
And the little Revenge ran on through the long
    sea-lane between.

VI

Thousands of their soldiers looked down from
    their decks and laughed,
Thousands of their seamen made mock at the
    mad little cra*f*t
Running on and on, till delayed
By their mountain-like San Philip that, of fif-
    teen hundred tons,   40
And up-shadowing high above us with her
    yawning tiers of guns,
Took the breath from our sails, and we stayed.

VII

And while now the great San Philip hung above us like a cloud
Whence the thunderbolt will fall
Long and loud, 45
Four galleons drew away
From the Spanish fleet that day,
And two upon the larboard and two upon the starboard lay,
And the battle-thunder broke from them all.

VIII

But anon the great San Philip, she bethought herself and went, 50
Having that within her womb that had left her ill content;
And the rest they came aboard us, and they fought us hand to hand,
For a dozen times they came with their pikes and musqueteers,
And a dozen times we shook 'em off as a dog that shakes his ears
When he leaps from the water to the land. 55

IX

And the sun went down, and the stars came out far over the summer sea,
But never a moment ceased the fight of the one and the fifty-three.
Ship after ship, the whole night long, their high-built galleons came,
Ship after ship, the whole night long, with her battle-thunder and flame;
Ship after ship, the whole night long, drew back with her dead and her shame. 60
For some were sunk and many were shattered, and so could fight us no more—
God of battles, was ever a battle like this in the world before?

X

For he said, 'Fight on! fight on!'
Though his vessel was all but a wreck;
And it chanced that, when half of the short summer night was gone, 65
With a grisly wound to be drest he had left the deck,
But a bullet struck him that was dressing it suddenly dead,
And himself he was wounded again in the side and the head,
And he said, 'Fight on! fight on!'

XI

And the night went down, and the sun smiled out far over the summer sea, 70
And the Spanish fleet with broken sides lay round us all in a ring;
But they dared not touch us again, for they feared that we still could sting,
So they watched what the end would be.
And we had not fought them in vain,
But in perilous plight were we, 75
Seeing forty of our poor hundred were slain,
And half of the rest of us maimed for life
In the crash of the cannonades and the desperate strife;
And the sick men down in the hold were most of them stark and cold,
And the pikes were all broken or bent, and the powder was all of it spent; 80
And the masts and the rigging were lying over the side;
But Sir Richard cried in his English pride:
'We have fought such a fight for a day and a night
As may never be fought again!
We have won great glory, my men! 85
And a day less or more
At sea or ashore,
We die—does it matter when?
Sink me the ship, Master Gunner—sink her, split her in twain!
Fall into the hands of God, not into the hands of Spain!' 90

XII

And the gunner said, 'Ay, ay,' but the seamen made reply:
'We have children, we have wives,
And the Lord hath spared our lives.
We will make the Spaniard promise, if we yield, to let us go;
We shall live to fight again and to strike another blow.' 95
And the lion there lay dying, and they yielded to the foe.

XIII

And the stately Spanish men to their flagship bore him then,
Where they laid him by the mast, old Sir Richard caught at last,
And they praised him to his face with their courtly foreign grace;
But he rose upon their decks, and he cried: 100
'I have fought for Queen and Faith like a valiant man and true;
I have only done my duty as a man is bound to do.
With a joyful spirit I Sir Richard Grenville die!'
And he fell upon their decks, and he died.

XIV

And they stared at the dead that had been so valiant and true, 105
And had holden the power and glory of Spain so cheap
That he dared her with one little ship and his English few;
Was he devil or man? He was devil for aught they knew,

But they sank his body with honor down into
    the deep,
And they manned the Revenge with a swarthier
    alien crew,   110
And away she sailed with her loss and longed
    for her own;
When a wind from the lands they had ruined
    awoke from sleep,
And the water began to heave and the weather
    to moan,
And or ever that evening ended a great gale
    blew,
And a wave like the wave that is raised by an
    earthquake grew,   115
Till it smote on their hulls and their sails and
    their masts and their flags,
And the whole sea plunged and fell on the shot-
    shattered navy of Spain,
And the little Revenge herself went down by
    the island crags
To be lost evermore in the main.
                                            (1878)

TO VIRGIL

ROMAN Virgil, thou that singest Ilion's lofty
    temples robed in fire,
Ilion falling, Rome arising, wars, and filial
    faith, and Dido's pyre;

Landscape-lover, lord of language more than he
    that sang the 'Works and Days,'
All the chosen coin of fancy flashing out from
    many a golden phrase;

Thou that singest wheat and woodland, tilth
    and vineyard, hive and horse and herd; 5
All the charm of all the Muses often flowering
    in a lonely word;

Poet of the happy Tityrus piping underneath
    his beechen bowers;
Poet of the poet-satyr whom the laughing
    shepherd bound with flowers;

Chanter of the Pollio, glorying in the blissful
    years again to be,
Summers of the snakeless meadow, unlaborious
    earth and oarless sea;   10

Thou that seest Universal Nature moved by
    Universal Mind;
Thou majestic in thy sadness at the doubtful
    doom of human kind;

Light among the vanished ages; star that gildest
    yet this phantom shore;
Golden branch amid the shadows, kings and
    realms that pass to rise no more;

Now thy Forum roars no longer, fallen every
    purple Cæsar's dome—   15
Though thine ocean-roll of rhythm sound for-
    ever of Imperial Rome—

Now the Rome of slaves hath perished, and the
    Rome of freemen holds her place,
I, from out the Northern Island sundered once
    from all the human race,

I salute thee, Mantovano, I that loved thee
    since my day began,
Wielder of the stateliest measure ever molded
    by the lips of man.   20
                                          (1882)

'FRATER AVE ATQUE VALE'

Row us out from Desenzano, to your Sirmione
    row!
So they rowed, and there we landed—'*O venusta
    Sirmio!*'
There to me through all the groves of olive in
    the summer glow,
There beneath the Roman ruin where the pur-
    ple flowers grow,
Came that '*Ave atque Vale*' of the Poet's hope-
    less woe,   5
Tenderest of Roman poets nineteen hundred
    years ago,
'*Frater Ave atque Vale*'—as we wandered to
    and fro,
Gazing at the Lydian laughter of the Garda
    Lake below,
Sweet Catullus's all-but-island, olive-silvery
    Sirmio!
                                          (1883)

CROSSING THE BAR

SUNSET and evening star,
    And one clear call for me!
And may there be no moaning of the bar,
    When I put out to sea,

But such a tide as moving seems asleep,   5
    Too full for sound and foam,
When that which drew from out the boundless
    deep
    Turns again home.

Twilight and evening bell,
    And after that the dark!   10
And may there be no sadness of farewell,
    When I embark;

For though from out our bourne of Time and
    Place
    The flood may bear me far,
I hope to see my Pilot face to face   15
    When I have crossed the bar.
                                          (1889)

ROBERT BROWNING (1812-1889)

BROWNING, born in Camberwell, a London suburb, was the son of a clerk in the Bank of England, who gave him a good education and encouraged his youthful inclination towards poetry. His first poem, *Pauline, the Fragment of a Confession*, was published anonymously in 1833; it is strongly marked by the influence of Shelley, and gives only a hint of its author's later style. After a visit to Russia, he produced *Paracelsus* (1835), which shows a considerable advance in artistic power, especially in the delineation of character. It brought about an invitation from Macready, the leading actor-manager of the day, to write a play, and in response *Strafford* was written and acted in 1837, with only moderate success. Browning wrote other plays, some for the stage and others for the study, *A Blot in the 'Scutcheon* being his best tragedy, and *Colombe's Birthday* his best comedy. Meanwhile he was working at a long narrative poem, *Sordello*, discussing the philosophic issues raised in connection with the life of a medieval troubadour; for the historical background he made elaborate studies in the British Museum and in Italy, to which he paid his first visit in 1838. *Sordello* was published in 1840, and had an unfavorable reception, owing to its extraordinarily concise and allusive style, which made it exceedingly difficult to understand. Browning was compelled to issue his next volumes in very cheap form at his own expense; the early numbers of the *Bells and Pomegranates* series, as he called it, could be bought for a few cents. The first issue, a dramatic poem entitled *Pippa Passes*, at once became popular, but many years elapsed before the injury done to the poet's reputation by *Sordello* was overcome.

The crucial event in Browning's life and in his poetic career was his marriage, in 1846, to the most gifted of English poetesses, Elizabeth Barrett. Owing partly to the state of her health and partly to her father's disapproval of the match, they lived in Italy, chiefly at Florence, till Mrs. Browning's death in 1861. During his married life Browning produced his best work—the dramatic monologues included in the volume known as *Men and Women* (1855). His wife's influence is also to be discerned in another collection of shorter poems, *Dramatis Personæ* (1864), and in his longest narrative poem, *The Ring and the Book* (1868-9), an elaborate treatment of a Roman murder trial, of which Browning found the pleadings in an old book he picked up from a second-hand book stall at Florence. He did not return to Florence after the death of his wife, but resided in London, and slowly won for himself a leading place in public esteem along with Tennyson, with whom he was on very friendly terms. His later work is marred by an excessive tendency to philosophical speculation and psychological analysis as well as grotesqueness of expression, but these defects are naturally most noticeable in his longer poems. He continued to produce beautiful lyrics and dramatic monologues of unsurpassed power and intensity until his death at Venice in 1889.

It is probably by his shorter rather than by his longer poems that Browning will hold his place among the leading English poets. He is unsurpassed as a master of the dramatic monologue—a short poem in which the speaker reveals his soul at some critical moment by telling his thoughts or his story to someone else. Although Browning had unusual metrical facility, he indulged at times in abrupt transitions and grotesque rimes which give to his work an appearance of oddity and sometimes of obscurity. The charge of intentional obscurity sometimes leveled against him is, of course, absurd. He wrote to an admirer who drew attention to this accusation: 'I can have little doubt that my writing has been in the main too hard for many I should have been pleased to communicate with; but I never designedly tried to puzzle people, as some of my critics have supposed. On the other hand, I never pretended to offer such literature as should be a substitute for a cigar or a game at dominoes to an idle man. So, perhaps, on the whole I get my deserts, and something over—not a crowd, but a few I value more.' Swinburne's comment was that Browning is 'something too much the reverse of obscure; he is too brilliant and subtle for the ready reader of a ready writer to follow with any certainty the track of an intelligence which moves with such incessant rapidity. . . . He never thinks but at full speed; and the rate of his thought is to that of another man's as the speed of a railway to that of a waggon, or the speed of a telegraph to that of a railway.' Fortunately for the ordinary reader, his best poems are not his most difficult ones, and the patient student will find that even his worst are marked by extraordinary intellectual vigor and insight into character. While his reputation has hardly kept the supreme place given to it by his admirers at the close of the Victorian era, he remains one of the greatest figures in English poetry, remarkable alike for his message to his time and for the skill and power with which he delivered it.

SONGS from 'PIPPA PASSES'

I

ALL SERVICE RANKS THE SAME WITH GOD

All service ranks the same with God:
If now, as formerly he trod
Paradise, his presence fills
Our earth, each only as God wills
Can work—God's puppets, best and worst,   5
Are we; there is no last nor first.

II

THE YEAR'S AT THE SPRING

The year's at the spring
And day's at the morn;
Morning's at seven;
The hill-side's dew-pearled;
The lark's on the wing;   5
The snail's on the thorn:
God's in his heaven—
All's right with the world!

III

GIVE HER BUT A LEAST EXCUSE TO LOVE ME

Give her but a least excuse to love me!
   When—where—
How—can this arm establish her above me,
If fortune fixed her as my lady there,
There already, to eternally reprove me?   5
('Hist!'—said Kate the Queen;
But 'Oh!'—cried the maiden, binding her tresses,
'*'T is only a page that carols unseen,
Crumbling your hounds their messes!*')

Is she wronged?—To the rescue of her honor,   10
   My heart!
Is she poor?—What costs it to be styled a
   donor?
Merely an earth to cleave, a sea to part.
But that fortune should have thrust all this
   upon her!
('Nay, list!'—bade Kate the Queen;   15
And still cried the maiden, binding her tresses,
'*'Tis only a page that carols unseen,
Fitting your hawks their jesses!*')

(1841)

MY LAST DUCHESS

FERRARA

That's my last Duchess painted on the wall,
Looking as if she were alive. I call
That piece a wonder, now: Frà Pandolf's hands
Worked busily a day, and there she stands.
Will 't please you sit and look at her? I said
'Frà Pandolf' by design, for never read   6
Strangers like you that pictured countenance,
The depth and passion of its earnest glance,
But to myself they turned (since none puts by
The curtain I have drawn for you, but I)   10
And seemed as they would ask me, if they
   durst,
How such a glance came there; so, not the first
Are you to turn and ask thus. Sir, 't was not
Her husband's presence only, called that spot
Of joy into the Duchess' cheek: perhaps   15
Frà Pandolf chanced to say, 'Her mantle laps
Over my lady's wrist too much,' or 'Paint
Must never hope to reproduce the faint
Half-flush that dies along her throat:' such
   stuff
Was courtesy, she thought, and cause enough   20
For calling up that spot of joy. She had
A heart—how shall I say?—too soon made
   glad,
Too easily impressed; she liked whate'er
She looked on, and her looks went everywhere.
Sir, 't was all one! My favor at her breast,   25
The dropping of the daylight in the West,
The bough of cherries some officious fool
Broke in the orchard for her, the white mule
She rode with round the terrace—all and each
Would draw from her alike the approving
   speech,   30
Or blush, at least. She thanked men,—good!
   but thanked
Somehow—I know not how—as if she ranked
My gift of a nine-hundred-years-old name
With anybody's gift. Who'd stoop to blame
This sort of trifling? Even had you skill   35
In speech—(which I have not)—to make your
   will
Quite clear to such an one, and say, 'Just this
Or that in you disgusts me; here you miss,
Or there exceed the mark'—and if she let
Herself be lessoned so, nor plainly set   40
Her wits to yours, forsooth, and made excuse,
—E'en then would be some stooping; and I
   choose
Never to stoop. Oh, sir, she smiled, no doubt,
Whene'er I passed her; but who passed without
Much the same smile? This grew; I gave commands;   45
Then all smiles stopped together. There she
   stands
As if alive. Will 't please you rise? We'll meet
The company below then. I repeat,
The Count your master's known munificence
Is ample warrant that no just pretense   50
Of mine for dowry will be disallowed;
Though his fair daughter's self, as I avowed
At starting, is my object. Nay, we'll go
Together down, sir. Notice Neptune, though,
Taming a sea-horse, thought a rarity,   55
Which Claus of Innsbruck cast in bronze for me!

(1842)

COUNT GISMOND

AIX IN PROVENCE

I

Christ God who savest man, save most
   Of men Count Gismond who saved me!
Count Gauthier, when he chose his post,
   Chose time and place and company
To suit it; when he struck at length
My honor, 't was with all his strength.

II

And doubtlessly ere he could draw
   All points to one, he must have schemed!
That miserable morning saw
   Few half so happy as I seemed,
While being dressed in queen's array
To give our tourney prize away.

III

I thought they loved me, did me grace
   To please themselves; 't was all their deed;
God makes, or fair or foul, our face;
   If showing mine so caused to bleed
My cousins' hearts, they should have dropped
A word, and straight the play had stopped.

IV

They, too, so beauteous! Each a queen
   By virtue of her brow and breast;
Not needing to be crowned, I mean,
   As I do. E'en when I was dressed,
Had either of them spoke, instead
Of glancing sideways with still head!

V

But no: they let me laugh, and sing
   My birthday song quite through, adjust
The last rose in my garland, fling
   A last look on the mirror, trust
My arms to each an arm of theirs,
And so descend the castle-stairs—

VI

And come out on the morning-troop
   Of merry friends who kissed my cheek,
And called me queen, and made me stoop
   Under the canopy—(a streak
That pierced it, of the outside sun,
Powdered with gold its gloom's soft dun)—

VII

And they could let me take my state
   And foolish throne amid applause
Of all come there to celebrate
   My queen's-day—Oh, I think the cause
Of much was, they forgot no crowd
Makes up for parents in their shroud!

VIII

Howe'er that be, all eyes were bent
   Upon me, when my cousins cast
Theirs down; 't was time I should present
   The victor's crown, but . . . there, 't will last
No long time . . . the old mist again
Blinds me as then it did. How vain!

IX

See! Gismond's at the gate, in talk
   With his two boys: I can proceed.
Well, at that moment, who should stalk
   Forth boldly—to my face, indeed—
But Gauthier, and he thundered, 'Stay!'
And all stayed. 'Bring no crowns, I say!

X

'Bring torches! Wind the penance-sheet
   About her! Let her shun the chaste,
Or lay herself before their feet!
   Shall she whose body I embraced
A night long, queen it in the day?
For honor's sake no crowns, I say!'

XI

I? What I answered? As I live,
   I never fancied such a thing
As answer possible to give.
   What says the body when they spring
Some monstrous torture-engine's whole
Strength on it? No more says the soul.

XII

Till out strode Gismond; then I knew
   That I was saved. I never met
His face before, but, at first view,
   I felt quite sure that God had set
Himself to Satan; who would spend
A minute's mistrust on the end?

XIII

He strode to Gauthier, in his throat
   Gave him the lie, then struck his mouth
With one back-handed blow that wrote
   In blood men's verdict there. North, South,
East, West, I looked. The lie was dead,
And damned, and truth stood up instead.

XIV

This glads me most, that I enjoyed
   The heart of the joy, with my content
In watching Gismond unalloyed
   By any doubt of the event:
God took that on him—I was bid
Watch Gismond for my part: I did.

XV

Did I not watch him while he let
   His armorer just brace his greaves,
Rivet his hauberk, on the fret
   The while! His foot . . . my memory leaves
No least stamp out, nor how anon
He pulled his ringing gauntlets on.

XVI

And e'en before the trumpet's sound
  Was finished, prone lay the false knight,
Prone as his lie, upon the ground:
  Gismond flew at him, used no sleight
O' the sword, but open-breasted rove,   95
  Cleaving till out the truth he clove.

XVII

Which done, he dragged him to my feet
  And said, 'Here die, but end thy breath
In full confession, lest thou fleet
  From my first, to God's second death!   100
Say, hast thou lied?' And, 'I have lied
  To God and her,' he said, and died.

XVIII

Then Gismond, kneeling to me, asked
  —What safe my heart holds, though no word
Could I repeat now, if I tasked   105
  My powers for ever, to a third
Dear even as you are. Pass the rest
  Until I sank upon his breast.

XIX

Over my head his arm he flung
  Against the world; and scarce I felt   110
His sword (that dripped by me and swung)
  A little shifted in its belt;
For he began to say the while
  How South our home lay many a mile,

XX

So 'mid the shouting multitude   115
  We two walked forth to never more
Return. My cousins have pursued
  Their life, untroubled as before
I vexed them. Gauthier's dwelling-place
  God lighten! May his soul find grace!   120

XXI

Our elder boy has got the clear
  Great brow; though when his brother's black
Full eye shows scorn, it . . . Gismond here?
  And have you brought my tercel back?
I just was telling Adela   125
  How many birds it struck since May.
                                    (1842)

INCIDENT OF THE FRENCH CAMP

I

You know, we French stormed Ratisbon;
  A mile or so away,
On a little mound, Napoleon
  Stood on our storming-day;
With neck out-thrust, you fancy how,   5
  Legs wide, arms locked behind,
As if to balance the prone brow
  Oppressive with its mind.

II

Just as perhaps he mused, 'My plans
  That soar, to earth may fall,   10
Let once my army-leader Lannes
  Waver at yonder wall,'—
Out 'twixt the battery-smokes there flew
  A rider, bound on bound
Full-galloping; nor bridle drew   15
  Until he reached the mound.

III

Then off there flung in smiling joy,
  And held himself erect
By just his horse's mane, a boy:
  You hardly could suspect—   20
(So tight he kept his lips compressed,
  Scarce any blood came through)
You looked twice ere you saw his breast
  Was all but shot in two.

IV

'Well,' cried he, 'Emperor, by God's grace 25
  We've got you Ratisbon!
The Marshal's in the market-place,
  And you'll be there anon
To see your flag-bird flap his vans
  Where I, to heart's desire,   30
Perched him!' The chief's eye flashed; his plans
  Soared up again like fire.

V

The chief's eye flashed; but presently
  Softened itself, as sheathes
A film the mother-eagle's eye   35
  When her bruised eaglet breathes;
'You're wounded!' 'Nay,' the soldier's pride
  Touched to the quick, he said:
'I'm killed, Sire!' And his chief beside,
  Smiling the boy fell dead.   40
                                    (1842)

THE ITALIAN IN ENGLAND

That second time they hunted me
From hill to plain, from shore to sea,
And Austria, hounding far and wide
Her blood-hounds through the country-side,
Breathed hot and instant on my trace,—   5
I made six days a hiding-place
Of that dry green old aqueduct
Where I and Charles, when boys, have plucked
The fire-flies from the roof above,
Bright creeping through the moss they love: 10
—How long it seems since Charles was lost!
Six days the soldiers crossed and crossed
The country in my very sight;
And when that peril ceased at night,
The sky broke out in red dismay   15
With signal fires; well, there I lay

Close covered o'er in my recess,
Up to the neck in ferns and cress,
Thinking on Metternich our friend,
And Charles's miserable end, 20
And much beside, two days; the third,
Hunger o'ercame me when I heard
The peasants from the village go
To work among the maize; you know,
With us in Lombardy, they bring 25
Provisions packed on mules, a string
With little bells that cheer their task,
And casks, and boughs on every cask
To keep the sun's heat from the wine;
These I let pass in jingling line. 30
And, close on them, dear noisy crew,
The peasants from the village, too;
For at the very rear would troop
Their wives and sisters in a group
To help, I knew. When these had passed, 35
I threw my glove to strike the last,
Taking the chance: she did not start,
Much less cry out, but stooped apart,
One instant rapidly glanced round,
And saw me beckon from the ground. 40
A wild bush grows and hides my crypt;
She picked my glove up while she stripped
A branch off, then rejoined the rest
With that; my glove lay in her breast.
Then I drew breath; they disappeared: 45
It was for Italy I feared.

  An hour, and she returned alone
Exactly where my glove was thrown.
Meanwhile came many thoughts; on me
Rested the hopes of Italy. 50
I had devised a certain tale
Which, when 't was told her, could not fail
Persuade a peasant of its truth:
I meant to call a freak of youth
This hiding, and give hopes of pay, 55
And no temptation to betray.
But when I saw that woman's face,
Its calm simplicity of grace,
Our Italy's own attitude
In which she walked thus far, and stood, 60
Planting each naked foot so firm,
To crush the snake and spare the worm—
At first sight of her eyes, I said,
'I am that man upon whose head
They fix the price, because I hate 65
The Austrians over us; the State
Will give you gold—oh, gold so much—
If you betray me to their clutch,
And be your death, for aught I know,
If once they find you saved their foe. 70
Now, you must bring me food and drink,
And also paper, pen and ink,
And carry safe what I shall write
To Padua, which you'll reach at night
Before the duomo shuts; go in, 75
And wait till Tenebræ begin;

Walk to the third confessional,
Between the pillar and the wall,
And kneeling whisper, *Whence comes peace?*
Say it a second time, then cease; 80
And if the voice inside returns,
*From Christ and Freedom; what concerns
The cause of Peace?*—for answer, slip
My letter where you placed your lip;
Then come back happy we have done 85
Our mother service—I, the son,
As you the daughter of our land!'

  Three mornings more, she took her stand
In the same place, with the same eyes:
I was no surer of sunrise 90
Than of her coming. We conferred
Of her own prospects, and I heard
She had a lover—stout and tall,
She said—then let her eyelids fall,
'He could do much'—as if some doubt 95
Entered her heart,—then, passing out,
'She could not speak for others, who
Had other thoughts; herself she knew;'
And so she brought me drink and food
After four days, the scouts pursued 100
Another path; at last arrived
The help my Paduan friends contrived
To furnish me: she brought the news.
For the first time I could not choose
But kiss her hand, and lay my own 105
Upon her head—'This faith was shown
To Italy, our mother; she
Uses my hand and blesses thee.'
She followed down to the sea-shore;
I left and never saw her more. 110

  How very long since I have thought
Concerning—much less wished for—aught
Beside the good of Italy,
For which I live and mean to die!
I never was in love; and since 115
Charles proved false, what shall now convince
My inmost heart I have a friend?
However, if I pleased to spend
Real wishes on myself—say, three—
I know at least what one should be. 120
I would grasp Metternich until
I felt his red wet throat distil
In blood through these two hands. And next
—Nor much for that am I perplexed—
Charles, perjured traitor, for his part, 125
Should die slow of a broken heart
Under his new employers. Last
—Ah, there, what should I wish? For fast
Do I grow old and out of strength.
If I resolved to seek at length 130
My father's house again, how scared
They all would look, and unprepared!
My brothers live in Austria's pay
—Disowned me long ago, men say;
And all my early mates who used 135

To praise me so—perhaps induced
More than one early step of mine—
Are turning wise: while some opine
'Freedom grows license,' some suspect
'Haste breeds delay,' and recollect 140
They always said, such premature
Beginnings never could endure!
So, with a sullen 'All 's for best,'
The land seems settling to its rest.
I think then, I should wish to stand 145
This evening in that dear, lost land,
Over the sea the thousand miles,
And know if yet that woman smiles
With the calm smile; some little farm
She lives in there, no doubt; what harm 150
If I sat on the door-side bench,
And, while her spindle made a trench
Fantastically in the dust,
Inquired of all her fortunes—just
Her children's ages and their names, 155
And what may be the husband's aims
For each of them. I 'd talk this out,
And sit there, for an hour about,
Then kiss her hand once more, and lay
Mine on her head, and go my way. 160

So much for idle wishing—how
It steals the time! To business now.
(1845)

THE LOST LEADER

I

Just for a handful of silver he left us,
    Just for a riband to stick in his coat—
Found the one gift of which fortune bereft us,
    Lost all the others she lets us devote;
They, with the gold to give, doled him out silver,
    So much was theirs who so little allowed: 6
How all our copper had gone for his service!
    Rags—were they purple, his heart had been proud!
We that had loved him so, followed him, honored him,
    Lived in his mild and magnificent eye, 10
Learned his great language, caught his clear accents,
    Made him our pattern to live and to die!
Shakespeare was of us, Milton was for us,
    Burns, Shelley, were with us,—they watch from their graves! 14
He alone breaks from the van and the freemen,
    —He alone sinks to the rear and the slaves!

II

We shall march prospering,—not through his presence;
    Songs may inspirit us,—not from his lyre;
Deeds will be done,—while he boasts his quiescence,
    Still bidding crouch whom the rest bade aspire; 20
Blot out his name, then, record one lost soul more,
    One task more declined, one more footpath untrod,
One more devil's-triumph and sorrow for angels,
    One wrong more to man, one more insult to God!
Life's night begins: let him never come back to us! 25
    There would be doubt, hesitation and pain,
Forced praise on our part—the glimmer of twilight,
    Never glad confident morning again!
Best fight on well, for we taught him—strike gallantly,
    Menace our heart ere we master his own; 30
Then let him receive the new knowledge and wait us,
    Pardoned in heaven, the first by the throne!
(1845)

HOME-THOUGHTS FROM ABROAD

I

Oh, to be in England,
Now that April 's there,
And whoever wakes in England
Sees, some morning, unaware,
That the lowest boughs and the brush-wood sheaf 5
Round the elm-tree bole are in tiny leaf,
While the chaffinch sings on the orchard bough
In England—now!

II

And after April, when May follows,
And the white-throat builds, and all the swallows! 10
Hark, where my blossomed pear-tree in the hedge
Leans to the field and scatters on the clover
Blossoms and dewdrops—at the bent spray's edge—
That 's the wise thrush; he sings each song twice over,
Lest you should think he never could recapture
The first fine careless rapture! 16
And though the fields look rough with hoary dew,
All will be gay when noontide wakes anew
The buttercups, the little children's dower
—Far brighter than this gaudy melon-flower! 20
(1845)

HOME-THOUGHTS FROM THE SEA

Nobly, nobly, Cape Saint Vincent to the Northwest died away;
Sunset ran, one glorious blood-red, reeking into Cadiz Bay;

Bluish 'mid the burning water, full in face Trafalgar lay;
In the dimmest Northeast distance dawned Gibraltar, grand and gray;
'Here and here did England help me: how can I help England?'—say, 5
Whoso turns as I, this evening, turn to God to praise and pray,
While Jove's planet rises yonder, silent over Africa.

(1845)

SAUL

I

Said Abner, 'At last thou art come! Ere I tell, ere thou speak,
Kiss my cheek, wish me well!' Then I wished it, and did kiss his cheek.
And he: 'Since the King, O my friend, for thy countenance sent,
Neither drunken nor eaten have we; nor until from his tent
Thou return with the joyful assurance the King liveth yet, 5
Shall our lip with the honey be bright, with the water be wet,
For out of the black mid-tent's silence, a space of three days,
Not a sound hath escaped to thy servants, of prayer nor of praise,
To betoken that Saul and the Spirit have ended their strife,
And that, faint in his triumph, the monarch sinks back upon life. 10

II

'Yet now my heart leaps, O beloved! God's child with his dew
On thy gracious gold hair, and those lilies still living and blue
Just broken to twine round thy harp-strings, as if no wild heat
Were now raging to torture the desert.'

III

Then I, as was meet,
Knelt down to the God of my fathers, and rose on my feet, 15
And ran o'er the sand burnt to powder. The tent was unlooped;
I pulled up the spear that obstructed, and under I stooped;
Hands and knees on the slippery grass-patch, all withered and gone,
That extends to the second enclosure, I groped my way on
Till I felt where the foldskirts fly open. Then once more I prayed, 20
And opened the foldskirts and entered, and was not afraid
But spoke, 'Here is David, thy servant!' And no voice replied.
At the first I saw naught but the blackness; but soon I descried
A something more black than the blackness—the vast, the upright
Main prop which sustains the pavilion; and slow into sight 25
Grew a figure against it, gigantic and blackest of all.
Then a sunbeam, that burst through the tent roof, showed Saul.

IV

He stood as erect as that tent-prop, both arms stretched out wide
On the great cross-support in the center, that goes to each side;
He relaxed not a muscle, but hung there as, caught in his pangs 30
And waiting his change, the king serpent all heavily hangs,
Far away from his kind, in the pine, till deliverance come
With the spring-time,—so agonized Saul, drear and stark, blind and dumb.

V

Then I tuned my harp,—took off the lilies we twine round its chords
Lest they snap 'neath the stress of the noontide—those sunbeams like swords! 35
And I first played the tune all our sheep know, as, one after one,
So docile they come to the pen-door till folding be done.
They are white and untorn by the bushes, for lo, they have fed
Where the long grasses stifle the water within the stream's bed;
And now one after one seeks its lodging, as star follows star 40
Into eve and the blue far above us,—so blue and so far!

VI

—Then the tune, for which quails on the cornland will each leave his mate
To fly after the player; then, what makes the crickets elate
Till for boldness they fight one another; and then, what has weight
To set the quick jerboa a-musing outside his sand-house— 45
There are none such as he for a wonder, half bird and half mouse!
God made all the creatures and gave them our love and our fear,
To give sign, we and they are his children, one family here.

VII

Then I played the help-tune of our reapers,
    their wine-song, when hand
Grasps at hand, eye lights eye in good friend-
    ship, and great hearts expand   50
And grow one in the sense of this world's life.—
    And then, the last song
When the dead man is praised on his journey—
    'Bear, bear him along
With his few faults shut up like dead flowerets!
    Are balm-seeds not here
To console us? The land has none left such as
    he on the bier.
Oh, would we might keep thee, my brother!'
    —And then, the glad chaunt   55
Of the marriage,—first go the young maidens,
    next, she whom we vaunt
As the beauty, the pride of our dwelling.—
    And then, the great march
Wherein man runs to man to assist him and
    buttress an arch
Nought can break; who shall harm them, our
    friends?—Then, the chorus intoned
As the Levites go up to the altar in glory en-
    throned.   60
But I stopped here: for here in the darkness
    Saul groaned.

VIII

And I paused, held my breath in such silence,
    and listened apart;
And the tent shook, for mighty Saul shuddered:
    and sparkles 'gan dart
From the jewels that woke in his turban, at once
    with a start,
All its lordly male-sapphires, and rubies
    courageous at heart.   65
So the head; but the body still moved not, still
    hung there erect.
And I bent once again to my playing, pursued
    it unchecked,
As I sang:—

IX

    'Oh, our manhood's prime vigor!
    No spirit feels waste,
Not a muscle is stopped in its playing nor
    sinew unbraced.
Oh, the wild joys of living! the leaping from
    rock up to rock,   70
The strong rending of boughs from the fir-tree,
    the cool silver shock
Of the plunge in a pool's living water, the hunt
    of the bear,
And the sultriness showing the lion is couched
    in his lair.
And the meal, the rich dates yellowed over with
    gold dust divine,
And the locust-flesh steeped in the pitcher, the
    full draft of wine,   75
And the sleep in the dried river-channel where
    bulrushes tell
That the water was wont to go warbling so
    softly and well.
How good is man's life, the mere living! how
    fit to employ
All the heart and the soul and the senses forever
    in joy!
Hast thou loved the white locks of thy father,
    whose sword thou didst guard   80
When he trusted thee forth with the armies, for
    glorious reward?
Didst thou see the thin hands of thy mother,
    held up as men sung
The low song of the nearly-departed, and hear
    her faint tongue
Joining in while it could to the witness, "Let
    one more attest
I have lived, seen God's hand through a life-
    time, and all was for best?"   85
Then they sung through their tears in strong
    triumph, not much, but the rest.
And thy brothers, the help and the contest, the
    working whence grew
Such result as, from seething grape-bundles,
    the spirit strained true:
And the friends of thy boyhood—that boyhood
    of wonder and hope,
Present promise and wealth of the future be-
    yond the eye's scope,—   90
Till lo, thou art grown to a monarch; a people
    is thine:
And all gifts, which the world offers singly, on
    one head combine!
On one head, all the beauty and strength, love
    and rage (like the throe
That, a-work in the rock, helps its labor and
    lets the gold go),
High ambition and deeds which surpass it,
    fame crowning them,—all   95
Brought to blaze on the head of one creature—
    King Saul.'

X

And lo, with that leap of my spirit,—heart,
    hand, harp and voice,
Each lifting Saul's name out of sorrow, each
    bidding rejoice
Saul's fame in the light it was made for—as
    when, dare I say,
The Lord's army, in rapture of service, strains
    through its array,   100
And upsoareth the cherubim-chariot—'Saul!'
    cried I, and stopped,
And waited the thing that should follow. Then
    Saul, who hung propped
By the tent's cross-support in the center, was
    struck by his name.
Have ye seen when Spring's arrowy summons
    goes right to the aim,

And some mountain, the last to withstand her, that held (he alone, 105
While the vale laughed in freedom and flowers) on a broad bust of stone
A year's snow bound about for a breast-plate,— leaves grasp of the sheet?
Fold on fold all at once it crowds thunderously down to his feet,
And there fronts you, stark, black, but alive yet, your mountain of old,
With his rents, the successive bequeathings of ages untold— 110
Yea, each harm got in fighting your battles, each furrow and scar
Of his head thrust 'twixt you and the tempest— all hail, there they are!
—Now again to be softened with verdure, again hold the nest
Of the dove, tempt the goat and its young to the green on his crest
For their food in the ardors of summer. One long shudder thrilled 115
All the tent till the very air tingled, then sank and was stilled
At the King's self left standing before me, released and aware.
What was gone, what remained? All to traverse 'twixt hope and despair;
Death was past, life not come: so he waited. Awhile his right hand
Held the brow, helped the eyes left too vacant, forthwith to remand 120
To their place what new objects should enter: 't was Saul as before.
I looked up, and dared gaze at those eyes, nor was hurt any more
Than by slow pallid sunsets in autumn, ye watch from the shore,
At their sad level gaze o'er the ocean—a sun's slow decline
Over hills which, resolved in stern silence, o'erlap and entwine 125
Base with base to knit strength more intensely; so, arm folded arm
O'er the chest whose slow heavings subsided.

XI

What spell or what charm
(For, awhile there was trouble within me), what next should I urge
To sustain him where song had restored him?— Song filled to the verge
His cup with the wine of this life, pressing all that it yields 130
Of mere fruitage, the strength and the beauty: beyond, on what fields,
Glean a vintage more potent and perfect to brighten the eye,
And bring blood to the lip, and commend them the cup they put by?

He saith, 'It is good;' still he drinks not: he lets me praise life.
Gives assent, yet would die for his own part. 135

XII

Then fancies grew rife
Which had come long ago on the pasture, when round me the sheep
Fed in silence—above, the one eagle wheeled slow as in sleep;
And I lay in my hollow and mused on the world that might lie
'Neath his ken, though I saw but the strip 'twixt the hill and the sky:
And I laughed—'Since my days are ordained to be passed with my flocks, 140
Let me people at least, with my fancies, the plains and the rocks,
Dream the life I am never to mix with, and image the show
Of mankind as they live in those fashions I hardly shall know!
Schemes of life, its best rules and right uses, the courage that gains,
And the prudence that keeps what men strive for!' And now these old trains 145
Of vague thought came again; I grew surer; so, once more the string
Of my harp made response to my spirit, as thus—

XIII

'Yea, my King,'
I began—'thou dost well in rejecting mere comforts that spring
From the mere mortal life held in common by man and by brute:
In our flesh grows the branch of this life, in our soul it bears fruit. 150
Thou hast marked the slow rise of the tree,— how its stem trembled first
Till it passed the kid's lip, the stag's antler; then safely outburst
The fan-branches all round; and thou mindest when these too, in turn
Broke a-bloom and the palm-tree seemed perfect: yet more was to learn,
E'en the good that comes in with the palm-fruit. Our dates shall we slight, 155
When their juice brings a cure for all sorrow? or care for the plight
Of the palm's self whose slow growth produced them? Not so! stem and branch
Shall decay, nor be known in their place, while the palm-wine shall stanch
Every wound of man's spirit in winter. I pour thee such wine.
Leave the flesh to the fate it was fit for! the spirit be thine! 160
By the spirit, when age shall o'ercome thee, thou still shalt enjoy

More indeed, than at first when inconscious,
    the life of a boy.
Crush that life, and behold its wine running!
    Each deed thou hast done
Dies, revives, goes to work in the world; until
    e'en as the sun
Looking down on the earth, though clouds
    spoil him, though tempests efface, 165
Can find nothing his own deed produced not,
    must everywhere trace
The results of his past summer-prime,—so,
    each ray of thy will,
Every flash of thy passion and prowess, long
    over, shall thrill
Thy whole people, the countless, with ardor,
    till they too give forth
A like cheer to their sons; who in turn, fill the
    South and the North 170
With the radiance thy deed was the germ of.
    Carouse in the past!
But the license of age has its limit; thou diest
    at last:
As the lion when age dims his eyeball, the rose
    at her height,
So with man—so his power and his beauty for
    ever take flight.
No! Again a long draft of my soul-wine! Look
    forth o'er the years! 175
Thou hast done now with eyes for the actual;
    begin with the seer's!
Is Saul dead? In the depth of the vale make
    his tomb—bid arise
A grey mountain of marble heaped four-square,
    till, built to the skies,
Let it mark where the great First King slumbers: whose fame would ye know?
Up above see the rock's naked face, where the
    record shall go 180
In great characters cut by the scribe,—Such
    was Saul, so he did;
With the sages directing the work, by the
    populace chid,—
For not half, they 'll affirm, is comprised there!
    Which fault to amend,
In the grove with his kind grows the cedar,
    whereon they shall spend
(See, in tablets 't is level before them) their
    praise, and record 185
With the gold of the graver, Saul's story,—the
    statesman's great word
Side by side with the poet's sweet comment.
    The river's a-wave
With smooth paper-reeds grazing each other
    when prophet-winds rave:
So the pen gives unborn generations their due
    and their part
In thy being! Then, first of the mighty, thank
    God that thou art!' 190

XIV

And behold while I sang . . . but O thou who
    didst grant me that day,
And before it not seldom hast granted thy help
    to essay,
Carry on and complete an adventure,—my
    shield and my sword
In that act where my soul was thy servant, thy
    word was my word,—
Still be with me, who then at the summit of
    human endeavor 195
And scaling the highest, man's thought could,
    gazed hopeless as ever
On the new stretch of heaven above me—till,
    mighty to save,
Just one lift of thy hand cleared that distance—
    God's throne from man's grave!
Let me tell out my tale to its ending—my voice
    to my heart
Which can scarce dare believe in what marvels
    last night I took part, 200
As this morning I gather the fragments, alone
    with my sheep,
And still fear lest the terrible glory evanish like
    sleep!
For I wake in the gray dewy covert, while
    Hebron upheaves
The dawn struggling with night on his shoulder,
    and Kidron retrieves
Slow the damage of yesterday's sunshine. 205

XV

    I say then,—my song
While I sang thus, assuring the monarch, and,
    ever more strong,
Made a proffer of good to console him—he
    slowly resumed
His old motions and habitudes kingly. The
    right hand replumed
His black locks to their wonted composure, adjusted the swathes
Of his turban, and see—the huge sweat that his
    countenance bathes, 210
He wipes off with the robe; and he girds now his
    loins as of yore,
And feels slow for the armlets of price, with the
    clasp set before.
He is Saul, ye remember in glory,—ere error
    had bent
The broad brow from the daily communion;
    and still, though much spent
Be the life and the bearing that front you, the
    same, God did choose, 215
To receive what a man may waste, desecrate,
    never quite lose.
So sank he along by the tent-prop, till, stayed
    by the pile
Of his armor and war-cloak and garments, he
    leaned there awhile,
And sat out my singing,—one arm round the
    tent-prop, to raise

His bent head, and the other hung slack—till I
touched on the praise 220
I foresaw from all men in all time, to the man
patient there;
And thus ended, the harp falling forward. Then
first I was 'ware
That he sat, as I say, with my head just above
his vast knees
Which were thrust out on each side around me,
like oak roots which please
To encircle a lamb when it slumbers. I looked
up to know 225
If the best I could do had brought solace: he
spoke not, but slow
Lifted up the hand slack at his side, till he laid
it with care
Soft and grave, but in mild settled will, on my
brow: through my hair
The large fingers were pushed, and he bent
back my head, with kind power—
All my face back, intent to peruse it, as men do
a flower. 230
Thus held he me there with his great eyes that
scrutinized mine—
And oh, all my heart how it loved him! but where
was the sign?
I yearned—'Could I help thee, my father, inventing a bliss,
I would add, to that life of the past, both the
future and this;
I would give thee new life altogether, as good,
ages hence, 235
As this moment,—had love but the warrant,
love's heart to dispense!'

XVI

Then the truth came upon me. No harp more—
no song more! outbroke—

XVII

'I have gone the whole round of creation: I saw
and I spoke:
I, a work of God's hand for that purpose, re-
ceived in my brain
And pronounced on the rest of his handwork
—returned him again 240
His creation's approval or censure: I spoke as I
saw,
I report, as a man may of God's work—all 's
love, yet all 's law.
Now I lay down the judgeship he lent me.
Each faculty tasked
To perceive him has gained an abyss, where a
dewdrop was asked.
Have I knowledge? confounded it shrivels at
Wisdom laid bare. 245
Have I forethought? how purblind, how blank,
to the Infinite Care!
Do I task any faculty highest, to image success?
I but open my eyes,—and perfection, no more
and no less,

In the kind I imagined, full-fronts me, and God
is seen God
In the star, in the stone, in the flesh, in the soul
and the clod. 250
And thus looking within and around me, I ever
renew
(With that stoop of the soul which in bending
upraises it too)
The submission of man's nothing-perfect to
God's all-complete,
As by each new obeisance in spirit, I climb to
his feet.
Yet with all this abounding experience, this
deity known, 255
I shall dare to discover some province, some gift
of my own.
There's a faculty pleasant to exercise, hard to
hoodwink,
I am fain to keep still in abeyance (I laugh as I
think)
Lest, insisting to claim and parade in it, wot ye,
I worst
E'en the Giver in one gift.—Behold, I could love
if I durst! 260
But I sink the pretension as fearing a man may
o'ertake
God's own speed in the one way of love; I ab-
stain for love's sake.
—What, my soul? see thus far and no farther?
when doors great and small,
Nine-and-ninety flew ope at our touch, should
the hundredth appal?
In the least things have faith, yet distrust in the
greatest of all? 265
Do I find love so full in my nature, God's
ultimate gift,
That I doubt his own love can compete with it?
Here, the parts shift?
Here, the creature surpass the Creator,—the
end, what Began?
Would I fain in my impotent yearning do all for
this man,
And dare doubt he alone shall not help him,
who yet alone can? 270
Would it ever have entered my mind, the bare
will, much less power,
To bestow on this Saul what I sang of, the
marvelous dower
Of the life he was gifted and filled with? to make
such a soul,
Such a body, and then such an earth for in-
sphering the whole?
And doth it not enter my mind (as my warm
tears attest), 275
These good things being given, to go on, and
give one more, the best?
Ay, to save and redeem and restore him, maintain at the height
This perfection,—succeed with life's dayspring,
death's minute of night?

Interpose at the difficult minute, snatch Saul the mistake,
Saul the failure, the ruin he seems now,—and bid him awake 280
From the dream, the probation, the prelude, to find himself set
Clear and safe in new light and new life,—a new harmony yet
To be run and continued, and ended—who knows?—or endure!
The man taught enough by life's dream, of the rest to make sure;
By the pain-throb, triumphantly winning intensified bliss, 285
And the next world's reward and repose, by the struggles in this.

XVIII

'I believe it! 'T is thou, God, that givest, 't is I who receive:
In the first is the last, in thy will is my power to believe.
All's one gift: thou canst grant it moreover, as prompt to my prayer
As I breathe out this breath, as I open these arms to the air. 290
From thy will, stream the worlds, life and nature, thy dread Sabaoth:
I will?—the mere atoms despise me! Why am I not loth
To look that, even that in the face too? Why is it I dare
Think but lightly of such impuissance? What stops my despair?
This;—'t is not what man Does which exalts him, but what man Would do! 295
See the King—I would help him but cannot, the wishes fall through.
Could I wrestle to raise him from sorrow, grow poor to enrich,
To fill up his life, starve my own out, I would—knowing which,
I know that my service is perfect. Oh, speak through me now!
Would I suffer for him that I love? So wouldst thou—so wilt thou! 300
So shall crown thee the topmost, ineffablest, uttermost crown—
And thy love fill infinitude wholly, nor leave up nor down
One spot for the creature to stand in! It is by no breath,
Turn of eye, wave of hand, that salvation joins issue with death!
As thy Love is discovered almighty, almighty be proved 305
Thy power, that exists with and for it, of being Beloved!
He who did most, shall bear most; the strongest shall stand the most weak.

'T is the weakness in strength, that I cry for! my flesh, that I seek
In the Godhead! I seek and I find it. O Saul, it shall be
A Face like my face that receives thee; a Man like to me, 310
Thou shalt love and be loved by, for ever: a Hand like this hand
Shall throw open the gates of new life to thee! See the Christ stand!'

XIX

I know not too well how I found my way home in the night.
There were witnesses, cohorts about me, to left and to right,
Angels, powers, the unuttered, unseen, the alive, the aware: 315
I repressed, I got through them as hardly, as strugglingly there,
As a runner beset by the populace famished for news—
Life or death. The whole earth was awakened, hell loosed with her crews;
And the stars of night beat with emotion, and tingled and shot
Out in fire the strong pain of pent knowledge: but I fainted not, 320
For the hand still impelled me at once and supported, suppressed
All the tumult, and quenched it with quiet, and holy behest,
Till the rapture was shut in itself, and the earth sank to rest.
Anon at the dawn, all that trouble had withered from earth—
Not so much, but I saw it die out in the day's tender birth; 325
In the gathered intensity brought to the gray of the hills;
In the shuddering forests' held breath; in the sudden wind-thrills;
In the startled wild beasts that bore off, each with eye sidling still,
Though averted with wonder and dread; in the birds stiff and chill
That rose heavily as I approached them, made stupid with awe: 330
E'en the serpent that slid away silent,—he felt the new law.
The same stared in the white humid faces upturned by the flowers;
The same worked in the heart of the cedar and moved the vine-bowers:
And the little brooks witnessing murmured, persistent and low,
With their obstinate, all but hushed voices—
'E'en so, it is so!' 335

(1845-1855)

LOVE AMONG THE RUINS

I

Where the quiet-colored end of evening smiles
    Miles and miles
On the solitary pastures where our sheep
    Half-asleep
Tinkle homeward through the twilight, stray or stop 5
    As they crop—
Was the site once of a city great and gay
    (So they say),
Of our country's very capital, its prince
    Ages since 10
Held his court in, gathered councils, wielding far
    Peace or war.

II

Now,—the country does not even boast a tree,
    As you see,
To distinguish slopes of verdure, certain rills 15
    From the hills
Intersect and give a name to (else they run
    Into one),
Where the domed and daring palace shot its spires
    Up like fires 20
O'er the hundred-gated circuit of a wall
    Bounding all,
Made of marble, men might march on nor be pressed,
    Twelve abreast.

III

And such plenty and perfection, see, of grass 25
    Never was!
Such a carpet as, this summer-time, o'erspreads
    And embeds
Every vestige of the city, guessed alone,
    Stock or stone— 30
Where a multitude of men breathed joy and woe
    Long ago;
Lust of glory pricked their hearts up, dread of shame
    Struck them tame;
And that glory and that shame alike, the gold 35
    Bought and sold.

IV

Now,—the single little turret that remains
    On the plains,
By the caper overrooted, by the gourd
    Overscored, 40
While the patching houseleek's head of blossom winks
    Through the chinks—
Marks the basement whence a tower in ancient time
    Sprang sublime,
And a burning ring, all round, the chariots traced 45
    As they raced,
And the monarch and his minions and his dames
    Viewed the games.

V

And I know—while thus the quiet-colored eve
    Smiles to leave 50
To their folding, all our many tinkling fleece
    In such peace,
And the slopes and rills in undistinguished gray
    Melt away—
That a girl with eager eyes and yellow hair 55
    Waits me there
In the turret whence the charioteers caught soul
    For the goal,
When the king looked, where she looks now, breathless, dumb
    Till I come. 60

VI

But he looked upon the city, every side,
    Far and wide,
All the mountains topped with temples, all the glades,
    Colonnades,
All the causeys, bridges, aqueducts,—and then,
    All the men! 66
When I do come, she will speak not, she will stand,
    Either hand
On my shoulder, give her eyes the first embrace
    Of my face, 70
Ere we rush, ere we extinguish sight and speech
    Each on each.

VII

In one year they sent a million fighters forth
    South and North,
And they built their gods a brazen pillar high 75
    As the sky,
Yet reserved a thousand chariots in full force—
    Gold, of course.
Oh heart! oh blood that freezes, blood that burns!
    Earth's returns 80
For whole centuries of folly, noise and sin!
    Shut them in,
With their triumphs and their glories and the rest!
    Love is best.

(1855)

A WOMAN'S LAST WORD

I

Let's contend no more, Love,
    Strive nor weep:
All be as before, Love,
    —Only sleep!

II

What so wild as words are?
    I and thou
In debate, as birds are,
    Hawk on bough!

III

See the creature stalking
    While we speak!
Hush and hide the talking,
    Cheek on cheek.

IV

What so false as truth is,
    False to thee?
Where the serpent's tooth is
    Shun the tree—

V

Where the apple reddens
    Never pry—
Lest we lose our Edens,
    Eve and I.

VI

Be a god and hold me
    With a charm!
Be a man and fold me
    With thine arm!

VII

Teach me, only teach, Love!
    As I ought
I will speak thy speech, Love,
    Think thy thought—

VIII

Meet, if thou require it,
    Both demands,
Laying flesh and spirit
    In thy hands.

IX

That shall be to-morrow,
    Not to-night:
I must bury sorrow
    Out of sight:

X

—Must a little weep, Love,
    (Foolish me!),
And so fall asleep, Love
    Loved by thee.

(1855)

A TOCCATA OF GALUPPI'S

I

Oh, Galuppi, Baldassare, this is very sad to find!
I can hardly misconceive you; it would prove me deaf and blind;
But although I take your meaning, 't is with such a heavy mind!

II

Here you come with your old music, and here's all the good it brings.
What, they lived once thus at Venice where the merchants were the kings,
Where St. Mark's is, where the Doges used to wed the sea with rings?

III

Ay, because the sea's the street there; and 't is arched by . . . what you call
. . . Shylock's bridge with houses on it, where they kept the carnival:
I was never out of England—it's as if I saw it all.

IV

Did young people take their pleasure when the sea was warm in May?
Balls and masks begun at midnight, burning ever to mid-day,
When they made up fresh adventures for the morrow, do you say?

V

Was a lady such a lady, cheeks so round and lips so red,—
On her neck the small face buoyant, like a bell-flower on its bed,
O'er the breast's superb abundance where a man might base his head?

VI

Well, and it was graceful of them—they'd break talk off and afford
—She, to bite her mask's black velvet—he, to finger on his sword,
While you sat and played Toccatas, stately at the clavichord?

VII

What? Those lesser thirds so plaintive, sixths diminished, sigh on sigh,
Told them something? Those suspensions, those solutions—'Must we die?'
Those commiserating sevenths—'Life might last! we can but try!'

VIII

'Were you happy?'—'Yes.'—'And are you still as happy?'—'Yes. And you?'
—'Then, more kisses!'—'Did *I* stop them, when a million seemed so few?'
Hark, the dominant's persistence till it must be answered to!

IX

So, an octave struck the answer. Oh, they praised you, I dare say!
'Brave Galuppi! that was music! good alike at grave and gay!
I can always leave off talking when I hear a master play!'

X

Then they left you for their pleasure: till in
    due time, one by one,
Some with lives that came to nothing, some
    with deeds as well undone,
Death stepped tacitly and took them where
    they never see the sun.   30

XI

But when I sit down to reason, think to take
    my stand nor swerve,
While I triumph o'er a secret wrung from na-
    ture's close reserve,
In you come with your cold music till I creep
    through every nerve.

XII

Yes, you, like a ghostly cricket, creaking where
    a house was burned:
'Dust and ashes, dead and done with, Venice
    spent what Venice earned.   35
The soul, doubtless, is immortal—where a soul
    can be discerned.

XIII

'Yours for instance: you know physics, some-
    thing of geology,
Mathematics are your pastime; souls shall rise
    in their degree;
Butterflies may dread extinction,—you'll not
    die, it cannot be!

XIV

'As for Venice and her people, merely born to
    bloom and drop,   40
Here on earth they bore their fruitage, mirth
    and folly were the crop:
What of soul was left, I wonder, when the kiss-
    ing had to stop?

XV

'Dust and ashes!' So you creak it, and I want
    the heart to scold.
Dear dead women, with such hair, too—what's
    become of all the gold
Used to hang and brush their bosoms? I feel
    chilly and grown old.   45

(1855)

MY STAR

    ALL that I know
      Of a certain star
    Is, it can throw
      (Like the angled spar)
    Now a dart of red,   5
      Now a dart of blue;
    Till my friends have said
      They would fain see, too,
My star that dartles the red and the blue!
Then it stops like a bird; like a flower, hangs
    furled: 10
They must solace themselves with the Saturn
    above it.
What matter to me if their star is a world?
    Mine has opened its soul to me; therefore I
    love it.

(1855)

THE LAST RIDE TOGETHER

I

I said—Then, dearest, since 't is so,
Since now at length my fate I know,
Since nothing all my love avails,
Since all, my life seemed meant for, fails,
  Since this was written and needs must be   5
My whole heart rises up to bless
Your name in pride and thankfulness!
Take back the hope you gave,—I claim
Only a memory of the same,
—And this beside, if you will not blame,   10
    Your leave for one more last ride with me.

II

My mistress bent that brow of hers;
Those deep dark eyes where pride demurs
When pity would be softening through,
Fixed me a breathing-while or two   15
    With life or death in the balance: right!
The blood replenished me again;
My last thought was at least not vain:
I and my mistress, side by side
Shall be together, breathe and ride,   20
So, one day more am I deified.
    Who knows but the world may end to-night?

III

Hush! if you saw some western cloud
All billowy-bosomed, over-bowed
By many benedictions—sun's   25
And moon's and evening-star's at once—
    And so, you, looking and loving best,
Conscious grew, your passion drew
Cloud, sunset, moonrise, star-shine too,
Down on you, near and yet more near,   30
Till flesh must fade for heaven was here!—
Thus leant she and lingered—joy and fear!
    Thus lay she a moment on my breast.

IV

Then we began to ride. My soul
Smoothed itself out, a long-cramped scroll 35
Freshening and fluttering in the wind.
Past hopes already lay behind.
    What need to strive with a life awry?
Had I said that, had I done this,
So might I gain, so might I miss.   40
Might she have loved me? just as well
She might have hated, who can tell!
Where had I been now if the worst befell?
    And here we are riding, she and I.

V

Fail I alone, in words and deeds? 45
Why, all men strive, and who succeeds?
We rode; it seemed my spirit flew,
Saw other regions, cities new,
 As the world rushed by on either side.
I thought,—All labor, yet no less 50
Bear up beneath their unsuccess.
Look at the end of work, contrast
The petty done, the undone vast,
This present of theirs with the hopeful past!
 I hoped she would love me; here we ride. 55

VI

What hand and brain went ever paired?
What heart alike conceived and dared?
What act proved all its thought had been?
What will but felt the fleshly screen?
 We ride and I see her bosom heave. 60
There 's many a crown for who can reach.
Ten lines, a statesman's life in each!
The flag stuck on a heap of bones,
A soldier's doing! what atones?
They scratch his name on the Abbey-stones. 65
 My riding is better, by their leave.

VII

What does it all mean, poet? Well,
Your brains beat into rhythm, you tell
What we felt only; you expressed
You hold things beautiful the best, 70
 And place them in rhyme so, side by side.
'T is something, nay 't is much: but then,
Have you yourself what 's best for men?
Are you—poor, sick, old ere your time—
Nearer one whit your own sublime 75
Than we who never have turned a rhyme?
 Sing, riding 's a joy! For me, I ride.

VIII

And you, great sculptor—so, you gave
A score of years to Art, her slave,
And that 's your Venus, whence we turn 80
To yonder girl that fords the burn!
 You acquiesce, and shall I repine?
What, man of music, you grown gray
With notes and nothing else to say,
Is this your sole praise from a friend, 85
'Greatly his opera's strains intend,
But in music we know how fashions end!'
 I gave my youth; but we ride, in fine.

IX

Who knows what 's fit for us? Had fate
Proposed bliss here should sublimate 90
My being—had I signed the bond—
Still one must lead some life beyond,
 Have a bliss to die with, dim-descried.
This foot once planted on the goal,
This glory-garland round my soul, 95
Could I descry such? Try and test!
I sink back shuddering from the quest.
Earth being so good, would heaven seem best?
 Now, heaven and she are beyond this ride.

X

And yet—she has not spoke so long! 100
What if heaven be that, fair and strong
At life's best, with our eyes upturned
Whither life's flower is first discerned,
 We, fixed so, ever should so abide?
What if we still ride on, we two, 105
With life for ever old yet new,
Changed not in kind but in degree,
The instant made eternity,—
And heaven just prove that I and she
 Ride, ride together, for ever ride? 110
(1855)

MEMORABILIA

I

Ah, did you once see Shelley plain,
 And did he stop and speak to you,
And did you speak to him again?
 How strange it seems and new!

II

But you were living before that, 5
 And also you are living after;
And the memory I started at—
 My starting moves your laughter!

III

I crossed a moor, with a name of its own
 And a certain use in the world no doubt, 10
Yet a hand's-breadth of it shines alone
 'Mid the blank miles round about:

IV

For there I picked up on the heather
 And there I put inside my breast
A moulted feather, an eagle-feather! 15
 Well, I forget the rest.
(1855)

'DE GUSTIBUS—'

Your ghost will walk, you lover of trees,
 (If our loves remain)
 In an English lane,
By a cornfield-side a-flutter with poppies.
Hark, those two in the hazel coppice— 5
A boy and a girl, if the good fates please,
 Making love, say,—
 The happier they!
Draw yourself up from the light of the moon,
And let them pass, as they will too soon, 10
 With the beanflowers' boon,
 And the blackbird's tune,
 And May, and June!

What I love best in all the world
Is a castle, precipice-encurled, 15
In a gash of the wind-grieved Apennine.
Or look for me, old fellow of mine,
(If I get my head from out the mouth
O' the grave, and loose my spirit's bands,
And come again to the land of lands)— 20
In a sea-side house to the farther South,
Where the baked cicala dies of drouth,
And one sharp tree—'t is a cypress—stands,
By the many hundred years red-rusted,
Rough iron-spiked, ripe fruit-o'ercrusted, 25
My sentinel to guard the sands
To the water's edge. For, what expands
Before the house, but the great opaque
Blue breadth of sea without a break?
While, in the house, forever crumbles 30
Some fragment of the frescoed walls,
From blisters where a scorpion sprawls.
A girl bare-footed brings, and tumbles
Down on the pavement, green-flesh melons,
And says there 's news to-day—the king 35
Was shot at, touched in the liver-wing,
Goes with his Bourbon arm in a sling:
—She hopes they have not caught the felons.
Italy, my Italy!
Queen Mary's saying serves for me— 40
  (When fortune's malice
  Lost her Calais)—
Open my heart and you will see
Graved inside of it, 'Italy.'
Such lovers old are I and she: 45
So it always was, so shall ever be!

(1855)

ANDREA DEL SARTO

CALLED 'THE FAULTLESS PAINTER'

But do not let us quarrel any more,
No, my Lucrezia; bear with me for once:
Sit down and all shall happen as you wish.
You turn your face, but does it bring your heart?
I 'll work then for your friend's friend, never fear, 5
Treat his own subject after his own way,
Fix his own time, accept too, his own price,
And shut the money into this small hand
When next it takes mine. Will it? tenderly?
Oh, I 'll content him,—but to-morrow, Love!
I often am much wearier than you think, 11
This evening more than usual, and it seems
As if—forgive now—should you let me sit
Here by the window with your hand in mine
And look a half-hour forth on Fiesolé, 15
Both of one mind, as married people use,
Quietly, quietly the evening through,
I might get up to-morrow to my work
Cheerful and fresh as ever. Let us try.
To-morrow, how you shall be glad for this! 20
Your soft hand is a woman of itself,
And mine the man's bared breast she curls inside.
Don't count the time lost, neither; you must serve
For each of the five pictures we require:
It saves a model. So! keep looking so— 25
My serpentining beauty, rounds on rounds!
—How could you ever prick those perfect ears,
Even to put the pearl there! oh, so sweet—
My face, my moon, my everybody's moon,
Which everybody looks on and calls his, 30
And, I suppose, is looked on by in turn,
While she looks—no one's: very dear, no less.
You smile? why, there 's my picture ready made,
There 's what we painters call our harmony!
A common grayness silvers everything,— 35
All in a twilight, you and I alike
—You, at the point of your first pride in me
(That 's gone you know),—but I, at every point;
My youth, my hope, my art, being all toned down
To yonder sober pleasant Fiesolé. 40
There's the bell clinking from the chapel-top;
That length of convent-wall across the way
Holds the trees safer, huddled more inside;
The last monk leaves the garden; days decrease,
And autumn grows, autumn in everything. 45
Eh? the whole seems to fall into a shape
As if I saw alike my work and self
And all that I was born to be and do,
A twilight-piece. Love, we are in God's hand.
How strange now looks the life he makes us lead; 50
So free we seem, so fettered fast we are!
I feel he laid the fetter: let it lie!
This chamber for example—turn your head—
All that 's behind us! You don't understand
Nor care to understand about my art, 55
But you can hear at least when people speak:
And that cartoon, the second from the door
—It is the thing, Love! so such thing should be—
Behold Madonna!—I am bold to say.
I can do with my pencil what I know, 60
What I see, what at bottom of my heart
I wish for, if I ever wish so deep—
Do easily, too—when I say, perfectly,
I do not boast, perhaps: yourself are judge,
Who listened to the Legate's talk last week, 65
And just as much they used to say in France.
At any rate, 't is easy, all of it!
No sketches first, no studies, that's long past:
I do what many dream of all their lives,
—Dream? strive to do, and agonize to do, 70
And fail in doing. I could count twenty such
On twice your fingers, and not leave this town,
Who strive—you don't know how the others strive
To paint a little thing like that you smeared
Carelessly passing with your robes afloat,— 75
Yet do much less, so much less, Someone says,

(I know his name, no matter)—so much less!
Well, less is more, Lucrezia: I am judged.
There burns a truer light of God in them,
In their vexed beating stuffed and stopped-up
  brain,   80
Heart, or whate'er else, than goes on to prompt
This low-pulsed forthright craftsman's hand of
  mine.
Their works drop groundward, but themselves,
  I know,
Reach many a time a heaven that's shut to me,
Enter and take their place there sure enough,   85
Though they come back and cannot tell the
  world.
My works are nearer heaven, but I sit here.
The sudden blood of these men! at a word—
Praise them, it boils, or blame them, it boils
  too.
I, painting from myself, and to myself,   90
Know what I do, am unmoved by men's blame
Or their praise either. Somebody remarks
Morello's outline there is wrongly traced,
His hue mistaken; what of that? or else,
Rightly traced and well ordered; what of that?
Speak as they please, what does the mountain
  care?   96
Ah, but a man's reach should exceed his grasp,
Or what's a heaven for? All is silver-gray
Placid and perfect with my art: the worse!
I know both what I want and what might gain,
And yet how profitless to know, to sigh   101
'Had I been two, another and myself,
Our head would have o'erlooked the world!'
No doubt.
Yonder's a work now, of that famous youth
The Urbinate who died five years ago.   105
('T is copied, George Vasari sent it me.)
Well, I can fancy how he did it all,
Pouring his soul, with kings and popes to see,
Reaching, that heaven might so replenish him,
Above and through his art—for it gives way;   110
That arm is wrongly put—and there again—
A fault to pardon in the drawing's lines,
Its body, so to speak: its soul is right,
He means right—that, a child may understand.
Still, what an arm! and I could alter it: 115
But all the play, the insight and the stretch—
Out of me, out of me! And wherefore out?
Had you enjoined them on me, given me soul,
We might have risen to Rafael, I and you!
Nay, Love, you did give all I asked, I think—
More than I merit, yes, by many times.   121
But had you—oh, with the same perfect brow,
And perfect eyes, and more than perfect mouth,
And the low voice my soul hears, as a bird
The fowler's pipe, and follows to the snare—
Had you, with these the same, but brought a
  mind!   126
Some women do so. Had the mouth there
  urged
'God and the glory! never care for gain.

The present by the future, what is that?
Live for fame, side by side with Agnolo!   130
Rafael is waiting: up to God, all three!'
I might have done it for you. So it seems:
Perhaps not. All is as God overrules.
Beside, incentives come from the soul's self;
The rest avail not. Why do I need you?   135
What wife had Rafael, or has Agnolo?
In this world, who can do a thing, will not;
And who would do it, cannot, I perceive:
Yet the will's somewhat—somewhat, too, the
  power—
And thus we half-men struggle. At the end,   140
God, I conclude, compensates, punishes.
'T is safer for me, if the award be strict,
That I am something underrated here,
Poor this long while, despised, to speak the
  truth.
I dared not, do you know, leave home all day,
For fear of chancing on the Paris lords.   146
The best is when they pass and look aside;
But they speak sometimes; I must bear it all.
Well may they speak! That Francis, that first
  time,
And that long festal year at Fontainebleau!
I surely then could sometimes leave the ground,
Put on the glory, Rafael's daily wear,   152
In that humane great monarch's golden look,—
One finger in his beard or twisted curl
Over his mouth's good mark that made the
  smile,   155
One arm about my shoulder, round my neck,
The jingle of his gold chain in my ear,
I painting proudly with his breath on me,
All his court round him, seeing with his eyes,
Such frank French eyes, and such a fire of souls
Profuse, my hand kept plying by those hearts,—
And, best of all, this, this, this face beyond, 162
This in the background, waiting on my work,
To crown the issue with a last reward!
A good time, was it not, my kingly days?   165
And had you not grown restless . . . but I
  know—
'T is done and past; 't was right, my instinct
  said;
Too live the life grew, golden and not gray,
And I'm the weak-eyed bat no sun should tempt
Out of his grange whose four walls make his
  world.   170
How could it end in any other way?
You called me, and I came home to your heart.
The triumph was—to reach and stay there;
  since
I reached it ere the triumph, what is lost?
Let my hands frame your face in your hair's
  gold,   175
You beautiful Lucrezia that are mine!
'Rafael did this, Andrea painted that;
The Roman's is the better when you pray,
But still the other's Virgin was his wife'—
Men will excuse me. I am glad to judge   180

Both pictures in your presence; clearer grows
My better fortune, I resolve to think.
For, do you know, Lucrezia, as God lives,
Said one day Agnolo, his very self,
To Rafael . . . I have known it all these
    years . . .   185
(When the young man was flaming out his
    thoughts
Upon a palace-wall for Rome to see,
Too lifted up in heart because of it)
'Friend, there 's a certain sorry little scrub
Goes up and down our Florence, none cares
    how,   190
Who, were he set to plan and execute
As you are, pricked on by your popes and kings,
Would bring the sweat into that brow of yours!'
To Rafael's!—And indeed the arm is wrong.
I hardly dare . . . yet, only you to see,   195
Give the chalk here—quick, thus the line should
    go!
Ay, but the soul! he 's Rafael! rub it out!
Still, all I care for, if he spoke the truth
(What he? why, who but Michel Agnolo?
Do you forget already words like those?),   200
If really there was such a chance, so lost,—
Is, whether you 're—not grateful—but more
    pleased.
Well, let me think so. And you smile indeed!
This hour has been an hour! Another smile?
If you would sit thus by me every night   205
I should work better, do you comprehend?
I mean that I should earn more, give you more.
See, it is settled dusk now; there 's a star;
Morello 's gone, the watch-lights show the wall,
The cue-owls speak the name we call them by.
Come from the window, Love,—come in, at last,
Inside the melancholy little house   212
We built to be so gay with. God is just.
King Francis may forgive me; oft at nights,
When I look up from painting, eyes tired out, 215
The walls become illumined, brick from brick
Distinct, instead of mortar, fierce bright gold,
That gold of his I did cement them with!
Let us but love each other. Must you go?
That Cousin here again? he waits outside? 220
Must see you—you, and not with me? Those
    loans?
More gaming debts to pay? you smiled for that?
Well, let smiles buy me! have you more to
    spend?
While hand and eye and something of a heart
Are left me, work 's my ware, and what 's it
    worth?   225
I 'll pay my fancy. Only let me sit
The gray remainder of the evening out,
Idle, you call it, and muse perfectly
How I could paint, were I but back in France,
One picture, just one more—the Virgin's face, 230
Not yours this time! I want you at my side
To hear them—that is, Michel Agnolo—
Judge all I do and tell you of its worth.

Will you? To-morrow, satisfy your friend.
I take the subjects for his corridor,   235
Finish the portrait out of hand—there, there,
And throw him in another thing or two
If he demurs; the whole should prove enough
To pay for this same Cousin's freak. Beside,
What 's better and what 's all I care about, 240
Get you the thirteen scudi for the ruff!
Love, does that please you? Ah, but what
    does he,
The Cousin! what does he to please you more?

I am grown peaceful as old age to-night.
I regret little, I would change still less.   245
Since there my past life lies, why alter it?
The very wrong to Francis!—it is true
I took his coin, was tempted and complied,
And built this house and sinned, and all is said.
My father and my mother died of want.   250
Well, had I riches of my own? you see
How one gets rich! Let each one bear his lot.
They were born poor, lived poor, and poor they
    died:
And I have labored somewhat in my time
And not been paid profusely. Some good son 255
Paint my two hundred pictures—let him try!
No doubt, there 's something strikes a balance.
    Yes,
You loved me quite enough, it seems to-night.
This must suffice me here. What would one
    have?
In heaven, perhaps, new chances, one more
    chance—   260
Four great walls in the new Jerusalem,
Meted on each side by the angel's reed,
For Leonard, Rafael, Agnolo and me
To cover—the three first without a wife,
While I have mine! So—still they overcome 265
Because there 's still Lucrezia,—as I choose.

Again the Cousin's whistle! Go, my Love.
                                                (1855)

THE GUARDIAN-ANGEL

A PICTURE AT FANO

I

Dear and great Angel, wouldst thou only leave
    That child, when thou hast done with him,
        for me!
Let me sit all the day here, that when eve
    Shall find performed thy special ministry,
And time come for departure, thou, suspend-
    ing,   5
Thy flight, may'st see another child for tending,
    Another still, to quiet and retrieve.

II

Then I shall feel thee step one step, no more,
    From where thou standest now, to where I
        gaze,

—And suddenly my head is covered o'er 10
  With those wings, white above the child who prays
Now on that tomb—and I shall feel thee guarding
Me, out of all the world; for me, discarding
  Yon heaven thy home, that waits and opes its door.

III

I would not look up thither past thy head 15
  Because the door opes, like that child, I know,
For I should have thy gracious face instead,
  Thou bird of God! And wilt thou bend me low
Like him, and lay, like his, my hands together,
And lift them up to pray, and gently tether 20
  Me, as thy lamb there, with thy garment's spread?

IV

If this was ever granted, I would rest
  My head beneath thine, while thy healing hands
Close-covered both my eyes beside thy breast,
  Pressing the brain, which too much thought expands, 25
Back to its proper size again, and smoothing
  Distortion down till every nerve had soothing,
  And all lay quiet, happy, and suppressed.

V

How soon all worldly wrong would be repaired!
  I think how I should view the earth and skies
And sea, when once again my brow was bared 31
  After thy healing, with such different eyes.
O world, as God has made it! All is beauty:
And knowing this, is love, and love is duty.
  What further may be sought for or declared? 35

VI

Guercino drew this angel I saw teach
  (Alfred, dear friend!)—that little child to pray,
Holding the little hands up, each to each
  Pressed gently,—with his own head turned away
Over the earth where so much lay before him 40
Of work to do, though heaven was opening o'er him,
  And he was left at Fano by the beach.

VII

We were at Fano, and three times we went
  To sit and see him in his chapel there,
And drink his beauty to our soul's content 45
  —My angel with me too: and since I care
For dear Guercino's fame (to which in power
And glory comes this picture for a dower,
  Fraught with a pathos so magnificent)—

VIII

And since he did not work thus earnestly 50
  At all times, and has else endured some wrong—
I took one thought his picture struck from me,
  And spread it out, translating it to song.
My love is here. Where are you, dear old friend?
How rolls the Wairoa at your world's far end? 55
  This is Ancona, yonder is the sea.

(1855)

A GRAMMARIAN'S FUNERAL

SHORTLY AFTER THE REVIVAL OF LEARNING IN EUROPE

Let us begin and carry up this corpse,
  Singing together.
Leave we the common crofts, the vulgar thorpes
  Each in its tether
Sleeping safe on the bosom of the plain, 5
  Cared-for till cock-crow:
Look out if yonder be not day again
  Rimming the rock-row!
That's the appropriate country; there, man's thought,
  Rarer, intenser, 10
Self-gathered for an outbreak, as it ought,
  Chafes in the censer.
Leave we the unlettered plain its herd and crop;
  Seek we sepulture
On a tall mountain, citied to the top, 15
  Crowded with culture!
All the peaks soar, but one the rest excels;
  Clouds overcome it;
No! yonder sparkle is the citadel's
  Circling its summit. 20
Thither our path lies; wind we up the heights:
  Wait ye the warning?
Our low life was the level's and the night's;
  He's for the morning.
Step to a tune, square chests, erect each head, 25
  'Ware the beholders!
This is our master, famous, calm, and dead,
  Borne on our shoulders.

Sleep, crop and herd! sleep, darkling thorpe and croft,
  Safe from the weather! 30
He, whom we convoy to his grave aloft,
  Singing together,
He was a man born with thy face and throat,
  Lyric Apollo!
Long he lived nameless: how should spring take note 35
  Winter would follow?
Till lo, the little touch, and youth was gone!
  Cramped and diminished,
Moaned he, 'New measures, other feet anon!
  My dance is finished?' 40

No, that's the world's way: (keep the mountain-side,
    Make for the city!)
He knew the signal, and stepped on with pride
    Over men's pity;
Left play for work, and grappled with the world
    Bent on escaping: 46
'What's in the scroll,' quoth he, 'thou keepest furled?
    Show me their shaping,
Theirs who most studied man, the bard and sage,—
    Give!'—So, he gowned him, 50
Straight got by heart that book to its last page:
    Learnèd, we found him.
Yea, but we found him bald too, eyes like lead,
    Accents uncertain:
'Time to taste life,' another would have said, 55
    'Up with the curtain!'
This man said rather, 'Actual life comes next?
    Patience a moment!
Grant I have mastered learning's crabbed text,
    Still there's the comment. 60
Let me know all! Prate not of most or least,
    Painful or easy!
Even to the crumbs I'd fain eat up the feast,
    Ay, nor feel queasy.'
Oh, such a life as he resolved to live, 65
    When he had learned it,
When he had gathered all books had to give!
    Sooner, he spurned it.
Image the whole, then execute the parts—
    Fancy the fabric 70
Quite, ere you build, ere steel strike fire from quartz,
    Ere mortar dab brick.
(Here's the town-gate reached; there's the market-place
    Gaping before us.)
Yea, this in him was the peculiar grace 75
    (Hearten our chorus!)
That before living he'd learn how to live—
    No end to learning.
Earn the means first—God surely will contrive
    Use for our earning. 80
Others mistrust and say, 'But time escapes:
    Live now or never!'
He said, 'What's time? Leave Now for dogs and apes!
    Man has Forever!' 84
Back to his book then: deeper drooped his head;
    Calculus racked him:
Leaden before, his eyes grew dross of lead:
    Tussis attacked him.
'Now, master, take a little rest!'—not he!
    (Caution redoubled, 90
Step two abreast, the way winds narrowly!)
    Not a whit troubled,
Back to his studies, fresher than at first,
    Fierce as a dragon

He (soul-hydroptic with a sacred thirst) 95
    Sucked at the flagon.
Oh, if we draw a circle premature,
    Heedless of far gain,
Greedy for quick returns of profit, sure
    Bad is our bargain! 100
Was it not great? did not he throw on God
    (He loves the burthen)—
God's task to make the heavenly period
    Perfect the earthen,
Did not he magnify the mind, show clear 105
    Just what it all meant?
He would not discount life, as fools do here,
    Paid by instalment.
He ventured neck or nothing—heaven's success
    Found, or earth's failure: 110
'Wilt thou trust death or not?' He answered 'Yes:
    Hence with life's pale lure!'
That low man seeks a little thing to do,
    Sees it and does it;
This high man, with a great thing to pursue, 115
    Dies ere he knows it.
That low man goes on adding one to one,
    His hundred's soon hit;
This high man, aiming at a million,
    Misses an unit. 120
That, has the world here—should he need the next,
    Let the world mind him!
This, throws himself on God, and unperplexed
    Seeking shall find Him.
So, with the throttling hands of death at strife,
    Ground he at grammar; 126
Still, through the rattle, parts of speech were rife:
    While he could stammer
He settled *Hoti's* business—let it be!—
    Properly based *Oun*— 130
Gave us the doctrine of the enclitic *De*,
    Dead from the waist down.
Well, here's the platform, here's the proper place:
    Hail to your purlieus,
All ye highfliers of the feathered race, 135
    Swallows and curlews!
Here's the top-peak, the multitude below
    Live, for they can, there:
This man decided not to Live but Know—
    Bury this man there? 140
Here—here's his place, where meteors shoot, clouds form,
    Lightnings are loosened,
Stars come and go! Let joy break with the storm,
    Peace let the dew send!
Lofty designs must close in like effects: 145
    Loftily lying,
Leave him—still loftier than the world suspects,
    Living and dying.

(1855)

ONE WORD MORE

TO E. B. B.

I

There they are, my fifty men and women
Naming me the fifty poems finished!
Take them, Love, the book and me together:
Where the heart lies, let the brain lie also.

II

Rafael made a century of sonnets, 5
Made and wrote them in a certain volume
Dinted with the silver-pointed pencil
Else he only used to draw Madonnas:
These, the world might view—but one, the volume.
Who that one, you ask? Your heart instructs you. 10
Did she live and love it all her lifetime?
Did she drop, his lady of the sonnets,
Die, and let it drop beside her pillow
Where it lay in place of Rafael's glory,
Rafael's cheek so duteous and so loving— 15
Cheek, the world was wont to hail a painter's,
Rafael's cheek, her love had turned a poet's?

III

You and I would rather read that volume,
(Taken to his beating bosom by it)
Lean and list the bosom-beats of Rafael, 20
Would we not? than wonder at Madonnas—
Her, San Sisto names, and Her, Foligno,
Her, that visits Florence in a vision,
Her, that's left with lilies in the Louvre—
Seen by us and all the world in circle. 25

IV

You and I will never read that volume.
Guido Reni, like his own eye's apple,
Guarded long the treasure-book and loved it.
Guido Reni dying, all Bologna
Cried, and the world cried too, 'Ours, the treasure!' 30
Suddenly, as rare things will, it vanished.

V

Dante once prepared to paint an angel:
Whom to please? You whisper 'Beatrice.'
While he mused and traced it and retraced it,
(Peradventure with a pen corroded 35
Still by drops of that hot ink he dipped for,
When, his left-hand i' the hair o' the wicked,
Back he held the brow and pricked its stigma,
Bit into the live man's flesh for parchment,
Loosed him, laughed to see the writing rankle, 40
Let the wretch go festering through Florence)—
Dante, who loved well because he hated.
Hated wickedness that hinders loving,
Dante, standing, studying his angel—
In there broke the folk of his Inferno. 45
Says he—'Certain people of importance'
(Such he gave his daily dreadful line to)
'Entered and would seize, forsooth, the poet.'
Says the poet—'Then I stopped my painting.'

VI

You and I would rather see that angel, 50
Painted by the tenderness of Dante,
Would we not?—than read a fresh Inferno.

VII

You and I will never see that picture.
While he mused on love and Beatrice,
While he softened o'er his outlined angel, 55
In they broke, those 'people of importance';
We and Bice bear the loss forever.

VIII

What of Rafael's sonnets, Dante's picture?
This: no artist lives and loves, that longs not
Once, and only once, and for one only 60
(Ah, the prize!), to find his love a language
Fit and fair and simple and sufficient—
Using nature that's an art to others,
Not, this one time, art that's turned his nature.
Ay, of all the artists living, loving, 65
None but would forego his proper dowry,—
Does he paint? he fain would write a poem,—
Does he write? he fain would paint a picture,—
Put to proof art alien to the artist's,
Once, and only once, and for one only, 70
So to be the man and leave the artist,
Gain the man's joy, miss the artist's sorrow.

IX

Wherefore? Heaven's gift takes earth's abatement!
He who smites the rock and spreads the water,
Bidding drink and live a crowd beneath him,
Even he, the minute makes immortal, 76
Proves, perchance, but mortal in the minute,
Desecrates, belike, the deed in doing.
While he smites, how can he but remember,
So he smote before, in such a peril, 80
When they stood and mocked—'Shall smiting help us?'
When they drank and sneered—'A stroke is easy!'
When they wiped their mouths and went their journey,
Throwing him for thanks—'But drought was pleasant.'
Thus old memories mar the actual triumph; 85
Thus the doing savors of disrelish;
Thus achievement lacks a gracious somewhat;
O'er-importuned brows becloud the mandate,
Carelessness or consciousness—the gesture,
For he bears an ancient wrong about him, 90
Sees and knows again those phalanxed faces,
Hears, yet one time more, the 'customed prelude—

'How shouldst thou, of all men, smite, and save us?'
Guesses what is like to prove the sequel—
'Egypt's flesh-pots—nay, the drought was better.'   95

X

Oh, the crowd must have emphatic warrant!
Theirs, the Sinai-forehead's cloven brilliance,
Right-arm's rod-sweep, tongue's imperial fiat.
Never dares the man put off the prophet.

XI

Did he love one face from out the thousands, 100
(Were she Jethro's daughter, white and wifely,
Were she but the Æthiopian bondslave)
He would envy yon dumb, patient camel,
Keeping a reserve of scanty water
Meant to save his own life in the desert,   105
Ready in the desert to deliver
(Kneeling down to let his breast be opened)
Hoard and life together for his mistress.

XII

I shall never, in the years remaining,   109
Paint you pictures, no, nor carve you statues,
Make you music that should all-express me;
So it seems: I stand on my attainment,
This of verse alone, one life allows me;
Verse and nothing else have I to give you,
Other heights in other lives, God willing: 115
All the gifts from all the heights, your own, Love!

XIII

Yet a semblance of resource avails us—
Shade so finely touched, love's sense must seize it.
Take these lines, look lovingly and nearly,
Lines I write the first time and the last time.   120
He who works in fresco, steals a hair-brush,
Curbs the liberal hand, subservient proudly,
Cramps his spirit, crowds its all in little,
Makes a strange art of an art familiar,
Fills his lady's missal-marge with flowerets.
He who blows through bronze may breathe through silver,   126
Fitly serenade a slumbrous princess.
He who writes, may write for once as I do.

XIV

Love, you saw me gather men and women,
Live or dead or fashioned by my fancy,   130
Enter each and all, and use their service,
Speak from every mouth,—the speech, a poem.
Hardly shall I tell my joys and sorrows,
Hopes and fears, belief and disbelieving:
I am mine and yours—the rest be all men's,   135
Karshish, Cleon, Norbert, and the fifty.
Let me speak this once in my true person,
Not as Lippo, Roland, or Andrea,
Though the fruit of speech be just this sentence:
Pray you, look on these my men and women,   140
Take and keep my fifty poems finished;
Where my heart lies, let my brain lie also!
Poor the speech; be how I speak, for all things.

XV

Not but that you know me! Lo, the moon's self!
Here in London, yonder late in Florence,   145
Still we find her face, the thrice-transfigured.
Curving on a sky imbrued with color,
Drifted over Fiesolé by twilight,
Came she, our new crescent of a hair's-breadth.
Full she flared it, lamping Samminiato,   150
Rounder 'twixt the cypresses and rounder,
Perfect till the nightingales applauded.
Now, a piece of her old self, impoverished,
Hard to greet, she traverses the house-roofs,
Hurries with unhandsome thrift of silver   155
Goes dispiritedly, glad to finish.

XVI

What, there 's nothing in the moon noteworthy?
Nay: for if that moon could love a mortal,
Use, to charm him (so to fit a fancy),
All her magic ('t is the old sweet mythos),   160
She would turn a new side to her mortal,
Side unseen of herdsman, huntsman, steersman—
Blank to Zoroaster on his terrace,
Blind to Galileo on his turret.   164
Dumb to Homer, dumb to Keats—him, even!
Think, the wonder of the moonstruck mortal—
When she turns round, comes again in heaven,
Opens out anew for worse or better!
Proves she like some portent of an iceberg
Swimming full upon the ship it founders,   170
Hungry with huge teeth of splintered crystals?
Proves she as the paved work of a sapphire,
Seen by Moses when he climbed the mountain?
Moses, Aaron, Nadab, and Abihu
Climbed and saw the very God, the Highest,   175
Stand upon the paved work of a sapphire.
Like the bodied heaven in his clearness
Shone the stone, the sapphire of that paved work,
When they ate and drank and saw God also!

XVII

What were seen? None knows, none ever shall know.   180
Only this is sure—the sight were other,
Not the moon's same side, born late in Florence,
Dying now impoverished here in London.
God be thanked, the meanest of his creatures
Boasts two soul-sides, one to face the world with,   185
One to show a woman when he loves her!

XVIII

This I say of me, but think of you, Love!
This to you—yourself my moon of poets!
Ah, but that's the world's side, there's the wonder,
Thus they see you, praise you, think they know you! 190
There, in turn I stand with them and praise you—
Out of my own self, I dare to phrase it.
But the best is when I glide from out them,
Cross a step or two of dubious twilight,
Come out on the other side, the novel 195
Silent silver lights and darks undreamed of,
Where I hush and bless myself with silence.

XIX

Oh, their Rafael of the dear Madonnas,
Oh, their Dante of the dread Inferno,
Wrote one song—and in my brain I sing it, 200
Drew one angel—borne, see, on my bosom!

R. B. (1855)

ABT VOGLER

AFTER HE HAS BEEN EXTEMPORIZING UPON THE MUSICAL INSTRUMENT OF HIS INVENTION

I

Would that the structure brave, the manifold music I build,
  Bidding my organ obey, calling its keys to their work,
Claiming each slave of the sound, at a touch, as when Solomon willed
  Armies of angels that soar, legions of demons that lurk,
Man, brute, reptile, fly,—alien of end and of aim, 5
  Adverse, each from the other heaven-high, hell-deep removed,—
Should rush into sight at once as he named the ineffable Name,
  And pile him a palace straight, to pleasure the princess he loved!

II

Would it might tarry like his, the beautiful building of mine,
  This which my keys in a crowd pressed and importuned to raise! 10
Ah, one and all, how they helped, would dispart now and now combine,
  Zealous to hasten the work, heighten their master his praise!
And one would bury his brow with a blind plunge down to hell,
  Burrow awhile and build, broad on the roots of things,
Then up again swim into sight, having based me my palace well, 15
  Founded it, fearless of flame, flat on the nether springs.

III

And another would mount and march, like the excellent minion he was,
  Ay, another and yet another, one crowd but with many a crest,
Raising my rampired walls of gold as transparent as glass,
  Eager to do and die, yield each his place to the rest: 20
For higher still and higher (as a runner tips with fire,
  When a great illumination surprises a festal night—
Outlining round and round Rome's dome from space to spire)
  Up, the pinnacled glory reached, and the pride of my soul was in sight.

IV

In sight? Not half! for it seemed, it was certain, to match man's birth, 25
  Nature in turn conceived, obeying an impulse as I;
And the emulous heaven yearned down, made effort to reach the earth,
  As the earth had done her best, in my passion, to scale the sky:
Novel splendors burst forth, grew familiar and dwelt with mine,
  Not a point nor peak but found and fixed its wandering star; 30
Meteor-moons, balls of blaze: and they did not pale nor pine,
  For earth had attained to heaven, there was no more near nor far.

V

Nay more; for there wanted not who walked in the glare and glow,
  Presences plain in the place; or, fresh from the Protoplast,
Furnished for ages to come, when a kindlier wind should blow, 35
  Lured now to begin and live, in a house to their liking at last;
Or else the wonderful Dead who have passed through the body and gone,
  But were back once more to breathe in an old world worth their new:
What never had been, was now; what was, as it shall be anon;
  And what is,—shall I say, matched both? for I was made perfect too. 40

VI

All through my keys that gave their sounds to
   a wish of my soul,
  All through my soul that praised as its wish
    flowed visibly forth,
All through music and me! For think, had I
   painted the whole,
  Why, there it had stood, to see, nor the
    process so wonder-worth:
Had I written the same, made verse—still, ef-
   fect proceeds from cause,   45
  Ye know why the forms are fair, ye hear how
    the tale is told;
It is all triumphant art, but art in obedience to
   laws,
  Painter and poet are proud in the artist-list
    enrolled:—

VII

But here is the finger of God, a flash of the will
   that can,
  Existent behind all laws, that made them and,
    lo, they are!   50
And I know not if, save in this, such gift be
   allowed to man
  That out of three sounds he frame, not a
    fourth sound, but a star.
Consider it well: each tone of our scale in itself
   is nought:
  It is everywhere in the world—loud, soft, and
    all is said:
Give it to me to use! I mix it with two in my
   thought: 55
  And there! Ye have heard and seen: con-
    sider and bow the head!

VIII

Well, it is gone at last, the palace of music I
   reared;
  Gone! and the good tears start, the praises
    that come too slow;
For one is assured at first, one scarce can say
   that he feared,
  That he even gave it a thought, the gone
    thing was to go.   60
Never to be again! But many more of the kind
   As good, nay, better perchance: is this your
    comfort to me?
To me, who must be saved because I cling with
   my mind
  To the same, same self, same love, same God:
    ay, what was, shall be.

IX

Therefore to whom turn I but to thee, the in-
   effable Name?   65
  Builder and maker, thou, of houses not made
    with hands!
What, have fear of change from thee who art
   ever the same?
  Doubt that thy power can fill the heart that
    thy power expands?
There shall never be one lost good! What was,
   shall live as before;
  The evil is null, is nought, is silence implying
    sound;   70
What was good shall be good, with, for evil, so
   much good more;
  On the earth the broken arcs; in the heaven
    a perfect round.

X

All we have willed or hoped or dreamed of good
   shall exist;
  Not its semblance, but itself; no beauty, nor
    good, nor power
Whose voice has gone forth, but each survives
   for the melodist   75
  When eternity affirms the conception of an
    hour.
The high that proved too high, the heroic for
   earth too hard,
  The passion that left the ground to lose itself
    in the sky,
Are music sent up to God by the lover and the
   bard;
  Enough that he heard it once: we shall hear
    it by and by.   80

XI

And what is our failure here but a triumph's
   evidence
  For the fullness of the days? Have we
    withered or agonized?
Why else was the pause prolonged but that
   singing might issue thence?
  Why rushed the discords in, but that har-
    mony should be prized?
Sorrow is hard to bear, and doubt is slow to
   clear,   85
  Each sufferer says his say, his scheme of the
    weal and woe:
But God has a few of us whom he whispers in
   the ear;
  The rest may reason and welcome: 't is we
    musicians know.

XII

Well, it is earth with me: silence resumes her
   reign:
  I will be patient and proud, and soberly
    acquiesce.   90
Give me the keys. I feel for the common chord
   again,
  Sliding by semitones till I sink to the minor,
    —yes,
And I blunt it into a ninth, and I stand on alien
   ground,
  Surveying awhile the heights I rolled from
    into the deep;

Which, hark, I have dared and done, for my
    resting-place is found,   95
  The C Major of this life: so, now I will try to
    sleep.

(1864)

RABBI BEN EZRA

I

Grow old along with me!
  The best is yet to be,
The last of life, for which the first was made:
  Our times are in His hand
  Who saith, 'A whole I planned,   5
Youth shows but half; trust God: see all, nor
    be afraid!'

II

Not that, amassing flowers,
  Youth sighed, 'Which rose make ours,
Which lily leave and then as best recall?'
  Not that, admiring stars,   10
  It yearned, 'Nor Jove, nor Mars;
Mine be some figured flame which blends,
    transcends them all!'

III

Not for such hopes and fears
  Annulling youth's brief years,
Do I remonstrate: folly wide the mark!   15
  Rather I prize the doubt
  Low kinds exist without,
Finished and finite clods, untroubled by a spark.

IV

Poor vaunt of life indeed,
  Were man but formed to feed   20
On joy, to solely seek and find and feast;
  Such feasting ended, then
  As sure an end to men;
Irks care the crop-full bird? Frets doubt the
    maw-crammed beast?

V

Rejoice we are allied   25
  To That which doth provide
And not partake, effect and not receive!
  A spark disturbs our clod;
  Nearer we hold of God
Who gives, than of his tribes that take, I must
    believe.   30

VI

Then, welcome each rebuff
  That turns earth's smoothness rough,
Each sting that bids nor sit nor stand but go!
  Be our joys three-parts pain!
  Strive, and hold cheap the strain;   35
Learn, nor account the pang; dare, never grudge
    the throe!

VII

For thence,—a paradox
  Which comforts while it mocks,—
Shall life succeed in that it seems to fail:
  What I aspired to be,   40
  And was not, comforts me:
A brute I might have been, but would not sink
    i' the scale.

VIII

What is he but a brute
  Whose flesh has soul to suit,
Whose spirit works lest arms and legs want
    play?   45
  To man, propose this test—
  Thy body at its best,
How far can that project thy soul on its lone
    way?

IX

Yet gifts should prove their use:
  I own the Past profuse   50
Of power each side, perfection every turn:
  Eyes, ears took in their dole,
  Brain treasured up the whole;
Should not the heart beat once 'How good to
    live and learn'?

X

Not once beat 'Praise be thine!   55
  I see the whole design,
I, who saw power, see now love perfect too:
  Perfect I call thy plan:
  Thanks that I was a man!
Maker, remake, complete,—I trust what thou
    shalt do!'   60

XI

For pleasant is this flesh;
  Our soul, in its rose-mesh
Pulled ever to the earth, still yearns for rest:
  Would we some prize might hold
  To match those manifold   65
Possessions of the brute,—gain most, as we
    did best!

XII

Let us not always say,
  'Spite of this flesh to-day
I strove, made head, gained ground upon the
    whole!'
  As the bird wings and sings,   70
  Let us cry, 'All good things
Are ours, nor soul helps flesh more, now, than
    flesh helps soul!'

XIII

Therefore I summon age
  To grant youth's heritage,
Life's struggle having so far reached its term: 75
  Thence shall I pass, approved
  A man, for aye removed
From the developed brute; a God though in
    the germ.

XIV

And I shall thereupon
Take rest, ere I be gone   80
Once more on my adventure brave and new:
Fearless and unperplexed,
When I wage battle next,
What weapons to select, what armor to indue.

XV

Youth ended, I shall try   85
My gain or loss thereby;
Leave the fire ashes, what survives is gold:
And I shall weigh the same,
Give life its praise or blame:
Young, all lay in dispute; I shall know, being old.   90

XVI

For, note when evening shuts,
A certain moment cuts
The deed off, calls the glory from the gray:
A whisper from the west
Shoots—'Add this to the rest,   95
Take it and try its worth: here dies another day.'

XVII

So, still within this life,
Though lifted o'er its strife,
Let me discern, compare, pronounce at last,
'This rage was right i' the main,   100
That acquiescence vain:
The Future I may face now I have proved the Past.'

XVIII

For more is not reserved
To man, with soul just nerved
To act to-morrow what he learns to-day: 105
Here, work enough to watch
The Master work, and catch
Hints of the proper craft, tricks of the tool's true play.

XIX

As it was better, youth
Should strive, through acts uncouth,   110
Toward making, than repose on aught found made:
So, better, age, exempt
From strife, should know, than tempt
Further. Thou waitedst age: wait death nor be afraid!

XX

Enough now, if the Right   115
And Good and Infinite
Be named here, as thou callest thy hand thine own,
With knowledge absolute,
Subject to no dispute
From fools that crowded youth, nor let thee feel alone.   120

XXI

Be there, for once and all,
Severed great minds from small,
Announced to each his station in the Past!
Was I, the world arraigned,
Were they, my soul disdained,   125
Right? Let age speak the truth and give us peace at last!

XXII

Now, who shall arbitrate?
Ten men love what I hate,
Shun what I follow, slight what I receive;
Ten, who in ears and eyes   130
Match me: we all surmise,
They, this thing, and I, that: whom shall my soul believe?

XXIII

Not on the vulgar mass
Called 'work,' must sentence pass,
Things done, that took the eye and had the price;   135
O'er which, from level stand,
The low world laid its hand,
Found straightway to its mind, could value in a trice:

XXIV

But all, the world's coarse thumb,
And finger failed to plumb,   140
So passed in making up the main account;
All instincts immature,
All purposes unsure,
That weighed not as his work, yet swelled the man's amount:

XXV

Thoughts hardly to be packed   145
Into a narrow act,
Fancies that broke through language and escaped;
All I could never be,
All, men ignored in me,
This, I was worth to God, whose wheel the pitcher shaped.   150

XXVI

Ay, note that Potter's wheel,
That metaphor! and feel
Why time spins fast, why passive lies our clay,—
Thou, to whom fools propound,
When the wine makes its round,   155
'Since life fleets, all is change; the Past gone, seize to-day!'

XXVII

Fool! All that is, at all,
Lasts ever, past recall;

Earth changes, but thy soul and God stand
    sure:
  What entered into thee,
    That was, is, and shall be:
Time's wheel runs back or stops: Potter and
    clay endure.

XXVIII

  He fixed thee mid this dance
    Of plastic circumstance,
This Present, thou, forsooth, wouldst fain ar-
    rest:
  Machinery just meant
    To give thy soul its bent,
Try thee and turn thee forth, sufficiently im-
    pressed.

XXIX

  What though the earlier grooves
    Which ran the laughing loves
Around thy base, no longer pause and press?
  What though about thy rim,
    Skull-things in order grim
Grow out, in graver mood, obey the sterner
    stress?

XXX

  Look not thou down but up!
    To uses of a cup!
The festal board, lamp's flash, and trumpet's
    peal,
  The new wine's foaming flow,
    The Master's lips a-glow!
Thou, heaven's consummate cup, what need'st
    thou with earth's wheel?

XXXI

  But I need, now as then,
    Thee, God, who moldest men;
And since, not even while the whirl was worst,
  Did I—to the wheel of life
    With shapes and colors rife,
Bound dizzily,—mistake my end, to slake thy
    thirst:

XXXII

  So, take and use thy work,
    Amend what flaws may lurk,
What strain o' the stuff, what warpings past
    the aim!
  My times be in thy hand!
    Perfect the cup as planned!
Let age approve of youth, and death complete
    the same!

                  (1864)

PROSPICE

Fear death?—to feel the fog in my throat,
    The mist in my face,
When the snows begin, and the blasts denote
    I am nearing the place,
The power of the night the press of the storm,
    The post of the foe;
Where he stands, the Arch Fear in a visible
    form,
    Yet the strong man must go:
For the journey is done and the summit at-
    tained,
    And the barriers fall,
Though a battle's to fight ere the guerdon be
    gained,
    The reward of it all.
I was ever a fighter, so—one fight more,
    The best and the last!
I would hate that death bandaged my eyes, and
    forbore,
    And bade me creep past.
No! let me taste the whole of it, fare like my
    peers
    The heroes of old,
Bear the brunt, in a minute pay glad life's ar-
    rears
    Of pain, darkness, and cold.
For sudden the worst turns the best to the
    brave,
    The black minute's at end,
And the elements' rage, the fiend-voices that
    rave,
    Shall dwindle, shall blend,
Shall change, shall become first a peace out of
    pain,
    Then a light, then thy breast,
O thou soul of my soul! I shall clasp thee again,
    And with God be the rest!

                  (1864)

HERVÉ RIEL

I

On the sea and at the Hogue, sixteen hundred
    ninety-two.
  Did the English fight the French,—woe to
    France!
And, the thirty-first of May, helter-skelter
    through the blue,
Like a crowd of frightened porpoises a shoal of
    sharks pursue,
  Came crowding ship on ship to Saint Malo
    on the Rance,
With the English fleet in view.

II

'T was the squadron that escaped, with the
    victor in full chase;
First and foremost of the drove, in his great
    ship, Damfreville;
  Close on him fled, great and small,
  Twenty-two good ships in all;
And they signaled to the place
'Help the winners of a race!
  Get us guidance, give us harbor, take us
    quick—or, quicker still,
  Here's the English can and will!'

III

Then the pilots of the place put out brisk and
    leapt on board;
'Why, what hope or chance have ships like
    these to pass?' laughed they:
'Rocks to starboard, rocks to port, all the
    passage scarred and scored,
Shall the "Formidable" here with her twelve
    and eighty guns
Think to make the river-mouth by the single
    narrow way,
Trust to enter where 't is ticklish for a craft
    of twenty tons,
    And with flow at full beside?
    Now, 't is slackest ebb of tide.
    Reach the mooring? Rather say,
While rock stands or water runs,
    Not a ship will leave the bay!'

IV

    Then was called a council straight.
    Brief and bitter the debate:
'Here 's the English at our heels; would you
    have them take in tow
All that 's left us of the fleet, linked together
    stern and bow,
    For a prize to Plymouth Sound?
    Better run the ships aground!'
(Ended Damfreville his speech.)
Not a minute more to wait!
Let the Captains all and each
Shove ashore, then blow up, blow up the vessels on
    the beach!
France must undergo her fate.

V

'Give the word!' But no such word
    Was ever spoke or heard;
For up stood, for out stepped, for in struck
    amid all these
—A Captain? A Lieutenant? A Mate—first,
    second, third?
No such man of mark, and meet
With his betters to compete!
But a simple Breton sailor pressed by Tour-
    ville for the fleet,
A poor coasting-pilot he, Hervé Riel the
    Croisickese.

VI

And 'What mockery or malice have we here?'
    cried Hervé Riel:
'Are you mad, you Malouins? Are you
    cowards, fools, or rogues?
Talk to me of rocks and shoals, me who took
    the soundings, tell
On my fingers every bank, every shallow, every
    swell
'Twixt the offing here and Grève where the
    river disembogues?

Are you bought by English gold? Is it love
    the lying 's for?
    Morn and eve, night and day,
    Have I piloted your bay,
Entered free and anchored fast at the foot of
    Solidor.
Burn the fleet and ruin France? That were
    worse than fifty Hogues!
Sirs, they know I speak the truth! Sirs,
    believe me there 's a way!
Only let me lead the line,
    Have the biggest ship to steer,
    Get this "Formidable" clear,
Make the others follow mine,
And I lead them, most and least, by a passage
    I know well,
    Right to Solidor past Grève,
    And there lay them safe and sound;
    And if one ship misbehave,
    —Keel so much as grate the ground,
Why, I 've nothing but my life,—here 's my
    head!' cries Hervé Riel.

VII

Not a minute more to wait.
'Steer us in, then, small and great!
Take the helm, lead the line, save the squadron!'
    cried its chief.
Captains, give the sailor place!
He is Admiral, in brief.
    Still the north-wind, by God's grace!
    See the noble fellow's face
    As the big ship, with a bound,
    Clears the entry like a hound,
Keeps the passage as its inch of way were the
    wide sea's profound!
See, safe through shoal and rock,
How they follow in a flock,
Not a ship that misbehaves, not a keel that
    grates the ground,
Not a spar that comes to grief!
    The peril, see, is past,
    All are harbored to the last,
And just as Hervé Riel hollas 'Anchor!'—sure
    as fate,
Up the English come—too late!

VIII

So, the storm subsides to calm:
    They see the green trees wave
    On the heights o'erlooking Grève.
Hearts that bled are stanched with balm.
'Just our rapture to enhance,
    Let the English rake the bay,
    Gnash their teeth and glare askance
    As they cannonade away!
'Neath rampired Solidor pleasant riding on the
    Rance!'
How hope succeeds despair on each Captain's
    countenance!

Out burst all with one accord,
　'This is Paradise for Hell!
　Let France, let France's King
　Thank the man that did the thing!'
What a shout, and all one word,
　'Hervé Riel!'
As he stepped in front once more;
　Not a symptom of surprise
　In the frank blue Breton eyes.
Just the same man as before.

IX

Then said Damfreville, 'My friend,
I must speak out at the end,
　Though I find the speaking hard.
Praise is deeper than the lips:
You have saved the King his ships.
　You must name your own reward
'Faith, our sun was near eclipse!
Demand whate'er you will,
France remains your debtor still.
Ask to heart's content and have! or my name's
　not Damfreville.'

X

Then a beam of fun outbroke
On the bearded mouth that spoke,
As the honest heart laughed through
Those frank eyes of Breton blue:
'Since I needs must say my say,
　Since on board the duty 's done,
　And from Malo Roads to Croisic Point, what
　　is it but a run?—
Since 't is ask and have, I may—
　Since the others go ashore—
Come! A good whole holiday!
　Leave to go and see my wife, whom I call the
　　Belle Aurore!'
That he asked and that he got,—nothing
　more.

XI

　Name and deed alike are lost:
　　Not a pillar nor a post
In his Croisic keeps alive the feat as it befell:
　Not a head in white and black
　On a single fishing-smack,
　In memory of the man but for whom had
　　gone to wrack
All that France saved from the fight whence
　England bore the bell.
Go to Paris: rank on rank
Search the heroes flung pell-mell
　On the Louvre, face and flank!
You shall look long enough ere you come to
　Hervé Riel.
So, for better and for worse,
　Hervé Riel, accept my verse!
In my verse, Hervé Riel, do thou once more
Save the squadron, honor France, love thy wife
　the Belle Aurore!
　　　　　(1871)

THE TWO POETS OF CROISIC
PROLOGUE

Such a starved bank of moss
　Till, that May-morn,
Blue ran the flash across:
　Violets were born!

Sky—what a scowl of cloud
　Till, near and far,
Ray on ray split the shroud:
　Splendid, a star!

World—how it walled about
　Life with disgrace
Till God's own smile came out:
　That was thy face!

EPILOGUE

I

What a pretty tale you told me
　Once upon a time
—Said you found it somewhere (scold me)!
　Was it prose or was it rhyme,
Greek or Latin? Greek, you said,
While your shoulder propped my head.

II

Anyhow there 's no forgetting
　This much if no more,
That a poet (pray, no petting!)
　Yes, a bard, sir, famed of yore,
Went where suchlike used to go,
Singing for a prize, you know.

III

Well, he had to sing, not merely
　Sing but play the lyre;
Playing was important clearly
　Quite as singing: I desire,
Sir, you keep the fact in mind
For a purpose that 's behind.

IV

There stood he, while deep attention
　Held the judges round,
—Judges able, I should mention,
　To detect the slightest sound
Sung or played amiss: such ears
Had old judges, it appears!

V

None the less he sang out boldly,
　Played in time and tune,
Till the judges, weighing coldly
　Each note's worth, seemed, late or soon,
Sure to smile 'In vain one tries
Picking faults out: take the prize!'

VI

When, a mischief! Were they seven
   Strings the lyre possessed?
Oh, and afterwards eleven,
   Thank you! Well, sir,—who had guessed   45
Such ill luck in store?—it happed
One of those same seven strings snapped.

VII

All was lost, then! No! a cricket
   (What 'cicada?' Pooh!)   50
—Some mad thing that left its thicket
   For mere love of music—flew
With its little heart on fire,
Lighted on the crippled lyre.

VIII

So that when (Ah, joy!) our singer   55
   For his truant string
Feels with disconcerted finger,
   What does cricket else but fling
Fiery heart forth, sound the note
Wanted by the throbbing throat?   60

IX

Ay, and ever to the ending,
   Cricket chirps at need,
Executes the hand's intending,
   Promptly, perfectly,—indeed
Saves the singer from defeat   65
With her chirrup low and sweet.

X

Till, at ending, all the judges
   Cry with one assent,
'Take the prize—a prize who grudges
   Such a voice and instrument?   70
Why, we took your lyre for harp;
So it thrilled us forth F sharp!'

XI

Did the conqueror spurn the creature,
   Once its service done?
That's no such uncommon feature   75
   In the case when Music's son
Finds his Lotte's power too spent
For aiding soul-development.

XII

No! This other on returning
   Homeward, prize in hand,   80
Satisfied his bosom's yearning:
   (Sir, I hope you understand!)
—Said 'Some record there must be
Of this cricket's help to me!'

XIII

So, he made himself a statue: 85
   Marble stood, life-size;
On the lyre, he pointed at you,
   Perched his partner in the prize;
Never more apart you found
Her, he throned, from him, she crowned.   90

XIV

That's the tale: its application?
   Somebody I know
Hopes one day for reputation
   Through his poetry that's—Oh,
All so learned and so wise   95
And deserving of a prize!

XV

If he gains one, will some ticket,
   When his statue's built,
Tell the gazer ''T was a cricket
   Helped my crippled lyre, whose lilt   100
Sweet and low, when strength usurped
Softness' place i' the scale, she chirped?

XVI

'For as victory was nighest,
   While I sang and played,—
With my lyre at lowest, highest   105
   Right alike,—one string that made
"Love" sound soft was snapt in twain,
Never to be heard again,—

XVII

'Had not a kind cricket fluttered,
   Perched upon the place   110
Vacant left, and duly uttered
   "Love, Love, Love," whene'er the bass
Asked the treble to atone
For its somewhat somber drone.'

XVIII

But you don't know music! Wherefore   115
   Keep on casting pearls
To a—poet? All I care for
   Is—to tell him that a girl's
'Love' comes aptly in when gruff
Grows his singing. (There, enough!)   120

(1878)

PHEIDIPPIDES

Χαίρετε, νικῶμεν

First I salute this soil of the blessed, river and
   rock!
Gods of my birthplace, dæmons, and heroes,
   honor to all!
Then I name thee, claim thee for our patron,
   co-equal in praise
—Ay, with Zeus the Defender, with Her of the
   ægis and spear!
Also, ye of the bow and the buskin, praised be
   your peer,   5
Now, henceforth and for ever,—O latest to
   whom I upraise

Hand and heart and voice! For Athens, leave pasture and flock!
Present to help, potent to save, Pan—patron I call!

Archons of Athens, topped by the tettix, see, I return!
See, 't is myself here standing alive, no specter that speaks! 10
Crowned with the myrtle, did you command me, Athens and you,
'Run, Pheidippides, run and race, reach Sparta for aid!
Persia has come, we are here, where is She?' Your command I obeyed,
Ran and raced: like stubble, some field which a fire runs through,
Was the space between city and city: two days, two nights did I burn 15
Over the hills, under the dales, down pits and up peaks.

Into their midst I broke: breath served but for 'Persia has come.
Persia bids Athens proffer slaves'-tribute, water and earth;
Razed to the ground is Eretria—but Athens, shall Athens sink,
Drop into dust and die—the flower of Hellas utterly die, 20
Die with the wide world spitting at Sparta, the stupid, the stander-by?
Answer me quick, what help, what hand do you stretch o'er destruction's brink?
How,—when? No care for my limbs!—there's lightning in all and some—
Fresh and fit your message to bear, once lips give it birth!'

O my Athens—Sparta love thee? Did Sparta respond? 25
Every face of her leered in a furrow of envy, mistrust,
Malice,—each eye of her gave me its glitter of gratified hate!
Gravely they turned to take counsel, to cast for excuses. I stood
Quivering,—the limbs of me fretting as fire frets, an inch from dry wood:
'Persia has come, Athens asks aid, and still they debate? 30
Thunder, thou Zeus! Athene, are Spartans a quarry beyond
Swing of thy spear? Phoibos and Artemis clang them "Ye must"!'

No bolt launched from Olumpos! Lo, they answer at last!
'Has Persia come,—does Athens ask aid,—may Sparta befriend?
Nowise precipitate judgment—too weighty the issue at stake! 35
Count we no time lost time which lags through respect to the gods!
Ponder that precept of old, "No warfare, whatever the odds
In your favor, so long as the moon, half-orbed, is unable to take
Full-circle her state in the sky!" Already she rounds to it fast:
Athens must wait, patient as we—who judgment suspend.' 40

Athens,—except for that sparkle,—thy name, I had moldered to ash!
That sent a blaze through my blood; off, off, and away was I back,
—Not one word to waste, one look to lose on the false and the vile!
Yet 'O gods of my land!' I cried, as each hillock and plain,
Wood and stream, I knew, I named, rushing past them again, 45
'Have ye kept faith, proved mindful of honors we paid you erewhile?
Vain was the filleted victim, the fulsome libation! Too rash
Love in its choice, paid you so largely service so slack!

'Oak and olive and bay,—I bid you cease to enwreathe
Brows made bold by your leaf! Fade at the Persian's foot, 50
You that, our patrons were pledged, should never adorn a slave!
Rather I hail thee, Parnes,—trust to thy wild waste tract!
Treeless, herbless, lifeless mountain! What matter if slacked
My speed may hardly be, for homage to crag and to cave
No deity deigns to drape with verdure?—at least I can breathe, 55
Fear in thee no fraud from the blind, no lie from the mute!'

Such my cry as, rapid, I ran over Parnes' ridge;
Gully and gap I clambered and cleared till, sudden, a bar
Jutted, a stoppage of stone against me, blocking the way.
Right! for I minded the hollow to traverse, the fissure across: 60
'Where I could enter, there I depart by! Night in the fosse?
Athens to aid? Though the dive were through Erebos, thus I obey—
Out of the day dive, into the day as bravely arise! No bridge
Better!'—when—ha! what was it I came on, of wonders that are?

There, in the cool of a cleft, sat he—majestical
    Pan! 65
Ivy drooped wanton, kissed his head, moss
    cushioned his hoof:
All the great god was good in the eyes grave-
    kindly—the curl
Carved on the bearded cheek, amused at a
    mortal's awe
As, under the human trunk, the goat-thighs
    grand I saw.
'Halt, Pheidippides!'—halt I did, my brain of
    a whirl: 70
'Hither to me! Why pale in my presence?' he
    gracious began:
'How is it,—Athens, only in Hellas, holds me
    aloof?

'Athens, she only, rears me no fane, makes me
    no feast!
Wherefore? Than I what godship to Athens
    more helpful of old?
Ay, and still, and forever her friend! Test Pan,
    trust me! 75
Go, bid Athens take heart, laugh Persia to
    scorn, have faith
In the temples and tombs! Go, say to Athens,
    "The Goat-God saith:
When Persia—so much as strews not the soil—
    is cast in the sea,
Then praise Pan who fought in the ranks with
    your most and least,
Goat-thigh to greaved-thigh, made one cause
    with the free and the bold!" 80

'Say Pan saith: "Let this, foreshowing the
    place, be the pledge!"'
(Gay, the liberal hand held out this herbage I
    bear
—Fennel,—I grasped it a-tremble with dew—
    whatever it bode)
'While, as for thee . . . ' But enough! He
    was gone. If I ran hitherto—
Be sure that the rest of my journey, I ran no
    longer, but flew. 85
Parnes to Athens—earth no more, the air was
    my road:
Here am I back. Praise Pan, we stand no more
    on the razor's edge!
Pan for Athens, Pan for me! I too have a
    guerdon rare!

Then spoke Miltiades. 'And thee, best runner
    of Greece,
Whose limbs did duty indeed,—what gift is
    promised thyself? 90
Tell it us straightway,—Athens the mother de-
    mands of her son!'
Rosily blushed the youth: he paused; but, lift-
    ing at length

His eyes from the ground, it seemed as he
    gathered the rest of his strength
Into the utterance—'Pan spoke thus: "For
    what thou hast done
Count on a worthy reward! Henceforth be
    allowed thee release 95
From the racer's toil, no vulgar reward in praise
    or in pelf!"

'I am bold to believe, Pan means reward the
    most to my mind!
Fight I shall, with our foremost, wherever this
    fennel may grow,—
Pound—Pan helping us—Persia to dust and,
    under the deep,
Whelm her away forever; and then,—no Athens
    to save,— 100
Marry a certain maid, I know keeps faith to the
    brave,—
Hie to my house and home: and, when my
    children shall creep
Close to my knees,—recount how the God was
    awful yet kind,
Promised their sire reward to the full—reward-
    ing him—so!'

Unforeseeing one! Yes, he fought on the
    Marathon day: 105
So, when Persia was dust, all cried 'To Akro-
    polis!
Run, Pheidippides, one race more! the meed is
    thy due!
"Athens is saved, thank Pan," go shout!' He
    flung down his shield,
Ran like fire once more: and the space 'twixt
    the Fennelfield
And Athens was stubble again, a field which a
    fire runs through, 110
Till in he broke: 'Rejoice, we conquer!' Like
    wine through clay,
Joy in his blood bursting his heart, he died—
    the bliss!
So, to this day, when friend meets friend, the
    word of salute
Is still 'Rejoice'—his word which brought re-
    joicing indeed.
So is Pheidippides happy forever,—the noble
    strong man 115
Who could race like a god, bear the face of a
    god, whom a god loved so well;
He saw the land saved he had helped to save,
    and was suffered to tell
Such tidings, yet never decline, but, gloriously
    as he began,
So to end gloriously—once to shout, thereafter
    be mute:
'Athens is saved!'—Pheidippides dies in the
    shout for his meed. 120

(1879)

CAVALIER TUNES

I. MARCHING ALONG

Kentish Sir Byng stood for his King,
Bidding the crop-headed Parliament swing:
And, pressing a troop unable to stoop
And see the rogues flourish and honest folk droop,
Marched them along, fifty-score strong,   5
Great-hearted gentlemen, singing this song.

God for King Charles! Pym and such carles
To the Devil that prompts 'em their treasonous parles!
Cavaliers, up! Lips from the cup,
Hands from the pasty, nor bite take nor sup   10
Till you're—

CHORUS

*Marching along, fifty-score strong,
Great-hearted gentlemen, singing this song.*

Hampden to hell, and his obsequies' knell.
Serve Hazelrig, Fiennes, and young Harry as well!
England, good cheer! Rupert is near!   15
Kentish and loyalists, keep we not here,

CHORUS

*Marching along, fifty-score strong,
Great-hearted gentlemen, singing this song?*

Then, God for King Charles! Pym and his snarls
To the Devil that pricks on such pestilent carles!
Hold by the right, you double your might;   21
So, onward to Nottingham, fresh for the fight,

CHORUS

*March we along, fifty-score strong,
Great-hearted gentlemen, singing this song!*

II. GIVE A ROUSE

King Charles, and who'll do him right now?   25
King Charles, and who's ripe for fight now?
Give a rouse: here's, in hell's despite now,
King Charles!

Who gave me the goods that went since?
Who raised me the house that sank once?   30
Who helped me to gold I spent since?
Who found me in wine you drank once?

CHORUS

*King Charles, and who'll do him right now?
King Charles, and who's ripe for fight now?
Give a rouse: here's, in hell's despite now,
King Charles!*   36

To whom used my boy George quaff else,
By the old fool's side that begot him?
For whom did he cheer and laugh else,
While Noll's damned troopers shot him?   40

CHORUS

*King Charles, and who'll do him right now?
King Charles, and who's ripe for fight now?
Give a rouse: here's, in hell's despite now,
King Charles!*

(1842)

ASOLANDO

EPILOGUE

At the midnight in the silence of the sleep time,
  When you set your fancies free,
Will they pass to where—by death, fools think, imprisoned—
Low he lies who once so loved you, whom you loved so,—
            —Pity me?   5

Oh, to love so, be so loved, yet so mistaken!
  What had I on earth to do
With the slothful, with the mawkish, the unmanly?
Like the aimless, helpless, hopeless, did I drivel
            —Being—who?   10

One who never turned his back but marched breast forward,
  Never doubted clouds would break,
Never dreamed, though right were worsted, wrong would triumph,
Held we fall to rise, are baffled to fight better,
            Sleep to wake.   15

No, at noonday in the bustle of man's worktime
  Greet the unseen with a cheer!
Bid him forward, breast and back as either should be,
'Strive and thrive!' cry 'Speed,—fight on, fare ever
            There as here!'   20

(1890)

MATTHEW ARNOLD (1822–1888)

From his father, Dr. Thomas Arnold, afterward headmaster of Rugby, Matthew Arnold may well have inherited the academic tastes that dominated his life. After a schooling at Winchester and Rugby, Arnold won a classical scholarship, in 1841, at Balliol College, Oxford. During his second year at the university, he gained the Newdigate prize by a poem on Cromwell, and in 1845 he was elected to a fellowship at Oriel College. Arnold abandoned Oxford presently, however, in order to become private secretary to the Marquis of Lansdowne, who procured for him, in 1851, an appointment as inspector of schools, from which he was released only a short time before his death. In 1848 he became known to a small circle of readers by his first volume of poems, *The Strayed Reveller and other Poems*, and during the next few years his poetical influence greatly increased, especially through the poems contained in *Poems by Matthew Arnold* (1853), a volume to which he prefaced a notable critical essay on poetry. In 1857 Arnold was elected to the professorship of poetry at Oxford, which he held for ten years, and which provided him the stimulus for writing certain of his best critical essays. The substantial classic *On Translating Homer: Three Lectures given at Oxford* (1861) was followed by *Essays in Criticism* (1865), which promptly fascinated and influenced English readers, as did also the published lectures, *On the Study of Celtic Literature* (1867). From pure literary criticism Arnold passed, for a time, to studies in religion, ethics, and politics, such as *Culture and Anarchy* (1869), *Friendship's Garland* (1871), *Literature and Dogma* (1873), and *Last Essays on Church and Religion* (1877). He returned subsequently, however, to literary criticism, occupying himself largely in editing, in making selections from poets, and in writing prefaces. In 1883 Arnold received a civil service pension of £250, which enabled him to retire from his duties as inspector of schools. In the winter of 1883–1884, he lectured in America, as he did also in 1886. The lectures delivered during his first American tour were published in 1885 as *Discourses in America*.

Arnold's poetry, small in volume, is of almost invariable excellence. Although it makes no strong popular appeal, it has always held a large audience through its grace, gravity, and melody. As a critic, Arnold is preëminent. For a generation or two his canons of poetry, securely expressed in a poised, gentle, and precise style, have dominated English literary criticism.

THE STUDY OF POETRY

'*The future of poetry is immense, because in poetry, where it is worthy of its high destinies, our race, as time goes on, will find an ever surer and surer stay. There is not a creed which is not shaken, not an accredited dogma which is not shown to be questionable, not a received tradition which does not threaten to dissolve. Our religion has materialized itself in the fact, in the supposed fact; it has attached its emotion to the fact, and now the fact is failing it. But for poetry the idea is everything; the rest is a world of illusion, of divine illusion. Poetry attaches its emotion to the idea; the idea is the fact. The strongest part of our religion to-day is its unconscious poetry.*'

Let me be permitted to quote these words of my own, as uttering the thought which should, in my opinion, go with us and govern us in all our study of poetry. In the present work it is the course of one great contributory stream to the world-river of poetry that we are invited to follow. We are here invited to trace the stream of English poetry. But whether we set ourselves, as here, to follow only one of the several streams that make the mighty river of poetry, or whether we seek to know them all, our governing thought should be the same. We should conceive of poetry worthily, and more highly than it has been the custom to conceive of it. We should conceive of it as capable of higher uses and called to higher destinies, than those which in general men have assigned to it hitherto. More and more mankind will discover that we have to turn to poetry to interpret life for us, to console us, to sustain us. Without poetry, our science will appear incomplete; and most of what now passes with us for religion and philosophy will be replaced by poetry. Science, I say, will appear incomplete without it. For finely and truly does Wordsworth call poetry 'the impassioned expression which is in the countenance of all science;' and what is a countenance without its expression? Again, Wordsworth finely and truly calls poetry 'the breath and finer spirit of all knowledge:' our religion, parading evidences such as those on which the popular mind relies now; our philosophy, pluming itself on its reasonings about causation and finite and infinite being; what are they but the shadows and dreams and false shows of knowledge? The day will come when we shall wonder at ourselves for having trusted to them, for having taken them seriously; and the more we perceive their hollowness, the more we shall prize 'the breath and finer spirit of knowledge' offered to us by poetry.

But if we conceive thus highly of the destinies of poetry, we must also set our standard for poetry high, since poetry, to be capable of fulfilling such high destinies, must be poetry of a high order of excellence. We must accustom ourselves to a high standard and to a strict judgment. Sainte-Beuve relates that Napoleon one day said, when somebody was spoken of in his presence as a charlatan: 'Charlatan as much as you please; but where is there *not* charlatanism?' 'Yes,' answers Sainte-Beuve, 'in politics, in the art of governing mankind, that is perhaps true. But in the order of thought, in art, the glory, the eternal honor is that charlatanism shall find no entrance; herein lies the inviolableness of that noble portion of man's being.' It is admirably said, and let us hold fast to it. In poetry, which is thought and art in one, it is the glory, the eternal honor, that charlatanism shall find no entrance; that this noble sphere be kept inviolate and inviolable. Charlatanism is for confusing or obliterating the distinctions between excellent and inferior, sound and unsound or only half-sound, true and untrue or only half-true. It is charlatanism, conscious or unconscious, whenever we confuse or obliterate these. And in poetry, more than anywhere else, it is unpermissible to confuse or obliterate them. For in poetry the distinction between excellent and inferior, sound and unsound or only half-sound, true and untrue or only half-true, is of paramount importance. It is of paramount importance because of the high destinies of poetry. In poetry, as a criticism of life under the conditions fixed for such a criticism by the laws of poetic truth and poetic beauty, the spirit of our race will find, we have said, as time goes on and as other helps fail, its consolation and stay. But the consolation and stay will be of power in proportion to the power of the criticism of life. And the criticism of life will be of power in proportion as the poetry conveying it is excellent rather than inferior, sound rather than unsound or half-sound, true rather than untrue or half-true.

The best poetry is what we want; the best poetry will be found to have a power of forming, sustaining, and delighting us, as nothing else can. A clearer, deeper sense of the best in poetry, and of the strength and joy to be drawn from it, is the most precious benefit which we can gather from a poetical collection such as the present. And yet in the very nature and conduct of such a collection there is inevitably something which tends to obscure in us the consciousness of what our benefit should be, and to distract us from the pursuit of it. We should therefore steadily set it before our minds at the outset, and should compel ourselves to revert constantly to the thought of it as we proceed.

Yes; constantly, in reading poetry, a sense for the best, the really excellent, and of the strength and joy to be drawn from it, should be present in our minds and should govern our estimate of what we read. But this real estimate, the only true one, is liable to be superseded, if we are not watchful, by two other kinds of estimate, the historic estimate and the personal estimate, both of which are fallacious. A poet or a poem may count to us historically, they may count to us on grounds personal to ourselves, and they may count to us really. They may count to us historically. The course of development of a nation's language, thought, and poetry, is profoundly interesting; and by regarding a poet's work as a stage in this course of development we may easily bring ourselves to make it of more importance as poetry than in itself it really is, we may come to use a language of quite exaggerated praise in criticizing it; in short, to overrate it. So arises in our poetic judgments the fallacy caused by the estimate which we may call historic. Then, again, a poet or a poem may count to us on grounds personal to ourselves. Our personal affinities, likings, and circumstances, have great power to sway our estimate of this or that poet's work, and to make us attach more importance to it as poetry than in itself it really possesses, because to us it is, or has been, of high importance. Here also we overrate the object of our interest, and apply to it a language of praise which is quite exaggerated. And thus we get the source of a second fallacy in our poetic judgments,—the fallacy caused by an estimate which we may call personal.

Both fallacies are natural. It is evident how naturally the study of the history and development of a poetry may incline a man to pause over reputations and works once conspicuous but now obscure, and to quarrel with a careless public for skipping, in obedience to mere tradition and habit, from one famous name or work in its national poetry to another, ignorant of what it misses, and of the reason for keeping what it keeps, and of the whole process of growth in its poetry. The French have become diligent students of their own early poetry, which they long neglected; the study makes many of them dissatisfied with this so-called classical poetry, the court-tragedy of the seventeenth century, a poetry which Pellison long ago reproached with its want of the true poetic stamp, with its *politesse stérile et rampante* [sterile and servile politeness], but which nevertheless has reigned in France as absolutely as if it had been the perfection of classical poetry indeed. The dissatisfaction is natural; yet a lively and accomplished critic, M. Charles d'Héricault, the editor of Clément Marot, goes too far when he says that 'the cloud of glory playing round a classic is a mist as dangerous to the future of a literature as it is intolerable for the purposes of history.' 'It hinders,' he goes on, 'it hinders us from seeing more than one single point, the culminating and exceptional point; the summary, fictitious and arbitrary, of a thought and of a work. It substitutes a halo for a physiognomy, it puts a statue where there was once a man, and hiding from us all trace of the labor, the attempts, the weaknesses, the failures, it claims not study but veneration; it does not show us how the thing is done, it imposes upon us a model. Above all, for the historian this creation of classic personages is inadmissible; for it withdraws the poet from his time, from his proper life, it breaks historical relationships, it blinds criticism by conventional admiration, and renders the investigation of literary origins unacceptable. It gives us a human personage no longer, but a God seated immovable amidst his perfect work, like Jupiter on Olympus; and hardly will it be possible for the young student, to whom such work is exhibited at such a distance from him, to believe that it did not issue ready made from that divine head.'

All this is brilliantly and tellingly said, but we must plead for a distinction. Everything depends on the reality of a poet's classic character. If he is a dubious classic, let us sift him; if he is a false classic, let us explode him. But if he is a real classic, if his work belongs to the class of the very best (for this is the true and right meaning of the word *classic, classical*), then the great thing for us is to feel and enjoy his work as deeply as ever we can, and to appreciate the wide difference between it and all work which has not the same high character. This is what is salutary, this is what is formative; this is the great benefit to be got from the study of poetry. Everything which interferes with it, which hinders it, is injurious. True, we must read our classic with open eyes, and not with eyes blinded with superstition; we must perceive when his work comes short, when it drops out of the class of the very best, and we must rate it, in such cases, at its proper value. But the use of this negative criticism is not in itself, it is entirely in its enabling us to have a clearer sense and a deeper enjoyment of what is truly excellent. To trace the labor, the attempts, the weaknesses, the failures of a genuine classic, to acquaint oneself with his time and his life and his historical relationships, is mere literary dilettantism unless it has that clear sense and deeper enjoyment for its end. It may be said that the more we know about a classic the better we shall enjoy him; and, if we lived as long as Methuselah and had all of us heads of perfect clearness and wills of perfect steadfastness, this might be true in fact as it is plausible in theory. But the case here is much the same as the case with the Greek and Latin studies of our schoolboys. The elaborate philological groundwork which we require them to lay is in theory an admirable preparation for appreciating the Greek and Latin authors worthily. The more thoroughly we lay the groundwork, the better we shall be able, it may be said, to enjoy the authors. True, if time were not so short, and schoolboys' wits not so soon tired and their power of attention exhausted; only, as it is, the elaborate philological preparation goes on, but the authors are little known and less enjoyed. So with the investigator of 'historic origins' in poetry. He ought to enjoy the true classic all the better for his investigations; he often is distracted from the enjoyment of the best, and with the less good he overbusies himself, and is prone to overrate it in proportion to the trouble which it has cost him.

The idea of tracing historic origins and historical relationships cannot be absent from a compilation like the present. And naturally the poets to be exhibited in it will be assigned to those persons for exhibition who are known to prize them highly, rather than to those who have no special inclination towards them. Moreover the very occupation with an author, and the business of exhibiting him, disposes us to affirm and amplify his importance. In the present work, therefore, we are sure of frequent temptation to adopt the historic estimate, or the personal estimate, and to forget the real estimate; which latter, nevertheless, we must employ if we are to make poetry yield us its full benefit. So high is that benefit, the benefit of clearly feeling and of deeply enjoying the really excellent, the truly classic in poetry, that we do well, I say, to set it fixedly before our minds as our object in studying poets and poetry, and to make the desire of attaining it the one principle to which, as the *Imitation* says, whatever we may read or come to know, we always return. *Cum multa legeris et cognoveris, ad unum semper oportet redire principium* [When you have read and known many things, you ought always to revert to the one beginning].

The historic estimate is likely in especial to affect our judgment and our language when we are dealing with ancient poets; the personal estimate when we are dealing with poets our contemporaries, or at any rate modern. The exaggerations due to the historic estimate are not in themselves, perhaps, of very much gravity. Their report hardly enters the general ear; probably they do not always impose even on the literary men who adopt them. But they lead to a dangerous abuse of language. So we hear Cædmon, amongst our own poets, compared to Milton. I have already noticed the enthusiasm of one accomplished French critic for 'historic origins.' Another eminent French critic, M. Vitet, comments upon that famous document of the early poetry of his nation, the *Chanson de Roland*. It is indeed a most interesting document. The *joculator* or *jongleur* Taillefer, who was with William the Conqueror's army at Hastings, marched before the Norman troops, so said the tradition, singing 'of Charlemagne and of Roland and of Oliver, and of the vassals who died at Roncevaux'; and it is suggested that in the *Chanson de Roland* by one Turoldus or Théroulde, a poem preserved in a manuscript of the twelfth century in the Bodleian Library at Oxford, we have certainly the matter, perhaps even some of the words of the chaunt which Taillefer sang. The poem has vigor and freshness; it is not without pathos. But M. Vitet is not satisfied with seeing in it a document of some poetic value, and of very high historic and linguistic value; he sees in it a grand and beautiful work, a monument of epic genius. In its general design he finds the grandiose conception, in its details he finds the constant union of simplicity with greatness, which are the marks, he truly says, of the genuine epic, and distinguish it from the artificial epic of literary ages. One thinks of Homer; this is the sort of praise which is given to Homer, and justly given. Higher praise there cannot well be, and it is the praise due to epic poetry of the highest order only, and to no other. Let us try, then, the *Chanson de Roland* at its best. Roland, mortally wounded, lays himself down under a pine tree, with his face turned toward Spain and the enemy:

> *De plusurs choses à remembrer li prist*
> *De tantes teres cume li bers cunquist,*
> *De dulce France, des humes de sun lign,*
> *De Carlemagne sun seignor ki l'nurrit.*[1]

That is primitive work, I repeat, with an undeniable poetic quality of its own. It deserves such praise and such praise is sufficient for it. But now turn to Homer:

> Ὣς φάτο, τοὺς δ' ἤδη κατέχεν φυσίζοος αἶα
> ἐν Λακεδαίμονι αὖθι, φίλῃ ἐν πατρίδι γαίῃ[2]

We are here in another world, another order of poetry altogether; here is rightly due such supreme praise as that which M. Vitet gives to the *Chanson de Roland*. If our words are to have any meaning, if our judgments are to have any solidity, we must not heap that supreme praise upon poetry of an order immeasurably inferior.

Indeed there can be no more useful help for discovering what poetry belongs to the class of the truly excellent, and can therefore do us most good, than to have always in one's mind lines and expressions of the great masters, and to apply them as a touchstone to other poetry. Of course we are not to require this other poetry to resemble them: it may be very dissimilar.

[1] 'Then began he to call many things to remembrance,—all the lands which his valor conquered, and pleasant France, and the men of his lineage, and Charlemagne his liege lord who nourished him.'—*Chanson de Roland*, iii. 939–942.

[2] 'So said she; they long since in Earth's soft arms were reposing,
There, in their own dear land, their fatherland, Lacedæmon.'
Iliad, iii. 243-4 (translated by Dr. Hawtrey).

But if we have any tact we shall find them, when we have lodged them well in our minds, an infallible touchstone for detecting the presence or absence of high poetic quality, and also the degree of this quality, in all other poetry which we may place beside them. Short passages, even single lines, will serve our turn quite sufficiently. Take the two lines which I have just quoted from Homer, the poet's comment on Helen's mention of her brothers; or take his

Ἀ δειλὼ τί σφῶϊ δόμεν Πηλῆϊ ἄνακτι
θνητῷ; ὑμεῖς δ' ἐστὸν ἀγήρω τ' ἀθανάτω τε.
ἦ ἵνα δυστήνοισι μετ' ἀνδράσιν ἄλγε' ἔχητον; [1]

the address of Zeus to the horses of Peleus; or, take finally, his

Καὶ σέ, γέρον, τὸ πρὶν μὲν ἀκούομεν ὄλβιον εἶναι [2]

the words of Achilles to Priam, a suppliant before him. Take that incomparable line and a half of Dante, Ugolino's tremendous words:

Io no piangeva; sì dentro impietrai.
Piangevan elli . . . [3]

take the lovely words of Beatrice to Virgil:

Io son fatta da Dio, sua mercè, tale,
Che la vostra miseria non mi tange,
Nè fiamma d'esto incendio non m'assale . . . [4]

take the simple, but perfect, single line:

In la sua volontade è nostra pace. [5]

Take of Shakespeare a line or two of Henry the Fourth's expostulation with sleep:

Wilt thou upon the high and giddy mast
Seal up the ship-boy's eyes, and rock his brains
In cradle of the rude imperious surge . . .

and take, as well, Hamlet's dying request to Horatio:

If thou didst ever hold me in thy heart,
Absent thee from felicity awhile,
And in this harsh world draw thy breath in pain
To tell my story . . .

Take of Milton that Miltonic passage:

Darkened so, yet shone
Above them all the archangel; but his face
Deep scars of thunder had intrenched, and care
Sat on his faded cheek . . .

[1] 'Ah, unhappy pair, why gave we you to King Peleus, to a mortal? but ye are without old age, and immortal. Was it that with men born to misery ye might have sorrow?'—*Iliad*, xvii. 443–445.
[2] 'Nay, and thou too, old man, in former days wast, as we hear, happy.'—*Iliad*, xxiv. 543.
[3] 'I wailed not, so of stone grew I within;—*they* wailed.'—*Inferno*, xxxiii, 39, 40.
[4] 'Of such sort hath God, thanked be his mercy, made me, that your misery toucheth me not, neither doth the flame of this fire strike me.'—*Inferno*, ii. 91–93.
[5] 'In His will is our peace.'—*Paradiso*, iii. 85.

add two such lines as:

And courage never to submit or yield,
And what is else, not to be overcome . . .

and finish with the exquisite close to the loss of Proserpine, the loss

. . . which cost Ceres all that pain
To seek her through the world.

These few lines, if we have tact and can use them, are enough even of themselves to keep clear and sound our judgments about poetry, to save us from fallacious estimates of it, to conduct us to a real estimate.

The specimens I have quoted differ widely from one another, but they have in common this: the possession of the very highest poetical quality. If we are thoroughly penetrated by their power, we shall find that we have acquired a sense enabling us, whatever poetry may be laid before us, to feel the degree in which a high poetical quality is present or wanting there. Critics give themselves great labor to draw out what in the abstract constitutes the characters of a high quality of poetry. It is much better simply to have recourse to concrete examples:—to take specimens of poetry of the high, the very highest quality, and to say: The characters of a high quality of poetry are what is expressed *there*. They are far better recognized by being felt in the verse of the master, than by being perused in the prose of the critic. Nevertheless if we are urgently pressed to give some critical account of them, we may safely, perhaps, venture on laying down, not indeed how and why the characters arise, but where and in what they arise. They are in the matter and substance of the poetry, and they are in its manner and style. Both of these, the substance and matter on the one hand, the style and manner on the other, have a mark, an accent, of high beauty, worth, and power. But if we are asked to define this mark and accent in the abstract, our answer must be: No, for we should thereby be darkening the question, not clearing it. The mark and accent are as given by the substance and matter of that poetry, by the style and manner of that poetry, and of all other poetry which is akin to it in quality.

Only one thing we may add as to the substance and matter of poetry, guiding ourselves by Aristotle's profound observation that the superiority of poetry over history consists in its possessing a higher truth and a higher seriousness (φιλοσοφώτερον καὶ σπουδαιότερον)

[more philosophic and more serious]. Let us add, therefore, to what we have said, this: that the substance and matter of the best poetry acquire their special character from possessing, in an eminent degree, truth and seriousness. We may add yet further, what is in itself evident, that to the style and manner of the best poetry their special character, their accent, is given by their diction, and, even yet more, by their movement. And though we distinguish between the two characters, the two accents, of superiority, yet they are nevertheless vitally connected one with the other. The superior character of truth and seriousness, in the matter and substance of the best poetry, is inseparable from the superiority of diction and movement marking its style and manner. The two superiorities are closely related, and are in steadfast proportion one to the other. So far as high poetic truth and seriousness are wanting to a poet's matter and substance, so far also we may be sure, will a high poetic stamp of diction and movement be wanting to his style and manner. In proportion as this high stamp of diction and movement, again, is absent from a poet's style and manner, we shall find, also, that high poetic truth and seriousness are absent from his substance and matter.

So stated, these are but dry generalities; their whole force lies in their application. And I could wish every student of poetry to make the application of them for himself. Made by himself, the application would impress itself upon his mind far more deeply than made by me. Neither will my limits allow me to make any full application of the generalities above propounded; but in the hope of bringing out, at any rate, some significance in them, and of establishing an important principle more firmly by their means, I will, in the space which remains to me, follow rapidly from the commencement the course of our English poetry with them in my view.

Once more I return to the early poetry of France, with which our own poetry, in its origins, is indissolubly connected. In the twelfth and thirteenth centuries, that seed-time of all modern language and literature, the poetry of France had a clear predominance in Europe. Of the two divisions of that poetry, its productions in the *langue d'oil* and its productions in the *langue d'oc*, the poetry of the *langue d'oc*, of southern France, of the troubadours, is of importance because of its effect on Italian literature;—the first literature of modern Europe to strike the true and grand note, and to bring forth, as in Dante and Petrarch it brought forth, classics. But the predominance of French poetry in Europe, during the twelfth and thirteenth centuries, is due to its poetry of the *langue d'oil*, the poetry of northern France and of the tongue which is now the French language. In the twelfth century the bloom of this romance-poetry was earlier and stronger in England, at the court of our Anglo-Norman kings, than in France itself. But it was a bloom of French poetry; and as our native poetry formed itself, it formed itself out of this. The romance-poems which took possession of the heart and imagination of Europe in the twelfth and thirteenth centuries are French; 'they are' as Southey justly says, 'the pride of French literature, nor have we anything which can be placed in competition with them.' Themes were supplied from all quarters; but the romance-setting which was common to them all, and which gained the ear of Europe, was French. This constituted for the French poetry, literature, and language, at the height of the Middle Age, an unchallenged predominance. The Italian Brunetto Latini, the master of Dante, wrote his *Treasure* in French because, he says, '*la parleure en est plus délitable et plus commune à toutes gens.*' In the same century, the thirteenth, the French romance-writer, Christian of Troyes, formulates the claims, in chivalry and letters, of France, his native country, as follows:

> Or vous ert par ce livre apris,
> Que Gresse ot de chevalerie
> Le premier los et de clergie;
> Puis vint chevalerie à Rome,
> Et de la clergie la some,
> Qui ore est en France venue.
> Diex doinst qu'ele i soit retenue,
> Et que li lius li abelisse
> Tant que de France n'isse
> L'onor qui s'i est arestée!

'Now by this book you will learn that first Greece had the renown for chivalry and letters; then chivalry and the primacy in letters passed to Rome, and now it is come to France. God grant it may be kept there; and that the place may please it so well, that the honor which has come to make stay in France may never depart thence!'

Yet it is now all gone, this French romance-poetry, of which the weight of substance and the power of style are not unfairly represented by this extract from Christian of Troyes. Only by means of the historic estimate can we persuade ourselves now to think that any of it is of poetical importance.

But in the fourteenth century there comes an Englishman nourished on this poetry, taught his trade by this poetry, getting words, rime, meter from this poetry; for even of that stanza which the Italians used, and which Chaucer derived immediately from the Italians, the basis and suggestion was probably given in France. Chaucer (I have already named him) fascinated his contemporaries, but so too did Christian of Troyes and Wolfram of Eschenbach. Chaucer's power of fascination, however, is enduring; his poetical importance does not need the assistance of the historic estimate, it is real. He is a genuine source of joy and strength which is flowing still for us and will flow always. He will be read, as time goes on, far more generally than he is read now. His language is a cause of difficulty for us; but so also, and I think in quite as great a degree, is the language of Burns. In Chaucer's case, as in that of Burns, it is a difficulty to be unhesitatingly accepted and overcome.

If we ask ourselves wherein consists the immense superiority of Chaucer's poetry over the romance-poetry, why it is that in passing from this to Chaucer we suddenly feel ourselves to be in another world, we shall find that his superiority is both in the substance of his poetry and in the style of his poetry. His superiority in substance is given by his large, free, simple, clear yet kindly view of human life,—so unlike the total want, in the romance-poets, of all intelligent command of it. Chaucer has not their helplessness; he has gained the power to survey the world from a central, a truly human point of view. We have only to call to mind the Prologue to *The Canterbury Tales*. The right comment upon it is Dryden's: 'It is sufficient to say, according to the proverb, that *here is God's plenty*.' And again: 'He is a perpetual fountain of good sense.' It is by a large, free, sound representation of things, that poetry, this high criticism of life, has truth of substance; and Chaucer's poetry has truth of substance.

Of his style and manner, if we think first of the romance-poetry and then of Chaucer's divine liquidness of diction, his divine fluidity of movement, it is difficult to speak temperately. They are irresistible, and justify all the rapture with which his successors speak of his 'gold dew-drops of speech.' Johnson misses the point entirely when he finds fault with Dryden for ascribing to Chaucer the first refinement of our numbers, and says that Gower also can show smooth numbers and easy rimes. The refinement of our numbers means something far more than this. A nation may have versifiers with smooth numbers and easy rimes, and yet may have no real poetry at all. Chaucer is the father of our splendid English poetry, he is our 'well of English undefiled,' because by the lovely charm of his diction, the lovely charm of his movement, he makes an epoch and founds a tradition. In Spenser, Shakespeare, Milton, Keats, we can follow the tradition of the liquid diction, the fluid movement, of Chaucer; at one time it is his liquid diction of which in these poets we feel the virtue, and at another time it is his fluid movement. And the virtue is irresistible.

Bounded as is my space, I must yet find room for an example of Chaucer's virtue, as I have given examples to show the virtue of the great classics. I feel disposed to say that a single line is enough to show the charm of Chaucer's verse; that merely one line like this:

O martyr souded[1] in virginitee!

has a virtue of manner and movement such as we shall not find in all the verse of romance-poetry;—but this is saying nothing. The virtue is such as we shall not find, perhaps, in all English poetry, outside the poets whom I have named as the special inheritors of Chaucer's tradition. A single line, however, is too little if we have not the strain of Chaucer's verse well in our memory; let us take a stanza. It is from *The Prioress's Tale*, the story of the Christian child murdered in a Jewry:—

My throte is cut unto my nekke-bone,
Saidë this child, and as by way of kinde
I should have deyd, yea, longë time agone;
But Jesu Christ, as ye in bookës finde,
Will that his glory last and be in minde
And for the worship of his mother dere
Yet may I sing *O Alma* loud and clere.

Wordsworth has modernized this Tale and to feel how delicate and evanescent is the charm of verse, we have only to read Wordsworth's first three lines of this stanza after Chaucer's:—

My throat is cut unto the bone, I trow,
Said this young child, and by the law of kind
I should have died, yea, many hours ago.

The charm is departed. It is often said that the power of liquidness and fluidity in Chaucer's verse was dependent upon a free, a licentious dealing with language, such as is now impos-

[1] The French *soudé;* soldered, fixed fast.

sible; upon a liberty, such as Burns too enjoyed, of making words like *neck, bird,* into a dissyllable by adding to them, and words like *cause, rime,* into a dissyllable by sounding the *e* mute. It is true that Chaucer's fluidity is conjoined with this liberty, and is admirably served by it; but we ought not to say that it was dependent upon it. It was dependent upon his talent. Other poets with a like liberty do not attain to the fluidity of Chaucer; Burns himself does not attain to it. Poets again, who have a talent akin to Chaucer's, such as Shakespeare or Keats, have known how to attain to his fluidity without the like liberty.

And yet Chaucer is not one of the great classics. His poetry transcends and effaces, easily and without effort, all the romance-poetry of Catholic Christendom; it transcends and effaces all the English poetry contemporary with it, it transcends and effaces all the English poetry subsequent to it down to the age of Elizabeth. Of such avail is poetic truth of substance, in its natural and necessary union with poetic truth of style. And yet, I say, Chaucer is not one of the great classics. He has not their accent. What is wanting to him is suggested by the mere mention of the name of the first great classic of Christendom, the immortal poet who died eighty years before Chaucer,—Dante. The accent of such verse as

In la sua volontade è nostra pace . . .

is altogether beyond Chaucer's reach; we praise him, but we feel that this accent is out of the question for him. It may be said that it was necessarily out of the reach of any poet in the England of that stage of growth. Possibly; but we are to adopt a real, not a historic, estimate of poetry. However we may account for its absence, something is wanting, then, to the poetry of Chaucer, which poetry must have before it can be placed in the glorious class of the best. And there is no doubt what that something is. It is the σπουδαιότης, the high and excellent seriousness, which Aristotle assigns as one of the grand virtues of poetry. The substance of Chaucer's poetry, his view of things and his criticism of life, has largeness, freedom, shrewdness, benignity; but it has not this high seriousness. Homer's criticism of life has it, Dante's has it, Shakespeare's has it. It is this chiefly which gives to our spirits what they can rest upon; and with the increasing demands of our modern ages upon poetry, this virtue of giving us what we can rest upon will be more and more highly esteemed. A voice from the slums of Paris, fifty or sixty years after Chaucer, the voice of poor Villon out of his life of riot and crime, has at its happy moments (as, for instance, in the last stanza of *La Belle Heaulmière*[1]) more of this important poetic virtue of seriousness than all the productions of Chaucer. But its apparition in Villon, and in men like Villon, is fitful; the greatness of the great poets, the power of their criticism of life, is that their virtue is sustained.

To our praise, therefore, of Chaucer as a poet there must be this limitation; he lacks the high seriousness of the great classics, and therewith an important part of their virtue. Still, the main fact for us to bear in mind about Chaucer is his sterling value according to that real estimate which we firmly adopt for all poets. He has poetic truth of substance, though he has not high poetic seriousness, and corresponding to his truth of substance he has an exquisite virtue of style and manner. With him is born our real poetry.

But for my present purpose I need not dwell on our Elizabethan poetry, or on the continuation and close of this poetry in Milton. We all of us profess to be agreed in the estimate of this poetry; we all of us recognize it as great poetry, our greatest, and Shakespeare and Milton as our poetical classics. The real estimate, here, has universal currency. With the next age of our poetry divergency and difficulty begin. An historic estimate of that poetry has established itself; and the question is, whether it will be found to coincide with the real estimate.

The age of Dryden, together with our whole eighteenth century which followed it, sincerely believed itself to have produced poetical classics of its own, and even to have made advance, in

---

[1] The name *Heaulmière* is said to be derived from a head-dress (helm) worn as a mark by courtesans. In Villon's ballad a poor old creature of this class laments her days of youth and beauty. The last stanza of the ballad runs thus:—

> *Ainsi le bon temps regretons*
> *Entre nous, pauvres vieilles sottes,*
> *Assises bas, à croppetons,*
> *Tout en ung tas comme pelottes;*
> *A petit feu de chenevottes*
> *Tost allumées, tost estainctes.*
> *Et jadis fusmes si mignottes!*
> *Ainsi en prend à maintz et maintes.*

'Thus amongst ourselves we regret the good time, poor silly old things, low-seated on our heels, all in a heap like so many balls; by a little fire of hemp-stalks, soon lighted, soon spent. And once we were such darlings! So fares it with many and many a one.'

poetry, beyond all its predecessors. Dryden regards as not seriously disputable the opinion 'that the sweetness of English verse was never understood or practised by our fathers.' Cowley could see nothing at all in Chaucer's poetry. Dryden heartily admired it, and, as we have seen, praised its matter admirably; but of its exquisite manner and movement all he can find to say is that 'there is the rude sweetness of a Scotch tune in it, which is natural and pleasing, though not perfect.' Addison, wishing to praise Chaucer's numbers, compares them with Dryden's own. And all through the eighteenth century, and down even into our own times, the stereotyped phrase of approbation for good verse found in our early poetry has been, that it even approached the verse of Dryden, Addison, Pope, and Johnson.

Are Dryden and Pope poetical classics? Is the historic estimate, which represents them as such, and which has been so long established that it cannot easily give way, the real estimate? Wordsworth and Coleridge, as is well known, denied it; but the authority of Wordsworth and Coleridge does not weigh much with the young generation, and there are many signs to show that the eighteenth century and its judgments are coming into favor again. Are the favorite poets of the eighteenth century classics?

It is impossible within my present limits to discuss the question fully. And what man of letters would not shrink from seeming to dispose dictatorially of the claims of two men who are, at any rate, such masters in letters as Dryden and Pope; two men of such admirable talent, both of them, and one of them, Dryden, a man, on all sides, of such energetic and genial power? And yet, if we are to gain the full benefit from poetry, we must have the real estimate of it. I cast about for some mode of arriving, in the present case, at such an estimate without offence. And perhaps the best way is to begin, as it is easy to begin, with cordial praise.

When we find Chapman, the Elizabethan translator of Homer, expressing himself in his preface thus: 'Though truth in her very nakedness sit in so deep a pit, that from Gades to Aurora and Ganges few eyes can sound her, I hope yet those few here will so discover and confirm, that, the date being out of her darkness in this morning of our poet, he shall now gird his temples with the sun,'—we pronounce that such a prose is intolerable. When we find Milton writing: 'And long it was not after, when I was confirmed in this opinion, that he, who would not be frustrate of his hope to write well hereafter in laudable things, ought himself to be a true poem,'—we pronounce that such a prose has its own grandeur, but that it is obsolete and inconvenient. But when we find Dryden telling us: 'What Virgil wrote in the vigor of his age, in plenty and at ease, I have undertaken to translate in my declining years, struggling with wants, oppressed with sickness, curbed in my genius, liable to be misconstrued in all I write,'—then we exclaim that here at last we have the true English prose, a prose such as we would all gladly use if we only knew how. Yet Dryden was Milton's contemporary.

But after the Restoration the time had come when our nation felt the imperious need of a fit prose. So, too, the time had likewise come when our nation felt the imperious need of freeing itself from the absorbing preoccupation which religion in the Puritan age had exercised. It was impossible that this freedom should be brought about without some negative excess, without some neglect and impairment of the religious life of the soul; and the spiritual history of the eighteenth century shows us that the freedom was not achieved without them. Still, the freedom was achieved; the preoccupation, an undoubtedly baneful and retarding one if it had continued, was got rid of. And as with religion amongst us at that period, so it was also with letters. A fit prose was a necessity; but it was impossible that a fit prose should establish itself amongst us without some touch of frost to the imaginative life of the soul. The needful qualities for a fit prose are regularity, uniformity, precision, balance. The men of letters, whose destiny it may be to bring their nation to the attainment of a fit prose, must of necessity, whether they work in prose or in verse, give a predominating, an almost exclusive attention to the qualities of regularity, uniformity, precision, balance. But an almost exclusive attention to these qualities involves some repression and silencing of poetry.

We are to regard Dryden as the puissant and glorious founder, Pope as the splendid high-priest, of our age of prose and reason, of our excellent and indispensable eighteenth century. For the purposes of their mission and destiny their poetry, like their prose, is admirable. Do you ask me whether Dryden's verse, take it almost where you will, is not good?

A milk-white Hind, immortal and unchanged,
Fed on the lawns and in the forest ranged.

I answer: Admirable for the purposes of the inaugurator of an age of prose and reason. Do you ask me whether Pope's verse, take it almost where you will, is not good?

To Hounslow Heath I point, and Banstead Down;
Thence comes your mutton, and these chicks my own.

I answer: Admirable for the purposes of the high-priest of an age of prose and reason. But do you ask me whether such verse proceeds from men with an adequate poetic criticism of life, from men whose criticism of life has a high seriousness, or even, without that high seriousness, has poetic largeness, freedom, insight, benignity? Do you ask me whether the application of ideas to life in the verse of these men, often a powerful application, no doubt, is a powerful *poetic* application? Do you ask me whether the poetry of these men has either the matter or the inseparable manner of such an adequate poetic criticism: whether it has the accent of

Absent thee from felicity awhile . . .

or of

And what is else not to be overcome . . .

or of

O martyr souded in virginitee!

I answer: It has not and cannot have them; it is the poetry of the builders of an age of prose and reason. Though they may write in verse, though they may in a certain sense be masters of the art of versification, Dryden and Pope are not classics of our poetry, they are classics of our prose.

Gray is our poetical classic of that literature and age; the position of Gray is singular, and demands a word of notice here. He has not the volume or the power of poets who, coming in times more favorable, have attained to an independent criticism of life. But he lived with the great poets, he lived, above all, with the Greeks, through perpetually studying and enjoying them; and he caught their poetic point of view for regarding life, caught their poetic manner. The point of view and the manner are not self-sprung in him, he caught them of others; and he had not the free and abundant use of them. But whereas Addison and Pope never had the use of them, Gray had the use of them at times. He is the scantiest and frailest of classics in our poetry, but he is a classic.

And now, after Gray, we are met, as we draw towards the end of the eighteenth century, we are met by the great name of Burns. We enter now on times where the personal estimate of poets begins to be rife, and where the real estimate of them is not reached without difficulty. But in spite of the disturbing pressures of personal partiality, of national partiality, let us try to reach a real estimate of the poetry of Burns.

By his English poetry Burns in general belongs to the eighteenth century, and has little importance for us.

Mark ruffian Violence, distained with crimes,
Rousing elate in these degenerate times;
View unsuspecting Innocence a prey,
As guileful Fraud points out the erring way;
While subtle Litigation's pliant tongue
The life-blood equal sucks of Right and Wrong!

Evidently this is not the real Burns, or his name and fame would have disappeared long ago. Nor is Clarinda's love-poet, Sylvander, the real Burns either. But he tells us himself: 'These English songs gravel me to death. I have not the command of the language that I have of my native tongue. In fact, I think that my ideas are more barren in English than in Scotch. I have been at *Duncan Gray* to dress it in English, but all I can do is desperately stupid.' We English turn naturally, in Burns, to the poems in our own language, because we can read them easily; but in those poems we have not the real Burns.

The real Burns is of course in his Scotch poems. Let us boldly say that of much of this poetry, a poetry dealing perpetually with Scotch drink, Scotch religion, and Scotch manners, a Scotchman's estimate is apt to be personal. A Scotchman is used to this world of Scotch drink, Scotch religion, and Scotch manners; he has a tenderness for it; he meets its poet half way. In this tender mood he reads pieces like the *Holy Fair* or *Halloween*. But this world of Scotch drink, Scotch religion, and Scotch manners is against a poet, not for him, when it is not a partial countryman who reads him; for in itself it is not a beautiful world, and no one can deny that it is of advantage to a poet to deal with a beautiful world. Burns' world of Scotch drink, Scotch religion, and Scotch manners, is often a harsh, a sordid, a repulsive world; even the world of his *Cotter's Saturday Night* is not a beautiful world. No doubt a poet's criticism of life may have such truth and power that it triumphs over its world and delights us. Burns may triumph over his world, often he does triumph over his world, but let us observe how and where. Burns is the first case we have had where the bias of the personal estimate tends to mislead; let us look at him closely, he can bear it.

Many of his admirers will tell us that we have Burns, convivial, genuine, delightful, here:

> Leeze me on drink! it gies us mair
>   Than either school or college;
> It kindles wit, it waukens lair,
>   It pangs us fou o' knowledge,
> Be 't whiskey gill or penny wheep
>   Or ony stronger potion,
> It never fails, on drinking deep,
>   To kittle up our notion
>   By night or day.

There is a great deal of that sort of thing in Burns, and it is unsatisfactory, not because it is bacchanalian poetry, but because it has not that accent of sincerity which bacchanalian poetry, to do it justice, very often has. There is something in it of bravado, something which makes us feel that we have not the man speaking to us with his real voice; something, therefore, poetically unsound.

With still more confidence will his admirers tell us that we have the genuine Burns, the great poet, when his strain asserts the independence, equality, dignity, of men, as in the famous song *For a' that and a' that*:

> A prince can mak' a belted knight,
>   A marquis, duke, and a' that;
> But an honest man 's aboon his might,
>   Guid faith he mauna fa' that!
> For a' that and a' that,
>   Their dignities, and a' that,
> The pith o' sense, and pride o' worth,
>   Are higher rank than a' that.

Here they find his grand, genuine touches; and still more, when this puissant genius, who so often set morality at defiance, falls moralizing:

> The sacred lowe o' weel-placed love
>   Luxuriantly indulge it;
> But never tempt th' illicit rove,
>   Tho' naething should divulge it.
>
> I waive the quantum o' the sin,
>   The hazard o' concealing,
> But och! it hardens a' within,
>   And petrifies the feeling.

Or in a higher strain:

> Who made the heart, t 'is he alone
>   Decidedly can try us;
> He knows each chord, its various tone;
>   Each spring, its various bias.
> Then at the balance let 's be mute,
>   We never can adjust it;
> What 's *done* we partly may compute,
>   But know not what 's resisted.

Or in a better strain yet, a strain, his admirers will say, unsurpassable:

> To make a happy fire-side clime
>   To weans and wife,
> That 's the true pathos and sublime
>   Of human life.

There is criticism of life for you, the admirers of Burns will say to us; there is the application of ideas to life! There is, undoubtedly. The doctrine of the last-quoted lines coincides almost exactly with what was the aim and end, Xenophon tells us, of all the teaching of Socrates. And the application is a powerful one; made by a man of vigorous understanding, and (need I say?) a master of language.

But for supreme poetical success more is required than the powerful application of ideas to life; it must be an application under the conditions fixed by the laws of poetic truth and poetic beauty. Those laws fix as an essential condition, in the poet's treatment of such matters as are here in question, high seriousness;— the high seriousness which comes from absolute sincerity. The accent of high seriousness, born of absolute sincerity, is what gives to such verse as

> *In la sua volontade e nostra pace* . . .

to such criticism of life as Dante's, its power. Is this accent felt in the passages which I have been quoting from Burns? Surely not; surely, if our sense is quick, we must perceive that we have not in those passages a voice from the very inmost soul of the genuine Burns; he is not speaking to us from these depths, he is more or less preaching. And the compensation for admiring such passages less, from missing the perfect poetic accent in them, will be that we shall admire more the poetry where that accent is found.

No; Burns, like Chaucer, comes short of the high seriousness of the great classics, and the virtue of matter and manner which goes with that high seriousness is wanting to his work. At moments he touches it in a profound and passionate melancholy, as in those four immortal lines taken by Byron as a motto for *The Giaour*, but which have in them a depth of poetic quality such as resides in no verse of Byron's own:

> Had we never loved sae kindly,
> Had we never loved sae blindly,
> Never met, or never parted,
> We had ne'er been broken-hearted.

But a whole poem of that quality Burns cannot make; the rest, in the *Farewell to Nancy*, is verbiage.

We arrive best at the real estimate of Burns, I think, by conceiving his work as having truth of matter and truth of manner, but not the accent or the poetic virtue of the highest masters. His genuine criticism of life, when the sheer poet in him speaks, is ironic; it is not:

> Thou Power Supreme, whose mighty scheme
> These woes of mine fulfil,
> Here firm I rest, they must be best
> Because they are Thy will!

It is far rather: *Whistle owre the lave o't!* Yet we may say of him as of Chaucer, that of life and the world, as they come before him, his view is large, free, shrewd, benignant,—truly poetic, therefore; and his manner of rendering what he sees is to match. But we must note, at the same time, his great difference from Chaucer. The freedom of Chaucer is heightened, in Burns, by a fiery, reckless energy; the benignity of Chaucer deepens, in Burns, into an overwhelming sense of the pathos of things; —of the pathos of human nature, the pathos, also, of non-human nature. Instead of the fluidity of Chaucer's manner, the manner of Burns has spring, bounding swiftness. Burns is by far the greater force, though he has perhaps less charm. The world of Chaucer is fairer, richer, more significant than that of Burns; but when the largeness and freedom of Burns get full sweep, as in *Tam o' Shanter,* or still more in that puissant and splendid production, *The Jolly Beggars,* his world may be what it will, his poetic genius triumphs over it. In the world of *The Jolly Beggars* there is more than hideousness and squalor, there is bestiality; yet the piece is a superb poetic success. It has a breadth, truth, and power which make the famous scene in Auerbach's Cellar, of Goethe's *Faust,* seem artificial and tame beside it, and which are only matched by Shakespeare and Aristophanes.

Here, where his largeness and freedom serve him so admirably, and also in those poems and songs, where to shrewdness he adds infinite archness and wit, and to benignity infinite pathos, where his manner is flawless, and a perfect poetic whole is the result,—in things like the address to the Mouse whose home he had ruined, in things like *Duncan Gray, Tam Glen, Whistle and I'll come to you, my lad, Auld lang syne* (the list might be made much longer), —here we have the genuine Burns, of whom the real estimate must be high indeed. Not a classic, nor with the excellent σπουδαιότης [seriousness] of the great classics, nor with a verse rising to a criticism of life and a virtue like theirs; but a poet with thorough truth of substance and an answering truth of style, giving us a poetry sound to the core. We all of us have a leaning towards the pathetic, and may be inclined perhaps to prize Burns most for his touches of piercing, sometimes almost intolerable, pathos; for verse like:

> We twa hae paidl't i' the burn
> From mornin' sun till dine;
> But seas between us braid hae roar'd,
> Sin auld lang syne . . .

where he is as lovely as he is sound. But perhaps it is by the perfection of soundness of his lighter and archer masterpieces that he is poetically most wholesome for us. For the votary misled by a personal estimate of Shelley, as so many of us have been, are, and will be,— of that beautiful spirit building his many-colored haze of words and images

> Pinnacled dim in the intense inane—

no contact can be wholesomer than the contact with Burns at his archest and soundest. Side by side with the

> On the brink of the night and the morning
> My coursers are wont to respire,
> But the Earth has just whispered a warning,
> That their flight must be swifter than fire . . .

of *Prometheus Unbound,* how salutary, how very salutary, to place this from *Tam Glen:*

> My minnie does constantly deave me
> And bids me beware o' young men;
> They flatter, she says, to deceive me;
> But wha can think sae o' Tam Glen?

But we enter on burning ground as we approach the poetry of times so near to us, poetry like that of Byron, Shelley, and Wordsworth, of which the estimates are so often not only personal, but personal with passion. For my purpose, it is enough to have taken the single case of Burns, the first poet we come to of whose work the estimate formed is evidently apt to be personal, and to have suggested how we may proceed, using the poetry of the great classics as a sort of touchstone, to correct this estimate, as we had previously corrected by the same means the historic estimate where we met with it. A collection like the present, with its succession of celebrated names and celebrated poems, offers a good opportunity to us for resolutely endeavoring to make our estimates of poetry real. I have sought to point out a method which will help us in making them so, and to exhibit it in use so far as to put any one who likes in a way of applying it for himself.

At any rate the end to which the method and the estimate are designed to lead, and from leading to which, if they do lead to it, they get their whole value,—the benefit of being able clearly to feel and deeply to enjoy the best, the truly classic, in poetry,—is an end, let me say once more at parting, of supreme importance. We are often told that an era is opening in which we are to see multitudes of a common sort of readers, and masses of a common sort of literature; that such readers do not want and could not relish anything better than such literature, and that to provide it is becoming a vast and profitable industry. Even if good literature entirely lost currency with the world, it would still be abundantly worth while to continue to enjoy it by oneself. But it never will lose currency with the world, in spite of momentary appearances; it never will lose supremacy. Currency and supremacy are insured to it, not indeed by the world's deliberate and conscious choice, but by something far deeper,—by the instinct of self-preservation in humanity.

(1880)

SHAKESPEARE

OTHERS abide our question. Thou art free.
We ask and ask: Thou smilest and art still,
Out-topping knowledge. For the loftiest hill
That to the stars uncrowns his majesty,

Planting his steadfast footsteps in the sea, 5
Making the heaven of heavens his dwelling-place,
Spares but the cloudy border of his base
To the foiled searching of mortality:

And thou, who didst the stars and sunbeams know,
Self-schooled, self-scanned, self-honored, self-secure, 10
Didst tread on earth unguessed at. Better so!
All pains the immortal spirit must endure,
All weakness that impairs, all griefs that bow,
Find their sole voice in that victorious brow.

(1849)

THE FORSAKEN MERMAN

COME, dear children, let us away,
Down and away below!
Now my brothers call from the bay,
Now the great winds shoreward blow,
Now the salt tides seaward flow, 5
Now the wild white horses play,
Champ, and chafe, and toss in the spray,
Children dear, let us away!
This way, this way!

Call her once before you go, 10
Call once yet!
In a voice that she will know:
'Margaret! Margaret!'
Children's voices should be dear
(Call once more!) to a mother's ear; 15
Children's voices, wild with pain:
Surely she will come again!
Call her once and come away;
This way, this way!
'Mother dear, we cannot stay; 20
The wild white horses foam and fret.'
Margaret! Margaret!

Come, dear children, come away down;
Call no more!
One last look at the white-walled town, 25
And the little gray church on the windy shore;
Then come down!
She will not come though you call all day:
Come away, come away!

Children dear, was it yesterday 30
We heard the sweet bells over the bay?
In the caverns where we lay,
Through the surf and through the swell,
The far-off sound of a silver bell?
Sand-strewn caverns, cool and deep, 35
Where the winds are all asleep;
Where the spent lights quiver and gleam,
Where the salt weed sways in the stream,
Where the sea-beasts, ranged all round,
Feed in the ooze of their pasture-ground; 40
Where the sea-snakes coil and twine,
Dry their mail and bask in the brine;
Where great whales come sailing by,
Sail and sail, with unshut eye,
Round the world for ever and aye; 45
When did music come this way?
Children dear, was it yesterday?

Children dear, was it yesterday
(Call yet once!) that she went away?
Once she sate with you and me, 50
On a red gold throne in the heart of the sea,
And the youngest sate on her knee.
She combed its bright hair, and she tended it well,
When down swung the sound of a far-off bell.
She sighed, she looked up through the clear green sea; 55
She said: 'I must go, for my kinsfolk pray
In the little gray church on the shore to-day!
'T will be Easter-time in the world, ah me.
And I lose my poor soul, merman! here with thee.'
I said: 'Go up, dear heart, through the waves:—
Say thy prayer, and come back to the kind sea-caves!'
61

She smiled, she went up through the surf in the bay.
Children dear, was it yesterday?

Children dear, were we long alone?
'The sea grows stormy: the little ones moan:—
Long prayers,' I said, 'in the world they say; 66
Come!' I said; and we rose through the surf in the bay.
We went up the beach, by the sandy down
Where the sea-stocks bloom, to the white-walled town;
Through the narrow paved streets, where all was still, 70
To the little gray church on the windy hill.
From the church came a murmur of folk at their prayers,
But we stood without in the cold blowing airs.
We climbed on the graves, on the stones worn with rains,
And we gazed up the aisle through the small leaded panes. 75
She sate by the pillar; we saw her clear:
'Margaret, hist! come quick, we are here!
Dear heart,' I said, 'we are long alone:
The sea grows stormy; the little ones moan.'
But, ah, she gave me never a look, 80
For her eyes were sealed to the holy book.
Loud prays the priest; shut stands the door.
Come away, children, call no more!
Come away, come down, call no more!

Down, down, down! 85
Down to the depths of the sea—
She sits at her wheel in the humming town,
Singing most joyfully.
Hark what she sings: 'O joy, O joy,
For the humming street, and the child with its toy! 90
For the priest, and the bell, and the holy well;
For the wheel where I spun,
And the blessèd light of the sun!'
And so she sings her fill,
Singing most joyfully, 95
Till the spindle drops from her hand,
And the whizzing wheel stands still.
She steals to the window, and looks at the sand,
And over the sand at the sea;
And her eyes are set in a stare: 100
And anon there breaks a sigh,
And anon there drops a tear,
From a sorrow-clouded eye,
And a heart sorrow-laden;
A long, long sigh 105
For the cold strange eyes of a little mermaiden
And the gleam of her golden hair.

Come away, away, children;
Come children, come down!—
The hoarse wind blows coldly; 110
Lights shine in the town.

She will start from her slumber
When gusts shake the door;
She will hear the winds howling,
Will hear the waves roar. 115
We shall see, while above us
The waves roar and whirl,
A ceiling of amber,
A pavement of pearl.
Singing: 'Here came a mortal, 120
But faithless was she!
And alone dwell for ever
The kings of the sea.'
But, children, at midnight,
When soft the winds blow, 125
When clear falls the moonlight,
When spring-tides are low;
When sweet airs come seaward
From heaths starred with broom,
And high rocks throw mildly 130
On the blanchèd sands a gloom;
Up the still, glistening beaches,
Up the creeks, we will hie,
Over banks of bright seaweed
The ebb-tide leaves dry. 135
We will gaze, from the sand-hills,
At the white, sleeping town;
At the church on the hill-side;
And then come back down,
Singing: 'There dwells a loved one, 140
But cruel is she!
She left lonely for ever
The kings of the sea.'

(1849)

THE BURIED LIFE

LIGHT flows our war of mocking words, and yet,
Behold, with tears mine eyes are wet!
I feel a nameless sadness o'er me roll.
Yes, yes, we know that we can jest,
We know, we know that we can smile! 5
But there's a something in this breast,
To which thy light words bring no rest,
And thy gay smiles no anodyne.
Give me thy hand, and hush awhile,
And turn those limpid eyes on mine, 10
And let me read there, love! thy inmost soul.
Alas! is even love too weak
To unlock the heart, and let it speak?
Are even lovers powerless to reveal
To one another what indeed they feel? 15
I knew the mass of men concealed
Their thoughts, for fear that if revealed
They would by other men be met
With blank indifference, or with blame reproved;
I knew they lived and moved 20
Tricked in disguises, alien to the rest
Of men, and alien to themselves—and yet
The same heart beats in every human breast!

But we, my love!—doth a like spell benumb 24
Our hearts, our voices?—must we too be dumb?

Ah! well for us, if even we,
Even for a moment, can get free
Our heart, and have our lips unchained;
For that which seals them hath been deep-ordained!

Fate, which foresaw 30
How frivolous a baby man would be—
By what distractions he would be possessed,
How he would pour himself in every strife,
And well-nigh change his own identity—
That it might keep from his capricious play 35
His genuine self, and force him to obey
Even in his own despite his being's law,
Bade through the deep recesses of our breast
The unregarded river of our life
Pursue with indiscernible flow its way; 40
And that we should not see
The buried stream, and seem to be
Eddying at large in blind uncertainty,
Though driving on with it eternally.

But often, in the world's most crowded streets,
But often, in the din of strife, 46
There rises an unspeakable desire
After the knowledge of our buried life;
A thirst to spend our fire and restless force
In tracking out our true, original course; 50
A longing to inquire
Into the mystery of this heart which beats
So wild, so deep in us—to know
Whence our lives come and where they go. 54
And many a man in his own breast then delves,
But deep enough, alas! none ever mines.
And we have been on many thousand lines,
And we have shown, on each, spirit and power;
But hardly have we, for one little hour, 59
Been on our own line, have we been ourselves—
Hardly had skill to utter one of all
The nameless feelings that course through our breast,
But they course on for ever unexpressed,
And long we try in vain to speak and act
Our hidden self, and what we say and do 65
Is eloquent, is well—but 't is not true!
And then we will no more be racked
With inward striving, and demand,
Of all the thousand nothings of the hour
Their stupefying power; 70
Ah, yes, and they benumb us at our call!
Yet still, from time to time, vague and forlorn,
From the soul's subterranean depth upborne
As from an infinitely distant land,
Come airs, and floating echoes, and convey 75
A melancholy into all our day.

Only—but this is rare—
When a belovèd hand is laid in ours,
When, jaded with the rush and glare
Of the interminable hours, 80
Our eyes can in another's eyes read clear,
When our world-deafened ear
Is by the tones of a loved voice caressed—
A bolt is shot back somewhere in our breast,
And a lost pulse of feeling stirs again. 85
The eye sinks inward, and the heart lies plain,
And what we mean, we say, and what we would, we know.
A man becomes aware of his life's flow,
And hears its winding murmur; and he sees
The meadows where it glides, the sun, the breeze. 90

And there arrives a lull in the hot race
Wherein he doth for ever chase
That flying and elusive shadow, rest.
An air of coolness plays upon his face,
And an unwonted calm pervades his breast. 95
And then he thinks he knows
The hills where his life rose,
And the sea where it goes.

(1852)

SELF-DEPENDENCE

Weary of myself, and sick of asking
 What I am, and what I ought to be,
At this vessel's prow I stand, which bears me
 Forwards, forwards, o'er the starlit sea.

And a look of passionate desire 5
 O'er the sea and to the stars I send:
'Ye who from my childhood up have calmed me,
 Calm me, ah, compose me to the end!

'Ah, once more,' I cried, 'ye stars, ye waters,
 On my heart your mighty charm renew; 10
Still, still let me, as I gaze upon you,
 Feel my soul becoming vast like you!'

From the intense, clear, star-sown vault of heaven,
 Over the lit sea's unquiet way,
In the rustling night-air came the answer: 15
 'Wouldst thou *be* as these are? *Live* as they.

'Unaffrighted by the silence round them,
 Undistracted by the sights they see,
These demand not that the things without them
 Yield them love, amusement, sympathy. 20

'And with joy the stars perform their shining,
 And the sea its long moon-silvered roll;
For self-poised they live, nor pine with noting
 All the fever of some differing soul.

'Bounded by themselves, and unregardful 25
 In what state God's other works may be,
In their own tasks all their powers pouring,
 These attain the mighty life you see.'

O air-born voice! long since, severely clear,
   A cry like thine in mine own heart I hear:
'Resolve to be thyself; and know that he,   31
   Who finds himself, loses his misery!'
                          (1852)

MORALITY

We cannot kindle when we will
The fire which in the heart resides;
The spirit bloweth and is still,
In mystery our soul abides.
      But tasks in hours of insight willed,   5
      Can be through hours of gloom fulfilled.

With aching hands and bleeding feet
We dig and heap, lay stone on stone;
We bear the burden and the heat
Of the long day, and wish 't were done.   10
      Not till the hours of light return,
      All we have built do we discern.

Then, when the clouds are off the soul,
When thou dost bask in Nature's eye,
Ask, how *she* viewed thy self-control,   15
Thy struggling, tasked morality—
      Nature, whose free, light, cheerful air,
      Oft made thee, in thy gloom, despair.

And she, whose censure thou dost dread,
Whose eye thou wast afraid to seek,   20
See, on her face a glow is spread,
A strong emotion on her cheek!
      'Ah, child!' she cries, 'that strife divine,
      Whence was it, for it is not mine?

'There is no effort on *my* brow—   25
I do not strive, I do not weep;
I rush with the swift spheres and glow
In joy, and when I will, I sleep.
      Yet that severe, that earnest air,
      I saw, I felt it once—but where?   30

'I knew not yet the gauge of time,
Nor wore the manacles of space;
I felt it in some other clime,
I saw it in some other place.
      'T was when the heavenly house I trod,
      And lay upon the breast of God.'   36
                          (1852)

SOHRAB AND RUSTUM

AN EPISODE

And the first gray of morning filled the east
And the fog rose out of the Oxus stream.
But all the Tartar camp along the stream
Was hushed, and still the men were plunged in
      sleep;
Sohrab alone, he slept not: all night long   5
He had lain wakeful, tossing on his bed;
But when the gray dawn stole into his tent,
He rose, and clad himself, and girt his sword,
And took his horseman's cloak, and left his
      tent,
And went abroad into the cold wet fog,   10
Through the dim camp to Peran-Wisa's tent.

   Through the black Tartar tents he passed,
      which stood
Clustering like bee-hives on the low flat strand
Of Oxus, where the summer floods o'erflow   14
When the sun melts the snows in high Pamere:
Through the black tents he passed, o'er that
      low strand,
And to a hillock came, a little back
From the stream's brink, the spot where first
      a boat,
Crossing the stream in summer, scrapes the
      land.
The men of former times had crowned the top
With a clay fort: but that was fall'n; and
      now   21
The Tartars built there Peran-Wisa's tent,
A dome of laths, and o'er it felts were spread.
And Sohrab came there, and went in, and stood
Upon the thick-piled carpets in the tent,   25
And found the old man sleeping on his bed
Of rugs and felts, and near him lay his arms.
And Peran-Wisa heard him, though the step
Was dulled; for he slept light, an old man's
      sleep;
And he rose quickly on one arm, and said: 30

   'Who art thou? for it is not yet clear dawn.
Speak! is there news, or any night alarm?'

   But Sohrab came to the bedside, and said:
'Thou knowest me, Peran-Wisa: it is I.
The sun is not yet risen, and the foe   35
Sleep; but I sleep not; all night long I lie
Tossing and wakeful, and I come to thee.
For so did King Afrasiab bid me seek
Thy counsel, and to heed thee as thy son,
In Samarcand, before the army marched;   40
And I will tell thee what my heart desires.
Thou know'st if, since from Ader-baijan, first
I came among the Tartars, and bore arms,
I have still served Afrasiab well, and shown,
At my boy's years, the courage of a man.   45
This too thou know'st, that, while I still bear on
The conquering Tartar ensigns through the
      world,
And beat the Persians back on every field,
I see one man, one man, and one alone—   49
Rustum, my father; who, I hoped, should greet,
Should one day greet, upon some well-fought
      field,
His not unworthy, not inglorious son.
So I long hoped, but him I never find.
Come then, hear now, and grant me what I ask.
Let the two armies rest to-day: but I   55

Will challenge forth the bravest Persian lords
To meet me, man to man; if I prevail,
Rustum will surely hear it; if I fall—
Old man, the dead need no one, claim no kin.
Dim is the rumor of a common fight, 60
Where host meets host, and many names are sunk:
But of a single combat Fame speaks clear.'

He spoke: and Peran-Wisa took the hand
Of the young man in his, and sighed, and said:

'O Sohrab, an unquiet heart is thine! 65
Canst thou not rest among the Tartar chiefs,
And share the battle's common chance with us
Who love thee, but must press forever first,
In single fight incurring single risk,
To find a father thou hast never seen? 70
That were far best, my son, to stay with us
Unmurmuring; in our tents, while it is war,
And when 't is truce, then in Afrasiab's towns.
But, if this one desire indeed rules all,
To seek out Rustum—seek him not through fight: 75
Seek him in peace, and carry to his arms,
O Sohrab, carry an unwounded son!
But far hence seek him, for he is not here,
For now it is not as when I was young,
When Rustum was in front of every fray: 80
But now he keeps apart, and sits at home,
In Seïstan, with Zal, his father old.
Whether that his own mighty strength at last
Feels the abhorred approaches of old age;
Or in some quarrel with the Persian King. 85

There go:—Thou wilt not? Yet my heart forebodes
Danger of death awaits thee on this field.
Fain would I know thee safe and well, though lost
To us: fain therefore send thee hence, in peace
To seek thy father, not seek single fights 90
In vain:—but who can keep the lion's cub
From ravening? and who govern Rustum's son?
Go: I will grant thee what thy heart desires.'

So said he, and dropped Sohrab's hand, and left
His bed, and the warm rugs whereon he lay, 95
And o'er his chilly limbs his woolen coat
He passed, and tied his sandals on his feet,
And threw a white cloak round him, and he took
In his right hand a ruler's staff, no sword;
And on his head he set his sheep-skin cap, 100
Black, glossy, curled, the fleece of Kara-Kul;
And raised the curtain of his tent, and called
His herald to his side, and went abroad.

The sun, by this, had risen, and cleared the fog
From the broad Oxus and the glittering sands:
And from their tents the Tartar horsemen filed
Into the open plain; so Haman bade; 107

Haman, Who next to Peran-wisa ruled
The host, and still was in his lusty prime.
From their black tents, long files of horse, they streamed: 110
As when, some gray November morn, the files,
In marching order spread, of long-necked cranes,
Stream over Casbin, and the southern slopes
Of Elburz, from the Aralian estuaries,
Or some frore Caspian reed-bed, southward bound 115
For the warm Persian sea-board: so they streamed.
The Tartars of the Oxus, the King's guard,
First, with black sheep-skin caps and with long spears;
Large men, large steeds; who from Bokhara come
And Khiva, and ferment the milk of mares. 120
Next, the more temperate Toorkmuns of the south,
The Tukas, and the lances of Salore,
And those from Attruck and the Caspian sands;
Light men, and on light steeds, who only drink
The acrid milk of camels, and their wells. 125
And then a swarm of wandering horse, who came
From far, and a more doubtful service owned;
The Tartars of Ferghana, from the banks
Of the Jaxartes, men with scanty beards
And close-set skull-caps; and those wilder hordes 130
Who roam o'er Kipchak and the northern waste,
Kalmuks and unkempt Kuzzaks, tribes who stray
Nearest the Pole, and wandering Kirghizzes,
Who come on shaggy ponies from Pamere.
These all filed out from camp into the plain. 135

And on the other side the Persians formed:
First a light cloud of horse, Tartars they seemed,
The Ilyats of Khorassan: and behind,
The royal troops of Persia, horse and foot,
Marshaled battalions bright in burnished steel,

But Peran-Wisa with his herald came 141
Threading the Tartar squadrons to the front,
And with his staff kept back the foremost ranks.
And when Ferood, who led the Persians, saw
That Peran-Wisa kept the Tartars back, 145
He took his spear, and to the front he came,
And checked his ranks, and fixed them where they stood.
And the old Tartar came upon the sand
Betwixt the silent hosts, and spake, and said:

'Ferood, and ye, Persians and Tartars, hear!
Let there be truce between the hosts to-day. 151
But choose a champion from the Persian lords
To fight our champion Sohrab, man to man.'

As, in the country, on a morn in June,
When the dew glistens on the pearlèd ears, 155

A shiver runs through the deep corn for joy—
So, when they heard what Peran-Wisa said,
A thrill through all the Tartar squadrons ran
Of pride and hope for Sohrab, whom they loved.

   But as a troop of peddlers, from Cabool, 160
Cross underneath the Indian Caucasus,
That vast sky-neighboring mountain of milk snow;
Crossing so high, that, as they mount, they pass
Long flocks of traveling birds dead on the snow,
Choked by the air, and scarce can they themselves 165
Slake their parched throats with sugared mulberries—
In single file they move, and stop their breath,
For fear they should dislodge the o'erhanging snows—
So the pale Persians held their breath with fear.

   And to Ferood his brother chiefs came up 170
To counsel. Gudurz and Zoarrah came,
And Feraburz, who ruled the Persian host
Second, and was the uncle of the King:
These came and counseled; and then Gudurz said:

   'Ferood, shame bids us take their challenge up, 175
Yet champion have we none to match this youth.
He has the wild stag's foot, the lion's heart.
But Rustum came last night; aloof he sits
And sullen, and has pitched his tents apart:
Him will I seek, and carry to his ear 180
The Tartar challenge, and this young man's name.
Haply he will forget his wrath, and fight,
Stand forth the while, and take their challenge up.'

   So spake he; and Ferood stood forth and cried:
'Old man, be it agreed as thou hast said. 185
Let Sohrab arm, and we will find a man.'

   He spake; and Peran-Wisa turned, and strode
Back through the opening squadrons to his tent.
But through the anxious Persians Gudurz ran,
And crossed the camp which lay behind, and reached, 190
Out on the sands beyond it, Rustum's tents.
Of scarlet cloth they were, and glittering gay,
Just pitched: the high pavilion in the midst 193
Was Rustum's, and his men lay camped around.
And Gudurz entered Rustum's tent, and found
Rustum: his morning meal was done, but still
The table stood before him, charged with food—
A side of roasted sheep, and cakes of bread, 198
And dark green melons; and there Rustum sate
Listless, and held a falcon on his wrist, 200
And played with it; but Gudurz came and stood
Before him; and he looked, and saw him stand;
And with a cry sprang up, and dropped the bird,
And greeted Gudurz with both hands, and said:

   'Welcome! these eyes could see no better sight. 205
What news? but sit down first, and eat and drink.'

   But Gudurz stood in the tent-door, and said:
'Not now: a time will come to eat and drink,
But not to-day: to-day has other needs.
The armies are drawn out, and stand at gaze:
For from the Tartars is a challenge brought 211
To pick a champion from the Persian lords
To fight their champion—and thou know'st his name—
Sohrab men call him, but his birth is hid.
O Rustum, like thy might is this young man's!
He has the wild stag's foot, the lion's heart. 216
And he is young, and Iran's chiefs are old,
Or else too weak; and all eyes turn to thee.
Come down and help us, Rustum, or we lose.'
He spoke: but Rustum answered with a smile:—
'Go to! if Iran's chiefs are old, then I 221
Am older: if the young are weak, the king
Errs strangely: for the king, for Kai-Khosroo,
Himself is young, and honors younger men,
And lets the agèd molder to their graves. 225
Rustum he loves no more, but loves the young—
The young may rise at Sohrab's vaunts, not I.
For what care I, though all speak Sohrab's fame?
For would that I myself had such a son,
And not that one slight helpless girl I have, 230
A son so famed, so brave, to send to war,
And I to tarry with the snow-haired Zal,
My father, whom the robber Afghans vex,
And clip his borders short, and drive his herds,
And he has none to guard his weak old age. 235
There would I go, and hang my armor up,
And with my great name fence that weak old man,
And spend the goodly treasures I have got,
And rest my age, and hear of Sohrab's fame,
And leave to death the hosts of thankless kings,
And with these slaughterous hands draw sword no more.' 241

   He spoke, and smiled; and Gudurz made reply:
'What then, O Rustum, will men say to this,
When Sohrab dares our bravest forth, and seeks,
Thee most of all, and thou, whom most he seeks,
Hidest thy face? Take heed, lest men should say, 246
"Like some old miser, Rustum hoards his fame,
And shuns to peril it with younger men."'
And, greatly moved, then Rustum made reply:
'O Gudurz, wherefore dost thou say such words?
Thou knowest better words than this to say. 251

What is one more, one less, obscure or famed,
Valiant or craven, young or old, to me?
Are not they mortal, am not I myself?
But who for men of naught would do great
    deeds?   255
Come, thou shalt see how Rustum hoards his
    fame.
But I will fight unknown, and in plain arms;
Let not men say of Rustum, he was matched
In single fight with any mortal man.'

   He spoke, and frowned; and Gudurz turned,
    and ran   260
Back quickly through the camp in fear and joy,
Fear at his wrath, but joy that Rustum came.
But Rustum strode to his tent-door, and called
His followers in, and bade them bring his arms,
And clad himself in steel: the arms he chose   265
Were plain, and on his shield was no device,
Only his helm was rich, inlaid with gold,
And from the fluted spine atop, a plume
Of horsehair waved, a scarlet horsehair plume.
So armed, he issued forth; and Ruksh, his horse,
Followed him, like a faithful hound, at heel,   271
Ruksh, whose renown was noised through all
    the earth,
The horse, whom Rustum on a foray once
Did in Bokhara by the river find   274
A colt beneath its dam, and drove him home,
And reared him; a bright bay, with lofty crest,
Dight with a saddle-cloth of broidered green
Crusted with gold, and on the ground were
    worked
All beasts of chase, all beasts which hunters
    know:
So followed, Rustum left his tents, and crossed
The camp, and to the Persian host appeared.   281
And all the Persians knew him, and with shouts
Hailed; but the Tartars knew not who he was.
And dear as the wet diver to the eyes
Of his pale wife who waits and weeps on shore,
By sandy Bahrein, in the Persian Gulf,   286
Plunging all day in the blue waves, at night,
Having made up his tale of precious pearls,
Rejoins her in their hut upon the sands—
So dear to the pale Persians Rustum came.   290

   And Rustum to the Persian front advanced,
And Sohrab armed in Haman's tent, and came.
And as afield the reapers cut a swath
Down through the middle of a rich man's corn,
And on each side are squares of standing corn,
And in the midst a stubble, short and bare;   296
So on each side were squares of men, with spears
Bristling, and in the midst, the open sand.
And Rustum came upon the sand, and cast
His eyes toward the Tartar tents, and saw   300
Sohrab come forth, and eyed him as he came.

   As some rich woman, on a winter's morn,
Eyes through her silken curtains the poor
    drudge
Who with numb blackened fingers makes her
    fire—
At cock-crow on a starlit winter's morn,   305
When the frost flowers the whitened window-
    panes—
And wonders how she lives, and what the
    thoughts
Of that poor drudge may be; so Rustum eyed
The unknown adventurous youth, who from
    afar
Came seeking Rustum, and defying forth   310
All the most valiant chiefs: long he perused
His spirited air, and wondered who he was.
For very young he seemed, tenderly reared;
Like some young cypress, tall, and dark, and
    straight,   314
Which in a queen's secluded garden throws
Its slight dark shadow on the moonlit turf,
By midnight, to a bubbling fountain's sound—
So slender Sohrab seemed, so softly reared.
And a deep pity entered Rustum's soul
As he beheld him coming; and he stood,   320
And beckoned to him with his hand, and said:

   'O thou young man, the air of heaven is soft,
And warm, and pleasant; but the grave is cold.
Heaven's air is better than the cold dead grave.
Behold me: I am vast, and clad in iron,   325
And tried; and I have stood on many a field
Of blood, and I have fought with many a foe:
Never was that field lost, or that foe saved.
O Sohrab, wherefore wilt thou rush on death?
Be governed: quit the Tartar host, and come
To Iran, and be as my son to me,   331
And fight beneath my banner till I die.
There are no youths in Iran brave as thou.'

   So he spake, mildly: Sohrab heard his voice,
The mighty voice of Rustum; and he saw   335
His giant figure planted on the sand,
Sole, like some single tower, which a chief
Hath builded on the waste in former years
Against the robbers; and he saw that head,
Streaked with its first gray hairs: hope filled
    his soul;   340
And he ran forwards and embraced his knees,
And clasped his hand within his own and said:

   'Oh, by thy father's head! by thine own soul!
Art thou not Rustum? Speak! art thou not he?'

   But Rustum eyed askance the kneeling youth,
And turned away, and spake to his own soul: 346

   'Ah me, I muse what this young fox may
    mean.
False, wily, boastful, are these Tartar boys.
For if I now confess this thing he asks,   349
And hide it not, but say, "Rustum is here,"
He will not yield indeed, nor quit our foes,
But he will find some pretext not to fight,

And praise my fame, and proffer courteous gifts,
A belt or sword perhaps, and go his way.
And on a feast-day, in Afrasiab's hall, 355
In Samarcand, he will arise and cry—
"I challenged once, when the two armies camped
Beside the Oxus, all the Persian lords
To cope with me in single fight; but they
Shrank; only Rustum dared: then he and I 360
Changed gifts, and went on equal terms away."
So will he speak, perhaps, while men applaud.
Then were the chiefs of Iran shamed through me.' 363

And then he turned, and sternly spake aloud:
'Rise! wherefore dost thou vainly question thus
Of Rustum? I am here, whom thou hast called
By challenge forth: make good thy vaunt, or yield.
Is it with Rustum only thou wouldst fight?
Rash boy, men look on Rustum's face and flee.
For well I know, that did great Rustum stand
Before thy face this day, and were revealed, 371
There would be then no talk of fighting more.
But being what I am, I tell thee this:
Do thou record it in thine inmost soul:
Either thou shalt renounce thy vaunt, and yield; 375
Or else thy bones shall strew this sand, till winds
Bleach them, or Oxus with his summer floods,
Oxus in summer wash them all away.'

He spoke: and Sohrab answered, on his feet:—
'Art thou so fierce? Thou wilt not fright me so. 380
I am no girl, to be made pale by words.
Yet this thou hast said well, did Rustum stand
Here on this field, there were no fighting then.
But Rustum is far hence, and we stand here.
Begin: thou art more vast, more dread than I,
And thou art proved, I know, and I am young—
But yet success sways with the breath of heaven. 387
And though thou thinkest that thou knowest sure
Thy victory, yet thou canst not surely know.
For we are all, like swimmers in the sea, 390
Poised on the top of a huge wave of Fate,
Which hangs uncertain to which side to fall.
And whether it will heave us up to land,
Or whether it will roll us out to sea,
Back out to sea, to the deep waves of death, 395
We know not, and no search will make us know·
Only the event will teach us in its hour.'

He spoke; and Rustum answered not, but hurled
His spear: down from the shoulder, down it came
As on some partridge in the corn a hawk 400
That long has towered in the airy clouds
Drops like a plummet: Sohrab saw it come,
And sprang aside, quick as a flash: the spear
Hissed, and went quivering down into the sand,
Which it sent flying wide:—then Sohrab threw
In turn, and full struck Rustum's shield: sharp rang, 406
The iron plates rang sharp, but turned the spear.
And Rustum seized his club, which none but he
Could wield: an unlopped trunk it was, and huge,
Still rough; like those which men in treeless plains 410
To build them boats fish from the flooded rivers,
Hyphasis or Hydaspes, when, high up
By their dark springs, the wind in winter-time
Has made in Himalayan forests wrack,
And strewn the channels with torn boughs; so huge 415
The club which Rustum lifted now, and struck
One stroke; but again Sohrab sprang aside
Lithe as the glancing snake, and the club came
Thundering to earth, and leapt from Rustum's hand.
And Rustum followed his own blow, and fell 420
To his knees, and with his fingers clutched the sand:
And now might Sohrab have unsheathed his sword,
And pierced the mighty Rustum while he lay
Dizzy, and on his knees, and choked with sand:
But he looked on, and smiled, nor bared his sword, 425
But courteously drew back, and spoke, and said:

'Thou strik'st too hard: that club of thine will float
Upon the summer-floods, and not my bones.
But rise, and be not wroth; not wroth am I:
No, when I see thee, wrath forsakes my soul. 430
Thou say'st thou art not Rustum: be it so,
Who art thou then, that canst so touch my soul?
Boy as I am, I have seen battles too;
Have waded foremost in their bloody waves,
And heard their hollow roar of dying men; 435
But never was my heart thus touched before.
Are they from heaven, these softenings of the heart?
O thou old warrior, let us yield to heaven!
Come, plant we here in earth our angry spears,
And make a truce, and sit upon this sand, 440
And pledge each other in red wine, like friends,
And thou shalt talk to me of Rustum's deeds.
There are enough foes in the Persian host
Whom I may meet, and strike, and feel no pang;
Champions enough Afrasiab has, whom thou
Mayst fight; fight them, when they confront thy spear. 446
But oh, let there be peace 'twixt thee and me!'

He ceased: but while he spake, Rustum had risen,
And stood erect, trembling with rage: his club
He left to lie, but had regained his spear, 450
Whose fiery point now in his mailed right-hand
Blazed bright and baleful, like that autumn star,
The baleful sign of fevers: dust had soiled
His stately crest, and dimmed his glittering arms.
His breast heaved; his lips foamed; and twice his voice 455
Was choked with rage: at last these words broke way:

'Girl! nimble with thy feet, not with thy hands!
Curled minion, dancer, coiner of sweet words!
Fight; let me hear thy hateful voice no more!
Thou art not in Afrasiab's gardens now 460
With Tartar girls, with whom thou art wont to dance;
But on the Oxus sands, and in the dance
Of battle, and with me, who make no play
Of war: I fight it out, and hand to hand.
Speak not to me of truce, and pledge, and wine!
Remember all thy valor; try thy feints 466
And cunning: all the pity I had is gone:
Because thou hast shamed me before both the hosts
With thy light skipping tricks, and thy girl's wiles.'

He spoke: and Sohrab kindled at his taunts,
And he too drew his sword: at once they rushed 471
Together, as two eagles on one prey
Come rushing down together from the clouds,
One from the east, one from the west: their shields
Dashed with a clang together, and a din 475
Rose, such as that the sinewy woodcutters
Make often in the forest's heart at morn,
Of hewing axes, crashing trees: such blows
Rustum and Sohrab on each other hailed.
And you would say that sun and stars took part
In that unnatural conflict; for a cloud 481
Grew suddenly in heaven, and darked the sun
Over the fighters' heads; and a wind rose
Under their feet, and moaning swept the plain,
And in a sandy whirlwind wrapped the pair. 485
In gloom they twain were wrapped, and they alone;
For both the on-looking hosts on either hand
Stood in broad daylight, and the sky was pure,
And the sun sparkled on the Oxus stream.
But in the gloom they fought, with bloodshot eyes 490
And laboring breath; first Rustum struck the shield
Which Sohrab held stiff out: the steel-spiked spear
Rent the tough plates, but failed to reach the skin,
And Rustum plucked it back with angry groan.
Then Sohrab with his sword smote Rustum's helm, 495
Nor clove its steel quite through; but all the crest
He shore away, and that proud horsehair plume,
Never till now defiled, sank to the dust;
And Rustum bowed his head; but then the gloom
Grew blacker: thunder rumbled in the air, 500
And lightnings rent the cloud; and Ruksh, the horse,
Who stood at hand, uttered a dreadful cry:
No horse's cry was that, most like the roar
Of some pained desert lion, who all day
Hath trailed the hunter's javelin in his side 505
And comes at night to die upon the sand:
The two hosts heard that cry, and quaked for fear,
And Oxus curdled as it crossed his stream.
But Sohrab heard, and quailed not, but rushed on, 509
And struck again; and again Rustum bowed
His head; but this time all the blade, like glass,
Sprang in a thousand shivers on the helm,
And in his hand the hilt remained alone.
Then Rustum raised his head; his dreadful eyes
Glared, and he shook on high his menacing spear, 515
And shouted, 'Rustum!' Sohrab heard that shout,
And shrank amazed: back he recoiled one step,
And scanned with blinking eyes the advancing form:
And then he stood bewildered; and he dropped
His covering shield, and the spear pierced his side. 520
He reeled, and staggering back, sank to the ground.
And then the gloom dispersed, and the wind fell,
And the bright sun broke forth, and melted all
The cloud; and the two armies saw the pair;
Saw Rustum standing, safe upon his feet, 525
And Sohrab, wounded, on the bloody sand.

Then with a bitter smile, Rustum began:
'Sohrab, thou thoughtest in thy mind to kill
A Persian lord this day, and strip his corpse,
And bear thy trophies to Afrasiab's tent. 530
Or else that the great Rustum would come down
Himself to fight, and that thy wiles would move
His heart to take a gift, and let thee go.
And then that all the Tartar host would praise
Thy courage or thy craft, and spread thy fame,
To glad thy father in his weak old age. 536
Fool! thou art slain, and by an unknown man!
Dearer to the red jackals shalt thou be,
Than to thy friends, and to thy father old.'

And, with a tearless mien, Sohrab replied: 540
'Unknown thou art; yet thy fierce vaunt is vain.
Thou dost not slay me, proud and boastful man!
No! Rustum slays me, and this filial heart.
For were I matched with ten such men as thee,
And I were he who till to-day I was, 545
They should be lying here, I standing there.
But that belovèd name unnerved my arm—
That name, and something, I confess, in thee,
Which troubles all my heart, and made my
   shield 549
Fall; and thy spear transfixed an unarmed foe,
And now thou boastest, and insult'st my fate.
But hear thou this, fierce man, tremble to hear!
The mighty Rustum shall avenge my death!
My father, whom I seek through all the world,
He shall avenge my death, and punish thee!' 555

   As when some hunter in the spring hath
      found
A breeding eagle sitting on her nest,
Upon the craggy isle of a hill-lake,
And pierced her with an arrow as she rose,
And followed her to find her where she fell 560
Far off;—anon her mate comes winging back
From hunting, and a great way off descries
His huddling young left sole; at that, he checks
His pinion, and with short uneasy sweeps
Circles above his eyry, with loud screams 565
Chiding his mate back to her nest; but she
Lies dying, with the arrow in her side,
In some far stony gorge out of his ken,
A heap of fluttering feathers: never more
Shall the lake glass her, flying over it; 570
Never the black and dripping precipices
Echo her stormy scream as she sails by:—
As that poor bird flies home, nor knows his
   loss—
So Rustum knew not his own loss, but stood
Over his dying son, and knew him not. 575

   But with a cold, incredulous voice, he said:
'What prate is this of fathers and revenge?
The mighty Rustum never had a son.'

   And, with a failing voice, Sohrab replied:
'Ah, yes, he had! and that lost son am I. 580
Surely the news will one day reach his ear,
Reach Rustum, where he sits, and tarries long,
Somewhere, I know not where, but far from
   here;
And pierce him like a stab, and make him leap
To arms, and cry for vengeance upon thee. 585
Fierce man, bethink thee, for an only son!
What will that grief, what will that vengeance
   be!
Oh, could I live, till I that grief had seen!
Yet him I pity not so much, but her,
My mother, who in Ader-baijan dwells 590
With that old king, her father, who grows gray
With age, and rules over the valiant Koords.

Her most I pity, who no more will see
Sohrab returning from the Tartar camp,
With spoils and honor, when the war is done. 595
But a dark rumor will be bruited up,
From tribe to tribe, until it reach her ear;
And then will that defenceless woman learn
That Sohrab will rejoice her sight no more:
But that in battle with a nameless foe, 600
By the far distant Oxus, he is slain.'

   He spoke; and as he ceased he wept aloud,
Thinking of her he left, and his own death.
He spoke; but Rustum listened, plunged in
   thought.
Nor did he yet believe it was his son 605
Who spoke, although he called back names he
   knew;
For he had had sure tidings that the babe,
Which was in Ader-baijan born to him,
Had been a puny girl, no boy at all:
So that sad mother sent him word, for fear 610
Rustum should seek the boy, to train in arms;
And so he deemed that either Sohrab took,
By a false boast, the style of Rustum's son;
Or that men gave it him, to swell his fame.
So deemed he; yet he listened, plunged in
   thought; 615
And his soul set to grief, as the vast tide
Of the bright rocking ocean sets to shore
At the full moon: tears gathered in his eyes;
For he remembered his own early youth,
And all its bounding rapture; as, at dawn, 620
The shepherd from his mountain-lodge de-
   scries
A far, bright city, smitten by the sun,
Through many rolling clouds;—so Rustum saw
His youth; saw Sohrab's mother, in her bloom;
And that old king, her father, who loved well 625
His wandering guest, and gave him his fair child
With joy; and all the pleasant life they led,
They three, in that long-distant summertime—
The castle, and the dewy woods, and hunt
And hound, and morn on those delightful hills
In Ader-baijan. And he saw that youth, 631
Of age and looks to be his own dear son,
Piteous and lovely, lying on the sand,
Like some rich hyacinth, which by the scythe
Of an unskilful gardener has been cut, 635
Mowing the garden grass-plots near its bed,
And lies, a fragrant tower of purple bloom,
On the mown, dying grass;—so Sohrab lay,
Lovely in death, upon the common sand.
And Rustum gazed on him with grief, and
   said:— 640

   'O Sohrab, thou indeed art such a son
Whom Rustum, wert thou his, might well have
   loved!
Yet here thou errest, Sohrab, or else men
Have told thee false;—thou art not Rustum's
   son.

For Rustum had no son: one child he had—
But one—a girl: who with her mother now   646
Plies some light female task, nor dreams of us—
Of us she dreams not, nor of wounds, nor war.'

But Sohrab answered him in wrath; for now
The anguish of the deep-fixed spear grew fierce,
And he desirèd to draw forth the steel,   651
And let the blood flow free, and so to die;
But first he would convince his stubborn foe—
And, rising sternly on one arm, he said:

'Man, who art thou who dost deny my words?
Truth sits upon the lips of dying men,   656
And falsehood, while I lived, was far from mine.
I tell thee, pricked upon this arm I bear
That seal which Rustum to my mother gave,
That she might prick it on the babe she bore.'

He spoke: and all the blood left Rustum's cheeks;   661
And his knees tottered, and he smote his hand,
Against his breast, his heavy mailèd hand,
That the hard iron corslet clanked aloud:
And on his heart he pressed the other hand, 665
And in a hollow voice he spake, and said:

'Sohrab, that were a proof which could not lie.
If thou show this, then art thou Rustum's son.'

Then, with weak hasty fingers, Sohrab loosed
His belt, and near the shoulder bared his arm,
And showed a sign in faint vermilion points. 671
Pricked: as a cunning workman, in Pekin,
Pricks with vermilion some clear porcelain vase,
An emperor's gift—at early morn he paints,
And all day long, and, when night comes, the lamp   675
Lights up his studious forehead and thin hands:—
So delicately pricked the sign appeared
On Sohrab's arm, the sign of Rustum's seal.
It was that Griffin, which of old reared Zal,
Rustum's great father, whom they left to die,
A helpless babe, among the mountain rocks. 681
Him that king creature found, and reared, and loved—
Then Rustum took it for his glorious sign.
And Sohrab bared that image on his arm,   684
And himself scanned it long with mournful eyes,
And then he touched it with his hand and said:

'How say'st thou? Is that sign the proper sign
Of Rustum's son, or of some other man's?'

He spoke: but Rustum gazed, and gazed, and stood   689
Speechless; and then he uttered one sharp cry—
'O boy—thy father!'—and his voice choked there.

And then a dark cloud passed before his eyes,
And his head swam, and he sank down to earth.
But Sohrab crawled to where he lay, and cast
His arms about his neck, and kissed his lips, 695
And with fond faltering fingers stroked his cheeks,
Trying to call him back to life: and life
Came back to Rustum, and he oped his eyes,
And they stood wide with horror; and he seized
In both his hands the dust which lay around, 700
And threw it on his head, and smirched his hair,
His hair, and face, and beard, and glittering arms:
And strong convulsive groanings shook his breast,
And his sobs choked him; and he clutched his sword,
To draw it, and forever let life out.   705
But Sohrab saw his thought, and held his hands,
And with a soothing voice he spake, and said:

'Father, forbear: for I but meet to-day
The doom that at my birth was written down
In heaven, and thou art heaven's unconscious hand.   710
Surely my heart cried out that it was thou,
When first I saw thee; and thy heart spoke too,
I know it: but Fate trod those promptings down
Under its iron heel; Fate, Fate engaged
The strife, and hurled me on my father's spear.
But let us speak no more of this: I find   716
My father; let me feel that I have found.
Come, sit beside me on this sand, and take
My head betwixt thy hands, and kiss my cheeks,
And wash them with thy tears, and say: "My son!"   720
Quick! quick! for numbered are my sands of life,
And swift; for like the lightning to this field
I came, and like the wind I go away—
Sudden, and swift, and like a passing wind.
But it was writ in heaven that this should be.'

So said he: and his voice released the heart 726
Of Rustum, and his tears broke forth; he cast
His arms round his son's neck, and wept aloud,
And kissed him. And awe fell on both the hosts
When they saw Rustum's grief: and Ruksh, the horse,   730
With his head bowing to the ground, and mane
Sweeping the dust, came near, and in mute woe
First to the one, then to the other moved
His head, as if inquiring what their grief
Might mean; and from his dark, compassionate eyes,   735
The big warm tears rolled down, and caked the sand.
But Rustum chid him with stern voice, and said:

'Ruksh, now thou grievest; but O Ruksh, thy feet
Should first have rotted on their nimble joints,
When first they bore thy master to this field.'

But Sohrab looked upon the horse and said:
'Is this then Ruksh? How often, in past days,
My mother told me of thee, thou brave steed!
My terrible father's terrible horse; and said, 744
That I should one day find thy lord and thee.
Come, let me lay my hand upon thy mane.
O Ruksh, thou art more fortunate than I;
For thou hast gone where I shall never go,
And snuffed the breezes of my father's home.
And thou hast trod the sands of Seïstan, 750
And seen the river of Helmund, and the Lake
Of Zirrah; and the agèd Zal himself
Has often stroked thy neck, and given thee food,
Corn in a golden platter soaked with wine,
And said—"O Ruksh! bear Rustum well!"—
    but I 755
Have never known my grandsire's furrowed face,
Nor seen his lofty house in Seïstan,
Nor slaked my thirst at the clear Helmund
    stream:
But lodged among my father's foes, and seen
Afrasiab's cities only, Samarcand, 760
Bokhara, and lone Khiva in the waste,
And the black Toorkmun tents; and only
    drunk
The desert rivers, Moorghab and Tejend,
Kohik, and where the Kalmuks feed their sheep,
The northern Sir; and this great Oxus stream—
The yellow Oxus, by whose brink I die.' 766

And, with a heavy groan, Rustum bewailed:
'Oh, that its waves were flowing over me!
Oh, that I saw its grains of yellow silt
Roll tumbling in the current o'er my head!' 770

And, with a grave mild voice, Sohrab replied:
'Desire not that, my father: thou must live.
For some are born to do great deeds, and live,
As some are born to be obscured, and die.
Do thou the deeds I die too young to do, 775
And reap a second glory in thine age.
Thou art my father, and thy gain is mine.
But come: thou seest this great host of men
Which follow me; I pray thee, slay not these:
Let me entreat for them: what have they done?
They followed me, my hope, my fame, my star.
Let them all cross the Oxus back in peace. 782
But me thou must bear hence, not send with
    them,
But carry me with thee to Seïstan,
And place me on a bed, and mourn for me, 785
Thou, and the snow-haired Zal, and all thy
    friends.
And thou must lay me in that lovely earth,
And heap a stately mound above my bones,
And plant a far-seen pillar over all;
That so the passing horseman on the waste 790
May see my tomb a great way off, and cry:
"Sohrab, the mighty Rustum's son, lies there,
Whom his great father did in ignorance kill"—
And I be not forgotten in my grave.' 794

And, with a mournful voice, Rustum replied:—
'Fear not; as thou hast said, Sohrab, my son,
So shall it be; for I will burn my tents
And quit the host, and bear thee hence with me,
And carry thee away to Seïstan.
And place thee on a bed, and mourn for thee, 800
With the snow-headed Zal, and all my friends,
And I will lay thee in that lovely earth,
And heap a stately mound above thy bones,
And plant a far-seen pillar over all:
And men shall not forget thee in thy grave. 805
And I will spare thy host: yea, let them go:
Let them all cross the Oxus back in peace.
What should I do with slaying any more?
For would that all whom I have ever slain
Might be once more alive; my bitterest foes, 810
And they who were called champions in their
    time,
And through whose death I won that fame I
    have;
And I were nothing but a common man,
A poor, mean soldier, and without renown;
So thou mightest live too, my son, my son! 815
Or rather would that I, even I myself,
Might now be lying on this bloody sand,
Near death, and by an ignorant stroke of thine,
Not thou of mine; and I might die, not thou;
And I, not thou, be borne to Seïstan; 820
And Zal might weep above my grave, not thine;
And say—"O son, I weep thee not too sore,
For willingly, I know, thou met'st thine end."
But now in blood and battles was my youth,
And full of blood and battles is my age; 825
And I shall never end this life of blood.'

Then, at the point of death, Sohrab replied:
'A life of blood indeed, thou dreadful man!
But thou shalt yet have peace; only not now.
Not yet: but thou shalt have it on that day, 830
When thou shalt sail in a high-masted ship,
Thou and the other peers of Kai Khosroo,
Returning home over the salt blue sea,
From laying thy dear master in his grave.'

And Rustum gazed in Sohrab's face, and
    said: 835
'Soon be that day, my son, and deep that sea!
Till then, if fate so wills, let me endure.'

He spoke; and Sohrab smiled on him, and
    took
The spear, and drew it from his side, and eased
His wound's imperious anguish; but the blood
Came welling from the open gash, and life 841
Flowed with the stream; all down his cold white
    side
The crimson torrent ran, dim now and soiled,
Like the soiled tissue of white violets
Left, freshly gathered, on their native bank, 845
By children whom their nurses call with haste
Indoors from the sun's eye; his head drooped
    low.

His limbs grew slack: motionless, white, he lay,
White, with eyes closed, only when heavy gasps,
Deep heavy gasps, quivering through all his
    frame,   850
Convulsed him back to life, he opened them.
And fixed them feebly on his father's face;
Till now all strength was ebbed; and from his
    limbs
Unwillingly the spirit fled away,
Regretting the warm mansion which it left, 855
And youth, and bloom, and this delightful world.

   So, on the bloody sand, Sohrab lay dead:
And the great Rustum drew his horseman's cloak
Down o'er his face, and sate by his dead son.
As those black granite pillars, once high-reared,
By Jemshid in Persepolis, to bear   861
His house, now 'mid their broken flights of steps,
Lie prone, enormous, down the mountain side:
So, in the sand, lay Rustum by his son.

   And night came down over the solemn waste,
And the two gazing hosts, and that sole pair, 866
And darkened all; and a cold fog, with night,
Crept from the Oxus. Soon a hum arose,
As of a great assembly loosed, and fires
Began to twinkle through the fog; for now 870
Both armies moved to camp, and took their
    meal:
The Persians took it on the open sands
Southward, the Tartars, by the river marge:
And Rustum and his son were left alone.

   But the majestic river floated on,   875
Out of the mist and hum of that low land,
Into the frosty starlight, and there moved,
Rejoicing, through the hushed Chorasmian
    waste,
Under the solitary moon: he flowed
Right for the polar star, past Orgunjè,   880
Brimming, and bright, and large; then sands
    began
To hem his watery march, and dam his streams,
And split his currents, that for many a league
The shorn and parceled Oxus strains along
Through beds of sand and matted rushy isles;
Oxus, forgetting the bright speed he had,   886
In his high mountain-cradle in Pamere,
A foiled circuitous wanderer: till at last
The longed-for dash of waves is heard, and wide
His luminous home of waters opens, bright 890
And tranquil, from whose floor the new-bathed
    stars
Emerge, and shine upon the Aral Sea.
                (1853)

THE SCHOLAR GIPSY

Go, for they call you, shepherd, from the hill;
   Go, shepherd, and untie the wattled cotes:
No longer leave thy wistful flock unfed,
   Nor let thy bawling fellows rack their throats,
Nor the cropped grasses, shoot another head. 5
   But when the fields are still,
And the tired men and dogs all gone to rest,
   And only the white sheep are sometimes seen
   Cross and recross the strips of moon-blanched
    green;
Come, shepherd, and again renew the quest. 10

Here, where the reaper was at work of late,
   In this high field's dark corner, where he
    leaves
His coat, his basket, and his earthen cruise,
   And in the sun all morning binds the sheaves,
Then here, at noon, comes back his stores to
    use;   15
   Here will I sit and wait,
While to my ear from uplands far away,
   The bleating of the folded flocks is borne;
   With distant cries of reapers in the corn—
All the live murmur of a summer's day.   20

Screened is this nook o'er the high, half-reaped
    field,
   And here till sun-down, shepherd, will I be.
Through the thick corn the scarlet poppies peep
   And round green roots and yellowing stalks
    I see
Pale blue convolvulus in tendrils creep;   25
   And air-swept lindens yield
Their scent, and rustle down their perfumed
    showers
   Of bloom on the bent grass where I am laid,
   And bower me from the August sun with
    shade;
And the eye travels down to Oxford's towers. 30

And near me on the grass lies Glanvil's book—
   Come, let me read the oft-read tale again,
The story of that Oxford scholar poor,
   Of shining parts and quick inventive brain,
Who, tired of knocking at preferment's door, 35
   One summer-morn forsook
His friends, and went to learn the gipsy lore,
   And roamed the world with that wild brother-
    hood,
   And came, as most men deemed, to little
    good,
But came to Oxford and his friends no more. 40

But once, years after, in the country lanes,
   Two scholars whom at college erst he knew,
Met him, and of his way of life enquired.
   Whereat he answered, that the gipsy crew,
His mates, had arts to rule as they desired, 45
   The workings of men's brains;
And they can bind them to what thoughts they
    will:
   'And I,' he said, 'the secret of their art,
   When fully learned, will to the world impart;
But it needs happy moments for this skill.' 50

This said, he left them, and returned no more,
  But rumors hung about the country side
That the lost scholar long was seen to stray,
  Seen by rare glimpses pensive and tongue-tied,
In hat of antique shape, and cloak of gray,   55
  The same the gipsies wore.
Shepherds had met him on the Hurst in spring:
  At some lone alehouse in the Berkshire moors,
On the warm ingle-bench, the smock-frocked boors
Had found him seated at their entering.   60

But, 'mid their drink and clatter, he would fly,
  And I myself seem half to know thy looks,
And put the shepherds, wanderer, on thy trace;
  And boys who in lone wheat fields scare the rooks
I ask if thou hast passed their quiet place;   65
  Or in my boat I lie
Moored to the cool bank in the summer heats,
  'Mid wide grass meadows which the sunshine fills,
  And watch the warm green-muffled Cumner hills,
And wonder if thou haunt'st their shy retreats.

For most, I know, thou lov'st retirèd ground.   71
  Thee, at the ferry, Oxford riders blithe,
Returning home on summer nights, have met
  Crossing the stripling Thames at Bablock-hithe,
Trailing in the cool stream thy fingers wet,   75
  As the punt's rope chops round:
And leaning backwards in a pensive dream,
  And fostering in thy lap a heap of flowers
  Plucked in shy fields and distant Wychwood bowers,
And thine eyes resting on the moonlit stream. 80

And then they land, and thou art seen no more.
  Maidens who from the distant hamlets come
To dance around the Fyfield elm in May,
  Oft through the darkening fields have seen thee roam,
Or cross a stile into the public way.   85
  Oft thou hast given them store
Of flowers—the frail-leafed, white anemone—
  Dark bluebells drenched with dews of summer eves—
  And purple orchises with spotted leaves—
But none hath words she can report of thee.   90

And, above Godstow Bridge, when haytime's here
  In June, and many a scythe in sunshine flames,
Men who through those wide fields of breezy grass
  Where black-winged swallows haunt the glittering Thames,

To bathe in the abandoned lasher pass,   95
  Have often passed thee near
Sitting upon the river bank o'ergrown;
  Marked thine outlandish garb, thy figure spare,
  Thy dark vague eyes, and soft abstracted air;
But, when they came from bathing, thou wast gone.   100

At some lone homestead in the Cumner hills,
  Where at her open door the housewife darns,
Thou hast been seen, or hanging on a gate
  To watch the threshers in the mossy barns.
Children, who early range these slopes and late
  For cresses from the rills,   105
Have known thee eying, all an April day,
  The springing pastures and the feeding kine;
  And marked thee, when the stars come out and shine,
Through the long dewy grass move slow away.

In Autumn, on the skirts of Bagley Wood—   111
  Where most the gipsies by the turf-edged way
Pitch their smoked tents, and every bush you see
  With scarlet patches tagged and shreds of gray,
Above the forest-ground called Thessaly—   115
  The blackbird picking food
Sees thee, nor stops his meal, nor fears at all;
  So often has he known thee past him stray,
  Rapt, twirling in thy hand a withered spray,
And waiting for the spark from heaven to fall.

And once, in winter, on the causeway chill   121
  Where home through flooded fields foot-travelers go,
Have I not passed thee on the wooden bridge
  Wrapt in thy cloak and battling with the snow,
Thy face toward Hinksey and its wintry ridge?
  And thou hast climbed the hill,   126
And gained the white brow of the Cumner range,
  Turned once to watch, while thick the snow-flakes fall,
  The line of festal light in Christ Church hall—
Then sought thy straw in some sequestered grange.   130

But what—I dream! Two hundred years are flown
  Since first thy story ran through Oxford halls,
And the grave Glanvil did the tale inscribe
  That thou wert wandered from the studious walls
To learn strange arts, and join a gipsy tribe: 135
  And thou from earth art gone
Long since, and in some quiet churchyard laid;
  Some country nook, where o'er thy unknown grave
  Tall grasses and white flowering nettles wave—
Under a dark red-fruited, yew-tree's shade.   140

—No, no, thou hast not felt the lapse of hours,
   For what wears out the life of mortal men?
'T is that from change to change their being rolls:
   'T is that repeated shocks, again, again,
Exhaust the energy of strongest souls,   145
   And numb the elastic powers.
Till having used our nerves with bliss and teen,
   And tired upon a thousand schemes our wit,
To the just-pausing Genius we remit
Our worn-out life, and are—what we have been.

Thou hast not lived, why should'st thou perish so?   151
   Thou had'st *one* aim, *one* business, *one* desire;
Else wert thou long since numbered with the dead—
Else hadst thou spent, like other men, thy fire.
The generations of thy peers are fled,   155
   And we ourselves shall go;
But thou possessest an immortal lot,
   And we imagine thee exempt from age,
   And living as thou liv'st on Glanvil's page,
Because thou hadst—what we, alas, have not!

For early didst thou leave the world, with powers   161
   Fresh, undiverted to the world without,
   Firm to their mark, not spent on other things;
   Free from the sick fatigue, the languid doubt,
Which much to have tried, in much been baffled, brings.   165
   O life unlike to ours!
Who fluctuate idly without term or scope,
   Of whom each strives, nor knows for what he strives,
   And each half lives a hundred different lives;
Who wait like thee, but not, like thee, in hope.

Thou waitest for the spark from heaven: and we,   171
   Light half-believers of our casual creeds,
   Who never deeply felt, nor clearly willed,
   Whose insight never has borne fruit in deeds,
Whose vague resolves never have been fulfilled;   175
   For whom each year we see
Breeds new beginnings, disappointments new;
   Who hesitate and falter life away,
   And lose to-morrow the ground won to-day—
Ah, do not we, wanderer, await it too?   180

Yes, we await it, but it still delays,
   And then we suffer; and amongst us one,
   Who most has suffered, takes dejectedly
   His seat upon the intellectual throne;
And all his store of sad experience he   185
   Lays bare of wretched days;
Tells us his misery's birth and growth and signs,
   And how the dying spark of hope was fed,
   And how the breast was soothed, and how the head,
And all his hourly varied anodynes.   190

This for our wisest: and we others pine,
   And wish the long unhappy dream would end,
And waive all claim to bliss, and try to bear
   With close-lipped patience for our only friend,
Sad patience, too near neighbor to despair,   195
   But none has hope like thine.
Thou through the fields and through the woods dost stray,
   Roaming the country side, a truant boy,
   Nursing thy project in unclouded joy,
And every doubt long blown by time away.   200

O born in days when wits were fresh and clear,
   And life ran gaily as the sparkling Thames;
Before this strange disease of modern life,
   With its sick hurry, its divided aims,
Its heads o'ertaxed, its palsied hearts, was rife—
   Fly hence, our contact fear!   206
Still fly, plunge deeper in the bowering wood!
   Averse, as Dido did with gesture stern
   From her false friend's approach in Hades turn,
Wave us away, and keep thy solitude.   210

Still nursing the unconquerable hope,
   Still clutching the inviolable shade,
With a free onward impulse brushing through,
   By night, the silvered branches of the glade—
Far on the forest skirts, where none pursue,   215
   On some mild pastoral slope
Emerge, and resting on the moonlit pales,
   Freshen thy flowers, as in former years,
   With dew, or listen with enchanted ears,
From the dark dingles, to the nightingales.   220

But fly our paths, our feverish contact fly,
   For strong the infection of our mental strife,
   Which, though it gives no bliss, yet spoils for rest;
   And we should win thee from thy own fair life,
Like us distracted, and like us unblest.   225
   Soon, soon thy cheer would die,
Thy hopes grow timorous, and unfixed thy powers,
   And thy clear aims be cross and shifting made:
   And then thy glad perennial youth would fade,
Fade, and grow old at last, and die like ours.   230

Then fly our greetings, fly our speech and smiles!
   —As some grave Tyrian trader, from the sea,
Descried at sunrise an emerging prow
   Lifting the cool-haired creepers stealthily,
The fringes of a southward-facing brow   235
   Among the Ægean isles;
And saw the merry Grecian coaster come,
   Freighted with amber grapes, and Chian wine,
   Green bursting figs, and tunnies steeped in brine;   239
And knew the intruders on his ancient home,

The young light-hearted masters of the waves;
  And snatched his rudder, and shook out
    more sail,
And day and night held on indignantly
O'er the blue Midland waters with the gale,
Betwixt the Syrtes and soft Sicily,   245
  To where the Atlantic raves
Outside the Western Straits; and unbent sails
  There, where down cloudy cliffs through
    sheets of foam,
Shy traffickers, the dark Iberians come;
And on the beach undid his corded bales.   250

(1853)

REQUIESCAT

Strew on her roses, roses,
  And never a spray of yew!
In quiet she reposes;
  Ah, would that I did too!

Her mirth the world required;   5
  She bathed it in smiles of glee.
But her heart was tired, tired,
  And now they let her be.

Her life was turning, turning,
  In mazes of heat and sound.   10
But for peace her soul was yearning,
  And now peace laps her round.

Her cabined, ample spirit,
  It fluttered and failed for breath.
To-night it doth inherit   15
  The vasty hall of death.

(1853)

RUGBY CHAPEL

NOVEMBER 1857

Coldly, sadly descends
The autumn evening. The field
Strewn with its dank yellow drifts,
Of withered leaves, and the elms,
Fade into dimness apace,   5
Silent;—hardly a shout
From a few boys late at their play!
The lights come out in the street,
In the school-room windows;—but cold,
Solemn, unlighted, austere,   10
Through the gathering darkness, arise
The chapel-walls, in whose bound
Thou, my father! art laid.

There thou dost lie, in the gloom
Of the autumn evening. But ah,   15
That word, *gloom,* to my mind
Brings thee back, in the light
Of thy radiant vigor, again;

In the gloom of November we passed
Days not dark at thy side;   20
Seasons impaired not the ray
Of thy buoyant cheerfulness clear.
Such thou wast! and I stand
In the autumn evening, and think
Of bygone autumns with thee.   25

Fifteen years have gone round
Since thou arosest to tread,
In the summer-morning, the road
Of death, at a call unforeseen,
Sudden. For fifteen years,   30
We who till then in thy shade
Rested as under the boughs
Of a mighty oak, have endured
Sunshine and rain as we might,
Bare, unshaded, alone,   35
Lacking the shelter of thee.

O strong soul, by what shore
Tarriest thou now? For that force,
Surely, has not been left vain!
Somewhere, surely, afar,   40
In the sounding labor-house vast
Of being, is practised that strength,
Zealous, beneficent, firm!

Yes, in some far-shining sphere,
Conscious or not of the past,   45
Still thou performest the word
Of the Spirit in whom thou dost live—
Prompt, unwearied, as here!
Still thou upraisest with zeal
The humble good from the ground,   50
Sternly repressest the bad!
Still, like a trumpet, dost rouse
Those who with half-open eyes
Tread the border-land dim
'Twixt vice and virtue; reviv'st,   55
Succorest! This was thy work,
This was thy life upon earth.

What is the course of the life
Of mortal men on the earth?
Most men eddy about   60
Here and there—eat and drink,
Chatter and love and hate,
Gather and squander, are raised
Aloft, are hurled in the dust.
Striving blindly, achieving   65
Nothing; and then they die—
Perish;—and no one asks
Who or what they have been,
More than he asks what waves,
In the moonlit solitudes mild   70
Of the midmost Ocean, have swelled,
Foamed for a moment, and gone.

And there are some, whom a thirst
Ardent, unquenchable, fires,
Not with the crowd to be spent,   75

Not without aim to go round
In an eddy of purposeless dust,
Effort unmeaning and vain.
Ah, yes! some of us strive
Not without action to die   80
Fruitless, but something to snatch
From dull oblivion, nor all
Glut the devouring grave!
We, we have chosen our path—
Path to a clear-purposed goal,   85
Path of advance!—but it leads
A long, steep journey, through sunk
Gorges, o'er mountains in snow.
Cheerful, with friends, we set forth—
Then, on the height, comes the storm.   90
Thunder crashes from rock
To rock, the cataracts reply,
Lightnings dazzle our eyes.
Roaring torrents have breached
The track, the stream-bed descends   95
In the place where the wayfarer once
Planted his footstep—the spray
Boils o'er its borders! aloft
The unseen snow-beds dislodge
Their hanging ruin! alas,   100
Havoc is made in our train!
Friends, who set forth at our side,
Falter, are lost in the storm.
We, we only are left!
With frowning foreheads, with lips   105
Sternly compressed, we strain on,
On—and at nightfall at last
Come to the end of our way,
To the lonely inn 'mid the rocks;
Where the gaunt and taciturn host   110
Stands on the threshold, the wind
Shaking his thin white hairs—
Holds his lantern to scan
Our storm-beat figures, and asks:
Whom in our party we bring,   115
Whom we have left in the snow?

Sadly we answer: We bring
Only ourselves! we lost
Sight of the rest in the storm.
Hardly ourselves we fought through,   120
Stripped, without friends, as we are.
Friends, companions, and train,
The avalanche swept from our side.

But thou would'st not *alone*
Be saved, my father! *alone*   125
Conquer and come to thy goal,
Leaving the rest in the wild.
We were weary, and we
Fearful, and we in our march
Fain to drop down and to die.   130
Still thou turnedst, and still
Beckonedst the trembler, and still
Gavest the weary, thy hand.

If, in the paths of the world,
Stones might have wounded thy feet,   135
Toil or dejection have tried
Thy spirit, of that we saw
Nothing—to us thou wast still
Cheerful, and helpful, and firm!
Therefore to thee it was given   140
Many to save with thyself;
And, at the end of thy day,
O, faithful shepherd! to come,
Bringing thy sheep in thy hand.

And through thee I believe   145
In the noble and great who are gone;
Pure souls honored and blest
By former ages, who else—
Such, so soulless, so poor,
Is the race of men whom I see—   150
Seemed but a dream of the heart,
Seemed but a cry of desire.
Yes! I believe that there lived
Others like thee in the past,
Not like the men of the crowd   155
Who all round me to-day
Bluster or cringe, and make life
Hideous, and arid, and vile;
But souls tempered with fire,
Fervent, heroic and good,   160
Helpers and friends of mankind.

Servants of God!—or sons
Shall I not call you? because
Not as servants ye knew
Your Father's innermost mind,   165
His, who unwillingly sees
One of his little ones lost—
Yours is the praise, if mankind
Hath not as yet in its march
Fainted, and fallen, and died!   170

See! In the rocks of the world
Marches the host of mankind,
A feeble, wavering line.
Where are they tending?—A God
Marshaled them, gave them their goal.   175
Ah, but the way is so long!
Years they have been in the wild!
Sore thirst plagues them, the rocks,
Rising all round, overawe;
Factions divide them, their host   180
Threatens to break, to dissolve.
—Ah, keep, keep them combined!
Else, of the myriads who fill
That army, not one shall arrive;
Sole they shall stray; on the rocks   185
Batter for ever in vain,
Die one by one in the waste.

Then, in such hour of need
Of your fainting, dispirited race,
Ye, like angels, appear,   190

Radiant with ardor divine!
Beacons of hope, ye appear!
Languor is not in your heart,
Weakness is not in your word,
Weariness not on your brow.   195
Ye alight in our van! at your voice,
Panic, despair, flee away.
Ye move through the ranks, recall
The stragglers, refresh the outworn,
Praise, re-inspire the brave!   200
Order, courage, return.
Eyes rekindling, and prayers
Follow your steps as ye go.
Ye fill up the gaps in our files,
Strengthen the wavering line,   205
Stablish, continue our march,
On, to the bound of the waste,
On, to the City of God.

(1867)

DOVER BEACH

The sea is calm to-night,
The tide is full, the moon lies fair
Upon the Straits;—on the French coast, the light
Gleams, and is gone; the cliffs of England stand,
Glimmering and vast, out in the tranquil bay. 5
Come to the window, sweet is the night air!
    Only, from the long line of spray
Where the ebb meets the moon-blanch'd sand,
Listen! you hear the grating roar
Of pebbles which the waves suck back, and fling,   10
At their return, up the high strand,
Begin, and cease, and then again begin,
With tremulous cadence slow, and bring
The eternal note of sadness in.

    Sophocles long ago   15
Heard it on the Ægæan, and it brought
Into his mind the turbid ebb and flow
    Of human misery; we
Find also in the sound a thought,
Hearing it by this distant northern sea.   20

    The sea of faith
Was once, too, at the full, and round earth's shore
Lay like the folds of a bright girdle furl'd;
    But now I only hear
Its melancholy, long, withdrawing roar,   25
    Retreating to the breath
Of the night-wind down the vast edges drear
And naked shingles of the world.

    Ah, love, let us be true
To one another! for the world, which seems   30
To lie before us like a land of dreams,
So various, so beautiful, so new,
Hath really neither joy, nor love, nor light,
Nor certitude, nor peace, nor help for pain;
And we are here as on a darkling plain   35
Swept with confused alarms of struggle and flight,
Where ignorant armies clash by night.

(1867)

DANTE GABRIEL ROSSETTI (1828–1882)

ALTHOUGH as a very young boy Rossetti showed a talent for versifying, he attained distinction first as a painter. After spending five years at King's College School and in art academies in London, he became a pupil of Ford Madox Brown, and later joined Holman Hunt, Millais, and others, in that revival of mystical interpretation and detailed elaboration in painting commonly called the Pre-Raphaelite movement. No considerable part of Rossetti's poems appeared in print before the publication of *Poems*, in 1870. The following year Robert Buchanan, in an article entitled *The Fleshly School in Poetry*, savagely attacked the alleged immorality of Rossetti's poems. Although Rossetti stoutly resisted the assault, it aggravated the mental depression which had begun with the death of his wife, and which persisted until his death. The last ten years of his life were tragically clouded by mental weakness and by the habit of taking chloral. Even during this period, however, creative flashes of his mind resulted in both poems and paintings of great beauty.

Poems (1870), *Dante and His Circle* (1874), and *Ballads and Sonnets* (1881) contain substantially all of Rossetti's poetry. The volume of 1881 brought out *The King's Tragedy*, and added sonnets to complete *The House of Life*, the first sonnets of which had appeared in 1870. Rossetti's only imaginative work in prose is *Hand and Soul* (1850). His poetry, though often subtly mystical in thought, is never primarily religious. Above all, it is sensuous, conveying beauty of form and color with a profuseness of detail natural to 'painter's poetry.'

MY SISTER'S SLEEP

SHE fell asleep on Christmas Eve:
  At length the long-ungranted shade
  Of weary eyelids overweighed
The pain nought else might yet relieve.

Our mother, who had leaned all day   5
  Over the bed from chime to chime,
  Then raised herself for the first time,
And as she sat her down, did pray.

Her little work-table was spread
  With work to finish. For the glare   10
  Made by her candle, she had care
To work some distance from the bed.

Without, there was a cold moon up,
  Of winter radiance sheer and thin;
  The hollow halo it was in   15
Was like an icy crystal cup.

Through the small room, with subtle sound
  Of flame, by vents the fireshine drove
  And reddened. In its dim alcove
The mirror shed a clearness round.   20

I had been sitting up some nights,
  And my tired mind felt weak and blank;
  Like a sharp strengthening wine it drank
The stillness and the broken lights.

Twelve struck. That sound, by dwindling years   25
  Heard in each hour, crept off; and then
  The ruffled silence spread again,
Like water that a pebble stirs.

Our mother rose from where she sat:
  Her needles, as she laid them down,   30
  Met lightly, and her silken gown
Settled: no other noise than that.

'Glory unto the Newly Born!'
  So, as said angels, she did say;
  Because we were in Christmas Day   35
Though it would still be long till morn.

Just then in the room over us
  There was a pushing back of chairs,
  As some who had sat unawares
So late, now heard the hour, and rose.   40

With anxious softly-stepping haste
  Our mother went where Margaret lay,
  Fearing the sounds o'er head—should they
Have broken her long watched-for rest!

She stopped an instant, calm, and turned,   45
  But suddenly turned back again;
  And all her features seemed in pain
With woe, and her eyes gazed and yearned.

For my part, I but hid my face,
  And held my breath, and spoke no word: 50
  There was none spoken: but I heard
The silence for a little space.

Our mother bowed herself and wept:
  And both my arms fell, and I said,
  'God knows I knew that she was dead.'   55
And there, all white, my sister slept.

Then kneeling, upon Christmas morn
  A little after twelve o'clock,
We said, ere the first quarter struck,
  'Christ's blessing on the newly born!'   60
          (1850)

THE BLESSED DAMOZEL

THE blessed damozel leaned out
  From the golden bar of heaven;
Her eyes were deeper than the depth
  Of waters stilled at even;
She had three lilies in her hand,   5
  And the stars in her hair were seven.

Her robe, ungirt from clasp to hem,
  No wrought flowers did adorn,
But a white rose of Mary's gift,
  For service meetly worn;   10
Her hair that lay along her back
  Was yellow like ripe corn.

Her seemed she scarce had been a day
  One of God's choristers;
The wonder was not yet quite gone   15
  From that still look of hers;
Albeit, to them she left, her day
  Had counted as ten years.

(To one, it is ten years of years.
  . . . Yet now, and in this place,   20
Surely she leaned o'er me—her hair
  Fell all about my face. . . .
Nothing: the autumn-fall of leaves
  The whole year sets apace.)

It was the rampart of God's house   25
  That she was standing on;
By God built over the sheer depth
  The which is Space begun;
So high, that looking downward thence
  She scarce could see the sun.   30

It lies in heaven, across the flood
  Of ether, as a bridge.
Beneath, the tides of day and night
  With flame and darkness ridge
The void, as low as where this earth   35
  Spins like a fretful midge.

Around her, lovers, newly met
  'Mid deathless love's acclaims,
Spoke evermore among themselves
  Their heart-remembered names;   40
And the souls mounting up to God
  Went by her like thin flames.

And still she bowed herself and stooped
  Out of the circling charm;
Until her bosom must have made   45
  The bar she leaned on warm,
And the lilies lay as if asleep
  Along her bended arm.

From the fixed place of Heaven she saw
  Time like a pulse shake fierce   50
Through all the worlds. Her gaze still strove,
  Within the gulf to pierce
Its path: and now she spoke as when
  The stars sang in their spheres.

The sun was gone now; the curled moon   55
  Was like a little feather
Fluttering far down the gulf; and now
  She spoke through the still weather.
Her voice was like the voice the stars
  Had when they sang together.   60

(Ah, sweet! Even now, in that bird's song,
  Strove not her accents there,
Fain to be hearkened? When those bells
  Possessed the mid-day air,
Strove not her steps to reach my side   65
  Down all the echoing stair?)

'I wish that he were come to me,
  For he will come,' she said.
'Have I not prayed in Heaven?—on earth,
  Lord, Lord, has he not prayed?   70
Are not two prayers a perfect strength?
  And shall I feel afraid?

'When round his head the aureole clings,
  And he is clothed in white,
I'll take his hand and go with him   75
  To the deep wells of light;
As unto a stream we will step down,
  And bathe there in God's sight.

'We two will stand beside that shrine,
  Occult, withheld, untrod,   80
Whose lamps are stirred continually
  With prayer sent up to God;
And see our old prayers, granted, melt
  Each like a little cloud.

'We two will lie i' the shadow of   85
  That living mystic tree
Within whose secret growth the Dove
  Is sometimes felt to be,
While every leaf that his plumes touch
  Saith his name audibly.   90

'And I myself will teach to him,
  I myself, lying so,
The songs I sing here; which his voice
  Shall pause in, hushed and slow,
And find some knowledge at each pause,   95
  Or some new thing to know.'

(Alas! We two, we two, thou say'st!
  Yea, one wast thou with me
That once of old. But shall God lift
  To endless unity   100
The soul whose likeness with thy soul
  Was but its love for thee?)

'We two,' she said, 'will seek the groves
    Where the lady Mary is,
With her five handmaidens, whose names   105
    Are five sweet symphonies,
Cecily, Gertrude, Magdalen,
    Margaret and Rosalys.

'Circlewise sit they, with bound locks
    And foreheads garlanded;   110
Into the fine cloth white like flame
    Weaving the golden thread,
To fashion the birth-robes for them
    Who are just born, being dead.

'He shall fear, haply, and be dumb: 115
    Then will I lay my cheek
To his, and tell about our love,
    Not once abashed or weak;
And the dear Mother will approve
    My pride, and let me speak.   120

'Herself shall bring us, hand in hand,
    To him round whom all souls
Kneel, the clear-ranged unnumbered heads
    Bowed with their aureoles:
And angels meeting us shall sing   125
    To their citherns and citoles.

'There will I ask of Christ the Lord
    Thus much for him and me:—
Only to live as once on earth
    With Love, only to be,   130
As then awhile, forever now
    Together, I and he.'

She gazed and listened and then said,
    Less sad of speech than mild,—
'All this is when he comes.' She ceased.   135
    The light thrilled towards her, filled
With angels in strong level flight.
    Her eyes prayed, and she smiled.

(I saw her smile.) But soon their path
    Was vague in distant spheres: 140
And then she cast her arms along
    The golden barriers,
And laid her face between her hands,
    And wept. (I heard her tears.)

(1850)

FRANCESCA DA RIMINI

From DANTE

* * *

When I made answer, I began: 'Alas!
  How many sweet thoughts and how much
    desire
  Led these two onward to the dolorous pass!'
Then turned to them, as who would fain inquire,
  And said: 'Francesca, these thine agonies   5
  Wring tears for pity and grief that they in-
    spire:—

But tell me,—in the season of sweet sighs,
  When and what way did Love instruct you so
  That he in your vague longings made you
    wise?'
Then she to me: 'There is no greater woe   10
  Than the remembrance brings of happy days
  In Misery; and this thy guide doth know.
But if the first beginnings to retrace
  Of our sad love can yield thee solace here,
  So will I be as one that weeps and says.   15
One day we read, for pastime and sweet cheer,
  Of Lancelot, how he found Love tyrannous;
  We were alone and without any fear.
Our eyes were drawn together, reading thus,
  Full oft, and still our cheeks would pale and
    glow;   20
  But one sole point it was that conquered us.
For when we read of that great lover, how
  He kissed the smile which he had longed to
    win,—
  Then he whom nought can sever from me now
Forever, kissed my mouth, all quivering.   25
  A Galahalt was the book, and he that writ:
  Upon that day we read no more therein.'
At the tale told, while one soul uttered it,
  The other wept: a pang so pitiable
That I was seized, like death, in swooning-fit,
And even as a dead body falls, I fell.   31

(1861)

LOVE'S NOCTURN

Master of the murmuring courts
    Where the shapes of sleep convene!—
Lo! my spirit here exhorts
    All the powers of thy demesne
For their aid to woo my queen.   5
      What reports
  Yield thy jealous courts unseen?

Vaporous, unaccountable,
    Dreamworld lies forlorn of light,
Hollow like a breathing shell.   10
    Ah! that from all dreams I might
Choose one dream and guide its flight!
      I know well
  What her sleep should tell to-night.

There the dreams are multitudes: 15
    Some that will not wait for sleep,
Deep within the August woods;
    Some that hum while rest may steep
Weary labor laid a-heap;
      Interludes,   20
  Some, of grievous moods that weep.

Poet's fancies all are there;
    There the elf-girls flood with wings
Valleys full of plaintive air;
    There breathe perfumes; there in rings   25
  Whirl the foam-bewildered springs;
      Siren there
  Winds her dizzy hair and sings.

Thence the one dream mutually
  Dreamed in bridal unison,   30
Less than waking ecstasy;
  Half-formed visions that make moan
  In the house of birth alone;
    And what we
At death's wicket see, unknown.   35

But for mine own sleep, it lies
  In one gracious form's control,
Fair with honorable eyes,
  Lamps of a translucent soul:
  O their glance is loftiest dole,   40
    Sweet and wise,
Wherein Love descries his goal.

Reft of her, my dreams are all
  Clammy trance that fears the sky;
Changing footpaths shift and fall;   45
  From polluted coverts nigh,
  Miserable phantoms sigh;
    Quakes the pall,
And the funeral goes by.

Master, is it soothly said   50
  That, as echoes of man's speech
Far in secret clefts are made,
  So do all men's bodies reach
  Shadows o'er thy sunken beach,—
    Shape or shade   55
In those halls portrayed of each?

Ah! might I, by thy good grace
  Groping in the windy stair
(Darkness and the breath of space
  Like loud waters everywhere),   60
  Meeting mine own image there
    Face to face,
Send it from that place to her!

Nay, not I; but oh! do thou,
  Master, from thy shadowkind   65
Call my body's phantom now:
  Bid it bear its face declined
  Till its flight her slumbers find,
    And her brow
Feel its presence bow like wind.   70

Where in groves the gracile Spring
  Trembles, with mute orison
Confidently strengthening,
  Water's voice and wind's as one
  Shed an echo in the sun.   75
    Soft as Spring,
Master, bid it sing and moan.

Song shall tell how glad and strong
  Is the night she soothes alway;
Moan shall grieve with that parched tongue   80
  Of the brazen hours of day:
  Sounds as of the springtide they,
    Moan and song,
While the chill months long for May.

Not the prayers which with all leave   85
  The world's fluent woes prefer,—
Not the praise the world doth give,
  Dulcet fulsome whisperer;—
  Let it yield my love to her,
    And achieve   90
Strength that shall not grieve or err.

Wheresoe'er my dreams befall,
  Both at night-watch (let it say),
And where round the sun-dial
  The reluctant hours of day,   95
  Heartless, hopeless of their way,
    Rest and call;—
There her glance doth fall and stay.

Suddenly her face is there:
  So do mounting vapors wreathe   100
Subtle-scented transports where
  The black fir-wood sets its teeth.
  Part the boughs, and look beneath—
    Lilies share
Secret waters there, and breathe.   105

Master, bid my shadow bend
  Whispering thus till birth of light,
Lest new shapes that sleep may send
  Scatter all its work to flight;—
  Master, master of the night,   110
    Bid it spend
Speech, song, prayer, and end aright.

Yet, ah, me! if at her head
  There another phantom lean
Murmuring o'er the fragrant bed,   115
  Ah! and if my spirit's queen
  Smile those alien prayers between,—
    Ah! poor shade!
Shall it strive, or fade unseen?

How should love's own messenger   120
  Strive with love and be love's foe?
Master, nay! If thus, in her,
  Sleep a wedded heart should show,—
  Silent let mine image go,
    Its old share   125
Of thy spell-bound air to know.

Like a vapor wan and mute,
  Like a flame, so let it pass;
One low sigh across her lute,
  One dull breath against her glass;   130
  And to my sad soul, alas!
    One salute
Cold as when death's foot shall pass.

Then, too, let all hopes of mine,
  All vain hopes by night and day,   135
Slowly at thy summoning sign
  Rise up pallid and obey.
  Dreams, if this is thus, were they:—
    Be they thine,
And to dreamworld pine away.   140

Yet from old time, life, not death,
  Master, in thy rule is rife;
Lo! through thee, with mingling breath,
  Adam woke beside his wife.
O Love, bring me so, for strife,   145
    Force and faith,
Bring me so not death but life!

Yea, to Love himself is poured
  This frail song of hope and fear,
Thou art Love, of one accord   150
  With kind Sleep to bring her near,
  Still-eyed, deep-eyed, ah, how dear!
    Master, Lord,
In her name implored, O hear!
        (1870)

THE CLOUD CONFINES

The day is dark and the night
  To him that would search their heart;
  No lips of cloud that will part
Nor morning song in the light:
  Only, gazing alone,   5
  To him wild shadows are shown,
  Deep under deep unknown,
And height above unknown height.
    Still we say as we go,—
    'Strange to think by the way,   10
    Whatever there is to know,
    That shall we know one day.'

The Past is over and fled;
  Named new, we name it the old;
  Thereof some tale hath been told,   15
But no word comes from the dead;
  Whether at all they be,
  Or whether as bond or free,
  Or whether they too were we,
Or by what spell they have sped.   20
    Still we say as we go,—
    'Strange to think by the way,
    Whatever there is to know,
    That shall we know one day.'

What of the heart of hate   25
  That beats in thy breast, O Time?—
  Red strife from the furthest prime,
And anguish of fierce debate;
  War that shatters her slain,
  And peace that grinds them as grain,   30
  And eyes fixed ever in vain
On the pitiless eyes of Fate.
    Still we say as we go,—
    'Strange to think by the way,
    Whatever there is to know,   35
    That shall we know one day.'

What of the heart of love
  That bleeds in thy breast, O Man!
  Thy kisses snatched 'neath the ban

Of fangs that mock them above;   40
  Thy bells prolonged unto knells,
  Thy hope that a breath dispels,
  Thy bitter forlorn farewells
And the empty echoes thereof?
    Still we say as we go,—   45
    'Strange to think by the way,
    Whatever there is to know,
    That shall we know one day.'

The sky leans dumb on the sea,
  Aweary with all its wings;   50
  And oh! the song the sea sings
Is dark everlastingly.
  Our past is clean forgot,
  Our present is and is not,
  Our future's a sealed seedplot,   55
And what betwixt them are we?—
    We who say as we go,—
    'Strange to think by the way,
    Whatever there is to know,
    That shall we know one day.'   60
        (1872)

THREE SHADOWS

I looked and saw your eyes
  In the shadow of your hair,
As a traveler sees the stream
  In the shadow of the wood;
And I said, 'My faint heart sighs,   5
  Ah me! to linger there,
To drink deep and to dream
  In that sweet solitude.'

I looked and saw your heart
  In the shadow of your eyes,   10
As a seeker sees the gold
  In the shadow of the stream;
And I said, 'Ah me! what art
  Should win the immortal prize,
Whose want must make life cold   15
  And heaven a hollow dream?'

I looked and saw your love
  In the shadow of your heart,
As a diver sees the pearl
  In the shadow of the sea;   20
And I murmured, not above
  My breath, but all apart,—
'Ah! you can love, true girl,
  And is your love for me?'
        (1881)

THE KING'S TRAGEDY

James I of Scots—20th February, 1437

I Catherine am a Douglas born,
  A name to all Scots dear;
And Kate Barlass they've called me now
  Through many a waning year.

This old arm's withered now. 'T was once 5
    Most deft 'mong maidens all
To rein the steed, to wing the shaft,
    To smite the palm-play ball.

In hall adown the close-linked dance
    It has shone most white and fair; 10
It has been the rest for a true lord's head,
    And many a sweet babe's nursing-bed,
    And the bar to a King's chambère.

Aye, lasses, draw round Kate Barlass,
    And hark with bated breath 15
How good King James, King Robert's son,
    Was foully done to death.

Through all the days of his gallant youth
    The princely James was pent,
By his friends at first and then by his foes, 20
    In long imprisonment.

For the elder prince, the kingdom's heir,
    By treason's murderous brood
Was slain; and the father quaked for the child
    With the royal mortal blood. 25

I' the Bass Rock fort, by his father's care,
    Was his childhood's life assured;
And Henry the subtle Bolingbroke,
Proud England's king, 'neath the southron yoke
    His youth for long years immured. 30

Yet in all things meet for a kingly man
    Himself did he approve;
And the nightingale through his prison-wall
    Taught him both lore and love.

For once, when the bird's song drew him close 35
    To the opened window-pane,
In her bower beneath a lady stood,
A light of life to his sorrowful mood,
    Like a lily amid the rain.

And for her sake, to the sweet bird's note, 40
    He framed a sweeter song,
More sweet than ever a poet's heart
    Gave yet to the English tongue.

She was a lady of royal blood;
    And when, past sorrow and teen, 45
He stood where still through his crownless years
    His Scottish realm had been,
At Scone were the happy lovers crowned,
    A heart-wed king and queen.

But the bird may fall from the bough of youth,
    And song be turned to moan, 51
And love's storm-cloud be the shadow of hate,
When the tempest-waves of a troubled state
    Are beating against a throne.

Yet well they loved; and the god of love, 55
    Whom well the king had sung,
Might find on the earth no truer hearts
    His lowliest swains among.

From the days when first she rode abroad
    With Scottish maids in her train, 60
I Catherine Douglas won the trust
    Of my mistress sweet Queen Jane.

And oft she sighed, 'To be born a King!'
    And oft along the way
When she saw the homely lovers pass 65
    She has said, 'Alack the day!'

Years waned,—the loving and toiling years:
    Till England's wrong renewed
Drove James, by outrage cast on his crown,
    To the open field of feud. 70

'T was when the king and his host were met
    At the leaguer of Roxbro' hold,
The queen o' the sudden sought his camp
    With a tale of dread to be told.

And she showed him a secret letter writ 75
    That spoke of treasonous strife,
And how a band of his noblest lords
    Were sworn to take his life.

'And it may be here or it may be there,
    In the camp or the court,' she said: 80
'But for my sake come to your people's arms
    And guard your royal head.'

Quoth he, ''T is the fifteenth day of the siege,
    And the castle's nigh to yield.'
'O face your foes on your throne,' she cried, 85
    'And show the power you wield;
And under your Scottish people's love
    You shall sit as under your shield.'

At the fair queen's side I stood that day
    When he bade them raise the siege, 90
And back to his court he sped to know
    How the lords would meet their liege.

But when he summoned his parliament,
    The louring brows hung round,
Like clouds that circle the mountain-head 95
    Ere the first low thunders sound.

For he had tamed the nobles' lust
    And curbed their power and pride,
And reached out an arm to right the poor
    Through Scotland far and wide; 100
And many a lordly wrong-doer
    By the headsman's axe had died.

'T was then upspoke Sir Robert Græme,
    The bold o'ermastering man:—
'O King, in the name of your Three Estates 105
    I set you under their ban!

'For, as your lords made oath to you
  Of service and fealty,
Even in like wise you pledged your oath
  Their faithful sire to be:—   110

'Yet all we here that are nobly sprung
  Have mourned dear kith and kin
Since first for the Scottish Barons' curse
  Did your bloody rule begin.'

With that he laid his hands on his king:— 115
  'Is this not so, my lords?'
But of all who had sworn to league with him
  Not one spake back to his words.

Quoth the King:—'Thou speak'st but for one Estate,
  Nor doth it avow thy gage.   120
Let my liege lords hale this traitor hence!'
  The Græme fired dark with rage:—
'Who works for lesser men than himself,
  He earns but a witness wage!'

But soon from the dungeon where he lay   125
  He won by privy plots,
And forth he fled with a price on his head
  To the country of the Wild Scots.

And word there came from Sir Robert Græme
  To the King of Edinbro':—   130
'No liege of mine thou art; but I see
From this day forth alone in thee
  God's creature, my mortal foe.

'Through thee are my wife and children lost,
  My heritage and lands;   135
And when my God shall show me a way,
  Thyself my mortal foe will I slay
  With these my proper hands.'

Against the coming of Christmastide
  That year the king bade call   140
I' the Black Friars' Charterhouse of Perth
  A solemn festival.

And we of his household rode with him
  In a close-ranked company;
But not till the sun had sunk from his throne 145
  Did we reach the Scottish Sea.

That eve was clenched for a boding storm,
  'Neath a toilsome moon, half seen;
The cloud stooped low and the surf rose high;
  And where there was a line of the sky,   150
  Wild wings loomed dark between.

And on a rock of the black beach-side
  By the veiled moon dimly lit,
There was something seemed to heave with life
  As the king drew nigh to it.   155

And was it only the tossing furze
  Or brake of the waste sea-wold?
Or was it an eagle bent to the blast?
When near we came, we knew it at last
  For a woman tattered and old.   160

But it seemed as though by a fire within
  Her writhen limbs were wrung;
And as soon as the king was close to her,
  She stood up gaunt and strong.

'T was then the moon sailed clear of the rack 165
  On high in her hollow dome;
And still as aloft with hoary crest
  Each clamorous wave rang home,
Like fire in snow the moonlight blazed
  Amid the champing foam.   170

And the woman held his eyes with her eyes:—
  'O King, thou art come at last;
But thy wraith has haunted the Scottish Sea
  To my sight for four years past.

'Four years it is since first I met,   175
  'Twixt the Duchray and the Dhu,
A shape whose feet clung close in a shroud,
  And that shape for thine I knew.

'A year again, and on Inchkeith Isle
  I saw thee pass in the breeze,   180
With the cerecloth risen above thy feet
  And wound about thy knees.

'And yet a year, in the Links of Forth,
  As a wanderer without rest,
Thou cam'st with both thine arms i' the shroud
  That clung high up thy breast.   186

'And in this hour I find thee here,
  And well mine eyes may note
That the winding-sheet hath passed thy breast
  And risen around thy throat.   190

'And when I meet thee again, O King,
  That of death hast such sore drouth,—
Except thou turn again on this shore,—
The winding-sheet shall have moved once more
  And covered thine eyes and mouth.   195

'O King, whom poor men bless for their king,
  Of thy fate be not so fain;
But these my words for God's message take,
And turn thy steed, O King, for her sake
  Who rides beside thy rein!'   200

While the woman spoke, the king's horse reared
  As if it would breast the sea,
And the queen turned pale as she heard on the gale
  The voice die dolorously.

When the woman ceased, the steed was still,
   But the king gazed on her yet,   206
And in silence save for the wail of the sea
   His eyes and her eyes met.

At last he said:—'God's ways are his own;
   Man is but shadow and dust.   210
Last night I prayed by his altar-stone;
To-night I wend to the Feast of His Son;
   And in him I set my trust.

'I have held my people in sacred charge,
   And have not feared the sting   215
Of proud men's hate,—to his will resigned
Who has but one same death for a hind
   And one same death for a king.

'And if God in his wisdom have brought close
   The day when I must die,   220
That day by water or fire or air
My feet shall fall in the destined snare
   Wherever my road may lie.

'What man can say but the Fiend hath set
   Thy sorcery on my path,   225
My heart with the fear of death to fill,
And turn me against God's very will
   To sink in his burning wrath?'

The woman stood as the train rode past,
   And moved nor limb nor eye;   230
And when we were shipped, we saw her there
   Still standing against the sky.

As the ship made way, the moon once more
   Sank slow in her rising pall;
And I thought of the shrouded wraith of the
   king,   235
   And I said, 'The heavens know all.'

And now, ye lasses, must ye hear
   How my name is Kate Barlass:—
But a little thing, when all the tale
   Is told of the weary mass   240
Of crime and woe which in Scotland's realm
   God's will let come to pass.

'T was in the Charterhouse of Perth
   That the king and all his court
Were met, the Christmas Feast being done, 245
   For solace and disport.

'T was a wind-wild eve in February,
   And against the casement-pane
The branches smote like summoning hands
   And muttered the driving rain.   250

And when the wind swooped over the lift
   And made the whole heaven frown,
It seemed a grip was laid on the walls
   To tug the housetop down.

And the queen was there, more stately fair 255
   Than a lily in garden set;
And the king was loth to stir from her side;
For as on the day when she was his bride,
   Even so he loved her yet.

And the Earl of Athole, the king's false friend,
   Sat with him at the board;   261
And Robert Stuart the chamberlain
   Who had sold his sovereign lord.

Yet the traitor Christopher Chaumber there
   Would fain have told him all,   265
And vainly four times that night he strove
   To reach the king through the hall.

But the wine is bright at the goblet's brim
   Though the poison lurk beneath;
And the apples still are red on the tree   270
Within whose shade may the adder be
   That shall turn thy life to death.

There was a knight of the king's fast friends
   Whom he called the King of Love;
And to such bright cheer and courtesy   275
   That name might best behoove.

And the king and queen both loved him well
   For his gentle knightliness;
And with him the king, as that eve wore on,
   Was playing at the chess.   280

And the king said, (for he thought to jest
   And soothe the queen thereby)—
'In a book 't is writ that this same year
   A king shall in Scotland die.

'And I have pondered the matter o'er,   285
   And this have I found, Sir Hugh,—
There are but two kings on Scottish ground,
   And those kings are I and you.

'And I have a wife and a newborn heir,
   And you are yourself alone;   290
So stand you stark at my side with me
   To guard our double throne.

'For here sit I and my wife and child,
   As well your heart shall approve,
In full surrender and soothfastness,   **295**
   Beneath your Kingdom of Love.'

And the knight laughed, and the queen too
   smiled;
   But I knew her heavy thought,
And I strove to find in the good king's jest
   What cheer might thence be wrought. 300

And I said, 'My Liege, for the queen's dear love
   Now sing the song that of old
You made, when a captive prince you lay,
And the nightingale sang sweet on the spray,
   In Windsor's castle-hold.'   305

Then he smiled the smile I knew so well
  When he thought to please the queen;
The smile which under all bitter frowns
  Of hate that rose between,
For ever dwelt at the poet's heart   310
  Like the bird of love unseen.

And he kissed her hand and took his harp,
  And the music sweetly rang;
And when the song burst forth, it seemed
  'T was the nightingale that sang.   315

'*Worship, ye lovers, on this May:*
  Of bliss your kalends are begun:
Sing with us, Away, Winter, away!
  Come, Summer, the sweet season and sun!
Awake for shame,—your heaven is won,—   320
And amorously your heads lift all:
Thank Love, that you to his grace doth call!'

But when he bent to the queen and sang
  The speech whose praise was hers,
It seemed his voice was the voice of the spring
  And the voice of the bygone years.   326

'*The fairest and the freshest flower*
  That ever I saw before that hour,
The which o' the sudden made to start
  The blood of my body to my heart.   330

* * *

Ah sweet, are ye a worldly creature
Or heavenly thing in form of nature?'

And the song was long, and richly stored
  With wonder and beauteous things;
And the harp was tuned to every change   335
  Of minstrel ministerings;
But when he spoke of the queen at the last,
  Its strings were his own heart-strings.

'*Unworthy but only of her grace,*
  Upon Love's rock that's easy and sure,   340
In guerdon of all my love's space
  She took me her humble creäture.
Thus fell my blissful aventure
In youth of love that from day to day
Flowereth aye new, and further I say.   345

'*To reckon all the circumstance*
  As it happed when lessen gan my sore,
Of my rancor and woful chance,
  It were too long,—I have done therefor.
And of this flower I say no more   350
But unto my help her heart hath tended
And even from death her man defended.'

'Aye, even from death,' to myself I said;
  For I thought of the day when she
Had borne him the news, at Roxbro' siege,   355
  Of the fell confederacy.

But Death even then took aim as he sang
  With an arrow deadly bright;
And the grinning skull lurked grimly aloof,
And the wings were spread far over the roof   360
  More dark than the winter night.

Yet truly along the amorous song
  Of Love's high pomp and state,
There were words of Fortune's trackless doom
  And the dreadful face of Fate.   365

And oft have I heard again in dreams
  The voice of dire appeal
In which the king then sang of the pit
  That is under Fortune's wheel.

'*And under the wheel beheld I there*   370
  An ugly pit as deep as hell,
That to behold I quaked for fear:
  And this I heard, that who therein fell
Come no more up, tidings to tell:
Whereat, astound of the fearful sight,   375
  I wist not what to do for fright.'

And oft has my thought called up again
  These words of the changeful song:—
'*Wist thou thy pain and thy travàil*
To come, well might'st thou weep and wail!'   380
  And our wail, O God! is long.

But the song's end was all of his love;
  And well his heart was graced
With her smiling lips and her tear-bright eyes
  As his arm went round her waist.   385

And on the swell of her long fair throat
  Close clung the necklet-chain
As he bent her pearl-tired head aside,
And in the warmth of his love and pride
  He kissed her lips full fain.   390

And her true face was a rosy red,
  The very red of the rose
That, couched on the happy garden-bed,
  In the summer sunlight glows.

And all the wondrous things of love   395
  That sang so sweet through the song
Were in the look that met in their eyes,
  And the look was deep and long.

'T was then a knock came at the outer gate,
  And the usher sought the king.   400
'The woman you met by the Scottish Sea,
  My Liege, would tell you a thing;
And she says that her present need for speech
  Will bear no gainsaying.'

And the king said: 'The hour is late;   405
  To-morrow will serve, I ween.'
Then he charged the usher strictly, and said:
  'No word of this to the queen.'

But the usher came again to the king.
   'Shall I call her back?' quoth he: 410
'For as she went on her way, she cried,
   "Woe! woe! then the thing must be!"'

And the king paused, but he did not speak.
   Then he called for the voidee-cup:
And as we heard the twelfth hour strike,   415
There by true lips and false lips alike
   Was the draught of trust drained up.

So with reverence meet to king and queen,
   To bed went all from the board;
And the last to leave of the courtly train   420
Was Robert Stuart the chamberlain
   Who had sold his sovereign lord.

And all the locks of the chamber-door
   Had the traitor riven and brast;
And that Fate might win sure way from afar,   425
He had drawn out every bolt and bar
   That made the entrance fast.

And now at midnight he stole his way
   To the moat of the outer wall,
And laid strong hurdles closely across   430
   Where the traitors' tread should fall.

But we that were the queen's bower-maids
   Alone were left behind;
And with heed we drew the curtains close
   Against the winter wind.   435

And now that all was still through the hall,
   More clearly we heard the rain
That clamored ever against the glass
   And the boughs that beat on the pane.

But the fire was bright in the ingle-nook,   440
   And through empty space around
The shadows cast on the arrased wall
'Mid the pictured kings stood sudden and tall
   Like specters sprung from the ground.

And the bed was dight in a deep alcove;   445
   And as he stood by the fire
The king was still in talk with the queen
   While he doffed his goodly attire.

And the song had brought the image back
   Of many a bygone year;   450
And many a loving word they said
With hand in hand and head laid to head;
   And none of us went anear.

But Love was weeping outside the house,
   A child in the piteous rain;   455
And as he watched the arrow of Death,
He wailed for his own shafts close in the sheath
   That never should fly again.

And now beneath the window arose
   A wild voice suddenly: 460
And the king reared straight, but the queen
   fell back
   As for bitter dule to dree;
And all of us knew the woman's voice
   Who spoke by the Scottish Sea.

'O King,' she cried, 'in an evil hour   465
   They drove me from thy gate;
And yet my voice must rise to thine ears;
   But alas! it comes too late!

'Last night at mid-watch, by Aberdour,
   When the moon was dead in the skies,   470
O King, in a death-light of thine own
   I saw thy shape arise.

'And in full season, as erst I said,
   The doom had gained its growth;
And the shroud had risen above thy neck   475
   And covered thine eyes and mouth.

'And no moon woke, but the pale dawn broke,
   And still thy soul stood there;
And I thought its silence cried to my soul
   As the first rays crowned its hair.   480

'Since then have I journeyed fast and fain
   In very despite of Fate,
Lest hope might still be found in God's will:
   But they drove me from thy gate.

'For every man on God's ground, O King,   485
   His death grows up from his birth
In a shadow-plant perpetually;
   And thine towers high, a black yew-tree,
   O'er the Charterhouse of Perth!'

That room was built far out from the house;
   And none but we in the room   490
Might hear the voice that rose beneath,
   Nor the tread of the coming doom.

For now there came a torchlight-glare,
   And a clang of arms there came;   495
And not a soul in that space but thought
   Of the foe Sir Robert Græme.

Yea, from the country of the Wild Scots,
   O'er mountain, valley, and glen,
He had brought with him in murderous league
   Three hundred armèd men.   501

The king knew all in an instant's flash,
   And like a king did he stand;
But there was no armor in all the room,
   Nor weapon lay to his hand.   505

And all we women flew to the door
   And thought to have made it fast;
But the bolts were gone and the bars were gone
   And the locks were riven and brast.

And he caught the pale, pale queen in his arms
    As the iron footsteps fell,—   511
Then loosed her, standing alone, and said,
    'Our bliss was our farewell!'

And 'twixt his lips he murmured a prayer,
    And he crossed his brow and breast;   515
And proudly in royal hardihood
Even so with folded arms he stood,—
    The prize of the bloody quest.

Then on me leaped the queen like a deer:—
    'O Catherine, help!' she cried.   520
And low at his feet we clasped his knees
    Together side by side.
'Oh! even a king, for his people's sake,
    From treasonous death must hide!'

'For *her* sake most!' I cried, and I marked   525
    The pang that my words could wring.
And the iron tongs from the chimney-nook
    I snatched and held to the king:—
'Wrench up the plank! and the vault beneath
    Shall yield safe harboring.'   530

With brows low-bent, from my eager hand
    The heavy heft did he take;
And the plank at his feet he wrenched and tore;
And as he frowned through the open floor,
    Again I said, 'For her sake!'   535

Then he cried to the queen, 'God's will be done!'
    For her hands were clasped in prayer.
And down he sprang to the inner crypt;
And straight we closed the plank he had ripped,
    And toiled to smooth it fair.   540

(Alas! in that vault a gap once was
    Wherethro' the king might have fled:
But three days since close-walled had it been
By his will; for the ball would roll therein
    When without at the palm he played.)   545

Then the queen cried, 'Catherine, keep the door,
And I to this will suffice!'
At her word I rose all dazed to my feet,
    And my heart was fire and ice.

And louder ever the voices grew,   550
    And the tramp of men in mail;
Until to my brain it seemed to be
As though I tossed on a ship at sea
    In the teeth of a crashing gale.

Then back I flew to the rest; and hard   555
    We strove with sinews knit
To force the table against the door
    But we might not compass it.

Then my wild gaze sped far down the hall
    To the place of the hearthstone-sill;   560
And the queen bent ever above the floor,
    For the plank was rising still.

And now the rush was heard on the stair,
    And 'God, what help?' was our cry.
And was I frenzied or was I bold?   565
I looked at each empty stanchion-hold,
    And no bar but my arm had I!

Like iron felt my arm, as through
    The staple I made it pass:—
Alack! it was flesh and bone—no more!   570
'T was Catherine Douglas sprang to the door,
    But I fell back Kate Barlass.

With that they all thronged into the hall,
    Half dim to my failing ken;
And the space that was but a void before   575
    Was a crowd of wrathful men.

Behind the door I had fall'n and lay,
    Yet my sense was widely aware,
And for all the pain of my shattered arm
    I never fainted there.   580

Even as I fell, my eyes were cast
    Where the king leaped down to the pit;
And lo! the plank was smooth in its place,
    And the queen stood far from it.

And under the litters and through the bed   585
    And within the presses all
The traitors sought for the king, and pierced
    The arras around the wall.

And through the chamber they ramped and stormed
    Like lions loose in the lair,   590
And scarce could trust to their very eyes,—
    For behold! no king was there.

Then one of them seized the queen, and cried,—
    'Now tell us, where is thy lord?'
And he held the sharp point over her heart: 595
She drooped not her eyes nor did she start,
    But she answered never a word.

Then the sword half pierced the true, true breast:
    But it was the Græme's own son
Cried, 'This is a woman,—we seek a man!'   600
    And away from her girdle-zone
He struck the point of the murderous steel;
    And that foul deed was not done.

And forth flowed all the throng like a sea,
    And 't was empty space once more;   605
And my eyes sought out the wounded queen
    As I lay behind the door.

And I said: 'Dear Lady, leave me here.
    For I cannot help you now;
But fly while you may, and none shall reck   610
    Of my place here lying low.'

And she said, 'My Catherine, God help thee!'
    Then she looked to the distant floor,
And clasping her hands, 'O God help *him*,'
    She sobbed, 'for we can no more!'   615

But God he knows what help may mean,
    If it mean to live or to die;
And what sore sorrow and mighty moan
On earth it may cost ere yet a throne
    Be filled in his house on high.   620

And now the ladies fled with the queen;
    And through the open door
The night-wind wailed round the empty room
    And the rushes shook on the floor.

And the bed drooped low in the dark recess   625
    Whence the arras was rent away;
And the firelight still shone over the space
    Where our hidden secret lay.

And the rain had ceased, and the moonbeams lit
    The window high in the wall,—   630
Bright beams that on the plank that I knew
    Through the painted pane did fall
And gleamed with the splendor of Scotland's crown
    And shield armorial.

But then a great wind swept up the skies,   635
    And the climbing moon fell back;
And the royal blazon fled from the floor,
    And naught remained on its track;
And high in the darkened window-pane
    The shield and the crown were black.   640

And what I say next I partly saw
    And partly I heard in sooth,
And partly since from the murderers' lips
    The torture wrung the truth.

For now again came the armèd tread,   645
    And fast through the hall it fell;
But the throng was less: and ere I saw,
    By the voice without I could tell
That Robert Stuart had come with them
    Who knew that chamber well.   650

And over the space the Græme strode dark
    With his mantle round him flung;
And in his eye was a flaming light
    But not a word on his tongue.

And Stuart held a torch to the floor,   655
    And he found the thing he sought;
And they slashed the plank away with their swords;
    And O God! I fainted not!

And the traitor held his torch in the gap,
    All smoking and smoldering;   660
And through the vapor and fire, beneath
    In the dark crypt's narrow ring,
With a shout that pealed to the room's high roof
    They saw their naked king.

Half naked he stood, but stood as one   665
    Who yet could do and dare:
With the crown, the king was stript away,—
The knight was reft of his battle-array,—
    But still the man was there.

From the rout then stepped a villain forth,   670
    Sir John Hall was his name;
With a knife unsheathed he leapt to the vault
    Beneath the torchlight-flame.

Of his person and stature was the king
    A man right manly strong,   675
And mightily by the shoulder-blades
    His foe to his feet he flung.

Then the traitor's brother, Sir Thomas Hall,
    Sprang down to work his worst;
And the king caught the second man by the neck   680
    And flung him above the first.

And he smote and trampled them under him;
    And a long month thence they bare
All black their throats with the grip of his hands
    When the hangman's hand came there.   685

And sore he strove to have had their knives,
    But the sharp blades gashed his hands.
Oh! James so armed, thou hadst battled there
    Till help had come of thy bands;
And oh! once more thou hadst held our throne
    And ruled thy Scottish lands!   691

But while the king o'er his foes still raged
    With a heart that naught could tame,
Another man sprang down to the crypt;
And with his sword in his hand hard-gripped,
    There stood Sir Robert Græme.   696

(Now shame on the recreant traitor's heart
    Who durst not face his king,
Till the body unarmed was wearied out
    With two-fold combating!   700

Ah! well might the people sing and say,
    As oft ye have heard aright:—
*O Robert Græme, O Robert Græme,
Who slew our king, God give thee shame!*
    For he slew him not as a knight.)   705

And the naked king turned round at bay,
    But his strength had passed the goal,
And he could but gasp:—'Mine hour is come;
But oh! to succor thine own soul's doom,
    Let a priest now shrive my soul!'   710

And the traitor looked on the king's spent strength
    And said:—'Have I kept my word?—
Yea, King, the mortal pledge that I gave?
No black friar's shrift thy soul shall have,
    But the shrift of this red sword!'   715

With that he smote his king through the breast;
   And all they three in the pen
Fell on him and stabbed and stabbed him there
   Like merciless murderous men.

Yet seemed it now that Sir Robert Græme, 720
   Ere the king's last breath was o'er,
Turned sick at heart with the deadly sight
   And would have done no more.

But a cry came from the troop above:—
   'If him thou do not slay, 725
The price of his life that thou dost spare
   Thy forfeit life shall pay!'

O God! what more did I hear or see,
   Or how should I tell the rest,
But there at length our king lay slain 730
   With sixteen wounds in his breast.

O God! and now did a bell boom forth,
   And the murderers turned and fled;—
Too late, too late, O God, did it sound?—
   And I heard the true men mustering round, 735
   And the cries and the coming tread.

But ere they came, to the black death-gap
   Somewise did I creep and steal;
And lo! or ever I swooned away,
Through the dusk I saw where the white face lay
   In the pit of Fortune's wheel. 741

And now, ye Scottish maids who have heard
   Dread things of the days grown old,—
Even at the last, of true Queen Jane
   May somewhat yet be told. 745
And how she dealt for her dear lord's sake
   Dire vengeance manifold.

'T was in the Charterhouse of Perth,
   In the fair-lit Death-chapelle,
That the slain King's corpse on bier was laid 750
   With chaunt and requiem-knell.

And all with royal wealth of balm
   Was the body purified;
And none could trace on the brow and lips
   The death that he had died. 755

In his robes of state he lay asleep
   With orb and scepter in hand;
And by the crown he wore on his throne
   Was his kingly forehead spanned.

And, girls, 't was a sweet sad thing to see 760
   How the curling golden hair,
As in the day of the poet's youth,
   From the king's crown clustered there.

And if all had come to pass in the brain
   That throbbed beneath those curls, 765
Then Scots had said in the days to come
That this their soul was a different home
   And a different Scotland, girls!

And the queen sat by him night and day,
   And oft she knelt in prayer, 770
All wan and pale in the widow's veil
   That shrouded her shining hair.

And I had got good help of my hurt:
   And only to me some sign
She made; and save the priests that were there
   No face would she see but mine. 776

And the month of March wore on apace;
   And now fresh couriers fared
Still from the country of the Wild Scots
   With news of the traitors snared. 780

And still as I told her day by day,
   Her pallor changed to sight,
And the frost grew to a furnace-flame,
   That burnt her visage white.

And evermore as I brought her word, 785
   She bent to her dead King James,
And in the cold ear with fire-drawn breath,
   She spoke the traitors' names.

But when the name of Sir Robert Græme
   Was the one she had to give, 790
I ran to hold her up from the floor;
   For the froth was on her lips, and sore
   I feared that she could not live.

And the month of March wore nigh to its end,
   And still was the death-pall spread; 795
For she would not bury her slaughtered lord
   Till his slayers all were dead.

And now of their dooms dread tidings came,
   And of torments fierce and dire;
And naught she spake,—she had ceased to speak, 800
   But her eyes were a soul on fire.

But when I told her the bitter end
   Of the stern and just award,
She leaned o'er the bier, and thrice three times
   She kissed the lips of her lord. 805

And then she said,—'My King, they are dead!'
   And she knelt on the chapel-floor,
And whispered low with a strange proud smile,
   'James, James, they suffered more!'

Last she stood up to her queenly height. 810
   But she shook like an autumn leaf,
As though the fire wherein she burned
Then left the body, and all were turned
   To winter of life-long grief.

And 'O James!' she said,—'My James!' she said,— 815
   'Alas for the woeful thing,
That a poet true and a friend of man,
In desperate days of bale and ban,
   Should needs be born a King!'

(1881)

SONNETS from THE HOUSE OF LIFE

A Sonnet is a moment's monument,—
Memorial from the Soul's eternity,
To one dead deathless hour. Look that it be,
Whether for lustral rite or dire portent,

Of its own arduous fulness reverent: 5
Carve it in ivory or in ebony,
As Day or Night may rule; and let Time see
Its flowering crest impearled and orient.

A Sonnet is a coin: its face reveals
The soul,—its converse, to what Power 't is due:—
Whether for tribute to the august appeals 11
Of Life, or dower in Love's high retinue
It serve; or, 'mid the dark wharf's cavernous breath,
In Charon's palm it pay the toll to Death.

IV. LOVE-SIGHT

When do I see thee most, belovèd one?
When in the light the spirits of mine eyes
Before thy face, their altar, solemnize
The worship of that Love through thee made known?

Or when in the dusk hours, (we two alone,) 5
Close-kissed and eloquent of still replies,
Thy twilight-hidden glimmering visage lies,
And my soul only sees thy soul its own?

O love, my love! if I no more should see
Thyself, nor on the earth the shadow of thee, 10
Nor image of thine eyes in any spring,—
How then should sound upon Life's darkening slope,
The ground-whirl of the perished leaves of Hope
The wind of Death's imperishable wing?

XIX. SILENT NOON

Your hands lie open in the long fresh grass,—
The finger-points look through like rosy blooms:
Your eyes smile peace. The pasture gleams and glooms
'Neath billowing skies that scatter and amass.

All round our nest, far as the eye can pass, 5
Are golden kingcup-fields with silver edge
Where the cow-parsley skirts the hawthorn-hedge.
'T is visible silence, still as the hour-glass.

Deep in the sun-searched growths the dragon-fly,
Hangs like a blue thread loosened from the sky:— 10
So this winged hour is dropt to us from above.
Oh! clasp we to our hearts, for deathless dower,
This close-companioned inarticulate hour
When two-fold silence was the song of love.

XXI. LOVE-SWEETNESS

Sweet dimness of her loosened hair's downfall
About thy face; her sweet hands round thy head
In gracious fostering union garlanded;
Her tremulous smiles; her glances' sweet recall

Of love; her murmuring sighs memorial; 5
Her mouth's culled sweetness by thy kisses shed
On cheeks and neck and eyelids, and so led
Back to her mouth which answers there for all:—

What sweeter than these things, except the thing
In lacking which all these would lose their sweet:— 10
The confident heart's still fervor; the swift beat
And soft subsidence of the spirit's wing,
Then when it feels in cloud-girt wayfaring
The breath of kindred plumes against its feet?

XXVI. MID-RAPTURE

Thou lovely and belovèd, thou my love;
Whose kiss seems still the first; whose summoning eyes,
Even now, as for our love-world's new sunrise,
Shed very dawn; whose voice, attuned above

All modulation of the deep-bowered dove, 5
Is like a hand laid softly on the soul;
Whose hand is like a sweet voice to control
Those worn tired brows it hath the keeping of:—

What word can answer to thy word,—what gaze
To thine, which now absorbs within its sphere 10
My worshipping face, till I am mirrored there
Light-circled in a heaven of deep-drawn rays?
What clasp, what kiss mine inmost heart can prove,
O lovely and belovèd, O my love?

LV. STILLBORN LOVE

The hour which might have been yet might not be,
Which man's and woman's heart conceived and bore
Yet whereof life was barren,—on what shore
Bides it the breaking of Time's weary sea?

Bondchild of all consummate joys set free, 5
It somewhere sighs and serves, and mute before
The house of Love, hears through the echoing door
His hours elect in choral consonancy.

But lo! what wedded souls now hand in hand
Together tread at last the immortal strand 10
With eyes where burning memory lights love home?
Lo! how the little outcast hour has turned
And leaped to them and in their faces yearned:—
'I am your child: O **parents**, ye have come!'

LXIII. INCLUSIVENESS

The changing guests, each in a different mood,
Sit at the roadside table and arise:
And every life among them in likewise
Is a soul's board set daily with new food.

What man has bent o'er his son's sleep, to brood
How that face shall watch his when cold it
    lies?—   6
Or thought, as his own mother kissed his eyes,
Of what her kiss was when his father wooed?

May not this ancient room thou sitt'st in dwell
In separate living souls for joy or pain?   10
Nay, all its corners may be painted plain?
Where heaven shows pictures of some life spent
    well;
And may be stamped, a memory all in vain,
Upon the sight of lidless eyes in hell.

LXV. KNOWN IN VAIN

As two whose love, first foolish, widening scope,
Knows suddenly, to music high and soft,
The holy of holies; who because they scoffed
Are now amazed with shame, nor dare to cope

With the whole truth aloud, lest heaven should
    ope;   5
Yet, at their meetings, laugh not as they laughed
In speech; nor speak, at length; but sitting oft
Together, within hopeless sight of hope

For hours are silent:—So it happeneth
When Work and Will awake too late, to gaze   10
After their life sailed by, and hold their breath.
Ah! who shall dare to search through what sad
    maze
Thenceforth their incommunicable ways
Follow the desultory feet of Death?

LXXI. THE CHOICE. I

Eat thou and drink; to-morrow thou shalt
    die.
Surely the earth, that 's wise, being very old,
Needs not our help. Then loose me, love, and
    hold
Thy sultry hair up from my face; that I

May pour for thee this golden wine, brim-high,   5
Till round the glass thy fingers glow like gold.
We 'll drown all hours; thy song, while hours are
    tolled,
Shall leap, as fountains veil the changing sky.

Now kiss, and think that there are really those,
My own high-bosomed beauty, who increase   10
Vain gold, vain lore, and yet might choose our
    way!
Through many years they toil; then on a day
They die not,—for their life was death,—but
    cease;
And round their narrow lips the mold falls close.

LXXII. THE CHOICE. II

Watch thou and fear; to-morrow thou shalt die.
Or art thou sure thou shalt have time for death?
Is not the day which God's word promiseth
To come man knows not when? In yonder sky,

Now while we speak, the sun speeds forth: can I
Or thou assure him of his goal? God's breath   6
Even at this moment haply quickeneth
The air to a flame; till spirits, always nigh

Though screened and hid, shall walk the day-
    light here.
And dost thou prate of all that man shall do?   10
Canst thou, who hast but plagues, presume to be
Glad in his gladness that comes after thee?
Will *his* strength slay *thy* worm in hell? Go to:
Cover thy countenance, and watch, and fear.

LXXIII. THE CHOICE. III

Think thou and act; to-morrow thou shalt die.
Outstretched in the sun's warmth upon the
    shore,
Thou say'st: 'Man's measured path is all gone
    o'er;
Up all his years, steeply, with strain and sigh,

Man clomb until he touched the truth; and I,   5
Even I, am he whom it was destined for.'
How should this be? Art thou then so much more
Than they who sowed, that thou shouldst reap
    thereby?

Nay, come up hither. From this wave-washed
    mound
Unto the furthest flood-brim look with me;   10
Then reach on with thy thought till it be
    drowned.
Miles and miles distant though the last line be,
And though thy soul sail leagues and leagues
    beyond,—
Still, leagues beyond those leagues, there is more
    sea.

LXXXVI. LOST DAYS

The lost days of my life until to-day,
What were they, could I see them on the street
Lie as they fell? Would they be ears of wheat
Sown once for food but trodden into clay?

Or golden coins squandered and still to pay?   5
Or drops of blood dabbling the guilty feet?
Or such spilt water as in dreams must cheat
The undying throats of hell, athirst alway?

I do not see them here; but after death
God knows I know the faces I shall see,   10
Each one a murdered self, with low last breath.
'I am thyself,—what hast thou done to me?'
'And I—and I—thyself,' (lo! each one saith)
'And thou thyself to all eternity!'

XCVII. A SUPERSCRIPTION

Look in my face; my name is Might-have-been;
I am also called No-more, Too-late, Fare-well;
Unto thine ear I hold the dead-sea shell
Cast up thy Life's foam-fretted feet between;

Unto thine eyes the glass where that is seen 5
Which had Life's form and Love's, but by my spell
Is now a shaken shadow intolerable,
Of ultimate things unuttered the frail screen.

Mark me, how still I am! But should there dart
One moment through thy soul the soft surprise
Of that winged Peace which lulls the breath of sighs,— 11
Then shalt thou see me smile, and turn apart
Thy visage to mine ambush at thy heart,
Sleepless with cold commemorative eyes.

XCIX. NEWBORN DEATH. I

To-day Death seems to me an infant child
Which her worn mother Life upon my knee
Has set to grow my friend and play with me;
If haply so my heart might be beguil'd

To find no terrors in a face so mild,— 5
If haply so my weary heart might be
Unto the newborn milky eyes of thee,
O Death, before resentment reconcil'd.

How long, O Death? And shall thy feet depart
Still a young child's with mine, or wilt thou stand 10
Fullgrown the helpful daughter of my heart,
What time with thee indeed I reach the strand
Of the pale wave which knows thee what thou art,
And drink it in the hollow of thy hand?

C. NEWBORN DEATH. II

And thou, O Life, the lady of all bliss,
With whom, when our first heart beat full and fast
I wandered till the haunts of men were pass'd,
And in fair places found all bowers amiss

Till only woods and waves might hear our kiss, 5
While to the winds all thought of Death we cast:—
Ah, Life! and must I have from thee at last
No smile to greet me and no babe but this?

Lo! Love, the child once ours; and Song, whose hair
Blew like a flame and blossomed like a wreath;
And Art, whose eyes were worlds by God found fair; 11
These o'er the book of Nature mixed their breath
With neck-twined arms, as oft we watched them there:
And did these die that thou mightst bear me Death?

CI. THE ONE HOPE

When vain desire at last and vain regret
Go hand in hand to death, and all is vain,
What shall assuage the unforgotten pain
And teach the unforgetful to forget?

Shall Peace be still a sunk stream long unmet,—
Or may the soul at once in a green plain 6
Stoop through the spray of some sweet life-fountain
And cull the dew-drenched flowering amulet?

Ah! when the wan soul in that golden air
Between the scriptured petals softly blown 10
Peers breathless for the gift of grace unknown,—
Ah! let none other alien spell soe'er
But only the one Hope's one name be there,—
Not less nor more, but even that word alone.

(1869, 1870, 1881)

WILLIAM MORRIS (1834–1896)

After a youth of wide reading and varied schooling, Morris reached Exeter College, Oxford, in 1853, with broad information and strongly developed intellectual tendencies. Aside from a notable achievement in general reading, the most important result of his Oxford residence was a close friendship with Edward Burne-Jones, with whom he continued to live in the closest intimacy. A propensity toward Romanism, and then toward Anglicanism, resolved itself ultimately into an enthusiasm for art, for social reform, and for the utterances of Carlyle, Ruskin, and Kingsley. Travels in northern France, in 1854 and 1855, together with his permanent love for French Gothic art, led to his decision to become an architect. After he had studied architecture sincerely for a year or so, Rossetti persuaded him to take a studio and devote himself to painting. Morris found his true vocation, however, when, in 1861, with Rossetti, Burne-Jones, and others, he established a firm in London for designing and manufacturing artistic furniture and household decorations. The scope of the enterprise was eventually enlarged to include the manufacture of textiles, dyeing, book-illumination, and printing. In 1890, Morris founded the famous Kelmscott Press, at Hammersmith. In advancing the minor arts and in sustaining the principle that every object and utensil should be beautiful, Morris did more than any other man of his time. In 1885, he became an active socialist, lecturing freely to workingmen, and contributing to *The Commonweal*, the organ of the Socialistic League.

Except during certain periods of interruption, Morris wrote voluminously throughout his life. *The Defence of Guinevere* (1858), his earliest considerable publication, is among his best. From the Arthurian themes of this work, he turned with facility to the Greek, Old French, and Norse stories seen in *Life and Death of Jason* (1867), *The Earthly Paradise* (1868–70), and *Sigurd the Volsung and the Fall of the Niblungs* (1876). Aside from these original poetical writings, Morris's chief works are his romances,—in prose, or in prose and verse,—of which the most important are *A Tale of the House of the Wolfings* (1889), *The Roots of the Mountains* (1890), *The Story of the Glittering Plain* (1891) and *The Well at the World's End* (1896). Of his translations the most notable are the *Grettis Saga* (1869) and the *Völsunga Saga* (1870). Morris stands preëminent in the literature of the nineteenth century as a charming story-teller. In his stories we find neither humor nor a dramatic grasp of situations, but rather, dreamy narrative idealizations of an alluring past.

THE EARTHLY PARADISE

Of Heaven or Hell I have no power to sing,
  I cannot ease the burden of your fears,
Or make quick-coming death a little thing,
  Or bring again the pleasure of past years,
  Nor for my words shall ye forget your tears,
Or hope again for aught that I can say,   6
The idle singer of an empty day.

But rather, when aweary of your mirth,
  From full hearts still unsatisfied ye sigh,
And, feeling kindly unto all the earth,   10
  Grudge every minute as it passes by,
  Made the more mindful that the sweet days die,—
Remember me a little then, I pray,
The idle singer of an empty day.

The heavy trouble, the bewildering care   15
  That weighs us down who live and earn our bread,
These idle verses have no power to bear;
  So let me sing of names rememberèd,
  Because they, living not, can ne'er be dead,
Or long time take their memory quite away   20
From us poor singers of an empty day.

Dreamer of dreams, born out of my due time,
  Why should I strive to set the crooked straight?
Let it suffice me that my murmuring rime
  Beats with light wing against the ivory gate,
  Telling a tale not too importunate   26
To those who in the sleepy region stay,
Lulled by the singer of an empty day.

Folk say, a wizard to a northern king
  At Christmas-tide such wondrous things did show,   30
  That through one window men beheld the spring,

And through another saw the summer glow,
And through a third the fruited vines arow,
While still, unheard, but in its wonted way,
Piped the drear wind of that December day. 35

So with this Earthly Paradise it is,
If ye will read aright and pardon me,
Who strive to build a shadowy isle of bliss
  Midmost the beating of the steely sea,
Where tossed about all hearts of men must be; 40
Whose ravening monsters mighty men shall slay,
Not the poor singer of an empty day.

ATALANTA'S RACE

Atalanta, daughter of King Schœneus, not willing to lose her virgin's estate, made it a law to all suitors that they should run a race with her in the public place, and if they failed to overcome her should die unrevenged; and thus many brave men perished. At last came Milanion, the son of Amphidamas, who, outrunning her with the help of Venus, gained the virgin and wedded her.

I

Through thick Arcadian woods a hunter went,
Following the beasts up, on a fresh spring day;
But since his horn-tipped bow, but seldom bent,
Now at the noontide nought had happed to slay,
Within a vale he called his hounds away, 5
Hearkening the echoes of his lone voice cling
About the cliffs and through the beech-trees ring.

But when they ended, still awhile he stood,
And but the sweet familiar thrush could hear,
And all the day-long noises of the wood, 10
And o'er the dry leaves of the vanished year
His hounds' feet pattering as they drew anear,
And heavy breathing from their heads low hung,
To see the mighty cornel bow unstrung.

Then smiling did he turn to leave the place, 15
But with his first step some new fleeting thought
A shadow cast across his sunburnt face:
I think the golden net that April brought
From some warm world his wavering soul had caught;
For, sunk in vague sweet longing, did he go 20
Betwixt the trees with doubtful steps and slow.

Yet howsoever slow he went, at last
The trees grew sparser, and the wood was done;
Whereon one farewell, backward look he cast,
Then, turning round to see what place was won,
With shaded eyes looked underneath the sun, 26
And o'er green meads and new-turned furrows brown
Beheld the gleaming of King Schœneus' town.

So thitherward he turned, and on each side
The folk were busy on the teeming land, 30
And man and maid from the brown furrows cried,
Or midst the newly blossomed vines did stand,
And as the rustic weapon pressed the hand
Thought of the nodding of the well-filled ear,
Or how the knife the heavy bunch should shear.

Merry it was: about him sung the birds, 36
The spring flowers bloomed along the firm dry road,
The sleek-skinned mothers of the sharp-horned herds
Now for the barefoot milking-maidens lowed;
While from the freshness of his blue abode, 40
Glad his death-bearing arrows to forget,
The broad sun blazed, nor scattered plagues as yet.

Through such fair things unto the gates he came,
And found them open, as though peace were there;
Wherethrough, unquestioned of his race or name, 45
He entered, and along the streets 'gan fare,
Which at the first of folk were wellnigh bare;
But pressing on, and going more hastily,
Men hurrying too he 'gan at last to see.

Following the last of these, he still pressed on, 50
Until an open space he came unto,
Where wreaths of fame had oft been lost and won,
For feats of strength folk there were wont to do.
And now our hunter looked for something new,
Because the whole wide space was bare, and stilled 55
The high seats were, with eager people filled.

There with the others to a seat he gat,
Whence he beheld a broidered canopy,
'Neath which in fair array King Schœneus sat
Upon his throne with councilors thereby; 60
And underneath his well-wrought seat and high,
He saw a golden image of the sun,
A silver image of the fleet-foot one.

A brazen altar stood beneath their feet
Whereon a thin flame flickered in the wind; 65
Nigh this a herald clad in raiment meet
Made ready even now his horn to wind,
By whom a huge man held a sword, intwined
With yellow flowers; these stood a little space
From off the altar, nigh the starting-place. 70

And there two runners did the sign abide,
Foot set to foot,—a young man slim and fair,
Crisp-haired, well-knit, with firm limbs often tried

In places where no man his strength may spare;
Dainty his thin coat was, and on his hair 75
A golden circlet of renown he wore,
And in his hand an olive garland bore.

But on this day with whom shall he contend?
A maid stood by him like Diana clad
When in the woods she lists her bow to bend, 80
Too fair for one to look on and be glad,
Who scarcely yet has thirty summers had,
If he must still behold her from afar;
Too fair to let the world live free from war.

She seemed all earthly matters to forget; 85
Of all tormenting lines her face was clear,
Her wide gray eyes upon the goal were set
Calm and unmoved as though no soul were near.
But her foe trembled as a man in fear,
Nor from her loveliness one moment turned 90
His anxious face with fierce desire that burned.

Now through the hush there broke the trumpet's clang
Just as the setting sun made eventide.
Then from light feet a spurt of dust there sprang,
And swiftly were they running side by side; 95
But silent did the thronging folk abide
Until the turning-post was reached at last,
And round about it still abreast they passed.

But when the people saw how close they ran,
When half-way to the starting-point they were, 100
A cry of joy broke forth, whereat the man 101
Headed the white-foot runner, and drew near
Unto the very end of all his fear;
And scarce his straining feet the ground could feel,
And bliss unhoped-for o'er his heart 'gan steal.

But midst the loud victorious shouts he heard
Her footsteps drawing nearer, and the sound 107
Of fluttering raiment, and thereat afeard
His flushed and eager face he turned around,
And even then he felt her past him bound 110
Fleet as the wind, but scarcely saw her there
Till on the goal she laid her fingers fair.

There stood she breathing like a little child
Amid some warlike clamor laid asleep,
For no victorious joy her red lips smiled, 115
Her cheek its wonted freshness did but keep;
No glance lit up her clear gray eyes and deep,
Though some divine thought softened all her face
As once more rang the trumpet through the place.

But her late foe stopped short amidst his course,
One moment gazed upon her piteously, 121
Then with a groan his lingering feet did force
To leave the spot whence he her eyes could see;
And, changed like one who knows his time must be
But short and bitter, without any word 125
He knelt before the bearer of the sword;

Then high rose up the gleaming deadly blade,
Bared of its flowers, and through the crowded place
Was silence now, and midst of it the maid
Went by the poor wretch at a gentle pace, 130
And he to hers upturned his sad white face;
Nor did his eyes behold another sight
Ere on his soul there fell eternal night.

II

So was the pageant ended, and all folk
Talking of this and that familiar thing
In little groups from that sad concourse broke;
For now the shrill bats were upon the wing,
And soon dark night would slay the evening, 5
And in dark gardens sang the nightingale
Her little-heeded, oft-repeated tale.

And with the last of all the hunter went,
Who, wondering at the strange sight he had seen,
Prayed an old man to tell him what it meant, 10
Both why the vanquished man so slain had been,
And if the maiden were an earthly queen,
Or rather what much more she seemed to be,
No sharer in the world's mortality.

'Stranger,' said he, 'I pray she soon may die 15
Whose lovely youth has slain so many an one!
King Schœneus' daughter is she verily,
Who when her eyes first looked upon the sun
Was fain to end her life but new begun,
For he had vowed to leave but men alone 20
Sprung from his loins when he from earth was gone.

'Therefore he bade one leave her in the wood,
And let wild things deal with her as they might;
But this being done, some cruel god thought good
To save her beauty in the world's despite: 25
Folk say that her, so delicate and white
As now she is, a rough root-grubbing bear
Amidst her shapeless cubs at first did rear.

'In course of time the woodfolk slew her nurse,
And to their rude abode the youngling brought,
And reared her up to be a kingdom's curse, 31
Who, grown a woman, of no kingdom thought,
But armed and swift, mid beasts destruction wrought,
Nor spared two shaggy centaur kings to slay,
To whom her body seemed an easy prey. 35

'So to this city, led by fate, she came,
Whom, known by signs, whereof I cannot tell,
King Schœneus for his child at last did claim;
Nor otherwhere since that day doth she dwell,
Sending too many a noble soul to hell.— 40
What! thine eyes glisten? what then! thinkest thou
Her shining head unto the yoke to bow?

'Listen, my son, and love some other maid,
For she the saffron gown will never wear,
And on no flower-strewn couch shall she be laid,
Nor shall her voice make glad a lover's ear; 46
Yet if of Death thou hast not any fear,
Yea, rather, if thou lovest him utterly,
Thou still may'st woo her ere thou comest to die,

'Like him that on this day thou sawest lie dead;
For, fearing as I deem the sea-born one, 51
The maid has vowed e'en such a man to wed
As in the course her swift feet can outrun,
But whoso fails herein, his days are done:
He came the nighest that was slain to-day, 55
Although with him I deem she did but play.

'Behold, such mercy Atalanta gives
To those that long to win her loveliness;
Be wise! be sure that many a maid there lives
Gentler than she, of beauty little less, 60
Whose swimming eyes thy loving words shall bless,
When in some garden, knee set close to knee,
Thou sing'st the song that love may teach to thee.'

So to the hunter spake that ancient man,
And left him for his own home presently; 65
But he turned round, and through the moonlight wan
Reached the thick wood, and there 'twixt tree and tree
Distraught he passed the long night feverishly,
'Twixt sleep and waking, and at dawn arose
To wage hot war against his speechless foes. 70

There to the hart's flank seemed his shaft to grow,
As panting down the broad green glades he flew,
There by his horn the Dryads well might know
His thrust against the bear's heart had been true,
And there Adonis' bane his javelin slew; 75
But still in vain through rough and smooth he went,
For none the more his restlessness was spent.

So wandering, he to Argive cities came,
And in the lists with valiant men he stood,
And by great deeds he won him praise and fame,
And heaps of wealth for little-valued blood; 81
But none of all these things, or life, seemed good
Unto his heart, where still unsatisfied
A ravenous longing warred with fear and pride.

Therefore it happed when but a month had gone
Since he had left King Schœneus' city old, 86
In hunting-gear again, again alone
The forest-bordered meads did he behold,
Where still mid thoughts of August's quivering gold
Folk hoed the wheat, and clipped the vine in trust 90
Of faint October's purple-foaming must.

And once again he passed the peaceful gate,
While to his beating heart his lips did lie,
That, owning not victorious love and fate,
Said, half aloud, 'And here too must I try 95
To win of alien men the mastery,
And gather for my head fresh meed of fame,
And cast new glory on my father's name.'

In spite of that, how beat his heart when first
Folk said to him, 'And art thou come to see 100
That which still makes our city's name accurst
Among all mothers for its cruelty?
Then know indeed that fate is good to thee,
Because to-morrow a new luckless one
Against the white-foot maid is pledged to run.'

So on the morrow with no curious eyes, 106
As once he did, that piteous sight he saw,
Nor did that wonder in his heart arise
As toward the goal the conquering maid 'gan draw,
Nor did he gaze upon her eyes with awe,— 110
Too full the pain of longing filled his heart
For fear or wonder there to have a part.

But O, how long the night was ere it went!
How long it was before the dawn begun 114
Showed to the wakening birds the sun's intent
That not in darkness should the world be done!
And then, and then, how long before the sun
Bade silently the toilers of the earth
Get forth to fruitless cares or empty mirth!

And long it seemed that in the market-place 120
He stood and saw the chaffering folk go by,
Ere from the ivory throne King Schœneus' face
Looked down upon the murmur royally;
But then came trembling that the time was nigh
When he midst pitying looks his love must claim, 125
And jeering voices must salute his name.

But as the throng he pierced to gain the throne,
His alien face distraught and anxious told
What hopeless errand he was bound upon,
And, each to each, folk whispered to behold 130
His godlike limbs; nay, and one woman old,
As he went by, must pluck him by the sleeve
And pray him yet that wretched love to leave.

For sidling up she said, 'Canst thou live twice,
Fair son? Canst thou have joyful youth again,
That thus thou goest to the sacrifice, 136

Thyself the victim? Nay, then, all in vain
Thy mother bore her longing and her pain,
And one more maiden on the earth must dwell
Hopeless of joy, nor fearing death and hell.   140

'O fool, thou knowest not the compact then
That with the three-formed goddess she has made
To keep her from the loving lips of men,
And in no saffron gown to be arrayed,
And therewithal with glory to be paid,   145
And love of her the moonlit river sees
White 'gainst the shadow of the formless trees.

'Come back, and I myself will pray for thee
Unto the sea-born framer of delights,
To give thee her who on the earth may be   150
The fairest stirrer-up to death and fights,
To quench with hopeful days and joyous nights
The flame that doth thy youthful heart consume:
Come back, nor give thy beauty to the tomb.'

How should he listen to her earnest speech,—155
Words such as he not once or twice had said
Unto himself, whose meaning scarce could reach
The firm abode of that sad hardihead?
He turned about, and through the market-stead
Swiftly he passed, until before the throne   160
In the cleared space he stood at last alone.

Then said the king, 'Stranger, what dost thou here?
Have any of my folk done ill to thee?
Or art thou of the forest men in fear?
Or art thou of the sad fraternity   165
Who still will strive my daughter's mates to be,
Staking their lives to win to earthly bliss
The lonely maid, the friend of Artemis?'

'O King,' he said, 'thou sayest the word indeed;
Nor will I quit the strife till I have won   170
My sweet delight, or death to end my need.
And know that I am called Milanion,
Of King Amphidamas the well-loved son;
So fear not that to thy old name, O King,
Much loss or shame my victory will bring.'   175

'Nay, Prince,' said Schœneus, 'welcome to this land
Thou wert indeed, if thou wert here to try
Thy strength 'gainst some one mighty of his hand;
Nor would we grudge thee well-won mastery.
But now, why wilt thou come to me to die,   180
And at my door lay down thy luckless head,
Swelling the band of the unhappy dead,

'Whose curses even now my heart doth fear?
Lo, I am old, and know what life can be,
And what a bitter thing is death anear.   185
O son! be wise, and hearken unto me;
And if no other can be dear to thee,
At least as now, yet is the world full wide
And bliss in seeming hopeless hearts may hide:

'But if thou losest life, then all is lost.'   190
'Nay, King,' Milanion said, 'thy words are vain.
Doubt not that I have counted well the cost.
But say, on what day wilt thou that I gain
Fulfilled delight, or death to end my pain?
Right glad were I if it could be to-day,   195
And all my doubts at rest forever lay.'

'Nay,' said King Schœneus, 'thus it shall not be,
But rather shalt thou let a month go by,
And weary with thy prayers for victory
What god thou know'st the kindest and most nigh.   200
So doing, still perchance thou shalt not die;
And with my good-will wouldst thou have the maid,
For of the equal gods I grow afraid.

'And until then, O Prince, be thou my guest,
And all these troublous things awhile forget.'   205
'Nay,' said he, 'couldst thou give my soul good rest,
And on mine head a sleepy garland set,
Then had I 'scaped the meshes of the net,
Nor shouldst thou hear from me another word;
But now, make sharp thy fearful heading sword.   210

'Yet will I do what son of man may do,
And promise all the gods may most desire,
That to myself I may at least be true;
And on that day my heart and limbs so tire,
With utmost strain and measureless desire,   215
That, at the worst, I may but fall asleep
When in the sunlight round that sword shall sweep.'

He went with that, nor anywhere would bide,
But unto Argos restlessly did wend;
And there, as one who lays all hope aside,   220
Because the leech has said his life must end,
Silent farewell he bade to foe and friend,
And took his way unto the restless sea,
For there he deemed his rest and help might be.

III

Upon the shore of Argolis there stands
A temple to the goddess that he sought,
That, turned unto the lion-bearing lands,
Fenced from the east, of cold winds hath no thought,
Though to no homestead there the sheaves are brought,
No groaning press torments the close-clipped murk,
Lonely the fane stands, far from all men's work.

Pass through a close, set thick with myrtle-trees,
Through the brass doors that guard the holy place,
And, entering, hear the washing of the seas 10
That twice a day rise high above the base,
And, with the southwest urging them, embrace
The marble feet of her that standeth there,
That shrink not, naked though they be and fair.

Small is the fane through which the sea-wind sings 15
About Queen Venus' well-wrought image white;
But hung around are many precious things,
The gifts of those who, longing for delight,
Have hung them there within the goddess' sight,
And in return have taken at her hands 20
The living treasures of the Grecian lands.

And thither now has come Milanion,
And showed unto the priests' wide-open eyes
Gifts fairer than all those that there have shown,—
Silk cloth, inwrought with Indian fantasies, 25
And bowls inscribed with sayings of the wise
Above the deeds of foolish living things,
And mirrors fit to be the gifts of kings.

And now before the sea-born one he stands, 29
By the sweet veiling smoke made dim and soft;
And while the incense trickles from his hands,
And while the odorous smoke-wreaths hang aloft,
Thus doth he pray to her: 'O thou who oft
Hast holpen man and maid in their distress,
Despise me not for this my wretchedness! 35

'O goddess, among us who dwell below,
Kings and great men, great for a little while,
Have pity on the lowly heads that bow,
Nor hate the hearts that love them without guile;
Wilt thou be worse than these, and is thy smile
A vain device of him who set thee here, 41
An empty dream of some artificer?

'O great one, some men love, and are ashamed;
Some men are weary of the bonds of love;
Yea, and by some men lightly art thou blamed,
That from thy toils their lives they cannot move, 46
And 'mid the ranks of men their manhood prove.
Alas! O goddess, if thou slayest me
What new immortal can I serve but thee?

'Think then, will it bring honor to thy head 50
If folk say, "Everything aside he cast,
And to all fame and honor was he dead,
And to his one hope now is dead at last,
Since all unholpen he is gone and past:
Ah! the gods love not man, for certainly 55
He to his helper did not cease to cry."

'Nay, but thou wilt help: they who died before
Not single-hearted, as I deem, came here;
Therefore unthanked they laid their gifts before
Thy stainless feet, still shivering with their fear, 60
Lest in their eyes their true thought might appear,
Who sought to be the lords of that fair town,
Dreaded of men and winners of renown.

'O Queen, thou knowest I pray not for this:
O, set us down together in some place 65
Where not a voice can break our heaven of bliss,
Where naught but rocks and I can see her face,
Softening beneath the marvel of thy grace,
Where not a foot our vanished steps can track,—
The golden age, the golden age come back! 70

'O fairest, hear me now, who do thy will,
Plead for thy rebel that she be not slain,
But live and love and be thy servant still:
Ah! give her joy and take away my pain,
And thus two long-enduring servants gain. 75
An easy thing this is to do for me,
What need of my vain words to weary thee?

'But none the less this place will I not leave
Until I needs must go my death to meet,
Or at thy hands some happy sign receive 80
That in great joy we twain may one day greet
Thy presence here and kiss thy silver feet,
Such as we deem thee, fair beyond all words,
Victorious o'er our servants and our lords.'

Then from the altar back a space he drew, 85
But from the queen turned not his face away,
But 'gainst a pillar leaned, until the blue
That arched the sky, at ending of the day,
Was turned to ruddy gold and changing gray,
And clear, but low, the nigh-ebbed windless sea 90
In the still evening murmured ceaselessly.

And there he stood when all the sun was down;
Nor had he moved when the dim golden light,
Like the far luster of a godlike town,
Had left the world to seeming hopeless night; 95
Nor would he move the more when wan moonlight
Streamed through the pillars for a little while,
And lighted up the white queen's changeless smile.

Nought noted he the shallow flowing sea,
As step by step it set the wrack a-swim; 100
The yellow torchlight nothing noted he
Wherein with fluttering gown and half-bared limb
The temple damsels sung their midnight hymn;
And nought the doubled stillness of the fane
When they were gone and all was hushed again.

But when the waves had touched the marble
    base,   106
And steps the fish swim over twice a day,
The dawn beheld him sunken in his place
Upon the floor; and sleeping there he lay,
Not heeding aught the little jets of spray   110
The roughened sea brought nigh, across him cast,
For as one dead all thought from him had passed.

Yet long before the sun had showed his head,
Long ere the varied hangings on the wall
Had gained once more their blue and green and
    red,   115
He rose as one some well-known sign doth call
When war upon the city's gates doth fall,
And scarce like one fresh risen out of sleep,
He 'gan again his broken watch to keep.   119

Then he turned round; not for the sea-gull's cry
That wheeled above the temple in his flight,
Not for the fresh south-wind that lovingly
Breathed on the new-born day and dying night,
But some strange hope 'twixt fear and great
    delight
Drew round his face, now flushed, now pale and
    wan,   125
And still constrained his eyes the sea to scan.

Now a faint light lit up the southern sky,—
Not sun or moon, for all the world was gray,
But this a bright cloud seemed, that drew anigh,
Lighting the dull waves that beneath it lay   130
As toward the temple still it took its way,
And still grew greater, till Milanion
Saw nought for dazzling light that round him
    shone.

But as he staggered with his arms outspread,
Delicious unnamed odors breathed around;   135
For languid happiness he bowed his head,
And with wet eyes sank down upon the ground,
Nor wished for aught, nor any dream he found
To give him reason for that happiness,
Or make him ask more knowledge of his bliss.   140

At last his eyes were cleared, and he could see
Through happy tears the goddess face to face
With that faint image of divinity,
Whose well-wrought smile and dainty change-
    less grace
Until that morn so gladdened all the place;   145
Then he unwitting cried aloud her name,
And covered up his eyes for fear and shame.

But through the stillness he her voice could hear
Piercing his heart with joy scarce bearable,
That said, 'Milanion, wherefore dost thou fear?
I am not hard to those who love me well;   151
List to what I a second time will tell,
And thou mayest hear perchance, and live to
    save
The cruel maiden from a loveless grave.

'See, by my feet three golden apples lie,—   155
Such fruit among the heavy roses falls,
Such fruit my watchful damsels carefully
Store up within the best loved of my walls,
Ancient Damascus, where the lover calls
Above my unseen head, and faint and light   160
The rose-leaves flutter round me in the night.

'And note that these are not alone most fair
With heavenly gold, but longing strange they
    bring
Unto the hearts of men, who will not care,
Beholding these, for any once-loved thing   165
Till round the shining sides their fingers cling.
And thou shalt see thy well-girt swiftfoot maid
By sight of these amid her glory stayed.

'For bearing these within a scrip with thee,
When first she heads thee from the starting-
    place   170
Cast down the first one for her eyes to see,
And when she turns aside make on apace,
And if again she heads thee in the race
Spare not the other two to cast aside
If she not long enough behind will bide.   175

'Farewell, and when has come the happy time
That she Diana's raiment must unbind,
And all the world seems blessed with Saturn's
    clime,
And thou with eager arms about her twined
Beholdest first her gray eyes growing kind,   180
Surely, O trembler, thou shalt scarcely then
Forget the helper of unhappy men.'

Milanion raised his head at this last word,
For now so soft and kind she seemed to be
No longer of her godhead was he feared;   185
Too late he looked, for nothing could he see
But the white image glimmering doubtfully
In the departing twilight cold and gray,
And those three apples on the steps that lay.

These then he caught up, quivering with de-
    light,   190
Yet fearful lest it all might be a dream,
And though aweary with the watchful night,
And sleepless nights of longing, still did deem
He could not sleep; but yet the first sunbeam
That smote the fane across the heaving deep   195
Shone on him laid in calm untroubled sleep.

But little ere the noontide did he rise,
And why he felt so happy scarce could tell
Until the gleaming apples met his eyes.
Then, leaving the fair place where this befell,   200
Oft he looked back as one who loved it well,
Then homeward to the haunts of men 'gan wend
To bring all things unto a happy end.

IV

Now has the lingering month at last gone by,
Again are all folk around the running-place.

Nor other seems the dismal pageantry
Than heretofore, but that another face
Looks o'er the smooth course ready for the race,
For now, beheld of all, Milanion
Stands on the spot he twice has looked upon.

But yet—what change is this that holds the maid?
Does she indeed see in his glittering eye
More than disdain of the sharp shearing blade,
Some happy hope of help and victory? 11
The others seemed to say, 'We come to die;
Look down upon us for a little while,
That, dead, we may bethink us of thy smile.'

But he—what look of mastery was this 15
He cast on her? Why were his lips so red?
Why was his face so flushed with happiness?
So looks not one who deems himself but dead,
E'en if to death he bows a willing head;
So rather looks a god well pleased to find 20
Some earthly damsel fashioned to his mind.

Why must she drop her lids before his gaze,
And even as she casts adown her eyes
Redden to note his eager glance of praise,
And wish that she were clad in other guise? 25
Why must the memory to her heart arise
Of things unnoticed when they first were heard,
Some lover's song, some answering maiden's word?

What makes these longings, vague, without a name,
And this vain pity never felt before, 30
This sudden languor, this contempt of fame,
This tender sorrow for the time past o'er,
These doubts that grow each minute more and more?
Why does she tremble as the time grows near,
And weak defeat and woful victory fear? 35

But while she seemed to hear her beating heart,
Above their heads the trumpet blast rang out,
And forth they sprang; and she must play her part.
Then flew her white feet, knowing not a doubt,
Though, slackening once, she turned her head about, 40
But then she cried aloud and faster fled
Than e'er before, and all men deemed him dead.

But with no sound he raised aloft his hand,
And thence what seemed a ray of light there flew
And past the maid rolled on along the sand; 45
Then trembling she her feet together drew,
And in her heart a strong desire there grew
To have the toy: some god she thought had given
That gift to her, to make of earth a heaven.

Then from the course with eager steps she ran,
And in her odorous bosom laid the gold. 51
But when she turned again, the great-limbed man
Now well ahead she failed not to behold,
And, mindful of her glory waxing cold,
Sprang up and followed him in hot pursuit, 55
Though with one hand she touched the golden fruit.

Note, too, the bow that she was wont to bear
She laid aside to grasp the glittering prize,
And o'er her shoulder from the quiver fair
Three arrows fell and lay before her eyes 60
Unnoticed, as amidst the people's cries
She sprang to head the strong Milanion,
Who now the turning-post had wellnigh won.

But as he set his mighty hand on it,
White fingers underneath his own were laid, 65
And white limbs from his dazzled eyes did flit;
Then he the second fruit cast by the maid,
But she ran on awhile, then as afraid
Wavered and stopped, and turned and made no stay
Until the globe with its bright fellow lay. 70

Then, as a troubled glance she cast around,
Now far ahead the Argive could she see,
And in her garment's hem one hand she wound
To keep the double prize, and strenuously
Sped o'er the course, and little doubt had she 75
To win the day, though now but scanty space
Was left betwixt him and the winning-place.

Short was the way unto such wingèd feet;
Quickly she gained upon him, till at last
He turned about her eager eyes to meet, 80
And from his hand the third fair apple cast.
She wavered not, but turned and ran so fast
After the prize that should her bliss fulfil,
That in her hand it lay ere it was still.

Nor did she rest, but turned about to win 85
Once more an unblest woful victory—
And yet—and yet—why does her breath begin
To fail her, and her feet drag heavily?
Why fails she now to see if far or nigh 89
The goal is? Why do her gray eyes grow dim?
Why do these tremors run through every limb?

She spreads her arms abroad some stay to find,
Else must she fall, indeed, and findeth this,
A strong man's arms about her body twined.
Nor may she shudder now to feel his kiss, 95
So wrapped she is in new unbroken bliss;
Made happy that the foe the prize hath won,
She weeps glad tears for all her glory done.

v

SHATTER the trumpet, hew adown the posts!
Upon the brazen altar break the sword,
And scatter incense to appease the ghosts

Of those who died here by their own award.
Bring forth the image of the mighty lord, 5
And her who unseen o'er the runners hung,
And did a deed forever to be sung.

Here are the gathered folk; make no delay,
Open King Schœneus' well-filled treasury,
Bring out the gifts long hid from light of day,—
The golden bowls o'erwrought with imagery, 11
Gold chains, and unguents brought from over sea,
The saffron gown the old Phœnician brought,
Within the temple of the goddess wrought.

O ye, O damsels, who shall never see 15
Her, that Love's servant bringeth now to you,
Returning from another victory,
In some cool bower do all that now is due!
Since she in token of her service new
Shall give to Venus offerings rich enow,— 20
Her maiden zone, her arrows, and her bow.

THE LADY OF THE LAND

A certain man having landed on an island in the Greek Sea, found there a beautiful damsel, whom he would fain have delivered from a strange and dreadful doom, but failing therein, he died soon afterwards.

It happened once, some men of Italy
Midst the Greek Islands went a sea-roving
And much good fortune had they on the sea:
Of many a man they had the ransoming,
And many a chain they gat, and goodly thing; 5
And midst their voyage to an isle they came,
Whereof my story keepeth not the name.

Now though but little was there left to gain,
Because the richer folk had gone away,
Yet since by this of water they were fain 10
They came to anchor in a land-locked bay,
Whence in a while some went ashore to play,
Going but lightly armed in twos or threes,
For midst that folk they feared no enemies.

And of these fellows that thus went ashore, 15
One was there who left all his friends behind;
Who going inland ever more and more,
And being left quite alone, at last did find
A lonely valley sheltered from the wind,
Wherein, amidst an ancient cypress wood, 20
A long-deserted ruined castle stood.

The wood, once ordered in fair grove and glade,
With gardens overlooked by terraces,
And marble-pavèd pools for pleasure made,
Was tangled now, and choked with fallen trees;
And he who went there, with but little ease 26
Must stumble by the stream's side, once made meet
For tender women's dainty wandering feet.

The raven's croak, the low wind choked and drear,
The baffled stream, the gray wolf's doleful cry, 30
Were all the sounds that mariner could hear,
As through the wood he wandered painfully;
But as unto the house he drew anigh,
The pillars of a ruined shrine he saw,
The once fair temple of a fallen law. 35

No image was there left behind to tell
Before whose face the knees of men had bowed;
An altar of black stone, of old wrought well,
Alone beneath a ruined roof now showed
The goal whereto the folk were wont to crowd, 40
Seeking for things forgotten long ago,
Praying for heads long ages laid a-low.

Close to the temple was the castle-gate,
Doorless and crumbling; there our fellow turned,
Trembling indeed at what might chance to wait
The prey entrapped, yet with a heart that burned 46
To know the most of what might there be learned,
And hoping somewhat too, amid his fear,
To light on such things as all men hold dear.

Noble the house was, nor seemed built for war,
But rather like the work of other days, 51
When men, in better peace than now they are,
Had leisure on the world around to gaze,
And noted well the past times' changing ways;
And fair with sculptured stories it was wrought,
By lapse of time unto dim ruin brought. 56

Now as he looked about on all these things,
And strove to read the moldering histories,
Above the door an image with wide wings,
Whose unclad limbs a serpent seemed to seize, 60
He dimly saw, although the western breeze,
And years of biting frost and washing rain,
Had made the carver's labor well-nigh vain.

But this, though perished sore, and worn away,
He noted well, because it seemed to be, 65
After the fashion of another day,
Some great man's badge of war, or armory;
And round it a carved wreath he seemed to see:
But taking note of these things, at the last
The mariner beneath the gateway passed. 70

And there a lovely cloistered court he found;
A fountain in the midst o'erthrown and dry,
And in the cloister briers twining round
The slender shafts; the wondrous imagery
Outworn by more than many years gone by;
Because the country people, in their fear 76
Of wizardry, had wrought destruction here;

And piteously these fair things had been maimed;
There stood great Jove, lacking his head of might;

Here was the archer, swift Apollo, lamed; 80
The shapely limbs of Venus hid from sight
By weeds and shards; Diana's ankles light
Bound with the cable of some coasting ship;
And rusty nails through Helen's maddening lip.

Therefrom unto the chambers did he pass, 85
And found them fair still, midst of their decay,
Though in them now no sign of man there was,
And everything but stone had passed away
That made them lovely in that vanished day;
Nay, the mere walls themselves would soon be gone 90
And nought be left but heaps of moldering stone.

But he, when all the place he had gone o'er,
And with much trouble clomb the broken stair,
And from the topmost turret seen the shore
And his good ship drawn up at anchor there, 95
Came down again, and found a crypt most fair
Built wonderfully beneath the greatest hall,
And there he saw a door within the wall,

Well-hinged, close shut; nor was there in that place
Another on its hinges, therefore he 100
Stood there and pondered for a little space,
And thought, 'Perchance some marvel I shall see,
For surely here some dweller there must be,
Because this door seems whole, and new, and sound,
While nought but ruin I can see around.' 105

So with that word, moved by a strong desire,
He tried the hasp, that yielded to his hand,
And in a strange place, lit as by a fire
Unseen but near, he presently did stand;
And by an odorous breeze his face was fanned,
As though in some Arabian plain he stood, 111
Anigh the border of a spice-tree wood.

He moved not for awhile, but looking round,
He wondered much to see the place so fair,
Because, unlike the castle above ground, 115
No pillager or wrecker had been there;
It seemed that time had passed on otherwhere,
Nor laid a finger on this hidden place,
Rich with the wealth of some forgotten race.

With hangings, fresh as when they left the loom, 120
The walls were hung a space above the head,
Slim ivory chairs were set about the room,
And in one corner was a dainty bed,
That seemed for some fair queen apparelèd;
And marble was the worst stone of the floor, 125
That with rich Indian webs was covered o'er.

The wanderer trembled when he saw all this,
Because he deemed by magic it was wrought;
Yet in his heart a longing for some bliss,

Whereof the hard and changing world knows nought, 130
Arose and urged him on, and dimmed the thought
That there perchance some devil lurked to slay
The heedless wanderer from the light of day.

Over against him was another door
Set in the wall; so, casting fear aside, 135
With hurried steps he crossed the varied floor,
And there again the silver latch he tried
And with no pain the door he opened wide,
And entering the new chamber cautiously
The glory of great heaps of gold could see. 140

Upon the floor uncounted medals lay,
Like things of little value; here and there
Stood golden caldrons, that might well outweigh
The biggest midst an emperor's copper-ware,
And golden cups were set on tables fair, 145
Themselves of gold; and in all hollow things
Were stored great gems, worthy the crowns of kings.

The walls and roof with gold were overlaid
And precious raiment from the wall hung down;
The fall of kings that treasure might have stayed, 150
Or gained some longing conqueror great renown,
Or built again some god-destroyed old town;
What wonder, if this plunderer of the sea
Stood gazing at it long and dizzily?

But at the last his troubled eyes and dazed 155
He lifted from the glory of that gold,
And then the image, that well-nigh erased
Over the castle-gate he did behold,
Above a door well wrought in colored gold
Again he saw; a naked girl with wings 160
Enfolded in a serpent's scaly rings.

And even as his eyes were fixed on it
A woman's voice came from the other side,
And through his heart strange hopes began to flit
That in some wondrous land he might abide 165
Not dying, master of a deathless bride,
So o'er the gold he scarcely now could see
He went, and passed this last door eagerly.

Then in a room he stood wherein there was
A marble bath, whose brimming water yet 170
Was scarcely still; a vessel of green glass
Half full of odorous ointment was there set
Upon the topmost step that still was wet,
And jeweled shoes and women's dainty gear,
Lay cast upon the varied pavement near. 175

In one quick glance these things his eyes did see,
But speedily they turned round to behold
Another sight, for throned on ivory

There sat a girl, whose dripping tresses rolled
On to the floor in waves of gleaming gold,   180
Cast back from such a form as, erewhile shown
To one poor shepherd, lighted up Troy town.

Naked she was, the kisses of her feet
Upon the floor a dying path had made
From the full bath unto her ivory seat;   185
In her right hand, upon her bosom laid,
She held a golden comb, a mirror weighed
Her left hand down, aback her fair head lay
Dreaming awake of some long vanished day.

Her eyes were shut, but she seemed not to sleep,
Her lips were murmuring things unheard and
   low,   191
Or sometimes twitched as though she needs
   must weep
Though from her eyes the tears refused to flow,
And oft with heavenly red her cheek did glow,
As if remembrance of some half-sweet shame 195
Across the web of many memories came.

There stood the man, scarce daring to draw
   breath
For fear the lovely sight should fade away;
Forgetting heaven, forgetting life and death,
Trembling for fear lest something he should say
Unwitting, lest some sob should yet betray   201
His presence there, for to his eager eyes
Already did the tears begin to rise.

But as he gazed, she moved, and with a sigh
Bent forward, dropping down her golden head;
'Alas, alas! another day gone by,   206
Another day and no soul come,' she said;
'Another year, and still I am not dead!'
And with that word once more her head she
   raised,
And on the trembling man with great eyes
   gazed.   210

Then he imploring hands to her did reach,
And toward her very slowly 'gan to move
And with wet eyes her pity did beseech,
And seeing her about to speak, he strove
From trembling lips to utter words of love;
But with a look she stayed his doubtful feet,   216
And made sweet music as their eyes did meet.

For now she spoke in gentle voice and clear,
Using the Greek tongue that he knew full well;
'What man art thou, that thus hast wandered
   here,   220
And found this lonely chamber where I dwell?
Beware, beware! for I have many a spell;
If greed of power and gold have led thee on,
Not lightly shall this untold wealth be won.

'But if thou com'st here, knowing of my tale,   225
In hope to bear away my body fair,
Stout must thine heart be, nor shall that avail
If thou a wicked soul in thee dost bear;

So once again I bid thee to beware,
Because no base man things like this may see,
And live thereafter long and happily.'   231

'Lady,' he said, 'in Florence is my home,
And in my city noble is my name;
Neither on peddling voyage am I come,
But, like my fathers, bent to gather fame;   235
And though thy face has set my heart a-flame
Yet of thy story nothing do I know,
But here have wandered heedlessly enow.

'But since the sight of thee mine eyes did bless,
What can I be but thine? what wouldst thou
   have?   240
From those thy words, I deem from some dis-
   tress
By deeds of mine thy dear life I might save;
O then, delay not! if one ever gave
His life to any, mine I give to thee;
Come, tell me what the price of love must be?

'Swift death, to be with thee a day and night 246
And with the earliest dawning to be slain?
Or better, a long year of great delight,
And many years of misery and pain?
Or worse, and this poor hour for all my gain?   250
A sorry merchant am I on this day,
E'en as thou willest so must I obey.'

She said, 'What brave words! nought divine am
   I,
But an unhappy and unheard-of maid
Compelled by evil fate and destiny   255
To live, who long ago should have been laid
Under the earth within the cypress shade.
Hearken awhile, and quickly shalt thou know
What deed I pray thee to accomplish now.

'God grant indeed thy words are not for nought!
Then shalt thou save me, since for many a day
To such a dreadful life I have been brought: 262
Nor will I spare with all my heart to pay
What man soever takes my grief away;
Ah! I will love thee, if thou lovest me   265
But well enough my savior now to be.

'My father lived a many years agone
Lord of this land, master of all cunning,
Who ruddy gold could draw from out gray stone,
And gather wealth from many an uncouth
   thing;   270
He made the wilderness rejoice and sing,
And such a leech he was that none could say
Without his word what soul should pass away.

'Unto Diana such a gift he gave,
Goddess above, below, and on the earth,   275
That I should be her virgin and her slave
From the first hour of my most wretched birth;
Therefore my life had known but little mirth
When I had come unto my twentieth year
And the last time of hallowing drew anear.   280

'So in her temple had I lived and died,
And all would long ago have passed away,
But ere that time came, did strange things betide,
Whereby I am alive unto this day;
Alas, the bitter words that I must say! 285
Ah! can I bring my wretched tongue to tell
How I was brought unto this fearful hell?

'A queen I was, what gods I knew I loved,
And nothing evil was there in my thought,
And yet by love my wretched heart was moved
Until to utter ruin I was brought! 291
Alas! thou sayest our gods were vain and nought;
Wait, wait, till thou hast heard this tale of mine,
Then shalt thou think them devilish or divine.

'Hearken! in spite of father and of vow 295
I loved a man; but for that sin I think
Men had forgiven me—yea, yea, even thou;
But from the gods the full cup must I drink,
And into misery unheard of sink,
Tormented, when their own names are forgot,
And men must doubt if they e'er lived or not. 301

'Glorious my lover was unto my sight,
Most beautiful,—of love we grew so fain
That we at last agreed, that on a night
We should be happy, but that he were slain 305
Or shut in hold; and neither joy nor pain
Should else forbid that hoped-for time to be;
So came the night that made a wretch of me.

'Ah! well do I remember all that night,
When through the window shone the orb of June, 310
And by the bed flickered the taper's light,
Whereby I trembled, gazing at the moon:
Ah me! the meeting that we had, when soon
Into his strong, well-trusted arms I fell,
And many a sorrow we began to tell. 315

'Ah me! what parting on that night we had!
I think the story of my great despair
A little while might merry folk make sad;
For, as he swept away my yellow hair
To make my shoulder and my bosom bare, 320
I raised mine eyes, and shuddering could behold
A shadow cast upon the bed of gold:

'Then suddenly was quenched my hot desire
And he untwined his arms; the moon so pale
A while ago, seemed changed to blood and fire,
And yet my limbs beneath me did not fail, 326
And neither had I strength to cry or wail,
But stood there helpless, bare, and shivering,
With staring eyes still fixed upon the thing.

'Because the shade that on the bed of gold 330
The changed and dreadful moon was throwing down
Was of Diana, whom I did behold,
With knotted hair, and shining girt-up gown,
And on the high white brow, a deadly frown
Bent upon us, who stood scarce drawing breath,
Striving to meet the horrible sure death. 336

'No word at all the dreadful goddess said,
But soon across my feet my lover lay,
And well indeed I knew that he was dead;
And would that I had died on that same day! 340
For in a while the image turned away,
And without words my doom I understood,
And felt a horror change my human blood.

'And there I fell, and on the floor I lay
By the dead man, till daylight came on me, 345
And not a word thenceforward could I say
For three years; till of grief and misery,
The lingering pest, the cruel enemy,
My father and his folk were dead and gone,
And in this castle I was left alone: 350

'And then the doom foreseen upon me fell,
For Queen Diana did my body change
Into a fork-tongued dragon, flesh and fell,
And through the island nightly do I range,
Or in the green sea mate with monsters strange,
When in the middle of the moonlit night 356
The sleepy mariner I do affright.

'But all day long upon this gold I lie
Within this place, where never mason's hand
Smote trowel on the marble noisily; 360
Drowsy I lie, no folk at my command,
Who once was called the Lady of the Land;
Who might have bought a kingdom with a kiss,
Yea, half the world with such a sight as this.'

And therewithal, with rosy fingers light, 365
Backward her heavy-hanging hair she threw,
To give her naked beauty more to sight;
But when, forgetting all the things he knew,
Maddened with love unto the prize he drew,
She cried, 'Nay, wait! for wherefore wilt thou die, 370
Why should we not be happy, thou and I?

'Wilt thou not save me? once in every year
This rightful form of mine that thou dost see
By favor of the goddess have I here
From sunrise unto sunset given me, 375
That some brave man may end my misery.
And thou—art thou not brave? can thy heart fail,
Whose eyes e'en now are weeping at my tale?

'Then listen! when this day is overpast,
A fearful monster shall I be again, 380
And thou may'st be my savior at the last;
Unless, once more, thy words are nought and vain.

If thou of love and sovereignty art fain,
Come thou next morn, and when thou seest here
A hideous dragon, have thereof no fear,   385

'But take the loathsome head up in thine hands,
And kiss it, and be master presently
Of twice the wealth that is in all the lands
From Cathay to the head of Italy;
And master also, if it pleaseth thee,   390
Of all thou praisest as so fresh and bright,
Of what thou callest crown of all delight.

'Ah! with what joy then shall I see again
The sunlight on the green grass and the trees,
And hear the clatter of the summer rain,   395
And see the joyous folk beyond the seas.
Ah, me! to hold my child upon my knees,
After the weeping of unkindly tears,
And all the wrongs of these four hundred years.

'Go now, go quick! leave this gray heap of stone;   400
And from thy glad heart think upon thy way,
How I shall love thee—yea, love thee alone,
That bringest me from dark death unto day;
For this shall be thy wages and thy pay;
Unheard-of wealth, unheard-of love is near,   405
If thou hast heart a little dread to bear.'

Therewith she turned to go; but he cried out,
'Ah! wilt thou leave me then without one kiss,
To slay the very seeds of fear and doubt,
That glad to-morrow may bring certain bliss?
Hast thou forgotten how love lives by this,   411
The memory of some hopeful close embrace,
Low whispered words within some lonely place?'

But she, when his bright glittering eyes she saw,
And burning cheeks, cried out, 'Alas, alas!   415
Must I be quite undone, and wilt thou draw
A worse fate on me than the first one was?
O haste thee from this fatal place to pass!
Yet, ere thou goest, take this, lest thou shouldst deem
Thou hast been fooled by some strange mid-day dream.'   420

So saying, blushing like a new-kissed maid,
From off her neck a little gem she drew,
That, 'twixt those snowy rose-tinged hillocks laid,
The secrets of her glorious beauty knew;
And ere he well perceived what she would do,
She touched his hand, the gem within it lay,   426
And, turning, from his sight she fled away.

Then at the doorway where her rosy heel
Had glanced and vanished, he awhile did stare,
And still upon his hand he seemed to feel   430
The varying kisses of her fingers fair;

Then turned he toward the dreary crypt and bare,
And dizzily throughout the castle passed,
Till by the ruined fane he stood at last.

Then weighing still the gem within his hand,   435
He stumbled backward through the cypress wood,
Thinking the while of some strange lovely land,
Where all his life should be most fair and good
Till on the valley's wall of hills he stood,
And slowly thence passed down unto the bay   440
Red with the death of that bewildering day.

The next day came, and he, who all the night
Had ceaselessly been turning in his bed,
Arose and clad himself in armor bright,
And many a danger he rememberèd;   445
Storming of towns, lone sieges full of dread,
That with renown his heart had borne him through
And this thing seemed a little thing to do.

So on he went, and on the way he thought
Of all the glorious things of yesterday,   450
Nought of the price whereat they must be bought,
But ever to himself did softly say,
'No roaming now, my wars are passed away;
No long dull days devoid of happiness,
When such a love my yearning heart shall bless.'

Thus to the castle did he come at last,   456
But when unto the gateway he drew near,
And underneath its ruined archway passed
Into a court, a strange noise did he hear,
And through his heart there shot a pang of fear;
Trembling, he gat his sword into his hand,   461
And midmost of the cloisters took his stand.

But for a while that unknown noise increased,
A rattling, that with strident roars did blend,
And whining moans; but suddenly it ceased,   465
A fearful thing stood at the cloister's end,
And eyed him for a while, then 'gan to wend
Adown the cloisters, and began again
That rattling, and the moan like fiends in pain.

And as it came on towards him, with its teeth
The body of a slain goat did it tear,   471
The blood whereof in its hot jaws did seethe,
And on its tongue he saw the smoking hair;
Then his heart sank, and standing trembling there,
Throughout his mind wild thoughts and fearful ran,   475
'Some fiend she was,' he said, 'the bane of man.'

Yet he abode her still, although his blood
Curdled within him; the thing dropped the goat,
And creeping on, came close to where he stood,

And raised its head to him, and wrinkled throat,
Then he cried out and wildly at her smote, 481
Shutting his eyes, and turned and from the place
Ran swiftly, with a white and ghastly face.

But little things rough stones and tree-trunks seemed,
And if he fell, he rose and ran on still; 485
No more he felt his hurts than if he dreamed,
He made no stay for valley or steep hill,
Heedless he dashed through many a foaming rill,
Until he came unto the ship at last
And with no word into the deep hold passed. 490

Meanwhile the dragon, seeing him clean gone,
Followed him not, but crying horribly,
Caught up within her jaws a block of stone
And ground it into powder, then turned she,
With cries that folk could hear far out at sea, 495
And reached the treasure set apart of old,
To brood above the hidden heaps of gold.

Yet was she seen again on many a day
By some half-waking mariner, or herd,
Playing amid the ripples of the bay, 500
Or on the hills making all things afeard,
Or in the wood, that did that castle gird,
But never any man again durst go
To seek her woman's form, and end her woe.

As for the man, who knows what things he bore?
What mournful faces peopled the sad night, 506
What wailings vexed him with reproaches sore,
What images of that nigh-gained delight!
What dreamed caresses from soft hands and white,
Turning to horrors ere they reached the best; 510
What struggles vain, what shame, what huge unrest?

No man he knew, three days he lay and raved,
And cried for death, until a lethargy
Fell on him, and his fellows thought him saved;
But on the third night he awoke to die; 515
And at Byzantium doth his body lie
Between two blossoming pomegranate trees,
Within the churchyard of the Genoese.

(1868)

ALGERNON CHARLES SWINBURNE (1837-1909)

The poet's parents were Admiral Charles Henry Swinburne and Lady Henrietta Jane, daughter of the third Earl of Ashburnham. After a schooling of five years at Eton, Swinburne went to Balliol College, Oxford, where he contributed prose and verse to *Undergraduate Papers*, distinguished himself in Latin, Greek, French, and Italian, and began friendships with William Morris, Dante Gabriel Rossetti, and Edward Burne-Jones. After leaving Oxford, in 1860, he traveled on the continent, visiting Landor in Florence. The greater part of his life Swinburne spent quietly in England. After living for a time in London, with the Rossetti brothers, he retired to spend most of his later years at Putney Hill.

Swinburne first distinguished himself in literature as a dramatist, by the publication of *Rosamond* (1860), *The Queen Mother* (1860), *Atalanta in Calydon* (1865), and *Chastelard* (1865). By the publication of *Poems and Ballads* (1866), he aroused a moral commotion that has never been equaled in the history of English literature. To his assailants,—some of whom admired his rhythmical mastery as genuinely as they deprecated his unbridled utterances of passion,— Swinburne replied scornfully in *Notes on Poems and Reviews* (1866). The huge volume of Swinburne's poetical production, in which the lapses from lyrical and dramatic power are only occasional, is best represented by such publications as *Songs before Sunrise* (1871), *Bothwell: a Tragedy* (1874), *Erechtheus* (1876), *Studies in Song* (1880), *Mary Stuart: a Tragedy* (1881), *Tristram of Lyoness, and Other Poems* (1882), *The Tale of Balen* (1896), and *A Channel Passage, and Other Poems* (1904). Swinburne's achievement in poetry, moreover, did not prevent his attaining a firm place in prose, chiefly through his critical studies of Elizabethan dramatists, such as *George Chapman* (1875), *A Study of Shakspere* (1880), *A Study of Ben Jonson* (1889), and *The Age of Shakspere* (1908).

Swinburne's earlier poems expressed, no doubt, a definite defiance of established social, political, and religious conventions that probably prevented, ultimately, his succession to the laureateship upon the death of Tennyson. His later poems are less defiant, and contain a more incisive appreciation of nature and more narrative charm. The severest of Swinburne's critics have never questioned his absolute mastery of the rhythmical possibilities of the English language, a mastery that resulted in his most serious poetical defect,—the substitution, in some cases, of a superb sonorousness for genuine ideas.

CHORUSES
From ATALANTA IN CALYDON

CHORUS

When the hounds of spring are on winter's traces,
   The mother of months in meadow or plain
Fills the shadows and windy places
   With lisp of leaves and ripple of rain;
And the brown bright nightingale amorous   5
Is half assuaged for Itylus,
For the Thracian ships and the foreign faces,
   The tongueless vigil, and all the pain.

Come with bows bent and with emptying of quivers,
   Maiden most perfect, lady of light,   10
With a noise of winds and many rivers,
   With a clamor of waters, and with might;
Bind on thy sandals, O thou most fleet,
Over the splendor and speed of thy feet;
For the faint east quickens, the wan west shivers,   15
   Round the feet of the day and the feet of the night.

Where shall we find her, how shall we sing to her,
   Fold our hands round her knees, and cling?
O that man's heart were as fire and could spring to her,
   Fire, or the strength of the streams that spring!
For the stars and the winds are unto her   21
   As raiment, as songs of the harp-player;
For the risen stars and the fallen cling to her,
   And the southwest-wind, and the west-wind sing.

For winter's rains and ruins are over,   25
   And all the season of snows and sins;
The days dividing lover and lover,
   The light that loses, the night that wins;
And time remembered is grief forgotten,
And frosts are slain and flowers begotten,   30
And in green underwood and cover
   Blossom by blossom the spring begins.

The full streams feed on flower of rushes,
   Ripe grasses trammel a traveling foot,
The faint fresh flame of the young year flushes   35
   From leaf to flower and flower to fruit;
And fruit and leaf are as gold and fire,

And the oat is heard above the lyre,
And the hoofèd heel of a satyr crushes
   The chestnut-husk at the chestnut-root.   40

And Pan by noon and Bacchus by night,
  Fleeter of foot than the fleet-foot kid,
Follows with dancing and fills with delight
  The Mænad and the Bassarid;
And soft as lips that laugh and hide   45
The laughing leaves of the trees divide,
And screen from seeing and leave in sight
  The god pursuing, the maiden hid.

The ivy falls with the Bacchanal's hair
  Over her eyebrows hiding her eyes;   50
The wild vine slipping down leaves bare
  Her bright breast shortening into sighs;
The wild vine slips with the weight of its leaves,
But the berried ivy catches and cleaves
To the limbs that glitter, the feet that scare   55
  The wolf that follows, the fawn that flies.

CHORUS

BEFORE the beginning of years
  There came to the making of man
Time, with a gift of tears;
  Grief, with a glass that ran;
Pleasure, with pain for leaven;   5
  Summer, with flowers that fell;
Remembrance fallen from heaven,
  And madness risen from hell;
Strength without hands to smite;
  Love that endures for a breath;   10
Night, the shadow of light,
  And life, the shadow of death.

And the high gods took in hand
  Fire, and the falling of tears,
And a measure of sliding sand   15
  From under the feet of the years
And froth and drift of the sea;
  And dust of the laboring earth;
And bodies of things to be
  In the houses of death and of birth;   20
And wrought with weeping and laughter,
  And fashioned with loathing and love,
With life before and after
  And death beneath and above,
For a day and a night and a morrow,   25
  That his strength might endure for a span
With travail and heavy sorrow,
  The holy spirit of man.

From the winds of the north and the south
  They gathered as unto strife;   30
They breathed upon his mouth,
  They filled his body with life;
Eyesight and speech they wrought
  For the veils of the soul therein,
A time for labor and thought,   35
  A time to serve and to sin;
They gave him light in his ways,
  And love, and a space for delight,
And beauty and length of days,
  And night, and sleep in the night.   40
His speech is a burning fire;
  With his lips he travaileth;
In his heart is a blind desire,
  In his eyes foreknowledge of death;
He weaves, and is clothed with derision;   45
  Sows, and he shall not reap;
His life is a watch or a vision
  Between a sleep and a sleep.

CHORUS

WE have seen thee, O Love, thou art fair; thou art goodly, O Love;
Thy wings make light in the air as the wings of a dove.
Thy feet are as winds that divide the stream of the sea;
Earth is thy covering to hide thee, the garment of thee.
Thou art swift and subtle and blind as a flame of fire;   5
Before thee the laughter, behind thee the tears of desire;
And twain go forth beside thee, a man with a maid;
Her eyes are the eyes of a bride whom delight makes afraid;
As the breath in the buds that stir is her bridal breath:
But Fate is the name of her; and his name is Death.   10

For an evil blossom was born
  Of sea-foam and the frothing of blood,
    Blood-red and bitter of fruit,
      And the seed of it laughter and tears,
And the leaves of it madness and scorn;   15
  A bitter flower from the bud,
    Sprung of the sea without root,
      Sprung without graft from the years.

The weft of the world was untorn
  That is woven of the day on the night,   20
    The hair of the hours was not white
      Nor the raiment of time overworn,
When a wonder, a world's delight,
  A perilous goddess was born;
    And the waves of the sea as she came   25
      Clove, and the foam at her feet,
        Fawning, rejoiced to bring forth
    A fleshly blossom, a flame
Filling the heavens with heat
  To the cold white ends of the north.   30

And in air the clamorous birds,
  And men upon earth that hear
Sweet articulate words
  Sweetly divided apart,
And in shallow and channel and mere   35
  The rapid and footless herds,
    Rejoiced, being foolish of heart.

For all they said upon earth,
   She is fair, she is white like a dove,
      And the life of the world in her breath   40
Breathes, and is born at her birth;
   For they knew thee for mother of love,
      And knew thee not mother of death.

What hadst thou to do being born,
   Mother, when winds were at ease,   45
As a flower of the springtime of corn,
   A flower of the foam of the seas?
For bitter thou wast from thy birth,
   Aphrodite, a mother of strife;
For before thee some rest was on earth,   50
   A little respite from tears,
   A little pleasure of life;
For life was not then as thou art,
   But as one that waxeth in years
Sweet-spoken, a fruitful wife;   55
   Earth had no thorn, and desire
No sting, neither death any dart;
   What hadst thou to do amongst these,
   Thou, clothed with a burning fire,
Thou, girt with sorrow of heart,   60
   Thou, sprung of the seed of the seas
As an ear from a seed of corn,
   As a brand plucked forth of a pyre,
As a ray shed forth of the morn,
   For division of soul and disease,   65
For a dart and a sting and a thorn?
What ailed thee then to be born?

Was there not evil enough,
   Mother, and anguish on earth
Born with a man at his birth,   70
Wastes underfoot, and above
   Storm out of heaven, and dearth
Shaken down from the shining thereof,
   Wrecks from afar overseas
And peril of shallow and firth,   75
   And tears that spring and increase
In the barren places of mirth,
That thou, having wings as a dove,
   Being girt with desire for a girth,
   That thou must come after these,   80
That thou must lay on him love?

Thou shouldst not so have been born:
   But death should have risen with thee,
   Mother, and visible fear.
      Grief, and the wringing of hands,   85
And noise of many that mourn;
   The smitten bosom, the knee
   Bowed, and in each man's ear
      A cry as of perishing lands,
A moan as of people in prison,   90
   A tumult of infinite griefs;
      And thunder of storm on the sands,
      And wailing of wives on the shore;

And under thee newly arisen
   Loud shoals, and shipwrecking reefs,   95
   Fierce air and violent light;
   Sail rent and sundering oar,
   Darkness, and noises of night;
Clashing of streams in the sea,
   Wave against wave as a sword,   100
   Clamor of currents, and foam;
   Rains making ruin on earth,
   Winds that wax ravenous and roam
   As wolves in a wolfish horde;
Fruits growing faint in the tree,   105
   And blind things dead in their birth;
   Famine, and blighting of corn,
   When thy time was come to be born.

All these we know of; but thee
   Who shall discern or declare?   110
In the uttermost ends of the sea
   The light of thine eyelids and hair,
   The light of thy bosom as fire
   Between the wheel of the sun
And the flying flames of the air?   115
   Wilt thou turn thee not yet nor have pity,
But abide with despair and desire
   And the crying of armies undone,
   Lamentation of one with another
   And breaking of city by city;   120
The dividing of friend against friend,
   The severing of brother and brother;
Wilt thou utterly bring to an end?
   Have mercy, mother!

For against all men from of old   125
   Thou hast set thine hand as a curse,
   And cast out gods from their places
   These things are spoken of thee.
Strong kings and goodly with gold
   Thou hast found out arrows to pierce,   130
   And made their kingdoms and races
   As dust and surf of the sea.
All these, overburdened with woes
   And with length of their days waxen weak,
   Thou slewest; and sentest moreover   135
   Upon Tyro an evil thing,
Rent hair and a fetter and blows
   Making bloody the flower of the cheek,
   Though she lay by a god as a lover,
   Though fair, and the seed of a king.   140
For of old, being full of thy fire,
   She endured not longer to wear
   On her bosom a saffron vest,
   On her shoulder an ashwood quiver;
Being mixed and made one through desire,   145
   With Enipeus, and all her hair
   Made moist with his mouth, and her breast
   Filled full of the foam of the river.

(1865)

THE GARDEN OF PROSERPINE

Here, where the world is quiet;
  Here, where all trouble seems
Dead winds' and spent waves' riot
  In doubtful dreams of dreams;
I watch the green field growing
For reaping folk and sowing,
For harvest-time and mowing,
  A sleepy world of streams.

I am tired of tears and laughter,
  And men that laugh and weep;
Of what may come hereafter
  For men that sow to reap:
I am weary of days and hours,
Blown buds of barren flowers,
Desires and dreams and powers
  And everything but sleep.

Here life has death for neighbor,
  And far from eye or ear
Wan waves and wet winds labor,
  Weak ships and spirits steer;
They drive adrift, and whither
They wot not who make thither;
But no such winds blow hither,
  And no such things grow here.

No growth of moor or coppice,
  No heather-flower or vine,
But bloomless buds of poppies,
  Green grapes of Proserpine,
Pale beds of blowing rushes,
Where no leaf blooms or blushes
Save this whereout she crushes
  For dead men deadly wine.

Pale, without name or number,
  In fruitless fields of corn,
They bow themselves and slumber
  All night till light is born;
And like a soul belated,
In hell and heaven unmated,
By cloud and mist abated
  Comes out of darkness morn.

Though one were strong as seven,
  He too with death shall dwell,
Nor wake with wings in heaven,
  Nor weep for pains in hell;
Though one were fair as roses,
  His beauty clouds and closes;
And well though love reposes,
  In the end it is not well.

Pale, beyond porch and portal,
  Crowned with calm leaves, she stands
Who gathers all things mortal
  With cold immortal hands;
Her languid lips are sweeter
Than love's who fears to greet her,
To men that mix and meet her
  From many times and lands.

She waits for each and other,
  She waits for all men born;
Forgets the earth her mother,
  The life of fruits and corn;
And spring and seed and swallow
Take wing for her and follow
Where summer song rings hollow
  And flowers are put to scorn.

There go the loves that wither,
  The old loves with wearier wings;
And all dead years draw thither,
  And all disastrous things;
Dead dreams of days forsaken,
Blind buds that snows have shaken,
Wild leaves that winds have taken,
  Red strays of ruined springs.

We are not sure of sorrow;
  And joy was never sure;
To-day will die to-morrow;
  Time stoops to no man's lure;
And love, grown faint and fretful,
With lips but half regretful
Sighs, and with eyes forgetful
  Weeps that no loves endure.

From too much love of living,
  From hope and fear set free,
We thank with brief thanksgiving
  Whatever gods may be
That no life lives for ever;
That dead men rise up never;
That even the weariest river
  Winds somewhere safe to sea.

Then star nor sun shall waken,
  Nor any change of light:
Nor sound of waters shaken,
  Nor any sound or sight:
Nor wintry leaves nor vernal,
Nor days nor things diurnal;
Only the sleep eternal
  In an eternal night.

(1866)

HERTHA

I am that which began;
  Out of me the years roll;
Out of me God and man;
  I am equal and whole;
God changes, and man, and the form of them bodily; I am the soul.

Before ever land was,
  Before ever the sea,
Or soft hair of the grass,
  Or fair limbs of the tree,
Or the flesh-colored fruit of my branches, I was, and thy soul was in me.

First life on my sources
    First drifted and swam;
Out of me are the forces
    That save it or damn;
Out of me, man and woman, and wild-beast and
    bird; before God was, I am.   15

Beside or above me
    Nought is there to go;
Love or unlove me,
    Unknow me or know,
I am that which unloves me and loves; I am
    stricken, and I am the blow.   20

I the mark that is missed
    And the arrows that miss,
I the mouth that is kissed
    And the breath in the kiss.
The search, and the sought, and the seeker,
    the soul and the body that is.   25

I am that thing which blesses
    My spirit elate;
That which caresses
    With hands uncreate
My limbs unbegotten that measure the length
    of the measure of fate.   30

But what thing dost thou now,
    Looking Godward, to cry
'I am I, thou art thou,
    I am low, thou art high?'
I am thou, whom thou seekest to find him;
    find thou but thyself, thou art I.   35

I the grain and the furrow,
    The plough-cloven clod
And the plough-share drawn thorough,
    The germ and the sod,
The deed and the doer, the seed and the sower,
    the dust which is God.   40

Hast thou known how I fashioned thee,
    Child, underground?
Fire that impassioned thee,
    Iron that bound,
Dim changes of water, what thing of all these
    hast thou known of or found?   45

Canst thou say in thine heart
    Thou hast seen with thine eyes
With what cunning of art
    Thou wast wrought in what wise,
By what force of what stuff thou wast shapen,
    and shown on my breast to the skies?   50

Who hath given, who hath sold it thee,
    Knowledge of me?
Hath the wilderness told it thee?
    Hast thou learnt of the sea?
Hast thou communed in spirit with night? have
    the winds taken counsel with thee?   55

Have I set such a star
    To show light on thy brow
That thou sawest from afar
    What I show to thee now?
Have ye spoken as brethren together, the sun
    and the mountains and thou?   60

What is here, dost thou know it?
    What was, hast thou known?
Prophet nor poet
    Nor tripod nor throne
Nor spirit nor flesh can make answer, but only
    thy mother alone.   65

Mother, not maker,
    Born, and not made;
Though her children forsake her,
    Allured or afraid,
Praying prayers to the God of their fashion, she
    stirs not for all that have prayed.   70

A creed is a rod,
    And a crown is of night;
But this thing is God,
    To be man with thy might,
To grow straight in the strength of thy spirit,
    and live out thy life as the light.   75

I am in thee to save thee,
    As my soul in thee saith;
Give thou as I gave thee,
    Thy life-blood and breath,
Green leaves of thy labor, white flowers of thy
    thought, and red fruit of thy death.   80

Be thy ways of thy giving
    As mine were to thee;
The free life of thy living,
    Be the gift of it free;
Not as a servant to lord, nor as master to slave,
    shalt thou give thee to me.   85

O children of banishment,
    Souls overcast,
Were the lights ye see vanish meant
    Always to last,
Ye would know not the sun overshining the
    shadows and stars overpast.   90

I that saw where ye trod
    The dim paths of the night
Set the shadow called God
    In your skies to give light;
But the morning of manhood is risen, and the
    shadowless soul is in sight.   95

The tree many-rooted
    That swells to the sky
With frondage red-fruited
    The life-tree am I;
In the buds of your lives is the sap of my leaves:
    ye shall live and not die.   100

But the gods of your fashion
  That take and that give,
In their pity and passion
  That scourge and forgive,
They are worms that are bred in the bark that
  falls off, they shall die and not live.   105

My own blood is what stanches
  The wounds in my bark;
Stars caught in my branches
  Make day of the dark,
And are worshipped as suns till the sunrise shall
  tread out their fires as a spark.   110

Where dead ages hide under
  The live roots of the tree,
In my darkness the thunder
  Makes utterance of me;
In the clash of my boughs with each other ye
  hear the waves sound of the sea.   115

That noise is of Time,
  As his feathers are spread
And his feet set to climb
  Through the boughs overhead,
And my foliage rings round him and rustles, and
  branches are bent with his tread.   120

The storm-winds of ages
  Blow through me and cease,
The war-wind that rages,
  The spring-wind of peace,
Ere the breath of them roughen my tresses, ere
  one of my blossoms increase.   125

All sounds of all changes,
  All shadows and lights
On the world's mountain-ranges,
  And stream-riven heights,
Whose tongue is the wind's tongue and language
  of storm-clouds on earth-shaking nights;

All forms of all faces,   131
  All works of all hands
In unsearchable places
  Of time-stricken lands,
All death and all life, and all reigns and all ruins,
  drop through me as sands.   135

Though sore be my burden
  And more than ye know,
And my growth have no guerdon
  But only to grow,
Yet I fail not of growing for lightnings above me
  or death-worms below.   140

These two have their part in me,
  As I too in these;
Such fire is at heart in me,
  Such sap is this tree's,
Which hath in it all sounds and all secrets of
  infinite lands and of seas.   145

In the spring-colored hours
  When my mind was as May's,
There brake forth of me flowers
  By centuries of days,
Strong blossoms with perfume of manhood, shot
  out from my spirit as rays.   150

And the sound of them springing
  And smell of their shoots
Were as warmth and sweet singing,
  And strength to my roots;
And the lives of my children made perfect with
  freedom of soul were my fruits.   155

I bid you but be;
  I have need not of prayer;
I have need of you free
  As your mouths of mine air;
That my heart may be greater within me, be-
  holding the fruits of me fair.   160

More fair than strange fruit is
  Of faiths ye espouse;
In me only the root is
  That blooms in your boughs;
Behold now your god that ye made you, to feed
  him with faith of your vows.   165

In the darkening and whitening
  Abysses, adored,
With dayspring and lightning
  For lamp and for sword,
God thunders in heaven, and his angels are red
  with the wrath of the Lord.   170

O my sons, O too dutiful
  Towards gods not of me,
Was not I enough beautiful?
  Was it hard to be free?
For behold, I am with you, am in you and of
  you; look forth now and see.   175

Lo, winged with world's wonders,
  With miracles shod,
With the fires of his thunders
  For raiment and rod,
God trembles in heaven, and his angels are white
  with the terror of God.   180

For his twilight is come on him,
  His anguish is here;
And his spirits gaze dumb on him,
  Grown gray from his fear;
And his hour taketh hold on him stricken, the
  last of his infinite year.   185

Thought made him and breaks him,
  Truth slays and forgives;
But to you, as time takes him,
  This new thing it gives,
Even love, the belovèd Republic, that feeds
  upon freedom and lives.   190

For truth only is living,
   Truth only is whole,
And the love of his giving
   Man's polestar and pole;
Man, pulse of my center, and fruit of my body,
   and seed of my soul.   195

One birth of my bosom;
   One beam of mine eye;
One topmost blossom
   That scales the sky;
Man, equal and one with me, man that is made
   of me, man that is I.   200
          (1871)

A FORSAKEN GARDEN

In a coign of the cliff between lowland and highland,
   At the sea-down's edge between windward and lee,
Walled round with rocks as an inland island,
   The ghost of a garden fronts the sea.
A girdle of brushwood and thorn encloses   5
   The steep square slope of the blossomless bed
Where the weeds that grew green from the graves of its roses
   Now lie dead.

The fields fall southward, abrupt and broken,
   To the low last edge of the long lone land.   10
If a step should sound or a word be spoken,
   Would a ghost not rise at the strange guest's hand?
So long have the gray bare walks lain guestless,
   Through branches and briers if a man make way,
He shall find no life but the sea-wind's restless   15
   Night and day.

The dense hard passage is blind and stifled
   That crawls by a track none turn to climb
To the strait waste place that the years have rifled
   Of all but the thorns that are touched not of time.   20
The thorns he spares when the rose is taken;
   The rocks are left when he wastes the plain;
The wind that wanders, the weeds wind-shaken,
   These remain.

Not a flower to be pressed of the foot that falls not;   25
   As the heart of a dead man the seed-plots are dry;
From the thicket of thorns whence the nightingale calls not,
   Could she call, there were never a rose to reply.
Over the meadows that blossom and wither,
   Rings but the note of a sea-bird's song.   30
Only the sun and the rain come hither
   All year long.

The sun burns sear, and the rain dishevels
   One gaunt bleak blossom of scentless breath,
Only the wind here hovers and revels,   35
   In a round where life seems barren as death.
Here there was laughing of old, there was weeping,
   Haply, of lovers none ever will know,
Whose eyes went seaward a hundred sleeping
   Years ago.   40

Heart handfast in heart as they stood, 'Look thither,'
   Did he whisper? 'Look forth from the flowers to the sea;
For the foam-flowers endure when the rose-blossoms wither,
   And men that love lightly may die—but we?'
And the same wind sang, and the same waves whitened,   45
   And or ever the garden's last petals were shed,
In the lips that had whispered, the eyes that had lightened,
   Love was dead.

Or they loved their life through, and then went whither?
   And were one to the end—but what end who knows?   50
Love deep as the sea as a rose must wither,
   As the rose-red seaweed that mocks the rose.
Shall the dead take thought for the dead to love them?
   What love was ever as deep as a grave?
They are loveless now as the grass above them 55
   Or the wave.

All are at one now, roses and lovers,
   Not known of the cliffs and the fields and the sea.
Not a breath of the time that has been hovers
   In the air now soft with a summer to be.   60
Not a breath shall there sweeten the seasons hereafter
   Of the flowers or the lovers that laugh now or weep,
When as they that are free now of weeping and laughter
   We shall sleep.

Here death may deal not again for ever;   65
   Here change may come not till all change end.
From the graves they have made they shall rise up never,
   Who have left nought living to ravage and rend.
Earth, stones, and thorns of the wild ground growing,
   While the sun and the rain live, these shall be;   70
Till a last wind's breath, upon all these blowing,
   Roll the sea.

Till the slow sea rise, and the sheer cliff crumble,
   Till terrace and meadow the deep gulfs drink,
Till the strength of the waves of the high tides
     humble   75
   The fields that lessen, the rocks that shrink,
Here now in his triumph where all things falter,
   Stretched out on the spoils that his own hand
     spread,
As a god self-slain on his own strange altar,
     Death lies dead.   80
                (1876)

THALASSIUS

Upon the flowery forefront of the year,
One wandering by the gray-green April sea
Found on a reach of shingle and shallower sand,
Inlaid with starrier glimmering jewelry
Left for the sun's love and the light wind's cheer
   Along the foam-flowered strand,   6
Breeze-brightened, something nearer sea than
   land,
Though the last shoreward blossom-fringe was
   near,
A babe asleep, with flower-soft face that
   gleamed
To sun and seaward as it laughed and dreamed,
Too sure of either love for either's fear,   11
Albeit so birdlike slight and light, it seemed,
Nor man, nor mortal child of man, but fair
As even its twin-born tenderer spray-flowers
   were,
That the wind scatters like an Oread's hair. 15

For when July strewed fire on earth and sea
   The last time ere that year,
Out of the flame of morn Cymothoë,
Beheld one brighter than the sun-bright sphere
Move toward her from its fieriest heart, whence
   trod   20
   The live sun's very god,
Across the foam-bright water-ways that are
As heavenlier heavens, with star for answering
   star;
And on her eyes and hair and maiden mouth
Felt a kiss falling fierier than the South,   25
   And heard above afar
A noise of songs and wind-enamored wings,
And lutes and lyres of milder and mightier
   strings,
And round the resonant radiance of his car
   Where depth is one with height,   30
 ight heard as music, music seen as light,
  d with that second moondawn of the spring's
   'hat fosters the first rose,
   -child whiter than the sunlit snows
   \rn out of the world of sunless things 35
   \nd the round earth flows and ebbs and

But he that found the sea-flower by the sea,
And took to foster like a graft of earth,
Was born of man's most highest and heaven-
   liest birth,
Free-born as winds and stars and waves are free;
A warrior gray with glories more than years, 41
Though more of years than change the quick
   to dead
Had rained their light and darkness on his head;
A singer that in time's and memory's ears
Should leave such words to sing as all his peers
Might praise with hallowing heat of rapturous
   tears,   46
Till all the days of human flight were fled.
And at his knees his fosterling was fed,
   Not with man's wine and bread,
Nor mortal mother-milk of hopes and fears, 50
But food of deep memorial days long sped;
For bread with wisdom, and with song for wine,
Clear as the full calm's emerald hyaline.
And from his grave glad lips the boy would
   gather
Fine honey of song-notes, goldener than gold, 55
More sweet than bees make of the breathing
   heather,
   That he, as glad and bold,
Might drink as they, and keep his spirit from
   cold.
And the boy loved his laurel-laden hair
As his own father's risen on the eastern air, 60
And that less white brow-binding bayleaf bloom,
More than all flowers his father's eyes relume,
   And those high songs he heard,
More than all notes of any landward bird,
   More than all sounds less free   65
Than the wind's quiring to the choral sea.

High things the high song taught him: how the
   breath,
Too frail for life, may be more strong than
   death;
And this poor flash of sense in life, that gleams
   As a ghost's glory in dreams,   70
More stable than the world's own heart's root
   seems,
By that strong faith of lordliest love, which
   gives
To death's own sightless-seeming eyes a light
Clearer, to death's bare bones a verier might,
Than shines or strikes from any man that lives;
How he that loves life overmuch shall die   76
   The dog's death, utterly;
And he that much less loves it than he hates
   All wrong-doing that is done,
Anywhere always underneath the sun,   80
Shall live a mightier life than time's or fate's.
One fairer thing he showed him, and in might
   More strong than day and night,
Whose strengths build up time's towering period;
Yea, one thing stronger and more high than
   God,   85

Which, if man had not, then should God not be:
  And that was Liberty.
And gladly should man die to gain, he said,
Freedom; and gladlier, having lost, lie dead.
For man's earth was not, nor the sweet sea-
    waves   90
His, nor his own land, nor its very graves,
Except they bred not, bore not, hid not slaves;
  But all of all that is,
Were one man free in body and soul, were his.

And the song softened, even as heaven by night
Softens, from sunnier down to starrier light, 96
And with its moon-bright breath
Blessed life for death's sake, and for life's sake
    death;
Till as the moon's own beam and breath con-
    fuse,
In one clear hueless haze of glimmering hues, 100
The sea's line, and the land's line, and the sky's,
And light for love of darkness almost dies,
As darkness only lives for light's dear love,
Whose hands the web of night is woven of:
So in that heaven of wondrous words were life
  And death brought out of strife;   106
Yea, by that strong spell of serene increase,
Brought out of strife to peace.

And the song lightened, as the wind at morn
Flashes, and even with lightning of the wind 110
  Night's thick-spun web is thinned,
And all its weft unwoven and overworn
  Shrinks, as might love from scorn,
And as when wind and light, on water and land,
Leap as twin gods from heavenward, hand in
    hand,   115
And with the sound and splendor of their leap
Strike darkness dead, and daunt the spirit of
    sleep,
  And burn it up with fire;
So with the light that lightened from the lyre,
Was all the bright heat in the child's heart
    stirred,   120
And blown with blasts of music into flame,
  Till even his sense became
Fire, as the sense that fires the singing bird,
  Whose song calls night by name.
And in the soul within the sense began   125
The manlike passion of a godlike man,
And in the sense within the soul again
Thoughts that make men of gods, and gods of
    men.

For love the high song taught him,—love that
    turns
God's heart toward man as man's to Godward;
    love   130
That life and death and life are fashioned of,
  From the first breath that burns
Half-kindled on the flower-like yeanling's lip
So light and faint that life seems like to slip,
  To that yet weaklier drawn   135
When sunset dies of night's devouring dawn;
But the man dying not wholly as all men dies
If aught be left of his in live men's eyes
Out of the dawnless dark of death to rise;
  If aught of deed or word   140
Be seen for all time, or of all time heard.
Love, that though body and soul were over-
    thrown,
Should live for love's sake of itself alone,
Though spirit and flesh were one thing doomed
    and dead.
  Not wholly annihilated   145
Seeing even the hoariest ash-flake that the pyre
Drops, and forgets the thing was once afire,
And gave its heart to feed the pile's full flame
Till its own heart its own heat overcame,   149
Outlives its own life, though by scarce a span,
As such men dying outlive themselves in man,
Outlive themselves for ever; if the heat
Outburn the heart that kindled it, the sweet
Outlast the flower whose soul it was, and flit,
  Forth of a body of it   155
Into some new shape of a strange perfume
More potent than its light live spirit of bloom,—
How shall not something of that soul relive,
That only soul that had such gifts to give
As lighten something even of all men's doom, 160
  Even from the laboring womb,
Even to the seal set on the unopening tomb?
And these the loving light of song and love
Shall wrap and lap round, and impend above,
Imperishable; and all springs born illume   165
Their sleep with brighter thoughts than wake
    the dove
To music, when the hillside winds resume
The marriage-song of heather-flower and broom
  And all the joy thereof.

And hate the song, too, taught him,—hate of all
  That brings or holds in thrall   171
Of spirit or flesh, free born ere God began,
The holy body and sacred soul of man.
And wheresoever a curse was, or a chain,
A throne for torment or a crown for bane   175
Rose, molded out of poor men's molten pain,
There, said he, should man's heaviest hate be set
Inexorably, to faint not or forget
Till the last warmth bled forth of the last vein
In flesh that none should call a king's again, 180
Seeing wolves and dogs and birds that plague-
    strike air
Leave the last bone of all the carrion bare.

And hope the high song taught him,—hope whose
    eyes
Can sound the seas unsoundable, the skies
Inaccessible of eyesight; that can see   185
What earth beholds not, hear what wind and
    sea
Hear not, and speak what all these crying in one
  Can speak not to the sun.

For in her sovereign eyelight all things are
Clear as the closest seen and kindlier star 190
That marries morn and even and winter and
    spring
   With one love's golden ring.
For she can see the days of man, the birth
Of good, and death of evil things on earth
Inevitable and infinite, and sure 195
As present pain is, or herself is pure.
Yea, she can hear and see, beyond all things
That lighten from before Time's thunderous
    wings
Through the awful circle of wheel-winged
    periods,
The tempest of the twilight of all gods; 200
And, higher than all the circling course they ran,
The sundawn of the spirit that was man.

And fear the song, too, taught him,—fear to be
Worthless the dear love of the wind and sea
That bred him fearless, like a sea-mew reared
   In rocks of man's foot feared, 206
Where nought of wingless life may sing or shine.
Fear to wax worthless of that heaven he had,
When all the life in all his limbs was glad,
And all the drops in all his veins were wine, 210
And all the pulses music; when his heart,
Singing, bade heaven and wind and sea bear part
In one live song's reiterance, and they bore;
Fear to go crownless of the flower he wore
When the winds loved him, and the waters
    knew 215
The blithest life that clove their blithe life
    through
With living limbs exultant, or held strife
More amorous than all dalliance aye anew
With the bright breath and strength of their
    large life,
With all strong wrath of all sheer winds that
    blew, 220
All glories of all storms of the air that fell
   Prone, ineluctable,
With roar from heaven of revel, and with hue
   As of a heaven turned hell.
For when the red blast of their breath had
    made, 225
All heaven aflush with light more dire than
    shade,
He felt it in his blood and eyes and hair
Burn as if all the fires of the earth and air
Had laid strong hold upon his flesh, and stung
The soul behind it as with serpent's tongue, 230
Forked like the loveliest lightnings; nor could
    bear
   hardly, half distraught with strong delight,
   joy that like a garment wrapped him round,
   lapped him over and under
      raiment of great light, 235
      pture of great sound
         oud leap earthward of the thunder
         ven's most furthest bound:

So seemed all heaven in hearing and in sight,
Alive and mad with glory and angry joy,
That something of its marvelous mirth and
    might 241
Moved even to madness, fledged as even for
    flight,
The blood and spirit of one but mortal boy.
* * *
(1880)

ÉTUDE RÉALISTE

I

A BABY's feet, like sea-shells pink,
   Might tempt, should heaven see meet,
An angel's lips to kiss, we think,
   A baby's feet.

Like rose-hued sea-flowers toward the heat 5
   They stretch and spread and wink
Their ten soft buds that part and meet.

No flower-bells that expand and shrink
   Gleam half so heavenly sweet
As shine on life's untrodden brink 10
   A baby's feet.

II

A BABY's hands, like rosebuds furled
   Whence yet no leaf expands,
Ope if you touch, though close upcurled,
   A baby's hands. 15

Then, fast as warriors grip their brands
   When battle's bolt is hurled,
They close, clenched hard like tightening bands.

No rosebuds yet by dawn impearled
   Match, even in loveliest lands, 20
The sweetest flowers in all the world—
   A baby's hands.

III

A BABY's eyes, ere speech begin,
   Ere lips learn words or sighs,
Bless all things bright enough to win 25
   A baby's eyes.

Love, while the sweet thing laughs and lies,
   And sleep flows out and in,
Sees perfect in them Paradise.

Their glance might cast out pain and sin, 30
   Their speech make dumb the wise,
By mute glad godhead felt within
   A baby's eyes.
(1883)

THE ROUNDEL

A ROUNDEL is wrought as a ring or a star-bright
    sphere,
With craft of delight and with cunning of sound
    unsought.
That the heart of the hearer may smile if to
    pleasure his ear
      A roundel is wrought.

Its jewel of music is carven of all or of aught— 5
Love, laughter, or mourning—remembrance of rapture or fear—
That fancy may fashion to hang in the ear of thought.
As a bird's quick song runs round, and the hearts in us hear
Pause answer to pause, and again the same strain caught,
So moves the device whence, round as a pearl or tear,   10
    A roundel is wrought.
              (1883)

ON A COUNTRY ROAD

ALONG these low pleached lanes, on such a day,
So soft a day as this, through shade and sun,
With glad grave eyes that scanned the glad wild way,
And heart still hovering o'er a song begun,
And smile that warmed the world with benison,
Our father, lord long since of lordly rime,   6
Long since hath haply ridden, when the lime
Bloomed broad above him, flowering where he came.
Because thy passage once made warm this clime,
Our father Chaucer, here we praise thy name.   10

Each year that England clothes herself with May,
She takes thy likeness on her. Time hath spun
Fresh raiment all in vain and strange array
For earth and man's new spirit, fain to shun
Things past for dreams of better to be won,   15
Through many a century since thy funeral chime
Rang, and men deemed it death's most direful crime
To have spared not thee for very love or shame;
And yet, while mists round last year's memories climb,
Our father Chaucer, here we praise thy name.   20

Each turn of the old wild road whereon we stray,
Meseems, might bring us face to face with one
Whom seeing we could not but give thanks, and pray
For England's love our father and her son
To speak with us as once in days long done   25
With all men, sage and churl and monk and mime,
Who knew not as we know the soul sublime
That sang for song's love more than lust of fame.
Yet, though this be not, yet, in happy time,
Our father Chaucer, here we praise thy name.   30

Friend, even as bees about the flowering thyme,
Years crowd on years, till hoar decay begrime
Names once beloved; but, seeing the sun the same,
As birds of autumn fain to praise the prime,
Our father Chaucer, here we praise thy name.   35
              (1884)

COR CORDIUM

O HEART of hearts, the chalice of love's fire,
Hid round with flowers and all the bounty of bloom;
O wonderful and perfect heart, for whom
The lyrist liberty made life a lyre;
O heavenly heart, at whose most dear desire   5
Dead love, living and singing, cleft his tomb,
And with him risen and regent in death's room
All day thy choral pulses rang full choir;
O heart whose beating blood was running song,
O sole thing sweeter than thine own songs were,
Help us for thy free love's sake to be free,   11
True for thy truth's sake, for thy strength's sake strong,
Till very liberty make clean and fair
The nursing earth as the sepulchral sea.
              (1871)

'NON DOLET'

IT does not hurt. She looked along the knife
Smiling, and watched the thick drops mix and run
Down the sheer blade: not that which had been done
Could hurt the sweet sense of the Roman wife,
But that which was to do yet ere the strife   5
Could end for each for ever, and the sun:
Nor was the palm yet nor was peace yet won
While pain had power upon her husband's life.
It does not hurt, Italia. Thou art more
Than bride to bridegroom: how shalt thou not take   10
The gift love's blood has reddened for thy sake?
Was not thy life-blood given for us before?
And if love's heart-blood can avail thy need,
And thou not die, how should it hurt indeed?
              (1871)

SONNET

ON THE DEATHS OF THOMAS CARLYLE AND GEORGE ELIOT

Two souls diverse out of our human sight
Pass, followed one with love and each with wonder:
The stormy sophist with his mouth of thunder,
Clothed with loud words and mantled in the might
Of darkness and magnificence of night;   5
And one whose eye could smite the night in sunder,
Searching if light or no light were thereunder,
And found in love of loving-kindness light.

Duty divine and Thought with eyes of fire
Still following Righteousness with deep desire 10
Shone sole and stern before her and above
Sure stars and sole to steer by; but more sweet
Shone lower the loveliest lamp for earthly
    feet,—
The light of little children, and their love.
(1881)

CHRISTOPHER MARLOWE

CROWNED, girdled, garbed, and shod with light
    and fire,
Son first-born of the morning, sovereign star!
Soul nearest ours of all, that wert most far,
Most far off in the abysm of time, thy lyre

Hung highest above the dawn-enkindled quire 5
Where all ye sang together, all that are,
And all the starry songs behind thy car
Rang sequence, all our souls acclaim thee sire.

'If all the pens that ever poets held
Had fed the feeling of their masters' thoughts,'
And as with rush of hurtling chariots 11
The flight of all their spirits were impelled
Toward one great end, thy glory—nay, not then,
Not yet mightst thou be praised enough of men.
(1882)

A MATCH

IF love were what the rose is,
  And I were like the leaf,
    Our lives would grow together
    In sad or singing weather,
Blown fields or flowerful closes, 5
  Green pleasure or grey grief;
If love were what the rose is,
  And I were like the leaf.

If I were what the words are,
  And love were like the tune, 10
    With double sound and single
    Delight our lips would mingle,
With kisses glad as birds are
  That get sweet rain at noon;
If I were what the words are, 15
  And love were like the tune.

If you were life, my darling,
  And I your love were death,
    We'd shine and snow together
    Ere March made sweet the weather 20
With daffodil and starling
  And hours of fruitful breath;
If you were life, my darling,
  And I your love were death.

If you were thrall to sorrow, 25
  And I were page to joy,
    We'd play for lives and seasons
    With loving looks and treasons
And tears of night and morrow
  And laughs of maid and boy; 30
If you were thrall to sorrow,
  And I were page to joy.

If you were April's lady,
  And I were lord in May,
    We'd throw with leaves for hours 35
    And draw for days with flowers,
Till day like night were shady
  And night were bright like day;
If you were April's lady,
  And I were lord in May. 40

If you were queen of pleasure,
  And I were king of pain,
    We'd hunt down love together,
    Pluck out his fly-feather,
And teach his feet a measure, 45
  And find his mouth a rein;
If you were queen of pleasure,
  And I were king of pain.
(1866)

GEORGE MEREDITH (1828-1909)

MEREDITH is perhaps most widely known by his novels, but during recent years his poetry has come in for an increasing share of attention. His radical ideas, especially with respect to the emancipation of women, which are suggested rather than openly advocated in the novels, are explicitly avowed in the poems; and the form of his poetry, while no less characteristic than the style of his prose, is equally distinguished, and at times exquisitely musical. Meredith had to wait a long time to come by his own; his first volume of poems was published as long ago as 1851, and his first work of fiction, *The Shaving of Shagpat*, appeared in 1856. *The Ordeal of Richard Feverel* (1859) established his position in the world of fiction, as *Modern Love* (1862) won him recognition as one of the leading poets of the day; an unappreciative review provoked Swinburne to a letter of vigorous protest, in the course of which he said: 'Mr. Meredith is one of the three or four poets now alive whose work, perfect or imperfect, is always as noble in design as it is often faultless in result.' But after winning the suffrages of contemporary men of letters, Meredith had still to conquer the public. *The Egoist* (1879) is usually regarded as turning the tide in his favor, but in reviewing the *Poems and Lyrics of the Joy of Earth* in 1883 Mark Pattison could still write: 'Mr. Meredith is well known, by name, to the widest circle of readers—the novel readers. By name, because his name is a label warning them not to touch.' *Diana of the Crossways* (1885) opened the way for a larger circle of readers not only of this, but of the earlier and later novels, especially in the United States; the poems have made their way much more slowly to any considerable popularity, if indeed they can be said, as a whole, to have won it yet. Except in a few love lyrics and wayside studies, Meredith makes large demands upon his readers' powers of comprehension. He has his own system of philosophy, which needs some familiarity with his modes of expressing it before it can be understood. 'Where other writers appeal to the Christian divinities or to humanity,' says a recent critic, 'he speaks, somewhat insistently, of the Earth, a term to which he attaches his own mystic meaning. The Earth is Nature, considered not as the malign stepmother which she is in pessimistic theory, but as a stern yet genial mother and instructress. The Earth gives us our bodies, our fund of power, and our basis of instinct. Life is an adjustment and realization of the inward forces that the Earth generates, and love it is that both tasks and rewards most completely our power of controlling these forces.' These are high themes for young readers, and they may well leave them till they are older and wiser. If they can appreciate Meredith's simpler poems, the understanding of the more difficult ones will come later.

Of the external events of Meredith's life there is little to be said. Of Welsh descent, he was born in Hampshire, and educated in Germany. During his early manhood he worked as a journalist, and in 1866 he was a war correspondent in Italy and Austria, his sympathy with the cause of Italian unity and independence being shown in his novel *Vittoria*, published the following year. The last thirty years of his life were spent in quiet retirement at Boxhill, near London, and the enjoyment of the admiration of an ever-widening circle of readers. In 1905 he received the Order of Merit, perhaps the most distinguished of British decorations, and in 1908, on his eightieth birthday, an address of congratulation was presented to him from the leading writers of the English-speaking world.

LOVE IN THE VALLEY

UNDER yonder beech-tree single on the greensward,
  Couched with her arms behind her golden head,
Knees and tresses folded to slip and ripple idly,
  Lies my young love sleeping in the shade.
Had I the heart to slide an arm beneath her, 5
  Press her parting lips as her waist I gather slow,
Waking in amazement she could not but embrace me:
  Then would she hold me and never let me go?

Shy as the squirrel and wayward as the swallow,
  Swift as the swallow along the river's light 10
Circleting the surface to meet his mirrored winglets,
  Fleeter she seems in her stay than in her flight.
Shy as the squirrel that leaps among the pine-tops,
  Wayward as the swallow overhead at set of sun,
She whom I love is hard to catch and conquer
  Hard, but oh, the glory of the winning were she won! 16

When her mother tends her before the laughing mirror,
    Tying up her laces, looping up her hair,
Often she thinks, were this wild thing wedded,
    More love should I have, and much less care.
When her mother tends her before the lighted mirror, 21
    Loosening her laces, combing down her curls,
Often she thinks, were this wild thing wedded,
    I should miss but one for many boys and girls.

Heartless she is as the shadow in the meadows 25
    Flying to the hills on a blue and breezy noon.
No, she is athirst and drinking up her wonder;
    Earth to her is young as the slip of the new moon.
Deals she an unkindness, 't is but her rapid measure,
    Even as in a dance; and her smile can heal no less: 30
Like the swinging May-cloud that pelts the flowers with hailstones
    Off a sunny border, she was made to bruise and bless.

Lovely are the curves of the white owl sweeping
    Wavy in the dusk lit by one large star.
Lone on the fir-branch, his rattle-note unvaried,
    Brooding o'er the gloom, spins the brown eve-jar. 36
Darker grows the valley, more and more forgetting:
    So were it with me if forgetting could be willed.
Tell the grassy hollow that holds the bubbling well-spring, 39
    Tell it to forget the source that keeps it filled.

Stepping down the hill with her fair companions,
    Arm in arm, all against the raying West,
Boldly she sings, to the merry tune she marches,
    Brave in her shape, and sweeter unpossessed.
Sweeter, for she is what my heart first awaking
    Whispered the world was; morning light is she. 46
Love that so desires would fain keep her changeless;
    Fain would fling the net, and fain have her free.

Happy happy time, when the white star hovers
    Low over dim fields fresh with bloomy dew, 50
Near the face of dawn, that draws athwart the darkness,
    Threading it with color, as yewberries the yew.
Thicker crowd the shades while the grave East deepens
    Glowing, and with crimson a long cloud swells.
Maiden still the morn is; and strange she is, and secret; 55
    Strange her eyes; her cheeks are cold as cold sea-shells.

Sunrays, leaning on our southern hills and lighting
    Wild cloud-mountains that drag the hills along,
Oft ends the day of your shifting brilliant laughter
    Chill as a dull face frowning on a song. 60
Ay, but shows the South-west a ripple-feathered bosom
    Blown to silver while the clouds are shaken and ascend
Scaling the mid-heavens as they stream, there comes a sunset
    Rich, deep like love in beauty without end.

When at dawn she sighs, and like an infant to the window 65
    Turns grave eyes craving light, released from dreams,
Beautiful she looks, like a white water-lily,
    Bursting out of bud in havens of the streams.
When from bed she rises clothed from neck to ankle
    In her long nightgown sweet as boughs of May, 70
Beautiful she looks, like a tall garden-lily,
    Pure from the night, and splendid for the day.

Mother of the dews, dark eye-lashed twilight;
    Low-lidded twilight, o'er the valley's brim,
Rounding on thy breast sings the dew-delighted skylark, 75
    Clear as though the dew-drops had their voice in him.
Hidden where the rose-flush drinks the rayless planet,
    Fountain-full he pours the spraying fountain-showers.
Let me hear her laughter, I would have her ever
    Cool as dew in twilight, the lark above the flowers. 80

All the girls are out with their baskets for the primrose;
    Up lanes, woods through, they troop in joyful bands.
My sweet leads: she knows not why, but now she loiters,
    Eyes the bent anemones, and hangs her hands.
Such a look will tell that the violets are peeping,
    Coming the rose; and unaware a cry 86
Springs in her bosom for odors and for color,
    Covert and the nightingale; she knows not why.

Kerchiefed head and chin she darts between her tulips,
    Streaming like a willow gray in arrowy rain:
Some bend beaten cheek to gravel, and their angel 91

She will be; she lifts them, and on she speeds
   again.
Black the driving raincloud breasts the iron
   gate-way;
She is forth to cheer a neighbor lacking mirth.
So when sky and grass met rolling dumb for
   thunder   95
   Saw I once a white dove, sole light of earth.

Prim little scholars are the flowers of her garden,
   Trained to stand in rows, and asking if they
      please.
I might love them well but for loving more the
   wild ones;
   O my wild ones! they tell me more than
      these,   100
You, my wild one, you tell of honied field-rose,
   Violet, blushing eglantine in life; and even
      as they,
They, by the wayside are earnest of your good-
      ness,
   You are of life's on the banks that line the
      way.

Peering at her chamber the white crowns the
   red rose,   105
   Jasmine winds the porch with stars two and
      three.
Parted is the window; she sleeps; the starry
   jasmine
   Breathes a falling breath that carries thoughts
      of me.
Sweeter unpossessed, have I said of her my
   sweetest?
   Not while she sleeps: while she sleeps the
      jasmine breathes,   110
Luring her to love; she sleeps; the starry jasmine
   Bears me to her pillow under white rose-
      wreaths.

Yellow with birdfoot-trefoil are the grass-
   glades;
   Yellow with cinquefoil of the dew-gray leaf;
Yellow with stonecrop; the moss-mounds are
   yellow;   115
   Blue-necked the wheat sways, yellowing to
      the sheaf.
Green-yellow, bursts from the copse the laugh-
   ing yaffle,
   Sharp as a sickle is the edge of shade and
      shine:
Earth in her heart laughs looking at the heavens,
   Thinking of the harvest: I look and think of
      mine.   120

This I may know: her dressing and undressing
   Such a change of light shows as when the
      skies in sport
Shift from cloud to moonlight; or edging over
   thunder
   Slips a ray of sun: or sweeping into port

White sails furl; or on the ocean borders   125
   White sails lean along the waves leaping green.
Visions of her shower before me, but from eye-
   sight
   Guarded she would be like the sun were she
      seen.

Front door and back of the mossed old farm-
   house
   Open with the morn, and in a breezy link 130
Freshly sparkles garden to stripe-shadowed
   orchard,
   Green across a rill where on sand the minnows
      wink.
Busy in the grass the early sun of summer
   Swarms, and the blackbird's mellow fluting
      notes
Call my darling up with round and roguish
   challenge: 135
   Quaintest, richest carol of all the singing
      throats!

Cool was the woodside; cool as her white dairy
   Keeping sweet the cream-pan; and there the
      boys from school,
Cricketing below, rushed brown and red with
   sunshine;
   O the dark translucence of the deep-eyed
      cool!   140
Spying from the farm, herself she fetched a
   pitcher
   Full of milk, and tilted for each in turn the
      beak.
Then a little fellow, mouth up and on tip-toe,
   Said, 'I will kiss you': she laughed and leaned
      her cheek.

Doves of the fir-wood walling high our red roof
   Through the long noon coo, crooning through
      the coo.   146
Loose droop the leaves, and down the sleepy
   roadway
   Sometimes pipes a chaffinch; loose droops the
      blue.
Cows flap a slow tail knee-deep in the river,
   Breathless, given up to sun and gnat and fly,
Nowhere is she seen; and if I see her nowhere, 151
   Lightning may come, straight rains and tiger
      sky.

O the golden sheaf, the rustling treasure-
   armful!
   O the nutbrown tresses nodding interlaced!
O the treasure-tresses one another over   155
   Nodding! O the girdle slack about the waist!
Slain are the poppies that shot their random
   scarlet
   Quick amid the wheat-ears: wound about the
      waist,
Gathered, see these brides of Earth one blush
   of ripeness!
   O the nutbrown tresses nodding interlaced! 160

Large and smoky red the sun's cold disk drops,
  Clipped by naked hills, on violet shaded snow:
Eastward large and still lights up a bower of
    moonrise,
  Whence at her leisure steps the moon aglow.
Nightlong on black print-branches our beech-
    tree   165
  Gazes in this whiteness: nightlong could I.
Here may life on death or death on life be
    painted.
  Let me clasp her soul to know she cannot die!

Gossips count her faults! they scour a narrow
    chamber
  Where there is no window, read not heaven
    or her.   170
'When she was a tiny,' one agèd woman quavers,
  Plucks at my heart and leads me by the ear.
Faults she had once as she learned to run and
    tumbled:
  Faults of feature some see, beauty not com-
    plete.
Yet, good gossips, beauty that makes holy   175
  Earth and air, may have faults from head to
    feet.

Hither she comes; she comes to me; she lingers,
  Deepens her brown eyebrows, while in new
    surprise
High rise the lashes in wonder of a stranger,
  Yet am I the light and living of her eyes.   180
Something friends have told her fills her heart
    to brimming,
  Nets her in her blushes, and wounds her, and
    tames.—
Sure of her haven, O like a dove alighting,
  Arms up, she dropped; our souls were in our
    names.

Soon will she lie like a white frost sunrise.   185
  Yellow oats and brown wheat, barley pale as
    rye,
Long since your sheaves have yielded to the
    thresher,
  Felt the girdle loosened, seen the tresses fly.
Soon will she lie like a blood-red sunset.
  Swift with the to-morrow, green-winged
    Spring!   190
Sing from the South-west, bring her back the
    truants,
  Nightingale and swallow, song and dipping
    wing.

Soft new beech-leaves, up to beamy April
  Spreading bough on bough a primrose moun-
    tain, you
Lucid in the moon, raise lilies to the skyfields,195
  Youngest green transfused in silver shining
    through:
Fairer than the lily, than the wild white cherry:
  Fair as in image my seraph love appears
Born to me by dreams when dawn is at my
    eyelids;
  Fair as in the flesh she swims to me on
    tears.   200

Could I find a place to be alone with heaven,
  I would speak my heart out: heaven is my
    need.
Every woodland tree is flushing like the dog-
    wood,
  Flashing like the whitebeam, swaying like the
    reed.
Flushing like the dogwood crimson in October;
  Streaming like the flag-reed south-west
    blown,   206
Flashing as in gusts the sudden-lighted white-
    beam:
  All seem to know what is for heaven alone.
    (1851–78)

THE LAST WORDS OF JUGGLING JERRY

Pitch here the tent, while the old horse grazes:
  By the old hedge-side we'll halt a stage.
It's nigh my last above the daisies:
  My next leaf 'll be man's blank page,
Yes, my old girl! and it's no use crying: 5
  Juggler, constable, king, must bow.
One that outjuggles all 's been spying
  Long to have me, and has me now.

We've traveled times to this old common:
  Often we've hung our pots in the gorse.   10
We've had a stirring life, old woman!
  You, and I, and the old gray horse.
Races, and fairs, and royal occasions,
  Found us coming to their call:
Now they'll miss us at our stations: 15
  There's a Juggler outjuggles all!

Up goes the lark, as if all were jolly!
  Over the duck-pond the willow shakes,
It's easy to think that grieving's folly,
  When the hand's firm as driven stakes!   20
Ay, when we're strong, and braced, and manful,
  Life's a sweet fiddle: but we're a batch
Born to become the Great Juggler's han'ful:
  Balls he shies up, and is safe to catch.

Here's where the lads of the village cricket: 25
  I was a lad not wide from here:
Could n't I juggle the bail off the wicket?
  Like an old world those days appear!
Donkey, sheep, geese and thatched ale-house—
  I know 'em!
They are old friends of my halts, and seem,   30
  Somehow, as if kind thanks I owe 'em:
Juggling don't hinder the heart's esteem.

Juggling 's no sin, for we must have victual:
    Nature allows us to bait for the fool.
Holding one's own makes us juggle no little; 35
    But, to increase it, hard juggling 's the rule.
You that are sneering at my profession,
    Have n't you juggled a vast amount?
There 's the Prime Minister, in one Session,
    Juggles more games than my sins 'll count. 40

I 've murdered insects with mock thunder.
    Conscience, for that, in men don't quail.
I 've made bread from the bump of wonder:
    That 's my business, and there 's my tale.
Fashion and rank all praised the professor; 45
    Ay! and I 've had my smile from the Queen:
Bravo, Jerry! she meant: God bless her!
    Ain't this a sermon on that scene?

I 've studied men from my topsy-turvy
    Close, and, I reckon, rather true. 50
Some are fine fellows: some, right scurvy;
    Most, a dash between the two.
But it 's a woman, old girl, that makes me
    Think more kindly of the race:
And it 's a woman, old girl, that shakes me 55
    When the Great Juggler I must face.

We two were married, due and legal:
    Honest we 've lived since we 've been one.
Lord! I could then jump like an eagle:
    You danced bright as a bit o' the sun. 60
Birds in a May-bush we were! right merry!
    All night we kissed, we juggled all day.
Joy was the heart of Juggling Jerry!
    Now from his old girl he 's juggled away.

It 's past parsons to console us; 65
    No, nor no doctor fetch for me:
I can die without my bolus;
    Two of a trade, lass, never agree!
Parson and Doctor!—don't they love rarely,
    Fighting the devil in other men's fields! 70
Stand up yourself and match him fairly:
    Then see how the rascal yields!

I, lass, have lived no gipsy, flaunting
    Finery while his poor helpmate grubs:
Coin I 've stored, and you won't be wanting: 75
    You sha 'n 't beg from the troughs and tubs.
Nobly you 've stuck to me, though in his kitchen
    Duke might kneel to call you Cook!
Palaces you could have ruled and grown rich in,
    But your old Jerry you never forsook. 80

Hand up the chirper! ripe ale winks in it;
    Let 's have comfort and be at peace.
Once a stout draft made me light as a linnet.
    Cheer up! the Lord must have his lease.
May be—for none see in that black hollow—
    It 's just a place where we 're held in pawn,
And, when the Great Juggler makes as to swallow, 87
    It 's just the sword-trick—I ain't quite gone.

Yonder came smells of the gorse, so nutty,
    Gold-like and warm: it 's the prime of May. 90
Better than mortar, brick, and putty,
    Is God's house on a blowing day.
Lean me more up the mound; now I feel it;
    All the old heath-smells! Ain't it strange?
There 's the world laughing, as if to conceal it!
    But He 's by us, juggling the change. 96

I mind it well, by the sea-beach lying,
    Once—it 's long gone—when two gulls we beheld,
Which, as the moon got up, were flying
    Down a big wave that sparked and swelled.
Crack went a gun; one fell: the second 101
    Wheeled round him twice, and was off for new luck:
There in the dark her white wing beckoned;—
    Give me a kiss—I 'm the bird dead-struck!
(1859)

THE OLD CHARTIST

Whate'er I be, old England is my dam!
    So there 's my answer to the judges, clear,
I 'm nothing of a fox, nor of a lamb;
    I don't know how to cheat, nor how to leer:
        I 'm for the nation! 5
That 's why you see me by the wayside here,
    Returning home from transportation.

It 's Summer in her bath this morn, I think
    I 'm fresh as dew, and chirpy as the birds:
And just for joy to see old England wink 10
    Thro' leaves again, I could harangue the herds:
        Is n't it something
To speak out like a man when you 've got words,
    And prove you 're not a stupid dumb thing?

They shipped me off for it: I 'm here again. 15
    Old England is my dam, whate'er I be.
Says I, I 'll tramp it home, and see the grain:
    If you see well, you 're king of what you see:
        Eyesight is having,
If you 're not given, I said, to gluttony. 20
    Such talk to ignorance sounds as raving.

You dear old brook, that from his Grace's park
    Come bounding! on you run near my old town:
My lord can't lock the water; nor the lark,
    Unless he kills him, can my lord keep down. 25
        Up, is the song-note!
I 've tried it, too:—for comfort and renown,
    I rather pitched upon the wrong note.

I 'm not ashamed: Not beaten 's still my boast:
    Again I 'll rouse the people up to strike. 30
But home 's where different politics jar most.
    Respectability the women like.
        This form, or that form—
The Government may be hungry pike,
    But don't you mount a Chartist platform! 35

Well, well! Not beaten—spite of them, I shout;
   And my estate is suffering for the Cause.—
Now, what is yon brown water-rat about,
     Who washes his old poll with busy paws?
         What does he mean by 't?   40
It 's like defying all our natural laws,
   For him to hope that he 'll get clean by 't.

His seat is on a mud-bank, and his trade
   Is dirt:—he 's quite contemptible; and yet
The fellow 's all as anxious as a maid   45
   To show a decent dress, and dry the wet.
       Now it 's his whisker,
And now his nose, and ear; he seems to get
   Each moment at the motion brisker!

To see him squat like little chaps at school,   50
   I can't help laughing out with all my might.
He peers, hangs both his fore-paws: bless that fool,
   He 's bobbing at his frill now! what a sight!
       Licking the dish up,
As if he thought to pass from black to white,   55
   Like parson into lawny bishop.

The elms and yellow reed-flags in the sun,
   Look on quite grave:—the sunlight flecks his side;
And links of bindweed-flowers round him run,
   And shine up doubled with him in the tide.   60
       I 'm nearly splitting,
But nature seems like seconding his pride,
   And thinks that his behavior 's fitting.

That isle o' mud looks baking dry with gold
   His needle-muzzle still works out and in,   65
It really is a wonder to behold,
   And makes me feel the bristles of my chin.
       Judged by appearance,
I fancy of the two I 'm nearer Sin,
   And might as well commence a clearance.   70

And that 's what my fine daughter said:—she meant:
   Pray hold your tongue, and wear a Sunday face.
Her husband, the young linendraper, spent
   Much argument thereon:—I 'm their disgrace.
       Bother the couple!   75
I feel superior to a chap whose place
   Commands him to be neat and supple.

But if I go and say to my old hen:
   I 'll mend the gentry's boots, and keep discreet,
Until they grow too violent,—why, then,   80
   A warmer welcome I might chance to meet:
       Warmer and better.
And if she fancies her old cock is beat,
   And drops upon her knees—so let her!

She suffered for me:—women, you 'll observe,   85
   Don't suffer for a Cause, but for a man,
When I was in the dock she showed her nerve:
   I saw beneath her shawl my old tea-can
       Trembling . . . she brought it
To screw me for my work: she loathed my plan,
   And therefore doubly kind I thought it.   91

I 've never lost the taste of that same tea:
   That liquor on my logic floats like oil,
When I state facts, and fellows disagree.
   For human creatures all are in a coil;   95
       All may want pardon.
I see a day when every pot will boil
   Harmonious in one great Tea-garden!

We wait the setting of the Dandy's day,
   Before that time!—He 's furbishing his dress—   100
He will be ready for it!—and I say
   That yon old dandy rat amid the cress,—
       Thanks to hard labor!—
If cleanliness is next to godliness,
   The old fat fellow' s Heaven's neighbor!   105

You teach me a fine lesson, my old boy!
   I 've looked on my superiors far too long.
And small has been my profit as my joy.
   You 've done the right while I 've denounced the wrong.
       Prosper me later!   110
Like you I will despise the sniggering throng,
   And please myself and my Creator.

I 'll bring the linendraper and his wife
   Some day to see you; taking off my hat.
Should they ask why, I 'll answer: in my life   115
   I never found so true a democrat.
       Base occupation
Can't rob you of your own esteem, old rat!
   I 'll preach you to the British nation.
                (1862)

FRANCE 1870

   We look for her that sunlike stood
      Upon the forehead of our day,
An orb of nations, radiating food
      For body and for mind alway.
   Where is the Shape of glad array;   5
      The nervous hands, the front of steel,
The clarion tongue? Where is the bold proud face?
      We see a vacant place;
      We hear an iron heel.

   O she that made the brave appeal   10
      For manhood when our time was dark,
And from our fetters struck the spark
      Which was as lightning to reveal

New seasons, with the swifter play
Of pulses, and benigner day; 15
She that divinely shook the dead
From living man; that stretched ahead
Her resolute forefinger straight,
And marched towards the gloomy gate
Of earths Untried, gave note, and in 20
The good name of Humanity
Called forth the daring vision! she,
She likewise half corrupt of sin,
Angel and Wanton! Can it be?
Her star has foundered in eclipse, 25
The shriek of madness on her lips;
Shreds of her, and no more, we see.
There is a horrible convulsion, smothered din,
As of one that in a grave-cloth struggles to be free.

Look not on spreading boughs 30
For the riven forest tree.
Look down where deep in blood and mire
Black thunder plants his feet and plows
The soil for ruin; that is France:
Still thrilling like a lyre, 35
Amazed to shivering discord from a fall
Sudden as that the lurid hosts recall
Who met in Heaven the irreparable mischance.
O that is France!
The brilliant eyes to kindle bliss, 40
The shrewd quick lips to laugh and kiss,
Breasts that a sighing world inspire,
And laughter-dimpled countenance
Whence soul and senses caught desire!

Ever invoking fire from Heaven, the fire 45
Has seized her, unconsumable, but framed
For all the ecstasies of suffering dire.
Mother of Pride, her sanctuary shamed:
Mother of Delicacy, and made a mark 49
For outrage: Mother of Luxury, stripped stark:
Mother of Heroes, bondsmen; through the rains,
Across her boundaries, lo the league-long chains!
Fond mother of her martial youth; they pass,
They are specters in her sight, are mown as grass!
Mother of Honor, and dishonored: Mother 55
Of Glory, she condemned to crown with bays
Her victor, and be fountain of his praise.
Is there another curse? There is another:
Compassionate her madness: is she not
Mother of Reason? she that sees them mown, 60
Like grass, her young ones! Yea, in the low groan,
And under the fixed thunder of this hour
Which holds the animate world in one foul blot
Tranced circumambient while relentless Power
Beaks at her heart and claws her limbs downthrown, 65
She, with the plunging lightnings overshot,
With madness for an armor against pain,
With milkless breasts for little ones athirst,
And round her all her noblest dying in vain,
Mother of Reason is she, trebly cursed, 70
To feel, to see, to justify the blow;
Chamber to chamber of her sequent brain
Gives answer of the cause of her great woe,
Inexorably echoing through the vaults,
' 'T is thus they reap in blood, in blood who sow:
This is the sum of self-absolvèd faults.' 76
Doubt not that through her grief, with sight supreme,
Through her delirium and despair's last dream,
Through pride, through bright illusion and the brood
Bewildering of her various Motherhood, 80
The high strong light within her, though she bleeds,
Traces the letters of returned misdeeds.
She sees what seed long sown, ripened of late,
Bears this fierce crop; and she discerns her fate
From origin to agony, and on 85
As far as the wave washes long and wan
Off one disastrous impulse: for of waves
Our life is, and our deeds are pregnant graves
Blown rolling to the sunset from the dawn.

Ah, what a dawn of splendor, when her sowers 90
Went forth and bent the necks of populations,
And of their terrors and humiliations
Wove her the starry wreath that earthward lowers
Now in the figure of a burning yoke!
Her legions traversed North and South and East, 95
Of triumph they enjoyed the glutton's feast:
They grafted the green sprig, they lopped the oak.
They caught by the beard the tempests, by the scalp
The icy precipices, and clove sheer through 100
The heart of horror of the pinnacled Alp,
Emerging not as men whom mortals knew.
They were the earthquake and the hurricane,
The lightnings and the locusts, plagues of blight,
Plagues of the revel: they were Deluge rain,
And dreaded Conflagration; lawless Might. 105
Death writes a reeling line along the snows,
Where under frozen mists they may be tracked,
Who men and elements provoked to foes,
And Gods: they were of God and Beast compact:
Abhorred of all. Yet, how they sucked the teats 110
Of Carnage, thirsty issue of their dam,
Whose eagles, angrier than their oriflamme,
Flushed the vext earth with blood, green earth forgets.
The gay young generations mask her grief;
Where bled her children hangs the loaded sheaf.
Forgetful is green earth; the Gods alone 116
Remember everlastingly: they strike
Remorselessly, and ever like for like.
By their great memories the Gods are known.

They are with her now, and in her ears, and
        known.   120
'T is they that cast her to the dust for Strength,
Their slave, to feed on her fair body's length,
That once the sweetest and the proudest shone;
Scoring for hideous dismemberment
Her limbs, as were the anguish-taking breath
Gone out of her in the insufferable descent   126
From her high chieftainship; as were she death,
Who hears a voice of justice, feels the knife
Of torture, drinks all ignominy of life.
They are with her, and the painful Gods might
        weep,   130
If ever rain of tears came out of Heaven
To flatter Weakness and bid Conscience sleep,
Viewing the woe of this Immortal, driven
For the soul's life to drain the maddening cup
Of her own children's blood implacably: 135
Unsparing even as they to furrow up
The yellow land to likeness of a sea:
The bountiful fair land of vine and grain,
Of wit and grace and ardor, and strong roots,
Fruits perishable, imperishable fruits;   140
Furrowed to likeness of the dim gray main
Behind the black obliterating cyclone.

Behold, the Gods are with her, and are known.
Whom they abandon misery persecutes
No more: them half-eyed apathy may loan   145
The happiness of the pitiable brutes.
Whom the just Gods abandon have no light,
No ruthless light of introspective eyes
That in the midst of misery scrutinize
The heart and its iniquities outright.   150
They rest, they smile and rest; they have earned
        perchance
Of ancient service quiet for a term;
Quiet of old men dropping to the worm;
And so goes out the soul. But not of France.
She cries for grief, and to the gods she cries, 155
For fearfully their loosened hands chastise,
And mercilessly they watch the rod's caress
Ravage her flesh from scourges merciless,
But she, inveterate of brain, discerns
That Pity has as little place as Joy   160
Among their roll of gifts; for Strength she yearns,
For Strength, her idol once, too long her toy.
Lo, Strength is of the plain root-Virtues born:
Strength shall ye gain by service, prove in scorn,
Train by endurance, by devotion shape.   165
Strength is not won by miracle or rape.
It is the offspring of the modest years,
The gift of sire to son, through those sound laws
Which we name Gods, which are the righteous
        cause,
The cause of man, and Manhood's ministers. 170
Could France accept the fables of her priests,
Who blest her banners in this game of beasts,
And now bid hope that Heaven will intercede
To violate its laws in her sore need,
She would find comfort in their opiates.   175

Mother of Reason! can she cheat the Fates?
Would she, the champion of the open mind,
The Omnipotent's first gift—the gift of
        growth—
Consent even for a night-time to be blind,
And sink her soul on the delusive sloth   180
For fruits ethereal and material, both,
In peril of her place among mankind?
The Mother of the many Laughters might
Call one poor shade of laughter in the light
Of her unwavering lamp to mark what things 185
The world puts faith in, careless of the truth:
What silly puppet-bodies danced on strings,
Attached by credence, we appear in sooth,
Demanding intercession, direct aid,
When the whole tragic tale hangs on a forfeit
        blade!   190

She swung the sword for centuries; in a day
It slipped her, like a stream cut from its source.
She struck a feeble hand, and tried to pray,
Clamored of treachery, and had recourse
To drunken outcries in her dream that Force 195
Needed but to hear her shouting to obey.
Was she not formed to conquer? The bright
        plumes
Of crested vanity shed graceful nods:
Transcendent in her foundries, Arts and looms,
Had France to fear the vengeance of the Gods?
Her Gods were then the battle-roll of names 201
Sheathed in the records of old war; with dance
And song she thrilled her warriors and her
        dames,
Embracing her Dishonorer: gave him France
From head to foot, France present and to come,
So she might hear the trumpet and the drum—
Bellona and Bacchante! rushing forth   207
On those stout marching Schoolmen of the
        North.
Inveterate of brain, well knows she why
Strength failed her, faithful to himself the first;
Her dream is done, and she can read the sky, 211
And she can take into her heart the worst
Calamity to drug the shameful thought
Of days that made her as the man she served,
A name of terror, but a thing unnerved;   215
Buying the trickster, by the trickster bought,
She for dominion, he to patch a throne.

Behold the Gods are with her now, and known:
And to know them, not suffering for their sake,
Is madness to the souls that may not take   220
The easy way of death, being divine.
Her frenzy is not Reason's light extinct
In fumes of foul revenge and desperate sense,
But Reason rising on the storm intense,
Three-faced, with present, past, and future
        linked;   225
Informed three-fold with duty to her line.
By sacrifice of blood must she atone,
(Since thus the foe decrees it) to her own:

That she who cannot supplicate, nor cease,
Who will not utter the false word for Peace, 230
May burn to ashes, with a heart of stone,
Whatso has made her of all lands the flower,
To spring in flame for one redeeming hour,
For one propitious hour arise from prone,
Athwart Ambition's path, and have and wrench
His towering stature from the bitter trench, 236
Retributive, by her taskmasters shown,—
The spectral trench where bloody seed was
    sown.

Henceforth of her the Gods are known,
Open to them her breast is laid, 240
Inveterate of brain, heart-valiant,
Never did fairer creature pant
Before the altar and the blade!

Swift fall the blows, and men upbraid,
And friends give echo blunt and cold, 245
The echo of the forest to the axe.
Within her are the fires that wax
For resurrection from the mold.

She snatched at Heaven's flame of old,
And kindled nations: she was weak: 250
Frail sister of her heroic prototype,
The Man; for sacrifice unripe,
She too must fill a Vulture's beak.

Once more, O earthly fortune, speak!
Has she a gleam of victory? one 255
Outshining of her old historic sun?
For a while! for an hour!
And sunlight on her banner seems
A miracle conceived in dreams,
The faint reflux of orient beams 260
Through a lifting shower.

Now is she in the vulture-grasp of Power,
And all her sins are manifest to men.
Now may they reckon with punctilious pen
Her list of misdemeanors, and her dower 265
Of precious gifts that gilded the rank fen
Where lay a wanton greedy to devour.

Now is she in the vulture-grasp of Power.
The harlot sister of the man sublime,
Prometheus, she, though vanquished will not
    cower. 270
Offending Heaven, she groveled in the slime;
Offending Man, she aimed beyond her time;
Offending Earth, her Pride was like a tower.

O like the banner on the tower,
Her spirit was, and toyed and curled 275
Among its folds to lure the world—
It called to follow. But when strong men
    thrust
The banner on the winds, 't was flame,
And pilgrim-generations tread its dust,

And kiss its track. Disastrously unripe, 280
Imperfect, changeful, full of blame,
Still the Gods love her, for that of high aim
Is this good France, the bleeding thing they
    stripe.

She shall rise worthier of her prototype
Through her abasement deep; the pain that
    runs 285
From nerve to nerve some victory achieves.
They lie like circle-strewn soaked Autumn-
    leaves
Which stain the forest scarlet, her fair sons!
And of their death her life is: of their blood
From many streams now urging to a flood, 290
No more divided, France shall rise afresh.
Of them she learns the lesson of the flesh:—
The lesson writ in red since first Time ran
A hunter hunting down the beast in man:
That till the chasing out of its last vice, 295
The flesh was fashioned but for sacrifice.
Cast hence the slave's delights, the wanton's
    lures,
O France! and of thy folly pay full price;
The limitary nature that immures
A spirit dulled in clay shall break, as thrice 300
It has broken on a night of blood and tears,
To give thy ghost free breath, and joy thy peers.

Immortal mother of a mortal host!
Thou suffering of the wounds that will not slay,
Wounds that bring death but take not life
    away!— 305
Stand fast and hearken while thy victors boast:
Hearken, and loathe that music evermore.
Slip loose thy garments woven of pride and
    shame:
The torture lurks in them, with them the blame
Shall pass to leave thee purer than before. 310
Undo thy jewels, thinking whence they came,
For what, and of the abominable name
Of her who in imperial beauty wore.

O Mother of a fated fleeting host
Conceived in the past days of sin, and born 315
Heirs of disease and arrogance and scorn,
Surrender, yield the weight of thy great ghost,
Like wings on air, to what the Heavens pro-
    claim
With trumpets from the multitudinous mounds
Where peace has filled the hearing of thy sons:
Albeit a pang of dissolution rounds 321
Each new discernment of the undying Ones,
Stoop to these graves here scattered thick and
    wide
Along thy fields, as sunless billows roll;
These ashes have the lesson for the soul. 325
'Die to thy Vanity, and to thy Pride,
And to thy Luxury: that thou may'st live,
Die to thyself,' they say, 'as we have died
From dear existence, and the foe forgive,

Nor pray for aught save in our little space 330
To warm good seed to greet the fair earth's face.'
O mother! take their counsel, and so shall
The broader world breathe in on this thy home,
Light clear for thee the counter-changing dome,
Fire lift thee to the heights meridional, 335
Strength give thee, like an ocean's vast expanse
Off mountain cliffs, the generations all,
Not whirling in their narrow rings of foam,
But like a river forward. Soaring France!
Now is Humanity on trial in thee: 340
Now may'st thou gather humankind in fee:
Now prove that Reason is a quenchless scroll;
Make of calamity thine aureole,
And bleeding lead us through the troubles of the sea.

(1871)

THE LARK ASCENDING

He rises and begins to round,
He drops the silver chain of sound,
Of many links without a break,
In chirrup, whistle, slur and shake,
All intervoled and spreading wide, 5
Like water-dimples down a tide
Where ripple ripple overcurls
And eddy into eddy whirls;
A press of hurried notes that run
So fleet they scarce are more than one, 10
Yet changingly the trills repeat
And linger ringing while they fleet,
Sweet to the quick o' the ear, and dear
To her beyond the handmaid ear,
Who sits beside our inner springs, 15
Too often dry for this he brings,
Which seems the very jet of earth
At sight of sun, her music's mirth,
As up he wings the spiral stair,
A song of light, and pierces air 20
With fountain ardor, fountain play,
To reach the shining tops of day,
And drink in everything discerned
An ecstasy to music turned,
Impelled by what his happy bill 25
Disperses; drinking, showering still,
Unthinking save that he may give
His voice the outlet, there to live
Renewed in endless notes of glee,
So thirsty of his voice is he, 30
For all to hear and all to know
That he is joy, awake, aglow,
The tumult of the heart to hear
Through pureness filtered crystal-clear,
And know the pleasure sprinkled bright 35
By simple singing of delight,
Shrill, irreflective, unrestrained,
Rapt, ringing, on the jet sustained
Without a break, without a fall,
Sweet-silvery, sheer lyrical, 40
Perennial, quavering up the chord

Like myriad dews of sunny sward
That trembling into fullness shine,
And sparkle dropping argentine;
Such wooing as the ear receives, 45
From zephyr caught in choric leaves
Of aspens when their chattering net
Is flushed to white with shivers wet;
And such the water-spirit's chime
On mountain heights in morning's prime, 50
Too freshly sweet to seem excess,
Too animate to need a stress;
But wider over many heads
The starry voice ascending spreads,
Awakening, as it waxes thin, 55
The best in us to him akin;
And every face to watch him raised,
Puts on the light of children praised,
So rich our human pleasure ripes
When sweetness on sincereness pipes, 60
Though nought be promised from the seas,
But only a soft ruffling breeze
Sweep glittering on a still content,
Serenity in ravishment.

For singing till his heaven fills, 65
'T is love of earth that he instils,
And ever winging up and up,
Our valley is his golden cup;
And he the wine which overflows
To lift us with him as he goes, 70
But not from earth is he divorced,
He joyfully to fly enforced;
The woods and brooks, the sheep and kine,
He is, the hills, the human line,
The meadows green, the fallows brown, 75
The dreams of labor in the town;
He sings the sap, the quickened veins,
The wedding song of sun and rains
He is, the dance of children, thanks
Of sowers, shout of primrose-banks, 80
And eye of violets while they breathe;
All these the circling song will wreathe,
And you shall hear the herb and tree,
The better heart of men shall see,
Shall feel celestially, as long 85
As you crave nothing save the song.

Was never voice of ours could say
Our inmost in the sweetest way,
Like yonder voice aloft, and link
All hearers in the song they drink: 90
Our wisdom speaks from failing blood,
Our passion is too full in flood,
We want the key of his wild note
Of truthful in a tuneful throat,
The song seraphically free 95
Of taint of personality,
So pure that it salutes the suns
The voice of one for millions,
In whom the millions rejoice
For giving their one spirit voice. 100

Yet men have we, whom we revere,
Now names, and men still housing here,
Whose lives, by many a battle-dint
Defaced, and grinding wheels on flint,
Yield substance, though they sing not, sweet 105
For song our highest heaven to greet,
Whom heavenly singing gives us new,
Enspheres them brilliant in our blue,
From firmest base to farthest leap,
Because their love of Earth is deep, 110
And they are warriors in accord
With life to serve and pass reward,
So touching purest, and so heard
In the brain's reflex of yon bird;
Wherefore their soul in me, or mine, 115
Through self-forgetfulness divine,
In them, that song aloft maintains,
To fill the sky and thrill the plains
With showerings drawn from human stores,
As he to silence nearer soars, 120
Extends the world at wings and dome,
More spacious making more our home,
Till lost on his aërial rings
In light, and then the fancy sings.

(1881)

THE WOODS OF WESTERMAIN

I

Enter these enchanted woods,
    You who dare.
Nothing harms beneath the leaves
More than waves a swimmer cleaves,
Toss your heart up with the lark, 5
Foot at peace with mouse and worm,
    Fair you fare.
Only at a dread of dark
Quaver, and they quit their form:
Thousand eyeballs under hoods 10
    Have you by the hair.
Enter these enchanted woods,
    You who dare.

II

Here the snake across your path
Stretches in his golden bath: 15
Mossy footed squirrels leap
Soft as winnowing plumes of Sleep:
Yaffles on a chuckle skim
Low to laugh from branches dim:
Up the pine, where sits the star, 20
Rattles deep the moth-winged jar,
Each has business of his own;
But should you distrust a tone,
    Then beware.
Shudder all the haunted roods, 25
All the eyeballs under hoods
    Shroud you in their glare.
Enter these enchanted woods,
    You who dare.

III

Open hither, open hence, 30
Scarce a bramble weaves a fence,
Where the strawberry runs red,
With white star-flower overhead;
Cumbered by dry twig and cone,
Shredded husks of seedlings flown, 35
Mine of mole and spotted flint:
Of dire wizardry no hint,
Save mayhap the print that shows
Hasty outward-tripping toes,
Heels to terror, on the mold. 40
These, the woods of Westermain,
Are as others to behold,
Rich of wreathing sun and rain;
Foliage lusterful around
Shadowed leagues of slumbering sound. 45
Wavy tree-tops, yellow whins,
Shelter eager minikins,
Myriads, free to peck and pipe:
Would you better? Would you worse?
You with them may gather ripe 50
Pleasures flowing not from purse,
Quick and far as Color flies
Taking the delighted eyes,
You of any well that springs,
May unfold the heaven of things; 55
Have it homely and within,
And thereof its likeness win,
Will you so in soul's desire:
This do sages grant t' the lyre.
This is being bird and more, 60
More than glad musician this;
Granaries you will have a store
Past the world of woe and bliss;
Sharing still its bliss and woe;
Harnessed to its hungers, no. 65
On the throne Success usurps,
You shall seat the joy you feel
Where a race of water chirps,
Twisting hues of flourished steel:
Or where light is caught in hoop 70
Up a clearing's leafy rise,
Where the crossing deerherds troop
Classic splendors, knightly dyes.
Or, where old-eyed oxen chew
Speculation with the cud, 75
Read their pool of vision through
Back to hours when mind was mud;
Nigh the knot, which did untwine
Timelessly to drowsy suns;
Seeing Earth a slimy spine, 80
Heaven a space for winging tons.
Farther, deeper, may you read,
Have you sight for things afield.
Where peeps she, the Nurse of seed,
Cloaked, but in the peep revealed; 85
Showing a kind face and sweet:
Look you with the soul you see 't.
Glory narrowing to grace,

Grace to glory magnified,
Following that will you embrace 90
Close in arms or aëry wide.
Banished is the white Foam-born
Not from here, nor under ban
Phœbus lyrist, Phœbe's horn,
Pipings of the reedy Pan. 95
Loved of Earth of old they were,
Loving did interpret her,
And the sterner worship bars
None whom Song has made her stars.
You have seen the huntress moon 100
Radiantly facing dawn,
Dusky meads between them strewn
Glimmering like downy awn;
Argent Westward glows the hunt,
East the blush about to climb; 105
One another fair they front,
Transient, yet outshine the time;
Even as dewlight off the rose
In the mind a jewel sows.
Thus opposing grandeurs live 110
Here if Beauty be their dower:
Doth she of her spirit give,
Fleetingness will spare her flower.
This is in the tune we play,
Which no spring of strength would quell, 115
In subduing does not slay;
Guides the channel, guards the well:
Tempered holds the young blood-heat,
Yet through measured grave accord,
Hears the heart of wildness beat 120
Like a centaur's hoof on sward.
Drink the sense the notes infuse,
You a larger self will find:
Sweetest fellowship ensues
With the creatures of your kind. 125
Ay, and Love, if Love it be
Flaming over *I* and *ME*,
Love meet they who do not shove
Cravings in the van of Love.
Courtly dames are here to woo, 130
Knowing love if it be true.
Reverence the blossom-shoot
Fervently, they are the fruit.
Mark them stepping, hear them talk,
Goddess, is no myth inane, 135
You will say of those who walk
In the woods of Westermain.
Waters that from throat and thigh
Dart the sun his arrows back;
Leaves that on a woodland sigh 140
Chat of secret things no lack;
Shadowy branch-leaves, waters clear,
Bare or veiled they move sincere;
Not by slavish terrors tripped;
Being anew in nature dipped, 145
Growths of what they step on, these;
With the roots the grace of trees.
Casket-breasts they give, nor hide,
For a tyrant's flattered pride,

Mind, which nourished not by light, 150
Lurks the shuffling trickster sprite:
Whereof are strange tales to tell;
Some in blood writ, tombed in bell.
Here the ancient battle ends,
Joining two astonished friends, 155
Who the kiss can give and take
With more warmth than in that world
Where the tiger claws the snake,
Snake her tiger clasps infurled,
And the issue of their fight 160
Peoples lands in snarling plight.
Here her splendid beast she leads
Silken-leashed and decked with weeds
Wild as he, but breathing faint
Sweetness of unfelt constraint. 165
Love, the great volcano, flings
Fires of lower Earth to sky;
Love, the sole permitted, sings
Sovereignly of *ME* and *I*.
Bowers he has of sacred shade, 170
Spaces of superb parade,
Voiceful. . . . But bring you a note
Wrangling, howsoe'er remote,
Discords out of discord spin
Round and round derisive din: 175
Sudden will a pallor pant
Chill at screeches miscreant;
Owls or specters, thick they flee;
Nightmare upon horror broods;
Hooded laughter, monkish glee, 180
    Gaps the vital air.
Enter these enchanted woods
    You who dare.

IV

You must love the light so well
That no darkness will seem fell. 185
Love it so you could accost
Fellowly a livid ghost,
Whish! The phantom wisps away,
Owns him smoke to cocks of day.
In your breast the light must burn 190
Fed of you, like corn in quern
Ever plumping while the wheel
Speeds the mill and drains the meal.
Light to light sees little strange,
Only features heavenly new; 195
Then you touch the nerve of Change,
Then of Earth you have the clue;
Then her two-sexed meanings melt
Through you, wed the thought and felt.
Sameness locks no scurfy pond 200
Here for Custom, crazy-fond:
Change is on the wing to bud
Rose in brain from rose in blood.
Wisdom throbbing shall you see
Central in complexity; 205
From her pasture 'mid the beasts
Rise to her ethereal feasts,
Not, though lightnings track your wit

Starward, scorning them you quit:
For be sure the bravest wing   210
Preens it in our common spring,
Thence along the vault to soar,
You with others, gathering more,
Glad of more, till you reject
Your proud title of elect,   215
Perilous even here while few
Roam the arched greenwood with you.
    Heed that snare.
Muffled by his cavern-cowl
Squats the scaly Dragon-fowl,   220
Who was lord ere light you drank,
And lest blood of knightly rank
Stream, let not your fair princess
Stray: he holds the leagues in stress,
    Watches keenly there.   225
Oft has he been riven; slain
Is no force in Westermain.
Wait, and we shall forge him curbs,
Put his fangs to uses, tame,
Teach him, quick as cunning herbs,   230
How to cure him sick and lame.
Much restricted, much enringed,
Much he frets, the hooked and winged,
    Never known to spare.
'T is enough: the name of Sage   235
Hits no thing in nature, nought,
Man the least, save when grave Age
From yon Dragon guards his thought.
Eye him when you hearken dumb
To what words from Wisdom come.   240
When she says how few are by
Listening to her, eye his eye.
    Self, his name declare.
Him shall Change, transforming late,
Wonderously renovate,   245
Hug himself the creature may:
What he hugs is loathed decay.
Crying, slip thy scales, and slough!
Change will strip his armor off;
Make of him who was all maw,   250
Inly only thrilling-shrewd,
Such a servant as none saw
Through his days of dragonhood.
Days when growling o'er his bone,
Sharpened he for mine and thine;   255
Sensitive within alone;
Scaly as in clefts of pine.
Change, the strongest son of Life,
Has the Spirit here to wife.
Lo, their young of vivid breed,   260
Bear the lights that onward speed,
Threading thickets, mounting glades,
Up the verdurous colonnades,
Round the fluttered curves, and down,
Out of sight of Earth's blue crown,   265
Whither, in her central space,
Spouts the Fount and Lure o' the chase.
Fount unresting, Lure divine!
There meet all: too late look most.

Fire in water hued as wine,   270
Springs amid a shadowy host;
Circled: one close-headed mob,
Breathless, scanning divers heaps
Where a Heart begins to throb,
Where it ceases, slow, with leaps.   275
And 't is very strange, 't is said,
How you spy in each of them
Semblance of that Dragon red,
As the oak in bracken-stem.
And, 't is said, how each and each: 280
Which commences, which subsides:
First my Dragon! doth beseech
Her who food for all provides.
And she answers with no sign;
Utters neither yea nor nay;   285
Fires the water hued as wine;
Kneads another spark in clay.
Terror is about her hid;
Silence of the thunders locked;
Lightnings lining the shut lid;   290
Fixity on quaking rocked.
Lo, you look at Flow and Drought
Interflashed and interwrought:
Ended is begun, begun
Ended, quick as torrents run.   295
Young Impulsion spouts to sink;
Luridness and luster link;
'T is your come and go of breath;
Mirrored pants the Life, the Death;
Each of either reaped and sown;   300
Rosiest rosy wanes to crone.
See you so? your senses drift;
'T is a shuttle weaving swift.
Look with spirit past the sense,
Spirit shines in permanence.   305
That is She, the view of whom
Is the dust within the tomb,
Is the inner blush above,
Look to loathe, or look to love;
Think her Lump, or know her Flame;   310
Dread her scourge, or read her aim;
Shoot your hungers from their nerve;
Or, in her example, serve.
Some have found her sitting grave;
Laughing, some; or, browed with sweat,   315
Hurling dust of fool and knave
In a hissing smithy's jet.
More it were not well to speak;
Burn to see, you need but seek.
Once beheld she gives the key   320
Airing every doorway, she.
Little can you stop or steer
Ere of her you are the seër.
On the surface she will witch,
Rendering Beauty yours, but gaze   325
Under, and the soul is rich
Past computing, past amaze.
Then is courage that endures
Even her awful tremble yours.
Then, the reflex of that Fount   330

Spied below, will Reason mount
Lordly and a quenchless force,
Lighting Pain to its mad source,
Scaring Fear till Fear escapes,
Shot through all its phantom shapes.   335
Then your spirit will perceive
Fleshly seed of fleshly sins;
Where the passions interweave,
How the serpent tangle spins
Of the sense of Earth misprised,   340
Brainlessly unrecognized;
She being Spirit in her clods,
Footway to the God of Gods.
Then for you are pleasures pure,
Sureties as the stars are sure: 345
Not the wanton beckoning flags
Which, of flattery and delight,
Wax to the grim Habit-Hags
Riding souls of men to night:
Pleasures that through blood run sane,   350
Quickening spirit from the brain.
Each of each in sequent birth,
Blood and brain and spirit, three
(Say the deepest gnomes of Earth),
Join for true felicity.   355
Are they parted, then expect
Some one sailing will be wrecked:
Separate hunting are they sped,
Scan the morsel coveted.
Earth that Triad is: she hides   360
Joy from him who that divides;
Showers it when the three are one
Glassing her in union.
Earth your haven, Earth your helm,
You command a double realm: 365
Laboring here to pay your debt,
Till your little sun shall set;
Leaving her the future task:
Loving her too well to ask.
Eglantine that climbs the yew,   370
She her darkest wreathes for those
Knowing her the Ever-new,
And themselves the kin o' the rose
Life, the chisel, axe and sword,
Wield who have her depths explored: 375
Life, the dream, shall be their robe,
Large as air about the globe;
Life, the question, hear its cry
Echoed with concordant Why;
Life, the small self-dragon ramped,   380
Thrill for service to be stamped,
Ay, and over every height
Life for them shall wave a wand;
That, the last, where sits affright,
Homely shows the stream beyond.   385
Love the light and be its lynx
You will track her and attain;
Read her as no cruel Sphinx
In the woods of Westermain.
Daily fresh the woods are ranged;   390
Glooms which otherwhere appal,

Sounded: here, their worths exchanged,
Urban joins with pastoral:
Little lost, save what may drop
Husk-like, and the mind preserves.   395
Natural overgrowths they lop,
Yet from nature neither swerves,
Trained or savage: for this cause:
Of our Earth they ply the laws,
Have in Earth their feeding root,   400
Mind of man and bent of brute.
Hear that song; both wild and ruled.
Hear it: is it wail or mirth?
Ordered, bubbled, quite unschooled?
None, and all: it springs of Earth.   405
O but hear it! 't is the mind;
Mind that with deep Earth unites,
Round the solid trunk to wind
Rings of clasping parasites.
Music have you there to feed   410
Simplest and most soaring need.
Free to wind, and in desire
Winding, they to her attached
Feel the trunk a spring of fire,
And ascend to heights unmatched,   415
Whence the tidal world is viewed
As a sea of windy wheat,
Momently black, barren, rude;
Golden-brown, for harvest meet;
Dragon-reaped from folly-sown;   420
Bride-like to the sickle-blade:
Quick it varies, while the moan,
Moan of a sad creature strayed,
Chiefly is its voice. So flesh
Conjures tempest-flails to thresh   425
Good from worthless. Some clear lamps
Light it; more of dead marsh-damps.
Monster is it still, and blind,
Fit but to be led by Pain.
Glance we at the paths behind,   430
Fruitful sight has Westermain.
There we labored, and in turn
Forward our blown lamps discern,
As you see on the dark deep
Far the loftier billows leap,   435
 Foam for beacon bear.
Hither, hither, if you will,
Drink instruction, or instil,
Run the woods like vernal sap,
Crying, hail to luminousness!   440
  But have care.
In yourself may lurk the trap:
On conditions they caress.
Here you meet the light invoked:
Here is never secret cloaked.   445
Doubt you with the monster's fry
All his orbit may exclude;
Are you of the stiff, the dry,
Cursing the not understood;
Grasp you with the monster's claws;   450
Govern with his truncheon-saws;
Hate, the shadow of a grain:

You are lost in Westermain;
Earthward swoops a vulture sun,
Nighted upon carrion:
Straightway venom wine cups shout
Toasts to One whose eyes are out:
Flowers along the reeling floor
Drip henbane and hellebore:
Beauty, of her tresses shorn,
Shrieks as nature's maniac:
Hideousness on hoof and horn
Tumbles, yapping in her track:
Haggard Wisdom, stately once,
Leers fantastical and trips:
Allegory drums the sconce,
Impiousness nibblenips.
Imp that dances, imp that flits,
Imp o' the demon-growing girl,
Maddest! whirl with imp o' the pits
Round you, and with them you whirl
Fast where pours the fountain-rout
Out of Him whose eyes are out;
Multitudes on multitudes,
Drenched in wallowing devilry:
And you ask where you may be,
  In what reek of a lair
Given to bones and ogre-broods:
  And they yell you Where.
Enter these enchanted woods,
  You who dare.

(1883)

From MODERN LOVE

XVI

In our old shipwrecked days there was an hour
When, in the firelight steadily aglow,
Joined slackly, we beheld the red chasm grow
Among the clicking coals. Our library-bower
That eve was left to us; and hushed we sat
As lovers to whom Time is whispering.
From sudden-opened doors we heard them sing;
The nodding elders mixed good wine with chat.
Well knew we that Life's greatest treasure lay
With us, and of it was our talk. 'Ah, yes!
Love dies!' I said: I never thought it less.
She yearned to me that sentence to unsay.
Then when the fire domed blackening, I found
Her cheek was salt against my kiss, and swift
Up the sharp scale of sobs her breast did lift:—
Now am I haunted by that taste! that sound.

XLIII

Mark where the pressing wing shoots javelin-like,
Its skeleton shadow on the broad-backed wave!
Here is a fitting spot to dig Love's grave;
Here where the ponderous breakers plunge and strike,
And dart their hissing tongues high up the sand:
In hearing of the ocean, and in sight
Of those ribbed wind-streaks running into white.
If I the death of Love had deeply planned,
I never could have made it half so sure,
As by the unblest kisses which upbraid
The full-waked senses; or failing that, degrade!
'T is morning: but no morning can restore
What we have forfeited. I see no sin:
The wrong is mixed. In tragic life, God wot,
No villain need be! Passions spin the plot:
We are betrayed by what is false within.

XLVII

We saw the swallows gathering in the sky
And in the osier-isle we heard them noise.
We had not to look back on summer joys,
Or forward to a summer of bright dye:
But in the largeness of the evening earth
Our spirits grew as we went side by side.
The hour became her husband and my bride.
Love that had robbed us so, thus blessed our dearth!
The pilgrims of the year waxed very loud
In multitudinous chatterings, as the flood
Full brown came from the West, and like pale blood
Expanded to the upper crimson cloud.
Love that had robbed us of immortal things,
This little moment mercifully gave,
Where I have seen across the twilight wave
The swan sail with her young beneath her wings.

L

Thus piteously Love closed what he begat;
The union of this ever-diverse pair!
These two were rapid falcons in a snare,
Condemned to do the flitting of the bat.
Lovers beneath the singing sky of May,
They wandered once; clear as the dew on flowers.
But they fed not on the advancing hours:
Their hearts held cravings for the buried day.
Then each applied to each that fatal knife,
Deep questioning, which probes to endless dole.
Ah! what a dusty answer gets the soul
When hot for certainties in this our life!—
In tragic hints here see what evermore
Moves dark as yonder midnight ocean's force,
Thundering like ramping hosts of warrior horse,
To throw that faint thin line upon the shore.

(1851–62)

OTHER VICTORIAN POETS

The imposing list of major Victorian poets from Tennyson to Meredith would be incomplete without the addition of other names which it would seem sacrilegious to classify as of minor importance. Elizabeth Barrett Browning was regarded by her own generation as more secure of immortality than her distinguished husband. The Fitzgerald version of *The Rubáiyát of Omar Khayyám*, on the other hand, has come to be one of the Victorian treasures most cherished by posterity, though its first edition lay neglected in the 'penny' boxes of second-hand bookstalls. In spite of all changes of opinion, however, Victorian poetry remains impressive by its mass and variety, whether we divide it into 'major' or 'minor' or regard it as a whole. The 'minors' and the 'majors' too, no longer win a willing ear for their greater, more serious work. Clough, Coventry Patmore, Christina Rossetti, James Thomson, and Francis Thompson may be regarded as too serious, or too sentimental, or too devotional, especially in their longer efforts, for present day use; but we still enjoy that nice blending of frivolity, easy cynicism, veiled sentiment, and good breeding, which characterize the lighter poetry of Thackeray, Locker-Lampson, Calverley, and Austin Dobson.

Of the later members of this group Davidson, Housman, Newbolt and Kipling, each in his own way, stretches out a hand to the future, and seems nearer, in spirit as well as in chronology, to our own time. Davidson gave poetic expression to the aspirations of the new science and the new industrialism; Housman, from the secure detachment of a Cambridge professorship, produced a small body of poetry, perfect in its bareness of form and concentrated bitterness of spirit; Newbolt, by way of contrast, sounded notes of national confidence in the 'public school' spirit which has been in part absorbed, in part discarded, by democracy triumphant; Kipling, with equal confidence, blew the trumpet of the new imperialism in resounding blasts of which the echoes were so soon to die away.

W. B. Yeats and 'A. E.' were pioneers in that Irish Literary Revival which in the last decade of the nineteenth century attempted to escape from the dreariness of actuality into the romance of Celtic mythology. Both were mystics, and both brought into the poetry of the time a beauty that was new and strange. The movement had many ramifications, of which perhaps the most important was the dramatic work of J. M. Synge.

ELIZABETH BARRETT BROWNING
(1806–1861)

SONNETS FROM THE PORTUGUESE

I

I thought once how Theocritus had sung
Of the sweet years, the dear and wished-for
    years,
Who each one in a gracious hand appears
To bear a gift for mortals, old or young:

And, as I mused it in his antique tongue,   5
I saw in gradual vision through my tears,
The sweet, sad years, the melancholy years,
Those of my own life, who by turns had flung

A shadow across me. Straightway I was 'ware,
So weeping, how a mystic Shape did move   10
Behind me, and drew me backward by the
    hair;
And a voice said in mastery while I strove,
'Guess now who holds thee?'—'Death!' I
    said. But there,
The silver answer rang: 'Not Death, but Love.'

V

I lift my heavy heart up solemnly,
As once Electra her sepulchral urn,
And looking in thine eyes, I overturn
The ashes at thy feet. Behold and see

What a great heap of grief lay hid in me,   5
And how the red wild sparkles dimly burn
Through the ashen grayness. If thy foot in scorn
Could tread them out to darkness utterly,

It might be well perhaps. But if instead
Thou wait beside me for the wind to blow   10
The gray dust up, . . . those laurels on thine
    head,
O my Belovèd, will not shield thee so,
That none of all the fires shall scorch and shred
The hair beneath. Stand farther off then! go.

VI

Go from me. Yet I feel that I shall stand
Henceforward in thy shadow. Nevermore
Alone upon the threshold of my door
Of individual life, I shall command

The uses of my soul, nor lift my hand   5
Serenely in the sunshine as before,
Without the sense of that which I forbore—
Thy touch upon the palm. The widest land

Doom takes to part us, leaves thy heart in mine
With pulses that beat double. What I do   10
And what I dream include thee, as the wine
Must taste of its own grapes. And when I sue
God for myself, he hears that name of thine,
And sees within my eyes the tears of two.

VII

THE face of all the world is changed, I think,
Since first I heard the footsteps of thy soul
Move still, oh, still, beside me, as they stole
Betwixt me and the dreadful outer brink

Of obvious death, where I, who thought to sink,
Was caught up into love, and taught the whole 6
Of life in a new rhythm. The cup of dole
God gave for baptism, I am fain to drink,

And praise its sweetness, Sweet, with thee anear.
The names of country, heaven, are changed away   10
For where thou art or shalt be, there or here;
And this . . . this lute and song . . . loved yesterday,
(The singing angels know) are only dear
Because thy name moves right in what they say.

XIII

AND wilt thou have me fashion into speech
The love I bear thee, finding words enough,
And hold the torch out, while the winds are rough,
Between our faces, to cast light on each?—

I drop it at thy feet. I cannot teach   5
My hand to hold my spirit so far off
From myself—me—that I should bring thee proof
In words, of love hid in me out of reach.

Nay, let the silence of my womanhood
Commend my woman-love to thy belief,—   10
Seeing that I stand unwon, however wooed,
And rend the garment of my life, in brief,
By a most dauntless, voiceless fortitude,
Lest one touch of this heart convey its grief.

XIV

IF thou must love me, let it be for nought
Except for love's sake only. Do not say
'I love her for her smile—her look—her way
Of speaking gently,—for a trick of thought

That falls in well with mine, and certes brought
A sense of pleasant ease on such a day'—   6
For these things in themselves, Belovèd, may
Be changed, or change for thee,—and love, so wrought,

May be unwrought so. Neither love me for
Thine own dear pity's wiping my cheeks dry,—
A creature might forget to weep, who bore   11
Thy comfort long, and lose thy love thereby!
But love me for love's sake, that evermore
Thou mayst love on, through love's eternity.

XX

BELOVÈD, my Belovèd, when I think
That thou wast in the world a year ago,
What time I sat alone here in the snow
And saw no footprint, heard the silence sink

No moment at thy voice, but, link by link,   5
Went counting all my chains as if that so
They never could fall off at any blow
Struck by thy possible hand,—why, thus I drink

Of life's great cup of wonder! Wonderful,
Never to feel thee thrill the day or night   10
With personal act or speech,—nor ever cull
Some prescience of thee with the blossoms white
Thou sawest growing! Atheists are as dull,
Who cannot guess God's presence out of sight.

XXXV

IF I leave all for thee, wilt thou exchange
And be all to me? Shall I never miss
Home-talk and blessing and the common kiss
That comes to each in turn, nor count it strange,

When I look up, to drop on a new range   5
Of walls and floors, another home than this?
Nay, wilt thou fill that place by me which is
Filled by dead eyes too tender to know change?

That's hardest. If to conquer love, has tried,
To conquer grief, tries more, as all things prove;
For grief indeed is love and grief beside.   11
Alas, I have grieved so I am hard to love.
Yet love me—wilt thou? Open thine heart wide,
And fold within the wet wings of thy dove.

XLIII

How do I love thee? Let me count the ways.
I love thee to the depth and breadth and height
My soul can reach, when feeling out of sight
For the ends of Being and ideal Grace.

I love thee to the level of everyday's   5
Most quiet need, by sun and candle-light.
I love thee freely, as men strive for Right;
I love thee purely, as they turn from Praise.

I love thee with the passion put to use
In my old griefs, and with my childhood's faith.
I love thee with a love I seemed to lose   11
With my lost saints,—I love thee with the breath,
Smiles, tears, of all my life!—and, if God choose,
I shall but love thee better after death.

(1850)

EDWARD FITZGERALD
(1809–1883)

From the RUBÁIYÁT of OMAR KHAYYÁM

Why, if the Soul can fling the dust aside,
And naked on the air of Heaven ride,
  Were 't not a shame—were 't not a shame for him
In this clay carcase crippled to abide?

'T is but a tent where takes his one-day's rest 5
A Sultán to the realm of Death addrest;
  The Sultán rises, and the dark Ferrásh
Strikes, and prepares it for another guest.

And fear not lest existence closing your
Account, and mine, should know the like no more; 10
  The Eternal Saki from that bowl has poured
Millions of bubbles like us, and will pour.

When you and I behind the veil are past,
Oh, but the long, long, while the world shall last,
  Which of our coming and departure heeds 15
As the Seven Seas should heed a pebble-cast.

A moment's halt—a momentary taste
Of Being from the well amid the waste—
  And lo!—the phantom caravan has reached
The Nothing it set out from—Oh, make haste!

* * *

The Moving Finger writes; and, having writ, 21
Moves on: nor all your Piety nor Wit
  Shall lure it back to cancel half a Line
Nor all your Tears wash out a Word of it.

* * *

Yet ah, that Spring should vanish with the rose!
That Youth's sweet-scented manuscript should close! 26
  The nightingale that in the branches sang,
Ah, whence, and whither flown again, who knows!

Would but the desert of the fountain yield
One glimpse—if dimly, yet indeed, revealed, 30
  To which the fainting traveler might spring,
As springs the trampled herbage of the field!

Would but some wingèd Angel ere too late
Arrest the yet unfolded roll of fate,
  And make the stern Recorder otherwise 35
Enregister, or quite obliterate!

Ah, Love! could you and I with him conspire
To grasp this sorry Scheme of Things entire,
  Would not we shatter it to bits—and then
Re-mold it nearer to the heart's desire! 40

* * *

(1859; 1872)

WILLIAM MAKEPEACE THACKERAY
(1811–1863)

AT THE CHURCH GATE

Although I enter not,
  Yet round about the spot
    Ofttimes I hover;
And near the sacred gate,
With longing eyes I wait, 5
    Expectant of her.

The minster bell tolls out
Above the city's rout,
    And noise and humming;
They 've hush'd the minster bell: 10
The organ 'gins to swell;
    She 's coming, she 's coming!

My lady comes at last,
Timid and stepping fast
    And hastening thither, 15
With modest eyes downcast;
She comes—she 's here, she 's past!
    May heaven go with her!

Kneel undisturbed, fair saint!
Pour out your praise or plaint 20
    Meekly and duly;
I will not enter there,
To sully your pure prayer
    With thoughts unruly.

But suffer me to pace 25
Round the forbidden place,
    Lingering a minute,
Like outcast spirits, who wait,
And see, through heaven's gate,
    Angels within it. 30

(1849–50)

THE END OF THE PLAY

The play is done—the curtain drops,
  Slow falling to the prompter's bell;
A moment yet the actor stops,
  And looks around, to say farewell.
It is an irksome word and task; 5
  And when he 's laughed and said his say,
He shows, as he removes the mask,
  A face that 's anything but gay.

One word, ere yet the evening ends:
  Let's close it with a parting rhyme, 10
And pledge a hand to all young friends,
  As fits the merry Christmas time;
On life's wide scene you, too, have parts,
  That fate ere long shall bid you play;
Good-night!—with honest gentle hearts 15
  A kindly greeting go alway!

Good-night!—I'd say the griefs, the joys,
    Just hinted in this mimic page,
The triumphs and defeats of boys,
    Are but repeated in our age;   20
I'd say your woes were not less keen,
    Your hopes more vain, than those of men,
Your pangs or pleasures of fifteen
    At forty-five played o'er again.

I'd say we suffer and we strive   25
    Not less nor more as men than boys,
With grizzled beards at forty-five,
    As erst at twelve in corduroys,
And if, in time of sacred youth,
    We learned at home to love and pray,   30
Pray heaven that early love and truth
    May never wholly pass away.

And in the world, as in the school,
    I'd say how fate may change and shift,
The prize be sometimes with the fool,   35
    The race not always to the swift;
The strong may yield, the good may fall,
    The great man be a vulgar clown,
The knave be lifted over all,
    The kind cast pitilessly down.   40

Who knows the inscrutable design?
    Blessèd be he who took and gave!
Why should your mother, Charles, not mine,
    Be weeping at her darling's grave?
We bow to heaven that willed it so,   45
    That darkly rules the fate of all,
That sends the respite or the blow,
    That's free to give or to recall.

This crowns his feast with wine and wit—
    Who brought him to that mirth and state? 50
His betters, see, below him sit,
    Or hunger hopeless at the gate.
Who bade the mud from Dives' wheel
    To spurn the rags of Lazarus?
Come, brother, in that dust we'll kneel,   55
    Confessing heaven that ruled it thus.

So each shall mourn, in life's advance,
    Dear hopes, dear friends, untimely killed,
Shall grieve for many a forfeit chance,
    And longing passion unfulfilled.   60
Amen!—whatever fate be sent,
    Pray God the heart may kindly glow,
Although the head with cares be bent,
    And whitened with the winter snow.

Come wealth or want, come good or ill,   65
    Let young and old accept their part,
And bow before the awful will,
    And bear it with an honest heart.
Who misses or who wins the prize—
    Go, lose or conquer as you can;   70
But if you fail, or if you rise,
    Be each, pray God, a gentleman.

A gentleman, or old or young!
    (Bear kindly with my humble lays;)
The sacred chorus first was sung   75
    Upon the first of Christmas days;
The shepherd heard it overhead—
    The joyful angels raised it then:
Glory to heaven on high, it said,
    And peace on earth to gentle men!   80

My song, save this, is little worth;
    I lay the weary pen aside,
And wish you health, and love, and mirth,
    As fits the solemn Christmas-tide.
As fits the holy Christmas birth,   85
    Be this, good friends, our carol still:
Be peace on earth, be peace on earth,
    To men of gentle will.

                      (1848)

ARTHUR HUGH CLOUGH
(1819–1861)

QUA CURSUM VENTUS

As ships, becalmed at eve, that lay
    With canvas drooping, side by side,
Two towers of sail at dawn of day
    Are scarce long leagues apart descried;

When fell the night, upsprung the breeze,   5
    And all the darkling hours they plied,
Nor dreamt but each the self-same seas
    By each was cleaving, side by side;

E'en so, but why the tale reveal
    Of those, whom year by year, unchanged, 10
Brief absence joined anew to feel,
    Astounded, soul from soul estranged?

At dead of night their sails were filled,
    And onward each rejoicing steered—
Ah, neither blame, for neither willed,   15
    Or wist, what first with dawn appeared!

To veer, how vain! On, onward strain,
    Brave barks! In light, in darkness too,
Through winds and tides one compass guides—
    To that, and your own selves, be true.   20

But O blithe breeze; and O great seas,
    Though ne'er, that earliest parting past,
On your wide plain they join again,
    Together lead them home at last.

One port, methought, alike they sought,   25
    One purpose hold where'er they fare,—
O bounding breeze, O rushing seas!
    At last, at last, unite them there!

                      (1849)

WHITHER DEPART THE BRAVE

Rome is fallen, I hear, the gallant Medici taken,
Noble Manara slain, and Garibaldi has lost *il Moro;*—
Rome is fallen; and fallen, or falling, heroical Venice.
I, meanwhile, for the loss of a single small chit of a girl, sit
Moping and mourning here,—for her, and myself much smaller.   5

Whither depart the souls of the brave that die in the battle,
Die in the lost, lost fight, for the cause that perishes with them?
Are they upborne from the field on the slumberous pinions of angels
Unto a far-off home, where the weary rest from their labor,
And the deep wounds are healed, and the bitter and burning moisture   10
Wiped from the generous eyes? or do they linger, unhappy,
Pining, and haunting the grave of their by-gone hope and endeavor?

All declamation, alas! though I talk, I care not for Rome nor
Italy; feebly and faintly, and but with the lips, can lament the
Wreck of the Lombard youth, and the victory of the oppressor.   15
Whither depart the brave!—God knows; I certainly do not.

(1858)

WHERE LIES THE LAND

Where lies the land to which the ship would go?
Far, far ahead, is all her seamen know.
And where the land she travels from?   Away,
Far, far behind, is all that they can say.

On sunny noons upon the deck's smooth face,   5
Linked arm in arm, how pleasant here to pace;
Or, o'er the stern reclining, watch below
The foaming wake far widening as we go.

On stormy nights when wild northwesters rave,
How proud a thing to fight with wind and wave!
The dripping sailor on the reeling mast   11
Exults to bear, and scorns to wish it past.

Where lies the land to which the ship would go?
Far, far ahead, is all her seamen know.
And where the land she travels from?   Away,   15
Far, far behind, is all that they can say.

(1862)

AH! YET CONSIDER IT AGAIN!

'Old things need not be therefore true,'
O brother men, nor yet the new;
Ah! still awhile the old thought retain,
And yet consider it again!

The souls of now two thousand years   5
Have laid up here their toils and fears,
And all the earnings of their pain,—
Ah, yet consider it again!

We! what do we see? each a space
Of some few yards before his face;   10
Does that the whole wide plan explain?
Ah, yet consider it again!

Alas! the great world goes its way,
And takes its truth from each new day;
They do not quit, nor can retain,   15
Far less consider it again.

(1862)

IN THE DEPTHS

It is not sweet content, be sure,
   That moves the nobler Muse to song,
Yet when could truth come whole and pure
   From hearts that inly writhe with wrong?

'T is not the calm and peaceful breast   5
   That sees or reads the problem true;
They only know, on whom 't has prest
   Too hard to hope to solve it too.

Our ills are worse than at their ease
   These blameless happy souls suspect,   10
They only study the disease,
   Alas, who live not to detect.

(1862)

THE LATEST DECALOGUE

Thou shalt have one God only; who
Would be at the expense of two?

No graven images may be
Worshipped, except the currency:

Swear not at all; for, for thy curse   5
Thine enemy is none the worse:

At church on Sunday to attend
Will serve to keep the world thy friend:

Honor thy parents: that is, all
From whom advancement may befall;   10

Thou shalt not kill; but need'st not strive
Officiously to keep alive:

Do not adultery commit;
Advantage rarely comes of it:

Thou shalt not steal; an empty feat,   15
When it's so lucrative to cheat:

Bear not false witness; let the lie
Have time on its own wings to fly:

Thou shalt not covet, but tradition
Approves all forms of competition.   20

(1862)

SAY NOT THE STRUGGLE NOUGHT AVAILETH

Say not the struggle nought availeth,
  The labor and the wounds are vain,
The enemy faints not, nor faileth,
  And as things have been they remain.

If hopes were dupes, fears may be liars;
  It may be, in yon smoke concealed,
Your comrades chase e'en now the fliers,
  And, but for you, possess the field.

For while the tired waves, vainly breaking,
  Seem here no painful inch to gain,   10
Far back, through creeks and inlets making,
  Comes silent, flooding in, the main.

And not by eastern windows only,
  When daylight comes, comes in the light,
In front, the sun climbs slow, how slowly,   15
  But westward, look, the land is bright.

(1862)

LIFE IS STRUGGLE

To wear out heart, and nerves, and brain,
And give oneself a world of pain;
Be eager, angry, fierce, and hot,
Imperious, supple—God knows what,
For what 's all one to have or not;   5
O false, unwise, absurd, and vain!
For 't is not joy, it is not gain,
It is not in itself a bliss,
Only it is precisely this
  That keeps us all alive.   10

To say we truly feel the pain,
And quite are sinking with the strain;—
Entirely, simply, undeceived,
Believe, and say we ne'er believed
The object, e'en were it achieved,   15
A thing we e'er had cared to keep;
With heart and soul to hold it cheap,
And then to go and try it again;
O false, unwise, absurd, and vain!
O, 't is not joy, and 't is not bliss,   20
Only it is precisely this
  That keeps us still alive.

(1869)

FREDERICK LOCKER-LAMPSON
(1821-1895)

TO MY GRANDMOTHER

Suggested by a picture by Mr. Romney

This relative of mine,
Was she seventy-and nine
  When she died?
By the canvas may be seen
How she looked at seventeen,   5
  As a bride.

Beneath a summer tree
Her maiden reverie
  Has a charm;
Her ringlets are in taste;   10
What an arm! and what a waist
  For an arm!

With her bridal-wreath, bouquet,
Lace farthingale, and gay
  Falbala,—   15
If Romney's touch be true,
What a lucky dog were you,
  Grandpapa!

Her lips are sweet as love;
They are parting! Do they move?   20
  Are they dumb?
Her eyes are blue, and beam
Beseechingly, and seem
  To say, 'Come!'

What funny fancy slips   25
From atween these cherry lips?
  Whisper me,
Fair Sorceress in paint,
What canon says I may n't
  Marry thee?   30

That good-for-nothing Time
Has a confidence sublime!
  When I first
Saw this Lady, in my youth,
Her winters had, forsooth,   35
  Done their worst.

Her locks, as white as snow,
Once shamed the swarthy crow;
  By-and-by
That fowl's avenging sprite   40
Set his cruel foot for spite
  Near her eye.

Her rounded form was lean,
And her silk was bombazine;
  Well I wot   45
With her needles would she sit,
And for hours would she knit,—
  Would she not?

Ah, perishable clay!
Her charms had dropt away   50
  One by one;
But if she heaved a sigh
With a burthen, it was, 'Thy
  Will be done.'

In travail, as in tears,   55
With the fardel of her years
  Overprest,
In mercy she was borne
Where the weary and the worn
  Are at rest.   60

Oh, if you now are there,
And sweet as once you were,
  Grandmamma,
This nether world agrees
You 'll all the better please   65
  Grandpapa.
                    (1862)

MY MISTRESS'S BOOTS

She has dancing eyes and ruby lips,
Delightful boots—and away she skips.

THEY nearly strike me dumb,—
I tremble when they come
  Pit-a-pat: 5
This palpitation means
These Boots are Geraldine's—
  Think of that!

O, where did hunter win
So delicate a skin   10
  For her feet?
You lucky little kid,
You perished, so you did,
  For my Sweet.

The faery stitching gleams   15
On the sides, and in the seams,
  And reveals
That the Pixies were the wags
Who tipt these funny tags,
  And these heels.   20

What soles to charm an elf!—
Had Crusoe, sick of self,
  Chanced to view
One printed near the tide,
O, how hard he would have tried   25
  For the two!

For Gerry's debonair,
And innocent and fair
  As a rose;
She 's an Angel in a frock,—   30
She 's an Angel with a clock
  To her hose!

The simpletons who squeeze
Their pretty toes to please
  Mandarins,   35
Would positively flinch
From venturing to pinch
  Geraldine's!

Cinderella's left and rights
To Geraldine's were frights: 40
  And I trow
The Damsel, deftly shod,
Has dutifully trod
  Until now.

Come, Gerry, since it suits   45
Such a pretty Puss (in Boots)
  These to don,
Set your dainty hand a while
On my shoulder, Dear, and I 'll
  Put them on.   50
                    (1868)

COVENTRY PATMORE
(1823–1896)

THE SPIRIT'S EPOCHS

NOT in the crises of events,
  Of compassed hopes, or fears fulfilled,
Or acts of gravest consequence,
  Are life's delight and depth revealed.
The day of days was not the day;   5
  That went before, or was postponed;
The night Death took our lamp away
  Was not the night on which we groaned.
I drew my bride, beneath the moon,
  Across my threshold; happy hour!   10
But, ah, the walk that afternoon
  We saw the water-flags in flower!
                    (1862)

THE MARRIED LOVER

WHY, having won her, do I woo?
  Because her spirit's vestal grace
Provokes me always to pursue,
  But, spirit-like, eludes embrace;
Because her womanhood is such   5
  That, as on court-days subjects kiss
The Queen's hand, yet so near a touch
  Affirms no mean familiarness;
Nay, rather marks more fair the height
  Which can with safety so neglect   10
To dread, as lower ladies might,
  That grace could meet with disrespect;
Thus she with happy favor feeds
  Allegiance from a love so high
That thence no false conceit proceeds   15
  Of difference bridged, or state put by,

Because although in act and word
  As lowly as a wife can be,
Her manners, when they call me lord,
  Remind me 't is by courtesy;   20
Not with her least consent of will,
  Which would my proud affection hurt,
But by the noble style that still
  Imputes an unattained desert;
Because her gay and lofty brows,   25
  When all is won which hope can ask,
Reflect a light of hopeless snows
  That bright in virgin ether bask;
Because, though free of the outer court
  I am, this Temple keeps its shrine   30
Sacred to Heaven; because in short,
  She's not and never can be mine.

(1862)

IF I WERE DEAD

'IF I were dead, you'd sometimes say, Poor
    Child!'
The dear lips quivered as they spake,
  And the tears brake
From eyes which, not to grieve me, brightly
    smiled.
  Poor Child, poor Child!   5
I seem to hear your laugh, your talk, your song.
It is not true that Love will do no wrong.
  Poor Child!
And did you think, when you so cried and
    smiled,
How I, in lonely nights, should lie awake, 10
And of those words your full avengers make?
  Poor Child, poor Child!
And now unless it be
That sweet amends thrice told are come to thee,
O God, have thou *no* mercy upon me!   15
  Poor Child!

(1877)

SIDNEY DOBELL
(1824–1874)

AMERICA

MEN say, Columbia, we shall hear thy guns.
But in what tongue shall be thy battle-cry?
Not that our sires did love in years gone by,
When all the Pilgrim Fathers were little sons
In merrie homes of Englaunde? Back, and see 5
Thy satcheled ancestor! Behold, he runs
To mine, and, clasped, they tread the equal lea
To the same village-school, where side by side
They spell 'our Father.' Hard by, the twin-pride
Of that gray hall whose ancient oriel gleams 10
Through yon baronial pines, with looks of light
Our sister-mothers sit beneath one tree.
Meanwhile our Shakspere wanders past and
    dreams
His Helena and Hermia. Shall we fight?

Nor force nor fraud shall sunder us! O ye   15
Who north or south, on east or western land,
Native to noble sounds, say truth for truth,
Freedom for freedom, love for love, and God
For God; O ye who in eternal youth
Speak with a living and creative flood   20
This universal English, and do stand
Its breathing book; live worthy of that grand,
Heroic utterance—parted, yet a whole,
Far, yet unsevered,—children brave and free
Of the great Mother-tongue, and ye shall be 25
Lords of an Empire wide as Shakspere's soul,
Sublime as Milton's immemorial theme,
And rich as Chaucer's speech, and fair as
    Spenser's dream.

(1855)

CHRISTINA ROSSETTI
(1830–1894)

SONG

WHEN I am dead, my dearest,
  Sing no sad songs for me;
Plant thou no roses at my head,
  Nor shady cypress-tree:
Be the green grass above me   5
  With showers and dewdrops wet;
And if thou wilt, remember,
  And if thou wilt, forget.

I shall not see the shadows,
  I shall not feel the rain;   10
I shall not hear the nightingale
  Sing on, as if in pain:
And dreaming through the twilight
  That doth not rise nor set,
Haply I may remember,   15
  And haply may forget.

(1862)

REMEMBER

REMEMBER me when I am gone away,
Gone far away into the silent land;
When you can no more hold me by the hand,
Nor I half turn to go yet turning stay.

Remember me when no more, day by day,   5
You tell me of our future that you planned:
Only remember me; you understand
It will be late to counsel then or pray.

Yet if you should forget me for a while
And afterwards remember, do not grieve: 10
For if the darkness and corruption leave
A vestige of the thoughts that once I had,
Better by far you should forget and smile
Than that you should remember and be sad.

(1862)

ABNEGATION

If there be any one can take my place
And make you happy whom I grieve to grieve,
Think not that I can grudge it, but believe
I do commend you to that nobler grace,

That readier wit than mine, that sweeter face; 5
Yea, since your riches make me rich, conceive
I too am crowned, while bridal crowns I weave,
And thread the bridal dance with jocund pace.

For if I did not love you, it might be 9
That I should grudge you some one dear delight;
But since the heart is yours that was mine own,
Your pleasure is my pleasure, right my right,
Your honorable freedom makes me free,
And you companioned I am not alone.

(1881)

TRUST

If I could trust mine own self with your fate,
Shall I not rather trust it in God's hand?
Without whose will one lily doth not stand,
Nor sparrow fall at his appointed date;

Who numbereth the innumerable sand, 5
Who weighs the wind and water with a weight,
To whom the world is neither small nor great,
Whose knowledge foreknew every plan we planned.

Searching my heart for all that touches you,
I find there only love and love's good-will 10
Helpless to help and impotent to do,
Of understanding dull, of sight most dim;
And therefore I commend you back to him
Whose love your love's capacity can fill.

(1881)

UP-HILL

Does the road wind up-hill all the way?
  Yes, to the very end.
Will the day's journey take the whole long day?
  From morn to night, my friend.

But is there for the night a resting-place? 5
  A roof for when the slow dark hours begin.
May not the darkness hide it from my face?
  You cannot miss that inn.

Shall I meet other wayfarers at night?
  Those who have gone before. 10
Then must I knock, or call when just in sight?
  They will not keep you standing at that door.

Shall I find comfort, travel-sore and weak?
  Of labor you shall find the sum.
Will there be beds for me and all who seek? 15
  Yea, beds for all who come.

(1862)

CHARLES STUART CALVERLEY
(1831–1884)

COMPANIONS

A TALE OF A GRANDFATHER

I know not of what we pondered
  Or made pretty pretence to talk,
As, her hand within mine, we wandered
  Toward the pool by the lime-tree walk,
While the dew fell in showers from the passion flowers 5
  And the blush-rose bent on her stalk.

I cannot recall her figure:
  Was it regal as Juno's own?
Or only a trifle bigger
  Than the elves who surround the throne 10
Of the Faëry Queen, and are seen, I ween,
  By mortals in dreams alone?

What her eyes were like I know not:
  Perhaps they were blurred with tears;
And perhaps in yon skies there glow not 15
  (On the contrary) clearer spheres.
No! as to her eyes I am just as wise
  As you or the cat, my dears.

Her teeth, I presume, were 'pearly:'
  But which was she, brunette or blonde? 20
Her hair, was it quaintly curly,
  Or as straight as a beadle's wand?
That I failed to remark: it was rather dark
  And shadowy round the pond.

Then the hand that reposed so snugly 25
  In mine,—was it plump or spare?
Was the countenance fair or ugly?
  Nay, children, you have me there!
My eyes were p'haps blurred; and besides I'd heard
  That it's horribly rude to stare. 30

And I,—was I brusque and surly?
  Or oppressively bland and fond?
Was I partial to rising early?
  Or why did we twain abscond,
When nobody knew, from the public view, 35
  To prowl by a misty pond?

What passed, what was felt or spoken,—
  Whether anything passed at all,—
And whether the heart was broken
  That beat under that shelt'ring shawl,— 40
(If shawl she had on, which I doubt),—has gone,
  Yes, gone from me past recall.

Was I haply the lady's suitor?
  Or her uncle? I can't make out;
Ask your governess, dears, or tutor. 45
  For myself, I'm in hopeless doubt
As to why we were there, who on earth we were,
  And what this is all about.

(1872)

AUSTIN DOBSON
(1840–1921)

A DEAD LETTER

I

I DREW it from its china tomb;—
  It came out feebly scented
With some thin ghost of past perfume
  That dust and days had lent it.

An old, old letter,—folded still!   5
  To read with due composure,
I sought the sun-lit window-sill,
  Above the gray enclosure,

That glimmering in the sultry haze,
  Faint flowered, dimly shaded,   10
Slumbered like Goldsmith's Madam Blaize,
  Bedizened and brocaded.

A queer old place! You'd surely say
  Some tea-board garden-maker
Had planned it in Dutch William's day   15
  To please some florist Quaker,

So trim it was. The yew-trees still,
  With pious care perverted,
Grew in the same grim shapes; and still
  The lipless dolphin spurted;   20

Still in his wonted state abode
  The broken-nosed Apollo;
And still the cypress-arbor showed
  The same umbrageous hollow.

Only,—as fresh young Beauty gleams   25
  From coffee-colored laces,—
So peeped from its old-fashioned dreams
  The fresher modern traces;

For idle mallet, hoop, and ball
  Upon the lawn were lying;   30
A magazine, a tumbled shawl,
  Round which the swifts were flying;

And, tossed beside the Guelder rose,
  A heap of rainbow knitting,
Where, blinking in her pleased repose,   35
  A Persian cat was sitting.

'A place to love in,—live,—for aye,
  If we too, like Tithonus,
Could find some God to stretch the gray
  Scant life the Fates have thrown us;   40

'But now by steam we run our race,
  With buttoned heart and pocket;
Our Love's a gilded, surplus grace,—
  Just like an empty locket!

"The time is out of joint." Who will,   45
  May strive to make it better;
For me, this warm old window-sill,
  And this old dusty letter.'

II

'DEAR *John* (the letter ran), it can't, can't be,
  For Father's gone to *Chorley Fair* with *Sam*,
And Mother's storing Apples,—*Prue* and *Me*   51
  Up to our Elbows making Damson Jam:
But we shall meet before a Week is gone,—
  "'T is a long Lane that has no turning," *John!*

'Only till Sunday next, and then you'll wait   55
  Behind the White-Thorn, by the broken Stile—
We can go round and catch them at the Gate,
  All to Ourselves, for nearly one long Mile;
Dear Prue won't look, and Father he'll go on,
  And *Sam*'s two Eyes are all for *Cissy*, *John!*   60

'*John*, she's so smart,—with every ribbon new,
  Flame-colored Sack, and Crimson Padesoy;
As proud as proud; and has the Vapors too,
  Just like My Lady;—calls poor *Sam* a Boy,
And vows no Sweet-heart's worth the Thinking-on   65
  Till he's past Thirty . . . I know better, *John!*

'My Dear, I don't think that I thought of much
  Before we knew each other, I and you;
And now, why, *John*, your least, least Finger-touch,   69
  Gives me enough to think a Summer through.
See, for I send you Something! There, 't is gone!
  Look in this corner,—mind you find it, *John!*'

III

THIS was the matter of the note,—
  A long-forgot deposit,
Dropped in an Indian dragon's throat,   75
  Deep in a fragrant closet,

Piled with a dapper Dresden world,—
  Beaux, beauties, prayers, and poses,—
Bonzes with squat legs undercurled,
  And great jars filled with roses.   80

Ah, heart that wrote! Ah, lips that kissed!
  You had no thought or presage
Into what keeping you dismissed
  Your simple old-world message!

A reverent one. Though we to-day   85
  Distrust beliefs and powers,
The artless, ageless things you say
  Are fresh as May's own flowers,

Starring some pure primeval spring,
  Ere Gold had grown despotic,—   90
Ere Life was yet a selfish thing,
  Or Love a mere exotic!

I need not search too much to find
  Whose lot it was to send it,
That feel upon me yet the kind,   95
  Soft hand of her who penned it;

And see, through twoscore years of smoke,
  In by-gone, quaint apparel,
Shine from yon time-black Norway oak
  The face of Patience Caryl,—   100

The pale, smooth forehead, silver-tressed;
  The gray gown, primly flowered;
The spotless, stately coif whose crest
  Like Hector's horse-plume towered;

And still the sweet half-solemn look   105
  Where some past thought was clinging,
As when one shuts a serious book
  To hear the thrushes singing.

I kneel to you! Of those you were,
  Whose kind old hearts grow mellow,—   110
Whose fair old faces grow more fair
  As Point and Flanders yellow;

Whom some old store of garnered grief,
  Their placid temples shading,
Crowns like a wreath of autumn leaf   115
  With tender tints of fading.

Peace to your soul! You died unwed—
  Despite this loving letter.
And what of John? The less that's said
  Of John, I think, the better.   120
                    (1883)

JAMES THOMSON
(1834–1882)

'MELENCOLIA'

From THE CITY OF DREADFUL NIGHT

ANEAR the center of that northern crest
  Stands out a level upland bleak and bare,
From which the city east and south and west
  Sinks gently in long waves; and thronèd there
An Image sits, stupendous, superhuman,   5
The bronze colossus of a wingèd Woman,
  Upon a graded granite base foursquare.

Low-seated she leans forward massively,
  With cheek on clenched left hand, the forearm's might
Erect, its elbow on her rounded knee;   10
  Across a clasped book in her lap the right
Upholds a pair of compasses; she gazes
With full set eyes, but wandering in thick mazes
  Of somber thought beholds no outward sight.

Words cannot picture her; but all men know
  That solemn sketch the pure sad artist wrought 16
Three centuries and three score years ago,
  With fantasies of his peculiar thought:
The instruments of carpentry and science
Scattered about her feet, in strange alliance 20
  With the keen wolf-hound sleeping undistraught;

Scales, hour-glass, bell, and magic-square above;
  The grave and solid infant perched beside,
With open winglets that might bear a dove,
  Intent upon its tablets, heavy-eyed;   25
Her folded wings as of a mighty eagle
But all too impotent to lift the regal
  Robustness of her earth-born strength and pride;

And with those wings, and that light wreath which seems
  To mock her grand head and the knotted frown 30
Of forehead charged with baleful thoughts and dreams,
  The household bunch of keys, the housewife's gown
Voluminous, indented, and yet rigid
As if a shell of burnished metal frigid,
  The feet thick-shod to tread all weakness down; 35

The comet hanging o'er the waste dark seas,
  The massy rainbow curved in front of it
Beyond the village with the masts and trees;
  The snaky imp, dog-headed, from the Pit,
Bearing upon its batlike leathern pinions   40
Her name unfolded in the sun's dominions,
  The 'MELENCOLIA' that transcends all wit.

Thus has the artist copied her, and thus
  Surrounded to expound her form sublime,
Her fate heroic and calamitous;   45
  Fronting the dreadful mysteries of Time,
Unvanquished in defeat and desolation,
Undaunted in the hopeless conflagration
  Of the day setting on her baffled prime.

Baffled and beaten back she works on still, 50
  Weary and sick of soul she works the more.
Sustained by her indomitable will:
  The hands shall fashion and the brain shall pore,
And all her sorrow shall be turned to labor,
Till Death the friend-foe piercing with his saber
  That mighty heart of hearts ends bitter war. 56

But as if blacker night could dawn on night,
  With tenfold gloom on moonless night unstarred,
A sense more tragic than defeat and blight,
  More desperate than strife with hope debarred, 60
More fatal than the adamantine Never
Encompassing her passionate endeavor,
  Dawns glooming in her tenebrous regard:

The sense that every struggle brings defeat
  Because Fate holds no prize to crown success;
That all the oracles are dumb or cheat   66
  Because they have no secret to express;

That none can pierce the vast black veil uncertain
Because there is no light beyond the curtain;
  That all is vanity and nothingness.   70

Titanic from her high throne in the north,
  That City's somber Patroness and Queen,
In bronze sublimity she gazes forth
  Over her Capital of teen and threne,
Over the river with its isles and bridges,   75
The marsh and moorland, to the stern rock-ridges,
  Confronting them with a coeval mien.

The moving moon and stars from east to west
  Circle before her in the sea of air;
Shadows and gleams glide round her solemn rest.   80
  Her subjects often gaze up to her there:
The strong to drink new strength of iron endurance,
The weak new terrors; all, renewed assurance
  And confirmation of the old despair.
                             (1874)

ARTHUR O'SHAUGHNESSY
(1844–1881)

HAS SUMMER COME WITHOUT THE ROSE?

Has summer come without the rose,
  Or left the bird behind?
Is the blue changed above thee,
  O world! or am I blind?
Will you change every flower that grows,   5
  Or only change this spot,
Where she who said, I love thee,
  Now says, I love thee not?

The skies seemed true above thee,
  The rose true on the tree;   10
The bird seemed true the summer through,
  But all proved false to me.
World, is there one good thing in you,
  Life, love, or death—or what?
Since lips that sang, I love thee,   15
  Have said, I love thee not?

I think the sun's kiss will scarce fall
  Into one flower's gold cup;
I think the bird will miss me,
  And give the summer up.   20
O sweet place, desolate in tall
  Wild grass, have you forgot
How her lips loved to kiss me,
  Now that they kiss me not?

Be false or fair above me;   25
  Come back with any face,
Summer!—do I care what you do?
  You cannot change one place,—

The grass, the leaves, the earth, the dew,
  The grave I make the spot,—   30
Here, where she used to love me,
  Here, where she loves me not.
                            (1874)

ODE

We are the music makers,
  And we are the dreamers of dreams,
Wandering by lone sea-breakers,
  And sitting by desolate streams;—
World-losers and world-forsakers,   5
  On whom the pale moon gleams:
Yet we are the movers and shakers
  Of the world for ever, it seems.

With wonderful deathless ditties
We build up the world's great cities,   10
  And out of a fabulous story
We fashion an empire's glory:
One man with a dream, at pleasure,
  Shall go forth and conquer a crown;
And three with a new song's measure   15
  Can trample a kingdom down.

We, in the ages lying
  In the buried past of the earth,
Built Nineveh with our sighing,
  And Babel itself in our mirth;   20
And o'erthrew them with prophesying
  To the old of the new world's worth;
For each age is a dream that is dying,
  Or one that is coming to birth.
                            (1874)

ROBERT BRIDGES
(1844–1930)

THE GROWTH OF LOVE
(SONNET NO. 50)

The world comes not to an end: her city-hives
Swarm with the tokens of a changeless trade,
With rolling wheel, driver and flagging jade,
Rich men and beggars, children, priests and wives.

New homes on old are set, as lives on lives;   5
Invention with invention overlaid:
But still or tool or toy or book or blade
Shaped for the hand, that holds and toils and strives.

The men to-day toil as their fathers taught,
With little better'd means; for works depend   10
On works and overlap, and thought on thought:
And thro' all change the smiles of hope amend
The weariest face, the same love changed in nought:
In this thing too the world comes not to an end.
                            (1876)

MOONLIGHT

May Marigold is frolic,
  She laughs till summer is done;
She hears the Grillie chirping
  All day i' the blazing sun.
But when the pale moon rises,   5
  She fain her face would hide;
For the high Queen of sorrows
  Disdains her empty pride.

Fair Primrose haunts the shadow
  With children of the Spring,   10
Till in the bloomy woodland
  The nightingale will sing.
And when he lauds the May-night
  And spirits throng the grove,
The moon shines thro' the branches   15
  And floods her heart with love.

ALICE MEYNELL
(1848–1922)

PARTED

Farewell to one now silenced quite,
Sent out of hearing, out of sight,—
  My friend of friends, whom I shall miss,—
  He is not banished, though, for this,—
Nor he, nor sadness, nor delight.   5

Though I shall talk with him no more,
A low voice sounds upon the shore.
  He must not watch my resting-place,
  But who shall drive a mournful face
From the sad winds about my door?   10

I shall not hear his voice complain,
But who shall stop the patient rain?
  His tears must not disturb my heart,
  But who shall change the years, and part
The world from every thought of pain?   15

Although my life is left so dim,
The morning crowns the mountain-rim;
  Joy is not gone from summer skies,
  Nor innocence from children's eyes,
And all these things are part of him.   20

He is not banished, for the showers
Yet wake this green warm earth of ours.
  How can the summer but be sweet?
  I shall not have him at my feet
And yet my feet are on the flowers.   25
(1893)

THE LADY POVERTY

The Lady Poverty was fair:
But she has lost her looks of late,
With change of times and change of air.
Ah, slattern! she neglects her hair,
Her gown, her shoes: she keeps no state   5
As once when her pure feet were bare.

Or—almost worse, if worse can be—
She scolds in parlors, dusts and trims,
Watches and counts. Oh, is this she
Whom Francis met, whose step was free   10
Who with obedience carolled hymns,
In Umbria walked with Chastity?

Where is her ladyhood? Not here,
Not among modern kinds of men;
But in the stony fields, where clear   15
Through the thin trees the skies appear,
In delicate spare soil and fen,
And slender landscape and austere.
(1901)

THE SHEPHERDESS

She walks—the lady of my delight—
  A shepherdess of sheep.
Her flocks are thoughts. She keeps them white;
  She guards them from the steep;
She feeds them on the fragrant height,   5
  And folds them in for sleep.

She roams maternal hills and bright,
  Dark valleys safe and deep.
Into that tender breast at night
  The chastest stars may peep.   10
She walks—the lady of my delight—
  A shepherdess of sheep.

She holds her little thoughts in sight,
  Though gay they run and leap.
She is so circumspect and right;   15
  She has her soul to keep.
She walks—the lady of my delight—
  A shepherdess of sheep.
(1901)

WILLIAM ERNEST HENLEY
(1849–1903)

OUT OF THE NIGHT THAT COVERS ME

Out of the night that covers me,
  Black as the pit from Pole to Pole,
I thank whatever gods may be
  For my unconquerable soul.

In the fell clutch of circumstance   5
  I have not winced nor cried aloud;
Under the bludgeonings of chance
  My head is bloody, but unbowed.

Beyond this place of wrath and tears
  Looms but the Horror of the shade,   10
And yet the menace of the years
  Finds and shall find me unafraid.

It matters not how strait the gate,
  How charged with punishments the scroll,
I am the master of my fate;   15
  I am the captain of my soul.

                    (1898)

PRO REGE NOSTRO

WHAT have I done for you,
  England, my England?
What is there I would not do,
  England, my own?
With your glorious eyes austere,   5
As the Lord were walking near,
Whispering terrible things and dear
  As the song on your bugles blown,
    England—
Round the world on your bugles blown!   10

Where shall the watchful Sun,
  England, my England,
Match the master-work you 've done,
  England, my own?
When shall he rejoice agen   15
Such a breed of mighty men
As come forward, one to ten,
  As the song on your bugles blown,
    England—
Round the world on your bugles blown!   20

Ever the faith endures,
  England, my England:—
'Take and break us: we are yours,
  England, my own!
Life is good, and joy runs high   25
Between English earth and sky:
Death is death; but we shall die
  To the Song on your bugles blown,
    England—
To the stars on your bugles blown!'   30

They call you proud and hard,
  England, my England:
You with worlds to watch and ward,
  England, my own!
You whose mailed hand keeps the keys   35
Of such teeming destinies,
You could know nor dread nor ease,
  Were the Song on your bugles blown,
    England—
Round the Pit on your bugles blown!   40

Mother of Ships whose might,
  England, my England,
Is the fierce old Sea's delight,
  England, my own,
Chosen daughter of the Lord,   45
Spouse-in-Chief of the ancient Sword,
There 's the menace of the Word
  In the Song on your bugles blown,
    England—
Out of heaven on your bugles blown!   50

SIR WILLIAM WATSON
(1856–1935)

WORDSWORTH'S GRAVE

II

POET who sleepest by this wandering wave!
  When thou wast born, what birth-gift hadst thou then?
To thee what wealth was that the Immortals gave,
  The wealth thou gavest in thy turn to men?

Not Milton's keen, translunar music thine;   5
  Not Shakespeare's cloudless, boundless human view;
Not Shelley's flush of rose on peaks divine;
  Nor yet the wizard twilight Coleridge knew.

What hadst thou that could make so large amends
  For all thou hadst not and thy peers possessed,   10
Motion and fire, swift means to radiant ends?—
  Thou hadst, for weary feet, the gift of rest.

From Shelley's dazzling glow or thunderous haze,
  From Byron's tempest-anger, tempest-mirth,
Men turned to thee and found—not blast and blaze,   15
  Tumult of tottering heavens, but peace on earth.

Nor peace that grows by Lethe, scentless flower,
  There in white languors to decline and cease;
But peace whose names are also rapture, power,
  Clear sight, and love: for these are parts of peace.   20

              (1890)

JOHN DAVIDSON
(1857–1909)

THIRTY BOB A WEEK

I COULD N'T touch a stop and turn a screw,
  And set the blooming world a-work for me,
Like such as cut their teeth—I hope, like you—
  On the handle of a skeleton gold key;
I cut mine on a leek, which I eat it every week;   5
  I 'm a clerk at thirty bob as you can see.

But I don't allow it 's luck and all a toss;
  There 's no such thing as being starred and crossed;
It 's just the power of some to be a boss,
  And the bally power of others to be bossed: 10

I face the music, sir; you bet I ain't a cur;
   Strike me lucky if I don't believe I 'm lost!

For like a mole I journey in the dark,
   A-traveling along the underground
From my Pillar'd Halls and broad Suburban
     Park,   15
   To come the daily dull official round;
And home again at night with my pipe all
     alight,
   A-scheming how to count ten bob a pound.

And it 's often very cold and wet,
   And my missis stitches towels for a hunks;
And the Pillar'd Halls is half of it to let—   21
   Three rooms about the size of traveling
     trunks.
And we cough, my wife and I, to dislocate a
     sigh,
   When the noisy little kids are in their bunks.

But you never hear her do a growl or whine,
   For she 's made of flint and roses, very odd; 26
And I 've got to cut my meaning rather fine,
   Or I 'd blubber, for I 'm made of greens and
     sod:
So p'r'aps we are in Hell for all that I can tell,
   And lost and damn'd and served up hot to
     God.   30

I ain't blaspheming, Mr. Silver-tongue;
   I 'm saying things a bit beyond your art:
Of all the rummy starts you ever sprung,
   Thirty bob a week 's the rummiest start!
With your science and your books and your
     the'ries about spooks,   35
   Did you ever hear of looking in your heart?

I didn't mean your pocket, Mr., no:
   I mean that having children and a wife,
With thirty bob on which to come and go,
   Is n't dancing to the tabor and the fife: 40
When it does n't make you drink, by Heaven!
     it makes you think,
   And notice curious items about life.

I step into my heart and there I meet
   A god-almighty devil singing small,
Who would like to shout and whistle in the
     street,   45
   And squelch the passers flat against the wall;
If the whole world was a cake he had the power
     to take,
   He would take it, ask for more, and eat them
     all.

And I meet a sort of simpleton beside,
   The kind that life is always giving beans; 50
With thirty bob a week to keep a bride
   He fell in love and married in his teens:

At thirty bob he stuck; but he knows it is n't
     luck:
   He knows the seas are deeper than tureens.

And the god-almighty devil and the fool   55
   That meet me in the High Street on the
     strike,
When I walk about my heart a-gathering wool,
   Are my good and evil angels if you like.
And both of them together in every kind of
     weather
   Ride me like a double-seated bike.   60

That 's rough a bit and needs its meaning curled.
   But I have a high old hot un in my mind—
A most engrugious notion of the world,
   That leaves your lightning 'rithmetic behind:
I give it at a glance when I say 'There ain't no
     chance,   65
   Nor nothing of the lucky-lottery kind.'

And it 's this way that I make it out to be
   No fathers, mothers, countries, climates—
     none;
Not Adam was responsible for me,
   Nor society, nor systems, nary one: 70
A little sleeping seed, I woke—I did, indeed—
   A million years before the blooming sun.

I woke because I thought the time had come;
   Beyond my will there was no other cause;
And everywhere I found myself at home,   75
   Because I chose to be the thing I was;
And in whatever shape of mollusc or of ape
   I always went according to the laws.

I was the love that chose my mother out;
   I joined two lives and from the union burst; 80
My weakness and my strength without a doubt
   Are mine alone forever from the first:
It 's just the very same with a difference in the
     name
   As 'Thy will be done.' You say it if you durst!

They say it daily up and down the land   85
   As easy as you take a drink, it 's true;
But the difficultest go to understand,
   And the difficultest job a man can do,
Is to come it brave and meek with thirty bob a
     week,
   And feel that that 's the proper thing for you.

It 's a naked child against a hungry wolf;   91
   It 's playing bowls upon a splitting wreck;
It 's walking on a string across a gulf
   With millstones fore-and-aft about your neck;
But the thing is daily done by many and many
     a one;   95
   And we fall, face downward, fighting, on the
     deck.

FRANCIS THOMPSON
(1859–1907)

THE HOUND OF HEAVEN

I FLED Him, down the nights and down the days;
   I fled Him, down the arches of the years;
I fled Him, down the labyrinthine ways
   Of my own mind; and in the mist of tears
I hid from Him, and under running laughter.   5
      Up vistaed hopes, I sped;
      And shot, precipitated,
   Adown Titanic glooms of chasmèd fears,
From those strong Feet that followed, followed after.
      But with unhurrying chase,   10
      And unperturbèd pace,
Deliberate speed, majestic instancy,
      They beat—and a Voice beat
      More instant than the Feet—
'*All things betray thee, who betrayest Me.*'   15
      I pleaded, outlaw-wise,
By many a hearted casement, curtained red,
   Trellised with intertwining charities;
(For, though I knew His love Who followèd,
      Yet was I sore adread   20
Lest, having Him, I must have nought beside.)
But, if one little casement parted wide,
   The gust of His approach would clash it to.
   Fear wist not to evade as Love wist to pursue.
Across the margent of the world I fled,   25
   And troubled the gold gateways of the stars,
   Smiting for shelter on their clangèd bars;
      Fretted to dulcet jars
And silvern chatter the pale ports o' the moon.
I said to dawn: Be sudden; to eve: Be soon—   30
   With thy young skyey blossoms heap me over
      From this tremendous Lover!
Float thy vague veil about me, lest He see!
   I tempted all His servitors, but to find
My own betrayal in their constancy,   35
In faith to Him their fickleness to me,
   Their traitorous trueness, and their loyal deceit.
To all swift things for swiftness did I sue;
   Clung to the whistling mane of every wind.
      But whether they swept, smoothly fleet,
The long savannahs of the blue;   41
      Or whether, Thunder-driven,
   They clanged His chariot 'thwart a heaven,
Plashy with flying lightnings round the spurn o' their feet:—
Fear wist not to evade as Love wist to pursue.   45
      Still with unhurrying chase,
      And unperturbèd pace,
Deliberate speed, majestic instancy,
      Came on the following Feet,
      And a Voice above their beat—   50
'*Nought shelters thee, who wilt not shelter Me.*'

I sought no more that after which I strayed
   In face of man or maid;
But still within the little children's eyes
Seems something, something that replies,   55
   They at least are for me, surely for me!
I turned me to them very wistfully;
But just as their young eyes grew sudden fair
   With dawning answers there,   59
Their angel plucked them from me by the hair.
'Come then, ye other children, Nature's—share
With me' (said I) 'your delicate fellowship;
      Let me greet you lip to lip,
      Let me twine with you caresses,
          Wantoning   65
   With our Lady-Mother's vagrant tresses,
          Banqueting
   With her in her wind-walled palace,
   Underneath her azured daïs,
   Quaffing, as your taintless way is,   70
      From a chalice
Lucent-weeping out of the dayspring.'
So it was done:
I in their delicate fellowship was one—
Drew the bolt of Nature's secrecies.   75
      I knew all the swift importings
      On the wilful face of skies;
      I knew how the clouds arise,
      Spumèd of the wild sea-snortings;
      All that 's born or dies   80
   Rose and drooped with; made them shapers
Of mine own moods, or wailful or divine—
      With them joyed and was bereaven.
      I was heavy with the even,
   When she lit her glimmering tapers   85
   Round the day's dead sanctities.
   I laughed in the morning's eyes.
I triumphed and I saddened with all weather,
   Heaven and I wept together,
And its sweet tears were salt with mortal mine;
Against the red throb of its sunset-heart   91
   I laid my own to beat,
   And share commingling heat;
But not by that, by that, was eased my human smart.
In vain my tears were wet on Heaven's gray cheek.   95
For ah! we know not what each other says,
   These things and I; in sound *I* speak—
Their sound is but their stir, they speak by silences.
Nature, poor stepdame, cannot slake my drouth;
   Let her, if she would owe me,   100
Drop yon blue bosom-veil of sky, and show me
   The breasts o' her tenderness:
Never did any milk of hers once bless
   My thirsting mouth.

      Nigh and nigh draws the chase,   105
      With unperturbèd pace,

Deliberate speed, majestic instancy,
    And past those noisèd Feet
    A Voice comes yet more fleet—   109
'Lo! nought contents thee, who content'st not Me.'

Naked I wait Thy love's uplifted stroke!
My harness piece by piece Thou hast hewn from me,
    And smitten me to my knee;
    I am defenseless utterly,
    I slept, methinks, and woke,   115
And, slowly gazing, find me stripped in sleep.
In the rash lustihead of my young powers,
    I shook the pillaring hours
And pulled my life upon me; grimed with smears,
I stand amid the dust o' the mounded years—120
My mangled youth lies dead beneath the heap.
My days have crackled and gone up in smoke,
Have puffed and burst as sun-starts on a stream.
    Yea, faileth now even dream
The dreamer, and the lute the lutanist;   125
Even the linked fantasies, in whose blossomy twist
I swung the earth a trinket at my wrist,
Are yielding: cords of all too weak account
For earth, with heavy griefs so overplussed.
    Ah! is Thy love indeed   130
A weed, albeit an amaranthine weed,
Suffering no flowers except its own to mount?
    Ah! must—
    Designer infinite!—
Ah! must Thou char the wood ere Thou canst limn with it?   135
My freshness spent its wavering shower i' the dust;
And now my heart is as a broken fount,
Wherein tear-drippings stagnate, spilt down ever
    From the dank thoughts that shiver
Upon the sighful branches of my mind.   140
    Such is; what is to be?
The pulp so bitter, how shall taste the rind?
I dimly guess what Time in mists confounds;
Yet ever and anon a trumpet sounds
From the hid battlements of Eternity: 145
Those shaken mists a space unsettle, then
Round the half-glimpsèd turrets slowly wash again;
    But not ere him who summoneth
    I first have seen, enwound
With glooming robes purpureal, cypress-crowned;   150
His name I know, and what his trumpet saith.
Whether man's heart or life it be which yields
    Thee harvest, must Thy harvest fields
    Be dunged with rotten death?

    Now of that long pursuit   155
    Comes on at hand the bruit;
That Voice is round me like a bursting sea:
    'And is thy earth so marred,
    Shattered in shard on shard?
Lo, all things fly thee, for thou fliest Me!'   160

    Strange, piteous, futile thing!
Wherefore should any set thee love apart?
Seeing none but I makes much of nought'
    (He said),
'And human love needs human meriting:
    How hast thou merited—   165
Of all man's clotted clay the dingiest clot?
    Alack, thou knowest not
How little worthy of any love thou art!
Whom wilt thou find to love ignoble thee,
    Save Me, save only Me?   170
All which I took from thee I did but take,
    Not for thy harms,
But just that thou might'st seek it in My arms,
    All which thy child's mistake
Fancies as lost, I have stored for thee at home: 175
    Rise, clasp My hand, and come!'

    Halts by me that footfall:
    Is my gloom, after all,
Shade of His hand, outstretched caressingly?
    'Ah, fondest, blindest, weakest,   180
    I am He Whom thou seekest!
Thou dravest love from thee, who dravest Me.'
    (1893)

ALFRED EDWARD HOUSMAN
(1859–1936)

A SHROPSHIRE LAD

IV—REVEILLE

WAKE: the silver dusk returning
    Up the beach of darkness brims,
And the ship of sunrise burning
    Strands upon the eastern rims.

Wake: the vaulted shadow shatters,   5
    Trampled to the door it spanned,
And the tent of night in tatters
    Straws the sky-pavilioned land.

Up, lad, up, 't is late for lying:
    Hear the drums of morning play;   10
Hark, the empty highways crying
    'Who 'll beyond the hills away?'

Towns and countries woo together,
    Forelands beacon, belfries call;
Never lad that trod on leather   15
    Lived to feast his heart on all.

Up, lad: thews that lie and cumber
    Sunlit pallets never thrive;
Morns abed and daylight slumber
    Were not meant for man alive.   20

Clay lies still, but blood 's a rover;
    Breath 's a ware that will not keep.
Up, lad: when the journey 's over
    There 'll be time enough to sleep.

V

Oh, see how thick the goldcup flowers
  Are lying in field and lane,
With dandelions to tell the hours
  That never are told again.
Oh, may I squire you round the meads   5
  And pick you posies gay?
—'T will do no harm to take my arm.
  'You may, young man, you may.'

Ah, spring was sent for lass and lad,
  'T is now the blood runs gold,   10
And man and maid had best be glad
  Before the world is old.
What flowers to-day may flower to-morrow,
  But never as good as new.
—Suppose I wound my right arm round—   15
  ''T is true, young man, 't is true.'

Some lads there are, 't is shame to say,
  That only court to thieve,
And once they bear the bloom away
  'T is little enough they leave.   20
Then keep your heart for men like me
  And safe from trustless chaps.
My love is true for all and you.
  'Perhaps, young man, perhaps.'

Oh, look in my eyes then, can you doubt?   25
  —Why, 't is a mile from town.
How green the grass is all about!
  We might as well sit down.
—Ah, life, what is it but a flower?
  Why must true lovers sigh?   30
Be kind, have pity, my own, my pretty,—
  'Good-by, young man, good-by.'

XXXI—THE NEW MISTRESS

'Oh, sick I am to see you, will you never let me be?
You may be good for something but you are not good for me.
Oh, go where you are wanted, for you are not wanted here.'
And that was all the farewell when I parted from my dear.

'I will go where I am wanted, to a lady born and bred,   5
Who will dress me free for nothing in a uniform of red;
She will not be sick to see me if I only keep it clean:
I will go where I am wanted for a soldier of the Queen.

'I will go where I am wanted, for a sergeant does not mind;
He may be sick to see me but he treats me very kind: 10
He gives me beer and breakfast and a ribbon for my cap,
And I never knew a sweetheart spend her money on a chap.

'I will go where I am wanted, where there's room for one or two,
And the men are none too many for the work there is to do;
Where the standing line wears thinner and the dropping dead lie thick;   15
And the enemies of England they shall see me and be sick.'

XLI

In my own shire, if I was sad,
Homely comforters I had:
The earth, because my heart was sore,
Sorrowed for the son she bore;
And standing hills, long to remain,   5
Shared their short-lived comrade's pain.
And bound for the same bourn as I,
On every road I wandered by,
Trod beside me, close and dear,
The beautiful and death-struck year: 10
Whether in the woodland brown
I heard the beechnut rustle down,
And saw the purple crocus pale
Flower about the autumn dale;
Or littering far the fields of May   15
Lady-smocks a-bleaching lay,
And like a skylit water stood
The bluebells in the azured wood.
Yonder, lightening other loads,
The seasons range the country roads,   20
But here in London streets I ken
No such helpmates, only men;
And these are not in plight to bear,
If they would, another's care.
They have enough as 't is: I see   25
In many an eye that measures me
The mortal sickness of a mind
Too unhappy to be kind.
Undone with misery, all they can
Is to hate their fellow man;   30
And till they drop they needs must still
Look at you and wish you ill.

XLIX

Think no more, lad; laugh, be jolly:
  Why should men make haste to die?
Empty heads and tongues a-talking
Make the rough road easy walking,
And the feather pate of folly   5
  Bears the falling sky.
Oh, 't is jesting, dancing, drinking
  Spins the heavy world around.
If young hearts were not so clever,
Oh, they would be young forever: 10
Think no more; 't is only thinking
  Lays lads underground.

(1896)

SIR HENRY NEWBOLT
(1862–)

DRAKE'S DRUM

Drake he 's in his hammock an' a thousand mile away,
  (*Capten, art tha sleepin' there below?*)
Slung atween the round shot in Nombre Dios Bay,
  An' dreamin' arl the time o' Plymouth Hoe.
Yarnder lumes the Island, yarnder lie the ships,
  Wi' sailor lads a-dancin' heel-an'-toe, 6
An' the shore-lights flashin', an' the night-tide dashin',
  He sees et arl so plainly as he saw et long ago.

Drake he was a Devon man, an' ruled the Devon seas,
  (*Capten, art tha sleepin' there below?*) 10
Rovin' tho' his death fell, he went wi' heart at ease,
  An' dreamin' arl the time o' Plymouth Hoe.
'Take my drum to England, hang et by the shore,
  Strike et when your powder 's runnin' low;
If the Dons sight Devon, I 'll quit the port o' Heaven, 15
  An' drum them up the Channel as we drummed them long ago.'

Drake he 's in his hammock till the great Armadas come,
  (*Capten, art tha sleepin' there below?*)
Slung atween the round shot, listenin' for the drum,
  An dreamin' arl the time o' Plymouth Hoe. 20
Call him on the deep sea, call him up the Sound,
  Call him where ye sail to meet the foe;
Where the old trade 's plyin' an' the old flag flyin'
  They shall find him ware an' wakin', as they found him long ago!
(1898)

VITAI LAMPADA

There 's a breathless hush in the Close to-night—
  Ten to make and the match to win—
A bumping pitch and a blinding light,
  An hour to play and the last man in.
And it 's not for the sake of a ribboned coat, 5
  Or the selfish hope of a season's fame,
But his Captain's hand on his shoulder smote—
  'Play up! play up! and play the game!'

The sand of the desert is sodden red,—
  Red with the wreck of a square that broke;—
The Gatling's jammed and the Colonel dead, 11
  And the regiment blind with dust and smoke.
The river of death has brimmed his banks,
  And England's far, and Honor a name,
But the voice of a schoolboy rallies the ranks: 15
  'Play up! play up! and play the game!'

This is the word that year by year,
  While in her place the School is set,
Every one of her sons must hear,
  And none that hears it dare forget. 20
This they all with a joyful mind
  Bear through life like a torch in flame,
And falling fling to the host behind—
  'Play up! play up! and play the game!'
(1898)

CLIFTON CHAPEL

This is the Chapel: here, my son,
  Your father thought the thoughts of youth,
And heard the words that one by one
  The touch of Life has turned to truth.
Here in a day that is not far, 5
  You too may speak with noble ghosts
Of manhood and the vows of war
  You made before the Lord of Hosts.

To set the cause above renown,
  To love the game beyond the prize, 10
To honor, while you strike him down,
  The foe that comes with fearless eyes;
To count the life of battle good,
  And dear the land that gave you birth,
And dearer yet the brotherhood 15
  That binds the brave of all the earth—

My son, the oath is yours: the end
  Is His, Who built the world of strife,
Who gave His children Pain for friend,
  And Death for surest hope of life. 20
To-day and here the fight 's begun,
  Of the great fellowship you 're free;
Henceforth the School and you are one,
  And what You are the race shall be.

God send you fortune: yet be sure, 25
  Among the lights that gleam and pass,
You 'll live to follow none more pure
  Than that which glows on yonder brass.
'*Qui procul hinc*,' the legend 's writ,—
  The frontier-grave is far away— 30
'*Qui ante diem periit:
  Sed miles, sed pro patriâ.*'
(1898)

RUDYARD KIPLING
(1865–1936)

THE BALLAD OF EAST AND WEST

Oh, East is East, and West is West, and never
    the twain shall meet,
Till Earth and Sky stand presently at God's great
    Judgment Seat;
But there is neither East nor West, Border, nor
    Breed, nor Birth,
When two strong men stand face to face, tho' they
    come from the ends of the earth!

Kamal is out with twenty men to raise the
    Border side,   5
And he has lifted the Colonel's mare that is
    the Colonel's pride:
He has lifted her out of the stable-door between
    the dawn and the day,
And turned the calkins upon her feet, and ridden
    her far away.
Then up and spoke the Colonel's son that led
    a troop of the Guides:
'Is there never a man of all my men can say
    where Kamal hides?'   10

Then up and spoke Mahommed Khan, the son
    of the Ressaldar,
'If ye know the track of the morning-mist, ye
    know where his pickets are.
'At dusk he harries the Abazai—at dawn he is
    into Bonair,
'But he must go by Fort Bukloh to his own
    place to fare,
'So if ye gallop to Fort Bukloh as fast as a bird
    can fly,   15
'By the favor of God ye may cut him off ere he
    win to the Tongue of Jagai,
'But if he be passed the Tongue of Jagai, right
    swiftly turn ye then,
'For the length and the breadth of that grisly
    plain is sown with Kamal's men.
'There is rock to the left, and rock to the right,
    and low lean thorn between,
'And ye may hear a breech-bolt snick where
    never a man is seen.'   20

The Colonel's son has taken a horse, and a raw
    rough dun was he,
With the mouth of a bell and the heart of Hell,
    and the head of the gallows-tree.
The Colonel's son to the Fort has won, they bid
    him stay to eat—
Who rides at the tail of a Border thief, he sits
    not long at his meat.
He's up and away from Fort Bukloh as fast as
    he can fly,   25
Till he was aware of his father's mare in the gut
    of the Tongue of Jagai,
Till he was aware of his father's mare with
    Kamal upon her back,
And when he could spy the white of her eye, he
    made the pistol crack.
He has fired once, he has fired twice, but the
    whistling ball went wide.
'Ye shoot like a soldier,' Kamal sa'd. 'Show
    now if ye can ride.'   30

It's up and over the Tongue of Jagai, as blown
    dust-devils go,
The dun he fled like a stag of ten, but the mare
    like a barren doe.
The dun he leaned against the bit and slugged
    his head above,
But the red mare played with the snaffle-bars,
    as a maiden plays with a glove.
There was rock to the left and rock to the right,
    and low lean thorn between,   35
And thrice he heard a breech-bolt snick tho'
    never a man was seen.
They have ridden the low moon out of the sky,
    their hoofs drum up the dawn,
The dun he went like a wounded bull, but the
    mare like a new-roused fawn.
The dun he fell at a water-course—in a woeful
    heap fell he,
And Kamal has turned the red mare back, and
    pulled the rider free.   40
He has knocked the pistol out of his hand—
    small room was there to strive,
'' T was only by favor of mine,' quoth he, 'ye
    rode so long alive:
'There was not a rock for twenty mile, there
    was not a clump of tree,
'But covered a man of my own men with his
    rifle cocked on his knee.
'If I had raised my bridle-hand, as I have held
    it low,   45
'The little jackals that flee so fast, were feasting
    all in a row:
'If I had bowed my head on my breast, as I
    have held it high,
'The kite that whistles above us now were
    gorged till she could not fly.'

Lightly answered the Colonel's son:—'Do good
    to bird and beast,
'But count who come for the broken meats
    before thou makest a feast.   50
'If there should follow a thousand swords to
    carry my bones away,
'Belike the price of a jackal's meal were more
    than a thief could pay.
'They will feed their horse on the standing crop,
    their men on the garnered grain,
'The thatch of the byres will serve their fires
    when all the cattle are slain.
'But if thou thinkest the price be fair,—thy
    brethren wait to sup,   55

'The hound is kin to the jackal-spawn,—howl,
  dog, and call them up!
'And if thou thinkest the price be high, in steer
  and gear and stack,
'Give me my father's mare again, and I 'll fight
  my own way back!'
Kamal has gripped him by the hand and set
  him upon his feet.
'No talk shall be of dogs,' said he, 'when wolf
  and gray wolf meet. 60
'May I eat dirt if thou hast hurt of me in deed
  or breath;
'What dam of lances brought thee forth to jest
  at the dawn with Death?'
Lightly answered the Colonel's son, 'I hold by
  the blood of my clan:
Take up the mare for my father's gift—by
  God, she has carried a man!'
The red mare ran to the Colonel's son, and nuzzled against his breast, 65
'We be two strong men,' said Kamal then,
  'but she loveth the younger best.
'So she shall go with a lifter's dower, my turquoise-studded rein,
'My broidered saddle and saddle-cloth, and
  silver stirrups twain.'

The Colonel's son a pistol drew and held it
  muzzle-end,
'Ye have taken the one from a foe,' said he;
  'will ye take the mate from a friend?' 70
'A gift for a gift,' said Kamal straight; 'a limb
  for the risk of a limb.
'Thy father has sent his son to me, I 'll send
  my son to him!'
With that he whistled his only son, that dropped
  from a mountain-crest—
He trod the ling like a buck in spring, and he
  looked like a lance in rest.
'Now here is thy master,' Kamal said, 'who
  leads a troop of the Guides, 75
'And thou must ride at his left side as shield on
  shoulder rides.
'Till Death or I cut loose the tie, at camp and
  board and bed,
'Thy life is his—thy fate it is **to guar**d him with
  thy head.
'So thou must eat the White Queen's meat, and
  all her foes are thine,
'And thou must harry thy father's hold for the
  peace of the Border-line, 80
'And thou must make a trooper tough and hack
  thy way to power—
'Belike they will raise thee to Ressaldar when I
  am hanged in Peshawur.'

They have looked each other between the eyes,
  and there they have found no fault,
They have taken the Oath of the Brother-in-
  Blood on leavened bread and salt:
They have taken the Oath of the Brother-in-
  Blood on fire and fresh-cut sod, 85
On the hilt and the haft of the Khyber knife,
  and the Wondrous Names of God.
The Colonel's son he rides the mare and Kamal's
  boy the dun,
And two have come back to Fort Bukloh where
  there went forth but one.
And when they drew to the Quarter-Guard, full
  twenty swords flew clear—
There was not a man but carried his feud with
  the blood of the mountaineer. 90
'Ha' done! ha' done!' said the Colonel's son.
  'Put up the steel at your sides!
'Last night ye had struck at a Border thief
  —to-night 't is a man of the Guides!'

Oh, East is East, and West is West, and never
  the two shall meet,
Till Earth and Sky stand presently at God's great
  Judgment Seat;
But there is neither East nor West, Border, nor
  Breed, nor Birth, 95
When two strong men stand face to face, tho' they
  come from the ends of the earth.

(1890)

DANNY DEEVER

'WHAT are the bugles blowin' for?' said Files-
  on-Parade.
'To turn you out, to turn you out,' the Color-
  Sergeant said.
'What makes you look so white, so white?' said
  Files-on-Parade.
'I 'm dreadin' what I 've got to watch,' the
  Color-Sergeant said.
  For they 're hangin' Danny Deever, you can
    'ear the Dead March play, 5
  The regiment 's in 'ollow square—they 're
    hangin' him to-day;
  They 've taken of his buttons off an' cut his
    stripes away,
  An' they 're hangin' Danny Deever in the
    mornin'.

'What makes the rear-rank breathe so 'ard?'
  said Files-on-Parade.
'It 's bitter cold, it 's bitter cold,' the Color-
  Sergeant said. 10
'What makes that front-rank man fall down?'
  says Files-on-Parade.
'A touch o' sun, a touch o' sun,' the Color-
  Sergeant said.
  They are hangin' Danny Deever, they are
    marchin' of 'im round,
  They 'ave 'alted Danny Deever by 'is coffin
    on the ground;

An' 'e 'll swing in 'arf a minute for a sneakin'
    shootin' hound—   15
O they 're hangin' Danny Deever in the
    mornin'!

''Is cot was right-'and cot to mine,' said Files-
    on-Parade.
''E 's sleepin' out an' far to-night,' the Color-
    Sergeant said.
'I 've drunk 'is beer a score o' times,' said Files-
    on-Parade.
''E 's drinkin' bitter beer alone,' the Color-
    Sergeant said.   20

They are hangin' Danny Deever, you must
    mark 'im to 'is place,
For 'e shot a comrade sleepin'—you must
    look 'im in the face;
Nine 'undred of 'is country an' the regiment's
    disgrace,
While they 're hangin' Danny Deever in the
    mornin'.

'What 's that so black agin the sun?' said Files-
    on-Parade.   25
'It 's Danny fightin' 'ard for life,' the Color-
    Sergeant said.
'What 's that that whimpers over'ead?' said
    Files-on-Parade.
'It 's Danny's soul that 's passin' now,' the
    Color-Sergeant said.

For they 're done with Danny Deever, you
    can 'ear the quickstep play,
The regiment 's in column, an' they 're
    marchin' us away;   30
Ho! the young recruits are shakin', an' they 'll
    want their beer to-day,
After hangin' Danny Deever in the mornin'.
                                       (1890)

RECESSIONAL

God of our fathers, known of old
    Lord of our far-flung battle-line—
Beneath whose awful hand we hold
    Dominion over palm and pine—
Lord God of Hosts, be with us yet,   5
Lest we forget—lest we forget!

The tumult and the shouting dies—
    The captains and the kings depart—
Still stands Thine ancient sacrifice,
    An humble and a contrite heart.   10
Lord God of Hosts, be with us yet,
Lest we forget—lest we forget!

Far-called our navies melt away—
    On dune and headland sinks the fire—
Lo, all our pomp of yesterday   15
    Is one with Nineveh and Tyre!
Judge of the Nations, spare us yet,
Lest we forget—lest we forget!

If, drunk with sight of power, we loose
    Wild tongues that have not Thee in awe—
Such boasting as the Gentiles use   21
    Or lesser breeds without the Law—
Lord God of Hosts, be with us yet,
Lest we forget—lest we forget!

For heathen heart that puts her trust   25
    In reeking tube and iron shard—
All valiant dust that builds on dust,
    And guarding calls not Thee to guard—
For frantic boast and foolish word,
Thy Mercy on Thy People, Lord!   30
                                     Amen.
                                     (1897)

WILLIAM BUTLER YEATS
(1865–   )

THE LAKE ISLE OF INNISFREE

I will arise and go now, and go to Innisfree,
And a small cabin build there, of clay and
    wattles made;
Nine bean rows will I have there, a hive for the
    honey bee,
And live alone in the bee-loud glade.

And I shall have some peace there, for peace
    comes dropping slow,   5
Dropping from the veils of the morning to
    where the cricket sings;
There midnight 's all a glimmer, and noon a
    purple glow,
And evening 's full of the linnet's wings.

I will arise and go now, for always night and day
I hear lake water lapping with low sounds by
    the shore;   10
While I stand on the roadway, or on the pave-
    ments gray,
I hear it in the deep heart's core.

INTO THE TWILIGHT

Out-worn heart, in a time out-worn,
    Come clear of the nets of wrong and right;
    Laugh heart again in the gray twilight,
Sigh heart again in the dew of the morn.

Your mother Eire is always young.   5
    Dew ever shining and twilight gray;
    Though hope fall from you and love decay
Burning in fires of a slanderous tongue.

Come heart, where hill is heaped on hill;
    For there the mystical brotherhood   10
    Of sun and moon and hollow wood
And river and stream work out their will.

And God stands winding his lonely horn,
　And time and the world are ever in flight, 14
　And love is less kind than the gray twilight,
And hope is less dear than the dew of the morn.

RED HANRAHAN'S SONG ABOUT IRELAND

The old brown thorn trees break in two high
　　over Cummen Strand,
Under a bitter black wind that blows from the
　　left hand;
Our courage breaks like an old tree in a black
　　wind and dies,
But we have hidden in our hearts the flame out
　　of the eyes
　Of Cathleen, the daughter of Houlihan.　5

The wind has bundled up the clouds high over
　　Knocknarea,
And thrown the thunder on the stones for all
　　that Maeve can say.
Angers that are like noisy clouds have set our
　　hearts abeat;
But we have all bent low and low and kissed
　　the quiet feet
　Of Cathleen, the daughter of Houlihan.　10

The yellow pool has overflowed high up on
　　Clooth-na-Bare,
For the wet winds are blowing out of the cling-
　　ing air;
Like heavy flooded waters our bodies and our
　　blood;
But purer than a tall candle before the Holy
　　Rood
　Is Cathleen, the daughter of Houlihan.　15

SONG

From The Land of Heart's Desire

The wind blows out of the gates of the day,
　The wind blows over the lonely of heart,
And the lonely of heart is withered away
　While the faeries dance in a place apart,
Shaking their milk-white feet in a ring,　5
　Tossing their milk-white arms in the air;
For they hear the wind laugh and murmur and
　　sing
Of a land where even the old are fair,
And even the wise are merry of tongue;
　But I heard a reed of Coolaney say,　10
'When the wind has laughed and murmured and
　　sung,
　The lonely of heart is withered away.'

　　　　　　　　　　　　　(1894)

'A. E.' [GEORGE RUSSELL]
(1862–1935)

THE EARTH BREATH

From the cool and dark-lipped furrows
　Breathes a dim delight
Through the woodland's purple plumage
　To the diamond night.
Aureoles of joy encircle　　　　　　　　5
　Every blade of grass
Where the dew-fed creatures silent
　And enraptured pass.
And the restless plowman pauses,
　Turns and, wondering,　　　　　　　　10
Deep beneath his rustic habit
　Finds himself a king;
For a fiery moment looking
　With the eyes of God
Over fields a slave at morning　　　　　15
　Bowed him to the sod.
Blind and dense with revelation
　Every moment flies,
And unto the Mighty Mother,
　Gay, eternal, rise　　　　　　　　　　20
All the hopes we hold, the gladness,
　Dreams of things to be.
One of all thy generations,
　Mother, hails to thee.
Hail, and hail, and hail forever,　　　　25
　Though I turn again
From thy joy unto the human
　Vesture of pain.
I, thy child who went forth radiant
　In the golden prime,　　　　　　　　30
Find thee still the mother-hearted
　Through my night in time;
Find in thee the old enchantment
　There behind the veil
Where the gods, my brothers, linger.　　35
　Hail, forever, hail!

　　　　　　　　　　　　　(1897)

THOMAS HENRY HUXLEY (1825-1895)

THE son of an assistant master in a school at Ealing near London, Huxley was a precocious student, and qualified for the practice of medicine before he was twenty-one. In 1846 he entered the medical service of the Royal Navy and was appointed assistant (research) surgeon to the surveying ship 'Rattlesnake,' on which he spent four years in marine investigations, chiefly off the coast of Australia. Returning to London in 1850, he was elected a Fellow of the Royal Society the following year in recognition of the scientific work he had done on the voyage, and in 1854 was appointed lecturer on natural history at the Royal School of Mines, which afterwards developed into the Royal College of Science; it was a well paid and important post, which he held for over thirty years. He became a close friend of Charles Darwin, of the botanist Hooker, who about the same time was appointed assistant director of Kew Gardens, and of John Tyndall, who a little earlier had been elected to the chair of natural philosophy at the Royal Institution. Of this famous band of scientists the one to obtain most enduring fame was Darwin, whose *Origin of Species* was published in 1859. But by a happy accident it fell to Huxley's lot to be the protagonist of the new theory of natural selection which held the excited attention not only of the scientific but of the intellectual world for the next few years. The *Times* reviewer to whom the *Origin of Species* was assigned, conscious of his own incapacity to deal with it, sent it on to Huxley, who had already received advance sheets from Darwin, and a long review of the new book, written by Huxley and published in the *Times*, gave the *Origin of Species* the send-off it deserved. At the Oxford meeting of the British Association in 1860, the Bishop of Oxford (Dr. Samuel Wilberforce, better known as 'Soapy Sam') was put up to 'smash Darwin' by his ecclesiastical colleagues, who felt that their authority and that of the first chapters of Genesis was being undermined by the new theory. Huxley repelled the attack, to which the Bishop gave a somewhat personal slant, with a skill and vigor which completely turned the tables upon his redoubtable antagonist. Darwin disliked controversy, preferring to continue his researches in the quiet of his country home at Down in Kent—since 1928 a national memorial to his fame. But Huxley was a born fighter, having as he himself acknowledged something of the 'wildcat' in his natural disposition, and in the long evolutionary controversy he enjoyed himself hugely in 'episcopophagy' (bishop-eating), tilting with Mr. Gladstone over 'the Gadarene pig affair,' and similar diversions in the intellectual arena. He was qualified for the leading position in the debate on evolution not only by a delight in battle but by keen intelligence, sound scientific knowledge, absolute devotion to the truth as he saw it, a wide acquaintance with literature, both English and foreign, and a literary style, which, at once vigorous and polished, was an admirable weapon in controversy. He interested himself in the philosophic aspect of modern science and especially in the application of scientific methods to education. He had already attained world-wide eminence when he came to the United States to give the inaugural address at the opening of Johns Hopkins University in 1876, and lectured on evolution at New York and other important centers. Beside his admirably clear expositions of the new scientific theory and its bearings upon life and opinion, he was an excellent essayist on general topics; one of his *Lay Sermons* is reproduced below. His eminence as an investigator was recognized by his election as President of the Royal Society in 1883, but the impression he made upon his generation was that of an eager and brilliant spirit who made the religion of science a potent influence in his own day. His aims were excellently outlined in the autobiographical fragment he wrote a year before his death:

'To promote the application of scientific methods of investigation to all the problems of life to the best of my ability; in the conviction, which has grown with my growth and strengthened with my strength, that there is no alleviation for the sufferings of mankind except veracity of thought and of action, and the resolute facing of the world as it is when the garment of make-believe by which pious hands have hidden its uglier features is stripped off. It is with this intent that I have subordinated any reasonable or unreasonable ambition for scientific fame which I may have permitted myself to entertain, to other ends: to the popularization of science; to the development and organization of scientific education; to the endless series of battles and skirmishes over evolution; to the untiring opposition to that ecclesiastical spirit, that clericalism, which in England, as everywhere else and to whatever denomination it may belong, is the deadly enemy of science. In striving for the attainment of these objects, I have been but one among many; and I shall be well content to be remembered, or even not remembered, as such.'

From LAY SERMONS

EMANCIPATION—BLACK AND WHITE

QUASHIE's plaintive inquiry, 'Am I not a man and a brother?' seems at last to have received its final reply—the recent decision of the fierce trial by battle on the other side of the Atlantic fully concurring with that long since delivered here in a more peaceful way.

The question is settled; but even those who are most thoroughly convinced that the doom is just, must see good grounds for repudiating half the arguments which have been employed by the winning side; and for doubting whether its ultimate results will embody the hopes of the victors, though they may more than realize the fears of the vanquished. It may be quite true that some negroes are better than some white men; but no rational man, cognizant of the facts, believes that the average negro is the equal, still less the superior, of the average white man. And, if this be true, it is simply incredible that, when all his disabilities are removed, and our prognathous relative has a fair field and no favor, as well as no oppressor, he will be able to compete successfully with his bigger-brained and smaller-jawed rival, in a contest which is to be carried on by thoughts and not by bites. The highest places in the hierarchy of civilization will assuredly not be within the reach of our dusky cousins, though it is by no means necessary that they should be restricted to the lowest. But whatever the position of stable equilibrium into which the laws of social gravitation may bring the negro, all responsibility for the result will henceforward lie between Nature and him. The white man may wash his hands of it, and the Caucasian conscience be void of reproach for evermore. And this, if we look to the bottom of the matter, is the real justification of the abolition policy.

The doctrine of equal natural rights may be an illogical delusion; emancipation may convert the slave into a pauperized man; mankind may even have to do without cotton shirts; but all these evils must be faced if the moral law, that no human being can arbitrarily dominate over another without grievous damage to his own nature, be, as many think, as readily demonstrable by experiment as any physical truth. If this be true, no slavery can be abolished without a double emancipation, and the master will benefit by freedom more than the freedman.

The like considerations apply to all the other questions of emancipation which are at present stirring the world—the multifarious demands that classes of mankind shall be relieved from restrictions imposed by the artifice of man, and not by the necessities of Nature. One of the most important, if not the most important, of all these, is that which daily threatens to become the 'irrepressible' woman question. What social and political rights have women? What ought they to be allowed, or not allowed to do, be, and suffer? And, as involved in, and underlying all these questions, how ought they to be educated?

There are philogynists as fanatical as any 'misogynists' who, reversing our antiquated notions, bid the man look upon the woman as the higher type of humanity; who ask us to regard the female intellect as the clearer and the quicker, if not the stronger; who desire us to look up to the feminine moral sense as the purer and nobler; and bid man abdicate his usurped sovereignty over Nature in favor of the female line. On the other hand, there are persons not to be outdone in all loyalty and just respect for womankind, but by nature hard of head and haters of delusion, however charming, who not only repudiate the new woman-worship which so many sentimentalists and some philosophers are desirous of setting up, but, carrying their audacity further, deny even the natural equality of the sexes. They assert, on the contrary, that in every excellent character, whether mental or physical, the average woman is inferior to the average man, in the sense of having that character less in quantity, and lower in quality. Tell these persons of the rapid perceptions and the instinctive intellectual insight of women, and they reply that the feminine mental peculiarities, which pass under these names, are merely the outcome of a greater impressibility to the superficial aspects of things, and of the absence of that restraint upon expression, which, in men, is imposed by reflection and a sense of responsibility. Talk of the passive endurance of the weaker sex, and opponents of this kind remind you that Job was a man, and that, until quite recent times, patience and long-suffering were not counted among the specially feminine virtues. Claim passionate tenderness as especially feminine, and the inquiry is made whether all the best love-poetry in existence (except, perhaps, the 'Sonnets from the Portuguese') has not been written by men; whether the song which embodies the ideal of pure and tender passion—Adelaida—was written by *Frau* Beethoven; whether it was the Fornarina, or Raphael, who painted the Sistine Madonna. Nay, we have known one such heretic go so far as to lay his hands upon the ark itself, so to speak, and to defend the startling paradox that, even in physical beauty, man is the superior. He admitted, indeed, that there was a brief period of early youth when it might be hard to say whether the prize should be awarded to the graceful undulations of the female figure, or the perfect balance and supple vigor of the male frame. But while our new Paris might hesitate between the youthful Bacchus and the Venus emerging from the foam, he averred that, when Venus and Bacchus had reached thirty, the point no longer admitted of a doubt; the male form having then attained its greatest nobility, while the female is far gone in decadence; and that, at this epoch, womanly beauty, so far as it is independent of grace or expression, is a question of drapery and accessories.

Supposing, however, that all these arguments have a certain foundation; admitting for a moment, that they are comparable to those by which the inferiority of the negro to the white man may be demonstrated, are they of any value as against woman-emancipation? Do they afford us the smallest ground for refusing to educate women as well as men? No mistake is so commonly made by clever people as that of assuming a cause to be bad because the arguments of its supporters are, to a great extent, nonsensical. And we conceive that those who may laugh at the arguments of the extreme philogynists, may yet feel bound to work heart and soul towards the attainment of their practical ends.

As regards education, for example. Granting the alleged defects of women, is it not somewhat absurd to sanction and maintain a system of education which would seem to have been specially contrived to exaggerate all these defects?

Naturally not so firmly strung, nor so well balanced, as boys, girls are in a great measure debarred from the sports and physical exercises which are justly thought absolutely necessary for the full development of the vigor of the more favored sex. Women are, by nature, more excitable than men—prone to be swept by tides of emotion, proceeding from hidden and inward, as well as from obvious and external causes; and female education does its best to weaken every physical counterpoise to this nervous mobility—tends in all ways to stimulate the emotional part of the mind and to stunt the rest. We find girls naturally timid, inclined to dependence, born conservatives, and we teach them that independence is unladylike; that blind faith is the right frame of mind; and that whatever we may be permitted, and indeed encouraged, to do to our brother, our sister is to be left to the tyranny of authority and tradition. With few insignificant exceptions, girls have been educated either to be drudges, or toys, beneath a man; or a sort of angels above him; the highest ideal aimed at oscillating between Clärchen and Beatrice. The possibility that the ideal of womanhood lies neither in the fair saint, nor in the fair sinner; that the female type of character is neither better nor worse than the male, but only weaker; that women are meant neither to be men's guides nor their playthings, but their comrades, their fellows and their equals, so far as Nature puts no bar to that equality, does not seem to have entered into the minds of those who have had the conduct of the education of girls.

If the present system of female education stands self-condemned, as inherently absurd; and if that which we have just indicated is the true position of woman, what is the first step towards a better state of things? We reply, emancipate girls. Recognize the fact that they share the senses, perceptions, feelings, reasoning powers, emotions, of boys, and that the mind of the average girl is less different from that of the average boy, than the mind of one boy is from that of another; so that whatever argument justifies a given education for all boys, justifies its application to girls as well. So far from imposing artificial restrictions upon the acquirement of knowledge by women, throw every facility in their way. Let our Faustinas, if they will, toil through the whole round of

'*Juristerei und Medizin,
Und lieder! auch Philosophie.*'

Let us have 'sweet girl graduates' by all means. They will be none the less sweet for a little wisdom; and the 'golden hair' will not curl the less gracefully outside the head by reason of there being brains within. Nay, if obvious practical difficulties can be overcome, let those women who feel inclined to do so descend into the gladiatorial arena of life, not merely in the guise of *retiariæ*, as heretofore, but as bold *sicariæ*, breasting the open fray. Let them, if they so please, become merchants, barristers, politicians. Let them have a fair field, but let them understand, as the necessary correlative, that they are to have no favor. Let Nature alone sit high above the lists, 'rain influence and judge the prize.'

And the result? For our parts, though loth to prophesy, we believe it will be that of other emancipations. Women will find their place, and it will neither be that in which they have been held, nor that to which some of them aspire. Nature's old salique law will not be repealed, and no change of dynasty will be effected. The big chests, the massive brains, the vigorous muscles and stout frames, of the best men will carry the day, whenever it is worth their while to contest the prizes of life with the best women. And the hardship of it is, that the very improvement of the women will lessen their chances. Better mothers will bring forth better sons, and the impetus gained by the one sex will be transmitted, in the next generation, to the other. The most Darwinian of theorists will not venture to propound the doctrine, that the physical disabilities under which women have hitherto labored, in the struggle for existence with men, are likely to be removed by even the most skilfully conducted process of educational selection.

We are, indeed, fully prepared to believe that the bearing of children may, and ought, to become as free from danger and disability, to the civilized woman, as it is to the savage; nor is it improbable that, as society advances towards its right organization, motherhood will occupy a less space of woman's life than it has hitherto done. But still, unless the human species is to come to an end altogether—a consummation which can hardly be desired by even the most ardent advocate of 'women's rights'—somebody must be good enough to take the trouble of annually adding to the world exactly as many people as die out of it. In consequence of some domestic difficulties, Sydney Smith is said to have suggested that it would have been good for the human race had the model offered by the hive been followed, and had all the working part of the female community been neuters. Failing any thorough-going reform of this kind, we see nothing for it but the old division of humanity into men potentially, or actually, fathers, and women potentially, if not actually, mothers. And we fear that so long as this potential motherhood is her lot, woman will be found to be fearfully weighted in the race of life.

The duty of man is to see that not a grain is piled upon that load beyond what Nature imposes; that injustice is not added to inequality.

(1865)

SAMUEL BUTLER (1835-1902)

BUTLER was the original Anti-Victorian, though his life was almost exactly coeval with the Victorian Age. Born of an ecclesiastical family and destined for the Anglican priesthood, he was on the point of taking holy orders when he was deterred by observing the lack of spiritual effect following the baptismal sacrament; the baptized and the unbaptized members of a boys' club in a London parish where he was working seemed to him equally unregenerate. So he disappointed his father, a clergyman in succession to a long line of distinguished clerics, and went off to New Zealand, where by diligent and successful sheep-farming he earned a competence (eked out by a legacy or two) sufficient to satisfy his modest needs for the rest of his life. From his bachelor chambers at Clifford's Inn, London, he sallied forth daily (when he was not travelling on the European or American Continent) to the British Museum Library, which now contains the numerous volumes of Note-Books, wherein he jotted down, not excerpts from other authors, but his own original reflections on men and things. Some, but not all, of these were included in his numerous books of satire on Victorian institutions, beliefs, and habits. His first satirical novel *Erewhon* (*Nowhere* spelled backward), beginning with a lively description of his New Zealand farm and the mountains near it, depicts an imagined Utopia in the spirit of Swift rather than of More. The English universities, the English Church, and many social conventionalities and foibles are satirized, though the main theme is the prevailing mechanization of modern life, which, combined with a reading of the *Origin of Species*, had spurred Butler to publish a playful fancy entitled *Darwin among the Machines* as early as 1863, when he was still in New Zealand. *Erewhon* was published in 1872 and made a considerable hit, but the author refused, for the time being, to gratify the popular demand for more of the same kind. He preferred to go his own way, antagonizing in turn the clergy (*The Fair Haven*), the scientists (*Life and Habit*), the colonies (*A Psalm of Montreal*), the classical scholars (*The Authoress of the Odyssey*) and the Shakespeare worshipers (*Shakespeare's Sonnets Reconsidered*). Having thus subjected to ridicule most of the things that his own time thought worthy of reverence, Butler was satisfied to leave for publication after his death *The Way of All Flesh*, a novel in which he satirized the family in general as an institution and the members of his own family in particular. Most of the heresies ascribed to the younger generation in the twentieth century were fathered by Samuel Butler in the nineteenth. Perhaps the difference is that what Butler got off half in jest is propounded by later writers in dead earnest.

From THE NOTE-BOOKS

YOUNG PEOPLE

WITH regard to sexual matters, the best opinion of our best medical men, the practice of those nations which have proved most vigorous and comely, the evils that have followed this or that, the good that has attended upon the other should be ascertained by men who, being neither moral nor immoral and not caring two straws what the conclusion arrived at might be, should desire only to get hold of the best available information. The result should be written down with some fullness and put before the young of both sexes as soon as they are old enough to understand such matters at all. There should be no mystery or reserve. None but the corrupt will wish to corrupt facts; honest people will accept them eagerly, whatever they may prove to be, and will convey them to others as accurately as they can. On what pretext therefore can it be well that knowledge should be withheld from the universal gaze upon a matter of such universal interest? It cannot be pretended that there is nothing to be known on these matters beyond what unaided boys and girls can be left without risk to find out for themselves. Not one in a hundred who remembers his own boyhood will say this. How, then, are they excusable who have the care of young people and yet leave a matter of such vital importance so almost absolutely to take care of itself, although they well know how common error is, how easy to fall into and how disastrous in its effects both upon the individual and the race?

Next to sexual matters there are none upon which there is such complete reserve between parents and children as on those connected with money. The father keeps his affairs as closely as he can to himself and is most jealous of letting his children into a knowledge of how he manages his money. His children are like monks in a monastery as regards money and he calls this training them up with the strictest regard to principle. Nevertheless he thinks himself ill-used if his son, on entering life, falls a victim to designing persons whose knowledge of how money is made and lost is greater than his own.

THE FAMILY

I

I BELIEVE that more unhappiness comes from this source than from any other—I mean from the attempt to prolong family connection unduly and to make people hang together who would never naturally do so. The mischief among the lower classes is not so great, but among the middle and upper classes it is killing a large number daily. And the old people do not really like it much better than the young.

II

ON my way down to Shrewsbury some time since I read the Bishop of Carlisle's *Walks in the Regions of Science*, then just published, and found the following on p. 129 in the essay which is entitled 'Man's Place in Nature.' After saying that young sparrows or robins soon lose sight of their fellow-nestlings and leave off caring for them, the bishop continues:

'Whereas "children of one family" are constantly found joined together by a love which only grows with years, and they part for their posts of duty in the world with the hope of having joyful meetings from time to time, and of meeting in a higher world when their life on earth is finished.'

I am sure my great-grandfather did not look forward to meeting his father in heaven—his father had cut him out of his will; nor can I credit my grandfather with any great longing to rejoin my great-grandfather—a worthy man enough, but one with whom nothing ever prospered. I am certain my father, after he was 40, did not wish to see my grandfather any more—indeed, long before reaching that age he had decided that Dr. Butler's life should not be written, though R. W. Evans would have been only too glad to write it. Speaking for myself, I have no wish to see my father again, and I think it likely that the Bishop of Carlisle would not be more eager to see his than I mine.

UNCONSCIOUS HUMOR

'WRITING to the Hon. Mrs. Watson in 1856, Charles Dickens says: "I have always observed within my experience that *the men who have left home very young* have, *many long years afterwards* had the tenderest regard for it. That's a pleasant thing to think of as one of the wise adjustments of this life of ours."'

HOMER'S ODYSSEY

FROM the description of the meeting between Ulysses and Telemachus it is plain that Homer considered it quite as dreadful for relations who had long been separated to come together again as for them to separate in the first instance. And this is about true.

MELCHISEDEC

HE was a really happy man. He was without father, without mother and without descent. He was an incarnate bachelor. He was a born orphan.

BACON FOR BREAKFAST

NOW (1893), when I am abroad, being older and taking less exercise, I do not want any breakfast beyond coffee and bread and butter, but when this note was written (1880), I liked a modest rasher of bacon in addition, and used to notice the jealous indignation with which heads of families who enjoyed the privilege of Cephas and the brethren of our Lord regarded it. There were they with three or four elderly unmarried daughters as well as old mama—how could they afford bacon? And there was I, a selfish bachelor—The appetizing, savory smell of my rasher seemed to drive them mad. I used to feel very uncomfortable, very small and quite aware how low it was of me to have bacon for breakfast and no daughters instead of daughters and no bacon. But when I consulted the oracles of heaven about it, I was always told to stick to my bacon and not to make a fool of myself. I despised myself but have not withered under my own contempt so completely as I ought to have done.

GOD AND MAN

TO love God is to have good health, good looks, good sense, experience, a kindly nature and a fair balance of cash in hand. 'We know that all things work together for good to them that love God.' To be loved by God is the same as to love Him. We love Him because He first loved us.

The Homeric Deity and the Pall Mall Gazette

A writer in the *Pall Mall Gazette* (I think in 1874 or 1875, and in the autumn months, but I cannot now remember) summed up Homer's conception of a god as that of a 'superlatively strong, amorous, beautiful, brave and cunning man.' This is pretty much what a good working god ought to be, but he should also be kind and have a strong sense of humor, together with a contempt for the vices of meanness and for the meannesses of virtue. After saying what I have quoted above the writer in the *Pall Mall Gazette* goes on, 'An impartial critic can judge for himself how far, if at all, this is elevated above the level of mere fetish worship.' Perhaps it is that I am not an impartial critic, but, if I am allowed to be so, I should say that the elevation above mere fetish worship was very considerable.

Good Breeding the Summum Bonum

When people ask what faith we would substitute for that which we would destroy, we answer that we destroy no faith and need substitute none. We hold the glory of God to be the summum bonum, and so do Christians generally. It is on the question of what is the glory of God that we join issue. We say it varies with the varying phases of God as made manifest in his works, but that, so far as we are ourselves concerned, the glory of God is best advanced by advancing that of man. If asked what is the glory of man we answer 'Good breeding'—using the words in their double sense and meaning both the continuance of the race and that grace of manner which the words are more commonly taken to signify. The double sense of the words is all the more significant for the unconsciousness with which it is passed over.

Advice to the Young

You will sometimes find your elders laying their heads together and saying what a bad thing it is for young men to come into a little money—that those always do best who have no expectancy, and the like. They will then quote some drivel from one of the Kingsleys about the deadening effect an income of £300 a year will have upon a man. Avoid any one whom you may hear talk in this way. The fault lies not with the legacy (which would certainly be better if there were more of it) but with those who have so mismanaged our education that we go in even greater danger of losing the money than other people are.

Religion

Is there any religion whose followers can be pointed to as distinctly more amiable and trustworthy than those of any other? If so, this should be enough. I find the nicest and best people generally profess no religion at all, but are ready to like the best men of all religions.

Heaven and Hell

Heaven is the work of the best and kindest men and women. Hell is the work of prigs, pedants and professional truth-tellers. The world is an attempt to make the best of both.

Priggishness

The essence of priggishness is setting up to be better than one's neighbor. Better may mean more virtuous, more clever, more agreeable or what not. The worst of it is that one cannot do anything outside eating one's dinner or taking a walk without setting up to know more than one's neighbors. It was this that made me say in *Life and Habit* that I was among the damned in that I wrote at all. So I am; and I am often very sorry that I was never able to reach those more saintly classes who do not set up as instructors of other people. But one must take one's lot.

Lohengrin

He was a prig. In the bedroom scene with Elsa he should have said that her question put him rather up a tree but that, as she wanted to know who he was, he would tell her and would let the Holy Grail slide.

Swells

People ask complainingly what swells have done, or do, for society that they should be able to live without working. The good swell is the creature towards which all nature has been groaning and travailing together until now. He is an ideal. He shows what may be done in the way of good breeding, health, looks, temper and fortune. He realizes men's dreams of themselves, at any rate vicariously. He preaches the gospel of grace. The world is like a spoilt child, it has this good thing given it at great expense and then says it is useless!

Science and Religion

These are reconciled in amiable and sensible people but nowhere else.

Gentleman

If we are asked what is the most essential characterization that underlies this word, the word itself will guide us to gentleness, to absence of such things as brow-beating, overbearing manners and fuss, and generally to the consideration for other people.

The Finest Men

I suppose an Italian peasant or a Breton, Norman or English fisherman, is about the best thing nature does in the way of men—the richer and the poorer being alike mistakes.

On Being a Swell All Round

I have never in my life succeeded in being this. Sometimes I get a new suit and am tidy for a while in part, meanwhile the hat, tie, boots, gloves and underclothing all clamor for attention and, before I have got them well in hand, the new suit has lost its freshness. Still, if ever I do get any money, I will try and make myself really spruce all round till I find out, as I probably shall in about a week, that if I give my clothes an inch they will take an ell.

(1880)

Money

Is the last enemy that shall never be subdued. While there is flesh there is money—or the want of money; but money is always on the brain so long as there is a brain in reasonable order.

A Luxurious Death

Death in anything like luxury is one of the most expensive things a man can indulge himself in. It costs a lot of money to die comfortably, unless one goes off pretty quickly.

Money, Health and Reputation

Money, if it live at all, that is to say if it be reproductive and put out at any interest, however low, is mortal and doomed to be lost one day, though it may go on living through many generations of one single family if it be taken care of. No man is absolutely safe. It may be said to any man, 'Thou fool, this night thy money shall be required of thee.' And reputation is like money: it may be required of us without warning. The little unsuspected evil on which we trip may swell up in a moment and prove to be the huge, Janus-like mountain of unpardonable sin. And his health may be required of any fool, any night or any day.

A man will feel the loss of money more keenly than loss of his bodily health, so long as he can keep his money. Take his money away and deprive him of the means of earning any more, and his health will soon break up; but leave him his money and, even though his health breaks up and he dies, he does not mind it so much as we think. Money losses are the worst, loss of health is next worse and loss of reputation comes in a bad third. All other things are amusements provided money, health and good name are untouched.

Solicitors

A man must not think he can save himself the trouble of being a sensible man and a gentleman by going to his solicitor, any more than he can get himself a sound constitution by going to his doctor; but a solicitor can do more to keep a tolerably well-meaning fool straight than a doctor can do for an invalid. Money is to the solicitor what souls are to the parson or life to the physician. He is our money-doctor.

Doctors

Going to your doctor is having such a row with your cells that you refer them to your solicitor. Sometimes you, as it were, strike against them and stop their food, when they go on strike against yourself. Sometimes you file a bill in Chancery against them and go to bed.

Priests

We may find an argument in favor of priests if we consider whether man is capable of doing for himself in respect of his moral and spiritual welfare (than which nothing can be more difficult and intricate) what it is so clearly better for him to leave to professional advisers in the case of his money and his body which are comparatively simple and unimportant.

(1912)

WALTER HORATIO PATER (1839-1894)

PATER began his life-long academic career at King's School, Canterbury, from which he proceeded to Queen's College, Oxford, where he took his bachelor's degree in 1862. As an undergraduate Pater knew few men, devoting himself closely to books, especially to Greek literature, in which Benjamin Jowett gave him much encouragement. After graduation he was elected to the Old Mortality, an essay society, through which he came into contact with the stimulating personalities of T. H. Green, A. C. Swinburne, and others. In 1864, he was elected fellow of Brasenose College, and except for visits to the Continent and a short residence in London, he remained in Oxford for the rest of his life. In 1865, a sojourn in Italy gave Pater those impressions of Renaissance art that appear conspicuously in his later writing. The quiet poise of his life as Oxford tutor and author was disturbed by nothing more eventful than an occasional vacation tour in France or Germany.

Pater's most significant mission was in interpreting to his age the spirit of the Renaissance in art and literature. His first essays, which had begun to appear in periodicals in 1867, were collected and published in a considerable volume, *Studies in the History of the Renaissance*, in 1873. In 1885 appeared Pater's finest single work, *Marius the Epicurean*, a historical romance expounding the best phases of Epicureanism. His *Imaginary Portraits* (1887) contains fine studies in philosophic fiction, and his *Appreciations, with an Essay on Style* (1889) reveals bits of his most subtle literary criticism. *Plato and Platonism* (1893) is a notable result of his early classical studies. Pater's somewhat painful seeking for precision of expression resulted in a style more delicate and rhythmical than direct and simple. His sensitive personality pervades his writing. His philosophy of temperance, discipline, and asceticism in art has had a permanent and refining influence upon English criticism.

STYLE

SINCE all progress of mind consists for the most part in differentiation, in the resolution of an obscure and complex object into its component aspects, it is surely the stupidest of losses to confuse things which right reason has put asunder, to lose the sense of achieved distinctions, the distinction between poetry and prose, for instance, or, to speak more exactly, between the laws and characteristic excellences of verse and prose composition. On the other hand, those who have dwelt most emphatically on the distinction between prose and verse, prose and poetry, may sometimes have been tempted to limit the proper functions of prose too narrowly; and this again is at least false economy, as being, in effect, the renunciation of a certain means or faculty, in a world where after all we must needs make the most of things. Critical efforts to limit art *a priori*, by anticipations regarding the natural incapacity of the material with which this or that artist works, as the sculptor with solid form, or the prose-writer with the ordinary language of men, are always liable to be discredited by the facts of artistic production; and while prose is actually found to be a colored thing with Bacon, picturesque with Livy and Carlyle, musical with Cicero and Newman, mystical and intimate with Plato and Michelet and Sir Thomas Browne, exalted or florid, it may be, with Milton and Taylor, it will be useless to protest that it can be nothing at all, except something very tamely and narrowly confined to mainly practical ends—a kind of 'good round-hand'; as useless as the protest that poetry might not touch prosaic subjects as with Wordsworth, or an abstruse matter as with Browning, or treat contemporary life nobly as with Tennyson. In subordination to one essential beauty in all good literary style, in all literature as a fine art, as there are many beauties of poetry, so the beauties of prose are many and it is the business of criticism to estimate them as such; as it is good in the criticism of verse to look for those hard, logical and quasi-prosaic excellences which that too has, or needs. To find in the poem, amid the flowers, the allusions, the mixed perspectives, of *Lycidas* for instance, the thought, the logical structure:—how wholesome! how delightful! as to identify in prose what we call the poetry, the imaginative power, not treating it as out of place and a kind of vagrant intruder, but by way of an estimate of its rights, that is, of its achieved powers, there.

Dryden, with the characteristic instinct of his age, loved to emphasize the distinction between poetry and prose, the protest against their confusion with each other, coming with somewhat diminished effect from one whose poetry was so prosaic. In truth, his sense of prosaic excellence affected his verse rather than his prose, which is not only fervid, richly figured, poetic, as we say, but vitiated, all unconsciously, by many a scanning line. Setting up correctness, that humble merit of prose, as the central literary excellence, he is really a less correct writer than he may seem, still with an imperfect mastery of the relative pronoun. It might have been foreseen that, in the rotations of mind, the province of poetry in prose would find its assertor; and, a century after Dryden, amid very different intellectual needs, and with the need therefore of great modifications in literary form, the range of the poetic force in literature was effectively enlarged by Wordsworth. The true distinction between prose and poetry he regarded as the almost technical or accidental one of the absence or presence of metrical beauty, or, say! metrical restraint; and for him the opposition came to be between verse and prose of course; but, as the essential dichotomy in this matter, between imaginative and unimaginative writing, parallel to De Quincey's distinction between 'the literature of power and the literature of knowledge,' in the former of which the composer gives us not fact, but his peculiar sense of fact, whether past or present.

Dismissing then, under sanction of Wordsworth, that harsher opposition of poetry to prose, as savoring in fact of the arbitrary psychology of the last century, and with it the prejudice that there can be but one only beauty of prose style, I propose here to point out certain qualities of all literature as a fine art, which, if they apply to the literature of fact, apply still more to the literature of the imaginative sense of fact, while they apply indifferently to verse and prose, so far as either is really imaginative— certain conditions of true art in both alike, which conditions may also contain in them the secret of the proper discrimination and guardianship of the peculiar excellences of either.

The line between fact and something quite different from external fact is, indeed, hard to draw. In Pascal, for instance, in the persuasive writers generally, how difficult to define the point where, from time to time, argument which, if it is to be worth anything at all, must consist of facts or groups of facts, becomes a pleading— a theorem no longer, but essentially an appeal to the reader to catch the writer's spirit, to think with him, if one can or will—an expression no longer of fact but of his sense of it, his peculiar intuition of a world prospective, or discerned below the faulty conditions of the present, in either case changed somewhat from the actual world. In science, on the other hand, in history so far as it conforms to scientific rule, we have a literary domain where the imagination may be thought to be always an intruder. And as, in all science, the functions of literature reduce themselves eventually to the transcribing of fact, so all the excellences of literary form in regard to science are reducible to various kinds of painstaking; this good quality being involved in all 'skilled work' whatever, in the drafting of an act of parliament, as in sewing. Yet here again, the writer's sense of fact, in history especially, and in all those complex subjects which do but lie on the borders of science, will still take the place of fact, in various degrees. Your historian, for instance, with absolutely truthful intention, amid the multitude of facts presented to him must needs select, and in selecting assert something of his own humor, something that comes not of the world without but of a vision within. So Gibbon molds his unwieldy material to a preconceived view. Livy, Tacitus, Michelet, moving full of poignant sensibility amid the records of the past, each, after his own sense, modifies— who can tell where and to what degree?—and becomes something else than a transcriber; each, as he thus modifies, passing into the domain of art proper. For just in proportion as the writer's aim, consciously or unconsciously, comes to be the transcribing, not of the world, not of mere fact, but of his sense of it, he becomes an artist, his work *fine* art; and good art (as I hope ultimately to show) in proportion to the truth of his presentment of that sense; as in those humbler or plainer functions of literature also, truth— truth to bare fact, there—is the essence of such artistic quality as they may have. Truth! there can be no merit, no craft at all, without that. And further, all beauty is in the long run only *fineness* of truth, or what we call expression, the finer accommodation of speech to that vision within.

—The transcript of his sense of fact rather than the fact, as being preferable, pleasanter, more beautiful to the writer himself. In literature, as in every other product of human skill, in the molding of a bell or a platter for instance, wherever this sense asserts itself, wherever the producer so modifies his work as, over and above its primary use or intention, to make it pleasing (to himself, of course, in the first instance) there, 'fine' as opposed to merely serviceable art, exists. Literary art, that is, like all art which is in any way imitative or reproductive of fact—form, or color, or incident—is the representation of such fact as connected with soul, of a specific personality, in its preferences, its volition and power.

Such is the matter of imaginative or artistic literature—this transcript, not of mere fact, but of fact in its infinite variety, as modified by human preference in all its infinitely varied forms. It will be good literary art not because it is brilliant or sober, or rich, or impulsive, or severe, but just in proportion as its representation of that sense, that soul-fact, is true, verse being only one department of such literature, and imaginative prose, it may be thought, being the special art of the modern world. That imaginative prose should be the special and opportune art of the modern world results from two important facts about the latter: first, the chaotic variety and complexity of its interests, making the intellectual issue, the really master currents of the present time incalculable—a condition of mind little susceptible of the restraint proper to verse form, so that the most characteristic verse of the nineteenth century has been lawless verse; and secondly, an all-pervading naturalism, a curiosity about everything whatever as it really is, involving a certain humility of attitude, cognate to what must, after all, be the less ambitious form of literature. And prose thus asserting itself as the special and privileged artistic faculty of the present day, will be, however critics may try to narrow its scope, as varied in its excellence as humanity itself reflecting on the facts of its latest experience—an instrument of many stops, meditative, observant, descriptive, eloquent, analytic, plaintive, fervid. Its beauties will be not exclusively 'pedestrian': it will exert, in due measure, all the varied charms of poetry, down to the rhythm which, as in Cicero, or Michelet, or Newman, at their best, gives its musical value to every syllable.

The literary artist is of necessity a scholar, and in what he proposes to do will have in mind, first of all, the scholar and the scholarly conscience—the male conscience in this matter, as we must think it, under a system of education which still to so large an extent limits real scholarship to men. In his self-criticism, he supposes always that sort of reader who will go (full of eyes) warily, considerately, though without consideration for him, over the ground which the female conscience traverses so lightly, so amiably. For the material in which he works is no more a creation of his own than the sculptor's marble. Product of a myriad various minds and contending tongues, compact of obscure and minute association, a language has its own abundant and often recondite laws, in the habitual and summary recognition of which scholarship consists. A writer, full of a matter he is before all things anxious to express, may think of those laws, the limitations of vocabulary, structure, and the like, as a restriction, but if a real artist, will find in them an opportunity. His punctilious observance of the proprieties of his medium will diffuse through all he writes a general air of sensibility, of refined usage. *Exclusiones debitæ naturæ*—the exclusions, or rejections, which nature demands—we know how large a part these play, according to Bacon, in the science of nature. In a somewhat changed sense, we might say that the art of the scholar is summed up in the observance of those rejections demanded by the nature of his medium, the material he must use. Alive to the value of an atmosphere in which every term finds its utmost degree of expression, and with all the jealousy of a lover of words, he will resist a constant tendency on the part of the majority of those who use them to efface the distinctions of language, the facility of writers often reinforcing in this respect the work of the vulgar. He will feel the obligation not of the laws only, but of those affinities, avoidances, those mere preferences, of his language, which through the associations of literary history have become a part of its nature, prescribing the rejection of many a neology, many a license, many a gipsy phrase which might present itself as actually expressive. His appeal, again, is to the scholar, who has great experience in literature, and will show no favor to short-cuts, or hackneyed illustration, or an affectation of learning designed for the unlearned. Hence a contention, a sense of self-restraint and renunciation, having for the susceptible reader the effect of a challenge for minute consideration; the attention of the writer, in every minutest detail, being a pledge that it is worth the reader's while to be attentive too, that the writer is dealing scrupulously with his instrument, and therefore, indirectly, with the reader himself also, that he has the science of the instrument he plays on, perhaps, after all, with a freedom which in such case will be the freedom of a master.

For meanwhile, braced only by those restraints, he is really vindicating his liberty in the making of a vocabulary, an entire system of composition, for himself, his own true manner; and when we speak of the manner of a true master we mean what is essential in his art. Pedantry being only the scholarship of *le cuistre* (we have no English equivalent), he is no pedant, and does but show his intelligence of the rules of language in his freedoms with it, addition or expansion, which like the spontaneities of manner in a well-bred person will still further illustrate good taste.—The right vocabulary! Translators have not invariably seen how all-important that is in the work of translation, driving for the most part at idiom or construction; whereas, if the original be first-rate, one's first care should be with its elementary particles, Plato, for instance, being often reproducible by an exact following, with no variation in structure, of word after word, as the pencil follows a drawing under tracing-paper, so only each word or syllable be not of false color, to change my illustration a little.

Well! that is because any writer worth translating at all has winnowed and searched through his vocabulary, is conscious of the words he would select in systematic reading of a dictionary, and still more of the words he would reject were the dictionary other than Johnson's; and doing this with his peculiar sense of the world ever in view, in search of an instrument for the adequate expression of that, he begets a vocabulary faithful to the coloring of his own spirit, and in the strictest sense original. That living authority which language needs lies, in truth, in its scholars, who recognizing always that every language possesses a genius, a very fastidious genius, of its own, expand at once and purify its very elements, which must needs change along with the changing thoughts of living people. Ninety years ago, for instance, great mental force, certainly, was needed by Wordsworth, to break through the consecrated poetic associations of a century, and speak the language that was his, that was to become in a measure the language of the next generation. But he did it with the tact of a scholar also. English, for a quarter of a century past, has been assimilating the phraseology of pictorial art; for half a century, the phraseology of the great German metaphysical movement of eighty years ago; in part also the language of mystical theology: and none but pedants will regret a great consequent increase of its resources. For many years to come its enterprise may well lie in the naturalization of the vocabulary of science, so only it be under the eye of sensitive scholarship —in a liberal naturalization of the ideas of science too, for after all, the chief stimulus of good style is to possess a full, rich, complex matter to grapple with. The literary artist, therefore, will be well aware of physical science; science also attaining, in its turn, its true literary ideal. And then, as the scholar is nothing without the historic sense, he will be apt to restore not really obsolete or really worn-out words, but the finer edge of words still in use: *ascertain, communicate, discover*—words like these it has been part of our 'business' to misuse. And still, as language was made for man, he will be no authority for correctnesses which, limiting freedom of utterance, were yet but accidents in their origin; as if one vowed not to say '*its*,' which ought to have been in Shakespeare; '*his*' and '*hers*,' for inanimate objects, being but a barbarous and really inexpressive survival. Yet we have known many things like this. Racy Saxon monosyllables, close to us as touch and sight, he will intermix readily with those long, savorsome, Latin words, rich in 'second intention.' In this late day certainly, no critical process can be conducted reasonably without eclecticism. Of such eclecticism we have a justifying example in one of the first poets of our time. How illustrative of monosyllabic effect, of sonorous Latin, of the phraseology of science, of metaphysic, of colloquialism even, are the writings of Tennyson; yet with what a fine, fastidious scholarship throughout!

A scholar writing for the scholarly, he will of course leave something to the willing intelligence of his reader. 'To go preach to the first passer-by,' says Montaigne, 'to become tutor to the ignorance of the first I meet, is a thing I abhor;' a thing, in fact, naturally distressing to the scholar, who will therefore ever be shy of offering uncomplimentary assistance to the reader's wit. To really strenuous minds there is a pleasurable stimulus in the challenge for a continuous effort on their part, to be rewarded by securer and more intimate grasp of the author's sense. Self-restraint, a skilful economy of means, *ascêsis*, that too has a beauty of its own; and for the reader supposed, there will be an esthetic satisfaction in that frugal closeness of style which makes the most of a word, in the exaction from every sentence of a precise relief, in the just spacing out of word to thought, in the logically filled space connected always with the delightful sense of difficulty overcome.

Different classes of persons, at different times, make, of course, very various demands upon literature. Still, scholars, I suppose, and not only scholars, but all disinterested lovers of books, will always look to it, as to all other fine art, for a refuge, a sort of cloistral refuge, from a certain vulgarity in the actual world. A perfect poem like *Lycidas*, a perfect fiction like *Esmond*, the perfect handling of a theory like Newman's *Idea of a University*, has for them something of the uses of a religious 'retreat.' Here, then, with a view to the central need of a select few, those 'men of a finer thread' who have formed and maintain the literary ideal, everything, every component element will have undergone exact trial, and, above all, there will be no uncharacteristic or tarnished or vulgar decoration, permissible ornament being for the most part structural, or necessary. As the painter in his picture, so the artist in his book, aims at the production by honorable artifice of a peculiar atmosphere. 'The artist,' says Schiller, 'may be known rather by what he *omits;*' and in literature, too, the true artist may be best recognized by his tact of omission. For to the grave reader words too are grave; and the ornamental word, the figure, the accessory form or color or reference, is rarely content to die to thought precisely at the right moment, but will inevitably linger awhile, stirring a long 'brain-wave' behind it of perhaps quite alien associations.

Just there, it may be, is the detrimental tendency of the sort of scholarly attentiveness of mind I am recommending. But the true artist allows for it. He will remember that, as the very word ornament indicates what is in itself non-essential, so the 'one beauty' of all literary style is of its very essence, and independent, in prose and verse alike, of all removable decoration; that it may exist in its fullest luster, as in Flaubert's *Madame Bovary*, for instance, or in Stendhal's *Le Rouge et Le Noir*, in a composition utterly unadorned, with hardly a single suggestion of visibly beautiful things. Parallel, allusion, the allusive way generally, the flowers in the garden:—he knows the narcotic force of these upon the negligent intelligence to which any *diversion*, literally is welcome, any vagrant intruder, because one can go wandering away with it from the immediate subject. Jealous, if he have a really quickening motive within, of all that does not hold directly to that, of the facile, the otiose, he will never depart from the strictly pedestrian process, unless he gains a ponderable something thereby. Even assured of its congruity, he will still question its serviceableness. Is it worth while, can we afford, to attend to just that, to just that figure or literary reference, just then?—Surplusage! he will dread that, as the runner on his muscles. For in truth all art does but consist in the removal of surplusage, from the last finish of the gem-engraver blowing away the last particle of invisible dust, back to the earliest divination of the finished work to be, lying somewhere, according to Michelangelo's fancy, in the rough-hewn block of stone.

And what applies to figure or flower must be understood of all other accidental or removable ornaments of writing whatever; and not of specific ornament only, but of all that latent color and imagery which language as such carries in it. A lover of words for their own sake, to whom nothing about them is unimportant, a minute and constant observer of their physiognomy, he will be on the alert not only for obviously mixed metaphors of course, but for the metaphor that is mixed in all our speech, though a rapid use may involve no cognition of it. Currently recognizing the incident, the color, the physical elements or particles in words like *absorb, consider, extract*, to take the first that occur, he will avail himself of them, as further adding to the resources of expression. The elementary particles of language will be realized as color and light and shade through his scholarly living in the full sense of them. Still opposing the constant degradation of language by those who use it carelessly, he will not treat colored glass as if it were clear; and while half the world is using figure unconsciously, will be fully aware not only of all that latent figurative texture in speech, but of the vague, lazy, half-formed personification—a rhetoric, depressing, and worse than nothing, because it has no really rhetorical motive—which plays so large a part there, and, as in the case of more ostentatious ornament, scrupulously exact of it, from syllable to syllable, its precise value.

So far I have been speaking of certain conditions of the literary art arising out of the medium or material in or upon which it works, the essential qualities of language and its aptitudes for contingent ornamentation, matters which define scholarship as science and good taste respectively. They are both subservient to a more intimate quality of good style: more intimate, as coming nearer to the artist himself. The otiose, the facile, surplusage: why are these abhorrent to the true literary artist, except because, in literary as in all other art, structure is all-important, felt, or painfully missed, everywhere?—that architectural conception of work, which foresees the end in the beginning and never loses sight of it, and in every part is conscious of all the rest, till the last sentence does but, with undiminished vigor, unfold and justify the first—a condition of literary art, which, in contra-distinction to another quality of the artist himself, to be spoken of later, I shall call the necessity of *mind* in style.

An acute philosophical writer, the late Dean Mansel (a writer whose works illustrate the literary beauty there may be in closeness, and with obvious repression or economy of a fine rhetorical gift) wrote a book, of fascinating precision in a very obscure subject, to show that all the technical laws of logic are but means of securing, in each and all of its apprehensions, the unity, the strict identity with itself, of the apprehending mind. All the laws of good writing aim at a similar unity or identity of the mind in all the processes by which the word is associated to its import. The term is right, and has its essential beauty, when it becomes, in a manner, what it signifies, as with the names of simple sensations. To give the phrase, the sentence, the structural member, the entire composition, song, or essay, a similar unity with its subject and with itself:—style is in the right way when it tends towards that. All depends upon the original unity, the vital wholeness and identity, of the initiatory apprehension or view. So much is true of all art, which therefore requires always its logic, its comprehensive reason—insight, foresight, retrospect, in simultaneous action—true, most of all, of the literary art, as being of all the arts most closely cognate to the abstract intelligence. Such logical coherency may be evidenced not merely in the lines of composition as a whole, but in the choice of a single word, while it by no means interferes with, but may even prescribe, much variety, in the building of the sentence for instance, or in the manner, argumentative, descriptive, discursive, of this or that part or member of the entire design. The blithe, crisp sentence, decisive as a child's expression of its needs, may alternate with the long-contending, victoriously intricate sentence; the sentence, born with the integrity of a single word, relieving the sort of sentence in which, if you look closely, you can see much contrivance, much adjustment, to bring a highly qualified matter into compass at one view. For the literary architecture, if it is to be rich and expressive, involves not only foresight of the end in the beginning, but also development or growth of design, in the process of execution, with many irregularities, surprises, and after-thoughts; the contingent as well as the necessary being subsumed under the unity of the whole. As truly, to the lack of such architectural design, of a single, almost visual, image, vigorously informing an entire, perhaps very intricate, composition, which shall be austere, ornate, argumentative, fanciful, yet true from first to last to that vision within, may be attributed those weaknesses of conscious or unconscious repetition of word, phrase, motive, or member of the whole matter, indicating, as Flaubert was aware, an original structure in thought not organically complete. With such foresight, the actual conclusion will most often get itself written out of hand, before, in the more obvious sense, the work is finished. With some strong and leading sense of the world, the tight hold of which secures true *composition* and not mere loose accretion, the literary artist, I suppose, goes on considerably, setting joint to joint, sustained by yet restraining the productive ardor, retracing the negligences of his first sketch, repeating his steps only that he may give the reader a sense of secure and restful progress, readjusting mere assonances even, that they may soothe the reader, or at least not interrupt him on his way; and then, somewhere before the end comes, is burdened, inspired, with his conclusion, and betimes delivered of it, leaving off, not in weariness and because he finds *himself* at an end, but in all the freshness of volition. His work now structurally complete, with all the accumulating effect of secondary shades of meaning, he finishes the whole up to the just proportion of that ante-penultimate conclusion, and all becomes expressive. The house he has built is rather a body he has informed. And so it happens, to its greater credit, that the better interest even of a narrative to be recounted, a story to be told, will often be in its second reading. And though there are instances of great writers who have been no artists, an unconscious tact sometimes directing work in which we may detect, very pleasurably, many of the effects of conscious art, yet one of the greatest pleasures of really good prose literature is in the critical tracing out of that conscious artistic structure, and the pervading sense of it as we read. Yet of poetic literature too; for, in truth, the kind of constructive intelligence here supposed is one of the forms of the imagination.

That is the special function of mind, in style. Mind and soul,—hard to ascertain philosophically, the distinction is real enough practically, for they often interfere, are sometimes in conflict, with each other. Blake, in the last century, is an instance of preponderating soul, embarrassed, at a loss, in an era of preponderating mind. As a quality of style, at all events, soul is a fact, in certain writers—the way they have of absorbing language, of attracting it into the peculiar spirit they are of, with a subtlety which makes the actual result seem like some inexplicable inspiration. By mind, the literary artist reaches us, through static and objective indications of design in his work, legible to all. By soul, he reaches us, somewhat capriciously perhaps, one and not another, through vagrant sympathy and a kind of immediate contact. Mind we cannot choose but approve where we recognize it; soul may repel us, not because we misunderstand it. The way in which theological interests sometimes avail themselves of language is perhaps the best illustration of the force I mean to indicate generally in literature, by the word *soul*. Ardent religious persuasion may exist, may make its way, without finding any equivalent heat in language: or, again, it may enkindle words to various degrees, and when it really takes hold of them doubles its force. Religious history presents many remarkable instances in which, through no mere phrase-worship, an unconscious literary tact has, for the sensitive, laid open a privileged pathway from one to another. 'The altar-fire,' people say, 'has touched those lips!' The Vulgate, the English Bible, the English Prayer-Book, the writings of Swedenborg, the Tracts for the Times:— there, we have instances of widely different and largely diffused phases of religious feeling in operation as soul in style. But something of the same kind acts with similar power in certain writers of quite other than theological literature, on behalf of some wholly personal and peculiar sense of theirs. Most easily illustrated by theological literature, this quality lends to profane writers a kind of religious influence. At their best, these writers become, as we say sometimes, 'prophets'; such character depending on the effect not merely of their matter, but of their matter as allied to, in 'electric affinity' with, peculiar form, and working in all cases by an immediate sympathetic contact, on which account it is that it may be called soul, as opposed to mind, in style. And this too is a faculty of choosing and rejecting what is congruous or otherwise, with a drift towards unity—unity of atmosphere here, as there of design—soul securing color (or perfume, might we say?) as mind secures form, the latter being essentially finite, the former vague or infinite, as the influence of a living person is practically infinite. There are some to whom nothing has any real interest, or real meaning, except as operative in a given person; and it is they who best appreciate the quality of soul in literary art. They seem to know a *person*, in a book, and make way by intuition: yet, although they thus enjoy the completeness of a personal information, it is still a characteristic of soul, in this sense of the word, that it does but suggest what can never be uttered, not as being different from, or more obscure than, what actually gets said, but as containing that plenary substance of which there is only one phase or facet in what is there expressed.

If all high things have their martyrs, Gustave Flaubert might perhaps rank as the martyr of literary style. In his printed correspondence, a curious series of letters, written in his twenty-fifth year, records what seems to have been his one other passion—a series of letters which, with its fine casuistries, its firmly repressed anguish, its tone of harmonious gray, and the sense of disillusion in which the whole matter ends, might have been, a few slight changes supposed, one of his own fictions. Writing to Madame X. certainly he does display, by 'taking thought' mainly, by constant and delicate pondering, as in his love for literature, a heart really moved, but still more, and as the pledge of that emotion, a loyalty to his work. Madame X., too, is a literary artist, and the best gifts he can send her are precepts of perfection in art, counsels for the effectual pursuit of that better love. In his love-letters it is the pains and pleasures of art he insists on, its solaces: he communicates secrets, reproves, encourages, with a view to that. Whether the lady was dissatisfied with such divided or indirect service, the reader is not enabled to see; but sees that, on Flaubert's part at least, a living person could be no rival of what was, from first to last, his leading passion, a somewhat solitary and exclusive one.

'I must scold you,' he writes, 'for one thing, which shocks, scandalizes me, the small concern, namely, you show for art just now. As regards glory be it so: there, I approve. But for art!—the one thing in life that is good and real—can you compare with it an earthly love?—prefer the adoration of a relative beauty to the *cultus* of the true beauty? Well! I tell you the truth. That is the one thing good in me: the one thing I have, to me estimable. For yourself, you blend with the beautiful a heap of alien things, the useful, the agreeable, what not?—

'The only way not to be unhappy is to shut yourself up in art, and count everything else as nothing. Pride takes the place of all beside when it is established on a large basis. Work! God wills it. That, it seems to me, is clear.—

'I am reading over again the *Æneid*, certain verses of which I repeat to myself to satiety. There are phrases there which stay in one's head, by which I find myself beset, as with those musical airs which are forever returning, and cause you pain, you love them so much. I observe that I no longer laugh much, and am no longer depressed. I am ripe. You talk of my serenity, and envy me. It may well surprise you. Sick, irritated, the prey a thousand times a day of cruel pain, I continue my labor like a true working-man, who, with sleeves turned up, in the sweat of his brow, beats away at his anvil, never troubling himself whether it rains or blows, for hail or thunder. I was not like that formerly. The change has taken place naturally, though my will has counted for something in the matter.—

'Those who write in good style are sometimes accused of a neglect of ideas, and of the moral end, as if the end of the physician were something else than healing, of the painter than painting—as if the end of art were not, before all else, the beautiful.'

What, then, did Flaubert understand by beauty, in the art he pursued with so much fervor, with so much self-command? Let us hear a sympathetic commentator:—

'Possessed of an absolute belief that there exists but one way of expressing one thing, one word to call it by, one adjective to qualify, one verb to animate it, he gave himself to superhuman labor for the discovery, in every phrase, of that word, that verb, that epithet. In this way, he believed in some mysterious harmony of expression, and when a true word seemed to him to lack euphony still went on seeking another, with invincible patience, certain that he had not yet got hold of the *unique* word. . . . A thousand preoccupations would beset him at the same moment, always with this desperate certitude fixed in his spirit: Among all the expressions in the world, all forms and turns of expression, there is but *one*—one form, one mode—to express what I want to say.'

The one word for the one thing, the one thought, amid the multitude of words, terms, that might just do: the problem of style was there!—the unique word, phrase, sentence, paragraph, essay, or song, absolutely proper to the single mental presentation or vision within. In that perfect justice, over and above the many contingent and removable beauties with which beautiful style may charm us, but which it can exist without, independent of them yet dexterously availing itself of them, omnipresent in good work, in function at every point, from single epithets to the rhythm of a whole book, lay the specific, indispensable, very intellectual, beauty of literature, the possibility of which constitutes it a fine art.

One seems to detect the influence of a philosophic idea there, the idea of a natural economy, of some preëxistent adaptation, between a relative, somewhere in the world of thought, and its correlative, somewhere in the world of language—both alike, rather, somewhere in the mind of the artist, desiderative, expectant, inventive—meeting each other with the readiness of 'soul and body reunited,' in Blake's rapturous design; and, in fact, Flaubert was fond of giving his theory philosophical expression.—

'There are no beautiful thoughts,' he would say, 'without beautiful forms, and conversely. As it is impossible to extract from a physical body the qualities which really constitute it—color, extension, and the like—without reducing it to a hollow abstraction, in a word, without destroying it; just so it is impossible to detach the form from the idea, for the idea only exists by virtue of the form.'

All the recognized flowers, the removable ornaments of literature (including harmony and ease in reading aloud, very carefully considered by him) counted certainly; for these too are part of the actual value of what one says. But still, after all, with Flaubert, the search, the unwearied research, was not for the smooth, or winsome, or forcible word, as such, as with false Ciceronians, but quite simply and honestly for the word's adjustment to its meaning. The first condition of this must be, of course, to know yourself, to have ascertained your own sense exactly. Then, if we suppose an artist, he says to the reader,—I want you to see precisely what I see. Into the mind sensitive to 'form,' a flood of random sounds, colors, incidents, is ever penetrating from the world without, to become, by sympathetic selection, a part of its very structure, and, in turn the visible vesture and expression of that other world it sees so steadily within, nay, already with a partial conformity thereto, to be refined, enlarged, corrected, at a hundred points; and it is just there, just at those doubtful points that the function of style, as tact or taste, intervenes. The unique term will come more quickly to one than another, at one time than another, according also to the kind of matter in question. Quickness and slowness, ease and closeness alike, have nothing to do with the artistic character of the true word found at last. As there is a charm of ease, so there is also a special charm in the signs of discovery, of effort and contention towards a due end, as so often with Flaubert himself—in the style which has been pliant, as only obstinate, durable metal can be, to the inherent perplexities and recusancy of a certain difficult thought.

If Flaubert had not told us, perhaps we should never have guessed how tardy and painful his own procedure really was, and after reading his confession may think that his almost endless hesitation had much to do with diseased nerves. Often, perhaps, the felicity supposed will be the product of a happier, a more exuberant nature than Flaubert's. Aggravated, certainly, by a morbid physical condition, that anxiety in 'seeking the phrase,' which gathered all the other small *ennuis* of a really quiet existence into a kind of battle, was connected with his lifelong contention against facile poetry, facile art—art, facile and flimsy; and what constitutes the true artist is not the slowness or quickness of the process, but the absolute success of the result. As with those laborers in the parable, the prize is independent of the mere length of the actual day's work. 'You talk,' he writes, odd, trying lover, to Madame X.—

'You talk of the exclusiveness of my literary tastes. That might have enabled you to divine what kind of a person I am in the matter of love. I grow so hard to please as a literary artist, that I am driven to despair. I shall end by not writing another line.'

'Happy,' he cries, in a moment of discouragement at that patient labor, which for him, certainly, was the condition of a great success.—

'Happy those who have no doubts of themselves! who lengthen out, as the pen runs on, all that flows forth from their brains. As for me, I hesitate, I disappoint myself, turn round upon myself in despite: my taste is augmented in proportion as my natural vigor decreases, and I afflict my soul over some dubious word out of all proportion to the pleasure I get from a whole page of good writing. One would have to live two centuries to attain a true idea of any matter whatever. What Buffon said is a big blasphemy: genius is not long-continued patience. Still, there is some truth in the statement, and more than people think, especially as regards our own day. Art! art! art! bitter deception! phantom that glows with light, only to lead one on to destruction.'

Again—

'I am growing so peevish about my writing. I am like a man whose ear is true but who plays falsely on the violin: his fingers refuse to reproduce precisely those sounds of which he has the inward sense. Then the tears come rolling down from the poor scraper's eyes and the bow falls from his hand.'

Coming slowly or quickly, when it comes, as it came with so much labor of mind, but also with so much luster, to Gustave Flaubert, this discovery of the word will be, like all artistic success and felicity, incapable of strict analysis: effect of an intuitive condition of mind, it must be recognized by like intuition on the part of the reader, and a sort of immediate sense. In every one of those masterly sentences of Flaubert there was, below all mere contrivance, shaping and afterthought, by some happy instantaneous concourse of the various faculties of the mind with each other, the exact apprehension of what was *needed* to carry the meaning. And that it fits with absolute justice will be a judgment of immediate sense in the appreciative reader. We all feel this in what may be called inspired translation. Well! all language involves translation from inward to outward. In literature, as in all forms of art, there are the absolute and the merely relative or accessory beauties; and precisely in that exact proportion of the term to its purpose is the absolute beauty of style, prose or verse. All the good qualities, the beauties, of verse also, are such, only as precise expression.

In the highest as in the lowliest literature, then, the one indispensable beauty is, after all, truth:—truth to bare fact in the latter, as to some personal sense of fact, diverted somewhat from men's ordinary sense of it, in the former; truth there as accuracy, truth here as expression, that finest and most intimate form of truth, the *vraie vérité*. And what an eclectic principle this really is! employing for its one sole purpose —that absolute accordance of expression to idea—all other literary beauties and excellences whatever: how many kinds of style it covers, explains, justifies, and at the same time safeguards! Scott's facility, Flaubert's deeply pondered evocation of 'the phrase,' are equally good art. Say what you have to say, what you have a will to say, in the simplest, the most direct and exact manner possible, with no surplusage:—there, is the justification of the sentence so fortunately born, 'entire, smooth, and round,' that it needs no punctuation, and also (that is the point!) of the most elaborate period, if it be right in its elaboration. Here is the office of ornament: here also the purpose of restraint in ornament. As the exponent of truth, that austerity (the beauty, the function, of which in literature Flaubert understood so well) becomes not the correctness or purism of the mere scholar, but a security against the otiose, a jealous exclusion of what does not really tell towards the pursuit of relief, of life and vigor in the portraiture of one's sense. License again, the making free with rule, if it be indeed, as people fancy, a habit of genius, flinging aside or transforming all that opposes the liberty of beautiful production, will be but faith to one's own meaning. The seeming baldness of *Le Rouge et Le Noir* is nothing in itself; the wild ornament of *Les Misérables* is nothing in itself; and the restraint of Flaubert, amid a real natural opulence, only redoubled beauty—the phrase so large and so precise at the same time, hard as bronze, in service to the more perfect adaptation of words to their matter. Afterthoughts, retouchings, finish, will be of profit only so far as they too really serve to bring out the original, initiative, generative, sense in them.

In this way, according to the well-known saying, 'The style is the man,' complex for simple, in his individuality, his plenary sense of what he really has to say, his sense of the world; all cautions regarding style arising out of so many natural scruples as to the medium through which alone he can expose that inward sense of things, the purity of this medium, its laws or tricks of refraction: nothing is to be left there which might give conveyance to any matter save that. Style in all its varieties, reserved or opulent, terse, abundant, musical, stimulant, academic, so long as each is really characteristic or expressive, finds thus its justification, the sumptuous good taste of Cicero being as truly the man himself, and not another, justified, yet insured inalienably to him, thereby, as would have been his portrait by Raphael, in full consular splendor, on his ivory chair.

A relegation, you may say perhaps—a relegation of style to the subjectivity, the mere caprice, of the individual, which must soon transform it into mannerism. Not so! since there is, under the conditions supposed, for those elements of the man, for every lineament of the vision within, the one word, the one acceptable word, recognizable by the sensitive, by others 'who have intelligence' in the matter, as absolutely as ever anything can be in the evanescent and delicate region of human language. The style, the manner, would be the man, not in his unreasoned and really uncharacteristic caprices, involuntary or affected, but in absolutely sincere apprehension of what is most real to him. But let us hear our French guide again.—

'Styles,' says Flaubert's commentator, '*Styles*, as so many peculiar molds, each of which bears the mark of a particular writer, who is to pour into it the whole content of his ideas, were no part of his theory. What he believed in was *Style:* that is to say, a certain absolute and unique manner of expressing a thing, in all its intensity and color. For him the *form* was the work itself. As in living creatures, the blood, nourishing the body, determines its very contour and external aspect, just so, to his mind, the *matter*, the basis, in a work of art, imposed necessarily, the unique, the just expression, the measure, the rhythm—the *form* in all its characteristics.'

If the style be the man, in all the color and intensity of a veritable apprehension, it will be in a real sense 'impersonal.'

I said, thinking of books like Victor Hugo's *Les Misérables*, that prose literature was the characteristic art of the nineteenth century, as others, thinking of its triumphs since the youth of Bach, have assigned that place to music. Music and prose literature are, in one sense, the opposite terms of art; the art of literature presenting to the imagination, through the intelligence, a range of interests, as free and various as those which music presents to it through sense. And certainly the tendency of what has been here said is to bring literature too under those conditions, by conformity to which music takes rank as the typically perfect art. If music be the ideal of all art whatever, precisely because in music it is impossible to distinguish the form from the substance or matter, the subject from the expression, then, literature, by finding its specific excellence in the absolute correspondence of the term to its import, will be but fulfilling the condition of all artistic quality in things everywhere, of all good art.

Good art, but not necessarily great art; the distinction between great art and good art depending immediately, as regards literature at all events, not on its form, but on the matter. Thackeray's *Esmond*, surely, is greater art than *Vanity Fair*, by the greater dignity of its interests. It is on the quality of the matter it informs or controls, its compass, its variety, its alliance to great ends, or the depth of the note of revolt, or the largeness of hope in it, that the greatness of literary art depends, as *The Divine Comedy*, *Paradise Lost*, *Les Misérables*, *The English Bible*, are great art. Given the conditions I have tried to explain as constituting good art; —then, if it be devoted further to the increase of men's happiness, to the redemption of the oppressed, or the enlargement of our sympathies with each other, or to such presentment of new or old truth about ourselves and our relation to the world as may ennoble and fortify us in our sojourn here, or immediately, as with Dante, to the glory of God, it will be also great art; if, over and above those qualities I summed up as mind and soul—that color and mystic perfume, and that reasonable structure, it has something of the soul of humanity in it, and finds its logical, its architectural place, in the great structure of human life.

(1888)

ROBERT LOUIS STEVENSON (1850-1894)

Stevenson's great-grandfather, grandfather, and father were engineers to the Board of Northern Lighthouses, and he was educated for the family profession. At twenty-one he asked to be allowed to give up engineering for literature, and his father consented on condition that he qualified for the Scottish Bar. Stevenson fulfilled the condition, but took as little interest in his legal as in his engineering studies, setting far more store 'by certain other odds and ends that he came by in the open street while he was playing truant.' At his chosen pursuit of literature, however, he toiled incessantly. He says: 'I imagine nobody had ever such pains to learn a trade as I had; but I slogged at it day in and day out; and I frankly believe (thanks to my dire industry) I have done more with smaller gifts than almost any man of letters in the world.' As a schoolboy he edited magazines and wrote essays, stories and plays; his first novel was turned into a historical essay and privately printed when he was sixteen. As an undergraduate at Edinburgh he established the *University Magazine* which 'ran four months in undisturbed obscurity and died without a gasp.' In 1873-4 he had half-a-dozen articles in various magazines, and his first book, *An Inland Voyage*, was published in 1878. It is an account of a canoe trip in Belgium and France made two years earlier. About this time Stevenson met and fell in love with Mrs. Fanny Osbourne, an American lady who came to study art in France. In 1878 she returned to California, and thither in 1879 Stevenson followed her. Some of his experiences in crossing the Atlantic and the American continent (though by no means all the sufferings he endured) are told in *The Amateur Emigrant* and *Across the Plains*. He arrived at San Francisco in desperate straits of health and pocket, and only Mrs. Osbourne's devoted nursing saved his life. After his recovery, they were married, and spent their honeymoon in the neighboring mountains, described in *The Silverado Squatters*. His first volume of essays, *Virginibus Puerisque*, was highly appreciated, but only by a few: it was a book for boys, *Treasure Island*, which made him suddenly famous. *Dr. Jekyll and Mr. Hyde* and *Kidnapped* were equally successful. During these years he was living in various health resorts in Europe and America; in 1888 he went for a long voyage in the Pacific, at the end of which he bought an estate and settled in Samoa. He endeared himself to the natives, and in spite of continued illness, did some of his best literary work. The year before his death he wrote: 'For fourteen years I have not had a day's real health; I have wakened sick and gone to bed weary; and I have done my work unflinchingly. I have written in bed, and written out of it, written in hemorrhages, written in sickness, written torn by coughing, written when my hand swam for weakness; and for so long, it seems to me I have won my wager and recovered my glove. I am better now, have been, rightly speaking, since first I came to the Pacific; and still, few are the days when I am not in some physical distress. And the battle goes on—ill or well, is a trifle: so as it goes. I was made for a contest, and the Powers have so willed that my battlefield should be this dingy, inglorious one of the bed and the physic bottle.' He was buried at the top of the mountain overlooking his Samoan home in a tomb inscribed with his own *Requiem*:

> Under the wide and starry sky,
> Dig the grave and let me lie.
> Glad did I live and gladly die,
> And I laid me down with a will.
> This be the verse you grave for me:
> Here he lies where he longed to be;
> Home is the sailor, home from sea,
> And the hunter home from the hill.

THE FOREIGNER AT HOME

'This is no my ain house;
I ken by the biggin' o 't.'

Two recent books,[1] one by Mr. Grant White on England, one on France by the diabolically clever Mr. Hillebrand, may well have set people thinking on the divisions of races and nations. Such thoughts should arise with particular congruity and force to inhabitants of that United Kingdom, people from so many different stocks, babbling so many different dialects, and offering in its extent such singular contrasts, from the busiest over-population to the unkindliest desert, from the Black Country to the Moor of Rannoch. It is not only when we cross the seas that we go abroad; there are foreign parts of England; and the race that has conquered so wide an empire has not yet managed to assimilate the islands whence she sprang. Ireland, Wales, and the Scottish mountains still cling, in part, to

[1] 1881.

their old Gaelic speech. It was but the other day that English triumphed in Cornwall, and they still show in Mousehole, on St. Michael's Bay, the house of the last Cornish-speaking woman. English itself, which will now frank the traveler through the most of North America, through the greater South Sea Islands, in India, along much of the coast of Africa, and in the ports of China and Japan, is still to be heard, in its home country, in half a hundred varying stages of transition. You may go all over the States, and—setting aside the actual intrusion and influence of foreigners, negro, French, or Chinese—you shall scarce meet with so marked a difference of accent as in the forty miles between Edinburgh and Glasgow, or of dialect as in the hundred miles between Edinburgh and Aberdeen. Book English has gone round the world, but at home we still preserve the racy idioms of our fathers, and every county, in some parts every dale, has its own quality of speech, vocal or verbal. In like manner, local custom and prejudice, even local religion and local law, linger on into the latter end of the nineteenth century—*imperia in imperio* [kingdoms within the kingdom], foreign things at home.

In spite of these promptings to reflection, ignorance of his neighbors is the character of the typical John Bull. His is a domineering nature, steady in fight, imperious to command, but neither curious nor quick about the life of others. In French colonies, and still more in the Dutch, I have read that there is an immediate and lively contact between the dominant and the dominated race, that a certain sympathy is begotten, or at the least a transfusion of prejudices, making life easier for both. But the Englishman sits apart, bursting with pride and ignorance. He figures among his vassals in the hour of peace with the same disdainful air that led him on to victory. A passing enthusiasm for some foreign art or fashion may deceive the world, it cannot impose upon his intimates. He may be amused by a foreigner as by a monkey, but he will never condescend to study him with any patience. Miss Bird, an authoress with whom I profess myself in love, declares all the viands of Japan to be uneatable—a staggering pretension. So, when the Prince of Wales's marriage was celebrated at Mentone by a dinner to the Mentonese, it was proposed to give them solid English fare—roast beef and plum pudding, and no tomfoolery. Here we have either pole of the Britannic folly. We will not eat the food of any foreigners; nor, when we have the chance, will we suffer him to eat of it himself. The same spirit inspired Miss Bird's American missionaries, who had come thousands of miles to change the faith of Japan, and openly professed their ignorance of the religions they were trying to supplant.

I quote an American in this connection without scruple. Uncle Sam is better than John Bull, but he is tarred with the English stick. For Mr. Grant White the States are the New England States and nothing more. He wonders at the amount of drinking in London; let him try San Francisco. He wittily reproves English ignorance as to the status of women in America; but has he not himself forgotten Wyoming? The name Yankee, of which he is so tenacious, is used over the most of the great Union as a term of reproach. The Yankee States, of which he is so staunch a subject, are but a drop in the bucket. And we find in his book a vast virgin ignorance of the life and prospects of America; every view partial, parochial, not raised to the horizon; the moral feeling proper, at the largest, to a clique of States; and the whole scope and atmosphere not American, but merely Yankee. I will go far beyond him in reprobating the assumption and the incivility of my countryfolk to their cousins from beyond the sea; I grill in my blood over the silly rudeness of our newspaper articles; and I do not know where to look when I find myself in company with an American and see my countrymen unbending to him as to a performing dog. But in the case of Mr. Grant White example were better than precept. Wyoming, is, after all, more readily accessible to Mr. White than Boston to the English, and the New England self-sufficiency no better justified than the Britannic.

It is so, perhaps, in all countries; perhaps in all, men are most ignorant of the foreigners at home. John Bull is ignorant of the States; he is probably ignorant of India; but considering his opportunities, he is far more ignorant of countries nearer his own door. There is one country, for instance—its frontier not so far from London, its people closely akin, its language the same in all essentials with the English—of which I will go bail he knows nothing. His ignorance of the sister kingdom cannot be described; it can only be illustrated by anecdote. I once traveled with a man of plausible manners and good intelligence,—a university man, as the phrase goes,—a man, besides, who had taken his degree in life and knew a thing or two about the age we live in. We were deep in talk, whirling between Peterborough and London; among other things, he began to describe some piece of legal injustice he had recently encountered, and I observed in my innocence that things were not so in Scotland. 'I beg your pardon,' said he, 'this is a matter of law.' He had never heard of the Scots law; nor did he choose to be informed. The law was the same for the whole country, he told me roundly; every child knew that. At last, to settle matters, I explained to him that I was a member of a Scottish legal body, and had stood the brunt of an examination in the very law in question. Thereupon he looked me for a moment full in the face and dropped the conversation. This is a monstrous instance, if you like, but it does not stand alone in the experience of Scots.

England and Scotland differ, indeed, in law, in history, in religion, in education, and in the very look of nature and men's faces, not always widely, but always trenchantly. Many particulars that struck Mr. Grant White, a Yankee, struck me, a Scot, no less forcibly; he and I felt ourselves foreigners on many common provocations. A Scotchman may tramp the better part of Europe and the United States, and never again receive so vivid an impression of foreign travel and strange lands and manners as on his first excursion into England. The change from a hilly to a level country strikes him with delighted wonder. Along the flat horizon there arise the frequent venerable towers of churches. He sees at the end of airy vistas the revolution of the windmill sails. He may go where he pleases in the future; he may see Alps, and Pyramids, and lions; but it will be hard to beat the pleasure of that moment. There are, indeed, few merrier spectacles than that of many windmills bickering together in a fresh breeze over a woody country; their halting alacrity of movement, their pleasant business, making bread all day with uncouth gesticulations, their air, gigantically human, as of a creature half alive, put a spirit of romance into the tamest landscape. When the Scotch child sees them first he falls immediately in love; and from that time forward windmills keep turning in his dreams. And so, in their degree, with every feature of the life and landscape. The warm, habitable age of towns and hamlets, the green, settled, ancient look of the country; the lush hedgerows, stiles and privy pathways in the fields; the sluggish, brimming rivers; chalk and smock-frocks; chimes of bells and the rapid, pertly sounding English speech—they are all new to the curiosity; they are all set to English airs in the child's story that he tells himself at night. The sharp edge of novelty wears off; the feeling is scotched, but I doubt whether it is ever killed. Rather it keeps returning, ever the more rarely and strangely, and even in scenes to which you have been long accustomed suddenly awakes and gives a relish to enjoyment or heightens the sense of isolation.

One thing especially continues unfamiliar to the Scotchman's eye—the domestic architecture, the look of streets and buildings; the quaint, venerable age of many, and the thin walls and warm coloring of all. We have, in Scotland, far fewer ancient buildings, above all in country places; and those that we have are all of hewn or harled masonry. Wood has been sparingly used in their construction; the window-frames are sunken in the wall, not flat to the front, as in England; the roofs are steeper-pitched; even a hill farm will have a massy, square, cold, and permanent appearance. English houses, in comparison, have the look of cardboard toys, such as a puff might shatter. And to this the Scotchman never becomes used. His eye can never rest consciously on one of these brick houses—rickles of brick, as he might call them—or on one of these flat-chested streets, but he is instantly reminded where he is, and instantly travels back in fancy to his home. 'This is no my ain house; I ken by the biggin' o't.' And yet perhaps it is his own, bought with his own money, the key of it long polished in his pocket; but it has not yet, and never will be, thoroughly adopted by his imagination; nor does he cease to remember that, in the whole length and breadth of his native country, there was no building even distantly resembling it.

But it is not alone in scenery and architecture that we count England foreign. The constitution of society, the very pillars of the empire, surprise and even pain us. The dull, neglected peasant, sunk in matter, insolent, gross, and servile, makes a startling contrast with our own long-legged, long-headed, thoughtful, Bible-quoting plowman. A week or two in such a place as Suffolk leaves the Scotchman gasping. It seems incredible that within the boundaries of his own island a class should have been thus forgotten. Even the educated and intelligent, who hold our own opinions and speak in our own words, yet seem to hold them with a difference or from another reason, and to speak on all things with less interest and conviction. The first shock of English society is like a cold plunge. It is possible that the Scot comes looking for too much, and to be sure his first experiment will be in the wrong direction. Yet surely his complaint is grounded; surely the speech of Englishmen is too often lacking in generous ardor, the better part of the man too often withheld from the social commerce, and the contact of mind with mind evaded as with terror. A Scotch peasant will talk more liberally out of his own experience. He will not put you by with conversational counters and small jests; he will give you the best of himself, like one interested in life and man's chief end. A Scotchman is vain, interested in himself and others, eager for sympathy, setting forth his thoughts and experience in the best light. The egoism of the Englishman is self-contained. He does not seek to proselytize. He takes no interest in Scotland or the Scotch, and, what is the unkindest cut of all, he does not care to justify his indifference. Give him the wages of going on and being an Englishman, that is all he asks; and in the meantime, while you continue to associate, he would rather not be reminded of your baser origin. Compared with the grand, tree-like self-sufficiency of his demeanor, the vanity and curiosity of the Scot seem uneasy, vulgar, and immodest. That you should continually try to establish human and serious relations, that you should actually feel an interest in John Bull, and desire and invite a return of interest from him, may argue something more awake and lively in your mind, but it still puts you in the attitude of a suitor and a poor relation. Thus even the lowest class of the educated English towers over a Scotchman by the head and shoulders.

Different indeed is the atmosphere in which Scotch and English youth begin to look about them, come to themselves in life, and gather up those first apprehensions which are the material of future thought and, to a great extent, the rule of future conduct. I have been to school in both countries, and I found, in the boys of the North, something at once rougher and more tender, at once more reserve and more expansion, a greater habitual distance checkered by glimpses of a nearer intimacy, and on the whole wider extremes of temperament and sensibility. The boy of the South seems more wholesome, but less thoughtful; he gives himself to games as to a business, striving to excel, but is not readily transported by imagination; the type remains with me as cleaner in mind and body, more active, fonder of eating, endowed with a lesser and a less romantic sense of life and of the future, and more immersed in present circumstances. And certainly, for one thing, English boys are younger for their age. Sabbath observance make a series of grim, and perhaps serviceable, pauses in the tenor of Scotch boyhood—days of great stillness and solitude for the rebellious mind, when in the dearth of books and play, and in the intervals of studying the Shorter Catechism, the intellect and senses prey upon and test each other. The typical English Sunday, with the huge midday dinner and the plethoric afternoon, leads perhaps to different results. About the very cradle of the Scot there goes a hum of metaphysical divinity; and the whole of two divergent systems is summed up, not merely speciously, in the two first questions of the rival catechisms, the English tritely inquiring, 'What is your name?' the Scottish striking at the very roots of life with, 'What is the chief end of man?' and answering nobly, if obscurely, 'To glorify God and to enjoy Him forever.' I do not wish to make an idol of the Shorter Catechism; but the fact of such a question being asked opens to us Scotch a great field of speculation; and the fact that it is asked of all of us, from the peer to the plowboy, binds us more nearly together. No Englishman of Byron's age, character, and history, would have had patience for long theological discussions on the way to fight for Greece; but the daft Gordon blood and the Aberdonian schooldays kept their influence to the end. We have spoken of the material conditions; nor need much more be said of these: of the land lying everywhere more exposed, of the wind always louder and bleaker, of the black, roaring winters, of the gloom of high-lying, old stone cities, imminent on the windy seaboard; compared with the level streets, the warm coloring of the brick, the domestic quaintness of the architecture, among which English children begin to grow up and come to themselves in life. As the stage of the university approaches, the contrast becomes more express. The English lad goes to Oxford or Cambridge; there, in an ideal world of gardens, to lead a semi-scenic life, costumed, disciplined, and drilled by proctors. Nor is this to be regarded merely as a stage of education; it is a piece of privilege besides, and a step that separates him further from the bulk of his compatriots. At an earlier age the Scottish lad begins his greatly different experience of crowded classrooms, of a gaunt quadrangle, of a bell hourly booming over the traffic of the city to recall him from the public-house where he has been lunching, or the streets where he has been wandering fancy-free. His college life has little of restraint, and nothing of necessary gentility. He will find no quiet clique of the exclusive, studious, and cultured; no rotten borough of the arts. All classes rub shoulders on the greasy benches. The raffish young gentleman in gloves must measure his scholarship with the plain, clownish laddie from the parish school. They separate, at the session's end, one to smoke cigars about a watering-place, the other to resume the labors of the field beside his peasant family. The first muster of a college class in Scotland is a scene of curious and painful interest; so many lads, fresh from the heather, hang round the stove in cloddish embarrassment, ruffled by the presence of their smarter comrades, and afraid of the sound of their own rustic voices. It was in these early days, I think, that Professor Blackie won the affection of his pupils, putting these uncouth, umbrageous students at their ease with ready human geniality. Thus, at least, we have a healthy democratic atmosphere to breathe in while at work; even when there is no cordiality there is always a juxtaposition of the different classes, and in the competition of study the intellectual power of each is plainly demonstrated to the other. Our tasks ended, we of the North go forth as freemen into the humming, lamp-lit city. At five o'clock you may see the last of us hiving from the college gates, in the glare of the shop windows, under the green glimmer of the winter sunset. The frost tingles in our blood; no proctor lies in wait to intercept us; till the bell sounds again, we are the masters of the world; and some portion of our lives is always Saturday, *la trève de Dieu* [the truce of God].

Nor must we omit the sense of the nature of his country and his country's history gradually growing in the child's mind from story and from observation. A Scottish child hears much of shipwreck, outlying iron skerries, pitiless breakers, and great sea-lights; much of heathery mountains, wild clans, and hunted Covenanters. Breaths come to him in song of the distant Cheviots and the ring of foraying hoofs. He glories in his hard-fisted forefathers, of the iron girdle and the handful of oatmeal, who rode so swiftly and lived so sparely on their raids. Poverty, ill-luck, enterprise, and constant resolution are the fibers of the legend of his country's history. The heroes and kings of Scotland have been tragically fated; the most marking incidents in Scottish history—Flodden, Darien, or the Forty-five—were still either failures or defeats; and the fall of Wallace and the repeated reverses of the Bruce combine with the very smallness of the country to teach rather a moral than a material criterion for life. Britain is altogether small, the mere taproot of her extended empire; Scotland, again, which alone the Scottish boy adopts in his imagination, is but a little part of that, and avowedly cold, sterile, and unpopulous. It is not so for nothing. I once seemed to have perceived in an American boy a greater readiness of sympathy for lands that are great, and rich, and growing, like his own. It proved to be quite otherwise: a mere dumb piece of boyish romance, that I had lacked penetration to divine. But the error serves the purpose of my argument; for I am sure, at least, that the heart of young Scotland will be always touched more nearly by paucity of number and Spartan poverty of life.

So we may argue, and yet the difference is not explained. That Shorter Catechism which I took as being so typical of Scotland, was yet composed in the city of Westminster. The division of races is more sharply marked within the borders of Scotland itself than between the countries. Galloway and Buchan, Lothian and Lochaber, are like foreign parts; yet you may choose a man from any of them, and, ten to one, he shall prove to have a headmark of a Scot. A century and a half ago the Highlander wore a different costume, spoke a different language, worshipped in another church, held different morals, and obeyed a different social constitution from his fellow-countrymen either of the South or North. Even the English, it is recorded, did not loathe the Highlander and the Highland costume as they were loathed by the remainder of the Scotch. Yet the Highlander felt himself a Scot. He would willingly raid into the Scotch lowlands; but his courage failed him at the border, and he regarded England as a perilous, unhomely land. When the Black Watch, after years of foreign service, returned to Scotland, veterans leaped out and kissed the earth at Port Patrick. They had been in Ireland, stationed among men of their own race and language, where they were well liked and treated with affection; but it was the soil of Galloway that they kissed at the extreme end of the hostile lowlands, among a people who did not understand their speech, and who had hated, harried, and hanged them since the dawn of history. Last, and perhaps most curious, the sons of chieftains were often educated on the continent of Europe. They went abroad speaking

Gaelic; they returned speaking, not English, but the broad dialect of Scotland. Now, what idea had they in their minds when they thus, in thought, identified themselves with their ancestral enemies? What was the sense in which they were Scotch and not English, or Scotch and not Irish? Can a bare name be thus influential on the minds and affections of men, and a political aggregation blind them to the nature of facts? The story of the Austrian Empire would seem to answer, No; the far more galling business of Ireland clenches the negative from nearer home. Is it common education, common morals, a common language, or a common faith, that joins men into nations? There were practically none of these in the case we are considering.

The fact remains: in spite of the difference of blood and language, the Lowlander feels himself the sentimental countryman of the Highlander. When they meet abroad, they fall upon each other's necks in spirit; even at home there is a kind of clannish intimacy in their talk. But from his compatriot in the South the Lowlander stands consciously apart. He has had a different training; he obeys different laws; he makes his will in other terms, is otherwise divorced and married; his eyes are not at home in an English landscape or with English houses; his ear continues to remark the English speech; and even though his tongue acquire the Southern knack, he will still have a strong Scotch accent of the mind.

(1882)

From A CHILD'S GARDEN OF VERSES

Whole Duty of Children

A CHILD should always say what's true,
And speak when he is spoken to,
And behave mannerly at table:
At least as far as he is able.

Bed in Summer

In winter I get up at night
And dress by yellow candle-light.
In summer, quite the other way,—
I have to go to bed by day.

I have to go to bed and see
The birds still hopping on the tree,
Or hear the grown-up people's feet
Still going past me in the street.

And does it not seem hard to you,
When all the sky is clear and blue,
And I should like so much to play,
To have to go to bed by day?

System

Every night my prayers I say,
And get my dinner every day;
And every day that I've been good,
I get an orange after food.

The child that is not clean and neat,
With lots of toys and things to eat,
He is a naughty child, I'm sure—
Or else his dear papa is poor.

Happy Thought

The world is so full of a number of things,
I'm sure we should all be as happy as kings.

To Auntie

Chief of our aunts—not only I,
But all your dozen of nurslings cry—
*What did the other children do?
And what were childhood, wanting you?*

(1885)

IN THE STATES

With half a heart I wander here
  As from an age gone by,
A brother—yet though young in years
  An elder brother, I.

You speak another tongue than mine,
  Though both were English born.
I towards the night of time decline,
  You mount into the morn.

Youth shall grow great and strong and free,
  But age must still decay:
To-morrow for the States,—for me,
  England and Yesterday.

(1887)

San Francisco.

HEATHER ALE

A GALLOWAY LEGEND

From the bonny bells of heather
  They brewed a drink long-syne,
Was sweeter far than honey,
  Was stronger far than wine.
They brewed it and they drank it,
  And lay in a blessed swound
For days and days together
  In their dwellings underground.

There rose a king in Scotland,
   A fell man to his foes,
He smote the Picts in battle,
   He hunted them like roes.
Over miles of the red mountain
   He hunted as they fled,
And strewed the dwarfish bodies
   Of the dying and the dead.

Summer came in the country,
   Red was the heather bell;
But the manner of the brewing
   Was none alive to tell.
In graves that were like children's
   On many a mountain head,
The Brewsters of the Heather
   Lay numbered with the dead.

The king in the red moorland
   Rode on a summer's day;
And the bees hummed, and the curlews
   Cried beside the way.
The king rode, and was angry,
   Black was his brow and pale,
To rule in a land of heather
   And lack the Heather Ale.

It fortuned that his vassals,
   Riding free on the heath,
Came on a stone that was fallen
   And vermin hid beneath.
Rudely plucked from their hiding,
   Never a word they spoke:
A son and his aged father—
   Last of the dwarfish folk.

And the king sat high on his charger,
   He looked on the little men;
And the dwarfish and swarthy couple
   Looked at the king again.
Down by the shore he had them;
   And there on the giddy brink—
'I will give you life, ye vermin,
   For the secret of the drink.'

There stood the son and father;
   And they looked high and low;
The heather was red around them,
   The sea rumbled below.
And up and spoke the father,
   Shrill was his voice to hear:
'I have a word in private,
   A word for the royal ear.

'Life is dear to the aged,
   And honor a little thing;
I would gladly sell the secret,'
   Quoth the Pict to the King.
His voice was small as a sparrow's,
   And shrill and wonderful clear;
'I would gladly sell my secret,
   Only my son I fear.

'For life is a little matter,
   And death is nought to the young;
And I dare not sell my honor
   Under the eye of my son.
Take *him*, O king, and bind him,
   And cast him far in the deep;
And it's I will tell the secret
   That I have sworn to keep.'

They took the son and bound him,
   Neck and heels in a thong,
And a lad took him and swung him,
   And flung him far and strong,
And the sea swallowed his body,
   Like that of a child of ten;—
And there on the cliff stood the father,
   Last of the dwarfish men.

'True was the word I told you:
   Only my son I feared;
For I doubt the sapling courage
   That goes without the beard.
But now in vain is the torture,
   Fire shall never avail:
Here dies in my bosom
   The secret of Heather Ale.'

(1891)

GEORGE MOORE (1852-1933)

Moore was born in County Mayo, the son of a well-known Irish orator and politician. He became an art student in London and Paris, and his first recognition by the British public was as an art critic, his early publications in verse, *Flowers of Passion* and *Pagan Poems*, attracting little attention. His experiments in fiction were not much more successful until in 1894 he produced *Esther Waters*, a study of an English racing stable and its dependents in the approved methods of modern French realism. It was about this time that the Irish literary renaissance was coming to fruition, and one of its leaders, Edward Martyn, drew Moore's attention to the importance of Erse as a literary medium. Up to that time Moore had 'thought nobody did anything in Irish except bring turf from the bog and say prayers,' but he was interested in the prospect of writing in a language 'revived and sharpened to literary usage for the first time'; after the Boer War he found England 'so beastly' that he accepted Lady Gregory's invitation to become her guest in order to write an Irish play in collaboration with W. B. Yeats, the leader of the new movement, which later culminated in the establishment of the Abbey Theatre in Dublin. Moore's wayward spirit did not lend itself easily to collaboration or organization, and he did not like the Yeats vocabulary, so he expressed casually a preference for writing his share of the play in French. To his astonishment Yeats agreed: 'Lady Gregory will translate your text into English. Taidh O'Donohue will translate the English text into Irish, and Lady Gregory will translate the Irish text back into English.' So Moore left Ireland for Paris to do his part; but the most important outcome of his share in the Irish revival was his impudently critical account of it in his autobiographical *Ave*, *Salve*, and *Vale*, three volumes published in 1911-14. The degree of its veracity may be judged from the remark—obviously his own invention—which Moore puts into the mouth of 'A. E.': 'A literary movement consists of five or six people, who live in the same town and hate each other cordially.'

After the Great War, Moore settled down again in London and busied himself with the revision of his earlier works for *de luxe* editions, the publication of further reminiscences and confessions, the retelling of the romance of *Héloïse and Abélard*, and a new (fictitious) version of the Gospel story in *The Brook Kerith*. His competence as a literary artist was beyond question and his style found many admirers, but he seldom took his work or his readers seriously, and his tricksiness of spirit, often too baffling even for his Irish compatriots, is too constant to command the continued respect of the British public, which likes wit in small doses, watered with an abundant supply of common sense.

From MODERN PAINTING

THE ORGANIZATION OF ART

No fact is more painful to the modern mind than that men are not born with equal brains; and every day we grow more and more determined to thwart Nature's desire of inequality by public education. Whether everybody should be taught to read and write I leave to politicians—the matter is not important; but that the nation should not be instructed in drawing, music, painting, and English literature I will never cease to maintain. Everything that has happened in England for the last thirty years goes to prove that systematized education in art means artistic decadence.

To the ordinary mind there is something very reassuring in the words institutions, professors, examinations, medals, and titles of all kinds. All these things have been given of late years to art, and parents and guardians need no longer have any fear for those confided to their charge: the art of painting has been recognized as a profession! The principal institution where this profession is practised is called the Royal Academy It owes its existence to the taste of a gentleman known as George the Third, and it has been dowered by the State to the extent of at least three hundred thousand pounds Professors from Oxford, even bishops, dine there. The members of this institution put R. A. after their names; the president has been made a baronet; there was even a rumor that he was to be made a lord, and that he was not we must consider as another blow dealt against the dignity of art.

Literature does not offer so much scope for

organization as painting; but strenuous efforts are being made to organize it, and, by the aid of academies, examinations, and crowns, hopes are entertained that, before long, it will be brought into line with the other professions. And the journalists too are anxious to 'erect their craft to the dignity of a profession which shall confer upon its members *certain social status* like that of the barrister and the lawyer.' Entrance is to be strictly conditional; no one is to have the right to practise without a diploma, and members are to be entitled to certain letters after their names. A movement is on foot to Churton-Collinise English literature at the universities, and every month Mr. Walter Besant raises a wail in the *Author* that the peerage is not as open to three-volume novelists as it is to brewers. He bewails the fact that no eminent man of letters, with the exception of Lord Tennyson, has been made the enforced associate of brewers and politicians. Mr. Besant does not think that titles in these democratic days are foolish and absurd, pitiful in the personality of those who own them by inheritance, grotesque in the personality of those on whom they have been conferred. Mr. Besant does not see that the desire of the baker, the brewer, the butcher, and I may add the three-volume novelist, to be addressed by small tradesmen and lackeys as 'yer lordship,' raises a smile on the lips of even the most *blasé*.

I am advocating an unpopular *régime* I know, for the majority believe that art is in Queer Street if new buildings are not being raised, if official recognition of merits is not proclaimed, and if the newspapers do not teem with paragraphs concerning the homes of the Academicians. The wailing and gnashing of teeth that were heard when an intelligent portion of the Press induced Mr. Tate to withdraw his offer to build a gallery and furnish it with pictures by Messrs. Herkomer, Fildes, Leader, Long, are not forgotten. It was not urged that the pictures were valuable pictures; the merit or demerit of the pictures was not what interested, but the fact that a great deal of money was going to be spent, and that titles, badges, medals, crowns, would be given to those whose pictures were enshrined in the new temple of art. The Tate Gallery touched these folk as would an imposing review of troops, a procession of judges, or a coronation in Westminster Abbey. Their senses were tickled by the prospect of a show, their minds were stirred by some idea of organization—something was about to be organized, and nothing appeals so much to the vulgar mind as organization.

An epoch is represented by a word, and to organize represents the dominant idea of our civilization. To organize is to be respectable, and as every one wants to be respectable, every one dreams of new schemes of organization. Soldiers, sailors, policemen, members of parliament, independent voters, clerks in the post office, bus drivers, dockers, every imaginable variety of worker, domestic servants—it is difficult to think of any class that has not been organized of late years. There is a gentleman in parliament who is anxious to do something in the way of social organization for the gipsies. The gipsies have not appealed to him; they have professed no desire to have their social status raised; they have, I believe, disclaimed through their king, whoever he may be, all participation in the scheme of this benevolent gentleman. Nor does any sense of the absurdity of his endeavor blight the worthy gentleman's ardor. How should it? He, like the other organizers, is an unreasoning instrument in a great tendency of things. To organize something—or, put it differently, to educate some one—is to-day every man's ambition. So long as it is not himself, it matters no jot to him whom he educates. The gipsy under the hedge, the artist painting under a hill, it matters not. A technical school of instruction would enable the gipsy to harness his horse better than he does at present; and the artist would paint much better if he were taught to stipple, and examined by salaried professors in stipple, and given prizes for stippling. The general mind of our century is with education and organization of every kind, and from this terrible general mind art seems unable to escape. Art, that poor little gipsy whose very condition of existence is freedom, who owns no code of laws, who evades all regulations, who groups himself under no standards, who can live only in disastrous times, when the world's attention is drawn to other things, and allows him life in shelter of the hedges, and dreams in sight of the stars, finds himself forced into a uniform—poor little fellow, how melancholy he looks on his high stool in the South Kensington Museum, and notwithstanding the professors his hand drops from the drawing-board, unable to accomplish the admired stipple.

But solemn members of parliament are certain that official recognition must be extended to art. Art is an educational influence, and the Kensington galleries are something more than agreeable places, where sweethearts can murmur soft nothings under divine masterpieces. The utilitarian M.P. must find some justification for art; he is not sensible enough to understand that art justifies its own existence, that it is its own honor and glory; and he nourishes a flimsy lie, and votes that large sums of money shall be spent in endowing schools of art and founding picture galleries. Then there is another class—those who have fish to fry, and to whom art seems a convenient frying-pan. Mr. Tate craves for a museum to be called Tate's; or, if his princely gift gained him a title, which it may, the museum would be called—What would be an appropriate name? There are men too who have trifles to sell, and they talk loudly of the glories of modern art, and the necessity of a British Luxembourg.

That France should have a Luxembourg is natural enough; that we should have one would be anomalous. We are a free-trading country. I pass over the failure of the Luxembourg to recognize genius, to save the artist of genius a struggle with insolent ignorance. What did the Luxembourg do for Corot, Millet, Manet, Degas, Monet, Renoir, Sisley, Pissaro? The Luxembourg chose rather to honor such pretentious mediocrities as Bouguereau, Jules Lefebvre, Jules Breton, and their like. What has our Academy done to rescue struggling genius from poverty and obscurity? Did it save Alfred Stevens, the great sculptor of his generation, from the task of designing fire-irons? How often did the Academy refuse Cecil Lawson's pictures? When they did accept him, was it not because he had become popular in spite of the Academy? Did not the Academy refuse Mr. Whistler's portrait of his mother, and was it not hung at the last moment owing to a threat of one of the Academicians to resign if a place was not found for it? Place was found for it seven feet above the line. Has not the Academy for the last five-and-twenty years lent the whole stress and authority of its name to crush Mr. Whistler? Happily his genius was sufficient for the fight, and it was not until he had conquered past all question that he left this country. The record of the Academy is a significant one. But if it has exercised a vicious influence in art, its history is no worse than that of other academies. Here, as elsewhere, the Academy has tolerated genius when it was popular, and when it was not popular it has trampled upon it.

We have Free Trade in literature, why should we not have Free Trade in art? Why should not every artist go into the market without title or masquerade that blinds the public to the value of what he has to sell? I would turn art adrift, title-less, R.A.-less, out into the street and field, where, under the light of his original stars, the impassioned vagrant might dream once more, and for the mere sake of his dreams.

(1893)

GEORGE BERNARD SHAW (1856–

BERNARD SHAW at the end of his career was probably the best known figure in Europe and America connected with the spoken drama; the first productions of his latest plays—*Back to Methuselah*, and *St. Joan*—by the Theatre Guild of New York were international events, and with all the world's dramatists to choose from the Guild found no surer attraction for American audiences than old favorites from the Shaw repertoire. But Shaw's success on the commercial stage dates back only to the beginning of this century. His first play, *Widowers' Houses*, put on at the Independent Theatre, London, in 1892, was not much more than a dramatized pamphlet on the iniquities of slum landlords and those dependent on their profits; it was applauded by the Socialists and hooted by their opponents, and as the latter were a large majority of the audience, it was speedily withdrawn. He says: 'It made a sensation out of all proportion to its merits and even its demerits, and I at once became infamous as a dramatist.' He had previously won notoriety as a socialistic soap-box orator, journalist and novelist, and he was well known in London as a brilliant critic of art, music, and the drama. His contributions to the *Saturday Review*, edited by James Huneker as *Dramatic Opinions and Essays* (1906), are still well worth the attention of the student.

Throughout his career, from the *Manifesto* of the Fabian Society (1884) to *The Intelligent Woman's Guide to Socialism and Capitalism* (1928), Shaw has consistently advocated the equal distribution of the national income among the whole population; and he began by regarding the stage as a pulpit from which he could propagate socialistic doctrine. But his gradual development of 'comedic talent'—dialogue sparkling with wit, situations pregnant with humor and even pathos—made his plays a delight to millions of people all the world over who had no sympathy with his opinions. Of the Irish Protestant training of his youth he kept a certain asceticism in practice—abstaining from alcohol, tobacco, and meat—and a detached point of view which enabled him to regard any issue with pure intelligence, free from any emotional sympathy. It is an attitude bound often to run counter to popular prejudices, but so rare that it is likely to secure for a long time respectful (if amused) attention to what Shaw has to say.

From DRAMATIC OPINIONS AND ESSAYS

THE CASE FOR THE CRITIC-DRAMATIST

A DISCUSSION has arisen recently as to whether a dramatic critic can also be a dramatic author without injury to his integrity and impartiality. The feebleness with which the point has been debated may be guessed from the fact that the favorite opinion seems to be that a critic is either an honest man or he is not. If honest, then dramatic authorship can make no difference to him. If not, he will be dishonest whether he writes plays or not. This childish evasion cannot, for the honor of the craft, be allowed to stand. If I wanted to ascertain the melting-point of a certain metal, and how far it would be altered by an alloy of some other metal, and an expert were to tell me that a metal is either fusible or it is not—that if not, no temperature will melt it; and if so, it will melt anyhow—I am afraid I should ask that expert whether he was a fool himself or took me for one. Absolute honesty is as absurd an abstraction as absolute temperature or absolute value. A dramatic critic who would die rather than read an American pirated edition of a copyright English book might be considered an absolutely honest man for all practical purposes on that one particular subject—I say on that one, because very few men have more than one point of honor; but as far as I am aware, no such dramatic critic exists. If he did, I should regard him as a highly dangerous monomaniac. That honesty varies inversely with temptation is proved by the fact that every additional penny on the income-tax yields a less return than the penny before it, showing that men state their incomes less honestly for the purpose of taxation at sevenpence in the pound than sixpence. The matter may be tested by a simple experiment. Go to one of the gentlemen whose theory is that a man is either honest or he is not, and obtain from him the loan of half a-crown on some plausible pretext of a lost purse or some such petty emergency. He will not ask you for a written acknowledgment of the debt. Return next day and ask for a loan of £500 without a promissory note, on the ground that you are either honest or not honest, and that a man who will pay back half-a-crown without compulsion will also pay back £500. You will find that the theory of absolute honesty will collapse at once.

Are we then to believe that the critic-dramatist who stands to make anything from five hundred to ten thousand pounds by persuading a manager to produce his plays, will be prevented by his honesty from writing about that manager otherwise than he would if he had never written a play and were quite certain that he never should write one? I can only say that people who believe such a thing would believe anything. I am myself a particularly flagrant example of the critic-dramatist. It is not with me a mere case of an adaptation or two raked up against me as incidents in my past. I have written half-a-dozen 'original' plays, four of which have never been performed; and I shall presently write half-a-dozen more. The production of one of them, even if it attained the merest success of esteem, would be more remunerative to me than a couple of years of criticism. Clearly, since I am no honester than other people, I should be the most corrupt flatterer in London if there were nothing but honesty to restrain me. How is it, then, that the most severe criticisms of managers come from me and from my fellow critic-dramatists, and that the most servile puffery comes from writers whose every sentence proved that they have nothing to hope or fear from any manager? There are a good many answers to this question, one of the most obvious being that as the respect inspired by a good criticism is permanent, whilst the irritation it causes is temporary, and as, on the other hand, the pleasure given by a venal criticism is temporary, and the contempt it inspires permanent, no man really secures his advancement as a dramatist by making himself despised as a critic. The thing has been tried extensively during the last twenty years; and it has failed. For example, the late Frank Marshall, a dramatist and an extravagantly enthusiastic admirer of Sir Henry Irving's genius, followed a fashion which at one time made the Lyceum Theatre a sort of court formed by a retinue of literary gentlemen. I need not question either their sincerity or the superiority of Canute to their idolatry; for Canute never produced their plays: 'Robert Emmet' and the rest of their masterpieces remain unacted to this day. It may be said that this brings us back to honesty as the best policy; but honesty has nothing to do with it: plenty of the men who know that they can get along faster fighting than crawling, are no more honest than the first Napoleon was. No virtue, least of all courage, implies any other virtue. The cardinal guarantee for a critic's integrity is simply the force of the critical instinct itself. To try to prevent me from criticizing by pointing out to me the superior pecuniary advantages of puffing is like trying to keep a young Irving from going on the stage by pointing out the superior pecuniary advantages of stockbroking. If my own father were an actor-manager, and his life depended on his getting favorable notices of his performance, I should orphan myself without an instant's hesitation if he acted badly. I am by no means the willing victim of this instinct. I am keenly susceptible to contrary influences—to flattery, which I swallow greedily if the quality is sufficiently good; to the need of money, to private friendship or even acquaintanceship, to the pleasure of giving pleasure and the pain of giving pain, to consideration of other people's circumstances and prospects, to personal likes and dislikes, to sentimentality, pity, chivalry, pugnacity and mischief, laziness and cowardice, and a dozen other human conditions which make the critic vulnerable; but the critical instinct gets the better of them all. I spare no effort to mitigate its inhumanity, trying to detect and strike out of my articles anything that would give pain without doing any good. Those who think the things I say severe, or even malicious, should just see the things I do *not* say. I do my best to be partial, to hit out at remediable abuses rather than at accidental shortcomings, and at strong and responsible people rather than weak and helpless ones. And yet all my efforts do not alter the result very much. So stubborn is the critic within me, that with every disposition to be as good-natured and as popular an authority as the worst enemy of art could desire, I am to all intents and purposes incorruptible. And that is how the dramatist-critic, if only he is critic enough, 'slates' the actor-manager in defiance of the interest he has in counciliating him. He cannot help himself, any more than the ancient mariner could help telling his story. And the actor-manager can no more help listening than the wedding guest could. In short, the better formula would have been, that a man is either a critic or not a critic; that to the extent to which he is one he will criticize the managers in spite of heaven and earth; and that to the extent to which he is not, he will flatter them anyhow, to save himself trouble.

The advantage of having a play criticized by a critic who is also a playwright is as obvious as the advantage of having a ship criticized by a critic who is also a master shipwright. Pray observe that I do not speak of the criticism of dramas and ships by dramatists and shipwrights who are not also critics; for that would be no more convincing than the criticism of acting by actors. Dramatic authorship no more constitutes a man a critic than actorship constitutes him a dramatic author; but a dramatic critic learns as much from having been a dramatic author as Shakespeare or Mr. Pinero from having been actors. The average London critic, for want of practical experience, has no real confidence in himself; he is always searching for an imaginary 'right' opinion, with which he never dares to identify his own. Consequently every public man finds that as far as the press is concerned his career divides itself into two parts: the first, during which the critics are afraid to praise him; and the second, during which they are afraid to do anything else. In the first, the critic is uncomfortably trying to find faults enough to make out a case for his timid coldness: in the second, he is eagerly picking out excellencies to justify his eulogies. And of course he blunders equally in both phases. The faults he finds are either inessential or are positive reforms, or he blames the wrong people for them: the triumphs of acting which he announces are stage tricks that any old hand could play. In criticizing actresses he is an open and shameless voluptuary. If a woman is pretty, well dressed, and self-satisfied enough to be at her ease on the stage, he is delighted; and if she is a walking monument of handsome incompetence, so much the better, as your voluptuary rarely likes a woman to be cleverer than himself, or to force him to feel deeply or think energetically when he only wants to wallow in her good looks. Confront him with an actress who will not condescend to attack him on this side—who takes her work with thorough seriousness and self-respect —and his resentment, his humiliation, his sense of being snubbed, break out ludicrously in his writing, even when he dare not write otherwise than favorably. No dramatist begins by writing plays merely as excuses for the exhibition of pretty women on the stage. He comes to that ultimately perhaps; but at first he does his best to create real characters and make them pass through three acts of real experiences. Bring a critic who has done this face to face with the practical question of selecting an actress for his heroine, and he suddenly realizes for the first time that there is not such a galaxy of talent on the London stage as he thought, and that the handsome walking ladies whom he always thought good enough for other people's plays are not good enough for his own. That is already an immense step in his education. There are other steps, too, which he will have taken before the curtain falls on the first public representation of his play; but they may be summed up in the fact that the author of a play is the only person who really wants to have it well done in every respect, and who therefore has every drawback brought fully home to him. The man who has had that awakening about one play will thenceforth have his eyes open at all other plays; and there you have at once the first moral with the first technical qualification of the critic—the determination to have every play as well done as possible, and the knowledge of what is standing in the way of that consummation. Those of our critics who, either as original dramatists or adapters and translators, have superintended the production of plays with paternal anxiety, are never guilty of the wittily disguised indifference of clever critics who have never seen a drama through from its first beginnings behind the scenes. Compare the genuine excitement of Mr. Clement Scott, or the almost Calvinistic seriousness of Mr. Wm. Archer with the gaily easy what-does-it-matterness of Mr. Walkley, and you see at once how the two critic-dramatists influence the drama, whilst the critic-playgoer only makes it a pretext for entertaining his readers. On the whole there is only as much validity in the theory that a critic should not be a dramatist, as in the theory that a judge should not be a lawyer nor a general a soldier. You cannot have qualifications without experience; and you cannot have experience without personal interest and bias. That may not be an ideal arrangement; but it is the way the world is built; and we must make the best of it.

(1906)

THE TWENTIETH CENTURY

QUEEN VICTORIA died in the first year of the twentieth century after a long and eventful reign, which seemed to constitute an epoch in itself. The reign of her successor, Edward VII, was comparatively short and uneventful (1901–10), except for the *entente cordiale* with France, which afterwards involved the British Empire in the Great War. This broke out in 1914 and cast before it a shadow which loomed ominously over the earlier years of the century. Otherwise the new reign continued the programme of peace, prosperity and reform which had begun under Victoria. The Conservative Ministry of Mr. Balfour (afterwards Lord Balfour) passed a useful Education Act, giving further state aid to secondary as well as to elementary education. The Liberal Government which came to power in 1906, backed by a considerable number of Labor members in the House of Commons, strengthened the legal position of the trades unions, provided small holdings, trade boards, old age pensions, and health insurance for the benefit of the working class, and proposed drastic land legislation which involved a conflict with the House of Lords, and the limitation of the veto hitherto exercised by the Peers upon legislation sent up to them by the Lower House.

In literature also the advent of the new century seemed to bring no new forces or new personalities. Samuel Butler died in 1902, and the publication of his posthumous novel *The Way of All Flesh* made a considerable impression upon subsequent fiction. Gissing died in 1903, Swinburne and Meredith in 1909. Hardy, who had published his great 'epic drama' *The Dynasts* in 1903–8, succeeded Meredith as a member of the Order of Merit, and held in popular esteem the position of the last of the Great Victorians until his death in 1928. Of their younger contemporaries who had begun to attract public attention in the nineteenth century, Kipling continued for a time—but only for a few years—to hold the place he had already won in popular favor. Bernard Shaw turned his *succès d'estime* of the nineteenth century into a popular triumph early in the twentieth, and became the most prominent figure in European drama. J. M. Barrie, who had in the nineteenth century won repute as a novelist, built up a second reputation in the twentieth century as a writer for the stage. John Galsworthy practised both arts with equal facility. H. G. Wells and Arnold Bennett, whose dramatic achievements were of little importance, did work of first rate quality in the novel; but all of these were not only born in the Victorian era but started their literary careers before it was over. During the reign of George V it was the fashion to call this group of novelists 'Edwardians,' but with the accession of Edward VIII this label ceased to be sufficiently distinctive to be useful. In the early years of George V it appeared for a time as if 'the Edwardians' might be superseded in popular favor by a younger school of novelists led by Hugh Walpole, Gilbert Cannan, Compton Mackenzie and D. H. Lawrence, but of these only the first named and the last succeeded in holding the attention of a predominant body of readers. Bennett, Galsworthy and Wells regained their supremacy until almost the end of the Georgian period, when D. H. Lawrence, James Joyce, Virginia Woolf and Aldous Huxley were being read by the younger generation and discussed by the middle-aged critics.

The bounds between journalism and literature had never been very clearly defined, for in the nineteenth century Coleridge, Lamb, Hazlitt, De Quincey, Macaulay, and Carlyle were in a sense journalists, though much that they wrote for periodical publication came soon to be recognized as of permanent interest and value. But in the twentieth century Shaw, Bennett, and Wells emphasized the necessity of dealing with issues of the day and the hour—even of the passing moment. This secured for them immediate popularity but is already putting limits to their abiding fame. Much of their work seems 'dated'—which really means out of date except for the antiquarian; the successive educational and informational books put out by Wells in his later years, beginning with the *Outline of History*, lost a good deal of the power of their appeal before the series was finished. The generation to which the author seemed an inspired and authoritative prophet had grown old or passed away.

The twentieth century up to the end of George V's reign was a period of good prose rather than of great poetry—but of this more anon.

NOTEWORTHY DATES

HISTORICAL

1901 EDWARD VII
    Australia federated
1903 Education Act
    Airplane invented
1904 *Entente Cordiale*
1905 Liberal Government
1909 Lloyd George Budget
1910 Union of South Africa
    GEORGE V
1911 Lords' Veto abolished
    National Insurance
1914 Great War Began
1915 Italy joined Allies
1917 United States entered War
    Russian Revolution
1918 War ended. Women enfranchised
1919 Treaty of Versailles
1920 League of Nations organized
1922 Irish Free State
1924 First Labor Government
1926 General Strike
1929 Adult franchise
    Second Labor Government
    Financial Crisis
1931 Coalition Government
    Social Legislation (Housing)
1935 Silver Jubilee
    Germany left League of Nations
    Italy invaded Ethiopia
1936 EDWARD VIII
    Germany abrogated Locarno Treaty

LITERARY

1902 Barrie *The Admirable Crichton*
1903 Butler *The Way of All Flesh*
    Shaw *Man and Superman*
    Synge *The Shadow of the Glen*
1903-8 Hardy *The Dynasts*
1905 Wells *Kipps*
1906 Galsworthy *The Man of Property*
1908 Bennett *The Old Wifes' Tale*
1909 Swinburne died
    Meredith died
    Synge died
1913 D. H. Lawrence *Sons and Lovers*
1915 Rupert Brooke died
1916 Wells *Mr. Britling Sees it Through*
    Masefield *Gallipoli*
1921 Shaw *Back to Methuselah*
    Strachey *Queen Victoria*
1922 T. S. Eliot *The Waste Land*
    Galsworthy *The Forsyte Saga*
1923 Shaw *Saint Joan*
1924 Conrad died
1928 Hardy died
    Virginia Woolf *Orlando*
    T. E. Lawrence *Revolt in the Desert*
1930 D. H. Lawrence died
1931 Bennett died
1932 Strachey died
    Huxley *Brave New World*
1933 Galsworthy died
1935 T. E. Lawrence died
1936 Kipling died

EARLY TWENTIETH-CENTURY PROSE

The predominant prose medium of the early twentieth century was the novel, which about that time reached its highest point of popularity and influence, and soon afterwards began to decline. From the period of its beginnings in the hands of Richardson, the English novel had rarely escaped for long from a didactic tendency, and this tradition, clearly marked in the work of the great Victorians—Dickens, Thackeray, the Brontës, Mrs. Gaskell, George Eliot, Anthony Trollope, Gissing, Meredith and Hardy—was faithfully maintained by their twentieth-century successors. Of the brilliant group which began to flourish about the turn of the century Joseph Conrad (Korzeniowski), the Polish aristocrat who became a British subject and master mariner, but hardly spoke English till he was twenty, paid the most attention to style, 'the shape and ring of sentences,' as he put it, and the least to teaching moral lessons; his task, as he conceived it, was to make his readers *see*, and the virtues he inculcated were the simple ones—solidarity and fidelity, courage and personal devotion.

Next in rank as a stylist stands John Galsworthy, and even he was reproached by Max Beerbohm for selling his birthright for 'a pot of message.' But Galsworthy's *Forsyte Saga* and its associated fictions (including half a dozen novels and four shorter stories) is of permanent value both as a work of art and as a social document, recording the changes in view and practice for a long and crucial period of recent history, especially as they affected the upper middle class to which Galsworthy himself belonged.

For the ideas and customs of the English middle class as modified by nineteenth-century industrialism we must turn to the studies by Arnold Bennett of that characteristic Midland center known as 'the Five Towns,' especially *The Old Wives' Tale* and the Clayhanger series. In *Riceyman's Steps* the scene shifts to London, but a London not of politics and finance but of grimy commercialism, and the spirit is still that of the Midland middle class. Bennett's work marks the entry into the novel of the methods of journalism. Much of his work is sheer reporting—by a reporter of genius. It is only when his imagination is warmed by sympathy that he becomes a supreme artist.

If Arnold Bennett is the reporter become novelist, H. G. Wells is the editorial writer endowed with the imaginative power and freedom of fiction. In an essay printed below Wells promised (or threatened) to 'bring all life within the scope of the novel,' and he went far toward fulfilling his own prediction. In the novels of his middle period the elements of imagination and propaganda were fairly balanced, but in his later work the editor in him has almost entirely overcome the novelist, in spite of his remarkable gift for lively and even thrilling narrative. *Joan and Peter* is practically a treatise on education with a background of fiction, and *The World of William Clissold* is a world of political discussion on all kinds of subjects, national and international. As a method of propaganda, this subordination of the traditional elements of the novel to the personal interests of the author may seem to justify itself, but from the reader's point of view it involves the decay of the novel as a mode of artistic enjoyment. As an instrument of instruction it is evident that it will command a much smaller audience.

JOSEPH CONRAD
(1857-1924)

From A PERSONAL RECORD

WITH THE MARSEILLES PILOTS

Shortly before midnight I walked down the quay of the *Vieux Port* to join the pilot-boat of my friends. I knew where she would be waiting for her crew, in the little bit of a canal behind the fort at the entrance of the harbor. The deserted quays looked very white and dry in the moonlight, and as if frost-bound in the sharp air of that December night. A prowler or two slunk by noiselessly; a custom-house guard, soldier-like, a sword by his side, paced close under the bowsprits of the long row of ships moored bows on opposite the long, slightly curved, continuous flat wall of the tall houses that seemed to be one immense abandoned building with innumerable windows shuttered closely. Only here and there a small, dingy café for sailors cast a yellow gleam on the bluish sheen of the flagstones. Passing by, one heard a deep murmur of voices inside—nothing more. How quiet everything was at the end of the quays on the last night on which I went out for a service cruise as a guest of the Marseilles pilots! Not a footstep, except my own, not a sigh, not a whispering echo of the usual revelry going on in the narrow, unspeakable lanes of the Old Town reached my ear—and suddenly, with a terrific jingling rattle of iron and glass, the omnibus of the Jolliette on its last journey swung round the corner of the dead wall which faced across the paved road the characteristic angular mass of the Fort St. Jean. Three horses trotted abreast, with the clatter of hoofs on the granite setts, and the yellow, uproarious machine jolted violently behind them, fantastic, lighted up, perfectly empty, and with the driver apparently asleep on his swaying perch above that amazing racket. I flattened myself against the wall and gasped. It was a stunning experience. Then after staggering on a few paces in the shadow of the fort, casting a darkness more intense than that of a clouded night upon the canal, I saw the tiny light of a lantern standing on the quay, and became aware of muffled figures making toward it from various directions. Pilots of the Third Company hastening to embark. Too sleepy to be talkative, they step on board in silence. But a few low grunts and an enormous yawn are heard. Somebody even ejaculates: 'Ah! Coquin de sort!' and sighs wearily at his hard fate.

The *patron* of the Third Company (there were five companies of pilots at that time, I believe) is the brother-in-law of my friend Solary (Baptistin), a broad-shouldered, deep-chested man of forty, with a keen, frank glance which always seeks your eyes. He greets me by a low, hearty '*Hé, l'ami. Comment va?*' With his clipped mustache and massive open face, energetic and at the same time placid in expression, he is a fine specimen of the southerner of the calm type. For there is such a type in which the volatile southern passion is transmuted into solid force. He is fair, but no one could mistake him for a man of the north even by the dim gleam of the lantern standing on the quay. He is worth a dozen of your ordinary Normans or Bretons, but then, in the whole immense sweep of the Mediterranean shores, you could not find half a dozen men of his stamp.

Standing by the tiller, he pulls out his watch from under a thick jacket and bends his head over it in the light cast into the boat. Time's up. His pleasant voice commands, in a quiet undertone, '*Larguez.*' A suddenly projected arm snatches the lantern off the quay—and, warped along by a line at first, then with the regular tug of four heavy sweeps in the bow, the big half-decked boat full of men glides out of the black, breathless shadow of the fort. The open water of the *avantport* glitters under the moon as if sown over with millions of sequins, and the long white breakwater shines like a thick bar of solid silver. With a quick rattle of blocks and one single silky swish, the sail is filled by a little breeze keen enough to have come straight down from the frozen moon, and the boat, after the clatter of the hauled-in sweeps, seems to stand at rest, surrounded by a mysterious whispering so faint and unearthly that it may be the rustling of the brilliant, overpowering moonrays breaking like a rain-shower upon the hard, smooth, shadowless sea.

I may well remember that last night spent with the pilots of the Third Company. I have known the spell of moonlight since, on various seas and coasts—coasts of forests, of rocks, of sand dunes—but no magic so perfect in its revelation of unsuspected character, as though one were allowed to look upon the mystic nature of material things. For hours I suppose no word was spoken in that boat. The pilots, seated in two rows facing each other, dozed, with their arms folded and their chins resting upon their breasts. They displayed a great variety of caps: cloth, wool, leather, peaks, ear-flaps, tassels, with a picturesque round *béret* or two pulled down over the brows; and one grandfather, with a shaved, bony face and a great beak of a nose, had a cloak with a hood which made him look in our midst like a cowled monk being carried off goodness knows where by that silent company of seamen—quiet enough to be dead.

My fingers itched for the tiller, and in due course my friend, the *patron*, surrendered it in the same spirit in which the family coachman lets a boy hold the reins on an easy bit of road. There was a great solitude around us; the islets ahead, Monte Cristo and the Chateau d'If in full light, seemed to float toward us—so steady, so imperceptible was the progress of our boat. 'Keep her in the furrow of the moon,' the *patron* directed me, in a quiet murmur, sitting down ponderously in the stern-sheets and reaching for his pipe.

The pilot station in weather like this was only a mile or two to the westward of the islets; and presently, as we approached the spot, the boat we were going to relieve swam into our view suddenly, on her way home, cutting black and sinister into the wake of the moon under a sable wing, while to them our sail must have been a vision of white and dazzling radiance. Without altering the course a hair's breadth we slipped by each other within an oar's length. A drawling, sardonic hail came out of her. Instantly, as if by magic, our dozing pilots got on their feet in a body. An incredible babel of bantering shouts burst out, a jocular, passionate, voluble chatter, which lasted till the boats were stern to stern, theirs all bright now, and, with a shining sail to our eyes, we turned all black to their vision, and drew away from them under a sable wing. That extraordinary uproar died away almost as suddenly as it had begun; first one had enough of it and sat down, then another, then three or four together; and when all had left off with mutters and growling half-laughs the sound of hearty chuckling became audible, persistent, unnoticed. The cowled grandfather was very much entertained somewhere within his hood.

He had not joined in the shouting of jokes, neither had he moved the least bit. He had remained quietly in his place against the foot of the mast. I had been given to understand long before that he had the rating of a second-class able seaman (*matelot léger*) in the fleet which sailed from Toulon for the conquest of Algeria in the year of grace 1830. And, indeed, I had seen and examined one of the buttons of his old brown, patched coat, the only brass button of the miscellaneous lot, flat and thin, with the words *Equipages de ligne* engraved on it. That sort of button, I believe, went out with the last of the French Bourbons. 'I preserved it from the time of my navy service,' he explained, nodding rapidly his frail, vulture-like head. It was not very likely that he had picked up that relic in the street. He looked certainly old enough to have fought at Trafalgar—or, at any rate, to have played his little part there as a powder-monkey. Shortly after we had been introduced he had informed me in a Franco-Provençal jargon, mumbling tremulously with his toothless jaws, that when he was a 'shaver no higher than that' he had seen the Emperor Napoleon returning from Elba. It was at night, he narrated vaguely, without animation, at a spot between Fréjus and Antibes, in the open country. A big fire had been lit at the side of the cross-roads. The population from several villages had collected there, old and young—down to the very children in arms, because the women had refused to stay at home. Tall soldiers wearing high, hairy caps stood in a circle, facing the people silently, and their stern eyes and big mustaches were enough to make everybody keep at a distance. He, 'being an impudent little shaver,' wriggled out of the crowd, creeping on his hands and knees as near as he dared to the grenadiers' legs, and peeping through discovered, standing perfectly still in the light of the fire, 'a little fat fellow in a three-cornered hat, buttoned up in a long straight coat, with a big, pale face inclined on one shoulder, looking something like a priest. His hands were clasped behind his back. . . . It appears that this was the Emperor,' the ancient commented, with a faint sigh. He was staring from the ground with all his might, when 'my poor father,' who had been searching for his boy frantically everywhere, pounced upon him and hauled him away by the ear.

The tale seems an authentic recollection. He related it to me many times, using the very same words. The grandfather honored me by a special and somewhat embarrassing predilection. Extremes touch. He was the oldest member by a long way in that company, and I was, if I may say so, its temporarily adopted baby. He had been a pilot longer than any man in the boat could remember; thirty—forty years. He did not seem certain himself, but it could be found out, he suggested, in the archives of the Pilot-office. He had been pensioned off years before, but he went out from force of habit; and, as my friend the *patron* of the company once confided to me in a whisper, 'the old chap did no harm. He was not in the way.' They treated him with rough deference. One and another would address some insignificant remark to him now and again, but nobody really took any notice of what he had to say. He had survived his strength, his usefulness, his very wisdom. He wore long, green, worsted stockings pulled up above the knee over his trousers, a sort of woolen nightcap on his hairless cranium, and wooden clogs on his feet. Without his hooded cloak he looked like a peasant. Half a dozen hands would be extended to help him on board, but afterward he was left pretty much to his own thoughts. Of course he never did any work, except, perhaps, to cast off some rope when hailed '*Hé, l'Ancien!* let go the halyards there, at your hand'—or some such request of an easy kind.

No one took notice in any way of the chuckling within the shadow of the hood. He kept it up for a long time with intense enjoyment. Obviously he had preserved intact the innocence of mind which is easily amused. But when his hilarity had exhausted itself, he made a professional remark in a self-assertive but quavering voice:

'Can't expect much work on a night like this.'

No one took it up. It was a mere truism. Nothing under canvas could be expected to make a port on such an idle night of dreamy splendor and spiritual stillness. We would have to glide idly to and fro, keeping our station within the appointed bearings, and, unless a fresh breeze sprang up with the dawn, we would land before sunrise on a small islet that, within two miles of us, shone like a lump of frozen moonlight, to 'break a crust and take a pull at the wine bottle.' I was familiar with the procedure. The stout boat emptied of her crowd would nestle her buoyant, capable side against the very rock—such is the perfectly smooth amenity of the classic sea when in a gentle mood. The crust broken and the mouthful of wine swallowed—it was literally no more then that with this abstemious race—the pilots would pass the time stamping their feet on the slabs of sea-salted stone and blowing into their nipped fingers. One or two misanthropists would sit apart, perched on boulders like manlike sea-fowl of solitary habits; the sociably disposed would gossip scandalously in little gesticulating knots; and there would be perpetually one or another of my hosts taking aim at the empty horizon with the long, brass tube of the telescope, a heavy, murderous-looking piece of collective property, everlastingly changing hands with brandishing and leveling movements. Then about noon (it was a short turn of duty—the long turn lasted twenty-four hours) another boatful of pilots would relieve us—and we should steer for the old Phœnician port, dominated, watched over from the ridge of a dust-gray, arid hill by the red-and-white striped pile of the Notre Dame de la Garde.

All this came to pass as I had foreseen in the fullness of my very recent experience. But also something not foreseen by me did happen, something which causes me to remember my last outing with the pilots. It was on this occasion that my hand touched, for the first time, the side of an English ship.

No fresh breeze had come with the dawn, only the steady little draught got a more keen edge on it as the eastern sky became bright and glassy with a clean, colorless light. It was while we were all ashore on the islet that a steamer was picked up by the telescope, a black speck like an insect posed on the hard edge of the offing. She emerged rapidly to her water-line and came on steadily, a slim hull with a long streak of smoke slanting away from the rising sun. We embarked in a hurry, and headed the boat out for our prey, but we hardly moved three miles an hour.

She was a big, high-class cargo-steamer of a type that is to be met on the sea no more—black hull, with low, white superstructures, powerfully rigged with three masts and a lot of yards on the fore; two hands at her enormous wheel—steam steering-gear was not a matter of course in these days—and with them on the bridge three others, bulky in thick blue jackets, ruddy-faced, muffled up, with peak caps—I suppose all her officers. There are ships I have met more than once and known well by sight whose names I have forgotten; but the name of that ship once seen so many years ago in the clear flush of a cold, pale sunrise I have not forgotten. How could I—the first English ship on whose side I ever laid my hand! The name —I read it letter by letter on the bow—was *James Westoll*. Not very romantic, you will say. The name of a very considerable, well-known, and universally respected ship-owner, I believe. James Westoll! What better name could an honorable hard-working ship have? To me the very grouping of the letters is alive with the romantic feeling of her reality as I saw her floating motionless and borrowing an ideal grace from the austere purity of the light.

We were then very near her and, on a sudden impulse, I volunteered to pull bow in the dinghy which shoved off at once to put the pilot on board while our boat, fanned by the faint air which had attended us all through the night, went on gliding gently past the black, glistening length of the ship. A few strokes brought us alongside, and it was then that, for the very first time in my life, I heard myself addressed in English—the speech of my secret choice, of my future, of long friendships, of the deepest affections, of hours of toil and hours of ease, and of solitary hours, too, of books read, of thoughts pursued, of remembered emotions—of my very dreams! And if (after being thus fashioned by it in that part of me which cannot decay) I dare not claim it aloud as my own, then, at any rate, the speech of my children. Thus small events grow memorable by the passage of time. As to the quality of the address itself I cannot say it was very striking. Too short for eloquence and devoid of all charm of tone, it consisted precisely of the three words 'Look out there!' growled out huskily above my head.

It proceeded from a big fat fellow (he had an obtrusive, hairy double chin) in a blue woolen shirt and roomy breeches pulled up very high, even to the level of his breast-bone, by a pair of braces quite exposed to public view. As where he stood there was no bulwark, but only a rail and stanchions, I was able to take in at a glance the whole of his voluminous person from his feet to the high crown of his soft black hat, which sat like an absurd flanged cone on his big head. The grotesque and massive aspect of that deckhand (I suppose he was that—very likely the lamp-trimmer) surprised me very much. My course of reading, of dreaming, and longing for the sea had not prepared me for a sea brother of that sort. I never met again a figure in the least like his except in the illustrations to Mr. W. W. Jacobs's most entertaining tales of barges and coasters; but the inspired talent of Mr. Jacobs for poking endless fun at poor, innocent sailors in a prose which, however extravagant in its felicitous invention, is always artistically adjusted to observed truth, was not yet. Perhaps Mr. Jacobs himself was not yet. I fancy that, at most, if he had made his nurse laugh it was about all he had achieved at that early date.

Therefore, I repeat, other disabilities apart, I could not have been prepared for the sight of that husky old porpoise. The object of his concise address was to call my attention to a rope which he incontinently flung down for me to catch. I caught it, though it was not really necessary, the ship having no way on her by that time. Then everything went on very swiftly. The dinghy came with a slight bump against the steamer's side; the pilot, grabbing the rope ladder had scrambled half-way up before I knew that our task of boarding was done; the harsh, muffled clanging of the engine-room telegraph struck my ear through the iron plate; my companion in the dinghy was urging me to 'shove off—push hard;' and when I bore against the smooth flank of the first English ship I ever touched in my life, I felt it already throbbing under my open palm.

Her head swung a little to the west, pointing toward the miniature lighthouse of the Jolliette breakwater, far away there, hardly distinguishable against the land. The dinghy danced a squashy, splashy jig in the wash of the wake; and, turning in my seat, I followed the *James Westoll* with my eyes. Before she had gone in a quarter of a mile she hoisted her flag, as the harbor regulations prescribe for arriving and departing ships. I saw it suddenly flicker and stream out on the flagstaff. The Red Ensign! In the pellucid, colorless atmosphere of that southern land, the livid islets, the sea of pale, glassy blue under the pale, glassy sky of that cold sunrise, it was, as far as the eye could reach, the only spot of ardent color—flame-like, intense, and presently as minute as the tiny red spark the concentrated reflection of a great fire kindles in the clear heart of a globe of crystal. The Red Ensign—the symbolic, protecting, warm bit of bunting flung wide upon the seas, and destined for so many years to be the only roof over my head.

(1912)

H. G. WELLS
(1866–)

From SOCIAL FORCES IN ENGLAND AND AMERICA

THE CONTEMPORARY NOVEL

It is no new discovery that the novel, like the drama, is a powerful instrument of moral suggestion. This has been understood in England ever since there has been such a thing as a novel in England. This has been recognized equally by novelists, novel-readers, and the people who would n't read novels under any condition whatever. Richardson wrote deliberately for edification, and *Tom Jones* is a powerful and effective appeal for a charitable, and even indulgent, attitude towards loose-living men. But excepting Fielding and one or two other of those partial exceptions that always occur in the case of critical generalizations, there is a definable difference between the novel of the past and what I may call the modern novel. It is a difference that is reflected upon the novel from a difference in the general way of thinking. It lies in the fact that formerly there was a feeling of certitude about moral values and standards of conduct that is altogether absent to-day. It was n't so much that men were agreed upon these things—about these things there have always been enormous divergences of opinion—as that men were emphatic, cock-sure, and unteachable about whatever they did happen to believe to a degree that no longer obtains. This is the Balfourian age, and even religion seeks to establish itself on doubt. There were, perhaps, just as many differences in the past as there are now, but the outlines were harder—they were, indeed, so hard as to be almost, to our sense, savage. You might be a Roman Catholic, and in that case you did not want to hear about Protestants, Turks, Infidels, except in tones of horror and hatred. You knew exactly what was good and what was evil. Your priest informed you upon these points, and all you needed in any novel you read was a confirmation, implicit or explicit, of these vivid, rather than charming, prejudices. If you were a Protestant you were equally clear and unshakable. Your sect, whichever sect you belonged to, knew the whole of truth and included all the nice people. It had nothing to learn in the world, and it wanted to learn nothing outside its sectarian convictions. The unbelievers, you know, were just as bad, and said their creeds with an equal fury—merely interpolating *nots*. People of every sort—Catholic, Protestant, Infidel, or what not—were equally clear that good was good and bad was bad, that the world was made up of good characters whom you had to love, help and admire, and of bad characters to whom one might, in the interests of goodness, even lie, and whom one had to foil, defeat and triumph over shamelessly at every opportunity. That was the quality of the times. The novel reflected this quality of assurance, and its utmost charity was to unmask an apparent villain and show that he or she was really profoundly and correctly good, or to unmask an apparent saint and show the hypocrite. There was no such penetrating and pervading element of doubt and curiosity—and charity, about the rightfulness and beauty of conduct, such as one meets on every hand to-day.

The novel-reader of the past, therefore, like the novel-reader of the more provincial parts of England to-day, judged a novel by the convictions that had been built up in him by his training and his priest or his pastor. If it agreed with these convictions he approved; if it did not agree he disapproved—often with great energy. The novel, where it was not unconditionally banned altogether as a thing disturbing and unnecessary, was regarded as a thing subordinated to the teaching of the priest or pastor, or whatever director and dogma was followed. Its modest moral confirmations began when authority had completed its direction. The novel was good—if it seemed to harmonize with the graver exercises conducted by Mr. Chadband—and it was bad and outcast if Mr. Chadband said so. And it is over the bodies of discredited and disgruntled Chadbands that the novel escapes from its servitude and inferiority.

Now the conflict of authority against criticism is one of the eternal conflicts of humanity. It is the conflict of organization against initiative, of discipline against freedom. It was the conflict of the priest against the prophet in ancient Judæa, of the Pharisee against the Nazarene, of the Realist against the Nominalist, of the Church against the Franciscan and the Lollard, of the Respectable Person against the Artist, of the hedgeclippers of mankind against the shooting buds. And to-day, while we live in a period of tightening and extending social organizations, we live also in a period of adventurous and insurgent thought, in an intellectual spring unprecedented in the world's history. There is an enormous criticism going on of the faiths upon which men's lives and associations are based, and of every standard and rule of conduct. And it is inevitable that the novel, just in the measure of its sincerity and ability, should reflect and coöperate in the atmosphere and uncertainties and changing variety of this seething and creative time.

And I do not mean merely that the novel is unavoidably charged with the representation of this wide and wonderful conflict. It is a necessary part of the conflict. The essential characteristic of this great intellectual revolution amidst which we are living to-day, that revolution of which the revival and restatement of nominalism under the name of pragmatism is the philosophical aspect, consists in the reassertion of the importance of the individual instance as against the generalization. All our social, political, moral problems are being approached in a new spirit, in an inquiring and experimental spirit, which has small respect for abstract principles and deductive rules. We perceive more and more clearly, for example, that the study of social organization is an empty and unprofitable study until we approach it as a study of the association and inter-reaction of individualized human beings inspired by diversified motives, ruled by traditions, and swayed by the suggestions of a complex intellectual atmosphere. And all our conceptions of the relationships between man and man, and of justice and rightfulness and social desirableness, remain something misfitting and inappropriate, something uncomfortable and potentially injurious, as if we were trying to wear sharp-edged clothes made for a giant out of tin, until we bring them to the test and measure of realized individualities.

And this is where the value and opportunity of the modern novel comes in. So far as I can see, it is the only medium through which we can discuss the great majority of the problems which are being raised in such bristling multitude by our contemporary social development. Nearly every one of those problems has at its core a psychological problem, and not merely a psychological problem, but one in which the idea of individuality is an essential factor. Dealing with most of these questions by a rule or generalization is like putting a cordon round a jungle full of the most diversified sort of game. The hunting only begins when you leave the cordon behind you and push into the thickets.

Take, for example, the immense cluster of difficulties that arises out of the increasing complexity of our state. On every hand we are creating officials, and compared with only a few years ago the private in a dozen fresh directions comes into contact with officialdom. But we still do practically nothing to work out the interesting changes that occur in this sort of man and that, when you withdraw him as it were from the common crowd of humanity, put his mind if not his body into uniform and endow him with powers and functions and rules. It is manifestly a study of the profoundest public and personal importance. The process of social and political organization that has been going on for the last quarter of a century is pretty clearly going on now if anything with increasing vigor—and for the most part the entire dependence of the consequences of the whole problem upon the reaction between the office on the one hand and the weak, uncertain, various human beings who take office on the other does n't seem even to be suspected by the energetic, virtuous and more or less amiable people whose activities in politics and upon the back stairs of politics bring about these developments. They assume that the sort of official they need, a combination of godlike virtue and intelligence with unfailing mechanical obedience, can be made out of just any young nephew. And I know of no means of persuading people that this is a rather unjustifiable assumption, and of creating an intelligent controlling criticism of officials and of assisting conscientious officials to an effective self-examination, and generally of keeping the atmosphere of official life sweet and healthy, except the novel. Yet so far the novel has scarcely begun its attack upon this particular field of human life, and all the attractive varied play of motive it contains.

Of course we have one supreme and devastating study of the illiterate minor official in Bumble. That one figure lit up and still lights the whole problem of Poor Law administration for the English reading community. It was a translation of well-meant regulations and pseudoscientific conceptions of social order into blundering, arrogant, ill-bred flesh and blood. It was worth a hundred Royal Commissions. You may make your regulations as you please, said Dickens in effect; this is one sample of the stuff that will carry them out. But Bumble stands almost alone. Instead of realizing that he is only one aspect of officialdom, we are all too apt to make him the type of all officials, and not an urban district council can get into a dispute about its electric light without being denounced as a Bumbledom by some whirling enemy or other. The burden upon Bumble's shoulders is too heavy to be borne, and we want the contemporary novel to give us a score of other figures to put beside him, other aspects and reflections upon this great problem of officialism made flesh. Bumble is a magnificent figure of the follies and cruelties of ignorance in office—I would have every candidate for the post of workhouse master pass a severe examination upon Oliver Twist—but it is not only caricature and satire I demand. We must have not only the fullest treatment of the temptations, vanities, abuses, and absurdities of office, but all its dreams, its sense of constructive order, its consolations, its sense of service, and its nobler satisfactions. You may say that is demanding more insight and power in our novels and novelists than we can possibly hope to find in them. So much the worse for us. I stick to my thesis that the complicated social organization of to-day cannot get along without the amount of mutual understanding and mutual explanation such a range of characteristics in our novels implies. The success of civilization amounts ultimately to a success of sympathy and understanding. If people cannot be brought to an interest in one another greater than they feel to-day, to curiosities and criticisms far keener, and coöperations far subtler, than we have now; if class cannot be brought to measure itself against, and interchange experience and sympathy with class, and temperament with temperament, then we shall never struggle very far beyond the confused discomforts and uneasiness of to-day, and the changes and complications of human life will remain as they are now, very like the crumplings and separations and complications of an immense avalanche that is sliding down a hill. And in this tremendous work of human reconciliation and elucidation, it seems to me it is the novel that must attempt most and achieve most.

You may feel disposed to say to all this: We grant the major premises, but why look to the work of prose fiction as the main instrument in this necessary process of, so to speak, sympathizing humanity together? Cannot this be done far more effectively through biography and autobiography, for example? Isn't there the lyrics; and, above all, isn't there the play? Well, so far as the stage goes, I think it is a very charming and exciting form of human activity, a display of actions and surprises of the most moving and impressive sort; but beyond the opportunity it affords for saying startling and thought-provoking things—opportunities like Mr. Shaw, for example, has worked to the utmost limit—I do not see that the drama does much to enlarge our sympathies and add to our stock of motive ideas. And regarded as a medium for startling and thought-producing things, the stage seems to me an extremely clumsy and costly affair. One might just as well go about with a pencil writing up the thought-provoking phrase, whatever it is, on walls. The drama excites our sympathies intensely, but it seems to me it is far too objective a medium to widen them appreciably, and it is that widening, that increase in the range of understanding, at which I think civilization is aiming. The case for biography, and more particularly autobiography, as against the novel, is, I admit, at the first blush stronger. You may say: Why give us these creatures of a novelist's imagination, these phantom and fantastic thinkings and doings, when we may have the histories of real lives, really lived—the intimate record of actual men and women? To which one answers: 'Ah, if one could!' But it is just because biography does deal with actual lives, actual facts, because it radiates out to touch continuing interests and sensitive survivors, that it is so unsatisfactory, so untruthful. Its inseparable falsehood is the worst of all kinds of falsehood—the falsehood of omission. Think what an abounding, astonishing, perplexing person Gladstone must have been in life, and consider Lord Morley's *Life of Gladstone*, cold, dignified—not a life at all, indeed, so much as embalmed remains; the fire gone, the passions gone, the bowels carefully removed. All biography has something of that post-mortem coldness and respect, and as for autobiography—a man may show his soul in a thousand half-unconscious ways, but to turn upon oneself and explain oneself is given to no one. It is the natural liars and braggarts, your Cellinis and Casanovas, men with a habit of regarding themselves with a kind of objective admiration, who do best in autobiography. And, on the other hand, the novel has neither the intense self-consciousness of autobiography nor the paralyzing responsibilities of the biographer. It is by comparison irresponsible and free. Because its characters are figments and phantoms, they can be made entirely transparent. Because they are fictions, and you know they are fictions, so that they cannot hold you for an instant as soon as they cease to be true, they have a power of veracity beyond that of actual records. Every novel carries its own justification and its own condemnation in its success or failure to convince you that *the thing was so*. Now history, biography, blue-book, and so forth, can hardly ever get beyond the statement that the superficial fact was so.

You see now the scope of the claim I am making for the novel; it is to be the social mediator, the vehicle of understanding, the instrument of self-examination, the parade of morals and the exchange of manners, the factory of customs, the criticism of laws and institutions and of social dogmas and ideas. It is to be the home confessional, the initiator of knowledge, the seed of fruitful self-questioning. Let me be very clear here. I do not mean for a moment that the novelist is to set up as a teacher, as a sort of priest with a pen, who will make men and women believe and do this and that. The novel is not a new sort of pulpit; humanity is passing out of the phase when men *sit under* preachers and dogmatic influences. But the novelist is going to be the most potent of artists, because he is going to present conduct, devise beautiful conduct, discuss conduct, analyze conduct, suggest conduct, illuminate it through and through. He will not teach, but discuss, point out, plead, and display. And this being my view you will be prepared for the demand I am now about to make for an absolutely free hand for the novelist in his choice of topic and incident and in his method of treatment; or, rather, if I may presume to speak for other novelists, I would say it is not so much a demand we make as an intention we proclaim. We are going to write, subject only to our limitations, about the whole of human life. We are going to deal with political questions and religious questions and social questions. We cannot present people unless we have this free hand, this unrestricted field. What is the good of telling stories about people's lives if one may not deal freely with the religious beliefs and organizations that have controlled or failed to control them? What is the good of pretending to write about love, and the loyalties and treacheries and quarrels of men and women, if one must not glance at those varieties of physical temperament and organic quality, those deeply passionate needs and distresses from which half the storms of human life are brewed? We mean to deal with all these things and it will need very much more than the disapproval of provincial librarians, the hostility of a few influential people in London, the scurrility of one paper, and the deep and obstinate silences of another, to stop the incoming tide of aggressive novel-writing. We are going to write about it all. We are going to write about business and finance and politics and precedence and pretentiousness and decorum and indecorum, until a thousand pretences and ten thousand impostures shrivel in the cold, clear air of our elucidations. We are going to write of wasted opportunities and latent beauties until a thousand new ways of living open to men and women. We are going to appeal to the young and the hopeful and the curious, against the established, the dignified, and defensive. Before we have done, we will have all life within the scope of the novel.

(1914)

JOHN GALSWORTHY
(1867–1933)

From A COMMENTARY

THE LOST DOG

It was the first October frost. Outside a half-built house, before a board on which was written, 'Jolly Bros., Builders,' I saw a man, whose eyes seemed saying: 'In the winter building will stop; if I am homeless and workless now, what shall I be in two months' time?' Turning to me he said: 'Can you give me a job, Sir? I don't mind what I do.'

His face was in mourning for a shave, his clothes were very ragged, and he was so thin that there seemed hardly any man behind those ragged clothes. He smelt, not indeed of whisky, but as though bereaved of it; and his blue and watery eyes were like those of a lost dog.

We looked at each other, and this conversation passed between our eyes:

'What are you? Where did you work last? How did you get into this condition? Are you married? How many children? Why don't you apply to the proper authorities? I have money, and you have none; it is my right to ask these questions.'

'I am a lost dog.'

'But I have no work for you; if you are really hungry I can give you sixpence; I can also refer you to a Society who will examine your affairs, but if they find you a man for whom life has been too much, they will tell me so, and warn me not to help you. Is that what you want?'

'I am a lost dog.'

'I dare say; but what can I do? I can't make work! I know nothing about you, I dare n't recommend you to my friends. No man gets into the condition you are in without the aid of his own folly. You say you fell ill; yes, but you all say that. Why could n't you look ahead and save some money? You see now that you ought to have? And yet you come to me! I have a great many calls—societies, old people, and the sick; the rates are very high—you know that— partly on your account!'

'I am a lost dog.'

'Ah! but I am told daily by the just, the orderly, the practical, who have never been lost or hungry, that I must not give to casuals. You know yourself it would be pure sentiment; you know yourself it would be mere luxury. I wonder you can ask me!'

'I am a lost dog.'

'You have said that before. It's not as if I did n't know you! I have seen and talked with you—with dozens of you. I have found you asleep on the Thames Embankment. I have given you sixpence when you were shambling empty away after running a mile behind a cab. One night, don't you remember, in the Cromwell Road—well, not you, but your twin brother —we talked together in the rain, and the wind blew your story against the shuttered windows of the tall, closed houses. Once you were with me quite six weeks, cutting up a dead tree in my garden. Day after day you sat there, working very slowly to keep the tree from coming to an end, and showing me in gratitude each morning your waistbelt filling out. With the saw in your hand and your weak smile you would look at me, and your eyes would say: "You don't know what a rest it is for me to come here and cut up wood all day." At all events, you *must* remember how you kept yourself from whisky until I went away, and how you excused yourself when I returned and found you speaking thickly in the morning: "I can't *help* rememberin' things!" It was not you, you say? No; it was your double.'

'I am a lost dog.'

'Yes, yes, yes! You are one of those men that our customs breed. You had no business to be born—or at any rate you should have seen to it that you were born in the upper classes. What right had you to imagine you could ever tackle the working-man's existence—up to the mark all day and every day? You, a man with a soft spot? You knew, or your parents ought to have known, that you could n't stand more than a certain pressure from life. You are diseased, if not physically, then in your disposition. Am I to excuse you because of that? Most probably I should be the same if life pressed hard enough. Am I to excuse myself because of that? Never—until it happens! Being what you are you chose deliberately—or was it chosen for you?—to run the risks of being born; and now you complain of the consequences, and come to me for help? To me—who may myself at some time be in need, if not of physical, of moral bread? Is it right, or reasonable?'

'I am a lost dog.'

'You are getting on my nerves! Your chin is weak—I can see that through your beard; your eyes are wistful, not like the professional beggar's pebbly eyes; you have a shuffling walk, due perhaps a little to the nature of your boots; yes, there are all the marks of amiability about you. Can you look me in the face and say it would be the slightest use to put you on your legs and thrust you again, equipped, into the ranks of battle? Can you, now? Ah! if you could only get some clothes on you, and some work to do! But don't you know that, three weeks hence, that work would be lost, those clothes in pawn, and you be on the drink? Why should I waste my charity on *you*—"the deserving" are so many! There's "something against you" too? Oh! nothing much—you 're not the sort that makes a criminal; if you were you would not be in such a state. You would be glad enough to do your fellows a good turn yourself; and you are not ungrateful, you would attach yourself to any one who showed you kindness. But you are hopeless, hopeless, hopeless —aren 't you now?'

'I am a lost dog.'

'You know our methods with lost dogs? Have you never heard of the lethal chamber? A real tramp, living from hand to mouth in sun and rain and dirt and rags, enjoys his life. But *you* don't enjoy the state you're in. You're afraid of the days when you 've nothing to eat, afraid of the nights when you 've nowhere to sleep, afraid of crime, afraid even of this begging; twice since we 've been standing here I 've seen you looking round. If you knew you 'd be afraid like this, what made you first desert the narrow path? Something came over you? How could you let it come like that? It still comes over you? You were tired, you wanted something new—something a little new. We all want that something, friend, and get it if we can; but we can't recognize that *your* sort of human creature is entitled, for you see what 's come of it?'

'I am a lost dog.'

'You say that as if you thought there were one law for the rich and another for the poor. You are making a mistake. If I am had up for begging as well as you, we shall both of us go to prison. The fact that I have no need to steal or beg, can pay for getting drunk and taking holidays, is hardly to the point—you must see that! Do not be led away by sentimental talk; if we appear before a judge, we both must suffer punishment. I am not so likely to appear as you perhaps, but that 's an accident. No, please don't say that dreadful thing again! I wish to help you. There is Canada, but they don't want you. I would send you anywhere to stop your eyes from haunting me, but they don't want you. Where do they want you? Tell me, and you shall go.'

'I am a lost dog.'

'You remind me of that white shadow with little liver spots that my spaniel dog and I picked up one night when we were going home.

'"Master," he said, "there 's such an amusing cur out there in the middle of the road."

'"Behave yourself! Don't pick up with anything you come across like this!"

'"Master, I know it is a thin and dirty cur, but the creature follows me."

'"Keep to heel! The poor dog will get lost if you entice him far from home."

'"Oh, master! that 's just what 's so amusing. He hasn't any."

'And like a little ghost the white dog crept along behind. We took him home—and how he ate, and how he drank! But my spaniel said to me:

'"Master, what is the use of bringing in a dog like this? Can't you see what he is like? He has eaten all my meat, drunk my bowl dry, and now he is sleeping in my bed."

'I said to him: "My dear, you ought to like to give this up to this poor dog."

'And he said to me: "Master, I *don't!* He is no good, this dog; I am cleaner and fatter than he. And don't you know there's a place the other side of the water for all this class of dog? When are we going to take him there?"

'And I said to him: "My dear, don't ask me; *I don't know.*" . . .

'And you are like that dog, standing there with those eyes of yours and that weak chin and those weak knees, before this half-built house with the winter coming on. And I am like my spaniel, who knows there is a proper place for all your kind of creature. Man! what shall I do with you?'

'I am a lost dog.'

(1908)

ARNOLD BENNETT
(1867–1931)

From OUR WOMEN

SALARY EARNING GIRLS

(Copyright, 1920, by George H. Doran Co., Publishers)

YOUNG girls have always been held to be very mysterious. To-day they are held to be more mysterious than ever. Such at any rate is the view taken by people of middle-age, both men and women, and their attitude to the 'typical' young girl has in it a certain amount of reproach. But whether young men regard their feminine contemporaries as specially mysterious I doubt. And the young are the best judges of the young. (Though old, I assert it.)

Before going further, let me interject that when I say 'young girl' I mean what the French mean when they say 'jeune fille,' that is, an unmarried adult virgin who is not old enough to be called a spinster. I will not attempt to determine at what age an unmarried virgin begins to incur the terrible imputation of spinsterhood; it varies, being dependent on a lot of things, such as color of hair, litheness of frame, complexion, ankles, chin (the under part), style of talk and of glance. I have known spinsters of twenty-five, and young girls of at least forty. Henceforward in this chapter I intend to discuss that very large middle class of girls whose members wholly or partly earn their own living. Unfortunately this class does not yet by a long way comprise all girls; nevertheless, its demeanor towards life influences and explains the demeanor towards life of the 'leisured class' of girls above it, and therefore in some degree it is representative of that class also.

The root of modern feminism is, of course, the desire for money—money that can be transformed into personal satisfactions. True, the pioneers of feminism did not think primarily of money when they set out on those adventurous careers which too often involved obloquy and even martyrdom. They thought primarily of freedom—freedom to fulfill themselves according to their individual instincts. But freedom includes, and must include, economic freedom; and economic freedom signifies the control of the means of living.

How many pioneers would, for example, have given up the fight against the medical societies for the right to practise as doctors if the medical societies had said to them: 'You may practise as doctors, but you must not charge fees?' None. The right to earn, to be economically free, was the essence of the struggle.

After the pioneers had turned the tide of the battle, and cleared many paths for the multitude, the multitude began to follow from no other motive than an economic motive. The mass of girls saw a chance of obtaining for themselves a share of that strange and delectable commodity, money, and they took it. If they did not take it of their own accord their parents little by little insisted on their taking it, and finally, in the middle-class under review, the general rule was established that girls must earn. A few of them go out into the world against their will. On the other hand, a few would have gone out even if no money had resulted from the process, simply to escape an oppressive atmosphere at home, and to breathe the fresh winds of the world. But the great mass, the all-but totality, go out solely in search of money and the economic freedom which money confers on its possessors.

The consequences were not entirely advantageous. The girls lost the old girlish air of ignorance, of being simpletons in the world. But that was an advantage. They lost the attractiveness of perfect inexperience. That, too, was an advantage, for such attractiveness appealed chiefly to the perverse and the Oriental in the male sex. They lost much futile leisure; that too was an advantage. They lost some of their ideals, and that, though not an unrelieved disadvantage, was a disadvantage. They lost, thousands of them, a measure of health; for, being raw and eager, they were, and still are, often exploited in the conditions of employment, overworked, and sweated. That was an unrelieved disadvantage, and all the more so because it filled them with a sense of resentment against the men who exploited them and against the innocent men who received (and still receive) more pay than they for precisely the same work.

But the gain on the whole was enormous. There was, at first, the novel and dignifying sensation of the performance of a useful function in society. Certainly the mere novelty of the sensation soon departed, and girls of the present and the future do not, and probably will not, recapture it. But the sensation itself remains, though it is chiefly subconscious, and though it may be mingled with the quite different sensation of the oppressiveness of work. People, even enthusiastic girls, as a rule start the week's work with the complaint uttered or unexpressed; 'Monday morning again! What a grind!' They do not rise on Monday morning with hearts full of heavenly gratitude for the privilege of being allowed to perform a useful function in society. Still, the gratitude vaguely persists and it gives birth to pleasurable pride.

Then, there is the advantage of meeting men other than near relatives. Under the old régime, middle-class and also lower-middle-class girls met men in a sort of ceremonial—except sometimes when they met them by ingenious and conspiratorial design. They elaborately prepared themselves for meeting men. Before meeting men they pondered long over the encounter, and after meeting men they pondered long over the encounter. Under the new régime girls who work meet as many men in a day as their predecessors of similar standing met in a month. Indeed, many of their predecessors met men (other than relatives) about as often as they met giraffes.

* * *

Lastly, the salary-earning girl gains knowledge of the world. This knowledge may be superficial, imperfect, one-sided, mischievous in certain respects, but it is far better than ignorance. She does get some sort of a notion of the structure and working of society; she does get some sort of a notion of real values; which notions, even if they be pitifully vague, do enable her on frequent occasions to reject the dangerous poison of sentimentality which would otherwise be poured into her by the older persons whose object in life seems to be to confuse that which ought to be with that which is. To anybody who demands skeptically: 'But after all can the girl teach her grandmother to suck eggs?' I would reply: 'As a rule, she can.'

How does she gain this knowledge of the world? It would be more reasonable to ask how she could avoid gaining it. All day the world is rubbing off information on to her. Even if she sits with a thousand girl-colleagues in some clacking interior of a Chicago mail-order house and does nothing for eight hours but tap out bills on a typewriter, she is learning about the kind of things that people really do want and how much they want them and what wild sums they are ready to pay for them. She cannot travel with regularity through a city on the top of a 'bus, or under a city in a tube, without effectively learning more about the world than she would learn from a hundred books and a hundred parents in a hundred years.

She reads the newspaper. It teaches her. She may read it simply for distraction on the daily journey. It teaches her. It may teach her badly. It teaches her. She may not read a newspaper, but only look at the pictures in a newspaper. The pictures teach her. I would sooner that she read the newspaper than any of the vast majority of novels. If she reads the latest old-fashioned sweet novels she is severely handicapped, for the latest old-fashioned novelists are still catering for the girl's grandmother, and the perusal of one of them may almost undo in half an hour's train journey at night all the solid educational work that contact with the world has accomplished in ten hours.

Then she visits restaurants, either public or private—not places where there is a conspiracy of waiters to convince her that she is a most high queen surrounded by slaves; but hurrying, realistic places where the principles which rule the world stand forth naked, and everybody not merely knows, but openly admits, what is what; and she will not obtain value for her money in such places until she has genuinely obtained a grasp of the aforesaid principles.

And when she reaches home and sits down to the family meal she finds that the conversation is much more instructive, candid, catholic, and interesting than it used to be before she went into the world. The most arrogantly male father, the most head-burying ostrich of a mother, cannot decently pretend that exactly the same girl has come home who went forth. And the conversation improves accordingly.

(1920)

GEORGIAN PROSE

The decay of the novel, already discussed, may be suggested as a contributing cause for the revival of the essay, sometimes, as in the work of Aldous Huxley, combined with fiction in the form of a novel. Like Bernard Shaw and G. K. Chesterton, who had preceded him in the attempt to make the theme of a novel more important than the story, Huxley succeeded best as a satirical essayist unhampered by the demands of fiction. Virginia Woolf made daring experiments with the form and method of the novel—encouraged no doubt by the example of James Joyce in *Ulysses*—and these attracted a great deal of attention at the time of their publication, but it seems likely that her permanent fame will rest rather upon the ready wit and deftness of style she has shown in her essays. As a literary critic she shares honors with T. S. Eliot, whose appreciations of the Metaphysical poets and Dryden made a distinct mark upon literary opinion, and also upon poetic production.

Max Beerbohm, in his writing as in his cartoons, conveyed the whimsical humor—and sometimes the pathos—of his own charming personality. W. H. Hudson gave the attraction of a distinguished style to the remarkable adventures of his youth. The most permanent contribution to the development of a literary form was that made by Lytton Strachey. By training a literary critic, historian, and biographer, he succeeded in investing biography and history with the allurements of fiction. He has had many imitators but none has as yet displayed his unusual combination of talents—the patience and acumen of the historical research student, the power of seizing upon the salient incidents and traits of character which give to history or biography the thrill of fiction, and the gift to embody these historical facts in an imaginative presentation which conveys to the reader an impression of the movement and reality of actual life.

GILBERT K. CHESTERTON
(1873-1936)

From A SHORT HISTORY OF ENGLAND

THE RETURN OF THE BARBARIAN

The only way to write a popular history, as we have already remarked, would be to write it backwards. It would be to take common objects of our own street and tell of how each of them came to be in the street at all. And for my immediate purpose it is really convenient to take two objects we have known all our lives, as features of fashion or respectability. One which has grown rarer recently, is what we call a top-hat; the other, which is still a customary formality, is a pair of trousers. The history of these humorous objects really does give a clue to what has happened in England for the last hundred years. It is not necessary to be an æsthete in order to regard both objects as the reverse of beautiful, as tested by what may be called the rational side of beauty. The lines of human limbs can be beautiful, and so can the lines of loose drapery, but not cylinders too loose to be the first and too tight to be the second. Nor is a subtle sense of harmony needed to see that while there are hundreds of differently proportioned hats, a hat that actually grows larger towards the top is somewhat top-heavy. But what is largely forgotten is this, that these two fantastic objects, which now strike the eye as unconscious freaks, were originally conscious freaks. Our ancestors, to do them justice, did not think them casual or commonplace; they thought them, if not ridiculous, at least rococo. The top-hat was the topmost point of a riot of Regency dandyism, and bucks wore trousers while business men were still wearing knee-breeches. It will not be fanciful to see a certain oriental touch in trousers, which the later Romans also regarded as effeminately oriental; it was an oriental touch found in many florid things of the time—in Byron's poems or Brighton Pavilion. Now, the interesting point is that for a whole serious century these instantaneous phantasies have remained like fossils. In the carnival of the Regency a few fools got into fancy dress, and we have all remained in fancy dress. At least, we have remained in the dress, though we have lost the fancy.

I say this is typical of the most important thing that happened in the Victorian time. For the most important thing was that nothing happened. The very fuss that was made about minor modifications brings into relief the rigidity with which the main lines of social life were left as they were at the French Revolution. We talk of the French Revolution as something that changed the world; but its most important relation to England is that it did not change England. A student of our history is concerned rather with the effect it did not have than the effect it did. If it be a splendid fate to have survived the Flood, the English oligarchy had that added splendor. But even for the countries in which the Revolution was a convulsion, it was the last convulsion—until that which shakes the world to-day. It gave their character to all commonwealths, which all talked about progress, and were occupied in marking time. Frenchmen, under all superficial reactions, remained republican in spirit, as they had been when they first wore top-hats. Englishmen, under all superficial reforms, remained oligarchical in spirit, as they had been when they first wore trousers. Only one power might be said to be growing, and that in a plodding and prosaic fashion—the power in the North-East whose name was Prussia. And the English were more and more learning that this growth need cause them no alarm, since the North Germans were their cousins in blood and their brothers in spirit.

The first thing to note, then, about the nineteenth century is that Europe remained herself as compared with the Europe of the great war, and that England especially remained herself as compared even with the rest of Europe. Granted this, we may give their proper importance to the cautious internal changes in this country, the small conscious and the large unconscious changes. Most of the conscious ones were much upon the model of an early one, the great Reform Bill of 1832, and can be considered in the light of it. First, from the standpoint of most real reformers, the chief thing about the Reform Bill was that it did not reform. It had a huge tide of popular enthusiasm behind it, which wholly disappeared when the people found themselves in front of it. It enfranchised large masses of the middle classes; it disfranchised very definite bodies of the working classes; and it so struck the balance between the conservative and the dangerous elements in the commonwealth that the governing class was much stronger than before. The date, however, is important, not at all because it was the beginning of democracy, but because it was the beginning of the best way ever discovered of evading and postponing democracy. Here enters the homœopathic treatment of revolution, since so often successful. Well into the next generation Disraeli, the brilliant Jewish adventurer who was the symbol of the English aristocracy being no longer genuine, extended the franchise to the artisans, partly, indeed, as a party move against his great rival, Gladstone, but more as the method by which the old popular pressure was first tired out and then toned down. The politicians said the working-class was now strong enough to be allowed votes. It would be truer to say it was now weak enough to be allowed votes. So in more recent times Payment of Members, which would once have been regarded (and resisted) as an inrush of popular forces, was passed quietly and without resistance, and regarded merely as an extension of parliamentary privileges. The truth is that the old parliamentary oligarchy abandoned their first line of trenches because they had by that time constructed a second line of defense. It consisted in the concentration of colossal political funds in the private and irresponsible power of the politicians, collected by the sale of peerages and more important things, and expended on the gerrymandering of the enormously expensive elections. In the presence of this inner obstacle a vote became about as valuable as a railway ticket when there is a permanent block on the line. The façade and outward form of this new secret government is the merely mechanical application of what is called the Party System. The Party System does not consist, as some suppose, of two parties, but of one. If there were two real parties, there could be no system.

But if this was the evolution of parliamentary reform, as represented by the first Reform Bill, we can see the other side of it in the social reform attacked immediately after the first Reform Bill. It is a truth that should be a tower and a landmark, that one of the first things done by the Reform Parliament was to establish those harsh and dehumanized workhouses which both honest Radicals and honest Tories branded with the black title of the New Bastille. This bitter name lingers in our literature, and can be found by the curious in the works of Carlyle and Hood, but it is doubtless interesting rather as a note of contemporary indignation than as a correct comparison. It is easy to imagine the logicians and the legal orators of the parliamentary school of progress finding many points of differentiation and even of contrast. The Bastille was one central institution; the workhouses have been many, and have everywhere transformed local life with whatever they have to give of social sympathy and inspiration. Men of high rank and great wealth were frequently sent to the Bastille, but no such mistake has ever been made by the more business administration of the workhouse. Over the most capricious operations of the *Lettres de Cachets* there still hovered some hazy traditional idea that a man is put in prison to punish him for something. It was a discovery of a later social science that men who cannot be punished can still be imprisoned. But the deepest and most decisive difference lies in the better fortune of the New Bastille, for no mob has ever dared to storm it, and it never fell.

The new Poor Law was indeed not wholly new in the sense that it was the culmination and clear enunciation of a principle foreshadowed in the earlier Poor Law of Elizabeth, which was one of the many anti-popular effects of the Great Pillage. When the monasteries were swept away and the medieval system of hospitality destroyed, tramps and beggars became a problem, the solution of which has always tended towards slavery, even when the question of slavery has been cleared of the irrelevant question of cruelty. It is obvious that a desperate man might find Mr. Bumble and the Board of Guardians less cruel than cold weather and the bare ground—even if he were allowed to sleep on the ground, which (by a veritable nightmare of nonsense and injustice) he is not. He is actually punished for sleeping under a bush on the specific and stated ground that he cannot afford a bed. It is obvious, however, that he may find his best physical good by going into the workhouse, as he often found it in pagan times by selling himself into slavery. The point is that the solution remains servile, even when Mr. Bumble and the Board of Guardians ceased to be in common sense cruel. The pagan might have the luck to sell himself to a kind master. The principle of the new Poor Law, which has so far proved permanent in our society, is that the man lost all his civic rights and lost them solely through poverty. There is a touch of irony, though hardly of mere hypocrisy, in the fact that the Parliament which effected this reform had just been abolishing black slavery by buying out the slave-owners in the British colonies. The slave-owners were bought out at a price big enough to be called blackmail, but it would be misunderstanding the national mentality to deny the sincerity of the sentiment. Wilberforce represented in this the real wave of Wesleyan religion which had made a humane reaction against Calvinism, and was in no mean sense philanthropic. But there is something romantic in the English mind which can always see what is remote. It is the strongest example of what men lose by being long-sighted. It is fair to say that they gain many things also, the poems that are like adventures and the adventures that are like poems. It is a national savor, and therefore in itself neither good nor evil, and it depends on the application whether we find a scriptural text for it in the wish to take the wings of the morning and abide in the uttermost parts of the sea, or merely in the saying that the eyes of a fool are in the ends of the earth.

Anyhow, the unconscious nineteenth-century movement, so slow that it seems stationary, was altogether in this direction, of which workhouse philanthropy is the type. Nevertheless, it had one national institution to combat and overcome; one institution all the more intensely national because it was not official, and in a sense not even political. The modern Trade Union was the inspiration and creation of the English; it is still largely known throughout Europe by its English name. It was the English expression of the European effort to resist the tendency of Capitalism to reach its natural culmination in slavery. In this it has an almost weird psychological interest, for it is a return to the past by men ignorant of the past, like the subconscious action of some man who has lost his memory. We say that history repeats itself, and it is even more interesting when it unconsciously repeats itself. No man on earth is kept so ignorant of the Middle Ages as the British workman, except perhaps the British business man who employs him, yet all who know even a little of the Middle Ages can see that the modern Trade Union is a groping for the ancient Guild. It is true that those who look to the Trade Union, and even those clear-sighted enough to call it the Guild, are often without the faintest tinge of medieval mysticism, or even of medieval morality. But this fact is itself the most striking and even staggering tribute to medieval morality. It has all the clinching logic of coincidence. If large numbers of the most hardheaded atheists had evolved, out of their own inner consciousness, the notion that a number of bachelors or spinsters ought to live together in celibate groups for the good of the poor, or the observation of certain hours and offices, it would be a very strong point in favor of the monasteries. It would be all the stronger if the atheists had never heard of monasteries; it would be strongest of all if they hated the very name of monasteries. And it is all the stronger because the man who puts his trust in Trades Unions does not call himself a Catholic or even a Christian, if he does call himself a Guild Socialist.

The Trade Union movement passed through many perils, including a ludicrous attempt of certain lawyers to condemn as a criminal conspiracy that Trade Union solidarity of which their own profession is the strongest and most startling example in the world. The struggle culminated in gigantic strikes which split the country in every direction in the earlier part of the twentieth century. But another process, with much more power at its back, was also in operation. The principle represented by the new Poor Law proceeded on its course, and in one important respect altered its course, though it can hardly be said to have altered its object. It can most correctly be stated by saying that the employers themselves, who already organized business, began to organize social reform. It was more picturesquely expressed by a cynical aristocrat in Parliament who said, 'We are all Socialists now.' The Socialists, a body of completely sincere men led by several conspicuously brilliant men, had long hammered into their heads the hopeless sterility of mere non-interference in exchange. The Socialists proposed that the State should not merely interfere in business but should take over the business, and pay all men as equal wage-earners, or at any rate as wage-earners. The employers were not willing to surrender their own position to the State, and this project has largely faded from politics; but the wiser of them were willing to pay better wages, and they were specially willing to bestow various other benefits so long as they were bestowed after the manner of wages. Thus we had a series of social reforms which, for good or evil, all tended in the same direction; the permission to employees to claim certain advantages *as* employees, and as something permanently different from employers. Of these the obvious examples were Employers' Liability, Old Age Pensions, and, as marking another and more decisive stride in the process, the Insurance Act.

The latter in particular, and the whole plan of the social reform in general, were modeled upon Germany. Indeed the whole English life of this period was overshadowed by Germany. We had now reached, for good or evil, the final fulfilment of that gathering influence which began to grow on us in the seventeenth century, which was solidified by the military alliances of the eighteenth century, and which in the nineteenth century had been turned into a philosophy—not to say a mythology. German metaphysics had thinned our theology, so that many a man's most solemn conviction about Good Friday was that Friday was named after Freya. German history had simply annexed English history, so that it was almost counted the duty of any patriotic Englishman to be proud of being a German. The genius of Carlyle, the culture preached by Matthew Arnold, would not, persuasive as they were, have alone produced this effect but for an external phenomenon of great force. Our internal policy was transformed by our foreign policy; and foreign policy was dominated by the more and more drastic steps which the Prussian, now clearly the prince of all the German tribes, was taking to extend the German influence in the world. Denmark was robbed of two provinces; France was robbed of two provinces; and though the fall of Paris was felt almost everywhere as the fall of the capital of civilization, a thing like the sacking of Rome by the Goths, many of the most influential people in England still saw nothing in it but the solid success of our kinsmen and old allies of Waterloo. The moral methods which achieved it, the juggling with the Augustenberg claim, the forgery of the Ems telegram, were either successfully concealed or were but cloudily appreciated. The Higher Criticism had entered into our ethics as well as our theology. Our view of Europe was also distorted and made disproportionate by the accident of a natural concern for Constantinople and our route to India, which led Palmerston and later premiers to support the Turk and see Russia as the only enemy. This somewhat cynical reaction was summed up in the strange figure of Disraeli, who made a pro-Turkish settlement full of his native indifference to the Christian subjects of Turkey, and sealed it at Berlin in the presence of Bismarck. Disraeli was not without insight into the inconsistencies and illusions of the English; he said many sagacious things about them, and one especially when he told the Manchester School that their motto was 'Peace and Plenty amid a starving people, and with the world in arms.' But what he said about peace and plenty might well be parodied as a comment on what he himself said about Peace with Honor. Returning from that Berlin Conference he should have said, 'I bring you Peace with Honor; peace with the seeds of the most horrible war of history; and honor as the dupes and victims of the old bully in Berlin.'

But it was, as we have seen, especially in social reform that Germany was believed to be leading the way, and to have found the secret of dealing with the economic evil. In the case of Insurance, which was the test case, she was applauded for obliging all her workmen to set apart a portion of their wages for any time of sickness; and numerous other provisions, both in Germany and England, pursued the same ideal, which was that of protecting the poor against themselves. It everywhere involved an external power having a finger in the family pie; but little attention was paid to any friction thus caused, for all prejudices against the process were supposed to be the growth of ignorance. And that ignorance was already being attacked by what was called education—an enterprise also inspired largely by the example, and partly by the commercial competition of Germany. It was pointed out that in Germany governments and great employers thought it well worth their while to apply the grandest scale of organization and the minutest inquisition of detail to the instruction of the whole German race. The government was the stronger for training its scholars as it trained its soldiers; the big businesses were the stronger for manufacturing mind as they manufactured material. English education was made compulsory; it was made free; many good, earnest, and enthusiastic men labored to create a ladder of standards and examinations, which would connect the cleverest of the poor with the culture of the English universities and the current teaching in history or philosophy. But it cannot be said that the connection was very complete, or the achievement so thorough as the German achievement. For whatever reason, the poor Englishman remained in many things much as his fathers had been, and seemed to think the Higher Criticism too high for him even to criticize.

And then a day came, and if we were wise, we thanked God that we had failed. Education, if it had ever really been in question, would doubtless have been a noble gift; education in the sense of the central tradition of history, with its freedom, its family honor, its chivalry which is the flower of Christendom. But what would our populace, in our epoch, have actually learned if they had learned all that our schools and universities had to teach? That England was but a little branch on a large Teutonic tree; that an unfathomable spiritual sympathy, all-encircling like the sea, had always made us the natural allies of the great folk by the flowing Rhine; that all light came from Luther and Lutheran Germany, whose science was still purging Christianity of its Greek and Roman accretions; that Germany was a forest fated to grow; that France was a dung-heap fated to decay—a dung-heap with a crowing cock on it. What would the ladder of education have led to, except a platform on which a posturing professor proved that a cousin german was the same as a German cousin! What would the guttersnipe have learnt as a graduate, except to embrace a Saxon because he was the other half of an Anglo-Saxon? The day came, and the ignorant fellow found he had other things to learn. And he was quicker than his educated countrymen, for he had nothing to unlearn.

He in whose honor all had been said and sung stirred, and stepped across the border of Belgium. Then were spread out before men's eyes all the beauties of his culture and all the benefits of his organization; then we beheld under a lifting daybreak what light we had followed and after what image we had labored to refashion ourselves. Nor in any story of mankind has the irony of God chosen the foolish things so catastrophically to confound the wise. For the common crowd of poor and ignorant Englishmen, because they only knew that they were Englishmen, burst through the filthy cobwebs of four hundred years and stood where their fathers stood when they knew that they were Christian men. The English poor, broken in every revolt, bullied by every fashion, long despoiled of property, and now being despoiled of liberty, entered history with a noise of trumpets, and turned themselves in two years into one of the iron armies of the world. And when the critic of politics and literature, feeling that this war is after all heroic, looks around him to find the hero, he can point to nothing but the mob.

(1917)

MAX BEERBOHM
(1872-   )

WILLIAM AND MARY

Memories, like olives, are an acquired taste. William and Mary (I give them the Christian names that were indeed theirs—the joint title by which their friends always referred to them) were for some years an interest in my life, and had a hold on my affection. But a time came when, though I had known and liked them too well ever to forget them, I gave them but a few thoughts now and then. How, being dead, could they keep their place in the mind of a young man surrounded with large and constantly renewed consignments of the living? As one grows older, the charm of novelty wears off. One finds that there is no such thing as novelty—or, at any rate, that one has lost the faculty for perceiving it. One sees every newcomer not as something strange and special, but as a ticketed specimen of this or that very familiar genus. The world has ceased to be remarkable; and one tends to think more and more often of the days when it was so very remarkable indeed.

I suppose that had I been thirty years older when first I knew him, William would have seemed to me little worthier of attention than a penny-halfpenny postage-stamp seems to-day. Yet, no; William really had some oddities that would have caught even an oldster's eye. In himself he was commonplace enough (as I, coeval though I was with him, soon saw). But in details of surface he was unusual. In them he happened to be rather ahead of his time. He was a Socialist, for example. In 1890 there was only one other Socialist in Oxford, and he not at all an undergraduate, but a retired chimney-sweep, named Hines, who made speeches, to which nobody, except perhaps William, listened, near the Martyrs' Memorial. And William wore a flannel shirt, and rode a bicycle—very strange habits in those days, and very horrible. He was said to be (though he was short-sighted and wore glasses) a first-rate 'back' at football; but, as football was a thing frowned on by the rowing men, and coldly ignored by the bloods, his talent for it did not help him: he was one of the principal pariahs of our College; and it was rather in a spirit of bravado, and to show how sure of myself I was, that I began, in my second year, to cultivate his acquaintance.

We had little in common. I could not think Political Economy 'the most exciting thing in the world,' as he used to call it. Nor could I without yawning listen to more than a few lines of Mr. William Morris's interminable smooth Icelandic Sagas, which my friend, pious young Socialist that he was, thought 'glorious.' He had begun to write an Icelandic Saga himself, and had already achieved some hundreds of verses. None of these pleased him, though to me they seemed very like his master's. I can see him now, standing on his hearth-rug, holding his MS. close to his short-sighted eyes, declaiming the verses and trying, with many angular gestures of his left hand, to animate them—a tall, broad, raw-boned fellow, with long brown hair flung back from his forehead, and a very shabby suit of clothes. Because of his clothes and his socialism, and his habit of offering beer to a guest, I had at first supposed him quite poor; and I was surprised when he told me that he had from his guardian (his parents being dead) an allowance of £350, and that when he came of age he would have an income of £400. 'All out of dividends,' he would groan. I would hint that Mr. Hines and similar zealots might disembarrass him of this load, if he asked them nicely. 'No,' he would say quite seriously, 'I can't do that,' and would read out passages from 'Fabian Essays' to show that in the present anarchical conditions only mischief could result from sporadic dispersal of rent. 'Ten, twelve years hence—' he would muse more hopefully. 'But by that time,' I would say, 'You'll probably be married, and your wife might n't quite—,' whereat he would hotly repeat what he had said many times: that he would never marry. Marriage was an anti-social anachronism. I think its survival was in some part due to the machinations of Capital. Anyway, it was doomed. Temporary civil contracts between men and women would be the rule 'ten, twelve years hence'; pending which time the lot of any man who had civil sense must be celibacy, tempered perhaps with free love.

Long before that time was up, nevertheless, William married. One afternoon in the spring of '95 I happened to meet him at a corner of Trafalgar Square. I wondered at the immense cordiality of his greeting; for our friendship, such as it was, had waned in our two final years at Oxford. 'You look very flourishing, and,' I said, 'you're wearing a new suit!' 'I'm married,' he replied, obviously without a twinge of conscience. He told me he had been married just a month. He declared that to be married was the most splendid thing in all the world;

but he weakened the force of this generalization by adding that there never was any one like his wife. 'You must see her,' he said; and his impatience to show her proudly off to some one was so evident, and so touching, that I could but accept his invitation to go and stay with them for two or three days—'why not next week?' They had taken and furnished 'a sort of cottage' in ——shire, and this was their home. He had 'run up for the day, on business—journalism' and was now on his way to Charing Cross. 'I know you 'll like my wife,' he said at parting. 'She 's—well, she 's glorious.'

As this was the epithet he had erst applied to 'Beowulf' and to 'Sigurd the Volsung' it raised no high hopes. And indeed, as I was soon to find, he had again misused it. There was nothing glorious about his bride. Some people might even have not thought her pretty. I myself did not, in the flash of first sight. Neat, insignificant, pleasing, was what she appeared to me, rather than pretty, and far rather than glorious. In an age of fringes, her brow was severely bare. She looked 'practical.' But an instant later, when she smiled, I saw that she was pretty, too. And presently I thought her delightful. William had met me in a 'governess cart,' and we went to see him unharness the pony. He did this in a fumbling, experimental way, confusing the reins with the traces, and profiting so little by his wife's directions that she began to laugh. And her laugh was a lovely thing; quite a small sound, but exquisitely clear and gay, coming in a sequence of notes that neither rose nor fell, that were quite even; a trill of notes, and then another, and another, as though she were pulling repeatedly a little silver bell. . . . As I describe it, perhaps the sound may be imagined irritating. I can only say it was enchanting.

I wished she would go on laughing; but she ceased, she darted forward and (William standing obediently aside, and I helping unhelpfully) unharnessed the pony herself, and led it into its small stable. Decidedly, she was 'practical,' but—I was prepared now to be lenient to any quality she might have.

Had she been feckless, no doubt I should have forgiven her that, too; but I might have enjoyed my visit less than I did, and might have been less pleased to go often again. I had expected to 'rough it' under William's roof. But everything thereunder, within the limits of a strict Arcadian simplicity, was well-ordered. I was touched, when I went to my bedroom, by the precision with which the very small maid had unpacked and disposed my things. And I wondered where my hostess had got the lore she had so evidently imparted. Certainly not from William. Perhaps (it only now strikes me) from a handbook. For Mary was great at handbooks. She had handbooks about gardening, and others about poultry, and one about 'the stable,' and others on cognate themes. From these she had filled up the gaps left in her education by her father, who was a widower and either a doctor or a solicitor —I forget which—in one of the smallest towns of an adjoining county. And I daresay she may have had, somewhere hidden away, a manual for young hostesses. If so, it must have been a good one. But to say this is to belittle Mary's powers of intuition. It was they, sharpened by her adoration of William, and by her intensity for everything around him, that made her so efficient a housewife.

If she possessed a manual for young househunters, it was assuredly not by the light of this that she had chosen the home they were installed in. The 'sort of cottage' had been vacant for many years—an unpromising and ineligible object, a mile away from a village, and three miles away from a railway station. The main part of it was an actual cottage, of seventeenth-century workmanship; but a little stuccoed wing had been added to each side of it, in 1850 or thereabouts, by an eccentric old gentleman who at that time chose to make it his home. He had added also the small stable, a dairy, and other appanages. For these, and for garden, there was plenty of room, as he had purchased and enclosed half an acre of the surrounding land. Those two stuccoed, very Victorian wings of his, each with a sash-window above and a French window below, consorted queerly with the old red brick and latticed panes. And the long wooden veranda that he had invoked did not unify the trinity. But one did n't want it to. The wrongness had a character all its own. The wrongness was right—at any rate after Mary had hit on it for William. As a spinster, she would, I think, have been happiest in a trim modern villa. But it was a belief of hers that she had married a man of strange genius. She had married him for himself, not for his genius; but this added grace in him was a thing to be reckoned with, ever so much; a thing she must coddle to the utmost in a proper setting. She was a year older than he (though, being so small and slight, she looked several years younger), and in her devotion the maternal instinct played a great part. William, as I have already conveyed to you, was not greatly gifted. Mary's instinct, in this matter, was at fault. But endearingly, rightly at fault. And, as William *was* outwardly odd, was n't it well that his home should be so, too? On the inside, comfort was what Mary always aimed at for him, and achieved.

The ground floor had all been made one room, into which you stepped straight from the open air. Quite a long big room (or so it seemed, from the lowness of the ceiling); well-freshened in its antiquity, with rush-mats here and there on the irregular red-tiles, and very white whitewash on the plaster between the rafters. This was the dining-room, drawing-room, and general focus throughout the day, and was called simply the Room. William had a 'den' on the ground floor of the left wing; and there, in the mornings, he used to write a great deal. Mary had no special place of her own: her place was wherever her duties needed her. William wrote reviews of books for the *Daily* ———. He did also creative work. The vein of poetry in him had worked itself out—or rather, it expressed itself for him in Mary. For technical purposes the influence of Ibsen had superseded that of Morris. At the time of my first visit, he was writing an extraordinarily gloomy play about an extraordinarily unhappy marriage. In subsequent seasons (Ibsen's disc having been somehow eclipsed for him by George Gissing's) he was usually writing novels in which everyone—or do I exaggerate?—had made a disastrous match. I think Mary's belief in his genius had made him less diffident than he was at Oxford. He was always emerging from his den, with fresh pages of MS., into the Room. 'You do n't mind?' he would say, waving his pages, and then would shout 'Mary!' She was always promptly forthcoming—sometimes from the direction of the kitchen, in a white apron, sometimes from the garden, in a blue one. She never looked at him while he read. To do so would have been lacking in respect for his work. It was on this that she must concentrate her whole mind, privileged auditor that she was. She sat looking straight before her, with her lips slightly compressed, and one hand beneath her chin. I used to wonder that there had been that first moment when I did not think her pretty. Her eyes were of a very light hazel, seeming all the lighter because her hair was of so dark a brown; and they were beautifully set in a face of that 'pinched oval' kind which is rather rare in England. Mary as listener would have atoned to me for any defects there may have been in dear old William's work. Nevertheless, I sometimes wished this work had some comic relief in it. Publishers, I believe, shared this wish; hence the eternal absence of William's name from among their announcements. For Mary's sake, and his, I should have liked him to be 'successful.' But at any rate he did n't need money. He did n't need, in addition to what he had, what he made by his journalism. And as for success—well, did n't Mary think him a genius? And was n't he Mary's husband? The main reason why I wished for light passages in what he read to us was that they would have been cues for Mary's laugh. This was a thing always new to me. I never tired of that little bell-like euphony; those funny little lucid and level trills.

There was no stint of that charm when William was not reading to us. Mary was in no awe of him, apart from his work, and in no awe at all of me: she used to laugh at us both, for one thing and another—just the same laugh as I had first heard when William tried to unharness the pony. I cultivated in myself whatever amused her in me; I drew out whatever amused her in William; I never let slip any of the things that amused her in herself. 'Chaff' is a great bond; and I should have enjoyed our bouts of it even without Mary's own special *obbligato*. She used to call me (for I was very urban in those days) the Gentleman from London. I used to call her the Brave Little Woman. Whatever either of us said or did could be twisted easily into relation to those two titles; and our bouts, to which William listened with a puzzled, benevolent smile, used to cease only because Mary regarded me as a possible purveyor of what William, she was sure, wanted and needed, down there in the country, alone with her: intellectual conversation, after his work. She often, I think, invented duties in garden or kitchen so that he should have this stimulus, or luxury, without hindrance. But when William was alone with me it was about her that he liked to talk, and that I myself liked to talk too. He was very sound on the subject of Mary; and so was I. And if, when I was alone with Mary, I seemed to be sounder than I was on the subject of William's wonderfulness, who shall blame me?

Had Mary been a mother, William's wonderfulness would have been less greatly important. But he was her child as well as her lover. And I think, though I do not know, she believed herself content that this should always be, if so it were destined. It was not destined so. On the first night of a visit I paid them in April, 1899, William, when we were alone, told me news. I had been vaguely conscious, throughout the evening, of some change; conscious that Mary had grown gayer, and less gay—somehow different, somehow remote. William said that her child would be born in September, if all went well. 'She's immensely happy,' he told me. I realized that she was indeed happier than ever. . . . 'And of course it would be a wonderful thing, for both of us,' he said presently,' to have a son—or a daughter.' I asked him which he would rather it were, a son or a daughter. 'Oh, either,' he answered wearily. It was evident that he had misgivings and fears. I tried to reason him out of them. He did not, I am thankful to say, ever let Mary suspect them. She had no misgivings. But it was destined that her child should live only for an hour, and that she should die in bearing it.

I had stayed again at the cottage in July, for some days. At the end of that month I had gone to France, as was my custom, and a week later had written to Mary. It was William that answered this letter, telling me of Mary's death and burial. I returned to England next day. William and I wrote to each other several times. He had not left his home. He stayed there, 'trying,' as he said in a grotesque and heart-rending phrase, 'to finish a novel.' I saw him in the following January. He wrote to me from the Charing Cross Hotel, asking me to lunch with him there. After our first greetings, there was a silence. He wanted to talk of—what he could not talk of. We stared helplessly at each other, and then, in the English way, talked of things at large. England was engaged in the Boer War. William was the sort of man whom one would have expected to be violently Pro-Boer. I was surprised at his fervor for the stronger side. He told me he had tried to enlist, but had been rejected on account of his eyesight. But there was, he said, a good chance of his being sent out, almost immediately, as one of the *Daily* ———'s special correspondents. 'And then,' he exclaimed, 'I shall see something of it.' I had a presentiment that he would not return, and a belief that he did not want to return. He did not return. Special correspondents were not so carefully shepherded in that war as they have since been. They were more at liberty to take risks, on behalf of the journals to which they were accredited. William was killed a few weeks after he had landed at Cape Town.

And there came, as I have said, a time when I did not think of William and Mary often; and then a time when I did more often think of them. And especially much did my mind hark back to them in the late autumn of last year; for on the way to the place I was staying at I had passed the little railway station, whose name had always linked itself for me with the names of those two friends. There were but four intervening stations. It was not a difficult pilgrimage that I made some days later—back towards the past, for that past's sake and honor. I had thought I should not remember the way, the three miles of way, from the station to the cottage; but I found myself remembering it perfectly, without a glance at the fingerposts. Rain had been falling heavily, driving the late leaves off the trees; and everything looked rather sodden and misty, though the sun was now shining. I had known this landscape only in spring, summer, early autumn. Mary had held to a theory that at other seasons I could not be acclimatized. But there were groups of trees that I knew, even without their leaves; and farmhouses and small stone bridges that had not at all changed. Only what mattered was changed. Only what mattered was gone. Would what I had come to see be there still? In comparison with what it had held, it was not much. But I wished to see it, melancholy spectacle though it must be for me if it were extant, and worse than melancholy if it held something new. I began to be sure it had been demolished, built over. At the corner of the lane that had led to it, I was almost minded to explore no further, to turn back. But I went on, and suddenly I was at the four-barred iron gate, that I remembered, between the laurels. It was rusty, and fastened with a rusty padlock, and beyond it there was grass where a winding 'drive' had been. From the lane the cottage never had been visible, even when these laurels were lower and sparser than they were now. Was the cottage still standing? Presently, I climbed over the gate, and walked through the long grass, and—yes, there was Mary's cottage; still there; William's and Mary's cottage. Trite enough, I have no doubt, were the thoughts that possessed me as I stood gazing. There is nothing new to be thought about the evanescence of human things; but there is always much to be felt about it by one who encounters in his maturity some such intimate instance and reminder as confronted me, in that cold sunshine, across that small wilderness of long rank wet grass and weeds.

Incredibly woebegone and lonesome the house would have looked even to one for whom it contained no memories; all the more because in its utter dereliction it looked so durable. Some of the stucco had fallen off the walls of the two wings; thick flakes of it lay on the discolored roof of the veranda, and thick flakes of it could be seen lying in the grass below. Otherwise, there were few signs of actual decay. The sash-window and the French window of each wing were shuttered, and, from where I was standing, the cream-colored paint of those shutters behind the glass looked almost fresh. The latticed windows between had all been boarded up from within. The house was not to be let perish soon.

I did not want to go nearer to it; yet I did go nearer, step by step, across the wilderness, right up to the edge of the veranda itself, and within a yard of the front door.

I stood looking at that door. I had never noticed it in the old days, for then it had always stood open. But it asserted itself now, master of the threshold.

It was a narrow door—narrow even for its height, which did not exceed mine by more than two inches or so; a door that even when it was freshly painted must have looked mean. How much meaner now, with its paint all faded and mottled, cracked and blistered! It had no knocker, not even a slit for letters. All that it had was a large-ish key-hole. On this my eyes rested; and presently I moved to it, stooped down to it, peered through it. I had a glimpse of—darkness impenetrable.

Strange it seemed to me, as I stood back, that there the Room was, the remembered Room itself, separated from me by nothing but this unremembered door . . . and a quarter of a century, yes. I saw it all, in my mind's eye, just as it had been: the way the sunlight came into it through this same doorway and through the lattices of these same four windows; the way the little bit of a staircase came down into it, so crookedly yet so confidently; and how uneven the tiled floor was, and how low the rafters were, and how littered the whole place was with books brought in from his den by William, and how bright with flowers brought in by Mary from her garden. The rafters, the stairs, the tiles, were still existing changeless in despite of cobwebs and dust and darkness, all quite changeless on the other side of the door, so near to me. I wondered how I should feel if by some enchantment the door slowly turned on its hinges, letting in light. I should not enter, I felt, not even look, so much must I hate to see those inner things lasting when all that had given to them a meaning was gone from them, taken away from them, finally. And yet, why blame them for their survival? And how know that *nothing* of the past ever came to them, revisiting, hovering? Something —sometimes—perhaps? One knew so little. How not be tender to what, as it seemed to me, perhaps the dead loved?

So strong in me now was the wish to see again all those things, to touch them and, as it were, commune with them, and so queerly may the mind be wrought upon in a solitude among memories, that there were moments when I almost expected that the door would obey my will. I was recalled to a clearer sense of reality by something which I had not before noticed. In the door-post to the right was a small knob of rusty iron—mocking reminder that to gain admission to a house one does not 'will' the door: one rings the bell—unless it is rusty and has quite obviously no one to answer it; in which case one goes away. Yet I did not go away. The movement that I made, in despite of myself, was towards the knob itself. But, I hesitated, suppose I did what I half meant to do, and there were no sound. That would be ghastly. And surely there *would* be no sound. And if sound there were, wouldn't that be worse still? My hand drew back, wavered, suddenly closed on the knob. I heard the scrape of the wire—and then, from somewhere within the heart of the shut house, a tinkle.

It had been the weakest, the puniest of noises. It had been no more than is a fledgling's first attempt at a twitter. But I was not judging it by its volume. Deafening peals from steeples had meant less to me than that one single note breaking the silence—in there. In there, in the dark, the bell that had answered me was still quivering, I supposed, on its wire. But there was no one to answer *it*, no footstep to come hither from those recesses, making prints in the dust. Well, *I* could answer it; and again my hand closed on the knob, unhesitatingly this time, pulling further. That was my answer; and the rejoinder to it was more than I had thought to hear—a whole quick sequence of notes, faint but clear, playful, yet poignantly sad, like a trill of laughter echoing out of the past, or even merely out of this neighboring darkness. It was so like something I had known, so recognizable and oh, recognizing, that I was lost in wonder.

And long must I have remained standing at that door, for I heard the sound often, often. I must have rung again and again, tenaciously, vehemently, in my folly.

W. H. HUDSON
(1841-1922)

From FAR AWAY AND LONG AGO

MY FIRST VISIT TO BUENOS AYRES
(By permission. Copyright 1918 by E. P. Dutton & Co.)

THE happiest time of my boyhood was at that early period, a little past the age of six, when I had my own pony to ride on, and was allowed to stay on his back just as long and go as far from home as I liked. I was like the young bird when on first quitting the nest it suddenly becomes conscious of its power to fly. My early flying days were, however, soon interrupted, when my mother took me on my first visit to Buenos Ayres; that is to say, the first I remember, as I must have been taken there once before as an infant in arms, since we lived too far from town for any missionary-clergyman to travel all that distance just to baptize a little baby. Buenos Ayres is now the wealthiest, most populous Europeanized city in South America; what it was like at that time these glimpses into a far past will serve to show. Coming as a small boy of an exceptionally impressionable mind, from that green plain where people lived the simple pastoral life, everything I saw in the city impressed me deeply, and the sights which impressed me the most are as vivid in my mind today as they ever were. I was a solitary little boy in my rambles about the streets, for though I had a younger brother who was my only playmate, he was not yet five, and too small to keep me company in my walks. Nor did I mind having no one with me. Very, very early in my boyhood I had acquired the habit of going about alone to amuse myself in my own way, and it was only after years, when my age was about twelve, that my mother told me how anxious this singularity in me used to make her. She would miss me when looking out to see what the children were doing, and I would be called and searched for, to be found hidden away somewhere in the plantation. Then she began to keep an eye on me, and when I was observed stealing off she would secretly follow and watch me, standing motionless among the tall weeds or under the trees by the half-hour, staring at vacancy. This distressed her very much; then to her great relief and joy she discovered that I was there with a motive which she could understand and appreciate: that I was watching some living thing, an insect perhaps, but oftener a bird—a pair of little scarlet flycatchers building a nest of lichen on a peach tree, or some such beautiful thing. And as she loved all living things herself she was quite satisfied that I was not going queer in my head, for that was what she had been fearing.

The strangeness of the streets was a little too much for me at the start, and I remember that on first venturing out by myself a little distance from home I got lost. In despair of ever finding my way back I began to cry, hiding my face against a post at a street corner, and was there soon surrounded by quite a number of passers-by; then a policeman came up, with brass buttons on his blue coat and a sword at his side, and taking me by the arm he asked me in a commanding voice where I lived—the name of the street and the number of the house. I couldn't tell him; then I began to get frightened on account of his sword and big black moustache and loud rasping voice, and suddenly ran away, and after running for about six or eight minutes found myself back at home, to my surprise and joy.

The house where we stayed with English friends was near the front, or what was then the front, that part of the city which faced the Plata river, a river which was like the sea, with no visible shore beyond; and like the sea it was tidal, and differed only in its color, which was a muddy red instead of blue or green. The house was roomy, and like most of the houses at that date had a large courtyard paved with red tiles and planted with small lemon trees and flowering shrubs of various kinds. The streets were straight and narrow, paved with round boulder stones the size of a football, the pavements with brick or flagstones, and so narrow they would hardly admit of more than two persons walking abreast. Along the pavements on each side of the street were rows of posts placed at a distance of ten yards apart. These strange looking rows of posts, which foreigners laughed to see, were no doubt the remains of yet ruder times, when ropes of hide were stretched along the side of the pavements to protect the foot-passengers from runaway horses, wild cattle driven by wild men from the plains, and other dangers of the narrow streets. As they were then paved the streets must have been the noisiest in the world, on account of the immense numbers of big springless carts in them. Imagine the thunderous racket made by a long procession of these carts, when they were returning empty, and the drivers, as was often the case, urged their horses to a gallop, and they bumped and thundered over the big round stones!

Just opposite the house we stayed at there was a large church, one of the largest of the numerous churches of the city, and one of my most vivid memories relates to a great annual festival at the church—that of the patron saint's day. It had been open to worshippers all day, but the chief service was held about three o'clock in the afternoon; at all events it was at that hour when a great attendance of fashionable people took place. I watched them as they came in couples, families and small groups, in every case the ladies, beautifully dressed, attended by their cavaliers. At the door of the church the gentleman would make his bow and withdraw to the street before the building, where a sort of outdoor gathering was formed of all those who had come as escorts to the ladies, and where they would remain until the service was over. The crowd in the street grew and grew until there were about four or five hundred gentlemen, mostly young, in the gathering, all standing in small groups, conversing in an animated way, so that the street was filled with the loud humming sound of their blended voices. These men were all natives, all of the good or upper class of the native society, and all dressed exactly alike in the fashion of that time. It was their dress and the uniform appearance of so large a number of persons, most of them with young, handsome, animated faces, that fascinated me and kept me on the spot gazing at them until the big bells began to thunder, at the conclusion of the service and the immense concourse of gaily-dressed ladies swarmed out, and immediately the meeting broke up, the gentlemen hurrying back to meet them.

They all wore silk hats and the glossiest black broadcloth, not even a pair of trousers of any other shade was seen; and all wore the scarlet silk or fine cloth waistcoat which, at that period, was considered the right thing for every citizen of the republic to wear; also in lieu of buttonhole, a scarlet ribbon pinned to the lapel of the coat. It was a pretty sight, and the concourse reminded me of a flock of military starlings, a black or dark-plumaged bird with a scarlet breast, one of my feathered favorites.

My rambles were almost always on the front, since I could walk there a mile or two from home, north or south, without getting lost, always with the vast expanse of water on one hand, with many big ships looking dim in the distance, and numerous lighters or belanders coming from them with cargoes of merchandise which they unloaded into carts, these going out a quarter of a mile in the shallow water to meet them. Then there were the water-carts going and coming in scores and hundreds, for at that period there was no water supply to the houses and every householder had to buy muddy water by the bucket at his own door from the watermen.

One of the most attractive spots to me was the congregating place of the lavenderas, south of my street. Here on the broad beach under the cliff one saw a whiteness like a white cloud, covering the ground for a space of about a third of a mile; and the cloud, as one drew near, resolved itself into innumerable garments, sheets and quilts, and other linen pieces, fluttering from long lines, and covering the low rocks washed clean by the tide and the stretches of green turf between. It was the spot where the washerwomen were allowed to wash all the dirty linen of Buenos Ayres in public. All over the ground the women, mostly negresses, were seen on their knees, beside the pools among the rocks, furiously scrubbing and pounding away at their work, and like all negresses they were exceedingly vociferous, and their loud gabble, mingled with yells and shrieks of laughter, reminded me of the hubbub made by a great concourse of gulls, ibises, godwits, geese, and other noisy water-fowl on some marshy lake. It was a wonderfully animated scene, and drew me to it again and again: I found, however, that it was necessary to go warily among these women, as they looked with suspicion at idling boys, and sometimes, when I picked my way among the spread garments, I was sharply ordered off. Then, too, they often quarrelled over their right to certain places and spaces among themselves; then very suddenly their hilarious gabble would change to wild cries of anger and torrents of abuse. By and by I discovered that their greatest rages and worst language were when certain young gentlemen of the upper classes visited the spot to amuse themselves by baiting the lavenderas. The young gentleman would saunter about in an absent-minded manner and presently walk right on to a beautifully embroidered and belaced nightdress or other dainty garment spread out to dry on the sward or rock, and, standing on it, calmly proceed to take out and light a cigarette. Instantly the black virago would be on her feet confronting him and pouring out a torrent of her foulest expressions and deadliest curses. He, in a pretended rage, would reply in even worse language. That would put her on her mettle; for now all her friends and foes scattered about the ground would suspend their work to listen with all their ears; and the contest of words growing louder and fiercer would last until the combatants were both exhausted and unable to invent any more new and horrible expressions of opprobrium to hurl at each other. Then the insulted young gentleman would kick the garment away in a fury and hurling the unfinished cigarette in his adversary's face would walk off with his nose in the air.

I laugh to recall these unseemly word-battles on the beach, but they were shocking to me when I first heard them as a small, innocent-minded boy, and it only made the case worse when I was assured that the young gentleman was only acting a part, that the extreme anger he exhibited, which might have served as an excuse for using such language, was all pretence.

Another favorite pastime of these same idle, rich young gentlemen offended me as much as the one I have related. The night-watchmen, called *serenos*, of that time interested me in an extraordinary way. When night came it appeared that the fierce policemen, with their swords and brass buttons, were no longer needed to safeguard the people, and their place in the streets was taken by a quaint, frowsy-looking body of men, mostly old, some almost decrepit, wearing big cloaks and carrying staffs and heavy iron lanterns with a tallow candle alight inside. But what a pleasure it was to lie awake at night and listen to their voices calling the hours! The calls began at the stroke of eleven, and then from beneath the window would come the wonderful long drawling call of *Las ón———ce han dá———do y se———ré———no*, which means eleven of the clock and all serene, but if clouded the concluding words would be *nu———blá———do*, and so on, according to the weather. From all the streets, from all over the town, the long-drawn calls would float to my listening ears, with infinite variety in the voices—the high and shrill, the falsetto, the harsh, raucous note like the caw of the carrion-crow, the solemn booming bass, and then some fine, rich, pure voice that soared heavenwards above all the others and was like the pealing notes of an organ.

I loved the poor night-watchmen and their cries, and it grieved my little soft heart to hear that it was considered fine sport by the rich young gentlemen to sally forth at night and do battle with them, and to deprive them of their staffs and lanterns, which they took home and kept as trophies.

Another human phenomenon which annoyed and shocked my tender mind, like that of the contests on the beach between young gentlemen and washerwomen, was the multitude of beggars which infested the town. These were not like our dignified beggar on horseback, with his red poncho, spurs and tall straw hat, who rode to your gate, and having received his tribute, blessed you and rode away to the next estancia. These city beggars on the pavement were the most brutal, even fiendish, looking men I had ever seen. Most of them were old soldiers, who, having served their ten, fifteen, or twenty years, according to the nature of the crime for which they had been condemned to the army, had been discharged or thrown out to live like carrion-hawks on what they could pick up. Twenty times a day at least you would hear the iron gate opening from the courtyard into the street swung open, followed by the call or shout of the beggar demanding charity in the name of God. Outside you could not walk far without being confronted by one of these men, who would boldly square himself in front of you on the narrow pavement and beg for alms. If you had no change and said, '*Perdón, por Dios*,' he would scowl and let you pass; but if you looked annoyed or disgusted, or ordered him out of the way, or pushed by without a word, he would glare at you with a concentrated rage which seemed to say, 'Oh, to have you down at my mercy, bound hand and foot, a sharp knife in my hand!' And this would be followed by a blast of the most horrible language.

One day I witnessed a very strange thing, the action of a dog, by the waterside. It was evening and the beach was forsaken; cartmen, fishermen, boatmen all gone, and I was the only idler left on the rocks; but the tide was coming in, rolling quite big waves on to the rocks, and the novel sight of the waves, the freshness, the joy of it, kept me at that spot, standing on one of the outermost rocks not yet washed over by the water. By and by a gentleman, followed by a big dog, came down on to the beach and stood at a distance of forty or fifty yards from me, while the dog bounded forward over the flat, slippery rocks and through pools of water until he came to my side, and sitting on the edge of the rock began gazing intently down at the water. He was a big, shaggy, round-headed animal, with a greyish coat with some patches of light reddish color on it; what his breed was I cannot say, but he looked somewhat like a sheep-dog or an otter-hound. Suddenly he plunged in, quite disappearing from sight, but quickly reappeared with a big shad of about three and a half or four pounds weight in his jaws. Climbing on to the rock he dropped the fish, which he did not appear to have injured much, as it began floundering about in an exceedingly lively manner. I was astonished and looked back at the dog's master; but there he stood in the same place, smoking and paying no attention to what his animal was doing. Again the dog plunged in and brought out a second big fish and dropped it on the flat rock, and again and again he dived, until there were five big shads all floundering about on the wet rock and likely soon to be washed back into the water.

The shad is a common fish in the Plata and the best to eat of all its fishes, resembling the salmon in its rich flavor, and is eagerly watched for when it comes up from the sea by the Buenos Ayres fishermen, just as our fishermen watch for mackerel on our coasts. But on this evening the beach was deserted by every one, watchers included, and the fish came and swarmed along the rocks, and there was no one to catch them— not even some poor hungry idler to pounce upon and carry off the five fishes the dog had captured. One by one I saw them washed back into the water, and presently the dog, hearing his master whistling to him, bounded away.

For many years after this incident I failed to find any one who had ever seen or heard of a dog catching fish. Eventually, in reading I met with an account of fishing-dogs in Newfoundland and other countries.

One other strange adventure met with on the front remains to be told. It was about eleven o'clock in the morning and I was on the Parade, walking north, pausing from time to time to look over the sea-wall to watch the flocks of small birds that came to feed on the beach below. Presently my attention was drawn to a young man walking on before me, pausing and peering too from time to time over the wall, and when he did so throwing something at the small birds. I ran on and overtook him, and was rather taken aback at his wonderfully fine appearance. He was like one of the gentlemen of the gathering before the church, described on a few pages back, and wore a silk hat and fashionable black coat and trousers and scarlet silk waistcoat; he was also a remarkably handsome young gentleman, with a golden-brown curly beard and moustache and dark liquid eyes that studied my face with a half-amused curiosity when I looked up at him. In one hand he carried a washleather bag by its handle, and holding a pebble in his right hand he watched the birds, the small parties of crested song sparrows, yellow house sparrows, siskins, field finches, and other kinds, and from time to time he would hurl a pebble at the bird he had singled out forty yards down below us on the rocks. I did not see him actually hit a bird, but his precision was amazing, for almost invariably the missile, thrown from such a distance at so minute an object, appeared to graze the feathers and to miss killing by but a fraction of an inch.

I followed him for some distance, my wonder and curiosity growing every minute to see such a superior-looking person engaged in such a pastime. For it is a fact that the natives do not persecute small birds. On the contrary, they despise the aliens in the land who shoot and trap them. Besides, if he wanted small birds for any purpose, why did he try to get them by throwing pebbles at them? As he did not order me off, but looked in a kindly way at me every little while, with a slight smile on his face, I at length ventured to tell him that he would never get a bird that way—that it would be impossible at that distance to hit one with a small pebble. 'Oh, no, not impossible,' he returned, smiling and walking on, still with an eye on the rocks. 'Well, you have n't hit one yet,' I was bold enough to say, and at that he stopped and putting his finger and thumb in his waistcoat pocket he pulled out a dead male siskin and put it in my hands.

This was the bird called 'goldfinch' by the English resident in La Plata, and to the Spanish it is also goldfinch; it is, however, a siskin, *Chrysomitris magellanica*, and has a velvet-black head, the rest of its plumage being black, green, and shining yellow. It was one of my best-loved birds, but I had never had one in my hand, dead or alive, before, and now its wonderful unimagined loveliness, its graceful form, and the exquisitely pure flower-like yellow hue affected me with a delight so keen that I could hardly keep from tears.

After gloating a few moments over it, touching it with my finger-tips and opening the little black and gold wings, I looked up pleadingly and begged him to let me keep it. He smiled and shook his head: he would not waste his breath talking; all his energy was to be spent in hurling pebbles at other lovely little birds.

'Oh, señor, will you not give it to me?' I pleaded still; and then, with sudden hope, 'Are you going to sell it?'

He laughed, and taking it from my hand put it back in his waistcoat pocket; then, with a pleasant smile and a nod to say that the interview was now over, he went on his way.

Standing on the spot where he left me, and still bitterly regretting that I had failed to get the bird, I watched him until he disappeared from sight in the distance, walking towards the suburb of Palermo; and a mystery he remains to this day, the one and only Argentine gentleman, a citizen of the Athens of South America, amusing himself by killing little birds with pebbles. But I do not know that it was an amusement. He had perhaps in some wild moment made a vow to kill so many siskins in that way, or a bet to prove his skill in throwing a pebble; or he might have been practising a cure for some mysterious deadly malady, prescribed by some wandering physician from Bagdad or Ispahan; or, more probable still, some heartless, soulless woman he was in love with had imposed this fantastical task on him.

Perhaps the most wonderful thing I saw during that first eventful visit to the capital was the famed Don Eusebio, the court jester or fool of the President or Dictator Rosas, the 'Nero of South America,' who lived in his palace at Palermo, just outside the city. I had been sent with my sisters and little brother to spend the day at the house of an Anglo-Argentine family in another part of the town, and we were in the large courtyard playing with the children of the house when some one opened a window above us and called out, 'Don Eusebio!' That conveyed nothing to me, but the little boys of the house knew what it meant; it meant that if we went quickly out to the street we might catch a glimpse of the great man in all his glory. At all events, they jumped up, flinging their toys away, and rushed to the street door, and we after them. Coming out we found quite a crowd of lookers-on, and then down the street, in his general's dress—for it was one of the Dictator's little jokes to make his fool a general—all scarlet, with a big scarlet three-cornered hat surmounted by an immense aigrette of scarlet plumes, came Don Eusebio. He marched along with tremendous dignity, his sword at his side, and twelve soldiers, also in scarlet, his bodyguard, walking six on each side of him with drawn swords in their hands.

We gazed with joyful excitement at this splendid spectacle, and it made it all the more thrilling when one of the boys whispered in my ear that if any person in the crowd laughed or made any insulting or rude remark, he would be instantly cut to pieces by the guard. And they looked truculent enough for anything.

The great Rosas himself I did not see, but it was something to have had this momentary sight of General Eusebio, his fool, on the eve of his fall after a reign of over twenty years, during which he proved himself one of the bloodiest as well as the most original-minded of the Caudillos and Dictators, and altogether, perhaps, the greatest of those who have climbed into power in this continent of republics and revolutions.

(1918)

LYTTON STRACHEY
(1880–1932)

From QUEEN VICTORIA

THE LAST YEARS
(Copyright by Harcourt, Brace & Co.)

THE final years were years of apotheosis. In the dazzled imagination of her subjects Victoria soared aloft towards the regions of divinity through a nimbus of purest glory. Criticism fell dumb; deficiencies which, twenty years earlier, would have been universally admitted, were now as universally ignored. That the nation's idol was a very incomplete representative of the nation was a circumstance that was hardly noticed, and yet it was conspicuously true. For the vast changes which, out of the England of 1837, had produced the England of 1897, seemed scarcely to have touched the Queen. The immense industrial development of the period, the significance of which had been so thoroughly understood by Albert, meant little indeed to Victoria. The amazing scientific movement, which Albert had appreciated no less, left Victoria perfectly cold. Her conception of the universe, and of man's place in it, and of the stupendous problems of nature and philosophy remained, throughout her life, entirely unchanged. Her religion was the religion which she had learnt from the Baroness Lehzen and the Duchess of Kent. Here, too, it might be supposed that Albert's views might have influenced her. For Albert, in matters of religion, was advanced. Disbelieving altogether in evil spirits, he had had his doubts about the miracle of the Gadarene Swine. Stockmar, even, had thrown out, in a remarkable memorandum on the education of the Prince of Wales, the suggestion that while the child 'must unquestionably be brought up in the creed of the Church of England,' it might nevertheless be in accordance with the spirit of the times to exclude from his religious training the inculcation of a belief in 'the supernatural doctrines of Christianity.' This, however, would have been going too far; and all the royal children were brought up in complete orthodoxy. Anything else would have grieved Victoria, though her own conceptions of the orthodox were not very precise. But her nature, in which imagination and subtlety held so small a place, made her instinctively recoil from the intricate ecstasies of High Anglicanism; and she seemed to feel most at home in the simple faith of the Presbyterian Church of Scotland. This was what might have been expected; for Lehzen was the daughter of a Lutheran pastor, and the Lutherans and the Presbyterians have much in common. For many years Dr. Norman Macleod, an innocent Scotch minister, was her principal spiritual adviser; and, when he was taken from her, she drew much comfort from quiet chats about life and death with the cottagers at Balmoral. Her piety, absolutely genuine, found what it wanted in the sober exhortations of old John Grant and the devout saws of Mrs. P. Farquharson. They possessed the qualities, which, as a child of fourteen, she had so sincerely admired in the Bishop of Chester's 'Exposition of the Gospel of St. Matthew'; they were 'just plain and comprehensible and full of truth and good feeling.' The Queen, who gave her name to the Age of Mill and of Darwin, never got any further than that.

From the social movements of her time Victoria was equally remote. Towards the smallest no less than towards the greatest changes she remained inflexible. During her youth and middle age smoking had been forbidden in polite society, and so long as she lived she would not withdraw her anathema against it. Kings might protest; bishops and ambassadors, invited to Windsor, might be reduced, in the privacy of their bedrooms, to lie full-length upon the floor and smoke up the chimney—the interdict continued. It might have been supposed that a female sovereign would have lent her countenance to one of the most vital of all the reforms to which her epoch gave birth—the emancipation of women—but, on the contrary, the mere mention of such a proposal sent the blood rushing to her head. In 1870, her eye having fallen upon the report of a meeting in favor of Women's Suffrage, she wrote to Mr. Martin in royal rage—'The Queen is most anxious to enlist everyone who can speak or write to join in checking this mad, wicked folly of "Woman's Rights," with all its attendant horrors, on which her poor feeble sex is bent, forgetting every sense of womanly feeling and propriety. Lady —— ought to get a *good whipping*. It is a subject which makes the Queen so furious that she cannot contain herself. God created men and women different—then let them remain each in their own position. Tennyson has some beautiful lines on the difference of men and women in "The Princess." Woman would become the most hateful, heartless, and disgusting of human beings were she allowed to unsex herself; and where would be the protection which man was intended to give the weaker sex? The Queen is sure that Mrs. Martin agrees with her.' The argument was irrefutable; Mrs. Martin agreed; and yet the canker spread.

In another direction Victoria's comprehension of the spirit of her age has been constantly asserted. It was for long the custom for courtly historians and polite politicians to compliment the Queen upon the correctness of her attitude towards the Constitution. But such praises seem hardly to be justified by the facts. In her later years Victoria more than once alluded with regret to her conduct during the Bedchamber crisis, and let it be understood that she had grown wiser since. Yet in truth it is difficult to trace any fundamental change either in her theory or her practice in constitutional matters throughout her life. The same despotic and personal spirit which led her to break off the negotiations with Peel is equally visible in her animosity towards Palmerston, in her threats of abdication to Disraeli, and in her desire to prosecute the Duke of Westminster for attending a meeting upon Bulgarian atrocities. The complex and delicate principles of the Constitution cannot be said to have come within the compass of her mental faculties; and in the actual developments which it underwent during her reign she played a passive part. From 1840 to 1861 the power of the Crown steadily increased in England; from 1861 to 1901 it steadily declined. The first process was due to the influence of the Prince Consort, the second to that of a series of great Ministers. During the first Victoria was in effect a mere accessory; during the second the threads of power, which Albert had so laboriously collected, inevitably fell from her hands into the vigorous grasp of Mr. Gladstone, Lord Beaconsfield, and Lord Salisbury. Perhaps, absorbed as she was in routine, and difficult as she found it to distinguish at all clearly between the trivial and the essential, she was only dimly aware of what was happening. Yet, at the end of her reign, the Crown was weaker than at any other time in English history. Paradoxically enough, Victoria received the highest eulogiums for assenting to a political evolution, which, had she completely realised its import, would have filled her with supreme displeasure.

Nevertheless it must not be supposed that she was a second George III. Her desire to impose her will, vehement as it was, and unlimited by any principle, was yet checked by a certain shrewdness. She might oppose her Ministers with extraordinary violence; she might remain utterly impervious to arguments and supplications; the pertinacity of her resolution might seem to be unconquerable; but, at the very last moment of all, her obstinacy would give way. Her innate respect and capacity for business, and perhaps, too, the memory of Albert's scrupulous avoidance of extreme courses, prevented her from ever entering an *impasse*. By instinct she understood when the facts were too much for her, and to them she invariably yielded. After all, what else could she do?

But if, in all these ways, the Queen and her epoch were profoundly separated, the points of contact between them also were not few. Victoria understood very well the meaning and the attractions of power and property, and in such learning the English nation, too, had grown to be more and more proficient. During the last fifteen years of the reign—for the short Liberal Administration of 1892 was a mere interlude— imperialism was the dominant creed of the country. It was Victoria's as well. In this direction, if in no other, she had allowed her mind to develop. Under Disraeli's tutelage the British Dominions over the seas had come to mean much more to her than ever before, and, in particular, she had grown enamoured of the East. The thought of India fascinated her; she set to, and learnt a little Hindustani; she engaged some Indian servants, who became her inseparable attendants, and one of whom, Munshi Abdul Karim, eventually almost succeeded to the position which had once been John Brown's. At the same time, the imperialist temper of the nation invested her office with a new significance exactly harmonizing with her own inmost proclivities. The English polity was in the main a common-sense structure; but there was always a corner in it where common-sense could not enter —where, somehow or other, the ordinary measurements were not applicable and the ordinary rules did not apply. So our ancestors had laid it down, giving scope, in their wisdom, to that mystical element which, as it seems, can never quite be eradicated from the affairs of men. Naturally it was in the Crown that the mysticism of the English polity was concentrated— the Crown, with its venerable antiquity, its sacred associations, its imposing spectacular array. But, for nearly two centuries, common-sense had been predominant in the great building, and the little, unexplored, inexplicable corner had attracted small attention. Then, with the rise of imperialism, there was a change. For imperialism is a faith as well as a business; as it grew, the mysticism in English public life grew with it; and simultaneously a new importance began to attach to the Crown. The need for a symbol—a symbol of England's might, of England's worth, of England's extraordinary and mysterious destiny—became felt more urgently than ever before. The Crown was that symbol; and the Crown rested upon the head of Victoria. Thus it happened that while by the end of the reign the power of the sovereign had appreciably diminished, the prestige of the sovereign had enormously grown.

Yet this prestige was not merely the outcome of public changes; it was an intensely personal matter, too. Victoria was the Queen of England, the Empress of India, the quintessential pivot round which the whole magnificent machine was revolving—but how much more besides! For one thing, she was of a great age —an almost indispensable qualification for popularity in England. She had given proof of one of the most admired characteristics of the race —persistent vitality. She had reigned for sixty years, and she was not out. And then, she was a character. The outlines of her nature were firmly drawn, and, even through the mists which envelop royalty, clearly visible. In the popular imagination her familiar figure filled, with satisfying ease, a distinct and memorable place. It was, besides, the kind of figure which naturally called forth the admiring sympathy of the great majority of the nation. Goodness they prized above every other human quality; and Victoria, who had said that she would be good at the age of twelve, had kept her word. Duty, conscience, morality—yes! in the light of those high beacons the Queen had always lived. She had passed her days in work and not in pleasure —in public responsibilities and family cares. The standard of solid virtue which had been set up so long ago amid the domestic happiness of Osborne had never been lowered for an instant. For more than half a century no divorced lady had approached the precincts of the Court. Victoria, indeed, in her enthusiasm for wifely fidelity, had laid down a still stricter ordinance: she frowned severely upon any widow who married again. Considering that she herself was the offspring of a widow's second marriage, this prohibition might be regarded as an eccentricity; but, no doubt, it was an eccentricity on the right side. The middle classes, firm in the triple brass of their respectability, rejoiced with a special joy over the most respectable of queens. They almost claimed her, indeed, as one of themselves, but this would have been an exaggeration. For, though many of her characteristics were most often found among the middle classes, in other respects—in her manners, for instance—Victoria was decidedly aristocratic. And, in one important particular, she was neither aristocratic nor middle-class: her attitude toward herself was simply regal.

Such qualities were obvious and important; but, in the impact of a personality, it is something deeper, something fundamental and common to all its qualities, that really tells. In Victoria, it is easy to discern the nature of this underlying element: it was a peculiar sincerity. Her truthfulness, her single-mindedness, the vividness of her emotions and her unrestrained expression of them, were the varied forms which this central characteristic assumed. It was her sincerity which gave her at once her impressiveness, her charm, and her absurdity. She moved through life with the imposing certitude of one to whom concealment was impossible—either towards her surroundings or towards herself. There she was, all of her—the Queen of England, complete and obvious; the world might take her or leave her; she had nothing more to show, or to explain, or to modify; and, with her peerless carriage, she swept along her path. And not only was concealment out of the question; reticence, reserve, even dignity itself, as it sometimes seemed, might be very well dispensed with. As Lady Lyttelton said: 'There is a transparency in her truth that is very striking—not a shade of exaggeration in describing feelings or facts; like very few other people I ever knew. Many may be as true, but I think it goes often along with some reserve. She talks all out; just as it is, no more and no less.' She talked all out; and she wrote all out, too. Her letters, in the surprising jet of their expression, remind one of a turned-on tap. What is within pours forth in an immediate, spontaneous rush. Her utterly unliterary style has at least the merit of being a vehicle exactly suited to her thoughts and feelings; and even the platitude of her phraseology carries with it a curiously personal flavour. Undoubtedly it was through her writings that she touched the heart of the public. Not only in her 'Highland Journals,' where the mild chronicle of her private proceedings was laid bare without a trace either of affectation or of embarrassment, but also in those remarkable messages to the nation which, from time to time, she published in the newspapers, her people found her very close to them indeed. They felt instinctively Victoria's irresistible sincerity, and they responded. And in truth it was an endearing trait.

The personality and the position, too—the wonderful combination of them—that, perhaps, was what was finally fascinating in the case. The little old lady, with her white hair and her plain mourning clothes, in her wheeled chair or her donkey-carriage—one saw her so; and then—close behind—with their immediate suggestion of singularity, of mystery, and of power—the Indian servants. That was the familiar vision, and it was admirable; but at chosen moments, it was right that the widow of Windsor should step forth apparent Queen. The last and the most glorious of such occasions was the Jubilee of 1897. Then, as the splendid procession passed along, escorting Victoria through the thronged re-echoing streets of London on her progress of thanksgiving to St. Paul's Cathedral, the greatness of her realm and the adoration of her subjects blazed out together. The tears welled to her eyes, and, while the multitude roared around her, 'How kind they are to me! How kind they are!' she repeated over and over again. That night her message flew over the Empire: 'From my heart I thank my beloved people. May God bless them!' The long journey was nearly done.

But the traveller, who had come so far, and through such strange experiences, moved on with the old unfaltering step. The girl, the wife, the aged woman, were the same: vitality, conscientiousness, pride, and simplicity were hers to the latest hour.

The evening had been golden; but, after all, the day was to close in cloud and tempest. Imperial needs, imperial ambitions, involved the country in the South African War. There were checks, reverses, bloody disasters; for a moment the nation was shaken, and the public distresses were felt with intimate solicitude by the Queen. But her spirit was high, and neither her courage nor her confidence wavered for a moment. Throwing herself heart and soul into the struggle, she labored with redoubled vigor, interested herself in every detail of the hostilities, and sought by every means in her power to render service to the national cause. In April 1900, when she was in her eighty-first year, she made the extraordinary decision to abandon her annual visit to the South of France, and to go instead to Ireland, which had provided a particularly large number of recruits to the armies in the field. She stayed for three weeks in Dublin, driving through the streets, in spite of the warnings of her advisers, without an armed escort; and the visit was a complete success. But, in the course of it, she began, for the first time, to show signs of the fatigue of age.

For the long strain and the unceasing anxiety, brought by the war, made themselves felt at last. Endowed by nature with a robust constitution, Victoria, though in periods of depression she had sometimes supposed herself an invalid, had in reality throughout her life enjoyed remarkably good health. In her old age, she had suffered from a rheumatic stiffness of the joints, which had necessitated the use of a stick, and, eventually, a wheeled chair; but no other ailments attacked her, until, in 1898, her eyesight began to be affected by incipient cataract. After that, she found reading more and more difficult, though she could still sign her name, and even, with some difficulty, write letters. In the summer of 1900, however, more serious symptoms appeared. Her memory, in whose strength and precision she had so long prided herself, now sometimes deserted her; there was a tendency towards aphasia; and, while no specific disease declared itself, by the autumn there were unmistakable signs of a general physical decay. Yet, even in these last months, the strain of iron held firm. The daily work continued; nay, it actually increased; for the Queen, with an astonishing pertinacity, insisted upon communicating personally with an ever-growing multitude of men and women who had suffered through the war.

By the end of the year the last remains of her ebbing strength had almost deserted her; and through the early days of the opening century it was clear that her dwindling forces were only kept together by an effort of will. On January 14, she had at Osborne an hour's interview with Lord Roberts, who had returned victorious from South Africa a few days before. She inquired with acute anxiety into all the details of the war; she appeared to sustain the exertion successfully; but, when the audience was over, there was a collapse. On the following day her medical attendants recognized that her state was hopeless; and yet, for two days more, the indomitable spirit fought on; for two days more she discharged the duties of a Queen of England. But after that there was an end of working; and then, and not till then, did the last optimism of those about her break down. The brain was failing, and life was gently slipping away. Her family gathered round her; for a little more she lingered, speechless and apparently insensible; and, on January 22, 1901, she died.

When, two days previously, the news of the approaching end had been made public, astonished grief had swept over the country. It appeared as if some monstrous reversal of the course of nature was about to take place. The vast majority of her subjects had never known a time when Queen Victoria had not been reigning over them. She had become an indissoluble part of their whole scheme of things, and that they were about to lose her appeared a scarcely possible thought. She herself, as she lay blind and silent, seemed to those who watched her to be divested of all thinking—to have glided already, unawares, into oblivion. Yet, perhaps, in the secret chambers of consciousness, she had her thoughts too. Perhaps her fading mind called up once more the shadows of the past to float before it, and retraced, for the last time, the vanished visions of that long history—passing back and back, through the cloud of years, to older and ever older memories—to the spring woods at Osborne, so full of primroses for Lord Beaconsfield—to Lord Palmerston's queer clothes and high demeanor, and Albert's face under the green lamp, and Albert's first stag at Balmoral, and Albert in his blue and silver uniform, and the Baron coming in through a doorway, and Lord M. dreaming at Windsor with the rooks cawing in the elm-trees, and the Archbishop of Canterbury on his knees in the dawn, and the old King's turkey-cock ejaculations, and Uncle Leopold's soft voice at Claremont, and Lehzen with the globes, and her mother's feathers sweeping down towards her, and a great old repeater-watch of her father's in its tortoise-shell case, and a yellow rug, and some friendly flounces of sprigged muslin, and the trees and the grass at Kensington.

(1921)

HUGH WALPOLE
(1884–)

From JOSEPH CONRAD

ROMANCE AND REALISM

I

THE terms, Romance and Realism, have been used of late years very largely as a means of escape from this business of the creation of character. The purely romantic novel may now be said to be, in England at any rate, absolutely dead. Mr. Frank Swinnerton, in his study of 'Robert Louis Stevenson,' said: 'Stevenson, reviving the never-very-prosperous romance of England, created a school which has brought romance to be the sweepings of an old costume-chest; . . . if romance is to be conventional in a double sense, if it springs not from a personal vision of life, but is only a tedious virtuosity, a pretence, a conscious toy, romance as an art is dead. The art was jaded when Reade finished his vociferous carpet-beating; but it was not dead. And if it is dead, Stevenson killed it!'

We may differ very considerably from Mr. Swinnerton with regard to his estimate of Stevenson's present and future literary value without denying that the date of the publication of St. Ives was also the date of the death of the purely romantic novel.

But, surely, here, as Mr. Swinnerton himself infers, the term 'Romantic' is used in the limited and truncated idea that has formed, lately, the popular idea of Romance. In exactly the same way the term 'Realism' has, recently, been most foolishly and uncritically handicapped. Romance, in its modern use, covers everything that is removed from reality: 'I like romances,' we hear the modern reader say, 'because they take me away from real life, which I desire to forget.' In the same way Realism is defined by its enemies as a photographic enumeration of unimportant facts by an observant pessimist. 'I like realism,' admirers of a certain order of novel exclaim, 'because it is so like life. It tells me just what I myself see every day—I know where I am.'

Nevertheless, impatient though we may be of these utterly false ideas of Romance and Realism, a definition of those terms that will satisfy everyone is almost impossible. I cannot hope to achieve so exclusive an ambition—I can only say that to myself Realism is the study of life with all the rational faculties of observation, reason and reminiscence—Romance is the study of life with the faculties of imagination. I do not mean that Realism may not be emotional, poetic, even lyrical, but it is based always upon truth perceived and recorded—it is the essence of observation. In the same way Romance may be, indeed must be, accurate and defined in its own world, but its spirit is the spirit of imagination, working often upon observation and sometimes simply upon inspiration. It is, at any rate, understood here that the word Romance does not, for a moment, imply a necessary divorce from reality, nor does Realism imply a detailed and dusty preference for morbid and unagreeable subjects. It is possible for Romance to be as honestly and clearly perceptive as Realism, but it is not so easy for it to be so because imagination is more difficult of discipline than observation. It is possible for Realism to be as eloquent and potential as Romance, although it cannot so easily achieve eloquence because of its fear of deserting truth. Moreover, with regard to the influence of foreign literature upon the English novel, it may be suggested that the influence of the French novel, which was at its strongest between the years 1885 and 1895, was towards Realism, and that the influence of the Russian novel, which has certainly been very strongly marked in England during the last years, is all towards Romantic-Realism. If we wished to know exactly what is meant by Romantic-Realism, such a novel as 'The Brothers Karamazov,' such a play as 'The Cherry Orchard' are there before us, as the best possible examples. We might say, in a word, that 'Karamazov' has, in the England of 1915, taken the place that was occupied, in 1890, by Madame Bovary. . . .

II

It is Joseph Conrad whose influence is chiefly responsible for this development in the English novel. Just as, in the early nineties, Mr. Henry James and Mr. Rudyard Kipling, the one potential, the other kinetic, influenced, beyond all contemporary novelists, the minds of their younger generation, so to-day, twenty-five years later, do Mr. Joseph Conrad and Mr. H. G. Wells, the one potential, the other kinetic, hold that same position.

Joseph Conrad, from the very first, influenced though he was by the French novel, showed that Realism alone was not enough for him. That is to say that, in presenting the case of Almayer, it was not enough for him merely to state as truthfully as possible the facts. Those facts, sordid as they are, make the story of Almayer's degradation sufficiently realistic, when it is merely recorded and perceived by any observer. But upon these recorded facts Conrad's imagination, without for a moment deserting the truth, worked, beautifying, ennobling it, giving it pity and terror, above all putting it into relation with the whole universe, the whole history of the cycle of life and death.

As I have said, the Romantic novel, in its simplest form, was used, very often, by writers who wished to escape from the business of the creation of character. It had not been used for that purpose by Sir Walter Scott, who was, indeed, the first English Romantic-Realist, but it was so used by his successors, who found a little optimism, a little adventure, a little color and a little tradition go a long way towards covering the required ground.

Conrad had, from the first, a poet's—that is to say, a romantic—mind, and his determination to use that romance realistically was simply his determination to justify the full play of his romantic mind in the eyes of all honest men.

In that intention he has absolutely succeeded; he has not abated one jot of his romance—'Nostromo,' 'Lord Jim,' 'Heart of Darkness' are amongst the most romantic things in all our literature—but the last charge that any critic can make against him is falsification, whether of facts, of inference or of consequences.

The whole history of his development has for its key-stone this determination to save his romance by his reality, to extend his reality by his romance. He found in English fiction little that could assist him in this development; the Russian novelists were to supply him with his clue. This whole question of Russian influence is difficult to define, but that Conrad has been influenced by Turgéniev a little and by Dostoievsky very considerably, cannot be denied. 'Crime and Punishment,' 'The Idiot,' 'The Possessed,' 'The Brothers Karamazov' are romantic realism at the most astonishing heights that this development of the novel is ever likely to attain. We will never see again the heroes of the Prince Myshkin, Dmitri Karamazov, Nicolas Stavrogin build, men so real to us that no change of time or place, age or sickness can take them from us, men so beautifully lit with the romantic passion of Dostoievsky's love of humanity that they seem to warm the whole world, as we know it, with the fire of their charity. That power of creating figures typical as well as individual has been denied to Conrad. Captain Anthony, Nostromo, Jim do not belong to the whole world, nor do they escape the limitations and confinements that their presentation as 'cases' involves on them. Moreover, Conrad does not love humanity. He feels pity, tenderness, admiration, but love, except for certain of his sea heroes, never, and even with his sea heroes it is love built on his scorn of the land. Dostoievsky scorned no one and nothing; as relentless in his pursuit of the truth as Stendhal or Flaubert, he found humanity, as he investigated it, beautiful because of its humanity—Conrad finds humanity pitiable because of its humanity.

Nevertheless he has been influenced by the Russian writer continuously and sometimes obviously. In at least one novel, 'Under Western Eyes,' the influence has led to imitation. For that reason, perhaps, that novel is the least vital of all his books, and we feel as though Dostoievsky had given him Razumov to see what he could make of him, and had remained too overwhelmingly curious an onlooker to allow independent creation. What, however, Conrad has in common with the creator of Raskolnikov is his thrilling pursuit of the lives, the hearts, the minutest details of his characters. Conrad alone of all English novelists shares this zest with the great Russian. Dostoievsky found his romance in his love of his fellow-beings, Conrad finds his in his love of beauty, his poet's cry for color, but their realism they find together in the hearts of men—and they find it not as Flaubert, that they may make of it a perfect work of art, not as Turgéniev, that they may extract from it a flower of poignant beauty, not as Tolstoi, that they may, from it, found a gospel—simply they pursue their quest because the breathless interest of the pursuit is stronger than they. They have, both of them, created characters simply because characters demanded to be created. We feel that Emma Bovary was dragged, painfully, arduously, against all the strength of her determination, out of the shades where she was lurking. Myshkin, the Karamazovs, and, in their own degree, Nostromo, Almayer, M'Whirr, demanded that they should be flung upon the page.

Instead of seizing upon Romance as a means of avoiding character, he has triumphantly forced it to aid him in the creation of the lives that, through him, demand existence. This may be said to be the great thing that Conrad has done for the English novel—he has brought the zest of creation back into it; the French novelists used life to perfect their art—the Russian novelists used art to liberate their passion for life. That at this moment in Russia the novel has lost that zest, that the work of Kouprin, Artzybashev, Sologub, Merejkovsky, Andreiev, shows exhaustion and sterility means nothing; the stream will soon run full again. Meanwhile we, in England, know once more what it is to feel, in the novel, the power behind the novelist, to be ourselves in the grip of a force that is not afraid of romance nor ashamed of realism, that cares for life as life and not as a means of proving the necessity for form, the danger of too many adjectives, the virtues of the divorce laws or the paradise of free love.

(1916)

ALDOUS HUXLEY

(1894–   )

From JESTING PILATE

AT SEA

(Copyright 1926 by George H. Doran Co.)

FAMILIARITY blunts astonishment. Fishes do not marvel at water; they are too busy swimming in it. It is the same with us. We take our Western civilization for granted and find nothing intrinsically odd or incongruous in it. Before we can realize the strangeness of our surroundings, we must deliberately stop and think.

But moments come when that strangeness is fairly forced upon our notice, moments when an anomaly, a contradiction, an immense incongruity is suddenly illumined by a light so glaring that we cannot fail to see it. Such a moment came to me as I was crossing the Pacific. It was the first morning out of Yokohama. Coming out of my cabin, I was handed the day's bulletin of wireless news. I unfolded the typewritten sheet and read: 'Mrs. X, of Los Angeles, girl wife of Dr. X, aged 79, has been arrested for driving her automobile along the railroad track, whistling like a locomotive.' This piece of information had been transmitted through the ethereal holes between the molecules of air. From a broadcasting station more than five thousand miles away it had come to our ship in rather less time than it would have taken the sound of my voice to travel from one end of the promenade deck to the other. The labors of half a dozen men of genius, of hundreds of patient and talented investigators, had gone to creating and perfecting the means for achieving this miracle. To what end? That the exploits of young Mrs. X, of Los Angeles, might be instantaneously known to every traveler on all the oceans of the globe. The ether reverberated with the name of Mrs. X. The wave that bore it broke against the moon and the planets, and rippled on toward the stars and the ultimate void. Faraday and Clerk Maxwell had not lived in vain.

The wise men of antiquity (so say the Indians) knew all that we have learned about nature, and a great deal more besides. But they kept their science to themselves, or revealed it only in enigmas which cannot be interpreted except in the light of a previous knowledge of the answers. They were afraid that—men being what they are—their discoveries might be put to bad or futile uses. The ordinary man, they argued, is not to be trusted with the power which comes of knowledge. They withheld their science.

Being prejudiced in favor of the West and of the present, I have no great belief in the scientific attainments of the ancient sages of the Orient. But their wisdom is undeniable. The fruits of knowledge are abused and wasted; it is, alas, only too obvious. Disinterested men have given their lives to the search for truth, and we have turned their discoveries to the service of murder, or employed them to create a silly entertainment. The modern civilization of the West, which is the creation of perhaps a hundred men of genius, assisted by a few thousand intelligent and industrious disciples, exists for the millions, whose minds are indistinguishable in quality from those of the average humans of the paleolithic age. The ideas of a handful of supermen are exploited so as to serve the profit and pleasure of the innumerable subtermen, or men *tout court*. The contemporary cave man listens in on instruments which he owes to the inspired labors of superior and, by comparison, divine intelligences. Negroid music shoots across the void into his ears, and the wisdom of such sages as Dr. Frank Crane; racing results and bedtime stories and the true tale of a young Mrs. X, of Los Angeles. The fire of Prometheus is put to the strangest uses. Gods propose, men dispose. The world in which we live may not be the best of all possible worlds: it is certainly the most fantastic.

Not being a superman myself, I took the liveliest interest in young Mrs. X. After being arrested for whistling like a locomotive—whether by means of an instrument or with the unaided vocal cords was never made clear—she was bailed out of prison by her husband, the aged doctor. The time came for the hearing of her case. Mrs. X told the doctor that she proposed to forfeit her (or rather his) recognizances and run away. The doctor protested. Mrs. X then began to smash the furniture. The aged doctor telephoned for the police; they came, and Mrs. X was re-arrested on charges of assault. We on the Pacific waited in a dreadful suspense. A few days later, as we were crossing the hundred and eightieth meridian, we learned to our profound relief that a reconciliation had taken place. Aged Dr. X had withdrawn his charge; the girl wife had gone home quietly. What happened about the whistling business we never learned. The anonymous powers which purvey wireless news are strangely capricious. The name of Mrs. X no longer rippled out toward Aldeboran and the spiral nebulæ. In the next morning's bulletin there was a little paragraph announcing the declaration of the General Strike. And Bébé Daniels had fallen off her horse and received contusions.

(1926)

T. S. ELIOT
THE CRITICISM OF POETRY

LET us declare at once that there is nothing peculiar either in endowment or training to designate the critic. The critic of poetry needs the same professional equipment as the poet: the same knowledge of poetry, the same enjoyment of it, the same ear and eye, the same philology, the same general education. If any poet asks himself what writings about poetry have been of any use to him, he finds that they are almost without exception the writings of poets —Campion, Dryden, Coleridge, Gourmont, even Boileau—and that almost the only exception is the man who wrote well on every subject: Aristotle.

I say again that there are a variety of points of view from which thoughtful and useful study of poetry can be made. Poetry is also a social document, and may be made use of by the historian, the moralist, the social philosopher or the psychoanalyst. Nor do I say that the critic should not be aware of these aspects. He is only required to know what he is doing. And as poetry is primarily an art, that is to say, a means of communicating those direct feelings peculiar to art, which range from amusement to ecstasy, the first impression it should make is to the feelings of art, and the first questions it should excite are questions of art. It is a social document afterwards. And since it is as a work of art that a poem should be first discussed, the critic of contemporary verse should be competent to discuss it as a work of art. Let us now consider what is the proper behavior for a critic when he meets with a poem that he genuinely believes to be a work of art, and whether our critics can be trusted to behave themselves properly.

I have in mind a sentence encountered recently in a literary periodical of the very highest standing—a periodical with which there is nothing to compare in *any* other country. This sentence was not in a leading article or in a review, but in a small book-notice, and a notice concerned with other poems by other writers as well. It ran, in what I believe is called diamond type, almost as follows: 'Mr. Honeydew's poem, *The Golden Hoopoe*, would give fame to any book or paper in which it appeared. It is a great poem. The song by Mr. Leadbeater is worthy of Mr. Leadbeater . . .' etc.

Consider the sentence 'It is a great poem,' and all that it implies. Assume that the critic is one for whose opinion you have vast respect: then he has told you all that you need to know. You read the poem, you become acquainted with a new work of art, and the literary periodical has served the most important purpose that literary periodicals can serve. But this never happens. Probably no one who read the notice really believed, or even entertained the thought, that the poem was a great poem. No one rose panting from the breakfast table and rushed hatless to the stationer's to procure a copy. The periodical itself did not come out with a leading article on the poem the next week. Perhaps the editor himself never noticed this little critic in his diamond type, and he too would not have believed. I could not believe either; I have never read the poem. The critic was believed by no one, incredulous eyes outstared him, and yet he was a brave little critic. For he dared to say the only sensible thing about a great poem: 'It is a great poem.' He was a great critic. Or else he was a very irresponsible, completely untrustworthy, poisonous little critic.

He took the honest course, the critic, if he really believed the poem was a great poem. What else is there to say? Who wants an analysis, an account of the man and his message, his vision of life, his place as a representative of something or other, his derivations, his relation to his colleagues Mr. Leadbeater and Mr. Spooner—*before he has read the poem?* But, as a matter of fact, it cannot be done in that way. It must be hammered. And so the good critic will merely say 'this is a good poem' in a hundred different ways. He will make a column of it. He will quote and quote. When he writes about someone else he will say, 'Here and there we find a slight suggestion of the bitter intensity of Mr. Honeydew,' or 'With the inevitable exception of Mr. Honeydew,' or a million such phrases. He will persuade the amiable Mrs. Saffron Walden to write a little article about Honeydew. The people who read Mrs. Walden's article will not read the poems, but they will be prepared to be impressed when they read another reference to Honeydew next week. Honeydew gets to know a few writers, and they will from time to time mention him. And after a time some of the important critics—the critics on important papers—will come to accept Honeydew. Not that they will *praise* him. But they will say, 'The bizarre work of Mr. Honeydew,' 'The acknowledged leader of the Febrilist school of younger writers, Mr. Honeydew.' No one will have praised him except the Good Critic and Mrs. Walden and a few private people with no influence. But he is all the safer for that: he escapes malice. Honeydew must not make himself too conspicuous, or he will sink to a depth at which even the diamond criticism will seem to be fame. He merely wants such degree of notoriety and such number of editions that the few intelligent people in each generation will be likely to come across his work. And in 100 years there will, perhaps, be popular lectures on English literature 'from Chaucer to Honeydew.'

So great is the value of good criticism, which is discreet advertisement.

I do not assert, by any means, that the only function of criticism is to advertise good poetry. But it cannot too often be insisted that the purpose—not of writing poetry, but of publishing it—should be primarily to give pleasure; and that the purpose for which we suppose reviewing was divinely intended was primarily to indicate such works as can give the best pleasure to the people who otherwise may fail to hear of their existence. This is the purpose, I say, not of criticism, but of reviewing; for criticism and reviewing are not to be confused. Reviewing, if it is to be done at all, should be done by critics, but critics have other things to do as well. Now the point at which a piece of writing ceases to be a review and becomes a critical article is difficult to determine. But if we isolate reviewing from criticism its only proper motive is to call attention to something good and new. And this is exactly the motive which least often animates the reviewer. That it should be so is not wholly the reviewer's fault. For reviewing is, unfortunately, a means of livelihood; though it is known to be one of the most corrupting, degrading, and badly-paid means of livelihood that a writing man can ply. The reviewers are merely the lowest wage-slaves in the modern literary system. Many intelligent men find themselves in this condition; it is part of the social organization or disorganization that writers who have honest work of their own to do find that this is the only work for which they can be paid. Consequently, it is hardly to be expected that the reviewer, unless he has become so depraved as to have no other function, should enjoy reviewing. From the point of view of any man of the slightest intellect or taste, there is not enough good verse to occupy a reviewer one week out of the year. There is not enough pernicious work worth attacking to occupy him another week. So that twenty-five twenty-sixths of the reviewer's time must be occupied with books that are perfectly colorless. And the dilemma is this: either a reviewer is a bad writer and bad critic, and he ought not to be allowed to intervene between books and the public; or he is a good writer and good critic, and therefore ought not to be occupied in writing about inferior books.

The other apparent dilemma is this: that if books of poetry are not reviewed, you must find some other way of introducing them to the public. If some other way be possible, the opportunity for criticism will if anything be greater, for it is the reviewer who kills the critic. And the harm done by the review-system is not only to the critic, not only to the public, but to the critic, the public, and the poet at once. In advance of the book comes always something which is not merely a statement that there is a good book to be read, and which is not, on the other hand to be taken as criticism, since to read *criticism* without having already read the book criticized is meaningless. A poet may legitimately take pleasure in his work in three ways. He may have the solitary joy of expression, of having turned his material into a work of art. He may have the pleasure of being enjoyed by a few people whose taste he respects and who, he believes, have more or less understood the poem. And he may have the satisfaction, equally legitimate, of having given entertainment, and the pleasure of which they are capable, to a large number of people who have not understood him at all. As for the review, every one is tickled by a 'good review.' But it is unimportant. Yet, as few writers of verse have so great conviction of the value of their work as to be indifferent to the pleasure they give others, and as in any case it is a pleasure to give pleasure to others, and as a poet only knows of the pleasure he gives others by what is written about him in print, the review comes to appear important. And the extraordinary result is that the greater number of poetry books are written, I am sure, only in order to be reviewed. The 'good review' replaces, in the writer's mind, the pleasure to be given to the public. The books are born, reviewed, and die. I do not know who reads them; I never see anyone or hear of anyone reading them. Some people glance at them. But the book never reaches the public in a *pure* state. We are so saturated in the review spirit that we are satisfied to read about books; in consequence, we are merely—well-informed. A few rebellious souls complain that we have too much criticism, and not enough 'creation.' But we have neither criticism nor creation.

If it were only possible first to abate this nuisance of reviewing, we might hope for some improvement in the condition of verse. If it were more difficult for young poets to spring into brief and meaningless notoriety, they might be more self-critical. There should be no reviewing of poetry in daily newspapers. In the periodicals which appear less frequently, no work should be discussed except from one of the several critical points of view approved: the historical, the philosophical, the expert-professional. From the last point of view, only the absolutely first-rate should be discussed at all. If the several legitimate types of criticism were recognized, and the public and the critic taught to distinguish between them, we might have more good criticism of each kind, where now there are only two or three critics who are not utterly confused about their own intentions. Let us come to look back upon reviewing as a barbarous practice of a half-civilized age. Let private presses multiply, and the advertisements of the great publishing houses be reduced in size. Let small books of new poets be circulated first among a private audience of the two hundred people who are most likely to be interested in them. The book, the price, and the address of the publisher, could be mentioned in the literary periodical. There is a great deal for these periodicals to do besides reviewing. If 'critical journalism' is an activity quite apart from creative activity, if critics are a race apart from artists who hold the artist's destiny in their hands, both criticism and art perish. Let the practitioners of any art or of several arts who have a sufficient community of interests and standards publish their conversation, their theories and their opinions in periodicals of their own. They should not be afraid of forming 'cliques,' if their cliques are professional and not personal. The friction will be stimulating. Certainly there is no more useful criticism and no more previous praise for a poet than that of another poet:

> Fu miglior fabbro del parlar materno. . .
>   e lascia dir gli stolti. . .

If we are really utterly sundered in spirit from the Pall Mall clubs, the country houses, and the provincial study-circles, it is a pity that we should have to depend upon them for support. If they purchase our works as a result of reviews in the dignified Press, and I am not sure that they do, they ought to be sufficiently aware of the difference between reviewing and criticism to be aware that a review is not a complete substitute for feeling and thinking on their part, and that good criticism is something which must itself be criticized by the reader.

How the man of letters is to be supported if he does not write reviews is an important social problem of which I have no solution to offer.

(1920)

VIRGINIA WOOLF

THE PATRON AND THE CROCUS

From THE COMMON READER

YOUNG men and women beginning to write are generally given the plausible but utterly impracticable advice to write what they have to write as shortly as possible, as clearly as possible, and without other thought in their minds except to say exactly what is in them. Nobody ever adds on these occasions the one thing needful: 'And be sure you choose your patron wisely,' though that is the gist of the whole matter. For a book is always written for somebody to read, and, since the patron is not merely the paymaster, but also in a very subtle and insidious way the instigator and inspirer of what is written, it is of the utmost importance that he should be a desirable man.

But who, then, is the desirable man—the patron who will cajole the best out of the writer's brain and bring to birth the most varied and vigorous progeny of which he is capable? Different ages have answered the question differently. The Elizabethans, to speak roughly, chose the aristocracy to write for and the playhouse public. The eighteenth-century patron was a combination of coffee-house wit and Grub Street bookseller. In the nineteenth century the great writers wrote for the half-crown magazines and the leisured classes. And looking back and applauding the splendid results of these different alliances, it all seems enviably simple, and plain as a pikestaff compared with our own predicament—for whom should we write? For the present supply of patrons is of unexampled and bewildering variety. There is the daily Press, the weekly Press, the monthly Press; the English public and the American public; the best-seller public and the worst-seller public; the high-brow public and the red-blood public; all now organized self-conscious entities capable through their various mouthpieces of making their needs known and their approval or displeasure felt. Thus the writer who has been moved by the sight of the first crocus in Kensington Gardens has, before he sets pen to paper, to choose from a crowd of competitors the particular patron who suits him best. It is futile to say, 'Dismiss them all; think only of your crocus,' because writing is a method of communication; and the crocus is an imperfect crocus until it has been shared. The first man or the last may write for himself alone, but he is an exception and an unenviable one at that, and the gulls are welcome to his works if the gulls can read them.

Granted, then, that every writer has some public or other at the end of his pen, the high-minded will say that it should be a submissive public, accepting obediently whatever he likes to give it. Plausible as the theory sounds, great risks are attached to it. For in that case the writer remains conscious of his public, yet is superior to it—an uncomfortable and unfortunate combination, as the works of Samuel Butler, George Meredith, and Henry James may be taken to prove. Each despised the public; each desired a public; each failed to attain a public; and each wreaked his failure upon the public by a succession, gradually increasing in intensity, of angularities, obscurities, and affectations which no writer whose patron was his equal and friend would have thought it necessary to inflict. Their crocuses in consequence are tortured plants, beautiful and bright, but with something wry-necked about them, malformed, shrivelled on the one side, overblown on the other. A touch of the sun would have done them a world of good. Shall we then rush to the opposite extreme and accept (if in fancy alone) the flattering proposals which the editors of the *Times* and the *Daily News* may be supposed to make us—'Twenty pounds down for your crocus in precisely fifteen hundred words, which shall blossom upon every breakfast table from John o' Groats to the Land's End before nine o'clock tomorrow morning with the writer's name attached'?

But will one crocus be enough, and must it not be a very brilliant yellow to shine so far, to cost so much, and to have one's name attached to it? The Press is undoubtedly a great multiplier of crocuses. But if we look at some of these plants, we shall find that they are only very distantly related to the original little yellow or purple flower which pokes up through the grass in Kensington Gardens about this time of year. The newspaper crocus is amazing but still a very different plant. It fills precisely the space allotted to it. It radiates a golden glow. It is genial, affable, warm-hearted. It is beautifully finished, too, for let nobody think that the art of 'our dramatic critic' of the *Times* or of Mr. Lynd of the *Daily News* is an easy one. It is no despicable feat to start a million brains running at nine o'clock in the morning, to give two million eyes something bright and brisk and amusing to look at. But the night comes and these flowers fade. So little bits of glass lose their lustre if you take them out of the sea; great prima donnas howl like hyenas if you shut them up in telephone boxes; and the most brilliant of articles when removed from its element is dust and sand and the husks of straw. Journalism embalmed in a book is unreadable.

The patron we want, then, is one who will help us to preserve our flowers from decay. But as his qualities change from age to age, and it needs considerable integrity and conviction not to be dazzled by the pretensions or bamboozled by the persuasions of the competing crowd, this business of patron-finding is one of the tests and trials of authorship. To know whom to write for is to know how to write. Some of the modern patron's qualities are, however, fairly plain. The writer will require at this moment, it is obvious, a patron with the book-reading habit rather than the play-going habit. Nowadays, too, he must be instructed in the literature of other times and races. But there are other qualities which our special weaknesses and tendencies demand in him. There is the question of indecency, for instance, which plagues us and puzzles us much more than it did the Elizabethans. The twentieth-century patron must be immune from shock. He must distinguish infallibly between the little clod of manure which sticks to the crocus of necessity, and that which is plastered to it out of bravado. He must be a judge, too, of those social influences which inevitably play so large a part in modern literature, and able to say which matures and fortifies, which inhibits and makes sterile. Further, there is emotion for him to pronounce on, and in no department can he do more useful work than in bracing a writer against sentimentality on the one hand and a craven fear of expressing his feeling on the other. It is worse, he will say, and perhaps more common, to be afraid of feeling than to feel too much. He will add, perhaps, something about language, and point out how many words Shakespeare used and how much grammar Shakespeare violated, while we, though we keep our fingers so demurely to the black notes on the piano, have not appreciably improved upon *Antony and Cleopatra*. And if you can forget your sex altogether, he will say, so much the better; a writer has none. But all this is by the way—elementary and disputable. The patron's prime quality is something different, only to be expressed perhaps by the use of that convenient word which cloaks so much—atmosphere. It is necessary that the patron should shed and envelop the crocus in an atmosphere which makes it appear a plant of the very highest importance, so that to misrepresent it is the one outrage not to be forgiven this side of the grave. He must make us feel that a single crocus, if it be a real crocus, is enough for him; that he does not want to be lectured, elevated, instructed, or improved; that he is sorry that he bullied Carlyle into vociferation, Tennyson into idyllics, and Ruskin into insanity; that he is now ready to efface himself or assert himself as his writers require; that he is bound to them by a more than maternal tie; that they are twins indeed, one dying if the other dies, one flourishing if the other flourishes; that the fate of literature depends upon their happy alliance—all of which proves, as we began by saying, that the choice of a patron is of the highest importance. But how to choose rightly? How to write well? Those are the questions.

(1925)

JOHN BUCHAN, LORD TWEEDSMUIR
(1875–   )

ENGLAND AFTER THE WAR

From THE PEOPLE'S KING

THE conditions of working-class life had on the whole been greatly improved by the War. Higher wages did not lead to waste, but higher standards of decency and comfort. The average household had better food, better clothing, more margin for amusements, wider horizons. Small wonder that they struggled to maintain what they had won. That was for those in employment: for the unemployed, who had now passed beyond the two million figure, there was a bare subsistence and a tragic idleness, a steady loss of their technical skill and a slow souring and dulling of mind. Yet in the very tragedy there were elements of hope. A problem of such magnitude required for its solution not only the energies of the State, but the thought and the good-will of every private citizen; and, largely owing to the work of the Prince of Wales, these were forthcoming. People began to recognize a personal duty. Also there was a stimulus to clearer thinking and to an effort to remake our whole industrial machine. Hitherto the task had been to remedy the defects of industrialism, now it was to transform industrialism itself.

One social danger was however forgotten—the embarrassed middle classes, especially their youth. When a young man of that class was unemployed, he was the care of nobody; when he was employed, it was too often on a job without light or horizon. From such natural discontent, fascism or some other authoritarian creed might draw many recruits.

Had some Rip van Winkle gone to sleep on the eve of the War, and awakened any time in the first decade of peace to cast an eye over our society, he would have been first impressed, I think, by the superficial levelling-up of classes. Men and women could no longer be judged by their clothes. These had become simpler and more uniform. A clerk was as well dressed, and in much the same way, as a Guards officer, and a village girl as the lady of the manor. People—the women especially—would have appeared to him slimmer and more vital. He would have missed the old stately ritual of London life. The capital now looked more like a provincial city, for the top-hat had largely gone, club life was a declining thing, the great mansions had become blocks of flats, and the 'season,' shorn of its old splendors, now lasted most of the year. He would have been struck by the trimness and the healthier appearance of youth. Parliament, perhaps, would have seemed to him rather a shabby assembly.

In the country he would have found towns spreading into mushroom suburbs, and ancient villages blotched with bungalows. He would have been amazed at the size and populousness of the roads and the scarcity of horses. Famous houses which he had known were now either pulled down or turned into schools and asylums, the parks had been ploughed up and built upon, and their owners had migrated to suburban or Continental lodgings with a few family heirlooms and the war-medals of their dead. But he would have found village life gayer and freer, if less idiomatic. He would have noted, too, that the hunt meets were as large as ever, and that a new gentry had made its appearance. As after the Wars of the Roses, a small squirearchy was growing up on the ruin of the grandees; and he would have consoled himself by reflecting that it was the new modest manors which had produced some of the greatest Elizabethans.

As he looked more closely into things, our Rip van Winkle would have been awed by the widespread passion for entertainment. He remembered that Disraeli more than half a century before had told Lord Rowton that the true revolution would come in Britain when the bourgeoisie took to amusing itself. After the War games bulked larger than ever in the nation's eyes. The cinema had become a universal habit; twenty millions visited it each week. There were now five million wireless sets, the remotest hamlets were forests of wireless poles, and daily about half the population were entertained and instructed from the air. Instructed!—that was what impressed him. The demand for a greater margin of leisure involved the means of filling that leisure, and almost every form of entertainment had its educative side. There would soon be no more pleasant oases of unsophistication. The workers and the peasants were getting to know how their neighbors lived and how the world lived. Knowledge was being diffused in the widest commonalty, shallow, perhaps, but still knowledge. A mighty transformation was in progress, managed by the people themselves and not by their Government. But the Government, too, was affected. The press might disparage or belaud a statesman, but that statesman now broadcast *urbi et orbi* [to the city and the world at large], and the whole nation could hear, and judge, his words.

The awakened sleeper would have observed another thing. The cities were straggling into the country as never before, but the nation was becoming alive to the loss. It was as if the perils and discomforts of war had made people more conscious of their heritage of ancient peace. The old distinction between town-dweller and country-dweller was less rigid. New means of transport took the urban population easily to remote places; the interest in wild nature was spreading; men and women, whose eyes had once looked scarcely beyond their own street, were now alive to the riches of their native land. But if Britain awoke to the consciousness of a great possession, this awakening would mean desecration unless the possession were protected. The countryside, so long neglected, was rediscovered and christened 'rural England,' and there was a vigorous movement to preserve rustic beauty, now badly scarred but not beyond hope, a movement springing, not from the few, but from the many.

* * *

After every great effort there is a natural expectation of some quickening and sublimation of the human soul. It may take the form of a religious revival or some splendid flowering of the creative mind. The war with Spain was followed by the Puritan kindling of the religious consciousness, by Shakespeare and Milton; the war with Napoleon by the romantic revival in letters and the zealous evangelicalism of the early nineteenth century. But the Great War had no such fruit. The instinct of men to huddle into groups for comfort did indeed produce a few mob-religions, and the dislocation of things and the breakdown of old standards brought forth a host of new literary modes. But there was no strong creative impulse to be discerned or any notable enlargement of spirit. The struggle had taken too heavy a toll of human vitality.

The characteristic note of the first post-War years was a certain peevishness. A thing had only to have won general acceptance in the past to be flouted. A starveling intellectualism discounted whatever to the ordinary mind seemed moving and heroic. A kind of minor history became popular, in which the writers strove to strip the aura from every great character or great drama of the past, like some Greek of the decadence who chipped the nose of an Apollo of Pheidias in order to make the Goths laugh. In fiction the fashion was for the cloacal or the minutely analytic; in poetry for a breakdown of all shape and a petulant defiance of the orthodox. At the same time an antiquarian spirit was abroad; obscure ancients were disinterred and deified, and the *pastiche* became a fashionable form. In belief, in morals, and in art there was a craze for disintegration, which sought to reduce solid things to mere nebulæ of atoms. The prevalent mood was one of bitterness and disillusion, and, since the older standards were rejected, of an extreme arrogance. To be modern was the only proof of quality, and the 'post-War mind,' brittle and insecure, was regarded as the ultimate flowering of the human spirit. All the familiar *clichés* of a decadence were in use, and an imperfect education prevented the users from realizing how hoary were their darling novelties. This intellectual temper was matched in social life by a kind of joyless gaiety, without manners or grace. Anxious elders in their haste set down the new youth as trivial in soul and shallow in mind.

The mood did not last. At first the younger generation, more demoralized by the War than those who had fought in it, clamored only for a safe niche and a 'soft option' in life. Ease and security seemed the only ends. But presently youth found its bearings again. In letters there appeared a manlier strain, a return of confidence, humanity, and hope. The writers might be extravagant and wildly empirical, but they were cheerfully facing a new world and striving after a new interpretation. If they had not found a gospel, they recognized the need of one. To those who had the chance of seeing much of the youth of Britain, the change between the beginning and the end of the post-War decade seemed little short of a miracle. In spite of growing difficulties in making a living, young men carried their heads high. It was as if they realized that they were living in a hard world, and must make certain that there was no hardship in it which they could not face. There was an honest craving for discipline and construction, for they had grown tired of the atomist and the disintegrator. The appeal to many of creeds like communism and fascism was simply the opportunity they gave for sacrifice. The new temper had its perils, but it had also its splendid promise. The idealism, which seemed to have gone to earth after peace, was now again abroad in the world. There was visible, too, one incontrovertible gain from the War. It had done much to break down class barriers and kill a shoddy gentility. The young man of the educated classes today is at home, as his father could never have been, in a Hull trawler, or working on the soil with unemployed miners, or lending a hand with the Canadian harvest. He is tougher in fibre, more resourceful, more human.

* * *

The older histories were built up on fortunes of Cabinets and Parliaments. Politics were 'decontrolled,' like other things, when the Coalition Cabinet fell in the autumn of 1922, but the Governments which ensued were not the milestones in the national progress which Governments had once been. Mr. Bonar Law succeeded Mr. Lloyd George, and, when ill-health compelled him to resign, he was followed by Mr. Baldwin. The election in the autumn of 1923 brought for the first time a Labor Government into office, a minority Government dependent on Liberal votes. It fell in the next autumn, and for five years the Conservatives were in power with a great majority. In 1929 a Labor Government was again installed, also a minority Government, and in 1931 came the economic crisis and the formation of a National Government under the Labor Prime Minister. But, except the last, these were changes of no profound significance. Any Government, whatever its election program, had to face the same problems as its predecessor, and very much in the same way. Urgent facts had played havoc with party creeds. At no time in our history, perhaps, has party interest sunk so low as in recent years. This is due in some degree to the fact that our democracy is now plebiscitary, and with universal franchise an election has become a scuffle and a gamble as compared with the old, well-planned contests. But it is largely due to the fact that in a crisis like war or impending bankruptcy the ordinary party business means little. Its use will come again, but that day is not yet.

Few of the men remain who were the foremost public figures before and during the War. The great sailors survive, but of the generals, Haig and three of his army commanders are gone. Asquith and Balfour, Curzon and Milner, have taken with them some of the high traditions of an earlier Britain, dignity in speech and demeanor, subtlety and precision of thought, a passionate belief in an imperial mission, and a supreme administrative talent. This is not the place to write of those who are left, except to say that the succession is not broken. War left a lamentable gap in our youth, but happily there are brilliant younger figures left to bridge that gap. One fact may be noted. The War and the first years of peace did not increase the prestige of Parliament, but the downfall of constitutional government in Europe has revived it. Once again Parliament means much to our people, a thing of their own contriving which they will defend against all attacks, since it is intertwined with their liberties. It is an opportune moment, if statesmen are wise, for that reform in its procedure and in its mode of election which will fit it to meet the stresses of a new age. Plebiscitary democracy, unless it be wisely regulated, may relapse into a meaningless see-saw.

In the disorder of the world every people has felt the need of concentration. This has been done elsewhere by nations surrendering their wills to dictators and camarilla. Britain, with a wiser instinct, has clung to her old institutions, but has modified them to meet new needs. The formation of a National Government in August, 1931, was typical of our land, which brought to the task all her constitutional resources. And not least the Throne. On August 21 the King arrived at Balmoral for his Scottish holiday: next day he returned to London. It was not for him to have any economic policy or any preference as between parties. The common procedure would have been for Mr. MacDonald to resign, and give place to the Conservatives. But, as the trustee of the nation, the King felt that a national emergency should be faced by a national front. His view was accepted by Ministers, and a National Government was formed. That it was also the desire of the people the ensuing election gave instant proof.

TWENTIETH-CENTURY POETRY

In the second year of the century, William Archer, a very competent critic, reviewing the 'Poets of the Younger Generation,' noted a 'general tendency among cultivated people to assume that English poetry has of late entered upon a temporary or permanent period of decadence.' This assumption seemed to be borne out in the following years by the fact that such poems as attracted general attention were written by men who had made their mark in the previous century—Rudyard Kipling, or W. B. Yeats, or John Davidson or Francis Thompson, George Meredith or Thomas Hardy. *The Dynasts* by the last mentioned was undoubtedly the greatest achievement in English poetry between the beginning of the century and the outbreak of the European War. Just before the War, the publication of *Georgian Poetry 1911-12* seemed to justify the belief that 'English poetry is now once again putting on a new strength and beauty, and that we are at the beginning of another "Georgian period" which may take rank in due time with the several great poetic ages of the past.' The little volume had a very favorable reception, but the hope of which it was the expression and the promise ended on August 4, 1914, when England entered the War. Rupert Brooke, the most promising of the young band of singing birds, died in April, 1915, on the ill fated expedition to the Dardanelles, and others followed him swiftly to the grave—Julian Grenfell, Charles Hamilton Sorley and Edward Thomas—to mention only those of whose work examples are given below. Nor did the War and the results of the War offer any spiritual compensation for the extinction of so much youthful promise. Many of the young fellows who had gone to the front with exalted devotion, if they returned at all, returned as physical or spiritual wrecks; faith in God and man dwindled, patriotism degenerated into selfish nationalism or sheer cynicism, the prevalent tone of the after-war poetry became one of discontent, disillusion and even despair—typified in T. S. Eliot's *The Waste Land*. The 'famous victory' was blunderingly exploited by the crass egotism of the Versailles Treaty. The England which the War Premier had promised to make a country 'fit for heroes to live in,' became the England of financial collapse, commercial disorganization, unemployment and 'the dole.' The saying of the ancient prophet was fulfilled: 'The fathers have eaten sour grapes and the children's teeth are set on edge.'

JOHN MASEFIELD
(1874-   )

SEA-FEVER

I must down to the seas again, to the lonely sea
    and the sky,
And all I ask is a tall ship and a star to steer
    her by,
And the wheel's kick and the wind's song and
    the white sail's shaking,
And a gray mist on the sea's face and a gray
    dawn breaking.

I must down to the seas again, for the call of the
    running tide   5
Is a wild call and a clear call that may not be
    denied;
And all I ask is a windy day with the white
    clouds flying,
And the flung spray and the blown spume, and
    the sea-gulls crying.

I must down to the seas again to the vagrant
    gipsy life,
To the gull's way and the whale's way where the
    wind's like a whetted knife;   10
And all I ask is a merry yarn from a laughing
    fellow-rover,
And quiet sleep and a sweet dream when the
    long trick's over.

(1903)

HILAIRE BELLOC
(1870-   )

THE SOUTH COUNTRY

When I am living in the midlands,
    That are sodden and unkind,
I light my lamp in the evening:
    My work is left behind;
And the great hills of the South Country   5
    Come back into my mind.

The great hills of the South Country
    They stand along the sea,
And it's there, walking in the high woods,
    That I could wish to be,   10
And the men that were boys when I was a boy
    Walking along with me.

The men that live in North England
  I saw them for a day:
Their hearts are set upon the waste fells, 15
  Their skies are fast and gray;
From their castle-walls a man may see
  The mountains far away.

The men that live in West England
  They see the Severn strong, 20
A-rolling on rough water brown
  Light aspen leaves along.
They have the secret of the rocks,
  And the oldest kind of song.

But the men that live in the South Country
  Are the kindest and most wise, 26
They get their laughter from the loud surf,
  And the faith in their happy eyes
Comes surely from our Sister the Spring
  When over the sea she flies; 30
The violets suddenly bloom at her feet,
  She blesses us with surprise.

I never get between the pines
  But I smell the Sussex air;
Nor I never come on a belt of sand 35
  But my home is there.
And along the sky the line of the Downs
  So noble and so bare.

A lost thing could I never find,
  Nor a broken thing mend: 40
And I fear I shall be all alone
  When I get towards the end.
Who will be there to comfort me
  Or who will be my friend?

I will gather and carefully make my friends 45
  Of the men of the Sussex Weald.
They watch the stars from silent folds,
  They stiffly plow the field.
By them and the God of the South Country
  My poor soul shall be healed. 50

If I ever become a rich man,
  Or if ever I grow to be old,
I will build a house with deep thatch
  To shelter me from the cold,
And there shall the Sussex songs be sung 55
  And the story of Sussex told.

I will hold my house in the high wood,
  Within a walk of the sea,
And the men that were boys when I was a boy
  Shall sit and drink with me. 60
(1916)

WALTER DE LA MARE
(1873-)

ALL THAT'S PAST

VERY old are the woods;
  And the buds that break
Out of the briar's boughs,
  When March winds wake,
So old with their beauty are— 5
  Oh, no man knows
Through what wild centuries
  Roves back the rose.

Very old are the brooks;
  And the rills that rise 10
Where snows sleep cold beneath
  The azure skies
Sing such a history
  Of come and gone,
Their every drop is as wise 15
  As Solomon.

Very old are we men;
  Our dreams are tales
Told in dim Eden
  By Eve's nightingales; 20
We wake and whisper awhile,
  But, the day gone by,
Silence and sleep like fields
  Of amaranth lie.
(1912)

MISS LOO

WHEN thin-strewn memory I look through,
I see most clearly poor Miss Loo,
Her tabby cat, her cage of birds,
Her nose, her hair—her muffled words,
And how she'd open her green eyes, 5
As if in some immense surprise,
Whenever as we sat at tea,
She made some small remark to me.

It's always drowsy summer when
From out the past she comes again; 10
The westering sunshine in a pool
Floats in her parlor still and cool;
While the slim bird its lean wires shakes,
As into piercing song it breaks;
Till Peter's pale-green eyes ajar 15
Dream, wake; wake, dream, in one brief bar;

And I am sitting, dull and shy,
And she with gaze of vacancy,
And large hands folded on the tray,
Musing the afternoon away; 20
Her satin bosom heaving slow
With sighs that softly ebb and flow,
And her plain face in such dismay.

It seems unkind to look her way:
Until all cheerful back will come   25
Her cheerful gleaming spirit home:
And one would think that poor Miss Loo
Asked nothing else, if she had you.

(1912)

RUPERT BROOKE
(1887–1915)

THE OLD VICARAGE, GRANTCHESTER
(Café des Westens, Berlin, May, 1912)

Just now the lilac is in bloom,
All before my little room;
And in my flower-beds, I think,
Smile the carnation and the pink;
And down the borders, well I know,   5
The poppy and the pansy blow . . .
Oh! there the chestnuts, summer through,
Beside the river make for you
A tunnel of green gloom, and sleep
Deeply above; and green and deep   10
The stream mysterious glides beneath,
Green as a dream and deep as death.
—Oh, damn! I know it! and I know
How the May fields all golden show,
And when the day is young and sweet,   15
Gild gloriously the bare feet
That run to bathe. . . .
                        Du lieber Gott!

Here am I, sweating, sick, and hot,
And there the shadowed waters fresh   20
Lean up to embrace the naked flesh.
Temperamentvoll German Jews
Drink beer around;—and *there* the dews
Are soft beneath a morn of gold.
Here tulips bloom as they are told;   25
Unkempt about those hedges blows
An English unofficial rose;
And there the unregulated sun
Slopes down to rest when day is done,
And wakes a vague unpunctual star,   30
A slippered Hesper; and there are
Meads towards Haslingfield and Coton
Where *das Betreten* 's not *verboten.*

εἴθε γενοίμην . . . would I were
In Grantchester, in Grantchester!—   35
Some, it may be, can get in touch
With Nature there, or Earth, or such.
And clever modern men have seen
A Faun a-peeping through the green,
And felt the Classics were not dead,   40
To glimpse a Naiad's reedy head,
Or hear the Goat-foot piping low: . . .
But these are things I do not know,
I only know that you may lie
Day long and watch the Cambridge sky,   45
And, flower-lulled in sleepy grass,
Hear the cool lapse of hours pass,
Until the centuries blend and blur
In Grantchester, in Grantchester. . . .
Still in the dawnlit waters cool   50
His ghostly Lordship swims his pool,
And tries the strokes, essays the tricks,
Long learnt on Hellespont, or Styx.
Dan Chaucer hears his river still
Chatter beneath a phantom mill.   55
Tennyson notes, with studious eye,
How Cambridge waters hurry by . . .
And in that garden, black and white,
Creep whispers through the grass all night;
And spectral dance, before the dawn,   60
A hundred vicars down the lawn;
Curates, long dust, will come and go
On lissom, clerical, printless toe;
And oft between the boughs is seen
The sly shade of a Rural Dean . . .   65
Till, at a shiver in the skies,
Vanishing with Satanic cries,
The prim ecclesiastic rout
Leaves but a startled sleeper-out,
Gray heavens, the first bird's drowsy calls,   70
The falling house that never falls.

God! I will pack, and take a train,
And get me to England once again!
For England's the one land, I know,
Where men with Splendid Hearts may go;   75
And Cambridgeshire, of all England,
The shire for Men who Understand;
And of *that* district I prefer
The lovely hamlet Grantchester.
For Cambridge people rarely smile,   80
Being urban, squat, and packed with guile;
And Royston men in the far South
Are black and fierce and strange of mouth;
At Over they fling oaths at one,
And worse than oaths at Trumpington,   85
And Ditton girls are mean and dirty,
And there's none in Harston under thirty,
And folks in Shelford and those parts
Have twisted lips and twisted hearts,
And Barton men make Cockney rhymes,   90
And Coton's full of nameless crimes,
And things are done you 'd not believe
At Madingley on Christmas Eve.
Strong men have run for miles and miles
When one from Cherry Hinton smiles;   95
Strong men have blanched, and shot their wives,
Rather than send them to St. Ives;
Strong men have cried like babes, bydam,
To hear what happened at Babraham.
But Grantchester! ah, Grantchester!   100
There's peace and holy quiet there,
Great clouds along pacific skies,
And men and women with straight eyes,
Lithe children lovelier than a dream,
A bosky wood, a slumbrous stream,   105

And little kindly winds that creep
Round twilight corners, half asleep.
In Grantchester their skins are white;
They bathe by day, they bathe by night;
The women there do all they ought;   110
The men observe the rules of Thought.
They love the Good; they worship Truth;
They laugh uproariously in youth;
(And when they get to feeling old,
They up and shoot themselves, I'm told) . . .

Ah God! to see the branches stir   116
Across the moon at Grantchester!
To smell the thrilling-sweet and rotten
Unforgettable, unforgotten
River-smell, and hear the breeze   120
Sobbing in the little trees.
Say, do the elm-clumps greatly stand
Still guardians of the holy land?
The chestnuts shade, in reverend dream,
The yet unacademic stream?   125
Is dawn a secret shy and cold
Anadyomene, silver-gold?
And sunset still a golden sea
From Haslingfield to Madingley?
And after, ere the night is born,   130
Do hares come out about the corn?
Oh, is the water sweet and cool,
Gentle and brown, above the pool?
And laughs the immortal river still
Under the mill, under the mill?   135
Say, is there Beauty yet to find?
And Certainty? and Quiet kind?
Deep meadows yet, for to forget
The lies, and truths, and pain? . . . oh! yet
Stands the Church clock at ten to three?   140
And is there honey still for tea?

(1914)

JAMES ELROY FLECKER
(1884–1915)

THE BALLAD OF ISKANDER

*Aflatun and Aristu and King Iskander
Are Plato, Aristotle, Alexander*

SULTAN Iskander sat him down
On his golden throne, in his golden crown,
And shouted 'Wine and flute-girls three,   5
And the Captain, ho! of my ships at sea.'

He drank his bowl of wine; he kept
The flute-girls dancing till they wept,
Praised and kissed their painted lips,
And turned to the Captain of All his Ships.   10

And cried, 'O Lord of my Ships that go
From the Persian Gulf to the Pits of Snow,
Inquire for men unknown to man!'
Said Sultan Iskander of Yoonistan.

'Daroosh is dead, and I am King   15
Of Everywhere and Everything:
Yet leagues and leagues away for sure
The lion-hearted dream of war

'Admiral, I command you sail!
Take you a ship of silver mail,   20
And fifty sailors, young and bold,
And stack provision deep in the hold.

'And seek out twenty men that know
All babel tongues which flaunt and flow;
And stay! Impress those learned two,   25
Old Aflatun, and Aristu.

'And set your prow South-western ways
A thousand bright and dimpling days,
And find me lion-hearted Lords
With breasts to feed Our rusting swords.'   30

The Captain of the Ships bowed low.
'Sir,' he replied, 'I will do so.'
And down he rode to the harbor mouth,
To choose a boat to carry him South.

And he launched a ship of silver mail,   35
With fifty lads to hoist the sail,
And twenty wise—all tongues they knew,
And Aflatun, and Aristu.

There had not dawned the second day
But the glittering galleon sailed away,   40
And through the night like one great bell
The marshalled armies sang farewell.

In twenty days the silver ship
Had passed the Isle of Serendip,
And made the flat Araunian coasts   45
Inhabited, at noon, by Ghosts.

In thirty days the ship was far
Beyond the land of Calcobar,
Where men drink Dead Men's Blood for wine,
And dye their beards alizarine.   50

But on the hundredth day there came
Storm with his windy wings aflame,
And drave them out to that Lone Sea
Whose shores are near Eternity.

* * *

For seven years and seven years   55
Sailed those forgotten mariners,
Nor could they spy on either hand
The faintest level of good red land.

Bird or fish they saw not one;
There swam no ship beside their own,   60
And day-night long the lilied Deep
Lay round them, with its flowers asleep.

The beams began to warp and crack,
The silver plates turned filthy black
And drooping down on the carven rails 65
Hung those once lovely silken sails.

And all the great ship's crew who were
Such noble lads to do and dare
Grew old and tired of the changeless sky
And laid them down on the deck to die. 70

And they who spake all tongues there be
Made antics with solemnity,
Or closely huddled each to each
Talked ribald in a foreign speech.

And Aflatun and Aristu 75
Let their Beards grow, and their Beards grew
Round and about the mainmast tree
Where they stood still, and watched the sea.

And day by day their Captain grey
Knelt on the rotting poop to pray: 80
And yet despite ten thousand prayers
They saw no ship that was not theirs.

* * *

When thrice the seven years had passed
They saw a ship, a ship at last!
Untarnished glowed its silver mail, 85
Windless bellied its silken sail.

With a shout the grizzled sailors rose
Cursing the years of sick repose,
And they who spake in tongues unknown
Gladly reverted to their own. 90

The Captain leapt and left his prayers
And hastened down the dust-dark stairs,
And taking to hand a brazen Whip
He woke to life the long dead ship.

But Aflatun and Aristu, 95
Who had no work that they could do,
Gazed at the stranger Ship and Sea
With their beards around the mainmast tree.

Nearer and nearer the new boat came, 99
Till the hands cried out on the old ship's shame—
'Silken sail to a silver boat,
We too shone when we first set float!'

Swifter and swifter the bright boat sped,
But the hands spake thin like men long dead—
'How striking like that boat were we 105
In the days, sweet days, when we put to sea.'

The ship all black and the ship all white
Met like the meeting of day and night,
Met, and there lay serene dark green
A twilight yard of the sea between. 110

And the twenty masters of foreign speech
Of every tongue they knew tried each;
Smiling, the silver Captain heard,
But shook his head and said no word.

Then Aflatun and Aristu 115
Addressed the silver Lord anew,
Speaking their language of Yoonistan
Like countrymen to a countryman.

And 'Whence' they cried, 'O Sons of Pride,
Sail you the dark eternal tide? 120
Lie your halls to the South or North,
And who is the King that sent you forth?'

'We live,' replied that Lord with a smile,
'A mile beyond the millionth mile.
We know not South and we know not North, 125
And SULTAN ISKANDER sent us forth.'

Said Aristu to Aflatun—
'Surely our King, despondent soon,
Has sent this second ship to find
Unconquered tracts of humankind.' 130

But Aflatun turned round on him
Laughing a bitter laugh and grim.
'Alas,' he said, 'O Aristu,
A white weak thin old fool are you.

'And does yon silver Ship appear 135
As she had journeyed twenty year?
And has that silver Captain's face
A mortal or Immortal grace?

'Theirs is the land (as well I know)
Where live the Shapes of Things Below: 140
Theirs is the country where they keep
The Images men see in Sleep.

'Theirs is the Land beyond the Door,
And theirs the old ideal shore.
They steer our ship: behold our crew 145
Ideal, and our Captain too.

'And lo! beside that mainmast tree
Two tall and shining forms I see,
And they are what we ought to be,
Yet we are they, and they are we.' 150

He spake, and some young Zephyr stirred,
The two ships touched: no sound was heard;
The Black Ship crumbled into air;
Only the Phantom Ship was there.

And a great cry rang round the sky 155
Of glorious singers sweeping by,
And calm and fair on waves that shone
The Silver Ship sailed on and on.

(1911)

POEMS OF THE GREAT WAR

FOR THE FALLEN

With proud thanksgiving, a mother for her children,
England mourns for her dead across the sea.
Flesh of her flesh they were, spirit of her spirit,
    Fallen in the cause of the free.

Solemn the drums thrill: Death august and royal
Sings sorrow up into immortal spheres.
There is music in the midst of desolation
    And a glory that shines upon our tears.

They went with songs to the battle, they were young,
Straight of limb, true of eye, steady and aglow.
They were stanch to the end against odds uncounted,
    They fell with their faces to the foe.

They shall grow not old, as we that are left grow old:
Age shall not weary them, nor the years contemn.
At the going down of the sun and in the morning
    We will remember them.

They mingle not with their laughing comrades again;
They sit no more at familiar tables of home;
They have no lot in our labor of the daytime;
    They sleep beyond England's foam.

But where our desires are and our hopes profound,
Felt as a well-spring that is hidden from sight,
To the innermost heart of their own land they are known
    As the stars are known to the Night;

As the stars that shall be bright when we are dust,
Moving in marches upon the heavenly plain;
As the stars that are starry in the time of our darkness,
    To the end, to the end, they remain.

                LAURENCE BINYON

THE SOLDIER

If I should die, think only this of me:
That there's some corner of a foreign field
That is forever England. There shall be
In that rich earth a richer dust concealed;
A dust whom England bore, shaped, made aware,
Gave, once, her flowers to love, her ways to roam,
A body of England's, breathing English air,
Washed by the rivers, blest by suns of home.
And think, this heart, all evil shed away,
A pulse in the eternal mind, no less
Gives somewhere back the thoughts by England given;
Her sights and sounds; dreams happy as her day;
And laughter, learnt of friends; and gentleness,
In hearts at peace, under an English heaven.

                RUPERT BROOKE

THE WIFE OF FLANDERS

Low and brown barns thatched and repatched and tattered
    Where I had seven sons until to-day,
A little hill of hay your spur has scattered . . .
    This is not Paris. You have lost the way.

You, staring at your sword to find it brittle,
    Surprised at the surprise that was your plan,
Who, shaking and breaking barriers not a little,
    Find never more the death-door of Sedan.

Must I for more than carnage call you claimant,
    Paying you a penny for each son you slay?
Man, the whole globe in gold were no repayment
    For what *you* have lost. And how shall I repay?

What is the price of that red spark that caught me
    From a kind farm that never had a name?
What is the price of that dead man they brought me?
    For other dead men do not look the same.

How should I pay for one poor graven steeple
    Whereon you shattered what you shall not know,
How should I pay you, miserable people?
    How should I pay you everything you owe?

Unhappy, can I give you back your honor?
    Though I forgave would any man forget?
While all the great green land has trampled on her
    The treason and terror of the night we met.

Not any more in vengeance or in pardon
    An old wife bargains for a bean that's hers,
You have no word to break; no heart to harden,
    Ride on and prosper. You have lost your spurs.

                GILBERT K. CHESTERTON

A HARROW GRAVE IN FLANDERS

Here in the marshland, past the battered bridge,
   One of a hundred grains untimely sown,
Here, with his comrades of the hard-won ridge
     He rests, unknown.

His horoscope had seemed so plainly drawn,   5
   School triumphs, earned apace in work and play;
Friendships at will; then love's delightful dawn
     And mellowing day.

Home fostering hope; some service to the State;
   Benignant age; then the lost tryst to keep   10
Where in the yew-tree shadow congregate
     His fathers sleep.

Was here the one thing needful to distil
   From life's alembic, through this holier fate,
The man's essential soul, the hero-will?   15
     We ask; and wait.
        Robert Offley Ashburton,
        Lord Crewe

'HOW SLEEP THE BRAVE'

Nay, nay, sweet England, do not grieve!
   Not one of these poor men who died
But did within his soul believe
   That death for thee was glorified.

Ever they watched it hovering near   5
   That mystery 'yond thought to plumb,
Perchance sometimes in loathèd fear
   They heard cold Danger whisper, Come!—

Heard and obeyed. Oh, if thou weep
   Such courage and honor, beauty, care,   10
Be it for joy that those who sleep
   Only thy joy could share.
        Walter de la Mare

THE DEFENDERS

His wage of rest at nightfall still
   He takes, who sixty years has known
Of plowing over Cotsall hill
   And keeping trim the Cotsall stone.

He meditates the dusk, and sees   5
   Folds of his wonted shepherdings
And lands of stubble and tall trees
   Becoming insubstantial things.

And does he see on Cotsall hill—
   Thrown even to the central shire—   10
The funnelled shapes forbidding still
   The stranger from his cottage fire?
        John Drinkwater

RAINING

The night I left my father said:
   'You'll go and do some stupid thing.
You've no more sense in that fat head
   Than Silly Billy Witterling.

'Not sense to come in when it rains—   5
   Not sense enough for that, you've got.
You'll get a bullet through your brains,
   Before you know, as like as not.'

And now I'm lying in the trench
   And shells and bullets through the night   10
Are raining in a steady drench,
   I'm thinking the old man was right.
        W. W. Gibson

THE QUESTION

I wonder if the old cow died or not.
   Gey bad she was the night I left, and sick.
Dick reckoned she would mend. He knows a lot—
   At least he fancies so himself, does Dick.

Dick knows a lot. But maybe I did wrong   5
   To leave the cow to him, and come away.
Over and over like a silly song
   These words keep bumming in my head all day.

And all I think of, as I face the foe
   And take my lucky chance of being shot,   10
Is this—that if I'm hit I'll never know
   Till Doomsday if the old cow died or not.
        W. W. Gibson

HIS FATHER

I quite forgot to put the spigot in.
   It's just come over me. . . . And it is queer
To think he'll not care if we lose or win
   And yet be jumping-mad about that beer.

I left it running full. He must have said   5
   A thing or two. I'd give my stripes to hear
What he will say if I'm reported dead
   Before he gets me told about that beer!
        W. W. Gibson

THE AIRMAN

Wild wind, and drear, beneath the pale stars blowing,
   Whom do you hunt to-night?
Out of the west into the storm-cloud glowing
   A biplane wings her flight.

In the gray day-dawn was there no returning, 5
  No homewards for the dead:—
Only a broken wing, a biplane burning,
  A shattered airship shed!

O Nation proud, on whose red altar gladly
  One more young Life is laid, 10
Scatter the news—flutter the posters madly—
  'Triumph of British raid!'

What of the Cross they brought to her—his Mother?
  Wanly her dumb lips smiled,
Then whispered: 'Give back *him*—I had no other— 15
  My Son—my only child.'
GREGG GODDARD

INTO BATTLE

THE naked earth is warm with Spring,
  And with green grass and bursting trees
Leans to the sun's gaze glorying,
  And quivers in the sunny breeze;

And Life is Color and Warmth and Light, 5
  And a striving evermore for these;
And he is dead who will not fight;
  And who dies fighting has increase.

The fighting man shall from the sun
  Take warmth, and life from the glowing earth; 10
Speed with the light-foot winds to run,
  And with the trees to newer birth;
And find, when fighting shall be done,
  Great rest, and fullness after dearth.

All the bright company of Heaven 15
  Hold him in their high comradeship,
The Dog-Star and the Sisters Seven,
  Orion's Belt and sworded hip.

The woodland trees that stand together,
  They stand to him each one a friend; 20
They gently speak in the windy weather;
  They guide to valley and ridges' end.

The kestrel hovering by day,
  And the little owls that call by night,
Bid him be swift and keen as they, 25
  As keen of ear, as swift of sight.

The blackbird sings to him, 'Brother, brother,
  If this be the last song you shall sing,
Sing well, for you may not sing another;
  Brother, sing.'

In dreary doubtful waiting hours, 30
  Before the brazen frenzy starts,
The horses show him nobler powers;
  O patient eyes, courageous hearts!

And when the burning moment breaks,
  And all things else are out of mind, 35
And only Joy-of-Battle takes
  Him by the throat, and makes him blind,

Through joy and blindness he shall know,
  Not caring much to know, that still
Nor lead nor steel shall reach him, so 40
  That it be not the Destined Will.

The thundering line of battle stands,
  And in the air Death moans and sings;
But Day shall clasp him with strong hands,
  And Night shall fold him in soft wings. 45
JULIAN GRENFELL
Flanders, April, 1915.

THE WYKHAMIST

IN the wake of the yellow sunset one pale star
Hangs over the darkening city's purple haze.
An errand-boy in the street beneath me plays
On a penny whistle. Very faint and far
Comes the scroop of tortured gear on a battered car. 5
A hyacinth nods pallid blooms on the window sill,
Swayed by the tiny wind. St. Catherine's Hill
Is a place of mystery, a land of dreams.
The tramp of soldiers, barrack-marching, seems
A thing remote, untouched by fate or time. 10
. . . A year ago you heard Cathedral's chime,
You hurried up to books—a year ago;
—Shouted for 'Houses' in New Field below.
. . . You . . . 'died of wounds' . . . they told me
      . . . yet your feet 15
Pass with the others down the twilit street.
NORA GRIFFITHS

SOLDIER, SOLDIER

SOLDIER, soldier, off to war,
Take me a letter to my sweetheart O.
  He's gone away to France
  With his carbine and his lance,
And a lock of brown hair of his sweetheart O. 5

*Fair maid of London, happy may you be
To know so much of your sweetheart O.
  There's not a handsome lad,
  To get the chance he's had,
But would skip, with a kiss for his sweetheart O.* 10

Soldier, soldier, whatever shall I do
If the cruel Germans take my sweetheart O?
  They'll pen him in the jail
  And starve him thin and pale,
With never a kind word from his sweetheart O.

Fair maid of London, is that all you see   16
Of the lad you've taken for your sweetheart O?
  He'll make his prison ring
  With his God Save the King
And his God bless the blue eyes of my sweetheart O!

Soldier, soldier, if by shot or shell   21
They wound him, my dear lad, my sweetheart O,
  He'll lie bleeding in the rain
  And call me, all in vain.
Crying for the fingers of his sweetheart O.   25

Pretty one, pretty one, now take a word from me:
Don't you grudge the life-blood of your sweetheart O.
  For you must understand
  He gives it to our land,
And proud should fly the colors of his sweetheart O.   30

Soldier, soldier, my heart is growing cold—
If a German shot kill my sweetheart O!
  I could not lift my head
  If my dear love lay dead
With his wide eyes waiting for his sweetheart O.

Poor child, poor child, go to church and pray,   36
Pray God to spare you your sweetheart O.
  But if he live or die
  The English flag must fly,
And England take care of his sweetheart O!   40
                MAURICE HEWLETT

THE SPIRES OF OXFORD

I saw the spires of Oxford
  As I was passing by,
The gray spires of Oxford
  Against a pearl-gray sky.
My heart was with the Oxford men   5
  Who went abroad to die.

The years go fast in Oxford,
  The golden years and gay,
The hoary Colleges look down
  On careless boys at play.   10
But when the bugles sounded war
  They put their games away.

They left the peaceful river,
  The cricket-field, the quad,
The shaven lawns of Oxford   15
  To seek a bloody sod—
They gave their merry youth away
  For country and for God.

God rest you, happy gentlemen,
  Who laid your good lives down,   20
Who took the khaki and the gun
  Instead of cap and gown.
God bring you to a fairer place
  Than even Oxford town.
                WINIFRED M. LETTS

MANY SISTERS TO MANY BROTHERS

When we fought the campaigns (in the long Christmas rains)
  With soldiers spread in troops on the floor,
I shot as straight as you, my losses were as few,
  My victories as many, or more.
And when in naval battle, amid cannon's rattle,
  Fleet met fleet in the bath,   6
My cruisers were as trim, my battleships as grim,
  My submarines cut as swift a path.
Or, when it rained too long, and the strength of the strong
  Surged up and broke a way with blows,   10
I was as fit and keen, my fists hit as clean,
  Your black eye matched my bleeding nose.
Was there a scrap of play in which you, the boy,
  Could better me? You could not climb higher,
Ride straighter, run as quick (and to smoke made you sick)
. . . But I sit here, and you're under fire   16
Oh, it's you that have the luck, out there in blood and muck:
  You were born beneath a kindly star;
All we dreamt, I and you, you can really go and do,
  And I can't, the way things are.   20
In a trench you are sitting, while I am knitting
  A hopeless sock that never gets done.
Well, here's luck, my dear;—and you've got it, no fear;
  But for me . . . a war is poor fun.
                ROSE MACAULAY

THE ISLAND OF SKYROS

Here, where we stood together, we three men,
Before the war had swept us to the East
Three thousand miles away, I stand again
And hear the bells, and breathe, and go to feast.

We trod the same path, to the self-same place,   5
Skyros whose shadows the great seas erase,
Yet here I stand, having beheld their graves,
And Seddul Bahr that ever more blood craves.

So, since we communed here, our bones have been
Nearer, perhaps, than they again will be,   10
Earth and the world-wide battle lie between,
Death lies between, and friend-destroying sea.
Yet here, a year ago, we talked and stood
As I stand now, with pulses beating blood.

I saw her like a shadow on the sky   15
In the last light, a blur upon the sea,
Then the gale's darkness put the shadow by,
But from one grave that island talked to me;

And, in the midnight, in the breaking storm,
I saw its blackness and a blinking light,   20
And thought, 'So death obscures your gentle form,
So memory strives to make the darkness bright;

And, in that heap of rocks, your body lies,
Part of the island till the planet ends,
My gentle comrade, beautiful and wise,   25
Part of this crag this bitter surge offends,
While I, who pass, a little obscure thing,
War with this force, and breathe, and am its king.'

JOHN MASEFIELD

THE SEARCHLIGHTS

Political morality differs from individual morality because there is no power above the state.—GENERAL VON BERNHARDI.

SHADOW by shadow, stripped for fight
   The lean black cruisers search the sea.
Night-long their level shafts of light
   Revolve, and find no enemy.
Only they know each leaping wave   5
May hide the lightning, and their grave.

And in the land they guard so well
   Is there no silent watch to keep?
An age is dying, and the bell
   Rings midnight on a vaster deep.   10
But over all its waves, once more
The searchlights move, from shore to shore.

And captains that we thought were dead,
   And dreamers that we thought were dumb,
And voices that we thought were fled,   15
   Arise, and call us, and we come;
And 'search in thine own soul,' they cry;
'For there, too, lurks thine enemy.'

Search for the foe in thine own soul,
   The sloth, the intellectual pride;   20
The trivial jest that veils the goal
   For which our fathers lived and died;
The lawless dreams, the cynic Art,
That rend thy nobler self apart.

Not far, not far into the night,   25
   These level swords of light can pierce;
Yet for her faith does England fight,
   Her faith in this our universe,
Believing Truth and Justice draw
From founts of everlasting law;   30

The law that rules the stars, our stay,
   Our compass through the world's wide sea

The one sure light, the one sure way,
   The one firm base of Liberty;
The one firm road that men have trod   35
Through Chaos to the throne of God.

Therefore a Power above the State,
   The unconquerable Power returns.
The fire, the fire that made her great
   Once more upon her altar burns,   40
Once more, redeemed and healed and whole,
She moves to the Eternal Goal.

ALFRED NOYES

REVENGE FOR RHEIMS

THOU Permanence amid all things that pass!
Unchanging Thought amid the drift of change;
Thou Rally of the Soul in days of dross;
   How art Thou fallen!

Thou Prayer, that ever-rising, yet remained,   5
That for seven hundred years didst sing and soar,
Spirit with wings outspread tip-toe on Earth,
   How art Thou fallen!

Thou Vision frozen, and Thou Sigh transfixed;
Thou Camp of dreams, Thou Fort of faith unstormed,   10
Time-worn, yet wearying t'ward Eternity,
   How art Thou fallen!

Thou wast to France her Inspiration old,
Thou hadst for ivy earliest memories;
From Thee her Knights, her Angels long looked down;   15
   How art Thou fallen!

What vengeance for Thy ruin shall She hurl?
Oh, be that vengeance, that the ruin stand,
Only those Choirs forever unrestored!
   Ever unfallen!   20

STEPHEN PHILLIPS

SOCKS

SHINING pins that dart and click
   In the fireside's sheltered peace
Check the thoughts that cluster thick—
   20 plain and then decrease.

He was brave—well, so was I—   5
   Keen and merry, but his lip
Quivered when he said good-by—
   Purl the seam-stitch, purl and slip.

Never used to living rough,
   Lots of things he 'd got to learn;   10
Wonder if he 's warm enough—
   Knit 2, catch 2, knit 1, turn.

Hark! The paper-boys again!
  Wish that shout could be suppressed;
Keeps one always on the strain—
Knit off 9, and slip the rest.

Wonder if he's fighting now,
  What he's done an' where he's been;
He'll come out on top, somehow—
Slip 1, knit 2, purl 14.

JESSIE POPE

'ALL THE HILLS AND VALES ALONG'

ALL the hills and vales along
Earth is bursting into song,
And the singers are the chaps
Who are going to die perhaps.
  O sing, marching men,
  Till the valleys ring again.
  Give your gladness to earth's keeping,
  So be glad, when you are sleeping.

Cast away regret and rue,
Think what you are marching to.
Little live, great pass.
Jesus Christ and Barabbas
Were found the same day.
This died, that went his way.
  So sing with joyful breath.
  For why, you are going to death.
  Teeming earth will surely store
  All the gladness that you pour.

Earth that never doubts nor fears,
Earth that knows of death, not tears,
Earth that bore with joyful ease
Hemlock for Socrates,
Earth that blossomed and was glad
'Neath the cross that Christ had,
Shall rejoice and blossom too
When the bullet reaches you.
  Wherefore, men marching
  On the road to death, sing!
  Pour your gladness on earth's head,
  So be merry, so be dead.

From the hills and valleys earth
Shouts back the sound of mirth,
Tramp of feet and lilt of song
Ringing all the road along.
All the music of their going,
Ringing, swinging, glad song-throwing,
Earth will echo still, when foot
Lies numb and voice mute.
  On, marching men, on
  To the gates of death with song
  Sow your gladness for earth's reaping,
  So you may be glad, though sleeping.
  Strew your gladness on earth's bed,
  So be merry, so be dead.

CHARLES HAMILTON SORLEY

A GIRL'S SONG

THE Meuse and Marne have little waves;
  The slender poplars o'er them lean.
One day they will forget the graves
  That give the grass its living green.

Some brown French girl the rose will wear
  That springs above his comely head;
Will twine it in her russet hair,
  Nor wonder why it is so red.

His blood is in the rose's veins,
  His hair is in the yellow corn.
My grief is in the weeping rains
  And in the keening wind forlorn.

Flow softly, softly, Marne and Meuse;
  Tread lightly all ye browsing sheep;
Fall tenderly, O silver dews,
  For here my dear Love lies asleep.

The earth is on his sealèd eyes,
  The beauty marred that was my pride;
Would I were lying where he lies,
  And sleeping sweetly by his side!

The Spring will come by Meuse and Marne,
  The birds be blithesome in the tree.
I heap the stones to make his cairn
  Where many sleep as sound as he.

KATHARINE TYNAN

FROM A FLEMISH GRAVEYARD

A YEAR hence may the grass that waves
O'er English men in Flemish graves,
Coating this clay with green of peace
And softness of a year's increase,
Be kind and lithe as English grass
To bend and nod as the winds pass;
It was for grass on English hills
These bore too soon the last of ills.

And may the wind be brisk and clean,
And singing cheerfully between
The bents a pleasant-burdened song
To cheer these English dead along;
For English songs and English winds
Are they that bred these English minds.

And may the circumstantial trees
Dip, for these dead ones, in the breeze,
And make for them their silver play
Of spangled boughs each shiny day.
Thus may these look above, and see
And hear the wind in grass and tree,
And watch a lark in heaven stand,
And think themselves in their own land.

IOLO ANEURIN WILLIAMS
(January, 1915)

AFTER THE WAR

G. W. ARMITAGE

LANCASHIRE

WHY does nobody write a poem about the cotton trade?
You'd think the poems would crowd up till they touched,
That big paunchy men on the Chamber would go lyrical all over,
And little clerks who work out consular invoices for Havana, and Antofagasta,
And go nights to the Tech. to learn about Crompton and his mule:
Or was it Arkwright? Who kept that mule anyway?
Well, they got to know about it because they mean to get on.
Mean to get on. In Manchester. In cotton. Some pluck, what?

I remember when I was beginning standing under our mill. It was evening.
What a thing! I was a speck under it. It towered over me
Like a black precipice, cut with square port-holes of light.
Out of the dark hull oozed the smell of warm oil:
In the air was that high-pitched hum every spinner knows:
And I stammered You monster! You monster!
Tearing the bales to death in the claws of your breaker,
Spinning them back to life in your racing fingers,
Racing, racing, every part of you racing,
Yet balanced, meticulously co-ordinated, plumb in line,
Biting off just what you chew, and chewing all you bite.
Only a white man could invent a monster like you. No other color could.
Now all the other colors have pinched it,
Rice eaters, grass eaters, smoke eaters. We want meat.
They say that round thing on the Jap flag is a sun. It's a plate of rice.
Below is written *In hoc signo vinces*.

My great-great-grandfather was a hand-loom weaver.
The yarn was so bad they couldn't use cotton for warp. The warp was linen.
There were forty yards to a piece and it took him a week to weave.
At week-end a little mester came,
And took what he'd woven away and gave him some weft and some money.
If no little mester came he clemmed.

In a clough below the fell is the wreck of an old, old mill,
Tiny, no bigger than a tennis court. How could they spin in that?
How could the long procession of ordered ideas march in that match-box?
The roof's gone, the floors are gone, there's nothing to tell you.
But the shell of the wheelhouse stands, and below the maidenhair that feathers the coolstone
In a thick brown stocking of rust the iron axle remains.
I swarmed down the race to know if some old foundryman,
Boulton and Watt perhaps, had cast his name on it.
But if there ever was a name the rust had eaten it:
Axle and bearing had become one flesh, and never will stir again.
The lade was a groove of grass, and I nearly trod on a lark
As she sat her nest in the conduit, the cheeky thing.
No one will ever spin in that valley again:
Sheep you shall find, and moorland grass, and sky,
And a curlew send you his exquisite rippling call.

970

That was the second stage, and then came steam,
And then came everything else. They kicked the lock off
Pandora's box and turned it upside down.
And they made everything right and everything wrong:
Machines that marched the floor with the measured precision of the planetary system,   50
And towns that sprawled in muddles of beastliness:
Had hands tender as a lover's for yarn and hard as Cain's for the children they enslaved.
Was there a bargain? They drove it. An ugliness? They made it.
An obstacle? They cursed at it, and battered at it, and either solved it or botched it,
Being neither demigods nor heroes,   55
But ingenious, hard-working descendants of *homo sapiens*,
Who had the luck to plant their seedlings in kind weather,
Not in the frost or the storm, but when the slow ripening of time, the felicitous crossings of circumstance
Presented unimagined opportunities,
Which they took. And prospered. And grew tall.   60

See that woman weaving in that steam-heated shed? There's a kid coming.
But the Act says she mustn't go on weaving after . . . Oh, it does, does it?
And the Act says the humidity mustn't exceed . . . Oh, it does, does it?
Mustn't exceed warm tea. She's stood eight hours: is she tired? Oh boy!
The kid's just flush with the breast-beam, and from shuttle-box to shuttle-box the racing dart flickers by, flickers by: 65
Do the tiny ears hear through her the roar of her bread-winning?
The warp that shivers and divides, shivers and divides, is Mississippi cotton,
And drifted on scows on cool November mornings, drifted through the somnolent misty opalescence, the far bank a faint pencilled line:
The piece she is weaving will go through the Great Wall of China and ride on a dromedary into Mongolia:
But she only knows it's making-up to-morrow and she'll miss her cut.   70
Race, little dart—*drat it, there's an end broke: leave it while cop end: they'll not fine me for that.*

Buyer on 'Change had a satin the Japs are shipping;
Thirty-two inches, pure rayon, nice colors, tuppence-farthing a yard.
Why, a dyer here would charge you that for the dyeing only;
If you pinched the gray for nothing off a lorry, the dyer, I tell you, would charge you that. And him losing money.   75
Then how the hell——
Here, cut that out. They've found how to save the cotton trade:
London chap, he found it. He spent a whole day in Manchester.
Lancashire must reduce her costs and recover the export trade.
Mister Compositor, have you no more brains than to print God's message to the worms in those measly italics? Stuff it up in capitals . . .   80
LANCASHIRE MUST REDUCE HER COSTS AND RECOVER THE EXPORT TRADE.
There! Does the eyesight good. Stand it on the desk where I can see it.
Lancashire must—— Oh, my God.

I know an economist lives in a library and studies trade.
It's the best place. Inside a library you see all trade, and outside you only see part, the part that hurts.   85
Demand, he said, *is satisfied from the cheapest supply. Productive energies which no longer conform to this condition should be transferred to alternative activities.*
What sheltered lives these long words lead. Never been soaked with sweat or cold with fear. Never been parts of men, like short words.
Productive energies which no longer—that's me and my mill. Are you getting it?
That's Oldham and—No! I won't have it. See here, Professor:
If all the light and heat of a million men is gathered through a burning-glass to one incandescent THIS: 90
If they did THIS before anybody and better than everybody:
If they spun THIS out of themselves and wove it through themselves and dyed it into themselves,
Till no one in the world could think of THIS without thinking of them;

After all that, do you dare, do you dare suddenly to flip them away,
Puff them off like greenfly off roses, discard them, efface them, expunge them, make a vacuum of them,
Merely because some sweltered Asiatic sells an imitation cheaper?
Demand, he said, is satisfied from the cheapest supply. Productive energies which no longer . . .
Oh, do you mind not saying that again? It's more . . . it's more . . .
What a nice library this is of yours.

The white races seem to me like rich kids sitting round a table,
Playing with wonderful toys of their own invention.
Clever as angels, the kids: they never stop inventing.
Down below, under the table, are swarms of dark little figures.
Are they dwarfs? Are they gnomes?
If anything falls from the table they snatch it with eagerness,
And copy it and copy it and copy it,
Murmuring, swarming, like insects, myriads and myriads.
If anything falls it never goes back again.

The cotton trade has fallen off the table.
It will never go back, and yet I keep on thinking
Of little gray mills, tucked into meadows, under beechwoods,
The only mill in the village. Meat, drink, father and mother to the whole village. And stopped.
And of Preston. There's many a weaver in Preston can save the life of a sick warp that in any other land would die.
I've heard tell of an old woman there when she had a fine warp and a bad one she pieced the ends with her hair.
And of Oldham, riding up its hill with all its lances in rest, more spires than Oxford, and lots of them as smokeless.
And of Stockport, with its Roman aqueduct;
And of Glossop, in its plover's nest of moor.

How can you change the flow of a people's life? How can you change the North?
Stubborn, conservative, stoical, proud, contemptuous of advice,
Having marched for a hundred and fifty years in one direction,
Known of all men, sought of all men, suddenly
It awakened to a world that no longer sought it as before.
In the barbarous age the test of the pluck of a bulldog
Was to hack off its leg and still it wouldn't let go.
Lancashire's been through that, and has not let go.
The stubborn millowner, spinning his last ducat down the drain,
The stubborn millhand sticking it, sticking it,
How can you change the set of a people's mind?

Rice eaters, grass eaters, smoke eaters, decent little beggars, I've nothing against them.
But I can't go on writing this because I keep seeing a ship.
Rotten old tramp in the gray dawn sullenly steaming.
Must be a popular boat: brown with passengers: brown as a skep with bees:
All men. All wearing brown. Her sides are funnily painted,
Futurist stuff. What's her name? RIVER CLYDE. River Clyde?
Don't speak that name: it frightens me. What is she doing?
Lancashire men are aboard and they're making a landing.
A landing? There? Not there? Oh Christ, not there?
They have reduced their cost and gained the export trade.
What do you mean? Nothing in the world is worth—Oh God, what have you sold them for?

For nothing.

(1935)

JOSEPH CAMPBELL
(1881–   )

I AM THE MOUNTAINY SINGER

I am the mountainy singer—
   The voice of the peasant's dream,
The cry of the wind on the wooded hill,
   The leap of the fish in the stream.

Quiet and love I sing—   5
   The carn on the mountain crest,
The cailin in her lover's arms,
   The child at its mother's breast.

Beauty and peace I sing—
   The fire on the open hearth,   10
The cailleach spinning at her wheel,
   The plough in the broken earth.

Travail and pain I sing—
   The bride on the childing bed,
The dark man laboring at his rhymes,   15
   The ewe in the lambing shed.

Sorrow and death, I sing—
   The canker come on the corn,
The fisher lost in the mountain loch,
   The cry at the mouth of morn.   20

No other life I sing,
   For I am sprung of the stock
That broke the hilly land for bread,
   And built the nest in the rock.

PADRAIC COLUM
(1881–   )

THE PLOUGHER

Sunset and silence! A man: around him earth savage, earth broken;
Beside him two horses—a plough!

Earth savage, earth broken, the brutes, the dawn-man there in the sunset,
And the Plough that is twin to the Sword, that is founder of cities!

'Brute-tamer, plough-maker, earth-breaker!
   Can'st hear? There are ages between us.   5
Is it praying you are as you stand there alone in the sunset?

'Surely our sky-born gods can be naught to you, earth child and earth master?
Surely your thoughts are of Pan, or of Wotan, or Dana?

'Yet, why give thought to the gods? Has Pan led your brutes where they stumble?
Has Dana numbed pain of the child-bed, or Wotan put hands to your plough?   10

'What matter your foolish reply! O man standing lone and bowed earthward,
Your task is a day near its close. Give thanks to the night-giving God.'

* * *

Slowly the darkness falls, the broken lands blend with the savage;
The brute-tamer stands by the brutes, a head's breadth only above them.

A head's breadth? Ay, but therein is hell's depth, and the height up to heaven,   15
And the thrones of the gods and their halls, their chariots, purples, and splendors.

WHAT THE SHUILER SAID AS SHE LAY BY THE FIRE IN THE FARMER'S HOUSE

I 'm glad to lie on a sack of leaves
By a wasted fire and take my ease.
For the wind would strip me bare as a tree—
The wind would blow old age upon me.
And I 'm dazed with the wind, the rain, and the cold.   5
If I had only the good red gold
To buy me the comfort of a roof,
And under the thatch the brown of the smoke!
I 'd lie up in my painted room
Until my hired girl would come;   10
And when the sun had warmed my walls
I 'd rise up in my silks and shawls,
And break my fast before the fire.
And I 'd watch them that had to sweat
And shiver for shelter and what they ate.   15
The farmer digging in the fields;
The beggars going from gate to gate;
The horses striving with their loads,
And all the sights upon the roads.

I 'd live my lone without clan or care,   20
And none about me to crave a share.
The young have mocking, impudent ways,
And I 'd never let them a-nigh my place.
And a child has often a pitiful face.

I 'd give the rambling fiddler rest,   25
And for me he would play his best.
And he 'd have something to tell of me
From the Moat of Granard down to the sea!
And, though I 'd keep distant, I 'd let in
Old women who would card and spin   30
And clash with me, and I 'd hear it said,
'Mór who used to carry her head
As if she was a lady bred—

Has little enough in her house, they say—
And such-a-one's child I saw on the way   35
Scaring crows from a crop, and glad to get,
In a warmer house, the bit to eat.
O! none are safe, and none secure,
And it's well for some whose bit is sure!'

I'd never grudge them the weight of their lands
If I had only the good red gold   41
To huggle between my breast and hands!

WILLIAM H. DAVIES
(1870-   )

LEISURE

What is this life if, full of care,
We have no time to stand and stare.

No time to stand beneath the boughs
And stare as long as sheep or cows.

No time to see, when woods we pass,   5
Where squirrels hide their nuts in grass.

No time to see, in broad daylight,
Streams full of stars, like stars at night.

No time to turn at Beauty's glance,
And watch her feet, how they can dance.   10

No time to wait till her mouth can
Enrich that smile her eyes began.

A poor life this if, full of care,
We have no time to stand and stare.

MONEY

When I had money, money, O!
  I knew no joy till I went poor;
For many a false man as a friend
  Came knocking all day at my door.

Then felt I like a child that holds   5
  A trumpet that he must not blow
Because a man is dead; I dared
  Not speak to let this false world know.

Much have I thought of life, and seen
  How poor men's hearts are ever light;   10
And how their wives do hum like bees
  About their work from morn till night.

So, when I hear these poor ones laugh
  And see the rich ones coldly frown—
Poor men, think I, need not go up   15
  So much as rich men should come down.

When I had money, money, O!
  My many friends proved all untrue;
But now I have no money, O!
  My friends are real, though very few.   20

SHEEP

When I was once in Baltimore,
  A man came up to me and cried,
'Come, I have eighteen hundred sheep,
  And we will sail on Tuesday's tide.

'If you will sail with me, young man,   5
  I'll pay you fifty shillings down;
These eighteen hundred sheep I take
  From Baltimore to Glasgow town.'

He paid me fifty shillings down,
  I sailed with eighteen hundred sheep;   10
We soon had cleared the harbor's mouth,
  We soon were in the salt sea deep.

The first night we were out at sea
  Those sheep were quiet in their mind;
The second night they cried with fear—   15
  They smelt no pastures in the wind.

They sniffed, poor things, for their green fields,
  They cried so loud I could not sleep:
For fifty thousand shillings down
  I would not sail again with sheep.   20

THE MUSE

I have no ale,
  No wine I want;
No ornaments,
  My meat is scant.

No maid is near,   5
  I have no wife;
But here's my pipe
  And, on my life:

With it to smoke,
  And woo the Muse,   10
To be a king
  I would not choose.

But I crave all,
  When she does fail—
Wife, ornaments,   15
  Meat, wine and ale.

T. S. ELIOT
(1888-   )

THE *BOSTON EVENING TRANSCRIPT*

The readers of the *Boston Evening Transcript*
Sway in the wind like a field of ripe corn.

When evening quickens faintly in the street,
Wakening the appetites of life in some
And to others bringing the *Boston Evening
  Transcript*,   5
I mount the steps and ring the bell, turning

Wearily, as one would turn to nod good-bye to
    Rochefoucauld,
If the street were time and he at the end of the
    street,
And I say, 'Cousin Harriet, here is the *Boston
    Evening Transcript*.'

AUNT HELEN

Miss Helen Slingsby was my maiden aunt,
And lived in a small house near a fashionable
    square
Cared for by servants to the number of four.
Now when she died there was silence in heaven
And silence at her end of the street.   5
The shutters were drawn and the undertaker
    wiped his feet—
He was aware that this sort of thing had oc-
    curred before.
The dogs were handsomely provided for,
But shortly afterwards the parrot died too.
The Dresden clock continued ticking on the
    mantelpiece,   10
And the footman sat upon the dining-table
Holding the second housemaid on his knees—
Who had always been so careful while her mis-
    tress lived.

COUSIN NANCY

Miss Nancy Ellicott
Strode across the hills and broke them,
Rode across the hills and broke them—
The barren New England hills—
Riding to hounds   5
Over the cow-pasture.

Miss Nancy Ellicott smoked
And danced all the modern dances;
And her aunts were not quite sure how they felt
    about it,
But they knew that it was modern.   10

Upon the glazen shelves kept watch
Matthew and Waldo, guardians of the faith,
The army of unalterable law.

JOHN FREEMAN
(1880-1929)

ENGLISH HILLS

Oh that I were
Where breaks the pure cold light
On English hills,
And peewits rising cry,
And gray is all the sky.   5

Or at evening there
When the faint slow light stays,
And far below
Sleeps the last lingering sound,
And night leans all around.   10

O then, O there
'T is English haunted ground.
The diligent stars
Creep out, watch, and smile;
The wise moon lingers a while.   15

For surely there
Heroic shapes are moving,
Visible thoughts,
Passions, things divine,
Clear beneath clear star-shine.   20

O that I were
Again on English hills,
Seeing between
Laborious villages
Her cool dark loveliness.   25

HAPPY IS ENGLAND NOW

There is not anything more wonderful
Than a great people moving towards the deep
Of an unguessed and unfeared future; nor
Is aught so dear of all held dear before
As the new passion stirring in their veins   5
When the destroying Dragon wakes from sleep.

Happy is England now, as never yet!
And though the sorrows of the slow days fret
Her faithfullest children, grief itself is proud.
Ev'n the warm beauty of this spring and sum-
    mer   10
That turns to bitterness turns them to gladness
Since for this England the beloved ones died.

What'er was dear before is dearer now,
There 's not a bird singing upon his bough
But sings the sweeter in our English ears: 15
There 's not a nobleness of heart, hand, brain
But shines the purer; happiest is England now
In those that fight, and watch with pride and
    tears.

ROBERT GRAVES
(1895-   )

NOT DEAD

Walking through trees to cool my heat and
    pain,
I know that David's with me here again.
All that is simple, happy, strong, he is.
Caressingly I stroke
Rough bark of the friendly oak.   5
A brook goes bubbling by: the voice is his.
Turf burns with pleasant smoke;
I laugh at chaffinch and at primroses.
All that is simple, happy, strong, he is.
Over the whole wood in a little while   10
Breaks his slow smile.

OVER THE BRAZIER

What life to lead and where to go
  After the War, after the War?
  We'd often talked this way before
But I still see the brazier glow
That April night, still feel the smoke
And stifling pungency of burning coke.

I'd thought: 'A cottage in the hills,
  North Wales, a cottage full of books,
  Pictures and brass and cozy nooks
And comfortable broad window-sills,
Flowers in the garden, walls all white,
I'd live there peacefully, and dream and write.'

But Willy said: 'No, Home's played out:
  Old England's quite a hopeless place:
  I've lost all feeling for my race:
The English stay-at-home's a tout,
A cad; I've done with him for life,
I'm off to Canada with my wee wife.

'Come with us, Mac, old thing,' but Mac
  Drawled: 'No, A Coral Isle for me,
  A warm green jewel in the South Sea.
Of course you'll sneer, and call me slack,
And Colonies are quite jolly . . . but—
Give me my hot beach and my cocoanut.'

So then we built and stocked for Willy
  A log-hut, and for Mac a calm
  Rockabye cradle on a palm—
Idyllic dwellings—but this silly
Mad War has now wrecked both, and what
Better hopes has my little cottage got?

THOMAS HARDY
(1840–1928)

FOR LIFE I HAD NEVER CARED GREATLY

For Life I had never cared greatly,
  As worth a man's while;
  Peradventures unsought,
Peradventures that finished in nought,
Had kept me from youth and through manhood till lately
  Unwon by its style.

In earliest years—why I know not—
  I viewed it askance;
  Conditions of doubt,
Conditions that leaked slowly out,
May haply have bent me to stand and to show not
  Much zest for its dance.

With symphonies soft and sweet color
  It courted me then,
  Till evasions seemed wrong,
Till evasions gave in to its song,
And I warmed, until living aloofly loomed duller
  Than life among men.

Anew I found nought to set eyes on,
  When, lifting its hand,
  It uncloaked a star,
Uncloaked it from fog-damps afar,
And showed its beams burning from pole to horizon
  As bright as a brand.

And so, the rough highway forgetting,
  I pace hill and dale
  Regarding the sky,
Regarding the vision on high,
And thus re-illumed have no humor for letting
  My pilgrimage fail.

AFTERWARDS

When the Present has latched its postern behind my tremulous stay,
  And the May month flaps its glad green leaves like wings,
Delicate-filmed as new-spun silk, will the neighbors say,
  'He was a man who used to notice such things'?

If it be in the dusk when, like an eyelid's soundless blink,
  The dewfall-hawk comes crossing the shades to alight
Upon the wind-warped upland thorn, will a gazer think,
  'To him this must have been a familiar sight'?

If I pass during some nocturnal blackness, mothy and warm,
  When the hedgehog travels furtively over the lawn,
Will they say, 'He strove that such innocent creatures should come to no harm,
  But he could do little for them; and now he is gone'?

If, when hearing that I have been stilled at last, they stand at the door,
  Watching the full-starred heavens that winter sees,
Will this thought rise on those who will meet my face no more,
  'He was one who had an eye for such mysteries'?

And will any say when my bell of quittance is
    heard in the gloom,
  And a crossing breeze cuts a pause in its out-
    rollings,
Till they rise again, as they were a new bell's
    boom,
  'He hears it not now, but used to notice such
    things'?   20

THE COMING OF THE END

  How it came to an end!
The meeting afar from the crowd,
And the love-looks and laughters unpenned,
The parting when much was avowed,
  How it came to an end!   5

  It came to an end;
Yes, the outgazing over the stream,
With the sun on each serpentine bend,
Or, later, the luring moon-gleam;
  It came to an end.   10

  It came to an end,
The housebuilding, furnishing, planting,
As if there were ages to spend
In welcoming, feasting, and jaunting;
  It came to an end.   15

  It came to an end,
That journey of one day a week:
('It always goes on,' said a friend,
'Just the same in bright weathers or bleak');
  But it came to an end.   20

  '*How* will come to an end
This orbit so smoothly begun,
Unless some convulsion attend?'
I often said. 'What will be done
  When it comes to an end?'   25

  Well, it came to an end
Quite silently—stopped without jerk;
Better close no prevision could lend;
Working out as One planned it should work
  Ere it came to an end.   30

RALPH HODGSON
(1879-   )

EVE

Eve, with her basket, was
Deep in the bells and grass
Wading in bells and grass
Up to her knees,
Picking a dish of sweet   5
Berries and plums to eat,
Down in the bells and grass
Under the trees.

Mute as a mouse in a
Corner the cobra lay,   10
Curled round a bough of the
Cinnamon tall . . .
Now to get even and
Humble proud heaven and
Now was the moment or   15
Never at all.

'Eva!' Each syllable
Light as a flower fell,
'Eva!' he whispered the
Wondering maid,   20
Soft as a bubble sung
Out of a linnet's lung,
Soft and most silverly
'Eva!' he said.

Picture that orchard sprite,   25
Eve, with her body white,
Supple and smooth to her
Slim finger tips,
Wondering, listening,
Listening, wondering,   30
Eve with a berry
Half-way to her lips.

Oh had our simple Eve
Seen through the make-believe!
Had she but known the   35
Pretender he was!
Out of the boughs he came,
Whispering still her name,
Tumbling in twenty rings
Into the grass.   40

Here was the strangest pair
In the world anywhere,
Eve in the bells and grass
Kneeling, and he
Telling his story low . . .   45
Singing birds saw them go
Down the dark path to
The Blasphemous Tree.

Oh what a clatter when
Titmouse and Jenny Wren   50
Saw him successful and
Taking his leave!
How the birds rated him,
How they all hated him!
How they all pitied   55
Poor motherless Eve!

Picture her crying
Outside in the lane,
Eve, with no dish of sweet
Berries and plums to eat,   60
Haunting the gate of the
Orchard in vain . . .
Picture the lewd delight
Under the hill to-night—
'Eva!' the toast goes round,   65
'Eva!' again.

THE BULL

See an old unhappy bull,
Sick in soul and body both,
Slouching in the undergrowth
Of the forest beautiful,
Banished from the herd he led,　　　5
Bulls and cows a thousand head.

Cranes and gaudy parrots go
Up and down the burning sky;
Tree-top cats purr drowsily
In the dim-day green below;　　　10
And troops of monkeys, nutting, some,
All disputing, go and come;

And things abominable sit
Picking offal buck or swine,
On the mess and over it　　　15
Burnished flies and beetles shine,
And spiders big as bladders lie
Under hemlocks ten foot high;

And a dotted serpent curled
Round and round and round a tree,　　　20
Yellowing its greenery,
Keeps a watch on all the world,
All the world and this old bull
In the forest beautiful.

Bravely by his fall he came;　　　25
One he led, a bull of blood
Newly come to lustihood,
Fought and put his prince to shame,
Snuffed and pawed the prostrate head
Tameless even while it bled.　　　30

There they left him, every one,
Left him there without a lick,
Left him for the birds to pick,
Left him there for carrion,
Vilely from their bosom cast　　　35
Wisdom, worth and love at last.

When the lion left his lair
And roared his beauty through the hills,
And the vultures pecked their quills
And flew into the middle air,　　　40
Then this prince no more to reign
Came to life and lived again.

He snuffed the herd in far retreat,
He saw the blood upon the ground,
And snuffed the burning airs around　　　45
Still with beevish odors sweet,
While the blood ran down his head
And his mouth ran slaver red.

Pity him, this fallen chief,
All his splendor, all his strength,　　　50
All his body's breadth and length
Dwindled down with shame and grief,
Half the bull he was before,
Bones and leather, nothing more.

See him standing dewlap-deep　　　55
In the rushes at the lake,
Surly, stupid, half asleep,
Waiting for his heart to break
And the birds to join the flies
Feasting at his bloodshot eyes,—　　　60

Standing with his head hung down
In a stupor, dreaming things:
Green savannas, jungles brown,
Battlefields and bellowings,
Bulls undone and lions dead　　　65
And vultures flapping overhead.

Dreaming things: of days he spent
With his mother gaunt and lean
In the valley warm and green,
Full of baby wonderment,　　　70
Blinking out of silly eyes
At a hundred mysteries;

Dreaming over once again
How he wandered with a throng
Of bulls and cows a thousand strong,　　　75
Wandered on from plain to plain,
Up the hill and down the dale,
Always at his mother's tail;

How he lagged behind the herd,
Lagged and tottered, weak of limb,　　　80
And she turned and ran to him
Blaring at the loathly bird
Stationed always in the skies,
Waiting for the flesh that dies,

Dreaming maybe of a day　　　85
When her drained and drying paps
Turned him to the sweets and saps,
Richer fountains by the way,
And she left the bull she bore
And he looked to her no more;　　　90

And his little frame grew stout,
And his little legs grew strong,
And the way was not so long;
And his little horns came out,
And he played at butting trees　　　95
And boulder-stones and tortoises,

Joined a game of knobby skulls
With the youngsters of his year,
All the other little bulls,
Learning both to bruise and bear,　　　100
Learning how to stand a shock
Like a little bull of rock.

Dreaming of a day less dim,
Dreaming of a time less far,
When the faint but certain star　　　105
Of destiny burned clear for him,
And a fierce and wild unrest
Broke the quiet of his breast,

And the gristles of his youth
Hardened in his comely pow,　　　　　110
And he came to fighting growth,
Beat his bull and won his cow,
And flew his tail and trampled off
Past the tallest, vain enough,

And curved about in splendor full　　115
And curved again and snuffed the airs
As who should say, Come out who dares!
And all beheld a bull, a Bull,
And knew that here was surely one
That backed for no bull, fearing none.　120

And the leader of the herd
Looked and saw, and beat the ground,
And shook the forest with his sound,
Bellowed at the loathly bird
Stationed always in the skies,　　　　125
Waiting for the flesh that dies.

Dreaming, this old bull forlorn
Surely dreaming of the hour
When he came to sultan power,
And they owned him master-horn,　　130
Chiefest bull of all among
Bulls and cows a thousand strong.

And in all the tramping herd
Not a bull that barred his way,
Not a cow that said him nay,　　　　135
Not a bull or cow that erred
In the furnace of his look
Dared a second, worse rebuke;

Not in all the forest wide,
Jungle, thicket, pasture, fen,　　　　140
Not another dared him then,
Dared him and again defied;
Not a sovereign buck or boar
Came a second time for more.

Not a serpent that survived　　　　　145
Once the terrors of his hoof
Risked a second time reproof,
Came a second time and lived,
Not a serpent in its skin
Came again for discipline;　　　　　150

Not a leopard bright as flame,
Flashing fingerhooks of steel,
That a wooden tree might feel,
Met his fury once and came
For a second reprimand,　　　　　　155
Not a leopard in the land.

Not a lion of them all,
Not a lion of the hills,
Hero of a thousand kills,
Dared a second fight and fall,　　　　160
Dared that ram terrific twice,
Paid a second time the price.

Pity him this dupe of dream,
Leader of the herd again
Only in his daft old brain,　　　　　165
Once again the bull supreme
And bull enough to bear the part
Only in his tameless heart.

Pity him that he must wake;
Even now the swarm of flies　　　　170
Blackening his bloodshot eyes
Bursts and blusters round the lake,
Scattered from the feast half-fed,
By great shadows overhead.

And the dreamer turns away　　　　175
From his visionary herds
And his splendid yesterday,
Turns to meet the loathly birds
Flocking round him from the skies,
Waiting for the flesh that dies.　　　180

D. H. LAWRENCE
(1885-1931)

THE BRIDE

(Copyright 1916 by B. W. Huebsch, New York)

My love looks like a girl to-night,
　But she is old.
The plaits that lie along her pillow
　Are not gold,
But threaded with filigree,　　　　　5
　And uncanny cold.

She looks like a young maiden, since her brow
　Is smooth and fair,
Her cheeks are very smooth, her eyes are closed,
　She sleeps a rare　　　　　　　　10
Still winsome sleep, so still, and so composed.

Nay, but she sleeps like a bride, and dreams her
　　dreams
　Of perfect things.
She lies at last, the darling, in the shape of her
　　dream,
　And her dead mouth sings　　　　15
By its shape, like the thrushes in clear evenings.

STUDY

(Copyright 1916 by B. W. Huebsch, New York)

Somewhere the long mellow note of the blackbird
Quickens the unclasping hands of hazel,
Somewhere the wind-flowers fling their heads back,
Stirred by an impetuous wind. Some ways 'll
All be sweet with white and blue violets.　　5
(*Hush now, hush, Where am I?—Biuret—*)

On the green wood's edge a shy girl hovers
From out of the hazel-screen on to the grass,
Where wheeling and screaming the petulant
    plovers
Wave frighted. Who comes? A laborer, alas! 10
Oh the sunset swims in her eyes' swift pool.
(*Work, work, you fool———!*)

Somewhere the lamp hanging low from the
    ceiling
Lights the soft hair of a girl as she reads,
And the red firelight steadily wheeling   15
Weaves the hard hands of my friend in sleep.
And the white dog snuffs the warmth, appealing
For the man to heed lest the girl shall weep.
(*Tears and dreams for them; for me
Bitter science—the exams. are near.*   20
*I wish I bore it more patiently.
I wish you did not wait, my dear,
For me to come: since work I must:
Though it's all the same when we are dead.—
I wish I was only a bust,*   25
  All head.)

SUSAN L. MITCHELL

From 'Secret Springs of Dublin Song' published by The
    Talbot Press, Ltd., Dublin)

AMBITION IN CUFFE STREET

When I grow big I'll smoke and swear
And drink like my old fellow there,
I'll smoke till all the air is thick,
I'll drink five pints and not feel sick,
And use bad language to my fill,   5
  I will!

On a high stool for hours I'll sit,
Or lean against the door and spit;
I'll drink each pint to the last sup,
And tell the man to hurry up,   10
Till I have had five tankards, yes,
  No less!

I'll talk with Jemmy Cassidy,
He'll have grown old and fat like me,
We'll talk of women and everything,   15
And then perhaps we'll start to sing,
We'll start to sing and fight and shout,
'T will take three men to chuck us out,
By God, the things that I could do—
  Whew!   20

HOW WOULD IT BE?

How would it be if we should fare,
  By whispering to the pillar-box.
A spell of which I am aware,
To some grey mountain whence the bear
May turn him to the West and stare   5
Nor yet see known land anywhere,
  And find there carven of the rocks
An idol that can answer prayer?

Or winding up a palace stair,
  Beyond the hills of Let's Pretend,   10
Come suddenly and unaware
Upon a monarch seated there,
Whose eyes were angry and whose hair
  Was frizzled there at World's End
By the sun's triumphant glare.   15

And now, indeed, how would it be
  If songs and little tales were true?
And we should find the jujube tree,
And galleons still should cross the sea,
And elves should lurk by every tree,   20
  And dragons amble two by two,
While nobody should cry 'Dear me!'

HAROLD MONRO
(1879–1932)

THE REBELLIOUS VINE

One day, the vine
  That clomb on God's own house
Cried, 'I will not *grow*,'
And, 'I will *not* grow,'
And, 'I *will* not grow.'   5
And, '*I* will not grow.'
So God leaned out his head,
And said:
'You need not,' Then the Vine
Fluttered its leaves, and cried to all the winds: 10
'Oh, have I not permission from the Lord
And may I not begin to cease to grow?'
But that wise God had pondered on the vine
Before he made it.
And, all the while it labored *not* to grow   15
It grew; it grew;
And all the time God knew.

CHANGE OF MIND

How the rain tumbles. Lord!—
Only last week I would have gone all night
Dripping and scurrying, of my own accord,
For just one sight
Of you. How can I be so bored   5
Now at your short imploring note?
I curse the ugly rain and you.
I know exactly how you wrote,
'Smiling—and sobbing too. . . .
I will stay here. I will not go to you.   10

I know precisely how you'll look;
I can imagine every word you'll say;
I want to close you like a finished book:
Please let me have my way.

Why must I tell you that our love is done?   15
It lasted well, but now you have begun
To sorrow me. Be wise and understand.

Whatever purpose can be served indeed
By going two enormous rainy miles
To hold your hand? 20
Or is there any need
To trudge the lane, and climb the slippery stiles,
When, by this fire, and snugly in my brain,
I, without effort, may
Press your dry lips and hold your hands again, 25
And answer every word you'll have to say?

But I'm forgetting something . . . Who was that
Loafing about your cottage all last week?
How cool he was, and always sat
Watching you, and would not speak. 30
Why was he there; and is he still?
It's raining less, I think. Who can he be?
Shall I put on my coat? I think I will.
He may—may not, be gone. I'll go and see.
I'll go and find out why you sent for me. 35

SUBURB

Dull and hard the low wind creaks
Among the rustling pampas plumes.
Drearily the year consumes
Its fifty-two insipid weeks.

Most of the grey-green meadow land 5
Was sold in parsimonious lots;
The dingy houses stand
Pressed by some stout contractor's hand
Tightly together in their plots.

Through builded banks the sullen river 10
Gropes, where its houses crouch and shiver.
Over the bridge the tyrant train
Shrieks, and emerges on the plain.

In all the better gardens you may pass,
(Product of many careful Saturdays), 15
Large red geraniums and tall pampas grass
Adorn the plots and mark the graveled ways.

Sometimes in the background may be seen
A private summer-house in white or green.
Here on warm nights the daughter brings 20
Her vacillating clerk
To talk of small exciting things.

And touch his fingers through the dark.
He, in the uncomfortable breach
Between her trilling laughters, 25
Promises, in halting speech,
Hopeless immense Hereafters.

She trembles like the pampas plumes,
Her strained lips haggle. He assumes
The serious quest. . . . 30

Now as the train is whistling past
He takes her in his arms at last.
It's done. She blushes at his side
Across the lawn—a bride, a bride.

* * *

The stout contractor will design, 35
The lazy laborers will prepare,
Another villa on the line;
In the little garden-square
Pampas grass will rustle there.

MILK FOR THE CAT

When the tea is brought at five o'clock,
And all the neat curtains are drawn with care,
The little black cat with bright green eyes
Is suddenly purring there.

At first she pretends, having nothing to do, 5
She has come in merely to blink by the grate,
But, though tea may be late or the milk may be sour,
She is never late.

And presently her agate eyes
Take a soft large milky haze, 10
And her independent casual glance
Becomes a stiff hard gaze.

Then she stamps her claws or lifts her ears
Or twists her tail and begins to stir,
Till suddenly all her lithe body becomes 15
One breathing trembling purr.

The children eat and wriggle and laugh;
The two old ladies stroke their silk:
But the cat is grown small and thin with desire,
Transformed to a creeping lust for milk. 20

The white saucer like some full moon descends
At last from the clouds of the table above;
She sighs and dreams and thrills and glows,
Transfigured with love.

She nestles over the shining rim, 25
Buries her chin in the creamy sea;
Her tail hangs loose; each drowsy paw
Is doubled under each bending knee.

A long dim ecstasy holds her life;
Her world is an infinite shapeless white, 30
Till her tongue has curled the last holy drop,
Then she sinks back into the night.

Draws and dips her body to heap
Her sleepy nerves in the great arm-chair,
Lies defeated and buried deep 35
Three or four hours unconscious there.

SIEGFRIED SASSOON
(1886–   )

THE OLD HUNTSMAN

(By permission. Copyright 1918 by E. P. Dutton & Co.)

I 've never ceased to curse the day I signed
A seven years' bargain for the Golden Fleece.
'T was a bad deal all round; and dear enough
It cost me, what with my daft management,
And the mean folk as owed and never paid me, 5
And backing losers; and the local bucks
Egging me on with whiskies while I bragged
The man I was when huntsman to the Squire.
I 'd have been prosperous if I 'd took a farm
Of seventy acres, drove by gig and haggled 10
At Monday markets; now I 've squandered all
My savings; nigh three hundred pound I got
As testimonial when I 'd grown too stiff
And slow to press a beaten fox.

                  The Fleece! 15
'T was the damned Fleece that wore my Emily out,
The wife of thirty years who served me well;
(Not like this beldam clattering in the kitchen,
That never trims a lamp nor sweeps the floor,
And brings me greasy soup in a foul crock.) 20

Blast the old harridan! What 's fetched her now,
Leaving me in the dark, and short of fire?
And where 's my pipe? 'T is lucky I 've a turn
For thinking, and remembering all that 's past.
And now 's my hour, before I hobble to bed, 25
To set the works a-wheezing, wind the clock
That keeps the time of life with feeble tick
Behind my bleared old face that stares and wonders.

                * * *

It 's queer how, in the dark, comes back to mind
Some morning of September. We 've been digging 30
In a steep, sandy warren, riddled with holes,
And I 've just pulled the terrier out and left
A sharp-nosed cub-face blinking there and snapping,
Then in a moment seen him mobbed and torn
To strips in the baying hurly of the pack. 35
I picture it so clear: the dusty sunshine
On bracken, and the men with spades, that wipe
Red faces: one tilts up a mug of ale.
And, having stooped to clean my gory hands,
I whistle the jostling beauties out o' the wood.

I 'm but a daft old fool! I often wish 41
The Squire were back again—ah, he was a man!
They don't breed men like him these days; he 'd come
For sure, and sit and talk and suck his briar
Till the old wife brings up a dish of tea. 45

Ay, those were days, when I was serving Squire!
I never knowed such sport as '85,
The winter afore the one that snowed us silly.

                * * *

Once in a way the parson will drop in
And read a bit o' the Bible, if I 'm bad,— 50
Pray the Good Lord to make my spirit whole
In faith: he leaves some 'baccy on the shelf,
And wonders I don't keep a dog to cheer me,
Because he knows I 'm mortal fond of dogs!

I ask you, what 's a gent like that to me, 55
As would n't know Elijah if I saw him,
Nor have the wit to keep him on the talk?
'T is kind of parson to be troubling still
With such as me; but he 's a town-bred chap,
Full of his college notions and Christmas hymns.

Religion beats me. I 'm amazed at folk 61
Drinking the gospels in and never scratching
Their heads for questions. When I was a lad
I learned a bit from mother, and never thought
To educate myself for prayers and psalms. 65

But now I 'm old and bald and serious-minded,
With days to sit and ponder. I 'd no chance
When young and gay to get the hang of all
This Hell and Heaven; and when the clergy hoick
And holloa from their pulpits, I 'm asleep, 70
However hard I listen; and when they pray
It seems we 're all like children sucking sweets
In school, and wondering whether master sees.

I used to dream of Hell when I was first
Promoted to a huntsman's job, and scent 75
Was rotten, and all the foxes disappeared,
And hounds were short of blood: and officers
From barracks over-rode 'em all day long
On weedy, whistling nags that knocked a hole
In every fence; good sportsmen to a man 80
And brigadiers by now, but dreadful hard
On a young huntsman keen to show some sport.

Ay, Hell was thick with captains, and I rode
The lumbering brute that 's beat in half a mile,
And blunders into every blind old ditch. 85
Hell was the coldest scenting land I 've known.
And both my whips were always lost, and hounds
Would never get their heads down; and a man
On a great yawing chestnut trying to cast 'em
While I was in a corner bounded by 90
The ugliest hog-backed stile you 've clapped your eyes on.
There was an iron-spiked fence round all the coverts,
And civil-spoken keepers I could n't trust,
And the main earth unstopp'd. The fox I found
Was always a three-legged 'un from a bag 95
Who reeked of aniseed and would n't run.

The farmers were all ploughing their old pasture
And bellowing at me when I rode their beans
To cast for beaten fox, or galloped on
With hounds to a lucky view. I 'd lost my
  voice   100
Although I shouted fit to burst my guts,
And could n't blow my horn.

       And when I woke,
Emily snored, and barn-cocks started crowing,
And morn was at the window; and I was glad
To be alive because I heard the cry   106
Of hounds like church-bells chiming on a
  Sunday,—
Ay, that 's the song I 'd wish to hear in Heaven!
The cry of hounds was Heaven for me: I know
Parson would call me crazed and wrong to
  say it,   110
But where 's the use of life and being glad
If God 's not in your gladness?

        I 've no brains
For book-learned studies; but I 've heard men
  say
There 's much in print that clergy have to
  wink at;   115
Though many I 've met were jolly chaps, and
  rode
To hounds, and walked me puppies; and could
  pick
Good legs and loins and necks and shoulders, ay,
And feet,—'t was necks and feet I looked at first.

Some hounds I 've known were wise as half
  your saints,   120
And better hunters. That old dog of the Duke's,
Harlequin; what a dog he was to draw!
And what a note he had, and what a nose
When foxes ran down wind and scent was
  catchy!
And that light lemon bitch of the Squire's, old
  Dorcas,—   125
She were a marvelous hunter, were old Dorcas!

Ay, oft I 've thought: 'If there were hounds in
  Heaven,
With God as Master, taking no subscription;
And all His blessed country farmed by tenants;
And a straight-necked old fox in every gorse!'
But when I came to work it out, I found   131
There 'd be too many huntsmen wanting
  places,—
Though some I 've known might get a job with
  Nick!

     *   *   *

I 've come to think of God as something like
The figure of a man the old Duke was   135
When I was turning hounds to Nimrod King,
Before his Grace was took so bad with gout,
And had to quit the saddle. Tall and spare,
Clean-shaved and grey, with shrewd, kind eyes,
  that twinkled,
And easy walk; who, when he gave good words,
Gave them whole-hearted; and would never
  blame   141
Without just cause. Lord God might be like
  that,
Sitting alone in a great room of books
Some evening after hunting.

        Now I 'm tired   145
With hearkening to the tick-tack on the shelf;
And pondering makes me doubtful.

         Riding home
On a moonless night of cloud that feels like frost
Though stars are hidden, (hold your feet up,
  horse!)   150
And thinking what a task I had to draw
A pack with all those lame 'uns, and the lot
Wanting a rest from all this open weather,—
That 's what I 'm doing now.

     *   *   *

        Now I know   155
It 's God that speaks to us when we 're be-
  witched,
Smelling the hay in June and smiling quiet;
Or when there 's been a spell of summer drought,
Lying awake and listening to the rain.

     *   *   *

I 'd like to be the simpleton I was   160
In the old days when I was whipping-in
To a little harrier-pack in Worcestershire,
And loved a dairymaid, but never knew it
Until she 'd wed another. So I 've loved
My life; and when the good years are gone
  down,   165
Discover what I 've lost.

        I never broke
Out of my blundering self into the world,
But let it all go past me, like a man
Half-asleep in a land that 's full of wars.   170

What a grand thing 't would be if I could go
Back to the kennels now and take my hounds
For summer exercise: be riding out
With forty couple when the quiet skies
Are streaked with sunrise, and the silly birds
Grown hoarse with singing; cobwebs on the
  furze   176
Up on the hill, and all the country strange,
With no one stirring; and the horses fresh,
Sniffing the air I 'll never breathe again.

     *   *   *

You 've brought the lamp then, Martha? I 've
  no mind   180
For newspaper to-night, nor bread and cheese.
Give me the candle, and I 'll get to bed.

JAMES STEPHENS
(1882–   )

WHAT TOMAS AN BUILE SAID IN A PUB

I saw God. Do you doubt it?
  Do you dare to doubt it?
I saw the Almighty Man. His hand
Was resting on a mountain, and
He looked upon the World and all about it: 5
I saw him him plainer than you see me now,
  You must n't doubt it.

He was not satisfied;
  His look was all dissatisfied.
His beard swung on a wind far out of sight   10
Behind the world's curve, and there was light
Most fearful from His forehead, and He sighed,
'That star went always wrong, and from the start
  I was dissatisfied.'

He lifted up His hand—   15
  I say He heaved a dreadful hand
Over the spinning Earth; then I said 'Stay,
You must not strike it, God; I'm in the way;
And I will never move from where I stand.'
He said, 'Dear child, I feared that you were dead,'   20
  And stayed His hand.

EDWARD THOMAS
(1878–1917)

SOWING

It was a perfect day
For sowing; just
As sweet and dry was the ground
As tobacco-dust.

I tasted deep the hour   5
Between the far
Owl's chuckling first soft cry
And the first star.

A long stretched hour it was;
Nothing undone   10
Remained; the early seeds
All safely sown.

And now, hark at the rain,
Windless and light,
Half a kiss, half a tear,   15
Saying good-night.

BRIGHT CLOUDS

Bright clouds of May
Shade half the pond.
Beyond,
All but one bay
Of emerald   5
Tall reeds
Like criss-cross bayonets
Where a bird once called,
Lies bright as the sun.
No one heeds.   10
The light wind frets
And drifts the scum
Of May-blossom.
Till the moor-hen calls
Again   14
Naught's to be done
By birds or men
Still the May falls.

THE GALLOWS

There was a weasel lived in the sun
  With all his family,
Till a keeper shot him with his gun
  And hung him up on a tree,
Where he swings in the wind and rain,   5
  In the sun and in the snow,
Without pleasure, without pain,
  On the dead oak tree bough.

There was a crow who was no sleeper,
  But a thief and a murderer   10
Till a very late hour; and this keeper
  Made him one of the things that were,
To hang and flap in rain and wind,
  In the sun and in the snow.
There are no more sins to be sinned   15
  On the dead oak tree bough.

There was a magpie, too,
  Had a long tongue and a long tail;
He could both talk and do—
  But what did that avail?   20
He, too, flaps in the wind and rain
  Alongside weasel and crow,
Without pleasure, without pain,
  On the dead oak tree bough.

And many other beasts   25
  And birds, skin, bone and feather,
Have been taken from their feasts
  And hung up there together,
To swing and have endless leisure
  In the sun and in the snow,   30
Without pain, without pleasure,
  On the dead oak tree bough.

NOTES
TO
CENTURY READINGS IN ENGLISH LITERATURE

Page 5. BEOWULF

The translation is that of William Ellery Leonard, published separately under the title, *Beowulf: A New Verse Translation*, The Century Co., 1923.

The general form of the verse used by Professor Leonard may be seen in the following familiar lines:

Síng a sóng of síx-pènce.   a bág fùll of rýe,
Fóur and twénty bláckbìrds   báked ìn a píe

In this illustration the syllables strongly accented are marked thus: ´. The syllables accented less strongly are marked thus: `. These marks may be applied to the opening lines of the translation as follows:

What hó! We've héard the glórỳ ·
Their déeds of ólden stórỳ,— · how fóught the aèthelíngs!

The relationships among the chief personages mentioned in the poem will be more readily understood through reference to the following:

GENEALOGICAL TABLES

I THE DANES (Scyldings, also called East-Danes, etc.)

Scyld Scefing
|
Beowulf (*not* the hero of our poem)
|
Halfdane (spelt Healfdene in Anglo-Saxon)

- Heorogar
- Heoroweard
- HROTHGAR, married WEALHTHEOW
  - Hrethric
  - Hrothmund
  - Freawaru, married Ingeld, the Heathobard
- Halga
  - Hrothulf
- a daughter, married a Swedish King (Onela?)

II THE GEATS (Weders)

Hrethel
- Herebeald
- Haethcyn
- HYGELAC (or Hyglac), married Hygd
  - a daughter, married Eofor
  - Heardred
- a daughter, married Ecgtheow
  - BEOWULF (the hero)

Waegmund, ancestor of
- Weohstan
  - WIGLAF

III THE SWEDES (Scylfings)

Ongentheow
- Onela
- Ohthere
  - Eanmund
  - Eadgils

985

The accompanying map shows the location of the important peoples and places. The Geats, the people to whom the hero, Beowulf, belonged, occupied the southern part of what is now Sweden. At this time the Swedes were settled north of Lakes Wenner and Wetter. The Danes lived in the easterly part of what is now Denmark. Heorot, the famous hall of the Danish king, Hrothgar, was on the island now called Zealand.

Page 5.

1. *clansmen-kings.* Such compound words are abundant in Anglo-Saxon poetry, and hence in the present translation.
2. *æthelings,* warriors of noble descent, princes, heroes.
3. *Scyld Scefing,* ancestor of King Hrothgar. See Genealogical Table above. *reft,* plundered.
4. *wassail,* drinking bout. *mead,* a fermented beverage made of water, honey, and malt.
5. *jarls,* thanes, retainers, noblemen. Pronounced 'yarl'.
6. *came a foundling.* The story runs that Scyld, the founder of the Danish royal house, drifted ashore as a lone child in a boat, in which he had used as a pillow a sheaf of grain. See l. 41 below.
7. *welkin,* sky.
9. *whale-road,* the sea. In Anglo-Saxon poetry objects and persons are often designated indirectly by compounds such as 'bone-house' for 'body', and 'glee-wood' for 'harp.' Such expressions are called *kennings.*

Page 5.

17. *Beowulf.* This Beowulf, son of Scyld, is *not* the hero of the poem, who was not a Dane (Scylding), but a Geat. See Genealogical Table.
18. *Scandia,* name of the southern part of the Scandinavian peninsula, here applied to the Danish kingdom.
20. *largesse,* liberal gifts.
22. *liegemen,* vassals, devoted followers.
30. *a rounded ring.* 'The wood of the prows of these old boats extended high above the gunwales and curved gracefully forward over the bow in a ring.' (Leonard.)

Page 6.

32. *Bracelet-Breaker,* prince, king, chief,—'one who breaks off and gives to his retainers bands of gold twisted about his arm.' (Leonard.)
36. *dight,* arranged, adorned.
37. *weeds,* garments, armor.
38. *byrnies,* coats of mail.
41. See note to l. 6 above.

Page 6.

47. *burg*, stronghold, town,—especially a walled town or castle.
49. *was ta'en elsewhere*, an allusion to the death and ship-burial of Scyld Scefing recounted earlier in the poem.
50. *Halfdane*, or Healfdene. See Genealogical Table.
55. *Heorogar, Hrothgar, Halga*. See Genealogical Table.
56. *queen*. This daughter may have married the Swedish king, Onela. See Genealogical Table.
67. *folkstead*, meeting-place of the people, or royal seat.
69. *Heorot*, a name meaning 'hart,' or 'stag.' It is supposed that the hall was so named from horns or antlers fastened to the gable-ends. The name may, however, be used symbolically, the hart signifying royalty. The hall was probably rectangular in shape, with a door at each end, benches along the side, and gilded pillars supporting the roof. In the middle of the floor was, presumably, an open hearth, with a 10le in the roof above it, for the escape of smoke. As has been said above, Heorot was probably located on the island now called Zealand, or Seeland. See Map above.
75-6. These lines refer to a feud between Hrothgar and his son-in-law, Ingeld. See Genealogical Table.
85. *fold*, the earth, the ground. *eke*, also.
90. *marches*, borderlands.
91. *wight*, creature, person.

Page 7.

95. *the monster-brood*. During the Middle Ages it was commonly believed that because of God's curse upon Cain (Genesis iv, 11-12) he became the progenitor of monsters, evil spirits, and giants.
96. *Ettins*, giants.
99. *Ring-Danes*, Danes wearing armor made of rings.
108. *mickle*, great, large.
114. *Eftsoons*, afterward, soon.
125. *dreed*, suffered, endured.
128. *gleemen's ballads*, poems recited by itinerant minstrels.
132. *compound for fee*, settle by payment.
133. *wot*, know.
135. *reaving*, robbing.
143. *gift-stool*, throne of Hrothgar.
147. *at rede*, in council.
152-4. Here the poet speaks of the Danes as not knowing God, whereas in other passages he credits them with this knowledge. The combination of pagan and Christian elements in the poem shows numerous inconsistencies. See note to l. 578 below.
153. *wist*, knew.

Page 8.

156. *ween*, think.
159. *carked*, worried.
163. *Geatish breeds*. The Geats occupied the southern part of the Scandinavian peninsula. See Map.
164. *Hyglac's thane and nephew*, Beowulf. See Genealogical Table.
167. *rider-of-the-sea*, ship.
168. *swan-road*, sea.
170. *carls*, men.
175. *kenned*, knew.
176. *abaft*, in the direction of the stern.
181. *eager voyage*. The sea journey of Beowulf from the land of the Geats to the Danish island on which Hrothgar's hall, Heorot, was situated is indicated on the Map above.
188. *Weder-clansmen*. Beowulf's people, the Geats, were also called Weders, or Wederas.
189. *sea-wood*, ship.
190. *sarks*, coats of mail.
193. *water-cliffs*, the cliffs of the Danish island on which Heorot was situated—now the island of Zealand.
207. *jarlman*, nobleman, retainer.
211. *bin*, be.

Page 9.

218. *Ecgtheow*. See Genealogical Table.
225. *wottest*, knowest.
229. *rede*, lesson, advice.
231. *teen*, grief, woe.
232. *seething*, boiling.
233. *tholeth*, suffereth.
243. *Weder-mark*, boundaries of the land of the Weders, or Geats. See Map.
247. *boar*. The crests of the helmets were formed by images of boars.

Page 10.

286. See note to l. 32 above.
304. *Hrethel*. See Genealogical Table.
310. *West-Danes*. The people of Hrothgar are called Scyldings, Danes, West-Danes, East-Danes, South-Danes, etc.
312. *derring-do*, high courage, valor.

Page 11.

342. *nicors*, water monsters.
368. *Hild*, personification of battle.
369. *Wyrd*, Destiny, Fate.
373. *Wylfings' land*, probably south of the Baltic Sea.
379. *Heorogar*. See Genealogical Table.

Page 12.

409. *Unferth*, spokesman of Hrothgar.
413. *Middle-Yard*, Middle-World, the earth.
415. *Breca*. Concerning this person we know only what is recounted here.
416. *enow*, enough.
422. *mere's path*, the sea.
425. *swinked*, toiled, struggled.
427. *Heathoreams*. See Map.
428. *Bronding-kith*, Unferth's people.
431. *son of Beanstan*, Unferth.

Page 13.

458. *Mere-Beast*, sea-monster.
463. *glaive*, sword.
470. *fey*, doomed, fated, marked for death.
480. *brands*, swords.
510. *Helmings' Dame*. Of the tribe of Helmings, to which Wealhtheow belonged, we know nothing.
511. *rich-beseen*, beautifully wrought, or ornamented.
513. *Crown-bedight*, adorned with a crown.

Page 14.

525. *dree*, suffer, endure.
550. *him*, probably Hrothgar.
578. *webs*, the webs woven by the Norns, the Fates of Germanic mythology. Note that these 'webs' are assigned to men by the Christian God. The mingling of Christian with pagan conceptions is characteristic of the poem.

Page 15.

587. *Darkness*, i.e., death.
613. *Kin of Hygelac*, Beowulf.
617. *bone-box*, body, trunk. One of the numerous 'kennings' in the poem.
621. *nim*, take, seize.
626. *Middle-World*, the earth.
637. *dingles*, secluded ravines.

Page 16.

652. *bone-bright*. Possibly this refers to the stag-antlers on the gable-ends. See note to l. 69 above.
666. *father's falchion*. Beowulf inherited his sword from his father.
671. *battle-bill*, sword.
680. *moe*, more.
683. *Ogreling*, descendant of an ogre.
713. *Nicor's mere*, pool, or lake, where water monsters dwelt.

Page 17.

728. *fallow bays*, horses.
733. *scop*, writer and reciter of poems, especially heroic poems.

Page 17.

735. *Linking words together.* The omitted story concerns Sigemund, who slew a dragon and rifled its hoard of gold. This story belongs to a large body of epic narratives known to-day chiefly through Wagner's operas and such poems as William Morris's *Sigurd the Volsung.* The scop tells also of an ancient Danish king Heremod (before the coming of Scyld), who was an evil ruler, and thus serves as a contrast to Sigemund and Beowulf.

Page 18.

799. *hest*, command.
810. *wanhope*, loss of hope, despair.
838. *files'-remainders*, swords,—the blade that *remains* after files have done their work.

Page 19.

848. *Ingwines*, another tribal name for the Danes.
864. *linked as one*, i.e., words sung to the accompaniment of the harp.
867. *his glee.* The "glee", or lay, sung by the scop, but omitted here, has to do with 'The Woe of Hildeburh.' This story is somewhat obscure, telling of feuds among Danes, Frisians, and Jutes. See Map.
873. *nephew, and the uncle*, Hrothulf and Hrothgar. See Genealogical Table.
891. *ween*, think.
893. *erst*, formerly.
895. *Hrethric and Hrothmund.* See Genealogical Table.
901. The brief passage omitted after this line tells of a famous collar, or necklace, which Hygelac wore when he made his last raid on the Frisians. This historical event of the sixth century is mentioned in the introductory note prefixed to *Beowulf* in the text above, and Hygelac's route on this occasion is indicated on the Map.

Page 20.

946. *Cain.* See note to l. 95 above.
948. *he*, Cain.
956. *Troll*, an ogre, a supernatural being of large size.
957. *a-cringing*, cringing, shrinking, cowering.

Page 21.

998. *Ingwines' Sire*, king of the Danes, *i.e.*, Hrothgar.

Page 22.

1092. *sail-road*, sea.

Page 23.

1098. *swam more sluggish.* This is an understatement characteristic of Anglo-Saxon poetry. The sea monster was more sluggish because he was dead!
1119. *twig and spray.* The blade was engraved with scroll-work.
1124. *aow*, succeed.
1125. *bairn of Ecglaf*, Unferth.
1126. *speech of late.* See ll. 409 ff. above.
1138. *fere*, companion, comrade.
1154. *ravin-fierce*, fierce for prey.

Page 24.

1157. *eldritch-wights*, weird or uncanny creatures.
1167. *tushes*, tusks.
1177. *flasher-in-the-fray*, gleaming sword.
1201. *wreak*, avenge.
1209. *bill*, sword.
1215. *ringèd blade.* 'Ringed' may designate scroll-work on the blade of the sword, or a loose ring attached to the hilt.

Page 25.

1240. *brave man*, Beowulf.
1244. *ninth hour*, probably the close of the day. *ness* promontory, headland.
1259. *eldritch*, weird, uncanny. Observe that before the poison-blood of Grendel's mother had melted Beowulf's sword, he had used it for cutting off Grendel's head.
1275. *bedene*, straightway.

Page 26.

1295. *Wardens*, Grendel and Grendel's mother.
1319. *runic stave*, stanza written in the runic, or early Germanic, alphabet.
1332. The latter part of Hrothgar's speech, omitted after this line, contains admonition to Beowulf, in the course of which a lesson is drawn from the wickedness of the ancient Danish king, Heremod. See note to l. 735 above.

Page 27.

1339. *list*, please.
1347. *Joy-of-Heaven*, the sun.
1352. *lief*, dear, beloved.
1370. The passage omitted after this line includes the latter part of Beowulf's speech, and Hrothgar's reply.
1388. *boon*, gift, kindness.
1390. *Eld*, old age. *scathes*, harms. The long passage omitted after this line recounts Beowulf's departure from Denmark, his arrival among his own people, the Geats, and his long report to King Hygelac of his adventures. In this report is repeated much of what is told in the preceding part of the poem. The omitted part speaks also of Beowulf's gifts to the king and queen, and of Hygelac's reward to Beowulf.
1394. *Scylfings*, Swedes. They dwelt north of the Geats. See Map.
1395. *grame*, sorrow, misery.
1396. *Nephew of Hereric*, probably the brother of Hygd, Hygelac's queen.

Page 28.

1401. *stone-barrow*, mound of stones.
1403. *nim*, seize. From the next sixty lines or so, it appears that this theft was committed by a nameless slave, fleeing from an unnamed master. Many years before this, some nobleman, the last of his race, had hidden the treasure in the mound (ll. 1404, 1421-30), and had laid a curse upon it, that it should never be meddled with. Eventually the dragon had assumed charge of the hoard, and is now enraged over its being disturbed.
1409. *Drake*, dragon.
1424. *ness*, promontory, headland.
1444. *glee-wood's game*, music of the harp.
1464. *boon*, request, reward.

Page 29.

1470. *fey*, marked for death.
1484. *wall*, i.e., wall of the dragon's cave in the mound.
1486. *kenned*, knew, learned.
1488. *gleeds*, glowing coals of fire.
1509. *water-land*, land bordering on the sea.
1510. *ledes*, people, nation.
1527. In the passage omitted here the poet recounts, among other things, Beowulf's part in Hygelac's historic raid upon the Frisians (see note to l. 901 above), his subsequent rôle in the governing of the deceased Hygelac's kingdom, and Beowulf's own reminiscences of his exploits in his youth. As printed in this book, the poem resumes the story at the conclusion of those reminiscences.

Page 30.

1540. *Reek*, smoke, smoky flame.
1543. *wall*, wall of the dragon's lair.
1549. *meed*, reward.
1553. *stark*, strong.
1563. *flare*, blaze of fire or light.
1571. *battle-fume*, smoke of battle.
1574. *Ring-Bow*, the dragon, with back arched like a bow.
1580. *bowed.* Pronounced bōd, meaning curved like a bow. *glode*, glided.
1590. *battle-swingeing*, clash of battle.

Page 31.
- 1606. *cark*, distress of mind.
- 1608. *Hight*, named, called. *Wiglaf*. See Genealogical Table.
- 1609. *Scylfings*. Wiglaf's relationship to the Swedes (Scylfings) is not entirely clear.
- 1610. *Liege-Lord*, i.e., Beowulf.
- 1611. *casque*, head-covering. *maw*, stomach, throat.
- 1613. *Waegmundings*, descendants of Waegmund. See Genealogical Table.
- 1616. The brief passage omitted after this line concerns Wiglaf's sword and a feud in which his father had been engaged.
- 1622. *dreed*, suffered, endured.
- 1627. *haply*, by chance.
- 1653. *prow*, valor, prowess.
- 1657. *boss*, protuberant parts of the buckler, or shield.
- 1658. *Spear-Wight*, spear-man, spear-bearer.

Page 32.
- 1716. *not many*. A characteristic understatement, for Beowulf means that he had sworn no false oaths at all.

Page 33.
- 1745. *wefted*, woven.
- 1763. *moor-stead*, place on the moor.
- 1767. *breast-hoard*, the thoughts and feelings in the breast.
- 1774. *fere*, comrade, companion.
- 1783. *doffed*, took off.
- 1787. *common line*. See Genealogical Table.

Page 34.
- 1811. *ring-hall*, treasure-room.
- 1827. *Deemster*, judge.
- 1849. *small the sum*. As a matter of fact, only *one*,—Wiglaf himself!

Page 35.
- 1878–83. Concerning the sea-raid of Hygelac into the land of the Hetwaras see note to l. 901 above.
- 1883. In the passage omitted after this line the herald sent by Wiglaf retells the story of old wars. When the text of the poem is resumed, the herald is still speaking.
- 1929. The brief passage omitted before this line provides a few somewhat confusing details concerning the ancient curse upon the dragon's hoard.

Page 36.
- 1944. *quick*, alive.
- 1972. *one*, Wiglaf (?).
- 1989. *swart*, black.
- 1995. *grame*, sorrow, misery.
- 1997. *rech*, smoke.

Page 38.
SIR GAWAIN AND THE GREEN KNIGHT
The translation is that of Miss Jessie L. Weston.
a.
- 7. *Romulus*. According to Roman tradition, Romulus founded Rome in 753 B. C.
- 9. *Ticius*. The person intended cannot be identified with certainty. *Langobard*. The Germans who, in 568, founded the kingdom of Lombardy in Northern Italy were called in Latin, Langobardi.
- 11. *Felix Brutus*, Brutus, the great-grandson of Æneas, the fabled founder of the kingdom of Britain. The name Felix may be the invention of the writer.
- 24. *Camelot*, a legendary spot in England where Arthur is said to have held his court.
- 30. *carols*, dances accompanied by song.

b.
- 25. *Tars*, a name of uncertain identification. This place is often mentioned in medieval literature as famous for silks and tapestries.

Page 39.
a.
- 20. *Agravain, à la dure main*, Agravain of the hard hand.

b.
- 8. *gauds*, ornaments.
- 35. *hauberk*, a part of the armor intended originally for the protection of the neck and shoulders.
- 36. *gorget*, a piece of armor protecting the throat.

Page 40.
a.
- 2. *mustered*, surveyed.
- 19. *doubt*, fear.

Page 41.
a.
- 25. *redest*, understandest or, perhaps, advisest.

Page 42.
a.
- 17. *dossal*, a hanging of rich, heavy cloth, against the wall.

b.
- 14. *Michaelmas*, Sept. 29.
- 17. *All Hallows Day*, Nov. 1.

Page 43.
a.
- 1. *cuisses*, armor for the thighs.
- 2. *byrnie*, coat of mail.
- 7. *surcoat*, an outer garment.
- 9. *bawdrick*, a kind of belt.
- 29. *ventail*, a movable piece of armor extending downward from the front of the helmet.
- 32. *turtle*, turtle-dove.
- 38. *pentangle*, a heraldic device with five corners.

b.
- 43. *Logres*, here used as a name for England in general.
- 48. *Anglesey*, an island off the northwest coast of Wales. See Map.
- 50. *foreland*, headland. *Holyhead*, a small island west of Anglesey.
- 51. *wilderness of Wirral*, in Cheshire.

Page 44.
a.
- 50. *matins*, the first of the series of eight daily devotional offices called collectively the Canonical Office.

b.
- 12. *Saint Julian*. This saint was noted for hospitality.
- 15. *hostel*, lodging.
- 26. *corbels*, ornamental brackets for supporting moldings.
- 28. *barbican*, an outwork of a castle or fortified place.

Page 45.
a. 51. *samite*, a heavy silk material.
b.
- 9. *sodden*, boiled.
- 24. *keep*, a stronghold.
- 42. *evensong*, vespers.

Page 46.
b.
- 2. *in his degree*, according to his rank.
- 15. *Saint John's Day*, Dec. 27.
- 33. *behest*, command, request.
- 46. *wend*, go.

Page 47.
a.
- 23. *solace*, pleasure.
- 31. *waked*, kept awake, sat up.

Page 48.
a. 36. *rede*, advise.

Page 49.
a. 27. *tale*, number, sum.

Page 51.
b.
- 3. *prime*, probably about 9 o'clock.
- 32. *spinney*, a clump of trees or shrubs.

Page 52.
b. 15. *marks*. A mark was reckoned at approximately 13 shillings.

Page 53.
a. 19. *assoiled*, absolved, shrived.
b. 40. *deal the doom of my weird*, to suffer the judgment of my fate.

Page 54.
a.
- 34. *did on*, put on.
- 36. *cognizance*, the crest by which a man in complete armor could be recognized.

Page 55.
a. 35. *let*, detain, hinder.
47. *greet*, weep.
b. 26. *kirk*, church.

Page 56.
a. 2. *bent*, field.

Page 57.
b. 8. *Samson . . . Delilah*. See Judges xvi.
9. *David . . . Bathsheba*. See 2 Samuel xi.

Page 58.
b. 18. *book of Brutus*. Works treating the early legendary history of Britain were sometimes called *Brut*. See, for example, in English, Layamon's *Brut*, written about the year 1200.

Page 59.
PEARL
The translation is by Dr. S. Weir Mitchell, The Century Co., 1906.
1. *pleasance*, delight. *enow*, enough.
43. *gromwell*, a plant.

Page 60.
63. *quick ghost*, live spirit.
75. *boles*, trunks of trees.
76. *blue of Inde*, indigo.
110. *beryl*, a precious mineral.
118. *gent*, elegant.
123. *hale*, safe, free from infirmity.
127. *mere*, water.
131. *wight*, person.

Page 61.
158. *lissome*, supple, lithe.
184. *empery*, the status of an emperor.
185. *amice*, a white linen cloth commonly worn about the head or neck by priests when celebrating the Roman Mass.
189. *ween*, think.
192. *bedight*, adorned.
194. *margerys*, pearls.
237. *weird*, fate.

Page 62.
246. *perdue*, lost.
275. *trow*, believe.
286. *yore-father*, ancestor, referring to Adam.
289. *dole*, grief.
301. *demoiselle*, maiden.
306. *misericorde*, pity, mercy.

Page 63.
358. *phenix of Araby*, a mythical bird, fabled to be the only one of its kind.
389. *pater*, the Lord's Prayer, or *Pater Noster*.
393. *par ma fay*, by my faith.
401. *Matthew*. See Matthew xx, 1–16.

Page 64.
433. *evensong*, Vespers.
442. *waxed*, grew.

Page 65.
THE CHESTER PLAYS
NOAH'S FLOOD

The text of the play is modernized from that of Deimling in the Early English Text Society, Extra Series, Vol. LXII. The stage-directions are translated from the Latin. Stage-directions not in the original text are enclosed in square brackets. *Noah's Flood* is the third play in the cycle, as may be seen in the following complete list of the Chester plays:

1. The Fall of Lucifer
2. The Creation of the World; Cain and Abel
3. Noah's Flood

Page 65.
4. Abraham and Isaac
5. King Balak and Balaam
6. Octavian and the Sibyl; the Nativity
7. The Adoration of the Shepherds
8. Herod and the Magi
9. The Adoration of the Magi
10. The Slaughter of the Innocents
11. Christ in the Temple
12. The Temptation of Christ; the Woman taken in Adultery
13. The Raising of Lazarus
14. Christ's Entry into Jerusalem
15. The Last Supper
16. The Trial and Scourging of Christ
17. The Crucifixion
18. The Harrowing of Hell
19. The Resurrection
20. The Journey to Emmaus
21. The Ascension
22. Pentecost
23. The Prophets
24. Antichrist
25. The Last Judgment

Noah's Flood should be compared with its Biblical source in Genesis vi–ix.
1. *Stage-direction*. In this stage-direction, and in others in the play, it will be observed that, although the stage was merely a large wagon, the stage-setting was in some respects ambitious. It is not safe, however, to speculate too closely upon the nature of the 'clouds' demanded in the present instance.
5. *ghost*, spirit.
6. *fone*, foe.
7. *six score years*. It will be noticed that the period of 120 years during which God promises to delay punishing mankind conforms to the period of 'a hundred winters and twenty' (line 149) occupied by Noah in building the Ark.
8. *blyn*, cease.
23. *slake*, slack.

Page 66.
27. *fonge*, take.
35. *flow*, flood.
43. *spill*, destroy.
44. *soothly*, truly.
46. *grill*, annoy.
53. *bowne*, prepared.
73. *slich*, pitch, or oily substance.
75. *stitch*, fragment.
78. *in fere*, all together.
79. *dight*, prepare.
95. *weete*, wet weather.
100. *frankish fare*, nonsense.
101. *rede*, advice.
103. *By Christ*. This asseveration, like that in line 112, is an obvious anachronism. See also lines 203 and 205.

Page 67.
109. *bere*, noise.
111. *ween*, think.
114. *hie*, make haste.
119. *make*, mate.
122. *mo*, more.
132. *bydene*, in haste.
145. *bayne*, ready.
149. *A hundred winters and twenty*. See note to line 7.
154. *Hie you*, make haste.
170. *fulmart*, polecat.
172. *cowle*, tub or similar large vessel.
178. *crowse*, lively, jolly.
182. *bittour*, bittern.

Page 68.
195. *on God's half*, for God's sake.
202. *gone*, go.

Page 68.
- 209. *wraw*, angry.
- 211. *trow*, trust.
- 224. *doubt*, fear.
- 225. *Stage-direction. gossips*, companions.
- 234. *childer*, children.
- 236. *bought*, redeemed. The reference to events of the New Testament is an obvious anachronism.
- 240. *Stage-direction*. This stage-direction is somewhat inadequate, for Noah's sons obviously apply force to their recalcitrant mother. The situation provides a notable opportunity for a scuffle on the stage.
- 242. *mote*, talking, chatter.
- 250. *wood*, mad.

Page 69.
- 257. *Stage-direction*. The Psalm sung is the fifty-fourth.
- 261. *again*, back.
- 262. *sayne*, say.
- 269. From this stanza one line has been lost.
- 271. *hend*, gentle. The second dove mentioned in the stage-direction after this line seems to be a mechanical contrivance.
- 286. *fay*, faith.
- 297. *hight*, haste.
- 298. *dight*, prepare.
- 307. *bowne*, ready.
- 312. *able*, pleasing.
- 315. *myn*, think.
- 324. *flytte*, swim.
- 325. *behite*, promise.
- 326. *let*, hesitate.
- 329. *bore*, born.
- 332. *in fere*, together.
- 335. *let*, leave alone.

Page 70.
- 344. *foreword*, covenant.
- 348. *hest*, promise.
- 351. *spill*, destroy.
- 352. *My bow*. On the origin of the rainbow, see Genesis ix, 12–15.
- 360. *been*, be.
- 362. *teen*, anger.

THE BANNS

The banns were the formal announcement, or prologue, of the play.
- 5. *Sir John Arnway*, mayor of Chester, 1268–77. It may be, however, that the reference intended is to Richard Erneis, or Herneys, who was mayor, 1327–29.
- 7. *device*, composition. *Don Rondall*. Don is a title of honor, like 'Sir.' According to persistent tradition, the Chester plays were written by Randulf Higden, a monk of St. Werburgh's Abbey, Chester, who entered the monastery in 1299 and died in 1364.
- 8. *seen*, versed.
- 10. *apparently*, openly.
- 15. *abbrevited*, condensed.
- 18. *all*, although.
- 30. *Pentecost*, called *Whitsuntide*, the seventh Sunday after Easter.
- 38. *awarrant*, give warrant for.
- 39. *erstly*, first. *rout*, crowd.
- 41. *your author his author hath*, your author has his authority. *your show let be*, let your show have.

Page 74.

CHAUCER — THE CANTERBURY TALES

PRONUNCIATION

THE following are a few practical suggestions as to pronunciation of Chaucer's language, comparisons being made to sounds in modern words:

Vowels

a long—as in f*a*ther (Example: face)
a short—as in *a*rdent (Example: whan)

Page 74.
e long ('open')—as in th*e*re (Example: heeth)
e long ('close')—as *a* in n*a*me (Example: slepen)
e short—as in m*e*n (Example: hem)
i (or *y*) long—as in mach*i*ne (example: shire)
i (or *y*) short—as in p*i*n (Example: his)
o long ('open')—as in l*o*rd (Example: cold)
o long ('close')—as in n*o*te (Example: rote)
o short—as in h*o*t (Example: croppes)
u (ou, ow) long—as *oo* in b*oo*t (Example: flour)
u short—as in f*u*ll (Example: us)

Diphthongs

ai, ay, ei, ey—as *ai* in str*ai*ght (Example: streit)
au, aw—as *ow* in n*ow* (Example: draughte)
ou, ow—as in through (Example: now)

Consonants

c (before a, o, u)—as *k* (Example: cop)
c (before e, i, y)—as *s* (Example: certes)
ch—as *tch* in i*tch* (Example: ich)
gg—usually as *dg* in ju*dg*e (Example: hegge)
h (not initial), *gh*—guttural as *ch* in German *Nacht* (Example: knight)
f (between vowels)—as *v* (Example: wyfes)
s (final)—as *s* in thi*s* (Example: was)
s (between vowels)—as *z* (Example: ese)

METER

THE poems of Chaucer printed in this book are written in a meter called iambic pentameter, best known to modern readers through the plays of Shakespeare and such poems as Milton's *Paradise Lost* and Tennyson's *Idylls of the King*. The single line contains five iambic feet. Each foot consists of an unaccented syllable followed by an accented one (Example: deláy). The following is a typical line of iambic pentameter from Milton:

Will ónce more líft us úp, in spíte of fáte

In reading Chaucer's lines according to this general pattern, however, one must remember that in his time a word often had at the end a syllable (such as *-en*, *-es*, or *-e*) which is no longer present in modern English, or is no longer sounded. Particular attention should be given to the large number of Chaucerian words ending in *-e* (Example: Chaucerian *smalë*; modern *small*). In Chaucer's verse this final *e* might be pronounced or not in accordance with the requirements of the meter. As a general rule, then, the reader may pronounce a final *e* whenever an unaccented syllable is needed to maintain the metrical alternation of accented and unaccented syllables. Final *e* is sometimes pronounced also as an extra unaccented syllable at the end of a line. According to these general principles, lines 9, 30, and 33 of the *Prologue* of the *Canterbury Tales* are read as follows:

And sma|llë fów|lës ma|kën me|lodý|ë
And shórt|ly, whán| the són|në wás| to rés|të
And ma|dë fór|ward ér|ly fór|to fy|së

THE PROLOGUE

1. *shoures soote*, sweet showers.
2. *droghte*, dryness.
3. *swich licour*, such liquor (sap).
4. *vertu*, power.
5. *Zephirus*, the west wind. *eek*, also.
6. *holt*, wood, grove. *heeth*, heath, open country.
7. *croppes*, shoots. *yonge sonne*, young sun,—young because it had recently entered upon its annual course through the signs of the zodiac.
8. *Hath . . . y-ronne. Ram*, one of the signs of the zodiac, Aries. 'Hath run his half-course in the Ram' means that it was past the eleventh of April.
9. *fowles*, birds in general.
10. *yë*, eye.
11. *So . . . corages*, so nature excites them in their hearts (feelings).

Page 74.

13. *palmers*, pilgrims to foreign parts. Originally, a palmer was one who made a pilgrimage to the Holy Land and brought home a palm-branch as a token. *strondes*, shores.
14. *ferne halwes couthe*, distant shrines known.
16. *wende*, go.
17. *blisful*, blessed. *martir*, Thomas à Becket. *seke*, seek.
18. *That . . . seke*, who hath helped them when they were sick. Notice the riming,—*seke . . . seke*,—of identical forms that have different meanings.
19. *bifel*, it befell.
20. *Southwerk*, Southwark, on the south bank of the Thames, across from London. *Tabard*, an inn, of which the sign was a tabard, or sleeveless jacket.
22. *corage*, heart.
24. *wel*, full, quite.
25–26. *by aventure . . . felawshipe*, by chance fallen into association.
27. *wolden ryde*, wished to ride.
28. *wyde*, spacious.
29. *esed atte beste*, accommodated in the best manner.
30. *to reste*, gone to rest, set.
31. *everichon*, every one.
32. *of hir felawshipe anon*, of their company immediately.
33. *forward*, agreement.
34. *ther . . . devyse*, to that place that I tell you of.
35. *natheles*, nevertheless.
37. *Me . . . resoun*, it seems to me reasonable.
38. *condicioun*, standing.
39–40. *Of . . . degree*, Of each of them, as it appeared to me, and of what sort they were, and of what social class.
41. *eek*, also. *array*, dress.
43. *worthy*, honorable.
45. *chivalrye*, knighthood.
46. *fredom*, liberality.
47. *werre*, war.
48. *therto*, besides that. *ferre*, **farther**.
49. *hethenesse*, heathen lands.
51. *Alisaundre*, Alexandria.
52–53. *Ful . . . Pruce*, Very many times, in Prussia, he had been placed at the head of the table above the knights of all other nations.
54. *Lettow*, Lithuania. *reysed*, made a military expedition. *Ruce*, Russia.
55. *degree*, rank.
56. *Gernade*, Granada.
57. *Algezir*, modern Algeciras. *Belmarye*, a Moorish kingdom in Africa.
58. *Lyeys*, in Armenia. *Satalye*, on the south coast of Asia Minor.
59. *Grete See*, the Mediterranean.
60. *aryve*, landing of troops.
62. *Tramissene*, a Moorish kingdom in Africa.
63. *In . . . foo*, In the lists (field of combat at a tournament) thrice, and always slain his antagonist.
64. *ilke*, same.
65. *Somtyme*, at one time. *Palatye*, in what was Asiatic Turkey.
66. *Ageyn*, against.
67. *sovereyn prys*, great renown.
68. *wys*, wise.
69. *port*, bearing.
70. *vileinye*, low speech or action.
71. *un-to no maner wight*, to no kind of man.
72. *verray parfit gentil knight*, very perfect noble knight.
73. *array*, dress, costume.
74. *hors*, horses. *gay*, gaudily dressed.
75. *fustian*, stout, coarse cloth. *wered*, wore. *gipoun*, a short coat worn over the armor.
76. *bismotered*, spotted. *habergeoun*, coat of mail.
77. *late y-come from his viage*, lately come from his journey.
79. *Squyer*, esquire, one who attended a knight.
80. *lovyer*, lover. *lusty*, joyful, gay. *bacheler*, a young candidate for knighthood.
81. *lokkes crulle*, locks curled.
83. *evene lengthe*, good stature.

Page 74.

84. *delivere*, active.
85. *chivachye*, military expedition.
86. *Flaundres*, Flanders, an ancient country of Europe, extending along the North Sea from the Strait of Dover to the mouth of the Scheldt. *Artoys, Picardye*, Artois, Picardy, ancient provinces of northern France.
87. *space*, length of time.
88. *lady*, genitive singular, without 's.
89. *embrouded*, embroidered. *mede*, mead.
91. *floytinge*, playing the flute.
95. *coude*. knew how. *endyte*, relate, compose.
96. *juste*, joust. *purtreye*, draw, paint.
97. *nightertale*, night-time.
98. *sleep*, slept.
99. *lowly*, modest. *servisable*, helpful.
100. *carf*, carved.
101. *yeman*, yeoman, a servant of the next degree above a groom. *namo*, no more.
102. *him liste ryde*, it pleased him to ride.
104. *A sheef of pecok arwes*, a sheaf of arrows fitted with peacocks' feathers.

Page 75.

106. *takel*, implements; here, arrows.
109. *not-heed*, hair closely cut.
111. *bracer*, a guard for the coat-sleeve, used by archers to avoid the friction of the string against the cloth.
112. *bokeler*, buckler, a small shield.
114. *harneised*, equipped.
115. *Cristofre*, 'a figure of St. Christopher, used as a brooch' (Wright).
116. *bawdrik*, baldric, belt.
117. *forster*, forester.
119. *coy*, quiet, modest.
120. *sëynt Loy*, Saint Eligius.
121. *cleped*, called.
124. *fetisly*, neatly, excellently.
125. *After . . . Bowe*, after the manner of Stratford-le-Bow. This was a monastery near London. The French of the prioress was dialectical, not Parisian.
132. *lest*, pleasure.
134. *ferthing*, a fourth part; hence a small bit.
136. *raughte*, reached.
137. *sikerly*, certainly. *of greet disport*, readily amused.
138. *port*, carriage.
139–141. *And peyned . . . reverence*, and took pains to imitate courtly behavior, and to be stately in her deportment, and to be esteemed worthy of reverence.
142. *conscience*, feeling, tenderness.
143. *pitous*, compassionate.
147. *wastel breed*, bread made of fine flour.
148. *weep*, wept.
149. *yerde*, rod.
150. *conscience*, tenderness.
151. *wimpel*, a covering for the neck. *pinched*, closely pleated.
152. *tretys*, long and well-proportioned.
153. *there-to*, besides.
156. *hardily*, certainly. *undergrowe*, undergrown, stunted.
157. *fetis*, neat, well-made.
159. *peire*, set. *gauded al with grene*, provided with green gawdies. Gawdies were the larger beads in the set.
160. *heng*, hung, *shene*, bright.
162. *Amor vincit omnia*, love conquers all things (Virgil *Eclôg*. x, 69).
164. *chapeleyne*. The prioress has a female chaplain.
165. *a fair for the maistrye*, a fair one for superiority.
166. *out-rydere*, outrider, the monastic officer who visited the outlying manors belonging to the house. *venerye*, hunting.
172. *Ther as*, where. *keper*, head. *celle*, cell, a monastery or nunnery dependent on another one.
173. *seint Maure*, St. Maur (d. 584). *seint Beneit*, St. Benedict (d. 543). St. Benedict founded the Benedictine order, and St. Maur was his later disciple.

Page 75.

174. *som-del streit*, somewhat narrow, strict.
175. *ilke*, same.
176. *space*, course.
177. *yaf*, gave. *pulled*, plucked.
182. *thilke*, that.
184. *What*, why. *wood*, mad.
185. *poure*, pore.
186. *swinken*, work.
187. *Austin*, St. Augustine (d. 604), after whom the Augustinian Canons were named. *bit*, contracted from 3d person singular present, *biddeth*.
188. *swink*, toil.
189. *pricasour*, a hard rider.
191. *priking*, riding.
193. *seigh*, saw. *purfiled*, fringed.
194. *grys*, costly gray fur.
199. *anoint*, anointed.
200. *in good point*, in good condition. Cf. French *en bon point*.
201. *stepe*, prominent.
202. *stemed*, shone. *Leed*, caldron.
203. *botes souple*, boots soft.
205. *for-pyned goost*, tormented ghost.
207. *palfrey*, riding-horse.
208. *frere*, friar. *wantown*, brisk, lively.
209. *limitour*, a begging friar to whom was assigned a certain district, within which he might solicit alms. *ful solempne*, very important.
210. *ordres foure*. The four orders of mendicant friars were: (1) the Dominicans, or Black Friars; (2) the Franciscans, or Gray Friars; (3) the Carmelites, or White Friars; (4) the Augustine, or Austin Friars. These orders arose in the early part of the thirteenth century. *can*, knows.
211. *daliaunce and fair language*, gossip and flattery.
216. *frankeleyns*, wealthy farmers. *over-al*, everywhere.
219. *curat*, parish priest.
220. *licentiat*, provided with a licence from the Pope to hear confession in all places.

Page 76.

223. *yeve*, give.
224. *Ther . . . pitaunce*, where he knew he was sure to have good returns.
225. *povre*, poor. *yive*, give.
226. *y-shrive*, confessed, shriven.
227. *yaf*, gave. *dorste make avaunt*, dared make boast, dared assert confidently.
228. *wiste*, knew.
230. *He . . . smerte*, He cannot weep, although it may pain him sorely.
232. *Men moot yeve*, one ought to give.
233. *tipet*, hood. *farsed*, stuffed.
236. *rote*, a kind of violin.
237. *yeddinges*, songs. *prys*, prize.
238. *flour-de-lys*, lily.
239. *champioun*, athlete.
241. *hostiler*, inn-keeper. *tappestere*, female tapster.
242. *Bet . . . beggestere*, better than a leper or a female beggar.
244. *as by his facultee*, considering his ability.
246. *honest*, becoming. *avaunce*, profit.
247. *poraille*, poor people, rabble.
248. *riche*, rich people. *vitaille*, victuals.
249–250. *And over-al . . . servyse*, And everywhere where profit was likely to arise, he was polite, and humble in offering his services.
251. *vertuous*, efficient.
253. *sho*, shoe.
254. *In principio*, In the beginning,—the opening words of the Gospel according to St. John.
256. *purchas*, proceeds from begging. *rente*, regular income.
257. *rage*, romp. *as . . whelpe*, exactly as if he were a puppy.
258. *love-dayes*, days fixed for settling differences by umpire, without having recourse to law or violence. *mochel*, greatly

Page 76.

260. *cope*, an outer vestment for a cleric.
262. *semi-cope*, short cope.
263. *presse*, mold.
264. *lipsed*, lisped.
271. *mottelee*, motley costume. *hye*, high.
273. *fetisly*, see l. 124.
274. *resons*, opinions.
275. *Sowninge . . . winning*, tending always to the increase of his profit.
276. *kept*, guarded.
277. *Middelburgh*, a port on an island off the coast of the Netherlands. *Orewelle*, an English port, across the North Sea from Middelburgh, at the mouth of the Orwell River. See Map.
278. *Wel . . . selle*, well knew how to sell crowns in exchange. *Sheeldes*, or crowns, were valued at 3 shillings 4 pence.
279. *bisette*, used.
280. *wiste*, knew.
281–282. *So estatly . . . chevisaunce*, So ceremoniously did he order his bargains and agreements for borrowing money.
283. *sothe*, truly.
284. *noot*, know not.
285. *Clerk*, scholar.
286. *y-go*, gone.
288. *nas*, was not.
289. *holwe*, hollow. *soberly*, adj. sad, solemn.
290. *overest courtepy* uppermost short cloak.
291. *benefice*, a church office endowed with a revenue.
292. *office*, secular office.
293. *him . . . have*, it was dearer to him to have.
295. *Aristotle*, Greek philosopher, 384–322 B. C.
296. *fithele*, fiddle. *sautrye*, psaltery, an instrument like a zither, having a sounding-box under the strings.
297–298. *philosophre*, used in the double sense of philosopher and alchemist. It was commonly believed that alchemists could produce gold.
299. *hente*, seize, get.
302. *Of hem . . . scoleye*, of those who gave him (money) with which to go to school.
303. *cure*, care.
304. *o*, one.
305. *in . . . reverence*, in due form and dignity.
306. *hy sentence*, lofty meaning.
307. *sowninge in*, conducive to.
309. *Sergeant of the Lawe*, a law officer of the crown. *war*, cautious.
310. *parvys*, porch or aisle of the church. It was customary for lawyers to meet for consultation at St. Paul's, London.
312. *reverence*, dignity.
313. *swich*, such.
314. *assyse*, session of a court.
315. *By patente . . . commissioun*, by letter patent (definite legal authorization) or by full (unlimited) authorization.
318. *purchasour*, conveyancer.
319. *fee simple*, held in absolute possession.
320. *purchasing*, conveyancing. *infect*, invalid.
323. *In termes . . . alle*, he had (in mind) exactly all the cases and decisions.
325. *Therto*, moreover. *endyte*, write. *make*, draw up.
326. *pinche at*, find fault with.
327. *coude . . . rote*, knew he fully by rote.
328. *medlee cote*, a coat of mixed stuff or color.
329. *ceint*, girdle. *barres*, ornaments, or studs, of a girdle.
330. *array*, costume.
331. *Frankeleyn*, a wealthy farmer.
332. *berd*, beard. *dayesye*, daisy.
333. 'The old school of medicine, following Galen, supposed that there were four "humours," *viz.* hot, cold, moist, and dry, and four complexions or temperaments of men, *viz.* the sanguine, the choleric, the phlegmatic, and the melancholy. The man of sanguine complexion abounded in hot and moist humours' (Skeat). See note to line 421.

Page 76.

334. *by the morwe*, in the morning. *a sop in wyn*, wine with pieces of cake in it.
335. *delyt*, pleasure. *wone*, custom.
336. *Epicurus* (d. 270 B. C.), a Greek philosopher who assumed pleasure to be the highest good.
337. *pleyn*, full.
340. *Seynt Iulian*. 'St. Julian was eminent for providing his votaries with good lodgings and accommodations of all sorts' (Chambers).
341. *alwey after oon*, always up to the standard.

Page 77.

342. *envyned*, stored with wine.
343. *bake mete*, meat pie.
344. *plentevous*, plenteous.
345. *snewed*, snowed.
347. *after*, according to.
348. *soper*, supper.
349. *mewe*, coop.
350. *breem*, bream, a fresh water fish. *luce*, pike. *stewe*, fishpond.
351. *but-if*, unless.
352. *gere*, utensils.
353. *table dormant*, a table fixed to the floor, irremovable. The Franklin kept open house.
355. *sessiouns*, meetings of the justices of the peace.
357. *anlas*, a knife or dagger. *gipser*, pouch.
358. *heng*, hung. *morne*, morning.
359. *shirreve*, 'governor of a county' (Skeat); our modern word *sheriff*. *countour*, accountant.
360. *vavasour*, a sub-vassal of a king's vassal.
362. *Webbe*, weaver. *Tapicer*, upholsterer.
363. *in o liveree*, in one livery.
364. *solempne*, dignified. *fraternitee*, gild.
365. *hir gere apyked*, their apparel trimmed.
366. *y-chaped*, provided with *chapes*, caps of metal at the end of the sheath.
368. *everydeel*, every part.
369. *burgeys*, burgess, citizen.
370 *To . . . deys*, to sit on a dais in a gildhall.
371. *Everich*, each. *can*, knows.
372. *shaply*, adapted, fit.
373. *catel*, property. *ynogh*, enough. *rente*, income.
376. *y-clept*, called.
377. *vigilyës*. 'It was the manner in times past, upon festival evens, called *vigiliæ*, for parishioners to meet in their church-houses or church-yards, and there to have a drinking-fit for the time' (Speght). *al bifore*, before all the others.
378. *roialliche y-bore*, royally borne.
379. *for the nones*, for the occasion.
380. *mary-bones*, marrow-bones.
381. *poudre-marchant*, a sharp flavoring powder. *galingale*, a root of sweet cyperus.
384. *mortreux*, a kind of soup.
385. *thoughte me*, seemed to me.
386. *mormal*, cancer, open sore.
387. *blankmanger*, 'a compound made of capon minced, with rice, milk, sugar, and almonds' (Skeat).
388. *woning . . . weste*, dwelling far westward.
389. *woot*, know. *Dertemouthe*, Dartmouth, an important sea-port on the southwest coast of England.
390. *rouncy*, nag. *couthe*, knew how.
391. *falding*, coarse cloth.
392. *laas*, cord, lace.
397. *Ful . . . sleep*, Very many a draught of wine had he drawn (stolen!) along Bordeaux-way, while the merchant slept.
398. *Of nyce . . . keep*, He had no regard for a fussy conscience.
400. *By water . . . lond*, i.e., he made them 'walk the plank.'
402. *stremes*, currents. *him bisydes*, near him.
403. *herberwe*, harbor. *mone*, moon. *lodemenage*, pilotage.
404. *Hulle*, Hull. *Cartage*, Carthage.
405. *undertake*, assume responsibility.

Page 77.

408. *Gootlond*, Gottland, an island in the Baltic sea. *Finistere*, Cape Finisterre, on the northern coast of Spain.
409. *cryke*, creek, inlet.
414. *astronomye*, astrology.
415. *kepte*, watched.
416. *houres*, astrological hours. A good deal of medical science during the middle ages depended upon astrological and other superstitious observances.
417. *fortunen*, predict. *ascendent*, the point of the zodiacal circle which happens to be ascending above the horizon at a given moment.
418. *images*. 'It was believed that images of men and animals could be made of certain substances and *at certain times*, and could be so treated as to cause good or evil to a patient, by means of magical and planetary influences' (Skeat).
421. *humour*. The four elementary qualities, or *humours*, were hot, cold, dry, and moist. The excess of some one humor was thought to cause disease. The mixture of humors in a man determined his *complexion*, or temperament. The *sanguine complexion* was thought to be hot and moist; the *phlegmatic*, cold and moist; the *choleric*, hot and dry; the *melancholy*, cold and dry.
422. *parfit practisour*, perfect practitioner.
424. *bote*, remedy.
426. *drogges*, drugs. *letuaries*, electuaries, syrups.
428. *Hir*, their.
429. *Esculapius*, Æsculapius, god of medicine.
430. *Deiscorides*, Dioscorides, a Greek physician of the 2d century. *Rufus*, a Greek physician of the 1st century.
431. *Ypocras*, Hippocrates, a Greek physician (460–c 377 B. C.). *Galien*, Galen, a Greek physician of the 2d century.
431–433. Haly, Serapion, Rhazis, Avicenna, Averroës, and John Damascene were Arabian medical authorities.
433–434. Constantinus Afer, Bernardus Gordonius, John Gatisden, and Gilbertus Anglicus were European medical authorities of the later middle ages.
435. *measurable*, moderate.
439. *sangwin*, red. *pers*, blue.
440. *taffata*, *sendal*, two kinds of thin silk.
441. *esy of dispence*, moderate in expenditure.
443. *For*, since, because.
445. *of bisyde Bathe*, from (a place) near Bath.
446. *som-del*, somewhat. *scathe*, misfortune.
447. *haunt*, practice, use.
448. *passed*, surpassed. *Ypres*, *Gaunt*, Ypres, Ghent, cities in Flanders.
450. *to the offring*. The people themselves offered bread and wine for consecration at Mass.
453. *coverchiefs*, coverings for the head. *ground*, texture.
454. *weyeden*, weighed.
456. *hosen*, leggings.
457. *streite y-teyd*, tightly fastened. *moiste*, soft.

Page 78.

460. *at chirche-dore*. The marriage ceremony took place at the church-porch.
461. *withouten*, besides.
462. *as nouthe*, now, at present.
465. *Boloigne*, Boulogne.
466. *In Galice at seint Iame*, the shrine of St. James at Compostella in Galicia. *Coloigne*, Cologne. The Wife of Bath had had wide experience in making pilgrimages.
467. *coude*, knew.
468. *Gat-tothed*, possibly goat-toothed, lascivious.
469. *amblere*, ambling horse.
470. *Y-wimpled*, provided with a wimple.
471. *targe*, target, shield.
472. *foot-mantel*, an outer skirt.
474. *carpe*, prate.
475. *remedies of love*, allusion to title and content of Ovid's *Remedia Amoris*.
476. *the olde daunce*, the old game.

Page 78.

478. *Persoun*, parish priest.
482. *parisshens*, parishioners.
485. *y-preved ofte sythes*, proved oftentimes.
486. *cursen for his tythes*, excommunicate for not paying the tithes that were due him.
487. *yeven, out of doute*, give, without doubt.
489. *offring*, voluntary gifts of his parishioners. *substaunce*, regular income derived from his benefice.
490. *suffisaunce*, a sufficiency.
492. *ne lafte not*, left not, ceased not.
493. *meschief*, mishap.
494. *ferreste*, farthest. *moche and lyte*, great and small
496. *ensamble*, example. *yaf*, gave.
497. *wroghte*, wrought, worked.
498. *Out of the gospel*, see Matthew v. 19. *tho*, the.
502. *lewed*, ignorant.
507. He did not leave his parish duties to be performed by a stranger.
508. *leet*, left.
509. *sëynt Poules*, St. Paul's.
510. *chaunterie*, chantry, 'an endowment for the payment of a priest to sing mass, agreeably to the appointment of the founder' (Skeat).
511. *bretherhed*, brotherhood, or gild. *withholde*, supported.
516. *despitous*, contemptuous.
517. *daungerous*, unapproachable. *digne*, full of dignity, repellent.
519. *fairnesse*, a fair life.
523. *snibben*, reprimand.
525. *wayted after*, looked for.
526. *spyced*, fussy.
530. *y-lad*, led, carried. *fother*, load.
531. *swinkere*, worker.
534. *thogh . . . smerte*, though it pleased him or hurt him.
535. *thanne*, then.
536. *dyke*, make ditches. *delve*, dig.
540. *his propre swink*, his own labor. *catel*, property.
541. *tabord*, sleeveless jacket. *mere*, mare. Persons of quality did not ride mares.
542. *Reve*, steward or bailiff of a manor.
543. *Somnour*, summoner for an ecclesiastical court. *Pardoner*, one who had the Pope's licence to sell pardons and indulgences.
544. *Maunciple*, manciple, a caterer or steward for a college or inn of court.
545. *carl*, fellow.
546. *braun*, muscle.
547. *over-al ther he cam*, everywhere where he came.
548. *ram*. A ram was a frequent prize at a wrestling-match.
549. *a thikke knarre*, a thick knotted fellow.
550. *nolde heve of harre*, would not heave off its hinge.
551. *renning*, running.
554. *cop*, top.
557. *nose-thirles*, nostrils.
560. *Ianglere*, loud talker. *goliardeys*, a teller of ribald stories.
561. *harlotryes*, scurrility.
562. *tollen thryes*. A part of the corn ground was legally taken by a miller in payment for grinding. Our miller took thrice the legal allowance.
563. *a thombe of gold*, a common expression to describe the value of a miller's skill in testing meal or flour between the thumb and finger. *pardee*, a common and mild oath.
564. *wered*, wore.
565. *sowne*, sound.
567. *temple*, an inn of court.
568. *which*, whom. *achatours*, purchasers.
570. *took by taille*, took by tally, took on credit.
571. *Algate . . . achat*, Always he watched so in his buying.
572. *ay biforn*, always before.
574. *switch a lewed*, such an unlearned.

Page 79.

577. *curious*, careful.
581. *his propre good*, his own income.
582. *dettelees*, without debt. *but he were wood*, unless he were mad.
583. *Or . . . desire*, Or live as economically as it pleased him to desire.
584. *al a*, a whole.
586. *sette . . . cappe*, cheated them all.
587. *colerik*, see note to l. 421.
588. *ny*, nigh, close.
592. *Y-lyk*, like. *y-sene* visible.
593. *gerner*, garner.
595. *wiste*, knew. *droghte*, drought. *reyn*, rain.
597. *neet*, cattle. *dayerye*, dairy.
598. *hors*, horses. *stoor*, farm stock.
599. *hoolly*, wholly.
600. *covenaunt*, contract. *yaf*, gave.
602. *Ther . . . arrerage*, No one could prove him to be in arrears.
603. *herde*, herdsman. *hyne*, hind, farm-laborer.
604. *sleighte*, trickery. *covyne*, deceit.
605. *adrad*, afraid. *the deeth*, pestilence.
606. *woning*, dwelling.
609. *astored*, provided with stores.
611. *lene*, lend.
613. *mister*, trade, craft.
614. *wel*, very. *wrighte*, wright, workman.
615. *stot*, stallion.
616. *pomely grey*, gray dappled with apple-like spots.
617. *surcote*, upper coat. *pers*, blue.
619. *Northfolk*, Norfolk. See Map.
621. *Tukked he was*, his long coat tucked up by means of a girdle.
622. *hindreste*, hindmost.
623. *Somnour*; see note to l. 543.
624. *cherubinnes*, cherub's.
625. *sawceflem*, afflicted with pimples. *narwe*, small.
627. *scalled*, scabby. *blake*, black. *piled*, scanty, thin.
629. *litarge*, litharge, white lead.
630. *boras*, borax. *ceruce*, ceruse, cosmetic made from white lead. *oille of tartre*, cream of tartar.
632. *whelkes*, pimples.
633. *knobbes*, large pimples.
636. *Thanne*, then. *wood*, mad.
644. *grope*, test.
646. *Questio quid iuris*, The question is, what law (is there)?
647. *harlot*, a fellow of low conduct.
651. *atte fulle*, fully.
653. *owher*, somewhere.
655. *erchedeknes curs*, archdeacon's curse, excommunication.
656. *But-if*, unless.
661. *wol slee*, will slay. *assoilling*, absolution.
662. *significavit*. A writ of excommunication usually began with this word.
663. *In daunger*, within his jurisdiction. *gyse*, manner.
664. *girles*, young people of both sexes.
665. *hir reed*, their adviser.
666. *gerland*, garland.
667. *ale-stake*, a support for a garland in front of an alehouse.
669. *Pardoner*; see note to l. 543.
670. *Rouncivale*, a hospital near Charing Cross, London.
673. *bar . . . burdoun*, sang bass to his treble.
675. *heer*, hair. *wex*, wax.
676. *heng*, hung. *strike of flex*, hank of flax.
677. *ounces*, thin clusters.
679. *colpons*, portions.
680. *for Iolitee*, for smartness. *wered*, wore.
681. *trussed up*, packed up.
682. *Him thoughte*, it seemed to him. *Iet*, fashion.
685. *vernicle*, 'a diminutive of *Veronike* (Veronica), a copy in miniature of the picture of Christ which is supposed to have been miraculously imprinted upon a handkerchief preserved in the church of St. Peter at Rome.'
687. *Bret-ful*, brimful.
692. *Berwik*, Berwick, on north east coast of England. *Ware*, in Hertfordshire. See Map.
694. *male*, bag. *pilwe-beer*, pillow-case.

Page 80.

695. *lady,* genitive singular.
696. *gobet,* a small piece.
697. *wente,* walked.
698. *hente,* caught hold of.
699. *latoun,* a mixed metal. *ful of,* set with.
702. *person,* parson. *up-on lond,* in the country.
703. *a,* one.
704. *tweye,* two.
705. *Iapes,* tricks.
706. *apes,* dupes.
709. *a lessoun or a storie,* a reading in a church service, or a whole series of such readings.
710. *alderbest,* best of all. *offertorie,* the offertory sung in the mass.
712. *affyle,* make smooth.
716. *Thestat,* the estate. *tharray,* the array, appearance.
719. *highte,* was called. *Belle,* probably another tavern.
721. *baren us,* conducted ourselves. *ilke,* same.
723. *viage,* journey.
726. *That . . . vileinye,* That you ascribe it not to my ill-breeding.
728. *chere,* appearance.
729. *hir wordes proprely,* their words exactly.
731. *shal telle,* has to tell. *after,* according to.
732. *moot,* must.
733. *Everich a,* every single. *charge,* undertaking.
734. *Al,* although. *rudeliche,* rudely. *large,* freely.
736. *feyne,* feign, distort.
739. *brode,* broadly.
740. *woot,* know. *vileinye,* ill-breeding.
744. *Al,* although.
747. *everichon,* every one.
750. *us leste,* it pleased us.
752. *marshal.* The 'marshal of the hall' assigned guests to their seats at public festivals according to their rank.
753. *stepe,* bright.
754. *burgeys,* burgess, citizen. *Chepe,* Cheapside in London.
757. *Eek therto,* also besides.
760. *our rekeninges,* our bills.
765. *herberwe,* inn.
766. *wiste,* knew.
768. *To doon yow ese,* to give you pleasure.
770. *The blisful . . . mede,* May the blessed martyr give you your reward.
772. *shapen yow,* intend. *talen,* tell tales.
775. *disport,* sport.
776. *erst,* first.
777. *And . . . alle,* And if it is pleasing to you all.
781. *fader,* genitive singular. *deed,* dead.
782. *But,* unless. *heed,* head.
784. *seche,* seek.
785. *Us . . . wys,* It seemed to us not worth while to make it a matter of deliberation.
786. *avys,* consideration.
787. *as him leste,* as it pleased him.
788. *herkneth,* listen, 2d pers. plur. imperative.
791. *shorte,* make short.
792. *viage,* journey. *tweye,* two.
795. *aventures,* occurrences. *whylom,* formerly. *han,* have.
798. *sentence,* meaning, content. *solas,* amusement.
799. *our aller cost,* the cost of us all.
805. *withseye,* oppose.
807. *vouche-sauf,* grant.
809. *shape me therfore,* prepare myself for it.

Page 81.

810. *othes swore,* oaths sworn.
816. *devys,* direction.
819. *fet,* fetched.
820. *echoon,* each one.
823. *our aller cok,* cock of us all.
824. *gadrede,* gathered.
825. *riden,* rode. *pas,* foot-pace.
826. St. Thomas a Watering was two miles from Southwark.
828. *herkneth;* see note to l. 788. *if you leste,* if it pleases you.

Page 81.

829. *woot,* know. *forward,* agreement. *yow recorde,* call to your mind.
830. *If . . . acorde,* If even-song (vespers) and matins agree; *i.e.,* if you are minded this morning as you were last night.
832. *As . . . ale,* As surely as I ever hope to be able to drink wine or ale.
835. *draweth,* draw, 2d pers. plur. imperative. *ferrer twinne,* farther depart.
838. *acord,* agreement.
839. *neer,* nearer.
842. *wight,* person.
844. *sort,* lot, destiny.
845. *fil,* fell.
847. *resoun,* reasonable.
848. *forward,* agreement. *composicioun,* compact.
850. *saugh,* saw.
854. *a,* in.
856. *riden,* rode.

THE NUN'S PRIEST'S TALE

1. *widwe,* widow. *stope,* advanced.
2. *whylom,* formerly. *narwe,* narrow, small.
5. *thilke,* that.
6. *ladde,* led.
7. *catel,* property. *rente,* income.
8. *housbondrye,* economy.
9. *fond,* found, supported. *doghtren,* daughters.
11. *highte,* was called.
12. *bour,* bower, inner room.
13. *sclendre meel,* slender meal.
14. *Of . . . deel,* Of poignant sauce she had not the slightest need.
15. *thurgh,* through.
17. *Repleccioun,* overeating.
19. *hertes suffisaunce,* heart's satisfaction.
20. *lette hir no-thing,* prevented her not at all.
21. *popleyxe shente,* apoplexy hurt.
25. *Seynd,* singed. *ey or tweye,* egg or two.
26. *deye,* dairy-woman.
28. *dich,* ditch.
30. *nas,* was not.
31. *merier,* pleasanter, sweeter.
32. *messe-dayes,* Mass-days.
33. *sikerer,* more certain. *logge,* lodging-place.
34. *orlogge,* clock.
35–8. The cock crew every hour, for fifteen degrees of the equinoctial make an hour. *Thanne,* then.
39. *fyn,* fine.
40. *batailed,* indented like a battlement.
41. *bile,* bill. *Ieet,* jet.
42. *toon,* toes.
47. *paramours,* lovers.
48. *as of,* as to.
50. *cleped,* called.
51. *debonaire,* gracious.
52. *compaignable,* companionable.
53. *thilke,* that same.
54. *in hold,* in possession.
55. *loken in every lith,* locked in every limb.
59. '*my lief . . . londe,*' 'my beloved has gone away.' Probably the refrain of a popular song.
61. *briddes,* birds.
62. *bifel,* happened.

Page 82.

67. *drecched,* troubled.
70. *eyleth,* ails.
71. *verray,* true.
73. *agrief,* amiss.
74. *me mette,* I dreamed. *meschief,* mishap.
76. *my . . . aright,* interpret my dream favorably.
78. *me mette,* I dreamed.
79. *saugh,* saw.
81. *deed,* dead.
85. *tweye,* two.
86. *deye,* die.

Page 82.

88. *Avoy,* fie. *herteles,* coward.
94. *free,* generous.
95. *secree,* secret, discreet.
96. *tool,* weapon.
97. *avauntour,* boaster.
99. *aferd,* afraid.
101. *swevenis,* dreams.
103. *replecciouns,* gluttony.
104. *fume,* vapor arising from gluttony. *complecciouns;* see note to *Prologue,* l. 421.
106. *met,* dreamed.
108. *rede colera,* 'red cholera caused by too much bile and blood' (Skeat).
110. *lemes,* gleams.
112. *contek,* strife.
113. *humour of malencolye, i.e.,* black choler.
115. *boles blake,* bulls black.
120. *Catoun,* Cato's *Disticks.* This collection of sayings, of uncertain authorship, was well known as early as the 4th century.
121. *do no fors,* pay no heed to.
122. *flee,* fly. *bemes,* beams, perches.
124. *Up,* upon.
130. *prow,* profit.
131. *tho,* the.
132. *kynde,* nature.
133. *binethe,* beneath.
135. *colerik of compleccioun;* see note to l. 104.
136. *Ware,* beware.
137. *humours hote;* see note to *Prologue,* l. 421.
138. *grote,* groat.
139. *fevere terciane,* tertian fever, a fever occurring every second day.
143. *lauriol,* laurel. *centaure,* the herb centaury. *fumetere,* the herb fumitory.
144. *ellebor,* hellebore.
145. *catapuce,* the herb spurge. *gaytres beryis,* dogwood berries.
146. *yve,* ivy. *mery,* pleasant. The herbs mentioned are disagreeable to the taste!
148. *fader kyn,* father's kinsmen.
149. *Dredeth,* 2d pers. plur. imperative.
150. *graunt mercy,* great thanks.
151. *daun,* dan, Lord, a title given to monks, and to many other sorts of persons.
156. *so moot I thee,* as I may prosper. An expletive phrase.
157. *sentence,* sense.
163. *verray preve,* true proof.
164. *Oon . . . auctours,* refers to Cicero's *De Divinatione.*
165. *whylom,* formerly.
169. *streit of herbergage,* cramped of lodging, lacking in quarters.
170. *o,* one.
173. *departen,* separate.
175. *as . . . falle,* as it chanced.
177. *Fer,* far.
179. *aventure,* chance.
180. *That . . . commune,* That governs us all alike.
182. *mette,* dreamed.

Page 83.

185. *ther,* where.
188. *abrayde,* started suddenly.
190. *took . . . keep,* paid no heed to this.
191. *Him thoughte,* it seemed to him. *nas,* was not.
194. *slawe,* slain.
196. *morwe-tyde,* morning-time.
198. *donge,* dung.
200. *Do . . . arresten,* have that cart stopped.
201. *sooth to sayn,* to say the truth.
206. *in,* inn.
210. *agon,* gone.
213. *mette,* dreamed.
214. *lette,* delay.
216. *to donge,* to put dung upon.
222. *upright,* lying flat on his back.
223. *ministres,* officers of justice.

Page 83.

224. *kepe and reulen,* guard and rule.
225. *Harrow,* a cry of distress. *lyth,* lies.
226. *What,* why.
227. *out-sterte,* started out.
231. *biwreyest,* makest known.
233. *wlatsom,* loathsome.
235. *it heled be,* it to be concealed.
238. *ministres,* officers of justice.
239. *han hent,* have seized. *pyned,* punished.
240. *engyned,* tortured.
241. *biknewe,* confessed.
246. *gabbe,* lie, jest.
247. *han,* have.
248. *fer,* far.
251. *mery,* pleasant.
252. *agayn,* toward.
253. *as hem leste,* as they desired.
254. *Iolif,* cheerful. *hir,* their.
255. *casten hem,* plan.
256. *oo,* one.
258. *mette,* dreamed. *agayn,* toward.
259. *Him thoughte,* it seemed to him.
260. *abyde,* wait.
261. *wende,* go away.
262. *dreynt,* drowned.
263. *wook,* woke. *mette,* dreamed.
264. *And . . . lette,* And urged him to abandon his journey.
265. *abyde,* stay.
268. *agaste,* terrify.
269. *lette . . . thinges,* give up doing my business.
271. *swevenes,* dreams. *Iapes,* deceptions.
273. *mase,* maze.
274. *shal,* shall be.
276. *for-sleuthen,* lose through sloth. *tyde,* time.
277. *God . . . me,* God knows it causes me sorrow.
279. *y-seyled,* sailed.
280. *eyled,* ailed.
281. *botme rente,* bottom burst.
286. *ensamples,* examples, *maistow lere,* mayest thou learn.
287. *recchelees,* careless.
290. *seint Kenelm.* 'Kenelm succeeded his father Kenulph on the throne of the Mercians in 821 at the age of seven years, and was murdered by order of his aunt, Quenedreda. He was subsequently made a saint' (Wright).
292. *Mercenrike,* Mercia. *mette,* dreamed.
293. *A lyte er,* a little while before.
294. *avisioun,* vision. *say,* saw.
295. *norice,* nurse. *del,* part, bit.
296. *kepe,* guard.
297. *For traisoun,* for fear of treason. *nas,* was not.

Page 84.

298. *litel . . . told,* little heed hath he paid.
300. *levere,* rather.
301. *legende,* life of a saint.
302. *yow,* to you.
303–304. *Macrobeus.* Macrobius (early 5th century) wrote a commentary on Cicero's *Somnium Scipionis.*
305. *Affermeth,* confirms.
307. *loketh,* look, 2d pers. plur. imperative.
308. *Daniel.* See Daniel ii.
310–315. *Joseph.* See Genesis xxxix–xli.
311. *Wher,* whether, or where.
312. *falle,* occur.
316. *actes,* history. *remes,* realms, kingdoms.
318. *Cresus.* Crœsus. *Lyde,* Lydia.
319. *Mette,* dreamed.
321. *heer,* here. *Andromacha.* The dream of Andromache, wife of Hector, is recorded not in Homer but in the *De Excidio Troiæ* of Dares Phrygius, a popular medieval authority on the Trojan war.
324. *lorn,* lost.
325. *thilke,* the same.
327. *natheles,* nevertheless.
330. *ny,* nigh.
331. *as for conclusion,* in conclusion.

Page 84.

334. *That . . . store*, That I have no confidence in laxatives.
335. *woot*, know.
336. *defye*, renounce. *del*, bit.
337. *stinte*, cease.
339. *o*, one.
343. *siker*, certain. *In principio*, In the beginning,—the opening words of the Gospel according to John in the Vulgate.
344. *Mulier . . . confusio*. Woman is the undoing of man.
345. *sentence*, meaning.
350. *solas*, mirth, pleasure.
355. *lay*, that lay.
356. *aferd*, afraid.
359. *leoun*, lion.
366. *aventure*, chance, misfortune.
367. *month . . . bigan*. According to medieval chronology, the world began at the vernal equinox.
368. *highte*, was called.
370. *Sin March bigan*, used parenthetically here. What we are really told is that all of March and 32 days more were gone,—an indirect way of indicating that it was May 3.
371. *Bifel*, it befell.
374. *Taurus*, the Bull, one of the signs of the zodiac. *y-ronne*, run.
376. *kynde*, nature.
377. *pryme*, prime, 9 o'clock. *stevene*, voice.
383. *solas*, pleasure, mirth.
384. *him fil*, befell him. *cas*, occurrence, chance.
386. *woot*, knows, *ago*, gone.
387. *rethor*, rhetorician. *endyte*, write, relate.
388. *chronique*, chronicle. *saufly*, safely.
389. *a sovereyn notabilitee*, a particularly worthy saying.
391. *undertake*, affirm.
392. *book of Launcelot de Lake*. The famous romance of Lancelot was full of incredible adventures.
394. *sentence*, meaning, thread of the story.
395. *col-fox*, a black-tipped fox.
396. *woned*, dwelt.
397. *heigh imaginacioun*, lofty calculation.
398. *hegges*, hedges.
399. *ther*, where.
401. *wortes*, herbs.
402. *undern*, here, about 11 o'clock A. M.
407. *Scariot*, Judas Iscariot. *Genilon*, Ganelon, the traitor who betrayed Roland. See *The Song of Roland*.
408. *dissimilour*, deceiver. *Sinon*, the spy who persuaded the Trojans to take the wooden horse into Troy.
409. *al outrely*, utterly.
410. *morwe*, morning.
411. *flough*, flew.
414. *forwot*, foreknows. *mot*, must.
416. *Witnesse . . . is*, Bring to witness any one who is a perfect scholar.

Page 85.

418. *disputisoun*, dispute.
420. *bulte it to the bren*, bolt it to the bran, *i.e.*, sift the matter.
421. *Augustyn*. St. Augustine (d. 430), a great theologian.
422. *Boece*, Boethius (d. 525), wrote *On the Consolation of Philosophy*, in which, among other things, he discusses God's foreknowledge and man's free will. *Bradwardyn*, Thomas Bradwardine, an Oxford theologian of the early 14th century, wrote *On the Cause of God*, in which he discusses the problem of free will and predestination.
423. *forwiting*, foreknowledge.
424. *streyneth me nedely*, constrains me necessarily.
428. *forwot*, foreknew.
429. *Or . . . del*, Or if his knowledge forces not at all.
430. *necessitee condicionel*, conditional necessity, *i.e.*, mere foresight, on God's part, of what man is going to do voluntarily.
431. *han*, have. *swich*, such.
433. *with sorwe*, sorrow take her!
436. *colde*, baneful.

Page 85.

440. *noot*, know not.
442. *in my game*, jokingly.
447. *sond*, sand.
448. *Lyth*, lyeth.
449. *Agayn*, against, in.
451. *Phisiologus*. A book, in Latin verse, describing the nature of certain animals, written by one Theobaldus, of uncertain date.
456. *no-thing . . . crowe*, Then it did not at all please him to crow.
457. *sterte*, started.
458. *affrayed*, frightened.
461. *erst*, first.
467. *vileinye*, rudeness.
471. *stevene*, voice.
474. *Boece*. See note to l. 422. Boethius wrote a treatise *De Musica*.
477. *ese*, pleasure.
478. *certes*, certainly. *fayn*, gladly.
480. *So mote I brouke*, so may I have the use of.
485. *peyne him*, take pains.
486. *winke*, close.
492. *daun Burnel the Asse*, a satirical poem, *Burnellus seu Speculum Stultorum*, written by Nigel Wireker in the late 12th century.
493. *vers*, verses.
494. *yaf*, gave.
495. *nyce*, foolish.
497. *nis*, is not.
500. *seinte*, holy.
501. *countrefete*, imitate, equal.
502. *bete*, beat.
505. *flatour*, flatterer.
506. *losengeour*, liar.
508. *soothfastnesse*, truth.
509. *Ecclesiaste*, Ecclesiasticus, in the *Apocrypha*, not Ecclesiastes. See Ecclesiasticus xii, 10, 11, 16.
513. *for the nones*, for the occasion.
514. *sterte*, started.
515. *gargat*, throat. *hente*, seized.
516. *wode*, wood. *beer*, bore.
517. *sewed*, followed.
518. *eschewed*, avoided, escaped.
519. *fleigh*, flew.
520. *roghte nat of*, paid no heed to.
522. *O Venus*. Friday was Venus' day.
522. *plesaunce*, pleasure.
523. *servant*, Venus's servant, *i.e.*, a lover.
527. *Gaufred*, Geoffrey de Vinsauf wrote, about the year 1200, an art of poetry, *Nova Poetria*, which contains an inflated lament against Friday, the day when Richard I was shot.
530. *sentence*, judgment.
533. *pleyne*, complain.
534. *drede*, fright.

Page 86.

537. *Pirrus*, Pyrrhus. *streite*, drawn.
538. *hent*, seized.
539. *Eneydos*; see *Æneid*, ii, 550–553.
542. *shrighte*, shrieked.
543. *Hasdrubales wyf*, Hasdrubal was king of Carthage when the Romans captured it, 146 B. C.
545. *brend*, burned.
547. *sterte*, started, rushed.
548. *brened hir-selven*, burned herself.
555. *sely*, simple, poor.
558. *syen*, see. *goon*, go.
566. *fered*, frightened.
568. *hem . . . breke*, it seemed to them their heart would break.
570. *as men*, as if men. *quelle*, kill.
573. *benedicite*, an expletive. Pronounce in three syllables ben-si-tā.
574. *Iakke Straw*. In 1381 Jack Straw led an uprising of peasants in an attack upon the Flemish weavers in England. *meynee*, company, crowd.

Page 86.

578. *bemes*, horns. *box*, boxwood.
579. *boon*, bone.
588. *as wis God helpe me*, as surely as God may help me.
589. *Turneth*, turn, 2d per. plur. imperative. *cherles*, churls.
592. *Maugree*, in spite of; French *malgré*.
596. *brak*, broke. *deliverly*, quickly.
597. *heighe*, high. *fleigh*, flew.
598. *sough*, saw.
601. *aferd*, afraid.
602. *hente*, seized.
603. *wikke entente*, wicked intention.
606. *shrewe*, curse.
610. *Do*, make. *winke with*, close.
612. *wilfully*, willingly. *thee*, prosper.
614. *undiscreet of governaunce*, indiscreet of conduct.
615. *iangleth*, babbles.
616. *recchelees*, reckless.
620. *Taketh*, take, 2d pers. plur. imperative.
621. *seint Paul seith;* see 2 Timothy iii, 16.
622. *doctryne*, teaching. *y-write, y-wis*, written certainly.
625. *my lord*, possibly the archbishop of Canterbury, William Courtenay, archbishop 1381–1396.
626. *heighe*, high.

CHAUCERS WORDES UNTO ADAM HIS OWNE SCRIVEYN

Written, probably, not long after 1383.

1. *scriveyn*, scrivener, scribe. *thee bifalle*, happens to thee.
2. *Boece*, Chaucer's prose translation of the *De Consolatione Philosophiæ* of Boethius (died c. 524). *Troilus*, Chaucer's *Troilus and Criseyde*, written about 1383.
3. *lokkes*, locks. *scalle*, scab.
4. *But . . . making*, unless according to my composition.
5. *mot*, must.
7. *rape*, haste.

LAK OF STEDFASTNESSE

Addressed to King Richard II some time between the years 1393 and 1399.

1. *Som tyme*, once, formerly.
3. *deceivable*, full of deceit.
5. *lyk*, alike. *up so doun*, modern English 'upside down.'
6. *mede*, meed, bribe.

Page 87.

9. *lust*, pleasure.
10. *unable*, wanting in ability.
12. *don*, do.
17. *merciable*, merciful.
18. *covetyse*, covetousness. *blent*, blinded.
19. *permutacioun*, change.
22. *Lenvoy*, the envoy. An envoy is a postscript to a composition, to enforce or recommend it.
26. *don*, to be done.
27. *castigacioun*, punishment.

THE COMPLEINT OF CHAUCER TO HIS EMPTY PURSE

This pleasant begging poem must have been addressed to Henry IV immediately after he became king, Sept. 30, 1399, for Chaucer received an answer in the form of an annual grant of forty marks, on Oct. 3 of the same year.

1. *wight*, creature, person.
4. *chere*, countenance.
7. *mot*, must.
8. *voucheth sauf*, grant (imperative). *or*, before.
9. *soun*, sound.
12. *stere*, rudder.
19. The line means, 'I am as bare of money as a friar's tonsure is of hair.'
22. *Lenvoy de*, see preceding poem, l. 22, note.
23. *conquerour*, Henry IV. *Brutes Albioun.* Albion is the old name of England, or Britain. According to legend, Brutus, a descendant of Æneas, was the first ruler of Britain.
25. *verray*, true.
26. *mowen*, can.

Page 87.

TRUTH

1. *prees*, press, crowd. *sothfastnesse*, truth.
2. *Suffyce unto thy good*, be content with thy property.
3. *hord*, hoard, store. *climbing*, ambition. *tikelnesse*, instability.
4. *wele blent overal*, prosperity blinds everywhere.
5. *Savour no more . . . bihove shal*, Have an appetite for no more than it shall behoove you [to eat].
6. *rede*, advise.
7. *drede*, doubt. Cf. John viii, 32: 'The truth shall make you free.'
8. *Tempest thee noght . . . to redresse*, Do not distress yourself by trying to straighten everything that is crooked.
9. *hir*, The reference is to Fortune, whose fickleness was symbolized by a revolving wheel upon which the affairs of a man were alternately raised and lowered.
10. *stant*, stands, is. 'Much repose consists in abstinence from fussiness.' (Skeat.)
11. *eek*, also. *sporne ageyn an al*, kick against an awl. Cf. Acts ix, 5: 'It is hard for thee to kick against the pricks.'
12. *crokke*, earthenware pot.
13. *Daunte*, subdue.
15. *buxumnesse*, submissiveness.
16. *axeth*, asks, requires, invites.
18. *beste*, beast.
19. *contree*, i.e., heaven. *of al*, for all things.
20. *hye wey*, highway. *gost*, spirit.
22. *Envoy*, see note to the corresponding line in the preceding two poems. *Vache*, probably a reference to Sir Philip la Vache, or de la Vache, who married Elizabeth, daughter of Chaucer's friend, Sir Lewis Clifford. Chaucer may intend a pun upon *vache* meaning cow (see line 18), and *Vache* as part of a proper name.
23. *leve*, cease. *thral*, slave.
27. *hevenlich mede*, heavenly reward.

Page 88.

MALORY — LE MORTE D'ARTHUR

a. 7. *ensamples*, examples. *doctrine*, teaching.
   10. *do . . . enprint*, had made and printed.
   11. *Sangreal*, Holy Grail.
   15. *to-fore*, before.
   18. *paynims*, pagans.
   21. *Hector*, son of Priam, and champion of the Trojans.

b. 1. *Alexander the Great* (356–323 B. C.), the famous king of Macedon.
   2. *Julius Cæsar* (100–44 B. C.), the famous Roman general, statesman, and writer.
   6. *Joshua*, the successor of Moses as leader of the Israelites. See the Book of Joshua.
   7. *behest*, promise.
   8. *David*, the second king of Israel, 1055–1015 B. C.
   9. *Judas Maccabæus* (d. 160 B. C.), a famous Jewish patriot and warrior.
   12. *stalled*, installed, placed.
   17. *Charlemagne*, king of the Franks and emperor of the Romans. Crowned emperor, 800 A. D.
   20. *Godfrey of Boloine*, Godefroy de Bouillon (1061–1100), a leader of the first Crusade.
   22. *King Edward the Fourth*, king of England 1461–1483.

Page 89.

a. 1. *instantly*, insistently, earnestly.
   20. *aretted*, reckoned.
   23. *Glastonbury*, a town in Somerset, England, seat of an abbey.
   24. *Polichronicon.* Ran·ulf Higden (died c. 1363), a monk of Chester, wrote *Polychronicon*, a general history, in Latin.
   27. *translated*, removed.
   29. *Bochas*, Boccaccio (1313–1375), a celebrated Italian novelist and poet. *De Casu Principum* [On the Fall of Princes] recounts the misfortunes of famous men.

NOTES TO MALORY; THE NUTBROWNE MAIDE

Page 89.
a. 31. *Galfridus*, Geoffrey of Monmouth (c. 1100–1152?), whose fabulous Latin *History of the Kings of Britain* purported to be based largely upon a 'British book.'
38. *Patricius . . . Imperator*, 'Noble Arthur, Emperor of Britain, Gaul, Germany and Dacia.'
53. *Camelot*, a legendary spot in England where Arthur was said to have had his court.
b. 17. *conning*, knowledge, skill.
19. *emprised*, undertaken.

Page 90.
a. 9. *did do make*, had made.
12. *made a parliament*, called a council.
21. *prefixed*, set, decided upon.
27. *longed*, belonged.
33. *garnished*, furnished, supplied.
34. *wist*, heard, learned.
41. *prevail*, avail.
47. *sithen*, afterward.
54. *book and bell and candle*, a reference to formal ecclesiastical curses.
b. 9. *orgulist*, most arrogant, insolent.
19. *sonds*, messages.
28. *made write*, had written.
34. *depraved*, calumniated, vilified.
48. *term*, length of time.

Page 91.
a. 3. *new-fangle*, fickle.
14. *carracks*, large, round-built vessels.
16. *let*, prevent.
25. *maugre*, in spite of. *power*, army.
41. *affiance*, trust, confidence.
53. *cankered*, inveterate.
54. *danger*, subjection, control.
b. 4. *cedle*, schedule, note.
8. *French book*. As Caxton explains in his preface, Malory's sources are chiefly French.
34. *straitly bestead*, hard pressed.
36. *let . . . king*, had him crowned king.

Page 92.
a. 6. *pight a new field*, prepared for another battle. *Barham Down*, a short distance south of Canterbury. See Map.
32. *Trinity Sunday*, the eighth Sunday after Easter.
44. *chaflet*, platform.
b. 8. *weened*, thought.
20. *an*, if.
23. *parties*, sides.
28. *as to-morn*, to-morrow.
30. *proffer you largely*, make liberal offers.
33. *worshipfully*, honorably, respectfully.
38. *wightly*, swiftly, strongly.
41. *avision*, vision.

Page 93.
a. 8. *everych*, each, every one.
31. *beams*, horns.
38. *foining*, thrusting.
45. *devoir*, duty, service.
47. *stinted*, ceased.
51. *wood*, mad.
b. 25. *Tide*, befall.
36. *foin*, thrust.
40. *bur*, an iron ring, to prevent the hand from slipping.
55. *wit*, know.

Page 94.
a. 3. *yede*, went.
4. *pillers*, pillagers.
12. *rede*, advice.
32. *brast*, burst.
53. *lightly*, quickly.
b. 21. *wap*, ripple.
22. *wan*, grow wan.

Page 95.
a. 12. *Avilion*, or Avalon, the Land of the Blessed in Celtic mythology.
19. *holt*, a hill with a grove on it.
30. *graven*, dug.
33. *flemed*, put to flight.
36. *deeming*, judging.
41. *besant*, a gold coin, first coined at Byzantium.
45. *still*, always.
b. 6. *read*, tell.

Page 96.
a. 19. *let*, prevent.
30. *hard bestead*, hard pressed.
40. *unhap*, misfortune.
52. *will my worship*, wish my honor.
b. 6. *spered*, asked, inquired.
23. *dole*, alms.
31. *Requiem*, the mass for the dead, the first words of the Introit being *Requiem æternam dona eis*.
36. *dured*, lasted.
44. *sithen*, since.
47. *disease*, trouble.

Page 97.
a. 10. *still*, always, constantly.
12. *boot*, use, advantage.
43. *wrack*, ruin.
b. 16. *perfection*, the religious or monastic life.
31. *gray or white*, referring to the habit, or costume.

Page 98.
a. 2. *assoil*, absolve.
16. *overthwart and endlong*, across and up and down.
32. *still*, continually.
34. *lust*, desire.
45. *took no force*, paid no heed.
51. *by then*, when.
54. *purvey*, provide. *horse bier*, bier drawn by horses.
b. 15. *yede*, went.
35. *Dirige*. An antiphon in the office for the dead begins with the word *Dirige* ('direct').
37. *brenning*, burning.
51. *cered cloth of Raines*, waxed cloth of Raines (in Brittany).

Page 99.
a. 11. *careful*, troubled.
13. *orgulity*, arrogance, pride.
29. *dwined*, dwindled.
44. *steven*, voice.
45. *longeth*, belong.
46. *need you*, be necessary to you.
50. *will into*, wills to go into.
53. *houseled*, given the Eucharist. *anealed*, anointed.
b. 24. *dretching of swevens*, tormenting of dreams.
45. *quire*, choir.
49. *worship*, honor, dignity.

Page 100.
a. 35. *rest*, a loop or hook attached to the armor, to steady the spear in a charge.
b. 11. *favor of makers*, fabrication of poets.
15. *quick*, alive.
50. *Caxton . . . fecit*, 'Caxton caused me to be made.'

Page 101.

THE NUTBROWNE MAIDE

It is to be observed that this poem is a dialogue in stanzas, between a lover and his lass. The man speaks the first stanza.

3. *dele*, bit. *agayne*, in return.
11. *mone*, moan.
20. *use*, practice.
27. *ton*, one.
29. *red*, advice, course. *can*, know.
33. *departe*, separate.

NOTES TO NUTBROWNE MAIDE; ENGLISH AND SCOTTISH BALLADS

Page 102.
- 37. *distrayne*, distress.
- 45. *leve*, stay, remain.
- 47. *anoon*, at once.
- 49. *rede*, advise.
- 58. *parte*, share.
- 59. *thoo*, those.
- 64. *lyeve*, live.
- 65. *than*, then.
- 71. *ony*, any.
- 75. *rescous*, rescue.
- 82. *greeve*, grieve, hurt, wound.
- 88. *rove*, roof.

Page 103.
- 89. *than*, then.
- 91. *Syth*, since.
- 93. *oo*, one.
- 94. *perdé*, French *par dieu*, less strong than 'by God.'
- 97. *lust*, desire, wish.
- 103. *dere*, animals.
- 104. *vitayle*, food.
- 106. *hele*, health.
- 110. *here*, hair. *ere*, ear.
- 127. *bee*, by, concerning.
- 131. *dey*, die.
- 135. *power*, poor. *yede*, should go.
- 136. *be*, by.
- 137. *red*, advice. *can*, know.

Page 104.
- 146. *purveid me*, provided myself.
- 153. *curteis*, courteous. *our*, hour.
- 165. *on the splene*. The meaning of this expression is uncertain.
- 172. *be*, by.
- 179. *echeon*, each one.

Page 105.

ENGLISH AND SCOTTISH POPULAR BALLADS
ROBIN HOOD AND GUY OF GISBORNE

Although tradition has persistently maintained that Robin Hood was actually a historical character of the early 14th century, the early historians seem to have had no information concerning him except what they found in the ballads themselves. In any case, whatever his origin, Robin Hood was the hero of ballads of outlawry as early as 1377. His generosity, fair-dealing, tenderness, and wit subsequently established him as a true English hero.

- 1. *shawes*, groves. *sheene*, beautiful. *shradds*, coppices.
- 5. *woodweele*, woodlark.
- 6. *a lyne*, of linden.
- 7. *wight*, stout.
- 10. *froe*, from.
- 12. *wrocken*, avenged. *towe*, two.
- 13. *Sweavens*, dreams.
- 17. *Buske*, dress, prepare. *bowne*, prepare.
- 29. *capull-hyde*, horse-hide.

Page 106.
- 36. *ffarley*, strange.
- 39. *ken*, know.
- 40. *And*, if.
- 43. *bale*, evil.
- 50. *slade*, valley.
- 52. *stockes*, wooden blocks, stumps.
- 56. *Crist his*, Christ's. *mayne*, strength.
- 58. *ffaine*, glad.
- 59. *veiwe*, yew.
- 60. *ffetteled*, prepared.
- 63. *Woe worth thee*, woe be to thee.
- 66. *boote*, help.
- 77. *tane*, taken.
- 88. *lyne*, linden.
- 95. *wilfull*, astray.
- 96. *tyde*, time.

Page 106.
- 103. *tow*, two. *whether*, which of the two.
- 107. *masteryes*, trials of skill.
- 110. *steven*, hour.
- 111. *shroggs*, wands.
- 113. *in twinn*, apart.
- 114. *prickes*, targets, bull's eyes.
- 122. *cold*, could.
- 124. *garlande*, 'the ring within which the prick (or bull's eye) was set.'
- 126. *pricke-wande*, pole, stick.

Page 107.
- 150. *ffettled*, made ready.
- 151. *reacheles*, careless.
- 156. *may*, maiden.
- 161. *awkwarde*, back-handed.
- 177. *capull-hyde*, horse-hide.
- 186. *lowe*, hill.
- 192. *tyde*, time.
- 208. *steven*, voice.
- 209. *loset*, loosed.
- 212. *belive*, quickly.
- 222. *boote*, help.
- 224. *rawstye*, rusty.

Page 108.
- 234. *in twinn*, in twain.

ROBIN HOOD'S DEATH AND BURIAL
- 3. *broom*, a kind of shrub.
- 12. *win*, go.
- 48. *dree*, endure, hold out.
- 53. *boon*, favor.

THE BATTLE OF OTTERBURN

During the reign of Richard II (1377–1399), the Scots frequently harried in the northern part of England. In 1388 an army of Scots, under James, Earl of Douglas, besieged Newcastle for three days. At this time Douglas met Harry Percy, 'Hotspur,' in single combat, captured his lance and banner, and boasted that he would raise the banner on the Scottish castle at Dalkeith. Percy collected a force, pursued the Scots, and attacked them at night in a hand to hand fight, at Otterburn, near the frontier. Although Douglas was killed, the English were defeated and Percy was taken prisoner.

- 1. *Lamasse*, Lammas, August 1st.
- 2. *wynnes*, dry.
- 3. *bowynd*, prepared.
- 4. *praye*, prey.

Page 109.
- 5. *yerlle of Fyffe*. The Earl of Fife, son of the Scottish king, was ravaging in the northwest of England, about Carlisle. He passed over the Solway Firth. See Map.
- 7. *wolde*, would.
- 8. *raysse*, raid.
- 9–11. The places mentioned are in old Northumberland.
- 12. *Styrande*, stirring.
- 13. *brente*, burned.
- 16. *bowyn*, prepared.
- 17. *berne*, man. *bent*, field.
- 31. *march-man*, warrior of the border.
- 32. *kepte Barwyke*, guarded Berwick upon Tweed.
- 34. *on hyght*, aloud.
- 35. *and thou byste*, if thou art.
- 39. *syne*, since. *logeyng*, lodging.
- 46. *envye*, injury.
- 48. *tone*, one.
- 52. *logeed*, lodged.
- 53. *roo*, roe. *rinnes*, runs.
- 59. *the tyll*, to thee.
- 65. *pype*, pipe, a measure for wine,—126 wine-gallons.
- 73. *pyght*, fixed.
- 74. *gettyng*, booty.
- 75. *syne*, afterwards.

Page 109.

76. *gresse*, grass.
77. *hoved*, tarried. *bent*, field.
78. *wache*, watch, sentinel.
79. *ware on*, aware of.
81. *prycked*, rode.
86. *wynne*, joy.
91. *brede*, broad.
92. *haylle*, hale, strong.
96. *garre*, make, cause.
98. *and . . . lesse*, if it were a lie.
100. *peysse*, peace.

Page 110.

101. *yerle of Mentaye*, Earl of Menteith. *eme*, uncle.
102. *forwarde*, van.
103. *cawte and kene*, wary and bold.
105. *Bowghan*, Buchan.
110. *bowen*, ready.
115. *can*, gan, did.
116. *hyght*, promised.
121. *agayne*, back.
122. *upon hye*, in a loud voice.
128. *schoote*, sent.
130. *ryall*, royal. *rowght*, rout, company.
132. *rowynde*, round.
138. *layne*, lie.
140. *agayne*, against.
155. *Wende*, go.
156. *yee*, eye.
161. *weynde . . . growende*, go from this ground.
162. *onfowghten*, not fought, without fight.
165. *rynde*, flayed.
166. *mykkel maye*, powerful maid.
168. *Wyth*, by.
171. *waryson*, reward.
174. 'And cross himself in the name of the Trinity.'
181. *perte*, part, side.
183. *lucettes*, pikes (fish).

Page 111.

199. *swapped*, smote. *whyll that the*, until they.
200. *collayne*, Cologne steel.
201. *bassonnettes*, steel caps, helmets.
202. *roke*, reek, steam.
210. *rede*, guessed.
215. *thee*, they. *beette*, beat.
218. *stounde*, hour, time.
225. *eke a*, every.
229. *freke*, man.
230. *stowre*, battle.
231. *drye*, endure.
238. *Grysely*, fearfully.
263. *Seyng*, seeing.
268. *makes*, mates, husband. *fette*, fetched.
276. *borowed*, ransomed.

CAPTAIN CAR OR EDOM O GORDON

Adam Gordon was deputy, in 1571, for Queen Mary in the north of Scotland, where he encountered the hostility of the Forbeses, who supported the king's party. On one occasion he sent his soldiers to take the castle of Towie in the queen's name. After the lady of the house had refused, the eager soldiers were commanded by their leader, Captain Ker, to set fire to the castle. Tradition has it that the lady and twenty-seven others were burned to death.

1. *Martynmas*, Nov. 11th.
4. *holde*, castle.
5. *Syck, sike*, sick. *to-towe*, too-too.

Page 112.

9. *wether*, whither.
17. *lend*, leaned.
34. *bande*, bond, agreement.
36. *ere*, possess.
38. *whitt and redde*, white and red.
45. *pestilett*, pistol.

Page 112.

50. *pellettes*, bullets.
54. *lowne*, servant, worthless person.
60. *eare*, heir.
64. *waran*, protection, surety.
70. *knet*, knotted.
80. *smoldereth*, smothers.
82. *ffee*, property.
86. *the*, thee.
101. *busk*, prepare. *bowne*, make ready.
104. *or*, before.
108. *dele*, deal, bit.

Page 113.

121. *ought*, had.

THE WIFE OF USHER'S WELL

7. *carline wife*, old woman, or perhaps, wealthy woman, low-born woman.
8. *gane*, gone.
14. *fashes*, troubles.
17. *Martinmass*, Nov. 11th.
20. *birk*, birch.
21. *syke*, ditch, trench.
22. *sheugh*, ditch, furrow.
27. *a'*, all.
41. *daw*, dawn.
42. *channerin*, fretting.
43. *Gin*, if.
44. *sair*, sore. *maun*, must.
46. *byre*, cow-house.

KEMP OWYNE

Kemp Owyne is Owain, one of King Arthur's knights. The adventure here ascribed to him is that of disenchantment through kisses.

6. *dee*, do.
12. *borrow*, set free, ransom.
34. *wi*, with.

Page 114.

THE DÆMON LOVER

20. *kend*, knew.
30. *baith*, both.
31. *ain*, own.
35. *taffetie*, fine silk.
40. *drumlie*, gloomy, frightened. *ee*, eye.
52. *win*, arrive.
57. *strack*, struck.

LORD RANDALL

4. *wald*, would.

Page 115.

11. *broo*, water in which something has been boiled.

SIR PATRICK SPENS

3. *guid*, good.
9. *braid*, broad.
14. *lauch*, laugh.
29. *laith*, loth.
31. *owre a'*, ere all.
32. *aboone*, above.
38. *kems*, coombs.
39. *ain*, own.
41. *owre*, over.

THOMAS RYMER

There is considerable evidence that Thomas the Rimer was one Thomas of Erceldoune, who lived in southern Scotland in the 13th century. Tradition has it that he was a prophet, as well as a poet, and that he was frequently visited by fairies.

4. *fernie brae*, ferny hill.
7. *ilka tett*, every lock.
10. *till*, to.
17. *maun*, must.
20. *wae*, woe.

Page 116.
44. *fairlies*, wonders.
49. *braid*, broad.
50. *lillie leven*, pleasant lawn.
56. *gae*, go.
59. *gin ae*, if one.
61. *even*, smooth.

BONNY BARBARA ALLAN
1. *Martinmass*, Nov. 11th.
8. *Gin*, if.
9. *hooly*, slowly.
17. *dinna*, do not.
19. *gae*, go.
28. *reft*, deprived.
31. *jow*, stroke. *geid*, gave.

THE TWA SISTERS
1. *bowr*, bower.
10. *brotch*, brooch.
12. *sair*, sore.

Page 117.
15. *brast*, burst.
22. *stane*, stone.
25. *jaw*, wave, current.
27. *Ise*, I shall. *mack*, make. *a' my lan*, all my land.
29. *goud*, gold.
32. *fa*, fall. *han*, hand.
33. 'It separated me and my world's mate.'
35. *Gars*, makes. *gae*, go.
46. *sma*, small.
47. *braw*, fine, handsome.
49. *sae gryte*, so great.
58. *nextin*, next. *syne*, afterwards.

THE CRUEL BROTHER
1. *ba*, ball.
5. *baith*, both.
18. *maun*, must. *frae a'*, from all.

Page 118.
31. *closs*, court-yard.
46. *pall*, cloak.
48. *gowden*, golden.
57. *sair*, sore.
58. *rive*, tear.

EDWARD
1. *dois*, does. *brand*, sword, knife.
4. *gang*, go.
7. *guid*, good.
8. *mair*, more.
13. *reid-roan steid*, red-roan steed.
16. *frie*, good.
20. *dule ye drie*, sorrow ye suffer.
25. *drie*, suffer.
35. *ha*, hall.
37. *tul*, till. *fa*, fall.
45. *thrae*, through.
53. *sall*, shall. *beir*, bear.

Page 121.
WYATT—A RENOUNCING OF LOVE
3. *Senec*, Lucius Annæus Seneca (4 B. C.–65 A. D.), a famous Roman Stoic philosopher and writer of tragedies. *Plato* (429 or 427–347 B. C.), a famous Greek philosopher.

Page 122.
8. *lever*, dearer.

AN EARNEST SUIT
4. *grame*, sorrow.

THE LOVER COMPLAINETH
7. *grave*, make an impression upon, engrave.
24. *playn*, to complain.

Page 123.
OF THE MEAN AND SURE ESTATE
John Poins (died 1558), an intimate friend of Wyatt, lived chiefly at the English court.
6. *souse*, drench.
10. *dight*, put in order.
14. *store*, supply, abundance. *stroyed*, destroyed.
26. *cater*, caterer.
28. *charge*, care, burden.
31. *jape*, jest.
53. *steaming*, gleaming.

Page 124.
61. *tho*, then.
88. *hay*, snare. *conies*, rabbits.
105. *dome*, judgment.

Page 125.
HENRY HOWARD—DESCRIPTION OF SPRING
1. *soote*, sweet.
2. *eke*, also.
4. *turtle*, turtle-dove. *make*, mate.
5. *spray*, branch, stem. *springs*, sprouts.
8. *flete*, float.
11. *mings*, mixes.

DESCRIPTION AND PRAISE OF HIS LOVE GERALDINE
1. *Tuscan*, Tuscany.
2. *her*, their.
3. *Western isle*. See line 5.
4. *Camber's cliffs*, the cliffs of Wales.
9. *Hunsdon*, in Hertfordshire, some 30 miles north of London. See Map.

Page 126.
11. *Hampton*, Hampton Court, a royal palace near London. See Map.
12. *Windsor*, Windsor Castle. See Map.
13. *kind*, nature.

COMPLAINT OF THE LOVER DISDAINED
1. *Cyprus*. The island of Cyprus was the especial home of Venus.

COMPLAINT OF THE ABSENCE OF HER LOVER
4. *eke*, also.
5. *wonted*, was accustomed.
14. *avail*, profit, advantage.
33. *drencheth*, drowns.
38. *doubtful*, full of fear.

Page 127.
A PRAISE OF HIS LOVE
4. *sayn*, say.
7. *troth*, fidelity.
8. *Penelope*, the proverbially faithful wife of Odysseus.
11. *mo*, more.
21. *kind*, nature.
25. *sith*, since.

DESCRIPTION OF THE RESTLESS STATE OF A LOVER
19. *list*, please.
24. *use*, practice.
31. *plain*, complain.
44. *agazed*, wrapt, amazed.
51. *teen*, sorrow.

OF THE DEATH OF SIR THOMAS WYATT
7. *stithe*, anvil.

Page 128.
14. *reft*, bereft.
17. *served in foreign realms*. See p. 121 above.
21. *none affect*, no affection.

Page 128.

VIRGIL'S ÆNEID

1. *whisted*, became silent.
6. *Phrygian*, of Phrygia, that country or division of Asia Minor in which Troy was situated. *wailful*, lamentable.
10. *Myrmidon*. The Myrmidons were led to the Trojan War by Achilles. *Dolopës*. The Dolopës came from Thessaly to fight on the Greek side before Troy.
17. *plaint eschews*, avoids complaint.
35. *fet*, fetched, reached.
40. *Pyrrhus*, a famous Greek hero of the Trojan War. *pight*, camped.
42. *scathful*, harmful.
43. *Behight*, promised.

Page 129.

SACKVILLE — THE INDUCTION

2. *treen*, trees.
3. *Saturnus*, Saturn, one of the planets, of unpropitious influence.
7. *tapets*, tapestries, figuratively used for foliage. *bloom*, flower.
10. *soote*, sweet.
11. *Boreas*, the north wind.
21. *whereas*, where.
24. *Venus*, goddess of love. *Hermes*, Mercury, messenger of Jupiter.
25. *Mars*, god of war. *will*, desire, urge.
27. *Virgo*, the Virgin, one of the constellations, and a sign of the zodiac.
28. *Thetis*, goddess of the sea.
29. *Scorpio, Sagittarius*, Scorpion and Archer, signs of the zodiac.
30. *prest*, ready.
32. *Bear*, a constellation.
36. *Phaëton*, son of the sun-god.
38. *prest*, ready.
40. *stent*, end.
42. *Titan*, the sun personified.
43. *Cynthea*, the moon.
48. *chare*, car, chariot.
51. *lusty*, pleasant.
53. *fade*, faded.

Page 130.

57. *leams*, flames, rays.
60. *Phœbus*, the sun-god.
68. *peers*, noblemen of especial dignity.
69. *descrive*, describe.
74. *wight*, creature, person. *forewaste*, completely wasted.
75. *brast*, burst.
76. *fold*, folded.
77. *ruth*, pity.
80. *welkèd*, withered, pale. *besprent*, sprinkled.
90. *doom*, judgment.
93. *distrained*, pained, torn.
96. *apart*, set aside.
97. *dewle*, lamentation, sorrow.
100. *stint*, cease. *spill*, destroy, kill.
102. *dure*, last, endure, *attaint*, tainted, afflicted.
103. *forefaint*, very faint.
106. *distrained*, distressed.
109. *Furies*, the Eumenides: Alecto, Megæra, and Tisiphone.
111. *Lethe*, the river of oblivion, in Hades.
112. *reave*, take away.
119. *dure*, last, endure.
120. *brayed*, started.
122. *shright*, shrieked.
123. *to-dashed*, dashed to pieces.
125. *eft*, again.
131. *avale*, abate.
134. *sith*, since.
141. *stike*, stich, verse, stanza.
143. *Æölus*, god of the winds.
145. *bedrent*, drenched.

Page 131.

161. *won*, dwelling.
166. *silly*, simple, innocent.
175. *shright*, shrieked.
176. *grisly*, dreadful.
179. *whilom*, formerly, once. *bare swing*, bore sway.
191. *unmeet*, unseemly, unusual.
202. *Astoined*, astounded.
208. *yeding*, going.
210. *clepèd*, called. *Avern*, a small lake near modern Naples, anciently believed to be the entrance to the infernal regions.
212. *swelth*, overflow.
219. *besprent*, sprinkled.
221. *stent*, cease.
223. *thoughtful*, sorrowful.
233. *proffered*, put forth.
236. *staring of his hair*, hair standing on end.
237. *'Stoined*, astounded.
243. *far forth*, extremely, excessively.

Page 132.

250. *fet*, fetched.
253. *somedeal*, somewhat.
257. *clouts*, tatters, rags.
258. *scrip*, wallet.
260. *for most*, chiefly.
262. *wot*, knows.
268. *ruth*, pity.
271. *breres*, briars.
284. *keep*, heed.
291. *Reaver*, robber, one who deprives.
292. *tide*, happen.
294. *Crœsus*, the fabulously wealthy king of Lydia, who came to the throne in 560 B. C. *Irus*, in Homeric legend, a beggar of gigantic stature.
297. *cheer*, countenance. *still*, ever, always.
299. *the sisters*, the fates: Clotho, Lachesis, and Atropos.
306. *forewaste*, wasted away.
308. *beseeck*, beseech.
309. *But and*, although.
313. *eld*, old age.
328. *fain*, eagerly.
333. *pilled*, bare. *with eld forlore*, wasted with age.
336. *For brief*, in brief.
340. *brook*, use, endure, enjoy.
342. *recure*, recovery.
346. *grisly*, terrible.

Page 133.

361. *maw*, stomach.
371. *Enthrilling*, forcing in. *reave*, deprive.
374. *daunts*, subdues (by fear).
376. *peers*, noblemen.
381. *eftsoons*, forthwith, immediately.
382. *affrayèd*, frightened.
383. *dight*, provided. *pardé*, French *par Dieu*.
389. *imbrued*, covered.
393. *whilom*, formerly, once.
398. *forehewed*, hewed to pieces.
399. *targe*, shield.
401. *Debate*, dispute, contest, war.
402. *fillet*, a band for tying about the hair.
405. *Darius*, king of Persia 521–486 B. C. *power*, army.
407. *Macedo*, Alexander the Great (356–323 B. C.), king of Macedonia.
409. *daunted*, subdued.
410–418. *Hannibal* (247–183 B. C.), a famous Carthaginian general, among those victories against the Romans are those of the Trebia, of Lake Trasimene, and of Cannæ. At Cannæ the Roman consul Paulus was killed. Hannibal was finally defeated by Scipio Africanus Major, at Zama, in 202 B. C.
419. *Cæsar . . . Pompey*. The civil war between Julius Cæsar and Pompey was ended by the total defeat of Pompey at Pharsalia in 48 B. C.
423. *Sulla and Marius*. The civil war between the Romans Marius and Sulla began in 88 B. C.

Page 133.

425. *Cyrus*, the Great (d. 529 B. C.), founded the Persian empire.
428. *Xerxes* (c. 519–464 B. C.), king of Persia.
432. *Thebes*, a city in Bœotia, Greece, destroyed by Alexander the Great.
433. *Tyrus*, Tyre, despoiled by Alexander the Great.
440. *Priam*, king of Troy.
441. *lin*, restrain myself.
442. *sith*, since.

Page 134.

445. *quail*, fall.
449. *Hector*, son of Priam.
451. *boot*, reward, outcome.
452. *hugy horse*, the wooden horse by means of which the Greeks gained entrance into Troy.
463. *Cassandra*, a prophetess, daughter of Priam. By command of Apollo, her prophecies, though true, were always descredited.
464. *Pallas' house*, temple of Pallas. *sperkled*, disheveled.
465. *rout*, mob. *empaled*, pierced.
467. *Pyrrhus*, the Greek who slew Priam.
468. *baign*, bath.
475. *Ilium*, the citadel of Troy. *gledes*, flames.
476. *Neptunus*, god of the sea.
480. *Acheron*, a river in Hades.
482. *grisly*, terrible. *Charon*, the ferryman who transported the souls of the dead over the rivers of the underworld.
486. *rout*, crowd.
491. *fraughted*, freighted, laden.
494. *hoise*, hoist.
499. *Cerberus*, the three-headed watch-dog at the entrance to the infernal regions.
501. *Foredinning*, filling with a din.
504. *peased*, held his peace, became silent.
512. *puled*, whined.
517. *yfear*, together.
527. *whilom*, formerly, once.
530. *erewhile*, a while ago.
532. *kesar*, emperor. *peer*, nobleman.

Page 135.

ROGER ASCHAM — THE SCHOOLMASTER

a. 4. *Circe's Court*. In Greek mythology Circe was an enchantress who, attended by four nymphs, feasted all persons who approached her dwelling. Anyone, however, who tasted the contents of her magic cup was turned into a beast.
27. *Inglese . . . incarnato*, 'An Englishman Italianate is a devil incarnate.'
b. 14. *policy*, cunning.
18. *discoursing*, reasoning, argumentative.
25. *fond*, foolish.
28. *honest*, virtuous.
32. *charge*, duty, office.
35. *Paul's Cross*, a cross situated near the northeast angle of old St. Paul's, in the churchyard. From it great public assemblies were addressed and sermons preached. The 'Paul's Cross Sermons' are still preached on Sunday morning.

Page 136.

a. 7. *Louvain*, a city in the province of Brabant, Belgium. Religious books were often printed here.
8. *wink*, close the eyes.
18. *St. Paul saith*, Galatians v, 19ff.
46. *canons*, ecclesiastics retained for the performance of divine service in a cathedral or collegiate church.
47. *Morte Arthur*, a compilation of prose romances on the life and death of King Arthur and the knights of the Round Table, translated largely from French romances by Sir Thomas Malory and printed by Caxton in 1485. See p. 88.

Page 136.

a. 52. *shifts*, tricks. *Sir Launcelot*, 'Launcelot of the Lake,' one of the most famous of the knights of the Round Table, who guiltily loved Arthur's queen, Guinevere.
53. *Wife of King Arthur*, Guinevere. *Sir Tristram*, of Lyonesse, another famous Knight of the Round Table. His love for Isolde, wife of King Mark of Cornwall, forms the subject of many romances.
55. *Sir Lamerock*, a knight of the Round Table. *wife of King Lot*. King Lot in Malory's *Morte d'Arthur* was a King of Orkney who married Margawse, sister of Arthur.
b. 12. *fond*, foolish.
48. *lewd*, unlearned, vulgar.

Page 137.

a. 1. *Plato* (429 or 427–347 B. C.), a famous Greek philosopher, disciple of Socrates and teacher of Aristotle.
3. *abominabiles . . . suis*, 'made detestable in their studies.'
5. *Dixit insipiens in corde suo, non est Deus*, 'The fool hath said in his heart there is no God,' Psalm xiv, i.
13. *Triumphs of Petrarch*, an allegorical work by the celebrated Italian poet Petrarch (1304–1374).
14. *Tully's Offices*. Marcus Tullius Cicero (106–43 B. C.) was a famous Roman orator, statesman, and philosopher. The work here referred to is his *De Officiis* (On Duties).
15. *Boccaccio* (1313–1375), eminent Italian writer, author of *The Decameron*, a collection of 100 tales.
25. *Whether*, which.
30. *general councils*, composed of bishops and theologians from different nations, convened to consider questions of church doctrine, discipline, and the like.
33. *Luther*, Martin Luther (1483–1546), leader of the Protestant Reformation in Germany.
38. *epicures*, those who held the opinions of the Greek philosopher Epicurus (342–270 B. C.), who taught that pleasure is the only possible end of rational action and that ultimate pleasure is freedom.
b. 1. *list*, like, choose.
2. *Mysteries of Moses*, the rites of the Jewish religion instituted by Moses. See the Book of Leviticus.
3. *Law and ceremonies*. See Deuteronomy.
7. *Horace*, Roman poet (65–8 B. C.). Quotation from *Satires*, i, 5, 100.
26. *Pygius*, Pighius (1490–1542), a theologian whose writings were opposed by Calvin. *Machiavelli* (1469–1527), celebrated Italian statesman and author. He was imprisoned and put to the torture on suspicion of conspiring against Giovanni de Medici, but was released and after retiring to his country estate wrote *The Prince*. His name is synonymous with all that is cunning and unscrupulous in diplomacy.
36. *where Christ's doctrine . . . special regard*, Germany.
47. *lust*, desire.
48. *pantocle*, a slipper.

Page 138.

a. 7. *bent enemy*, cf. 'bent on mischief.'
21. *Bridewell*, a celebrated London prison or house of detention. The name has become a generic term for a house of correction or lock-up.
26. *present Pope*, Pius V (1566–1572).
27. *meed*, a reward, gift.
b. 24. *lust*, desire.
26. *Guelph*, the papal and popular party in Italy during the struggle between the papacy and the Empire in the Middle Ages. *Ghibelin*, the imperial and aristocratic party in the same struggle.
33. *let*, hindrance; archaic except in the common phrase 'without let or hindrance.'

Page 139.
JOHN LYLY — EUPHUES AND HIS ENGLAND
a. 1. *This queen.* Mary was queen from 1553 to 1558.
2. *age of twenty-two years.* At her accession to the throne, in 1558, Elizabeth (born 1533) was actually twenty-five years of age.
4. *a prisoner.* Queen Mary had imprisoned Elizabeth in the Tower of London.
5. *Prince,* used properly, by extension of meaning, to designate a royal personage of either sex.
22. *Zeno,* a philosopher of Elea (born c. 488 B. C.), was mentioned in classical times as an example of patience. *Eretricus,* apparently Lyly's own invention.
23. *Lycurgus,* either the Spartan legislator (9th century B. C.), or the Athenian orator (c. 396-c. 323 B. C.).
b. 4. *spill,* destroy.
5. *proffer,* offer.
9. *Aristides* (d. 468? B. C.), an Athenian general and politician, was exiled through the influence of his great rival, Themistocles.
11. *Alexander.* Lyly's reference is uncertain.
15. *bills,* requests.
16. *resembling Julius Cæsar.* There is no authority for this comparison.
25. *government,* reign.
27. *racking,* stretching.
30. *Antoninus* (emperor of Rome 138-161 A. D.), surnamed 'Pius.'

Page 140.
a. 6. *gun that was shot off.* This was, for Lyly, a recent occurrence, of the summer of 1579.
15. *close,* secret.
20. *in the whale's belly.* An allusion to the story of Jonah. See Jonah i-ii.
22. *in the hot oven.* An allusion to the story of Shadrach, Meshach, and Abednego. See Daniel iii.
29. *list,* please.
32. *Theodosius,* an allusion, perhaps, to the repentance of Theodosius I (c. 346-395), Emperor of the East, after his massacre of the rebels of Thessalonica in 390.
34-6. *Augustus . . . write.* This anecdote is recounted not of Augustus, but of Nero, emperor of Rome 54-68.
35. *we,* royal use of plural for singular.
b. 5. *Praxitiles,* born at Athens near the end of the 5th century B. C. A famous sculptor. His statues of Venus and Cupid are known, but not his paintings.
6. *her son,* Cupid.
14. *Zeuxis,* a famous Greek painter who flourished at the end of the 5th century B. C.
21. *table,* probably a slab, or tablet.
24. *Apelles,* a famous Greek painter who flourished in the early part of the 4th century B. C.
36. *narrowly,* closely.
45. *mold,* pattern, model.
53. *forty years,* actually forty-seven years!

Page 141.
a. 7. *tickle,* uncertain.
8. *twist,* thread.
15. *the bird Ibis.* There is a slender tradition that this bird was distinguished for sweetness of odor.
29. *Nicaulia the queen of Saba.* A Nicaul is mentioned in Josephus' *Antiquities of the Jews,* Bk. viii, Ch. 6.
31. *Nicostrata,* a legendary or mythological Greek prophetess.
34. *Amalasunta,* ruled at Ravenna as queen of the Ostrogoths 522-530 A. D. Tradition ascribes to her numerous literary accomplishments. *Aspasia . . . Pericles.* Aspasia was an accomplished woman to whom the famous Athenian statesman, Pericles (c. 495-429 B. C.), was notoriously attached.

Page 141.
a. 36. *Themistoclea . . . Pythogoras.* Pythagoras (c. 582-c. 500 B. C.), a famous Greek philosopher and mathematician, is said to have received instruction from one Aristocleia, a priestess.
40. *escapes,* mistakes.
53. *twice . . . universities.* Queen Elizabeth visited Cambridge for a few days in 1564, and Oxford for a few days in 1566. In both places she attended disputations, and made speeches in Greek and Latin.
b. 12. *Sybarites,* inhabitants of Sybaris in southern Italy, who were noted for luxurious living.
20. *withal,* with.
28. *whenas,* since.
31. *gallery of Olympia.* Reference to a famous echoing gallery at Olympia, in Greece.

Page 142.
a. 2. *curses of the Pope.* Pope Pius V directed a bull of excommunication and deposition against Elizabeth in 1570.
37-8. *Alexander,* 'the Great' (356-323 B. C.), king of Macedon. *Galba* (3 B. C.-69 A. D.), a Roman emperor.
40. *queen of Navarre,* Margaret d' Angouleme (1492-1549), queen of Henry II of Navarre. Elizabeth, while princess, translated a small book of religious meditations from the French of Margaret.
46. *bound . . . palm tree,* i.e., was victorious in Egypt.
b. 4. *silly,* innocent.
8. *whist,* silent.
9. *bird Attagen.* The habits of this bird here recounted are vouched for by Pliny (23-79 A. D.), the celebrated Roman naturalist.
11. *wade,* go.
36. *weams,* blemishes, scars.

Page 143.
SONG (FROM GALLATHEA)
1. *O yes, O yes!* A development from French *oiez,* 'hear ye,' a summons to court.

Page 144.
SIDNEY — AN APOLOGY FOR POETRY
a. 1. *so long a career.* Up to this point, Sidney has considered at length the nature and value of poetry, its superiority to history, and the kinds of poetry.
10. *Musa . . . læso,* Virgil, *Æn.* i. 8.
16-17. *David.* See, for example, 2 Samuel xxii. *Adrian,* the emperor Hadrian (117-138 A. D.), who wrote both prose and verse. *Sophocles,* the Greek tragic poet (495?-406 B. C.). *Germanicus* (15 B. C.-19 A. D.), nephew of the Emperor Tiberius, took his name from Germany (*Germania*), where he distinguished himself in military service. He wrote prose and poetry.
19. *Robert, King of Sicily,* king of Naples, 1309-1343. He wrote prose and poetry.
20. *King Francis,* Francis I (1515-1547), a generous patron of letters. *King James of Scotland,* James I of Scotland (1405-1436). His *King's Quair* is a pleasant poem in the Chaucerian style.
21. *Bembus,* Pietro Bembo (1470-1547), a cardinal and papal secretary, wrote poetry and prose in both Latin and Italian.
22. *Bibiena,* Bernardo da Bibbiena (1470-1520), one of the tutors of Pope Leo X.
23. *Beza,* Theodore Beza (1519-1605), a French Calvinistic controversialist, composed numerous Latin poems. *Melanchthon,* Philip Melanchthon, (1497-1560), a German supporter of Luther, and a Latin poet.
24. *Fracastorius,* Hieronymus Fracastorius (1483-1553), an Italian poet, philosopher, and scientist. *Scaliger,* Julius Cæsar Scaliger (1484-1558) was an Italian literary critic. Sidney appears to have studied diligently his treatise on poetry.

NOTES TO SIDNEY: AN APOLOGY FOR POETRY

Page 144.

b. 1. *Pontanus*, Johannes Jovius Pontanus (1420–1503), an Italian, wrote both prose and distinguished poetry in Latin. *Muretus*, Marc Antoine Muret (1526–1585), a French orator, jurist, and poet.
    2. *George Buchanan* (1506–1582), a distinguished Scotch Latinist.
    4. *Hospital of France*, Michael de l'Hospital (1505–1573), a distinguished French lawyer and statesman, wrote numerous Latin poems.
    16. *when . . . loudest.* Chaucer, for example, served in the English army under Edward III (1327–1377).
    17. *over-faint quietness.* Under Queen Elizabeth England had been at peace for some 25 years.
    18. *strew the house,* a figure derived from the practice of strewing rushes on the floor.
    19. *mountebanks at Venice,* peddlers of quack medicines, notorious at Venice.
    23. *troubled . . . Mars.* Vulcan, jealous over his wife, forged a net for her.

Page 145.

a. 1. *a piece of a reason,* a considerable reason.
    6. *Epaminondas* (418–362 B. C.), a Theban general and statesman, who began his career modestly but effectively as a sort of commissioner of sewers.
    15. *Helicon,* a mountain in Bœotia haunted by the Muses.
    18. *Queis . . . Titan,* Juvenal, *Sat.* xiv. 36.
    29. *Pallas,* Minerva, goddess of wisdom and war.
    52. *Dædalus,* invented wings for himself and for his son Icarus.
b. 3. *withal,* with.
    13. *Ovid's verse.* Cf. Ovid, *Tristia,* iv. 10. 26.
    21. *Troilus and Criseyde.* See p. 73.
    26. *Mirror for Magistrates.* See p. 129.
    28. *Earl of Surrey's lyrics.* See p. 125.
    30. *Shepherd's Calendar.* See p. 161.
    31. *eclogues,* pastoral poems.
    34. *Theocritus,* a Greek idyllic poet of the 3d century B. C.
    35. *Sannazaro* (1458–1530), a famous Italian poet.
    48. *Gorboduc, or Ferrex and Porrex,* a tragedy by Thomas Sackville (see p. 129) and Thomas Norton, was first acted in 1561.
    51. *Seneca's style.* Lucius Annæus Seneca (c. 4 B. C.–65 A. D.), a Roman philosopher and writer of tragedies.

Page 146.

a. 2. *faulty both in place and time,* i.e., a violation of the 'unity of place,' which required that all the action of a play occur in one place, and of the 'unity of time,' which required that the time represented by the action should not exceed one revolution of the sun.
    7. *Aristotle's precept.* Aristotle (384–322 B. C.) was the most influential of Greek philosophers. The principles of dramatic writing are discussed in his *Poetics.*
    29. *traverses,* difficulties.
    37. *Eunuch in Terence.* Terence (c. 185–c. 159 B. C.), a Roman comic poet. The *Eunuchus* is not the only play of Terence that violates the 'unity of time.'
    41. *Plautus . . . amiss.* Plautus (died 184 B. C.), a Roman writer of comedies. We cannot be certain as to the particular play here referred to.
b. 1. *Calicut,* the capital of Malabar, India.
    2. *Pacolet's horse,* the magic horse of Pacolet, a dwarf in the French romance, *Valentine et Orson.* By turning a pin in the horse's head, the rider could convey himself instantly to any part of the world.
    4. *Nuntius.* In Greek and Roman tragedy the catastrophe was not usually presented on the stage, but was reported by a messenger.

Page 146.

b. 7. *Horace,* a Roman poet (65–8 B. C.), wrote a work called, *The Art of Poetry. Ab ovo* means, 'from the remotest origin.'
    11–24. *Polydorus . . . Euripides.* Polydorus was the youngest son of Priam, king of Troy. The story is told in the *Hecuba* of Euripides, a Greek tragic poet (480–406 B. C.).
    17. *Hecuba,* second wife of Priam, and mother of Polydorus.
    18. *sleight,* trick.
    38. *Apuleius* (born c. 125 A. D.), a Roman philosopher and rhetorician, best known for his romance *The Golden Ass.* The exact significance of Sidney's reference is not clear.
    42. *Amphitruo.* This is pure comedy, except for the introduction of gods and heroes.
    44. *daintily,* with discrimination.
    50. *tract,* course.

Page 147.

a. 7. *conveniency,* suitability.
    22. *go . . . bias,* take an unexpected turn. The figure is taken from the game of bowls. *Bias* means 'slope.'
    30–33. *Spinning . . . commandment.* Hercules, in his infatuation for Omphale, queen of Lydia, allowed himself to be dressed as a female slave, and spun wool.
    42. *forbidden plainly by Aristotle,* in his *Poetics.*
    52. *Nil . . . facit,* Juvenal, *Sat.* iii. 152–3. The translation is that of Samuel Johnson.
b. 2. *Thraso,* a bragging, swaggering captain. See the *Eunuchus* of Terence, referred to above.
    3. *a wry-transformed traveler,* a traveler who unwisely affects foreign manners.
    7. *Buchanan.* See note to page 144, b. 2.
    17. *lyrical . . . sonnets,* a reference to such miscellanies as *Tottel's Miscellany.* See p. 121.
    50. *coursing of a letter,* such devices as the acrostic, in which the first letters of the several lines spell a word.
    52. *with figures and flowers,* the printing of the lines in such a way as to form geometrical figures, flowers, and the like.

Page 148.

a. 6. *Tully,* Marcus Tullius Cicero (106–43 B. C.), the Roman orator, philosopher, and statesman. *Demosthenes* (384?–322 B. C.), the greatest of the Greek orators.
    8. *Nizolian paper-books,* note-books containing collections of phrases, such as the *Ciceronian Thesaurus* of Marius Nizolius, an Italian professor (born 1498).
    17. *Catiline,* the Roman conspirator against whom Cicero directed certain of his most famous orations.
    20. *Vivit . . . venit,* from Cicero's first oration against Catiline.
    26. *choler,* anger.
    30. *'similiter cadences,'* 'endings of similar sound or arrangement,' such as rime in poetry, or repetition.
    33. *daintiness,* discrimination.
    36. *sophister,* a university term for students qualified for disputations.
    42. *stories . . . fishes.* Notice the use of curious illustrations from natural history in Lyly's *Euphues,* above.
    55. *Antonius and Crassus.* Marcus Antonius (145–87 B. C.), grandfather of the famous Antony of the Triumvirate, was a distinguished Roman orator, and was so honored by Cicero. Publius Licinius Crassus (175–131 B. C.) was a celebrated orator and lawyer.
b. 2. *As Cicero testifieth,* in his dialogue *On Oratory.*
    3. *not to set by it,* not to value it.
    8. *knacks,* tricks, ornaments.
    24. *pounded,* put in a 'pound,' or enclosure.
    34. *awry,* out of a straight line, wrong.

Page 148.

b. 46. *Tower of Babylon.* See Genesis, Chap. xi.
  52. *compositions . . . together,* compound words.

Page 149.

a. 8. *Whether,* which.
  31. *Now for rime.* Rime is here used in the sense of rhythm.
  42. *sdrucciola,* means 'slippery,' 'sliding.' This is the regular Italian term for trisyllabic rime.
b. 7. *toy,* trifle.
  15. *Bembus.* See note above.
  16. *Scaliger.* See note above.
  19–20. *Clauserus . . . Cornutus.* Lucius Annæus Cornutus (fl. 1st. century A. D.) wrote a treatise in Greek *On the Nature of the Gods,* which was translated into Latin by one Clauserus and published about the middle of the 16th century. Sidney is drawing from the preface of this work.
  21. *Hesiod,* a Greek poet assigned to the 8th century B. C.
  27. *Landin,* Cristofero Landino (1424–1504), an Italian poet and critic, is here referred to for the critical precepts of his *Disputations.*
  38. *Libertino patre natus,* Horace, *Satires,* i. 6. 45.
  40. *Herculea proles,* descendant of Hercules, i.e., royal, noble.
  41. *Si . . . possunt,* Virgil, *Æneid,* ix. 446.
  45. *with Dante's Beatrice, or Virgil's Anchises,* that is, in heaven, or in the Elysian fields.
  47. *dull-making,* deafening. *Nilus,* the River Nile.
  48. *planet-like music,* the music of the spheres produced by the rotation of the planets.
  52. *Mome,* stupid person. *Momus,* the son of Night, used as a personification of the critical spirit.
  54. *Midas,* king of Phrygia. Having been chosen to judge between the musical abilities of Apollo and Marsyas, he awarded the prize to Marsyas. Apollo changed his ears into those of an ass.
  55. *Bubonax.* The story goes that Hipponax, an Ephesian poet (c. 500 B. C.), so savagely satirized the sculptor Bupalus that he hanged himself. The spelling Bubonax is the error either of Sidney or of his printer.

Page 150.

a. 2. *done in Ireland.* It is said that the Irish peasants had a superstitious fear of the bards.

ASTROPHEL AND STELLA

XV, 2. *Parnassus,* a mountain-ridge in Greece, near ancient Delphi, frequented by Apollo, the muses, and the nymphs, and hence the seat of music and poetry.
  7. *Petrarch's long-deceasèd woes.* The celebrated Italian poet Petrarch (1304–1374) wrote sonnets to his Laura which later set the fashion for Elizabethan sonneteers.
  8. *denizened,* made a citizen, naturalized, adopted.
  9. *far-fet,* far-fetched.
  10. *bewray,* reveal.
  14. *endite,* compose.
XXI, 1. *caustics,* medical substances which burn animal tissue.
  2. *windlass,* bewilder.
  5. *Plato,* Athenian philosopher (429?–347 B. C.). *but-if,* unless.

Page 151.

LXIV, 9. *Aristotle's wit.* Aristotle (384–322 B. C.), the most famous of Greek philosophers.
  10. *Cæsar's bleeding fame.* Julius Cæsar 102–44 B. C. assassinated by Brutus, Cassius, and others in the senate-house at Rome.

ELEVENTH SONG

Page 152.

a. 42. *Argus' eyes.* In Greek legend, Argus is famed to have had 100 eyes.

Page 152.

SONG: THE NIGHTINGALE

8. *Tereus.* Tereus abandoned his wife Procné in order to dishonor her sister Philomela.
9. *Philomela.* After having been dishonored by Tereus, Philomela was metamorphosed into a nightingale.

LOVE IS DEAD

8. *franzie,* frenzy.

DORUS TO PAMELA

3. *sterve,* die.
6. *weeds,* clothes.

Page 153.

HAKLUYT'S VOYAGES
DEDICATORY EPISTLE

Francis Walsingham (1536–1590) was a noted English statesman and patron of learning. He served his government as member of parliament, as ambassador to France, as secretary of state, and as special ambassador to several Continental courts.

a. 4. *Westminster,* Westminster School, established in Westminster Abbey by Henry VIII, and reëstablished by Elizabeth.
  6. *Middle Temple,* one of the legal societies in London which provide instruction and examinations for admitting candidates to the bar.
  18. *commodities,* articles of merchandise.
b. 8. *Christ Church,* one of the largest and most fashionable of the Oxford colleges.
  28. *Sir Edward Stafford* (1552?–1605), a distinguished English diplomatist, much in favor with Queen Elizabeth.
  29. *Ligier* (spelled also *lieger, leger. ledger*), an ordinary or resident ambassador.
  30. *chargeable,* weighty, onerous.

Page 154.

b. 11. *Aleppo,* in Asiatic Turkey. *Balsara,* Balsar, or Bulsar, a town of British India, on the Gulf of Cambray.
  12. *Goa,* on the western coast of India.
  14. *river of Plate,* the Rio de la Plata, between Uruguay and the Argentine Republic.
  17. *Nova Hispania,* Mexico.
  20. *South Sea,* the Pacific Ocean. *Luzones,* islands in the Malay Archipelago in the South Pacific.
  24. *Bona Speranza, Cape of Good Hope. St. Helena,* an island off the west coast of Africa.

THE LAST FIGHT OF THE REVENGE

33. *armada,* a fleet of war-vessels.
35. *Sir Walter Raleigh* (1552–1618), an English courtier, soldier, colonizer, and writer. After a short residence at Oxford, he took up military service. He became a favorite of Elizabeth. In 1584 he began his efforts towards colonizing Virginia. In 1588 he took an active part against the Armada. In 1595 he explored the Orinoco. In 1596 and 1597 he took part in the naval expeditions against the Spanish. Charged with plotting to put Arabella Stuart on the throne, Raleigh was imprisoned in 1603. In 1616 he was released to command an expedition to Guiana and the Orinoco. The expedition failed, and on his return he was condemned and executed.
36. *Lord Thomas Howard* (1561–1626), a distinguished naval officer and statesman.
38. *pinnaces,* large ship's boats.
55. *pestered,* crowded. *rummaging,* making a disturbance.

Page 155.

a. 10. *recovered,* regained, returned to.
  23. *shrouded,* covered, concealed.
  27. *Sir Richard Grenville* (c. 1541–1591), a British naval hero, cousin of Sir Walter Raleigh. In 1585 he commanded a fleet of seven vessels which

Page 155.

shared in the colonization of Virginia. In 1591 he served as vice-admiral in the fleet of 16 vessels under Lord Thomas Howard which sailed to Azores to intercept the Spanish treasure-ships. He died a few days after the battle recounted in the present text.

a. 44. *sprang their luff*, sailed nearer to the wind.
55. *charged*. The sense of this word is unknown. It may mean 'timbered.'
b. 5. *admiral*, the ship that carries the commander-in-chief.
6. *Biscayans*, inhabitants of Biscay, a province of northern Spain.
10. *right out of her chase*, directly ahead from her bow.
47. *galleons*, large unwieldy ships, usually having three or four decks.
55. *Lima*, a city of Peru, in South America.

Page 156.

a. 19. *armadas*, single war-vessels.
b. 55. *galley*, i.e., service as prisoner on a galley.

Page 157.
LINSCHOTEN'S TESTIMONY

Jean-Hugues van Linschoten (1563–1611) was a Dutch voyager who cruised widely in the Pacific, in the Indian Ocean, and in the northern seas.

a. 13. *Corvo*, the most northerly of the Azores.
19. *Lord Thomas Howard*, see note above.
40. *Sir Richard Grenville*, see note above.

THE LOSS OF SIR HUMPHREY GILBERT

Sir Humphrey Gilbert (c. 1539–1583) was an English navigator and soldier, a stepbrother of Sir Walter Raleigh. After military services in Ireland and the Netherlands, he began (1578) his voyages of exploration and discovery. On June 11, 1583, he set out for North America, and on Aug. 5 landed at St. John's, where he established the first English colony in North America. On the return voyage his vessel, the *Squirrel*, foundered in a storm.

Page 158.

a. 4. *large*, fair, favorable.
9. *Cape Race*, the southeastern extremity of Newfoundland.
b. 11. *St. John's*, a town on the island of Newfoundland.

Page 159.

a. 2. *fights*, screens designed for the protection of men during a battle.
42. *Castor and Pollux*, a name given to the electric phenomenon known as St. Elmo's Fire. The phenomenon consists of the appearance, especially in southern climates, during thunder storms, of a brush or star of light.
b. 19. *flaw*, a sudden gust of wind.

A REPORT OF VIRGINIA

30. *Sir Walter Raleigh*, see note above.
43. *humors*, bodily fluids.

Page 160.
DRAKE IN CALIFORNIA

a. 25. *Sir Francis Drake*, see p. 261.
37. *the Line*, the equator.
53. *cauls*, nets for confining the hair.

Page 161.
SPENSER — THE SHEPHEARDES CALENDAR
FEBRUARIE

2. *tasswage*, to subside.
4. *gryde*, pierce.
5. *rontes*, young bullocks
6. *doen*, do.
7. *wont*, are accustomed. *wrigle*, wriggling.
8. *Perke*, pert, brisk. *avales*, subsides, droops.
9. *Lewdly*, foolishly.
10. *wracke*, violence.
16. *lusty prime*, pleasant spring-time.

Page 162.

22. *that*, that which.
24. *mought*, might.
26. *cheare*, countenance.
27. *nie*, nigh.
28. *wrye*, awry, crooked.
30. *Good Fryday*, Friday before Easter.
32. *unwont*, unaccustomed.
35. *heardgroomes*, herdsmen.
36. *broomes*, a kind of shrub.
38. *deemen*, deem, judge.
39. *fond*, foolish.
42. *eft*, afterwards.
43. *breme*, rough.   *chamfred*, wrinkled, furrowed.
46. *cruddles*, curdles.
47. *corage accoied*, heart daunted.
49. *surquedrie*, arrogance, pride.
52. *spil*, mar, ruin.
54. *elde*, old age.
55. *sicker*, certainly.   *tottie*, tottering.
56. *corbe*, crooked.
57. *lopp*, branch.
58. *Als*, also.   *cropp*, cut off
62. *hery*, praise.
65. *gelt*, gold.
66. *buegle*, bead-work.
67. *faine*, glad.
69. *fon*, a foolish fellow.
71. *brag*, ostentatious.
72. *smirke*, smart.
74. *dewelap*, throat-wattle.   *lythe*, pliant.
75. *venteth*, snuffs.
77. *can*, knows.
78. *lustlesse*, listless, feeble.
80. *flocks father*, ram.
82. *crags*, necks.
83. *rather lambes*, lambs born early in the year.
86. *headlessehood*, heedlessness.
89. *ynne*, inn, abode.
90. *stoopegallaunt age*, age which subdues gallantry.
92. *cond*, learned.   *Tityrus*, Chaucer. The tale that follows is, of course, not from Chaucer.
95. *novells*, news, or tales.   *devise*, telling.
96. *thewed*, founded in morality.
97. *bespake*, spoke of.
98. *meete*, fitting.
104. *largely*, widely.
106. *pight*, fixed, planted.
107. *throughly*, thoroughly.
108. *Whilome*, formerly.
109. *mochell mast*, many acorns.   *husband*, master of the house.
110. *larded*, fattened.
111. *rine*, rind, bark.
114. *honor*, i.e., foliage.
115. *Brere*, briar.
117. *threat*, threaten.
119. *wonned*, were wont.
121. *peinct*, paint, decorate.

Page 163.

122. *shrowde*, take shelter.
124. *wexe*, wax, grow.
125. *cast him*, planned.
126. *snebbe*, snub, reprove.   *for*, because.
131. *engrained*, dyed.   *lusty*, pleasant.
133. *wast*, waste.
134. *dirks*, darkens.
135. *accloieth*, encumbers.
140. *againe*, back.
141. *adawed*, subdued.
145. *survewe*, oversee, survey.
146. *trees of state*, stately trees.
151. *Pleaseth*, 2d pers. plur. imperative.   *ponder*, weigh, consider.
154. *recure*, cure, heal.
155. *doole*, grief.
157. *aghast*, amazed.

Page 163.
160. *painted*, false.
162. *colowred*, colored, disguised.
167. *prime*, spring-time.
169. *falls*, happens.
178. *coronall*, garland.
182. *defast*, defaced, destroyed.
184. *goodlihead*, goodness.
185. *ranckorous*, sharp.
187. *sufferance*, patience.
189. *cast him*, prepared.
190. *couth*, knew.
192. *noulde*, would not.
195. *hent*, seized.
200. *enaunter*, lest. *mought*, might, should.
202. *wast*, waste.
203. *againe*, back.
206. *eld*, old age.
209. *crewe*, cruet, cruise, vessel.
211. *sike*, such.
213. *quitten*, free.
223. *pleasaunce*, pleasure.
225. *eftsones*, forthwith.
226. *Boreas*, north-wind.

Page 164.
242. *graffed*, grafted.
243. *frorne*, frozen.
244. *galage*, wooden shoe.
245. *ease*, pleasure. *lewd*, foolish, rude.
248–9. 'God, since he is old, makes his own in his own likeness.'
251–2. 'No old man fears God.'

OCTOBER
3. *lingring Phœbus race*, lingering daylight.
4. *Whilome thou wont*, formerly thou used.
5. *bydding base*, the game of prisoners'-base.
11. *pleasaunce*, pleasure.
12. *ligge so layd*, lie so subdued.
13. *wont*, used to.
14. *fry*, children, youth.
15. *what ... forthy*, how am I the better for that?
23. *pleasaunce of thy vaine*, pleasure of thy vein.
24. 'To whatever it pleases thee to entice their allured wills.'
26. *routes*, crowds.
28. *shepheard*, i.e., Orpheus. *dame*, i.e., Eurydice.
29. *Plutoes balefull bowre*, i.e., Hades.
32. *Argus blazing eye*. The spots in the peacock's tail are said to be Argus' hundred eyes.
33. *forthy*, for that.
35. *sike*, such. *sheddeth*, disperses.
37. *clowne*, lout, low fellow.
39. *giusts*, jousts.
41. *doubted*, dreaded.
42. *wexen*, wax, grow.
45. *Whither thou list*, whether thou choose. *Elisa*, Queen Elizabeth.
47. *the worthy*, the hero, i.e., the Earl of Leicester.
48. *white beare*, Leicester's cognizance was a bear and a ragged staff.
49. *stounds*, efforts.
50. *slackt the tenor of*, lowered the pitch of.
51. *lustihead*, pleasure. *tho*, then.
52. *the myllers*, a kind of dance.
53. *All*, although. *thilke*, that.
54. *mought*, might.
55. *Romish Tityrus*, Virgil.
56. *Mecœnas*, Mæcenas, patron of Virgil.
59. *eft*, afterwards.
62. *Augustus*, the Roman emperor.
63. *liggen*, lie.
65. *derring doe*, daring deeds.
66. *hem*, them.
68. *brought ... ease*, brought to a bed of ease.
69. *found ... preace*, found nothing worth putting forth for competition.

Page 165.
72. *pend*, penned.
75. *mote*, must. *fayne*, feign.
76. *rybaudrye*, ribaldry.
78. *Tom Piper*, the piper who accompanied Morris-dancers.
87. *peeced*, patched, imperfect.
88. *Colin*, i.e., Spenser. *scanne*, mount.
89. *bedight*, dressed.
90. *soote*, sweetly.
91. *fon*, foolish fellow.
95. *caytive corage*, base mind.
98. *tyranne fell*, baneful tyrant.
101. *wont*, are accustomed.
103. 'Whoever thinks to accomplish great things.'
105. 'Let him pour down plentiful draughts and nourishing food.'
106. *Bacchus fruite*, wine. *Phœbus*, god of poetry.
113. *buskin*, the high-heeled boot worn by actors in tragedy.
114. *queint*, elegant. *Bellona*, goddess of war.
115. *corage*, mind, heart.
116. *Forthy*, therefore.
117. *han us assayde*, have attacked us.
118. *charme*, temper.
119. *gates*, goats.
122. 'With his urging we become inflamed, etc.'

THE FAERIE QUEENE BOOK I
1. *whylome*, formerly. *maske*, go disguised.
2. *shephards weeds*, a graceful reference to Spenser's own earlier *Shepherd's Calendar.*
7. *areeds*, counsels.
10. *holy virgin*, refers to Clio, the muse of history.
12. *scryne*, chest for papers.
14. *Tanaquill*, a British princess, daughter of Oberon, king of fairyland. In the allegory Tanaquill is probably Queen Elizabeth.
15. *Briton Prince*, Prince Arthur, representing in the allegory, probably, the Earl of Leicester.
17. *rue*, pity.
19. *dreaded impe*, Cupid, god of love.
21. *rove*, shoot an arrow with an elevation, not point blank.
23. *heben*, ebony.
25. *Mart*, Mars.

Page 166.
28. *Goddesse*, Queen Elizabeth.
31. *Phœbus*, Apollo, the sun-god.
32. *eyne*, eyes.
34. *type of thine*, Una, who represents truth in the allegory.
35. *afflicted*, cast down.
36. *dearest dread*, dearest object of reverence.

CANTO I
1. *knight*, the Redcross Knight, representing the English church militant. *pricking*, riding.
6. *chide*, chafe, grind.
9. *giusts*, jousts.
14. *scor'd*, traced.
15. *For soveraine hope*, as a sign of supreme hope.
17. *cheere*, countenance.
18. *ydrad*, dreaded, feared.
20. *Gloriana*, Queen Elizabeth.
22. *worshippe*, honor.
24. *earne*, yearn.
25. *puissance*, power, prowess.
27. *dragon*, 'the great dragon ... called the devil.' Revelation xii, 9.
28. *ladie*, Una.
31. *wimpled*, pleated.
36. *in a line*, by a cord. *lambe*, symbolizing innocence.
44. *Forwasted*, utterly wasted.
45. *compeld*, summoned.
46. *dwarfe*, symbolizing prudence, or common sense.
52. *lemans*, sweet-heart's.
53. *wight*, person, creature. *shrowd*, take shelter.
54. *fain*, glad.
55. *covert*, hiding-place.
56. *shadie grove*, the wood of Error.

Page 166.

60. *Not perceable with*, impervious to.
63. 'A fair shelter it seems to them when they have entered.'
69. *sayling pine*, pine used for building ships.
70. *poplar never dry*, never dry because it grows especially well in moist soil.
71. *builder oake*, oak used for building.
72. *cypresse funerall*, the cypress, emblematic of death.
73. *meed*, reward.
74. *weepeth still*, weeps always. The fir exudes a resinous substance.
75. *paramours*, lovers.

Page 167.

76. *eugh*, yew.
77. *sallow*, a kind of willow.
78. *The mirrhe*. The Arabian myrtle exudes a bitter but fragrant gum. The allusion is to the wounding of Myrrha by her father and her metamorphosis into a tree.
79. *warlike beech*. Lances and other arms were made of beech. *ash for nothing ill*. The ash served many purposes.
80. *platane*, plane-tree.
81. *carver holme*. The evergreen oak was good for carving.
84. *weening*, thinking.
88. *doubt*, fear.
94. *about*, out of.
95. *by tract*, by trace.
98. *Eftsoones*, forthwith.
103. *doubts*, fears.
106–7. *shame . . . shade*, 'it were shameful to check forward steps for fear of an unseen danger.'
108. *wade*, walk, go, pass.
110. *wot*, know.
114. *wandering wood*, wood that causes men to go astray.
118. *greedy hardiment*, eager boldness.
122. *glooming*, gloaming, twilight.
126. *full . . . disdain*, full of vileness that breeds disgust in the beholder.
129. *boughtes*, folds, coils.
130. *bred*, were born.
133. *ill favored*, of ugly appearance.
134. *uncouth*, unknown, strange.
136. *upstart*, started up. *effraide*, frightened.
139. *entraile*, fold, coil.
141. *Armed to the point*, completely armed.
143. *Ay wont*, ever accustomed.
145. *Elfe*, so called because he was reputed to be the son of an elf or fairy.
147. *trenchand*, sharp, cutting.
152. *enhaunst*, raised.
154. *dint*, stroke.
158. *Tho*, then. *wrethed*, twisted.

Page 168.

161. *That*, so that.
163. *constraint*, distress.
168. 'His anger was aroused because of pain and great disgust.' *grate*, chafe.
170. *gorge*, throat.
172. *maw*, stomach.
174. *gobbets*, lumps, pieces.
175. *vildly*, vilely.
177. *bookes and papers*, allegorically the scurrilous Catholic pamphlets that had been launched against Elizabeth and the reformed Church of England.
180. *parbreake*, vomit.
183. *outwell*, pour out.
185. *avale*, subside.
189. *reed*, perceive.
194. *sinke*, hoard, deposit.
200. *welke*, fade, grow dim.
206. *clownish*, rough, rude.
208. *bestedd*, situated.
212. *lin*, cease.
213. *manly*, human.
215. *rafi*, struck away.

Page 168.

216. *corse*, body.
225. *eke*, also.
227. *unkindly*, unnatural.
233. *needeth him*, needs he.
234. *should contend*, should have had to contend.
239. *armory*, armor.
243. *like succed it may*, similar successful adventures may follow.

Page 169.

248. *still*, ever, always.
250. *to frend*, as friend.
254. *aged sire*, Archimago, the false enchanter. In general he represents hypocrisy and the Church of Rome.
259. *shew*, appearance.
262. *louting*, bowing.
263. *him quited*, paid him back, responded.
267. *silly*, simple, innocent.
268. *Bidding his beades*, praying his prayers.
270. *sits not*, is not fitting. *Mell*, mingle, meddle.
277. *weare*, spend.
279. *space*, time.
280. *wastefull*, barren.
282. *thorough*, through.
285. *forwearied*, greatly wearied.
288. *baite*, feed, refresh.
295. *take up your in*, take lodging.
301. *a little wyde*, a little way off.
302. *edifyde*, built.
303. *wont*, was wont.
315. *Ave-Mary*, Hail Mary, a prayer to the Virgin.
317. *Sad humor*, heavy moisture.
318. *Morpheus*, god of sleep.
319. *deaw*, dew.
320. *riddes*, removes.
322. *amiddes*, amid.
328. *Plutoes griesly dame*, Proserpine.
332. *Great Gorgon*, Demogorgon, whose name was not to be uttered, and who had magical power over the spirits of the lower world.
333. *Cocytus*, the river of wailing. *Styx*, the river of hate. Both rivers were in Hades.

Page 170.

338. *fray*, frighten.
343. *spersed*, dispersed.
348. *Tethys*, the ocean.
349. *Cynthia*, the moon.
360. *takes keepe*, pays heed.
367. *still*, always.
372. *mought*, might.
373. *paine*, effort.
376. *dryer braine*, too dry brain. It was supposed that a dry brain was slow in physiological processes.
378. *all*, entirely.
381. *Hecate*, queen of demons in Hades, and ruler of witches on earth.
382. *lompish*, dull.
387. *sent*, sense.
389. *diverse*, perverse.
391. *carke*, care, anxiety.
392. *starke*, stiff.
396. *afore*, before.
405. *like*, likely. *seeme for*, represent.
409. *fantasy*, fancy.
410. 'In the way in which he schooled him secretly.'
411. *without her dew*, in an unnatural manner.

Page 171.

429. *leman*, lover.
431. *Hymen iö Hymen*, refrain of a Roman nuptial song. Hymen was god of marriage.
432. *Flora*, goddess of flowers.
443. *guise*, appearance.
444. *despight*, indignation.
445. *sufferance*, patience.
447. 'To test his perception and prove her feigned truth.'

Page 171.
449. *Tho can*, then did. *ruth*, pity.
454. *blind god*, Cupid. *amate*, dismay, dishearten.
462. *bereave*, take away.
468. *frayes*, frightens.
469. *deare constraint*, grievous distress.
473. *redoubted*, terrible.
476. *shend*, revile, reproach. *rew*, pity, regret.
483. *appease*, cease from.
484. *beguiled of*, disappointed in.
491. *irksome*, troubled. *spright*, spirit.

CANTO II
1. *northerne wagoner*, constellation of Boötes, situated behind the Great Bear.
2. *sevenfold teme*, seven stars of Ursa Major, the Great Bear. *stedfast starre*, the pole-star.

Page 172.
6. *Chaunticlere*, the cock.
7. *Phoebus fiery carre*, the sun.
13. *bootelesse*, useless.
16. *Proserpine*, queen of the infernal regions.
19. *Eftsoones*, presently.
22. *squire*, an attendant on a knight. *lustyhed*, pleasure.
26. *misdeeming*, misleading.
30. *repast*, rest, refreshment.
34. *wex*, wax, grow.
37. *start*, started.
40. *ment*, mingled.
43. *yblent*, blinded.
49. *wast*, waste. *despight*, anger.
50. *Yrkesome*, weary.
51. *Hesperus*, the evening star.
56. *aged Tithones*. Tithonus is 'aged' because Aurora gave him immortality, but not eternal youth.
58. *Titan*, the sun-god.
59. *drousyhed*, drowsiness.
62. *wont to wait*, was accustomed to watch.
63. *stowre*, distress.
84. *in seeming wise*, in the way of appearance
85. *Proteus*, a sea-god.
87. *fell*, destructive.

Page 173.
97. *jolly*, handsome.
99. *Saint George*, patron saint of England.
100. *semblaunt*, semblance.
104. *him chaunst*, he happened.
105. *Sarazin*, used for pagans in general. *armde to point*, completely armed.
107. *Sans foy*, faithless.
108. *a point*, a speck, a bit.
109. *faire companion*, Duessa, or Falsehood, who calls herself Fidessa. She probably represents Mary, Queen of Scots and the Church of Rome.
111. *Purfled*, embroidered on the edge. *assay*, quality, value.
113. *owches*, jewels.
115. *palfrey*, lady's riding-horse.
117. *bosses*, ornamental studs or knobs.
118. *disport*, play.
128. *dispiteous*, cruel.
129. *couch*, level, adjust.
130. *fell*, destructive.
135. *rebutte*, recoil.
144. *broken reliques*, shivered lances.
145. *buffe*, blow.
147. *quyteth*, pays.
148. 'Each vies with the equal power of the other.'
150. *repining*, indignant. *courage*, heart.
155. *bitter fitt*, death agony.
156. *wote*, know.
157. *forwarned*, warded off.
158. *assured sitt*, sit firm.
159. *hide thy head*, i.e., behind thy shield for protection.
160. *rigor so outrageous*, force so violent.
162. *from . . . blest*, fairly preserved him from harm.

Page 173.
164. *eftsoones*, forthwith.
166. *rive*, split.
171. *Whether*, whither.
174. *funerall*, death.
176. *scowre*, run fast.
181. *ruefull*, sad.
183. *silly*, innocent.

Page 174.
188. *rueth*, touches with pity.
196. *emperour*, the Pope.
198. *Tiberis*, River Tiber.
200. *onely haire*, only heir, the dauphin of France, the first husband of Mary Queen of Scots.
203. *debonaire*, gracious, courteous.
206. *fone*, foes.
212. *assaid*, tried.
213. *corse*, body.
224. *Sansjoy*, without happiness.
225. *Sansloy*, without law.
233. *rew*, pity.
239. *chear*, countenance.
241. *gainsaid*, denied, opposed.
243. *dainty . . . derth*, coyness, they say, creates desire.
250. *fearefull*, timid.
251. *ne wont*, nor was accustomed to.
258. *abide*, endure, tolerate.
261. *tide*, time.
262. *seemely pleasaunce*, pleasant courtesies.
269. *rifte*, fissure.
270. *gory bloud*, clotted blood.
273. *rynd*, bark. *embard*, imprisoned.

Page 175.
278. *Astond*, astonished. *hove*, rise.
280. *dreadfull passion*, passion of fear.
284. *Limbo lake*, abode of the damned.
287. *rare*, thin, faint.
288. *ruefull*, piteous.
291. *Fradubio*, 'Brother Doubtful.'
295. *Boreas*, the north-wind.
316. *take in hand*, maintain.
328. *Whether*, which of the two.
329. *meede*, reward.
332. *mote*, might.
336. *cast*, planned.
342. *in place*, in that place.
348. *Eftsoones*, forthwith.
351. *treën mould*, form of a tree.
353. *unweeting*, not knowing.
355. *prime*, springtime.
358. *origane*, wild marjoram.
360. *rew*, regret.

Page 176.
370. *cheare*, countenance.
374. *bereaved*, taken away. *quight*, quite.
376. *pight*, placed, fixed
378. *wights*, men.
382. *living well*, a flowing well.
385. *wonted well*, accustomed well-being.
386. *suffised*, satisfied. *kynd*, nature.
391. *dreriment*, sorrow.
398. *unweeting*, unaware.
404. *all passed feare*, all fear having passed.

AMORETTI

I, 6. *lamping*, shining.
   7. *spright*, spirit.
  10. *Helicon*, a mountain in Bœotia, Greece, famous in mythology as the haunt of the muses.

XXIV, 8. *Pandora*, according to Greek mythology, the first woman, created by command of Zeus in revenge for the theft of fire from heaven by Prometheus. The gods endowed her with such attributes as should bring misfortune to man.

NOTES TO SPENSER: EPITHALAMION; PROTHALAMION

Page 177.
XXXIV, 10. *Helice*, the Great Bear.
LXX, 2. *cote-armour*, a herald's tabard.
12. *amearst*, punished.

EPITHALAMION

1. *learned sisters*, the muses.
8. *wreck*, violence.
11. *dreriment*, sorrow.

Page 178.
22. *lustyhed*, vigor.
25. *Hymen*, god of marriage.
27. *tead*, torch. *flake*, flash.
28. *bachelor*, one in the first stage of knighthood.
30. *dight*, dress.
35. *solace*, pleasure.
40. *well beseene*, very comely.
44. *riband*, ribbon.
45. *poses*, flowers.
51. *diapred*, variegated. *discolored*, many-colored.
56. *Mulla*, river Awbeg, on Spenser's Irish estate.
75. *Tithones*, Tithonus, consort of Aurora.
77. *Phœbus*, the sun-god.
80. *mattins*, morning service.
81. *mavis*, song-thrush. *descant*, an accompanying melody.
82. *ouzell*, blackbird. *ruddock*, redbreast.
83. *consent*, harmony.
86. *meeter*, more fitting.
87. *make*, mate.
95. *Hesperus*, the evening star, and also the morning star.
98-99. *Houres*, Horæ, goddesses who presided over the changes of the seasons, and of day and night.
102. *still*, always, ever.
103. *three handmayds of the Cyprian Queene*, the Graces, who were especially associated with Venus.
104, 106. *still*, ever, always.
108. 'And as you are accustomed to sing to Venus, sing to her (my bride).'
113. *strayt*, presently, soon.
121. *Phœbus*, Apollo.
123. *mote*, may.

Page 179.
124. *boone*, boon, prayer, favor.
131. *tabor*, drum. *croud*, fiddle.
140. *Hymen, Iö Hymen*, the refrain of a Roman nuptial song. Hymen is god of marriage.
148. *portly*, dignified.
151. *seemes*, befits.
152. *weene*, think.
165. *nathlesse*, nevertheless. *still*, ever, always.
175. *uncrudded*, uncurdled.
186. *spright*, spirit.
189. *red*, saw.
190. *Medusaes mazeful hed*. Medusa was a beautiful maiden whose hair was transformed into serpents. *mazeful*, confounding.
228. *dyde in grayne*, dyed in cochineal.

Page 180.
234. *sad*, grave. *still*, ever.
239. *band*, tie.
257. *Graces*, the three daughters of Zeus,—Euphrosyne, Aglaia, and Thalia,—who personified grace and beauty.
265. ff. *This day*. June 11th, St. Barnabas' day, was, according to Spenser's calendar, the day of the summer solstice.
269. *Crab*, one of the signs of the zodiac.
272. *weare*, were.
282. *fayrest planet*, the sun.
285. *gloome*, become twilight.
299. *boures*, bowers.
304. *Arras*, a town in northern France formerly noted for its manufacture of tapestries.
307. *Maia*, mother of Hermes by Zeus.
308. *Tempe*, a beautiful valley in the north of Thessaly.

Page 180.
310. *Acidalian brooke*, the fountain Acidalius, in Bœotia, Greece.
316. *defray*, pay for.
328. *Alcmena*, mother of Hercules by Zeus.
329. *Tirynthian groome*. Hercules is said to have lived for many years at the city of Tiryns, in Greece.
331. *Majesty*. By ancient poets, Night was called the mother of all things, and she was worshipped with great solemnity.
337. *dout*, fear.
340. *helplesse*, irremediable.
341. *Pouke*, Puck, or Robin Goodfellow.

Page 181.
346. *still*, ever, continually.
348. *griesly*, horrible.
374. *Cinthia*, the moon.
376. *envy*, begrudge.
380. *Latmian shepard*, Endymion, loved by Cynthia.
388. *hap*, fortune, lot.
390. *Juno*, sister and wife of Jove, and protectress of marriage.
398. *Genius*, a high power that maintains life and assists at the begetting and birth of each individual.
405. *Hebe*, cup-bearer to the gods.
414. *fayne*, imagine.
421. *guerdon*, reward.
429. *Hasty accidents*, accidents due to haste.
430. *expect*, await.
433. *for*, instead of.

PROTHALAMION

Written on the occasion of the marriage, on the same day, of the two daughters of the Earl of Worcester to Henry Guilford and William Peter.

2. *Zephyrus*, the west wind.
4. *Titans beames*, the sun. *glyster*, glitter, shine.

Page 182.
8. *still*, always.
11. *Themmes*, Thames.
12. *rutty*, rooty.
16. *paramours*, lovers.
25. *entrayled*, intertwined.
26. *flasket*, a long, shallow basket.
27. *cropt*, cut, clipped. *featously*, neatly
33. *vermeil*, vermilion.
38. *lee*, stream.
40. *Pindus*, a range of mountains in northern Greece.
43. *Leda*. Leda was amorously approached by Zeus in the form of a swan.
55. *Eftsoones*, forthwith.
63. *Venus silver teeme*, team of swans, according to Ovid, Metamorphoses, x. 708.
67. *Somers-heat*, Somerset.
78. *Peneus*, a river in Thessaly that traverses the Vale of Tempe.
79. *Tempes shore*. Tempe is a valley in Thessaly celebrated for its beauty.
100. *assoile*, absolve.

Page 183.
110. *undersong*, burden, refrain, chorus.
119. *foule*, fowl.
121. *Cynthia*, the moon. *shend*, shame.
128. *kyndly nurse*. Spenser was born in London.
132. *whereas*, where.
132-5. *bricky towres . . . Templer Knights*. A reference to the Temple. After the order of the Knights Templars had been suppressed in the reign of Edward II (1307-1327), their property on the bank of the Thames passed eventually into the hands of the students of the common law.
137-140. *a stately place . . . that great lord*. The reference is to Leicester House, where Spenser's patron, the Earl of Leicester, dwelt for some years. See the life of Spenser, above, p. 104.

Page 183.
145. *a noble peer*, the Earl of Essex. After the death of Leicester, in 1588, the Earl of Essex occupied his house and gave it the name, Essex House.
147. *through all Spaine did thunder.* A reference to the capture of Cadiz in 1596. Essex commanded the land forces.
148. *Hercules two pillars*, the rocks on either side of the strait of Gibraltar.
153-4. Probably a pun on Essex's family name, *Devereux*, as if it were connected with the French *heureux*, 'happy.'
157. *Elisaes glorious name*, Queen Elizabeth.
164. *Hesper*, the evening, and also the morning, star.
173. *twins of Jove*, Castor and Pollux, who became the constellation Gemini.

Page 184.
ELIZABETHAN LYRICS
GASCOIGNE — A STRANGE PASSION
1. *bale*, suffering.
15. *eschew*, avoid.
16. *grutch*, ill-will.
25. *Philomene*, the nightingale.
28. *wray*, reveal.
29. *bewray*, reveal.

Page 185.
DYER — MY MIND TO ME A KINGDOM IS
4. *kind*, nature.
35. *fawn*, cringe to.

RALEIGH — HIS PILGRIMAGE
1. *scallop-shell*, shell of a kind of mollusk. The scallop-shell was the badge of a pilgrim.
3. *scrip*, wallet.

Page 186.
25. *suckets*, dried sweetmeats, or delicacies of any kind.
57. *palmer*, a pilgrim. Specifically, a pilgrim to Jerusalem who brought back a palm-branch as a token.

A VISION UPON THIS CONCEIT OF THE FAERY QUEEN
1. *Laura*, celebrated in Petrarch's sonnets.
2. *vestal flame.* Vesta was goddess of the hearth. The sacred fire, which was her symbol, was kept burning in her temple at home by six stainless virgins, called *vestals.*
7. *Petrarch* (1304-1374), a celebrated Italian poet.
13. *sprite*, spirit.

Page 188.
GREENE — THE SHEPHERD'S WIFE'S SONG
18. *curds*, the thickened part of sour milk, eaten as food.
36. *spill*, destroy.
37. *snort*, snore.
42. *tide or sithe*, time or occasion.
44. *broils*, disturbances.

Page 189.
DANIEL — SONNETS FROM DELIA
XIX, 2. *Cytherea's son*, Cupid.
    8. *Thetis*, chief of the sea-nymphs.
   10. *Hermonius' spheres*, an allusion to the music supposed to be made by the planets in their revolutions. Perhaps this line should read: And thy sweet voice give back unto the spheres.
   12. *Hyrcan*, pertaining to Hyrcania, a region in Asia bordering on the Caspian Sea.
XXXVIII, 3. *Laura . . . Petrarch.* Petrarch's sonnets were inspired by his Laura.
   13. *limnèd*, described.
L, 1. *Paladins*, the knights of Charlemagne, and hence, heroic champions in general.
   2. *untimely*, archaic, obsolete.
   9. *arcs*, arches.

Page 190.
DRAYTON — SONNETS FROM IDEA
IX, 9. *Bedlam*, the hospital of St. Mary of Bethlehem in London, originally a priory, but afterward used as an asylum for lunatics.
XLIV, 6. *Medea-like.* Medea was granted the power of conferring immortality upon her children.

Page 191.
ODE XI. TO THE VIRGINIAN VOYAGE
16. *Eolus*, god of the winds.
37. *Golden Age*, a fabled period of simplicity, plenty, and eternal spring.
49. *kenning*, recognition.
52. *frolic*, merry.
68. *Industrious Hakluyt.* See above, p. 91.

ODE XII. TO THE CAMBRO–BRITONS
The Cambro-Britons were the Welsh.
The battle of Agincourt was fought near the northern coast of France on Oct. 25, 1415. Henry V, with about 15,000 men, defeated 50,000 or more French soldiers under the Constable d'Albret.
5. *main*, sea.
8. *King Harry*, Henry V.
16. *power*, army.

Page 192.
41. *Poitiers and Cressy*, famous victories of the English in France, during the Hundred Years' War. The battle of Crécy was fought on Aug. 26, 1346; the battle of Poitiers, on Sept. 19, 1356.
45. *our Grandsire.* The grandfather of Henry V was John of Gaunt, son of Edward III.
49. *Duke of York*, Edward, Duke of York, who fell at Agincourt.
50. *vanward*, advance-guard.
53. *Exeter*, the Duke of Exeter, uncle of Henry V.
66. *Erpingham*, Sir Thomas Erpingham, steward of the king's household.
82. *bilboes*, swords.
91. *ding*, strike.
94. *besprent*, sprinkled.
97-112. *Gloucester . . . Clarence . . . Warwick . . . Oxford . . . Suffolk . . . Beaumont . . . Willoughby . . . Ferrers . . . Fanhope*, English noblemen and gentlemen who fought in the battle of Agincourt.
111. *doughtily*, mightily, forcibly.
113. *Saint Crispin's Day*, Oct. 25.

MARLOWE — HERO AND LEANDER
THE FIRST SESTIAD
Leander, a youth of Abydos, in love with Hero, a priestess of Aphrodite at Sestos, swam the Hellespont every night to visit her, until he perished one night in a storm. When his body was cast up on the shore of Sestos next morning, Hero threw herself into the sea.
Sestiad is really a Latinized adjective meaning 'belonging to Sestos.'
1. *Hellespont*, the Strait of Dardanelles.
14. *Adonis*, a youth of model beauty loved by Venus.
15. *kirtle*, close-fitting gown.

Page 193.
31. *buskins*, shoes laced to a point above the ankle.
49. *wrack*, destruction.
52. *Musæus*, a Greek author of the 5th century B. C., author of a celebrated poem on Hero and Leander, upon which Marlowe's poem is based.
56. *Colchos*, Colchis was the region in Asia to which the Argonautic expedition was directed in quest of the golden fleece.
59. *Cynthia*, the moon.
61. *Circe's wand.* Circe was an enchantress who, with her wand, could transform men into beasts.
65. *Pelops.* According to a tradition, one of Pelops' shoulders was made of ivory.
77. *Hippolytus*, son of Theseus and Hippolyta.

NOTES TO ELIZABETHAN LYRICS; SEVENTEENTH–CENTURY LYRICS 1015

Page 193.
98. *glistered*, glistened.
101. *Phaëton*, son of the sun-god, obtained permission of his father to drive his chariot across the heavens; but, being unable to check the horses, he nearly set the earth on fire.
107. *that . . . star*, the moon.
108. *thirling*, quivering.
109. *Latmus' mount*, a mountain in Asia Minor, the scene of the story of Cynthia's love for Endymion.
114. *Ixion's shaggy-footed race*, the Centaurs.

Page 194.
137. *Proteus*, a sea-god.
146. *Vulcan and his Cyclops*. Vulcan, the god of fire and of the working of metals, had the giant Cyclops for his workmen.
148. *Silvanus*, god of the fields and forests.
152. *turtles*, turtle-doves.
153. *Vailed*, bowed.

SHAKESPEARE — VENUS AND ADONIS
Adonis was a beautiful youth beloved by Venus. In spite of her favor, he died from a wound received from a boar in the chase. The flower anemone sprang from his blood. Moved by the grief of Venus, the gods of the lower world allowed Adonis to spend six months of the year with her on earth, and the remaining six among the shades.
18. *coasteth*, proceeds, goes.

Page 195.
43. *ecstasy*, excitement.
54. *rate*, scold, upbraid.
55. *spleens*, passionate impulses.
57. *mated*, bewildered.
59. *respects*, considerations, thoughts.
60. *In hand with*, undertaking.
62. *caitiff*, wretch.
78. *exclaims on*, cries out against.
81. *worm*, serpent.
94. *crop*, pick.
104. *vailed*, lowered.
112. *still*, ever, always.

Page 196.
141. *all to naught*, good for nothing.
143. *clepes*, calls.
144. *Imperious*, imperial.
148. *still*, ever.
152. *wreaked*, revenged.
158. *suspect*, suspicion.
160. *With . . . insinuate*, try to ingratiate oneself with.
169. *fond*, foolish.
175. *lure*, a call or decoy, used to attract a falcon.
200. *trenched*, gashed.
207. *passions*, grieves.

Page 197.
231, 234. *fair*, beauty.
242. *fear*, frighten.
246. *silly*, innocent, helpless.
253. *urchin-snouted*, with snout like that of a hedgehog.
263. *nuzzling*, thrusting his nose in.
305. *toward*, fitting.

Page 198.
311. *Sith*, since.
316. *A purple flower*, the anemone.
323. *crops*, plucks, breaks off.
341. *Paphos*, a town in Cyprus, the chief seat of the worship of Venus.

SONNETS
XII, 2. *brave*, beautiful.
    9. *question make*, consider.
XV, 9. *conceit*, conception.
    11. *debateth*, combats.
XVIII, 7. *fair*, beauty.

Page 199.
XXX, 6. *dateless*, endless.
    8. *moan the expense*, lament the loss.
    10. *tell*, count.
XXXIII, 6. *rack*, mass of floating clouds.
LIV, 5. *canker-blooms*, dog-roses.
    8. *discloses*, uncloses.
    9. *for*, because.
    10. *unrespected*, unregarded.
LV, 3. *in these contents*, in the contents of these verses.
LX, 7. *Crooked*, malignant.
    8. *confound*, destroy.
    9. *flourish*, decoration.
    10. *delves the parallels*, digs the furrows.
    13. *times in hope*, future times.

Page 200.
LXV, 4. *action*, perhaps in the sense of 'legal action.'
LXVI, 11. *simplicity*, folly.
LXXVI, 5. *still*, always.
XCVII, 7. *prime*, spring.
    10. *hope of orphans*, such hope as orphans bring.

Page 201.
XCVIII, 2. *proud-pied*, gaily variegated.
    4. *That*, so that. *Saturn*, a planet of melancholy influence.
    6. *different flowers in*, flowers different in.
XCIX, 6. *for thy hand*, for stealing the whiteness of thy hand.
    13. *canker*, canker-worm.
CIV, 10. *Steal from his figure*, creep away from the figure on the dial.
CVI, 8. *master*, control, possess.
CVII, 10. *subscribes*, yields, submits.
    12. *insults o'er*, exults over.
CIX, 2. *qualify*, temper, moderate.
    7. *Just . . . time*, punctual. *exchanged*, altered.
CX, 2. *motley*, fool.

Page 202.
    6. *strangely*, distantly, distrustfully.
    7. *blenches*, startings-aside.
    10. *grind*, whet.
CXI, 10. *eisel*, vinegar.
CXIX, 2. *limbecks*, alembics.
CXXVIII, 5. *jacks*, here used in the sense of 'keys' of the virginal or the harpsichord.
CXXX, 5. *damasked*, variegated.
CXLVI, 10. *aggravate*, increase.

Page 203.
SONG FROM LOVE'S LABOR'S LOST
8. *keel*, skim.

SONG FROM THE MERCHANT OF VENICE
1. *fancy*, love.

ENGLAND'S HELICON
PHYLLIDA AND CORYDON

Page 205.
21. *silly*, innocent, simple.

AS IT FELL UPON A DAY
23. *King Pandion*, father of Philomela (the nightingale).

THE SHEPHERD'S COMMENDATION
19. *Cynthia's silver light*, moonlight.
26. *damask-rose*, a species of pink rose.
31. *Phœbus*, god of the sun.
32. *Thetis*, goddess of the sea.
40. *Dea*, an early Roman goddess.

Page 210.
SEVENTEENTH CENTURY LYRICS
CAMPION — WHEN THOU MUST HOME
4. *White Iope*, referred to by the Latin poet, Propertius, as among the beautiful women in the underworld.

Page 210.
A RENUNCIATION
3. *mere*, absolute, pure.

Page 211.
JONSON — HYMN TO DIANA
This song is from *Cynthia's Revels*, Act V, scene iii. In Elizabethan symbolism, Cynthia, goddess of the moon, patroness of hunting and of chastity, is emblematic of Queen Elizabeth.
5. *Hesperus*, the evening star.
7. *Earth let not thy envious shade*, Let there be no eclipse of the moon.

AN EPITAPH ON SALATHIEL PAVY
11. *three filled zodiacs*, three full years.
12. *The stage's jewel*. Salathiel Pavy was a child of Queen Elizabeth's Chapel, and, apparently, a boy actor of great talent.
15. *Parcæ*, the Fates.

Page 212.
TO THE MEMORY OF MY BELOVED MASTER WILLIAM SHAKESPEARE
20. *Beaumont*. Francis Beaumont (1584–1616), an English dramatist and lyrist.
29. *Lyly*. John Lyly (1554?–1606), an English dramatist and lyrist.
30. *Kyd*. Thomas Kyd (1558–1594), an English dramatist who wrote 'tragedies of blood.' *Marlowe's mighty line*. Christopher Marlowe (1564–1593), an English poet and dramatist. Marlowe's plays are written in sonorous blank verse.
33. *Æschylus, Euripides, and Sophocles*, the great Greek writers of tragedy, of the 5th century B. C.
35. *Pacuvius*, a Roman tragic poet (c. 220–c. 129 B. C.). *Accius*, a Roman tragic poet (born c. 170 B. C.). *him of Cordova*, Seneca (c. 4 B. C.–65 A. D.), a Roman Stoic philosopher and writer of tragedy.
36. *buskin*, the cothurnus, or high boot, anciently worn by actors in tragedy.
37. *socks*. The sock (Latin *soccus*) was a light shoe worn by the ancient actors of comedy.
45. *Apollo*. Apollo, the god of light, was also patron of music and poetry.
46. *Mercury*, the messenger of the gods, noted for his versatility and power of fascination.
51. *Aristophanes*, greatest of the Greek comic poets (c. 448–c. 380 B. C.).
52. *Terence*, a celebrated Roman writer of comedy (c. 185–c. 159 B. C.). *Plautus*, a Roman writer of comedy (died 184 B. C.).
71. *Swan of Avon*, a reference to Shakespeare's birthplace, Stratford-upon-Avon.
74. *Eliza*, Queen Elizabeth. *James*, James I.

DONNE — SONG
2. *mandrake root*. The root of the mandrake somewhat resembles the human body in shape. It was used in amorous incantations, and was the focus of numerous superstitions.

Page 213.
THE CANONIZATION
23. *The phœnix riddle*. It was said that the phœnix, after living 500 (or 1,000) years, made a nest of spices, burned itself to ashes, and came forth with renewed life for another similar period.

Page 215.
FORGET
11. *Lethean flood*. Lethe was one of the streams of Hades, the waters of which caused those who drank of them to forget their previous existence.

Page 215.
FLETCHER — SONG TO BACCHUS
1. *Lyæus*, a surname of Bacchus.
3. *lusty*, pleasant, healthy.
5. *mazer's brim*. A mazer is a bowl or large drinking cup.

Page 217.
WILLIAM BROWNE
ON THE COUNTESS DOWAGER OF PEMBROKE
Mary Sidney, Countess of Pembroke (1561–1621), was a sister of Sir Philip Sidney. To her he dedicated his *Arcadia*.
10. *Niobe*. Too proud of her numerous progeny, Niobe provoked the anger of Apollo and Artemis, who slew her children with arrows. Zeus metamorphosed Niobe into stone.

ROBERT HERRICK
THE ARGUMENT OF HIS BOOK
3. *hock-carts*, harvest-home carts. *wassails*, drinking parties.
8. *ambergris*, a product of the sperm-whale, used in perfumery.

Page 218.
12. *Mab*, queen of the fairies.

CORINNA'S GOING A-MAYING
10. *matins*, the first of the ecclesiastical services for the day.
17. *Flora*, goddess of the spring and of flowers.
25. *Titan*, the sun personified.
28. *beads*, prayers.
66. *shade*, ghost.

Page 219.
THE NIGHT-PIECE, TO JULIA
7. *slowworm*, a harmless, small, limbless lizard, resembling a snake.

AN ODE FOR BEN JONSON
5–6. *Sun, Dog, Triple Tun*, names of taverns.
7. *clusters*, gatherings of persons.

A THANKSGIVING TO GOD
Page 220.
12. *state*, show, formality.
22. *unflead*, not stripped.
28. *pulse*, seeds of leguminous plants.
31. *worts*, plants, greens. *purslain*, purslane, a plant often used in salads.
39. *wassail bowls*, bowls for drinking healths.

GRACE FOR A CHILD
3. *paddocks*, toads.
5. *benison*, blessing.

Page 221.
GEORGE HERBERT — THE COLLAR
5. *store*, abundance.
14. *bays*, garlands or crowns bestowed as prizes.

THE WORLD
Page 222.
14. *summers*, the main planks or girders in a floor.

JAMES SHIRLEY
THE GLORIES OF OUR BLOOD AND STATE
From the masque, *The Contention of Ajax and Ulysses*, printed in 1659.

CAREW — SONG
3. *orient*, bright and clear.
18. *Phœnix*. See note to Donne, *The Canonization*, p. 213, l. 23.

SONG
6. *orbs*, spheres. An allusion to the music made by the revolving of the spheres.

Page 223.
THE PROTESTATION
11. *Lethe,* one of the streams of Hades, the waters of which caused those who drank to forget their previous existence.

Page 224.
WALLER — THE STORY OF PHŒBUS AND DAPHNE
3. *Phœbus,* Apollo, god of light, poetry, and music.
4. *Daphne,* a nymph.
20. *bays,* garlands.

SUCKLING — A DOUBT OF MARTYRDOM
5. *Whether,* which. *chaplets,* wreaths.

Page 225.
19. *Elysium,* the abode of the souls of the good.
23. *Sophonisba,* a Carthaginian woman (died c. 204. B. C.) who was betrothed to a Numidian prince Masinissa, afterwards married Syphax, and later married Masinissa, after he had conquered her husband.
26–8. *Philoclea* . . . *Pirocles* . . . *Amphialus,* characters in Sir Philip Sidney's pastoral romance *Arcadia*. See p. 144.

RICHARD CRASHAW
IN THE HOLY NATIVITY OF OUR LORD GOD
15–16. *Tityrus* . . . *Thyrsis,* conventional names for shepherds.

Page 226.
46. *phœnix.* See note to Donne, *The Canonization,* p. 213, l. 23.
98. *Maia,* an old Italian goddess of spring.

Page 227.
SIR JOHN DENHAM
ON MR. ABRAHAM COWLEY'S DEATH
For selections from Cowley, see p. 228.
7. *Aurora,* the dawn. *Spenser.* See above, pp. 104 ff.
10. *Phœbus,* Apollo, god of poetry and music.
16. *bays,* wreaths.
35. *Horace,* Quintus Horatius Flaccus (65–8 B. C.), a famous Roman lyric and satirical poet. *state,* stateliness.
40. *Jason.* Jason with other Argonauts made an expedition to Colchis, in Asia, to obtain the Golden Fleece.
43. *Flaccus,* the Roman poet Horace.
44. *The Theban Swan,* Pindar (c. 522–443 B. C.) the greatest of the Greek lyric poets.

Page 228.
LOVELACE — THE ROSE
5. *Flora,* goddess of spring and flowers.
6. *Aurora,* the dawn.
11. *coverled,* coverlet.
14. *Silenus,* the foster-father of Bacchus, and leader of the satyrs.

COWLEY — THE SWALLOW
4–5. *Tereus* . . . *Philomel.* Tereus, after dishonoring his sister-in-law, Philomela, deprived her of her tongue. Philomela was afterward metamorphosed into a nightingale.

Page 229.
MARVEL — THE GARDEN
2. *bays,* wreaths, often of laurel.
5. *narrow-verged,* of narrow margin.
29. *Apollo* . . . *Daphne.* Daphne, daughter of the river-god Peneus, was pursued by Apollo, who had been charmed by her beauty. She prayed for aid, and was metamorphosed into a laurel-tree.
31. *Pan* . . . *Syrinx.* Syrinx, an Arcadian maid, when pursued by Pan was, as the result of her own prayer, metamorphosed into a reed.

TO HIS COY MISTRESS
5. *Ganges,* the sacred river of India.

Page 230.
7. *Humber,* an estuary on the eastern coast of England.
40. *slow-chapt,* slowly cracked, or, perhaps, slowly devouring.

SACKVILLE — SONG
Page 232.
27. *Whitehall,* a royal palace in London.
32. *Goree,* on the west coast of Africa.
45. *ombre,* a game played with cards.

FRANCIS BACON — ESSAYS OF TRUTH
Page 233.
a. 3. *jesting Pilate.* See John xviii, 38.
 5. *in giddiness,* in quick change of opinion.
 18. *at a stand,* at a loss.
b. 4–5. *masques, mummeries, triumphs,* shows or entertainments.
 17. *One of the fathers.* Both Jerome and Augustine have a similar saying; neither uses exactly these words.

Page 234.
a. 19. *The poet,* Lucretius (1st century B. C.) in the Latin poem *On the Nature of Things*.
 20. *the sect,* of the Epicureans.
 38. *round,* straightforward, or as we should say, square.
 47. *Montaigne.* Essays ii, 18.
b. 2. *it being foretold.* Luke xviii, 8.

OF ADVERSITY
8. *Seneca.* The Roman philosopher and tutor of Nero (4 B. C.–65 A. D.). Both the passages quoted are from his Epistles.
21. *transcendencies,* hyperboles, exaggerations.
32. *in a mean,* in a moderate or prosaic style.
33. *temperance,* moderation.

Page 235.
OF PARENTS AND CHILDREN
a. 24. *Solomon saith.* Proverbs x, 1.
 34. *shifts,* subterfuges.
b. 4. *the precept.* Ascribed by Plutarch to the Pythagoreans. Plutarch (1st century A. D.) wrote in Greek, but Bacon doubtless read him in a Latin translation.

OF MARRIAGE AND SINGLE LIFE
13. *impediments,* hindrances, in the sense that they may deter a man from taking big risks.
37. *humorous,* subject to humors, or moods.
44. *churchmen,* clergymen.
50. *hortatives,* exhortations.

Page 236.
a. 2. *exhaust,* exhausted. The form Bacon uses is taken directly from the Latin past participle.
 7. *Ulysses* refused to share immortality with the goddess Calypso, and returned home to his wife Penelope.
 17. *a quarrel,* a pretext or excuse.
 18. *one of the wise men.* The saying quoted is ascribed by Plutarch and Montaigne to the Greek philosopher, Thales.

OF LOVE
42. *Marcus Antonius* (83–30 B. C.), the lover of Cleopatra.
43. *Appius Claudius,* the Roman decemvir who became enamored of Virginia 449 B. C. See Macaulay's *Lays of Ancient Rome*.
51. *saying of Epicurus.* Quoted by Seneca, Epistle vii.
b. 5. *braves,* exaggerates.
 8. *it hath been well said.* By Plutarch.
 14. *it was well said.* The reference may be to Publius Syrus, or to Plutarch.
 20. *the reciproque,* mutual affection.

Page 236.

25. *he that preferred Helena.* Paris, who awarded the apple to Venus in return for the gift of Helen, rejecting the offers of Juno (the sovereignty of Asia) and Pallas (renown in war).
35. *keep quarter,* keep within bounds.
37. *check,* interfere.

OF BOLDNESS

55. *Demosthenes.* The story of the great Greek orator (385–322 B. C.) is told by Cicero and by Plutarch.

Page 237.

a. 24. *popular,* democratic.
28. *mountebanks,* quacks who sell their medicines from public stages.
32. *grounds,* principles.
45. *slight it over,* make nothing of it.
b. 3. *stale at chess,* a drawn game which neither party wins.

OF SUPERSTITION

38. *Augustus Cæsar,* Emperor of Rome 31 B. C.–14 A. D. *civil,* peaceful.
41. *primum mobile,* the origin or cause of motion, according to the old astronomy.
46. *Council of Trent,* a great ecclesiastical council of the Roman Catholic Church held 1545–1563.
48. *schoolmen,* medieval philosophers.

Page 238.

OF WISDOM FOR A MAN'S SELF

a. 29. *shrewd,* harmful. Bacon is wrong as to the fact.
31. *waste,* injure.
35. *right earth,* exactly like the earth.
46. *crooketh,* distorts, perverts.
47. *eccentric to,* having a different center or motive from.
51. *accessory,* secondary.
b. 5. *bias,* a weight inserted in a bowl to make it run in a curve.
14. *and,* if.
18. *respect,* consideration.

OF DISPATCH

38. *Affected,* excessively desired.
50. *false periods,* apparent conclusions, which do not really end the matter.

Page 239.

a. 1. *a wise man,* Sir Amyas Paulet.
2. *byword,* proverb.
21. *moderator,* presiding officer.
22. *actor,* speaker.
27. *curious,* elaborate, highly wrought.
29. *passages,* transitions.
32. *bravery,* extravagance of dress, meant for show, not use.
33. *being too material,* keeping too close to the point.

OF SEEMING WISE

b. 7. *the Apostle,* Paul, 2. Timothy iii, 5.
11. *magno conatu nugas.* Quoted from Terence, the Roman writer of comedies.
15. *prospectives,* stereoscopes.
30. *bear it,* carry their point.
31. *by admittance,* for granted.
32. *make good,* prove.
35. *curious,* trifling.
37. *difference,* distinction.
38. *blanch the matter,* gloss over or shirk the issue.

Page 240.

a. 2. *opinion,* credit.
4. *you were better,* it would be better for you.

OF EXPENSE

a. 11. *worth,* importance.
13. *kingdom of heaven.* See Matthew xix, 24.

Page 240.

a. 20. *of even hand.* His outgo equal to his income.
27. *broken,* bankrupt.
28. *searching,* probing.
31. *new.* Servants.
34. *certainties,* fixed amounts.
44. *disadvantageable,* disadvantageous.

OF DISCOURSE

b. 9. *want,* lack.
19. *jade,* spur, overdrive.
27. *would be bridled,* ought to be restrained.
28. *Parce . . . loris,* Ovid, *Metamorphoses* ii, 127.
32. *saltness,* wit.
42. *poser,* an examiner putting questions.
47. *galliard,* a lively dance.

Page 241.

a. 3. *himself pretendeth,* he himself lays claim.
4. *of touch,* reflecting upon or wounding.
5. *as a field,* open, general.
11. *flout or dry blow,* an insulting jest or hard knock.

OF RICHES

38. *conceit,* fancy, imagination. *saith Solomon,* Ecclesiastes v, 11.
43. *dole and donative,* gifts small and large.
45. *feigned,* fictitious.
51. *Solomon saith.* Proverbs xviii. 11.
55. *sold,* betrayed.
b. 11. *Solomon,* Proverbs xxviii, 20.
14. *poets,* The saying quoted is found in the Greek prose writer Lucian (2nd century A. D.).
26. *enrich,* become rich.
34. *husbandry,* industry.
36. *audits,* accounts.
38. *collier,* owner of coal mines.
42. *observed by one.* In Plutarch.
46. *expect the prime,* wait for the most favorable condition. *overcome,* take advantage of.
50. *mainly,* greatly.
55. *broke,* do business, negotiate.

Page 242.

a. 2. *chapmen,* buyers.
4. *chopping of bargains,* speculation by middlemen.
28. *co-emption,* the modern trust.
33. *service,* to a monarch or nobleman.
54. *glorious,* ostentatious.
b. 3. *advancements,* gifts.

OF YOUTH AND AGE

22. *Septimius Severus,* Roman Emperor 193–211 A. D.
23. *it is said.* By Spartianus.
28. *Cosmos,* usually called Cosimo de' Medici, made Grand Duke of Tuscany, 1570.
29. *Gaston de Foix,* a celebrated French general, made Duke of Nemours in 1505.
31. *composition,* disposition, temperament. *Young men,* &c. Suggested by an observation of Plutarch.
36. *them,* old men (implied in *age*). *abuseth,* deceives.
41. *manage,* management.
45. *absurdly* qualifies *pursue. care,* hesitate.
53. *period,* conclusion.

Page 243.

a. 5. *extern,* external.
9. *A certain rabbin.* Isaac Abrabanel (1437–1508).
22. *Hermogenes,* a famous rhetorician of the second century B. C.
28. *Tully.* Cicero. Hortensius was his great rival at the Roman bar.
33. *Scipio Africanus.* Roman general (234–183 B. C.).
34. *Livy.* Roman historian (59–17 B. C.). *Ultima primis.* Quoted from Ovid. What Livy says is that Scipio in his later life had no opportunity for the military exploits for which he was naturally fitted.

Page 243.
OF NEGOTIATING
a. 47. *tender*, delicate or difficult.
    55. *success*, result.
b. 4. *affect*, are inclined to.
    6. *quickeneth*, spurs on, encourages.
    14. *prescription*, prestige, reputation previously won.
    19. *in appetite*, eager for advancement.
    20. *upon conditions*. A. agrees to do something if B. will do something. Who is to do his part first? A. must unless (1) B.'s part necessarily comes first; or (2) A. will still need B. for some other part of the scheme; *or* (3) A. is known to be more trustworthy and B. can therefore depend on him.
    27. *practice*, negotiation.
    28. *discover*, to ascertain a man's plans or character. *work*, to induce a man to do something.
    32. *know*. This verb governs *nature, fashions, ends, weakness, disadvantages, those*

OF STUDIES
    50. *expert*, practised, experienced.

Page 244.
a. 2. *humor*, fanciful peculiarity, foible.
    18. *curiously*, with elaborate care.
    22. *would*, should.
    25. *flashy*, tasteless.
b. 3. *confer*, converse.
    8. *moral grave*, studies in moral philosophy make men serious and dignified.
    10. *stond*, drawback, hindrance.
    14. *stone and reins*, bladder and kidneys.
    23. *beat over matters*, take a broad general view of many things.
    26. *receipt*, prescribed remedy.

Page 245.
BROWNE — RELIGIO MEDICI
a. 5. *general scandal of my profession*. According to the old saying, 'Where there are three physicians, there are two atheists.'
b. 10. *nothing but the name*. 'Protestant, as carrying with it an insinuation of enmity and discord, inconsistent with the peace and harmony prescribed by the gospel.'
    20. *the person*. Luther.
    25. *shaken hands with*, parted from.
    26. *desperate resolutions*. These words, with the dependent relative clauses up to *what they have been*, refer to the Roman Catholics.

Page 246.
a. 1. *bottom*, ship.
    3. *all* (doctrines).
    5. *in diameter*, in diametrical opposition.
    8. *improperations*, taunts, reproaches.
    9. *difference*, show the difference of.
    13. *am not scrupulous*, do not hesitate.
    15. *in defect of ours*, where ours do not exist.
    34. *morosity*, moroseness.
    38. *violate*, injure.
b. 4. *consorts*, companions.
    6. *questionless*, unquestionably.
    22. *mediocrity*, moderation.
    32. *difference myself*, distinguish my opinions.
    44. *humor*, mood.
    46. *disproving*, disapproving.
    47. *disavouched*, disavowed.
    48. *Council of Trent*. See page 237. b. 46, note.
    49. *Dort*. In the Netherlands, where a great Protestant Synod was held in 1618-19.
    53. *Geneva*. The center of Protestantism on the European Continent.
    54. *scandal*, objection.

Page 247.
a. 6. *the state of Venice* had a dispute with Pope Paul V in 1606.

Page 247.
a. 17. *reaction*, recrimination.
    54. *Œdipus* solved the riddle of the Sphinx.
b. 32. *Diogenes*, the Cynic, a Greek philosopher (412-323 B. C.).
    33. *Timon*, of Athens, a famous misanthrope, contemporary with Socrates.
    42. *pia mater*, a membrane enveloping the brain.
    43. *impossibilities*, apparent impossibilities, difficulties calling for the exercise of faith.
    48. *O altitudo*. A height beyond human comprehension

Page 248.
a. 1. *Tertullian of Carthage*, one of the fathers of the Church (2nd and 3rd centuries).
    33. *expansed*, spread out.
    38. *admire*, wonder at.
    41. *the other* (people), *i.e.*, the Israelites.
b. 44. *the chaos*, *i.e.*, before the Creation.

Page 249.
a. 29. *away with*, put up with.
    52. *temper*, constitution. *crows and daws*, proverbially long-lived birds.
b. 3. *revolution of Saturn*. The year of Saturn is 10,759 days.
    11. *canicular days*, dog days. Latin. *dies caniculares*, the hottest days of summer, ascribed in ancient astrology to the malignant influence of the dog star.
    14. *pantalones and antics*, pantaloons and clowns.
    27. *Methuselah* lived 969 years. See Genesis v, 27.
    28. *rectify*, straighten, improve. *incurvate*, deteriorate.
    49. *Cicero* says in his treatise *On Old Age:* I am not sorry to have lived: since I have so lived that I do not think I was born in vain.

Page 250.
a. 5. *Æson*, an old man in classical mythology whom Medea restored to youth by a magical bath.
    6. *providence*, foresight.
    8. *able temper*, sound constitution.
    9. *radical humor*, vital juice.
    16. *glome or bottom*, a ball of thread.
b. 17. *climate*, a space measured on the earth's surface; England was in the eighth.
    36. *Hydra*, a many-headed monster slain by Hercules.
    38. *Solomon*. See Proverbs i, 7, 22, &c.
    51. *Doradoes*, rich men; literally 'the gilded' [ones].
    54. *politicians*, statesmen.

Page 251.
a. 31. *as the world* (is one).
    36. *buffet*, box.
    37. *at sharp*, with pointed weapons.
    39. *Lepanto*, a battle between the Italians and Turks, 1571.
    43. *dastards*, intimidates.
b. 3. *epidemical*, common to all people.
    29. *the world*, the macrocosm which man, the microcosm, resembles.
    47. *grammarian*, student of Latin grammar.
    49. *construction*, construing.
    55. *Babel*. See Genesis xi, 1-9.

Page 252.
a. 4. *chorography*, description of countries.
    13. *pointers*, the Dipper.
    19. *simpled*, collected simples, or herbs. *Cheapside*, a famous London herb market.
    31. *Euripus*, a strait dividing Attica from Euboea, where the tide, according to classical tradition, ebbed and flowed seven times a day. The story that Aristotle drowned himself there because he could not discover the cause of the phenomenon is discussed by Browne, along with the fable as to the death of Homer because he could not guess the fisherman's riddle, in *Pseudodoxia Epidemica*, Bk. VII, ch. 13.

Page 252.

a. 37–38. *Peripatetics, Stoics, Academics.* Classical schools of philosophy.
40. *Janus*, facing both ways.
52. *attending*, waiting.
53. *which* (knowledge).

b. 5. *glorification* (in heaven).
8. *disallow*, disapprove.
26. *music of the spheres*. The ancients had a fancy that the rotation of the planets produced music; this kept its place in poetry after it had been denied by the astronomers. See *Merchant of Venice,* V. i, 60–62.
38. *first composer.* God.

Page 253.

a. 6. *ephemerides*, astrological tables.

HYDRIOTAPHIA, URN-BURIAL

b. 7. *ossuaries*, receptacles for bones. In this essay Browne discourses about some urns containing bones, dug up in Norfolk and supposed to be of Roman origin.
14. *tutelary observators*, guardian spirits of the place.
19. *pyramidally*, by means of a tombstone.
28. *Atropos*, the Greek Fate who cut the thread of human life.
32. *meridian*, the noon of the world's lifetime.
39. *Charles V* (1500–1558), Emperor of Germany.
47. *Janus*, facing past and future.

Page 254.

a. 26. *Gruter*, Dutch philologist (1560–1627).
36. *Cardan*, a celebrated Italian (1501–1576).
38. *Hippocrates*, famous Greek physician (460–357 B. C.).
41. *entelechia*, actual being, a term in the philosophy of Aristotle.
44. *Canaanitish woman.* See Matthew x, 4. Mark iii, 18.
45. *Herodias.* See Matthew xiv, 1–12.
46. *good thief.* See Luke xxiii, 39–43.

b. 3. *Herostratus . . . Diana.* At Ephesus 356 B. C.
5. *Adrian* (76–138 A. D.), Emperor of Rome.
11. *Thersites*, the foul-mouthed rogue of Homer's *Iliad*, in which *Agamemnon* is one of the heroes.
21. *the first story.* See Genesis v.
22. *one living century* a hundred people still remembered.
28. *Lucina*, the goddess of childbirth.

Page 255.

a. 16. *Cambyses*, king of Persia and conqueror of Egypt, d. 521 B. C.
18. *Mizraim*, the brother of Cush, is the Hebrew name of Egypt.
19. *Pharaoh*, the title of many kings of ancient Egypt. In Browne's time Egyptian mummies were used for medical prescriptions.
27. *Nimrod*, the founder of the Babylonian Empire. See Genesis x, 8–12. In Hebrew astronomy he corresponds to the Greek constellation Orion. *Osiris*, an Egyptian deity.
32. *perspectives*, telescopes.

b. 8. *scape*, a momentary chance.
18. *Sardanapalus*, the last Assyrian king of Nineveh, unable to withstand a siege there, burnt himself and his household on a huge funeral pile 876 B. C.
25. *Gordianus.* Emperor of Rome, third century. *The Man of God.* Moses. See Deuteronomy xxxiv, 1–6.
29. *Enoch.* See Genesis v, 24. *Elias*, Elijah. See 2 Kings ii, 1–11.
40. *Lazarus.* See John xi.
42. *die but once.* See Revelation xxi, 8.
45. *coverings of mountains.* See Revelation vi, 15–17

Page 256.

WALTON — THE COMPLETE ANGLER

This chapter is in the form of an open-air dialogue between the Angler (Piscator), who represents the author, and the Hunter, who is his pupil. The Angler continues the discourse he had begun in Chapter III, on the chub.

a. 10. *generous*, originally high born, and hence full of spirit, rich and full of strength, invigorating.
14. *Gesner*, a Swiss physician and naturalist who wrote a book *On Animals* (1551–8). *offspring*, origin; there is little doubt, however, that the word *trout* comes through the Latin *trutta* from the Greek τρώκτης.
35. *three cubits*, 4½ feet. The trout of the Great American Lakes is sometimes even larger.
36. *Mercator*, a Flemish scientist who died in 1594.

b. 17. *Fordidge trout* are salmon trout and live in the ordinary way: so do grasshoppers. Walton's aspersions on the mother raven are groundless.

Page 257.

a. 29. *Michaelmas*, September 29.
35. *Albertus*, Magnus (1193–1280), a German Dominican monk, who wrote more than twenty volumes on natural philosophy.

Page 258.

b. 25. *the best.* Men were readier at sharing a bed in those days.
27. *catch*, a short part-song for three or more voices.

Page 259.

a. 44. *verjuice*, acid of the crab-apple, or other fruits.
b. 7. *Troy Town*, a ballad about Dido and Æneas.

Page 260.

a. 4. *Overbury's . . . wish.* In the 'characters' subjoined to *The Wife* (1604).
17. *Philomel*, the nightingale.
Walton found both these songs in *England's Helicon* (1600). The first is ascribed with some certainty to Christopher Marlowe, the second, more doubtfully, to Sir Walter Raleigh.

Page 261.

FULLER — LIFE OF SIR FRANCIS DRAKE

a. 9. *Six Articles of Faith*, which Henry VIII required the clergy to sign.

Page 262.

a. 30. *chapmen*, merchants, i.e.. adventurers.
40. *admire*, wonder.
53. *Cabo-verd*, Cape Verde.
b. 36. *Portugals*, Portuguese.

Page 263.

a. 8. *caudle*, a warm drink, consisting of weak gruel, mixed with ale or wine, sweetened and spiced.
22. *curious*, careful.
42. *half moon*, the power of Spain, which was broken by the destruction of the Armada in 1588.
b. 1. *caraval of adviso*, a messenger-ship.
8. *vent*, outlet, i.e., publicly.

Page 264.

a. 27. *fresh water . . . Plymouth.* It is indeed one of the striking instances of Drake's public-spirited enterprise that in the intervals of adventure he devised a municipal water supply.

Page 265.

TAYLOR — THE PATIENCE OF THE SAINTS

a. 21. *my text.* 'For the time is come that judgment must begin at the house of God: and if it first begin at us, what shall the end be of them that obey not the Gospel of God? And if the righteous scarcely be saved, where shall the ungodly and the sinner appear?'—1 Peter iv, 17, 18.
32. *Dives*, the rich man of Luke xvi, 19–31.

Page 266.
a. 17. *renegadoes*, renegades, those who have denied the true faith.
b. 2. *rainbow . . . grace.* See Genesis ix, 13–17.
   15. *consequent*, consequence.

Page 267.
a. 36–37. *green tree . . . dry.* See Luke xxiii, 31. This is a good example of the way in which Taylor's whole phraseology is colored by reminiscences of Scripture.

JOHN BUNYAN — PILGRIM'S PROGRESS

Page 270.
a. 19. *fat*, vessel, tub, vat.

Page 271.
a. 52. *going*, walking.

Page 272.
a. 2. *fact*, deed.

Page 275.
a. 22. *conversation*, manner of life.
   33. *tenderness in*, sensitiveness about, scrupulous care against.

Page 279.

JOHN MILTON — ON SHAKESPEARE

Printed among the commendatory verses prefixed to the Shakespeare folio of 1632.
4. *star-ypointing*, pointing to the stars; not a correctly formed word, *y* being properly a prefix for the past participle only.
11. *unvalued*, invaluable.
12. *Dephic*, oracular. The oracle of Apollo was at Delphi.

Page 280.

L'ALLEGRO

Published 1645; written probably at Horton about 1634.
2. *Cerberus*, the three-headed monstrous dog which guarded the classic hell.
3. *Stygian*, belonging to the Styx, i.e., infernal.
5. *uncouth*, unknown, hence strange, monstrous.
8. *ebon*, black.
10. *Cimmerian desert*, according to Homer, a land of perpetual darkness 'beyond the ocean-stream.'
12. *yclept*, called. *Euphrosyne*, Mirth, one of the three Graces of classical mythology.
19. *Zephyr*, the West Wind. *Aurora*, the Dawn.
29. *Hebe*, goddess of Youth, Jove's cupbearer.
62. *dight*, decked.
67. *tells his tale*, counts his sheep.
80. *cynosure*, center of attraction; in Greek the name of the constellation containing the pole-star.
83–88. *Corydon, Thyrsis, Thestylis, Phyllis*, conventional names in pastoral poetry.
94. *rebecks*, fiddles.
102. *fairy Mab.* See *Romeo and Juliet*, I, iv. 95.
103. *she—he*, members of the group of story-tellers.
104. *friar's lantern*, will o' the wisp.
105. *drudging goblin*, Robin Goodfellow, the Puck of *Midsummer Night's Dream*, a mischievous but helpful fairy.
110. *lubber*, clumsy, awkward.

Page 281.
120. *weeds*, garments.
122. *rain influence*, like the stars.
125. *Hymen*, the god of marriage.
132. *sock*, Latin *soccus*, the low-heeled shoe worn in classical comedy. For tragedy the buskin was used.
136. *Lydian*, the softest and sweetest kind of Greek music.
139. *bout*, turn.

Page 281.
145. *Orpheus* with his music won Pluto to release his wife Eurydice from hell on condition that he did not look back to see if she were following him to the upper world: he could not withstand the temptation, and she was lost.
147. *elysian*, heavenly.

IL PENSEROSO

A companion poem to the foregoing, written and printed with it.
3. *bested*, avail, profit.
10. *Morpheus*, god of dreams.
18. *Memnon*, a handsome Ethiopian prince who fought in the Trojan war.
19. *starred Ethiop Queen*, Cassiope, changed into the constellation Cassiopœia.
23. *Vesta*, goddess of the fireside.
24. *Saturn*, father of Jupiter.
29. *Ida*, a mountain near Troy.
39. *commèrcing*, having commerce or intercourse with.
56. *Philomel*, the nightingale.
59. *Cynthia*, the moon.
74. *curfew*, the evening bell.

Page 282.
87. *Bear*, the Great Bear which never sets in the latitude of Great Britain. To *outwatch the Bear* is therefore to stay awake till all the stars have faded in the light of day.
88. *Hermes*, an ancient Egyptian philosopher.
95. *consent*, sympathy.
99. *Thebes . . . Troy*, subjects of classical tragedy.
102. *buskined*, tragic. See 238. 132, note.
109. *him that left half told*, Chaucer in the Squire's Tale.
113. *virtuous*, magical.
124. *Attic boy.* Cephalus, beloved of Aurora.
134. *Sylvan*, the god of woods.
148. *his*, of sleep.
154. *genius*, guardian spirit.
156. *pale*, enclosure.
159. *storied*, adorned with stories from Scripture.
170. *spell*, read slowly.

LYCIDAS

The purpose of the poem is best explained in Milton's own words:—'In this monody the author bewails a learned friend, unfortunately drowned in his passage from Chester on the Irish seas, 1637, and by occasion foretells the ruin of our corrupted clergy, then in their height.' Milton's friend was Edward King, of Christ's College, Cambridge. *Lycidas* was written in 1637 and published along with other elegies in a memorial volume for King in 1638.
8. *Lycidas*, a name used in the Seventh Idyll of Theocritus, the founder of pastoral poetry. *ere his prime.* King was 25.

Page 283.
15. *sacred well*, the fountain of the Muses on Mount Helicon.
27. *drove* (our flocks).
29. *battening*, fattening.
36. *Damætas*, a conventional name in pastoral poetry. Possibly Milton's college tutor is meant. Both Milton and King wrote Latin verse of merit.
46. *weanling*, weaned.
52–55. The Welsh hills, Mona (Anglesea), and the River Dee bound the Irish sea on the east. See Map.
59. *the Muse*, Calliope, mother of Orpheus; he was torn to pieces by Thracian women, and his head floated down the river Hebrus to Lesbos.
64. *boots*, profits.
68. *Amaryllis, Neæra*, maidens of classical pastoral.
75. *blind Fury.* More properly the Fate Atropos, who cuts the thread of human life.
77. *Phœbus*, Apollo, the god of poetry.
79. *glistering foil*, glittering tinsel.
82. *Jove.* God.

Page 283.

85. *Arethuse, Mincius*, rivers of Greek and Latin pastoral poetry.
88. *oat*, oaten pipe.
91. *felon*, criminal, cruel.
95. *his*, of Lycidas. *Hippotades*, Æolus, who controlled the winds.
99. *Panope*, a nymph, one of the fifty daughters of Nereus.
100. *fatal*, fated to destruction. *perfidious*, treacherous, unworthy of trust.
101. *the eclipse*, a time of evil omen.
103. *Camus*, the river at Cambridge personified as a god. *footing slow*. The Cam flows gently.
106. *sanguine flower*, the hyacinth which the ancients held to be marked 'Ai, Ai,' in lamentation for Hyacinthus.
107. *reft*, bereaved me of.
109. *pilot of the Galilean lake*, St. Peter.
110. *keys*. See Matthew xvi, 19.
112. *mitered*. St. Peter was the first bishop of Rome. The miter is the official headdress of a Roman bishop.
114. *Enow*, enough.

Page 284.

120. *sheep-hook*. Milton has now turned from the shepherd as poet to the shepherd as pastor.
122. *recks*, concerns. *sped*, provided for.
123. *flashy*. See 199. b. 25, note.
124. *scrannel*, screeching.
130. *two-handed engine*, the axe.
132. *Alphëus*, a classical river, lover of Arethusa.
133. *Sicilian Muse*, Theocritus. Milton is returning to the more conventional tone of pastoral poetry.
138. *swart star*, the dog-star, which was supposed to blast vegetation.
142. *rathe*, early. *forsaken*, unsought for, or perhaps there is an allusion to an old myth of the wooing of certain flowers by the sun. See Shakespeare's *Winter's Tale*, IV, iv, 122–5.
144. *freaked*, freckled, sprinkled.
149. *amaranthus*, emblem of immortality.
151. *laureate*, adorned with the poet's laurel. *hearse*, a platform adorned with black hangings and containing an effigy of the deceased.
152. *so*, by imagining that the body of Lycidas has been recovered.
156. *Hebrides*, islands to the far north of Scotland.
160. *Bellerus*. Land's End, the most western point of England, was anciently called Bellerium. Near it is St. Michael's Mount, a rocky island with a fortress on top and a craggy seat from which visions of St. Michael were seen.
162. *Namancos*, in Spain, near Cape Finisterre and the Castle of Bayona.
163. *ruth*, pity.
169. *anon*, immediately. *repairs*, refreshes.
170. *tricks*, sets in order, adorns. *ore*, brightness.
173. *Through . . . waves*. See Matthew xiv, 22–3.
176. *unexpressive*, inexpressible.
183. *genius*, protecting deity, guardian angel.
186. *uncouth*, unknown, uncultivated.
188. *quills*, reeds.
189. *Doric*, pastoral, rude, or as a shepherd.
193. A forecast of the very different occupations of the poet during the next few years.

SONNETS
WHEN THE ASSAULT WAS INTENDED

Written Nov., 1642; pub. 1645.
10. *Emathian conqueror*. Alexander of Macedon, when he sacked Thebes in 333 B.C. spared the house of the poet Pindar, who died almost a century before.
13. *Electra*, one of the tragedies of Euripides, the recital of whose verses is said to have saved the walls of Athens from destruction after the capture of the city by Lysander, the Spartan, in 404 B.C.

Page 284.
TO A VIRTUOUS YOUNG LADY
2. *the broad way*. See Matthew vii, 13.

Page 285.
5. *Mary . . . Ruth*. See Luke x, 42; Ruth i, 14–17.
12. *the Bridegroom*. See Matthew xxv, 1–13.

ON THE DETRACTION
1. *Tetrachordon*, one of Milton's pamphlets in favor of divorce, the full title being *Tetrachordon: Expositions upon the four chief places of Scripture which treat of marriage*.
7–8. *Mile-End Green*, in Milton's time, one of the London suburbs.
8–9. *Gordon . . . Galasp*, names of Scottish generals during the war of 1644–5, soon after which apparently this sonnet was written. This and the following sonnet were not included in the edition of 1645; they first appeared in 1673.
10. *our like*, like ours.
11. *Quintilian*, the great Latin writer on literary style.
12. *Sir John Cheke* (1514–1557), first professor of Greek at Cambridge and tutor of Edward VI.

ON THE SAME
6. *Latona's twin-born progeny*, Apollo and Diana.

TO THE LORD GENERAL CROMWELL
The Puritan Parliament had a committee for *propagation of the gospel*, to which proposals were submitted by certain ministers that the Puritan preachers should be maintained at the public expense. Milton was a strong believer in the voluntary system, and objected to any interference of the government with religious matters.
7. *Darwen stream*, in Lancashire, the scene of Cromwell's victory over the Scots, Aug. 17–19, 1648.
8. *Dunbar field*, another victory, Sept. 30, 1650.
9. *Worcester's laureate wreath*. Cromwell was accustomed to speak of his success at Worcester (Sept. 3, 1651) as the 'crowning mercy' of God.
11. *new foes*, a section of the Independents who proposed to accept state aid, as Milton's old foes, the Anglicans and Presbyterians, wished to do.
12. *secular chains*, government control.
14. *maw, stomach*. Compare *Lycidas*, ll. 114–125, p. 241.

ON THE LATE MASSACRE
The Protestants of Piedmont were in 1655 subjected to a cruel persecution by the Court of Turin, whose soldiery evicted them from their homes with extraordinary ferocity. The English government, through Milton, who was then Latin secretary, sent a solemn protest against the massacre to the Duke of Savoy. The sonnet expresses Milton's personal feeling.
7–8. The English agent in Piedmont narrated the following incident: 'A mother was hurled down a mighty rock with a little infant in her arms; and three days after was found dead with the child alive, but fast clasped between the arms of the mother, which were cold and stiff, insomuch that those that found them had much ado to get the child out.'
12. *The triple Tyrant*, the Pope, from his wearing a triple tiara.
14. *Babylonian woe*. The Puritans identified Rome with the Babylon of *Revelation* and of 1 Peter v, 13.

ON HIS BLINDNESS
Milton became completely blind about 1653: this sonnet was probably written not long after.

Page 286.
ON HIS DECEASED WIFE
1. *late espousèd saint*. Catherine Woodcock, Milton's second wife, died in childbirth, in February, 1658, fifteen months after their marriage.
2. *like Alcestis*. According to the classical myth, Alcestis, who gave her life to save her husband, was rescued from death by Hercules.

Page 286.

6. *the old law.* Leviticus xii.
10. *her face was veiled.* Although Milton was devotedly attached to his wife, probably he had never seen her. See above as to his blindness.

PARADISE LOST, BOOK I

2. *forbidden tree.* See Genesis iii.
4. *one greater Man.* The Messiah. See Romans v, 19.
7. *Sinai,* the lower part of the mountain range of Horeb, where God appeared to Moses. See Exodus iii and xix.
8. *first taught.* In Genesis i.
12. *fast,* close. *oracle,* the temple at Jerusalem.
15. *Aonian mount,* Helicon in Bœotia, the seat of the Greek muses. *pursues,* treats of—a classical usage.
19–22. See Genesis i, 2.
21. *Dove-like.* See Luke iii, 22.
25. *assert,* vindicate.

Page 287.

29. *grand,* first.
32. *For,* because of; or (perhaps) but for.
36. *what time,* when; a Latin construction.
39. *peers,* equals. Latin *pares.*
45–6. See Luke x, 18.
48. See 2 Peter ii, 4.
58. *obdurate.* Accent on second syllable.
66–7. Reminiscent of Euripides and Dante.
73–4. Milton's ideas of cosmography were founded on the Ptolemaic system, and are illustrated in the accompanying figures. Fig. 1 represents the Universe before the fall, and Fig. 2 after the fall of the Angels. Fig. 3 shows the stellar world, hanging by a golden chain from the floor of heaven. At the center of this is the earth, and around it the planets revolve in their several spheres, enclosed by the *primum mobile.* The distance from heaven to hell is three times the radius of the stellar universe.

Fig. 1—Before the fall of the Angels

Fig. 2—After the fall of the Angels

Fig. 3—After the creation of the World

81. *Beelzebub,* the sun-god of the Philistines.
82. *Satan,* 'the adversary.'

Page 287.

84. See Isaiah xiv, 12.
114. *Doubted,* feared for.
120. *successful hope,* hope of success.
130. *conduct,* command.

Page 288

148. *suffice,* satisfy.
167. *if I fail not,* if I am not mistaken. Latin construction.
172. *laid* (to rest).
178. *slip,* let slip.
187. *offend,* harm. Latin *offendere.*
193. *uplift,* uplifted.
197. *whom,* those whom.
197–200. *fables,* of classical mythology, according to which the Titans rebelled against their father Uranus, as the Giants did later against Zeus or Jove. *Briareos* was a Titan, *Typhon* a Giant. The latter is described by the Greek poets as living in a 'Cilician den.' *Tarsus* is the capital of Cilicia.
201. *Leviathan,* a Hebrew word meaning any huge monster. The translators of the Bible identified it with the whale, as Milton does here.
204. *night-foundered,* overtaken and enveloped by night.
226. *incumbent on,* lying on, supported by.
232–3. *Pelorus,* N. E. promontory of Sicily near Mt. Etna.

Page 289.

244. *change for,* take in exchange for.
257. *all but,* only.
266. *astonished,* astounded, thunderstruck. *Oblivious,* making forgetful.
268. *mansion,* abiding place.
281. *amazed,* confounded.
282. *pernicious,* destructive, dreadful.
288. *optic glass,* the telescope, developed by the Florentine astronomer Galileo, whom Milton saw during his Italian tour (1638–9).
289–290. *Fesolè, Valdarno,* near Florence.
296. *marl,* soil.
299. *Nathles,* nevertheless.
303. *Vallombrosa,* eighteen miles from Florence in Tuscany, anciently named Etruria.
305. *Orion armed.* The rising and setting of the constellation Orion the Hunter were traditionally attended with storms.
306. *Red Sea,* called by the Hebrews the Sea of Sedge, on account of the quantity of seaweed in it.
307. *Busiris,* Pharaoh. See Exodus xiv, 5–29. *Memphian* Egyptian.
309. *Goshen.* See Genesis xlvii, 27.
313. *Under amazement of,* utterly confounded by.
317. *If,* dependent on *lost.*
320. *virtue,* valor. Latin *virtus.*
335. *not perceive,* failed to perceive.
338–343. See Exodus x, 12–15.
339. *Amram's son,* Aaron. See Exodus vi, 20.
341. *warping,* advancing with an undulating motion.
351–5. The northern tribes which invaded the Roman empire from the third century onwards crossed from Spain into Africa and captured Carthage 439 A. D.

Page 290.

355. *beneath,* south of.
360. *erst,* formerly.
363. *books.* Milton probably dictated '*Book*' and was misunderstood by his amanuensis. See Revelation iii, 5.
372. *religions,* religious ceremonies.
392. *Moloch.* See 1 Kings xi, 7; 2 Kings xxiii, 10; Psalm cvi, 37, 38. Sandys, whose book of travels in Palestine was known to Milton, describes the idol as 'hollow within, filled with fire,' the children offered for sacrifice being placed in his arms. 'And lest their lamentable shrieks should sadden the hearts of their parents, the priests of Moloch did deafen their ears with the continual clang of trumpets and timbrels.'
397. *Rabba,* capital of Ammon, 'the city of waters'.

Page 290.

398–9. *Argob, Basan, Arnon*, east of the river Jordan.
401. *Solomon*. See 1 Kings xi, 5–7; 2 Kings xxiii, 13.
403. *opprobrious hill.* The Mount of Olives, where Solomon established the worship of Moloch, was later called the 'Mount of Corruption' and 'Mount of Offence.'
404. *Hinnom*, south of Olivet.
405. *Gehenna*, the Greek form of the Hebrew *Ge Hinnom*, valley of Hinnom.
406. *Chemos*, the god of Moab, the neighbors of Ammon.
409. *Seon*, king of the Amorites. See Numbers xxi, 26.
410. *Sibma.* See Isaiah xvi, 8.
411. *the asphaltic pool*, the Dead Sea.
413. *Sittim.* See Numbers xxv.
416. *scandal*, offence.
418. *good Josiah.* See Kings xxiii, 10.
420. *the brook*, Besor, 'the river of Egypt.'
422. *Baälim and Ashtaroth*, the collective names of the various manifestations of the deities of the sun and moon respectively.
438. *Astoreth*, the same as the Assyrian Istar, the Greek Aphrodite, and the Latin Venus.
441. Sidon was the oldest city of Phenicia.
444. *uxorious king*, Solomon.
446. *Thammuz*, 'Sun of Life,' the Greek Adonis, god of the solar year.
450. *Adonis*, the name of a river flowing from the heights of Lebanon, and colored in spring by the red mud gathered there.
455. *Ezekiel.* See Ezekiel viii, 14.
457. *came one*. Dagon, god of the Philistines. See 1 Samuel v, 4.

Page 291.

460. *grunsel*, threshold.
464–6. *Azotus . . . Gaza*, the five chief cities of the Philistines.
467. *Rimmon*, god of Damascus.
471. *leper*, Naaman. See 2 Kings v.
472. *Ahaz.* See 2 Kings xvi. *sottish*, foolish.
478. *Osiris, Isis, Orus*, Egyptian deities, worshipped under the shape of the bull, cow, and sun.
479. *abused*, deceived.
483. *borrowed*, from the Egyptians. See Exodus xii, 35–6.
484. *calf in Oreb.* See Exodus xxxii. *rebel king*, Jeroboam. 1 Kings xii, 20, 28, 29.
487. *he*, Israel. See Exodus xii.
495. *Eli's sons.* See 1 Samuel ii, 12–17.
498. *luxurious*, lustful.
502. *flown*, flushed.
503–4. *Sodom, Gibeah.* Genesis xix, Judges xix.
506. *prime*, leaders.
508. *Ionian*, Greek. *Javan*, son of Japhet. Genesis x, 2.
509. *Heaven and Earth*, Uranus and Ge, whose 12 giant children were Titans. One of them, Cronos (Saturn in Roman mythology), deposed Uranus, and was in turn deposed by his own son Zeus (Jove), whose mother was Rhea.
515–6. *Ida* in Crete was the birthplace of Zeus. *Olympus*, north of Thessaly, his abode, according to Greek mythology.
517. *Delphian cliff*, Apollo's oracle on Mt. Parnassus.
518. *Dodona*, an oracle of Zeus, in Epirus.
519. *Doric*, Greek.
520. *Adria*, the Adriatic. *Hesperian*, western, i.e., Italy.
521. *Celtic*, France and Spain. *utmost isles*, of Britain.
523. *damp*, depressed.
528. *recollecting*, recovering.
534. *Azazel.* Leviticus xvi, 8.
536. *advanced*, raised.
538. *emblazed*, emblazoned.
546. *orient*, bright.
547. *helms*, helmets.
548. *serried*, overlapping in compact order.
550. *Dorian mood*, the kind of Greek music adapted to military exercises.
551. *recorder*, a kind of flute.
556. *'suage*, assuage.

Page 292.

563. *horrid*, bristling with spears. Latin *horridus*.
568. *traverse*, across.
573. *since created man*, after the creation of man.
574. *embodies*, assembled in a body. *named*, compared.
575. *small infantry*, the Pygmies. Homer's *Iliad* iii, 5.
577. *Phlegra*, in Macedonia where the Gods defeated the Giants. See l. 509.
578. *Thebes and Ilium*, the chief battle grounds of Greek tradition.
580. *fable*, Geoffrey of Monmouth's History of the Britons. *romance*, Malory's *Morte D'Arthur*.
581. *Armoric*, Breton.
583–6. The references are to scenes famous in medieval romances.
586. *peerage*, the twelve peers of the *Chanson de Roland*.
588. *observed*, obeyed.
596–9. Curiously enough, this was the only passage in the poem objected to by the official Licenser for the Press (chaplain to the Archbishop of Canterbury), when the book was first printed. Either he did not like the suggestion of a 'change' of government, or he would not admit that Charles II could be 'perplexed' even by an eclipse.
597. *disastrous*, threatening disaster.
603. *considerate*, thoughtful, reflective.
605. *remorse and passion*, pity and suffering.
609. *amerced*, condemned to loss.
613. *scathed*, injured.
615. *blasted*, withered.
624. *event*, outcome.
632. *exile.* Accent on second syllable.
646. *work*, accomplish.
656. *eruption*, expedition, sortie.
662. *understood*, agreed on secretly.

Page 293.

670. *grisly*, horrible.
675. *brigade.* Pronounce brigad.
678. *Mammon*, riches (Syriac). See Matthew vi, 24.
686. *ransacked the center*, dug into the earth.
690. *ribs*, bars. *admire*, wonder.
694. *Babel.* See Genesis xi, 1–9. *Memphian*, Egyptian, i.e., the Pyramids.
703. *founded*, melted.
704. *severing*, separating.
713. *pilasters*, pillars set in a wall and lightly projecting from it. *overlaid*, surmounted.
715. *architrave*, the main beam.
716. *cornice, frieze*, adornments of the architrave. *Bossy*, in relief, projecting.
717. *fretted*, worked in designs.
720. *Belus*, the Assyrian god Bel or Baal. *Serapis*, an Egyptian god.
728. *cresset*, an iron lantern.
738. *his name*, Hephaistos or Vulcan.
739. *Ausonian land*, Italy.
740. *Mulciber*, the welder of metals.
746. *Lemnos*, sacred to Hephaistos. The story of his fall is told in Homer's *Iliad* i, 591.
750. *engines*, machines, contrivances.
756. *Pandemonium*, the place of all the demons.
764. *wont*, were wont to. *soldan*, sultan.
765. *paynim*, pagan.
769. The sun is in *Taurus* (one of the signs of the zodiac) April 19–May 20.
774. *expatiate*, walk abroad. Latin use. *confer*, discuss.

Page 294.

780–1. Pliny placed the Pygmies beyond the source of the Ganges.
781–5. Reminiscent of *A Midsummer Night's Dream* and the *Æneid*.
785. *arbitress*, witness. The moon was supposed to be influenced by fairy incantations.
795. *recess*, retirement. *conclave*, the name given to a meeting of Cardinals in the Roman Church.
797. *frequent*, crowded. Latin use.
798. *consult*, consultation.

Page 294.
BOOK II
2. *Ormus*, Persia.
9. *success*, result, experience.
16. *from no fall*, if they had not fallen.
27. *whom*, him whom.
29. *Your bulwark*, as your defence.
50. *recked*, cared.
52. *unexpert*, inexperienced.
59. *of*, imposed by.
60. *By*, in consequence of.
63. *our tortures*, what tortures us.
69. *Tartarean*, infernal.

Page 295.
73. *such*, those who think so.
74. *forgetful*, making forgetful.
75. *proper*, natural.
77. *who but felt*, who did not feel?
82. *event*, outcome.
83. *stronger*, superior in strength.
89. *exercise*, harass, torment. Latin usage.
97. *essential*, substance.
100. *at worst*, as badly off as we can be short of annihilation.
101. *proof*, experience.
104. *fatal*, established by fate.
106. *denounced*, betokened, threatened.
113. *manna*. See Exodus xvi, 31.
124. *fact*, deed.
127. *scope*, mark, aim, its original meaning in the Greek.
130. *watch*, watchmen; hence the plural verb.
132. *obscure*. Accent on first syllable.
133. *Scout*, act as scouts, reconnoiter.
139. *mold*, substance. Milton imagines the angels as made of fire (see Psalm civ, 4) and the argument is that the fiery substance of the angels would expel the *baser fire* of hell.
143. *flat*, absolute.
156. *Belike*, probably. Used ironically. *impotence*, lack of self-restraint. Latin use.
165. *amain*, with all speed.
175. *Her*, of hell.
176. *cataracts*, torrents, floods.

Page 296.
203. *fall*, befall, happen.
210. *supreme*. Accent on first syllable.
216. *inured*, accustomed to it.
224. *For happy*, in point of happiness.
231–2. *then . . . when*, i.e., never.
234. *former*, 'to disenthrone.' *argues*, proves.
235. *latter*, 'to regain.'
245. *Ambrosial*, divinely excellent.
249. *pursue*, seek to regain.
251. *unacceptable*. Accent on second syllable.
263–5. See Psalms xvii, 11, 13; xcvii, 2.
277. *needs*, of necessity.
278. *sensible*, sense; adj. for noun.
281. *Compose*, arrange, adjust.
288. *o'er-watched*, worn out with watching.

Page 297.
294. *Michael*, the leading archangel, whose discomfiture of Satan and his followers is described later: vi, 320–327.
301. *aspect*. Accent on second syllable.
303. *public care*, care for the common weal.
305. *Majestic* qualifies face.
306. *Atlantean*, worthy of Atlas, a Titan condemned by Zeus to bear the skies on his shoulders.
324. *first and last*. See Revelation i, 11.
330. *determined*, made an end of.
336. *to*, to the extent of.
337. *untamed reluctance*, invincible resistance.
341. *want*, be wanting.
346. *fame*, report. Latin *fama*.
367. *puny*, literally, later born; hence, weaker.
375. *original*, origin, or perhaps originator.

Page 297.
376. *Advise*, consider.
380. *By Satan*. See I, 650–654.
382. *confound*, utterly destroy.
387. *states*, authorities, or bodies of representatives, as in the phrase, 'the three estates of the realm,' meaning the King, Lords, and Commons in Great Britain.
391. *Synod*, assembly, meeting.

Page 298.
404. *tempt*, try.
406. *obscure*, obscurity. Adj. for noun.
407. *uncouth*, unknown.
409. *abrupt*, abyss, i.e., between hell and the world. *arrive*, reach.
410. *isle*, the World, hung like a globe in Chaos from the floor of Heaven.
413. *had need*, would have need of.
415. *Choice*, careful selection.
418. *suspense*, in suspense. Latin form.
423. *Astonished*, astounded.
425. *hardy*, bold, courageous.
429. *unmoved*. Contrasted with *Astonished*, l. 423.
431. *demur*, hesitation.
434. *convex*, circle.
441. *abortive*, monstrous.
443. *remains*, awaits.
452. *Refusing*, if I refuse.
457. *intend*, consider, devise.
461. *deceive*, beguile. Latin use. *slack*, mitigate.
462. *mansion*, abode.
467. *prevented*, forestalled.
468. *raised*, encouraged. Refers to *Others*.
470. *erst*, before.
471. *opinion*, reputation.
478. *awful*, full of awe.
485. *close*, concealed. *varnished o'er*, speciously covered with.
490. *louring element*, dark and threatening sky.
491. *Scowls*, covers the face of nature with a dark cloud of rain or snow.
492. *If chance*, if it chances that.
503. *accord*, agreement.

Page 299.
AREOPAGITICA

In November, 1644, when this pamphlet was published, the parliamentary cause was triumphant in the field, and high hopes were entertained for its future success in the promotion of 'real and substantial liberty—whose existence depends not so much on the terror of the sword as on sobriety of conduct and integrity of life.' But Parliament was already showing an inclination to adopt the intolerant and tyrannical measures which it had condemned in its adversaries, and it was against one of these—an order that books should not be printed without license—that Milton was here directing his efforts. His object was to secure the free publication of thought,—'that the power of determining what was true and what was false; what ought to be published and what to be suppressed, might no longer be entrusted to a few illiterate and illiberal individuals, who refused their sanction to any work which contained views or sentiments at all above the level of the vulgar superstition.' Beside Milton's general devotion to the cause of liberty, he had a special incentive in the attempt which was being made by the Stationers' Company to suppress his divorce pamphlets, which had aroused a good deal of hostile feeling.

a. 17. *Julius Agricola*, governor of Britain 78–85 A. D.
18. *Cæsar*, a general name for the Roman Emperor. *preferred . . . French*. This statement is made on the authority of Tacitus.
23. *Hercynian*, a name given by the Romans to the mountainous and wooded region in the south and center of Germany; the country beyond it.

Page 299.

    Transylvania, which became part of the Austrian Empire in 1689, had during the Commonwealth friendly relations with England.
28. *propending*, inclining.
30. *as out of Sion.* See Joel ii, 1.
35. *Wyclif*, the English ecclesiastical reformer of the fourteenth century.
37–38. *Huss, Jerome* (of Prague), *Luther, Calvin*, leaders of the Protestant Reformation on the Continent.
41. *demeaned*, conducted, managed.
43. *of whom*, of those of whom.

b. 3. *mansion house*, abiding place, manorial seat.
6. *plates*, armor, *instruments*, weapons.
13. *trying*, testing.
22. *white already.* See John iv, 35.
27. *fantastic*, fancied, imaginary.
33. *ill-deputed*, i.e., to the clergy.
47. *Pyrrhus*, after fighting against the Romans at Heraclea (280 B. C.) is said to have exclaimed: 'How easy it would be for me to conquer the world if I had Roman soldiers.'

Page 300.

a. 4. *schisms, dissections*, literally, cuttings.
19. *Moses.* See Numbers xii, 29.
26. *Joshua.* See Numbers xii, 28.
35. *maniple*, a company in the Roman army, consisting of about 60 men serving under the same ensign.
40. *vex*, worry.
44. *besieged.* Two years before the publication of Milton's pamphlet the Royalists had advanced almost to the gates of London. See Milton's first sonnet printed on p. 284.
48. *suburb trenches.* The suburbs were defended by trenches made by the loyal citizens, even women and children helping.
53. *to a rarity*, to an extraordinary extent or degree.
54. *argues*, proves.

b. 2. *derives itself to*, develops into.
6. *nigh*, closely. The incident here referred to is recounted by Livy xxvi, 11.
13. *to*, as to.
14. *pertest*, sprightliest.
17. *sprightly up*, lively and excited.
23. *old and wrinkled skin.* Like a snake.
29. *strong man.* Samson. See Judges xvi, 13, 14.
31. *mewing*, renewing; originally used of a hawk molting.
35. *noise*, noisy crew. *flocking*, not daring to act independently.
38. *prognosticate*, foretell, like the astrologers and almanac makers.
43. *engrossers*, merchants who dealt in large quantities, and often made a corner to raise prices. Milton compares to these the Licensers of Printing, who will set up a monopoly in knowledge.
55. *purchased*, obtained.

Page 301.

a. 3. *influence*, mystic power; the original reference is to astrology.
20. *law.* The Roman law gave fathers power of life and death over children. *despatch*, slay.
22. *stick closest*, be most faithful. See Proverbs xviii, 24.
23–24. *for coat . . . danegelt*, merely to resist illegal taxation, the former part of the phrase referring to the clothing and conveyance of troops, the latter to ship-money. Milton is arguing for a nobler freedom than that of not paying unjust taxes.
27. *utter*, publish.
30. *unequal*, unjust.
43. *vote*, solemn wish.
47. *last testament.* See John xiv, 27.
55. *dis-conformity*, dissent.

b. 10. *controversal*, opposite. The temple was open in war, closed in peace.

Page 301.

b. 18. *Her confuting*, confutation by her.
22. *the discipline of Geneva*, the form of faith and of church government accepted as perfect by the Presbyterians.
23. *fabricked*, fabricated, manufactured.
26. *casements*, windows. *collusion*, deception.
27. *wise man*, Solomon. See also Matthew xiii, 44.
33. *equipage*, equipment.
34. *battle*, army.
47. *shifts*, sleights, contrivance.
55. *Micaiah.* See 1 Kings xxii, 1–2.

Page 302.

a. 7. *nailed to the cross.* See Colossians ii, 14.
8. *purchase*, boon, achievement.
10. *His doctrine.* Romans xiv, 5–9.
16. *outward conformity*, under royal and episcopal government.
18. *linen decency*, the outward conformity of a white surplice is abolished, but the spirit remains.
24. *care not*, do not take care, *truth separated from truth*, i.e., essentials from non-essentials.
30. *wood, and hay, and stubble.* See 1 Corinthians iii, 12.
33. *subdichotomies*, sub-divisions.
37. *wheat from the tares.* See Matthew xiii, 24–43.
38. *fry*, small fish; properly, spawn.
47. *extirpate*, extirpated.

b. 1. *unity of Spirit.* Ephesians iv, 3.
7. *bejesuited*, made into Jesuits.
14. *unplausible*, unappreciated.
16. *see to*, look upon.
43. *Convocation House*, where the governing body of the Church of England met.
44. *Chapel.* The Puritan Assembly of Divines met in Henry VII's Chapel at Westminster in 1643, and drew up a Confession of Faith and two Catechisms.
46. *canonized*, embodied in canons or rules.
47. *convincement*, argument and conviction.
48. *supple*, cure.
49. *edify*, build up, establish.
53. *liege tombs.* Henry VII's Chapel contains several royal tombs beside his own.

Page 303.

a. 3. *that we do not give*, from giving. Latin construction.
11. *manage*, handle.
19–20. *Priests, Pharisees.* See Matthew v, 20.
21. *precipitant*, precipitate.
28. *the beginning of this Parliament.* Nov. 3, 1640.
31. *Imprimatur.* The Licenser's stamp or inscription 'Let it be printed.'
37. *Moses.* See Numbers xi, 28–29.
39. *young John.* See Luke ix, 50.
41. *Elders*, the leaders of the Presbyterians.
45. *let*, hindrance.
48. *Inquisition.* One of the duties of the Inquisition was the prohibition of heretical books. The Dominican Order was especially active in the campaign against heresy. Both the Inquisition and the Dominicans were especially unpopular as Roman Catholic institutions to the Puritan readers to whom Milton was appealing.

b. 3. *next before this.* The earlier order was passed on Jan. 20, 1642.
7. *fire . . . executioner.* Seditious books were burnt in public by the hangman.
10. *authentic*, genuine, so-called and really so.
14. *Star Chamber*, abolished by the Puritans in 1641 owing to its unjust exactions. It had charge, among other things, of licensing.
17. *Lucifer.* See Isaiah xiv, 12.
22. *bind*, by recognizances, as people enter into bonds for their good behavior in the English courts.
24. *precedent*, of Jan. 29, 1642.
27. *doubted*, suspected.

NOTES TO MILTON; DRYDEN: ABSALOM AND ACHITOPHEL

Page 303.

b. 28. *monopolizers.* The order of 1643 recognized the monopoly of the Stationers' Company, who applied the fees for licensing in part to the 'relief and maintenance of their poor.'
33. *divers glossing colors,* various specious misrepresentations.
35. *exercise a superiority,* exert authority, have an advantage. *neighbors,* fellow booksellers.
36–38. *therefore . . . that,* to the end that.
38. *vassals,* subjects.
41. *malignant,* seditious, royalist.
43. *sophisms and elenchs of merchandise,* trade sophistries and fallacies.
44. *skill not,* am not versed in or concerned about.
46. *incident,* inevitable.
50. *what hath been erred,* the mistakes that have been made. Latin construction. *in,* for those in.
51. *advertisement,* warning.

Page 304.

DRYDEN—ABSALOM AND ACHITOPHEL
PART I

This satirical poem, written, it is said, at the suggestion of Charles II, was directed against Shaftesbury, the minister whom Charles had dismissed, and who had retaliated by arousing public alarm in connection with the Popish Plot and by furthering the claims of the Duke of Monmouth, the king's illegitimate son, to the throne, in opposition to the lawful heir, Charles's brother, the Duke of York, who later succeeded as James II. In November, 1681, when the poem was published, Shaftesbury was a prisoner in the Tower on a charge of high treason, and Dryden's attack was no doubt meant to influence public feeling (and the jury) against him. In this respect it failed, for Shaftesbury was acquitted; but it made a great sensation and remains the most remarkable example of political satire in the English language. The scriptural allegory is not closely adhered to and serves as a transparent veil for personal vituperation.

2. *Absalon,* a variant of Absalom, introduced, apparently, merely for sake of the rime. Absalom represents the Duke of Monmouth, illegitimate son of Charles II.
15. *indulgent David,* King Charles II. Monmouth was his favorite son and Charles forgave him many indiscretions.
18. *Annabel,* Anne Scott, Countess of Buccleugh, Monmouth's wife.
23. *Ammon's murther.* Probably a reference to a savage attack upon Sir John Coventry by ruffians supposed to have been hired by Monmouth to perpetrate the outrage.
29. *The Jews,* the English people.

Page 305.

41. *Saul,* Oliver Cromwell.
42. *Ishbosheth,* Cromwell's son, Richard Cromwell.
69. *Jerusalem,* London.
70. *Jebusites,* Catholics.
82. *heathen,* Roman Catholic.
88. *Jewish rabbins,* leading clergy of the Church of England.
92. *Plot,* the Popish Plot, a Jesuit conspiracy, which if it ever existed, was greatly exaggerated for political purposes.
102. *Egyptian,* French.
103–105. This blasphemous sneer at the Roman Catholic doctrine of transubstantiation must have been regretted by Dryden after his conversion.
111. *court and stews.* The king was (justly) suspected of being a Roman Catholic; his mistresses were known to be; so was the Duke of York, his brother.
112. *Hebrew priests,* Church of England clergymen.
114. *God's anointed,* the king. One of the reports circulated about the Popish Plot was that the conspirators had planned the assassination of Charles II and the placing of his brother, who was a Roman Catholic, on the throne.

Page 305.

125. *threat,* threaten.
134. *Achitophel,* Anthony Ashley Cooper, Earl of Shaftesbury, formerly Lord Chancellor, at this time the leader of the party in favor of making the Duke of Monmouth the next heir to the throne and excluding the Duke of York as a Roman Catholic.
136. *close,* secret.
141. *pigmy body.* Shaftesbury was of small stature and his frame was enfeebled by disease.
146. *boast his wit,* show off his skill.

Page 306.

154. *unfeathered two-legged thing.* A humorous description of man ascribed to Plato. Shaftesbury's heir was a man of 'no ability and insignificant character.'
155. *huddled,* confused.
159. *the triple bond,* the Triple Alliance of England, Holland, and Sweden against France, made in 1668 and exceedingly popular in England. It was broken in 1670 without Shaftesbury's knowledge by Charles II, who made a secret treaty with the French king.
164–175. Added in the second edition, after Shaftesbury's acquittal.
172. *abbethdin,* president of the Jewish judicature. Shaftesbury was Lord Chancellor 1672–3.
179. *cockle,* weed.
181. *wanted,* lacked. Dryden's compliment to himself as David, the sweet singer of Israel, is shameless, but true. His poem has proved 'immortal.'
188. *manifest,* convicted. A Latinism.
193. *more he makes.* The charge that Shaftesbury invented the Plot is absurd; but he undoubtedly used it for political purposes by fomenting public agitation.
197. *Jebusite.* One of the stories current at the time was that the king himself had become a Roman Catholic. It is now known that it was true.
203. *instinct.* Accent on second syllable.
208. *title not allowed.* Monmouth's claim to the succession was barred by his illegitimacy.
211. *democracy,* then a form of government in disfavor. Dryden was so fond of this line that he repeated it in *The Hind and the Panther.*
234. *the Solymæan rout,* the London rabble.
238. *an Ethnic plot,* a plot of the Gentiles, that is, of the Catholics.
240. *hot Levites,* the Presbyterian clergy.

Page 307.

265. *Zimri* George Villiers, Duke of Buckingham. He had been a patron and part author of *The Rehearsal,* a burlesque drama in which Dryden's heroic plays were travestied and Dryden himself held up to ridicule. Dryden here takes revenge.

ABSALOM AND ACHITOPHEL
PART II

2. *a tun,* a great cask or vat for storing or brewing liquors.
6. *Og,* Thomas Shadwell (c. 1640–1692), a rival dramatist. Dryden here attacks his old enemy chiefly for his personal and political characteristics, having already ridiculed his literary pretentions in *Mac Flecknoe.*
15. *What 'twas of old to pamper up a Jew.* See Deuteronomy xxxii,15: 'But Jeshurun waxed fat,' etc.
38. *Doeg,* Elkanah Settle (1648–1724). Dryden had ridiculed Settle's *Empress of Morocco,* and Settle had retaliated by attacking his *Conquest of Granada.* Recently, Settle had renewed the unpleasantness with a dull parody of the first part of *Absalom and Achitophel.*
41. *for writing treason,* Shadwell was a violent Whig; cf. 'treason-tavern,' l. 3 above.
47. *the Lord's anointed,* the king.

ALEXANDER'S FEAST

This ode was written for a London musical society, which held an annual festival on Nov. 22, the day of

Page 307.

St. Cecilia, reputed the inventor of the organ and the patron saint of music.

1. *for Persia won*, for the winning of Persia.
2. *By Philip's warlike son*, Alexander, son of Philip of Macedon, and the conqueror of Persia.
9. *Thais*, a famous Athenian courtesan who accompanied Alexander into Asia, and, according to the tradition which Dryden makes use of in this poem, induced him to fire the palace of Persepolis.

Page 308.

17. *Timotheus*, Alexander's favorite musician.
22. *from*, with.
64. *Darius*, the Persian king whom Alexander had conquered.
83. *Lydian*, soft, sensuous.
113–4. *rear . . . hair*. Correctly rimed according to the pronunciation of the time.

Page 309.

139. *vocal frame*, organ.
147. The tradition was that Cecilia, owing to her virtue and piety, was visited by an angel.

ESSAY OF DRAMATIC POESY

a. 1. *that memorable day*, June 3, 1665.
10. *conduct*, leadership. *his royal highness*, the Duke of York, afterwards James II.
21–22. *Eugenius*, Sackville, Lord Buckhurst, who later became Earl of Dorset. *Crites*, Sir Robert Howard, Dryden's brother-in-law. *Lisideius*, Sir Charles Sedley. *Neander*, Dryden himself.
31. *the bridge*, London bridge.

Page 310.

b. 35. *Sir John Suckling*. See p. 224.
36. *Mr. Waller*. See p. 224.
37. *Sir John Denham*. See p. 226.
39. *Mr. Cowley*. See p. 228.

Page 311.

a. 27. *a genere et fine*, a definition of class and object.
42. *Thespis* (c. 540 B. C.), the somewhat fabulous inventor of Greek drama.
43. *Aristophanes* (448–c. 388 B. C.), the great Greek comic writer.
54. *virtuosi*, those skilled in the fine arts.
b. 12. *pretend*, lay claim.
45. *want*, lack.
55. *remember*, remind.

Page 312.

a. 27. *fable*, plot.
b. 42. *Corneille* (1606–84), the great French dramatist, contemporary with Dryden.

Page 313.

a. 15. *intended*, aimed at.
41. wanted, fell short.
b. 5. *Macrobius*, c. beginning of fifth century A. D.
11. *Tully*, Marcus Tullius Cicero (106–43 B. C.).

Page 314.

b. 16. *lively*, lifelike.

Page 315.

b. 15. *Scaliger* (Julius Cæsar Scaliger), 1484–1558.

Page 316.

a. 9. *inartificial*, inartistic.
43. *shadow*, palliate.
54. *sock and buskin*, the stage shoe of comedy and tragedy respectively.
b. 24. *the author*, Ben Jonson.
50. *clenches*, playing upon words.

Page 317.

a. 3. *Mr. Hales* (1584–1656), Greek Professor at Oxford and Fellow of Eton College.
17. *precedent*, predecessor, model.
21. *censure*, opinion.
41. *apt*, inclined.
b. 27. *taxed*, accused.
41. *comply with*, observe.

Page 318.

SAMUEL PEPYS—THE DIARY

THE LANDING OF CHARLES II

a. 5. *the two Dukes*, James, Duke of York, afterward King James II, and Henry, Duke of Gloucester, the king's youngest brother. The latter's death, from small-pox, is recorded by Pepys, September 13, 1660.
11. *my Lord*, Admiral Sir Edward Montagu, later Earl of Sandwich, was for many years Pepys' chief on the Admiralty Board. He is styled 'my Lord' throughout the *Diary*.

Page 319.

a. 12. *Sir W. Batten*, William Batten had been a naval commander in the parliamentary service, but deserted, with his ship, to the service of Prince Charles, afterwards Charles II. He was rewarded with a baronetcy and made Rear-Admiral by the Prince. After the Restoration he became a Commissioner of the Navy. His death October 5, 1667, is recorded by Pepys.
18. *a Crown and C. R.*, The king's initials, 'C. R,' for Carolus Rex, surmounted by a crown.
19. *the coach table*, the table in the Captain's cabin ('the coach'), located on the quarter-deck of the ship.

PLAYS AND PLAYERS

40. *Burt*, Nicholas Burt, one of the leading actors after the Restoration.
49. *to White-fryars*, The Salisbury Court Theater was in the section of the city known as Whitefriars.
50. *The Bondman*, a play by Philip Massinger.
52. *Betterton*, Thomas Betterton, the most eminent Restoration actor.
b. 10. *The Red Bull*, This old theater in St. John Street, Clerkenwell, had been reopened immediately after the Restoration.
19. *All's Lost by Lust*, a tragedy by William Rowley.
25. *the Cockpitt*, The Cockpit, in Drury Lane, was one of three theaters that were opened immediately after the Restoration.
30. *The Humersome Lieutenant:* 'The Humorous Lieutenant,' a tragi-comedy by Beaumont and Fletcher.
37. *The Joviall Crew*, a comedy by Richard Brome.
52. *The Cardinal*, a tragedy by James Shirley.

Page 320.

a. 11. *Nell*, the famous actress, Mrs. Nell Gwynne, a mistress of Charles II.
42. *The Silent Woman*, a comedy by Ben Jonson.
43. *Knipp*, Mrs. Knipp, a minor actress whose society Pepys cultivated. The *Diary* has frequent references to their meetings, which were not always enthusiastically approved by Mrs. Pepys.
46. *Moone*, Michael Mohun, a leading actor of the day.
53. *Pierce*, Mrs. Pierce, a friend and boon-companion of Mrs. Knipp, called by Pepys (Mar. 24, 1662) 'La Belle Pierce.'

ROYALTY ABROAD

b. 35. *a boy*, James, Duke of Cambridge.

Page 321.

THE GREAT FIRE

b. 21. *steeple*, of the church called St. Lawrence Poultney. See the Map at the beginning of this volume.
36. *Lord Mayor*, Sir Thomas Bludworth.

Page 325.

DEFOE—THE TRUE-BORN ENGLISHMAN

This poem was a reply to an attack on William III and the Dutch nation, entitled *The Foreigners*. It was so successful in turning popular opinion in the king's favor that he had Defoe sent for to express his obligations to the writer.

11-14. See Matthew xxviii, 19.

Page 326.

THE SHORTEST WAY WITH THE DISSENTERS

The succession of Queen Anne in 1702 disappointed Defoe and his nonconformist friends, while it correspondingly encouraged the Tory and High Church party. The latter pressed for severe measures against the dissenters, who had been tolerated under William III, and allowed to compromise by 'occasional conformity,' i.e., by going to church on official occasions and attending their own place of worship at other times. Defoe in his pamphlet endeavored to show the absurdity of the high church position by making extravagant claims on their behalf, although he took occasion to aim a blow now and then at the inconsistency of his own side. The result was that he offended both parties, although for a while the high church clergy were so deceived that according to Defoe, one of them wrote to him that next to the Holy Bible and Sacred Comments he held *The Shortest Way with the Dissenters* 'as the most valuable thing I can have. I look upon it as the only Method! and I pray God to put it into the heart of our most gracious Queen, to put what is there proposed in execution.'

a. 1. *Sir Roger L'Estrange* a prolific pamphleteer, the founder in 1665 of the *Gazette*, the first English newspaper which has continued to appear regularly ever since. It is the official organ of the British Government.
11. *some people*, the Nonconformists.
20. *fourteen years*, from the Revolution of 1688 to 1702.
22. *church*, the Church of England.
23. *sort*, set, lot.
27. *reproach of the wicked*. Writing in the character of a high church clergyman, Defoe imitates Scripture phraseology.
b. 16. *Act of Toleration* (1689), relieving the nonconformists from penalties for not attending the services of the Church of England.
21. *abjurations*. The clergy were required to take an oath of fidelity to William III and abjure their allegiance to James. Many refused and were deprived of their livings.
33-34. *a war*. William engaged, with varying success in a prolonged struggle against Louis XIV of France.

Page 327.

a. 4. *in France*. After the Revocation of the Edict of Nantes in 1685, the Huguenots were forced to conform or leave the country.
8-9. *one king . . . another . . . a third*, Charles I, James II, William III.
11. *the fourth*, Anne.
b. 5. *a sordid impostor*, Oliver Cromwell.
41-43. *Just such measure . . . again*. See Matthew vii, 2.

Page 328.

a. 2. *regicides*, the judges who condemned Charles I.
11. *Rye House Plot* (1682-3), a conspiracy to assassinate Charles II and his brother James.
15. *unusual favor*. James was in favor of toleration to both Puritan and Roman Catholic dissenters; but the Puritans, suspecting that his designs were really directed to Roman Catholic supremacy, joined in the movement against him.
35. *a king of their own*, William III.
44. *Scotland*. The Church of Scotland, with the consent of William III, abolished episcopacy, and has ever since been presbyterian in its form of government.

Page 328.

b. 38. *the right heir*. The high church Tories who had remained loyal to James II looked forward to putting his son on the throne at the death of Anne. The Elector of Hanover, who became George I, was not in the direct line of succession.
40. *ridiculous settlements*. The Act of Settlement, passed by Parliament in 1701, vested the succession in the House of Hanover.
53. *French king*. Louis XIV expelled 400,000 Huguenots.

Page 329.

a. 9. *some animals*, rats.
27. *the common enemy*, France.
b. 17. *Monmouth*, beheaded after the rebellion of 1685.
18. *Shaftesbury*, died in exile 1683. *Argyle*, head of a Scottish rising against James; executed 1685.
26. *experimentally*, as a result of experience.
50. *impossible* (if the dissenters are tolerated).

Page 330.

a. 12-13. *What will . . . spoken for?* See Song of Solomon viii, 8.
16. *enthusiasm* was associated with dissenters, and generally regarded with disfavor in the eighteenth century.
36. *sensitive*, of the senses, physical. *these*, the dissenters.
b. 13-14. *Amalekite race*. The enemies of Israel in Canaan. See 1 Samuel xv.
29-32. *Moses . . . Israelites*. See Exodus xxxii, 28. The number given there is, however, three thousand.
43. *gallows instead of the counter*, hanging instead of imprisonment. *counter*, a city prison. *galleys*, enslavement to the oar in a galley.
45. *conventicle*, a gathering of dissenters for worship.
48. *sheriffs and mayors*. It was the custom of dissenters to go to church on their appointment to official positions, in accordance with the law.

Page 331.

a. 18. *hang men for trifles*. Hanging was the punishment for stealing in England up to 1823.

Page 332.

a. 24. *humor*, spirit, influence.
b. 21. *religious houses*, convents, which were at this time illegal.
22. *meeting houses*, for nonconformist worship.

PREFACE TO THE REVIEW

The *Review*, begun on Feb. 19, 1704, and published first once, then twice a week, for nine years gave Defoe scope for his talents as a journalist. The original title was *A Review of the Affairs of France and of all Europe, as influenced by that Nation*, France being at that time the center of European politics. Defoe discussed not only politics but trade and current gossip; he invented not only editorial comment, which was before unknown, but personal interviews, scandalous personalities, answers to correspondents, and many other features of the modern newspaper. The numbers of the *Review* were issued afterwards in annual volumes, and in this preface to Vol. I, Defoe sets forth his motives and aims in the undertaking.

Page 333.

a. 5. *the Wise Man*, Solomon.
10. *first design*. See the original title, as given above.
31. *Marlborough*, the great English general who defeated the French at Blenheim, Aug. 13, 1704. The war continued for several years.
b. 34. *negoce*, commerce.

Page 334.

a. 6. *its birth*. The design of the *Review* was conceived by Defoe in prison.

Page 335.
a. 8. *D. F.* Daniel Foe. The name Defoe was adopted by the author a year later.

THE EDUCATION OF WOMEN

The *Essay upon Projects*, from which this paper is taken, was written in 1692, but first printed in 1697.
a. 23. *conversible*, fit for human intercourse.
b. 10. *wit*, intellectual ability.
   22. *more tongues than one.* Milton is reported to have said that one tongue was enough for any woman.
   31. *genius*, natural ability.

Page 336.
b. 9. *female government*, government by women.

Page 337.

SWIFT — A TALE OF A TUB

'Seamen have a custom, when they meet a whale, to fling him out an empty tub by way of amusement, to divert him from laying violent hands upon the ship . . . the whale was interpreted to be Hobbes's *Leviathan* . . . whence the wits of our age are said to borrow their weapons . . . and it was decreed, that, in order to prevent these Leviathans from tossing and sporting with the Commonwealth . . . they should be diverted from that game by a Tale of a Tub.' (Swift's Preface.)

Page 338.
a. 21. *d'Argent*, of wealth. *de Grands Titres*, of distinguished titles.
   22. *Orgueil*, of pride.
   36. *Locket's*, a famous ordinary, or tavern, at Charing Cross. *Will's* coffee-house.
b. 9. *grande monde*, world of fashion.
   20. *Jupiter Capitolinus.* From his temple on the Capitoline Hill, Rome.
   42–43. *They held the universe to be a large suit of clothes, etc.* Compare Carlyle's *Sartor Resartus*.
   46. *primum mobile.* In the Ptolemaic cosmogony, the outer or tenth revolving sphere.

Page 339.
a. 47. *ex traduce.* From the root: from the original stock.
b. 50. *shoulder-knots.* This fashion had been introduced from France in the reign of Charles II. See *Tatler*, No. 82.

Page 340.
a. 1. *ruelles*, bedsides.
b. 40. *nuncupatory and scriptory*, verbal and written.

Page 341.
b. 10. *my lord C— and Sir J. W.* have not been identified.

Page 342.
b. 19. *fonde*, fund, stock, capital.

Page 344.
a. 7–11. *Varias inducere . . . piscem.* Horace, *Ars Poetica*, 2 and 4.

Page 347.

A MEDITATION UPON A BROOMSTICK

a. 3. *Hon. Robert Boyle* (1627–1691). A celebrated scientist, 'The father of chemistry and brother to the Earl of Cork.' One of the original members of the Royal Society. Swift's essay travesties the platitudinous moralizing of his religious meditations.

A MODEST PROPOSAL

Page 349.
a. 53. *the famous Psalmanazar.* George Psalmanazar, a notorious impostor, pretended to be a native of Formosa, of which he published a *Description* in 1705

Page 349.

STEELE — THE TATLER

Page 352.
a. 14. *White's Chocolate-house.* In St. James's Street. Famous for gambling.
   15. *Will's Coffee-house.* No. 1, Bow Street, Covent Garden. Originally kept by William Urwin. Pepy's *Diary* mentions it, Feb. 3, 1663, as a resort of Dryden and notable for 'very witty and pleasant discourse.'
   16. *Grecian.* Coffee-house in the Strand, originally kept by a Greek named Constantine, had been a resort of Newton, other members of the Royal Society, and Templars.
   18. *Saint James's Coffee-house.* Near St. James's Palace. A resort of Whig statesmen, military men, and men of fashion.
   25. *plain Spanish.* A simple wine.
   28. *kidney*, temper, humor. A pun on the name of one of the waiters.
   37. *casting a figure.* Determining the horoscope.

Page 353.

THE SPECTATOR

a. 11. *Lord Rochester.* John Wilmot, Earl of Rochester (1647–80), a fashionable rake and poet of the Restoration period. Sir George Etherege (1639–94). The Restoration dramatist. Like Rochester, a courtly rake.
   13. *Bully Dawson.* d. 1699. A notorious swaggerer and gamester.
   40. *Inner Temple.* One of the Inns of Court.
   47. *Aristotle*, etc. The reference is to his *Poetics*. *Longinus*. Greek Philosopher, third century A. D., to whom the essay, *On Sublimity*, is doubtfully ascribed.
   48. *Littleton or Coke.* Sir Thomas Littleton (1402–1481) and Sir Edward Coke (1552–1634) were members of the Inner Temple (above, a. 40). A work of the first with commentary by the second used to be the English authority on the law of real property.
b. 2. *Demosthenes*, the greatest Greek orator (384–322 B. C.). *Tully*, Marcus Tullius Cicero (106–43 B. C.), Roman orator and philosopher.
   21. *The Rose.* A tavern adjoining Drury Lane Theater.
   26. *the city of London.* The central or business district is so called.

Page 354.
a. 18. *Duke of Monmouth.* The Absolom of Dryden's *Absalom and Achitophel*. See above, p. 304.

Page 355.
b. 35. *Sir Richard Blackmore* (c. 1650–1729). Physician to William III, and a poet of repute in his day.

Page 358.
a. 41. *Martial* (Bk. I, 69), Latin poet, first century A. D.

Page 359.
a. 6. *Strand Bridge.* A landing pier at the foot of Strand Lane, giving access to the Strand.
   25. *The Vainloves.* Vainlove is 'a capricious lover' in Congreve's comedy, *The Old Bachelor*.

Page 360.
a. 36. *Robin's.* A coffee-house in Exchange Alley, frequented by brokers.
b. 7. *the city.* See above, note to p. 353. b. 26.

Page 361.

ADDISON — THE SPECTATOR

Page 362.
b. 2. *Child's.* Coffee-house in St. Paul's Churchyard.
   9. *the Cocoa-tree.* A chocolate-house frequented by Tories as St. James's by Whigs. The *Spectator* pretends to patronize both.

Page 362.
b. 10–11. *Drury Lane and the Haymarket.* The two principal theaters of London. The Theater Royal in Drury Lane, designed by Sir Christopher Wren, had been opened in 1674. The Haymarket Opera House, designed and built by Sir John Van Brugh, had been opened in 1705.
14. *Jonathan's* Coffee-house in Cornhill. 'The general mart for stock-jobbers.' (*Tatler*, No. 38.)

Page 363.
a. 35. *Mr. Buckley's.* Buckley was the publisher. *Little Britain.* A street in London.

Page 366.
b. 13. *Moll White.* The witch described in *Spectator*, No. 117.

Page 367.
a. 49. *The Committee* (1665). Comedy by Sir Robert Howard.
53. *Distressed Mother.* Adaptation, by Ambrose Philips, of Racine's *Andromaque.* Produced 1712.
b. 5. *The Mohocks.* Some ruffianly carousers of the upper classes assumed this name. They committed a series of outrages in 1712.
41. *plants,* sticks, staves.

Page 370.
b. 39. *Mr. Cowley,* etc. See Cowley's *Davideis* iii, 403–4.

Page 372.
a. 2. *Gallus,* Caius Cornelius (c. 69–26 B. C.). Roman poet and general. *Propertius,* Sextus (c. 50–16 B. C.), poet. *Horace,* Quintus Horatius Flaccus (65–8 B. C.), the Roman poet.
3. *Varius.* Lucius Varius Rufus, 1st century B. C. *Tucca.* Plotius Tucca and Lucius Varius were Virgil's literary executors. *Ovid,* Publius Ovidius Naso (43 B. C.–c. 17 A. D.).
3–4. *Bavius and Mævius.* Inferior Roman poets mentioned by Virgil (*Ecl.* iii) and Horace (*Epode* x).
14. *Sir John Denham.* See p. 226.
25. *The Art of Criticism.* Pope's *Essay on Criticism.* See p. 375.
42. *Boileau* (1636–1711). French critic and poet.
b. 13. *Petronius Arbiter,* Roman satirical author. Died c. 66 A. D., *Quintilian,* Marcus Fabius Quintilianus (c. 35–c. 95 A. D.), Roman rhetorician. *Longinus.* See note to p. 353, a. 47.

Page 373.
a. 9. *Essay on Translated Verse.* By Wentworth Dillon, Earl of Roscommon (1634–85).
10. *Essay on the Art of Poetry.* By John Sheffield, Duke of Buckinghamshire (1649–1721).
49. *The path of an arrow.* Wisdom of Solomon v, 12–13. The quotation is inaccurate.
b. 45. *Sir Cloudesley Shovel.* Commander of the British fleets from 1705. Drowned 1707.

Page 375.
POPE — AN ESSAY ON CRITICISM

Page 376.
34. *Mævius.* See Addison's comment, p. 372.
129–30. *the Mantuan Muse . . . young Maro.* Virgil.

Page 377.
138. *the Stagirite,* Aristotle.
180. *Homer nods.* Allusion to Horace, *Ars Poetica,* 359.
216. *the Pierian Spring.* Pieria in Thessaly was the reputed birthplace of the Muses.

Page 378.
248. *E'en thine, O Rome.* St. Peter's.
267. *La Mancha's Knight.* Don Quixote.
270. *Dennis . . . stage.* John Dennis, the critic and playwright, made sententious references to the dramatic precepts of Aristotle. This allusion and another, lines 585–591, initiated Pope's quarrel with him.

Page 378.
328. *Fungoso.* A character in Ben Jonson's *Every Man Out of His Humour,* who tries, without success, to keep up with court fashions.

Page 379.
356. *Alexandrine.* The succeeding line is an example.
361. *Denham.* See p. 226. *Waller.* See p. 224.
372. *Camilla.* In Virgil's *Æneid* vii, 808–11.
374–383. Compare Dryden's *Alexander's Feast,* p. 307.
376. *Son of Libyan Jove.* Alexander the Great.
391. *Approve,* test, put to the proof.

Page 380.
441. *Sentences.* The *Sententiæ* of Peter Lombard, 12th century.
444. *Scotists and Thomists.* Followers of the thirteenth century schoolmen, Duns Scotus and Thomas Aquinas.
463. *Blackmores.* Blackmore attacked Dryden in 'A Satire on Wit.'
463. *Milbourns,* Luke Milbourn, a clergyman, attacked Dryden's translation of Virgil.
465. *Zoilus.* Greek critic of the 4th century B. C., said to have been put to death for criticizing Homer.
483. *Such as Chaucer is.* Pope and his generation regarded Chaucer as obsolete.
527. *Spleen,* anger, ill-temper.
536. *love was all an easy Monarch's care.* The reign of Charles II is referred to.
544. *a foreign reign.* That of William III.
545. *Socinus.* Italian Unitarian of the sixteenth century.

Page 381.

THE RAPE OF THE LOCK

CANTO I

3. *Caryl.* John Caryl, a friend and correspondent of Pope.
4. *Belinda.* Miss Arabella Fermor, a belle of the period, from whom the lock celebrated in the poem was stolen.
8. *a well-bred lord.* Lord Petre, who had stolen the curl.
17. *the slipper knocked the ground.* Rapping for the servant.
56. *ombre,* a game at cards. See Canto III, lines 27 ff.
73. *Spark.* A beau, a lady-killer.

Page 382.

CANTO II

25. *springes.* Snares. Cf. *Hamlet,* I. iii, 115.

Page 383.
113. *drops,* earrings.
133. *Ixion.* For an offense to Zeus, fastened to an eternally revolving wheel in Hades.

Page 384.

CANTO III

3. *a structure of majestic frame,* Hampton Court, one of the royal residences. See Map.
27. *ombre.* A game of cards, of Spanish origin, usually played by three persons.
47. *Matadores.* The three highest cards at ombre.
49. *Spadillio.* Ace of Spades.
51. *Manillio.* The two of a black, the seven of a red, trump.
53. *Basto.* Ace of clubs.
61. *Pam.* Knave of clubs, the highest card in the game of loo.
92. *codille.* Failure to get the requisite tricks.

Page 385.
122–24. *Scylla's fate . . . Nisus' injured hair.* Pope's note refers to Ovid, *Metam.* viii.
151. *cut the sylph in twain.* Compare *Par. Lost* vi, 330.
165. *Atalantis.* A book of contemporary scandal by Mrs. Manley, *The New Atalantis* (1709).

CANTO IV

16. *Spleen,* anger, ill-temper.

Page 386.

24. *Megrim*. Tired feeling, the blues.
89. *Thalestris*. One Mrs. Morley.
118. *the sound of Bow*. St. Mary Le Bow, in Cheapside, the heart of the city, was famous for its peal of bells.
121. *Sir Plume*, Sir George Brown. He threatened Pope with violence for this delightfully malicious caricature.

Page 387.

156. *bohea*. A kind of tea, from the Chinese province whence it was first imported in 1666.

CANTO V

5. *The Trojan*. Æneas. See *Æneid* iv, 296 ff.

Page 388.

62. *Dapperwit*. 'A brisk, conceited, half-witted fellow of the town' bears this name in Wycherley's *Love in a Wood*.
63. *Sir Fopling*. Suggested, perhaps, by Sir Fopling Flutter in Etherege's *The Man of Mode*.
65. *Meander*, a river of Asia Minor frequently mentioned in classical poetry. Celebrated for its windings.
125. *Rome's great founder*, Romulus.
126. *Proculus*. The legend is given in Livy I, 6.
136. *Rosamonda's lake*. A pond in St. James's Park.
137. *Partridge*, an astrologer and almanac maker ridiculed by Swift in his Bickerstaff papers.
138. *Galileo's eyes*, the telescope.
140. *Louis*, Louis XIV, King of France. *Rome*, the Papacy.

EPISTLE TO DR. ARBUTHNOT

'This paper is a sort of bill of complaint, begun many years since, and drawn up by snatches, as the several occasions offered.' Dr. John Arbuthnot was a very learned Scotch physician, residing in London, and through his numerous satirical and political writings, associated with most of the literary wits of his time.

1. *good John*, John Searle, Pope's old household servant.

Page 389.

3. *Dog-star*, Sirius, the most brilliant of the stars.
4. *Bedlam*, corrupted form of *Bethlehem*, a London hospital for the insane. *Parnassus*, a mountain in Greece, regarded in ancient mythology as sacred to Apollo and the Muses.
12. *Sabbath day*, day of rest.
13. *Mint*, a place in Southwark to which insolvent debtors retired to escape their creditors.
21. *Twit'nam*, Pope's villa at Twickenham. See Map, 'Environs of London.'
23. *Arthur*, Arthur Moore, a politician.
25. *Cornus*, Sir Robert Walpole (1676-1745), prime minister.
40. *'Keep your piece nine years.'* See Horace, *Ars Poetica*, l. 388.
41. *Drury Lane*, a street near the Strand. Not far away was Drury Lane Theater.
43. *term*, the London social 'season.'
49. *Pitholeon*, a foolish poet of Rhodes in ancient times.
53. *Curll*, Edmund Curll, a piratical bookseller.
62. *Lintot*, Bernard Lintot, publisher of many of Pope's works.
69. *Midas*, a king who had ass's ears given him, for preferring Pan's music to Apollo's.
85. *Codrus*, an inferior poet referred to by Juvenal.
96. *Parnassian*, Parnassus was a mountain in central Greece celebrated as the haunt of Apollo and the Muses.

Page 390.

99. *Grub Street*, formerly noted as the abode of 'small authors.'
105. *Ammon's great son*, Alexander the Great.
110. *Maro*, the poet Virgil.
123. *Granville*. George Granville, Lord Lansdowne (1667-1735), who suggested Pope's publishing *Windsor Forest* in 1713.
124. *Walsh*, William Walsh (1663-1709), a friend of Dryden and Pope.
125. *Garth*, Samuel Garth (1661-1719), physician and poet.
127. *Talbot, Somers, Sheffield*, noblemen and politicians who had encouraged Pope in his early literary work.
128. *mitred Rochester*, Francis Atterbury, Bishop of Rochester.
129. *St. John*, Henry St. John, Viscount Bolingbroke (1678-1751), orator and politician.
134. *Burnet, Oldmixon, Cooke*, writers, as Pope alleged, of disreputable historical works.
137. *gentle Fanny*, Lord Hervey (1696-1743).
139. *Gildon*, Charles Gildon, an abusive pamphleteer.
141. *Dennis*, John Dennis (1657-1734), an English critic.
152. *Bentley*, Richard Bentley (1662-1742), a famous classical scholar and critic, who produced a murderous edition of Milton. *Tibbald*, Lewis Theobald (1688-1744), a notable Shakespearean editor, and a hero of Pope's *Dunciad*.
168. *a Persian tale*. Ambrose Philips (1671-1749) wrote *Pastorals*, and translated a book called *Persian Tales*.
178. *Tate*, Nahum Tate (1652-1715), poet, playwright, and, at one time, poet laureate.
181. *were there one*, the characterization of Addison (Atticus) which begins here is particularly famous.
202. *Atticus*, a Roman scholar and bookseller of the first century before Christ, here means Addison.

Page 391.

210. *great George*, George II, king of England (1727-1760).
218. *Bufo*, probably Charles Montagu, Earl of Halifax (1661-1715), statesman, financier, and poet. *Castalian state*, kingdom of poetry. Castalia was a spring on the slope of Mt. Parnassus.
238. *Bavius*, an inferior ancient Latin poet.
244. *Gay*, John Gay (1685-1732), a poet.
248. *Queensbury*. Gay died in the house of the Duke and Duchess of Queensbury. They gave him a monument in Westminster Abbey.
264. *Balbus*, the Earl of Kinnoul.
268. *Sir Will*, Sir William Yonge. *Bubo*, George Bubb Dodington (1691-1762), a politician and patron of letters.
287. *Dean and silver bell*. This refers to the unknown person 'who would have persuaded the Duke of Chandos that Mr. Pope meant him in those circumstances ridiculed in the epistle on "Taste."'
288. *Canons*, the house of the Duke of Chandos.
293. *Sporus*, Lord Hervey. Sporus was an effeminate hero of Nero.

Page 392.

351. *Japhet in a jail*. Japhet Crook was imprisoned for forgery.
357. *Sappho*, Lady Mary Wortley Montagu (1689-1762), a brilliant woman of letters.
361. *Cibber*, Colley Cibber (1671-1757), actor, playwright, and minor poet. He superseded Theobald as hero of Pope's *Dunciad*. *Moore*, James Moore-Smythe, a versifier and playwright.
363. *Welsted*, Leonard Welsted, a Whig pamphleteer.
366. *Budgell*, Eustace Budgell (1686-1737), a miscellaneous writer, was notorious through being charged with forging a will.
375. *Bestia*, probably the Duke of Marlborough. Bestia, a Roman proconsul, accepted bribes from Jugurtha for a dishonorable peace.

Page 395.

JAMES THOMSON — SUMMER

50. *Stygian*, dark. From Styx, one of the rivers of Hades.

THE CASTLE OF INDOLENCE

Page 397.

32. *Philomel*, the nightingale.
75. *the rural poets*, those who treated pastoral subjects.

Page 397.

76. *Arcadian.* See *Life of Sidney,* p. 144. *Sicilian,* Sicily was the home of a group of pastoral poets of whom the chief was Theocritus.
98. *Lorraine,* Claude Lorrain (1600–82), French landscape painter.
99. *Rosa,* Salvator (c 1615–1673). Neapolitan painter noted for his battle pieces. *Poussin,* doubtless Nicholas Poussin (1594–1665), French landscape and historical painter.

Page 398.

131. *mell,* mingle, mix.
136. *Morpheus,* god of sleep.
138. *Elysian,* associated with Elysium, and hence blessed or delightful.
141. *Titian,* famous Italian painter (1477–1576).

Page 399.

THOMAS GRAY
ON THE DEATH OF MR. RICHARD WEST

Richard West, son of the Lord Chancellor of Ireland, had been Gray's most intimate friend at Eton, and his constant correspondent while they were at Oxford and Cambridge respectively. See also the sketch of Gray, p. 399.

AN ODE ON A ... PROSPECT OF ETON COLLEGE

4. *Her Henry's holy Shade.* Eton College was founded by King Henry VI in 1440.
6. *Windsor's heights.* Windsor Castle, overlooking Eton, is one of the royal residences.

Page 401.

HYMN TO ADVERSITY

35. *Gorgon,* the terror-inspiring image on the shield of Pallas Athene, goddess of wisdom.

ELEGY WRITTEN IN A COUNTRY CHURCH-YARD

57. *Hampden* (John 1594–1643). One of the chief heroes of the Puritan revolt. Resisted the collection of shipmoney, 1637–38.

Page 402.

THE PROGRESS OF POESY

1. *Æolian lyre.* The lyre of Pindar who belonged to the Æolian division of the Greek race. See, also, p. 163, *A Pindaric Ode,* note.
3. *Helicon,* a mountain in central Greece, celebrated as the seat of Apollo and the Muses.
9. *Ceres' golden reign,* fields ruled by Ceres, goddess of grain and harvest.
17. *On Thracia's hills.* Thrace was thought to be a favorite haunt of Mars.
21. *the feathered king,* Jove's eagle, symbolical of the thunderbolt.

Page 403.

27. *Idalia,* an ancient town in Cyprus consecrated to Venus.
29. *Cytherea's day,* the day for the worship of Venus.
53. *Hyperion's march,* the sunrise.
66. *Delphi's steep,* the seat of the Greek oracle.
68. *Ilissus,* a small stream flowing through Athens.
69. *Mæander,* the river Mæander in Asia Minor.
83–94. Shakespeare.
95–102. Milton.
112. *what daring spirit,* Gray himself.
115. *the Theban Eagle.* 'Pindar compares himself to that bird, and his enemies to ravens that croak and clamor in vain below, while it pursues its flight, regardless of their noise.' (Gray.)

Page 404.

THE BARD

'The following ode is founded on a tradition current in Wales, that Edward the First, when he completed the conquest of that country, ordered all the bards that fell into his hands to be put to death.' (Gray.) 'The massacre of the bards is a mere fable.' (J. R. Green.)

Page 404.

5. *Hauberk's twisted mail,* a close-fitting shirt of steel ringlets.
8. *Cambria,* Wales.
11. *Snowdon,* the highest mountain in England or Wales. The name applies also to the mountainous tract of which this peak is a part. See Map.
13. *Gloster.* 'Gilbert de Clare, surnamed the Red, Earl of Gloucester and Hertford, son-in-law to King Edward.' (Gray.)
14. *Mortimer.* 'Edmond de Mortimer, Lord of Wigmore. A Lord Marcher.' (Gray.)
28. *high-born Hoel.* Son of Prince Owain Gwynedd of north Wales. A warrior and poet. *Llewellyn,* possibly Llewellyn ap Jorwerth, the Welsh leader, is meant.
29. *Cadwallo,* a common Welsh bardic name.
31. *Urien,* a Welsh warrior and bard of the sixth century.
33. *Modred.* No bard of this name is known.
34. *Plinlimmon,* a mountain on the border of Cardigan and Montgomery, in Wales. See Map.
35. *Arvon's shore,* the shores of Carnarvonshire opposite Anglesey. (Gray.) See Map.
54–56. *When Severn ... an agonizing King.* Edward II was murdered in Berkeley castle in September, 1327.
57. *She-Wolf of France,* Isabel of France, Edward the Second's adulterous queen.
59–66. King Edward III.
67. *the sable Warrior,* The Black Prince.
71–82. Reign of Richard II.

Page 405.

85. *Long years of havoc,* Wars of the Roses.
87. *Towers of Julius,* the Tower of London, according to tradition, built by Julius Cæsar. See Shakespeare's *Richard III,* iii, i. There is no authority to confirm the tradition. (Wheatley and Cunningham: *London Past and Present.*)
89. *his Consort's faith,* Margaret of Anjou. *His Father's fame,* the military glory of Henry V.
90. *the meek Usurper's holy head.* Henry VI was noted for his piety.
93. *The bristled Boar,* the insignia of Richard III. *infant gore,* i.e., of the murdered princes.
110. *ye genuine Kings.* The Tudor line, beginning with Henry VII.
111–124. *The reign of Queen Elizabeth.*
121. *Taliessin,* Cymric bard of the sixth century.
125–27. Spenser.
128–30. Shakespeare.
131–34. Milton and succeeding poets.

THE FATAL SISTERS

Written in 1761. The text of the poem from which Gray derived these stanzas may be found, with a prose translation, in *Corpus Poeticum Boreale,* Vol. I, pp. 281–83. It is an Icelandic poem of the eleventh century celebrating an invasion of Ireland by a Norse hero, Sictrygg, who was assisted by Sigurd, Earl of the Orkneys. Sigurd and Brian, the Irish king, fall in the battle. The Valkries are imagined weaving the web of battle. The title of the original is *Darradar-Liod* [*Lay of the Darts*].

8. *Orkney's woe.* The woe of Sigurd, Earl of Orkney. *Randver's bane,* Direct from the original. Randver's destruction.
17–31. *Mista ... Sangrida ... Hilda ... Gondula ... Geira.* The names of the Valkyries in the original are Hilda, Hiorthrimol, Sangrida, and Swipol.

Page 406.

44. *Soon a King,* etc. Brian, King of Dublin.
45. *Eirin,* Ireland.
62. *falchion,* a short sword, bellied near the tip.

LETTER TO RICHARD WEST

a. 3. *I do not take degrees.* Gray, at this time, apparently rebelled against the curriculum and intended to

Page 406.

quit Cambridge, but afterward changed his mind, or was over-ruled.

a. 30. *The wild beasts . . . a place of rest.* This is a medley and parody of passages in *Isaiah* and *Jeremiah*, with a hint of Job xxx, 29, 'I am a brother to dragons, and a companion to owls.'

LETTER TO MRS. DOROTHY GRAY

This letter is noteworthy for the evidence it contains of Gray's early sensitiveness to what we should now call 'romantic' wild scenery.

Page 407.

a. 38. *St. Bruno.* St. Bruno founded 'the aforesaid convent' about 1086.

LETTER TO THOMAS WHARTON

Dr. Thomas Wharton was one of Gray's oldest and best friends. This letter describes, somewhat sardonically, Gray's first meeting with Horace Walpole after a quarrel which had taken place during their travels on the Continent, some three years earlier.

b. 24. *to see the party (as Mrs. Foible says).* An allusion to Congreve's *The Way of the World*, Act III, scene 1, where Foible says to Lady Wishfort, 'Madam, I have seen the party.'

35. *Ashton.* Thomas Ashton (d. 1775) had been intimate with Gray, Walpole, and Richard West, at Eton.

Page 408.

LETTER TO HORACE WALPOLE

a. 14. *having put an end to a thing.* Gray had finished the *Elegy in a Country Church-yard*, and evidently sent it to Walpole with this letter.

30. *against Middleton.* Conyers Middleton (1683–1750) published, in 1748, *A Free Inquiry into the Miraculous Powers which are supposed to have Existed in the Christian Church*, attacking the Deists from a theological position very close to their own.

LETTER TO WILLIAM MASON

With William Mason (1735–1797), Gray corresponded copiously on literary subjects. This letter is mainly concerned with the poet-laureateship, which Gray had been offered and had refused.

b. 48. *Rowe*, Nicholas Rowe (1673–1718), dramatist, and editor of Shakespeare.

50. *Settle*, Elkanah Settle (1646–1724), a dramatist and poetaster ridiculed by Dryden and Pope.

51. *Eusden*, Lawrence Eusden (d. 1730).

Page 409.

LETTER TO THOMAS WHARTON

Dr. Wharton had been prevented from joining Gray on his excursion into the Highlands. Gray therefore wrote a very full account of his travels.

a. 18. *dismal heath . . . witches.* This letter was written from Glamis Castle, and Shakespeare's *Macbeth* naturally suggested itself to Gray's mind.

Page 410.

a. 42. *Vestibulum ante ipsum primisque in faucibus Orci.* Before the vestibule itself and in the first jaws of Hell (Virgil's *Æneid*, VI, 272).

47. *Fingal and all his family*, an allusion to Macpherson's *Ossian*, by which Gray had been greatly impressed and interested.

b. 4. *since I saw the Alps.* Compare Gray's letter to his mother, pp. 406–7 above.

LETTER TO NORTON NICHOLLS

One of the deepest attachments of Gray's entire life was his friendship for young Norton Nicholls, whom he first met in 1760, when Nicholls was an undergraduate at Cambridge. The depth of their intimacy is indicated by

Page 410.

Gray's unguarded revelation of his personal feelings in this letter about their respective mothers.

b. 40. *Mr. Palgrave.* The Reverend William Palgrave was a member of Pembroke College, and intimately associated with Gray.

Page 411.

COLLINS — DIRGE IN CYMBELINE

See Shakespeare's *Cymbeline*, Act IV, scene 2.

Page 412.

ODE TO SIMPLICITY

14. *Hybla's thymy shore.* Mount Hybla in Sicily is celebrated in classical poetry for the sweetness of its honey.

16–18. *By her . . . Electra's poet's ear.* 'The nightingale for which Sophocles seems to have entertained a peculiar fondness.' (Collins.)

19. *Cephisus.* A river of Attica.

35. *One distinguished throne.* Augustus Cæsar.

52. *reed.* The symbol of pastoral poetry.

THE PASSIONS

Page 413.

75. *chaste-ey'd queen*, Diana.

86. *Tempe*, a valley adjacent to Olympus in Thessaly.

104. *Devote*, devoted.

Page 414.

114. *Cecilia's mingled world of sound.* See Dryden's poem, *Alexander's Feast*, line 138, p. 309 above.

ODE ON THE DEATH OF MR. THOMSON

6. *His airy harp.* 'The harp of Æolus, of which see a description in the *Castle of Indolence*.' (Collins.)

19. *yon whitening spire.* Richmond church, [in which Thomson was buried]. (Collins.) See Map.

Page 415.

THOMAS CHATTERTON
AN EXCELLENT BALLAD OF CHARITY

This poem was sent by Chatterton to the *Town and Country Magazine*, July 4, 1770, with the following letter: 'If the Glossary annexed to the following piece will make the language intelligible; the Sentiment, Description, and Versification, are highly deserving the attention of the literati.' The letter was signed with the initials 'D. B.' which Chatterton frequently used as his pseudonym. The present text is largely modernized.

1. *Virgine*, the zodiacal sign of Virgo. *sheene*, shine.

5. *chelandry*, goldfinch.

7. *eke*, also. *dight*, clothed. *deft aumere*, neat robe.

15. *holm*, oak tree.

18. *weed*, clothing.

21. *housen*, house.

22. *gloomèd*, dejected. *sprite*, spirit.

24. *church-glebe-house*, grave.

31. *ghastness*, ghostliness, terror.

34. *levin*, lightning.

35. *flame-lowe*, flame.

38. *dispended*, lost.

40. *swangs*, swings.

45. *chapournette*, small round hat.

46. *mickle*, much, great.

47. *bederoll*, beads, rosary.

50. *cope*, outer cloak.

52. *autremete*, a loose white robe.

Page 416.

63. *crouch*, cross, crucifix.

64. *varlet*, low-born person.

70. *eftsoons*, immediately.

74. *jape*, short surplice.

75. *Limitour*, a licensed begging friar.

89. *aborde*, went on.

90. *gloure*, glory.

Page 416.
MYNSTRELLES SONGE
3. *hallie*, holy.
10. *Rodde*, red.
11. *cale*, cold.
15. *Swote*, sweet.
25. *heie*, they.
38. *Seyncte*, Saint.
39. *celness*, coldness.
43. *dente*, fasten.
44. *gre*, grow.
45. *Ouphante*, elfin.
46. *bee*, bow.
58. *leathalle*, lethal, deadly.

Page 418.
GOLDSMITH — THE DESERTED VILLAGE
39. *One only master*, etc. The system of enclosures is referred to.

Page 421.
344. *wild Altama*. The river Altamaha in Georgia, U. S. A.
418. *Torno's cliffs*. Lake Tornea in northern Sweden. *Pambamarca's side*. A mountain in Ecuador.

THE RETALIATION
1. *Edmund*. Edmund Burke.
6. *Tommy Townshend*. Thomas Townshend, Viscount Sidney (1733-1780), a prominent Whig statesman.

Page 422.
15. *David Garrick*, the actor. See Boswell's Johnson, p. 427.
37. *Hickey*, 'honest Tom Hickey,' a jovial Irish attorney.
49. *Reynolds*, Sir Joshua Reynolds, the eminent portrait painter.
57. *Raphael, Correggio*, famous Italian painters of the Renaissance.

JOHNSON — THE LIFE OF ADDISON
Page 424.
a. 13. *the Chartreux*. Originally a Carthusian monastery in London. Endowed in 1611 as a hospital and boys' school. Usually known as the Charterhouse.
b. 14. *Boileau*. See note to p. 372, a. 42.
16. *Tickell*. Thomas Tickell (1686-1740), Addison's friend, contributed a biographical preface to the collective edition of Addison's works published by Jacob Tonson in 1721.

Page 428.
b. 19. *Cibber*. In his *Apology for the Life of Mr. Colley Cibber* (1740).

Page 429.
a. 9. '*heavily in clouds . . . day*.' Quoted from the opening lines of *Cato*.
16. *The Distressed Mother*. See note to p. 367, a. 53.
23. *Bolingbroke*. Henry St. John, Viscount Bolingbroke, the Tory leader.
24. *Booth*. Barton Booth (1681-1733), who played Cato.
33. *Mrs. Porter*. An excellent actress who played the part of Lucia.

Page 431.
a. 39. *Milton against King Charles II.*, from the *Defense of England against Salmasius*, Chap. viii.
45. *Oldmixon*, John (1653-1742), has a prominent place in Pope's *Dunciad*.

Page 433.
b. 40. *Chesterfield*. Philip Stanhope, Earl of Chesterfield (1694-1773). For Johnson's relations with him, see note to p. 436 below.

Page 434.
a. 13. *Terence*, Publius Terentius Afer, Roman comic poet of the second century B. C. *Catullus*, Caius Valerius. Brilliant Roman poet, contemporary with Julius Cæsar.

Page 435.
a. 10. *Mandeville*, Bernard (1670-1733), author of *Fable of the Bees*.
b. 14. '*above all Greek . . . fame*.' Pope, *To Augustus*, 26.
22. '*turned many to righteousness*.' Dan, 12, 3.
53. *Mille . . . habet*. Tibullus, 4, 2, 14.

Page 436.
LETTERS
To the . . . Earl of Chesterfield. Of the occasion of this famous letter Johnson said to Boswell: 'Sir, after making great professions, he had, for many years, taken no notice of me; but when my *Dictionary* was coming out, he fell a-scribbling in *The World* about it. Upon which, I wrote him a letter expressed in civil terms, but such as might shew him that I did not mind what he said or wrote, and that I had done with him.' (Hill's Boswell, I, 301.)
a. 32. *the proprietor of The World*. Edward Moore, an old acquaintance of Johnson's.
b. 10. *The shepherd in Virgil*. Eclogue viii, 43 ff.
19. *tili I am solitary*. Johnson's wife had died three years before.
38. *Mr. James Macpherson*. Johnson had publicly declared that the poems of Ossian which Macpherson claimed to have translated from the Gaelic were forgeries. Macpherson threatened physical vengeance, and this celebrated letter, Johnson said, 'put an end to our correspondence.'

Page 437.
THE VANITY OF HUMAN WISHES
37. *Wolsey*. This passage is largely based on the picture of Cardinal Wolsey in Shakespeare and Fletcher's *Henry VIII*.

Page 438.
68. *Swedish Charles*. Charles XII (1682-1718), defeated by Peter the Great, at Pultowa, July 8, 1709. Killed at Frederikshald, Norway.

Page 439.
JAMES BOSWELL — THE LIFE OF JOHNSON
a. 3. *The accession of George the Third*. October 25, 1760.
b. 13. *Mr. Thomas Sheridan*. The father of the dramatist, Richard Brinsley Sheridan.

Page 441.
a. 15. *Collins*. See p. 411.

Page 443.
b. 6-7. *Messieurs Thornton, Wilkes, Churchill, and Lloyd*. Wits of the time, all of whom except Wilkes had been members, with William Cowper, of the Nonsense Club.

Page 445.
b. 22. *Colley Cibber*. Poet laureate, 1730-57.
41. *Whitehead*, William (1715-85). He succeeded Cibber as poet laureate.

Page 446.
a. 2. *His Ode which begins. The Bard*. See p. 404.

Page 447.
a. 28. *Dr. Goldsmith*. See above, p. 417.
b. 39. *Mr. Burke*. See below, p. 457.
42. *Mr. Malone*. Edmond Malone (1741-1812), the great Shakespeare scholar, assisted Boswell in preparing the *Life of Johnson* for the press.

Page 448.
a. 19-20. *Nihil quod tetigit*, etc. Inaccurate and often quoted in this form. Johnson wrote *Qui nullum ferè scribendi genus non tetigit, nullum quod tetigit non ornavit*. [Who left hardly any species of writing untouched and touched none that he did not adorn it.]

Page 448.
a. 35. *un étourdi*, a rattle-head.
49. *Fantoccini*, puppets.
b. 31. *Mrs. Piozzi*. Formerly the wife of Henry Thrale (d. 1781), one of Johnson's most intimate friends. She published *Anecdotes of Dr. Johnson* (1786), *Letters to and from Dr. Johnson* (1788). *Sir John Hawkins*, a member of Johnson's Club, published a *Life* in 1787.

Page 449.
a. 48. *Miss Williams*. One of the many recipients of Johnson's eccentric charity.

Page 451.
a. 38. *Dr. Adam Smith* (1723–1790). Author of *The Wealth of Nations*.

Page 452.
b. 41. *The Old Swan*, Swan Stairs. The landing here and the walk to Billingsgate beyond London Bridge were made in order to avoid the risk of 'shooting the bridge.'

Page 453.
b. 41. *Turk's Head coffee-house*. In the Strand. Johnson said, on an earlier occasion, 'I encourage this house, for the mistress of it is a good civil woman and has not much business.'

Page 456.
b. 7. *Bishop Berkeley's ingenious sophistry*. In his *Principles of Human Knowledge* (1710).

BURKE — SPEECH FOR CONCILIATION
Page 458.
a. 4. *sensible*, concrete, such as the senses can perceive.

Page 459.
a. 35. *Gothic*. We should say Teutonic.
b. 3. *Blackstone's Commentaries*. The great law treatise published (1765–1769) by Sir William Blackstone.
4. *General Gage*, Governor of Massachusetts, 1774.
23. *Abeunt studia*, etc. Compare Bacon, page 244, b. c.

Page 460.
a. 46. *with all its imperfections on its head*. *Hamlet* I, v. 79.
b. 32. *Lord Dunmore*. Governor of New York, and later of Virginia.

Page 462.
a. 2. '*Increase and multiply*.' Inaccurate. See Gen. i, 22 and 28.
51–2. *Spoliatis arma supersunt*. Juvenal, *Sat.* viii, 124.
b. 35. *advocates and panegyrisis*. For example, Dr. Johnson in *Taxation no Tyranny*.

Page 463.
a. 16. *ye gods annihilate*, etc. This piece of bombast has never been traced beyond *The Art of Sinking in Poetry*, by Arbuthnot, Swift, and Pope, where it is ostensibly quoted.
48. *Sir Edward Coke*. Public prosecutor in 1603, when Raleigh was tried.
54. *The very same title*. Popular election.

Page 464.
a. 35. *juridical*, abstractly legal.

Page 465.

GIBBON — THE DECLINE AND FALL OF THE ROMAN EMPIRE

The extract is from Chapter lxviii of the *Decline and Fall*. It presents the first grand culmination of Gibbon's massive study, the fall of the Eastern Empire. The remaining three chapters of the last volume deal with the disintegration of the empire in Italy from the eleventh to the fifteenth century. Other striking passages are the accounts of Petrarch and of Rienzi, Chapter lxx, and the 'Prospect of the Ruins of Rome in the Fifteenth Century,' Chapter lxxi.
a. 8. *Phranza*. The minister and friend of the Emperor Constantine.

Page 466.
a. 43. *seven times in one day*. Near an hundred years after the siege of Constantinople, the French and English fleets in the Channel were proud of firing 300 shot in an engagement of two hours. (Gibbon.)
b. 4. *fascines*, bundles of sticks.
49. *Justiniani*. John Justiniani, 'a noble Genoese,' was in command of 2,000 'strangers.'

Page 467.
a. 8. *generosity*, spirit.
b. 21. *The passions of his soul*, etc. I must confess that I have before my eyes the living picture which Thucydides (i. vii, c. 71) has drawn of the passions and gestures of the Athenians in a naval engagement in the great harbor of Syracuse. (Gibbon.)

Page 468.
a. 19. *the divan*. The Turkish council of state.
b. 21–2. *the boasted miracle . . . our own times*. I particularly allude to our own embarkations on the lakes of Canada, in the years 1776 and 1777, so great in the labor, so fruitless in the event. (Gibbon.)

Page 469.
a. 21. *Gabours*. Unbelievers.
49. *bashaws*, dignitaries, here probably generals. *Janizaries*, members of the central standing army of the Sultan.
54. *oda*, the unit of janizary organization.

Page 470.
b. 5. *sanjaks* were, formerly, bashaws of the rank entitled to wear one horse-tail.
26. *attaballs*, oriental tambours.

Page 471.
a. 44. *Cantacuzene*. Byzantine emperors of the fourteenth century.
b. 14. *Chosroes*, Khusrau I, a powerful Persian king of the sixth century. *the Chagan*, the Khan. The Tartar regal title. The reference here is to Jenghiz Khan, who conquered central Asia and threatened Europe early in the thirteenth century. *the caliphs*, successors of Mohammed.

Page 472.
a. 6. *Ducas*. A Byzantine historian who was an eye witness of the first siege of Constantinople. His history was first printed at Paris in 1649.
b. 40. *ducats*. The ducat, as a money of account, was about two dollars and thirty cents.

Page 473.
b. 29. *imam*. The officiating priest in Mohammedan worship.
31. *namaz*. The canonical prayer of the Moslems.
36. *the great Constantine*. Constantine I (272–337) transferred the seat of the Roman Empire in the year 330 to Byzantium, which was thereafter known as Constantinople.

Page 475.

THOMAS KEN — DOXOLOGY

This stanza, often sung at the close of other hymns, or, by itself, to open or conclude religious exercises, was appended by Bishop Ken to each of his three hymns, 'Morning,' 'Evening,' and 'Midnight.'

Page 475.

ISAAC WATTS — PSALM XC

In many hymn-books, the opening of this hymn is changed to read: 'O God, our help,' etc.

Page 477.

CHARLES WESLEY — CHRISTMAS CAROL

The two opening lines of this hymn, as given in the text, were contributed by one Martin Madan while Wesley was still living, and Wesley accepted the change. In Wesley's original version the hymn opens as follows:

'Hark how all the welkin rings
Glory to the King of Kings.'

JESU, LOVER OF MY SOUL

The first line was so written by Wesley. In most modern versions, 'Jesu' is changed to 'Jesus.'

Page 478.

FAWCETT — BLEST BE THE TIE

Like many hymns that have found almost universal acceptance, this hymn was inspired by a particular occasion. Its author, an English Baptist pastor, had been called from a small rural parish to an important London church and had made all preparations for departure, when he abruptly reversed his decision and determined to remain with his people. Thereupon, he wrote this hymn.

TOPLADY — ROCK OF AGES

The original version of this famous hymn is here given. Its phraseology has often been revised by hymn-book editors, so that it exists in many versions.

PERRONET — CORONATION

This hymn has undergone many alterations since originally published by Perronet in *Occasional Verses, Moral and Sacred* (1785). It is here given in a modern version.

Page 480.

WILLIAM COWPER — THE TASK

BOOK I

The general title of Book I is *The Sofa.* See line 18.
55. *Ouse.* See Map (near York).

Page 481.

BOOK II

Twenty-two years after the publication of Cowper's *Task* his view of slavery prevailed, and the English slave-trade was abolished by Act of Parliament (1807).

BOOK IV

3. *Arcadian scenes that Maro sings.* Virgil in his *Eclogues.*
4. *Sidney.* See p. 144.

Page 482.

57. *Tityrus,* a shepherd in the first *Eclogue* of Virgil.
73. *Cowley.* See p. 228.
78. *Chertsey's silent bowers,* a village in Surrey, not far from London.

ON THE RECEIPT OF MY MOTHER'S PICTURE

Written in 1788. Cowper's mother died in 1737, when he was little more than six years of age; yet fifty years afterward he wrote, 'Not a week passes (perhaps I might with equal veracity say a day) in which I do not think of her.' The picture which suggested this poem was sent to him 'out of Norfolk,' by his cousin Anne Bodham. See the letter to Mrs. Bodham on p. 487 below.

Page 483.

ON THE LOSS OF THE ROYAL GEORGE

The Royal George was the flagship of Rear-Admiral Kempenfelt. While being refitted, off Spithead, she heeled and went down with crew and admiral aboard, Aug. 29, 1782. The poem was probably written the same year, though not published until after Cowper's death. The meter was determined by a tune which Cowper had in mind, and the poem, therefore, must be regarded as a ballad.

Page 484.

THE CASTAWAY

The Castaway, Cowper's last original poem, was based upon his recollection of an incident in Anson's voyages. Its deepest source, however, was the profound despair which clouded the poet's mind near the end of his life.

52. *Is wet with Anson's tear.* Admiral George Anson (1697–1762), created Baron Anson, 1747, was the most distinguished British seaman of his time. His expedition to the South Sea and circumnavigation of the globe (1740–1744) were described in *A Voyage Round the World . . . by G. A.,* Compiled from papers and other materials . . . of Lord A., and published under his direction, by Richard Walter (1748)

LETTER TO JOSEPH HILL

Joseph Hill virtually managed Cowper's financial affairs from the time of the latter's release from St. Albans Asylum until his death, a period of thirty-five years. With him Cowper had an unbroken and affectionate friendship, and to him wrote many of his brightest letters.

Page 485.

a. 2. *Parson Adams,* a famous character in Fielding's novel *Joseph Andrews.*

13–14. *Rousseau's description of an English morning.* There is a famous description of a *matinée Anglaise* in the *Nouvelle Héloise* (Part V, Letter III).

LETTER TO JOHN NEWTON

September 18, 1781

After Newton left Olney in 1779, his intimacy with Cowper was continued by correspondence and many of Cowper's most important letters were written to him. The letter from which this extract is taken has to do mainly with Cowper's first volume of poems, published in 1782.

Page 486.

a. 6. *his animadversions on Dr. Watts.* Johnson's *Lives of the Poets* had just appeared. Dr. Johnson was, perhaps, less 'severe' than Cowper in his criticism of Watts, although, in general, he condemned devotional poetry, declaring that 'the sanctity of its matter rejects the ornaments of figurative diction.' Of Watts, in particular, he had recently written in his *Lives of the Poets:* 'Dr. Watts was one of the first authors that taught the Dissenters to court attention by the graces of language. . . He showed them that zeal and purity might be expressed and enforced by polished diction.'

31. *Sir Richard Blackmore:* His reputation had been 'generously cleared by Johnson,' says Boswell, 'from the cloud of prejudice which the malignity of contemporary wits had raised around it.'

LETTER TO JOHN NEWTON

Jan. 26, 1783

b. 53–4. *the Americans, at length declared independent.* The war for American independence had just been concluded.

Page 487.

LETTER TO MRS. BODHAM

As the contents of this letter disclose, the lady to whom it is addressed was a cousin of Cowper on his mother's side of the family. Compare the poem, *On the Receipt of My Mother's Picture,* p. 482 above.

b. 43–4. *more of the Donne than of the Cowper.* Cowper's mother was the daughter of Roger Donne of Ludham, in Norfolk, a family related to that of John Donne, the poet, Dean of St. Paul's.

Page 488.
LETTER TO LADY HESKETH
Lady Hesketh was a cousin whom Cowper had known in youth, and with whom he again became intimate toward the end of his life. The extract here given refers to the 'Reign of Terror', then at its height in France.

a. 18. *pauvre misérable*, poor wretch.
23. *Mrs. Unwin*, wife of Cowper's friend, the Reverend Mr. Unwin, with whom the poet made his home. After the sudden death of Mr. Unwin, in 1767, Cowper continued to live with Mrs. Unwin, and they were to have been married, but for the recurrence of the poet's attacks of insanity.
33. *Joseph Hill*, an old school-fellow and life-long friend of Cowper.
41. *Walter Bagot*, Reverend W. B., 1731–1806, a former school mate and later patron of the poet.
43. *author . . . Maids*, William Hayley, 1745–1820, a poet of some fame in his day, and an intimate friend of Cowper.
46–7. *Joseph . . . has two*, Theodora and Frances. They are the 'Modern Antiques' of Miss Mitford's *Our Village*.

b. 15. *Miltonic trammels*, refers to *The Task*, his long poem in blank verse.
18. *Romney*, George, 1734–1802, the famous portrait painter.
18–19. *mortuary . . . verses*, the poem beginning 'Thankless for favors from on high.'
22. *Johnson, Joseph*, bookseller, and publisher of Cowper's poems.
28. *Abbott's picture*, Lemuel Abbot, or Abbott, who painted Cowper's portrait in July, 1792, at Weston.

Page 489.
GEORGE CRABBE — THE VILLAGE
12. *Corydons*. Conventional shepherds of pastoral poetry, from a character of this name in Virgil's *Eclogues*.
15. *Mincio's banks*. See below, 18. *Cæsar's bounteous reign*. The reign of Augustus.
16. *If Tityrus found the Golden Age again*. Virgil, in his *Eclogues*, particularly *Eclogue IV*.
18. *Mantuan song*. Mantua, situated on an island in the river Mincio, was the home of Virgil.
27. *honest Duck*. Possibly Stephen Duck, a poor thresher who was patronized by Queen Caroline, wife of George II. He is mentioned by Johnson in his *Life of Savage* (*Lives*, London, 1821, Vol. II, p. 149).

Page 490.
97. *Ajax*. Homer's 'strong man.'

Page 492.
303. '*passing rich with forty pounds a year.*' Goldsmith's *Deserted Village*, line 142. See page 419 above.
330. *the moping owl*. Compare Gray's *Elegy*, line 10, page 401 above.

Page 497.
ROBERT BURNS — MARY MORISON
The subject of this song (written in 1781) was Ellison Begbie. Burns proposed marriage to her and was refused.
5. *bide*, await, endure. *stoure*, dust, struggle.
13. *braw*, fine, handsome.

Page 498.
SONG: MY NANIE, O
Written in 1782.
1. *Lugar*, fanciful for Stinchar.
5. *shill*, shrill, keen.
7. *plaid*, highland shawl or wrap.
15. *gowan*, daisy.
21. *penny-fee*, wages paid in money.
23. *gear*, stuff, wealth.
25. *guidman*, master.

Page 498.
SONG: GREEN GROW THE RASHES
Written in 1783.
1. *rashes*, rushes.
13. *cannie*, well considered, clever.
17. *douce*, solemn.
19. *The wisest man*, etc. Solomon.

LINES TO JOHN LAPRAIK
Written in 1785. The recipient of the verses was a rustic wit and poet of local reputation. When they were written Burns was still unknown to the world and quite unaware of the greatness of his own gift.
14. *horns*, probably ink-horns.
16. *sairs*, serves.
17. *shools*, shovels.
18. *knappin-hammers*. Hammers for breaking stone.
19. *hashes*, fools, weak-minded persons.
21. *stirks*, yearling steers.
23. *syne*, afterwards.

TO A MOUSE
Written in 1785.
4. *brattle*, sudden sound or scamper.
6. *pattle*, paddle for scouring the plow.

Page 499.
13. *whyles*, at times.
15. *daimen icker*, occasional ear. *thrave*, 'shock.'
17. *lave*, remainder.
21. *big*, build.
22. *foggage*, aftermath.
34. *but*, without.
40. *a-gley*, awry.

THE COTTER'S SATURDAY NIGHT
Written in 1785.
23. *ingle*, chimney-corner.
26. *kiaugh*, worry.
28. *Belyve*, soon, directly.
30. *ca*, drive. Literally, call.
31. *toun*, a farm with its collection of buildings.
34. *braw*, fine, handsome.
35. *sair-won*, hard-earned.
38. *spiers*, inquires.
40. *uncos*, news.
44. *Gars*, causes, makes.
48. *eydent*, attentive.
49. *jauk*, trifle, 'soldier.'

Page 500.
62. *hafflins*, halfway, partly.
67. *cracks*, chats, holds forth.
69. *blate*, bashful, embarrassed.
92. *halesome parritch*, healthful porridge (oatmeal).
93. *sowpe*, liquid.
94. *hallan'*, partition.
96. *well-hain'd kebbuck fell*. well-saved cheese, and ripe.
99. *towmond*, twelve month. *lint*, flax. *bell*, blossom.
105. *lyart haffets*, grayish temples.
107. *wales*, chooses.
111–113. *Dundee's, . . . Martyrs, . . . Elgin*. Sacred melodies.
113. *beets*, kindles.
133–135. *How he, who lone in Patmos*, etc. John. See Revelation.
138. Pope's *Windsor Forest*, 112, is quoted.

Page 501.
166. Pope's *Essay on Man*, iv, 248.
182. *Wallace's undaunted heart*. Sir William Wallace, one of the chief national heroes of Scotland, maintained a sturdy resistance to England for several years at the close of the 13th century, but was finally captured and executed at London in 1305.

Page 501.
ADDRESS TO THE DEIL
Written the winter of 1784–5.
1–2. Imitated from the opening of Pope's *Dunciad*.
2. *Clootie*. Cloot is hoof.
5. *Spairges*, splashes. *cootie*, foot-tub.
11. *skelp*, slap.
15. *lowin heugh*, flaming cavern (gully).
17. *lag*, slow. Compare verb, to lag behind.
18. *blate*, bashful, embarrassed. *scaur*, scary, timorous.
22. *Tirlin*, stripping. *kirks*, churches.
30. *eldritch*, uncanny, elvish.
32. *douce*, sober.
35. *boortrees*, elder bushes.
38. *sklentin*, slanting.
40. *lough*, lake, pond.
41. *rush-buss*, bush of rushes.
43. *neive*, fist.
45. *stoor*, harsh.
49. *warlocks*, wizards.
50. *ragweed nags*. Horses fed on ragweed, hence neglected, wild.
54. *howket*, dug up.
56. *kirn*, churn.
59. *dawtet*, petted. *Twal-pint hawkie*, twelve-pint white face. The Ayrshire breed of cattle has white markings.
60. *yell 's the bill*, dry as the bull.
62. *crouse*, bold.
64. *cantrip*, maliciously magical.

Page 502.
69. *water-kelpies*. Malevolent water-spirits in the form of black horses. Compare the 'White Horses' of Ibsen's *Rosmersholm*.
73. *spunkies*, will-o-the-wisps.
91. *sneck-drawin*, latch-lifting, intruding.
93. *brogue*, trick.
97. *bizz*, bustling hurry.
98. *reeket*, smoky. *reestet gizz*, singed face.
101. *the man of Uz*. Job. See i, 1.
107. *lows'd*, let loose. *scaul*, scold.
108. *ava*, of all.
113. *ding*, knock, be too much for. *Lallan*, Low land. *Erse*, the form of Gaelic spoken in the Scottish Highlands.
117. *linkin*, skipping.
119. *jinkin*, dodging.
123. *aiblins*, possibly.
124. *hae a stake*, have something to gain.

A BARD'S EPITAPH
Written in 1786.
3. *blate*, bashful. *snool*, snivel, cringe.
5. *dool*, sorrow.

OF A' THE AIRTS THE WIND CAN BLAW
Written in 1788.
1. *airts*, quarters, directions.
3. *bonie*, winsome. This favorite Scotch word combines the ideas of good, good-looking, and good-tempered.
5. *row*, roll.
8. *my Jean*. Jean Armour, Burns's wife.

Page 503.
14. *shaw*, grove, woodland dell.

GO FETCH TO ME A PINT O' WINE
Written in 1788.
2. *tassie*, goblet.
4. *bonie*, winsome.
5. *Leith*, the port of Edinburgh.
7. *Berwick-law*. Berwick hill, a landmark to seamen cruising in that region.

AULD LANG SYNE
Written in 1788. The phrase 'auld lang syne' was an ancient one and there were other songs embodying it,

Page 503.
the first line of the poem, and the tune, when Burns took them up. His version of the song is immeasurably superior to any which preceded it.
9. *pint-stowp*, flagon, drinking vessel.
13. *braes*, hill-sides.
14. *gowans*, daisies.
15. *fit*, foot.
17. *paidl't i' the burn*, dabbled in the brook.
21. *fier*, comrade.
23. *waught*, draught.

JOHN ANDERSON, MY JO
Written in 1789.
1. *jo*, sweetheart.
4. *brent*, straight, steep, firm.
7. *pow*, poll, head.
11. *canty*, cheerful.

TAM GLEN
Written in 1789.
1. *tittie*, sister.
5. *braw*, handsome, fine.
6. *poortith*, poverty. *fen'*, shift.
9. *laird*, landlord.
10. *ben*, the interior of the house.
11. *siller*, money.
13. *minnie*, mother. *deave*, deafen, bother with noise.
17. *gin*, if (given).
18. *marks*, silver coins, each worth 26 2-3 cents.
19. *ordain'd* a humorous allusion to the prevalent Scottish belief in foreordination.
22. *sten*, bounce.
25. *waukin*, watching, keeping awake over.
26. *my droukit sark-sleeve*. Drenched sleeve of my chemise.
28. *breeks*, breeches.

Page 504.
TO MARY IN HEAVEN
The subject of this poem was Mary Campbell and the parting described took place in the spring of 1788. Mary died the following autumn and the poem was written on the first anniversary of her death, after a night of agitated recollection.

TAM O' SHANTER
Written in 1790.
1. *chapman billies*, peddler fellows.
4. *tak the gate*, leave town, take the road, go home.
5. *nappy*, ale.
6. *unco*, very.
7. *lang Scots miles*. The ancient Scottish mile was 1,976 yards.
8. *slaps*, openings.
16. *bonie*, winsome.
19. *skellum*, scamp.
20. *blellum*, 'loud-mouth,' 'blow-hard.'
23. *ilka melder*, every grist.
24. *siller*, silver, money.
25. *ev'ry naig*, etc. Every horse that was shod. *ca'd*, driven.
28. *Kirkton*, the village near any church.
30. *Doon*, a charming little river near Burns's birthplace. Compare *Bonie Doon*, p. 507.
31. *warlocks*, wizards.
33. *gars me greet*, makes me grieve.
39. *ingle*, chimney-corner.
40. *reamin swats*, foaming ale.
41. *Souter*, cobbler.
65. *like*, as.

Page 505.
81. *skelpit*, clattered. *dub*, puddle.
86. *bogles*, goblins.
93. *whins*, boulders, basaltic rocks. *cairn*, heap of stones.
103. *bore*, crevice.
107. *tippenny*, twopenny ale.
108. *usquebae*, whiskey.
110. *a boddle*, a copper.
116. *brent-new*, brand new.

Page 505.

117. *strathspeys*, Scotch dances with a peculiar catch in the time.
119. *winnock bunker*. Window box, bench.
121. *towzie tyke*, touseled cur.
123. *gart them skirl*. Made them shriek.
124. *dirl*, tingle.
127. *cantraip sleight*, magic trick.
131. *airns*, irons.
134. *gab*, mouth.
147. *cleekit*, linked.
148. *carlin*, fellow. *reekit*, smoked.
149. *duddies*, duds, clothes.
150. *linket at it*. Went at it energetically. *sark*, chemise.
151. *queans*, wenches.
153. *creeshie*, greasy.
154. *seventeen-hunder linen*. Very fine linen.
155. *Thir breeks*. These breeches.
157. *hurdies*, hips.
158. *burdies*, brides, girls.
160. *walie*, vigorous.
162. *Carrick shore*, the southern district of Ayrshire.
165. *corn*, wheat. *bear*, barley.
167. *cutty sark*, short under-dress. *Paisley harn*, coarse linen.
170. *vauntie*, vain.
172. *coft*, bought.
173. *twa pund Scots*. The pound Scots was one-twelfth of the English pound sterling.
182. *hotch'd*, hitched.
184. *tint*, lost.

Page 506.

189. *fyke*, fuss.
190. *byke*, nest.
191. *pussie*, the hare.
196. *eldritch*, uncanny, elvish.
197. *fairin*, reward, a present from the fair.
209. *ettle*, intention.
210. *wist*, knew.

WILLIE BREWED A PECK O' MAUT
Written in 1789.

1. *Willie*, William Nichol, a schoolmaster.
2. *Rob and Allan came to see*. Burns and Allan Masterton celebrated the occasion by composing this song, Masterton contributing the music.
8. *bree*, brew.
14. *lift*, sky.

A WINTER NIGHT
Written in 1786.

1. *Boreas*, the north wind. *doure*, grim.
4. *lift*, sky.
9. *burns*, brooks.
11. *bocked*, poured with a rush.
13. *winnocks*, windows.
14. *ourie*, drooping.
15. *brattle*, clamor.
17. *deep-lairing*, foundering. *Sprattle*, sprawl.
18. *scaur*, scar, jutting rock.
23. *chittering*, shivering.

HIGHLAND MARY
Written in 1792. See note upon *To Mary in Heaven* above.

1. *braes*, hill-sides.
9. *birk*, birch.

Page 507.

FLOW GENTLY, SWEET AFTON
The identification of the stream addressed in this poem is uncertain. The heroine was probably some casual fancy of the poet.

1. *braes*, slopes.
16. *birk*, birch.

BONIE DOON
Written in 1791. There are three versions of this poem, of which this is the second and best. The third version, which is the most popular, was written in 1792, and was published in Johnson's *Musical Museum*. It is given below:

THE BANKS O' DOON

YE banks and braes o' bonie Doon,
  How can ye bloom sae fresh and fair?
How can ye chant, ye little birds,
  And I sae weary fu' o' care!
Thou'll break my heart, thou warbling bird,
  That wantons thro' the flowering thorn!
Thou minds me o' departed joys,
  Departed never to return.

Aft hae I rov'd by bonie Doon
  To see the rose and woodbine twine,
And ilka bird sang o' its luve,
  And fondly sae did I o' mine.
Wi' lightsome heart I pu'd a rose,
  Fu' sweet upon its thorny tree!
And my fause luver staw my rose—
  But ah! he left the thorn wi' me.

1. *bonie*, winsome. *Doon*, a charming small river near Burns's birthplace.
6. *bough*, pronounced in Scotch fashion this rimes perfectly with 'true,' below.
12. *wist*, knew.
19. *staw*, stole.

DUNCAN GRAY
Written in 1792. Like many of Burns's songs of this period it is an old Scotch ditty completely transformed by his rehandling. Of its tune, he wrote, 'Duncan Gray is a light-horse gallop of an air which precludes sentiment.'

2. *o't*, of it.
5. *heigh*, high.
6. *asklent*, askance. *skeigh*, skittish.
7. *Gart*, made. *abeigh*, aside, aloof.
9. *fleech'd*, flattered.
11. *Ailsa Craig*, a small rocky island in the Firth of Clyde.
14. *Grat his e'en*, etc. Wept his eyes both bleared and blind.
15. *lowpin*, leaping. *Linn*, waterfall.
17. *but a tide*, that is, they ebb and flow.
19. *sair*, sore, hard. *bide*, bear, endure.

Page 508.

31. *sic*, such.
38. *smoor'd*, smothered.
39. *crouse*, brisk. *cantie*, cheerful.

SCOTS WHA HAE
Written in 1793. In 1314, 100,000 Englishmen under Edward II were met on the field of Bannockburn by Robert Bruce with 30,000 Scots. Bruce's force was overwhelmingly victorious. Burns 'threw into a kind of Scotch ode' what Bruce might be supposed to have said 'on that eventful morning.'

23. *Liberty's in every blow*. By this victory the Scotch achieved their independence.

A MAN'S A MAN FOR A' THAT
Written in 1795. Burns was strongly republican in his sentiments. His burning sense of personal worth as opposed to the privileges of station are best expressed in this piece which he called 'no song, but . . . two or three pretty good prose thoughts put into rime.'

7. *guinea's stamp*. That is, merely the statement of its value which is intrinsic.
8. *gowd*, gold.
10. *hodden-gray*, coarse woollen cloth, undyed.
17. *birkie*, a fellow (usually implying conceit).
20. *coof*, stupid lout.
28. *mauna fa' that*, must not get that.
36. *gree*, prize.

Page 512.
WORDSWORTH — PREFACE TO LYRICAL BALLADS
This preface, in which Wordsworth sets forth his theory of poetry, was prefixed to the second edition of *Lyrical Ballads* in 1800, and enlarged and modified in subsequent issues to the shape in which it is here given.

A full commentary upon Wordsworth's poetic dogma will be found, considerably scattered, in Coleridge's *Biographia Literaria*. For Chapter XIV, see *Century Readings*, pp. 550–553.

Coleridge believed that Wordsworth's theories, rather than his practice, were responsible for much of the early hostility to Wordsworth's poems. 'A careful and repeated examination of these confirms me in the belief, that the omission of less than a hundred lines would have precluded nine-tenths of the criticism on this work.... The men of business who had passed their lives chiefly in cities, and who might therefore be expected to derive the highest pleasure from acute notices of men and manners conveyed in easy, yet correct and pointed language; and all those who, reading but little poetry, are most stimulated with that species of it, which seems most distant from prose, would probably have passed by the volumes altogether. Others more catholic in their taste, and yet habituated to be most pleased when most excited, would have contented themselves with deciding that the author had been successful in proportion to the elevation of his style and subject....

'In the critical remarks, therefore, prefixed and annexed to the Lyrical Ballads, I believe, we may safely rest, as the true origin of the unexampled opposition which Mr. Wordsworth's writings have been since doomed to encounter.' (*Biographia Literaria*, Chap. IV.)

b. 5–6. *Catullus* (87–47 B. C.), *Terence* (c. 195–158 B. C.) and *Lucretius* (95–55 B. C.) belong to the earlier, or classical, period of Roman poetry; *Statius* (61–96 A. D.) and *Claudian* (fl. c. 400 A. D.) to the later, or 'Silver Age.'

42. *a selection of language*, etc. 'To this I reply; that a rustic's language, purified from all provincialism and grossness, and so far re-constructed as to be made consistent with the rules of grammar—(which are in essence no other than the laws of universal logic, applied to psychological materials)—will not differ from the language of any other man of common sense, however learned or refined he may be, except as far as the notions, which the rustic has to convey, are fewer and more indiscriminate. This will become still clearer, if we add the consideration—(equally important though less obvious)—that the rustic, from the more imperfect development of his faculties, and from the lower state of their cultivation, aims almost solely to convey insulated facts, either those of his scanty experience or his traditional belief; while the educated man chiefly seeks to discover and express those connections of things, or those relative bearings of fact to fact, from which some more or less general law is deducible. For facts are valuable to a wise man, chiefly as they lead to the discovery of the indwelling law, which is the true being of things, the sole solution of their modes of existence, and in the knowledge of which consists our dignity and our power.

'As little can I agree with the assertion, that from the objects with which the rustic hourly communicates the best part of language is formed. For first, if to communicate with an object implies such an acquaintance with it, as renders it capable of being discriminately reflected on, the distinct knowledge of an uneducated rustic would furnish a very scanty vocabulary. The few things and modes of action requisite for his bodily conveniences would alone be individualized; while all the rest of nature would be expressed by a small number of confused general terms. Secondly, I deny that the words and combinations of words derived from the objects, with which the rustic is familiar, whether with distinct or confused knowledge, can be justly said to form the best part of language. . . . The best part of human language, properly so called, is derived from reflection on the acts of the mind itself. It is formed by a voluntary appropriation of fixed symbols to internal acts, to processes and results of imagination, the greater part of which have no place in the consciousness of uneducated men; though in civilized society, by imitation and passive remembrance of what they hear from their religious instructors and other superiors, the most uneducated share in the harvest which they neither sowed, nor reaped, If the history of the phrases in hourly currency among our peasants were traced, a person not previously aware of the fact would be surprised at finding so large a number, which three or four centuries ago were the exclusive property of the universities and schools; and, at the commencement of the Reformation, had been transferred from the school to the pulpit, and thus gradually passed into common life.' (*Biographia Literaria*, Chap. XVII.)

Page 515.
a. 40. *the language of prose and metrical composition.* See *Biographia Literaria*, Chap. XVIII, for Coleridge's correction of this doctrine.

Page 517.
b. 36. *Shakespeare hath said.* Hamlet IV, iv, 37.

Page 519.
b. 39. *Clarissa Harlowe* (1748), Richardson's novel. *The Gamester* (1753). A tragedy by Edward Moore portraying the horrors of gambling.

Page 522.
THE PRELUDE
This poem is so called because it was intended to be introductory to a great philosophical poem Wordsworth planned on retiring to the Lake District in 1799, 'with the hope of being enabled to construct a literary work that might live.' As a preliminary it seemed to him a reasonable thing that 'he should take a review of his own mind, and examine how far Nature and education had qualified him for such an employment. The philosophical poem was to be divided into three parts, and only one of these, *The Excursion*, was ever finished. But the introductory work, in which Wordsworth 'undertook to record, in verse, the origin and progress of his own powers, as far as he was acquainted with them,' was completed in 1805, although it was not published till 1850, after the poet's death, when it was given the title, *The Prelude, or Growth of a Poet's Mind; an Autobiographical Poem.* Our extract is taken from Book I, which was begun at Goslar, in Germany, and finished in the first year or two of Wordsworth's settlement at Grasmere. Lines 101–163 were published in 1809 in Coleridge's periodical *The Friend*. The whole poem was addressed to Coleridge as 'a dear friend, most distinguished for his knowledge and genius, and to whom the author's intellect is deeply indebted.'

2–4. Wordsworth was born at Cockermouth, in Cumberland, and in his ninth year was sent to Hawkshead Grammar School in the Vale of Esthwaite.

10. *springes*, snares. Hamlet I, iii, 115: 'Ay, springes to catch woodcocks.'

26. *the cultured Vale*, identified by Professor Knight with the neighboring valley of Yewdale.

29. *object*, what we aimed at. *end*, what actually resulted.

40. *Dust as we are*, in spite of our mortal bodies.

Page 523.

57. *her*, Nature.
73. *elfin pinnace*, fairy bark. The 'craggy ridge' was probably Ironkeld, the 'huge peak' behind it Wetherlam; but there are other ridges and peaks about Esthwaite answering to Wordsworth's description. A similar impression may be obtained by rowing out into any lake surrounded by ridges with higher mountains behind them. It is the moral and spiritual interpretation of the impression that is Wordsworth's own.
80. *struck* with the oars.
101-163. When Wordsworth published these lines in 1809 he gave them the title *Growth of Genius from the Influence of Natural Objects on the Imagination in Boyhood and Early Youth*.
101-114. The nominative of this whole sentence is 'thou,' referring to the 'Wisdom and Spirit of the universe,' addressed in the opening lines; the verb is 'didst intertwine,' and lines 108-114 are an extension of this predicate. By intertwining the passions with Nature, the Divine Spirit purifies and ennobles them, the very emotions of pain and fear, awakened by contact with Nature, gain a touch of Nature's grandeur.
143. *an alien sound*. The weird echo from the distant hills seemed to come from another world.
150. *reflex*, the reflection of a star in the ice.
155. *spinning still*. To the swift skater, aided by the wind, the banks seem to be moving in the contrary direction, and their motion seems to continue for a moment or two even after he has stopped, the mental impression being retained.

Page 524.

LINES COMPOSED ABOVE TINTERN ABBEY

Wordsworth wrote of this poem, originally published in *Lyrical Ballads*:—'No poem of mine was composed under circumstances more pleasant for me to remember than this. I began it upon leaving Tintern, after crossing the Wye, and concluded it just as I was entering Bristol in the evening, after a ramble of four or five days with my sister. Not a line of it was altered, and not any part of it written down till I reached Bristol.'

The importance of this poem as an illustration of Wordsworth's view of Nature has been already touched on in the Introduction; but it cannot be urged too strongly. Myers says:—'To compare small things with great—or, rather, to compare great things with things vastly greater —the essential spirit of the *Lines near Tintern Abbey* was for practical purposes as new to mankind as the essential spirit of the Sermon on the Mount. Not the isolated expression of moral ideas, but their fusion into a whole in one memorable personality, is that which connects them for ever with a single name. Therefore it is that Wordsworth is venerated; because to so many men— indifferent, it may be, to literary or poetical effects, as such—he has shown by the subtle intensity of his own emotion how the contemplation of Nature can be made a revealing agency, like Love or Prayer—an opening, if indeed there be any opening, into the transcendent world.'

1-2. Wordsworth's earlier visit was made, alone and on foot, in 1793.
3-5. The Wye Valley, above Tintern Abbey, is, perhaps, the most beautiful river scenery in England. Although only a few miles from the sea, the stream is free from the influence of the tide; and rocks, meadows, and wooded cliffs combine to make the scene one of romantic loveliness.
23-50. The memory has been a consolation to the poet amid the noise and loneliness of city life (23-31); it has given him, too, feelings of pleasure, which he no longer remembers, but which, he is sure, have had their influence on his moral character (31-36); and, finally, when perplexed by the mysteries of human life, he has been uplifted by the recollection of Nature's loveli-

Page 524.

ness to a mood, in which the soul, endowed with spiritual insight, penetrates beyond material things to the secret of life, and sees with joy the divine harmony underlying the apparent contradictions of the world (36-50).
66-111. Wordsworth in this passage distinguishes three periods in his relation to Nature. In the first, Nature merely offered opportunity for boyish pleasures, such as bird-nesting, rowing, and skating, described in the extract from *The Prelude;* in the second he took delight in the forms and colors of the woods and mountains and the sound of the waterfalls—a delight of eye and ear only, for he was as yet insensible

to the moods
Of time and season, to the moral power,
The affections and the spirit of the place.

In the third period, Nature had a moral and spiritual significance and helped him to understand the mystery of human life. The best commentary is a passage in *The Prelude;* (Book VIII, 340-356), in which he sets forth the same succession of his delight in Nature—first, animal, second, sensuous; third, moral and contemplative.

Page 525.

108. Wordsworth noted the resemblance of this line to Young's *Night-Thoughts*, in which it is said that 'Our *senses* as our *reason*, are divine,' 'And half-create the wondrous world they see.'
110. In nature as revealed and interpreted by the senses.
114-122. Dorothy Wordsworth was a little younger than her brother, and even in her childhood was a refining influence in his life. See what he writes of her in *The Sparrow's Nest*, p. 531. From childhood they were separated until they were both over twenty, when Dorothy became, not only her brother's constant companion and helper, but a hallowing influence in the crisis of his life.
125. *inform*, mold, inspire.
149. *Of past existence*, of my own past life. Cf. 119-123.

STRANGE FITS OF PASSION

This and the four following poems belong to what is known as the 'Lucy' group of lyrics, written in Germany in 1799. Nothing is known of the English maiden so beautifully and devoutly enshrined; she may have existed only in the poet's imagination.

SHE DWELT AMONG THE UNTRODDEN WAYS

2. *Dove*, a river in the English Midlands.

Page 526.

MICHAEL

This poem was written in Oct.–Dec., 1800, largely at the sheep-fold in Green-head Ghyll, round which the subject is centered. Wordsworth said to Mr. Justice Coleridge that there was some foundation in fact, however slight, for every poem he had ever written of a narrative kind. '*Michael* was founded on the son of an old couple having become dissolute, and run away from his parents; and on an old shepherd having been seven years in building up a sheep-fold in a solitary valley.' He wrote on another occasion:—'In the two poems, *The Brothers* and *Michael*, I have attempted to draw a picture of the domestic affections, as I know they exist amongst a class of men who are now almost confined to the north of England. They are small independent *proprietors* of land, here called 'statesmen,' men of respectable education, who daily labor on their own little properties. The domestic affections will always be strong amongst men who live in a country not crowded with population, if these men are placed above poverty. But if they are proprietors of small estates which have descended to them from their ancestors, the power which these affections acquire amongst such men is inconceivable by those who have only had an opportunity of observing

Page 526.

hired laborers, farmers, and the manufacturing poor. Their little tract of land serves as a kind of permanent rallying point for their domestic feelings, as a tablet on which they are written, which makes them objects of memory in a thousand instances, when they would otherwise be forgotten. It is a fountain fitted to the nature of social man, from which supplies of affection, as pure as his heart was intended for, are daily drawn. This class of men is rapidly disappearing.'

Page 531.

MY HEART LEAPS UP WHEN I BEHOLD

Wordsworth adopted the last three lines of this little poem (written in 1802) as the motto of the great Ode on Immortality, which was begun about a year later. 'Piety' is used in its original sense of 'reverence, affection.' The meaning is that the man should cherish the love of Nature he feels as a child, so that it may be a continuous inspiration, running through all his life. The sense in which 'the child is father of the man' is explained more fully in the Ode. (See p. 537.)

THE SPARROW'S NEST

Written at Grasmere in 1801. The nest was in the hedge of the garden at Cockermouth in which William and Dorothy Wordsworth played as children. In the poem as originally composed, l. 9 read: 'My sister Dorothy and I.' As to Dorothy Wordsworth see note on *Tintern Abbey*, 114–122 above.

RESOLUTION AND INDEPENDENCE

Written at Grasmere, 1802, 'This old man I met a few hundred yards from my cottage; and the account of him is taken from his own mouth. I was in the state of feeling described in the beginning of the poem, while crossing over Barton Fell from Mr. Clarkson's, at the foot of Ullswater, towards Askham. The image of the hare I then observed on the ridge of the fell.' (Wordsworth's note.)

Page 532.

12. *plashy*, marshy, swampy, boggy.
43. *Chatterton*. See p. 415.
45. *Him*. Burns. See p. 497.

Page 533.

TO A YOUNG LADY

Written 1802. The poem refers either to Dorothy Wordsworth or to Mary Hutchinson—probably to the former.

17. *a Lapland night*. In the far north at a certain season of the year the sun does not sink below the horizon. The winter nights are often calm and still.

SHE WAS A PHANTOM OF DELIGHT

The subject of this poem, written in 1804, is Mary Hutchinson, whom Wordsworth had married two years before.

22. *machine*. This word has been objected to as unpoetical. But cf. *Hamlet* II, ii, 124: 'whilst this machine is to him?'

YARROW UNVISITED

'At Clovenford, being so near to the Yarrow, we could not but think of the possibility of going thither, but came to the conclusion of reserving the pleasure for some future time, in consequence of which, after our return, William wrote the poem which I shall here transcribe.'—From Dorothy Wordsworth's *Recollections of a Tour made in Scotland*, 1803.

When Scott sent *The Lay of the Last Minstrel* to Wordsworth, the latter returned a copy of these verses by way of acknowledgment. Scott in reply said: 'I by no means admit your apology, however ingeniously and artfully stated, for not visiting the bonny holms of Yarrow, and certainly will not rest until I have prevailed upon you to compare the ideal with the real stream. . . .

Page 533.

I like your swan upon St. Mary's Lake. How came you to know that it is actually frequented by that superb bird?'

Wordsworth subsequently complained that Scott in one of his novels mis-quoted lines 43–44 of this poem, printing 'swans' instead of 'swan.' He added 'Never could I have written "swans" in the plural. The scene, when I saw it with its still and dim lake, under the dusky hills, was one of utter loneliness: there was *one swan*, and one only, stemming the water, and the pathetic loneliness of the region gave importance to the one companion of that swan, its own white image in the water, It was for that reason that I recorded the Swan and its Shadow. Had there been many swans and many shadows, they would have implied nothing as regards the character of that place: and I should have said nothing about them.'

Page 534.

6. *Marrow*, companion. Dorothy Wordsworth.
20. *lintwhites*, linnets, small singing birds.
33. *holms*, flat and low-lying pieces of ground by a river, surrounded or submerged in time of flood.
37. *Strath*, valley.

THE SOLITARY REAPER

Suggested to Wordsworth by the following sentence in the MS. of his friend Wilkinson's *Tours to the British Mountains*: 'Passed a female who was reaping alone; she sang in Erse, as she bended over her sickle; the sweetest human voice I ever heard; her strains were tenderly melancholy, and felt delicious long after they were heard no more.'

I WANDERED LONELY AS A CLOUD

Wordsworth says: 'The daffodils grew and still grow on the margin of Ullswater, and probably may be seen to this day as beautiful in the month of March, nodding their golden heads beside the dancing and foaming waves.'

Dorothy Wordsworth's *Journal* has the following entry under April 15, 1802: 'When we were in the woods beyond Gowbarrow Park we saw a few daffodils close to the water-side. . . . As we went along there were more, and yet more; and, at last, under the boughs of the trees, we saw there was a long belt of them along the shore. . . . I never saw daffodils so beautiful. They grew among the mossy stones, about and above them; some rested their heads on these stones as on a pillow for weariness; and the rest tossed, and reeled, and danced, and seemed as if they verily laughed with the wind that blew upon them over the lake. They looked so gay, ever glancing, ever changing.'

Page 535.

21–2. These lines, said by Wordsworth to be the best in the poem, were contributed by his wife. For the thought of this stanza cf. *Tintern Abbey*, lines 23–36.

TO A SKY-LARK

Cf. Shelley's poem with the same title (p. 618) and Meredith's *The Lark Ascending* (p. 854).

ELEGIAC STANZAS

There are two Peele Castles, one in the Isle of Man, the other on the coast of Lancashire. The latter is the one referred to in the poem, Wordsworth being known to have spent a four weeks' vacation in its neighborhood.

Page 537.

ODE ON IMMORTALITY

Of this poem the very highest opinions have been expressed by competent judges. Principal Shairp says it 'marks the highest limit which the tide of poetic inspiration has reached in England . . . since the days of Milton.' It is, therefore, worthy of the most careful study. The best help to understanding it is given in Words-

Page 537.

worth's own note:—'This was composed during my residence at Townend, Grasmere. Two years at least passed between the writing of the first four stanzas and the remaining part. To the attentive and competent reader the whole sufficiently explains itself; but there may be no harm in adverting here to particular feelings or *experiences* of my own mind on which the structure of the poem partly rests. Nothing was more difficult for me in childhood than to admit the notion of death as a state applicable to my own being. I have said elsewhere:—

> A simple child,
> That lightly draws its breath,
> And feels its life in every limb,
> What should it know of death?

'But it was not so much from feelings of animal vivacity that *my* difficulty came as from a sense of the indomitableness of the spirit within me. I used to brood over the stories of Enoch and Elijah, and almost to persuade myself that, whatever might become of others, I should be translated, in something of the same way, to heaven. With a feeling cogenial to this, I was often unable to think of external things as having external existence, and I communed with all that I saw as something not apart from, but inherent in my own immaterial nature. Many times while going to school have I grasped at a wall or tree to recall myself from this abyss of idealism to the reality. At that time I was afraid of such processes. In later periods of life I have deplored, as we have all reason to do, a subjugation of an opposite character, and have rejoiced over the remembrances, as is expressed in the lines:—

> Obstinate questionings
> Of sense and outward things
> Fallings from us, vanishings, etc.

'To that dream-like vividness and splendor which invest objects of sight in childhood, every one, I believe, if he would look back, could bear testimony, and I need not dwell upon it here; but having in the poem regarded it as presumptive evidence of a prior state of existence, I think it right to protest against a conclusion, which has given pain to some good and pious persons, that I meant to inculcate such a belief. It is far too shadowy a notion to be recommended to faith as more than an element in our instincts of immortality. But let us bear in mind that, though the idea is not advanced in revelation, there is nothing there to contradict it, and the fall of man presents an analogy in its favour. Accordingly, a pre-existent state has entered into the popular creeds of many nations, and, among all persons acquainted with classic literature, is known as an ingredient in Platonic philosophy. Archimedes said that he could move the world if he had a point whereon to rest his machine. Who has not felt the same aspirations as regards the world of his own mind? Having to wield some of its elements when I was impelled to write this poem on the "Immortality of the Soul," I took hold of the notion of pre-existence as having sufficient foundation in humanity for authorizing me to make for my purpose the best use of it I could as a poet.'

Wordsworth's view of childish reminiscences of a previous existence was, however, probably not suggested by Plato, but by the seventeenth century poet Vaughan, in *Childhood* and *The Retreat*. See p. 230.

4. Cf. lines 4–5 of the *Sonnet Composed upon Westminster Bridge* (p. 539), and *Elegiac Stanzas* 14–16 (p. 535).
13. *bare*, of clouds.
21. *tabor*, a small drum.
22. *a thought of grief*, the thought expressed in the last two lines of the preceding stanza.
26. *wrong*, offend by lack of sympathy.
28. *the fields of sleep*, 'from the dark beyond the dawn,' or possibly 'from the sleeping [i.e., quiet] fields.'
40. *coronal*, garland.

Page 538.

56–7. Cf. lines 4–5 and note above.
72. *Nature's Priest*, the Minister and Interpreter of the Divinity.
81. *homely*, humble—in contrast with the glories of man's divine origin.
85–9. Probably suggested by the sight of Hartley Coleridge, to whom Wordsworth addressed a poem *To H. C., Six Years Old*, beginning: 'O thou! whose fancies from afar are brought.'
102–7. Referring to Shakespeare's well-known lines in *As You Like It*, II, vii, 139–166, 'All the world's a stage,' etc.
112. *the eternal deep*, the deep mysteries of eternity.
126. *earthly freight*, 'burden of earthly cares.' (Webb.)
132. *fugitive*, evanescent, quickly disappearing.
141–5. Professor Bonamy Price, walking one day with Wordsworth by the side of Rydal Water, asked him the meaning of these lines:—'The venerable old man raised his aged form erect; he was walking in the middle, and passed across me to a five-barred gate in the wall which bounded the road on the side of the lake. He clenched the top bar firmly with his right hand, pushed strongly against it, and then uttered these ever-memorable words, "There was a time of my life when I had to push against something that resisted, to be sure that there was anything outside of me. I was sure of my own mind; everything else fell away and vanished into thought." Thought he was sure of; matter for him, the moment, was an unreality.'

Page 539.

181. *primal sympathy*, the child's intuitive sympathy with nature.
183–4. Cf. *Tintern Abbey*, lines 92–5.
185. *through*, beyond.
189. *yet*, still, even now.
196–9. The sunset has no longer 'a celestial light, the glory and the freshness of a dream,' but suggests serious reflections to the Man who has pondered on the issues of Life and Death. The poet's final thought is that acquaintance with the world, while robbing Nature of its first glory, increases its significance by awakening sympathy with the joys and sorrows of humanity. Professor Dowden has well observed that the last two lines of the *Ode* are 'often quoted as an illustration of Wordsworth's sensibility to external nature; in reality, they testify to his enriching the sentiment of nature with feeling derived from the heart of man and from the experience of human life.'

NUNS FRET NOT

3. *pensive citadels*, refuges in which they can think, secure from interruption.
6. *Furness-fells*, the hills of the district of Furness, in or near which Wordsworth spent the greater part of his life.
8–9. Cf. Lovelace, *To Althea from Prison*, pp. 227–8.

COMPOSED UPON WESTMINSTER BRIDGE

Wordsworth appears to have been mistaken as to the date he assigned to this sonnet, which was written when he left London for Dover on his way to Calais early in the morning of July 30th, 1802. The following is the entry in his sister's diary under that date: 'Left London between five and six o'clock of the morning outside the Dover coach. A beautiful morning. The city, St. Paul's, with the river—a multitude of little boats, made a beautiful sight as we crossed Westminster Bridge; the houses not overhung by their clouds of smoke, and were spread out endlessly; yet the sun shone so brightly, with such a pure light, that there was something like the purity of one of Nature's own grand spectacles.'

Page 540.

IT IS A BEAUTEOUS EVENING

9. *Dear Child*, Wordsworth's daughter in France. See p. 511, column 1.

Page 540.

12. *Abraham's bosom*. In the presence of God. See Luke xvi, 22.

ON THE EXTINCTION OF THE VENETIAN REPUBLIC

1–2. At the beginning of the thirteenth century the Venetians, with the help of France, captured Constantinople, and added to their dominions a large part of the Eastern Empire. They protected Western Europe from the incursions of the Turks for centuries.

4. Venice was founded in the fifth century in the marshes of the Adriatic by inhabitants of the mainland who fled before the conquering Huns under Attila.

7–8. The Venetians having protected Pope Alexander III against the German Emperor, whom they defeated in a sea fight in 1177, the Pope gave the Doge a ring and bade him wed with it the Adriatic that posterity might know that the sea was subject to Venice, 'as a bride is to her husband.' The ceremony was observed annually by a solemn naval procession, after which the Doge threw a ring into the sea.

9–14. Venice was robbed of much of her power in 1508 by the League of Cambrai, but the real cause of her decay was the discovery of the New World, which made the Atlantic the highway of trade instead of the Mediterranean, and shifted the commercial center from Italy to England and Holland. The Republic, however, remained free and independent, though greatly enfeebled, until 1797, when Austria and France divided its territory between them. Venice remained under Austrian dominion (except for brief intervals) until it became a part of the kingdom of Italy in 1866.

TO TOUSSAINT L'OUVERTURE

This sonnet was written in August, 1802, when Toussaint L'Ouverture, the liberator of San Domingo, was lying in prison at Paris, where he died a few months later. He was born in 1743, the child of African slaves, and showed great political and military ability; but he was unable to resist the French fleet sent against him by Napoleon, who reëstablished slavery in the island in 1801.

Page 541.

TO THE MEN OF KENT

Written when Britain was in fear of a Napoleonic invasion.

4. *hardiment*, hardihood, courage.
10. *from the Norman*, at the battle of Hastings, 1066.

ON THE SUBJUGATION OF SWITZERLAND

Switzerland was conquered by the French in 1798, and three of its cantons were annexed to the Republic. The sonnet appears to have been suggested by the Act of Mediation, by which Napoleon arranged for the government of Switzerland in 1803; he became Emperor a few months afterwards, and at the time the sonnet was written had made himself master of Europe, England alone having resisted him successfully. It was the attack upon the liberties of Switzerland which gave the final blow to the French sympathies of both Coleridge and Wordsworth, and united them with their fellow-countrymen in antagonism to Napoleon.

THE WORLD IS TOO MUCH WITH US

13–14. Proteus and Triton were sea-deities in the old Greek mythology. Wordsworth means that he would rather be a heathen with some sense of the Divinity in Nature than a professed Christian whose heart is so given to the pursuit of wealth and worldly ambition that he is out of harmony with the beautiful sights and sounds of land and sea.

TO THE RIVER DUDDON

This is the concluding sonnet of a beautiful series which Wordsworth wrote under the above title. The Duddon is a small stream which rises on the borders of Westmoreland, Cumberland, and Lancashire, and flows into the Irish Sea.

KING'S COLLEGE CHAPEL

This beautiful chapel was built by Henry VI for the scholars of the College, which up to a few years ago was reserved to students from Eton.

Page 542.

CONTINUED

4. *Westminster* Abbey.
8. *younger Pile*. St. Paul's Cathedral, built by Sir Christopher Wren in the seventeenth century. It is a more modern structure than the Abbey, and contains the ashes of many great men for whom room could not be found in the older national burial place. It is surmounted by a great dome and cross.

ON THE DEPARTURE OF SIR WALTER SCOTT

This was the journey which Scott took in the hope of recovery from what proved to be his last illness. Abbotsford, on the Tweed, was his home. See Map.

3. *Eildon*, three hills near Abbotsford, famous in Scottish legend.
14. *Parthenope*, one of the Sirens, said to be buried at Naples.

'THERE!' SAID A STRIPLING

'Mossgiel was thus pointed out to me by a young man on the top of the coach on my way from Glasgow to Kilmarnock.' (Wordsworth's note.)

9. *bield*, lodging, dwelling, place of shelter.

CONCLUSION

This and the former sonnet were among the 'Poems composed or suggested during a tour in the summer of 1833,' published two years later.

Page 544.

COLERIDGE — BIOGRAPHIA LITERARIA

a. 20. *The Friend*. A periodical published by Coleridge in 1809–10.

Page 545.

b. 16. *stamp tax*, levied at this time upon all newspapers and weekly periodicals.
17. *a war against freedom*, against France.
30. *ad normam Platonis*, after the rule of Plato, the Greek philosopher.
53. κατ' ἔμφασιν, in appearance rather than reality.
55. *pingui-nitescent*, shining with fat.

Page 546.

a. 27. *Phileleutheros*, lover of freedom.
48. *ambrosial*, heavenly.
b. 32. *Orpheus*, the musician of classical mythology whose strains persuaded even stones and trees to follow him.
36. *illuminati*, illuminated or inspired ones.

Page 547.

b. 3. *Jacobinism*, revolutionary principle. Jacobin means, originally, a friar of the order of St. Dominic. Hence one of a faction in the French revolution, so called from the *Jacobin* club, which first met in the hall of the Jacobin friars in Paris, Oct., 1789.
10. *The Watchman* ran from March 1 to May 13, 1796.
28. *text from Isaiah*. 'My bowels shall sound like an harp.' xvi, 11.
34. *psilosophy*. See above, p. 545, col. 2.
42. *gagging bills*. The bills introduced into Parliament to restrict public meetings and the freedom of the press.
52. *melioration*, improvement.

Page 548.

a. 14. *a dear friend.* Thomas Poole.
22. *first revolutionary war,* against the French revolutionists.
35. *Stowey.* In Somersetshire. See Map.
37. *morning paper.* The Post.
b. 12. *a poet.* Wordsworth came to Stowey in July, 1797.
38. *Quidnunc,* an idle gossip, continually asking 'What now?'
40. *Dogberry,* the pompous, ignorant constable of *Much Ado about Nothing.*
42. *pour surveillance of,* to exercise supervision over.

Page 549.

a. 7. *Spy Nozy,* the great Jewish philosopher Spinoza (1632–1677), in whose teaching Wordsworth and Coleridge were greatly interested.
8. *a remarkable feature,* a red nose.

Page 551.

b. 54. *Anacrean,* Greek lyric poet of the sixth century B. C.

Page 552.

b. 18. *Bishop Taylor.* See p. 265.
19. *Burnet* (1635–1715), a distinguished philosopher and divine. His *Sacred Theory of the Earth* is a fanciful and ingenious speculation.

Page 553.

a. 22–23. *Sir John Davies* (1570–1626).

THE ANCIENT MARINER

The circumstances under which this poem was written and published have been already related (see p. 511). Some further particulars of the suggestions made by Wordsworth may here be given, from his own account:

'In the autumn of 1797 Mr. Coleridge, my sister and myself started from Alfoxden pretty late in the afternoon with a view to visit Linton and the Valley of Stones near to it; and as our united funds were very small, we agreed to defray the expense of the tour by writing a poem, to be sent to the *New Monthly Magazine.* Accordingly we set off and proceeded along the Quantock Hills towards Watchet; and in the course of this walk was planned the poem of the "Ancient Mariner," founded on a dream, as Mr. Coleridge said, of his friend Mr. Cruikshank. Much the greatest part of the story was Mr. Coleridge's invention, but certain parts I suggested.

'For example, some crime was to be committed which should bring upon the Old Navigator, as Coleridge afterwards delighted to call him, the spectral persecution, as a consequence of that crime, and his own wanderings. I had been reading in Shelvocke's *Voyages* a day or two before that, while doubling Cape Horn, they frequently saw albatrosses in that latitude, the largest sort of seafowl, some extending their wings twelve or thirteen feet. "Suppose" said I, "you represent him as having killed one of these birds on entering the South Sea, and that the tutelary spirits of these regions take upon them to avenge the crime." The incident was thought fit for the purpose, and adopted accordingly. I also suggested the navigation of the ship by the dead men, but do not recollect that I had anything more to do with the scheme of the poem. The gloss with which it was subsequently accompanied was not thought of by either of us at the time; at least not a hint of it was given to me, and I have no doubt it was a gratuitous afterthought. We began the composition together on that, to me, memorable evening. I furnished two or three lines at the beginning of the poem, in particular:—

> And listened like a three years' child:
> The Mariner had his will.'

Coleridge seems later to have had doubts whether Wordsworth's suggestion of moral responsibility was consistent with the imaginative character of the poem as a whole. He is reported as saying in his *Table Talk* on

Page 553.

May 31, 1830:—'Mrs. Barbauld once told me that she admired *The Ancient Mariner* very much, but that there were two faults in it,—it was improbable, and had no moral. As for the probability, I owned that that might admit some question; but as to the want of a moral, I told her that in my own judgment the poem had too much; and that the only, or chief fault, if I might say so, was the obtrusion of the moral sentiment so openly on the reader as a principle or cause of action in a work of pure imagination. It ought to have had no more moral than the *Arabian Nights'* tale of the merchant's sitting down to eat dates by the side of a well and throwing the shells aside, and lo! a genie starts up and says he *must* kill the aforesaid merchant *because* one of the date shells had, it seems, put out the eye of the genie's son.'

A marginal gloss was added by Coleridge in the edition of 1817, together with a Latin motto from Burnet, of which the following is a translation:—'I readily believe that there are more invisible beings in the universe than visible. But who shall explain to us the nature, the rank and kinship, the distinguishing marks and graces of each? What do they do? Where do they dwell? The human mind has circled round this knowledge, but never attained to it. Yet there is profit, I do not doubt, in sometimes contemplating in the mind, as in a picture, the image of a greater and better world: lest the intellect, habituated to the petty details of daily life, should be contracted within too narrow limits and settle down wholly on trifles. But, meanwhile, a watchful eye must be kept on truth, and proportion observed, that we may distinguish the certain from the uncertain, day from night.'

11. *loon,* an idle, stupid, worthless fellow.
12. *eftsoons,* forthwith, immediately. These obsolete words are used to recall the style of the old ballads, which Coleridge was trying to revive, and to suggest that the time of the story was somewhat remote.
23–4. As the ship sailed farther away from the harbor, first the church, then the hill, and last the top of the lighthouse upon the hill disappeared from view.
25. If the sun rose on the left, in what direction was the ship sailing?
29–30. At the equator the noon sun is never far out of the perpendicular, and during the equinoxes it is directly overhead. See lines 111–114.
32. *bassoon.* This particular detail was probably suggested to Coleridge by the fact that during his residence at Stowey, his friend, Poole, added a bassoon to the instruments used in the village church.
36. *minstrelsy,* band of minstrels.

Page 554.

55–57. *clifts,* cliffs. *sheen,* brightness, splendor. *ken,* see, discern.
58. *between* the ship and the land.
62. *in a swound,* heard in a swoon.
75. *shroud,* a rope running from the mast-head to the ship's side.
76. *vesper,* (Latin) evening; in its plural form the term is usually applied to the evening service of the Roman Catholic church.
81. *crossbow.* This suggests that the time of the story was at the end of the sixteenth or beginning of the seventeenth century, when the crossbow was still in common use.
83. Why 'upon the right?' The reader should trace the voyage of the ship on a map; it must have been now about nine days' sail from a point between Cape Horn and the South Pole.
98. *uprist,* used instead of 'uprose' (as 'eat' instead of 'eaten' in line 67) to give the suggestion of language of the olden time.
104. In the edition of 1817 Coleridge altered this line to read

> The furrow streamed off free,

and added in a footnote: 'In the former edition the line was—

Page 554.

The furrow followed free;

but I had not been long on board a ship before I perceived that this was the image as seen by a spectator from the shore, or from another vessel. From the ship itself the *wake* appears like a brook flowing off from the stern.' But in 1828 and after, the original reading was restored.

107. Notice the sudden check in the verse at the end of this line, and the contrast with the swift movement of the preceding stanza.
128. *death-fires*, phosphorescent lights, to which the sailors attached a superstitious significance.
139. *well-a-day*, an antique exclamation of lament, as 'gramercy' in line 164 is of joy and thankfulness.

Page 555.

152. *wist*, knew. See notes above on use of old words.
164. 'I took the thought of "*grinning for joy*" from poor Burnett's remark to me, when we had climbed to the top of Plinlimmon, and were nearly dead with thirst. We could not speak for the constriction, till we found a little puddle under a stone. He said to me, "You grinned like an idiot!" He had done the same.' (*Table Talk*.)
184. *gossameres*, fine spider-threads.
185–9. Coleridge made considerable alterations, omissions and additions in this part of the poem after it was first published. Another version of this stanza reads:

'Are those *her* ribs which flecked the sun
 Like bars of a dungeon grate?
Are these two all, all of the crew,
 That woman and her mate?'

And he left the following additional stanza in manuscript:

'This ship it was a plankless thing
 A bare Anatomy!
A plankless Spectre—and it moved
 Like a being of the Sea!
The woman and a fleshless man
 Therein sate merrily.'

199–200. A fine description of the sudden darkness of the tropics.
209–11. A star within the lower tip of the crescent moon is never seen. This is Coleridge's imaginative way of using what he describes in a manuscript note as the 'common superstition among sailors that something evil is about to happen whenever a star dogs the moon.'
226–7. 'For the last two lines of this stanza I am indebted to Mr. Wordsworth. It was on a delightful walk from Nether Stowey to Dulverton, with him and his sister, in the autumn of 1797, that this poem was planned and in part composed.'—Coleridge's note in the edition of 1817.

Page 556.

254. *reek*, give off vapor.
267–8. The white moonlight, as if in mockery, covered the hot sea with a sheen like that of April hoar frost.
294. Note this and other indications that the religious setting of the poem is medieval.
297. The buckets looked *silly*, because they had stayed so long dry and useless.
302. *dank*, wet.
314. *sheen*, bright. The reference seems to be to the Polar Lights, known in the Northern Hemisphere as the Aurora Borealis.
319. *sedge*, coarse grass growing in a swamp.
333. *had been* (subjunctive mood), would have been.

Page 557.

394. *I have not* the power; I cannot.
435. *charnel-dungeon*, a vault for the bones of the dead.

Page 558.

489. *rood*, cross.
512. *shrieve* (usually pronounced and written 'shrive') to absolve after confession.
524. *trow*, trust, believe, think.
535. *ivy-tod*, ivy-bush.

Page 559.

575. *crossed his brow*, made the sign of the cross on his forehead to ward off evil spirits.
623. *of sense forlorn*, one who has lost his senses.

CHRISTABEL

Christabel was begun in 1797–8, and continued in 1800. Scott heard it recited while it was still in manuscript, and the melody of the verse made such an impression on his mind that he adopted it for *The Lay of the Last Minstrel*. *Christabel* in its fragmentary state was printed in 1816; Coleridge said in 1821, 'Of my poetic works I would fain finish *Christabel*,' but he never succeeded in doing so. It remains, however, one of the most wonderful and beautiful poems of the Romantic Revival.

Page 563.

408–426. Said by Coleridge to be 'the best and sweetest lines I ever wrote.'

Page 565.

KUBLA KHAN

In a note to this poem on its publication in 1816, Coleridge relates the circumstances of its composition. Being in ill-health, he had retired to a lonely farmhouse on Exmoor, and an anodyne had been prescribed, from the effects of which he fell asleep in his chair at the moment that he was reading the following sentence from the old book of travels known as *Purchas his Pilgrimage*:—'In Xamdu did Cublai Can build a stately palace, encompassing sixteen miles of plain ground with a wall, wherein are fertile meadows, pleasant springs, delightful streams, and all sorts of beasts of chase and game, and in the midst thereof a sumptuous house of pleasure.' Coleridge adds:—'The Author continued for about three hours in a profound sleep, at least of the external senses, during which time he has the most vivid confidence that he could not have composed less than from two to three hundred lines; if that indeed can be called composition in which all the images rose up before him as *things*, with a parallel production of the correspondent expressions, without any sensation or consciousness of effort. On awaking he appeared to himself to have a distinct recollection of the whole, and taking his pen, ink, and paper, instantly and eagerly wrote down the lines that are here preserved. At this moment he was unfortunately called out by a person on business from Porlock, and detained by him above an hour, and on his return to his room, found, to his no small surprise and mortification, that though he still retained some vague and dim recollection of the general purport of the vision, yet, with the exception of some eight or ten scattered lines and images, all the rest had passed away like the images on the surface of a stream into which a stone had been cast, but, alas without the after restoration of the latter!'

Kubla Khan in the thirteenth century founded the Mogul dynasty in China, and made Pekin the capital of his empire, which was the largest that has ever existed in Asia. He was an enlightened but ambitious ruler, very fond of pomp and splendor.

13. *athwart a cedarn cover*, across a cedar wood.
41. *Abora*, apparently a mountain of Coleridge's imagination.

FROST AT MIDNIGHT

Mrs. Coleridge was wont to complain to her friends that her husband '*would* walk up and down composing poetry instead of coming to bed at proper hours.' This poem was the outcome of a midnight meditation in his cottage at Stowey in February, 1798, and was published in the same year.

Page 566.

27. *stranger*, a film of soot sticking to the bars of the grate, which, according to a common English superstition, betokens the coming of a visitor.

29-30. As to Coleridge's birth and school days, see Life, p. 543.

38 *stern preceptor*. Coleridge, in his *Biographia Literaria*, says: 'At school I enjoyed the inestimable advantage of a very sensible, though at the same time, a very severe master.' He goes on to speak at length of Boyer's merits as a teacher, 'whose severities, even now, not seldom furnish the dreams, by which the blind fancy would fain interpret to the mind the painful sensations of distempered sleep; but neither lessen nor dim the deep sense of my moral and intellectual obligations.' Coleridge writes also in his *Table Talk:* 'The discipline at Christ's Hospital in my time was ultra Spartan; all domestic ties were to be put aside. "Boy!" I remember Boyer saying to me once when I was crying the first day of my return after the holidays, "Boy! the school is your father! Boy! the school is your mother! Boy! the school is your brother! Boy! the school is your sister! the school is your first cousin, and your second cousin, and all the rest of your relations! Let's have no more crying!"' Coming under the influence of Voltaire, Coleridge professed himself an infidel. 'So, sirrah, you are an infidel, are you?' said Boyer; 'then I'll flog your infidelity out of you!' Coleridge said it was the 'only just flogging he ever received.'

43-44. Coleridge was very fond of his sister Ann, who was five years older than himself and had been his playmate when he was still in petticoats. She died in 1791, to his great grief.

52-54. At Christ's Hospital Coleridge used to lie on the roof and gaze upon the clouds and stars.

55-65. There was no likelihood at this time that Coleridge would live in the Lake District, but he fulfilled his own prophecy in 1800 by removing to Greta Hall, Keswick, from which he writes, soon after his settlement there, of his little son's enjoyment of nature: 'I look at my doted-on Hartley—he moves, he lives, he finds impulses from within and from without, he is the darling of the sun and the breeze. Nature seems to bless him as a thing of her own. He looks at the clouds, the mountains, the living beings of the earth, and vaults and jubilates.'

HUMILITY THE MOTHER OF CHARITY

The date appended to this poem is that of composition.

EPITAPH

This poem like the preceding bears the date of its composition.

Page 567.

LAMB — THE OLD FAMILIAR FACES

This was written in Jan., 1798, at the time of the central tragedy of Lamb's life, the poem in its original form beginning:—

'Where are they gone, the old familiar faces?
I had a mother, but she died and left me,
Died prematurely in a day of horrors—
All, all are gone, the old familiar faces.'

The last stanza began with the word 'For,' and the words 'And some are taken from me' in l. 20 were italicized, referring no doubt to Mary Lamb, whose illness was probably the occasion of the poem. The 'friend' of l. 10 was Charles Lloyd, with whom Lamb had a temporary difference about this time; the 'more than brother' of l. 16, Coleridge.

MACKERY END, IN HERTFORDSHIRE

All these essays appeared in the *London Magazine*, 1821-22, and were afterwards included in the *Essays of Elia*.

Page 567.

Mackery End may now be easily reached from Wheathampstead Station on the Great Northern Railway. The old farmhouse, with some additions since Lamb's day, is still standing.

b. 1. *Bridget Elia*, Mary Lamb. See biographical sketch, p. 567.

Page 568.

a. 2. *the rash king's offspring*, Jephthah's daughter. Judges xi, 30-40.
4. '*with a difference.*' Ophelia in *Hamlet* IV, v. 183, 'O, you must wear your rue with a difference.'
14. *Burton*, the author of *The Anatomy of Melancholy* (1621).
20. *a story*. Mary Lamb's passion for novel-reading is spoken of by others.
25. *humors*, eccentricities.
29. *bizarre*, whimsical, fantastic.
31. '*holds Nature more clever*'—a quotation from Gay, *Epitaph of Byewords*.
33. *obliquities*, irregularities. *Religio Medici*, the chief work of Sir Thomas Browne, whose curious notions and elaborate style made him a favorite with Lamb. See p. 245.
36. *intellectuals*, reasoning powers, intelligence.
40. *Margaret Newcastle*, an eccentric Restoration noblewoman, of high character and remarkable talents, for whom Lamb often expressed his admiration.

b. 19. *stuff of the conscience*, quoted from *Othello* I, ii, 2.
27. *good old English reading*, in the library of Samuel Salt of the Inner Temple.
47. *beat up the quarters of*, arouse, disturb, visit unceremoniously. The expression is used in exactly the same way by Richardson in *Pamela*.
49. *corn country*. Hertfordshire is mainly agricultural and grows a large quantity of wheat.

Page 569.

a. 7. *substantial yeoman*, well-to-do farmer.
36. '*heart of June*,' quoted from Ben Jonson.
37. *the poet*, Wordsworth. See *Yarrow Visited*, stanza 6, 'than which' (Lamb wrote to Wordsworth) 'I think no lovelier stanza can be found in the wide world of poetry.'
42. *waking bliss*, conscious enjoyment, less like a dream; quoted from Milton's *Comus*.

b. 20-21. *gossamer*, spider thread. *rending*, separating.
29. *the two scriptural cousins*, Mary and Elizabeth. Luke i, 39-40.
35-6. *B. F.*, Baron Field, an English barrister, who in 1816 became Judge of the Supreme Court of New South Wales. To him Lamb addressed the Elia essay entitled *Distant Correspondents*.
38. *The fatted calf*. See the Parable of the Prodigal Son, Luke xv, 23.
53. *astoundment*, intense surprise.

Page 570.

a. 3-4. *I forget all this*. A reminiscence of Psalm cxxxvii, 5: 'If I forget thee, O Jerusalem, let my right hand forget her cunning.'

DREAM-CHILDREN: A REVERIE

The death of Lamb's brother John on Oct. 26, 1821, appears to have suggested the tender vein of reminiscence and musing on 'what might have been' in this essay, which is justly regarded as one of the most delicate in pathos and perfect in workmanship Lamb ever wrote. But this kind of reverie was not unusual with him. He writes in an earlier essay (*New Year's Eve*): 'Being without wife or family . . . and having no offspring of my own to dally with, I turn back upon memory, and adopt my own early idea, as my heir and favorite.'

a. 13. *Norfolk*. Lamb's grandmother, Mary Field, was housekeeper for more than fifty years at Blakesware in Hertfordshire, the seat of the Plumers, described in the Elia essay, *Blakesmoor in H——*

Page 570.

shire. William Plumer, who lived in another family seat (also in Hertfordshire), and dismantled Blakesware, was still living when *Dream-Children* was published, and this may have been the reason why Lamb altered the name of the county to Norfolk, the scene of the legend of the children in the wood.

a. 23. *Robin Redbreasts*, which at the end of the ballad cover the bodies of the murdered children with leaves.

b. 8. *Psaltery*, the Psalms. Psalter is the more usual and correct form.

10. *spread her hands*, in amazement at such learning.
17. *cancer*, the actual cause of Mrs. Field's death.
24. *apparition of two infants*. There was a legend in the Plumer family about the mysterious disappearance of two children in the seventeenth century.
36. *the old busts*. These were among the things removed by Mr. Plumer from Blakesware.
48. *nectarines*, a variety of peach thought particularly delicious.
50. *forbidden fruit*. See Genesis ii, 16–17, and the opening lines of *Paradise Lost*.

Page 571.

a. 12. *impertinent*, because the pike eats dace. It is a sluggish fish, while dace are very lively.
28. *mettlesome*, high-spirited.
39–40. *a lame-footed boy*. It is not known whether Lamb was ever temporarily lame in boyhood. John Lamb's lameness was caused by the fall of a stone in 1796, just before the tragedy which made such a difference in Charles Lamb's life. Writing to Coleridge just afterwards he says: 'I had the whole weight of the family thrown on me; for my brother, little disposed (I speak not without tenderness for him) at any time to take care of old age and infirmities, had now, with his bad leg, an exemption from such duties, and I was now left alone.' John Lamb was self-indulgent, and in manhood they saw little of each other, but Charles felt his loss severely, as is shown by the letters he wrote at the time. A fuller account of John Lamb, written before his death, will be found in the Elia essay, *My Relations*.

b. 15. *took off his limb*. This is a detail supplied from Lamb's imagination.

23. *Alice W——n*, Winterton in Lamb's Key, but he adds that it is a feigned name. The real name of the village girl 'with the bright yellow Hertfordshire hair, and eye of watchet hue' was probably Ann Simmons. She seems to have lived in one of the cottages near Blakesware and married Mr. Bartram, or Bartrum, a London pawnbroker. Lamb probably idealized this youthful passion, which, if his 'seven long years' are to be taken literally, must have begun when he was a boy of fourteen. He writes in *New Year's Eve:* 'I would scarce now have any of those untoward accidents and events of my life reversed. I would no more alter them than the incidents of some well-contrived novel. Methinks it is better that I should have pined away seven of my goldenest years, when I was thrall to the fair hair, and fairer eyes, of Alice W——n, than that so passionate a love-adventure should be lost.'

25. *difficulty*, shyness, reserve, reluctance to be won.
28. *representment*, re-incarnation.
30. *whose*, i.e., the first or the second Alice's.
40. *might have been*, if he had married Alice.
41. *Lethe*, the river of Hades, which made those who drank of it completely forget their past life. Virgil in the *Æneid* (VI, 703–751) says that after thousands of years the soul, having drunk of Lethe, returns to earth in another body. Some such far-off incarnation is all that is possible for the creations of the dreamer's imagination.

Page 571.

b. 45–6. *Bridget . . . James Elia*, the names given by Lamb to his sister and brother in *My Relations*.
46. *gone for ever*. This was the only part of the dream that remained true.

A CHAPTER ON EARS

Lamb exaggerates his lack of appreciation for music in this essay, as in his verses, *Free Thoughts on Several Eminent Composers*, beginning:

'Some cry up Haydn, some Mozart,
Just as the whim bites; for my part
I do not care a farthing candle
For either of them, or for Handel.'

As a matter of fact he was a fervent admirer of Braham, whose singing of Handel's oratorio, *Israel in Egypt*, is commended in the essay on *Imperfect Sympathies*. Lamb wrote of this great singer: 'He was a rare composition of the Jew, the gentleman, and the angel; yet all these elements mixed up so kindly in him that you could not tell which preponderated.'

a. 52. *volutes*, spiral ornaments at the sides of the capital or top of Ionic and Corinthian columns.

b. 50. *conduits*, channels, usually for water, here for sound.
52. *the mole* has small ears but keen hearing.

Page 572.

a. 1. *side-intelligencers*, side passages, conveying information to the brain.
5. *to draw upon assurance*, to rely upon impudence.
6. '*quite unabashed*.' Lamb gave the reference in a foot-note in the *London Magazine* to Pope's *Dunciad* (II, 147):

'Earless on high stood unabashed Defoe.'

6–7. *upon that article*, in that particular.
8. *pillory*, a frame in which the offender's head and hands were fixed in an uncomfortable and helpless position while he was exposed to the jeers and insults of the mob. This mode of punishment was practised in Great Britain up to the beginning of Queen Victoria's reign.
12–13. *concourse of sweet sounds*. *The Merchant of Venice* V, i, 83–5.
14–15. '*Water parted from the sea*.' This and '*In infancy*' are both songs from Arne's opera *Artaxerxes*, Lamb's *First Play*.
16. *harpsichord*, the forerunner of the modern pianoforte.
20. *Mrs. S——*, not identified beyond the name 'Spinkes' given in Lamb's Key.
28. *Alice W——n.* See notes to *Dream-Children* above.
39. *A.*, William Ayrton, a well-known musical critic of the time.

b. 12. *Sostenuto and adagio*, Italian musical terms indicating that a passage is to be played in a 'sustained' or 'leisurely' manner.
13. *Sol, Fa, Mi, Re*, names of notes used in singing.
14. *conjuring*, mysterious, magical. *Baralipton*, a meaningless word invented by the scholastic philosophers for the purpose of exercises in logic.
18. *Jubal* 'was the father of all such as handle the harp and organ'—Genesis iv, 21.
19. *gamut*, the scale, from Gamma-ut, the ancient name of the first note.
20. *singly unimpressible to*, alone incapable of receiving impressions from.
22. *stroke*, effect.
26. *cried-up*, extravagantly praised.
29. *midsummer madness*. Olivia, in *Twelfth Night* III, iv, 61: 'Why, this is very midsummer madness.' The midsummer moon was believed a cause of insanity.
33. *con*, learn by heart.
36. *thrid*, thread, follow all the windings of.

Page 572.

b. 41. *follow*, with the mind, in the attempt to connect what went before with what comes after.
45. *the Enraged Musician*, a picture by Hogarth of a musician almost driven mad by street noises.
47. *Oratorio*, a sacred musical performance without scenery or special dress.
49. *pit*, the part of the theatre on the ground floor, a little removed from the stage, chiefly frequented by devoted theatre-goers who cannot afford to pay for dearer seats.
50. *Laughing Audience*, a wonderful picture by Hogarth representing varieties of mirth as seen on different human faces at a play. There is a good description of it in Dowden, *Shakspere's Mind and Art*, pp. 338–9.

Page 573.

a. 3. *Party in a parlor*, etc. Quoted from the first edition of Wordsworth's *Peter Bell*. The stanza was omitted from subsequent editions, but in the meantime Shelley had taken it for the motto of his burlesque *Peter Bell the Third*.
5. *concertos*, elaborate pieces of music for one or more instruments, accompanied by an orchestra.
16. *all stops*, all punctuation marks, no words.
19. *mime*, a mimic actor of farces. Latin *mimus*.
27. *book in Patmos*. See Revelation x, 10.
28. *Burton. Anatomy of Melancholy* I, ii, 2, 6.
30. *melancholy given*, given or inclined to melancholy.
34. *amabilis insania*, delightful ecstasy. Horace, *Odes* III, iv, 5.
35. *mentis gratissimus error*, a most welcome deception of the mind, a pleasing hallucination. Horace, *Epistles* II, ii, 140.
40. *toys*, trifles, innocent amusements.
51. *subrusticus pudor*, awkward bashfulness. Cicero, *Epistolæ ad Familiares* V, xii, first sentence.

b. 8. *Nov——*, Vincent Novello, a well-known organist and composer.
16. *abbey*, Westminster.
21. *dove's wings*. Psalm lv, 6: 'Oh that I had wings like a dove!' Barron Field says that Lamb was especially fond of the setting of these words by Kent, the English composer of the previous century. Mendelssohn's anthem, 'O for the wings of a dove,' was not yet composed.
24. *cleanse his mind*. Psalm cxix, 9: 'Wherewithal shall a young man cleanse his way?' Anthems to these words were written by the English composers Cook and Boyce.
26. *rapt above earth*, etc. Walton's *Complete Angler* I, iv. See p. 256.
33. '*earthly*' . . . '*heavenly*.' See 1 Corinthians xv, 48–9.
35. *German ocean*, of music by German composers.
37. *Arion* (long i), a musician of Lesbos, who, according to the Greek legend, when threatened with death by pirates, obtained permission to play one last tune. This attracted a shoal of dolphins, and upon the back of one of these he escaped to land.
38. *Tritons*, sea gods, half men, half fishes. Modern opinion would not agree with Lamb in making Bach and Beethoven subordinate to Haydn and Mozart.
44. *dazzle*, gleam confusedly. This is a curious use of the word, which is a diminutive of 'daze,' and means to make or become confused. *his*, Novello's.
46. *tiara*, an elaborate head-dress; originally Persian, now used with special reference to the triple crown worn by the Pope on ceremonial occasions.
47. *naked*, unadorned, frank.
50. *malleus hereticorum*, the heretics' hammer, the title of an attack upon Luther and other early Protestants.
51. *heresiarch*, chief of heretics.

Page 573.

b. 52–3. *Marcion, Ebion, Cerinthus*, heretics of the first century, each of whom had a view inconsistent with the opinions of the other two.
53. *Gog and Magog.* See Revelation xx, 8, where they stand for all unbelievers.

Page 574.

a. 2. *dissipates the figment*, dispels the vision.
3. *Lutheran*, Protestant. Ben Jonson has a jesting reference to 'Luther's beer' (*Epigram* 101). Ollier in his reminiscences of Lamb says: 'Once at a musical party at Leigh Hunt's, being oppressed with what to him was nothing better than a prolonged noise . . . he said—"If one only had a pot of porter, one might get through this." It was procured for him, and he weathered the Mozartian storm.'

b. 1. *rationalities of a purer faith*, reasonable views of Protestantism.

A DISSERTATION UPON ROAST PIG

'The idea of the discovery of roasting pigs I borrowed from my friend Manning,' Lamb says in a letter written six months later. Manning had been in China for some years, and this fact may have suggested to Lamb his fantastic setting of the story, which in its bald outlines is a commonplace of literature going back to the third century. With the exception of the name of the Chinese philosopher Confucius (sixth century B. C.), the details are, of course, Lamb's own invention.

a. 15–16. *broiling*, exposing to a fierce heat; roasting, to a moderate one.
16. *the elder brother*, of earlier date.
20. *mast*, beech nuts, used to feed pigs.
23. *younker*, a Shakespearean word conveying the idea of youth associated with either gaiety or greenness.
30. *new-farrowed*, new-born.
35. *tenement*, habitation.
48. *firebrand*, used in the double sense of 'incendiary' and 'mischievous rogue.'
50. *premonitory moistening*. He was forewarned of the delicacies in store for him by his mouth watering.
51. *nether*, lower.

b. 11. *crackling*, the crisp skin of roast pork.
22. *retributory*, avenging, punishing.
27. *lower regions*, stomach.
29. *remote quarters*, his shoulders, on which the blows were raining.
32. *sensible*, conscious, aware.
37. *me*, the indirect object of advantage or disadvantage, often used in Shakespeare. See *Taming of the Shrew*, beginning of I, ii: 'Knock me at this gate.'
42. *eats*, quasi-passive. Goldsmith, *Vicar of Wakefield*: 'If the cakes at tea eat short and crisp.' Used in the same sense by Shakespeare.
49. *the lesser half*, keeping the larger share for himself.

Page 575.

a. 15. *litter*, of nine pigs.
26. *farrowed*, brought forth young.
33. *assize town*, in England a county town to which the judges come to hold the assizes. Used here to give a burlesque effect of historic detail. So with the whole circumstances of the trial, which are distinctively modern and English.
43. *charge*, direction as to the law of the case given by an English judge.
46. *box*, the shut-in benches where the jury sit during an English trial. After hearing the evidence, they are conducted to a private room for consultation, unless they are ready to give a unanimous verdict offhand, as Lamb imagines to have been the case in this instance. The taste of the burnt pig had such an effect upon their minds that they at once agreed upon a verdict in direct contradiction to the judge's charge and the evidence.

Page 575.

a. 49. *winked at*, shut his eyes to. This meaning is common in the Bible and Shakespeare.
55. *took wing*, was noised abroad.
b. 9. *Locke*, the great English philosopher (1632–1704).
16. *dynasty*, succession of sovereigns of the same family. Lamb is still writing in the mock-historic style.
27. *mundus edibilis*, world of eatables.
29. *princeps obsoniorum*, chief of dainties.
31. *between pig and pork*, too old to roast and too young to salt. *hobbydehoy* (or hobbledehoy), a clumsy youth, 'neither a man nor a boy.'
32. *suckling*, babe at the breast. *moon*, month.
33. *guiltless . . . of*, unpolluted by.
34. *amor immunditiæ*, love of filth. The allusion is to the doctrine of original sin, the fall of Adam which involved all his offspring.
36. *broken*, commonly used only of the passage of a boy's voice to the deeper tones of manhood.
38. *præludium*, prelude, music played by way of introduction.
41. *exterior tegument*, outer skin. The longer words are used in mock seriousness for comic effect.
47. *oleaginous*, oily.
53. *manna*, the food sent from heaven to the Israelites in the wilderness. See Exodus xvi, 14, 15.
54. *if it must be so*, if we must use terms so gross.

Page 576.

a. 1. *ambrosian*, heavenly, like ambrosia, the food of the Greek gods.
3. *doing*, being cooked.
5. *passive*, submissive. *equably*, smoothly, evenly, with mind undisturbed.
7. *sensibility*, sensitiveness.
8–9. *radiant jellies—shooting stars*. There is an ancient superstition that shooting stars leave jellies where they fall. The prosaic fact is, of course, that the young pig's eyes drop out because of the heat to which they are exposed.
16. *conversation*, manner of life, as in 2 Peter ii, 7, 'the filthy conversation of the wicked.'
18. *Ere sin could blight*, etc. This couplet is quoted, with exquisite humor, from Coleridge's *Epitaph on a Young Infant*, published in 1796 in a little volume of poems to which Lamb himself contributed.
24. *epicure*, one devoted to the pleasures of the table. The modern use of the word is a slander on the philosopher Epicurus, who was devoted to the pleasures of the intellect. *for such a tomb might be content to die*, probably a reminiscence of the last line of Milton's verses on Shakespeare, 'that kings for such a tomb would wish to die.' See p. 279.
26. *sapors*, tastes, flavors.
31. *excoriateth*, takes the skin off—an exaggeration of the keenness of the flavor.
34. *stoppeth at the palate*, satisfies the taste, not the stomach.
41. *batten*, fatten.
47–8. *helpeth . . . all around*, may be served and do good to everybody.
49. *is the least envious*, excites the least envy, because all parts are equally good.
50. *neighbors' fare*, food promoting neighborly or friendly feeling.
51. *I am one of those*, etc. This paragraph and the next are merely the elaboration of a letter Lamb wrote to Coleridge on March 9, 1822—six months before the essay was published. The story of the old gray impostor and some other hints are to be found in the letter, which was evidently the foundation of the essay, the main addition being the fable of the origin of the art of roasting, suggested by Manning.

b. 3. *proper*, peculiar to himself. Latin, *proprius*, one's own.

Page 576.

b. 4. *Absents*, those absent. The odd form adds force to the pun.
6. '*tame villatic fowl*,' quoted from Milton, *Samson Agonistes*. *villatic*, of the village.
7. *brawn*, boar's flesh pickled or potted.
11. '*give everything*.' *Lear* II, iv, 253: 'I gave you all.'
13. *extra-domiciliate*, a word of Lamb's own invention, from the Latin, *extra*, outside, and *domicilium*, a dwelling-house.
17. *insensibility*, lack of feeling.
20. *nice*, discriminating.
24. *The age of discipline*, of the use of the rod. The clause echoes a famous phrase of Burke's, 'the age of chivalry is gone.'
27. *intenerating and dulcifying*, making tender and sweet.
29. *refining a violet*. See *King John* IV, ii, 11.
32. *gusto*, relish, flavor.
34. *St. Omer's*, a Jesuit college in France. Lamb was never there. Canon Ainger remarks upon this as an instance of Lamb's 'audacious indifference to fact.' The phrase on the preceding page 'over London Bridge' has also been regarded as a wilful mystification; but this is at least doubtful. Lamb had certainly no hesitation in adding fictitious details according to his fancy.
38. *per flagellationem extremam*, by whipping to death.
43. *I forget the decision*. This is the final touch of affected seriousness, the whole incident being, of course, a playful invention.
48. *barbecue*, to roast whole after splitting and stuffing. The derivation '*barbe à queue*' sometimes given is fanciful and erroneous. It comes from an Indian word, meaning a wooden frame for smoking or roasting meat. *to your palate*, with stuffing to your taste.
49. *shalots*, strong onions.
50. *rank*, strong-smelling. *guilty*, harmful, poisonous, a translation of Horace's phrase (*Epodes* III, 3) *cicutis allium nocentius*.
51. *stronger*, in scent and flavor.

Page 577.

SCOTT — MARMION

16. *Tantallon's towers*. Tantallon Castle on the coast of Haddingtonshire, Scotland.

Page 578.

82. *Save Gawain*. Gawain Douglas (c. 1474–1522), poet, scholar, and translator of Virgil's *Æneid*.
107. *Old Bell-the-Cat*. A phrase applied to persons of acknowledged intrepidity. From the fable of the mice and the cat.

Page 579.

194. *The Till by Twisel Bridge*. On the evening previous to the memorable battle of Flodden, Surrey's headquarters were at Barmorewood, and King James held an inaccessible position on the ridge of Flodden-hill, one of the last and lowest eminences detached from the ridge of Cheviot. The Till, a deep and slow river, winded between the armies. On the morning of the 9th September, 1513, Surrey marched in a northwesterly direction, and crossed the Till, with his van and artillery, at Twisel-bridge, nigh where that river joins the Tweed, his rearguard column passing about a mile higher, by a ford. This movement had the double effect of placing his army between King James and his supplies from Scotland and of striking the Scottish monarch with surprise, as he seems to have relied on the depth of the river in his front. But as the passage, both over the bridge and through the ford, was difficult and slow, it seems possible that the English might have been attacked to great advantage, while struggling with these natural obstacles. (Scott).

Page 580.
364. *gilded spurs.* The rewards of victory.

Page 583.
618. *vaward,* vanguard.
620–625. *O for a blast . . . Roncesvalles.* A reference to the battle of Roncesvalles in the Pyrenees Mountains, where the rearguard of Charlemagne's army, commanded by his nephew Roland, was surprised and defeated by the Saracens. Roland had a magic horn with which he might have summoned Charlemagne to his aid. *Fontarabia* was a Spanish town near Roncesvalles. *Oliver* was one of Charlemagne's renowned knights.
639. *Tweed.* See Map.
705. *Beseem'd,* became, suited.
711. *Lichfield's lofty pile,* Lichfield Cathedral. See Map.
718. *Saint Chad,* patron saint of Lichfield.

Page 584.
719. *guerdon,* reward.
721. *couchant,* reclining.
725. *feats,* deeds, achievements. *blazed,* blazoned, set forth.
732. *wede away.* The reference is to an old ballad.

Page 585.

BYRON — SONNET ON CHILLON

13. *Bonnivard.* François de Bonnivard (1496–1570) was held for six years as a political prisoner in the dungeon of the Castle of Chillon, near Geneva. Byron's well-known tale, *The Prisoner of Chillon,* presents an imaginary history of his confinement.

Page 586.

CHILDE HAROLD, CANTO III

39. *Morat.* The Swiss gained a decisive victory at the village of Morat in 1476.
42. *Burgundy.* Charles the Bold, Duke of Burgundy.
44. *the Stygian coast,* etc. An allusion to the Greek superstition that the shades of unburied men could not pass the river Styx which bounded Hades.
46. *Waterloo.* The Battle of Waterloo which ended the military career of Napoleon was fought June 18, 1815. It is described in an earlier section of this canto. *Cannæ.* A battle in which Hannibal defeated the Roman army, 216 B. C.
47. *Marathon.* The Greeks defeated the Persians on the plains of Marathon, 490 B. C.
54. *Draconic.* Because of its free use of the death penalty, the code of Draco, an Athenian law-giver of the seventh century, is proverbially said to have been written in blood.
63. *Adventicum.* The Roman name for Avenches, the ancient capital of Helvetia, or Switzerland.
65. *Julia.* This passage is based upon the epitaph of Julia Alpinula 'Deæ Aventiæ Sacerdos [Priestess of the goddess Aventia]' now known to be a modern forgery.
80. *like yonder Alpine snow.* Byron records that Mont Blanc was visible in the distance.
82. *Lake Leman.* Lake Geneva, the largest lake in Switzerland.

Page 587.
163. *Rousseau.* Jean Jacques Rousseau (1712–1778), a Swiss-French philosopher of brilliant though morbid originality whose writings are held to have been a strong influence in precipitating the French Revolution.
181. *Julie.* The heroine of Rousseau's *New Héloïse* (1761).
193. *the kind.* Civilized man.

Page 588.
200. *Pythian's mystic cave.* The prophetess of the Delphic oracle was called 'The Pythia'; while the god she served was known as the Pythian Apollo.
274. *Jura.* A mountain chain in France and Switzerland, visible from Geneva.
286. *Cytherea's zone.* The zone or girdle of the Cytherean Aphrodite, or Venus.

Page 589.
361. *Clarens.* A village on Lake Leman celebrated in Rousseau's *New Héloïse* and in his *Confessions.*

Page 590.
410. *Love his Psyche's zone,* etc. An allusion to the legend of Cupid and Psyche.
420. *Titan-like.* The Titans piled the hills on each other, attempting to ascend the sky, in their war with Zeus.
424. *The one.* Voltaire.
429. *Proteus.* The son of Oceanus who could assume any shape at will.
433. *The other.* Gibbon. See p. 465.

Page 591.

CHILDE HAROLD, CANTO IV

10. *Niobe.* According to the Greek myth Niobe brought upon her children the wrath of Artemis and Apollo, by boasting over their mother Leto who had only those two.
14. *The Scipio's tomb.* A group of tombs on the Appian Way is called 'The tombs of the Scipios.' The most famous Roman generals of this name flourished at the beginning of the second century B. C.
39. *when Brutus,* etc. An allusion to the assassination of Julius Cæsar.
41. *Tully's voice.* The oratory of Cicero.
42. *Livy's pictured page.* Titus Livius (B. C. 59–17 A. D.). The greatest Roman historian.
47. *Sylla.* Lucius Cornelius Sulla (c. 138–78 B. C.). Famous for his wholesale proscription of Roman citizens.

Page 592.
88. *Nemesis.* The Greek personification of fortune and hence retribution.
89. *Pompey.* Gnæus Pompeius Magnus (106–48 B. C.).
92. *She-wolf.* Allusion to a bronze group which is supposed to represent Romulus and Remus, the founders of Rome, suckled by a wolf.
107. *Save one vain man.* Napoleon, at the time this was written, a prisoner on the island of St. Helena.
116. *Alcides with the distaff.* Hercules, in expiation of the murder of Iphitus, sold himself for three years to Omphale, queen of Lydia. During this time according to some poets he sat among women and spun wool.
135. *Renew thy rainbow, God!* Compare Gen. ix, 13–17.
166. *Sprung forth a Pallas.* The goddess of wisdom sprang, full-armed, from the brain of Jove.
173. *Saturnalia.* A Roman feast in honor of Saturn in which great license was customary.

Page 593.
211. *Cornelia's,* etc. Celebrated Roman matron, daughter of Scipio Africanus the Elder.
212. *Egypt's graceful queen.* Cleopatra.
252. *There woos no home.* Allusion to his separation from his wife and exile from England.
258. *the Palatine.* One of the 'seven hills' of Rome. It is adjacent to the site of the Forum, and was a favorite place of residence with the Roman emperors.

Page 594.
294. *Titus or Trajan's.* It is now believed to have been erected by Trajan, 113 A. D.
304. *A mere Alexander.* A mere military conqueror.
337. *Ruins of years, though few.* Byron was thirty.
347. *Orestes,* the son of Agamemnon and Clytemnestra and brother of Electra. After the return of Agamemnon from the Trojan Wars he was murdered by Clytemnestra and her paramour, Ægisthus. They were in turn slain by Orestes and he was tormented by the Furies for the killing of his mother. The *Agamemnon* and *The Furies* of Æschylus, the

NOTES TO BYRON: VISION OF JUDGMENT; DON JUAN 1053

Page 594.

Electra and the *Orestes* of Euripides, and the *Electra* of Sophocles, are based upon this legend.

353. *For my ancestral faults.* The parallel with Orestes is here continued.

Page 595.

384. *Janus.* The Roman guardian of doors and gateways was represented with two faces.

415. *the Gladiator.* The statue in the Museum of the Capitol upon which this passage is based is now usually called 'The Dying Gaul,' not as formerly, 'The Dying Gladiator,' and is believed to represent a warrior wounded in battle.

429. *their Dacian mother.* The region north of the Lower Danube was conquered by Trajan and made into the Roman province of Dacia, 101 A. D.

432. *Arise! ye Goths*, etc. Alludes to the taking of Rome by the Barbarians, in 410 A. D.

456. *the bald first Cæsar's head.* 'Suetonius informs us that Julius Cæsar was particularly gratified by that decree of the senate which enabled him to wear a wreath of laurel on all occasions. He was anxious, not to show that he was the conqueror of the world, but to hide that he was bald.' (Byron.) This stroke of bold bathos is very characteristic of Byron and anticipates his manner in *Don Juan*.

Page 596.

463. *Thus spake the pilgrims.* Byron refers in his note on this passage to Gibbon's *Decline and Fall*.

THE VISION OF JUDGMENT

This poem is an indignant parody upon a poem of the same title in which Robert Southey, poet laureate, had celebrated the passing of George III. Byron's anger was augmented by the fact that Southey had arraigned him in his preface as the chief of a 'Satanic School' of English poetry. Southey had been a strong radical in his earlier years, but had now become a complacent servant of the government.

36. *A German will.* Probably this means only obscure, difficult. Byron's jibes at Germans were frequent.

37. *his son*, George IV.

Page 597.

160. *Captain Parry's crew.* A narrative of Parry's arctic expedition had appeared in 1821.

168. *Johanna Southcote.* A fanatical Englishwoman of low birth who created a popular religious sensation at the beginning of the nineteenth century. Died 1814.

Page 598.

200. *champ clos*, closed field, lists.

Page 599.

281. *He came to his scepter young; he leaves it old.* George III reigned from 1760 to 1820.

308. *Apicius' board.* Marcus Gabius Apicius, the most celebrated Roman epicure, flourished in the time of Augustus and Tiberius.

327. *The foe to Catholic participation.* The political disability of Catholics was not removed until 1829.

DON JUAN, CANTO III

2. *Sappho.* Greek poetess (c. 600 B. C.).

4. *Delos.* An island of the Cyclades, Apollo's birthplace, hence Apollo. *Phœbus.* One of the epithets of Apollo, god of poetry.

7. *Scian.* The island of Scio was a home of epic poetry and laid claim to Homer. *the Teian muse.* Anacreon. See below, 63-64.

13. *Marathon.* See note to p. 586, line 47.

20. *Salamis.* An island off Attica, near which the Greeks won their decisive naval victory over the fleet of Xerxes, 480 B. C.

Page 600.

55. *Pyrrhic dance.* An ancient martial dance in quick time.

63-64. *Anacreon's song . . . Polycrates.* From his birthplace, Teos in Asia Minor, Anacreon went to the court of the tyrant, Polycrates (d. 522 B. C.), in the island of Samos. His poetry celebrates the pleasures of love and wine.

67-69. *Chersonese . . . Miltiades.* Miltiades whom Peisistratus had appointed master of the Chersonesus in Crete was the leader to whom the Greeks owed much of their success in Marathon.

74. *Suli's rock.* Suli, a mountain district in Albania, was the home of a warlike race, Suliotes. They played an important part in the Greek rebellion with which Byron was later associated. *Parga's shore.* Parga was an Albanian sea-port.

76. *Doric.* One of the divisions of the Greek race. Here, Spartan.

78. *Heracleidan blood.* Race of Hercules, Spartans.

79. *Franks.* Western Europeans generally.

91. *Sunium's marbled steep.* Cape Colonna with its ruins of a temple of Athene.

99. *Orpheus.* The earliest poet in Greek legend.

Page 601.

127. *the great Marlborough's skill.* He won the battle of Blenheim, 1704.

128. *Life by Archdeacon Coxe.* Like many of Byron's allusions, this one is strictly 'up-to-date.' The Memoirs of Marlborough appeared in 1818-19.

133. *his life . . . Johnson's way*, etc. Dr. Johnson's life of Milton in his *Lives of the English Poets* (1779-80).

138. *Bacon's bribes.* See p. 233.

139. *Titus' Youth.* The reign of Titus Vespasianus (A. D. 79-81) was popular; but his youth, though brilliant, had been marked by luxury and indiscretion. *Cæsar's earliest acts.* The youth of Julius Cæsar is said to have been voluptuous.

140. *Doctor Currie.* James Currie (1756-1805), a Scottish physician, edited the first collective edition of Burns's works (1800).

146. *Pantisocracy.* See the sketch of Coleridge, p. 542.

148. *peddler poems.* A hit at the humbleness of Wordsworth's characters.

152. *Milliners of Bath.* The implication is false. The Misses Fricker were respectable young women of Bristol, although they had lived for a time at Bath.

154. *Botany Bay.* An inlet near Sydney, Australia, the seat of a colony of transported criminals.

198. *Boccaccio's lore.* The reference is to the eighth tale of the fifth day of the *Decameron*.

199. *Dryden's lay.* Dryden's *Theodore and Honoria*, is an adaptation of the above-mentioned tale by Boccaccio.

205. *Onesti's line.* Boccaccio's Nastagio degli Onesti is Dryden's Theodore.

Page 602.

239. *Cantabs.* Those associated with the University of Cambridge.

DON JUAN, CANTO IV

21. *'falls into the yellow leaf.'* From *Macbeth* V, 3, 23.

55. *Apollo plucks me by the ear.* Compare *Lycidas*, 'and touched my trembling ears,' above, p. 283, line 77.

Page 604.

249. *Cognac*, a French brandy.

250. *Naiad*, a water nymph. *Phlegethontic rill*, playful allusion to Phlegethon, the river of fire in Hades.

Page 605.

263. *Fez*, a province of Morocco.

288. *Simoom*, a hot wind of the desert.

317. *Laocoön's . . . throes*, a group of sculpture in the Vatican, Rome.

318. *Gladiator.* See page 595, line 415, note.

Page 609.

SHELLEY — PROMETHEUS UNBOUND, ACT IV

The conception of *Prometheus Unbound* was suggested to Shelley by the *Prometheus Bound* of Æschylus. The Titan, Prometheus, having offended Zeus by his gift to man of fire and the arts, is bound to a rocky mountainside and subjected to appalling tortures. Nothing can subdue his will and he disappears at the end in a tremendous storm. Shelley represents Prometheus, after the lapse of ages, adding love to power and endurance; whereupon he is released by Hercules and united with Asia, who typifies the generative principle in nature. Act IV is purely lyrical and portrays the elements rejoicing in the overthrow of Jupiter, the evil potency which has hitherto ruled the universe and the bulk of humanity.

Page 611.

197. *Æolian*, wind-born. From Æolus, god of winds.

Page 612.

291. *valueless*, priceless, beyond valuation.

Page 613.

348. *Sceptered curse.* Jupiter.

Page 614.

426. *Dædal*, cunningly contriving or creative.

Page 615.

483. *Mœnad*, Bacchante.
484. *Agavë*, the daughter of Cadmus.
485. *Cadmeian*, Theban; from Cadmus, the mythical founder of Thebes. A world of oriental mystery envelops the Cadmeian legend.
521. *A mighty Power.* Demogorgon, who seems to represent, in Shelley's mythology, the ultimate force which presides over the destinies of the universe.

Page 616.

ODE TO THE WEST WIND

21. *Mœnad.* See note to page 615, line 483 above.
32. *pumice*, a light, porous, volcanic substance.
32. *Baiæ's bay.* Modern Baja, in Campania, Italy. Baiæ was a favorite resort of the luxurious in the days of the Early Empire.

Page 617.

THE INDIAN SERENADE

11. *Champak.* An Indian tree, planted about temples. The perfume of its flowers is often celebrated in Hindu poetry.

Page 618.

THE CLOUD

81. *cenotaph.* An honorary tomb to a person whose remains are lost, or who is buried elsewhere.

Page 619.

ADONAIS

This elegy was written in memory of John Keats, for whom, see p. 627.
12. *Urania.* The celestial Muse. She is the Heavenly Muse of Milton's *Paradise Lost.* Shelley's conception has been influenced by that of Milton.

Page 620.

55. *that high Capital.* Rome.

Page 621.

127–35. *Lost Echo*, etc. Narcissus, insensible to love, was caused to fall in love with his own image and pined away until he was turned into a flower. The nymph Echo, disappointed of his love, died from grief.
140. *to Phœbus was not Hyacinth.* Apollo fell in love with a beautiful youth, Hyacinthus, who died and was turned into a flower.
141. *Narcissus.* See above, 127–35, note.
160. *brere*, brier.

Page 622.

238. *the unpastured dragon.* The selfish and greedy world.
244. *The herded wolves.* The banded critics who execute the will of successful politicians.
250. *The Pythian of the age.* Lord Byron in his *English Bards and Scotch Reviewers*, by allusion to the Pythian Apollo, slayer of the Python.
264. *The Pilgrim of Eternity.* The author of *Childe Harold's Pilgrimage*, Byron.
268. *Ierne*, Ireland. Thomas Moore is meant.
271. *Midst others of less note*, etc. Shelley himself.
276. *Actæon-like.* According to a Greek myth the hunter Actæon, having seen Diana bathing, was changed into a stag and destroyed by his own hounds.
280. *pardlike*, leopardlike.

Page 623.

307–15. *What softer voice*, etc. Keats's nearest friend among literary men, Leigh Hunt.
325. *Live thou, whose infamy*, etc. The unknown critic who had assailed Keats in the *Quarterly Review.*

Page 624.

399. *Chatterton.* See p. 415.
401. *Sidney.* Sir Philip Sidney (1554–86). See p. 144.
404. *Lucan.* Marcus Annæus Lucanus (39–65 A. D.), Roman poet. He committed suicide to prevent his execution for joining a conspiracy against Nero.
439. *A slope of green access.* The Protestant burial ground at Rome, where Keats was buried, and where Shelley's ashes were placed a few months after these lines were written.

Page 625.

WITH A GUITAR, TO JANE

1. *Ariel to Miranda.* The reference is, of course, to the characters in Shakespeare's *Tempest.* Ariel is Shelley, and Miranda is Mrs. Williams.
10. *Prince Ferdinand.* Edward Williams, a young English officer with whom Shelley was intimate towards the end of his life. He and Shelley were drowned together. See Life, p. 607.

Page 627.

KEATS — KEEN, FITFUL GUSTS ARE WHISPERING HERE AND THERE

10. *a little cottage.* Leigh Hunt's home at Hampstead Heath. Hunt was deeply interested in Italian poetry.
12. *gentle Lycid drowned.* For Milton's Lycidas, see p. 282.
13. *Laura.* The lady to whom Petrarch addressed his sonnets. According to one theory she was the wife of Hugues de Sade and mother of eleven children.
14. *Petrarch gloriously crowned.* Francesco Petrarca (1304–1374). He was crowned poet laureate, at Rome, in 1341.

ON FIRST LOOKING INTO CHAPMAN'S HOMER

4. *Apollo.* As patron of poetry.
8. *Chapman.* George Chapman published his translation of Homer in instalments between 1598 and 1616. It is still prized as one of the greatest of English poetical translations.
11. *stout Cortez.* Not Cortez, but Balboa actually discovered the Pacific Ocean.
14. *Darien.* The mountain from which Balboa first sighted the Pacific was nearly a month's journey from his base at Darien.

Page 628.

ENDYMION, BOOK I

35. *the story of Endymion.* The most famous English treatment of the legend before Keats was that of John Lyly in his drama, *Endymion* (1579).

THE EVE OF ST. AGNES

1. *St. Agnes' Eve*, January 20, in popular opinion, apt to be the coldest night of the year. St. Agnes suffered mar-

Page 628.

tyrdom under Diocletian. The chief superstitions connected with the Eve of St. Agnes are given in the course of the poem, especially ll. 47–55.

Page 630.

171. *Since Merlin paid his Demon.* According to the legend with which Keats was familiar, Merlin had been begotten by demons. He was beguiled by an enchantress who employed one of his own spells to imprison him forever in a tree in the forest of Broceliande. Immediately afterward, a terrific tempest swept the forest. The legend forms the basis of Tennyson's *Merlin and Vivien* in *The Idylls of the King*.

241. *missal where swart Paynims pray.* A prayer-book bearing upon its margin pictures of converted heathen in the act of prayer. Possibly it means a missal protected carefully in a heathen land.

Page 631.

269. *Fez*, a province of Morocco.
270. *Samarcand.* A city in Turkestan, more important in the middle ages than now. It was the capital of the conqueror Tamerlane. *cedared Lebanon.* A mountain range in Syria, famed from remote antiquity for its cedars.
292. *In Provence called*, 'La belle dame sans mercy.' This is the title of a poem by Alain Chartier, a translation of which Keats had seen in a volume of Chaucer. The ascription of it to Provence is fanciful. The same words suggested to Keats the poem of this title, p. 639.

Page 632.

349. *Rhenish*, wine from the vineyards of the Rhine. *mead*, a liquor made by fermenting honey, much prized by the ancient Teutons.

ROBIN HOOD

For the ballads of Robin Hood, see above, pp. 105–8.

Page 633.

LINES ON THE MERMAID TAVERN

4. *the Mermaid Tavern.* A favorite resort of Elizabethan dramatists, Shakespeare, Ben Jonson, Beaumont, etc.
6. *Canary wine.* Wine made in the Canary islands. It was the 'sack' of Shakespeare and his contemporaries.

ODE ON A GRECIAN URN

7. *Tempe*, the beautiful vale of Tempe in Thessaly.
7. *Arcady*, Arcadia, celebrated in pastoral poetry as the home of a carefree shepherd life.

Page 634.

41. *brede*, embroidery. Strictly, braid.

ODE TO A NIGHTINGALE

4. *Lethe-wards.* Towards the river of oblivion.
7. *Dryad*, a tree nymph.
13. *Flora*, goddess of the flowers and the spring.
14. *Provençal song.* Medieval lyric began in Provence.
16. *Hippocrene*, the Muses' fountain on Mount Helicon.
32. *Bacchus and his pards.* The leopard or, more strictly, the panther, was associated with the god of wine. He was sometimes represented in a chariot drawn by leopards.
37. *Fays*, fairies.
66. *Ruth.* See Ruth ii.

Page 635.

ODE ON MELANCHOLY

1. *Lethe.* The river of oblivion, in Hades.
4. *Proserpine.* Queen of the infernal regions.
7. *Psyche*, the soul. Her symbol was the butterfly.

HYPERION

Of the design of this poem Keats's friend, Woodhouse, wrote in his annotated copy: 'The poem, if completed,

Page 635.

would have treated of the dethronement of Hyperion, the former god of the sun, by Apollo — and incidentally of those of Oceanus by Neptune, of Saturn by Jupiter, etc., and of the war of the Giants for Saturn's reëstablishment — with other events, of which we have but very dark hints in the mythological poets of Greece and Rome.'

4. *Saturn*, an Italic deity, supposed to have ruled in the golden age; he was identified with the Greek Cronus, father and predecessor of Zeus.
23. *there came one.* Thea, sister of Hyperion, one of the female Titans.

Page 636.

30. *Ixion's wheel.* For an offense to Zeus, he was fastened to an eternally revolving wheel in Hades.
31. *Memphian sphinx.* A purely hypothetical sphinx. Memphis was an early capital of Egypt.

Page 637.

147. *The rebel three.* Jupiter, Neptune, and Apollo.
166. *Blazing Hyperion.* Hyperion was the pre-Olympian god of the sun. He was supplanted by Apollo.
181. *Aurorian.* Of Aurora, goddess of the dawn.

Page 638.

246. *Tellus*, the earth goddess.
274. *broad-belting colure.* The colures are the two great circles which belt the celestial sphere, intersecting each other at right angles at the poles of the equator.
307. *Cœlus*, god of the firmament.

Page 639.

LA BELLE DAME SANS MERCI

See note to page 631, line 292 above.

ON SEEING THE ELGIN MARBLES

Between 1801 and 1803 the Earl of Elgin brought from Athens and deposited in the British Museum a superb collection of Greek sculptures. Keats derived not a little of his sympathy with Greek conceptions of beauty from the study of these antiquities.

Page 640.

TO CHATTERTON

8, *amate*, subdue destroy.

BRIGHT STAR! WOULD I WERE STEADFAST AS THOU ART

This is believed to have been the last poem written by Keats. It was composed on shipboard just before his departure for Italy and written across a blank page of Shakespeare's poems.

4. *eremite*, hermit.

Page 641.

OTHER POETS OF THE ROMANTIC REVIVAL
ROBERT SOUTHEY
THE BATTLE OF BLENHEIM

Page 642.

56. *Prince Eugene.* François Eugene de Savoie-Carignan (1663–1736), a distinguished Austrian general, in alliance with Marlborough defeated the French and Bavarians at Blenheim, Aug. 13, 1704.

WALTER SAVAGE LANDOR — ROSE AYLMER

The subject of this poem was a beautiful Welsh girl who had died in Italy. She was of an ancient and titled family; hence, 'the sceptred race.'

PAST RUINED ILION

1. *Ilion*, Troy.
2. *Alcestis*, the heroine of Euripides' drama of that name.

Page 642.

THE DEATH OF ARTEMIDORA

11. *Iris stood over her dark hair.* Iris the messenger of the gods was supposed to loosen the hair of dying persons and, until she did so, their spirits were unable to depart.

DIRCE

1. *Stygian*, of the river Styx; here, destined for Hades.
3. *Charon.* The ferryman of the river Styx.

ON LUCRETIA BORGIA'S HAIR

Lucretia Borgia (1480–1519), Duchess of Ferrara was famed for beauty, wit, and wickedness.

MEMORY AND PRIDE

3. *Ianthë*, Sophia Jane Swift, afterwards Countess de Molandé, Landor's early 'flame' and life-long friend. Many of his lyrics of gallantry were addressed to her.

Page 643.

TO ROBERT BROWNING

10–14. *But warmer climes*, etc. Browning had just married Elizabeth Barrett and left England for Italy.

TO AGE

3. *The Fates . . . shears.* Compare p. 283, line 75, and note.

THOMAS CAMPBELL
YE MARINERS OF ENGLAND

15. *Blake.* Robert Blake, the famous admiral of the Commonwealth, died at sea, 1657. *Nelson fell.* Killed in action at Trafalgar in 1805. This reference was a later addition by the poet. The version of 1801 read: 'Where Blake (the Boast of Freedom) fell.' For the solution of this difficulty we are indebted to Professor G. R. Elliott.

Page 644.

THOMAS MOORE
THE HARP THAT ONCE THROUGH TARA'S HALLS

Tara, the ancient capital of one branch of the Irish race, is frequently named in early Irish poetry.

LEIGH HUNT — RONDEAU

The Jenny of this poem is Jane Welsh Carlyle, wife of Thomas Carlyle. The incident occurred in 1838.

Page 646.

JOHN KEBLE — UNITED STATES

1. This poem had been preceded in the *Lyra Apostolica* by John Henry Newman's similar apostrophe to England, beginning 'Tyre of the West.'
23. *Tyre*, the great trading center of ancient Phenicia, was constantly execrated by the Hebrew prophets for its worldliness and commercial prosperity. *Salem*, Jerusalem.

Page 649.

PRAED — THE BELLE OF THE BALL-ROOM

31. *Locke.* John Locke (1632–1704), author of *Essay Concerning Human Understanding*, etc.
32. *Little.* A pseudonym of Thomas Moore.
61. *Handel.* Georg Friederich Händel lived for a long time in London and died there in 1759. His compositions were popular in England.
62. *the Catalani.* Angelica Catalani, an Italian singer.
70. *Fierce odes*, etc. Probably an allusion to Coleridge's *Fire, Famine, and Slaughter*.
71. *Prince Leboo.* Jean Louis Joseph Lebeau (b. 1794) was a distinguished Belgian diplomat who carried on important negotiations in England, 1830–31.

Page 650.

A LETTER OF ADVICE

67. *the vapors*, a 'Queen Anne' term for the blues.
71. *Werther.* Goethe's sentimental novel, *The Sorrows of Werther*.
73. *The City.* The business district of London.

Page 650.

WILLIAM BARNES — BLACKMWORE MAIDENS

The peculiarities of the spelling are intended to suggest the Dorsetshire pronunciation.
4. *clote*, waterlily.

Page 651.

7. *bricken tuns.* Brick-built vats.
37. *tweil*, toil.

Page 653.

WILLIAM HAZLITT
ON GOING ON A JOURNEY

Published first in the *New Monthly Magazine*, in 1822. Reprinted in the second edition of Hazlitt's *Table Talk* (1824).

a. 8. *The fields . . . his book*, from Robert Bloomfield's *The Farmer's Boy* (1800).
20. *a friend . . . is sweet*, from *Retirement*, by William Cowper (1731–1800).
b. 6. *May plume her feathers*, etc., Milton's *Comus*, ll. 378–80.
12. *Tilbury*, a gig, or two-wheeled open carriage.

Page 654.

a. 2. *Sunken wrack . . . treasuries*, Shakespeare's *Henry V*, I, ii, 165.
10. *Leave, oh . . . repose*, from Thomas Gray's *The Descent of Odin*.
13. *very stuff of the conscience*, *Othello*, I, ii, 2.
29. *Out upon . . . fellowship*, Shakespeare's *1 Henry IV*, I, iii, 208.
33. *Mr. Cobbett's.* William Cobbett (1763–1835), essayist and politician.
40. *says Sterne.* The quotation is taken, somewhat inaccurately, from the *Sermons* of Laurence Sterne (1713–68).
b. 35. *give it . . . tongue*, Shakespeare's *Hamlet*, I, ii, 250.
36. *friend C——*, Coleridge.
40. *Pindaric ode.* For an example see Gray's *The Progress of Poesy* above, p. 402. *He talked . . . singing.* See Beaumont and Fletcher's *Philaster*, V, v, 165–6.
46. *All-Foxden*, in Somersetshire, where Wordsworth was living in 1797. Coleridge lived in the neighboring village of Nether Stowey. See Map.
47. *That fine madness . . . poets had.* See ll. 105–10 of *To Henry Reynolds — of Poets and Poesie* by Michael Drayton (1563–1631).
51. *Here be woods*, etc., John Fletcher's *The Faithful Shepherdess*, I, iii, 26 ff.

Page 655.

a. 5. *Endymion*, the shepherd boy who was beloved of Phœbe, the moon-goddess, on Mt. Latmor in Asia Minor. See Keats's *Endymion*, above, p. 628.
21. *L——*, Charles Lamb.
36. *take one's ease*, etc. See *1 Henry IV*, III, iii, 92–3.
45. *The cups . . . inebriate.* See Cowper's *The Task*, IV, 39–40.
49. *Sancho.* For the incident see Cervantes' *Don Quixote*, Part II, Chap. lix. Sancho Panza was Don Quixote's squire.
53. *Shandean*, a reference to the random and whimsical reflections of Walter Shandy in Sterne's novel, *Tristram Shandy*.
b. 10. *West Riding.* Yorkshire is subdivided into three parts called the North, East, and West Ridings.
26. *unhoused free . . . and confine*, *Othello* I, ii, 26–7.
29. *lord of . . . a name*, Dryden's *To My Honoured Kinsman, John Dryden*, l. 18.
53. *Witham-common, St. Neot's*, towns within twenty or thirty miles from London. See Map.

Page 656.

a. 3. *Gribelin's engravings of the Cartoons.* A cartoon is a full-sized drawing or painting prepared for re-

NOTES TO HAZLITT; DE QUINCEY: CONFESSIONS – PP. 656–661

Page 656.

production in tapestry, mosaic, fresco, or the like. Hazlitt refers to cartoons by Raphael now in the Victoria and Albert Museum, London. From these Gribelin made some engravings in 1707.

a. 6. *Westall's*, Richard Westall (1765–1836) was a prominent English historical painter.
10. *Severn*, a river in the west of England. See Map.
14. *Paul and Virginia*, a romantic tale by Bernardin de Saint Pierre published in 1788.
15. *Bridgewater*, a town in Somersetshire. See Map.
18. *Madame D'Arblay's Camilla*, a novel published in 1795.
20. *New Eloise*, *La Nouvelle Héloïse* (1761), written in the form of letters by Jean Jacques Rousseau. The reference here is to Letter No. 17 of Part IV. *Llangollen*, a town in northern Wales. See Map.
24. *Jura, Pays de Vaud*. The Jura mountains are in the Swiss canton of Vaud.
25. *bon bouche*, choice morsel. The correct expression is *bonne bouche*.
29. *Chirk, Wrexham*, towns in northern Wales. See Map.
33. *green upland . . . of flocks*, from Coleridge's *Ode on the Departing Year*.
35. *river Dee*, flows through Chester into the Irish Sea. See Map.
37. *glittered green with sunny showers*, from Coleridge's *Ode on the Departing Year*.
48. *faded into the light of common day*, Wordsworth's *Ode on Intimations of Immortality*, l. 76. See above, p. 538.
51. *The beautiful . . . returns not*, Coleridge's translation (1799–1800) of Schiller's *Death of Wallenstein*, V, i, 68.
b. 9–10. *Yet will I turn*, etc. In this sentence are combined passages from Wordsworth's *Tintern Abbey*, ll. 56–8, and from *Revelation* xxi, 6; xxii, 1–2, 17.
40. *says Sir Fopling Flutter*, in Sir George Etherege's comedy, *The Man of Mode*, V, ii.
54. *China orange*, a term for the sweet orange.

Page 657.

a. 29–30. *Salisbury Plain, Stonehenge*. Near the town of Salisbury is Stonehenge, a group of prehistoric stones arranged in concentric circles.
35. *The mind is its own place*, Milton's *Paradise Lost*, I, 254.
39. *éclat*, ostentation. Hazlitt refers to his taking Charles and Mary Lamb on a visit to Oxford in 1810.
41. *With glistening . . . adorn'd*, *Paradise Lost*, III, 550.
45. *Bodleian*, the great library at Oxford, named after a benefactor, Sir Thomas Bodley.
46. *Blenheim*, the seat of the Duke of Marlborough, near Oxford.
47. *cicerone*, guide.
b. 16. *when I first set*, etc. Hazlitt went to Paris in 1802.
25. *the vine-covered . . . of France*, from a song by the English historian, William Roscoe (1753–1831).
33. *Bourbons*, the French royal house which reigned continuously from the sixteenth century until the French Revolution.
47. *Dr. Johnson remarked*. See Boswell's *Life*, under the year 1778.

Page 658.

DE QUINCEY
CONFESSIONS OF AN ENGLISH OPIUM EATER

The version of the 'Confessions' adopted in the text is that of the original issue of the *London Magazine* (1821), which has been generally preferred, both by the critics and the public, to the enlarged edition published by De Quincey in his collected works thirty-five years later. On account of his tendency to digression, De Quincey's second thoughts are sometimes less effective than his first. The additional details given in the later version have been used in the notes and are distinguished by quotation marks.

b. 8. *an affection of the stomach*. Opium is said to be a remedy for gastrodynia, or neuralgia of the stomach.

Page 659.

a. 11. *My father*. Thomas Quincey, merchant, of Manchester, d. July 18, 1793.
37. *'and a ripe and good one.'* See *Henry VIII*, IV, ii, 51–2. The master in question was a Mr. Morgan, of Bath Grammar School.
41. *a blockhead*. The master of Winkfield, a small private school.
44. *a respectable scholar*. Mr. Lawson, head of Manchester Grammar School.
46. —— *College*, Brasenose.
51. *Etonian*. Up to 1851 the curriculum at Eton was entirely classical.
b. 11. *Archididascalus*. Greek for head master.
46. *a woman of high rank*, Lady Carbery. 'A young woman some ten years older than myself, and who was remarkable for her intellectual pretensions as she was for her beauty and her benevolence.'
49. *five guineas*, twenty-five dollars.

Page 660.

a. 11. *of Dr. Johnson's*, at the end of the last article in his periodical, *The Idler*.
18. *I had not been happy*. The chief reasons of De Quincey's unhappiness at Manchester Grammar School were (1) the state of his health, the school hours not permitting him to take sufficient exercise; (2) his dislike of the head master; (3) the refusal of his guardian to allow him to go to Oxford, as explained above.
32. *valediction*, farewell.
46. *towers of* ——, the 'old church,' now the cathedral of the modern diocese of Manchester.
b. 15. *'pensive citadel.'* See Wordsworth's sonnet *Nuns fret not*, page 539, line 3, and note.
29. *eighteen years ago*, when De Quincey wrote the 'Confessions' about Christmas, 1820; really nineteen when they were published, the following September and October.
33. *lovely* ——. A portrait of an unknown lady, reputed in the school to be a copy from Vandyke (1598–1641).
41. —— *clock*, 'the old church clock.'

Page 661.

a. 13–14. See *Paradise Lost* II, 306–7, p. 297.
15. *Salisbury Plain*, in Wiltshire.
36. *contretemps*, mishap, unlucky accident.
38. *canorous*, resonant, ringing.
39. *the Seven Sleepers*, seven Christian youths of Ephesus, who took refuge in a cave from persecution, and, according to the legend, slept there for 230 years.
43. *étourderie*, heedless, giddy behaviour.
51. *Dr* ——. 'The head-master at that time was Mr. Charles Lawson. In former editions of this work I created him a doctor; my object being to evade too close an approach to the realities of the case, and consequently to personalities, which (though indifferent to myself) would have been in some cases displeasing to others.'
b. 4. *'with Providence my guide.'* *Paradise Lost*, closing lines:

'The world was all before them, where to choose
Their place of rest, and Providence their guide.
They, hand in hand, with wandering steps and slow,
Through Eden took their solitary way.'

Page 661.

b. 24. *lustrum*, period of five years.
43. νυχθήμερον, a night and a day.
47. *That moveth*. See Wordsworth's *Resolution and Independence*, p. 532, line 77.

Page 662.

a. 1. *Now, then, I was again happy*. This was in 1816, the year of De Quincey's marriage, which induced him to suddenly cut down from 8,000 to 1,000 drops his daily allowance of opium. 'Instantaneously, and as if by magic, the cloud of profoundest melancholy which rested upon my brain, like some black vapors that I have seen roll away from the summit of a mountain, drew off in one week.' De Quincey began to take opium in 1804 as a remedy for 'excruciating rheumatic pains of the head and face;' but he did not become a regular and confirmed opium eater till 1813, when he was attacked by 'a most appalling irritation of the stomach.' De Quincey made repeated efforts to free himself from thraldom to the drug, which brought on severe depression and made him at times incapable of mental exertion, but he never entirely succeeded.
6. *Kant*, Immanuel Kant (1724–1804), the founder of 'Transcendental' Philosophy.
22. *Malay*. There has been an inclination to regard this as a fictitious personage invented by De Quincey to give variety and color to his narrative; he himself protested that he had recorded the incident 'most faithfully.' He adds a note to the later edition: 'Between the sea-faring populations on the coast of Lancashire and the corresponding populations on the coast of Cumberland (such as Ravenglass, Whitehaven, Workington, Maryport, etc.) there was a slender current of interchange constantly going on, and especially in the days of press-gangs—in part by sea, but in part also by land.'
28. *a young girl*. 'This girl, Barbara Lewthwaite, was already at that time a person of some poetic distinction, being (unconsciously to herself) the chief speaker in a little pastoral poem of Wordsworth's. That she was really beautiful, and not merely so described by me for the sake of improving the picturesque effect, the reader will judge from this line in the poem, written perhaps ten years earlier, when Barbara might be six years old:—

'Twas little Barbara Lewthwaite, a child of beauty rare!'

De Quincey adds in an appendix that subsequently, when a young woman, she entered unconsciously into the composition of Wordsworth's Ode, *Intimations of Immortality from Recollections of Early Childhood*. Wordsworth, however, writing in 1843, when Barbara Lewthwaite was still living at Ambleside, says that she was not in fact the child whom he had seen and overheard as described in *The Pet Lamb*. Within a few months after the publication of the poem, it came to Barbara's knowledge, 'and alas! I had the mortification of hearing that she was very vain of being thus distinguished: and, in after-life, she used to say that she remembered the incident and what I said to her upon the occasion.'

b. 24. *Anastasius*, a novel published in 1819, and in 1821 'both of high reputation and of great influence amongst the leading circles of society.' Its hero was a Greek who ate opium, and it included a glossary of the Oriental terms used in the story.
26. *Mithridates*, King of Pontus, was said to be able to speak the twenty-two dialects of his kingdom. For this reason the German philologer Adelung gave this title to a universal dictionary of languages he published in 1806.

Page 663.

a. 16. '*a-muck*,' Malay *amoq*, 'rushing in a state of frenzy to the commission of indiscriminate murder.'
18. *intercalary*, interpolated, intervening. An intercalary day is one inserted to make the calendar agree with the solar year, as the 29th of February in leap year. *happiness*, i.e., opium.

b. 3. *didactically*, in the way of teaching, by direct instruction.
7. *elixir*, the philosopher's stone, which the alchemists imagined would confer perpetual youth.
11. *a cottage standing in a valley*. 'The cottage and valley concerned in this description were not imaginary: the valley was the lovely one, *in those days*, of Grasmere: and the cottage was occupied for more than twenty years by myself, as immediate successor, in the year 1809, to Wordsworth. Looking to the limitation here laid down—viz. *in those days*—the reader will inquire in what way *Time* can have affected the beauty of Grasmere. Do the Westmoreland valleys turn grey-headed? O reader! this is a painful memento for some of us! Thirty years ago, a gang of vandals (nameless, I thank heaven, to me), for the sake of building a mail coach road that never would be wanted, carried, at a cost of £3,000 to the defrauded parish, a horrid causeway of sheer granite masonry, for three-quarters of a mile, right through the loveliest succession of secret forest dells and shy recesses of the lake, margined by unrivalled ferns, amongst which was the *Osmunda regalis*. This sequestered angle of Grasmere is described by Wordsworth, as it unveiled itself on a September morning, in the exquisite poems in the "*Naming of Places*." From this also—viz. this spot of ground, and this magnificent crest (the *Osmunda*)—was suggested that unique line, the finest independent line through all the records of verse:

Or lady of the lake,
Sole-sitting by the shores of old romance.

Rightly, therefore, did I introduce this limitation. The Grasmere before and after this outrage were two different vales.'
21. *a witty author*, Coleridge in *The Devil's Thoughts*.

He saw a cottage with a double coach-house,
A cottage of gentility!
And the Devil did grin, for his darling sin
Is pride that apes humility.

49. *The Castle of Indolence*, by Thomson, Canto I, Stanza 43. See p. 396.
52. *a high latitude*, far north. Lord Dufferin's travels in Iceland are described in *Letters from High Latitudes*.

Page 664.

a. 3. '*particular*,' precise, exactly. De Quincey puts the word in quotation marks because this use of it is a Northern provincialism.
5. Mr.——, 'Anti-slavery Clarkson,' the author of a *History of the Abolition of the Slave Trade*.
13. *a Canadian winter*. De Quincey seems to have been in earnest in this preference. At one time he thought of retiring to the woods of Lower Canada to devote himself to philosophic studies, and he had even fixed upon the situation for a cottage and a considerable library seventeen miles below Quebec. He gives the following reasons for this choice: 'My object was simply profound solitude, such as cannot now be had in any part of Great Britain—with two accessory advantages, also peculiar to countries situated in the circumstances and under the climate of Canada: viz. the exalting presence in an under-consciousness of forests endless and silent, the everlasting sense of living amongst forms so ennobling and impressive, together with the pleasure attached to natural agencies, such as

Page 664.

frosts, more powerfully manifested than in English latitudes, and for a much longer period. I hope there is nothing fanciful in all this. It is certain that in England and in all moderate climates, we are too slightly reminded of nature or the forces of nature. Great heats or great colds (and in Canada there are both) or great hurricanes, as in the West Indian latitudes, recall us continually to the sense of a powerful presence, investing our path on every side: whereas in England it is possible to forget that we live amongst greater agencies than those of men and human institutions.'

a. 16. *fee-simple*, a legal phrase for absolute ownership.
19. *St. Thomas's day*, December 21.
20. *vernal*, spring
32-3. *bellum internecinum*, war to the death. Hanway wrote an *Essay on Tea* (1756), which Dr. Johnson reviewed and condemned, declaring himself 'a hardened and shameless tea-drinker, ... whose kettle has scarcely time to cool.' A lively controversy resulted. See Boswell's *Life of Johnson* (Macmillan's edition—Library of English Classics), I, pp. 224-5.
47. '*a double debt to pay*.' Goldsmith's *Deserted Village*. See page 419, ll. 229-30.

b. 15-16. *eternal à parte ante and à parte post*, from everlasting to everlasting, having no beginning and no end.
21-2. *Aurora ... Hebe*, beautiful Greek goddesses, the former the personification of Dawn, the latter of Youth.
22. *dear M——*, Margaret, De Quincey's wife.
31. '*little golden receptacle, etc.*,' quoted from the *Anastasius* mentioned above.
38. '*stately Pantheon*,' a London theatre, so described by Wordsworth, near which was the druggist's shop from which De Quincey first obtained opium, as described in an earlier passage in the 'Confessions' not included in our extracts.

Page 665.

MACAULAY—THE ROMANCE OF HISTORY

The article of which the latter part is here printed was professedly a review in the *Edinburgh*, May, 1828, of a new book by a popular writer of that day, Henry Neele, entitled, 'The Romance of History. England'; but this served Macaulay merely as an opportunity to set forth his own ideas as to how history should be written. He had stated the same opinions before in a review of Mitford's *History of Greece*, and he re-stated them in reviews of the historical works of Hallam and Mackintosh before he was able to put them into practice in his own *History of England from the Accession of James II*. In spite of his extraordinary aptitude for the undertaking, he carried out his scheme for only fifteen years of the century and a half for which the work was planned; no one man, even in a long life, could have executed the design with such a broad canvas and in such minute detail as Macaulay attempted. Much of the higher side of life was omitted, and many of his judgments have not stood the test of subsequent investigation. The modern historian aims at far greater accuracy as well as a more profound inquiry into causes; but no one has been more successful than Macaulay in writing a historical narrative of unfailing interest to the general reader.

b. 14. *Laud*, Archbishop of Canterbury, 1633-45, and the director of Charles I's ecclesiastical policy. Curiously enough, the very faults of which Macaulay here accuses other historians have since been urged against himself, and Laud is one of the instances cited. Professor Montague says: 'Macaulay, who regarded this period of English history in a peculiarly partisan spirit, uniformly wrote of Laud's personal character with a loathing, and of his abilities with a contempt, unbecoming the gravity of a historian.'

Page 666.

a. 3. *Herodotus*, 'the father of history' and the first important writer of Greek prose. Macaulay says of him earlier in this same article: 'Of the romantic historians Herodotus is the earliest and the best. His animation, his simple-hearted tenderness, his wonderful talent for description and dialogue, and the pure, sweet flow of his language, place him at the head of narrators. . . . He has written something better perhaps than the best history; but he has not written a good history; he is, from the first to the last chapter, an inventor.' Fuller knowledge has proved that Herodotus is much more accurate and trustworthy than Macaulay here makes out.
28. *Hume's History of England* was published in 1754-61 and still retained its popularity in 1825, as Macaulay admits in his essay on Milton, in which he says that Hume 'hated religion so much that he hated liberty for having been allied with religion, and has pleaded the cause of tyranny with the dexterity of an advocate, while affecting the impartiality of a judge.' This comment Professor Montague describes as 'mere childish petulance,' adding that 'Hume sympathized with the Stuarts because he was a Scotchman and distrusted popular government because he was a skeptic.' The fact is, as Professor Huxley points out in his essay on Hume, that Hume wrote history from the Tory point of view, Macaulay from that of the Whigs.
32. *obnoxious*, open, liable. *Gibbon* published his *Decline and Fall of the Roman Empire* in 1776-88. It has stood the test of time much better than Macaulay's own work and has still a very high reputation for impartiality and accuracy.
35. *Mitford*, who died the year before this criticism appeared, published his *History of Greece* in 1784-1818. Macaulay had reviewed it with some severity in 1824, with the object, to use his own words, of 'reducing an over-praised writer to his proper level.'
54. *Plutarch* (first century A. D.) wrote the Lives of 46 eminent Greeks and Romans, arranged in pairs so as to bring out contrasts of character and point moral and political lessons. Sir Thomas North's English version, made from Amyot's French translation of the Greek original, was the foundation of Shakespeare's Roman tragedies. *Thucydides*, the second great Greek historian (fifth century B. C.), wrote the history of the long struggle between Athens and Sparta which ended in the ruin of the former. Macaulay says earlier in this essay that 'Thucydides has surpassed all his rivals in the art of historical narration, in the art of producing an effect on the imagination, by skilful selection and disposition, without indulging in the license of invention.'

b. 6. *Calcutta . . . Bombay* both in India, but at opposite ends of it. So, it is said, English people coming to Montreal are charged with messages for friends in Vancouver.
7. *Rollin and Barthelemi*, French historians of the seventeenth and eighteenth centuries, who in Macaulay's time had not ceased to be read.
49-50. *make the worse appear the better reason*. Milton of Belial in *Paradise Lost*, II, 112-4. See p. 295.

Page 667.

a. 1. *the poet laureate*, Southey, who wrote excellent biographies of Nelson and Wesley, but no historical works of any value. His *Book of the Church*, Macaulay wrote a year or two later, 'contains some stories very prettily told; the rest is mere rubbish.' Southey was a copious writer of reviews and miscellaneous articles, in which he frequently attacks Lingard, who was a Roman Catholic. The latter's *History of England* (first edition 1819-25) at once became a standard work on account of its learning and insight; it is still held in high esteem.
2. *Brodie*, author of *A History of the British Empire from the Accession of Charles I to the Restoration* (1822).

Page 667.

In 1836 he was appointed Historiographer Royal for Scotland.

a. 5. *about to be reheard.* Macaulay no doubt refers to the *History of Greece* by George Grote, written with much more sympathy for democracy than Mitford's. It was not published till 1846–56, but the author began to collect materials as early as 1823.

11. *neglect the art of narration.* This was Macaulay's repeated complaint about the historians of his day; it was an art in which he himself excelled.

22. *the most frivolous and indolent.* This passage is an instance, not only of Macaulay's exaggeration of statement, but of his misconception of popular tastes. He writes in his review of Sir James Mackintosh:—'A history of England, written throughout in this manner, would be the most fascinating book in the language. It would be more in request at the circulating libraries than the last novel.' In his own History Macaulay went further than any one else towards justifying the claim he here puts forward; but he could not altogether succeed. The comparison with the historical novel, on which Macaulay so often insisted, is misleading, as Professor Montague points out. 'A novel and a history can never really be occupied with the same matter. Imaginative writing, whether in prose or verse, is always and above all concerned with the individual, and everything else is only accessory. History concerns itself with the great organized masses of men known as people or states and treats of individuals only in relation to such masses and the effect produced upon them by uncommon personal qualities.' Moreover, history deals with what actually happened, the historical novel with what might have happened.

38. *conventional decencies . . . of the French drama,* the rules of classical tragedy which forbid the introduction of comic or commonplace elements and the representation of acts of violence on the stage, all the murders, etc., being reported by messengers. The bane of the French drama, from the English point of view, has been rather the observance of the Unities of Time and Place, the restriction of the plot to one critical event, and the consequent exclusion of incident.

42. *too trivial for the majesty of history.* This is a favorite idea with Macaulay. In 1824 he wrote that the true historian 'will not think anything too trivial for the gravity of history which is not too trivial to promote or diminish the happiness of man.' In the opening of his History (1846) he says: 'I shall cheerfully bear the reproach of having descended below the dignity of history, if I can succeed in placing before the English of the nineteenth century a true picture of the life of their ancestors.'

44. *King of Spain,* Philip III, who was said to have died from a fever brought on by the excessive heat of a fire, which the courtiers refused to damp because it was contrary to etiquette, the nobleman whose office it was being absent. But Lafuente in his *History of Spain* says the story was a pure invention of the French Ambassador, Bassompierre.

54. *The knowledge of it is valuable,* etc. It is characteristic of Macaulay that he has no appreciation of knowledge for its own sake.

b. 4. *turnpike,* tollgate.

5. *Sir Matthew Mite,* the principal character in Foote's farce *The Nabob* (1772), described by Macaulay in his essay on Clive as 'an Anglo-Indian chief, dissolute, ungenerous, and tyrannical, ashamed of the humble friends of his youth, hating the aristocracy, yet childishly eager to be numbered among them, squandering his wealth on panders and flatterers, tricking out his chairmen with the most costly hot-house flowers, and astounding the ignorant with jargon about rupees, lacs, and jaghires. He uses the fortune he has made in India to bribe his way into Parliament, becomes a member of the Antiquarian Society, and commits scores of extravagant follies similar to that referred to in the text.'

b. 6. *Lord Clarendon,* Charles II's chief minister and author of the *History of the Great Rebellion.*

13. *Hampden,* Oliver Cromwell's cousin and the man on the Parliamentary side whom Macaulay most admired. In his essay, *John Hampden,* he describes him as 'the first of those great English commoners whose plain addition of Mister has, to our ears, a more majestic sound than the proudest of the feudal titles.'

18. *Vane* was 'a singular combination of the statesman and the mystic.' According to Clarendon 'he did at some time believe that he was the person deputed to reign over the saints upon earth for a thousand years.' He was at one time Governor of Massachusetts, and his statue adorns the entrance hall of the Boston Public Library. He was a leading member of the Long Parliament and after the Restoration was put to death as a traitor.

27. *Rupert* (Prince), nephew of Charles I and commander of the Royalist cavalry in the Civil War.

28. *Harrison and Fleetwood,* leaders on the Parliamentary side, who were famous for their religious zeal.

Page 668.

a. 3. *Bishop Watson* (1737–1816), a distinguished defender of revealed religion against Tom Paine and other skeptical writers.

14. *at the close of the Seven Years' War* (1763), when France gave up Canada to Great Britain and acknowledged British supremacy in India.

16. *American war* of Independence.

25. *late ministerial interregnum,* in 1827, on the death of Canning, when Goderich kept the ministry together for a few months, giving place in January, 1828, to a new government under Wellington and Peel.

Page 669.

a. 12. *Sir Walter Scott,* whose novels Macaulay praises in this and the following pages, is not now so highly esteemed as a historical authority for the customs and phraseology of the sixteenth and seventeenth centuries.

33. *Froissart* was the chronicler, as Chaucer was the poet, of fourteenth century chivalry. The Tabard Inn, in Southwark, is the scene of the opening of the *Canterbury Tales.*

38. *Legate,* the ambassador of the Pope.

40. *palmers,* strictly, pilgrims who had been to the Holy Land and were therefore entitled to carry a branch or leaf of palm, but often used of pilgrims generally, and especially of those who gave all their lives to pilgrimage.

41. *refectory,* dining-hall.

50. *villain* (Low Latin *villanus*), a medieval villager or serf, who was bound to the soil and subject to the lord of the manor.

b. 9. *Tacitus* is described by Macaulay earlier in this essay as unrivaled for the delineation of character and certainly the greatest of the Latin historians.

35. *keep,* the central tower or stronghold of a medieval castle.

37. *oriel,* a window built out so as to form a recess. It is one of the features of Elizabethan domestic architecture, of which Longleat and Burleigh were conspicuous examples. The houses of the nobility built at this time surpassed all that had been built before in comfort and magnificence and all that have been built since in beauty.

Page 670.

a. 10. *Fifth-monarchy-man,* one of those who in the seventeenth century believed that the second coming of Christ was immediately at hand, and that it was the duty of Christians to be prepared to assist in

Page 670.

establishing his reign by force, and in the meantime to repudiate all allegiance to any other government. The allusion is to the fifth kingdom foretold in Daniel ii, 44.

THE HISTORY OF ENGLAND

This short extract cannot give any adequate impression of the scope and methods of the great history, but it may be enough to suggest some idea of the way in which Macaulay carried out his conception of how history should be written.

b. 35. *Danby's administration.* 1674–9.

Page 671.

a. 16. *clown*, country bumpkin.
31–2. *Perrault* (1628–1703), a member of the French academy, the advocate of the superiority of modern literature against *Boileau*, who upheld the classics.
36. *Venice Preserved* (1682), a tragedy by Thomas Otway.
40. *Templars*, barristers or law students, of the inner or Middle Temple.
47. *Racine* (1660–1699).
48. *Bossu* (1631–1680).
b. 46–7. *Lord Mayor's show*, a magnificent allegorical procession through the streets of London made every year when the Lord Mayor assumes office. *Money-droppers*, coiners or distributors of false money. *cart's tail*, at which they were whipped through the city.

Page 672.

b. 37. *Thoresby* (1658–1725).
41. *Pepys* (1632–1703), the great diarist. See p. 318.

Page 673.

a. 17. *higgler*, a wandering dealer in poultry and dairy produce.
b. 23. *parochial*, levied on the parish, the smallest territorial division in England.
37. *turnpike acts*, acts of parliament establishing trusts for the maintenance of roads on which tolls were collected. The toll-gates or toll-bars were abolished about the middle of the nineteenth century.

Page 674.

a. 16. *seven pounds*, nearly $35.
17. *fifteen pence*, 30 cents.
b. 25. *Vanbrugh* (1666–1726), writer of witty and licentious comedy.

Page 678.

NEWMAN — THE IDEA OF A UNIVERSITY

This discourse is one of a series given before the University of Dublin and addressed primarily to Catholic educators.

Page 681.

a. 6. '*the world is all before it where to choose.*' *Paradise Lost*, XII, 646.
b. 23. *St. Thomas.* Thomas Aquinas, the famous schoolman of the thirteenth century.

Page 682.

a. 36. *Pompey's Pillar*, a shaft of the Corinthian order near Alexandria. Its traditional association with Pompey is no longer believed to have any foundation in fact.

Page 683.

a. 12. *the Peripatetic*, an epithet applied to the school of Aristotle, traditionally because his discussions were carried on while *walking about* in the Lyceum.
14. *the Stoic*, the school of Greek philosophy founded by Zeno, about 340–265 B. C.
15–17. *Felix qui potuit*, etc. Virgil's *Georgics* II, 490–92.
50. *the music of the spheres.* A proverbial phrase founded on the old belief that the celestial spheres were of crystal and made a harmonious sound as they revolved.

Page 683.

b. 27. *Salmasius.* A Dutch scholar, chiefly remembered by Englishmen for his controversy with Milton. *Burman.* François Burmann, Dutch theologian of the seventeenth century.
28. *Imperat aut servit* collecta pecunia cuique [a man's money is either his master or his servant]. Horace, *Ep.* 1, x, 48.
32. *Vis consili*, etc. Horace, *Odes* 3. iv, 65.
35. *Tarpeia.* According to legend, she betrayed the Roman citadel to the Sabines for promised treasure, but was crushed to death by the shields they threw upon her.
47. *Mosheim.* Johann Lorenz von Mosheim (1694–1755).
48. *Du Pin*, Louis Ellies (1657–1719), French ecclesiastical historian.

Page 685.

a. 51. *a so-called university*, etc. The University of London, a corporation for the giving of examinations and conferring of degrees had been founded in 1836.
b. 4–5. *the University of Oxford . . . some sixty years since* One may read in this connection Gibbon's account of Oxford, in his *Memoirs*.

Page 686.

a. 31. *genius loci.* Spirit of the place.
b. 52. '*tongues in the trees . . . brooks.*' Slightly inaccurate quotation of *As You Like It*, II, i, 16.

Page 687.

CARLYLE — THE FRENCH REVOLUTION

As has been noted in the biographical introduction, this was Carlyle's first attempt to present history as romance, with the poetry, color, and excitement which Scott had put into historical fiction. In the opinion of many critics, it remains his most successful effort in this kind.

a. 4. *Bastille*, an ancient fortress, used as a prison, which dominated the Suburb Saint-Antoine. In this suburb the working-class lived. To this prison many persons had been committed without trial under orders from the King (*lettres de cachet*). It was therefore, to the popular mind, a symbol of the iniquities and oppressions of monarchical government.
7. *Fourteenth*, of July, still celebrated in Paris as the National Festival, with a great military review and dancing in the streets.
8. *nodus*, knot or culmination—the height of the action as Aristotle defined it in his treatise on tragedy (*The Poetics*).
b. 7. *Charleville Boxes*, expected to contain arms, for when seized they were marked *Artillerie;* but when opened they were found to contain only 'rags, foul linen, candle-ends, and bits of wood.'
12–13. *whiffed with grapeshot*, dispersed by 'a whiff of grapeshot.'

Page 688.

a. 5. *Besenval's Camp.* Besenval commanded the foreign troops concentrated outside Paris by the royal party to overawe Paris and disperse the National Assembly. His headquarters were at the Hôtel des Invalides.
15. *Priam's curtains.* Priam was King of Troy. See Homer's *Iliad*.
23. *Camille Desmoulins*, lived 1760–94, a brilliant journalist whose pamphlets disseminated revolutionary doctrines.
26. *Palais Royal*, property of the Duke of Orleans. Its gardens, cafés, and arcades provided a meeting-place for those who resisted the revolution.
35. *Clerks of the Basoche.* The Basoche was the association of students and clerks connected with the Paris law-courts.

Page 688.

a. 40. *M. de Sombreuil*, governor of the Hôtel des Invalides.
42. *skills*, avails.
45. *grunsel*, ground-sill, foundation.
b. 16. *De Launay*, Marquis, governor of the Bastille.
17 *Sunday*. July 14th in 1789 fell on Tuesday. The news of the dismissal of Necker, a popular prime minister, got about on the previous Sunday (the 12th), and the tumult culminating in the taking of the Bastille began on that day.
25. *Swiss*, mercenaries from Switzerland used as a body-guard by French sovereigns.
46. *générale*, the general alarm. *Suburb Saint-Antoine*, the laborers' quarter on the eastern side of the city, near the Bastille.
52. *Que voulez-vous*, What mean you? or What do you want?

Page 689.

a. 48. *felloe*, rim of a wheel, in allusion to Tournay's trade of cartwright.
49. *Orcus*, the world of the dead.
b. 41. *Maelstrom*, a dangerous whirlpool off the west coast of Norway.

Page 690.

a. 21. *paillasse*, straw mattress.
28. *Tophet*, hell.
53. *Spinola-Santerre*, a leader of the revolutionary mob in Paris, and later a general in the National Guard. Spinola was a famous Spanish general, who captured Ostend in 1604.
b. 17. *Broglie*, Duke and Marshal, in command of the royal troops.
33. *this same day come four years*. Marat, having become a revolutionary leader, was assassinated by Charlotte Corday at Paris, July 13, 1793.
49. *canaille*, mob.

Page 691.

a. 32. *chamade*, parley, surrender.

CARLYLE — PAST AND PRESENT

This pamphlet, written during the first seven weeks of 1843, and published in April, has two sides: its historical side is founded on the twelfth century *Chronical of Jocelin de Brakelonde*, describing the government of the Abbey of St. Edmund's, which had been printed in 1840 by the Camden Society; its social and political side is concerned with the England of 1842, alarmed by Chartist riots and at a loss which way to turn for relief of popular discontent. Carlyle was not in sympathy with any of the existing political parties; his pamphlet aimed at arousing the laboring classes, their employers, and the landed aristocracy to nobler ideals and a sense of their obligations to each other.

LABOR

b. 11. *Mammonish*, done merely to get money.
55. *Ezechiel*. There is no reference to the potter's wheel in Ezechiel. Carlyle probably trusted to his remembrance of Jeremiah xviii, 1–6, and ascribed the passage to the wrong prophet.

Page 692.

a. 5. *amorphous*, shapeless.
14–16. *shambling*, unable to stand straight. *squint-cornered*, irregular. *vessel of dishonor*. Romans ix, 21: 'Hath not the potter power over the clay, of the same lump to make one vessel unto honor, and another unto dishonor?'
25. *festering*, stagnant, decaying.
28. *How blessed*, etc., blessed for the man's life, no matter what kind of work it is.
34. *awakens*, nominative 'force' two lines above.
42. *schools*, of philosophy.
43. *vortices*, whirlpools.
54. *Sir Christopher* Wren, after St. Paul's was destroyed by the great fire of London (1666) was appointed architect of the new Cathedral, and carried his design to accomplishment in 1710, in spite of the many difficulties Carlyle here refers to. Nell Gwyn was a popular actress of the time, a great favorite with Charles II, who spoke of her on his deathbed. 'Defender of the Faith' is a title conferred by the Pope upon Henry VIII for his answer to Luther, and retained by all the English sovereigns since.
b. 14. *architectonics*, the principles of building.
30. *monument*. Sir Christopher Wren's tomb in St. Paul's bears the inscription: '*Si monumentum quaeris, circumspice*.' 'If you seek his monument, look around you.'

Page 693.

a. 15. *Ursa Major*, the Great Bear, a group of stars near the North Pole, popularly known as Charles's Wain or the Dipper.

REWARD

49. '*Religion*.' Carlyle now returns to the thought of the last paragraph but one.
51–2. *Brahmins*, the highest caste in the Hindoo religion. *Antinomians*, a sect who maintained that the moral law was not binding upon Christians. *Spinning Dervishes*, Mohammedan friars who whirl round and round in a state of religious excitement 'till collapse ensue and sometimes death.'
b. 9. *immethodic*, without method, irregular.
25. *Shovel-hat*, a broad-brimmed hat, turned up at the sides and projecting in front, worn by some clergymen.
26. *Talfourd-Mahon Copyright Act* (1842) gave the author copyright for forty-two years. The meaning is that people should attack Ignorance, without waiting to be invested with authority, or promised reward and legal protection.
34. *Sinai thunders*. See Exodus xix, 16–19.
35. *speech of Whirlwinds*. See 1 Kings xix, 11–12.
45. *work*, etc. John ix, 4: 'I must work the works of him that sent me, while it is day: the night cometh, when no man can work.'
52–3. *Kepler* (1571–1630), *Newton* (1642–1727), two of the world's greatest mathematicians and astronomers.
55. '*Agony of bloody sweat*.' See Luke xxii, 44.

Page 694.

a. 22. *denizen*, one born in the country, having rights of citizenship; opposed to 'foreigner.'
29. *Mayfair*, the fashionable quarter of London.
37. *Phantasm*, an appearance, not a reality.
42. *unprofitable servants*. See Luke xvii, 10.
b. 6. *Eldorado*, 'the golden' land dreamed of by the Spanish explorers of America.
12. *St. Stephen's*, The Houses of Parliament.
28. *Owen*, Robert (1771–1858), a socialist reformer, who, amid many other projects intended to benefit working people, established in 1832 an 'Equitable Labor Exchange.' It proved a failure.
36. *Downing-street*, where many of the government offices are in London.

Page 696.

RUSKIN — TRAFFIC

a. 2. *carelessness*, lack of interest.
b. 9. *pitch farthing*, 'pitching pennies.'
48. ***Teniers*** (1582–1649), the great Dutch realist painter.

Page 697.

a. 2. *Titian* (1477–1576), the leading artist of the Venetian school.
3. *Turner* (1775–1851), the greatest of English landscape painters and Ruskin's particular favorite. See introductory biography, 733, **4**.
19. *Fleet Street*, a great London thoroughfare, where many London publishers have offices.

Page 697.
a. 23. *classifying*, dividing into classes.
   31–2. *costermonger*, peddler of apples ('costards') and other small fruits. *Newgate Calendar*, a publication giving accounts of sensational crimes. Newgate is a London prison.
b. 20–23. Quoted from Scott's *Lay of the Last Minstrel*, Canto I.
   46. *steel-traps . . . spring guns*. Appliances used against poachers, but here allegorically signifying the armaments of modern nations.

Page 698.
a. 5. *Bedlam*, the monastery of St. Mary of Bethlehem in London, later used as an asylum for the insane.
   18. *Armstrongs*, big guns manufactured by the great English firm of Armstrong.
   23. *black eagles* of Austria. Ruskin means that the English let the great military nations alone.
   50–52. *Inigo Jones . . . Sir Christopher Wren*, the great English architects of the seventeenth century. The former planned the royal palace of Whitehall in London, the latter St. Paul's Cathedral, both in Italian style.
b. 43. *This is none other than the house of God.* See Genesis xxviii, 10–17.

Page 699.
a. 15. *Thou, when thou prayest.* See Matthew vi, 5–6.
   36. *Lares*, Latin gods of the hearth, household gods.
   47. *The Seven Lamps.* See introductory biography, p. 695.

Page 700.
a. 23. *Bosphorus*, the strait dividing Europe from Asia.
   36. *to the Jews.* See 1 Corinthians i, 23.

Page 701.
a. 12. *Tetzel*, a seller of papal indulgences who provoked the indignation of Luther.
   15. *bals masqués*, masked balls. They were a feature of the French frivolity which preceded the Revolution and the guillotine.
   22. *Revivalist*, of classical architecture, as seen in the royal palace of Versailles, near Paris, and the papal palace of the Vatican at Rome.
   32. *sevenths of time*, Sunday, one-seventh of the week.
   49. *Acropolis*, the hill overlooking Athens; the site of the Parthenon and other Greek temples.
   50–52. *walls of Babylon . . . temple of Ephesus*, monuments of antiquity.
b. 29. *affairs of exchange.* See Matthew xxi, 12–13.
   39. *quartering.* As armies do when they occupy a country.
   43. *color*, pretence.

Page 702.
a. 3. '*carry.*' At the point of the bayonet.
   49. *St. George*, the English national saint.
b. 1–2. *semi-fleeced . . . proper . . . fields*, terms of heraldry.
   18. *Comforter*, the Holy Ghost. See John xiv, 16–17.
   21. *Agora*, market.
   47–8. *Olympus . . . Pelion . . . Ossa.* Mountains of classical antiquity. See *Hamlet* V, i, 304–7.

Page 704.
b. 25. *plain of Dura*, where Nebuchadnezzar set up a golden image. See Daniel iii, 1.
   40–41. *pleasantness . . . peace.* See Proverbs iii, 17.
   48. *not made with hands.* See 2 Corinthians v, i.

Page 705.
TENNYSON — MARIANA
8. *moated grange.* Tennyson printed, as the motto of this poem, the phrase, 'Mariana in the moated grange,' adapted from a passage in Shakespeare's *Measure for Measure*, III, i. The situation of Shakespeare's Mariana, then, probably furnished the germ of Tennyson's conception.

Page 706.
THE POET
15. *Calpe*, Gibraltar. *Caucasus*, the Caucasian Mountains.

Page 707.
THE LADY OF SHALOTT
This was probably Tennyson's earliest study from the Arthurian legend. It may be compared with his later embodiment of the story in *Lancelot and Elaine*.
5. *Camelot.* In Cornwall. The legendary seat of King Arthur's court.
9. *Shalott.* Malory's Astolat. According to Palgrave, this poem was suggested to Tennyson by an Italian romance upon the *Donna di Scalotta*. This would account for the form, Shalott.

Page 708.
84. *the golden Galaxy.* The Milky Way.
107. '*Tirra Lirra.*' Tirelirer, in French, signifies to sing like a lark.

THE PALACE OF ART
The ethical burden of this poem has been well stated by Tennyson's friend, James Spedding. The poem 'represents allegorically the condition of a mind which, in the love of beauty and the triumphant consciousness of knowledge and intellectual supremacy, in the intense enjoyment of its own power and glory, has lost sight of its relation to man and God.'

Page 710.
99. *Saint Cecily.* Compare page 309, lines 138–147, and note.
105. *Uther's deeply-wounded son*, King Arthur.
111. *The wood-nymph*, Egeria. *The Ausonian king*, Numa Pompilius.
115. *Indian Cama.* The Hindu god of love.
117. *Europa.* According to the Greek myth, Europa, sister of Cadmus, was carried to Crete by Zeus who assumed the form of a white bull. 'Europa and the Bull' is the subject of a famous painting by Paolo Veronese.
121. *Ganymede*, the cup-bearer of Zeus, who was conveyed to Olympus by an eagle.
137. *the Ionian father*, etc. Homer.
163. *Verulam.* Francis Bacon was created Baron Verulam in 1618. See pp. 187–199.
171–2. *as morn from Memnon*, etc. A colossus near Thebes, Egypt, was believed by the Greeks to represent this solar deity and to give forth a musical sound when reached by the rays of the rising sun.

Page 711.
219. *Like Herod*, etc. See Acts xii, 21–23.
226. *The airy hand*, etc. See Daniel v, 24–27.

Page 712.
A DREAM OF FAIR WOMEN
2. *The Legend of Good Women.* For its place among Chaucer's works, see p. 73.
27. *tortoise*, the roof formed by the shields of Roman soldiers held over their heads.

Page 713.
87. *a daughter of the gods*, etc. Helen.
100. *One that stood beside.* Iphigenia, the daughter of Agamemnon. Part of the details are drawn from Aeschylus' *Agamemnon*, 225–49, and from Lucretius' *De Rerum Natura*, I, 85–100.
123. *Sudden I heard*, etc. The description of Cleopatra is based chiefly on Shakespeare's *Antony and Cleopatra*, though there are touches from Horace, *Ode* i.
146. *Canopus.* One of the brightest of the first magnitude stars. It is not visible in our middle northern latitudes.
155. *the other.* Octavius Cæsar.

Page 714.

177. *Then I heard*, etc. Jephthah's daughter. See Judges xi.
251. *Rosamond*, illicitly loved by King Henry II.

Page 715.

255. *Eleanor*, Henry II's queen. She is said to have slain Rosamond with her own hand or to have forced her to drink poison.
259. *Fulvia*. Antony's first wife. Cleopatra means, 'You should have slain your rival.'
263. *The captain of my dreams*. The morning star, an allusion to l. 3.
266–7. *her, who clasped . . . father's head*, Margaret Roper, the daughter of Sir Thomas More, is said to have rescued his head from London Bridge where it had been placed after his execution for high treason, and to have kept it until she died.
269–72. *Or her who knew*, etc. Eleanor, wife of Edward I, who saved his life by applying her lips to his wound after he had been stabbed with a poisoned dagger.

ST. AGNES EVE

See page 628, line 1, note.

Page 716.

OF OLD SAT FREEDOM ON THE HEIGHTS

15. *the triple forks*. The trident of Neptune, symbolic of maritime supremacy.

SIR GALAHAD

25. *stormy crescent*, the moon in storm.
53. *the leads*. The roofs of lead.

Page 717.

84. *Until I find the holy Grail*. The sacred vessel in which the blood of the Lord was caught as he hung upon the Cross, was said to have been carried to Britain by Joseph of Arimathea. It was an object of quest among the knights of the Round Table, but only Galahad was pure enough to achieve it. See Tennyson's *Holy Grail* in *The Idylls of the King* and Malory's *Morte d'Arthur*.

A FAREWELL

The Tennysons left their old home at Somersby in 1837. There are references to the incident and to the same brook in *In Memoriam*.

MORTE D'ARTHUR

For Malory's *Morte d'Arthur*, Bk. XXI, upon which this poem is based, see p. 90. The poem was afterward incorporated, with additions, into *The Idylls of the King*.

4. *Lyonnesse*. A mythical region, off the shores of Cornwall, now supposedly submerged by the sea.
15. *The goodliest fellowship*, etc. The Round Table.
21. *Camelot*, the legendary seat of Arthur's court:
23. *Merlin*. The wise magician of Arthur's court.
31. *samite*, a kind of silk.
43. *hest*, behest, command.

Page 718.

139. *the northern morn*. Aurora borealis.
140. *isles of winter*, icebergs.

Page 719.

186. *harness*, armor.
215. *greaves*, shin pieces. *cuisses*, thigh pieces.
259. *the island valley of Avilion*. Tennyson's description is influenced by classical conceptions of the Fortunate Islands. See page 720, line 63, note.

Page 720.

ULYSSES

The germ of this poem is to be found in Dante's *Inferno*, xxvi, 85–142.

2. *these barren crags*, the bleak island of Ithaca.
3. *mete*, measure.
10. *the rainy Hyades*. A part of the constellation Taurus, supposed to bring rain. Virgil's *pluvias Hyadas*.

Page 720.

63. *the Happy Isles*. Vaguely thought of by the ancients as somewhere in the Atlantic off the west coast of Africa, perhaps the Cape Verde or the Canary Islands. Tennyson's description of Avilion borrows from classical sources. See page 719, line 259, note.

LOCKSLEY HALL

Suggestions for this poem were derived from the *Amriolkais*, an Arabian poem translated by Sir William Jones. *Works*, Vol. IV, pp. 247–57.

8. *Orion*. A conspicuous constellation often mentioned by Tennyson.
9. *the Pleiads*. A group of stars in the constellation Taurus. A similar reference occurs in the *Amriolkais*.

Page 722.

75. *Comfort scorned of devils*. The reference is to *Paradise Lost*, Books I and II, *passim*.
75–76. *this is truth the poet sings*, etc. *Nessun maggior dolore, Che ricordarsi del tempo felice Nella miseria.*—Dante, *Inferno*, v, 121–3.

Page 723.

155. *Mahratta-battle*. With the Mahrattas, a warlike and powerful Hindu people of mid-India, the British had a number of serious wars between 1750 and 1818.

Page 724.

180. *Joshua's moon in Ajalon*. See Joshua x, 12–13.
182. *the ringing grooves of change*. Tennyson has explained that when he traveled by the first train from Liverpool to Manchester in 1830 it was night and he thought that the wheels ran in a groove. 'Then I wrote this line.'
184. *Cathay*, China.

BREAK, BREAK, BREAK

Composed 'in a Lincolnshire lane at five o'clock in the morning between blossoming hedges.' (Tennyson.)

Page 725.

IN MEMORIAM A. H. H.

Arthur Henry Hallam died at Vienna, in September, 1833. He had been Tennyson's most intimate friend at Cambridge and was betrothed to Tennyson's sister. He was a youth of great intellectual promise and exceptional purity of spirit. The 'elegies,' as they were called, which made up *In Memoriam*, were composed at various times during the seventeen years which intervened between Hallam's death and their publication in 1850.

5. *orbs of light and shade*. The eyes.
8. *the skull*. As symbolizing death.

Page 726.

35. *merit lives from man to man*. That is, in men's relations to one another, not in their relation to God.
42. *Confusions of a wasted youth*. This section of the poem was written in 1849, while much of the poem had been composed years before.

XIX

1–4. *The Danube to the Severn*, etc. Vienna, where Hallam died, is on the Danube; while Clevedon Church, where he is buried, is on the river Severn near its confluence with Bristol Channel.
5–8. *There twice a day the Severn fills*, etc. The tide pushes back into the Severn and up the tributary Wye.

LV

7–8. *So careful of the type*, etc. Type, species. In lvi, Tennyson points out that types, as well as individuals, become extinct.

LXIV

1. *thou*, the spirit of Hallam.

Page 727.

LXVII

3. *that broad water of the west.* The mouth of the Severn. See xix, 1–4, note.

LXXXVIII

2. *quicks*, hedges. Literally, living things.

Page 728.

MAUD: A MONODRAMA

37. *vitriol madness.* The frenzy produced by chemicalized liquor.
41. *center-bits.* The drills of the safe-blower.
44. *poisoned poison.* Adulterated drugs.
46. *Timour-Mammon.* Timour (Tamerlane), 'the Scourge of the World,' is united with the god of riches to name an evil potency of the modern world.

Page 729.

90. *Orion.* Compare *Locksley Hall*, page 720, line 8, and note.
133. *Birds in the high Hall-garden*, etc. Tennyson called attention to the imitation of the cries of the rooks, ll. 134 and 158, and of the smaller birds, l. 142.

Page 730.

209. *Lebanon.* The cedars of Lebanon are said to have been brought into England by the crusaders, on their return from the Holy Land.
228. *A sad astrology.* The old astrology was based upon a belief that the movements of stars controlled the destiny of men; but modern science teaches us that they have no such significance.

Page 731.

298. *the planet of love.* Venus, as morning star.

Page 732.

393. *the Breton Strand.* The coast of Brittainy, in France.
412. *that of Lamech.* 'I have slain a man to my wounding, and a young man to my hurt.' Genesis iv, 23.
457. *O that 't were possible*, etc. This section of the poem, in slightly different form, had been published in *The Tribute*, 1837. Tennyson's friend, Sir John Simeon, who greatly admired the verses, suggested that they needed some introduction to make them fully intelligible. Tennyson undertook to carry out the suggestion, and *Maud* was the result.

Page 734.

TITHONUS

Although not published until 1860, this poem was written at about the same time as *Ulysses*. It is based upon the Greek myth according to which Tithonus, a mortal, being beloved by Eos, goddess of the dawn, the gods conferred upon him the gift of immortality. As they had neglected the gift of immortal youth, he gradually dwindled away and was metamorphosed into a grasshopper. The poem should be read as a myth of the dawn.

MILTON

This is one of a group of poems which Tennyson styled 'experiments in quantity.' It imitates the Alcaic stanza of Alcæus, Horace and other classical poets. To those who are unacquainted with classical prosody perhaps the best advice is that which Tennyson gave in regard to a similar experiment: 'Read it as prose and the meter will come right.'

The following time scheme may, however, be found useful in interpreting the meter:

— | ́‿ ∪ | ́‿ — || ́‿ ∪ ∪ | ́‿ ∪ | ́‿
— | ́‿ ∪ | ́‿ — || ́‿ ∪ ∪ | ́‿ ∪ | ́‿
— | ́‿ ∪ | ́‿ — | ́‿ ∪ | ́‿ ∪ |
́‿ ∪ ∪ | ́‿ ∪ ∪ | ́‿ ∪ | ́‿ ∪

Page 735.

NORTHERN FARMER

This poem is written in the Lincolnshire dialect with which Tennyson was familiar from childhood. It will be more easily understood if read aloud.

1. *'asta*, hast thou. *liggin'*, lying.
2. *nowt*, nothing.
10. *issen*, himself.
11. *towd*, told. *toithe*, tithe.
14. *barne*, bairn, child.
16. *raäte*, tax.
18. *buzzard-clock*, cockchafer.
23. *'Siver*, howsoever.
27. *thaw summun said it*, though some may have said it.
28. *stubb'd*, grubbed, cleared.
30. *boggle*, goblin, bogle.
31. *butter-bump*, bittern.
32. *raäved*, rived, tore. *rembled*, removed.
34. *'enemies*, anemones.
35. *toaner*, the one or the other.
36. *'soize*, the assizes.
37. *Dubbut*, do but.
38. *bracken*, brake, fern. *fuzz*, furze, goise.
41. *nobbut*, only.
49. *'aapoth*, half-penny's worth.
52. *hoalms*, flats, lowlands.
54. *sewerloy*, surely.

Page 736.

61. *kittle o' steam*, steam-engine.
62. *Huzzin' an' maäzin'.* Buzzing and amazing.
65. *atta*, art thou.
66. *'toattler*, teetotaler. *a's hallus i' the owd taäle*, he's always at the old story.

THE REVENGE

Compare the account from Hakluyt, above, page 154.

Page 738.

TO VIRGIL

1. *Ilion's . . . fire.* The reference is to Æneas's description of the burning of Troy. *Æneid*, II.
3. *he that sang the 'Works and Days.'* Hesiod.
5. *Thou that singest . . . herd.* Reference to the *Georgics*.
7. *Tityrus.* See *Eclogue* I.
8. *the poet-satyr.* See *Eclogue* VI.
9. *the Pollio.* See *Eclogue* IV.
11. *Thou that seest Universal Nature*, etc. See *Æneid*, VI, 727.
14. *Golden branch*, etc. See *Æneid*, VI, 208.
18. *the Northern Island*, etc. See *Eclogue* I, 67.
19. *Mantovano*, Mantuan. From Mantua, Virgil's birthplace.

FRATER AVE ATQUE VALE

The refrain, 'Brother, hail and farewell,' is from Catullus's invocation at his brother's tomb. See Catullus, ci.

1. *Desenzano . . . Sirmione.* Villages on the Lago di Garda, largest of the northern Italian lakes.
2. *O venusta Sirmio* [O lovely Sirmio]. See Catullus, xxxi.
8. *Lydian laughter of the Garda Lake.* See Catullus, xxxi.

CROSSING THE BAR

Tennyson requested of his son that these verses should be placed at the close of all collections of his poems. They were written in his eighty-first year and 'came in a moment.'

3. *moaning of the bar.* The poem was suggested by the popular superstition that the tide moans in going out, whenever a death has occurred.
15. *my Pilot*, 'that Divine and Unseen who is always guiding us.' (Tennyson.)

Page 739.

BROWNING — SONGS FROM 'PIPPA PASSES'

Browning was walking alone in a wood on the outskirts of London when the image flashed upon him of 'someone

Page 739.

walking thus alone through life; one apparently too obscure to leave a trace of his or her passage, yet exercising a lasting, though unconscious, influence at every step of it.' This original conception is charmingly worked out in the character of Felippa or Pippa, the little silk winder of Asolo, a hill town in North Italy which had taken Browning's fancy during his first visit. Pippa is introduced in her humble room springing out of bed on her one holiday—New Year's Day, and singing the first of her songs, as here given. During the day she passes in and out of the village, singing her artless songs, and unconsciously influencing the lives of those about her. The second song, 'The year's at the Spring,' awakens two wicked people to a sense of their guilt and the divine government of the world. The third, 'Give her but a least excuse to love me,' rouses a young painter to a higher conception of love and art. The explanation of this song is given in the lines which follow in the original:—

What name was that the little girl sang forth?
Kate? The Cornaro, doubtless, who renounced
The crown of Cyprus to be lady here
At Asolo, where still her memory stays,
And peasants sing how once a certain page
Pined for the grace of her so far above
His power of doing good to 'Kate the Queen—
She never could be wronged, be poor,' he sighed,
'Need him to help her!'

Browning gives us in the first five lines of each stanza the page's song; in the last four the comments of the Queen and her maid, who overhear him. Caterina (or Kate) Cornaro was a Venetian citizen who married the King of Cyprus, and after his death, resigning her authority to the Republic, retired to keep a small court at the Venetian village of Asolo, where she 'wielded her little sceptre for her people's good, and won their love by gentleness and grace.'

Page 740.

18. *jesses.* Straps for hawks' legs.

MY LAST DUCHESS

Ferrara, which Browning gives as the scene of this poem, is a town in North Italy, not far from Venice. It was the capital of the House of Este, who were among the most accomplished and the most cruel of the tyrants of the Italian Renascence. Symonds says in his *Age of the Despots:* 'Under the House of Este, Ferrara was famous throughout Italy for its gaiety and splendor. No city enjoyed more brilliant or more frequent public shows. Nowhere did the aristocracy retain so much feudal magnificence and chivalrous enjoyment. The square castle of red brick, which still stands in the middle of the town, was thronged with poets, players, fools who enjoyed an almost European reputation, court flatterers, knights, pages, scholars, and fair ladies. But beneath its cube of solid masonry, on a level with the moat, shut out from daylight by the sevenfold series of iron bars, lay dungeons in which the objects of the Duke's displeasure clanked chains and sighed their lives away.'

3. *Frà.* The painter, who is an imaginary character, was a monk like Fra Angelico and other Italian artists of the Renaissance.
45-6 There has been much discussion as to whether these two lines imply that the Duke gave orders for his wife's execution. Professor Corson put the question to Browning himself, and quotes his answer thus: '"Yes, I meant that the commands were that she should be put to death." And then after a pause he added with a characteristic dash of expression, as if the thought had just started in his mind, "Or he might have had her shut up in a convent."'
56. *Claus of Innsbruck.* An imaginary artist. Innsbruck is in the Tyrol. It is famous for the bronze work on the tomb of the emperor Maximilian.

Page 741.

COUNT GISMOND

This stirring narrative, in which Browning concentrates the heroic spirit of medieval chivalry, tells in the very words of the heroine of the incident a straight-forward story which needs no comment; but the reader should not miss the charming equivocation with which the heroine avoids telling her husband that she has been boasting to her friend of his prowess.

Page 742.

INCIDENT OF THE FRENCH CAMP

Ratisbon is in Bavaria, on the right bank of the Danube. It was stormed by Napoleon in 1809, after an obstinate defence by the Austrians. Mrs. Orr says: 'The story is true; but its actual hero was a man.'

1. *we French,* The story is told by a spectator.
7. *prone.* Bending or leaning forward.
11. *Lannes.* One of Napoleon's generals.
29. *flag-bird.* The Napoleonic standard was a tricolor powdered with golden bees, with an eagle on the central stripe.
vans. Wings. Latin *vannus,* a fan for winnowing grain.
34-5. *film* is nominative to *sheathes.*

THE ITALIAN IN ENGLAND

Browning was proud to remember that the Italian patriot Mazzini used to read this poem to his fellow exiles in England to show how an Englishman could sympathize with them. (Mrs. Orr.)

8. *Charles.* Charles Albert, Prince of Carignano belonged to the royal house of Savoy, but was brought up among the people, and as a young man expressed sympathy with revolutionary principles. He was afterward accused of betraying Italy, and was bitterly denounced by his former friends.

Page 743.

19. *Metternich our friend.* Said ironically. Metternich, the Austrian statesman and diplomatist, was the most determined enemy of Italian independence.
20. See note above on Charles Albert.
41. *crypt.* Place of concealment; commonly used of a place for burial.
46. My fears were not for myself, but for my country; 'on me Rested the hopes of Italy.'
75. *duomo.* (Italian) Cathedral.
76. *Tenebræ.* A service of the Roman Catholic Church, which involves the gradual extinction of the lights on the altar. The Latin word literally means 'darkness.'
81. It was not unusual for a priest to render service to the cause of Italian liberty.
125-7. Charles Albert became King of Sardinia in 1831 and resigned the crown to his son, Victor Emmanuel, in 1849. He retired to Portugal, where he died in the same year, 'broken-hearted and misunderstood.' The patriot's wish as expressed by Browning was, therefore, fulfilled four years after the poem was published. Charles Albert's position was a very difficult one, and historians generally take a more favorable view of his conduct than is here given. Browning has merely given characteristic expression to the sentiment of the ardent Italian patriots of the time.

Page 744.

138-44. These lines forcefully represent the division of opinion in Italy during the apparently fruitless struggles for independence.

THE LOST LEADER

The suggestion for this early poem was undoubtedly Wordsworth's abandonment of the Liberal principles of his youth for the reactionary Conservatism of his old age; but it was only a suggestion. 'Once call my fancy portrait Wordsworth,' Browning wrote, 'and how much

NOTES TO BROWNING, PP. 744-752

Page 744.

more ought one to say.' In another letter he speaks of Wordsworth's 'moral and intellectual superiority,' and protests against taking this poem as an attempt to draw his real likeness. It is really a character study from Browning's own imagination, and should be so regarded, in justice to both poets.

29-30. It is best for him to fight for the side he has chosen as well as he can, to fight so well indeed as to threaten us with defeat before the hour of our final triumph.

HOME THOUGHTS FROM ABROAD

It is interesting to contrast Browning's preference for English birds and flowers, expressed in this poem after his earlier visits to the Continent, with the love of Italy breathed in '*De Gustibus*—' p. 754, which was written after his settlement with his wife in Florence.

HOME THOUGHTS FROM THE SEA

Written off Gibraltar during Browning's first voyage to Italy in 1838.

1-7. *Cape St. Vincent, Cadiz Bay, Trafalgar* are all associated with English victories. *Gibraltar*, the famous rock-fortress which guards the entrance to the Mediterranean, has been held by Great Britain since its capture in 1704. These glorious memories inspire the poet with a sense of his duty to his country, and he mingles prayer for the future with praise for the past. *Say* is imperative 'Whoso turns, etc. . . . let him say "How can I help England?"'

Page 745.

SAUL

Browning found the suggestion for this, one of his finest religious poems, in the Old Testament narrative of Saul's depression and its relief by the harping of David, the shepherd boy—1 Samuel xvi, 14-23, which the teacher would do well to read to the class in order to show how the poet has filled with life and color the mere hints of the original. Browning has read into the ancient story not only doctrines and ideas taken from the New Testament, but modern religious views and sentiments.

1. *Abner.* The son of Ner, captain of Saul's host. See 1 Samuel xxvi, 5.
36-41. Professor Albert S. Cook suggests that Browning obtained his hints for these tunes from Longus's romance of *Daphnis and Chloe*. The first is found on pp. 303-4 (Smith's Translation, Bohn ed.), 'He ran through all variations of pastoral melody, he played the tune which the oxen obey, and which attracts the goats—that in which the sheep delight,' etc.; pp. 332-4, '. . . . standing under the shade of a beech-tree, he took his pipe from his scrip and breathed into it very gently. The goats stood still, merely lifting up their heads. Next he played the pasture tune, upon which they all put down their heads and began to graze. Now he produced some notes soft and sweet in tone; at once his herd lay down. After this he piped in a sharp key, and they ran off to the wood, as if a wolf were in sight.' In answer to the question as to whether there is any historical foundation for David's songs, Rabbi Charles Fleischer of Boston replied in a letter to the editors: 'I believe that David's songs in Browning's poem *Saul* are the inspired melodies of our nineteenth century David rather than the songs of Israel's poetic shepherd-king. . . . While, then, I believe that these melodies in *Saul* were not current among the Jews of old, I know that they would serve well to express beliefs and ideals characteristic of the best minds among the Jews of to-day.'—Porter and Clarke.
45. *Jerboa.* The jumping hare.

Page 748.

203. *Hebron* was one of the cities of refuge, but Browning evidently takes it as the name of a mountain.

Page 748.

204. *Kidron.* A brook near Jerusalem.

The first nine stanzas of this poem (to line 96) were published in *Dramatic Romances and Lyrics* in 1845; the later stanzas were written after his marriage, and published in *Men and Women* (1855). The latter part shows a marked advance in intensity of religious conviction, probably due to Mrs. Browning's influence. The student should note that David first played on his harp (36-60); then sang (68-190); and finally spoke (237-312). The inner structure of the poem should be carefully studied so as to bring out the gradual rise of theme from external nature to human activities and sympathies, from the glory of kingship to the glory of fame, and so to the culmination of Divine Love as manifested in the Incarnation.

Page 751.

LOVE AMONG THE RUINS

This poem was written when Browning was in Rome in the winter of 1853-4, and is said to have been suggested by the contrast between the present desolation of the Campagna and its former magnificence; but the scene is imaginatively treated, and cannot be identified with any place in particular. The living love, even of an obscure boy and girl, counted for more with Browning than all the dead glories of the earth.

A WOMAN'S LAST WORD

The title refers to the old proverb, 'a woman will always have the last word in a quarrel.' This 'woman's last word,' however, is not one of recrimination, but of reconciliation and submission. She will even sacrifice what she believes to be true (st. iv), lest she should lose her domestic peace as Eve lost Paradise.

Page 752.

A TOCCATA OF GALUPPI'S

Baldassare Galuppi (1706-85), a musical composer of some note in his day, who was for the last years of his life organist at St. Mark's Cathedral, Venice, is here taken by Browning as an exponent and critic of the frivolous, empty life with which the name of this Italian city has long been associated. But the toccata speaks to the man who plays it—a student of science—not only of the emptiness of life at Venice in the eighteenth century, but of the emptiness of life in general, for st. xiii is, of course, to be taken ironically; as he thinks of the beauty and gaiety of Venice all turned to 'dust and ashes,' he feels 'chilly and grown old,' for even so all human activities seem to pass away into nothingness.

The *toccata* is marked by the repetition of phrases calculated to display a peculiar facility of touch (It. *toccare*, to touch) on the musician's part.

6. 'The ceremony of wedding the Adriatic was instituted in 1174 by Pope Alexander III, who gave the Doge a gold ring from his own finger in token of the victory achieved by the Venetian fleet at Istria over Frederick Barbarossa, in defense of the Pope's quarrel. When His Holiness gave the ring, he desired the Doge to throw a similar ring into the sea annually, in commemoration of the event.' (Brewer.)
8. *Shylock's bridge.* The Rialto.
18. *clavichord.* An old-fashioned instrument, with keys and strings, the predecessor of the modern pianoforte.

The musical technicalities made use of are thus elucidated by Porter and Clarke, *Poems of Robert Browning*:—'The technical musical allusions in the poem are all to be found in the 7th, 8th, and 9th stanzas. The *lesser thirds* (line 19) are minor thirds (intervals containing three semitones), and are of common occurrence, but the diminished sixth is an interval rarely used. Ordinarily a *diminished sixth* (seven semitones), exactly the same interval as a perfect fifth, instead of giving a plaintive, mournful, or minor impression, would suggest a feeling of rest and satisfaction. There is one way, however, in

Page 752.

which it can be used—as a suspension, in which the root of the chord on the *lowered* super-tonic of the scale is suspended from above into the chord with added seventh on the super-tonic, making a diminished sixth between the root of the first and third of the second chord. The effect of this progression is most dismal, and possibly Browning had it in mind. *Suspensions* (line 20) are notes which are held over from one chord into another, and must be made according to certain strict musical rules. This holding over of a note always produces a dissonance, and must be followed by a concord—in other words, a *solution*. Sevenths are very important dissonances in music, and a *commiserating seventh* (line 21) is most likely the variety called a minor seventh. Being a somewhat less mournful interval than the lesser thirds and the diminished sixths, whether real or imaginary, yet not so final as "those solutions" which seem to put an end to all uncertainty, and therefore to life, they arouse in the listeners to Galuppi's playing a hope that life may last, although in a sort of dissonantal, Wagnerian fashion. The "commiserating sevenths" are closely connected with the "dominant's persistence" (line 24). The dominant chord in music is the chord written on the fifth degree of the scale, and it almost always has a seventh added to it, and in a large percentage of cases is followed by the tonic, the chord on the first degree of the scale. Now; in fugue form a theme is first presented in the tonic key, then the same theme is repeated in the dominant key, the latter being called the answer; after some development of the theme the fugue comes to what is called an episode, after which the theme is presented first, in the dominant. "Hark! the dominant's persistence" alludes to this musical fact; but according to rule this dominant must be answered in the tonic an octave above the first presentation of the theme, and "So an octave struck the answer." Thus the inexorable solution comes in after the dominant's persistence. Although life seemed possible with commiserating sevenths, the tonic, a resistless fate, strikes an answer that all must end.'

Page 753.

MY STAR

This poem has been interpreted as having personal reference to Mrs. Browning; but there is no reason to set it apart from the other poems described by Browning as 'always dramatic in principle, and so many utterances of so many imaginary persons.'

4. *angled spar*. 'A prism of Iceland spar has the property of polarizing or dividing a ray of light into two parts. Suppose this polarized ray be passed through a plate of Iceland spar, at a certain angle, and a second prism of Iceland spar be rotated in front of it, different colors will be given out, complementary tints being ninety degrees apart, and four times during the rotation the light will vanish completely. Some such experiment as this was probably in the poet's mind when he made the comparison with the angled spar.' (Porter and Clarke.)

THE LAST RIDE TOGETHER

The utter devotion of this poem is, in Browning's view, characteristic of true love.

Page 754.

62. *Ten lines*. Of history or biography.
65. *the Abbey*. Westminster Abbey, where England's heroes are commemorated.
67-88. Cf. *In a Balcony*, 664-7:—

 'We live, and they experiment on life—
 Those poets, painters, all who stand aloof
 To overlook the farther. Let us be
 The thing they look at!'

MEMORABILIA

'Things worth remembering.' This poem is said to have been suggested to Browning by overhearing a man

Page 754.

say in a shop that he had met and spoken to Shelley. By the metaphor of the eagle's feather, Browning conveys to the reader that if such a piece of good fortune had happened to him, it would have been enough to blot out all other incidents.

'DE GUSTIBUS'

The Latin proverb '*De gustibus non est disputandum*,' corresponds to the English one 'There's no accounting for tastes.' Browning says that if our preferences persist after death, his will be, not for England, but for Italy.

Page 755.

22. *cicala*, the cicada, commonly called 'locust,' often heard in Italy in the heat of summer.
36. *liver-wing*, right arm. The Bourbon rule in Southern Italy was exceedingly unpopular, and numerous attempts were made to cast it off; the king here referred to was Ferdinand II, whose cruelties were denounced by Gladstone in 1851. He was succeeded by his son, who was expelled in 1860, and Naples was incorporated with the new kingdom of Italy. Browning sympathized with all the Italians' attempts to regain their liberty and independence, even when they went the length of assassination.

ANDREA DEL SARTO

This is one of the most remarkable of Browning's shorter poems, whether regarded as a study of character or of art. It was written when he was living in Florence, in answer to a request from a friend in England for a copy of the portrait of Andrea del Sarto and his wife in the Pitti Palace. Browning could not get one, and sent the poem instead. Mr. Ernest Radford thus describes the picture:—'The artist and his wife are presented at half length. Andrea turns towards her with a pleading expression on his face. . . . His right arm is round her; he leans forward as if searching her face for the strength that has gone from himself. . . . She holds the letter in her hand, and looks neither at that nor at him, but straight out of the canvas. And the beautiful face with the red-brown hair is passive and unruffled, and awfully expressionless. There is silent thunder in this face if there ever was, but there is no anger. It suggests only a very mild, and at the same time immutable determination to have her own way.'

Browning develops, in his favorite form of the dramatic monologue, the suggestion given by Andrea's portrait of himself; for the details he is chiefly indebted to Vasari's *Life of Andrea del Sarto*, as will be seen from the following extracts (translation by Blashfield and Hopkins, with Mrs. Foster's notes):

'Had this master possessed a somewhat bolder and more elevated mind, had he been as much distinguished for higher qualifications as he was for genius and depth of judgment in the art he practised, he would, beyond all doubt, have been without an equal. But there was a certain timidity of mind, a sort of diffidence and want of force in his nature, which rendered it impossible that those evidences of ardor and animation, which are proper to the more exalted character, should ever appear in him; nor did he at any time display one particle of that elevation which, could it but have been added to the advantages wherewith he was endowed, would have rendered him a truly divine painter. . . . At that time there was a most beautiful girl in the Via di San Gallo, who was married to a cap-maker, and who, though born of a poor and vicious father, carried about her as much pride and haughtiness as beauty and fascination. She delighted in trapping the hearts of men, and among others ensnared the unlucky Andrea, whose immoderate love for her soon caused him to neglect the studies demanded by his art, and in great measure to discontinue the assistance which he had given his parents. Now it chanced that a sudden and grievous illness seized the husband of this woman, who rose no more from his bed, but died thereof. Without taking counsel of his friends therefore; without

Page 755.

regard to the dignity of his art or the consideration due to his genius, and to the eminence he had attained with so much labor; without a word, in short, to any of his kindred, Andrea took this Lucrezia di Baccio del Fede, such was the name of the woman, to be his wife; her beauty appearing to him to merit thus much at his hands, and his love for her having more influence over him than the glory and honor towards which he had begun to make such hopeful advances. But when this news became known in Florence the respect and affection which his friends had previously borne to Andrea changed to contempt and disgust, since it appeared to them that the darkness of this disgrace had obscured for a time all the glory and renown obtained by his talents. But he destroyed his own peace as well as estranged his friends by this act, seeing that he soon became jealous, and found that he had besides fallen into the hands of an artful woman, who made him do as she pleased in all things. He abandoned his own poor father and mother, for example, and adopted the father and sisters of his wife in their stead; insomuch that all who knew the facts mourned over him, and he soon began to be as much avoided as he had previously been sought after.' Andrea found this mode of life so oppressive that, on the advice of his friends, he put his wife in safe keeping and went to Paris, where he was richly rewarded by the King of France for his work. But a pitiful letter from his wife induced him to return. 'Taking the money which the king confided to him for the purchase of pictures, statues and other fine things, he set off, therefore, having first sworn on the gospels to return in a few months. Arrived happily in Florence, he lived joyously with his wife for some time, making large presents to her father and sisters, but doing nothing for his own parents, whom he would not even see, and who, at the end of a certain period, ended their lives in great poverty and misery.' Having spent the money entrusted to him in building a house and indulging himself in various other pleasures, Andrea was afraid to return to France, and remained in Florence in the very lowest position, 'procuring a livelihood and passing his time as he best might.'

So says Vasari, who at one time was Andrea's pupil, and published his *Lives of the Painters* while Andrea's widow was still in Florence; but recent investigation has failed to reveal the slightest evidence in support of the charge of embezzlement made by Vasari against Andrea, and it has been generally discredited.

15. *Fiesolë*. The village on the top of the ridge overlooking the quarter of Florence in which Andrea lived.
25. *It saves a model*. 'Andrea rarely painted the countenance of a woman in any place that he did not avail himself of the features of his wife, and if at any time he took his model from any other face there was always a resemblance to hers in the painting, not only because he had this woman constantly before him and depicted her so frequently but also and what is still more, because he had her lineaments engraven on his heart; it thus happens that almost all his female heads have a certain something which recalls that of his wife.' (Vasari.)
32. *no one's*. Not even his.
36–45. Lucrezia has lost only her first pride in her husband; he has lost all his youthful ambitions and aspirations, as the day loses its noontide splendor, and the glory of summer changes to the decay of autumn.
43. *huddled more inside*. The trees are huddled together within the convent wall, and have no room to grow; but they are, perhaps, safer—so, perhaps, too, is the painter in his own home, though he misses the inspiration and development that comes from contact with the world. Andrea acquiesces in his seclusion, but he cannot help regretting his lost opportunities.

Page 756.

93. *Morello*. A mountain near Florence.
105. *the Urbinate*. Raphael of Urbino, the most famous of Italian painters; he died in 1520, ten years before

Page 756.

Andrea. Vasari says that Andrea copied a portrait by Raphael with such exactness that Raphael's own pupils, who had helped in the painting, could not tell the copy from the original.
130. *Agnolo*. The great Italian painter usually called Michael Angelo in English; he was doubtless the 'Someone' of line 76; Andrea refers to him again in line 184.
150. *Fontainebleau*. A royal palace not far from Paris.
166. See quotation from Vasari above for Andrea's recall from France by his wife's importunities.
173. *there*, in your heart.
174. *ere the triumph*. Of my genius in art.

Page 757.

189–193. Bocchi, in his *Beauties of Florence*, states that Michael Angelo said to Raphael, referring to Andrea:—'There is a little man in Florence, who, if he were employed upon such great works as have been given to you, would bring the sweat to your brow.'
199. Lucrezia has interrupted to ask Andrea about whom and what he is talking. She is evidently paying no attention.
209–10. Mount Morello can no longer be seen, the lights on the city wall are lit, and the little owls, named in Italy from their call, *Chiu*, are crying; darkness is falling on the house as on Andrea's life.
212–18. See above for the charge against Andrea of building a house for himself with the money entrusted to him by King Francis to buy pictures with.
220. The cousin (or lover) who waits outside is the third character in the little drama—silent and unseen, but profoundly affecting the situation.
263. *Leonard*. Leonardo da Vinci, the third great Italian painter of the time; he died the year before Raphael.
266. Andrea at last acknowledges to himself that his wife has been a hindrance instead of a help, a drag preventing his ascent from the second rank to the first: but he prefers this to the sacrifice of giving her up.

THE GUARDIAN ANGEL

In the Church of St. Augustine at Fano, on the Adriatic, there is a picture called 'The Guardian Angel,' by Guercino, an Italian painter of the seventeenth century. It represents an angel with outspread wings embracing a kneeling child, whose hands he folds in prayer.

6. *another child*. The poet himself.
7. *retrieve*. Bring back to the right way.

Page 758.

14–16. In the picture cherubs point to the opened heaven, and the child looks upward past the angel's head.
18. *bird of God*. This beautiful expression is translated from Dante's *Purgatorio*.
20–21. The angel seems to be enfolding the child with the skirt of his robe, held in his left hand.
39–40. The angel's head is turned away, but the reason given is Browning's own.
46. *My angel with me, too*. His wife. See line 54.
54. *dear old friend*. Alfred Domett, a much-prized friend of Browning's youth, who in 1842 settled in New Zealand.
56. *Ancona*. On the Italian coast, near Fano. Browning and his wife visited both places soon after their first settlement in Italy in 1846, and the poem was doubtless written at the time. Mrs. Browning writes of the visit to her friend, Miss Mitford:—'So we went to Ancona—a striking sea city, holding up against the brown rocks, and elbowing out the purple tides—beautiful to look upon. An exfoliation of the rock itself you would call the houses that seem to grow there—so identical is the color and character.'

A GRAMMARIAN'S FUNERAL

This poem 'exhibits something of the life of the Scaligers and the Casaubons, of many an early scholar, like

Page 758.

Roger Bacon's friend Pierre Maricourt, working at some region of knowledge, and content to labor without fame so long as he mastered thoroughly whatever he undertook.' (*Contemporary Review*, IV, 135.)

The scholars are bearing their master to his tomb in one of the Italian hill-cities, perched on the top of the rocks, like Orvieto or Perugia.

3. *croft.* Enclosed tilled or pasture land. *thorpe.* Little village.
34. *Apollo.* The classical ideal of manly beauty. His statues usually represent him holding the lyre.
39 *Moaned he.* Did he moan?

Page 759.

45. *the world.* Of classical lore, which was bent on escaping.
56. *the curtain.* Of the play of life.
68. *Sooner.* Before he had gathered all books had to give.
86. *Calculus.* The stone.
88. *Tussis.* Cough.
95. *soul-hydroptic.* 'Every lust is a kind of hydropic distemper, and the more we drink the more we shall thirst.' (Tillotson, quoted by Webster.) *hydroptic,* dropsical.
96–100. Cf. *Abt Vogler,* l. 72, 763.
113–124. Cf. *Rabbi ben Ezra,* stanzas xxiii-xxv, p. 815.
129–131. *Hoti, . . . Oun, . . . De.* Greek particles, meaning respectively 'that,' 'therefore,' 'towards.' As to the last, Browning wrote to the editor of the *London Daily News* on Nov. 20, 1874, as follows:— 'In a clever article you speak of "the doctrine of the enclitic *De*"—"which with all deference to Mr. Browning, in point of fact, does not exist." No, not to Mr. Browning: but pray defer to Herr Buttmann, whose fifth list of "enclitics" ends "with the inseparable *De*"—or to Curtius, whose fifth list ends also with "*De* (meaning '*towards,*' and as a demonstrative appendage)." That this is not to be confounded with the accentuated "*De,* meaning but," was the "Doctrine" which the Grammarian bequeathed to those capable of receiving it.'

Page 760.

ONE WORD MORE

A special interest attaches to this poem because it is the only one addressed by Browning, directly and avowedly, to his wife, Elizabeth Barrett Browning. It was originally appended to the collection of poems, called *Men and Women* (1855). Browning uses the sonnets written by Raphael and a portrait painted by Dante to illustrate the desire of the artist to show his personal affection in some other way than that of his familiar craft, which has become professional and belongs to the world, so that everybody feels entitled to criticize. But as the poet cannot paint pictures, or carve statues, or make music to show his love, a semblance of resource remains in the use of a slightly different form of art from that which he commonly practises. Instead of writing dramatically, he may write, for once in his own person; for just as, according to the ancient myth, the moon would turn to her lover a side unseen by other mortals, so the poet has two soul-sides, 'one to face the world with, One to show a woman when he loves her.' While he says this of himself, he likes to think it of her, his 'moon of poets.' Her poetry is the world's side, and he too admires her from that point of view; but the best is when he leaves the standpoint of literary appreciation for the more intimate relation of personal knowledge and affection. Then it is that he realizes the love that Raphael sought to express by his sonnets and Dante by his picture.

5. *a century of sonnets.* Guido Reni had a book of 100 drawings of Raphael's, but Raphael is only known to have made four sonnets. Raphael never married, but he was very much in love with a certain lady, who has been identified, not very convincingly, with

Page 760.

the original of one or other of the portraits attributed to his hand.

22–24. The Sistine Madonna is now in the Dresden Art Gallery, the Madonna di Foligno is in the Vatican at Rome. 'The Madonna at Florence is that called del Granduca, which represents her as "appearing to a votary in a vision"—so say the describers; it is in the earlier manner, and very beautiful. I think I meant La Belle Jardinière—but am not sure—for the picture in the Louvre.' (Browning to W. J. Rolfe.) The Louvre Madonna is seated in the midst of a garden, in which there are lilies. All these are among the most famous works of Raphael.
27. *Guido Reni.* A celebrated Italian painter about a century later than Raphael. See note on line 5.
32. *Dante.* The first great Italian poet (1265–1321), who in *The Divine Comedy* attached eternal opprobrium to his enemies by assigning to them conspicuous places in Hell. Stanzas v, vi, and vii refer to a passage of his *Vita Nuova,* in which he has idealized his love for Beatrice, whom he had known as a young girl:—'On that day which fulfilled the year since my lady had been made of the citizens of eternal life; remembering me of her as I sat alone, I betook myself to draw the resemblance of an angel upon certain tablets. And while I did thus, chancing to turn my head, I perceived that some were standing beside me to whom I should have given courteous welcome, and that they were observing what I did: also I learned afterwards that they had been there a while before I perceived them. Perceiving whom, I rose for salutation and said: "Another was with me." Afterwards, when they had left me, I set myself again to the same occupation, to wit, to the drawing figures of angels.' (Section 35, Rossetti's translation.) It will be noticed that Browning's interpretation of the incident goes somewhat beyond the original, which gives no indication that those who interrupted Dante were people he scarified in the *Inferno.*
33. *Beatrice.* Four syllables—*bā-ah-trē-tshe.*
57. *Bice.* Two syllables—*bē-tshe.* A contraction of endearment of Beatrice.
74–93. There are two accounts in the Pentateuch of the smiting of the rock by Moses.—Exodus xvii 1–7, and Numbers xx, 10–12. The latter reads: 'And Moses and Aaron gathered the congregation together before the rock, and he said unto them, Hear now, ye rebels; must we fetch you water out of this rock? . . . And the LORD spake unto Moses and Aaron, Because ye believed me not, to sanctify me in the eyes of the children of Israel, therefore ye shall not bring this congregation into the land which I have given them.' Here, again, Browning has allowed his imagination to play round the original record.

Page 761.

94–5. When the children of Israel were rebellious against Moses, they cried, 'Would to God we had died by the hand of the LORD in the land of Egypt, when we sat by the flesh pots' (Exodus xvi, 3).
97. Exodus xxxiv, 29–35. *cloven,* because, following the Latin translation of this passage, the early painters represented Moses with two horns on his forehead. The original means to shine out or dart forth like rays of light.
101–2. Moses married Zipporah, Jethro's daughter (Exodus ii, 16–21), and an Ethiopian woman (Numbers xii, 1).
121. *fresco.* Painting in fresh plaster, usually done on the inside wall of a church.
125. *missal-marge.* The margin of a prayer book.
136–8. *Karshish, Cleon, Norbert, Lippo, Roland* and *Andrea* were among the characters in *Men and Women,* originally fifty in number.
143. *how I speak.* The personal instead of the dramatic mode of expression.
145. *Here in London.* The poem was written in London in September, 1855.

Page 761.

150. *Samminiato.* The common pronunciation of San Miniato, an old church, surrounded by cypress trees, overlooking Florence.
160. *mythos.* The old myth or story of the love of Diana, the moon-goddess, for the mortal Endymion.
163. *Zoroaster* (589–513 B. C.), founder of the Persian religion and a famous astronomer.
164. *Galileo* (1564–1642). Professor at Padua, and one of the founders of modern science. After being condemned by the church, he continued his studies in his house at Florence, which overlooks the city from the same side as San Miniato.
165. *Homer.* In allusion to the *Hymn to the Moon.* Keats, the author of *Endymion.* Browning expressed special admiration for him in the poem entitled *Popularity.*
172–9. Exodus xxiv, 9–11: 'Then went up Moses and Aaron, Nadab and Abihu, and seventy of the elders of Israel: And they saw the God of Israel: and there was under his feet as it were a paved work of a sapphire stone, and as it were the body of heaven in his clearness . . . also they saw God, and did eat and drink.'

Page 762.

ABT VOGLER

George Joseph Vogler (1749–1814), the priest-musician, composer, and teacher of Weber and Meyerbeer, was especially celebrated as an improviser, and traveled all over Europe giving performances on his orchestrion.

7. *Name,* Jehovah, used by Solomon as a talisman, according to oriental tradition.
22. *festal night.* Easter at St. Peter's, Rome.
32. *no more near nor far.* 'Music frees us from the phenomena of time and space.'
34. *Protoplast.* 'The thing first formed as a model to be imitated.' The *presences* are either of the future or of the past.

Page 763.

70. *The evil is null.* The teaching of Spinoza, Hegel, and Emerson, as well as of the Kabbalists, founded on that of the Gnostics and Neo-Platonists.
91. *the common chord* 'consists of the fundamental, with a major (four semitones), or minor (three semitones) third, and a perfect fifth (seven semitones) over it.
93. *a ninth* 'if major, contains an octave and two semitones; if minor, an octave and one semitone. These last lines of the poem, stripped of their symbolic meaning, may be taken as an exact explanation of a simple harmonic modulation.' (Porter and Clarke.)

Page 764.

RABBI BEN EZRA

Ibn Ezra, or Abenezra (1092–1167), was a great Jewish scholar, poet, philosopher, and physician, who wandered over Europe, Asia, and Africa in pursuit of knowledge. As will be seen from the notes, his writings contain some of the views expressed by Browning's sage.

1. The Rabbi seems to be at the end of middle age, just where old age begins. He looks back to youth, forward to old age.
4. A poem of Abenezra's, quoted by Dr. Michael Sachs, has the same thought: 'In deiner Hand leigt mein Geschick.'

Stanzas ii and iii should be taken together. The sense is: 'I do not remonstrate because youth, amassing flowers, sighed. . . .' He does not find fault with the foolish ambitions of his youth, for these aspirations, though they are vain, are what distinguish man from the beasts. This thought is expressed by Abenezra in his Commentary on Job xxxv, 11: 'Man has the sole privilege of becoming superior to the beast and the fowl.'

25–30. Stanza v expresses a favorite thought of Browning's. Cf. *A Death in the Desert,* 576–578:—

Progress, man's distinctive mark alone,
Not God's and not the beasts': God is, they are;
Man partly is and wholly hopes to be.

40–42. Cf. *Saul,* lines 160 and 295.
48. *soul on its lone way.* 'The soul of man is called lonely because it is separated during its union with the body from the universal soul.' (Abenezra's Commentary on Psalm xxii, 22.)
57. Cf. *Saul,* line 242.

Page 765.

151. *Potter's wheel.* Cf. Isaiah lxiv, 8: 'We are the clay and thou our Potter.' This is a favorite scriptural and oriental metaphor, used also by Quarles and in Fitzgerald's translation of the *Rubaiyat* of Omar Khayyam, but by no previous poet with such deep significance as here.

Page 766.

PROSPICE

'Look forward.' This noble defiance of death was written in the autumn after Browning lost his wife, and appeared first in the *Atlantic Monthly* for June, 1864.

19. *life's arrears.* All the pain that a man might fairly have expected to suffer in life, but missed.
23. *fiend-voices.* The ancient belief was that the soul at the moment of separation from the body is the object of a struggle between the angels, whose office is to bear away the freed spirit (Luke xvi, 22) and the powers of darkness who strive to snatch it from salvation. For this reason fervent prayers are offered for a soul on the point of departure.
27–28. Browning had a strong faith in immortality, and repeatedly expressed it in both prose and verse. He said: 'I know I shall meet my dearest friends again.'

HERVÉ RIEL

Browning was in France when it was invaded by Prussia in 1870, and escaped from the country with some difficulty before the outbreak of the disorders which followed the collapse of the French resistance. Desiring to express his sympathy for the sufferers by the siege of Paris, he sold this poem to *Cornhill Magazine* for £100, which he gave as a subscription to the Relief Fund. It was written in 1867 and first published in 1871. The incident it relates was first denied in France, but the records of the admiralty of the time proved that Browning was correct, except in one small detail: the reward Hervé Riel asked and received was '*un congé absolu*'— a holiday for the rest of his life.

1. *the Hogue.* Cap La Hogue, where the French fleet was attacked in 1692 by the English and Dutch, and forced to retire. The expedition aimed at the restoration of James II, who watched the defeat from the Norman coast.
5. *St. Malo,* at the mouth of the Rance River, in Brittany, has a harbor which is described as 'safe, but difficult of approach.' In the sixteenth and seventeenth centuries it was a flourishing port, and from it Jacques Cartier sailed in 1535 to explore the River St. Lawrence. *the Rance.* A small stream with picturesque steep banks. The town is situated on a rock between the harbor and the mouth of the river.

Page 767.

18. *twelve and eighty.* French, quatre-vingt-douze.
30. *Plymouth Sound.* In the West of England, an important harbor and naval station.
43. *pressed,* forced to serve. *Tourville,* the French admiral.
44. *Croisickese.* Of Croisic, a little fishing village of Brittany, where Browning liked to stay. See the title of the next poem in this selection. It was no doubt at Croisic that Browning picked up the story.
46. *Malouins.* Men of St. Malo.
49. *Grève.* La Grande Grève, the sandy shallows of the coast about St. Malo, especially to the east.

Page 767.

53. *Solidor.* A small harbor near the mouth of the Rance, beside the town of St. Servan. A fort of the same name defends it.
75. *profound* (here used as a noun). Depths.
92. *rampired.* Protected by ramparts or fortifications.

Page 768.

95. *for.* Instead of.
135. *the Louvre.* A famous palace at Paris, now used as an art museum. On its external walls there are eighty-six statues of notable Frenchmen, but not, of course, one of the forgotten hero, Hervè Riel.

THE TWO POETS OF CROISIC

The Prologue and the Epilogue are connected with the main poem (which is here omitted) only by the thought, common to all three, that love is a necessary part of the poet's life and art. The Prologue may cause a little difficulty to begin with by its extraordinary conciseness, but this only adds to its charm when the meaning has been grasped. The grammatical construction and the relation of the stanzas to each other are indicated in the following prose rendering: 'As a bank of moss stands bare till some May morning it is made beautiful by the sudden growth of the violets; as the night sky is dark and louring till a bright star pierces the concealing clouds; so the world seemed to hem in my life with disgrace till your face appeared to brighten it with the smile of God— the divine gift of love.'

In the Epilogue it is a young girl who repeats to the poet the 'pretty tale' he has once told her, and makes her own application of its significance. The story is found in Greek literature both in prose and in verse.

Page 769.

50. Here, as in lines 15 and 21, the poet has attempted to interrupt.
77. *Lotte.* The pet name of Charlotte Buff, upon whom Goethe modelled the heroine of *The Sorrows of Young Werther.* The reference here, however, is rather to Goethe's way of treating women in general than to the particular case of Lotte, for she was already engaged to be married when he met her.
100-2. The sweet lilt of the treble was supplied by the chirping of the cricket, when its absence would have allowed the predominance of the sombre bass. Cf. lines 112–114.

PHEIDIPPIDES

This is Browning's romantic setting of an incident of the Persian war which is thus recounted by the Greek historian Herodotus (VI, 105. Rawlinson's translation):—

'And first, before they left Athens, the generals sent off to Sparta a herald, one Pheidíppides, who was by birth an Athenian, and by birth and practice a trained runner. This man, according to the account which he gave to the Athenians on his return, when he was near Mount Parthenium, above Tegea, fell in with the god Pan, who called him by his name, and bade him ask the Athenians 'wherefore they neglected him so entirely, when he was kindly disposed towards them, and had often helped them in times past, and would do so again in time to come?' The Athenians, entirely believing in the truth of this report, as soon as their affairs were once more in good order, set up a temple to Pan under the Acropolis, and, in return for the message which I have recorded, established in his honor yearly sacrifices and a torch-race.

'On the occasion of which we speak, when Pheidippides was sent by the Athenian generals, and, according to his own account saw Pan on his journey, he reached Sparta on the very next day after quitting the city of Athens. Upon his arrival he went before the rulers, and said to them:—

'"Men of Lacedæmon, the Athenians beseech you to hasten to their aid, and not allow that state, which is the most ancient in all Greece, to be enslaved by the barbarians. Eretria, look you, is already carried away captive, and Greece weakened by the loss of no mean city."

'Thus did Pheidippides deliver the message committed to him. And the Spartans wished to help the Athenians, but were unable to give them any present succor, as they did not like to break their established law. It was the ninth day of the first decade, and they could not march out of Sparta on the ninth, when the moon had not reached the full. So they waited for the full of the moon.'

It will be seen that the original story makes no mention of a reward promised by Pan to Pheidippides. This was Browning's own invention, following a later tradition. In connection with the Marathon race at the Olympic games this was the subject of a considerable discussion, to which Professor Ernest A. Gardner contributed the following note as to Pheidippides: 'His great exploit, as recorded by Herodotus, was to run from Athens to Sparta within two days, for the practical purpose of summoning the Spartans to help against the Persian invader. The whole Athenian army made a forced march back to Athens immediately after the battle, also for a practical purpose; but there is no reason to suppose that Pheidippides or any one else ran the distance. The tale of his bearing the message of victory and falling dead when he arrived is probably an invention of some later rhetorician; it is referred to by Lucian, as well as by Robert Browning, but the two authorities are about of equal value for an occurrence of the fifth century B. C. It is most unlikely that Herodotus would have omitted such a story if it had been current in his time.'

χαίρετε, νικῶμεν, the Greek words prefixed by Browning to the poem, form the message which Plutarch and Lucian attribute to the dying runner after Marathon. Browning translates them 'Rejoice; we conquer!' and in lines 113–114 makes effective use of the fact that χαίρετε ('Hail!' or 'be of good cheer!') was also the customary form of salutation with the Greeks. Here again he was indebted to a suggestion derived from Lucian.

4. *Her of the ægis and spear.* Athene. *ægis,* shield.
5. *ye of the bow and the buskin.* Apollo and Artemis. *buskin,* laced boot.

Page 770.

9. *Archons.* Rulers or magistrates. *tettix.* The golden cicada ('locust') worn by Athenians to show that they were autochthons (natives of the country).
11. *Crowned with the myrtle.* This still refers to *Archons.* Browning is strictly accurate in these points of detail.
18. *water and earth.* The emblems of subjection. This demand was made in 493 B. C. The invading Persians were defeated at Marathon three years later.
19. *Eretria.* The chief city of the island of Eubœa, a little north of Athens.
20. *Hellas.* Greek civilization regarded as a whole.
25–40. Herodotus, as quoted above, says: 'So they waited for the full of the moon.' Grote ascribes the delay of the Spartans to conservatism, Rawlinson to envy; there was long-standing jealousy between Athens and Sparta, who were rivals for the leadership of Hellas. Sparta later sent 2,000 men, who arrived after the battle.
32–33. *Phoibos. Olumpos.* Browning preferred to retain the Greek spelling instead of the Latinized forms 'Phœbus' and 'Olympus.'
47. *filleted.* Adorned for sacrifice with wreaths and ribbons.
52. *Parnes.* In North Attica. But according to Herodotus as quoted above, Pan appeared to Pheidippides near Mount Parthenium in Argolis. This would be on his way from Athens to Sparta: Parnes would not. Professor John Macnaughton suggests that Browning made the change deliberately. 'He must have an Attic hill at all costs, when what he wants to say is that it is the spirit of her own mountains, her own autochthonous vigor, which is going to save Athens.

Page 770.

He consciously sacrifices, in a small and obvious point, literal accuracy to the larger truth.' (*Queen's Quarterly*, April, 1903.)

62. *Erebos*. The darkness under the earth—Erebus.

Page 771.

72–80. After Marathon, the Athenians built a temple to Pan and established yearly sacrifices and a torch-race in acknowledgment of the help the god had given them in the battle by affecting the Persians with 'panic'—the headlong fear Pan was supposed to inspire.

83. *Fennel*. Marathon, the name of the place where the battle was fought, is also Greek for fennel. This touch is Browning's own.

87. *on the razor's edge*. In a critical position—a proverbial phrase in Greek.

89. *Miltiades*. The leading Athenian citizen of the time and commander of the forces at Marathon.

106. *Akropolis*. The citadel of Athens.

109. *the Fennelfield*. Marathon. See note on line 83.

Pheidippides is in a measure of Browning's own, composed of dactyls and spondees, each line ending in a half foot or pause. It gives the impression of firm, continuous, and rhythmic emotion, and is generally fitted to convey the exalted sentiment and heroic character of the poem. (Mrs. Orr.)

The metrical scheme should be carefully analysed. Dr. D. G. Brunton uses this poem as an illustration of Browning's employment of rime 'merely as a means of heightening his secondary rhythm. The riming words are so far apart that we are aware only of a faint melodious echo. The always artificial and somewhat mechanical effect of rime is thus avoided, while its rhythmic essence is retained.'

Page 772.

CAVALIER TUNES

These two songs express the temper of those who supported Charles I (1625–1649) in his struggle with Parliament.

7. *Pym*, John (1584–1643), a leader of the Parliament party. *carles*, low-born men, churls.

13. *Hampden*, John (1594–1643), resisted the king's ship-money tax.

14. *Hazelrig*, Sir Arthur, one of the five members whom the king tried to impeach in 1642. *Fiennes*, Nathaniel (1608–1669), a Presbyterian member of Parliament in favor with Cromwell. *Young Harry*, son of the king's Secretary of State, Sir Henry Vane, who opposed his father.

15. *Rupert*, Prince Robert (1619–1682), grandson of James I. He supported Charles I.

22. *Nottingham*. See Map.

40. *Noll's damned troopers*, Oliver Cromwell's well-disciplined cavalry.

EPILOGUE TO ASOLANDO

We have given at the foot of each poem the date of its publication, and the volume to which this little poem is the Epilogue bears the date 1890; it was actually issued in London on Dec. 12, 1889, the day of Browning's death at Venice. 'The report of his illness had quickened public interest in the forthcoming work, and his son had the satisfaction of telling him of its already realized success, while he could still receive a warm, if momentary pleasure from the intelligence.' (Mrs. Orr.) Browning prepared the volume for publication while staying in the Asolo villa of his friend Mrs. Arthur Bronson, to whom it is dedicated. The fanciful title is derived from the Italian verb *asolare*—'to disport in the open air, amuse one's self at random'—popularly ascribed, Browning tells us, to Cardinal Bembo, who was Queen Cornaro's secretary, and in his dialogue, *Gli Asolani*, described the discussions on Platonic love and kindred subjects the little court at Asolo used to indulge in. To Mrs. Bronson Browning justified the title in the following sentence: 'I use it for love of the place and in requital of your pleas-

Page 772.

ant assurance that an early poem of mine first attracted you thither.' This was no doubt, *Pippa Passes*.

The Epilogue is a final expression of Browning's profound belief in a future life of hopeful activity. When reading the poem in proof, he said of the third stanza:— 'It almost looks like bragging to say this, and as if I ought to cancel it, but it's the simple truth; and as it's true, it shall stand.'

As in life he had faith in right, so in death—which only fools think of as a prison of the soul—he would be, not pitied, but encouraged by the good wishes of those who are working in the world.

17. *the unseen*. The poet himself after death.

Page 773.

ARNOLD — THE STUDY OF POETRY

This essay was published as the *Introduction* to *The English Poets*, edited by T. H. Ward, London, 1880.

a. 16. *these words of my own*, quoted—not quite exactly—from Arnold's introduction to *The Hundred Greatest Men*, Vol. I, London, 1879.

19. *In the present work*, in *The English Poets*, edited by Ward.

b. 20. *Wordsworth . . . Again Wordsworth*. These two quotations are taken from the *Preface* to the Second edition of *Lyrical Ballads*, 1800.

Page 774.

a. 23. *Sainte-Beuve*, Charles Augustin Sainte-Beuve (1804–1869), an eminent French critic.

Page 775.

a. 18. *Pellisson*, Paul Pellisson (1624–1693), a French man of letters and politician.

25. *Charles d' Héricault* (born 1823), French historian, novelist, and editor.

26. *Clément Marot*, a noted French poet (1497–1544).

29. *Methuselah*, see Genesis v, 25–27.

Page 776.

b. 19. *the Imitation, The Imitation of Christ*, a religious treatise commonly ascribed to Thomas à Kempis (1380–1471). The passage quoted is found in Bk. iii, Ch. 43, § 2.

36. *Cædmon*, an Anglo-Saxon poet who is said to have flourished about the year 670. The Biblical paraphrases long ascribed to Cædmon are now regarded as of uncertain authorship.

40. *M. Vitet*, a French critic and politician (1802–1873).

42. *Chanson de Roland*, the oldest French national epic, written, probably, during the closing years of the 11th century.

43. *joculator or jongleur*, well enough understood by our English word *minstrel*.

45. *Hastings*, battle of Hastings, in 1066.

48. *Roncevaux*, a pass in the Pyrenees, in Spain, notable as the scene of the events recounted in the *Chanson de Roland*.

50. *Turoldus or Théroulde*. The last line of the *Chanson* in the Oxford manuscript may be translated, 'Here ends the geste that *Turoldus* tells.' Turoldus may be the name of the minstrel who sang or recited the poem rather than that of the poet who composed it.

Page 777.

a. 21. *Dante*, Dante Alighieri (1265–1321), the greatest of Italian poets. His great work, *The Divine Comedy*, consisted of three parts: *Hell, Purgatory*, and *Paradise*. *Ugolino*, Ugolino della Gherardesca (d. 1289), a partisan leader in Pisa. With his two sons and two nephews he was starved to death in prison.

24. *Beatrice to Virgil*. According to *The Divine Comedy*, Virgil guided Dante through Hell and Purgatory. In Paradise, Beatrice became Dante's guide.

Page 777.

a. 31. *Henry the Fourth's expostulation, 2 Henry IV*, Act iii, Scene 1.
　36. *Hamlet's dying request.* In the closing scene of the play.
　41. *that Miltonic passage, Paradise Lost*, I, 599–602.
　44. *intrenched*, cut, furrowed.
b. 1. *two such lines, Paradise Lost*, I, 108–9.
　4. *exquisite close, Paradise Lost*, IV, 271–2.

Page 778.

b. 18. *Southey*, Robert Southey (1774–1843), an English poet and prose-writer.
　27. *Brunetto Latini* (1230–1294), an Italian poet, scholar, and orator. His chief work is an encyclopedia, *Trésor* (Treasure), in French.
　32. *Christian of Troyes.* The passage here quoted is from *Cliges*, lines 30–39.

Page 779.

a. 7. *that stanza.* To which of the Chaucerian stanzas Arnold refers we cannot be certain.
　13. *Wolfram of Eschenbach*, a German poet (fl. c. 1200).
　41. *Dryden's.* Quoted from the *Preface to the Fables.* See edition of Scott and Saintsbury, Vol. XI, p. 230.
b. 3. *Gower*, John Gower (1325?–1408), an English poet.
　43. *worship*, honor.
　44. *O Alma*, the beginning of a hymn to the Virgin.

Page 780.

b. 3. *Villon*, François Villon (1431–1484?), a French poet of irregular life.

Page 781.

a. 4. *Cowley*, Abraham Cowley (1618–1667), an English poet. See p. 183.
　6–11. *Dryden . . . there . . . perfect.* See *Preface to the Fables*, edition of Scott and Saintsbury, Vol. XI, p. 224.
　44. *Chapman*, George Chapman (1559?–1634), an English poet and dramatist, best known for his translation of Homer.
　47. *Gades*, a Phenician colony on the spot where Cadiz now stands, on the western coast of Spain.
　48. *Aurora*, the dawn, the East. *Ganges*, the sacred river of India.
　53–4. *Milton writing.* See Milton's *An Apology for Smectymnuus*, Prose Works (ed. Bohn), Vol. III, pp. 117–118.
b. 6. *Dryden telling us.* See the *Postscript to the Reader* appended to Dryden's translation of the *Æneid*.
　16. *Restoration*, the reëstablishment of the English monarchy with the return of Charles II in 1660.
　54. *A milk-white Hind . . . ranged*, the opening lines of *The Hind and the Panther.*

Page 782.

a. 5. *To Hounslow Heath . . . my own, Second Satire*, lines 143–4.
　34. *Gray.* See p. 399.
b. 8. *Mark ruffian Violence*, etc., from *On the Death of Robert Dundas, Esq.*
　16. *Clarinda's love-poet Sylvander.* Over the name Sylvander, Burns carried on a correspondence with Mrs. Maclehose, whom he called Clarinda.
　18. *gravel*, vex.

Page 783.

a. 3. *Leeze me on*, dear to me is. The quotation is from *The Holy Fair.* *gies*, gives. *mair*, more.
　5. *waukens lair*, wakes learning.
　6. *pangs*, crams, stuffs. *fou*, full.
　7. *gill*, a pint of ale. *penny wheep*, small ale.
　9. *kittle*, tickle, enliven.
　27. *aboon*, above.
　28. *mauna fa'*, may not get.
　34. *falls moralizing.* See *Epistle to a Young Friend.*
　35. *lowe*, flame.

Page 783.

a. 37. *rove*, roving.
　39. *quantum*, quantity.
　43. *Who made*, etc., from *Address to the Unco Guid.*
　52. *To make*, etc., from *To Dr. Blacklock.*
　53. *weans*, children.
b. 6. *Xenophon . . . Socrates.* In his *Memorabilia*, the Greek historian and essayist, Xenophon (born about 430, died after 357 B. C.), defends the memory of his master Socrates.

Page 784.

a. 2. *Thou Power Supreme*, etc., from *Winter.*
　6. *lave*, remainder.
　33. *Auerbach's Cellar of Goethe's Faust.* Johann Wolfgang von Goethe (1749–1832) is the greatest name in German literature. The scene in Auerbach's Cellar is to be found near the beginning of the First Part of *Faust.*
　36. *Aristophanes* (c. 450–c. 380 B. C.), the greatest of the Greek writers of comedy.
b. 4. *We twa*, etc., from *Auld Lang Syne.* *paidl't*, paddled. *burn*, stream, brook.
　5. *dine*, dinner-time.
　6. *braid*, broad.
　7. *Sin auld lang syne*, since old times.
　16. *Pinnacled . . . inane*, Shelley's *Prometheus Unbound*, Act III, Sc. iv, l. 204.
　21. *On the brink*, etc., from Shelley's *Prometheus Unbound*, Act. II, Sc. v.
　27. *minnie*, mother. *deave*, pester.

Page 788.

SOHRAB AND RUSTUM

　2. *Oxus*, the chief river of central Asia, flowing northwest into the Aral Sea.
　3. *Tartar camp.* The Tartars were nomadic tribes of central Asia and southern Russia.
　11. *Peran-Wisa*, a chief of central Asia, in command of Afrasiab's army of various Tartar tribes.
　15. *Pamere*, a plateau region of central Asia.
　38. *Afrasiab*, king of the Tartars.
　40. *Samarcand*, a city in Turkestan.
　42. *Ader-baijan*, the northwest province of Persia.

Page 789.

　60. *common fight*, general engagement.
　82. *Seistan*, a province of southwest Afghanistan bordering on Persian territory.
　85. *Persian King*, Kai Khosroo. See line 223.
　101. *Kara-Kul*, a district in the southern part of central Asia.
　107. *Haman*, a leader of the Tartars, next to Peran-Wisa in command.
　113. *Casbin*, a fortified city in the northern part of Persia.
　114. *Elburz*, mountains on the northern border of Persia. *Aralian*, on the Aral Sea, in central Asia.
　115. *frore*, frozen.
　119. *Bokhara*, a large district in central Asia, of which Bokhara, is the capital.
　120. *Khiva*, a district in the valley of the lower Oxus.
　121. *Toorkmuns*, a branch of the Turkish race, living in central Asia, east of the Caspian Sea.
　122. *Tukas*, from northwest Persia. *Salore*, a tribe living east of the Caspian Sea.
　123. *Attruck*, a river in northern Persia.
　128. *Ferghana*, a district in Turkestan.
　129. *Jaxartes*, an ancient name of the Sir-Daria River, which flows northwest through Turkestan into the Aral Sea.
　131. *Kipchak*, a district in central Asia.
　132. *Kalmucks*, Mongolian nomads dwelling in western Siberia. *Kuzzaks*, Cossacks, a warlike people in southern Russia and in various parts of Asia.
　133. *Kirghizzes*, a nomadic people in northern Turkestan.
　138. *Ilyats of Khorassan.* Khorassan is a province in northeastern Persia.

Page 790.

156. *corn*, grain.
160. *Cabool*, an important commercial city of northern Afghanistan.
161. *Indian Caucasus*, a range of mountains on the boundary between Turkestan and Afghanistan.
217. *Iran's*, Persia's.

Page 791.

257. *plain arms*, arms not emblazoned with devices. See line 266.
277. *Dight*, adorned, harnessed.
286. *Bahrein*, or Aval Islands, in the Persian Gulf, celebrated for their pearl-fisheries.
288. *tale*, reckoning, count.

Page 792.

412. *Hyphasis, Hydaspes*, two rivers in northern India.
414. *wrack*, ruin.

Page 793.

452. *autumn star*, Sirius, the Dog Star.
497. *shore*, cut.
508. *curdled*, thickened.

Page 794.

590. *Ader-baijan*. See l. 42.
592. *Koords*, a semi-independent people of western Persia.
596. *bruited up*, noised abroad.
613. *style*, name.

Page 796.

750. *Seistan*. See l. 82.
751. *Helmund*, a river in Seistan, in Afghanistan.
752. *Zirrah*, a lake in Seistan.
763-764. *Moorghab, Tejend, Hohik*, rivers in Turkestan.
765. *The northern Sir*, the Maxartes. See l. 129.

Page 797.

861. *Jemshid*, a legendary king. *Persepolis*, an ancient capital of Persia.
878. *Chorasmian waste*, a region of Turkestan.
880. *Right . . . star*, i.e., due north. *Orgunje*, a village near the delta of the Oxus.
887. *Pamere*. See l. 15.
890. *luminous home*, the Aral Sea.

THE SCHOLAR GIPSY

'There was very lately a lad in the University of Oxford who was by his poverty forced to leave his studies there and at last to join himself to a company of vagabond gipsies. Among these extravagant people, by the insinuating subtilty of his carriage, he quickly got so much of their love and esteem that they discovered to him their mystery. After he had been a pretty while exercised in the trade, there chanced to ride by a couple of scholars who had formerly been of his acquaintance. They quickly spied out their old friend among the gipsies, and he gave them an account of the necessity which drove him to that kind of life, and told them that the people he went with were not such impostors as they were taken for, but that they had a traditional kind of learning among them, and could do wonders by the power of imagination, their fancy binding that of others; that himself had learned much of their art, and when he had compassed the whole secret, he intended, he said, to leave their company, and give the world an account of what he had learned.' (Glanvil's *Vanity of Dogmatizing*, 1661.)

2. *wattled cotes*, sheep-folds.
19. *corn*, grain.
31. *Glanvil's book*. See note above.
42. *erst*, formerly.

Page 798.

57. *Hurst*, Cumner Hurst, a hill a few miles southwest of Oxford.
58. *Berkshire*, a county south of Oxford.
59. *ingle-bench*, bench in the chimney-corner.

Page 798.

74. *Bablock-hithe*, a village about four miles southwest of Oxford.
79. *Wychwood bowers*, Wychwood Forest, ten miles or so northwest of Oxford.
83. *Fyfield elm in May*, the May-pole dance at Fyfield, some six miles southwest of Oxford.
91. *Godstow Bridge*, about two miles up the Thames from Oxford.
95. *lasher pass*, mill race.
111. *Bagley Wood*, southwest of Oxford.
114. *tagged*, marked.
115. *Thessaly*, the name of the northeastern district of ancient Greece, here given to a ground near Bagley Wood.
125. *Hinksey*, a village a short distance south of Oxford.
129. *Christ-Church*, a large and fashionable college in Oxford.
133. *Glanvil*, Joseph Glanvil (1636-1680), an English clergyman and writer.

Page 799.

147. *teen*, sorrow.
182. *amongst us one*, perhaps Carlyle.
208-9. *Averse . . . turn*. Dido, queen of Carthage, deserted by her lover Æneas, slew herself. When Æneas encountered her on his journey through Hades, she turned scornfully away from him.
220. *dingles*, wooded dells.
232. *Tyrian*, a city of Phenicia, anciently an important commercial center.
236. *Ægean isles*, islands of the Ægean Sea, east of Greece.
238. *Chian wine*. Chios, an island in the Ægean, was noted for its wine.
239. *tunnies*, a kind of fish.

Page 800.

244. *Midland waters*, Mediterranean Sea.
245. *Syrtes*, Gulf of Sidra, on northern coast of Africa.
247. *western straits*, Strait of Gibraltar.
250. *Iberians*, inhabitants of Spain and Portugal.

RUGBY CHAPEL

Written in memory of the poet's father, Dr. Thomas Arnold (1795-1842), head-master of Rugby, whose remains are interred in Rugby Chapel.

Page 802.

DOVER BEACH

For the location of Dover see Map.

15. *Sophocles*, a great tragic poet of Greece, 495 or 496-406 B. C.
16. *Ægæan*, the part of the Mediterranean Sea which lies between Greece and Asia Minor.
28. *shingles*, coarse, rounded gravel found on the sea-shore.
35. *darkling*, dimly seen.

Page 805.

ROSSETTI — FRANCESCA DA RIMINI

Francesca da Rimini, an Italian lady of the thirteenth century, became the wife of Giovanni Malatesta. Having discovered the love between Francesca and his young brother Paolo, Giovanni killed them both. An incident in the love-story of Paolo and Francesca is put into the mouth of Francesca in Dante's *Divine Comedy*, *Hell*, Canto v, whence it is here rendered by Rossetti.

17. *Lancelot*, the lover of Queen Guenevere, in several medieval romances.
26. *A Galahalt*. Galahalt was the go-between for Lancelot and Guenevere. Hence the book that brought Paolo and Francesca together is here called 'a Galahalt.'

Page 807.

THE KING'S TRAGEDY

'Tradition says that Catherine Douglas, in honor of her heroic act when she barred the door with her arm against the murderers of James the First of Scots, received popularly the name of "Barlass." This name

Page 807.

remains to her descendants, the Barlas family, in Scotland, who bear for their crest a broken arm. She married Alexander Lovell of Bolunnie.

'A few stanzas from King James's lovely poem, known as *The King's Quair*, are quoted in the course of this ballad. The writer must express regret for the necessity which has compelled him to shorten the ten-syllabled lines to eight syllables, in order that they might harmonize with the ballad meter.' (Rossetti.)

The passages from *The King's Quair* quoted in the present poem are printed in italics.

James I was murdered at Perth, Feb. 20, 1437, by the Earl of Atholl and Robert Graham (Græme).

Page 808.

8. *palm-play ball*, an old kind of tennis in which the ball was struck with the hand rather than with a racket.
26. *Bass Rock*, an islet at the entrance of the Firth of Forth.
29. *England's king*, Henry IV.
30. *long years immured*. In 1405, on his way from Scotland to France, James was captured by the English, and detained in one English prison or another until 1424.
37. *a lady*, Joan Beaufort, daughter of the Earl of Somerset. She became the wife of James in 1424.
41. *a sweeter song*, a reference to King James' poem, *The King's Quair*.
45. *teen*, sorrow, grief.
48. *At Scone . . . crowned*. Scone, in Perthshire, Scotland, was the traditional scene of Scottish coronations. The coronations of James I and Joan occurred on May 21, 1424.
72. *leaguer*, siege. *Roxbro' hold*, Roxburgh Castle, on the Tweed, near the English border, besieged by James I in 1436.
105. *Three Estates*, that is, the nobility, the clergy, and the common people.

Page 809.

122. *Græme*. See introductory note above.
157. *sea-wold*, open land.
162. *writhen*, twisted.
165. *rack*, floating mass of clouds.
176. *Duchray . . . Dhu*. The Duchray is probably the smallest stream west of Loch Lomond. A Loch Dhu is found in southwest Aberdeenshire.
179. *Inchkeith Isle*, a small island in the Firth of Forth.
181. *cerecloth*, waxed cloth, used in burial.
183. *Links of Forth*, slightly undulating land on the Firth of Forth.
192. *drouth*, thirst, lack.

Page 810.

217. *hind*, peasant.
246. *solace and disport*, pleasure and entertainment.
251. *lift*, sky, air.
305. *Windsor's castle-hold*. During the period of his detention in England, James was for a time imprisoned in Windsor Castle.

Page 811.

316. *Worship, ye lovers*. The lines printed in italics are adapted from King James' *The King's Quair*.
343. *blissful aventure*, happy chance.
388. *pearl-tired*, attired in pearls.

Page 812.

414. *voidee-cup*, a drink of spiced wine served well after dinner-time and before bed-time.
424. *riven and brast*, torn and broken.
430. *hurdles*, narrow boards.
440. *ingle-nook*, a corner by the fire.
442. *arrased wall*, hung with tapestries from Arras.
445. *dight*, prepared, placed.
448. *doffed*, took off.
462. *dule to dree*, sorrow to suffer.
469. *Aberdour*, north of Edinburgh, on the north shore of the Firth of Forth.

Page 813.

532. *heft*, handle.
585. *litters*, movable bed-frames.

Page 815.

751. *requiem-knell*, the bell at requiem-mass for the dead.

Page 819.

MORRIS — THE EARTHLY PARADISE

The Earthly Paradise is a collection of stories related, supposedly, at fortnightly feasts alternately by the Wanderers, who are Norwegian mariners, and by certain men of a 'Western land' whose guests they have become. Twenty-four tales are eventually told in the course of the year. *Atalanta's Race* and *The Lady of the Land* are the first and eighth stories, respectively.

Page 820.

ATALANTA'S RACE

I

1. *Arcadian woods*. Arcadia was an inland country of Peloponnesian Greece.
14. *cornel*, the tough wood of the cornel-tree.
28. *King Schœneus' town*, probably Tegea or Mantinea, these being two of the larger towns of Arcadia.
63. *the fleet-foot one*, Hermes, Mercury.

Page 821.

79. *Diana*, patroness of hunting and woodland sports.

Page 822.

II

51. *the sea-born one*, Venus.
65. *presently*, at once.
73. *Dryads*, wood-nymphs.
75. *Adonis' bane*. Adonis was killed by a wild boar that he had wounded.
78. *Argive cities*, cities of the Grecian state of Argolis.
91. *must*, new wine not yet fermented.

Page 823.

142. *three-formed goddess*, Diana.
149. *framer of delights*, Venus.
168. *Artemis*, Diana.
207. *sleepy garland*, poppy wreath.
210. *heading*, beheading.

III

1. *Argolis*, one of the states of Greece.
2. *the goddess*, Venus.
6. *murk*, what is left of fruit after the juice has been extracted.

Page 824.

8. *close*, enclosure.
54. *unholpen*, unhelped.
70. *the golden age*, a fabled age of innocence and plenty.
100. *wrack*, seaweeds cast up on the shore.

Page 825.

169. *scrip*, wallet.

Page 826.

IV

72. *the Argive*, Milanion, whose father was king of Argolis.

V

1. *the posts*, the starting and turning posts

Page 827.

5. *mighty lord*, Zeus.
6. *her*, Venus.
16. *Love's servant*, Milanion.
21. *maiden zone*, a girdle worn by maidens before marriage.

THE LADY OF THE LAND

35. *law*, belief, religion.

Page 829.

182. *poor shepherd*, Paris.

Page 830.
310. *orb of June*, the moon.

Page 831.
389. *Cathay*, a medieval name for a vague region in eastern Asia.
467. *wend*, go.

Page 833.
SWINBURNE—ATALANTA IN CALYDON
FIRST CHORUS
5–8. *nightingale . . . Thracian ships . . . tongueless vigil.* Philomela and Procne were daughters of Pandion, king of Attica, who gave Procne in marriage to his ally, the Thracian king Tereus. After Procne had borne a son, Itys (Itylus), Tereus concealed her in the country, that he might dishonor her sister Philomela. Having accomplished his purpose, he deprived Philomela of her tongue. By embroidering her story on a robe, however, Philomela communicated the truth to Procne, whereupon Procne killed her son and served his flesh on a dish before Tereus. When Tereus pursued the fleeing sisters, the gods granted them an escape by transforming Procne into a swallow and Philomela into a nightingale.
10. *Maiden most perfect*, Artemis.

Page 834.
41. *Pan*, god of flocks and shepherds.
44. *Mænad*, a female worshipper of Bacchus. *Bassarid*, a Lydian or Thracian bacchanal.

Page 835.
THIRD CHORUS
49. *Aphrodite*, Venus, goddess of love.
136, 146. *Tyro, Enipeus.* Tyro was the wife of Cretheus, beloved by the river-god Enipeus in Thessaly.

Page 836.
THE GARDEN OF PROSERPINE
28. *Proserpine*, queen of the infernal regions. During the six months of the year that she passed in Olympus she was considered an amiable and propitious divinity; but during the six months in Hades she was stern and terrible. She personified the changing seasons.
HERTHA
Hertha, or Nerthus was the Germanic goddess of the earth, of fertility, and of growth.

Page 839.
A FORSAKEN GARDEN
The scene of this poem is East Dene, Bonchurch, Isle of Wight.

Page 840.
THALASSIUS
15. *Oread*, a nymph of the hills.
18. *Cymothoë*, a nereid, or nymph of the sea.
37. *he*, Walter Savage Landor. See p. 642.

Page 841.
88–9. *And gladly . . . dead.* A rendering of the epitaph written by Landor for the Spanish troops who died resisting the invasion of Napoleon:

    Emeriti lubenter quiescerimus
    Libertate parta;
    Quiescimus amissa perlubenter.

Page 842.
THE ROUNDEL
The roundel in Swinburne's sense is illustrated by this poem. It consists of nine complete lines arranged as follows: *a b a, b a b, a b a*, part of the first line being repeated as a refrain after the third and ninth lines. The refrain is usually so selected as to rime with the *b* lines.

Page 843.
COR CORDIUM
Cor cordium, 'Heart of Hearts,'—the words on Shelley's tomb in Rome.
NON DOLET
4. *the Roman wife.* 'Pætus Cæcina was ordered by the Emperor Claudius to take his own life; and when he hesitated, his wife Arria stabbed herself, crying, "*Pæte, non dolet*" (Pætus, it does not hurt).' (Beatty.)
ON THE DEATHS OF THOMAS CARLYLE AND GEORGE ELIOT
Carlyle and George Eliot died in the same year, 1881.

Page 844.
CHRISTOPHER MARLOWE
9–10. These two lines are quoted from Marlowe's *Tamburlaine*, Part I, Act v, Scene 1.

Page 845.
MEREDITH — LOVE IN THE VALLEY
First published in 1851; here printed in the fuller and more perfect version of 1878.

Page 846.
24. *for*, in return for, instead of.
32. *Off a sunny border*, the sunlit edge of the cloud.
50. *bloomy*, like blossom.
77. *the rose-flush drinks the rayless planet.* The rising sun absorbs the morning star in its brighter rays.
88. *Covert*, thick wood.

Page 847.
117. *yaffle*, the European green woodpecker, noted for its loud laugh-like note.
128. *like the sun.* By her blinding beauty.
132. *wink*, flash with quick darting motion.
134. *Swarms*, quivers like a swarm of bees.
148. *blue* (sky).
152. *tiger*, striped like a tiger, or, perhaps, fierce.
154. *nutbrown tresses*, of the wheat.
156. *girdle*, of straw about the sheaf.

Page 848.
162. *Clipped*, cut off, or, perhaps, embraced. *violet shaded*, by the purple shadows of the setting sun. *snow*, the season has changed from autumn to winter.
165. *black print-branches*, the shadows of the branches printed black on the snow in the moonlight.
178. *Deepens*, towers.
179. *of*, at.
183. *in our names*, as we greeted each other.
188. *girdle . . . tresses.* See ll. 154 and 156.
193. *beamy*, with sunbeams between the showers.
200. *tears*, evoked by the vision seen before waking.
203. *dogwood*, which has red branches.
204. *whitebeam*, a tree with leaves white underneath, which are suddenly lighted up by a gust of wind.
208. *what is for heaven alone*, the secret which I wish to breathe to heaven. See ll. 120–2.
JUGGLING JERRY
7. *One that outjuggles all.* Death.
25. *cricket*, play at cricket.
27. *bale*, a small piece of wood placed on top of the wickets, and whipped off by the wicket keeper to put the batsman 'out.'

Page 849.
33. *victual*, pronounced 'vittle.'
39. *session* (of Parliament).
41. *mock thunder* of the juggler's pistol.
45. *professor* of juggling.
67. *bolus*, a large pill.
70. *fields*, souls or bodies.
81. *chirper*, glass.
88. *sword-trick*, by which a sword appears to be swallowed.

Page 849.

THE OLD CHARTIST

The Chartists were political revolutionaries, whose agitation came to a head in 1848. Some of them were transported on charges of sedition. The hero of the poem has returned to England after serving his sentence.

7. *transportation,* imprisonment beyond the seas.
22. *his Grace's,* the Duke's.
28. *wrong note,* too high, in advance of the time.

Page 850.

39. *poll,* head.
56. *parson . . . bishop,* from the black-gowned parson into the bishop with his sleeves of white lawn.
65. *needle-muzzle,* sharp nose.
76. *place,* situation as a linen draper or dry goods salesman.
87. *dock.* At the police court.

FRANCE 1870

This ode was written in the hour of France's bitter humiliation by Germany, when Paris was in the hands of the enemy. Meredith regards France as the nation which brought political enlightenment and freedom to the world at the Revolution, but surrendered her ideals at the instigation of Napoleon III, whom he despises as a trickster. The Franco-Prussian war, he thinks, did France a service by showing her the hollowness of the pretensions of her sham-hero, and by recalling her to the path of light and freedom from which she had been beguiled by the Emperor's dreams of military glory. France is treated throughout under the similitude of the mythological Prometheus, who brought fire from heaven for the service of man, and was punished by Zeus by being chained on a rock with a vulture perpetually tearing his vitals: being immortal, he suffered unending agony, although the bringer of light and fire—the foundation of all the arts—to men. He is first mentioned by name in l. 270.

11. *when our time was dark.* Before the Revolution of 1788.
12. *fetters,* of feudal serfdom. *spark,* of freedom.

Page 851.

24. *Angel and Wanton.* Half an angel of light, and half sunk in vice. The state of private and public morality under Napoleon III was low.
31. *riven,* split by lightning.
37–8. *the lurid hosts who . . . irreparable mischance.* The Fallen Angels in Milton's *Paradise Lost.*
45. *fire from heaven.* Here the Prometheus metaphor begins.
48. *Mother of Pride.* The past is contrasted with the present, which is pictured in the words that follow.
51. *Heroes, bondsmen.* The contrast continued.
56. *crown with bays.* The King of Prussia was made Emperor of Germany in the Palace of Versailles, on the outskirts of Paris.
64. *Tranced circumambient.* The world is imaged as a circle of spectators, struck dumb with astonishment.
65. *Beaks.* As the vulture tore the entrails of Prometheus with its beak.
72. *Chamber* (gives answer) to chamber. *sequent,* logical, reasoning.
74. *vaults* (of the brain).
84. *long,* long ago.
100. *pinnacled Alp.* A reference to the crossing of the Alps by Napoleon I, a feat up to that time thought impossible.
106. *along the snows.* Napoleon I's retreat from Moscow.
112. *oriflamme,* the banner of ancient France, which gave place to the imperial eagle under Napoleon I.
113. *forgets,* how they sucked, etc. (l. 110), during the wars of Napoleon I. Earth covers the slain with the green grass, but the gods do not forget; they punish after the lapse of many years.

Page 852.

120. *They,* the gods.
133. *Immortal.* Again the Prometheus metaphor.
136. *Unsparing.* The gods are merciless as were the children of France in their hour of triumph over Europe under Napoleon I.
140. *perishable,* material, the vine and grain of l. 138. *imperishable,* spiritual.
153. *worm,* grave.
161. *their,* the gods'.
171. *fables of her priests.* Napoleon III had the support of the Roman Catholic clergy, who, when the tide of battle went against France, prayed for a special intervention of Providence.
182. *In peril of,* at the risk of losing.
190. *a forfeit blade.* Meredith changed this afterwards to 'a broken blade.' His point is that France was defeated because of the insufficiency of her military organization, which, under the laxity and corruption of the administration of Napoleon III, had been allowed to fall into decay.
194. *Clamored of treachery.* At the surrender of Sedan, which was the turning point of the war, there were outcries that France had been betrayed to the Germans by the leaders.
204. *her Dishonorer,* Napoleon III.
207. *Bellona and Bacchante,* the goddesses of War and Bacchic Frenzy.
208. *Schoolmen of the North,* the Germans, who planned the campaign scientifically long before it began.
210. *faithful to himself,* to the law of strength. See ll. 161–170.
215. *A name of terror.* Napoleon III was much dreaded in Europe, but was suffering from severe illness, and showed a lack of self-control at critical moments.
216. *trickster.* Napoleon III.
217. *for dominion.* Napoleon had gained military successes and territory in previous wars. *to patch a throne.* The war against Germany was said to be undertaken to divert the public attention from internal misgovernment and secure the succession of Napoleon III's son, the Prince Imperial.
220. *for their sake,* i.e., in a righteous cause.
221. *divine,* and therefore immortal.
228. *her own* (line).

Page 853.

229. *That,* so that. *cease,* die.
231. *burn . . . Whatso.* Destroy her charms with a resolute heart, which is left unconsumed.
234. *from prone,* from the position of humiliation, to which she has been stricken down.
236. *His,* Ambition's.
237. Shown by her taskmasters (the Germans) to be the retribution for her misdeeds in the past.
252. *The Man.* Prometheus.
284. *prototype.* Prometheus, the light-bringer. See l. 251.
302. *ghost,* spirit.
322. *the undying Ones.* The gods, or eternal principles of right.

Page 854.

334. *counter-changing,* interchanging, checkered.
335. *meridional,* of the sun at noon.
341. *in fee,* in lordship, placing them under an everlasting obligation.
343. *aureole,* crown of glory.

THE LARK ASCENDING

Cf. Wordsworth (p. 535) and Shelley, *To a Sky Lark* (p. 618). The different ways in which the subject is treated by the three poets should not be overlooked.

13. *quick o' the ear,* inmost nerve of the ear.
14. *her,* the brain.
16. *dry* (referring to springs), unresponsive. *he,* the lark.
44. *argentine,* silvery.
46. *choric,* dancing in the wind.

Page 854.

48. *shivers wet*. In a storm of wind and rain.
49. *chime* (of a waterfall).
56. *him*, the lark.
64. The sentence here ended runs on continuously from the beginning of the poem, like the lark's song.
75. *fallows*, fields lying fallow.

Page 855.

101-124. In associating the lark's song with human intellectual activities, Meredith strikes a characteristic note, different from that of the older poets of the nineteenth century.
110. *Earth*. See biographical sketch, p. 845.

THE WOODS OF WESTERMAIN

This is more difficult than the preceding poems, and had perhaps better not be attempted by students who have not attained some mastery of Meredith's habits of thought and modes of expression.

The first three stanzas are similar in structure, the first part in each indicating the consequences of an attitude of trustfulness towards Nature, the second part the consequences of an attitude of distrust. At the beginning of each stanza, the poet says: 'You may enter the enchanted woods safely, if you do so trustingly;' at the end, 'If you enter distrustfully, you do so at your own risk.' The fourth stanza passes into a general discussion of the conduct of life, considered allegorically under the similitude of a wood.

5-7. If you toss your heart up—you fare successfully.
8-9. But if you show a sign of fear, they change their form.
15. *golden bath*, of sunlight.
17. *winnowing* plumes, fanlike wings.
18. *on a chuckle*, chuckling.
21. *jar*, a bird with wings mottled like those of a moth.
23. Note the change of thought.
25. *rood*, a small plot of ground, a fraction of an acre.
30-40. The wood opens in various directions with bramble bushes, and wild strawberries, topped by the starflower; the ground is encumbered by fallen twigs, fir cones, seed pods, mole hills, and parti-colored flint stones; here and there in the earth are to be seen the foot prints of small animals that have fled in fear.
46. *whins*, low shrubs.
47. *minikins*, small birds.
51. *flowing not from purse*, not dependent upon the power of money.
58. If you desire it with all your soul.
59. *t' the lyre*, to the poet.
62. *Granaries*, treasures.
65. Not enslaved to worldly appetites.
66-73. In the place too often usurped by mere worldly success, you will enthrone the joy evoked by such natural beauties as a brook or a waterfall, or a clearing in the wood, where the light shines through, and the deer pass, stately and magnificent as the knights of old.
74-81. Or the dull eyes of cattle chewing the cud may take your mind back to the primeval ages, before mind was developed, when Earth was mere rocks and slime, and the sky was a place for ungainly winged creatures—the pterodactyls.
84. *The Nurse of seed*. The principle of reproduction.
88-91. If you follow Nature, you will embrace closely her glory narrowed down to beauty, or take in arms spread wide as air her beauty enlarged to magnificence.

Page 856.

92. *white Foam-born*, Venus, the goddess of Love.
94. *Phœbus*, Apollo, the god of song. *Phœbe*, Diana the huntress, goddess of chastity.
95. *Pan*, the god of untamed Nature.
97. *her*, Nature.

Page 856.

98. *sterner worship*, of modern science, which regards them not as deities but as natural forces.
99. *her*, Nature.
103. *awn*, the delicate silky growth that terminates the grain-sheath of barley, oats, etc.
104. *Argent*, silvery. The moon is imaged as Diana the huntress.
105. *the blush*, of sunrise.
107. Passing, and eternally recurring.
110. *opposing grandeurs*, as of moonlight and sunrise. The spirit of beauty saves their glory from death ('fleetingness').
114-121. The divine harmony of Nature destroys no spring (fountain) of strength; it subdues, but does not slay, guiding the course of the stream, but preserving its source; it tempers the heat of young blood, but hears the heart of its wildness beat through self-restraint, like the solemn yet ardent dance of centaurs on the greensward.
122-129. If you catch the sense of Nature's harmony, it will open the way to a larger fellowship with humanity, and to a Love, instinct with passion, soaring beyond egotism, if you do not put the sensual appetites in the foreground.
132-133. Womanhood, the supreme triumph of Nature, demands reverence for Nature's earlier developments.
138. *throat and thigh*. The waterfall, reflecting the rays of the sun, is pictured as a human being.
143. *Bare or veiled*. The 'courtly dames' are compared to the open waters and whispering leaves, with which they share the sincerity of Nature.
146. Part of the Nature, by which they are surrounded and of which they are the outcome.
147. They have the surety of the tree's roots and the grace of its branches.
148-151. They reveal the treasures of their hearts, and do not conceal those of their minds, in order to flatter the pride of the tyrant, Man; for when the mind is not open to the light of day, darkness breeds trickery. Of woman's wiles when oppressed and their consequences, strange and terrible stories are told.
154. *the ancient battle*, between the sexes.
155. *astonished friends*, man and woman, astonished at the charm of the new relation of friendship.
158. *the tiger*, man. *the snake*, woman.
162-165. Now the woman leads the man in a silken leash, decked with wild flowers, and unconscious of the constraint, though feeling its sweetness.
166-169. Love ennobles the senses, and develops individuality.
172. The dots indicate the change of thought.
181. *Gaps*, rends.
185. *fell*, savage, dreadful.
187. *Fellowly*, in the spirit of comradeship.
189. *cocks of day*, harbingers of dawn.
191. *quern*, mill.
199. *thought and felt*, what is thought and what is felt.
200-201. Nature flows on, ever-changing, like the brook, not foolishly standing still in established customs, like a stagnant pool.

Page 857.

209. *them you quit*, the fellow mortals you leave behind.
210-211. The most soaring spirit gains by contact with common humanity.
215-216. The sense of superiority to one's fellows is always dangerous.
218. Again the thought changes.
220. *Dragon-fowl*, of selfishness. See l. 243.
226-227. No force, not even that of egotism, is destroyed, but is controlled and turned to noble uses.
235-238. Nothing in nature is philosophically wise, least of all man, except when long experience has freed his mind from egotism.
239. *him*. The dragon of selfishness. *dumb*, with astonishment. Beware of self-esteem, even when you seem to be drinking in wisdom.

Page 857.

241. *she*, wisdom. When you feel that you only are wise, then above all beware.
244. *late* in the history of the race.
250. *Maw*, stomach, material desires.
251. Shrewd only for his own material interests.
256. *within*. See l. 251.
257. Like the pine, soft within, but obdurate to all outside himself.
265–267. Out of sight of heaven, to the very heart of Earth, the source of her activity and the spring of progress.
270–287. Humanity is imagined as a crowd gazing on the source of Nature, and discovering in the history of the race the slow beginnings of human sensibility. In all these beginnings are described the efforts of man to demand of Nature the satisfaction of material and selfish desires. But Nature cares nothing for the individual, and gives no sign in answer to the cravings of egotism. She proceeds with her task of developing the human spirit out of sensual desires.
293–305. Regarded merely from the physical side, the history of the race appears only a constant interchange of beginnings and endings, darkness and light, life and death, youth and age; but regarded spiritually, beyond the mere senses, Nature is seen to be permanent.
306–309. We may regard Nature with loathing, gazing on the dust in the tomb, or with love, keeping in mind the spiritual sense of living men.
312–313. Yield to the sensual appetites, or, like Nature, give yourself to service.
321. *Airing*, opening.
323. *seer*, the prophet or beholder of Nature.
324. *witch*, bewitch, play the witch, charming you with external beauty.
329. *her awful tremble*. What is dreadful in Nature, as well as what appears beneficent.
330. *Fount*. The source of Nature. See ll. 266–7.

Page 858.

346–349. Not the pleasures of sense, which, wantonly followed, grow into habits, and like hags ride the souls of men to destruction.
350–351. Pleasures that keep the senses under the control of the intellect.
352. *sequent birth*. Body, mind, and spirit developed in orderly succession.
356–363. 'It is fatal to neglect either blood, or brain, or soul. If we part company with any one of these three we shall be wrecked. The attempt to develop soul without blood, or worse still, without brain, is to court certain disaster, of which the chronicles of religion are full. The athletic craze for training the blood alone, is no better; and if the brain of the mere intellectual be a higher development, it is not in itself perfect, or satisfying, or secure.' (G. M. Trevelyan.)
363. *Glassing her*, mirroring Earth or Nature.
370. *Eglantine*, the wild-rose.
371. *darkness*. Dark eglantine is thought most beautiful.
372. *Knowing*, who know.
373. *kin o' the rose*. Short-lived, but beautiful while it lasts.
374. Those who have explored the depths of Nature use life as a tool or weapon.
379. If they ask the secret of life, the answer is the same as the question 'Why?' With this answer they are content. See l. 369.
380. *ramped*, held in check. Selfishness being subdued, they will thrill to be marked for service.
384–385. So that in the hour of death, where fear sits, they will still see the stream of life flowing on.
386. *lynx*. Eyeing it without fear. *her*, Nature.
388. *Sphinx*. Riddle.
396. *lop*, trim, keep within bounds.
418. *Momently*, for a moment.
430. *at the paths behind*, at the past history of the race.
441. Again the note of warning.

Page 858.

446–452. If with the sons of selfishness you fear all that is outside of your personal interests. All these are conditional clauses, dependent on l. 453.

Page 859.

455. *Nighted*, descending by night, like a vulture.
457. *One whose eyes are out*. Ignorance.
463. *yapping*, barking.
466. *drums the sconce*, confuses the intelligence.
467. *nibblenips*, pinches, torments.
469. *demon-growing girl*, the girl being transformed into a demon.
479. *yell you Where*, yell to you where you are.

MODERN LOVE

This beautiful series of sixteen-line stanzas in its entirety tells the tragedy of an ill-assorted pair. In the first here given, the husband looks back to an evening before the shipwreck of their love. The second describes a meeting by the sea after a hollow though well-meant reconciliation. The third commemorates a moment of peaceful companionship. The last analyses the causes of their failure, and contrasts the immense forces of passion with their pitiful outcome when not wisely guided and controlled.

Page 860.

ELIZABETH BARRETT BROWNING
SONNETS FROM THE PORTUGUESE

The sonnet series is based upon the courtship of Robert Browning and Elizabeth Barrett (see p. 739). When the poems were published the description 'from the Portuguese' was adopted for the sake of disguising their personal import.

I

1–2. *Theocritus had sung . . . years*. Idyl xv, 104–5.
13. '*Death*'! *I said*. Miss Barrett had been for years an invalid.

V

2. *As once Electra*, etc. An allusion to a passage in the *Electra* of Sophocles in which the heroine, holding as she supposes the urn containing the ashes of her brother Orestes, experiences a sudden revulsion of feeling when she finds him alive before her.
11. *those laurels*, etc. Browning's poetical fame.

Page 861.

XXXV

1. *If I leave all*, etc. The marriage with Browning, because of the character and attitude of Miss Barrett's father, involved the severing of all home ties.

Page 862.

EDWARD FITZGERALD — THE RUBÁIYÁT

7. *the dark Ferrásh*, servant, camp-follower.
11. *Saki*, wine-bearer.

Page 867.

SIDNEY DOBELL — AMERICA

These sonnets are from a series published during the Crimean War, when America was supposed to be hostile to Great Britain.
6. *satcheled*. Compare *As You Like It*, II, 7, 145, 'the schoolboy with his satchel,' etc.

Page 869.

AUSTIN DOBSON — A DEAD LETTER

11. *Goldsmith's Madam Blaize*. An allusion to Goldsmith's ridiculous poem *An elegy on the Glory of her Sex, Mrs. Mary Blaize*.
14. *tea-board garden-maker*. Apparently, one designing a garden on the scale of a tea-tray.
15. *Dutch William's day*. William of Orange's time, 1688 and after.
38. *Tithonus*. See p. 778 and note.
52. *Damson Jam*. Jam made of the damson, or damask plum.

NOTES TO OTHER VICTORIAN POETS, PP. 869–881

Page 869.
62. *Padesoy*, paduasoy, a rich heavy silk from Padua.
63. *the Vapors*, 'the blues.'
79. *Bonzes*, images of Buddhist priests.

Page 870.
112. *Point and Flanders.* Lace.

JAMES THOMSON — MELENCOLIA
16. *the pure sad artist.* Albrecht Dürer (1471–1528), Nuremberg, painter and engraver. The sketch here described is one of his works on copper.

Page 871.
74. *teen and threne*, sorrow and lamentation.

Page 872.

BRIDGES — MOONLIGHT
3. *Grillie*, from the French *grillon*, a cricket.
7. *Queen of Sorrows*, the moon.

Page 873.

WILLIAM ERNEST HENLEY
OUT OF THE NIGHT THAT COVERS ME
13. *strait*, narrow.

PRO REGE NOSTRO
The title means, 'For our King.'

WATSON — WORDSWORTH'S GRAVE
Wordsworth was buried at Grasmere in the Lake District which he loved. He was born near and lived in the District for the greater part of his life. See Map.
5. *translunar*, literally, beyond the moon; figuratively, ethereal, visionary.
17. *Lethe*, a river of Hades whose waters brought oblivion and forgetfulness of former existence to the dead.

DAVIDSON — THIRTY BOB A WEEK
Bob, a shilling, rather less than 25 cents.

Page 875.

THOMPSON — THE HOUND OF HEAVEN
8. *Titanic*, the Titans, a race in Greek Mythology, were taken as types of enormousness.
12. *instancy*, insistency.
17. *hearted casement*, heart-shaped window.
24. *wist*, knew.
25. *margent*, margin.
41. *savannahs*, in reality, flat treeless plains.
44. *Plashy*, speckled as if splashed with color.
66. *Lady-Mother*, Nature.
100. *owe*, own.

Page 876.
112. *harness*, armor.
117. *Shook the pillaring hours*, as Samson made an end.
123. *sun-starts*, reflections of the sun.
129. *overplussed*, overweighted.
131. *amaranthine.* The amaranth was a fabulous flower supposed never to fade.
159. *shard*, fragment.

HOUSMAN — A SHROPSHIRE LAD
IV
17. *thews*, sinews.

Page 877.
XXXI
8. *soldier of the Queen*, Queen Victoria.
XLI
7. *bourn*, destination.
16. *ladysmocks*,

> 'Daisies pied and violets blue
> And lady-smocks all silver-white.'
>   Shakespeare, *Love's Labour Lost.*

Page 878.

NEWBOLT — DRAKE'S DRUM
3. *Nombre Dios*, a Spanish port on the Caribbean coast of the Isthmus of Panama, near which Drake died on his own ship.
4. *Plymouth Hoe*, a promenade running out between two inlets at Plymouth, where the Elizabethan Admirals were playing bowls when word was brought that the Armada had been sighted. The Hoe has now a fine statue of Drake.
15. *Dons*, the Spaniards.

VITAI LAMPADA
The title means 'The Torch of Life.'
1. *Close*, the school yard.
11. *Gatling*, a machine-gun.

CLIFTON CHAPEL
This is the chapel of the school where Newbolt was educated.
28. '*Qui procul hinc*' etc. 'Who far away, dies before his time, but dies a soldier for his country.'

Page 879.

KIPLING — THE BALLAD OF EAST AND WEST
5. *Kamal*, a border chief of the Punjab.
8. *turned the calkins on her feet*, turned the horse-shoes round so that the mare's footprints would point in the opposite direction.
9. *the Guides*, a distinguished corps in the Indian army.
11. *Ressaldar*, a title given to a native captain in an Indian regiment of cavalry.
13. *Abayai, Bonair*, districts of the Punjab about forty miles apart.
42. ''*Twas only by favor of mine*,' etc. The Afghans have a generous admiration for courage in a foe.
54. *byres*, stables.

Page 880.
57. *gear*, equipment or goods.
74. *ling*, heath.
82. *Peshawur*, the principal military station of the North-West Frontier.
86. *Wondrous Names of God.* According to the Mohammedan belief, the real name of God is known only to prophets and apostles, to whom it gives miraculous powers. His name being a secret, He is known by 99 other epithets given in the 7th chapter of the Koran.

DANNY DEEVER
1. *Files-on-Parade*, a term applied to the common soldier.
2. *Color-Sergeant*, the senior sergeant of a regiment who has charge of the colors.
6. *regiment's in 'ollow-square.* The ceremonial formation with the regiment forming three sides of a square is used for capital punishment of a soldier.
7. *They've taken of his buttons off an' cut his stripes away.* All military insignia are removed from the uniform of a soldier who is disgraced.

Page 881.
29. *you can 'ear the quickstep play.* The quickstep is the lively air which replaces slow music after a military funeral.

RECESSIONAL
Originally published in the London *Times*, July 17, 1897, at the time of the Diamond Jubilee, a brilliant and glorious celebration attended by representatives from all the British possessions.

YEATS — THE LAKE ISLE OF INNISFREE
2. *wattles*, thatching.

INTO THE TWILIGHT
5. *Eire*, Ireland.

Page 882.
RED HANRAHAN'S SONG ABOUT IRELAND
5. *Cathleen, the daughter of Houlihan,* Ireland in poetry and legend.
6. *Knocknarea,* the place where Queen Maeve is said to be buried under a cairn.

Page 884.
HUXLEY
EMANCIPATION — BLACK AND WHITE
a. 5. *Quashie,* a nickname at one time applied to the negro.
7. *fierce trial by battle,* the American Civil War, which was just finished when the essay was written.
39. *Caucasian,* the white division of mankind.

Page 885.
a. 1. *Adelaida,* a Beethoven song for soprano.
2. *Fornarina,* literally, baker's daughter. Marguerita, a baker's daughter with whom Raphael was in love, is said to have been the model for some of his pictures. The Sistine Madonna is now in the Dresden gallery.
b. 13. *Clärchen,* a simple cottage girl in Goethe's tragedy, *Egmont.* She is in love with the hero and takes poison when he dies. *Beatrice,* the idealized object of Dante's Platonic devotion.
39. *Faustinas,* mother and daughter, wives of Roman emperors, who founded schools for orphan girls in their honor.
41. *Juristerei etc.*
    'Jurisprudence and Medicine,
    And even, alas! Philosophy'
These lines are taken from the first scene in Goethe's *Faust.*
51. *retiariae.* A *retiarius* was a gladiator who endeavored to hold his adversary by throwing a net over his head—hence a fighter with feeble weapons.
52. *sicariae.* A *sicarius* was an assassin armed with a curved dagger. Huxley is exhorting women to fight with effective weapons.

Page 886.
a. 9. *salique law.* The Salic Law provided for inheritance in the male line only.
b. 13. *Sydney Smith,* a well-known wit of the early nineteenth century.

Page 887.
BUTLER — THE NOTE BOOKS
Butler began, while still young, to make jottings of his experiences and impressions, as well as his thoughts. As time passed, the number of notes grew tremendous. They were intended for his own use, but after his death they were arranged and edited by his literary executor, Henry Festing Jones.

Page 888.
THE FAMILY
a. 51. *R. W. Evans,* archdeacon of Westmoreland and author of the time, who was educated under Dr. Butler at Shrewsbury, where Samuel Butler was also a pupil.

UNCONSCIOUS HUMOR
b. 2. *the Hon. Mrs. Watson* and her husband were intimate friends of Dickens, and *David Copperfield* was dedicated to them.

HOMER'S ODYSSEY
11–12. *meeting between Ulysses and Telemachus. Odyssey,* xvi, 180–320 describes the meeting of Ulysses after his long absence with his son, Telemachus. Both father and son wept.

MELCHISEDEC
This personage is described in Hebrews vii, 3, as being 'without father, without mother, without descent.'

Page 888.
BACON FOR BREAKFAST
b. 31. *privilege of Cephas and the brethren of our Lord* Cephas, the Greek for Peter, was the surname given by Christ to Simon. I Corinthians ix, 5: 'Have we not power to lead about a sister, a wife, as well as the Brethren of the Lord, and Cephas.'

Page 889.
GOOD BREEDING THE SUMMUM BONUM
The words *summum bonum* mean 'the highest good.'
ADVICE TO THE YOUNG
a. 49. *the Kingsleys,* popular writers of the time.
LOHENGRIN
Wagner's opera, *Lohengrin,* is founded on the medieval legend of the search for the Holy Grail, the vessel from which Christ ate the Last Supper, and in which Joseph of Arimathea caught the blood of Our Lord. In the opera, Elsa, whom Lohengrin has married, asks his name in spite of the fact that he has forbidden it. Owing to a spell, it would be impossible for him to find the Grail if he answered her. He refuses to do so and leaves her.

Page 890.
MONEY, HEALTH AND REPUTATION
b. 4. *Janus-like mountain of unpardonable sin.* In Roman mythology, Janus was a god with two faces, one looking east, the other west. The unpardonable sin, mentioned in Matthew xii, 31–32, may be variously interpreted; hence, it also seems to look both ways.

DOCTORS
36–37. *file a bill in Chancery.* The Chancery Court in England was at one time notorious for delays.

Page 891.
PATER — STYLE
b. 1. *Bacon.* See above, p. 233. *Livy,* Titus Livius (59 B. C.–17 A. D.), greatest of the Roman historians.
2. *Carlyle.* See p. 687. *Cicero,* Marcus Tullius Cicero (106–43 B. C), the celebrated orator, philosopher, and statesman. *Newman.* See p. 677.
3. *Plato* (429 or 427–347 B. C.), a famous Greek philosopher. *Michelet,* Jules Michelet (1798–1874), French historian and man of letters.
4. *Sir Thomas Browne.* See p. 245.
5. *Milton.* See p. 279. *Taylor.* See p. 265.
22. *Lycidas.* See p. 282.

Page 892.
a. 4. *Dryden.* See p. 304.
30. *dichotomy,* a division into two parts.
31. *De Quincey.* See p. 658.
54. *Pascal,* Blaise Pascal (1623–1662), French mathematician, philosopher, and man of letters.
b. 30. *Gibbon.* See p. 465.
32. *Tacitus,* Cornelius Tacitus (c. 55–after 117 A. D.), an eminent Roman historian and orator.

Page 893.
b. 43. *neology,* innovation in language.

Page 894.
a. 12. *le cuistre,* the pedantic fellow.
35. *Johnson.* See p. 423.
b. 44. *Montaigne,* Michel Eyquem de Montaigne (1533–1592), a famous French essayist.
54. *ascêsis,* a transliteration of a Greek word meaning 'exercise, training, art.'

Page 895.
a. 15. *Esmond,* a historical novel, *Henry Esmond,* by William Makepeace Thackeray (1811–1863).
16. *Newman's Idea of a University.* See p. 703.

Page 895.
a. 28. *Schiller*, Johann Christoph Friedrich von Schiller (1759–1805), a celebrated German poet, dramatist, and historian.
   48. *Flaubert's Madame Bovary*, a novel by the French man of letters, Gustave Flaubert (1821–1880).
   49. *Stendhal's Le Rouge et Le Noir*, a novel by Marie Henri Beyle (1783–1842), best known by his pseudonym 'De Stendhal.'
b. 18. *Michelangelo*, Michelagnolo Buonarroti (1475–1564), a famous Italian sculptor, painter, architect, and poet.

Page 896.
a. 19–20. *Dean Mansel*, Henry Longueville Mansel (1820–1871), dean of St. Paul's, an English metaphysician.
b. 45. *ante-penultimate*, immediately preceding that one of a series which is next to the last one.

Page 897.
a. 11. *Blake*. See p. 493.
   43. *Swedenborg*. Emanuel Swedenborg (1688–1772), a Swedish philosopher and theosophist. *Tracts of the Times*, a series of 90 pamphlets published at Oxford from 1833–1841, to which Newman, Pusey, and others contributed. See p. 702.
b. 29–36. *series of letters. . . . Madame X.* Flaubert's letters to Madame X., in which he so often disparages human love and exalts the love of art, were written during the latter half of the year 1846. *Madame X.* was Madame Colet.

Page 898.
a. 43. *a sympathetic commentator*, Guy de Maupassant, who wrote an introduction to *Lettres de Gustave Flaubert à George Sand*. The passage here quoted will be found in the edition of Paris, 1884, pp. lxii–lxv.
b. 30. *Blake's rapturous design*. See p. 493.

Page 899.
a. 35. *ennuis*, wearinesses, vexations.
b. 9. *Buffon*, the Comte de Buffon (1707–1788), a celebrated French naturalist. Especially known to literary criticism for his *Discours sur le style* (1853).

Page 900.
a. 8. *Scott's facility*. See p. 577.
   33. *Les Misérables*, a famous novel by Victor Marie Hugo (1802–1885).
b. 5. *Raphael*, Raphael Santi (1483–1520), a famous Italian painter.
   24. *Flaubert's commentator*, Guy de Maupassant. See *Lettres de Gustave Flaubert à George Sand*, Paris, 1884, pp. lxi–lxii.
   46. *Bach*, Johann Sebastian Bach (1685–1750), one of the greatest of German musicians.

Page 901.
a. 19. *The Divine Comedy*, the greatest work of the greatest of Italian poets, Dante Alighieri (1265–1321).

Page 902.

STEVENSON—THE FOREIGNER AT HOME
a. 3. *biggin'*, building.
b. 5. *Black Country*. In the English Midlands. *Moor of Rannoch*. In Perthshire.

Page 903.
a. 46. *Miss Bird*. Isabella L. Bird, author of a popular book of travel, *Unbeaten Tracks in Japan*.
b. 51. *plausible*, pleasing, acceptable.

Page 904.
a. 9. *roundly*, plainly, flatly.
   11. *a Scottish legal body*. The Society of Scottish Advocates, whose examinations Stevenson passed at his father's request, though he never practiced law. See his *Apology for Idlers*.
a. 39. *bickering*, flushing, quivering.
b. 17. *harled*, rough-cast with lime mingled with small gravel.

Page 905.
a. 7. *commerce*, conversation, intercourse.
   11. *counters*, remarks that mean nothing, not true coin.
   21. *Give him the wages of going on.* A reminiscence of Tennyson's poem entitled *Wages*, in which the poet says of Virtue, 'Give her the wages of going on, and not to die.'
b. 27. *Byron* did actually discuss theology on his way to take part in the Greek war of independence. As to his descent and schooldays, see the biographical sketch on p. 585.
   47. *proctors*, officers who supervise the behavior of students at Oxford and Cambridge.

Page 906.
a. 5. *rotten borough*. The constituencies which before the Reform Act were in the gift of great patrons were so called; they were regarded as safe refuges for unknown or unpopular politicians, and some of the greatest of English statesmen made their entrance into Parliament—Gladstone for instance—in this way.
   7. *raffish*, fashionable.
   19. *Professor Blackie* (1809–95), a popular professor of Greek at the University of Edinburgh.
   20. *umbrageous*, suspicious, shy.
   42. *iron skerries*, rocks projecting from the sea, hard as iron.
   48. *girdle*, griddle, gridiron.
   54. *Flodden* Field, where James IV of Scotland was defeated in 1513. *Darien*, an attempt in 1698 to plant Scottish settlers on the Isthmus of Panama, which caused considerable loss of life and widespread disappointment.
   55. *Forty-five*, the rebellion of 1745, which was crushed by the defeat of the Scotch at Culloden the following year.
b. 1. *Wallace*, the Scottish hero who was defeated by the English at Falkirk in 1298.
   2. *Bruce* defeated the English at Bannockburn in 1314; he was King of Scotland, 1306–29, and suffered many reverses.
   21. *Shorter Catechism*, adopted at an Assembly of Puritan divines held at Westminster during the Commonwealth.
   32. *another church*. The Highlanders were, for the most part, Roman Catholics.
   37. *Highland costume*, the kilt, a short plaited skirt, coming to the knees.
   42. *Black Watch*, a famous Highland regiment.

Page 907.
a. 12. *Ireland*, though in the 'political aggregation' of the British Empire, retains its own religion and customs.

A CHILD'S GARDEN OF VERSES

Stevenson began this collection of 'Rimes for Children' (as he once intended to call them—another rejected title was 'Penny Whistles') in 1881. They were dedicated when published in 1885 to his old nurse Alison Cunningham, the 'Cummy' of his own childhood.

HEATHER ALE

Among the curiosities of human nature, this legend claims a high place. It is needless to remind the reader that the Picts were never exterminated, and form to this day a large proportion of the folk of Scotland: occupying the eastern and the central parts, from the Firth of Forth, or perhaps the Lammermoors, upon the south, to the Ord of Caithness on the north. That the blundering guess of a dull chronicler should have in-

Page 907.

spired men with imaginary loathing for their own ancestors is already strange: that it should have begotten this wild legend seems incredible. Is it possible the chronicler's error was merely nominal? that what he told, and what the people proved themselves so ready to receive, about the Picts, was true or partly true of some anterior and perhaps Lappish savages, small of stature, black of hue, dwelling underground—possibly also the distillers of some forgotten spirit? See Mr. Campbell's *Tales of the West Highlands.* (Stevenson's own Note.)
    2. *long-syne,* long ago.
    6. *Swound,* swoon.
    8. *underground.* The ballad tells of the early race of men who dwelt in caves.

Page 908.
10. *feld,* fierce, dreadful.
12. *roes,* deer.
15. *dwarfish.* This ancient race was of small stature.
21. *like children's.* They were so small.
23. *Brewsters.* Brewers.
27. *curlews.* Characteristic birds of the Scottish moorlands, with a peculiarly piercing, haunting cry.
33. *fortuned,* happened.
34. *free.* Not on the road.
36. *vermin.* The despised cave-dwellers.
43. *swarthy.* It was a small dark race.

Page 909.

GEORGE MOORE — THE ORGANIZATION OF ART
b. 7. *Royal Academy,* founded by George III in 1768.

Page 910.
a. 14. *Churton-Collinise.* John Churton Collins, journalist and scholar, lectured in 1880 for the London Extension Society and later for the American University Extension Society, both organizations for the popularization of learning.
    15. *Mr. Walter Besant,* novelist and first chairman of the Society of Authors.
    33. *in Queer Street,* colloquial expression meaning 'in a hole.'
    40. *Mr. Tate,* a wealthy merchant, had a large art collection which he wished to give to the National Gallery. As some of his pictures were thought mediocre, his offer could not be accepted, and he then built the Tate Gallery, with part of his collection as a nucleus.
    42. *Herkomer, Fildes, Leader, Long,* popular painters of their day.
b. 48. *South Kensington Museum,* includes the National Art Training Schools.

Page 911.
a. 19. *Luxembourg,* an art gallery in Paris, second only to the Louvre.
    25–6. *Corot, Millet, Manet, etc.,* modern painters, mainly of the impressionistic school.

Page 913.

SHAW — THE CASE FOR THE CRITIC–DRAMATIST
a. 48. *Frank Marshall,* a playwright and dramatic critic, who, with others, edited 'The Henry Irving Edition' of Shakespeare.
    50. *Sir Henry Irving,* a distinguished actor and manager. The Lyceum Theatre was at one time under his entire control.
    55. *Canute,* the king of England whose flattering courtiers declared that even the tide would obey him.
b. 1. *Robert Emmet.* Marshall's play which deals with the Irish patriot, Emmet, has never been produced.

Page 914.
a. 18. *Mr. Pinero,* Sir Arthur Pinero, a successful English playwright, whose first connection with the stage was as an actor.
b. 36–9. *Mr. Clement Scott, Mr. Wm. Archer and Mr. Walkley,* all London dramatic critics, the two first also playwrights.

Page 917.

CONRAD — WITH THE MARSEILLES PILOTS
a. 9. *Vieux Port,* Marseilles.

Page 918.
a. 27. *patron,* coxswain.
    33. *'Hé, l'ami, Comment va?'* Hey, friend, how goes it?
    50. *'Larguez,'* cast off.
b. 1. *avant-port,* outer harbor.
    27. *béret,* a sort of Tam o' Shanter.

Page 919.
a. 28. *Equipages de ligne,* Crews of the Line.
    38. *Franco-Provençal jargon,* a mixture of French and the Romance tongue of Provence, the *Langue d'oc* of southern France.
    44. *Fréjus and Antibes.* Antibes is a seaport of southern France and Fréjus is a town not far away.
b. 44. *l'ancien,* Old Nick.

Page 920.
a. 34. *old Phœnician port.* Marseilles was founded by Greek colonists from Phocæa about 600 B. C. and was used by Phœnician traders.

Page 921.
a. 16. *Mr. W. W. Jacobs,* an author of humorous short stories which deal largely with 'old salts.'
b. 9. *The Red Ensign,* the merchant ensign of Great Britain.

WELLS — THE CONTEMPORARY NOVEL
b. 30. *Samuel Richardson,* 1689–1761, called 'the founder of the English domestic novel.' His heroes and heroines were Sunday-School perfections, and he took care always to reward virtue.
    31. *Tom Jones,* the title of a novel by Fielding, one of the first realists, who began the writing of novels to satirize Richardson's sentimentality and moralizing.
    50. *Balfourian Age.* A. J., later Lord Balfour, published in 1879 a *Defence of Philosophic Doubt.*

Page 922.
a. 49. *Mr. Chadband,* a hypocritical minister much given to platitudes, in Dickens's *Bleak House.*
b. 5. *the Realist against the Nominalist.* In philosophy realism denotes the medieval metaphysical theory that universals have an existence independent of individual objects. Directly opposed to this is nominalism, the philosophical theory that only individual objects have real existence, and that the universals are nothing but names given in common to actually different objects having nothing else in common.
    6. *the Church against the Franciscan and the Lollard.* The founding of these orders by St. Francis and Wyclif was a protest against the greed and unworthiness of the clergy.

Page 923.
a. 55. *Bumble,* a self-important and officious beadle in *Oliver Twist.*

Page 924.
b. 1. *Cellinis.* Benvenuto Cellini, an Italian sculptor and worker in gold of the sixteenth century, has left in his *Autobiography* accounts of his own courage and success in amorous adventure. *Casanovas.* Casanova was an Italian poet and adventurer of the eighteenth century, the author of scandalous memoirs in which he gleefully exposes his immorality.

Page 925.

GALSWORTHY — THE LOST DOG
b. 36. *Thames Embankment,* a street with sidewalks on either side running along the north bank of the Thames in London—like Riverside Drive in New York City.

Page 929.

G. K. CHESTERTON
THE RETURN OF THE BARBARIAN

b. 13. *Regency*, the period in English history during which George IV, then Prince of Wales, was Regent. Socially, it was a time which followed its leader, Beau Brummel, in fashion and elegance.
20. *Brighton Pavilion*. The Royal Pavilion at Brighton, a fashionable watering place, was founded by the Regent.

Page 930.

b. 55. *Hood*, Thomas Hood, nineteenth-century poet, author of the *Song of the Shirt*. See p. 648 of this work.

Page 931.

a. 15. *Lettres de Cachet*, written orders for imprisonment without trial, which in France before the Revolution could be secured against innocent men, for personal revenge.
29. *the Great Pillage*. In 1536 Henry VIII dissolved the monasteries in England and confiscated their property.
b. 8. *Wilberforce*, the English humanitarian whose fight against slavery resulted in the final passage of the bill for abolition, 1807.

Page 932.

b. 18. *Freya*, in Norse mythology the wife of Odin.
31-2. *Denmark was robbed of two provinces*, Schleswig and Holstein.
32. *France was robbed of two provinces*, Alsace and Lorraine.
40. *Augustenburg claim*. The duchies of Schleswig and Holstein had been fiefs of the King of Denmark. When the royal house became extinct at the death of Frederick VII, Prince Frederick of Augustenburg put forward claims of his house to the succession to the duchies. The German Diet supported this claim, and from that time on the two provinces became pawns in the game of German Unification, being finally ceded to Austria and Prussia.
41. *Ems telegram*. In 1870 Bismarck was anxious to bring about a war with France over the succession to the Spanish throne. France demanded that the King of Prussia withdraw the name of his cousin, Prince Leopold, as candidate, and this was done. Then the French ambassador visited the King of Prussia at the watering-place of Ems and asked for a promise that Leopold's name should never be brought up in the future. The King refused courteously and telegraphed what he had done to Bismarck, who deliberately condensed the despatch so that the King's words seemed insulting to the French and made the Prussians feel that their sovereign had been insulted. When the despatch was published the French fell into the trap and declared war.
48. *Palmerston*, Foreign Secretary and Prime Minister during the Eastern crisis and Crimean War, in which England supported Turkey against Russia.

Page 933.

a. 3-4. *Manchester School*, a group of English economic and political writers and speakers, who, under the leadership of Cobden and Bright, advocated a policy of Free Trade and Laissez-faire.
53. *Higher Criticism*, inquiry into the origin, authorship and meaning of the various books of the Bible.

Page 934.

BEERBOHM — WILLIAM AND MARY

a. 28. *Fabian Essays*. The Fabian Society was a moderate Socialistic group formed in London in 1884, by young literary men, including H. G. Wells, Bernard Shaw, and Sidney Webb. The Fabian Essays, its most important publication, began to appear in 1889.
47. *Trafalgar Square*, one of the principal squares in London, which contains the Nelson Monument.

Page 935.

a. 15. *Beowulf*, the Anglo-Saxon epic. *Sigurd the Volsung*, hero of the Norse sagas, corresponding to the later German Siegfried.
48. *feckless*, shiftless.

Page 936.

a. 27. *Ibsen*, the great Norwegian dramatist whose plays are serious and often gloomy. *Morris*, William Morris, the poet, who, in his later years, was interested in spreading Socialism.
32. *George Gissing*, the novelist, whose effort to depict 'the ignobly decent' often results in dreariness.
b. 30. *obbligato*, an accompaniment.

Page 940.

HUDSON — MY FIRST VISIT TO BUENOS AYRES

b. 19. *lavenderas*, wash-women.

Page 941.

b. 18. *estancia*, farm, or ranch.
35. *Perdón, por Dios*, Pardon, in God's name.

Page 943.

a. 35. *Rosas, the Nero of South America* governed Buenos Ayres about the middle of the nineteenth century as an absolute dictator and with tyrannical cruelty.
b. 20. *Caudillo*, commander or leader.

LYTTON STRACHEY — THE LAST YEARS

b. 50. *Albert*, Prince Consort, died 1861.

Page 944.

a. 3. *Baroness Lehzen*, Victoria's Governess.
Duchess of Kent, her mother.
8. *Gadarene Swine*. See Mark v.
9. *Stockmar*, one of Victoria's early advisors.
b. 11. *Mr. Martin*, afterwards Sir Theodore Martin, the author of *The Life of the Prince Consort* (1875-80) and *Queen Victoria as I Knew Her* (1908).

Page 945.

b. 5. *John Brown*, a favorite personal attendant, who died in 1883.

Page 946.

b. 4. *Lady Lyttleton* (1787-1870), governess to Victoria's children and lady of the bedchamber.

Page 948.

a. 2. *Lord M.*, Lord Melbourne, Victoria's first Prime Minister.
4. *Archbishop of Canterbury on his knees*, on June 20, 1837, when he came to inform the Princess Victoria of the death of William IV and her accession to the throne.
6. *Uncle Leopold, Prince of Saxe-Coburg*, who married Princess Charlotte, only child of the Prince Regent (afterwards George IV), and lived at Claremont near Esher in Surrey.

Page 948.
- 12. *Kensington*, a London suburb, where the Princess Victoria grew up with her mother, the Duchess of Kent.

WALPOLE — ROMANCE AND REALISM
- a. 39. *Reade*, Charles Reade, novelist and dramatist, author of *The Cloister and the Hearth*.
  - 47. *St. Ives*, a story by Stevenson, finished by Sir Arthur Quiller-Couch and published after Stevenson's death.
- b. 49. '*The Brothers Karamazov*,' a novel by Dostoievsky.
  - 50. '*The Cherry Orchard*,' a play by Chekhov.
  - 54. *Madame Bovary*, Flaubert's great realistic novel.

Page 949.
- a. 16. *Almayer*, the chief character in Conrad's first novel, *Almayer's Folly*.
- b. 5. '*Crime and Punishment*,' '*The Idiot*,' '*The Possessed*,' '*The Brothers Karamazov*,' works of Dostoievsky.
  - 10. *Prince Myshkin*, a character in *The Idiot*. Dmitri Karamazov, one of the Brothers Karamazov.
  - 11. *Nicolas Stavrogin*, a character in Dostoievsky's *The Possessed*.
  - 19. *Captain Anthony*, a character in Conrad's *Chance*.
  - 29. *Stendhal*, the pseudonym of Marie Henri Beyle, distinguished French critic and novelist.
  - 39. *Razumov*, a character in Conrad's novel *Under Western Eyes*, which deals with Russian revolutionaries.
  - 43. *Raskolnikov*, a character in *Crime and Punishment*.

Page 950.
- a. 10. *M'Whirr*, the sea captain in Conrad's *Typhoon*.
  - 23. *Kouprin, Artzybashev, Sologub, Merejkovsky, Andreiev*, modern and contemporary Russian writers.

ALDOUS HUXLEY — AT SEA
- b. 28. *Faraday* (1791–1867) and *Clerk Maxwell* (1831–1879) were English scientists whose discoveries made the invention of wireless possible

Page 951.
- a. 10. *Frank Crane* (1861–1928), a popular newspaper writer.
  - 12. *Prometheus*. According to the Greek myth on which Æschylus founded his celebrated tragedy, Prometheus stole fire from heaven concealed in a reed and thus communicated to mortals the secret of the inventions upon which modern civilization is founded.
  - 43. *Bébé Daniels*, a well-known motion picture actress.

T. S. ELIOT — THE CRITICISM OF POETRY
- b. 5. *Gourmont*, Remy de (1858–1915), French critic, one of the founders of the *Mercure de France*, to which he contributed many articles on æsthetics.
  - 6. *Boileau*, Nicolas (1636–1711), French poet and critic, whose *L'Art Poétique* expresses his literary creed, setting up standards of elegance and dignity. Through his influence French prose became more lucid and precise.

Page 952.
- a. 1. *stationer's*, bookseller's.
  - 44. *Febrilist*, febrile, feverish, a made up word intended to ridicule a certain school of poetry.

Page 953.
- b. 36. *Fu miglior . . . stolti* — 'He was a better craftsman with the mother-tongue . . . and let the fools chatter.' The passage from which these words are quoted is in Dante's *Divine Comedy*, Purgatory XXVI, 117–119. They are spoken to Dante by Guido Guinizelli, a Provençal poet who preferred above himself Arnaldo Daniello as superior to all others in verses of love and prose romances.
  - 40. *Pall Mall*, a fashionable London street, where the leading West End clubs are situated.

Page 954.

VIRGINIA WOOLF — THE PATRON AND THE CROCUS
- a. 29. *Grub Street*, the street of literary hacks in the eighteenth century.
  - 31. *half-crown*, an English coin worth two shillings and sixpence, a high price for a magazine.
- b. 13. *Henry James*, born in New York, 1843, naturalized in England, 1915, died 1916, after Meredith the leading intellectual novelist of his time.
  - 33. *John O'Groats . . . Land's End*, the northernmost and furthest southwestern points in Great Britain.
  - 50. '*our dramatic critic*.' At the time this essay was written, the dramatic critic of *The Times* was A. B. Walkley, and the assistant critic Charles Morgan, who succeeded Walkley on the latter's death in 1926.
  - 51. *Lynd*, Robert, born 1879, well known essayist and critic.

Page 955.

JOHN BUCHAN — ENGLAND AFTER THE WAR
- b. 49. *Prince of Wales*, now Edward VIII.

Page 956.
- a. 17. *Guards*, the fashionable regiment.
  - 46. *Wars of the Roses*, in the fifteenth century, ending in the establishment of the Tudor dynasty.
  - 54. *Disraeli*, Benjamin (1804–1881), Earl of Beaconsfield, the leading Conservative Minister of his time.
  - 55. *Lord Rowton*, a Victorian politician and philanthropist.

Page 957.
- a. 25. *Apollo of Pheidias*, famous statue by the great Athenian sculptor of the age of Pericles.
  - 27. *cloacal*, of the sewer (Latin *cloaca*).
  - 32. *pastiche*, imitation.
  - 42. *clichés*, hackneyed sayings.
  - 53. *soft option*, easy job.
- b. 29. *Hull trawler*, fishing steamer from Hull in Yorkshire.

Page 958.
- a. 7. *plebiscitary*, founded on the votes of the entire adult population.
- b. 14. *camarilla*, a political clique.
  - 21. *Balmoral*, a royal palace in Scotland.
  - 25. *MacDonald*, Ramsay, Premier of the Labor Government.

Page 959.

BELLOC — THE SOUTH COUNTRY
- 20. *Severn*, an English river flowing down through the west counties. See Map.
- 46. *Sussex Weald* was covered long ago with the forest of Andredsweald—the forest without habitations—but is now a rich agricultural district. See Map.

NOTES TO TWENTIETH-CENTURY POETRY

Page 961.
BROOKE — THE OLD VICARAGE, GRANTCHESTER
Grantchester is a village near Cambridge, where Brooke once lived and this poem is a cry of homesickness, written when the poet was in Germany. See Map.
18. *Du Lieber Gott*, Good God.
22. *Temperamentvoll*, temperamental.
23. *and there the dews*. In the next few lines Brooke suggests the contrast between the English and German attitudes of mind toward Nature.
32. *Haslingfield and Coton*. These, and the towns named in lines 82-100, are small places round about Cambridge.
33. *das Betreten's not verbotem*, Walking on the grass is not forbidden.
34. εἴθε γενοίμην, would I were.
41. *Naiad*, a water nymph.
42. *Goat-foot*, Pan, the Greek god of pastures, forest and flocks, represented with the head and body of an elderly man and the hindquarters of a goat, whose horns and ears he wore. The original place of his worship was Arcadia.
51. *ghostly Lordship*, Lord Byron.
53. *Hellespont*, the name given in ancient geography to the Dardanelles, which were swum by Byron, once a student at Trinity College, Cambridge. *Styx*, river in Hell—an allusion to Byron's diabolic reputation.
54. *Dan Chaucer*, Dan, archaic title of honor, equivalent to master or sir. 'Dan Chaucer, well of English undefiled,' he is called by Spenser in the *Faerie Queene*.

Page 962.
127. *Anadyomene*, a surname for Aphrodite, meaning 'rising from the sea.'

FLECKER — THE BALLAD OF ISKANDER
1. *Aflatun, Aristu,* and *Iskander* are the Turkish forms for Plato, Aristotle and Alexander.
44. *Isle of Serendip*, an ancient name for Ceylon.
50. *alizarine*, a dye which produces Turkey reds, shades of orange, violet, etc.

Page 963.
151. *Zephyr*, a personification of the west wind.

Page 964.
POEMS OF THE GREAT WAR
CHESTERTON — THE WIFE OF FLANDERS
8. *Sedan*, the battle at which the French suffered an overwhelming defeat by the Germans in the war of 1870.

Page 965.
CREWE — A HARROW GRAVE IN FLANDERS
Harrow is one of the great public schools of England.
14. *alembic*, a vessel used in chemistry for distillation.

GIBSON — THE QUESTION
2. *gey*, very.

HIS FATHER
1. *spigot*, a plug fitting into a tap to draw off liquor.

Page 966.
GRENFELL — INTO BATTLE
17. *The Dog-Star and the Sisters Seven, Orion's Belt*, the most brilliant of the stars and constellations.
23. *kestrel*, falcon.

GRIFFITHS — THE WYKHAMIST
Wykhamist, student of Winchester College, founded by William of Wykeham, Bishop of Winchester in the fourteenth century.

Page 967.
MASEFIELD — THE ISLAND OF SKYROS
Skyros is an island of Greece in the Ægean Sea, where Rupert Brooke was buried. See Introduction, p. 929.
8. *Seddul Bahr*, a fortified village on the Gallipoli peninsula, taken by the British with enormous casualties in 1915.

Page 968.
PHILLIPS — REVENGE FOR RHEIMS
The Cathedral of Rheims, built in the thirteenth century and one of the most beautiful buildings in the world, was irreparably damaged by the German bombardment of the city in 1914.

Page 969.
SORLEY — ALL THE HILLS AND VALES ALONG
12. *Barabbas*, the robber, who, by the choice of the people, was released instead of Christ.
22. *Hemlock for Socrates*. The great Greek philosopher was accused of impiety, condemned and forced to drink hemlock.

TYNAN — A GIRL'S SONG
1. *Meuse and Marne* are rivers flowing through that part of France which saw the death and devastation of the Western Front.

WILLIAMS — FROM A FLEMISH GRAVEYARD
15. *circumstantial*. The word is used in its literal sense, surrounding.

Page 970.
ARMITAGE — LANCASHIRE
3. *Chamber*, of Commerce.
6. *Tech.*, technical school.
Crompton, Samuel, a native of Bolton, Lancashire, inventor of the spinning mule.
7. *Arkwright*, Sir Richard, another Lancashire inventor, who established the first spinning mill.
15. *bales*, of cotton.
breaker, a machine performing the first operation in carding cotton.
22. *smoke*, opium.
24. *In hoc signo vinces*, 'In this sign thou shalt conquer,' a motto embroidered on the standards of Constantine, the Roman Emperor who established Christianity as the state religion after a vision in which he saw in the sky a flaming cross inscribed with these words in Greek.
28. *mester*, master, employer.
30. *clemmed*, starved.
31. *clough*, wood.
fell, mountain, moorland.
37. *race*, of water.
38. *Boulton and Watt*, Birmingham engineers who manufactured the early spinning machinery. James Watt of Glasgow applied the use of steam to industry.
41. *lade*, the channel leading water to the mill wheel.
45. *curlew*, lapwing.

Page 971.
48. *Pandora's box* of human evils, according to the old myth.
56. *homo sapiens*, man arrived at the stage of intelligence.
62. *Act*, of Parliament.
70. *cut*, a length of cloth about 100 yards long, cut from the warp. If she does not finish it, she will not be paid for it, next day, when her wages are made up.
71. *cop end*, end of the cop or length of thread wound on a spindle.

Page 971.
73. *tuppence-farthing*, four and a half cents.
89. *Oldham*, center of the coarse cotton manufacture.

Page 972.
113. *Preston*, birthplace of Arkwright and an important weaving center.
116. *Stockport*, now a busy manufacturing town, formerly a station on the Roman road.
117. *Glossop*, center of Derbyshire cotton trade.
132. *skep*, beehive.
134. *River Clyde*, where the shipbuilding industry of Glasgow was, at the date of the poem (1935), in an almost worse state of depression than the Lancashire cotton trade.

Page 973.
CAMPBELL — I AM THE MOUNTAINY SINGER
6. *carn*, a rock or heap of rocks.
7. *cailin*, maiden.
11. *cailleach*, crone.
18. *canker*, rust.

COLUM — THE PLOUGHER
8. *Pan*, see note for p. 932, line 42. *Wotan*, Woden or Odin, the chief god of northern mythology who created the world. *Dana*, a great nature goddess of the Celts, identified with the Greek Artemis.

WHAT THE SHUILER SAID AS SHE LAY BY THE FIRE IN THE FARMER'S HOUSE
Shuiler, a beggar.
20. *clan*, crowd, tribe.

Page 974.
42. *huggle*, cuddle.

ELIOT — THE *BOSTON EVENING TRANSCRIPT*
The *Boston Evening Transcript* is the organ of the intellectuals of Boston, Mass. Eliot was a student at Harvard University.

Page 975.
7. *Rochefoucauld*, François, Duc de (1613–1680), whose *Mémoires* were the record of a life of sophisticated political and love intrigue. His *Maximes* are extremely cynical.

COUSIN NANCY
12. *Matthew and Waldo*, Matthew Arnold and Ralph Waldo Emerson (1803–1882), held in high honor by Victorian New Englanders.
13. *The army of unalterable law*. A quotation from a well known sonnet by George Meredith, also a favorite with the New England intellectuals.

Page 976.
HARDY — AFTERWARDS
6. *dewfall-hawk*, night hawk.

Page 977.
HODGSON — EVE
48. *The Blasphemous Tree*, the tree of knowledge of good and evil.
64. *under the hill*. Elves and other spirits have their abode under mounds.

Page 978.
THE BULL
55. *dewlap-deep*, up to the dewlap, a fold of skin which hangs from the neck of cattle.

Page 979.
110. *pow*, head.

LAWRENCE — STUDY
6. *Biuret*, a chemical term. The young man drags himself from dreams to study his chemistry.

Page 980.
MITCHELL — AMBITION IN CUFFE STREET
Cuffe Street, a street in Dublin.

HOW WOULD IT BE?
18. *jujube tree*, a small tree which grows in Syria, India and China. Jujube paste is a favorite confection.
19. *galleons*, ships used by the Spaniards especially for treasure.

Page 982.
SASSOON — THE OLD HUNTSMAN
2. *Golden Fleece*, his public house.
69. *hoick*, a call used in hunting to incite the hounds.

Page 984.
JAMES STEPHENS
WHAT TOMAS AN BUILE SAID IN A PUB
Pub, a public-house, or saloon.

INDEX OF AUTHORS AND TEXT

AUTHORS	PAGE
Addison, Joseph	361
'A. E.' [George Russell]	882
Armitage, G. W.	970
Arnold, Matthew	773
Ascham, Roger	135
Ashburton, Robert Offley, Lord Crewe	965
Bacon, Francis	233
Ballads, English and Scottish Popular	105
Barnes, William	650
Beaumont, Francis	216
Beddoes, Thomas Lovell	651
Beerbohm, Max	934
Belloc, Hilaire	959
Bennett, Arnold	927
Beowulf	5
Binyon, Laurence	964
Blake, William	493
Boswell, James	439
Breton, Nicholas	204
Bridges, Robert	871
Brooke, Rupert	961, 964
Browne, Sir Thomas	245
Browne, William	217
Browning, Elizabeth Barrett	860
Browning, Robert	739
Buchan, John	955
Bunyan, John	269
Burke, Edmund	457
Burns, Robert	497
Butler, Samuel	887
Byron, George Noel Gordon	585
Calverley, Charles Stuart	868
Campbell, Joseph	973
Campbell, Thomas	643
Campion, Thomas	210
Carew, Thomas	222
Carlyle, Thomas	687
Chatterton, Thomas	415
Chaucer, Geoffrey	73
Chester Plays, The	65
Chesterton, Gilbert K.	929, 964
Clough, Arthur Hugh	863
Coleridge, Samuel Taylor	543
Collins, William	411
Colum, Padraic	973
Conrad, Joseph	917
Cowley, Abraham	228
Cowper, William	479
Crabbe, George	489
Crashaw, Richard	225
Crewe, Lord	965
Daniel, Samuel	189
Davenant, Sir William	223
Davidson, John	873
Davies, William H.	974
Defoe, Daniel	325
Dekker, Thomas	204

AUTHORS	PAGE
Denham, Sir John	226
De Quincey, Thomas	658
Dobell, Sidney	867
Dobson, Austin	869
Donne, John	212
Drayton, Michael	190
Drinkwater, John	965
Dryden, John	304
Dyer, Sir Edward	185
Eliot, T. S.	951, 974
England's Helicon	204
Fawcett, John	478
Fitzgerald, Edward	862
Flecker, James Elroy	962
Fletcher, John	215
Freeman, John	975
Fuller, Thomas	261
Galsworthy, John	925
Gascoigne, George	184
Gibbon, Edward	465
Gibson, W. W.	965
Goddard, Gregg	965
Goldsmith, Oliver	417
Graves, Robert	975
Gray, Thomas	399
Greene, Robert	187
Grenfell, Julian	966
Griffiths, Nora	966
Hakluyt's Voyages	153
Hardy, Thomas	976
Hazlitt, William	653
Henley, William Ernest	872
Herbert, George	220
Herrick, Robert	217
Hewlett, Maurice	966
Hodgson, Ralph	977
Hood, Thomas	646
Housman, Alfred Edward	876
Howard, Henry, Earl of Surrey	125
Hudson, W. H.	939
Hunt, Leigh	644
Huxley, Aldous	950
Huxley, Thomas Henry	883
Hymns of the Eighteenth Century	474
Johnson, Samuel	423
Jonson, Ben	210
Keats, John	627
Keble, John	646
Ken, Thomas	475
Kipling, Rudyard	879
Lamb, Charles	567
Landor, Walter Savage	642
Lawrence, D. H.	979

INDEX OF AUTHORS AND TEXT

AUTHORS	PAGE
Letts, Winifred M.	967
Locker-Lampson, Frederick	865
Lodge, Thomas	206
Lovelace, Richard	227
Lyly, John	139
Macaulay, Rose	967
Macaulay, Thomas Babington	665
Malory, Sir Thomas	88
Mare, Walter de la	960, 965
Marlowe, Christopher	192
Marvel, Andrew	229
Masefield, John	959, 967
Meredith, George	845
Meynell, Alice	872
Milton, John	279
Mitchell, Susan L.	980
Monro, Harold	980
Moore, George	909
Moore, Thomas	644
Morris, William	819
Newbolt, Sir Henry	878
Newman, John Henry, Cardinal	677
Noah's Flood	65
Noyes, Alfred	968
Nutbrowne Maide, The	101
O. M.	943
O'Shaughnessy, Arthur	871
Pater, Walter Horatio	891
Patmore, Coventry	866
Peacock, Thomas Love	644
Pearl	59
Peele, George	186
Pepys, Samuel	318
Perronet, Edward	478
Phillips, Stephen	968
Pope, Alexander	375
Pope, Jessie	968
Praed, Winthrop Mackworth	648
Quarles, Francis	220
Raleigh, Sir Walter	185
Rossetti, Christina	867
Rossetti, Dante Gabriel	803
Ruskin, John	695
Russell, George ['A. E.']	882
Sackville, Charles, Earl of Dorset	231
Sackville, Thomas, Lord Buckhurst	129
Sassoon, Siegfried	982
Scott, Sir Walter	577
Shakespeare, William	194
Shaw, George Bernard	912
Shelley, Percy Bysshe	607
Shirley, James	222
Sidney, Sir Philip	144
Sir Gawain and the Green Knight	38
Sorley, Charles Hamilton	969
Southey, Robert	641
Southwell, Robert	188
Spenser, Edmund	161
Steele, Sir Richard	351
Stephens, James	984
Stevenson, Robert Louis	902
Strachey, Lytton	943
Suckling, Sir John	224
Swift, Jonathan	337
Swinburne, Algernon Charles	833
Taylor, Jeremy	265
Tennyson, Alfred, Lord	705
Thackeray, William Makepeace	862
Thomas, Edward	984
Thompson, Francis	875
Thomson, James (1700–1748)	393
Thomson, James (1834–1882)	870
Toplady, Augustus Montague	478
Tynan, Katharine	969
Vaughan, Henry	230
Waller, Edmund	224
Walpole, Hugh	948
Walton, Isaak	256
Watson, Sir William	873
Watts, Isaac	475
Wells, H. G.	921
Wesley, Charles	476
Williams, Iolo Aneurin	969
Wilmot, John, Earl of Rochester	232
Wither, George	216
Wolfe, Charles	645
Woolf, Virginia	954
Wordsworth, William	511
Wyatt, Sir Thomas	121
Yeats, William Butler	881

INDEX OF TITLES

	PAGE		PAGE
Abnegation	868	Blackmwore Maidens	650
Absalom and Achitophel	304	Blessed Damozel, The	804
Abt Vogler	762	Blest be the Tie that Binds	478
Adam Scriveyn	86	Blow, Blow, Thou Winter Wind	203
Address to the Deil	501	Bonie Doon	507
Adonais	619	Bonny Barbara Allan	116
Advertisement, The (Steele: *The Tatler*)	351	*Boston Evening Transcript*, The	974
Ælla	416	Break, Break, Break	724
After-thought to the River Duddon	541	Bride, The	979
Afterwards	976	Bridge of Sighs, The	647
Against Idleness and Mischief	476	Bright Clouds	984
Against Quarrelling and Fighting	476	Bull, The	978
Ah Sunflower	496	Burial of Sir John Moore, The	645
Ah! Yet Consider It Again!	864	Buried Life, The	786
Airman, The	965	Burning Babe, The	188
Alexander's Feast	307		
All Service Ranks the Same with God	740	Canonization, The	213
All That's Past	960	Canterbury Tales, The	74
'All the Hills and Vales Along'	969	Captain Car or Edom O Gordon	111
A Man's a Man for A' That	508	Case for the Critic-Dramatist, The	912
Ambition in Cuffe Street	980	Castaway, The	484
America	867	Castle of Indolence, The	396
Amoretti	176	Cavalier Tunes	772
Andrea del Sarto	755	Celia, Song to	210
An Earnest Suit to His Unkind Mistress	122	Change of Mind	980
Apelles' Song	142	Chapter on Ears, A	571
Apology for Poetry, An	144	Character of the Happy Warrior	536
Areopagitica	299	Chaucers Wordes unto Adam His Owne Scriveyn	86
Argument of His Book, The	217	Chester Plays, The	65
Arraignment of Paris, The	186	Childe Harold	586
As It Fell Upon a Day	205	Child's Garden of Verses, A	907
Ask Me No More (Carew)	222	Chimney Sweeper, The	496
Ask Me No More (Tennyson)	725	Choice, The	817
A Slumber did my Spirit Seal	526	Christabel	559
Asolando	772	Christ Crucified	475
Aspatia's Song	216	Christmas Carol	477
Astrophel and Stella	150	Christopher Marlowe	844
Atalanta in Calydon	833	City of Dreadful Night, The	870
Atalanta's Race	820	Clifton Chapel	878
At Sea	950	Clod and the Pebble, The	496
At the Church Gate	862	Cloud, The	617
Auld Lang Syne	503	Cloud Confines, The	807
Aunt Helen	975	Club, The (Steele: *The Spectator*)	352
Autumn	394	Collar, The	221
		Coming of the End, The	977
Ballad of East and West, The	879	Commentary, A	925
Ballad of Human Life	652	Companions	868
Ballad of Iskander, The	962	Complaint by Night, A	126
Bard, The	404	Complaint of the Absence of Her Lover	126
Bard's Epitaph, A	502	Complaint of the Lover Disdained	126
Bards of Passion and of Mirth	632	Complaint of a Lover Rebuked	125
Basia	210	Compleint of Chaucer to His Empty Purse	87
Battle of Blenheim, The	641	Complete Angler, The	256
Battle of Otterburn, The	108	Computation, The	214
Beauty Clear and Fair	215	Conciliation with the Colonies, The Speech for	457
Bed in Summer	907	Conclusion, The (Raleigh)	186
Before the Beginning of Years	834	Conclusion (Wordsworth)	542
Belle of the Ball-Room, The	648	Confessions of an English Opium Eater	658
Beowulf	5	Constant Lover, The	225
Biographia Literaria	544	Contemporary Novel, The	921

1091

INDEX OF TITLES

Title	PAGE
Cooper's Hill	226
Cor Cordium	843
Corinna's Going A-Maying	218
Coronation	478
Cotter's Saturday Night, The	499
Count Gismond	741
Country Sunday, A (Addison: *The Spectator*)	363
Cousin Nancy	975
Cradle Hymn, A	476
Cradle Song (from *Songs of Experience*)	495
Cradle Song (from *Songs of Innocence*)	495
Criticism of Poetry, The	951
Crossing the Bar	738
Cruel Brother, The	117
Dæmon Lover, The	114
Danny Deever	880
Day in London, A (Steele: *The Spectator*)	358
Dead Letter, A	869
Death	215
Death of Artemidora, The	642
Death of Sir Roger, The	368
Death's Jest Book	652
Decline and Fall of the Roman Empire, The	465
Dedicatory Epistle (Hakluyt's Voyages)	153
Defenders, The	965
'De Gustibus'	754
Delia, Sonnets from	189
Departed Friends	231
Description and Praise of His Love, Geraldine	125
Description of Spring	125
Description of the Restless State of a Lover	127
Deserted Village, The	417
Detraction Among Poets	371
Diary of Samuel Pepys, The	318
Dirce	642
Dirge (Beddoes)	652
Dirge, A (Shelley)	626
Dirge in Cymbeline	411
Dissertation Upon Roast Pig, A	574
Ditty, A	152
Divine Image, The	495
Don Juan	599
Dorus to Pamela	152
Doubt of Martyrdom, A	224
Dover Beach	802
Doxology	475
Drake in California	160
Drake's Drum	878
Dramatic Opinions and Essays	912
Dream, A (Blake)	495
Dream, The (Donne)	213
Dream-Children: A Reverie	570
Dream of Fair Women, A	712
Dream-Pedlary	651
Duncan Gray	507
Earnest Suit to His Unkind Mistress, An	122
Earth Breath, The	882
Earthly Paradise, The	819
Economic Consequences of the Peace, The	978
Ecstasy, An	220
Education of Women, The	335
Edward	118
Elegiac Stanzas	535
Elegy Written in a Country Churchyard	401
Emancipation—Black and White	884

Title	PAGE
End of the Play, The	862
Endymion	627
England after the War	955
England's Helicon	204
English Hills	975
Epistle to Dr. Arbuthnot	388
Epitaph, An (Carew)	223
Epitaph (Coleridge)	566
Epitaph on Elizabeth L. H.	212
Epitaph on Salathiel Pavy, An	211
Epithalamion	177
Essay of Dramatic Poesy, An	309
Essay on Criticism, An	375
Essay on Projects	335
Étude Réaliste	842
Euphues and His England	139
Eve	977
Eve of St. Agnes, The	628
Excellent Ballad of Charity, An	415
Faerie Queene, The	165
Fair Ines	646
Faith and Patience of the Saints, The	265
Far Away and Long Ago	973
Farewell, A	717
Farewell to Folly, The	187
Fatal Sisters, The	405
Fear No More the Heat o' th' Sun	204
Flow Gently, Sweet Afton	507
Foreigner at Home, The	902
Forget	214
'Forget not Yet!'	122
For Life I Had Never Cared Greatly	976
Forsaken Garden, A	839
Forsaken Merman, The	785
For the Fallen	964
France 1870	850
Francesca da Rimini	805
'Frater Ave Atque Vale'	738
French Revolution, The	687
Friar's Song, The	645
From a Flemish Graveyard	969
Frost at Midnight	565
Full Fathom Five Thy Father Lies	204
Funeral, The	214
Gallathea	143
Gallows, The	984
Garden, The	229
Garden of Proserpine, The	836
Gawain and the Green Knight, Sir	38
Girl's Song, A	969
Glories of Our Blood and State, The	222
Go Fetch to Me a Pint o' Wine	503
Goliath and David	951
Go, Lovely Rose!	224
Grace for a Child	220
Grammarian's Funeral, A	758
Green Grow the Rashes	498
Growth of Love, The	871
Guardian Angel, The	757
Guinevere	733
Hakluyt's Voyages	155
Happy is England Now	975
Happy Thought	907
Hark, Hark! the Lark	204

INDEX OF TITLES

Title	PAGE
Harp That Once Through Tara's Halls, The	644
Harrow Grave in Flanders, A	965
Harvestmen A-Singing	187
Has Summer Come Without the Rose?	871
Heather Ale	907
Herdman's Happy Life, The	206
Hero and Leander, The First Sestiad	192
Hertha	836
Hervé Riel	766
Highland Mary	506
His Father	965
His Pilgrimage	185
His Prayer for Absolution	220
History of England, The	670
Holy State, The	261
Home They Brought Her Warrior Dead	725
Home-Thoughts from Abroad	744
Home-Thoughts from the Sea	744
Hound of Heaven, The	875
House of Life, The	816
How Sleep the Brave (Collins)	411
'How Sleep the Brave' (de la Mare)	965
How Would It Be?	980
Humility the Mother of Charity	566
Hydriotaphia, Urn-burial	253
Hymn, A (Thomson)	395
Hymn to Adversity	400
Hymn to Diana	211
Hymn to God the Father, A	215
Hymn to Intellectual Beauty	607
Hymns of the Eighteenth Century	474
Hyperion	635
I Am the Mountainy Singer	973
Idea, Sonnets from	190
Idea of a University, The	678
If I Were Dead	867
Il Penseroso	281
In a Drear-Nighted December	639
Incident of the French Camp	742
Inclusiveness	817
Indian Serenade, The	617
Indifferent, The	213
Induction, The (Mirror for Magistrates)	129
Ingrateful Beauty Threatened	223
In Memoriam A. H. H.	725
In the Depths	864
In the Holy Nativity of our Lord God	225
In the States	907
Into Battle	966
Into the Twilight	881
Island of Skyros, The	967
Italian in England, The	742
I Traveled among Unknown Men	526
I Wandered Lonely as a Cloud	534
Jesting Pilate	987
Jesu, Lover of My Soul	477
John Anderson My Jo	503
Johnson, The Life of	439
Joseph Conrad	981
Keen, Fitful Gusts Are Whispering	627
Kemp Owyne	113
King's Tragedy, The	807
Known In Vain	817
Kubla Khan	565
La Belle Dame Sans Merci	639
Lady of the Land, The	827
Lady of Shalott, The	707
Lady Poverty, The	872
Lake Isle of Innisfree, The	881
Lak of Stedfastnesse	86
L'Allegro	280
Lament, A	619
Lancashire	970
Land of Heart's Desire, The	882
Lark Ascending, The	854
Last Fight of the *Revenge*, The	154
Last Ride Together, The	753
Last Words of Juggling Jerry, The	848
Last Years, The	943
'Late, late, so late' (Tennyson)	733
Latest Decalogue, The	864
Lay Sermons	884
Leisure	974
Le Morte D'Arthur	88
Letter of Advice, A	649
Letters (Cowper)	484
Letters (Gray)	406
Letters (Johnson)	436
Life Is Struggle	865
Life of Addison, The	423
Life of Sir Francis Drake, The	261
Life of Johnson, The	439
Lines (When the lamp is shattered)	626
Lines Composed a Few Miles Above Tintern Abbey	524
Lines on the Mermaid Tavern	633
Lines on the Tombs in Westminster	216
Lines to John Lapraik	498
Linschoten's Testimony	157
Little Black Boy, The	494
Locksley Hall	720
London, 1802	540
Lord Randal	114
Loss of Sir Humphrey Gilbert, The	157
Loss of the Royal George, On the	483
Lost Days	817
Lost Dog, The	925
Lost Leader, The	744
Love	221
Love Among the Ruins	751
Love Divine	476
Love in the Valley	845
Love is Dead	152
Love of Other Years, The	643
Love's Deity	214
Love's Emblems	215
Love's Nocturn	805
Lover Compareth His State, The	121
Lover Complaineth, The	122
Lover for Shamefastness, The	121
Lover Having Dreamed, The	121
Lover Sendeth His Complaints, The	123
Lover's Resolution, The	216
Love-Sight	816
Love-Sweetness	816
Lycidas	282
Lyrical Ballads (Preface)	512
Mackery End in Hertfordshire	567
Mad Song	494
Many Sisters to Many Brothers	967

INDEX OF TITLES

	PAGE
Mariana	705
Marmion	577
Married Lover, The	866
Mary Morison (Song)	497
Match, A	844
Maud; a Monodrama	727
Meditation Upon a Broomstick, A	347
Melancholy	215
'Melencolia'	870
Memorabilia	754
Memory and Pride	642
Menaphon	187, 188
Men of Gotham, The	644
Michael	526
Mid-Rapture	816
Mild Is the Parting Year	642
Milk for the Cat	981
Milton (Blake)	496
Milton (Tennyson)	734
Mirror for Magistrates, The (The Induction)	129
Miss Loo	960
Modern Love	859
Modern Painting	909
Modest Proposal, A	347
Money	974
Moonlight	872
Morality	788
Morte D'Arthur, Le (Malory)	88
Morte D'Arthur (Tennyson)	717
Muse, The	974
Music, When Soft Voices Die	619
My First Visit to Buenos Ayres	939
My Heart Leaps Up When I Behold	531
My Last Duchess	740
My Mind to Me a Kingdom Is	185
My Mistress's Boots	866
My Nanie, O	498
Mynstrelles Songe	416
My Sister's Sleep	803
My Star	753
Newborn Death	818
Nightingale, The (Song: Sidney)	152
Night-Piece to Julia, The	219
Noah's Flood	65
'Non Dolet'	843
Northern Farmer, Old Style	735
Not Dead	975
Note-books, The (Butler)	887
Nuns Fret Not	539
Nun's Priest's Tale, The	81
Nurse's Song	496
Nutbrowne Maide, The	101
Nymph's Disdain of Love, A	206
Ode (Keats)	632
Ode ('How Sleep the Brave')	411
Ode (O'Shaughnessy)	871
Ode for Ben Jonson, An	219
Ode, Intimations of Immortality	537
Ode on a Distant Prospect of Eton College, An	399
Ode on a Grecian Urn	633
Ode on Melancholy	635
Ode on the Death of Mr. Thomson	414
Ode to a Nightingale	634
Ode to Duty	536
Ode to Evening	411

	PAGE
Ode to Simplicity	412
Ode to the West Wind	616
Of Adversity	234
Of A' the Airts the Wind Can Blaw	502
Of Boldness	236
Of Discourse	240
Of Dispatch	238
Of Expense	240
Of Love	236
Of Marriage and Single Life	235
Of Negotiating	243
Of Old Sat Freedom on the Heights	716
Of Parents and Children	235
Of Riches	241
Of Seeming Wise	239
Of Studies	243
Of Superstition	237
Of the Death of Sir T[homas] W[yatt]	127
Of the Mean and Sure Estate	123
Oft in the Stilly Night	644
Of Truth	233
Of Wisdom for a Man's Self	238
Of Youth and Age	242
Old Adam, the Carrion Crow	652
Old Chartist, The	849
Old Familiar Faces, The	567
Old Huntsman, The	982
Old Vicarage, Grantchester, The	961
O Mistress Mine	203
On a Country Road	843
On a Girdle	224
On Charles II	232
One Hope, The	818
One Word More	760
On First Looking into Chapman's Homer	627
On Going a Journey	653
On His Blindness	285
On His Deceased Wife	286
On His Seventy-fifth Birthday	643
On Lucretia Borgia's Hair	642
On Mr. Abraham Cowley's Death and Burial	227
On Seeing the Elgin Marbles	639
On Shakespeare	279
On the Countess Dowager of Pembroke	217
On the Death of Mr. Richard West	399
On the Deaths of Thomas Carlyle and George Eliot	843
On the Departure of Sir Walter Scott	542
On the Detraction which Followed	285
On the Extinction of the Venetian Republic	540
On the Late Massacre in Piedmont	285
On the Life of Man	216
On the Loss of the Royal George	483
On the Receipt of My Mother's Picture	482
On the Sea	639
On Timely Death	643
Organization of Art, The	909
O Sweet Content	204
Our Women	927
Out of the Night That Covers Me	872
Over the Brazier	976
Ozymandias	608
Palace of Art, The	708
Paradise Lost	286
Parted	872
Party Patches	370

INDEX OF TITLES

Title	PAGE
Passions, The	412
Past and Present	691
Past Ruined Ilion	642
Patrick Spens, Sir	115
Patron and the Crocus, The	954
Pearl	59
People of Destiny	972
Personal Record, A	917
Persuasions to Joy: a Song	223
Pheidippides	769
Philomela's Ode	187
Phyllida and Corydon	204
Pilgrim's Progress, The	269
Piper, The	494
Pippa Passes	740
Plougher, The	973
Poet, The	706
Poet's Song, The	724
Praise and Prayer	223
Praise of His Love, A	127
Prayer of Old Age, The	217
Preface to *Lyrical Ballads*	512
Preface to *The Review*	332
Prelude, The	522
Princess, The	724
Progress of Poesy, The	402
Prologue, The (Canterbury Tales)	74
Prometheus Unbound	609
Pro Rege Nostro	873
Prospice	766
Protestation, The	223
Prothalamion	181
Psalm LXXII	475
Psalm XC	475
Pulley, The	222
Qua Cursum Ventus	863
Queen Victoria	983
Question, The	965
Quip, The	221
Rabbi Ben Ezra	764
Raining	965
Rape of the Lock, The	381
Rebellious Vine, The	980
Recessional	881
Recollection, A (Steele: *The Tatler*)	352
Red Hanrahan's Song About Ireland	882
Religio Medici	245
Remember	867
Renouncing of Love, A	121
Renunciation, A	210
Report of Virginia, A	159
Requiem ('Under the wide and starry sky')	902
Requiescat	800
Resolution and Independence	531
Retaliation, The	421
Retreat, The	230
Return of the Barbarian, The	929
Revenge, The	736
Revenge for Rheims	968
Review, The, Preface to	332
Rime of the Ancient Mariner, The	553
Robin Hood	632
Robin Hood and Guy of Gisborne	105
Robin Hood's Death and Burial	108
Rock of Ages	478
Romance and Realism	948
Romance of History, The	665
Rondeau	644
Rosalind's Madrigal	206
Rose, The	228
Rose Aylmer	642
Roundel, The	842
Rubáiyát of Omar Khayyám, The	862
Rugby Chapel	800
Saint Agnes' Eve	715
Salary Earning Girls	927
Samuel Butler, a Critical Study	971
Sappho's Song	143
Saul	745
Say Not the Struggle Nought Availeth	865
Scholar Gypsy, The	797
Schoolmaster, The	135
Scots Wha Hae	508
Sea-Fever	959
Searchlights, The	968
Seasons, The	393
Self-Dependence	787
September, 1802, near Dover	540
Shakespeare	785
She Dwelt Among the Untrodden Ways	525
Sheep	974
Shepheardes Calendar, The	161
Shepherd, The	494
Shepherd's Commendation of His Nymph, The	205
Shepherd's Wife's Song, The	188
Shepherdess, The	872
She Was a Phantom of Delight	533
Short History of England, A	961
Shortest Way With the Dissenters, The	326
Shropshire Lad, A	876
Sic Transit	210
Sigh No More, Ladies	203
Silent Lover, The	185
Silent Noon	816
Sir Galahad	716
Sir Gawain and the Green Knight	38
Sir Patrick Spens	115
Sir Roger at the Assizes	364
Sir Roger at the Play	367
Sir Roger in Love	356
Sir Roger on Men of Parts	355
Social Forces in England and America	921
Socks	968
Sohrab and Rustum	788
Soldier, The	964
Soldier, Rest!	584
Soldier, Soldier	966
Solitary Reaper, The	534
Song ('Ask me no more')	222
Song ('A spirit haunts')	706
Song ('Go and catch')	212
Song ('Green Grow the Rashes')	498
Song ('Old Adam')	652
Song ('The lark now leaves')	223
Song ('To all you ladies')	231
Song ('When I am dead')	867
Song ('When lovely woman stoops')	417
Song ('Would you know')	222
Song from *Gallathea*	143
Song from *Guinevere*	733
Song from *Menaphon* ('Some say Love')	188

INDEX OF TITLES

	PAGE
Song from *Menaphon* ('Weep not')	187
Song from *The Farewell to Folly*	187
Song from *The Land of Heart's Desire*	882
Song from *The Arraignment of Paris*	186
Song of the Shirt, The	648
Song: Mary Morison	497
Song: My Nanie, O	498
Songs from *Pippa Passes*	740
Songs from Shakespeare's plays	203
Songs from *The Princess*	724
Song to Bacchus	215
Song to Celia	210
Song: To Celia	210
Sonnet ('Bright star! would I were steadfast')	640
Sonnet ('It is a beauteous evening')	540
Sonnet ('It is not to be thought of')	540
Sonnet ('Keen, fitful gusts')	627
Sonnet ('Nuns fret not')	539
Sonnet ('"There!" said a stripling')	542
Sonnet ('The world is too much with us')	541
Sonnet ('To one who has been long')	640
Sonnet ('When I have borne in memory')	541
Sonnet ('When I have fears')	640
Sonnet Composed by the Sea-side	539
Sonnet Composed upon Westminster Bridge	539
Sonnet: Inside of King's College Chapel	541
Sonnet on Chillon	585
Sonnet: On First Looking into Chapman's Homer	627
Sonnet on the Death of Mr. Richard West	399
Sonnet: On the Deaths of Thomas Carlyle and George Eliot	843
Sonnet: On the Departure of Sir Walter Scott	542
Sonnet: On the Extinction of the Venetian Republic	540
Sonnets (Shakespeare)	198
Sonnets from the Portuguese	860
Sonnet: Thought of a Briton	541
Sonnet: To Chatterton	640
Sonnet: To Mrs. Unwin	483
Sonnet: To Toussaint l'Ouverture	540
South Country, The	959
Sowing	984
Sparrow's Nest, The	531
Spectator, The	352, 361
Spectator Introduces Himself, The	361
Speech for Conciliation with the Colonies, The	457
Spires of Oxford, The	967
Spirit's Epochs, The	866
Spring's Welcome	143
Stanzas Written in Dejection, Near Naples	608
Stillborn Love	816
Story of Phœbus and Daphne Applied, The	224
Strange Fits of Passion Have I Known	525
Strange Passion of a Lover, A	184
Study	979
Study of Poetry, The	773
Style	891
Suburb	981
Summer	393
Superscription, A	818
Surprise, The	651
Swallow, The	228
Sweet Afton	507
System	907
Table Talk	479
Take, O Take Those Lips Away	204
Tale of a Tub, A	337
Tam Glen	503
Tam O'Shanter	504
Task, The	480
Tatler, The	351
Tears, Idle Tears	724
Tell Me, Where is Fancy Bred	203
Thalassius	840
Thanksgiving to God for His House, A	219
There is a Land	475
'There!' Said a Stripling	542
Thirty Bob a Week	873
Thomas Rymer	115
Thought of a Briton on the Subjugation of Switzerland	541
Three Shadows	807
Three Years She Grew in Sun and Shower	526
Thy Voice is Heard	725
Tiger, The	496
Tithonus	734
To ——	619
To ——	625
To Age	643
To Althea, from Prison	227
To a Mouse	498
To a Skylark (Shelley)	618
To a Skylark (Wordsworth)	535
To Auntie	907
To Autumn	635
To a Virtuous Young Lady	284
To a Young Lady	533
Toccata of Galuppi's, A	752
To Colin Clout	205
To Cyriack Skinner	286
To Daffodils	219
To Heaven	211
To His Coy Mistress	229
To Lucasta	228
To Lucasta, Going to the Wars	227
To Mary in Heaven	504
To Music	219
To My Grandmother	865
To Night	625
To Phyllis	224
To Robert Browning	643
To Sea, To Sea!	652
To Spring	493
To the Cambro-Britons and Their Harp	191
To the Cuckoo	531
To the Lord General Cromwell, May, 1652	285
To the Memory of My Beloved, Master William Shakespeare	212
To the Men of Kent	541
To the Muses	493
To Toussaint l'Ouverture	540
To the Virginian Voyage	191
To the Virgins to Make Much of Time	218
To Virgil	738
Town and Country (Addison, *The Spectator*)	366
Traffic	695
Triumph of Charis, The	211
True-Born Englishman, The	325
Trust	868
Truth	87
Twa Sisters, The	116
Two Poets of Croisic	768

INDEX OF TITLES

Title	PAGE
Ulysses	720
Under the Greenwood Tree	203
United States	646
Up-Hill	868
Upon Julia's Clothes	218
Vanity of Human Wishes, The	437
Venus and Adonis	194
Village, The	489
Virgil's Æneid, Book II	128
Virtue	220
Vision of Judgment, The	596
Vision Upon This Conceit of the Faery Queen, A	186
Vitai Lampada	878
Vow to Love Faithfully	126
Walking with God	479
War-Song of Dinas Vawr, The	645
We Are the Music Makers	871
Weep No More	216
We Have Seen Thee, O Love	834
Westminster Abbey	373
What the Shuiler Said	973
What Tomas An Buile Said in a Pub	984
When I Am Dead, My Dearest	867
When Icicles Hang By the Wall	203
When I Have Borne in Memory	541
When I Have Fears That I May Cease to Be	640
When the Assault was Intended to the City	284
When the Hounds of Spring	833
When the Lamp is Shattered	626
When Thou Must Home	210
When We Are Upon the Seas	217
Where Lies the Land	864
Whither Depart the Brave	864
Who Is Sylvia?	203
Whole Duty of Children, The	907
Why So Pale and Wan?	225
Wife of Flanders, The	964
Wife of Usher's Well, The	113
William and Mary	934
Willie Brewed a Peck O' Maut	506
Winter	394
Winter Night, A	506
Wish, The	228
With a Guitar, to Jane	625
With the Marseilles Pilots	917
Woman's Last Word, A	751
Woods of Westermain, The	855
Wordsworth's Grave	873
World, The (Herbert)	221
World, The (Vaughan)	230
Wykhamist, The	966
Yarrow Unvisited	533
Ye Mariners of England	643
You Ask Me, Why, Though Ill at Ease	715

INDEX OF ILLUSTRATIONS

	PAGE		PAGE
Arnold, Matthew	lviii	Keats, John	li
		Kipling, Rudyard	lxi
Bacon, Francis	xxviii		
Bacon's Essays	xxix	Lamb, Charles	xlviii
Bennett, Arnold	lxi	Lawrence, D. H.	lxiv
Beowulf MS.	xvii	*Lyrical Ballads*	xliv
Boswell, James	xl		
Boswell's *Johnson*	xli	Macaulay, Lord	lii
Browning, Robert	lvii	Masefield, John	lxiv
Bunyan, John	xxxii	Milton, John	xxx
Burke, Edmund	xl		
Burns, Robert	xliii	Newman, Cardinal	liv
Byron, Lord	xlix	*Paradise Lost*	xxxi
		Pepys, Samuel	xxxv
Carlyle, Thomas	liii	*Pilgrim's Progress*	xxxiii
Caxton's Malory	xix	Pope, Alexander	xxxviii
Chaucer	xviii		
Coleridge, Samuel Taylor	xlvi	Raleigh, Sir Walter	xxi
Cowper, William	xlii	Ruskin, John	lv
		Scott, Sir Walter	xlvii
Defoe, Daniel	xxxvi	Shakespeare's Bust	xxiv
Donne, John	xxvii	Shaw, Bernard	lxii
Dryden, John	xxxiv	Shelley, Percy Bysshe	l
		Sidney, Sir Philip	xxvi
Faerie Queene	xxiii	Spenser, Edmund	xxii
First Folio Shakespeare	xxv	Stevenson, Robert Louis	lx
		Strachey, Lytton	lxiii
Galsworthy, John	lxi	Swift, Jonathan	xxxvii
Goldsmith, Oliver	xl	Swinburne, Algernon Charles	lix
Gray, Thomas	xxxix		
		Tennyson, Lord	lvi
Hakluyt's *Voyages*	xx		
Huxley, Aldous	lxiv	Wells, H. G.	lxi
		Woolf, Virginia	lxiv
Johnson, Samuel	xl	Wordsworth, William	xlv

INDEX OF FIRST LINES

	PAGE
A baby's feet, like the sea-shells pink,	842
A book was writ of late called *Tetrachordon*,	285
Adam scriveyn, if ever it thee bifalle	86
After long stormes and tempests sad assay	177
A gentle knight was picking on the plaine	166
Ah, Ben!	219
Ah, did you once see Shelley plain,	754
Ah for pittie! will rancke winters rage	161
Ah Sunflower, weary of time,	496
Ah, what avails the sceptered race,	642
Ah, what is love? It is a pretty thing,	188
Alas, so all things now do hold their peace!.	126
Alas, 't is true I have gone here and there.	201
A little black thing among the snow	496
All hail the power of Jesus' name!.	478
All service ranks the same with God.	740
All that I know	753
All the hills and vales along	969
All ye that lovely lovers be,	187
Along these low pleached lanes, on such a day,	843
Although I enter not,	862
Amid my bale I bathe in bliss,	184
And the first gray of morning filled the east,	788
And thou, O Life, the lady of all bliss	818
And wilt thou leave me thus?.	122
An evil Spirit (your Beauty) haunts me still,	190
A povre widwe somdel stope in age.	81
Ariel to Miranda.—Take.	625
A roundel is wrought as a ring or a star-bright sphere,	842
'Artemidora! Gods invisible,'	642
Art thou poor, yet hast thou golden slumbers.	204
As I in hoary winter's night stood shivering in the snow,	188
As it fell upon a day.	205
Ask me no more; the moon may draw the sea.	725
Ask me no more where Jove bestows,	222
A slumber did my spirit seal;	526
A sonnet is a moment's monument,	816
As other men, so I myself, do muse	190
A spirit haunts the year's last hours	706
As ships, becalmed at eve, that lay	863
As there I left the road in May,	651
As this my carnal robe grows old,	217
As two whose love, first foolish, widening scope,	817
At Flores in the Azores Sir Richard Grenville lay,	736
A thing of beauty is a joy for ever:	627
A trouble not of clouds, or weeping rain,	542
At the midnight in the silence of the sleep time,	772
Avenge, O Lord, thy slaughtered saints, whose bones.	285
Awake, Æolian lyre, awake,	402
A year hence may the grass that waves	969
Bards of Passion and of Mirth,	632
Beauty clear and fair,	215
Beauty sat bathing in a spring.	205
Behind yon hills where Lugar flows,	498
Behold her, single in the field,	534

	PAGE
Behold, within the leafy shade,	531
Be it right or wrong, these men among on women do complaine.	101
Blest be the tie that binds.	478
Blow, blow, thou winter wind!	203
Borgia, thou once wert almost too august	642
Break, break, break,	724
Bright clouds of May.	984
Bright Star of Beauty, on whose eyelids sit.	190
Bright star! would I were steadfast as thou art	640
But do not let us quarrel any more,	755
By this the northerne wagoner had set.	171
Calme was the day, and the trembling ayre.	181
Captain or colonel, or knight in arms,	284
Care-charmer Sleep, son of the sable Night,	189
Charm me asleep, and melt me so.	219
Christ God who savest man, save most	741
Coldly, sadly descends.	800
Come, cheerful day, part of my life to me;	210
Come, dear children, let us away,	785
Come, live with me, and be my love,	259
Come, my Celia, let us prove,	210
Come Sleep! O Sleep, the certain knot of peace,	151
Come, we shepherds, whose blest sight.	225
Comrades, leave me here a little, while as yet 't is early morn:	720
Cromwell, our chief of men, who through a cloud.	285
Crowned, girdled, garbed, and shod with light and fire,	844
Cuddie, for shame hold up thy heavye head,	164
Cupid and my Campaspe played	142
Cyriack, this three years' day these eyes, though clear,	286
Daughter of Jove, relentless power	400
Dear and great Angel, wouldst thou only leave.	757
Dear child of nature, let them rail!	533
Dear love, for nothing less than thee.	213
Death, be not proud, though some have called thee.	215
Deep in the shady sadness of a vale	635
Deep on the convent-roof the snows.	715
Does the road wind up-hill all the way?.	868
'Do you remember me? or are you proud?'.	642
Drake he 's in his hammock an' a thousand mile away,	878
Drink to me only with thine eyes,	210
Dull and hard the low wind creaks	981
Duncan Gray came here to woo,	507
Earth has not anything to show more fair:	539
Eat thou and drink; to-morrow thou shalt die.	817
E'en like two little bank-dividing brooks	220
Enter these enchanted woods,	855
Eternal Spirit of the chainless Mind!	585
Eve, with her basket was.	977
Even such is time, that takes in trust	186

1099

INDEX OF FIRST LINES

	PAGE
Fair and fair, and twice so fair;	186
Fair Daffodils, we weep to see	219
Fair Star of evening, Splendor of the west,	539
Fair stood the wind for France,	191
False Hope prolongs my ever certain grief	189
Farewell, Love, and all thy laws for ever	121
Farewell to one now silenced quite,	872
Fear death? to feel the fog in my throat	766
Fear no more the heat o' th' sun,	204
First I salute this soil of the blessed, river and rock	769
Five years have passed; five summers, with the length	524
Flee fro the prees, and dwelle with sothfastnesse.	87
Flow down, cold rivulet, to the sea,	717
Flow gently, sweet Afton, among thy green braes.	507
Foolish Prater, what do'st thou	228
Forget not yet the tried intent	122
For God's sake hold your tongue, and let me love;	213
For Life I had never cared greatly,	976
For my first twenty years, since yesterday,	214
For those my unbaptizèd rimes,	220
Frail creatures are we all! To be the best	566
Fresh Spring, the herald of loves mighty king,	177
From Stirling Castle we had seen	533
From the bonny bells of heather	907
From the cool and dark-lipped furrows	882
From Tuscan came my lady's worthy race.	125
From you have I been absent in the spring,	201
Full fathom five thy father lies	204
Full many a glorious morning have I seen	199
Gather ye rosebuds while ye may,	218
Get up, get up for shame, the blooming morn	218
Give her but a least excuse to love me!	740
Give place, ye lovers, here before	127
Give me my scallop-shell of quiet	185
Go and catch a falling star,	212
God Lyæus, ever young,	215
God of our fathers, known of old	881
Go fetch to me a pint o' wine,	503
Go, for they call you, shepherd, from the hill;	797
Go, lovely Rose!	224
Good and great God, can I not think of thee,	211
Green grow the rashes, O!	498
Grow old along with me!	764
Had we but world enough, and time,	229
Hail to thee, blithe spirit!	618
Happy those early days, when I.	230
Happy ye leaves! when as those lilly hands.	176
Hark, hark! the lark at heaven's gate sings,	204
Hark! the herald angels sing	477
Has summer come without the rose,	871
Having this day my horse, my hand, my lance	151
Hence, all you vain delights,	215
Hence, loathèd Melancholy,	280
Hence, vain deluding joys,	281
Here, a little child, I stand,	220
Here in the marshland, past the battered bridge,	965
Here lies our Sovereign Lord and King	232
Here, where the world is quiet;	836
Here, where we stood together, we three men,	967
Her eyes the glowworm lend thee,	219
He rises and begins to round,	854
Her mother died when she was young	113
'Hey down, a down!' did Dian sing,	206

	PAGE
High on a throne of royal state, which far	294
His wage of rest at nightfall still	965
Home they brought her warrior dead	725
How doth the little busy bee	476
How it came to an end!	977
How like a winter hath my absence been	200
How oft, when thou, my music, music play'st	202
How sleep the brave who sink to rest	411
How sweet is the shepherd's sweet lot!	494
How the rain tumbles. Lord!—	980
How vainly men themselves amaze,	229
How would it be if we should fare,	980
Hush! my dear, lie still, and slumber.	476
I am that which began;	836
I am the mountainy singer—	973
I arise from dreams of thee.	617
I bring fresh showers for the thirsting flowers,	617
I built my soul a lordly pleasure-house,	708
I can love both fair and brown	213
I Catherine am a Douglas born,	807
I could n't touch a stop and turn a screw,	873
I did but prompt the age to quit their clogs.	285
I drew it from its china tomb;	869
If all the world and love were young	260
If from the public way you turn your steps;	526
If I could trust mine own self with your fate,	868
If I should die, think only this of me:	964
'If I were dead, you'd sometimes say, Poor child!'	867
I fled Him, down the nights and down the days;	875
If love were what the rose is,	844
If ought of oaten stop, or pastoral song,	411
If poisonous minerals, and if that tree.	214
If the quick spirits in your eye.	223
If there be any one can take my place	868
If there were dreams to sell,	651
If thou wilt ease thine heart.	652
I, God, that all the world have wrought.	65
I hate the dreadful hollow behind the little wood,	727
I have had playmates, I have had companions,	567
I have no ale,	974
I know not of what we pondered	868
I long to talk with some old lover's ghost	214
I looked and saw your eyes.	807
I met a traveler from an antique land.	608
I'm glad to lie on a sack of leaves	973
I must down to the seas again, to the lonely sea and the sky,	959
In a coign of the cliff between lowland and highland.	839
In a drear-nighted December,	639
In Cyprus springs, whereas dame Venus dwelt,	126
Inland, within a hollow vale, I stood;	540
In my own shire, if I was sad,	877
In the merry month of May,	204
In the wake of the yellow sunset one pale star	966
Into these loves, who but for passion looks,	190
In vain to me the smiling mornings shine.	399
In Virgine the sultry Sun 'gan sheene.	415
In Xanadu did Kubla Khan	565
In yonder grave a druid lies	414
I quite forgot to put the spigot in	965
I read, before my eyelids dropped their shade,	712
I said—Then, dearest, since 't is so,	753
I saw Eternity the other night,	230
I saw God. Do you doubt it?	984
I saw the spires of Oxford	967

INDEX OF FIRST LINES

	PAGE		PAGE
I sing of books, of blossoms, birds and bowers	217	Lucasta, frown, and let me die!	228
Is it not better at an early hour	643	Lyke as a ship, that through the ocean wyde	177
Is there a whim-inspirèd fool,	502		
Is there, for honest poverty,	508	Mary! I want a lyre with other strings;	483
I strove with none; for none was worth my strife,	643	Master of the murmuring courts	805
I struck the board, and cried, 'No more; I will abroad!	221	May Marigold is frolic,	872
It befell at Martynmas	111	Men call you fayre, and you doe credit it	177
It does not hurt. She looked along the knife	843	Men say, Columbia, we shall hear thy guns,	867
It happened once, some men of Italy	827	Methought I saw my late espousèd saint	286
I thought of Thee, my partner and my guide	541	Methought I saw the grave where Laura lay	186
I thought once how Theocritus had sung	860	Mild is the parting year, and sweet	642
It is a beauteous evening, calm and free	540	Milton! thou shouldst be living at this hour:	540
It is an ancient Mariner	553	Miss Helen Slingsby was my maiden aunt	975
It is not sweet content, be sure,	864	Miss Nancy Ellicott	975
It is not to be thought of that the Flood	540	More then most faire, full of the living fire	176
It keeps eternal whisperings around	639	Morpheus, the lively son of deadly Sleep,	151
It little profits that an idle king,	720	Mortality, behold and fear!	216
I traveled among unknown men,	526	Most sweet it is with unuplifted eyes	542
It was a perfect day	984	Much have I traveled in the realms of gold,	627
It was a summer evening,	641	Music, when soft voices die,	619
It was in and about the Martinmas time	116	My eye, descending from the hill, surveys	226
I 've never ceased to curse the day I signed	982	My galley chargèd with forgetfulness	121
I wandered lonely as a cloud	534	My good blade carves the casques of men,	716
I was thy neighbor once, thou rugged Pile!	535	My heart aches, and a drowsy numbness pains	634
I weep for Adonais—he is dead!	619	My heart is a-breaking, dear tittie,	503
I will arise and go now, and go to Innisfree,	881	My heart leaps up when I behold	531
I wonder if the old cow died or not	965	My lov'd, my honored, much respected friend!	499
		My love looks like a girl to-night,	979
Jenny kissed me when we met,	644	My lute, awake, perform the last	122
Jesu, lover of my soul	477	My mind to me a kingdom is,	185
Jesus shall reign where'er the sun	475	My mistress' eyes are nothing like the sun;	202
John Anderson my jo, John,	503	My mother bore me in the southern wild,	494
Just for a handful of silver he left us,	744	My mother's maids, when they did sew and spin,	123
Just now the lilac is in bloom,	961	My sheep are thoughts, which I both guide and serve;	152
Keen, fitful gusts are whispering here and there	627	My spirit is too weak—mortality	639
Kentish Sir Byng stood for his King	772	My true-love hath my heart and I have his,	152
King Charles, and who 'll do him right now?	772		
Know, Celia, since thou art so proud,	223	Nay, nay, sweet England, do not grieve!	965
		Nobly, nobly, Cape Saint Vincent to the Northwest died away;	744
Lady, that in the prime of earliest youth	284	No longer mourn for me when I am dead	200
Lay a garland on my hearse	216	No more, My Dear, no more these counsels try!	151
Let dogs delight to bark and bite	476	No more shall meads be decked with flowers,	223
Let me not to the marriage of true minds	202	No! my own love of other years!	643
Let observation, with extensive view	437	No, no, go not to Lethe, neither twist	635
Let others sing of Knights and Paladins	189	Not a drum was heard, not a funeral note,	645
Let 's contend no more, Love,	751	Not in the crises of events	866
Let those who are in favor with their stars	198	Not marble, nor the gilded monuments	199
Let us begin and carry up this corpse,	758	Not mine own fears nor the prophetic soul	201
Light flows our war of mocking words, and yet,	786	No! those days are gone away,	632
Like as the waves make towards the pebbled shore,	199	Now the lusty spring is seen;	215
Like to the falling of a star	216	Now the storm begins to lower,	405
Lo, here the gentle lark, weary of rest,	194	Nuns fret not at their convent's narrow room;	539
Lo! I the man, whose muse whylome did maske	165		
Look in my face; my name is Might-have-been;	818	O blithe New-comer! I have heard,	531
Lord, thou hast given me a cell	219	Obscurest night involved the sky	484
Love bade me welcome; yet my soul drew back,	221	O Chatterton! how very sad thy fate	640
Love built a stately house, where Fortune came;	221	O cruel Love! on thee I lay,	143
Love divine, all love excelling	476	Of a' the airts the wind can blaw	502
Love in my bosom like a bee,	206	Of all this numerous progeny was none	304
'Love seeketh not itself to please,'	496	Of Heaven or Hell I have no power to sing,	819
Love, that liveth and reigneth in my thought	125	Of Man's first disobedience, and the fruit	286
Loving in truth, and fain in verse my love to show,	150	Of old sat Freedom on the heights,	716
Low and brown barns thatched and repatched and tattered	964	O, for my sake do you with Fortune chide,	202
		O for some honest lover's ghost,	224
		Oft do I marvel, whether Delia's eyes	189
		Oft, in the stilly night,	644

INDEX OF FIRST LINES

	PAGE
Oft when my spirit doth spred her bolder winges.	177
O happy dames! that may embrace.	126
O Heart of hearts, the chalice of love's fire,	843
O, how much more doth beauty beauteous seem.	199
Oh, East is East, and West is West, and never the twain shall meet,	879
Oh! for a closer walk with God.	479
Oh, Galuppi, Baldassare, this is very sad to find!	752
Oh, see how thick the goldcup flowers.	877
'Oh, sick I am to see you, will you never let me be?	877
Oh that I were.	975
Oh, that those lips had language! Life has passed	482
Oh, to be in England,	744
Old Adam, the carrion crow,	652
Old Chaucer, like the morning star,	227
'Old things need not be therefore true,'	864
O Mary, at thy window be,	497
O mighty-mouthed inventor of harmonies,	734
O Mistress mine, where are you roaming?	203
O mortal man, who livest here by toil,	396
Once a dream did weave a shade.	495
Once an earlier David took.	951
Once did she hold the gorgeous east in fee;	540
One day, the vine.	980
On either side the river lie.	707
One more Unfortunate,	647
O, never say that I was false of heart.	201
One word is too often profaned.	625
On Hellespont, guilty of true love's blood,	192
On the sea and at the Hogue, sixteen hundred ninety-two.	766
On those great waters now I am,	217
O saw ye not fair Ines?.	646
O! synge untoe mie roundelaie,	416
Others abide our question. Thou art free.	785
O Thou, by nature taught.	412
O thou! whatever title suit thee,	501
O thou with dewy locks, who lookest down.	493
Our God, our help in ages past.	475
Out of the night that covers me,	872
Out upon it, I have loved.	225
Out-worn heart, in a time out-worn,	881
O what can ail thee, knight-at-arms!.	639
O where hae ye been, Lord Randal, my son?.	114
O where have you been, my long, long, love,	114
O, wild West Wind, thou breath of Autumn's being,	616
O, Willie brew'd a peck o' maut,	506
O world! O life! O time!	619
O yes, O yes! If any maid.	143
Pass forth, my wonted cries.	123
Passions are likened best to floods and streams.	185
Past ruined Ilion Helen lives,	642
Phyllis! why should we delay	224
Piping down the valleys wild,	494
Pitch here the tent, while the old horse grazes:.	848
Poet who sleepest by this wandering wave!.	873
Poor soul, the center of my sinful earth,	202
Praise God from whom all blessings flow.	475
Praise is devotion fit for mighty minds,	223
Queen and Huntress, chaste and fair.	211
Remember me when I am gone away,	867
Restore thy treasure to the golden ore;	189
Ring out your bells, let mourning shows be spread.	152

	PAGE
Rock of Ages, cleft for me.	478
Roman Virgil, thou that singest Ilion's lofty temples robed in fire,	738
Rome is fallen, I hear, the gallant Medici taken.	864
Rough wind, that moanest loud.	626
Row us out from Desenzano, to your Sirmione row!.	738
'Ruin seize thee, ruthless King!.	404
Said Abner, 'At last thou art come! Ere I tell, ere thou speak,'	745
Say not the struggle nought availeth,	865
Scots, wha hae wi' Wallace bled,	508
Seamen three! what men be ye?.	644
Season of mists and mellow fruitfulness,	635
See an old unhappy bull.	978
See the chariot at hand here of Love,	211
Set me whereas the sun doth parch the green,	126
Shadow by shadow, stripped for fight.	968
Shall I compare thee to a summer's day?.	198
Shall I, wasting in despair,	216
She dwelt among the untrodden ways.	525
She fell asleep on Christmas Eve:.	803
She has dancing eyes and ruby lips,	866
She walks—the lady of my delight—.	872
She was a Phantom of delight.	533
Shining pins that dart and click.	968
Should auld acquaintance be forgot,	503
Sigh no more, ladies, sigh no more!.	203
Since brass nor stone, nor earth, nor boundless sea.	200
Since there's no help, come, let us kiss and part!.	190
Sitting by a river's side,	187
Sleep! sleep! beauty bright,	495
So all day long the noise of battle rolled.	717
Soldier, rest! thy warfare o'er,	584
Soldier, soldier, off to war,	966
Some say Love,	188
Somewhere the long mellow note of the blackbird.	979
Som tyme this world was so stedfast and stable.	86
Souls of Poets dead and gone,	633
St. Agnes' Eve—Ah, bitter chill it was!.	628
Stand close around, ye Stygian set,	642
Stella since thou so right a princess art.	151
Stern Daughter of the Voice of God!.	536
Stop, Christian passer-by!—Stop, child of God,	566
Strange fits of passion have I known:	525
Strew on her roses, roses.	800
Strong Son of God, immortal Love,	725
Such a starved bank of moss.	768
Sultan Iskander sat him down.	962
Sunset and evening star,	738
Sunset and silence! A man: around him.	973
Sweet Auburn! loveliest village of the plain;	417
Sweet are the thoughts that savor of content;	187
Sweet day, so cool, so calm, so bright,	220
Sweet dimness of her loosened hair's down fall.	816
Sweet dreams, form a shade.	495
Sweet, serene, sky-like flower,	228
Swiftly walk over the western wave,	625
Take, O, take those lips away,	204
Tax not the royal saint with vain expense,	541
Tears, idle tears, I know not what they mean.	724
Tell me not, Sweet, I am unkind,	227
Tell me, where is fancy bred.	203
That second time they hunted me.	742

INDEX OF FIRST LINES 1103

	PAGE
That's my last Duchess painted on the wall,...	740
That time of year thou mayst in me behold:....	200
That which her slender waist confined,........	224
The awful shadow of some unseen Power.......	607
The blessed damozel leaned out...............	804
The changing guests, each in a different mood,...	817
The Curfew tolls the knell of parting day,......	401
The day is dark and the night.................	807
The forward violet thus did I chide............	201
The frost performs its secret ministry,.........	565
The glories of our blood and state.............	222
The harp that once through Tara's halls.......	644
The hour which might have been, yet might not be,..	816
The isles of Greece, the isles of Greece.........	599
The king sits in Dumferling toune.............	115
The Lady Poverty was fair:...................	872
The lark now leaves his wat'ry nest,...........	223
The long love that in my thought I harbor,....	121
The lost days of my life until to-day,..........	817
The merry World did on a day................	221
The Meuse and Marne have little waves;.......	969
The mountain sheep are sweeter,..............	645
The naked earth is warm with Spring..........	966
The night I left my father said:...............	965
The nightingale, as soon as April bringeth......	152
The old brown thorn trees break in two high over Cummen Strand,...........................	882
The pale stars are gone!.....................	609
The play is done—the curtain drops,..........	862
The poet in a golden clime was born,..........	706
The primrose in the sheäde do blow,...........	750
The rain had fallen, the Poet arose,............	724
The readers of the *Boston Evening Transcript*...	974
There is not anything more wonderful.........	975
There's a breathless hush in the Close tonight—.	878
There is a land of pure delight................	475
There is delight in singing, though none hear...	643
There lived a wife at Usher's Well.............	113
'There!' said a Stripling, pointing with meet pride	542
There they are, my fifty men and women......	760
There was a roaring in the wind all night;.....	531
There was a time when meadow, grove and stream,...................................	537
There was a weasel lived in the sun............	984
There was three ladies played at the ba,.......	117
There was twa sisters in a bowr...............	116
The sea is calm to-night......................	802
These, as they change, Almighty Father, these...	395
The soote season that bud and bloom forth brings.	125
The splendor falls on castle walls..............	725
The sun hath twice brought forth his tender green,...................................	127
The sun is warm, the sky is clear,.............	608
The Village Life, and every care that reigns....	489
The wild winds weep,........................	494
The wind blows out of the gates of the day,....	882
The woods decay, the woods decay and fall,....	734
The world comes not to an end: her city-hives..	871
The world is too much with us: late and soon,..	541
The wrathful Winter, 'proaching on apace,.....	129
They are all gone into the world of light!......	231
They dreamt not of a perishable home.........	542
The year's at the spring......................	740
They whisted all, with fixèd face attent,.......	128
Think no more, lad; laugh, be jolly:...........	877
Think thou and act; to-morrow thou shalt die..	817

	PAGE
This little vault, this narrow room,............	223
This is the Chapel: here, my son..............	878
This relative of mine,........................	865
Thou art not fair, for all thy red and white,....	210
Thou canst not die, whilst any zeal abound.....	189
Though I be now a gray, gray friar,...........	645
Thou ling'ring star, with less'ning ray,........	504
Thou lovely and beloved, thou my love;.......	816
Thou Permanence amid all things that pass!....	968
Thou shalt have one God only; who...........	864
Thou still unravished bride of quietness,.......	633
Three years she grew in sun and shower,......	526
Through thick Arcadian woods a hunter went,..	820
Thyrsis, a youth of the inspired train,.........	224
Thy voice is heard through rolling drums......	725
Tiger! Tiger! burning bright.................	496
Tired with all these, for restful death I cry.....	200
'T is hard to say, if greater want of skill.......	375
'T is the middle of night by the castle clock....	559
To all you ladies now at land..................	231
To-day Death seems to me an infant child.....	818
To draw no envy, Shakespeare, on thy name,...	212
To fair Fidele's grassy tomb...................	411
To me, fair friend, you never can be old,......	201
To sea, to sea! The calm is o'er;..............	652
Toll for the brave...........................	483
To Mercy, Pity, Peace, and Love..............	495
To one who has been long in city pent.........	640
Toussaint, the most unhappy man of men!.....	540
To wear out heart, and nerves, and brain,.....	865
To you, my purse, and to non other wight......	87
True Thomas lay oer yond grassy bank,........	115
'T was at the royal feast for Persia won........	307
Turn back, you wanton flyer..................	210
Two souls diverse out of our human sight......	843
Two Voices are there; one is of the sea,........	541
Tyre of the farther West! be thou too warned....	646
Underneath this sable hearse..................	217
Under the greenwood tree.....................	203
Under the wide and starry sky................	902
Under yonder beech-tree single on the greensward,...................................	845
Unstable dream, according to the place,.......	121
Upon the flowery forefront of the year,........	840
Up with me! up with me into the clouds!......	535
Vanguard of Liberty, ye men of Kent,.........	541
Very old are the woods;......................	960
Wake: the silver dusk returning...............	876
Walking through trees to cool my heat and pain,..	975
Watch thou and fear; to-morrow thou shalt die.	817
We are the music makers,.....................	871
Weary of myself, and sick of asking...........	787
We cannot kindle when we will...............	788
Weep no more, nor sigh, nor groan,...........	216
Weep not, my wanton, smile upon my knee....	187
Weep with me all you that read...............	211
Wee, sleekit, cow'rin, tim'rous beastie,.........	498
Welcome, old friend! These many years.......	643
Well then! I now do plainly see..............	228
We look for her that sunlike stood.............	850
Whan that Aprille with his shoures soote.......	74
'What are the bugles blowin' for?' said Files-on-Parade...................................	880
What bird so sings, yet so does wail?..........	143
What dire offense from amorous causes springs,..	381

INDEX OF FIRST LINES

	PAGE
Whate'er I be, old England is my dam!	849
What have I done for you,	873
What is this life if, full of care,	974
What life to lead and where to go	976
What needs my Shakespeare for his honored bones.	279
What pleasure have great princes	206
What potions have I drunk of Siren tears,	202
What shepherd can express.	205
Wheer 'asta beän saw long and meä liggin' 'ere aloän?	735
Whenas in silks my Julia goes,	218
When biting Boreas, fell and doure,	506
When chapman billies leave the street,	504
When do I see thee most, belovèd one?	816
When God at first made man,	222
When I am dead, my dearest,	867
When I am living in the midlands,	959
When I behold that beauties wonderment	176
When icicles hang by the wall,	203
When I consider every thing that grows	198
When I consider how my light is spent.	285
When I do count the clock that tells the time,	198
When I grow big I 'll smoke and swear	980
When I had money, money, O!	974
When I have borne in memory what has tamed.	541
When I have fears that I may cease to be	640
When I have seen by Time's fell hand defaced	199
When I made answer, I began: 'Alas!	805
When in disgrace with fortune and men's eyes	199
When in the chronicle of wasted time.	201
When I survey the wondrous cross	475
When I was once in Baltimore,	974
When Love with unconfinèd wings	227
When lovely woman stoops to folly,	417
When Music, heav'nly maid, was young,	412
When Nature made her chief work, Stella's eyes,	150
When Robin Hood and Little John.	108
When shawes beene sheene, and shradds full fayre	105
When the hounds of spring are on winter's traces.	833
When the lamp is shattered.	626
When the Present has latched its postern behind my tremulous stay,	976
When the tea is brought at five o'clock,	981
When the voices of children are heard on the green.	496
When thin-strewn memory I look through,	960
When thou must home to shades of underground.	210
When to the sessions of sweet silent thought.	199
When vain desire at last and vain regret	818
When we fought the campaigns (in the long Christmas rains)	967
When we were girl and boy together,	652
Where lies the land to which the ship would go?	864
Where the quiet-colored end of evening smiles.	751
Whether on Ida's shady brow,	493
Whilst thus my pen strives to eternize thee,	190
Whoever comes to shroud me, do not harm.	214
Who is it that this dark night.	151
Who is Silvia? what is she,	203
Who is the happy Warrior? Who is he.	536
Why does nobody write a poem about the cotton trade?	970
Why dois your brand sae drap wi bluid,	118
Why, having won her, do I woo?.	866
Why is my verse so barren of new pride,	200
Why so pale and wan, fond lover?.	225
Wild wind, and drear, beneath the pale stars blowing,	965
Wilt thou forgive that sin where I begun,	215
With blackest moss, the flower-plots.	705
With fingers weary and worn,	648
With half a heart I wander here.	907
With how sad steps, O moon, thou climb'st the skies!	150
With proud thanksgiving, a mother for her children,	964
Would'st thou hear what man can say	212
Would that the structure brave, the manifold music I build,	762
Would you know what 's soft? I dare.	222
W. resteth here, that quick could never rest.	127
Years—years ago, ere yet my dreams.	648
Ye banks, and braes, and streams around	506
Ye distant spires, ye antique towers,	399
Ye flowery banks o' bonie Doon,	507
Ye mariners of England.	643
Yet once more, O ye laurels, and once more,	282
Ye learnèd sisters, which have oftentimes	177
You ask me, why, though ill at ease,	715
You brave heroic minds,	191
You know, we French stormed Ratisbon;	742
Your ghost will walk, you lover of trees,	754
Your hands lie open in the long fresh grass,	816
Your words, my friend, right healthful caustics, blame.	150
You tell me you 're promised a lover,	649
You that do search for every purling spring	150
Yt felle abowght the Lamasse tyde	108

(15)

INDEX OF PLACES

Abbotsford D 2
Aberdour C 1
Aldborough (Aldeburgh) H 5
Aldwinkle F 5
Aldworth E 6
Alfoxden C 6
Alnwick E 2
Anglesey (Mona) B 4
Annan C 3
Arundel F 7
Ashestiel D 2
Auchinleck B 2
Avon (River) E 5
Ayr B 2
Ayr (River) B 2

Baldeswelle (Bawdeswell) H 5
Balloch B 1
Bamborough D 2
Bannockburn C 1
Barham H 6
Bath D 6
Bedford F 5
Berwick D 2
Birmingham E 5
Blean Forest H 6
Blee (See Blean)
Boughton Street G 6
Bow H 2
Box Hill G 3
Bradford E 4
Brantwood C 3
Bridgewater C 6
Brighton F 7
Bristol D 6
Brummagen (See Birmingham)
Brunanburgh C 2
Bury St Edmunds G 5

Cader Idris (Mt.) C 5
Camberwell H 2
Cambridge G 5
Canterbury H 6
Charlecote E 5
Chester D 4
Chichester F 7
Chirk C 5
Clevedon D 6
Clyde, Firth of B 2
Cockermouth C 3
Colchester G 6
Conway (River) C 4
Coventry E 5
Craigenputtock C 2

Dalkeith C 2
Dartford G 6
Dartmouth C 7
Denmark Hill H 2
Deptford H 2, F 6
Derby E 5
Dertemouthe (See Dartmouth)
Doon (River) B 2
Dorchester D 7
Dover H 6
Duddon (River) C 3
Dumfermline (Dumferling) C 1
Dumfries C 2
Dunbar D 1

Earlston D 2
Ecclefechan C 2
Edinburgh C 2
Ellisland C 2
Elstow F 5
Elwy (River) C 4
Erceldoune (See Earlston)

Eton F 2
Exeter C 7

Farringford E 7
Felpham F 7
Field Place F 6
Flodden Field D 2
Fordidge H 6
Fordwich (See Fordidge)
Forth, Firth of C 1

Glasgow B 2
Glastonbury D 6
Gloucester D 6
Grantchester G 5
Grasmere C 3
Great Berkhampstead F 6
Greenwich H 1, F 6
Grongar Hill B 6

Hagley D 5
Hammersmith G 2
Hampstead G 2
Hampton G 2
Hampton Court G 2
Harbledown H 6
Harrow G 2
Harwich H 6
Hastings G 7
Hatfield E 4
Hawkshead D 3
Herne Hill H 2
Highgate H 2
Horton F 2, F 6
Hull (Hulle) F 4
Humber (River) F 4
Hunsdon G 6
Huntingdon F 5
Huntington C 5

Irvine B 2

Jarrow E 3

Katrine (Lake) B 1
Keswick C 3
Kilgerran B 5
Kilmarnock B 2
Kirk Alloway B 2

Laleham F 2
Lasswade C 2
Leasowes D 5
Leeds E 4
Lichfield E 5
Lincoln F 4
Lindisfarne E 2
Littlemore E 6
Liverpool D 4
Llangollen C 4
Lochlea B 2
London F 6
Louth F G 4
Lynmouth C 6

Maidstone G 6
Maldon G 6
Manchester D 4
Medway (River) G 6
Mona (See Anglesey)
Monmouth D 6
Moor Park F 6
Mossgiel B 2

Nether Stowey C 6
Newbold E 5
Newcastle E 3

Newstead Abbey E 4
Norwich H 5
Nottingham E 5

Olney F 5
Orwell (Orewelle) H 6
Osprínge G 6
Otterburn D 2
Ottery St. Mary C 7
Oxford (Oxenford) E 6

Penshurst G 6
Plinlimmon (Mt.) C 5
Plymouth B 7
Portsmouth E 7
Putney G 2

Quantock Hills (Mt.) C 6

Racedown D 7
Richmond G 2
Rochester G 6
Rothley Temple E 5
Rugby E 5
Rydal Mount D 3

St. Neot's B 7
Salisbury E 6
Scarborough F 3
Severn (River) D 5-6
Sheffield E 4
Shrewsbury D 5
Sittingbourne G 6
Snowdon (Mt.) B 4
Solway Firth C 3
Somersby G 4
Southampton E 7
Southwark F 6, H 2
Staines F 2
Stirling C 1
Stoke Poges F 2
Stonehenge E 6
Stour (River) D 7
Stowey (See Nether Stowey)
Stratford-at-Bow (See Bow)
Stratford-on-Avon E 5
Strawberry Hill G 2
Sussex Weald G 6

Tavistock B 7
Teifi (River) B 5
Thames (River) E 6-G 6
Tintagel B 7
Tintern Abbey D 6
Towy (River) B 6
Trossachs B 1
Tweed (River) D 2
Twickenham G 2
Tyne (River) D 3

Wakefield E 4
Ware F 6
Wedmore D 6
Wem D 5
Whitby F 3
Wilton E 6
Wimborne E 7
Winchester E 6
Windermere D 3
Windermere (Lake) D 3
Windsor F 2
Witham D 6
Worcester D 5
Wrexham C 4
Wye (River) D 5

Yarrow (River) C 2
York E 4